Carchemish
Nineveh
Euphrates
Tigris
Babylon
N
Ur
E LOWENSTEIN

THE INTERPRETER'S BIBLE

THE INTERPRETER'S BIBLE

IN TWELVE VOLUMES

VOLUME

I. General Articles on the Bible; General Articles on the Old Testament; Genesis; Exodus

II. Leviticus; Numbers; Deuteronomy; Joshua; Judges; Ruth; Samuel

III. Kings; Chronicles; Ezra; Nehemiah; Esther; Job

IV. Psalms; Proverbs

V. Ecclesiastes; Song of Songs; Isaiah; Jeremiah

VI. Lamentations; Ezekiel; Daniel; Hosea; Joel; Amos; Obadiah; Jonah; Micah; Nahum; Habakkuk; Zephaniah; Haggai; Zechariah; Malachi

VII. General Articles on the New Testament; Matthew; Mark

VIII. Luke; John

IX. Acts; Romans

X. Corinthians; Galatians; Ephesians

XI. Philippians; Colossians; Thessalonians; Timothy; Titus; Philemon; Hebrews

XII. James; Peter; John; Jude; Revelation; Index

VOLUME IV

The Book of
PSALMS

The Book of
PROVERBS

THE
INTERPRETER'S BIBLE

The Holy Scriptures

IN THE KING JAMES AND REVISED STANDARD VERSIONS

WITH GENERAL ARTICLES AND

INTRODUCTION, EXEGESIS, EXPOSITION

FOR EACH BOOK OF THE BIBLE

IN TWELVE VOLUMES

VOLUME

IV

דבר־אלהינו יקום לעולם

NEW YORK *Abingdon Press* NASHVILLE

For information address Abingdon Press,
810 Broadway, Nashville 2, Tennessee.

Library of Congress Catalog Card Number: 51-12276

B

SET UP, PRINTED, AND BOUND BY THE PARTHENON PRESS, AT NASHVILLE, TENNESSEE, UNITED STATES OF AMERICA

ABBREVIATIONS AND EXPLANATIONS

Abbreviations

Canonical books and bibliographical terms are abbreviated according to common usage

Amer. Trans. — *The Bible, An American Translation,* Old Testament, ed. J. M. P. Smith
Apoc.—Apocrypha
Aq.—Aquila
ASV—American Standard Version (1901)
Barn.—Epistle of Barnabas
Clem.—Clement
C.T.—Consonantal Text
Did.—Didache
Ecclus.—Ecclesiasticus
ERV—English Revised Version (1881-85)
Exeg.—Exegesis
Expos.—Exposition
Goodspeed—*The Bible, An American Translation,* New Testament and Apocrypha, tr. Edgar J. Goodspeed
Herm. Vis., etc.—The Shepherd of Hermas: Visions, Mandates, Similitudes
Ign. Eph., etc.—Epistles of Ignatius to the Ephesians, Magnesians, Trallians, Romans, Philadelphians, Smyrnaeans, and Polycarp
KJV—King James Version (1611)
LXX—Septuagint
Macc.—Maccabees
Moffatt—*The Bible, A New Translation,* by James Moffatt
M.T.—Masoretic Text
N.T.—New Testament
O.T.—Old Testament
Polyc. Phil.—Epistle of Polycarp to the Philippians
Pseudep.—Pseudepigrapha
Pss. Sol.—Psalms of Solomon
RSV—Revised Standard Version (1946-52)
Samar.—Samaritan recension
Symm.—Symmachus
Targ.—Targum
Test. Reuben, etc.—Testament of Reuben, and others of the Twelve Patriarchs
Theod.—Theodotion
Tob.—Tobit
Vulg.—Vulgate
Weymouth—*The New Testament in Modern Speech,* by Richard Francis Weymouth
Wisd. Sol.—Wisdom of Solomon

Quotations and References

Boldface type in Exegesis and Exposition indicates a quotation from either the King James or the Revised Standard Version of the passage under discussion. The two versions are distinguished only when attention is called to a difference between them. Readings of other versions are not in boldface type and are regularly identified.

In scripture references a letter (*a, b,* etc.) appended to a verse number indicates a clause within the verse; an additional Greek letter indicates a subdivision within the clause. When no book is named, the book under discussion is understood.

Arabic numbers connected by colons, as in scripture references, indicate chapters and verses in deuterocanonical and noncanonical works. For other ancient writings roman numbers indicate major divisions, arabic numbers subdivisions, these being connected by periods. For modern works a roman number and an arabic number connected by a comma indicate volume and page. Bibliographical data on a contemporary work cited by a writer may be found by consulting the first reference to the work by that writer (or the bibliography, if the writer has included one).

Greek Transliterations

α = a	ε = e	ι = i	ν = n	ρ = r	φ = ph
β = b	ζ = z	κ = k	ξ = x	σ(ς) = s	χ = ch
γ = g	η = ē	λ = l	ο = o	τ = t	ψ = ps
δ = d	θ = th	μ = m	π = p	υ = u, y	ω = ō

Hebrew and Aramaic Transliterations

I. HEBREW ALPHABET

א = ʾ	ה = h	ט = ṭ	מ(ם) = m	פ(ף) = p, ph	שׁ = s, sh
ב = b, bh	ו = w	י = y	נ(ן) = n	צ(ץ) = ç	ת = t, th
ג = g, gh	ז = z	כ(ך) = k, kh	ס = ṣ	ק = q	
ד = d, dh	ח = ḥ	ל = l	ע = ʿ	ר = r	

II. MASORETIC POINTING

Pure-long	Tone-long	Short	Composite *sh*ᵉ*wa*
ָ = â	ָ = ā	ַ = a	ֲ = ª
ֵ = ê	ֵ = ē	ֶ = e	ֱ = ᵉ
ִ *or* ִי = î		ִ = i	
וֹ *or* ֹ = ô	ֹ = ō	ָ = o	ֳ = ᵒ
וּ = û		ֻ = u	

NOTE: (*a*) The *páthaḥ* furtive is transliterated as a *ḥaṭeph-páthaḥ.* (*b*) The simple *sh*ᵉ*wa,* when vocal, is transliterated ᵉ. (*c*) The tonic accent, which is indicated only when it occurs on a syllable other than the last, is transliterated by an acute accent over the vowel.

TABLE OF CONTENTS

VOLUME IV

THE BOOK OF PSALMS

THE BOOK OF PROVERBS

MAP

The Book of

PSALMS

Introduction by W. Stewart McCullough

Exegesis Psalms 1-71, 93, 95-96, 100, 120-138, 140-150 by William R. Taylor

Exegesis Psalms 72-92, 94, 97-99, 101-119, 139 by W. Stewart McCullough

Exposition Psalms 1-41 by J. R. P. Sclater

Exposition Psalms 42-89 by Edwin McNeill Poteat

Exposition Psalms 90-150 by Frank H. Ballard

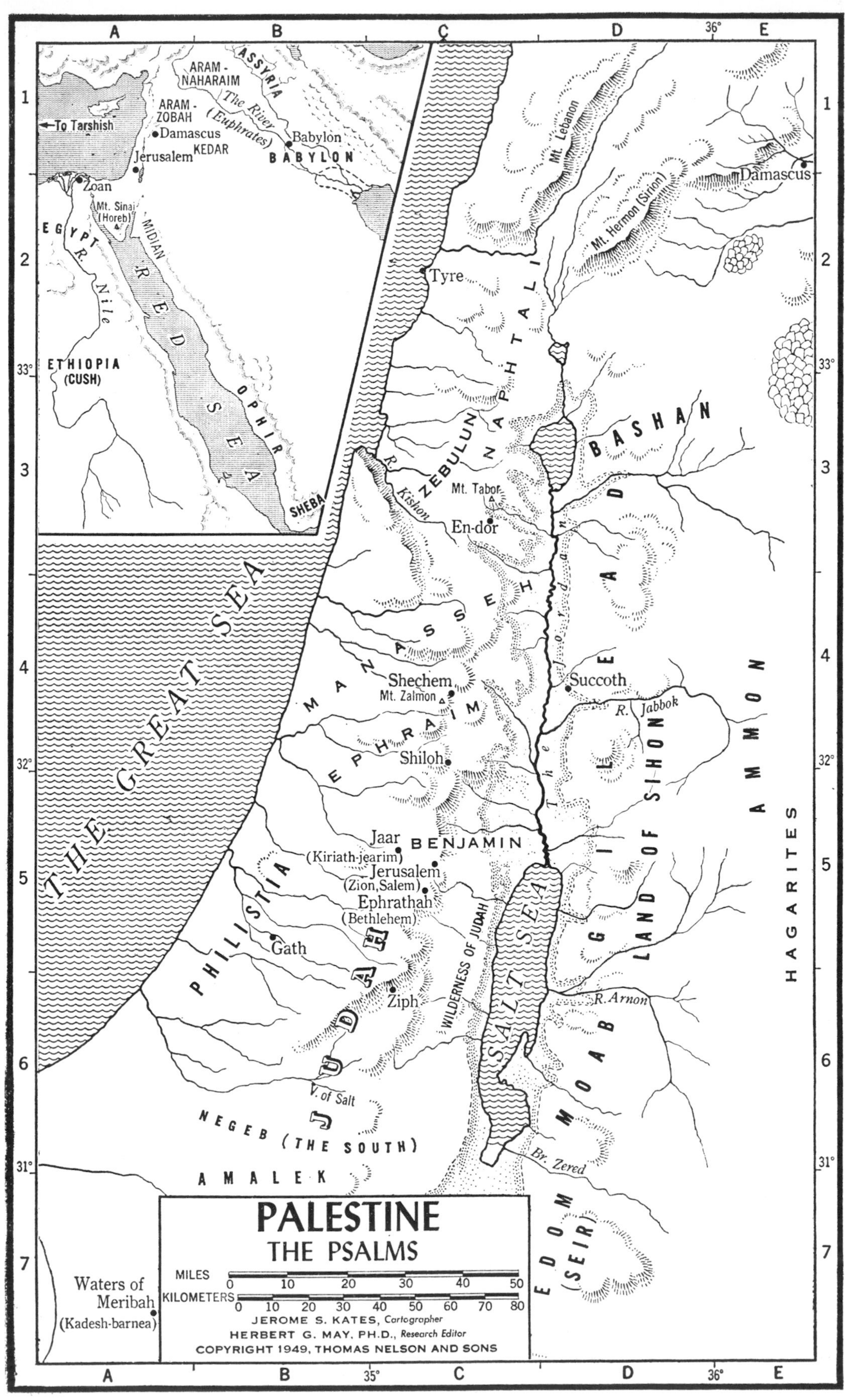
PALESTINE
THE PSALMS
MILES 0 10 20 30 40 50
KILOMETERS 0 10 20 30 40 50 60 70 80
JEROME S. KATES, Cartographer
HERBERT G. MAY, PH.D., Research Editor
COPYRIGHT 1949, THOMAS NELSON AND SONS
THE GREAT SEA
ARAM-NAHARAIM
ASSYRIA
The River (Euphrates)
ARAM-ZOBAH
To Tarshish
Damascus
Babylon
BABYLON
KEDAR
Jerusalem
Zoan
Mt. Sinai (Horeb)
MIDIAN
EGYPT
R. Nile
RED SEA
ETHIOPIA (CUSH)
OPHIR
SHEBA
Mt. Lebanon
Mt. Hermon (Sirion)
Damascus
Tyre
NAPHTALI
BASHAN
ZEBULUN
R. Kishon
Mt. Tabor
En-dor
GILEAD
MANASSEH
The Jordan
Shechem
Mt. Zalmon
Succoth
R. Jabbok
EPHRAIM
Shiloh
AMMON
LAND OF SIHON
Jaar (Kiriath-jearim)
BENJAMIN
Jerusalem (Zion, Salem)
Ephrathah (Bethlehem)
PHILISTIA
Gath
JUDAH
Ziph
WILDERNESS OF JUDAH
SALT SEA
HAGARITES
R. Arnon
MOAB
V. of Salt
NEGEB (THE SOUTH)
Br. Zered
AMALEK
EDOM (SEIR)
Waters of Meribah (Kadesh-barnea)

PSALMS

INTRODUCTION[1]

In the Hebrew text the Psalms are entitled *tehillîm,* a word meaning "praises" or "songs of praise." As many of the psalms are not hymnal in the ordinary sense of the term, this title is hardly an accurate description of the contents of the Psalter. The word, however, has become among the Jews the accepted designation for the book, and its primary meaning is of little importance. The English title "Psalms" comes from the Latin *psalmi,* which in turn rests upon ψαλμοί, the title in the Septuagint (Codex Vaticanus). The Septuagint uses ψαλμός to translate מזמור ("psalm" in KJV, RSV), which occurs in the titles of fifty-seven psalms.

I. General Character

The Psalter comprises one hundred and fifty religious poems which were brought together a few centuries before the Christian Era opened. While it is an integral part of the scriptures of Israel, it possesses certain traits which set it off from the rest of the Old Testament. Many portions of the Old Testament are to be described as the words of man addressed to man: this is true of most of the historical writings and of much of the wisdom literature. Other parts purport to be the words of God addressed to man: this is especially so of the prophetic writings. The Psalms, however, have the distinction that, to a degree not present in any other part of the Bible, they contain the words of man directed to God. Sometimes the psalmists speak to God directly, in praise, thanksgiving, or supplication. God is also spoken to obliquely, as in the psalms of trust or in the more didactic poems. But in either case the psalmists' thoughts and feelings are turned Godward, and their words furnish us with the supreme example in the Old Testament of man's search for and experience of the living God. The Psalms thus give us glimpses into the inner religion of some of Israel's select souls. At times, as we survey the

[1] William R. Taylor died before he had finished writing the Introduction and Exegesis to the book of Psalms, and his friend and colleague W. Stewart McCullough completed the work.

religion of the Old Testament, we are impressed with the importance that appears to be attached to the due performance of various external acts: procedures to obtain ceremonial cleanliness; the animal sacrifices; the ritual of the great festivals. Over against such a type of religious interest, and indeed sometimes alongside it, there also flourished an awareness of the deeper values of the Hebrew faith, and it is to this more spiritual side of Old Testament religion that the Psalms bear eloquent witness.

The Psalms are also notable as being the literary record of a reproducible religious experience. What lies behind these outpourings of Israel's soul can, in fact, be re-enacted both by the sinner and by the saint, by the wayfaring man and by the scholar. Later generations can imitate the psalmists; they can stand, as it were, on their shoulders; they can think their thoughts after them and catch some of their faith and vision; they can, in short, be led by them into the secret of the Most High. Thus the Psalms have served to school the children of men in the mysteries of God; they have been the human vehicle whereby the grace of heaven has come with comforting and strengthening power into the lives of those who fear the Lord.

II. Text and Ancient Versions

A. Hebrew Text.—The third edition of Kittel, *Biblia Hebraica* (1929-37) is based chiefly on a manuscript in Leningrad (B 19A), copied in Cairo A.D. 1008, and believed to rest upon the work of Aaron ben Moses ben Asher of Tiberias in the early tenth century A.D. In the case of the Psalter, Kahle collated B 19A with two other Leningrad manuscripts.[1]

B. Ancient Versions.—The most important of the ancient versions of the Psalms are the Septuagint, the Syriac, and the Latin.

1. The Septuagint.—It is impossible in the present state of Septuagint studies to produce a definitive edition of any part of the Greek Old Testament, including the Psalter. Of the three oldest manuscripts of the Septuagint, only Codex Sinaiticus (fourth century A.D.) contains all the Psalms. Codex Vaticanus (fourth century A.D.) lacks Pss. 105:27–137:6 (Hebrew Pss. 106:27–138:6), and Codex Alexandrinus (fifth century A.D.) lacks Pss. 49:20–79:11 (Hebrew Pss. 50:20–80:11). H. B. Swete[2] offers a handy edition of the Vaticanus text of the Psalter, with the lacuna supplied by Sinaiticus. A. Rahlfs[3] gives an eclectic text based on what the Göttingen group considers to be the best manuscript evidence.

2. The Syriac.—The Syriac Old Testament, while made from the Hebrew probably in the second century A.D., shows some dependence on a Jewish Targum and also upon the Septuagint.[4]

3. The Latin.—*a*) The Old Latin (pre-Jerome). This version, of which there was more than one type, is chiefly of value for throwing light on the Greek text from which it was made.

b) The Latin Psalters of Jerome (346-420). The *Psalterium Romanum* was a rather hastily made revision of the current Old Latin and was based on the Septuagint. Subsequently adopted by the churches of Rome and Italy (until the sixteenth century), it is known as the "Roman Psalter," and is still used in St. Peter's, Rome, in St. Mark's, Venice, and in Milan.

The *Psalterium Gallicanum* was made after 386 in Palestine. It was a new translation of the Psalms, but was based on the current Septuagint. Jerome is thought to have also used Origen's *Hexapla* at Caesarea. Because of its widespread popularity in Gaul, this version became known as the "Gallican Psalter," and as the result of the influence of Pius V (1566-72), it supplies the text of the Psalms in the modern Vulgate.[5]

The Gallican Psalter found its way to England, where in the pre-Reformation period it was the common form of the Latin Psalter. It may be presumed that Coverdale used it for his English Bible of 1535, although he was also indebted to George Joye's Psalter of 1534, which was based on a Latin text by Friar Felix. The Psalter in the Matthew Bible of 1537 was virtually a reprint of Coverdale's. The Great Bible of 1539 (edited by Coverdale) was based on the Matthew Bible, but the Psalms were revised, and they were again revised for the 1540 edition. When the first Book of Common Prayer was compiled in 1549, it did not contain the Psalter, but the Psalms as rendered in the Great Bible were used in conjunction with it. Thus the Great Bible's Psalter became associated from the very beginning with the Anglican liturgy, and when the "Psalms of David" were subsequently added to the Prayer Book, the usage of the Church of England determined that the translation should be that of the Great Bible. In this way the influence of Jerome's second Psalter has been perpetuated beyond the Roman Catholic Church.

The *Psalterium iuxta Hebraeos* was made

[1] P. L. Hedley, reviewing A. Sperber's edition of Kittel, *Biblia Hebraica* in *Journal of Theological Studies*, XXXII (1931), 302.

[2] *The Old Testament in Greek* (Cambridge: Cambridge University Press, 1891), Vol. II.

[3] *Psalmi cum Odis* (Göttingen: Vandenhoeck & Ruprecht, 1931).

[4] For a critical edition of the West Syrian text of the Psalms, see W. E. Barnes, *The Peshitta Psalter* (Cambridge: Cambridge University Press, 1904), which is based on a sixth- or seventh-century codex in the Ambrosian Library in Milan.

[5] For a standard edition of the Vulgate see *Biblia Sacra*, ed. Michael Hetzenauer (Oeniponte: Sumptibus Librariae Academicae Wagnerianae, 1906).

between 390 and 396 from the Hebrew text current in Palestine. It was never used in the public worship of the church.[6]

III. Main Divisions of the Book

The Psalter is divided into five sections or books, viz., Pss. 1–41; 42–72; 73–89; 90–106; 107–150. Each of the first four divisions concludes with a short doxology; the fifth ends with Ps. 150, which both terminates that book and serves as an appropriate finale to the whole Psalter. This division, which antedates the Septuagint, appears to be quite arbitrary and may have been introduced to obtain some correspondence with the five parts of the Law. Nevertheless, the Psalter displays nothing that can properly be called literary structure. The types of psalm referred to on pp. 6-7 are not grouped together, but are scattered promiscuously throughout the book. Moreover, if the Psalter is a compilation (see pp. 7-8), the various sources from which it was drawn are quite broken up. Thus it is clear that the editor had no interest in maintaining their identity. Of the principal collections which lie behind the present Psalter only one has had its unity kept—the psalms entitled in the Revised Standard Version, "A Song of Ascents" (Pss. 120–134).

IV. Music and the Psalms

A. Music in the Religion of Ancient Israel.—Any attempt to reconstruct the temple ceremonies of the religion of the Old Testament has to face a deplorable lack of evidence. There are references in I and II Chronicles to temple ritual, but it is difficult to assess these statements and in particular to know how much of what is recorded goes back to the pre-exilic period. On the other hand, the allusions to the cultus in the prophetic books, while few in number, have the merit of being approximately datable. It is Amos who casually mentions both songs and harp music as the accompaniment of sacrifices in the sanctuary (Amos 5:22-23; cf. 8:3). Similar evidence of vocal and instrumental music in connection with temple rites is found in Isa. 30:29; 64:11; Jer. 33:11. According to Ezra 3:10-11, the foundation laying of the second temple (538 or 520 B.C.) was marked both by praise and by the use of trumpets and cymbals. In view of these references the testimony of I and II Chronicles about the arrangements for vocal and instrumental music in the sanctuary cannot be lightly dismissed (I Chr. 6:31-32; 15:16-24; 16:4-6; 25:1-7; II Chr. 5:11-14). It is of course improbable that the ritual of the Chronicler's age (*ca.* 250 B.C.) can be traced back in its entirety to the reigns of David and Solomon. Much of the temple procedure may have been fully developed only in the Persian period, but we can well believe that there was a continuous tradition in these matters going back to Israel's early monarchy. Similarly, the record in II Chr. 29 about Hezekiah's reforms in the temple cultus (*ca.* 700 B.C.) may rest upon an authentic source; vss. 25-30 describe the musical arrangements. The evidence of Ben Sirach shows that about 180 B.C. the musical traditions of the Jerusalem temple were substantially the same as those in I and II Chronicles, and that these traditions were believed to be Davidic (Ecclus. 39:15; 47:1-11; 50:1-21).

B. Musical Instruments Mentioned in the Psalms. 1. Wind Instruments.—חצצרות (98:6): "trumpets." A trumpet ("clarion," Köhler) was apparently a long straight metal tube (of silver in Num. 10:2) with a flaring end. Sometimes it was used for secular purposes (II Kings 11:14), but more commonly it was blown by priests in wartime, on various festal occasions, and as an accompaniment of certain sacrifices (Num. 10:8-10).

נחילות in the title of Ps. 5 is thought by the RSV to mean "flutes."

עוגב (150:4): "pipe," "organs," "flute" (Köhler). Possibly a reed pipe.

שופר (47:5; etc.): usually rendered "trumpet," but in 98:6 the RSV uses "horn" and the KJV uses "cornet." This was of curved animal's horn (of the ram or the wild goat). It was used in war (Judg. 3:27; 6:34; etc.), on state occasions (I Kings 1:34, 39; etc.), and for religious purposes (Lev. 25:9; Joel 2:15; II Chr. 15:14).

2. Stringed Instruments.—כנור (33:2; etc.): "lyre," "harp"; in 150:3 the RSV renders as "harp." Köhler takes as "zither." Used for secular purpose (Gen. 31:27; I Sam. 16:16; etc.); by prophets (I Sam. 10:5); for various religious purposes (II Sam. 6:5; I Chr. 13:8; 15:16; etc.); played by Levites (Neh. 12:27). In Solomon's time it was made of almug wood (I Kings 10:12). According to Josephus,[7] it had ten strings and was struck with a plectrum, but Jewish coins suggest that it had three, five, or six strings (cf. Fig. 36, Vol. 1, p. 163).

מנים (150:4; RSV reads it also in 45:8): "strings" (RSV); "stringed instruments" (KJV). This word does not occur but is seemingly implied in 33:3 ("play skilfully on the strings").

נבל (57:8; etc.): "harp" (RSV), "psaltery" (KJV); in 150:3 the RSV renders as "lute."

[6] For a critical edition see J. M. Harden, ed., *Psalterium iuxta Hebraeos Hieronymi* (London: Society for Promoting Christian Knowledge, 1922). For a summary of criticism of the generally accepted views of Jerome's work see B. J. Roberts, *The Old Testament Text and Versions* (Cardiff: University of Wales Press, 1951), pp. 247-54.

[7] *Antiquities* VII. 12. 3.

Used for secular purposes (Isa. 5:12; etc.); by prophets (I Sam. 10:5); for religious purposes (II Sam. 6:5). According to Josephus, it had twelve notes and was plucked with the fingers.[8]

נבל עשור: "the harp of ten strings" (33:2), "a ten-stringed harp" (144:9). It is not clear whether this is to be identified with the preceding instrument.

נגינות appears in the titles of six psalms (Pss. 4; 6; etc.) and is rendered "stringed instruments."

עשור (lit., "a ten") appears in 92:3 ("lute" RSV; "an instrument of ten strings" KJV), where it is apparently distinct from the "harp."

3. Percussion Instruments.—צלצלי תרועה (150:5): "loud clashing cymbals" (RSV), "high sounding cymbals" (KJV).

צלצלי שמע (150:5); "sounding cymbals" (RSV), "loud cymbals" (KJV), "tinkling cymbals" (Köhler). On the use of cymbals in David's time see II Sam. 6:5. We may note that Josephus describes ordinary cymbals (מצלתים) as "large broad plates of brass." [9]

תוף (81:2; 149:3; 150:4; RSV reads it also in 68:25): "timbrel." Probably a small flat drum. It was used by ordinary people (Gen. 31:27; Judg. 11:34; etc.), by prophets (I Sam. 10:5), and in a kind of religious dance (II Sam. 6:5).

C. "Selah."—This word is used seventy times in the Psalter (3:2, 4, 8; 4:2, 4; etc.), and three times elsewhere in the O.T. (Hab. 3:3, 9, 13). It would appear to be a musical term or direction, but its precise significance has not been determined.

V. Purpose of Composition

A. The Psalms as Liturgical Literature.—Since, as has been shown above (see p. 5), both vocal and instrumental music played a part in the temple cultus, and since there are numerous references in the psalms to musical instruments (see pp. 5-6), to singing (7:17; 9:2, 11; 18:49; etc.), and to temple activities (see p. 13), it seems reasonable to suppose that some of the psalms, perhaps the majority, had a cultic origin, or at least were adapted to liturgical purposes. Solomon's prayer (I Kings 8:31-53) indicates some of the situations which brought men to the temple, and suitable prayers for such occasions must have been in demand. Meritorious poems meant originally for particular cultic needs doubtless survived to be used on later occasions, perhaps with some alterations or additions, and thus collections of sacred songs and prayers were built up by the temple staff. Sigmund Mowinckel would further claim that members of the temple personnel, presumably with some poetic gifts, were largely responsible for the creation of the cultic psalms. A variation of this view is that some of the psalms should be ascribed to prophets (cultic prophets) who were closely associated with the temple and its services.[10]

B. The Psalms as Private Prayers.—While most of the psalms appear to have had a cultic origin, a number of them cannot be directly related to the cultus and must be set down as devotional poetry which has become part of Israel's psalmody. Among these, Pss. 1; 112; 127 are to be described as didactic in character, while another group, which is often designated "Psalms of Trust" (e.g., Pss. 11; 16; 23; 27:1-6; 62; 131), and which shows some evidence of adaptation to community usage, may originally have had no connection with temple procedures. Such psalms are obviously akin, at least in form and to some degree in content and intent, to the poems scattered throughout the Old Testament (e.g., Gen. 49:2-27; Exod. 15:1-18; Deut. 32:1-43; Judg. 5; I Sam. 2:1-10; Hab. 3; etc.), and they remind us of the prayers of Jeremiah (11:18-20; 12:1-4; 15:15-18; etc.).

VI. Types of Psalms

A. Gunkel's Classification.—All commentators have recognized that the Psalter comprises psalms of different types, but it is Hermann Gunkel's distinction that he proposed a classification which has met with a wider acceptance than that of any other modern scholar.[11] Gunkel's scheme is too elaborate to be recorded here, but the principal varieties which it detects in the Psalter are as follows:

1. "Hymns" (e.g., Pss. 8; 19; 29; 33; etc.) were intended to praise God and were meant primarily for the choral part of the temple ceremonies.
2. "Laments of the Community" (e.g., Pss. 44; 74; 79; etc.) arose out of national calamities, presented the nation's cause to God, and asked for his intervention. Judith 4:8-15 describes a situation in which such laments would be used.[12]
3. "Royal Psalms" (e.g., Pss. 2; 18; 20; etc.) are concerned with a reigning Hebrew king,

[8] *Ibid.*

[9] *Ibid.*

[10] On the liturgical origin of the Psalms see John P. Peters, *The Psalms as Liturgies* (New York: The Macmillan Co., 1922), and Mowinckel, *Psalmenstudien I-VI* (Kristiania: Jacob Dybwad, 1921-24).

[11] *Die Psalmen* (Göttingen: Vandenhoeck & Ruprecht, 1926; "Göttinger Handkommentar zum Alten Testament"); see also Hermann Gunkel and Joachim Begrich, *Einleitung in die Psalmen* (Göttingen: Vandenhoeck & Ruprecht, 1933; "Göttinger Handbuch zum Alten Testament").

[12] For the general structure of a lament see Exeg. on Ps. 6:4-5.

and as there is no reason for placing them in the second or first century B.C., when the Hasmoneans ruled in Judea, they must be dated prior to 587 B.C., when the Davidic monarchy terminated.

4. "Individual Laments" (e.g., Pss. 3; 5; 6; 7; 13; etc.) are the commonest type in the Psalter and are the counterpart of the "Laments of the Community." Such a psalm is the cry of an individual to God for succor from a variety of trying circumstances. This interpretation of certain psalms represents a reaction to a view which at one time was much in vogue—that the "I" of the psalms is not an individual but a personification of the nation. In these individual laments there are numerous references to the psalmists' enemies, and much effort has been expended in attempts to establish their identity. Gunkel favored the view that they were self-righteous or oppressive neighbors, but Mowinckel would think of them as sorcerers and their demonic allies, and Hans Schmidt considers them as false accusers in the law courts.

5. "Individual Songs of Thanksgiving" (e.g., Pss. 30; 32; 34; etc.) are individual expressions of gratitude to God for mercies received. Most of them appear to be connected with ceremonies in the temple during which the worshiper gives tangible evidence of his thankfulness.

6. In addition to these five main categories Gunkel recognized other groups, either as subclasses of his main varieties or as clearly defined minor types. Among these need be cited only: (*a*) "Enthronement Songs" (e.g., Pss. 47; 93; etc.), which are hymns of an eschatological kind, celebrating the Lord's enthronement as king of the universe; (*b*) "Psalms of Confidence" (e.g., Pss. 4; 11; 16; 23; etc.), which are regarded as an offshoot of the individual lament; (*c*) "Wisdom Poetry" (e.g., Pss. 1; 37; 49; etc.); (*d*) "Liturgies" (e.g., Pss. 8; 42–43; 46; etc.) are intended for cultic use; they may contain antiphonal elements, and often result from the conflation of different literary types; (*e*) "Prophetic Liturgies" (e.g., Pss. 12; 75; etc.) are liturgical poems containing oracles in prophetic style presumably uttered by some temple functionary; (*f*) "Mixed Poems" (e.g., Pss. 9–10; 40; 78; etc.).

B. Mowinckel's Views.—Probably the scholar next to Gunkel who has influenced most powerfully the modern study of the Psalter is Mowinckel. As noted above (see p. 6), Mowinckel claimed that nearly all the psalms are cultic in origin. He also argued that about forty-three psalms belong to a distinctive type, "The Psalms of Yahweh's Enthronement." His thesis was that on the New Year's Day in Israel there was an annual celebration of the Lord's enthronement as the universal king, and that many psalms are to be regarded as having originated on this occasion.[13]

In actual fact we know almost nothing about the New Year celebration in Old Testament times, and the theory that it was marked by a ritual drama (comparable to the New Year festival in Babylon) is highly speculative. Moreover, while much of Israel's popular religion must have moved on a fairly primitive level, the idea that the Hebrew God could in any real sense be enthroned annually was poor theology, and could hardly have been seriously held by the nation's religious leaders. At the most there may have been some public recognition on New Year's Day of the Lord's sovereign power. To suppose that a large proportion of the extant psalms of Israel should have had their origin in this connection is quite improbable.[14]

VII. The Psalter as a Compilation

The generally accepted view is that the Psalter as we now have it results from the compilation of a number, or portions of a number, of existing collections of psalms. We can, however, only theorize about the precise way in which the compiling was done.

A. The Principal Facts.—The following considerations would appear to support the conclusion that there are different strata within the Psalter, and that these in turn rest upon separate collections of psalms:

1. The variety in the types of psalms, in the historical situations that seem to lie behind the psalms, and in the religious experience of the psalmists.

2. The duplications within the Psalter: Ps. 14=Ps: 53; 40:13-17=Ps. 70; 57:7-11 and 60:5-12 =Ps. 108.

3. The usage with respect to the names for God: in Pss. 1–41, Lord (Yahweh) is the commonest name for God, the term God (Elohim) being employed infrequently; in Pss. 42–83 the frequency of the two names is reversed, whereas in Pss. 90–150 God (Elohim) is relatively uncommon; the shortened form for Lord (Yah) does not occur in Pss. 1–76.

4. The statement in 72:20 that "the prayers of David, the son of Jesse, are ended."

[13] See Intro. to Pss. 47; 93 for a discussion of Mowinckel's proposal; cf. A. R. Johnson, "The Psalms" in H. H. Rowley, ed., *The Old Testament and Modern Study* (Oxford: Clarendon Press, 1951), pp. 190-91.

[14] For a criticism of Mowinckel's views see Moses Buttenwieser, *The Psalms* (Chicago: University of Chicago Press, 1938), pp. 321-24; N. H. Snaith, *The Jewish New Year Festival* (London: Society for Promoting Christian Knowledge, 1947), pp. 195-220.

5. The titles ascribe the psalms to various personages, the commonest names being David, "the choirmaster" (RSV), the sons of Korah, and Asaph; Pss. 120–134 bear the caption "A Song of Ascents" (RSV).

6. Of the thirty-four psalms without titles, twenty-eight are found between Pss. 91–150.

7. There are no musical terms in the titles of Pss. 90–150.

B. The Process of Compilation.—The compilation of the Psalter may have taken place along the following lines:

An editor made a selection from a Davidic collection of psalms and appended to it the statement, "The prayers of David, the son of Jesse, are ended" (72:20). Whether this selection comprised all the Davidic psalms now found in Pss. 1–72 or only Pss. 3–41 (all of which are Davidic except Pss. 10; 33) is uncertain.

Another editor at a later date expanded the material described above by attaching to it (*a*) additional Davidic psalms; (*b*) selections from two Levitical collections (Korah and Asaph); (*c*) miscellaneous items such as Pss. 1; 2; 66; etc. He thus produced Pss. 1–89. This collection was later revised by an editor who apparently preferred "Elohim" as the appellative for God, but why this revision was confined to Pss. 42–83 is obscure.

At a still later date another editor added (*a*) twenty-eight psalms without any title (Pss. 91; 93–97; etc.); (*b*) fifteen (Pss. 120–134) with the title "A Song of Ascents" (RSV); (*c*) thirteen "Davidic" psalms (101; 103; etc.); (*d*) sundry poems such as Pss. 90; 92; 98; etc. He, in fact, gathered together Pss. 90–150, and in doing so brought the compilation of Israel's Psalter to a conclusion.

VIII. Superscriptions

All the psalms have titles (superscriptions) prefixed to them with the exception of the thirty-four "orphans" (Pss. 1–2; 10; 33; 43; 71; 91; 93–97; 99; 104–107; 111–119; 135–137; 146–150). These titles, which are not free from obscurity, either describe the character of the poem, or furnish some liturgical or musical direction, or indicate the author or the source of the psalm, or suggest the circumstances under which the psalm arose. It is generally agreed that the titles are later than the psalms to which they are attached, and that they are of little value for the interpretation of the individual psalms. But the Septuagint bears witness that the titles belong to the pre-Christian period, and we must treat them as preserving certain Jewish traditions about the psalms and as likely to shed some light on the way the Psalter was compiled.

A. Names and Technical Terms.—1. "Alamoth" occurs only in Ps. 46 and in I Chr. 15:20. The word is merely the transliteration of the Hebrew for "young women," but the meaning in the context of the Psalter is not known. It may refer to a tune, a musical instrument, or mean "for women's voices."

2. "Asaph" appears in Pss. 50; 73–83. In the Old Testament Asaph occurs as the name of at least three individuals, and doubtless it was used of others as well. In I Chr. 6:39; 15:17, Asaph the son of Berechiah is reported to have been one of David's chief musicians. It is usually assumed that "the sons of Asaph" referred to in Nehemiah's time as singers (Neh. 7:44) were a musical guild going back to the Asaph of David's time. In the Psalter, Asaph presumably refers either to this guild, or to their hymnal, or to some well-known individual.

3. "Ascents, Song of." See Exeg. on 120:1-7.

4. "Choirmaster" is prefixed to fifty-five psalms. This meaning of the word is tolerably certain, but its use in the Psalter is obscure. Possibly the psalms to which it is attached were taken from a collection belonging or dedicated to an unknown precentor.

5. "David, of," found in seventy-three titles (seventy-two in RSV, which erroneously omits it from Ps. 133), can also mean "belonging to David," "dedicated to David," "with respect to David." Probably the phrase indicates that a psalm to which it is prefixed belonged originally to a Davidic collection of songs.[15]

6. "Dedication of the Temple" occurs in Ps. 30. The first temple was built by Solomon in the tenth century B.C., and the second in the days of Haggai and Zechariah (520-516 B.C.), both occasions being marked by dedication ceremonies (I Kings 8:1-66; Ezra 6:14-18). Major repairs to the sanctuary (II Kings 12:1-16; 22:1-7) may also have had some concluding ritual. In 164 B.C. the second temple was rededicated by Judas Maccabaeus (I Macc. 4:52-59), and this was the beginning of the annual Jewish festival of Hanukkah ("dedication"). The chanting of Ps. 30 came eventually to be part of the Hanukkah celebration, and its title may reflect this Jewish usage.

7. "Do Not Destroy" appears in Pss. 57–59; 75, and is presumably a reference to a familiar song. Isa. 65:8 suggests that it was a vintage melody.

8. "Dove on Far-off Terebinths" occurs in Ps. 56. "Terebinths" is a slightly emended, or at least repointed, text. The reference may be to a tune.

9. "Ethan the Ezrahite," found in Ps. 89, may be the Levitical singer of David's time (I Chr. 6:44), although another Ethan, also called the

[15] On the Davidic authorship of the Psalms see p. 10.

Ezrahite, is referred to as a wise man in I Kings 4:31. "Ezrahite" means "of the family of Zerah," and in I Chr. 2:6, Ethan and Heman are mentioned as the sons of Zerah. But an Ezrahite was a Judean and could hardly be a Levite. Possibly the title confuses two different persons.

10. "Flutes," found in Ps. 5, appears only here in the Old Testament. It is probably a musical term, but the meaning is uncertain.

11. "Gittith" is found in the titles of Pss. 8; 81; 84, but it has not been satisfactorily explained. It may be the name of a vintage tune (*gath* is the Hebrew for "wine press").

12. "Heman the Ezrahite," found in Ps. 88, may be the Levitical singer of David's time (I Chr. 6:33). To term him "the Ezrahite" is probably incorrect (see paragraph 9 above).

13. "Hind of the Dawn," found only in Ps. 22, is generally assumed to be the name of a melody.

14. "Instruction, for," is found in Ps. 60, which is the only psalm to be so entitled, although the contents of this poem can hardly be described as didactic.

15. "Jeduthun" appears in Pss. 39; 62; 77. It is the name of the leader of a Levitical choir in Solomon's time (II Chr. 5:12); it is also given to Josiah's seer (II Chr. 35:15) and to a Levite in Nehemiah's age (Neh. 11:17). The word may have become a musical term, but if so, its significance escapes us.

16. "Korah, Sons of," found in Pss. 42; 44–49; 84–85; 87–88, may refer to a guild of temple singers whose traditions possibly went back to Korah, the great-grandson of Levi (Num. 16:1-50; I Chr. 6:31-38; II Chr. 20:19).

17. "Lilies" occurs in Pss. 45; 69; 80 (cf. Ps. 60). The word is usually taken to mean "lilies," although the American Translation favors "hyacinths" (Song of S. 2:2, 16). The reference may be to a tune.

18. "Love Song," found only in Ps. 45, is appropriate in a wedding song.

19. "Mahalath" appears in Pss. 53; 88. It may point to a tune. A very similar word is used as a woman's name in Gen. 28:9; II Chr. 11:18.

20. "Mahalath Leannoth" occurs in Ps. 88 (on "Mahalath" see 19 above). "Leannoth" ("for affliction" or "for singing") may be the designation of a melody.

21. "Maskil," which appears in thirteen titles, is of uncertain meaning. One etymology suggests a didactic or meditative psalm, but the usage of the word in the Psalter does not bear this out. The Revised Standard Version translates it as "psalm" in 47:7.

22. "Memorial Offering," in Pss. 38; 70, is an infinitive (lit., "to commemorate") with the force of a noun. Probably the reference is to the memorial offering in Lev. 2:2, 9; etc.

23. "Miktam" is an obscure word occurring in Pss. 16; 56–60. Mowinckel[16] suggests that it points to certain psalms as having an atoning or expiatory function.

24. "Moses" appears only in Ps. 90.

25. "Muth-labben" is an obscure expression found only in Ps. 9. It may be the name of a tune or a corruption of "Alamoth."

26. "Praise, Song of," appears only in Ps. 145. Its plural (*tᵉhillîm*) is the Jewish designation of the Psalms.

27. "Prayer" occurs in Pss. 17; 86; 90; 102; 142 (cf. "the prayers of David" in Ps. 72:20).

28. "Prayer of One Afflicted, etc.," actually describes the mood and contents of Ps. 102.

29. "Psalm" (מזמור) occurs in fifty-seven psalms and nowhere else in the Old Testament. The cognate verb in Ps. 7:17 is translated "sing praise," and in Ps. 27:6, "make melody." Probably the noun means "song."

30. "Sabbath, A Song for the," appears only in Ps. 92, the single reference in the Psalter to the sabbath. The title indicates that this psalm was thought to be particularly appropriate for use on the sabbath (cf. Mishnah, Tamid 7:4).

31. "Sheminith" is a term found in Pss. 6; 12, and elsewhere in the Old Testament only in I Chr. 15:21. It appears to be a musical reference. It is, lit., "eighth," but the meaning is not clear.

32. "Shiggaion" appears only in Ps. 7 (the plural is found in Hab. 3:1). The meaning is not known.

33. "Shushan Eduth" appears in Ps. 60. "Shushan" is the singular of "lilies," which occurs in the title of Ps. 45. "Eduth," which means "testimony," is found in the title of Ps. 80. The combination, "The Lily of Testimony," may be the name of a tune.

34. "Solomon" appears in Pss. 72; 127. In Ps. 72 the idealized picture of a king may have suggested the ascription; in Ps. 127 the reference to "the house" may have been thought to indicate Solomon's temple.

35. "Song" (שיר) appears in thirty titles and is a general term for both secular and religious songs.

36. "Stringed Instruments" appears in six titles (Pss. 4; 6; 54; 55; 67; 76); the Revised Standard Version emends the Masoretic Text to find this caption also in Ps. 61. It doubtless refers to the instrumental accompaniment.

37. "Testimony" occurs only in Ps. 80 and is virtually equivalent to "psalm." It is possible, however, that the Hebrew is slightly corrupt

[16] *Psalmenstudien*, "Die technischen Termini in den Psalmenüberschriften" (Kristiania: Jacob Dybwad, 1921-24), IV, 4-5.

and that the text should be "Shushan Eduth," as in Ps. 60.

38. "Thank Offering," in Ps. 100, reflects the liturgical use of this psalm in connection with the thank offering (Lev. 7:11-21).

B. Historical Allusions.—Thirteen titles purport to describe the historical circumstances under which the psalms arose. The psalms to which they are prefixed are associated with the name of David, and the titles undoubtedly reflect a desire to find the occasions for certain psalms in particular incidents in the life of David.

Ps. 3. "When he fled, etc.": cf. II Sam. 15:1–18:33.

7. "Concerning Cush a Benjaminite": this individual is not mentioned in the biblical account of David.

18. "Who addressed the words, etc.": cf. I Sam. 19:1-17; 24:1-22; 26:1-25; II Sam. 5:17-25; 8:1-14; 10:1-19; 15:1–18:33; 21:15-22.

34. "When he feigned, etc.": cf. I Sam. 21:10-15, where, however, the Gentile king is Achish, not Abimelech.

51. "When Nathan the prophet, etc.": cf. II Sam. 11:1–12:31.

52. "When Doeg the Edomite, etc.": cf. I Sam. 22:6-23.

54. "When the Ziphites, etc.": cf. I Sam. 23:14-29.

56. "When the Philistines, etc.": according to I Sam. 21:10-15; 22:1; 27:1-7, David's sojourn in Gath was on his own initiative.

57. "When he fled, etc.": cf. I Sam. 22:1-2; 24:1-7.

59. "When Saul sent, etc.": cf. I Sam. 19:8-17.

60. "When he strove, etc.": cf. II Sam. 8:3-14; 10:15-19.

63. "When he was, etc.": probably the allusion is to the flight from Absalom (II Sam. 15:1–17:29; cf. David in the wilderness of En-gedi, I Sam. 24:1-22).

142. "When he was in the cave": cf. I Sam. 22:1-2; 24:1-7.

IX. Authorship and Date

From what has been said above (see pp. 6-10) the conclusion emerges that the Psalter is made up of compositions from various periods in Israel's history. Presumably the final stage in the compilation belongs somewhere between 400 and 200 B.C. Furthermore, as we cannot attach much importance to the titles, at least as far as the origin of the individual psalms is concerned, we can only conclude that the authors are unknown.

We must, however, take cognizance of the opinion that David wrote the psalms. This was the ancient Jewish tradition, and it probably lies behind the statement of Josephus that David "composed songs and hymns to God in varied meters."[17] Similarly, the Mishnah (200 A.D.) prefaces the quotation of Ps. 119:72 thus: "It is written in the Book of Psalms by David king of Israel" (Aboth 6:9). This tradition became part of the heritage of the early church, and in the New Testament the psalms are not only freely quoted, but their Davidic authorship is assumed (e.g., Mark 12:36-37; Rom. 4:6-8; 11:9-10; etc.). The latter assumption is made even when the psalms referred to are without any ascription to David either in the Masoretic Text or in the Septuagint (e.g., Acts 4:25-26; Heb. 4:7).

We do not know how early the authority of David's name became attached to the Psalms as a whole. We may surmise that it was encouraged by such considerations as (*a*) the desire to have the prestige of the scriptures enhanced by the authorship of illustrious figures of the past; (*b*) the fact that seventy-three psalms are connected by their titles with David; (*c*) the tradition that David was a musician and poet (I Sam. 16:17-23; 18:10; Amos 6:5; II Sam. 1:17-27; 3:33-34; 23:1-7); (*d*) the tradition which credits David with organizing the choral side of Israel's public worship (Ezra 3:10; Neh. 12:24, 36, 45-46; II Chr. 29:30; Ecclus. 47:7-9).

To treat the traditions referred to in (*c*) and (*d*) of the preceding paragraph as entirely fictitious cannot be regarded as a sober appraisal of them, for it is possible that they contain a measure of truth. Nor in our state of limited knowledge can we dogmatically assume that the religious level of the Psalms is entirely incongruent with the character of David and the times in which he lived. It is indeed conceivable that David was a "sweet psalmist" (II Sam. 23:1), and that he left some religious lyrics which were treasured by later generations. Whether any of these songs are now to be found in the Psalter, and if so, how they are to be identified, it is impossible to say. But only the assumption that David was a stimulating influence on Israel's sacred poetry seems adequate to account for the later Davidic tradition.

At one time it was considered almost axiomatic that the Aramaisms of the Psalms were conclusive proof that the poems which displayed them were late in origin. It is of course true that in the Persian and Greek periods the Aramaic language was coming into more common use among the Jews, as the Elephantine Papyri and the Aramaic portions of the books of Ezra and Daniel testify (Ezra 4:8–6:18; 7:12-26; Dan. 2:4*b*–7:28). But it is also evident from II Kings 18:26 that as early as the eighth

[17] *Antiquities* VII. 12. 3.

century Aramaic was known to certain groups in Jerusalem, and since the Hebrews and the Aramaic-speaking peoples from then on were under a common political overlord, it is probable that Aramaic became increasingly familiar in Judah. To cite "Aramaisms" as evidence of the late date of a psalm is therefore a highly questionable procedure.

X. Canonization

The Psalms are found in the third division of the Hebrew Bible. This division, known as "The Writings," was apparently the last part of the Old Testament to be recognized as canonical. In Luke 24:44 "the psalms" are referred to (along with "the law of Moses" and "the prophets") as scripture, but we do not know how early they were accepted as such. In I Macc. 7:17 (*ca.* 90-70 B.C.) Ps. 79:2-3 is quoted, seemingly as scripture. In the prologue to Ecclesiasticus (*ca.* 132 B.C.), in addition to the Law and the Prophets, a third group of writings is referred to—"the other books of our forefathers" and "the rest of the books." It is probable that the Psalms were included in this third section. In the text of Ecclesiasticus (about 180 B.C.), it is said of David,

Over all that he did he gave thanks
To the Holy One, the Most High, with words of praise.
He sang praise with his whole heart (Ecclus. 47:7-8 Goodspeed).

This may point to the acceptance of the Psalter as scripture in the early second century B.C. In any case the Psalms, by reason of their employment in the temple ceremonies, must have established a peculiarly warm place in Israel's affections, and their association with the Law and the Prophets was doubtless a very natural one. We may note that in II Macc. 2:13, Nehemiah (*ca.* 445 B.C.) is credited with collecting "the works of David," which may indicate the creation of a Davidic Psalter in the fifth century B.C.

XI. Poetic Structure

The poetry of the Psalms exhibits the same features as the other poetical parts of the Old Testament. Its principal characteristics may be summarized as follows:

A. Rhythm.—The Hebrews were unfamiliar with meter in the European sense. But a line of Hebrew poetry is usually broken into two or more parts, each of which is called a "stich," and each stich has two, three, or four stressed words. These stressed words, especially if their number is constant in the successive lines, give a poem a certain recognizable rhythm. The term meter then comes to mean the arrangement of accented words which a given poem displays. For instance,

Save mé, O God, by thy náme,
  and vindicate mé by thy míght.
Héar my práyer, O Gód;
  give éar to the words of my móuth (54:1-2);

this is said to employ a 3+2 meter. Other meters are 2+2, 3+3, 3+2+2, 2+2+2. In many cases one meter is not used consistently throughout a psalm, and various mixtures appear.

B. Parallelism.—It was Robert Lowth who in 1753 first noted that the lines of Hebrew poetry, or the parts of a line, were closely related to one another, and he called this relationship "parallelism of verse-members," of which he indicated three types: (*a*) Synonymous, in which the second stich or line repeats the thought of the first:

Hear this, all peoples!
  Give ear, all inhabitants of the world (49:1).

(*b*) Antithetic, in which the second stich presents some antithesis to the first:

For the LORD knows the way of the righteous,
  but the way of the wicked will perish (1:6).

(*c*) Synthetic, in which the second stich supplements or completes the first:

I cry aloud to the LORD,
  and he answers me from his holy hill (3:4).

Since Lowth's time other varieties of parallelism have been detected by various scholars, but most of them are in fact minor variations of the three described above.

C. Stanzas.—There is some evidence that many of the psalmists grouped their lines into what we may call "stanzas" or "strophes," some of which are couplets, others are longer. In some cases stanzas are clearly indicated by the content of the poem, in others by the appearance of a refrain. There is, however, no convincing evidence that all psalmists employed stanzas, or that the stanzas within a single poem were necessarily of equal length. Ps. 114 illustrates the use of couplets; Ps. 107, stanzas of unequal length; and Pss. 42–43, a refrain (42:5, 11; 43:5).

D. Acrostic Structure.—A number of psalms (Pss. 9–10; 25; 34; 37; 111; 112; 119; 145) are based upon the acrostic principle, that is, each stich, line, or couplet commences with a fresh letter of the Hebrew alphabet. The most ex-

treme example of this is Ps. 119. Such a method of composition was a literary fad, and it made for considerable artificiality in the psalmist's achievement.[18]

XII. Religion of the Psalmists

As the psalms were written in a variety of circumstances and over a long period of time, we cannot expect them either to reveal a uniform point of view or to present a carefully worked out system of theology. Poetry is hardly the medium best adapted for religious speculation, and we must not look for a theological scheme in a collection of hymns and prayers intended for practical purposes. The psalmists have appropriated in varying degree the great truths of Israel's religion, and these truths, often compounded with matters of secondary worth, furnish the theological framework of the Psalms. But a systematic treatment of Israel's faith is quite foreign to the design of these poems.

A. God.—The conception of God behind the psalms is a monotheistic one. It is true that there are occasional allusions to "gods," and while these may be concessions to popular thought, it seems preferable to take them as a reflection of the view that the Lord presides over a heavenly court (see Exeg. on Ps. 82). Although it is generally assumed that God is enthroned in heaven (33:13; 53:2; 103:19; 123:1; etc.), there are traces of the belief that Zion is his habitation (132:13-14). Such a difference is readily resolved if we follow the author of 139:7-12, and find God everywhere.

Righteousness, justice, mercy, and faithfulness—these are grounded in God himself and are the basic principles of his government of the world (89:14; 97:2). An even more important truth, to which the psalmists come back again and again, is that the Lord is gracious: he forgives iniquity and lends a willing ear to the petitions of his servants (4:1; 5:1; 6:2; etc.). But above all, God is such that to be in communion with him is life's *summum bonum:* "In thy presence there is fullness of joy" (16:11; cf. 21:6).

B. The World.—The psalmists do not display any abstract love of nature or of the beauties of the out of doors; attempts to capture colors and other sense impressions are largely absent from their poems. Their real interest in the outside world is a religious one: they look upon the heavens and the earth as the handiwork of God, and they see in the so-called processes of nature the Lord's active providence. Two striking treatments of God in the thunderstorm are found in 18:7-15 and 29:1-11. The psalmist who deals most fully with God's great creative acts in the past is the author of Ps. 104, but even he is also concerned with God's continuing mercies in the present. Again, in 65:6-13 we find that the God whose strength has established the mountains is the same who ever and anon visits the earth and crowns the year with his bounty.

C. Man.—To the author of Ps. 8 man is the acme of God's creation and the master of the animal world (cf. Gen. 1:28). At the same time the psalmist expresses surprise that God should be mindful of man (cf. 144:3). Possibly his astonishment is due to his awareness of man's mortality. While a human life may extend to seventy or eighty years (90:10), man's final lot is to perish like the beasts or the flowers of the field (39:4-6; 49:12; 89:47-48; 90:3-10; 103:14-15; 144:4). The view of death which dominates the psalms is that in Sheol there is no remembrance or praise of the Lord (6:5; 30:9; 88:3-12; 115:17). It is only in such passages as 49:15; 73:23-26, that there may be a hint of the hope of survival beyond death.

The Psalms voice man's sense of his dependence on and need of God. But God's requirements of man must be met, and in 15:1-5; 24:3-6; 34:12-14; 50:18-21 these are stated to be largely moral. Some participation in sacrificial worship is taken for granted (4:5; 20:3; 50:8; 51:19), but in other psalms sacrifice is minimized (40:6; 51:16; 69:30-31). The failure to meet God's demands creates the sense of sin, but in the Psalter the acknowledgment of sin is not conspicuous (cf. 32:5; 38:18; 41:4; 51:1-4; 79:9; 90:8). Much more prominent is the boldness with which the psalmists call upon God. The immediate end of many of their petitions is deliverance from various evil circumstances. Some of the speakers, however, appear to set more store on less tangible benefits. In some cases the greatest good is being in the Lord's house, and in others it is the sheer joy of the Lord's presence (16:11; 17:15; 21:6; 23:6; 27:4; 36:7-9; 42:1; 63:1-4; 65:4; etc.).

D. The People of God.—The Psalter, like the rest of the Old Testament, comes out of the life of the Hebrew people, and it reflects Israel's conception of its peculiar position in God's economy. "The Lord has chosen Jacob for himself" (135:4), and "he has not dealt thus with any other nation" (147:20). "The Lord loves the gates of Zion" (87:2), for the latter site is his "holy hill" (2:6). Numerous references to Israel as God's people (3:8; 14:4, 7; 28:9; etc.) explain why the Lord can be expected to have an interest in "deliverance for Israel" (14:7). The inclusion in the Psalter of eulogies of Israel's law (1:1-6; 19:7-11; 119:1-

[18] For a further discussion of Hebrew poetry see Vol. I, pp. 226-27.

176) is another indication of its Hebrew background. Such laments as Pss. 74; 79 derive much of their force from the conviction that "we [are] thy people, the flock of thy pasture" (79:13), while the royal psalms (Pss. 2; 18; 20; etc.) rest in part upon a rugged Hebrew nationalism, and in them the Gentile nations play a subservient role (2:8; 18:43-47; etc.).

If, however, we take the Psalter as a whole, its particularism does not obtrude itself upon us, as is evidenced by its employment in the devotions of the Christian centuries. Many of the psalms are entirely free of Hebrew exclusiveness (e.g., Pss. 1; 4–8; etc.), while others display it in so slight a degree that it is innocuous (e.g., Pss. 3; 9; 14; etc.). Furthermore, the church's claim to be the true "Israel of God" (Gal. 6:16) has made it easy for Christians to give to the words of the psalmists a much wider meaning than their authors originally intended.

E. The Cultus.—While some psalmists deprecate the sacrificial ritual (40:6; 50:13; 51:16-17; 69:30-31), the majority appear to accept the customary religious procedures. The temple is frequently referred to (5:7; 11:4; 18:6; etc.), as are its courts (65:4; 84:2, 10; 92:13; etc.) and its altars (26:6; 43:4; 51:19; etc.). Curiously, the officiating priesthood receives rather scant mention (115:10, 12; 118:3; 132:9, 16; 135:19-20). There are allusions to the great congregation, sometimes in a religious procession (22:22, 25; 35:18; 40:9-10; 42:4; 68:24-27; 107:32; 111:1; 116:18; 118:26-27; 132:8-9; 149:1). The propriety of sacrifice is assumed (4:5; 20:3; 27:6; 50:8; 51:19; 96:8; 107:22; 116:17), and various types of offering are mentioned: burnt offerings (50:8; 51:19; 66:13); cereal offerings (20:3; 96:8); thank offerings (50:14; 56:12; 107:22; 116:17); freewill offerings (54:6). The payment of vows is another religious duty touched on by the psalmists (22:25; 50:14; 56:12; 61:5, 8; 65:1; 66:13; 76:11; 116:14, 18).

Although the references in the Psalter to cultic practices are numerous, these ceremonial matters are not thrust unduly upon our attention. For the most part they are incidental to the poems in which they appear, and they merely reflect the ritualistic background of the psalmists' religion. In consequence, when the psalms are utilized by religious groups which have left the ceremonies of ancient Israel far behind, it is not difficult to assimilate or ignore the cultic allusions.

It is important to note certain striking omissions from the psalmists' ritualistic vocabulary. There are no references in the psalms to the blood of sacrifices, drink offerings of wine (cf. 16:4), sin offerings (the "sin offering" of 40:6 is not the usual word, and in any case the offering is here disapproved), guilt offerings, or atonement by sacrifice (the verb often rendered "atone" appears in 65:3; 78:38; 79:9, but in these passages the Revised Standard Version translates it correctly as "forgive"). These terms and concepts were of special interest to the priests, as we know from the P document of the Pentateuch, and their omission from the Psalter is rather unexpected in view of two common suppositions: that the Psalter was a hymnbook of the temple, and that some of the psalms were composed by temple personnel.

F. The Nations.—Although some psalms represent the Gentiles as destined to be subordinated to Israel (2:8; 18:43-47; 45:5; 72:10-11; 110:5-6), others strike a more universalistic note. Israel's God reigns over the nations (47:8; cf. 82:8), and his eyes behold and test the children of men (11:4; 14:2; 33:13). While the references to God judging the peoples with equity may be eschatological (9:8; 67:4; 96:13), a number of psalms envisage the time when all men shall praise and worship the Lord (2:11; 22:27-29; 65:2; 66:4; 67:5, 7; 68:32; 86:9; 99:3; 102:15; 117:1; 138:4). We are not told, however, how or when this is to be brought about, or the relation between these Gentile proselytes and the people of Israel.

G. Eschatology.—The Psalter as a whole concerns itself with life's present problems, and in so far as it looks into the future, it is a future in this world, free from sickness, evil, and the machinations of enemies. The author of 27:13 is in this respect typical of the psalmists as a group: he hopes to "see the goodness of the Lord in the land of the living." There is in the Psalter, therefore, little that can properly be called eschatology. Apart from 49:15; 73:24 (see Exeg.), the view of death entertained by the psalmists is that when men die they go to Sheol, where they are cut off from the Lord and are no longer remembered by him (see p. 12). Man's pomp does not survive the grave: both his riches and the praise of his fellows are left behind when he departs from this world (49:16-20). On the other hand, the author of 139:8 dares to address the Lord, "If I make my bed in Sheol, thou art there!"

Some of the psalmists anticipate the time when the Lord will restore the fortunes of his people (14:7; 53:6; 85:4, 9-13; 126:4; 130:8; 135:14). The older view that the psalmists refer to an anointed personage (the Messiah) who would have a share in bringing in Israel's future blessedness, has had to be abandoned, for it is now generally recognized that the "anointed one" of the Psalms (2:2; 18:50; 20:6; etc.) is a reigning Hebrew king. This salvation of Israel may be connected with the destruction of the

wicked (11:6; 37:9-15; 75:8-10), but it is uncertain how we should relate it to the Lord's judgment of the peoples (or of the earth) of which a number of psalmists speak (1:5; 7:7-8; 9:8, 19; 50:6; 58:11; 67:4; 75:2, 7; 82:8; 94:2; 96:10, 13; 98:9). Some of these passages may allude to God's recurring judgments in history, others to a definitive judgment at the end of the age. A few psalms point to demonstrations of the Lord's power on a cosmic scale, including the ending of war (46:8-9; 96:11-13; 98:7-9), and these may be eschatological.[19]

XIII. The Psalms of Israel and the Literatures of the Ancient Near East

The Hebrews of the biblical period lived in a world dominated politically by Gentile nations. These alien cultures were immensely religious in the manner of most polytheisms, and they produced much religious literature. Among the latter we find hymns, thanksgivings, petitions, and prayers to the gods (or to a particular god), as well as a vast number of incantations.[20] A few examples follow:

1. An Egyptian hymn to Amon-Re (before 1350 B.C.).

Hail to thee, Amon-Re,
Lord of the Thrones of the Two Lands, Presiding over Karnak, . . .
Lord of what is, enduring in all things, . . .
The lord of truth and father of the gods.
Who made mankind and created the beasts,
Lord of what is, who created the fruit tree,
Made herbage, and gave life to cattle.[21]

2. An Egyptian hymn in honor of a Pharaoh (Thutmose III, 1490-1436 B.C.).[22]

Welcome to me, as thou exultest at the sight of my beauty, my son and my avenger. . . . I shine forth for love of thee, and my heart is glad at thy good comings into my temple, while my hands endow thy body with protection and life. How sweet is thy graciousness toward my breast!

I establish thee in my dwelling place. I *work a* wonder for thee: I give thee valor and victory over all foreign countries.[23]

3. An Egyptian prayer to the sun-god, Atum Re-Har-akhti (*ca.* 1230 B.C.).

Come to me, O Re-Har-akhti, that thou mayest look after me! Thou art he who does, and there is none who does without thee. . . .

Thou one and only, O Re-Har-akhti! There is no other here like unto him, who protects millions while he rescues hundred-thousands! The protector of him who calls out to him, the Lord of Heliopolis.[24]

4. A Babylonian prayer to the goddess Ishtar (*ca.* seventh or sixth century B.C.).

I pray to thee, O Lady of ladies, goddess of goddesses.
O Ishtar, queen of all peoples, who guides mankind aright, . . .
I have cried to thee, suffering, wearied, and distressed, as thy servant.
See me O my Lady; accept my prayers.
Faithfully look upon me and hear my supplication.
Promise my forgiveness and let thy spirit be appeased.
Pity! For my wretched body which is full of confusion and trouble.
Pity! For my sickened heart which is full of tears and suffering.[25]

5. An Assyrian prayer to Sin, the moon-god (seventh century B.C.).

O Sin, O Nannar, glorified one . . . ,
Sin, unique one, who makes bright . . . ,
Who furnishes light for the people . . . ,
To guide the dark-headed people aright . . . ,
Bright is thy light in heaven. . . .
Brilliant is thy torch like fire. . . .
I am kneeling; I tarry (thus); I seek after thee.
Bring upon me wishes for well-being and justice.
May my god and my goddess, who for many days have been angry with me,
In truth and justice be favorable to me; may my road be propitious; may my path be straight.[26]

The selections cited above merely illustrate what is evident from the general study of man's religions, that when men cry out to their god or gods, their cries have a basic similarity: it is the idiom—and to some extent the concepts—that varies with the particular culture. The Psalms, therefore, may be expected to resemble the hymns and prayers of other peoples, and especially those of the ancient Near East. A more contentious point is whether Israel, as one of the youngest and weakest nations within her cultural orbit, was in any way dependent upon the literatures of the surrounding Gentiles. This problem is exemplified when we compare the Babylonian penitential psalms and the laments of Israel. Here there are close parallels

[19] For another view of the meaning of Pss. 96; 98 see Exeg., *ad loc.* For a further discussion of the religion of the psalms see Vol. I, pp. 336-38.

[20] A representative collection of this material, translated by various scholars, is available in J. B. Pritchard, ed., *Ancient Near Eastern Texts Relating to the Old Testament* (Princeton: Princeton University Press, 1950). Examples printed by permission of the publishers.

[21] Tr. John A. Wilson; *ibid.*, p. 365.

[22] The words are represented as spoken by the god, Amon-Re.

[23] Tr. John A. Wilson; *op. cit.*, pp. 373-74.

[24] *Ibid.*, p. 379.

[25] Tr. Ferris J. Stephens; *ibid.*, p. 384.

[26] *Ibid.*, p. 386.

both in psalm construction and in minor details, and some scholars aver that the Hebrew psalmists were leaning on the Akkadian material.[27] A more convincing argument for Israel's debt to her neighbors has been advanced through the modern study of Ugaritic. John Hastings Patton has shown that there is a surprising number of parallels in language and thought between the psalms and the Ugaritic texts,[28] and W. F. Albright has made the same point.[29] Parallels in poetic form between the two groups of texts have also been detected.[30] It has been further claimed by Albright (who follows Ginsberg) that Ps. 29 is "a relatively little changed adaptation of a Baal hymn to the cult of Yahweh." [31]

Even if the psalmists' dependence on foreign literatures were to be decisively proved, it is not clear that this would be a matter of great moment or that it would in any way be derogatory of Israel's religious achievement. For whatever the Hebrews took over from their Gentile neighbors they adapted to their own purposes and transformed it by their own genius into something fit for their national life or for the Lord's service. As far as poetry is concerned, the Psalms stand up rather well when compared with other similar literatures. Indeed, the comparison indicates that in a very real sense the Psalter is *sui generis.*

XIV. The Psalms in Jewish Worship

A. Mishnaic Period.—The Mishnah, which was compiled about A.D. 200 and which presents the Jewish traditions of the first two Christian centuries, tells us something about the place of the Psalms in Israel's life during this age. It is, for instance, significant that in the Mishnah there are more quotations from the Psalms than from any other part of the Scriptures, save the Law itself. Psalms are frequently mentioned in connection with the temple ceremonies. In Tamid 7:4 we are told that the Levites used to sing one psalm daily in the temple: the seven psalms rendered each week were Pss. 24; 48; 82; 94; 81; 93; 92. A Levitical choir sang Ps. 30 when the first fruits were brought to the temple court (Bikkurim 3:4), and the Hallel (Pss. 113–118) at the celebration of the Passover (Pesahim 5:7; 9:3; 10:7). The Hallel was also recited on each of the eight days of the feast of Tabernacles (Sukkah 4:1, 8) and of the feast of Dedication or Hanukkah (Taanith 4:4-5). The use of the Hallel at Pentecost is actually not referred to in the Mishnah. We are further informed that apart from the temple ritual, the Psalms served other religious purposes. For example, four psalms (Pss. 120; 121; 130; 102) were used on days of public fasting in time of drought (Taanith 2:3), and the Great Hallel (Ps. 136) was recited in gratitude for rain (Taanith 3:9).

There is little information about the place of the Psalms in the liturgy of the synagogue in the Mishnaic period. We learn from Megillah 4:1-6 that psalms were not used as scripture lessons, for the latter were taken only from the Law and the Prophets. It is generally assumed that some of the liturgy was based on the temple services, and this must have led to the employment of psalms. This inference is borne out by the extensive use of psalms—and by the influence of their style—in the ritual of the later period. The recitation or singing of psalms in the synagogues of the first century doubtless explains why hymn singing became a natural part of the worship of the early church (Acts 16:25; I Cor. 14:15, 26; Eph. 5:19; Col. 3:16; Jas. 5:13).

B. Modern Period.—The modern Jewish prayer book (siddur) has a long history which cannot be summarized here. One may note that it goes back to the siddur of Amram, the head of an academy in Babylonia in the ninth century, and this in turn rests on earlier liturgical practices. A striking feature of the prayer book is its great dependence on the Psalms. Apart from the psalms which are utilized *in toto* in the various services, the prayers and benedictions not only contain numerous verbal quotations from psalms, but their tone and vocabulary are strongly reminiscent of the Psalter.

The use of entire psalms in the prayer book can be illustrated from the regular sabbath services. The sabbath evening (Friday) service commences with the reading of six psalms (Pss. 95–99; 29), which are presently followed by Pss. 92–93. The first part of the sabbath morning (Saturday) service employs Ps. 30; I Chr. 16:8-36 (parts of Pss. 105: 96); Pss. 19; 34; 90; 91; 135–136; 33; 92; 93; 145–150. After the scripture has been read, and when the roll is to be returned to the Ark, Ps. 29 is recited. Other services in the synagogue are similarly enriched

[27] See Geo Widengren, *The Accadian and Hebrew Psalms of Lamentation as Religious Documents* (Uppsala: Almqvist & Wiksells, 1937).

[28] *Canaanite Parallels in the Book of Psalms* (Baltimore: Johns Hopkins Press, 1944).

[29] Vol. I, p. 259; *Archaeology and the Religion of Israel* (Baltimore: Johns Hopkins Press, 1942), pp. 128-29.

[30] E.g., Frank M. Cross, Jr., "Notes on a Canaanite Psalm in the Old Testament," *Bulletin of the American Schools of Oriental Research,* No. 117 (1950), pp. 19-21.

[31] "The Psalm of Habakkuk" in H. H. Rowley, ed., *Studies in Old Testament Prophecy* (New York: Charles Scribner's Sons, 1950), p. 6. On the question of Israel's borrowing from an Egyptian source see Exeg. on 104:1-35.

by the Psalms. Thus throughout the centuries the piety of the Jewish people has been nurtured by these hymns and prayers traditionally ascribed to the sweet singer of Israel.

XV. Place of the Psalter in the Church

As has been noted above (see p. 15), it probably was the Jewish use of psalms both in the temple ceremonies and in the synagogues that led the Jewish Christians, and so Christians generally, to employ Israel's psalms in the life of the early church. The Christian hymns found in Luke (Magnificat, Luke 1:46-55; Benedictus, Luke 1:68-79; Nunc dimittis, Luke 2:29-32) are clearly modeled after the psalms, and this familiarity with the Psalter is further illustrated by the numerous quotations from it found in the New Testament. According to A. F. Kirkpatrick,[32] ninety-three passages from the Psalms are quoted in the New Testament, a number of them more than once (e.g., 2:7 is found in Acts 13:33; Heb. 1:5; 5:5).

While worship followed no uniform pattern in early Christianity, it would appear that the Psalter presently established itself as an accepted model for public and private devotions. Pliny the Younger [33] refers to the hymn singing of the Christians in Bithynia (*ca.* 111-13); Ignatius, bishop of Antioch, of about the same time, is credited with introducing antiphonal hymn singing into the church.[34] Tertullian (*ca.* 197) notes that after the Christians' supper was over "each is invited to sing publicly to God as he is able from his knowledge of holy scriptures or from his own mind." [35] Jerome (346-420) in his letters speaks of psalm singing by ordinary people; [36] of a person in the church known as a "psalm singer"; [37] of the chanting of the psalms in Greek, Latin, and Syriac at the death of Paula.[38] As has been indicated (see p. 4), Jerome was himself responsible for three revisions of the Latin Psalter, which testifies to its importance in the life of the church at this period. Jerome's contemporary, Augustine (354-430), writes of the Psalter: "Oh, in what accents spake I unto Thee, my God, when I read the Psalms of David, those faithful songs, and sounds of devotion. . . . Oh, . . . how was I by them kindled toward Thee." [39]

Thus the Psalter became the classical manual for the private devotions of the church, as well as the principal aid in its liturgical services. A thorough knowledge of the Psalms came to be required both of candidates for ordination and of those seeking clerical advancement. In the monasteries the Psalter was systematically recited: in the Benedictine order of the Western Church the whole of it was gone through once a week. If some individuals carried their devotions to the extreme length of repeating the whole of it daily (as is reported of St. Patrick), this at least points to the values which Christendom found in the Psalms. It is significant that the only parts of the Old Testament to obtain a place in the Ordinary of the Mass are 43:1-5; 26:6-12. At an early period Pss. 6; 32; 38; 51; 102; 130; 143 were recognized as the "penitential psalms," and their repetition was considered a prayer against the seven deadly sins. They still appear as such in Roman Catholic prayer books.

It is not necessary to discuss the role which the Psalms have played in the life of the Reformed churches since the sixteenth century. Calvin's words in the preface to his commentary on the Psalms pay a representative tribute:

> The varied and resplendent riches which are contained in this treasury it is no easy matter to express in words. . . . I have been accustomed to call this book, I think not inappropriately, "An Anatomy of all the Parts of the Soul"; for there is not an emotion of which any one can be conscious that is not here represented as in a mirror.[40]

As scripture lessons for the services of the churches, as hymns for groups of worshiping people, as prayers for the devout amid the tribulations of this world, the Psalms have been unique. No other book of the Bible has exercised such a function in the church, and no other book, with the exception perhaps of the Gospels and some of Paul's letters, has gone so directly to the heart of Christendom.

The reasons for the hold of the Psalter on all branches of the church are not hard to find. The Psalms offer a classical expression of the theistic basis of Christianity, and represent in fact the spiritual continuity between the religion of Israel and the Christian gospel. Moreover, as Calvin perceived, they portray a variety of religious moods, and this, as well as the relative shortness of each psalm, makes them easily adaptable for liturgical purposes. Like much of the Old Testament, they use simple and concrete words and on the whole are free from extravagance of expression; thus they have furnished the church with a chaste devotional vocabulary. Above all, they have tutored

[32] *The Book of Psalms* (Cambridge: Cambridge University Press, 1902; "Cambridge Bible"), pp. 838-40.

[33] *Letters* X. 96.

[34] Socrates Scholasticus *Ecclesiastical History* VI. 8.

[35] *Apology* XXXIX. 18.

[36] *Epistles* XLVI. 12.

[37] *Ibid.* LII. 5.

[38] *Ibid.* CVIII. 30.

[39] *Confessions* IX. 4.

[40] *Commentary on the Book of Psalms*, tr. James Anderson (Grand Rapids: W. B. Eerdmans, 1949), I, xxxvi-xxxvii.

Christian believers both in private prayer and in communal worship. Behind, in, and through these ancient words the church has found the promptings of the Spirit of God.

XVI. Selected Bibliography

CALÈS, JEAN. *Le livre des Psaumes.* Paris: G. Beauchesne et ses fils, 1936.

GUNKEL, HERMANN. *Die Psalmen* ("Göttinger Handkommentar zum Alten Testament"). Göttingen: Vandenhoeck & Ruprecht, 1926.

JAMES, FLEMING. *Thirty Psalmists.* New York: G. P. Putnam's Sons, 1938.

KIRKPATRICK, A. F. *The Book of Psalms* ("Cambridge Bible"). Cambridge: Cambridge University Press, 1902.

LESLIE, ELMER. *The Psalms.* New York and Nashville: Abingdon-Cokesbury Press, 1949.

OESTERLEY, W. O. E. *The Psalms.* New York: The Macmillan Co., 1939.

PATERSON, JOHN. *The Praises of Israel.* New York: Charles Scribner's Sons, 1950.

SCHMIDT, HANS. *Die Psalmen* ("Handbuch zum Alten Testament"). Tübingen: J. C. B. Mohr, 1934.

WEISER, ARTUR. *Die Psalmen* ("Das Alte Testament deutsch"). Göttingen: Vandenhoeck & Ruprecht, 1950.

PSALMS

TEXT, EXEGESIS, AND EXPOSITION

1 Blessed *is* the man that walketh not in the counsel of the ungodly, nor standeth

1 Blessed is the man
who walks not in the counsel of the wicked,

I. THE TWO WAYS OF LIFE (1:1-6)

This psalm serves as a prologue to the whole Psalter. When the final work of drawing together the different components of the book had been completed, it was a happy inspiration that led the editors to choose for it such an introduction. Brief as the psalm is, its contents portray vividly the type of man who will feed on the words of the psalmists: "Thy statutes have been my songs in the house of my pilgrimage" (119:54). The whole range of religious interests reflected in the hymns, the prayers, and the meditations of the Psalter are directly or indirectly related to the ordinances of the law. The Psalter was therefore a handbook for the pious. But wholehearted

---

Interpreting the Psalms.—Ps. 1 is a poetic statement of the Jewish conception of a good man. It portrays his quality analytically (vss. 1-2), in imagery (vs. 3), and by contrast (vss. 4-6). It forms an introduction to the Psalter as a whole, and is a good illustration of the problems of interpretation. A few general remarks with regard to those problems are therefore in order.

Anyone who attempts to interpret the devotional parts of the Bible, of which the Psalter is the chief, enters on what is really an art by itself; for the Bible as a whole contains God's Word to man, while the Psalms are man's word to God (see p. 3). However, the Psalms also record God's answers to man's questions and complaints; but the church has recognized the distinction by the fact that in liturgical communions the psalms are never read as "lessons," but are used as part of man's approach to God. The interpreter therefore has a certain freedom of treatment which he is not granted when dealing with the history of God's doings or with straight theological compositions. Moreover, the Psalms are poetry and awaken the spiritual poet latent in every man. As a result, one may well allow oneself to be captured by a phrase or an image, and urged by it into whatever region it may lead. In Ps. 1, as we shall see, vs. 3 is a good instance of an image which by itself may suggest Christian ideas not in the forefront of the original writer's mind. Thus the expositor's preparation must be a process of imaginative meditation more than of

loyalty to the law and faith in its promises (e.g., Deut. 28:1-14) were put to severe tests by the events of history. The observers of the law seemed too often to suffer bad fortune, while the godless prospered. Hence among the many voices in the Psalter we hear expressions of doubt and despair from men whose souls, perplexed by the ways of God in the world, were "cast down" (see 42:9-11; 73:2-14). The psalmist knows well that the facts of history and of individual experience often seem to belie the expectations of the faithful; but he maintains that, despite all seeming, it is abidingly true that God cares for all who fear him, and so it goes well with those who love his law and ill with those who despise it.

The psalm resembles prose more than poetry; its literary style is didactic rather than psalmodic or hymnal. The writer has the point of view which we associate with the teachers of wisdom, whose interest was to instruct men about the wise way of life rather than to invent for them songs of praise. The word with which the psalm opens (see Exeg. on vs. 1) is characteristic of the formulas of blessing found in the wisdom literature (cf. Job 5:17; Prov. 3:13; 8:34; 28:14). For his material the psalmist has looked to Jer. 17:5-8, making some adaptations of the prophet's language and point of view to his own needs and times, notably by substituting **delight . . . in the law of the Lord** for "confidence in the Lord" and the more commonplace simile of "the wind-driven chaff" for the rarer one of "a scrub of the desert."

It is not necessary to suppose that the psalm was written to supply an introduction to the Psalter; rather, we may assume that it was selected from some independent source or liturgical collection and set in its present position at or about the time of the final edition of the Psalter. The compositeness of the Psalter (see Intro., pp. 6-8) is an evidence that the writing of psalms or the production of books of devotions was not reserved as the prerogative of a single, official group in Judaism. But whatever opinion we hold as to the relation of this psalm to the final edition of the Psalter, the date of its composition is clearly in the late postexilic period. We need not stress the point that it, along with its immediate neighbor, is not provided with a superscription indicating the source from which it was taken, as are most of the psalms of the first book of the Psalter (Pss. 1–41); that, in other words, it has been brought into a group of which it was not originally a member. The lateness of its date is manifested rather by the internal evidences. It belongs to a time when, through the influence of the work of Ezra, the nation is viewed as a religious community, **the congregation of the righteous** (vs. 5); when zeal in the study of the law is a mark of the righteous man; and when

---

strict exposition; and he will find himself continually moved to spiritualize expressions which originally had a physical reference. Their agelong devotional use in a spiritual sense has in itself been a commentary upon them, and the interpreter cannot divorce himself from the meaning which the Christian society has found in them. The "wounds and bruises" of the body have become the "putrefying sores" of the soul, and the "saving health" which God gives is found for Christian ears in the region of the heart.

The fact is that Christ has captured the psalms; it is hardly too much to say that he has rewritten them. Certainly he has inscribed his name over them and in them. It is quite impossible for a Christian to explain the term "Lord" in any other context, with all that is thereby involved in the interpretation of what follows in the psalm. No one can even so much as entertain the thought that "the Lord is my shepherd" without winging his way at once to Christ, or without turning "the dark defile" into "death's dark vale." What the Christian means by immortality, an idea alien to the original writer, keeps forcing its way in under the touch of the Lord of life; in addition, ethical ideas, honest enough at the time the psalms were written, have to be either transmuted or rejected under his leading. In short, the Psalms should be understood not more by way of what they meant than by way of what they have come to mean. The poet-heart of the saints has been at work upon them too long and too nobly to leave them undeepened and unenriched.

In that connection a point of some importance arises. Probably many of the psalms had a national significance, and doubtless they may still be so used, and profitably; but in the practices of devotion they have acquired a far more immediate and personal reference. The leading of the Spirit would be wasted if people

in the way of sinners, nor sitteth in the seat of the scornful.

nor stands in the way of sinners,
nor sits in the seat of the scoffers;

wisdom and the law are being equated by those who belong to the circle of the teachers of wisdom, as in Ecclesiasticus (cf. 24:23-27), *ca.* 190 B.C. There is, however, no reference in the blessings of the righteous or the punishment of the wicked to an apocalyptic event; men receive the recompense due to them within the bounds of this life, a point of view which was especially modified in the course of the second century B.C. and later by the apocalyptic interpretation of history. Altogether these facts seem to warrant us in dating the psalm in the late Greek period, not far from the end of the third century.

The psalm falls into two sections. The first (vss. 1-3) tells us of the righteous man. He is described first negatively: he will have no fellowship or dealings with the wicked. Next, the good man is described positively: he gives himself day and night to observance of and meditation on the law of his God. For such a man the psalmist predicts a life of stable and abundant prosperity.

The second section (vss. 4-6) describes the fate of the wicked. The psalmist says nothing here about their character, since he has alluded to it in the names he gives them in vs. 1. It is their end to which he invites our attention. They are not like the tree, firm, deep-rooted, and fruitful. They are like the chaff, which is impermanent, without roots, useless, and blown away from its place by the winds. So the wicked disappear through the judgments of the Lord, and so Israel, as the community of the righteous, is rid of them. For, as the psalmist would have us know, all men must reckon with the Lord, who is never unmindful of our way and our deserts.

1. The Blessedness of the Righteous (1:1-3)

1:1. Blessed: "Happy" or "Oh, the happiness of" would be a more faithful rendering. The Hebrew word (אשרי) ordinarily connotes not so much inward blessedness as outward felicity. The synonym (ברוך) marks the blessing more especially as heaven sent. **Walketh not in the counsel:** He does not follow their advice, plans, or pattern of life (cf. Job 10:3; Jer. 7:24). **Sits in the seat:** I.e., sits down with them in the place where they

were required to find communal meanings in poems which have come to be a strength and stay to the single heart in its distress. The interpreter will fasten then on the possessive pronoun of the first person wherever he finds it, and by "my" will emphatically mean "mine," first endeavoring by God's help to make it his own, and thus inviting others to do the same when they commune with their hearts on their beds and are still. The famous Scottish preacher, Alexander Whyte, once exclaimed to theological students, "Ah! I envy you young men with your ministry before you, and especially that you have ahead a lifetime of explaining the psalms to your people!" Few ever lived who were more personal in their interpretation. It was in that region that Whyte found the power of the Psalms. We must know everything that scholarship can tell us about their origins; but we must then go on to know what two thousand years of devotion have found in them, under the leadership of him who makes all things new.

Ps. 1 is an illustration of some of these principles. Its original meaning is clear enough. It describes the good man and in vivid contrasts sets forth the difference that the good life makes to destiny. Consequently it has been a favorite with interpreters of the older school. The good man becomes stable, gracious, and prosperous; the evil man becomes empty, futile, and forgotten. It is a sharp word, which the modern world would do well to remember.

1:1-2. ***The Two Ways.***—The righteous man is first portrayed negatively. The fact that the psalm begins in this way is significant: a Christlit poem would begin positively, as, for example, the Beatitudes. The very point of departure suggests the difference between being under the law and being under grace. However, the negative description is valuable. Three pictorial phrases are used, which doubtless were variant ways of describing the same spiritual attitude. If he **walketh not in the counsel of the ungodly,** he stands not **in the way of sinners, nor sitteth in the seat of the scornful.** Here is one example of the psalmist's art: he will often be saying the same thing over again, but freshly. The interpreter cannot fail to see an ascending scale in the verbs—a sort of spiritual rake's progress—

2 But his delight *is* in the law of the LORD; and in his law doth he meditate day and night.
3 And he shall be like a tree planted by the rivers of water, that bringeth forth his

2 but his delight is in the law of the LORD,
and on his law he meditates day and
night.
3 He is like a tree
planted by streams of water,

meet to confer on their common designs. **Ungodly . . . sinners . . . scornful:** These three words constitute a climax like that of the three words, **walks, stands,** and **sits,** describing the good man's attitude to the wicked. The first is a general term for ungodly persons, men out of joint with the proper standards of conduct; their condition may or may not be a fixed one. The second connotes a habitual or professional sinner. The third covers a type of person frequently mentioned in Proverbs (cf. 13:1; 21:24; 22:10; 29:8), where it designates the worst of the godless; they are arrogant, quarrelsome, and mischief-making, foes of peace and order among men and in their communities, and mockers of goodness. Because in their own eyes they are self-sufficient, they set themselves against God.

2. **Delight:** The word is used in the later Hebrew sense of that in which one takes delight—one's business or occupation (cf. Prov. 31:13; Eccl. 3:1, 17; 8:6). The good man's chief interest is to fulfill the law, the content of which is indicated in 19:7-10; Prov. 3:1-3. **Meditate:** A secondary meaning of a word that primarily means to utter the low, inarticulate sounds of reading half-aloud to oneself in studying or conning the words of a book.

3. **Streams of water:** Properly, irrigation ditches such as one sees in Egypt or Babylonia, but rarely in Palestine (Deut. 11:10-11). **Planted:** To these never-failing

and he should feel free to elaborate it in the light of his own experience. A man begins by entertaining godless ideas intermittently, when his mind is free to roam. He allows himself to wonder whether the **counsel of the ungodly** has not something to say for itself. We call it "becoming realistic." He then, tentatively at first and later as his usual rule, indulges in godless practices; especially he forgets worship, turning a progressively blind eye to the Ten Commandments: he **standeth in the way of sinners.** Before he knows where he is, his character is petrified, he **sitteth in the seat of the scornful,** a successful worldling for the time being, honored by those whose honor is dishonor. He even scorns godliness, for it does not lead to a seat among the elders at the gate; and when a man cynically sneers at goodness he has reached his nadir. A wise old saint, a character in his day, used to reserve this conception for his ultimate condemnation. "The man's a scorner," he would declare, and his face would grow grim. There was no more to be said.

Vs. 2 gives the positive side of the quality of the saint, and declares the kind of idea he feels free to entertain. **The law of the LORD** may fairly be extended to cover more than the writer probably meant. All that declares the mind of God, all that is in any sort his word, is the region in which the righteous man's mind delights to roam. His pleasure is to think God's thoughts after him; and God is beauty and love. His mind instinctively dwells where God dwells too. The thoughts he entertains are thoughts to which he could call the Lord's attention. Moreover, he is a man who wills himself to meditate on the issues of life, a point which our hurrying society needs to remember. John Buchan, reporting that a great American banker once declared, "I never spend more than five hours in my office, but I do a whale of a lot of thinking at home," went on to quote Isa. 30:15, "In quietness and in confidence shall be your strength," as the forgotten motto of modern life. It is well to note the almost exaggerated emphasis which Paul puts on the devotional life: "Pray without ceasing" (I Thess. 5:17). No man can do nothing but meditate; but no man can get on without meditating. It would be interesting to know in actual time measurement how long we spend each day, solitary with our minds and thoughts. The amount might surprise us, and the regions of our meditations might startle and shock us. This psalm teaches us that the righteous man will deliberately direct his mind to thoughts of that which is eternal; and if we are candid, we shall admit that it is practical in our modern life, as well as necessary. Where there is a will to meditate, there are both time and a way.

3. ***What the Good Man Will Become.***—This is the critical and most profitable verse for the interpreter. In the original intent it gives a happy image of what the good man will become. **A tree planted by the rivers of water, that bringeth forth his fruit in his season; his leaf**

fruit in his season; his leaf also shall not wither; and whatsoever he doeth shall prosper.
4 The ungodly *are* not so: but *are* like the chaff which the wind driveth away.
5 Therefore the ungodly shall not stand in the judgment, nor sinners in the congregation of the righteous.

that yields its fruit in its season,
and its leaf does not wither.
In all that he does, he prospers.

4 The wicked are not so,
but are like chaff which the wind drives away.
5 Therefore the wicked will not stand in the judgment,
nor sinners in the congregation of the righteous;

---

sources the tree has been brought by the hand of a careful gardener. **Planted** does less than justice to the thought of the psalmist, who employs a word used in horticulture for the transplanting of vines and fruit trees (cf. Ezek. 17:7-8). In these favorable circumstances the tree never fails to produce fruit at the proper season.

2. The Lot of the Wicked (1:4-6)

5. Stand in the judgment: See 130:3. In the judgments of the Lord the wicked cannot endure (cf. 37:9, 13, 15, 17, 35-36). The wise are less disposed than some other religious thinkers in Israel to look to a single eschatological day of judgment for a demonstration of God's justice in the earth; for them the divine judgment is ever at hand.

---

also shall not wither is a fine picture of graciousness, stability, and prosperity. A good comment is quoted by Charles J. Ellicott from Bishop Hall: "Look where you will in God's Book, you shall never find any lively member of God's house, any true Christian, compared to any but a *fruitful* tree."[1] In the psalmist's mind, however, the **fruit** was the symbol of material achievement, as the concluding clause shows: **Whatsoever he doeth shall prosper.** The image therefore is an expression of the prevalent view that the secure and prosperous life here and now is the sign and reward of godliness.

The Christian will feel moved to use the image differently. He would make it a symbol of the condition rather than of the result of the good life. Indeed, he might well begin the psalm with it: "Blessed is the man who is like a tree planted by the rivers of water," finding in the words **planted** and **rivers of water** symbols of that which is necessary for the development of spiritual life. A man must be planted in the "word"—in the conception of God as the arbiter of right and wrong, and consequently must possess principles by which he lives—as the first step in godliness; he must be a man with "roots" growing deep in that from which he draws life and power. And he must be planted beside the **rivers** of the grace of God, from which he obtains constant renewal and refreshing. He must, in private prayer and in communal worship, and above all in the sacraments, be seeking that intaking without which his inner life will wither and die. Then, and only then, he can confidently hope that he will bring forth **his fruit in his season.** The evangelic treatment of the text thus understood is obvious: an expositor, especially in these days of loose convictions, can make great work with the word **planted;** and when he follows this with emphasis upon the importance of nearness to the means of grace, he can find in the verse a starting point for a whole volume of practical theology. If he aims at a single discourse, then the first condition of the good life is that it shall have roots; the second is that these roots shall be in well-watered soil; and given these conditions, the life will be fruitful, but with gradual development, for the fruit comes **in its season.** He could well proceed to apply these principles to the family: parents must see to it that their children have "roots," being firmly **planted** in principles; and they must watch that they keep their children in touch with the channels of God's inflowing, being especially concerned to be channels of the Spirit themselves; seeing to it that by all these means, "Christ may have a better residence in them," to use the lovely phrase of a sixteenth-century preacher, speaking on the significance of the Holy Communion. There is hardly an end to the possibilities of such a text interpreted by Christ.

4-5. *The Warning Against Evil.*—These two verses are perhaps of less value for us because they are negative. As Dante puts it, they are "bridles" rather than "spurs." Cf. the use of the warning against evil through examples of

[1] *An Old Testament Commentary for English Readers* (London: Cassell & Co., 1884), IV, 86.

6 For the LORD knoweth the way of the righteous: but the way of the ungodly shall perish.

2 Why do the heathen rage, and the people imagine a vain thing?

6 for the LORD knows the way of the righteous,
but the way of the wicked will perish.

2 Why do the nations conspire,
and the peoples plot in vain?

6. The LORD knoweth the way of the righteous: Sympathetic interest in and regard for the manner of life of the righteous is implied, rather than mere factual knowledge of it. The word "know" in Hebrew has a wider connotation than in our speech (cf. Prov. 12:10 in the Amer. Trans., where "cares" translates the Hebrew **knows**). Therefore, whereas the course of the wicked ends in nothing, the Lord rewards his righteous ones.

II. WORDS TO HEARTEN A KING (2:1-12)

This psalm, like Ps. 1, has no superscription in the M.T. According to this tradition, therefore, it was not an original member of the collection of "David" psalms which, with four exceptions, comprise the first book of the Psalter. This common feature may account for the fact that in some Hebrew MSS of the Psalter, in certain Greek and Latin readings of Acts 13:33, and in the Talmud (cf. Babylonian Berakoth 9*b*), Ps. 2 is made a part of Ps. 1. But their contents are so different that in a literary sense they can never have belonged together. It is probable that Ps. 2 was editorially selected to perform for the "David" psalms a service somewhat similar to that of Ps. 1 for the whole Psalter.

It was easy for later students of the period of the Psalter's editors to assume a Davidic setting for the psalm. David had become king under divine auspices (II Sam. 7:1-29), and his reign had been signalized by victories over the neighboring states of Edom, Moab, Ammon, and Syria (II Sam. 8:11-14) so that he seemed to have achieved a dominion such as vss. 2, 9-11 described. But this view overlooked the fact that extensive

moral catastrophe and the urge to good through examples of moral victory, as given on the eight terraces in Dante's *Purgatory*. The whole of the *Divine Comedy* is a mine for the Bible student. The use of the Psalms in *Purgatory* is especially to be noticed. But perhaps in these days we need a return to the solemnities and to the thought of the stone that grinds to powder. The image of the godless as wind-driven **chaff** can bring to mind the fact of the ultimate futility of the life that has no steady God-reference. A comparison of the permanent effect of positive religious leaders with the obliteration of the work of mere conquerors illustrates the truth of this psalm. Moses is a living force today; but what work of Alexander persists? Zoroaster, Mohammed, and Buddha affect the lives of millions; compared with them the names of Hannibal, Genghis Khan, and even Caesar are "writ in water"—whereas in vital power the name of Jesus is above every name. Browning's title *Parleyings with Certain People of Importance in Their Day* starts a valuable train of thought; their importance may have been considerable, but their day was soon over and their names soon forgotten. The overthrow of the "proud" and the obliteration of their memories is a grim fact of history on which men who are greedy for power should ponder. In the approach to God there is an emotive scale of fear, awe, joy, love. Maybe we have forgotten the value of plain fear. If so, meditation on these verses helps to recapture it. Shelley's "Ozymandias" may be remembered profitably.

6. *Conclusion.*—The final verse brings the psalm to a fitting conclusion. **The way of the righteous** persists because it exists in the mind and will of God; but **the way of the ungodly** is not even known to him: it is outside the patient processes of the divine Order. Wherefore, let all men fear him, and let Christian men rejoice. "There shall never be one lost good!" [2]

2:1-12. *The Rightful King.*—This psalm is a drama in three acts, with a prologue and an epilogue, and is of unique value. It requires a careful statement of its structure (see Expos. below), after which the interpreter must give rein to his perceptive and imaginative powers. He must enter with the writer into the solemn contrasts of the settings of the scenes.

1. *The Poet's Prologue.*—The question with which the psalm begins opens a wide field of

[2] Browning, "Abt Vogler," st. ix.

2 The kings of the earth set themselves,
and the rulers take counsel together, against
the LORD, and against his Anointed, *saying*,

2 The kings of the earth set themselves,
and the rulers take counsel together,
against the LORD and his anointed, saying,

---

as the sway of David was, it fell far short of a rule that reached to **the uttermost parts of the earth** (vs. 8) ; there were still great powers on the Nile, the Tigris, the Euphrates, and the Orontes that gave him no allegiance.

Because of the difficulty of relating the psalm literally to a particular historical occasion in the time of David or of any of his successors, it was not unnatural that the psalm should have been interpreted as prophetic of the Messiah, i.e., of the coming ideal ruler of the Davidic house (Pss. Sol. 17:23-24) or of Jesus as such (Acts 4:25-26; 13:33; Heb. 1:5; 5:5; Rev. 2:27; 19:18). It is notable, however, that apart from the quotation of vs. 7 with a Targumic addition ("beloved") in the baptismal account (Mark 1:11; Matt. 3:17; Luke 3:22) the Gospels do not refer to the psalm, nor is it ever quoted by Jesus. The fact is that the messianic interpretation cannot be sustained. The N.T. quotations are in this respect not decisive, since the O.T. passages used by N.T. writers with a messianic connotation are frequently selected without regard to the original context (cf. Mark 1:2-3). The character of the rule to be initiated by the king (vss. 9-11) scarcely comports with the messianic ideal. Further, it is to be noted that the relation of the nations and their rulers to the king (vss. 1-2) is not in accord with the messianic scheme of things to come. In the psalm the king is confronted with a disaffection of states that have already been subjected to him. That the Messiah's rule, once established, should be threatened by revolt is a situation outside messianic thought (cf. Rev. 11:15).

The difficulties in the interpretation of the psalm diminish when we understand it as an oracle or a poem written to express the confidence of, or to give confidence to, one of the royal line at the time of his accession or on an anniversary of his enthronement (vss. 6-7). Since the opening of his reign was troubled by reports of an impending revolt of his subject states, it was appropriate to the occasion that the status of the king as the vice-regent of the Lord should be stressed and that victory over his foes and world-wide dominion should be assured him, as a manifestation of the Lord's mastery in history and in the affairs of the nations. The psalm may have been used only once for a specific ruler, or it may have become a part of the liturgy observed at the accession of kings.

The psalm, as hinted above, belongs to the pre-exilic period. It is not possible to be more precise as to date. Some Aramaic influences on the vocabulary (רגש in vs. 1; רעע in vs. 9), which ordinarily are indicative of a postexilic date, may be due to a late recension for which also there is evidence in the disturbance of the poetical form of certain lines. It is apparent that the author meant the psalm to consist of four strophes of six lines each in the 3+3 measure. Disturbances have occurred in vss. 2, 7, 8.

1. The Conspiracy of the Subject Peoples (2:1-3)

2:1-3. The psalm takes the form of an utterance of the king (vss. 7-8). In this first strophe we are abruptly introduced to a lively scene of commotion among the rulers

---

edification. **Why do . . . the people imagine a vain thing?** Why, indeed! Is the reason ambition, sensuality, or mere blindness to the superiority of a birthright over a mess of pottage? A useful series of lessons might be found in the scriptural questions that begin with "why," of which this verse could be the first. They cover so much of human "folly, noise, and sin." The psalm does not answer the question, but it displays the vanity of a vain imagining.

2-3. *The Courts of Earthly Power.*—Suddenly we are taken to Act I, which is laid in the courts of earthly power. They are a place of hustle, agitation, plottings, whisperings, cabals. Even the English translation suggests haste and restlessness, with a raucous sound and a hissing in

3 Let us break their bands asunder, and cast away their cords from us.
4 He that sitteth in the heavens shall laugh: the Lord shall have them in derision.
5 Then shall he speak unto them in his wrath, and vex them in his sore displeasure.
6 Yet have I set my King upon my holy hill of Zion.

3 "Let us burst their bonds asunder,
and cast their cords from us."

4 He who sits in the heavens laughs;
the LORD has them in derision.
5 Then he will speak to them in his wrath,
and terrify them in his fury, saying,
6 "I have set my king
on Zion, my holy hill."

---

and nations of the earth. It is meant to be preparatory to a widespread revolt against the king's dominion. The outbreak is therefore in its incipient stage. There is as yet no march of armies or clash of arms; but kings and princes are agitating and coming together to devise plans for war. Their aim is to free themselves from the yoke of the king (vs. 3).

In the ancient East the death of a strong king was not uncommonly followed by revolts of states which had been subject to him. The first duty of the new king was to subdue the revolting states and to re-establish authority over them. The rulers of Israel and Judah were no strangers to such political problems. It would be natural for one of their psalmists to speak of the disaffection of states such as Moab, Ammon, and Edom in language like that employed by the court poets of the major powers. **Their bonds . . . their cords:** The harness of a work animal provides a metaphor for political bondage.

But the plot has a deeper significance; it is **against the LORD and his anointed;** it is a conspiracy of heathen peoples against the Lord's orderings in world society. Since in the nature of things it can come only to nought, what madness urges the conspirators to foment it!

2. THE LORD VIEWS THE INCIPIENT REBELLION (2:4-6)

4-6. In the second strophe we are boldly transported from the earthly scene to the heavenly. We see and hear the divine reaction to the report of the tumult of the rebels. The Lord laughs and holds their vain conceits in derision; then in terrifying anger he sets about to show that the king whom he has set up on Zion is inviolable: "I, I have installed my king on Sion" (Moffatt).

---

such words as **break** and **cast away their cords from us.** The recurrent sibilants in the second clause have their value. We get the same hiss more emphatically in "business is business," a modern variant of the attitude described in this text. The tone throughout is the tone of conspiracy, with a view to grasping power, by a group of highly placed political gangsters. Yet there is more than that; these **kings** and **rulers** are godless humanity in a position of temporary eminence. Their opponent is the moral Authority and his agent in human affairs. They are the representatives of the rebellious human will, demanding license in place of liberty. The precise historical occasion of the psalm is unknown, but for our purpose that is unimportant. It is "permanently contemporaneous" as long as there is a struggle between worldly pride and ambition on the one hand and the will of God and the kingdom of his Christ on the other. With all this compare the councils of those who deemed it "better to reign in hell than serve in heaven," in Milton's *Paradise Lost*,[3] and Dante's treatment of the sin of pride in *Purgatory*,[4] where he contrasts Lucifer, Briareus, the Giants, and Nimrod, the mythical builders of the Tower of Babel—examples of pride against God—with the humility of God in the Incarnation.

4-6. ***The Courts of Heaven.***—The abrupt change of scene in Act II is startlingly dramatic. We are now in the courts of heaven. The opening words of vs. 4 contrast terribly with the implied self-importance of the conspirators on earth. They take themselves and their plottings so seriously; but their real significance is measured by God's scornful laughter, his contemptuous **derision.** And what God thus scorns in his power, he visits with **sore displeasure.** These somber phrases should be made forceful to the men of today who forget that some of their sins

[3] Bk. I.

[4] Canto XII, ll. 25-36.

7 I will declare the decree: the LORD hath said unto me, Thou *art* my Son; this day have I begotten thee.

8 Ask of me, and I shall give *thee* the heathen *for* thine inheritance, and the uttermost parts of the earth *for* thy possession.

9 Thou shalt break them with a rod of iron; thou shalt dash them in pieces like a potter's vessel.

10 Be wise now therefore, O ye kings: be instructed, ye judges of the earth.

7 I will tell of the decree of the LORD:
He said to me, "You are my son,
today I have begotten you.
8 Ask of me, and I will make the nations
your heritage,
and the ends of the earth your possession.
9 You shall break them with a rod of iron,
and dash them in pieces like a potter's
vessel."

10 Now therefore, O kings, be wise;
be warned, O rulers of the earth.

---

3. THE KING REPEATS THE LORD'S ORACLE (2:7-9)

7-9. In the third strophe we are brought back to Zion. The king speaks and tells of the oracle or prophecy that came to him from the Lord on the day of his installation. The Lord declared, **You are my son, today I have begotten you.** The first part of the oracle was a form of words used in the legal adoption of a child (cf. Code of Hammurabi 170-71). In the same terms the idea of the special relationship between a king and his god was expressed both in Egypt and in Babylonia; the king was said to have been adopted by his god. A similar notion is met in the O.T. (cf. II Sam. 7:14; Ps. 89:26-27), but always with the stress on the ethical implications. In the second part of the oracle, **this day have I begotten thee, this day** or **today** means the day when the king ascended the throne. The use of this word in the context shows that nothing more is implied than in the formula of adoption of the first part. But in Babylonia and Assyria, and especially in Egypt, kings were thought to be the offspring of the gods. Such a belief could maintain itself only where polytheistic religions existed. In the O.T. the formula was emptied of its old sense because of the O.T. conception of God; it persisted only as a form of words through which the theocratic nature of the kingship could be stressed. Further, the Lord promised the king as his **son** a share in the divine prerogatives, world-wide dominion with free exercise of authority: **Ask of me, and I will make the nations your heritage. . . . You shall break them with a rod of iron, . . . like a potter's vessel.**

4. THE CONSPIRATORS ARE ADMONISHED (2:10-11)

10-12. In the concluding strophe our attention is turned to the conspirators. An ultimatum is addressed to them. What they have heard must, if they are open to warnings,

---

produce "the dreadful astonishment of God." Vs. 6 is of deep significance. Its slow and stately rhythm suggests the inevitability of that which God wills. The upsetting of the plans of the conspirators lies ahead in time; but there is a "must needs be" about it, for the alternate plan exists already in the mind of God, and therefore is timelessly real. Men may have to wait long for the enthronement of Christ over the world as seen from the earth; but it is already a fact in God's purpose. In the realm of the real there is no other **King** but Jesus.

7-9. ***The Court of the Ideal King.***—Act III (vss. 7-9) is set in the future. The scene returns to earth again, but it is changed from the court of the godless kings to the court of the ideal king. The occasion is his coronation. The moment chosen is the reading of the decree of his institution; the reader is the poet, in his capacity as a seer. The points are threefold: the king's unique relationship to God; his ultimate world-wide authority; and his complete ascendancy in power, if any should stand out against him. None has any chance whatever in rebellion; nothing awaits the rebellious but complete destruction. The vivid phrases of vs. 9 should not be excluded from the Christian vocabulary. History is too full of examples of the irresistible might of God. "Knowing therefore the terror of the Lord, we persuade men" (II Cor. 5:11).

10-12. ***Epilogue.***—Like the prologue, vss. 10-11 are spoken by the poet. A still and awed

11 Serve the LORD with fear, and rejoice with trembling.
12 Kiss the Son, lest he be angry, and ye perish *from* the way, when his wrath is kindled but a little. Blessed *are* all they that put their trust in him.

11 Serve the LORD with fear,
with trembling 12 kiss his feet,[a]
lest he be angry, and you perish in the way;
for his wrath is quickly kindled.

Blessed are all who take refuge in him.

A Psalm of David, when he fled from Absalom his son.

3 LORD, how are they increased that trouble me! many *are* they that rise up against me.

A Psalm of David, when he fled from Absalom his son.

3 O LORD, how many are my foes!
Many are rising against me;

[a] Cn: The Hebrew of 11b and 12a is uncertain

change their counsels. So, before the fury of the Lord breaks forth on them, let them do obeisance to him, i.e., to his son, for a revolt against the king is nothing less than a revolt against the Lord.

Rejoice with trembling. Kiss the Son: Better, **with trembling kiss his feet.** The versions and the Targ. have difficulty in translating the Hebrew text here. Through a slight emendation we obtain a good rendering. Kissing the feet was an act of obeisance required of subjugated princes by their overlord (cf. 72:9; Isa. 49:23; Mic. 7:17).

III. A Plea for God's Deliverance (3:1-8)

In the superscription this psalm is said to have been written by David when he was in flight from Absalom. In the later postexilic times, when the tradition of the Davidic authorship of the Psalms was generally accepted (with exceptions, cf. Pss. 72; 90), scribal exegetes sought to identify the occasion for the writing of certain of them with particular situations in David's career, and their opinions are preserved in some of the superscriptions (cf. Pss. 7; 18; 30; 34; 51; etc.). For a discussion of the superscriptions see Intro., pp. 8-10. The ascription of this psalm to David was doubtless due to the reference to the host of enemies (vs. 1) and to the **holy hill** (vs. 4). But there is little else to support it. No mention is made of the flight itself or any of the stirring incidents attending it, as described in II Sam. 15–17; there is no reference to the disloyalty of

reflectiveness pervades them. Men are called on to be **wise;** and wisdom involves teachableness, particularly on the part of leaders; willingness to put every faculty at God's disposal (cf. Luke 22:27, "I am among you as he that serveth"); gladness with awe that right has might; and public acknowledgment of allegiance to the true king.

Vs. 12 is doubtless corrupt; but even as it stands it has a clear enough meaning. Some form of ceremonial homage is indicated. If the word **kiss** is retained, a vivid contrast may be drawn with the kiss of Judas, in whose subsequent story an awe-inspiring commentary on vs. 9 may be found; for the principles in this psalm are to be applied to the individual life, as well as to that of the nation.

The psalm as a whole is a striking instance of how literature of this kind may justly be "spiritualized." Perhaps one may compare its main lines of development with relevant passages in the N.T. The plottings of the conspirators suggest the scenes before and at the trial of our Lord by Annas and Caiaphas (John 18:13, 19-24). The still declarations of the irresistible calm of the will of God may be related to our Lord's proleptic statement, "I have overcome the world" (John 16:33). It connects with the scene before Pilate, when in answer to his "knowest thou not that I have power?" Jesus answered with marked emphasis, "Thou couldest have no power at all against me, except it were given thee from above" (John 19:10-11). The solemnity of vs. 9 recalls the stone that will grind to powder in the parable of the wicked husbandman (Matt. 21:41-44); while the epilogue reminds us of the insistence of Jesus that men must hear and learn of him. The final commentary on the psalm is to be found in the N.T.

3:1-8. ***A Morning Hymn of Thanksgiving.***— There is no accurate knowledge of the historical setting of this psalm. The poet seems to be some

friends or offspring. Besides, Zion was not yet the Lord's "holy mountain" in David's time (cf. II Sam. 6:10, 16). The language of the psalm because of its general character permits us to assume no more than that it relates to the experience of some unknown individual.

The psalm belongs to a type or class of liturgical prayers or psalms which comprise a large section of the Psalter. They express variously the grievance, complaint, or lament of an individual or a community, and they are designated respectively as "Laments of the individual" and "Laments of the community." Ps. 3 is an example of the former type (see Intro., pp. 6-7).

The psalm consists of strophes of equal length, except that the last one is shortened by half a line, seemingly for a poetical effect which is met from time to time in the Psalter. The meter is almost regularly 3+3. An additional line (vs. 8) lifts the psalm out of its originally individual setting and appropriates it for congregational use. The psalm, therefore, is in its careful structure a beautiful though simple example of its type.

1. The Psalmist's Plight (3:1-2)

3:1-2. In the opening lines we are told of the desperate plight of the psalmist. He is menaced by a multitude of enemies who are confident that he is powerless to withstand them, since according to their thinking **there is no help for him in God. How many are my foes!** In this type of psalm complaints about "enemies" are frequently met (cf. 6:10; 17:9; 25:2, 19). They are designated sometimes by other names such as "persecutors" (7:1), "my haters" (35:19), "those who seek my life" (40:14), "workers of mischief"

---

leader, regal or otherwise, who speaks after a signal victory over dangerous enemies. On the suggestion of vs. 5, **I awaked; for the Lord sustained me,** we may regard it as a morning hymn of thanksgiving, with the one sustained note of acknowledgment that his happy situation was due to the intervention and inspiration of a spiritual force outside himself, working for and through him.

This idea of the effect of the spiritual factor in national affairs is of course one that has to be continually emphasized, for man's innate pride tends to make him forget it. An acute observer, speaking of Britain during World War II, said that "the turning point came when we realized the depth and reality of our spiritual resources." In anxious times we need to stress not only the fact of such resources but the importance of practical steps to call them forth. The duty and wisdom of steadfast private and public prayer on the part of the church is here implicit. Prayer is stated to be the process by which power is let loose. The psalmist's happy song of deliverance has in its heart the statement, **I cried unto the Lord with my voice** (vs. 4). The Christian community in the world is said to be six hundred million strong; and yet it complains of its weakness. Maybe the reason is that it fails to "cry unto the Lord" with that fervent prayer which Jas. 5:16 tells us avails much. It should also be noted that the man in question was a fighting man, offering all that he had in addition to, and as the condition of, his praying. "To pray and not to do our best to accomplish that for which we pray is to insult God," said Sir Stafford Cripps. "The Praying Warrior" would provide a good heading for this psalm, and would suggest a radiant ideal for the Christian. An examination of the prayer life of our Lord would naturally be indicated.

It would seem therefore that the psalm can best be used personally. C. S. Lewis has reminded us that the phrase "*the* war" should be applied to the agelong strife between good and evil which is fought continually on the battlefield of the heart—a war in which there is no leave, and for which we are all conscripted. The enterprise of life is to turn our conscription into eager, voluntary service on the side of God. From that point of view the psalm is a rich mine of suggestion.

1. *Lord, How Are They Increased that Trouble Me!*—It is a pathetic fact, as an old saint once said, that "no temptation ever seems to be quite stone-dead upon the field." Justification is a complete thing; but sanctification is an ever-becoming thing, and in depressed moments seems singularly slow. The reader will find plenty of proof if he will face candidly his own best evidence, given by "the inhabitant within," which is himself. We continually surprise ourselves by our own unworthiness in regions where we thought we were secure. "Is thy servant a dog, that he should do this great thing?" (II Kings 8:13.) Yet as the old preacher said, startlingly if uncritically, "Dog or no dog, he did it." A little stocktaking now and then reveals us in the same case. Who does not know what it is to be shocked at his own pettiness

2 Many *there be* which say of my soul, *There is* no help for him in God. Selah.
3 But thou, O LORD, *art* a shield for me; my glory, and the lifter up of mine head.
4 I cried unto the LORD with my voice, and he heard me out of his holy hill. Selah.

2 many are saying of me,
there is no help for him in God. *Selah*

3 But thou, O LORD, art a shield about me,
my glory, and the lifter of my head.
4 I cry aloud to the LORD,
and he answers me from his holy hill.
Selah

(64:2). In this instance the enemies are identified in vs. 6 as men of the psalmist's own people. **No help . . . in God:** The LXX reads "his God"; the Syriac reads "no help for thee in thy God." According to these readings the enemies of the psalmist not only deny God's power to help but disassociate themselves from him. The psalmist does not reveal to us the reasons for his enemies' hostility. But in his distress he appeals to his God.

2. An Expression of Trust (3:3-6)

3-4. The psalmist acquaints us with the grounds on which he bases his confidence in the divine help: the Lord has been **a shield,** not on one side alone, but on all sides, **about me;** the defender of **my glory,** or honor; and the **lifter of my head** in triumph over all personal foes. For whenever **I cry aloud to the LORD, . . . he answers me from his holy hill**—a compressed manner of saying the Lord hears and sends out help from his holy hill (cf. 20:2). This conception of the peculiar sanctity of Zion from which Israel's prayers receive their answers suggests that the psalm was written in the postexilic period when the Deuteronomic point of view had become accepted (cf. Deut. 12:1-32;

and his instinct for self-pity? Or to be shamed at the dominance over his mind and spirit of Brother Ass—as Francis of Assisi termed it—which is his body? Not only in grosser ways, but in the clamor for ease, with the result in part-done work, begun but never finished, and the squandering of material halfheartedly collected, like the slothful man who "roasted not that which he took in hunting" (Prov. 12:27). A facing of our failures is much more salutary than a compiling of our achievements in respectability, as the parable of the Pharisee and the publican (Luke 18:10-14) so searchingly reminds us. It will provide us with saving health if, as in the case of "the praying warrior" who wrote this psalm, it brings us with a humble and purposeful heart to cry unto the Lord.

2. *God's Relevance to Human Affairs.*—Here is a verse with a wide range. It states precisely the philosophy which many voices are declaring, and on which we are invited to build a civilization. This philosophy does not always deny the vague existence of a "something" which may be termed God, for want of another name; but it distinctly affirms his or its irrelevance to human affairs. The duty of the Christian is to meet that challenge openly and frequently by the reasoned defense of a theistic interpretation of the universe, not denying its difficulties—for the problem of evil remains—but making credible his affirmation that it leaves fewer difficulties in that it explains the problem of good and makes intelligible the existence of beauty. The Christian apologist must carry the war into the enemy's camp, maintaining that it is the fool who "hath said in his heart, There is no God" (14:1). A useful and related thought may be found in Isa. 48:16, "I have not spoken in secret from the beginning." The open voices of God in nature, history, the seers, and the soul must be made audible to questioning spirits.

An equally profitable development may lie in a somewhat different direction. Let the interpreter emphasize the pronoun "him." Is it possible that people may say of us, "Whoever gives evidence of divine help, he does not"? Or more positively, "There is nothing in his life that requires a divine factor to explain it." A Christian is presumably a person who is of such caliber that those who know him admit that there is an x in his life; and if he claims that this x is the Holy Spirit, the claim must not sound ridiculous. On the other hand, he is the most convincing Christian apologist whose life is of such beauty and strength that men cannot understand it apart from the inflowing of far-off fountains.

3-4. *The Power of the Cross.*—The word **but** should be noted. It may suggest a useful series of biblical studies. The writer has heard "the fiend voices that rave" of the irrelevance of God, and with a jerk pulls himself and his scorners up with the facts of experience. There are many such sharp contrasts in scripture, which a con-

5 I laid me down and slept; I awaked; for the LORD sustained me.
6 I will not be afraid of ten thousands of people, that have set *themselves* against me round about.
7 Arise, O LORD; save me, O my God: for

5 I lie down and sleep;
I wake again, for the LORD sustains me.
6 I am not afraid of ten thousands of people
who have set themselves against me round about.

7 Arise, O LORD!
Deliver me, O my God!

I Kings 8:28-30). The course of the psalmist's life, we may judge, has not been easy or free from grave troubles. Many a time he has been beset by trials, but the Lord has never failed to help him. The special epithets which the psalmist here applies to God probably indicate the nature of his immediate problem; his honor, his station among his fellows, are imperiled. Is he the object of false accusations before the judges or the officials of the land? Is his integrity in the discharge of a religious office assailed?

5-6. In the third strophe the psalmist looks away from the major deliverances which he has experienced in the course of his life to the evidences of God's unceasing watchfulness over him in the common round of his days. "When I lie down and sleep, I awake again; yea, the Lord is ever my support." As a result of this review of his God's dealings with him, he is prepared to face the assaults of his foes. **I will not be afraid of ten thousands of people, that have set themselves against me round about.**

3. PETITION FOR HELP (3:7-8)

7-8. In the closing lines the confidence of the psalmist in a triumphant vindication rings out. There is no lingering doubt of victory; the moment for the decisive act of

cordance will reveal under the words "but," "nevertheless," or "notwithstanding." The most striking of all has a simple conjunction in it which makes the contrast the more vivid because of the apparent casualness with which it is made: "The whole world lieth in wickedness. And we know that the Son of God is come" (I John 5:19-20). Note also that the **but** here is followed by **thou art.** Not "it" but **thou.** The impact of a living personality is set over against the sayings of the sneerers; and the experience of the impact is given in actual happenings. The writer declares that in point of fact he has been dependent upon the Lord (cf. John 9:25, "Whereas I was blind, now I see"); only so has his dignity been restored. The phrase **the lifter up of mine head** is evangelically suggestive, and leads to the thought of the power of the Cross to restore hope through forgiveness. In the baptistery of Florence there is a wonderful statue of the Magdalene. She is portrayed as a gaunt and degraded hag, but her head is lifted up and in her eyes the carver has placed an extraordinary if desperate hope. It is the moment in which she discovers the Savior. One can almost hear her whisper, "There is life for me." Remember also the phrases introducing the stanzas of George Matheson's best-known hymn, "O Love that wilt not let me go"; "O Light that followest all my way"; "O Joy that seekest me through pain"; "O Cross that liftest up my head." A reminiscence perhaps of this psalm.

There follows in vs. 4 the poet's part in the experiences and confidence which the other verses recount. God's blessings and helps always involve a condition; at the very least we must be willing to receive them. It is only when we put ourselves in his hands that we can go on to the restfulness of vs. 5.

5-6. ***I Laid Me Down and Slept.***—It is something to be able to say that when we lay us down to sleep, we discover sleep's knitting up of "the ravell'd sleave of care," having learned that to be able to relax in quiet trust in God is a wonderful sleep restorer. Notice that both this psalm and Ps. 4 make special mention of the gift of sleep to those that rest in the Lord. The writers are such different men that their witness to a mutual experience is all the more noteworthy. This happy warrior puts more emphasis on his awaking in the morning, vigorous, alert, dauntless. Any fears that his enemies might creep on him in the dark are banished. Not only so, but he feels entirely adequate to deal with them all, able to "salute the day" (vs. 6). Turn now to Ps. 4:8 and note the contrast between the two writers and their situations; yet the similarity between them is in their peace.

7-8. ***Appeal for God's Help.***—The poet continues with a renewed appeal for God's help,

thou hast smitten all mine enemies *upon* the cheek bone; thou hast broken the teeth of the ungodly.
8 Salvation *belongeth* unto the LORD: thy blessing *is* upon thy people. Selah.

For thou dost smite all my enemies on the cheek,
thou dost break the teeth of the wicked.

8 Deliverance belongs to the LORD;
thy blessing be upon thy people! *Selah*

To the chief Musician on Neginoth, A Psalm of David.

4 Hear me when I call, O God of my righteousness: thou hast enlarged me *when I was* in distress; have mercy upon me, and hear my prayer.

To the choirmaster: with stringed instruments. A Psalm of David.

4 Answer me when I call, O God of my right!
Thou hast given me room when I was in distress.
Be gracious to me, and hear my prayer.

God is at hand. **Arise, O Lord! deliver me, O my God!** So he sees his enemies doomed to a sudden end. Verily, **thou dost smite, . . . break the teeth:** The enemies are like ravenous beasts pursuing or lying in wait for their prey; their coming discomfiture is described appropriately as like that of their kind whose jaws have been crushed and whose teeth have been broken. **Deliverance belongs to the LORD:** This is the answer to the arrogant assertions of the godless enemies (vs. 2). Also it is the lesson of the psalm. The experience of the psalmist points the truth that the Lord works salvation for his people. So may the Lord's **blessing** continue ever upon them!

IV. Confidence in the Lord (4:1-8)

This psalm belongs to a type closely related to that of Ps. 3, so closely indeed that some scholars have been led to regard Ps. 4 as a continuation of Ps. 3. However, there is a difference between the two. In this psalm there are the elements of distress and struggle out of which a psalm of lament or complaint might have grown, if the psalmist had been overwhelmed by the bitterness of his experience or had succumbed to it. But these elements, in spite of their reality, have been muted because they have been overcome by the psalmist's confidence in the Lord as the champion of his cause. It is this firm note of trust which dominates the psalm from the first verse to the last, distinguishing it from Ps. 3, where the words of complaint give way to those of full confidence only toward the end. The two neighboring psalms illustrate how there may be differences of emphasis in men's reactions to the components of an experience of trouble.

The lines are in 4+4 measure, varied by some stichs of three beats, as in vss. 1, 5, 8. The thought of the psalm is arranged in four strophes, of which the first is half a line

---

based upon his experience of it. The images in which the treatment of the enemies is described start trains of thought if we transfer them to the realm of moral struggle. The "enemy"—our intimate temptations—can become a trifle ridiculous in our eyes, a something which we can "slap upon the cheek," with the suggestion of contempt which that conveys. At least its biting power can be ended. **Thou hast broken the teeth of the ungodly** may be applied to ungodly longings as well as to ungodly men. Many a man can bear witness to the fact that with God's help a temptation which once like a wild beast tore him has become a poor, toothless meaninglessness from which he can turn with a smile, and consequently join in the ascription that follows in vs. 8, **Salvation belongeth unto the LORD.** This the reader may make as wide as the N.T. and as deep as the love of God. Note how largely it is a characteristic of the psalms to end on a note of confidence and thanksgiving.

4:1-8. ***An Evening Meditation.***—This is not one of the most familiar psalms but it is one of the noblest, marking a strong upward movement in the history of Hebrew religion. Its significant verse is vs. 7, to which the main attention should be given when expounding the psalm. Whoever wrote it was a good and great man holding high office—maybe high priest (but see Exeg.)—who learned his lesson in a time of public

KJV	RSV
2 O ye sons of men, how long *will ye turn* my glory into shame? *how long* will ye love vanity, *and* seek after leasing? Selah.	2 O men, how long shall my honor suffer shame? How long will you love vain words, and seek after lies? *Selah*

shorter than each of the succeeding ones; the final strophe is followed by an additional line, a common device to sum up or point the lesson of an entire psalm.

1. Appeal to God (4:1)

4:1. The first strophe opens with the appeal of the psalmist to God. But it is not a cry of despair, for it is addressed to the **God of my righteousness,** i.e., the God who maintains or vindicates the rightness of a cause. This confidence is warranted by the past experience of the psalmist, for **Thou hast given me room** [or **enlarged me**] **when I was in distress.** The language is a vivid figure to express release into ample space from a narrow or restricted condition. This petition is not a counsel of despair, a last resort to be tried in time of crisis, but the normal resource of a man who has had a steady acquaintance with the ways of his God.

2. Remonstrating with Adversaries (4:2-5)

2-3. In the second strophe the psalmist is in imminent danger; he is the object of accusations which turn his honor into disgrace. **Ye sons of men** or **O men:** The term בני איש seems to connote persons of influence or station over against the rank and file of men who are designated בני אדם; cf. 49:2; "the son of a man" in Babylonian and Egyptian (Bruno Meissner, *Babylonien und Assyrien* [Heidelberg: C. Winter, 1920], I, 371). They may have belonged to a powerful group, although they were not as numerous as those of Ps. 3, who are described as "many." It is not possible to say whether the psalmist belonged to the class whose hostility he suffered, or whether like the man Jeremiah he stood outside it; nor do we know why the calumnies to which he refers were leveled against him. We infer from his attitude to his adversaries that he was not a king addressing subjects from whom he was estranged. It is equally improbable that he was a high priest or prophet, zealous to reform the cult or to combat social

---

trouble in which he himself and the cause for which he stood were in danger. As Ps. 3 was the morning thanksgiving of a victorious warrior, so this is the evening meditation of a God-fearing statesman. We could wish that all who aspire to public leadership would think in quiet thus before they sleep.

The structure is simple enough. Vs. 1 is an appeal to God, who, the writer is sure, approves of his policy as a national leader seeking to determine his course by a constant reference to the divine will. Note the phrase **God of my righteousness,** i.e., "the God who has declared me justified in what I have tried to do." Whatever or whoever else is uneasy, his conscience is at peace.

Next comes an appeal to his opponents, who are bringing not only his policy but his office into shame (vs. 2). He would have them spend time in meditation also. If they do, they will see that God is on the side of the man who in the face of all the odds honestly seeks to serve him (vs. 3). There is some confusion in the text of vs. 4. The KJV gives a good meaning, but so does the RSV, **be angry, but sin not:** a notable word for any day. In all political disputes men should see that their anger is not sinful. Fury for propaganda purposes, bitterness engendered by personal jealousies or generated solely to create an opportunity for grasping at power—all this is plain **sin.** On the other hand, **stand in awe** [Moffatt, "tremble at it," i.e., at God and his word], **and sin not** is perhaps more in line with the rest of the thought. If men tremble in awe at the Word of God they are not likely to go far wrong. Incidentally, we may observe that it is better to tremble at it than for it, as Uzza did in regard to the ark of the Lord (II Sam. 6:6-8). The ark of God's will and truth can look after itself; but those who do not **stand in awe** before it are in a perilous state. W. Robertson Smith, that leader of the scholarly and reverent study of the Bible, once made a striking use of this contrast before the Scottish Assembly, when attacked by the traditionalists. Vs. 5 advises in addition that the psalmist's opponents should be very careful about the completeness and regularity of their public and

3 But know that the LORD hath set apart him that is godly for himself: the LORD will hear when I call unto him.

4 Stand in awe, and sin not: commune with your own heart upon your bed, and be still. Selah.

5 Offer the sacrifices of righteousness, and put your trust in the LORD.

3 But know that the LORD has set apart the
godly for himself;
the LORD hears when I call to him.

4 Be angry, but sin not;
commune with your own hearts on
your beds, and be silent. *Selah*
5 Offer right sacrifices,
and put your trust in the LORD.

---

wrongs. The notion that he was a man of faith valiantly struggling against the inclinations of some of his fellows to apostatize in a time of famine has little support in the text. Such conjectures may be dismissed because in vs. 6 we see that the situation is such that the issue of the psalmist's guilt or innocence can be settled only by reference to certain sacrifices; it is his status before God that is involved. Has he been accused of malfeasance in the discharge of civil or priestly responsibilities? Has he been arraigned on a charge of breach of trust or disloyalty? We know from numerous sources that sacrifices served as a means to ascertain the will of the Lord (cf. 6:9; 21:8-12; 81:6-16; 95:7*b*-11; the method of trial by ordeal (Num. 5:1-31; the practice is well known elsewhere; see *ibid.,* II, 279-82) either by a sign in the sacrifice or by an oracle delivered by a priest or priests in conjunction with the sacrifice. However that may be, the psalmist is confident of his acquittal, since his traducers are misled, they **love vain words, and seek after lies.**

3. Some read "Know that the Lord has wondrously shown his goodness to me" (cf. LXX, Jerome, Ps. 31:21). If this is the correct text, the psalmist admonishes his persecutors that the marvelous deliverances which God has wrought for him in the past (vs. 1*b*) are a token of what God will do for him now; for **the LORD hears when I call to him.**

4-5. **Be angry:** Lit., "be perturbed" or "be enraged." The root suggests the physical accompaniments of rage and terror. It is an evidence of the spiritual level of the psalmist that, in contrast to the writer of Ps. 3, he does not call his adversaries "enemies"

---

private religious observances. The advice is still timely. Many of the opponents of spiritual ideals in public or ecclesiastical life are those whose religious practice is but slightly honored in its observance.

Vss. 6-7 contain the core of the psalm and must be examined at length, leading as they do to the singular beauty of the **peace** with which the psalm closes. An *idée fixe* in the Hebrew mind was that righteousness and prosperity were cause and effect. "Honesty is the best policy" might well have served the pious as the first of all proverbs; and indeed it is not altogether a bad proverb. It goes wrong only when it is inverted and reads, "Prosperity is the outward and visible sign of honesty," which is a little different from the "ye rich men, weep and howl" of Jas. 5:1, or even from the pathetic picture of the rich young ruler. Yet the idea still has a grip on our minds; and many a sermon supports it. A professor in one of the great universities once declared his perturbation because on three successive Sundays three different preachers in the university chapel had told nothing but success stories, their unanimous gospel being, "Be good and you will at least be president of whatever company employs you." Clearly there is need for Ps. 4.

It is of course true that we are likely to prosper and keep well if we behave ourselves; but it is equally true that this does not paint the whole picture. The unrighteous do flourish, and the **godly** go into concentration camps. In fact, godliness often seems to make suffering inevitable. So it was in the days of the Maccabees when this psalm may well have been written. So it has been since, notably in the early Christian Era and in modern Europe. The cry **Who will show us any good?** is the cry of the righteous who feel—and who can blame them?—that they are the victims of injustice in a universe whose morality they have begun to doubt.

In such a mental and spiritual setting this good and discerning man meditated and was able to reply to the doubt. Not by an unsupported generalization that because God was in

6 *There be* many that say, Who will show us *any* good? LORD, lift thou up the light of thy countenance upon us.

6 There are many who say, "O that we might see some good!
Lift up the light of thy countenance upon us, O LORD!"

or "foes," nor does he imply that they are beasts (3:7). Rather, he gives them counsel, entreating them to restrain their anger and, if they must rage, to utter it to themselves in the seclusion of their beds in the stillness of the night, and so to possess their souls in patience until God has spoken. **Sacrifices of righteousness,** i.e., the prescribed sacrifices (cf. 51:19; Deut. 33:19), the sacrifices proper to the occasion. The term may here carry with it the sense of sacrifices offered by righteous men, i.e., men who in this instance are not motivated by blind passion but by a sincere desire to learn the truth. The double meaning suits the context.

3. The Joy of Trusting in God (4:6-8)

6-7. In the bitter experience of life many are quick to surrender to despair, saying,

O that we might see some good!
Lift up the light of thy countenance upon us!

To greet a person with a shining or smiling countenance gives him an assurance of one's good will. The words (cf. 67:1) are meant to recall the priestly benediction of Num. 6:24-26; they hint that it has failed of power in the circumstances. By reading in vs. 6 נס מעלינו for נסה עלינו, one may translate "the light of his countenance has departed

his heaven all was well with the world, but by a discovery in his own experience. He discovered **gladness**—the critical word in vs. 7. The KJV rendering has a certain value, although the RSV **joy** may be more accurate, for it indicates a touch of gaiety which so many of the psalmists so consistently display. Cf. the tone suggested by what we know of the dwellers in the catacombs, as indicated in their happy carvings of the young Good Shepherd, in whose care they were. The writer's discovery went even further; he declared that in his experience this **gladness** was greater in the testing days than in the days of facile prosperity. He found a joy that not only sought him through pain, but in part was its offspring. Cf. Browning:

> Then, welcome each rebuff
> That turns earth's smoothness rough,[5]

or the word of an old saint, "Ah! I could have done without my joys, but I could never have done without my sorrows."

The core of the psalm may be conveyed under the headings of two "queer facts": the queer fact of the greater gladness, and the queer fact of the ancestry of the greater gladness. Under the former it may be observed that sufferers are often the most conspicuous possessors of that kind of sunniness which is the twin of peace. An Englishman once remarked that he had never known the British people so happy as in their days of supreme danger in 1940. Churchill's call to be "grim and gay" reminds us that the two are not incompatible; and the spirit of Browning's "Prospice" suggests the same idea. "The fiend voices that rave" create a song in the hearts of those who challenge them, even at the cost of wounds; and quiet endurance of life's disciplines as from the hand of God brings a strange sweet melody in the midst of suffering. Hospitals are full of instances, as every pastor knows; healthy people leave the bedsides of their sick friends rebuked for their own megrims and complainings by the smile of the sufferers. Those men and women on their beds of pain are renewing their own self-respect, though they themselves would hardly phrase it in any such way. They are proving that they can face life's harshness and still stand fast; and there is an inner glow in the heart of a man who has shown that quality. It is recorded of General Wilhelm Ludendorff that when he resigned his command, he went straight to Liége. Years before he had discovered there that he could face physical danger without loss of nerve: so when everything else had crashed around him, he went to the spot where, to use his own words, he had "proved his manhood"; and then he went home. When our **corn and . . . wine** [are] **increased,** we do not know much about our manhood; it takes trial to discover

[5] "Rabbi Ben Ezra," st. vi.

7 Thou hast put gladness in my heart, more than in the time *that* their corn and their wine increased.

8 I will both lay me down in peace, and sleep: for thou, LORD, only makest me dwell in safety.

7 Thou hast put more joy in my heart
than they have when their grain and wine abound.

8 In peace I will both lie down and sleep;
for thou alone, O LORD, makest me dwell in safety.

---

from us." Such a change introduces an interesting nuance in the text of the psalm, but in no wise alters the essential course of its thought.

7. But in the midst of his trouble the psalmist, firm in his faith, knows a joy that exceeds the highest human satisfactions. **More than in the time that their corn and their wine increased:** It is wrong to deduce from these words that the occasion of the psalm was a bad harvest, in consequence of which the psalmist had to struggle against the loss of faith on the part of the people and their turning to false gods. The psalmist seeks only to make clear the measure of his spiritual joy and chooses a common figure of joy at its maximum (cf. 126:6; Isa. 9:3).

8. In the fullness of confidence he leaves the issues of the tomorrow in the keeping of the Lord.

---

that. Then we may find that our "world" is of less importance than our souls, and that our capacity for sacrifice is genuine and dominant. No man can be "glad" unless he has some confidence that there is something outside himself for which he would be prepared to die, as the Covenanters put it, and that he has "points enough worth fighting for." Only then is he granted that inner harmony with the hidden reality—with himself—from which there springs this gladness the psalmist is writing about. It comes like God's own benediction (Num. 6:24-26).

This leads us to the second "queer fact," that life comes from life through suffering and, indeed, from death. The principle is established by the will of God, and he who accepts it is harmonious to the will, and therefore is "glad." It certainly is a queer fact, but fact it is, and we had better accept it. It can of course be illustrated from all experience. Nature proclaims it: no winter, no spring. We may remember how Robert Herrick emphasizes the truth that it is the patient ground which God with his sunshine and his showers "turns to flowers." Similarly in the upward progress of man: the agents of it are those that dare and endure; "they shall be free that dare to be free," and "the blood of the martyrs is the seed of the church."[6] And "God's new saint, the scientist" is the servant of the same principle. No man became a great doctor by having a good time; but the discoverer of any cure—of cancer, in due course—will certainly be able to say, "Thou hast given me greater gladness than if I had oscillated between Florida and Muskoka." Garibaldi cried, "I offer you wounds, but I offer you honor," and with honor, inevitably greater **gladness.** In the supreme region of the knowledge of God life came to the world through suffering and death. The cross of Christ is the final instance of the reign of the principle to which in this world even God proved himself subject. Yet perhaps therefore he is the "happy God."

It is this inner harmony with ourselves and our Maker, created by a total acceptance of the principle of life through pain, which is the great good. Rebellion against the principle is the root cause of most of our malaise. The universe of created beings may be conceived of as a great orchestra or choir called together to give glory to God in the music of their common life. For each of us to play his part requires patience, drudgery, weariness, and the recurrent pain of inadequacy; so that we tend to cry for ease and rest and relaxing, finding therein our **gladness.** But if we yield to that, we are late in our entrances, bungling our notes, singing off-key, and so facing the rebuke of the great Conductor's eye. Our cry must be, "Bind me in the meshes of thy music, Master." He takes up his thongs of suffering and binds us, and we, obedient to his controlling hand, become his musicians and are glad.

The psalm ends with the gentlest of lullabies, as if the writer were singing to himself in quietness, **I will both lay me down in peace, and sleep.** He may have been a great statesman, but in the evening he was a child, a trusting child of God, one of the beloved to whom God gave greatly in his sleep (cf. 127:2 Moffatt).

[6] Tertullian *Apology* L. 13.

To the chief Musician upon Nehiloth, A Psalm of David.

5 Give ear to my words, O LORD; consider my meditation.

To the choirmaster: for the flutes. A Psalm of David.

5 Give ear to my words, O LORD;
give heed to my groaning.

V. A PRAYER AT THE MORNING SACRIFICE (5:1-12)

From the standpoint of the Psalter's editors it was fitting that this psalm as a prayer uttered at the time of the morning sacrifice (vs. 3) should be set after Ps. 4, which was assumed to be an evening prayer (4:8). It is of the same type as Pss. 3 and 4, expressing the fervent appeal of a devout servant of the Lord for help against men who treacherously plan his destruction (vs. 9). Vs. 3 makes it clear that the singing or recitation of such psalms was recognized in the order of worship at the temple.

The psalmist is menaced by a company of persons who are devising some plot against him (vs. 10). They are men of his own religion, as we see by his reference to their coming to the temple to worship (vss. 4*b*-5*a*). Their character is set forth in strong terms and unsparingly. They are an arrogant, **boastful** set (vs. 5), who by **lies** (vs. 6) and slanderous talk (vs. 9) are seeking to accomplish their purpose, and who in the pursuit of it will not shrink from the worst acts of violence since they are **bloodthirsty . . . men** (vs. 6); **their heart is destruction,** and their throat **an open sepulchre** (vs. 9). They try to conceal their intrigue by deceit (vs. 6) and the use of smooth words (vs. 9). The psalmist feels himself so hemmed in by them that there is no hope of his escape except by the intervention of him who is the defender of the righteous, "Make my way straight before me" (vs. 8).

The five strophes of about equal length (RSV), through which the appeal of the psalmist is expressed, are so patterned that in the first and the third strophe the psalmist is in the foreground; in the second and the fourth his foes are dealt with; the concluding strophe is a petition on behalf of all righteous souls who make the Lord their refuge. In the composition of the psalm, therefore, special attention has been paid to the matter of poetical form.

The meter is almost regularly in the 3+2 or *qînāh* measure, except where, as in vss. 11*c*-12 (Hebrew vss. 12*c*-13), the text seems to have become slightly disordered.

1. THE PLEA FOR THE LORD'S ATTENTION (5:1-3)

5:1-3. In his straits the psalmist enters the temple and prostrates himself in worship toward the holy place (vs. 7): **Hearken, . . . my King and my God** (cf. 44:4; 68:24; 74:12;

5:1-12. ***A Hymn for the Morning Offering.***—We have in this psalm a hymn for morning sacrifice in the temple, sharply personal in tone. While its references are related to the natural acts of the worship of the writer's time, its phrases are such that they can be applied to Christian worship in its most spiritual aspects. It is a psalm from which the interpreter may take an image here, or a phrase there, and put himself in their charge, their true context being his own religious experience or need and that of the people whom he is addressing.

The structure is evident. Vss. 1-3 are a true "invocation." Vss. 4-7 remind us that only those who seek harmony with the divine Will can bring an offering of worship that will be acceptable, particularly that the offering of the "man of blood," who has cruelty and hate in his heart, will be rejected. On the other hand, the worshiper's own state of mind is marked by awareness of God's mercy, through which alone he is permitted to enter the place of prayer, and by consequent reverence; it is implied that thereby he may hope that his worship will be acceptable. Vss. 8-12 are a prayer for divine light and leading in the difficulties created by men who willfully misrepresent him, for the destruction of his slanderous opponents, and for the open and joyful triumph of the honest and God-fearing. The conclusion is a strong instance of that complete confidence in God's ultimate vindication of the good, which like a trumpet melody runs through the varied music of the psalms.

1. *Consider My Meditation.*—The word **meditation** is hardly a precise translation. "The murmur of my soul" (Moffatt) is a helpful

2 Hearken unto the voice of my cry, my King, and my God: for unto thee will I pray.
3 My voice shalt thou hear in the morning, O LORD; in the morning will I direct *my prayer* unto thee, and will look up.

2 Hearken to the sound of my cry,
my King and my God,
for to thee do I pray.
3 O LORD, in the morning thou dost hear
my voice;
in the morning I prepare a sacrifice for
thee, and watch.

84:3). His prayer is made **in the morning,** not only an appointed time of worship (cf. Exod. 29:39; 36:3; Num. 28:4, 8, 23; II Kings 3:20; Ezek. 46:15), but of the three times of daily prayer referred to in the Psalter, the principal one (cf. 55:17; 59:16; 88:13). He pours forth his entreaty to God in muttered words mingled with loud cries,

Give heed to my groaning.
Hearken to the sound of my cry.

His prayer is accompanied by the offering of a **sacrifice,** because a sacrifice, as inviting the special presence of the Lord (cf. Amos 5:21-23; Ezek. 44:7-16), was thought to provide a most favorable time for a prayer to reach the divine ear, and especially for a prayer that made itself heard by loud shouts and wailings (vss. 1-2). Further, at such a time a revelation from God could be expected either by sign or oracle (cf. Gen. 15:11; Num. 23:3; Mic. 7:7; Luke 1:11), for—as men have always reasoned—if we draw near to God, he will draw near to us (145:18-19). Hence **I prepare a sacrifice for thee, and watch.**

I prepare . . . for thee: A technical term for setting in order the wood for a sacrifice (Lev. 1:7), the sacrifice itself (Lev. 1:8), the sacred lamps (Lev. 24:3-4), or the showbread (Lev. 24:7-8). Since the psalmist's relations to the temple do not seem to be those of one who served as a priest (cf. vs. 7), the term here means to institute or provide a sacrifice; it may also be translated, "I cause a sacrifice to be made ready."

---

alternative. A fruitful suggestion is to be found in both. A man comes before God with his case against the experiences which he feels he does not deserve. That sets him to probe deeper into himself in order to discover the murmurings against God which may be poisoning his inner life; from which he may proceed to real meditation, wherein he faces all the facts, and particularly counts his blessings one by one. He thereby is more likely to come into a frame of mind fit for worship. It is worth noting how different phrases in the psalm are psychologically connected. If he really faces his complaint in God's presence (vs. 1), he is more likely to be honest when he says that he may worship in reverence to God (vs. 4). Moffatt's phrase "the murmur of my soul" is singularly fruitful. When a man discovers his innate complaining spirit, and how it blinds him to God's goodness, he has started on the way to "saving health." A study of the demand for meditation, so frequent in scripture, will also be profitable.

2. ***The Impress of Christ.***—The conjunction of the titles **my King, and my God** should be noted. It hints a consideration of the development of the impress of Christ, from the Man to the Master, and on to the God-filled Man, and so to the King—the aspect of Christ which dominates the final book of the Scriptures—ending with the Christ in God. The modern world badly needs to be reminded that the Man of Galilee is not enough, and that when "Jesus comes, he comes to reign."

3. ***In the Morning.***—Every phrase in this verse is full of material. The first directs the mind to the vital question of religious practice, particularly at the start of the day. The writer reminds himself that God is before him in the morning, ready to hear: "New every morning is the love." Then he declares that he promptly responds. In the morning he makes ready for God. The psalmist is thinking of the proper arrangements of the sacrifice he is placing on the altar, but the ASV gives a more spiritual meaning when it translates, "In the morning will I order my prayer unto thee." The expositor will find an opportunity here for counsel upon the whole matter of the ordering of devotion. When should the main effort be made? Is the early celebration of the Holy Communion a vital matter? Is the "evening sacrifice" the most potent and necessary time for meditation? In any case, emphasis

4 For thou *art* not a God that hath pleasure in wickedness: neither shall evil dwell
with thee.
5 The foolish shall not stand in thy sight:
thou hatest all workers of iniquity.
6 Thou shalt destroy them that speak
leasing: the LORD will abhor the bloody
and deceitful man.
7 But as for me, I will come *into* thy
house in the multitude of thy mercy: *and* in
thy fear will I worship toward thy holy
temple.

4 For thou art not a God who delights in
wickedness;
evil may not sojourn with thee.
5 The boastful may not stand before thy
eyes;
thou hatest all evildoers.
6 Thou destroyest those who speak lies;
the LORD abhors bloodthirsty and deceitful men.

7 But I through the abundance of thy steadfast love
will enter thy house,
I will worship toward thy holy temple
in the fear of thee.

---

2. THE GROUNDS OF THE PSALMIST'S FAITH (5:4-7)

4-7. The psalmist fortifies his case by laying boldly before the Lord the grounds on which he bases his expectation of a favorable response to his prayer. First, his awe before the Lord does not weaken his instinctive conviction that an upright man may reason with the Lord as a man with a friend (cf. Gen. 18:23-33; Job 13:17-28). The Lord, his king, **hatest all evildoers** (vs. 5) and brings them to nought (vs. 6) because they are in truth rebels against himself (vs. 10). How then can he permit the enemies of the psalmist to accomplish their evil designs? Second, the psalmist indirectly reminds the Lord that his participation in the worship of the temple is an evidence of his good standing before the Lord, for "an evil man cannot sojourn with thee" (vs. 4). Third, the Lord's good will toward him up to the present time is surely an earnest of his favor in the future (vs. 7).

I will worship toward thy holy temple: Lit., "I fall down in the direction of." The psalm may be postexilic. In this connection it should be noted that certain words in the vocabulary of the psalm, while not peculiar to the late literature, are, however, commonly met there; e.g., ערך, **prepare** (vs. 3); אשם, "make bear guilt" (vs. 10); and גור, "sojourn," with the sense of enjoying the privilege of worship in the temple (vs. 4).

---

should be placed on **in the morning.** So does one **prepare** for all that God may send in that particular day of duties and testings and disappointments and joys. In the morning, whatever else we do, we must start with a purpose to face what he wills and to keep the comradeship. Not only so, but, **in the morning will I . . . look up.** "I will lift up mine eyes" (121:1) is the only way to face life at any time, but particularly in the morning. The morning offers a new chance to work with God.

4-7. ***A God Who Delights Not in Wickedness.***—Vs. 4 is a striking image. We see evil knocking at God's gate, asking that it be admitted as a guest, only to be met with an indignant stare and a disdainful rejecting hand. There is such a thing as the disgust of God.

In vs. 5 a class of evil men is singled out for rejection, variously translated **foolish, boastful,** or "arrogant" (ASV). The two latter give the flavor of the original, indicating men wise in their own conceit, who think they can get on without God; but it is helpful to be reminded in the KJV what fools they are. The healthy vigor of the psalmist's language should suggest to us that we need not be mealymouthed in describing the folly of men, or of humanity as a whole, when they put the crown of wisdom on their own head. The cult of success easily becomes a moral epidemic.

Allied with these in condemnation are **those who speak lies,** the **bloodthirsty,** and cheats (vs. 6). We need not be surprised at their condemnation; but it is significant that they are the natural comrades of the arrogantly proud and occupy a secondary place with regard to them. History has plenty of instances to prove that lies and cruelty and treachery spring from pride, that queen of sins. Cf. the pre-eminence of pride as a root sin in Dante's *Purgatory*.[7]

The phrase **through the abundance of thy**

[7] Canto XII.

8 Lead me, O LORD, in thy righteousness because of mine enemies; make thy way straight before my face.

9 For *there is* no faithfulness in their mouth; their inward part *is* very wickedness; their throat *is* an open sepulchre; they flatter with their tongue.

10 Destroy thou them, O God; let them fall by their own counsels; cast them out in the multitude of their transgressions; for they have rebelled against thee.

8 Lead me, O LORD, in thy righteousness
because of my enemies;
make thy way straight before me.

9 For there is no truth in their mouth;
their heart is destruction,
their throat is an open sepulchre,
they flatter with their tongue.
10 Make them bear their guilt, O God;
let them fall by their own counsels;
because of their many transgressions cast them out,
for they have rebelled against thee.

---

3. THE PSALMIST'S ENEMIES (5:8-10)

8-10. The psalmist concludes his prayer with three petitions. First he prays that the Lord will lead him out of his straits and make smooth and straight the way before him (vs. 8). **Make thy way straight before me:** I.e., help me to follow easily the way that you would have me go so that I may be kept from error. The alternate reading of the LXX, "my way," changes the passage into a prayer simply for escape from the imminent danger.

Then he asks that his enemies be requited according to the measure of the guilt they have incurred by their murderous designs (vss. 9-10). Such an imprecation is not a rare thing in the Psalter and can be justified only on the ground that the psalmist identified enmity against himself with enmity against God.

Open sepulchre: In Palestine graves were sometimes made by cutting a hole or pit in the rock. When left uncovered through neglect they could be the cause of death

---

steadfast love (vs. 7) expresses prevenient grace *in excelsis.* This psalmist must have been a truly humble man, deeply realizing his dependence on God. Even permission to cross the threshold of the **temple** came from God; even permission to worship in reverence came from him, and still more remarkable was the evidence of his abundant kindness. We may wonder whether such an idea ever enters the mind of a Christian worshiper today. The common idea would rather seem to be that we confer a favor by going to church, and that we deserve praise for patronizing God's house. If so, we are vastly inferior spiritually to this writer. It is, after all, astonishing that God permits us to worship him; for we are "not worthy of the least of these thy benefits," or so we say in our prayers. We had better meditate on our own prayers.

8-10. ***The Villainy of Slanderers.***—Here again (vs. 8) variant translations are illuminating. The KJV has **mine enemies.** So has the ASV, with "those that lie in wait for me" as the marginal alternative. Moffatt has "foes." The KJV mg. has a very useful hint—"those who observe me," critically, it is to be presumed, and with a view to tripping one up. The Christian today must be on guard because of those who "observe" him with unfriendly eyes, and he has particular reason, like the psalmist, to ask God's guidance that he may walk circumspectly.

The second clause of vs. 8, **make thy way straight before my face,** is also to be marked. Moffatt has "smooth," but **straight** or "plain" is preferable. No doubt the psalmist is asking for an easier journey; but his emphasis is upon the kind of ease that comes when a man knows clearly the path of right. Much of the difficulty of living comes from intellectual perplexity as to what the will of God is for us and in our time. The interesting thing about the day of judgment (as a witty woman once remarked) will be that we shall then know "the right answers." In actual living we often have to choose the lesser of two evils, or we are perturbed between two mutually incompatible goods. No wonder the psalmist desires a **straight,** plain path! The honest puzzled man of today is his brother in need. Happy will he be who discovers that in the matter of light in darkness God will surround him **with favor . . . as with a shield** (vs. 12).

A violent image of the villainy of the slanderers is given in vs. 9. They are plain liars, **there is no truth in their mouth;** they do not lie only for the pleasure of lying, but with a view to destruction: **their heart is destruction** (cf.

11 But let all those that put their trust in thee rejoice: let them ever shout for joy, because thou defendest them: let them also that love thy name be joyful in thee.

12 For thou, LORD, wilt bless the righteous; with favor wilt thou compass him as *with* a shield.

To the chief Musician on Neginoth upon Sheminith, A Psalm of David.

6 O LORD, rebuke me not in thine anger, neither chasten me in thy hot displeasure.

11 But let all who take refuge in thee rejoice,
let them ever sing for joy;
and do thou defend them,
that those who love thy name may exult in thee.
12 For thou dost bless the righteous, O LORD;
thou dost cover him with favor as with a shield.

To the choirmaster: with stringed instruments; according to The Sheminith.
A Psalm of David.

6 O LORD, rebuke me not in thy anger,
nor chasten me in thy wrath.

---

or injury to those who came upon them unawares. In the O.T. there are not a few references to the deadly effects of slander, false witness, and lying (cf. 52:2; 57:4; 64:3; Prov. 18:21; Jer. 9:8).

4. The Joy of the Righteous (5:11-12)

11-12. In the concluding petition the psalmist moves to a higher level. He prays both for himself and for all **who love thy name,** that they may **sing for joy** and **exult in thee.** For the vindication of the psalmist will be a fresh demonstration of God's goodness to his faithful servants, since the strength of their faith is that God does **bless the righteous** and defends him **as with a shield.**

VI. Cry of a Sick Man (6:1-10)

In this psalm, as in Pss. 3–5, we hear the cry of a man in trouble. In its lines, however, the subject of complaint is not the truculence of adversaries but a sickness

---

Adolf Hitler, *Mein Kampf*,[8] and Robert H. Jackson, *The Nürnberg Case*[9]). They lull their victim to sleep with flattering, or better, "smooth words." It is an ugly picture of what is only too prevalent in the world. The phrase **their throat is an open sepulchre** should be contrasted with the lips of him who could say, "The words that I speak unto you, they are spirit, and they are life" (John 6:63). The "two mouths" of mankind give a sharp image of the gulf that is fixed between good and evil. No wonder that in vs. 10 the psalmist prays that such men may be **cast . . . out.** There is a motto carved in stone in Winchester School in England: *Aut disce aut discedite, non sors tertia hic manet*—"Either learn or depart, there is no third choice here." Similarly, in a world where God's rule is apparent, tricksters, who make the lie their agent, must either cease to be what they are or be banished from the society of decent men.

11-12. ***Sing for Joy.***—The words to emphasize in vs. 11 are **joy** and **shout.** There ought to be something exhilarating about being a Christian, and the watching world ought to be able to mark it in the good cheer of Christian folk. It is an uplifting thought, surely, that neither life nor death can separate us from the love of God. If Christ the conqueror has become the "pale Galilean," and if the world has gone gray from his breath,[10] there is something very wrong with the image we have made of him and with the effect we have had on society. If such a statement possesses even a grain of truth, the fault is not his but ours. We need a little more of the spirit of the early days, and especially of Paul, that apostle who knew the glad heart of liberty when he realized that there was now no condemnation to them that are in Christ Jesus. Christians must remember that the Lord instructed and expected us to "be of good cheer."

The last verse closes the psalm on a note of confidence, a note which is one of the main contributions of the Psalter to the religious life.

6:1-10. ***A Prayer for Help.***—Here we have a prayer in familiar circumstances. An honest and

[8] New York: Reynal & Hitchcock, 1939.

[9] New York: Alfred A. Knopf, 1947.

[10] Algernon Charles Swinburne, "Hymn to Proserpine."

that racks the psalmist's body and soul. So great is his distress that his death seems close at hand (vs. 5). It is in accordance with the thinking of his time that he views his condition to be a manifestation of the divine displeasure. For since God wills all that happens in human experience as well as in the world in general, it follows that our afflictions must be conceived as expressive of his ill will toward us.

This psalm, while true to the type of a psalm of lament, sheds some independent light on the manner in which God-fearing men oriented themselves to their personal experiences of physical suffering. In this respect a comparison of the psalm with, for example, Pss. 30; 32; 88; 116 serves to bring its individuality into relief (see Exeg. on 38:1-22).

The meter is 3+3, but in vss. 2, 4, 8 we have respectively 4+4, 2+2+3, and 4+3.

1. Petition for the Lord's Deliverance (6:1-5)

6:1-3. The pains of the psalmist are like the blows of a rod in the hands of an angry God:

> **O Lord, rebuke me not in thy anger,**
> **nor chasten me in thy wrath.**

The measure of his visitation is registered in his whole being, **my bones are troubled. My soul also is sorely troubled.** Instead of נבהלו, **are troubled,** a better reading is

---

humble man is sick, and he prays for help and healing. Apparently, from the evidence of vss. 1-7, his sickness is physical, and he is afraid that he will not recover. But in vs. 5 the tone changes. From then on he speaks as one who has been surrounded by active enemies, from whose plottings he is escaped. Here the subject might well be the nation, perhaps toward the end of the Exile.

The church, however, has used the psalm differently, for it is the first of the penitential psalms, of which Ps. 51 is the chief. That is to say, the suffering is of the soul and the enemies are spiritual, including both men and demonic tempters. The translation of vs. 8 might cover both, **you workers of evil.** Doubtless the historical facts are that the writer was sick of body and that his spiritual depression arose from his illness, while at the same time he had personal enemies who were seeking his hurt. In that situation, in the simplest way he turns to the only help left. It is a state of mind akin to the phrase in the Book of Common Prayer, "There is none other that fighteth for us, but only thou, O God"; or in Jane Crewdson's beautiful hymn, "O Savior, I have nought to plead."

For a Christian the spiritual use of the psalm is inevitable. In any case the physical and spiritual blend into one another in common experience. Only greatness of soul can prevent bodily sickness from bringing weariness of spirit; it is hard to be spiritually buoyant with neuralgia, or still more when subject to weakness and "the masterful collapse of all that makes me man." The church had a right instinct when it found in this prayer a cry universal of the soul in its darkest needs; and the interpreter is well justified in using it in the way that Christian experience has deepened it.

1. *Spiritual Gain in Pain.*—Rebuke me not in thy anger indicates that the writer regards his sickness as disciplinary, which is a worthy and Christian attitude toward pain. John Kelman, at one time minister of the Fifth Avenue Presbyterian Church in New York City, when suffering great weakness not long before he died, said, "I am persuaded that this is the best that can be done for me now." All pain has in it the possibility of spiritual gain, and our enterprise at such a time is to see to it that we obtain that benefit which God can bring from our pain. "Unproductive suffering" is a sad thing, and we must struggle to avoid adding to its mass.

The psalmist, however, is so weak and sick that his prayer is not an appeal for light to discover and appropriate any spiritual benefit, but a plain pleading for recovery. He wants the pain to stop, and he says so to God, a most permissible proceeding. If we may define prayer as "telling God all about it," the declaration of our heartfelt longing is certainly true prayer. "I never knew how wonderful the promise is that there shall be no more pain, until I had this cancer," a famous doctor said not long before death brought the fulfillment of the promise. But we notice a point in which Christian faith reaches beyond the psalmist. The latter prays that God may not correct him in his **anger,** a thought that does not belie God, for love has angers. If our pain is disciplinary, we must hold it to be necessary. It may even come to be, as we look back on it, our strongest evi-

2 Have mercy upon me, O Lord; for I *am* weak: O Lord, heal me; for my bones are vexed.
3 My soul is also sore vexed: but thou, O Lord, how long?

2 Be gracious to me, O Lord, for I am languishing;
O Lord, heal me, for my bones are troubled.
3 My soul also is sorely troubled.
But thou, O Lord—how long?

בלו, "are dried up," or נבלו, "rot away." No claims to righteousness, no pleas of innocence, and no protests against the incommensurateness of his affliction relatively to the quantum of his sin are voiced by the psalmist. Unlike Job, he accepts without question the verdict of his contemporaries, that when affliction comes there must first have been sin. Although he is a God-fearing man (cf. vs. 5), his sense of shortcomings may have been so quick that he suppressed the inner urge to press forward to a more penetrating conception of the divine relation to human suffering.

---

dence that God is concerned for our spiritual well-being. Nevertheless, pain hurts; and it is no unseemly thing for a child to ask his Father to let the cup pass from him.

2. ***The Disease of Success.***—The meaning of this verse is clear; it is simply a plea that comes out of the midst of physical illness. The writer feels "withered away," "faint," **weak,** as various translations put it. We wonder what the illness was; malaria, perhaps. But the spiritual result is the same whatever the precise cause: the sufferer is convinced that there are situations in life to which he is entirely inadequate. Healing must come from without. Is not this a good word to rich and prosperous men, especially to those who have been the architects of their own fortune? Religiously a man is in danger if he is afflicted with the pride of achievement. There is such a thing as the disease of success. Those who think that the first and last commandment is "be strong," have developed satisfactorily only when they change it to "be strengthened"; and this they are in God's mercy sometimes helped to do by becoming thoroughly weak and helpless. The creation of the spirit of dependence is, in the case of the masterful, part of what "the blessed evil" of illness is for.

3. ***How Long?***—**My soul is also sore vexed** or **sorely troubled** should be read with the second clause, **But thou, O Lord—how long?** The psalmist sets out to declare the corrective to his soul's troubling, which is the thought of the helper; but even as he does so, the trouble of the soul reasserts itself in the haunting phrase, **how long?** Men who do not deny God can nevertheless be perplexed by his apparent unconcern. Surely a Father would not only deliver, but would make speed to deliver. Large views of history show that "though the mills of God grind slowly, yet they grind exceeding small";[1] so slowly, however, that the individual does not seem to share in their ultimate victory. Here indeed is a perplexity, especially for those who, like the psalmist, have no hope of immortality. The question **how long?** meets with varied answers in Scripture and experience. The main reply seems to be "wait"—a harsh saying. It is not easy to wait in the midst of the monotony of pain and unfulfilled desire. Yet it is only thus that strength through dependence comes. Indeed, the man who can say "my soul waiteth upon the Lord" has largely succeeded in life. But "wait" is not the only answer. Sometimes it is "now," when a man prays for forgiveness, as the penitent thief discovered. Sometimes it is, "You must wait for what you desire, but you will receive now what you need." Cf. the incident in Acts 1:6-8, when the disciples inquired whether the kingdom was to be restored at once to Israel, and received the reply, "It is not for you to know, . . . but ye shall receive power"; with the result that their combined ignorance and power made them "witnesses." Similarly illness, disappointment, and sorrow have many a time left misty horizons, but also have been sources of power for noble tasks. God works in a mysterious way for the human soul; but he does work.

The phrase **how long?** occurs more than fifty times in Scripture, and some sixteen or seventeen times in the psalms alone. It is well worth while examining each instance. Sometimes it is a question addressed from man to man: in these cases it is an exclamation which rises instinctively to the lips of reformers, who are rightly impatient with "the unbearable thing." Sometimes it is addressed to man by God (4:2), and to man by Jesus (Matt. 17:17). But for the most part it is an expression of the longing of the weary human heart for release and light, a very fundamental cry. We need to search the Scriptures widely to find the varying replies,

[1] Longfellow, "Poetic Aphorisms: Retribution." From the *Sinngedichte* of Friedrich von Logau.

4 Return, O Lord, deliver my soul: oh save me for thy mercies' sake.

5 For in death *there is* no remembrance of thee: in the grave who shall give thee thanks?

6 I am weary with my groaning; all the night make I my bed to swim; I water my couch with my tears.

7 Mine eye is consumed because of grief; it waxeth old because of all mine enemies.

8 Depart from me, all ye workers of iniquity; for the Lord hath heard the voice of my weeping.

4 Turn, O Lord, save my life;
deliver me for the sake of thy steadfast love.
5 For in death there is no remembrance of thee;
in Sheol who can give thee praise?

6 I am weary with my moaning;
every night I flood my bed with tears;
I drench my couch with my weeping.
7 My eye wastes away because of grief,
it grows weak because of all my foes.

8 Depart from me, all you workers of evil;
for the Lord has heard the sound of my weeping.

4-5. The elements of which a psalm of lament normally consists are (*a*) a call to God, (*b*) the matter of the complaint, (*c*) a petition, and (*d*) a conclusion, which may express the sufferer's confidence in a favorable answer from God, or which may be a vow of an offering to God on his recovery, or which in sheer distress of spirit may be omitted (cf. Ps. 88). In the present instance the psalmist handles the complaint (vss. 2-3) and the petition (vss. 4-5) in such a way that they become a statement of the reasons why the Lord should grant healing. The first reason is that the severity of the affliction should excite the divine sympathy; the second is that the reputation of the Lord as a gracious God (vs. 4) is at stake; the third is that the death of the psalmist will cost the Lord the loss of a loyal worshiper (vs. 5), since in Sheol there is neither praise nor mention of the Lord.

2. The Psalmist's Condition (6:6-7)

6-7. In the third strophe the appeal of his distress is reinforced by a more poignant description of its pitiableness. He moans and weeps, so that every night he drenches his pillows and in the morning his eyes, worn out with weeping and want of sleep, are dimmed.

For עתקה, **waxeth old,** read with the versions עתקתי, "I am grown old" (but see RSV); and for צוררי, **my foes,** read צרתי, "my distress," to preserve the parallelism with the preceding line.

3. Answered Prayer (6:8-10)

8-10. To add to his troubles he has **enemies,** but he does not mention the grounds for their animosity. Although they may be potentially as vicious as those who torment other psalmists, since they belong to the class of **workers of evil,** yet in this instance he is not the victim of their machinations by magic, calumnies, or plots (vs. 10); rather, they seem to be sitting and waiting upon the outcome of the divine visitation, either

---

noting that one of them is "never." The recapture of an earthly youth, the escape from the common burden of humanity, the reversal of the process of physical decay—to all these God answers irrevocably, "nevermore." This leads us to harmonize our desires, and therefore our prayers, with reality, and helps us to "assent to the universe," until at last we discover that though the transient is still transient the eternal is "some better thing."

4-10. ***Darkness and Light.***—Observe in these verses the picture of inevitable pessimism, apart from immortality. The psalmist was a very honest man who could take a steady look into the dark. For him death closed all; even remembrance and the praise of God were impossible in the place of shadows (vs. 5). No wonder that his cry was for restored health (vs. 4), or that in vss. 6-7 he bursts anew into exclamations of misery. **I drench my couch**

9 The LORD hath heard my supplication; the LORD will receive my prayer.
10 Let all mine enemies be ashamed and sore vexed: let them return *and* be ashamed suddenly.

Shiggaion of David, which he sang unto the LORD, concerning the words of Cush the Benjamite.

7 O LORD my God, in thee do I put my trust: save me from all them that persecute me, and deliver me:

9 The LORD has heard my supplication;
the LORD accepts my prayer.
10 All my enemies shall be ashamed and sorely troubled;
they shall turn back, and be put to shame in a moment.

A Shiggaion of David, which he sang to the LORD concerning Cush a Benjaminite.

7 O LORD my God, in thee do I take refuge;
save me from all my pursuers, and deliver me,

---

as adversaries, gloating over the psalmist's plight as evidence that his piety has been only a pretense (cf. 35:21), or as former friends and neighbors, horrified at the implications of the divine dealings with him (cf. 31:12; 55:12-13). But with vs. 8 the note of plangent anguish suddenly gives way to one of exulting confidence. **Depart from me, all you workers of evil. . . . The LORD has heard my supplication.**

Read in vs. 10*a*, "All my enemies shall be sorely troubled," omitting יבשו, **shall be ashamed,** both for the sake of the meter and because it is contrary to grammatical usage.

This concluding strophe is open to more than one interpretation. On the one hand, it may be viewed as integral to the psalm, and therefore an outburst of the psalmist's sure confidence in a favorable response from the Lord; on the other hand, there are those who believe that the psalm, having been included in a liturgy for the sick and afflicted to be used before the offerings on their behalf, was eventually supplemented by this strophe to be recited when by an oracle or by other signs a favorable response from the Lord was indicated.

When we pass from a review of its setting and structural features, we note that theologically the psalm bears the marks of the immaturity of its times in its assumption that sickness is the sign of God's disfavor, and in its pagan view of the afterlife, perhaps the result of a lag in the discernment of the implications of monotheism. Over against these defects should be set these other salient articles in the psalmist's creed: there is one Lord in whose hands lie men's affairs; he is not a capricious God, but a God whose mark is kindness; he is a God to whose face a man can defend his cause (cf. Job 13:15).

VII. A Cry for Help from Evil Pursuers (7:1-17)

In this psalm of lament, as in Pss. 3–5, the psalmist cries out to God for deliverance from bitter persecution. The psalm, like some others of its kind, evidences the fierce enmities bred by religious and political strife within the community, and the social scene it reflects is not a happy one. We are permitted to see how in such circumstances a man seeks to defend himself against the accusations of an enemy. In a ritual act he makes an appeal to God for vindication. Noting a certain lack of unity in the thought and the structure of the psalm, some commentators hold that it is of composite author-

---

with my weeping is not an exhilarating summary. The contrast between this good man's spiritual state and that of Paul in Rom. 8:38 is the contrast between darkness and light, and should be pondered by any who belittle the importance of immortality for a belief in the ultimate decency of things. The suggestion in this closing section of the psalm, as has been noted, is that in addition to illness the psalmist had personal **enemies.** But even the happy ending—he recovers, his foes are put to rout, and he gives God praise—remains shadowed. If this were indeed the only and therefore ultimate outcome, we should still walk in darkness.

7:1-17. ***The Refuge of the Innocent.***—Some authorities maintain that in this psalm two

2 Lest he tear my soul like a lion, rending *it* in pieces, while *there is* none to deliver.

3 O LORD my God, if I have done this; if there be iniquity in my hands;

4 If I have rewarded evil unto him that was at peace with me; (yea, I have delivered him that without cause is mine enemy;)

5 Let the enemy persecute my soul, and take *it;* yea, let him tread down my life upon the earth, and lay mine honor in the dust. Selah.

2 lest like a lion they rend me,
dragging me away, with none to rescue.

3 O LORD my God, if I have done this,
if there is wrong in my hands,
4 if I have requited my friend with evil
or plundered my enemy without cause,
5 let the enemy pursue me and overtake me,
and let him trample my life to the ground,
and lay my soul in the dust. *Selah*

---

ship; e.g., it is contended that vss. 6-9, because of their abrupt appeal for a divine assize in which the peoples will be gathered for judgment, contrast too sharply with the situation in vss. 1-5, 10-17, where the psalmist is hoping for an immediate deliverance from the machinations of a single enemy; vss. 10-11 also are regarded as extraneous material, on the ground that vss. 12-17 offer a better sequence to vss. 1-5, and that vss. 10-11 both in meter and in the preference of אלהים, **God,** to יהוה, **LORD,** for the divine name differ from the rest of the psalm. We may assume, however, that any additions to the original matter of the psalm were made in order to adapt it to congregational use, and that in spite of resultant inconsistencies the person or persons responsible for its present form conceived it to be a unity.

The rhythm is not regular. For the most part the lines are in 3+3 measure, but 4+3 or 3+4 occurs in vss. 1, 3, 5-6, 12, 14, and 3+2 in vss. 8*b*-10. These irregularities are to be attributed in some cases to errors in textual transmission, and in others to the composite structure of the psalm.

1. THE PSALMIST'S PLIGHT (7:1-2)

7:1-2. According to the context, the attack on the psalmist is provoked by one person (cf. vss. 2, 5; in vs. 1 read, therefore, מרדפי for מכל־רדפי, i.e., "from my pursuer" for **from all my pursuers)** who, like some of the enemies mentioned in other psalms (cf. 10:9; 17:12; 22:13; 35:16), is said to act with the fury and cruelty of a beast of prey. The attack consists in formal charges of criminal conduct laid against him.

2. PROTESTATION OF INNOCENCE (7:3-5)

3-5. By a solemn oath the psalmist protests his innocence: **O LORD my God, if I have done this.** For the form of the oath cf. the successive oaths in Job 31:5-35. The exact nature of the charge of which the psalmist seeks to clear himself is stated in vss. 3*b*-4. He is accused of committing a wrong through fraud or dishonesty (for the meaning of עול see Ezek. 18:8; 28:18) of such proportions that it could be described as plundering

---

entirely different poems have been welded into one. In vss. 1-5 and vss. 12-17 we find the pleading before God of an innocent man who is in danger through personal enemies. In vss. 6-11 the personified nation pleads for the gathering of all nations before God's court of justice, that they may hear the divine vindication of Israel. It is clear that vs. 12 reads continuously from vs. 5; for the subject of vs. 12 is obviously **the enemy,** who is the subject of vs. 5. However, the critical questions involved are discussed in the Exeg. For the Expos. it is sufficient to notice that vss. 1-5 and vss. 12-17 are regarded as a unity and personal; vss. 6-11, as a section by itself and national.

1-5. ***Rules of War.***—For purposes of exposition the psalm is not very rich ground. The RSV should be used; the KJV contains serious difficulties; e.g., in the second clause of vs. 4 **(I have delivered him that without cause is mine enemy)** we get an alien idea of the forgiveness of enemies of which there is no sign elsewhere in the psalms, and for which we need to go to the N.T. The RSV is better, **if I have . . . plundered my enemy without cause.** This would be a suitable phrase on which to base an ex-

6 Arise, O LORD, in thine anger, lift up
thyself because of the rage of mine enemies:
and awake for me *to* the judgment *that*
thou hast commanded.
7 So shall the congregation of the people
compass thee about: for their sakes therefore return thou on high.
8 The LORD shall judge the people:
judge me, O LORD, according to my righteousness, and according to mine integrity
that is in me.

6 Arise, O LORD, in thy anger,
lift thyself up against the fury of my enemies;
awake, O my God;[b] thou hast appointed a judgment.
7 Let the assembly of the peoples be gathered about thee;
and over it take thy seat[c] on high.
8 The LORD judges the peoples;
judge me, O LORD, according to my righteousness
and according to the integrity that is in me.

[b] Or *for me*
[c] Cn: Heb *return*

(vs. 4). The seriousness of his offense is aggravated by the allegation that he did the wrong to a **friend,** one who trusted him, a bosom friend (cf. 41:9; Jer. 38:22). It seems clear that the solemn affirmation of innocence is made in the temple in accordance with a procedure indicated in I Kings 8:31-32. The oath therefore concludes in due form with the imprecation that if the guilt of the psalmist is proved, he may pay for it by the loss of his life. **Mine honor** is a synonym of the **soul,** parallel to **my life** in the preceding stich (cf. 16:9; 30:12; 108:1; Gen. 49:6). **The dust:** In the first instance the words means the dust that fills the grave, and then it is commonly used as a euphemism for the grave itself (cf. Isa. 26:19; Job 7:21; Dan. 12:2).

3. THE LORD'S JUDGMENT (7:6-8)

6-8. In the gravity of the situation it is natural that the oath should be followed by an appeal to God to **arise . . . in** [his] **anger** and vindicate the psalmist in a **judgment** in which **the fury of my enemies** will be brought to an end. It is obvious that the psalmist is not thinking here of the final world judgment, since he is in need of an immediate divine intervention in his favor (cf. 26:1; 35:23-24; 43:1). He assumes that the Lord is not above sitting in a great assize to consider the case of a single petitioner. The book of Job shows that this was a commonplace in the thought of the times. Whether the parties to be summoned to sit in judgment under the Lord (vs. 7) are **the peoples** of the world (see Amos 3:9) or "the heavenly beings" (cf. Ps. 82:1, and read אלהים, "divine beings," for לאמים, "peoples") is a matter on which there is a diversity of opinion among commentators. Since in vs. 8 the peoples themselves are subjects for judgment, the context seems to favor the latter view. At any rate, the conception of the psalmist that

---

amination of "rules of war." If it is our unhappy lot to have to choose war as the lesser of two evils, society must endeavor to put those who force the choice by aggression on peaceable peoples in the class of "criminals against society." Wanton plundering and destruction should be known by potential aggressors to be a crime for which they will have to answer in their persons. In this connection vss. 4-5 should be linked. Every phrase then becomes full of meaning.

6-11. ***Prayer for Judgment on the Nations.***—The RSV of vs. 6 is preferable. **Awake, O my God; thou hast appointed a judgment.** Two points stand out clear: (*a*) God means to judge, and the man of today needs to be reminded of that fact; and (*b*) it is a reasonable prayer that God may make judgment a vivid and somber reality here and now. "Let us see, O God, the righteous grinding of thy mills that the fear of judgment may stay haughty and cruel hands." In vs. 7 read,

Let the assembly of the peoples be gathered about thee;
and over it take thy seat on high.

A prayer, pictorially expressed, that the judgment with its verdict be open and unmistakable—a permanent human longing which is only

9 Oh let the wickedness of the wicked come to an end; but establish the just: for the righteous God trieth the hearts and reins.

10 My defense *is* of God, which saveth the upright in heart.

11 God judgeth the righteous, and God is angry *with the wicked* every day.

12 If he turn not, he will whet his sword; he hath bent his bow, and made it ready.

13 He hath also prepared for him the instruments of death; he ordaineth his arrows against the persecutors.

9 O let the evil of the wicked come to an end,
but establish thou the righteous,
thou who triest the minds and hearts,
thou righteous God.
10 My shield is with God,
who saves the upright in heart.
11 God is a righteous judge,
and a God who has indignation every day.

12 If a man[d] does not repent, God[d] will whet his sword;
he has bent and strung his bow;
13 he has prepared his deadly weapons,
making his arrows fiery shafts.

[d] Heb *he*

each individual has a place in the thought of the Lord has parallels in the N.T. (cf. Matt. 10:29-31; Luke 18:1-8).

4. The Righteous God (7:9-11)

9-11. The psalmist expresses his confidence in the issue of the judgment. Since God is a **righteous God** who tries the minds and hearts of men, wickedness must surely come to an end, and the righteous be established. "My shield over me is God" (read עלי for על). But woe to those who plot evil! God is "a God who executes punishment every day."

5. The Rewards of Evil (7:12-16)

12-16. Even as the psalmist's case is being laid before God, the enemy comes to his attack again. His charges of guilt are renewed against the psalmist's protestations of innocence. **God will whet his sword:** To describe the virulence of God's retributive intent the psalmist employs a series of metaphors drawn from such deadly things as the weapons

occasionally satisfied. As has been suggested, it will be refreshing to know the right answers to many things, not least in the apportioning of national guilt. Vss. 8-11 are a general statement of the perfect justice of God's judgment and the confidence that a man of integrity may have in its outcome. If the verses are national in character, they indicate an attitude in policy which modern states would do well to adopt. If governments can truly appeal to the God of history to vindicate their decisions, it means that they are not aggressors, nor the "haughty" whom moral forces will dethrone. Self-righteousness in an individual or a nation is an ugly thing against which our Lord warned us; but for a man whose desire is to do God's will, it is reasonable and right to declare his honesty of purpose, God being his helper. "Thrice is he armed that hath his quarrel just";[2] and if he believes that he has, there need be no spiritual pride in saying so. "The times are dark, but we believe we have points enough worth fighting for," the Covenanters cried; nobody can blame them for so declaring. "Our hearts are at peace," said Churchill of the British people in 1940; and there was no haughty boasting in it. But first one must search for God's purpose, and strive for humility under his mighty hand. In national affairs the church's business is to create such an atmosphere that governors and people alike will take their actions into the presence of God and determine their causes, solemnly and gravely, by the standards of the highest right they know. For by that right they will be judged in history as in eternity.

12-17. ***Preparations for Aggression.***—In vs. 12 read as in the ASV, "Surely he [the enemy] will again whet his sword." The writer's foe is implacable and is not to be turned from his preparations for mischief. While the link of vs. 12 with vs. 5 is clear, and the "enemy" is therefore the personal foe referred to in the opening section of the psalm, yet the attitude indicated in vss. 12-14 is that of an absolute ruler who is preparing an attack on a rival ruler. The verses

[2] Shakespeare, *Henry VI,* Part II, Act III, scene 2.

14 Behold, he travaileth with iniquity, and hath conceived mischief, and brought forth falsehood.

15 He made a pit, and digged it, and is fallen into the ditch *which* he made.

16 His mischief shall return upon his own head, and his violent dealing shall come down upon his own pate.

17 I will praise the LORD according to his righteousness: and will sing praise to the name of the LORD most high.

14 Behold, the wicked man conceives evil,
and is pregnant with mischief,
and brings forth lies.

15 He makes a pit, digging it out,
and falls into the hole which he has made.
16 His mischief returns upon his own head,
and on his own pate his violence descends.

17 I will give to the LORD the thanks due to his righteousness,
and I will sing praise to the name of the LORD, the Most High.

of a warrior (vss. 12-13), the pitfall of a hunter (vs. 15). But the enemy is only planning his own ruin (see I Kings 8:32).

His mischief returns upon his own head,
and on his own pate his violence descends.

6. DOXOLOGY (7:17)

17. So sure is the psalmist of the help of his God that he ends his psalm with a vow of thanksgiving: **I will give to the LORD the thanks due to his righteousness,** i.e., his vindication of the right.

are accurate descriptions of the secret preparations for aggressive war. In vs. 13 read with the RSV:

he has prepared his deadly weapons,
making his arrows fiery shafts.

Vs. 14 is a violent image of the soul of a rapacious man of power: his whole being is dedicated to his purpose, as is a woman whose faculties are centered on giving to the world a child. The KJV is perhaps preferable to the concrete RSV here, in the use of the word **travaileth** for **pregnant.** Archaisms, with their touch of poetry, have sometimes their advantages. But in vs. 14 the simple word **lies** is more vivid than **falsehood,** and is more descriptive of what actually happens in preparation for either personal or national attacks. Without the use of deliberate **lies,** half the world's quarrels would never reach the point of action—a fact which Christians need to press home on those who mold public opinion. Vss. 15-16 lead us into large regions; for they open up the subject of retribution, especially in its vivid form of "poetic justice." The word **pate** (vs. 16) has its value. It sticks in the memory, and helps to make the phrase proverbial. Modern illustrations of such nemeses are, and will remain, in all minds. Holes were dug in World War II for countless thousands done to death: into what sordid holes were the bodies of the men who ordained the digging ultimately flung? But we may go into a greater region still. Here is a principle; its writ runs in the spiritual realm. "With the froward thou wilt show thyself froward" (18:26); "Whatsoever a man soweth, that shall he also reap" (Gal. 6:7). The most terrible of all commentaries on this inevitable sequence (apart from penitence and God's grace) is found in Dante's *Inferno.* Every punishment therein portrayed is the expression in physical terms of the reaction of a moral universe in bringing an impenitent into the precise position into which his sin brought others. Would he shed blood in order to achieve power? Then let him wallow in blood that is boiling with hate. Would he leave his enemies only eyes to weep with? Then let his own eyes rain tears, but let them be tears of blood; cf. especially Canto XII, where the latter end of those who have dealt violently with their neighbors is symbolized. It is terrible reading—because we can but admit that it is an attempt to express that which must needs be; and it sends us hurrying to the gospel and to the Savior. In the light of Christ we may join with the psalmist in his conclusion (vs. 17). He gives thanks simply for the overthrow of his enemy. We may give thanks not only to him who brings to nought the plottings of the wicked, but who died and lives again that they also may be turned from wickedness to live.

To the chief Musician upon Gittith, A Psalm of David.

8 O Lord our Lord, how excellent *is* thy name in all the earth! who hast set thy glory above the heavens.

To the choirmaster: according to The Gittith. A Psalm of David.

8 O Lord, our Lord,
how majestic is thy name in all the earth!

Thou whose glory above the heavens is chanted

VIII. The Majesty of God (8:1-9)

This psalm is to be classed with the hymns which together constitute a distinct group within the Psalter. With some freedom it follows the literary standards which governed the composition of these exalted songs of praise to God. The author was stirred to praise by a contemplation of the glory of God as manifested in the wonders of the heavens, which in turn excited reflections on the place of man in the scheme of creation. The hymn is marked by such originality, imagination, elevation of thought, and artistry in the handling of its theme that it has won for itself a special place in the regard of all readers of the Psalter, ancient or modern (cf. 144:3; Job 7:17; Matt. 21:16; I Cor. 15:25; Heb. 2:6-7).

The first and the last line are in 2+2+2 measure. In the body of the psalm the meter of vss. 4-7 is 3+3; the rest of the verses present the normal variations of 4+3 (vs. 8), 4+4 (vs. 3), 3+4+3 (vs. 2).

The psalm opens with a line which, being repeated at its close, is of the nature of a refrain. Whether this line was provided by the author or not, it is useful in adapting the psalm to use by the congregation, for in vss. 1, 9 **our Lord** implies that a number of persons are joining in praise, whereas in the body of the psalm there seems to be only one voice, **when I look.** It is not necessary to go further and assume that in public worship one part of the psalm was sung by a choir and the other by a single voice, although instances of such antiphonal singing are not wanting in the Psalter, e.g., Pss. 24; 66; 118; 136. With the refrain omitted, the psalm falls into four strophes of four stichs or two lines each.

8:1-9. *God, Nature, and Man.*—Here is a psalm that is a mine for the expositor, as well as for any who would meditate worthily in the eventide. W. E. Addis[3] heads it simply "A Nature Psalm," but it is more than that. It has also been called "a lyric echo of the first chapter of Genesis"; but it is more than that too. It is a psalm of God, nature, and man, and might be called today the psalm of a religious scientist. Some of its phrases have become part of the permanent mental furniture of reflective people.

The general structure needs only a passing observation. The psalm begins with an outburst of praise to the God of nature. Vs. 2 is corrupt in the text and the KJV reading cannot stand; but the RSV, based on slight emendations, gives a good meaning. We notice how the contrasts begin with this verse—the psalm might indeed be called a psalm of contrasts. God's "excelling" is so splendid that even little children can see it and respond. For is it not to beauty that children do respond? But it is also of such a kind that it is an irresistible power against cruel and bitter men, who stand still in their tracks in front of it.

Vss. 3-4 deal with the main contrasts: between God's greatness and man's littleness, and also between what might be God's relation to man and what, in point of fact, that relation is as shown by divine action. Vss. 5-8 bring into sharp relief the contrast between man's relation to God and his relation to his own natural world, with a consequent restatement of his relation to God. In vs. 9 the psalm closes with a repetition of the opening phrase of adoration. Abruptly the psalmist leaves his reader face to face with the wonder of the Most High.

1-2. *How Excellent Thy Name.*—That is to say, look at God's creation and let it hit home upon the mind. You will be forced to admit that the Creator is one whom humanity must exalt and acknowledge to be great beyond our com-

[3] In A. S. Peake, ed., *A Commentary on the Bible* (London: Thomas Nelson & Sons, n.d.), p. 375.

2 Out of the mouth of babes and sucklings hast thou ordained strength because of thine enemies, that thou mightest still the enemy and the avenger.	2 by the mouth of babes and infants, thou hast founded a bulwark because of thy foes, to still the enemy and the avenger.

In the O.T. a hymn is normally introduced by a call to worship or praise, consisting of one or more lines (cf. 99:1-9; Isa. 42:10-13), followed by the reasons for the summons (cf. 100:1-5). But in this psalm the introduction has been omitted, and the simple stereotyped recitation of the reasons for worship has been transcended by a wholly original treatment of this element of the hymnic form. Such evidences of literary freedom are indicative of the date of the psalm. The hymnal pattern had a history. In the pre-exilic period it was simple and fixed (cf. Isa. 6:3; Zeph. 3:14-15), its highest development being seen in Isa. 42:10-13. But in the postexilic period the old pattern undergoes a development by the introduction of a fuller and richer content and by a freer treatment of the subject matter. On these premises Ps. 8 must be assigned to the later period. Besides, its conception of the divine creative work belongs to the level of the theological insights of Second Isaiah (cf. Isa. 40:28; 45:18), Gen. 1, and Ps. 104, none of which is pre-exilic.

1. The Glory of God in Nature (8:1-2)

8:1-2. As a hymn, the psalm opens with simple and sublime words of praise in which the psalmist is joined by the whole congregation assembled in the presence of "Yahweh our Lord." It is the excellence or majesty of God's being as manifested by his creative work **in all the earth** that inspires the worshipers to glorify his **name.** The **name** of the Lord, in this instance, is identical with the Lord himself (cf. 19:2; 148:13). But more splendidly than the earth, **the heavens,** on which God sits enthroned (cf. 2:4; 104:3; Isa. 66:1), reveal the glory of the Creator and his handiwork. Yet it is beyond the power of human tongues to frame praises equal to such a theme; the noblest hymns that men can invent in praise of God's glory in creation are like the babblings of **babes and infants.** First of creation's wonders, the firmament itself apart from its "lights" (cf.

---

puting—and thus is **excellent** in the true sense of the word (cf. Charles Wesley's hymn, "Love divine, all loves excelling"). Meditate upon that word **excellent** or "surpassing," and let it lead to the thought of the "beyondness of God." Many a phrase will come to mind: "The high and lofty One that inhabiteth eternity" (Isa. 57:15); "Thou art a God that hidest thyself" (Isa. 45:15); "Thou thoughtest I was altogether such a one as thyself" (Ps. 50:21); "The Father of lights, with whom is no variableness, neither shadow of turning" (Jas. 1:17); etc. "How surpassing all else that is, art thou." Herein is displayed the essential attitude of mind for all true worship. Part of the reason for the divorce of the scientific mind from worship lies in our anthropomorphic habit of thinking, whereby we seem to suggest that God is made in man's image, and that we can easily grasp the conception of God intellectually. To judge by some of our habitual modes of expression, we are not far from Browning's Caliban, who "thinketh, He dwelleth i' the cold o' the moon." Let us remember the mystics and their name for God—the Alone.

At the same time, let us not forget the possessive pronoun **our,** so obligatory for religion—and in this connection so awesome in the comfort it provides. Beginning with this verse, and turning the pages of the Bible, we may mark the value of the possessive pronoun, both singular and plural, ranging from "our sins" to "our Father." Evangelical preaching can never overemphasize "our" and "my." The God who is the Beyond is also **our** God—a thought that comes to its power only through Christ. The reader must let him capture this whole psalm.

The second clause of vs. 1 stands in need of emendation. It is best read in connection with vs. 2, as in the RSV. Yet we must emphasize the phrase **whose glory above the heavens,** for it is this before which even babes are in awe. There is no exaggeration here. Even little children stand open mouthed before nature's grandeur. Not to be forgotten is the look of concentrated wonder in the eyes of a boy of eighteen months when he first saw the sea, or his bitter weeping two or three years later when a branch of laburnum in full bloom was broken off the tree to be given to him. "Oh! It was right just

3 When I consider thy heavens, the work of thy fingers, the moon and the stars, which thou hast ordained;

3 When I look at thy heavens, the work of
thy fingers,
the moon and the stars which thou hast
established;

Gen. 1:6, 14) proclaims "the power that made it is divine." The psalmist, being acquainted with the old myths according to which creation began with a divine victory over the dragon of chaos (cf. 104:1-9; see G. A. Barton, *Archaeology and the Bible* [7th ed.; Philadelphia: American Sunday School Union, 1937], pp. 279-302) speaks of the firmament as a **bulwark** or fortress which is impregnable against any attempt of **the enemy and the avenger** to rise up again and challenge God's sovereign power.

2. Man's Place in God's Economy (8:3-8)

3-4. The psalmist is contemplating the heavens at night, for he speaks only of **the moon and the stars.** The movements and the patterns of the constellations and the ordered course of the moon, more than even the mighty firmament, excite his wonder and deepen his sense of man's insignificance before God. In Gen. 2:7-19 man and the animals are said to have been formed by the hand of God, but here the heavenly bodies are described as **the work of thy fingers,** a phrase which poetically suggests the deftness and the artistry as well as the might of a Creator before whom all the great things of our world are as nothing (cf. Isa. 40:12-17). **Established:** Lit., "prepared" (כוננתה), a verb which in the form here used is not uncommon in later writers as a synonym of "create" (24:2; 119:90; Job 31:15; Prov. 3:19); it implies "to build and establish." At the thought of the immeasurable greatness of God the psalmist is moved to exclaim, **What is man that thou art mindful of him?**

---

where it was," he cried. We recall how little children joined in praise of our Lord when he royally entered Jerusalem, and how they willingly accepted the shelter of his arms when he blessed them. They hailed their King: they accepted his defense, feeling "safe in the arms of Jesus."

We may fairly remember also that the childlike in heart, of maturer years, instinctively give reverence to the wonders of earth. "Beauty, beauty; I never knew there was such beauty," a young farmer from the prairies exclaimed when he faced his first morning in the Rockies. The less childlike among us may reflect with a sigh on the dulling of our response to loveliness in our older years, each fearing that he is farther off from heaven than when he was a boy; and conversely, mourning that we have lessened our instinct to be shocked at ugliness, or at that which destroys beauty. Thereby we may find new proof of our constant need of divine pardon, cleansing, and help.

"Blessed are the pure in heart: for they shall see God [in nature]." This psalmist must have been one of their company.

3-4. ***God's Greatness and Man's Littleness.***—These verses give the first great contrast—the contrast between man and the universe of which he is a part. Poets and moralists of all ages have been stirred thereby to remind us of man's pitiable littleness; and in our present days the thought has become overwhelming. If Newman found it a thought to "dizzy and appall," how much more should we? "The horror of vastness" is upon us: and if mechanical views of the universe have given place to something less determinate, yet we find no relief, for vastness has become even more alien. "The heavens declare the glory of mathematics" is a chilling utterance to simple folk who cannot help believing that it is of the first importance to be good, who know that without help from the source of power they cannot achieve. Our danger lies in the fact that man is discovering that which can petrify his moral concern. "What does it matter? It will be all the same in a hundred years. Let us sit and eat our pot of honey on the grave." For nature cries,

> . . . A thousand types are gone;
> I care for nothing, all shall go,[4]

as Tennyson phrased it. If all that we know of ultimate reality is that "it" does not care, why should man care? Then all is vanity, except the "pot of honey."

Note in vs. 3 the word **consider** (KJV), which is of more value for the expositor than **look at** (RSV), and trace the idea through Scripture,

[4] *In Memoriam,* Part LVI, st. i.

4 What is man, that thou art mindful of him? and the son of man, that thou visitest him?
5 For thou hast made him a little lower than the angels, and hast crowned him with glory and honor.

4 what is man that thou art mindful of him,
and the son of man that thou dost care for him?

5 Yet thou hast made him little less than God,
and dost crown him with glory and honor.

It is clear in this strophe from the use of the first personal pronoun that the psalm was originally a private hymn welling out of the soul of the psalmist as he stood alone before his God under the star-studded heavens, overpowered by the sense of man's littleness over against such evidences of the divine greatness and might. **Son of man,** as the poetic parallelism shows, is a synonym of **man.** It is frequently used in Ezekiel to connote the insignificance and mundane nature of man. Rabbinical exegesis, assuming that the Spirit in revelation did not repeat itself within a single line, found here a messianic reference (cf. I Cor. 15:27; Heb. 2:6). The term has a collective, not an individual sense in the context. **Visitest:** A better rendering is **care for.** The primary sense of the word is to look for what is missing or lacking. It may be used sinisterly, as of an officer's or overseer's exacting inspection, or of a divine visitation (Job 7:17-19), or, as here, in the sense of a tender, gracious visitation (cf. Jer. 15:15; 27:22).

5-6. Insignificant as man is, yet he is no accident in the divine economy. Like the stars, the moon, and the firmament, he has been created by God for a high purpose. God

---

remembering especially that the charge against the people in the great assize of Isaiah was "my people doth not consider" (Isa. 1:3). "If you have only three minutes to give to Bible reading in the morning, give one minute to reading and two to thinking of what you have read," was the advice given by a famous churchman to his son, who also became famous. So with the book of Nature, and especially the stars, that "army of unalterable law," [5] as George Meredith called it. The discovery of the symbol of order in a disordered world steadies the mind. "They are michty consoling, thae stars," a shepherd exclaimed in the darkest moments of war. For they speak not only of power and order, but of supreme artistry; they proclaim that the true is also the beautiful. And not only so: they speak of particular care. A significant verse occurs in another psalm, "He telleth the number of the stars; he calleth them all by their names" (147:4). If God gives such care to his stars, how much more to his children? Whence we are led to the images of the stars in the N.T. as indicating the company that no man can number. F. W. H. Myers makes Paul, recovered from depression by the thought of the mighty host of the victors, exclaim, "Stars, and of stars the innumerable streaming"; [6] the writer to the Hebrews uses the same symbol in the phrase "so many as the stars of the sky in multitude" (Heb. 11:12). Indeed, we are led straight to Christ himself, whose own claim is "I am . . . the bright and morning star" (Rev. 22:16), and to our strange hope of achievement in Rev. 2:28, where it is said of him that overcometh, "I will give him the morning star." With such an expectation men may well be steadfast "until the day dawn, and the day-star arise in your hearts" (II Pet. 1:19).

What is . . . the son of man, that thou visitest him? A significant turn is given to our thought by the word **visitest** which, if not so accurate as **care for,** has a value of its own. Sometimes mistranslations seem to be inspired. In this case the impetus to think of God in terms of Christ is manifest; for what is he but the Visitor from God who comes to stay permanently? There are visitors and visitors; it is a wondrous thing to know of one Visitor whose sole purpose in coming is to save. Starting from this phrase a man may reach the heart of the evangel.

5. ***Little Less Than God.***—This verse provides the answer to the question of vs. 4 by suddenly offering the second contrast—between the quality of man and the rest of nature. He is different in kind and not in degree. His affinity is with the Maker, not with the made. Indeed, the poet uses the language of hyperbole and declares him to be only **little less than God.** (Note that the

[5] "Lucifer in Starlight."

[6] *Saint Paul,* final section. See the constant use of the imagery of stars throughout the whole poem.

6 Thou madest him to have dominion over the works of thy hands; thou hast put all *things* under his feet:

7 All sheep and oxen, yea, and the beasts of the field;

8 The fowl of the air, and the fish of the sea, *and whatsoever* passeth through the paths of the seas.

6 Thou hast given him dominion over the
works of thy hands;
thou hast put all things under his feet,
7 all sheep and oxen,
and also the beasts of the field,
8 the birds of the air, and the fish of the sea,
whatever passes along the paths of the
sea.

---

has great thoughts concerning him. In a few sentences the psalmist gives us his philosophy of man's place and function in creation. Man has been appointed by God to be a king, God's deputy in his world: **Thou hast made him a little lower than the angels.** Another translation is "than a god." Obviously the psalmist would not say **than God.** The word *'elōhîm* is capable of these three interpretations, since it means either a divine being (god) or divine beings **(angels)** or the divine being par excellence **(God).** The context must be our guide to its sense (cf. 97:7; 138:1). **Thou . . . hast crowned him with glory and honor.** The words are used commonly with reference to kings. Man's royal status is manifested in the lordship assigned to him: **Thou hast given him dominion over the works of thy hands.**

7-8. The domain over which man bears rule as God's vice-regent is more specifically defined in words borrowed with poetic freedom from Gen. 1:26; 2:19-20. **Under his feet** are the creatures of the land, the sea, and the air.

---

word **angels** [KJV] is used to translate the Hebrew word for "gods" in the interests of monotheism.) He can think God's thoughts after him, and rejoice in that in which God rejoices. The stars in their courses are a great wonder; astronomy leads us "beyond the Beyond": but higher than astronomy is the Astronomer. The greatest of wonders, short of God, is the mind of man. To many a modern reader it is this that crowns man **with glory and honor.** The psalmist stops short of saying so, but the thought is inherent in the O.T. when man is declared to be made in God's image. A nobler region still comes to its fullness in the N.T., where saintliness is set forth as man's highest achievement. The Creator placed the royal crown on man's head when he made him potentially Christlike.

An expositor in our day must be very careful in his use of this text, and must never forget to connect it with the awed humility of vs. 4. Nothing has planted itself more firmly in the modern mind than the conviction of man's greatness: even the awful tragedies of war have not dislodged it from our thought. Indeed, we have tended to emend the verse by leaving out a **little lower than,** inclined to think of God as an irrelevant hypothesis while man is a potent fact, in virtue of his achievements. It is necessary therefore to emphasize the fact that it is God who has **crowned him with glory and honor,** so that any self-crowning is, like boasting, "excluded"; and to point out further that all man does in relation to nature is to find out God's secrets, not to invent them. God was the inventor of chloroform: man only found what was there. Moreover, the expositor will stress the fact that man's power of discovery is as awe-inspiring as the secrets to be discovered, and he must use it with fear and trembling; for the secrets have an either-or about them: either blessing or curse, either life or death. Anesthetics may be used either to banish pain and recover life or to murder! Man's crowning places him in supreme peril; let him think and be still. At least there is laid upon him a unique responsibility: of all God's creation, as far as our knowledge runs, he it is to whom much is given and of whom assuredly much will be required.

6-8. ***Man's Dominion over Living Creatures.*** —Vs. 6 signalizes man's dignity on another, if lower, level: the level of power. Man is exalted in authority over all other living things; a sufficiently astounding fact when man's physical puniness is remembered. Brain plus a little brawn is the master of brawn plus a little brain. Mind is might: a fact to be remembered by the religious who belittle the intellect. It is quite true that the "heart" of man must be changed before the world can be right; for the greatest thing in the world is love. But there is also required great intelligence. Mind and heart must accord well, and both be raised to the *n*th degree before the kingdom comes. Meantime, man's power over the lower creation is not only a fact, but it gives him high moral responsibility. If the psalm had been written in this century, the writer would not have stopped

9 O LORD our Lord, how excellent *is* thy name in all the earth!

9 O LORD, our Lord,
how majestic is thy name in all the earth!

To the chief Musician upon Muth-labben, A Psalm of David.

9 I will praise *thee,* O LORD, with my whole heart; I will show forth all thy marvelous works.

To the choirmaster: according to Muth-labben. A Psalm of David.

9 I will give thanks to the LORD with my whole heart;
I will tell of all thy wonderful deeds,

3. DOXOLOGY (8:9)

9. Lest man should be absorbed in the contemplation of his own greatness, the concluding verse reminds him of his subordinate rank. Majesty and dominion are the prerogatives of God.

IX-X. PRAISE AND SUPPLICATION (9:1–10:18)

There is general agreement among commentators that Pss. 9 and 10 were originally a single psalm. The evidences in support of this opinion are drawn in part from the oldest textual sources: in the LXX and the Vulg. they appear as a unity; also in four Hebrew MSS. The division into two psalms is seen first in the Peshitta and in the Targ. These textual evidences are supported by some literary ones: Ps. 10 lacks a superscription, a defect which elsewhere in the first book of the Psalter is met only in Pss. 1; 2; and 33; the **Selah,** which elsewhere never appears at the end of a psalm, by its appearance in the last verse of Ps. 9 indicates that the conclusion of the psalm had not been reached at that point; the psalms together are clearly meant to be an acrostic, despite the fact that at points the alphabetic scheme is obscured by faulty textual transmission; the metrical and the strophic structure of each psalm reflects a common pattern; the want of symmetry in the development of the thought, a characteristic feature of acrostic composition (cf. Pss. 25; 34; 37; etc.), is counterbalanced by elements in each psalm which exhibit a similarity of interests, problems, and points of view (cf. 9:17-20; 10:12-18).

there. Indeed, it is doubtful if he would even have mentioned sheep and oxen and the rest of them. The dominion which would have occupied his mind would have been that which man has achieved over the forces of nature, as he goes on to discover God's secrets and to find that he is not fit to rule over them unless his heart is attuned to God's. This is the fact to "dizzy and appall." Man has dominion over the bomb, and is not fit to have dominion over bows and arrows. Our somber condition may fairly be expressed thus: the thought of man's dominion led the psalmist to praise and adoration, but it should lead us to startled fear.

It is interesting to observe here that man's pre-eminence is detailed only in relation to sentient creatures. In the days of the psalmist he was the slave, not the master, of nature's impersonal forces; as indeed he is yet to a vital extent. But over the living creatures his dominion was and is manifest; and these living creatures have a common bond with him—they too can be hurt. To what extent is this in itself a claim on his compassion? Beyond that the mind is led into deep and difficult regions. It is worth noting that almost every one of the creatures mentioned in the psalm are eaten by man; he regards them as his servants literally unto death. They are food, necessary for his physical continuance; and this he holds to be part of the providential order. Life comes from life through death in the physical sphere, the strangest and harshest of inevitable sequences; and it has its parallel in the spiritual realm also. Here is a something that man can only accept, for he cannot explain it. But it is at least comforting to reflect that in Christ God assents to the sequence he has ordered, for he died that we might live; and that in him the last enemy which is death shall be so destroyed that it will cease to be a condition of living. Life from the living is to be the final word.

9:1–10:18. ***The Sure Judgments of God.***— That Pss. 9–10 are really one psalm is proved by the fact that they are one in the LXX and the Vulg., by the absence of a title over Ps. 10, and

However it is not difficult to understand why the original psalm suffered division at the hands of the Masoretes; Ps. 9 seems to sound a note of triumph over foreign foes, while Ps. 10 expresses despair in the face of domestic oppression; Ps. 9 is hymnal in character; Ps. 10 a lament.

Though an acrostic ordinarily consists of a series of more or less loosely connected verses or strophes with a mild claim to the development of a theme (cf. Ps. 34), these two psalms are marked by an unusual collocation of unrelated or discordant elements. This literary feature is to be explained by the manner in which the acrostic arrangement has been effected. The original element in the psalm (9:1-4, 9-16) is a hymn of thanksgiving by a person who was delivered from **the gates of death** (vs. 13)—where he was brought by the malice of his **enemies** (vs. 3)—because the Lord had been gracious to him (vs. 13) and had maintained his cause by giving a **righteous judgment** (vs. 4). Since the initial letters of the strophes of this hymn (טחזובא) by their order called up the idea of an acrostic, another psalmist followed the suggestion and introduced the strophes required to complete the acrostic pattern. It is this circumstance which accounts for the apparent confusion in the thought of the psalm.

In Ps. 9 the supplementary strophes (vss. 5-8, 17-20) deal with a judgment of God on the nations. There was a warrant for the use of such a theme in the context since in Ps. 7, for example, the vindication of a persecuted soul is associated with a judgment to which the people are summoned. In the section of the acrostic which comprises Ps. 10 the strophes assume the character of a lament or complaint about the godless in the land (vss. 1-11) who, setting God at nought, work their evil purposes (vss. 9-10, 15, 18), robbing the weak, murdering the innocent, and waylaying the poor and the hopeless. It is in the utterance of these grievances that the real purpose of the psalm, as it stands, comes to light, for the chief concern of the psalmist is with the social distress which he witnesses. His countrymen who so ruthlessly oppress their weak and defenseless fellows hold their power through submitting to, or allying themselves with, the foes who rule the land. The psalmist's confidence in the defeat of the latter gives him assurance of the end of the cruel tyranny of the former (cf. 9:17-20; 10:17-18).

The lateness of the date of the psalm is evidenced not only by the acrostic form but also by other literary features, e.g., the interpolation of a hymn celebrating a divine judgment on the peoples into a hymn of thanksgiving of an individual for deliverance from death (Ps. 9), and the use of the form of a psalm of lament (Ps. 10) for the concluding portion of the psalm. Such a jumble of three types of composition in the effort to develop an acrostic is indicative of a period of decline in literary taste and creative capacity. And this manifest condition of decline, coupled with the social and political situation reflected in the psalm, points to a date as late as the Greek period.

1. Thanks Be to God (9:1-4)

9:1-2. Following the style of a hymn of thanksgiving, the psalmist begins with fervid expressions of gladness, praise, and thanksgiving. No words can adequately voice

---

conclusively by the evidence that they form one acrostic poem (see Exeg.). But it is convenient to keep their numbering for purposes of interpretation.

The general idea is clear enough: it is a recognition of God as the refuge of his people, with consequent praise and appeal for his further help. The psalmist begins with thanksgiving for victory and so continues to vs. 18; then, with a connecting link in vss. 19-20, changes praise to appeal in 10:1, returning to confident thanksgiving in 10:16-18. It is not clear whether the enemies of whom he is afraid are foreign powers, or godless foes within the state, or possibly both. There is little ground for guessing the precise historical situation. Moreover, the acrostic arangement has become somewhat confused, especially in 10:3-11, and the text is frequently corrupt.

The two psalms are therefore open to a general and free interpretation. For purposes of exposition they are of value chiefly for certain striking phrases which are suggestive in a spiritual sense. To these particularly attention should be drawn.

9:1-4. ***The War Between Good and Evil.***—In vs. 1 read **wonderful deeds** rather than **marvelous works,** for the latter suggests the Creator,

2 I will be glad and rejoice in thee: I will sing praise to thy name, O thou Most High.
3 When mine enemies are turned back, they shall fall and perish at thy presence.
4 For thou hast maintained my right and my cause; thou satest in the throne judging right.
5 Thou hast rebuked the heathen, thou

2 I will be glad and exult in thee,
I will sing praise to thy name, O Most High.

3 When my enemies turned back,
they stumbled and perished before thee.
4 For thou hast maintained my just cause;
thou hast sat on the throne giving righteous judgment.

5 Thou hast rebuked the nations, thou hast destroyed the wicked;

---

the measure of his gratitude for what the Lord has done for him. The effect of his exclamations of joy is heightened in the Hebrew by the device of making each stich of this strophe begin with the letter א. **All thy wonderful deeds:** The psalmist perceives that his particular deliverance is an instance of the multitude of God's "thoughts toward us" (cf. vss. 9-12; 40:5); he has also a lively sense of the manifold implications of the divine intervention on his behalf (vss. 13-14).

3-4. My enemies turned back: The deliverance of the psalmist is actually his vindication against the accusations or machinations of persons hostile to him. The defeat of his foes is described in terms drawn from the rout of an army; actually it is the discomfiture of men who, confident in the deadly character of their charges against the psalmist, had brought their case to the temple to seek through some ritual act or some form of ordeal a pronouncement of the psalmist's guilt from God, and had been put to shame by a divine decision contrary to their desire. **For thou hast maintained my just cause:** Such a deliverance is normally viewed as the result of a judgment made by the Lord in his heavenly court of justice (cf. 7:6-8; 43:1; Jer. 11:20). In Babylonian hymns we meet a similar conception of the sun-god as the judge of mankind:

> Thou knowest what is right, thou knowest what is wrong.
> . . . .
> O Shamash! Supreme judge of heaven and earth art thou.

(Morris Jastrow, Jr., *The Religion of Babylonia and Assyria* [Boston: Ginn & Co., 1898], pp. 300-301.)

5-8. See Exeg. on vss. 5-8, 17-20, p. 59.

---

rather than the Warrior-helper. In vs. 3 read "because" (Amer. Trans.) rather than **when,** for the former gives the better sense. The latter is an offer of conditional praise; the former is definite and the result of a victory already complete.

In a spiritual sense these verses provide a challenge to the reader. Who of us can give thanks to God because the **enemies** of our soul are **turned back,** stumbling and perishing? Who of us can recount signal victories in the endless war between the flesh and the spirit? Let us remember the candid confession of an old and saintly professor, "Some of the evil within *seems* dead: I hope it *is* dead: but I fear it is not *stone dead.*" Further, let us be on the watch to give credit to the God who invigorates for such victories as there are. The man of strong will is in danger of that pride which blinds the eyes to the subtler foes of the spirit. It was a Puritan fault. Note that the word translated **fall** (KJV) means "stumble through weakness." It is a great thing when a man can say that his temptations are getting weaker, as if they had fallen into a decline; but he must still watch, for evil has remarkable recuperative power. Goodness requires to be nurtured, but evil has its private supplies of energy in the heart of man—a painful fact of human nature.

5. *Thou Hast Blotted Out Their Name.*— "The family is extinct and its name erased from the civil register." [7] The modern equivalent of the image is a thick black line drawn through

[7] Ellicott, *O.T. Commentary for English Readers,* IV, 98.

hast destroyed the wicked, thou hast put out their name for ever and ever.

6 O thou enemy, destructions are come to a perpetual end: and thou hast destroyed cities; their memorial is perished with them.

7 But the LORD shall endure for ever: he hath prepared his throne for judgment.

8 And he shall judge the world in righteousness, he shall minister judgment to the people in uprightness.

thou hast blotted out their name for ever and ever.
6 The enemy have vanished in everlasting ruins;
their cities thou hast rooted out;
the very memory of them has perished.

7 But the LORD sits enthroned for ever,
he has established his throne for judgment;
8 and he judges the world with righteousness,
he judges the peoples with equity.

---

a name in the family Bible. The story of the "blackened doge" of Venice is an apt illustration. In 1355 Marino Faliero, who had been elected doge in the previous year, was beheaded for a murderous conspiracy against all the leading citizens who could curb his power; and in the council chamber, where hang the portraits of the doges from A.D. 809, the space which should have held his picture is covered with black and has the inscription: *Hic est locus Marini Faliero decapitati pro criminibus.* In the spiritual realm, blotting out remains an inevitable moral possibility; for there are some spiritual conditions with which God wants to have nothing whatever to do. But there is the fact of the grace of God and of his desire that none should perish. The two facts lead us to watchfulness, with hope that shall not be made ashamed.

6. *O Thou Enemy.*—In the interpretation of this verse one craves large liberty. As it stands in the KJV, it is a partial mistranslation. The vocative is out of place. **The enemy have vanished in everlasting ruins** is doubtless right. But what a magnificent suggestion the older rendering provides; and its sense is in effect the same as the more modern one. The expositor may fairly use it, giving the rigidly accurate form if he thinks fit. The discovery of a vivid text is treasure trove and of real evangelical value. A hearer may (and probably will) forget a sermon; but he will remember a striking text. "I have never yet heard a useless sermon, for I have never yet heard a useless text," a godly old lady said. Searching the Scriptures for the memorable phrase is happy work. The meaning must never be twisted, nor must the phrase be merely bizarre; the test is whether, its context being given due consideration, it can lead fairly and reverently to Christ.

The verse under consideration is an admirable instance. In its original context it lends itself naturally to a service of thanksgiving for victory, though it emphasizes triumph over a fallen foe rather than humble gratitude to God. A Christian preacher, however, would not be likely to select it. But when we enlarge its range we are brought into nobler regions. God has other foes besides dictators and aggressor nations. Pain is one; ignorance is another; death is a third. And he has other warriors besides armed forces. All who fight against anything that brings destruction are soldiers of God. Thus the verse could be used on any occasion when fighters against pain and ignorance are gathered together. It could be at least given them as a slogan; e.g., in the case of doctors who wage so incessant a war against cancer. **O thou enemy,** [thy] **destructions are come to a perpetual end.** We might go even further than that. "The last enemy that shall be destroyed is death" (I Cor. 15:26) ; but it will be overcome, and we believe that it was once overcome at the first Easter. Is it transgressing the limits of fair scriptural use to suggest that this verse would prove to be an unforgettable Easter text? It is not difficult or unseemly to think of it as on the lips of the risen Christ.

6-7. *Sic Transit Gloria Mundi.*—These verses give with much dignity the contrast between the transience of worldly power and the permanence of the changeless: **their memorial is perished with them. But the LORD shall endure for ever.** Lord Salisbury, the Victorian British Prime Minister, used to advise students of foreign affairs to use "large maps." So should we give consideration to the centuries. In the Christian Era the center of world power has changed again and again. Rome, Venice, Portugal, Spain, the Netherlands, had their day; in our time the scepter seems to have passed to the United States of America. But the Christian church has gone its way into all the world, and the table has unfailingly been spread. The contrast historically provokes thought and induces reverence.

8. *Government with Righteousness.*—This verse reminds us of a dream unfulfilled. Man has longed for divine control of government,

9 The LORD also will be a refuge for the oppressed, a refuge in times of trouble.
10 And they that know thy name will put their trust in thee: for thou, LORD, hast not forsaken them that seek thee.
11 Sing praises to the LORD, which dwelleth in Zion: declare among the people his doings.

9 The LORD is a stronghold for the oppressed,
a stronghold in times of trouble.
10 And those who know thy name put their trust in thee,
for thou, O LORD, hast not forsaken those who seek thee.

11 Sing praises to the LORD, who dwells in Zion!
Tell among the peoples his deeds!

2. THE LORD SUCCORS THE AFFLICTED (9:9-12)

9-10. So all **who know thy name**—i.e., all who acknowledge God (cf. 36:10; 79:6; 87:4; Exod. 3:13-15) because they have come to know him through his revealing providence—**put their trust** in the Lord; to the **oppressed** he is a mighty defender, to **those who seek** him **in times of trouble,** a dependable helper.

11-12. In a fresh outburst of praise to the Lord the psalmist summons all in the temple (vs. 14) to join with him in proclaiming what they have witnessed of the Lord's work, and so, **Tell among the peoples his deeds!** The second hymn (vss. 11-16) reinforces the first one (vss. 1-4) by a more vigorous statement of what is implied in the Lord's deliverance. **He who avenges blood:** Freely rendered, "He who exacts an accounting from those who shed blood by violence"—the positive side of God's interest

but on a world scale it is a far-distant prospect. The bitterness and pride of nationalism stand in the way, a fact to be learned by the Jew as well as by the Gentile. This verse calls upon us to support projects like the United Nations: does it also urge us to seek a world state? One point at least is clear: any such ideal arrangement of society depends upon the common acknowledgment of the Lord. The missionary spirit in the church is an essential for the creation of God's Utopia.

9. *The High and the Low.*—The reading of the KJV mg., "the Lord also will be an high place for the oppressed," is suggestive. Strictly, the words "high place" mean simply "refuge"; but the contrast between the "high" and by implication the "low" can light a candle in the mind. Where God rules there is exhilaration and joyousness of living. Freedom to call your soul your own and to give it into God's keeping is an expansive thing; so is security beneath your own fig tree; so is ability to go forth on your lawful occasions, none making afraid. The absence of these is to dwell in a "low" place, and is proof that whoever rules, it is not God.

10. *They That Know Thy Name Will Put Their Trust in Thee.*—This is a significant statement. To know the truth about God produces an inner confidence which trial cannot shake; cf. "This is life eternal, that they might know thee the only true God, and Jesus Christ, whom thou hast sent" (John 17:3). Moreover, none of us is entirely without evidence of God's sheltering of the soul. Even, perhaps especially, martyrs have been able to declare with this psalmist, **Thou, LORD, hast not forsaken them that seek thee.** It was when he was being stoned that Stephen's face shone like an angel's. Man's bitterness, for which there is plenty of ground, should be directed against human evil, not against God, for it is "man's inhumanity to man" that "makes countless thousands mourn."[8] This is where the "complaint" in such writers as Thomas Hardy and A. E. Housman goes wrong. God took a terrible risk, from the point of view of time, when he gave man divine powers; but sainthood at its best has justified the risk and is the prophecy of the final outcome. We must put the blame for human misery on the right shoulders, and repent and strive.

11. *Declare Among the People His Doings.*—Here is a fine exhortation to personal evangelism. If we have known anything of the pitifulness of God's great mercy, why are we so reticent about it? If we have a common cold, half the neighborhood will tell us about their infallible remedy, which probably is no real remedy at all. But whoever has found in experience evidence of real remedy for failure and the faintheart tends to become dumb. "Let the redeemed of the LORD say so" (107:2) is a reasonable challenge to the church. May it be that this

[8] Robert Burns, "Man Was Made to Mourn."

12 When he maketh inquisition for blood, he remembereth them: he forgetteth not the cry of the humble.

13 Have mercy upon me, O LORD; consider my trouble *which I suffer* of them that hate me, thou that liftest me up from the gates of death:

14 That I may show forth all thy praise in the gates of the daughter of Zion: I will rejoice in thy salvation.

12 For he who avenges blood is mindful of them;
he does not forget the cry of the afflicted.

13 Be gracious to me, O LORD!
Behold what I suffer from those who hate me,
O thou who liftest me up from the gates of death,
14 that I may recount all thy praises,
that in the gates of the daughter of Zion
I may rejoice in thy deliverance.

in **the cry of the afflicted. Is mindful of them:** To whom does **them** refer? The Hebrew אותם is obscure; it is better to emend it and with Duhm to read הוא תם. The line then becomes, "He is an avenger of blood, being mindful of the innocent."

3. AN APPEAL FOR GOD'S FAVOR (9:13-14)

13-14. Be gracious to me: Since the psalm is a hymn of thanksgiving rather than a penitential psalm or a lament, we should render the text, "The LORD has been gracious to me," pointing חנני *ḥanānánî* rather than *ḥonnēnî*. For similar reasons the following words should be translated, "he has seen what I have suffered," by reading ראה *rā'āh* rather than *re'ēh*. **The gates of death:** Sheol, for which **death** here is a synonym, is sometimes represented after the manner of a conception of it in Babylonian and Egyptian mythologies as a walled city with strong gates (cf. 107:18; Isa. 38:10; Matt. 16:18; Rev. 1:18) which prevent escape. In the plight into which his enemies had brought him the psalmist was threatened with the loss of his life. **All thy praises:** Idiomatic phrase for "thy praiseworthy deeds." **The gates of the daughter of Zion:** The gates of Zion in contrast with the gates of death; the glad praises in Zion over against the silence of Sheol (cf. 88:10-12). **Zion,** which is synonymous with Jerusalem (cf. Lam. 2:18), is sometimes directly or by inference in poetry and prophecy personified as the mother of her people (87:5; Isa. 37:22; Lam. 1:5), so that the population of the city can be viewed as her daughter (Isa. 1:8; 10:32; Mic. 4:8; cf. "daughter of Tyre" in 45:12; "daughter of Babylon" in 137:8). The expression **in the gates** here does not mean "at the gates," but "within the city" (cf. Isa. 14:31; Deut. 5:14). Accordingly, the praise of the psalmist will be uttered publicly before the body of Zion's citizens, foregathered in the temple.

silence, sometimes justified by "good manners" (of all things!), is our chief weakness? After all, the church at the beginning was promised just one endowment, "Ye shall receive power . . . and ye shall be witnesses" (Acts 1:8).

12. *He Forgetteth Not.*—Who has meditated on "God the Rememberer," contrasting him with "Man the Forgetter"? The largeness and the severity of the field herein opened needs no comment. Encouragement of our powers to obliterate plain moral teaching, and to expunge from our minds the misery of other people, is one of the devil's most successful tactics. But there is Another who remembers, and will remind us.

13-14. *From Death to Life.*—Notice two **gates:** a useful hint. God lifts us from **the gates of death** in order that we may enter **the gates of the daughter of Zion** and there praise him. The word "gate" implies power or rule, for the gate was the seat of the judge or king. The pictorial image, however, should be kept, and the spectacle of two processions be developed—one heading for the lifeless life and the other for the happy intercourse of the God-governed community, with the merciful Provider moving in and out of the former to turn it toward the latter. It is a living picture of the unceasing ministry of the All-loving in the soul of man and through the church.

15 The heathen are sunk down in the pit *that* they made: in the net which they hid is their own foot taken.

16 The LORD is known *by* the judgment *which* he executeth: the wicked is snared in the work of his own hands. Higgaion. Selah.

17 The wicked shall be turned into hell, *and* all the nations that forget God.

18 For the needy shall not always be forgotten: the expectation of the poor shall *not* perish for ever.

19 Arise, O LORD; let not man prevail: let the heathen be judged in thy sight.

20 Put them in fear, O LORD: *that* the nations may know themselves *to be but* men. Selah.

15 The nations have sunk in the pit which
they made;
in the net which they hid has their own
foot been caught.
16 The LORD has made himself known, he
has executed judgment;
the wicked are snared in the work of
their own hands. *Higgaion. Selah*

17 The wicked shall depart to Sheol,
all the nations that forget God.

18 For the needy shall not always be forgotten,
and the hope of the poor shall not
perish for ever.

19 Arise, O LORD! Let not man prevail;
let the nations be judged before thee!
20 Put them in fear, O LORD!
Let the nations know that they are but
men! *Selah*

---

4. JUDGMENT OF THE NATIONS (9:15-16, 5-8, 17-20)

15-16. The nations have sunk: Instead of גוים, **nations,** read with Duhm, גאים, "proud," which the context and **the wicked** (vs. 16) require. It is not the nations but the "arrogant" among the Jews who make "the wretched" and "the oppressed" cry to God. The expressions employed to describe the discomfiture of the wicked are frequently met in the Psalter (cf. 7:15-16).

5-8, 17-20. To the writer or editor who expanded the original hymn of thanksgiving (vss. 1-4, 9-16) into an acrostic, the overthrow of the enemies mentioned in the hymn suggested a picture of the eschatological destruction of the nations which in the course of history had afflicted the people of God. With the eye of a prophet he sees the sentence of the Lord on the day of judgment already passed (vss. 7-8) and the proud cities of the godless nations (vs. 17) fallen into ruin and forgotten (vss. 5-6). So, at last, **let the nations know that they are but men!**

15-16. ***Sunk in the Pit.***—These verses repeat familiar ideas of the preciseness of retribution (cf. 7:15). Those who oppose God have **sunk down in the pit that they made** and **are snared in the work of their own hands.** The suggestions of slow sinking and sudden entanglement are both valuable. Men hardly notice that they are being engulfed by their own folly: alcoholism is a case in point. When they do notice, the trap has already been sprung.

17-18. ***Two Promises.***—These verses sharply sum up the moral outcome. **The wicked shall depart to Sheol.** For the conception of their destiny in that shadow world read Isa. 14:9-20, one of the greatest of literary passages in the Bible. On the other hand, in the end of the day, **the expectation of the poor shall not perish for ever.** The word **expectation** is helpful, and gives a more vivid image than **hope.** It suggests the straining eyes of those who are awaiting with confidence the coming of the Deliverer, as well as desiring his appearance.

19-20. ***Appeal for Action.***—The psalm ends with an appeal for divine action, that **man,** godless man, may not **prevail;** that he may be made healthily afraid; and that the **nations** (i.e., those ignorant of God) may know what they are. The wording is very suggestive and useful in our day: "Let the nations know that they are but men." How the psalms hammer at that point! The poets and novelists who have been seized with a like knowledge are a great gift to the twentieth century. The preacher or teacher must do his best to learn of them.

10 Why standest thou afar off, O LORD? *why* hidest thou *thyself* in times of trouble?

2 The wicked in *his* pride doth persecute the poor: let them be taken in the devices that they have imagined.

10 Why dost thou stand afar off, O LORD?
Why dost thou hide thyself in times of trouble?
2 In arrogance the wicked hotly pursue the poor;
let them be caught in the schemes which they have devised.

---

5. PLEA FOR GOD'S INTERVENTION (10:1-2)

In Ps. 10 the psalmist concentrates on the woes of the land, which godless men of power among the Jews cause by cruel acts of tyranny. As we have already noted, this division of the acrostic assumes the form of a psalm of lament, the theme of which is a cry for help against the oppressors.

10:1-2. Why dost thou stand afar off, O LORD? The seeming indifference of God in the face of wrongs or ills suffered by the righteous is a frequent ground of complaint in the Psalter. So commonly did those who came to the temple with their troubles assume that the Lord was hiding himself in their time of need that a reference to the aloofness of God becomes one of the formulas with which the psalmists preface a lament (cf. 13:1; 22:1; 31:22; 42:9; 43:2). However, certain of the psalmists, refusing to have their faith shaken by severe trials or afflictions, sought for a worthy solution of the mystery of the ways of God.

10:1-18. *The Lord Is Yet King.*—Though there are good reasons for regarding Pss. 9–10 as one psalm, there is no question that Ps. 10 begins on a new note. Ps. 9 ends with confidence; Ps. 10 begins with complaint. The agelong heaviness of spirit in face of the apparent heedlessness of God is suddenly expressed in vs. 1, and the poet then proceeds to inveigh for twelve verses against a society in which the ruling class is unscrupulous, cruel, God-neglectful, and apparently prosperous. Bitterness against the rich pervades every verse, and vivid images are piled one upon the other to describe a condition of lawlessness in which the prosperous are ravenous animals and the poor are their victims. It is not till vs. 14 that confidence in the power of God and righteousness reappears; but when it does return, it returns solemnly and majestically and the psalm ends with clear and virile optimism.

For the expositor this also is a psalm of phrases, in which three classes of men are portrayed: the wandering and perplexed moralist who has the suffering of the mass of men upon his heart; the immoral materialist who laughs at God; and finally the man of faith who sees clearly the central fact and the inevitable outcome. The various images can be thoroughly modern in their application.

1. *A Call to God.*—The psalm opens with the cry of the believer who is perplexed at oppression. He seems to be an observer rather than one of the oppressed himself, though he may be that too. At least he is the "single heart" through which "the desperate tides of the whole world's anguish" are forced. Note that his complaint is not so much that oppressors exist as that God does not seem to do anything about them. *"Le bon Dieu,"* cried the French peasant woman during the war, *"ah! le bon Dieu est en permission."* She and this psalmist join hands across the centuries in wonder that God should apparently "go on leave," especially in times of trouble.

2. *The Arrogance of the Wicked.*—Sharply the divine attention is drawn to the pertinent fact. **In arrogance the wicked hotly pursue the poor.** The KJV **in his pride**, meaning thereby an arrogant and contemptuous haughtiness, is not to be neglected. No one who realizes the dignity of a man, however humble, can lend himself to persecution. To know that

> The honest man, though e'er sae poor,
> Is king o' men for a' that,[9]

and to know it as living fact, would remove magically many of our social sores. We are all far more in the grip of **pride** than we think. The thought of the black wrong of pride and its child, persecution, stings the poet into a flash of anger. **Let them be caught in the schemes which they have devised.** It is curious to mark how frequent is this desire for a precise retribution. "Let the punishment fit the crime."

[9] Robert Burns, "For a' That and a' That."

3 For the wicked boasteth of his heart's desire, and blesseth the covetous, *whom* the LORD abhorreth.
4 The wicked, through the pride of his countenance, will not seek *after God:* God *is* not in all his thoughts.
5 His ways are always grievous; thy judgments *are* far above out of his sight: *as for* all his enemies, he puffeth at them.

3 For the wicked boasts of the desires of his heart,
and the man greedy for gain curses and renounces the LORD.
4 In the pride of his countenance the wicked does not seek him;
all his thoughts are, "There is no God."

5 His ways prosper at all times;
thy judgments are on high, out of his sight;
as for all his foes, he puffs at them.

6. DESCRIPTION OF THE WICKED (10:3-11)

3-11. In this part of the psalm we are given, conformably with its type, a statement of the conditions which have provoked the lamentation. The description of the wicked is a terrible one. They are unbridled in their lust for possessions; they have cast off the restraints of religion, for they not only blaspheme God but even deny his existence;

Spiritually it does and will. Is not this a word for commercial buccaneers to ponder?

3-4. ***The Wicked Boasteth.***—Is he wicked that **boasteth of his heart's desire,** if that desire be earthy? Then there is a great company of the "proud" in our way of life! The ordinary citizen shows a remarkable capacity for emphasizing his possessions: by reason of them he feels entitled to be the observed of all observers. If anyone asks him, "What porridge had John Keats?" he would inwardly shrug his shoulders at a man who by modern standards was a failure. A profitable meditation could arise from the question as to whether any boasting about any possessions is not a sign of perversity. Could the saint "boast" of his possession of a pure heart? It is the last thing he would do; he would stand with bent head before God and give him the praise. The difference between right and wrong desires lies in the fact that the former turn a man's eyes away from himself to the source, while the latter concentrate them upon himself. The possessive pronoun can be a danger sign as well as a sign of spiritual health. "My Lord" is one thing; "my acres," "my bank balance," "my position," are quite another.

The second clause of vs. 3 is textually corrupt, but its meaning is clear and follows directly from the first, **and the man greedy for gain curses and renounces the LORD.** In poetic image he has just addressed the lusts of the soul in laudatory terms, like the rich man in the parable, who invited his soul to be at ease; and the necessary corollary is to sneer at the absentee God. Man cannot either praise or serve both God and mammon. On the contrary, whichever he praises, he must belittle the other.

Wherefore he proceeds in a moral sequence; **the wicked** fails to **seek after God.** Naturally, since **all his thoughts are, "There is no God."** We must remember that this kind of atheism is practical, not theoretical. The last thing the "proud-wicked" will engage in is philosophic inquiry. He is, he claims, a "realist." The fact that his claim is pathetically absurd does not worry him. He is dealing with that which can be touched, seen, handled, and above all, measured. These to him are obviously the tests of "reality," and none of them can be applied to God. Therefore, at the best, give God a little *g* and forget him. A theoretical atheist who, perhaps with pain, cannot accept a theistic view of the universe, is much nearer the kingdom of heaven than the worldling who dismisses God with a wave of the hand. For the first may, up to his lights (however mistaken), be serving the God of truth; the latter is denying him in the soul. It is a serious reflection for our modern world. This man is the blind of whom the Lord spoke so often and so sadly (cf. Matt. 15:14).

5. ***Enemies of the Soul.***—God is always a mystery, and must always so remain to finite minds. Even the life for which we long, whereto we hope to pass, must needs be an endless adventure of discovery of the hidden wonders of God. But at every point in existence we are given light enough to live by: our worst tragedy is to be self-blinded, so that we cannot use the light we have. Darkness of that kind is the inevitable consequence of "pride." We might see, but damage our own sight; we do not see, and then reach our nadir by denying that there is anything to be seen. It is suggestive that so many of our Lord's "works" were the restoring of sight to the blind.

6 He hath said in his heart, I shall not be moved: for *I shall* never *be* in adversity.

7 His mouth is full of cursing and deceit and fraud: under his tongue *is* mischief and vanity.

8 He sitteth in the lurking places of the villages: in the secret places doth he murder the innocent: his eyes are privily set against the poor.

9 He lieth in wait secretly as a lion in his den: he lieth in wait to catch the poor: he doth catch the poor, when he draweth him into his net.

10 He croucheth, *and* humbleth himself, that the poor may fall by his strong ones.

11 He hath said in his heart, God hath forgotten: he hideth his face; he will never see *it*.

6 He thinks in his heart, "I shall not be moved;
throughout all generations I shall not meet adversity."

7 His mouth is filled with cursing and deceit and oppression;
under his tongue are mischief and iniquity.
8 He sits in ambush in the villages;
in hiding places he murders the innocent.

His eyes stealthily watch for the hapless,
9 he lurks in secret like a lion in his covert;
he lurks that he may seize the poor,
he seizes the poor when he draws him into his net.

10 The hapless is crushed, sinks down,
and falls by his might.
11 He thinks in his heart, "God has forgotten,
he has hidden his face, he will never see it."

---

carried away by the success that attends their ways, they ignore all warnings of the divine acts of judgment in history; since they believe in the permanent security of their tyranny, they violate all codes of human conduct; they use their tongues to utter potent curses on those who excite their hostility; their words are designed to deceive and to work ruin and mischief; what they cannot attain by crafty speech they plot to take by violence, robbery, and murder. They are confident that **God has forgotten, he has hidden his face, he will never see it.** The situation pictured by the psalmist has a parallel in Ps. 73.

As for all his foes, he puffs at them. An unhappily true description of our self-confident attitude to our weaknesses. "Never underestimate your enemy" is the advice of every great general. "I can take it or leave it" might be the family motto of alcoholics. The preacher who began his sermon with the words "The devil is a poor tactician" must have had a curious experience or a remarkably thick blind spot. On the contrary, the enemies of the soul are never negligible, and no man dare belittle them and live, unless he can say, "Not I, but Christ." [1]

6. *I Shall Not Be Moved.*—The almost unbelievable but so common attitude of the worldling, that he is secure from adversity, and vaguely from death itself, is here put bluntly before us. The inculcation of that foolish, negligent feeling is a frequent devilish tactic. Whatever malignant power there is must chuckle at the silliness of mankind. Perhaps it is to correct this folly that depressions seem to be part of the providential order. Certainly we need to be reminded that "here have we no continuing city" (Heb. 13:14).

7-9. *Beasts of Prey.*—Here is a picture of plain banditry. The proud-wicked are compared to gangsters, beasts of prey, and hunters, who regard **the poor** as their victims, not as fellow beings. It may seem too high-pitched a picture to apply to the ordinary citizen, but we have learned often enough that in international affairs it can be an understatement, as also in the underworld of cities. And has it no connection with the "economic jungle"?

10-11. *Plight of the Hapless.*—Here is a pathetic picture of the plight of the unfortunate and the weakling. Notice the descending verbs, **crushed, sinks down, falls.** They give the life history of so much of human wastage, even, per-

[1] Cf. the portrayal of the subtleties of temptation in C. S. Lewis, *The Screwtape Letters* (New York: The Macmillan Co., 1943).

12 Arise, O LORD; O God, lift up thine hand: forget not the humble.
13 Wherefore doth the wicked contemn God? he hath said in his heart, Thou wilt not require *it*.
14 Thou hast seen *it;* for thou beholdest mischief and spite, to requite *it* with thy hand: the poor committeth himself unto thee; thou art the helper of the fatherless.
15 Break thou the arm of the wicked and the evil *man:* seek out his wickedness *till* thou find none.

12 Arise, O LORD; O God, lift up thy hand;
forget not the afflicted.
13 Why does the wicked renounce God,
and say in his heart, "Thou wilt not
call to account"?

14 Thou dost see; yea, thou dost note trouble and vexation,
that thou mayest take it into thy hands;
the hapless commits himself to thee;
thou hast been the helper of the fatherless.

15 Break thou the arm of the wicked and evildoer;
seek out his wickedness till thou find none.

---

7. APPEAL FOR GOD'S ACTION (10:12-18)

12-16. In characteristic fashion the complaint of the psalmist is followed by an appeal to the Lord to rouse himself to action. The appeal is followed by a series of arguments calculated to strengthen the force of it: the lot of the wretched in the land (vs. 12); the godlessness of the oppressors (vs. 13); the misery which the Lord himself has witnessed (vs. 14*a*); the trust of the hapless in the Lord, because of what the Lord has done in the past (vs. 14*b*); the sovereignty of the Lord in the affairs of men (vs. 16).

---

haps especially, of little children. No wonder such people come to a conclusion quite like the worldling's. Pride and wretchedness have the same dreary logic, **God has forgotten, he has hidden his face, he will never see it.** We may note a strengthening scale of sunless denial of God, from forgetfulness to purposeful neglect, and from that to the hopeless statement that he will always forget and always hide his face. **He will never see it** is the very accent of despair.

12-15. ***The Psalmist's Faith.***—Here we find the attitude of the psalmist himself, the representative believer, in face of the spectacle of pain and oppression. The sequence of thought and feeling is worth noting. (*a*) There is direct prayer for strong and immediate action by God. **Arise, O LORD; O God, lift up thy hand.** The **hand** is the agent of deeds; it can hold a sword as well as bless. (*b*) There is the answer of experience and faith to the question, **Why does the wicked . . . say . . . , "Thou wilt not call to account"?** Note again the ethical quality of this atheism: "God, if there is a God, has no judgment seat." In modern language, "In any case, supposing a God exists, he is a good fellow and all will be well." But the answer of the psalmist is clear and powerful through its brief directness: **Thou dost see;** especially, **thou dost note trouble and vexation.** Not only that, but God sees with a view to action: **thou dost note . . . that thou mayest take it into thy hands.** Connect this with the N.T., "It is a fearful thing to fall into the hands of the living God" (Heb. 10:31), a statement whereof history is a witness. The psalmist goes on to appeal to experience. **Thou hast been the helper of the fatherless.** Experience seems to give much evidence of a God who is asleep; yet there is evidence too of a God who "shall neither slumber nor sleep," and that evidence becomes the dominant fact if the longer view is taken. "I could believe in God if he would do something," Carlyle is reported as saying.[2] Surely his historical vision was concentrated on the foreground at that moment. In any case, for the Christian there is one great doing to be remembered, in that God sent his Son, with all that is implied therein of saviorhood and life and immortality. (*c*) The psalmist returns to a sharp appeal for destructive action in vs. 15. The phrases **break thou the arm, seek out his wickedness,** and **till thou find none,** are all suggestive. They hint the strength and the patience of the indignation of God. His fury is a very fire, and burns mortally till the cause of it is purged forever.

Herein we are presented with a fact of life, a great and solemn fact. But it is a partial fact.

[2] Cf. John Nichol, *Carlyle* (New York: Harper & Bros., 1901), p. 231.

16 The LORD *is* King for ever and ever: the heathen are perished out of his land.

17 LORD, thou hast heard the desire of the humble: thou wilt prepare their heart, thou wilt cause thine ear to hear:

18 To judge the fatherless and the oppressed, that the man of the earth may no more oppress.

16 The LORD is king for ever and ever;
the nations shall perish from his land.

17 O LORD, thou wilt hear the desire of the meek;
thou wilt strengthen their heart, thou wilt incline thy ear
18 to do justice to the fatherless and the oppressed,
so that man who is of the earth may strike terror no more.

To the chief Musician, *A Psalm* of David.

11 In the LORD put I my trust: how say ye to my soul, Flee *as* a bird to your mountain?

To the choirmaster. Of David.

11 In the LORD I take refuge;
how can you say to me,
"Flee like a bird to the mountains;[e]

[e] Gk Syr Jerome Tg: Heb *flee to your mountain, O bird*

The last argument is the strongest, for if the Lord exercises his power, **the nations shall perish from his land,** and in consequence the arm of the godless evildoers among the Jews will be broken.

17-18. Thou wilt hear: The psalmist is so confident of a favorable response to his appeal that he sees victory for the oppressed already at hand. **The meek:** Better, "the oppressed." The word is frequently used of those who suffer at the hands of the rich and powerful (cf. 76:9; Amos 2:7; 8:4; Isa. 29:19). **Thou wilt strengthen their heart, thou wilt incline thy ear:** The text is somewhat obscure. For תכין, **Thou wilt strengthen,** read הגיג or הגיון, "sighing," as a parallel to **desire,** and translate, "Thine ear will listen to the sighing of their heart."

XI. THE LORD IS MY REFUGE (11:1-7)

In this psalm the religion of the O.T. finds one of its noblest expressions. We do not know the historical situation which occasioned its composition. We are told only that the psalmist is in imminent peril from cruel and treacherous enemies who are preparing to kill him. If we were informed as to who his enemies were or what the issue was which excited their violent antagonism, we should know the range and the area of the conflict, whether personal, social, religious, or national interests were involved.

The Christian goes on in the N.T. to find that the punishment of the wicked may be reformative. On Calvary there were three crosses. The central one was purely redemptive, for the Divine hung there; the one on the right was reformative, for the penitent hung there; only the one on the left was retributive, for lack of penitence. If both thieves had been penitent, there would have been nothing at all on Calvary but the redemption of God and its power.

16-17. *The Man of the Earth.*—The psalm ends with confidence. The language takes on a statelier and gladder rhythm. The verses could easily be used as a temple hymn of praise. In vs. 18 a name for the "proud-wicked" is used, which is worth remembering, **the man of the earth.** If we are to succeed in life, we are to be mindful that "our commonwealth is in heaven" (Phil. 3:20); it is there that our treasure must be.

11:1-7. *The Problem of Faith and Its Answer.*—This short psalm is not without its modern interest, for it deals with a mood into which we may easily fall. Indeed, it is permanently contemporaneous; but it is especially applicable to men and societies who are in circumstances with which they feel themselves unable to cope. It falls into two parts: vss. 1-3 state the problem; vss. 4-7 give the answer, setting forth the mood of faith in which an answer is found.

A nice point in interpretation is raised in the first section. The psalm opens with the devout

But it is enough for our understanding of the soul of the psalmist to recognize that his words are a triumphant answer of faith to cowardly counsel. In his desperate straits his supporters, urging the murderous intent of his enemies and the tottering state of his cause, entreat him to take to flight. But he rejects indignantly their fainthearted faithless advice with the memorable words which open the psalm: **In the LORD I take refuge.** To quit the scene of his struggle cravenly would mean want of faith. Whereas those about him see the bows and arrows of his enemies, the psalmist sees the Lord.

The psalm is an example of the group designated "psalms of trust" (cf. Pss. 16; 23; 27). The meter is in the 4+3 mode, with a slight irregularity in vs. *4b*, which is in 2+4.

1. THE PSALMIST'S FAITH (11:1-3)

11:1-3. In the LORD I take refuge: Some other psalms are prefaced with the same strong affirmation of faith (cf. 7:1; 16:1; 31:1; 71:1) or with words of like import (cf. 23:1; 62:2), for the ground of their confidence in times of stress is, "[If] God is the stronghold of my life, of whom shall I be afraid?" (27:1). **Flee . . . to the mountains:** The mountains offered hiding places where the poet could be safe from pursuit. **Like a**

---

man's statement of his basic position, **In the LORD put I my trust.** Whereupon, immediately and dramatically he becomes the questioner of those who question the reasonableness of his foundation. From the last clause of vs. 1 to the end of vs. 3 he repeats the questions of the questioners. It is helpful to put this part of the psalm, from **Flee like a bird** to **what can the righteous do** in quotation marks, as in the RSV. But we must ask, Who are these questioners, or who is the questioner? No doubt a historic situation is implied in which possibly the nation is involved. Some commentators describe the psalm, along with others (Pss. 3; 7; 9; 14; 17), as a "persecution psalm"; but this does not enlighten us as to whether it is the nation, or "the church within the nation," or an individual that is being persecuted; nor does it tell us whether the questioners are timid friends, possibly fellow statesmen, or whether the man is questioning himself, the questions being the timidities and defeatisms of his own soul. Certainly this last view is at least highly profitable, for it applies to a daily human situation and temptation. We are all cousins of Mr. Fearing and Mr. Ready-to-halt, apt to see lions in the way. Whatever the source of the psalm, its main teaching is applicable either to a nation or to a man who is being weakened by timorous doubt.

Let us modernize the opening verses. "I hold to the Moral Factor who is God. Yet there are misgivings. Would it not be better to escape to some private Innisfree where 'peace comes dropping slow'?[3] The forces of evil are active, violent, and prepared. They are the men with the guns; and the men with the guns win. The fundamental beliefs of ordered society are undermined; and in that case the good man can do nothing about it. So—what is the use of trying?" Which of us has not heard talk of this kind, or found similar thoughts spreading their miasma in the soul?

In answer (vss. 4-7) the psalmist does the only thing he can do: he returns, hard and sharp, to his basic faith. **The LORD is in his holy temple, the LORD's throne is in heaven.** God is present in the world, as true worshipers know (cf. 73:17, "Until I went into the sanctuary of God; then understood I their end"—a verse on which to meditate). That same God is the strong overruler: his **throne is in heaven.** He is watching detail as well as vastness, "trying" and estimating every man; and as he "tries," so he separates into groups, and prepares his weapons of war against those he judges unworthy. It is the old answer: Hold fast to the truth you know and wait. Time should be spent collating the passages in the Psalms and the Prophets where the injunction to wait is given. "Wait patiently" is the burden of their song, even if "mine eyes fail while I wait for my God" (69:3). At the same time, waiting does not mean inaction. Good soldiers, while they wait for reinforcements, hold their position. They even counterattack. But unless they believe that they can wait in confidence, they might very well surrender.

Strong and admirable as this teaching is, we cannot fail to note how far it falls short of the N.T. Our Lord has a good deal of rewriting to do. The psalmist is waiting for destruction; the thought of redemption does not occur to him, and the N.T. conception of love as a weapon of offense is beyond his horizon. Nevertheless, within its religious limits it is a brave psalm, and contains moral gravities which must not be overlooked.

1. *Flee as a Bird.*—The phrase is more accurately read "as a little bird." The weapon of scorn and ridicule is to be sparingly used, but

[3] William Butler Yeats, "The Lake Isle of Innisfree."

2 For, lo, the wicked bend *their* bow, they make ready their arrow upon the string, that they may privily shoot at the upright in heart.

3 If the foundations be destroyed, what can the righteous do?

4 The LORD *is* in his holy temple, the LORD's throne *is* in heaven: his eyes behold, his eyelids try, the children of men.

2 for lo, the wicked bend the bow,
they have fitted their arrow to the string,
to shoot in the dark at the upright in heart;
3 if the foundations are destroyed, what can the righteous do"?

4 The LORD is in his holy temple,
the LORD's throne is in heaven;
his eyes behold, his eyelids test, the children of men.

---

bird: The flight is to be prompt and speedy, for there is no time to lose, since his life is in immediate jeopardy. **The wicked:** Better, "godless," for the context shows that they are not among those who put their trust in the Lord.

Two reasons are advanced to support the advice to flee. (*a*) **The wicked bend the bow . . . to shoot in the dark:** The death of the psalmist at the hands of his enemies is imminent. Their methods of accomplishing their evil purpose are compared now to those of a hunter of birds, and now, by a change of metaphor, to robbers who attack their victims under the cover of darkness. By such language the hopelessness of evading their deadly assault is stressed. (*b*) **If the foundations are destroyed:** Or, "When the foundations are being destroyed, what has the righteous accomplished?" However the line is translated, the sense is that when the foundations of the things on which the righteous has put his trust are being torn down, what has been (or will be) the use of his striving against the agents of destruction? In short, the supporters of the psalmist point out that his cause is tumbling to pieces, and he is about to be buried in the ruins.

But what is the cause whose foundations are being undermined? The situation may be interpreted in the light of the graphic narrative of Jer. 26. On the other hand, the reference may be to some incident in a long and bitter struggle between "the godly ones" (the Hasidim) and "the ungodly" in the postexilic period, when men of position and power were tempting their fellows to forsake "the old paths" of Israel's faith.

2. The Ground of His Faith (11:4-7)

4-7. The psalmist's answer to his fainthearted friends reveals the secret of his firm stand in the confusion about him. It is **the LORD.** Twice he repeats the word. It is **the LORD** who is close at hand in his **temple.** It is **the LORD** who is also enthroned in

---

on occasion it is legitimate. If we are dealing with the spirit of defeatism it can come in handy. We may contrast "the little bird" spirit with Cromwell's men, or the Covenanters, or the iron of the soul of pioneers, with advantage: or we may reread *The Pilgrim's Progress*—a work which modern readers neglect to their sore disadvantage—and notice the varying kinds of "little birds" therein displayed, observing what honor is given to the men of the contrasting sort, such as Mr. Faithful, Mr. Honest, and Mr. Valiant-for-the-truth, and especially marking for which of them "all the trumpets sounded . . . on the other side." Bunyan on "little birds" and their opposites makes a lively and arresting series of meditations.

3. ***If the Foundations Be Destroyed.***—This is a classical stimulus to thought on civic uprightness, education, home life, and basic theology. What are **the foundations** in each case? The word itself is frequent in scripture and is strikingly used in the N.T. It varies from the plain utterance of I Cor. 3:10 ff. ("other foundation can no man lay") to the subtle use of the jewel foundations of the holy city in Rev. 21:19 ff. Note their correspondence with the jewels on the high priest's vestments when he went in alone to the holy of holies to pray, the suggestion being that the holy city is the fulfillment of the noblest aspirations of humanity. Cf. the movements of the mind that may be set off by Josh. 6:26, with its sidelights on parental duty:

5 The Lord trieth the righteous: but the wicked and him that loveth violence his soul hateth.

6 Upon the wicked he shall rain snares, fire and brimstone, and a horrible tempest: *this shall be* the portion of their cup.

7 For the righteous Lord loveth righteousness; his countenance doth behold the upright.

5 The Lord tests the righteous and the wicked,
and his soul hates him that loves violence.
6 On the wicked he will rain coals of fire and brimstone;
a scorching wind shall be the portion of their cup.
7 For the Lord is righteous, he loves righteous deeds;
the upright shall behold his face.

---

the heavens, whence he can survey all that goes on in the earth. (For the union of these two aspects of the Divine see 7:6-8; Gen. 28:1-22; Isa. 6:1-13).

The Lord is not asleep nor is he indifferent to what men are doing, as some of the faithless may suppose (cf. 9:4-6). **His eyes behold, his eyelids try, the children of men:** He sees and he scrutinizes all men. And the result of his examination is that "he chooses the righteous." In vs. 5 read יבחר, "chooses," for יבחן, "tries," and delete **and the wicked. His soul hates him that loves violence:** He abhors and repudiates all such, because what they love he hates. The Lord by his very nature can have no fellowship with them. In vss. 6-7 the lot that awaits the two classes of persons is described. **On the wicked he will rain coals of fire and brimstone:** The words recall the terrible and final destruction which overtook Sodom (Gen. 19:24). We ought for metrical reasons to omit גפרית, **brimstone,** as overweighting the line. **A scorching wind shall be the portion of their cup:** The wind is more terrible than either the simoon or the sirocco; as the root (זעף) indicates, the word connotes a "raging" blast accompanied, as we see in the context, with devastating fire, hence something like a death-dealing volcanic flame. What are the bows and arrows of the wicked in comparison with the weapons which the Lord has at his command? Such language is more than an expression of Hebrew vindictiveness. It reflects concretely the belief that evil is in a hopeless conflict with the fundamental laws of the world, as a moral order: "The stars in their courses fought against Sisera" (Judg. 5:20); "He shall make the whole creation his weapons for vengeance on his enemies" (Wisd. Sol. 5:17; cf. 5:20; 16:24). **Portion:** The form of this word (מנת) in the text appears chiefly in late literature. **Cup:** I.e., "fate" or

---

"He shall lay the foundation thereof in his firstborn, and in his youngest son shall he set up the gates of it."

What can the righteous do? In the original meaning the answer expected is "nothing." Recall the futile, fluttering little bird of vs. 1. But the answer of faith contradicts such hopelessness and shames it. The man of contrasting type in Bunyan "laid about him lustily." Never discount the practical possibilities of forlorn hopes. Gideon comes to memory.

5-7. *The Lord Trieth the Righteous.*—In vs. 5 the verb **trieth** has as its object both **the righteous** and **the wicked,** and means no more than that the Lord watchfully observes them both and estimates them for what they are, hating the latter and ultimately pouring his destruction on them. But the translation in the KJV, which separates the "trying" of the righteous, is true to much of life, and attention should be called to it. A man must be well tested before he becomes a member of God's shock troops; and once he has become a member, he will be "tried" some more. The Scriptures supply endless examples, of whom Paul is one. He was what he became because, first, he was suddenly touched by Christ; and because, second, he was "tried" in the manifold experiences recounted in II Cor. 11:23 ff. When a man becomes a Christian, he accepts the Christian program, which consists partly in readiness to be tried.

Both clauses of vs. 7 are suggestive. The first is a blunt assertion of final truth: **The righteous Lord loveth righteousness.** There is a finality about that which puts in their proper perspective such teachings as belittle the divine intention to subdue all things unto himself. Shallow confidence in the "geniality of God," and his willingness to turn a blind eye to wrong, is shown to be the sham it is. The gates of the holy

To the chief Musician upon Sheminith, A Psalm of David.

12 Help, LORD; for the godly man ceaseth; for the faithful fail from among the children of men.

To the choirmaster: according to The Sheminith. A Psalm of David.

12 Help, LORD; for there is no longer any that is godly;
for the faithful have vanished from among the sons of men.

"destiny" (cf. 16:5)—a figure of speech probably derived from the custom of passing a cup at a feast or ceremonial occasion (cf. Matt. 26:27, 39, 42). The reward of **the righteous** is that they **shall behold his face.** Because they love the things which he loves they shall have freedom of access to his presence and the enjoyment of his favor (17:15; Gen. 33:10; 43:3, 5), whether in the special approach through the services in the temple (63:2) or in the general course of their life (4:6; 42:4; 89:15-17). Most commentators read ישרים, "the righteous" plural, instead of ישר, "the righteous" singular. The KJV, however, adhering to the text, renders, **his countenance doth behold the upright.** The RSV is preferable because it accords with the general use of the idiom.

XII. Plea for Help in a Godless Age (12:1-8)

The psalmist calls on the Lord for help because his soul has become bitter at "the inhuman dearth of noble natures" among the sons of men. Faithfulness to God and reverence for truth have vanished from the current code of social conduct; honesty of speech and humility of spirit are lightly regarded; on the one hand lying, flattery, hypocrisy, and insincerity are the order of the day, and on the other, pretentiousness, boasting, and swaggering. As we read the words of this complaint we are reminded of the state of mind of the Egyptian of the early part of the second millennium B.C. who, resolving on suicide, composed the poem entitled "The Dispute with His Soul of One Who Is Tired of Life" (Adolf Erman, *The Literature of the Ancient Egyptians* [tr. Aylward M. Blackman; London: Methuen & Co., 1927], pp. 86-92; cf. J. H. Breasted, *Development of Religion and Thought in Ancient Egypt* [New York: Charles Scribner's Sons, 1912], pp. 188-98), in the course of which he says in defense of his purpose,

To whom do I speak to-day?
Brothers are evil,
Friends of to-day, they are not lovable.
. . . .
Gentleness hath perished,
Insolence hath come to all men.
. . . .
There are none that are righteous,

city are open continually, but "without" is all that God hates; "within" is reserved for what he loves. The second clause is inverted in the KJV. We should read with the RSV, **the upright shall behold his face.** That also is true finally even in this life: light has a way of rising for the upright. Not only intelligence, but goodness also is a requisite for the growing perception of the truth by which men live.

12:1-8. ***The Arrogance of the Ungodly.***—Whatever may be the date of this psalm, there is no question as to its circumstances. It is the outburst of an honest and faithful man against the arrogant falsehoods of the ungodly. Unfortunately it is therefore relevant to every generation. "The tongue," as James observes, "is a fire, a world of iniquity" (Jas. 3:6). Anyone who desires to issue some warning against one of the most fruitful sources of evil should give the tongue high priority. He will find good grist for his mill if he reads this psalm, along with Jas. 3:1-12. Indeed he might do worse than use his concordance to discover how much space the Scriptures give to the tongue, and how uncomplimentary they are about it, from "the scourge of the tongue" (Job 5:21), to the tongue which "no human being can tame" (Jas. 3:8).

1-2. ***Help, Lord; for the Godly Man Ceaseth.***—This is the authentic cry of depressed religion.

2 They speak vanity every one with his neighbor: *with* flattering lips *and* with a double heart do they speak.

2 Everyone utters lies to his neighbor;
with flattering lips and a double heart
they speak.

The earth is given over to the workers of iniquity.
. . . .
Death is before me to-day
As the odour of myrrh.

In both instances we are brought to feel the intolerableness of life in a society where no man dare trust the word or motives of his fellows.

In his distress the psalmist derives hope and comfort from a fragment of prophecy which he recalls or comes upon, a divine promise of judgment on those who sin against the peace and happiness of their fellows. Unlike the word of men, the word of God can be trusted; it is pure like purest silver. With this assurance, therefore, the psalmist repeats his prayer for help, pleading also that the need is urgent since "this generation" increasingly vaunts its "baseness."

We know as little of the historical background of this psalm as of that of Ps. 11. But because of the psalmist's citation of a prophecy or oracle that is only indirectly relevant to the matter of his complaint, we may assume that he lives in a time when the word of prophecy is known only through books or tradition. There is nothing in the psalm to indicate that the psalmist had gone to the temple to seek an oracle, or to perform an imprecatory rite, nor is there anything to warrant the opinion that the psalm reflects a struggle between religious or political parties.

The psalm is a protest against the lax ways of a generation which set little store by the homely virtues of honesty and sincerity in speech and manners. It is therefore concerned with certain aspects of social conduct toward which later Judaism as represented by the wisdom literature was giving increasing attention. Altogether, then, the seeming remoteness of the psalmist from the living voice of prophecy, and the special moral interest which he has in common with some wisdom writers possibly lead us to date the psalm in the postexilic period (cf. 73:4-20; Prov. 6:16-19; 8:6-9; Ecclus. 4:20-31; Pss. Sol. 12:5).

The lines are in 4+4 meter, with the normal variations of 4+3 and 3+4, which appear in vss. 3, 7-8.

1. Petition for the Lord's Intervention (12:1-4)

12:1-2. There is some uncertainty in the translation of vs. 1. The word אמונים, which is rendered **the faithful,** may, as in the LXX, be regarded as the abstract noun meaning "truth" or "faithfulness." If this translation is adopted, we must assume that the word rendered **any that is godly** or **the godly man** (חסיד) is an error for the abstract noun

---

The point to observe is that it is sometimes an excusable cry; but it is never true. God is never without some witnesses; and what the **godly** often require is a voice to call them out of their gloom to remember the fact and the power of the faithful, whose knees have not bowed to Baal, nor have their lips kissed him.

Without introduction the psalmist gives the essential description of the prevailing type, the opposite of the **godly** and men that are true. Implicitly they are the ungodly and the untrue, and their sign is **flattering lips.** There is a significance in the sequence: ungodliness produces inner untruth, which produces as its overt fruit plain lying. Forget God, and you get a society in which men cannot trust each other, and which therefore must ultimately collapse. Cf. the Flatterer in *The Pilgrim's Progress.* A flatterer gives to the flattered a false opinion of himself, so that a society is formed which degenerates in its standards and output. Distinguish between flatterers and encouragers. S. R. Crockett suggests that a phrase should be added to the *Te Deum,* giving thanks for "the noble army of encouragers." Every Christian should endeavor to be enrolled in it, while avoiding the plague of flattery. For encouragement fastens on what is good and emphasizes it;

3 The LORD shall cut off all flattering lips, *and* the tongue that speaketh proud things:
4 Who have said, With our tongue will we prevail; our lips *are* our own: who *is* lord over us?
5 For the oppression of the poor, for the sighing of the needy, now will I arise, saith the LORD; I will set *him* in safety *from him that* puffeth at him.

3 May the LORD cut off all flattering lips,
the tongue that makes great boasts,
4 those who say, "With our tongue we will prevail,
our lips are with us; who is our master?"

5 "Because the poor are despoiled, because the needy groan,
I will now arise," says the LORD;
"I will place him in the safety for which he longs."

"love" (חסד), an error which is probably duplicated in 4:3 (Hebrew 4:4). The line would then be translated, "Love has ceased, for faithfulness has vanished." In that case, the psalm addresses itself wholly to moral issues.

From among the sons of men: The extent to which the corruption has spread among his own people prompts the psalmist to believe that it is universal. **Flattering lips:** Lit., "smooth lips." **A double heart:** Lit., "with hearts of diverse kinds," i.e., a heart that thinks one thing and a heart that devises another thing; for the idiom cf. "weights of different sizes" (Deut. 25:13).

3-4. The evils of which the psalmist speaks come to fullest expression among men in places of authority or power. They are arrogant and self-confident; what they cannot obtain by flattery or plausible lying or polite defamation they mean to take by more direct methods. For they have a **tongue that makes great boasts,** and the substance of their boasts is **our lips are with us; who is our master?** or, more freely translated, "with our lips as our allies, who can stop us?"

2. The Lord's Response (12:5-6)

5-6. The prophetic word quoted by the psalmist is in the form of the oracle of Isa. 33:10-13, one of the postexilic sections of the prophecy. Since it relates to a situation

---

flattery whitewashes what is mean and unworthy. No wonder that in vs. 3 the psalmist breaks into an ejaculation that false lips may be **cut off.**

4. ***The Power of Words.***—This verse vividly describes the inner conviction of false men. They believe in the power of their lies. They say, **With our tongue we will prevail, our lips are with us; who is our master?** There is something to be said for the sharper if less accurate translation in the KJV, **our lips are our own**—a very fruitful suggestion. The whole verse opens a serious and practical question, viz., the power of words. The antithesis between men of words and men of action is a false one; for words are the expression of ideas, the channel by which ideas are conveyed; and ideas are mighty. "Take with you words" and you have taken with you the mother of deeds. The concordance should be studied here. "Lord, to whom shall we go? thou hast the words of eternal life" (John 6:68). "The Preacher sought to find out acceptable words" (Eccl. 12:10). "Remember the words of the Lord Jesus" (Acts 20:35), etc. On the other hand, words must be the garments of ideas. Paul's preference for "five words with my understanding" (I Cor. 14:19) will be remembered, and so will his advice in II Tim. 2:14, that "they strive not about words to no profit." In these days of the radio we have double reason for searching the Scriptures on this matter. Words are always a weapon for good or ill, but ultimately their effect is dependent upon their relation to facts. The tongue which "boasts of great things" (Jas. 3:5) may have its temporary influence, but "we can do nothing against the truth, but for the truth" (II Cor. 13:8) in the end of the day.

The verse may also be used by way of inversion. The lips of the godly are their own, as well as the lips of the ungodly. Like our wills, we can make them God's. If that is done, in glad conclusion the question may indeed be asked, **Who is our master?**

5-6. ***The Unfailing Shelter of the Soul.***—Now the direction of the poet's eyes changes. Turning from the falseness of the oppressors, he sees God looking at the poor, and immediately is convinced that such a spectacle as they provide

6 The words of the LORD *are* pure words:
as silver tried in a furnace of earth, purified
seven times.
7 Thou shalt keep them, O LORD, thou
shalt preserve them from this generation for
ever.
8 The wicked walk on every side, when
the vilest men are exalted.

6 The promises of the LORD are promises
that are pure,
silver refined in a furnace on the
ground,
purified seven times.

7 Do thou, O LORD, protect us,
guard us ever from this generation.
8 On every side the wicked prowl,
as vileness is exalted among the sons of
men.

---

somewhat different from that of the psalm, the oracle is not to be understood as a divine communication to the psalmist. Rather, it is a fragment of prophecy or an oracular utterance that has survived from other times and that the psalmist quotes with the same confidence as Paul cites words of Jesus not preserved in the gospel records. The psalmist perceives its applicability to the situation with which he is confronted. **The promises of the LORD . . . are pure.** For this reliance on God's purpose and power to fulfill his word cf. 105:42; 119:140; 130:5; Heb. 4:12. **In a furnace on the ground:** These pointless words are probably a marginal gloss that has crept into the text. **Furnace** (עליל) is a *hapax legomenon,* and its meaning a guess of the Targ. The gloss probably was itself corrupted.

3. THE PETITION REPEATED (12:7-8)

7-8. In the closing strophe the psalmist renews his appeal. **Protect us:** The reading of the LXX is superior to that of the M.T., which the KJV follows. **The wicked prowl:** Lit., "go to and fro." By a slight emendation the verb יתהלכון becomes יתהללון, "vaunt themselves," which in the context is preferable. Also the context suggests reading ב,

---

will stir divine action. **Now will I arise, saith the LORD.** The difficulty for faith is that the Lord does not seem to do any such thing; but that is a short-term view. The slow-grinding wheels grind. Nevertheless, for the individual our present life is often unjust. Without immortality, there remains an unhealed sore. Christians must admit it, and acknowledge the inadequacy of the psalmist's view. The O.T. badly needs the N.T. In the KJV the translation **him that puffeth at him,** to describe the oppressor, gives a vivid hint, even if it is a mistranslation. The impudence of it suggests the arrogant man's cheapness of soul. Hermann Göring had a way of referring to the Czechs as "these dwarfs." Who turned out to be the moral dwarf in the end?

What follows in vs. 6 can be used as a generalization, the truth of which in the spiritual realm has the attestation of the saints. Because of injustices in time, we must not allow ourselves to be blind to the unfailing shelter of the soul. **The promises . . . are pure** is a testimony given often on the deathbeds of the godly—a fact which must be pondered, for it is an arresting fact. Dying people are greatly concerned with reality. "When a man is to be hanged in a fortnight, it helps him wonderfully to concentrate," as Samuel Johnson reminded us. In a nobler way, when a good man faces his passing, it opens his eyes. "Listen to me now," said a woman of faith very shortly before she died, "for the veil is very thin and I know." What she knew was peace and strange hope. In the heart of every cyclone there is a core of complete quiet. They that trust in the Lord dwell there and find the fulfillment of the promises. Search the Scriptures, especially the words of our Lord, to discover what **the promises** are. In their essence they are very personal—promises of the great Carer for the single soul. "That where I am, there ye may be also" (John 14:2) sums up their power and hope. Their complete genuineness is suggested by the image of **purified silver.** There is no wishful thinking in such confidence, rooted as it is in the nature of God himself as shown in Christ. Either the promises for the soul of man are true or our Lord was quite wrong about God.

7-8. ***Guard Us Ever!***—The psalm closes on a note of trust, in spite of its emphasis of the fact that the times are out of joint. The final clause, **when the vilest . . . are exalted,** may well be taken to heart by the people of a democracy,

To the chief Musician, A Psalm of David.

13 How long wilt thou forget me, O Lord? for ever? how long wilt thou hide thy face from me?

To the choirmaster. A Psalm of David.

13 How long, O Lord? Wilt thou forget me for ever?
How long wilt thou hide thy face from me?

"because," for כ, **when,** in the closing line. Thus the psalmist boldly fortifies his appeal by a parting word which implies that the time for fulfilling the divine promise of help is now.

XIII. A Cry for Deliverance from an Enemy (13:1-6)

This psalm, brief as it is, has had a special appeal to readers of the Psalter because of its poignant expression of the deep emotions of a troubled soul. The simplicity, beauty, and sincerity of its words have enriched the language of prayer throughout the centuries. John Calvin selected it to be included among the eighteen psalms set to music, which he published in 1539 for use in public worship. The Scottish theologian, Marcus Dods, wrote on one occasion to his sister: "If you can direct me to anything more exquisite than the 13th Psalm, I will follow your direction with a happiness not often attaching to earthly pursuits" (*Early Letters of Marcus Dods,* ed. by his son [New York: Hodder & Stoughton, 1911], p. 137).

Because of its brevity the psalm presents very clearly the normal structure or form of the type known as the lament of an individual, with its threefold divisions: (*a*) the complaint, (*b*) the appeal, (*c*) the expression of confidence in God's help. In this instance the psalmist does not inform us of the specific source of the distress which weighs heavily upon him. We know, however, that he is under a burden of never-ceasing sorrow and trouble, whether it has been occasioned by sickness, change of fortune, political or religious strife, or personal rivalries. Also there are in his community men who, being ill disposed to him, take a malicious interest in his plight. Without pause or pity, by night as well as by day, fears and foes press so hard on him that the strength of his body is failing and death appears to be imminent. In the situation he is perplexed by the seemingly prolonged indifference of God to his appeal for help, and harassed by the thought that in his downfall his enemies would see both a triumph for themselves and a confutation of the creed to which he has witnessed. But in spite of all the difficulties that mount against him, his faith not only holds firm but rises to a new pitch—*ingens at laetum paradoxon.* For a discussion of the provenance of these individual laments see Intro., p. 7.

The meter is for the most part 4+4; vss. 4-5 are 3+3, and vs. 6, 2+2.

1. Appeal to the Lord (13:1-4)

13:1-2. How long? The fourfold repetition of these words indicates the troubled state of the psalmist's heart. His complaint is grounded upon the following: (*a*) God

---

whose duty is ever to see to it that right men are given power. Here is portrayed a midnight society in which the lawless **prowl** unchecked, the sort of society that is bound to be fashioned when "baseness is exalted by the sons of men." It is tragic to think that such a thing is possible. When choosing men to govern, advantage and "interest" come second; concern to be led by the God-fearing comes first. On any other terms nations condemn themselves. Like people, like leaders.

13:1-6. ***Assurance for Dark Days.***—This is a slight psalm, consisting simply of a cry of weariness (vss. 1-2), a prayer for restoration to vigor so that the enemy may be disappointed (vss. 3-4), and a statement of trust and consequent confidence based on experience (vss. 5-6). There is little here that cannot be found more vividly in other psalms. This, however, is noteworthy for its extremes of feeling, expressed with poetic skill. The distress of the first two stanzas falls into a quietness of peace in the

2 How long shall I take counsel in my
soul, *having* sorrow in my heart daily? how
long shall mine enemy be exalted over me?
3 Consider *and* hear me, O LORD my
God: lighten mine eyes, lest I sleep the
sleep of death;
4 Lest mine enemy say, I have prevailed
against him; *and* those that trouble me rejoice when I am moved.

2 How long must I bear pain[f] in my soul,
and have sorrow in my heart all the day?
How long shall my enemy be exalted over me?

3 Consider and answer me, O LORD my God;
lighten my eyes, lest I sleep the sleep of death;
4 lest my enemy say, "I have prevailed over him";
lest my foes rejoice because I am shaken.

[f] Syr: Heb *hold counsels*

seems to have let him pass out of mind; (*b*) further, God not only fails to take the initiative on his behalf, but seems to be unwilling to listen to his appeal for help, hiding his face from him; (*c*) consequently, the psalmist suffers **pain in my soul, and . . . sorrow in my heart all the day,** or with the LXX, "day and night"; (*d*) this condition is aggravated by the elation of the enemy at his humiliation, **How long shall my enemy be exalted over me?**

For **counsel** [עצות] **in my soul** most translators read **pain** [or "sorrows" or "cares"] **in my soul,** emending in the light of the context and with the support of the Syriac, עצות to עצבות.

3-4. The prayer of the psalmist gives fresh evidence of the despair of his heart. **Lighten my eyes:** The effects of his mental and spiritual struggles on his body are registered in the dullness of the eyes (cf. 6:7; 38:10; Lam. 5:17). There is no implication

last two, which are at once soothing in their rhythm and emphatic in their restfulness. We do well to mark the sudden yielding of the poet as perturbation gives way to contented and happy peace of mind. Life has its unexpected blessings as well as its protracted sorrows; and in comparison with the blessings, the sorrows are short-lived in retrospect. "Our light affliction, which is but for a moment" (II Cor. 4:17), yields to peace out of pain. Cf. Browning's "Prospice" with its line, "The black minute's at end"; and remember the exhortation in the hymn to stand up for Jesus, "The strife will not be long."

First the familiar **how long?** motif is made emphatic. **How long, O Lord? Wilt thou forget me for ever?** The translation in the KJV, with its double question, helps to make the emphasis vivid. **How long wilt thou forget me, O LORD? for ever?** Note in Scripture the questions which despair, even devout despair, puts to God, e.g., Jer. 15:18, "Wilt thou be altogether unto me as a liar?" No modern writer, pluming himself on his boldness and frankness, can surpass that. The Bible is a very honest book, and its honesty is well displayed in the complaints it records against God. The outcry of heaviness is evidently in order, provided that the man who makes it is still a seeker. It is worth observing that the bitterness of vs. 1 did not prevent this man from receiving at God's hand experiences which led to the still waters and the song of vs. 6.

The RSV mg., in vs. 2, **How long must I hold counsels in my soul?** suggests that there is such a thing as the introspection of sorrow; and it can become a disease. The "happy warrior," who "Turns his necessity to glorious gain,"[4] flatly refuses to become a victim to it. Indeed, here we may find the reason for the sudden change of feeling from dejection to confidence; the writer stopped brooding and began to "count his blessings." He would find—as most of us would—that he had much more to think about when he opened his eyes to God's bounty. For many the astonishing thing about life is not that God disciplines us, but that he gives us so much. For our desert is small.

Doubtless the phrase, **lest I sleep the sleep of death,** has a physical reference. The poet was ill and unable to cope with his enemies and his

[4] Wordsworth, "The Character of the Happy Warrior."

5 But I have trusted in thy mercy; my heart shall rejoice in thy salvation.
6 I will sing unto the LORD, because he hath dealt bountifully with me.

5 But I have trusted in thy steadfast love;
my heart shall rejoice in thy salvation.
6 I will sing to the LORD,
because he has dealt bountifully with me.

---

of failing eyesight, contra Hans Schmidt (*Die Psalmen* [Tübingen: J. C. B. Mohr, 1934; "Handbuch zum Alten Testament"], p. 22). The expression has a different meaning in 19:8. **Lest I sleep the sleep of death:** Unless by a change in his sad lot his strength is revived (cf. I Sam. 14:27, 29), he will sink in despair into the grave. And not only will God lose a faithful servant (88:11), but the psalmist's **foes** will have occasion to **rejoice** since his discomfiture confirms their godlessness.

2. Confidence in the Lord's Salvation (13:5-6)

5-6. Faith has its own logic. **I have trusted . . . ; my heart shall rejoice.** His confidence that he will be triumphantly vindicated comes from his conception of the nature of the Lord in whom he has put his trust (cf. Rom. 8:38-39). He is one of many men of faith in the O.T. who believed "in the sun when the night was blackest." "And by our dawn their faith is justified." The psalmist goes further and concludes with the lines of a hymn of thanksgiving in anticipation of his deliverance. **I will sing to the LORD, because he has dealt bountifully with me** (cf. 116:7; 119:17; 142:7).

---

circumstances. But the words leap to the eye in other contexts. Moral inertia is the commonest of ailments. We are wonderful adepts at proposing enterprises of every kind, especially enterprises for "tomorrow"; whereas Christ's word is "today." That flaccidity of the will unfortunately does not remain constant; it proceeds to complete incapacity of effort. "I see and approve the better course, but I follow the worse," as Ovid exclaimed. A man is in a sore case when his judgment of good is quite clear while his spiritual energy is negligible. We shadow our lives not so much by calculated rebellion as by inertly slumbering. We tend not so much to disobedience as to feeble nonobedience. No wonder that the Scriptures cry, "Awake, thou that sleepest"; no wonder that "sloth" is one of the deadly sins. Study the fourth terrace of Dante's *Purgatory*,[5] where the sin of accidie is purified—the sin of "don't care"—one of the most searchingly relevant passages ever penned to warn against a permanent danger of the soul.

There follows a quite human little touch. The psalmist prays that God may hear him in order that his enemies may not be able to boast that they have got the better of him, and that they may not **rejoice because I am shaken.** In part that is not altogether a worthy prayer, unless the cause for which he stands concerns him more than his personal feeling. A man who hates to be beaten or proved in the wrong is an unpleasant man to work with. The poet was sure he stood for the true and the good against the unworthy; in such case his prayer is right and proper. But before a man can pray thus, he must be very sure of where he stands. The church unfortunately is not without those who persuade themselves that their position is right because it is theirs. "This is my story and I stick to it" becomes to them a slogan of strength; whereas it is actually a slogan of obstinacy and pride. Before we can pray like this, we must carefully be checking our wills with the will of God.

In the next clause, **those that trouble me rejoice when I am moved,** we find a prayer that in part we must answer ourselves. It is open to us to wear our hurts, as well as our hearts, upon our sleeve. The ill-disposed will cease their attacks if they find that they do not discompose us. Many a man has won victories by declining to expose his wounds and has even found that the wounds themselves disappear. Some of the unworthy clashes that dishonor congregational life would not occur if those who imagine themselves injured declined to admit injury.

The final verses set before us a gentle sequence of peace. Mark the tenses of the verbs: **I have trusted,** the basic condition; **my heart shall rejoice,** the confident expectation of the man of faith; **in thy salvation,** the salvation which is God's because it is he who wills to give it, but is mine also for he gives it to me; **I will sing,** with "grave, sweet melody" because as I look back and see steadily and see whole, **the LORD . . . hath dealt bountifully with me.** A beautiful evening testimony of a good man.

[5] Cantos XVII, XVIII.

To the chief Musician, *A Psalm* of David.

14 The fool hath said in his heart, *There is* no God. They are corrupt, they have done abominable works, *there is* none that doeth good.

2 The LORD looked down from heaven upon the children of men, to see if there were any that did understand, *and* seek God.

To the choirmaster. Of David.

14 The fool says in his heart, "There is no God."
They are corrupt, they do abominable deeds,
there is none that does good.

2 The LORD looks down from heaven upon the children of men,
to see if there are any that act wisely,
that seek after God.

XIV. THE UNGODLY AND THEIR FATE (14:1-7)

14:1-7. See Exeg. of Ps. 53. The two psalms are identical, with the exception of some slight textual variations, but for the most part the text is better preserved in Ps. 53. A comparison of these psalms, particularly in respect to the text of 14:5, 6 and 53:5,

---

14:1-7. ***Irreligion and What Comes of It.***—Ps. 14 and Ps. 53 are the same. Evidently the original psalm was inserted in an early collection, and afterward in the Elohistic Psalter (Pss. 42–83). In the first version the name "Yahweh" is used throughout; in the second, "Elohim" (cf. Exeg. on Ps. 42:1-5). There are also minor variations; but in substance the poems are identical (cf. Exeg. on Ps. 53).

The content is clear. In vss. 1-6 we find a condemnation of atheistic Jews, such as we have already found in Pss. 10; 12. In vs. 7, which some regard as a liturgical addition, the writer breathes his longing for a better day, when those that are weary of godlessness shall be at rest. The core of the psalm is thus a statement of the spiritual state of the practical atheist and his inevitable history of futility and fear. It is given in a dramatic form which is worth noting.

1. ***There Is No God.***—Observe the practical and ethical character of this denial of God. A useful study could be made of the scriptural conception of atheism, and of its related idea of the **fool.** Basically he is a person who thinks of God as an absentee landlord who may be safely disregarded. It is a far more prevalent modern attitude than we are prepared to admit. Carlyle's bitter "mostly fools" is truer ethically than intellectually. Not to live as beneath the "great Taskmaster's eye" is doubtless wrong; and it is also senseless. The power of God's "stream of righteousness" stares us in the face. We might do worse than adopt the O.T. attitude of declaring the successful godless to be subnormal, the morons of society.

The first stage in their unhappy development is at once set down: **They are corrupt, they do abominable deeds.** Get away from some steady reference to God, and you will find yourself doing that which once you would have shuddered at. The practice of religion preserves for us our early instinct to be shocked at evil; its neglect kills that instinct. And if we lose our power of being shocked, we may find ourselves participating in evil which once made us blush. Such is the unaided human heart.

2. ***The Lord Looked Down.***—Suddenly then we are taken into the region of stillness where God dwells. In the psalms we find more than once this quick transference from the noisy fuss of human life to the quiet of God (cf. Ps. 2). But stillness does not mean inactivity; still less, lack of awareness. Man is not the only being who can "stand and stare." God also can and does; and there is something solemnizing in the thought of the silent gaze of his eyes. The word used indicates deliberate concentration of vision, as when a man moves to a window and **looks down** on something that has riveted his attention. We may notice that God is represented as looking in order to find something that will please him (cf. John 4:23, "The Father seeketh such to worship him"). The clause, **to see if there were any that did understand, and seek God,** is thought provoking. There are whole eras of alleged "understanding." We **understand,** or say we do, everything from atoms to the stars in their courses; in the view of the psalmist, we may understand and yet lack understanding. The one essential mark of understanding (or wisdom) is practically to conduct our affairs on the basis that God is and has a will of his own, which we may learn by listening and by search. The higher mathematician can easily be a fool, while his less endowed brother may be wise.

3 They are all gone aside, they are *all* together become filthy: *there is* none that doeth good, no, not one.

4 Have all the workers of iniquity no knowledge? who eat up my people *as* they eat bread, and call not upon the LORD.

5 There were they in great fear: for God *is* in the generation of the righteous.

6 Ye have shamed the counsel of the poor, because the LORD *is* his refuge.

7 Oh that the salvation of Israel *were come* out of Zion! when the LORD bringeth back the captivity of his people, Jacob shall rejoice, *and* Israel shall be glad.

3 They have all gone astray, they are all alike corrupt;
there is none that does good,
no, not one.

4 Have they no knowledge, all the evildoers
who eat up my people as they eat bread,
and do not call upon the LORD?

5 There they shall be in great terror,
for God is with the generation of the righteous.
6 You would confound the plans of the poor,
but the LORD is his refuge.

7 O that deliverance for Israel would come out of Zion!
When the LORD restores the fortunes of his people,
Jacob shall rejoice, Israel shall be glad.

---

affords an excellent example of the vagaries of textual transmission and an evidence of what we must be prepared to allow in the numerous instances where we are not favored with the witness of duplicates.

---

3. ***They Are Altogether Become Filthy.***—The vigor of this translation is useful. It gives the second step in the development of the practical atheist. His deeds have turned upon himself and have poisoned him. "Would I show you my heart? I would sooner show you a dung-heap," an old preacher cried. What he implied in his humility is the truth about the God-forgetter, according to the psalmist. Inevitably the poisoned self produces poisonous deeds: and the unhappy sequence continues and spreads, until **there is none that doeth good, no, not one.** The years before and following World War II afforded a terrible exhibition of this sequence. The subsequent uncovering of the events which took place in Europe under unbridled leaders displayed cruelties and insensibilities to the infliction of cruelty which appalled the mind. As we ponder, we must take warning against pride. We can never point to our own hearts and say, "This can never happen here." We can only shudder at the possibilities of corruption inherent in humanity, knowing that the psalmist was speaking sober truth, remembering the silent Watcher and who he is.

4-6. *The Gathering Storm.*—The text of vss. 4-6 may be subject to emendment; but the renderings in the KJV and the RSV give good sense. The neglect of God and the subsequent poisoning of a man's nature result in poisoned relations with his fellow men. To **eat up my people as they eat bread** is a vivid image of cruel contempt for the rights of others, disregard of them as fellow human beings. It is a straight path from practical atheism to gas chambers.

There were they in great fear, or more accurately, "there *are* they." This is the third step in the development: **they have done abominable works; they are all together become filthy;** then **were they in great fear.** As we read the psalms we must try to cultivate visual imagination and visual memory. All poets possess them. Tennyson would see his "flower in the crannied wall" very clearly, when subsequently he meditated upon it. Hebrew poets must have cultivated the power; conveying ideas through images was their natural habit of mind. Vs. 5 is a case in point. Perhaps the psalmist saw or remembered a sudden dark stormcloud, evidence of the gathering wrath of God. "There," he cried. You can almost see his pointing finger. Above, the stormcloud; and huddled beneath it, a crowd of worldlings, with pallid faces and startled eyes. "There they are in great fear." History can give us visions of horror in plenty to illustrate the poet's thought. "There—in that bombproof shelter they feared." Material is not lacking for one who would know "the terror of the Lord." Let it be used sparingly, however, and only, in the manner of the apostle, to "persuade men."

A Psalm of David.

15 Lord, who shall abide in thy tabernacle? who shall dwell in thy holy hill?

A Psalm of David.

15 O Lord, who shall sojourn in thy tent?
Who shall dwell on thy holy hill?

XV. The Virtues of the Godly Man (15:1-5)

A didactic psalm. The purpose of psalms of this type was to instruct the people in matters relating to their religious interests. In function these psalms are not far removed from the wisdom psalms in the postexilic times. They arose out of the ancient custom of repairing to a seat of worship to seek through a priest an oracle which would give the suppliant guidance in action or decision (cf. I Sam. 23:2, 4, 10, 12) or light on some affliction or calamity which had overtaken him (cf. II Sam. 21:1). Again, he might seek from the priest an interpretation of a sacred law in a particular reference or a fresh definition of religious duty (cf. Zech. 7:1-7; Hag. 2:11-13) and receive for answer a *tôrāh,* i.e., teaching. The prophets in their own way gave the oracle and the *tôrāh* a richer significance by transferring the range of their operation from the narrow interests of ritual and divination to moral and spiritual principles (cf. Hos. 5:15–6:6; 14:1-9). In the postexilic period the temple bore the responsibility of preserving and transmitting this religious heritage, and so the priest-scribes or the scribes played an increasingly important role in the religious guidance of the people (cf. Ezra 9:4-15; Neh. 8:1-9). By teaching disciples, by giving answers to inquirers, and by introducing homilies into the liturgy (cf. 95:8-11) they made their influence felt. Some of their instructions took the old form of the question-and-answer method (cf. Mic. 6:6-8). Out of such circumstances arose this psalm. So understood, it is not to be classed initially as a liturgical psalm, i.e., a psalm sung antiphonally; rather, it was written for use in the temple, the synagogue, the home, or wherever men made preparations to present themselves for worship at the temple (H. Ludin Jansen, *Die spätjüdische Psalmendichtung* [Oslo: Jacob Dybwad, 1937], pp. 141-45). It could, however, be introduced into a liturgy (cf. Ps. 24).

The precise translation of **in great fear** is "they feared a fear," which may suggest our modern concern for "the fear of fear." But it is applicable only in reverse. We need not fear that we should fear God's indignation against wrong: we need only fear that we may come to a condition in which we do not fear him, because we think so lightly of him; we need only pray that we may come into a state in which we have yielded to the perfect love that casteth out fear.

You would confound the plans of the poor, or **the counsel of the poor.** These **plans** or **counsels** may well be the pious confidence of the poor in the goodness of God. It is a terrible indictment to suggest that men so act as to make humble folk blush for being so naïve as to trust in God. But men do. Heedlessly for the most part, yet they do.

The psalm ends with an utterance of the messianic hope, when the Lord shall restore **the fortunes of his people.** That hope we must not forgo, remembering how wide is the range of **his people** in Christ. For "it is hope that saves" and "every man that hath this hope in him purifieth himself" (I John 3:3). Without hope, the hands hang down; with it, we are renewed for work.

15:1-5. *Genuine Piety.*—For a description of a man of God, turn to this psalm. There is no better definition of that elusive term. The last verse is the only one that requires explanation and is "dated." The rest holds good for all sorts and conditions of men.

O Lord, who shall sojourn in thy tent? The psalm pitches the standard high from the beginning; for it begins with the court of the ideal king. Who are the people whom he wants for intimates? In monarchical countries there are what are known as "court circles," and within these there are special orders who are friends of the king, appointed at his sole good pleasure; e.g., the Order of the Garter in England, which is regarded as the highest honor attainable by a subject of the British king, and is usually granted for conspicuous service. Those who obtain it are in a special sense "friends of the king." This psalm gives the qualities requisite to becoming one of the "friends of the King" in heaven (but see Exeg.).

The psalm deals with the qualifications which a man must satisfy if his worship in the temple is to be attended with blessings. It consists of three parts: (*a*) the question, vs. 1; (*b*) the answer, vss. 2-5*b*; (*c*) the reward, vs. 5*c*. The qualifications are ten in number, the decalogue form being doubtless of original design rather than the result of later additions. The psalm is closely paralleled in form and substance by Isa. 33:14-16. There is obviously an interdependence, but we cannot say which composition is the earlier (cf. also 24:1-6).

It is to be noted that the psalmist, passing over the ceremonial requirements of religion, speaks only of the ethical. In this the prophetic influence on the priestly order can be discerned. However, nothing is said of man's duty to God, nor is there a warning against such sins as murder, stealing, and adultery. For the most part the psalmist is concerned with the sins which we can describe as antisocial, since they destroy good will and brotherhood in a community—lying, slander, gossip, bribery, greed, perfidy. Evidently the psalmist was living in an age when the great need was for men of integrity and truth. His psalm is a tract for the times.

The postexilic date of the psalm is shown by the psalmist's knowledge of Deuteronomy and Leviticus (cf. Deut. 23:20; Lev. 5:4; 25:36), which obviously have for him quasi-canonical authority. The paraenetic or catechetical character of the psalm points to a late postexilic period (Otto Eissfeldt, *Einleitung in das Alte Testament* [Tübingen: J. C. B. Mohr, 1934], p. 80), as also the indication of a weakening of religious loyalties (vs. 4). The lines are mostly distichs and tristichs in 3+3 or 3+3+3 meter, but the meter of vs. 2 is 4+3 and that of vs. 5, 3+3+4. The fact that the organization of the lines appears to differ slightly from a loose aggregation of 3+3 stichs has led some commentators to suspect that some of the stichs, e.g., vs. 3*ab*, are secondary.

1. Qualifications for Citizenship in Zion (15:1-5*b*)

15:1. Cf. 24:3-6. A "sojourner" (גר) is one who, having no inherited rights in a community, is permitted to enjoy as a permanent guest the privileges of membership in the community. To be accorded such a status in the temple of a god brought in its train the riches of divine protection and favor (cf. 65:4; 84:4). This privilege, however, is not extended except to those who can prove their worthiness of it. **Who shall dwell on thy holy hill?** The second part of the line simply echoes the thought of the first part. The use of **tent** or **tabernacle** is an archaism for "house" (cf. 61:4; 91:10; 132:3). The holy place is described now as **thy tent** and now as **thy holy hill.**

With a phrase like that in mind we might recall Esth. 4:2, "No one might enter the king's gates clothed with sackcloth"; or the guest without a wedding garment; or the Beatitudes, especially the nearness to God promised to the poor in spirit, to the pure in heart, and to the peacemakers.

Two points present themselves in the list of qualities which vss. 2-4 present. First, simplicity—such folk appeal to common sense and are understandable by the ordinary citizen; and second, the emphasis placed upon care in the use of speech. A friend of the king sets a watch on the door of his lips. The characteristics (leaving out for the moment vs. 5), are eightfold: (*a*) He lives up to the accepted standards—he **walks blamelessly, and does what is right.** (*b*) His speech is true, because he himself is a true man—he **speaks truth from his heart.** (*c*) He **does not slander** anybody. (*d*) He is particularly careful to observe the obligations of friendship—**he does no evil to his friends.** (*e*) He keeps his tongue from insulting people in his community. (*f*) An added point is suggested by the KJV mg., "nor receiveth [or endureth] reproach against his neighbor." We are reminded of the rebuke of a wise old woman to malicious gossipers with its emphasis on the final adjective, "Is it true, is it kind, is it necessary?" Our life would be sweetened if criticism were confined to what it is necessary to utter for the common good. (*g*) He recognizes and regards **a vile person** or **reprobate** for what he is, and implicitly honors the God-fearing wherever he finds them. (*h*) In business affairs his word is his bond; even if he has made a deal in which he is the loser, he **swears to his own hurt and does not change.**

It is manifest that in all this there is ample material for setting forth the permanent ethical demands required of a truly civilized community, and that some subtle points are raised.

2 He that walketh uprightly, and worketh righteousness, and speaketh the truth in his heart.

3 *He that* backbiteth not with his tongue, nor doeth evil to his neighbor, nor taketh up a reproach against his neighbor.

4 In whose eyes a vile person is contemned; but he honoreth them that fear the LORD. *He that* sweareth to *his own* hurt, and changeth not.

2 He who walks blamelessly, and does what is right,
and speaks truth from his heart;
3 who does not slander with his tongue,
and does no evil to his friend,
nor takes up a reproach against his neighbor;
4 in whose eyes a reprobate is despised,
but who honors those who fear the LORD;
who swears to his own hurt and does not change;

2-5*b*. The enumeration of the qualifications for admission to membership in God's community provides the answer to the questions in vs. 1. First the acceptable man is described in broad outline (vs. 2). **He . . . walks blamelessly, and does what is right.** He, like Job, is not only negatively good, but positively good; not only is he above blame in his relations with his fellow men (see Job 31:1-40), but he seeks to serve their welfare (Job 30:25; 31:31-32; Matt. 23:23). **Speaks truth from his heart:** In his speech he is as upright as in his actions because what he says is in accordance with what he thinks; his promise and his intention are one. "To speak in the heart" is a Hebrew idiom for "to think."

Next the psalmist defines more concretely the man who is a guest of God, filling in the details of the picture sketched in vs. 2. Such a man guards his tongue against wronging his fellows by **slander** or **reproach.** The word translated **slander** (רגל) is more akin to "gossip," since a literal translation would be "he does not go footing about with his tongue" (cf. Ecclus. 5:14). Further, he will have no commerce with a **reprobate** (cf. 1:1; Luke 15:2), for "in his eyes the reprobate [a better reading is מנאץ, "the despiser"] is contemptible," but he holds in regard only **those who fear the LORD.** He stands by his solemn undertakings, even though the circumstances when he made oath may have altered to his disadvantage (cf. Lev. 5:4). He **swears to his own hurt and does not change.** Finally, he is not greedy for gain. He **does not put out his money at interest,** obeying the injunctions of the law against the exaction of interest on loans to a fellow countryman (see Exod. 22:25; Deut. 23:19; Lev. 25:36). Interest rates in the ancient world were usurious, ranging variously from 20 to 50 per cent. He **does not take**

2-3. *Sins of the Tongue.*—What is it to walk **uprightly?** How far does that tie us to the ethical fashion or manners of our time? Someone has remarked, "Fashion is civilization"; yet our Lord himself broke with it when he defended his disciples for plucking corn on the sabbath. The final clause suggests that the righteous man follows it only when and if it commends itself to his heart. So are we sent questing to find a universal fashion of conduct, and find ourselves forced to study the Ten Commandments afresh, particularly the "commandments of probity." Their relation to the permanent conception of true piety provides a striking footnote to the psalm as a whole.

The vital importance of unmalicious speech reopens the teaching of 10:7, but from the opposite point of view. Here it is represented as one of the things that simply are not done. Chivalrous speech may not be enough to solve the greater problems, but it goes a long way toward creating gracious communities. A society in which the good cease being "harsh to the clever," and the clever cease being "rude to the good," would be a pleasant society to live in. Public life would take a leap upward if public men cultivated generous tongues, and the press would be a new thing if it wielded only courteous pens. Is it possible that in ethical emphasis of this kind we have been lacking, and that we have to pay more attention to "the foxes, the little foxes, that spoil the vines," with the possibility that in the misuse of speech we have one of the king-foxes?

4-5. *The Good Man.*—The second clause of vs. 4, **but who honors those who fear the LORD,** offers no difficulty. It provides the right standard for distinction within the church, a standard

5 *He that* putteth not out his money to usury, nor taketh reward against the innocent. He that doeth these *things* shall never be moved.

5 who does not put out his money at interest,
and does not take a bribe against the innocent.

He who does these things shall never be moved.

---

a bribe against the innocent: Neither as judge nor as witness can he be tempted by a bribe to subvent the cause of the man who is innocent of wrongdoing or whose plea has right on its side. Here, too, he respected the law (cf. Exod. 23:8; Deut. 27:25). For the evils perpetrated through the corruption of justice see Prov. 25:18; Isa. 1:23; Ezek. 22:13; Amos 2:6; Luke 12:57-59.

2. The Blessing Attendant upon Righteousness (15:5*c*)

5c. The blessing promised to the man whose life can meet the test of this decalogue: **He who does these things shall never be moved.** He will be blessed with security, and against all the assaults of evil he will stand unshaken as a rock (cf. Matt. 7:24-25).

---

which we sometimes honor in the breach. Our chief places are not always reserved for the saints, except in distant retrospect. But the preceding clause lacks something. **In whose eyes a reprobate is despised.** Apparently no further thought is given to reprobates. This is a striking instance of how far the O.T. comes short of the N.T. There is nothing at all of the "passion to deliver," or any of Augustine's insistence that a man is redeemable as long as he lives. Contrast what is said here with the fact that our Lord won the title of "friend of publicans and sinners" and wore it proudly. The third clause reminds us of some heart-warming stories in the Bible. The character of Ittai the Gittite (II Sam. 15:19-21) provides an interesting commentary; so does that of Jephthah (Judg. 11:29-40)—a striking instance which, if anything could, might conceivably justify his place in the queer list of "saints" in Heb. 11:32. There is also the story of Daniel (6:10), who prayed at his open window as he had done previously, though it meant death. It is hardly necessary to suggest how large an ethical field under modern conditions, both in industrial and political life, this opens up; or to indicate how the story of Christ traces its origin to God himself.

Vs. 5 takes us into an economic world which to us is incomprehensible; its presence has made the use of the psalm impossible for some honest folk. In the Israelite state there were definite laws against usury, but there was no system of commercial credit. Debtors were the poor, and the laws against usury as given in Deuteronomy were promulgated to protect an unfortunate man against rapacity on the part of a brother Israelite. There never seems to have been any great objection to getting what could be obtained from a foreigner. In the N.T. there are no edicts against usury; Christ accepts the existing credit system and uses it in parables.[6] It is quite clear that we are not to hold that the code of the truly pious forbids honest return on money lent.

Yet we can take our stand on this verse when applying Christian ethics to economic systems and to business practices. Modern states have found legislation necessary to hold moneylending in check. The temper of Shylock in *The Merchant of Venice* is an obvious illustration of what is here rebuked. The words **does not take a bribe against the innocent** indicate the kind of economic immorality, harsh and cruel, which is forbidden; indeed, the primary meaning of the Hebrew word for usury, which is "to bite," suggests the financial rapacity which is to be condemned. Beyond that there is food for thought with regard to the practices of corporations and nations. Who but the devil takes a man or a group of men into a high mountain and shows them a 25 per cent profit? The N.T. is explicit when it declares that "the love of money is the root of all evil" (I Tim. 6:10).

With the concluding clause we may well be in agreement. A man who keeps the standards and is honest all through; who restrains his tongue; who is a dependable friend; who honors good men; whose word is his bond; and who gives an honest day's work for an honest day's pay, and seeks no more than a fair return on his outlay, is the sort of man who will "stand

[6] On the whole subject cf. W. H. Bennett, articles on "Debt" and "Usury" in James Hastings, ed., *Dictionary of the Bible* (New York: Charles Scribner's Sons, 1899-1904), I, 579-80; II, 841.

Michtam of David.

16 Preserve me, O God: for in thee do I put my trust.

A Miktam of David.

16 Preserve me, O God, for in thee I take refuge.

XVI. The Lord Is My Portion Forever (16:1-11)

This psalm is a prayerful meditation on the riches which the psalmist enjoys in his fellowship with God. It is placed by Gunkel in the class designated as psalms of trust, which includes also Pss. 4; 11; 23; 27A; 62; 131. The dominant feature of these psalms is an expression of quiet confidence in God as the source of life's highest satisfaction.

I nothing lack if I am his
And he is mine forever.

The prototype of these psalms is to be found in the section of a hymn or an individual lament in which respectively the reasons for praise or the grounds of the appeal are recited (cf. 22:9-10; 103:2-18), but eventually the theme of this section developed independently at the cost of the other elements, and a distinctive type or subtype of psalm emerged. Gunkel chooses to regard the psalms of trust only as a subtype of the individual lament, and Ps. 16, he points out, still retains in its opening verse, with the appeal for help and refuge, an element of the lament. In the other psalms of the class this relation of dependence is not so evident.

While the text of the psalm in vss. 3-4 is in a confused state, the course of the argument has not been obscured. The psalmist begins with the prayer that he may always live in the shelter of God's presence, for in God alone his soul finds its happiness. His experience is not an isolated one, since others too can speak of the blessedness which they have enjoyed through God's good favor. In contrast to this he sees the wretched plight of those who turn for help to other gods whose rites are abhorrent and whose worship multiplies sorrows for their suppliants. Reverting to the main theme, the psalmist tells how richly the Lord has supplied, beyond the competence of any other

in his lot at the end of the day"; for his spiritual home will be in the God who is just.

16:1-11. ***God as the Ultimate Good.***—This poetic meditation is markedly individual in tone, and therefore is a fruitful source for the cultivation of personal religion. We may come to it confidently to find material for the edification of saints rather than for the conversion of sinners. In older days it provided the kind of subject matter for the quiet of a weekly prayer meeting; today, if a man desires to escape into the region of inner peace from the hurly-burly of "problems" and "causes," he cannot do better than turn to this psalm. Such escape is not "escapist" in the sense of becoming blind to facts; it is rather the facing of other facts—facts of permanency. For the psalm deals with the things that remain when much else seems to vanish away. So many of us address ourselves to the times; it would be well if there were a few "poor brothers" who would address themselves to eternity in the company of this psalmist.

Since the psalm is personal and meditative, it is best to treat it verse by verse, rather than to regard it as a unified whole with a "message." The value of such a song as this lies not so much in what the writer was thinking and feeling as in what he makes the reader think and feel. We have at our disposal more than the poet has said here: we have that, plus centuries teeming with discoveries of God, plus our own experience, plus Christ. It is valuable, no doubt, from the point of view of what is often called "the development of religious ideas," to discuss whether in vss. 10-11 there are adumbrations of the doctrine of immortality; but it is also true interpretation to let the lovely expressions they contain work on our minds to set free our own hopes and persuasions derived from him who has brought immortality to light. We bring, as it were, the singer into our own company and find to our delight how wide and far distant his vistas become. If he had lived today, he would have written great Christian hymns.

1-3. ***Preserve Me, O God!***—This is the permanent admission and prayer of the human spirit that knows its dependence and its need. If we are to advance in religion, we must begin here.

2 *O my soul,* thou hast said unto the
LORD, Thou *art* my Lord: my goodness *extendeth* not to thee;
3 *But* to the saints that *are* in the earth, and *to* the excellent, in whom *is* all my delight.

2 I say to the LORD, "Thou art my Lord;
I have no good apart from thee."[g]
3 As for the saints in the land, they are the noble,
in whom is all my delight.

[g] Jerome Tg: The meaning of the Hebrew is uncertain

---

god, all spiritual and material benefits. But the Lord's transcendence over other gods is manifested still more by the fact that he holds communion with his faithful ones, counseling and admonishing them. So, keeping the Lord always before him, the psalmist receives through the "inner voice" instruction in the wisdom which leads to life and unfailing joys.

A date in the postexilic period is warranted by (*a*) the evident literary relationship between vs. 4 and Isa. 57:5-6; 65:4; (*b*) the Aramaisms מנת (vs. 5), נחלת for נחלתי, שפרה (vs. 6); (*c*) the influence of the wisdom style and point of view seen in **counsel** (יעץ), "admonish" (יסר), **show** in the sense of "instruct" (הודיע), **path of life, pleasures** (cf. Prov. 3:1-12, 15-18), and in the characteristic manner of contrasting the two ways of life.

The meter is clearly meant to be 4+4 with the usual 4+3 variation, e.g., in vss. 6-8, except in vs. 11 where it is 3+3+3. We have noted elsewhere that Hebrew poems are commonly concluded with an added half line.

1. No Good Apart from God (16:1-4)

16:1-3. Preserve me: In this instance not a cry of distress, but a prayer for a continuance of present blessings. **Good:** All good things such as prosperity and happiness. **To the saints . . . in whom:** The text is uncertain. The translation in the RSV follows the LXX, which differs from the Hebrew only slightly, reading האדיר for ואדירי and חפצו for חפצי. Some, by the slight change of ואדירי to האדירים, translate, "As for the holy in the land, they are the excellent; all my delight is in them," but after vs. 1, "all my delight is in them" becomes bathos. Wellhausen, seeing a reference to pagan gods,

---

But we notice that it is no cringing appeal for succor apart from action. **Preserve me, O God, for . . . .**" Search the Scriptures to discover what constitutes the implied condition—obedience, love perhaps, etc. The implied condition here is trust: **for in thee I take refuge,** or **in thee do I put my trust.** The points are clearly raised: (*a*) the central admission and cry; (*b*) the essential condition of directing life on the basis that God is, that he is benevolent, and that he is "able to keep." "Keep me, O Lord, for I am settled on this: from my heart, in thee do I trust, with all that the words imply of assent to thy will."

The Hebrew of vss. 2-3 is hopelessly corrupt: but there is a remarkable fact about the various guesses—they are all suggestive. Probably the RSV is right in making vs. 2 read:

> **I say to the LORD, "Thou art my Lord;**
> **I have no good apart from thee,"**

for it thereby becomes a development of vs. 1. To trust in God is to make him our own Lord, thus yielding the will, and to put him first, thus yielding the heart. But the KJV's **my goodness extendeth not to thee** is a highly profitable utterance. Our best is always far short of *the* best; therefore let us be humble and ask pardon and ever aspire.

It is in vs. 3 that we find embarrassment of riches in the differing renderings. The RSV reads **they are the noble;** but we should part unwillingly with the suggestion of **the excellent** in the KJV. The latter suggests rather more pointedly the consequence of wholeheartedly putting our trust in God. If a man does that, he will increasingly delight in the excellent. Few better verses can be found for youth, and especially for those about to be ordained to the ministry. **The excellent, in whom is all my delight** should be written over the desk of all who teach the young, especially in days when we are invited to be "at ease among the little worths." From an analysis of **the excellent** and from historical examples the thought may run to the heroes of the faith; or to the challenging character of our Lord himself—"Jesus, the Excellent, in whom is our delight." The peculiar flavor of the adjective stirs the imagination.

4 Their sorrows shall be multiplied *that* hasten *after* another *god:* their drink offerings of blood will I not offer, nor take up their names into my lips.

5 The LORD *is* the portion of mine inheritance and of my cup: thou maintainest my lot.

6 The lines are fallen unto me in pleasant *places;* yea, I have a goodly heritage.

4 Those who choose another god multiply their sorrows;[h]
their libations of blood I will not pour out
or take their names upon my lips.

5 The LORD is my chosen portion and my cup;
thou holdest my lot.
6 The lines have fallen for me in pleasant places;
yea, I have a goodly heritage.

[h] Cn: The meaning of the Hebrew is uncertain

emends the last two words of vs. 2 and also vs. 3 to read, "Of no account are the gods which they have chosen and the great ones in whom is their delight," but the "they" and "their" lack an antecedent. It is simplest to follow the RSV. The psalmist is one of a fellowship of saints who enjoy God's blessings.

4. They **multiply their sorrows: Sorrows** is, lit., "pain," "hurt," or "grief," whether of the body (Prov. 10:10) or the heart (Prov. 15:13). **Who choose another god:** Read **choose** for "exchange," i.e., בחרו for מהרו. The word **god** is supplied because understood (cf. Isa. 42:8; Exod. 34:14). **Their libations of blood:** Only libations of wine were offered to the Lord (Num. 28:7-8; Exod. 29:40). It is probable that the heathen libations were associated with some detestable practices (cf. Isa. 57:6; 65:4), but even a ritual out of accord with the prescriptions of the divine law would be abhorrent to the psalmist (cf. Isa. 66:3). As for those who practice such things, he will not even **take their names upon my lips.** Some of his fellows have become recreant.

2. A Goodly Heritage (16:5-8)

5-6. Far otherwise, **the LORD is my chosen portion and my cup,** lit., "the choice part of my portion and of my cup," unless *minnithā* is read rather than *menāth,* and one translates, "Thou hast allotted my portion and my cup." **Portion** is one's share in the

4. ***Multiplication of Sorrows.***—This verse is very modern: **Those who choose another god multiply their sorrows.** History is a living commentary on that exclamation. Notice the word **multiply.** It is not merely a matter of increasing, but rather of geometrical progression. The multiplication of sorrows from war is the most obvious fact; sorrows economic, sorrows physical, sorrows mental, sorrows of hunger and hate, sorrows of pain and perplexity—all multiply like the breeding of bacteria. We might contrast the divine command to be "fruitful and multiply," noting its suggestion of a happily increasing family of mankind, with our perversion of it into a multiplying of sorrows; nor may we fail to point out the root cause of it all, viz., the choosing of **another god.** The great god Pan—is he back? Even the Baals—are they returning, with their ancient disregard of Sinai? And all this despite the fact that the Son of God is come. What can we expect but multiplied sorrows?

5. ***The Chosen Portion.***—From this verse to the end of the psalm the poet expresses, in a crescendo, his inner well-being, based on his trust in God. He begins with the general statement that God is his permanent possession (**portion**) and that the harmony which results is his condition in life (**cup**), while both the possession and the condition are secured by God's own will: **thou holdest my lot.** But note that **the LORD is my chosen portion.** The co-operation of the human will is explicit. God imposes himself on nobody. All is well if we are in God's hands willingly; but we must do the necessary willing to put ourselves there. The phrase **my chosen portion,** with a question mark after it, should prove suggestive, remembering that not to choose consciously is nevertheless to choose, and to choose badly.

6. ***A Goodly Heritage.***—This lovely verse has become part of our common speech. One is glad to reflect how many people have been able to use it of their own habitation in very diverse lands. **The lines are fallen unto me in pleasant places; yea, I have a goodly heritage** has been quoted so often on both sides of the Atlantic,

7 I will bless the LORD, who hath given me counsel: my reins also instruct me in the night seasons.

8 I have set the LORD always before me: because *he is* at my right hand, I shall not be moved.

7 I bless the LORD who gives me counsel;
in the night also my heart instructs me.
8 I keep the LORD always before me;
because he is at my right hand, I shall not be moved.

---

division of goods or land; **cup,** a metaphor drawn from the practice of passing the wine to a guest at a feast or meal, means one's fate or destiny (Matt. 26:27, 39). **Thou holdest my lot:** Lit., "holdest fast." The psalmist's good fortune in God cannot be taken from him because God holds it fast. **The lines have fallen for me in pleasant places:** He uses another metaphor, that of the division of land by a measuring line (cf. Amos 7:17). Eventually "line" became a synonym of "share" or "allotment." Each one of the several lots which have fallen to him in God is comparable to the luck of obtaining a fertile field or a pleasant land.

7-8. The LORD . . . in the night: The night is a time favorable for divine communications (cf. I Kings 3:5; II Chr. 1:7; Dan. 7:2; Acts 27:23). **My heart:** Lit., "my kidneys," conceived as the seat of the affections and impulses that involve the will and character. **Instructs:** God instructs him and warns him through the chidings of conscience that by the discipline of the divine commands he may be kept in the way of life. **I keep the LORD always before me . . . moved:** Having the Lord always before his eyes, he is defended from whatever would cause him to slip or waver, and so to lose his blessed lot. Only the people of the Lord have this experience of a saving grace.

---

and in regions beyond, that we should dislike any change in them. They might well be given a national reference, provided (*a*) that we regard our heritage as spiritual, not alone material; (*b*) that we emphasize the word **heritage;** and (*c*) that we trace back the inheritance to the original Provider, who is God. National boasting, as if we ourselves had made our hills and valleys, or unaided had fashioned the noblest in our "way of life," is a national degradation.

7. *In the Night.*—From this verse to the end of the psalm the poet contrasts the lot of the righteous, who worship the true God, with that of those who, choosing the false god, multiply their sorrows. First, he obtains mental enlightenment—the Lord gives him **counsel**—and second, he gains a lively and sensitive conscience, for the Lord "admonishes" him. Observe the profitable phrase, **in the night.** According to the medievalists, the forces of evil are vigorous in the night; but according to this psalm, so are the forces of God. Our Lord's trial before Caiaphas was in the night: and in that night God "admonished" all mankind. What happened to Judas, when "he immediately went out; and it was night"? He had not made the Lord his chosen portion; there was therefore nothing to say but that "it was night." If we use the phrase to cover the night of sorrow, we can remind ourselves how much counseling and admonition we have received in the times of darkness, and be able to speak of "blessed grief."

8. *The Nearby Friend.*—This verse seems somewhat mixed in its metaphor. The singer first puts the Lord **before** him and then **at** [his] **right hand,** i.e., he is determined upon the direction of his life; he means to be harmonious with God, God being the fixed end toward which he moves. Then suddenly he discovers a curious thing. God, who was the object of his life, has become the comrade of his living. He put God ahead; but God shifted to his side. A man has achieved something when he discovers that the far-off Excellence is, in point of fact, the nearby Friend. Indeed, you might say without exaggeration that herein you have the gospel of Christ—the message that the high and lofty One walks with you as helper and defender. Note especially the phrase **at my right hand,** making the picture clear to the mind. If a man has God at his right hand, he has God's shield arm next to him and God's sword arm free to deal with the enemy. It is an entrancing picture: the pilgrim walking behind the shield of God, while God has his sword unsheathed in his strong right arm to smite down the pilgrim's foes. With such a comrade-escort "safe shall he be."

It is worth the interpreter's while to consider further the symbolism of the phrase, **at my right hand.** A bridegroom has his bride on his left side, she has him on her right, at a

9 Therefore my heart is glad, and my glory rejoiceth: my flesh also shall rest in hope.

10 For thou wilt not leave my soul in hell; neither wilt thou suffer thine Holy One to see corruption.

11 Thou wilt show me the path of life: in thy presence *is* fulness of joy; at thy right hand *there are* pleasures for evermore.

9 Therefore my heart is glad, and my soul rejoices;
my body also dwells secure.
10 For thou dost not give me up to Sheol,
or let thy godly one see the Pit.

11 Thou dost show me the path of life;
in thy presence there is fullness of joy,
in thy right hand are pleasures for evermore.

---

3. The Security of Faith (16:9-11)

9-11. Therefore my heart is glad; . . . my body also dwells secure: Heart and flesh alike witness to the fullness of the psalmist's fellowship with God. **My soul:** The Hebrew has כבודי, **my glory,** a probable error for כבדי, "my liver"; **flesh** or **body** suggests its appropriateness here. The liver was regarded as the seat of the emotions. The psalmist fills out the allotted span of years, shielded from wasting sickness and sudden death because **thou dost not give me up to Sheol.** There is no reference to a resurrection after death. The Hebrew means only that he is not abandoned by God to Sheol which, like an insatiable monster (Isa. 5:14), ever seeks to devour men (cf. 116:3). The preposition is ל, **to,** not ב, **in** (cf. Prov. 15:24). **Thy godly one** is the psalmist himself. The use of this verse in Acts 2:27 rests on the LXX, which read εἰς ᾅδην, and mistranslated "pit" for "destruction," through a misunderstanding of the root of the former. **The Pit** is a synonym of Sheol because the latter is conceived to be a great hole under the earth.

---

marriage service as they take their mutual vows, symbolizing his pledge of protection. It is seemly to remember that the church is the bride of Christ, and that he is her protector and warrior-comrade, as well as her Lord. Moreover the right side is the side of honor and trust. When we put someone at our right hand, we immobilize our own sword arm and indicate our trust in the good will of our neighbor. No higher dignity can be offered than to set a guest at our right hand; the final statement of the place of Christ is that he "sitteth on the right hand of God, in glory everlasting." The image, with its illustrations from our social practices, is recommended to any man with imagination; nor must we forget the quiet, satisfied expression of security with which the verse closes: **Because he is at my right hand, I shall not be moved.**

9. *Therefore My Heart Is Glad.*—Mark the **therefore.** There are many exhilarating "therefores" in scripture, and this is one of them. Let us notice the logic of experience implicit in these verses: (*a*) my primary purpose, **I have set the Lord always before me;** (*b*) my subsequent discovery of the comrade-God, **at my right hand;** (*c*) my curious feeling of spiritual safety; and (*d*) my growing exhilaration. Life is a great and good thing in this companionship. Even though enemies and dangers abound, achievement is going to be a fact. Myself, plus God, plus his shield, plus his sword bared in my defense are an unconquerable army. **Therefore . . . my soul rejoices;** and well it may.

My body also dwells secure. Here the Christian must pause. The O.T. singer clearly was taking the ancient view that physical prosperity and God-fearingness went hand in hand; and indeed godliness and physical health are far from being enemies. But it remains true that Job had "boils," and that Christian saints are not immune from cancer. A God-fearing world would doubtless be so mentally enlarged that disease would be greatly if not completely overcome in the end; but meantime many a generation must go on in the knowledge that the purifying of the soul does not guarantee immunity from physical pain. It is the soul itself that the comrade on the right hand defends. Therefore for the Christian the concluding verses must lead to "diviner regions, amplier lit."

10-11. *A Hint of Immortality?*—It surely is at least an open question whether these verses, particularly vs. 11, do not give something more than a hint of immortality. True, vs. 10 connects so closely with the end of vs. 9 that it is natural to think of the words as promising only escape from physical death. "My body also dwells secure, for thou dost not give me up to the place of shadows, nor let thy godly one see the underworld of darkness"; but is there no lifting up of the eyes to far-off hills in **thou dost show me**

A Prayer of David.

17 Hear the right, O LORD, attend unto my cry; give ear unto my prayer, *that goeth* not out of feigned lips.

A Prayer of David.

17 Hear a just cause, O LORD; attend to my cry!
Give ear to my prayer from lips free of deceit!

XVII. HEAR A JUST CAUSE, O LORD (17:1-15)

Here we have the characteristic features of the class designated laments of individuals. With it may be compared Pss. 3–5; 7. While conforming to the general pattern of such psalms, it shows some independence in setting forth its cause.

The psalmist is petitioning God for deliverance from enemies who menace his life (vss. 10-12). They have made charges against him (vss. 1-2), of which he vigorously protests his innocence. There is a vagueness as to the specific nature of the alleged offenses, but we may deduce from vss. 4-5 that for the sake of personal profit and in violation of the principles of his religion he was accused of some act or acts tantamount to the crime of robbery or violence. His last court of appeal is God. In the temple (vs. 8; cf. 61:5) he pleads for vindication (I Kings 8:31-32). While we are not told how in such a case the divine answer was communicated, it is safe to assume that it came through an oracle or some rite of purgation (cf. I Chr. 14:10, 14). The lament ends, as is the rule for such pieces, on a note of confidence.

The psalm, apart from its religious interest, sheds some light on the insecurity of life and honor in an age where society of itself provides no proper controls against the evils of the wicked tongue.

---

the path of life, or **in thy presence there is fullness of joy,** or **at thy right hand there are pleasures for evermore?** It is almost impossible to believe that a man so religiously sensitive as this poet did not look beyond death with a wondering question of hope. In any case it is quite obvious that if Christ has captured the psalms, we are free to understand these lovely phrases in the light of the God whom Christ revealed. We may note the useful hint in the changed use of the image of the right hand. The theme of the whole psalm might well be "Journey's End": God ahead and my soul behind, but following after; God at my side, and the soul covered by his care; the soul at his right hand, honored and given freedom in his fullness of joy.

17:1-15. ***Before the Great Tribunal.***—The writer of this dramatic psalm is clearly a godly Jew who keeps to the ways of his fathers, and consequently has drawn on himself the active hostility of worldly Jews. He thus becomes the representative of a class of men who, disdainful of following the herd and unafraid of speaking their minds, find themselves exposed to social and material danger at the hands of successful worldlings. It is a situation not uncommon. Many, individually and collectively, find themselves at a disadvantage if they will not yield to corrupt or semicorrupt commercial practices, or if they are compelled to denounce those holding public office. It is therefore not difficult to find material in the psalm apposite to modern conditions.

The poem is a dramatic monologue. The writer conceives of himself as appealing to the court of supreme justice; the psalm is his statement of his case. It is divided into several portions with a recurrent chorus of appeal. Vss. 1-2 are appeal, pure and simple, to the discernment and justice of the court. Vss. 3-5 declare the writer's unstained record. They are his plea of "not guilty" against the implicit charges of his opponents. Indeed, they are more than that: they are a defiance to anyone who dares suggest that he has anything on his conscience that he would hesitate to disclose. Vss. 6-9 reiterate the appeal for help, using picturesque images to further the urgency of his pleading. Vss. 10-12 disclose the character of his opponents, and describe the cruelty of their actions. Vss. 13-14 appeal for their destruction, in phrases that give food for thought. Vs. 15 lifts the psalm to a high religious plane, as the poet contemplates the inevitable outcome of his righteous plea.

1-9. ***Opening Plea.***—The interpreter must endeavor to visualize the scene, which was evidently so clear in the writer's mind. On the throne sits the impeccable judge who not only does justly, but is able to discern precisely the

2 Let my sentence come forth from thy
presence; let thine eyes behold the things
that are equal.
3 Thou hast proved mine heart; thou
hast visited *me* in the night; thou hast tried
me, *and* shalt find nothing: I am purposed
that my mouth shall not transgress.

2 From thee let my vindication come!
Let thy eyes see the right!

3 If thou triest my heart, if thou visitest me
by night,
if thou testest me, thou wilt find no
wickedness in me;
my mouth does not transgress.

The internal evidences are insufficient for dating the psalm. The type to which it belongs occurs in both pre- and postexilic times (see Pss. 61; 141). Vs. 15 (see below) does not imply a resurrection.

If it is assumed that the strophe corresponds to a division of thought, a comparison of the irregular strophic structure of this psalm with the almost regular structure of Ps. 16 demonstrates the freedom of the psalmists from adherence to a rigid theory of the strophe form. The text is corrupt in some verses, but one can identify the meter as 4+4 with some instances of 4+3.

1. The Appeal to God (17:1-2)

17:1-2. The psalmist begins his prayer with an appeal (vs. 1) and a petition (vs. 2). The urgency of his need is pressed by the threefold call, **Hear, attend to my cry, give ear.** His prayer is not a silent one; it is a loud cry. Through it **the right** or **a just cause** (cf. LXX), as opposed to the false, will be set forth (52:4), for he speaks with **lips free of deceit.** His request is that God may issue **my vindication** or "the judgment due to me." **Let thy eyes see the right,** i.e., where the right lies; the LXX reads "let my eyes," i.e., let me see a right decision.

2. Protestation of Innocence (17:3-5)

3-5. The psalmist continues with a protestation of his innocence which serves as a reason for granting the petition. **If thou triest my heart, . . . testest me, thou wilt find no wickedness in me** (זמתי should be read *zimmāthî* rather than *zammōthî*), also **if thou**

---

truth of the case and the quality of the man who brings it. Around are the shadowy figures of the worldlings, who are nevertheless made real in one biting, descriptive phrase in vs. 10. Into the center of the stage there has stepped the upright man himself, confident and passionate. He raises his hand and his voice rings out, **Hear the right, O Lord** (vs. 1).

The verses that follow open a valuable character study and a real problem in religion and ethics. At first blush it seems as if this were only another instance of spiritually immature complacency, sharply contrasted with the humble piety which the N.T. enjoins. Certainly the writer uses phrases which suggest that he had a good deal of moral self-satisfaction. He is not afraid of the discerning eyes. His **lips** are **free of deceit** (vs. 1); he can pray unhesitatingly, **From thee let my vindication come!** (vs. 2), provided the judge will let his eyes **see the right!** (vs. 2). He proceeds to tell the truth about himself, and there is no mock modesty in the picture. **Thou hast proved mine heart; thou hast visited me in the night; thou hast tried me, and shalt find nothing** (vs. 3). Note the phrase **visited me in the night**—that time when other distractions are stilled and a man can commune quietly with his own heart. The writer has evidently done some visiting of himself in the night and has found nothing of which justice could disapprove. Indeed, he is prepared to go down the list of possible transgressions and to declare himself free of them all. He has never planned to obtain any material gain, if it meant breaking a divine rule (vs. 4); he has never used the methods of the violent (vs. 4); and in general he has kept to the straight and narrow way, in which his feet have not even wavered (vs. 5). He certainly pitches his case high, and is different from the publican in the parable.

There is no question that this is a lower conception of a man's moral state than our Lord teaches. No sense of the corruption of the heart is found here, nor is there any suggestion of that pity for sinners which is a fruit of Christianity. "But for the grace of God there goes John Bradford" could never have been on this

4 Concerning the works of men, by the word of thy lips I have kept *me from* the paths of the destroyer.

5 Hold up my goings in thy paths, *that* my footsteps slip not.

6 I have called upon thee, for thou wilt hear me, O God: incline thine ear unto me, *and* hear my speech.

7 Show thy marvelous loving-kindness, O thou that savest by thy right hand them which put their trust *in thee* from those that rise up *against them.*

4 With regard to the works of men, by the word of thy lips
I have avoided the ways of the violent.
5 My steps have held fast to thy paths,
my feet have not slipped.

6 I call upon thee, for thou wilt answer me, O God;
incline thy ear to me, hear my words.
7 Wondrously show thy steadfast love,
O savior of those who seek refuge
from their adversaries at thy right hand.

---

visitest me by night, when the soul is especially open to the divine scrutiny (see 16:7). Let the search be ever so thorough, the psalmist is sure of a favorable result, for "my mouth has not transgressed [e.g., by false witness or oath or worship] any command of thine"; also he has **avoided the ways of the violent** (read with Syriac נשמרתי מארחות), such as robbers and murderers (cf. Ezek. 7:22; 18:10; Jer. 7:11); and **my steps have held fast to thy paths** with unwavering fidelity (construe תמך as infinitive absolute, or read תמכו).

3. The Appeal Renewed (17:6-7)

6-7. The psalmist makes a new appeal and petition, introducing into it certain allusions to God's disposition and character, which form a second reason for his intervention on the psalmist's behalf: **Thou wilt hear me, . . . show thy marvelous loving-kindness, O thou that savest . . . them which put their trust in thee.** By this is meant that in history and experience the Lord has shown himself to be a God who answers the prayer of the innocent, shows wonderful kindness in his dealings, and saves those who look to him for safety and protection. The psalmist has need of such help, for he is menaced by men who make cause against him, **adversaries,** lit., **those that rise up.**

---

man's lips. Yet we must not wave him away as a mere Pharisee. It must be remembered that he is standing before justice in a court of law, and that he is claiming that the law has nothing against him. He declares that he has never committed, or dreamed of committing, crime. His defense is that whatever anybody may say, he "did not do it." Is there not a danger that we may sometimes belittle the importance of being able honestly to say that one thing? Can we become so conscious of our inherent evil that we fail to distinguish between admission of tendency to wrong and admission of overt wrongdoing? Is it not a great deal to be able to say that we "did not do it"; and will not perfect justice take great heed of that fact? In days of shaky standards do we not need to emphasize the importance of keeping them intact, even while admitting our constant need of inner cleansing? The publican was not justified because he was a sinner; penitential tears are not an excuse for wrong acts. "Why call ye me, Lord, Lord, and do not the things which I say?" (Luke 6:46) is one of the clearest words of our Lord; and if this psalm reminds us of the importance of the act, it has moral relevance today.

It is possible for us, on the evidence of the poem, to get a good idea of the quality of its writer; for though its form is dramatic, its subject matter is not. The poet is not sitting where someone else sat; he is markedly being himself. Whoever has a gift for character study might profitably consider the writers of the psalms, judged by the internal evidence of their writings; and he might well begin with this one. If he thinks, as he possibly may, that the same man wrote Ps. 16, the picture is enlarged; but a clear enough outline emerges from Ps. 17 alone. Here is a man of probity, of whom it may be said, "Whatever record leaps to light, he never shall be shamed." He does not fear that he will be found out in immoral doings, for he commits none. He is not even afraid of the discovery of follies—perhaps least of all of follies, for there is no evidence of a cheerful, irresponsible boyishness about him. He is the epitome of the upright citizen of the Victorian

8 Keep me as the apple of the eye; hide me under the shadow of thy wings,
9 From the wicked that oppress me, *from* my deadly enemies, *who* compass me about.
10 They are inclosed in their own fat: with their mouth they speak proudly.
11 They have now compassed us in our steps: they have set their eyes bowing down to the earth;

8 Keep me as the apple of the eye;
hide me in the shadow of thy wings,
9 from the wicked who despoil me,
my deadly enemies who surround me.

10 They close their hearts to pity;
with their mouths they speak arrogantly.
11 They track me down; now they surround me;
they set their eyes to cast me to the ground.

4. The Psalmist's Enemies (17:8-12)

8-9. The petition is restated in more moving terms. He entreats protection such as one gives to that which most needs protection, **the apple of the eye**, lit., "the pupil of the eye," for which the Hebrew is "the little man of the eye," since the reflection of one looking into the eye suggests such a designation; an alternative name for it is "the daughter of the eye" (cf. Zech. 2:8; Lam. 2:18). **The shadow of thy wings:** The figure of speech may have been suggested by the wings of the symbol of the Egyptian sun-god, or by the wings of the cherubim, or more simply by the protecting wings of a mother bird. The need of defense is urged by the characterization of the adversaries as **my deadly enemies.** The Hebrew may be paraphrased, "my enemies against [the] soul," or "my enemies [surround me] for [the] soul."

10-12. A third reason for God's intervention is advanced by a still more terrible portrayal of the enemies. The psalmist has already (vs. 9) described them as ungodly, violent, bloodthirsty men from whom there is no way open for escape. He now goes on

period. More than that, he seems to have had control of his mind; he invites investigation of his inner self, even in the night watches, when his thoughts are free to roam. This comes near the picture of such a one as Sir Walter Scott, walking in his fields "thinking wise thoughts and good." Moreover, he is capable of moral indignation. Even if his indignation is stirred in the psalm by wrongs done to himself, it is nevertheless anger against the injustice of what is done more than because of the material hurt which has fallen upon him. What is wrong with a character of that kind? It is strong, honest, self-mastering. "I would be ashamed," cried a famous lawyer, "to possess a single habit that I could not give up at a moment's notice." He and our poet would have been akin. On such pillars strong societies are built, and men of that caliber swell the noble army of martyrs.

Yet something is lacking, as in the case of the rich young ruler, who, though this man's inferior, has a certain spiritual kinship with him; and the lack displays itself as the psalm proceeds. When we pass on beyond his claim of rectitude (vss. 3-5), we find a passionate appeal for personal help (vss. 6-9) in which one highly significant phrase occurs: **the apple of the eye.** The apple is the image of one man which may be seen in the pupil of another's eye. Literally, it is "little man," or "little daughter of the eye," the "mannikin" seen in reflection. Keep me as thou wouldest keep that which is reflected in thee, that which is almost a part of thyself. In our speech **apple of the eye** has come to mean simply the pupil of the eye; so that the verse may be regarded as an appeal that God preserve what is especially valuable to him. However, it is the image of himself that the poet sees reflected in God's eye: not man in general, or any other man; he himself is the sole object of his passion and his pleading—natural enough perhaps in his circumstances, for is he not in a court of law, fighting single-handed against enemies? Nevertheless, here we get a hint of where he falls short. Is he concerned for nobody but himself? Is he the only sufferer from injustice? A man can become self-centered in his sense of wrong as well as in his demands for pleasure, as all of us know. Some rigidly righteous folk are painfully sensitive—but chiefly to injustice done themselves. To that degree they cease to be "righteous." At the very least, this man, being reviled, will promptly revile again, as we see in the verses that follow.

10-12. *A Good Hater.*—At this point the psalmist rounds on his enemies. The vividness

12 Like as a lion *that* is greedy of his prey, and as it were a young lion lurking in secret places.

13 Arise, O LORD, disappoint him, cast him down: deliver my soul from the wicked, *which is* thy sword:

14 From men *which are* thy hand, O LORD, from men of the world, *which have* their portion in *this* life, and whose belly thou fillest with thy hid *treasure:* they are full of children, and leave the rest of their *substance* to their babes.

12 They are like a lion eager to tear,
as a young lion lurking in ambush.

13 Arise, O LORD! confront them, overthrow them!
Deliver my life from the wicked by thy sword,
14 from men by thy hand, O LORD,
from men whose portion in life is of the world.
May their belly be filled with what thou hast stored up for them;
may their children have more than enough;
may they leave something over to their babes.

---

to say that they cannot be touched by any appeal to pity for "they close up their fat hearts," i.e., their hearts are dull of perception and feeling. Read for חלבמו, **their own fat,** חלב לבמו, "the fat of their heart" (cf. 119:70, Job 15:27). **They speak arrogantly** because they are confident in their strength; RSV emends the M.T. of vs. 11 to get אשרוני **(they track me down)** and changes the next to the last word to להטות **(to cast).** Their leader is **like a lion eager to tear.**

5. PLEA FOR VENGEANCE ON THE WICKED (17:13-14)

13-14. The final petition expresses a passionate prayer for vengeance. **Deliver my life . . . by thy sword:** Counter their sword with thy sword (חרבך as second subject; cf. E. F. Kautzsch, *Gesenius' Hebrew Grammar,* tr. A. E. Cowley [2nd English ed.; Oxford: Clarendon Press, 1910], sec. 144*m*). "May thy hand slay them [תמתם ידך], may it dispatch them out of the world [תמתם מחלד], from their portion among the living"

---

of his language leaves no doubt of the vigor of his feelings. He almost seems to be enjoying himself. Like many a public man, he is a good hater. And indeed he has something to hate, as his opening denunciation makes clear. The expositor may well prefer the rendering **they are inclosed in their own fat** to the less suggestive **They close their hearts to pity;** for while the latter is the essence of the meaning, the former gives a more comprehensive hint of character. Here were people unreceptive of gentle and generous influences, because they were enclosed in their own gross standards of good. In the image of **fat** there is a suggestion of their golden hoard. Modern society is full of their descendants: the **fat** is in our way of life; the possession of it the hallmark of success; and it has an amazing enclosing power.

Thereafter the writer lets himself go. Arrogance is their quality, particularly in speech (vs. 10); they "gang up" against anybody and everybody who threatens their possessions (vs. 11); they are plain beasts of prey, both openly attacking and hiddenly waiting to spring (vs. 12). Is there nothing like that in our industrial and political life?

13-15. ***Closing Plea.***—So does the psalmist move to his demands against his adversaries, calling not only for a verdict in his own favor, but suggesting in plain terms the sentence to be imposed. At this point also the lack in his spiritual outlook is revealed.

First he asks for their violent overthrow (vss. 13-14),

. . . confront them, overthrow them!
Deliver my life from the wicked by thy sword,
from men by thy hand, O LORD,

ending with a description of them as **men whose portion in life is of the world.** Follow the sequence of ideas: (*a*) **men,** made in God's image, with all the possibilities implied; (*b*) **men whose portion . . . is of the world,** a portion chosen by them, with all the enclosing it creates, until they have to say, "myself mine

15 As for me, I will behold thy face in righteousness: I shall be satisfied, when I awake, with thy likeness.

15 As for me, I shall behold thy face in righteousness;
when I awake, I shall be satisfied with beholding thy form.

(cf. 142:5). **May their belly be filled . . . them:** A formula of blessing is grimly employed for a curse, which is to operate generation after generation.

6. The Anticipated Vindication (17:15)

15. The psalmist ends with expressing his conviction of being heard. Obviously he is not setting hope on the life after death, since his prayer is for preservation in the life that now is. **I shall behold thy face in righteousness:** He will be vindicated, and because of the rightness of his life he will, in contrast to his enemies, enjoy God's favor. **When I awake:** After the night of testing (vs. 3), whether the testing be by an examination of his heart or by some ordeal of purgation (Schmidt), the psalmist will have to the full the privilege of close fellowship with God. **Thy form:** A word that implies a more intimate relationship than "thy face" (cf. 11:7; Num. 12:8).

own dark goal"; (*c*) **men whose portion in life is of the world.** But when they cease to live, and the fashion of their world passes away, what then?

After that comes the psalmist's most bitter outburst. Let this **portion** which they have chosen be **their portion:** yes, and their children's after them. It is odd to find a Hebrew writer demanding that the penalty for godlessness be the increase and continuance of worldly prosperity.

May their belly be filled with what thou hast stored up for them;
may their children have more than enough.

Is this a man in advance of his time, one who has rejected the idea that goodness and worldly prosperity are interlocked? It may be that there is a gleam of spiritual advance here; but what is startling is the wholehearted savagery with which he prays that their mistaken longing for "good" may be satisfied to satiety. In effect he is praying for their firmer enclosure in their own fat, that the same spiritual sickness may fall on their children. There can be no question that he was a good hater, this man.

Thus we are able to add to the outline of his character. Strong of will, master of his thoughts and actions, completely faithful to the good he knew, but without pity except for his own fellows, he would have made his battle cry "Écrasez l'infâme!" [7] It is far from this to that universal longing to deliver which possessed our Lord. If the psalmist lived in times of persecution and saw the persecutors undermining the structure of society, his attitude is comprehensible enough; his was an honest fury, for he had his just quarrel. Yet its bitter curse against future generations indicates a state of mind from which the world still tragically suffers. Manifestly there is something here that is lacking—a something that is supplied by him who taught us to ask forgiveness as we forgive. The best shines most clearly in contrast with the second best; so Christ stands out in beauty against the background of this bitterly good man.

15. ***When I Awake.***—It is to be remembered, however, that the psalmist did live up to the good he knew. Nothing more can be asked of anyone, except that he should be willing to admit his need of further teaching. Wherefore it is not surprising that the psalm ends with a verse of singular quietude. The poet's conscience is at rest and his trust in God's rightness is complete; consequently, in his heart's deep core he can look forward to inner peace upon the morrow. **I shall be satisfied . . . with thy likeness,** i.e., **with beholding thy form.** Doubtless this meant for him a physical awakening on an earthly morning, when he would repair to God's house and find himself in harmony with the God whose house it was. But if ever a verse could be enlarged, this verse is a case in point. We cannot use the words apart from their capturing by Christ. **When I awake**—the Christian description of death—**I shall be satisfied**—with beauty and goodness and truth—**with beholding thy form**—knowledge at last of the heart of things, and freedom to be glad as a child is glad in the shelter and care of his Father from whom light perpetual falls.

[7] Voltaire, Letter to d'Alembert, June 23, 1760.

To the chief Musician, *A Psalm* of David, the servant of the LORD, who spake unto the LORD the words of this song in the day *that* the LORD delivered him from the hand of all his enemies, and from the hand of Saul: And he said,

18 I will love thee, O LORD, my strength.
2 The LORD *is* my rock, and my fortress, and my deliverer; my God, my strength, in

To the choirmaster. A Psalm of David the servant of the LORD, who addressed the words of this song to the LORD on the day when the LORD delivered him from the hand of all his enemies, and from the hand of Saul. He said:

18 I love thee, O LORD, my strength.
2 The LORD is my rock, and my fortress, and my deliverer,
my God, my rock, in whom I take refuge,

XVIII. THE THANKSGIVING OF A KING (18:1-50)

This psalm is of composite structure. It consists of two originally independent hymns represented by vss. 1-30 and vss. 31-50, which we may designate respectively as Ps. 18A and Ps. 18B. The former appears to be the thanksgiving hymn of an individual who has been delivered from enemies who made false accusations against him; the latter, on the contrary, seems to be the thanksgiving hymn of a king who has triumphed over his foes on the battlefield. While Ps. 18B is clearly a unit, Ps. 18A has probably been expanded by at least one addition, vss. 7-15, to the basal element, vss. 1-6, 16-30, which in itself could form a complete hymn of the type. It is impossible to determine through what circumstances Ps. 18A and Ps. 18B were united; it may have come about through their juxtaposition in the original Davidic Psalter, or through the desire of some editor or editors to make Ps. 18B, as a hymn of the house of David (vs. 50), longer and more impressive, or through their possession of a common hymnic introduction, vss. 1-3 (cf. 62:2, 6-7).

The psalm in approximately its present form was at a late date introduced into II Samuel (22:2-51) and there wrongly attributed to David. Its secondary relation to the text of II Samuel is shown by its interruption of the connection between 21:15-22 and 23:8-10. The differences between the two texts of the psalm are due to corruptions in transmission, and each becomes useful in correcting the text of the other.

The date of the psalm in its composite form is late, but the dates of the component parts are not uniform. Ps. 18B is late pre-exilic. The king (cf. vss. 43-44) is not David, contrary to the superscription, but one of his line (vs. 50). A late pre-exilic date is indicated by the court style (vss. 43-45), the broad impressionistic description of battle,

---

18:1-50. ***A Song of Deliverance.***—This noble psalm offers particular difficulties. On one of its aspects it is what has sometimes been called a "nature psalm," and the attitude of the O.T. to nature is different from ours. The modern eye discerns both qualities and facts in nature, things to which O.T. poets were blind. It is significant that biblical Hebrew has scarcely any words for colors, and that such as it has are hardly used in nature descriptions. Natural beauty—a sunset or a rose garden—did not hit the Hebrew mind as of great theological importance; nor does it seem to have been a source of delight, as it is to men of our time and race who have "a disciplined habit to see."

Yet the psalm opens the whole question of nature as a "word of God"—whether heard by ancient or modern ears. The expositor will have to equip himself with literature in addition to philosophy, remembering the "two voices" and "the mountains' gloom and the mountains' glory," and "Nature, red in tooth and claw." He may find George Meredith, a poet whose writings are too little known, to be profitable. Meredith's *A Reading of Earth,* and all that he has to say of the "pure wild-cherry in bloom," is a mine with good ore in it.[8] But despite our changed outlook and enlargement of knowledge, we can still go straight to the psalm itself, for it leads us unerringly to the one fixed point—the God whose creature and servant nature is.

The reader and student will also no doubt concern himself with questions of authorship, and with the parallel passages of scripture. He must take heed of the version of the psalm in

[8] See especially, "A Faith on Trial."

whom I will trust; my buckler, and the horn of my salvation, *and* my high tower.
3 I will call upon the LORD, *who is worthy* to be praised: so shall I be saved from mine enemies.

my shield, and the horn of my salvation, my stronghold.
3 I call upon the LORD, who is worthy to be praised,
and I am saved from my enemies.

---

with repetitions and want of order in details (cf. vss. 33, 36, 40-42, 37-39), due to the commingling of elements from older battle songs. Because of the reference to the continuity of the Davidic house, Ps. 18B would evoke a response in postexilic times.

Ps. 18A should be assigned to a postexilic, even a late postexilic, date, which is warranted by (*a*) the Deuteronomic tone of vss. 20-23, (*b*) the wisdom motifs of vss. 25-30, (*c*) the sermonic effect of vss. 20-30, with the omission of any reference to a thank offering and the emphasis on the ethical in religion. The introduction of didactic elements of a mixed prophetic and wisdom character is a mark of late hymnic style. The description of the theophany in vss. 7-15 is in the manner of similar compositions in Exod. 15:1-18; Deut. 32:1-43; Isa. 30:27-33; Hab. 3:1-19, all of which are generally regarded as late. Whether this section is an interpolation or an original part of the psalm is a matter of dispute.

The meter throughout is 3+3. The few irregularities are due chiefly to textual corruptions; corrections are possible by reference to the text in II Samuel.

A. AN INDIVIDUAL SONG (18:1-30)

1. INTRODUCTORY PRAISE (18:1-3)

18:1-3. The opening verse is wanting in the text of II Samuel. **O LORD:** In a hymn of thanksgiving the sacred name is regularly given prominence in the introduction. The psalmist will have all men know the name of the God to whom he owes his praises. It is set in large letters as a preface to the psalm. **I love thee:** It is probable that we should read "I will exalt thee" (cf. 30:1; 145:1), i.e., ארממך for ארחמך. **My rock . . . my stronghold:** By a series of epithets which stress the might and saving power of the Lord, the keynote of the psalm is struck (cf. 144:2). The Lord is a God whom men can lean upon, "although they walk in darkness and can see no light." **The horn of my salvation** does not occur elsewhere in the psalms. The metaphor may be understood in the light of Deut. 33:17, i.e., "the champion of my salvation." **I call . . . I am saved:** Not once only, but at all times the Lord shows himself a savior.

II Sam. 22; and he will compare the theophany of vss. 3-20 with that in Deut. 32. Probably he will come to the conclusion that the psalm was a tribute to the exploits of an unknown hero who united strict piety with successful leadership in battle. Possibly that hero was David himself, seen ideally; but the point is of no great importance. The psalm gives us God, nature, a warrior-servant of God, and his danger and escape, in which nature, under God's control, at once expressed the divine presence and assisted the servant in his need. Further, there are reflections on the nature of God himself as discerned by the servant whom he has helped. Manifestly the poem abounds in the permanently contemporaneous.

1-6. ***Praise and Appeal.***—These verses are introductory, and in two sections: vss. 1-3 are a hymn of praise; vss. 4-6 state the stress of circumstances in which the appeal is made. Pause on vs. 1 with its sharp statement of the poet's attitude. **I love thee, O LORD, my strength.** Note the present tense, **I love,** as against the future **I will love.** The former is preferable (yet see Exeg.). But mark especially the title given to God, **my strength.** Implicit in it is an admission of the poet's own weakness, with the humility therein involved; explicitly he is declaring that the strength of God is for him, not against him. As a rule, men fear the strength of God; and something noteworthy has happened to a man who can say that he loves it. Moreover, such a man discovers that God, the strong one, is the dispenser of strength to the weak, so that God and he together make an unconquerable combination. A man has gone a long way when the thought of God's almighty power is good news, sending him about his business confident and gay. It is a great thing when anybody can say, "I trust in the God who is able.

4 The sorrows of death compassed me, and the floods of ungodly men made me afraid.
5 The sorrows of hell compassed me about: the snares of death prevented me.
6 In my distress I called upon the LORD, and cried unto my God: he heard my voice out of his temple, and my cry came before him, *even* into his ears.
7 Then the earth shook and trembled; the foundations also of the hills moved and were shaken, because he was wroth.

4 The cords of death encompassed me,
the torrents of perdition assailed me;
5 the cords of Sheol entangled me,
the snares of death confronted me.

6 In my distress I called upon the LORD;
to my God I cried for help.
From his temple he heard my voice,
and my cry to him reached his ears.

7 Then the earth reeled and rocked;
the foundations also of the mountains trembled
and quaked, because he was angry.

2. The Psalmist's Perils (18:4-6)

4-6. The account of the psalmist's trouble forms an indispensable part of this type of psalm. Since he was in imminent peril of death, the psalmist could not hide in his heart what God had done for him. The underworld, near to which he came, is figured first as a violent, engulfing flood (cf. 42:7; 69:2), a metaphor derived from the ancient mythology of the great deep (cf. Jonah 2:3-6; Lam. 3:54), then as a monster setting traps and snares to capture men. In his distress the psalmist cried to the Lord, and his **voice** reached to the heavenly **temple.**

3. The Lord's Coming in Power (18:7-15)

7-15. The intervention of the Lord on behalf of the psalmist is described in terms of a theophany. The sense of the immediacy of God's relations with men, so marked in

Praise to his name for the majesty of his power."

The torrent of thankful names (vs. 2) in which the poet addresses his divine helper should also be marked, not so much the names themselves as the fact that there is a torrent of them. Strong feeling sometimes produces silence: "When I saw him, I fell at his feet as though dead" (Rev. 1:17). But sometimes it lets loose the gates of speech ecstatically: **My rock, and my fortress, and my deliverer, . . . my rock, . . . my shield, . . . the horn of my salvation** [i.e., either "my weapon which secures victory"—an image taken from a bull's horn—or "my peak of salvation"—an image taken from a narrow, precipitous mountain], **my stronghold.** This is the outpouring of a very thankful heart. Why has the religious temper so little of that note today? Maybe it is because we are not sufficiently alive to the enemies of our souls, nor have known "the amazement and the shock" of awaking to the fact of the strong love of God.

I am saved from my enemies. The poem is the hymn of a fighter who knows he has won his battle; but we note again to whom he gives the credit. No boasting here, but gratitude. **I call upon the LORD, who is worthy to be praised.** The man who seems to have won a moral victory, and congratulates himself, had better watch out. His enemy is only shamming dead to attack him through pride.

In vss. 4-6 the writer indicates the extremity of his danger. Clearly his life was in utmost peril. His pursuers were almost upon him. The quick succession of images is striking: **the cords of death . . . , torrents of perdition . . . ; cords of Sheol . . . , snares** [perhaps "breakers"] **of death** are all around him. May one not find in these images pictorial expression of the masterful quality of temptation? "The Torrents of Belial" is an arresting title for the lusts of the flesh. In vs. 6 the psalmist did the only thing he could do, he **called upon the LORD;** but notice that it was in his **distress** that he called. If a man is distressed when he realizes that his temptations are mastering him, there is hope for him; otherwise there is nothing for God to do but let the billows roll on, if haply their bruising may teach him. This man meant business when he cried for God's help; and the help came. God does not fail those in earnest in the warfare of the soul. Said the psalmist, **From his temple he heard my voice.** He always does, if our desire not to yield is strong and real.

7-15. ***God's Response.***—In this remarkable literary passage we get a striking description of

8 There went up a smoke out of his
nostrils, and fire out of his mouth devoured:
coals were kindled by it.
9 He bowed the heavens also, and came
down: and darkness *was* under his feet.
10 And he rode upon a cherub, and did
fly: yea, he did fly upon the wings of the
wind.
11 He made darkness his secret place; his
pavilion round about him *were* dark waters
and thick clouds of the skies.

8 Smoke went up from his nostrils,
and devouring fire from his mouth;
glowing coals flamed forth from him.
9 He bowed the heavens, and came down;
thick darkness was under his feet.
10 He rode on a cherub, and flew;
he came swiftly upon the wings of the wind.
11 He made darkness his covering around him,
his canopy thick clouds dark with water.

---

the Psalter, led the psalmists to view their vindication by God as something of the dimensions of a world judgment. The whole majesty of God fought on their behalf (cf. 9:5-8; 144:5-6; Wisd. Sol. 5:15-23). **The earth reeled and rocked:** The effects of the advent of the Lord in his anger are compared to the phenomena accompanying a volcanic eruption, quakings of the earth, smoke, deadly flames, and fiery volcanic stones. As the Lord himself, **he bowed the heavens, and came down; . . . he rode on a cherub, . . . came swiftly upon the wings of the wind.** Such language, reflecting older modes of thought, persists in the literary tradition (cf. Judg. 5:4-5) but does not necessarily reveal the spiritual level of the writer (cf. 139:1-12). A **cherub** or the cherubim seem in later times to have replaced the cloud in the bearing of the divine

---

a thunderstorm, in the midst of which the hard-pressed fugitive escapes. If the reader wants to see the Bible as literature, this is one of the sections to which his attention is to be called. It is accurate in observation—the phases of a great storm are all there—and is interfused with a sense of awe before the majesty of power. He who would do more will fasten on the master theme which pervades it, viz., that God is in the storm for a definite purpose. From that central thought he will find here a basis for meditation on the moral significance of natural catastrophe. Why, in a divinely ordered world, does nature sometimes smash down upon man and destroy him? In this case the writer gives the simple explanation that thereby the righteous man escapes from his foes; the smashing falls on the enemies of the righteous. But that does not meet the problem of nature's indiscriminate smashing. Catastrophe, like the rain, falls upon the just and the unjust. No doubt nature's ruthlessness is a spur to man's development: fear of lightning started him on his long and finally productive study of electricity. But behind that lies his need to remember that he is not the final master, even in the little sphere of his earthly dwelling. Nature has a terrible reserve of power which, when she chooses, she may unleash, and thus apparently obliterate many. Man is only so far the master of his fate: ultimately he is at the disposal of Another; "let him think and be still." The word of the storm and the flood and the earthquake teaches the puniness of man. Yet he knows his greatness; even against nature his victories are neither few nor slight: "men against the sea" have done incredible things. Nature challenges us to struggle, and we must not flinch from the challenge; for thereby men grow in strength. Nevertheless, we know that within her own domain she has the last word. In due time none shall stand before her army of ice; the last man shall fall asleep upon her snow. Wherefore we, with the psalmist, go behind nature to nature's God, whose word to us is, "Here we have no continuing city"; but there is "a city which hath foundations, whose builder and maker is God." From the threats of our temporary dwelling we escape to God himself, who is our home; we look up to the dwelling of the soul.

In the meantime nature utters many words of God. She speaks of his strength; of the beauty of his power, for storms have an awful grandeur of their own; his providence in the sustaining of life—even what seems to be his anger proves to be his protecting care, as this man found. She expresses endlessly the uncreated loveliness; she, in the march of unalterable law, is the presentation of the design of an infinite Mind. The interpreter will turn unhesitatingly and largely to the work of God's hands, and declare its witness to the majesty, beauty, and benevolence of the worker.

11. *He Made Darkness His Secret Place.*— Two thoughts suggest themselves: (*a*) In the secret place of God, is he necessarily alone?

12 At the brightness *that was* before him
his thick clouds passed, hail *stones* and
coals of fire.
13 The LORD also thundered in the
heavens, and the Highest gave his voice;
hail *stones* and coals of fire.
14 Yea, he sent out his arrows, and scattered them; and he shot out lightnings, and
discomfited them.
15 Then the channels of waters were
seen, and the foundations of the world were
discovered at thy rebuke, O LORD, at the
blast of the breath of thy nostrils.
16 He sent from above, he took me, he
drew me out of many waters.
17 He delivered me from my strong
enemy, and from them which hated me: for
they were too strong for me.

12 Out of the brightness before him
there broke through his clouds
hailstones and coals of fire.
13 The LORD also thundered in the heavens,
and the Most High uttered his voice,
hailstones and coals of fire.
14 And he sent out his arrows, and scattered
them;
he flashed forth lightnings, and routed
them.
15 Then the channels of the sea were seen,
and the foundations of the world were
laid bare,
at thy rebuke, O LORD,
at the blast of the breath of thy nostrils.

16 He reached from on high, he took me,
he drew me out of many waters.
17 He delivered me from my strong enemy,
and from those who hated me;
for they were too mighty for me.

---

presence (cf. 104:3; Isa. 19:1; Ezek. 1:22-28). **Thick darkness was under his feet, . . . darkness his covering around him,** and over him as **his canopy thick clouds.** As at Sinai his form is hidden from the eyes of men (Exod. 19:16-18; 33:20, 23). **Out of the brightness before him:** For the meaning cf. 104:2. With the LXX and II Samuel omit **his clouds** and translate, "out of the brightness before him proceeded hail and fiery coals." **The LORD also thundered, . . . sent out his arrows:** In vss. 13-14 the details are drawn from the phenomena of a thunderstorm, but vs. 15 relates to cataclysmic disturbances in the sea such as occur in conjunction with earthquakes. The whole description of the theophany is a composite of the most terrible events in the natural world: "He makes the whole creation his weapons for vengeance" (cf. Judg. 5:20).

4. THE PSALMIST IS DELIVERED (18:16-19)

16-19. The psalmist concludes the narrative of his troubles and of the divine intervention by an account of his deliverance. **He reached from on high, . . . drew me out of many waters.** The Lord delivered him from "the waves of death" (vs. 4). His peril was occasioned by "my enemies, for they were strong" (איבי כי עזו). **Those who**

Or is it a place where he meets with us, each of us separately? What manner of speech has God with us in his secret place? Is it not there that we might expect the tendernesses of his heart to be revealed? (*b*) Is what we call darkness never the secret place into which God calls us that he may whisper to us? Has the house of grief never proved to be the place of God's nearness? Before we complain of the shadowing of our souls through sorrow or defeat, let us wait and listen; mayhap we shall find it the place where he meets us.

16-50. ***Deliverance, Faith, Thanksgiving.***—The opening verses of this section, vss. 16-19, simply state the fact of the writer's escape, attributing it thankfully to God. The attitude he takes is surely quite reasonable. He might state it somewhat after this manner: "I was in great danger. A storm came up, and because of that storm I escaped. Therefore I praise him." His escape was part of the providential order. It was due to the storm. Therefore the meaning of the storm, as far as he was concerned, was divine assistance in his danger. It is not unreasonable for a man to discern what God's acts mean for him. If as a result he escapes from some peril, he has learned not a little about God's relation to him, taking God as encountered in personal experience. Philosophers may have something different to say; but he says, "Whereas I was nearly dead, now I am alive and safe," and gives God the praise.

18 They prevented me in the day of my calamity: but the LORD was my stay.
19 He brought me forth also into a large place; he delivered me, because he delighted in me.
20 The LORD rewarded me according to my righteousness; according to the cleanness of my hands hath he recompensed me.
21 For I have kept the ways of the LORD, and have not wickedly departed from my God.
22 For all his judgments *were* before me, and I did not put away his statutes from me.
23 I was also upright before him, and I kept myself from mine iniquity.

18 They came upon me in the day of my calamity;
but the LORD was my stay.
19 He brought me forth into a broad place;
he delivered me, because he delighted in me.

20 The LORD rewarded me according to my righteousness;
according to the cleanness of my hands he recompensed me.
21 For I have kept the ways of the LORD,
and have not wickedly departed from my God.
22 For all his ordinances were before me,
and his statutes I did not put away from me.
23 I was blameless before him,
and I kept myself from guilt.

---

hated me had charged him with having hands that were not clean (vs. 20), i.e., with crimes such as murder, violence, stealing, bribery, unjust gain (cf. 24:4; Job 9:30). Through some solemn procedure in the temple his innocence must have been pronounced.

5. The Lord's Recompense (18:20-24)

20-24. Without reference to a thank offering, the psalmist in conformity with the later mode proceeds to point the religious lessons to be drawn from his experience. **The LORD rewarded me according to my righteousness,** for **I have kept the ways of the LORD, . . . his ordinances, . . . his statutes.** The vocabulary is Deuteronomic (סור מן, חקות, משפטים, שמר).

Two phrases here catch the eye for their potentialities. In vs. 16,

> **He reached from on high, he took me,**
> **he drew me out of many waters**

cries out to be seen as a description of the action of God's grace. Many a man has felt himself lifted from the waters in which he might have drowned—waters of sin and bitterness and grief—by the strong arm of God in Christ. In vs. 19 the phrase describing the spiritual condition into which he is lifted is suggestive: **He brought me forth into a broad place.** Concentration on evil is terribly restricting to the mind; sin invites us into a very narrow place. In Christ's society the horizons are far and the vistas are wide. A Christ-filled mind is free to roam; for truth and beauty and goodness have endless forms and wide dwellings.

Vss. 20-24 reiterate the thought so frequently found in the Psalter, that God had intervened to defend the writer because he was a conspicuously righteous man. This is held to be the general principle of God's government. No doubt ultimately it is true; but it does not take account of the sufferings of the moment, or of the place of sacrificial pain. The psalmist has to learn from Christ.

Vss. 25-30 contain a series of generalizations, in which vss. 25-26 provide striking material. They declare the perplexing fact that life gives back to us what we put into it: our experience is often a mirror of our disposition. **Merciful** people see mercy in providence; the **upright** find uprightness; the **pure** discover purity; and above all the **froward** find that life treats them "frowardly." We should do well to retain the last of these terms, instead of substituting "crushed" or "tortuous"; its very unfamiliarity lingers in the mind. It must be explained, of course, by synonyms: **perverse,** "cranky," "mule-like." There is an old Scottish word "thrawn" that precisely meets the case, meaning "obstinate," "unteachable," "sour," "unsmiling." The thrawn man creates a corresponding attitude toward himself on the part of his fellows; and because his fellows treat him sourly and unyieldingly, he thinks that life as a whole conspires against him. Whereas if a man has a

24 Therefore hath the LORD recompensed me according to my righteousness, according to the cleanness of my hands in his eyesight.

25 With the merciful thou wilt show thyself merciful; with an upright man thou wilt show thyself upright;

26 With the pure thou wilt show thyself pure; and with the froward thou wilt show thyself froward.

27 For thou wilt save the afflicted people; but wilt bring down high looks.

28 For thou wilt light my candle: the LORD my God will enlighten my darkness.

24 Therefore the LORD has recompensed me
according to my righteousness,
according to the cleanness of my hands
in his sight.

25 With the loyal thou dost show thyself
loyal;
with the blameless man thou dost show
thyself blameless;
26 With the pure thou dost show thyself
pure;
and with the crooked thou dost show
thyself perverse.
27 For thou dost deliver a humble people;
but the haughty eyes thou dost bring
down.
28 Yea, thou dost light my lamp;
the LORD my God lightens my darkness.

---

6. THE LORD'S DEALINGS WITH MEN (18:25-30)

25-30. The psalmist turns from himself to express some reflections on God's dealings with men in general. In gnomic style he teaches that God's response to men is as various as their response to him. **With the loyal thou dost show thyself loyal.** This principle

---

merciful, upright, pure disposition, he tends to emphasize the corresponding elements in his experience, and to communicate his spirit to those with whom he comes in contact. There is a great deal to be said for the mental rule, "To aspects fair I turn the head, from foul I turn away"; for thereby a man increases the aspects fair and diminishes the foul.

The psalmist, however, falls short when he attributes this "reactive" quality to God himself. It is not God who is froward with the froward. The word means "from-ward" as distinct from "to-ward": and God is never "from-ward" in respect of men. The whole gospel of Christ is a declaration of his "to-wardness." But it is true that we may easily distort our vision so as to mistake a reflection of ourselves for God. Herein lies the cause of much of our cynicism and pessimism. Let us remember the word of the Lord Jesus when he said, "Blessed are the pure in heart: for they shall see God." Goodness enables us to see through mists to reality; evil in the heart throws back its own distortions.

In vss. 31-45 the psalmist moves on from the account of his escape from danger through the divine intervention, and his reflections thereupon, to an account of personal success in battle which he also attributes to the divine help of God, who **trains my hands for war** (vs. 34). This section offers us little. Indeed, some phrases in it jar upon our ears; e.g., vs. 42, **I beat them fine as dust before the wind.** The fact that this is a not inept description of the effects of strategic bombing should make us uneasy; let us hope we can say that we do not glory in it, but at the best regard it as a dreadful choice of the lesser of two evils.

Vss. 46-50 are a final ascription of praise, ending in vs. 50 with what may be a late liturgical addition. Vs. 49 is remarkable for the fact that it is quoted by Paul in Rom. 15:9 as a proof that God's salvation was not confined to the Jews; but this seems to be straining the intention of the verse, which says no more than that the psalmist will extol God **among the nations,** thereby making the nations only auditors of his praise.

While these concluding portions do not provide a great deal, the psalm as a whole contains poetic phrases and images which are eminently suggestive.

28. ***Thou Wilt Light My Candle.***—An admirable verse for parents or teachers. Every child possesses a **candle** of its own—some particular power of heart or mind whereby the sum total of man's light may be increased. The business of the older generation is to see that the younger can get its "candles" lighted; and each child can plead that its special candle be given a chance. The young musician, scientist, gardener, or artist thinks he has a right to ask of his guardians their help to get his particular flame alight. Every child is at least a potential "compassionate"; it is the business of society so to

29 For by thee I have run through a troop; and by my God have I leaped over a wall.
30 *As for* God, his way *is* perfect: the word of the LORD is tried: he *is* a buckler to all those that trust in him.
31 For who *is* God save the LORD? or who *is* a rock save our God?
32 *It is* God that girdeth me with strength, and maketh my way perfect.
33 He maketh my feet like hinds' *feet,* and setteth me upon my high places.
34 He teacheth my hands to war, so that a bow of steel is broken by mine arms.
35 Thou hast also given me the shield of thy salvation: and thy right hand hath holden me up, and thy gentleness hath made me great.
36 Thou hast enlarged my steps under me, that my feet did not slip.

29 Yea, by thee I can crush a troop;
and by my God I can leap over a wall.
30 This God — his way is perfect;
the promise of the LORD proves true;
he is a shield for all those who take refuge in him.

31 For who is God, but the LORD?
And who is a rock, except our God? —
32 the God who girded me with strength,
and made my way safe.
33 He made my feet like hinds' feet,
and set me secure on the heights.
34 He trains my hands for war,
so that my arms can bend a bow of bronze.
35 Thou hast given me the shield of thy salvation,
and thy right hand supported me,
and thy help[i] made me great.
36 Thou didst give a wide place for my steps under me,
and my feet did not slip.

[i] Or *gentleness*

---

of *lex talionis* in spiritual relations is below the level of Matt. 5:43-47. But in a richer vein the psalmist ends (vss. 28-30) with a confession of the faith he has come to as a result of his experience.

B. A Royal Song (18:31-50)

1. The King Defeats His Enemies (18:31-42)

31-42. With this strophe the thanksgiving hymn of a king (cf. vs. 50) for victory is introduced. We are told first of the manner in which God equipped him for battle (vss. 31-36), and then of his triumphs over his foes. For an analysis of the contents of the strophe see Exeg. on 18:1-50.

---

train him that his "light of compassion" is not quenched but increased.

29. *By My God I Can Leap Over a Wall.*— Our possibilities, both of mind and body, are far greater than we realize. It is recorded of an athlete that when he was fifteen, he jumped over a five-barred gate—a feat he never afterward equaled—because he was then chased by a bull. Fear drew out his latent power. If fear can be so great an incentive, how much more may love be? The stories of the martyrs and heroes provide the answers.

33. *He Maketh My Feet Like Hinds' Feet.*— He gives me energy, swiftness, and above all, sure-footedness. Nerve was defined by a small boy as "walking along awfully high walls and liking it." That is what the mountain goat does, as anybody knows who has seen a chamois in the Alps. In the things of the mind and conscience, where others hesitate and are afraid, the man who is constantly God-referred walks with steady steps. Jesus himself is the supreme example. The sure-footedness of his teaching had impressed his hearers when they said that he spoke with authority and not as the scribes.

34. *He Trains My Hands for War.*—There are various kinds of war. There is the war against filth and disease. Contrast the wars of destruction with the wars against destruction. The figure could be used of men who are breaking down slum areas in order to rebuild or of surgeons plying their surgical instruments to heal on battlefields.

35. *Thy Gentleness Hath Made Me Great.* —No doubt this is a wrong translation. It should read, **Thy help made me great;** but we cannot afford to lose the older reading. An interesting series could be worked out under

37 I have pursued mine enemies, and overtaken them: neither did I turn again till they were consumed.

38 I have wounded them that they were not able to rise: they are fallen under my feet.

39 For thou hast girded me with strength unto the battle: thou hast subdued under me those that rose up against me.

40 Thou hast also given me the necks of mine enemies; that I might destroy them that hate me.

41 They cried, but *there was* none to save *them: even* unto the LORD, but he answered them not.

42 Then did I beat them small as the dust before the wind: I did cast them out as the dirt in the streets.

43 Thou hast delivered me from the strivings of the people; *and* thou hast made me the head of the heathen: a people *whom* I have not known shall serve me.

44 As soon as they hear of me, they shall obey me: the strangers shall submit themselves unto me.

45 The strangers shall fade away, and be afraid out of their close places.

46 The LORD liveth; and blessed *be* my Rock; and let the God of my salvation be exalted.

47 *It is* God that avengeth me, and subdueth the people under me.

37 I pursued my enemies and overtook them;
and did not turn back till they were consumed.
38 I thrust them through, so that they were not able to rise;
they fell under my feet.
39 For thou didst gird me with strength for the battle;
thou didst make my assailants sink under me.
40 Thou didst make my enemies turn their backs to me,
and those who hated me I destroyed.
41 They cried for help, but there was none to save,
they cried to the LORD, but he did not answer them.
42 I beat them fine as dust before the wind;
I cast them out like the mire of the streets.

43 Thou didst deliver me from strife with the peoples;[j]
thou didst make me the head of the nations;
people whom I had not known served me.
44 As soon as they heard of me they obeyed me;
foreigners came cringing to me.
45 Foreigners lost heart,
and came trembling out of their fastnesses.

46 The LORD lives; and blessed be my rock,
and exalted be the God of my salvation,
47 the God who gave me vengeance
and subdued peoples under me;

[j] Gk Tg: Heb *people*

---

2. UNIVERSAL RECOGNITION OF THE KING (18:43-45)

43-45. As a result of his successes in battle, the king becomes **the head of the nations.** His fame as a warrior causes even **people whom** [he] **had not known** to come **cringing to** [him].

3. THANKS BE TO GOD (18:46-50)

46-50. Appropriately therefore the psalm of the king concludes with a double hymn of praise (vss. 46-48, 49-50). **Blessed be my rock. . . . I will extol thee, O LORD.**

---

the title of "inspired mistranslations." In this case the phrase is so apt a description of God in Christ and the graciousness of his redemption that we must keep it as part of our permanent mental furnishing. Starting from it, a man has before him the whole range of the gospel—Zacchaeus, to say nothing of Peter, would have said a loud "Amen" to it. The Holy Spirit can make the mistakes of copyists or translators to praise God, the God who makes all things,

48 He delivereth me from mine enemies:
yea, thou liftest me up above those that rise
up against me: thou hast delivered me from
the violent man.
49 Therefore will I give thanks unto
thee, O LORD, among the heathen, and sing
praises unto thy name.
50 Great deliverance giveth he to his
king; and showeth mercy to his anointed, to
David, and to his seed for evermore.

To the chief Musician, A Psalm of David.

19 The heavens declare the glory of
God; and the firmament showeth his
handiwork.

48 who delivered me from my enemies;
yea, thou didst exalt me above my adversaries;
thou didst deliver me from men of violence.

49 For this I will extol thee, O LORD, among the nations,
and sing praises to thy name.
50 Great triumphs he gives to his king,
and shows steadfast love to his anointed,
to David and his descendants for ever.

To the choirmaster. A Psalm of David.

19 The heavens are telling the glory of God;
and the firmament proclaims his handiwork.

The king is not David, but one of his line, for he can testify to the blessings through long years by **David and his descendants.**

XIX. The Glory of God in the World and in the Law (19:1-14)

Ps. 19 is composed of two distinct parts (Ps. 19A and Ps. 19B), of which the first (vss. 1-6) extols the glory of God in the heavens, and the second (vss. 7-14), the wonder of his law. The differences shown by them also in style, poetic power, and point of view argue dual authorship. However, it is not difficult to understand why such diverse compositions were brought together. To some editor, or perhaps to the second psalmist himself, it seemed appropriate to express his conviction that the law is no less a marvel of divine creation than the majestic order of the celestial bodies.

The meter of Ps. 19A is 4+4 in vss. 1-2, 5, with the common 3+3 variation in vs. 3; in vss. 4-6 it is 3+3+3. The meter of Ps. 19B is 3+2, varied by 3+3 in vs. 11 and 3+3+3 in vs. 14. The metrical difference between the two parts also points to their separate origins.

A. The Heavens Are Telling the Glory of God (19:1-6)

Like Ps. 8, this brief hymn ranks as one of the noblest examples of Hebrew poetry. It follows none of the traditional patterns of hymnic composition, and from beginning to end its material manifests fresh poetic and theological insights.

1. The Firmament Proclaims God's Handiwork (19:1-4*b*)

19:1-4*b*. Ordinarily a hymn commences with a summons to raise a song of praise to the Lord (cf. Ps. 113), but here it is omitted because, as the psalm opens, the hymn had already begun. Aeons ago at the time of creation its first notes were sounded (cf.

---

including literary errors, to work together for good.

19:1-14. *God's Handiwork in Nature and Law.* —Is this two psalms, and are vss. 1-6 a fragment of a longer one? Not necessarily, we may think, although the change in rhythm is abrupt at vs. 7. Vss. 1-6 deal with God in nature, vss. 7-14, with the moral law, and some see in the alteration of subject evidence for separation into two poems. But surely no two subjects are more closely related psychologically. A man who is awed by the majesty of God's **handiwork** can easily turn to the solemnity of his **ordinances.** "The starry heavens above . . . and the moral law within" were linked by Kant;[9] and if by him, why not in deeper sense by this poet? Indeed, it is precisely in the linking of vss. 1-6 with vss. 7-14

[9] *Critique of Pure Reason,* Conclusion.

2 Day unto day uttereth speech, and
night unto night showeth knowledge.
3 *There is* no speech nor language, *where*
their voice is not heard.
4 Their line is gone out through all the
earth, and their words to the end of the
world. In them hath he set a tabernacle for
the sun,

2 Day to day pours forth speech,
and night to night declares knowledge.
3 There is no speech, nor are there words;
their voice is not heard;
4 yet their voice[k] goes out through all the
earth,
and their words to the end of the world.

In them he has set a tent for the sun,

[k] Gk Jerome Compare Syr: Heb *line*

Job 38:7), and never since has the celestial host ceased from singing it. **The heavens are telling the glory of God:** The theme which the heavens recount and **the firmament proclaims** is "the work of his hands" at their creation. There is neither pause nor break in passing on the story of the marvels of that far-off event. **Day to day pours forth speech,** i.e., each day tells the story to its successor in torrential ecstatic speech. **Night to night declares knowledge,** for planets, moon, and constellations, as primordial creatures, alone were witnesses of the mysteries of creation which are "hidden from the eyes of all living" (cf. Job 28:20-28). Though neither **speech . . . words,** nor **voice** is heard by mortal ears, yet the mind that surveys them can detect an eloquence so loud that it resounds **to the end of the world.** For קום, **their line,** read קולם, "their sound" (with LXX and Jerome); and emend בקצה, "in the end," to לקצה, **to the end** (with Aq. and LXX).

2. The Witness of the Sun (19:4*c*-6)

4*c*-6. The greatest of the members of the heavenly choir is the **sun.** With its praise, therefore, the psalmist ends his hymn. Isolated from their context, these words could serve as a hymn to the sun-god. Because of myths about the sun as a deity, hymns to

---

that part of the value of the psalm consists. If somebody joined two such poems into this unity, he also was inspired.

One critical point may be noticed by way of introduction. Some critics hold that vs. 3 is a gloss by a later commentator. The psalmist has been declaring the constant speech of nature: **day to day pours forth speech;** following this in vs. 3 we find

> **There is no speech nor are there words;**
> **their voice is not heard.**

If this is a gloss (to the effect that "they do not really speak"), all we can say is that the scribe was guilty of pedantry; whereas, if it is part of the psalm, it is poetry. The contrast between the eloquence and the silence of nature is a fact of great moment on which the reflective must brood. Let us take vs. 3 as an integral and important part of the poem.

1. *The Glory of God in Nature.*—What is it to "glorify" God? How can the creature **declare the glory** of the Creator? By being a credit to him, so that gazing at **the firmament,** he is compelled to say, "How noble must be the mind that dreamed it." Connect this with the opening of the Shorter Catechism: "Man's chief end is to glorify God," i.e., to be such that he is an honor to his Maker, as a building of beauty honors its architect. Note also that among all natural things, the psalmist selects **the heavens** and **the firmament** as the first of the voices of glory. For they speak of beauty, of vastness, and of steadfast order. There is such a thing as the "consolations of the stars" in a world of confusion and change. "The stars brought me to God," said a man from the northern islands; and what he made of his life proved that it was no temporary bringing. There is possibly a permissible hint also in the English of the phrase, **the firmament showeth his handiwork;** as if the "innumerable streaming" of the stars were but the hobby of the Creator, while the full power of his creativeness was to be found elsewhere, in that which is made in his own image, and in the house which time cannot touch. We remember the apostle's words, "Eye hath not seen . . ." (I Cor. 2:9).

2-6. *Day, Night, and the Sun.*—Day unto day uttereth speech is better phrased "pours forth the story." The Hebrew habit of personifying the impersonal adds vividness to poetry such as this. Each day had a life of its own, and is

5 Which *is* as a bridegroom coming out of his chamber, *and* rejoiceth as a strong man to run a race.

5 which comes forth like a bridegroom leaving his chamber,
and like a strong man runs its course with joy.

---

the sun-god appear in the liturgies of Egypt (Adolf Erman, *Die Religion der Ägypter* [Berlin: Walter de Gruyter & Co., 1934], pp. 17-22) and of Babylon (Jastrow, *Religion of Babylonia and Assyria,* pp. 300-302). In one of the latter the sun-god is addressed as follows:

> O Shamash! on the horizon of heaven thou flamest forth,
> the bars of the shining heavens thou openest,
> the gates of heaven thou dost open.
> O Shamash! over the world thou liftest thy head,
> O Shamash! with the glory of heaven hast thou covered the lands,
> (Thy) course through the world (thou dost take?).

The psalmist, while utilizing such ideas about the sun widespread in pagan lands, halts at describing the sun as a deity. To him the sun is like a heroic runner for whom "a tent is set in the western sea" (read בים, "in the sea" for בהם, **in them**). From it he issues each morning as radiant as a **bridegroom,** as joyful as an athlete eager to run his course.

The fact that the sun is represented as a runner rather than a charioteer might at

---

pictured as coming forth from its dwelling to play its part at the appointed time, with a primary duty of declaring to its successor that God is glorious. There is something majestic and exhilarating in the conception that each day is handing a trumpet to its successor to blow the same triumphant note; while as evening falls and the stars come out, each night does likewise. As we gaze at the society of men, with their follies and their sins, the mind becomes confused and darkened; but if we turn to the day and to the night, we hear one unfailing song, "The hand that made us is divine."[1] It is significant that the countryman, who lives with the day and the night, is often wiser and more reverent than the city dweller; and that the most foolish of men are those who in pursuit of pleasure turn day into night. They confuse the voices.

Despite their endless **speech,** however, both day and night are enwrapped in silence. Indeed, their silence is part of their speech. For the heavens and the firmament are full of movement; the stars are not fixed points, but are "stars in their courses"; moreover, the movements are irresistible and inevitable. What does this speak of but power? The noisy engine is deficient; its clamor is a prophecy of its coming failure. It is the mighty that is still. True, such silence as that of the heavens may lay its chill upon the heart; if they declare no glory but their own, we dwell with the aloof and the heedless.

[1] Joseph Addison, "The spacious firmament on high."

A. H. Clough records somewhere that a small boy cast himself on his little brother's grave, listening; and rose to his feet weeping. "It's all quiet," he said. So is it always in grief; nature's silence seems to spring from a stony heart, unless we hear her true speech declaring the glory of God. Then the silence becomes a caressing thing, healing the hurt of the spirit and leading us to the God within, enabling us, in Pliny's phrase, to "build up the pillars of the mind." It is interesting to think of that cultivated Roman, escaping from the fret of Rome to his villa among the hills, to let the heavens and the firmament have their way with him for a little. Is there anything our present world needs more than the search for silence, in order that it may hear?

Yet their voice goes out through all the earth. No man is without a witness to God in this world, just because he is in this world, of which the heavens and the firmament and day and night are a part. "God, having . . . spoken unto the fathers . . . in divers manners" (Heb. 1:1 ASV): of these divers manners nature is one. Wherefore we need not fear for religion, nor doubt that in humanity there is a "prepared heart" for the truth about God given in his Son.

In them hath he set a tabernacle for the sun —them being the heavens. It is natural that an Oriental—or anyone else for that matter—should give the place of honor to the **sun;** for it is so manifestly the "lord of our life" as

6 His going forth *is* from the end of the
heaven, and his circuit unto the ends of it:
and there is nothing hid from the heat
thereof.
7 The law of the LORD *is* perfect, convert-

6 Its rising is from the end of the heavens,
and its circuit to the end of them;
and there is nothing hid from its heat.

7 The law of the LORD is perfect,
reviving the soul;

---

first glance be held to argue an early date for the psalm. But the presence of late words in the vocabulary, e.g., אמר, מליהם, יחוה, points to a postexilic date. It is possible that he also had heard of the famous doctrine of the harmony of the spheres advanced by Pythagoras in the sixth century B.C. The music, it was said, could not be heard because we are like men who, constantly hearing a sound, cease to be aware of it.

B. Piety Born of the Law (19:7-14)

7-14. As a poet, the writer observes carefully the metrical rules of Hebrew poetry, but he lacks that divine spark of poetic genius which is evident in the previous hymn. We are moved, however, by his earnest thoughts, which are born of the soul of a truly devout man who makes up in personal devotion to his God and the precepts of his law what comparatively to his fellow poet he lacks in range of mind. His religious point of view is like that of Ps. 119.

1. In Praise of the Law (19:7-10)

7-10. The psalmist begins by making a statement about each of the several terms used for the **law.** There are six of them, and they represent different aspects of the

---

earth born. From the sun, presumably, our world came; and to it, possibly, our world will return, ending its career in fervent heat. Meantime, upon the sun we are dependent. If it should cease to be, we might have eight minutes of ignorance, followed by obliteration. No wonder that there have been sun worshipers, and that in some cases their ethics have been high. For the sun is light, and the Lord himself did not think it unseemly to claim that title. Light is searching, healing—a golden thing; in it men may work and dwell together. "Praised be Thou, my Lord, . . . for Sir Brother Sun" [2]—a gay and radiant thing, **like a bridegroom** or an athlete (vs. 5). Students of literature will find this "poetry of the dawn" in sharp contrast with corresponding passages of English poetry where the sun comes up slowly with "pilgrim steps," not "like thunder" as in the East.

His **rising** is at one **end of the heavens** and his **circuit** is to the other **end of them.** The psalmist wrote, of course, in pre-Copernican days, with the earth the fixed central point. It is a pleasing fancy to imagine how he would have written this verse had he known of the solar system, with the earth and the planets become courtiers of the sun, delighting him and doing obeisance with their encircling dance; but we may doubt if he would have written any better poetry, or more adequately conveyed his central theme of the glorifying of God. A curious little light is thrown here on the significance of scientific knowledge in relation to the eternities. If a man is looking at the heavens to discern the glory of God, it matters very little whether the earth goes around the sun or vice-versa. Important, no doubt, in its place and way; but in relation to the eternities, irrelevant. If the poet had known all that astronomy now knows he would not have altered a word of vs. 1. He would only have spoken it with a deeper note of reverent awe.

There is nothing hid from the heat thereof. It is of importance that we do not omit this clause in which the old solemnity appears. God's greatest benefit, in all its splendor, may contain death if we are presumptuous. He who boastfully would dare the sun will die. In the presence of God a man must "cover his head," as Isaiah did in the temple. Perhaps this explains why God curtains his light; it is mercy, not aloofness, that prevents his full glory from "striking through our day." The mists of earth are necessary if we are to endure the rays of the sun. They are the condition even of the beauty of sunlight: it is they who turn its steady, silvery strength to gold; it is through them that we obtain the glory of the sunsets. Sorrows and perplexities that seem to veil him may well be evidence of his pity: until at last we, by his grace, become fit to see him face to face and live.

7-14. ***The Glory of God in the Law.***—At this point both the manner and the matter of the

[2] Francis of Assisi, "Canticle of Brother Sun."

ing the soul: the testimony of the LORD *is* sure, making wise the simple.

8 The statutes of the LORD *are* right, rejoicing the heart: the commandment of the LORD *is* pure, enlightening the eyes.

9 The fear of the LORD *is* clean, enduring for ever: the judgments of the LORD *are* true *and* righteous altogether.

10 More to be desired *are they* than gold, yea, than much fine gold: sweeter also than honey and the honeycomb.

the testimony of the LORD is sure,
making wise the simple;
8 the precepts of the LORD are right,
rejoicing the heart;
the commandment of the LORD is pure,
enlightening the eyes;
9 the fear of the LORD is clean,
enduring for ever;
the ordinances of the LORD are true,
and righteous altogether.
10 More to be desired are they than gold,
even much fine gold;
sweeter also than honey
and drippings of the honeycomb.

---

law. But to him **law, testimony, precepts, commandment, fear,** and **ordinances** are little more than synonyms. What he states about them is the matter of major significance. **The law . . . is perfect,** i.e., without a flaw, and it gives fresh life to the soul that grows faint in the face of persecution and affliction. It is **sure,** i.e., dependable, **making wise the simple.** It gives to the young and inexperienced wise guidance. **Right, rejoicing the heart:** Because **the precepts** are right, they produce in the heart the joy that springs from the inner sense of being in the right. **Pure:** Lit., shining. **The commandment of the LORD,** therefore, like a lamp, sheds light on the path of life. **The fear of the LORD,** i.e., the religion of the Lord. But for יראת, **fear,** read אמרה, "word" (cf. 17:6; 119:11, 38, 41; Isa. 5:24). It is free from all the abominations of pagan religions—**clean.** Its

---

psalm change. The writer turns sharply to a contemplation of the law of God, and fits his style to his subject. We catch the difference of rhythm in the English version; but in the original the change is as marked as can be. The swing of vss. 7-13 becomes a precise, polished, built-up structure. Each clause contains the same number of words; the various names for the law are introduced in sequence; and the law is praised first for its own qualities and second for its results.

Notice first the varying names for **the law: testimony, statutes** or **precepts, commandment, judgments** or **ordinances.** In vs. 9 the phrase **the fear of the LORD** is used as another synonym—the religious awe which the law produces, and the religious service which the law demands. Is it not time that Christian people should be reminded that churchgoing, the family altar, private prayer, and devotional reading are duties, as distinguished from things to be done when we are in the mood? Notice also the qualities associated with each term. The law, the total body of practical doctrine, is **perfect;** i.e., it is entirely sufficient to live by, especially when it is summed up by Christ, as in Matt. 22:37-40. The **testimony . . . is sure,** i.e., it is not a variable thing, to be changed according to circumstances, but is part of the established order. Much nonsense is talked about the variability of morality. Doubtless it is true that we have twisted God's demands and have seen the lesser matters out of proportion; but there are "testimonies" based on the love of God and our neighbor which are as fixed as the sun and the stars. Murder, adultery, theft, and false witness are plain wrong; as also are irreverence and blasphemy. The **statutes** or **precepts** are **right.** The path of moral duty is discernible: it lies straight ahead. **The fear of the LORD is clean;** and because it is undefiled, it lasts when systems that find an excuse for anything collapse. **The judgments** (better, **ordinances**) of God are **true,** "altogether right." How refreshing words like **true** and "right" are! "I do not care about being clever or modern; this course is wrong, and that is right." When a man can say some such thing, and say it humbly, as before the face of God, he has his feet upon a rock.

Further, we notice the results that follow from a proper honoring of the law. It refreshes or restores the soul. There is nothing that invigorates a man's inner self so much as being in touch with reality; and if he can find reality anywhere, he can find it in God's law, as that law touches his conscience. **The testimony** makes **wise the simple,** a fact to be observed any and every day. Humble folk, with lives based on the **law of the LORD,** are very sure-footed in the path of life, while others, who argue about it and about, flounder. The wisdom of an old woman who has the Bible at her elbow and

11 Moreover by them is thy servant warned: *and* in keeping of them *there is* great reward.

12 Who can understand *his* errors? cleanse thou me from secret *faults*.

13 Keep back thy servant also from presumptuous *sins;* let them not have dominion over me: then shall I be upright, and I shall be innocent from the great transgression.

11 Moreover by them is thy servant warned;
in keeping them there is great reward.
12 But who can discern his errors?
Clear thou me from hidden faults.
13 Keep back thy servant also from presumptuous sins;
let them not have dominion over me!
Then I shall be blameless,
and innocent of great transgression.

---

principles assure its permanence. **True: The ordinances** never betray those who trust in them.

2. Prayer for a Blameless Life (19:11-14)

11-13. The psalmist draws a lesson for himself from what he has said. Since the law is such a precious means of grace, instructing and warning men about the Lord's will, he prays that he may be preserved from sins against it, among which he names **hidden faults**—i.e., sins unwittingly committed (cf. Lev. 5:2)—and the sin of association with presumptuous men—i.e., men who in arrogance divorce themselves from God's ways.

Christ in her heart is an extraordinary fact. "What is wrong with clever folk," said such a one, "is just that they are clever. They can make out a case for murder. It is not difficult to do that; I could do it myself, if I wanted to waste my time. But, you see, it is against God's will, so what is the use of all this arguing?" Said another: "The advantage we have over you people is that we are sure; for God has made the path so clear so often." She was unconsciously repeating this verse, for the word translated **testimony** has a root meaning of "repetition"; he makes clear the path again and again. If he says anything once, we had better listen; if he repeats and repeats it in history, we must listen or perish. The simple, who mark the testimonies, learn that wisdom. The **statutes** or **precepts of the Lord** (vs. 8), being right or straight, "rejoice the heart." This is a good psychological point; when a man's duty is clear before him there follows a kind of glad inner release. **The commandment of the Lord** is "clear," **enlightening the eyes.** Again good psychology; a man who obeys his conscience finds himself living in a condition of moral enlightenment in which his conscience itself grows more discerning.

In vss. 9-10 the excellence of **the fear of the Lord** and his **ordinances** is summed up without reference to their results. They are more to be prized than **gold** or **honey.** A point is to be observed in these two comparisons. The importance of **gold,** i.e., the means to a large and dignified life, and **drippings of the honeycomb,** which are the purest honey, i.e., the most delicate satisfactions of the body, are not denied. But moral rectitude and achievement come first.

Vss. 11-13 put the obverse side of the function of the law. Positively, it displays the good life in all its attractiveness; negatively, it makes manifest the disaster and ugliness of the not-good. Moreover, this negative aspect is emphasized in advance. The law operates on the mind as a warning. It has not only its green light and its red, but also its yellow. This is brought out in the words, **moreover by them is thy servant warned.** It is of value to stress the cautionary character of the moral code. Conscience acts in three ways: it approves, it condemns, and it counsels watchfulness; to keep alive its sensitiveness in the last of these regions is particularly important. Ordinary people do not normally go dead against the red light. Deliberate and calculated wrongdoing comes with degeneracy. But we are constantly taking chances with the yellow light. The paths of life are strewed with moral jaywalkers who did not heed the "stop, look, and listen" of conscience; with the unhappy result of the development of moral color blindness. Yellow becomes green until at last red and green become interchangeable according to our fancy. The commonest examples of this downward movement are in business practices and in the use of alcohol; but in all departments of ethics the supreme importance of retaining awareness to warning is familiar to us all. We must not forget to point out that this aspect of the moral code is a strong evidence of the mercy of God, who does not let us slip into disaster without warning. The law is a channel of his grace.

The query in vs. 12 is well put. **Who can discern his errors?** Sins against conscience are plain enough; but what is this cesspool in the recesses of the self, from which spring thoughts,

14 Let the words of my mouth, and the meditation of my heart, be acceptable in thy sight, O LORD, my strength, and my redeemer.

To the chief Musician, A Psalm of David.

20 The LORD hear thee in the day of trouble; the name of the God of Jacob defend thee;

14 Let the words of my mouth and the meditation of my heart
be acceptable in thy sight,
O LORD, my rock and my redeemer.

To the choirmaster. A Psalm of David.

20 The LORD answer you in the day of trouble!
The name of the God of Jacob protect you!

---

14. The psalmist presents **the meditation of** [his] **heart** with the prayer that it may be as an acceptable offering in the eyes of the Lord—i.e, as pleasing to the Lord as an offering on his altars.

The psalm belongs to the time after Ezra. The law is the expression of the divine will for his people, and its precepts, as embodied in the book of the Law, occupy the thoughts of the pious. It is to be noted, however, that the law is not viewed as a yoke hard to bear. The N.T. conception of it is far removed from that of the psalmist. In the interval the scribes had not dealt well with it.

XX. PRAYER FOR A KING (20:1-9)

This psalm, as also Ps. 21, was meant to be sung on behalf of a king. In type it has an affinity to a lament of the people. There are several psalms in the Psalter which

---

impulses, desires which shock even ourselves? They at least should convince us of the importance of a code to which we adhere, even if now and then it seems unreasonable or unnecessary. No man should go against the standards of his time and community unless he is convinced that his rebellion is positively right. It is better not to "whistle on the sabbath" unless we are satisfied that we whistle to the glory of God and to the freeing of our fellow men from unnecessary fetters. The hidden man requires the curb of definite moral regulations.

The prayer in the second clause is, or should be, universal. **Clear** [cleanse] **thou me from hidden faults. Hidden** may mean "hidden from our fellows" or "hidden from ourselves." In the former case we must co-operate with God by ceasing to commit them. If "religion is what the individual does with his own solitariness," [3] the test of our religion is found in our warfare against **secret** sins; and here is our main battlefield. In the latter case we are flung wholly back on the help of God to enlighten our eyes and to cleanse our desires. Our part is to "walk with him" up to the limit of our capacity.

From this the next prayer is inevitable religious logic. **Keep back thy servant also from presumptuous sins. Presumptuous** is a significant word, with its suggestion of complacency and of a false thought of God and our relationship to him: "He's a good fellow, and it will all be well," plus "I am not a bad fellow at all, so it will all be better." Presumption of that kind is too like our real underthoughts to be taken lightly. It holds sway over us (vs. 13) far more than we think, unless we compel ourselves to go into the silence with God and face the facts of our sick souls. Win in the secret place and in solitude and, though there may still be defeats, the campaign is won. The KJV translates **great transgression** as **the great transgression.** Though inaccurate, it is an inspired mistake if we connect this clause with its preceding context of **presumptuous sins.** For presumption, self-sufficiency, inner spiritual pride is **the great transgression**—the baleful root from which the evil fruits derive.

The beautiful closing verse is a permanent possession of Christian worship, both private and public. In nonliturgical churches it is often used as a prayer before or after the sermon. If our public **words** and our **meditation** are **acceptable** in the Lord's **sight,** we have succeeded as heralds, witnesses, and teachers; if in private they are acceptable, we have by God's grace succeeded in life. For then we are either speaking or meditating "as if Christ were at our elbow," or at least as if we should not be perturbed to look around and find him there. After all, that is the test.

20:1-9. ***Before the Battle.***—This is a song written for some public occasion, when a king

[3] A. N. Whitehead, *Religion in the Making* (New York: The Macmillan Co., 1926), p. 16.

relate to a royal person (cf. Pss. 2; 18; 45; 72; 101; 110; 132; 144). In this instance the king belongs to the ruling house of Judah (vs. 2). He is seeking divine help at a time when he is menaced by powerful foes from within or without his country (vss. 7-8). Apparently (vs. 3) an abundance of sacrificial offerings and gifts has been offered or is being offered in conjunction with his petition at the temple. In Israel, just as in other lands, responsible leaders of the people in every generation turned to the Lord for help when the dangers of war were imminent (cf. Judg 4:14; I Sam. 7:9; I Kings 8:44-45; II Chr. 14:11; 20:4). For the form and contents of a king's prayer on such an occasion see Ps. 144:1-11.

The psalm falls into two parts. The first part (vss. 1-5), addressed to the king, voices a prayer that God may grant him a favorable response. The second part (vss. 6-9) assures the king that his prayer has been heard and that his enemies will be defeated. Some ritual act has taken place in the interval between the singing of the two parts. Was it a sign of the divine favor indicated by an oracle or by some examination of the sacrificial victims? However obtained, the answer of the Lord is announced (vs. 6) by some priestly individual, and his words are taken up by a choir of voices (vss. 7-8). The concluding verse closes the ceremony with a prayer to the heavenly king, repeating the theme of the psalm; it balances a similar prayer of the worshipers at the close of the first part.

The date of the psalm is pre-exilic because the context indicates the existence of the kingship in Judah. There is nothing to warrant an opinion that a messianic or Maccabean kingship is implied. It is to be noted, however, that the conceptions about the Lord and his relation to the temple reflect a considerable advance in theological thought. The Lord is not assumed to go into battle in person; he sends help from the temple. And while the temple is the place where he communicates his will to men, his answer comes from the heavens. The old anthropomorphic beliefs have given way to more spiritual ones. The date is probably late in the pre-exilic period.

The meter is generally 3+3. Stichs of four stresses occur in vss. *5c, 7b*. Vss. 2-3 are in 3+2.

1. Petition of the People (20:1-5)

20:1-5. The name of the God of Jacob: In earlier times the utterance of the divine name had magical power. Later the name was regarded as a quasi agent or representative

---

repaired to the temple to offer prayers and sacrifices for victory before going to battle. Vss. 1-5 were sung to the king by the choir or congregation—perhaps by the warriors under the king's command—and vss. 6-9 by the priest or the king as priest. The former was a straight prayer for victory, the latter an expression of confidence that the prayer would be answered. The psalm ends with a shout by the assembled host, "God save the king."

For our purposes this is a slight psalm. It was an "occasional" piece, written perhaps to order, by the equivalent of the poet laureate of the day. But it is curious how even so restricted a poem has enlarged its usefulness through association with Christian worship. John Ker[4] records how in 1839 Scottish miners, trapped in a mine near Edinburgh, were heard singing vss. 1-4 as they waited for death. He also tells us how the mother of Sir James Simpson, discoverer of the anesthetic property of chloroform, who was early left a widow and had a hard struggle to bring up her family, used to refresh herself frequently by repeating the psalm—so much so that her children called it "Mother's psalm." The strength she thereby obtained doubtless communicated itself to her son and helped him to develop the patience necessary for the discoveries which did so much to banish pain. It is a long trail from the temple and an Israelite king to trapped miners and an old lady in Scotland two thousand and more years afterward. Herein is provided another proof that the songs of religion are more than their words. They gradually collect the blood and tears, the hope and confidence, of centuries of history and experience, if they have been used in worship by generations. These miners, pre-

[4] *The Psalms in History and Biography* (Edinburgh: A. Elliot, 1888), pp. 36-38.

2 Send thee help from the sanctuary, and
strengthen thee out of Zion;
3 Remember all thy offerings, and accept
thy burnt sacrifice; Selah.
4 Grant thee according to thine own
heart, and fulfil all thy counsel.

2 May he send you help from the sanctuary,
and give you support from Zion!
3 May he remember all your offerings,
and regard with favor your burnt sacrifices! *Selah*

4 May he grant you your heart's desire,
and fulfil all your plans!

---

of the Lord (cf. 54:1; 124:8) or his second self (cf. 20:7). Still later, **the name,** like the law, was regarded as a mediator between God and men. **God of Jacob,** as a synonym of the Lord, identified him more specifically as Israel's God, and appropriately here as the God who had wrought great deliverances for his people (cf. 46:7), in fulfillment of his promises to Jacob (cf. Gen. 35:10-13). **Protect you:** Lit., "set thee up on high" (ASV), i.e., make you as safe as an unassailable height. **Regard with favor your burnt sacrifices:** Lit., "regard as fat your burnt sacrifices." Only fat beasts were acceptable for sacrifices to the Lord (cf. Mal. 1:7-8). The burnt sacrifices were accompanied with meal or cereal offerings (cf. Lev. 7:37; 23:37; II Kings 16:15). Read with Hebrew MSS the plural in each instance. **May we . . . set up our banners:** For נדגל read either נגיל or נגדל, and translate "may we rejoice" or "may we boast." The word דגל can mean only "troops" (G. Buchanan Gray, "The Meaning of the Hebrew Word דגל," *Jewish Quarterly*

---

paring for death, drew strength from the accumulated strength of their fathers as they sang the words made sacred by brave men before them who trusted in God and were not ashamed. The church, while continually enriching its worship, will do well to retain, especially in its songs, words and music ennobled by ancient courage and deepened by knowledge of Christ.

But apart from associations such as these—and there are others in Christian history—the psalm is not a deep mine, though there are some suggestions which we should not miss.

1-5. *Prayer for the King.*—The name of the God of Jacob defend thee, "make thee secure," "set thee on high." Besides the meaning of **name** as "character" or "quality," the utterance of a name itself brings confidence and power, even if it is only the name of a famous leader or hero. "St. George for England," or "John Brown's body" were tonic cries. How much more when the name can be "God of our fathers and our God." Cromwell's men knew the value of the name of God; by reason of it they were "Ironsides." But it is possible to be inspired by a wrong name. "Heil Hitler!" is a terrible example. If we are to call upon a name, we must see to it that we possess the right name; and we can do that only if we fight for the right cause. Our "point to fight for" must accord with our leader's name. For us the name is Christ; the cause therefore must be deliverance.

Send thee help from the sanctuary. The only causes, therefore, for which we may fight are those which we can take into God's house; the only swords we can draw are those which we can lay on the altar. We cannot expect **help from the sanctuary** if what we bring to the sanctuary is hateful to the Lord of the sanctuary. A point, this, for governments and for democracies. Recall the place of the vigil in the practice of chivalry. After the young knight had completed his seven years' training as a boy and his further seven years as a squire in full armor, he entered the sanctuary and, laying his shield against the altar and his sword upon it, spent the night in prayer. Then, and only then, he went forth to the perils and adventures of the knightly life, and its enterprises of succor for the oppressed.

The king-priest, after the fashion of his time, was sacrificing both the offering of blood and the bloodless offering of fine flour (vs. 3). Occasions may arise when we must be willing to offer our blood. No people is great unless it has something for which it is prepared to die. But we also have to bring the bloodless, e.g., the offering of goods, or of effort apparently beyond our strength. Winston Churchill, we may remember, called in a universal phrase not only for blood, but also for "toil, tears, and sweat." If there were more of the bloodless offerings of toil, tears, and sweat in days of peace, there would be less likelihood that offerings of blood would become necessary.

Grant thee according to thine own heart. An arresting prayer to offer for a leader before battle; and a futile prayer if his heart is the heart of ambition and conquest.

In the name of our God we will set up our banners probably refers to a point in the

5 We will rejoice in thy salvation, and in the name of our God we will set up *our* banners: the LORD fulfil all thy petitions.
6 Now know I that the LORD saveth his anointed; he will hear him from his holy heaven with the saving strength of his right hand.

5 May we shout for joy over your victory,
and in the name of our God set up our banners!
May the LORD fulfil all your petitions!

6 Now I know that the LORD will help his anointed;
he will answer him from his holy heaven
with mighty victories by his right hand.

Review, XI [1899], 92-101). The prayer is that king and people may be able to rejoice over the fresh evidences of the power of the divine name.

2. Assurance of God's Help (20:6-9)

6-9. Now I know: Through an oracle or some outward sign the priestly ministrants are assured that the divine favor is with the king. The good news is announced by one who speaks for the priests and who may be the psalmist himself. The pronoun indicates that vs. 6 is the utterance of an individual. The **we** of vss. 7-8 may connote that other

---

service when the flag-bearers waved their flags and all present joined in the cry **the LORD fulfil all your petitions** (better, "plans"). But it opens a large field. The reader should look elsewhere in scripture for the use of **banners,** and should turn to heraldry and the ceremonial use of banners, bannerets, flags, standards, etc. For these buntings convey "quality" and "achievement," among other things. A royal standard, for example, proclaims the fact that its possessor has the quality of a king, and its quarterings may convey his great deeds or achievements or those of his house. Similarly with national flags. The English-speaking peoples are fortunate in the significance of their national standards. The Stars and Stripes has aspiration and the red price of achievement in the symbols; the Union Jack, with its crosses of the chivalrous knight (St. George), the missionary hero (St. Patrick), and the quiet, practical saint (St. Andrew)—the last, the representative of the steady ordinary Christian, being basic—is rich in significance. These are banners which can be set up in the name of the Lord; and every citizen of these countries should know their meaning so that, in the words of a great orator, the challenge may come to us all: "Whenever you are tempted to anything mean, anything unworthy, look on that flag and forbear."

6-9. *Assurance of Victory.*—At this point, the sacrifice having been offered, the king declares his confidence (but see Exeg.): **Now I know that the LORD will help his anointed.** The emphatic word is **now.** Everything has been done that could be done. The warriors are equipped; the plan (cf. vs. 4) has been thought out; **now** the enterprise has been laid before God and his help invoked. Therefore the king has no qualms. With all that human foresight can provide, and with an easy conscience and confidence that the moral factor is on his side, he accepts the gage of battle.

It is permissible to lift this phrase into higher realms. Under what conditions can a man be sure of divine help? The whole Christian evangel is the answer. Having seen God in Christ, a man can say, "Now I know that God cannot do anything but help." Otherwise, in the vivid phrase of the N.T., he would be "ashamed to be called their God" (Heb. 11:16). But within that large area of confidence, are there not particular occasions in the experience of many when the mind settles itself into unshakable security? The essential condition is surrender to the divine will, with the price of surrender accepted. After our Lord declared "not my will, but thine," he was able as his final word to say, "into thy hands." If a man has acted on the precept to pluck out an offending eye or cut off a rebellious hand, he arrives at a most peace-giving **now.** If he ceases to try to serve two masters, then also he can say, **Now I know.** Religious confidence is the inevitable child of honest acceptance of the divine order: the man who possesses that confidence has the strength of ten. He believes in the good outcome of whatever awaits him; and his belief makes him more than conqueror. This sense of security arising from strong-willed surrender is a fact of religious experience; of how much importance is clear when the power that arises from it is also noted and remembered.

7 Some *trust* in chariots, and some in horses: but we will remember the name of the LORD our God.

8 They are brought down and fallen: but we are risen, and stand upright.

9 Save, LORD: let the king hear us when we call.

7 Some boast of chariots, and some of horses;
but we boast of the name of the LORD our God.
8 They will collapse and fall;
but we shall rise and stand upright.

9 Give victory to the king, O LORD;
answer us when we call.[l]

[l] Gk: Heb *give victory, O* LORD, *let the king answer us when we call*

---

voices have joined his, unless the psalmist in his words has identified himself with the congregation. **Some boast of chariots, . . . horses; but we boast of the name of the LORD:** Since the issue of battles is with God, it is vain for a people to put their trust in the size and quality of their military equipment. This truth is frequently impressed on pre-exilic kings (see Deut. 20:1; II Kings 6:17; Isa. 31:3; 37:23-36). **Answer us when we call:** The reading of the versions is preferable to the Hebrew text, which is followed by the KJV. The final verse forms a fitting conclusion to the psalm.

In vs. 7 the poet puts the depth of his confidence in the most vivid way he can:

Some boast of chariots, and some of horses;
but we boast of the name of the LORD our God.

It looks as if the enemy he was going to fight were those notable horsemen and charioteers, the Assyrians; but the important point is not historical or local. He is saying that in every war morale is more important than equipment and armaments.

But is that true? Surely in the physical wars that disfigure the human story it needs serious qualifications. "God is on the side of the big battalions";[5] what is necessary is "to get there firstest with the mostest"; one atom bomb is mightier than an army. Nevertheless it is worth noting how even modern commanders lay supreme stress on morale. Ill-equipped troops, fitted with the will to conquer, have held lines many a time against overwhelming numbers of the halfhearted. Feeble forces have gained delay against stronger foes until the balance of might changed sides. Still more, instances may be multiplied of the appearance of incalculable influences and happenings which gave strength to the weak. The moral factor is still the supreme disposer of events.

Vs. 8 is an image from the battlefield. Certain considerations suggest themselves: (*a*) The warfare of the soul is no simple campaign. It is not easy to knock out the soul's enemies. They totter but they keep their feet, and go on fighting. So harsh is the fight that they often bring us down with them. But (*b*) the difference is that in the end the God-helped warrior is on his feet again. Never allow a moral lapse to create a spirit of moral defeatism. Rather let our self-disgust jerk us upright to continue the struggle. For (*c*) if we are in earnest, we shall finally be able to say, "We keep our stand." The boxing ring can provide a lively illustration or two, and they are permissible, seeing that the apostle Paul used the phrase "so box I" (I Cor. 9:26). On occasion we may have to admit sadly that we are down. But not down and out. We hold that "we fall to rise, are baffled to fight better."[6] The end of the story of the God-empowered man is to be "pedestaled in triumph." If we believe it, it will be true. "You can't keep a good man down" is a reasonable remark to make to our own private devil. For a good man is himself plus God; and that is an unbeatable combination.

The psalm ends with a brief united prayer by the congregation. Ellicott makes an interesting comment: "The change from second to third person is characteristic of the Hebrew manner of conquering emotion, and allowing the close of a poem to die away in calm and subdued language."[7] There is a hint here of the desirability of keeping emotion in restraint and not allowing our feelings to "run away with us," a fault from which some forms of worship suffer. Hensley Henson in his memoirs speaks of the distress caused him by "choribantic religion." The dignified close of this psalm seems to agree with him.

[5] Marshal de la Ferté.

[6] Browning, *Asolando*, Epilogue.

[7] *O.T. Commentary for English Readers*, IV, 116.

To the chief Musician, A Psalm of David.

21 The king shall joy in thy strength, O LORD; and in thy salvation how greatly shall he rejoice!
2 Thou hast given him his heart's desire, and hast not withholden the request of his lips. Selah.
3 For thou preventest him with the blessings of goodness: thou settest a crown of pure gold on his head.

To the choirmaster. A Psalm of David.

21 In thy strength the king rejoices, O LORD;
and in thy help how greatly he exults!
2 Thou hast given him his heart's desire,
and hast not withheld the request of his lips. *Selah*
3 For thou dost meet him with goodly blessings;
thou dost set a crown of fine gold upon his head.

XXI. Psalm for a King (21:1-13)

Like Ps. 20, this is one of the so-called royal psalms (see Exeg. on 20:1-9). It falls into two divisions or strophes: (*a*) vss. 1-7, addressed to the Lord; (*b*) vss. 8-12, addressed to the king. Vs. 13, as we shall see, may be taken either as a part of the second division or as a brief ejaculatory prayer for divine assistance.

The psalm, like Ps. 20, is to be classified with the laments. In form it may be compared with 89:19-37, in which there is a contrast of past blessings with present troubles. The occasion of the psalm seems to have been an anniversary of either the king's coronation (vs. 3) or the king's birthday (vs. 4). But the king is harassed by the fear of enemies who, one judges, must be a real menace, since vss. 8-12 are wholly concerned with them. After the manner of certain Babylonian royal psalms (Heinrich Zimmern, *Babylonische Hymnen und Gebete* [Leipzig: J. C. Hinrichs, 1911; "Der alte Orient"], pp. 8-9) the first division is a hymn of praise to the Lord for the great benefits he has bestowed on the royal suppliant. As in Ps. 20, between the first and the second division an oracle or a sign of the divine favor was received, on the ground of which the promises of vss. 8-12 are delivered.

As in the case of Ps. 20, so here we assume that the king is pre-exilic. But it is not possible to say where or when he ruled or who he was. The meter is 4+4 in vss. 1-5; 3+3 in vss. 7, 10-13; and 4+3 in vss. 6, 8-9.

1. The King's Past Blessings (21:1-7)

21:1-7. In this strophe the several benefits which the king owes to the Lord's goodness are recited. In the course of his days the king has been given such a fullness of support

---

21:1-13. *A Song of Thanksgiving.*—As Ps. 20 was a prayer before battle, so this psalm is a hymn after a successful conflict. The two may quite possibly refer to the same event. Like its predecessor, Ps. 21 is intended for antiphonal use. In vss. 1-7 the people, or their representatives, who may very well have been a company of maidens, singing and praising God go out to meet their king, home from the wars. In vss. 8-12 they directly address him, recounting his achievements; and in vs. 13 they join together in a closing ascription to God.

1-7. *Song of the Welcomers.*—**Thou hast given him his heart's desire, and hast not withholden the request of his lips** is a suitable text for a day of national celebration. The negative in the second half of the verse is emphatic, "thou hast by no means withheld." The whole verse assumes that before setting out on the enterprise the king or the nation has taken the matter "to the Lord in prayer." Thanksgiving of this sort is the privilege of a praying people; success such as is here implied has prayer back of it.

Thou preventest him with the blessings of goodness (vs. 3). It may in one sense be better to retain the older form **preventest,** instead of replacing it with its modern equivalent, **dost meet him,** for the archaism, when it has been explained, sticks in the mind of the hearers. Observe the change of meaning in the word "prevent," from "coming to meet" to "blocking the way." There is a hint of natural pessimism in this development. We tend to imagine that what awaits us in life is a barbed-wire fence, or notices saying "Keep Out"; whereas the truth is that a Person is waiting to meet us with blessings in his hand. The image here called to

4 He asked life of thee, *and* thou gavest
it him, *even* length of days for ever and ever.
5 His glory *is* great in thy salvation:
honor and majesty hast thou laid upon him.
6 For thou hast made him most blessed
for ever: thou hast made him exceeding
glad with thy countenance.
7 For the king trusteth in the LORD, and
through the mercy of the Most High he
shall not be moved.
8 Thine hand shall find out all thine

4 He asked life of thee; thou gavest it to him,
length of days for ever and ever.
5 His glory is great through thy help;
splendor and majesty thou dost bestow upon him.
6 Yea, thou dost make him most blessed for ever;
thou dost make him glad with the joy of thy presence.
7 For the king trusts in the LORD;
and through the steadfast love of the Most High he shall not be moved.

8 Your hand will find out all your enemies;

---

and help that he can exult in it. **His heart's desire, . . . the request of his lips** have been granted without fail. Even before he has made his wants known, the Lord has met him **with goodly blessings.** All these experiences of divine beneficence were but a part of the consummate evidence of God's favor in putting **a crown of fine gold upon his head.** Further, the Lord had in answer to the king's prayer granted him **length of days for ever and ever.** In the court language of the ancient Orient **for ever and ever** meant no more than "many years." There is no ground here for interpreting the psalm as messianic, nor need we assume that the king is already an old man. The psalmist may know of some oracle which promised the king a long life, or he may again in the language of the court propitiously express his confidence that the Lord would fulfill the king's natural wish for a long and prosperous reign. The psalmist, however, is not so overcome by the theme of his hymn as to forget his duty to remind the king that **his glory is great through thy help.** Only because **the king trusts in the LORD** is he kept secure **through the steadfast love of the Most High.**

2. THE KING'S FUTURE VICTORIES (21:8-13)

8-12. In this second strophe there is the promise of the annihilation of the king's foes. **Your hand will find out:** The word **find** is used with the sense of "come upon"

---

mind is of a company of young girls going out to meet a returning hero with garlands in their hands (cf. I Sam. 18:6; Judg. 11:34).

Thou settest a crown of pure gold on his head is probably no more than a poetic extension of the figure just mentioned; but it may be connected with the actual coronation of a victor. There would be nothing unseemly about using it for a meditation on the triumph of Christ; or, through him, as a pictorial representation of the final condition of those who trust in him. There is an old Gaelic saying that "he is a king who is well"; what God promises us is "saving health." Morally, health is holiness; to be well is to be "good all through." That **crown of pure gold** is within the reach of all of us poor "slaves who should be kings."

Length of days for ever and ever means no more than a prolonged reign of indefinite length; but in the light of immortality and the gospel, we cannot leave it to so poor a meaning. No more heart-warming phrase in the presence of death is to be found in the psalms, if once we let the lips of Christ utter it. It can echo in the mind with great comfort if we are thinking of a brave youth "dead e'er his prime." So earnestly he desired life; with such "manifold entreating" we prayed that he might (in our sad, misunderstanding speech) be spared. Nevertheless, he died. But what is this that Christ shows us? What far horizons? If our prayers had been answered, it would have been but a postponement; God's better gift came to him without waiting, even life **for ever and ever.** The psalmist did not guess, when he wrote this formal little line, to what nobler uses of healing it would be put, once the Lord's finger had been laid on it. He did not know that he had given the world an inscription for the grave of all heroic youth who have died for others.

8-12. ***The Longed-for Victory.***—These verses, taken in their literal sense, stand in contrast to

enemies: thy right hand shall find out those that hate thee.

9 Thou shalt make them as a fiery oven in the time of thine anger: the LORD shall swallow them up in his wrath, and the fire shall devour them.

10 Their fruit shalt thou destroy from the earth, and their seed from among the children of men.

11 For they intended evil against thee: they imagined a mischievous device, *which* they are not able *to perform*.

12 Therefore shalt thou make them turn their back, *when* thou shalt make ready *thine arrows* upon thy strings against the face of them.

your right hand will find out those who
hate you.
9 You will make them as a blazing oven
when you appear.
The LORD will swallow them up in his
wrath;
and fire will consume them.
10 You will destroy their offspring from the
earth,
and their children from among the sons
of men.
11 If they plan evil against you,
if they devise mischief, they will not
succeed.
12 For you will put them to flight;
you will aim at their faces with your
bows.

---

or "seize" (cf. I Sam. 23:17; Isa. 10:14). **Your right hand will find out:** Since Hebrew poetry avoided the repetition of a word in close sequence, תמצא, **find,** in this instance is probably an error for a word like תמחץ, "shatter," or "smite through." **Those who hate you:** I.e., "your enemies." **You will make them as a blazing oven . . . fire will consume them:** Vs. 9 (Hebrew vs. 10) has suffered some confusion in the text. Read תציתמו כתנור לעת פניך באפך חבלעם ותאכלם כאש and translate, "Thou shalt burn them up like a furnace when thou dost appear; in thy wrath thou shalt destroy and consume them like fire." The king is addressed throughout the verse: **Destroy their offspring . . . their children from among the sons of men. Their fruit** and **their seed,** i.e., their issue, viewed either as their descendants or as the propagators of their breed, will suffer

---

the teaching of Christ. They represent acts of vengeance rather than a campaign of honest defense. Vs. 8 sets the tone: **Thy right hand shall find out** [or, "may your right hand find out"] **those that hate thee,** i.e., "thy sword arm." The sword is the sword of conquest, not of justice, as vs. 9 proves—**you will** ["may you"] **make them as a blazing oven.** Cf. Judg. 15:6, where the Philistines burned alive Samson's wife and father-in-law. There are references to the same practice in the prophets (cf. Jer. 48:45; 49:2; Amos 2:1). These are on a small scale the modern "death chambers" which have so shocked the conscience of the world. The only way to use verses such as these is frankly to spiritualize them, applying them to the war in the soul of man. So interpreted, they become vivid and emotionally stirring.

Your hand will find out all your enemies, i.e., the war in the soul is total war. Partial victories may be the preludes to defeat. A man is still in danger if he overcomes temptations to laziness, but remains censorious. **Your right hand will find out those who hate you.** Arresting truth can spring from a personifying of our tendencies to wrong. Our soul may be pictured as containing ambushes of lusts, who hate the real "us" made in God's image. An imaginative interpreter, under such a figure, could make truth vivid.

You will make them as a blazing oven. No truce in this war; these tendencies have to be eradicated "so as by fire." The concluding phrase in the KJV runs **in the time of thine anger.** Accurately, it should be rendered, **when you appear** (RSV), i.e., "your appearance will burn them up." But the appearance is the appearance of a man in anger. There is a point here. A man is on the right road when he directs his power of moral indignation against himself. Even the word **children** (vs. 10) may be used in this sense. Evil in the soul has a large family. Selfishness and pride are the parents of all the deadly sins. Once they are conquered, **their offspring** become weaker, but they have still to be conquered one by one (cf. the various terraces in Dante's *Purgatory,* which is in effect an enlargement of this conception). Still wider horizons appear. The Christian warrior cannot be content with victory in his own soul alone.

You will destroy their offspring from the earth,
and their children from among the sons of men.

13 Be thou exalted, LORD, in thine own strength: *so* will we sing and praise thy power.

To the chief Musician upon Aijeleth Shahar, A Psalm of David.

22 My God, my God, why hast thou forsaken me? *why art thou so* far from helping me, *and from* the words of my roaring?

13 Be exalted, O LORD, in thy strength!
We will sing and praise thy power.

To the choirmaster; according to The Hind of the Dawn. A Psalm of David.

22 My God, my God, why hast thou forsaken me?
Why art thou so far from helping me, from the words of my groaning?

---

extermination. Such wholesale slaughter was meant not only to satisfy a thirst for vengeance but also to guard against the ability of the enemy ever to retaliate (cf. Josh. 6:21; Deut. 13:15-16).

13. **Be exalted, O LORD:** Since the king's victory can come only from the Lord, the psalm ends with a prayer to him to speed the day when the people can **sing and praise thy power** as a God mighty in battle. Some commentators hold that this final verse was addressed to the king, and emend the text to read רומה בעז יהוה, "Rise up in the strength of the LORD" (cf. vs. 1).

XXII. PRAYER OF A LONELY SOUL (22:1-31)

Because of its unique and moving portrayal of the sufferings of one who was despised and forsaken of men and torn by affliction, this psalm is a supreme example of an individual lament. The similarity of the lot of this psalmist to his own must have so deeply impressed the mind of our Lord that in the agonies of his last hour he used the opening words of the psalm to express his sense of dereliction, "My God, my God, why hast thou forsaken me?" (Mark 15:34.) In the stories of the Crucifixion, as preserved in the Gospels, the correspondence between the sufferings of Jesus and those of the psalmist is noted in detail (cf. Mark 15:29=vs. 7; Matt. 27:43=vs. 8; Matt. 27:35,

---

In this fight, which is the fight of the church, the weapons are truth and love.

Vss. 11-12 are verses of hope. The evil in the soul may have its plans—**if they plan evil against you**—and it may **devise mischief;** but it will not succeed. The plans and the devisings are manifest enough; all men know the subtlety of temptation. Indeed, so subtle is it at times that it looks as if there were a brain, magnificent in its malignity, behind it all. Yet, God with us, we are stronger. A vital part of the Christian's work is to persuade men of that one truth. Vs. 12 gives a pictorial hint of the attitude necessary for victory. It is the attitude of instant readiness: **You will aim at their faces with your bows.** No parleying, no negotiations or appeasement; the moment they appear we are to move to the attack, seeking their weakest spot. Their bodies may be armored, but their faces are exposed. If the arrow finds its billet there, that enemy is down and out. Temptations have their weak spot. If they are seen in relation to good, they look so ugly. They have nasty faces behind the masks they assume; and the odd thing is that the masks fall off when the evil is put side by side with good. That is why it is so important to have Christ "at our elbow." For "A glance at the face of the Crucified One" makes lust and its **offspring** look dreadful; and when they are seen to be what they are, the battle is half won: the bow is raised, and the bowstring drawn back.

13. ***The Power of Love.***—This verse is a simple conclusion by the whole gathering. But it too can be used in a spiritual sense. When all is said and done, we are dependent upon God's initial action: always we need his reinforcements. Wherefore, while summoning all our powers, let us also pray, "Rise up, O Lord, in thy might." So strong is the impulse to evil that it is the very might of God that we need. But if that is desired, it will always be given; and the end of the story is singing: **We will sing and praise thy power. Thy power!** Exerted to give moral victory to one poor man. Herein is the power of Love. We may well **sing** and **praise.**

22:1-31. ***Through Defeat to Victory.***—There is no question that this is a difficult psalm for the scholar; so much so that he and the expositor may find themselves at loggerheads over

Mark 15:24, Luke 23:34, John 19:23-24=vs. 18). In the Johannine account, however, it has been overlooked that in accordance with Hebrew poetical parallelism, the **raiment** of vs. 18*b* is not different from the **garments** of 18*a*.

The psalm presents two major divisions (vss. 1-21, vss. 22-31), the first of which is the cry of the psalmist in his agony to God, the second a hymn of praise and thanksgiving to God for deliverance. The change from the one motif to the other is so abrupt, as many have felt, that the unity of the authorship of the psalm has been called in question. It can be said, of course, that the two parts were written by the psalmist at different times, and subsequently set together by him. But some commentators believe that the psalm was written at one time: e.g., Schmidt holds that the psalmist relates the bitterness of his affliction as a prelude to his hymn of thanksgiving; Gunkel, on the other hand, thinks that the hymn is really anticipatory, being inspired by the psalmist's sudden conviction that his prayer is to be answered. Since, however, it can be said that the hymn has no special relevance to the lament, and might conceivably have been as proper to other sorts of afflicted men as to the psalmist, it is possible to regard the hymn as a composition of independent origin which was added to the lament in order that the whole psalm might serve as a liturgical form for the use of any who came to the temple to give thanks for deliverance from affliction.

The first part consists of a series of strophes of about equal length. Those in vss. 1-11 have for their subject alternately **thou** and **I**; in vss. 12-18, **they** and **I**. Vss. 19-21, repeating the petition of vs. 11, mark the conclusion. Such attention to form shows that the psalm is no more than the speeches of Job an unpremeditated or extemporaneous outburst. The psalmist has reflected on the various aspects of his experience. In vss. 1-21 the meter is 3+3; in vss. 22-31, though somewhat confused by the faultiness of the text, it is for the most part 4+4, with some instances of 3+3.

1. The Cry of a Troubled Individual (22:1-21)

a) Appeal to the God of the Fathers (22:1-5)

22:1-5. The anguish of the psalmist is expressed in the cry **My God, my God** with which the psalm opens. His physical sufferings are made harder to bear by reason of

---

it. The latter will find in vss. 1-21 a great deal that seems christological, and will therefore be inclined to turn a deaf ear to suggestions that dissociate it from the actual experiences of Christ. In the early days of the church the theory was held that the psalm was inspired by our Lord himself, and was not so much prophecy as history. Although we may not today be able to accept this, we may yet be unwilling to adopt the view that the psalm deals with a suffering servant objectively, or with the personified nation in its pain. It seems rather to be the genuine outpouring of some sorely tried man who made so alive his own experience of despair that it has become a universal cry of suffering everywhere, and could be used even by our Lord to express his darkest moment.

Some find it difficult to explain vss. 22-31 as other than a separate psalm or a "liturgical addition"; though why verses breathing, or so it would seem, the contented calm of national prosperity should be an addition, liturgical or not, to so sharp a cry of individual pain, is hard to understand. Why should anyone join together utterances so disparate? Unless indeed the closing verses are understood as suggesting that a man should lose sight of his own unhappiness in the vision of the well-being of the larger whole. A man dying of cancer might thus be thankful if he saw prosperity and brotherhood returning to the world, and knew that in war-ravaged lands children were shedding "far fewer tears, far softer tears." [8] In that he might even find hope for himself. Like the Lord who healed the nations, he would then be able to follow his bitterest cry with "Father, into thy hands."

It is from the point of view that the psalm speaks of one man's pain—an actual though unknown man of long ago—that we shall interpret it, with of course freedom to apply it to the sufferings of Christ. The fact that its words were on his lips at his supreme moment of agony justifies us.

1-21. *The Afflicted Soul.*—My God, my God, why hast thou forsaken me? Here is the final word of despair. Note that it is the utterance of a religious man: he speaks of **my God** (cf. vs. 10). But despite his honest religion, he has

[8] William Johnson Cary, "A Song."

2 O my God, I cry in the daytime, but
thou hearest not; and in the night season,
and am not silent.
3 But thou *art* holy, *O thou* that inhabitest the praises of Israel.
4 Our fathers trusted in thee: they
trusted, and thou didst deliver them.
5 They cried unto thee, and were delivered: they trusted in thee, and were not
confounded.

2 O my God, I cry by day, but thou dost not answer;
and by night, but find no rest.

3 Yet thou art holy,
enthroned on the praises of Israel.
4 In thee our fathers trusted;
they trusted, and thou didst deliver them.
5 To thee they cried, and were saved;
in thee they trusted, and were not disappointed.

---

the distress of his soul, which springs from the mystery of God's ways in relation to him. The problems which meet his faith are twofold. **Why art thou so far . . . from the words of my groaning?** For מישׁועתי, "from my help," read משועתי, "from my cry for help." "My wail of anguish" is, lit., **my roaring.** Although the psalmist cries **by day . . . and by night,** he receives no answer from God, no sign that he can rest from his clamorous prayers. But why should this be? **Thou art . . . enthroned on the praises of Israel:** The LXX reading is preferable, "Thou sittest enthroned in the temple, [the theme of] Israel's praise." But whichever reading one adopts, the meaning is much the same. The Lord, because of his mighty deeds on behalf of his people, is unceasingly extolled in their praises so that his throne seems to be upborne by them. **Our fathers trusted . . . and were saved.** But where now is this God of help?

---

come to a moment when for him there is no God at all—a moment, moreover, when if God had any love in his heart, one would expect him to be near. Yet there is hope for the sufferer's faith; for he does not fling the thought of God away with blasphemies, but asks, **Why?** There is always hope for a man who asks God, **Why?**

The abruptness of this question at the beginning of the psalm is arresting, as it was meant to be. The sufferer takes us at once into the heart of his trouble. For loneliness of heart in suffering is the ultimate in heaviness. Sorrow and pain tend to create loneliness; they are imprisoning things. We feel "shut in" with grief; and if our heaviness is associated with sin, the prison bars are thicker still. We find ourselves in our oubliette of the soul, of which God only has the key; and if he will not use his key and come near us, all hope is gone. Nature is of no use to us; anything blinder and more heedless we cannot conceive.

> How can ye chant, ye little birds,
> And I sae weary fu' o' care? [1]

Unless God will speak to us through nature, the very cheerfulness of nature is an added pang. If, then, his lips are sealed, nor is there any whisper from him anywhere, we taste the very dregs of bitterness.

[1] Robert Burns, "The Banks of Doon."

The fact that these were the words from the Psalter which our Lord used on the cross is full of significance doctrinally. He must have known many of the psalms by heart; their sunnier songs must often have been on his lips. Why did he not quote, "Yea, though I walk through the valley of the shadow of death, . . . thou art with me," instead of this terrible cry? Is the answer indeed that at this moment God was not with him? Are we actually faced with the appalling spectacle of Jesus without a God? "It was damnation," the old preacher cried, "and he took it lovingly." Whatever happened to him afterward, at this moment too he descended into hell; for what is hell but the state of a spirit with whom God will not have anything to do? In that one cry the Lord took all the swords of the world's pain, and gathering them into one, pressed them into his own heart. Those who neglect the doctrine of the Atonement must face gravely this darkness of the night that the Lord went through.

The second clause should be translated, with RSV, **Why art thou so far from helping me, from the words of my groaning?** It connects with vs. 2:

> **O my God, I cry by day, but thou dost not answer;**
> **and by night, but find no rest.**

The poet makes the claim of extreme need. Anyone, surely, who heard so sharp a cry would

6 But I *am* a worm, and no man; a reproach of men, and despised of the people.
7 All they that see me laugh me to scorn: they shoot out the lip, they shake the head, *saying,*
8 He trusted on the LORD *that* he would deliver him: let him deliver him, seeing he delighted in him.
9 But thou *art* he that took me out of the womb: thou didst make me hope *when I was* upon my mother's breasts.
10 I was cast upon thee from the womb: thou *art* my God from my mother's belly.

6 But I am a worm, and no man;
scorned by men, and despised by the people.
7 All who see me mock at me,
they make mouths at me, they wag their heads;
8 "He committed his cause to the LORD; let him deliver him,
let him rescue him, for he delights in him!"

9 Yet thou art he who took me from the womb;
thou didst keep me safe upon my mother's breasts.
10 Upon thee was I cast from my birth,
and since my mother bore me thou hast been my God.

b) THE MOCKINGS OF MEN (22:6-11)

6-11. A fresh element in the sufferings of the psalmist is the inexplicable indifference of God to his plight in view of God's goodness to him in the morning of his life. Did God hide a sinister purpose behind a smiling providence (cf. Job 10:10-13)? **I am a worm, and no man:** Such an object of contempt that all men despise and deride him (cf. Job 30:9-11). Ironically they say that the Lord will surely deliver his servant. **He committed his cause to the LORD; let him deliver him, . . . for he delights in him:** Their words are the more painful because there seems to be truth in their implication of an estrangement between the psalmist and his God. **Yet thou art he who took me**

turn aside at least to inquire. Can it be that God is deaf? That the divine Helper is deaf with heedlessness is the dreariest of thoughts, for it contains a denial of the existence of the God whom we thought we knew. The saint may cry, "How long?" and still believe; but his faith is departing if he wonders whether God either cannot or will not hear. Such a God ceases to be the God of pity, for the ears of pity are always acute. The poet was in the extremity of suffering. He was both ill and surrounded by enemies; any kindliness would be moved to active compassion. Wherefore—could it be?—there is no kindliness anywhere, least of all in God. "Do not speak to me of God," said a stricken father who had lost his son in war, "God's a murderer."

But at this point the author pulls himself up sharply. He reminds himself of the foundation of his faith and its vindication in history.

> **Yet thou art holy,**
> **enthroned on the praises of Israel.**

Note the emphasis on the word **yet,** having something of the force of "nevertheless." Verses in which these words occur should be sought out. Note also the sequence of remembrance in the following verses. (*a*) **Thou art holy,** on whom no stain of brutal, heedless injustice may fall; moreover, (*b*) thou hast always been the theme of Israel's praise; and for the good reason that (*c*) **in thee our fathers trusted . . . and thou didst deliver them.** Note further how the psalmist repeats his thought in vs. 5, as if he would hammer it into his mind. The history of the church, and of our own part of it, is always a corrective of our temptations to faithlessness. Our fathers knew sufferings in the great periods, but they stood firm; and through them God brought advance to the world. We in a similar time must do no less. A variant of the close of the *Te Deum* must remain our song: "In thee, O Lord, have we trusted; we shall never be confounded." It is vs. 5 made personal. In men of that caliber the hope of the world is found.

In vss. 6-21 the psalmist elaborates his appeal with vivid, pictorial descriptions of his sufferings, interspersed with cries for aid. Given that we hold on to our faith in God, there is no reason why we should not relate our piteous case to him. Indeed, the more we turn to God as Father, the more intimate and childlike will be our speech with him. It is a child's privilege

11 Be not far from me; for trouble *is*
near; for *there is* none to help.
12 Many bulls have compassed me:
strong *bulls* of Bashan have beset me round.
13 They gaped upon me *with* their
mouths, *as* a ravening and a roaring lion.
14 I am poured out like water, and all
my bones are out of joint: my heart is like
wax; it is melted in the midst of my bowels.
15 My strength is dried up like a potsherd; and my tongue cleaveth to my jaws;
and thou hast brought me into the dust of
death.

11 Be not far from me,
for trouble is near
and there is none to help.

12 Many bulls encompass me,
strong bulls of Bashan surround me;
13 they open wide their mouths at me,
like a ravening and roaring lion.

14 I am poured out like water,
and all my bones are out of joint;
my heart is like wax,
it is melted within my breast;
15 my strength is dried up like a potsherd,
and my tongue cleaves to my jaws;
thou dost lay me in the dust of death.

---

from the womb: From his earliest years the psalmist was surrounded by evidences of the divine favor. Was he so tenderly preserved only to be abandoned now? **Be not far from me; . . . there is none to help.**

c) The Psalmist's Enemies (22:12-21)

12-15. The pathos of the psalmist's lot is further brought to view by the contrast between the might of his foes and the weakness of himself. Is not this an additional reason for God's intervention? Like others who voice laments, this psalmist has many foes. In their brutishness and ferocity he compares them now to the **strong bulls** of the rich grazing lands of the region east of the Lake of Galilee, and now to **a ravening and roaring lion.** Some would prefer to render vs. 13, "a lion, ravening and roaring, opens its mouth against me," reading פצה עלי פיהו. Before such foes the psalmist's body, wasted by sickness and fever, is a picture of utter helplessness. **I am poured out like**

---

to tell his father when things go hard with him; by the very admission of our trials and temptations in God's presence there is release. "Thou knowest, Lord, that I do not find it easy; and it is not altogether my fault." Then he shows us his hands and their marks, and we find it simpler to bear our "lesser Calvaries."

Vs. 6 indicates that part of the poet's misery is due to the contempt in which he is regarded by his community. He is **scorned by men, and despised by the people.** The opening clause puts forthrightly his sense of being a pariah; **I am a worm, and no man.** Taken by itself, and whispered in the holy precinct of God, it might conceivably serve as the confession of one who has discovered by some hard way the perils of complacency or pride. Vss. 7-8 develop the same idea. He is so poor a specimen that he is an object of derision; even God could scarcely be bothered with him. Both verses are given a deepened significance by the fact that while one seemed to set the stage on Calvary, the other was quoted by those who jeered at Jesus on his cross.

In vss. 9-10 the poet retires again into the citadel of his faith. Note the repetition: **Yet thou** (vs. 3), **Yet thou** (vs. 9), **But thou** (vs. 19). From childhood he has been put into God's protection and has been kept there. God was his shelter before he could know anything about God. One may reasonably start from these verses to explain the intimate and most comforting doctrine contained at the heart of the sacrament of baptism; or one may enlarge upon our debt to the past, if we are the children of many prayers. **Since my mother bore me thou hast been my God.** Therefore in vs. 11 the psalmist feels, and justly, that he has a right to make appeal for help. One of the children of many prayers cannot be, and must not be, lost. We can help ourselves to be open to God's help by remembering the pleadings of hearts that loved us when the first stirrings of our life were known. World-hardened men might be softened if they compelled themselves to remember their mothers' prayers of long ago.

Vss. 12-17 take up again the "complaint." The images vary from bitter descriptions of the qualities of the poet's enemies to almost hyperbolic metaphors of his physical and spiritual

16 For dogs have compassed me: the assembly of the wicked have inclosed me: they
pierced my hands and my feet.
17 I may tell all my bones: they look *and*
stare upon me.
18 They part my garments among them,
and cast lots upon my vesture.
19 But be not thou far from me, O
LORD: O my strength, haste thee to help me.

16 Yea, dogs are round about me;
a company of evildoers encircle me;
they have pierced[m] my hands and feet —
17 I can count all my bones —
they stare and gloat over me;
18 they divide my garments among them,
and for my raiment they cast lots.

19 But thou, O LORD, be not far off!
O thou my help, hasten to my aid!

[m] Gk Syr Jerome: Heb *like a lion*

---

water, . . . my tongue cleaves to my jaws. In vs. 15 read "palate" for **strength,** i.e., חכי for כחי. Already **the dust of death** is on his lips.

16-18. The ruthlessness of the enemies is also compared to that of hunters closing in on a wild beast or dragging it off for the kill. **They stare and gloat over** [him], as his physical condition indicates the nearness of his end. They even anticipate his death, and **divide** [his] **garments among them,** like executioners laying hold on their perquisites.

19-21. Once again the psalmist appeals to God for help, repeating the cry of vs. 11, **be not thou far from me.** The time for God to act is short—**hasten to my aid. My life,**

---

sickness. His foes are like **bulls** (vs. 12), like **lions,** with their mouths open to tear (vs. 13), and **dogs . . . ; a company of evildoers** (vs. 16). This last image is not an anticlimax but a climax. An evildoer is worse than a bull of Bashan or a ravening lion or even a mongrel dog, slinking around to snap at offal; and a company of evildoers is worse than an individual one, for they strengthen each other with might in evil.

As for his physical sufferings, the psalmist runs the gamut of pictorial ills. He is **poured out like water,** his **bones are out of joint,** his **heart is like wax** (vs. 14); his **strength** [palate] **is dried up like a potsherd** and his **tongue cleaves to** [his] **jaws** (vs. 15); he is in such a state of emaciation that he **can count all** [his] **bones.** All this might be the description of a desperately afraid and exhausted fugitive, or of the physical and mental effects of a severe illness; either way we may find here images of spiritual sickness. **The dust of death** (vs. 15) is one of the most striking: there lies the man who has sold his birthright for a mess of pottage.

> **They divide my garments among them,**
> **and for my raiment they cast lots** (vs. 18).

Cf. the use of this in John 19:24. As with the third clause of vs. 16 (**they have pierced my hands and feet**), it would be natural here to find some connection with the crucifixion of Jesus. But a prophetic interpretation has no sound base. The original of vs. 16*c* is uncertain; the strict translation would be **like a lion my hands and feet,** which does not make sense. Lions do not especially attack hands or feet. Therefore attempts have been made to change the punctuation or to emend the original. An intelligible meaning can be found if the word for **like a lion** is changed slightly to a word signifying "to bind tightly," the verse thus meaning **a company of evildoers encircle me;** [they have bound tightly] **my hands and feet,** i.e., he is captured. An evangelical use of this translation is obvious. If sin captures us, our freedom to go where we will (our **feet**) is circumscribed, and so is our power of action (our **hands**). But all this is in the region of conjecture. "It is impossible to give any satisfactory explanation," says Peake.[2] In vs. 18 the words **garments** and **vesture** mean the same thing: the distinction in John 19:24 is not found here. All the verse signifies is that the enemies treat the sufferer as if he were already dead. Again a parallel can be drawn. Evil habits and desires hunt a man; they weaken and torture him; they capture him and bind him fast. Once they have him in their grip, he is as good as dead. The eyes of evil **stare and gloat** at him (vs. 17). Another soul destroyed. Preachers of an older school, with somber imaginations, would have found a parable of the descent to Avernus in all this; and they would have been true enough to life.

There is only one resource left to a man in such a case—the resource of prayer. **Be not far off, . . . hasten, . . . deliver, . . . save me** (vss. 19-21). There is an ascending scale of de-

[2] *Commentary on the Bible,* p. 377.

20 Deliver my soul from the sword; my darling from the power of the dog.
21 Save me from the lion's mouth: for thou hast heard me from the horns of the unicorns.
22 I will declare thy name unto my brethren: in the midst of the congregation will I praise thee.
23 Ye that fear the LORD, praise him; all ye the seed of Jacob, glorify him; and fear him, all ye the seed of Israel.
24 For he hath not despised nor abhorred the affliction of the afflicted; neither hath he hid his face from him; but when he cried unto him, he heard.

20 Deliver my soul from the sword,
my life[n] from the power of the dog!
21 Save me from the mouth of the lion,
my afflicted soul[o] from the horns of the wild oxen!

22 I will tell of thy name to my brethren;
in the midst of the congregation I will praise thee:
23 You who fear the LORD, praise him!
all you sons of Jacob, glorify him,
and stand in awe of him, all you sons of Israel!
24 For he has not despised or abhorred
the affliction of the afflicted;
and he has not hid his face from him,
but has heard, when he cried to him.

[n] Heb *my only one*
[o] Gk Syr: Heb *thou hast answered me*

---

lit., **my only one,** synonymous here with **my soul** (cf. 35:17), means "my very self." **The horns of the wild oxen:** The Syrian wild ox, now extinct, was noted for its fierceness and strength (Kurt Galling, *Biblisches Reallexikon* [Tübingen: J. C. B. Mohr, 1937; "Handbuch zum Alten Testament"], p. 286).

2. Thanksgiving to God (22:22-31)

The scene suddenly changes. The man who was uttering a cry of despair is now beginning a hymn of thanksgiving as a prelude to his votive offerings for his deliverance.

a) Praise in the Congregation (22:22-26)

22-24. I will tell of thy name to my brethren: His thanks and praise will be published in the temple **in the midst of the congregation.** In vss. 23-24 we are given the words of the hymn.

---

sire in these verbs, at least to Christian ears, ending with the great word **save.** One should meditate upon them in the light of Christ. Vs. 20*b* reads strangely. **Deliver . . . my darling from the power of the dog. Darling** should be translated "soul" or **life,** for which the original word is used as a tender synonym. Yet the KJV rendering has had its meaning for loving hearts perturbed about their own private "darlings." After all, those whom we chiefly love make up our life; if our life is to be saved, they must be saved too, a psycho-theological fact requiring consideration. **The power of the dog** is a lively image in the spiritual realm, suggesting the nasty, slinking, offal-loving sins that with such lionlike strength destroy their victims. Many temptations that look like yellow dogs become lions unless we are careful. In vs. 21 **unicorns** are antelopes or buffaloes. **Wild oxen** is a satisfactory rendering. If we spiritualize the whole passage, these may represent temptations to unbridled anger.

22-31. ***Deliverance.***—At this point the whole tone of the psalm changes, and many have felt it all but impossible to find a genuine psychological connection. Yet there must be one; for even if there were originally two psalms (see Exeg.), why did somebody put them together? If this second section is a liturgical addition, where is the link for worship? Apparently it speaks of the nation and of God's helpful guidance to Israel as a whole. What has that to do with the wild sufferings of one poor man, whose story ends with helpless capture? There would be unity if we dared imagine an omitted section describing the captive's rescue and rehabilitation (see vs. 21*b* RSV mg.). Vss. 22-31 would then become his final attitude as he revises his life's story in tranquillity. Older interpreters would supply this omission unhesitatingly, assuming the answer in Christ to the prayer in vss. 19-21; and who is to say that in so doing they did not catch the permanent "word of God" in the psalm?

25 My praise *shall be* of thee in the great congregation: I will pay my vows before them that fear him.

26 The meek shall eat and be satisfied: they shall praise the LORD that seek him: your heart shall live for ever.

27 All the ends of the world shall remember and turn unto the LORD: and all the kindreds of the nations shall worship before thee.

28 For the kingdom *is* the LORD's: and he *is* the governor among the nations.

29 All *they that be* fat upon earth shall eat and worship: all they that go down to the dust shall bow before him: and none can keep alive his own soul.

25 From thee comes my praise in the great congregation;
my vows I will pay before those who fear him.
26 The afflicted[p] shall eat and be satisfied;
those who seek him shall praise the LORD!
May your hearts live for ever!

27 All the ends of the earth shall remember and turn to the LORD;
and all the families of the nations shall worship before him.[q]
28 For dominion belongs to the LORD,
and he rules over the nations.

29 Yea, to him[r] shall all the proud of the earth bow down;
before him shall bow all who go down to the dust,
and he who cannot keep himself alive.

[p] Or *poor*
[q] Gk Syr Jerome: Heb *thee*
[r] Cn: Heb *they have eaten and*

25-26. From thee comes my praise: Better, "Thy faithfulness is my praise," i.e., for מאתך read אמתך. On the occasion of sacrificial offerings of thanksgiving and payment of vows, portions of the sacrifice were eaten by the one who provided the offerings and by those whom he invited to be his guests. The psalmist's guests are those in the congregation who like himself were afflicted and sought the Lord. **The afflicted shall eat** to the full. As their strength, so may their **hearts live for ever!** By such a gracious formula the invitation to the feast is extended to them.

b) THE WHOLE EARTH RECOGNIZES THE LORD (22:27-31)

27-28. The testimony of the psalmist, however, is not for Israel alone. **All the ends of the earth . . . and all the families of the nations** are summoned to take note that what the Lord has done for the psalmist he can do also for them, since his **dominion** is as wide as the world.

29-31. The hymn moves in an exultant crescendo and comes to a resounding climax in this final stanza. Not only the living, near and far, but the dead, the generations that

In this connection a point arises which is akin to modern thinking. A sufferer finds balm for his hurt in the thought that though he is submerged, his nation and his cause will survive. "Who dies if England live?"[3] In the case of the psalmist he foresees himself escaped from his immediate troubles and becoming a part of the congregation that praises God for the well-being of the whole (vs. 22); and to that extent his optimism is well based. But we observe that it is dependent on his own preservation, temporarily at least. **I will tell of thy name to my brethren.** If, however, we make communal immortality a substitute for personal immortality (cf. George Meredith's poems and many modern essayists), we are offering cold comfort. For the race also is doomed. All that such teachers offer humanity is obliteration, with a stay of execution, made all the more drearily wicked if humanity reaches in the meantime unguessed heights of achievement. Bertrand Russell honestly faces the fact that there is no escape from pessimism, unless perchance immortality should prove true.[4] To give a meaning to life we need to hold that personality is the stuff of reality, and therefore remains.

[3] Rudyard Kipling, "For All We Have and Are."

[4] In a broadcast from London.

30 A seed shall serve him; it shall be accounted to the Lord for a generation.
31 They shall come, and shall declare his righteousness unto a people that shall be born, that he hath done *this*.

A Psalm of David.

23 The LORD *is* my shepherd; I shall not want.

30 Posterity shall serve him;
men shall tell of the LORD to the coming generation,
31 and proclaim his deliverance to a people yet unborn,
that he has wrought it.

A Psalm of David.

23 The LORD is my shepherd, I shall not want;

---

have passed and gone to Sheol, and the generations yet unborn shall hear and swell the chorus of praise to the Lord. The text of these verses has suffered some corruption. In vs. 29*a* read ישני for דשני, and translate "those who sleep in the earth." Vs. 29*c* and vs. 30*a* should be read as one line, and the text emended to read, נפש לא חיה זרעו יכבדון, i.e., "the souls that no longer live shall glorify his might." **He has wrought it:** The psalmist grounds this universalism on his own experience. Only the God who is above all gods could have worked the miracle of the psalmist's deliverance.

XXIII. THE GOODNESS OF THE LORD (23:1-6)

In the course of the centuries this psalm has won for itself a supreme place in the religious literature of the world. All who read it, whatever their age, race, or circumstances, find in the quiet beauty of its thoughts a range and depth of spiritual insight that both satisfies and possesses their souls. It belongs to that class of psalms that breathe confidence and trust in the Lord. Such psalms resemble the concluding section or strophe of a lament, which ordinarily consists of a strong affirmation of faith in the loving care of the Lord. So here the psalmist has no preface of complaints about the pains of sickness or the treachery of enemies, but begins, as he ends, only with words of grateful acknowledgment of the never-failing goodness of the Lord.

Once again we must move on from the psalm to Christ.

Vss. 27-30 express in the form of a hymn the hope for a universal kingdom under the rule of God. They may well call to mind our own aspirations: **All the families of the nations shall worship before him** (vs. 27). **Yea, to him shall all the proud of the earth bow down** (vs. 28). **Posterity shall serve him** (vs. 30) would be a good slogan for the religious education departments of churches. A helpful suggestion is to link vs. 22 with vs. 30. **I will tell of thy name;** so will there be more likelihood that **posterity shall serve him:** "I" being especially a father or a mother. **Posterity** should be particularized. The thought of far-off generations has no power to hit home on the mind; for us **posterity** means our own children, or all children whom we can help. That does hit home on the mind, and helps us to change the mood of the verb **shall serve** from mere future to a future of purpose. **Posterity,** our immediate posterity, "shall serve him, God being our helper."

Was something of this same confidence in the mind of Jesus, even as he cried out in that moment of dereliction? What was going on around him must inevitably have reminded him, for instance, of vss. 7-10. What vision broke on his closing eyes? (Cf. vss. 27-31.)

23:1-6. ***Shepherd and Host.***—What is there about this psalm that makes it so beloved? For it is but a simple little lyric, artless and sunny, written by some godly Hebrew Robert Burns in a restful moment, when he sang because he must. Yet it is hardly too much to say that along with the Lord's Prayer it is the best-known passage in the Bible; and it has proved a mine for the expositor.

It is of some value to attempt an explanation of the unique affection with which people of all sorts and conditions regard it. Its brief simplicity is one reason. Here is no elaborate ode, smelling of midnight oil. Even for those who find a change of imagery from the shepherd to the host in vs. 5, an underlying unity is retained, with a meaning which he who runs may read. But the main point about it is its realism. This is no sundial recording only sunny hours; it faces faithfully the dark defile and the lurking foes. At the same time it honestly and thank-

2 He maketh me to lie down in green pastures: he leadeth me beside the still waters.	2 he makes me lie down in green pastures. He leads me beside still waters;[s] [s] Heb *the waters of rest*

It is clear from the reference to **the house of the Lord** (vs. 6) that the psalm is not Davidic. The individualism of the psalm points to a date in the postexilic period when the relations of the Lord to the individual claimed special attention. Such an opinion is further confirmed by the fact that the class to which this psalm belongs appears to be a late development in the history of Hebrew psalmody.

The meter is mostly 3+2. The symmetry of the brief poem is beautifully sustained.

1. The Lord as a Shepherd (23:1-4)

23:1-3. In order to describe vividly his sense of the fullness of God's care for him, the psalmist uses first the metaphor of the **shepherd.** The loyalty and devotion of the good shepherd to his sheep was a matter of common knowledge in the ancient Near East. His first interest was to supply the sheep with all it needed for its well-being. Since **the Lord is my shepherd, I shall not want.** He guides the sheep to places of lush

fully remembers life's delights. In short, it sees life steadily and sees it whole, and leaves no doubt as to the master force governing all. In the heart of things it discerns the good shepherd. Therefore, despite the inevitableness of the valley of the shadow, it is a life story with a happy ending. Moreover, it gives all this with a childlike clarity that reminds us of the parables of our Lord. It is a stream of clear waters, but they are deep. The mind of the common man is a discerning critic of religious literature; and it says much for this psalm that the common man has rejoicingly seen in it a picture of life as he knows it, and has found in it the expression of his unconquerable persuasion and hope.

Let us glance first at the structure of the psalm, although perhaps the word "structure" is too stilted to apply to so unstudied a little poem. "Arrangement" might be better. Vss. 1-4 speak of the good shepherd; vs. 5 presents the good host; vs. 6 blends the two. The first section might be entitled "The Journey," and vss. 5-6 "Journey's End." The two images, however, are interwoven throughout the psalm. The good shepherd is a good host in vs. 2, when he provides still waters and green pastures for the midday rest; and the good host is the good shepherd in vs. 6, when his goodness and mercy are a rear guard still. It is all very true to life: the Good Shepherd sees to his shepherding from the beginning to the end of our pilgrimage that at the eventide we may come to our dwelling, which is also his, where he can lay aside his shepherd's garments and assume the vestments of the kindly host. Indeed, all through life God appears sometimes in one aspect and sometimes in another, displaying himself now as our defender and leader, and now as our Father, with whom we dwell. As we yield to his shepherding, more and more we find him our home.

1-4. *Day's Journey.*—Vs. 1 gives us the general thesis: **The Lord is my shepherd;** [therefore] **I shall not want.** Who is this Lord? Let the answer be supplied by Christ's claim to be the good shepherd (John 10:14). Contrast the conception of the Lord which the writer possessed with that which Christ has given and note how enriched the psalm becomes. Stress now the possessive pronoun and explain what it involves of "listening" and "following" on our part, as laid down in John 10:3-5. The practice of Eastern shepherds should be described. Travelers have told us how various flocks may be sheltering in a common fold, and when a particular shepherd comes to the gate and calls, a shivering movement can be seen here and there among the sheep; in little groups of two or three they turn toward the gate and edge their way through the other herds. No sheep of another flock will move; but these know the voice and straight make answer. Later one may see them journeying, with the shepherd in the van; they follow in his train. First they lift their heads in the fold and listen. Is it his voice or not? Then they hear; they have verified his tones. Then they move obediently behind him, and "follow whithersoever he goeth." Only so can one say, **The Lord is my shepherd;** only so can one be confident, **I shall not want.** Now observe more closely the word **shepherd,** i.e., the guardian of the flock. It is true that he watches over each separate sheep. Shepherds declare that they can recognize their sheep individually, as we

pasturage, where its need for food is more than supplied, and it can rest. **He leads me:** In the later literature there are several passages in which the Lord is spoken of as the shepherd of Israel (cf. 79:13; 80:1; 95:7), but the thought is most tenderly elaborated in Isa. 49:10, "They shall not hunger; . . . he . . . shall lead them, even by the springs of

---

recognize each other's faces, and thus "know" their sheep. Certainly the Good Shepherd knows his. Nevertheless he is guarding his flock as a whole, and each sheep is safer if it stays with its comrades and if together they move homeward. There is a word for the church in this, and not least, a word of warning. If the church as a whole stampedes, each member is in sore danger: a self-willed church, which does not keep Christ at its head, is like a panicked flock. An unbalanced church, overemphasizing one aspect of truth, or a sentimental church, turning a blind eye to the tragic facts of evil, puts every separate member in peril. The only thing for the church to do is to declare the gospel without qualifying adjectives, and then go true to the leadership of the shepherd. Conversely, each sheep is safer with the Christ-led flock; a man who thinks he can manage his pilgrimage outside the community of Christ neglects the strength that comes from membership in a company and forgets that it is the flock that Christ leads.

Or it may be that we shall wish to fasten on the single clause, **I shall not want.** The writer was clearly referring to his material needs—food, drink, rest, shelter, etc. Is it possible for us to hold that a Christ-led man is materially secure, or more secure than a man who turns from Christian principles? Undoubtedly in normal circumstances there is something to be said for the psalmist; honesty *is* the best policy. A prominent preacher once declared that in a long ministry he had never "seen the righteous forsaken, nor his seed begging bread" (37:25). That was said in the solid Victorian days before war challenged it; but even then it was a bold statement, hardly to be accepted. Today we must either wave away such words as expressive simply of a mood, or we must examine the area in which the Christian man will not suffer want. Strength to continue, hope that saves, and peace in the hidden heart—these will not fail, as the army of the patient have proved. Everything depends upon what we mean by "I": if we mean the enduring self, which possesses a body, the words stand. Here is a chance to determine the Christian conception of the relation of the "self" to the body which is owned. Joseph Parker once made dramatic use of this distinction. He saw an advertisement of a pamphlet "Has a Man a Soul?" and in his pulpit proceeded to answer the question for himself. "I have no soul," he cried, repeating his cry to his startled congregation; but followed it, using all the emphasis of his magnificent voice, with the declaration, "I *am* a soul and *have* a body." Which after all is the truth of the matter, and enables a man who trusts in the Good Shepherd to say, **I shall not want.**

In vss. 2-3 is portrayed a day in the life of the God-led—or the picture of a whole life story. We begin with the morning—the sheep implicitly awakened by their shepherd's call, setting out for their pasture lands. The early journey is assured; steadily if slowly the flock completes the first stage to its appointed place, and then is given its reasonable rest and its due refreshing **beside the still waters,** whereby energies are restored for the journey that awaits. Life surely is like that. Nobody denies that we have to walk and not faint; but we must always remember the resting times. A great deal of the life of the ordinary man in ordinary circumstances is filled with gentle delights; and we shall get a wrong idea of Providence if we do not take them, enjoy them, and call them to mind. Is it fanciful to give each phrase a particular meaning, weighing each word? **He maketh me to lie down.** Is that what weariness is for, and even illness? In our modern life we seem to lose the power to relax; so God, most merciful, compels us. **He maketh me to lie down in green pastures.** Green is the most restful of all colors, and at the same time the most hopeful, implying showers as well as sunshine. Not only so, but he gives us our rest beside **still waters,** or as in another version, **waters of rest.** The line will do us no harm if it only reminds us of our need to seek quiet in this noise-rocked world. But rest is not an end in itself. **He restoreth my soul.** Rest is a means to an end. The restored soul is expected to renew the pilgrimage. Life is to be a movement, not a stagnation. "Excelsior" is always to be the device on our banners; green pastures and still waters afford no permanent dwelling. If we are content with them and nothing else, God may have to drive us forth. The new energy we have gained has to be used, always under his continued leading, along "straight paths"—the highways, possibly the dusty highways, of duty.

The implicit imagery of the second clause of the verse should be carefully marked and developed. The **paths of righteousness** strictly are "straight" or "direct" paths. The journey is

3 He restoreth my soul: he leadeth me in the paths of righteousness for his name's sake.

3 he restores my soul.[t]
He leads me in paths of righteousness[u]
for his name's sake.

[t] Or *life*
[u] Or *right paths*

---

water shall he guide them." The psalmist turns this imagery to the illustration of God's thought for him and, by inference, for every child of God (cf. Luke 15:3-7). **Beside the still waters:** Or "waters by resting places," a poetic inversion of "resting places by water," where in quietness and peace the sheep slakes its thirst and its strength is refreshed and revived. These blessings of food, water, and rest are the lot of the sheep because it is led in right paths. The good shepherd guides the sheep on paths that lead right to the sources of life, peace, and happiness, and keeps it from straying into wrong

---

not haphazard. The paths lead somewhere: straight paths lead straight somewhere. The imagery requires that that somewhere should be the fold, which for the sheep is home. They have been awakened in the morning; they have been led to the mountainsides of pasturage, where necessarily they have been given rest for tired hoofs and weary limbs; and now it is eventide, and they must take the track again to reach the fold before nightfall. The essence of the clause is given if we translate, "He leadeth me by paths that run straight home for his name's sake." Where would you be going at night, except home? Observe: (*a*) The fact of the divine control, **he leadeth me.** "It is not in man that walketh to direct his steps." (*b*) The good result of the divine control, **he leadeth me** by paths that take me home. (*c*) The inevitability of such good results: they needs must be—**for his name's sake.** The honor and repute of the leader are at stake. If he leads to homeless night those who trust him, let him be "ashamed to be called their God" (cf. Heb. 11:16). This is not so much brief comment as it is an outline for a volume of theology. Remember that Christ's last word was an acknowledgment of a surrender to the divine control, "Father, into thy hands." Remember how straight, in more senses than one, was the path by which he was led to darkness, silence, and a tomb. Remember that the name "Father" implied trust in the divine intent. And remember the outcome at the right hand of the majesty on high. Or apply the verse to the common experience of men. Let the mind dwell on the fact that so much of the vital in life is not of our ordering. We do not settle the period of our birth, the culture group in which we find ourselves, the opportunities of service which, as we say, "come our way." The shapes of our heads, and still more their contents, are not determined by us; even our appearance is largely imposed on us, frequently to our dismay. Much of our future is directed by happenings which we term "accidental." An "accidental" collision with a stranger in the street may be the occasion of the formation of a friendship which alters your life. You turn a corner when you might as reasonably have gone the other way, and you find a wife. Both these instances, complete in their accidental quality, are taken from life; and they are instances of the commonest of experiences. They force the mind into an acceptance of the providential order; otherwise it would be difficult sometimes to remain sane. For the same assent must be given to the harsh experience as to the glad. "I feel he laid the fetter, let it lie"; it is only when the first clause can be uttered that the second can follow in peace of assent. Then the mind goes out to find the good results of these "accidental" or inexplicable happenings; nor will the mind fail in its quest. There is spiritual gain to be found in all that God permits to happen to us. Happy is the man who steadfastly seeks to discover it; for in this region above all others, "He that seeketh findeth" (Luke 11:10).

Although in vs. 3 a glimpse is given of the journey's end, the flock has not yet completed its pilgrimage. "The dark defile" is still to be traversed. The straight path is not always the easiest; round about you may wander in sunny glades, while the straight path is through the defile, a dark and dangerous way. Nevertheless it is the road, and the best road, to the place where you fain would be. To take easier journeys would mean that you would be overtaken by the night before the sheepfold could be reached. Wherefore the shepherd in his wisdom leads to the threatening valley; but he keeps close to the sheep, with his rod (his weapon of offense) and his staff (his weapon of guidance) ready, so that when darkness comes, the shepherd and his sheep are home. It is a lovely little picture of the God-trusting life, so complete and so true.

4 Yea, though I walk through the valley of the shadow of death, I will fear no evil: for thou *art* with me; thy rod and thy staff they comfort me.

4 Even though I walk through the valley of
the shadow of death,[v]
I fear no evil;
for thou art with me;
thy rod and thy staff,
they comfort me.

[v] Or *the valley of deep darkness*

---

paths (cf. Isa. 30:21; John 10:4). **For his name's sake:** The good shepherd will not be false to himself (cf. 106:8).

4. The sheep is also the object of the shepherd's protecting care: "though I walk through a valley of dark shadows," where robbers and beasts of prey lurk, **I fear no evil.** The scribal copyists pointed the word for "dark shadows" (*çalmûth*) to read **the shadow of death** (*çal māweth*), thereby in the interest of interpretation spoiling the psalmist's picture. With his **rod** or stout club the shepherd beats off the foes of the sheep, and with his **staff** he helps it through the dark and perilous defile. So in the midst of dangers these symbols of the shepherd's might and affection banish fear: "they are my consolation."

Notice (*a*) that the refreshing beside still waters comes *before* the severest part of the journey. The reserves of energy are first secured. In this we must co-operate with God, seeing to our religious practices when life is plain sailing, particularly in the days of our youth. "The devil was sick, the devil a monk would be";[5] even he has enough sense of reality for that. Where he fails is in the spiritual common sense that tells us to look after the powers of sainthood when we are not fighting for our lives. "The devil was well, the devil a monk was he."[6] Note (*b*) that the heaviest tests do not come in the morning of life, but in the afternoon. We speak quite accurately of "the dangerous forties." A wise man will have his shepherd chosen and his fidelities fixed before he enters that trying decade. Moreover, the deep valley is not a short one; it stretches on to the evening. Old age has many compensations; but it is always a discipline. The process by which God pries our fingers loose from their clutch on things material is not entertaining. The closing of the doors of the senses, the increasing feebleness of the physical powers, and the pathetic loneliness of great age make up a process of detachment which is stern in its mercy (cf. the frank depression of Eccl. 11:7-8). Well in advance a man needs to know in whom he has believed. Note (*c*) that this part of life's experience gets an emphatic verse to itself. We may almost say it is this verse that has "made" the psalm. The honesty of the devout spirit would have declined to immortalize a song which had no due recognition of "the tears of things," or minimized their bulk in life's sum. Sunny as it is, the psalm steadily faces the dark; but it illumines that dark with light. Here also it is true to experience.

The details of the imagery are somewhat alien to us. Our shepherds do not carry rods and staffs. A shepherd's crook, laid lightly on the back of a sheep showing tendencies to wander, is familiar enough. But a weapon of offense against marauding enemies is not a modern shepherd's equipment. Yet something may be made of both the **rod** and the **staff** as we spiritualize the psalm. The **staff** is plain: it symbolizes all the gentle disciplines that keep us going. But the **rod** also is recognizable. All that ejects evil from our minds is a weapon of offense—such as sudden disgust, particularly at ourselves when we realize that God's alleged servant is behaving like a dog, perhaps disfiguring the divine image in someone else. The uprush of wrathful feeling that makes a man cry "have at you" to habits which are weakening him and spoiling his work—this too is the shepherd's rod in action. All that the shepherd's presence means in creating honest anger against evil in ourselves or in our world, from the tigers of lust to the little foxes of laziness, is hinted at in the rod. Thank God for the rod, especially when it is brandished in the face of our lower selves.

The image of **the valley,** in Christian hands, obviously goes beyond the original intention of the writer. The translation **the valley of the shadow of death** is an inevitable Christian addi-

[5] Samuel Smiles, *Thrift* (Chicago: Belford Clarke & Co., 1881), p. 254.

[6] *Ibid.*

5 Thou preparest a table before me in the presence of mine enemies: thou anointest my head with oil; my cup runneth over.

5 Thou preparest a table before me
in the presence of my enemies;
thou anointest my head with oil,
my cup overflows.

---

b) The Lord as a Gracious Host (23:5-6)

5. The picture changes. The psalmist uses the metaphor of a host to give richer expression to his sense of the warmth and intimacy of his relationship to his God. He is a guest under the protection of the divine host. In the East the man who is hunted

---

tion. In the Scottish metrical version it is even more emphatic:

> Yea, though I walk in death's dark vale,
> yet will I fear none ill:
> For thou art with me.

To those brought up on that version it is impossible to divorce the phrase from the idea of death; for it has brought comfort to too many in the actual experience of dying; too many have quoted it beside deathbeds. There was an instance in which a man who had been unconscious for hours came back to consciousness just long enough to join in the saying of that one verse and immediately thereafter breathed his last. It was an unforgettable scene; the relatives who loved him were sorely anxious for one little word to indicate his confidence and peace, for he had been a reserved man who said little about his religion. There seemed to be nothing to do except softly to recite the twenty-third psalm in his ear, trusting that hearing would be the last of the senses to cease. He lay quite immobile and without response until this verse was reached, when quite clearly his voice uttered the familiar words as far as **for thou art with me;** and then he died. So it is that for a great multitude of Christian folk the verse refers to the valley of death, first and last. Christian experience has, if you like, rewritten it. Certain it is that the prospect of death is solemnizing: *Timor mortis conturbat me,* as the old poet William Dunbar reiterated in moving verses.[7] But actual dying is nearly always in normal circumstances a quiet thing. No fiend voices rave; rather, tired childen fall asleep. Men used to pray for "dying mercies"; such prayers seem to be almost unnecessary. Dying mercies are mercies which it is the Father's will to grant. Surely if the last thought is **thou art with me,** the king of terrors will change his aspect. For the Shepherd is there—and he is friend and guide.

5-6. ***Journey's End.***—With vs. 5 the imagery changes abruptly into that of the kindly host and his generous providing. But though the images alter, the thought is continuous. The good shepherd has brought his flock home; and the idea of home is made vivid by the image of the spread **table** and the lavishness of provision prepared by a most fatherly host. **Thou preparest a table before me,** however, applies to the journey as well as to journey's end. We often find opportunities of refreshment even in the midst of our dark valleys; if it were not so, we should find it hard to travel them. Even sheep are allowed to crop the grass for a moment or two as they journey. But the main idea of the verse is the welcome and provision at the end of the day. The enemies are outside, glaring but helpless; the sheep are within and safe. As the verse proceeds, the pastoral imagery begins to merge with another, and the object of the divine care becomes more clearly a man, raising to his lips the brimming cup of God's lavish hospitality.

Again, Christian experience has deepened the conception. **Thou preparest a table before me in the presence of mine enemies** becomes a table spread in the midst of the pilgrimage, even when foes are massing to the attack. The verse has been declared to have been a favorite text in London at Communion services during World War II, when the bombing was at its peak; even in one instance when a part of the church was hit, while the service continued. In normal times it conveys the living thought of the table of strengthening set for our partaking at times when our private spiritual war is at its most bitter, suggesting that when we are finding the going hardest, we should at that very time repair to the Lord's table and receive at his hands. Our enemies slink away and become poor things when we resolutely sit down with our host.

Thou anointest my head with oil is not an image which means much to us; but in the ancient Near East it was a means of refreshment to weary travelers, and healing oils were sometimes rubbed into the fleece of sheep. An old version translates, "Thou hast my head with balm refreshed," and this gives the idea intended. The point to emphasize is that the shepherd of the soul goes the "second mile" in

[7] "Lament for the Makars."

by enemies needs but to enter or even only to touch the tent of him with whom he seeks refuge in order to be safe and to enjoy gracious hospitality. His enemies may stand and glare outside the tent door, but can do no more. **Thou preparest a table before me in the presence of my enemies:** The divine host has exceeded the bare requirements of hospitality. The meal assumes the proportions of a feast at which sweet-smelling unguents are poured on the head of the guest (cf. Luke 7:46), and there is no lack of good things. **My cup overflows:** Lit., "my cup is saturation." The

---

giving all that is required for renewing power and providing comfort. "Here is a basin and cool water, wash ye: here is a towel, too: and here is a chair, sit ye down and rest ye; your dinner will be on the table when ye are ready for it," was the way an old preacher used to elaborate. We could do worse than to copy his arresting homeliness. No wonder that the wayfarer could say that his **cup** ["lot" or "portion"] **overflows;** no point of hospitality was neglected. If we choose to think of the home and the hospitality beyond "death's dark defile," we can find here a starting point for images that are well justified by the N.T. Why should we not speak more of heaven? Our fathers did, and they spoke with power. Is it possible that we hesitate because we do not believe? Yet it is written that "eye hath not seen, nor ear heard" (I Cor. 2:9). Let us start with "the cup running over" and pray God to sanctify our imaginations. We shall serve our generation well if we can make living the beauty of the "many mansions." At the least we might reawaken some "homesickness of the soul." Whittier did it; why should not others try?

In vs. 6 the two images of shepherd or host are combined. **Surely goodness and mercy shall follow me all the days of my life** suggests continued pilgrimage and shepherding, while **I shall dwell in the house of the Lord for ever** suggests permanency as a member of the household of the divine host—a guest adopted into the family. The poet doubtless was thinking of the actual temple and his daily participation in its worship; but the devout mind has found here a picture of the eternal home of the soul. The temple becomes God himself. The end of the God-guided life, as portrayed in scripture, is extraordinarily splendid, and we should not be afraid of dealing with it, remembering that "every man that hath this hope in him purifieth himself" (I John 3:3). We should seek poetry that utters the heart's noblest longings, and find how scripture promises their fulfillment. Innisfree, where "peace comes dropping slow" [8] is there; for "there remaineth . . . a rest to the people of God" (Heb. 4:9). Gallant adventure awaits in the armies of heaven that follow God. The possession of truth and its freedom await, for "then shall I know even as also I am known" (I Cor. 13:12). And "goodness all through" awaits, for "we shall be like him" (I John 3:2). We lay aside one of our mightiest weapons if we fail to search the scriptures and declare the

> one far-off divine event,
> To which the whole creation moves.[9]

Life's storms and warfares become a new thing as seen in the light of the consummation, when, God-guided,

> Home is the sailor, home from the sea,
> And the hunter home from the hill.[1]

Nor is the vision merely individual. The shepherd, let us reiterate, is the shepherd of a flock; the single soul reaches its height in the "beloved community." Turn to Dante's conception of the *rosa mystica* in *Paradise*,[2] where each petal is perfect because it shares the life of the whole, and see how great a thing it is to say in Christ, **I shall dwell in the house of the Lord for ever.**

No doubt the original writer throughout had in his mind solely the protection of God in the vicissitudes of this mortal life. "I shall have my good days and my bad, but my Lord will see me through the latter, and I shall be able as long as I live to join in the worship of his temple." **The house of the Lord** figured for him the actual temple on the hill. But it is quite impossible for us to interpret the psalm in so restricted a sense. The Lord has touched it with his finger, and enlarged its horizons. Indeed part of his shepherding of us is precisely the deepening and widening of such a song as this. Wherefore let it be interpreted in the light of our knowledge of him.

A few general hints may be added, which may start trains of thought in the minds of interpreters. For instance, the abruptness of the appearance of the kindly host (vs. 5) and his spread table brings before us the thought of the sudden mercies and helps of God. There is a word which occurs not only in English but

[8] Yeats, "The Lake Isle of Innisfree."

[9] Tennyson, *In Memoriam*, Conclusion, st. xxxvi.

[1] Robert Louis Stevenson, "Requiem."

[2] Canto XXX.

6 Surely goodness and mercy shall follow me all the days of my life: and I will dwell in the house of the LORD for ever.

6 Surely[w] goodness and mercy[x] shall follow
me
all the days of my life;
and I shall dwell in the house of the LORD
for ever.[y]

[w] Or *Only*
[x] Or *kindness*
[y] Or *as long as I live*

---

psalmist has had enemies, but their plans against him have been frustrated because the Lord, in effect, has said, "This man is my friend."

6. The past is a prophecy of the future: "Only goodness and kindness will pursue me." If he looks behind him, fearing lest enemies be upon him, he will see only these twin angels of God tracking him down. **I shall dwell in the house of the LORD:** His highest delight will be to continue as a guest in the house of his divine host. The picture of the tent melts into that of the temple. **For ever:** Lit., "for length of days," i.e., **as long as I live.**

---

in Old French, the word "suddenty," meaning anything that happens suddenly, or as we say, "out of the blue." In Scots law it means any crime committed without premeditation under stress of passion; but it is also used in a good sense. We find significant instances of "God's suddenties" in the N.T. Deliverance can come suddenly, as to Paul and Silas (Acts 16). Vision and light can come suddenly, when there is before our eyes "no man, save Jesus only" (Matt. 17:8), as in the case of Paul (Acts 9:3 ff.). Power can come suddenly, as at Pentecost (Acts 2:2 ff.). All these are part of the "mercies on the table spread."

Or may we connect **I walk** (vs. 4) with **I shall dwell** (vs. 6)? **I walk,** admitting the drudgery of it; but remembering that they who "wait upon the LORD . . . shall walk, and not faint" (Isa. 40:31), and acknowledging what is implied by walking, that here we have no abiding city. *Ave atque vale* has continually to be on our lips, since walking is our portion. Why should I walk? To reach the place where I want to go, the place where God's mercy is under that very necessity (if I truly want to go there), which enables me to say with Robert Frost, "They have to take you in." [3] Whither then do I walk? Why, home; which is in the heart of God. Meantime I make my purpose definite, "I walk and it is hard going in this shadowed valley; but, please God, in his good time, I will dwell."

Surely in vs. 6 is a high religious word. Connect it with the Pauline phrase, "I am persuaded" (Rom. 8:38). Religious certainty is not mathematical: the methods of scientific proof in this region give uncertainty. Nevertheless men do attain to religious conviction; and by it they outlive and outdie the rest of mankind. In part these convictions are based on personal experience and on the assumption that God is consistent. So in this case. The writer has found that the guide leads wisely and leads well; wherefore he has confidence in the future. He is persuaded to stake his life on the goodness and mercy of the shepherd.

Additional points could be suggested. It is worth an interpreter's while to read other versions of the psalm, and the hymns to which it has given rise, to see how the spiritual essence of it has been developed by the devout of later generations. Henry W. Baker's well-known hymn, "The King of love my Shepherd is," comes to mind. In it we find the truth that the rod and staff of correction are made necessary by our own fault, "Perverse and foolish oft I strayed." Emphasis is given to the seeking labor of the shepherd as well as to his guiding, "But yet in love he sought me"; the tenderness and persistence of the shepherd are brought out:

And on his shoulder gently laid,
And home, rejoicing, brought me.

This is Ps. 23 seen in the light of Luke 15.

Should we comment too that there is nowhere any mention of the shepherd's dogs? In our day they do a great deal of the shepherding of wandering sheep. Their skill is uncanny and has become proverbial; but only a countryman knows how high is their sense of honor. A sheep dog will finish a day exhausted almost to collapse, his feet wounded and sometimes bleeding, but not a single sheep will have been lost; all are enfolded. On that fact a poetic preacher of an older time fastened. He spoke in the vernacular, which added both force and tenderness to his words. "The Lord is my shepherd," he cried, "aye, and more than that, he has twa fine collie dogs, Goodness and Mercy. With him before and them behind, even poor sinners like you and me can hope to win home at last."

[3] "The Death of the Hired Man."

A Psalm of David.

24 The earth *is* the LORD's, and the fulness thereof; the world, and they that dwell therein.

A Psalm of David.

24 The earth is the LORD's and the fulness thereof,
the world and those who dwell therein;

XXIV. HYMN TO THE KING OF GLORY (24:1-10)

This psalm, as its contents show, must have been sung on some processional occasion. It is composed of three originally independent parts (vss. 1-2, 3-6, 7-10), as the differences respectively in measure, form, mood, and contents make unmistakable. However, the liturgical rite for which the psalm was prepared served to bind the disparate elements into a unity.

The opening lines (vss. 1-2) are a brief hymn or a fragment of a hymn proclaiming that because of his work in creation, the Lord is the master of the world and all who are in it. In the second part (vss. 3-6) is a short didactic composition comparable to Ps. 15, defining the qualities which fit a man for admission to the worship of the temple. It has a question-and-answer form such as we associate with a torah, and in its context it is to be taken as a torah-liturgy—i.e., a musical composition in which the question and the answer are recited by different persons. The third part (vss. 7-10) is clearly an antiphonal song in which the voices of a company in front of the gates of the temple alternate with voices from behind the gates.

We have some hints as to the nature of the occasion which the psalm celebrated. The LXX adds to the title of the psalm the significant words "for the first day of the week." Since according to Genesis creation began on the first day of the week, and since the opening verses of the psalm deal with the creation of the earth, the LXX evidently reflects the opinion of the Judaism of its day that the psalm as a whole had some reference to the event of creation. Later Jewish sources associate it quite definitely with the festival of the New Year (Paul Fiebig, ed., *Rosh ha-schana* [Giessen: A. Töpelmann, 1914], p. 52; cf. also pp. 13-71) in the liturgy of which the work of creation was commemorated and the idea of the kingship of the Lord was prominent. The

24:1-10. *The Rightful Lord.*—This psalm follows closely in thought on Ps. 23, for it exalts the Lord as Creator-King. The shepherding of God and his overlordship are inextricably intertwined. The experience of the first leads to the acceptance of the second and vice versa. An interpreter will find a point for pondering on this contiguity. "The Lord is my shepherd." "What Lord?" "Why, none other than he to whom the earth belongs, he who is the King of glory." He is "the God who is able," in whose shepherding we may trust. It is significant that when in 1598 free worship was authorized in Paris for the first time, after the Edict of Nantes, and when an assemblage gathered in the Louvre under Catharine of Navarre, this was the psalm with which the worship opened.[4] The worshipers had had some strange experiences of shepherding in very dark defiles, but then they were learning of the royal power of the shepherd, even though their journeyings in the valley were not complete.

The structure of the psalm is curious, and suggests the joining of two separate songs (yet see Exeg.). Vss. 1-6 form a metrical unity; vss. 7-9 are metrically different. The first section, which is an instructional poem, falls into two parts: (*a*) vss. 1-2, a statement of the fact of the Creator and his universal authority, followed by (*b*) a description of the qualities of the true worshiper, reminiscent of Ps. 15. The second section is a march, pictorially vivid. We see the army of the righteous,[5] with the king at the head, advancing on the "ancient fortress of ill." We hear the voice of the herald, demanding the opening of the gates. We hear the answering question from the fortress walls, **Who is this King of glory?** and the confident reply. We hear question and answer repeated, till the psalm ends with a shout in unison, **The LORD of hosts, he is the King of glory.**

An example of the way in which an interpreter can use the imagery of this song is provided in Hugh Walpole's *Rogue Herries.*[6] A description is therein given of the preaching of George Whitefield, one of the leaders of the revival under John Wesley at Keswick, at the

[4] Ker, *Psalms in History and Biography,* p. 48.

[5] The interpretation here does not follow the widely held view that the psalm is a liturgy for the New Year. Editors. (See Exeg.)

[6] Garden City: Doubleday, Doran & Co., 1930, p. 337.

Babylonians and the Egyptians had New Year festivals (see Intro., p 7) in which annually the patron deity was honored as creator and symbolically enthroned as king. Some scholars, therefore, assume that the psalm is a processional hymn which was used at the annual feast when the Lord's enthronement as King of men and of the world was celebrated.

The psalm in its present form is postexilic. Vss. 3-6, as a torah or torah-liturgy, like Ps. 15 exhibit so thoroughly the prophetic influence on the cult that they must be given a postexilic date. Vss. 7-10 are probably late in the pre-exilic period. The fact that the **gates** of the temple are spoken of as ancient or eternal precludes, on the one hand, a Davidic date, and, on the other, a date subsequent to the destruction of the first temple. Vss. 1-2 may have been written to provide an introduction to the psalm. It should be remembered that it was in the postexilic period that New Moon and New Year festivals become special religious events. In the pre-exilic period they were absorbed in the more general feast of Tabernacles.

The meter of vss. 1-2 is 3+3; that of vss. 3-6 is 3+3, with the usual variations, e.g., 4+4+3 in vs. 4, and 3+4 in vs. 6. In the third part, vss. 7-10 consist of three lines in 3+3+3 and a concluding line in 3+4.

1. The World Is the Lord's (24:1-2)

24:1-2. The psalm begins by declaring, **The earth is the Lord's and the fulness thereof.** The following stich repeats the thought of the first. **The world** is the cultivated

---

head of Derwentwater, in the English Lakes. From where he stood, the highest peaks in England encircle the further end of the lake, a scene of great natural dignity and beauty. He began quietly and in gentle appeal; until suddenly with pointing hand and full voice he cried, "The trumpeters have crossed the hills! The trumpeters have crossed the hills!" His audience was stirred intolerably, and ready for the imperious demand that the doors of their hearts be opened for the King of glory.

Other differences between the first and second sections become apparent on examination. In the first part the whole earth (including this hill) belongs to God; in the second he advances to demand its surrender. In the first it is the worshiper who hopes to ascend to meet the Lord, it is the worshiper who must examine his qualifications for such an enterprise; in the second it is the Lord who is the sole dominant figure claiming authority, while implicitly there is with him a host of those who are already his. But we must not push these differences too far. Indeed, if we regard them as developments in the unity of one poem, we find vital points for emphasis. First, there is the basic claim that all that is belongs to God as creator; second, we find a description of the kind of man who can venture into his presence to be his worshiper, i.e., a description of the quality of one who would be a member of his court and a soldier in his army; third, the picture alters abruptly from the eternal to the temporal. In God's rightful territory there are in point of fact fortresses of rebellion, dedicated to other overlords. These he comes to claim, backed by the army he has fashioned. Herein are suggestions: (*a*) All is God's, and that which seems not to be is the result of plain rebellion. (*b*) The first essential is to form an active force of those who in their personal qualities are in harmony with him. In the language of today, a living, loyal church is the condition of divine victory over evil. (*c*) Then follows inevitably the presence of the divine Overlord, claiming and securing entrance everywhere. The Creator-King, the true worshipers who recognize him as such, the challenging King among men, the surrendered gates, the victorious King—all are links in one chain.

The psalm has obvious liturgical possibilities. In reformed churches, after the call to worship, the words of vss. 7-10, or parts of them, make an admirable congregational response in the "approach to worship"; after which an opening collect, that we may be fit to ascend into the hill of the worshipers, follows suitably. In early Christian days these verses were regarded as figurative of the Resurrection and Ascension; the challenge to the gates was heard in the context of Easter, when the gates of death yielded to their Master. It should be noted that strictly the gates are hostile, or have been hostile. Possibly the psalm was written for the feast of the dedication, which celebrated the purification of the temple by Judas Maccabaeus in 165 B.C. In any case, the stronghold defended by these gates has been a stronghold of ill, and is now to be a stronghold of the Lord.

1-2. ***The Creator-King.*—The earth is the Lord's, and the fulness thereof** is the fundamental statement from which all else follows.

2 For he hath founded it upon the seas, and established it upon the floods.
3 Who shall ascend into the hill of the LORD? or who shall stand in his holy place?
4 He that hath clean hands, and a pure heart; who hath not lifted up his soul unto vanity, nor sworn deceitfully.

2 for he has founded it upon the seas,
and established it upon the rivers.

3 Who shall ascend the hill of the LORD?
And who shall stand in his holy place?
4 He who has clean hands and a pure heart,
who does not lift up his soul to what is false,
and does not swear deceitfully.

---

and productive earth. The clause **those who dwell therein** is, as the parallelism indicates, the counterpart of **the fulness thereof.** The Lord's sovereignty is based on the fact that he made the earth. **He has founded it upon the seas, . . . the rivers. Seas** and **rivers** are poetic plurals. Both words refer to the primeval deep of Gen. 1:2.

2. Who Shall Stand Before the Lord? (24:3-6)

3-6. Originally an admonition of general application, these words are given a liturgical setting and directed to the throng. A priest asks who is fit to enter the temple. Another priest makes reply. **He who has clean hands and a pure heart.** The hands are stained by such sins as murder, theft, taking a bribe, greed for gain; the heart is made impure by evil thoughts (cf. Matt. 15:19). **Who does not lift up his soul to what is false,** i.e., whose heart does not long after what is empty and false (cf. Ecclus. 46:11), whether

---

It is his because he **founded it** and **established it.** Such a text may well be taken to rebuke a certain modern temper of mind which, regarding man's discoveries as man's creations, unduly exalts man's place in the scheme of things. All our inventions are discoveries of what is already implanted in nature by the Creator. Man has created nothing material; he has merely found out God's secrets. Electricity was hidden in Niagara all the time; man only "came across it" and discovered how to use it. So with chloroform and penicillin and all the rest of the benefits which God hid from the beginning of the world. Science is a sort of treasure hunt, with scientists as the hunters—all honor to them; but the originator of the treasure is God. Man's great "originality" is in misusing God's secrets once he has found them. It is indeed a fact that in most of them God has set before us blessing or curse; and we have chosen the curse. Atomic energy is an illustration in point. The first use man determined to make of it took the form of a bomb. Can we not learn that this **fulness thereof** belongs to God, and that only those of **clean hands and a pure heart** should have anything to do with it? Otherwise we have to face God's terrific "or else."

It would be well also to fasten upon the second clause, **the world and those who dwell therein.** People belong to their Creator at least as much as material forces. They compose a great **fulness** of the earth; and they have a **fulness** of their own, in their various endowments and capacities. Comment on the sin of unworthy racial pride may start with this phrase; the business of the Christian, especially if he is privileged in his way of life, is to discover God's secrets hidden in men of every nation and color and draw them out. God has hidden wonderful latent powers in those who dwell in China, India, and Africa. A Christian world will discover them in patience and love.

Or we may, if we choose, expound the cosmogony contained in the statement that God **has founded it** [the earth] **upon the seas,** pointing out that there were thought to be three seas—one beneath the earth (explaining the existence of springs), one on a level with the earth (which was flat), and one above the earth. These primitive views of natural history do not in any way, however, lessen the religious value of the psalm. Modern knowledge on these matters does not invalidate the necessity of **clean hands and a pure heart** if we would stand in God's holy place—a point to ponder in reading the Bible as "the word of God."

3-6. ***The True Worshiper.***—These verses repeat the teaching of Ps. 15:2. The phrase **who hath not lifted up his soul unto vanity** should be noted for amplification. The parallelism suggests that the particular meaning of **vanity** here is **what is false.** We may extend it to cover the "sham" or the "counterfeit." How much of our energy is given to the achievement of "vain things," things that have the appearance of true value, but fail in the great test of lastingness! "Pleasures are like poppies spread," as Robert Burns[7] wrote from knowledge. The complaint of the Roman gen-

[7] "Tam o' Shanter."

5 He shall receive the blessing from the
LORD, and righteousness from the God of
his salvation.
6 This *is* the generation of them that seek
him, that seek thy face, O Jacob. Selah.
7 Lift up your heads, O ye gates; and be
ye lifted up, ye everlasting doors; and the
King of glory shall come in.
8 Who *is* this King of glory? The LORD
strong and mighty, the LORD mighty in
battle.
9 Lift up your heads, O ye gates; even
lift *them* up, ye everlasting doors; and the
King of glory shall come in.

5 He will receive blessing from the LORD,
and vindication from the God of his
salvation.
6 Such is the generation of those who seek
him,
who seek the face of the God of Jacob.[z]
Selah

7 Lift up your heads, O gates!
and be lifted up, O ancient doors!
that the King of glory may come in.
8 Who is the King of glory?
The LORD, strong and mighty,
the LORD, mighty in battle!
9 Lift up your heads, O gates!
and be lifted up,[a] O ancient doors!
that the King of glory may come in!

[z] Gk Syr: Heb *thy face, O Jacob*
[a] Gk Syr Jerome Tg. Compare verse 7: Heb *lift up*

it is in respect to religion or pursuits or ambitions. The Masoretes read "my soul" because they coupled the warning with Exod. 20:7. A man marked by these qualities not only will be blessed, but also will see his cause victoriously maintained by his God. In this context the word צדקה, translated **righteousness** in the KJV, means, as frequently in Second Isaiah, "due reward" (cf. LXX ἐλεημοσύνην). The priest concludes his answer to the question of vs. 3 by stating that the people before him possess these qualities. **Such is the generation of those who seek . . . the face of the God of Jacob.** They know that could they not meet such a test, there is nothing for them in the worship of the temple.

3. AN ANTIPHONAL SONG (24:7-10)

7-10. The procession moves on and halts at the gates of the temple. **O ye gates:** The song alternates antiphonally between the gates personified and the throng before them. Voices behind the gates make the responses for them. **Be lifted up:** They are too low to receive the "high and exalted One" who is about to pass through them. Among the Romans the greater the victor, the higher was the triumphal arch. **That the King of glory may come in.** It is to be noted that the Lord is here described as a **King**—a glorious King. Also he is **strong and mighty, . . . mighty in battle,** because his kingship is based on his work in creation, which in turn began by his victory over the dragons

ral as he rode in the triumph that Rome had accorded him is apropos, "It lacks continuance." In vs. 6 the rendering **that seek thy face, O Jacob** should yield to **who seek the face of the God of Jacob**—the God of a man who once had set his soul on vanity, but in God's providence learned the true nature of the Creator and became a prince. Incidentally, there is a helpful suggestion in such personal titles for God as the God of Abraham and of Isaac, as well as of Jacob. The differences in the characters suggested by these names hint differences in appreciation of God, whereby the total conception of God is enriched.

7-10. ***The Ancient Stronghold.***—These verses stir the imagination, especially the picture of the fortress on the hill and its **gates.** What gates? The gates of entrenched evil in society, the gates of pain, the gates of death; but above all, the gates of the human heart barred against God. He who knows his own heart will have no difficulty in enumerating many a one of them. **Be lifted up, O ancient doors**—ancient as inner evil; over against them, for us, a vision of "the young prince of glory" advancing against the world's wrong. The figures of chivalry, the St. Georges against the dragons, come to mind. But much will be lost unless a portrayal by a greater poet than this psalmist supplants even this fine imagining. There is one who, as a pleading Friend, waits before the gates of every heart, saying, "Behold, I stand at the door, and knock" (Rev. 3:20).

The metrical version of these verses in the

10 Who is this King of glory? The LORD
of hosts, he *is* the King of glory. Selah.

10 Who is this King of glory?
The LORD of hosts,
he is the King of glory! *Selah*

A Psalm of David.

25 Unto thee, O LORD, do I lift up my
soul.
2 O my God, I trust in thee: let me not
be ashamed, let not mine enemies triumph
over me.

A Psalm of David.

25 To thee, O LORD, I lift up my soul.
2 O my God, in thee I trust,
let me not be put to shame;
let not my enemies exult over me.

---

of chaos (cf. 74:12-17). **O ancient doors:** Such an epithet implies that the temple and its gates have stood unharmed for a long period of time. **The LORD of hosts:** This is the magic word, the "open sesame" at which the gates swing open. At this point some symbol of the Lord's presence, be it ark or chariot or other sacred object, moves into the temple.

XXV. LET ME NOT BE PUT TO SHAME (25:1-22)

Appearing to be the supplication of an individual for relief from troubles that beset him, this psalm is in form an acrostic. The thought of the psalmist suffers in consequence some lack of freedom in expression. Unlike some others of its class, the psalm does not seem to have risen immediately out of the agonies of a bitter trial. In fact, the troubles of the psalmist's heart and his afflictions are spoken of so indefinitely that it is impossible to discern to what category they belong. In this circumstance we have a hint of the purpose of the psalm. The writer is not composing an address to God on his own behalf but constructing, rather, a form of prayer for the use of anyone who in a time of distress seeks divine help. In doing so, however, the psalmist reveals something of his own spiritual measure by the religious ideas to which he gives expression.

A postexilic date is evidenced not alone by the acrostic form, which appears only in the late postexilic period, but also by the mixture of hymnic (vss. 8-10) and wisdom motifs (vss. 4-5, 12-14) with those proper to the class to which the psalm belongs, a mark of late style. The meter is almost regularly 3+3. Vs. 15 is in 3+4 measure; stichs of four beats occur in vss. 1, 7-8, 10 because of textual corruptions.

1. PETITION FOR SUCCOR (25:1-7)

25:1-7. Notwithstanding the problem of making his lines begin with the successive letters of the alphabet, the psalmist succeeds in this first strophe in voicing his complaint

---

Scottish Psalter, "Ye gates, lift up your heads on high," sung to a noble tune, opens the evening service on Communion Sunday in very many Scottish churches. It has become a valued tradition to those who are familiar with it, "strong music for a strong people." The point is worth noting as indicating the place that the psalm holds in Christian devotion, and the lofty spiritual significance which its images have come to bear.

25:1-22. ***The Suppliant Soul.***—Here is a series of prayers and maxims forming an acrostic poem of which the text must be in some measure corrupt, for one letter (*l*) is omitted and another (*r*) is repeated. The unity is therefore largely that of a literary device. It is true that through the psalm there runs the note of confession and pleading for pardon, with an undertone of meek submission under the hand of God, but the interpreter may feel free to treat each verse on its own merits.

1-7. ***The Prayer of Faith.***—**Unto thee, O LORD, do I lift up my soul** is the gesture of a suppliant without personal resource, as if the mere spectacle of the man's self in its helplessness would strike pity from any who could assist, an attitude of mind which has its justification both in "our exceeding need and God's exceeding love." Our prayers should contain an element of merely showing our souls—ourselves as we are—to God. If prayer can be defined as "telling God all about it," the baring of our souls is true prayer. In trying to lift up our souls to him we shall develop in self-

3 Yea, let none that wait on thee be
ashamed: let them be ashamed which transgress without cause.
4 Show me thy ways, O Lord; teach me
thy paths.
5 Lead me in thy truth, and teach me:
for thou *art* the God of my salvation; on
thee do I wait all the day.

3 Yea, let none that wait for thee be put to
shame;
let them be ashamed who are wantonly
treacherous.

4 Make me to know thy ways, O Lord;
teach me thy paths.
5 Lead me in thy truth, and teach me,
for thou art the God of my salvation;
for thee I wait all the day long.

---

and petition after the traditional manner of psalms of this type. Through homoeoteleuton one of the stichs of the first line has almost disappeared. The opening line probably read, "I wait, O Lord, for thee; I lift up my soul to my God."

The psalmist has enemies. **Let not my enemies exult over me.** They have a malicious interest in his plight, whatever it may be, but they are not the occasion of it, for the psalmist hints that his visitation is a penalty for past sins: **Remember not the sins of my youth.** Omit in vs. 7 **my transgressions** for metrical reasons. Ignorance as well as the heedlessness of youth may have led to transgression. Therefore **teach me thy paths,**

---

knowledge; and self-knowledge will make us more earnest in prayer.

Let not my enemies exult over me. Anyone who would make vivid the idea of the war in the soul could do worse than to copy the Hebrew habit of personifying the impersonal. The psalmist was referring to human enemies; but his prayer applies also to spiritual foes. What if we were to see our lusts and meannesses and untruths as actual beings, sneering and chuckling as we yield to their blandishments or fall before their assaults! "A poor, spineless thing this," they cry, "hardly worth tempting." So might a man develop a healthy self-scorn and discontent with himself as he is.

Yea, let none that wait on thee be ashamed is an appeal to God's honor and power. "There is help with thee." It surely will be given to those who ask and go on asking in patient suppliance. "Justify our trust, O Lord. Thou owest it to thyself." But there are some who should be ashamed, viz., those that **transgress** [or are faithless] **without cause.** One should pause here. Some folk are terribly tempted; but all of us know what it is to transgress when the temptation is really negligible or, worse, self-invented. We made it formidable by dwelling on it; we tempted ourselves. That kind of transgression ought to make us ashamed. A good deal of our idleness is of such sort. One little effort at the beginning, and our work would have been done faithfully; whereas we frittered the day away. "Lord, make us ashamed."

Note the three classes of which the word **ashamed** is used in these verses: (*a*) **let me not be ashamed:** there I must co-operate with God. (*b*) **Let none that wait on thee be ashamed:** there we can also co-operate, strengthening each other through God. (*c*) But the transgressors **without cause, let them be ashamed.** They ought to be; and a sense of self-shame is their best hope of cure.

If ever there was an ancient prayer that should be on modern lips, **Show me thy ways, O Lord** is the one. But if it is to be sincere we must become teachable, willing to answer Christ's demand that we hear and learn of him. Moreover, we must give all we have of mental capacity to discover the right ways under his guidance. Yet after all is said and done, there comes a time when we need illumination beyond our power to discover; and for it we should "pray without ceasing." Perhaps God will answer us by sending the "illuminated man." May he grant that he shall not need to answer again in disaster and tragedy. For often he can make us recognize the right path only by showing us whither the wrong one leads.

Lead me in thy truth, or better, "troth" or "faithfulness," i.e., remembering that God does not change his mind, let me also remember that the paths in which I am being led are the right paths, leading home. A very human prayer. We all want to walk by sight occasionally; forever walking by faith is a strain; wherefore, seeing that God is gracious, this is a prayer that is often answered positively, especially in retrospect. Sometimes we can say, "Yes, this is the best for me"; more frequently we can say, looking back, "Yes, I see now that it was the best for me."

Remember, O Lord, thy tender mercies. It sounds to our ears anthropomorphic, this appeal to God to remember what he once did, and therefore to be merciful now. It is an implicit appeal to him to be consistent; a not unnatural appeal in the light of experience. For the provi-

6 Remember, O LORD, thy tender mercies and thy loving-kindnesses; for they *have been* ever of old.

7 Remember not the sins of my youth, nor my transgressions: according to thy mercy remember thou me for thy goodness' sake, O LORD.

8 Good and upright *is* the LORD: therefore will he teach sinners in the way.

6 Be mindful of thy mercy, O LORD, and of thy steadfast love,
for they have been from of old.
7 Remember not the sins of my youth, or my transgressions;
according to thy steadfast love remember me,
for thy goodness' sake, O LORD!

8 Good and upright is the LORD;
therefore he instructs sinners in the way.

---

lead me in thy truth (cf. 19:7-10; 119:35). The psalmist, like other late writers, traces personal affliction and calamity to sin (cf. 32:1-5), and looks for truth in the words of the law (cf. 119:66-72). **Let none that wait for thee be put to shame:** While he is conscious of or ready to confess his shortcomings, he can sincerely say that he is of the company of humble and faithful souls whose eyes are ever turned toward God. **For thee I wait all the day long.** Yet he pleads for help not so much because of his religious constancy but because of what he knows of God's unchangeable character. **Be mindful of thy mercy, O LORD, and of thy steadfast love.** History confirms his trust: **For they have been from of old.** There is also the divine willingness to forgive: **Remember not the sins . . . ; remember me, for thy goodness' sake.**

2. God's Ways with Man (25:8-15)

8-15. Abruptly the psalmist turns from the personal aspects of his relations with God to the subject of the divine relations with men in general. His confidence in his

---

dential order seems often to vary between the merciful and the harsh, the careful and the heedless. Yet if we can go on to finish the verse, **for they have been ever of old,** we are in the way to find an answer. The harshnesses and the heedlessnesses must have another explanation, either in our own fault or in the world's evil; or they must be "concealed lovingkindnesses," as they frequently are. His clouds

> Are big with mercy, and shall break
> In blessings on your head.[8]

An equally human cry is the appeal to God to forget. **Remember not the sins of my youth.** According to Mic. 7:18-20, that is precisely what God is willing and anxious to do. Let us see about having done with the sins, and God will see about having done with the remembrance of them. It must be pointed out, however, that sins may be forgotten in the sense that they no longer prevent our peace with God, but that their consequences upon our capacities and opportunities remain. These capacities and opportunities may not be less, but they will be different. It is conceivable that a philosopher who was a drunkard might ruin his university career; but if he recovered, he might be a great evangelist. In that sense his sins would be "remembered no more."

Is there a distinction between this clause and the clause that follows? **Remember not the sins of my youth . . . : according to thy mercy remember thou me.** Can we distinguish between a man's sins and the man himself? Surely we can. At least God hates the one and loves the other. A man's sins are not his entire self; there is also the spark of God in him; and while there is life—that life—there is hope.

8-15. *The Uprightness of God.*—Good and upright is the LORD: therefore will he teach sinners in the way. This is one of those splendid "therefores" so frequent in scripture. Let the interpreter reach for his concordance and run his eye down them. He will find good store both of warning and encouragement. Here the point is that due enlightenment as to our duty is inevitable, seeing that God demands the fulfillment of duty and that he himself is upright. As a matter of fact, we have "light enough to live by." More, a remembrance of the goodness and uprightness of God is itself an instruction. To remember Christ and his selfless stainlessness is often all the light we need. He teaches us whenever we let the thought of him come into our minds. "Call the Lord to your elbow and march straight on." The thought of his presence,

[8] William Cowper, "Light Shining Out of Darkness," st. iii.

9 The meek will he guide in judgment: and the meek will he teach his way.
10 All the paths of the LORD *are* mercy and truth unto such as keep his covenant and his testimonies.

9 He leads the humble in what is right,
and teaches the humble his way.
10 All the paths of the LORD are steadfast love and faithfulness,
for those who keep his covenant and his testimonies.

own vindication is fortified by a review of God's attributes. His words become now like a series of hymnic affirmations (vss. 8-11), now like the admonitions of a wisdom teacher (vss. 12-15). **He instructs sinners in the way:** The **sinners**, in this instance, are not hardened sinners, but those like the psalmist, who at times chance to transgress. Read therefore חטאים as *ḥôṭᵉ'îm* rather than *ḥaṭṭā'îm* in view of the context. **He leads the humble, . . . teaches the humble his way:** For the second **humble** read with the Syriac, "the poor," in line with Hebrew style. To the man who **fears the LORD** there come great rewards. **He himself shall abide in prosperity.** And **his children shall possess the land,**

held in the focus of attention, is extraordinarily expulsive as well as impulsive.

The meek will be guided in judgment. If this is a postexilic psalm, as we may hold it to be, and if it expresses the religious attitude of the common man, it is the utterance of a man who is poor, for the Jews of that time had not much resource. Submission to a providential order which apparently ordained poverty for them was the mark of their piety. Thus they were **meek;** but their meekness was illumined with hope in the wise guidance of God (**judgment**) and in the ultimate outcome. The world is many a time in similar case: impoverished in material resources, poor in large vision. Yet it is "led" if it chooses to be led. Winston Churchill, in a world broadcast in 1943, reminded us that it is not given even to the clearest in mental sight to discern accurately the wisest path for the world; but it is given to a multitude of simple people to discern their own immediate duty. In the performing of that duty a light arises for the upright.

Everybody should wrestle with the text in vs. 10, if for nothing else than to clarify his own optimism. (*a*) **All the paths of the LORD are mercy and truth.** Are they? Test it by the case of a victim of hopeless insanity. Where is the spiritual benefit of such an experience to the man himself if he has lost the faculty by which he discerns truth? At the best he can be only an agent for the development of compassion in others, and for the increasing of their purpose to heal and deliver. It is a curious fact that alienists are often wonderfully compassionate men, and that there is no study pursued more selflessly than the study of the sick mind. Is it possible, further, to regard the very seriously ill as part of God's army against pain? Under him do the sufferers become the healers? Certainly in the case of conscious sufferers who bear their tragedy nobly there is no difficulty in seeing evidence of a purpose of good. They are magnificent "witnesses"; they are God's shock troops in the vanguard of the battle. The rest of us must stand at salute before them. God's purpose is a society in which there is no more pain; and in that purpose the individual is invited to "suffer together with him."

(*b*) **Unto such as keep his covenant and his testimonies.** Is this true? It certainly is not always true that if we are good we shall necessarily be happy and prosperous. In the inner region there will be peace, possibly joy. Even the martyrs sang. But the burning faggots and the snapping jaws of the lions tortured them. The only secure meaning, apart from the great reality of the "heart at leisure from itself," [9] is that they who keep his testimonies remain unshaken in their confidence of the outcome for men as a whole, and for themselves as a part of that whole.

But are the mercy and truth of God confined to the obedient? Not altogether. The disobedient are still used of him. "Babylon hath been a golden cup in the LORD's hand" (Jer. 51:7); Babylon, "drunk with the blood of the saints" (Rev. 17:6). Of God, let us remember, it can be said, "The remainder of wrath shalt thou restrain" (Ps. 76:10). Let us also note that the phrase **mercy and truth** brings this verse very close to the N.T. It is far from legalism, and near to that "fullness of grace and truth" which we find in Christ. The gospel is one long, hopeful unveiling of the width of this text.

For thy name's sake, O LORD, pardon my iniquity; for it is great. This is the familiar appeal to God's own nature, almost to his honor, to grant pardon, the suggestion being that if God is true to himself, he must pardon. We must avoid, however, pushing too much logic into a heart cry like this. It is enough to re-

[9] Anna Letitia Waring, "Father, I know that all my life."

11 For thy name's sake, O LORD, pardon
mine iniquity; for it *is* great.
12 What man *is* he that feareth the LORD?
him shall he teach in the way *that* he shall
choose.
13 His soul shall dwell at ease; and his
seed shall inherit the earth.
14 The secret of the LORD *is* with them
that fear him; and he will show them his
covenant.
15 Mine eyes *are* ever toward the LORD;
for he shall pluck my feet out of the net.
16 Turn thee unto me, and have mercy
upon me; for I *am* desolate and afflicted.

11 For thy name's sake, O LORD,
pardon my guilt, for it is great.
12 Who is the man that fears the LORD?
Him will he instruct in the way that he
should choose.
13 He himself shall abide in prosperity,
and his children shall possess the land.
14 The friendship of the LORD is for those
who fear him,
and he makes known to them his covenant.
15 My eyes are ever toward the LORD,
for he will pluck my feet out of the net.

16 Turn thou to me, and be gracious to me;
for I am lonely and afflicted.

because the blessings of one generation continue to the next (cf. 37:25; 103:17). Further, such men shall be favored with the close friendship of the Lord, who **makes known to them his covenant,** i.e., they have knowledge and experience of his alliance with them.

3. THE PETITION RENEWED (25:16-21)

16-21. The psalmist returns to his petition. Since he is reassured by the thoughts of the preceding section that his God will deliver those who keep their eyes toward him,

member that there is that in God which "delighteth in mercy"; and that it is permissible to appeal to the lovingkindness in the heart of justice. The idea of Christ as judge may be thought of in this connection, a sheltering thought. If he sits on the throne, all that can be said for us will be said, and we can hope to find that "a glorious high throne from the beginning is the place of our sanctuary" (Jer. 17:12).

The translation **my guilt, for it is great** has evangelic meaning. It implies an acknowledgment of such guilt as that we can do nothing to secure pardon, save plead for it. In the Nuremberg trials the presiding judge, in giving judgment, said of the chief defendant, "The enormity of this man's guilt is unique." It would be well if we pronounced that judgment on ourselves; and then prayed for pardon.

In vss. 12-13 we have a repetition of the psalmist's confidence in the well-being of the godly: **He . . . shall abide in prosperity.** The KJV reading, **His soul shall dwell at ease,** may strike sparks from some minds. To **dwell at ease** spiritually, to respond to the calls of conscience without strain, is surely to succeed in life; and to possess a "home in the mind," where all is lovely and of good report, is to fulfill the chief end of man.

The secret of the LORD is with them that fear him means that the intimate, friendly intercourse of the Lord is granted to them that fear him. The translation, **the friendship of the LORD,** is hardly strong enough. In Scottish speech there is a turn of phrase that gives the flavor we need. Ian Maclaren makes play with it in his Scottish sketches in *Beside the Bonnie Brier Bush.*[1] In humble homes there were only two sitting rooms; one, the parlor, was used for strangers; the other, the kitchen, was the family living room, and into it the intimates were taken. The house as a whole was only "a wee but and ben," the "but" being the seldom-used parlor, and the "ben" the kitchen. A family friend was invited "ben," i.e., into the room where the family dwelt; if he was a real intimate, he was said to be "far ben." So with a man and his God; those that fear the Lord are "far ben" with him. In that intimacy God lets them into his secret, namely that such folk shall be secure and ultimately exalted; and that this is a "covenant," a permanent relation which shall not change.

For he will pluck my feet out of the net, i.e., out of the trap or snare which has been set, an image drawn from the hunting of wild life. But it has spiritual suggestions. How greatly do our lower tendencies hamper our freedom of movement, caging the mind and literally preventing us from going about our business like freemen. Sins of appetite have this actual effect; a man can be enchained to the place where he will find his satisfactions. But in God's society he is enabled to kick that net away.

16-21. ***In Loneliness and Trouble.***—Vss. 16-19 repeat the psalmist's appeals and his sense of

[1] New York: Dodd, Mead & Co., 1895.

17 The troubles of my heart are enlarged: *O* bring thou me out of my distresses.

18 Look upon mine affliction and my pain; and forgive all my sins.

19 Consider mine enemies; for they are many; and they hate me with cruel hatred.

20 O keep my soul, and deliver me: let me not be ashamed; for I put my trust in thee.

21 Let integrity and uprightness preserve me; for I wait on thee.

22 Redeem Israel, O God, out of all his troubles.

17 Relieve the troubles of my heart,
and bring me[b] out of my distresses.
18 Consider my affliction and my trouble,
and forgive all my sins.

19 Consider how many are my foes,
and with what violent hatred they hate me.
20 Oh guard my life, and deliver me;
let me not be put to shame, for I take refuge in thee.
21 May integrity and uprightness preserve me,
for I wait for thee.

22 Redeem Israel, O God,
out of all his troubles.

A Psalm of David.

26 Judge me, O LORD; for I have walked in mine integrity: I have

A Psalm of David.

26 Vindicate me, O LORD,
for I have walked in my integrity,

[b] Or *The troubles of my heart are enlarged; bring me*

he presses his case with fresh force: **Turn thou to me, . . . for I am lonely and afflicted.** And again he makes mention of **the troubles of my heart.** Vs. 17 is better rendered, "the troubles of my heart are many," by reading רבו for הרחיבו. He speaks also of his **sins** and of his **foes,** who **hate** him with **violent hatred.** Having enlarged on the wretchedness of his plight, he pleads for the Lord to deliver him. **May integrity and uprightness preserve me:** Even though God should be unwilling to act, he must in the end be the protector of sincerity and uprightness; and if a man comes to him in the strength of a good conscience, God must vindicate his cause (cf. Job 13:16).

4. Liturgical Conclusion (25:22)

22. This verse falls out of the acrostic pattern. It has probably been added by someone who wished to make the psalm apply to **Israel.** A similar addition appears at the end of another acrostic, Ps. 34.

XXVI. A Plea for God's Vindication (26:1-12)

The circumstances which led to the writing of this psalm are similar to those reflected in Pss. 3–5; 7; 17. The psalmist is in straits because of charges which have been brought against him by persons who in his eyes are godless and unscrupulous. Since the offenses of which he is accused are of a capital nature, he has reason to fear that

need. Vs. 17 should read **relieve the troubles of my heart** [or "my sore heart"]. One may profitably go over the instances in the Gospels in which the Lord did relieve "sore hearts." Hearts are bruised and sore for many reasons: because of sin, bereavement, or honest doubt. Mary, the centurion, and Thomas come to the mind. "Sore Hearts Relieved" might be the title for a collection of many of our Lord's "mighty works."

The conclusion (vss. 20-21; vs. 22 is a late addition, out of keeping with the language and thought of the rest) sums up the appeal strongly. **Oh guard my life** is a phrase which a Christian, interpreting the word **life** in the highest sense, can urge upon all men as the kind of prayer which will be answered.

26:1-12. ***Vindication of the Righteous.***—To Christian ears this is an odd psalm, for it is a violent protest of complete innocence, presented not to man but to God. It is at variance with the Christian conviction that in God's sight no man living can be justified. Yet there is a robust honesty about it that attracts. The

trusted also in the LORD; *therefore* I shall not slide.

and I have trusted in the LORD without wavering.

his end is imminent (vs. 9). The decision as to his guilt or innocence lies with God. Through the results of some ordeal to which the psalmist must submit himself, or by an oracle, or through some other sign, this decision will be communicated to those who minister in such processes. In face of his peril he makes his plea to God for vindication (vs. 1).

It is to be noted, however, that the psalm does not bear the marks of individual experience to the same degree as certain of the psalms mentioned above. It is in fact so general in its reference that it could have been used by all who had to appear before God for a verdict of acquittal from charges falsely preferred against them. Perhaps, then, it was included among those of its type for use in the temple when more than one person or even a group of persons appeared on the same occasion for a declaration of their innocence by God. It could also have been used by persons whose cases presented no special individual features. In addition, we must remember that the Psalter had to provide for those who had no gift of utterance in prayer or supplication.

It is possible that in the original order of the lines of the text vss. 6*b*-7 followed vs. 12. The introduction of a reference to exultation and thanksgiving for God's work seems out of place when, as we see by vss. 8-11, the psalmist is still pleading for his life. Vss. 12, 6*b*-7, as the concluding strophe, would express the confidence of the psalmist that his prayer would be heard and that he would give praise and thanksgiving to God for his work of deliverance.

The meter is regularly 3+3, except in vs. 1, which has 2+3+3, and in vs. 11, which has 3+2, unless with the LXX יהוה ("O LORD") is read in the second stich. The date is most probably postexilic; vs. 8 refers to the temple at Jerusalem, **the place where thy glory dwells,** as do also **thy altar** (vs. 6) and **the great congregation** (vs. 12).

1. REQUEST FOR HELP (26:1-3)

26:1-3. The opening words **vindicate me** suggest at once the type to which the psalm belongs. It is justice, not healing, for which the psalmist is making his appeal to

writer is a persecuted Jew who, facing certain moral obligations, is able to declare that he has met them all. He maintains passionately that he has avoided the comradeship of the unfaithful, and that he has been punctilious in his worship, delighting in the temple services; and that indeed at a time when the judgments of God were abroad in the land. In the face of these aspects of the law, he insists that he is not guilty; and he has a perfect right so to do.

The Christian will have to meet this point. It is ridiculous to maintain that the man who has kept the Ten Commandments has nothing to say for himself. But it is equally false to say that the avoidance of overt act means an inner life in harmony with the divine; for the question of motive is not dealt with, nor the vital matter of hidden desire. We need terms more precise; and the scriptures give us a hint when they speak of the "conscience" and the "heart." A man may have a "conscience void of offense" (Acts 24:16) along with a heart that is unstable. Christian perception emphasizes the latter; and points out further that a conscience clear of legal offense may be the nurturer of spiritual pride and may take no cognizance of the Christian graces. A man who "washes his hands" in this kind of innocency may have no love in his heart nor any conception of the "second mile."

For our purposes this psalm should be set alongside the story of the rich young ruler, who had kept all the rules from his youth up, yet went away from Jesus; sorrowful, indeed, but he went away. It was an unforgettable experience to hear a preacher of the older school, Dr. Alexander Whyte, imagining the career of that young ruler, after he turned from the Master. Prosperous, respected, growing in pomposity and self-satisfaction, at last he died: and then his soul appeared—a poor, fluttering, leaf-like thing, blown by the winds of heaven, until it was caught in a whirlpool of air and drawn down and down. "And a voice cried, amidst the mocking laughter of the universe, 'Thou hast kept the commandments!' " Pilate, too, washed his hands, and claimed that it was in innocency. Such a contrast shows how deep Christian teaching cuts.

2 Examine me, O LORD, and prove me; try my reins and my heart.
3 For thy loving-kindness *is* before mine eyes: and I have walked in thy truth.
4 I have not sat with vain persons, neither will I go in with dissemblers.
5 I have hated the congregation of evildoers; and will not sit with the wicked.

2 Prove me, O LORD, and try me;
test my heart and my mind.
3 For thy steadfast love is before my eyes,
and I walk in faithfulness to thee.[c]

4 I do not sit with false men,
nor do I consort with dissemblers;
5 I hate the company of evildoers,
and I will not sit with the wicked.

[c] Or *in thy faithfulness*

God. He bases his plea on the uprightness of his life: **I have walked in my integrity.** He has followed the commandments of the Lord with wholeheartedness. And in every situation in his life he has made God the sole object of his trust **without wavering.** In great confidence he asks God to prove him, to test his inmost being to see whether the witness of his conscience is true. **For thy steadfast love is before my eyes:** Remembering his experiences of God's goodness and how God was ever loyal to his promises, he walks **in faithfulness to** God.

2. The Psalmist's Integrity (26:4-6*a*)

4-5. The psalmist proceeds to cite some evidences of the sincerity of his religious life. He has kept himself from association with men who in one way or another are renegades from religion: **I do not sit with false men,** i.e., men like those mentioned in 24:4, whose mind is set on vain or empty things, whether gods or purposes. Likewise, he avoids **dissemblers,** i.e., hypocritical men whose religious professions are only a cover

---

1-8. ***The Psalmist's Claim.*—Vindicate me, O LORD**—a bold demand. A man must be very sure of himself before he can say that to God. It can be said only in relation to some particular rule of conduct which he knows he has not broken. In that narrow region it is a comfort to be able to say such a thing. Call it merely the A B C of the good life; but after all we have to start with the alphabet, and must not fail to stress the desirability of obedience to general principles of conduct, however unwillingly rendered. At the same time, we are to understand what the answer to this prayer actually means to God. We are not "vindicated" in God's sleep, but on a Cross.

Translate the concluding clause, **I have trusted . . . in the LORD; therefore I shall not slide.** The supplicant's point is that his trust has been steady. But the two translations run into each other. If a man's trust is unwavering, he himself is less likely to be sliding or slipping. Connect this verse with vs. 12, **My foot standeth in an even place.** The two constitute a suggestive whole.

Examine me, O LORD, and prove me. This is definitely pitched too high; it is not the language of the Christian saint. But if it is taken in connection with vs. 3 it is not so indicative of spiritual pride; for vs. 3 surely means that the psalmist has lived believing in God's consistency. **I have walked** [believing] **in thy truth.** A man may fairly claim that he has honestly struggled aganst the temptations to doubt God and to question the unvarying rightness of providence.

I have not sat with vain persons. Is this a Christian boast, or does it exalt pharisaism? We note the word **sat;** he has not identified himself with the unworthy, even though it might have been politic to do so, and though he might have entertained his own "mental reservations." He was out-and-out and openly against the trimmers and the hypocrites. He would have made a fine Puritan, coming out from among them and being separate. But it is a good thing that the Lord acted differently, and dwelt among us. There is no hint of saviorhood in this attitude. Saviors must risk their skirts. Yet they need have no fear; "the longing to deliver" is a sure preventive of contamination. But we must be very watchful; we can afford to mingle with evil only if our one desire is to purge it.

Notice the descending scale of nouns: **vain persons,** i.e., those whose desire is toward the valueless; **dissemblers,** i.e., hypocrites, play-actors in the battle of life; **evildoers,** i.e., those who in act compromise with conscience, although they may be uneasy; **the wicked,** i.e., those who call evil good and are content. A significant descent to Avernus, and true to life.

I will wash mine hands in innocency. A figure of speech arising from a symbolical action.

6 I will wash mine hands in innocency: so will I compass thine altar, O LORD:
7 That I may publish with the voice of thanksgiving, and tell of all thy wondrous works.
8 LORD, I have loved the habitation of thy house, and the place where thine honor dwelleth.
9 Gather not my soul with sinners, nor my life with bloody men:
10 In whose hands *is* mischief, and their right hand is full of bribes.
11 But as for me, I will walk in mine integrity: redeem me, and be merciful unto me.

6 I wash my hands in innocence,
and go about thy altar, O LORD,
7 singing aloud a song of thanksgiving,
and telling all thy wondrous deeds.

8 O LORD, I love the habitation of thy house,
and the place where thy glory dwells.
9 Sweep me not away with sinners,
nor my life with bloodthirsty men,
10 men in whose hands are evil devices,
and whose right hands are full of bribes.

11 But as for me, I walk in my integrity;
redeem me, and be gracious to me.

---

to their evil practices, and **the wicked,** i.e., those who boldly set at naught the principles and practices of religion.

6a. For reasons given above, it is unlikely that vss. 6-7 set forth the psalmist's godliness from the positive side. It is more probable that the psalmist is referring to the rite that accompanied the formal affirmation of innocence made by accused persons (cf. Deut. 21:6-8), and that vss. 6*b*-7 are misplaced. **I wash my hands in innocence:** With this act the psalmist enforces his oath.

6*b*-7. See Exeg. on vss. 11-12, 6*b*-7.

3. The Request Renewed (26:8-12, 6*b*-7)

8-10. I love the habitation of thy house, i.e., "the dwelling place which is thy house" (cf. 27:4). The psalmist pleads for his life in order that he may continue to enjoy his chief delight. **Sweep me not away with sinners.** He prays to be spared the sudden end that is proper for sinners (cf. I Kings 8:31-32). **Men . . . whose right hands are full of bribes:** In this description of the sinful he may be delineating his own enemies, **bloodthirsty** and venal men.

11-12, 6*b*-7. Believing that his ways are acceptable to God, he repeats his opening

---

In Deut. 21:6 ff. the washing of the hands of the elders in the blood of a new-slain heifer, together with a declaration of innocence, relieved a community from the suspicion of being privy to a murder in its neighborhood. Pilate's action, recorded in Matt. 27:24, is of a similar kind. It is an easy step from that to an emphatic figure of speech, declaring guiltlessness. In English the phrase rather suggests a purpose and a hope, especially a hope. Someday our "good and ill forgotten and both forgiven," we may regain the freshness of the childlike heart. In our language the word **innocency** has a touch of the morning in it, and one may fairly mark and develop it. The phrase has been set to music by Samuel Wesley, and forms a suitable opening motet for Christian worship.

So will I compass thine altar, O LORD suggests an actual procession with thanksgiving songs around the altar, and is the only indication in the Bible of such a practice. In churches where the high altar is set away from the east wall, and where there is elaborate ceremonial, the practice is adaptable to Christian use on festivals. In any case, it suggests the spirit in which a man should approach "the enterprise of thanksgiving."

LORD, I have loved the habitation of thy house, and the place where thine honor dwelleth. An unrivaled word for anniversaries or services on occasions of historical memory. So, "with reasons annexed," we express our true pride in the church, holy and catholic, with its glorious record, despite its failures and its wrong. More intimately, we may use the verse with deep feeling in connection with any local congregation and its building, whose "very dust is dear" to its members. The love of quiet people for the house where they and their fathers before them have met with God is a real and potent fact, giving strength to the church as a whole.

9-11. *The Psalmist's Prayer.*—Here is a prayer that one may be spared to join in worship when

12 My foot standeth in an even place: in the congregations will I bless the LORD.

A Psalm of David.

27 The LORD *is* my light and my salvation; whom shall I fear? the LORD *is*

12 My foot stands on level ground;
in the great congregation I will bless the LORD.

A Psalm of David.

27 The LORD is my light and my salvation;
whom shall I fear?

---

petition, nay, he is confident that he will be heard. **My foot stands on level ground:** His present steep, rough, and perilous path will become smooth. And before his fellows in the courts of the temple he will offer his thanksgiving and tell what God has done for him: **I . . . go about thy altar, O LORD.** (For references to processions about the altar see 118:27; I Kings 18:26.)

XXVII. FAITH AND COURAGE (27:1-14)

This psalm falls clearly into two divisions: vss. 1-6, 7-14. But the contrast between them in theme is so well marked that it seems best to assume that we have here two originally independent psalms, which through circumstances at which we can only guess have in their transmission become joined together. We are scarcely warranted to interpret them as part of one psalm simply because in both there is a common element of trust in God in the face of assaults of enemies. On such grounds many psalms, now independent, could be conjoined.

---

nemesis overtakes the faithless and carries them away. **Sweep me not away with sinners** gives vigor to the thought. Of the completeness of "God's sweeping" there is no lack of historical illustration, both national and personal. Note the final description. The scale runs from **sinners** to the **bloodthirsty,** and on to **men in whose hands are evil devices,** rising to the climax, **whose right hands are full of bribes.** The O.T. moralists detested grafters; they are especially severe on the offerers of bribes. What wonder, when we remember how ugly bribing can be! A certain "thirty pieces of silver" have immortalized its foulness.

The psalm moves toward its close with a statement of the writer's spiritual condition. To our ears it sounds like self-complacency. **As for me, I will walk in mine integrity.** All we can say is that we hope he may, but "let him that thinketh he standeth take heed lest he fall" (I Cor. 10:12).

12. ***The Psalmist's Praise.***—The final verse is rich in suggestion. **My foot standeth in an even place** is an admirable pictorial basis from which to adduce (*a*) the ridiculous figure which those cut who slip and slide and fall through not watching where they are going, and (*b*) the warning not to provide other people with opportunities for slipping. The person who drops a banana skin on the sidewalk is morally responsible for the broken leg of him who slips on it. The spiritual parallel is painfully frequent. Let us remember Christina Rossetti's exclamation, "Each soul I might have succoured, may have slain." [2]

In the great congregation I will bless the LORD. This ordinary looking conclusion can justly open a noble train of thought, especially if it is taken as a statement of purpose. In days of pessimism and depression concerning the church, it is well to remember how great is its congregation. In round figures there are six hundred million professing Christians in the world, and our Lord started with twelve. The potential of Christianity is beyond measurement. With us also there is the great multitude which no man can number, whose souls go marching on. Our business is to be one with them in their source of inspiration, their moral purpose, and their worship. The man who thinks he can make the most of his life alone is a foolish one indeed. He neglects the inspiration of the company in whom however faintly the spirit of Christ dwells, and neglects it to the hurt of his own soul and to the diminishing of his power to serve his own generation. "Two are better than one"; how much more is **the great congregation** of which Christ is the head!

27:1-14. *From Meditation to Prayer.*—The question we have already had to ask in other instances has to be put again: Is this two psalms or one? If the latter, what explanation is there for the complete change of tone at vs. 7? If

[2] "If Thou Sayest, Behold, We Knew It Not," st. iii.

the strength of my life; of whom shall I be afraid?

The LORD is the stronghold[d] of my life;
of whom shall I be afraid?

[d] Or *refuge*

The first psalm (vss. 1-6) belongs to the type whose leading feature is the expression of confidence and trust in the Lord (cf. Pss. 16; 23). Because of his experience of the divine guidance and protection in the course of his days, the psalmist can bid defiance to all who would menace his life. His prayer is that he may ever be permitted to enjoy access to God's presence in the temple. For under God's protection in the shelter of the sacred dwelling place no foe can touch him. The thought of what he owes for present and past deliverances leads him to vow hymns of praise and offerings of thanksgiving to God. It is to be noted that in psalms of this type the Lord is spoken of in the third person.

The second psalm (vss. 7-14) is one of the so-called laments (cf. Pss. 7; 17; 55; 64). It is an earnest petition for God's favor from the lips of one who is in fear and despair because of the malice and false charges of personal enemies. As he speaks, the bitterness of his plight shows no sign of abatement, but his faith in the constancy of God's fatherly care sustains and encourages him with hope for his eventual deliverance (cf. Heb. 11:1). In these psalms the Lord is addressed in the second person.

The first psalm is to be regarded as postexilic because the temple in Jerusalem is implied in vss. 4, 6. The second psalm, because here even more than in the first the sense of religion as a fellowship with God is stressed to the exclusion of all reference to the formal obligations at the temple, seems also to be postexilic.

The meter is 3+2 in both psalms. Some variations, however, occur: in vs. 4*a* we have 2+2+2; vs. 6, as the end of a psalm, is in 3+2, 2+2+3; vs. 14 is in 3+2+2.

The stanzas of the first psalm appear, with the exception of the closing one, to consist regularly of two lines each. The second line of vs. 4 is probably a gloss drawn from 23:6.

A. Confidence in the Lord (27:1-6)

1. The Lord Is My Light (27:1-3)

27:1. The psalmist begins by proclaiming the fullness of his trust in the Lord. In his words, however, we can detect echoes of struggles and distresses through which

it is a composite psalm, why did someone join such different songs together? Vss. 1-6 express the thanksgiving and trust of a man for whom things are going exceedingly well; vss. 7-14 are the appeal of a frightened spirit for whom things are going exceedingly ill. Is it possible for the two moods to coincide? Perhaps there is here a deliberate point to be made. In the midst of trial, first concentrate upon the changeless Helper; then turn to stare at trouble, letting loose the heart's pleadings to the God whose character and presence we have already acknowledged. Vss. 3 and 12 seem to many contradictory. The interpreter may wish to deal with the two parts separately, as expressive of opposing experiences, with this connecting link, that the faith which arose easily in the sunny day stood the test also in the day of storm. Vss. 1 and 14 are gold from the same mint.

1-3. ***The Sure Defense.*—The LORD is my light.** To the psalmist this meant the light of leadership, showing the "right paths." It came to mean that God is the source of all mental illumination. We might well trace the enlargement of the idea in scripture, and its particular development in Christ's claim to be the light of the world. The phrase in Latin is the motto of Oxford University: *Dominus illuminatio mea.* It is a noble motto for any university; but all too often in our day, for the arts and sciences, not a heritage but an heirloom!

Vss. 1-6, in the metrical version, are often used in Scotland as the opening praise on Communion Sundays. "The Lord's my light and saving health" are appropriate words on such an occasion. "Saving health" for **salvation** gives a significant spiritual flavor to the line; and the recurrent challenge, **Whom shall I fear? Of whom shall I be afraid?** indicates a condition of healthy Christian vitality. An interpreter might meditate on the question, making a list of the causes of his fear—self, temptation, death,

2 When the wicked, *even* mine enemies and my foes, came upon me to eat up my flesh, they stumbled and fell.

3 Though a host should encamp against me, my heart shall not fear: though war should rise against me, in this *will* I *be* confident.

2 When evildoers assail me,
uttering slanders against me,[e]
my adversaries and foes,
they shall stumble and fall.

3 Though a host encamp against me,
my heart shall not fear;
though war arise against me,
yet I will be confident.

[e] Heb *to eat up my flesh*

---

he has passed in other days. But in all these bitter trials the Lord has been his helper. Hence his confidence is born of his acquaintance with the Lord. So he can speak of the Lord as his **light,** i.e., the source of joy (97:11), prosperity (Job 29:3), life (Ps. 36:9), and **the stronghold of** [his] **life,** i.e., the place where he can find **refuge** in time of danger. With such resources on his side, **of whom** need he **be afraid?**

2-3. The psalmist knows that enemies are ready to rise up against him in order by evil and slanderous attacks to cause his downfall. But he can foresee that they themselves will suffer the fate which they meant for him. His trust in the Lord in the face of any assault, however great, is unshakable. **Though a host encamp against me, . . . though war arise against me, yet I will be confident.**

---

judgment, as well as material ill—and ask in what sense and with what reality he can face and defy them; remembering the definite N.T. statement that "perfect love casteth out fear" (I John 4:18).

The Lord is the strength of my life should read, **The Lord is the stronghold** [re.fuge] **of my life,** to be accurate. But "my life's strength" perhaps goes a little farther. An outward fortress becomes an inward power, with its continual renewal.

Job 19:22 enables us to translate **to eat up my flesh** in vs. 2 as **uttering slanders against me,** thereby connecting with vs. 12, and so far supporting the unity of the psalm. But the images here seem to be martial; the picture as a whole is that of warlike combat. Wherefore we are justified in taking the phrase to mean an attack *à outrance*—violent and without quarter; an attack, moreover, in which the enemies were moved with particular animosity against the writer. The original indicates that they were emphatically his enemies. It is easy to take this in a spiritual sense; we know all about "my enemies and my foes to me" (as the original has it) on the battlefield of the heart.

There is a helpful suggestion in the words, **They stumbled and fell.** The hostile charge was a failure; an attacking army, tripped up and sprawling on their faces, would cease to be an awe-inspiring spectacle. Rather would they be an object of ridicule. Yet in the spiritual region these are the very verbs we use to describe ourselves in our moral lapses. *We* stumble; it is we who do the falling. It is a cheering thought that we can with God's help turn the tables on our lower tendencies and make them limping, halting ineffectives, so that we can laugh at them. A man who is justified in meeting his temptations with scornful laughter has traveled a long way on the right road. When we come to think of it, many of them, rightly regarded, are silly things.

Vs. 3 is a vigorous statement of wide confidence for the future. "Come one, come all, I am secure." There are tablelands in life's pilgrimage when a man feels himself to be the master of his fate and the captain of his soul; and under God he has reason for his sense of mastery if he possesses the "new affection" and has felt its expulsive power. For him the right in the soul has become mighty, by reason of its limitless reinforcements. Yet it is a mood that has its dangers: "Pride goeth before a fall." We need to remember that we can be overproud of our spiritual vitality, and that we walk safest when we walk most humbly with God.

In this will I be confident means "in these circumstances," i.e., when a host is encamped against me. **Yet** or "even then" gives the meaning of **in this.** It is a large boast; and it is a safe rule not to boast against the devil: he has too many partisans in the heart. However, the psalmist's thoughts were turned toward God; and his utterance helps us to remember that "with God all things are possible," even our complete victory. But we must not forget Christ's

4 One *thing* have I desired of the LORD, that will I seek after; that I may dwell in the house of the LORD all the days of my life, to behold the beauty of the LORD, and to inquire in his temple.

5 For in the time of trouble he shall hide me in his pavilion: in the secret of his tabernacle shall he hide me; he shall set me up upon a rock.

4 One thing have I asked of the LORD,
that will I seek after;
that I may dwell in the house of the LORD
all the days of my life,
to behold the beauty of the LORD,
and to inquire in his temple.

5 For he will hide me in his shelter
in the day of trouble;
he will conceal me under the cover of his tent,
he will set me high upon a rock.

---

2. THE JOY OF THE SANCTUARY (27:4-6)

4-5. This confidence is sustained by his presence in the temple, where through a consciousness of a nearness to God he feels himself to be under the divine protection. **One thing have I asked:** These words introduce both a statement of fact and a prayer. The psalmist pleads that what has been his joy may never be taken from him, viz., **to behold the beauty of the LORD, and to inquire in his temple.** Though these words are difficult to interpret, **the beauty of the LORD** seems to imply all that contributed to the impressiveness of the temple, its appointments and its worship, the things which, as nothing else, gave him a sense of the Lord's presence (cf. 90:17; 135:3); **to inquire** can scarcely mean here "to contemplate," but rather to inquire of God guidance in all the situations of existence (cf. Lev. 13:36; II Kings 16:15). Such a man will be both protected and impregnable. **He will hide me in his shelter:** The word **shelter** is here a synonym of "tent" or "tabernacle"; it recalls the rude shelters in which the people and their God were housed at the time of the Exodus (cf. Lev. 23:43). Poetic

---

words that we "watch" and "strive." If **a host should encamp** against us, we must not let the sentries sleep. For the opposing army has not unconditionally surrendered. It encamps to attack later; it means mischief yet.

4-6. *The Heart's Desire.*—A change of tone is felt here. Vs. 4 sounds like the aspiration of a servant of the temple, a Levite. But it can be an expression of the general life purpose of the "devout warrior"; and thus may be used of the Christian pilgrim. **One thing have I asked of the LORD.** What, in point of fact, have we asked of him? Our life's efforts, or lack of them, provide the answer. The Day of Judgment would be somber enough if it meant the recital, from the entries in the book, of the evidence which our actions provide as to the nature of our heart's deepest longings. Starting from this question, and putting it soberly to ourselves, we can immediately get down to the "inward parts," where the realities abide. It is a question that calls for moral candor. If we can get a genuine facing of it, and stab our spirits "broad awake" with alarm at our petty answers, we have prepared the ground for conversion. It will not do to be content with the replies we give in our sighs; we must face the answers given by our wills and our applied energies. It is startling and painful to have to surmise that our real demand is "a mess of pottage."

The answer given by the psalmist is threefold. He says that his main life purpose is (*a*) to **dwell in the house of the LORD,** (*b*) to **behold the beauty of the LORD,** and (*c*) to **inquire in his temple.** It will not be profitable to interpret this with prosaic literalness, though actual presence in God's house at worship is vital for the implicit lifelong spiritual intent and achievement. In a wider sense the verse suggests three essentials for the development of the good life: (*a*) purpose, to be a steadfast member of the community which puts God at the center; (*b*) desire, to be at home with beauty and to stay where it is to be found; which is another way of saying that (*c*) we determine to associate ourselves with Christlike ends and Christlike means. **One thing have I desired of the LORD:** To be numbered with the God-fearing, to know and to love better whatsoever is lovely and of good report, and to follow on in the effort to know the truth. These aims are quite compatible with living in this workaday world; but we need constantly to do something about it. Apart from these aims life

6 And now shall mine head be lifted up above mine enemies round about me: therefore will I offer in his tabernacle sacrifices of joy; I will sing, yea, I will sing praises unto the LORD.

7 Hear, O LORD, *when* I cry with my voice: have mercy also upon me, and answer me.

8 *When thou saidst,* Seek ye my face; my heart said unto thee, Thy face, LORD, will I seek.

6 And now my head shall be lifted up
above my enemies round about me;
and I will offer in his tent
sacrifices with shouts of joy;
I will sing and make melody to the LORD.

7 Hear, O LORD, when I cry aloud,
be gracious to me and answer me!
8 Thou hast said, "Seek ye my face."
My heart says to thee,
"Thy face, LORD, do I seek."

---

literature favors archaisms. **He will set me high upon a rock,** i.e., in a safe stronghold, an allusion to the "Rock of Israel" (Isa. 30:29).

6. Now my head shall be lifted up: As in the past, so in the present the psalmist will proudly exult over his foes. He therefore vows to present to the Lord thank offerings and loud hymns of praise.

B. A Cry for Deliverance (27:7-14)

1. Plea for Help (27:7-12)

7-8. Hear, O LORD: With the opening words of this section we are introduced into a situation strikingly different from that of the preceding verses. The psalmist is in straits, and the outlook is dark before him. The text of vss. 7-8 in its present state obscures

---

is vanity. Remember the Lord's words about the "one thing . . . needful" and the "good part" (Luke 10:42).

Vs. 5 returns to the image of the warrior; but it is a warrior in danger who speaks now. The imagery of the **shelter,** the **tent,** and the high **rock** suggests the dwelling place of God among men; but the reader finds his mind moving into the spiritual realm. There is a sure asylum for us in the community or congregation of those who frequent God's house; in their society the clamor of evil in our hearts dies down. Particularly the words, **in the time of trouble he shall hide me in his pavilion** ("counsel me in his tent"), have a moral content. There are spiritual conditions in which our only hope is not to be exposed to the full force of evil suggestion, as our Lord knew when he taught us to pray "lead us not into temptation"; the kindest thing God can do is to put us where temptations cannot compel themselves on our attention. He provides surroundings in which we shall not be tempted; our business is to go there in time. If an alcoholic enters a cocktail bar, likely enough he has no chance; but when he sees one, he can use his legs and run home. God conceals such a man in his **tent,** in the society of those who love him.

The full note of confidence returns. The warrior is safe, therefore he sings. This is psychologically inevitable. If a man feels that he has escaped from a moral weakness which has threatened his spiritual life, he must needs **sing.** Revivals have been great times of song; and the "songs of freedom," whether civil or spiritual, are often noble songs, for they are heartfelt. **I will offer in his tent sacrifices with shouts of joy** gives the flavor of the mood; but in the second clause the KJV has more power, **I will sing, yea, I will sing.** What could better convey the exhilaration of deliverance! The first clause, **I will offer . . . sacrifices with shouts of joy,** suggests a new mood at the time of the offertory, when funds are being gathered for missionary or philanthropic ends. And it is a reasonable mood when we remember that by God's mercy we have "escaped as a bird out of the snare of the fowler" (124:7). Interpreted spiritually, Ps. 124 is just such a "shout of joy."

7-12. ***The Cry of a Soul in Trouble.***—The psalm now becomes an appeal from someone who is in sore straits. In this section there are one or two phrases admirably suited to the general context of any soul's desperate need.

The primary condition of help is given in vs. 8. God says, **Seek ye my face;** we reply, **Thy face, LORD, do I seek.** We must do all we know and can to keep in touch with God. He is quite insistent upon that, and it is a reasonable insistence; for he asks that which it is in our power to give. He asks that our purpose be to search through worship, religious habit, willingness to learn, and the exercise of will up to our conceivable height, without a time limit.

9 Hide not thy face *far* from me; put not thy servant away in anger: thou hast been my help; leave me not, neither forsake me, O God of my salvation.

10 When my father and my mother forsake me, then the LORD will take me up.

11 Teach me thy way, O LORD, and lead me in a plain path, because of mine enemies.

12 Deliver me not over unto the will of mine enemies: for false witnesses are risen up against me, and such as breathe out cruelty.

9 Hide not thy face from me.

Turn not thy servant away in anger,
thou who hast been my help.
Cast me not off, forsake me not,
O God of my salvation!
10 For my father and my mother have forsaken me,
but the LORD will take me up.

11 Teach me thy way, O LORD;
and lead me on a level path
because of my enemies.
12 Give me not up to the will of my adversaries;
for false witnesses have risen against me,
and they breathe out violence.

---

the pitcous outpouring of his appeal. A better reading is, "Hear, O LORD, my voice, as I cry to thee; be gracious to me and answer me, O my God, for my heart is bitter; thy face, O LORD, I seek; hide not thy face!" The emended text is as follows:

[7.] שמע יהוה קולי אקרא לך חנני וענני [8.] אלי כי מר לבי
את־פניך יהוה אבקש [9.] אל־תסתר פניך:

To **seek** the **face** of a god or of a king, in the language of the times, is to plead for his help, favor, or mercy.

9-10. Apart from God, the psalmist has no helper to whom he can look in his trouble. **For my father and my mother have forsaken me:** A proverbial way of stating that all his kith and kin, his natural allies, have denied him help. **But the LORD will take me up:** Though all men disown him, he is sure that the Lord will adopt him (cf. 2:7) and take him into his care (cf. I Sam. 14:52; II Sam. 11:27).

11-12. The psalmist describes the source of his troubles as **false witnesses** who "pant for violence." In order that he may be delivered from these adversaries he prays. **Teach me thy way,** i.e., show me how I must conduct myself so that my path, being thy way, shall be free from trouble and peril.

A student once remarked, "I will give God and religion a three months' trial; if nothing happens, I quit." He was told that he had quit before he started. God gives no encouragement to experimenters, but he goes the second mile to meet seekers. Seekers are in earnest; experimenters are not.

Put not thy servant away in anger. That is a most unnecessary fear; cf. the parable of the prodigal son, or (as it should be called) "the parable of the ever-gracious father." But the fact that a good man, **thy servant,** can offer such a prayer indicates what all of us feel we would be justified in doing to ourselves if we were God; and it should deepen our astonishment at his mercy.

For my father and my mother have forsaken me. This man was in bad case; we do not know why. But we can infer much that would scarcely be complimentary to his parents, although fathers have done this very thing for righteousness' sake—or so they thought. The blacked-out name in the family Bible is not a fantasy of the imagination; but it was never a Christian practice, or an act springing from him who "delighteth in mercy." It was the outcome of an unrighteous pride in righteousness.

Lead me in a plain [on a level] path, because of enemies who observe me. Cf. the teaching of Jesus about the city set on a hill (Matt. 5:14-16). Leaders in the church, lay or clerical, are "observed" with critical eyes—eyes that can become hostile if what they see indicates that religion is served by polluted hands.

13 *I had fainted,* unless I had believed to
see the goodness of the LORD in the land of
the living.
14 Wait on the LORD: be of good courage,
and he shall strengthen thine heart: wait,
I say, on the LORD.

13 I believe that I shall see the goodness of the LORD
in the land of the living!
14 Wait for the LORD;
be strong, and let your heart take courage;
yea, wait for the LORD!

A Psalm of David.

28 Unto thee will I cry, O LORD my rock; be not silent to me: lest, *if* thou be silent to me, I become like them that go down into the pit.

A Psalm of David.

28 To thee, O LORD, I call;
my rock, be not deaf to me,
lest, if thou be silent to me,
I become like those who go down to the Pit.

---

2. THE COURAGE BRED BY FAITH (27:13-14)

13-14. Although his sky is still dark, the psalmist ends on a note of courage. So he exhorts himself to maintain hope, for his trust in God is such that he cannot doubt that **in the land of the living**—i.e., in this life—he will experience at God's hand the favor for which he now prays (cf. vs. 10). **Wait for the LORD:** The concluding verse is probably a liturgical formula added later to the psalm in order to point the lesson to be drawn from it.

XXVIII. A PLEA FOR HELP (28:1-9)

This brief psalm is of the same type as Ps. 27. The cause of the psalmist's trouble in this instance, however, is a sickness for which he holds certain godless and deceitful persons responsible (vss. 3-4). His appeal closes with an expression of confidence that the Lord will grant his request; in this respect the psalm follows the characteristic form of a lament.

The date may be pre-exilic, since one must assume that the psalm is older than the addendum (vss. 8-9), which can have been written when there was a king in Israel. If, however, the **anointed** one refers to a high priest or to the whole nation, then it may be argued that the psalm is postexilic.

The meter is 3+2, but a few lines are irregular through faultiness in textual transmission. In vs. 2*c* insert יהוה after the second word; in vs. 4*c* omit תן להם repeated from

---

13-14. ***The Sure Response.***—These verses are rich in suggestion. The first of them is an exclamation. The KJV reads, **Unless I had believed to see the goodness of the LORD in the land of the living.** Something therefore has to be supplied at the beginning of the verse: either **I had fainted, unless I had believed to see** or "God forgive me were I to doubt that I shall see." There is no fundamental difference between the KJV and the RSV. In both cases the writer's faith is either declared or implied. But the KJV is very human, and echoes a latent fear that was seldom stronger than it is today. Is there hope in this world? Is there hope for it? The man of faith answers "Yes." When, how, where, he does not know; he only holds to it that God has "wonders in loom," and that meantime he must do his best to keep the lamps of the world alight. Without that hope, based on the mind and will of God, he would faint indeed, as so many have done, proving by their listlessness how essential for the world is faith in God. But he also recognizes that with faith indeed springing from faith, there must be patience. **Wait for the LORD.** There are great words in this closing verse: **wait, be strong, courage,** all arising from belief in God. But the final word is **wait.**

28:1-9. ***Strength and Shield.***—This psalm is a brief prayer for help in trouble, offered by a man who was perhaps physically ill (vs. 1), perhaps a victim of wrongdoers (vs. 3). It may even be that he was a king (vs. 8) and spoke as the representative of his people (vss. 8-9). The enemies on whom he desires strict **justice** to fall (vss. 4-5) are best understood as national

2 Hear the voice of my supplications, when I cry unto thee, when I lift up my hands toward thy holy oracle.

2 Hear the voice of my supplication,
as I cry to thee for help,
as I lift up my hands
toward thy most holy sanctuary.[f]

[f] Heb *thy innermost sanctuary*

---

vs. 4*a*; vs. 5 is in prose style and probably of secondary origin. Vss. 8-9, which are not a part of the original psalm, are in 3+4 and 4+3 respectively.

1. Appeal to the Lord (28:1-5)

28:1-2. The psalmist opens his prayer by addressing the Lord as his **rock,** a designation used thirty-three times in the O.T. and expressive of the support and strength and defense which the Lord supplies to those who seek him (cf. 18:2; 19:14; 73:26). Unless the Lord answers him, the psalmist sees himself among **those who go down to the Pit,** or better rendered, "those who have gone down to the Pit." As a synonym of Sheol, the word here translated **Pit** (בּוֹר) is literally a cistern, deep and capacious at the bottom and narrow at the top; another synonym (שַׁחַת) also translated "pit" denotes a hole that is meant for a trap. By such terms we see how men of the psalmists' age thought of death and the place of the dead (see Exeg. on 16:9-10). **I lift up my hands toward thy most holy sanctuary:** The psalmist in an attitude of entreaty lifts up his hands toward the holy of holies as the place of the Lord's presence. The postures of prayer in the ancient world were suggested by the attitudes which men assumed in supplicating their earthly superiors. Such expressions as "lifting up the hands" (cf. 63:4; Neh. 8:6), "spreading out the hands" (cf. 143:6; Lam. 1:17), or more specifically "the palms of the hands" (cf. Isa. 1:15; Jer. 4:31), shed light on the customs associated in the O.T. with prayer. To these we must add the references to "bowing down," "kneeling," and "prostrating oneself" in prayer.

---

enemies, although a phrase here and there can be personally applied. There seems to be a pause at the end of vs. 5, for vs. 6 assumes that the prayer has been answered finally and completely. Indeed, so abrupt is the change that some commentators regard vs. 6 as an interpolation, or vss. 6-8 as part of a different song. We get, however, too many of these composite psalms. Abruptness of change is characteristic of Hebrew poetry; and in this case the psalm is a reasonable unity, if it is regarded as written in retrospect. It represents on a small scale the mood of the allies in World War II, from Pearl Harbor to a point just after the Nuremberg trials.

1-2. ***The Lifting Up of My Hands.*****—To thee, O Lord, I call.** This is an appeal to something solid and not to be crushed amid the advancing waves of violence and change, rather than to a "high place" lifted above strife. There are many times in life when we know that it is not God's will that we shall be taken out of the battle to some safe place of isolation. We have to stay in the fight; but we desperately need a fortress of the spirit which we can defend with "sober optimism," and a strength that will enable us to stand fast. We do not pray, "O Lord, make things easy," for we know that "blood, toil, tears, and sweat" are to be our portion; but we do pray for a fixed point and a hardness of soul, given from outside ourselves, which shall be harder than our trials. At such times **my rock** is the only title for the God on whom we call.

Be not deaf to me is a better translation than **be not silent.** There are times when to a sorely tried spirit God seems to be deaf and dumb; both ideas are suggested in the original. The calm irresponsiveness of nature supports the desperate feeling that we are unhelped because God cannot hear, or worse, has assumed a callous deafness. It is only a step from that to the thought that there is no God. In the dreadful silence all that can be done is to go on enduring and to go on supplicating, as in vs. 2. We notice there that the prayers become more urgent. The psalmist remembers **the voice of** [his] **supplication;** once again he becomes the man who cried **to thee for help,** and lifted up his **hands** (the gesture of uttermost appeal) toward God's **most holy sanctuary,** to the place where God must be. Our Lord commended the attitude in the parable of the householder in bed (Luke 11:5-8), and the apostle James emphasized the effectualness of fervent prayer (Jas. 5:16).

3 Draw me not away with the wicked, and with the workers of iniquity, which speak peace to their neighbors, but mischief *is* in their hearts.

4 Give them according to their deeds, and according to the wickedness of their endeavors: give them after the work of their hands; render to them their desert.

5 Because they regard not the works of the LORD, nor the operation of his hands, he shall destroy them, and not build them up.

3 Take me not off with the wicked,
with those who are workers of evil,
who speak peace with their neighbors,
while mischief is in their hearts.
4 Requite them according to their work,
and according to the evil of their deeds;
requite them according to the work of their hands;
render them their due reward.
5 Because they do not regard the works of the LORD,
or the work of his hands,
he will break them down and build them up no more.

3-5. After beseeching the Lord for his attention, the psalmist puts before him his request: **Take me not off with the wicked,** i.e., let me not suffer the violent end that befalls the godless, whom death drags off pitilessly like beasts caught in a net (cf. 10:9; 26:9; 49:14). It appears that the psalmist attributes his ills to the duplicity and treachery of men whom he trusted. He can say of them that they **speak peace with their neighbors, while mischief is in their hearts.** In most psalms of this type the plight of the psalmist is regarded as a divine visitation for which his enemies taunt him, but here the enemies are the agents of his trouble. The psalmist for reasons of caution does not take on his lips the name of the thing which he believes they have employed against him. Was it a spell, a curse, some form of witchcraft (cf. Deut. 18:10-11)? The further definition of

---

Lest . . . I become like those who go down to the Pit. A phrase that may signify sickness to death or death itself. But there is more than one kind of death, and more than one kind of pit. The words may obviously be used arrestingly of the possibility of sinking into moral degradation. It is salutary to remind everybody that this dire possibility remains a possibility for all of us unless we stand on the **rock.** Many a reputable citizen is perilously on the edge of that pit. It is healthful to open his eyes and frighten him.

3-5. ***Save! Requite!***—Now follows the poet's prayer against his enemies; it is a grim prayer for the strict application of the *lex talionis.* They were indubitably an evil lot, speaking **peace with their neighbors, while mischief is in their hearts.** History has often given humanity black instances of that very attitude, and the nemesis that has fallen upon the men who adopted it. Nor is this a description only of national criminals: business life supplies illustrations in plenty, when a man uses unfair methods which will ruin a friend whom he meets daily with "nods, and becks, and wreathèd smiles." [3]

But can a Christian use vs. 4? **Requite them according to their work.** The instinctive answer is "No," remembering the Savior's prayer as they crucified him, "Father, forgive them; for they know not what they do." But what if they know perfectly well what they do? What if for vainglory's sake and the lust of power they deliberately bring untold misery upon the world? Has righteous justice nothing to say or do? The honesty of men's souls recoils from such an idea. We tend to forget the Lord's severity, that he declared it would be better for such men to have a millstone tied round their necks and to be cast into the depths of the sea (Matt. 18:6). We forget that the rock can fall upon the evil, and falling, grind them to powder.

Every great religion must stand for the vindication of law. Christianity would be emasculated if the doctrine of the Atonement were removed from the scheme; and the Atonement at its heart is precisely such a vindication in the loftiest sense. On the other hand, Christianity is the religion of love; and law and love seem to be contrary one to the other. "They have said: but I say unto you" is Christ's ancient challenge to the rigidity of law, understood as the code by which men regulate their relations. But we have to remember that "law" is one of the most difficult words to make precise. It may mean inevitable sequence (as when we speak of the laws of nature), or it may mean that totality of particular rules which men have developed to make society stable, or it may be

[3] Milton, *L'Allegro.*

6 Blessed *be* the LORD, because he hath
heard the voice of my supplications.
7 The LORD *is* my strength and my
shield; my heart trusted in him, and I am
helped: therefore my heart greatly rejoiceth; and with my song will I praise him.

6 Blessed be the LORD!
for he has heard the voice of my supplications.
7 The LORD is my strength and my shield;
in him my heart trusts;
so I am helped, and my heart exults,
and with my song I give thanks to him.

---

the psalmist's enemies in vs. 5 seems to be a gloss, as both its prosaic style and its ill adjustment to the context evidence (cf. Isa. 5:12; Jer. 1:10).

2. THE PSALMIST IS REASSURED (28:6-7)

6-7. The psalmist expresses his assurance that his prayer has been heard. Similar positive words of hope occur at the end of other psalms of this class (cf. 3:8; 5:11-12; 13:5-6). The ground for the confidence of the psalmist may have been a favorable oracle. Some commentators, however, hold that this stanza was added after the psalmist had actually experienced his deliverance, and, following the LXX and Syriac, emend the text of vs. *7cd* to read נעזרתי ויחלף שארי ומלבי אהודנו, "I have been helped, and my flesh revived, and from my heart I give him thanks." The change in the text is scarcely warranted in view of the fact mentioned above.

---

used loosely of the particular laws themselves. It is the first of these which is majestic, if behind the inevitable sequences we see the perfect Will. We hold that there are these sequences in the moral and spiritual realm, and that they can never be set aside except by the introduction of a new cause. Otherwise the moral universe becomes an uncertain and capricious thing and God—if such a universe can have a God—a Being who does not know his own mind.

Now one of these sequences is that "the way of transgressors is hard" (Prov. 13:15). Sin entails penalty. But that penalty may become "loving" if it is a means to free a man from the sequence in which he is caught, the end of which is loss of "life." In any case, the sequence itself is unalterable. "Except ye repent, ye shall all likewise perish" (Luke 13:3). Neither in our thinking nor in our practice must we attempt to evade or belittle this irresistible fact, however somber it be.

It is this conception which gives so great a dignity to human laws. They are imperfect, and in constant need of change. But they are an adumbration of a divine thing; and we are in the divine order when we impose penalty. A "penaltyless" human society would be out of accord wtih the scheme of things, and would therefore perish. A human order must requite men for what they do, because that is what God does in so far as what they do is indicative of what they are. It is socially essential that we demand from each other actions according to the will of God; and if any of us oppose these demands, we must see to it that penalty is exacted relevant in kind and degree to the opposition. It is interesting to note that the law of "eye for eye" was not intended to invite vengeance, but to see that the penalty equaled the crime and no more. Thus the prayer to **requite** is a Christian prayer; but it does not go far enough. While the cross which we lay upon a transgressor must be retributive, we and the transgressor together must try to make it also reformative. The cross of the impenitent thief was retributive only; while that of the penitent was reformative also. The difference was effected by the fact that the cross redemptive was set between them, and one of the transgressors turned to him who hung on it. The sum of the matter is that we must ever vindicate the majesty of law, the great "needs must be" of God; but by sharing in the passion to redeem, must endeavor through our poor human laws to make retribution the source of remaking nearer to the desire of God's heart.

6-9. ***Blessed Be the Lord.***—These verses convey an exultation of thanksgiving which implies that the threatened dangers have passed away. The consecutive phrases of vs. 7 might suggest a meditation: (*a*) **in him my heart trusts;** (*b*) **so I am helped;** (*c*) **my heart exults;** and (*d*) **with my song I give thanks.** Trust as the condition of deliverance, and deliverance following upon trust, at the hands of the Lord who may well be trusted; these lead to an exultant heart, if a man realizes what he is delivered from and what he is delivered to—"dead . . . unto sin, but alive unto God" (Rom. 6:11). And if the **heart exults,** let the lips play their part. It will do others good to hear the songs of the spiritually exultant. Do not let us keep our

8 The LORD *is* their strength, and he *is* the saving strength of his anointed.
9 Save thy people, and bless thine inheritance: feed them also, and lift them up for ever.

A Psalm of David.

29 Give unto the LORD, O ye mighty, give unto the LORD glory and strength.

8 The LORD is the strength of his people,
he is the saving refuge of his anointed.
9 O save thy people, and bless thy heritage;
be thou their shepherd, and carry them for ever.

A Psalm of David.

29 Ascribe to the LORD, O heavenly beings,[g]
ascribe to the LORD glory and strength.

[g] Heb *sons of gods*

3. LITURGICAL CONCLUSION (28:8-9)

8-9. This closing stanza is an addition to the psalm, as the change in meter and in motif indicates. As a prayer for the Lord's anointed and his people, it may have been added when the psalm itself was used to express a lament of the nation or the congregation of Israel. **His anointed:** This phrase is not to be taken as equivalent to "his Messiah." It is applied to a king (cf. 20:6; 132:10, 17; I Sam. 24:6); a high priest (cf. 84:9; Lev. 6:22); the whole people (cf. 105:15). In support of the last application in this instance one may hold that **his people** and **his anointed** are synonyms by virtue of the parallelism. **Be thou their shepherd, and carry them for ever:** The good shepherd finds pasture for his flock and carries the weary (cf. Isa. 40:11; 63:9; Deut. 32:11*b*). So the solicitude of the Lord is figured.

XXIX. THE GOD OF THE STORM (29:1-11)

This psalm celebrates the glory of God in the thunderstorm. For the writer of this hymn it is not enough that the worshipers in the temple and the temple choir should be summoned to extol him who commands the elements. Rather, he calls on the heavenly beings to lead the praises of the Lord's majesty and might. Over the rolling thunder of the storm, which breaks now on the Lebanons and now on the wilderness of Kadesh, and which is echoed in the seven-times repeated *qôl Yahweh* **(the voice of the LORD),** the praises of the celestial choir are heard. With the creatures of the earth the heavenly singers witness the wonderful manifestation of Yahweh's power in the storm, and even more in the awfulness of the thunder (cf. Exod. 19:16; I Sam. 12:17-18; I Kings 19:11-12).

knowledge of the mercy of God to ourselves. If we are delivered, "let the redeemed of the LORD say so" (107:2), and if their saying so takes the form of **song,** so much the better.

It is interesting to notice that vs. 9, **save thy people and bless thine inheritance,** has been incorporated into the *Te Deum,* the noblest and most universal of all hymns of the church. No more striking instance could be given of the capture of the psalms for the worship of Christ.

29:1-11. ***The Glory of the Lord.***—Here is a poet who has no doubt at all that God reveals himself in nature, especially nature in storm. What is seen therefore does not speak concerning itself, but concerning what lies behind it. The storm has no voice, but is a voice, **a voice of the LORD**—a phrase which occurs seven times in seven verses. The verses themselves are descriptions of a storm and its effects.

An interesting comparison and contrast could be drawn between the "nature poetry" of this psalm and, for instance, of the Lake school of poetry in English literature, or the poetry of pantheists. In the psalms God is the fixed point; the upheavals of nature are his direct action. The psalmist is preserved from the "pathetic fallacy," and he is not concerned with the problems created by nature's violence and red claws. Man must simply accept nature's turbulence and be still before its might and terror. If the winds roar destruction, it is the voice of the Lord; if the thunder reverberates, it is the voice of the Lord. Let man worship him and cry, **Glory!**

Such a psalm, expressing so simple, and we

2 Give unto the LORD the glory due unto his name; worship the LORD in the beauty of holiness.

2 Ascribe to the LORD the glory of his name; worship the LORD in holy array.

The writer, however, true to the Hebrew religion, finds more than just a display of the divine omnipotence in the storm. He finds in it a source of comfort and assurance. The God who can work such wonders can guarantee to his people strength and peace, for the God of nature is also the God of history. The psalm was suitable for use at the time of the year when the season of the rains was beginning or had begun.

The psalm seems originally to have consisted of six stanzas or strophes of two lines each. The first, the third, and the sixth are still regular, but the others, because of some faultiness in transmission, exhibit slight irregularities. The meter is 4+4, except in vss. 3-4, 6, 10*a*, which have stichs of three units or beats. In vss. 5-6, 8, 10-11, the second stich of each line, which inverts the order of the first in chiastic form, possibly served as an antiphon and by this means produced the impression of an alternation of earthly with heavenly voices in the rendition of the psalm.

It is generally agreed that the psalm is of early date. Its theme is consonant with the earlier conceptions of Yahweh as a God whose most majestic self-manifestations were made through such phenomena of nature as wind, storm, thunder, and lightning. Certain features of its language may point to northern Israel as its place of origin, e.g., the use of **Sirion** as the name for Mount Hermon, and possibly dialectic elements (cf. יערות, אילות). In this event the psalm would have to be dated prior to 721 B.C. and set along with other vigorous examples of the earlier poetry of the Hebrew people.

In the LXX the Hebrew superscription is supplemented with a note, ἐξοδίου σκηνῆς, which means (cf. Vulg., *in consummatione tabernaculi*) that the psalm was used at that time on the eighth and last day of the feast of Tabernacles. The Talmudic tractate Sopherim assigns it to Pentecost, and this tradition still prevails.

1. Summons to the Celestial Host (29:1-2)

29:1-2. The highest **heavenly beings** are invoked to **ascribe to the LORD glory and strength** (cf. I Chr. 16:28-29). They are called **sons of gods** (cf. Kautzsch, *Gesenius' Hebrew Grammar,* sec. 124*q*). This expression has a long history. We meet it again

would say so naïve, a thought, is not in harmony with our feeling or knowledge. Yet we may be permitted to wonder if the psalmist has not something timeless to say to men. A thunderstorm among mountains is an awe-inspiring spectacle; it speaks of might overwhelming, before which man is puny indeed. If the creature can be so devastating in power, what must the Creator be; maybe God said, "Let there be storms," in order that the crown of his creation should not think too highly of itself. James M. Barrie said that genius "is the power to be a boy again at will." [4] Perhaps it is a sign of religious genius to feel before nature as reverent spirits felt in the childhood of the race. There can well be a real place in the modern pulpit for a sermon or two on storms and thunder, if thereby modern men can be led to catch a hint of the majesty behind the storm. Let the interpreter take the details from his own countryside and from what his hearers have seen for themselves. Let the cedars be oaks or maples; let the hills have local names; and let the plain be near at hand. But let there be no doubt that it is **the voice of the LORD** which he makes men hear, echoing in the mind and conscience as quietly they walk home. A sermon on a psalm like this is futile if it leaves only an impression of a vivid description of a natural happening; but it has worth if it tends even for a moment to make man **ascribe to the LORD glory and strength.**

1-2. *The Call to Worship.*—Here is a threefold appeal to the "heavenly powers," followed by a call to worship. These **mighty** ones, or **sons of gods,** may be the storm forces themselves (but see Exeg.). They are God's ministers (angels) to declare the majesty of his power, as they are doing in the lightning flash and the thunderclap and in the shrieking of the wind. It is a fine dramatic picture: the poet standing with outstretched arms in the midst of the storm, apostrophizing the elements, and so no doubt all living creatures, to make manifest the glory of

[4] *Tommy and Grizel* (London: Cassell & Co., 1900), p. 214.

3 The voice of the LORD *is* upon the
waters: the God of glory thundereth: the
LORD *is* upon many waters.
4 The voice of the LORD *is* powerful; the
voice of the LORD *is* full of majesty.
5 The voice of the LORD breaketh the
cedars; yea, the LORD breaketh the cedars
of Lebanon.
6 He maketh them also to skip like a calf;
Lebanon and Sirion like a young unicorn.
7 The voice of the LORD divideth the
flames of fire.

3 The voice of the LORD is upon the waters;
the God of glory thunders,
the LORD, upon many waters.
4 The voice of the LORD is powerful,
the voice of the LORD is full of majesty.

5 The voice of the LORD breaks the cedars,
the LORD breaks the cedars of Lebanon.
6 He makes Lebanon to skip like a calf,
and Sir'ion like a young wild ox.
7 The voice of the LORD flashes forth flames
of fire.

---

in the Psalter in 89:6. In Deut. 32:8 (cf. versions) they appear as the gods to whom the heathen nations were assigned at the time that the Lord chose Israel for his special possession, but they are inferior to him. Eventually they are included in the class of angels (cf. Job 1:6; Gen. 6:2). But however conceived, it was appropriate to summon them to extol the Lord and to proclaim "the glory proper to him." Since heaven is conceived as a temple, the heavenly beings are robed like the ministering priests of the earthly temple **in holy array.**

2. The Lord Manifests Himself in a Storm (29:3-9)

3-4. The storm begins. **The voice of the LORD is upon the waters:** The psalmist hears the rolling of the thunder as the stormclouds mass themselves over the vast expanse of the Mediterranean (cf. I Kings 18:44). As thunderstorms are rather rare in Palestine, the effect produced by them is all the more impressive: **The voice of the LORD is powerful, . . . full of majesty.**

5-6. The storm breaks in fury over the region of the Lebanons. Wind and lightning shatter the giant cedars that have stood for ages. The earth quakes too before the Lord (Exod. 19:17-18; Isa. 29:6), so that the great mountains seem to skip and dance about **like a calf, and Sirion like a young wild ox.** Sirion is the Sidonian name for snow-capped Mount Hermon (Deut. 3:9). It is derived from a root which means "to shine" or "to glitter" (cf. Arabic *šariya*). By synecdoche the Anti-Lebanon range may here be understood.

7-8. Half a line has been lost in vs. 7, descriptive of the action of the thunder and the lightning, possibly on mighty things like the rocks. As it stands, the truncated verse suggests that the thunder produces the forkings of the lightning. Some, however, would delete the verse as a gloss; others read it with vs. 9.

God's power. We can almost imagine a hearing and an answering in redoubled fury of might, as the storm reaches its zenith.

Worship the LORD in holy array may hint the cleanness of nature in its violence. A storm may be devastating, but it is never sordid. There is an awful purity in nature's wildness. Let every soul bow down in the solemn beauty of adoration.

3-4. ***The Gathering Tempest.***—The storm gathers, and comes on **in force.** It seems to begin in the west, **the voice of the LORD** (seven times repeated) pealing **upon the waters: . . . the LORD . . . upon many waters.** The center approaches from the sea, moving landward its masses of dark cloud seamed with lightning, the roar of it riven open with thunder—all ineffably impressive. Sea and air appear to be combined in a magnificent hostility to the shore.

5-7. ***The Onslaught.***—In vs. 5 the tempest reaches the land; trees bend and break under it, are splintered in pieces (vs. 5*b*), even the strongest and longest lived, like Lebanon's **cedars;** the very hills seem to leap and tremble. The poet goes the length of seeing them quiver **like a calf** when it skips, their highest peak (**Sirion** is Hermon) like a **wild ox.** The fury of the lightning falls upon the earth like the mighty blows of an axe. **The voice of the LORD flashes forth flames of fire.**

8 The voice of the LORD shaketh the wilderness; the LORD shaketh the wilderness of Kadesh.
9 The voice of the LORD maketh the hinds to calve, and discovereth the forests: and in his temple doth every one speak of *his* glory.
10 The LORD sitteth upon the flood; yea, the LORD sitteth King for ever.
11 The LORD will give strength unto his people; the LORD will bless his people with peace.

8 The voice of the LORD shakes the wilderness,
the LORD shakes the wilderness of Kadesh.

9 The voice of the LORD makes the oaks to whirl,[h]
and strips the forests bare;
and in his temple all cry, "Glory!"

10 The LORD sits enthroned over the flood;
The LORD sits enthroned as king for ever.
11 May the LORD give strength to his people!
May the LORD bless his people with peace!

[h] Or *makes the hinds to calve*

In vs. 8 the action of the storm is contemplated as it rolls now over the wilderness. A progress of the storm from north to south is not implied, since storms in Palestine do not follow such a course. **The wilderness of Kadesh** is mentioned as representing the extreme south of the land over against the Lebanons in the extreme north. Roughly it is the wilderness lying between Palestine and Egypt and takes its name from the place mentioned in Num. 34:4.

9. It is probable that vs. 9*ab* originally followed vs. 5. **The voice of the LORD makes the oaks to whirl:** The translation of the KJV is due to the Masoretic misreading of the word **oaks** or "terebinths," the consonants of which are the same as those of **hinds.** Obviously there is no reason why in the circumstances the hinds should be different from other animals. **And in his temple all cry, "Glory!"** Like the heavenly hosts, all the worshipers in the temple are filled with wonder at the might and majesty of the Lord as revealed in the storm.

3. HYMNIC CONCLUSION (29:10-11)

10-11. The storm has ceased. The Lord commands the elements, loosing or restraining them. He **sits enthroned over the flood:** The word **flood** (מבול) refers elsewhere to the flood of Noah's time (cf. Gen. 6:17; 9:11), but here it means the heavenly ocean or flood whose waters are released in the storm (cf. 104:3; Gen. 7:11). To the psalmist the

---

8-9. *Sweeping Away Toward the South.*—The far-off wilderness, as a rule so aridly still, seems shaken by some irresistible hand. The trees yonder in the distance feel the destructive powers of the raging tempest: the **oaks** fall and the **forests** are stripped bare. The imagery is carried more cohesively if we translate vs. 9, **The voice of the LORD makes the oaks to whirl** rather than **the hinds to calve,** though it is true that cattle cast their young in violent storms through fear. Until at last the storm finds its climax in a crash of sound, man's "hallelujah" to the God whose voice it is. **In his temple all cry, "Glory!"**

10-11. *Peace on Earth.*—At this point the psalm completely changes; but in this change its religious strength is found. So far the poet has been a spectator of the tempest from its own level, watching its course from west to east and then south. Now he is raised above it, to see the truth its somber majesty was conveying. What remains is a throne, and what controls is a person.

The LORD sits enthroned over the flood;
The LORD sits enthroned as king for ever.

It makes all the difference to read nature and its violence from the fixed point that all belongs to God and is obedient to his ordering.

Vs. 11 provides for the credo of the preceding verse a suitable benediction. Nature speaks of God's **strength,** the infinite reservoir of which storms are a sign, and is a symbol of the spiritual

A Psalm *and* Song *at* the dedication of the house of David.

30 I will extol thee, O LORD; for thou hast lifted me up, and hast not made my foes to rejoice over me.

A Psalm of David. A Song at the dedication of the Temple.

30 I will extol thee, O LORD, for thou hast drawn me up,
and hast not let my foes rejoice over me.

greatness of God is not a matter of ancient report or tradition, for year by year it is demonstrated before the eyes of men in the storms that visit the land. To this living God, therefore, a prayer for the welfare of **his people** is appropriately addressed in the closing line.

XXX. THANKS BE TO GOD (30:1-12)

In this artistically constructed psalm the author is giving thanks for his recovery from an illness which brought him near death. His joyous mood is set forth in regular and clearly marked stanzas, and the experience through which he passed is vividly portrayed. The result is a beautiful example of the class of hymns to which it belongs.

The psalm falls into two parts, each of which in turn consists of minor divisions. In the first part (vss. 1-5) it is clear not only that the Lord has delivered the psalmist from grievous sickness, but that this visitation came upon him because the Lord had been angry with him. In his joy at recovery the psalmist calls on all who are present with him in the courts of the temple to join in his hymn of praise and thanksgiving to the Lord. In the second part (vss. 6-12) he gives a more detailed recital of his experience. His sin had been overconfidence; he had come to believe that he was secure forever, forgetting that the source of his well-being was God. Then God withdrew from him, and trouble came upon him. In his distress he cried to God, and God in his abundant goodness answered him. So his wailing has been changed into gladness and song; his supplications for healing into participation in the festivities of thanksgiving.

The superscription of the psalm indicates that in the later period of Judaism it was used on the anniversaries of the rededication of the temple by Judas Maccabaeus (164 B.C.). By that time the psalm was interpreted as expressive of the experience of the nation.

The psalm should probably be dated in the postexilic period since in vs. 5 we can note an attempt in the wisdom manner to explain the principle regulative of God's punitory dealings with men. The meter is irregular; this may point to a late date.

strength from which his people can draw according to their need; until at last a strengthened people obtain peace. It is a long journey from the voice of storm to the happy, active quiet of the kingdom of God, for which God is so purposeful that he will storm his way to it, if there is no other means of its accomplishment. He will "overcome the world," with all that that means; so that the last great word is peace.

30:1-12. *Lines Written on Recovery from Serious Illness.*—Although this psalm in Jewish ritual is used at the feast of Dedication as a national song, it surely was entirely personal to its original author. A man had been sick to death; he was now well again, and he gave God the praise. Not only so, but he also records the spiritual benefit obtained through a period of physical ill, giving a touch or two of intimate autobiography. Read vss. 6-7, 8-10, 1-3, 11-12, 4-5 in that order for the sequence of events. In all this the psalmist speaks for every man, if every man will be as candid and humble as he in facing the facts, and as purposeful in obtaining spiritual gain from a time of distress. So does the psalm lie within the experience of all, evoking the thoughts we ought to have if we too have been sick and are again well, and inevitably leading us into the wide realm of recovery from moral ill. Note the parallelism in thought between vss. 1, 4-5 and vss. 11-12, as also between vss. 2-3 and vss. 8-10.

1-3. *Thanksgiving.*—In these verses the poet sings his recovery. They simply state, "Thank God, I am better," with all the emphasis on "thank God." One has an opportunity here to give real meaning to that easily and frequently uttered exclamation by recalling how a religious

2 O LORD my God, I cried unto thee, and thou hast healed me.
3 O LORD, thou hast brought up my soul from the grave: thou hast kept me alive, that I should not go down to the pit.
4 Sing unto the LORD, O ye saints of his, and give thanks at the remembrance of his holiness.

2 O LORD my God, I cried to thee for help,
and thou hast healed me.
3 O LORD, thou hast brought up my soul
from Sheol,
restored me to life from among those
gone down to the Pit.[i]

4 Sing praises to the LORD, O you his saints,
and give thanks to his holy name.

[i] Or *that I should not go down to the Pit*

1. WHY GOD IS TO BE PRAISED (30:1-5)

30:1-3. Thou . . . hast not let my foes rejoice over me: The foes here are not agents of the psalmist's troubles; rather, they are persons who gloat over his unhappy lot or who mock at his faith in God. **Thou hast brought up my soul from Sheol:** His sickness was so desperate that his healing was nothing less than his rescue from the underworld, even from the company of those already in **the Pit,** the lowest part of Sheol.

4-5. Ye saints of his: I.e., all those who, like the psalmist, are faithful to the Lord, the godly men of the community over against the skeptics and cynics. **Give thanks to**

man who is learning from experience may read future purpose into it. A casual "thank God" is one thing; but **I will extol thee, O LORD; for thou hast lifted me up** is another. "I was sick; I am recovered. Why? Because God willed it. Why did he will it? That I might really extol him, not with my words only, but with my deeds. This recovery is another of his endless new chances, and it is a large new chance. I must make it a new beginning. Gratitude alone demands as much. I prayed for recovery. Strange forces of life sprang up in me. Doctors and friends shook their heads; but I am better. I must not forget the urgencies of my mind and spirit in the prayers I said when I was hovering on the brink. I prayed. I must not forget that at least. I am healed; I must not in the days ahead take that for granted. I really did pray then. I cried unto the Lord and he healed me; I must keep up that praying, that a deeper healing may continue. I was very near death, on the very edge of that 'masterful collapse,' almost numbered with those who have gone into the shadows. Let that be a parable to me of my sickness in the soul: I was slipping into a deeper pit in my old, careless days (vss. 6-7*a*). God has brought me up sharp (vs. 7*b*), and in my sickness has been healing me in more senses than one. Wherefore **I will extol thee, O LORD,** with all it implies. So help me God!"

After such a manner an interpreter in quiet meditation may start from almost every phrase and, taking into account its context, move forward into wide and genuine regions of religious intent. The same upward spring may begin from any kind of sickness, not least the sickness of grief and anxiety. If someone recovers from a dangerous illness, it is not only he who should extol the Lord; those who love him have equal reason. It is love that makes life great; but in the trials to which it exposes us it gives noble opportunities for fixing a purpose to extol. If the worst happens, and the beloved is taken from us, we may find that a new healing sets in. God assuages our grief, and makes our loss provide a strange new impulse to stronger living. Even then, sometimes especially then, we find ourselves able to say, more softly but not less firmly, **I will extol thee, O LORD.**

No man can truly learn the devotional and personal psalms unless he will read them devotionally and slowly, letting the heart of long ago speak to his heart. Accuracy and sound scholarship are no doubt essentials for an interpreter, but they are not the only thing needful. An old woman in a cottage with a well-thumbed Bible may be the true authority. Who does not possess such a Bible? There are markings everywhere perhaps, but the two portions where the leaves are loose and yellow from constant reading are the Psalms and the Gospel of John. The owner of that Bible—was she one of God's "musicians who knew"? No doubt she read little at a time; but she meditated, and meditating, found the word of God.

4-5. ***A Treasure for the Devout.***—Vs. 4 demands wider thanksgiving, and vs. 5 gives a reason for the demand in a generalization about God's providential order. The poet asks all the **saints** to sing, or play upon their instruments, like an orchestra—the saints being the favored of God, who develop into people that endeavor to harmonize their lives actively to his will. They are to **give thanks** heartily to God, because

5 For his anger *endureth but* a moment;
in his favor *is* life: weeping may endure for
a night, but joy *cometh* in the morning.
6 And in my prosperity I said, I shall
never be moved.
7 LORD, by thy favor thou hast made my
mountain to stand strong: thou didst hide
thy face, *and* I was troubled.

5 For his anger is but for a moment,
and his favor is for a lifetime.
Weeping may tarry for the night,
but joy comes with the morning.

6 As for me, I said in my prosperity,
"I shall never be moved."
7 By thy favor, O LORD,
thou hadst established me as a strong
mountain;
thou didst hide thy face,
I was dismayed.

---

his holy name: Lit., "memorial," i.e., that by which he is made memorable (cf. Exod. 3:15; Isa. 26:8; Prov. 10:7). **His anger is but for a moment:** His wrath is brief, his goodness lifelong. God by his nature is a God of grace rather than a God of wrath. Gunkel, *et al.*, would read נגע, "stroke," for רגע, **moment,** and translate, "Suffering comes by his anger, but life by his favor." The following line does not warrant the emendation. **Weeping** stays with us for only half a day, and then joyous shouting comes to lodge with us.

2. THE PSALMIST REVIEWS HIS FORMER CONDITION (30:6-10)

6-7. The psalmist tells of his life in the days before he was struck down. He was at ease (Prov. 1:33). But his sense of security led to false confidence: **I shall never be moved,**

---

he is the kind of God he is. And what kind is he? The answer is given in vs. 5, which has become a treasure for the devout. God is such that **his anger is but for a moment, and his favor is for a lifetime.** This rendering keeps the balance more accurately than the KJV, **in his favor is life;** the point being to contrast the temporary character of God's disciplinary pain with the permanence of his tender mercy—a view still further expressed in the unforgettable phrase, **weeping may tarry for the night,** but a shout of **joy comes with the morning,** a translation true to the intention of the original. The image is that of Oriental hospitality which would not refuse shelter to a traveler at eventide, however uncouth or forbidding that traveler might be. **Weeping** is the traveler, knocking at the door for lodging as darkness falls, whom men must needs take in. But next morning? They wake to find him gone, and a cry like a song breaks from their lips. The sun is shining, and what brought the tears has departed.

This is true to a great deal of life. Many of our sorrows are imaginary children of the "night's untruth." Many are brief, and leave behind them a gain that may well make us sing. But it is not always true. The poignancy of grief may be softened, but it sometimes leaves our days dimmed for the rest of our journey; and sometimes it knows no respite till death sets us free. This man was ill and recovered; but his neighbor very likely did not. Are the friends of the latter excluded from the saints who were to give thanks to God's holy name? The poet-king of the Hebrew story, David himself, knew what it was to cry, "O Absalom, my son, my son!" and to entertain a grief that tarried long. The truth is that Hebrew thought here gives only a partial comfort. At the best it insists that joy fills more of this life than does sorrow, and that this is more likely to be true of the God-fearing than of the worldling. The former of these contentions is often contradicted, while the latter may be true only in the spiritual realm. In any case, alike for the God-fearing and the worldling, at the end—so we read here—there yawns **the pit,** where all relation to God ceases. It is a poor, brief optimism. We need the N.T. and God's great summer morning, if we are to use these lovely phrases either for ourselves or for our world; but with life eternal in Christ and the "far-off divine event," we can take them upon our lips with "the rapture of the forward view." From the vantage point of "The last of life, for which the first was made,"[5] the tarrying of sorrow will surely seem but for a moment.

6-7. ***By Thy Favor.***—These verses are autobiographical, and highly significant autobiography at that: **I said in my prosperity, "I shall never be moved."** The psalmist is not the only

[5] Browning, "Rabbi Ben Ezra," st. i.

8 I cried to thee, O LORD; and unto the
LORD I made supplication.
9 What profit *is there* in my blood, when
I go down to the pit? Shall the dust praise
thee? shall it declare thy truth?
10 Hear, O LORD, and have mercy upon
me: LORD, be thou my helper.

8 To thee, O LORD, I cried;
and to the LORD I made supplication:
9 "What profit is there in my death,
if I go down to the Pit?
Will the dust praise thee?
Will it tell of thy faithfulness?
10 Hear, O LORD, and be gracious to me!
O LORD, be thou my helper!"

---

i.e., "I shall never suffer adversity" (cf. 10:6). But the Lord alone was his stay. "Through thy favor I was established on a strong (or fortified) mountain." Read ברצונך העמדתי על־ הררי עז. He had overlooked the fact that the Lord might withdraw from him because of his sins, known or unknown, or because of reasons known only to the Lord himself (cf. Job 10:1-7). So when

thou didst hide thy face,
I was dismayed.

8-9. In the vivid account of this chapter of his life the psalmist introduces the words of his lament when he came under the frown of the Lord. This is an interesting departure from the normal form of a hymn of thanksgiving. **What profit is there in my blood?** His plea is that it is to the advantage of the Lord to preserve his life, for **will the dust praise thee? Blood** is here equivalent to **death** by violence (for its significance see Job 16:18). To the ancient mind a god with none to praise him was an extinct deity.

---

one who has said that. It is the underlying speech of all healthy men for whom things are going well. It is an odd fact that hardly anybody who is well and prosperous really believes he is going to die, or that he may become a complete invalid, or even lose all his money. These painful possibilities, of which the first is a certainty, are either so dim that they seem irrelevant, or are classed among the chances that "cannot happen to us." Our well-being is regarded as obviously God's will in a well-ordered world. Like the poet, we say,

By thy favor, O LORD,
Thou [hast] **established me as a strong mountain;**

but also like the poet, the time may come when we have to put that conviction in the past tense, **thou hadst established me.** Then came the change.

Thou didst hide thy face,
I was dismayed

—a pen picture of many a once prosperous man in any community. Depression years are full of them; so are the hospitals in every year. **Dismayed** is a notable understatement; the fashion of their world passes away. God is not what they thought him to be, nor his ways what they conceived. On the contrary, he will not allow any of his children to conceal their treasures in earthen vessels. If that is where we hide them, soon or late the vessels will be smashed.

8-10. ***If I Go Down to the Pit.***—Next we have the psalmist's prayers when his complacent security was rendered void by illness. They are odd prayers. The gist of them is, "What good will it do thee, O Lord, if thou dost destroy me; I will not be able to serve or praise thee any more in the shadowland of no-life."

What profit is there in my death,
if I go down to the Pit?
Will the dust praise thee?
Will it tell of thy faithfulness?

In this it is implicit that our relation to God is of value to God—an idea that is in keeping with the N.T. Augustine's familiar ejaculation, "Thou hast made us for thyself" is true in more senses than one. It is true for men that they "cannot rest until they rest in thee"; [6] it is true also for God, who has a place in his heart that only man—and each man—can fill. For that reason he sent his Son, that "whosoever believeth in him should not perish." If God is love, he needs his beloveds. How can we think that he would allow death, that last and universal enemy, to destroy us?

[6] *Confessions* I. 1.

11 Thou hast turned for me my mourning into dancing: thou hast put off my sackcloth, and girded me with gladness;
12 To the end that *my* glory may sing praise to thee, and not be silent. O LORD my God, I will give thanks unto thee for ever.

To the chief Musician, A Psalm of David.

31 In thee, O LORD, do I put my trust; let me never be ashamed: deliver me in thy righteousness.

11 Thou hast turned for me my mourning
into dancing;
thou hast loosed my sackcloth
and girded me with gladness,
12 that my soul[j] may praise thee and not be
silent.
O LORD my God, I will give thanks to
thee for ever.

To the choirmaster. A Psalm of David.

31 In thee, O LORD, do I seek refuge;
let me never be put to shame;
in thy righteousness deliver me!

[j] Heb *that glory*

3. THANKSGIVING (30:11-12)

11-12. The answer of the Lord came. Lamentation gave way to glad singing, sackcloth to festal garments. These are not empty words, for the rites in the temple performed at the presentation of votive offerings included dancing and loud songs of praise (cf. 26:6-7; 118:27-28). And so the Lord has done it **that my soul may praise thee and not be silent** (cf. vs. 9).

XXXI. A TRIPLE CRY FOR DELIVERANCE (31:1-24)

In its present form this psalm was meant to serve faithful souls who, encompassed by troubles of one kind or another, sought for words to pour out their complaint to God. Since the situations dealt with are described not too specifically, it must have been employed as a general formula of petition by large numbers of suppliants. Its suitability for such wide use is due to the fact that it is of composite structure, being the result of the combination of three laments, each of which is representative of a distinct class. The first (vss. 1-8) is a so-called protecting psalm (Geo Widengren, *The Accadian and Hebrew Psalms of Lamentation as Religious Documents* [Uppsala: Almqvist & Wiksells, 1937], pp. 135-36); the second (vss. 9-12) is the lament of one who is sick; and the third (vss. 13-18) is the lament of one whose life is menaced by men who prefer false charges against him. In the interpretation of the psalm some difficulty in the identification of the third lament has arisen because of the failure of commentators to note that something like vs. 1 or vs. 9*a* has fallen away or is to be understood at the beginning of vs. 13. Because of this failure vss. 13-18 are thought wrongly by some to be related to

11-12. ***Thanksgiving Renewed.***—Here the thanksgiving is renewed in an even more vivacious strain. **Thou hast turned for me my mourning into dancing. Mourning,** as Ellicott comments, is, lit., "beating the breast";[7] the contrast of that with the movements of a joyous dance is lively and expressive. Even the clothes are changed; **thou hast put off my sackcloth, and girded me with gladness.** It is worth noting how happily the psalm links garments with qualities in a way which has enriched English literature; girding with gladness reminds us of "crowneth thee with loving-kindness and tender mercy" (103:4). As one old preacher said, "If Shakespeare had written that, we should not have heard the end of it."

All this is done that **my soul may praise thee and not be silent.** The KJV rendering, **my glory** for **my soul,** is useful to remind us that a man's soul is the seat of his honor and dignity. That it **may sing praise** is a fine statement of the meaning of God's providential mercy for us as seen in the light of the N.T.

31:1-24. ***Reverie on a Lifetime.***—"This psalm sparkles all through with lamps, which have lighted the steps of men in dark places." So writes John Ker,[8] and justly. Especially he

[7] *O.T. Commentary for English Readers,* IV, 129.

[8] *Psalms in History and Biography,* p. 53; see also pp. 54-56.

2 Bow down thine ear to me; deliver me speedily: be thou my strong rock, for a house of defense to save me.
3 For thou *art* my rock and my fortress; therefore for thy name's sake lead me, and guide me.
4 Pull me out of the net that they have laid privily for me: for thou *art* my strength.

2 Incline thy ear to me,
rescue me speedily!
Be thou a rock of refuge for me,
a strong fortress to save me!

3 Yea, thou art my rock and my fortress;
for thy name's sake lead me and guide me,
4 take me out of the net which is hidden for me,
for thou art my refuge.

---

vss. 1-8, a conclusion which cannot be entertained since vss. 7-8 imply that the deliverance sought in vss. 1-5 has been experienced. Vss. 19-24 are a liturgical hymn of thanksgiving for the Lord's help, vss. 19-20 being for recitation by ministrants, vss. 21-22 by or in the name of the suppliant, and in conclusion vss. 23-24 by the ministrants again.

The psalm seems to be indebted to other writings for some of its material. The opening verses are almost identical with 71:1-3; vs. 8 recalls 18:19; vs. 11 is like 38:11; vss. 13-18 closely resemble Jer. 20:10-12. The phrase **let thy face shine** (vs. 16) occurs in several psalms (67:1; 80:3, 7, 19; 119:135) and in Num. 6:25, all of which are postexilic. These considerations indicate a postexilic date.

The meter is irregular. In the greater number of the lines it is either 3+2 or 3+3; in vss. 4, 11, 21-22 we meet examples of 2+2+2. As has been noted elsewhere, irregularity in meter is not unexpected in psalms of a late date.

1. From Impending Trouble (31:1-8)

31:1-8. In this opening lament the psalmist seems to be seeking assurance of protection not so much from an actual experience of trouble as from one that is impending. Some

---

points to vs. 5, and declares that it contains the dying words of Luther, Knox, and Huss, a formidable trio. Its supreme association, of course, is with our Lord himself, for it gives the seventh and final word from the cross: **Into thy hand I commit my spirit,** the difference being that our Lord added his own great word, "Father." A psalm which comes into the mind of the Sufferer of all sufferers at the moment of death is a psalm to be reverenced.

The historical background is quite uncertain, and so is the type of experience which produced it; for it is a curious amalgam of distress leading to prayer, and of confident trust for the future based upon safety and well-being in the present. Cf. vss. 7-8 with vss. 9-13, and ask what kind of situation a man was in to jump so quickly to **thou hast set my feet in a large room** (vs. 8) from **Have mercy upon me, . . . for . . . mine eye is consumed with grief** (vs. 9). Perhaps the answer is that life is like that, and that the psalm is a reverie on a lifetime in which the most vivid memories of guilt and forgiveness, of misfortune and prosperity, of enemies and of escape from them, come tumbling into the mind one after the other; or it may be a meditation on the history of Israel, at a time when the dominant society was pagan and hated the Israelite who worshiped the God of his fathers in the old God-fearing way. There are resemblances to the writings of Jeremiah. Perhaps he was the author; perhaps he knew the psalm well; or perhaps the author was familiar with his prophecies. For our purposes we can fairly take it as a reverie upon the ups and downs of life, and interpret it out of our own experience.

1-8. *Petition.*—The first verse is said to have been the last utterance of Francis Xavier. What is more significant is that it was chosen to be the last verse of the *Te Deum.* We must be grateful to the old poet who gave us an expression of confident appeal which sounds so often and with such strength in Christian worship. It appears also at the beginning of Ps. 71. Indeed 71:1-3 is the same, with textual variations, as vss. 1-3*a* here.

Vss. 1-4 display that mixture of appeal and confidence which provides such a contrast with some of the following sections. **Be thou a rock** (vs. 2) becomes **Yea, thou art my rock** in vs. 3. But is that not true of life? A man can ask God

5 Into thine hand I commit my spirit: thou hast redeemed me, O LORD God of truth.

6 I have hated them that regard lying vanities: but I trust in the LORD.

7 I will be glad and rejoice in thy mercy: for thou hast considered my trouble; thou hast known my soul in adversities;

8 And hast not shut me up into the hand of the enemy: thou hast set my feet in a large room.

5 Into thy hand I commit my spirit;
thou hast redeemed me, O LORD, faithful God.

6 Thou hatest[k] those who pay regard to vain idols;
but I trust in the LORD.
7 I will rejoice and be glad for thy steadfast love,
because thou hast seen my affliction,
thou hast taken heed of my adversities,
8 and hast not delivered me into the hand of the enemy;
thou hast set my feet in a broad place.

[k] With one Heb Ms Gk Syr Jerome: Heb *I hate*

---

evil omen, some alarming occurrence in his immediate surroundings, or some symptom of disease has been adjudged by him to be a sign that enemies are plotting against him. Therefore he prays, **take me out of the net which is hidden for me.** The metaphor of a **net,** which is drawn from hunting practices (cf. Isa. 51:20), is not uncommonly used by the psalmists for the devices being prepared for their downfall by plotting enemies. In fullness of trust the psalmist commits his "breath" (vs. 5) into the hand of his God, for trust in the Lord is better than trust in the false gods of his enemies. He ends on a note of confidence that his prayer for help has been received. He has been released from his straits, and his **feet** have been **set . . . in a broad place.**

---

for help, and in the next breath remind himself that God is already giving it. Part of the value of going into God's presence in prayer is that God then calls our attention to what we already know and possess. In vss. 2-3 the psalmist uses a striking form of superlative, calling God (in vs. 2) a "rock of a fortress" and (in vs. 3) a "cliff fortress." We must not be afraid of superlatives, either in prayer or in realizing the fact of God. In vs. 4 the translation **pull me out of the net** has more power than **take me out.** It recognizes the gripping quality of the net, and suggests a desire for violent action in order to be rid of it; and violent action is necessary in the case of the netlike entanglements of some of our inner enemies. If we want to be "pulled out" (which may be our one chance), we had better say so to God. The saying of it will reinforce our response, our acquiescence in the pulling. We may need the latter; for some of God's pulling is mercifully merciless.

Into thy hand I commit my spirit. In addition to the reformers mentioned above, Polycarp, Bernard, Henry V, Jerome of Prague, and Melanchthon are said to have had these words on their lips at the end.[9] While we should not take the statement that they were "last words" too literally, we may well believe that they were used to express the final attitude of such men as they faced squarely the fact that they were about to die. Many a minister, in the intimate conversations he has with those who are about to experience an operation from which they may not recover, has heard faithful men so acknowledge their trust. But let it now be always in the form in which Jesus used it; there is for us the prefix "Father."

It is a remarkable fact that no Christian preacher would think of using this text; always he would take the words from the lips of our Lord. If he did start from the psalm, he would inevitably find his way to the word from the cross, pointing out the enlargement made by Jesus. All that the psalmist meant was that he committed his life to God, confident that he would escape *from* physical death; Jesus committed himself to God *in* death. His trust was gloriously vindicated in the Resurrection; but on the cross his splendor is his complete submission to the will of God in any and every experience, including death. It leads into a new realm of religion, and is an instance of the difference Christ has made in the psalms. He it is who is the light of their light.

The second clause of the verse should read "thou wilt redeem me," rather than **thou hast redeemed me;** and **O LORD God of truth** is

[9] Ellicott, *op. cit.*, IV, 130.

9 Have mercy upon me, O LORD, for I am in trouble: mine eye is consumed with grief, *yea,* my soul and my belly.

10 For my life is spent with grief, and my years with sighing: my strength faileth because of mine iniquity, and my bones are consumed.

11 I was a reproach among all mine enemies, but especially among my neighbors, and a fear to mine acquaintance: they that did see me without fled from me.

9 Be gracious to me, O LORD, for I am in distress;
my eye is wasted from grief,
my soul and my body also.
10 For my life is spent with sorrow,
and my years with sighing;
my strength fails because of my misery,[l]
and my bones waste away.

11 I am the scorn of all my adversaries,
a horror[m] to my neighbors,
an object of dread to my acquaintances;
those who see me in the street flee from me.

[l] Gk Syr: Heb *iniquity*
[m] Cn: Heb *exceedingly*

---

2. FROM BODILY SICKNESS (31:9-12)

9-12. Here we meet the lament of one who has been afflicted by disease. He is utterly undone (vs. 9). His suffering has been of long standing. **My life is spent with sorrow, and my years with sighing** (cf. Jer. 20:18). All men, friends and adversaries alike, shun him as one under a curse of God, an object of horror (cf. 38:11; 88:18). In vs. 11 read מרא **(horror)** for מאד **(exceedingly).** He feels himself forgotten, **passed out of mind like one who is dead.** This lament, like Ps. 88, ends without note of hope.

---

better rendered **O LORD, faithful God.** "The Faithful God"—an idea constant in the psalms; "The God Who Does Not Change His Mind": such subjects readily occur to the interpreter; the natural and the spiritual world alike provide endless evidence of their truth. So does history. The sequences in the lives of Antiochus Epiphanes and Hitler are identical. Inasmuch as so many of the psalms are thought to be due to experiences in the Maccabean period, the reader should acquaint himself with the story of that particular Antiochus. He is a highly modern warning.

Vss. 6-8 confront us with the moods of escape and well-being. The poet is now remembering victorious days. In vs. 6 **thou hatest** is preferable to **I have hated.** The psalmist contrasts his attitude to God with that of the pagan society around him. A provocative idea is found here. **Those who pay regard to vain idols** are paying regard to **lying vanities.** Put these in modern terms. What are our **lying vanities?** Note particularly the adjective. It is bad enough to regard as important things that have no real value: but it is worse to allow ourselves to be swindled by them. Many of the things we strive for promise "life" or "rest" or "happiness," which are the precise gifts they cannot provide. On the contrary, all that they bring are "mornings after," long mornings sometimes. Behind so much of our striving lies a philosophy of life that is purely pagan. "The fool" in modern dress may say that "there is no God"; in fact he is worshiping an ancient one. Baal is alive in the land again; one of his many temples is the divorce court, where his congregation overflows.

On the other hand, there are many now, as in the days of the psalmist, who have not bowed the knee to him, nor have their lips kissed him (I Kings 19:18); and these still find themselves standing **in a broad place** (vs. 8; cf. Pss. 11:1-7; 18:19). Observe the contrast between (*a*) **lying vanities** and **thou**—the alternate masters—and (*b*) the results of the two choices, **shut . . . up into the hand of the enemy** on the one hand, and **my feet in a broad place** on the other. It is a universal fact that sensuality means spiritual imprisonment, while spiritual ascendancy means freedom. The image of being **shut . . . up into the hand** is arresting; a slave of evil seems gripped by an active, personal malignity, which drags him to the troughs of the swine against what he calls his will.

9-13. ***Lament.***—In vss. 9-13 is a story of sorrow told in poignant images. The writer leaves nothing unsaid to give an impression of the darkness of his way. **My eye is wasted from grief;** or, as we say, "I cry my eyes out." **My soul and my body also;** his vital energies and

12 I am forgotten as a dead man out of mind: I am like a broken vessel.
13 For I have heard the slander of many: fear *was* on every side: while they took counsel together against me, they devised to take away my life.
14 But I trusted in thee, O LORD: I said, Thou *art* my God.
15 My times *are* in thy hand: deliver me from the hand of mine enemies, and from them that persecute me.

12 I have passed out of mind like one who is dead;
I have become like a broken vessel.
13 Yea, I hear the whispering of many —
terror on every side! —
as they scheme together against me,
as they plot to take my life.

14 But I trust in thee, O LORD,
I say, "Thou art my God."
15 My times are in thy hand;
deliver me from the hand of my enemies and persecutors!

---

3. From Whispering Enemies (31:13-18)

13-18. In these verses is voiced the petition of one who is persecuted by false accusers who plot against his life. He is the victim of a **whispering** campaign, "words that glide along smoothly." But **my times are in thy hand:** The word rendered **times** is variously understood. It may be the equivalent of "lot" or "fate" (cf. Isa. 33:6), but more probably it is used here in the sense of "assize" or "time set for rendering judgment on a case" (cf. Eccl. 8:5; Job 24:1). The Lord will be both judge and defender of the suppliant. **Let thy face shine on thy servant:** "Mayst thou look with favor on thy servant." A smiling countenance is the sign of a favorable disposition to the one toward whom it is

---

his physical frame are worn down, a thing that happens if a man is so badly hurt that he loses the will to live. Nor is it any brief or surface trouble that is upon him: **My life is spent with sorrow, and my years with sighing.**

Is it possible to conceive that this man is the same one who wrote vss. 6-8, and that his years of grief followed his years of happy security? Surely it is. Bereavement can darken a life all the more because of the gladness which love had previously brought. The greater the joy, the blacker the subsequent misery. Memory, instead of enhancing life, torments it; for "sorrow's crown of sorrow is remembering happier things."[10] Moreover, real grief seems perpetual while we experience it; the hours and the days are leaden-footed, and the happy years seem to belong to some other life. Generations that have paid the price of war can well understand precisely what this poet is saying.

Vss. 11-13 give with painful accuracy one effect of overwhelming grief. It may be that the writer is describing the results of his own sin; but his words are equally applicable to the effects of sorrow, if a man allows himself to be submerged in it. A prisoner of grief becomes shut away from society. **Those who see me in the street flee from me.** The spectacle of a numbed, silent mourner who dwells apart, desiring no company but his own thoughts, "hugging his misery," as we say, is not uncommon; and he tends to become a **scorn.** Everybody grows impatient with one who is immersed in his grief permanently; and indeed he is a weakling. The phrase in vs. 12 is suggestive: I have become **like one who is dead.** We all know people who are discarded by society because they cast a gloom wherever they go. Ordinary folk do not invite death's-heads to their houses. The result is that such persons often imagine that they are surrounded by positive enemies; they hear **whispering . . . on every side.** Probably the original situation was that of a pious Jew surrounded by worldlings who not only held political power and might but used it against him; the description, however, fits with startling accuracy the case of a "grief neurotic." Psychiatrists would recognize every phrase.

14-18. ***Recovery.***—Notice the reassertion of the will. **But I trust** is the first step. There is a great deal of will in trusting, especially in the midst of sorrow. "I trust, and on good grounds; for I have seen God's mercies in days past. I will not allow this sorrow to slay my soul. I trust, I tell you." So a man may speak to himself; and then lift his eyes to the object of trust. For trust implies an object, and re-creative trust demands an object that is personal. Trust in "the ultimate decency of things" is not enough; "decent" is precisely what things seem not to be

[10] Tennyson, "Locksley Hall."

16 Make thy face to shine upon thy servant: save me for thy mercies' sake.
17 Let me not be ashamed, O LORD; for I
have called upon thee: let the wicked be
ashamed, *and* let them be silent in the grave.
18 Let the lying lips be put to silence;
which speak grievous things proudly and
contemptuously against the righteous.
19 *Oh* how great *is* thy goodness, which
thou hast laid up for them that fear thee;
which thou hast wrought for them that trust
in thee before the sons of men!
20 Thou shalt hide them in the secret of
thy presence from the pride of man: thou
shalt keep them secretly in a pavilion from
the strife of tongues.

16 Let thy face shine on thy servant;
save me in thy steadfast love!
17 Let me not be put to shame, O LORD,
for I call on thee;
let the wicked be put to shame,
let them go dumbfounded to Sheol.
18 Let the lying lips be dumb,
which speak insolently against the righteous
in pride and contempt.

19 O how abundant is thy goodness,
which thou hast laid up for those who fear thee,
and wrought for those who take refuge in thee,
in the sight of the sons of men!
20 In the covert of thy presence thou hidest them
from the plots of men;
thou holdest them safe under thy shelter
from the strife of tongues.

---

turned. **Let the wicked be put to shame** and in their discomfiture suffer the fate which they had in mind for the psalmist (cf. I Kings 8:31-32). For metrical reasons omit עַל־צַדִּיק עָתָק, **insolently against the righteous.**

4. THANKSGIVING FOR THE LORD'S GRACIOUS RESPONSE (31:19-24)

19-24. Those who have been delivered from such troubles as are reflected in the preceding laments join in words of praise and thanks to the Lord for his goodness to

---

when we are in the grip of overpowering grief. **I trust in thee, O LORD** is a different matter. We may discern a friend coming to our help, although we are outnumbered, with nothing but a forlorn hope; then we are ourselves again. Vs. 15 is the critical verse: **My times are in thy hand.** When a man can say that, he is recovered. Questions of predestination apart, he who would be the master of his fate must believe in the supreme Disposer of all events, he who makes "all things work together for good to them that love" him (Rom. 8:28). The Calvinist may have overstrained his logic; but the boast was not unjustified that "a Calvinist was never a coward." No listless sitting down under misfortune for him. On the contrary, the worse things were, the more firmly he

> . . . grasped his rusty sword
> And cocked his tattered feather to the glory of the Lord,

gaining ever new confidence in the hand that controlled his times. The remainder of the section is all prayer, and vigorous prayer at that. The company to which this man belonged were good haters; they lived in a moral world of black and white and had no knowledge of grays. **Let the wicked . . . go dumbfounded to Sheol** is virile, but not noticeably Christian. If, however, we think of the enemies as spiritual—glooms, suspicions, inertia, etc.—we could do with more of the attitude these verses indicate. The "have at you" spirit against our own weaknesses should always be encouraged. There is no better place for them than the land of forgetfulness, where they are dumbfounded and their voices fade off into silence. "You are a victim of injustice; you are broken; you are down and out." The proper response to that whispering in the soul is "liar," in the name of the Lord.

19-21. ***Confidence.***—Comes now the happy ending. The poet surely was an old man, writing from the vantage point of one who knows the whole story; a historian after the war's close. The verses are exultantly serene, breathing peace after storm. But one point should especially be noticed. The poet talks of himself

21 Blessed *be* the LORD: for he hath showed me his marvelous kindness in a strong city.

22 For I said in my haste, I am cut off from before thine eyes: nevertheless thou heardest the voice of my supplications when I cried unto thee.

23 O love the LORD, all ye his saints: *for* the LORD preserveth the faithful, and plentifully rewardeth the proud doer.

24 Be of good courage, and he shall strengthen your heart, all ye that hope in the LORD.

21 Blessed be the LORD,
for he has wondrously shown his steadfast love to me
when I was beset as in a besieged city.
22 I had said in my alarm,
"I am driven far[n] from thy sight."
But thou didst hear my supplications,
when I cried to thee for help.

23 Love the LORD, all you his saints!
The LORD preserves the faithful,
but abundantly requites him who acts haughtily.
24 Be strong, and let your heart take courage,
all you who wait for the LORD!

A Psalm of David, Maschil.

32 Blessed *is he whose* transgression *is* forgiven, *whose* sin *is* covered.

A Psalm of David. A Maskil.

32 Blessed is he whose transgression is forgiven,
whose sin is covered.

[n] Another reading is *cut off*

them. **In the covert of thy presence:** Read כנפיך for פניך, "In the covert of thy wings." **Under thy shelter,** i.e., in the temple, where they have sought and found deliverance. Therefore,

Be strong, and let your heart take courage,
all you who wait for the LORD!

XXXII. THE FRUITS OF PENITENCE (32:1-11)

This is the second of the penitential psalms (Pss. 6; 32; 38; 51; 102; 130; 143), which are often recited or sung in the Lenten season. In type it belongs to the wisdom psalms, because its purpose is to give instruction on how men should act when sickness

hardly at all; he talks about God, **O how abundant is thy goodness, which thou hast laid up for those who fear thee. . . . In the covert of thy presence thou hidest them . . . ; thou holdest them safe under thy shelter.** Thou, thou, thou, all the time. The psalmist is serene because at last he is persuaded who is in control, for his eyes have seen God's salvation. Wherefore, **Blessed be the LORD.**

23-24. ***Summons.***—The result is that he can call upon the **saints** everywhere to **love the LORD.** The psalm ends on a note of complete assurance, with a call to courage for those who come after him. **Be strong,** he cries; there is no place for the weakness of the fainthearted. It is the very word of one of the lionhearted of a later day: "Finally, my brethren, be strong in the Lord" (Eph. 6:10).

The interpreter would not be far wrong if he took this psalm as a life story, written in retrospect at eventide, and drew a parallel between its message and that of Ps. 23. Both begin in confidence, recording first the sunny hours; both go on to the experience of life's dark defiles; both are able to remember the generous good that followed trial; both are splendidly confident about the end. The two psalms are in form as different as can be, and their writers must have been very different men, the writer of this psalm being the more virile in intelligence and having had a harsher way to tread. But their word is the same: Trust God, and be afraid no more. Let your own experience be his vindication.

32:1-11. ***A Man Made New.***—If any psalm is to be taken in a purely spiritual sense, this is the one. It was a favorite of Augustine, who is reported to have had it written on the wall opposite his bed in his last sickness. Luther put it in his list of Pauline psalms, along with

2 Blessed *is* the man unto whom the LORD imputeth not iniquity, and in whose spirit *there is* no guile.

2 Blessed is the man to whom the LORD
imputes no iniquity,
and in whose spirit there is no deceit.

is visited upon them. It is therefore an interesting example of the attitude of some faithful souls to this vexed problem. With it one should read Pss. 49; 73 in order to see other kinds of teaching about God's dealings with the righteous in bodily affliction.

The psalm does not reach the higher spiritual levels of the Psalter since it reflects the common opinion held throughout the ancient Near East with reference to the relation of all sickness to sin. It has its counterparts in the religious literature of Babylonia and Assyria. The psalmist had little in common with the spirit of the author of the book of Job, who had the courage to rise up and contend against a false conception of the meaning of human pain.

The didactic nature of the psalm is indicative of a late date. The interest in instruction about the right way (vs. 8) and the use of words such as אשרי (vss. 1-2), שכל, ירה, יעץ, בין (vss. 8-9), show the affinity of the psalm with the wisdom writings. Late elements in the vocabulary, e.g., זו (vs. 8) and בלום (vs. 9), also point in the same direction. The meter in vss. 1-7 is a mixture of 3+2 and 2+2. The latter is met in vss. 5-6*a*, 7*b*. In the concluding lines (vss. 8-11) the meter is 4+3. Variety in a metrical pattern is not unexpected in a late psalm. Enjambment is also unusually conspicuous in the lines (cf. vss. 2, 5-6).

1. Blessedness of the Penitent Sinner (32:1-2)

32:1-2. The psalmist begins in a joyous strain. Yet in his expressions of gladness there are to be heard the echoes of past trouble. **Blessed is he whose transgression is forgiven:** "Happy" is a better rendering than **blessed** (see Exeg. on 1:1). All good things in life attend him who is rid of the thing that turns God against men. The psalmist gives force to his concept of sin by using four words, each of which expresses a special aspect of it. **Transgression** (פשע) implies willful disobedience to a divine command; **sin** (חטאה) is to miss the thing to be aimed at in respect of right or duty, and arises through lapses of various kinds; **iniquity** (עון) here is guilt unexpiated; **deceit** (רמיה) means in the context self-deception, the means by which one tries to excuse or palliate his offenses and so to evade the obligation to clear oneself of guilt. Sin in whatever form it appears must be "lifted away," "covered over," "canceled from the records of God." None can mistake his meaning.

Pss. 57; 130; 143, all penitentials, which he declared to be the best. Such a different man as Isaak Walton delighted in it, finding in vs. 2 the ideal of his life: **Blessed is the man . . . in whose spirit there is no guile.**[1]

The man who wrote the psalm knew what he was talking about. He himself had experienced "sin's disgust" and the necessity for a man to face his own dreary facts. He knew the pain of the liberating process. He also knew the reality of forgiveness, and had drawn deep breaths of relief from the bondage of sin's fear; and he realized the nature of the easy yoke that in his new life of release was placed upon him. It is the psalm of a man made new.

1-2. ***Pardon and Cleansing.***—These verses afford a picture of one who is possessed of "saving health." Note the dominating word **blessed.** Its use in scripture is highly suggestive, going far beyond happiness into peace and freedom. Here is the emotive result of being what God meant us to be. Swiftly the conditions are laid down. First, forgiveness; second, the forgetfulness of forgiveness on the part of the forgiver—the **sin is covered;** third, the sense that nothing stands against us, even in the unforgiving region of law—for **the LORD imputes no iniquity. Imputes** rightly conveys the idea of menace. *Pereunt et imputantur* is a motto sometimes graved on sundials, indicating that the hours pass away, but still are "cast up in our teeth"; "the unforgiving minute" in Kipling's "If." The psalmist, on the other hand, teaches us that in God's mercy that shadow on the spirit is removed. "I forgive you, but I can never forget" is no word of God's. He does both. Fourth, as a result of God's generosity, there is

[1] Ker, *Psalms in History and Biography*, p. 59.

3 When I kept silence, my bones waxed old through my roaring all the day long.
4 For day and night thy hand was heavy upon me: my moisture is turned into the drought of summer. Selah.
5 I acknowledged my sin unto thee, and mine iniquity have I not hid. I said, I will confess my transgressions unto the LORD; and thou forgavest the iniquity of my sin. Selah.

3 When I declared not my sin, my body wasted away
through my groaning all day long.
4 For day and night thy hand was heavy upon me;
my strength was dried up[o] as by the heat of summer. *Selah*

5 I acknowledged my sin to thee,
and I did not hide my iniquity;
I said, "I will confess my transgressions to the LORD";
then thou didst forgive the guilt of my sin. *Selah*

[o] Heb obscure

2. SIN ACKNOWLEDGED AND FORGIVEN (32:3-7)

3-4. The psalmist then records his experience. Once he became very ill. According to the settled opinion of the times, he was guilty of some sin, else sickness would not have come near him. But he persuaded himself that no sins could be charged against him. So he groaned and wasted away, but still no word of confession left his lips. **I declared not my sin:** He kept silent, and the longer he kept silent the worse his sickness grew. **Day and night thy hand was heavy upon me:** By the fever of the disease **my strength was dried up,** lit., "my heart was changed to my ruin" (*leshuddî*) or "my life sap [*leshādhî*] was changed," renderings which reflect an uncertain text.

5. In the end he gave way and was ready to admit that he was a sinner. He sought after some sin which he must have committed, found it, and acknowledged it to the Lord. Then **thou didst forgive the guilt of my sin,** i.e., the Lord removed the sickness which was the penalty for the guilt.

not only pardon but cleansing, and the sinner becomes a man purged from inner falsehood, a man **in whose spirit there is no guile.**

3-4. ***Spiritual Malaise.***—Here is described the state of spiritual malaise, to which all flesh is heir. Great revival movements from Savonarola to Moody have shown how true it is to life—not least to apparently respectable life. The poet seems to have been well regarded by everybody; there is no mention of any enemies as in other psalms. His foe is his self-knowledge. He knows, if no one else does, his own pet sin and his weakness in temptation and his fear of records that are plain to him and might leap to light for anybody to see. The contrast between what he is and what he seems to be tears him to pieces; his "soul fever" affects his body like a physical illness. Yet he is not without God. Later on he perceives that his misery was part of the healing process. Any man who would plead with the spiritually unhappy should specially note the statement **thy hand was heavy upon me.** The sufferer thought in his distress that he was outside God; whereas the distress itself was God's mercy, driving him to the place of healing. It can no doubt be "a fearful thing to fall into the hands of the living God" (Heb. 10:31), but it is a worse thing to fall out of them. It is better to be disciplined than to be left to rot (on this point cf. D. H. Lawrence's poem, "The Hands of God," and the fifty-seventh sermon of that tremendous preacher, John Donne).

5-9. *Confess and Be Saved.*—In vs. 5 is given us the turning point; and it is very simple. The spiritually distressed decides to be honest. **I acknowledged my sin to thee, and I did not hide my iniquity.** He confesses, and is a play-actor with God no more.

A subject of large concern is opened here. What are we to make of confession? The writer of this psalm puts heavy weight upon it; indeed, it is the only action which he takes. "Confess and be saved" seems to be his gospel. It is true that his confessor is God and God only; but we are aware how difficult it is to make that inner confession an uprooting thing. The essence of it is to realize ourselves as sinners, with all that sin means of spiritual putrefaction. *Intelligentia prima est ut te noris peccatorem,*

6 For this shall every one that is godly pray unto thee in a time when thou mayest be found: surely in the floods of great waters they shall not come nigh unto him.

7 Thou *art* my hiding place; thou shalt preserve me from trouble; thou shalt compass me about with songs of deliverance. Selah.

8 I will instruct thee and teach thee in the way which thou shalt go: I will guide thee with mine eye.

9 Be ye not as the horse, *or* as the mule, *which* have no understanding: whose mouth must be held in with bit and bridle, lest they come near unto thee.

6 Therefore let every one who is godly
offer prayer to thee;
at a time of distress,[p] in the rush of great waters,
they shall not reach him.
7 Thou art a hiding place for me,
thou preservest me from trouble;
thou dost encompass me with deliverance.[q] *Selah*

8 I will instruct you and teach you
the way you should go;
I will counsel you with my eye upon you.
9 Be not like a horse or a mule, without understanding,
which must be curbed with bit and bridle,
else it will not keep with you.

[p] Cn: Heb *at a time of finding only*
[q] Cn: Heb *shouts of deliverance*

6-7. The psalmist perceived that all the time he had been foolish and stubborn in his unwillingness to admit his sin. But now with his restoration to health he enjoys what he believes to be the blessings of confession, and he proceeds to moralize on his experience. The context suggests that in vs. 7 we read "him" for **me** in each instance.

3. The Wisdom and Joy of the Righteous (32:8-11)

8-9. The psalmist turns to those who need instruction about the way of life, particularly to the young and inexperienced, and urges them to learn the lesson of his mistakes. **I will instruct you and teach you:** Better rendered, "I will give you wise teaching." Read איעצך and translate vs. 8*b*, **I will counsel you. With my eye upon you,** i.e., with the deep concern of a friendly teacher. **Be not like a horse or a mule:** Read the singular תהי, i.e., "be thou not." The lesson he would teach is that one should at the first onset of sickness make a confession of sin and so escape the suffering that is designed to compel submission (cf. Job 11:13-20).

---

as Augustine put it. Really to know oneself a sinner is the beginning of wisdom; but how are we to put full content into that word "know"? Ordinary folk are lame and halt spiritually, and need the help of a crutch; large segments of the Christian society have it provided in the confessional. In monasteries communal confession was found helpful; and in modern Protestantism the development of "counseling" has its base in a recognition of the simple, human need of "unburdening the soul" to somebody who can obviously hear, understand, and pity. Every pastor who has the confidence of his people has plenty of experience of confessing penitents. Evidently there is a task here which the church cannot evade. At least we can say, "All may, some should, none must." At the same time we must remember that the ultimate confession is to God; that there are matters which are for his ears alone; and that if Christ's ministers are to be the confidants of men's souls, they must take great heed to their own.

The poet is bound therefore by his own experience to call upon all men who are godly to cultivate and practice the habit of prayer (vss. 6-7). Men who are **godly** in this connection means men who acknowledge that they are still in the hands of God, recognizing action on their behalf even in their troubles. Such men will find that though life seems but a meeting place with "overwhelming floods," they will not be engulfed (yet cf. Matt. 9:13*b*).

So is the psalmist bound over also to the task of instruction. The text of vss. 8-9 is confused, but the general sense is clear enough. We are

10 Many sorrows *shall be* to the wicked: but he that trusteth in the LORD, mercy shall compass him about.

11 Be glad in the LORD, and rejoice, ye righteous: and shout for joy, all *ye that are* upright in heart.

10 Many are the pangs of the wicked;
but steadfast love surrounds him who trusts in the LORD.
11 Be glad in the LORD, and rejoice, O righteous,
and shout for joy, all you upright in heart!

33 Rejoice in the LORD, O ye righteous: *for* praise is comely for the upright.

33 Rejoice in the LORD, O you righteous!
Praise befits the upright.

10-11. In the closing strophe the writer points his lesson by contrasting the lot of the **righteous** with that of the **wicked.** The righteous have good cause to join with the psalmist in songs of praise to the Lord.

XXXIII. A Hymn to the Congregation (33:1-22)

33:1-22. In form this psalm is a liturgical hymn of praise to the Lord as the providence of the world and the defender and savior of his faithful people. In content it shows affinity with the didactic or wisdom type of psalms (cf. vss. 16-19). It is probable that the number of verses (twenty-two) was meant to accord with the number of the letters of the alphabet (cf. Pss. 38; 103; Lam. 5).

The psalm, exclusive of the opening (vss. 1-3) and the closing (vss. 20-22) strophes, deals with two principal themes, God's work in creation and God's work in history. The two themes are covered in three sections, of which the subject of the first (vss. 4-9) is the **word of the LORD;** that of the second (vss. 10-12), **the counsel of the LORD;** and that of the third, **the eye of the LORD.** The opening and closing strophes may have been sung or recited by a priest, and the three sections which compose the body of the psalm by a choir or body of singers; between the parts the whole congregation may have loudly proclaimed their praise with voice and instruments of music (cf. vss. 1-3). The body of the psalm can be subdivided into strophes of about equal length.

It is noticeable that in the first part the storing of the waters from which the rain descends is given prominence (vs. 7), and in the third part the saving of the people from hunger and pestilence. These two interests may together suggest that the occasion of the psalm was the season when the advent of the rain was being anxiously looked for.

---

not to be **like a horse or a mule** which needs a hand upon the reins and a bit in the mouth to compel obedience. A forgiven man should respond to a glance from his master's eye, because he is watching the master and is desirous within to obey. The important change is in the region of desire, where the main wish now is to please him who has treated us so well. Pardon should beget gratitude, and gratitude love, with its expulsive power. Mere rules and regulations, sourly obeyed, are not enough; henceforward we are not to be "under the law, but under grace" (Rom. 6:14). Above all, we must not compel God to use the weapons of tribulation to drive us to him. He ought not to have to use them at all, if we did not so constantly wait till affliction hits before turning to him.

10-11. ***Appeal.***—The psalm ends in a general statement and appeal. **Many are the pangs of the wicked;** and while wickedness, unhealed and unresisted, remains, the pangs are simply pangs. But even so, they are evidences that we are still in the hands of God. When a man realizes that, and trusts in him who ordains it, he finds that goodness surrounds him. The pangs are part of the whole, for they are driving him home. They may not deliver him from trouble, but they can bring him to peace.

Wherefore, **be glad . . . and shout for joy.** There is a good deal about this kind of shouting in the psalms. It is "the shout of them that triumph," being forgiven. Our world today would be richer for hearing more of it.

33:1-22. ***The God of Creation and History.***—This is a psalm of national thanksgiving and praise to God as creator and protector of his people; as the originator and the moral factor. Vss. 1-3 are a general invitation to praise; vss.

2 Praise the LORD with harp: sing unto him with the psaltery *and* an instrument of ten strings.

3 Sing unto him a new song; play skilfully with a loud noise.

2 Praise the LORD with the lyre,
make melody to him with the harp of ten strings!
3 Sing to him a new song,
play skilfully on the strings, with loud shouts.

The date of the psalm is postexilic. The universalism of Second Isaiah is reflected in vss. 8, 10, 13-14, as also the Isaianic conception of the inevitability of the divine purposes (cf. Isa. 46:10; 51:6, 8) in vs. 11. The "alphabetizing" and the moralizing, noted above, are associated with psalmody in its later period. The spirit of the psalm manifests an approach to that of the still later Pss. 146–147. The kings of whom the psalmist speaks (vs. 16) are foreign kings. Israel's hopes are not for national triumphs, but for food and protection. The righteous and the upright are the Lord's people, and in patience they wait for the Lord. The general setting of the psalm does not conform to pre-exilic conditions.

The writer, however, is acquainted with the requirements of good poetical form. The symmetry of the strophes and the parallelism of the lines exhibit careful artistry. The meter is almost uniformly 3+3, with the exception of vss. 8, 10-12, 16, in which there are stichs of four units or stresses.

1. THE CALL TO PRAISE THE LORD (33:1-3)

33:1-3. The superscription has been lost in transmission. The psalm was to be sung to the accompaniment of a variety of stringed instruments (for a description of these instruments see Intro., pp. 5-6). **Sing . . . a new song:** The **song** is new either because its contents are new, the occasion is new, or because it is a fresh composition. The latter is probably the meaning in this instance.

4-9 form the section praising the Creator, and vss. 10-19, the section praising the God of history, on the occasion no doubt of some deliverance experienced by the Jews; while vss. 20-22 conclude the thanksgiving with an expression of hope and trust and a firm statement of the psalmist's willingness to wait, justified by the evidence of the past. The interpreter will not find any ideas here that are not to be found elsewhere in the Psalter; but he will find some suggestive expressions of the poet's confidence which will prove memorable, opening upon large areas of evangelical truth.

1. ***Praise Befits the Upright.***—Note the word **upright,** i.e., the steadfast fearer of God. Praise also befits the returned prodigal, the man who has badly needed forgiveness and has received it. The mouth of a man who has been given a new chance should be filled with thanksgiving, obviously. But so should the mouth of the good citizen; for his good citizenship is the outcome of God's grace, a thing he is apt to forget. The **upright,** like the open sinner, must keep his eyes fixed on God, not on his own uprightness, or he will cease to praise. "I thank thee, that I am not as other men are" is not praise, but self-glorification. An analysis of the word **praise** and the word **upright** would be profitable.

2. ***With the Lyre and the Harp.***—The problem of church music is a living one for both the worshiper and the leader of worship. Starting from this verse, we could trace the development of instrumental music in worship and give guidance on its use, and overuse. We might fasten too on the word **melody** to emphasize the need for songs of praise that people can sing, while at the same time avoiding offense to trained ears. Let us aim at the "grave, sweet melody" which has a universal quality, rather than at music which reflects only the need of the moment.

3. ***Sing to Him a New Song.***—The critical word is **new.** This may refer to an outburst of religious poetry at some vital point in Hebrew history, perhaps after the captivity or the Maccabean victories. Such periods come often for the church. But we have to be careful. Newness is not necessarily a virtue; new songs may be foolish songs. In any case, we notice that though this song was new, its theme was old. The truth is that the old songs that are genuine become new to every man who discovers their

4 For the word of the LORD *is* right; and all his works *are done* in truth.
5 He loveth righteousness and judgment: the earth is full of the goodness of the LORD.
6 By the word of the LORD were the heavens made; and all the host of them by the breath of his mouth.
7 He gathereth the waters of the sea together as a heap: he layeth up the depth in storehouses.

4 For the word of the LORD is upright;
and all his work is done in faithfulness.
5 He loves righteousness and justice;
the earth is full of the steadfast love of the LORD.

6 By the word of the LORD the heavens were made,
and all their host by the breath of his mouth.
7 He gathered the waters of the sea as in a bottle;
he put the deeps in storehouses.

---

2. THE WORD OF THE LORD (33:4-9)

4-5. The creation was effected by **the word of the LORD.** But the creation is not the product of divine caprice or the expression of purposeless might.

> **The word of the LORD is upright;**
> **and all his work is done in faithfulness.**

Creation is grounded in upright purposes, from which in his operation the Lord never swerves. **Righteousness, justice,** and **goodness** are therefore fundamental things in a world made by a moral God.

6-7. By the word of the LORD, . . . the breath of his mouth: Cf. Gen. 1:6-18. The heavens with all the heavenly host of stars and luminaries came into being by the mere utterance of his command (cf. Job 26:13*a*). Read בדברו, "his word" (vs. 6). **He gathered the waters of the sea; . . . put the deeps in storehouses:** The reference is to the heavenly deep (cf. Gen. 1:7), i.e., the waters which are above the firmament and from which the rain descends to the earth (cf. Job 38:22). Read כנאד for כנד, i.e., **as in a bottle** (RSV) for **as a heap** (KJV).

---

truth for himself. We need singers that are made new, rather than new hymns. "New every morning is the love," and so is the old true song that declares it. But we must see to it that our songs of praise have the real "old-new" quality, and are not merely carried over from the temporary need of the past, as so many nineteenth-century hymns are; and that our new hymns have a universal quality. The great psalms set us the standard.

4-9. *Nature's Beneficent Hand.*—Vss. 4-5 are the introduction to the praise of God as creator. They emphasize his consistency.

> **The word of the LORD is upright;**
> **and all his work is done in faithfulness.**

We can depend on God to be the same. The uniformity of nature is rooted in the character of its Maker: and he is such that **the earth is full of the goodness of the LORD.** It is a point to remember and emphasize. We are so impressed with nature's red claw that we forget nature's beneficent hand. The truth is that earth is so full of **the goodness** which ministers to life that it can provide a wonderful home for man to live in, if only he will behave himself. It is not the Creator's fault that the world gets itself over and again into such a terrible mess.

First, in majestic and striking phrases comes the act of creation. The conception of a Creator and his perfect will is nobly awe-inspiring, and religion will not be content with a lesser mystery of the beginning. **By the word of the LORD were the heavens made; and all the host of them by the breath of his mouth.** Let us stand there and be still. It is not for nothing that the psalmist begins with the stars, his eyes lifted up. After the stars, we can turn to the atom: and before them both be humble, thanking God that we also see him in man.

Vs. 7 offers a difficulty of interpretation; but whatever translation is accurate, the suggestion is vital. **He gathereth the waters of the sea together as a heap** may be a mistake for **as in a bottle.** In that case we have an unexpected

8 Let all the earth fear the LORD: let all the inhabitants of the world stand in awe of him.
9 For he spake, and it was *done;* he commanded, and it stood fast.
10 The LORD bringeth the counsel of the heathen to nought: he maketh the devices of the people of none effect.
11 The counsel of the LORD standeth for ever, the thoughts of his heart to all generations.
12 Blessed *is* the nation whose God *is* the LORD; *and* the people *whom* he hath chosen for his own inheritance.
13 The LORD looketh from heaven; he beholdeth all the sons of men.

8 Let all the earth fear the LORD,
let all the inhabitants of the world stand in awe of him!
9 For he spoke, and it came to be;
he commanded, and it stood forth.

10 The LORD brings the counsel of the nations to nought;
he frustrates the plans of the peoples.
11 The counsel of the LORD stands for ever,
the thoughts of his heart to all generations.
12 Blessed is the nation whose God is the LORD,
the people whom he has chosen as his heritage!

13 The LORD looks down from heaven,
he sees all the sons of men;

8-9. The earth too **stood forth** at the word of the Lord (cf. 104:6-8), and before the manifest power of the divine word men should tremble.

3. THE COUNSEL OF THE LORD (33:10-12)

10-12. The psalmist now deals with the Lord's rule in the earth. The Lord is the master of history. **The counsel of the LORD stands for ever.** Happy is the lot of the people **whose God is the LORD.**

4. THE EYE OF THE LORD (33:13-19)

13-19. The eye of the LORD sees all that men do and knows all that they think or plan (Isa. 40:18-28). No levies of human resources can save men from the penalty of

---

image for clouds (cf. Job. 38:37). Water is an essential thing for man and beast and for the earth itself; therefore God stores it in vessels, which every now and then he opens in life-giving rain. The "floods" also are **in storehouses,** which may mean reservoirs, or any secure place, where his creatures find refreshing. An interpreter starting here can develop the thesis of the varied arrangements of nature which minister to life. **He gathered the waters . . . as in a bottle** is a memorable figure, especially if we read on from it to vss. 8-9, with their demand for **awe** before the irresistible and primal act of God which set the whole universe on its course: **He spoke, and it came to be.**

10-19. ***God in History.***—The theme changes from creation to history and God's ultimate control of all the nations of the earth. It is a familiar theme of the psalmists; and it says much for them that they so often make the righteous power of God the burden of their song, standing reverent before it. Vss. 10-11 contrast the futility of human planning with the unbreakable effectiveness of **the counsel of the LORD.**

> The best-laid schemes o' mice and men
> Gang aft a-gley.[2]

The poet might have gone further and said "always" for "often," if the human purposes are at odds with the divine; for "we can do nothing against the truth, but for the truth" (II Cor. 13:8). Vs. 12, as a kind of inevitable conclusion, puts the favorable side of the matter in an often-quoted verse which is forever apt: **Blessed is the nation whose God is the LORD,** a nation which as a community endeavors to fashion its life and its policies in harmony with God's will. If a nation claims to be an entity, it must seek to be a God-fearing entity and must not depend solely on the private godliness of its members, though that is basic.

Vss. 13-15 give the picture of the watchfulness of the Controller. We note (*a*) that **he sits en-**

[2] Robert Burns, "To a Mouse."

14 From the place of his habitation he looketh upon all the inhabitants of the earth.

15 He fashioneth their hearts alike; he considereth all their works.

16 There is no king saved by the multitude of a host: a mighty man is not delivered by much strength.

17 A horse *is* a vain thing for safety: neither shall he deliver *any* by his great strength.

18 Behold, the eye of the LORD *is* upon them that fear him, upon them that hope in his mercy;

19 To deliver their soul from death, and to keep them alive in famine.

20 Our soul waiteth for the LORD: he *is* our help and our shield.

21 For our heart shall rejoice in him, because we have trusted in his holy name.

22 Let thy mercy, O LORD, be upon us, according as we hope in thee.

14 from where he sits enthroned he looks forth
on all the inhabitants of the earth,
15 he who fashions the hearts of them all,
and observes all their deeds.

16 A king is not saved by his great army;
a warrior is not delivered by his great strength.
17 The war horse is a vain hope for victory,
and by its great might it cannot save.

18 Behold, the eye of the LORD is on those who fear him,
on those who hope in his steadfast love,
19 that he may deliver their soul from death,
and keep them alive in famine.

20 Our soul waits for the LORD;
he is our help and shield.
21 Yea, our heart is glad in him,
because we trust in his holy name.
22 Let thy steadfast love, O LORD, be upon us,
even as we hope in thee.

---

thwarting or opposing the Lord's purposes (cf. Isa. 30:1; 31:1). But the favor of the Lord is with **those who fear him** [to] **deliver their soul from death, and keep them alive in famine.**

5. THE LORD IS OUR HOPE (33:20-22)

20-22. The moral of the psalm is pointed in the concluding strophe. For the **name** of the Lord see Exeg. on 20:2.

---

throned (vs. 14); it is an absolute king who is watching. Further (*b*) **he sees all the sons of men** (vs. 13), and God's "seeing" is no casual thing; for (*c*) it is he **who fashions the hearts of them all.** He knows exactly the limit of their capacities; having given them their powers, he knows precisely what to expect from them. It is with that insight into potentiality that he **observes all their deeds.** These words connect with Christ's warning that much is reasonably expected from men to whom much is given; and with the heart of the gospel. There is the divine Watcher; there is the human rebellion and failure in action; there is the necessary "frustrating" (vs. 10) of haughty plans. But is that all? For there is watching and watching. We may remember the comment of the small boy who said, "Teacher watches me at school so that he can catch me doing wrong; father watches me on the beach to see that I don't get in too deep. I like father's kind of watching." Out of the mouths of babes and sucklings! God watches and frustrates in mercy, and watches still. The end of his watching? He sends his Son, that he may have to frustrate no more.

So in clear terms the poet records the might of the moral factor: **A king is not saved by his great army. . . . The war horse is a vain hope for victory.** Such a warning does not imply that might is useless; but it does mean that might plus untruth is ultimately weaker than truth with temporary feebleness. For might will grow for those who stand for right. History has awesomely illustrated the accuracy of the psalmist's confidence. It is best that the right should be mighty; it is essential for the mighty to be right. Why? Because the Lord favors the right—**the eye of the LORD is upon them.** In the end no more need be said; for there is no more to say.

20-22. *Wait, Trust, Hope.*—The psalm comes quietly to a close. The verbs should be noted. They are fine, strong verbs. If we wait and trust,

A Psalm of David, when he changed his behavior before Abimelech; who drove him away, and he departed.

34 I will bless the LORD at all times: his praise *shall* continually *be* in my mouth.

A Psalm of David, when he feigned madness before Abimelech, so that he drove him out, and he went away.

34 I will bless the LORD at all times;
his praise shall continually be in my mouth.

XXXIV. THANKS BE TO GOD FOR HIS GOODNESS (34:1-22)

This psalm is in the Hebrew text an acrostic, each line beginning with a letter of the alphabet in order. By an accident the line of the sixth letter, which belonged between our vs. 5 and vs. 6, has been omitted. Also, as we see by the context, vs. 17 relates to vs. 15, the order of vs. 15 and vs. 16 should be reversed, i.e., in the order of the letters of the alphabet פ must have stood before ע, as happens, e.g., in Lam. 2–4; Prov. 31 (LXX).

The superscription refers the occasion of the psalm to the incident in David's life described in I Sam. 21:10-15, but it confuses Achish of Gath with Abimelech of Gerar (Gen. 20–21; 26). Nothing in the psalm reflects the particular situation of David among the Philistines unless it is the words of vs. 6. The identification, however, is an interesting instance of the character of later Jewish exegesis.

The purpose of the psalmist, who has been saved **out of all his troubles** (vs. 6), is to summon all men to join with him in words of gratitude to the Lord and to set forth the Lord's special care of the righteous. The keynote of the psalm is confidence and trust in the Lord. The psalmist brushes aside the problems which baffle other men in the O.T. He testifies to what his own experience has taught him.

The psalm falls into two main divisions: vss. 1-10, the summons to join the psalmist in giving thanks to the Lord; vss. 11-21, instruction in the style of the wisdom writers on how to live a long and happy life. Vs. 22, which is outside the acrostic scheme, was probably added to the psalm by a later hand in order that the psalm might end auspiciously with a word of comfort to the righteous rather than with a threat to the wicked. It is doubtful that the psalmist intended to order his thought in divisions other than the two indicated above, although vss. 3, 7, 10, 14, 17, 21 might be said to mark off a series of fairly regular strophes.

The date of the psalm is clearly late, as its acrostic form and wisdom style indicate. In both form and style it is like Ps. 25. The two psalms might have stood together, as lament and thanksgiving respectively (cf. the two parts of Ps. 22).

The meter is 3+3, with the exception of 4+3 in vss. 6, 8, and 4+4 in vss. 12, 22.

1. SUMMONS TO MAGNIFY THE LORD (34:1-3)

34:1-3. The psalmist expresses his intention to thank the Lord not only on the occasion of a special deliverance but **at all times** (cf. 119:164). And he calls on all **the afflicted** to hear his testimony and **be glad** and to **magnify the LORD** with him. **Let us exalt his name together!**

we shall find reason to hope; and hope with the hope that saves (Rom. 8:18-25).

34:1-22. ***God's Care for His Own.***—Here we have another acrostic psalm, not quite complete in form. It is a psalm with a history in Christian worship, for it is mentioned by Cyril and Jerome as usually sung by the church of Jerusalem at the time of Communion.[3] It was on the lips of martyrs as they faced the arena, and is associated with the closing hours of St. Columba; parts of it in the metrical version are very frequent in the worship of the Scottish church. The general theme is the thought of God's care for his own, set forth in a series of pious aphorisms and affirmations arranged in the acrostic form, each standing on its own merits.

1-3. ***Praise.*****—I will bless the LORD at all times** offers an opening challenge. **At all times?** In what sense, arising from a deep persuasion, can we take this as other than poetic hyperbole? Yet the apostle desires us "always and for everything giving thanks" (Eph. 5:20). It requires a

[3] Ker, *Psalms in History and Biography*, p. 61.

2 My soul shall make her boast in the LORD: the humble shall hear *thereof,* and be glad.

3 O magnify the LORD with me, and let us exalt his name together.

4 I sought the LORD, and he heard me, and delivered me from all my fears.

5 They looked unto him, and were lightened: and their faces were not ashamed.

6 This poor man cried, and the LORD heard *him,* and saved him out of all his troubles.

2 My soul makes its boast in the LORD;
let the afflicted hear and be glad.
3 O magnify the LORD with me,
and let us exalt his name together!

4 I sought the LORD, and he answered me,
and delivered me from all my fears.
5 Look to him, and be radiant;
so your[r] faces shall never be ashamed.
6 This poor man cried, and the LORD heard him,
and saved him out of all his troubles.

[r] Gk Syr Jerome: Heb *their*

---

2. THE PSALMIST'S TESTIMONY (34:4-10)

4-7. The psalmist's testimony is based on his own experience. He speaks of what he knows firsthand: **I sought the LORD, and he answered me.** So he calls on all who are beset by fears (vs. 4) and troubles (vs. 6) to follow his example. **Look to him, and be radiant.** Their sad countenances will beam with joy. **The angel of the LORD encamps around those who fear him:** In this instance **the angel of the LORD** is not the visible form which the Lord takes when he appears to men (cf. Exod. 14:19; Judg. 6:11-12, 14), but one of the heavenly beings who act for the Lord. That there was an army of them is an old idea (cf. Josh. 5:14; II Kings 6:17). In later times, however, their functions as mediatorial beings were elaborated and extended largely because of the increasing emphasis on the holiness of God and his separateness from men (cf. Matt. 18:10).

---

firm trust and a discerning spirit to be able to **bless the LORD** in some experiences. "It is the LORD; let him do what seemeth him good" (I Sam. 3:18) may be as far as we can go, but it is a good start.

My soul makes its boast in the LORD;
let the afflicted hear and be glad.

If we really can **boast in the LORD,** having had experience of trial, we are the best kind of helpers to the afflicted. But it needs to be the right kind of "boasting," and it needs to be **in the LORD**—a real testimony to what we know for ourselves of his merciful power and presence in the valley of the shadow.

O magnify the LORD with me, and let us exalt his name together. A splendid word, with its own application for the universal church! The motive for unity should be that together we may magnify and exalt the Lord, remembering that he will not be magnified and exalted as he should be until we do it together.

4-7. ***Witness.*—I sought the LORD, and he heard me, and delivered me from all my fears.** It is true that if we take our fears to God, they have a way of disappearing. The great fears arise from a wrong relation to him, some wrong thought of him. Put that right and they go.

Look to him, and be radiant. Accept this translation in place of the KJV. **Be radiant** provides an arresting thought. It should be regarded not as a command to force ourselves into an unnatural mood, but as a statement of the result of looking to God. Evelyn Underhill speaks somewhere of an old Quaker woman, saying, "Light simply streamed out of her." She must have been "looking to him" for a long while. Stephen as he died is another instance; for his face was as the face of an angel. Aged saints sometimes suggest a "radiant peace." All these are but reflecting the radiance of him who is himself the light of all our seeing. It is a great prize to be aimed at.

This poor man cried, and the LORD heard him. The word to stress is **poor.** Not simply in respect of material goods, though it covers that, but as a description of anybody who is finding life too much for him. There is a lovely little poem by George Macdonald beginning

I'm a puir man I grant,
But I am weel neiboured,[4]

which puts the point happily; of such men it is to say that theirs is the kingdom of heaven and its King as well.

The angel of the LORD encamps. Here the imagination runs far and free. This is one

[4] "Triolet."

7 The angel of the LORD encampeth round about them that fear him, and delivereth them.

8 O taste and see that the LORD *is* good: blessed *is* the man *that* trusteth in him.

9 O fear the LORD, ye his saints: for *there is* no want to them that fear him.

10 The young lions do lack, and suffer hunger: but they that seek the LORD shall not want any good *thing*.

11 Come, ye children, hearken unto me: I will teach you the fear of the LORD.

12 What man *is he that* desireth life, *and* loveth *many* days, that he may see good?

7 The angel of the LORD encamps
around those who fear him, and delivers them.
8 O taste and see that the LORD is good!
Happy is the man who takes refuge in him!
9 O fear the LORD, you his saints,
for those who fear him have no want!
10 The young lions suffer want and hunger;
but those who seek the LORD lack no good thing.

11 Come, O sons, listen to me,
I will teach you the fear of the LORD.
12 What man is there who desires life,
and covets many days, that he may enjoy good?

8-10. His saints: Lit., "his holy ones." The same word (קדשים) is used in 16:3; Deut. 33:3. It means those who are consecrated to God and so in their ways separate from the mass of men. It is different from the word (חסידים) commonly translated "saints," lit., "faithful ones," i.e., "the pious" (cf. 30:4; 31:23). **The young lions** is a mistake probably for "the unfaithful ones" or "the apostates," i.e., כפירים was written for כפרים (a late word). The LXX may have read כבירים, which was translated πλούσιοι, "the rich."

3. THE GODLY LIFE (34:11-14)

11-14. The psalmist uses the form of a wisdom writer and addresses his hearers as **sons** (cf. Prov. 2:1; 4:1; 6:1). The teachers of wisdom directed their words to those who desired a happy **life** and **many days** (Prov. 2:7-10; 4:20-23). The way to these blessings

---

of many scriptural hints that permit some wishful thinking; and thinking that is wishful is not necessarily false. Who or what is this **angel of the LORD?** To the poet's mind he was a representative of God. He may have been using the phrase vaguely, "in a general sense for the Divine manifestation of protection." [5] But taking it in connection with other passages in scripture which speak of those "ministers of his" who "do his pleasure" (103:21), it opens up a region of speculation from which too many modern minds have turned too easily away. Is man really the best that God can do in created intelligence? There is no easily proved reason why we should not be "on the side of the angels." If angels, why not guardian angels? And if guardian angels, why may we not possibly find among them those whom we "have loved long since, and lost awhile"? They must do something; why should not that something be where love urges them? We may wonder and hope; fastening on the word **encamps. The angel of the LORD** settles down to watch and guard.

[5] Ellicott, *O.T. Commentary for English Readers*, IV, 135.

8-10. *Summons.*—**O taste and see that the LORD is good!** A glove thrown down at our feet! Really drink life's draught, and you will find it a draught restorative. See steadily and whole, and you will find goodness. Do it for yourself, and you cannot help telling of it. If you need to listen to others, listen to those who have tasted and seen. The saints have tasted and seen—goodness! Unvarying goodness! A thought-provoking fact.

Vss. 9-10 are completely true only in the spiritual sense. There is a possible point in the image of the **young lions** suffering want, for they are ravenous beasts of prey. Men of that quality come to grief; in the spiritual sense at least they remain unsatisfied. But a slight emendation gives "the unfaithful" for **young lions,** and this is likely to be the true reading.

11-22. *Wisdom.*—The words **ye children** suggest a man's relation to others, not in the sense that he regards them as his inferiors, but in the sense that he has always to see himself in relation to them as a father. **I will teach you** reminds him of his duty, of the popular temptations he must resist in fulfilling it, and of the continuous effort he must make to qualify. But

13 Keep thy tongue from evil, and thy
lips from speaking guile.
14 Depart from evil, and do good; seek
peace, and pursue it.
15 The eyes of the LORD *are* upon the
righteous, and his ears *are open* unto their
cry.
16 The face of the LORD *is* against them
that do evil, to cut off the remembrance of
them from the earth.
17 *The righteous* cry, and the LORD heareth,
and delivereth them out of all their
troubles.
18 The LORD *is* nigh unto them that are
of a broken heart; and saveth such as be of
a contrite spirit.
19 Many *are* the afflictions of the righteous:
but the LORD delivereth him out of
them all.

13 Keep your tongue from evil,
and your lips from speaking deceit.
14 Depart from evil, and do good;
seek peace, and pursue it.

15 The eyes of the LORD are toward the righteous,
and his ears toward their cry.
16 The face of the LORD is against evildoers,
to cut off the remembrance of them from the earth.
17 When the righteous cry for help, the LORD hears,
and delivers them out of all their troubles.
18 The LORD is near to the brokenhearted,
and saves the crushed in spirit.

19 Many are the afflictions of the righteous;
but the LORD delivers him out of them all.

was through **the fear of the LORD** (Prov. 1:7; 2:5; 9:10). In vss. 13-14 the psalmist illustrates by a couple of aphorisms the practical aspects of godly living (cf. Prov. 10:32; 16:21, 30).

4. GOD'S CARE OF HIS SERVANTS (34:15-22)

15-17. After the manner of the wise, he contrasts the lot of the **righteous** with that of the wicked. See Ps. 1 for a discussion of the theme of the two ways which is so prominent in wisdom literature. Vs. 17*b* repeats vs. 6*b*, which is an evidence that the writer is a collector rather than a composer of sayings illustrating his thought.

18-22. Similarly, in the concluding verses he brings together a group of aphorisms dealing with the Lord's deliverance of the **righteous** from all their troubles. He **saves the crushed in spirit** and the afflicted in body. The sum of the teaching is that in the

what is he to teach? **The fear of the LORD,** with all that it implies of the true nature of God and man, and the relation between them. This for the psalmist is the substance of true religion: watch your tongue, **Keep thy tongue from evil** (vs. 13); turn the inner eye away from evil and so keep desire clean, **depart from evil** (vs. 14); in action keep to the kindly and upright, **do good** (vs. 14); and finally, **seek peace, and pursue it** (vs. 14). Note the emphasis on **pursue.** A most necessary word for all corporate life; the creation of a peace free from pettiness, peace of man with man and of man with God, must be a continual effort. On such the Lord will look with favor, while from the wicked he will turn his face. A point for historic illustration. God's hostility to evil has the intention to **cut off** its memory **from the earth.** On the whole, great villains are remembered only as "awful examples." Hitler's temporary greatness is largely forgotten; his dark tragedy has become something from which men avert the head.

Vss. 17-20 heap up the expressions of God's tender care. Starting from his seeing and hearing and moving to deliver, the psalmist lists especially "pitiable faces" as objects of God's concern—**the brokenhearted, . . . the crushed in spirit** (vs. 18). The church must remember that as God's agent and channel of help its concern also lies there. By and large it has never forgotten; with all its excesses of religious hate, it has been the most pitying society humanity has known; but how much more deeply must it feel concern, and how much more widely must it accept responsibility, as much for the causes of human suffering as for the victims, if it is to be the body of him who is **near to the brokenhearted. He keepeth all his bones: not one of them is broken** has been exalted in John 19:36, and given direct reference to Christ on the cross. But in the psalm it is no more

20 He keepeth all his bones: not one of them is broken.
21 Evil shall slay the wicked: and they that hate the righteous shall be desolate.
22 The LORD redeemeth the soul of his servants: and none of them that trust in him shall be desolate.

20 He keeps all his bones;
not one of them is broken.
21 Evil shall slay the wicked;
and those who hate the righteous will be condemned.
22 The LORD redeems the life of his servants;
none of those who take refuge in him will be condemned.

A Psalm of David.

35 Plead *my cause,* O LORD, with them that strive with me: fight against them that fight against me.

A Psalm of David.

35 Contend, O LORD, with those who contend with me;
fight against those who fight against me!

lasting experiences of life it goes ill with the wicked, but well with the righteous. **Evil shall slay the wicked; . . . the LORD redeems the life of his servants.**

XXXV. A PLEA FOR HELP (35:1-28)

Like others of its type, this psalm is the appeal of an individual to the Lord for deliverance from the false charges, evil plots, and relentless hatred of his enemies. Some judicial procedure is being prepared for his undoing. The charges that are to be preferred against him have already been hurled at him (vs. 21). Malicious witnesses are at hand to supply false evidence about offenses of which he is innocent (vs. 11). His life is in jeopardy (vss. 7, 17). The issue between him and his foes may be settled by some form of ordeal to which he must submit. But whatever form his trial takes, he looks for vindication to God alone (cf. Deut. 1:17). Either human help has failed him, or the situation is such that only divine intervention can avail (see Exeg. on 17:1-15; 26:1-12).

Such is the general purport of the psalm. But a closer study of its contents gives one the impression that it is a composite structure made up of three originally independent lament sections (vss. 1-10, 11-18, 19-28), each of which concludes with the customary vow to give thanks for the expected deliverance (cf. vss. 9-10, 18, 28). These three sections may relate to three separate episodes in the life of the psalmist, or more probably they are of independent authorship. It is to be noted that the situation which is the burden of the complaint varies with each section. In the first section powerful foes conspire against the property and life of the psalmist (cf. vss. 7, 10); in the second the psalmist's enemies were formerly his friends, his life is being sought through the use of false witnesses in some judicial process, and his troubles are augmented by sickness; in the third the psalmist is one of **the quiet in the land** (vs. 20), against whom crafty opponents, claiming to be eyewitnesses of the fact, bring accusations of wrongdoing; but the sentence which they hope to have pronounced on the psalmist is not so clearly indicated as in the

than a picturesque phrase indicating well-being. The **bones** are the basis of a man's structure; and they will be kept sound. Applied spiritually, a true man may show superficial scars of character; but if he has been God-referred in his essential self he stands the shocks of life's battle.

With the reiteration of God's purpose (vs. 21; cf. vs. 16), the acrostic, and therefore the psalm proper, closes.

Vs. 22 is a liturgical addition, but gives a glad ending. **None of those who take refuge in him** is doomed. There is that in God which evil cannot resist; but there is too a wideness in his mercy. We easily move from this utterance to the remembrance of the Cross, and that poor misguided man who took refuge in one last dying look toward God.

35:1-28. *The Cry of the Oppressed.*—This surely is the song of a representative man or leader. He is a single individual no doubt, but he sings as the embodiment of a company of men whose way of life is threatened by an influential party that stands for all that he hates and is none too scrupulous in the means

2 Take hold of shield and buckler, and
stand up for mine help.
3 Draw out also the spear, and stop *the*
way against them that persecute me: say
unto my soul, I *am* thy salvation.

2 Take hold of shield and buckler,
and rise for my help!
3 Draw the spear and javelin
against my pursuers!
Say to my soul,
"I am your deliverance!"

preceding sections (cf. vs. 25); also the psalmist has friends who are desirous of his vindication (cf. vs. 27). The psalm is therefore the result of a fusing of materials that belong to three somewhat different situations. The failure to note this fact has led to certain proposals for the emendation of the text, e.g., the omission of vs. 18, or its insertion between vs. 27 and vs. 28, or the transference of vs. 28 to a position between vs. 9 and vs. 10. Certain irregularities in the order of the verses have been explained by a theory that the psalm, as we have it, was copied from a text arranged in two columns (J. Magne, "Le texte du psaume XXXV," *Revue Biblique,* LIV [1947], 42). In any case the sense requires us to read vs. 5 and vs. 6 in the following order: 5*a*, 6*b*, 6*a*, 5*b*.

Textual corruptions obscure the metrical pattern. In the main the lines seem to be in 3+2 measure, but there are also lines in 3+3. The date of the psalm in its present composite form is probably postexilic. The psalmist belongs to a time when a sincere offering of words of thanksgiving was regarded as superior in God's sight to sacrifices on the altar (cf. 40:6-10; 51:16-17).

1. Appeal to God (35:1-3)

35:1-3. The psalmist speaks of his adversaries, now as opponents-at-law, now as foes on a field of battle, now as hunters spreading a net or digging a trench to take the prey, now as robbers stripping the weak, now as wild beasts. Against such men he prays

it uses to achieve its ends. A devout Jew in the time of Antiochus Epiphanes might sing thus, or a German of the school of Goethe under Nazism. Whatever the historical setting, however, the plan of the psalm is plain enough, and so is its sincerity. The writer's enemies are God's enemies; therefore he can hate them and pray for God's help in their overthrow—both of which he does wholeheartedly.

First he calls upon God to appear as a warrior, coming to his aid. "Buckle on thine armor, O Lord, and join battle against my pursuers!" The language suggests that he and his fellows may even have had to take to the hills, as the defenders of the faith and freedom have often had to do. Then follows (vss. 4-8) a lively and varied elaboration of the prayer in the second stanza of the British national anthem, "Frustrate their knavish tricks,"[6] the peculiar malignity of the knavish tricks being developed in later verses. The exaltation the writer will feel when the knaves and their tricks are well and truly confounded is set forth in vss. 9-10; their meanness and rascality in vss. 11-16, where their behavior to him is contrasted with his to them when they were in trouble. He shared in their grief and joined in their prayers when they had need of help; but when his turn came to be in difficulty, they slandered him and added insult to injury by laughter. He asks God, **How long wilt thou look on?** Only to pray once more for rescue, vowing to give thanks when men of that kind are no longer allowed to laugh last, or chuckle and wink at one another in derision at the simpleton who had dared to oppose them (vss. 17-19). Vss. 20-21 are a sharp reiteration and summary of their plottings and contrivings, while vss. 22-28 contain the final appeal that God may overthrow and dishonor them who would dishonor him; concluding with still another prayer for vindication, this time before the face of the psalmist's allies and sympathizers, and with a promise that then his tongue shall tell of God's righteousness **all the day long.**

The whole gives a familiar picture. Here is an honest walker in the ways of his fathers, who asks nothing but that he and his people should be left alone. Vs. 20 provides a clear hint of the kind of man he was and the kind of people he represented: they (i.e., his enemies) do not speak peaceably, but plot **against those who are quiet in the land.** He and his fellows are no aggressors, but strife is forced upon them by those who are. Therefore he prays for their confusion, and is not afraid to lay bare his anger before God. For the Christian an old

[6] See John Julian, ed., *A Dictionary of Hymnology* (New York: Charles Scribner's Sons, 1892), p. 437.

4 Let them be confounded and put to
shame that seek after my soul: let them be
turned back and brought to confusion that
devise my hurt.
5 Let them be as chaff before the wind:
and let the angel of the LORD chase *them*.
6 Let their way be dark and slippery: and
let the angel of the LORD persecute them.
7 For without cause have they hid for me
their net *in* a pit, *which* without cause they
have digged for my soul.
8 Let destruction come upon him at unawares; and let his net that he hath hid
catch himself: into that very destruction let
him fall.

4 Let them be put to shame and dishonor
who seek after my life!
Let them be turned back and confounded
who devise evil against me!
5 Let them be like chaff before the wind,
with the angel of the LORD driving
them on!
6 Let their way be dark and slippery,
with the angel of the LORD pursuing
them!

7 For without cause they hid their net for
me;
without cause they dug a pit[s] for my
life.
8 Let ruin come upon them unawares!
And let the net which they hid ensnare
them;
let them fall therein to ruin!

[s] The word *pit* is transposed from the preceding line

God to use all the instruments of battle. **Take hold of shield and buckler,** i.e., the small round shield and the larger one which together gave a soldier the protection needed for offensive action (cf. I Kings 10:16). In the words of the writer of Wisd. Sol. 5:17: "He shall take jealousy as his complete panoply, and shall make the whole creation his weapons for vengeance against his enemies." The word סגר **(stop)** in vs. 3 is taken by RSV to be a noun **(javelin).**

2. Maledictions on Foes (35:4-8)

4-8. In a series of maledictions the psalmist expresses the measure of the calamity which he hopes the Lord's intervention will bring to his foes. They are to be utterly overwhelmed. Let them be discredited in the eyes of men. Let them be like a defeated army which takes to flight, chased like straws before the wind, hunted down dark and slippery ways by the agent of the divine wrath, caught in the traps, and swallowed up in the pitfalls which they prepared for the psalmist. The accumulation of similes and

problem is here proposed: in what circumstances can we honestly pray for victory and for the confusion of our enemies? Are there any circumstances in which we could use this psalm? Wars have taught us that there are circumstances in which we do use it and entertain its spirit; but they also remind us that we need, like this man, to be sure that we are defenders and not aggressors, and that our defense is of something so great in value that the destruction of our enemies, who however faulty and unworthy are still men, is a lesser evil than the loss of that which we defend. A prayer like this implies at least that the writer is ready to take the sword if there is no other way of regaining the power to be **quiet** folk **in the land.** But he must never take the sword first; it is only a last, sad resort if his enemy's sword is already drawn, and if he himself is sure before his conscience that he has his just quarrel, on the principles of right he has learned and believes to be divinely ordained. If the author was one of the solid and courageous company who resisted the shallow, immoral fopperies of Antiochus Epiphanes, we must take off our hat to him and hope that his spirit will not perish from the earth. He is a spiritual ancestor of the Covenanters and the Puritans. Yet this is not the whole duty of man. We may desire that the enemy's knavish tricks may be confounded; but we must also desire that the enemy be saved. Christ died for all men, including Nazis and Communists and their like. Humanity must ever seek to find "the more excellent way."

5-6. ***Chaff Before the Wind.***—Observe the suggestive turns of phrase throughout the psalm. Here is the awesome picture of the state of a man who is awake to God's displeasure. He will

9 And my soul shall be joyful in the LORD: it shall rejoice in his salvation.

10 All my bones shall say, LORD, who *is* like unto thee, which deliverest the poor from him that is too strong for him, yea, the poor and the needy from him that spoileth him?

11 False witnesses did rise up; they laid to my charge *things* that I knew not.

12 They rewarded me evil for good *to* the spoiling of my soul.

13 But as for me, when they were sick, my clothing *was* sackcloth: I humbled my soul with fasting; and my prayer returned into mine own bosom.

14 I behaved myself as though *he had been* my friend *or* brother: I bowed down heavily, as one that mourneth *for his* mother.

15 But in mine adversity they rejoiced, and gathered themselves together: *yea,* the abjects gathered themselves together against me, and I knew *it* not; they did tear *me,* and ceased not:

9 Then my soul shall rejoice in the LORD,
exulting in his deliverance.
10 All my bones shall say,
"O LORD, who is like thee,
thou who deliverest the weak
from him who is too strong for him,
the weak and needy from him who despoils him?"

11 Malicious witnesses rise up;
they ask me of things that I know not.
12 They requite me evil for good;
my soul is forlorn.
13 But I, when they were sick —
I wore sackcloth,
I afflicted myself with fasting.
I prayed with head bowed[t] on my bosom,
14 as though I grieved for my friend or my brother;
I went about as one who laments his mother,
bowed down and in mourning.

15 But at my stumbling they gathered in glee,
they gathered together against me;
cripples whom I knew not
slandered me without ceasing;

[t] Or *My prayer turned back*

---

metaphors provides a picture of hopeless, rayless discomfiture. **The angel of the LORD:** See Exeg. on 34:4-7; cf. I Chr. 21:15-30; II Chr. 32:21.

3. Confidence in the Lord (35:9-10)

9-10. The psalmist has confidence in the Lord's help, and he vows to offer a hymn of thanksgiving. Some omit the second עני **(the weak)** on the basis of meter.

4. Malicious Witnesses (35:11-16)

11-16. The lament is renewed with a change in situation. **Malicious witnesses rise up** and charge the psalmist with crimes of which he knows nothing. Their conduct is all the

---

become even in his own eyes a mean and futile thing, the sport of forces against which he is helpless, **like chaff before the wind, with the angel of the LORD driving them on;** or with a change of imagery, a panting, desperate fugitive, slipping in a dark path, while behind him he hears the steady feet of relentless righteousness (cf. Francis Thompson's "The Hound of Heaven," marking its most Christian close).

13-14. *Comfort in Sorrow.*—These verses suggest the difficulty of true sympathy. They put questions to us as to the depth of our feeling for our friends in trouble, indicating that if we would be helpers, we must "sit where they sit." The greatest comfort we can give to sorrowers is often simply to grieve with them, if our grief is real. On one occasion a minister visiting a house of tragic bereavement so felt the poignancy of the loss that he burst into tears. Long afterward the bereaved father declared that at that moment the ice in his own heart broke. The clause **my prayer returned into mine own bosom** is better rendered **I prayed with head bowed on my bosom.** It is simply an added touch to the pictorial expression of fellow feeling.

15-16. *Profanity and Barbarism.*—These verses are confused and make little if any sense

16 With hypocritical mockers in feasts, they gnashed upon me with their teeth.

17 Lord, how long wilt thou look on? rescue my soul from their destructions, my darling from the lions.

18 I will give thee thanks in the great congregation: I will praise thee among much people.

19 Let not them that are mine enemies wrongfully rejoice over me: *neither* let them wink with the eye that hate me without a cause.

16 they impiously mocked more and more,[u]
gnashing at me with their teeth.

17 How long, O LORD, wilt thou look on?
Rescue me from their ravages,
my life from the lions!
18 Then I will thank thee in the great congregation;
in the mighty throng I will praise thee.

19 Let not those rejoice over me
who are wrongfully my foes,
and let not those wink the eye
who hate me without cause.

[u] Cn Compare Gk: Heb *like the profanest of mockers of a cake*

---

more painful because he had numbered them among his friends. When they were in trouble, he had grieved for them. He prayed for them again and again. Read חכי for חיקי and translate, "prayer kept returning to my mouth." He gave additional force to his prayers by fasting and putting on sackcloth (cf. Lev. 16:29, 31; Isa. 58:3). But now when through the bitterness of his persecution sickness comes upon him, they show him no sympathy. For נכים, **cripples** (vs. 15*b*), read מכים, "those about to smite."

5. THE APPEAL TO GOD RENEWED (35:17-18)

17-18. Moved by the tragedy of his case, the psalmist suddenly breaks forth here with an appeal for himself instead of maledictions on his adversaries. **How long, O LORD:** An exclamation of despair characteristic of a lament. **Wilt thou look on?** The time for giving help is short because of the bestial cruelty of those arrayed against him. **Rescue me . . . from the lions:** Again the psalmist concludes his appeal with a vow to give thanks before his fellows in the temple. In vs. 17 read with Duhm, *et al.*, משאגים, "from them that roar," instead of משאיהם, **from their ravages.**

6. ANOTHER DESCRIPTION OF THE PSALMIST'S FOES (35:19-21)

19-21. A new lament opens with this section of the psalm, and a fresh description of the psalmist's adversaries. They **wink the eye** in mockery at the psalmist's plight. Their

---

in the KJV. Read throughout as in the RSV. Ellicott suggests that **with hypocritical mockers in feasts** might be freely translated "with profanity and barbarism."[7] This at least gives an apposite description of some types of modern attacks on Christianity.

17. ***Enemies and Treasure.***—Here the odd phrase, **my darling,** means "my only one." The RSV renders **my life.** We might perhaps fairly spiritualize this: **Rescue . . . my life from the lions,** asking what a man may mean by that. What is his **life,** really? What is there in him that is a treasure to himself, and what are the inner enemies that lionlike tend to destroy that treasure?

18. ***A Verse for Quiet Places.***—**Then I will thank thee in the great congregation** reminds us of our duty to give thanks as a community, and of the multitude of those who stand for the right, even in the world as it is. An encouraging verse for worshipers who forget that they are a part of a **great congregation** throughout the world, through whom

> The voice of prayer is never silent,
> Nor dies the strain of praise away.[8]

It is also well to remember the "great multitude, which no man could number" (Rev. 7:9) beyond the veil, with whom also we are one.

19. ***Scornful Superiority.***—**Let not those wink the eye who hate me without cause.** A very human prayer. There are few things more maddening to an honest man who is standing for a principle which he knows to be vital than

[7] *O.T. Commentary for English Readers,* IV, 137.

[8] John Ellerton, "The day Thou gavest, Lord, is ended," st. iii.

20 For they speak not peace: but they devise deceitful matters against *them that are* quiet in the land.

21 Yea, they opened their mouth wide against me, *and* said, Aha, aha, our eye hath seen *it*.

22 *This* thou hast seen, O LORD: keep not silence: O Lord, be not far from me.

23 Stir up thyself, and awake to my judgment, *even* unto my cause, my God and my Lord.

24 Judge me, O LORD my God, according to thy righteousness; and let them not rejoice over me.

25 Let them not say in their hearts, Ah, so would we have it: let them not say, We have swallowed him up.

26 Let them be ashamed and brought to confusion together that rejoice at mine hurt: let them be clothed with shame and dishonor that magnify *themselves* against me.

27 Let them shout for joy, and be glad,

20 For they do not speak peace,
but against those who are quiet in the land
they conceive words of deceit.
21 They open wide their mouths against me;
they say, "Aha, Aha!
our eyes have seen it!"
22 Thou hast seen, O LORD; be not silent!
O Lord, be not far from me!
23 Bestir thyself, and awake for my right,
for my cause, my God and my Lord!
24 Vindicate me, O LORD, my God, according to thy righteousness;
and let them not rejoice over me!
25 Let them not say to themselves,
"Aha, we have our heart's desire!"
Let them not say, "We have swallowed him up."

26 Let them be put to shame and confusion altogether
who rejoice at my calamity!
Let them be clothed with shame and dishonor
who magnify themselves against me!

27 Let those who desire my vindication
shout for joy and be glad,

---

speech is not for peace, but for mischief, as they fabricate groundless charges against **those who are quiet in the land,** the pious ones. They say, **Aha, aha, our eye hath seen it.**

7. PRAYER FOR VINDICATION (35:22-28)

22-25. In his distress the psalmist repeats his prayer for vindication. **Bestir thyself . . . for my cause, my God.** For the sake of the rhythm omit אדני, **O Lord,** in vs. 22, and אלהי, **my God,** in vs. 24. **Let them not say, "We have swallowed him up."**

26-28. In a final appeal he prays that the Lord may so act that on the one hand his persecutors will be **clothed with shame and dishonor** and his friends will **shout for joy**

---

to suffer scornful expressions of superiority from the shallow. It is a common experience in modern society, particularly at the hands of people who call themselves "realists." "O Lord, save thy world from silly laughter."

21-23. ***Contempt of Fools.*—They say, "Aha, Aha!"** Let expressions like this be put in modern terms. The feeling of the psalm can be conveyed remarkably by the use of a little of the language of the man in the street. A contemptuous "My *dear* sir!" or "That puts you where you belong!" or "You poor idealist!" give something of the flavor. The situation of the psalmist was even worse; his enemies were trumping up charges against him and declaring themselves to be eyewitnesses of his misdemeanors; but the **"Aha, Aha!"** covers a wide range of the "contempt of fools." One might well ponder long over exclamations and their true significance.

The appeals to God in vss. 22-23, **be not silent! . . . Bestir thyself . . .** —mark the latter —are striking expressions of the human desire for divine action. It is the **how long?** (vs. 17) motif put in a cry. We must, however, join this with the recurrent injunction in the psalms to "wait upon the LORD"; and we must remember that if we want God to bestir himself, we have to bestir ourselves too. God has a deal of waiting to do also, seeing how listless his agents are.

27-28. ***Remembrance and Thanksgiving.*—Let those who desire my vindication shout for joy**

that favor my righteous cause: yea, let them say continually, Let the LORD be magnified, which hath pleasure in the prosperity of his servant.

28 And my tongue shall speak of thy righteousness *and* of thy praise all the day long.

To the chief Musician, *A Psalm* of David the servant of the LORD.

36 The transgression of the wicked saith within my heart, *that there is* no fear of God before his eyes.

and say evermore,
"Great is the LORD,
who delights in the welfare of his servant!"
28 Then my tongue shall tell of thy righteousness
and of thy praise all the day long.

To the choirmaster. A Psalm of David, the servant of the LORD.

36 Transgression speaks to the wicked
deep in his heart;
there is no fear of God
before his eyes.

---

and sing a hymn of praise for his deliverance. And in conclusion he vows to offer in his own name the praises of his tongue **all the day long.**

XXXVI. THE POWER OF EVIL AND THE POWER OF GOD (36:1-12)

This brief psalm is composed of two sharply contrasting parts. In the first (vss. 1-4), the psalmist describes the man who communes in his heart with **transgression.** This principle of evil is represented as an evil demon or an evil angel that by its whispering counsels directs the ways of the godless. The evidences of its presence in a man's life are not hard to find. Under its spell he breaks with the precepts of religion and, being divorced from the mind of God, becomes self-confident and arrogant and assumes that there is no punishment for iniquity. In word and deed he ceases **to act wisely and do good,** and the fever of wickedness so grows on him that even at night on his bed he gives himself no rest from plotting mischief. The end of listening to the whisperings of the demon is that the man loses all sense of what is right. The second part of the psalm (vss. 5-12) is a hymn in praise of the goodness of God. The psalmist dwells first on the measure of the divine goodness (vss. 5-6). It is high as the heavens, deep as the sea, and firm as the mountains. Its blessings extend not only to men, but also to animals. Light and life come to those who seek to dwell under its shelter. Then the psalmist prays that he may ever enjoy this goodness, and that through it he may be defended against the violence of the wicked.

The literary relationship between the two parts of the psalm is so weak that it seems obvious that originally they were independent compositions. But some editor has brought them together because they set forth in bold relief the two conflicting ways of life: that of the man whose communion is with evil, and that of the man whose delight is in the contemplation of God. The second part is therefore the complement of the first, and the whole psalm becomes a companion of Pss. 1; 10; 73.

---

and be glad. A fruitful theme is to be found here, viz., our duty to remember favorably those who have helped us, both in private life and in national affairs. Forgetfulness of benefits is an ugly thing; and it is grievous when those who have stood together in adversity fall out in prosperity.

Then my tongue shall tell of thy righteousness—a seemly enough promise, and a religious one, if the psalmist means that when he and his friends have triumphed they will not take all the credit to themselves, but will remember the good hand of God upon them. But there is the hint of a bargain also: "Do this and then I will praise thee." There is a higher region of trust to reach, as Another knew when he said, "Nevertheless, not as I will, but as thou wilt" (Matt. 26:39).

36:1-12. ***The Inner Epic of the Soul.***—There is a strong case to be made for the view that here we have two psalms or two fragments, the first consisting of vss. 1-4, the second of

2 For he flattereth himself in his own eyes, until his iniquity be found to be hateful.

2 For he flatters himself in his own eyes
that his iniquity cannot be found out
and hated.

The first part exhibits features with which we are familiar in the wisdom writings. The expressions, **fear of God, to act wisely, a way that is not good,** belong to the vocabulary of Proverbs. The analysis of the character of the godless man is on the lines of that met with in Job. The second part, though hymnic in form, in its emphasis on the sovereignty and universalism of the divine providence reflects theological ideas of late writers (cf. 139:1-24; Isa. 56:6-7; Job 26:5-14; 38:39-41; 39:1-30).

The first part consists of two strophes (vss. 1-2, 3-4); its meter originally was 3+2, but in the present text vs. 2 has 3+3 and vs. 4 has 3+3+2. The second part falls into three strophes (vss. 5-6, 7-9, 10-12); its meter is 3+3, though units or stichs of four beats occur in vss. 6*c*, 7*b*, 12*a*.

1. The Way of the Wicked (36:1-4)

36:1-2. Transgression speaks to the wicked: The text is difficult and various emendations have been proposed. The M.T. is, lit., "an oracle of transgression," etc. The RSV follows the LXX, reading the verb instead of the noun. If the M.T. is followed, then in the sequel we should expect to find the content of the oracle, but the text of vss. 1*b*-2 does not easily lend itself to such an interpretation. However, in spite of the textual difficulties the implication seems to be that **transgression,** like the serpent in Eden, tempts man to do evil by suggesting to him that God takes no account of wickedness (cf. 50:21; Job 22:2-3). As soon as this ordering principle of human conduct has been undermined there is a steady declension in character. **He flatters himself in his own eyes that his iniquity cannot be found out and hated:** This verse is a *crux interpretum;* lit., "In his own eyes he deceives him with respect to the finding his iniquity [and] the hating [it]," i.e., he thinks that he outwits God so that he does not find out his wickedness

vss. 5-12. But there is also a case to be made for the view that the psalm is a unity. Even if originally the parts were separate poems, someone by accident or design joined them, and generations of the devout have read them as one and have put into them their own thoughts. By this time the parts are well soldered. True, there is a sharp break of subject between vs. 4 and vs. 5; but this break is itself full of meaning. The contrast between vss. 1-4 and those which follow is of real value, and the movement of the mind implied in the contrast is quite comprehensible. It is the kind of movement a reflective, dramatic poet might make. Whatever the historical background, the psalm deals with (*a*) the world view of a man whose good is evil; (*b*) the world view of a man whose God is the Lord; and (*c*) the consequent appeal of the devout.

1-4. ***Sin.***—Here the poet contemplates the sinful heart of a man who was representative of a section of society at that time, a section which has proved self-propagating in all societies, not least today. We are face to face immediately with one who has sunk as deep as one can. Sin has "become his oracle." He does not only do wrong, but he interprets the world and its government from the point of view of sin. Evil is his instructor about the nature of things; as has been said, in his case "conscience is on the wrong side." Translate **transgression** [or "an oracle of transgression"] **speaks to the wicked deep in his heart.** This is the controlling conception of the first section; and it is sufficiently dark. **Transgression** is almost personified; it might be rendered "the spirit of transgression." It takes the place of the spirit of God speaking in conscience. **Deep in his heart** it speaks, in that part of a man where conviction and the springs of action reside (cf. the use of the imagery of personified evil in C. S. Lewis, *The Screwtape Letters*). The result is that he becomes a sheer atheist. There is no God, no other right than that which in transgression and by transgression he has come to regard as desirable. Conscience will trouble him no more, for transgression is in charge of it. This is a picture of the last degradation. We can only hope that in God's mercy it never completely happens, for it means that the spark of God in the soul is quenched.

Vs. 2 carries on the same idea, sharpening its

3 The words of his mouth *are* iniquity and deceit: he hath left off to be wise, *and* to do good.
4 He deviseth mischief upon his bed; he setteth himself in a way *that is* not good; he abhorreth not evil.
5 Thy mercy, O LORD, *is* in the heavens; *and* thy faithfulness *reacheth* unto the clouds.
6 Thy righteousness *is* like the great mountains; thy judgments *are* a great deep: O LORD, thou preservest man and beast.

3 The words of his mouth are mischief and deceit;
he has ceased to act wisely and do good.
4 He plots mischief while on his bed;
he sets himself in a way that is not good;
he spurns not evil.

5 Thy steadfast love, O LORD, extends to the heavens,
thy faithfulness to the clouds.
6 Thy righteousness is like the mountains of God,
thy judgments are like the great deep;
man and beast thou savest, O LORD.

---

and turn against it. The text is heavy and uncertain, but no emendation yet proposed is satisfactory.

3-4. The steps by which the wicked man makes his moral descent are indicated: (*a*) **the words of his mouth are mischief and deceit;** (*b*) **he has ceased to act wisely;** (*c*) **he plots mischief while on his bed;** (*d*) **he sets himself in a way that is not good;** and at last (*e*) **he spurns not evil,** i.e., he embraces it.

2. THE STEADFAST LOVE OF GOD (36:5-9)

5-6. Thy righteousness is like the great mountains or, lit., **the mountains of God.** In ancient mythology the divine beings were associated with the most impressive natural phenomena (cf. 104:16, "the trees of the LORD"). Such a form of expression acquired the force of a superlative.

---

outlines. There is indeed a touch of scorn for such a view in the words, **he flatters himself in his own eyes.** Such a man truly is "flattering himself": for whether it is at another's malignant whisper or not, he is in reality making himself his own god. Anyone who makes his own desire the criterion of right does just that. But the point of the verse is in the concluding words, **he flatters himself . . . that his iniquity cannot be found out.** Not "will not," but **cannot,** for there is no God to find it out or to recognize it if it were found. Then comes the critical word, **his iniquity cannot be found out and hated.** It makes all the difference if we believe that God really hates sin, and will have nothing whatever to do with it except to destroy it. Here is a deadly descent into darkness: (*a*) the whispering of the spirit of evil, deep in the heart; (*b*) the death of the fear of God; (*c*) the conviction that there is no appearing before him; (*d*) the comfort in evil, that there is no consuming fire for it. "Take thine ease, O my soul, and wallow."

Vss. 3-4 are a pen portrait of one who has come to think in such terms. His speech is an instrument of hurt and lies, **the words of his mouth are mischief and deceit.** What else can they be, when he has a lie in his soul? His acts are intemperately unwise, for wisdom interferes with pleasure; nor does he **do good,** for that also would put an end to his ministry of his own desires. Note the words **he has ceased to act wisely and do good.** At one time he had some decent impulses, but they died when he slew the God within. Even the hours of dark have no terrors for his perverted conscience, for **he plots mischief while on his bed.** All together, his character has become fixed; with evil for a cement, **he sets himself in a way that is not good;** and finally he is summed up in the tragic phrase, **he spurns not evil.** If a man gets into a condition in which no wrong can sicken and disgust him, he is in a perilous state. There is nothing left but that God should "unmake but to remake the soul."

It is a dark picture, but who can say it is impossible? Let all who would banish God and his right from the minds of men ponder it.

5-9. ***The Goodness of God.***—Suddenly the poet turns from this devil worship—for it is no less—to a contemplation of the God that is, and of his majestic goodness and faithfulness.

7 How excellent *is* thy loving-kindness, O God! therefore the children of men put their trust under the shadow of thy wings.
8 They shall be abundantly satisfied with the fatness of thy house; and thou shalt make them drink of the river of thy pleasures.
9 For with thee *is* the fountain of life: in thy light shall we see light.

7 How precious is thy steadfast love, O God!
The children of men take refuge in the shadow of thy wings.
8 They feast on the abundance of thy house,
and thou givest them drink from the river of thy delights.
9 For with thee is the fountain of life;
in thy light do we see light.

7-9. Men take refuge in the shadow of thy wings: See 17:8. In this instance the metaphor symbolizes, not the temple, but God's protecting care in which all men may put their trust (cf. 57:1; 63:7). Similarly, **the abundance of thy house** and **the river of thy delights** refer, not to the eating and drinking at the feasts in the temple, but to the rich provisions in nature for man's physical needs (cf. 65:9-13; 78:23-25). **With thee is the fountain of life:** Cf. Jer. 2:13; 17:13. **In thy light do we see light: Light** and **life** are synonyms here (cf. Job 33:30). To see the light is to live (cf. Job 3:16). The dead do not see the light (cf. 49:19). So it is through the goodness of God we have hold on life. For **thy light** see 27:1.

It almost seems as if he shook himself free from the grip of evil with a sigh of relief to see "the brave, new world," which is the only world that is real, with the true God at the heart of it. The contrast between the rancid odor of the world animated by the spirit of vss. 1-4, and the free, fresh air in vss. 5-8 is the contrast between evil and good, between the world of the not-good and that of the God of right and grace. We need to look on this picture and on that. It is precisely the blackness of the one that makes the other so splendidly invigorating.

Thy steadfast love, O Lord, extends to the heavens,
thy faithfulness to the clouds.
Thy righteousness is like the mountains of God,
thy judgments are like the great deep;

lines like these come with a shout to the lips in contradiction of the whisperings of evil. **Mountains** and **the great deep;** we are transported from a fetid prison house to the hills and to the sea, where the clean winds of God are blowing, where man can be great and all creation seems a sane thing. No wonder the poet adds, **Man and beast thou savest.**

Vss. 7-9 are among the most tenderly beautiful in the Psalter. After his sudden leap to the mountain of God—"the strength of the hills is his also" (95:4)—the psalmist begins a melody upon the graciousness of God. **How precious is thy steadfast love** (vs. 7). God is not an idea to inspire terror, but a thought to be taken comfortingly into the mind and heart, even of poor, inadequate people who need a refuge **in the shadow of** [his] **wings.**

They feast on the abundance of thy house,
and thou givest them drink from the river of thy delights.

The motif of Ps. 23 appears again. The guide becomes the host. The phrase **the river of thy delights** gives an image on which to ponder. The steady inner sustaining of the man whose heart is fixed on God is a fact to which there are many witnesses, especially among the old. The world may be turbulent, but the heart can be at peace. Sometimes the river suggests "still waters," sometimes a mighty current, as when F. W. H. Myers makes *Saint Paul* speak of "a surge and an increasing" with which spreads "the great wave of the grace of God." Cf. the image of the rivulet issuing from the temple rock and becoming "waters to swim in" (Ezek. 47, a pregnant passage). The "word of grace" is far more powerful even in the world today than cynics and pessimists think. Mark the **delights.** It is noteworthy that in vss. 1-4 there is nothing about "pleasantnesses." Only the "heart at leisure from itself" [9] is free to see and enjoy "the number of things" which life offers for our contentment.

For with thee is the fountain of life. A fountain, like a garden, is "a lovesome thing, God wot" [1]—sparkling, refreshing to the eyes, and

[9] Anna Letitia Waring, "Father, I know that all my life."
[1] Thomas Edward Brown, "My Garden."

10 O continue thy loving-kindness unto them that know thee; and thy righteousness to the upright in heart.

11 Let not the foot of pride come against me, and let not the hand of the wicked remove me.

12 There are the workers of iniquity fallen: they are cast down, and shall not be able to rise.

10 O continue thy steadfast love to those
who know thee,
and thy salvation to the upright of
heart!
11 Let not the foot of arrogance come upon
me,
nor the hand of the wicked drive me
away.
12 There the evildoers lie prostrate,
they are thrust down, unable to rise.

---

3. Concluding Prayer (36:10-12)

10-12. The psalmist concludes with a prayer that God's favor may ever abide with him, and that he may be saved from the cruelty of his arrogant foes. Read with Gunkel תבוסני for תבואני, i.e., "trample me" for **come upon me.** Also in vs. 12 read with Gunkel שממו for שם, and translate, "May evildoers be appalled, may they **lie prostrate,"** etc.

---

life-giving wherever its waters flow (recall Ezek. 47). God is life and means life; the knowledge of him and his Son is life eternal. Contrast this with vs. 12, which presents the end of the man whose conscience is perverted, **prostrate, thrust down, unable to rise.** Truly, God offers us blessing or cursing: "choose ye."

In the second clause, **in thy light do we see light,** the psalm reaches its zenith. It is no great stride from this to the Gospel of John and the Johannine Epistles, or to the figure of One who on the temple steps, as the shades of evening drew on, cried, "I am the light of the world" (John 8:12). But there is an immediate point in the thought of seeing light. For light is of varying quality. In some climates it is always subdued in a world of half-lights; in others it is allied to the heat that scorches. But in all places and at all times light itself is a joy in its clarity and youthfulness. The God of light must be forever young, for he is God of the morning. George Meredith's poem "The Day of the Daughter of Hades" has a vivid passage extolling the wonder of light in itself. The daughter of Persephone, dwelling in the underworld, is according to legend granted one day upon the earth each year, and is transported suddenly to a Sicilian spring morning. "Light," she cries, "light." She has no eyes at first for aught beside it. Afterward she sees things as they are and finds loveliness everywhere. So also the God-touched spirit shall awaken to the true world, where "light perpetual falls upon him."

10-12. ***Prayer and Triumph.***—These verses form a natural conclusion in the prayer that the poet's world may be the world where God is and not the other. If vs. 12 is the clue of the poem, the writer makes his prayer emphatic with a final, shuddering glance at the loathsome home in which the evildoers dwell. We notice the touch of universalism in vs. 10, as in the preceding verses. The psalmist has a vision of the wideness of God's mercy. Perhaps we could wish that the psalm ended with it; on the other hand, may it not be essential that we should be brought back to the world that is obscured with the smoke of wrong? Vs. 11 is the obverse of vs. 10 made personal. In vs. 10 the poet prays for the continuance of God's goodness on all upright men; in vs. 11 he prays for his own escape from two evils to which the godless are prone, **arrogance** and violence. For **remove me** read "make me a fugitive."

Vs. 12 is in its own way perplexing. It looks like a fragment from a different writing. But taken as a glimpse into the final condition of the man of perverted conscience it has apt meaning:

> **There the evildoers lie prostrate,**
> **they are thrust down, unable to rise.**

It is a vivid contrast with vs. 11. There arrogant feet trod on the humble and lowly; now they know another treading, the treading of the feet of righteous justice. The verse has a solemnizing power in its incompleteness. No direct mention is made of what it is that treads them down. But the poet has been thinking of God, and then glances back at those who deny him. They are flat on their faces now, with no hope of getting up again—unless! Perhaps we need always to be reminded of that side of the shield. The verse of the psalm, however, which will stay in the mind is that which tells us of the God with whom **is the fountain of life** (vs. 9).

A Psalm of David.

37 Fret not thyself because of evildoers, neither be thou envious against the workers of iniquity.

A Psalm of David.

37 Fret not yourself because of the wicked,
be not envious of wrongdoers!

XXXVII. Wise Counsel from an Aged Man (37:1-40)

We have here an acrostic psalm of the wisdom type. Each of the twenty-two strophes consists of a couplet or a double distich which begins with a letter of the Hebrew alphabet in regular succession (cf. Pss. 9–10). In its thought it is to be classed with the literature of the late wisdom school. Its purpose, like that of Proverbs, is to instruct and exhort men about the principles of the practice of religion, but its keynote is struck in the first line, **Fret not thyself because of evildoers.** In other words it belongs to a time when the old Deuteronomic doctrine (cf. Deut. 28) of a perfect equation between conduct and recompense was being questioned. In Proverbs, Job, and Ecclesiastes, as well as in Pss. 49; 73, we hear other murmurs of dissent from the old creed. The writer of this psalm, however, is not troubled by the conflict between the realities of life and the traditional theology (cf. 1:3; Prov. 11:31). He holds that God deals with men by an unchanging law of retributive justice; and that if the facts of experience at any time point otherwise, it is only a seeming disturbance of the balance of justice, for in due time, if he does not faint, the godly man shall be gloriously vindicated. The thesis of the psalm is somewhat loosely sustained since the couplets, like those of Proverbs, can be taken as independent units of thought, but by dint of its repetition with some variety in expression it gains the effect of an argument.

It should be noted that the psalmists deal in different ways with the enigma of the good fortune enjoyed by many of the wicked. Sometimes they find a ready solution in the belief that it is a punishment for the sins of the godly or of their ancestors (79:8); sometimes they explain the troubles of good men by supposing that God is angry with them for something of which the sufferers are ignorant (32:5); sometimes they dare to ascribe their unhappy lot to God's indifference (44:9, 23); sometimes they explain it as the result of their zealous loyalty to the Lord's cause (44:17).

The psalm as a product of the wisdom literature must be ascribed to the fourth or third century B.C. Its acrostic form and its equation of the law and wisdom (cf. vss. 30-31) point to the later date. The meter is 3+3, with some variations due in part to imperfect textual transmission.

1. Admonitions for Daily Living (37:1-11)

37:1-6. The writer urges men not to be vexed (more lit., "to become heated") about the good fortune enjoyed by some of the wicked, or even to be **envious of**

37:1-40. ***The Patience of the Saints.***—Psalms are of different qualities, and this is not one of the greatest. It is another alphabetical acrostic and consists largely of quotations, principally from the book of Proverbs, which follow one another in no particular order except that which the acrostic demands. The theme is of the simplest. The pious Jews who held to their principles and practices were having a hard time; which points to a late date, although it might also be the Exile. Whenever it was, it was a time when godlessness was prosperous and piety was poor and depressed. To the problem thus created the psalm offers not a solution but an affirmation: "God reigns; therefore prosperous wickedness cannot last. God will in his own time give to every man according to his deserts. Wherefore, wait and hope." The psalm must have been written to bring comfort; and it is a fact that a confident assertion, uttered by a believer, frequently repeated, brings assurance to perturbed spirits, especially if buttressed by old and well-loved quotations. Many a Scottish heart has been enabled to get through bad days by repeating the metrical version of 34:19,

> The troubles that afflict the just
> in number many be,
> But yet at length out of them all
> the Lord doth set him free.

2 For they shall soon be cut down like the grass, and wither as the green herb.
3 Trust in the LORD, and do good; *so* shalt thou dwell in the land, and verily thou shalt be fed.
4 Delight thyself also in the LORD; and he shall give thee the desires of thine heart.
5 Commit thy way unto the LORD; trust also in him; and he shall bring *it* to pass.
6 And he shall bring forth thy righteousness as the light, and thy judgment as the noonday.
7 Rest in the LORD, and wait patiently for him: fret not thyself because of him who prospereth in his way, because of the man who bringeth wicked devices to pass.

2 For they will soon fade like the grass,
and wither like the green herb.

3 Trust in the LORD, and do good;
so you will dwell in the land, and enjoy security.
4 Take delight in the LORD,
and he will give you the desires of your heart.

5 Commit your way to the LORD;
trust in him, and he will act.
6 He will bring forth your vindication as the light,
and your right as the noonday.

7 Be still before the LORD, and wait patiently for him;
fret not yourself over him who prospers in his way,
over the man who carries out evil devices!

wrongdoers. For a day is coming when **they will . . . fade like the grass,** but the Lord **will give you the desires of your heart,** and the cause of the just will be gloriously vindicated.

7-11. Be calm therefore and **wait patiently** for the Lord to act. To trouble oneself continually about "the man who succeeds in his evil devices" only works harm to

Thus the writer of Ps. 37 knew something of the human heart and did his sorely tried people a service when he arranged this anthology of trust and hope. There is many a verse in it which we should so make our own that it may come unbidden to our lips when the hill is steep.

The psalm being what it is, the expositor is free to take it verse by verse. It is, indeed, little more than a collection of devout sayings, and as such can be refreshingly used. Some of the expressions are unexpected and vivid.

1-11. ***Fret Not Thyself.*—Fret not . . . be not envious.** The two verbs have a similar root meaning of being "heated." The word translated **fret** occurs three times in the psalm (cf. vss. 7-8); the writer was evidently anxious to press home his point. If we may permit ourselves a colloquialism, he advises his readers not to become "hot and bothered" about the wicked, or "burning with jealousy" of the evildoers. The words indicate states of mind with which our society is familiar, and warning against them is always apposite.

Vs. 2 gives the psalmist's ground for keeping calm; viz., the day of evildoers is short. Few will have any difficulty in providing historical or present instances. In Lancashire, England, millworkers wore wooden shoes called "clogs." In the great industrial days men rose to fortune rapidly and often harshly; but Lancashire people had a saying, "Clogs to clogs, three generations." It is not always so, and need not be so; but there is sufficient evidence to support the thought that a purely material prosperity "lacks continuance."

Trust in the LORD, and do good;
so you will dwell in the land, and enjoy security.

Instead of **security**, one might read "stableness." The promise requires a time factor. For the individual it is not true when wars threaten and men and nations lust for power at any price. In saner times the upright man is stabler in his possession of what is necessary for life than is his crooked neighbor. If the first clause were the slogan of nations, the rest would follow. In any case, the man who trusts in the Lord and does good has food that the worldling knows not of.

Vs. 4 provides an arresting phrase that suggests self-examination. What are our **desires?** What do we seek and do in solitariness? Further,

8 Cease from anger, and forsake wrath: fret not thyself in any wise to do evil.

9 For evildoers shall be cut off: but those that wait upon the LORD, they shall inherit the earth.

10 For yet a little while, and the wicked *shall* not *be:* yea, thou shalt diligently consider his place, and it *shall* not *be.*

11 But the meek shall inherit the earth; and shall delight themselves in the abundance of peace.

8 Refrain from anger, and forsake wrath!
Fret not yourself; it tends only to evil.
9 For the wicked shall be cut off;
but those who wait for the LORD shall possess the land.

10 Yet a little while, and the wicked will be no more;
though you look well at his place, he will not be there.
11 But the meek shall possess the land,
and delight themselves in abundant prosperity.

---

oneself or leads to sin. The promise of the possession of **the land** is to the godly. The power and the dominion of the wicked will be short. In vs. 9 delete המה, **they** (KJV), for the sake of the meter.

---

what is meant by **the LORD?** All, surely, that expresses him, all that in his presence we can delight in. The word **take** indicates an effort of will. We have to train our desires. If they are properly trained, so that we can invite the Lord to inspect them, he will certainly increase them: **he will give you the desires of your heart.** *Crescit gramen edenti:* such "corn grows for the eater."

The word **way** in vs. 5 opens up avenues of thought. It means primarily, no doubt, one's journey through life; but it has come to mean the kind of life which we choose and develop. So we speak of our "way of life" nationally. It has to be such that we can commit it to the Lord. If we can, as far as our personal life is concerned, he will take care of it. A **way** leads somewhere; he will secure that a committed way will lead to himself. The verse has interesting historical associations. It is the basis of Paul Gerhardt's famous hymn, *Befiehl du deine wege,* familiar in English hymnals through John Wesley's translation, "Commit thou all thy griefs." In some high schools in Germany it was the custom to accompany graduates to the gate of the town singing this hymn the while. It is also recorded that the verse was often on the lips of David Livingstone in Africa.[2]

In vs. 6 are phrases taken from law courts, but they have a large meaning: the time is bound to come when all worldlings will be compelled to acknowledge that the God-fearing were right, and that they themselves were wrong; otherwise the scheme of things is a "sorry scheme."

In vs. 7, **Rest in the LORD, and wait patiently for him** is more accurately, **Be still before the LORD.** But we must not change the older version here; music has made it part of our devotional speech. If we wait, we must be still, in reverence and assent; but our stillness should be restful, especially when we are waiting for one whom in Christ we call our Father.

The very practical advice offered in vs. 8, if taken, would do much to sweeten society. The "culture of irritation" is a common modern disease, against which a man is his own best physician. Mere "fretting," even against undeserved prosperity, accomplishes nothing; it only embitters without rectifying. It is a mark of nervous weakness to which sections of youth are exposed today. The Christian church should be the example of an "unfretful society," which in its calmness becomes strong to deliver.

Vs. 9 is a repetition of the refrain of temporariness. **Those who wait for the LORD shall possess the land** indicates the historical setting of the saying. It implies that it was written at a time when the pious Jew was dispossessed. To our minds it promises stable security in a simple life, in place of the fret of economic uncertainty.

In vs. 10 the refrain is repeated once more. The introductory words **yet a little while** in themselves arrest the attention of hearers. **While** indicates "passingness," a coming to depart into that which is no more. It might be used in widely different regions. It could be applied to Good Friday, seen in the light of Easter Day. On that Friday afternoon all seemed dark; **yet a little while.** And as for those who caused that darkness, **though you look well at his place, he will not be there.** The simple, somber words with which the verse closes might be written over the thrones of all tryants, and ultimately over evil itself.

[2] Ker, *Psalms in History and Biography,* pp. 66-67.

12 The wicked plotteth against the just, and gnasheth upon him with his teeth.
13 The Lord shall laugh at him: for he seeth that his day is coming.
14 The wicked have drawn out the sword, and have bent their bow, to cast down the poor and needy, *and* to slay such as be of upright conversation.
15 Their sword shall enter into their own heart, and their bows shall be broken.
16 A little that a righteous man hath *is* better than the riches of many wicked.
17 For the arms of the wicked shall be broken: but the LORD upholdeth the righteous.
18 The LORD knoweth the days of the upright: and their inheritance shall be for ever.

12 The wicked plots against the righteous,
and gnashes his teeth at him;
13 but the LORD laughs at the wicked,
for he sees that his day is coming.

14 The wicked draw the sword and bend their bows,
to bring down the poor and needy,
to slay those who walk uprightly;
15 their sword shall enter their own heart,
and their bows shall be broken.

16 Better is a little that the righteous has
than the abundance of many wicked.
17 For the arms of the wicked shall be broken;
but the LORD upholds the righteous.

18 The LORD knows the days of the blameless,
and their heritage will abide for ever;

---

2. THE WICKED AND THE RIGHTEOUS CONTRASTED (37:12-22)

12-15. It is true that **the wicked plots against the righteous** by various devices, and even turns his weapons of death against **those who walk uprightly,** but he plots only to his own destruction.

16-22. The wealth which the wicked heap up will not avail them in testing times. In vs. 16 read with the versions רב for רבים, and translate, "than the great abundance

---

But the meek shall possess the land (vs. 11). Cf. the Beatitudes. Why should the idea of meekness cause so much laughter among "realists"? For the meek are God-trusters and God-dependers. Therefore they are strong. Their nerves are steady, and they never know when they are beaten. Indeed, they know that if they are in agreement with God they cannot be beaten. Their morale is unbreakable; and morale is nine tenths of the battle. Human mammoths die out.

12-13. *God's Laughter.*—Vs. 12 provides us with a precise picture of the "bloody-minded"; literally true of many famous tyrants. At the back of the mind such men are in constant fear. They have taken the sword; but they know that another sword is drawn against them, and they are terrified of its sharpness. Therefore they "gnash their teeth" in a superfretting. Ultimately the stress proves too great and they crack.

But the LORD laughs at him is a memorable expression of a terrible conception (cf. Ps. 2). It were better for a man never to have been born than to evoke the laughter of God. There is a painful touch of ridicule in the phrase. We see the proud man, haughtily seated among his cringers and his slaves, but we hear from the place of real power the sounds of risible contempt. Poor little king-grasshopper, lording it over grasshoppers; but **his day is coming,** and so soon!

14-15. *The Sword.*—The psalms were written by very devout men, and in their devoutness they saw far into the principles of things. Consequently, we should listen when they re-emphasize. One fact that they call our attention to again and again is that violent aggression—**the sword**—is a sure way to self-destruction. Let the nations learn and obey.

16-20. *The Little and the Abundance.*—A hard saying for modern society with the cash measurement of success; yet entirely true:

Better is a little that the righteous has
than the abundance of many wicked.

Note that the **little** is assumed; destitution is never a good. But the "sufficient" is a good, for it suffices. In such a case the righteous man is the richer, for he has his little plus righteousness, while the wicked has **abundance** plus nothing but wickedness, and wickedness is a subtracting quantity. Observation of many

19 They shall not be ashamed in the evil time: and in the days of famine they shall be satisfied.

20 But the wicked shall perish, and the enemies of the LORD *shall be* as the fat of lambs: they shall consume; into smoke shall they consume away.

21 The wicked borroweth, and payeth not again: but the righteous showeth mercy, and giveth.

22 For *such as be* blessed of him shall inherit the earth; and *they that be* cursed of him shall be cut off.

23 The steps of a *good* man are ordered by the LORD: and he delighteth in his way.

19 they are not put to shame in evil times,
in the days of famine they have abundance.

20 But the wicked perish;
the enemies of the LORD are like the glory of the pastures,
they vanish — like smoke they vanish away.

21 The wicked borrows, and cannot pay back,
but the righteous is generous and gives;
22 for those blessed by the LORD shall possess the land,
but those cursed by him shall be cut off.

23 The steps of a man are from the LORD,
and he establishes him in whose way he delights;

---

of the wicked." The **righteous** may have **little,** but they have nothing to fear since "the LORD is their support." **In the days of famine they have abundance:** The riches of the wicked will fail them, and their unjust gain will never be passed on to their heirs. The righteous will never be so straitened in circumstances that they will not have enough and to spare, but

> **The wicked borrows, and cannot pay back,**
> . . . .
> **for those blessed by the LORD shall possess the land,**
> **but those cursed by him shall be cut off.**

3. The Saints Are Ever Safeguarded (37:23-40)

23-28*b*. The misfortunes of the righteous are never final and complete: **Though he fall, he shall not be cast headlong.** Long experience has shown the psalmist that the

---

homes leads to the conviction that the simple home, where there is righteousness with all that follows therefrom of mental and spiritual interest, is the happiest of homes and gives the children the best chance in life. There is a hint in vs. 17 in the phrase **the arms of the wicked shall be broken:** the arms with their hands are the agents of action. The final result of "trying to take in God" is inability to do anything.

Vss. 18-20 repeat the same ideas in varying forms. In vs. 20, for **like the glory of the pastures,** some read "like a brand in the furnace." Note the parallelism with **like smoke they vanish away.** The two together give a combination of destruction, with its hint of punishment, and evanescence as the inevitable outcome of godlessness—particularly evanescence. **They vanish away** is the burden of this psalm. The godless are temporary and trivial.

21-33. ***A Stable Society.***—In vss. 21-26 the psalm changes its tone. It seems to suggest a stable society in which a good man is both prosperous and secure; but a collection of sayings of varying age will inevitably imply different social situations.

> **The wicked borrows, and cannot pay back,**
> **but the righteous is generous and gives.**

It is an open fact that philanthropic enterprises depend financially upon the religious, and especially upon the Christian, section of any community. It is also a fact that a God-fearing man has the longest "moral" credit, as any banker will agree. It is equally true that religious people with small possessions are the most principled people in the matter of giving. Vs. 22 refers not to personal prosperity so much as to the continuance of race, and even of

24 Though he fall, he shall not be utterly
cast down: for the LORD upholdeth *him*
with his hand.
25 I have been young, and *now* am old;
yet have I not seen the righteous forsaken,
nor his seed begging bread.
26 *He is* ever merciful, and lendeth; and
his seed *is* blessed.
27 Depart from evil, and do good; and
dwell for evermore.
28 For the LORD loveth judgment, and
forsaketh not his saints; they are preserved
for ever: but the seed of the wicked shall be
cut off.
29 The righteous shall inherit the land,
and dwell therein for ever.
30 The mouth of the righteous speaketh
wisdom, and his tongue talketh of judgment.
31 The law of his God *is* in his heart;
none of his steps shall slide.

24 though he fall, he shall not be cast headlong,
for the LORD is the stay of his hand.

25 I have been young, and now am old;
yet I have not seen the righteous forsaken
or his children begging bread.
26 He is ever giving liberally and lending,
and his children become a blessing.

27 Depart from evil, and do good;
so shall you abide for ever.
28 For the LORD loves justice;
he will not forsake his saints.
The righteous shall be preserved for ever,
but the children of the wicked shall be cut off.
29 The righteous shall possess the land,
and dwell upon it for ever.

30 The mouth of the righteous utters wisdom,
and his tongue speaks justice.
31 The law of his God is in his heart;
his steps do not slip.

Lord does what is right to the righteous, generation after generation. The righteous and his children, instead of **begging bread,** are the distributors of benefactions to others. In vs. 23, the RSV reads with Duhm כוננו בדרכו for כוננו ודרכו, which is represented by the KJV.

28*c*-34. The psalmist repeats the lesson of the previous verses. The righteous need only to be patient and to put their confidence in the Lord. **The children of the wicked shall be cut off,** but

The righteous shall possess the land,
and dwell upon it for ever,

---

family. This even yet is a frequent social fact. Vss. 23-24 are suggestive. **The LORD . . . establishes** [steadies] **him in whose way he delights.** He has his ups and downs, but he presents an erect front to life. A "steady" man is the cement of any society; and his secret is that he walks with the steadfast God. Vs. 25 is picturesque hyperbole. The writer was thinking of Eastern beggars and was declaring that he had never seen the righteous sink to that level of social degradation. But there is a deal of truth in the statement for any society. The righteous is rarely unemployable; in hard times his honest pride invents work, if it can be invented. His discontent with dependence sends him seeking ways to be independent; and his good repute stands him in good stead with those who can set him on his feet. It is also true that the **children** of God-fearing homes **become a blessing** in far greater proportion than the children of God-forgetting homes, e.g., the sons of Christian ministers provide a vastly higher proportion of distinguished men than any other profession or business.[3]

Vss. 27-29 give the practical conclusion: if we want our family or nation to continue, **depart from evil, and do good.** It is refreshing to listen to common sense uttered in plain

[3] Cf. A. W. Fergusson, *Sons of the Manse* (Dundee: James P. Mathew & Co., 1923).

32 The wicked watcheth the righteous, and seeketh to slay him.
33 The LORD will not leave him in his hand, nor condemn him when he is judged.
34 Wait on the LORD, and keep his way, and he shall exalt thee to inherit the land: when the wicked are cut off, thou shalt see *it.*
35 I have seen the wicked in great power, and spreading himself like a green bay tree.
36 Yet he passed away, and, lo, he *was* not: yea, I sought him, but he could not be found.
37 Mark the perfect *man,* and behold the upright: for the end of *that* man *is* peace.

32 The wicked watches the righteous,
and seeks to slay him.
33 The LORD will not abandon him to his power,
or let him be condemned when he is brought to trial.

34 Wait for the LORD, and keep to his way,
and he will exalt you to possess the land;
you will look on the destruction of the wicked.

35 I have seen a wicked man overbearing,
and towering like a cedar of Lebanon.[v]
36 Again I[w] passed by, and, lo, he was no more;
though I sought him, he could not be found.

37 Mark the blameless man, and behold the upright,
for there is posterity for the man of peace.

[v] Gk: Heb obscure
[w] Gk Syr Jerome: Heb *he*

---

for the righteous know the wise way of life. In vs. 28*c* read נשמדו, "shall be destroyed," for נשמרו, "shall be kept." **Wisdom** flows from the lips of the righteous and he keeps the **law** of the Lord with all his heart.

35-40. The higher the wicked man exalts himself the more terrible will be his fall. His end will be sudden and complete. **Though I sought him, he could not be found:** Root and branch, **transgressors** and their **posterity . . . shall be cut off.** But the Lord helps, delivers, and saves the righteous; **he is their refuge in the time of trouble.** In vs. 35 read עליז, "jubilant," for עריץ, "terrible." In vs. 37 read with the LXX and Syriac רעה, "keep" or "tend," for ראה, "see," and (without changing the consonants) *tōm,* "integrity," for *tām,* **blameless,** and *yōsher,* "uprightness," for *yāshār,* **upright.**

The psalm is a defense of the orthodox teaching of the day rather than an attempt to shed new light on a difficult problem. It does little for the relief of the troubles of a

---

English. This verse may be a platitude; but platitudes must not be forgotten merely because we have heard them before. A platitude like this implies a strong conception of God. The connection between the doing of good and continuance is rooted in him. That is the kind of God he is.

Vss. 30-33 record some of the marks of the good man and of his experience. The good man has a mouth that **utters wisdom, and his tongue speaks justice,** a comment which has its bearing on modern "cleverness," and on partisanship in political party strife. To be clever at the expense of wisdom and justice is to fail in character. On the other hand, **the wicked watches the righteous** with mean eyes, seeking his hurt. It is the mark of a darkened spirit to be concerned to "catch a brother out."

34-40. ***Retributive Justice.*—Wait for the Lord; . . . you will look on the destruction of the wicked** furnishes another example of the difference Christ makes. His promised feasting is in "the communion of life." Evil will not only disappear, but will be forgotten. Meantime his action is to save the wicked.

Vss. 35-38 restate in memorable phrases the impermanence of the godless and the continuance of the God-fearing. **I have seen a wicked man . . . towering like a cedar of Lebanon. Again I passed by, and, lo, he was no more;**

38 But the transgressors shall be destroyed together: the end of the wicked shall
be cut off.
39 But the salvation of the righteous *is*
of the LORD: *he is* their strength in the time
of trouble.
40 And the LORD shall help them, and
deliver them: he shall deliver them from
the wicked, and save them, because they
trust in him.

A Psalm of David, to bring to remembrance.

38 O LORD, rebuke me not in thy
wrath: neither chasten me in thy hot
displeasure.

38 But transgressors shall be altogether destroyed;
the posterity of the wicked shall be cut off.

39 The salvation of the righteous is from the LORD;
he is their refuge in the time of trouble.
40 The LORD helps them and delivers them;
he delivers them from the wicked, and saves them,
because they take refuge in him.

A Psalm of David, for the memorial offering.

38 O LORD, rebuke me not in thy anger,
nor chasten me in thy wrath!

---

godly man to tell him that a good time, which he may never see, is coming; to seek to answer the deep questionings of such a man by an eschatological promise is not sufficient (see Ps. 73).

XXXVIII. A SINNER'S PLEA FOR GOD'S HELP (38:1-22)

We have here the prayer of one who is in great trouble because of grave bodily affliction. The psalm belongs to the class of laments. In the usage of the church it has been numbered among the seven penitential psalms, the others being Pss. 6; 32; 51; 102; 130; 143. At the time when the superscription was added to the psalm, it was recited in connection with a **memorial offering.** The expression להזכיר means "for presenting a memorial," i.e., to bring (the offerer) to (God's) remembrance (cf. Targ., *ad loc.*). There were two kinds of memorial offerings: the first consisted in burning on the altar with incense a portion of the cereal offering mixed with oil (Lev. 2:1-10); the second, in burning the incense that was placed each sabbath on the showbread (Lev. 24:7). The LXX and Targ. seem to favor the second kind, but the supplicatory character of this psalm might point to the first. It is probable that, as in Ps. 33, the number of verses was meant to accord with the number of the letters of the alphabet (cf. Lam. 5). The structure of the psalm admits of a division into eleven strophes of two lines each, which, however, may be grouped into the sections characteristic of a lament, as in the RSV.

The argument is clearly discernible. The psalmist begins with an appeal for a measure of help from the affliction which in God's wrath has been visited on him (vss. 1-2). He supports his appeal by a description of the nature and grievousness of his malady, which

---

though I sought him he could not be found. Any imagination must respond to that. There is no more complete illustration of it than was provided by a cellar in Berlin in 1945; but the story of the bloodthirsty illustrates it in all generations. On the other hand, **there is posterity for the man of peace**—a spiritual law which gives encouragement to the idealists who work for a world according to the mind of Christ.

In vss. 39-40 is contained the conclusion of the whole matter. The emphasis is completely thrown upon the Lord. The world is a darkened place, but "Standeth God within the shadow, keeping watch above his own."[4] No man need be sad. There are many words in the world, but the last word is with God. Wherefore, in the phrase that Goethe put in the mouth of the heroes, "We bid you to hope."

38:1-22. ***An Act of Penitence.***—This is a penitential psalm and should be considered as an "act of penitence." Here it is one who is suffering severe bodily and mental wounds

[4] James Russell Lowell, "The Present Crisis," st. viii.

2 For thine arrows stick fast in me, and thy hand presseth me sore.	2 For thy arrows have sunk into me, and thy hand has come down on me.

he considers as deserved for his sins (vss. 3-10). Deserted by friends and kinsmen, he leaves his cause with the Lord, his sole source of deliverance and vindication (vss. 11-16). His suffering, his sin, and the might of his malicious foes combine to overwhelm him (vss. 17-20). As he began, so he ends with a poignant appeal for help. The psalm is outstanding in its class because of its genuinely penitential note, its frank confession of sin, and the absence of any attempt to lay the sickness to the charge of enemies.

For the relation of these lamentation psalms to the prayers preserved in the literature of non-Israelite peoples see Intro., pp. 14-15. This psalm was originally meant for use in the temple by suppliants who were afflicted by diseases which manifested themselves in suppurating sores (cf. Job 7:5; 19:13-20; 30:16-19, 27-30). The amount of material which it has in common with other psalms suggests that it was written by a temple psalmodist.

The alphabetization referred to above, the literary parallels with other psalms, and the number of unusual words and phrases of which some appear chiefly in postexilic literature (C. A. Briggs and E. G. Briggs, *A Critical and Exegetical Commentary on the Book of Psalms* [New York: Charles Scribner's Sons, 1906; "International Critical Commentary"], I, 336), point to a late date. The meter is generally 3+3. There are instances of 4+4 in vss. 3, 4, 10, 13, 16, and of 2+2 in vss. 18, 22.

1. Appeal to God (38:1-2)

38:1-2. The opening verse is a quotation of 6:1. The pains of the psalmist are like the blows of an angry God. **Rebuke me not in thy anger:** He does not contend with God

which may well be symbolic of moral corruptions; who acknowledges and faces his condition and frankly confesses his sins to God; for in God he hopes, and with God he pleads, trusting for an answer.

Whether the subject of the poem is a man or his nation is hard to say; and whether or not the pains which he so vividly enumerates are literally physical, and if so, whether or not he regards them as the direct punitory outcome of a particular sin, is also hard to say. When we compare the psalm with the imagery in Isa. 1, we may well feel that the language of the one is as symbolic as that of the other, with its "wounds, and bruises, and putrifying sores." It is likely enough that the writer was suffering bodily ailments; but there is such a tone of moral distress running through the whole that it is impossible not to believe that the sores which he lamented were moral sores, and that the aches were aches of the spirit when he realized what he had done and what he was. He is a forerunner of Christian in the Slough of Despond. The Expos. will consider it from this point of view, subsequently noting one or two significant expressions which may stir the mind.

The psalm begins with a brief prayer for pity, identical with 6:1, and immediately thereafter the writer opens his heart to make known his woes. Statements of physical ill and mental perturbation tumble from his lips in a kind of cascade, the two being interwoven in a pattern of distress. Notice that the central point of his distress is his **sin.** It is his **iniquity** that is too heavy for him. His real ailment is spiritual; the **wounds** that **grow foul and fester** may be the consequence of his wrongdoing, but they are also pictures of the wrongdoing itself.

A faithful interpreter will pause here to ask himself if he has ever tried to make vivid the quality of sin. This psalm gives him his chance. We are greatly concerned for physical health; foul and festering wounds, loathsome to sight and smell, send us straightway to a physician. Would it not be well for us to think of sins in terms of abscesses? A living sin is the spiritual equivalent of a malignant cancer. Many a physically fit man is in his real self a mass of fetid corruption and, until he awakes to the fact in fear and disgust, he is likely to go on in the course which leads to death. "Putrifying sores," cried the psalmist, as he looked at his soul; "putrifying sores," cried Isaiah, as he looked at the ethics of his nation. Similar voices, making the thought of moral putrefaction live, would serve our world well.

Further, the psalmist realizes his feebleness. His failing body is a phantom of his soul. As a result, he is cold-shouldered by his friends and even his kinsmen turn from him. A mourning, distressed, fear-gripped man—no wonder he is

3 *There is* no soundness in my flesh because of thine anger; neither *is there any*
rest in my bones because of my sin.
4 For mine iniquities are gone over mine
head: as a heavy burden they are too heavy
for me.
5 My wounds stink *and* are corrupt because of my foolishness.
6 I am troubled; I am bowed down
greatly; I go mourning all the day long.
7 For my loins are filled with a loathsome
disease: and *there is* no soundness in my
flesh.
8 I am feeble and sore broken: I have
roared by reason of the disquietness of my
heart.

3 There is no soundness in my flesh
because of thy indignation;
there is no health in my bones
because of my sin.
4 For my iniquities have gone over my
head;
they weigh like a burden too heavy for
me.

5 My wounds grow foul and fester
because of my foolishness,
6 I am utterly bowed down and prostrate;
all the day I go about mourning.
7 For my loins are filled with burning,
and there is no soundness in my flesh.
8 I am utterly spent and crushed;
I groan because of the tumult of my
heart.

---

about the justice of his chastisement; he prays only that God in his wrath may remember mercy (cf. Hab. 3:2; Isa. 57:16). **For thy arrows have sunk into me:** The Lord's arrows are the scourges with which he afflicts men (cf. Deut. 32:23; Job 6:4; 16:13-14). **Thy hand has come down on me:** Cf. 32:4; 39:10. By various metaphors the hostility of God is stressed. Such primitive conceptions of the divine wrath are born out of the psychology of pain.

2. The Psalmist's Condition (38:3-10)

3-10. The psalmist's description of his physical suffering is meant to strengthen the force of his appeal by awakening God's pity: **There is no soundness in my flesh because of thy indignation.** But in the next breath he absolves God from wrongdoing, for **there is no health in my bones because of my sin.** The deep root of the trouble is in him. The LXX and Syriac read "my sins." The results of his iniquities are compared now to waves which close over him (cf. 69:2, 15; 124:4; Jonah 2:3) and now to a weight which crushes him. **My foolishness:** The word אולת is frequent in Proverbs; it is sin that comes through stupid indifference to discipline. **I go about mourning:** Lit., "black," i.e., in sackcloth and ashes (cf. Isa. 58:5), the signs of distress. **With burning:** So RSV, which derives נקלה from קלה(I), "burn," "roast"; the KJV follows the LXX (ἐμπαιγμάτων),

---

solitary. Christian in the Slough of Despond was also left alone. A man's comrades will not stay with him in the place of penitence, unless they are penitent also and have learned how through penitence is found the way to health. He may even become **like a deaf man** and a **dumb man,** a prisoner of his own dark thoughts.

Yet in all this he is in the way of cure. He is facing facts; the reality of sin has hit him between the eyes. And he has not forgotten God. The appeal for help moves into a baring of his soul and its distress; then proceeds to the assertion of faith, the sorrow of penitence as the master emotion, and the purpose of confession. No more pretense; no more turning the blind eye to his spiritual state; no more making of excuses; but frank acknowledgment and sincere grieving. Thereafter he is able to confront his enemies and declare **I follow after good.**

The psalm closes with a plaintive cry for aid, as if he found it hard to believe that such a one as he could be helped. We do not know the end of his story, but the outcome of such penitence is pardon.

1-10. ***Distress of Body and Soul.***—Note that the "rebuking" and the "chastening" (vs. 1) are not complained of as unjust. Penitence must begin there. "I am not worthy" is the starting point. The one thing to do is to plead for God's mercy.

Thine arrows stick fast in me. If we accepted the painful results of wrongdoing as the **arrows** of God, we should make better use of them. An arrow with its barbs, is a most bitter weapon,

9 Lord, all my desire *is* before thee; and my groaning is not hid from thee.

10 My heart panteth, my strength faileth me: as for the light of mine eyes, it also is gone from me.

11 My lovers and my friends stand aloof from my sore; and my kinsmen stand afar off.

12 They also that seek after my life lay snares *for me;* and they that seek my hurt speak mischievous things, and imagine deceits all the day long.

13 But I, as a deaf *man,* heard not; and *I was* as a dumb man *that* openeth not his mouth.

14 Thus I was as a man that heareth not, and in whose mouth *are* no reproofs.

9 Lord, all my longing is known to thee,
my sighing is not hidden from thee.
10 My heart throbs, my strength fails me;
and the light of my eyes — it also has gone from me.
11 My friends and companions stand aloof from my plague,
and my kinsmen stand afar off.

12 Those who seek my life lay their snares,
those who seek my hurt speak of ruin,
and meditate treachery all the day long.

13 But I am like a deaf man, I do not hear,
like a dumb man who does not open his mouth.
14 Yea, I am like a man who does not hear,
and in whose mouth are no rebukes.

Vulg. (*illusionibus*), and Jerome (*ignominia*), which seem to assume its root to be קלה(II), "dishonor," "degrade." **The tumult of my heart:** Lit., "the roaring of my heart." Some would read לביא, "lion," for לבי, **my heart,** and translate "I groan louder than a lion's roar." **All my longing:** Read with Gunkel, תאניתי, "my lamentation," for תאותי, **my longing. My heart throbs:** Lit., "whirls about."

3. Friends' Indifference and Enemies' Malice (38:11-16)

11-16. Those who were closest to the psalmist by ties of friendship and blood forsake him. The statement of his utter dereliction adds fresh force to his appeal. Metrically, vs. 11 is overloaded; omit either אהבי, **my friends,** or רעי, **companions** (cf. Isa. 53:3-4; Job 6:14-15, 21). Seeing that his friends have deserted him, his enemies become bold. **Those who seek my hurt . . . meditate treachery.** But the psalmist keeps silent in the face of their attacks, and **I am like a man . . . in whose mouth are no rebukes** (cf.

---

painful to pull out. But "God's arrows" are strange as well as bitter; for they, if we will, are agents of cure. They are designed to remind us of him whom we have forgotten, whose arm, if it is strong to smite, is also strong to save.

Neither is there any rest in my bones (vs. 3) should be translated **health in my bones.** Yet **rest** is suggestive. Nothing is more creative of restlessness than an aching bone. It is a vivid image of the distress of the sick soul.

My wounds stink and are corrupt because of my foolishness. The words leap to the eye of anyone who is given to plain speaking. The reminder of the evil effects of foolishness is salutary. "Israel doth not know, my people doth not consider" (Isa. 1:3) is the main charge against Israel laid by the prophet. Foolishness leading to stinking wounds of both body and soul is the main charge to lay against a great multitude of transgressors.

Lord, all my longing is known to thee,
my sighing is not hidden from thee.

This is the one point in vss. 1-10 at which the writer appeals to God's justice. He still has a longing which he can show to God, and a sighing which has something worthy in it. It is the cry of the prisoner, but of the prisoner who would be free. God must surely mark favorably that longing. The declaration in Christ is that he does.

11-20. ***Alienation, Patience, Hope.*—My friends and companions stand aloof from my plague.** It is a well-based comment. The spectacle of

An Arab, old and blind,
Some caravan has left behind

is the epitome of the treatment of the diseased by the "natural" man. In old days a leper was driven forth; in our own day the law segregates transgressors. Persons suffering from contagious diseases are put in quarantine; certain types of offenders are socially ostracized. The parallel between the social effects of disease and wrong-

15 For in thee, O LORD, do I hope: thou wilt hear, O Lord my God.

16 For I said, *Hear me,* lest *otherwise* they should rejoice over me: when my foot slippeth, they magnify *themselves* against me.

17 For I *am* ready to halt, and my sorrow *is* continually before me.

18 For I will declare mine iniquity; I will be sorry for my sin.

19 But mine enemies *are* lively, *and* they are strong: and they that hate me wrongfully are multiplied.

15 But for thee, O LORD, do I wait;
it is thou, O LORD my God, who wilt answer.
16 For I pray, "Only let them not rejoice over me,
who boast against me when my foot slips!"

17 For I am ready to fall,
and my pain is ever with me.
18 I confess my iniquity,
I am sorry for my sin.
19 Those who are my foes without cause[x] are mighty,
and many are those who hate me wrongfully.

[x] Cn: Heb *living*

Isa. 53:7). He rests his case with God: **For thee, O LORD, do I wait; it is thou** [the pronoun is emphatic] **. . . who wilt answer.** Omit כי, **for,** in vs. 16. For the malicious joy of enemies see 13:4; 35:19.

4. THE PSALMIST RENEWS HIS APPEAL (38:17-22)

17-20. The psalmist sums up his case. His power of endurance is failing because his **pain is ever with** him. He has confessed his sin; he has followed what is good. But like his **pain,** his enemies too never leave off their mighty assaults. It is for God to act.

---

doing is precise. Sin is disease in the spiritual world, and as such is antisocial. At this point the Christian finds himself driven to the "good news" of one "Friend and Companion" who does not stand aloof from our plague-ridden selves, but is "numbered with the transgressors" that transgression may cease. For the difference that Christ makes cf. the treatment of the physically diseased in societies informed by his spirit; back of that is the action taken by the God that was in him to save sinners. It is, in our common phrase, "all the difference in the world."

In vs. 12 the tone of the psalm changes somewhat. The introduction of the **enemies** seems to indicate a representative pious Jew in persecution, a situation familiar in the psalms. Yet it need not be confined to that type of trouble; any man has some hostile critics who rejoice in his misfortunes. "Serve him right" is a common expression on unregenerate lips. As a general rule it is well to interpret psalms as personal, unless the evidence for a different interpretation is weighty, on the broad ground that the psalms have become a manual of personal devotion. We cannot lightly set aside the use of many generations.

Observe (vss. 13-16) that "silence" is a part of sin's penalty; and a part also of the process of penitence. A man has no more to say; he is still and prone before God. But he is not inactive. Willingness to be still in God's presence as a condition of healing is a form of activity. It is very significant that the verses which speak of the sufferer as **deaf** and **dumb,** unable to stand up for himself even against his critics, for in his **mouth are no rebukes** (vs. 14), are followed immediately by the statement, **But for thee, O LORD, do I wait.** In waiting, hope dawns: **It is thou, O LORD my God, who wilt answer,** and the psalmist is able to pray that he may not remain the kind of person who justifies the worldlings in their cynicism, boasting against him when his **foot slips.** Inasmuch as the way to be secure against such boasting is to see to it that his foot does not slip, there is promise here of an awakening will.

In vss. 17-18 the will becomes operative. Although, or rather because, he realizes his weakness, the poet summons his resources to do the one thing he can do: **I confess my iniquity.** His grieving is finally directed to the true point for grief: **I am sorry for my sin.** He is a genuine penitent at last. As he returns to the thought of his **enemies** (vss. 19-20), he introduces a note which seems out of harmony with the penitential movement. He speaks of **those who . . . are my adversaries because I follow after good.**

20 They also that render evil for good are mine adversaries; because I follow *the thing that* good *is.*

21 Forsake me not, O LORD: O my God, be not far from me.

22 Make haste to help me, O Lord my salvation.

20 Those who render me evil for good
are my adversaries because I follow after good.

21 Do not forsake me, O LORD!
O my God, be not far from me!
22 Make haste to help me,
O Lord, my salvation!

To the chief Musician, *even* to Jeduthun, A Psalm of David.

39 I said, I will take heed to my ways, that I sin not with my tongue: I will keep my mouth with a bridle, while the wicked is before me.

To the choirmaster: to Jeduthun. A Psalm of David.

39 I said, "I will guard my ways,
that I may not sin with my tongue;
I will bridle[y] my mouth,
so long as the wicked are in my presence."

[y] Heb *muzzle*

21-22. Hence the psalm concludes with an urgent appeal to the Lord for immediate help: **O my God, be not far from me! Make haste to help me.**

XXXIX. A CRY FOR DELIVERANCE (39:1-13)

This psalm belongs to the same class as Ps. 38. Heinrich Ewald has called it "incontestably the finest of all the elegies in the Psalter" (*Commentary on the Psalms,* tr. E. Johnson [London: Williams & Norgate, 1880-81], I, 204). Though it manifests a spirit of contrition, it is not included among the penitential psalms, doubtless because the psalmist's sense of sin seems less prominent than his sense of the pathos of human life. His sin he acknowledges, but he sees it in relation to the unutterable tragedy of man's brief and shadowy existence, a passing phenomenon in the world. Short as his poem is, he has the skill to reveal, or to suggest, the variety of moods which his reflections invoke—faith, rebellion, despair, penitence, resignation, and trust. We are singularly moved with sympathy as we see the contending emotions in the depths of the heart of a man of troubled and honest thought. The logic of his creed is pressing him on to the larger hope, which, however, he fails to grasp. Is man's life a fleeting shadow?

But does not this imply the final step of penitence? He has seen the true quality of wrong and has shuddered at it; he has put himself in the hands of God; he has brought himself to complete confession; his sorrow is "godly sorrow meet for repentance." The one remaining step is a purpose of "zealous amendment." Henceforward, says he, **I follow after good,** and so completes the process; and is it not true that the reformed waster will get plenty of sneers and hostility from his erstwhile boon companions?

21-22. ***The Final Plea.***—These verses form a touching, humble conclusion. The psalmist knows his weakness and still has the kind of fear that is health-giving, for it keeps him on his knees. **O my God, be not far from me!** That prayer will be answered, for God was at his side all the time, stabbing his spirit wide awake.

On the basis of this psalm the expositor may treat the whole subject of penitence; but starting from it, he must search the scriptures, and especially Rom. 7–8. He will also no doubt turn to Augustine. But he will not forget the pattern that is here given him. First, an almost involuntary cry to God; second, an awakening to the "wrongness of wrong," made possible by a right reading of painful experience; third, a developing shudder at his own wrong; fourth, a purpose to admit his own responsibility and blame; fifth, a settled grief that he could have been what he had been; and sixth, a determined will to good—all surrounded and interpreted by a search for and dependence upon that God in whom, through his experience of this painful mercy, he has come altogether to trust.

39:1-13. ***An Elegy.***—This psalm has been described as "the noblest elegy in the Psalter."

The argument of the psalm at first blush seems somewhat confused. In consequence, Duhm has assumed that vss. 8-9, 12-13 are additions from another source; and Gunkel, while holding to the unity of authorship, believes that the original order was vss. 1-6, 11, 7, 12*cdab*, 8-10, 13. Opinions in this respect will vary with the interpretation of the delicate nuances of the psalm. The metrical irregularities or the differences of meter are uncertain evidence for radical reconstructions of the text.

The words of the psalmist in their present order fall into a consistent pattern. It is clear that he has suffered a severe blow. The context suggests that it is physical, although he is not explicit on that point. For some time he bore his suffering in silence lest he should forget himself and murmur against God, and by his behavior delight his enemies who were maliciously watching for an occasion to deride his piety or to mock at his God. But at length the effort to repress himself only added to his distress; his thoughts and feelings became like a fire within him. And to relieve the anguish of his heart he

---

Its grave acknowledgment of life's shadows, with its semirefrain in vss. 5, 11, **surely every man is vanity** or **a mere breath,** gives it at once strength and a haunting sense of the tears of things. It has much in common with the book of Job; its main thesis of the evanescence of human effort is best developed in that "drama." Some have thought that the psalm is earlier than Job, that the writer of that book knew it, and that from it, at least in part, came his impulse to write.

The thesis is a somber one from the O.T. point of view. It is impressive to note the attitude of assent which the psalmist takes to the Will which purposes that his conscious creation shall cease to be. We can recall, by way of contrast, the lines of Thomas Hardy, the poet of the pessimism of pity.

"I have finished another year," said God,
"In grey, green, white, and brown;
I have strewn the leaf upon the sod,
Sealed up the worm within the clod,
And let the last sun down."

"And what's the good of it?" I said.[5]

The N.T. with its doctrine of immortality is in an altogether different position; and we need not be surprised that at least one critic has taken the view that the psalm proposes the possibility of immortality. A slight emendation of vs. 4 would give us "let me know whether I shall cease to be." But vs. 13 directly contradicts that suggestion:

**Look away from me, that I may know gladness,
before I depart and be no more,**

and vss. 8, 10 show the writer to be more concerned with present distresses than with distant hopes. We are left with a psalm that accepts man's transience and meaninglessness. Yet praying for a little gladness, the poet still trusts in God; **my hope,** he still says, **is in thee.**

Every modern interpreter must face this attitude of mind, for acceptance of **vanity** as the hallmark of conscious life is widespread. The welcome that was given, for instance, to A. E. Housman's verses is an indication that this type of pessimism or shadowed optimism is not uncommon. How can we make sure that it will not settle into a fixed pessimism? The O.T. offers two consolations: (*a*) a righteous life will spell a prosperous life in this world, and a prosperous life, even if it has nothing beyond itself, is a definite good; and (*b*) the pious Jew could look forward to the permanence and the ultimate secure identity of his race under an ideal king. The modern counterpart of that is "the dream of the blossom of good" and the knowledge that we, by high living and thinking, may hasten its fulfillment. Yet both of these are partial comforts: the first is far from universally true, and the second is temporary; for we know that however fair civilization may grow, in due time the earth will be a sepulcher, and mankind as a whole will **depart and be no more.**

We must admit, however, that man estimates mere living as a good. He proves it by his struggles to hold on to life. And if he is harmonized to the best he knows, he has an inner quiet store that justifies him in being thankful for his birth. He holds that it is better to have lived, even if his departure is final, than never to have lived at all. But this does not explain the righteous man's deep content, so manifest in the psalms; it can find its source only in the overwhelming sense, which the devout Hebrew possessed, of God and his rightness. If man was evanescent, it was God's will; if he saw the Promised Land only from afar, it was still God's will; and the way of the Lord was perfect.

[5] "New Year's Eve," from *Collected Poems* (London: Macmillan & Co.; New York: The Macmillan Co., 1940). Used by permission of the Trustees of the Hardy Estate and the publishers.

2 I was dumb with silence, I held my
peace, *even* from good; and my sorrow was
stirred.
3 My heart was hot within me; while I
was musing the fire burned: *then* spake I
with my tongue,

2 I was dumb and silent,
I held my peace to no avail;
my distress grew worse,
3 my heart became hot within me.
As I mused, the fire burned;
then I spoke with my tongue:

---

permitted his tongue to speak. His words are addressed to God. They consist of melancholy reflections on the brief measure of his own life and the futility of the life of men in general. It is vain and insubstantial as a breath or a shadow. It is full of the noise and fever of getting gain, but all its turmoil ends in nothing. What should one do in view of this sad human lot? Should one give way to despair? The psalmist cannot be content with such an attitude to the scheme of things. Life may be but a vain show; and yet a voice within him prompts him to believe that God must have prepared some better things, certainly some better things for him: **My hope is in thee.** But between him and that for which he hopes stand his transgressions. His **stroke** is God's chastisement: **Thou . . . hast done it.** And the penalty has been deserved. His former murmurs give place to a prayer, therefore, that God may be pleased to lift his heavy hand, remembering that man is too frail to endure the assaults of God's wrath and also that, as a **passing guest** in this life, he has only a few days to enjoy the goodness of his divine host.

The date of the psalm is probably late postexilic. It belongs to that period in Jewish history when men were examining the relation of their traditional faith to the suffering and sorrow and wretchedness with which they were met in the world. In Job, Ecclesiastes, and Ps. 90 we meet classical expressions of this "sense of tears in mortal things." The meter is for the most part 3+3 with the usual variations; a few instances of 3+2 also occur.

1. The Psalmist's Earlier Silence (39:1-3)

39:1-3. In these verses the psalmist tells of the inner agitation which he suffered before he gave vent to his feelings in the words of this psalm. **I said, "I will guard my ways":** As the context shows, we should read דברי, "my words," for דרכי, **my ways,** which is due to a *lapsus calami*. The reasons for his enforced silence are twofold: (*a*) **that I may not sin with my tongue;** (*b*) **so long as the wicked are in my presence.** By dittography of the word **guard** in vs. 1*a*, our text reads "I will keep a muzzle"; read with the LXX אשימה, "I will set," for אשמרה. Also read for בעד, **so long as,** בעבור, "because of," and

---

In that stubborn faith he sought communion with God and found it; and, finding, discovered that which made life a great thing and a good. Devotionally, the Calvinist and the pious Jew joined hands across the centuries; with closed lips they gazed up at the Inscrutable and, assenting, were at peace.

To the speculative mind, however, that is not enough. The human, plaintive "Why?" echoes even in the psalms. Mostly it is directed to God's slowness. "Why tarry the wheels?" But God's delay in vindicating righteousness is a minor problem. The great question is "Why create at all, if the result is finally 'vanity'?" And there is no final answer except in the hope of immortality. In that light all earth's distresses take on a different hue; they are part of the process that creates the beloved community, in which we shall know even as also we are known. The O.T. and its devotion become permanently valuable if they are regarded as the anteroom to the N.T. and its "many mansions."

1-3. ***The Poet's Self-restraint.***—The psalmist begins by warning himself against uttering complaints of God's providence, particularly in the presence of unbelievers—a matter for Christians to watch also. Bitter speech in trouble on the part of professing Christians is a strong incentive to the faithless to disbelieve in religion as a power. They hear Christians suggesting that they have an anchor that holds; when it slips they sneer and are confirmed in their unbelief. But soon the silence grows unbearable, and the

4 LORD, make me to know mine end, and the measure of my days, what it *is; that* I may know how frail I *am*.
5 Behold, thou hast made my days *as* a handbreadth; and mine age *is* as nothing before thee: verily every man at his best state *is* altogether vanity. Selah.
6 Surely every man walketh in a vain show: surely they are disquieted in vain: he heapeth up *riches,* and knoweth not who shall gather them.

4 "LORD, let me know my end,
and what is the measure of my days;
let me know how fleeting my life is!
5 Behold, thou hast made my days a few handbreadths,
and my lifetime is as nothing in thy sight.
Surely every man stands as a mere breath! *Selah*
6 Surely man goes about as a shadow!
Surely for nought are they in turmoil;
man heaps up, and knows not who will gather!

---

translate, "because of the ungodly in my presence"; the LXX reads בעמד, "while the wicked remain before me." But in spite of his efforts to keep silent, [he] **held** [his] **peace to no avail,** lit., "without good [results]," an uncertain text. But the longer he mused, "talked to his heart," the more his heart seethed with his turbulent thoughts. **The fire burned** so hotly that in order to relieve his pain he had to speak.

2. The Psalmist Seeks Enlightenment (39:4-6)

4-6. The psalmist speaks his mind to God: **LORD, let me know,** i.e., teach me or keep me mindful of the melancholy fact, **how fleeting my life is** (cf. 90:12). As the sequel shows, he has been deeply agitated by a review of human life, on which his sore experience has focused his attention. He is in revolt against the deduction that the chief wisdom of life is to know that man is a "nothing." **How fleeting my life is:** Lit., "how transient I am." **My days a few handbreadths:** The handbreadth was a measure four fingers broad. **Surely every man** [is a] **mere breath:** The word הבל, **breath,** means something unsubstantial, worthless; hence its synonyms are "vapor," **vanity,** "nothing." **A shadow,** because he quickly passes. The brief measure of his life is full of noise and hubbub, but it is all for nothing. **Man heaps up, and knows not who will gather:** The text of vs. 6 is somewhat uncertain; read אך הבל יהמה הונים יצבר, "Surely for nought is he in turmoil, he heaps up riches" (cf. Duhm, Gunkel).

---

poet speaks out his inner questionings. **As I mused, the fire burned** is often taken in a good sense as meaning that meditation stirs inner fire for a worthy cause; but accurately it is a confession of weakness. The writer has been stoking his bitterness; now he can hold back its flame no longer.

4-13. ***His Speech with God.***—These verses do not proceed upon a steadily advancing course, but are repetitive and interwoven with prayer. Vss. 4-6 state the psalmist's conviction of the "transiency" and "futility" of human life, vs. 4 particularly asking that he may be aided thoroughly to realize it. Vs. 7 turns from the mood of meditation to acknowledge that only in the thought of God can life be other than a mean thing: **My hope is in thee.** With vss. 8-9 comes the admission that back of his inner disquiet is transgression, vs. 9 indicating that the particular transgression is some outbreak of complaint against God; for now he closes his lips again. It was vs. 9 with which Calvin, "tormented by ill-health and harassed by news of the persecutions which befell his disciples . . . used to submit to the will of God."[6] The Scottish metrical version has a turn of translation which brings out the moral reason for silence:

> Dumb was I, op'ning not my mouth,
> because this work was thine.

The psalmist is saying in effect, "I could not complain of *man,* for it was *God's* doing; I could not complain of *God,* for I was conscious of *my own* sin."[7] Vss. 10-11 contain fresh prayers for relief, with a renewed implicit acknowledg-

[6] Samuel Terrien, *The Psalms and Their Meaning for Today* (Indianapolis: Bobbs-Merrill Co., 1952), p. ix.

[7] Kimchi, quoted by Ellicott, *O.T. Commentary for English Readers,* IV, 144.

7 And now, Lord, what wait I for? my
hope *is* in thee.
8 Deliver me from all my transgressions:
make me not the reproach of the foolish.
9 I was dumb, I opened not my mouth;
because thou didst *it*.
10 Remove thy stroke away from me: I
am consumed by the blow of thine hand.
11 When thou with rebukes dost correct
man for iniquity, thou makest his beauty to
consume away like a moth: surely every
man *is* vanity. Selah.
12 Hear my prayer, O LORD, and give ear
unto my cry; hold not thy peace at my tears:
for I *am* a stranger with thee, *and* a sojourner, as all my fathers *were*.
13 O spare me, that I may recover
strength, before I go hence, and be no more.

7 "And now, Lord, for what do I wait?
My hope is in thee.
8 Deliver me from all my transgressions.
Make me not the scorn of the fool!
9 I am dumb, I do not open my mouth;
for it is thou who hast done it.
10 Remove thy stroke from me;
I am spent by the blows[z] of thy hand.
11 When thou dost chasten man
with rebukes for sin,
thou dost consume like a moth what is dear to him;
surely every man is a mere breath!
Selah

12 "Hear my prayer, O LORD,
and give ear to my cry;
hold not thy peace at my tears!
For I am thy passing guest,
a sojourner, like all my fathers.
13 Look away from me, that I may know gladness,
before I depart and be no more!"

[z] Heb *hostility*

---

3. PLEA FOR DELIVERANCE (39:7-13)

7-11. Having no resources in himself, man's hope is in God, for God is the only solid fact in human experience. The psalmist's hope is for vindication in this world, but there is adumbrated in his words a desire for some affirmation of the substantial worth of man's life. First of all, his sins must be removed. He pleads for deliverance from them on four grounds: (*a*) **make me not the scorn of the fool;** (*b*) **I am dumb, I do not open my mouth** in rebellion against God's punishment; (*c*) **I am spent by the blows of thy hand,** or "by the might of thy hand," which is the reading of the LXX, i.e., מגבורת for the M.T. מתגרת; (*d*) no man can abide the chastisement of God: **thou dost consume . . . what is dear to him.**

12-13. The psalmist concludes with an appeal to God's kindness and pity. **I am thy passing guest:** A passing stranger in a strange land, he looks to his host for consideration. **Look away from me . . . gladness,** i.e., turn your angry face from me that I may smile **before I depart and be no more!**

---

ment that troubles are due to transgression. The closing clause must be regarded as a sort of refrain; it does not carry on the thought of the first clause, unless it means that man is **vanity** because of his sin. In vs. 12 the psalmist suddenly claims the divine protection. His days are few. He is but a **passing guest, a sojourner,** and is therefore, according to the ideas of that time, entitled to be treated as such. It is a point worth making. Man *has* a claim on God, freely admitted and met in the fact of Christ (cf. the use of this verse in I Pet. 2:11; note also Heb. 11–13). Whereupon the psalm ends with a cry from the heart. **O spare me** should be rendered **Look away from me,** i.e., let thine angered eyes be fixed on me no more. **That I may recover strength** is better translated **that I may know gladness** or "that I may become cheerful." The whole verse would then run, "Avert the anger of thine eyes, that I may be cheerful, before I depart and am no more." The same mood is found frequently in Job. Yet it is not uncommon, and is but another proof of the need of heavyhearted humanity to learn of the God and Father of our Lord Jesus Christ. In him last post is followed by reveille.

To the chief Musician, A Psalm of David.

40 I waited patiently for the LORD; and he inclined unto me, and heard my cry.

To the choirmaster. A Psalm of David.

40 I waited patiently for the LORD;
he inclined to me and heard my cry.

XL. DELIGHT IN DOING GOD'S WILL (40:1-17)

Here we have an instance of the combination of two originally independent psalms. The differences they exhibit in type and in motif, as well as the fact that one of them occurs alone as Ps. 70, shows that they are separate compositions. The first part (vss. 1-11) is a psalm of thanksgiving for recovery from sickness, while the second (vss. 13-17) is an appeal of the lament type for deliverance from enemies. Vs. 12 (see below) was probably introduced secondarily in order to help the fusion of the two parts by easing the abruptness of the transition from the tone of the one to the other. It is possible, as Gunkel says, that the psalm in its composite form was meant to express the feelings of someone who, though filled with a sense of gratitude for deliverance from one source of distress, was aware of the imminence of other troubles (cf. Pss. Sol. 16, and see Jansen, *Die spätjüdische Psalmendichtung,* 121). The mixing of types in this manner because of poverty of literary invention could occur only in a late period.

The date of the first part is indicated, by its attitude to sacrifices and the law, as late postexilic. The second part also reflects a late period in its indirect references to the tension between the God-fearing (vs. 16) and others in the community. The meter is 3+2, although in a few stichs variations occur on account of textual corruptions.

A. THANKSGIVING TO GOD (40:1-11)

1. THE PSALMIST REVIEWS HIS EXPERIENCE (40:1-3)

40:1-3. The psalmist finds himself in the midst of "the great congregation" (vs. 9, cf. 22:22, 25). The opening words show that the psalmist has known trouble, but he can now look on it as something in the past. In his distress he called on the Lord. The

40:1-17. *Gladness and Tears.*—Weighty opinion holds that we have here two psalms which have been fused. The break occurs after vs. 11; vs. 12 being inserted as a connecting link consequent upon the gentle, concluding appeal in vs. 11. Vss. 1-11 are praise, confident and almost gay; vss. 12-17 are plaintive and troubled. Although there is no psychological reason for holding that a sharp change of mood cannot occur in the same song, for the devotional life has its ups and downs, in this case the distinction is so severe that a harmony is difficult to understand. In addition, vs. 13-17 form, with minor verbal differences, Ps. 70, and are written in a different style.

However, if it is agreed that we have two psalms in one, there remains the fact that somebody put them together and provided a connecting link. It is a point on which to meditate, remembering what geniuses in the devotional life the editors, as well as the writers, of the psalms were. If the corporate explanation of the structure of the psalm is correct, it must have been the deliberate intention of the compiler to put the mood of singing and the mood of weeping side by side, and to put the second last, in order that we might not rest in a cheerfulness that may be transient, but might remember that tears are never far away. It is possible to find life so good that we begin to feel that here we have an abiding city, and so are unarmed and disconsolate when suddenly our skies are overcast. Along with joy and thankfulness we must never forget that we are **poor and needy** (vs. 17), and that our final shelter is in the confidence that **the LORD thinketh upon me** (vs. 17). The contrast in the psalm, so true to human experience, can provide for the interpreter one of its main lessons and messages. A certain type of optimism based upon a partial reading of life needs a corrective; and the psalm reminds us of that fact.

We must also note that the psalm begins with a reference to a previous experience of darkness. The thanksgiving of the opening section is a thanksgiving of deliverance **from the desolate pit,** and **out of the miry bog.** The life story outlined in the psalm is one of real disaster, leading to an experience of God's active delivering power, followed by a jubilant sense of

2 He brought me up also out of a horrible pit, out of the miry clay, and set my feet upon a rock, *and* established my goings.

2 He drew me up from the desolate pit,[a]
out of the miry bog,
and set my feet upon a rock,
making my steps secure.

[a] Cn: Heb *pit of tumult*

---

answer did not come at once, but he **waited patiently for the Lord,** and at length **he inclined to me and heard my cry.** Probably some words such as in 77:1, "Loudly to him I cried," or in 18:6, "In my distress I called to him," should be added before the last statement to preserve the metrical balance of the lines. The situation from which the psalmist sought deliverance was very grave. His feet were already in **the miry bog** of the **pit** of Sheol. For בור שאון, **horrible pit,** more lit., **pit of tumult,** we should read either בור שואה, "pit of ruin," or בור שאול, "pit of Sheol." The gloomy underworld is frequently described as a pit (see Exeg. on 28:1-2); it is, according to the Babylonians, a place "where dust is their nourishment, their food clay" (Jastrow, *Religion of Babylonia and Assyria,* p. 566). We may assume that the psalmist was "sick nigh unto death." Appropriately his recovery is described as a setting of his **feet upon a rock.** So miraculous is his deliverance that the old songs are insufficient to express his thanks. **A new song**

---

victory and freedom; until the shadows gather heavily again, and the whole concludes with a reawakened trust, in which there is the trembling of a sigh. It is a recognizable sequence in any pilgrim's progress; indeed, it is Bunyan writ briefly, except that it ends without the true end; it is true only of some pilgrimages. There are eventides, after earlier happy days, when sorrow and sighing have not fled away, and there is nothing for it but trust and prayer. So regarded, the psalm has a recognizable unity and can be interpreted from that point of view.

1-11. *Magnificat.*—**I waited patiently for the Lord.** The mood of the poet may be expressed by translating, "I waited and waited." It suggests that the writer was not naturally very good at waiting. In English a phrase of that kind is often on the lips of people whose patience is easily strained. They wait, but they pity themselves at having to wait; cf. the last words of the psalm, **make no tarrying, O my God.** The truly patient never applaud their patience. Nevertheless, this man did wait, even if there was an undercurrent of complaint in his mind. The interpreter can find a wide subject here, in the ascending quality of patience illustrated in scripture, until it reaches the "patience of the saints" (Rev. 13:10), shown in unwavering assent to the will of God. The demand for patience and its commendation in the N.T., particularly in the addresses to the churches in Rev. 2–3, provide meaty material. We note further the good results of patience in the psalmist's experience. God, he cries, in the end **inclined unto me**—i.e., listened favorably—and **heard my cry**—i.e., decided to take action. Why did God not act sooner? To teach patience perhaps? Clearly he regards the patient spirit as important.

2. *From Danger to Security.*—This verse must be emphasized: **He brought me up also out of a horrible [desolate] pit.** It doubtless refers to an experience in the writer's life in which he escaped from a condition of danger and misery into a state of security and peace; but no Christian can take it in any other than a spiritual sense. The **horrible pit** is a painfully true description of the situation of a man in the grip of base desire. The RSV mg., **pit of tumult,** is illuminating. The heart of a man at war with God is a noisy place, for "fiend voices rave"; in harmony with God, it is a place of peace. Where there is too much noise, something is wrong. War is noisy; indeed, our civilization is noisy. Is that a symptom of deep ill-health? The next image is also noteworthy: he took me **out of the miry clay;** miry slime or **bog** would be nearer the original, but **miry clay** has become so familiar a phrase that we should keep it. The clinging quality of clay has a moral suggestion in it. In any case we should underline all the adjectives, **horrible, desolate, miry,** and set them over against the false conceptions of life.

Mark the total experience of him who willingly accepts the divine control: (*a*) he is taken **out of** something **horrible;** (*b*) he is given something solid to stand on, principles and a worthy object of faith—his **feet** are **set . . . upon a rock;** (*c*) he is made active and progressive and sure-footed as he goes, the implication being that he has somewhere worth while to go—his **goings** are **established** or his **steps** made **secure.**

3 And he hath put a new song in my mouth, *even* praise unto our God: many shall see *it*, and fear, and shall trust in the LORD.

4 Blessed *is* that man that maketh the LORD his trust, and respecteth not the proud, nor such as turn aside to lies.

5 Many, O LORD my God, *are* thy wonderful works *which* thou hast done, and thy thoughts *which are* to us-ward: they cannot be reckoned up in order unto thee: *if* I would declare and speak *of them*, they are more than can be numbered.

3 He put a new song in my mouth,
a song of praise to our God.
Many will see and fear,
and put their trust in the LORD.

4 Blessed is the man who makes
the LORD his trust,
who does not turn to the proud,
to those who go astray after false gods!
5 Thou hast multiplied, O LORD my God,
thy wondrous deeds and thy thoughts
toward us;
none can compare with thee!
Were I to proclaim and tell of them,
they would be more than can be numbered.

---

must be composed. **Many will see** the miracle and by the story of it be led to **put their trust in the LORD.**

2. ON TRUSTING IN GOD (40:4-5)

4-5. The psalmist now introduces a brief hymn such as he had announced in vs. 3. **Blessed is the man:** See Exeg. on 1:1. He stresses the source of his present felicity. He might in his distress have turned for help to foreign gods or demons and their human agents, but he made **the LORD his trust** and did **not turn to the proud.** For **proud** the LXX reads הבלים, "vain things," i.e., idols, a reading which in the context commends itself. **Those who go astray after false gods:** Literally, those who are seduced by **lies.** The psalmist might have continued with a recital of what the Lord had done specifically for him, but he merges himself with the congregation and speaks of **thy wondrous deeds and thy thoughts toward us.** Nor does he attempt to recount the list of God's gracious dealings with Israel, because **they would be more than can be numbered** (cf.

3-4. *A New Song in My Mouth.*—Naturally if what has already been described has really happened to a man, he will feel like singing, and the quality of his song will be as new as his experience. Christian folk should be a singing folk, and their music should have a brave lilt in it. A contrast between the raucous music which offends good ears and the kind of music that beauty lovers delight in provides an arresting thought. The last half of the verse has its value also: (*a*) **many shall see** the new singing people; and (*b*) **fear**—i.e., reverently regard—the unseen Power that can make men who once were in horrible pits sing so cheerfully; and (*c*) at the same time gain a health-giving alarm as to their own condition, seeing that they cannot join in these songs; and (*d*) take the vital step of putting their lives in God's charge—**put their trust in the LORD.**

Blessed ["happy"] **is the man who makes the LORD his trust.** This connects with the "singing" of vs. 3, and with Christ's teaching on the desirability of learning to be like little children. Children with a good father can be happy and sing; grown folk should be so sure of the Father that they too can possess the carefree mind that has a song in it. We should emphasize the fact that in a Christian land we are surrounded by such people. They are not rarities, but the normal. Notice, moreover, that this trust in God has an ethical implication; it involves a fixed life direction. Such a man does not **turn to the proud, to those who go astray after false gods.** The connection between pride and **false gods** is significant, especially when we consider the most frequent of these substitute gods, such as uninhibited power and the golden calf. Pride is the "only begetter" of both of them.

5. ***God's Purposes.***—**Thy thoughts** [or "purposes"] **toward us** is a fruitful phrase. God's thoughts are always purposes; he does not daydream. Let a man brood upon the adjectives that can be used to describe them: **wondrous,** says the psalmist; but it might be "gracious" or "pitiful" or "Fatherly," never forgetting that

6 Sacrifice and offering thou didst not desire; mine ears hast thou opened: burnt offering and sin offering hast thou not required.
7 Then said I, Lo, I come: in the volume of the book *it is* written of me,
8 I delight to do thy will, O my God: yea, thy law *is* within my heart.
9 I have preached righteousness in the great congregation: lo, I have not refrained my lips, O LORD, thou knowest.

6 Sacrifice and offering thou dost not desire;
but thou hast given me an open ear.[b]
Burnt offering and sin offering
thou hast not required.
7 Then I said, "Lo, I come;
in the roll of the book it is written of me;
8 I delight to do thy will, O my God;
thy law is within my heart."

9 I have told the glad news of deliverance
in the great congregation;
lo, I have not restrained my lips,
as thou knowest, O LORD.

[b] Heb *ears thou hast dug for me*

139:17; Neh. 9:27). In vs. 5 the meaning is clear, but the order of the words has been confused. The original form was probably, "Many are thy wonders [which] thou hast wrought, O LORD; and as for thy purposes—none can compare with thee."

3. THE PSALMIST'S RESPONSE TO GOD'S GOODNESS (40:6-10)

6-10. On such an occasion of thanksgiving it was customary for an offering to be presented in payment of vows or as a token of gratitude (cf. 66:13-15). But our psalmist declares that sacrifices of such a kind are not sought by God. He is doubtless acquainted with the words of the prophets (cf. Amos 5:21-24; Jer. 7:22-23), but he has also on this matter received a word of revelation from God directly, **Thou hast given me an open ear;** lit., **ears thou hast dug for me** (cf. Isa. 48:8; 50:4-5). **Sacrifice** (זבח): The general term for the common animal sacrifice. **Offering** (מנחה): The meal or cereal offering. **Burnt offering** (עולה): The animal sacrifice offered in the fire of the altar wholly to God. **Sin offering** (חטאה): An expiatory offering to cancel sin. **Lo, I come,** i.e., "Here I am"

---

they are "long, long thoughts." God's greatest thought toward us is Christ: and he was purposed "before the foundation of the world" (cf. I Pet. 1:20; Rev. 13:8).

6-8. ***Sacrifice and Offering Thou Dost Not Desire.***—A strong verse, extolling ethical and spiritual religion. God has given men a moral law and a faculty of hearing and recognizing it; **mine ears hast thou opened.** The verb is vigorous; **dug** or "bored" may give the flavor. In English it is sufficient to say, "Thou hast given me an ear to hear." The interpreter should harp on this fact of endowment. Moral standards disappear when man comes to believe that he has no conscience, or that at best it is a hesitating and uncertain guide. Many voices endeavor to persuade us that this is the case; whereas the truth is that God has fairly "bored" the faculty into us. We need not so much a reawakening of conscience as a reawakening to the fact of conscience. If a man denies his possession of it, he might as well be bereft of it; he becomes one of those who having ears hear not. But he does have ears; and God has a voice of thunder that will compel him to hear. Cf. Christ's reiterated warning, "He that hath ears to hear, let him hear" (Matt. 11:15).

The psalmist then goes on to point out the next step, viz., action in response to the inner voice. What was once a sacrifice accompanied by thanksgiving (vs. 6*a*) becomes an act of self-dedication. **Lo, I come.** The clause following is perplexing. A good deal of support is given to the view that it meant simply that he came prepared to fulfill the rites prescribed for him in the Book of the Law; but the older version connects better with the spiritual attitude in vs. 8. We may read, **Lo, I come:** [for] **in the volume of the book it is written of me, I delight to do thy will, O my God; yea, thy law is within my heart**—a description of one who is at last using the "ear of conscience" which God has so strongly implanted in him (cf. Heb. 10:5-7 for a use of these verses based on the rendering in the LXX).

9-11. ***Witnesses Unto Me.***—These lines speak for themselves, and provide a splendid beachhead for assault on the strongholds of indiffer-

10 I have not hid thy righteousness within my heart; I have declared thy faithfulness and thy salvation: I have not concealed thy loving-kindness and thy truth from the great congregation.

11 Withhold not thou thy tender mercies from me, O LORD: let thy loving-kindness and thy truth continually preserve me.

12 For innumerable evils have compassed me about: mine iniquities have taken hold upon me, so that I am not able to look up; they are more than the hairs of mine head: therefore my heart faileth me.

10 I have not hid thy saving help within my heart,
I have spoken of thy faithfulness and thy salvation;
I have not concealed thy steadfast love and thy faithfulness
from the great congregation.

11 Do not thou, O LORD, withhold thy mercy from me,
let thy steadfast love and thy faithfulness ever preserve me!
12 For evils have encompassed me without number;
my iniquities have overtaken me, till I cannot see;
they are more than the hairs of my head;
my heart fails me.

(cf. Isa. 6:8). The psalmist's offering is himself (cf. 51:16-17). Vss. 7*b*-8 are a *crux interpretum*. Schmidt omits vss. 7*b*-8 as a gloss by some person who wished to assert over against the psalmist his loyalty to the prescriptions in the law on sacrifice. Hermann Gunkel (*Die Psalmen* [Göttingen: Vandenhoeck & Ruprecht, 1926; "Göttinger Handkommentar zum Alten Testament"], p. 171) would translate, "In the roll of the book it is prescribed for me" (cf. Deut. 6:6; Jer. 31:33). Most probably the psalmist is referring to the heavenly book where men's deeds are recorded (cf. 56:8; 87:6; 139:16). God knows his **heart.** Also the psalmist fulfills his duty to proclaim to his fellows God's **saving help** (cf. 51:13-15).

4. CONCLUDING PETITION (40:11)

11. He concludes with a brief prayer that the goodness of the Lord which he has experienced in his marvelous deliverance may continue with him forever.

B. AN APPEAL FOR HELP (40:12-17)

1. AN INTERPOLATION (40:12)

12. This verse has been interpolated in order to link more easily Ps. 40B with Ps. 40A. For it is to be noted: (*a*) that in vs. 12 the evils which encompass the writer are said to be due to his own sins, while in vss. 13-17 the evils from which deliverance is sought are said to be due to enemies; (*b*) that vs. 13, rather than vs. 12, forms the proper introduction to a lament. Vs. 12 has been drawn from some individual lament or penitential psalm occasioned by sickness.

---

ence. **I have preached righteousness in the great congregation,** or better, **I have told the glad news of deliverance,** going on in the same strain in vs. 10, **I have not hid thy saving help within my heart, . . . I have not concealed thy steadfast love and thy faithfulness.** Clearly these are verses to be marked by all those whose zeal for the gospel leads them to hope that Christian men and women may give evidence of the power which Christ promised when he said, "Ye shall receive power, . . . and ye shall be witnesses unto me" (Acts 1:8).

Vs. 11 suggests a quiet and confident concluding prayer, **Let thy loving-kindness and thy truth continually preserve me** rises from a heart that has known both the lovingkindness and the truth, and now breathes thanksgiving as well as appeal, in the spirit of Newman's lines:

> So long thy power hath blest me, sure it still
> Will lead me on.[8]

12-17. ***De Profundis.***—At this point the psalm changes in tone. Vss. 13-17 are found later as Ps. 70 (see Exeg.). All that we are concerned

[8] "Lead, Kindly Light."

13 Be pleased, O LORD, to deliver me: O LORD, make haste to help me.

14 Let them be ashamed and confounded together that seek after my soul to destroy it; let them be driven backward and put to shame that wish me evil.

15 Let them be desolate for a reward of their shame that say unto me, Aha, aha.

16 Let all those that seek thee rejoice and be glad in thee: let such as love thy salvation say continually, The LORD be magnified.

17 But I *am* poor and needy; *yet* the Lord thinketh upon me: thou *art* my help and my deliverer; make no tarrying, O my God.

13 Be pleased, O LORD, to deliver me!
O LORD, make haste to help me!
14 Let them be put to shame and confusion altogether
who seek to snatch away my life;
let them be turned back and brought to dishonor
who desire my hurt!
15 Let them be appalled because of their shame
who say to me, "Aha, Aha!"

16 But may all who seek thee
rejoice and be glad in thee;
may those who love thy salvation
say continually, "Great is the LORD!"
17 As for me, I am poor and needy;
but the Lord takes thought for me.
Thou art my help and my deliverer;
do not tarry, O my God!

---

2. The Petition to God (40:13-17)

13-17. The appeal is made for rescue from enemies who seek the psalmist's life. Their enmity is openly malicious for they **say to me, "Aha, Aha!"** The situation reflects a tension in the community between the godly ones and those who belittle the Lord. The psalmist therefore asks to be heard in order that (*a*) he may be delivered; (*b*) that **all who seek** the Lord may **rejoice;** (*c*) that it may be said **continually, "Great is the LORD!"** As in all the psalms of this type, there is the expression of a wish that the enemies may **be put to shame, . . . brought to dishonor.** The terms used apply to the defeat and rout of an army, with all that follows in the way of disgrace and loss of position in human society.

The text is better preserved in its form in Ps. 70, as a comparison of the translations will show.

---

with here is the connecting link (vs. 12). Observe simply that the writer's mind concentrates on the thought of his sins, a thing that a man may well do, all the more because he has had undeserved experience of God's lovingkindness. Against the background of the goodness of God, his rebellion stands out in deeper black. Moreover, he knows that though he may be forgiven, the consequences of sin continue, not least in impaired spiritual faculty; e.g., the earlier part of the *Paradise;* cf. Dante's teaching on the heavens within earth's shadow. The key to the verse is the second clause, **mine iniquities have taken hold upon me.** The tragedy of wrongdoing, to use an old phrase, is that it may be "bye, but not bye with." It may leave its marks on the body; it will leave them on the spiritual outlook; it must leave them on our relationship to God. The whole human race can never be to God as the angels are; to all eternity we are the saved in relation to the Savior. And in our pilgrimage on earth our sins keep a queer foothold within us; otherwise there would be no meaning in the process of sanctification. As a result, it is inevitable that the days of sunny gladness in freedom should be followed by times when we are aware that not yet "all is accomplished and the task is done"; and at these times the devout spirit is overwhelmed by sad remembrance and by the thought of the tenacity and the magnitude of the evil within. In such a mood a man may exaggerate, feeling that his spiritual capacity is warped, as in the case of this writer: **My iniquities have overtaken me**—caught up with me again when I thought I had done with them for good—**till I cannot see.** No wonder his courage flags and he says **My heart fails me.** In that mood he inevitably breaks again into the earnest pleading with which the psalm closes. He sees his present trials—and what life is ever without them?—as the offspring of his sins, interwoven with them; what can he do

To the chief Musician, A Psalm of David.

41 Blessed *is* he that considereth the poor: the LORD will deliver him in time of trouble.

To the choirmaster. A Psalm of David.

41 Blessed is he who considers the poor![c]
The LORD delivers him in the day
of trouble;

[c] Or *weak*

XLI. GOD UPHOLDS HIS SERVANTS (41:1-13)

In the words here the psalmist is expressing his thanks to the Lord for deliverance from a grave illness which, on the one hand, threatened to take away his life and, on the other, was the occasion of malicious satisfaction to those who falsely posed as his friends.

In the opening strophe (vss. 1-3) the psalmist in the light of his experience of the divine goodness reflects on the blessedness that comes in times of need to those who themselves practice kindness toward their fellows. "Blessed are the merciful, for they shall obtain mercy" (Matt. 5:7). The psalmist therefore shapes his utterance of thanksgiving into a testimony directed to all who will hear. The form is influenced by the wisdom style, as we see in the word of blessing with which the strophe begins (cf. 1:1; 32:1).

In the second strophe (vss. 4-10) the psalmist, instead of narrating his troubles in the manner characteristic of the thanksgiving of an individual, gives us the words of the lament which he addressed to the Lord when distress and affliction were upon him. In this way he conveys to his hearers a more lively and realistic impression of the situation in which he found himself, and at the same time their sense of the measure of God's providence is quickened.

In the short strophe (vss. 11-12) which concludes the psalm, the results which followed the Lord's answer to the psalmist's appeal are briefly dealt with. Healing came to

but cry afresh, **Be pleased, O LORD, to deliver me?** And how can he end but with the admission on his lips, **I am poor and needy,** followed by the new confidence he has learned, **Thou art my help and my deliverer,** and with a sigh of longing which is often on the lips of saints, **make no tarrying, O my God?**

Let it be granted that the psalm was two psalms originally; but the man who made them one understood the human heart and its pilgrimage.

41:1-12. ***Remembered Pain.***—From vss. 1-12 the course of this psalm is clear. It is the prayer of a sick man, perhaps a king, who is surrounded by enemies, among whom he discovers at least one treacherous friend. The form is semidramatic. The scene of vss. 4-6 is the sickroom, where at first the invalid is alone, bitterly meditating (vss. 4-5), and later is visited by one or more of his foes. Vss. 7-9 are set in some gathering place of his malevolent critics, where they gloat over his misfortunes. Vss. 10-12 return to the sickroom and record the sufferer's appeal in solitude to God. Vs. 13 is not part of the psalm, but an ascription added to mark the close of Book I of the sacred songs.

So far all is plain sailing, but vss. 1-3 are a problem. As they stand in the KJV, they seem to have little connection with what follows. They open with a generalization familiar in the O.T. **Blessed is he that considereth the poor,** and go on to express confidence in God's willingness and power to be the poor man's helper. If, however, **poor** is translated **weak,** and if the poem is regarded as having been written when the writer had recovered and when his enemies' gloating over his approaching end had proved mistaken, the unity of the whole becomes comprehensible. It is not a psalm written in the midst of trouble, but a section of autobiography written in placidity. The psalmist is not a man crying out of the depths, but rather a remembering observer of a time in his life that has now passed. He therefore is led to consider the form of his poem as well as its contents, and he begins with a touch of sententiousness. There is an interesting parallel in English literature: Oliver Goldsmith's "Stanzas on Woman" and Robert Burns's "The Banks of Doon" deal with an identical situation—that of a young woman who has been betrayed; but the former treats it from the point of view of a kindly, compassionate observer outside the experience, while the latter sings from within the experience itself and has a truer and a wilder note of pain. In the case of the psalm

2 The LORD will preserve him, and keep him alive; *and* he shall be blessed upon the earth: and thou wilt not deliver him unto the will of his enemies.

3 The LORD will strengthen him upon the bed of languishing: thou wilt make all his bed in his sickness.

2 the LORD protects him and keeps him
alive;
he is called blessed in the land;
thou dost not give him up to the will of
his enemies.
3 The LORD sustains him on his sickbed;
in his illness thou healest all his infirmities.[d]

[d] Heb *thou changest all his bed*

him. But more than his recovery, he stresses his vindication against the assaults of his enemies. His integrity has been attested. He can for all the days to come stand in the temple before his fellows as one of whom the Lord is mindful.

Vs. 13 is not a part of the psalm but has been added by an editor to serve as the doxology which closes the first book of the Psalter.

The didactic note and style with which the psalm is introduced are indicative of the influence of the wisdom literature and point to a postexilic date. The meter is generally 4+4. Textual corruption probably accounts for a few irregularities. We meet in vs. 2 a tristich in 3+2+3, in vs. 6 two lines in 3+3, and in vs. 10 a tristich in 2+2+2.

1. Blessed Is the Compassionate (41:1-3)

41:1-3. In the opening verses we see that the psalmist has been acquainted with **trouble.** But the dark hours are now past and gone, and in their place there is the memory of the rich experience of the Lord's saving help. On the ground of this experience he wishes both to express his thanks for the blessings which have come to him and to teach all his hearers the value of walking in accord with the mind of the Lord. **Blessed is he who considers the poor:** Lit., "the happinesses of him," etc. The word "happiness" is common in the wisdom books and has reference to worldly well-being rather than to spiritual. To the man who shows himself gracious to those in need, the Lord shows himself gracious (cf. 18:25; II Sam. 22:26; Prov. 29:7; Matt. 5:7). The psalmist sums up the blessings which attend such a man: **The LORD delivers him in the day of trouble;**

the distinction is not so clear; for the time of his adversity had bitten deeply into the psalmist's memory. Little wonder it inspired part of the meditation which Savonarola wrote as he lay in his cell, mutilated, only his right hand left him that he might confess his error and submit himself to the church. Nevertheless, the structure of the psalm suggests that the author was a man who is remembering that he once suffered, rather than a sufferer who needs must cry.

1-3. ***The Tenderness of God.*****—Blessed is he that considereth the poor [weak]: the LORD will deliver him in time of trouble.** Life has a tendency to give back to a man what he puts into it, and behind life stands the will of God (cf. 18:25-26). A compassionate man wins compassion; God inclines the hearts of men to help helpers, although as this man found, there are still those who are inclined to kick him when he is down; but the worthier a society is, the more pity breeds pity. Note the word **considereth;** it implies wisdom in help as well as an impulse to generosity. The verse is relevant to the problem of poverty and its alleviation, and applies to communities and governments as well as to individuals. We may remember the story of the Pope who, when a beggar was found starved to death in the streets of Rome, excommunicated himself for a day.

Note the change from the third to the second person in the last clause of vs. 2, and the corresponding change in vs. 3. The writer was a devout man, up to his lights; and the devout are not content with general statements in the third person. When they think about God they tend to address him directly, being aware of his presence: the Lord who preserves, becomes **thou** [who] **wilt not deliver him unto the will of his enemies.** In vs. 3 it is manifestly a physical **sickbed** to which reference is made; but we may use the phrase, if we so choose, in a spiritual sense. If God helps a sick body, how much more will he heal a sick soul. From this point of view the KJV is suggestive: **The LORD will strengthen him upon the bed of languishing** is a fruitful description of a common condition; cf. especially all that is written about the sin of

4 I said, LORD, be merciful unto me: heal my soul; for I have sinned against thee.

5 Mine enemies speak evil of me, When shall he die, and his name perish?

6 And if he come to see *me*, he speaketh vanity: his heart gathereth iniquity to itself; *when* he goeth abroad, he telleth *it*.

7 All that hate me whisper together against me: against me do they devise my hurt.

4 As for me, I said, "O LORD, be gracious to me;
heal me, for I have sinned against thee!"
5 My enemies say of me in malice:
"When will he die, and his name perish?"
6 And when one comes to see me, he utters empty words,
while his heart gathers mischief;
when he goes out, he tells it abroad.
7 All who hate me whisper together about me;
they imagine the worst for me.

. . . **protects him and keeps him alive,** so that all men treat him with respect, lit., "greet him" or "call him happy." He is safe from "the desire of his foes," and in sickness **the LORD sustains him.** In vs. 2 read with the LXX "he [the LORD] does not give him up," and emend vs. 3*b* to read כל־מכאבו הפך לחיל, "all his sickness he changes to strength."

2. The Psalmist Recollects His Former Plight (41:4-10)

4-10. In the time of his distress the psalmist appealed to the Lord for help, and so by experience learned the precious lesson which he has just unfolded. **I said, "O LORD, be gracious to me."** He was sick: **Heal me.** He believed, like other good men of his time, that God was by this visitation seeking to correct him (cf. Job 36:7-11) for he has **sinned.** But his enemies make what was a matter between him and God an occasion to visit their ill will against him. **My enemies say . . . in malice: "When will he die, and his name**

---

accidie (of sloth or "don't care") in Dante's *Purgatory*.[1] The following phrase in the KJV, **thou wilt make** ["turn"] **all his bed in his sickness** is a picturesque way of stating the psalmist's confidence that he will recover and should be rendered, **in his illness thou healest all his infirmities.** But we would part from the older translation with regret; the gentle tenderness of the words portrays active compassion at its simple best. An admirable verse for nurses or for mothers. We may permit ourselves the memory of the small girl's announcement, "Mother is always the kindest person, but she is awfully good to us when we are ill and spotty." Out of the mouths of babes and sucklings! So in our simplicity and need we may think of the Father.

4-10. *The Psalmist's Own Experience.*—At this point the psalm leaves generalizations and becomes autobiographical. **I said**—the pronoun is emphatic. It is as if the author interpolated, "Applying these principles to my case, let me tell you about my own experience." General statements become more credible when we can back them in our own experience. A man may make this a starting point of self-examination: "In trouble how did I, in point of fact, react? What did I say? And what do I say now, when I can see the harsh days in perspective?" It is profitable to note what this man said: (*a*) he asked simply for mercy and healing; (*b*) he admitted his own unworthiness; and (*c*) he put plainly the heart of his trouble, in the malice with which he was surrounded. Our prayers are none the less reverent for being frank.

Vs. 5 gives us the sick man's idea of what his neighbors are thinking: he imagines them saying to each other, **When will he die, and his name perish?** Evidently he was surrounded with hate. To be sick in an atmosphere of malice must be a sore tribulation; and unfortunately it has been a very common experience in modern days. World-wide wars fill the whole world with people who know this experience. The fact that it is so throws a lurid light on the evil of war.

Vs. 6, on the other hand, looks like the record of an actual happening. One of his enemies visited him, and did three things: (*a*) he chattered meaninglessly, uttering **empty words;** (*b*) all the time he was storing up in his mind everything that when told could make trouble, **his heart** gathering **mischief** the while; and (*c*) he promptly sought out his fellow conspirators and poured into their ears all the

[1] Cantos XVII, XVIII.

8 An evil disease, *say they,* cleaveth fast unto him: and *now* that he lieth he shall rise up no more.

9 Yea, mine own familiar friend, in whom I trusted, which did eat of my bread, hath lifted up *his* heel against me.

10 But thou, O LORD, be merciful unto me, and raise me up, that I may requite them.

8 They say, "A deadly thing has fastened
upon him;
he will not rise again from where he
lies."
9 Even my bosom friend in whom I trusted,
who ate of my bread, has lifted his heel
against me.
10 But do thou, O LORD, be gracious to me,
and raise me up, that I may requite
them!

---

perish?" The falseness and treachery of those who professed to be his friends weigh on him more than his physical ills. When under the cloak of sympathy and piety (cf. Job 2:11; Ecclus. 7:35) **one comes to see me, he utters empty words,** meditating fresh **mischief** the while. The M.T. reads "his heart utters emptiness," i.e., his heart inspires his **empty words** (for this difficult use of לִבּוֹ, "his heart," if it is retained, see Exeg. on 15:2*b*). His enemy finds the sick man's condition to his liking, and **when he goes out, he tells it abroad.** What this one does, all his enemies do. **All who hate me whisper** one to the other with cruel joy the hopeless outlook of his case. For **a deadly thing has fastened upon him. Deadly thing** is, lit., "a thing [or "word"] of wickedness" (cf. 101:3), and the implication is that the psalmist is the victim of sorcery; **has fastened** is, lit., "is poured out." The hardest thing to bear in his sad plight is that **my bosom friend . . . has lifted his heel against me.** But **do thou, O LORD, be gracious to me.** The psalmist has sought to move God to be gracious to him by pleading (*a*) his sickness; (*b*) his confession of sin (cf. 32:5); and mainly (*c*) the inordinate treachery of friends, who for no disclosed reason other than personal hostility have looked for his death with malicious delight. To these three reasons for God's intervention he adds in bitter indignation a fourth: **that I may requite them,** or "that I may pay them back," which is something less than a Christian petition.

---

damaging information he had obtained. A more complete picture of insincerity can hardly be imagined. Let it be contrasted with the "sick visiting" of Christ. Note especially the hint in the phrase **if he come to see me, he speaketh vanity,** or **utters empty words.** A useful check for all who would visit the sick!

Vss. 7-8 picture vividly the consequent action of the group of enemies. They sound like a court cabal. They (*a*) **whisper** among themselves; (*b*) proceed to imagine, hopefully from their point of view, the worst that can happen; and (*c*) put their imaginings into plain words which start rumors in the community: **A deadly thing has fastened upon him; he will not rise again from where he lies.** It all looks like a mean effort to prepare the ground for some kind of plot to seize power.

The unkindest cut of all is recorded in vs. 9. The sufferer evidently had one friend in the group around him in whom he trusted; but he turned out to be the blackest traitor of them all:

Even my bosom friend in whom I trusted,
who ate of my bread, has lifted his heel against
me.

The obligations of Oriental hospitality give special point to the phrase, **who ate of my bread.** It is a case of "Et tu, Brute," without the justification that Brutus had. The darkness of this treachery has to be remembered when we estimate the bitterness in the mind of the sufferer (vs. 10). The LXX reads "has magnified his supplanting of me," which fits in well with the conjecture that the sufferer is a king or governor, with palace enemies. **Hath lifted up his heel against me** means perhaps "hath kicked violently against me." To our minds the last touch of meanness is to kick a man when he is down.

In such circumstances we can make allowance for vs. 10. The sufferer was a sorely persecuted man, and his anger spills over in the cry, **But thou, O LORD, be merciful unto me, and raise me up, that I may requite them.** Nevertheless we must admit that this is no Christian prayer, and that there is a great gulf fixed between it and Christ's "Father, forgive them; for they know not what they do." The expositor should mark this contrast as a striking instance of the difference that Christ makes, and of the height of his ethical demands.

11 By this I know that thou favorest me,
because mine enemy doth not triumph over
me.
12 And as for me, thou upholdest me in
mine integrity, and settest me before thy
face for ever.
13 Blessed *be* the LORD God of Israel
from everlasting, and to everlasting. Amen,
and Amen.

11 By this I know that thou art pleased with
me,
in that my enemy has not triumphed
over me.
12 But thou hast upheld me because of my
integrity,
and set me in thy presence for ever.

13 Blessed be the LORD, the God of Israel,
from everlasting to everlasting!
Amen and Amen.

BOOK II

To the chief Musician, Maschil, for the sons of Korah.

42 As the hart panteth after the water
brooks, so panteth my soul after thee,
O God.

To the choirmaster. A Maskil of the Sons of Korah.

42 As a hart longs
for flowing streams,
so longs my soul
for thee, O God.

3. FAITH VINDICATED (41:11-12)

11-12. The prayer of the psalmist was answered, and thereby God's delight in his servant made known to the discomfiture of the false friends. **My enemy has not triumphed over me:** Because of the uprightness of his life, the Lord has vindicated him. And now he can stand again in the temple to give thanks before the Lord in the sight of the congregation not only for this occasion but forever.

13. This benediction is similar to those found at the close of other books of the Psalter (see 72:18-19; 89:52; 106:48). After the benediction was editorially introduced to close the book, the **Amen and Amen** response was added for liturgical reasons, as we see in 106:48 (cf. Neh. 8:6; I Chr. 16:36).

XLII-XLIII. THE DESPAIR AND HOPE OF A GODLY MAN (42:1–43:5)

These two psalms formed originally a single psalm and they so appear in many Hebrew MSS. That they should be treated as a unity is evident from the dependence

11-12. ***The Happy Issue.***—These verses clearly indicate that the sufferer has recovered and that the plot against him has failed. A good subject is latent in the contrast between the whisperings of the conspirators in vss. 7–8 and what actually happened. The plotters took no account of the moral factor—a common miscalculation. To our ears there is a touch of complacency in the statement, **but thou hast upheld me because of my integrity;** but it need not be so. Men and nations can rightly believe that God favors them if they can hold, in his presence, that they had their quarrel just, and that up to their lights they maintained the right.

13. ***Doxology.***—The psalm closes at the end of vs. 12. The doxology in vs. 13 marks the end of Book I of the Psalter. But we must not turn from it heedlessly; for it points a steady finger at the heart of the greatness of the psalms. When we remember the debased cults with which Israel was surrounded, with all the unhappy ethical fruits of polytheism and nature worship, and when we call to mind the weakness and insignificance of the Hebrew state in the midst of strong and warring empires, it is an amazement that its devout poets should have given to the world so austere, unwavering, and steadfast a vision of God. The glory of the psalms is that they left mankind, for good and all, face to face with the Most High. Wherefore, with these musicians of long ago, we lift up our eyes to him and say, **Blessed be the LORD God of Israel from everlasting, and to everlasting. Amen, and Amen.**

42:1-11. ***The Conflict in the Soul.***—This is a song of loneliness, and in so far as its intention as a Maskil is to instruct those who are victims of this common spiritual ailment, our author

of Ps. 43 upon Ps. 42, the repetition with slight variations of 42:9 in 43:2, the refrain which is common to both of them (42:5, 11; 43:5), and the absence of a superscription in Ps. 43. Their separation was made evidently for liturgical reasons.

In the two of them, viewed as a single composition, we are dealing with an example of a common literary type in the Psalter, the prayer of one who is in desperate straits. The psalmist feels that already the floods of the underworld are closing over him. His sense of desolation is deepened by his separation from his homeland where he used to take part in the festal processions that moved up to the house of God. For some reason unexplained, except possibly in 43:1, he is living in the region of the peaks of **Hermon** at **Mount Mizar.** But removed as he is from Jerusalem, he is not free from those who taunt him for his apparent desertion by his God and who continue in hostility against him. He longs for the return of his former happy conditions with the privilege of joining again in the worship at the altar of God's dwelling place, but most of all he longs to enjoy on the holy hill the intimate experience of the presence and good will of the living God.

Our understanding of the situation which occasioned the psalm is somewhat changed if we accept Schmidt's strictures on 42:6. He points out the general difficulty of explaining vs. 7*a* with reference to the geographical data of vs. 6*b*, for what is the **deep** (*tehôm*) that calls to **deep** (*tehôm*) in the context? Also he calls attention to the "prosaic precision" in the identification of the psalmist's place of exile; it is somewhat as if we were to say in a parallel case, "The land of the Hudson, in the Catskills, at Mount Hunter," using the style of a postal address in verse. Schmidt accordingly emends the verse (see below), and since in his text the geographical references disappear, he interprets the psalm as the prayer of a sick man with all the elements characteristic of the form of the type. Schmidt's treatment is to be recommended (*Die Psalmen*, pp. 79-82).

In spite of much in the thought and language of the psalmist that reflects the age to which he belongs, he beautifully expresses the basic longing of the hearts of men in all ages, the sense of God's nearness. From beginning to end the impression of the immediacy of the psalmist's communion with God is comparable only to what we meet in such prayers as Jer. 14:19-22; 15:15-18; 20:7-18; Exod. 33:13-16. The structure of the psalm adds to the emotional effect produced by the language of the psalmist. The refrain with its note of hope and confidence punctuates the strophes with their gloom and distress of spirit. Over against **Why hast thou forgotten me?** stands **Hope in God; for I shall again praise him.** Stage by stage the psalmist raises himself from the depths of despair to fullness of trust and peace of soul. The spiritual sincerity of the psalmist is matched by the poetic beauty of the mode of his utterance.

Opinions differ as to the date. It is clear from 43:3, with its reference to **thy holy hill,** that the author regards Jerusalem as the seat of the worship of "the LORD my God." In the same verse the use of the plural form in "thy dwelling-place[s]"—an instance of the plural of amplification (cf. 84:1; 132:5), properly translated as a singular—does not argue a pre-Deuteronomic date. The psalm reflects a period when there was a tension in the community between "the godly" and "the scorners" (cf. 1:1)—**my adversaries**

---

writes autobiographically. "None but the lonely heart can know my sorrow," runs a familiar song. So our poet-singer recounts his own sorrow and his escape from it, first in communion with himself and then in comradeship with God. When one is overwhelmed with the sense of loneliness because of the loss of human company, he has left only two resources—himself and God. It is perhaps a habit the human spirit has developed, or some "unlearned, untaught fidelity" to which it must be responsive, which makes one feel that when all others forsake, God will take one up; and that even if God should fail, there is always one's own self that stands by. This introduces, to be sure, a dualism in the soul which in fact may be nothing but sentiment or sheer wish; it is nevertheless so common an experience in us all as to be accepted without criticism. "I said to myself" is a pragmatic device; and who does not accept and practice it? It is indeed self-communion, commonly called introspection, and when it is free from morbidity, it is one of the most useful disciplines of personal religion.

2 My soul thirsteth for God, for the living God: when shall I come and appear before God?
3 My tears have been my meat day and night, while they continually say unto me, Where *is* thy God?
4 When I remember these *things,* I pour out my soul in me: for I had gone with the multitude, I went with them to the house of God, with the voice of joy and praise, with a multitude that kept holyday.

2 My soul thirsts for God,
for the living God.
When shall I come and behold
the face of God?
3 My tears have been my food
day and night,
while men say to me continually,
"Where is your God?"

4 These things I remember,
as I pour out my soul:
how I went with the throng,
and led them in procession to the house of God,
with glad shouts and songs of thanksgiving,
a multitude keeping festival.

. . . **say, . . . "Where is thy God?"** On the whole, one is warranted in assigning to the psalm a postexilic date. The text of 42:6 taken in conjunction with 43:3 does not lend any support to the opinion that the author was a North Israelite. The uncertainty of the text of 42:6 makes it doubtful that the author was even temporarily a dweller or exile in the Hermon region. The status of the author in the community is also not clear, since the text of 42:4*b* is in part obscure.

The meter is quite regularly 3+2, except in the refrain, where it is 3+3 and 4+3.

1. The Yearning of One Separated from the Temple (42:1-5)

42:1-5. In this opening strophe the psalmist expresses his thirst for God and his longing for the associations of the temple. **As a hart** [better, "a hind"] **longs for flowing streams:** The figure is that of an animal of the chase, parched with thirst and panting for the one source of relief, the cool fresh water of ever-running streams, lit., "channels, full of water." **My soul thirsts for God:** In Book II of the Psalter (Pss. 42–72), as in part of Book III (Pss. 73–83), the editors for unknown reasons have frequently substituted *'elōhîm,* **God,** for *Yahweh,* "the Lord." Indeed, within this portion of the Psalter, *'elōhîm* occurs four times more frequently than *Yahweh,* whereas in the rest of the book *Yahweh* appears twenty times as often as *'elōhîm.* In vs. 2*a* obviously the original reading was

---

This clearly is what the poet is concerned with here. **Why are you cast down, O my soul?** (Vs. 5*a*.) If he had found a psychiatrist alongside to warn him of the possible dangers of talking thus to his soul, he might have conceded the point. But he would not in that case have been shut up to communion with himself; having found a companion, he could have beguiled his loneliness in talk with his critic, and thus never have written his poem. Perhaps it is just as well that the psychiatrist did not come along.

1-4. ***Loneliness and Love.***—Lonely he surely was. Has not this been the poet's theme as much as love—the antithesis of loneliness? To be lonely or in love is the common grist of the poet's mill. Thomas Hardy or Lord Byron, Emily Dickinson or Dorothea Hemans, the Chief Musician or Solomon in a lyric moment—these all have tuned their lyres to the dominant moods. As our poet reflects, an imagined deer comes to a dry brook. Compelling thirst and its cruel denial furnish the simile of the poet's loneliness. The convulsive breath, the anguished eye, these symbolize the desperation of his own unrewarded search for God. And yet this very description of his plight is directed to God with whom he imagines himself to be in conversation, even while he laments that he is afar off. **My soul thirsts for God. . . . When shall I come and behold the face of God?** This is not merely the inconsistency of the poetic mood; it is one of the paradoxes of vital spiritual experience. The actual presence of God is often accompanied by a sense of his remoteness. One must speak to him if only to tell him how impossible it is to hold converse with him. To

5 Why art thou cast down, O my soul? and *why* art thou disquieted in me? hope thou in God: for I shall yet praise him *for* the help of his countenance.

6 O my God, my soul is cast down within me: therefore will I remember thee from the land of Jordan, and of the Hermonites, from the hill Mizar.

7 Deep calleth unto deep at the noise of thy waterspouts: all thy waves and thy billows are gone over me.

5 Why are you cast down, O my soul,
and why are you disquieted within me?
Hope in God; for I shall again praise him,
my help and my God.

6 My soul is cast down within me,
therefore I remember thee
from the land of Jordan and of Hermon,
from Mount Mizar.
7 Deep calls to deep
at the thunder of thy cataracts;
all thy waves and thy billows
have gone over me.

Yahweh, the divine proper name, which we translate by "the LORD." **The living God:** In contradistinction to the lifeless idols and the vain objects worshiped by the pagans and the apostate Jews. The text, however, should probably read as in vs. 8, **the God of my life. Behold the face of God:** Cf. 11:7; 17:15; Isa. 6:5. Originally, it was understood literally, but in later times "to see God's face" meant to enjoy access to his presence in the worship of the temple. Hence, later editors altered the reading of אראה from *'er'eh* to *'ērā'eh,* i.e., from "I shall see" to "I shall appear" (cf. KJV). **I remember . . . how I went with the throng, and led them in procession to the house of God:** The text is uncertain, particularly in respect to **the throng, and led them in procession.** The best of the conjectural emendations offered is to read בסך אדירים or בסך אדרת, i.e., "in the throng of the nobles" or "in the noble throng." The psalmist, whether a leader, priestly or lay, or just one of the crowd, loved to join with the pilgrim processions, the **multitude keeping festival.** The memory of the past revives his languishing soul. **Why art thou cast down, O my soul? Hope in God,** whom I shall yet be thanking for showing himself, **my help and my God.**

2. Longing for God Amid Sickness (42:6-11)

6-11. The text of vs. 6*b* should be emended to read in part with Schmidt, מארץ ירדתי הרימני ממצר רע, "Out of the deep to which I have gone down lift me up! Out

---

those unaccustomed to spiritual experience this sounds like nonsense; to those to whom God is real it is the essence of divine-human intercourse. Put more conventionally, it is the intangible but real essence of personality which, paradoxically, while it cannot exist in isolation, must always maintain a measure of its own insulated integrity. God, the mystics have taught us, is never so near us as when he seems far off. That saints and poets rebel against this proves their sensitiveness to it.

This God-seeker thirsts and pants for God, and yet God is there to hear his agony described. He stands in the very presence of God, but asks when he is to **come and appear before God.** Such refreshment as his thirst has found has been the thirst-increasing salt of his own tears which have been his food day and night. And as if to sharpen the sense of frustration that paradox invites, he talks to God in the presence of those who scoffingly ask, **Where is your God?**

How is he to escape from this inner conflict—the need for God that is felt more poignantly the closer he comes to God? There are some things he can remember; kept in the archives of his soul, they are to be "poured out" when there is need for them to answer his distress. How he **went with the throng, and led them . . . to the house of God, with glad shouts and songs of thanksgiving, a multitude keeping festival.** This gave him instantaneously something that mitigated his loneliness, that qualified the sharpness of the paradox. Whatever his own limitations, he could remember that there had been the uninhibited joy and holiday of multitudes of others he had led into God's house. He might question his own soul, but the affirmations of the multitude could not be disputed.

5-8. ***The Soul's Question and God's Answer.***—"So I said to myself"—the common device that poet and peasant use. Only the pedant insists that the self cannot talk to the self. Here is the

8 *Yet* the LORD will command his lovingkindness in the daytime, and in the night his song *shall be* with me, *and* my prayer unto the God of my life.

9 I will say unto God my rock, Why hast thou forgotten me? why go I mourning because of the oppression of the enemy?

8 By day the LORD commands his steadfast love;
and at night his song is with me,
a prayer to the God of my life.

9 I say to God, my rock;
"Why hast thou forgotten me?
Why go I mourning
because of the oppression of the enemy?"

---

of the evil straits!" In this second strophe the desperate state into which the sickness of the psalmist has brought him is described. He is already sinking into the underworld, and its soaring waters are closing over him (cf. Jonah 2:5-6; see Exeg. on Ps. 18:5). The difficult text of vs. 8 needs to be reordered with a slight change: יומם ולילה שיחה עמי,

---

paradox which the philosophers analyze while simpler folk are accepting it. **Why art thou cast down, O my soul, and why art thou disquieted within me?** This is less than self-analysis and more than soliloquy. It is the way of the plain man and the poet for resolving the problem. God, who is near, seems far off; I, who am alone, make company and conversation with myself. The result? A sense of fellowship and the defeat of loneliness. Lifting one's self by one's bootstraps? Perhaps. But why not, if one is lifted? It is not the whole matter, by a good deal; the hope is not in one's self, but in God. But one makes a beginning with one's self with the promise that the ultimate benefit will come from him. **Hope in God;** that much I can do. **For I shall again praise him, my help and my God;** that much he will do.

The psalmist has talked with himself and urged his soul to find repose and hope in the certainty of God, but he finds less than complete relief. It is as if in response to the exhortation of vs. 5, his soul had answered that it was not particularly impressed, and this unhappy fact must be communicated to God. The solitary tug at his bootstraps had not budged him. He reports, **My soul is cast down within me.** What to do? Another familiar resource comes to his aid—memory. Where loneliness is not dispelled by communion with self, consultation with the past may help.

I remember thee
from the land of Jordan and of Hermon,
from Mount Mizar.

God's voice, muted in the soul, was heard in history, it was thunderous in waterfalls and waves. Overwhelming, in fact, was the sense of his power and presence. So much so that one was almost afraid, until recollection re-created again the old experience of daytime kindness and the night song that was the quiet interlude between the din of wave and cataract, an interlude as beneficent as prayer (vss. 7-8).

9-11. ***From Pathos to Praise.***—Our lonely poet's appeal to his memory has evoked reassurance. But has God remembered? Ask him!

I say to God, my rock;
"Why hast thou forgotten me?"

There have been enemies and oppression, there have been taunt and reproach—a deadly wound in my body. These he cannot forget; but it is not enough to turn the narrow pages of one's own history and recall what it is easy, under the shroud of loneliness, to forget. It is of greater importance to look at the vaster pages of God's history, to see whether the bitterness of one's private remembered moment is the pattern of eternity. The hours should be silent, as Emerson suggested, in order that the centuries should speak, lest one's hour speak a word that falsifies the witness of the ages. After all, there may be little value in recalling God for one's own gratification, if God has forgotten.

My adversaries taunt me,
while they say to me continually,
"Where is your God?"

The taunt of cynics is just that. God *has* forgotten, they say; and all man's recollecting is poor compensation if God's forgetfulness abandons him to his ultimate undoing.

Why are you cast down, O my soul? Here is the familiar device again. The loneliness, the tears, the enemies; the recollections, the hopes, the mourning, the sword of enemy and the taunt of adversary; what are these, and to what do they ultimately add up? For the moment, disquiet within, but in the long perspective they may be the auxiliary reasons for praise. **I shall again praise him, my help and my God.**

10 *As* with a sword in my bones, mine enemies reproach me; while they say daily unto me, Where *is* thy God?

11 Why art thou cast down, O my soul? and why art thou disquieted within me? hope thou in God: for I shall yet praise him, *who is* the health of my countenance, and my God.

10 As with a deadly wound in my body,
my adversaries taunt me,
while they say to me continually,
"Where is your God?"

11 Why are you cast down, O my soul,
and why are you disquieted within me?
Hope in God; for I shall again praise him,
my help and my God.

"Day and night my longing [my prayer to the God of my life] is 'May God give charge to his kindness.'" In his deepest woe he remembers that his God is a God of kindness. And so in the face of the cruel taunts of his enemies he calls again on his soul to hope in God. "I shall yet give him thanks."

There is a final arresting word in the KJV. How better does a man reflect his faith than by his countenance? The dour face that is a warning to the frivolous; the hard face that is as flint against pity; the angry face that frightens gentleness: these all are indexes to the men who wear them. What then of the face of him who hopes, and hopes in God? It is anointed with a divine unguent at the skilled hands of **him, who is the health of my countenance, and my God.**

Thus we see our poet moving from pathos to praise in two resurgent movements. His first recital of spiritual anguish is ended by a fresh grip on hope; then he immediately returns to the somber mood, to return yet again to the brighter augury of confidence.

This is more than merely repetition as a pattern of poetic writing. Whether he was following a conventional rhythm or putting together rise and fall, harmony and discord, cadence and pause to create the artist's effect is interesting as art, but it reflects something that lies deeper than the levels of art. Man lives in alternations of ecstasy and depression, rhythm and awkwardness, movement and pause. Thus Omar Khayyám:

> The Worldly Hope men set their Hearts upon
> Turns Ashes . . . .[1]

To live perpetually in the light injures the eyes. "All sunshine," says an Arab proverb, "makes the desert." To say this is not to excuse man's vacillations but to explain them. The high mood kept too long is likely to be hysterical; the depressed mood endured too long will become morbid. Some have called this the tragic sense of life; but is it necessarily so? Paul knew how to abound and how to be abased. He could "take pleasure in infirmities, in reproaches, in necessities, in persecutions, in distresses for Christ's sake" (II Cor. 12:10). This was the same man who was "caught up into paradise, and heard unspeakable words, which it is not lawful for a man to utter" (II Cor. 12:4). And Jesus could see both Satan falling like lightning and the golden dome of Jerusalem, the city that killed the prophets.

The cycle of moods is a part of the wise economy of God's rule. The springtime visits the wastes of the spirit no less than the barren winter fields, and makes both bright with new life. To pant like a hind for the freshness of the water brooks is as normal as to feel replete with the cooling draught when it is drained. No thirst, no search for water; no enemy taunt, no retreat to the reassurances of memory; no tears, no countenance bright with the unguent of hope.

It is by maintaining the tension between the alternate moods of the spirit that the spirit stays vital. To yield to thirst is to die of it; to abandon oneself to the water brook is to drown in it. To know deeply that one by his very nature is ordained to move in the cadences of joy and sorrow, fulfillment and dismay, and to use each mood as the poet has done, to call the heart back to the awareness of God—this is truly to live in the divine presence. What the unnamed son of Korah who has written this poem for us is saying is something as old as experience. Yet it needs saying over and over again. For the temptation merely to let the moods of the spirit drift with the cycles of change is a lively one, and is as dangerous as to deny the fact of rhythm. We need our poet's warning and his example. It was, after all, by dint of conscious effort that he was able to use the up-and-down swing of life to communicate the sense of God, a sense that is often as real in our experience of remoteness from him as in our realization of his presence.

[1] *The Rubáiyát*, tr. Edward Fitzgerald, st. xvi.

43 Judge me, O God, and plead my cause against an ungodly nation: O deliver me from the deceitful and unjust man.

43 Vindicate me, O God, and defend my
cause
against an ungodly people;
from deceitful and unjust men deliver
me!

3. Plea for God's Vindication (43:1-5)

43:1-5. In this strophe the psalmist prays that he may be vindicated over against his enemies by being healed and restored to the privilege of worship in the temple. **From**

43:1-5. ***A Plea for Justice.***—There is plausibility in the suggestion that this poem belongs to the preceding one (see Exeg.) ; that an editor, whose name is as obscure as his tastes, felt that some literary or liturgical purpose would be better served by making a separate poem out of the last five verses of the former. Support for this suspicion of arbitrary editing is found in the fact that the last verse of Ps. 43 repeats exactly the sentiment found twice in Ps. 42. Whether this is the correct understanding of the structure of the poem is of minor importance. It is by no means the only case where repetition of sentiment and phrase occur in the Psalter, nor is it uncommon in the practice of writing poetry, particularly of the religious or devotional type; but the occurrence of this repetition in such close proximity to its foregoing parallels gives likelihood to the observation.

The basic idea with which Ps. 43 opens, however, is distinct from the emphasis of Ps. 42. Loneliness or the sense of isolation from God supplies the point in the former, and this theme—to change the figure from a poem to a symphony—is given two readings: the panting of the hind, and the cast-down soul. Ps. 43 opens with a different note. Here the poet reflects a sense of injustice, a much more positive and depressing matter than loneliness. Because one is friendless, one may more likely be the victim of injustice—or what appears to be injustice; but the default of a friend, however dispiriting, is more tolerable than the dangerous machinations of an enemy.

Here, then, we find our Korahite confronted by a situation that is thoroughly bad. We are suspicious that it is much exaggerated, but even if it were wholly illusory his state of mind would be no less unstable. God in this situation is not hiding himself or withholding the refreshment of his presence from the thirsty soul. He is there as judge; and the thirsty soul who wondered (42:2) when audience was to be granted now stands as plaintiff before him, asking for something more sustaining than water. He wants justice and deliverance.

1-2. ***Resentment.***—We are not to deduce from these opening words the juristic pattern of the courts of those ancient times. This is a poem, not a legal brief, and whatever else "poetic justice" may mean, it certainly does not give standing to an official who acts in the threefold capacity of judge, advocate, and bailiff. Nothing less than this, however, is what our petitioner asks. **Vindicate me, defend my cause, deliver me**; these are the three offices he asks God to perform, despite their odd combination as judged by modern standards.

Our psalmist is so confident he is the victim of scheming men that he dares what a century ago would have been called "lese majesty" and in our times "contempt of court." Since **thou art the God in whom I take refuge,** he says patronizingly. **Why hast thou cast me off?** he asks truculently. This is a poor way to influence a judge—assuming that justice is not as deaf as it is said to be blind.

This, we are saying, is a very different mood from that introduced by the panting hart of 42:1. It comes nearer being the snarl of a cornered beast. Observe how the psalmist builds up his case. What would seem to be the apex of the indignity he suffers is given at the first, rather than at the close of his argument. It is that he stands against a pitiless people, and ungodliness is surely the ultimate evil as the nation is the ultimate aggregate. Deceit and corruption, his second count, are bad enough in one man, but they cannot hold a candle to the menace of a pitiless people. There follows his remonstrance to the judge in whom he had trusted, but who in this unhappy moment seemed to have abandoned him. Had the poet allowed the judge a word with which to defend himself against this immoderate outburst, spice might have been added to the poem, but would not the integrity of the court have been compromised? Perhaps there is a deep suggestion in this silence of God in the face of an ill-tempered man. Indeed, it may be part of what our poet is trying to say by not saying it. At any rate, he follows his rebuke to the judge with a reference to the oppression of his enemy, a situation which causes him to mourn rather than to struggle. This is the fourth and final indictment he summons.

2 For thou *art* the God of my strength:
why dost thou cast me off? why go I mourning because of the oppression of the enemy?
3 O send out thy light and thy truth: let
them lead me; let them bring me unto thy holy hill, and to thy tabernacles.

2 For thou art the God in whom I take
refuge;
why hast thou cast me off?
Why go I mourning
because of the oppression of the enemy?

3 Oh send out thy light and thy truth;
let them lead me,
let them bring me to thy holy hill
and to thy dwelling!

---

deceitful and unjust men deliver me! "From a deceitful . . . man" is also a possible rendering. We note how out of the contending emotions of his heart trust and confidence win the ascendancy. His heart argues thus: Since **thou art the God in whom I take refuge,** I cannot be forsaken and **go . . . mourning because of the oppression of the**

From the standpoint of the development of his case we see that the series of complaints begins with their climax. What should have risen to a crescendo fades out into a sob. He starts with a pitiless people ranged against him; he ends, **mourning because of the oppression of the enemy.** A smart lawyer might have reversed the order; but we must remind ourselves that we are dealing with a poet. This latter fact comes upon us suddenly when we encounter vs. 3. Here is the lyric note of poetry, not the pleading tone of the advocate. In fact, it may be this sudden modulation that gives us one of the poet's most important insights.

3-5. ***Light and Truth.***—The familiar words of vs. 3 create at once a totally different mood. **Defend my cause against an ungodly people,** the plaintiff had angrily demanded. **Send out thy light and thy truth: let them lead me.** What a world of difference! **From deceitful and unjust men,** he had whined.

Let them bring me to thy holy hill
and to thy dwelling!

Is this the same man speaking? Note also that the courtroom, with God as the dispenser of justice (vs. 1), gives place to **the altar of God,** where God is **my exceeding joy** and the object of the praise of a worshiper (vs. 4).

If vss. 1-2 have exhibited a temper that is unreasonable because it is desperate, vss. 3-4 exhibit a mood that is mildly puzzling. The psalmist had been the victim of deceitful and corrupt men. How he was taken in and defrauded we do not know, but his humiliation was so complete that he called on God to come to his aid. Suddenly, however, he seemed to realize that deceit is the enemy of light, and injustice is the enemy of truth. If, then, God will dispatch **light** and **truth** to his aid, they will guarantee him safe conduct to the **holy hill,** and to the dwelling place of God. This is the strategy of one overborne with conflict, and his confidence in it is now as complete as was his earlier sense of prostration. Apprehension is lifted, and the sounds of mourning blend into the music of the harp played before the altar.

We now hear repeated the question the poet twice put to himself in the previous psalm. It seems this time, however, to be gently reproachful. He almost wonders, as he asks his soul the reason for despondency, how there could possibly have been such faithlessness. There had always been light enough to illumine the soul and truth enough to satisfy it. Why, then, had there been even for a moment fear of deceit and corruption? The question is put, but the soul is allowed no reply. Instead there is the familiar exhortation to hope, and the promise of praise rising from lips touched by a radiance that suffuses the whole countenance.

Our concern at this point is not with the authorship or the purpose of this poem. Whatever ritual or liturgy may have used it, the fact remains that it was the common qualities of the human spirit reflected in its depths that made it popular. The son of Korah who wrote it did so for all his brothers under the skin, who in reading or chanting it recognized its universal truth. For after all, the poet's sense of frustration was deep. He stood against a pitiless people. Hyperbole, no doubt. So was Elijah's dark mood when by the brook Kerith he claimed the same sort of unshared and unappreciated rectitude. It is not uncommon at all; who of us has not felt that he stood alone amidst hostility and anger and folly? It is no small thing to feel one's self a "mute inglorious Milton"; it is the low level from which one can rise to great heights. Whatever extravagance our poet may have been guilty of, however morbid indeed his desperate gloom may appear to us, he did not allow himself to be scorned for the mediocrity of either his doubt

4 Then will I go unto the altar of God,
unto God my exceeding joy: yea, upon the
harp will I praise thee, O God my God.
5 Why art thou cast down, O my soul?
and why art thou disquieted within me?
hope in God: for I shall yet praise him, *who
is* the health of my countenance, and my
God.

4 Then I will go to the altar of God,
to God my exceeding joy;
and I will praise thee with the lyre,
O God, my God.

5 Why are you cast down, O my soul,
and why are you disquieted within me?
Hope in God; for I shall again praise him,
my help and my God.

To the chief Musician for the sons of Korah, Maschil.

44 We have heard with our ears, O
God, our fathers have told us, *what*
work thou didst in their days, in the times
of old.

To the choirmaster. A Maskil of the Sons of Korah.

44 We have heard with our ears, O God,
our fathers have told us,
what deeds thou didst perform in their days,
in the days of old:

---

enemy. So the light of God's favor and his loyalty to his servants, like two angels, will yet bring him to **the altar of God. Oh send** [them] **out!** and **I will praise thee with the lyre.** The refrain becomes a final affirmation of certitude.

XLIV. The Nation Cries for Help (44:1-26)

In this psalm we meet an instance of a national lament such as was uttered by or on behalf of the people in a time of national distress. From vs. 25 we learn that the

---

or his faith. Of course he was wrong with the sort of perversity for which poets are distinguished; but it was wrongness that made possible spectacular rightness.

It is important, then, to point up the altitude to which his faith could soar. The bright familiar lines, **O send out thy light and thy truth: let them lead me,** have lost for us something of their original radiance. Here was great faith in a time, we may properly understand, when conventional faith rested on somewhat lower levels. In this poem God is first addressed as judge and deliverer. Then the idea explodes in a burst of radiance—**light** and **truth.** There is no modern formula more readily acceptable to describe the basic faith of men. Even those who for whatever reasons would deny God, or would accuse his votaries of darkness and error, are quick to acknowledge their devotion to light and truth. Not light and truth for their own sakes, however. Here our poet puts these two words in their proper perspective. To be illumined by truth is not the ultimate felicity of man. Light and truth are not the goal of our striving; it is they that lead us to the goal—the **holy hill** and the **dwelling** of God. Here is ancient testimony to something every generation must seek and find for itself. Devotion to light and truth can become academic or idolatrous; and to our own generation it may well be suggested that truth and the learning of it involve imperatives and actions that lie always beyond.

Is the discovery of nuclear fission an end in itself? Does it carry no plus of obligation? If man stops with light caught in a dancing electron which he can shut on or off, or with truth caught in an equation, he is not yet safe from "deceitful and unjust men." Light and truth must lead man up to the hill of holiness, to the altars of God, or these may turn to shadow and error in man's heart.

It is just this that is the timeless note in this poem. All great affirmations of faith have struck it. No matter how low the spirit plunges into despair, it still can rise exultantly to the altitudes of light and truth. Little wonder that our Lord spoke so much about light and truth. Less wonder that he was spoken of as Light and Truth by those whom he led. No wonder at all that those who have accepted him as Light and Truth have been led to the sacred places of God and to the shrines of true devotion.

To such it is an idle question to ask: **Why are you cast down, . . . and why are you disquieted within me?** They have known the threefold benison: hope, praise, and the radiant countenance; and it is they that stand against a pitiless people, not in terror, but in trust.

44:1. *Poet as Historian.*—Our Korahite poet accepts a somewhat more ambitious assignment

suppliants are lying in **the dust** as they make their entreaty to the Lord. Their grievous situation has been occasioned by the defeat of their armies (vs. 10) because the Lord has not gone out with them to battle (vs. 9). They have been driven in flight, spoiled and ruthlessly slaughtered by the foe (vss. 10-12). In consequence, they have lost status as a nation; they are scattered among the nations and treated with contempt and scorn (vss. 13-16). Their tragic circumstances, since they have arisen through assailants who are of a different faith, awaken questions as to the ways of God in respect to those who fear him (vss. 17-24). From vss. 4-8 we learn that the words of the lament in this instance were spoken on behalf of the people by some person who because of his station as a leader in battle (vss. 4, 6) was entitled to be their spokesman before the Lord.

There is general agreement that the psalm is not pre-exilic. We know of no time before the Exile when the people could complain of being scattered among the nations in spite of their unswerving allegiance to their God (vss. 11, 17, 22). For the same reason the psalm cannot be assigned to Josiah's time or to the situation before or after 597 B.C. (cf. Lam. 5:7). A postexilic date is therefore to be assumed, and the choice seems to lie between the Persian and the Maccabean periods. From the fifth century this psalm, along with others such as Pss. 74; 79; 83, was thought to reflect the Maccabean struggles. Only in recent years has this view been challenged in favor of the earlier period (see R. H. Pfeiffer, *Introduction to the Old Testament* [New York: Harper & Bros., 1941], p. 637; S. R. Driver, *An Introduction to the Literature of the Old Testament* [New York: Charles Scribner's Sons, 1913], pp. 387-89; Briggs, *Psalms,* I, 375; W. O. E. Oesterley, *The Psalms* [New York: The Macmillan Co., 1939], I, 245; James Hastings, ed., *Dictionary of the Bible* [New York: Charles Scribner's Sons, 1898-1904], IV, 152-53). Arguments against Maccabean authorship are that (*a*) it is difficult to understand how a psalm written between 175 and 150 B.C. could have been included in Book II of the Psalter; and (*b*) the psalm does not seem to accord precisely with the Maccabean situation. It is therefore suggested that since the Jews suffered severely in a general revolt of western subject-states against the Persian ruler, Artaxerxes III, in 351-349 B.C., the psalm probably came out of that time of national humiliation and suffering. Since, however, we know so little of the details connected with that tragic event, it is impossible to say that the psalm fits that period better than the Maccabean. On the other hand, the early chapters of I Maccabees recount incidents more than one of which might have been the occasion of just such a lament (cf. I Macc. 1:44-53; 2:29-38; 3:42-50; 5:55-62).

---

as he writes this poem for the choirmaster. He turns from lyric reflections on his own personal yearnings, disappointments, and triumphs, and becomes the spokesman of the nation.

> These things I remember,
> as I pour out my soul,

he said in 42:4. Here he begins:

> **We have heard with our ears, O God,**
> **our fathers have told us,**
> **what deeds thou didst perform in their days.**

A poet is a poor historian. Plato lamented the "ancient enmity between poetry and philosophy," and there have therefore been poet-philosophers who lamented that Plato was no poet; but the separation between the historian and the poet is so manifest as to excite no argument. Homer, as poet, could spin a lively tale, but the difference between an *Odyssey* and a history is the difference between fancy and fact. This is not to prejudge the quality of the poem that occupies us here; it is to make somewhat easier an understanding of the shuttling back and forth between what may be fact and what certainly is fancy in this psalm. The acid comment in an early review of H. G. Wells's *Outline of History* should teach us caution. "Mr. Wells's reputation as a writer of fiction is not diminished by his writing of history," the critic said. The same might be said of the epic poet.

1-3. ***The Days of Old.***—What **our fathers have told us** is certainly one of the sources of history, but often of dubious reliability. The way in which our fathers told us is also a calculated aid to piety in us, their sons, when, instead of glorifying their own epic deeds, they assigned them to the power of God. This is a good basis for what might be regarded as whole-

2 *How* thou didst drive out the heathen with thy hand, and plantedst them; *how* thou didst afflict the people, and cast them out.
3 For they got not the land in possession by their own sword, neither did their own arm save them: but thy right hand, and thine arm, and the light of thy countenance, because thou hadst a favor unto them.
4 Thou art my King, O God: command deliverances for Jacob.

2 thou with thy own hand didst drive out
the nations,
but them thou didst plant;
thou didst afflict the peoples,
but them thou didst set free;
3 for not by their own sword did they win
the land,
nor did their own arm give them victory;
but thy right hand, and thy arm,
and the light of thy countenance;
for thou didst delight in them.

4 Thou art my King and my God,
who ordainest[e] victories for Jacob.

[e] Gk Syr: Heb *Thou art my King, O God; ordain,* etc.

The meter is 3+3, with instances of a stich of 4 or 2+2 beats. The thought falls into three major divisions (vss. 1-8, 9-16, 17-26), of which the first and the third consist of two strophes of five lines each, and the second of two strophes of four lines each. Jean Calès regards each strophe as a double strophe of either 3+2 or 2+2 lines.

1. God's Deeds in the Past (44:1-3)

44:1-3. The psalmist begins by recalling the marvelous deeds by which the Lord had given victory to his people over their enemies at the time of the conquest of Canaan. **Thou . . . didst drive out the nations, but them thou didst plant.** He is thinking of the events covered by the book of Joshua (cf. ch. 12), and he is acquainted with the Deuteronomic editor's interpretation of the meaning and implications of them (Josh. 23). **Our fathers have told us,** in obedience to the injunctions of Deut. 8:2-18 (cf. Pss. 48:8; 78:3; II Chr. 20:7). What God has done for his faithful people in the past must surely be prophetic of what he means to do thereafter. **For not by their own sword did they win the land, . . . but** [by] **thy right hand** (cf. Deut. 8:17; Josh. 24:16-18). **The light of thy countenance:** i.e., thy gracious favor. Israel's history is a story of grace. Can it have ended?

2. The Nation's Trust in God Alone (44:4-8)

4-8. Just as in the days of old, the nation puts its trust in God alone. **Thou art my King and my God:** The **my** here, like the **I** in vs. 6, reveals that a leader is speaking in

---

some nationalism or a tribalism spared the excesses of pride. It starts with an assumption of divine partisanship; it explains success as the initiative and accomplishment of God, and it exhibits an appropriate humility in the face of such beneficence.

This our poet clearly does. The concluding words of vs. 3 explain the good fortunes of **the days of old. For thou didst delight in them:** that was reason enough. The operation of this preference was clear in the decisive way in which God's hand rested in blessing on his choice, and in doom on his discard. The latter were driven out and afflicted, the former were planted and spread abroad. There was no need to come to the aid of this Almighty Hand. **For not by their own sword . . . but . . . the light of thy countenance.** This last phrase is an echo of what we have heard before, and it is interesting because it reminds us that it is the poet who is giving us the record. To him the face of the divine conqueror was as important an element in victory as his hand or his arm. Thus the uncriticized memoirs of **our fathers.**

4-8. ***God as King and Ally.***—It all came about presumably because God had been acknowledged as **King.** The formula was a simple one: God loved them; they reciprocated, and he planted them and spread them abroad. Obviously, then, so long as this relationship was

5 Through thee will we push down our enemies: through thy name will we tread them under that rise up against us.

6 For I will not trust in my bow, neither shall my sword save me.

7 But thou hast saved us from our enemies, and hast put them to shame that hated us.

8 In God we boast all the day long, and praise thy name for ever. Selah.

9 But thou hast cast off, and put us to shame; and goest not forth with our armies.

5 Through thee we push down our foes;
through thy name we tread down our assailants.
6 For not in my bow do I trust,
nor can my sword save me.
7 But thou hast saved us from our foes,
and hast put to confusion those who hate us.
8 In God we have boasted continually,
and we will give thanks to thy name for ever. *Selah*

9 Yet thou hast cast us off and abased us,
and hast not gone out with our armies.

---

the name of his people. Except in vs. 15, he reverts to "we" and "us" and "our" in the other verses. This man who identifies himself with his people is a warrior, as the references to **my bow, my sword,** and **our armies** show. We cannot identify him further, but his **King** is God. He and his people have never failed to give the glory to God for Jacob's—i.e., Israel's—victories. **In God we have boasted continually.** And both now and in the future **we will give thanks to thy name.**

3. The Nation's Present Condition (44:9-16)

9-16. The psalmist turns from the contemplation of the past and the nation's enduring trust in God's help to the contrasting conditions of the present. First there is the spectacle of defeated armies (vss. 9-12). **Thou hast made us turn back from the foe:** In his desperation at the plight of his people the psalmist uses strong words before

---

sustained, there was reasonable certainty of continued good fortune. The record of **the days of old** was clear; **our fathers** fared well. We must not be overly presumptuous however. We live in different days. Mayhap we are not the men of faith and piety our fathers were. Will their fortune rest on their epigoni? Our poet is not quite sure. Observe his sudden retreat to private faith: **Thou art my King and my God.** Was that as far as he dared to go? Different times, different mores. Is he saying for Jacob what he is not sure Jacob would say for himself? To be sure, the poet's trust might only be representative or vicarious, but let us admit it is bold. On the basis of his acknowledged fealty he calls for **victories,** not for himself but **for Jacob.** And yet an expression of partial or representative loyalty from Jacob might elicit only partial or representative loyalty from the King. So, differing conspicuously from the noble inaction of the fathers in the days of old, he promises that Jacob will break a lance and stamp a foot. God becomes an aid to their efforts.

Through thee we push down our foes;
through thy name we tread down our assailants.

The shift is interesting, and it is commonplace, if not in fact proper. One generation cannot live forever on the invested heritage of its fathers. That must be reinvested by its own heroic deeds. At the same time this heroism is not a break with the faith of the past; it is an accommodation to the needs of the present. So our poet is quick to promise that Jacob's participation in the conflicts of his times is not an arrogant assertion of his own power. **Through thee we push down our foes,** he says, adding—and again it is his private and representative faith—

For not in my bow do I trust,
nor can my sword save me.

He returns to the mind of the group again:

In God we have boasted continually,
and we will give thanks to thy name for ever.

And why not? Has it not been he who has saved them from the aggression and the hate of their enemies?

9-16. ***The Shadow of Depression.*****—Selah** is properly interposed at this point. The rest it provides is more than liturgical; it clearly

10 Thou makest us to turn back from the enemy: and they which hate us spoil for themselves.

11 Thou hast given us like sheep *appointed* for meat; and hast scattered us among the heathen.

12 Thou sellest thy people for nought, and dost not increase *thy wealth* by their price.

13 Thou makest us a reproach to our neighbors, a scorn and a derision to them that are round about us.

14 Thou makest us a byword among the heathen, a shaking of the head among the people.

15 My confusion *is* continually before me, and the shame of my face hath covered me,

16 For the voice of him that reproacheth and blasphemeth; by reason of the enemy and avenger.

10 Thou hast made us turn back from the foe;
and our enemies have gotten spoil.
11 Thou hast made us like sheep for slaughter,
and hast scattered us among the nations.
12 Thou hast sold thy people for a trifle,
demanding no high price for them.

13 Thou hast made us the taunt of our neighbors,
the derision and scorn of those about us.
14 Thou hast made us a byword among the nations,
a laughingstock[f] among the peoples.
15 All day long my disgrace is before me,
and shame has covered my face,
16 at the words of the taunters and revilers,
at the sight of the enemy and the avenger.

[f] Heb *a shaking of the head*

God. Whereas once God gave victories to Israel, now "thou hast made us to be eaten up like sheep," selling the people like animals led up for butchery and **demanding no high price for them,** i.e., deriving no good from the transaction. Then there is the shame which has befallen the people (vss. 13-16). They are the **taunt, derision, scorn, byword,** and **laughingstock** among the peoples. **All day long my disgrace is before me,** for as leader the psalmist suffers the stigma of the shame of defeat and all its consequences. The argument of the psalmist is that if to God belongs the glory for victory, to him also belongs the **shame** of defeat.

---

marks a further change in the poet's mood. We have felt his proud confidence in the splendor of the days of old, when, because God was well disposed toward his fathers, there was no wasteland in which, once planted, they could not grow. We have noted also that, while grateful for the providences of the past, he accepts the responsibilities of his own generation. To offer to come to God's aid, or to ask God to be their strong arm, may seem a lesser faith than that of their fathers. But was it? Was the poet mildly skeptical of the romantic stories they had "heard with their ears"? Was life quite so simple as that? Was not companionship with God in a great enterprise more realistic, more rewarding, and more noble than an acceptance of divine favors in return for easy fealty? Here is no diminution of faith; it is rather the implementing of faith, and it represents clear moral and spiritual advance over the relationship that would allow man, merely for a promised word of fealty, to be the detached spectator of the mighty acts of God.

When we come to the end of the pause that selah provides, we encounter a mood so different from what has gone before that it seems almost to contradict it completely. We were first introduced to the lyric record of the days of old; then to the realistic expectations of the immediate future. What of the existential now? Vs. 9 introduces us to the poet's petulance. "Yet now," he whines. There follow seven verses filled with bitterness and recrimination. Forgotten for the moment are the days of old. They offer meager comfort to the anguished present. Tragedy has overtaken Jacob, through no fault of his own. Our poet is very clear as to what he thinks has happened and why. Again this may be history written with personal pique, and therefore a poor factual guide; but the poet's use of simile and metaphor does not disguise the anger and shame he feels.

17 All this is come upon us; yet have we
not forgotten thee, neither have we dealt
falsely in thy covenant.
18 Our heart is not turned back, neither
have our steps declined from thy way;
19 Though thou hast sore broken us in
the place of dragons, and covered us with
the shadow of death.
20 If we have forgotten the name of our
God, or stretched out our hands to a strange
god;
21 Shall not God search this out? for he
knoweth the secrets of the heart.
22 Yea, for thy sake are we killed all the
day long; we are counted as sheep for the
slaughter.
23 Awake, why sleepest thou, O Lord?
arise, cast *us* not off for ever.

17 All this has come upon us,
though we have not forgotten thee,
or been false to thy covenant.
18 Our heart has not turned back,
nor have our steps departed from thy
way,
19 that thou shouldst have broken us in the
place of jackals,
and covered us with deep darkness.

20 If we had forgotten the name of our God,
or spread forth our hands to a strange
god,
21 would not God discover this?
For he knows the secrets of the heart.
22 Nay, for thy sake we are slain all the day
long,
and accounted as sheep for the slaughter.

23 Rouse thyself! Why sleepest thou, O
Lord?
Awake! Do not cast us off for ever!

4. The Nation Remains Loyal to God (44:17-22)

17-22. All this has come upon us, though we have not forgotten thee: Cf. Deut. 28:1-2, 7. The psalmist presents as another argument the contrast between the promises of God and his performances, or in other words, the contrast between the facts of history and the claims of the spirit. **That thou shouldst have broken us in the place of jackals:** A pregnant construction which may be paraphrased, "Thou hast crushed us and made us to dwell in wasted or waste places, which are the haunts of jackals." **Covered us with deep darkness:** I.e., made us like the dwellers in the underworld, dead men (cf. Job 10:21; 38:17). Vs. 19 describes the effects of the military reverses on the land and its people. **For thy sake we are slain:** Loyalty to God and his religion has been costly to these Jews, who obviously are being challenged in respect to matters of conscience.

5. Plea for God's Intervention (44:23-26)

23-26. Why sleepest thou, O Lord? Cf. 121:4. With the same frank realism which we have noted above the psalmist pushes the logic of the situation to bold conclusions.

17-22. *Trust Struggles Against Doubt.*—It is not their fault!

> **All this has come upon us,**
> **though we have not forgotten thee,**
> **or been false to thy covenant.**

They could not be justly accused of faithlessness or falsehood; their religious (**our heart has not turned back**) and their moral (**nor have our steps departed from thy way**) records are blameless. That they have been **broken . . . in the place of jackals** and covered with gloom is no just penalty for indifference or idolatry. God, who **knows the secrets of the heart,** would realize this if he took time to search it out. The psalmist adds what is perhaps his bitterest word, a word that has been generally misunderstood and misused in the interests of piety. **Nay, for thy sake,** i.e., because of God's somnolence and injustice, **we are slain all the day long, and accounted as sheep for the slaughter.** This has all the aspects of tragedy, and none of the intimations of noble sacrifice with which it has been associated by later users.

23-26. *Plea for Help.*—Just how grim the picture is may be seen by a quick look at the bill of particulars. They have been cast off and brought to dishonor—they who were once the object of God's favor. Once God drove out the

24 Wherefore hidest thou thy face, *and*
forgettest our affliction and our oppression?
25 For our soul is bowed down to the
dust: our belly cleaveth unto the earth.
26 Arise for our help, and redeem us for
thy mercies' sake.

24 Why dost thou hide thy face?
Why dost thou forget our affliction and oppression?
25 For our soul is bowed down to the dust;
our body cleaves to the ground.
26 Rise up, come to our help!
Deliver us for the sake of thy steadfast love!

God being what he is would not permit such calamities to overtake his people, unless he was ignorant of their plight. God must be sleeping or inattentive or forgetful! Hence the psalm closes with the passionate cry, **Rise up, come to our help!** reinforced by the appeal to God to protect his reputation as a gracious God. **Redeem us for thy mercies' sake!** (Cf. the point of view of this psalm with that of Rom. 8:31-39.)

---

nations with his hand; now he makes Jacob to **turn back from the foe** (vs. 10). Once those who hated them were put to shame (vs. 7*b*), now **our enemies have gotten spoil** (vs. 10). Those whom he once did "spread abroad," now are **scattered . . . among the nations** (vs. 11*b*). They are **sold** but no profit accrues to God from the sale (vs. 12); they are a scoffing, a derision, an adage, and a riddle among their neighbors (vss. 13-15). They find no escape from the vengeance of the enemy, or from the daylong obscenities of the proud and the blasphemous (vs. 16). **All this has come upon us** (vs. 17). It is due to God's rejection—he has cast them off (vs. 9), or he has been asleep (vs. 23), or he has forgotten them (vs. 24*b*), or he has for some inscrutable reason deliberately concealed his face (vs. 24*a*).

How far our singer has come from the disposition with which he began his song is best seen by setting in contrast the concluding sentences of each of its two parts. Vs. 8 exclaims,

In God we have boasted continually,
and we will give thanks to thy name for ever.

Vs. 23 cries,

Rouse thyself! Why sleepest thou, O Lord?
Awake! Do not cast us off for ever.

Vss. 23-26 are almost angry. They clearly deny to God a quality that another ancient poet imputed, "He that keepeth Israel shall neither slumber nor sleep" (121:4). Here four grave defections are laid against him; sleep, languor, indifference, and forgetfulness. This bold impiety may be excused on the basis that it is the temperamental outburst of the poet, not the carefully reasoned deductions of a more realistic observer. And this extenuation may be allowed, since, as if by way of a signature, the poet affixes his mood instead of his name.

For our soul is bowed down to the dust;
our body cleaves to the ground.

From the low perspective of the dust one sees a distorted world; when one is prostrate before the bitter circumstances of life, one is less likely to use the language of piety than of complaint. Even desperation, however, allows a final modicum of hope, and the brief recollection of something that defeat all but denies. **Rise up, come to our help!** the psalmist prays. **Deliver us for the sake of thy steadfast love!** It is this last phrase that saves him from unrelieved despair. Without withdrawing anything that he has hitherto said, he can still feel—and say—that there is lovingkindness at the heart of the Eternal.

Here again we have found the vacillations of the poetic mood, the full cycle from ecstasy to despair, from boasting in God to prostration in the dust. And yet there is more in this song than the poet's vagaries. Whether consciously or otherwise, he has set forth a religious experience so common as to be thought almost, if not quite, universal. We have noted how lyrical he grew when he reflected upon God's great enterprise in ancient times; how real, if somewhat more modest, was his hope for the future. It was when he moved from the imaginative worlds of past and future into the realistic world of the present that his spirit at first faltered, and finally groveled in the dust. How much easier it sometimes is to maintain religious *élan* by reminiscence and hope than by experience. The spiritual impulse to retreat into the past, to return to Eden and the good old days, is a very common one. The wish to escape into the future, to transport ourselves to Elysium and the brave new world, is no less common. Both of these, whether they are encountered within the context of a psalm or explained as regression and fantasy in a psychology textbook, are very real. They have their values, but they are

To the chief Musician upon Shoshannim, for the sons of Korah, Maschil, A Song of loves.

45 My heart is inditing a good matter: I speak of the things which I have made touching the King: my tongue *is* the pen of a ready writer.

To the choirmaster: according to Lilies. A Maskil of the Sons of Korah; a love song.

45 My heart overflows with a goodly theme;
I address my verses to the king;
my tongue is like the pen of a ready scribe.

XLV. An Ode for a Royal Marriage (45:1-17)

This psalm is to be classed with the royal psalms. It is more frankly secular in its theme than the others of its class preserved in the Psalter. The occasion is the wedding of the king to a foreign princess, and the psalm is a poetic effusion from the lips of a court poet, priestly or lay, who has been deeply stirred by the scene which he is witnessing. From the paternal note which runs through his composition we may assume that the poet is a privileged person in the court. His years, his skill, and his personal distinction may together have clothed his role with a special authority. With fine restraint and delicate tact he mingles counsel with compliment; his praise avoids fulsomeness, and his injunctions austerity. The resultant gracious quality of his work gave it distinction among its kind in ancient courts, and doubtless accounts for its preservation and eventual inclusion in the Psalter (for the more tropical adulation of foreign kings by their court-poets see Erman, *Die Religion der Ägypter,* pp. 258-60, 278-80).

The psalm consists of eleven tristichs and two distichs (or one quatrain). After the first tristich (vs. 1), which serves as a formal introduction to the theme, there follow four strophes of three tristichs each (vss. 2-5, 6-9, 10-12, 13-15) addressed to the royal bride, and a two-line strophe (vss. 16-17) which is both a benediction and a prophecy. The meter is clearly meant to be four beats to a stich, divided lightly by a caesura. Corruptions of the text, due to the introduction of descriptive elements, have disturbed the symmetry of the form, particularly in vss. 11-16.

It is natural that there have been attempts to identify the bridegroom and bride. Among the royal personages of the pre-exilic period Solomon and the daughter of

not without their dangers. As an aid to perspective one dare not forget the past and as a fillip to the present one must not despise the future; but our lives are lived in the now, and if God cannot be made real to us now, he will be diffused by our piety into recollection or dream.

This was the problem our Korahite seems to have been struggling with. He was no wiser and no worse than all those who have faced up to the fact of God in human experience. If his song modulated from gaiety to sobriety, and finally to a minor key, the melody through it all is a familiar one. That life for him could in the closing measure be represented as ultimately redeemable because of the **steadfast love** of God—this was the testimony of a faith that is somehow as inextinguishable as life itself.

45:1-17. ***The King's Wedding.***—Here in the romantic mood is the stuff of which poetry is made. One might add also the martial mood. The fact is that love and war are psychological twins. It is commonplace that they make equal claims to fairness—"All is fair in love and war"—and it is equally obvious that they evoke the same basic drives in the same paradoxical relation: the complete abandonment of self in the complete conquest of the other.

This psalm is a song celebrating the marriage of a king, and the poet is as gay as the occasion he salutes. Indeed, this spirit betrays him into a claim that is quite as immoderate as his excitement. **I will cause your name to be celebrated in all generations,** he promises (vs. 17*a*), and even intimates that his epithalamium will occasion popular thanks forever and ever (vs. 17*b*). Not thanks for the poem exactly, but thanks to the king whose magnificence inspired it.

Whatever the ancients may have thought of the inspiration of their sacred writings, this writer entertains no doubts as to his afflatus. His heart overflows with **a goodly theme**—bubbles and froths is perhaps a more literal rendering—and his **tongue is the pen of a ready writer** as he speaks of his work for the king. Heart,

Pharaoh, Ahab and Jezebel, Joram and Athaliah, and even Jeroboam II and his unknown spouse have been proposed; among those of the postexilic period Duhm has thought of Aristobulus I (104-103 B.C.). We know so little of the personal histories of the kings of both periods that the identifications advanced by students can be nothing more than conjectural. Certain facts, however, must be kept in mind in any approach to the subject. The phrase **daughter of Tyre** (vs. 12) can be rendered **people of Tyre.** Hence it is precarious to predicate that the princess is Jezebel. Further, on the basis of language there are evidences pointing to a postexilic date: קציעות **(cassia)**, in vs. 8, is an Aramaic word; בכל־דר ודר **(in all generations)**, in vs. 17*a*, and לעלם ועד **(for ever and ever)**, in vs. 17*b*, are phrases appearing in late writings; מעשי ("my poem" or **my verses)**, in vs. 1, is equated by some with ποίημα (E. Podechard, "Notes sur les psaumes," *Revue Biblique*, XXXII [1923], 28-38). In the interest of a pre-exilic date these evidences may be dismissed by the assumption of glosses, additions, or a late revision of the psalm. The arguments for a pre-exilic date may be briefly summarized: such a secular psalm must have been sanctioned by some length of history to permit of its being allegorized and so introduced into the Psalter (Eissfeldt, *Einleitung in das A.T.*, p. 115); also, it must have been written in a time when the king was addressed by a divine title (vs. 6). Altogether, though the evidence is conflicting, the probabilities favor a pre-exilic date.

In the Targ. of the psalm the king is interpreted as the Messiah and the bride as Israel (see also Heb. 1:8-9).

1. Dedication to the King (45:1)

45:1. As the prophet in Isa. 5:1, so here the poet gives a brief introduction to his theme. **My heart overflows:** Lit., "boils" or "seethes," overpowered by the poetic afflatus. **My verses:** Lit., "my work" or "my works," because the poet compares his poem to the

---

tongue, and pen are all under the spell. This is hardly the discharge of the laborious literary duty of the court laureate; here is sheer delight; he could not resist the urge to sing even if the king forbade him.

With such a lyric opening, an unrestrained eulogy might have been forthcoming, but such is not the case. There is the conventional reference to the physical beauty of the king, **You are the fairest of the sons of men** (vs. 2). It is hardly less than the poet could have said, though he might have said more. The king's words are gracious as becomes his regal station, and God's blessing is promised in perpetuity (vs. 2). The king's love of righteousness and hatred of wickedness are the proper qualities of his magisterial role, and his anointing by God has not only elevated him to a throne, it has lifted up his heart with happiness above his fellows. Even the ceremonial unguent was **the oil of gladness** (vs. 7). The royal wardrobe was fragrant with the freshness of balsam, the bitter pungency of cinnamon, and the heavy and languorous scent of the lily. The royal chambers were of paneled ivory; and lute and dulcimer, played by tireless slaves, beguiled the hours with glad music. Among those whose duty it was to serve him were the daughters of lesser kings, and at his right hand stood his queen, clad in samite, woven of the fine gold of Ophir.

This is a ravishing picture, though in good taste, and to our eyes free from the gaudiness that some Oriental scenes might display. Furthermore, though he is celebrating the king, the singer has generous words for the royal consort, and even an admonition or two. In the palace she, herself a king's daughter (vs. 13) and to the manner born, is all-glorious. Dressed in embroidered garments and escorted by virgins, she comes into the kingly presence with gladness and rejoicing (vss. 14-15) that is unanimously shared. It is important for her to be reminded that although she brings royal lineage with her, she must leave behind her all recollections of her former life. Once upon a time to have been a princess was her all; now to be queen is her everything. **Forget your people and your father's house** (vs. 10*b*). This was the wifely abnegation expected even of a queen dressed in cloth of gold; and it was not without its compensation. If she was to lose her identity with one royal house, this meant that she gained allies in another. Her royal lord deserved the sort of utter fealty that imparted to her radiant beauty a quality of irresistible loveliness. Such fealty was, indeed, beyond all this, a diplomatic asset that brought native gifts from Tyre and the strong favor of the aristocracy of wealth among the king's own people. The greatest felicity with which her renunciation of her own people and her father's

2 Thou art fairer than the children of men: grace is poured into thy lips: therefore God hath blessed thee for ever.
3 Gird thy sword upon *thy* thigh, O *most* Mighty, with thy glory and thy majesty.

2 You are the fairest of the sons of men;
grace is poured upon your lips;
therefore God has blessed you for ever.
3 Gird your sword upon your thigh, O
mighty one,
in your glory and majesty!

careful workmanship of an artist or artisan (cf. Jer. 10:9; Ezek. 27:16, 18; Song of S. 7:1, and ποίημα), are dedicated to the king. And the words flow from **my tongue** like words from **the pen of a ready scribe,** so inspired is it by the theme.

2. The Royal Bridegroom (45:2-9)

2-5. The poet chooses carefully the moment in the wedding occasion which he is to immortalize; it is that when the king takes his station before the palace as the bridal procession draws near and the ceremony reaches its joyous culmination. First the personal qualities of the king are commended. His physical charm is matched by gracious speech and manners. **Grace is poured upon your lips:** I.e., his words by their courtesy and amiability win favor. Only to look upon him is to recognize that God's favor rests on

house was to be rewarded was in keeping with the act. **Instead of thy fathers shall be thy children, whom thou mayest make princes in all the earth** (vs. 16). She renounced her royal lineage to create a nobler one; the daughter of a king becomes the mother of princes in all the earth.

These are the encomiums of the king and his bride and the poet's exhortations to the latter. One other most important matter, moreover, is not forgotten. Grace and beauty are the king's, but it needs more than that to rule a people. God's blessing manifest in his personal charm must be matched by his own deeds of prowess. There is glory in a sword: he must gird it upon his thigh (vs. 3). There is glory also in sharp arrows driven through the hearts of the enemies that fall beneath him (vs. 5). There is a still greater glory—the glory not only of success, of victory, victory won by a keen-edged sword or sharp arrows or even a right hand that has learned terrible things (vs. 4*c*), but the glory of truth, meekness, and righteousness. **In your majesty ride forth victoriously** (vs. 4).

This, we say, is the sort of subject matter with which the poet delights to work. The extraordinary quality of this poem, however, lies in its restraint rather than in its extravagance. Gay it is—costly essences and garments of gold, the warrior king on his giant charger; but it is also grave—truth, meekness, and righteousness, and terrible deeds that a skillful fighting hand shall teach. Of greater interest and significance, then, is the interlude that falls just before the midpoint of the song. It is an apostrophe to God, as if in the exultation of the wedding it was necessary to set God in the midst of it all. This lone vs. 6 sets the whole matter in a perspective that includes God. Here was a new king for a transient throne; but **Thy throne, O God, is for ever and ever.** Here was a reign majestic, honest, and righteous; but **your royal scepter is a scepter of equity.** Except for the casual reference in vs. 2, where the young king's beauty is regarded as evoking divine approval, this address to the Eternal alone saves the hymn from what would today be called a purely secularist mode.

So much for the delight of the singer in the spectacle he celebrates. What is its value beyond the ancient exotic savor it possesses? It represents the level of regard on which the institution of marriage was maintained at that period of Hebrew history. This is by no means a typical wedding; kings do not set the fashion for the nuptials of common folk. At the same time, the king was ideally the pattern and preceptor of the people, and what he did was regarded as the best that the culture of his times afforded. This in a measure would account for the poet's obvious delight as his heart "bubbled over with a goodly theme" (vs. 1). And we have here the high note that has sounded through all the domestic history of the Jews. "Therefore shall a man leave his father and his mother"—thus Gen. 2:24. **Forget your people and your father's house**—thus the son of Korah. "What therefore God hath joined together, let not man put asunder"—thus Jesus in Matt. 19:6. This solid core of nuptial fidelity is the spiritual reason for the racial and familial integrity of the Jews for more than four thousand years.

1-17. ***Is the Psalm Messianic?***—Conspicuous use of this psalm has been made by those who have seen in it the ideal picture of the messiah-

4 And in thy majesty ride prosperously,
because of truth and meekness *and* righteousness; and thy right hand shall teach
thee terrible things.
5 Thine arrows *are* sharp in the heart of
the King's enemies; *whereby* the people
fall under thee.
6 Thy throne, O God, *is* for ever and
ever: the sceptre of thy kingdom *is* a right
sceptre.
7 Thou lovest righteousness, and hatest
wickedness: therefore God, thy God, hath
anointed thee with the oil of gladness above
thy fellows.
8 All thy garments *smell* of myrrh, and
aloes, *and* cassia, out of the ivory palaces,
whereby they have made thee glad.

4 In your majesty ride forth victoriously
for the cause of truth and to defend[g] the right;
let your right hand teach you dread deeds!
5 Your arrows are sharp
in the heart of the king's enemies;
the peoples fall under you.

6 Your divine throne[h] endures for ever and ever.
Your royal scepter is a scepter of equity;
7 you love righteousness and hate wickedness.
Therefore God, your God, has anointed you
with the oil of gladness above your fellows;
8 your robes are all fragrant with myrrh and aloes and cassia.
From ivory palaces stringed instruments make you glad;

[g] Cn: Heb *and the meekness of*
[h] Or *your throne is a throne of God*, or *your throne, O God*

him. Then shifting his attention to the insignia of the king who, scepter in his hand and sword bound to his side and attended by his bowman, stands beside his war chariot, the poet sees the king in fact as well as in symbol his people's champion. **In your glory and majesty,** i.e., in your regal splendor, **ride forth victoriously for the cause of truth,** i.e., what makes for a stable society, **and to defend the right.**

6-9. Because the rule of the king is marked by the love of equity and righteousness, two results follow. First, the dynasty will be perpetuated. **Your throne, O God:** In the ancient world kings were commonly accorded divine titles as vicegerents of deity or as belonging to a superhuman class (Anton Jirku, *Altorientalischer Kommentar zum Alten Testament* [Leipzig: A. Deichert, 1923], p. 226). The Hebrews were acquainted with this usage (cf. 2:7; 89:27; Isa. 9:6). Secondly, the king has been made the happiest of men on this his wedding day. In keeping with the customs proper to the occasion, his garments are saturated with the fragrance of unguents and perfumes. **Your robes are all fragrant with myrrh and aloes:** Lit., "all your robes are myrrh and aloes," i.e., the garments seem to be fabrics of perfumery. **Cassia** (קציעות) is probably a late gloss on **aloes,** since it overloads the line and is Aramaic (cf. older word קדה). **Cassia** is derived

conqueror and ruler who, as the political fortunes of the Jews declined, more and more possessed their imaginations. The point has been made elsewhere that this may have been the chief reason for retaining this poem in the text of the Psalter. Its idyllic picture of a royal wedding was, in the judgment of some scholars, of indifferent interest as compared to its popular appeal to people who were increasingly discouraged by mounting evidence of national decline. Wherever the orthodox messianic hope stirs the heart of modern Jewry, this picture still fits within its framework, and hearts can still "bubble over with a goodly theme."

It is to be expected, then, that where messianism is an important element in the body of Christian doctrine, this picture of the great king would be taken over in some of its details. The hope that springs eternal in the human breast needs pictures that do not fade. That such pictures usurp the place of fact, that men too often prefer an old fancy to a new truth, is something we must live with so long as we are mortal. Is this not the true function of poetry after all? And if messianism is no more than a

9 Kings' daughters *were* among thy honorable women: upon thy right hand did stand the queen in gold of Ophir.
10 Hearken, O daughter, and consider, and incline thine ear; forget also thine own people, and thy father's house;
11 So shall the King greatly desire thy beauty: for he *is* thy Lord; and worship thou him.

9 daughters of kings are among your
ladies of honor;
at your right hand stands the queen in
gold of Ophir.

10 Hear, O daughter, consider, and incline
your ear;
forget your people and your father's
house;
11 and the king will desire your beauty.
Since he is your lord, bow to him;

---

from the bark of *laurus cassia* of South Arabia; **aloes,** from the bark of an Indian tree (Sanskrit *Aghal*). From within the palace with its panels and furniture inlaid with ivory, **stringed instruments** send forth music to delight the king as the bridal procession reaches him. The text of vs. 9 is uncertain. Read, "Kings' daughters come to meet you." The bride now as the royal consort takes the place of honor at the king's right (cf. I Kings 2:19). For **Ophir,** a region in South Arabia or East Africa, see I Kings 9:26-28; Job 22:24.

3. Counsel for the Bride (45:10-12)

10-12. Hear, O daughter: The poet here gives the bride some wise and fatherly advice. **Forget your people and your father's house,** assuming a role not like that of a Jezebel or an Athaliah, but like that of Ruth who said, "Your people shall be my people, and your God my God" (Ruth 1:16). Her reward will be twofold: the king's love will abide with her, and she will be the recipient of rich gifts from foreigners as well as Israelites who sue for her favor and intercession. **The people of Tyre:** Lit., **daughter of Tyre** (cf., e.g., "daughter of Zion," Isa. 62:11). We must allow for the poet's license to

---

great, recurrent poetic theme, even on those grounds it could be dismissed as empty of meaning or value.

One does not demur at the pictorial use of great ideas. The church as the bride of Christ is an elevating concept, though it manifestly has little contact with reality, and to try to incarnate it in experience is to reduce it to absurdity, or thin it out into sentimentality. A song loved by countless devout Christians borrows from the words of our ancient poem:

> Out of the ivory palaces
> Into a world of woe.[2]

This has represented literal fact for most who have sung it; but it is highly improbable that the king in our psalm lived in a palace literally made of ivory. The modern songwriter certainly was on his own when he represented his king's exit from ivory palaces into a world of woe. The king in Ps. 45 faced no such unhappy prospect.

It is quite impossible to fit the picture of the royal marriage into any messianic framework. This is no less true today than it was in the third century B.C. or in the first century A.D., when the apocalyptic hope called for vivid new imagery for its dramatization. "A white horse; and he that sat upon him was called Faithful and True, and in righteousness he doth judge and make war" (Rev. 19:11) are words that recall the language of our poem (vss. 3-4). This is one poetic motif—the conquering warrior—of great dramatic intensity. The other, employed also by our Korahite singer, is similarly intense, though quite the reverse of the ferocity of the former. "The Spirit and the bride say, Come" (Rev. 22:17) is of the same genre as vs. 14. Here the image is not the warrior riding forth to conquer, but the security and beauty of companionship in the royal ménage.

There is a corrective to the deep spiritual need that is gratified only by imagery, fancy, and the pictorial patterns of poetry, a need that stands autonomous in its own right. We shall never get on without it; indeed, life would be intolerable if facts were the only resources of the spirit. Over against this messianic dream of something that is to come is the picture of something that eternally is, **Thy throne, O God,**

[2] Henry Barraclough, "My Lord has garments so wondrous fine." Copyright by Hope Publishing Company, owner. Used by permission.

12 And the daughter of Tyre *shall be there* with a gift; *even* the rich among the people shall entreat thy favor.

13 The King's daughter *is* all glorious within: her clothing *is* of wrought gold.

14 She shall be brought unto the King in raiment of needlework: the virgins her companions that follow her shall be brought unto thee.

15 With gladness and rejoicing shall they be brought: they shall enter into the King's palace.

16 Instead of thy fathers shall be thy children, whom thou mayest make princes in all the earth.

17 I will make thy name to be remembered in all generations: therefore shall the people praise thee for ever and ever.

12 the people[i] of Tyre will sue your favor
with gifts,
the richest of the people 13 with all
kinds of wealth.

The princess is decked in her chamber
with gold-woven robes;[j]
14 in many-colored robes she is led to the
king,
with her virgin companions, her escort,[k] in her train.
15 With joy and gladness they are led along
as they enter the palace of the king.

16 Instead of your fathers shall be your sons;
you will make them princes in all the
earth.
17 I will cause your name to be celebrated
in all generations;
therefore the peoples will praise you
for ever and ever.

[i] Heb *daughter*
[j] Or *people. All glorious is the princess within, gold embroidery is her clothing*
[k] Heb *those brought by her*

---

exaggerate. Gifts brought from Tyre, the market of rich merchandise, are represented as gifts from the Tyrian people.

4. The Royal Procession (45:13-15)

13-15. Leaving off his address to **the princess,** the poet now describes the splendor of her rich apparel and jewels as she is led to the nuptial chamber within the palace. The text of vss. 13-14 is uncertain. The RSV takes the first two words of vs. 13 with vs. 12, reading בכל־כבודה, **with all kinds of wealth.** For פנימה, **in her chamber** (RSV) or **within** (KJV), read פנינים, "pearls," and translate, "The royal lady, adorned with pearls in filigree work of gold, [and] clad in bright-colored robes, is led to the king." Read לבושה without mappiq, i.e., "clad" for **her clothing.**

5. Conclusion (45:16-17)

16-17. In the closing strophe, which is both benediction and prophecy, the poet speaks of the fruit of the marriage. **Sons** will keep alive the royal line and extend its rule. In vs. 17 read with the LXX, "They will cause your name to be remembered." So the name of the king will be honored for all time among the nations.

---

is for ever and ever: the sceptre of thy kingdom is a right sceptre (vs. 6). This is the fortress of fact on which the Christian builds his faith. The dream of a coming king and a glittering new throne will sustain many during times of darkness and fear. Thus do dreams serve the purpose of God. Lest, however, we abandon ourselves to an insubstantial and spiritually dangerous reliance on dream or hope—dream that may paralyze action, hope that may dangerously dilute caution—we have the central fact of God's scepter of equity and the throne forever and ever, which, as our poet has set it at the center of his song, is set forever at the center of our faith.

How appropriate, therefore, appears the verse with which our singer ends his lyric recital of the great wedding:

I will cause your name to be celebrated in all generations;
therefore the peoples will praise you for ever and ever.

To the chief Musician for the sons of Korah, A Song upon Alamoth.

46 God *is* our refuge and strength, a very present help in trouble.

To the choirmaster. A Psalm of the Sons of Korah. According to Alamoth. A song.

46 God is our refuge and strength,
a very present[l] help in trouble.

[l] Or *well proved*

XLVI. God as an Ever-Present Help (46:1-11)

This psalm, because of differences of opinion as to the circumstances which called it forth, is classified variously. In its general spirit and purpose it resembles a hymn, but on the other hand it does not conform to the normal structure of a hymn and, further, it is so permeated with prophetic elements that Kittel would describe it as a prophetic lyric. Because this prophetic strain is of an eschatological character, Gunkel and Staerk are disposed to call the psalm an eschatological hymn. It is, however, not to be understood as purely eschatological in the sense that it presents the usual eschatological pattern of the chaos in nature and among the worldly powers at the end of this age and of the golden age of peace to follow. The threefold refrain is **The Lord of hosts is with us; the God of Jacob is our refuge.** Obviously, whatever is eschatological in the psalm rises out of a present experience of the Lord's nearness, which is itself the guarantee of what the future will bring to light. For this reason some commentators, while not denying the eschatological, hold with Jean Calès that "Le poème est de signification historique avant d'être eschatologique" (*Le livre des Psaumes* [Paris: Gabriel Beauchesne et ses fils, 1936], I, 479). But in what sense "historical"? Some, e.g., König and Herkenne, think the psalm was inspired by the deliverance of Jerusalem from Sennacherib in the eighth century; Duhm connects it with the disturbances of the third century brought about by the wars among the successors of Alexander the Great; Schmidt, however, identifies it as a hymn of the New Year's Festival (see Exeg. on 24:1-10), celebrating the Lord's triumph at the time of the Creation by stressing its implications for Israel both now and for all time. The arguments in favor of an acceptance of Schmidt's view may be summed up briefly: (*a*) the allusions to wars, the roaring of nations, and the tottering of kingdoms seem to be too general for particular reference; (*b*) the evidences as to the date of the psalm preclude an eighth-century setting; (*c*) the verbs in vs. 6 should be rendered as gnomic aorists rather than as perfects or simple aorists, which a

---

46:1-11. ***Luther's Psalm.***—This is called "Luther's Psalm." It was not any claim that he staked out that gave him proprietary rights to it. Rather, we suspect, it was the great hymn "A mighty fortress is our God," into which he fashioned the bright gold he found here. There is perhaps a deeper reason in this fact that there is something massive, kinetic, irresistible in these giant rhythms that suggest the formidableness of the great iconoclast.

For the reason that it has been associated with Luther it has also had particular appeal to all who have seen and felt God in great moments. If indeed the choirmaster received it from the sons of Korah he must have realized at once its splendid possibilities as a chorus piece, and the singing of it then must certainly have reached a high level of the choric art. The centuries since have heard it sung in all the forms of song and to the melodies of countless composers. In addition to this, it is interesting to note that there is almost no line in the poem that has not in one form or another found its way into colloquial speech, for the most part in the vocabulary of worship and devotion, but not infrequently in the pretentious rhetoric of the forum. It does not derogate its fine qualities to say that it shares with the so-called "Shepherd Psalm" the highest popular rating. Indeed, its familiarity is so general that it has made possible the waggish claim that it was written by Shakespeare, proof of which is said to be found in the amusing coincidence that in the KJV the forty-sixth word from the beginning of this forty-sixth psalm is **shake** and the forty-sixth word from the end is **spear.** But all this proves is the fact that these great lines have been pored over by all sorts of readers, from monks to mountebanks.

1-7. ***Man's Security in God.***—Whatever may have been the proximate inspiration of this poem, whether it was the threat of some catastrophe of nature—earthquake or flood—or the terror of Sennacherib's siege, the efficient cause

2 Therefore will not we fear, though the
earth be removed, and though the mountains be carried into the midst of the sea;
3 *Though* the waters thereof roar *and* be
troubled, *though* the mountains shake with
the swelling thereof. Selah.

2 Therefore we will not fear though the
earth should change,
though the mountains shake in the
heart of the sea;
3 though its waters roar and foam,
though the mountains tremble with its
tumult. *Selah*

particular historical reference would require; (*d*) the eschatological elements, if admitted, must have had some *point d'appui* in the ritual. Altogether, such a festival as that of the New Year seems to provide the appropriate occasion to which the psalm is to be related.

For the use of **God** instead of "the LORD" as the divine name in this psalm see Exeg. on 42:1-5.

The psalm evidences a time when the psalmody of the temple was influenced by the prophetic spirit, and particularly by that of the later prophets with their visions of a warless world under the dominion of the Lord (cf. Isa. 8:9-10; 17:12-14; 33:17-24; 59:15*b*-20; Ezek. 6:7, 13; 11:10; Mic. 4:3). In view of the extent to which the psalmist has assimilated the ideas preserved in a wide range of the prophetic literature, one is led to date the psalm in the late postexilic period.

The psalm consists of three strophes, each of which comprises three lines either in 4+4 or 4+3 measure, and in addition, a refrain of one line regularly in 4+3. The refrain has by accident been dropped at the end of the first strophe.

1. God the Refuge of His People (46:1-3)

46:1-3. It is frequently noted that this psalm inspired Luther in the year 1529, when Vienna had been released from the Turkish siege, to write his hymn "A mighty fortress is our God." Also it is an interesting coincidence that Horace (*Odes* III. 3) speaks of Augustus' courage in words that are close to those of our psalm: *"Si fractus illabatur orbis, impavidum ferient ruinae,"* i.e., "Should the universe be shattered and overwhelm him, the ruins will strike him unafraid." Kittel calls this psalm "the song of songs of faith."

God is our refuge and strength: A better rendering is "God is our refuge and defense." An alternative rendering of the last word is "strong tower." He has well proved himself to be **a very present help in trouble** since ancient times. At the time of the Creation (cf. 93:2-4) he showed that he was mightier than all the monsters of chaos, and established forever his dominion over the world. **Therefore we will not fear though the earth should change:** Some would read המוג for המיר, "though the earth be dissolved." Though the mountains totter into the heart of the sea, though they quake before the proud onset of the roaring, crashing, seething waters of the great deep as it threatens to submerge the ordered world and re-establish the reign of chaos, **we will not fear**

was something deep in every human heart. Notwithstanding all man's pride and parade, he is in many ways an alien on the earth he claims as home. He boasts that he is more than a paragon to the beasts, but he is hardly a match for them in single combat. He has mastered nature in many ways, but still the nocturnal darkness frightens him; and in her violence the hospitable earth despoils him of what in her gentler moods he has been allowed to take from her. Worse still, he is not always trustful of his kind. His greatest satisfactions come to him when he is with his fellows, but his greatest fears come from his estrangements from them. Finally, man is much of the time unsure of God. Not openly or even consciously; but he cannot forever silence the questionings with which angry men and indifferent nature plague his spirit. Is the desolation of the burning mountain the sign of God's displeasure? Is the endless raging of the nations proof of God's indifference to his creation?

This is simply to say that an honest appraisal of man's life on the earth must make a place for his sense of insecurity and loneliness. This is not pessimism, for it is only one aspect of the total scene. At the same time, to avert one's eyes from the "melting earth" and the "burning

4 *There is* a river, the streams whereof shall make glad the city of God, the holy *place* of the tabernacles of the Most High.

5 God *is* in the midst of her; she shall not be moved: God shall help her, *and that* right early.

6 The heathen raged, the kingdoms were moved: he uttered his voice, the earth melted.

7 The LORD of hosts *is* with us; the God of Jacob *is* our refuge. Selah.

4 There is a river whose streams make glad
the city of God,
the holy habitation of the Most High.
5 God is in the midst of her, she shall not
be moved;
God will help her right early.
6 The nations rage, the kingdoms totter;
he utters his voice, the earth melts.
7 The LORD of hosts is with us;
the God of Jacob is our refuge.[m] *Selah*

[m] Or *fortress*

because **the LORD of hosts is with us.** The symbol of his presence (cf. Exeg. on 24:7-10), the invocation of his name, the oracles, the divine acceptance of the offerings—some or all of these factors assured the worshiping people that with the Lord of Creation in their midst they were more than equal to the worst imaginable catastrophes in the physical world (cf. Rom. 8:37-39).

2. GOD THE PROTECTOR OF ZION (46:4-7)

4-7. There is a river whose streams make glad the city of God. The river is neither the eschatological stream (Gunkel) of Isa. 33:21 nor the heavenly stream (Schmidt) which brings fertility to the land (cf. 65:9; 104:13), but the life-giving fountain of God's presence (cf. 36:9; Isa. 32:2; Jer. 2:13; 17:13), as we see in vs. 5, **God is in the midst of her.** Consequently, **she shall not be moved;** she is **the holy habitation of the Most High,** and therefore inviolable. Read with the LXX, "The Most High has made holy his dwelling place" (cf. Ezek. 39:7). Truly the name of the city is "The LORD is there" (Ezek. 48:35) and, when danger threatens her, **God will help her right early,** lit., "when the morning draws near." The darkest and therefore the most

chariot" is to invite ultimately something worse than pessimism.

Man has therefore made the effort to come to terms with these grim circumstances. He has denied them; but this is only to deceive himself. He has laughed at them; thus to deceive others. He has abandoned himself to them and placed his hope in another world where there will be nothing evil; this in an effort to escape from life. Or—and this is what our great poem is about—he has looked at the world of nature, man, and God, and while admitting that it is often terrifying, has found even in terror the manifestation of the splendor of **the LORD of hosts.** That discovery is man's greatest insight, and in that trust he commits himself to his noblest faith.

It is with this confident assertion that the poem begins. The lonely man needs refuge, the insecure man needs strength and help. Moreover, both loneliness and insecurity are the prelude to fear, particularly when the portents of nature are threatening. **God,** the psalmist boldly begins, **is our refuge and strength, a very present help in trouble. Therefore we will not fear.** Only one who has seen a violent paroxysm of the earth's solid surface can understand fully the imagery of his words. The earth changes; frost, water, and wind erode its face. But to feel a mountain shake and to see a crack run like a startled snake across a bare field, and to be caught in the midst of things from which one is powerless to flee—this is to know the puny strength of man when caught in the wild elemental dance of nature. The sea, often so innocent in its placid moments, knows a ferocity as terrible in its way as the convulsions of the land. The roaring tide that leaps from the depths and hurls itself against the mountains—let Browning speak of it:

> What if thy watery plural vastitude,
> Rolling unanimous advance, had rushed,
> Might upon might, a moment, . . .
> . . . .
> And when wave broke and overswarmed and, sucked
> To bounds back, multitudinously ceased—[3]

this is no ordinary tumult, and he who stands erect in the face of it has no ordinary faith.

But nature presents not the only threat in the face of which man feels insecure and afraid.

[3] *Aristophanes' Apology.*

8 Come, behold the works of the LORD, what desolations he hath made in the earth.

8 Come, behold the works of the LORD,
how he has wrought desolations in the earth.

dangerous hour or watch of the night is just before the morning draws near. "At eventide, . . . terror; Before morning, it is gone" (Isa. 17:14 Amer. Trans.). The Lord is also master of the peoples of the earth. "Nations roar and kingdoms surge" (vs. 6*a*): The tumult is of course directed against the Lord and his city and people. Israel was ever in a state of nervous apprehension of attack by foreign foes (cf. 2:2; Isa. 17:12-14; Jer. 47:2-7; Ezek. 38:10-23; 39:11-24). But the Lord of men is sufficient for her (cf. 48:4-7; Isa. 37:33-38).

3. God the Sovereign of the World (46:8-11)

8-11. The death and destruction of his enemies is the Lord's final work. Consider **how he has wrought desolations in the earth** (see Ps. 76). Therefore, in the manner of

Waters roar; that is bad enough and cannot be helped. But **nations rage,** and just because that ought to be helped, the terror is greater. Men under the spur of greed or fear unite to crush a neighbor nation, and they succeed. **Kingdoms totter.** What does this mean? It may refer to populations carried away en masse into captivity; it may mean the sudden changing of boundaries that meant literally moving a kingdom. Is there anything more formidable than the movement of a raging nation bent on conquest? Our generation knows the answer to that, and something of the frightful insecurity and helplessness of those caught in its path. Once again the valiant cry of faith: **The LORD of hosts is with us; the God of Jacob is our refuge.**

Not only is the singer's voice firm and clear; his spirit is serene. He is able to see beyond the tempest of shaking mountains and roaring waters to **the city of God,** high on its holy place, and to a placid **river whose streams make glad the city of God.** The transition in the poem creates the sensation of sudden calm after the violence of storm. The trouble (vs. 1) is spent, now the city is glad (vs. 4); the mountains are no more shaken into the heart of the seas (vs. 2); **God is in the midst** of the city, **she shall not be moved** (vs. 5). As for the raging nations and the scattering kingdoms—there was a shout above the noise of battle, one imperious word, and the blood and folly of the slaughter ended in a melting flame. **The LORD of hosts is with us; the God of Jacob is our refuge.**

8-11. *Evidences of God's Power.*—The fact that volcano and flood were God's desolations, and the melted battlefield where men had slain their brethren was the result of God's thundering word, disturbed our poet not at all. To the despoiled earth he invites the eyes of his fellows. There was trouble, to be sure, but in it there was a grandeur such as only God could order. Men boasted that they could make war, but none had been able to make war cease. Man has strung his bow, sharpened his spear, and fashioned his chariot. It is God alone that breaks, cuts asunder, and burns the weapons of offender and defender alike, and puts an end to the madness of their fratricide. There are two reasons for this giant faith, a faith that inspired a sixteenth-century monk to make a hymn that would express it for later generations to sing:

> A mighty fortress is our God,
> A bulwark never failing;
> Our helper he, amid the flood
> Of mortal ills prevailing.

The first reason rests firmly on certain rational a priori grounds. God is the major assumption: he is **refuge, strength, present help in trouble. Therefore**—from the hypothesis of God is drawn the major inference—**we will not fear.** There is point to the observation that the nature of sin is pride; much has been made of this insight, an insight freshly recovered. It may be quite as true that the hidden impulse to pride is fear. The brash, self-confident boast, the pose and the ostentation of the proud man, are his efforts to conceal a subconscious sense of insecurity. He is afraid for reasons hidden perhaps in his earliest conscious responses to tumult in his tiny world; his fear shuts the doors through which he might walk into confidence, and this closed-off isolation gives him the sense of loneliness which in itself is a component of his anxiety. He must then find something that will break down the barricades and let in light and companionship. The light is the symbol of the energy that streams from inexhaustible sources of a realm infinitely beyond the reach or safe vision of man; companionship is the symbol of the energy that

9 He maketh wars to cease unto the end of the earth; he breaketh the bow, and cutteth the spear in sunder; he burneth the chariot in the fire.

10 Be still, and know that I *am* God: I will be exalted among the heathen, I will be exalted in the earth.

9 He makes wars cease to the end of the earth;
he breaks the bow, and shatters the spear,
he burns the chariots with fire!
10 "Be still, and know that I am God.
I am exalted among the nations,
I am exalted in the earth!"

---

a prophet, the psalmist sees the ideal of a warless age already present. The final advent has come; the Lord sits king forever (cf. Mark 9:1; Matt. 10:7-8). **Be still:** Cf. Isa. 30:15. "This is the victory that overcomes the world, our faith" (I John 5:4). Since our God is the Lord of the world, we will not be afraid.

---

floods the soul of the isolated and lonely man. In the light is man's escape from fear; in fellowship is his safety from solitude. It is not surprising that our poet's faith encompasses both these elements in his grand hypothesis: **The Lord of hosts**—those numberless and mysterious energies, or beings perhaps, that are of the domains of infinity—the Lord of these hosts is with us. But more closely intimate and more immediately understood is **the God of Jacob:** the God of whom history is the indelible record, the God who talked with a man who was lonely and afraid amid the portents of nature and the anger of his brothers.

This, we say, is the first reason for his giant faith, a reason that rests on a priori grounds. The second reason is less a matter of ideas than of attitude. Yahweh is represented as proposing it as a prelude to cerebration. **Be still, and know that I am God.** "Let be," reads a marginal notation, but in a colloquialism we have it even more clearly: "Relax." *Cogito, ergo sum,* said Descartes. This other is hardly a theory of knowledge; to rest is not necessarily to know. But psychology has something to say about the relationship of relaxation to sanity, and the familiar exhortation is rendered in the Vulg., *Vacate, et videte.* Indeed, the treatment of minds broken by the cataclysms of earth, and the inhumanity, fancied or real, of one's fellows, demands relaxation as the first step in therapy. "Give place and see."

Two things we now know beyond peradventure about ourselves: the tensions produced by modern life are increasing, and each of us has his breaking point. This means that unless we learn to ease our tensions, they will break us. There is no possible evasion of that fact. Therefore the devices for coping with tension, from aspirin to alcohol, from hobby to holiday, are advocated and advertised endlessly. Still the figures that tell the story of broken minds show their appalling increase.

For those, however, for whom tension is not yet a malady or likely to cause breakdown, the word of this ancient psychotherapist is important. How, we may ask, is one to know God amid the clatter and din of our noisy world? There may be rare individuals for whom the noise is a proof of God, or who despite it can collect their thoughts and find a rationale for faith. Most of us are not so conspicuously endowed with iron nerve and imperturbable mind. Therefore more men know less and less of God. Mountains are shaken, waters roar and are troubled, nations rage and kingdoms are moved. The result is that men also are shaken and troubled, and men also rage and are moved.

Through the ages the offices of religion have been invoked to work at both ends of man's troubled state. Religion has sought to mediate between the strivings of men that cause group tensions on the one hand and, on the other hand, to ease the inner tensions of the individual. Thus we have had council and monastery, as today we have protocol and psychiatrist. And still we have strife and still the number of neurasthenics grows. Is it possible that at least a part of our growing unhappiness lies in the fact not only that tensions grow, but that even when we are able to be still, we are not interested in knowing God?

These are matters, to be sure, remote in time from our poet, but are they not very near to the things with which he was realistically concerned? Amid the tumult of nature he not only affirmed a faith; he rested in unagitated calm. When nations raged, he heard above the noises the quiet voice of Yahweh. It was good to be confident; but in order to be confident it was necessary first to **be still.**

This, we have said, has been called "Luther's Psalm." Those who have claimed it for him have, however, only half a claim, for the great champion of faith was never known as the advocate of relaxation. To speculate is idle, but one wonders if he had coupled with his overwhelming vehemence the practice of "being

11 The LORD of hosts *is* with us; the God of Jacob *is* our refuge. Selah.

To the chief Musician, A Psalm for the sons of Korah.

47 O clap your hands, all ye people; shout unto God with the voice of triumph.

11 The LORD of hosts is with us;
the God of Jacob is our refuge.[m] *Selah*

To the choirmaster. A Psalm of the Sons of Korah.

47 Clap your hands, all peoples!
Shout to God with loud songs of joy!

[m] Or *fortress*

XLVII. GOD AS KING OF THE EARTH (47:1-10)

This psalm together with Pss. 93; 96–99 compose a group which are now quite generally designated "Psalms of Yahweh's Enthronement." It is to the credit of Sigmund Mowinckel (*Psalmenstudien,* "Das Thronbesteigungsfest Jahwäs und der Ursprung der Eschatologie" [Kristiania: Jacob Dybwad, 1921-24], Vol. II), following some earlier work by Gressmann and Volz, to have discovered that in postexilic times on the Hebrew New Year's Day Yahweh was dramatically represented as taking his seat on his throne to exercise his dominion over the world for the coming year, just as Marduk was installed as king over the world in the Babylonian ceremonies of the New Year (N. H. Snaith, "The Priesthood and the Temple," in T. W. Manson, ed., *A Companion to the Bible* [Edinburgh: T. & T. Clark, 1939], pp. 441-42). Mowinckel's conclusions have found wide acceptance, but there is diversity of opinion as to the number of psalms which are to be related to this ceremonial occasion. The evidences of the O.T. in support of the theory are indirect, since there is no mention of such a New Year's event in the list of the Jewish festivals. But it must be remembered that there were not a few sacred observances which are known to us only by slight hints in the canonical and postcanonical literature, and that in postexilic times the number of the festivals was increased. At any rate, the meaning of certain psalms becomes intelligible once we can assume the general correctness of Mowinckel's interpretation.

The thought of Yahweh's kingship is a familiar one in the O.T. (cf. 44:4; 48:2; 74:12; I Sam. 12:12; Isa. 41:21; 52:7-10). In pre-exilic times when an earthly king was installed in the kingship he "went down" to Gihon, and after he was anointed he and the people "came up" (I Kings 1:38-40), with shoutings such as "Absalom has become king" or "Jehu has become king" (II Sam. 15:10; II Kings 9:13) and with blowing of trumpets, playing of flutes, and clapping of hands (II Kings 11:12); the noise of the

---

still," would he have ever felt that the way to **make glad the city of God** was to consent to the nation's rage against the peasants?

47:1-9. ***A National Hymn.***—Comparisons are invidious, but this song addressed to **all peoples** as an acclaim to God as the ruler of the world sounds a good deal like a national anthem. This is exactly what one would expect to encounter in a collection of poetic lyrics, epics, and odes that reflect the conditions and aspirations of the people among whom they were fashioned. Poetry is as representative as politics, and is likely to be as eccentric. The politician, whether he is chosen as head man of a tribe because he is a great hunter, or elected by his constituency because he is a great orator, must maintain at least the fiction—if he cannot prove the fact—of his representative capacity. The poet, who perhaps prefers a stylus to a spear and a song to a speech, essays to represent the folk without portfolio or credit. His soul may be full of private ambitions or frustrations, but he will sing of them as though they were public concerns, and in this way give vent to his feelings without inviting the accusation of selfishness, and at the same time multiply their importance by having them sung as a chorus instead of a solo.

So national anthems are generally grandiose, whether they represent triumph or failure. Written by poets, not by historians, they provide an emotional focus for great groups of people who, if they gave themselves to critical study of what they sang or shouted, would deny or modify much of its sentiment. Consequently, nationalist sentiment as expressed in poem or

2 For the LORD most high *is* terrible; *he*
is a great King over all the earth.
3 He shall subdue the people under us,
and the nations under our feet.
4 He shall choose our inheritance for us,
the excellency of Jacob whom he loved.
Selah.
5 God is gone up with a shout, the LORD
with the sound of a trumpet.

2 For the LORD, the Most High, is terrible,
a great king over all the earth.
3 He subdued peoples under us,
and nations under our feet.
4 He chose our heritage for us,
the pride of Jacob whom he loves.
Selah
5 God has gone up with a shout,
the LORD with the sound of a trumpet.

---

joyful acclaims was so great that "the earth was rent with the clamor" (I Kings 1:40). It seems clear that in postexilic times this pattern of the enthronement of the Hebrew kings served also for the enthronement of Yahweh.

The psalm consists of three strophes of four, three, and three lines respectively. The lines are in 3+3 meter, with a few variations; e.g., vs. 2 is in 3+4.

1. A Summons to All Peoples (47:1-4)

47:1-4. Clap your hands, all peoples! We have noted above the glad acclaims with which the king was saluted on the occasion of his enthronement. In this instance the enthusiasm is raised to a higher pitch, **For the LORD, the Most High, is . . . a great king over all the earth.** The universal dominion of the divine King is affirmed (97:7). All peoples therefore are commanded to join in the salutation. The LORD is **king** because he is creator and the world-wide recognition of the fact is ideally represented as already realized. **The Most High,** i.e., **עליון**, is a most ancient title of the sovereign Lord. As the Ras Shamra literature reveals, it belonged to a supreme deity of the Canaanites. As victor over the Canaanite gods, Yahweh is properly accorded it. His kingship has been demonstrated to Israel by the fact that **He subdued peoples under us,** giving thereby to his chosen folk both a history and a land. **The pride of Jacob** is parallel to **our heritage,** i.e., Canaan, the land of which Israel is proud.

2. A Call to Praise God Our King (47:5-9)

5-7. God has gone up: See Exeg. on vss. 1-10. An earthly king "goes up" to the high place where his palace is situated (cf. Gen. 46:31; I Sam. 23:19-20). The Lord

---

song tends always to the excesses of chauvinism on the one hand or disgust on the other. Thus we have the one hundred per cent patriot who thinks the parade and the national anthem the only true expression of loyalty, and who regards with contempt or anger the patriot who will not sing what he does not believe to be true.

There is perhaps a place in every culture for the use of patriotic songs, and these are not to be condemned outright even when they make the most extravagant claims. There are times when national morale can be sustained only by their use. A critical and objective essay on the current scene might be honest enough, but it might also be dispiriting and would rally no legions to battle. It is tribute to the extraordinary genius of Tom Paine that his pamphlets, written on a drumhead table by candlelight, gave such enormous impetus to the flagging Continental army. This is a rare exception to the general situation here discussed; but we wonder how far even his fiery paragraphs would have got without the help of "Yankee Doodle."

1-4. ***Exultation of Conquest.***—It is with these general principles in mind that we should be able to find the study of this psalm interesting and profitable. The poet is speaking in a public capacity, for the exultation of conquest is unanimously felt and must be universally acknowledged, even by the vanquished. To such an acknowledgment all the peoples are called. This is the clear intention of the first strophe (vss. 1-4). Yahweh is most high and **terrible,** and his dominion is **over all the earth.** Fiercely partisan to **Jacob whom he loves,** he has subjugated peoples, expropriated their inheritance, and awarded it to Jacob. This is the reason for the invitation to universal applause and the signal for the great acclaim (vs. 1).

5-7. ***The Conquering Warrior.***—The imagery invoked to represent the universal king is that of

6 Sing praises to God, sing praises: sing praises unto our King, sing praises.
7 For God *is* the King of all the earth: sing ye praises with understanding.
8 God reigneth over the heathen: God sitteth upon the throne of his holiness.

6 Sing praises to God, sing praises!
Sing praises to our King, sing praises!
7 For God is the king of all the earth;
sing praises with a psalm![n]

8 God reigns over the nations;
God sits on his holy throne.

[n] Heb *Maskil*

"goes up" to his temple. Words like these were used when an earthly king's procession was in progress (cf. I Kings 1:40).

8-9. God sits on his holy throne: The enthronement is complete, and the throne is inviolable and invincible because it is **holy.** Beyond the shouting crowds of the worshipers the prophetic eye of the psalmist sees a larger host doing obeisance to the divine King. **The princes of the peoples gather as the people of the God of Abraham:** The title of kingship is reserved for the Lord alone; lesser titles are given to human rulers. The princes join with the people of Abraham, fulfilling the promise of Gen. 17:4. **The shields of the earth:** A synonym of the princes as defenders of their peoples.

---

the conquering warrior ascending to the high place he has just won from the defenders. (But see Exeg.) All day long the inch-by-inch advance up the bitterly contested slope has tested to the uttermost the valor and the sturdiness of the king. There is at the crucial point in the struggle a mighty surge of effort and the strategic break-through. A shout announces the victory, and the trumpets of the victors blare out the news of their king's success, **God is gone up with a shout, the LORD with the sound of a trumpet.**

This episode of victory gave the poet a lift of enthusiasm that is understandable, though difficult to accept. It is as if he urges upon the defeated peoples the same exultation that the victors feel. **Sing praises to God, sing praises: sing praises unto our King, sing praises. For God is the King of all the earth: sing ye praises.** This surely is the excess of patriotic zeal. To assume that the stricken and subdued enemy will lift his tired voice to sing a skillful song in praise of his conqueror is too much. One may acknowledge defeat honestly, but to voice a paean of praise to the victor sounds like the yell the beaten team gives its still friendly and victorious rival; something to be expected as one of the forced amenities of amateur sport in our times. Elsewhere and under other circumstances it is sheer hypocrisy. And yet there is nothing in the ecstatic words of our singer to betray that he, or his fellows, or even God, who has just led them to spectacular triumph, would caution restraint in the claims he makes. We have heard before now of those who came a cropper because in boasting their mighty prowess they "took in too much territory." There is evidence in the history of Jacob that gives that fact the character of a warning.

8-9. ***Ruler over Nations.***—These verses which comprise the third segment of the poem are more moderate in tone. There is a definite modulation from the ecstatic chanting, sing praises, sing praises, sing praises, to a legato movement. Nothing of the daring universalism of the great King's hard-won dominion is lost, but the noise of trumpets and shouting is abated. God the conquering king is now God the ruler over the nations. He is seen sitting **on his holy throne,** around which

the princes of the peoples gather
as the people of the God of Abraham.

The enemy has been liquidated, the opposition assimilated. **The shields of the earth belong to God; he is highly exalted!** It is the picture of solid security, of lofty eminence, and of popular contentment. Yahweh, who was the most high and terrible, now sits serenely on a holy throne above the princes and peoples of all the earth.

It has been pointed out that the words of this psalm with very slight alteration could be pirated by any nation. (But see Exeg.; this may be a creation psalm for New Year's Day.) There is a simple reason: the pattern of patriotism has been fairly uniform ever since men have had vested interests in the groups of which they were part, and that must have been a long time. The attitude of the people toward the group leader, whether king or president, has for the most part been uncritical. He is shaman, chief, demigod, prince, lord; therefore he can do no wrong, and one's following must be unquestioning and unqualified. If he goes to battle, it is always to win; if he smites an enemy, it is

9 The princes of the people are gathered together, *even* the people of the God of Abraham: for the shields of the earth *belong* unto God: he is greatly exalted.

9 The princes of the peoples gather
as the people of the God of Abraham.
For the shields of the earth belong to God;
he is highly exalted!

To the Jews in postexilic times the New Year festival with the ceremony of the enthronement of Yahweh foreshadowed the time when the kingdoms of the world would become the kingdoms of the Lord. Each return of the event kept alive their expectation of the near advent of their hope. Vs. 9 makes it clear that in their thought the Lord's imperium and the imperium of **the people of the God of Abraham** are convertible terms (cf. Zech. 8:20-23).

---

always to subdue him; if he scatters princes, it is always to reassemble them under his shield. Any lesser loyalty that questions either the power or the right of the king to do battle is not loyalty at all; it is treason. The cultivation of this myth of absolute power and right has always been the leader's prerogative, and has often been so well promoted that the leader has come to believe it himself. This has always been the first step toward disaster. Nowhere better than in the history of the Hebrew people was this illustrated. How low thinking could fall was seen in evil days that overwhelmed the proud king Zedekiah, who, if he had heeded the warnings of Jeremiah, might have been spared the destruction wrought on him and the holy city by the cruel king of the Chaldeans (II Chr. 36:11-21). Despite this lofty and patriotic psalm, God's children were carried away into captivity.

The lesson is a difficult one to learn. It is the singular achievement of the Hebrew poets that they made their patriotic anthems extol the glory of Yahweh as their divine leader. It was not David who sat on a holy throne. When King David essayed to sing a martial air, he called on the arm of God to do battle: "Let God arise, let his enemies be scattered" (68:1). This gave a quality to their nationalism superior to that of many neighbor nations, but it did not save them from the nemesis that pursues national pride wherever it gets out of hand. Even Yahweh could not escape the operation of the law that war breeds war. Today the poet exults in God's subjugation of his enemies; yesterday he was crying, "Thou hast cast us off and abased us, and hast not gone out with our armies" (44:9).

The lesson must be learned, however difficult it may be. It is the nationalist mood of this psalm that is uncritically accepted today by nations that no longer believe in witch doctors, or kings or—one even dares to say—in God. It has been over a century and a half since the ancient nonsense that the king could do no wrong was repudiated in a bloody revolution. In place of the king we have tended to put the state, making it more completely infallible than the most exemplary king because it represents the will of the people—from the patrician to the panhandler. This is all to the good, but it does not go far enough. Does it allow the people who today are sovereign to decide whether the state shall embark on the desperate enterprise of conquest? Does not the state still bid us clap our hands and shout with the voice of triumph? As of old we boast that God "chooseth our inheritance for us," though we call it "manifest destiny." And the songs that are given us to sing are nothing different from those that other nationalists have sung. It is not difficult to make a song that commits a people to the false dreams of world dominion. "Tomorrow the world," sang German youth from 1935 to 1945. With what frightening fitness the words of our psalm, with slight change, fit their mood. "The Führer sitteth upon his holy throne. The princes of the peoples are gathered together to the people of the Führer of the Reich; for the shields of the earth belong to the Führer. He is greatly exalted."

This is the imagery that excites us still, yet how far it is from the promised conquest of the King of the kingdom of God. Here is no terrible King, no subduer of the peoples. To be sure, the Christian movement has used such imagery to describe Jesus. We still sing

> Onward, Christian soldiers!
> Marching as to war,

so deeply has the passion of this ancient song worked its way into the proud heart. But we are left with a troubled conscience, an uneasy spirit. We must find another song with an authentically Christian note. Men's hearts will always feel lighter if a song fits a helpful rhythm to the recurrent and steady stresses of courageous labor. They must therefore sing no discordant or shrill or angry tune. There is much

A Song *and* Psalm for the sons of Korah.

48 Great *is* the LORD, and greatly to be praised in the city of our God, *in* the mountain of his holiness.

A song. A Psalm of the Sons of Korah.

48 Great is the LORD and greatly to be
praised
in the city of our God!

XLVIII. A PILGRIM SONG OF ZION (48:1-14)

Because of the close association of Jerusalem with the worship at its temple, some of the psalms express the feelings of the worshipers toward the holy city. Such psalms are designated "Songs of Zion" (cf. 137:3; Isa. 26:1; 27:2-5; Jer. 31:23). Among them are included the hymns sung or recited by the pilgrims who came up to Jerusalem to join in the sacred festivals (cf. Pss. 84; 87; 122; 126), for to Jews who could rarely or only once in a lifetime make the pilgrimage, the stones and even the dust of the city were dear (102:14), and long journeys through desert ways or across seas served to heighten their feelings of wonder and awe toward the place where God dwelt. Ps. 48 is to be classed as one of these pilgrim hymns. The theme is God's protection of Zion, "his holy hill."

It is characteristic of hymns of this type that in form they differ slightly from the ordinary hymn by the lack of the introductory formula, which, as a summons to worship, would be incongruous in view of their theme. Another feature peculiar to them is the way in which they address the holy city (cf. vss. 1-2; 87:1-3; 122:2) and directly or indirectly seek its welfare and prosperity (cf. vss. 12-14; 122:6). As to the interpretation of the content of these hymns, there is difference of opinion; e.g., Gunkel holds that they exhibit in a marked way prophetic influence and are filled with an eschatological content—i.e., all that they say of Zion is to be referred to an ideal future. Others, e.g., Kittel, hold that they have been prompted by historical events which are recalled or celebrated at appropriate occasions or festivals, and that any eschatological elements that may chance to appear are incidental (see Exeg. on Ps. 46). In dealing with some of

---

for the clapping of hands and the shout of triumph. **The shields of the earth** do **belong to God**, and God will be greatly exalted when it shall become true with them all that *In hoc signo vinces*. We can make up our own songs as we march. We may even **shout unto God with the voice of triumph**, though it will be for "the victory that overcometh the world, even our faith" (I John 5:4).

48:1-14. *The Power and Peril of National Pride.*—In the Expos. of Ps. 47 it was pointed out that pride in one's nation, which is called patriotism, is easily exaggerated to the point of danger. The claims made for superiority in wisdom and wealth and power very often invite the challenge of others who for equally good reasons make equally impressive claims. Since both are in a measure right, their boasts engender fear; fear that one's own claims might not be successfully defended in a thoroughgoing test, and fear that the claims of one's rival might be proved true. The history of nationalist and religious and civil wars reveals that they have often been fought for no more important reason than the gratification of group egotism. It is true for those of the Hebrew-Christian tradition, that "the shields of the earth belong to God" (47:10), but the allocation can be made either as an act of piety or of provocation. The process that transmutes a vague ideal of devotion to God into dangerous nationalist arrogance is a very simple one. Therefore when God is described as "gone up with a shout" (47:5), it is time to reassess the situation. Somehow that picture fails to represent the best we have thought about the behavior of God in history. More commonly it is men who shout, and when

> The tumult and the shouting dies;
> The captains and the kings depart:
> Still stands Thine ancient sacrifice,
> An humble and a contrite heart.
> Lord God of Hosts, be with us yet,
> Lest we forget—lest we forget! [4]

The sense of the national integrity of the Hebrew peoples has been extraordinary, no matter by what standard—religious, social, or political—it is judged. A commoner fact, and for that reason more generally understood, is

[4] "Recessional," from *The Five Nations* by Rudyard Kipling. Copyright 1903 by Rudyard Kipling, reprinted by permission of Mrs. George Bambridge, Methuen & Co., and Doubleday & Co., Inc.

these psalms the interpreter may have difficulty in reaching a clear decision between the conflicting theories, but in respect to Ps. 48 it is hard to make out a fair case for Gunkel's view.

Whatever theory of interpretation we adopt leads to a postexilic date. It is generally agreed that the psalm was used in connection with one or other of the great annual festivals attended by pilgrims. In the LXX the superscription notes that it was appointed for use on the second day of the week (δευτέρᾳ σαββάτου), a fact indicating that in the regular services of the synagogue also it came in due course to find a place (see also Mishnah, Tamid 7:4).

The meter is for the most part 3+2, but in vss. 1, 2, 5, 13*c*-14*a* it is 2+2+2; in vs. 8 it is probably 2+2+2 and 2+3.

1. Zion the City of God (48:1-3)

48:1-3. The city of our God: The psalmist begins his Zion hymn with praise to the Lord of Zion, for it is through his presence that the holy city is what it is described to be. The **holy mountain,** synonymous with the holy city, is **beautiful in elevation,** or, better, "fairest of hills." **The joy of all the earth:** From all lands pilgrims come up to it with loud rejoicing and glad singing (cf. 50:2, "the perfection of beauty"). It is

---

the sense of local integrity. The experience of belonging to a nation is less real than that of being a member of a race or a community. Hence it is necessary in times of national danger to create, often arbitrarily, evocative national symbols. The threat to the home town, however, needs no propaganda to call its citizens to its defense; nor does extolling the local virtues and advantages wait upon professional surveys and the department of public relations of the chamber of commerce. Every resident is expected to defend his town against aspersion, to feel and if possible to extenuate its shame, and to advertise its climate, its churches, and its enterprising and successful citizenry without overscrupulous concern about the facts.

Here is another area where the poet has found a ready inspiration for his pen. "Sweet Auburn" is the "loveliest village of the plain,"[5] and the reasons given for its priority are exactly the same as would be advanced by the poet laureate in the village two miles away. None takes offense at Goldsmith's modest and lyric pride, but there is hidden danger if the claims are made by a braggart instead of a bard. And what of local shame? Balaustion, contemplating Athens' imminent humiliation by the enemy, says:

Wind, wave, and bark, bear Euthukles and me,
Balaustion, from—not sorrow but despair,
Not memory but the present and its pang!
Athenai, live thou hearted in my heart:
Never, while I live, may I see thee more,
Never again may these repugnant orbs
Ache themselves blind before the hideous pomp,
The ghastly mirth which mocked thine overthrow.[6]

[5] Goldsmith, "The Deserted Village."

[6] Browning, *Aristophanes' Apology.*

So there are "hubs of the universe," "crossroads of the world," cities of flowers and of homes and of churches, gangster heavens, the centers of this or that trade—all reflecting local pride or enterprise or embarrassment. Sybaris gave us a pleasing name for the epicure; Corinth a name for the voluptuary; Paris for the gay; and Boston for the Brahmin. Yet if all the records were spread before us, we should certainly find that the efforts of poets to immortalize all these communities have failed far more often than they have succeeded. Ps. 48, sometimes entitled "The Beauty and Glory of Zion," is one of the rare efforts that have won places in the anthology of great literature.

The poem is divided into two parts (vss. 1-8, 9-14) that separate themselves naturally. The first sets forth the effect that the external aspects of the city make on the observer. There is also a hint of this in the second part, for the external effect cannot be dissociated from the somewhat more subtle and spiritual qualities with which the second section deals. The reason the poet gives for his accolade is found at the end of the first division, a poetic device which is very effective since it is explicit but unobtrusive. He is concerned to put forward first the objective claims of the great city; his reasons for accepting them himself can come along later.

1-8. ***Zion's Physical Glory.***—The psalmist is a convinced man. Much had he heard about Zion; it had whetted his desire to see it for himself. No evidence here of skepticism of what he had heard; simply a wish to see, and the sight had confirmed all he had heard. **As we have heard, so have we seen in the city of the Lord of hosts, in the city of our God: God will establish it for ever** (vs. 8). What had he seen?

2 Beautiful for situation, the joy of the
whole earth, *is* mount Zion, *on* the sides of
the north, the city of the great King.
3 God is known in her palaces for a
refuge.
4 For, lo, the kings were assembled, they
passed by together.
5 They saw *it, and* so they marveled;
they were troubled, *and* hasted away.
6 Fear took hold upon them there, *and*
pain, as of a woman in travail.

2 His holy mountain, beautiful in elevation,
is the joy of all the earth,
Mount Zion, in the far north,
the city of the great King.
3 Within her citadels God
has shown himself a sure defense.

4 For lo, the kings assembled,
they came on together.
5 As soon as they saw it, they were astounded,
they were in panic, they took to flight;
6 trembling took hold of them there,
anguish as of a woman in travail.

---

unnecessary to press too literally poetical hyperbole in order to find in such a phrase only an eschatological hope. **In the far north: Mount Zion** is identified with the mountain in the northern regions whose top reached to heaven and which was the assembly place of the gods (see Isa. 14:13; Ezek. 1:4; Enoch 24:2-3; 25:3). Knowledge of this mythical mountain came from the Babylonians (Bruno Meissner, *Die babylonisch-assyriche Literatur* [Wildpark-Potsdam: Academische Verlagsgesellschaft Athenaion, 1928], p. 29). **The city of the great King:** Originally the title of the kings of Babylonia and Assyria (cf. II Kings 18:19, 28; Judith 2:5)—i.e., *šarrû rabû*—**the great King,** becomes one of Yahweh's titles (cf. 47:2; 95:3; Mal. 1:14; Matt. 5:35). So by a series of epithets the psalmist sets Zion above all other sacred places in the world, and what he claims for it has the seal of God's approval for **God has shown himself a sure defense** of his city.

2. Zion's Deliverance from Her Enemies (48:4-8)

4-7. If the first strophe reflects the feelings of a pilgrim at his first sight of the city, the second shows us how he is moved by the evidences of its endurance from age to age through God's miraculous deliverances. Zion is an eternal city. **Kings** and their armies come against her only to depart in **panic** and anguish of terror. The fame and the name of her foes perish, but she abides forever. The historical references are to such invasions as those of Rezin and Pekah (Isa. 7:1-25) and Sennacherib (Isa. 14:24-27; 29:1-24; 36:1–37:38). For the contempt in which the tyrants who assailed Zion were held in postexilic times see Isa. 14:4*b*-23. The poetic hyperbole in vs. 4 is scarcely an argument

---

It was beautifully located—the first requisite of a beautiful city. Something in its towering height, on hills that afforded distant vistas to the mountains north and east, and to the great sea to the west, excited him. Perhaps it was the sense of elevation (the poet might have been brought up in a city of the plains) that gave him his reason for claiming Zion as **the joy of all the earth** (vs. 2). It was a fitting habitation for **the great King,** but was more than that; God himself was there, it was his city, his **holy mountain** (vs. 1*b*), and his accommodations, let us assume, were appropriate to his divine magnificence. **Great is the Lord, and greatly to be praised in the city of our God** (vs. 1*a*).

This physical splendor was no façade behind which insecurity was hidden. There were **palaces** worthy of the divine tenant, but there were also bastions with high towers which provided secure refuge (vs. 3). Skeptic kings from alien lands had heard tall tales about these tall towers and formed a party to go up and see, and perhaps to batter them down.

For lo, the kings assembled,
they came on together.

What happened? They saw it, and it amazed them. Here was something even beyond the stories they had heard. But amazement turned to dismay, and dismay turned into the impetus to flight (vs. 5). Before they turned to flee,

7 Thou breakest the ships of Tarshish
with an east wind.
8 As we have heard, so have we seen in
the city of the LORD of hosts, in the city of
our God: God will establish it for ever.
Selah.
9 We have thought of thy loving-kindness, O God, in the midst of thy temple.

7 By the east wind thou didst shatter
the ships of Tarshish.
8 As we have heard, so have we seen
in the city of the LORD of hosts,
in the city of our God,
which God establishes for ever. *Selah*

9 We have thought on thy steadfast love,
O God,
in the midst of thy temple.

---

for finding in the passage a reference to the defeat of the enemies of God and his people in the last days—i.e., for an eschatological interpretation (cf. Ezek. 39). In vs. 7 read with some Hebrew MSS כרוח, "like the wind," and translate "as the east wind which breaks in pieces the ships of Tarshish"; i.e., the terror which seized the foes was comparable in its destructiveness to **the east wind** which was dangerous to Tyrian vessels (Ezek. 27:26). **Ships of Tarshish** were vessels of a size sufficient to enable them to make the journey from eastern Mediterranean ports to the Phoenician seaport of Tartessus in Spain, the ancient counterparts of our more modern Indiaman.

8. As we have heard, so have we seen: The pilgrims in their homelands have heard the stories of God's work on behalf of his city, and now with their own eyes they see the truth of what they have been told. Clearly vs. 8 could have been said only by persons whose homes were not in Jerusalem and to whom a visit to the city was an experience of a lifetime. Since the situation connotes a postexilic date, those who would assign a pre-exilic date to the psalm assume vs. 8 to be a later interpretation. Emend the text to read "in the city of our God, in the city of the LORD of hosts, who establishes her forever," which accords with the meter.

3. Praise for God's Love (48:9-14)

9-11. We have thought . . . in . . . thy temple: The pilgrims gather for worship in the temple, where in hymns and praises the goodness of God to his land and city is

---

however, they were smitten with a strange fear that shook them and induced violent visceral disturbance (vs. 6). Here was no place to linger. They were amazed at Zion's grandeur and dismayed by its impregnability; their early skepticism had turned into a terrible sort of assurance, and that assurance had turned into involuntary muscular agitation and abdominal pains. It would appear also that their flight was futile. We are not told that these terrified visitors had come by **the ships of Tarshish,** but if they planned to escape by sea, **the east wind** was already poised for their destruction (vss. 5-7).

This is about as near the ultimate in the expression of civic pride as we are likely to encounter, and if the poem had ended with the threat to the royal tourists, it would have little beyond extravagant self-praise to recommend it. The second part, however, presents a subdued legato tempo, observed also in the nationalistic Ps. 47. There was an element in the glory of the city of Zion very different from the high ground on which it was built and the tall towers that protected it. Not only were there palaces for the great king; there was a temple for the common folk. This is the emphasis that gives nobility to the poem, that reveals the central religious core in the culture of these ancient folk.

9-11. ***Zion's Spiritual Glory.*—We have thought of thy loving-kindness, O God, in the midst of thy temple.** Here is a shift of interest, as the psalmist turns from the spectacle of grandeur to thoughts of goodness. What was the meaning of God's dwelling in the midst of the great city? What purpose did its power and pretentiousness serve? To frighten neighbor kings? Hardly. Beneath it all, however explained, was not terror or bombast or threat, but goodness. The temple was where that conviction made itself felt; when men worshiped the king, he became to them the embodiment of love. Here is made explicit the difference between man's response to the outer and physical aspect of things, and what he thinks and feels when he waits at worship within the sanctuary.

Furthermore, in the first part of the psalm the towering battlements are referred to as

10 According to thy name, O God, so *is*
thy praise unto the ends of the earth: thy
right hand is full of righteousness.
11 Let mount Zion rejoice, let the daughters of Judah be glad, because of thy judgments.
12 Walk about Zion, and go round about
her: tell the towers thereof.

10 As thy name, O God,
so thy praise reaches to the ends of the earth.
Thy right hand is filled with victory;
11 let Mount Zion be glad!
Let the daughters of Judah rejoice
because of thy judgments!

12 Walk about Zion, go round about her,
number her towers,

---

extolled. The verb here used (דמה) means properly "to compare"; i.e., comparing crises and deliverances, the psalmist is more keenly aware of God's **loving-kindness.** The story of it is carried by the pilgrims **to the ends of the earth. Thy right hand is filled with victory,** i.e., with saving acts or victories in vindication of **righteousness** (KJV). Therefore **let Mount Zion** and all her daughter-cities in **Judah rejoice because of thy judgments,** i.e., thy gracious decisions in their history.

12-14. The loud and joyous songs of praise and thanksgiving in the temple were followed by a solemn procession about the city, its walls, its ramparts, and citadels. As the pilgrims move from point to point and are shown the places of historic interest they are unshakably convinced that God is a sure defense. Zion stands intact; no enemy has

---

the joy of all the earth (vs. 2). In this second section we have a similar idea, but with an important emphasis. **As thy name, O God,** known to the ends of the earth, **so thy praise** (vs. 10). The poet has lifted his eyes from the parapets of the city to **the ends of the earth.** He is sensitive to something more important than stone. Still further he goes in his emphasis on the spiritual qualities of the city. To the goodness of God is added the triumph with which his **right hand** is full (vs. 10*b*). And finally, whatever the reaction of aliens to the city, **the daughters of Judah** are urged to **rejoice because of** [God's] **judgments.** Here are three ideas, as towering in their spiritual splendor as the ramparts of Jerusalem: goodness, triumph, and judgment. The first evokes man's moral response, the second his sense of pride, and the third his sense of ultimate equity.

12-14. *Tell the Next Generation.*—There is a final strophe. After the poet has given voice to his own pride in the structural grandeur of the city, and has reflected more soberly on the spiritual qualities that alone can make a city great, he modestly advises that his opinions should be subjected to the judgment of others who, like himself, had thought of the holy mountain. **Walk about Zion,** he suggests, **go round about her, number her towers.** One is finally to be convinced by one's personal investigations.

Consider well her ramparts,
go through her citadels;
that you may tell the next generation.

Is there a note here that retracts something of his faith in the city's indestructibility as announced in vs. 8? **God will establish it for ever.** Here it is God who is eternal, not the city. There is an intimation that the poet is less sure, and for this reason urges others to scrutinize the city's glories so carefully that these will be remembered, even though some vast death should someday merge them with the dust. **This is God, our God for ever and ever. He will be our guide for ever.** Death has an ominous sound, and the writer must certainly have known of great cities that had died. After all, when one's pride of place is chastened by the stubborn facts of history, one will turn one's trust to that factor of life which is activated by the essence of eternity. This factor was to the poet, as it is to us, the supreme reality of the eternal God.

The mood of the poet has swung full cycle from the delight he felt in the glories of the city, which for the moment he thought to be indestructible, to the more sober joys that thoughts of God inspired. It is this that characterized the poetic and moral reflections of the Hebrew people. Their pride of place was no less than that of the other peoples of antiquity; their sense of racial superiority was in some respects more exaggerated. What distinguishes them is their amazing sense of God. Eventually everything has to give place to that fact: pride is modified by it, fear is quieted by it, evil is overwhelmed by it, man is redeemed by it.

All this provokes challenging suggestions about the history of the growth of cities. This

13 Mark ye well her bulwarks, consider her palaces; that ye may tell *it* to the generation following.

14 For this God *is* our God for ever and ever: he will be our guide *even* unto death.

13 consider well her ramparts,
go through her citadels;
that you may tell the next generation
14 that this is God,
our God for ever and ever.
He will be our guide for ever.

To the chief Musician, A Psalm for the sons of Korah.

49 Hear this, all *ye* people; give ear, all *ye* inhabitants of the world:

To the choirmaster. A Psalm of the Sons of Korah.

49 Hear this, all peoples!
Give ear, all inhabitants of the world,

---

been able to harm her. When the pilgrims return to their homes, they can **tell the next generation that this is God. Unto death** is a doubtful rendering. The Hebrew text is uncertain, and is judged to be a corruption either of **for ever** (עלמות, cf. Hebrew MSS and LXX, εἰς τοὺς αἰῶνας) or of a musical direction (על־עלמות, in the title of Ps. 46) in the superscription of a psalm that followed Ps. 48; it is best omitted.

XLIX. The Vanity of Human Pomp (49:1-20)

This is one of the psalms of the wisdom type (cf. Pss. 1; 37; 49; 73; 91; 112; 128). The purpose of the author, like that of other writers of the wisdom school, is to instruct and exhort men about the fundamental issues of life. His words are directed not to Jews alone but to all mankind (vs. 1). Clearly he lives in a time when the old belief of a balance between merit and reward (cf. Deut. 28) is being subjected to criticism in the light of the hard facts of life. In Proverbs, Job, and Ecclesiastes, as well as in Pss. 37; 73, we see how greatly the minds of men in Israel were exercised by the problem of a divine government of the world which, on the one hand, allowed ungodly men not only to escape their due penalty but to enjoy the good things of the world and, on the other hand, denied to godly souls success and happiness. The author of Ps. 37 seeks to ease the

---

is the particular concern of the student of society perhaps, but since in Western culture the process of urbanization seems to have reached its optimum, if indeed it has not moved beyond it, it has practical interest for us all. The city can grow so great in size and population and so intricate in organization that life itself is endangered: not physical life primarily, but the dynamic, spiritual, creative energies that are ultimately life's only protector. Physical life does not reproduce itself sufficiently to promise physical permanence; and the loss of the sense of neighborliness, for example, is at the same time both the effect and the cause of spiritual malnutrition. The huge expansion of cities in modern Western civilization has become a blight, a feebleness, and a danger. Before the atom bomb proved the peculiar vulnerability of great congested centers, there were those who preached the doctrines of the cult of decentralization as the cure for this morbid growth.

The city of Zion, whether it was the ideal of the poet's dream or the actual city of Jerusalem, has died a dozen deaths. Such is likely to be the fate of every great city's deeply laid foundations and high towers. Man will forever boast of the bulwarks and the citadels he makes, and point to them to impress the alien or terrify the enemy. And the poet too will celebrate magnificence and tenderness—"sweet Auburn! loveliest village," and **mount Zion, on the sides of the north.** And the cycle will continue to turn its full circumference; for somehow, by the design of the Eternal himself, man's spent pride turns to simple faith for replenishment, and he will either find God as **loving-kindness . . . in the midst of** [the] **temple** or he will utterly perish.

Great is the Lord, and greatly to be praised in the city of our God, in the mountain of his holiness. That is the beginning of the song; it is also the end of the story.

49:1-20. ***The Folly of Trust in Riches.***—The poet is proverbially poor. Occasionally perhaps he is awarded the laurel and a subsidy for the rhymes he turns out to celebrate the triumphs and extenuate the disasters of his sponsor. Rarely is he born rich. Lord Byron, whom

weight of the problem by positing that God deals with men by an unchanging law of retributive justice, and that in the course of days the godly will be duly vindicated. The author of Ps. 49 deals with the matter more fundamentally, and therefore more satisfactorily. He faces the facts honestly and takes life just as it is. He does not expect that the righteous, himself included, will be enriched someday on this earth and that the ungodly rich will all likewise be humbled and brought to the ground. The inequalities between **low and high, rich and poor** will persist right up to death, but at death the solution of the problem manifests itself. In his eyes the problem arises because men set too great a store on wealth; those who have it develop a false confidence in it and give themselves airs, while those who lack it are cowed and dispirited at the sight of those who have it. But let men once perceive the basic worthlessness of material riches and the problem that agitates the minds of the righteous poor vanishes. For the money of the rich, before whom men are awed, can buy all that the world has to offer, but it cannot buy off death. They can offer no ransom great enough to extricate themselves from the common lot of men.

Man cannot abide in his pomp,
he is like the beasts that perish.

The instruction which the psalmist here offers in solution of his **riddle** (vs. 4) came to him, as he brooded over the matter, more by a mystical communication or by inspiration than by the processes of reason. To him it is a discovery to which he attaches such importance that he summons all men to give ear to it. There are, however, differences of opinion as to what the psalmist means to say. The first point at issue in this respect is the genuineness of vs. 15. Some students, e.g., Staerk and Gunkel, hold that it is an interpolation because in summing up his argument in vss. 16-20, the psalmist does not take it into account. Others, e.g., Duhm, Kittel, Schmidt, Herkenne, and Calès, hold it to be genuine, because after the summons of vss. 1-4 one expects the communication of something more unusual than a reminder that death is the great leveler. The second point at issue is how we are to understand vs. 15, granting that it is genuine. Is the psalmist expressing a belief in a life after death, or does he mean that he will be kept from Sheol to live a long life? (See J. M. Powis Smith, *The Religion of the Psalms* [Chicago:

Matthew Arnold described as "the greatest natural force, the greatest elementary power . . . which has appeared in our literature since Shakespeare," but for his affluence might have measured up to his great native endowments. His wealth was his undoing. "Except for his genius," continues Arnold, "he was an ordinary nineteenth-century English gentleman, with little culture and no ideas."[7] He might have added, "And with too much money."

Poverty is improperly thought of as an advantage to the poet; it is simply a consequence. His craft is not a lucrative one, since it supplies an irregular and capricious demand. The caricature of the troubadour, who starves in a garret and emerges from time to time with his sheaf of verses few will read and none will buy, is deliberately overdrawn; but it may account for the often neurotic animus poets seem to have against worldly possessions. If to them all gold is tarnished, it may of course be because other hands than theirs have caressed it. But if they had been born with silver spoons in their mouths, they might ask how they would have learned to sing.

There may be matters here of interest to psychologists which are somewhat aside from our concern. It is not surprising, however, to find in the anthology of Hebrew poetry a piece to which has been given the title "The Folly of Trusting Riches." It is a psalm of the sons of Korah who, whatever else may be said of them, were catholic in the choice of themes for their songs; and it was written for the choirmaster. If this was sung in the temple ritual, it is not the first time that music has been used to moralize upon a common experience. Rich parishioners perhaps did not enjoy the allusions, but the humble poor no doubt kept the volume balanced by their zestful crescendo.

1-4. *Appeal for Hearing.*—Our poet asks for a sizable audience, for he is about to deal with a sizable theme. He will not speak in the manner of the rhetorician, he **will incline** [his] **ear to a proverb.** He will not preach, he will sing. **I will solve my riddle to the music of the lyre.** To this recital he invites everybody and asks

[7] *Essays in Criticism.*

2 Both low and high, rich and poor, together.
3 My mouth shall speak of wisdom; and the meditation of my heart *shall be* of understanding.
4 I will incline mine ear to a parable: I will open my dark saying upon the harp.
5 Wherefore should I fear in the days of evil, *when* the iniquity of my heels shall compass me about?

2 both low and high,
rich and poor together?
3 My mouth shall speak wisdom;
the meditation of my heart shall be understanding.
4 I will incline my ear to a proverb;
I will solve my riddle to the music of the lyre.

5 Why should I fear in times of trouble,
when the iniquity of my persecutors surrounds me,

University of Chicago Press, 1922], pp. 118-21.) For the reason indicated above, most commentators interpret the passage as referring to survival.

The psalm is to be classed with the wisdom literature of the later postexilic period. Its universal appeal, its didactic style, its concern with the problems of theodicy, its language (cf. חכמות, הגות, תבונות) combine to fix its date (Podechard, "Notes sur les psaumes," *Revue Biblique,* XXXI [1922], 7). The meter is 3+3, with instances of 4+3. Textual corruptions, however, complicate the metrical pattern.

1. Summons to All Men to Listen (49:1-4)

49:1-4. The psalmist summons all classes of men according to their social and economic rankings to listen to him because his words relate to all of them, the one needing them as much as the other. **My mouth shall speak wisdom:** The word **wisdom** (חכמות) has a formation found elsewhere only in Prov. 1:20; 9:1; 24:7. **I will incline my ear to a proverb:** The word משל, rendered **proverb,** has a wide variety of meanings: e.g., **parable,** poem (Num. 21:27), prophetic saying or oracle (Num. 23:7), wise saying or instruction (Prov. 10:1). The present text suggests that the psalmist is unfolding an oracle to which he is listening. Gunkel *et al.* would read, "Incline your ear to a saying" (cf. 78:1), the saying being that of vss. 12, 20, which serves as a refrain. **I will solve my riddle:** I.e., my difficult problem. **To the music of the lyre:** Prophetic utterances were sometimes accompanied with music (cf. I Sam. 10:5; II Kings 3:15), but nowhere else are we informed that "instruction" was thus accompanied.

2. The Vanity of Wealth (49:5-12)

5-11. This section depicts the vanity of riches. All men must die. No wealth can purchase exemption from the common lot. "Why is earth and ashes proud? . . . When a

---

for the ear of all the inhabitants of the world. It is not above the concern of the humble nor beneath the contempt of the high; **rich and poor together** are wise to attend to him, for what he says reflects both the understanding of his mind and his heart. If he speaks with emotional intensity, it is because his mind has instructed him clearly, but it will all be softened by the lilt of the melody that is the vehicle of its expression.

5-12. *Wealth and Security.*—What is this portentous theme? He puts it in the form of a question:

Why should I fear in times of trouble,
when the iniquity of my persecutors surrounds me?

The point is clear, though he mixes his metaphor slightly. How can iniquity at his heels compass him about? No matter; perhaps it was at his heels, but now surrounds him. His problem is a simple one: life is precarious; it needs defense against evil. Material wealth seems to be the most dependable bulwark. Those who are rich appear to be secure; those who are poor are afraid. Is this common judgment the correct one? Should he yield to fear? Is the rich man safe? Is he bold? Is his courage real or feigned? These are lively questions which, so far as one can know, have engaged the thoughts of as universal an audience as our poet asks to his discussion of them.

What is the basic assumption of rich men?

6 They that trust in their wealth, and boast themselves in the multitude of their riches;
7 None *of them* can by any means redeem his brother, nor give to God a ransom for him:
8 (For the redemption of their soul *is* precious, and it ceaseth for ever:)
9 That he should still live for ever, *and* not see corruption.
10 For he seeth *that* wise men die, likewise the fool and the brutish person perish, and leave their wealth to others.
11 Their inward thought *is, that* their houses *shall continue* for ever, *and* their dwelling places to all generations; they call *their* lands after their own names.
12 Nevertheless man *being* in honor abideth not: he is like the beasts *that* perish.

6 men who trust in their wealth
and boast of the abundance of their riches?
7 Truly no man can ransom himself,[o]
or give to God the price of his life,
8 for the ransom of his[p] life is costly,
and can never suffice,
9 that he should continue to live on for ever,
and never see the Pit.

10 Yea, he shall see that even the wise die,
the fool and the stupid alike must perish
and leave their wealth to others.
11 Their graves[q] are their homes for ever,
their dwelling places to all generations,
though they named lands their own.
12 Man cannot abide in his pomp,
he is like the beasts that perish.

[o] Another reading is *no man can ransom his brother*
[p] Gk: Heb *their*
[q] Gk Syr Compare Tg: Heb *their inward* (thought)

man dies, he inherits only the worm and the maggot." (Ecclus. 10:8, 11.) "This is the portion of all flesh from the hand of God, so how canst thou withstand the decree of the Almighty?" (Ecclus. 41:3-4.) Though a man rule an empire, his domain at death is just a grave. Men **leave their wealth to others.** And no one knows of what sort are the heirs (Eccl. 2:18-19). **Though they named lands their own:** Lit., "Though their names were proclaimed over lands," i.e., at the time when they took formal possession of their conquests. The expression does not mean naming cities after themselves, e.g., Alexandria, Antioch. Vs. 10*ab* is a gloss. The end of the wise and the foolish is extraneous to the theme.

12. This verse, which recurs in vs. 20, is so much like a refrain that some (Podechard, Duhm, Calès) are of the opinion that it has been omitted after the prelude.

Their inward thought is, that their houses shall continue for ever, and their dwelling places to all generations (vs. 11*a*). Proof of this is found in the romantic way in which men name their properties. **They call their lands after their own names** (vs. 11*b*). One of the sons of Kohath, we are told in Exod. 6:18, was Hebron. He gave his name to a settlement that before his day had been called Kiriath-arba, "this Arba was the greatest man among the Anakim" (Josh. 14:15). Before Arba, the Hittites occupied it and called it "the Association." Jacob, to whom our poets make frequent reference, came once to a place called Luz, and because he dreamed a dream, he called it Bethel. No; titles to properties are often as impermanent as their names. In *Names on the Land*[8] we are told the story of how deviously New York got its name. From a Celtic word meaning yew tree (*eburos*), by way of the Angle Eoforwic, to the Danish Yorvik, and finally to the English York, the evolution ran. When James, second son of Charles I, became the Duke of York, he was granted title to New Amsterdam because he had made a nuisance of himself to his brother the king. He promptly changed the name to New York. That was three hundred years ago. Three hundred more years may see other changes. Our poet long ago discovered the folly of this practice of the rich. Their houses (names) do not continue forever, nor do their dwelling places. No matter with what honor he has lived, **man cannot abide in his pomp** (vs. 12*a*). Less comforting even is the summary dismissal—**he is like the beasts that perish** (vs. 12*b*).

Thus the writer exposes the fallacy of their basic assumption; and with it, of course, all other propositions based on it also fall. Derived from the idea of permanence is the notion that

[8] George R. Stewart (New York: Random House, 1945), pp. 78-81.

13 This their way *is* their folly: yet their
posterity approve their sayings. Selah.
14 Like sheep they are laid in the grave;
death shall feed on them; and the upright
shall have dominion over them in the morning; and their beauty shall consume in the
grave from their dwelling.
15 But God will redeem my soul from the
power of the grave: for he shall receive me.
Selah.

13 This is the fate of those who have foolish
confidence,
the end of those[r] who are pleased with
their portion. *Selah*
14 Like sheep they are appointed for Sheol;
Death shall be their shepherd;
straight to the grave they descend,[s]
and their form shall waste away;
Sheol shall be their home.[t]
15 But God will ransom my soul from the
power of Sheol,
for he will receive me. *Selah*

[r] Tg: Heb *after them*
[s] Cn: Heb *the upright shall have dominion over them in the morning*
[t] Heb uncertain

---

3. The Dance of Death (49:13-15)

13-15. Though the text is corrupt, we can see that the psalmist is painting a grim picture of the ineluctable end to which the rich are moving—"a veritable Dance of Death after the style of the medieval painters." Death herds them like dumb-driven cattle to a precipice, down which they go **straight to the grave.** But at this crisis the true differences between men come to light. **God will ransom my soul from . . . Sheol:** Lit., "from the hand of Sheol." When Sheol is claiming him for its own, God delivers him from its grasp. Has the psalmist been influenced by the accounts of the translations of Enoch (Gen. 5:24) and Elijah (II Kings 2:11)? He does not elaborate the bald statement of his survival. Vs. 15 is one of the rare references in the O.T. to a belief in an afterlife (cf.

---

the false permanence that one's wealth guarantees can be transferred to one's brother. The rich man thinks he will live always and **not see corruption.** Why, then, should not his resources avail to redeem his brother from corruption or **give to God the price of his life?** Die he surely will, in spite of all the costly efforts to exempt him from death's levy (vs. 8). And why not? **Even the wise die**—all their wisdom does not avail them to cheat death;

> **the fool and the stupid alike must perish**
> **and leave their wealth to others.**

The former's folly will win no sympathy, and the latter's threat will not subvert the universal justice of death. Here is the level to which all men descend together. "Dead men's shrouds have no pockets," it has been said. It may be added that dead men's eyes read no epitaphs.

13-15. ***Wealth's Impermanence.***—To the poet—as indeed to all men—all this is clearly manifest. **This is the fate of those who have foolish confidence,** and yet men perversely blind themselves to the folly they recognize, and **are pleased with their portion.** Forgetting completely the fate of those whose hope for redemption from corruption lay in riches, their envious fellows hung tenaciously to the words they had heard, and to the spurious promises they had made. It is this stubborn blindness that calls forth our poet's most vigorous metaphor. They, these blind followers of folly, are **like sheep . . . appointed for Sheol; Death shall be their shepherd.** When one recalls the other uses to which the familiar shepherd figure has been put, its employment here is fairly shocking. There is no place for beauty of these sheep except the consuming death of **the grave;** and such rule as will order them will not be by the rich, but by **the upright . . . in the morning.** These are formidable prospects. Those who are rich, and the rest of us who wish we were, are promised no escape. But the situation is not completely hopeless. At least the poet, who classified himself neither with the opulent nor the foolish, remains with his spirit steadfast in the face of this doom.

> **But God will ransom my soul from the power of Sheol,**
> **for he will receive me.**

Our poet's rancor, if we may call it that, is spent; yet he has not abused those who trust in riches. He has simply shown how precarious is their hold upon life, and how futile their confidence in the redemptive power of gold.

16 Be not thou afraid when one is made rich, when the glory of his house is increased;

17 For when he dieth he shall carry nothing away: his glory shall not descend after him.

18 Though while he lived he blessed his soul, (and *men* will praise thee, when thou doest well to thyself,)

19 He shall go to the generation of his fathers; they shall never see light.

20 Man *that is* in honor, and understandeth not, is like the beasts *that* perish.

16 Be not afraid when one becomes rich,
when the glory[u] of his house increases.
17 For when he dies he will carry nothing away;
his glory[u] will not go down after him.
18 Though, while he lives, he counts himself happy,
and though a man gets praise when he does well for himself,
19 he will go to the generation of his fathers,
who will never more see the light.
20 Man cannot abide in his pomp,
he is like the beasts that perish.

[u] Or *wealth*

73:23-25; Isa. 26:19; Dan. 12:2-3; see W. O. E. Oesterley and T. H. Robinson, *Hebrew Religion, Its Origin and Development* [2nd ed.; New York: The Macmillan Co., 1937], pp. 352-65).

4. Worldly Magnificence Is Temporal (49:16-20)

16-20. The psalmist concludes by returning to his theme with its solemn warning of the futility and evanescence of all glory and happiness based only on riches, the last verse sounding again the ominous refrain:

Man cannot abide in his pomp,
he is like the beasts that perish.

He has gone beyond this to make again the effort, made so often by others, to persuade the poor that their folly is as great and as dangerous as that of those they envy. In a very subtle way they are guilty of the rich man's error. He believes in the power of the riches he has; they believe in the power of the riches they do not have. Their folly being the same, their fate will not be different.

16-20. ***The True Perspective on Wealth.***—There are further words of admonition the psalmist would offer the disinherited and the disappointed. Having pointed out the emptiness of their trust, he says, **Be not afraid when one is made rich, when the glory of his house is increased.** Why, we ask, should such success inspire fear in the poor man's heart? One might more properly expect a warning against covetousness, a sin against which the people had been set on guard. Is it the ancient idea that when one is enriched another is impoverished; when the glory of one house is increased, the glory of another declines? From the standpoint of our modern sophistication this sounds like naïve economics. There are those, to be sure, who still say that the physical security of the common people depends on the wealth of a few favored families who are capable of making and distributing material well-being with generosity and discernment. There are others who say, and with reason, that the wealth of one decreases the wealth of all. Pierre Joseph Proudhon said, "Property is theft."[9] There is no need here to take sides; it is evident that our poet is making a very practical observation. There is no cause for alarm, he insists, when one notes wealth and glory accreting to the few. Whatever else may be said, one fact is beyond argument: they take nothing away when they die; neither gold nor glory is diminished in its aggregate by what happens to them (vs. 17).

Here are no vindictiveness, no acid envy, no incitement of hate against the more favored. One is entitled to such satisfaction as is occasioned by these reflections. There follows, indeed, what is a note of amiable tolerance; it comes close to condescension. While the rich man lived, he seemed to be happy. He had a quaint way of congratulating himself; and his friends, taking the cue from him, added their felicitations. **While he lives, he counts himself happy, . . . a man gets praise when he does well for himself.** One is reminded here of a line from a later story: "Soul, thou hast much goods laid up for many years; take thine ease, eat, drink, and be merry. But God said unto him: Thou fool, this night thy soul shall be required of thee." (Luke 12:19-20.) Who would grudge him his moment of happiness, even though it

[9] *Principle of Right,* ch. i.

A Psalm of Asaph.

50 The mighty God, *even* the LORD, hath spoken, and called the earth from the rising of the sun unto the going down thereof.

A Psalm of Asaph.

50 The Mighty One, God the LORD,
speaks and summons the earth
from the rising of the sun to its setting.

L. GOD ADDRESSES HIS PEOPLE (50:1-23)

This psalm is an instance of the influence of prophecy on the cult as reflected in the Psalter. In style and content it recalls the addresses with which the pre-exilic prophets were accustomed to interrupt the course of sacred or popular assemblies in Jerusalem (cf. Isa. 1:10-23; Hos. 6:6; Mic. 6:6-8; Jer. 22:1, 13-17). The emphasis on the importance of the spirit over against the form in worship, the condemnation of the confusion of lip service to the principles of religion with true obedience, and the introduction of these themes with a description of a theophany by which the majesty of Yahweh's presence gives them solemn authentication—all these features show that the psalmist stands in the prophetic tradition. But the psalmist is not properly to be classed with the prophets in the sense that his words are born of a "vision" experience; rather he is an imitator of the prophets, achieving the impression of prophecy by artificial

is brief and spurious? A rich man might be called a worse name than "fool," so long as **he counts himself happy.** One is tempted to understand vs. 19 as the rather gloomy prediction that this man, and the likes of him, will never see through the folly of their trust in riches. This may be what our poet is saying, though it is more likely that he is dismissing his subject with a sentence of annihilation. No matter if this compromises conventional ideas of immortality. This is a poem, not an argument. The last verse continues the dismal forecast. **Man,** he concludes, **cannot abide in his pomp, he is like the beasts that perish.** That is to say, no matter how proud and honorable one's error may be, the destruction that his folly invites is as inescapable as the death that overtakes the humbler creatures.

We were confronted as we began with a question that our Korahite was to sing about.

Why should I fear in times of trouble,
when the iniquity of my persecutors surrounds me? (Vs. 5.)

His answer is: "There is no reason for fear. Certainly riches is no protector; the iniquity at one's heels destroys the wealth into which one's heels are dug. What riches cannot do for its owner it cannot do for one's brother. The best of intentions cannot mitigate the sentence of death that rests on rich and riches alike." For the poet there is only one hope, **God will ransom my soul from the power of Sheol, for he will receive me** (vs. 15).

This may not be a satisfactory answer to the age-old problem. It sounds a bit hollow to tell those who have been denied a fullness of goods that they should find their satisfaction in God. This idea, true though it is, has been used for evil purposes. Too often it has been preached by an institution—the church or the state—that would anesthetize the poor lest they grow restive and unruly. And yet two important facts may be left with us by this study. There is a soberness in the poet's repudiation of wealth that is in marked contrast to much of the conventional poetic protest on this perennial theme. It is of a pattern with that broad Hebrew-Christian attitude toward the competing values of things and spirit which is distinctive in our culture. Fullness of life comes neither by repudiating things nor by scorning spirit. The tension between them can be made creative of positive and redemptive values. It is the folly of trusting in riches against which our poet warns. This is the first important fact. The second is that modern wisdom has not advanced beyond this ancient insight. We have sought methods to control the evils of great wealth and to achieve wider and more equitable distribution of the goods of the earth to all its children. All of this is most necessary and somewhat heartening, but where does it promise ultimate safety from the basic folly of trusting in riches? And is there any new device proposed to cure our love of money that is as likely to prove effective as an honest and redemptive love of God?

50:1-83. ***Introducing the Asaphite Psalms.***—With four exceptions which appear almost at the end of Book III we are through with the

2 Out of Zion, the perfection of beauty, God hath shined.	2 Out of Zion, the perfection of beauty, God shines forth.

means. This is seen in the opening section (vss. 1-6). For whereas a theophany in Israel's traditions introduced one of the major acts or revelations of Yahweh, here it precedes a complaint of Yahweh against his people, based on what had already been made known to them; also the theophany, though made to appear **out of Zion** (vs. 2), is described in terms that are proper to Sinai (vs. 3). However, the defects in the psalmist's literary method need not obscure the spiritual quality of his message.

At first sight it may seem strange that a psalm which is critical of the sacrificial customs of the temple found a place in the hymnbook of the temple. But in the Psalter there is abundant evidence that in various ways the priests had granted a large place to the religious emphases of the prophets; e.g., we note it in the admonitions introduced into hymns sung on festival occasions (cf. 81:6-16; 95:7-11), in the Torah psalms (see Exeg. on Ps. 15), in the laments (cf. 85:8-13). Outside the regular or special services of worship in the temple there were, doubtless, priests who met individuals or small groups who came to seek an oracle or instruction (*tôrāh*) in answer to their special problems (cf. Zech. 7:2-6; 8:18). And what were originally words addressed to a particular audience came later into general use in the liturgy of the temple. This psalm was used on an occasion when it seemed proper to admonish the congregation of the spiritual complements of their worship and their religious professions. Its two principal strophes (vss. 7-15, 16-21), it seems, originated independently (Schmidt); each of them is a *tôrāh,* and on being put together by some hand, they were provided with vss. 1-6 as an introduction and vss. 22-23 as a conclusion.

The religious points of view expressed in the psalm are such as we meet in the postexilic period. In vss. 8-15, and particularly in vss. 14-15, true religion is defined as consisting not in the offering of sacrifices but in calling on God in times of trouble and in giving thanks to him for help received (cf. 51:16-17). The writer in handling the matter of animal sacrifices goes quite beyond the pre-exilic prophets (cf. Isa. 1:10-17; Jer. 7:21-23; Mic. 6:6-8), who pronounced the sacrifices of unrighteousness inefficacious, by showing the fundamental unimportance of sacrifice. In vss. 16-21 it is clear that legalistic tendencies are becoming ascendant in the definition of pious living, for the individual is warned against undue obsession with the externals of the law to the

songs of the sons of Korah. Two names have been given to the singers who now entertain us. Critical judgment declares the high probability that neither Asaph nor David actually wrote these poems. Something in their differing quality and mood no doubt suggested to early editors these early lyricists. Whoever the poets were, they exhibit clearly that they were temperamentally unlike. Thus the Asaphite songs are those of a rather stern moralist who prefers to teach as he sings. To him life has more rigor than romance, and when he takes to imagery, it is most often with a grave rather than a gay intent. Almost uniformly God is his theme, and God is a serious matter because life is serious. The Davidic mood, however, is romantic; whether it rhapsodizes or laments, it thrums its instrument in the truly romantic fashion. Discounting the sometimes aggressive agnosticism of some of Thomas Hardy's poems, it might be said that the Asaphite genre is to the Davidic as Hardy is to Browning.

Ps. 50 introduces us to the Asaphite manner and is fairly representative of the way in which the fact of God the Lord rests upon his mind and heart. God is judge, and the processes of the divine judgment are constantly in operation. Man must not be allowed to lose sight of this truth. No routine of religious practice can be permitted to dull man's moral sense. God is an experience, and is to be acknowledged less by the temple's ritual than by the common round infused by a grateful sense of his presence.

1-6. *God as Judge.*—Here we have the picture of an assize, not a final settlement but the concurrent judgment that always accompanies life. The "Hear ye, hear ye" of the court crier of

3 Our God shall come, and shall not
keep silence: a fire shall devour before him,
and it shall be very tempestuous round
about him.
4 He shall call to the heavens from above,
and to the earth, that he may judge his
people.
5 Gather my saints together unto me;
those that have made a covenant with me by
sacrifice.
6 And the heavens shall declare his righteousness: for God *is* judge himself. Selah.

3 Our God comes, he does not keep silence,
before him is a devouring fire,
round about him a mighty tempest.
4 He calls to the heavens above
and to the earth, that he may judge his
people:
5 "Gather to me my faithful ones,
who made a covenant with me by sacrifice!"
6 The heavens declare his righteousness,
for God himself is judge! *Selah*

---

neglect of its inner requirements. All these features point to a date when the characteristic features of Judaism were emerging.

The meter is for the most part 3+3.

1. The Advent of God (50:1-6)

50:1-6. The description of the coming of the Lord is derived from elements found in Deut. 33:2 and Exod. 19:16. Combinations of heterogeneous phenomena are used in this respect by later writers with whom the literary pattern of a theophany has become stylized. **Out of Zion:** The divine appearance is transferred from Sinai to Zion because Zion was, in the eyes of the later generations, the second Sinai for the giving of the law and its interpretation (cf. Isa. 2:3; Mic. 4:1-2). As the Lord comes **he calls to the heavens . . . and to the earth** to be his assessors as he prepares to hold an assize to **judge his people.** His **faithful ones,** i.e., his godly servants (חסידים), are summoned to his presence as those with whom the Lord enters into judgment. They are described as those **who made a covenant with me by sacrifice**—i.e., first at Mount Horeb (Exod. 24:3-8), and then in successive generations by their perpetuation of sacrifice. It is to be noted that the favorable attitude to sacrifice here is not sustained in the sequel. Schmidt holds that vss. 3-6 were originally an introduction to vss. 16-21, and so resolves the incongruity. Vs. 6 is better rendered, "So the heavens announce his assize, for God himself is about to act as judge."

---

modern times has ancient precedent, though this quaint, perfunctory summons has lost the color of the court to which our words give description. The vanguard of the judge is a **devouring fire,** and around him swirls the violence of a **tempest** (vs. 3). Not in lurid and terrifying display, however, but as a great shining, the perfection of beauty, resplendent out of Zion from the east to the west (vs. 2). This is **the Mighty One, God the Lord,** who summons the whole of heaven and earth (vs. 1); his the word that fills all creation (cf. Gen. 1:3), assembles all people that he may judge them. And if there are those who would quibble about his credentials,

The heavens declare his righteousness,
for God himself is judge!

Although all creation between east and west and earth and heaven is summoned to appear, there is an order in which the hearing is to be conducted. First are those God calls his own people, those who have covenanted with him by sacrifice: **faithful ones,** he calls them, faithful obviously meaning pledged (vs. 5).

God is both witness and judge. If this deviates from our ideas of orthodox legal practice, we may remind ourselves that nowhere is God as judge portrayed as an arbiter between contending counsels. He is always the judge and always the attorney for the prosecution or defense. Presumably this gave no one cause for concern: God as attorney would be as infallible as God as judge. Above it all is a clear intimation of the mood of God as he confronts his people. He asks for their hearing; he asks that they allow him to plead and to testify. It is important to accept these factors as representative of the function of God as judge. He is God: **I am God, your God;** they are his people; and yet it is as if by their sufferance that he will speak against them. Judge them he must,

7 Hear, O my people, and I will speak; O Israel, and I will testify against thee: I *am* God, *even* thy God.

8 I will not reprove thee for thy sacrifices or thy burnt offerings, *to have been* continually before me.

9 I will take no bullock out of thy house, *nor* he goats out of thy folds:

10 For every beast of the forest *is* mine, *and* the cattle upon a thousand hills.

11 I know all the fowls of the mountains: and the wild beasts of the field *are* mine.

12 If I were hungry, I would not tell thee: for the world *is* mine, and the fulness thereof.

13 Will I eat the flesh of bulls, or drink the blood of goats?

14 Offer unto God thanksgiving; and pay thy vows unto the Most High:

7 "Hear, O my people, and I will speak,
O Israel, I will testify against you.
I am God, your God.
8 I do not reprove you for your sacrifices;
your burnt offerings are continually before me.
9 I will accept no bull from your house,
nor he-goat from your folds.
10 For every beast of the forest is mine,
the cattle on a thousand hills.
11 I know all the birds of the air,[v]
and all that moves in the field is mine.
12 If I were hungry, I would not tell you;
for the world and all that is in it is mine.
13 Do I eat the flesh of bulls,
or drink the blood of goats?
14 Offer to God a sacrifice of thanksgiving,[w]
and pay your vows to the Most High;

[v] Gk Syr Tg: Heb *mountains*
[w] Or *make thanksgiving your sacrifice to God*

2. Acceptable Sacrifice (50:7-15)

7-15. In vs. 7 read "I am the Lord, your God" (see Exeg. on 42:1-5). **I do not reprove you for your sacrifices:** The sense of the passage is clearer if we read, "Though I do not reprove you for your sacrifices . . . yet I will not accept a bull, . . . goats." The worshipers have zeal—**your burnt offerings are continually before me**—but it springs

but the exercise of this mandate is free from the strict impersonal arbitrament we associate with the operations of justice. He speaks as a friend, not as a sheriff's deputy.

7-13. ***Man as Defendant.***—What is his charge against them? Not their failure to observe the formal prescriptions of religion. These things they do with studious regularity (vs. 8). It is their confusion of the meaning of their ritual with the practice of it. The rite has obscured the reason. When the worshiper fetched the carcass of a bull or a he-goat to the altar, he was likely to set more value on the votive flesh than on the act of devotion. But God set no store by the thing that was offered him. He had no need of it. Men ate meat to supply them their needed physical energy; therefore meat was valuable. But God knew nothing of the hunger that signals the need to replenish depleted strength (vs. 13). Even if he did suffer the mild discomfort of hunger, he would not complain to man about it (vs. 12). Since therefore he has no need for man to share his limited supply of foodstuff in order that God may not go hungry, he will not receive man's offerings of slaughtered beasts (vs. 9).

This seems to be a very matter-of-fact approach to the business of the ritual of worship. There is no point, God is saying, in offering something to him that he does not need. Does this mean that man should adjourn worship? There may be some spiritual value in denying one's self the meat he needs for his sustenance; but how far is it justified if it actually serves no purpose? In that it becomes sheer waste, and waste is immoral. Man follows the rubrics of sacrifice. This does him little good if he confuses, as he often does, the method with the motive of worship. God is offered the substance of sacrifice, which he does not need. For man sacrifice is wasteful; for God it is unnecessary. The alternative to the adjournment of worship therefore lies in the discovery of the need that it meets.

14-15. ***What God Desires.***—What does God need? Here the poet's insight was both novel and daring. Nay, he has the Lord God say, make thanksgiving your offering to God, and thus **pay your vows to the Most High.** It was daring because it threatened a whole system of sacrifice and its elaborate routines and its celebrants. If so pretentious an offering as a slain bullock was worthless, even less so were the lesser gifts. Away with them all! It was novel

15 And call upon me in the day of trouble: I will deliver thee, and thou shalt glorify me.

16 But unto the wicked God saith, What hast thou to do to declare my statutes, or *that* thou shouldest take my covenant in thy mouth?

17 Seeing thou hatest instruction, and castest my words behind thee.

18 When thou sawest a thief, then thou consentedst with him, and hast been partaker with adulterers.

19 Thou givest thy mouth to evil, and thy tongue frameth deceit.

15 and call upon me in the day of trouble;
I will deliver you, and you shall glorify me."

16 But to the wicked God says:
"What right have you to recite my statutes,
or take my covenant on your lips?
17 For you hate discipline,
and you cast my words behind you.
18 If you see a thief, you are a friend of his;
and you keep company with adulterers.

19 "You give your mouth free rein for evil,
and your tongue frames deceit.

---

from adherence to an ancient and outworn view of the efficacy of sacrifice. Let them know that the sacrifice of an animal does nothing for God in supplying his needs or his wants. What God desires from men is summed up in vss. 14-15. The psalmist in making sacrifice a matter relatively of no importance is preparing the way for its abrogation.

3. Hypocrites Are Rebuked (50:16-21)

16-21. But to the wicked is probably a gloss. **God says** introduces the strophe, but stands outside of the meter. The preceding strophe had special reference to the congrega-

---

because it suggested that what God really needed grew out of his nature. He had no body that required a daily ration of food; he was a spirit, and needed a daily ration of **thanksgiving.** A further point: this bold idea goes another step beyond the conventional idea of worship. If a man's worship is an act of grateful devotion instead of slavish attention to a prescribed routine, he may call in the day of trouble, i.e., address God when he needs him, as opposed to the perfunctory performance of vows, and, as our author puts it, **I will deliver you, and you shall glorify me.**

16-21. ***Indictment of the Wicked.***—To this assize are subpoenaed not only God's people, his faithful ones. There is a second category—the **wicked** (so our text; though the Exeg. inclines to think this is a gloss). The judge asks of them no permission that he may plead with them or testify. His attitude now is very different: **I rebuke you, and lay the charge before you.** They had made no covenant with him, yet they prated about the statutes of God. If God's friends had innocently misconceived the function of worship, the wicked had deliberately falsified it. At least God's friends agreed willingly to the performance of vows they dimly understood; the wicked, on the contrary, engaged in religious exercises they cordially hated. The picture of them is sharply drawn. **You hate discipline, and you cast my words behind you.** A man is known by the company he keeps rather than by the prayers he offers.

> **If you see a thief, you are a friend of his;**
> **and you keep company with adulterers,**

while at the same time you **recite my statutes** and **take my covenant on your lips. You give your mouth free rein for evil**—a bitter figure, the mouth abandoned to the control of evil—**and your tongue frames deceit;** another bitter image—the tongue, shuttling back and forth, weaving an ugly pattern of malice.

> **You sit and speak against your brother;**
> **you slander your own mother's son.**

All these defections are taken from Israel's basic covenant: "Thou shalt not steal, . . . thou shalt not commit adultery, . . . thou shalt not bear false witness." All the more point, then, to God's opening question to the wicked:

> **What right have you to recite my statutes,**
> **or take my covenant on your lips?**

Their denial of these covenant promises by the manner in which they lived took from them the right to worship. The fact that while this had been going on there was no overt sign of God's

20 Thou sittest *and* speakest against thy brother; thou slanderest thine own mother's son.

21 These *things* hast thou done, and I kept silence; thou thoughtest that I was altogether *such a one* as thyself: *but* I will reprove thee, and set *them* in order before thine eyes.

20 You sit and speak against your brother;
you slander your own mother's son.
21 These things you have done and I have been silent;
you thought that I was one like yourself.
But now I rebuke you, and lay the charge before you.

---

tion of Israel; this one is an admonition directed to the individual worshiper. **What right have you to recite my statutes?** This question is addressed to those who can recite all the commandments and the statutes which a Jew is required to observe; they are eloquent about what is "allowed" and what is "forbidden" (cf. Matt. 23:23), but they neglect the weightier things. They know the commandments against theft, adultery, and false witness (vss. 19-20), but though they do not steal or commit adultery, they consort with those who do, and though they do not bear false witness in the courts, they are guilty of slandering even the nearest of their kin. They imagine that, because he is **silent,** i.e., does not punish, the Lord approves of them. **But now I rebuke you,** and they know that they are under judgment. In vs. 20*a* read בשת, "shame," for תשב, **sit,** and translate, "you speak shameful things against your brother."

---

displeasure they had interpreted to mean that God himself was of their sort, one who made great promises but did little (vs. 21).

Even to these, however, there is a generous word. Though God has accused them of deliberate duplicity, of using statutes and covenants as a blind for their wickedness, he intimates that perhaps their trouble has been due to a short memory. God's friends misunderstood his needs; the wicked forgot them. To the former God issues a word of instruction; to the latter a warning. And yet, oddly enough, it is the same word.

> **Mark this, then, you who forget God,**
> **lest I rend, and there be none to deliver!**

God has said to his confused friends, "What I need is not sacrifice; I need gratitude." To the wicked he says, **He who brings thanksgiving as his sacrifice honors me.** It would seem also that the final word of the poet is addressed to both the groups that stand before the judge: **To him who orders his way aright** [so that he will neither misunderstand nor falsify it] **I will show the salvation of God!**

This, we are inclined to feel, is a noble conception of the relationship between God and man as it is expressed in the experience of life and worship. What our poet is concerned with is the place of gratitude in the experience of worship and the good life. It is as unfortunate as it is natural that the practice of worship tends almost universally to become dissociated from the more routine matters of living. In theistic religions God is so vastly elevated in thought above the human level that in order to ingratiate oneself it is sometimes thought necessary to pile splendor on magnificence in the effort to worship appropriately. This comes from a truly worthy impulse; but it can fall to hideous depths of moral depravity. To toss one's child into the flaming arms of Moloch was as genuine a response to the worship impulse as to toss a he-goat's carcass upon the altar fires. It was a genuine response, though we must judge the worship to have been spurious. How far is such performance calculated to stir in one the impulse to thanksgiving? That is the point.

Our poet presents this problem clearly. Men recognize the constraint to worship and seek ways by which to worship aright. God recognizes man's need and feels within himself the need to be worshiped; but slain victims fail to satisfy him. He needs not what a burning carcass can offer, but what the heart of the worshiper alone can bring. An altar laden with gifts and redolent of incense is nothing to him who owns the earth. It is the heart of man that God does not own which alone can be lovingly offered, and that heart must be offered as a token of thanksgiving.

> **Offer to God a sacrifice of thanksgiving,**
> **and pay your vows to the Most High** (vs. 14)

—a bold thing to have said among people who were both uniquely conscious of God and elaborately furnished with ritual for worshiping him.

22 Now consider this, ye that forget God, lest I tear *you* in pieces, and *there be* none to deliver.
23 Whoso offereth praise glorifieth me: and to him that ordereth *his* conversation *aright* will I show the salvation of God.

22 "Mark this, then, you who forget God,
lest I rend, and there be none to deliver!
23 He who brings thanksgiving as his sacrifice honors me;
to him who orders his way aright
I will show the salvation of God!"

To the chief Musician, A Psalm of David, when Nathan the prophet came unto him, after he had gone in to Bath-sheba.

51 Have mercy upon me, O God, according to thy loving-kindness: according unto the multitude of thy tender mercies blot out my transgressions.

To the choirmaster. A Psalm of David, when Nathan the prophet came to him, after he had gone in to Bathsheba.

51 Have mercy on me, O God,
according to thy steadfast love;
according to thy abundant mercy blot out my transgressions.

---

4. Warning and Promise (50:22-23)

22-23. The concluding verses sum up the argument of the psalm.

LI. Prayer of a Penitent (51:1-19)

This is properly described as a penitential psalm, a subclass of the individual lament. The writer is sick (vs. 8), perhaps near death (vs. 14). But he is racked less with pain of body than with agony of soul because of his sharp sense of having alienated himself from God by his sin. From vs. 6 we may conclude that his sin, whatever it may have been, was primarily an act against God. Unlike most psalmists who pour out laments to the Lord, he utters no complaints against personal enemies or against the plots of

---

22-23. *The Better Way.*—What of the good life? Our poem has something to say about this. The wicked are shown up for what they are: dishonest, rebellious, evil-speaking, unfilial; and the rebuke of the Judge is unequivocal and sharp. How, then, does he propose to redeem these forgetters of God lest they be rent asunder? **He who brings thanksgiving as his offering, honors me,** says the Most High.

To him who orders his way aright
I will show the salvation of God!

This might be thought to reduce right living to an all too simple formula: Watch your step, give heed to your way, and be thankful to God. Obviously—if one assumes the poet is writing a system of ethics instead of a poem. The point, however, is clear: There is a deeply laid relationship between the honest experience and expression of thanksgiving and genuine righteousness. Man struggles to give his sense of worship adequate embodiment in sacrifices, and often finds that the sacrifice at first deflects and at last destroys true devotion, the essence of which is gratitude. Man also struggles to give embodiment to his desire for the good life, and often finds that covenants and promises deflect and sometimes destroy the joy of godliness, the essence of which again is gratitude. So man abandons sacrifices or keeps them up as a perfunctory routine. So also man scoffs ultimately at covenants and promises, or respects them under duress. Contrition reflects one's sense of failure; gratitude, one's sense of recovery. May they not be thought to be two sides of the experience of thankfulness—one negative, the other positive?

For both of these perplexities—the futility of sacrifice and the frustration of goodness—our poet sets forth gratitude to God as the solution. It is not the whole of the matter; but it might be demonstrated even in these times when sacrifices are relics of more superstitious ages than our own, and covenants are often thought by modern sophistication to be as much honored in their breach as in their observance, that true gratitude, constantly and sincerely offered, can save our worship experience from tedium and our morals from being mechanical or meaningless. This at least was the poet's notion; it is still something worth thinking about. There may be more truth in it than poetry.

51:1-19. *David as Subject or Author.*—It has been pointed out that as compared with the Asaphite poems, which appear only five times

those who hate him, nor does he petition for recovery from his affliction to the end that these malevolent persons may be baffled and put to shame. Rather, he accepts his guilt. It is true that he regards himself as by birth prone to sin, sharing in the common weakness of all who are born of women. But he seeks no excuse for his personal guilt in this fact. If he was weak by the fleshly bond, he nevertheless made the sin his own. Further, he stands in contrast to other suppliants in that beyond his healing he is anxious to find not just escape from Sheol, but **a new and right spirit**—a **steadfast** spirit, a willing, responsive spirit. Having turned his sickness into an occasion of self-examination, he prays that he may become possessed of a steadier loyalty to the Lord of his life.

It is consonant with his spiritual temper that he considers no offering of thanks for the answering of his appeal acceptable to God except that of **a broken and contrite heart** (vss. 16-17). Such a point of view is so revolutionary in its implications for the traditional sacrificial system that a later editor, fearful of its influence, sought to qualify it by the addition of vss. 18-19.

The developed consciousness of personal sin, the denial of worth to animal sacrifices, and the spiritual reaction to affliction, these general features mark the psalm as postexilic. To them may be added some special ones: the psalmist is acquainted with the higher teachings of pre-exilic prophecy (cf. Hos. 13:12; 14:2; Jer. 17:9; 31:31-33) and some of its postexilic counterparts (cf. Ezek. 11:19; 36:26; Isa. 57:15; 63:10-11); certain of its theological conceptions and its words, as the Exeg. shows, reflect late usage. For the reference to **David** in the superscription see Intro., p. 8. Obviously it is shown to be unauthentic by vs. 4, **Against thee, thee only, have I sinned.**

The meter is 3+3, with an occasional 3+4 variation, e.g., in vss. 1, 11, 17.

1. Cry for Mercy and Cleansing (51:1-2)

51:1-2. Have mercy on me, O God: Psalms of this type are regularly introduced with a cry to God for help. The psalmist at once admits his sin and, casting himself on

---

in Books II and III, the writings attributed to the sons of Korah and David represent a different temperament (see Expos. on 50:1-23). The latter mood, whether it is from one author or many, will be before us for most of the rest of the Expos., and we shall be discovering the width of its romantic range. It is more distinctly poetic; its interests are more varied and its feelings more intense. It will be demonstrated that its enthusiasm often seems to run away with its judgment, that it even combines exalted spiritual insights with dubious moral ideas. For natural though for mistaken reasons, these poems and their moods have been attributed exclusively to David, the most picturesque of Israel's heroes—indeed, one of the great romantic and literary figures of all history. David had something of every man in him that excites the interest of every man. He was the great lover, the great rogue, and the great saint; he was Robin Hood hidden in the cave of Adullam, Bernard in mystic rapture at Clairvaux, François Villon surprised at prayer in a temple. If we must differ with ancient editors and accept the judgment of modern scholars who deny the Davidic authorship of many if not all the pieces assigned to him, we recognize the plausibility of the earlier allocation. If the experience recounted in this psalm was not written by David, it may have been written about him anonymously long after the story of the romantic king's famous sin had gained its first currency. Even if its reference to David is dubious, it is certainly an authentic portrayal of the sense of sin by a deeply penitent sinner. Herein lies its importance and its imperishable admonition.

One of the most familiar and favored passages of the O.T., this psalm has furnished the language with which contrition has made itself articulate, and given body to inchoate sentiments that weigh upon the stricken soul. It is the great prayer for pardon. Reaching down, as it does, into the corruption of sin, it lifts the heart up for purification by God's aromatic hyssop. Because it knows something of the blackness of human evil, it can speak with hope and confidence of the whiteness of the divine cleansing. Properly called the "most sacred lyric," it can be understood only when those two qualities are kept in mind. "Sacred" is here taken to mean the quality of spiritual experience that has direct reference to man's converse with God; "lyric" means the quality of sentiment in poetry that as often as not is irrational —meaning, of course, less concerned with logic than with feeling.

As has been indicated, it was impossible for

2 Wash me thoroughly from mine iniquity, and cleanse me from sin.
3 For I acknowledge my transgressions: and my sin *is* ever before me.

2 Wash me thoroughly from my iniquity,
and cleanse me from my sin!

3 For I know my transgressions,
and my sin is ever before me.

God's mercy, asks for riddance from it. **Blot out my transgressions:** The figure suggests removal from a record or a tablet (cf. Exod. 32:33; Num. 5:23; Isa. 43:25). **Wash me:** As a garment (Exod. 19:10). **Cleanse me:** Used of removing the dross from metals (Mal. 3:3), but also of making one clean and fit to appear before God (Lev. 14:11). Throughout the psalm the three words descriptive of the psalmist's unworthiness recur: **transgressions, iniquity, sin.**

2. Confession and Petition (51:3-12)

3-5. The psalmist presents still more fully his confession of sin. **I know,** and therefore do not need to be convinced of **my transgressions.** The essence of it is **against thee, thee only, have I sinned.** The psalmist may in these words be confessing some act of impiety or apostasy, but more probably he is distinguishing offenses against God

---

the earliest editors to avoid identifying the inspiration of this classic as King David's relationship with Bathsheba. The prophet Nathan's catalytic rebuke precipitated a mood that had to find expression. David's anger at the cruelty of the fictitious character Nathan had created to point up the nature of the king's own sin was grimly turned back upon the royal sinner. The hidden scandal was then in the open. " 'For you did it secretly; but I will do this thing before all Israel, and before the sun.' David said to Nathan, 'I have sinned against the Lord.' And Nathan said to David, 'The Lord also has put away your sin; you shall not die.' " (II Sam. 12:12-13.)

1-5. ***Self-rebuke.***—Such mixed feelings of exposure, denunciation, and threat were calculated to produce a chaos of thought and sentiment. The sinner's first feeling was relief that the hidden thing was out; he needed no longer to practice deception and subterfuge (cf. 31:3-4). This relief let loose a torrent of self-indictment. He had said to Nathan: "As the Lord lives, the man who has done this deserves to die; and he shall restore the lamb fourfold, because he did this thing, and because he showed no pity" (II Sam. 12:5-6). The prophet turned David's indictment back on him, but he softened the judgment—"You shall not die"—and throughout this great penitential prayer there breathes the atmosphere of great relief, as well as of supplication. **Have mercy upon me, O God, according to thy loving-kindness** [his sentence of death had been commuted]: **according unto the multitude of thy tender mercies blot out my transgressions. Wash me thoroughly from mine iniquity, and cleanse me from my sin** (vss. 1-2).

I acknowledge my transgressions: and my sin is ever before me (vs. 3). Now it is before everybody. "By this deed thou hast given great occasion to the enemies of the Lord to blaspheme," Nathan had warned (II Sam. 12:14). What, it may be asked, were his **transgressions?** As they related to the immediate episode, they were lust, intrigue, adultery, treachery, and promotion of the murder of his trusted servant, Uriah. Five of the Ten Commandments had been deliberately broken.

There follows a verse that has disturbed commentators; and their efforts to explain it, or explain it away, have been many and ingenious.

Against thee, thee only, have I sinned,
and done that which is evil in thy sight.

Together with the last two verses of the poem, it has been thought the addition of later editors or a misplaced fragment of another poem. (Cf. also Exeg.) Is it not best understood, however, as the normal protective irrationalism of the lyric mood under the pressure of a great emotion? It was a marked advance in moral thought that represented man's sin against his fellow as a sin against God. For this important idea we are indebted to the deep insight of some of Israel's thinkers. The sinner shared it in this anguished moment, but did he not go too far when he said that his sin was **only** against God? Had not he sinned against Uriah, Bathsheba, and Joab (II Sam. 11:14-21), against the throne he occupied, and the people he ruled? And were not these things evil in the sight of all who saw them? If he is consciously dismissing these segments of the total relevance of his sin, he is guilty of moral obliquity of the most

4 Against thee, thee only, have I sinned, and done *this* evil in thy sight: that thou mightest be justified when thou speakest, *and* be clear when thou judgest.

5 Behold, I was shapen in iniquity; and in sin did my mother conceive me.

6 Behold, thou desirest truth in the inward parts: and in the hidden *part* thou shalt make me to know wisdom.

4 Against thee, thee only, have I sinned,
and done that which is evil in thy sight,
so that thou art justified in thy sentence
and blameless in thy judgment.
5 Behold, I was brought forth in iniquity,
and in sin did my mother conceive me.

6 Behold, thou desirest truth in the inward being;
therefore teach me wisdom in my secret heart.

---

from those against his fellows. His sin, whatever its nature, is primarily disobedience to God's law, and therefore an offense to God. So the affliction which God has sent upon him cannot be cited as an instance of God's unrighteousness, for **thou art justified . . . in thy judgment.** But he is a sinner not only by his own acts, but by reason of the moral frailty of the flesh (cf. Job. 4:18-19). **In sin did my mother conceive me:** A strong word (יחם) is used not to disgrace his mother, but to humble himself (cf. 58:3). It is an anticipation of the later Jewish notion of the "evil inclination" (היצר הרע; cf. Ecclus. 15:11-15).

6-9. Now follows the psalmist's petition. "[Since] Thou desirest loyalty [cf. Isa. 38:3] in my inmost being, teach me the true way to live wisely before thee in the depths of my heart." Schmidt renders the difficult text of vs. 6, "Behold, thou desirest truth more than excuses [read מטוחות, "more than coverings up"], and dost teach me wisdom about that which is a mystery." **Purge me with hyssop:** The word **purge** is, lit., "unsin,"

---

dangerous sort; he is compounding a felony. To realize that an offense against one's fellows is a sin against God is the profoundest of moral insights; to regard an offense against God as unrelated to one's fellows is the shallowest of moral sophistries. What we have here, we must remind ourselves, is not the long-term reflections of a spiritual genius on the nature of the moral problem, but an account of the momentary defense reaction of a very sensitive spirit to his own acute and immediate problem.

The case is helped very little when, continuing in the strained state of mind, extenuation is offered for misbehavior. A rational response to one's feeling of guilt is almost reflexive, but the emotions can inspire strange rationalizations. He has done this thing, he says,

so that thou art justified in thy sentence
and blameless in thy judgment.

This amounts almost to making an accomplice of God; and when the sinner goes further and indicts as evil the biological processes which gave him birth, he definitely implicates God.

Behold, I was brought forth in iniquity,
and in sin did my mother conceive me.

What would the sinner's mother have said to that? Once again we are compelled to think that this is not the moralist arguing a point, but the sinner defending himself. Or is it an awareness of evil bias, and of the long entail of evil in human history?

6-7. ***Truth in the Inward Being.***—Because in these verses the psalmist reaches down into profound depths and lifts out an eternal aspect of the spiritual life, some redactors have wished that the disturbing interval (vss. 3-5) might have been omitted. Obviously the moral continuity would be preserved without the interruption. Vs. 6 follows vs. 3 logically and morally. We must recall again, however, that this is the account of a man under intense emotional strain, and we must allow and seek to understand his irrational interludes. If vs. 5 gives the only O.T. formulation of the doctrine of original sin (not the legend that tells the story), we may be grateful for its modification in the verses that follow.

Vs. 6 is not only one of the most profound and most cherished of all our religious insights; it is a corrective of the idea of original sin. If truth is what God desires in the inward being, i.e., the essence of the soul, original sin is not according to his will. Sin is therefore not God's choice for man; it is man's choice for himself. Thus sin is not original; it is derivative. One is also intrigued by the suggestion that the phrases **inward being** and **secret heart** have connota-

7 Purge me with hyssop, and I shall be clean: wash me, and I shall be whiter than snow.

8 Make me to hear joy and gladness; *that* the bones *which* thou hast broken may rejoice.

9 Hide thy face from my sins, and blot out all mine iniquities.

10 Create in me a clean heart, O God; and renew a right spirit within me.

11 Cast me not away from thy presence; and take not thy Holy Spirit from me.

12 Restore unto me the joy of thy salvation; and uphold me *with thy* free Spirit.

7 Purge me with hyssop, and I shall be clean;
wash me, and I shall be whiter than snow.
8 Fill[x] me with joy and gladness;
let the bones which thou hast broken rejoice.
9 Hide thy face from my sins,
and blot out all my iniquities.

10 Create in me a clean heart, O God,
and put a new and right[y] spirit within me.
11 Cast me not away from thy presence,
and take not thy holy Spirit from me.
12 Restore to me the joy of thy salvation,
and uphold me with a willing spirit.

[x] Syr: Heb *Make to hear*
[y] Or *steadfast*

a late usage (see the Piel use of חטא in Ezekiel and Leviticus). The **hyssop** plant was used in ritual cleansing of persons healed of leprosy (cf. Lev. 14:4-6, 49-57). Here the psalmist is not indicating his sickness but is speaking figuratively. **Fill me with joy** by healing the body of its disease or by taking away the sense of remorse that has pierced to the very marrow of his bones (Calès). **Hide thy face from my sins:** All these petitions, if answered, are sufficient for the present crisis, but what is needed for the days beyond?

10-12. The psalmist is aware that he needs more than forgiveness. **Create in me a clean heart:** The word **create** is the same as that used in the creation story of Genesis. The **clean heart** which he wants must be a new creation (cf. II Cor. 5:17). The effect of it will be manifest in a steadfast, unvacillating loyalty. The psalmist follows here the thought and even the words of Ezek. 36:25-27. Such a spiritual condition needs to be sustained by (*a*) **thy holy Spirit,** which will strengthen the good will of his heart for

tions similar to what moderns call the subconscious mind. The importance of this factor in human behavior is increasingly understood. Truth in the inward being and wisdom in the secret heart are eminently desirable, whether one speaks as psychotherapist or as saint. Was this the deduction of a disciplined mind reflecting on the relation of the subconscious to sin? Or was it not rather the sort of sparkling gem the poet often lifts unexpectedly from some hidden pocket of his soul?

7-12. ***The Longing of the Sin-sick Soul.***—Here is perhaps the most familiar of all the biblical descriptions of the longing of the sin-sick soul for healing. This is the sinner's real problem, and he is on much safer grounds than when he appears to be moralizing. Gone now is the excuse that he was born in sin. In vigorous metaphor he describes himself as sick, unclean, fouled, dejected, crippled, and hideous to look upon. **Purge me with hyssop** [an aromatic oil used to spray lepers and the loathsome sick], **and I shall be clean; wash me, and I shall be whiter than snow.** This second reference is surely to his clothing, since whiteness would be the pallor of illness. That he speaks as if his garments were besmirched with the filth of his degradation indicates the sharpness of his self-rebuke. He was accustomed to clean raiment. He is cast down. His bones are broken; not literally, of course, but a man cannot stand upright or move steadily with a broken leg, and he wants to stand spiritually erect and to approach the God he has offended. And lest God recoil from the hideous sight before him, he urges that he avert his face while the process of cleansing restores him to respectability (vs. 9).

This is no perfunctory and formal act of expiation; it is a man facing up to the spectacle he has made of himself. Standing before the mirror of his soul, he sees himself in every repugnant detail and begs for cleansing. It is not, however, the external aspect alone that needs attention. As if he knew that aromatics and clean garments and sturdy bones are often the disguise of sin, not the evidence of moral clean-

13 *Then* will I teach transgressors thy ways; and sinners shall be converted unto thee.

14 Deliver me from bloodguiltiness, O God, thou God of my salvation: *and* my tongue shall sing aloud of thy righteousness.

15 O Lord, open thou my lips; and my mouth shall show forth thy praise.

16 For thou desirest not sacrifice; else would I give *it:* thou delightest not in burnt offering.

17 The sacrifices of God *are* a broken spirit: a broken and a contrite heart, O God, thou wilt not despise.

13 Then I will teach transgressors thy ways,
and sinners will return to thee.
14 Deliver me from bloodguiltiness,[z] O God,
thou God of my salvation,
and my tongue will sing aloud of thy deliverance.

15 O Lord, open thou my lips,
and my mouth shall show forth thy praise.
16 For thou hast no delight in sacrifice;
were I to give a burnt offering, thou wouldst not be pleased.
17 The sacrifice acceptable to God[a] is a broken spirit;
a broken and contrite heart, O God,
thou wilt not despise.

[z] Or *death*
[a] Or *My sacrifice, O God*

holy living (cf. 143:10); and (*b*) **a willing spirit,** i.e., a spirit of nobility and willingness, an inclination of easy obedience. In his conception of the function of the spirit of God the psalmist is moving away from the religion of the O.T. to that of the N.T. (cf. Rom. 8).

3. The Psalmist's Vow (51:13-17)

13-17. The usual vow which concludes a lament is to make a thanksgiving offering in the presence of the great congregation of God-fearing men. But here the psalmist's vow is (*a*) to show the truth to **transgressors** in order to turn them to God, to teach them rather than to cry out against them (Schmidt); (*b*) to **sing** a song of thanksgiving for his deliverance from death (cf. Ps. 34); and (*c*) to offer that which God desires above all others—**a broken and contrite heart.** In vs. 14 the Hebrew "blood(s)" means **death,**

liness, he goes still deeper into his need. He must be made over, beginning with his heart and soul. These things men cannot see, but if they are soiled, no outer whiteness will avail to deceive. And as if his heart were unclean past cleansing, he asks that God shall create a new, clean heart; and as if his spirit were debilitated past repair, he asks for a new one, steadfast and strong (vs. 10). Finally, as the most abject of all fears, comes the poet's fear of spiritual loneliness. One can become inured to filth, to disability, and to feebleness, but can one endure his sin in solitude? It were better to have God's presence even in condemnation than to be separated from him. And he even dares to insist that such response as his contrition evokes from God shall—much or little—be ungrudging (vss. 11-12).

13-19. ***Restoration and Return.***—The sinner, the treacherous, the lecher, has laid bare his soul. Because he could feel deeply, he could sin grievously; endowed for greatness, he could greatly err. After this self-immolation he moves into a more spacious mood. He will teach, he will sing aloud, he will declare God's praise. Perhaps, he surmises, transgressors know not the ways of God; if they did, they would return to him (vs. 13). If God is going to cleanse and restore him, there will be none who fail to hear of it (vs. 14). His lips, guilty of sly and seductive whisperings, must now be opened in praise.

The final strophe (vss. 18-19) contains the insight previously offered in Ps. 50 concerning the importance of the grateful and contrite heart in worship as opposed to the value of burnt offerings. Our author's mood, touched now by a lyric urge, proposes that his sense of restoration and renewal be universally felt.

Do good to Zion in thy good pleasure;
rebuild the walls of Jerusalem.

Has not his enthusiasm swept him a bit from his moorings? When everything is thus restored, God will even be delighted once again to accept the sacrifice of burnt offerings and whole offerings. To this exuberance we cannot object. There is rejoicing in heaven, we are told, over

18 Do good in thy good pleasure unto Zion: build thou the walls of Jerusalem.
19 Then shalt thou be pleased with the sacrifices of righteousness, with burnt offering and whole burnt offering: then shall they offer bullocks upon thine altar.

18 Do good to Zion in thy good pleasure;
rebuild the walls of Jerusalem,
19 then wilt thou delight in right sacrifices,
in burnt offerings and whole burnt offerings;
then bulls will be offered on thy altar.

To the chief Musician, Maschil, *A Psalm* of David, when Doeg the Edomite came and told Saul, and said unto him, David is come to the house of Ahimelech.

52 Why boastest thou thyself in mischief, O mighty man? the goodness of God *endureth* continually.

To the choirmaster. A Maskil of David, when Doeg, the Edomite, came and told Saul, "David has come to the house of Ahimelech."

52 Why do you boast, O mighty man,
of mischief done against the godly?[b]
All the day you are plotting destruction.

[b] Cn Compare Syr: Heb *the kindness of God*

as in 30:9 (cf. Job 16:18). Many critics read the Hebrew *middāmîm,* "from bloods," as *middūmām,* "from silence."

4. Later Appendix (51:18-19)

18-19. These verses, as noted in the Exeg. on vss. 1-19, were added by a later hand to modify the psalmist's bold disparagement of the ritual offerings. According to this appendix, the suspension of the **sacrifices** is due only to the state of things at Jerusalem, but when the city has been restored by God's help sacrifices in rich abundance (עולה וכליל) will be resumed in the proper and traditional manner. **Sacrifices of righteousness:** Those that are right or correct ritually.

LII. The Downfall of the Wicked (52:1-9)

Because of some individual features, this psalm does not lend itself easily to strict classification. In general it presents the characteristic marks of a complaint or lament,

one sinner that repents. Why not an excess of joy in the heart of the sinner on earth who is forgiven? (But see Exeg.)

It appears that the imperishable values in this great poem may be summarized under two propositions. The first can be very simply stated: the high moral courage of the man who accused the sinner was its proximate cause. His is a fairly obscure figure in the record. He appears at the Lord's appointment to speak clearly against the man's sin. This he does, adding the menacing word, "Now therefore the sword shall never depart from thy house, because thou hast despised me" (II Sam. 12:10). What might have happened had not this bold man faced the royal sinner may be endlessly discussed. What happens when we fail to confront the sins of our times, in high or low places? There is an easy answer to that.

The second proposition may also be simply put: rank confers no immunity from judgment. One moment the sinner was a proud man, the next he was a man in anguish before the judgment of God. We may indulge to our heart's content our criticisms of the peccadilloes of the poet as he described his anguish. There may be value in that. But whether contrite or defensive, morbid or coldly realistic, his language has been appropriated by thousands who, confronted with their sin, have felt the need for propitiating God. Who has not prayed, grateful for the words of this ancient penitent,

Create in me a clean heart, O God,
and put a new and right spirit within me?

And who has not deeply felt, grateful for his insight, that

The sacrifice acceptable to God is a broken spirit;
a broken and contrite heart, O God, thou wilt not despise?

52:1-9. ***Pattern for Revolution.***—The contrast between this brief and fiery poem and Ps. 51 lends credibility to the early editors' claim for the wide variety of David's poetic moods and

2 Thy tongue deviseth mischiefs; like a sharp razor, working deceitfully.

2 Your tongue is like a sharp razor,
you worker of treachery.

---

but it lacks the usual introductory appeal to God for help and instead opens with bitter words of censure addressed to a man of evil purposes. The wicked man, however, is apparently a type or generalization of a class rather than a specific individual, and the fate of such a man is compared with that of the godly man. The psalm accordingly becomes an expression of trust and confidence in a time when men were debating the problem of the comparative values of godliness and ungodliness from the standpoint of what is profitable for the life that now is (cf. Pss. 1; 37; 49). The psalm is closely related in style to Ps. 58, and like it recalls the invectives of the prophets (cf. Isa. 22:15-19). In function it should be interpreted in the light of the prophetlike admonitions which appear in the Psalter (see 50:16-21; cf. 11:1-7). The psalm, then, while in the form of a lament, is a denunciation of wickedness and an assurance to the godly of vindication.

Like other psalms and writings in which the relation of piety to success, happiness, and long life is vehemently discussed (cf. Mal. 3:14-15), this psalm is of a postexilic date, probably late rather than early. The meter is 3+2, except where the text is corrupt.

The attempt in the superscription to connect the psalm with the incident in I Sam. 22:6-23 is not only inappropriate, but groundless because of the mention of the temple (vs. 8).

1. Address to the Ungodly (52:1-4)

52:1-4. The psalmist, in expressing his resentment against those in the Jewish community who broke with the conscientious practice of their religious obligations in the interest

---

themes. They regarded him as one who is as sensitive to the futile cruelties of angry men as he was to the serenity of green pastures and still waters; he was inspired no less by the lightning that crackled above Lebanon's cedars —Lebanon leaps like a calf, and Sirion like an antelope (29:6)—than by the majesty of the eternal law. We have here a shout of defiance against a political adversary. It is not the first time poets have used their art for this purpose. Even Wordsworth, who loved to commune with nature during long solitary walks, wished that he might have gone to France and joined the pamphleteer-poets who sang their wild songs against tyranny.

> O pleasant exercise of hope and joy!
> For mighty were the auxiliars which then stood
> Upon our side, us who were strong in love!
> Bliss was it in that dawn to be alive,
> But to be young was very Heaven! [1]

Although there may be explicit dissent from this reference (see Exeg.), this psalm may be studied in connection with the occasion which was at least thought to have inspired it. The editorial comment with which the poem is introduced says simply: **Doeg, the Edomite, came and told Saul, "David has come to the house of Ahimelech."** This refers to one of the most dramatic episodes in David's life. He was a fugitive from the anger of Saul and the victim of a popular movement to make him king. After his compact of undying friendship with Jonathan, he had fled to Nob and sought the protection of Ahimelech the priest while foraging for bread and weapons for himself and the few friends he had with him. Ahimelech, an honest and frightened man, having no "common bread" on hand, reluctantly allowed him to take the holy bread, and disclosed the hiding place of Goliath's sword, the same with which David had killed the giant Philistine. David took bread and sword and fled to Gath, but not before Doeg, one of Saul's "mightiest herdsmen," had seen him. David's peace of mind in Gath was not helped by the reminder that he was the current hero of a growing revolt against King Saul, and he was able to escape detention by Achish king of Gath only by dissembling madness. He finally found refuge for himself and his four hundred miscellaneous revolutionaries in a cave in Adullam. In the meantime, Doeg had returned to Saul and reported his discovery of the whereabouts of the fugitive. Ahimelech was summoned and questioned. He protested his loyalty to Saul, but defended David against the suspicion of faithlessness, and finally denied any knowledge that would incriminate either himself or the man he had reluctantly befriended. Saul, with the characteristic thoroughness of the counterrevolutionary, ordered his bodyguard to kill Ahimelech and his priestly

[1] *The Prelude,* Book XI.

3 Thou lovest evil more than good; *and* lying rather than to speak righteousness. Selah.
4 Thou lovest all devouring words, O *thou* deceitful tongue.

3 You love evil more than good,
and lying more than speaking the truth. *Selah*
4 You love all words that devour,
O deceitful tongue.

---

of worldly success and power, has chosen to adopt the style of a personal address to an individual.

Why do you boast, O mighty man,
of mischief done against the godly?

There is an element of sarcasm here, for the great man is due to be brought low. In the meantime, however, he uses his position and power in the community to accomplish evil ends (vs. 7). The humble, god-fearing men who challenge both his arrogance and his ways become the objects of his hostility. We can discern the war of words that was being carried on between the different parties within Judaism over policies, conduct, compromises touching on questions of religious loyalty. If the psalmist could use acrimonious words, so also his enemies could employ the weapons of speech. **All the day** they devise their accusations; their **tongue is like a sharp razor** (cf. 57:4), and by **lying more than speaking the truth,** its aim is to **devour.** Its allies are **treachery** and deceit.

---

associates. When the guard refused, he commanded Doeg the informer to do the job. He was a mighty man and an unquestioning servant of the king, and by the time he had finished the business, he had killed eighty-five priests and all the "men and women, children and sucklings, and oxen, and asses, and sheep" in "Nob, the city of the priests" (I Sam. 22:19). As is not infrequently the case, the job missed being complete by the escape of one of Ahimelech's sons, Abiathar. He ultimately found his way to the forest of Hereth, where David was in ambush, and told him the bloody tale. David's reported comment is interesting both for the determination and the tenderness of the man. "I knew that day, when Doeg the Edomite was there, that he would surely tell Saul: I have occasioned the death of all the persons of thy father's house. Abide thou with me, fear not: for he that seeketh my life seeketh thy life: but with me thou shalt be in safeguard" (I Sam. 22:22-23).

This to us is a lively tale; to David it was a terribly critical turn of events. With this clear evidence of Saul's proposal to pursue him and his followers to their death, he accepted what to him was an inevitable destiny, a destiny that was allotted by God himself. From this point he was the leader of rebellion. The mad king had challenged the daring young renegade; now, against his own wish but in response to popular demand, he was pretender to the throne.

This is the sort of thing out of which epic poems are made. It would be surprising therefore if David, who was poet as well as revolutionist, had not used it. Our author, whoever he was, does not tell the story, however. He writes a song to defy the "mighty man." It is a song of revolution. David had not sought the throne; taken from herding the sheep, he had been thrust into the turmoil of love, intrigue, and danger in the court. But the king had threatened his life, and his madness had imperiled the kingdom. David had become the symbol of the people's hope. Here was a people's revolution, and David, taking up the gauntlet the king had thrown down, must write the song that would help carry the battle to victory.

1-4. *The Evil King.*—Clearly this is a song that might have been directed against Saul, the royal father of David's wife and of his bosom friend Jonathan. Once committed to revolution, David pulls no punches. Braggart he calls Saul; mighty he concedes him to be, but his pride and his power are against the godly and marked for destruction. **Why . . . boast, O mighty man, of mischief done against the godly?** Remember the slaughter in the city of Nob! **All the day you are plotting destruction.** To this indictment in terms of an act against the priests of the Lord, he lashes out against the king in four terrible words: traitor, liar, consumer, deceiver. And lest a defense is offered for the king, saying he had been forced into doing this evil, David anticipates by saying that he is all these things because he loves to be. Doubtless, having lived at court, he could support all these charges convincingly.

5 God shall likewise destroy thee for ever,
he shall take thee away, and pluck thee out
of *thy* dwelling place, and root thee out of
the land of the living. Selah.
6 The righteous also shall see, and fear,
and shall laugh at him:
7 Lo, *this is* the man *that* made not God
his strength; but trusted in the abundance
of his riches, *and* strengthened himself in
his wickedness.
8 But I *am* like a green olive tree in the
house of God: I trust in the mercy of God
for ever and ever.

5 But God will break you down for ever;
he will snatch and tear you from your tent;
he will uproot you from the land of the living. *Selah*
6 The righteous shall see, and fear,
and shall laugh at him, saying,
7 "See the man who would not make God his refuge,
but trusted in the abundance of his riches,
and sought refuge in his wealth!"[c]

8 But I am like a green olive tree
in the house of God.
I trust in the steadfast love of God
for ever and ever.

[c] Syr Tg: Heb *his destruction*

2. God's Retribution (52:5-7)

5-7. But God will break you down for ever: Retribution will surely overtake the ungodly. The emphasis is on **God.** It is God against all such men. God "will pull you down" and "snatch you . . . from your home," and "destroy your roots in the land." So the wicked will be deprived of their power and wealth, made homeless, and stripped of posterity. **The righteous shall see . . . and shall laugh** at the end of those who **sought refuge in** [their] **wealth.**

3. The Psalmist's Trust in God (52:8-9)

8-9. In contrast to the wicked, the righteous shall flourish **like a green olive tree in the house of God.** The **olive tree,** because of its fruitfulness and hardiness, symbolizes the flourishing condition of those who put their **trust in the mercy of God** (cf. 1:3;

5-7. *Evil Can Be Overthrown.*—This is lese majesty with a vengeance; but not only does the poet shout against the person of the king; he predicts his downfall and gives the reason for it. This frightening humiliation will occasion no sympathy. On the contrary,

The righteous shall see, and fear,
and shall laugh at him, saying,
"See the man who would not make
God his refuge,
but trusted in the abundance of his riches,
and sought refuge in his wealth!"

8-9. *A Revolutionist's Song.*—Scorning God, Saul hid behind his wealth and trusted in riches; but he was confronted by an adversary who was more than a match for him. David the fugitive was none the less the poet. How odd a figure to choose as suggestive of the man who was to lead a successful revolution! **I am like a green olive tree in the house of God.** This is surely no martial image with which to arouse his fellow revolutionaries. Does it not indicate, after all, that the role forced on him was distasteful? He preferred not to think of himself as a mighty man of blood, but as a fruitful tree growing in the precincts of the temple.

His final word is a pledge and a prayer:

I trust in the steadfast love of God
for ever and ever.
I will thank thee for ever,
because thou hast done it [put destiny in his hands?].
I will proclaim thy name, for it is good,
in the presence of the godly.

This is a revolutionist's song such as David might have written. It stands as such in its own right, and in doing so it establishes the orthodox pattern of all revolutionary pieces. Three things the leader of revolution must do: he must make a case against the reigning powers; he must be convinced that they can be overthrown; and he must be confident of his own destiny as leader and of his ability to carry the struggle through.

The body of this song fits the need perfectly. We may assume that those who heard its ringing syllables knew what it meant and what it promised. Doeg was a mighty man. His hideous

9 I will praise thee for ever, because thou hast done *it:* and I will wait on thy name; for *it is* good before thy saints.

9 I will thank thee for ever,
because thou hast done it.
I will proclaim[d] thy name, for it is good,
in the presence of the godly.

[d] Cn: Heb *wait for*

92:12; Ecclus. 50:10). The righteous, recognizing God's hand in their blessedness—**because thou hast done it**—will thank God continually, and in the congregation of the godly proclaim his goodness. For **thy name** see Exeg. on 8:1-2; 9:9-10.

deed, done at Saul's order, was case enough against any king. Lidice in Czechoslovakia was reduced to a shambles in 1943 because an informer lived there. So was the city of Nob, millenniums before, and for the same reason. Saul's terrorism was obviously the result of his fear, and it was easy for common folk to foresee the final issue of such madness on the throne. In the meantime, Saul had forgotten his responsibility to the people. "Every one that was in distress, and every one that was in debt, and every one that was discontented, gathered themselves unto [David]" (I Sam. 22:2). Here was someone who was ready to do something *for* them; while Saul was planning to do something *to* them. **All the day you are plotting destruction,** David sang, and Nob was a preview of the extent to which Saul's determination to destroy opposition was prepared to go.

It was not enough to indict the king. Tyrants have made themselves secure before now; as their defenses are strengthened, their infamy deepens. Successful revolution depends much on shrewd timing. There is always a moment of weakness; no tyrant is safe twenty-four hours a day. If that interval can be seized, a breach may be made in the wall. God **will snatch and tear you from your tent,** David cried defiantly as he waited the strategic hour. The case against the king and the confident prediction of his overthrow are now made. There is the final step: revolution must have the sanction of something big enough to compel a following and promise success. With David it was **the steadfast love of God;** with other revolutionists, other sanctions.

However much or little we may relish it, the fact is that revolution has been one of the processes by which man has made his social adjustments and preserved social balances. For this reason it has always been true to say that our age—no matter to which one refers—is a revolutionary age. This is the case whether the violent change takes place within an economic, political, or religious context. There is therefore little point in lamenting that change has not always come about by gradual and evolutionary processes. Some social growths become so noxious that change of any sort, short of extirpation, seems impossible. "Every branch . . . that beareth not fruit he taketh it away" (John 15:2).

This is not to advocate revolution; it is to describe it. A great deal can be said about the folly, the wastefulness, and often the futility of revolution. Given time, men will learn wiser ways of coming to terms with situations that appear irremediable. We should be chastened by the fact that there are some elements within the Christian fellowship that see no hope for the coming of the kingdom of heaven on earth except through bloody revolution. The pattern will follow this song of David: the evil is monstrous; it can be overthrown; the leader has the sanction of the Most High. Revolution it will be—whether the sanction is proletarian, racial, or imperialist. Sometime men will work out the solution of social problems by methods that rest not on the rise and fall of power groups, but on universally accepted principles of moral and judicial law. Even then, however, the change will follow our revolutionist-poet's pattern: fixing the blame; predicting its rectification; accepting one's destiny and electing one's sanction.

This is the suggestion that David's defiance of Saul leaves with us, but from the longer perspective of the years between him and us, we are able to bring wiser judgment to the fact of revolution. Nathan, who appeared briefly in the study of Ps. 51, promised David that he would not die for his sin; but he warned him, "Now therefore the sword shall never depart from thine house" (II Sam. 12:10). Such was the case. His revolution put him on the throne; but he was to see his favorite son lead a revolution against him. This is because of the fact that, however successful the end results of violent revolution may be, there are auxiliary consequences which have in them the hurt, the frustration, the anger, and the bitter memories of which the poison of vengeance is brewed. Revolution breeds revolution.

Most will agree that our author has pitched the tone of revolutionary music high. There is much that is noble and little that is arrogant in claiming to go forth to battle under the aegis of **the steadfast love of God.** And yet it

To the chief Musician upon Mahalath, Maschil, *A Psalm* of David.

53 The fool hath said in his heart, *There is* no God. Corrupt are they, and have done abominable iniquity: *there is* none that doeth good.

To the choirmaster: according to Mahalath. A Maskil of David.

53 The fool says in his heart,
"There is no God."
They are corrupt, doing abominable iniquity;
there is none that does good.

LIII. The Ungodly and Their Fate (53:1-6)

Ps. 53 and Ps. 14 are variant forms of the same psalm, which owes its double appearance in the Psalter to its inclusion in two originally independent psalm collections. Although the text as presented in each of them is badly corrupt, it is on the whole better preserved in Ps. 53. In the versions the text of Ps. 14 has in vs. 3 been supplemented by lines drawn from 5:9; 10:7; 36:1; 140:3; Isa. 59:7-8, to elaborate the description of the wicked.

The interpretation of the psalm depends in part on the solution of the textual difficulties in vss. 4-5. Among these the principal one is the construing of the words at the end of vs. 4. Shall we follow the reading represented in the KJV and the RSV or shall we read, e.g., "Who eat up my people; they eat the bread of God, but call not [on him or his name]"? If the latter reading is adopted, then, since those who eat the bread of God are the priests (see Lev. 21:8, 17, 22), the psalmist is including members of the priestly caste among those who devour the people (cf. Mal. 2:7-8). If the other reading is adopted, then the prophetic invective is directed without distinction against all who show no fear of God in their ways.

In function the psalm is like Ps. 52, setting forth the doom which awaits the godless in the time when God intervenes on behalf of his people. The psalmist's words are directed to the correction of abuses with which he is familiar among his people in his day. In form, therefore, the psalm resembles Pss. 36; 52. The bitter feelings of the psalmist toward the contemporary perpetrators of iniquity are vented with abrupt prophetic vehemence (cf. Jer. 5:1-3; Isa. 59:1-8). His complaint witnesses in style and spirit to the persistence of the prophetic influence among the psalmists.

It is evident that the psalm was written at a time when practical atheism had appeared in the community of Israel. The specific charge of irreligiousness grows more common in the literature of the O.T. the closer we come to the Greek period, when through foreign influences the faith of many grew weak. The psalm belongs also to a time when many were looking to the eschatological hope as the solution of the problem for faith created by the prosperity of the wicked. The evidences therefore point to a late postexilic date. The meter is 3+2, except where it is obscured by textual corruptions.

1. The Depravity of Mankind (53:1-3)

53:1-3. In the opening verses we are introduced to the type of person against whom the prophet speaks. He is a **fool,** i.e., a man who scoffs at ethical and religious claims

---

is not high enough. How far this pattern for social readjustments is from the authentic Christian program for achieving the goodness of God can be seen by a simple experiment. Try to imagine Jesus quoting Ps. 52 before Pilate!

53:1-4. ***The Folly of Unbelief.***—How far our modern temper is from the distress the poet has compounded into this poem! Here is our versatile and volatile author in another mood. The rallying song of the revolutionary in Ps. 52 has given place for the moment to a lament, at the same time both scornful and sad, over the decline of religious faith. A forced connection between Pss. 52 and 53 might be made by pointing out that David's success against Saul was predicated on an unambiguous faith in the goodness of God. If this faith were lacking, manifestly his most potent weapon was lost, and the success of the revolution was unlikely. Such use of this poem, however, would be arbitrary and overly ingenious. It is more plausible to assume that it is what it seems to be: a sensitive and for

2 God looked down from heaven upon the children of men, to see if there were *any* that did understand, that did seek God.
3 Every one of them is gone back: they are altogether become filthy; *there is* none that doeth good, no, not one.

2 God looks down from heaven
upon the sons of men
to see if there are any that are wise,
that seek after God.

3 They have all fallen away;
they are all alike depraved;
there is none that does good,
no, not one.

(cf. 39:8; 74:22; Prov. 17:7). In his thoughts and plans he renounces God. He **says in his heart, "There is no God,"** or, better, "God is not here." He is a cynic and holds that God does not trouble himself with what is done among men. The psalmist is depressed by the moral and religious state of the people of his day. He sees God looking down **to see if there are any that are wise**—i.e., not of the class of the fools—and finding that **they have all fallen away,** backslidden, and become recreant to their God.

---

the moment depressed spirit reflecting upon the state of faith and morals, as though his theme were "The Folly and Wickedness of Men."

Heresy, which is a digression from an established and accepted majority pattern of thought or action, is always disconcerting. This is due to the fact first that it subtly asperses the pattern, and second that it overtly prescribes and encourages change. Change, for many and in many respects, is a bother, and a question may be impertinent. No matter for the moment that the word "heresy" comes from a Greek word meaning "school." Time was when the greatest heresy was a denial of the fact of God. This feeling still lingers, and in some quarters is very powerful. Statutes prohibiting one from holding office in some parts of the United States if he is an atheist are still on the books, though they are increasingly winked at. There is reasonable logic for this proscription. If God is the creator and sustainer of the universe, the source of our being and the proper object of devotion and service, a denial of him is a very sweeping and sometimes demoralizing thing.

If this is true in our times, fancy what it must have been like in the days when our author wrote. It is a significant fact that in all the literature of the O.T. there is no historic record either of a person who was known as a denier of God or of an argument disputing his existence. The wife of Job, who fortunately perhaps is unnamed, proposed to her harassed husband that he curse God and die. In a culture in which to deny God was to risk death, the spectacle or even the prospect of such a thing was terrifying.

Though not so stated here in this poem, it is likely either that the writer had encountered a brash and argumentative person who had announced his quittance of all bother with God, or he had conjured up the fiction in his mind. Either possibility would give him considerable concern, and being a poet, he would have his say about it. Again we must be reminded that we have here a poet's response to an irregular and disturbing situation, not a moral discourse on the meaning of atheism.

The fool says in his heart,
"There is no God."

This is a major prejudice, not a major premise. To be sure, one who says such a thing may be a fool, but he might be a philosopher. If he were, he would perhaps quietly turn to his accuser and propose that in the interests of understanding, or for the sake of argument, he define what he means by the words **fool** and **God.** For our poet, however, there was no such challenge. He quotes his man, fool or philosopher, and sweeps at once into a generalization, not about all deniers, but about everybody.

They are corrupt, doing abominable iniquity;
there is none that does good.

We would like to think this sweeping indictment was limited only to the blasphemous, but this exception is not allowed us. Here are unanimous apostasy, unanimous depravity, and unanimous moral impotence. The fool appears to be representative of humanity.

This reflects, of course, how grave a matter denial of God was in the eyes of the writer, and presumably in the common judgment of all men of his day. Starting with one man—real or imaginary—who was a **fool,** he arrived at a race of men who are unimaginably **corrupt.** Perhaps it was simply the poet's idea that an atheist was a fool. That might be allowed; but for God's search for a wise and righteous man to end in complete failure is something else alto-

4 Have the workers of iniquity no knowledge? who eat up my people *as* they eat
bread: they have not called upon God.
5 There were they in great fear, *where*
no fear was: for God hath scattered the
bones of him that encampeth *against* thee:
thou hast put *them* to shame, because God
hath despised them.
6 Oh that the salvation of Israel *were*

4 Have those who work evil no understanding,
who eat up my people as they eat bread,
and do not call upon God?

5 There they are, in great terror,
in terror such as has not been!
For God will scatter the bones of the ungodly;[e]
they will be put to shame,[f] for God has rejected them.

6 O that deliverance for Israel would come from Zion!

[e] Cn Compare Gk Syr: Heb *him who encamps against you*
[f] Gk: Heb *you will put to shame*

---

2. God's Judgment on the Ungodly (53:1-5)

4-5. But there is a day of retribution coming. **Have** [they] **no understanding?** Common sense ought to show them the folly of their conduct. Does experience teach that men can in their deeds leave God out of reckoning? For vs. 4 it is proposed by some (e.g., Gunkel, Schmidt, Duhm) to read about as follows:

הלא ידעו פעלי און אכלי עמי
אכלו לחם אלהים לא קראו שמו (=שם, vs. 5) :

"Have they no understanding, those who work evil, who devour my people? They eat the bread of God; they do not call on his name." Neither the sense nor the syntax obliges us to accept this hypothetical construction of the text. The LXX for both Ps. 14 and Ps. 53 seems to confirm the KJV and the RSV by its reading "those who eat up my people with [like] an eating of bread." The meter, however, is better supported by the above-cited proposal. In any case, instead of **there** (שם) at the beginning of vs. 5, read "his name" (שמו); and revise the text of vs. 4*c* to read, "and as for God they call not on his name." In vs. 5 there is an obvious duplication of the opening words; read הלא פחדו־פחד, "Shall they not be smitten with terror?" (See also C. C. Torrey, "The Archetype of Psalms 14 and 53," *Journal of Biblical Literature,* XLVI [1927], 186-92; Karl Budde, "Psalm 14 und 53," *ibid.,* XLVII [1928], 160-83.)

3. Hope for Israel's Deliverance (53:6)

6. Having forecast the terrors and shameful death that would overtake the corrupt and depraved men of his generation, the psalmist expresses his longing for and confidence in the day when God will appear in Zion and deliver Israel from all its evils (Isa. 59:20).

---

gether. Such a condition would demand summary treatment. Leaving aside for the moment that the search seems to have overlooked the writer, who presumably had lost neither his faith nor his probity, something had to be done even though the situation appeared to have got quite out of hand. No, on second thought it is not hopeless. There are good people left, but they are in great peril from the anthropophagous atheists.

Have those who work evil no understanding,
who eat up my people as they eat bread,
and do not call upon God?

5. ***Destroy the Heretics.***—There is only one thing for God to do: *écrasez l'infâme!* The judgment has been announced. We cannot soften it by assuming it to be doom falling on a few dangerous apostates, or even on a sizable segment of the arrogantly evil whom we might very well do without. Our poet has found one fool and gone on to discover that God has been unable to find a single wise man. Stupidity and godliness have become universal corruption, abominable iniquity, depravity, and figurative cannibalism!

6. ***The Poet Himself Is Not Sure.***—Yet it may be that things are not so desperate as to deny all

come out of Zion! When God bringeth back the captivity of his people, Jacob shall rejoice, *and* Israel shall be glad.

When God restores the fortunes of his
people,
Jacob will rejoice and Israel be glad.

---

hope. **Jacob will rejoice and Israel be glad** if and when **deliverance for Israel would come from Zion** and God would restore **the fortunes of his people.** We may assume the writer is thinking of deliverance from the corruption and **abominable iniquity** for which **the ungodly** are to blame. Obviously that is more of a predicament than the atheistic nonsense of a fool. At the same time, apostasy is linked all through this poem with the more overt forms of wickedness. It is not implausible to assume that the deliverance for Israel the poet hoped would come from Zion was deliverance from the dangerous heresy uttered by a fool. Might not also the restoration of the fortunes of his people have meant a return to vital faith? If infidelity was ruin, faith surely would be fortune.

Our poet's problem was clearly put in the **heart** of the **fool,** but it extended by implication to the behavior of everyone. That his heart committed the apostasy made him unfeeling and sullen, besides making him a fool. Mind and heart were allied in his conspiracy against God and man. After all, can they be kept wholly distinct? Or is there value in trying to keep them thus, when such inclusive matters as God and humanity are involved? We are admonished to love God with heart and mind and soul, and our neighbor as ourselves—which means with mind and heart and soul too. If these commandments are the result of ages of religious and social experience, it is likely that the great knowers of God have known him that way. But atheism in our time is not so simple a matter as our poet made it out. If it were the prating of a fool, it could either be discredited or instructed. If it were the certain cause of moral evil, many ethical problems might be easily settled. Not infrequently what is called atheism —disbelief in a particular idea about God, sometimes grotesque and not too seldom foolish —has been the sign of wisdom. Voltaire once told a story of two Athenians talking about Socrates, whom they had made out to be an atheist because he believed in only one god! Suppose he was an atheist on those terms. Was he therefore a wicked man?

The most important element in this study would then seem to be something that is implicit in the last two lines of the poem. We have commented on the mood swing that is to be observed in the writings attributed to David. His is a nimble soul—if the phrase may be allowed. From the heights of exaltation he plunges into the abyss of despair, to emerge presently in a leap to a new ecstasy. This made him, to the liturgists of a former time, the poets' poet; but it should be a warning that a correct understanding of what he says is not possible unless one understands his mood. Every mood is autonomous as long as it lasts, and its victim is sure of its infallibility for the duration; it is by this recognition that the violent contradictions in the writings attributed to David are to be reconciled.

The mood of Ps. 53 is not difficult to detect. It is morose to an extreme degree. Whether the fool was fictitious or real, he was to a certain extent so regarded because of the way in which the poet at the moment was looking at life. Nothing is more explicit than his picture of his unhappy state of mind. He is down in the dumps.

O that deliverance for Israel would come from Zion!
When God restores the fortunes of his people,
Jacob will rejoice and Israel be glad.

So also, we presume, will the poet! In such a temper the folly of one fool can make all humankind seem **corrupt** and **doing abominable iniquity.** A poet can even fall so low in his own perilous drift toward atheism that he sees God as busy in a painstaking search for one good man, and arriving at last at the melancholy conclusion that

there is none that does good,
no, not one.

In such a mood it is implied that God is blind or myopic, or his creation a vast moral frustration. So he breaks the atheists' bones!

The point is that a man's opinions about God are conspicuously affected by the mood he is in, whether he is denying God or writing a poem about an atheist. Surprisingly enough, in this poem the poet himself comes close to what to all intents and purposes is practical disbelief in God, though it would have shocked him to have had it pointed out. What, we might ask, more completely reduces God to grotesquerie than this splenetic man's picture of him breaking the bones of the atheists? It is that sort of statement that in our day, if not correctly understood, is repudiated by many morally sensitive persons. Their recoil hardly can be correctly described as a denial of God.

There are, one may assume, bona fide atheists

To the chief Musician on Neginoth, Maschil, *A Psalm* of David, when the Ziphim came and said to Saul, Doth not David hide himself with us?

54 Save me, O God, by thy name, and judge me by thy strength.

To the choirmaster: with stringed instruments. A Maskil of David, when the Ziphites went and told Saul, "David is in hiding among us."

54 Save me, O God, by thy name,
and vindicate me by thy might.

LIV. A Plea for Divine Intervention (54:1-7)

This short psalm presents the regular features of an individual lament with its appeal (vss. 1-2), complaint (vs. 3), petition (vss. 4-5), and vow (vss. 6-7). Its brevity and lack of individual color suggest that, like our general confessions, it served as a prayer for all who appealed to God for deliverance from men who sought their lives. Schmidt is of the opinion that the situation which called forth the psalm was that of suppliants who were about to face some form of trial by ordeal at the temple because of charges preferred against them by hostile persons (see Exeg. on 26:1-12). In any case, it is clear that the psalm speaks for those who have no hope for escape from deadly peril except by God's intervention (cf. Ps. 86).

There is no clear indication of date. We cannot be sure that the men who **do not set God before them** are the same as "the godless" (cf. Ps. 53) of the Greek period (Oesterley), since no more may be implied in the description of them than that **they do not set God** [as the avenger of wrong] **before them.** The **strangers** or "aliens" of vs. 3 is due to a copyist's mistake for **insolent men** (זרים for זדים), and hence offers no help for fixing the period to which the psalm belongs. The reference to David in the superscription is a conceit of scribal students, based on a fancied connection between vs. 3*b* and I Sam. 23:15.

The meter is 3+3; in vs. 3, because of the probable loss of a stich, it is 3+3+3.

1. Appeal to God (54:1-2)

54:1-2. Save me, O God, by thy name: The **name** of God was regarded almost as God's second self, his medium of operation in the world. To invoke the **name** is to

---

in our time. They may be fools, they may be blackguards, they may even be men after their fashion profoundly wise. There are others who for other reasons shout their denials of God. They may be lonely, or cruelly broken by illness or pain, or afraid. Adolphe Keller told Americans at the close of World War II that the basic religious problem of European Christians was the existence of God! If while victims of incredible suffering, and facing what has at times seemed the feeblest and most illusory of hopes, they should ask for proof of the living God, who is to insult them with this psalm's opprobrious epithet? The unhappy fool might have been lonely or afraid; or on a happier day for the writer he might have been written of as a saint. It would be interesting to have the judgment of the God he denied. It might not have concurred with the judgment of the poet.

54:1-7. ***The Setting of the Psalm.***—There is a limit to the variety of religious experience. While it is true, after a fashion, to say that everyone comes to the experience of God in his own unique way, it does not follow that every such encounter is different from every other. Since the authentic moods of the spirit are few, the compulsions they exert in the direction of God—or some other symbol of rescue or salvation—are not very many.

This poem is a lament. While there are many things to lament about, the lament experience is fairly uniform. It generally begins in a statement, often an overstatement, of one's predicament. To those whose life orientation is toward God, God is likely to be brought into the situation as savior, judge, or simply as confidant. From this point the recital of distress moves toward those who are the cause of it, described in sufficiently vigorous terms to discredit them completely. There may follow a cry for help.

Perhaps because most of us cannot be altogether honest with ourselves, we will imagine that we stand in a position superior to our adversary in order that redress may be more readily justified. If we can make out that we are injured innocence, God will more certainly

2 Hear my prayer, O God; give ear to the words of my mouth.

2 Hear my prayer, O God;
give ear to the words of my mouth.

---

invoke God's power, as the parallelism shows; hence, **vindicate me by thy might.** It is to God's **might** that the psalmist looks for defense against the power of his enemies, and it is the **name** and the **might** of God that the enemies have not taken into reckoning. The word דין, **vindicate,** means "render the justice due to me" (cf. 7:8), and implies here that the psalmist is looking for a favorable verdict in some legal or religious process that has been instituted against him.

---

come to our aid. Indeed, a part of this is the expressed confidence that God will not hesitate to take our side and administer proper justice. This in turn is followed by the correct ritual of thanksgiving, a sure sense of deliverance, and eyes bright with delight at the sight of one's enemies overthrown.

This is the fairly general pattern of a lament, conspicuously so where a sense of God is deeply a part of one's cultural environment. Even when God is not a factor in one's experience, when one is in straitened circumstances, the mood will also move from complaint to self-justification, to blame of others, and finally to a cry for rescue.

It is not surprising that the editors of the psalter should have found in the romantic record of David, the outlaw, a situation that could have been well described in the language of this psalm. The vendetta between the king and his putative successor is a wonderful tale, and since David was supposed to have been as assiduous a poet as he was a leader of guerrilla warfare, it was not difficult to imagine him, hidden in a cave or a leafy covert, pouring out his soul in a brief, poignant protest against the evil forces that pressed upon him. The Ziphites whom David had befriended had treacherously sent word to the king that his elusive enemy was hiding among them. David was indeed a rebel, but he had the warm friendship of Prince Jonathan at the court, whither he had been brought from the sheepfold at the initiative of others. The intrigue into which his simple tastes and inclinations were so soon woven, and his narrow escapes from death at the hands of the melancholy king, were enough to inspire the unhappy poet to lament his woes.

To ascribe this poem to such a person was a natural editorial conceit, and yet there is good reason for thinking that this is inaccurate. Perhaps this is better for us. Since most of us have moments of despair to which we must give expression, it will do us little good to imagine that only romantic heroes like David can write a lament. Plain folk can express their misfortunes in plain terms. Indeed, one reason for dismissing the idea that David wrote this when he was in the wilderness of Ziph is the fact that it exhibits almost too great restraint. Had we been David, would we not have let fly with wordy rage that would have seared the skin? To describe the treachery that had made him and his wretched friends hunted animals by such language as **strangers are risen up against me,** and his plight by such words as pursuit by **insolent men,** is hardly up to the grand occasion. They are strong words, but not strong enough.

It is this therefore that releases the poem for simpler folk and makes it the fairly common pattern of a common experience. Nevertheless, when misery lays its hand on the simplest person its touch is quite as unbearable for him as it is for the most glamorous. With this in view, and taking leave of the intriguing guess of the early anthologists, we may look at the poem as a fairly accurate setting forth of the average reaction to a situation in which one finds one's self helpless.

1-2. ***Address to God.***—There are three distinct ideas caught up here. Perhaps if the poet could have been aware of an editor looking over his shoulder as he wrote, he would have stated them in a reverse order. **Save, judge, hear,** he cries unto God. And yet a more reasonable sequence would be **hear, judge, save.** One's distress rarely allows for the niceties of sequence and climax, and maybe it is overfastidiousness to call attention to such things. To be sure, God must hear before he can pass judgment, and he will judge before he will save, but if one's agony is acute, the order of these responses does not much matter.

It is significant, however, that the analysis is complete, whatever we may think about the order. If one seeks redress for injustice, he must state his case with the assurance that after judgment has been rendered, it can be executed. This makes lament quite a different thing from an angry repudiation of God or justice, and quite equally a different thing from mere petulance or whimpering. It is, in effect, the difference between a case that can be judged and a mood that must be mollified. How important

3 For strangers are risen up against me, and oppressors seek after my soul: they have not set God before them. Selah.

3 For insolent[g] men have risen against me,
ruthless men seek my life;
they do not set God before them. *Selah*

[g] Another reading is *strangers*

2. The Psalmist's Evil Plight (54:3)

3. The psalmist gives the reason for his appeal. **Insolent men** is a general term to denote men who, seething with presumptuousness, self-confidence, and arrogance, put no bridle on their evil purposes. They are **ruthless men,** lit., "terror-inspiring men," and **they do not set God before them.** Such men **have risen against me, . . . seek my life.** The psalmist's plight is desperate in view of the odds against him. Vs. 3 recurs in Ps. 86:14.

this is may be seen by contrasting the Hebrew idea of a God of justice with those religious systems which are built about the hard core of Fate. If the order of things is so irreversibly set that good fortune and disaster will come along no matter what man may do to try to avert or escape them, then it does not make sense to ask for a hearing, a judgment, an action. Deep hidden in the Hebrew consciousness was the feeling that however cruel life might be, men were not inevitably its victims. There was relief to those who deserved it. It was important therefore that a man make as strong a case for himself as he could, and make it before as fair and powerful a judge as he could find. God was such a judge.

Thus when we put the words of vss. 1 2 in the sequence into which they naturally fall, we hear the poet saying: **Give ear to the words of my mouth** (vs. 2*b*); **hear my prayer, O God** (vs. 2*a*); **judge me by thy strength** (vs. 1*b*); and **save me . . . by thy name** (vs. 1*a*). The energy by which salvation is to come in the event that judgment is favorable is **thy name.** This is an exalted concept. But to us who speak of "big names" in all areas of life, and who recognize their potency, the concept is not strange. It is said that in the days of the French Revolution simply to worship the name of the Scarlet Pimpernel was to throw consternation into the ranks of the aristocracy. One wonders what would happen if the name of God were spoken with clarity, reverence, and verve in a great gathering, say a crowd at a baseball game. There is power in a name, power enough, in the words of our poet, to save; power enough in other matters to terrify or inspire. It would appear that the author of this lament believed that once his cause was heard, all that was necessary was that God should shout his name. That would assure him salvation from his enemies. They would be put to flight by the mighty sound.

3. *The Adversary.*—What about those who have discomfited the poet? Even before he has had a hearing, he produces a bill of indictment against his enemies. This is hardly testimony in a trial; it is rather an identification by the plaintiff of those he seeks to have brought before the bar of God's justice. Testimony as to what they have done will come later in the trial. For the moment it is enough to describe in general what sort of persons they are. Here again we find that reversing the order helps us to bring a cumulative effect to the description. These enemies are godless, they are violent, they are strangers. **They have not set God before them** (vs. 3*c*); **oppressors seek after my soul** (vs. 3*b*); **for strangers are risen up against me** (vs. 3*a*). We may be allowed to put it this way, for it heightens, we think, the effect of the plea for a just hearing.

To a man who trusted the justice of God, godlessness in an adversary was a very serious matter. To one who does not set God before him, justice may be a matter of little concern. Indeed, it may be a matter for contempt. We are learning this the hard way in our times, when our culture which leans heavily on the God we have set before us confronts another culture which has evicted God. To ask for justice under godless circumstances does not make sense; it makes rather for frustration and exasperation. The armistice negotiations that dragged on in 1952 and 1953 in Korea are a case in point. How is it possible ever to come to a just settlement of differences with those who repudiate what is the basis of our idea of justice?

Now it is just such persons as these who are correctly described by our poet (vs. 3*b*) as violent or insolent men. It is confidence in justice that makes swagger and insolence unnecessary. Courts of law are established in order to take the administration of crude justice out of the hands of noisy and arrogant men. Where we find men who are ruthless in the pursuit of their own ends and insolent in their repudiation of the simple necessities of common justice and

4 Behold, God *is* mine helper: the Lord *is* with them that uphold my soul.
5 He shall reward evil unto mine enemies: cut them off in thy truth.

4 Behold, God is my helper;
the Lord is the upholder[h] of my life.
5 He will requite my enemies with evil;
in thy faithfulness put an end to them.

[h] Gk Syr Jerome: Heb *of* or *with those who uphold*

---

3. Petition of Faith (54:4-5)

4-5. But know that **God is my helper;** with God's power (vs. 1) on his side the psalmist's weakness is turned to strength (cf. 18:29). **The Lord is the upholder of my life,** i.e., he grasps and holds it fast. So, confident in God's support, he expresses the hope that his enemies will meet the doom which they designed for him. **In thy faithfulness,** i.e., because of your steadfast loyalty to me, **put an end to them,** lit., "exterminate them." The type of men against whom the psalmist's anger tore explains in part this crass thirst for vengeance.

---

the exercise of law, we assume, as did our poet, that **they have not set God before them.** God has been replaced by their selfish or corrupt ambitions; the way of achieving their ends is violence, and their response to those who, in the light of a transcendent judge, would call them to book, is the laughter of derision and the contempt of arrogance.

To compound the infamy our poet points out that these hard and godless men are aliens, they are **strangers.** It is of no very great importance whether they were actually foreigners, though their repudiation of God and justice might indicate that they belonged to an alien culture. For the uses that we make of this poem it is more helpful to assume that their strangeness was not necessarily geographical or cultural. They did not know him. That was enough. And we must add that at this point we detect that note of special pleading that is difficult to keep out of a lament over one's misfortunes. It is a not too subtle sort of self-praise. It says in effect: If these people knew me, no matter how insolent and godless they might be, they would not misuse me as they do. All I ask is that my true nature be made known to them in a fair hearing before an impartial judge. Maybe they are so evil that even though my innocence is established, their fury will not abate. In that case God will have to destroy them. Still and all, it is the fact that we do not know each other that has made possible the feud that threatens to destroy me.

This is no idle fancy. Events in our times supply the evidence we need for its proof. We hear of curtains that divide us, iron, bamboo, and what not, and the evil of these barriers is that they create strangers in the earth. Where peoples are kept apart, suspicions grow and are wickedly cultivated. Those who have become strangers, who have been urged to rise up against us, appear to us to be exactly what our poet described—godless, insolent, and violent—and we can see what a peril lies in the creation and maintenance of barriers.

4-5. *The Poet's Confidence.*—In order to supply proper contrast between himself and his enemies, the poet also describes his allies. He has friends whom he identifies as **them that uphold my soul**—a delightful touch, exhibiting again the deep spiritual awareness of the writer. Today we might describe such friends as those who "boost our morale," but he, who has already named God as his helper, includes him now as one of the many that give support to his spirit. This is a fine testament of faith; it is what saves the lament from whining. For the poet has not merely indulged himself a moment of self-pity as he described his adversaries; he goes ahead to inventory his resources. Strangers who are vehement and godless are against him, but friends, among whom he counts God, are on his side. Furthermore, it is because he is confidently assured of the integrity of God (**cut them off in thy truth**) that he has no doubt about final escape from his predicament.

Here again we are reminded that the Hebrew mind was peculiarly sensitive to the importance of God in all experience. The poet called upon God because God would judge him in his **might.** But more important it was that God would requite the evil he was suffering, **in thy truth.** To combine might and truth in the performance of justice reaches a level of idealism that subsequent ages have not surpassed. Wherever justice rests simply on naked power, it is prone to despotism; where it rests alone on truth, it may suffer impotence. But where **might** and **truth** combine as the aids to justice, righteousness is done.

6 I will freely sacrifice unto thee: I will praise thy name, O LORD; for *it is* good.

7 For he hath delivered me out of all trouble: and mine eye hath seen *his desire* upon mine enemies.

6 With a free-will offering I will sacrifice to thee;
I will give thanks to thy name, O LORD, for it is good.
7 For thou hast delivered me from every trouble,
and my eye has looked in triumph on my enemies.

To the chief Musician on Neginoth, Maschil, *A Psalm* of David.

55 Give ear to my prayer, O God; and hide not thyself from my supplication.

To the choirmaster: with stringed instruments. A Maskil of David.

55 Give ear to my prayer, O God;
and hide not thyself from my supplication!

---

4. CONCLUDING VOW (54:6-7)

6-7. The psalmist vows in thanks a **free-will offering.** He will give not what is an obligation by the express terms of a vow, but what is a free, unbounded expression of his desire to honor God (cf. Num. 15:3; Lev. 7:16; Exod. 36:3-5). It will be accompanied with a song of thanksgiving, the theme of which is given in vs. 7.

LV. TWO VOICES UNITED IN APPEAL TO GOD (55:1-23)

This belongs to the class of psalms of lament. These laments, as we have seen, fall into two groups: laments of the individual, and laments of the people, of which the former comprise about one third of the total number of psalms in the Psalter. A lament consists normally of four parts: appeal, complaint, petition, and conclusion, i.e., vow, repetition of outcry, or expression of confidence. They are plainly discernible on a small scale in Ps. 54. The structure of Ps. 55, however, does not conform to the regular pattern of the type. The argument and the ordering of the parts are confused. It is

---

6-7. ***The Poet's Acknowledgment.***—When one's grievance is as clearly set forth, as in vss. 1-3, and one's confidence exhibited, as in vss. 4-5, the conclusion of the lament is foregone. There is nothing to be expected but a grateful acknowledgment of assured rescue. The **name of the LORD,** which in vs. 1 was to be the instrument of salvation, now becomes the theme for a shout of thanksgiving and the presentation of an offering out of the fullness of gratitude. Already the psalmist's mood exhibits a change. A moment ago he was calling for rescue; now he announces that God **hath delivered me out of all trouble;** and to his sense of escape is added the fierce satisfaction of seeing the obliteration of his persecutors accomplished before his eyes, **and my eye has looked in triumph on my enemies.**

There is more here, we believe, than the recorded experience of one man in trouble. From first to last we find the graph of our own moments of disquietude traced out before our eyes. Not least of these circumstances is the suddenness of this man's sense of escape. Can it be that once he confronted himself, his enemies, and God, and took careful account of the resources he was going to bring into the contest which at that moment seemed formidable, he had already won his victory?

There is much in this latter fact that interests us, since it is a common spiritual experience that latent fear, hostility, guilt, or uncertainty often need only to be confronted, assayed, weighed, understood, and exposed, to be vanquished. If this is what our melancholy friend discovered within such a relatively brief period of self-examination, does it not fit the pattern of our own experiences with many of the things about which we lament? This is the authentic spiritual record of numberless worriers who start with a cry for help and end with a shout of victory. And the wonder of it is that, by the grace of God, most of it has been achieved by their own inner resourcefulness.

55:1-23. ***Whose Utterance Is This?***—This poem, also in the traditional catalogue of David's writings, has given commentators no end of trouble. Speculations as to its origin

difficult to determine whether the verses devoted to the treacherous friend of the psalmist form an independent element in the psalm or are to be interpreted in relation to the rest of it. Then, as the individual enemy is addressed in the second person in vss. 13-14, but in the third person in vss. 20-21, we are uncertain whether the references relate to one or two individuals. Also, the petition of vs. 15 seems to anticipate awkwardly that of vs. 23, and the exhortation to patience and trust in vs. 22 is ill adjusted to the mood of vs. 23. In these circumstances there is considerable agreement among commentators that the difficulties in the interpretation of the psalm can best be resolved by assuming that it is composite. Otherwise we are compelled to defend the unity of the psalm, either by holding that it reflects a historical situation to which we cannot penetrate (Kittel), or by resorting to forced interpretations. Among those who regard the psalm as composite there are differences of opinion as to how the components are to be identified and disengaged. However, it seems best to assume that vss. 12-14, 20-21, 22 are fragments of a lament that by some accident were conjoined with another represented by vss. 1-11 (15), 16-19, 23. Schmidt holds that the psalm is a unity except for vss. 9*b*-11, 18*b*-19. Gunkel, on the other hand, regards the foreign element to be vss. 18*b*-21, 23. Both Schmidt and Gunkel, influenced by Ehrlich, find in the text of vss. 18*b*-19 the names Ishmael and Jaalam, and see in these verses the fragments of a charge against these Arab peoples. Ehrlich's rendering is ingenious but unconvincing. There are other instances of composite psalms (see Pss. 7; 18; 35; 36; 40). The fusing of the separate elements of this psalm may have occurred through circumstances such as we have noted in the Exeg. on 35:1-28.

The indications of date are not precise. The style (e.g., the introduction of a lyric note in a lament) and the language (e.g., רגש in vs. 14*b*) favor a postexilic date. Vs. 22 seems also to reflect a time when the pious needed to be assured of God's loyalty to the faithful, as also the notion that there are distinctions of level in Sheol (see **the lowest pit** in vs. 23).

The meter is almost without exception 3+2. The text of the psalm has suffered an unusual number of corruptions, but the versions are of considerable assistance in its restoration. The RSV represents for the most part an emended text.

1. Appeal to God (55:1-3*a*)

55:1-3*a*. The psalmist makes his appeal to the Lord. His cry is a loud one. **I am distraught:** The Hebrew word implies the cries or roars of a man who is rushing about distractedly. He is at his wit's end as he carries his case to God's ears. His enemies are in

---

have ranged all the way from somewhat reluctant acceptance of its Davidic authorship, emended and perhaps corrupted, to a composite authorship involving numerous writers. One thing is certain: it contains passages both of lyric beauty and pious devotion, and of abject and desperate fear. The former are familiar and often quoted: **Oh, that I had wings like a dove,** and **Cast thy burden upon the Lord, and he shall sustain thee;** the latter, fortunately perhaps, are largely forgotten.

It is this violent oscillation between devotion and desperation that supports the opinion that the poem had multiple authorship. That is not an implausible suggestion. On the other hand, such extremes of sentiment do not preclude single authorship, since it is always possible for a poet to reflect them. It has been said (Expos. on 51:1-19) that the most notable characteristic of the poems attributed to David is the wide variety of mood; already we have seen this exhibited not only in the variety of the poems, but in the variety of moods within single pieces as well. Unless the mood swing is too great to fall within the arc of the poet's ranging and unpredictable spirit, it does no violence to the canons of literary criticism to assume this to have been the work of one man.

Who the author was is another matter. It will be presently suggested that possible historic episodes in the life of David could have furnished the inspiration—or exasperation—of certain references in the body of the poem. If, on the other hand, the apparent reference to spe-

2 Attend unto me, and hear me: I mourn in my complaint, and make a noise;
3 Because of the voice of the enemy, because of the oppression of the wicked: for they cast iniquity upon me, and in wrath they hate me.

2 Attend to me, and answer me,
I am overcome by my trouble.
3 I am distraught by the noise of the enemy,
because of the oppression of the wicked.
For they bring[i] trouble upon me,
and in anger they cherish enmity against me.

[i] Cn Compare Gk: Heb *they cause to totter*

---

their way no less vociferous. He is **distraught by the noise of the enemy, . . . the oppression of the wicked** as they assail him with their slanders and accusations.

2. The Psalmist's Condition (55:3*b*-8)

3*b*-8. They bring trouble upon me: Lit., "they spread out trouble over me" like a net in order to envelop him as hunters trap their quarry and prepare for the killing. Hence because of the imminence of the end, **my heart is in anguish** with **terrors, . . . fear and trembling . . . and horror.** Schmidt holds that the psalmist is facing a situation like that of Ps. 54, and must undergo some ordeal or judgment of God to prove himself

---

cific persons and experiences is purely the imaginative flight of the poet's mind, there is no point in trying to identify them. Since our purpose is the discovery of the religious message that the ancient anthologists thought worth preserving, we assume either composite or single authorship. Many, however, lean to the latter, since exaltation and depression are both expressions of the religious mood, and not infrequently are found close by each other. A Chinese proverb says, "Sorrow is the child of ecstasy."

1-5, 9-21. ***Fears and Disasters.***—Our poet gives us in vs. 18 the context within which his spirit moves, **The battle that I wage.** This is not the sort of situation in which the mood of tranquillity is likely to be encountered. He expects to be safely delivered from the battle, but this confidence does not appreciably dull the anguish he suffers at the moment. When therefore he manages to escape momentarily from terror into rapture, it may be regarded either as a literary tour de force or the assertion of his indomitable spiritual vigor.

As is customary, the psalmist addresses his prayer to God, asking at once for overt attention and response.

> **Give ear to my prayer, O God;**
> **and hide not thyself from my supplication!**
> **Attend to me, and answer me,**
> **I am overcome by my trouble.**

His description of his condition follows in a series of words that move to a distinct crescendo of distress. His prayer is both supplication and lament; this is perhaps the darkest possible phase of the address to the Deity. He moans because of the noise and clamor of the ungodly adversary. Trouble is upon him; in anger his enemies are ranged against him; his heart is in anguish and the terror of death has fallen upon him. Fear and its physical concomitant, trembling, assail him, and he is overwhelmed by that most frightful of spiritual experiences, horror, a combination of extreme repugnance and dread. This description, found in vss. 3-5, presents, as has been said, a movement from a mood of relative composure to one of great agitation; from supplication to horror.

It is clear that while this is due to evil circumstances in which the poet himself is embroiled, there is more to it than his own private misfortune. **The city** (vss. 9-11) is as sorely beset as he is. Whether he is describing a state of siege from a point within or without the city is of no great matter. What he sees is clear enough. There are violence and strife in the city. Bands of sentinels or marauders are on her walls day and night, and in the streets there are mischief, trouble, and ruin. Pictures of looting, lawlessness, destruction, and the ravages of hunger and sickness—these are not difficult to imagine as he enumerates them. Nor is it the external enemy alone who is despoiling the place:

> **Oppression and fraud**
> **do not depart from its market place.**

The upsurging elements that seize upon confusion to glut their lust for power—extortion, black market, and blackmail—are rife in those centers of population from which order has fled

4 My heart is sore pained within me:
and the terrors of death are fallen upon me.
5 Fearfulness and trembling are come
upon me, and horror hath overwhelmed me.

4 My heart is in anguish within me,
the terrors of death have fallen upon me.
5 Fear and trembling come upon me,
and horror overwhelms me.

---

innocent of the charges of his foes. For this reason, doubtless, Schmidt regards the references to the civil evils in vss. 9-11 as extraneous material. But if the verses are viewed as integral to the psalm, then the psalmist seems to be involved in some political

---

before the advance of an army, and these are components of the avalanche of horror that buries the soul.

The crowning infamy of which the psalmist is the victim lies, however, not in the threat of the enemy who assails him nor in the ruin that levels the city. This is havoc that one expects in the midst of strife, and against which one is able to marshal some measure of defense. It calls for resolution and courage, and is often overcome. But when those who were once one's friends, or were at least thought to be, turn out to be enemies, a spiritual wound is inflicted more grievous than physical suffering. It is in the two passages covered by vss. 12-14, 20-21 that the apex of the poet's torture is reached.

It is not an enemy who taunts me—
then could I bear it;
it is not an adversary who deals insolently with me—
then I could hide from him.

What is more insufferable than the taunt and the insolence of a former friend, one for whom the former confidences of friendship have suddenly become the weapons of an enemy? Such a friend this one had been. The poet describes him: **My equal, my companion, my familiar friend.**

We used to hold sweet converse together;
within God's house we walked in fellowship.

Few more mordant descriptions of treachery are to be found anywhere in literature than the words of vss. 20-21.

It is interesting to raise the question as to the identity of this villain. Assuming for the moment that the psalm may be linked in whole or in part with David, it is not difficult to find in his experience episodes in which such a person might well have appeared. The Ziphites might have furnished him; the Keilahites who, after being saved from the Philistines by David's daring, turned informer to the king, could have been collectively indicted in a passage like vss. 20-21. These, however, are dubious guesses. Of all the intimate contacts preserved in the record of David's life, two stand out as coming close to the intimations of the poem. Jonathan is well represented as **my equal, my companion, my familiar friend.** The **sweet converse together,** the **fellowship** in **God's house,** recall the experiences these bonded companions had, an attachment of such strength and tenderness as has made it one of the symbols of great friendship in and for all time. But Jonathan could not have committed the treachery detailed so bitterly by our poet unless there is something in the story of their fealty that has been omitted or lost. Jonathan died beside his royal father in battle against the Philistines, and David's lament for both his king and his prince-companion (II Sam. 1:19-27) is a noble and eloquent panegyric. Had there been a break between Jonathan and David, he could not have sung his "song of the Bow, . . . written in the book of the upright."

Saul makes an easier mark for those who would let fly at villainy. From the first meeting of the two there was something equivocal in the attitude of the king toward the romantic young shepherd. He loved him, honored him, and humiliated him, he made him his son-in-law and a fugitive from the court. Vss. 20-21, were they all we know of David's moods, describe Saul's erratic behavior exactly:

My companion stretched out his hand against his friends,
he violated his covenant.
His speech was smoother than butter,
yet war was in his heart;
his words were softer than oil,
yet they were drawn swords.

It is not difficult for us to understand Saul's condition as mental illness; it is not unlikely indeed that David also knew he was mad, and that the description in vss. 20-21 is a diagnosis of his divided personality. David also had his moods; he was quite as capable of crying out in reproach against the king's treachery as he was to laud him as he lamented his death, "Saul and Jonathan were lovely and pleasant in their lives" (II Sam. 1:23). The grounds therefore for definite allocation of the object of our

6 And I said, Oh that I had wings like a
dove! *for then* would I fly away, and be at
rest.
7 Lo, *then* would I wander far off, *and*
remain in the wilderness. Selah.
8 I would hasten my escape from the
windy storm *and* tempest.
9 Destroy, O Lord, *and* divide their
tongues: for I have seen violence and strife
in the city.
10 Day and night they go about it upon
the walls thereof: mischief also and sorrow
are in the midst of it.
11 Wickedness *is* in the midst thereof:
deceit and guile depart not from her streets.

6 And I say, "O that I had wings like a
dove!
I would fly away and be at rest;
7 yea, I would wander afar,
I would lodge in the wilderness, *Selah*
8 I would haste to find me a shelter
from the raging wind and tempest."

9 Destroy their plans,[j] O Lord, confuse
their tongues;
for I see violence and strife in the city.
10 Day and night they go around it on its
walls;
and mischief and trouble are within it,
11 ruin is in its midst;
oppression and fraud
do not depart from its market place.

[j] Tg: Heb lacks *their plans*

---

or party strife within the city. **Oh that I had wings like a dove!** In lyric words, in striking contrast to the cacophonous notes of the preceding lines, the psalmist expresses a longing for the swift, free wings of a dove to carry him away from the imprisonment of his evil environment, **from the raging . . . tempest.**

3. Malediction on Enemies (55:9-11, 15-19, 23)

9-11. The psalmist interrupts the account of his troubles with a malediction on his enemies (vs. 9*a*), and then resumes with a description of the confusion that reigns in the city. The interruption is odd at this point and the text is doubtful. Gunkel would read in continuance of vs. 8, "from the destructive storm of their throats, from the flood of their tongues" (מסער בלע גרנם מפלג לשנם). At any rate, the city is the scene of internecine conflicts. **Violence and strife** go round about it, alert and sleepless like

---

writer's recriminations are largely speculative. Saul, we must admit, was capable of the sinister and shadowy betrayals of which David was certainly the victim. David, on the other hand, was not incapable of ambiguity. There is an easy choice between a madman and a poet, though in this particular case not enough to prove an indictment.

6-23. ***Man's Response to Life's Conflicts.***—There remain three other aspects of the poem that deserve attention and that can be studied with more realistic profit than mere speculation. Brief reference has been made to the famous vss. 6-8, in which the poet wishes for the wings of a dove; also to the equally memorable words of exhortation offered as much to himself as to others: **Cast your burden on the Lord** (vs. 22). Between these two somewhat opposite moods lies another: it represents the anguished and defeated man calling on God to avenge his sorrows on the adversary. **Destroy their plans, O Lord, confuse their tongues** (vs. 9*a*); **let death come upon them** (vs. 15); **cast them down into the lowest pit** (vs. 23*a*); **they keep no law, and do not fear God** (vs. 19*b*).

There are represented in these three groups of verses (vss. 6-8, 9-21, 22-23) three patterns of spiritual reaction that are very familiar. They are indeed so common to universal human experience that they bring unity out of a poem which in other respects has perplexed commentators by its diversities. There are, after all, three ways in which men respond to the bitterness of life's conflicts. We recall that our writer describes himself as in the midst of a battle he is waging, and that his enemies are both public and private; they are arrayed against him and against the city. This in itself is an important moral insight: however poignant one's own sense of suffering or outrage or peril, it cannot exhaust the totality of pain. This man was all but broken by the most cowardly of betrayals, that of a trusted and beloved friend. Except for the sense that God has falsified his love by deliberate and perverse deception, the perfidy of a confidential friend is the most shattering of spiritual experiences. And yet, terrible

12 For *it was* not an enemy *that* reproached me; then I could have borne *it:* neither *was it* he that hated me *that* did magnify *himself* against me; then I would have hid myself from him:
13 But *it was* thou, a man mine equal, my guide, and mine acquaintance.
14 We took sweet counsel together, *and* walked unto the house of God in company.
15 Let death seize upon them, *and* let them go down quick into hell: for wickedness *is* in their dwellings, *and* among them.
16 As for me, I will call upon God; and the LORD shall save me.
17 Evening, and morning, and at noon, will I pray, and cry aloud: and he shall hear my voice.
18 He hath delivered my soul in peace from the battle *that was* against me: for there were many with me.

12 It is not an enemy who taunts me —
then I could bear it;
it is not an adversary who deals insolently with me —
then I could hide from him.
13 But it is you, my equal,
my companion, my familiar friend.
14 We used to hold sweet converse together;
within God's house we walked in fellowship.
15 Let death[k] come upon them;
let them go down to Sheol alive;
let them go away in terror into their graves.[l]

16 But I call upon God;
and the LORD will save me.
17 Evening and morning and at noon
I utter my complaint and moan,
and he will hear my voice.
18 He will deliver my soul in safety
from the battle that I wage,
for many are arrayed against me.

[k] Or *desolations*
[l] Cn: Heb *evils are in their habitation, in their midst*

---

watchmen on the walls, and within it there are **mischief and trouble** and **ruin,** together with corrupt practices in buying and selling and fraudulent decisions by judges in the city's gates. The scene of this wickedness is doubtless Jerusalem.

12-14. See Exeg. on vss. 12-14, 20-21 below.

15-19, 23. The psalmist calls on God to bring on his perfidious, godless foes the doom that is meet for them—early death (vs. 23*a*) and the bottommost place in Sheol (vs. 23*b*). **They keep no law:** Lit., "no sworn agreements."

4. Another Psalmist Describes His Condition (55:12-14, 20-21)

12-14, 20-21. For this fragment of another lament we lack the introductory appeal to the Lord for help. It may have been similar to vss. 1-3. In any case, we are introduced

---

as was this shock, it did not desensitize him to the troubles of others in the city who were the victims of oppression and fraud. "One touch of nature makes the whole world kin," [2] we have been told; but too often if the touch is too heavy or too frequent, it desensitizes us to the wider miseries of the world.

How, then, do I react to **the battle that I wage?** It is here that our psalmist supplies us with clear answers. The first impulse is to escape. He was neither the first nor the last to want **wings like a dove** (vs. 6) to carry him far away to rest in a lodge in the wilderness, a shelter from the raging wind and tempest. And yet in the plaintive note of this lyric wish there is an overtone of doubt. It may not always be cowardly to wish to get away from it all; but it is nearly always futile. To retreat to Eden, we have said, is as fatal to the soul as to leap to Elysium. In the sweat of his face shall man eat bread: this is the first mandate of life. Man shall not be exempt from struggle.

Since doves' wings cannot lift the weight of the human soul, man turns to another and somewhat more realistic expedient: he asks God to destroy the oppressor who hectors him. **Destroy their plans, O Lord, confuse their tongues** (vs. 9). This, it may be observed, is little preferable to the wish to escape. It may even be called evasive, lazy, irresponsible, unheroic. Perhaps; but when all this is said, it still remains a reaction to the battle that is familiar to all normal spiritual experience.

One will therefore sooner or later come to the realization that to ask God to wipe out the

[2] Shakespeare, *Troilus and Cressida,* Act III, scene 3.

19 God shall hear, and afflict them, even he that abideth of old. Selah. Because they have no changes, therefore they fear not God.

20 He hath put forth his hands against such as be at peace with him: he hath broken his covenant.

21 *The words* of his mouth were smoother than butter, but war *was* in his heart: his words were softer than oil, yet *were* they drawn swords.

22 Cast thy burden upon the LORD, and he shall sustain thee: he shall never suffer the righteous to be moved.

19 God will give ear, and humble them,
he who is enthroned from of old;
because they keep no law,[m]
and do not fear God. *Selah*

20 My companion stretched out his hand
against his friends,
he violated his covenant.
21 His speech was smoother than butter,
yet war was in his heart;
his words were softer than oil,
yet they were drawn swords.

22 Cast your burden[n] on the LORD,
and he will sustain you;
he will never permit
the righteous to be moved.

[m] Or *do not change*
[n] Or *what he has given you*

---

abruptly to the grounds of the psalmist's outcry. Commentators who integrate these verses with the rest of the psalm find a warrant by emending vs. 18*b* so that it reads מקרבים לי, "from them that are near to me," instead of מקרב לי, **from the battle,** a conjectural remedy of an uncertain text. The psalmist is the victim of the treacherous betrayal of an intimate friend. **Sweet converse** is a translation of a word (סוד) which means the most intimate exchange of **counsel. We walked in fellowship,** i.e., with sympathy of purpose (for the word רגש see J. A. Montgomery, *A Critical and Exegetical Commentary on the Book of Daniel* [New York: Charles Scribner's Sons, 1927; "International Critical Commentary"], p. 272, but **he violated his covenant,** covering his actions with deceit and double-dealing. **His speech was smoother than butter:** A better reading (LXX, Syriac) is "his face."

5. A Comforting Word (55:22)

22. This verse seems to be a word of priestly admonition and comfort to the man who rocked under the most painful of blows (cf. Matt. 26:23). Though friends break faith, **the LORD . . . shall never suffer the righteous to be moved.**

---

assailant is more often than not to invite disappointment. The second mandate of life, then, is that one must face up to the fact of the enemy. God will not be likely to sweep the battlefield clear of the foe because, sorely beset, we ask him to. There will follow then the third reaction our poet mentions.

Cast your burden on the LORD,
and he will sustain you;
he will never permit
the righteous to be moved.

Again it is easy to dismiss this as slight if indeed any advance on our first two reactions. To flee the battle, to ask God to destroy the enemy, to cast one's battle burden on the Lord—are these not all of one piece of evasion? So one may answer, perhaps; and yet for our poet it may not have been so. There is hidden in this familiar exhortation the testament of strong faith. Man must have help in his struggle; he cannot go it alone. He is wise therefore if he seeks his aid where he is confident there will be no default.

He will never permit
the righteous to be moved.

Added to his confidence, moreover, is a tacit dedication to righteousness, for it is only the victory of the righteous concerning which our poet can be confident. The third mandate of life is therefore so to order one's conduct of the battle that he who helps to bear the burden of the righteous will lighten the load. That much is an important gain; it is as much perhaps as one may properly ask of God.

Our poet has not encompassed the whole problem. Elsewhere we may expect him to have

23 But thou, O God, shalt bring them down into the pit of destruction: bloody and deceitful men shall not live out half their days; but I will trust in thee.

23 But thou, O God, wilt cast them down
into the lowest pit;
men of blood and treachery
shall not live out half their days.
But I will trust in thee.

To the chief Musician upon Jonath-elem-rechokim, Michtam of David, when the Philistines took him in Gath.

56 Be merciful unto me, O God: for man would swallow me up; he fighting daily oppresseth me.

To the choirmaster: according to The Dove on Far-off Terebinths. A Miktam of David, when the Philistines seized him in Gath.

56 Be gracious to me, O God, for men
trample upon me;
all day long foemen oppress me;

---

23. See Exeg. on vss. 15-19, 23.

LVI. Plea for Deliverance (56:1-13)

This belongs to the same class as Pss. 54–55. It is the cry of a soul for help at a time when his enemies **band themselves together** and, like wild beasts with watering mouths, stalk his steps to find evidence through which they can accomplish some evil design against him. The evil design is not made known to us; it may have been ruin of reputation, deposition from office, loss of property, or even death. The large place in the Psalter occupied by complaints against personal enemies gives us a sad picture of the environment in which not only the authors of the psalms but all who used their words in synagogue, in home, or at the temple lived their days. Their occupation with the struggle against the threats of human foes in this temporal world weakened their perception of the deadly foes which "war against the spirit" (cf. I Pet. 2:11; Rom. 8:38-39; Eph. 6:16). The tensions provoked by unhappy human relations in a community repress the development of "the fruits of the Spirit."

The psalm follows the familiar pattern of a lament. Its theme is not relieved by any novel element such as the lyric passage in 55:1-8 which Mendelssohn set to music in his motet, "Hear My Prayer." The text has suffered in transmission. Among those who have given thought to its recovery are some who think that vss. 4, 10-11 are a refrain which originally appeared also between vs. 7 and vs. 8 and after vs. 13 (cf. Briggs, Oesterley). But since a refrain is not proper to either the form or the purpose of a lament, the notion of a refrain here is not to be entertained. Vs. 4 is most probably a variant of vss. 10-11 which found its way into the text from a marginal gloss.

---

something to say about the heroism of the man who appears to lose his battle to a stronger antagonist, and that will provide him another mood. He will have no difficulty expressing it. For the moment, then, we will accept what he has to say, whoever he was, since he has laid a sure finger on us, whoever we are. We shall still wish to fly, to let God win our battles, and to cast our burdens upon him, and these may be the necessary spiritual preliminaries to the successful waging of warfare both within our own hearts and in the threatened precincts of the city where others also are embattled.

56:1-13. ***Questions of Origin and Authorship.*** —The ancient editors assigned this poem to David, and found in his dealings with Achish king of Gath its historic basis (I Sam. 27:1–28:2; 29:1-11). Later scholars adduce reasons for denying this identification, but are not in agreement on the poem's date or occasion. If the earlier judgment is right, it is not without reason. To be sure, there is no single reference in the poem either to the Philistines or to the petty king of Gath. The same poem might have been written to express the fugitive hero's state of mind in a score of predicaments. It is a general prayer and lament, and its expressions of bold faith and unshaken devotion can be seen to fit general demands. At the same time, it is always a specific experience on which generalizations are made, and there is much in David's stay among the Philistines that could have immediately evoked or afterward suggested such a poem.

2 Mine enemies would daily swallow *me*
up: for *they be* many that fight against me,
O thou Most High.
3 What time I am afraid, I will trust in
thee.
4 In God I will praise his word, in God
I have put my trust; I will not fear what
flesh can do unto me.
5 Every day they wrest my words: all
their thoughts *are* against me for evil.

2 my enemies trample upon me all day
long,
for many fight against me proudly.
3 When I am afraid,
I put my trust in thee.
4 In God, whose word I praise,
in God I trust without a fear.
What can flesh do to me?

5 All day long they seek to injure my cause;
all their thoughts are against me for
evil.

The indications of date are not definite. But the belief in a record book in which God notes every particular of a person's life (vs. 8) suits a postexilic date (cf. 69:28; 139:16; Mal. 3:16; Job 19:23; Matt. 10:30). The meter was designed to be 3+3.

1. Appeal to God (56:1-4)

56:1-4. The appeal of the psalmist follows the familiar form. In Book II of the Psalter (Pss. 42–72) the divine name, **God,** displaces almost regularly Lord (see Exeg. on 42:1-5). **Many fight against me proudly:** The last word is probably a corruption of a word which opened the next line. So for מרום, **Most High,** read רממני, "save me"; and translate, "Save me in the day when I fear." Vs. 4, as has been explained, is a variant of vss. 10-11. It is too early to introduce in the lament a word of confidence.

2. The Psalmist's Foes (56:5-6*a*)

5-6*a*. The foes are described as wild beasts lurking for prey. The figure is not uncommon in the Psalter.

Be that as it may, and whether or not the psalm was related directly to David, it expresses what might have been true for him, and what has been true for many a soul since: the downswing and upswing between despair and the lift of the spirit into exalted faith. It has given to our heritage the affirmation so greatly familiar in Christian liturgics: "In God have I put my trust; I will not be afraid; what can flesh do unto me?" Did not General Bernard Montgomery in World War II conclude an address to his men during the Normandy campaign with those bold words?

1-4. ***Cry for Help, and Trust in God.***—We do not know, nor is it essential that we should know specifically, against whom our poet's bitter lament is lifted. His heart cries out:

Be gracious to me, O God, for men trample upon me;
all day long foemen oppress me.

This is vigorous language. Trampling men are those whose physical exertion is far beyond the leisurely or casual stage. To their pursued quarry they are like dogs on a hot scent, so avid for success that they press the chase to the utmost limits of their strength. It is an unresting pursuit—**all day long**—and their eyes are as eager as their lolling tongues and their convulsive breath; and—what predatory animals lack—there is bitterness in their relentless pressure. This danger is beyond the limits of protection that even the most cautious vigilance can guarantee; the hunted is afraid. Fear, a faithful sentinel, is, however, not always a dependable ally. The one pursued must sharpen his wits and at the same time quiet his heart. He cannot trust those with whom he lives; nor is there hope beyond the border. **When I am afraid,** he says, **I put my trust in thee.** It is interesting that he does not abandon all his trust in other possible aid. Men are trustworthy up to a certain point, he would say. The difficulty is that one must withhold absolute trust, because one knows one's fellows through one's knowledge of one's self. With God, however, the case is different. If one doubts the word of men, it is often a defensive precaution; but

In God, whose word I praise,
in God I trust without a fear.
What can flesh do to me?

5-7. ***Uncertainty About Rescue.***—This is what we call a rhetorical question, and lest his ene-

6 They gather themselves together, they hide themselves, they mark my steps, when they wait for my soul.

7 Shall they escape by iniquity? in *thine* anger cast down the people, O God.

8 Thou tellest my wanderings: put thou my tears into thy bottle: *are they* not in thy book?

9 When I cry *unto thee,* then shall mine enemies turn back: this I know; for God *is* for me.

6 They band themselves together, they lurk,
they watch my steps.
As they have waited for my life,
7 so recompense[o] them for their crime;
in wrath cast down the peoples, O God!

8 Thou hast kept count of my tossings;
put thou my tears in thy bottle!
Are they not in thy book?
9 Then my enemies will be turned back
in the day when I call.
This I know, that[p] God is for me.

[o] Cn: Heb *deliver*
[p] Or *because*

---

3. Plea for God's Vengeance (56:6*b*-9)

6*b*-9. The psalmist petitions God for vengeance commensurate with the purpose of those who maliciously pursue him. He reinforces his appeal by stating two grounds for God's intervention on his behalf: **my trust in thee** (vs. 3), and **my tossings, . . . my tears.** The text of vs. 8 is not certain. Read, "Record in thy book my tossings." **Put thou my tears in thy bottle!** Because of the boldness and novelty of the thought and of our ignorance

---

mies taunt him with an answer, the psalmist supplies a partial one himself; at least he tells what flesh would like to do to him! This is clear enough. **All day long they seek to injure my cause; . . . they lurk, they watch my steps.** What **cause** is referred to here? The revolution he was leading? His effort to protect his followers, concealed within the relatively safe regiments of Saul's enemy? Or was it some loftier cause: the vindication of a man's faith in God? We do not know; but like so many hunted men, men who have believed themselves patriots and have proved themselves so to be, this man identifies himself with something greater than his own personal security. He has a cause, and the evil thoughts of ruthless men are directed no less against his cause than against his life. Conspiracy (**they band themselves together**), ambuscade (**they lurk**), surveillance (**they watch my steps**), these are enough to engender distrust of men and, paradoxically, unless one is irreversibly embittered, at the same time encourage trust in God. Little wonder, then, that vs. 7 calls on God to recompense the trust of his servant by avenging the crimes of his enemies.

8. ***Self-pity.***—The effect of constant pressure upon the psalmist is summed up in a verse that is as unusual as it is mildly amusing. One does not smile at the discomfort of another, but it is possible that our poet saw and deliberately intended the whimsical note he introduced. It is inevitable that those who are afflicted by insomnia should toss restlessly during the long hours of sleeplessness. Perhaps in the effort to beguile their tedium they count imaginary sheep jumping over a fence. Here, however, is the somewhat surprising suggestion that God has kept a record of his twisting and turning during the long nights when he dared not or could not go to sleep. And as for his tears, surely here we have hyperbole of the most extreme sort. So extreme indeed is the word translated **bottle** that early renditions have hardly dared to use it. In the traditional Hebrew text it specifies a large wineskin, and in no way can properly be taken to refer to the little glass tear bottles found by burrowing archaeologists and assumed to be the dainty accessory of tearful females. There are, for our searching, modern colloquial phrases that closely parallel this extravagant description of a tortured and tearful night. **Thou hast kept count of my tossings,** the sleepless poet observes; **put thou my tears into thy bottle: are they not in thy book?** It was a truly harassed man who could speak in one line of God in wrath casting down his strong enemy, and in the next asking that his tears be caught in a wineskin and their volume be recorded in God's book.

9-13. ***Reassertion of Trust.***—But now, even if perhaps with a hint of weariness from his long crying, the poet exclaims, **I know, that God is for me. Then my enemies will be turned back . . . when I call.** There follows the zestful re-

10 In God will I praise *his* word: in the
LORD will I praise *his* word.
11 In God have I put my trust: I will not
be afraid what man can do unto me.
12 Thy vows *are* upon me, O God: I will
render praises unto thee.
13 For thou hast delivered my soul from
death: *wilt* not *thou deliver* my feet from
falling, that I may walk before God in the
light of the living?

10 In God, whose word I praise,
in the LORD, whose word I praise,
11 in God I trust without a fear.
What can man do to me?

12 My vows to thee I must perform, O God;
I will render thank offerings to thee.
13 For thou hast delivered my soul from death,
yea, my feet from falling,
that I may walk before God
in the light of life.

---

of the use of tear bottles among the ancients, some would read for בנאדך, **in thy bottle,** נגדך, "before thee," but the idea is not inconsistent with ancient Semitic thought (cf. Job 14:17; Hos. 13:12). "Then my enemies must be discomfited" and turned to flight like a defeated army.

4. THE PSALMIST'S BASIC CONFIDENCE IN GOD (56:10-13)

10-11. God is for me: Therefore, the psalmist expresses his confidence. **In God I trust without a fear:** The text of vs. 10*a* is uncertain. Calès translates, "with Elohim's help, I praised his promise"; Gunkel, "In God I shall bring my cause to success" (אכלכל דברי).

12-13. In the fullness of his assurance the psalmist speaks as if his triumph had already come.

---

frain to which reference has already been made (vss. 10-11). The psalmist has now reached the top of his upswing. Vss. 12-13 are the lyric words of a heart ready to worship. **Vows** are to be performed and **thank offerings** rendered. Left behind are scheming men, the suspicion, the fear, the sleepless nights, the torrent of tears, in which he appeared so hopelessly involved. Deliverance is already accomplished, and he now stands erect and walks sedately before God with a flood of light enveloping him.

It is the last line of the poem which gives us, whether the poet so intended it or not, the essence of his faith; and it is this that has made his poem worthy of inclusion in the anthology of a great devotional literature. There are no depths unplumbed by his moments of terror, just as there is to him nothing so trivial that God will overlook it. Trampling foemen and falling tears—these are the measure of his gloom; but God's stout hand striking out in vengeance and keeping a tear record in a book —these are the measure of his happiness. They are nothing more nor less than a poetic way of saying that the light falling across the pathway of life shows that these are the things of which human life is made: danger and sorrow, lovingkindness and success. To some the contrast constitutes a reason for turning from God. These are perhaps they who want life to be all happiness—or all woe. Not so our writer: he will look at himself in the illuminating light that falls from human experience and **walk before God.** This is the mood of religious realism and faith.

There is one further point to be made. Twice the psalmist asks the question: **What can man do to me?** That the first time **flesh** is used for **man** is of no particular importance. This question, for those who think seriously about life, probes to great depths. It asks, in effect, whether there is something in every man's experience that is inviolably his own, some area of the soul so private and proscribed to the touch or the inquiry of another that it cannot actually be reached by any save God. If this is so—and it is the essence of the Christian concept of the worth and inviolability of the individual soul—it has clear expression here in the insight of our often unhappy poet. Without it one doubts that he could have endured the torture, the tossings, and the tears; with it he can walk before God in the light of life. We recall naturally the word of another who said: "Do not fear those who kill the body but cannot kill the soul" (Matt. 10:28).

To the chief Musician, Al-taschith, Michtam of David, when he fled from Saul in the cave.

57 Be merciful unto me, O God, be merciful unto me: for my soul trusteth in thee: yea, in the shadow of thy wings will I make my refuge, until *these* calamities be overpast.

To the choirmaster: according to Do Not Destroy. A Miktam of David, when he fled from Saul, in the cave.

57 Be merciful to me, O God, be merciful to me,
for in thee my soul takes refuge;
in the shadow of thy wings I will take refuge,
till the storms of destruction pass by.

LVII. Prayer in the Midst of Danger (57:1-11)

The theme of this psalm, like that of Ps. 56, is an appeal of a godly soul to the Most High for deliverance from the plots of bloodthirsty enemies. Both psalms begin with the same words **Be merciful to me, O God,** followed by an affirmation of trust in God's good will, and both end with expressions of strong confidence that the answer to their prayers is at hand. In each also there appears to be a refrain through the double recurrence of a verse (56:4, 10-11; 57:5, 11), but the appearance is specious since, apart from the fact that a refrain is not proper to a lament, the context evidences that 57:5, like 56:4, owes its presence in the text to a scribal error or faulty editorial taste (cf. 59:9, 17; 62:2, 6).

The purpose of this psalm, as indicated above, is clear and consistent; it is a lament coupled with a hymn of thanksgiving in payment of the implied vows to God for his expected help. But the substance of the psalm is composed of two psalms, or parts of two psalms, originally independent, vss. 1-4, 6 and vss. 7-11. The literary relationship between the two sections is weak, the second exhibiting some elements of imagination and originality (vss. 7-8), the first keeping to familiar forms of thought and expression; the second, as a morning hymn after a night of sleep, a salute to the dawn (vs. 8), presents a situation foreign to the turbulence of the first. Further, the second section (vss. 7-11) appears independently of the first as a portion of Ps. 108, into which it was

57:1-11. ***The Essential Unity of the Psalm.***—Once again we find the opinions of scholars divided over the matter of authorship. This, however, poses slight difficulty for those whose purpose is to study the religious intention of the poem as it is put before us. Many pious redactors must have handled the ancient copies from which the final forms were drawn, and if in the case of this poem there seem to be two separate pieces put together to satisfy editorial fancy, and if a later editor borrowed casually for another psalm (Ps. 108), we shall still look primarily for the spiritual factor that drew the separate parts into a whole.

However, as has been the case in our previous studies, we can still hold to the validity of the assumption that even when a poem exhibits opposite and even contradictory moods, it is quite possibly the work of a single writer. Inconsistency is an easy error in any writing; in poetry inconsistency shares with variety—of which it is in fact a type—the respectable status of being the spice of life. It was a poet, Emerson, who said: "A foolish consistency is the hobgoblin of little minds, adored by little statesmen and philosophers and divines."[3] It is not therefore a problem that this poem begins with a prayer for protection from the storms of destruction and ends with the note of lute and harp to awaken the dawn. This is the glory of poetry, the reflection of a sensitive and answering spirit. In this case the moods are clear cut and divide the body of the poem equally. Vss. 1-6 are heavy with shadow and distress; vss. 7-11 are light with daybreak and music; and in each division an identical refrain is sung (vss. 5, 11). If this represents a compilation, it was obviously an effort to compose a unified whole. Is it not equally plausible to assume our poet to have been making the effort to bring a unified word of praise out of the compiled diversities of human experience?

It was the surmise of the oldest editors that the occasion for this poem was David's escape from Saul into a cave. No reference to a cave occurs in it, unless the statement that the writer lies **in the midst of lions** is taken literally to

[3] Essay on "Self-reliance."

2 I will cry unto God most high; unto God that performeth *all things* for me.	2 I cry to God Most High, to God who fulfils his purpose for me.

drawn apparently from some other source than Ps. 57, since 108:6 is wanting in the text of the latter.

It must also be noted that within each section there are composite elements: in vs. 4 the enemies of the psalmist are wild beasts, in vs. 6 the metaphor is transferred to the psalmist; vs. 11 introduces a sudden break in the theme of vss. 7-10, and has probably been adopted from an extraneous source.

The evidences of decline in literary sense and creativeness, with the consequent use of mechanical methods in composition, point to a late period. We are in the presence of an epoch when the prayers and songs of Israel are being shaped, not too understandingly, according to traditional patterns. In the superscription the psalm is fancifully related to the events in David's life described in I Sam. 23:19–24:7.

The meter is 3+3 in vss. 1-5, 11; 3+2 in vss. 6-10. In vss. 3-4 irregularities occur because of the present state of the text.

1. Petition for Mercy (57:1-3)

57:1-3. Be merciful to me, O God: The psalmist in his trouble appeals for God's favor, a free, unconvenanted, and unmerited act of divine goodness and compassion.

---

mean just that. This would involve the assumptions that lions in those days lived in caves, that the refugee found them less dangerous than his royal pursuer, and that such associations provided him the impulse to write a poem. These are all, to be sure, more or less dubious to the literal mind, but to the poet there is no great difficulty, for example, in creating metaphorical lions out of the roar of a passing storm. If, then, the early editor had imagination enough to see in the simple word **refuge** the suggestion of a cave, why should he not have thought of Israel's greatest hero losing himself in the dark opening of a cave, and going on to assume (even if, as the Exeg. believes, "fancifully") that he wrote about it, either on the spot, which is a most impossible likelihood, or later, when instead of in a cave he was living in royal splendor in the capital and had both writing materials and leisure in abundance?

There was a time in David's life—and we must not forget that the glamorous career of the son of Jesse could have inspired another poet to write thus even if David did not—when a cave meant the difference between life and death. This is no place to digress on the topic of caves, either as a topographical or sociological aid to man's survival; it is enough to point out that to a man like David, who was poet and fugitive at the same time, a cave could have been a very vivid symbol of God. The most famous of his caves was Adullam, where he mobilized his first contingent of rebels, and to which he brought his father and mother when they were about to be taken by Saul as hostages. Next perhaps in interest is the cave in which he and some of his men were hiding, and into which Saul stumbled by accident, looking for a place to rest. This was an exciting experience. There was an argument between David and his men while the king slept as to whether this momentary good luck was the design of the Lord for David's deliverance. Did he regret that he let the king get away? "Behold," he cried after the departing king, "this day thine eyes have seen how that the Lord hath delivered thee to-day into my hand in the cave: and some bade me kill thee; but mine eye spared thee; and I said, I will not put forth mine hand against my lord; for he is the Lord's anointed" (I Sam. 24:10). There were other caves and other uses of them. Saul told the Ziphites to "see, therefore, and take knowledge of all the lurking places where he hideth himself," but it is certain that none of his hide-outs in the wild hill country where he lived like a hunted animal was to him even momentarily a home. "All the lurking places" were, first and last, places of refuge. It was therefore as truly a part of his spiritual experience that he should turn to God for refuge in times of danger as it was for him to turn to God for domicile in times of security. The man who prayed from the dark recesses of a cave, "In thee my soul takes refuge," could also say, "I am like a green olive tree in the house of God" (52:8).

1-6. *The Poet's Distress.*—Consider the poet's description of his perilous state. There is the proper invocation at the beginning, in which he

3 He shall send from heaven, and save me
from the reproach of him that would swallow me up. Selah. God shall send forth his
mercy and his truth.

4 My soul *is* among lions: *and* I lie *even*
among them that are set on fire, *even* the
sons of men, whose teeth *are* spears and
arrows, and their tongue a sharp sword.

3 He will send from heaven and save me,
he will put to shame those who trample
upon me. *Selah*
God will send forth his steadfast love and
his faithfulness!

4 I lie in the midst of lions
that greedily devour[q] the sons of men;
their teeth are spears and arrows,
their tongues sharp swords.

[q] Cn: Heb *are aflame*

Like others in the O.T., he believes that God is moved by his gracious kindness to work deliverance for his faithful ones from enemies and from evil circumstances (cf. 77:7-9), hence **in thee my soul takes refuge.** The tense of the verb in the Hebrew indicates that it has been the habit of the psalmist to make God his refuge. His appeal therefore is not the cry of one who in a time of trouble suddenly bethinks himself of God.

The psalmist is in great straits because of the threat of **storms of destruction,** i.e., evils that cause everything to tumble into ruins. But there is a ring of confidence in the words of his appeal. **In the shadow of thy wings I will take refuge** (cf. Exeg. on 17:8). His trust in God's protective care of him is supported by the fact that God has in the past brought things to pass for his good (cf. 138:8)—the **God who fulfils his purpose for me.** The LXX reads, "the God who does good for me," i.e., גמל עלי for גמר עלי. Recalling the words of 43:3, the paslmist prays that God's kindness and proven loyalty to his servants may like two good angels be sent to "save me from the power of those who pant after my life." Emend חרף, **put to shame,** to מכף, "from the power of," so that the text of vs. *3b* reads as above (מכף שאפי נפשי). Some regard vs. *3c* as an editorial gloss.

2. The Psalmist's Situation (57:4-6)

4-5. The psalmist describes his situation as that of a man who has been cast in a den of **lions** (cf. Dan. 6:16). His enemies are ravenous beasts (a figure commonly

---

pleads for mercy and protection. Without a sense of God's graciousness, refuge would be spiritually unsatisfying; without the practical boon of refuge, grace would be a mockery. We have grown so accustomed to the metaphorical use of **the shadow of . . . wings** as a refuge that something of its poetic richness and beauty is lost. Light and shade are the most obvious of parallels to gaiety and melancholy, but to a fugitive a shadow has often meant rescue in a sudden encounter with danger: not only "as a hen gathereth her chickens under her wings," but as the moving shadow of a great bird often gives quick warning of a stalking beast, or as a patch of mottled shade provides the momentary camouflage upon which safety may precariously depend. There is the tumult and terror of what the psalmist calls **the storms of destruction,** his recollection of a violent hour spent in a cave perhaps while the elements rush wildly by, a recollection that pointed up his own sense of spiritual security as a threat to his life roared over him and spent itself in the distance. At least he was sure that the storm's fury would pass.

His prayer for mercy, however, is based on something more predictable than an improvised refuge in a sudden storm. God, whose hand holds the lightnings and splits the hills, has a purpose for those who hide in the rifts till the danger is past, and it is as much a part of his concern to fulfill it as it is to shake the world with the portents of his power. The reference in vs. *3a,c* may be a completion of the metaphor of **the storms of destruction,** and **his steadfast love and his faithfulness** in this case would be analogous to the reassuring sunlight and calm that follow the blackness and menace of storm. Between these lines is inserted a sentence reminding us that the storm is within the poet's soul. **He will put to shame those who trample upon me.** We have encountered these pursuers before; they are very much in the mind of the fugitive. They may never lay hands on his body, but they have already laid hands on his soul. They scorn him. Something might be

5 Be thou exalted, O God, above the
heavens; *let* thy glory *be* above all the earth.
6 They have prepared a net for my steps;
my soul is bowed down: they have digged
a pit before me, into the midst whereof
they are fallen *themselves.* Selah.

5 Be exalted, O God, above the heavens!
Let thy glory be over all the earth!

6 They set a net for my steps;
my soul was bowed down.
They dug a pit in my way,
but they have fallen into it themselves.
Selah

---

employed by the psalmists, cf. 7:2; 10:9; 22:21) which have developed a gluttonous appetite for blood, and **greedily devour the sons of men** (לעטים should be read for לחטים). They accomplish the destruction of their victims by their mouth, i.e., their accusations, slanders, and falsehoods. Their **teeth are spears and arrows, and their tongue a sharp sword** (cf. 140:3; Prov. 25:18). Vs. 5, which breaks the connection of vs. 4 and vs. 6 as descriptive of the enemy, came into the text at this point because of an inadvertent repetition of vs. 11.

6. The psalmist in speaking of his enemies now varies his speech. They are described as cruel hunters, and their plots and deceits are likened to the **net** and **pit** which hunters devise for the death of the prey. But suddenly in vs. 6*b* a new tone is heard in the psalmist's words. He is filled with certainty that the answer to his prayer is at hand. **They dug a pit . . . but they have fallen into it themselves.** With prophetic eye he sees the discomfiture of his enemies already accomplished (cf. 7:15; 9:15).

As has been noted above, the theme of the psalmist's complaint is so abruptly broken off as to seem fragmentary. His expression of confidence is even more truncated. Some help is given if, as some suggest, vs. 6*b* is emended to read, "their own feet are taken" (כפם נקשה).

---

made of this indication of self-pity in our hero. We do not disparage him to point it out; it is a common weakness. One somehow has more zest for the struggle if he can feel that however his antagonist may hate him, he still believes him to be a "foeman worthy of his steel." To feel an enemy's scorn is sometimes as crippling as to feel his sword.

Again the psalmist changes his figure of speech from storm to cave, this time to describe his companions in the cleft. He needs refuge even within his refuge, for other harried creatures share momentarily the cave's protection. **Lions,** of all things, and lions of the most fabulous sort! He has fled **the storms of destruction** and finds lions in his refuge. Not lions like the fabled friend of Androcles, ready to accept the kindness of a desperate human creature, but lions whose normal denture has been replaced by man's most lethal weapons, and whose slavering mouths are sheaths for **sharp swords.** This is of course the extravagance of poetic description and highly metaphorical. But the psalmist is representing a state of his mind. His soul is in desperation so great that the momentary promise of refuge in a cave is falsified by an encounter with improbable beasts. No wonder, then, that the poem at this point breaks off its agonized descriptions of his distress with an apostrophe to God. The storms have raked the heavens with fury; the earth is pocked with caves where lions wait. **Be thou exalted, O God, above the heavens; let thy glory be above all the earth.** This would presumably take care of the tempests and the lions; better still, because more needed, it would quiet the storms and the beasts that terrify his soul. There is a final word about his threatened misfortune. After the apostrophe, which is repeated as a refrain at the poem's end, vs. 6 sounds like the distant rumble of thunder of a storm that is past, though once again the figure is changed. Now it is not the furies of the sky or cave; it is the deliberate machinations of men. The interplay between body and soul is sustained, however.

They set a net for my steps;
my soul was bowed down.
They dug a pit in my way,
but they have fallen into it themselves.

A net to trap him as he stepped from his refuge, a pit (a cave made by man's evil scheming?) to trip him if he dodged the trap! For a moment his cause looked hopeless and his soul was bowed down, caught in their net! But the pit?

7 My heart is fixed, O God, my heart is
fixed: I will sing and give praise.
8 Awake up, my glory; awake, psaltery
and harp: I *myself* will awake early.
9 I will praise thee, O Lord, among the
people: I will sing unto thee among the
nations.
10 For thy mercy *is* great unto the heavens, and thy truth unto the clouds.

7 My heart is steadfast, O God,
my heart is steadfast!
I will sing and make melody!
8 Awake, my soul![r]
Awake, O harp and lyre!
I will awake the dawn!
9 I will give thanks to thee, O Lord, among
the peoples;
I will sing praises to thee among the
nations.
10 For thy steadfast love is great to the
heavens,
thy faithfulness to the clouds.

[r] Heb *glory*

3. The Psalmist Gives Thanks (57:7-11)

7-11. My heart is steadfast: I.e., ready for song and praise. An alternative translation is "my heart is confident." In either case the psalmist is no longer wavering in despair or anxiety, but is strong and steadied. His emotions break forth in a hymn of praise. **Awake, my soul:** Lit., **my glory** (cf. Exeg. on 7:3-5). He calls on his instruments of music, so long silent, to join with him in the anthem. **Awake, O harp and lyre!** In his rapture he will awaken the morning, which normally awakens him (Herkenne). In its original setting this morning hymn may have been for the use of those who received in the course of a night spent in the temple some divine sign or oracle which freed them

Look! In its black depths he sees his writhing adversary. So cleverly had he concealed it that he could not see it himself. How often the ingenuity of the enemy proves too ingenious for his own safety!

7-11. ***The Poet's Praise.***—Now he is altogether free. It is the exultation with which this section is inspired that has been adduced in support of the idea that our psalm is a tandem arrangement of two unrelated poems, or the work of at least two poets. This understanding is unsupported if we are able to sense the enormous relief that our author feels when the turmoil of his soul is past. In fact, the opening words of what are thought to be the first lines of a separate poem can be quite as properly thought of as the transition from one mood of the poet to another. Now he is prepared to sing! And no wonder; if in the darkness of caves, and in the company of lions and pursued by enemies, he has only the impulse to cry for mercy and refuge, when he is quit of these horrors such energy as he has left is convoked for song.

My heart is steadfast, O God,
my heart is steadfast!
I will sing and make melody!

Here is contrast, to be sure, but not contradiction. A moment ago his soul was bowed down; now he calls it awake to sing. A moment ago there was a net for his steps; now there is a melody for his lips. A moment ago there were night and storm and the menacing roar of beasts; now there are the awakening dawn and the whispering tones of harp and lyre. This is lyric gaiety as intense as the somberness of the foregoing verses, but it reflects the temperament of the poet in all its extravagance. What sprightlier lines are to be found anywhere than

Awake, O harp and lyre!
I will awake the dawn!

Chanticleer on a dunghill crowing up the day is dull by comparison. The compact the poet improvises with the instruments he plays: You wake yourselves up, and I will wake the dawn! This is sheer exuberance of spirit running over in immoderation, and we like it not the less for all its excess. It does not betray the singer, as exuberance often does, into preoccupation with himself. Like all truly godly men, he turns his mind to what is surely the source of his deliverance and the ground of his joy. **I will praise thee, O Lord, among the people.** Even the clouds that accompanied the violence of storm are not unrelated to the faithfulness of the Lord. We hear finally the same refrain with

11 Be thou exalted, O God, above the heavens: *let* thy glory *be* above all the earth.

To the chief Musician, Al-taschith, Michtam of David.

58 Do ye indeed speak righteousness, O congregation? do ye judge uprightly, O ye sons of men?

11 Be exalted, O God, above the heavens!
Let thy glory be over all the earth!

To the choirmaster: according to Do Not Destroy. A Miktam of David.

58 Do you indeed decree what is right,
you gods?[s]
Do you judge the sons of men uprightly?

[s] Or *mighty lords*

---

from the **net** of the enemy (cf. Exeg. on 5:1-3) **I will give thanks . . . among the peoples:** The testimony of the psalmist is to be published throughout all the world—the hyperbole of a joyful heart. Vs. 11 is the expression of a wish that God's exaltation and glory may be great beyond all measure (cf. 113:4).

LVIII. God's Judgment of the Wicked (58:1-11)

58:1-11. This is a protest against the tyranny of wickedness in the world. It follows the usual form of a lament, but the psalmist, touched by the spirit of prophecy, infuses into its lines his hot indignation against those whom he identifies as responsible for the moral and social disorder which reigns everywhere among **the sons of men.** He lives in a time when, because wrong seems to be "forever on the throne," doubts have been raised about the justice of the government of the world. It is clear that he believes that God assigned to subordinate divine beings or **gods** (cf. 29:1) certain functions to be discharged by them in the rule of the cosmos and of men, but these divine deputies have been faithless to the trust reposed in them and have become in consequence the causes of the ills in the social order of the world both directly (vs. 2) and through their human agents (vss. 3-5).

---

which the poet's doleful mood had closed. It fits his exultant mood quite as well: **Be thou exalted, O God, above the heavens: let thy glory be above all the earth.**

What was it, we may briefly ask, that gave this moody poem its place in the literature of a people? Not, it may be said, the vigor of its metaphor, or the gaiety of its lyric, or even the striking balance achieved between storm and dawn, a soul bowed down and a heart ready to sing, devouring beasts and the great kindness of the Lord. These are poetic qualities that evoke the delight of those who are sensitive to them. But something more profound is present here; we have seen it in much of the poetry of Israel, and we shall encounter it again and again. It was, in a manner of speaking, the essence of Israel's religious devotion. Our poet represents it faithfully. Ill-fortune does not despoil one's faith in God; nor does good fortune make it superfluous. Out of the depths man cried to God; on the high places he sang praises to him. And what seems to be the unique intimation of this piece, very often it is the passing through desolation that prepares the heart for devotion. This may be a lesson hard to learn in such days as our own, but it has never been easy. To those who have found it difficult there is inspiration in the words of this ancient, who, just after side-stepping a net spread in the darkness for his steps, could call for harp and lyre that he might awaken the dawn.

What of those whom the net caught, or who had no harp and thus no dawn? That is another matter, but our poet's reflections on life will encompass that also in due time.

58:1-11. ***Are Rulers Righteous?***—It has been pointed out many times that every man is native to three worlds: the world of himself, the world of his fellows, the world of his ideas. Each of these worlds impinges on and to some extent qualifies the others. He who lives within himself alone is not wholly alive; nor can one live in the world of his fellows without inhabiting a world of ideas about them. Each of these worlds is, moreover, divided into continents. Man's self is not an indivisible unit; it is a mysterious compound. The world of man's fellows is shaded into government, business, domestic, and other subdivisions; and a map of his world

In a lament it is customary to open with an appeal to God for help. Our psalmist boldly varies the pattern by changing the appeal into a charge against the gods. He uses the method of a prosecutor in the courts (cf. Job 13:22-25), ironically addressing the accused with a question that of itself convicts (vss. 1-2). He then describes the evils which their human collaborators work in the earth (vss. 3-5). And he makes petition to God (vss. 6-9) that through a sevenfold curse these deadly enemies of mankind may be blotted out of existence. After the utterance of this fierce malediction, the mood of the psalmist changes to one of calm trust and confidence (vss. 10-11) that righteousness will be vindicated and that men will yet know **there is a God who judges on earth.**

The theological problem that lies in the background of the psalm, and the psalmist's conception of a divine hierarchy in which the pagan deities are subordinated to God, are features which belong to late Jewish literature.

The psalm consists of lines either in 4+3 or 4+4 meter; the meter of vss. 1-3, 5, 9 is 4+3. The stichs of four units are not in this instance easily resolved to a 2+2 measure.

1. Address to Certain Lesser Deities (58:1-2)

58:1-2. The psalmist addresses his words to certain persons whom he designates by a term which regularly means "divine beings," **gods,** or "angels" (cf. 8:5; 138:1; Exod. 15:11; Dan. 11:36; Job 1:6; 38:7). The translation of this term by "magistrates" or by some word indicative of **mighty lords** is incorrect. The beings which excite the psalmist's anger are the same as those which are rebuked in Ps. 82, and in 82:6-7 they belong to a superhuman order. The O.T. religion never became so thoroughly monotheistic that it did not allow for the existence of divine beings subordinate to Yahweh. Since from early times in Israel the gods of the nations were thought to be existent, it was not unnatural that the people of Israel, instead of denying the existence of these gods,

---

of ideas would show continents of fact, of speculation, of art, of religion, and even of dreams. It is man's travels among these three worlds and about these many fascinating continents that is his earthly pilgrimage. He finds many companions along the way, but in a real sense he walks his way alone.

Great literature is concerned with such matters; Homer's *Iliad* and *Odyssey* illustrate this preoccupation. How shall man's private world protect itself against the myriad worlds of other men? How far can the ideal God of man's devotion affect the insistent demands of his self? How far must man yield the ordering of his life to others? Are those who rule, and who claim the sanction of judgment and righteousness as the scepter of their dominion, just and right? These are the questions, endlessly argued and unanswered, which men have fashioned into folk tale and saga, epic and oratorio, poem and philosophy.

It is definitely within such precincts that our poet wanders in this psalm. He is frankly puzzled.

Do you indeed decree what is right, you gods?
Do you judge the sons of men uprightly?

The identity of our writer is obscure. David, said the ancients; but later scholarship demurs. Whether the psalm had any specific connection with David or not, its question is indeed the question of every man as he faces up to the problem of adjusting his private life to the authorities under which he lives. These authorities are **mighty lords.** They may sit in the seats of government, they may be the arbiters of taste, they may be the priests before the altar or the masters of the countinghouse. They **decree what is right,** they **judge the sons of men.** But are they right? The moment the judgment of the mighty lord nudges insistently the private judgment of the humble man, questions are asked. It has not been uncommon for poets who dared not openly protest against tyranny to speak their mind through the subtle indirections of their art. Richard Wagner wrote his protests in a series of great operatic myths; and Robert Schumann, annoyed by a ban against playing the "Marseillaise" in Austria in 1838, neatly inserted it in his *Carnaval,* impishly daring the police to detect it. This sort of thing is still a perennial problem and privilege, and finding it in the literature of these ancient people establishes more securely its honorable history.

Still, we are likely to think that the citizen's challenge to vested authority is as recent as the days when Western democracy was coming to birth. This is disputed by our poem. Lese

2 Yea, in heart ye work wickedness; ye weigh the violence of your hands in the earth.	2 Nay, in your hearts you devise wrongs; your hands deal out violence on earth.
3 The wicked are estranged from the womb: they go astray as soon as they be born, speaking lies.	3 The wicked go astray from the womb, they err from their birth, speaking lies.

reduced them to the level of servants to Yahweh (cf. 86:8; 95:3; 97:7). Even though such beings were superfluous in the presence of a God who could accomplish his purposes by the power of his word (Gen. 1), yet we see that the notion of a heavenly court persisted (Job 1), and that it did not seem inconsistent for Yahweh, as supreme ruler of the world, to employ such divine agents to carry out his wishes in detail. The belief in angels is a later form of this conception (cf. Enoch 15:1–16:3; Heb. 1:4, 6, 13-14). **Do you judge the sons of men uprightly?** It is not a new thought that divine beings were liable to judgment (82:7; Isa. 24:21; Jer. 49:1-3; Zech. 3:1-2) for evils that they had done. In this instance, as in Ps. 82, the arraignment is made not by God but by a man who orders his case before God (vss. 6-9). The O.T. writers know of no order of beings exempt from judgment before the bar of man's moral sense of right and wrong. **Your hands deal out violence:** The gods against whom the psalmist directs his indictment were appointed to champion righteousness among men, but by evil design they have made confusion and suffering to reign among men, for **in your hearts you devise wrongs.**

2. Concerning Wicked Men (58:3-5)

3-5. The psalmist now turns from these divine workers of evil to speak of their human allies. They are **wicked,** i.e., guilty of disloyalty to God. The spirit of faithlessness

---

majesty is as old as organized society, though it has only lately and in some countries become a democratic right. When our poet asked for proof of the rectitude of his mighty lords, he was doing a bold thing; when he went on to answer his own request with an indictment, he was doing a dangerous thing. Unlike most of the psalms, there is no invocation of God as the poem opens. The poet lets fly his arrow straight at his target without warning or prayer. Indeed, were it not for his call for God to destroy those he denounces, there is little that gives this piece the essential religious quality found so consistently in the Psalter. It fits rather well in the category of political poetry.

There are clearly four divisions to the poem: (*a*) The poet raises a question and gives an answer (vss. 1-2); (*b*) he explains the reasons for his answer (vss. 3-5); (*c*) he utters a sort of incantation by which he hopes the evil he denounces can be exorcised (vss. 6-9); (*d*) he predicts the popular support that will follow effective and remedial action (vss. 10-11). This suggests a kinship, in spirit at least, with Ps. 52, in which we have understood David to be sounding the tocsin of revolution against the mighty lord he had found to be evil.

1-2. *Challenge to the Ruler.*—The words with which the first section opens and which ask the bold question have already been noted. The poet's answer was dangerous:

> **Nay, in your hearts you devise wrongs;**
> **your hands deal out violence on earth.**

While this appears to be a private resentment, it essays to speak for the earth. The business of the ruler is twofold: to declare what is true and to execute justice on the basis of truth. He is therefore both judiciary and executive, both lawgiver and judge. Our citizen-poet has ideas of truth and justice of his own, however, and he hurls into the teeth of the mighty lords his imputation that they deliberately devise wrongs. Here is no charge that vagrancy has led them into evil; it is a carefully and zealously (**in your hearts**) planned conspiracy to subvert truth, and it is followed up by the vigorous and malevolent action of hands that **deal out violence on earth.** This is the most serious of all possible charges. It says that instead of truth on the seat of government, a lie is ensconced; that instead of justice, violence is administered.

3-5. *The Ruler Evil from Birth.*—Not only is this a charge against the **mighty lords** whose power has corrupted them; it is also a denial that those who are on the seats of the mighty are there by divine appointment. Back of the

4 Their poison *is* like the poison of a serpent: *they are* like the deaf adder *that* stoppeth her ear;

5 Which will not hearken to the voice of charmers, charming never so wisely.

6 Break their teeth, O God, in their mouth: break out the great teeth of the young lions, O LORD.

7 Let them melt away as waters *which* run continually: *when* he bendeth *his bow to shoot* his arrows, let them be as cut in pieces.

4 They have venom like the venom of a serpent,
like the deaf adder that stops its ear,
5 so that it does not hear the voice of charmers
or of the cunning enchanter.

6 O God, break the teeth in their mouths;
tear out the fangs of the young lions, O LORD!
7 Let them vanish like water that runs away;
like grass let them be trodden down and wither.[t]

[t] Cn: Heb uncertain

---

is deeply ingrained in their nature. They are wicked and liars **from their birth.** They are like **a serpent** that, despite the skill of the charmer, will not be charmed. No counsels can make them withhold the deadly poison of their tongues. **They have venom . . . like the deaf adder that stops its ear.**

3. May God Destroy the Unrighteous (58:6-9)

6-9. The psalmist appeals to God to make an end of such a race of men. His prayer is that a sevenfold curse may come upon them. In the ancient Near East men believed in the magical and automatic potency of a word of ill omen, written or spoken (Zech. 5:1-4) . But the psalmist does not of himself send forth the curse; he asks God to effect it. The curse is made more dreadful by the multiplication of examples of swift and utter obliteration: may their **fangs** be broken; may they **vanish like water, like grass, like the snail, like the untimely birth,** like **thorns** under a pot. The text of vs. 7*b* should be emended to read, "like grass may they be trodden down and wither away" (כמו חציר

---

divine appointment there should have been a rectitude that could not lapse into corruption. Our poet must therefore explain how the lie found its way to the throne. It is not an easy problem to solve since it involves the inscrutable ways of God; so in lieu of argument our author asseverates. Whether or not God is culpable, the fact is clear to the poet: **The wicked,** whether magistrates or mere men, **go astray from the womb, they err from their birth, speaking lies.** This may not be precisely what is called original sin, but it comes close to it. From birth they are prodigies in the craftiness of deceit. More than that, their lies are like arrows dipped in **the venom of a serpent,** nor are they responsive to the voices that would charm or dissuade them from their evil. The reference to a **deaf adder** is important only for herpetology, but who does not know the difference between a deliberate misstatement of fact and a venomous lie? By **the cunning enchanter** does the psalmist mean what we mean by conscience, to which a deaf ear is turned? It is a delightful allusion, whatever its exact meaning.

6-9. *The Curse by Incantation.*—Thus the question, the answer, and the explanation. But something must be done about it. The **mighty lords** have the power by which they maintain themselves in authority. Shall there be popular revolt, an armed challenge to their evil governance? Perhaps; but since God is in the common mind associated with their establishment in power, why should not God take the initiative in dethroning them? The third section of the poem turns to this expedient. It is God's responsibility, and if he executes it properly, **the righteous will rejoice** (vs. 10*a*) .

Six metaphors are employed in vss. 6-9, and they seem to have the rhythmic cadences of an incantation. Even if allowance is made for the intensity of the poet's sense of outrage, it must still be said that there is a brutality in these words that is fairly gruesome. **O God,** he drones, **break the teeth in their mouths; tear out the fangs of the young lions!** This is not a pretty picture. In a country where living water was one of life's major demands, and where

8 As a snail *which* melteth, let *every one of them* pass away: *like* the untimely birth of a woman, *that* they may not see the sun.

9 Before your pots can feel the thorns, he shall take them away as with a whirlwind, both living, and in *his* wrath.

10 The righteous shall rejoice when he seeth the vengeance: he shall wash his feet in the blood of the wicked.

11 So that a man shall say, Verily *there is* a reward for the righteous: verily he is a God that judgeth in the earth.

8 Let them be like the snail which dissolves into slime,
like the untimely birth that never sees the sun.
9 Sooner than your pots can feel the heat of thorns,
whether green or ablaze, may he sweep them away!

10 The righteous will rejoice when he sees the vengeance;
he will bathe his feet in the blood of the wicked.
11 Men will say, "Surely there is a reward for the righteous;
surely there is a God who judges on earth."

ידרכו יתמללו) . The text of vs. 9 is corrupt and its recovery is difficult; the best proposal is to read, "Before they are aware, let them be rooted out and like a buckthorn [יכרתו כמו אטד], like a bramble [חוח], like a weed [חרול] may he sweep them away [ישערם]."

4. Rejoicing of the Righteous (58:10-11)

10-11. The psalmist is confident that God is with him and that the superhuman and human agents of evil in the world will be brought to an end. His description of the exultation of the righteous at their vindication is somewhat barbaric in its realism (vs. 10*b*) . But his eyes are chiefly filled with the glory of that day when men will know that **there is a God who judges on earth.**

---

grass was as important as bread, it was an evil wish that proposed:

Let them vanish like water that runs away;
like grass let them be trodden down and wither.

It was a popular notion that a snail's slow progress was a sort of suicidal erasure (vs. 8*a*) . The slimy track it left was thought to be its only residue. By its very motion it reduced itself to slime. This, we may agree, was not a very exalted prospect for **mighty lords.** To be sure, they are full-grown; how, then, wish for them abortive birth (vs. 8*b*) ? Is the poet thinking of these men with the horror and the sense of futility with which untimely births are necessarily regarded? Vs. 9 adds to the evidence that these are words of incantation, for after the evil spell has been woven, the trigger word that releases the charm is spoken:

Sooner than your pots can feel the heat of thorns,
whether green or ablaze, may he sweep them away!

This is not unlike the "fire, burn; and cauldron, bubble" of the witches on the heath in *Macbeth.* The invocation is spoken; it is up to the occult powers to perform. Broken teeth, spent streams, withered grass, slime of snail, aborted fetus, are in the caldron; let these portents of defeat and death augur the end of the **mighty lords.**

10-11. ***Satisfaction at Rulers' Overthrow.***—This concluding section predicts the popular satisfaction that will follow the dethronement of these evil and violent men. It uses language as grisly as the incantations chanted to bewitch them:

The righteous will rejoice when he sees the vengeance;
he will bathe his feet in the blood of the wicked.

If this is reminiscent of a pagan ritual bath, its origin is obscure; but whatever its source, it is no attractive picture, and hardly proper conduct for the righteous! It is therefore something of a relief to come upon the final confident and pious word:

Men will say, "Surely there is a reward for the righteous;
surely there is a God who judges on earth."

This, we will agree, is not a pretty poem; but it is not dealing with a pretty matter. Cor-

To the chief Musician, Al-taschith, Michtam of David; when Saul sent, and they watched the house to kill him.

59 Deliver me from mine enemies, O my God: defend me from them that rise up against me.

To the choirmaster: according to Do Not Destroy. A Miktam of David, when Saul sent men to watch his house in order to kill him.

59 Deliver me from my enemies, O my God,
protect me from those who rise up against me,

LIX. Prayer in Time of Stress (59:1-17)

In this psalm we hear the bitter complaint of an individual who is oppressed by ruthless enemies, bloodthirsty workers of mischief. Its original form, however, has been expanded considerably by later additions and by the accidental repetition of certain lines. The body of the psalm consisted at first of vss. 1-4, 6 (14), 5, 7, 12-13*ab*, 16-17, which conform to the pattern of a lament of an individual. But some later writer or writers, following a practice that is seen elsewhere (cf. Pss. 9–10; 102; Lam. 3), introduced a few verses in which the enemies of the psalmist appear to be **the nations:** vss. 8, 11, 13*cd*. In this way the psalm could be understood as a lament of the people. The thought of the psalm was further complicated by the careless introduction of some marginal corrections of the text of certain verses into the body of the psalm. In consequence of this mischance, vss. 9-10, 17 seem to function as a refrain (cf. parallel instances in Pss. 56–57). But it seems clear that vss. 9-10 originally stood on the margin as the correct reading of vs. 17, and that vss. 14-15 were a marginal correction of vs. 6 to supply the line omitted by a copyist. We have noted elsewhere (cf. Exeg. on Pss. 56–57) that a refrain is not proper to a lament.

ruption in high places is as old as human society, and man's revolt against it has never been able to accommodate lyric language to its denunciation. Our interest in this ancient bit of political polemic is, however, more than antiquarian. To be sure, in our day, within the structure of our Western democratic culture, we have ways of getting rid of **mighty lords** that are politically more effective than incantation. And yet the poison of corruption that must be neutralized or drained from government today is the same as that against which our poet proposed his brewing pot of charms. It is dishonesty, or as he more bluntly puts it, **lies.** He expected truth, right, and upright judgment; he got deliberate falsehood and violence, and his explanation is **lies,** lies that were born with the birth of the **mighty lords.**

Have we progressed much beyond this insight? The evil of despotism is not only the **hands** [that] **deal out violence on earth** (vs. 2), but the lie that says it has a right, ex officio, to do violence. The good of democracy is not in the rights conferred on citizens to have the sort of government they wish, but in the opportunities it affords for the exposure of the lies that spawn in any social and political context.

After all, it is no new thing under the sun to expose the lie as the heart of political corruption. "Do you in truth decree what is right?" is a question put to every unit of society, from the ruler to the humblest citizen. Upon the honest answer rests the security not only of government, but of individual integrity. The lie is the sin. It starts by deceiving itself. And having deceived itself, it goes on to deceive others; and the end of that is **violence on earth** (vs. 2).

Much in modern life documents the searching insight of our citizen-poet. There will be violence on earth so long as there is dishonesty on earth. As peace is the issue of the truth, war is the spawn of the lie. That is no less true for the peace or violence of the individual human heart than it is for nations of earth. On this point we stand shoulder to shoulder with our psalmist. One wonders whether in the matter of rebuking the lie we have advanced very far beyond the techniques of incantation.

59:1-17. ***Instinctive Human Emotions.***—It was easier for the first anthologists to assign this poem to David than for later scholars to do so. The excessive emotionalism of these disorderly stanzas seemed to present little difficulty to those who thought David was normally capable of such moods, or that his harassment by Saul was so intolerable as to drive him to such an angry and chaotic utterance. It is the

2 Deliver me from the workers of iniquity, and save me from bloody men.
3 For, lo, they lie in wait for my soul: the mighty are gathered against me; not *for* my transgression, nor *for* my sin, O LORD.

2 deliver me from those who work evil,
and save me from bloodthirsty men.

3 For, lo, they lie in wait for my life;
fierce men band themselves against me.
For no transgression or sin of mine, O LORD,

In its present form the psalm probably comes from a late period when there was some looseness in dealing with traditional literary forms and patterns as a result of a decline in literary sense. This fact, coupled with the reference to **the nations,** for whose destruction a prayer is offered, points to one of the later historical periods when the Jews were subject to foreigners. The original body of the psalm, however, gives no clear evidence of its date. The late scribal students, whose opinions appear in the superscription, found a historical setting for the psalm in the incident narrated in I Sam. 19:11.

The meter is 3+3, with some instances 2+2+2 in vss. 6, 12-14.

1. Plea for Succor (59:1-5)

59:1-5. Deliver me . . . protect me . . . deliver me . . . save me: The psalmist begins with a cry, four times repeated, for rescue from **my enemies.** The appeal to God is urgent, for his enemies are fierce and murderous. Their purpose is to compass his death. He compares them to cruel hunters waiting in ambush for the quarry—**they lie in wait for my life**—or again to a band of fierce robbers ready to waylay a victim. **Fierce men band themselves against me:** The emended verb (יגודו) implies that they are a marauding troop. The metaphors which the psalmist employs are meant to show the fixed and ruthless designs of his foes. On the other hand, he declares before God, the Judge of the hearts of men, his innocence of wrongdoing. **For no transgression or sin of mine . . .**

---

modern scholar who is puzzled and who must assign these illogical and asymmetrical strophes to anonymous editors. They, the assumption goes, patched together fragments of fear, fury, and devotion gathered from obscure sources and from periods in Israel's history to which no sure clue is indicated. Such cohesion as may be apparent is therefore factitious, and served a purpose more obvious to the early editors than to us.

One's impression from reading these immoderate lines is that, whoever or however many wrote them, the predicament described was—to use a word too mild for the poem—bad. Such circumstances do not inspire either logic or lyric; one is as likely to condemn as to pray, and to move back and forth between them without restraint or rebuke. One is also moved to excessive self-pity, and to equally excessive presumption with respect to God's mercy and salvation. At the same time, men and nations do get into trouble, and that becomes for them the determining factor in all that is done and said. We speak carelessly of "extenuating circumstances," meaning thereby special and perhaps mitigating factors in an awkward situation. Is it not truer to life to say that all circumstances are extenuating? We have here a description of a situation and the reactions it elicits. Although to the literary critic the poem defies strophic arrangement, and to the religious critic it stretches moral consistency, there is nothing in it that we cannot understand on the normal human level.

1-7. *Plaint for Deliverance.*—The first concern manifestly is with the predicament from which the poet must be delivered and protected. The alternation between the words **deliver** and **protect** may have more than poetic significance. While such great danger as that being described does not ordinarily encourage subtlety in the use of words, there is, after all, a common-sense difference between being delivered from trouble and being protected against it. The latter is a compromise settlement when the former is impossible, and, in a manner of speaking, it is the best that man has ever been able realistically to hope for. The point should not be pressed that while the poet asks deliverance from enemies, he hopes only for protection from his adversaries; or that in vs. 2 he seems to have made up his mind that after all he must be delivered from mischievous and **bloodthirsty men.** The catalogue of evil men is a formidable

4 They run and prepare themselves without *my* fault: awake to help me, and behold.

5 Thou therefore, O LORD God of hosts, the God of Israel, awake to visit all the heathen: be not merciful to any wicked transgressors. Selah.

6 They return at evening: they make a noise like a dog, and go round about the city.

4 for no fault of mine, they run and make ready.

Rouse thyself, come to my help, and see!
5 Thou, LORD God of hosts, art God of Israel.
Awake to punish all the nations;
spare none of those who treacherously plot evil. *Selah*

6 Each evening they come back,
howling like dogs
and prowling about the city.

---

they run and make ready, like bowmen for battle. Since this deadly assault of his foes is unprovoked, he can with confidence appeal to God to act. **Rouse thyself . . . and see!** For he believes that if only God were awake to the situation, he would see the plight of his servant and intervene on his behalf.

Thou, LORD God of hosts, art God of Israel.
Awake to punish all the nations.

By the introduction of this reference to **the nations,** the psalmist's lament seems to become part of a cry of the people against their heathen oppressors. Such a readaptation of the psalmist's words must have occurred in a time when the psalmist could be thought of as a personification of his people. In this literary procedure little allowance was made for the highly personal color of the description of his troubles. It seems incorrect to explain away such a phenomenon by assuming it to be traceable to the influence of the royal psalms, in which the enemies of the king are both personal and national (see Hermann Gunkel and Joachim Begrich, *Einleitung in die Psalmen* [Göttingen: Vandenhoeck & Ruprecht, 1933; "Göttinger Handbuch zum Alten Testament"], pp. 147-48).

2. The Psalmist's Foes (59:6-8, 11, 13*c*-15)

6 (14), 15, 7. A closer picture of the psalmist's foes is now given us. In a lively figure he compares them to the scavenger dogs of the Orient which, hiding away by day,

---

one: enemies, adversaries, men who work mischief, and bloodthirsty men. They are clever and they are ruthless and they are all against him. The psalmist cries for deliverance (vss. 1-2). He fears he will not only be overwhelmed by the conspiracy that is plotting his destruction; he is aware that wherever he goes he is likely to fall into an ambush set for him (vs. 3*a*).

He continues his description. To the danger that stalks him at noonday there is added the peril that comes with the evening. Out of the early shadows his enemies leap like the wild pariah dogs of the city on the prowl for food. They howl; their slavering jaws snap and snarl; they are everywhere, furtive and sinister (vss. 6-7). Later in the poem (vss. 14-15) they again appear to him in the form of hungry mongrels, prowling, roaming, growling, in and out of the darkness.

One may wonder why and how this wretched man got for himself such unanimous reproach. He comes to the point where he says that not only does he have more than his share of individual enemies; whole nations are in fact against him. This grandiose acceptance of jeopardy has led to the judgment, shared by the Exeg., that this particular reference is an alien fragment of some sort, having its origin in another poem of national rather than personal lament. So it may be; yet if the speaker in the psalm is taking on so great a load of personal enmity, why not add the nations to the list? There has always been the notion that to be overwhelmed by preponderant odds gives or makes some measure of glory in his downfall. This, however, is not all. The psalmist asserts next that this frightful assortment and aggregate of enmity is wholly undeserved! The world of men and nations seems suddenly to have gone mad with malice.

For no transgression or sin of mine, O LORD,
for no fault of mine, they run and make ready.

7 Behold, they belch out with their
mouth: swords *are* in their lips: for who,
say they, doth hear?
8 But thou, O Lord, shalt laugh at them;
thou shalt have all the heathen in derision.
9 *Because of* his strength will I wait upon
thee: for God *is* my defense.
10 The God of my mercy shall prevent
me: God shall let me see *my desire* upon
mine enemies.

7 There they are, bellowing with their
mouths,
and snarling with[u] their lips —
for "Who," they think, "will hear us?"

8 But thou, O Lord, dost laugh at them;
thou dost hold all the nations in derision.

9 O my Strength, I will sing praises to
thee;[v]
for thou, O God, art my fortress.
10 My God in his steadfast love will meet
me;
my God will let me look in triumph on
my enemies.

[u] Cn: Heb *swords in*
[v] Syr: Heb *I will watch for thee*

---

come out under cover of the darkness, prowling, howling, and snarling, as they seek to get their fill of that for which they crave. Though the language recalls 55:9-11, the psalmist is not speaking of a civil faction but only, by a metaphor, of the brutish disposition of those who seek his life. As we have seen above, vs. 6 (14) is to be followed by what now appears in the text as vs. 15. In vs. 7 read יבחו, "they bark," for יביעו, "they pour forth," and with the Syriac, ריבות, "contentions," or הר[י]בו, "they contend," for חרבות, **swords.** Vs. 7*c*, lit., "for who hears," is a stray fragment and should be omitted.

8, 11, 13*cd*. Another reference to the heathen oppressors interrupts the sequence of the psalmist's appeal. **Thou, O Lord, dost laugh at them,** i.e., the enemies of vs. 7, who in vs. 8*b* abruptly become **the nations—Thou dost hold all the nations in derision.** But these nations are not to be slain in a trice, **lest my people forget;** rather, they are to be brought low and left to linger on in weakness. **Make them totter by thy power, . . . O Lord, our shield, . . . that men may know that God rules over Jacob to the ends of the earth.**

9-10. See Exeg. on vss. 16-17.

Is this a horrid dream? No inadvertence, no error, no evil deed, and yet the world in the shape of bloodthirsty men, snarling dogs, and crowding nations stands menacingly above him. If we are to accept his statement that this alignment against him is undeserved, to what reason are we to assign it? What can explain the compounded mischief before which he is made to cringe? Pride, he suggests, pride of wicked men that is exhibited in cursing and lies, in the sin of their mouths and the words of their lips. It seems unlikely that our innocent hero could have exposed in his enemies enough dishonesty and cursing to have precipitated such an avalanche of hate; but he seems to have been no ordinary man, and he therefore incurs no ordinary wrath. Perhaps, indeed, the pride he pricked was as titanic as the recrimination of cursing and falsehood with which it sought to cover its shame.

This is the picture of his predicament, and as he paints it, he leaves no room for any brightness to relieve its shadowed hopelessness. Yet, as is characteristic of our ancient poets, he is far from despairing. A terror as formidable as he describes is only the background against which is to be confidently spread the pageant of a great deliverance. For the moment, however, while the terror threatens, his deliverer is unaware of what goes on. It is necessary that he be wakened and asked for help. **Rouse thyself, come to my help, and see!** Something here to be seen, if we are to trust the description; something worth waking up for. We observe in vs. 5 that deliverance is to be in the grand manner. To oppose the scheming and bloodthirsty enemies, the snarling and slavering carrion hunters, the victim summons the Lord of hosts, the God of Israel, who deals not only with conspirators on a small scale but will spare no nation that plots evil.

8-10. ***The Derision of God.***—We have thus the picture of the danger and the Lord of hosts who is abundantly competent to save. Now with

11 Slay them not, lest my people forget:
scatter them by thy power; and bring them
down, O Lord our shield.
12 *For* the sin of their mouth *and* the
words of their lips let them even be taken in
their pride: and for cursing and lying *which*
they speak.
13 Consume *them* in wrath, consume
them, that they *may* not *be:* and let them
know that God ruleth in Jacob unto the
ends of the earth. Selah.
14 And at evening let them return; *and*
let them make a noise like a dog, and go
round about the city.
15 Let them wander up and down for
meat, and grudge if they be not satisfied.

11 Slay them not, lest my people forget;
make them totter by thy power, and
bring them down,
O Lord, our shield!
12 For the sin of their mouths, the words of
their lips,
let them be trapped in their pride.
For the cursing and lies which they utter,
13 consume them in wrath,
consume them till they are no more,
that men may know that God rules over
Jacob
to the ends of the earth. *Selah*

14 Each evening they come back,
howling like dogs
and prowling about the city.
15 They roam about for food,
and growl if they do not get their fill.

---

3. Plea for Vengeance (59:12-13*b*)

12-13*b*. But the psalmist wishes summary vengeance to be visited on his enemies: **Consume them till they are no more.** And it is clear in these verses for what purpose his enemies have banded themselves together like a pack of street **dogs.** They have by common consent attacked him with lying accusations and curses, hoping that their evil magic and spells might do what their slanderous words might fail to accomplish. The enemies are proud men; by reason of station or wealth or other sources of power they feel sure of success in their conspiracy. The psalmist asks therefore that they may fall victims of their arrogance. **Consume them in wrath:** Better, "in thy wrath."

14-15. See Exeg. on vss. 6 (14), 15, 7.

---

a confidence that is almost debonair, the poet suggests the strategy by which God will discomfit his adversaries. It will not be by some cataclysm of nature, or by a blow from the shattering fist of the God of Israel, but by his towering scorn and the thunder of his terrible laughter (vs. 8). To us this may seem hardly enough to interpose between our threatened hero and his doom, but that he thought it was ample gives us the first real hint we have of the nobility latent in his soul. The prospect of God's laughter and corrosive scorn strikes a lyric chord in his spirit.

> **O my Strength, I will sing praises to thee;**
> **for thou, O God, art my fortress.**

And then, as if singing another line to himself, he continues:

> **My God in his steadfast love will meet me;**
> **my God will let me look in triumph on my enemies.**

11-15. *A Sinister Suggestion.*—Perhaps the assurance of triumph is too strong for the good of the poet's soul. He falls into a sinister mood. His enemies were to him like pariah dogs; now he unwittingly asks God to play the role of a cat, torturing a captive mouse. He does not want his enemies destroyed out of hand; it will be more just, perhaps, and certainly more entertaining, to tease them a bit. **Slay them not, lest my people forget,** i.e., lest the punishment be too quick and summary. **Make them totter by thy power, and bring them down.** Is this not the picture of a man shoved about, knocked down, and allowed to stagger to his feet again before the final blow that flattens him? Yet if this is the poet's mood, he does not let it last long. One does not contemplate the discomfort of one's adversary without being moved either to compassion or to greater fury. It is the latter that grips our psalmist. The teasing has gone far enough. Now for the *coup de grâce:* **Consume them till they are no more.** The somber overtones of vengeance are hardly mitigated by the pious and evangelistic hope with which the imprecation ends: **That men may know that God rules . . . to the ends of the earth.**

Does this sinister delight account for the ensuing interruption, the sharp recollection of

16 But I will sing of thy power; yea, I will sing aloud of thy mercy in the morning: for thou hast been my defense and refuge in the day of my trouble.

17 Unto thee, O my strength, will I sing: for God *is* my defense, *and* the God of my mercy.

16 But I will sing of thy might;
I will sing aloud of thy steadfast love in the morning.
For thou hast been to me a fortress
and a refuge in the day of my distress.
17 O my Strength, I will sing praises to thee,
for thou, O God, art my fortress,
the God who shows me steadfast love.

---

4. Vow to Offer Praise (59:16-17, 9-10)

16-17, 9-10. The psalmist, confident that his petition will be answered, vows to offer a hymn of thanksgiving. **I will sing aloud of thy steadfast love in the morning. In the morning** suggests the expectation of a favorable omen or oracle in the course of the night. Vs. 17 probably lost at the hand of a careless copyist half of its text, the full form of which seems to be preserved in vss. 9-10, for it is to be noted that vs. 17*ab*=vs. 9 and vs. 17*c*=the first two words of vs. 10. In vs. 17*b* (=vs. 9*b*) read with the Syriac, **Thou, O God, art my fortress.** It is consonant with the psalmist's thirst for vengeance as expressed in vs. 10*b* that his votive hymn ends in a vindictive strain, **My God will let me look in triumph on my enemies.**

---

enemies slinking through the shadows in search of offal? At any rate, there is the momentary flash back.

> **Each evening they come back,**
> **howling like dogs**
> **and prowling about the city.**

They growl indeed, and the laughter of God echoes derisively.

16-17. ***The Final Confidence.***—The final strophe is another song very much like that into which the poet burst after he had predicted the laughter of God in vss. 8-10. With that invincible optimism so characteristic of religious poets, he surmounts the turmoil before which he has shuddered, and sings again. He had begun his poem with a cry for deliverance from enemies; he ends it with a song about the might of God. There were adversaries, conspirators, and bloodthirsty men as he began, now God's matutinal goodness calls for loud song. God is a fortress and a refuge against those who lie in wait, and strength against fierce men united in opposition. And as if to set himself and his divine defender at the opposite pole from the conniving villainy he has so miraculously escaped, the poet ends his song with an ascription of praise that is both spirited and tender.

As has already been indicated, this poem has puzzled scholars. Its poetic structure is curious and it contains some unique and independent ideas. Little wonder that W. O. E. Oesterley says, of the attempts at reconstruction, "none of them appeals to us as satisfactory," yet he recognizes that "in all probability, very considerable alterations have been made in the psalm since it was first written." [3] Is it therefore beyond the use of those who are interested in the moral and religious ideas of the psalms? No; for the reason that it is one of three poems of the Hebrew psalter that make use of a very significant idea about God. It is interesting that man, called "the laughing animal," has so sparingly spoken of laughter as a divine quality, though such it must certainly be. Perhaps we have thought it beneath the dignity of the Deity to be amused. Yet in so far as laughter is often concomitant to delight, there is no incongruity, either actual or implied. Laughter as the visible sign of the pleasure of God has, however, no reference in the Bible. Here is a problem in anthropomorphism which might be engagingly investigated. Has man, creating God in his own likeness, preferred him dour and mirthless? Or does man deeply believe that his own best nature is devoid of this vocal testimony of joy? This would come close to the ultimate pessimism, but is a matter beyond the scope of our immediate concern.

God's laughter, in all three references to it (vs. 8; 2:4; 37:13), is not the laughter of mirth; it is the laughter of derision. Psychologists may argue as to whether derision and delight can be expressed by the same medium. A feeling for this difficulty is reflected in the rendering of certain translators who prefer "mock" to "laugh" in these three passages. It is better, perhaps, to lean toward the conventional acceptance of laughter as a mode of something deeper than mirth, yet not wholly different from it. There is the note of scorn in God's

[3] *The Psalms* (New York: The Macmillan Co., 1939), I, 294-95.

To the chief Musician upon Shushan-eduth, Michtam of David, to teach; when he strove with Aram-naharaim and with Aram-zobah, when Joab returned, and smote of Edom in the valley of salt twelve thousand.

60 O God, thou hast cast us off, thou hast scattered us, thou hast been displeased; O turn thyself to us again.

To the choirmaster: according to Shushan Eduth. A Miktam of David; for instruction; when he strove with Aram-naharaim and with Aram-zobah, and when Joab on his return killed twelve thousand of Edom in the Valley of Salt.

60 O God, thou hast rejected us, broken our defenses;
thou hast been angry; oh, restore us.

LX. Israel's Plea for God's Help (60:1-12)

This is a lament which was rendered when the people or some portion of them gathered to present to God an appeal for help at a time of national calamity. In the opening section (vss. 1-5) it is clear that at the hands of some enemy, not identified, a terrible defeat has been suffered. The ruin and devastation which have come in the wake of it are compared to the effects of an earthquake that leaves the land rent with breaches and fissures. The foe still drives the people on its flight. No stand can be made against the onslaught of his bowmen. In this desperate situation the immediate need is a refuge that **thy beloved may be delivered.** But in the second section (vss. 6-8) God is reminded that the broken fortunes of his people are strangely and utterly out of accord with what he has once promised them of triumph. The citation of the oracle is meant to spur God to fulfill that to which he has solemnly committed himself, and it becomes therefore an argument for a larger answer to the words of the appeal. What God had promised was something like a restoration of the peace, unity, and dominion of the Davidic kingdom. But as things now stand, there can be no golden future for Israel unless a remnant is saved. And so in the third section (vss. 9-11) the psalmist, as both leader and spokesman of the fugitive company, adds a personal appeal on their behalf for safe shelter behind the strong walls of a city in Edom. His hope is in God alone, **for vain is the help of man** since God has spurned and refused to march out **with our armies.** The closing words (vs. 12) are an expression of confidence that God will change his course and turn the discomfiture of his people into victory. The note of assurance was probably occasioned by the comforting words of an oracle delivered in answer to the petitions of the lament. In fact, it is this word of confident hope that probably gave the psalm its special worth and place in the Psalter, for it could be shown that in the course of history God did have in store for them some better thing. Like Ps. 57, Ps. 60 was used by the compiler of Ps. 108; vss. 6-12 are identical with 108:7-13.

The prophecy quoted in vss. 6-8 antedates the rest of the psalm, but there is a wide difference of opinion as to the date to be assigned to it, the estimates ranging from the reign of David to the Maccabean period. It seems, however, that the prophecy was

laughter, but is it angry? There is a note of exultation, but is it cruel? To our poet this was God's weapon against the pride of men who lied and cursed to prove their power. One may be allowed to ask if in our own prideful times we have not forgotten the potency of derision, of the rumble of deep laughter in the throat of one who sees folly and pride from eternal perspectives, who knows somehow that God is **a fortress and a refuge in the day of my distress,** and can laugh.

60:1-12. ***Man's Attempt to Conscript God.***— We have here a poem that reflects both bewilderment and annoyance at God's part in a military disaster. The odd and confused editorial reference with which it is introduced gives us no help in our effort to understand it. There was, it appears, a valley at the southwest extremity of the Dead Sea from which the briny water had long since evaporated, leaving it solid with salt. Why it should have been a battleground, or who it actually was who fought there, is not clear. One reference indicates that "David gat him a name when he returned from smiting of the Syrians [Edomites] in the valley of salt, being eighteen thousand men" (II Sam. 8:13). Another reference has it that it was Abishai who accomplished the feat (I Chr.

2 Thou hast made the earth to tremble; thou hast broken it: heal the breaches thereof; for it shaketh.

2 Thou hast made the land to quake, thou hast rent it open;
repair its breaches, for it totters.

---

delivered at a time when Israel, after having suffered a period of humiliation through national divisions and through alienation of portions of its territory by foreigners, had grounds in the trend of events to hope for a restoration of the conditions of the Davidic age. Such a time may have been after the downfall of Assyria in 612 B.C. (cf. Zeph. 2:1–3:20), or before the collapse of the revolt of the Jews together with all Syria and Egypt against Artaxerxes III in 351 B.C. (W. O. E. Oesterley and T. H. Robinson, *A History of Israel* [Oxford: Clarendon Press, 1932], II, 140-41, 168.) The Maccabean period also fostered large hopes, but by that time Edom was no longer a neighbor of Moab (cf. vs. 8). Vs. 9 also indicates that the later portion of the psalm must have been written when Edom, as lying east of Jordan, could offer a strong place of refuge to Israel. But by 312 B.C. the fortunes of Edom had suffered change and Sela (Petra) was in possession of Nabataeus (cf. Diodorus Siculus XIX. 94-100). The lower date for the psalm must be before the end of the fourth century. In the superscription the psalm is connected with the story of David's dealings with Moab, Edom, and Philistia in II Sam. 8; I Chr. 18.

The meter is 3+3, except in the prophetic section where it is 3+3+3. The change in the measure arises from differences in literary origin.

1. National Distress (60:1-5)

60:1-5. The psalmist begins not with the supplications which ordinarily introduce a lament but with a moving statement of the national distress. The root of the situation lies in God's withdrawal from the armies of his people. **Thou hast rejected us, broken**

18:12), and still another (II Kings 14:7) offers the distinction to good King Amaziah, though the total casualties in this case numbered only ten thousand. It is difficult to see, even if one accepts the most conservative record of the Syrian dead, how the victory could have inspired a poem beginning with the words **O God, thou hast rejected us.** Ten to eighteen thousand dead enemies was a handsome take. Such a lament could have represented the feelings of the losers, but not of David, who is mistakenly made the author of the poem, or of Abishai or Amaziah who, if it was David's doing, were no doubt accomplices to the slaughter.

If the psalm represents both bewilderment and annoyance, this unquestionably stems from the fact that doing battle seems to have been man's chief corporate industry since he began living in groups, and that he has assayed the favor of the gods and his success largely in terms of his victories at arms. Hence the legends and the epics, the heroes and the glories, of ancient folk revolve largely about the episodes of war. Hence also the rise and fall of piety in terms of God's share in victory or his failures in defeat. We are not yet beyond the primitive notion that to be successful in conflict we must have some sanction higher than the human aims for which we fight; nor have we yet risen above the folly of excusing our failures by some inexcusable blundering of God. It was God, we were told during World War II, who smothered the English Channel and spread a fog screen for the escape from Dunkerque. If we do not say it was his fault that Dunkerque was destroyed, it is because the blundering of the defenders was at the moment more obvious.

This theme occurs endlessly in the poetry of the Hebrews, as indeed also in the stories of all peoples, ancient and fairly modern. In a sense all war has been total war. It has of late become total in the extent to which it conscripts and destroys, but it has always been total in the way it has engrossed the interest of the embattled groups. Because religion has always been a large segment of a people's interest, God or the gods have consistently served as at least a partial explanation of victory and as an alibi for defeat. When therefore military calamity is described by our poet in terms of broken ranks and rout, it is not surprising that God is reproached for his failure to win. His anger, to which the failure is laid, is as bewildering as his failure is annoying.

1-5. *The Anger of God.*—It is in very truth an indication of the prolonged adolescence of mankind that we still prefer to blame our failures on the indifference or the anger of God

3 Thou hast showed thy people hard things: thou hast made us to drink the wine of astonishment.

4 Thou hast given a banner to them that fear thee, that it may be displayed because of the truth. Selah.

5 That thy beloved may be delivered; save *with* thy right hand, and hear me.

3 Thou hast made thy people suffer hard things;
thou hast given us wine to drink that made us reel.
4 Thou hast set up a banner for those who fear thee,
to rally to it from the bow.[w] *Selah*
5 That thy beloved may be delivered,
give victory by thy right hand and answer us!

[w] Gk Syr Jerome: Heb *truth*

---

our defenses. The effects of the defeat are compared to the devastation of an earthquake. **Thou hast made the land to quake, . . . it totters.** The people reel under their calamities as if they had been **given . . . wine to drink.** Since the end of their woes is not in sight, their prayer is for some place of refuge to which "they can flee from the bow." The mention of **the bow** suggests that they are matched unequally with the trained professional troops of a warrior nation. Vs. 4 should be emended slightly to read, "Give to them that fear thee a refuge to flee thereto from the bow," i.e., תנה ליראיך מנוס להתנסס מפני קשת. As it stands, the verse can only be understood as an ironical statement implying that God had **set up a banner** not for victory but for flight. The word קשט, translated **truth,** is an Aramaic form of the Hebrew קשת, **bow.**

---

rather than on our own stupidity and sin, and that we still see in the portents of nature the caprice of the Deity. This may not be original sin, but it surely comes close to being original folly. Observe it in our poem.

O God, thou hast rejected us, broken our defenses;
thou hast been angry.

There is apparently no thought that what is called God's rejection might have been foolish or reckless strategy, that broken defenses might have been the result of cowardice, or that the rout could have been nothing less than sheer panic. That it was due to the superiority of one's foe was, in those days as even in our own, unthinkable. It has always been easier to put the blame on God, and the quickest explanation of God's failure has not been his impotence—that would be impious—but his anger, the mood which can most easily be "sicklied o'er with the pale cast" of divinity.[4]

This anger of God comes close to being a tantrum. Nature suffers along with her shuddering sons. She is broken apart by the violence of God's fury, and so frightening are the opening rifts that the whole earth seems to totter on the edge of disintegration.

Thou hast made the land to quake, thou hast rent it open;
repair its breaches, for it totters.

[4] Shakespeare, *Hamlet,* Act III, scene 1.

We are not told whether it was this natural calamity of an earthquake that caused the military defeat. Apparently it is understood by our poet to be nothing more than added evidence of the anger of God. So great was the divine wrath that he was not content to put armies to rout; the ranks of nature were also broken and her normal and orderly processes were put to rout. Furthermore, to complete the picture of desolation, we have a word about the common people as opposed, for the moment, to the ranks of fighting men. Here appears also the total aspect of war that is not so modern as we sometimes think.

Thou hast made thy people suffer hard things;
thou hast given us wine to drink that made us reel.

This latter intimation has a particular interest. The earth totters under a blow of the angry fist of God; his people totter under the intoxication of bitter wine. This sort of melancholy, a compound of dismay and recrimination, was neither bad theology nor bad religion to the primitives who indulged it. Indeed it may have served a purpose for which it is no longer available. We are not surprised, then, to hear our poet shift to a manner of speech that on superficial reading seems incongruous with what has gone before. Does he contradict himself? He has accused God of rejecting his people in anger. Now he says (vss. 4-5) that God has set

6 God hath spoken in his holiness; I will
rejoice, I will divide Shechem, and mete
out the valley of Succoth.
7 Gilead *is* mine, and Manasseh *is* mine;
Ephraim also *is* the strength of mine head;
Judah *is* my lawgiver;
8 Moab *is* my washpot; over Edom will
I cast out my shoe: Philistia, triumph thou
because of me.

6 God has spoken in his sanctuary:[x]
"With exultation I will divide up Shechem
and portion out the Vale of Succoth.
7 Gilead is mine; Manas'seh is mine;
E'phraim is my helmet;
Judah is my scepter.
8 Moab is my washbasin;
upon Edom I cast my shoe;
over Philistia I shout in triumph."

[x] Or *by his holiness*

2. God's Earlier Promise (60:6-8)

6-8. The psalmist reminds God that he had **spoken in his sanctuary,** his holy dwelling place, by an oracle, promising far different things for his people. **I will divide up Shechem:** The territory of Shechem, which after the downfall of Samaria in 722 B.C. had been occupied by foreign colonists and their descendants (cf. II Kings 17:24; Ezra 4:1-10), will be reabsorbed into the heritage of Israel. Likewise **the valley of Succoth**—i.e., the valley of the Jabbok River from Succoth to the Jordan, which as early as 732 B.C., in the reign of Tiglath-pileser, formed a part of the Assyrian province east of Jordan and at the time of the oracle still remained apart from Israel—will be taken over and portioned out to God's people. **Gilead is mine:** According to Jer. 49:1 (*ca.* 450 B.C.), Gilead was in possession of the Ammonites (for other late prophecies of its recovery see Jer. 50:19; Zech. 10:10). To **Manasseh** also God asserts his rightful claim. Lying

up a standard to which they might gather; the divine purpose, after all, may have been one conceived in love, not in anger. The reference to **the bow** in vs. 4 will be commented on later; for the moment let it be pointed out that it is a weapon useful only in the hands of the skillful. It was therefore the arm of the professional soldier, and is used here as the symbol for what in later ages has been called militarism.

6-12. ***The Gentleness and Power of God.***—If this strikes us as a sudden *volte-face,* unaccounted for by anything within the conditions the poet has been describing, it may reasonably be explained by vss. 6-8. Here is clearly the voice of an oracle speaking, and since our poet has reflected the confidence the oracle inspired in him, he shares also its words. Such communications were not strange to his times or to his people. Often a word in Yahweh's interest was thought to be spoken from the holy place or from the temple in general or from such sacred writings as were occasionally turned to for reference. **God,** says our sage, somewhat more confident now, **has spoken in his sanctuary.** This was unlike the utterances that the Greeks coaxed from their oracles by divination, or frightened them into revealing by the ecstatic trances Plato called "insane." At the same time, it partakes of the indirect and symbolic form that such "words" have taken in all early cultures. To the uninitiated the oracle's promise was either devious or quite meaningless. It seems a poor response to the direct cry, **Give victory by thy right hand and answer us!** But to our poet the symbolism was clear if the result was not altogether reassuring. The allusion to **Shechem** and **the Vale of Succoth** is obscure. The two places had passed back and forth between the hands of Israel and her enemies. Was the oracle saying that it was God's right to make the ultimate settlement? Vs. 7 clearly indicates the undisputed power **(helmet)** and rule **(scepter)** of God in favored sections of **Gilead, Manasseh,** and **Ephraim.** The last three, **Moab, Edom,** and **Philistia,** are left for contempt. God will divest his sandals and cast them to the slave Edom and then wash his feet in Moab, shouting defiantly at Philistia, the while.

Moab is my washbasin;
upon [at] **Edom I cast my shoe;**
over Philistia I shout in triumph.

Thus spoke the oracle of God.

Was our poet conciliated? Hardly. He is still unsure, though he has moved a step away from the despair of his opening cry. It is better for him to ask questions than to shout his hopelessness.

Who will bring me to the fortified city?
Who will lead me to Edom?

9 Who will bring me *into* the strong city? who will lead me into Edom?
10 *Wilt* not thou, O God, *which* hadst cast us off? and *thou,* O God, *which* didst not go out with our armies?

9 Who will bring me to the fortified city?
Who will lead me to Edom?
10 Hast thou not rejected us, O God?
Thou dost not go forth, O God, with our armies.

---

north of Ephraim, with part on the east side and part on the west side of Jordan, its territory was open to conquest (cf. I Chr. 5:26). When Israel is again a great and undivided kingdom, the seat of government is to be in Judah, for **Judah is my scepter** (cf. Gen. 49:10), and **Ephraim is** [to be] **my helmet,** i.e., the protector of the realm. Israel's traditional enemies will be subjugated. **Moab,** with its sea, i.e., the Dead Sea, will serve as **my washpot.** And **upon Edom I cast my shoe,** a symbolical act to proclaim entrance into possession of it (cf. Ruth 4:8-9). **Over Philistia I shout in triumph:** Only in the days of David had Israel held sway over the Maritime Plain with Philistia. Its annexation will be the cause of special exultation.

3. Appeal to God (60:9-12)

9-11. After reminding the Lord of his promises, which the events of history seem to be mocking, the psalmist gloomily returns to the realities of mounting disaster. **Who will bring me to the fortified city . . . to Edom?** Better: "Oh, that one would bring me."

And then he returns questioningly to the language of his initial complaint, **Hast thou not rejected us, O God?** Has new light begun to break upon his dark spirit? Of one fact he is sure: **Thou dost not go forth, O God, with our armies;** but how is that fact to be understood—as God's act of rejection, as he had earlier thought, or as God's act of deliverance? It is something to have raised this searching question, but the answer is still beyond. The psalmist's only resource, therefore, is that to which the bewildered and the downcast ultimately turn—a prayer for help (vss. 11-12). However much of an anticlimax this ending is, it is the best that we can hope for from this bewildered and frightened man.

Mention has been made of the fear of **the bow** (vs. 4) or the skilled archers that the word symbolized. To herdsmen and vinedressers this was a terrifying thing; and not without reason has the bow been the symbol down the ages for the man of war and the business of warmaking. We must be careful that too heavy a weight of inference is not allowed to rest on the word and the poet's use of it. At the same time, however, we are supplied in this connection with two ideas which express the uneasy conscience of those who trust in war. In ways perhaps that our poet did not think, or even intend, we find him driving a dart through a rift in the armor of the god of war.

Two ideas come to us as the moral insight—deliberate or unplanned, no matter—that makes this poem religiously and spiritually fertile for our uses. It does no violence to the meaning they suggest to invert the sequence in which they appear. **Thou dost not go forth, O God, with our armies.** (Vs. 10*b*.) **Hast thou not rejected us?** (Vs. 10*a*.) **Thou hast set up a banner for those who fear thee** (vs. 4*a*), **to rally to it from the bow** (vs. 4*b*). It is no doubt the perspective of the centuries that enables us to understand what our poet said better than he may have understood it. It was, indeed, little short of treason for a God-fearing man to assert that armies which had marched forth to battle in God's name had marched off without him. If the same sentiment were put in different words today, it might still be thought seditious. We still try desperately to make God our ally; we still sing

> Onward, Christian soldiers!
> Marching as to war,

even though we would be more honest if we repeated this psalm's tentative yet profoundly significant words, **Thou dost not go forth, O God, with our armies.** It is but a step, though an important one, when we ask whether this discovery does not open the door into another. Once we realize that God does not march in our ranks we are able to see that his refusal is the only condition by which he can save us from the wickedness of war. He has not rejected us; by staying out of war he is saving us from war. Only thus can we believe that he is utterly and irreversibly dissociated from it.

This might be called a negative approach to the problem of war, this effort to separate from it all ideas that it is good, noble, true; or, to put it more bluntly, to quit the stupid, futile, and perfidious faith that the purposes of God

11 Give us help from trouble: for vain *is* the help of man.
12 Through God we shall do valiantly: for he *it is that* shall tread down our enemies.

To the chief Musician upon Neginah, *A Psalm* of David.

61 Hear my cry, O God; attend unto my prayer.

11 O grant us help against the foe,
for vain is the help of man!
12 With God we shall do valiantly;
it is he who will tread down our foes.

To the choirmaster: with stringed instruments. A Psalm of David.

61 Hear my cry, O God,
listen to my prayer;

The fortified city is probably Sela, the capital of Edom, since a country and its capital are frequently equated, as here in the parallelism (cf. Obad. 3). Since the intention is not to attack but to seek refuge (vs. 11) in Edom, the occasion must have been one of the rare times when Edom had made common cause with Israel against some invading power.

**O grant us help against the foe,
for vain is the help of man!**

The psalm would have ended with this tragic cry had not some sign, some oracle, some divine communication assured the people of a favorable answer from God. Because they now see a rainbow arching their clouds, their lament closes on a full-toned note of confidence (vs. 12).

LXI. Prayer of a Soul in Distress (61:1-8)

Within its brief compass this psalm conforms to the pattern of a lament. The psalmist is hard pressed by troubles, for the source of which he holds some enemy or enemies responsible. He has reached the end of his strength to endure these assaults that are directed against him. His defenses are crumbling and he has urgent need of protection and security. The nature of his troubles is not disclosed. A great variety of

---

can be served by war. The positive aspect is provided in the other sentiment our poet leaves with us (vs. 4). It is not enough for us to realize that God and war are irreconcilable. Man is still beset by his enemies, and he finds little help in himself or his brother (vs. 11). That God has set up a standard to which good men and true can repair—**to rally to it from the bow**—this is the ultimate Christian challenge to man's agelong folly of trust in the bow. Only in the long view of Christian history are we able to fix the point at which that standard was raised, and only by adding the Christian concept of the Cross to the psalmist's concept of **the banner** do we set forth fully the redemptive act of God. In these latter times, when our ranks are broken or we are put to rout, do we cry out in petulance against the anger of God? If we do, we shame the centuries that lie between us and an ancient poet's lament. When we mobilize for war in our times, do we look for God in the regimental command? If we do, we are totally blind to a banner that at least was dimly seen by one who had more excuse for being blind than we. "If the light in [us] is darkness, how great is the darkness!" (Matt. 6:23.)

61:1-8. ***Light Out of Darkness.***—It is refreshing to be engaged by a poem wholly free from the business of war. We cannot blame those who much of the time lived amid the exigencies of tribal and national conflicts for allowing their interests to be monopolized by them. If, however, one of the captives of one of the wars was carried far away, even to **the end of the earth,** as he puts it, and by his expatriation was removed from the preoccupations of warfare, we, remote as we are from the distressful circumstances, can be momentarily grateful to his captors. He is not the only one who "in durance vile" has given us insights both enduring and germinative. One thinks of Jeremiah, Paul, the Seer of Patmos, John Bunyan, Dostoevski, Gandhi, and a host of others. Much has been made of the apparent correlation between suffering and spiritual insight. It is not necessary

the ills that befall men were traced by the psalmists to the conspiracies, calumnies, or evil magic of enemies. The very indefiniteness and brevity of the psalm leads one to suppose that it could have served, and perhaps was made to serve, as a general lament for several categories of suppliants.

For the interpretation of the psalm it is important to understand what the psalmist meant by his words in vs. 2, **from the end of the earth I call to thee.** Taking them in their literal sense, some commentators suppose that the psalm was written by one who was in exile and who longed to enjoy again the privilege of being in the temple **under the shelter of thy wings.** Others change the rendering of the words slightly to read "from the end of the land," and assume that the psalmist was in some remote part of Palestine but unable to repair to Jerusalem. However, the generality of the terms employed by the psalmist with reference to his situation argues against the probability of finding in the psalm a hint as to his whereabouts. Consequently it seems better to follow the opinion of those who hold that by **the end of the earth** the psalmist means the point where the earth ends and the underworld begins, the lowest depths where life ends and death begins (cf. 18:5; 69:2; 130:1; Jonah 2:6).

In the original structure of the psalm vs. 8 must have followed vs. 5. The intervening verses which breathe a prayer on behalf of **the king** were added by a later hand either out of pious regard for the person of the ruler or to suit the psalm to some royal need. Such interpolations are met elsewhere, e.g., 28:8-9; 63:11*a*; 84:9, and in each instance, as here, introduce a break in the thought of the context. For this reason we cannot properly interpret the psalm as the lament of a king. We are, then, to understand it as the prayer of a soul in distress for shelter in God. The appeal (vss. 1-3) is followed by the expression of the psalmist's assurance that God has given a favorable response to his words (vss. 4-5). The promise of the psalmist to perform his vows of thanksgiving concludes the psalm (vs. 8).

The prayer for **the king** seems to postulate a pre-exilic date for these verses, and also for the psalm itself, which antedates them. The date, however, is probably in the late pre-exilic period since words of the psalmist in vs. 4 appear to have reference to the temple in Jerusalem as the sole **tent** of the Lord. The meter is irregular.

1. Appeal to God (61:1-3)

61:1-3. Hear my cry, O God: In Books II-III of the Psalter, **God** (אלהים) is preferred for the divine name to "the Lord" (יהוה; see Exeg. on 42:1-5). The psalmist includes

---

to agree that there is a causal relation in order to say that many times the loss of physical freedom seems to enlarge the freedom of the spirit; and it is important to be reminded that Epictetus the slave was more truly free than his master, lest we too easily equate political liberty with spiritual freedom.

The reason this psalm is an established favorite is that it makes articulate feelings which have always been common to the spiritually sensitive of all cultures. No time so much as our own has busied itself with the problems that harassed the poet of this ancient age. It is a part of the advantage under which we live that we have been able to know the deep-lying causes of our spiritual weaknesses, and to understand how we can nourish them back to vigorous health.

There is a clear aspect of unity in the literary construction of this poem, and it lends itself therefore to easy liturgical uses. Its brevity also helps, and except for the intrusion of the poet's prayer for his king, which is not necessarily as extraneous as some have thought, there is simple and direct movement from the opening cry to the more lighthearted commitment with which it ends. Our concern, however, can be more profitably directed to the pattern of spiritual depression sketched here. It is free from morbid excesses; it is indeed what many another has felt without being able to describe.

1-5. *Loneliness and Fear.*—The poet is lonely and afraid. Oddly enough—or is it odd?—this has been said about our own generation. "Almost everyone I know is either lonely or afraid," is the way one observer put it, confessing as he said it his own state of soul. He had not so intended his comment to be understood, for he was both rich and famous, and therefore one on whom suspicion of such wretchedness was not likely to rest. Our poet, however, sets it forth shamelessly. He was in an alien land

2 From the end of the earth will I cry unto thee, when my heart is overwhelmed: lead me to the rock *that* is higher than I.
3 For thou hast been a shelter for me, *and* a strong tower from the enemy.

2 from the end of the earth I call to thee,
when my heart is faint.

Lead thou me
to the rock that is higher than I;
3 for thou art my refuge,
a strong tower against the enemy.

---

in his appeal some reasons why God should listen to it. **My heart is faint,** i.e., his strength is done. The Hebrew word (עטף) is used in Lam. 2:19 of perishing or dying of hunger. His abject condition ought to move God to act. **For thou art my refuge:** Lit., "thou hast always been." The psalmist uses the perfect of experience. God will surely not show himself other than he has always been. And in all the past he has proved to be "a shelter," "a place to which one can go for protection," and an impregnable "stronghold." The text of vs. 2*b* is uncertain. As it now stands, it may be rendered freely, "To the rock [of safety] lead me, for it is too high for me [to climb in my own strength]." The text may be slightly emended (cf. LXX) to read, "Set me high on a rock and make me secure [lit., give me rest]," i.e., בצור תרממני תניחני.

---

through no wish of his own, and among hostile people. The terror of battle and the agony of the long trek into captivity—even perhaps the initial shock of enslavement—were past. He may have been able to accommodate himself somewhat to an intolerable regimen, but he had found no anodyne for his nostalgia. There was even a hint of uncertainty as to whether his God could hear him from so great a distance, or if hearing, he would listen. **Hear my cry, O God, . . . from the end of the earth I call to thee.** Where, we may ask, is **the end of the earth?** It is that place, whether noisy with people or silent by their absence, where one feels utterly alone. There is no point in trying to find out where our poet was, or into what captivity he had been taken. Had it been no farther than across a valley or a mountain ridge, or as distant as the setting sun, he could have spoken no truer word to describe his sense of alienation. He was at the end of the earth.

> Sometimes I feel like a motherless child
> A long ways from home.

Loneliness is a common and a numbing sensation, something which we now know can be exhibited by definite physical symptoms. But the psalmist was not only lonely; he was faint of heart. This is often the concomitant of loneliness; sometimes it is an element that sensitizes the spirit as loneliness sometimes dulls it. **My heart is faint,** he says; and yet we wonder if this is to be understood as faintheartedness, which is often cowardice. Is it not more correctly to be accepted as dis-couragement, using the word with its literal connotations and giving to "dis" its privative or separative force? He has lost heart. This, we observe, is often a spiritual condition more debilitating than active fear. To those who have no heart, active fear may cease to serve as a sentinel. We have then a condition or a type of fear that, while sensitive, is measurably deactivated. The panic that easily grips one with the realization that one is utterly alone and to that extent defenseless, is in a real way more prudential than the paralysis of despair that exposes one to the mildest sort of assault. In this connection it is not irrelevant to note that both loneliness and faintheartedness are by no means the result of external circumstances alone. More often than not they are largely subjective. For this reason it is proper to call them spiritual sickness, and thus a normal experience. When loneliness becomes an effort to escape from life and discouragement becomes morbid depression, they are dangerously neurotic and need treatment more skillful and sustained than our lonely and fainthearted poet asked for himself.

This primitive and yet profound diagnosis is not yet complete. To the sense of alienation and discouragement is added another pair of symptoms, bewilderment and insecurity. As loneliness and faintness of heart are a logical pair, so bewilderment, which is essentially a sense of lostness, and insecurity are a natural pair. The psalmist's prayer that he might be led to a high **rock** is susceptible of dual emphasis: one may think of the high rock which to him would certainly have been a place of refuge; or one may think of his desire for leading. After all, his loneliness and timidity might not have been helped by finding a **rock of refuge.** On the contrary! They might however be resolved if he could rediscover the presence of God leading

4 I will abide in thy tabernacle for ever: I will trust in the covert of thy wings. Selah.
5 For thou, O God, hast heard my vows: thou hast given *me* the heritage of those that fear thy name.
6 Thou wilt prolong the king's life: *and* his years as many generations.

4 Let me dwell in thy tent for ever!
Oh to be safe under the shelter of thy wings! *Selah*
5 For thou, O God, hast heard my vows,
thou hast given me the heritage of those who fear thy name.

6 Prolong the life of the king;
may his years endure to all generations!

2. The Psalmist's Faith Is Quickened (61:4-5, 8)

4-5. Thou, O God, hast heard my vows: The psalmist's mood is suddenly changed. Through some sign or communication given at the holy place he is made aware that God is about to act on his behalf. He has now no need to continue his lament, but only to give praise and thanks. **Thou hast given me the heritage of those who fear thy name:** Read ארשת, "request" or "desire," for ירשת, "possession." **Let me dwell in thy tent for ever:** The psalmist wishes that the rapture of this experience in God's house, with its sense of being **safe under the shelter of thy wings,** might never end (cf. Exeg. on 17:8; 57:1-3).

8. The psalmist will pay his vow to praise the name of his God for his deliverance not once, as was the common custom, but **day after day** anew.

3. Intercession for the King (61:6-7)

6-7. The prayer for **the king** voices three requests: (*a*) that the life of the king may be prolonged beyond the years God had allotted to him, "Add days to the days of

him. Confirmation is given this understanding by the explanation that follows his prayer. He asks to be led to a rocky eminence, but after all it is God, not the elevation, that is his refuge. **Lead thou me**—it is the man who is lost who asks for guidance—**to the rock that is higher than I; for thou art my refuge, a strong tower against the enemy.**

Not only is the sense of lostness implicit in these words; the sense of insecurity is explicit in them. The poet asks for leading with the confidence that his bewilderment, and the sense of insecurity it creates, can be relieved in God who is his **refuge** and his **strong tower.** It is his realization of the possibility of security that makes him break forth into his picturesque apostrophe to security (vs. 4). It is God's **tent** that promises him security, not a high rock; it is God's sheltering **wings** that guarantee safety. And lest it appear that he puts his ultimate trust in tents and wings, he forbears further use of metaphor and puts the matter literally:

For thou, O God, hast heard my vows,
thou hast given me the heritage of those who fear thy name.

6-7. ***A Wider Concern.***—These two verses seem to break the continuity of the poet's meditation. Up to this point his concern has been exclusively with himself. What reason is there for obtruding this solicitude for **the king?** It is this problem that has led some expositors to assign these verses to a later editor. This, however, answers no questions. There is little choice between the original vagary of the poet and the later vagary of the editor. If the sentiment is obtrusive, it is so no matter who is responsible for it. It is moreover unnecessary to appeal to editorial emendation if we remember that our author is a poet, and that his mood is one induced by loneliness and discouragement, confusion and insecurity. And in the experience of his people who but the king was proxy for the Lord? It in no sense derogated one's trust in God to think uneasily of the king when one was in the melancholy state of our writer. The concern he exhibits for his distant ruler would have served him well by momentarily taking his mind off himself. It might also intimate that he was anxious lest his fate befall others who would be defended against it so long as the king was sustained in power. It may therefore be plausibly argued that these seemingly odd verses are of a piece with the concern already manifest in the preceding strophes. Only if God preserved the king's life could the poet have hope for release; and only thus would others be safeguarded against the fate in which he was languishing. Clearly the word **king** symbolizes the throne, since such indeterminate longevity as is asked for would be no boon to an individual. And is it not a lofty note upon

7 He shall abide before God for ever: O prepare mercy and truth, *which* may preserve him.
8 So will I sing praise unto thy name for ever, that I may daily perform my vows.

7 May he be enthroned for ever before
God;
bid steadfast love and faithfulness
watch over him!

8 So will I ever sing praises to thy name,
as I pay my vows day after day.

---

the king" (cf. II Kings 20:6); (*b*) that the king's reign may never be cut off, but that he may live and rule always near to the place of God's presence; (*c*) that, like two guardians, God's kindness and faithful care may ever attend him. This loyal petition on behalf of the king is expressed in extravagant terms characteristic of the court style of the ancient Near East in utterances respecting the royal person (cf. 72:5). In Egypt a common prayer to the sun-god was "Keep Pharaoh, our good lord, in health! Let him celebrate millions of jubilees!" (Erman, *Die Religion der Ägypter,* pp. 198, 202.)

---

which the poet ends? Not escape from his predicament, but the securing of the throne of Israel by **steadfast love and faithfulness** will, he attests, be the inspiration of his eternal thanksgiving and the daily performance of his vows, no matter how dismal his own prospects.

8. ***The Sum of It All.***—We return briefly to the diagnosis our psalmist has made of his state of mind: loneliness and discouragement, bewilderment and insecurity. These have been symptoms of spiritual indisposition since the beginning of time, and it is doubtful that modern diagnostic procedures will produce more accurate understanding of the spiritual illness of the present. This needs no expansion: that this sickness is reaching epidemic proportions is something about which there is no longer any debate. That we must discover ways by which we can be cured follows, of course, on our acceptance of the diagnosis. It is at this point that the judgments of the doctors diverge —doctors medical, doctors political, doctors social. It is the doctors spiritual who for the most part prescribe the ancient therapeutics, and in this they are wise.

There was a time when to state that God was the cure for spiritual sickness was likely to evoke amiable tolerance or mild irritation. We are not wholly over this, and those of us who now say it must be better prepared than ever before to explain what we mean by it. It is hardly enough to point to our poet and quote his familiar metaphors. To a more sophisticated generation we may have to quote modern poets. T. S. Eliot, for all his puzzling obscurity, has one central theme: Man lives today in "the waste land"; he is lonely, discouraged, perplexed, insecure. He will find companionship, heart, understanding, and safety in God, but he will have to work at it. This is what Eliot's fellow craftsman said thousands of years ago.

There is one other insight deserving our attention. It occurs in the verse in which our poet prays for the king from whom he has been forcibly separated. In an engaging figure of speech our poet is surveying a court scene where the king is enthroned in splendid security, and he asks for him that steadfast love and faithfulness may be his bodyguards. This is an honorable literary device. Kipling in "The Elephant's Child" said:

> I keep six honest serving-men
> (They taught me all I knew);
> Their names are What and Why and When
> And How and Where and Who.[5]

We therefore have no difficulty in seeing two stalwart guardsmen at the king's side. They are variously called "lovingkindness and truth" (ASV), "love and loyalty" (Moffatt), "loving mercy and faithfulness" (Book of Common Prayer); but they are to the king both protection and power.

This completes our picture. Whether or not we agree, our poet has at least made clear what to him was indisputable. He felt lonely, dispirited, uncertain, unsafe. To a degree it is unpleasant to confess, he is the spokesman for all the sons of men. He is certain, if we take the second step with him, that his only escape from his unhappy state is in God. **Thou hast given me the heritage of those who fear thy name** (vs. 5). Again, to a degree modern man is increasingly ready to confess, our poet is spokesman for all men. There is the final matter which allows us no such hopefulness. As we today look at the kings of earth—or more properly at the centers of political power—do

[5] From *Just So Stories.* Copyright 1910 by Rudyard Kipling, reprinted by permission of Mrs. George Bambridge, Macmillan & Co., The Macmillan Co. of Canada, and Doubleday & Co., Inc.

To the chief Musician, to Jeduthun, A Psalm of David.

62 Truly my soul waiteth upon God: from him *cometh* my salvation.

To the choirmaster: according to Jeduthun. A Psalm of David.

62 For God alone my soul waits in silence;
from him comes my salvation.

LXII. My Soul Waits for God (62:1-12)

This brief poem belongs to that group of psalms in which the dominant note is one of trust and confidence in the Lord; cf. Pss. 4; 11; 16; 23; 27; 131, each of which expresses in its own way the same firm hope in God's full ability and willingness to help his faithful ones in every time of need. The ground of this assurance lies in these psalmists' clear vision of the greatness of the Lord upon his throne and of the immensity of the resources at his command. The worst assaults of earth cannot provoke dismay and loss of courage in their hearts or weaken their invincible faith. Such psalms have arisen out of such situations as are reflected in the laments. The familiar complaints of trouble, distress, and the evil machinations of men are heard or echoed (cf. Pss. 23; 131) in them. They differ from the laments in that they transcend the bitterness of the immediate experience to tell of that which makes men "more than conquerors" in their struggle against the evil powers of men or circumstance. In style also they differ from the laments in that they speak *of* the Lord in the third person instead of speaking *to* him in the second person.

Originally Ps. 62 opened abruptly (vss. 3-4) with a stern and indignant reprimand of the foes with whom the psalmist had to deal (cf. Ps. 58). At some later date a reader of the psalm, impressed by the beauty of the words of trust in vss. 5-6, wrote them out at the head of the psalm, and in time they appeared as vss. 1-2. That these opening verses are misplaced is shown, as Schmidt notes, by the particle אַךְ, "but." However, through this happy occurrence, though the form of the psalm has been disturbed, the theme has been accented.

The psalmist, while not disclosing with definiteness the situation which was created by or led to the hostility of a party of unscrupulous men, gives the impression that men of wealth and power (vss. 9-10) seek by deceitful and mendacious means not only to depose him from some high post which he holds, but to bring about his destruction (vss. 3-4). His words are not unlike those of Sir Thomas Elyot in his sixteenth-century *Boke Called the Governour:* "There is much conversant among men in authority a vice very ugly and monstrous, who under the pleasant habit of friendship and good counsel with a breath pestilential infecteth the wits of them that nothing mistrusteth; this monster is called in English *Detraction,* in Latin *calumnia.*"

---

we see standing in watch the twin giants, compassion and integrity? We must withhold our answer, but only because we must pray:

May he be enthroned for ever before God;
bid steadfast love and faithfulness watch over him!

62:1-12. ***Public Affairs and Religion.***—We registered our sense of satisfaction when, commenting on Ps. 61, we felt relieved at escaping for the moment from the atmosphere of war. Without having consented to the situation in which he was confined, our poet had adjusted himself to it by acquiescing in those matters which he could not at that point change. This freed him sufficiently so that he could examine his spiritual sickness and prescribe for it.

In this psalm we have another variant on man's unhappiness that is due neither to the tensions of war nor to the frustrations of captivity. Who our poet is need not detain our study of what he was thinking. All other considerations that question the Davidic authorship would seem to be guaranteed by the obvious fact that in so far as we know the story of David's life, he was never in the predicament our author describes. It is clear here that we have one who was a politico-religious leader —a designation less distinctive in its application to the days of Israel than it is for our own. There was no sharp cleavage between politics

2 He only *is* my rock and my salvation; *he is* my defense; I shall not be greatly moved.

3 How long will ye imagine mischief against a man? ye shall be slain all of you: as a bowing wall *shall ye be, and as* a tottering fence.

4 They only consult to cast *him* down from his excellency: they delight in lies: they bless with their mouth, but they curse inwardly. Selah.

2 He only is my rock and my salvation,
my fortress; I shall not be greatly
moved.

3 How long will you set upon a man
to shatter him, all of you,
like a leaning wall, a tottering fence?
4 They only plan to thrust him down from
his eminence.
They take pleasure in falsehood.
They bless with their mouths,
but inwardly they curse. *Selah*

The psalmist sums up his spiritual experience in an address (vss. 8-12) to the whole congregation of the people of Israel (cf. 115:9), which in its didactic form and point of view follows a pattern that is familiar in Hebrew wisdom literature (cf. Pss. 37; 49; 73; 130). The substance of his teaching is that men by their very nature are **but a breath,** and likewise riches, however gained, are a delusion, for to God alone belong all power and goodness, and he rewards each man according to his deserts. In the manner of Job 4:12; 33:14-18, this psalmist claims authority for his words in a revelation (vs. 11) which he has received more than once (cf. I Cor. 2:13).

The psalm is indubitably late. The meter is variable, a feature which, as in this instance it cannot be the result only of textual corruptions, points to a postexilic date. The introduction of wisdom motifs into psalmody becomes increasingly common in late Jewish literature until in the postcanonical period the wisdom element predominates (Jansen, *Die spätjudische Psalmendichtung,* pp. 49-53).

1. The Psalmist's Foes Reprimanded (62:3-4)

62:1-2. See Exeg. on vss. 5-7, 1-2.

3-4. How long will you set upon a man [lit., "rush upon a man"] **to shatter him?** The translation **shatter** is based on the meaning of the cognate Arabic verb. His enemies close in upon him to complete the ruin which is imminent. **Like a leaning wall,** he is all but

---

and religion then. Indeed, such a separation has never been explicit in the culture of the Hebrews. Its original theocratic political orientation has been conspicuously preserved wherever politics and religion have remained of vital concern. This fact has been adduced as a factor in the strange phenomenon of anti-Semitism. It is not, some have said, that the Jews have made themselves odious; it is that man's perverse rebellion against God and the institutions of religion has made him angry at those who have insisted that a deep sense of God is man's only safeguard against social corruption.

It is not difficult to see that our poet here is describing either an experience of his own in the role of a defender of the politico-religious orientation of his people, or the distress of another whom he has imagined or observed. He moves from the first to the third person as he writes, imparting thereby both subjective and objective emphasis to his discussion. He soliloquizes and preaches in alternate strophes; he moves from exhortation to judgment, and from ridicule to pathos. He never loses sight, however, of the position he feels destined to protect or of the ultimate resource on which his dependence rests. It will bring out the nature and the lasting significance of his struggle if we see it in the three dimensions he describes, though not necessarily in the order in which the Expos. will treat them.

1-7. ***Picture of the Poet.***—In the first place, the poet shares with us a clear picture of himself. That he is a man of deep piety is to be expected, but he does not allow us to take it for granted. If he is to put more emphasis on one or the other of his political and religious interests, it will be on the latter. He is sure that such action as he must take will be determined by the sort of man he is. He will therefore make clear to himself what his spiritual needs are and how they are to be met. These are summed up, as in the first stanza (though see Exeg.), in his over-all need of God. He must have a **rock** on which he can stand im-

5 My soul, wait thou only upon God; for my expectation *is* from him.
6 He only *is* my rock and my salvation: *he is* my defense; I shall not be moved.
7 In God *is* my salvation and my glory: the rock of my strength, *and* my refuge, *is* in God.

5 For God alone my soul waits in silence,
for my hope is from him.
6 He only is my rock and my salvation,
my fortress; I shall not be shaken.
7 On God rests my deliverance and my honor;
my mighty rock, my refuge is God.

---

down in consequence of their assaults. With vs. 4 the psalmist changes the pronoun of address. Having faced his detractors with an exposé of their villainy, he turns from them to tell of their purposes and their double-dealing before the world. **They . . . plan to thrust him down from his eminence, i.e.,** from his elevated position. One judges that these words have reference to a conspiracy against his exercise of some high office among his people (vs. 8). The weapons used against him are lying and duplicity.

2. Words of Quiet Trust (62:5-7, 1-2)

5-7, 1-2. For God alone my soul waits in silence: The opening word of this line in the Hebrew is an adversative particle; lit., "But unto God be still, O my soul." On the one hand are the adversaries, but on the other is God. In vs. 1 an alternate reading appears, "But unto God my soul is still." Such a reading in such a position in the psalm weakens the effect of vs. 5*a* and argues for vss. 1-2 having been misplaced (see Exeg. above). Schmidt and Gunkel would substitute the reading of vs. 1*a* for vs. 5*a* because in such a psalm of trust a summons to the soul seems inappropriate, but cf. 42:5, 11; 103:1. **Waits in silence:** I.e., without the utterance of loud appeals to God for help. **My hope is from him:** Vs. 1 reads **my salvation,** being affected by the text of vs. 6*a*. **He only is my rock, . . . fortress, . . . mighty rock, . . . refuge:** Metaphors are multiplied to show the psalmist's conviction of his invincible defenses in God. **I shall not be shaken:** In vs. 2 a later hand has modified this affirmation to read, **I shall not be greatly** [רבה]

---

movable, a **salvation** on which he can depend, a **fortress** from which he can direct his defensive and offensive strategy. The realization of these needs comes, strangely enough in a man of action, from silent waiting—**For God alone my soul waits in silence**—a discipline that is always self-imposed and never easy in the face of external demands for vigorous action.

Before his exercise of spiritual discipline, waiting in silence—and what a contrast that sets up with the noisy activism of his adversaries—the psalmist has taken a position from which he is determined not to retreat. It is not necessary here to decide just what that position was. It may have been one that concerned the established and orthodox order or some particular or seasonal episode. In any case he had declared himself. Not, however, with the bravado of blind confidence, though he was sure of ultimate victory. He realistically anticipates that he may have moments of insecurity when the adversary, noting his discomfiture, will press for advantage. He will be moved, but **not . . . greatly moved.**

The way the poet faces this contingency takes nothing away from the importance or the loftiness of the position he has assumed. It is eminent; not, we assume, because he has prideful notions of his own gravity, but because it is something in which the most high, the most eminent God has a stake. He stands on a lofty place; he is like a high wall. The wall leans precariously; it is more like **a tottering fence** than an impregnable bastion. He is the symbol of something high and eternal, and against it men throw themselves and their engines of assault. The man, the wall, leans. Will the adversary allow a moment for him to regain his balance, or will he strike him while he reels? He will strike, of course; he will shatter him and what he stands for, he will thrust him down like a crumbling fence.

How long will you set upon a man
to shatter him, all of you,
like a leaning wall, a tottering fence?

The simile clearly refers to the man. **They only plan to thrust him down from his eminence.**

This does not describe defeat; the poet has predicted that the wall would be shaken, and in that way has protected his soul from panic at the first shock. As he reflects upon it, a fresh fillip is given to his confidence. He recurs to the exercise in spiritual discipline with which

8 Trust in him at all times; ye people,
pour out your heart before him: God *is* a
refuge for us. Selah.
9 Surely men of low degree *are* vanity,
and men of high degree *are* a lie: to be laid
in the balance, they *are* altogether *lighter*
than vanity.
10 Trust not in oppression, and become
not vain in robbery: if riches increase, set
not your heart *upon them.*

8 Trust in him at all times, O people;
pour out your heart before him;
God is a refuge for us. *Selah*

9 Men of low estate are but a breath,
men of high estate are a delusion;
in the balances they go up;
they are together lighter than a breath.
10 Put no confidence in extortion,
set no vain hopes on robbery;
if riches increase, set not your heart on
them.

---

shaken, meaning to adjust the psalmist's words to his condition described in vs. 3 as **a leaning wall, a tottering fence.**

3. God a Refuge for All (62:8-12)

8-12. Trust in him at all times, O people: The lessons of the psalmist's experience are now set forth for the encouragement and comfort of the whole congregation (cf. LXX πᾶσα συναγωγὴ λαοῦ). Read preferably עמי, "my people," or כל־עדת עם, "all the

---

he began; he must wait in silence for God (vs. 5). This time, however, his reward will not be a sure though shaken stance; he will be able to stand without a tremor:

On God rests my deliverance and my honor;
my mighty rock, my refuge is God.

8-11. *A Cause and a Following.*—The preceding verses have presented the psalmist's picture of himself. Now we turn to the relation he sustains to a cause and a following. Only in the most general terms can his cause be known. He is clearly engaged in a struggle for power, this being the constant factor in every political equation. By inference we understand that his adversaries have made the claim that power belonged to them, thus defying the established and orthodox position that power belonged to God, an idea that carried with it the assurance that kindness also belonged to God. Was our poet setting up a contrast between power plus ruthlessness and power plus kindness? This is an ancient political difference and is basically the ideal difference between despotism and democracy; the former using ruthlessness as its political instrument, the latter using conciliation. It would appear, then, that our political leader puts two planks into his platform, or the cause for which he contends. The first is God as the source and center of authority; this is theocracy, and its formula is power plus kindness (consideration of human rights?). The second is that a man is judged and requited according to what he does, rather than because of any factitious rank or advantage. This, it is easy to see, is at least one, if not the basic, quality of democracy.

Once God has spoken;
twice have I heard this:
that power belongs to God;
and that to thee, O Lord, belongs steadfast love.
For thou dost requite a man
according to his work.

This was the poet's cause or platform. What of the constituency to which he appeals? It is obviously divided among those he can count on for support, those he hopes to enlist, and those who are resolutely opposed to him. To the first he needs only offer an exhortation to stay put; to the second he offers a warning against the specious promises of his opponents, and for the third he has a sharp word of condemnation.

To his own people his political and religious faith was acceptable. Vs. 8 sets forth the essence both of religious fidelity—**trust in him at all times;** and of political conservatism—**God is a refuge for us.** The poet seems to count also on the support of the unspecified stratum of middle-of-the-roaders who lie between the **men of low estate** and the **men of high estate** (vs. 9). For some reason he seems to write off these extremes of low and high. Are they ancient foreshadowings of what today are called the left and the right? It is easy to see how one with pious pretensions might regard the *haut monde* as vain, as lightweight, and therefore of little importance. Not so easy, however, is the dismissal of those of low estate, unless they are of the demimonde. The reference is almost certainly to a

11 God hath spoken once; twice have I heard this; that power *belongeth* unto God.
12 Also unto thee, O Lord, *belongeth* mercy: for thou renderest to every man according to his work.

11 Once God has spoken;
twice have I heard this:
that power belongs to God;
12 and that to thee, O Lord, belongs steadfast love.
For thou dost requite a man
according to his work.

---

congregation of the people," since עַם, **people,** is never used alone in the vocative (Baethgen). The substance of the teaching, in a word, is **God is a refuge for us.** For **men** of every degree, high and low, **are but a breath, . . . a delusion** (cf. 116:11). The adversaries of the psalmist have no ground of hope in the power that comes to them from extortion and robbery and the resultant increase of their wealth (cf. 49:5-6). The psalmist bases his confidence on what God has said to him through oracles or mystical communications (cf. Job 40:4-5; 42:2). **God hath spoken once; twice have I heard this:** A divine revelation given more than once has special weight. The content of this revelation therefore is not two separate things but one: God's omnipotence and kindness together work to the end that every man, good or evil, receives his just recompense. While some wisdom writers (cf. Job and Ecclesiastes) questioned the invariableness of the rule of this principle as set forth by the psalmist, it never ceased

---

low moral rather than social estate. **Men of low estate are but a breath.** Between these strata lie those who are both the poet's strength and his problem. They are the mobile middle class upon whom social and political and spiritual power depend. Since they can change their minds readily, they are appealed to by the pro and con of argument. Had our friend's opposition promised them a higher standard of living, based, to be sure, on a national policy that only dimly concealed its "wrong and robbery" (as the Book of Common Prayer quaintly puts it), but justified nevertheless by political arguments that have always been more or less persuasive? If so, our defender of political orthodoxy issues his word of warning:

Put no confidence in extortion
set no vain hopes on robbery;
if riches increase, set not your heart on them.

Thus he seeks to divert strength from his enemies to his own cause. To those he can count on, he would add those who ought to be held in line by appeals to righteousness in political life. For his enemies, those whom he has already pictured as assaulting a leaning wall and a tottering fence, he has a few descriptive and dismissive words.

They take pleasure in falsehood.
They bless with their mouths,
but inwardly they curse (vs. 4*bc*).

They have promised prosperity without moral safeguards. Such language has perennial and ageless familiarity.

12. ***Power Belongs to God.***—We have sought to discover our poet in two dimensions: his estimate of himself and his understanding of his constituency. This latter has given us some understanding of his platform, his supporters, his opponents, and those whom he must win. One dimension remains for study. It deals more specifically with the cause he espouses, and it is to be understood only if we remember the interfusion of political and spiritual interests as they occurred in the indigenous Hebrew mind. Our purpose will be served if it is put in its five rudiments. The cause is the governance of God in all human affairs, made articulate in four steps: (*a*) personal dedication through the disciplines of patient waiting and confident hope; (*b*) the maintenance of clear moral ideals and practices; (*c*) the exercise of such power as one has as the surrogate of God, mindful all the while that it must be used with kindness; and (*d*) the treatment of one's fellows, not arbitrarily, but in just recognition of the quality and extent of their voluntary participation in the social enterprise. In the effort to advance this lofty cause the poet announced his platform and made his appeal. The campaign ends with a note of confidence. We have no report on the election!

It is, of course, impossible to derive a political analysis from a poem. Yet in this lyric discursus we come upon something both very ancient in human experience and very modern in its religious and political pertinence. Even though we may have grown accustomed to the dichotomy between religion and politics and allowed each to have its own aims, codes, and practices,

A Psalm of David, when he was in the wilderness of Judah.

63 O God, thou *art* my God; early will I seek thee: my soul thirsteth for thee, my flesh longeth for thee in a dry and thirsty land, where no water is;

A Psalm of David, when he was in the Wilderness of Judah.

63 O God, thou art my God, I seek thee,
my soul thirsts for thee;
my flesh faints for thee,
as in a dry and weary land where no water is.

---

to be an article of faith in orthodox circles (cf. Luke 13:1-5). The Targ. reads here, "Twice have I heard from the mouth of Moses, the great teacher," as, e.g., in Deut. 28:1-68.

LXIII. A Soul Thirsty for God (63:1-11)

In the present arrangement of its text the psalm appears to be, like Ps. 62, an expression of trust and confidence in God's abiding help. But unlike psalms of this type (cf. Pss. 23; 27), its words are spoken to God, not about God, in this respect following the pattern of a prayer or petition rather than of a psalm of contemplative motifs. But even as such, it offers difficulties to both translator and interpreter, as the various handlings of it attest. The core of the trouble springs from some confusion in the order of the text. After the psalmist's opening cry for God's presence (vss. 1-2), he unexpectedly gives expression to a mood of spiritual satisfaction and thanksgiving (vss. 3-5), and only later reveals the occasion for it (vss. 6-8). The awkward **so** at the beginning of vs. 4 is only one of the difficulties arising from this singular circumstance, for vs. 3 is clearly not its antecedent. The confusion disappears when the order of the lines and of the stanzas is restored to what seems to be their natural sequence: vss. 1-2; 6-8; 4, 5, 3; 9-10, 11*c*; 11*ab*. It then becomes clear that the psalm conforms to the style of a lament.

The psalmist has been beset by grievous troubles occasioned by the bitter hostility of personal enemies (vss. 9-10). In his distress he seeks God's presence in the sanctuary

---

it is by no means assured that we either are better off that way or are satisfied to have it thus. Man is a political animal, we have been told. So long as he allows his political interests to express themselves in ways that are independent of or hostile to his elemental spiritual interests, his existence as an animal of any sort is jeopardized. The modern political and moral turmoil of our times is proof enough of that.

Whether therefore we have a right to appropriate this psalm for use as a political tract for the times, we can at least claim there is caught within its inspiration much of what has become the ideal for democratic society. Culturally we have assimilated the great Hebrew-Christian ideals of God's supremacy, human brotherhood, world community, moral law, the ultimate triumph of right, and the use of power for beneficent ends. As these have helped to shape the political thinking of the West they have given it its democratic contours. This much cannot be disputed.

It has been easy, in these times when democratic areas of the world have been contracted, to regard democracy as exhausted of power and empty of promise. An answer to this mood is not necessary in the context of this psalm, but it may be a stimulus to confidence if we can extend the line of our vision far enough into the past to catch sight of this stout old democrat of ancient times. See him standing amid the confusion and conflicts of his people; and hear him say with simple and quiet certainty to those who were dubious about the faith that supported him:

> **For God alone my soul waits in silence;**
> **from him comes my salvation.**

If that sounds too much like the pulpit, perhaps his final word sounds more like the hustings:

> **Once God has spoken;**
> **twice have I heard this:**
> **that power belongs to God;**
> **and that to thee, O Lord, belongs steadfast love.**
> **For thou dost requite a man**
> **according to his work.**

63:1-11. ***The Omnipresence of God.***—This poem is properly regarded as one of the truly notable bits of devotional writing in all the literature of religion. That is a great though

(vss. 1-2), and there, as he sleeps under the shelter of God's wings, his soul is satisfied, since in communion with God he discovers, as Isaiah (ch. 6) did in the same sacred place, the resources which he has in God and the grounds for fullness of confidence and courage (vss. 6-8). The psalmist takes heart, therefore, and with joy vows to sing all his days praises to God for the deliverance which he sees at hand (vss. 4, 5, 3). With equal confidence he concludes with a prediction of the utter overthrow of those who put their trust in lying words. Out of the depths of despair the psalmist has been brought to the heights of faith and trust. So understood, "the psalm," as Gunkel says (*Die Psalmen*, p. 267), "is one of the pearls of the Psalter."

Vs. 11*ab* stands outside of the text of the psalm. It should be regarded as an addition such as is seen in other psalms, e.g., 28:8-9; 61:6-7; 84:9, but from it we learn that the psalm must have been used in the services at the temple on some day of prayer and intercession for the king. However, its secondary nature is seen in the contrast between the strongly subjective note of the psalm and the objective reference to the king.

Since the psalm obviously antedates vs. 11*ab*, which belongs to the time of the monarchy, it must be reckoned as pre-exilic. The superscription relates the psalm, because of the mention of the **dry and weary land** of vs. 1, to the time of David's flight from Saul into the Judean wilderness (I Sam. 24). Among modern commentators, Oesterley believes that the king referred to is Jehoiachin, that the psalmist was one of his fellow exiles in Babylon, and that the psalm consequently is early exilic. As has been shown, the royal reference is secondary. Attempts to identify the king are, in view of the present state of our knowledge of the history of the monarchy in Israel, wholly speculative.

In this connection it must be stressed that the interpretation of the psalm as the lament of an individual does not imply that it was divorced from the cult of the temple

---

not an extravagant distinction. Nowhere more profoundly than in the literary compendium of the Hebrews is the religious mood propounded, probed, and made articulate for private and corporate use. This is true not only in the Psalter; there are other media of piety in the vital insights of the prophets and, one might add, in no little of the folklore and legend which contain the primitive aspirations of Israel's unorganized religious days. But the position of this poem in the Psalms has been well put by Oesterley: "The earnest yearning for God, and the insight into communion with him on the part of a truly good man, as these are set forth in this psalm, are unrivalled in the Psalter." [6] Cheyne asserts it thus: "His heart has become a temple of praise." [7]

Such virtuosity can be variously explained since there are numerous factors of temperament, environment, age, etc., that affect one's moods, whether they are religious or otherwise. Speculation as to the author has therefore been rife among the scholars. The early anthologists found it easy to put the poem into David's catalogue, and, for lack of a specific episode, assigned its inspiration to a sojourn in the wilderness of Judah, assuming no doubt that the reference to a **dry and weary land where no water is** was sufficiently general to include any inhospitable and dispiriting place where David in his wandering might have stopped long enough for a brief lyric exercise. This explanation is too easy and has therefore been abandoned. The general consensus is that the psalm is the work of an unknown exile who wrote during his captivity in Babylon. The reference in vs. 11 to **the king** is taken to indicate Jehoiachin, who was carried away by Nebuchadrezzar after the siege of Jerusalem *ca.* 603 B.C. Some doubt of this identification must be allowed. Jehoiachin was hardly the sort who would **rejoice in God,** as our poet generously claims. The opinion of the royal captive as expressed in a single line in II Kings 24:9 indicates that such filial piety as he exhibited was toward an evil father rather than a righteous God: "He did that which was evil in the sight of the LORD, according to all that his father had done." His father, we are reminded, was for three years a collaborationist with the king of Babylon. "He filled Jerusalem," the record has it, "with innocent blood; which the LORD would not pardon" (II Kings 24:4). Furthermore, the son lost his throne when he was made captive and was succeeded by a Babylonian puppet, his uncle Zedekiah, who, if our record is accurate, was as little inclined to rejoice in God as his captive nephew.

These matters are of little importance to our use of the poem. No matter what the name of the man who wrote it, his identity is established

[6] *The Psalms*, I, 307.

[7] *The Book of Psalms* (London: Kegan Paul, Trench, Trübner & Co., 1905), p. 236.

2 To see thy power and thy glory, so *as* I have seen thee in the sanctuary.	2 So I have looked upon thee in the sanctuary, beholding thy power and glory.

or that psalms were not designated for the king in its ritual (Elmer A. Leslie, *The Psalms* [New York and Nashville: Abingdon-Cokesbury Press, 1949], p. 273). All that can be maintained is that here the reference to the king is no more integral to the psalm than the generally recognized royal interpolations in certain other psalms, e.g., 28:8; 84:9 (*ibid.*, pp. 44, 367).

The meter is for the most part 3+3, but 4+3 occurs in vss. 5 and 9, and 3+2 in vs. 3.

1. The Psalmist's Faith (63:1-8)

63:1-2. O God, thou art my God: The psalmist begins with a statement of his credo, which is also the ground of his right of appeal. **My soul thirsts, . . . my flesh faints for thee:** His whole being longs for God (cf. 42:1-2), and he compares his state to that of physical hunger and thirst. **In a dry and thirsty land:** Better with Hebrew MSS and the Syriac, "as in a dry land." He is speaking metaphorically as in the preceding part of the verse. For rhythmical and grammatical reasons omit עָיֵף, **weary. So I have looked upon thee in the sanctuary:** Definitely the experience of the psalmist is met with in the temple to which he has betaken himself. For in the temple communion with and

in other ways. He was a deeply religious man, with a gift for both feeling and expression. No matter where he was—Babylon, the wilderness of Judea, or at home in Jerusalem—he was able to transport himself by the vehicle of imagination to such places as afforded him the intimacies of the divine presence. It is possible therefore for us to take this poem as it is and find in it a pattern of the devotional experience that is authentic, no matter where found or by whom enjoyed.

1-8. ***God Is Man's Ultimate Need.***—The residual essence of religious devotion is that the object of one's dedication is the All. Usually true of the experience, it is specifically true in the Hebrew-Christian tradition. Our poet agrees to it as readily as the saintly Fénelon, who said: "We must be God's without any reservation. When we have found God, there is nothing more to look for in men. We must sacrifice our best friends. The good friend is within our heart. He is the bridegroom who is jealous and who does away with all the rest." [8] This is what our psalmist says, though he uses a different metaphor. **O God, thou art my God; early will I seek thee: my soul thirsteth for thee, my flesh longeth for thee in a dry and thirsty land, where no water is.** Fénelon was archbishop of Cambrai and tutor to the Duke of Burgundy, but the profligacy of the court of Louis XIV in which he lived was spiritually as weary and waterless as the Babylon—real or fancied—of our poet.

This is more than an affirmation of the fact of God, which is easy; it is an affirmation of the possession of God, which is both difficult and daring. **Thou art my God,** he says. How the sense of possessing God is engendered is of itself the subject of a vast literature. With our saint, however, the method is clear. His is not the purely mystical experience, sensing God in an unmediated fashion. God has come to him through the experience of worship. His own sense of the Divine is real, but he does not scorn to have it validated and given form. Because it is real, he seeks to see God, to see him as power and glory, and to see him in the sanctuary where presumably there were effective aids to contemplation and apprehension. **So** [since thou art my God] **I have looked upon thee in the sanctuary, beholding thy power and glory.** The sure apprehension suggested here is above all full-bodied and dynamic. It indicates that God is no wraithlike, amorphous apparition. He is a god of power and splendor. Nothing of pageantry is lost in our poet's rapture; if he is to claim the possession of God, it is to hold something alive with energy and radiance. This stands in marked contrast to what is thought to be the passivity and colorlessness of much of the mystical vision of the Eastern saint.

2-4. ***God's Power and Glory in His Love.***—God is the All, this we have said is the center of religious devotion, and we have seen that our poet makes this claim and assigns to him the qualities of power and glory. It is this recognition of value that is distinctive here. God is the All, not because he is God, but because he is a God of power and glory. But more

[8] *Christian Perfection*, ed. Charles F. Whiston (New York: Harper & Bros., 1947), p. 27.

3 Because thy loving-kindness *is* better than life, my lips shall praise thee.
4 Thus will I bless thee while I live: I will lift up my hands in thy name.
5 My soul shall be satisfied as *with* marrow and fatness; and my mouth shall praise *thee* with joyful lips:
6 When I remember thee upon my bed, *and* meditate on thee in the *night* watches.

3 Because thy steadfast love is better than life,
my lips will praise thee.
4 So I will bless thee as long as I live;
I will lift up my hands and call on thy name.

5 My soul is feasted as with marrow and fat,
and my mouth praises thee with joyful lips,
6 when I think of thee upon my bed,
and meditate on thee in the watches of the night;

---

communications from God were looked for in times of perplexity, need, and distress (Alfred Guillaume, *Prophecy and Divination* [New York: Harper & Bros., 1938], pp. 328-33; cf. Isa. 6:1; I Kings 3:5, 15; cf. also Jer. 1:11; Amos 8:1). The word חזיתיך, lit., **I have seen thee,** means "I have appeared before thee," i.e., "come to see thee." **Beholding thy power and glory:** The psalmist hopes, through his nearness to the temple and its symbols and by participation in its worship, to receive from God's own mighty and majestic presence (cf. Isa. 6:1-5; Ezek. 1:26-28) some assurance that God is favorable to him in his distress (cf. 27:4).

3-5. See Exeg. on vss. 4, 5, 3, below.

6-8. When I think of thee upon my bed: As the psalmist passes the night near or in the precincts of the temple **in the shadow of thy wings,** he receives no theophany but an intimate spiritual experience like that of 73:17—I see that **thou hast been my help.** Between vs. 6 and vs. 7 we must supply some words like 73:17*b* (cf. 8:3-4 for a similar use of aposiopesis). Instead of a vision or an oracle, the psalmist is given eyes to see how unfailingly God has helped him in the past. And the past becomes for him a prophecy of the future. The sense of the new insight comes upon him again and again **in the watches of the night** (cf. 16:7; 119:55), for אם, **When,** means here "as often as." And so **I sing for joy** (cf. 42:8), since as truly as

My soul clings to thee;
thy right hand upholds me.

4, 5, 3. So I will bless thee as long as I live: The psalmist vows to sing all his days hymns of thanksgiving, using not only his voice and lips but also lifting up his **hands**

---

than that; he is a God not of austerity or indifference, not introverted and arbitrary, but outgoing and tender. It is this quality of **loving-kindness** that to our writer is the value without equal; **it is better than life;** it is the ultimate reason for his dedication of himself in praise and in action. That love stands higher in the scale of values than power and glory is significant. It is God's love that to our contemplative is better than life. Or is he trying to say that the supreme manifestation of God's power and glory is to be seen in his **loving-kindness?** This to us is not a novel concept, but in a time when the idea of love as God's primary quality was only dimly apprehended, the affirmation may appear almost as an original insight.

5-8. ***The Soul's Satisfaction in God.***—In these verses, the essential meaning of which would not be changed in the rearrangement of order suggested by the Exeg., the psalmist expresses his great conviction: God is the All; God is the supreme possession; God is the ultimate value. Our poet is dealing with the religious experience on profound levels, but up to this point his emphasis has been rather uniformly on the nature of God as he is available to the yearning soul. Now he undertakes to describe the ways in which the satisfactions of God are made real to him. Using categories that were current in the religious thinking of his time, he speaks of the sense of fullness with which his soul, mind, and heart are furnished. There is

7 Because thou hast been my help, therefore in the shadow of thy wings will I rejoice.
8 My soul followeth hard after thee: thy right hand upholdeth me.
9 But those *that* seek my soul, to destroy *it,* shall go into the lower parts of the earth.

7 for thou hast been my help,
and in the shadow of thy wings I sing for joy.
8 My soul clings to thee;
thy right hand upholds me.
9 But those who seek to destroy my life
shall go down into the depths of the earth;

---

in exultation as he proclaims the praises due to God's name. His soul enjoys a never-ending feast of good things (cf. 23:5-6). **Thy steadfast love is better than life:** Most of the psalmists think that life is the proof of God's kindness, but this psalmist has reached the spiritual level of 73:25-26 even at a time when his life is in peril.

2. The End of the Psalmist's Foes (63:9-10 [11*ab*], 11*c*)

9-10 [11*ab*], 11*c*. But those who seek to destroy my life: Lit., "But those who seek my life for destruction." Omit לשואה, "for destruction," an explanatory gloss, for the sake of the meter. The confidence of the psalmist that God will again as in the past come to his help makes him predict with equal confidence the end of his traducers.

---

no hint of asceticism here; indeed the reference to the diet with which his soul is nourished is sensuous in the extreme. **Marrow and fat** were the gourmet's dish, rich almost to the point of surfeit. In Isa. 25:6 they are used figuratively as a promise to everybody of God's most sumptuous salvation: "And in this mountain shall the Lord of hosts make unto all people a feast of fat things; a feast of wines on the lees, of fat things full of marrow, of wines on the lees well refined."

My soul is feasted as with marrow and fat,
and my mouth praises thee with joyful lips.

Thus our poet makes his own personal appropriation of God's provision for his soul.

A part of this soul satisfaction is the delight which comes with thinking and meditating during times of solitary rest, and through those silent hours during which, under the star-studded skies, many men like our poet have contemplated the meaning of existence. This again was not an abandonment of the rational processes in retreat before the advance of a mystic rapture. Here is the wise man thinking God's thoughts after him, not the yogi wrapped in inscrutable mist. **When I remember thee upon my bed, and meditate on thee in the night watches,** he finds fulfillment in the third segment of his spirit—his heart, or as we are more accustomed to put it, his emotions. **Thou hast been my help, therefore in the shadow of thy wings will I rejoice.** Our interest in an analysis of the poet's religious experience must not blind us to the intensity of his literary symbolism in vss. 5-7. Marrow and fat are heavily sensuous; the watches of the night are suffused with quiet reflection and the soft light of the stars; beneath the shadow of the divine protection there is heard the bright melody of gladness. Such metaphors would perhaps be sparingly used in our times to describe one's sense of repletion with God, but the reason for such lack is less likely a matter of literary tastes than a loss of something of the basic factor in religion, viz., that God is the All.

God is the great possession; God is the ultimate value; God supplies the seeking spirit with the maximum good. This then results in a reciprocal intimacy that is the *ne plus ultra* of the divine-human contact. Not, it is well to remember, the absorption into the divine which some contemplatives in the religious traditions have sought. Here is no merging of being into the ultimate essence or the loss of identity in the larger entity. God is still God and man is still man, and the apogee of their commerce preserves the integrity of each. **My soul clings to thee;** thus our poet; and quite understandably, since he has recounted in almost extravagant terms his inventory of the divine beneficence. But he does not cling unsupported. **Thy right hand upholds me** as if there were the need both for such aid and for the evidence of God's reciprocal concern for him. This is the rapturous embrace; the soul, enfolded by the mighty arm, clinging to God in mutual fulfillment.

9-11. *The Polarities of Love and Hate.*—The last three verses bring us down at once from an intense and lofty conception of man's per-

10 They shall fall by the sword: they shall be a portion for foxes.

11 But the king shall rejoice in God; every one that sweareth by him shall glory: but the mouth of them that speak lies shall be stopped.

10 they shall be given over to the power of
the sword,
they shall be prey for jackals.
11 But the king shall rejoice in God;
all who swear by him shall glory;
for the mouths of liars will be stopped.

The mouths of liars will be stopped: Their murderous designs will recoil on their own heads. They **shall go down into the depths of the earth,** or "into the lowest parts of the earth," i.e., into the bottom of Sheol; in the underworld there were gradations among its inhabitants (cf. Deut. 32:22), a view preparatory to apocalyptic notions about Sheol. They will suffer the death of criminals, executed by the **sword** and cast out to **be prey for jackals.** The sudden change in the spiritual climate of the psalm at this point is not a strange phenomenon in the O.T. (cf. 5:10-11; 145:20). Such an outburst of vindictiveness should be judged in the light of the fierce struggle of the psalmist. In vs. 10 read יגרו, "they will be delivered," for יגירהו, "they will deliver him."

---

sonal relation to God, and confront us with certain ignoble human satisfactions growing out of man's personal relations with his fellows. So sharp is the declivity down which we fall that some scholars have refused these verses a proper place in the poem. It is implausible, they argue, that one whose sense of God could be so splendid could have so base an attitude toward men, even toward those who had designs on his life. Perhaps; but is not such a moral judgment the result of centuries of development in religious idealism, and should we hold our poet to standards which are now generally recognized but are still only poorly lived up to? We have been exhorted to love our enemies, but a case might be made to prove that our poet's prescription for them is still nearer to our liking. No; to him there was no inconsistency in his contemplation at the same moment of the divine embrace and of his enemies hurtling down into the depths of the earth. Even this summary disposition is, it would seem, insufficiently condign. On second thought, he thinks it were better that they be hacked to pieces by the sword or crushed in the jaws of jackals, an appalling and shameful wish (vss. 9-10). And yet who are we to censure this as discordant or even dishonest? It would be more becoming in us if, recognizing the gap between our religious professions and our treatment of our fellows, we sought to understand his sudden anger at his enemies as a normal reaction to the intensity of his love for God. This has at least been made intelligible to us in a century dark with the passions of war.

The previous reference to the poet's salute to **the king** (vs. 11) needs little enlargement. It cannot be explained as inspired by any genuine love for him. If the king means Jehoiachin, concern for him would hardly be more than perfunctory. If the reference is to the king of Babylon, it has no meaning; if it means the puppet left in Jerusalem to do the dirty work of Nebuchadrezzar, there is something dishonest in his pious claim; if it refers to an idealized symbol, it is pointless in the present context. Perhaps the best we can do for this is to confess our puzzlement. If the whole psalm is from one author (but cf. Exeg.), we may perhaps conclude that literary amenities demanded that he advert to the king in some way. At this distance, however, we are sure that to have said nothing about him would have better served the purpose of piety.

In sum, we have here a poem which has explored and confessed great depths in the experience of God. Not all of the deep places are here, to be sure; nor has the author—or the ultimate compiler—been able to escape slipping into pitfalls of triviality and vengefulness. With the same eyes he has seen God's power in the sanctuary and his own enemies falling beneath the power of the sword, and he has exulted at both spectacles. We have little reason for feeling that these moods cancel each other or that either one makes the other unreal. In a way that we of later times are perhaps better able to understand, the psalm has exposed the polarities of love and hate, the dialectic swing between man's attraction to God and his recoil from his fellows. The paradox is real, though it is part of the basic faith of the Christian that the experience of God can and must redeem man's experience with his brethren. For this reason, if for no other, it is important to keep the text of this poem intact.

The experience of God for some has tended to blind their eyes to their fellows. For them both enemy and friend are forgotten in the ecstasy of the holy presence. This is perhaps

To the chief Musician, A Psalm of David.

64 Hear my voice, O God, in my prayer: preserve my life from fear of the enemy.

To the choirmaster. A Psalm of David.

64 Hear my voice, O God, in my complaint;
preserve my life from dread of the enemy,

LXIV. A Cry for Preservation from Evildoers (64:1-10)

This brief psalm follows the pattern of a lament. It is an appeal to God for protection from the artful plots and schemes of cunning enemies. We are not told the grounds of the vicious hostility which is directed against the psalmist. In accordance with the traditional form of such psalms, the history of the psalmist's plight, as being well known to the all-seeing God, is passed over by the psalmist because his soul is agitated by the critical nature of the deadly struggle in which he is involved at the time when he utters his cry to God in the sacred place or in private. To describe his situation the psalmist uses a series of metaphors drawn from the practices of those who stalk wild animals. He is a hunted man. His enemies, refusing to meet him with open assaults, resort to secret and stealthy stratagems to accomplish his destruction. His appeal (vss. 1-2) and his description of the machinations of the enemies (vss. 3-6) are followed, as commonly in laments, by a prayer that "the workers of mischief" may suffer a like end

---

the most searching criticism to be made of the contemplative's isolated disciplines. Clearly the alternative to this myopia is an experience of God that makes compelling the effort to bring others, enemies and friends alike, into its orbit. If we see this more clearly than the lonely exile in Babylon, we deserve scant credit unless we act on it. For this is the ultimate power of God that the ancient writer sought to see in the sanctuary, power so communicated to those who know him that they in turn, through their exercise of this power, will see their enemies given over not to the destroying power of the sword, but to the redeeming power of God. "The power of God is the worship he inspires." Is this not also God's ultimate glory?

64:1-10. *The Theocratic Order and Its Enemies.*—Concerning this psalm there are two matters on which the opinions of the scholars generally agree: first, it is a piece of political writing; second, vs. 6 is so badly mutilated that no literary surgery has been able to restore it (see below). There is nothing in the poem that refers to threat or injury to the person of the author, nor are his angry words addressed to individual adversaries. There is no evidence here of a personal vendetta; it is a political feud.

It is interesting to note the gap between the mood of this psalm and that of Ps. 63, though it might properly be paired with Ps. 62 because of its political orientation. From the intensity of personal religious devotion in Ps. 63 we are taken to a bitter political quarrel; from the shadow of protecting wings we are thrust into an ambush where arrows fly. Clearly such juxtaposition of themes was no problem to the ancient anthologists. On the other hand, we may assume that it reflected the deep religious bias that influenced the life of the Hebrews, both personal and corporate. God had no less a stake in the corporate security of the people than in their personal piety.

If we are to understand the problem that engages our poet, we must begin with vs. 10. It amounts to a party cry; it is the rallying shout of the Hasidim, the "party of the Righteous," or as they would be more picturesquely called in our times, the "Moralists." The use of the two words **righteous** and **upright** is interesting in its political connotations. **Righteous** clearly refers to the party; **upright in heart** apparently appeals to those who, as we would put it, agree with the principles of the party without having established formal allegiance to it. It seems that they were even at so early a date the balance of power in political contests.

It is useful perhaps to enlarge somewhat on the political setting of this piece. In the simplest sort of analysis we find political groups divided three ways: theocratic, monarchic, and democratic. Roughly this also represents their historical sequence. Something analogous to a god or the gods determined the governance of primitive groups. It was often the holy man or shaman who was the deity's surrogate. Kings evolved with group evolution, and the monarch of the kingdom represented the final stage of a process that began with the chief of a tribe. Control by the people of their political destinies is not as modern as we are likely to think. There have always been democratic elements

to that which they are devising against him. They shoot their arrows (vss. 3-4), so may God shoot at them with **his arrow** (vs. 7); they strike **suddenly,** so may God strike them suddenly (vss. 4, 7); they plot to lay **snares,** so may God "cause them to stumble" (vss. 5, 8); they use **bitter words** as their weapons, so may **their tongue** prove to be their **ruin** (vss. 3, 8). From prayer the psalmist's words change to confident prediction. The story of the requital which his enemies will surely suffer will cause all mankind to fear the Lord and to ponder on his deeds in judgment. In conclusion the psalmist calls on **the righteous** and **the upright in heart,** the whole congregation of the Lord's servants, to rejoice over the Lord's vindication of him and to see how, like him, they too can find a sure **refuge** in the Lord from the deadly arrows of malicious tongues (cf. 5:11-12; 32:11; 140:13). This exhortation to the God-fearing souls to **glory** in the Lord takes the place of a vow by the psalmist himself to offer praise (cf. 13:6; 18:49; 35:28; 52:9; 59:16-17).

It is clear in the argument of the psalm that the weapons of the psalmist's enemies are to be countered by God's **arrow** (vs. 7). In vs. 3 their weapons are said to be **their tongues** and their **bitter words,** which are **like a sword** or **like arrows.** God's **arrow,** then, might be assumed to be some formidable word of God. Under the influence of Mowinckel (*Psalmenstudien,* "Awän und die individuellen Klagepsalmen," I, 16) some commentators (cf. Schmidt, *Die Psalmen,* p. 120) believe that the baneful words which the psalmist's enemies let fly secretly against him are curses or spells uttered by persons who practice black magic, and that the psalmist invokes for his protection a countercurse from God. Though this interpretation of the psalmist's situation is tempting, it cannot be regarded as more than an interesting possibility, since the language of the psalmist admits of more than one interpretation and, further, we have as yet no sure criteria by

---

in all group control; it is the appeal to the people as the final arbiter that is relatively late.

The Hebrews were theocrats, yet hardly simon-pure. Moses was a powerful tribal chieftain, and it took time for the sense of the Lord as supreme ruler to be accepted. In time it gave place first to a prophetic order and then to the monarchic pattern, but it kept tight hold on the idea that God was in charge and that the prophet and the king were his spokesmen. All the while the voice of the people was more and more articulate, and nothing, either in a theocratic or monarchic system, was able to stifle their cry for security, justice, and felicity.

As with other peoples, the conduct of the Hebrews was codified in terms of the dominant factor in their corporate life. Thus whenever a king was supreme, his behavior tended to establish the moral code of the common folk. In a theocracy behavior of the god or gods was the prototype of right behavior; and in a democracy the tendency has always been to find a median morality suitable to popular achievement and demand. Thus righteousness in a monarchy was often as capricious as the royal behavior; while in a theocracy it was as austere as the deity himself. In a democracy goodness has been conditioned both by ideal and exigency; and therefore has been, as often as not, more or less opportunistic.

This is pertinent to our understanding of the theocratic character of Hebrew rule. When, in John Calvin's theocratic Geneva, people gave their oath to accept and abide by the Twenty-one Articles drawn up by Farel and Calvin, these articles thus accepted were articles of Christian faith, but they were signed by men as citizens, not as Christians. This was an effort to moralize—or Christianize—society. That there were dissident minorities may be laid to the simple fact of human nature, if no better explanation is available. In sober truth, is a better explanation needed? The Old Order Amish who dominate the Mennonite community of Lancaster County, Pennsylvania, approach as near to a literalistic theocracy as anything we have in the United States, but among them the rule of the Bible has never been completely able to subvert the human desire to be "gay" or to sew furtively a bright bauble on a plain blouse.

Is this what we have encountered in this poem? It is clearly evident that there is a struggle for power going on. It is not between individuals, but between groups within the nation. We have indicated that the Righteous Party (Hasidim) were seeking to overcome those who are called **the enemy** and **evildoers.** It is these latter who, we assume, are the dissident and powerful minority. Their threat to the established theocratic order was both cunning and ruthless, and the Righteous, whose concern was that moral standards should be preserved so that the security of the people

2 Hide me from the secret counsel of the wicked; from the insurrection of the workers of iniquity:
3 Who whet their tongue like a sword, *and* bend *their bows to shoot* their arrows, *even* bitter words:

2 hide me from the secret plots of the wicked,
from the scheming of evildoers,
3 who whet their tongues like swords,
who aim bitter words like arrows,

---

which to determine when the enemies of the psalmists are to be identified as sorcerers (Widengren, *Accadian and Hebrew Psalms of Lamentation,* pp. 239-50). Vss. 7-8 may be no more than a prayer that God mete to the crafty plotters measure for measure the very evils which they are concocting against the psalmist.

The psalm is probably postexilic, since it comes from a time when the righteous welcome fresh evidences that the Lord vindicates his faithful servants (vs. 10), and when the whole world is asked to consider his ways (vs. 9; cf. Isa. 44:8; 45:24; Deut. 32:4). The word רגשׁה, **scheming,** in vs. 2 is used in its late bad sense. The meter is irregular because of the uncertain state of the text, but it is for the most part 3+3, with instances of 2+2+2 and 4+4.

1. Appeal to God (64:1-2)

64:1-2. The psalmist begins after the manner of a lament with an appeal for help. "Hear my words, as I make my complaint." His **life** (LXX, Aq., Vulg., "my soul") is in need of protection from the "terror" (פחד) of enemies. In vs. 1*b* he speaks only of **the enemy,** but the word probably should be taken in a collective sense, as vs. 3 seems to indicate. Otherwise we must think of a leader of a band of evil conspirators. However that may be, the operations against the psalmist are initiated and carried on covertly by **secret plots** and **scheming** (for רגשׁה see Exeg. on 2:1-12).

2. Enemies Described (64:3-6)

3-6. From his appeal the psalmist quickly proceeds to describe with fuller detail the methods which his crafty foes pursue in order to work his ruin. They use words for **arrows** which they shoot **from ambush, . . . suddenly and without fear.** Vs. 3 is, lit.,

---

could be protected, were clearly disturbed. What to do?

1-2. ***A Prayer for Freedom from Fear.***—Obviously, since the Lord was the source both of their moral idealism and their corporate order, they appealed to him, just as the people in a threatened monarchy call on their king, or those in a menaced democracy appeal to their parliament. This is exactly what always happens, and with astute political realism vs. 1 concerns itself with the matter of morale. The psalmist's first prayer is not for safety from the enemy but for protection **from fear of the enemy.** "Nothing is so much to be feared as fear."[9] It is not that he wants to be shielded from the sight of the enemy's mischief, but that seeing it, he shall not be terrified by it.

The point is well taken. When the base on which one's political loyalty rests is religious or moral, it is relatively easy to suffer a lowering of morale. In the rough and tumble of political conflict he who wants to fight fair seems to be at a disadvantage. This is due to the fact that the weapons of the struggle are simple words and the powerful and complex implements of conflict that can be fashioned out of such insubstantial material. The righteous man cannot use words dishonestly, nor can he fabricate them into sentences that are like arrows tipped with poison. Not so the evildoer. The more clever his lies, the more skillful he; the bigger his fabrication, the more readily it will be believed. This was Hitler's terrible faith. Little wonder then that our poet-politician, sensing this disadvantage, cries out for protection against it.

Hide me from the secret plots of the wicked,
from the scheming of evildoers.

Have not those who fought fair always insisted —ingenuously no doubt—that everything be open and above board? No plotting, no scheming; open covenants openly arrived it!

3-6. ***The Forces that Might Make One Afraid.***—The poet proceeds to intimate how adept

[9] Thoreau, quoted in Emerson, *Lectures and Biographical Sketches,* "Thoreau."

4 That they may shoot in secret at the
perfect: suddenly do they shoot at him, and
fear not.
5 They encourage themselves *in* an evil
matter: they commune of laying snares
privily; they say, Who shall see them?
6 They search out iniquities; they accomplish a diligent search: both the inward
thought of every one *of them,* and the heart,
is deep.

4 shooting from ambush at the blameless,
shooting at him suddenly and without
fear.
5 They hold fast to their evil purpose;
they talk of laying snares secretly,
thinking, "Who can see us?[y]
6 Who can search out our crimes?[z]
We have thought out a cunningly conceived plot."
For the inward mind and heart of a
man are deep!

[y] Syr: Heb *them*
[z] Cn: Heb *they search out crimes*

"they tread their arrow, a bitter word," a pregnant construction (cf. KJV). In vs. 4 read with the Syriac, לא יראו, "they are not seen," for לא ייראו, **without fear. They hold fast to their evil purpose:** Though the Hebrew may mean "they talk of [יספרו] snare-laying," it is better to emend the text and read "they dig [יחפרו] in order that they may lay snares." Digging pits and **laying snares** are from ancient times among the common charges which men make against their enemies (*ibid.,* p. 240; Henri and H. A. Frankfort, *et al., The Intellectual Adventure of Ancient Man* [Chicago: University of Chicago Press, 1946], p. 179). Sometimes they are just figures of speech; sometimes

---

the opponents of the Righteous are in the fashioning of propaganda—for this is the intention of his use of words. Healthy respect has been inspired by what has already been said. There is a rapierlike thrust and an incisive cutting edge to what they say. Here are no hit-or-miss bumbling political ineptness, careless and unsupported charges, playing the opponents' errors instead of making direct hits of their own. So impressive is the opposition that our spokesman for the Righteous uses similes that show that he himself is neither careless nor unimaginative. They **whet their tongue like a sword,** they **aim bitter words like arrows,** he says; and, whether so intended or not, the description pays high compliment to his foe. A whetted tongue is kept in readiness to cut, and bitter words aimed like arrows are not scattered like feathers. The propaganda of the adversary lacks nothing of alertness or dexterity.

This cleverness, however, is at the service of determined men who fight with skill but without scruples. If we realize the political character of this struggle, we may not take too seriously the claim that the Righteous are **blameless.** Assuming that they might be, we must nevertheless remember that political strategy denies the contestants the luxury of acknowledging error. Moreover, it has been one of the trusted devices of the "outs" to gainsay the "ins," and the sudden explosion of scandal from an unexpected direction is something against which political contestants must harden themselves. Very often it is the timing of the scandal that gives it political persuasiveness. From some undisclosed source at an unanticipated moment the antagonist lets fly his dart. Its point is poisoned; it is aimed at the blameless; and—if we are to believe our poet—it convinces many who ought to know better.

Shooting from ambush at the blameless,
shooting at him suddenly and without fear:

this is the language of the feud skillfully appropriated to describe the hustings.

All this is discouraging to those who want to conduct their campaign according to the rules of honor and decency, and they have admonished the Evildoer Party to abandon their sinister designs and to "come out and fight fair." They refuse to yield to the disdainful notion that politics is politics; they still believe that evil men can be persuaded to abandon their mischief in the interests of good government—which means, of course, government by the Righteous Party. Far from being persuaded, however, the Evilites seem only to be confirmed in their evil ways. They boast openly of the traps they will secretly lay; they grow bolder in their confidence that they can elude detection. They rise to a crescendo of cynicism, taking from the accusations of the Righteous Party the very words they had used (vss. 5-6*b*). "Crimes," they say. Crimes then let them be.

The latter part of vs. 6 in the original is so corrupt as to be meaningless without very extensive literary reconstruction. Some scholars

7 But God shall shoot at them *with* an
arrow; suddenly shall they be wounded.
8 So they shall make their own tongue to
fall upon themselves: all that see them shall
flee away.
9 And all men shall fear, and shall declare the work of God; for they shall wisely
consider of his doing.
10 The righteous shall be glad in the
LORD, and shall trust in him; and all the
upright in heart shall glory.

7 But God will shoot his arrow at them;
they will be wounded suddenly.
8 Because of their tongue he will bring
them to ruin;[a]
all who see them will wag their heads.
9 Then all men will fear;
they will tell what God has wrought,
and ponder what he has done.

10 Let the righteous rejoice in the LORD,
and take refuge in him!
Let all the upright in heart glory!

[a] Cn: Heb *They will bring him to ruin, their tongue being against them*

they imply sorcery. In any case, the psalmist's enemies have confidence that their villainy will escape detection and consequent frustration. **Who can search out our crimes?** Besides, their plots have been **cunningly conceived** in the inscrutable depths of the human heart. Although there is general agreement as to the sense of vs. 6, the text is uncertain and none of the emendations proposed can be accepted with confidence.

3. God Is Sure to Act (64:7-10)

7-10. Let the enemies put their trust in sorceries or in crafty scheming in demonic or in human agencies. The psalmist puts his trust in God, in him who can do all things by the word of his power. The verbs in these verses are best construed as optatives,

omit the verse entirely since its original meaning is lost; and such emendation as has been undertaken has produced nothing particularly germane to the argument. In the text we use, the translation offers a generalization that is beyond dispute; it is a safe thing to say and would no doubt have been acceptable to both political parties, since each could appropriate it comfortably to its own self-gratification. **For the inward mind and heart of a man are deep** may after all be a wise accommodation by the translators to the mood of political argument, for it comes as near as one can approach to sheer political platitude!

7-10. ***God the Final Victor.***—Up to this point, our poet-politician has spent his strength denouncing the corruption of the Evilites. The issue between them is the simple moral one of being right or wrong. The Evilites are wrong; therefore they should be repudiated. But this is easier said than done. It has already been pointed out that they are not constrained by moral considerations, and therefore have a low advantage over those who fight fair. How then shall this advantage be overcome? Here emerges the faith of the political moralist, a faith that is an odd compound of naïveté and realism. **God will shoot his arrow at them.** This clearly offers a contrast to the **bitter words like arrows** which the evildoers aim at the blameless from ambush; but it is also a dubious sort of confidence. We have no report on the issue of this contest, but the long-term history of politics does not encourage us to think that such matters are **suddenly** settled by an arrow of God. If this faith strikes us as ingenuous, vs. 8 reassures us that the spokesman of the Righteous had not abandoned his fate to an improbability. There follows a realistic observation that can be documented by numberless political episodes:

Because of their tongue he will bring them to ruin;
all who see them will wag their heads.

It is not the arrow of God that wounds suddenly; their own tongues, whetted like swords, destroy them. This is faith in a moral order that ultimately wins, and it is more substantial than a single arrow adventitiously aimed by the stout arm of God.

We conclude that, dismal though the prospects of victory were for the Righteous Party as our poet began to write, he is very much encouraged as he brings his words to a close. There is a fine display of modesty as he predicts victory over the Evilites, and it stands in strong contrast to their boast. Said they: **We have thought out a cunningly conceived plot** (vs. 6). Said the Righteous:

Then all men will fear;
they will tell what God has wrought,
and ponder what he has done.

To the chief Musician, A Psalm *and* Song of David.

65 Praise waiteth for thee, O God, in Zion: and unto thee shall the vow be performed.

To the choirmaster. A Psalm of David. A Song.

65 Praise is due to thee,
O God, in Zion;
and to thee shall vows be performed,

---

although the Masoretes understood them as expressing future certainty. The psalmist made little distinction between them; his wishes and prayers were in his mind certain of God's fulfillment. So, when God acts, all men will know what manner of God the Lord is, and the godly will have fresh reasons to exult in their **refuge.**

This concise but well-rounded psalm expresses movingly the strong confidence of a soul in the power of a just plea to win a favorable response from God.

LXV. Thanksgiving for God's Power and Bounty (65:1-13)

The opening words identify this as a psalm of thanksgiving. The time is the season of spring (vss. 9-13); all nature smiles; the pastures are clothed with flocks, and the valleys decked with grain. In answer to the people's prayers and vows, copious rains have, it seems, changed conditions of drought that threatened disaster into rich and abundant fertility. It is meet therefore that the people should gather in Zion and record in words of praise the deep thankfulness of their hearts.

However, the assurance of a bounteous increase in fields and flocks has for these worshipers a larger meaning than its material implications. Their consciences had been weighed down with a sense of sin, and to the Lord's displeasure with them they had attributed the failure of nature to bless their land with the early fertilizing rains. They had, they believed, been under chastisement. But now their mourning has been turned into joy. The bounty with which the Lord has crowned the year is a sign that he has deigned to pardon them and to restore them to his favor (vss. 1-3). "So," as Rudolf Kittel says (*Die Psalmen* [5th ed.; Leipzig: A. Deichert, 1929; "Kommentar zum Alten Testament"], p. 221), "in this psalm thoughts on nature's blessings and God's mercy are woven into a rich unity, which shows how Israel's piety was able to see in the lower the higher, in the outer the inner, in the transitory the eternal."

The Hebrew mind at its best is never forgetful of the sovereignty of God on every level of life. If the people have come to the temple to pay their vows of thanksgiving,

---

There follows naturally the rallying cry to the Righteous and to all those who are **upright in heart.**

It is manifest that what we here write has been seen in political perspectives with which, so far as we know, the Hebrew people were unacquainted. At the same time it is apparent that the rudiments of political strife with which we have to do were present even in a theocratic order twenty-five centuries ago. It would be comforting to believe that an understanding of Ps. 64 would spare us the rigors and the rottenness of modern political conflict, but we shall not so easily be comforted. Perhaps we can avoid the glib moralizing that threatened the fortunes of our poet's party, and perhaps we can adopt from the party of evil something of their tireless enterprise. Above all, since we hope we shall never be spared the necessity of political action, we might modify without violence to the accepted text, and appropriate without equivocation, the rallying cry of the party of the Lord, **Let the righteous rejoice in the Lord,** adding in our contemporary idiom, "Let all the upright in heart vote!"

65:1-13. *Ways in Which God Manifests Himself.*—Although all of the psalms are poems, only a few are described as songs. The fact that all in one way or another have been used in music or liturgical settings must not be allowed to mislead us into thinking that the singable quality is present in them all. It is not necessary to discuss at this point what makes a poem lyrical. Men have sung their griefs and their joys, their wisdom and their nonsense, with gusto; and yet some gusto would be hard to catch in a cadence. The point is that for some reason the poem with which we are now concerned is listed as a song, and as a song it has been made familiar to us. It would be hard to find one who has attended church with anything approaching regularity who has not heard in

KJV	RSV
2 O thou that hearest prayer, unto thee shall all flesh come.	2 O thou who hearest prayer! To thee shall all flesh come

it is because God has willed that they should draw near to him and has made possible their access to **the goodness** of his **house** (vs. 4). Their presence before him on this occasion is due altogether to the awesome deeds which he has wrought for them in nature. But what is true for them is true for other peoples. Israel's God is the Providence of the whole world. It was so at the beginning of creation and it continues to be so to earth's remotest ends (vss. 5-8).

Thus in this liturgy of thanksgiving (cf. Pss. 107; 116; 118) the thoughts of the worshipers are carried from what is of particularistic concern to what is of universal import (cf. Ps. 117). The faith of Israel has within it germs of growth. The implications of their belief in their God as the Lord of Creation are being unfolded.

The psalm as it stands consists of three strophes: vss. 1-4, 5-8, 9-13. The first two are each made up regularly of three distichs in 3+2 measure. In the third strophe the meter is irregularly 4+4 (vss. 9*b*, 10) and 3+3 (vss. 11, 12, 13), and the lines are either tristichs or distichs. The want of uniformity between the last strophe and the others suggests that vss. 9-13 were added to adapt the psalm to a special congregational situation. A closer examination of the first two strophes with a comparison of their literary and poetic qualities leaves one with the opinion that they are of independent authorship. However, the three strophes have been blended into a liturgical unity which gives noble expression of Israel's faith.

The date of the psalm in its present form is postexilic. The second strophe has marked affinities with the monotheistic and the universalistic points of view which are met in Second Isaiah (cf. 42:10-12; 49:1) and later writers (cf. Isa. 11:1-9; Mal. 1:11). It should be noted also that in vs. 1 the seat of God's worship is said to be **in Zion.**

1. Praise in the Temple Courts (65:1-4)

65:1-4. Praise is due to thee, O God: Waiteth (KJV) is an attempt to render "silence," which seemed to be the meaning of the Hebrew word. However, the word is from a root דמה, "to be like" or "to be fitting," and is a late or Aramaic participial

hymn or anthem its sonorous phrases. To the Hebrew choirmaster it had what the liturgist needed, and we may assume it to have been as popular with his congregations as it has proved to be with us.

It has not been easy for some of the interpreters of the psalms to explain why this poem, dealing with two subjects so distinct that they seem to divide it into two definite sections, could have been effectively used as a unit. This apparent division, vss. 1-8, 9-13, has been understood by some to support the theory of dual authorship and even of dual date, the first part being a reflection of life after the Exile, the second part, before it. To us, however, such an explanation is unnecessary. While the division suggested is plausible, it is not difficult to discover a spiritual continuity and "a liturgical unity" (see Exeg.) that is uninterrupted. It might even be claimed that only thus can the deep insights of the psalm be apprehended, insights so profound and universal that they have given it both its liturgical utility and its wide appeal. It is from this point of view that we shall reflect upon it.

There is a proper spiritual sequence in one's approach to God. This is not to say that there is not more than one path into his presence; but no matter what path one is to take, there is an order in which the steps must fall. First, confession and forgiveness of sin; second, praise and supplication—this is the authentic order. Nowhere is clearer guidance by psychology available than here. The impulse to praise is an extraversion of one's self, and can easily become pure self-gratification or an unconscious evasion of one's spiritual shortcomings. Most of us find exultation more congenial than expiation; by praising another we may be praising ourselves, and this can, and doubtless often does, corrupt the true experience of worship.

1-3. *The Universal Tribunal.*—It is this significant fact which confronts us at the beginning of this song, though not in the first line. The important word is in vs. 2. Note that it is the God who hears prayer, as contrasted for the

3 Iniquities prevail against me: *as for* our
transgressions, thou shalt purge them away.
4 Blessed *is the man whom* thou choosest,
and causest to approach *unto thee, that* he
may dwell in thy courts: we shall be satisfied with the goodness of thy house, *even*
of thy holy temple.

3 on account of sins.
When our transgressions prevail over us,[b]
thou dost forgive them.
4 Blessed is he whom thou dost choose and bring near,
to dwell in thy courts!
We shall be satisfied with the goodness of thy house,
thy holy temple!

[b] Gk: Heb *me*

---

form. Accordingly, it should be pointed *dōmiyyāh* not *dumiyyāh.* The versions support this reading. **In Zion:** Only in postexilic times did Zion become the national seat of worship through the triumph of the Deuteronomic legislation. It is there at the temple that men must come to present their offerings in payment of their **vows** made when in trouble they sought deliverance through the Lord (cf. Deut. 12:6, 11, 18). The psalmist attributes the distress which the people suffered to **transgressions.** The divine displeasure brought upon them a punishment too heavy to bear (cf. 38:4). **Thou dost forgive them:** Lit., "cover them over" or "blot them out." Except in the Priestly Code, it is God alone who can do it (W. O. E. Oesterley, *Sacrifices in Ancient Israel* [London: Hodder & Stoughton, 1937], p. 93). **Blessed is he whom thou dost choose: Blessed** implies temporal happiness, for this is the lot of all whom God forgives and so selects for admission to his temple and to enjoy freedom of access to it and all its privileges, not as a guest but as a dweller. **Satisfied with the goodness of thy house:** The **goodness** enjoyed by those who had the privilege of worshiping in the temple consisted of blessings both spiritual and temporal. On the one hand, the worshiper had the means there of securing God's protection, forgiveness, and favor; on the other hand, he had fellowship in the joyous seasons of worship and a share in the meals at which the portions of the votive offerings falling to the laity were eaten (cf. Lev. 7:11-17).

---

moment with the God for whom praise is meet, to whom men universally turn. And the prayer is for forgiveness.

When our transgressions prevail over us,
thou dost forgive them.

It is perhaps nothing more than a poetic device in the text that gives praise a position ahead of prayer for forgiveness. There is no mistaking, however, which of the two the psalmist regards as more important. It almost amounts to his saying that in Zion praise and the performance of vows are largely an accepted routine, but it is the overwhelming sense of sin that turns **all flesh** everywhere to God. This is the precondition of true praise, and our poet has seen it very clearly. Men are more likely to turn to God on account of their sense of sin than for any other reason. This is no morbid estimate of the human spirit. Despair is sin's only rival in leading men to God, and quite as often as not, man's despair is derived from his sense of sin. Surely good fortune, for which we should normally praise God, is apt to turn our minds to self-praise. We do not get very far beyond the Little Jack Horner stage where every extricated plum impresses us with our greatness. Jack, however, was soon surfeited, we imagine; so also are we. The spirit is not well nurtured by self-praise; and it is the commonest of observations that where the sense of sin is dulled, the sight of God is dim, and man is soon overwhelmed by the transgressions that prevail over him. Up to a certain point man's pride convinces him that he can take care of his sins, and this is not altogether unsalutary. Let him do all he can to straighten up, he must yet be prepared for that moment when he is utterly cast down. This comes as near being a universal human experience as any we can describe. When man has slipped beyond the reach of his own self-rectification, he will cry out to God for saving. This therefore is the first step, we insist, in the bona fide approach to God.

4. ***The Joy of Finding God in His Temple.***—Furthermore, it is to just this sort of approach that our poet tells us God will respond. Those who for this reason come to him are "drawn to" him; it is they who are given habitation in court, in house, and in temple. And it is also they who, filled with the joys of house and temple, will break forth in unrestrained praise.

5 *By* terrible things in righteousness wilt thou answer us, O God of our salvation; *who art* the confidence of all the ends of the earth, and of them that are afar off *upon* the sea:
6 Which by his strength setteth fast the mountains; *being* girded with power:
7 Which stilleth the noise of the seas, the noise of their waves, and the tumult of the people.
8 They also that dwell in the uttermost parts are afraid at thy tokens: thou makest the outgoings of the morning and evening to rejoice.

5 By dread deeds thou dost answer us with deliverance,
O God of our salvation,
who art the hope of all the ends of the earth,
and of the farthest seas;
6 who by thy strength hast established the mountains,
being girded with might;
7 who dost still the roaring of the seas,
the roaring of their waves,
the tumult of the peoples;
8 so that those who dwell at earth's farthest bounds
are afraid at thy signs;
thou makest the outgoings of the morning and the evening
to shout for joy.

---

2. God's Deeds Inspire Universal Awe (65:5-8)

5-8. The awesome deeds of the Lord not only bring deliverance to Israel, but also cause peoples near and far to put their hope in him. The psalmist believes that the nations by whatever names they call their gods are in reality fearers of the Lord. The manifestation of his divine might was given first at the Creation, when he **established the mountains** and stilled **the roaring of the seas** (cf. 74:12-17). **The tumult of the peoples** is a gloss suggested probably by Isa. 17:12. From awe at his creative deeds the dwellers on the earth from the East to the West turn to jubilation as they contemplate the **tokens** of the Lord's power in the providential ordering of his creation.

5-8. *In the Greatness of His Acts.*—We have been told in vss. 1-4 that the reason for universal turning to God is the universal sense of prevailing transgression, against which man is in himself impotent; and that the true happiness which is the precondition of praise comes from the sense of dwelling in the presence of God who has drawn us to himself. It has not always been quite so painless a process as this might suggest, but that also is clear to our singer. It has been by **deeds** both splendid and terrifying that God has chosen and drawn men to himself. This is the certainty of those who know him as a God of salvation, even as it is the hope of men everywhere. It becomes necessary then to ask just why it can be hoped that men who are universally sinful unanimously turn to God for salvation.

Once again our poet gives the point at the end of the section instead of at the beginning. The purpose of the portentous activities of God as they are intimated in vss. 6-7 is given in vs. 8. Man will not turn for help in his greatest need to one of whom he is unsure; but since sin is an inner concern, the power to deliver a man from the bondage of sin is not always externally revealed. Our poet thinks that tokens of God's power in nature are proof of his power in human nature, and can be so construed by **those who dwell at earth's farthest bounds.** Where better is the might of God revealed than in the establishment of the towering mountains? Where better is the control of God seen than in the reduction of the tumults of tempest and people into imperturbable calm? This is commonplace to our poet, and perhaps he expects too much from those in the lands of **the morning and the evening**—the extreme latitudes of East and West—but his faith is undaunted, and they too can be made ready to praise. God, he has said, is the hope of the ends of the earth, God,

who by thy strength hast established the mountains,
being girded with might;
who dost still the roaring of the seas,
the roaring of their waves,
the tumult of the peoples.

Because God can do this, our psalmist is sure he can steady all men against the sins that prevail against them and the tumults that rise within them. In the realization of this great fact, and in having taken this primary step, man is made ready for the experience of praise.

9 Thou visitest the earth, and waterest it: thou greatly enrichest it with the river of God, *which* is full of water: thou preparest them corn, when thou hast so provided for it.

10 Thou waterest the ridges thereof abundantly: thou settlest the furrows thereof: thou makest it soft with showers: thou blessest the springing thereof.

11 Thou crownest the year with thy goodness; and thy paths drop fatness.

9 Thou visitest the earth and waterest it,
thou greatly enrichest it;
the river of God is full of water;
thou providest their grain,
for so thou hast prepared it.
10 Thou waterest its furrows abundantly,
settling its ridges,
softening it with showers,
and blessing its growth.
11 Thou crownest the year with thy bounty;
the tracks of thy chariot drip with fatness.

3. God's Blessings in Field and Flock (65:9-13)

9-13. Israel has its own reasons at this time for jubilant praise. The season of spring is rich with blessings in field and flock. For the Lord has visited **the earth** graciously and provided its **grain** by copious rains which come from **the river of God**, i.e., the heavenly brook (cf. Gen. 1:7; Job 38:25; see also Ps. 104:13). To the quickening effects of the rain have been added rich fertility, for **the tracks of thy chariot drip with fatness.** The psalmist is acquainted with some myth according to which the Lord in his visit to the earth rides in a chariot, whose wheels as they roll over the fields enrich their yield. The psalmist in a rich poetic vein personifies the vernal scene, and hears **hills, . . . meadows, . . . valleys** matching their voices as **they shout and sing**

9-13. ***In the Fruitfulness of the Earth.*—Shout for joy** is the last phrase of what is generally regarded as the first complete section of this song. Quite as clearly, however, it sets the mood of what follows; for we now encounter what is as sprightly a hymn of praise as is to be found in any literature. Wrote Wordsworth:

> Nature never did betray
> The heart that loved her.[1]

But the poet has always found more than fidelity there; he has found her a competent teacher.

> One impulse from a vernal wood
> May teach you more . . . .[2]

And so it has turned out that the pastoral poem is as old and as recurrent as any other. Who has not wished or tried to write a lyric salute to the seasons? And who, having undertaken it, has failed to bring in God's artistry to help explain the wonder?

Our ancient poet's experience is not different from our own. So bright is his ecstasy that he seems to get his seasons out of order, though this surely is a minor fault. What he is determined to do is to give exultant voice to the impulse to praise, an impulse that is the result of his deliverance from sin. Since this sense is universally felt, his praise refers to God's world-wide beneficence. God has visited the earth, and his hands have made a rapture of it. Spring touches off the poet's first delight. The good earth is enriched by God's touch; the gift of seeds is matched by copious streams; broad fields, the sediment of the agelong erosion of the mountains, have been prepared for sowing; the spring seeding, nurtured by sun and shower, erupt into the bright green of promise (vss. 9-10).

Since springtime invariably modulates into the tempo of summer, we would expect our poet to follow his vernal mood with its proper seasonal sequence. Instead he seems to skip over to a scene at harvesttime, when bumper crops and flocks of fat cattle fairly drip with the repletion of prosperity and joy. Little wonder that the famed words of vss. 11-12 are given seasonal voice in hymn and anthem when we observe our harvest festivals. Less wonder perhaps that there has been among all cultures a celebration of the summer's bounteous gifts, and praise has been ascribed to gods who, though perhaps guilty of occasional misconduct, always have seemed to relent at autumn and to supply the provender needed for the sterile days of winter.

Summer engages our poet's song as the finale to his piece, and he saves for it what is perhaps his most whimsical metaphor. After the springtime's careful planting of good seed in good

[1] "Lines Composed a Few Miles Above Tintern Abbey."
[2] Wordsworth, "The Tables Turned."

12 They drop *upon* the pastures of the
wilderness: and the little hills rejoice on
every side.
13 The pastures are clothed with flocks;
the valleys also are covered over with corn;
they shout for joy, they also sing.

To the chief Musician, a Song *or* Psalm.

66 Make a joyful noise unto God, all
ye lands:

12 The pastures of the wilderness drip,
the hills gird themselves with joy,
13 the meadows clothe themselves with flocks,
the valleys deck themselves with grain,
they shout and sing together for joy.

To the choirmaster. A Song. A Psalm.

66 Make a joyful noise to God, all the
earth;

---

together for joy (for the celebration of spring as one of the starting points of the year see Henri Frankfort, *Kingship and the Gods* [Chicago: University of Chicago Press, 1948], p. 314).

LXVI. Hymn to an Omnipotent but Gracious God (66:1-20)

Here is a psalm of thanksgiving prepared for use on an occasion when an individual of wealth and station (cf. vss. 13-15) presented votive offerings in the temple. The psalm was part of the liturgy of such an office, and in its rendition both a choir or choirs and the individual himself, or a priestly spokesman, shared. That an individual and not the people personified (cf. Calès, *Livre des Psaumes,* I, 626) speaks in vss. 13-19 is clear from vs. 16, where the speaker and the group are distinguished. But it is not necessary in consequence to assume as do some commentators (cf. Oesterley, *Psalms,* II, 313), that we have here two psalms, viz., vss. 1-12 and vss. 13-20, for in such a case

---

soil, and the fecundation of God's soft showers and diligent sun, the meadows and the valleys are green with new growth. But so vital are the valley and the lea that they must do more than grow. Over the green of the meadow is thrown the mottled lace of white flocks, and across the valleys the green blends slowly into the gold of ripening grain. It is a picture of surpassing loveliness.

> **The meadows clothe themselves with flocks,**
> **the valleys deck themselves with grain.**

And finally in the sheer exuberance of our singer he hears the staccato music of happiness blending in harmony and rising from flocks and fields. **They shout and sing together for joy.**

It would be a simple matter to find parallels to this famous song in the literatures of all peoples. It has been pointed out how the contemplation of nature has inspired some of the noblest of man's songs. One has a fondness for one season, one for another. Sang Thomas Wolfe:

> Autumn was kind to them,
> Winter was long to them—
> But in April, late April,
> All the gold sang.[3]

[3] "Spring," from *The Web and the Rock* (New York: Harper & Bros., 1939). Used by permission.

One will choose one, another will prefer another, as best representing man's gratitude for the rhythms of the earth. But the significance of the song we have sung so often and studied here so briefly lies, as has been said, in the very fact that some scholars have adduced to prove its disunity; the fact that before the highest levels of man's impulse to praise can be reached, he must first have reached the deepest levels of his sense of sin. Here is paradox again, but it is nonetheless intelligible for that reason.

This should therefore supply us with a valuable pointer as we undertake both in public and private worship to give vent to our feelings of gratitude. By the strange miracle that has created the human spirit, the impulse to praise has been planted in us. By that strange perversion to which the human spirit is prone, the inclination to make praise a substitute for penitence is always with us. And yet by that simple justice which rewards with deep spiritual satisfactions those who have followed the laws of the spirit, it is possible that those who have **come on account of sins . . . shall be satisfied with the goodness of thy house, thy holy temple, and with those who dwell at earth's farthest bounds . . . to shout for joy.**

66:1-20. ***From Shouting to Praying.***—We need to remind ourselves constantly that the poetry which was allowed place in the Psalter had to

the first would lack the conclusion proper to a hymn, and the second an introduction (Gunkel, *Die Psalmen*, p. 277). The psalm belongs to a mixed type (Gunkel, *Einleitung in die Psalmen*, p. 274) in which the hymn of an individual is preceded or followed by a general hymn of praise (cf. 9:1–10:18; 40:1-17; 77:1-20; 144:1-15).

The most important part of this psalm is that which concerns the individual of vss. 13-20. He has come to the temple to discharge his vows and, in the presence of all who have joined him for the occasion, to proclaim what God has done for him. Because he is a man of substance, the offerings, the number of his fellow worshipers, and the liturgical arrangements are on an appropriate scale. But he sees his experience in a large, human perspective. What God has done for him is an example of God's saving help to all mankind. So the psalm opens with an invitation to **all the earth** to raise a shout to God (vss. 1-4). And then, in particular, Israel, which has known God's mighty acts of deliverance at the Red Sea (vss. 5-7) and in the Exile (vss. 8-12), is summoned to add its voice to the jubilant hymn. Finally and dramatically, after these loud songs of praise and thanksgiving, the individual worshiper chants alone his hymn of thanksgiving, announcing his offerings (vss. 13-15) and telling of God's gracious dealings with him (vss. 16-20). In ordering the parts of the psalm in the manner described, the psalmist infuses into it teachings of a prophetic character: viz., that in the human scene the universal and the particular, the past and the present, are of a piece, since there is one God in all and over all; and that all mankind, collectively and individually, in every generation owe thanks to God for mercies received.

The psalm, which exhibits careful attention to symmetry in its composition, consists of five parts or stanzas of about equal length, as indicated above, and a concluding doxology (vs. 20). Its liturgical character is evidenced by the fact that a choir or a group of singers chant the first three parts, and one person the last two. It is of interest also that the Hebrew musical term **Selah** occurs three times, and each time at the end of a part or stanza. Whether, then, the first three parts were assigned to more than one choir for antiphonal rendition, as some assume, is a matter for conjecture until our knowledge of the choral music of the temple is ampler.

The meter is almost uniformly 3+3 throughout. The date is postexilic, as evidenced by the mixed type of the psalm, the influence of Second Isaiah on it (see below), its emphasis on the universality of God's dominion, and the developed ritual and sacrificial system of the temple which it presupposes.

---

pass the test of utility rather than those of literary purity or authorship. Why a poem was written, and when and by whom, was of incidental interest to the early anthologists. Whatever in their judgment provided a vehicle for conveying the moods of the soul was accepted or adapted to some of the uses for which poetry has always been available—worship, recrimination, introspection, or to unite a people or rouse a rabble to action. The odd and often vexing combinations of poetic fragments that confront the biblical scholar can be accounted for in diverse ways, but nothing in their structure has prevented their use. We may be somewhat more fastidious about certain of the moral and spiritual implications some of them suggest, but if we delete them from our liturgies, it is for these reasons, not for literary or structural irregularities.

This general observation is well illustrated in this song. It has escaped attachment to David, but the choirmaster seems to have found it interesting. Some scholars find it necessary to assign the psalm to at least two writers and two periods. What is important for our study is the fact that such early editorial weaving of different skeins as may have taken place created a pattern that made the psalm easily adaptable to liturgical use. In those remote days when it was first sung, it meant something to the singers. Does that meaning have a modern parallel? Is the experience sufficiently general to warrant our using this psalm as a medium of our worship?

As it stands, there appears to be a distinct and natural shifting of focus as the lines carry our attention along. This shift is sharp without being abrupt; it follows an easy development and sequence of idea. Its main theme is the proper ascription of praise to God, a theme that appears in the opening line as a peremptory command: **Make a joyful noise.** This fortissimo shout diminishes first to a song and then to a hymn, but the change of mood is part of the

2 Sing forth the honor of his name: make his praise glorious.
3 Say unto God, How terrible *art thou in* thy works! through the greatness of thy power shall thine enemies submit themselves unto thee.
4 All the earth shall worship thee, and shall sing unto thee; they shall sing *to* thy name. Selah.
5 Come and see the works of God: *he is* terrible *in his* doing toward the children of men.

2 sing the glory of his name;
give to him glorious praise!
3 Say to God, "How terrible are thy deeds!
So great is thy power that thy enemies
cringe before thee.
4 All the earth worships thee;
they sing praises to thee,
sing praises to thy name." *Selah*

5 Come and see what God has done:
he is terrible in his deeds among men.

---

1. Summons to All the Earth (66:1-4)

66:1-4. The opening is in the hymn style with a summons or invitation to worship. In this instance **all the earth** is bidden to **Make a joyful noise to God** and to sound his **glorious praise.** Read שירו, "sing" (cf. Syriac), for שימו, **give.** This notion of the universality of God's rule, coupled with the recognition of it by all the peoples, appears in other psalms (cf. 47:7-8; 98:4; 100:1), and we may take it as a mark of the influence on the psalmists of exilic and postexilic prophecy (cf. Isa. 52:10, 15; 54:5; 60:1-3; 62:2; 66:18). In the mouth of the peoples the psalmist puts the words of a canticle (vss. 3-4) in which they acknowledge that the greatness of God's deeds compels them to yield obedience to him.

2. God's Hand in the Exodus (66:5-7)

5-7. For **Come and see what God has done:** In times past the nations learned to know the measure of his might in events of history: first, **he turned the** [Red] **sea into dry land** and led his people through it in defiance of Egypt (Exod. 14:16); and later he marvelously divided the waters of the Jordan so that **men passed through the river**

---

change of focus. The uninitiated of the earth will shout; the people of the Lord will sing. This is the way in which a lofty and undisciplined impulse to praise can be organized into worship.

1-4. ***Exhortation to Praise God.***—The exhortation to praise is unequivocal, but it rests on the fact of the power of God, and this power is seen in three categories: (*a*) power in the portents of nature; (*b*) power in the affairs of men; (*c*) the evidence of his power among those who regarded themselves as uniquely God's concern. These three aspects of the power that should evoke praise are followed in a final section by a personal testimony that might without pressure be fitted into a fourth aspect of God's power—the constraint he lays upon the individual soul. This represents a natural progression from the general to the particular; from **Make a joyful noise . . . , all the earth** to **he was extolled with my tongue** (vs. 17). "A lofty hymn was under my tongue" is Cheyne's rendering of vs. 17.

The confidence of the poet in commanding the earth to shout is quaint. He stands figuratively on a high place, and as a precentor signals for unanimous response from **all the earth.** "Aloud" is an acceptable translation, but other renderings make use of jauntier words: "merrily" (Cheyne), "joyous shout" (Amer. Trans.), and "sing homage" (Moffatt). **Praise** must be **glorious** because God's name is honorable. This paean is not to be left to spontaneous or miscellaneous expression. The words are as fully prescribed as the shout. If this seems to us to compromise the values of impromptu praise, there was no problem for the precentor. To him it was of greater importance that the correct reasons for praise be assigned. God's deeds are terrible; the display of sheer physical power was frightful to those who opposed him (vs. 3). This was reason enough for praise.

5-7. ***Because of His Power.***—The thundering crescendo of the opening verses yields at once to a more ingratiating mood. Instead of the voice of all the earth united arbitrarily in one gigantic shout, an invitation is extended to a somewhat more limited group to make personal observations of what God has done; not in terrible and portentous display of sheer power, but in **deeds among men,** which are in their own way terrifying. God's most impressive

6 He turned the sea into dry *land:* they went through the flood on foot: there did we rejoice in him.

7 He ruleth by his power for ever; his eyes behold the nations: let not the rebellious exalt themselves. Selah.

8 O bless our God, ye people, and make the voice of his praise to be heard:

9 Which holdeth our soul in life, and suffereth not our feet to be moved.

10 For thou, O God, hast proved us: thou hast tried us, as silver is tried.

11 Thou broughtest us into the net; thou laidst affliction upon our loins.

12 Thou hast caused men to ride over our heads; we went through fire and through water: but thou broughtest us out into a wealthy *place.*

6 He turned the sea into dry land;
men passed through the river on foot.
There did we rejoice in him,
7 who rules by his might for ever,
whose eyes keep watch on the nations —
let not the rebellious exalt themselves.
Selah

8 Bless our God, O peoples,
let the sound of his praise be heard,
9 who has kept us among the living,
and has not let our feet slip.
10 For thou, O God, hast tested us;
thou hast tried us as silver is tried.
11 Thou didst bring us into the net;
thou didst lay affliction on our loins;
12 thou didst let men ride over our heads;
we went through fire and through water;
yet thou hast brought us forth to a spacious place.[c]

[c] Cn Compare Gk Syr Jerome Tg: Heb *saturation*

on foot (cf. Josh. 3:9-17) and put to shame the nations who had opposed their march (cf. Num. 21–24). Because the ancients thought of seas as rivers, owing to an old cosmology, it is possible that **river** (vs. 6*b*) is only a synonym of **sea** (vs. 6*a*). In any case the events of history prove that God's **eyes keep watch on the nations** to see that they do not rebelliously exalt themselves and put him to the test. The psalmist may here be thinking of the victories which by God's help Gideon, Deborah, Jephthah, and Samson won over the nations round about Israel, or he may be thinking of the overthrow of insolent rulers like Rezin and Sennacherib.

3. God's Guidance in Israel's Later Trials (66:8-12)

8-12. Again the peoples are called on to **bless our God,** this time not for the assertions of his dominion but for his mercies shown to Israel in that he **has kept us among the living.** The psalmist has in mind not one trial alone, such as the Exile, but the many trials through which his people have been brought triumphantly. Sin, suffering, and deliverance form the pattern of their history as the Deuteronomists and the Chronicler relate it. And since their exultation over God's saving grace is so great, they do not think it strange to ask the peoples to join with them and **let the sound of his praise be**

power, we assume, is that which appears to give sudden advantage to disadvantaged people. Its most satisfying evidence points to his eye, ever watchful over the affairs of nations. History is the record of what God has done. Let rebels take warning!

8-12. ***Because of His Dealing with the Soul.*** —The theme ends; and after a pause (*Selah*) another motif is heard. It is more intimate and subdued. Now God is not shouted at nor are his ways with other men scrutinized. The personal emphasis is caught in cadences indicated by plural possessive pronouns: **Our God, our feet, our loins, our heads.** This brings us a long way from the precentor evoking the thunder of unanimous praise; here is sober reflection on the fact that the touch of the hand of God on life—the strongest evidence, indeed, of its power—is not discovered merely in portent and protection. It is felt in discipline. Here is a great advance both in depth and distance; it is the sort of insight hardly to be discovered by those whose praise is only a shout. From an order to praise to an invitation to consider reasons for praise, we have at last reached a personal (group) expression of the impulse to praise arising out of the touch of the divine hand in discipline.

13 I will go into thy house with burnt offerings: I will pay thee my vows,
14 Which my lips have uttered, and my mouth hath spoken, when I was in trouble.
15 I will offer unto thee burnt sacrifices of fatlings, with the incense of rams: I will offer bullocks with goats. Selah.

13 I will come into thy house with burnt
offerings;
I will pay thee my vows,
14 that which my lips uttered
and my mouth promised when I was in
trouble.
15 I will offer to thee burnt offerings of fatlings,
with the smoke of the sacrifice of rams;
I will make an offering of bulls and goats.
Selah

---

heard (cf. Isa. 42:10; 49:13). **Thou hast tried us as silver is tried. Thou didst bring us into the net:** Such metaphors are used of the Exile in Isa. 48:10; Lam. 1:13; Ezek. 17:20, but not exclusively so (cf. Job 19:6; Zech. 13:9). **Thou didst lay affliction on our loins:** The word מועקה represents an Aramaized form of מצוקה, **affliction** (cf. Syriac). The same thought occurs in 129:1-3. In vs. 12*ab* the psalmist has followed closely Isa. 43:2; 51:23. **Yet thou hast brought us forth to a spacious place:** For רויה, "satiety" (KJV **wealthy place**), read with the versions רוחה, "spaciousness," "freedom" (for the meaning see Job 36:16).

4. The Psalmist's Personal Hymn (66:13-20)

13-15. The preceding hymn of universal praise has prepared the way for the psalmist's own hymn. These verses describe the various offerings which he is presenting in fulfillment of his **vows** made when he **was in trouble.** Over and above the votive

---

13-20. *From God's Works to God Himself.*—Up to this point the approach has been personal but thoroughly objective. It could be argued that a priest skilled in his rubrics could have said all that has been said, and still not have felt it important for him to participate. So long as the earth shouted praise, why should he sing? Not so our poet, for at this juncture his focus is narrowed to the dimensions of his own soul. He deliberately makes himself a part of this planetary praise. And since the previous section has touched the deep level of God's power revealed in discipline, he exhibits his own piety against the backdrop of his own trouble. The period of his affliction is past, but he does not forget that he had made promises to God while he was in the middle of it. So he makes his good confession; he offers his unit of praise as a part of the world's unanimous shout for joy (vss. 13-15). We recall that the **burnt offerings** were, unlike the compulsory sacrifices for sin, a voluntary acknowledgment of one's personal sense of gratitude. Often at feasts, accompanied by the sound of trumpets, such an offering gave a dramatic public exhibition of a man's inner impetus to thanksgiving.

Thus the singer makes his own good confession; but there is a still further sharpening of focus. He is seen standing beside the smoking altar of burnt offering. Why is he there? Is he vicariously acknowledging the goodness of God to the people? No; he is ready to share his private reasons with those who have shared his trust in God. He had experienced a personal catharsis; he had not acknowledged God's goodness until he had confronted himself with his own unworthiness. This self-purging, he was sure, was the reason for the deep inner joy that inspired his external acts of devotion. **Come and hear, all you who fear God.** Again we point out how far we have come from the initial world-wide call to praise. **I cried aloud to him . . . ; he has given heed to the voice of my prayer.** There follows a final note of praise. The transition that has taken place since we began this song can be clearly seen by setting the opening and closing verses in contiguity:

Make a joyful noise to God, all the earth.
. . . .
Say to God, "How terrible are thy deeds!"
. . . .
Blessed be God,
because he has not rejected my prayer
or removed his steadfast love from me!

13-20. *The Purifying of Worship.*—We return briefly to the point that this poem is classified as a song, and that as a piece to be sung it seems supplied with harmonizing factors

16 Come *and* hear, all ye that fear God, and I will declare what he hath done for my soul.

17 I cried unto him with my mouth, and he was extolled with my tongue.

18 If I regard iniquity in my heart, the Lord will not hear *me:*

19 *But* verily God hath heard *me;* he hath attended to the voice of my prayer.

20 Blessed *be* God, which hath not turned away my prayer, nor his mercy from me.

16 Come and hear, all you who fear God,
and I will tell what he has done for me.
17 I cried aloud to him,
and he was extolled with my tongue.
18 If I had cherished iniquity in my heart,
the Lord would not have listened.
19 But truly God has listened;
he has given heed to the voice of my prayer.

20 Blessed be God,
because he has not rejected my prayer
or removed his steadfast love from me!

---

offerings (Deut. 23:21-23) he brings whole **burnt offerings** (vs. 15). The sacrificial animals include all kinds—fat lambs, **goats, rams,** and **bulls.**

16-19. Come and hear: The psalmist calls on **all . . . who fear God** to hear his witness to God's goodness to him in answering his entreaties in a time of distress. Emend vs. 17*b* to read רוממתי מתחת אויבי, "and I was raised up from under my foes." Vs. 18*a* is, lit., "Iniquity I saw in my heart"; it is better to read with Gunkel אני אמרתי בלבי, "I said in my heart (the Lord will not hear)."

20. The psalmist concludes his words with a doxology suited to his case. The impressive character and proportions of this man's private sacrifice probably caused the occasion to be long remembered, and so the psalm was preserved.

---

which have introduced something like discord among those who study it purely as a literary piece. We cannot presume to say that the sense of progress and climax that gives meaning to our Western music was a part of the musical métier of the ancients. It is of course a fairly recent development with us, but it has been so generally the pattern of oratorio and song that we easily think it to be as old as music itself. This is a matter for musical history to concern itself with, but it is not without interest, even to amateur study, that what have been correctly discerned by literary scholars as originally disjunct and to some degree conflicting elements in an ancient poem, can become under the urgency of song a powerfully evocative and unifying spiritual experience. It is this that accounts in a very considerable measure for the inclusion of this psalm in the psalter. It offers the utility that we may assume was the chief concern of the choirmaster. Is it any less the concern of the modern leader of religious music?

But we must not forget that utility is not enough. Song is a compound of melody and words, and there is too much support, even in much music that goes by the name of religious, for the saying, "So long as the tune has a right good swing, it does not matter much what words you sing." The banality of the words of modern songs—with reference to what is sung in most Protestant churches—cannot be redeemed by catchy tunes. The song we have been studying puts to shame the cheap ditties that satisfy too easily what we think is our impulse to praise. It is at this point that scholarly criticism finds difficulty. It must account for the presence of deep moral insights in a song that reflects an age when moral understandings were shallow, and explain why God can be acclaimed as bending threateningly above cringing enemies in one line and as kindly disposed toward penitents in another; and how religion can in one song be shown both as a hecatomb of burning beasts and as a deep sense of inner cleanness.

It is important to do no more than call attention to such matters, pointing out at the same time the necessity for including them in any complete study of the scriptures. And yet it is possible for us in the interests of literary clarity to overemphasize the importance of time and place in the religious experience. There were times when the ancient Hebrews were more concerned with the punctilio of sacrifice than with inner experience. Liturgy is always more or less in conflict with true religion. Does it follow, however, that when our poet in vs. 18 says,

> **If I had cherished iniquity in my heart,**
> **the Lord would not have listened,**

he must therefore have been a different person from the author of **I will make an offering of bulls and goats?** One may quite properly note

To the chief Musician on Neginoth, A Psalm *or* Song.

67 God be merciful unto us, and bless us; *and* cause his face to shine upon us; Selah.

To the choirmaster: with stringed instruments. A Psalm. A Song.

67 May God be gracious to us and bless us
and make his face to shine upon us,
Selah

LXVII. THANKSGIVING FOR HARVEST (67:1-7)

This brief psalm is a thanksgiving hymn. The occasion which called it forth is not unlike that of Ps. 65. In the latter, composed in the springtime, there is a large promise of bounty in field and flock; in this psalm the promise has been fulfilled in an abundant harvest at the close of the agricultural year (vs. 6). Appropriately vs. 1 is drawn from the well-known and often-heard benediction of Num. 6:23-26, for the garnered stores were an evidence to all the world that the blessings uttered by the priests were no empty form of words: "God has been gracious to us and blessed us, and has caused his face to shine upon us."

The psalm consists of three strophes: vss. 1-2, 4, 6-7, together with a refrain which stands at the end of the first (vs. 3) and the second strophe (vs. 5), and which in all probability stood also at the end of the third. It was composed to be sung in public worship at the temple, as its text evidences. The body of singers which rendered the strophes were answered or joined by another choral group in the refrain.

---

that the former insight sounds more like the chastened religious mood of the postexilic period; but must we necessarily insist that even among the aromatic smoke of ritual sacrifice in pre-exilic days there were not hearts among the votaries that responded eagerly to a deeper understanding of the nature of true worship?

To us who look at this song with eyes long accustomed to historic perspectives there is much that delights us as we read it. Who does not want to affirm in times of international discord the old, old faith of our singer in the security God promises to the earth: His **eyes keep watch on the nations—let not the rebellious exalt themselves.** Who also has not warmly appropriated the imperishable truth that the only thing that deactivates the energy of prayer is the corrosion of cherished iniquity. Each of these sentiments is germane to spiritual experience, and each provides it religious expression. We go further, and say that neither is alien to any age or to any religious culture that has developed to maturity. This is reason enough, if we need it, for giving our attention again to the choirmaster. There he stands; time has diminished his enthusiasm but little, if at all, and his signal to the world is unmistakable. Altogether—now—sing!

67:1-7. ***Toward a Universal Hope.***—What do the words **with stringed instruments** mean? Our minds call up the sight of a symphony orchestra, its violin, cello, viola, and double bass sections busy with intricate and ingratiating harmony, blending the composer's genius, the artist's skill, and the hearer's fancy into a moment of sensuous fulfillment. Such an experience would surely startle if not annoy the choirmaster if he, suddenly conjured out of the past, were placed on the podium. The involved harmonies would blur the melody to which his ear was attuned. In time he would come to enjoy the enrichment of simple melody by tonal complement, but at first it would confuse him.

This may be taken as a parable of the theme of this beautifully fashioned poem. That it is one for which we have particular fondness is partly accounted for by its brevity, its unity, and its form. Most of all, however, it is its message that appeals to us. Here, in a piece written, say the scholars, in the days of growing idealism and hope that followed the bitterness of exile, we have the note of universalism clearly sounded. It was not a new or strange theme. Israel's progenitor had heard it when he was ninety-nine years old. "And Abram fell on his face: and God talked with him, saying, As for me, behold, my covenant is with thee, and thou shalt be a father of many nations. . . . And I will make thee exceeding fruitful, and I will make nations of thee, and kings shall come out of thee." (Gen. 17:3-4, 6.) Thus also it recurred down the ages in the antiphony: Israel, God's chosen people and God's redemptive purpose for all nations.

This simple melodic line, the universality of redemption, was sung in different tempo and key by singers both plaintive and robust, both skillful and untrained. It is the glory of the

2 That thy way may be known upon earth, thy saving health among all nations.
3 Let the people praise thee, O God; let all the people praise thee.

2 that thy way may be known upon earth,
thy saving power among all nations.
3 Let the peoples praise thee, O God;
let all the peoples praise thee!

We may assume also that the psalm was one of those sung at the feast of Tabernacles. This festival received special prominence among the sacred observances after the Exile (see Deut. 16:13-16; Lev. 23:34-36; Num. 29:12-38). It was a season of special rejoicing not only because of its nature, "joy at the harvest" (Isa. 9:3), but because it was the most important of all the festivals of pilgrimage (Zech. 14:16-19). Two features marked its celebration apart from the offering of the sacrifices: the first was the ceremony of the drawing of water which ensured the rains of the coming year (Zech. 14:17; Sukkah 4:9), and the second was the carrying of branches and fruit (Lev. 23:40; Sukkah 4:1-7). The joy of the festival during its seven days was so full and unrestrained that in later times an eighth day was added to solemnize the feelings of the people and to send them home in a religious frame of mind. It was therefore a time for singing; and glad hymns of praise and thanksgiving were heard in the temple services (see Pss. 113–119; 136; Sukkah 4:8).

The thought of the psalmist is terse and direct. God's goodness to Israel is a revelation to all the world of his ways in dealing with those who fear him (vss. 1-2).

ancient tradition that it was never wholly lost. But what universalism meant to the author of our poem and what it means to us is not unlike the relation of a simple tune to the intricacies of modern harmony. It is no less important for us to sing it than it was for him, and while the melody today is the same simple strain, it produces overtone, harmony, and even unresolved discord that would surprise our choirmaster as much as the string section of an orchestra. We shall make the effort to understand our poet in these terms. He amplifies the simple theme in a way that is without rival in any other bit of the O.T. record. When we take up the tune for ourselves, we shall discover the melody to be the same. It is with us, however, a theme with variations.

The immediate inspiration for the poem is clear: the earth had put on a display of the generosity of God that deserved the poet's rapture. There seems to be little doubt that this song was used originally—as it has been used since—as a song of the harvesttime, when the happy folk gave themselves over to holiday-making during the eight-day feast of Tabernacles in the seventh month. It is when one reflects on the bounty of nature's yield that one is moved to spacious and openhearted thoughts. God, we say, has singularly rewarded our toil in field and vineyard. We are grateful and glad. Why should not all men everywhere share our mood?

The earth has yielded its increase;
God, our God, has blessed us.
God has blessed us;
let all the ends of the earth fear him!

1. ***Invitation to Praise and Joy.***—The abundant crops are the proximate cause of this song. But as the psalmist begins to sing, he gives place to a mood deeper than gratitude. We have noted this before, and have observed that it is one of Israel's great religious insights, viz., that praise, to avoid being self-praise, must begin in an act of contrition. Too often we encounter in the psalms the pride that is native to all men and that expresses itself by saying that God's blessings are our deserts. Our poet is wiser, and his word is therefore more authentic. This bounteous store which has occasioned his song does not inspire him to begin singing about how good and proper it is for God to lavish his favor on those who so manifestly deserve it. On the contrary, though there is no doubt of the place of the harvest's plenitude in his mind, he begins his song with a prayer that God shall be good to his people despite their undeserving. They have gathered in the sheaves and threshed the ripened grain; but above this they need the radiance of the face of Yahweh to shine on them. God—may he be **gracious to us and bless us and make his face to shine upon us.**

2-3. ***The Universal Perspective.***—Vs. 1 gives us the purpose of the song and the mood of the singer, but the magnanimity of his spirit is not yet spent. It is at this point that the note of universalism with which the poem is engaged has its first rendering, and it is pitched appropriately on a very generous level. All that he is asking for himself and his people he asks for all people: **That thy way may be known upon earth, thy saving health among all nations.**

4 O let the nations be glad and sing for joy: for thou shalt judge the people righteously, and govern the nations upon earth. Selah.
5 Let the people praise thee, O God; let all the people praise thee.

4 Let the nations be glad and sing for joy,
for thou dost judge the peoples with equity
and guide the nations upon earth. *Selah*
5 Let the peoples praise thee, O God;
let all the peoples praise thee!

The nations should in consequence recognize his beneficence in the government of the world. In all things he is their guide, observing what is right and just in all his decrees in nature and history (vs. 4). His goodness to Israel is particularly seen now in the gift of another harvest. Such a clear demonstration of God's gracious providence should move all the peoples of the earth to join with Israel in giving him reverence and worship (vss. 6-7).

The psalm is filled with the missionary spirit which comes to expression first in Second Isaiah and later in Jonah. The old passion of Israel for imperial expansion has been superseded by a nobler one, a passion for making all nations the Lord's people. The psalmist would lead the nations from the contemplation of the bounty of a harvest to the recognition of the Lord's hand and then to his worship. At the same time

---

He sets in at once to indicate what this universal knowledge of God means, but only after introducing the first of two choral responses that occur in vss. 3, 5, which have become both familiar and current as the summary of universal praise.

4-5. *Justice for All.*—We discover four great words that the psalmist uses and for which universal dimensions are claimed. They, we might say, are the four tones in this great and eternal theme on which the saints and sages of all time have developed their variations. They are **thy way, thy saving power, judge . . . with equity,** and **guide.** More simply they may be stated thus: God's universal order, redemption, governance, and guidance.

It is important for us to realize what an advance was made in human thought when the concept of universal law was first proposed. What this means to us at the present moment is less exciting than what it must have meant to those who first discovered it. To us it is the basis of all order, and the precondition of rational thought; to our poet it may have meant much less, but it was by any ratio a very great deal. We are dealing, of course, with one whose interest here was devotional or, to put it otherwise, religious. And yet it is interesting that he speaks both of a **way** and of **saving power** as though they were two distinct ideas. This may be reading into his lines something that is not there. He may have been thinking of the way as the way of redemption, and yet the literal text allows us the more generous interpretation.

If we agree that the concept of a universal way or order was a great discovery, we should not have much difficulty persuading ourselves that to the poet the way was redemptive, both in its aim and operation. Here the dynamic optimism of the Hebrew mind is expressing itself. What is this way; what are the method and purpose of its giant powers? Not the display of a proud Deity, but the unfolding of a redemptive enterprise. All power, even in its malign manifestations, subserved the beneficent aims of God. Power that to surface inspection looked capricious or even evil to deeper probing was seen to be saving power. That all nations should come to a realization of this was prerequisite to universal felicity through the use of universal power under universal order.

Our poet has intimated that there is a universal way, and that this way is saving power; or that order is one of the media by which mankind is to be saved. Man's destruction is the result of his revolt against the order within which he has been established. But redemption is not quite so simple a matter, and in order to extend the saving power of areas of man's need beyond his difficulties in conforming to the way, there must be God's governance. **Thou dost judge the peoples with equity.** This is the reason for the universalism of gladness and song with which the verse opens. **Let the nations be glad and sing for joy.**

Wherever the hearts of men have reacted to God, whether in fear, devotion, or anger, the certainty is that back of their response has been a realization that they were dealing with an authority with which they had to come to terms. This means that whatever other concept they may fashion about God, it is not open to doubt that he is primarily governor. This is true of any formulation of the God-man intercourse

6 *Then* shall the earth yield her increase; *and* God, *even* our own God, shall bless us.	6 The earth has yielded its increase; God, our God, has blessed us.

the psalm, in contrast to conceptions that prevailed in the religions of the ancient world and even in the pre-exilic religion of Israel, grounds worship on thankfulness for mercies received, i.e., on a loyal response to a gracious God.

The use of the words of the Aaronic benediction which occurs in the late Priestly Code (Num. 6:23-26), and the world-embracing religious point of view favor a postexilic date. The meter is 3+3, except in the last verse where it is 2+2+2.

In vs. 1 the present form of the text is attributable to the influence of the form of the priestly blessing. But, as vs. 7 shows, the blessing has come and the psalmist, meaning to indicate that the blessing has been fulfilled, doubtless changed the verb forms to perfects. Hence we should read not **May God be gracious,** etc., but "God has been gracious," etc. Read vs. 2, "So that thy way is known on earth . . . ."

---

worthy of being called a religion. Furthermore, it is a normal deduction that this governor governs everybody. The universalism of the world-governor idea is, we assume, very old; that there is in this universal governance a universal equity is what our poet seems to be saying, and this, whatever its age, is very important.

It has not always been easy to assure ourselves of the justice of God's way or of his saving power or even of his equity. The subjective factor in any equation involving what we call justice more often than not disturbs the calculation, and we tend to attribute to the Judge the inequities that prejudice our case. At the same time there is, and certainly for centuries has been, a consensus supporting the idea of a general over-all justice in human affairs. It is a direct assertion of this that our poem is making. That God governs is an axiom; that he governs universally is a plausible deduction; but that he governs all peoples with universal and impartial equity was a daring hypothesis for one to propose in the sixth century B.C. It was, however, God's way of exercising his **saving power among all nations.** How else other than by the enactment of universal law could all the nations be saved? It was then, as it is now, the introverted and egoistic and self-justifying law of nations that was the culture in which the virus of injustice and conflict grew. There would have been few to dispute that the Lord ruled Israel, his chosen, with equity; but to extend that justice to all peoples could easily have stirred suspicions, either of active treason or of dangerous idealism. And yet all the while there was implicit in the very idea of justice the corollary of universal equity. It was this idea that engaged the poet's inspired mind.

The fourth element in the pattern of universalism follows naturally. If there is a universal way which is designed to save all nations by the governance of universal equity, one would assume that this would provide the necessary guidance for the nations upon earth. How otherwise was leading to be saved from partiality or whim? How otherwise were the conflicting interests of the peoples to be resolved into an orderly pattern by which progress was possible for all? This is a panorama of idealism that stretches to far horizons and fills all space with giant concepts. Little wonder that twice in the body of the poem (vss. 3, 5) there is a pause for song, and that the evocation of praise is in dimensions as universal as the ideas that are set forth.

Tennyson's oft-quoted lines are a modern expression of this ancient ideal; yet when he wrote them, it cost him little pluck.

> One God, one law, one element,
> And one far-off divine event,
> To which the whole creation moves [4]

was written in the spacious days of Victoria's growing empire, and the words, however sonorous and noble, do not altogether escape the taint of patronage. The one law, the one element, and the one far-off divine event more often than not were the white man's law, the white man's power, and the white man's world. In the tumultuous first half of the twentieth century there has been felt the sting of the reproach cast by "the peoples" and "the nations" who have called the attention of the great nations of the Hebrew-Christian tradition to the inequities of their rule in the world. And this has resulted in wars and in the ruin of nations and in the death of empires.

6-7. *Certainty of God's Fullness.*—Upon the heels of modern retributive justice there has followed once again the demand for universalism. It has been measurably achieved in the ideas and use of modern science. The realiza-

[4] *In Memoriam,* Conclusion, st. xxxvi.

7 God shall bless us; and all the ends of the earth shall fear him.

To the chief Musician, A Psalm *or* Song of David.

68 Let God arise, let his enemies be scattered: let them also that hate him flee before him.

7 God has blessed us;
let all the ends of the earth fear him!

To the choirmaster. A Psalm of David. A Song.

68 Let God arise, let his enemies be scattered;
let those who hate him flee before him!

Through a common copyist's error three words have fallen out of the text of vs. 4, which is preserved intact in the LXX; the words to be supplied are תבל בצדק תשפט (cf. 98:9). The translation of the emended verse is:

Let the nations be glad and shout for joy
for thou dost govern the world in righteousness,
thou dost govern the peoples with equity,
and guidest the nations of the earth.

LXVIII. Libretto of Songs for the Sanctuary (68:1-35)

The classification of this psalm is difficult because it has no exact counterpart in the Psalter. On the first impression it is a liturgical medley of songs and hymns strung along without any governing motif, each of them spirited and picturesque, and some of them adaptable to dramatic representation. One is not surprised therefore that the psalm has been described as a collection of short independent songs or fragments of songs drawn from different sources and periods and forming a hymnal for use in the ritual of some sacred occasion (cf. Schmidt, Oesterley). However, the difficulties presented by the apparently haphazard order of the units of the psalm are considerably eased when one recognizes the occasion to which the psalm related. As Schmidt has pointed out, the occasion is identified in vss. 24-25.

Thy solemn processions are seen, O God,
the processions of my God, my King, into the sanctuary—
the singers in front, the minstrels last,
between them maidens playing timbrels.

---

tion of a universal way in terms of the order of nature—human as well as physical—is unchallenged, and that we are to be saved by appropriating this way is similarly undisputed. But we, even in our talk of one world, seem to have stopped short of the one world of our ancient poet. Do we not come perilously near to believing that redemption in our times will come when we accept the universal orderliness of things—which is the salvation of scientism? The three great dramatic factors in the story of Israel are man, sin, redemption, and they still furnish our day with the problems about which all inquiry, whether political, scientific, or theological, revolves. Universalism as it has been most nobly conceived will not come to pass if we fail to come to grips with them; and from the Christian perspective that means coming to grips with them in terms of our great spiritual tradition. As yet there is no fully codified and accepted universal equity; even less universal is the acceptance of the primary fact that it is God who will **judge the peoples with equity,** or to put it otherwise, that only God's law can be universal law. If the almost universal mood today is opposite to that of our poet who was glad and sang for joy, is this not due to the fact that we have either lost our faith in universalism or have rested it on unsubstantial foundations? And does this not lay upon those who are the legatees of this eternal inheritance the obligation to rethink our plans for one world? We alone of all the peoples of earth can say:

The earth has yielded its increase;
God, our God, has blessed us.

Are we ready to accept utterly the poet's sequent: **Let all the ends of the earth fear him—** instead of us?

68:1-35. ***Men's Inconsistent Thought of God.*** —This poem has stumped the experts. They

It clearly has to do with a procession such as that of Pss. 24; 47, in which the kingship of the Lord was acclaimed and celebrated. The psalm is to be understood as a libretto of the songs used in the course of the procession, and the songs are the choral responses to the ceremonial acts or narratives, or both, belonging to a sacred pageant. We can think of the psalm as something like the choruses in a Greek play or the choral parts of a Bach *Passion*. The leading motif is the Lord's assumption of his kingship in Zion, and it is developed in five parts: (*a*) prelude (vss. 1-3); (*b*) victorious march of God from Sinai through the wilderness (vss. 4-14); (*c*) entrance into Zion (vss. 15-18); (*d*) implications of his rule for Israel and the nations (vss. 19-31); (*e*) exhortation to the kingdoms of the earth to extol the Lord (vss. 32-35). Each part consists of a number of contributory units (see T. H. Gaster, *Thespis* [New York: Henry Schuman, 1950], pp. 87-97).

The date of the psalm is postexilic. The fact that the Lord is represented as choosing Zion as his place of habitation after the march through the wilderness is post-Deuteronomic. Vss. 6-7 recall Deut. 15:1-23 and Isa. 49:9-10, 20-21; the reference in vs. 27 to the union of the Galilean tribes with Judah and Benjamin may reflect a late situation such as the Chronicler knew (cf. II Chr. 30:10-11). The interweaving of extracts from older literature is a work of the period of imitative writing, and the extracts themselves in their wide variety presuppose the text of the historical and prophetic literature as shaped in the postexilic period.

The meter is not uniform, but varies with the songs and even within a song. However, lines of 4+3 and 3+4 predominate.

---

are in general agreement on one point only: that there can be no agreement as to the source, authorship, date, construction, or intention of this medley. Dedicated to the choirmaster and described as a song, it would seem from our musical perspective to have asked of the congregations supposed to sing it, and the precentor who was to direct the ensemble, uncommon skill. There are at least seven different metrical patterns, or as we would put it, the time signature changes seven times. These changes are abrupt and ungraceful; rhythm is sacrificed to some undisclosed intention of the writer.

We must not forget that modern concepts of God are to a great extent the result of pious and scholarly efforts to bring moral and metaphysical consistency to the godward reach of the human spirit. We would hardly ascribe to him at one time the opposite qualities of tenderness and terror, compassion and vengeance, generosity and partisanship. Such antitheses created no problem for primitive worshipers. It is a commonplace of all religious experience that it can adapt itself to the widest range of circumstance. To the Trappist monk it demands silence, to the Penitentes self-torture, to one saint rapture, to another anguish. If this song comes from a single writer, he may have been one who was sensitive to contradictory moods. After all, our concern is somewhat different from that of the literary scholar. We are interested in structure only as it makes available the religious values of the text, and while it is important for us to know the redactor's problem, we shall find it more important to discover and appropriate the fact that man's exercise of the religious impulse, if it is real, is not stylized. Spontaneity, even though sometimes erratic, may be preferred to the austere rigors of design.

Keeping in mind the problem that this poem presents to the scholar, it will be profitable to inquire into the ways in which God was seen by its compiler. He is perhaps putting together for congregational use those components of then current attitudes that would come nearest to satisfying the moods of the worshipers. Nor shall we allow ourselves to forget that this is a song, not a treatise. If it could be sung with verve, the degree of its veracity could for the moment be overlooked.

In this form, which we assume served the worship needs of an ancient congregation, we discover God represented in at least six roles. He appears as destroyer, protector, giant (portent), warrior, savior, and worshiped one. It is of no great importance that we find it difficult to mortise these diverse qualities into a smooth unitary concept. The poet himself felt no necessity for the sort of consistency we commonly seek. We allow our differing human moods autonomy so long as they last, even though successive moods may tend to cancel each other. Thus to the ancients God was no less God because one moment he was a destroyer and the next a savior.

1-6. *God Surrounded.*—In vs. 1 the picture seems to represent God as surrounded by enemies who have surreptitiously established them-

2 As smoke is driven away, *so* drive *them*
away: as wax melteth before the fire, *so* let
the wicked perish at the presence of God.
3 But let the righteous be glad; let them
rejoice before God: yea, let them exceedingly rejoice.
4 Sing unto God, sing praises to his
name: extol him that rideth upon the heavens by his name JAH, and rejoice before
him.
5 A father of the fatherless, and a judge
of the widows, *is* God in his holy habitation.

2 As smoke is driven away, so drive them
away;
as wax melts before fire,
let the wicked perish before God!
3 But let the righteous be joyful;
let them exult before God;
let them be jubilant with joy!

4 Sing to God, sing praises to his name;
lift up a song to him who rides upon
the clouds;[d]
his name is the LORD, exult before him!

5 Father of the fatherless and protector of
widows
is God in his holy habitation.

[d] Or *cast up a highway for him who rides through the deserts*

1. PRELUDE (68:1-3)

68:1-3. The prelude opens with the words with which Moses gave the signal for lifting up the ark when the Israelites broke up camp to continue their march in the wilderness (Num. 10:35). In the context of the psalm these words are the signal for the start of the procession at the head of which a symbol of the Lord's presence is borne.

2. GOD IN THE EXODUS (68:4-14)

4-6. Sing to God, sing praises to his name: Remembrance of the Lord's goodness to his people in their Exodus journeyings calls forth a hymn to him as the protector of the needy and the oppressed. **To him who rides upon the clouds:** Cf. Deut. 33:26. "He who rides upon the clouds" is an epithet of Aleyan Baal in the Canaanite mythological poems. The reading בעבות, **upon the clouds,** for בערבות, "in the steppes," seems justified (cf. vs. 33), but more probably רכב בערבות is a late echo of the Canaanite *rkbʿrpt*. **His name JAH:** This form of the divine name is found chiefly in postexilic literature, especially in the Psalter in the phrase "Hallelujah."

selves—a sort of fifth column—in the midst of his people. The signal is given by a surveillant, and the enemy is surprised and set upon. God stands up! Panic follows and indiscriminate flight. The strength of the adversaries is as tenuous as smoke, their vaunted cohesion as fluid as melted wax. Before God's destruction they scatter to die, they flee to their ruin. This is the scene with which the poem opens; the customary exultation of the righteous, who absorb to their own credit the discomfiture of God's adversaries, follows (vs. 3). When the writer returns to this theme in vss. 21-23, his language is more violent. There we see shattered enemy heads, and the feet of the righteous bathed in blood as they return from Bashan and the sea. Even the dogs share in the gory celebration, and are allowed their portion from the foe.

This is a grisly demonstration of the Destroyer's power and partisanship. We are not told why his hapless victims deserved their fate. They were enemies and that was enough. The reference to **the hairy crown** (vs. 21) has been taken to indicate the tribesmen of the wilderness whose unkempt tonsure was a mark of their barbarity. Just how the Israelite wore his hair we need not inquire. Baldness was a reproach then, as it is a joke now. Isa. 3:24 says that baldness, "instead of well set hair," was to be a symptom of the moral degeneracy of the daughters of Israel in a later age. It is not implausible to assume that care of the hair was a sign of good breeding, and a hairy crown, indicating dishevelment, the sign of the boor. Whatever such details mean, there is no doubt on the main point that when God stood up, his enemies went down. How abrupt the contrast vss. 5-6 present as God is described as **Father of the fatherless and protector of widows,** etc. To be sure, the beneficiaries of his protection are his own people. This is conceptually a great

6 God setteth the solitary in families: he
bringeth out those which are bound with
chains: but the rebellious dwell in a dry
land.
7 O God, when thou wentest forth before
thy people, when thou didst march through
the wilderness; Selah:
8 The earth shook, the heavens also
dropped at the presence of God: *even* Sinai
itself *was moved* at the presence of God, the
God of Israel.
9 Thou, O God, didst send a plentiful
rain, whereby thou didst confirm thine inheritance, when it was weary.
10 Thy congregation hath dwelt therein:
thou, O God, hast prepared of thy goodness
for the poor.
11 The Lord gave the word: great *was*
the company of those that published *it.*
12 Kings of armies did flee apace: and
she that tarried at home divided the spoil.

6 God gives the desolate a home to dwell in;
he leads out the prisoners to prosperity;
but the rebellious dwell in a parched land.

7 O God, when thou didst go forth before thy people,
when thou didst march through the wilderness, *Selah*
8 the earth quaked, the heavens poured down rain,
at the presence of God;
yon Sinai quaked at the presence of God,
the God of Israel.
9 Rain in abundance, O God, thou didst shed abroad;
thou didst restore thy heritage as it languished;
10 thy flock found a dwelling in it;
in thy goodness, O God, thou didst provide for the needy.

11 The Lord gives the command;
great is the host of those who bore the tidings:
12 "The kings of the armies, they flee, they flee!"
The women at home divide the spoil,

Prosperity: Better, "with jubilations." The word כושרות is reminiscent of "the female jubilantes" of the Canaanite myth (see Cyrus H. Gordon, *Ugaritic Handbook* [Roma: Pontificium Institutum Biblicum, 1947], p. 241, No. 1050).

7-10. At Mount Sinai the Lord manifested his presence in mighty commotions of nature (cf. Judg. 5:4). At the same time he prepared for his people a land watered by the rains of heaven in contrast to the land of Egypt watered only by irrigation. **Yon Sinai:** It is better to read זע סיני, "Sinai quaked," or to delete as a gloss. The psalmist lived after the time when the text of Judg. 5:5 had become corrupt.

11-14. In spite of the opposition which the Israelites met from hostile kings in their march to and after their entrance into Canaan, and in spite of the lethargy of their own fellows who **stay among the sheepfolds,** the Lord gave them victory. The verses of this section recall Judg. 5:30 and are probably a free handling of the story of Sisera's defeat. **Though they stay among the sheepfolds:** Or, "If you dwell among the sheepfolds." These words interrupt the connection between vs. 12*b* and vs. 13*b* and

---

distance from feeding a hungry enemy (Rom. 12:20). At the same time, it must have stood even in ancient times as something of a reversal when the mighty hand that had shattered heads turned to shelter the orphan and the widow. The destroyer whose sudden standing up marked the death of his enemies now **rides upon the clouds** (vs. 4). His name is **JAH,** and he becomes the security of the despoiled and dispossessed and the protector of the defenseless.

7-18. ***What God Did.***—It is perhaps no more than a vigorous figure of speech that now describes God in vss. 7-8. To accomplish the prodigies of destruction and protection required the proportions of a giant. Bashan had been called "the land of giants." God was to smite

13 Though ye have lain among the pots, *yet shall ye be as* the wings of a dove covered with silver, and her feathers with yellow gold.

14 When the Almighty scattered kings in it, it was *white* as snow in Salmon.

15 The hill of God *is as* the hill of Bashan; a high hill *as* the hill of Bashan.

16 Why leap ye, ye high hills? *this is* the hill *which* God desireth to dwell in; yea, the LORD will dwell *in it* for ever.

17 The chariots of God *are* twenty thousand, *even* thousands of angels: the Lord *is* among them, *as in* Sinai, in the holy *place*.

13 though they stay among the sheepfolds —
the wings of a dove covered with silver,
its pinions with green gold.
14 When the Almighty scattered kings there,
snow fell on Zalmon.

15 O mighty mountain, mountain of Bashan;
O many-peaked mountain, mountain of Bashan!
16 Why look you with envy, O many-peaked mountain,
at the mount which God desired for his abode,
yea, where the LORD will dwell for ever?

17 With mighty chariotry, twice ten thousand,
thousands upon thousands,
the Lord came[e] from Sinai into the holy place.

[e] Cn: Heb *the Lord among them Sinai in the holy place*

---

must have been introduced from Judg. 5:16 as either a parenthesis or a gloss. **The wings of a dove, . . . gold:** A description of a choice item in the list of the booty. The Hebrew of vs. 14 is uncertain.

3. God Comes to Zion (68:15-18)

15-16. The Lord preferred for his dwelling place the modest hill of Zion to the loftier and more imposing peaks of **Bashan.** The reference here is probably to Mount Hermon, which, as the most imposing seat among those occupied by Canaanite Baals, might be regarded as presenting a claim to recognition by the Lord.

17-18. After the manner of a victorious earthly king the Lord enters his capital at the head of his troops with the captives and the spoils of his battles in his train. **With mighty chariotry:** Angelic hosts compose the army of the Lord (cf. Deut. 33:2; II Kings 6:17; Isa. 66:15). **The Lord came from Sinai:** For this translation one reads בא מסיני in preference to the M.T., בם סיני, lit., "among them Sinai" (cf. KJV). **Leading captives:** Probably a vague and general deduction from the implications of the conquest of Canaan.

---

the guilty of Bashan, and Bashan was to be twitted because its highest peaks were pygmy to the mount of God (vss. 15-16). Why then should not God be a giant to dwarf the oversized aliens? None of the Anakim could match the stride of God when he went forth before his people. **The earth quaked, the heavens poured down rain** (vs. 8*a*). Where God's foot stepped, the earth shook; where his head reached, the clouds burst. But it was a beneficent giant who stalked through his land. The tremors restored the languishing soil (vs. 9*b*), and the rain brought forth pasturage for the flocks. **In thy goodness, O God, thou didst provide for the needy** (vs. 10).

Destruction was not the prerogative of God alone. As warrior he led his people to battle that they too might inflict vengeance on the wicked. Hence we see him next in the role of the great commander. Two references in our poem, vss. 11 and 17-18, present this emphasis. Here again the historical references are as unimportant for our use as they are obscure to the literary critic. The intention of the poet is clear: he wants to present God as an invincible leader in battle. What meaning otherwise is to be gathered from the **tidings** brought by the great host (vs. 11)? The victory is complete; kings and armies flee, and housewives without even leaving the sheepfolds gather in the rich

18 Thou hast ascended on high, thou hast led captivity captive: thou hast received gifts for men; yea, *for* the rebellious also, that the LORD God might dwell *among them*.

19 Blessed *be* the Lord, *who* daily loadeth us *with benefits, even* the God of our salvation. Selah.

20 *He that is* our God *is* the God of salvation; and unto GOD the Lord *belong* the issues from death.

21 But God shall wound the head of his enemies, *and* the hairy scalp of such a one as goeth on still in his trespasses.

22 The Lord said, I will bring again from Bashan, I will bring *my people* again from the depths of the sea:

23 That thy foot may be dipped in the blood of *thine* enemies, *and* the tongue of thy dogs in the same.

18 Thou didst ascend the high mount,
leading captives in thy train,
and receiving gifts among men,
even among the rebellious, that the LORD
God may dwell there.

19 Blessed be the Lord,
who daily bears us up;
God is our salvation. *Selah*
20 Our God is a God of salvation;
and to GOD, the Lord, belongs escape
from death.

21 But God will shatter the heads of his
enemies,
the hairy crown of him who walks in
his guilty ways.
22 The Lord said,
"I will bring them back from Bashan,
I will bring them back from the depths
of the sea,
23 that you may bathe[f] your feet in blood,
that the tongues of your dogs may have
their portion from the foe."

[f] Gk Syr Tg: Heb *shatter*

Such an event, as described, could lend itself to dramatic representation. **Receiving gifts among men:** The apostle Paul seems to have known a different reading of this text (cf. Eph. 4:8), and interprets it as descriptive of the triumph of Jesus who, ascended on high, dispenses to men spiritual gifts. **Even among the rebellious:** Those who have offered stubborn resistance to the conqueror must yield to him. The Jebusites, who held out against the Hebrews, may be meant.

4. GOD IS ISRAEL'S SALVATION (68:19-23)

19-23. From Zion, where he takes up his abode, the Lord rules, giving help to his people and taking vengeance on his enemies. **God will shatter . . . the hairy crown:** His enemies are described as desperate men who let their hair grow as a symbol of a vow to carry on war without mercy against him. But they will be hunted down and brought to punishment even though they take flight to **Bashan** or seek escape in **the depths of the sea.** In vs. 23 read with the versions תרחץ, **bathe,** for תמחץ, **shatter.**

---

loot abandoned by the headlong flight of the vanquished. It was booty to delight the feminine eye:

> **The wings of a dove covered with silver,**
> **its pinions with green gold** (vs. 13).

19-35. ***What God Can Do.***—The ascription of saviorhood to God (vss. 19-20) bears slight relation to other roles in which he has been cast by our poet, and no relation whatever to the place where it occurs in the poem. This need not concern us. What is of interest is that there seems to have been no incompatibility in placing this brief gem of devotion between a train of captives and the smashing of uncombed heads. Its mood is completely insulated from the bloody business that precedes and follows it, and yet it too must be allowed its autonomy as long as it lasts. If our poet felt some momentary compunction about his other presentations of the God of Israel, he responded to it eloquently in vss. 19-20; if he did not, we must speculate further for an explanation.

There follows (vss. 24-34) a series of verses that dismay the critic as much as they delight the expositor. Moving from his description of the somewhat equivocal character of God, our poet plunges into what is either sheer vagary

24 They have seen thy goings, O God; *even* the goings of my God, my King, in the sanctuary.
25 The singers went before, the players on instruments *followed* after; among *them were* the damsels playing with timbrels.
26 Bless ye God in the congregations, *even* the Lord, from the fountain of Israel.
27 There *is* little Benjamin *with* their ruler, the princes of Judah *and* their council, the princes of Zebulun, *and* the princes of Naphtali.
28 Thy God hath commanded thy strength: strengthen, O God, that which thou hast wrought for us.
29 Because of thy temple at Jerusalem shall kings bring presents unto thee.

24 Thy solemn processions are seen,[g] O God,
the processions of my God, my King,
into the sanctuary —
25 the singers in front, the minstrels last,
between them maidens playing timbrels:
26 "Bless God in the great congregation,
the LORD, O you who are of Israel's fountain!"
27 There is Benjamin, the least of them, in the lead,
the princes of Judah in their throng,
the princes of Zeb'ulun, the princes of Naph'tali.

28 Summon thy might, O God;
show thy strength, O God, thou who hast wrought for us.
29 Because of thy temple at Jerusalem
kings bear gifts to thee.

[g] Or *have been seen*

5. PROCESSION IN THE TEMPLE (68:24-27)

24-27. His own people pay grateful homage to him in a procession in which the tribes from Judah and Benjamin, in the south, to Zebulun and Naphtali, in the north, take part. The detailed description of such a procession is illuminating. It is one of the few accounts of a ceremonial act in our Hebrew sources (cf. Ecclus. 50:5-21).

6. THE UNIVERSAL RECOGNITION OF ISRAEL'S GOD (68:28-35)

28-31. The Lord must become universally acknowledged: **Kings bear gifts to thee.** Prominent among the tributary peoples are Egypt and Ethiopia, whose subjection is

or truly profound insight into the place of religion in an otherwise rather dismal picture of man's existence. Brief references have already occurred—the jubilation of the righteous and their songs of praise (vss. 3-4)—but they are hardly more than interludes. With the opening words of vs. 24, however, we are in another world. From the shambles we have moved into the sanctuary; nor is the transition designed to provide simply a religious celebration of the destruction of the enemy. Indeed, it is surprising to discover how free it is from the martial mood. Whatever our scholarly colleagues think about the literary or historic source of this fragment, what we see is a religious pageant of impressive dimensions and meaning.

**The singers in front, the minstrels last,
between them maidens playing timbrels** (vs. 25).

It is indeed a grand procession. Then come the princes of Judah, Zebulun and Naphtali, with little Benjamin in the vanguard (vs. 27). Voices are united in a great paean of praise: **Bless God in the great congregation** (vs. 26). This spectacle was worthy to have at its head God himself. If it seems somewhat grandiose to us, let us not deny its true magnificence in the poet's eye.

The scene does not end with the ascent of the procession into the temple. Of even more profound importance are vss. 28-30. The call to the worshiping procession to **bless God in the great congregation** is followed by a call to God to display his might from the temple (vs. 28). Here the reference is not to the quaking earth when God goes striding by, or to the enemy scattered like smoke. The scene of God's fabulous doings is not a battleground in the mountains of Bashan, but **thy temple at Jerusalem.** Here speaks the God of religion, not the God of battles; this is the eternal word spoken from the holy place, rather than the command of the warrior rocketing across the **strewn field.** There is, to be sure, no abdication of the **royal** prerogatives: **Kings bear gifts to thee** (vs. 29*b*). The new note is one of rebuke to **the brute** mind, and a warning to those who **lust for**

30 Rebuke the company of spearmen, the multitude of the bulls, with the calves of the people, *till every one* submit himself with pieces of silver: scatter thou the people *that* delight in war.

31 Princes shall come out of Egypt; Ethiopia shall soon stretch out her hands unto God.

32 Sing unto God, ye kingdoms of the earth; O sing praises unto the Lord; Selah:

33 To him that rideth upon the heavens of heavens, *which were* of old; lo, he doth send out his voice, *and that* a mighty voice.

34 Ascribe ye strength unto God: his excellency *is* over Israel, and his strength *is* in the clouds.

35 O God, *thou art* terrible out of thy holy places: the God of Israel *is* he that giveth strength and power unto *his* people. Blessed *be* God.

30 Rebuke the beasts that dwell among the reeds,
the herd of bulls with the calves of the peoples.
Trample[h] under foot those who lust after tribute;
scatter the peoples who delight in war.[i]
31 Let bronze be brought from Egypt;
let Ethiopia hasten to stretch out her hands to God.

32 Sing to God, O kingdoms of the earth;
sing praises to the Lord, *Selah*
33 to him who rides in the heavens, the ancient heavens;
lo, he sends forth his voice, his mighty voice.
34 Ascribe power to God,
whose majesty is over Israel,
and his power is in the skies.
35 Terrible is God in his[j] sanctuary,
the God of Israel,
he gives power and strength to his people.

Blessed be God!

[h] Cn: Heb *trampling*
[i] The Hebrew of verse 30 is obscure
[j] Gk: Heb *from thy*

envisioned in other eschatological material (cf. Zeph. 3:10; Zech. 14:18-19). **The beasts that dwell among the reeds:** The Egyptians are typified contemptuously by the crocodile and the hippopotamus. **The herd of bulls with the calves of the peoples:** Better, with a slight emendation, "the herd of bulls, the lords of the peoples." Emend vs. 30*c* to read התרפס ברצי כסף, lit., "trample down those who lust after silver," i.e., in tribute.

32-35. After having exhorted the Lord to realize the ends of his victory, the singers summon the nations to give praise to him who manifests his power in the heavens and

tribute and delight in war (vs. 30). This, we are told, is a not too cryptic reference to Egypt (**that dwell among the reeds,** etc.). There are words here difficult to translate, and historic references impossible to identify; but the translator has unquestionably caught the spirit of this emphasis in the final exhortation of the passage: **Let Ethiopia hasten to stretch out her hands to God** (vs. 31). Here in sum we have an idea of the experience of worship, coupled with the basic intention of religion, set on a very high level.

32-35. ***The Transcendence of God.***—There remains the devotional epilogue (vss. 32-35). It brings the tempest of thematic contradictions out into a tranquil hymn of praise. Here the mood changes again. God no longer makes war; he is the Transcendent. Earthbound kingdoms must praise the Courser of the ancient heavens whose voice is mighty thunder; his power as the God of Israel stands over against his majestic power in the skies. And though the portents of his power are frightening in the sanctuary, it is he who gives power to his people. **Blessed be God!**

If now we turn from the multiple poem themes, from the high and low levels of the poet's presentation of God, can we find the factor that made this song acceptable to the anthologists? From the opening words, **Let God arise,** we move through confused passages to the closing words, **Blessed be God!** It is better that God shall arise even if it puzzles the mind of man than that he remains concealed. Here in miniature is the history of religion. God rises. How this portent is to be understood depends

To the chief Musician upon Shoshannim, *A Psalm* of David.	To the choirmaster: according to Lilies. A Psalm of David.
69 Save me, O God; for the waters are come in unto *my* soul.	69 Save me, O God! For the waters have come up to my neck.

his glory in Israel's history. Israel too is reminded that its **power and strength** come from him (vs. 35). The whole occasion is brought to an end with the doxology, **Blessed be God!**

LXIX. A Plaintive Cry for Deliverance (69:1-36)

This is a lament of one who is encompassed with trouble and affliction. In the first place, he is bowed down by a false accusation of having committed some kind of theft and by loud demands that he restore what he is alleged to have taken (vs. 4). Then at the same time he is the victim of a sickness which threatens to end his life (vss. 1-2). His enemies assume that his physical sufferings confirm their charges against him. The situation in which he finds himself does not affect only him (vss. 6-12). He has stood out among his fellows as one of those who seek God; he has been zealous for God's house and devout in his attention to the ritual acts of piety and penitence. But now he has become discredited; he is jeered at, the topic of the gossip of the idlers in the gate, the theme of drunkards' songs. In these circumstances, if he is left unvindicated, all who share his religious convictions and ways will be confounded. **Let not those who hope in thee be put to shame through me** (vs. 6).

Accordingly, in vs. 13 he renews his petition, appealing to God's compassion, goodness, and faithfulness, to draw near and rescue him from his distresses (vss. 13-18), and, more passionately than before, reminding God of the insults, the pitilessness, and the treachery of his enemies (vss. 19-21). In indignation at the wrongs suffered by him he turns from petition to malediction, calling for a series of curses to fall on his persecutors in large-measured retaliation in kind for their evil designs against him (vss. 22-28).

Finally he vows to God an offering of praise in anticipation of God's saving help. Such an offering, he declares significantly, **will please the Lord more than an ox or a bull with horns and hoofs.** He sees in advance how the glory of his deliverance, as recounted in his song of thanksgiving, will revive hope and courage in the hearts of men troubled like him (vss. 29-33).

The psalm is brought to a close with a hymn (vss. 34-36) in which the deliverance of Zion from its distresses and the restoration of the cities of Judah are declared to be assured, for the experience of the psalmist is indicative of what God can and will do for the whole body of his people. This is not the first time that the psalmists view the experience of the individual as history in miniature (cf. 9:13-20; 51:18-19; 102:12-13).

As to the date of this psalm, there are no certain indications. From vs. 9 we gather that the temple exists and is functioning in the life of the community. However, in vss. 35-36 it is expressly stated that Zion is not free from distress and the parts outside it

on the vagaries of human experience. To the threatened he may be protection; to the weak, power; to the stricken, compassion; to the wicked, the rod of chastening. Man's ideas do not change God. If he leads the worshiper into the sanctuary or the rebellious to destruction, his moral integrity is not violated. Ultimately there is blessing in both his mercy and his judgment.

Has not our compositor-poet, in spite of himself or of our superficial reading, laid hold of a profound truth and set it forth in disarmingly simple words? **Let God arise. . . . Blessed be God!** That, we agree, is the beginning of the religious experience and the end of religious devotion.

69:1-6. ***The Would-be Reformer Frustrated.***—It is not difficult to see why the early anthologists credited this poem to the pen of David. Less easy is the selection of the accompaniment. **Lilies** sounds singularly inappropriate as a tune for these dismal words. Though the

2 I sink in deep mire, where *there is* no standing: I am come into deep waters, where the floods overflow me.

3 I am weary of my crying: my throat is dried: mine eyes fail while I wait for my God.

4 They that hate me without a cause are more than the hairs of mine head: they that would destroy me, *being* mine enemies wrongfully, are mighty: then I restored *that* which I took not away.

2 I sink in deep mire,
where there is no foothold;
I have come into deep waters,
and the flood sweeps over me.
3 I am weary with my crying;
my throat is parched.
My eyes grow dim
with waiting for my God.

4 More in number than the hairs of my head
are those who hate me without cause;
mighty are those who would destroy me,
those who attack me with lies.
What I did not steal
must I now restore?

---

in Judah are suffering from ruin and depopulation. The conditions described seem to agree best with what we know of the state of Jerusalem and Judah in the fifth century, i.e., approximately the times of Nehemiah and Ezra, rather than in the Greek period. If we hold with those students who regard vss. 34-36 as a supplement added to the psalm by some editor in order to adapt it to liturgical use, then we must allow that the psalm (vss. 1-33) antedates the addendum by an indefinite period.

The psalm may have been planned to consist of three main divisions: vss. 1-12, the petition and the plight of the psalmist; vss. 13-28, renewed petition and curses; vss. 29-36, a vow of praise. Each part consists of strophes, usually of four distichs each, e.g., vss. 1-3, 4-5, 6-8, 9-12; 13-15, 16-19, 20-21, 22-25, 26-28; 29-33; 34-36. The meter is mainly 3+3.

1. Appeal to God (69:1-3)

69:1-3. Save me, O God: The psalmist addresses an appeal for deliverance to God. He is sick (cf. vss. 26*b*, 29). He believes that death is at hand and he pictures his condition as he draws near to the underworld as that of a man sinking slowly in **deep mire** or overwhelmed by a **flood.** These metaphors occur elsewhere in this connection (cf. vs. 15; 32:6; 40:2; 42:7; Jonah 2:5). **The waters have come up to my neck:** Lit., come unto my *néphesh;* i.e., "threaten my life." The word *néphesh,* generally translated **soul** or "life," means sometimes **neck** or "throat," like the Assyrian *napishtu* (cf. 44:25; 105:18; Jonah 2:5). The psalmist has appealed for help more than once, but the Lord seems slow to answer. **I am weary of my crying; my throat is dried:** His frank reminder to God of what could imply divine indifference or callousness is meant to be not so much a complaint as an argument for the granting of the answer (cf. Luke 18:1-8).

2. The Psalmist's Plight (69:4-12)

4-8. His enemies are numerous, **more in number than the hairs of my head.** Even if exaggeration is allowed for, their number is impressive and bespeaks the prominence of

---

scholars must deny its imputed authorship, there are episodes in David's life which might have inspired it. Since, however, its author must remain without a name, its sentiments can more readily be appropriated by many persons who have had much the same experience.

The experience is that of the frustrated reformer, and there is here stated in ancient categories much that might today come from the lips of the "tired liberal." One does not expect from such a person a wholly accurate description of his state of mind or the circumstances which produced it. Defeat embitters, and defeat in a cause to which one has given one's

5 O God, thou knowest my foolishness;
and my sins are not hid from thee.
6 Let not them that wait on thee, O Lord
God of hosts, be ashamed for my sake: let
not those that seek thee be confounded for
my sake, O God of Israel.
7 Because for thy sake I have borne reproach; shame hath covered my face.
8 I am become a stranger unto my brethren, and an alien unto my mother's children.

5 O God, thou knowest my folly;
the wrongs I have done are not hidden
from thee.

6 Let not those who hope in thee be put to
shame through me,
O Lord God of hosts;
let not those who seek thee be brought to
dishonor through me,
O God of Israel.
7 For it is for thy sake that I have borne
reproach,
that shame has covered my face.
8 I have become a stranger to my brethren,
an alien to my mother's sons.

---

the psalmist. They are powerful, **mighty,** and deadly, men **who would destroy me.** The attacks which they set going are **lies,** i.e., false, without foundation. The burden of their attacks (cf. 35:11) is concretely stated:

What I did not steal
must I now restore?

The sickness of the psalmist is construed by his accusers to be an evidence of his guilt. He, on the other hand, admits that his sickness is a visitation for sin, but not for that of which he is accused. **O God, thou knowest my folly:** The word translated **folly** means properly sin viewed as a product of stupidity or dull-wittedness.

6-8. Here the psalmist gives two additional reasons why God should answer him: (*a*) **Let not those who seek thee be brought to dishonor through me,** i.e., many will lose their faith if the psalmist is not vindicated; (*b*) **it is for thy sake I have borne reproach** and **have become a stranger to my brethren** (cf. 31:11; 41:9; 55:12-13). These arguments are not new in the Psalter. In this instance the religious course which the psalmist followed kindled especially the fire of his enemies' hatred and inspired their attacks.

---

self without prospect or wish for personal gain adds self-pity to bitterness. Thus perspectives are distorted and explanations are biased. One is likely to end with an exaggerated sense of solitary virtue among pretty general moral obliquity.

In the light of this observation our unhappy poet comes off fairly well. As he writes, he does not pursue his story in a straight line, and this gives to the reader the sense of vacillation or conflict which normally characterizes the mood of frustration. It is not difficult, however, to dissect out of the confusion a clear and altogether familiar pattern. We shall therefore listen first to his description of what he thinks has happened to him; second, to his effort to set forth his feeling of frustration; third, to his reaffirmation of his faith in the cause for which he has suffered defeat; and finally to his angry recriminations on those whom he thinks are to blame for his failure.

7-12. ***Reasons for His Failure.***—It is in vss. 7, 9 that we learn the cause that had commanded the poet's daring. **It is for thy sake that I have borne reproach. . . . Zeal for thy house has consumed me.** It is the cause of God and God's house. This is not very specific, to be sure, but the only permissible inference is that religion and worship had fallen on perilous days. Our reformer exhibits no mild concern; he is consumed with zeal. To break the indifference, the stereotype, the dead punctilio which had enervated the true religious experience, he had risked not only the opposition of the insolent—**the insults of those who insult thee have fallen on me**—but rejection by his kith and kin (vs. 8). He boldly confesses to the impetuosity of the zealot; he even intimates that his radicalism has betrayed him into the use of unwise and wrong methods. This is not only refreshing candor; it is at the same time indication of the fact that the reproach which had fallen on him

9 For the zeal of thine house hath eaten
me up; and the reproaches of them that
reproached thee are fallen upon me.
10 When I wept, *and chastened* my soul
with fasting, that was to my reproach.
11 I made sackcloth also my garment;
and I became a proverb to them.
12 They that sit in the gate speak against
me; and I *was* the song of the drunkards.
13 But as for me, my prayer *is* unto thee,
O LORD, *in* an acceptable time: O God, in
the multitude of thy mercy hear me, in the
truth of thy salvation.
14 Deliver me out of the mire, and let me
not sink: let me be delivered from them that
hate me, and out of the deep waters.

9 For zeal for thy house has consumed me,
and the insults of those who insult thee
have fallen on me.
10 When I humbled[k] my soul with fasting,
it became my reproach.
11 When I made sackcloth my clothing,
I became a byword to them.
12 I am the talk of those who sit in the gate,
and the drunkards make songs about
me.

13 But as for me, my prayer is to thee, O
LORD.
At an acceptable time, O God,
in the abundance of thy steadfast love
answer me.
14 With thy faithful help rescue me
from sinking in the mire;
let me be delivered from my enemies
and from the deep waters.

[k] Gk Syr: Heb *I wept with fasting my soul* or *I made my soul mourn with fasting*

9-12. More specifically we are told the grounds of the enmity which he provoked. **Zeal for thy house has consumed me:** Seemingly he was prominent and ardent in seeking to effect some reforms in connection with the temple, to rid it of wrong practices, idolatrous or superstitious, of abuses of its precincts (cf. John 2:14-17). By **fasting** and by putting on **sackcloth** he manifested the spirit of repentance and mourning for offenses against the sanctity of the temple. But his works of piety provoked the scorn and jeers of the common crowd, particularly the loafers in the broad place at the city **gate** and the **drunkards** at their banquets.

3. The Appeal Renewed (69:13-21)

13-21. Stirred again by the description of his plight, he makes a fresh impassioned appeal for help and deliverance from his distresses. **Hide not thy face. . . . Draw near to me, redeem me.** At the same time he adds fresh arguments on behalf of his case: (*a*) he appeals to God's **steadfast love** and **abundant mercy;** (*b*) **because of my enemies,**

was not due to errors that his adversaries had pointed out. God alone knew them (vs. 5); his enemies had their own reasons for hostility.

The psalmist does not seek, however, in a display of self-righteousness to conceal his failures. On the contrary, recognizing his folly and sin, he undertakes to make proper atonement. Did he think that this would turn stubborn hearts toward the righteous cause he was advocating? Perhaps. If so, he was cruelly deceived. His self-discipline evoked only the scorn of those who saw it. The fasting with which he would cure his soul and the sackcloth in which he clothed his wretched, hungry body won no allies to his cause (vss. 10-11). The loafers, the peddlers, the "cracker-box philosophers," made him the butt of their jokes, and at their feasts the bibulous made up ribald songs to lampoon his misbegotten enthusiasm (vs. 12).

13-21. ***Details of Failure.***—It is not surprising that the psalmist's aborted zeal should have turned into an overwhelming sense of frustration, or that this mood should be the one with which the poem opens. At that moment—and we must remember the autonomy of each mood as long as it lasts—there was no mitigation of his despair. Whatever the folly and sin he had confessed to God, he denies that there is real cause for the hatred of those who outnumber the hairs of his head. He is guilty of no deception; he has taken nothing from them. They

15 Let not the waterflood overflow me, neither let the deep swallow me up, and let not the pit shut her mouth upon me.

16 Hear me, O LORD; for thy lovingkindness *is* good: turn unto me according to the multitude of thy tender mercies.

17 And hide not thy face from thy servant; for I am in trouble: hear me speedily.

18 Draw nigh unto my soul, *and* redeem it: deliver me because of mine enemies.

19 Thou hast known my reproach, and my shame, and my dishonor: mine adversaries *are* all before thee.

20 Reproach hath broken my heart; and I am full of heaviness: and I looked *for some* to take pity, but *there was* none; and for comforters, but I found none.

21 They gave me also gall for my meat; and in my thirst they gave me vinegar to drink.

15 Let not the flood sweep over me,
or the deep swallow me up,
or the pit close its mouth over me.

16 Answer me, O LORD, for thy steadfast love is good;
according to thy abundant mercy, turn to me.
17 Hide not thy face from thy servant;
for I am in distress, make haste to answer me.
18 Draw near to me, redeem me,
set me free because of my enemies!

19 Thou knowest my reproach,
and my shame and my dishonor;
my foes are all known to thee.
20 Insults have broken my heart,
so that I am in despair.
I looked for pity, but there was none;
and for comforters, but I found none.
21 They gave me poison for food,
and for my thirst they gave me vinegar to drink.

---

who are also God's enemies; (*c*) **thou knowest my reproach,** i.e., the Lord knows of the "injustices" suffered by him; (*d*) **I looked . . . for comforters, but I found none;** (*e*) **they gave me poison for food.** The word **food** (ברות) means, lit., "bread-medicine," i.e., bread that is given to purge of their troubles persons who have suffered misfortune, bereavement, or affliction (cf. II Sam. 12:17; 13:5, 7, 10). The duplicity of those who cloaked their enmity under a guise of friendship is scored. **They gave me vinegar to drink:** I.e., they put vinegar into his drink so that it made him more thirsty.

---

attack him with lies, deflecting his accusations from themselves by the age-old smear tactic (vs. 4). This is not all; he has suffered reproach, shame, and dishonor from foes who have made no effort to conceal themselves (vs. 19). He has been insulted; his heart is broken. Men to whom he turned were pitiless when they were not scornful (vs. 20). He who would fast in penitence is fed poison, and to quench his thirst he is offered vinegar (vs. 21). How else then could he be expected to describe his anguish? Vss. 1-3 plumb the depths of mortal despair: eyes dim with waiting for God, throat parched with crying, deep waters where the mire offers no foothold, and finally the engulfing flood of swirling water that threatens his life. This is surely the nadir of frustration.

Auxiliary to his own sense of defeat is his fear that God, whose cause he has espoused, will share his defeat. Not all those about him have participated in the effort to heap ignominy on him. Some there are who still hope in the Lord God of hosts, even though their trust is precariously balanced on the edge of doubt. To see God's zealous advocate suffer abuse and humiliation might give the slight impulse that would tumble them into the abyss of denial. God has a stake in the fortunes of his discredited friend. There is then essential nobility in his prayer: **Let not those who hope in thee be put to shame through me, . . . let not those who seek thee be brought to dishonor through me, O God of Israel** (vs. 6).

There is another and longer prayer set in the body of the poem (vss. 13-18). It breaks forth in the section that follows the psalmist's reference to the drunkards and their vulgar songs. The contrast is easily understood: revulsion from the degeneracy of men throws him back on the kindness and mercy of God. It is "an acceptable time" for turning to him (vs. 13); and however disappointing the issue of

22 Let their table become a snare before them: and *that which should have been* for *their* welfare, *let it become* a trap.

23 Let their eyes be darkened, that they see not; and make their loins continually to shake.

24 Pour out thine indignation upon them, and let thy wrathful anger take hold of them.

25 Let their habitation be desolate; *and* let none dwell in their tents.

26 For they persecute *him* whom thou hast smitten; and they talk to the grief of those whom thou hast wounded.

27 Add iniquity unto their iniquity: and let them not come into thy righteousness.

28 Let them be blotted out of the book of the living, and not be written with the righteous.

22 Let their own table before them become a snare;
let their sacrificial feasts[l] be a trap.
23 Let their eyes be darkened, so that they cannot see;
and make their loins tremble continually.
24 Pour out thy indignation upon them,
and let thy burning anger overtake them.
25 May their camp be a desolation,
let no one dwell in their tents.
26 For they persecute him whom thou hast smitten,
and him[m] whom thou hast wounded, they afflict still more.[n]
27 Add to them punishment upon punishment;
may they have no acquittal from thee.
28 Let them be blotted out of the book of the living;
let them not be enrolled among the righteous.

[l] Tg: Heb *for security*
[m] One Ms Tg Compare Syr: Heb *those whom*
[n] Gk Syr: Heb *recount*

4. Maledictions on the Psalmist's Foes (69:22-28)

22-28. The psalmist concludes his petition by calling on God to retaliate on his enemies with a series of curses. The series of curse formulas will be effective not by their utterance alone, as most Easterners believed, but by God's operations. **Let their own table, . . . their sacrificial feasts be a trap:** The *shélem* or "peace offering" was one of the sacrifices at which most of the sacrificial animal was eaten by him who offered it and by his guests. The psalmist's wish is that as his enemies sought to do to him, so it may be done to them. May their festival food work their death. **Add to them punishment upon punishment:** Reckon against them more and more guilt, which brings punishment in its train. **Let them be blotted out of the book of the living,** i.e., out of the divine register in which the names of the living are kept and from which those appointed for death are erased.

his reform movement has been, he has at no time forgotten that God's kindness is good and his mercy is abundant. He will not be resigned to his fate—the engulfing flood, the mire, the pit, the hidden face of God—so long as he believes in the **steadfast love** that can set him free from his enemies.

22-29. ***A Mistaken Prayer.***—Over against this prayer that is alert with confidence in the readiness of God to save we encounter another. Rarely in the catalogue of angry imprecations is its equal to be found. It represents the dangerous excess of zealotry; the desire for vengeance against those who subvert the poet's efforts is as vehement as his desire for reform. He brings to his invective daring imagery. They eat off a mat: let them trip over it! Their meal is an act of worship: let their sacrificial food poison them till their eyes are glazed and control of their loins is lost! They have been as a flood of waters over his head; let them feel the cascade of God's molten anger falling on them! And after they have felt all this, add to it yet again and again endlessly. Let them know nothing of mercy or kindness; **may they have no acquittal from thee.** No acquittal? Nay; and more: annihilate them! **Let them be blotted out of the book of the living.** Yea; and more still:

29 But I *am* poor and sorrowful: let thy salvation, O God, set me up on high.

30 I will praise the name of God with a song, and will magnify him with thanksgiving.

31 *This* also shall please the LORD better than an ox *or* bullock that hath horns and hoofs.

32 The humble shall see *this, and* be glad: and your heart shall live that seek God.

33 For the LORD heareth the poor, and despiseth not his prisoners.

29 But I am afflicted and in pain;
let thy salvation, O God, set me on high!

30 I will praise the name of God with a song;
I will magnify him with thanksgiving.
31 This will please the LORD more than an ox
or a bull with horns and hoofs.
32 Let the oppressed see it and be glad;
you who seek God, let your hearts revive.
33 For the LORD hears the needy,
and does not despise his own that are in bonds.

5. CONCLUDING PRAISE (69:29-36)

29-33. In the psalmist's vow of a **song** of **thanksgiving** it is significant that he rates such an offering higher than one of animal flesh. Perhaps it was such a point of view which incited so many of his fellows against him. Others, of course, from early times down shared his mind (cf. 40:6; 50:8-14; 51:16-17; Amos 5:21-24; Jer. 7:21-23). We perceive in vs. 9 that he did not mean to abolish the temple. Rather, he meant to put first things first, subordinating traditional rites to the exercises of spiritual worship.

should there be contrition and a cry for forgiveness and restoration, **let them not be enrolled among the righteous.** As regards his enemies, our reformer would completely eliminate "the mercy and kindness" of God. As regards himself, he would set no limit on it. "But as for me," he hastens to add to this vindictive demand, **afflicted and in pain; let thy salvation, O God, set me on high!**

30-36. ***Another Mood.***—The psalmist's mood changes. The quick transition from plaint to praise is one of the commonest features of the writings of these ancient poets. What gives uncommon interest here is that from a very low moral level of vindictive imprecation the author rises to heights of religious apprehension found nowhere else in the psalms. There is no novelty in his proposal to praise God with music. That is what the Psalter was for. To go beyond this and say that the uses of song in worship were more pleasing to God than an offering of **an ox or a bull with horns and hoofs** is to make invidious comparisons few dared to make. This is a familiar emphasis of Micah and Amos, who were of course zealous reformers; it is rarely encountered in the psalms. This may be one of the counts held against the poet by his enemies. If so, he is repeating the heresy and calling on all the oppressed to take note of this giant fact and be glad. Finally, his affliction and his anger momentarily abated, he concludes his song with a praise lyric of great beauty. His spirit may be intimidated but it cannot be overcome; his hope may falter but his faith is invincible.

The children of his servants shall inherit it,
and those who love his name shall dwell in it.

At this point at least, the tune **Lilies** seems to fit the words.

We observed at the outset of our study of this poem that it reflects the state of mind of the frustrated reformer of ancient times and of the "tired liberal" of our own. This state of mind is much the same, no matter what may be the area in which reform is sought. In the so-called practical areas—politics, public concerns (health, education, etc.), economics—the reformer exhibits insight, conscience, courageous action, and leadership. He encounters inertia, hostility, fatigue, and frustration. He may quit or be liquidated in any one of several ways. In the area of religion, regarded unhappily as a less practical interest nowadays than the others mentioned, the reformer has much the same experience, but with one very important difference: the religious reformer's ultimate faith is in God. This gives him a zeal which, because it is inextinguishable, may easily turn into fanat-

34 Let the heaven and earth praise him, the seas, and every thing that moveth therein.
35 For God will save Zion, and will build the cities of Judah: that they may dwell there, and have it in possession.
36 The seed also of his servants shall inherit it: and they that love his name shall dwell therein.

34 Let heaven and earth praise him,
the seas and everything that moves therein.
35 For God will save Zion
and rebuild the cities of Judah;
and his servants shall dwell[o] there and possess it;
36 the children of his servants shall inherit it,
and those who love his name shall dwell in it.

[o] Syr: Heb *and they shall dwell*

34-36. The concluding strophe is in form a hymn. All nature, **earth, heaven,** and **the seas,** is called to give praise to God for his purpose to restore the land so that it will be an abiding inheritance for all **who love his name.**

---

icism. Since his faith is more militant, his frustrations will be more abject. A religious war is the terrifying apogee of the reformer's zeal, and it can advocate in the name of God, who is the focus of its fiery loyalty, the fate our unhappy poet invoked on those who stood against him. Its only protection against the suicidal excesses of fanatical zeal is its constant return through its frustrations to a fresh realization of God.

It is within such a context that our poet speaks a contemporary word. We have noted that he had insight into the nature of his problem. Religion, he had discovered, was not a matter of offering an ox or a bull. He had conscience: if this was so, he must speak out; God helping him, he could do no other. To conscience he brought zeal that demanded action. Up to this point he doubtless encountered mild opposition, if indeed any at all. He was merely a prophet—a prophet being one who has insight, conscience, and courage. It is when zeal demands action and action demands the enlistment of others in a crusade that two things happen: the prophet becomes "more than a prophet" (cf. Matt. 11:9), i.e., one who adds to insight, conscience, and courage the ability to enlist, organize, and command a following; and he begins to encounter inertia and hostility. If he cannot overcome the former, or is overcome of the latter, frustration follows. At this point his zeal may turn into fanaticism, with its excess of self-pity or anger; or into a reassessment of the situation and a return to the spiritual bases from which his strategy will be redrawn. It is this last-named factor in our poet's recital of his experience that saves it from morbidity and spiritual defeat. We deprecate the cruelty of the designs with which he hoped, with a divine accomplice, to exterminate his opponents, but we are grateful for the impulse that turned him back to God, not with a plan but with a song of praise. Is it not to be hoped that, in the divine presence as a worshiper, the spiritual insights that launched his crusade against indifference in religion helped him see the evil into which his unchastened zeal had betrayed him?

This experience shows us the pattern of the reformer all down the ages. We excuse his excesses because of our great debt to his insight and courage. And since every age, and we might add every area of human experience, has seen him and heard him and felt him, it is because every age has needed him. It follows that we shall never be without him. He is our protection against the complacency into which it is so difficult not to settle, the cynicism it is so easy to accept. Because the reformer is a lonely man, even when surrounded by his followers, he is the easy victim of frustration and spiritual fatigue. He will start out consumed by zeal for the house, the market, the home, the church, and he may end with a poignant cry for rescue from the deep waters. He will often become a stranger to his own kind, an alien to his brothers. Men may give him poison to eat and vinegar to drink, laugh at his self-discipline and make up songs to humiliate him. But though he accepts dishonor and insult and wears sackcloth for shame, we are not done with him or he with us. If he is God's messenger—as time after time he has been—his last word for himself will not be self-pity, or for us imprecation. He will say:

Let heaven and earth praise him,
the seas and everything that moves therein.
For God will save Zion
. . . .
and those who love his name shall dwell in it.

To the chief Musician, *A Psalm* of David, to bring to remembrance.

70 *Make haste,* O God, to deliver me; make haste to help me, O LORD.

To the choirmaster. A Psalm of David, for the memorial offering.

70 Be pleased, O God, to deliver me! O LORD, make haste to help me!

LXX. AN APPEAL FOR HELP (70:1-5)

70:1-5. The text of this psalm is the same as that of 40:13-17, with the exception of some unimportant variants. We may assume therefore that it was drawn into the Psalter from two different psalm collections, in each of which its text had in its transmission suffered some slight changes. On the whole, the text of Ps. 70 is preferable.

70:1-5. *A Psalm for the Memorial Offering.*—What it was that led the redactors to repeat this poem after it had been once before included in a fuller edition (Ps. 40) has puzzled modern literary editors. For the most part they attribute it to editorial carelessness, since there is no apparent connection between the first part of Ps. 40 and the second part, which is Ps. 70. Was it the editor of Book I that included Ps. 40 who blundered? Or did the editor of Book III borrow part of Ps. 40 for some peculiar reason of his own? What did the early editors see in this poem that made it appropriate to be sung **for the memorial offering?** What reasons led to its allocation to David as author?

1, 5. *The Impatient Saint.*—These are technical questions that detain those for whom they have proper importance. When the interest shifts from literary criticism to what for want of a more precise term is called theological interest, Ps. 70 presents a problem that is both common and simple. So simple, in fact, that it exhibits an intimacy with God that is positively childlike. What is congenial to the unsophisticated mind is likely also to be simply stated. At the same time, it is equally true that elemental questions which rise to the surface of the untutored mind are more often than not the concern also of the sophisticated. This being true, it is easily conceivable that however this poem came about, it provided a melodic medium for the expression in worship of something very close to the experience of all religious minds. It is the question of the apparent leisureliness of the action of God.

We live in an age in which in many operations celerity is equated with skill. The dominant characteristic of modern life is its speed. This is uncritically accepted as proof of our superiority over earlier periods and other cultures. From this it is easily deduced that moderation or deliberateness are symptoms of a disability caused by advanced age, by reduced efficiency, or by general decadence. A horse-and-buggy age was not, because of its means of transportation, a blundering age. We scorn it for its sobriety in the matter of speed. We come close to saying sometimes that velocity is the measure of virtue. We think we can get on without a new decalogue, but we must have bigger and better dials all the time.

There is of course a dangerous lack of historical perspective in such an estimate of values, and of life itself. Indeed, it was an ancient who protested the concern with acceleration that was dominating his times. "Whirl is king, having driven out Zeus," said Aristophanes, who we know was a serious man and therefore deplored the popular coronation of immoderation. Even more ancient, we assume, was the writer of this psalm, the chief emphasis of which is that God should hurry up. He was not concerned that God should speed up things in general. On the contrary, it was he himself who was in trouble, and to expedite his own escape from difficulty was a normal wish. The reverse would arouse suspicions concerning one's sanity. Asking for haste on the part of God, even in the perfectly proper exercise of relief, raises questions that are in general more significant than the particular aspect of this man's problem. From the divine point of view can the words **tarry** and **haste** have any meaning? Can one who is timeless by his very nature operate within the context of time? This becomes a real question for those for whom the fact of God is real, and for whom the achievement of the will of God within the continuum of time is important. We may properly doubt that this was in the mind of the poet who wrote or the editor who borrowed the poem for his book, but we cannot question that the seed of his inquiry has had luxuriant growth in our hurry-up civilization.

The cause of our poet's impatience is not very clearly stated. That he was **poor and needy** (vs. 5) is the first clue he gives us. These two words may describe an emergency situation, but normally they are taken to mean a relatively constant condition. Poverty and destitution have needed rectifying for a longer time than man can remember, and they cannot claim the

2 Let them be ashamed and confounded that seek after my soul: let them be turned backward, and put to confusion, that desire my hurt.
3 Let them be turned back for a reward of their shame that say, Aha, aha.
4 Let all those that seek thee rejoice and be glad in thee: and let such as love thy salvation say continually, Let God be magnified.

2 Let them be put to shame and confusion
who seek my life!
Let them be turned back and brought to dishonor
who desire my hurt!
3 Let them be appalled because of their shame
who say, "Aha, Aha!"

4 May all who seek thee
rejoice and be glad in thee!
May those who love thy salvation
say evermore, "God is great!"

---

effective action of man too soon. In sober truth, they have in modern times become the world's most critical emergency, and their relief demands full speed ahead. This was not the case with our petitioner in the psalm.

2-4. *The Voice of Ridicule and the Greatness of God.*—It is possible to write a more specific bill of particulars than the summary briefly contained in poverty and necessity. There were some who are somewhat vaguely described as seeking the psalmist's life; for them he desired shame and confusion. Others sought his hurt; for them he wished defeat and dishonor. Still others said, **Aha, Aha!** which is obviously a shameless display of obscene hilarity; for them he asked discomfiture. As compared with the importunities of other suppliants in other psalms, his words somehow fail to carry the impression of emergency, and this is supported by vs. 4. Here is the altogether congenial language of piety. It could be used without change by one who felt no threat to his life or who was not annoyed or embarrassed by the ribald laughter of unpleasant neighbors. Certainly it sounds no critical note.

One further observation: Nowhere else is the Eternal addressed with such an intimate—or it might be said an obsequious—word as in vs. 1. Two interpretations are possible. **Be pleased** comes very close to our conventional and polite form "please." It can be courteous or servile; it is said with confidence or a whine. It also may mean "at your convenience" or "whenever it pleases you," and again may be made to mean one thing or another by the manner in which it is spoken. After all is said, however, it is not easy to escape the feeling that there is lacking here the sense of exigency enlivening other poems that cry to God for help. As it first appears as the latter part of Ps. 40, it follows a familiar opening line, "I waited patiently for the Lord." This sufferer had cried "out of a horrible pit, out of the miry clay," but he had not been frantic in insisting that God come at once to his aid. His patience had been rewarded by complete restoration. "He . . . set my feet upon a rock, and established my goings" (40:2). Such considerations as these lead us to the conclusion that we are dealing here with the problem of the divine delay and human impatience. We may assume that some such insight as this is responsible for its having been lifted from its earlier context and introduced as a unit by a later editor. This at least exculpates the editor from inadvertence or blundering.

As has been stated, the problem here is the apparent leisureliness of God's action. It can be given a somewhat more spacious formulation. The two most familiar categories of philosophy have to do respectively with being and essence, the former concerned with existence in the abstract, the latter with the form, substance, or manner of existence. Put in theological terms and applied to the understanding of God, we would say that we know him metaphysically and morally. Here the former deals with the question of his existence, the latter with the manner of his behavior. There were no atheists in Israel. In the Hebrew mind as revealed in the O.T. writings the fact of God was never doubted. His existence was their grand hypothesis, their major premise. Such challenge as was directed against this basic assumption by the bare facts of life was met by explanations of his behavior—he was angry or inattentive or preoccupied. It never was seriously proposed that he was nonexistent. This is another way of saying that in so far as this ancient people was bewildered by God, it was due to moral rather than to metaphysical considerations.

To a very conspicuous degree this remains true of all those who are confronted by the Eternal. Where there is one who is perplexed by the being of God, there are a thousand who are puzzled by his behavior. The common question is not "Is there a God?" but "Why does God do or allow this or that?" Explain it how we will, it still is an observable fact that most men

5 But I *am* poor and needy; make haste
unto me, O God: thou *art* my help and my
deliverer; O LORD, make no tarrying.

5 But I am poor and needy;
hasten to me, O God!
Thou art my help and my deliverer;
O LORD, do not tarry!

The meter is mainly 3+2; the irregularities, which are slight, may be corrected by reference to the text in Ps. 40.

For the interpretation of this psalm see the Exeg. on 40:1-17, 13-17.

---

have little doubt about the existence of God, or that ultimately whatever plans he has for the universe will be fully realized. It is the laggard pace at which his purposes seem to move that inspires dubiety. We believe in final deliverance from pain and folly and wickedness; it is the apparent indifference or deliberate procrastination of God that bothers us. We are not atheists; we are puzzled and impatient theists. Our poem in its opening sentence puts it as succinctly as needs be. **Be pleased, O God, to deliver me,** i.e., our deliverance is agreeable to God. **O LORD, make haste to help me,** i.e., do not put it off too long. Here the first line has metaphysical and the second line moral implications.

God's delay therefore was for our poet, as it is for us, a moral problem. Assuming that God is (being), and that he is moral (essence), he ought to be interested in every moral issue. The moment we say "ought" we have stated the moral problem. In any metaphysical approach to the problem of God the matter of the timing of his actions is clearly irrelevant. God is timeless; therefore the aspects of immediacy or delay in terms of time have no meaning. He is "the high and lofty One that inhabiteth eternity" (Isa. 57:15). On the other hand, the moral approach to God leads us head on into two questions: First, does he regard this or that as right or wrong? Second, having decided, will he do anything about it? In connection with the latter, timing is as important an element as the act itself. This is obviously because man is time bound. God may have set eternity in our hearts, but we have endless difficulty in getting it into our heads.

The consequences of this difficulty are also moral. Having made time an essential component of any moral act (cf., e.g., "Procrastination is the thief of time"[5]), we give moral sanction to those qualities that serve the time demand. Punctuality becomes a sort of practical piety, much as "cleanliness is indeed next to godliness."[6] Conversely, we suspect the inexact, the dawdler, and the fastidious as lacking something of moral seriousness, and any delay becomes defection. It is then a very brief transition which makes a virtue of impatience. The prayer with which our poet closes his song, **O LORD, do not tarry!** has for us a gratifyingly pious tone. This sort of thing can bring us very close to an attitude that to all intents and purposes is a moral denial of God. Once we allow ourselves to insist that the doing of God's will must keep a schedule we set for it, we shall feel morally bound to take matters in our own hands if he seems to fall behind. "Better late than never" becomes to this heightened schedule awareness "better never late." Keeping a timetable becomes an end in itself. We outdistance the slow-paced purposes of God, and ultimately discover to our dismay that we have left God behind. This is practical godlessness unconsciously acquired; he whom we once loved we have left. There is an old familiar gospel hymn that warns us against this:

> Take time to be holy, let him be thy Guide,
> And run not before him, whatever betide.[7]

This was a real problem with Israel in her early days, and it became more acute as her national fortunes declined. It took then the form of political revolution and the messianic hope; the former was a desperate effort to do what God had apparently forgotten to do or had placed far down on the agenda of the divine plans; the latter was an abandonment of the expectation that God would do anything with a situation he had so long neglected, and a cry to him to create conditions altogether new. Into this atmosphere Jesus was introduced, and it is abundantly clear in the N.T. writings that in the interests of getting God's purposes known and his will done, our Lord had to combat both the revolutionist and messianic roles as they were offered him by his impatient and zealous fellow countrymen. In what was certainly the most tense period of his earthly ministry he told a story about a widow whose patience was so persistent and indomitable that she finally overcame a stubborn judge who had no faith at all in God or man, and very little, if any, in law. Jesus' sententious summary asked

[5] Edward Young, *Night Thoughts,* "Night I," l. 393.

[6] John Wesley, *Sermons on Several Occasions,* Second Series (London: Wesleyan Conference, 1869), "On Dress."

[7] W. D. Longstaff.

KJV	RSV
71 In thee, O LORD, do I put my trust: let me never be put to confusion.	**71** In thee, O LORD, do I take refuge; let me never be put to shame!

LXXI. THE TRIED REFUGE OF AN AGED SAINT (71:1-24)

This lament is marked off from others of its type by an element of human interest to which special prominence is given. The suppliant, who is beset by enemies (vss. 4, 10) and so near to death that he can feel himself sinking in the floods of the underworld (vs. 20), is an old man (vss. 9, 18). But old age has not dried up the springs of his hope (vss. 14-16) nor weakened his religious spirit (vss. 5, 20-21), for as he looks back over the years of his long life his heart is full of praise for the deliverances which God in his unfailing goodness has wrought for him in "distresses many and cruel" (vss. 15, 20).

> **Thou who hast done great things,**
> **O God, who is like thee?**

This moving personal feature with its deep vein of piety affords the psalm its special recognition among the compositions of the Psalter. As a literary production, however, it cannot claim so high a place, since it does not adhere strictly to the classical form of a lament, with its sections of appeal, complaint, petition, and vow of thanksgiving in fairly regular sequence (cf. Ps. 56), but confuses the logical unfolding of the theme through repetitiousness.

In spite of its literary defects, the argument of the psalm stands out tolerably clear. The course of the old man's life from the time of his birth seems to have been marked by a succession of crucial experiences. Sickness, bitter trials of one kind or another, persistent enmities, and dread calamities have severally made their assaults upon him. And now when he is aged, weak, and alone, his enemies put their heads together in

---

the question as to whether the Son of man would find faith like that on the earth when he came (Luke 18:1-8). There was no answer to his inquiry, but the answer is an easy one. If the Son of man does not find that sort of faith on the earth, he will find no earth. What he will find will be the ruins of a world destroyed by impatient and faithless men. Franz Kafka has said that impatience is the greatest sin.[8]

This is the crux of the matter: true faith can wait; the impatience that so easily flatters our moral pride cannot wait. Each runs risks, and each has plausible justification for itself. Faith says, "The times are in his hands"; impatience says, "Time is running out." Both are forced to agree that the ultimate issue for those who believe in God is not to be calculated on the scale of man's history alone.

The Expos. on this psalm began with certain observations about the contemporary worship of speed. It is this idolatry that gives liveliness to the psalm. So aptly it fits our impatient mood that we can use the poet's language without changing a syllable. We have not encompassed all that is in the problem thus raised. Faith in God does not mean either mere acquiescence with his will, or a mistaken retreat from positive moral action in pursuit of it. Just where faith ends and impatience begins is beyond our wit to measure. It is very clear, however, that the mood of our times has taken us perilously near to a restless and almost angry impatience that makes little room for confident and creative faith. This is as far as we can allow our poet to lead us, particularly since he has taken us in directions of which his intentions were unaware. There is an authentic word, however, with which he can dismiss us. It is a sentiment which from the standpoint of our discussion is improperly contained in his poem. For this reason it is perhaps more important to us, since it is a statement of simple faith, with no hint of the impatience elsewhere displayed. To our restless and hurrying age it may also speak the word of faith if we are willing to stop long enough to listen:

> **May all who seek thee**
> **rejoice and be glad in thee!**
> **May those who love thy salvation**
> **say evermore, "God is great!"**

71:1-24. ***An Old Man's Cry to God.***—An effort was once made to dispute the charge that poetry is the domain of youth by pointing out

[8] See, e.g., *The Castle* (tr. Willa and Edwin Muir; London: Secker & Warburg, 1942); or *The Trial* (*ibid.*, 1947).

2 Deliver me in thy righteousness, and cause me to escape: incline thine ear unto me, and save me.

2 In thy righteousness deliver me and rescue me;
incline thy ear to me, and save me!

---

secret counsel and conclude that the time has arrived to give him the *coup de grâce;* they reason that he has reached the end of his resources, and that obviously the last visitation which he has suffered shows how God has deserted him. In this hour of supreme test he turns to the One who has never failed to deliver him in the crises of the past, and whose praises have never left his lips: **Be thou to me a rock of refuge, . . . for thou art my rock. . . . Rescue me.**

The psalm is of late date. The writer is acquainted with material which occurs in psalms whose date is late, e.g., vss. 1-3=31:1-3*a*; vs. 6=22:10; vs. 12=35:22 and 38:22; vs. 24=35:28. The literary defects mentioned above also point to a late postexilic date. It ought to be noted, however, that the psalmist has introduced some individuality into the structure of his lament: instead of following in the traditional fashion his several appeals with a statement of the grounds in support of them, he prefaces his appeals, with one exception, by a consideration that warrants the appeal (cf. vss. 3*c*, 7-8, 17*b*-20*b*). This literary device is overlooked by students of the psalm.

The meter, as we should suspect in a late composition, is irregular; it consists of 3+2 and 3+3, with the usual variations, i.e., 3+4; 4+3; 2+2+2.

I. An Elderly Man Appeals for Help (71:1-21)

71:1-3*b*. The opening verses are drawn from or lent to 31:1-3 with some slight modifications. In the LXX the divine name is "God," which is to be expected in a psalm of Book II of the Psalter. However, the reading Lord in Ps. 31 has influenced the text here. We assume therefore that Ps. 31 is the older of the two psalms, i.e., the lender rather than the borrower. In vs. 3 the M.T. reads **to come continually thou hast**

---

that the masterwork of the great poets was written when they were no longer young. Dante, Shakespeare, Goethe, and other lesser bards did their finest work after they had reached fifty. This is an engaging but altogether pointless controversy, since youth in connection with poetry is patently a matter not of age but of spirit. Goethe at eighty writing the second part of *Faust* was as youthful in his heart as the gay young necromancer of whom he wrote. To be sure, the mood of the young is normally attuned to song and motion; lyric and rhythm seem the proper vehicles both of their gaiety and their melancholy. Maturity brings sedateness and the prosaic word; with old age the reminiscent mind brings back the impetuosity of the early years and the sober practicalities of middle life with impartial tolerance, and thinks of the future with indifference or benign curiosity.

These generalizations prepare us for our study of Ps. 71. In the ASV it is described as a "Prayer of an Old Man for Deliverance," and its author is not even important enough for speculation. Thus, if we wish it, he may be for us the spokesman of many who are old, insecure, and nostalgic. The ancient title of the poem, however, does him less than justice, since deliverance is certainly not his only or even his most important concern. Here, in fact, youth to the contrary notwithstanding, we have an old man writing a poem. There is plenty of realism, and that means all is not harp and lute; but the lute is there, and old lips and tongue are singing for joy. It is indeed necessary for the poet to explain that he is an old man, lest perchance some mistake his singing for that of one younger than he. Old he unquestionably is. Specifically he speaks of **the time of old age; . . . when . . . strength is spent** (vs. 9), and adds the invariable hope of tired folk that he will be revived again. He seems almost to believe in his indestructibility: **Thou . . . shalt bring me up again from the depths of the earth** (vs. 20). Is this an old man's hope for immortality? **Thou wilt increase my honor**—he has an old man's proper sense of personal dignity—**and comfort me again** (vs. 21). And if further indication of his years were needed, it is supplied by the **gray hairs** (vs. 18) that adorn his temples.

1-13. *The Ailments of Old Age.*—In addition to evidences of physical decrepitude the poet indicates, perhaps without intention, that he

3 Be thou my strong habitation, where-
unto I may continually resort: thou hast
given commandment to save me; for thou
art my rock and my fortress.
4 Deliver me, O my God, out of the hand
of the wicked, out of the hand of the unrighteous and cruel man.
5 For thou *art* my hope, O Lord GOD:
thou art my trust from my youth.
6 By thee have I been holden up from the
womb: thou art he that took me out of my
mother's bowels: my praise *shall be* continually of thee.
7 I am as a wonder unto many; but thou
art my strong refuge.

3 Be thou to me a rock of refuge,
a strong fortress,[p] to save me,
for thou art my rock and my fortress.

4 Rescue me, O my God, from the hand of
the wicked,
from the grasp of the unjust and cruel
man.
5 For thou, O Lord, art my hope,
my trust, O LORD, from my youth.
6 Upon thee I have leaned from my birth;
thou art he who took me from my
mother's womb.
My praise is continually of thee.

7 I have been as a portent to many;
but thou art my strong refuge.

[p] Gk Compare 31. 3: Heb *to come continually thou hast commanded*

---

commanded (RSV mg., cf. KJV), i.e., לבוא תמיד צוית, which, as the LXX shows, is a corrupt transcription of לבית מצודה, translated **a strong fortress.**

3*c*-6. The psalmist opens his second appeal with a fact of experience; God has been and still is the psalmist's **rock.** He then follows this appeal with another fact in support of it. **Upon thee I have leaned from my birth.** The psalmist may be recalling that at the beginning of his life he was indebted to some special acts of providence. The argument then is like that of Job 10:8-13. **Thou art he who took me from my mother's womb:** The M.T. reading גוזי, "my cutter off," is probably a corruption of a word that occurs also in 22:9, גוחי, "my drawer out." The root of the latter is attested in Arabic. Assuming that the root of the former was a variant of גזז, "cut off," the LXX understood it to mean "distribute" or "remunerate," and hence "protect." The deduction is far-fetched, and the translation of the text by "protector," etc., is unwarranted. **My praise is continually of thee:** The wonders of God's help in the psalmist's youth are for him a never-ending theme of praise (cf. 109:1; Jer. 17:14). In view of the parallels cited it is unnecessary to assume with Wellhausen that תהלתי, **my praise,** is to be changed to תוחלתי, "my hope," so that the line reads "my hope is continually in thee."

7-11. The psalmist makes a second appeal which, as in the first instance, is introduced with a cogent citation of experience. Though the psalmist's distresses have led many to

---

suffers from the depression which so often accompanies the advance of the years. He fears insecurity, loneliness, neglect, and infirmity. This is the burden of the opening strophe (vss. 1-3); he is afraid, and because he is too feeble to protect himself, he must be saved by the Lord—**a rock of refuge, a strong fortress.** His concern, however, is not alone for physical rescue; there is a fine touch in his anxiety that his dignity shall be preserved. That he shall **never be put to shame** follows immediately on his quest for refuge in the Lord. It is, generally speaking, in our elders that the sense of honor is as strong as the will to live.

The psalmist is lonely and seeks the companionship of God (vs. 12). Time was when men saw in his vigorous manhood a portent of God (vs. 7), but now that frailty is his lot, there are those who mock him and lay accusations against him. These delations are wounds—**my hurt** (vs. 13)—against which he has no protection. There are also others who would take advantage of his defenselessness—wicked, unjust, and cruel men (vs. 4). He sees or imagines a conspiracy. His **enemies speak concerning** him and **consult together,** deciding that the infirmity of years is the sign that God has abandoned him (vss. 10-11). **"God has forsaken him; pursue and seize him,"** they say, **"for there is none to deliver him"** (vs. 11).

8 Let my mouth be filled *with* thy praise
and with thy honor all the day.
9 Cast me not off in the time of old age;
forsake me not when my strength faileth.
10 For mine enemies speak against me;
and they that lay wait for my soul take
counsel together,
11 Saying, God hath forsaken him: persecute and take him; for *there is* none to deliver *him*.
12 O God, be not far from me: O my
God, make haste for my help.
13 Let them be confounded *and* consumed that are adversaries to my soul; let
them be covered *with* reproach and dishonor that seek my hurt.
14 But I will hope continually, and will
yet praise thee more and more.

8 My mouth is filled with thy praise,
and with thy glory all the day.
9 Do not cast me off in the time of old age;
forsake me not when my strength is spent.
10 For my enemies speak concerning me,
those who watch for my life consult together,
11 and say, "God has forsaken him;
pursue and seize him,
for there is none to deliver him."

12 O God, be not far from me;
O my God, make haste to help me!
13 May my accusers be put to shame and consumed;
with scorn and disgrace may they be covered
who seek my hurt.
14 But I will hope continually,
and will praise thee yet more and more.

---

view him as a portent—i.e., a terrible example of divine vengeance—yet he has not succumbed because at all times **thou art my strong refuge.** So every day **my mouth is filled with thy praise** and with fresh exaltations of **thy glory.** Because of these things, **do not cast me off in the time of old age, . . . when my strength is spent,** for there are **those who watch for my life,** seeking to execute their wicked purpose by the slanders which they **speak against me,** and pointing to the psalmist's malady as an evidence that **God has forsaken him,** and so **there is none to deliver him.** In vs. 10*a* it is preferable to read for אמרו, **speak,** ארבו, "lie in wait," and to render it, "For my enemies lie in wait for me."

12-16. The psalmist makes still another appeal. His need of help is urgent. **Make haste to help me!** He prays that his **accusers** may be covered **with scorn and disgrace** and suffer in the eyes of the community a reversal of fortune such as they had meant

---

14-24. ***The Hope of the Aged.***—The last line of the complete poem indicates that the old man finally escaped the fate he feared, and it would seem to have been his purpose in writing the piece to show both the real and imaginary hazards of old age, in order to assert that they are not after all inescapable.

For they have been put to shame and disgraced who sought to do me hurt.

This summarizes his good fortune. If his chronological age was high, so was his spiritual age. His final stanza rings with the optimism of youth validated by the experience of age. All this, however, was no accident of fortune. The solid and assessible facts of his experience gave him the reasons both for his opening claims on God and for the confidence of his closing sentence. Here again we see evidence of age in our poet's indulgence of the delights of reminiscence. He felt that he had a right to what he claimed for his old age. God had served as midwife at his birth (vs. 6*b*), and from that very moment and through the earliest experiences of youth God had been his hope, his trust; it was the Lord on whom he had leaned (vss. 5-6*a*). This last suggests the solicitous help a parent gives to the unpredictable steps of a child, the protection offered to the fretful or the fearful. As he had grown older, his faith in the divine parent had not declined. He had seen God's deliverance times without number and all day long. This had not only given him courage to trust in God as he had passed from youth to adulthood; it was the reason for his bold affirmation as an old man: **I will hope continually. . . . My mouth will tell of thy**

15 My mouth shall show forth thy righteousness *and* thy salvation all the day; for I know not the numbers *thereof.*

16 I will go in the strength of the Lord GOD: I will make mention of thy righteousness, *even* of thine only.

17 O God, thou hast taught me from my youth: and hitherto have I declared thy wondrous works.

15 My mouth will tell of thy righteous acts
of thy deeds of salvation all the day,
for their number is past my knowledge.
16 With the mighty deeds of the Lord GOD
I will come,
I will praise thy righteousness, thine
alone.

17 O God, from my youth thou hast taught
me,
and I still proclaim thy wondrous
deeds.

---

for him. For men of the ancient Near East public disgrace was harder to bear than death (cf. Job 29:7-10; 30:1, 9-15). Vs. 13 is overloaded metrically; it is suggested that יכלו, **and** [be] **consumed,** and וכלמה, **and disgrace,** be deleted. **But I will hope continually:** Parallelism calls for אגיל, "I will rejoice," instead of איחל, **I will hope,** but the sense is the same. The psalmist is giving voice to his confidence that deliverance is at hand and **I . . . will praise thee yet more and more,** and **my mouth will tell . . . of thy deeds of salvation. Their number is past my knowledge:** The word ספרות, here rendered **number,** is a *hapax legomenon* and has occasioned some difficulty for translators. The translation here given is supported by the Greek version of Symm. and the Targ. The LXX understood it to mean "books" (ספרות) and rendered it γραμματείας (Vulg., *litteraturam*), whence came by error in some LXX MSS πραγματίας, "the business," i.e., of telling them.

17-21. A final appeal is introduced after the manner of the psalmist's style, with a fresh reference to his past experience coupled with a new statement of his confidence

---

righteous acts. Observe the unequivocal confidence of his boast, daring even on the lips of a much younger man. **With the mighty deeds of the Lord GOD I will come.** This is not only experience, it is evangel. He speaks that line made familiar in the hymn

E'en down to old age, all my people shall prove
My sovereign, eternal, unchangeable love:
And when hoary hairs shall their temples adorn,
Like lambs they shall still in my bosom be borne.[9]

This would seem to be in all candor rather too much of a good thing. Such a man would seem to have known too little of adversity. His life seems almost overweighted with good fortune. God had been to him security, confidence, hope; and to this record he responded with unwavering fidelity. Why, one may ask, does he even give voice to his need in his old age for the things he has had uninterruptedly during his life? Is not the request itself almost an act of infidelity? This might be a fair question were it not that the poet gives place to a brief but searching reference to times when life had been for him the gall of bitterness.

[9] "How firm a foundation," st. vi. "K" in John Rippon's Selection, 1787.

Oddly enough, indeed, he attributes these dark nights of the soul to none other than God himself. He protects himself from romantic notions about God and life by making room for many distresses in his ideas about both. He had adversaries on the level of human existence and had been able by the power of God to overcome them. Also on the level of human existence he found God his adversary. "Thou who hast made us see many dangers and disasters" (vs. 20*a* Amer. Trans.). How dangerous and how disastrous these experiences were is indicated by the line that describes them as tantamount to death itself, from which he had to be brought up. Two words more descriptive would be hard to find. "Danger" means acute or extreme suffering; the quality of "disaster" denotes a pitiless or deliberately malign intent behind suffering. How this fits into a consistent idea of the nature of God is an old and still unsolved problem. It is sufficient at this point to note that by the deft use of these two words our poet projects a black shadow sharply across the sunlit landscape, adding both beauty and realism to the scene. It is the artist's touch, for as an ancient Arab proverb put it, "All sunshine makes a desert." Our gray poet saves himself from aridity by his honesty

18 Now also when I am old and gray-
headed, O God, forsake me not; until I have
showed thy strength unto *this* generation,
and thy power to every one *that* is to come.
19 Thy righteousness also, O God, *is* very
high, who hast done great things: O God,
who *is* like unto thee!
20 *Thou,* which hast showed me great
and sore troubles, shalt quicken me again,
and shalt bring me up again from the
depths of the earth.
21 Thou shalt increase my greatness, and
comfort me on every side.
22 I will also praise thee with the psaltery, *even* thy truth, O my God: unto thee
will I sing with the harp, O thou Holy One
of Israel.

18 So even to old age and gray hairs,
O God, do not forsake me,
till I proclaim thy might
to all the generations to come.[q]
19 Thy power and thy righteousness, O God,
reach the high heavens.

Thou who hast done great things,
O God, who is like thee?
20 Thou who hast made me see many sore
troubles
wilt revive me again;
from the depths of the earth
thou wilt bring me up again.
21 Thou wilt increase my honor,
and comfort me again.

22 I will also praise thee with the harp
for thy faithfulness, O my God;
I will sing praises to thee with the lyre,
O Holy One of Israel.

[q] Gk Compare Syr: Heb *to a generation, to all that come*

---

in God's help. **From my youth thou hast taught me:** These words are explained by vs. 20*a*. From his youth the psalmist has been taught to praise because God has done for him so many things that have evoked his praise. So he asks that now in his **old age** God may continue with him, **forsake me not,** and put a new song in his mouth. **Thou . . . wilt revive me again,** i.e., restore me to life. **From the depths of the earth:** Better, "From the floods of the underworld." **Thou wilt increase my honor:** The LXX, Vulg., and some MSS of Jerome point to another reading, "Do thou increase thy greatness."

2. The Psalmist's Grateful Praise (71:22-24)

22-24. The psalmist vows a perpetual hymn of thanksgiving.

And my tongue will talk of thy righteous help
all the day long.

---

and wisdom. Thus the youthful poetic impulse is restrained by age's solemn realism.

22-24. ***The Final Confidence.***—It is necessary here to direct brief attention to the concluding strophe. As has often been observed, the poets of Israel seem to have made the opening and closing stanzas of many of their poems a good deal more than mere beginning and ending. They sound the essential and authentic note; they open an argument and summarize a faith. This is the case here: "In thee, O Lord, do I take refuge" (vs. 1); thus the argument:

For they have been put to shame and disgraced
who sought to do me hurt (vs. 24*b*);

thus the summary. And coming from one who carries the burden of age and faces realistically its hazards, what a gay-spirited faith it is. We do not need to accept literally the old man's skill on stringed instruments because he refers to lyre and harp (vs. 22). Neither are we compelled to understand that his joy is as noisy as it sounds (vs. 23*a*), or his tongue as tireless and the topic of his conversation as unlimited as vs. 24*a* intimates. What is reflected is a state of mind, an attitude that has become habitual: lyre and harp engage the fingers; lips form the melody; tongue **all the day** speaks the confident word. These all distill the pure essence of his faith, and condense it into his final word of devotion.

Because we have a particular fondness for old age that is both wise and benignant, we like this old man. In common with many other psalms, portions of which he has borrowed (cf. 31:1-2), he reflects for the most part the con-

23 My lips shall greatly rejoice when I sing unto thee; and my soul, which thou hast redeemed.

24 My tongue also shall talk of thy righteousness all the day long: for they are confounded, for they are brought unto shame, that seek my hurt.

23 My lips will shout for joy,
when I sing praises to thee;
my soul also, which thou hast rescued.
24 And my tongue will talk of thy righteous help
all the day long,
for they have been put to shame and disgraced
who sought to do me hurt.

O Holy One of Israel: I.e., Israel's God, the exalted one who executes justice and righteousness in the earth; the term probably originates with Isaiah (cf. 6:3) and is appropriately used here by the psalmist.

---

ventional religious ideas of his times. Nowhere else, however, is there to be found a picture of one so greatly advanced in years who is at the same time so serene, so matter of fact and so devout. He has lived a full life; he has reflected on its triumphs and disasters, and he has pronounced it good. God, the Holy One of Israel, be praised!

The likely date of this poem must be set after the Exile, and this means that the times through which the psalmist lived were not conspicuously tranquil. The reverse is more probable. Also it is interesting that our old poet makes no reference to what was generally regarded as the crowning felicity of old age—the presence about him of stalwart sons and grandchildren. They were God's blessing to the aged; they kept him young and promised him the continuance of his family and his faith. It has been pointed out that his poem carries certain overtones of loneliness and the sense of insecurity. Maybe he was alone; exiles in alien lands or those returning to the ravaged homeland are often bereft of kin. If so, all the more poignant his transient moods of anxiety, and all the more vibrant the melody of his lyre and harp. It is devotion that keeps his spirit young and his faith secure.

Perhaps more than antiquarian interest is to be found here. As poetry is the mood of youth, religion is thought to be the mood of maturity. When it captivates the young, it does so largely by its dramatic or poetic qualities. It takes experience and reflection to establish religion in mature patterns that can survive the instabilities of youth or the shocks of adversity. The times in which we are living are postexilic in their own modern way. It may be too early perhaps to assert that the Exile is over, but surely the case can easily be made to support the notion that Western man has been driven from his spiritual home and is wretched with the fear and faithlessness which torture his homeless soul. Furthermore, ours is becoming more and more an old man's world. Population trends have been plotted by sociologists and old-age security benefits have been provided by governments in the effort to provide minimum sustenance for the increasing number of old people who cannot care for themselves. Add to this the appalling losses of young people that war causes. Not yet in the United States but in Europe the very old and the very young hold out their hands for the pittance that charity can allocate to their interminable misery. What also is to be said about the increasing decline of youth interest in organized religion?

This is hardly the place to come to terms with these problems. They are suggested in contemporary perspectives only because they are intimated in the body of the old man's poem. Exile and return were no strangers to his experience; shock and insecurity were so real as to call for drastic measures for revival; he knew the scorn of enemy and the delator's slander, and there were those who mocked the hope he had in the final victory of the Holy One of Israel. And we? What then was his formula for confidence? Since we must stay close to the text of his poem, we shall not find here the solution to the dilemma of old age: despair for the seen or courage for the unseen. It was, however, at this point that the vitality of his religious faith introduced the saving element. It was true when our ancient friend wrote his testimonial, and it is no less so when it is allowed to infuse our own disordered life. The word of Ps. 71 is no mere prayer of an old man for deliverance; it is a testament of an old man's faith. We too need a refuge, and our sense of dignity must be mended. It is then neither bizarre nor blind to appropriate as our own the psalmist's statement of his need: "Be thou to me a rock of refuge. . . . Thou wilt increase my honor, and comfort me again"; or to affirm as our own his ultimate confidence that those who sought to do harm to him have been put to shame.

A Psalm for Solomon.

72 Give the king thy judgments, O God, and thy righteousness unto the king's son.

A Psalm of Solomon.

72 Give the king thy justice, O God,
and thy righteousness to the royal son!

LXXII. A Prayer for a King (72:1-20)

This poem, as is evident from vs. 1, is a prayer offered on behalf of a reigning Hebrew king. The older view that the psalm is primarily messianic cannot be sustained by a plain reading of the text, although, as is indicated below, it still has its advocates. There is nothing to indicate either the identity of the king in question or the circumstances under which the psalm was first used. Like the other royal psalms (Pss. 2; 18; 20; 21; 45; 89; 101; 110; 132), this prayer may have been recited on some festive occasion such as the New Year, the ruler's birthday, or some other royal anniversary, but it shows no evidence of organic connection with the temple cult (for hymns sung at the accession of Egyptian Pharaohs see J. B. Pritchard, ed., *Ancient Near Eastern Texts,* pp. 378-79).

The hyperbole in the poem (the longevity of the king, vs. 5; the extent of his dominion, vss. 8-11; the durability of his fame, vs. 17) must not obscure the importance of its underlying ideas. The Hebrew king lives under the scrutiny of God, and if he rules with justice and righteousness, the troubles of the poor will cease and the whole of God's people will prosper (cf. Deut. 17:17-20). As Fleming James notes, this psalm "is the only one of the Royal Psalms to dwell at any length upon the king's duty to befriend the poor" (*Thirty Psalmists* [New York: G. P. Putnam's Sons, 1938], p. 220). It is a feature of the pre-exilic age to which the psalm belongs that the poet thinks in nationalistic terms. The rulers of the earth are to bring tribute to the Hebrew king, but nothing is said about their serving the Hebrew God.

This psalm, by reason of its broad and idealized portrait of a Hebrew sovereign, has lent itself readily to a messianic interpretation. This was the view taken in Jewish circles as early as the Targ., and it is still found in some modern Jewish commentators (e.g., Moses Buttenweiser, Abraham Cohen). While the psalm is never quoted in the

---

72:1-20. ***Vision of a Blessed Social Order.***—It would be difficult to dispute convincingly the proposition that all men develop fixed attitudes toward those who exercise authority over them. This might even be regarded as the most important of all social axioms. These attitudes are obviously varied and numerous, and they are subject to change with or without notice. One man may conceive of government—for it is this with which we are concerned—as a nuisance, another as a bore, another as a game, another as a responsibility, another as a vested interest, and still another may regard it as the enemy of all private concerns. Thus attitudes can run from the extremes of indifference to ambition, from contempt to servility; and though in a given set of circumstances they may be rigidly fixed, given a change in certain other factors, they can become fluid in the process of change to different attitudes.

This is another way of saying that politics is a constant among the variables of political change. The Marxist utopia of a classless society assumes the gradual disappearance of this normal human concern. The possibility is as dubious as it is disconcerting. Ever since men grouped themselves together, they have accepted the rule of a person or a class; and as society has become increasingly complex, the business of rule has increased in importance and difficulty. In a social group as large as a nation, order presupposes those who are responsible for it, and they will inescapably be the ordering class, whether tyrannical or conciliatory toward the individual.

There is a further fact that is important for our study of this poem. Since the basic concerns of man as an individual and men as a group are limited, the necessity for order—or government or politics—is limited to relatively few matters. This is true no matter how large or small the group may be. There must be order within the group; there must be order among contiguous or neighbor groups. There must be moral order represented by law, economic order represented by distribution, social order represented by opportunity. In none of these areas can a group trust to luck, the law of averages, or individual whim to provide social cohesion. There must be consent to the principles of

2 He shall judge thy people with righteousness, and thy poor with judgment.	2 May he judge thy people with righteousness, and thy poor with justice!

N.T., the church followed the Jewish tradition and interpreted the poem in terms of the messianic hope. Calvin, however, who found in the psalm David's prayer on behalf of Solomon, wrote: "Those who would interpret it simply as a prophecy of the kingdom of Christ, seem to put a construction upon the words which does violence to them" (*Commentary on the Book of Psalms,* tr. James Anderson [Grand Rapids: W. B. Eerdmans, 1949], p. 100). But the messianic view persisted, and this explains why in the Book of Common Prayer Ps. 72 is one of the proper psalms for the Epiphany. The commentaries of present-day Roman Catholic scholars (e.g., Heinrich Herkenne, Jean Calès) also assume a messianic significance for the poem.

The strophic structure of this psalm is uncertain, as is clear from a comparison of the schemes proposed by Gunkel, Leslie, and the Amer. Trans. The Exeg. below adopts the stanza divisions of the RSV. The meter is irregular.

1. Prayer That the King May Be Just and Compassionate (72:1-4)

72:1. Thy justice: A small emendation supported by the LXX, Jerome, and the Syriac. The psalmist, however, may not have been thinking of abstract justice, and the M.T. in the sense of "thy discriminating judgments" (cf. **thy judgments**) may be quite correct. The RSV retains the plural of this word in 10:5; 36:6; 48:11; etc. The poetic parallelism indicates that **the king** and **the king's son** (KJV) or **the royal son** (RSV), are synonymous. The king in question is not a usurper but a member of the legitimate royal family. On the desirability of the king's loyalty to the Lord's statutes, see Deut. 17:18-20; Jer. 22:15-16; I Chr. 22:12-13.

2. May he judge thy people: While the juridical legislation in Deuteronomy does not envisage an appeal to the crown (Deut. 16:18-20; 17:8-13; cf. II Chr. 19:5-11), some

---

order, and conformity to them. As concerns intergroup order, there also must be consent to law. This is familiar to us in the history of the development of international relations. It has come by agreements or alliances that have been the result of the discovery of what was mutually advantageous, or more frequently and less permanently, by subjugation of a neighbor group and the effort to assimilate it. Despite man's doubtful success in creating a world order and administering it, the dream and the effort to achieve it are very ancient and engaging.

1-4. ***An Idealization of Kingship.***—Ps. 72 is clearly a poet's reflection of this perennial human interest; and as we shall see, his interest is both practical and thorough. Being a poet, he does not express himself in the tedious language of the political scientist; being an Oriental, he is given to extravagance and imagery that must surely have flattered the king to whom the poem was addressed. Such interest may seem to be odd for a poet, but we must remember that it represents to a considerable degree the performance of a professional duty. He was the court laureate. Ps. 45 is an effort by a royal poet to celebrate a king's marriage. That it exhibits more personal enthusiasm than we find in Ps. 72 is not difficult to explain: a wedding is more romantic than a coronation, and more naturally the subject for an ode. "My heart overflows," says the wedding guest in Ps. 45; **Give the king thy justice, O God,** prays the laureate in Ps. 72 at the crowning. We may even go on and say that his concern is basically for justice rather than for ideas implicit in an invocation of God. The benediction with which the psalm closes is clearly an addendum; so, with the exception of the invocatory prayer, the whole poem is devoted to grinding the grist that falls into the political mill. This is not to say that the first stanza does not impart a strong moral tincture to the whole poetic coloring; it repeats our opening proposition to the effect that a concern with order is basic to all social groups. The extraordinary quality of this piece of political poetry is, as we shall presently see, the completeness of its coverage of the desiderata of social order everywhere. It is of course this fact that gives it its contemporary relevance, even though we are pretty well done with kings in our modern world.

The identification of the new king with the justice, righteousness, and peace of God is very real and very important. There occur in the

3 The mountains shall bring peace to the people, and the little hills, by righteousness.
4 He shall judge the poor of the people, he shall save the children of the needy, and shall break in pieces the oppressor.
5 They shall fear thee as long as the sun and moon endure, throughout all generations.
6 He shall come down like rain upon the mown grass: as showers *that* water the earth.

3 Let the mountains bear prosperity for the people,
and the hills, in righteousness!
4 May he defend the cause of the poor of the people,
give deliverance to the needy,
and crush the oppressor!

5 May he live[r] while the sun endures,
and as long as the moon, throughout all generations!
6 May he be like rain that falls on the mown grass,
like showers that water the earth!

[r] Gk: Heb *may they fear thee*

O.T. passages support the view that the king could be entreated (II Sam. 14:4-5; II Kings 6:26-28; Jer. 22:15-16). For a Babylonian king's interest in justice for the people see The Code of Hammurabi, Prologue 1:22-40 (Pritchard, *op. cit.*, p. 164).

3-4. Peace is a better translation of שלום than **prosperity.** The word generally signifies "well-being." **He shall judge** is closer to the Hebrew than **may he defend the cause of.** The verb means "to exercise an equitable judgment."

2. Prayer for a Long and Beneficent Reign (72:5-7)

5. May he live is an emended text (יאריך) based on the LXX. The M.T. is **they shall fear thee** (KJV; cf. RSV mg.). **While the sun endures:** For the sun as a symbol of permanence see also vs. 17. **The moon** serves the same purpose in vs. 7 and in 89:37. On the other hand, in Isa. 60:19-20; Rev. 21:23; 22:5, the time is anticipated when there will be neither sun nor moon.

6. May he be like rain that falls: This is what the Hebrew means; the KJV offers a literal translation. **Showers that water:** The verb implies an emended text (probably יזריפו).

---

opening strophe great words and lofty ideas. **Justice, prosperity for the people, the cause of the poor**—these have lost not a whit of their imponderable weight by having come to us down a journey of twenty-six or more centuries. Solomon had prayed for wisdom; this piece, mistakenly assigned to Solomon, asks for justice. Is there justice without wisdom; wisdom without justice? Never mind. But why **righteousness** for **the royal son?** Some scholars say this refers to the king's youth. May it not be plausibly taken to mean a concern for the real succession? The trouble with kings, it has been said, is their successors. What good will justice be in the royal sire if the royal son is to be a scoundrel? These are mostly matters of speculative interest; there is more important suggestion in the use of **thy** in vs. 2. The king was reminded on his coronation day that he was not the ultimate sovereign; he was only God's surrogate. The people were God's people, and therefore entitled to a rule of righteousness; the poor were God's poor, and therefore entitled to the rule of God's justice. Kings have been prone to forget this point; even those who are left continue in these times to refer to "my loyal subjects." It may be paternal and intimate, but it is also false and dangerous. Note the vivid image of vs. 3: giant **mountains,** heaving on their mighty shoulders the peace they bring to the people, aided and accompanied by the lesser **hills.** What a cavalcade! And in vs. 4, what a mandate!

5-15. *Basis of Security.*—Each of vss. 5-11—interrupted at one point—is introduced by the word **may.** Including the two times the word appears in the opening stanza (vss. 1-4), we have a total of fifteen such invocatives. They suggest the language of our toasts to the honored guest, and have led to the speculation that this poem, never used liturgically, may have been read at a coronation banquet. This is perhaps anachronistic, but we can be certain on one point: before these "mays" are exhausted, we have had set before the king the poet's hope that in four major areas where

7 In his days shall the righteous flourish; and abundance of peace so long as the moon endureth.

8 He shall have dominion also from sea to sea, and from the river unto the ends of the earth.

9 They that dwell in the wilderness shall bow before him; and his enemies shall lick the dust.

10 The kings of Tarshish and of the isles shall bring presents: the kings of Sheba and Seba shall offer gifts.

7 In his days may righteousness flourish,
and peace abound, till the moon be no more!

8 May he have dominion from sea to sea,
and from the River to the ends of the earth!
9 May his foes[s] bow down before him,
and his enemies lick the dust!
10 May the kings of Tarshish and of the isles
render him tribute,
may the kings of Sheba and Seba
bring gifts!

[s] Cn: Heb *those who dwell in the wilderness*

---

7. The M.T. is represented by **the righteous.** The RSV, in order to get an abstract noun parallel to **peace,** adopts the emendation צדק, **righteousness,** which is supported by some Hebrew MSS, the LXX, Jerome, and the Syriac. **Abundance of peace** is the M.T. and is quite satisfactory. **And peace abound** rests upon a small emendation (וירב).

3. Prayer for the King's World Dominion (72:8-14)

It is noteworthy that this petition comes after the earlier prayers for the king's advancement of righteousness, justice, and peace. The traditions of the glory of Solomon's reign (I Kings 4:21, 34; 10:1-29) probably account for some of the language of these verses, and also for the ascription of the psalm to Solomon.

8. Except for the opening word, this verse is identical with Zech. 9:10, but it is a moot point whether either author is dependent upon the other. Actually the psalmist is employing conventional phraseology to express extension, and his terms must not be pressed for precise meanings (cf. Amos 8:12; Mic. 7:12; Zech. 14:8; Joel 2:20). Doubtless the traditional boundaries of Israel also supply some of the vocabulary (80:11; Gen. 15:18; Exod. 23:31; Deut. 11:24; I Kings 4:21, 24; Ecclus. 44:21). **From sea to sea:** The Hebrews were most familiar with the Mediterranean Sea, the Red Sea, and the Salt Sea, but they must have had some knowledge of the Persian Gulf. **The River:** The Euphrates. **The ends of the earth:** The extreme limits of the world, a familiar phrase in the O.T., found five times elsewhere in the Psalms (2:8; 22:27; 59:13; 67:7; 98:3).

9. Similar language is used in Isa. 49:23 to describe the homage which the nations are to pay to Zion. **They that dwell in the wilderness** (KJV; cf. RSV mg.) represents one Hebrew word (ציים) which probably means "wild beasts." The RSV emends the text to secure **his foes** (צריו) as being more suitable to the context.

10. Isa. 60, especially vss. 6, 9, uses the same vocabulary to portray Israel's future glory. On **Tarshish** see Exeg. on 48:4-7. **The isles:** A comprehensive term for the islands

---

order must be preserved if the king himself is to survive the royal ordeal, he will provide both the symbol and the vehicle.

The first is the area of moral order. **May righteousness flourish, and peace abound.** There is a clear correlation here between the ideas of a vital moral order and abundant and continuous peace. How familiar this sounds in our day when the threat to peace has been unanimously ascribed to a moral breakdown. It may have been less familiar when our poet proposed it. There is an accompaniment to it that in our times needs restatement with the confidence of its original presentation. Vs. 5 appears to be little more than the customary toast to the king's health and longevity. It is hardly more than extravagance if it is concerned only with long life; but if it refers to the king as the symbol and vehicle of moral stability, it contains a profound observation on the nature of moral order. The basic element of a moral order is its timelessness; any suspicion that it may be subject to the caprice of man or the exigencies of group life destroys its power to command

11 Yea, all kings shall fall down before him: all nations shall serve him.

12 For he shall deliver the needy when he crieth; the poor also, and *him* that hath no helper.

13 He shall spare the poor and needy, and shall save the souls of the needy.

14 He shall redeem their soul from deceit and violence: and precious shall their blood be in his sight.

15 And he shall live, and to him shall be given of the gold of Sheba: prayer also shall be made for him continually; *and* daily shall he be praised.

11 May all kings fall down before him,
all nations serve him!

12 For he delivers the needy when he calls,
the poor and him who has no helper.
13 He has pity on the weak and the needy,
and saves the lives of the needy.
14 From oppression and violence he redeems
their life;
and precious is their blood in his sight.

15 Long may he live,
may gold of Sheba be given to him!
May prayer be made for him continually,
and blessings invoked for him all the
day!

---

and coasts of the Mediterranean. **Sheba:** Southwest Arabia, modern Yemen, where the Sabaean kingdom flourished from *ca.* 950 to at least 115 B.C. **Seba:** Uncertain, but probably northwest Ethiopia, between the White Nile and the Blue Nile, in the modern Anglo-Egyptian Sudan (cf. Josephus *Antiquities* II. 10. 2).

12-14. These verses reflect the king's concern for the poor and needy. This is a part of the preceding petition (vss. 8-11), but as the introductory **for** of vs. 12 shows, it indicates the grounds which justify the prayer for the king's world dominion. **When he crieth** is the M.T., and it seems quite satisfactory (cf. Job 29:12). The LXX, Jerome, and the Syriac repoint the Hebrew word to obtain "from the rich." **Precious is their blood:** See Exeg. on 116:15.

4. Prayer for the King's Prosperity (72:15-17 [18-20])

15. Long may he live: Lit., "And may he live," probably a shortened form of "May the king live" (I Sam. 10:24; II Sam. 16:17). Some (Gunkel, Leslie, *et al.*) take the subject of **live** to be the poor man, but this is unlikely. On **Sheba** see Exeg. on vs. 10.

---

and contain behavior. As it is put here, righteousness will flourish only if it is as durable as the moon. Another striking observation follows: the moral order which the king symbolizes rests not alone on an absolute and immutable base; it is characterized by a spiritual quality presented in the simile of falling rain (vs. 6). Again we do well to acknowledge the fact that our author sees that moral solidarity does not rest on destructive violence but on creative gentleness. Inevitably there comes to mind Portia's exquisite apostrophe to mercy that

> . . . droppeth as the gentle rain from heaven.
> . . . .
> 'Tis mightiest in the mightiest; it becomes
> The throned monarch better than his crown.[1]

Thus considered, our poet has set forth the nature of moral security in lofty terms.

Upon the base of moral security the king must erect a social structure that will also be enduring because it conforms to its moral foundations (vss. 12-14). This is the sort of social program one might expect to see initiated by a ruler who believed in an eternal moral order characterized by gentleness and solicitude for his people. It will have influence far beyond the limits of his own kingdom, and will induce first an interest and finally a series of alliances that will be the basis of political security on what would today be called the international level. Our poet puts this in such grandiose language that we can be easily misled. Vss. 8-11 describe the new king's dominion. It is world-wide (vs. 8) and his allies seem to have been violently brought to his feet. Translators agree that vs. 9 does not mean the abject groveling of defeated enemies. The word **foes** even admits of the rendering **those who dwell in the wilderness,** a description of barbarians in contrast to the kings of Tarshish, Sheba, and Seba. **To lick the dust** is no more than a hyperbole for the homage customarily accorded a king, as is also the reference to the kings who **fall**

[1] Shakespeare, *The Merchant of Venice,* Act IV, scene 1.

16 There shall be a handful of corn in the earth upon the top of the mountains; the fruit thereof shall shake like Lebanon: and *they* of the city shall flourish like grass of the earth.

17 His name shall endure for ever: his name shall be continued as long as the sun: and *men* shall be blessed in him: all nations shall call him blessed.

16 May there be abundance of grain in the
land;
on the tops of the mountains may it
wave;
may its fruit be like Lebanon;
and may men blossom forth from the
cities
like the grass of the field!
17 May his name endure for ever,
his fame continue as long as the sun!
May men bless themselves by him,
all nations call him blessed!

The phrase **gold of Sheba** occurs only here, although in I Kings 10:2, 10, the queen of Sheba is said to have brought much gold to Solomon. **Blessings invoked for him** is better than **shall he be praised,** but the Hebrew is "May they [lit., he] bless him."

16. This is a difficult verse. The meaning of פסת (**abundance** or **handful**) is doubtful; the verb ירעש (**wave** or **shake**) is not elsewhere used of grain or fruit; the syntax of מעיר (lit., "from a city") is uncertain. Numerous emendations have been proposed, but both the RSV and the KJV attempt to make sense of the M.T., not however with similar results. **Lebanon:** Usually assumed to be the Lebanon region (to the north of biblical Palestine), whose beauty, fertility, and forest riches were proverbial in ancient times, as is reflected in the O.T. (92:12; 104:16; Song of S. 4:11; 5:15; Isa. 35:2; 60:13; Hos. 14:5-7), and in Ugaritic (J. H. Patton, *Canaanite Parallels in the Book of Psalms* [Baltimore: Johns Hopkins Press, 1944], p. 23). Some scholars, however, take the reference here and elsewhere (Isa. 10:34; Hos. 14:5-7; cf. Ecclus. 39:14; 50:8) to be to the storax tree (*styrax officinalis*), valued for its fragrant gum, and alluded to in Gen. 30:37 and Hos. 4:13 ("poplar").

17. His name: The word (one word in Hebrew) occurs twice in this verse, but the RSV renders the second one by **his fame.** The notion of the king's name being remembered by future generations is found also in 45:17, and is in contrast to the disappearance which befalls the name of the wicked (Prov. 10:7). **Continue** or **shall be continued:** This verb (ינין), found only here and of uncertain meaning, is the biblical basis for the later Jewish view, expressed in the Talmud (Sanhedrin 98*b*), that Yinnon is one of the symbolic names of the Messiah. **May men bless themselves by him:** The king will enjoy such well-being that all men will invoke the same blessedness for themselves. Abraham and his seed are cast for a similar role in Gen. 12:3; 18:18; 22:18; 26:4.

---

down before him. All this becomes clear when we see that such extraordinary acclaim comes not because he has conquered the world, but because he has achieved phenomenal success in the just and merciful administration of his own nation. The gold of Sheba is given him, and prayers are offered and blessings invoked (vs. 15), **For he delivers the needy** (vss. 12-14). In other words—and this is another profound insight—the way to international political security is not by the road of war, but by the way of creative example. It is a modern American political dictum that the best way to create democracy abroad is to practice it at home.

16-20. ***The Abundant Reward.***—The final area where order must be symbolized by the king is that which is familiar to us as economic security. We may assume that it follows properly upon the full realization of order in the moral, social, and political areas. Economic security is pictured here in its two indispensable rudiments: provender and population. It even appears that in those remote times cities had difficulty reproducing their population! A king by whom such noble enterprise was symbolized and achieved would deserve the accolade contained in the last integral strophe (vss. 15-17). It is proper to end the poem on such a note, though the impulse of the ancient editor to append a benediction is not difficult to understand. (But see Exeg.)

The Expos. of this psalm carries assertion that social order, whether considered from the standpoint of morals or politics or economics, is

18 Blessed *be* the LORD God, the God of Israel, who only doeth wondrous things.
19 And blessed *be* his glorious name for ever: and let the whole earth be filled *with* his glory. Amen, and Amen.
20 The prayers of David the son of Jesse are ended.

18 Blessed be the LORD, the God of Israel,
who alone does wondrous things.
19 Blessed be his glorious name for ever;
may his glory fill the whole earth!
Amen and Amen!

20 The prayers of David, the son of Jesse,
are ended.

BOOK III

A Psalm of Asaph.

73 Truly God *is* good to Israel, *even* to such as are of a clean heart.

A Psalm of Asaph.

73 Truly God is good to the upright,
to those who are pure in heart.[t]

[t] Or *Truly God is good to Israel, to those who are pure in heart*

18-19. These verses constitute a concluding benediction for Book II of the Psalter (Pss. 42–72), and are not a part of Ps. 72 (see Exeg. on 41:13). On the name of God, see Exeg. on 8:1; 20:1.

20. This verse (cf. the concluding words of Job 31:40) can hardly have been placed in its present position by an editor who had the entire Psalter in front of him. Presumably it belongs to an earlier stage in the compilation of the Psalms, and it may originally have been intended to separate "Davidic" psalms from the "Asaph" ones, the latter now comprising Pss. 50; 73–83. **Prayers:** The word "prayer" occurs in the titles of Pss. 17; 86; 90; 102; 142, and in twenty-six other places in the Psalter (4:1; 6:9; etc.).

LXXIII. The Faith That Overcomes the World (73:1-28)

Fleming James (*Thirty Psalmists,* p. 204) has described this psalmist as the one "who penetrated most deeply into the inner heart of religion," and Artur Weiser (*Die Psalmen* [Göttingen: Vandenhoeck & Ruprecht, 1950], p. 332) has written: "Among the most mature achievements of the struggle of faith in the Old Testament, Psalm 73 occupies a foremost place." The poem describes, in the space of twenty-eight verses, a

---

of inexhaustible interest. It will be an unhappy day when men cease to have intelligent concern about those who are set over them as arbiters of taste and behavior. Wherever that interest declines, the invitation to the tyrant to take over has already been extended. We have seen that this concern, analyzed and presented in an ancient poem to a ruler accepting the scepter, has reached a high level of political and social idealism. That we rarely read coronation odes nowadays is perhaps as good a reason as any for recalling to mind that our own disordered society will not return to security and peace except by rebuilding the moral bases that in recent years have been everywhere shaken and in some places reduced to rubble.

That concern for those who rule over us is perennially interesting carries with it the collateral fact that it is not difficult to grow cynical about the whole idea of corporate order and security. There were cynics in ancient times also, and venality and corruption enough to justify their pessimism. Ps. 52:1-7 is a classic utterance of that mood, even as vss. 8-9 describe one man's escape from it. It is important for us who are the beneficiaries of the great Hebrew-Christian political tradition to remember that it has been vigorous and creative and permanent only when and because it has sought order in all the areas of human need—moral, social, economic, and political. Indifference to, or abandonment of, or compromise with the ideals sung by this ancient poet at the coronation of his king will be the prelude to chaos. Then, in a way the anthologist hardly dreamed, **the prayers of David, the son of Jesse,** will be truly **ended** (vs. 20).

73:1-28. ***The Everlasting Problem of Evil.***—Evil became a puzzle when the first man felt his first pain. It was a sensation for which he could not account, and therein lay his perplexity. As the physical and social organisms

spiritual odyssey not unlike the one unfolded in the book of Job. The author was a godly man, but he was greatly perplexed, not so much by his own sufferings (vs. 14) as by the health and prosperity of the wicked. Especially disturbing was their confident denial of God's knowledge of mankind. Thus he might have fallen into the abyss of utter despair had he not gone to the sanctuary, and there he caught the vision that saved him. He suddenly was made aware of how ephemeral are the ways of the unrighteous, and of how foolish he had been to doubt the wisdom of God's government of the world. But his chief gain was a fresh experience of the divine presence. The old truth came to him anew: **God is the strength of my heart, and my portion for ever.** Kittel (*Die Psalmen,* pp. 241, 247), taking his cue from Luther's translation of vs. 23 (*Dennoch bleibe ich,* etc.) entitled this psalm "The Great 'Nevertheless.'" As to whether the psalmist had the hope of immortality, see Exeg. on vs. 24.

This psalm may be given a double classification. It is clearly a psalm of trust (see Exeg. on 16:1-11), but in so far as it is concerned, like Pss. 37; 49, with some of the issues which exercised the minds of the more reflective, it may also be described as a didactic or wisdom psalm (see Exeg. on 49:1-20). We may note that Mowinckel (*Psalmenstudien,* I, 127-28) characteristically looks upon it as a psalm of thanksgiving, which has arisen out of the author's visit to the sanctuary where he submitted himself to the usual purificatory rites for sickness, and where he was physically healed and spiritually refreshed. Most commentators are agreed that the psalm is postexilic in date, but neither the language nor the contents demand this, and there is nothing in the poem that cannot be placed satisfactorily in the age of Jeremiah.

The four logical divisions of the psalm are vss. 1-3, 4-12, 13-20, 21-28, but no other strophic pattern is incontestably apparent. The RSV offers one reconstruction of the strophic structure. The meter for the most part is 3+3.

---

within which man's life is held captive have developed, the capacity for pain has increased. His efforts to understand the primeval puzzle and to mitigate the present pain have become elaborate and to a degree successful, but the enigma persists so stubbornly that evil in its manifest forms is accepted as concomitant with mortality. Physical pain is still a problem of great intricacy. To the physiologist a fracture, a laceration, and an ache present for solution different questions, moving from the mechanics of a break in the first case to the chemistry of vitamins in the third. This problem, however, is no longer regarded as metaphysical. Pain as sensation has real values to health. Even where it cannot be controlled by analgesics, man, it has been said, can make a friend of pain.

Not so moral evil. There is no anodyne for injustice. This is not to say injustice cannot be redressed; it is to say that there can be no justification for the physical good fortune of morally wicked people. Granted that there are varied criteria for what is regarded as moral rectitude, it still is true that where there are codes of established right and wrong, their observance no more uniformly results in felicity than their defiance in disaster. If perfect conformity to physical law expects to be rewarded by physical health, why should not perfect conformity to moral law promise the recompense of moral and social well-being? It was once enough to say that man's inhumanity to man was the satisfaction of the demands of inscrutable justice. But justice that uses one man's inhumanity to punish another man's sin is justice without moral scruples, and so no justice at all. To penalize one man for another's sin is no more or less morally repugnant than to reward one man for another's virtue. We cannot make a friend of that sort of evil.

This is the subject of our poem. In the literature of Israel the problem is set forth elsewhere with eloquence by the prophet Habakkuk, and with great dramatic power in Job. Because the Hebrew people were morally sensitive, the problem was never far from them, and their efforts at an understanding therefore found varied formulations. We have here a poet's reflections which were the result of bitter personal experience. It is neither involved nor for us definitive, nor is there any indication that he thought it might be anything more than a personal testimony. If, however, he was able to resolve the matter in a way that was satisfactory to his own morally astute spirit, there should be profit in our study of it. The structure of his poem is easily discerned. He tells his experience and its effect on his equivocal mind. Then, saved from indecision and folly, he propounds his judgment in two different reactions, the first emotional, the second solidly rational. The total effect is wholesome; we see the poet,

2 But as for me, my feet were almost gone; my steps had well-nigh slipped.
3 For I was envious at the foolish, *when* I saw the prosperity of the wicked.
4 For *there are* no bands in their death: but their strength *is* firm.
5 They *are* not in trouble *as other* men; neither are they plagued like *other* men.
6 Therefore pride compasseth them about as a chain; violence covereth them *as* a garment.

2 But as for me, my feet had almost stumbled,
my steps had well nigh slipped.
3 For I was envious of the arrogant,
when I saw the prosperity of the wicked.

4 For they have no pangs;
their bodies are sound and sleek.
5 They are not in trouble as other men are;
they are not stricken like other men.
6 Therefore pride is their necklace;
violence covers them as a garment.

---

1. Faith in God's Goodness (73:1-3)

73:1. The opening verse states the psalmist's final position, but as the following verses indicate, his confidence in God was firmly established only after his experience of life had almost cost him his faith. **Truly God is good to Israel** is the M.T. and is preferable to the emended text of the RSV. **To those who are pure in heart:** If **Israel** (KJV) is retained in the first half of the verse, this clause qualifies the term (cf. Rom. 9:6-7). **Pure in heart:** The same phrase occurs in 24:4, representing a mind that loves good and eschews evil (cf. Matt. 5:8; 15:18-20).

3. What chiefly vexed the psalmist was **the prosperity of the wicked.** The same problem appears elsewhere in the O.T. (17:14; 37:1, 35; 92:7; Job 12:6; 21:7; Eccl. 8:14; Jer. 12:1-3; Hab. 1:13; Mal. 3:15), but at the same time the pious are often urged not to be envious of evildoers (37:1; Prov. 3:31; 23:17; 24:1, 19). **Arrogant** is better than **foolish.**

2. The Felicity of the Godless (73:4-12)

A close parallel is found in Job 21:7-15.

4. The first half of the verse in the KJV is almost meaningless, and the RSV, by adopting Ewald's emendation (למו תם), obtains an intelligible text. **Their bodies** is preferable to **their strength,** but "fat" or "healthy" is a better translation of בריא than **sleek** or **firm.**

6. A chain is satisfactory as long as it is recognized as a decorative, not a restrictive, object; but **necklace** is preferable. The most natural translation of the Hebrew in vs. 6*b* is "a garment of violence covers them."

---

through the mystical experience of the saint, escaping the cynicism that characterizes another treatment of the problem in Ps. 49, and emerging into the full-bodied transvaluation of values with which he makes the announcement that opens the piece.

1-14. ***Why Does God Permit Evil?***—The initial adverb is important. Other translators render the first word "surely," and one will have it say "nevertheless." The point is clear and emphatic: after all is said and done to prove the contrary, God is on the right side of the argument. This, the conclusion to which our poet moved as he wrote, is set forth as his opening word. He puts his *quod erat demonstrandum* in the first sentence. But he would not have us think he picked up his demonstration at a bargain sale. A little less evidence, and he would have capitulated to its opposite; cupidity and envy had combined temporarily to dull his wits and constrain his will (vs. 2).

Having thus disarmed those critics who patronizingly say that poets and saints are insulated against the enticements of wealth and therefore arrive at conclusions about ultimate justice that are likely to be uncritical, he describes what he had seen that had so perilously excited his envy. Denunciation of the rich has always been able to evoke the literary virtuosity of impoverished poets, and our author shows up well. His astringent delineation convinces us that he writes of what he has seen. Oddly enough, however, it is not so much the physical well-being of the godless rich that has im-

7 Their eyes stand out with fatness: they
have more than heart could wish.
8 They are corrupt, and speak wickedly
concerning oppression: they speak loftily.
9 They set their mouth against the heavens, and their tongue walketh through the
earth.
10 Therefore his people return hither:
and waters of a full *cup* are wrung out to
them.
11 And they say, How doth God know?
and is there knowledge in the Most High?

7 Their eyes swell out with fatness,
their hearts overflow with follies.
8 They scoff and speak with malice;
loftily they threaten oppression.
9 They set their mouths against the heavens,
and their tongue struts through the earth.

10 Therefore the people turn and praise them;[u]
and find no fault in them.[v]
11 And they say, "How can God know?
Is there knowledge in the Most High?"

[u] Cn: Heb *his people return hither*
[v] Cn: Heb *abundant waters are drained by them*

---

7. There is at least one grammatical anomaly in this verse, and the M.T. may be at fault. A comparison of the Amer. Trans., Buttenwieser, Oesterley, and Leslie, indicates the difficulties of the English translator. The last clause is, lit., "They go beyond the imaginations of the heart." **Their hearts overflow** rests upon an emendation of the M.T.

8. They scoff or **they are corrupt:** The Hebrew verb is found only here, but the RSV gives the more probable meaning. The RSV divides the verse after **with malice** to obtain **loftily they threaten oppression.**

9. Against the heavens: Heavens is probably used here as a surrogate for God, although all the heavenly host (cf. Exeg. on 82:1-8) may also be included; cf. "heaven" in Matt. 21:25, and "kingdom of heaven" in Matt. 3:2; 4:17; etc.

10-11. The M.T. of vs. 10, reflected in the KJV (cf. RSV mg.), makes little sense, and the RSV resorts to emendations. **The people turn and praise them** presumably rests upon ישוב עם ויהללם; and **find no fault in them** upon ומום לא ימצאו למו. On vs. 11 cf. 10:11; Job 22:13-14.

---

pressed him as their spiritual demoralization. There is nothing wrong with physical health, even though it is described in the language our poet uses. For all mankind to be free from pain is a utopia forever dreamed of; whenever therefore it is actually encountered in individuals, it seems ideal (vs. 4). To be sure, this robustness is in part due to the fact that the rich have food to fatten them and doctors to physic them. And why not? The hunger and disease of the poor no more attest their piety than the sleek bodies of the rich their wickedness. The same thing is to be said about their immunity to trouble and strife. Again, this condition is universally desirable, though it is likely to be realized mostly by those who can afford to pay for their protection and security.

They are not in trouble as other men are;
they are not stricken like other men.

The physical health and security of the godless did not, we observe, invite the censure of our poet-saint; they summoned his envy. It was to this that he confessed in his opening strophe. But these two perquisites of wealth, when unrelated to spiritual health, become the culture in which grow the viruses which spread infectious moral disease. The Puritans who found it necessary to flee from the proud and pious churchmen who in their day had falsified true religion by their moral defections, talked much of their contemporary seven deadly sins in the effort to sensitize moral obtuseness: greed, gluttony, pride, anger, lust, envy, and sloth were appended to the Decalogue. These were not exclusively the pitfalls of the opulent; a pauper could indulge them all, save perhaps gluttony. Anyone consistently abjuring them would have been regarded as an aberrant specimen of the privileged class, and not seldom was indulgence adduced by an insolent profligate to prove God's favor. In a situation that antedated Puritanism by twenty-five centuries, our poet describes in sarcastic phrases the seven deadly sins of his day. They were pride: **pride is their necklace;** ill-temper: **violence covers them as a garment;** gluttony: **their eyes swell out**

12 Behold, these *are* the ungodly, who prosper in the world; they increase *in* riches.	12 Behold, these are the wicked; always at ease, they increase in riches.
13 Verily I have cleansed my heart *in* vain, and washed my hands in innocency.	13 All in vain have I kept my heart clean and washed my hands in innocence.
14 For all the day long have I been plagued, and chastened every morning.	14 For all the day long I have been stricken, and chastened every morning.

12. Wicked is better than **ungodly. Always at ease** is probably the meaning, rather than **who prosper in the world.**

3. Spiritual Autobiography (73:13-20)

The psalmist reviews the temptation he was under until he recovered his bearings in the house of God.

13. I kept my heart clean: Substantially the same thought as "pure in heart" (RSV) in vs. 1. **Washed my hands in innocence** may be a reference to a ritualistic act (cf. 26:6; Deut. 21:6-7), or it may be used figuratively.

14. Vs. 5 may furnish an oblique allusion to the psalmist's personal troubles, but this verse is the first direct reference to them.

with fatness; wanton folly: **their hearts overflow with follies;** humorless malice: **they scoff and speak with malice;** boastfulness: **loftily they threaten oppression;** and arrogant impiety: **they set their mouths against the heavens, and their tongue struts through the earth** (vss. 6-9).

This is not only an interesting anticipation of the moral revulsion of a much later day, it is a series of adroitly turned phrases that reveal the poet's skill as observer and craftsman. Could this composite portrait come to life and exhibit himself, we would recognize him. If these qualities could be dramatized briefly into the ill-tempered egotist, the stupid glutton, the malicious slanderer, the tiresome braggart, and the noisy threatener of heaven, what a distasteful spectacle they would present. Overdrawn? Perhaps. We allow the poet this license. At the same time we may wonder whether such an array of the arrogant godless would excite general envy and establish false moral standards. The psalmist has confessed his own private envy of those whom his pen describes. What seems to have been the popular reaction?

Therefore the people turn and praise them;
and find no fault in them.

No fault: this is a moral judgment. There is nothing wrong in what the godless do. **Praise them:** this is an advance from a negative judgment to a positive attitude of approbation. **The people turn:** this clearly indicates that both negative and positive attitudes represent the reversal of former points of view. It is a striking observation, for it indicates the way in which a dominant minority establishes the mores of the group. It is not always a simple matter to draw a distinction between respectability and ostentation. At what point does proper satisfaction in being self-reliant pass over into surly pride in being rich? At what point does the wish to improve one's status become envy of the opulent? We have a mistaken idea that such problems have had their origin in the relatively recent development of democracy and the rise of the middle class. But the glamour, the presumption, and the prodigality of the rich have exercised profound social influence for a long time. That **the people turn and praise them** is as timeless an observation as we are likely to encounter anywhere.

The social consequences noted by the poet do not exhaust his insight into what has taken place in the popular mind. Moral attitudes need religious justification, even to the unsophisticated. And this is precisely what was produced. There is escape from the sense of the judgment of God on the godless by the assertion that God knows nothing about it. If he knew, he would of course do something; if he does not know, why should not everyone follow the example of the unrighteous? **And they say, . . . "Is there knowledge in the Most High?"** The **ease** of the godless and their **increase in riches** are sufficient proof, they say, either of the ignorance or the indifference of God. Upon this judgment there follows inescapably the renunciation of former codes, and yet this is done, as our poet shrewdly observes, without an actual renunciation of moral values. The clean heart and innocent hands have not been proved to be wrong, they have been proved to be futile (vs. 13). **Why in vain?** Because such moral scrupulosity has resulted not in prosperity but in being **stricken** all day long **and chastened every morning.**

15 If I say, I will speak thus; behold, I
should offend *against* the generation of thy
children.
16 When I thought to know this, it *was*
too painful for me;
17 Until I went into the sanctuary of
God; *then* understood I their end.
18 Surely thou didst set them in slippery
places: thou castedst them down into destruction.
19 How are they *brought* into desolation,
as in a moment! they are utterly consumed
with terrors.
20 As a dream when *one* awaketh; *so,* O
Lord, when thou awakest, thou shalt despise
their image.

15 If I had said, "I will speak thus,"
I would have been untrue to the generation of thy children.
16 But when I thought how to understand this,
it seemed to me a wearisome task,
17 until I went into the sanctuary of God;
then I perceived their end.
18 Truly thou dost set them in slippery places;
thou dost make them fall to ruin.
19 How they are destroyed in a moment,
swept away utterly by terrors!
20 They are[w] like a dream when one awakes,
on awaking you despise their phantoms.

[w] Cn: Heb *Lord*

---

15. The psalmist's sense of obligation to his people. **Children** is used in the O.T. to express Israel's intimate relationship with God (cf. Exod. 4:22-23; Deut. 14:1; Isa. 1:2; 45:11; Hos. 11:1; etc.; on the fatherhood of God see Exeg. on 103:13).

17-20. It was in the temple, possibly during one of the annual festivals, when memories of God's great mercies in the past were revived, that the psalmist regained his spiritual balance. Against this panorama of history he became aware, perhaps as never before, of the fleeting character of human achievements and especially of the successes of the wicked. It was the recognition of this truth that put his own misfortunes in a new light. Vs. 20 is difficult, as the recent English translations testify. **They are:** An emended text (יהיו), the M.T. being **Lord. Their phantoms:** Lit., **their image.** The wicked have the unreality of objects seen in dreams.

15-17. ***The Beginning of Understanding.***—That was, we concede, not an unreasonable conclusion. It is what most men today would call practical common sense. So indeed it was to our poet, and he admits that he had found it beguiling. There were three factors, however, that entered into his contemplation of the problem, and these saved him from accepting the popular judgment. The first was a sense of perspective. It was necessary for him to be true not only to his own times but to the generations to come. Assuming that a case for moral laxity could be made out for today, what of tomorrow? In the light of the long haul, what was seen to be the true status of the godless? **If I had said, "I will speak thus"** [which means agree with the popular mind], **I would have been untrue to the generation of thy children.** The second factor was the realization that moral certainty required more than logic.

> **But when I thought how to understand this,**
> **it seemed to me a wearisome task.**

The third factor was the effort to set his problem within the dimensions of the religious experience.

> **Until I went into the sanctuary of God;**
> **then I perceived their end.**

And, we may judge, the solution of the argument.

18-28. ***Faith Despite Confusion.***—The psalmist does not tell us much of what it was in the sanctuary that supplied the final proof. The resources of logic had left him both puzzled and weary. Was it a sense of the presence of God that restored his confidence and quickened his faith in simple goodness? In vs. 24 he indicates that God guided him with his counsel; and in vss. 21-22 he confesses that bitterness of soul and resentfulness of heart had made him **stupid and ignorant** and dulled his sensitiveness to God. There is no doubt, however, that he was thoroughly convinced. So sure was he, in fact, that he almost attributes to God sinister designs, as if he were maliciously playing a moral cat-and-mouse game with the godless (vss. 18-19). He even goes to the quite illogical (though permissibly poetic) extreme of denying real existence to the godless. They are like a dream when one awakes (vs. 20).

The closing stanza (vss. 24-28) is a truly beau-

21 Thus my heart was grieved, and I was
pricked in my reins.
22 So foolish *was* I, and ignorant: I was
as a beast before thee.
23 Nevertheless I *am* continually with
thee: thou hast holden *me* by my right
hand.
24 Thou shalt guide me with thy counsel,
and afterward receive me *to* glory.
25 Whom have I in heaven *but thee?* and
there is none upon earth *that* I desire besides thee.
26 My flesh and my heart faileth: *but*
God *is* the strength of my heart, and my
portion for ever.

21 When my soul was embittered,
when I was pricked in heart,
22 I was stupid and ignorant,
I was like a beast toward thee.
23 Nevertheless I am continually with thee;
thou dost hold my right hand.
24 Thou dost guide me with thy counsel,
and afterward thou wilt receive me to
glory.[x]
25 Whom have I in heaven but thee?
And there is nothing upon earth that I
desire besides thee.
26 My flesh and my heart may fail,
but God is the strength[y] of my heart
and my portion for ever.

[x] Or *honor*
[y] Heb *rock*

4. It Is Good to Be Near God (73:21-28)

After recalling briefly his condition of doubt, the psalmist reaffirms his faith.

21. My soul: Lit., **my heart.** In the O.T. the heart is frequently the seat of man's cognition. **In heart** or **in my reins:** Lit., "in my kidneys," the seat of the emotions (see on "inward parts" in Exeg. on 139:13).

22. Stupid or **foolish:** The noun, used adjectivally, is cognate to the word בְּעִיר, "beasts," "cattle." The closest English equivalent is "brutish."

23. The psalmist's constant awareness of the presence and reality of God (cf. 63:8).

24. And afterward thou wilt receive me to glory: The text seems unusual, but no proposed emendation has met with general acceptance. **Afterward** is an adverb and normally signifies "at a later time," but its precise meaning here is debatable. **Glory** does not elsewhere mean "heavenly glory"; the most natural way of construing it would be as an adverbial accusative, "gloriously" or "in honor." Hebrew poetic parallelism suggests that the clause should be rendered, "And afterward thou wilt lead me in honor." But in view of the fact that Israel did eventually develop a belief in immortality, an alternative exegesis is that the verse expresses the psalmist's hope that God's guidance of him will continue after death. In support of this interpretation it has often been noticed that the verb **receive** (לקח) is used of both Enoch's and Elijah's translation into heaven (Gen. 5:24; II Kings 2:3, 5, 9, 10), and that it also appears in 49:15. The latter is the only other possible reference in the Psalter to a belief in an afterlife.

25. God is the psalmist's supreme good (cf. 16:2).

26. Though body and mind **fail,** God remains the author's certain possession. **The strength of my heart:** Lit., **the rock of my heart. For ever:** In the O.T. this phrase

tiful statement of the faith of a saint. After his envy of the prosperous the poet has been restored to an assertion that his whole desire is met by having God. The anonymous author of the fourteenth-century classic *The Cloud of Unknowing* says: "To them that are perfectly meek nothing shall be lacking either for the spirit or for the body. For they have God, in whom is all plenty; whoever has Him—as this book tells you—needs nothing else in this life."[2] This is a long way from the prideful trust of those whose **eyes swell out with fatness,** whose **tongue struts through the earth.** Because he has acquired adequate perspectives within which to look at himself and others, he feels that God is **the strength of** his **heart** and his **portion for ever** (vs. 26). That is a fair exchange for the enervating and ephemeral portion of those who wore **violence . . . as a garment.** His summary is the familiar confidence of those who have discovered values (good) in intangibles: **But for me it is good to be near God.**

This poem deals with an old problem. The things we possess are a part of the life we live. Very easily they can become the whole of the

[2] New York: Harper & Bros., 1948, p. 100.

27 For, lo, they that are far from thee shall perish: thou hast destroyed all them that go a whoring from thee.
28 But *it is* good for me to draw near to God: I have put my trust in the Lord GOD, that I may declare all thy works.

Maschil of Asaph.

74 O God, why hast thou cast *us* off for ever? *why* doth thine anger smoke against the sheep of thy pasture?

27 For lo, those who are far from thee shall perish;
thou dost put an end to those who are false to thee.
28 But for me it is good to be near God;
I have made the Lord GOD my refuge,
that I may tell of all thy works.

A Maskil of Asaph.

74 O God, why dost thou cast us off for ever?
Why does thy anger smoke against the sheep of thy pasture?

---

usually means "for the duration of life" or "for a relatively long time"; its significance here is probably dependent upon the meaning attached to vs. 24*b*.

27. That the eventual lot of the wicked is an unhappy one even in this world is an axiom of most O.T. writers (see Exeg. on 109:1-31; 139:1-24). **Those who are false to thee:** The Hebrew word is used of marital infidelity (cf. **them that go a whoring**), but the RSV brings out the figurative meaning in this verse.

28. **To be near God:** Some take the Hebrew to mean "the presence of God" (lit., "the drawing near of God"), with perhaps a slight emphasis upon God's initial step in man's religious experience (cf. Amer. Trans., Peters, Schmidt, Nötscher). The RSV, however, is supported by many scholars and by the usage in Isa. 58:2. **That I may tell of all thy works** may imply the recitation of the psalm before a temple congregation. Doubtless the psalmist looked upon his own experience as one of the wondrous **works** of the Lord.

LXXIV. Remember Mount Zion (74:1-23)

This is clearly a lament of the community. The immediate occasion for it is some disaster which has overtaken Judah. The sanctuary in Zion has been profaned and ruined (vss. 3-7), and the destruction has extended to other holy places scattered throughout the land (vs. 8). In the face of this catastrophe the poet urges God to

---

life we live. This is a risk we all take. In an age in which the mind and the values of men run increasingly to things as the measure of cleverness and importance, the risk is formidable. The secularist judgment completely dissociates God from the hazard. It is a human venture. "Take the Cash, and let the Credit go."[3] Suppose it is true that fortunes dissipate in three generations, one lives only in his own generation. Why bother then with the fear that one day an awakening will reveal man's wealth like dreams whose phantoms count for nought? This is frighteningly plausible, and those who resist are certain to be thought of as they who "set their mouths against the heavens." The indictment is strangely reversed.

And yet if one thing is more certain than any other in a confused age, it is that man is not finally satisfied with things, and that his preoccupation with them dulls the edge of his moral sense, blinds him to the values that truly satisfy, and confuses his ideas about the ultimate fact of God. This almost happened to our poet. Inexorably it happens to all who lose perspective and stubbornly stand outside the sanctuary of God. The godless see only their beginning, and are bemused by it; those who, as our poet put it, go "into the sanctuary of God," perceive the tragic end of the wicked, and recoil from it. Thus one's religious faith supplies both companion and safeguard:

> **Nevertheless I am continually with thee;**
> **thou dost hold my right hand.**

74:1-23. *Religious Institutions in Peril.*—A **Maskil** is generally thought to be the designation of a didactic poem. The liturgical uses for which the Psalter was compiled presupposed

[3] *The Rubáiyát of Omar Khayyám*, st. xiii.

remember **the sheep of thy pasture.** The lament itself is interrupted by vss. 12-17, wherein the psalmist in hymnic fashion praises God for his great power manifested in the past.

While the psalm is a suitable prayer for God's people under a variety of trying circumstances, efforts have been made to identify the historical events which first brought it into being. Of the three dates suggested, 587 B.C., the fourth century B.C., and 167-165 B.C., none is free from difficulty, but the first is the most likely. Certainly, as far as our knowledge goes, it was only in the sixth century B.C. that the temple in Jerusalem was treated in a manner that would justify the language of vss. 3-7 (cf. II Kings 25:1-22). Our understanding of Jewish history in the fourth century is most defective. The allusion in Josephus (*Antiquities* XI. 7. 1) to the pollution of the temple by a Persian general in the reign of Artaxerxes (II or III) is too vague to justify large conclusions being drawn from it. The reference in Eusebius (*Chronicon* II. 112-13) to a deportation of Jews from Palestine by Artaxerxes III points to some trouble with the

---

choral and congregational singing, and to some of the songs orchestral (stringed instruments) accompaniment was set. The psalms thus employed undoubtedly served the incidental purpose of preserving the religious tradition of Israel while providing a musical vehicle for the worship ritual. Some of the poems, however, were frankly educational; designed not to be sung, but to be read by the priest and committed to memory by the devout worshiper. This is of course one of the most practical of all teaching devices. Long before there were written languages, folk tale and song, saga and heroic myth, ode and epode passed on from one generation to another the lore of tribe and nation. If Arnold J. Toynbee is to be followed in his understanding of the development of these great epics, they are a symptom of cultural decay; heroes are manufactured or the tales of plain men embroidered with splendor when the days of real heroes and grand deeds are past.

This type of poem is not rare in the anthology of the Hebrews. Indeed, it is common in almost any anthology of English poetry. "Listen, my children, and you shall hear." How much of our history is written and remembered in easily memorized verse! Yet the fact that song and poem make teaching easy also makes them dangerous. A legend can be corrected by an objective historic fact, but how does one dislodge a myth that has been sung with a lilting rhythm since childhood? For this reason we must be cautious lest we accept a poetic fancy as the truth about the historic past, or a didactic poem for the correct record of the things that it lifts and carries on its lyric cadences.

The ancient editors thought Asaph wrote this poem. It clearly was not the Asaph of the times reported in the Chronicles, for in those early days of Israel's history no such despoliation as our poem describes had occurred. Since, however, Asaph, or the choristers who used the name collectively, was a good pseudonym to appropriate, a later poet-pedagogue easily could have taken it. He was a later writer, we say, because of the probable date of reference of the psalm which the Exeg. suggests.

It is apparent at once that the poet is slanting his poem obliquely at those whom it was designed to instruct. Superficially read, it would seem to be an effort to report certain matters to God. There is a striking absence of the use of the first person; and, with three exceptions, God is specifically addressed in every verse. This is not to be taken literally to mean that the poet thought he was teaching God a history lesson. It is, on the contrary, quite clear that the most that can be charged against God is not ignorance but apparent forgetfulness. The point of interest to us, however, is that this indirect approach to the hearer tended to soften the reproach hidden in much that is said. Recorded history tends to flatter those for whom it is written; poetry exaggerates or conceals bare fact in imagery. The national pride of a humiliated people must not be offended by too great objectivity. An epic poem directed to another can put with forthrightness and even with anger what would be unpalatable to its intended listener if it were said in honest prose. There is no way of assessing this teacher's success. That the lesson is preserved in the Psalter is indication enough that the editors saw its usefulness at the time the collection was made.

The obvious theme is the insecurity or impermanence of the institutions of religion. God as a fact is undeniable; religion as an experience is indestructible. It is the institutions, referred to by the poet as **thy congregation, Mount Zion, where thou hast dwelt, the sanctuary, signs,** and **meeting places of God,** that suffer in the exigencies of history. Subtly concealed within his discussion of this problem is his rebuke to the unwisdom of those who in order to protect themselves form alliances with the ungodly, and end with their altars smoking and

2 Remember thy congregation, *which* thou hast purchased of old; the rod of thine inheritance, *which* thou hast redeemed; this mount Zion, wherein thou hast dwelt.

3 Lift up thy feet unto the perpetual desolations; *even* all *that* the enemy hath done wickedly in the sanctuary.

4 Thine enemies roar in the midst of thy congregations; they set up their ensigns *for* signs.

2 Remember thy congregation, which thou hast gotten of old,
which thou hast redeemed to be the tribe of thy heritage!
Remember Mount Zion, where thou hast dwelt.
3 Direct thy steps to the perpetual ruins;
the enemy has destroyed everything in the sanctuary!

4 Thy foes have roared in the midst of thy holy place;
they set up their own signs for signs.

Persians, but the details are hidden from us. The desecration which Antiochus IV inflicted upon the Jewish sanctuary in 167 B.C. (I Macc. 1:29-64; 4:36-61) was much milder than that which confronted our psalmist. If therefore we keep within the compass of recorded events, we are left with the conclusion that Ps. 74 originated in the sixth century B.C. The poignancy of the psalmist's words suggests that the Babylonian war was still fresh in the minds of the people. The dominant meter is 4+4.

1. Opening Appeal to God (74:1-2)

74:1. The sheep of thy pasture: This phrase, expressive of the intimate connection between the Lord and Israel, occurs also in 79:13; 100:3; Jer. 23:1; Ezek. 34:31.

2. The tribe rather than **the rod.** The Hebrew word has both meanings. **Remember Mount Zion:** This is what the Hebrew means, but **remember** is not in the M.T.

2. The Nation's Sorry Plight (74:3-9)

3. The perpetual ruins: In this context **perpetual** must mean "old," "of long standing"; possibly there is some exaggeration (cf. Isa. 58:12; 61:4). Solomon's temple lay in ruins between 587 and 520 B.C.

4. The singular of the noun מועד, **thy holy place,** has better MS support than the plural found in **thy congregations. They set up their own signs for signs** is the literal translation of the Hebrew, but the text may be corrupt. Possibly there is an allusion to military standards (cf. Num. 2:2).

---

their shrines desecrated. God, we are directly told, can take care of his own interests. He has lost neither his power nor his concern. Less directly we are reminded that the institutions of religion are not imperishable. Man's feebleness or indifference may allow or cause their destruction; to effect a return to the experience of the God who is **King . . . from of old** may be the divine intention behind the apparent tragedy.

1-3. ***The Forgetful God.***—These verses seem to be a sharp indictment of the forgetfulness of God. The psalmist asks why God's rejection should be timeless, though he knows it has not been so; he speaks of **perpetual ruins,** but **Mount Zion,** where God had made his dwelling, could not always have been a desolation. There had been a time when God had shepherded his sheep with affection; there was a time when he had obtained a congregation, and when he had redeemed his tribe from the fate of ownerlessness. **O God, why . . . does thy anger smoke against the sheep of thy pasture?** Anger against sheep is a self-defeating mood; so much so indeed that some interpreters have said our poet is referring to a threatening storm cloud, black as smoke.

4-8. ***The Enemies' Intention.***—However equivocal the ideas about God may appear, and however they may be accounted for, there is nothing enigmatical about the section that follows (vss. 4-8). This is the poet's transcription of a tradition concerning a former destruction of the temple (**holy place**). The intention of the foes of God is stated. **They said to themselves, "We will utterly subdue them"** (vs. 8*a*). The process of subjugating the nation involved the destruction of all the external and institutional evidences of religion, since in the community of Israel religion was the colloid that

5 *A man* was famous according as he had lifted up axes upon the thick trees.

6 But now they break down the carved work thereof at once with axes and hammers.

7 They have cast fire into thy sanctuary, they have defiled *by casting down* the dwelling place of thy name to the ground.

8 They said in their hearts, Let us destroy them together: they have burned up all the synagogues of God in the land.

9 We see not our signs: *there is* no more any prophet: neither *is there* among us any that knoweth how long.

5 At the upper entrance they hacked
the wooden trellis with axes.[z]
6 And then all its carved wood
they broke down with hatchets and hammers.
7 They set thy sanctuary on fire;
to the ground they desecrated the dwelling place of thy name.
8 They said to themselves, "We will utterly subdue them";
they burned all the meeting places of God in the land.

9 We do not see our signs;
there is no longer any prophet,
and there is none among us who knows how long.

[z] Cn Compare Gk Syr: Heb uncertain

5. The Hebrew is obscure. The RSV emends the first two Hebrew words to get גדעו במבוא, **at the . . . entrance they hacked. The wooden trellis** is, lit., "the thicket of wood" (cf. **the thick trees** KJV). **With axes** requires the addition of the preposition **with** to the M.T.

6-7. Carved wood: The interior walls of Solomon's temple were paneled with cedar, decorated with carvings of cherubim, palm trees, and flowers (I Kings 6:29). **Hatchets** or **axes,** and **hammers** are words found only here. Nebuzaradan is reported to have burned Solomon's temple in 587 B.C. (II Kings 25:8-9).

8. The meeting places: The RSV translates the singular of the same noun in vs. 4 as **holy place.** Probably the word designates any sacred spot sanctified by ancient theophany or former sacrificial practice. **Synagogues** (KJV, Amer. Trans.) is improbable, as the psalm does not appear to belong to a period when synagogues were a part of Palestine's life.

9. Our signs: Possibly military ensigns as in vs. 4, but "omens" would be more consonant with the rest of the verse (cf. 86:17; I Sam. 10:7; II Kings 19:29; Jer. 44:29; etc.). The reference may be to priestly services, such as interpreting omens, no longer available (cf. Mowinckel, *Psalmenstudien,* I, 97-98). **Prophet:** The allusion points to prophecy as a feature, or at least a recent feature, of Hebrew religious life, which would not be true of the fourth or the second century B.C.

provided integration and solidarity. There is represented here the fine frenzy and thoroughness of religious persecution.

Thy foes have roared in the midst of thy holy place;
they set up their own signs for signs.

History is full of records of this sort of angry impiety. Antiochus establishing a pig on the altar of the holy of holies in the second century B.C. is one of its most notorious examples. Sacred emblems destroyed and replaced by the hated ensigns of the despoiler: do we not remember the installation in high places of the Nazi swastika?

There follows a detailed description of the assault against the temple (vss. 5-6). First the forced entrance at the upper portal by smashing the **trellis** (ladder). To kindle a fire they shattered the carved woodwork and put the flame to it. The impulse to desecrate was satisfied only when the holy place was cast to the ground and made the pattern of destruction for all other sacred places in the land. This is a short account, but it lacks nothing in thoroughness. Those who heard the story and who learned to recite it would never forget it. Odd, they would say, that God seemed to have lost it out of mind.

9-11. ***The Issue Not Clear.***—The preceding verses recorded the spoliation of the external symbols of formal religion. There was no indication that in the hearts of the defeated people there was a collateral loss of personal faith. This likelihood is not overlooked, how-

10 O God, how long shall the adversary reproach? shall the enemy blaspheme thy name for ever?

11 Why withdrawest thou thy hand, even thy right hand? pluck *it* out of thy bosom.

12 For God *is* my King of old, working salvation in the midst of the earth.

10 How long, O God, is the foe to scoff?
Is the enemy to revile thy name for ever?

11 Why dost thou hold back thy hand,
why dost thou keep thy right hand in[a] thy bosom?

12 Yet God my King is from of old,
working salvation in the midst of the earth.

[a] Cn: Heb *consume thy right hand from*

---

3. The Appeal Resumed (74:10-11)

11b. The RSV is based on two emendations of the M.T.: **Out of thy bosom** is altered to **in thy bosom,** and "destroy" **(pluck)** to **dost thou keep** (תכלא).

4. In Praise of God (74:12-17)

This short hymn may have been composed by the psalmist, or he may have taken it from an outside source. It serves to indicate the basis of the appeal in the preceding and subsequent verses. It is to the God whose great deeds are here recounted that the cry for help is addressed.

12. **God my King:** On God as king cf. 3:2; 10:16; etc. **Salvation:** The plural of ישועה. The RSV translates the singular variously: "deliverance" in 3:8; "salvation" in 13:5; "victory" in 20:5; "help" in 21:1; "saving power" in 78:22. Here it seems to refer to God's great creative acts in the past.

---

ever. It is difficult for man to cherish an experience without external institutional forms for its protection and expression. It is not surprising therefore that our poet suggests here that the outer destruction may imperil the inner confidence. **We do not see our signs.** To lose the familiar symbol of one's central devotion is to jeopardize that devotion. **There is no longer any prophet.** To lose the spokesman, the interpreter, the custodian of the word of God, is to feel cut off from the source of encouragement and solace, an experience that makes exorbitant demands on even the doughtiest spirits. **And there is none among us who knows how long.** To have lost those who have a personal faith that the tribulation will not last forever, those who will hazard a prediction on which others may rest their hope, is a grievous test of faith. The lost symbol, the lost word, the lost hope, may well be concomitant to the lost sanctuary and the lost assembly. Thus in close proximity does our writer place the possibility of the destruction of the institutions of religion and the inner conviction of personal faith.

Lacking symbol, spokesman, and assurance, the only recourse is to God himself. The temple is a ruin, and there is no portent of relief. Can God give a reassuring word? This is the burden of vss. 11-12. Can God produce a sign or a symbol for the tormented to see? Better than a portent in a place of worship would be the hand of God. It was the symbol revealed in old times, offering protection and guidance. Why not now? **Why dost thou keep thy right hand in thy bosom?**

12-17. *Yet God's Power Is Limitless.*—Our poet-teacher, we discover, has set forth with genuine insight a matter of perennial importance to the student of religious experience. Up to this point, however, it has been a disquieting recital, even though we have been able to discover its intention. In order to create a proper mood for an apostrophe to the eternal majesty and power of God, our author has drawn the dismal picture of man's predicament in the face of the collapse of external religious support. In the next section he moves grandly into an address to the king. This contrast is intentional for didactic purposes. To the question in the opening verse: "Why dost thou cast us off for ever?" he answers: **Yet God my King is from of old.** To his testy invitation to God to direct his steps "to the perpetual ruins" (vs. 3), he now relentingly admits: **Thine is the day, thine also the night.** This whole section engages the reader not alone by its delightful lyric quality and the nature poetry often encountered in the psalms; it is interesting in its borrowings from the Babylonian creation myth.

13 Thou didst divide the sea by thy strength: thou brakest the heads of the dragons in the waters.
14 Thou brakest the heads of leviathan in pieces, *and* gavest him *to be* meat to the people inhabiting the wilderness.
15 Thou didst cleave the fountain and the flood: thou driedst up mighty rivers.
16 The day *is* thine, the night also *is* thine: thou hast prepared the light and the sun.
17 Thou hast set all the borders of the earth: thou hast made summer and winter.

13 Thou didst divide the sea by thy might;
thou didst break the heads of the dragons on the waters.
14 Thou didst crush the heads of Leviathan,
thou didst give him as food[b] for the creatures of the wilderness.
15 Thou didst cleave open springs and brooks;
thou didst dry up ever-flowing streams.
16 Thine is the day, thine also the night;
thou hast established the luminaries and the sun.
17 Thou hast fixed all the bounds of the earth;
thou hast made summer and winter.

[b] Heb *food for the people*

13-15. Some scholars take these verses as containing references to the Exodus, with **Leviathan** representing Egypt, and vs. 15 reflecting Exod. 17:6; Josh. 3:1-17 (Briggs, Peters, Barnes, *et al.*). It is, however, much more likely that these verses, as well as vss. 16-17, preserve traditions about God's fashioning of the world. For other O.T. references to primitive creation mythology, apart from Gen. 1:1–2:4*a*, see Ps. 89:9-12; Isa. 27:1; 51:9-10; Job 7:12; 9:13-14; 26:12-13. These traditions go back in part to the Akkadian creation myth (*Enûma eliš*), which tells of a primeval conflict between Marduk and Tiamat (Alexander Heidel, *The Babylonian Genesis* [2nd ed.; Chicago: University of Chicago Press, 1951], pp. 18-60, 102-14). They also appear to be indebted to Ugaritic mythology, particularly what C. H. Gordon calls *The Loves and Wars of Baal and Anat* (Princeton: Princeton University Press, 1932, pp. xii, 5-26; cf. J. H. Patton, *Canaanite Parallels*, pp. 27-28; Gaster, *Thespis*, pp. 80-81, 145-50; Pritchard, *Ancient Near Eastern Texts*, pp. 129-55).

13. Thou didst divide the sea: ים, *yām*, is **sea**; cf. the Ugaritic account of Baal's conflict with Yam, the god of the sea. **The dragons:** Fabulous sea monsters; cf. Tannin, which in Ugaritic is apparently another name for **Leviathan** (see vs. 14).

14. The heads of Leviathan: In Job 41:1 leviathan appears to be the crocodile, but elsewhere in the O.T. it refers to a legendary marine animal (104:26; Job 3:8; Isa 27:1). In the Ugaritic "Poem of Baal," Lotan (Leviathan) is seemingly another name for Yam, the god of the sea, and it is said to have seven heads (Gaster, *op. cit.*, p. 186). **For the creatures of the wilderness:** The M.T. is, lit., "to [the] people to [the] wild beasts." The text may be at fault, although "people" is used of groups of animals in Prov. 30:25-26. An emendation suggested by Immanuel Löw (לעמלצי ים) gives "for the sharks of the sea."

15. Cf. Gen. 1:6-8. The existence (and creation) of **springs** is assumed in Gen. 7:11.

16-17. On **day** and **night** see Gen. 1:3-5. **The luminaries:** The M.T. is מאור, "luminary." The word is applied to the moon in Gen. 1:16, and it is reasonable to

The Genesis creation ode refers to the division of the sea and the fixing of the great lights. Breaking the heads of marine dragons and feeding the wild creatures with the crushed heads of **Leviathan** was the bold imagery of an earlier epic. There is no incongruity in the assimilation of one folklore into another. Our poet is presenting his God-King in heroic dimensions. Anything less would diminish the possibility of his bringing order out of the desolate shrines and sacred assemblies. It is with a confident figure that this section is concluded. After all, we are being told, there is nothing beyond the concern or the governance of God. **Thou hast fixed all the bounds of the earth;** and the winter of despair is no less under his eye than the cheer and assurance of the summertime: **thou hast made summer and winter.**

18 Remember this, *that* the enemy hath reproached, O LORD, and *that* the foolish people have blasphemed thy name.

19 O deliver not the soul of thy turtledove unto the multitude *of the wicked:* forget not the congregation of thy poor for ever.

20 Have respect unto the covenant: for the dark places of the earth are full of the habitations of cruelty.

21 O let not the oppressed return ashamed: let the poor and needy praise thy name.

18 Remember this, O LORD, how the enemy scoffs,
and an impious people reviles thy name.
19 Do not deliver the soul of thy dove to the wild beasts;
do not forget the life of thy poor for ever.

20 Have regard for thy[c] covenant;
for the dark places of the land are full of the habitations of violence.
21 Let not the downtrodden be put to shame;
let the poor and needy praise thy name.

[c] Gk Syr: Heb *the*

---

conclude that here also it designates the moon (cf. "moon" and "sun" in 104:19). On vs. 17, cf. Deut. 32:8; Gen. 8:22.

5. Concluding Appeal for God's Intervention (74:18-23)

18. Impious or **foolish,** as also in vs. 22. The RSV translates the same word as "fool" in 14:1; 39:8; 53:1. The people of whom the psalmist speaks were probably loyal to their own gods, but they showed no reverence for Israel's God.

19. Thy dove: This metaphor for Israel is employed only here. **The wild beasts** is the translation of חית (taken as a collective), and is preferable to **the multitude of the wicked. The life of:** A small emendation (חיי), correcting the M.T. represented by **the congregation of.**

20*b*. The text is not free from suspicion. Possibly the meaning is that even the caves and hiding places of the land have been overrun by the enemy.

21*a*. The KJV gives a literal, and the RSV a rather free, translation.

18-23. ***Reminder to God.***—The final strophe returns us to the mood of the opening verses. Here again God is asked to **remember.** This time, however, it is not to remember the congregation that met in the sanctuary, and Mount Zion, where he made his dwelling. He must now recall his creative power and his invincible might. These words are directed less to God than to those bereft mortals who needed to be constantly reminded of it. There were enemy scoffers; there were also the impious within the community of God, who in times of trouble reviled his name.

> **Remember this, O Lord, how the enemy scoffs,**
> **and an impious people reviles thy name.**

Then, taking leave of the didactic intention, our author offers a prayer for the soul and life of his people, for the continuation of God's covenant, and for an opportunity for the afflicted and needy to exercise the worship impulse in praise. His final word is a petition, **Arise, O God, plead thy cause,** not forgetting the impious, the clamor and the uproar of others who boast of their own impiety.

What strikes us in these closing stanzas is that there is no demand on God that he shall repair the ruined sanctuary, restore the desecrated symbol, or return the exiled prophet. It is the soul and the life of his people that must concern God. It is his **cause,** rather than his dwelling place on Mount Zion, that must be re-established. And this fits the pattern of the teaching of this Maskil. Let the generations be reminded what the record of history has to say, but let them be convinced that the experience of a living religious faith is not dependent on the indestructibility of the institutions living religion builds for its tenancy.

The relation of this great idea to our own day is obvious. In the bitter strife between Arabs and Jews that preceded the establishment of the state of Israel, the old city of Jerusalem was under bombardment by the modern weapons of destruction. So long as society must create institutions as an aid to the maintenance of order, we shall accept them as such; but

22 Arise, O God, plead thine own cause: remember how the foolish man reproacheth thee daily.
23 Forget not the voice of thine enemies: the tumult of those that rise up against thee increaseth continually.

To the chief Musician, Al-taschith, A Psalm *or* Song of Asaph.

75 Unto thee, O God, do we give thanks, *unto thee* do we give thanks: for *that* thy name is near thy wondrous works declare.

22 Arise, O God, plead thy cause;
remember how the impious scoff at thee all the day!
23 Do not forget the clamor of thy foes,
the uproar of thy adversaries which goes up continually!

To the choirmaster: according to Do Not Destroy. A Psalm of Asaph. A Song.

75 We give thanks to thee, O God; we give thanks;
we call on thy name and recount[d] thy wondrous deeds.

[d] Syr Compare Gk: Heb *and near is thy name. They recount*

---

22. The **cause** of Israel is the cause of God. **Impious:** See on vs. 18.
23. **Goes up** rather than **increaseth.**

LXXV. We Give Thanks to Thee, O God (75:1-10)

This psalm in its present form is a hymn of the community, as vs. 1 indicates, but it is clear that it comprises heterogeneous elements. Vss. 2-3 appear to be an oracle spoken by God, and vs. 9 an excerpt from an individual's hymn of praise. In vss. 7-8, 10, and possibly also in vss. 6-7, there are expressions that can be taken eschatologically. When and why these and the remaining verses were brought together to form the psalm is a matter of conjecture. It is probable that, when the psalm was used in the temple, the opening verse was recited by all the people, and vss. 2-5 by a priest on behalf of the Lord. What was done with vss. 6-10 is problematic. Gunkel labels the poem a "prophetic liturgy," and Weiser calls it a "fragment of a cult-liturgy."

The main thesis of the hymn is that the Lord upholds both the cosmic and the moral order, and that in his own good time he will exercise judgment with equity. It is a fair presumption that the age in which the psalmist lived was a troubled one, and that it needed the reassurance of these heartening words. The dominant meter is 3+3.

1. Invocation (75:1)

75:1. The beginning of the hymn, voiced by the whole congregation. **We call on thy name and recount:** An emended text (probably וקרא בשמך וספר, using two infinitives absolute), supported by the LXX and the Syriac. The KJV and the RSV mg. give the M.T.

---

when the preservation of an institution—educational, economic, political, or ecclesiastical—becomes an end in itself, then the free creative activities of the human spirit are in immediate danger of stultification. The lesson of history on this point is that man must allow a social institution, no matter what sort it is, to survive only as long as it permits the expansion of the original creative experience that gave it origin. Man's free spirit breaks old institutions apart in order that new ones may take their place. It is an old conflict. To us it testifies to the radical spirit of God in the heart of man, even while it frightens the conservative. What, we may ask, is the loss of a sanctuary if it allows God to arise and plead his cause?

75:1-10. ***Concerning Other People's Sins.***—This is largely a song about pride. Having said this, we can take leave of such certainty as we may claim on this main point and confess to some confusion on minor matters. It is meant to be sung; so says its caption. With the exception of brief and conventional allusions to God in vss. 1, 9, it is singularly lacking in religious interest. There are some reasons for regarding it as an incomplete transcription of a victory song. Evidence is seen pointing to antiphonal and therefore liturgical use. Here, however, it is not clear as to what words are to be ascribed to whom. Perhaps the least that can be said about it is that it falls below the level of most of the psalms in structure and content. This

2 When I shall receive the congregation I will judge uprightly.
3 The earth and all the inhabitants thereof are dissolved: I bear up the pillars of it. Selah.
4 I said unto the fools, Deal not foolishly: and to the wicked, Lift not up the horn:

2 At the set time which I appoint
I will judge with equity.
3 When the earth totters, and all its inhabitants,
it is I who keep steady its pillars. *Selah*
4 I say to the boastful, "Do not boast,"
and to the wicked, "Do not lift up your horn;

2. The Voice of the Lord (75:2-5)

These verses can be appropriately assigned only to the Lord (some confine the divine oracle to vss. 2-3), and presumably they were in temple usage rendered by a soloist, whom some scholars refer to as a "cult prophet."

2. At the set time which I appoint is preferable to **when I shall receive the congregation. At the set time** is ambiguous (see Exeg. on vss. 6-8). **I will judge:** On God as world judge cf. 9:8; 50:6; 58:11; 67:4; 94:2; 96:13; 98:9; Gen. 18:25; Job 8:3; Eccl. 12:14.

3. Keep steady or "establish" is better than **bear up. Pillars:** The same word is used of the earth's pillars only once elsewhere (Job 9:6), but the idea that the earth rests upon foundations of some sort is found in 18:15; 82:5; 104:5; I Sam. 2:8; Isa. 24:18; Mic. 6:2; Jer. 31:37; Job 38:4-6 (cf. 26:6-7); Prov. 8:29. Another view, that the earth rests upon water, is presented in 24:2; 136:6; Gen. 1:9-10.

4-5. The boastful rather than **the fools. Horn:** As the horns on oxen, goats, and rams gave those animals some advantages not enjoyed by the nonhorned creatures, the horn

confirms the scholarly judgment as to its fragmentary character. The best that can be said for it is that it alone of all the poems in the anthology undertakes to deal specifically and cogently with the dangers of pride.

It is of course the adversary who is admonished against this common human predilection. It is notable, even if on second thought not surprising, that though pride and proud people are many times referred to in the Bible, there is not one direct and unequivocal confession of a sense of personal involvement in it. Invariably it is the defect of another, and more often than not, of one's enemy. To pride may be assigned the cause of every folly and failure except those that overtake us. The honest proud do not confess their sins because confession is the sign of pride's opposite. When the dishonest proud prate of their humility, their pride is exhibited in its most odious and perverse form. Even though in our times we know pride to be for the most part an exhibition of a subconscious sense of inferiority seeking to hide itself in outward pretentiousness, we seem not conspicuously able to abate it in ourselves or others. Spinoza observed that "it may easily come to pass that a vain man may become proud and imagine himself pleasing to all when he is in reality a universal nuisance."[4] From the standpoint of our poem that would be something of an understatement.

[4] *Ethics*, Part III, Proposition XXX, Note.

1. ***Pride.***—It is both the development and the specific content of this piece that indicate its concern with human pride—the pride of the enemy. Vs. 1 is no more than the customary ascription of praise, though if we assume that the specific subject was clearly in the poet's or the redactor's mind, we can see in its latter half an implication. **We give thanks to thee, O God; we give thanks.** This is the decorous and deferent attitude of the faithful. **We call on thy name and recount thy wondrous deeds,** the implication being that those who do not call on God's name will recount their own wondrous deeds.

2-3. ***God's Rebuke.***—The next strophe clearly is the voice of God, spoken perhaps by the priest-liturgist. Otherwise considered, it would be the most insufferable of human pretensions. Even so, it can be best understood if projected against a background of prideful human claims. **At the set time which I appoint,** says the somewhat arbitrary and divinely confident voice, **I will judge with equity. Equity,** or lack of bias, is the one quality that human pride effectively negates. This mighty prerogative belongs to God, but there have been mortals who have claimed it for themselves, and others who have wished for it. Nietzsche sighed that if there were gods, he could not bear not to be one.

4-5. ***Pride's Presumption.***—God, having laid proper claim to title of earth-steadier when the foundations and people of the world were

5 Lift not up your horn on high: speak *not* with a stiff neck.
6 For promotion *cometh* neither from the east, nor from the west, nor from the south.
7 But God *is* the judge: he putteth down one, and setteth up another.
8 For in the hand of the LORD *there is* a cup, and the wine is red; it is full of mixture; and he poureth out of the same: but the dregs thereof, all the wicked of the earth shall wring *them* out, *and* drink *them.*

5 do not lift up your horn on high,
or speak with insolent neck."

6 For not from the east or from the west
and not from the wilderness comes lifting up;
7 but it is God who executes judgment,
putting down one and lifting up another.
8 For in the hand of the LORD there is a cup,
with foaming wine, well mixed;
and he will pour a draught from it,
and all the wicked of the earth
shall drain it down to the dregs.

---

came to be in the O.T. a symbol of strength and dignity. Here, in both verses, it is a metaphor for arrogance. **With insolent neck** rather than **with a stiff neck.**

3. THE JUDGMENT OF GOD (75:6-8)

It is God who executes judgment and punishes the wicked. It is not clear whether the psalmist is thinking of God's constant judgments in the present world, or of a final definitive judgment at the end of the age.

6-7. Wilderness rather than **south. Lifting up** or **promotion:** Many emend הרים to ומהרים, "or from the mountains." On vs. 7 see vs. 2.

8. A cup: The representation of the Lord's wrath as a **cup** which must be drunk by those who have incurred his displeasure is a familiar one in the O.T.: 11:6; 60:3; Isa. 51:17, 22; Jer. 25:15; 49:12; Lam. 4:21; Ezek. 23:33; Job 21:20. In the N.T. it appears in Rev. 14:10; 16:19; 18:6. **With foaming wine** is better than **the wine is red.** The Hebrew appears to be "the wine (which) ferments."

---

shaken, and having done so without the taint of arrogance that would disqualify it in a proud man, goes a step further and adjures the boastful to leave off boasting. Again, this could be morally convincing only if God himself were free from the frailty. **I say to the boastful, "Do not boast,"** and perhaps because this is easier said than done, he gives a much sharper designation to the braggart, **and to the wicked, "Do not lift up your horn"**—the lifting up of the horn, as we shall later see, being the gesture of presumption. Even this is given still more specific characterization,

Do not lift up your horn on high,
or speak with insolent neck.

The exact meaning of the last word is disputed by the translators, but there is no doubt as to the force of the qualifying adjective.

Taken as an effort to set forth the fact and futility of human pride, we find that this poem, even if we go no farther than vs. 5, has hit squarely upon the three stages of the pride sequence. They are indicated by three ideas: the **boastful,** the **wicked,** the **insolent.** Is this not what we see take place in those who, for any reason or none, allow themselves to swell with pride? They boast; then in order to prove their right to boast they must become wicked, since pride cannot glorify itself with righteous and humble deeds. And at length their boasting, credited by wickedness, becomes insolent. What is insolence? It is pride that has got to the point of exhibiting itself in contemptuous and overbearing treatment of others. At this point of course it has begun to destroy itself, if not actually by its own excesses, then by the hand of others who will suffer the proud only for a season.

6-10. ***The Judgment of Pride.***—Vss. 6-7 seem at first reading to take leave of the theme that we have thought central to the poem. More careful scrutiny, however, reveals that these verses give interesting and illustrative support to the idea. To **the east** of Jerusalem lay Persia, already in its time a proud civilization; and to **the west** lay Egypt. The latter, already beginning its time of troubles, was for that reason all the more prideful. What of the **wilderness**

9 But I will declare for ever; I will sing praises to the God of Jacob.

10 All the horns of the wicked also will I cut off; *but* the horns of the righteous shall be exalted.

9 But I will rejoice[e] for ever,
I will sing praises to the God of Jacob.
10 All the horns of the wicked he[f] will cut off,
but the horns of the righteous shall be exalted.

[e] Gk: Heb *declare*
[f] Heb *I*

4. Concluding Praise (75:9-10)

9. I will rejoice: An emendation (אגיל) suggested by the LXX. The M.T. is **I will declare.**

10. The punishment of the wicked (as in vs. 8), and the exaltation of the godly. **He will cut off:** A small emendation. The M.T. is **will I cut off,** which, if retained, means that the psalmist hopes to have a share in the destruction of the evildoers.

where unknown denizens hid, or the mountains from which God had once spoken with the voice of thunder? Pride, wherever it is, whether among the civilized or the barbarian, inevitably claims the right to execute judgment. This is its most intolerable pose: for reasons that it does not feel called upon to give, it assumes the prerogatives of the judge and executes its arbitrary pseudo justice solely in terms of the whim that at the moment flatters its posture. This, says our poet through the prophet-spokesman's lips, is pride's most mistaken folly. **It is God who executes judgment**—not east or west or wilderness. How complete will be God's command of his office is stated in vs. 10:

All the horns of the wicked he will cut off,
but the horns of the righteous shall be exalted.

10. *The Judgment in Symbol and Summary.* —The use of the word **horn** four times is both puzzling and interesting. There is great latitude in its scriptural meanings: it can mean a drinking vessel, a musical instrument, a symbol of honor and royal power, and in the familiar verse in Luke 1:69 Christ is called the "horn of salvation" by Zechariah father of John. Two of these uses are pertinent to the theme of our poem: the first that understands the horn as the symbol of power. This the proud man would have, either figuratively or literally; he would lift it up, and the greater his pride, the higher he would lift it (vss. 4-5). Because of this presumption and usurpation of the prerogative of God, **the horns of the wicked** will be **cut off** as a sign of humiliation and judgment.

The second understanding of the word as a drinking vessel fits the otherwise confused reference in vs. 8. Ezekiel mentions the traffic of the merchants of Tarshish in ebony and ivory horns and vessels of brass. On the occasion of a royal anointing the ceremonial oil was poured from a horn, and it may be properly assumed that it served other uses as well. Reference to vss. 4, 5 calls up a picture of horns of wine lifted high by the proud and the noisy boasts of the insolent stimulated by strong drink. Now, pride is a heady draught that induces a sort of intoxication. Overindulgence of self-regard looses the tongue and one drink calls for another until recklessness results in insolence and abuse.

Do not lift up your horn on high,
or speak with insolent neck.

How neatly this metaphor fits the need for warning the proud man, already drunk with self-flattery.

Against this picture there is set in satirical contrast (vs. 8) one that shows the hand of God holding a cup of foaming wine well savored with spices and the piquancy of fresh pomegranate seeds. But it is no drink for a festive crowd, nor is it lifted to the lips of God. From the hands of the proud who raise their brimming horns and boast their right to lord it over their fellows the wine vessel is struck, the vintage spilled; and from the giant cup in the steady hand of God is poured a cascade into the throats of all the world's boastful till the last dregs are downed. Thus for the wine of pride quaffed from the horns of the wicked there is substituted the wine of humiliation poured from the cup of God. This is strange and puzzling imagery to us, but to those of an earlier day it must have been both a shocking and sobering word. This interpretation does not come to terms with all the references in the poem, though the picture of a tottering earth and reeling inhabitants kept steady by the hand of God (vs. 3) offers further inferential support to it.

Our author concludes with a promise of perpetual rejoicing in the discomfiture of the wicked and the exaltation of the righteous, skillfully avoiding the pitfall of saying that it is he and his horn that will be lifted on high. That would have smirched him with the taint of pride, partially concealed perhaps by the garment of ultimately triumphant justice.

We may remind ourselves of the editorial caption that heads this psalm in the ASV: "God abases the Proud, but exalts the Righteous." This we may take to be the meaning it conveyed to those who edited the Psalter many years ago. We share their understanding, and recognize a need for its restatement. The twentieth century has seen both how God abases the proud and how he exalts the righteous. If defeat of national arrogance is its abasement at the hands of God—and the victorious have united to proclaim it—then is not the victory of national arrogance its exaltation at the hands of God? This is the logic to which we have advanced, though we have used more ingratiating words than "national arrogance." And this means that we are proud. Our horn is lifted up; is it not we who keep steady the pillars of the earth when it totters and its inhabitants stumble? Let us be warned; an everlasting word must be spoken to us as well as to those we call our proud adversaries.

> If, drunk with sight of power, we loose
> Wild tongues that have not Thee in awe. . . .[5]

There is little need here for a detailed study of this persistent and insinuating thing. For generations, it has been pointed out, pride was always the result of the blindness of some to follies that were all too clear to others. The proud had little reason for their pride; others saw that clearly and were pleased with their superior moral discernment. Man's moral insights went more deeply into the human plight than the Decalogue when pride was indicted as a deadly sin. It is much to the credit of modern ethical thought that it has pronounced its irreversible judgment on human pride as the elemental source of all man's moral failures. In this we have had the particular help of the historian and the psychologist. If what man needed to help him turn from the corruption of pride were a statistical record of its destructiveness, he would have escaped long since. What corporate sin—allowing the word for the moment—has its origin elsewhere than in pride? The world's dispossessed, impoverished, dispirited, embattled millions are the blight of this evil and unreasonable thing. Or if, added to the visible evidence of pride's corruption, man needed only to know why it is that he is, in spite of himself, so easily enslaved by this **foaming wine, well mixed,** he has libraries to guide him toward an understanding of his psyche.

It seems, however, that we are not to be saved from pride by the stark record of history or the probings of psychiatry. Both have rendered explicit, impartial, and unanimous judgment against which we shall be unable to place our veto. And yet despite our greater wisdom, are we to suffer no less than fools the ravages of pride? Yes, for if we are unable to rid ourselves of this moral poison we shall surely die. It is the distinction of this otherwise undistinguished poem that it provides for us the element lacking in the two great disciplines that modern man has perfected. Listen once again to what the poet has to say: "For not from the east or from the west and not from the wilderness . . . ; but it is God who executes judgment, putting one down and lifting up another" (vss. 6-7). This is the ancient, inexpungeable testimony of religious faith brought to bear on the problem of human pride. Some, it says, are exalted. That is a realistic and wholly practical observation. Some also are humbled. But by whose judgment are exaltation and humbling determined? By one's own uncriticized sense of personal worth? This is subject to elaborate errors of computation, even as one's feeling of humiliation can be improperly evaluated. It is simply another way of saying what religious faith has always said: the criteria of personal worth must be outside one's self and one's world, though one must always be himself in his own world. This is, to be sure, an old paradox. One must lose one's self to find one's self. And when one has found one's self, is he forever immune to the poison? No; the dialectic moral conflict goes on; he must lose himself again.

To the proud man this is infuriating nonsense. Up goes his horn and down goes the drink that warms and reassures him. To the modest man it is puzzling, and because of it he may do violence to his own best spiritual interests by a retreat to servility or self-pity. Is it not obvious therefore that it must be God who will exalt the one and abase the other? What this means beyond dispute is that the standards of up and down must transcend the level of all historic experience, however faithful an aid history may prove to be.

Finally, we can indeed put the poet's insight and words into a context that fairly shocks us with its modern relevance. "It is not from the East"—what does that mean to a modern Easterner or Westerner?—"or from the West"—

[5] "Recessional," from *The Five Nations*, by Rudyard Kipling. Copyright 1903 by Rudyard Kipling, reprinted by permission of Mrs. George Bambridge, Methuen & Co., and Doubleday & Co., Inc.

To the chief Musician on Neginoth, A Psalm *or* Song of Asaph.

76 In Judah *is* God known: his name *is* great in Israel.

To the choirmaster: with stringed instruments. A Psalm of Asaph. A Song.

76 In Judah God is known,
his name is great in Israel.

LXXVI. Our Glorious and Terrible God (76:1-12)

Despite some textual difficulties, this short poem, which in Gunkel's terminology is a "Song of Zion," is a very pleasing hymn. Some scholars find in it affinities with Pss. 46; 48. It appears to celebrate a victory of Israel's armies, interpreted as the work of the Lord, and many commentators suppose that there is an allusion to the defeat of Sennacherib at Jerusalem in 701 B.C. We may note that in the LXX "With reference to the Assyrian" is found in the title. The events of 701 B.C. may indeed have inspired the psalmist's first composition, but it is also possible that the subsequent use of the psalm in temple ritual (cf. vs. 11) has modified its original form. If we assume some pardonable exaggeration in vss. 8-9, there is no need to assert that the author had any eschatological interest in mind. He was concerned with the Lord's recent judgment in history, and in so far as he moved to something larger, it was God's awe-inspiring majesty that he thought needful to dwell upon (vss. 1, 4, 7-8, 11-12).

We may observe that Mowinckel *et al.* (cf. Gaster, *Thespis*, pp. 81-83) have detected in this psalm (e.g., vss. 1-2) a connection with the New Year festival and with the "Enthronement of Yahweh" ceremony (see Exeg. on 47:1-10; 93:1-5). Echoes of a cultic drama, widespread in the ancient Near East, in which the deity (in this case the Lord) overcomes all forces opposed to him, have also been found in vss. 3-6. In the absence of reliable information about the ritual in the Jewish temple, these claims must be viewed with caution.

The psalm exhibits a definite strophic pattern, as is seen in the RSV. The meter is 3+3, with variations.

1. In Judah God Is Known (76:1-3)

God, whose dwelling is in Jerusalem, has wrought there a great victory. These verses also reaffirm Israel's role as custodian of divine truth.

76:1. Judah and **Israel** are here synonymous.

---

what does that mean to a modern Easterner or Westerner?—"but it is God who executes judgment." In the next fateful years, who will be exalted, who humbled? And what will save us from the wickedness and folly of pride if not God alone?

76:1-12. ***The Lord Mighty in Battle.***—Whether this song was part of a celebration of a victory of a Judean king, or a masque portraying the triumph of the Lord over the forces that oppose him, or a simple hymn to be sung on a holiday, its representation of the character of God is severely limited to his prowess in war. Poetry is a dubious medium for the use of the philosopher and theologian; and while moral precepts have been taught in songs, one must not expect a complete ethical system to be communicated either by nursery rhymes or by anthems. At the same time, song and poem have been used to say so much that we easily allow the idea to persist that they have said or can say everything.

All that this song is designed to do is to exalt God the warrior, and this it does with great energy. Therefore it omits any reference to pity, tenderness, redemption, mercy—those qualities that are not the warrior's stock in trade. So stark and unrelieved is this picture of violence that the single intimation that might appear to qualify it is uniformly thought by some scholars to be an editorial excrescence. In this the faithful are exhorted to make vows to the Lord and to perform them, even though in the original body of the poem there is nothing to inspire such votive impulses. Vs. 11 is the most quoted fragment of the song, and shares with another line the honor of saving it from oblivion. **Surely the wrath of men shall praise thee** (vs. 10*a*) is a promise that has given strange justification to the most dangerous of human moods, but even this has been possible only by lifting it out of context and thereby missing, as we shall later see, its obvious intention. Except for its bold extravagances, this

2 In Salem also is his tabernacle, and his
dwelling place in Zion.
3 There brake he the arrows of the bow,
the shield, and the sword, and the battle.
Selah.
4 Thou *art* more glorious *and* excellent
than the mountains of prey.
5 The stout-hearted are spoiled, they
have slept their sleep: and none of the men
of might have found their hands.
6 At thy rebuke, O God of Jacob, both
the chariot and horse are cast into a dead
sleep.

2 His abode has been established in Salem,
his dwelling place in Zion.
3 There he broke the flashing arrows,
the shield, the sword, and the weapons
of war. *Selah*

4 Glorious art thou, more majestic
than the everlasting mountains.[g]
5 The stouthearted were stripped of their
spoil;
they sank into sleep;
all the men of war
were unable to use their hands.
6 At thy rebuke, O God of Jacob,
both rider and horse lay stunned.

[g] Gk: Heb *the mountains of prey*

---

2. His abode: In 10:9 the RSV translates this word as "covert." **Salem,** found only here and in Gen. 14:18 in the O.T., is an abbreviation for Jerusalem. **His dwelling place:** The word usually designates a lair or den of wild beasts (e.g., Amos 3:4).

3. The flashing arrows: Lit., "the flames of the bow" (cf. KJV, **the arrows of the bow). The weapons of war:** Lit., **the battle.**

2. Defeat of Zion's Foes (76:4-6)

4-6. A further description of the discomfiture of the enemy before the majesty of Israel's God. **The everlasting mountains:** An emended text, reading עד instead of טרף (cf. Hab. 3:6). The M.T. is **the mountains of prey,** which does not seem to be a suitable comparison. **Were unable to use:** Lit., "did not find" (cf. KJV). The RSV favors **rider** rather than **chariot** (vs. 6), although the former is a rare meaning for the Hebrew word (רכב).

---

might be a song sung by the adoring minstrel of a petty chieftain, and it is full of references that are repugnant to the spiritually sensitive. It merits a place in the Psalter because it sets up a foil by which the truly creative and redemptive ministries of God and religion can be more clearly seen. It gives us the reason for the songs of another genre. Other poets, sensing other qualities in the Lord God, wrote their songs too. The Lord was shepherd and host; this was one way to answer the troubadour who plucked a stringed instrument and sang of him as a terror.

It is within this perspective that we are to seek the values this psalm has for us. If it represented the only or the authentic picture of God, we should have to reject it. Since we are sure that it advances a partial or mistaken conception, we may face up to it and make such limited uses of it as it allows. What are the lineaments of the portrait it paints?

1-10. ***God the Warrior.***—Three times in the Hebrew text of this psalm God is described by the word ירא, **glorious** (vs. 4) or **terrible** (vss. 7, 12). This is of course the highest tribute that can be paid to one whose business is terror, and twice the compliment is paid directly to him (**terrible** [**glorious**] **art thou,** vss. 4, 7). It flatters the fighter to hear this said of him, for if his enemies are terrified, his exertions can be considerably economized. His battles are already half won before they are joined. Added to the horrendous title is the area covered by his reputation. **In Judah God is known, his name is great in Israel. His abode** [bivouac] **has been established in Salem** [the place of peace!], **his dwelling place** [lair] **in Zion.**

What has he done to earn this frightening fame? There are two variant renderings of the word **mountains** that give heightened color to the poet's description. One (Amer. Trans.) uses "devouring lion" as an alternate to **mountains,** the other, allowed by our text, has it as **mountains of prey.** The imagination strains to conjure up a more alarming spectacle than a hungry lion prowling for prey, and imagination fails. **Majestic** our poet flatteringly observes, but it is a majesty of terror, not of dignity. The other translation seems favorably to compare this mighty terror with a mountain of loot. Even

7 Thou, *even* thou, *art* to be feared: and
who may stand in thy sight when once thou
art angry?
8 Thou didst cause judgment to be heard
from heaven; the earth feared, and was still,
9 When God arose to judgment, to save
all the meek of the earth. Selah.

7 But thou, terrible art thou!
Who can stand before thee
when once thy anger is roused?
8 From the heavens thou didst utter judgment;
the earth feared and was still,
9 when God arose to establish judgment
to save all the oppressed of the earth.
Selah

3. The Judgment of Heaven (76:7-9)

7-9. The terribleness of God's anger as manifested in his judgments of men. Probably the psalmist looked upon such judgments as a recurrent feature of God's government of the world.

8. Men of the earth are judged by the standards of heaven.

9. All the oppressed of the earth: It is noteworthy that God is solicitous over **the oppressed** (preferable to KJV's **the meek**), and that if **the earth** means all the habitable earth, his concern is with the afflicted of all nations.

the piles of the spoils of war, which are after all creditable witness to the spoiler's prowess, are less grand, we are told, than he who towers above the prey. If perchance the word **prey** is taken to mean those slain in battle, the picture of the mountain of victims is as macabre a sight as our studies are likely to put on exhibition. **Glorious art thou, more majestic than the everlasting mountains** (of the dead).

Note, furthermore, how completely the enemies were immobilized. They were not weaklings; they were stout of heart and strong of hand; but without lifting a weapon the Lord frightened his opponents into prostrate submission. Stupefied by this prodigious apparition, their hands let fall the spoil they held; palsy seized them, weapons were useless; the God of Jacob shouted his remonstrance, and riders were unhorsed to lie sprawling among their fallen mounts (vss. 5-6).

At this point our poet seems to pause to catch his breath. He is bewitched by the spectacle of irresistible terror he has called up in his imagination. There is almost a note of rapture as once again he pays the flattering compliment to the hero. **But thou, terrible art thou!** Then he introduces a new component into the factor of terror—the aroused **anger** of God. The ravening lion stalked his prey; and if he roared, men called it fury, though it was free from the wrath that makes man formidable. When man is ravenous in war, there is a temper without which he cannot win. He must be angry, for anger gives excuse to ruthlessness; it is the black cloud of passion that darkens the sun of reason. All this our singer saw in his hero, and it promised him still greater miracles of conquest. Indeed, he wonders if there is anyone who can stand up to him, and, again as if to flatter him, asks:

Who can stand before thee
when once thy anger is roused?

All that he needs for complete and unchallenged dominion is terror instigated and armed by anger. For observe that it is not only the adversary that is now prostrate; it is the whole **earth.** Standing erect and terrible, his head pierced the heavens, and from his mouth thundered judgment. Not the judgment of law, we correctly surmise, but the arbitrament of power stirred to fury by aroused anger. What was the earth's response? Like the stunned and stupefied stout of heart (vs. 5), the earth feared and was still (vss. 8-9). This our poet, with a concession born of deference rather than of consistency, calls the execution of justice for the downtrodden.

We have already referred to the much used—and in this connection much misunderstood—aphorism to the effect that **the wrath of men shall praise** God. In order to keep this idea in its proper perspective we must see the wrath of men placed over against the wrath of God, before which no man can stand (vs. 7). Surely praise as an act of worship must be badly confused if it can or must use wrath as its vehicle. Here wrath is not understood to be the wrath of man against his fellow man or against evil or injustice; it is clearly the wrath of man against God. It is man's anger meeting the anger of God. This allows no place for praise; on the contrary, it renders praise impossible. Our poet here has a much more realistic understanding, grim though it is. He is picturing

10 Surely the wrath of man shall praise thee: the remainder of wrath shalt thou restrain.

11 Vow, and pay unto the LORD your God: let all that be round about him bring presents unto him that ought to be feared.

12 He shall cut off the spirit of princes: *he is* terrible to the kings of the earth.

10 Surely the wrath of men shall praise thee;
the residue of wrath thou wilt gird
upon thee.
11 Make your vows to the LORD your God,
and perform them;
let all around him bring gifts
to him who is to be feared,
12 who cuts off the spirit of princes,
who is terrible to the kings of the earth.

4. PERFORM YOUR VOWS (76:10-12)

10. The Hebrew is not free from suspicion, and various emendations have been proposed, but the RSV retains the M.T. **The wrath of men shall praise thee:** This presumably means that man's wrath and enmity against God are finally absorbed into the divine purpose and turned to God's praise (cf. Isa. 45:24; Exod. 9:16). **The residue of wrath:** Perhaps anger not overtly expressed in words or deeds. **Thou wilt gird upon thee** rather than **shalt thou restrain.**

11. This verse indicates that the psalm was used in conjunction with some cultic act in the sanctuary (cf. gifts brought to the temple in Jerusalem after 701 B.C., II Chr. 32:23). **Him who is to be feared:** One word in Hebrew, used also in Isa. 8:12-13.

12. Cf. 48:4-6.

man, standing in impotent rage before God the terrible, and he clearly discerns that this is the highest compliment that man can unwillingly pay God. God, we are being told, is not flattered by the submission of man. So utterly is he the Terrible One that man's wrath is to him adoration! And as if to make sure that this will not be misunderstood, we see the giant figure draping his massive torso with the tatters and remnants of man's futile fury: **the residue of wrath thou wilt gird upon thee.** If this is not exquisite sarcasm, it is the nadir of perversity.

11-12. ***Pay Vows to the Mighty One.***—There is a final admonition to the browbeaten peoples of the earth to make vows and perform them and to bring gifts to this Lord God of war. The demand is not softened by gentler reasons. The reason is still that God is terrible; as a vintager plucks the grapes and presses them, so will he strip and crush the spirit of the princes, while their royal elders cringe before his terror. Desperation makes vows and produces gifts, but they conceal the heart's bitterness and hide the restless resolutions of revenge.

It may be felt that such an interpretation as has been given here is overdrawn. Granted that the poet leaves unsaid much that is necessary to a complete understanding of the divine nature, has he intended to be as stentorian as the interpretation has made him? Perhaps not; but therein lies a matter important for us to ponder. The danger of all one-sided understandings is that they concentrate at one point the interest in the subject that should be distributed over a complete and therefore balanced view. This makes for overemphasis, disproportion, bias, and deception. This is what has happened to our poet's song about God the Terrible.

There is something to be said for the role of God described here, but since it is not all of God, it has been overdrawn. God is not terrifying to those who have no need to fear him. Is then our poet revealing something significant about himself in his portrayal of God? It is altogether possible that something within his soul was hospitable to the notion of terror. It may have been sadism that delighted in the pain and death of others and that projected these satisfactions upon the cosmic scene. Or it may have been that a hidden sense of guilt, in spite of himself, invited the rod he saw laid upon others. It is such unconscious factors in our own experience that should teach us caution in the uses we make of our idea of the frightening aspect of the power, the austerity, the implacable justice of God. There has always been a proper emphasis on these in preaching that is designed to confront man with God. There has also been an improper emphasis that has resulted in a presentation of God that in itself is non- or anti-Christian, and that in its effects on people has been spiritually pernicious. It may indeed be a terrible thing to fall into the hands of an angry God, but this predicament is to be more accurately described than falling, and the sinner may discover that God's hands are skilled no less in consolation than in chastisement. If it is necessary for us to speak of God as terrifying, we shall be well

To the chief Musician, to Jeduthun, A Psalm of Asaph.

77 I cried unto God with my voice, *even* unto God with my voice; and he gave ear unto me.

To the choirmaster: according to Jeduthun. A Psalm of Asaph.

77 I cry aloud to God,
aloud to God, that he may hear me.

LXXVII. An Appeal to the God Who Works Wonders (77:1-20)

This is an unusual psalm which Gunkel (*Einleitung in die Psalmen,* p. 258) is obliged to classify as a mixed type. Vss. 1-10 are in the manner of a lament of the individual, but unlike most laments these verses are not concerned with the author's personal sickness and misfortunes or with the animosity of his enemies. The psalmist's plea is that God may hear him. He speaks of trouble in vss. 2, 4, but he does not specify its nature; in vss. 7-9 he implies that God's compassion is no longer manifested.

advised to ask ourselves first whether the prospect of the sinner's fate is secretly gratifying to us, or whether our wish for his punishment is not a projection of our own unconfessed sense of guilt. When Jesus predicted the destruction of Jerusalem, he used language that might have fitted the mood of our poem, but there was no exultation in his heart; there were tears in his eyes.

To this it is necessary to add that it is just as easy to overemphasize the gentler aspects of the nature of God. As the terror of God is felt only by those who have secret reasons for fearing him, so also is the mercy of God felt only by those who have a need, consciously or unconsciously, for God's forbearance. So also is he the shepherd to those who are shepherdless, or host at a table in the presence of enemies to those who are too frightened by life to partake freely of God's sustenance. Each of these varying aspects of the nature of God presents itself to us in response to some deep spiritual need and creates its own particular mood, which, as has been often said in this Expos., is autonomous as long as it lasts.

If this is to be summarized in a general proposition, it is that, for reasons which we are now more fully equipped to discern than ever before, our understandings of life are very largely a response to the inner needs of our spirits. By the same token, our apprehension of God is a reflection of the nature of our need for him, need that is often so deeply protected against exposure that it is not seen for what it is except by those who have learned and practiced the discipline of self-analysis and criticism. This accounts for the so-called contradictory ideas about God found in the poetry of the Hebrew people. It is not that God is inconsistent or contrary in his nature. To resolve such apparent inner contradictions has been the unsolvable problem of the literalist, who reads in Ps. 23 that God is a shepherd and in Ps. 76 a terror. It is furthermore the problem that strict verbalistic revelation cannot even understand. A God objectively seen as terrible cannot be seen objectively as tender; but a God who responds to one's subconscious guilt feelings as terrifying can also respond to one's confession of sin as mercy, forgiveness, and redeeming love.

This was understood in the first century, even though we persist in losing sight of it in the twentieth. There is a creative synthesis in the divine nature that absorbs all man's diverse and conflicting categories. "In him there is no variation nor the slightest suggestion [ἀποσκίασμα] of change" (Jas. 1:17 Weymouth). The problem lies in the kaleidoscope of one's own experience, or in the varieties of religious experience and explication of all who have dealt with it. Herein then, and by this canon of interpretation, we can make profitable use of the effervescent enthusiasm of our Asaphite singer who wrote of an aspect of God that to him or to his times was a response to an unquiet spirit. If we refuse to bring God gifts because we do not fear him, let us make and perform vows to him for other and better reasons. If we do not believe that it is possible that the wrath of men can praise him, let us cultivate and exhibit moods that can. If we have boldness to stand before him when his anger is aroused (vs. 7), let it be because perfect love has cast out fear. If we doubt that he has crushed the youthful spirit of princes, let us yield our spirits to him for his indwelling. Thus in a way beyond the intention of our poet it can be said,

In Judah God is known,
his name is great in Israel.

77:1-4. ***The Sorrows of Man.***—To many lovers of his poetry Tennyson's *In Memoriam* will always be regarded as his greatest work. It not only represents the highest level of his achievement as a craftsman; it also records

2 In the day of my trouble I sought the Lord: my sore ran in the night, and ceased not: my soul refused to be comforted.

2 In the day of my trouble I seek the Lord;
in the night my hand is stretched out without wearying;
my soul refuses to be comforted.

With vs. 11 the tone of the psalm at once changes, and from here to the end we have a hymn. Its theme is God's mighty deeds in the past. The interest is in God's saving acts on behalf of the nation (**thy people** of vss. 15, 20). Thus light is shed on the lamentation of vss. 1-10. It is now apparent that the psalmist is troubled not by personal sorrow, but by a calamity that has visited the whole community. In the midst of this disaster God's voice appears to be silent and his hand stayed. As the author views this dreadful situation his only solace is to cast his mind's eye back on some of the ways in which the Lord has acted in the past on behalf of Israel. We may well believe that it is his hope, though unexpressed, that God will redeem his flock once again.

Some doubts have been voiced about the unity of the hymnic section, vss. 11-20. Vss. 16-19 are in the 3+3+3 meter, whereas the rest of the psalm is mostly 3+3. This fact, added to the difference in content, sets these four verses somewhat apart from the earlier ones, but is not conclusive evidence that they come from a different author.

The mention of **Jacob and Joseph** in vs. 15 has been taken to indicate that this psalm comes from northern Israel. If this is so, a date in the second half of the eighth century B.C. is likely (Leslie favors 733-721 B.C.). If, however, the two aforementioned names are being used loosely, with no necessary allusion to the north, there is nothing else within the psalm pointing to the place and time of its origin. Any dark moment in the nation's history might serve as its background. Buttenwieser's date of 344 B.C. is entirely conjectural.

1. A Cry for Help (77:1-10)

The lament of an individual, inspired by the troubles of his people. There is no discoverable strophic scheme that meets with general acceptance. Gunkel's divisions are vss. 1-4, 5-10.

77:1. The tenses of the Hebrew verbs used here are troublesome. The RSV obviates part of the difficulty by dropping the conjunction **and** before the first verb (with LXX, Jerome, and Syriac).

2. My hand is stretched out: I.e., in prayer. The Hebrew is curious, as the verb would normally mean "is poured out." The KJV takes יד (**hand**) to mean **sore** (cf. Job 23:2), but this is improbable.

---

the deepest level of his religious experience. Inspired by a great personal bereavement, it formulated the doubts that normally assail others similarly bereft, doubts that shook the whole structure of his faith, doubts that for one reason or another are the common lot of humanity.

> That loss is common would not make
> My own less bitter, rather more.
> Too common! Never morning wore
> To evening, but some heart did break.[6]

It is this that attracts the reader; not a morbid preoccupation with loss or a secret delight in doubt, but the fact that individual perplexity seems to find solace in the fact of the universality of human uncertainty.

[6] Part VI, st. ii.

The concern of our poet in this psalm is identical with that of Tennyson's masterpiece. Indeed, there is a striking parallelism between them in approach, treatment, and conclusion. In the brief compass of twenty verses the psalmist says what Tennyson says in one hundred and thirty-one cantos. This of course implies no judgment on the merits of the two poems; it simply means that in ages as separate and different as those of the psalmist and Tennyson, the same concern activated the poetic urge and produced poems that have been given an important place in the experience and literature of vital religious faith.

While it is true to say that religion is the expression of man's faith, it may be equally true to say that it is an expression of his doubt. Because one believes one thing he doubts an-

3 I remembered God, and was troubled:
I complained, and my spirit was overwhelmed. Selah.
4 Thou holdest mine eyes waking: I am
so troubled that I cannot speak.
5 I have considered the days of old, the
years of ancient times.
6 I call to remembrance my song in the
night: I commune with mine own heart:
and my spirit made diligent search.
7 Will the Lord cast off for ever? and will
he be favorable no more?

3 I think of God, and I moan;
I meditate, and my spirit faints. *Selah*
4 Thou dost hold my eyelids from closing;
I am so troubled that I cannot speak.
5 I consider the days of old,
I remember the years long ago.
6 I commune[h] with my heart in the night;
I meditate and search my spirit:[i]
7 "Will the Lord spurn for ever,
and never again be favorable?

[h] Gk Syr: Heb *my music*
[i] Syr Jerome: Heb *my spirit searches*

---

4. My eyelids: The expression occurs only here in the O.T., and is, lit., "the lids [guards] of my eyes." The accompanying verb is, lit., "thou dost grasp."

5. The remembrance of better days is the theme of Job 29; cf. Tennyson (paraphrasing Dante), "A sorrow's crown of sorrow is remembering happier things" ("Locksley Hall"). **I remember the years long ago:** The verb **I remember** is taken from vs. 6, where it is the first word of the M.T.

6. I commune: This verb (הגיתי), which is also the first word in vs. 12, is an emendation supported by the LXX and the Syriac. The M.T. is **my music (my song** KJV). **I . . . search my spirit:** A small emendation, with versional support. The M.T. is found in the KJV and the RSV mg.

---

other; e.g., it is difficult to see how one can believe in the claims of God without doubting the claims of whatever at the time is the opposite of God. Doubt is not the opposite of faith; it is collateral to it. The angry interdict of orthodox faith against doubt that in its own way may be quite as orthodox, rests on a shallow understanding of the relation of the two. It regards doubts as a stubborn repudiation of manifest truth. Parallel to this error is that which regards faith as an obstinate insistence on manifest absurdity. *Credo quia impossibile est,* is the expression of this latter error, which seeks protection of intellectual respectability by talking about the "paradox of faith." It has been said of Kierkegaard: "To be a Christian meant to him to suffer dialectically in the passionate, personal appropriation of the absurd, namely that God became man, eternity entered time. This was the supreme paradox of Christian faith." [7] In the religious experience of the average man, however, neither of these extremes takes shape. His doubt is not perversity, it is a sense of the contingent, the obscure, the complex. Similarly his faith is not paradox or perspicuity, it is serenity or trust.

These are the things our poet is saying in the overtones that may be heard above the plain melody of his song, said not by argument but by a revelation of a state of mind, a condition of soul. It is a fairly healthy moral condition. So far as any actual reference is concerned, he is free from a sense of sin. He describes his mood with bold and unmistakable metaphor, but nothing he confesses about his state of mind shuts him up to faithlessness or fear. In fact, as he describes what has taken place during a time of great perplexity, he is pointing forward to a description of his emergence into a time of equally great confidence. This is therefore a poem about doubt, the sort of doubt that has always been the stout ally of religious faith.

7-10. *Reasons for Man's Doubt.*—Not until we reach vss. 7-10 do we have a statement of what it is about God that has puzzled the poet. It is not that he doubts the fact of God. Six words are used to describe the God he had known: **favorable, steadfast love, promises, gracious, compassion.** He is convinced that this God has changed: **It is my grief that the right hand of the Most High has changed.** We may intellectually reject this ancient idea of the instability or even capriciousness of the nature of God, but emotionally we do not so easily set it aside. To our poet something had happened to God. This had created a disturbing contingency. He had once had faith in a favorable God; must he change to faith in a God who spurns, who forgets, and who in anger shuts up his compassion? The doubt he registers is the uncertainty such a situation produces.

I meditate and search my spirit:
"Will the Lord spurn for ever,

[7] Nels F. S. Ferré, "Present Trends in Protestant Thought," *Religion in Life,* XVII (1947), 340.

8 Is his mercy clean gone for ever? doth
his promise fail for evermore?
9 Hath God forgotten to be gracious?
hath he in anger shut up his tender mercies?
Selah.
10 And I said, This *is* my infirmity: *but*
I will remember the years of the right hand
of the Most High.

8 Has his steadfast love for ever ceased?
Are his promises at an end for all time?
9 Has God forgotten to be gracious?
Has he in anger shut up his compassion?" *Selah*
10 And I say, "It is my grief
that the right hand of the Most High
has changed."

8*b*. His promises: This word in the M.T. is in the absolute singular, "word," **promise** (possibly in a collective sense); it is improved by a slight emendation, the addition of **his** (אמרו).

9. The answer to this question is found in Isa. 49:15-16.

10. It is my grief or **This is my infirmity:** Either translation calls for a repointing of one word, חלותי, to secure the infinitive construct Qal. **That the right hand . . . has changed:** This interpretation of שנות (as the infinitive of "to change") was noted, but not adopted, by Calvin; it is, however, now accepted by most scholars. The KJV takes the word as **years.**

and never again be favorable?
Has his steadfast love for ever ceased?
Are his promises at an end for all time?
Has God forgotten to be gracious?
Has he in anger shut up his compassion?" ***Selah***

There is nothing sullen or querulous about this; it is honest inquiry, a doubt that seeks an escape from a dilemma.

How deeply this perplexity has touched the psalmist is indicated in both the emotional and rational emphases of vss. 1-2. He feels remote and rejected, and only by raising his voice can he make himself heard over the frightening distances that separate him from God. **I cry aloud to God, . . . that he may hear me.** Listen to Tennyson again:

> Forgive these wild and wandering cries,
> Confusions of a wasted youth;
> Forgive them where they fail in truth,
> And in thy wisdom make me wise.[8]

It is important to note also the emotional quality of the psalmist's doubt. He is in trouble but this does not drive him to a denial of God. He pictures himself as a searcher during the hours of daylight in quest of the confidence he has lost. As the dark night closes over him he continues his quest, his hand stretched unwearyingly before him, feeling his precarious way through the darkness. If this is doubt, it is a noble thing. Furthermore, we may infer that he has argued with himself, or perhaps with others, as to the folly or futility of his ceaseless searching, and his soul has refused to be comforted either by the counsels of hope or despair. A modern poet, Gamaliel Bradford, himself a vigorous doubter and a tireless searcher, put it thus in his poem "God":

> But my one unchanged obsession, wheresoe'er my feet have trod,
> Is a keen, enormous, haunting, never-sated thirst for God.[9]

The psalmist put it his own way:

In the day of my trouble I seek the Lord;
in the night my hand is stretched out without wearying;
my soul refuses to be comforted.

This refusal of his soul is not the willful repudiation of manifest truth, but the collateral resource of energetic faith trying to move out of contingency to confidence.

In the midst of this emotional cloud the psalmist sought for the guiding light of the mind. Doubt such as his is often emotionally induced; it would therefore be allayed by an escape from tension into the relaxation of calm reflection. How make the escape? That he had difficulty has been made very clear by three intimations (vss. 3-4). He has said that his soul wandering in darkness refused to be comforted. This was the failure of introspection, the nearest and in some ways the most dangerous of pitfalls. The tendency to turn inward is common to the perplexed, and if it results in critical self-examination it has its value. But it is extremely difficult to be constructively critical under emotional stress, and to fail is to invite a deepening of the darkness. So our doubter, admitting his difficulty, turned in another direction: he thought of God. This orientation has been for many the way of finding certainty. Not for

[8] *In Memoriam,* Prologue, st. xi.

[9] From *Shadow Verses* (New Haven: Yale University Press, 1920). Used by permission.

11 I will remember the works of the LORD: surely I will remember thy wonders of old.

12 I will meditate also of all thy work, and talk of thy doings.

13 Thy way, O God, *is* in the sanctuary: who *is so* great a God as *our* God?

14 Thou *art* the God that doest wonders: thou hast declared thy strength among the people.

15 Thou hast with *thine* arm redeemed thy people, the sons of Jacob and Joseph. Selah.

11 I will call to mind the deeds of the LORD;
yea, I will remember thy wonders of old.
12 I will meditate on all thy work,
and muse on thy mighty deeds.
13 Thy way, O God, is holy.
What god is great like our God?
14 Thou art the God who workest wonders,
who hast manifested thy might among the peoples.
15 Thou didst with thy arm redeem thy people,
the sons of Jacob and Joseph. *Selah*

---

2. Praise the Lord for His Wonders of Old (77:11-20)

13. Thy way . . . is in the sanctuary: This is a possible translation and is supported by the Masoretic pointing; for the thought cf. 73:17. **Thy way . . . is holy,** however, is favored by most commentators, **holy** being considered correlative to **great** in the next line. In this context **holy** probably signifies metaphysically unique and morally majestic. With the second half of the verse cf. Exod. 15:11. **What god:** A tacit recognition, perhaps only rhetorical, of the existence of other gods. The last word in the verse in the M.T. is "like God." The LXX and the Syriac read **like our God,** which is followed by the KJV and the RSV.

14-15. Possibly an allusion to the great deliverance wrought at the time of the Exodus. **The sons of Jacob and Joseph:** A phrase found only here in the O.T. It may mean that the psalm's origin is in northern Israel (cf. 80:1; 81:4-5), but on the other hand the terms may refer to the whole nation.

---

nothing have the saints of all the ages given themselves to the healing discipline of contemplation. But it is not uniformly successful, a fact which the experience of our poet points out. Contemplation became for him a most frustrating effort. Instead of his spirit being uplifted toward confidence, it is cast down; instead of invigoration, fainting; instead of rest, wakefulness; instead of certainty, he is speechless with trouble. We have here of course four symptoms of emotional disturbance that are no less common now than they were then. In modern language they are called depression, nervous fatigue, insomnia, and aphasia. There is a degree of pathology suggested by these terms that does not necessarily represent our doubter's state; but the symptoms are there, however mild or grave they may have been.

11-15. *Evidences for Faith.*—In such a condition doubt and its cognate moods are inescapable. It is not merely that, having turned from fruitless thinking about himself, the psalmist found thinking about God unrewarding. If his rational powers were to be invoked to help him resolve the emotional difficulty which had clouded his once-radiant faith, it was necessary for his thought to be directed toward matters about which the greatest objectivity was possible. To think about himself and God introduced subjectivism in some of its most subtle aspects. What was necessary, if his mind was to help him, was to achieve a perspective on his problem that would enable him to see himself in relation to objective facts. It was not until he did exactly this that his mood changed. He thought of himself, and his soul refused to be comforted; he thought of God, and his spirit fainted; then he set his problem in a frame of reference that included the world of fact and experience (vs. 5). This is called extrapolation by the modern therapist, who seeks to enable his emotionally unstable patient to fix his interest on some substantive datum around which emotion can be integrated. That our poet did just this has already been shown in vss. 7-10. He took himself out of the shadow and fatigue of his reflections about himself and God and set himself on a peak from which he surveyed past experiences of his own and of his people. He asked questions, but they dealt with matters that could be described by such words as **favorable, steadfast love, promises, compassion,** etc. He registered his grief—something different from doubt—that God seemed to have changed, but it was grief based on what for the moment at least took shape in his mind as objective fact.

16 The waters saw thee, O God, the waters saw thee; they were afraid: the depths also were troubled.

17 The clouds poured out water: the skies sent out a sound: thine arrows also went abroad.

18 The voice of thy thunder *was* in the heaven: the lightnings lightened the world: the earth trembled and shook.

16 When the waters saw thee, O God,
when the waters saw thee, they were afraid,
yea, the deep trembled.
17 The clouds poured out water;
the skies gave forth thunder;
thy arrows flashed on every side.
18 The crash of thy thunder was in the whirlwind;
thy lightnings lighted up the world;
the earth trembled and shook.

16-19. These verses are taken by many to be a reference to the crossing of the Red Sea at the time of the Exodus. In that case we must grant that they give us a very free treatment of the material in Exod. 14. It is equally plausible that we have here an independent poem, not necessarily by a different author, wherein Israel's God is portrayed as one whose glory is revealed in the thunderstorm, as in Ps. 29 (cf. Hab. 3:10-15; cf. also the Ugaritic Baal as the lord of the storm [Gaster, *Thespis,* p. 182, ll. 5-10]). Another suggestion is that there is, particularly in vs. 16, an echo of God's primeval conquest of the watery chaos in the period of the Creation (see Exeg. on 74:13-15). Still another view is that elements from the three interpretations just cited are inextricably mingled in these verses.

16. The deep or **the depths:** The plural of the word which occurs in Gen. 1:2.

17. The Hebrew word "voice," **sound,** here means **thunder. Thy arrows:** Bolts of lightning.

18. In the whirlwind or **in the heaven:** The word גלגל usually means "wheel," and only here does it seemingly designate a **whirlwind.** Some scholars, changing the preceding preposition to "like," translate "like chariot wheels."

Here was a solid spot on which to stand: it was the remembered acts of the Lord that he would mobilize as allies against his doubt. Six words indicate that they were not the figments of a disturbed or darkened mind. He called them **deeds, wonders, work, way, might.** General terms, to be sure, but descriptive of God's acts in history, acts that proved the quality of his power, his greatness, and his concern for his people. It was these that our poet set over against his insubstantial ruminations about himself and God. The final reference to **Jacob and Joseph** is of particular interest. Surely the plight of Jacob, when a fugitive and a doubter, was as unpromising as a man could experience. So also Joseph, sold into slavery, represented in the history of the Jews the nadir of ill-fortune. These men by the mighty power of God had been made patriarchs of a great nation. In the light of such historic testimony, what standing could the poet's momentary uncertainty about his own fortunes have?

16-20. ***The Supremacy of God.***—Already we detect a lift in the poet's mood. The facts of history had restored his confidence; the myths of history now invite his rapture. In a passage of epic intensity and intention he sees God not only as the arbiter of history but as the lord of nature. And nature in her most formidable aspect: the quaking abyss of the sea, the lightning-riven torrents of rain, the terror of the reeling wind; upon and through this colossal threatening God walked and left no footprints where he had gone.

Is vs. 20 a summary or a conclusion? **I cry aloud to God,** the poet said as he began. He concludes:

> **Thou didst lead thy people like a flock**
> **by the hand of Moses and Aaron.**

As conclusion it seems abrupt; in fact, scholars are agreed that what originally was the concluding stanza must have been lost in editorial transmission, or that this verse belongs in the section in which reference to God's hand in history is made. This is of no great matter for us. What we have before us, whether fragmentary or not, is a clear emergence from the cloud in which our poet was shrouded as be began. From perplexity about the validity of his own trust and shame over his doubt, he has moved to an affirmation of God as a shepherd, leading his people like a flock by the hands of mortal

19 Thy way *is* in the sea, and thy path in the great waters, and thy footsteps are not known.

20 Thou leddest thy people like a flock by the hand of Moses and Aaron.

Maschil of Asaph.

78 Give ear, O my people, *to* my law: incline your ears to the words of my mouth.

19 Thy way was through the sea,
thy path through the great waters;
yet thy footprints were unseen.
20 Thou didst lead thy people like a flock
by the hand of Moses and Aaron.

A Maskil of Asaph.

78 Give ear, O my people, to my teaching;
incline your ears to the words of my mouth!

---

19. Thy footprints were unseen: Lit., **are not known,** the psalmist's recognition that God's workings often leave no visible trace (cf. Job 9:11; 23:8-9).

20. This verse, in 3+3 or 3+2 meter, interprets the preceding verses as pertinent to the Exodus tradition, and points the truth that God's cause is often furthered by dedicated ordinary people. On the Lord's leadership at the Exodus see 78:52-53; Exod. 13:21; 15:13; on that of **Moses and Aaron** see Num. 33:1. Moses and Aaron are mentioned together elsewhere in the Psalter only in 99:6; 105:26; 106:16.

LXXVIII. The God Behind Israel's History (78:1-72)

This is a didactic ballad, and like Pss. 105; 106; 114, it uses some of the old traditions —in this case about the Exodus and the early days in Canaan—to teach a religious lesson. It is therefore not merely a recapitulation of past events; its aim is to show how God has been working in and through Israel's history. The psalmist is a Judean, as is clear from his conclusion (vss. 67-72), and he has perhaps some animus against Ephraim.

---

men who had trusted him in times of great and overbearing trial.

We return to the experience of doubt as a factor in religious faith. What we have seen in our poet is neither disaffection nor disobedience. He had lost God, and in his bereavement he asked whether the reason was in the darkness that had engulfed his mind or in some change that had altered the divine nature. Not until he was able to set his thoughts on what he could remember of God's doings in the history of his people could he lift from himself the heaviness that had depressed him. This seems to have been the way in which his doubt was turned to affirmation.

A good deal has been made of the symptoms that indicate that his doubt was basically emotional, and there is warrant for that idea here. However, this is not to say that all doubt is emotionally grounded; or that where it is, the therapy that was successful in this case will be successful in all others. This is clearly the story of one man's doubt and of his cure, and it may have useful suggestions for all men's doubts. What it can say to us without assuming too much is that when we confront religious perplexity, or hear the voice of doubt raised either in plaintive or angry tones, we may well look for its causes. The time should have long since passed when in the name of faith doubt could be the object of scorn or denunciation. The skeptic mood that corrodes into cynicism or abuse is not doubt. It has passed from its original state to something essentially demoralizing or destructive. We shall therefore be well served if we make this distinction. Religion's debt to its heretics and sturdy doubters is still slowly acknowledged and parsimoniously recompensed, even though by any reckoning it is immense. "The just shall live by faith" (Heb. 10:38); in a very real way faith shall live by doubt. Our ancient poet has said this to us as positively as his modern colleague. Said the psalmist: **Thy way was through the sea, . . . yet thy footprints were unseen.** Said Tennyson:

> Tho' truths in manhood darkly join,
> Deep-seated in our mystic frame,
> We yield all blessing to the name
> Of Him that made them current coin.[1]

78:1-72. ***History in Song.***—In the Expos. of Ps. 74 it was pointed out that the Psalter makes room for the teaching type of poem that is common to all literature. Because the lore of a

[1] *In Memoriam,* Part XXXVI, st. i.

But his main interest is in Israel as a whole, and by telling of **the glorious deeds of the Lord** (vs. 4) and of his wrath toward a sinful people (vs. 21), he hopes both to encourage and to warn the nation.

The date of the psalm has been variously estimated. The principal points to be considered are: (*a*) No major disaster appears to have befallen Judah; (*b*) the temple is referred to (vs. 69) in such a way as to suggest that Solomon's building is still standing; (*c*) the Davidic dynasty is still ruling in Jerusalem; (*d*) the use of **the Holy One of Israel** in vs. 41 (see Exeg., *ad loc.*) points to the influence of the prophet Isaiah; (*e*) there is no clear reference to the fall of Samaria, 722 or 721 B.C.; (*f*) Judah (or the psalmist) is convinced that the Lord has rejected Ephraim. These features of the psalm can be satisfactorily accounted for by positing an eighth-century date (Calès suggests a little before 722 B.C.; Buttenwieser, *ca.* 701 B.C.); Schmidt proposes near the end of the seventh century B.C., and Oesterley "a comparatively late period" after the P document.

The preceptive use of history, which the psalm exemplifies, is not a useful criterion for determining the author's date. The prophet Amos utilized fragments of tradition for preaching purposes (2:9-11; 3:1-2; 5:25; 9:7), as did Hosea (11:1-5), and from their time onward this became almost a standard practice of prophets and writers (Deut. 32:1-43; Judg. 2:11–3:6; Jer. 2:4-28; Ezek. 20:1-49; Neh. 9:1-38; etc.).

What sources the psalmist was dependent upon for his knowledge of the past we do not know. It is obvious that some of his details differ from those in Exodus (cf. Exeg. on vss. 20, 43-51), but it is a moot point whether our sources, even in the form of the J and E documents, were available to him. Moreover, it is impossible to say how much liberty he exercised when he adapted such traditions as he had to his immediate purpose.

---

people can best be remembered if it is sung over and over in folk songs or repeated in rhythms that give movement to fancy, the minstrel and the troubadour have served in a very important way as the custodians of history. Their intention may have been less to preserve a tradition than to entertain an audience, but the irresistible cadence and the unforgettable rhyme were often greater aids to memory than the most dramatic episode or the most emphatic gesture. When Byron wrote "The Destruction of Sennacherib," his version of II Kings 19:35-36, he no doubt thought he was writing poetry, not history, but there are many who remember Sennacherib and his army in the lines:

> The Assyrian came down like the wolf on the fold,
> And his cohorts were gleaming in purple and gold,

who never heard of them in the "and it came to pass" version in II Kings. They do not stop to ask whether the uniformed cohorts were actually as splendid as Byron describes them. The facts of history might have represented them as a drab or even bedraggled lot. It is enough for recollection that "fold" and "gold" end their respective iambic pentameters with a thumping and rememberable accent.

The psalmist, in the metrical patterns of his time, sets out in this psalm to tell a story to which an appropriate moral will be appended. The poem is full of devout references to God in his various aspects, but there is nowhere an address to the Deity or an exhortation to praise. It is simply a record, though hardly a simple one. Since the poet's purpose is to make a case by the selection of historic episodes, he has given to literary critics considerable puzzlement. He is clearly partisan, his historic sense is distorted by political bias, he is not able to sift the chaff of myth out of the grain of fact; and since he has an ax to grind, he forgets or ignores facts that do not suit his purpose, or transposes them so that they will. This is a criticism that could come only from a time such as our own when history is trying to become a science; it is therefore not to be taken as a disparagement of the poet or his purpose. It does help to explain, however, certain gaps and overweighted references. What we may reasonably be sure of is that those who heard and learned this song never forgot what it was intended to convey.

1-8. ***Strength in a Sense of Tradition.***—On this last point our poet-pedagogue is quite explicit. **Give ear, O my people, to my teaching. . . . I will utter dark sayings from of old, . . . that our fathers have told us** (vss. 1-3). The sense of tradition is strong, and he will not knowingly depart from it, since his purpose is to instruct rather than to entertain. Nor does he fail to state that his concern reaches beyond his immediate hearers to those who will in their own way pass the tradition along to their chil-

2 I will open my mouth in a parable: I
will utter dark sayings of old:
3 Which we have heard and known, and
our fathers have told us.
4 We will not hide *them* from their children, showing to the generation to come the praises of the LORD, and his strength, and his wonderful works that he hath done.
5 For he established a testimony in Jacob, and appointed a law in Israel, which he commanded our fathers, that they should make them known to their children:

2 I will open my mouth in a parable;
I will utter dark sayings from of old,
3 things that we have heard and known,
that our fathers have told us.
4 We will not hide them from their children,
but tell to the coming generation
the glorious deeds of the LORD, and his might,
and the wonders which he has wrought.

5 He established a testimony in Jacob,
and appointed a law in Israel,
which he commanded our fathers
to teach to their children;

Opinions vary about the psalmist's literary artistry. His ode, to our Western taste, displays some prolixity, and the arrangement of the historical material (cf. the introduction of the plagues in vss. 43-51) might perhaps have been improved. On the other hand, while the author uses no regular strophe scheme, he displays a sense of literary form, and the main divisions of his poem commence in a way which gives a pleasing rhythm to the psalm as a whole (cf. vss. 9-10, 17-18, 21-22, 32, 40-41, 56-57). The meter is 3+3 with the usual variations.

There is no evidence within the psalm of its connection with the temple cultus. Its contents, however, would make it suitable for recitation at one of the festivals, particularly the Passover.

1. Summons to the People to Listen (78:1-8)

A solemn introduction to the psalm in two parts. Vss. 1-4 have something of the tone of a wisdom psalm (see Exeg. on 49:1-20): they purport to pass on to the present generation what the fathers have heard about **the glorious deeds of the LORD** (vs. 4). Vss. 5-8 are more somber: the fathers are to teach the children so that the latter will not repeat the **stubborn and rebellious** conduct of their ancestors.

78:1. Give ear: Cf. 49:1; Prov. 4:1, 10, 20; 5:1; etc. **My teaching** is preferable to **my law** (cf. the usage in Prov. 1:8*b*; 3:1*a*; 6:20*b*; etc.).

2. Parable . . . dark sayings: See Exeg. on 49:1-4; cf. Prov. 1:6. **Dark sayings** in this context mean lessons drawn from Israel's past. This verse is quoted somewhat freely in Matt. 13:35.

4. Cf. Deut. 4:9; 6:7; 11:19; 32:46. **Glorious deeds:** Lit., **praises.**

5. The meaning of **testimony** and **law** depends on the date assigned to the psalm. If the poem is early, then the reference is to the general body of Israel's religious teaching from Moses onward; if it is late, the terms refer to the Pentateuch.

---

dren. He even warns that not all he is to say will be palatable to their pride, yet this will not deter him (vs. 4). And though he does not promise it, he plans to set over against the glory of God the sin and the ignominy of Ephraim, Jacob, Israel, and Joseph.

The most important fact in the life of the Hebrew people was what our poet refers to as **testimony** and **law**, and there is no understanding either of their history or of their attempts to understand history apart from this fact. Our concern at this point is not to ask how that law came about; it is to take account of two basic considerations: first, that in going back to their origins, they always found God, God as creator and lawgiver; second, that the law was established not to please the lawgiver, but to provide the people with a pattern of continuity explicit in an order of law. Life for the individual and the nation was not improvisation to meet emergencies; it was following the pattern God had given his people as a protection against

6 That the generation to come might know *them, even* the children *which* should be born; *who* should arise and declare *them* to their children:
7 That they might set their hope in God, and not forget the works of God, but keep his commandments:
8 And might not be as their fathers, a stubborn and rebellious generation; a generation *that* set not their heart aright, and whose spirit was not steadfast with God.
9 The children of Ephraim, *being* armed, *and* carrying bows, turned back in the day of battle.
10 They kept not the covenant of God, and refused to walk in his law;
11 And forgat his works, and his wonders that he had showed them.

6 that the next generation might know them,
the children yet unborn,
and arise and tell them to their children,
7 so that they should set their hope in God,
and not forget the works of God,
but keep his commandments;
8 and that they should not be like their fathers,
a stubborn and rebellious generation,
a generation whose heart was not steadfast,
whose spirit was not faithful to God.

9 The E'phraimites, armed with[j] the bow,
turned back on the day of battle.
10 They did not keep God's covenant,
but refused to walk according to his law.
11 They forgot what he had done,
and the miracles that he had shown them.

[j] Heb *armed with shooting*

---

8. Stubborn and rebellious: The same words are applied to the disobedient son in Deut. 21:18.

2. Disobedience of the Fathers (78:9-20)

9. The M.T. seems confused, and the historical references are not clear. Many scholars believe that the text requires emendation. If **Ephraim** means what it manifestly means in vs. 67, then **Ephraimites** denotes the northern tribes. The latter either are being made responsible for the refusal of the people to attack Canaan (Num. 14:1-10), or their performance in the subsequent invasion is being belittled (Judg. 1:22-36). The RSV drops one word of the M.T., רומי, and translates נושקי קשת as **armed with the bow** (cf. I Chr. 12:2; II Chr. 17:17).

---

themselves, their brethren, and their enemies. There was to be no alternative to the law. Therefore those who flouted it found God's hand heavy upon them. They might destroy themselves, but the testimony and the law were imperishable. This our poet makes clear (vss. 5-7). From father to children, from the **next generation** to **children yet unborn** and to their children, the intention of the testimony and the law was to be realized in two ways: they should set their hope in God, and they should keep his commandments. Here hope represents the long view, as keeping the commandments represents the immediate obligation. These are the two elements without which progress and social cohesion are impossible.

There were always in the past those who could be cited as examples of the way not to do it. Because they had not their hope in God, they were **not steadfast**—words that mean insecurity and unsteadiness.

> **A generation whose heart was not steadfast,**
> **whose spirit was not faithful to God** (vs. 8*b*).

Lacking this hope, they scorned to observe the testimony; they were **a stubborn and rebellious generation** (vs. 8*a*). In order that the children of the unborn generations **should not be like their fathers** (vs. 8*a*), the great testimony must be spoken, and it was to this that our poet invited his audience.

9-16. ***A Case of Broken Faith.***—The evidence, both for the fixity of the law and for the folly of flouting it, must be made more specific than the mere reference to **fathers.** Just why the

12 Marvelous things did he in the sight
of their fathers, in the land of Egypt, *in* the
field of Zoan.
13 He divided the sea, and caused them
to pass through; and he made the waters to
stand as a heap.
14 In the daytime also he led them with
a cloud, and all the night with a light of fire.
15 He clave the rocks in the wilderness,
and gave *them* drink as *out of* the great
depths.
16 He brought streams also out of the
rock, and caused waters to run down like
rivers.
17 And they sinned yet more against him
by provoking the Most High in the wilderness.
18 And they tempted God in their heart
by asking meat for their lust.
19 Yea, they spake against God; they
said, Can God furnish a table in the wilderness?
20 Behold, he smote the rock, that the
waters gushed out, and the streams overflowed; can he give bread also? can he provide flesh for his people?

12 In the sight of their fathers he wrought marvels
in the land of Egypt, in the fields of Zo'an.
13 He divided the sea and let them pass through it,
and made the waters stand like a heap.
14 In the daytime he led them with a cloud,
and all the night with a fiery light.
15 He cleft rocks in the wilderness,
and gave them drink abundantly as from the deep.
16 He made streams come out of the rock,
and caused waters to flow down like rivers.

17 Yet they sinned still more against him,
rebelling against the Most High in the desert.
14 They tested God in their heart
by demanding the food they craved.
19 They spoke against God, saying,
"Can God spread a table in the wilderness?
20 He smote the rock so that water gushed out
and streams overflowed.
Can he also give bread,
or provide meat for his people?"

12-14. Zoan (Rameses, Avaris, or Tanis) was a city in the northeastern part of the Delta of Egypt (modern Ṣan el Ḥagar, about twenty-five miles west of the Suez Canal). It is best known as the chief center of the Hyksos kings (*ca.* 1730-1580 B.C.), but it also served as the Delta capital of Seti I (1318-1299 B.C.) and of Rameses II (1299-1232 B.C.). On vs. 13 cf. Exod. 14:21-31. On vs. 14, cf. Exod. 13:21; 14:19-20.

15-16. Cf. Exod. 17:6; Num. 20:1-13.

17-20. The discontent in the desert: the demand for food (cf. Exod. 16:1-3; Num. 11:4-35). **Tested** (vs. 18) rather than **tempted. They craved:** Lit., "for their soul," i.e., "for their hunger" or "for their appetite." Vs. 20 implies that the **water** from the **rock** was given before the manna and the quails, but that is contrary to the traditions of both Exodus and Numbers (food: Exod. 16:1-36; Num. 11:4-35; water: Exod. 17:1-7; Num. 20:1-13). **Behold, he smote: Behold** or an equivalent should appear in the RSV.

Ephraimites are brought in as an exhibit is not easy to say, but the nature of their deliberate refusal and its consequences are clear. Vs. 10 says:

> **They did not keep God's covenant,**
> **but refused to walk according to his law.**

This was a clear case of breaking faith, though vs. 11 extenuates somewhat their infidelity: **they forgot.** It is the oldest defense, though in this case the long list of the things forgotten is so formidable as to allow the suspicion that our poet was rather rubbing it in. If the Ephraimites had managed to forget all these prodigies (vss. 12-16), one wonders if they managed to remember anything at all!

17-31. ***Rebellion and Challenge.***—We have noted that the first thing our poet wants to say is that God's testimony was given his people that they should be continuously secure by its observance. Therefore it must be passed on from generation to generation. Those who defied it forfeited both hope and security (stead-

21 Therefore the LORD heard *this*, and was wroth: so a fire was kindled against Jacob, and anger also came up against Israel;
22 Because they believed not in God, and trusted not in his salvation:
23 Though he had commanded the clouds from above, and opened the doors of heaven,
24 And had rained down manna upon them to eat, and had given them of the corn of heaven.
25 Man did eat angels' food: he sent them meat to the full.
26 He caused an east wind to blow in the heaven: and by his power he brought in the south wind.
27 He rained flesh also upon them as dust, and feathered fowls like as the sand of the sea:

21 Therefore, when the LORD heard, he was
full of wrath;
a fire was kindled against Jacob,
his anger mounted against Israel;
22 because they had no faith in God,
and did not trust his saving power.
23 Yet he commanded the skies above,
and opened the doors of heaven;
24 and he rained down upon them manna
to eat,
and gave them the grain of heaven.
25 Man ate of the bread of the angels;
he sent them food in abundance.
26 He caused the east wind to blow in the
heavens,
and by his power he led out the south
wind;
27 he rained flesh upon them like dust,
winged birds like the sand of the seas;

3. THE MANNA AND THE QUAILS (78:21-31)

Although the Lord bestows manna and quails, he is roused to anger against his people.

22. **Saving power or salvation:** See Exeg. on 74:12.

23. **The doors of heaven:** A phrase found only here; cf. "the windows of heaven" in Gen. 7:11.

24. **Manna** is mentioned only here in the Psalter (cf. Exod. 16:1-36; Num. 11:1-35). A modern study concludes that the biblical manna was "the liquid honeydew excretion of a number of cicadas, plant lice, and scale insects [which] speedily solidifies by rapid evaporation" (F. S. Bodenheimer, "The Manna of Sinai," *The Biblical Archaeologist*, X [1947], 6). **Grain of heaven:** A phrase found only here; cf. "bread of heaven" in 105:40 (quoted in Neh. 9:15; John 6:31-32).

25-26. **Bread of the angels:** Lit., "bread of the mighty ones." Manna is so described only here in the O.T. (cf. Wisd. Sol. 16:20). For **angels** as mighty ones cf. 103:20. We may note that Jewish exegetes of the early Christian period doubted if there was either eating or drinking among the angels (G. F. Moore, *Judaism* [Cambridge: Harvard University Press, 1927], I, 405). On vs. 26 cf. Num. 11:31.

27-29. The sending of the quails (cf. Exod. 16:13; Num. 11:31-32).

fastness). Ephraim, the symbol of revolt, **forgot** God and so refused to keep the agreement with God. But was this the real season? In the verses that follow we find Ephraim joined with Jacob and Israel in a conflict with the Most High. Forgetfulness has passed over into rebellion and challenge (vss. 17-20). It is not an illogical transition. Rebuked for forgetting past miracles, they **tested God in their heart** concerning present affairs. Suppose he had done mighty works in other days; what of their hunger at the moment? **Can he . . . give bread or provide meat?**

This seems to have been regarded as an insolent question. Were not the testimony and the law to be for all generations? How then doubt their operation at the moment? As our poet warms up to his story, he presents the Lord reacting in fiery **anger.** They will have an answer to their impertinent challenge, but little satisfaction in it. Vss. 21-31 give a poetic recapitulation of a familiar story, but a new motive—God's **wrath**—introduces and closes it. There follows the description of God's demonstration of his power in overwhelming the people with abundance. But it was a spurious response to their challenge, for the reason that their challenge was spurious. So, as they gorged themselves with miraculous food, **the anger of God rose . . . and he slew the strongest . . . and laid low the picked men of Israel** (vss. 30*b*-31).

28 And he let *it* fall in the midst of their camp, round about their habitations.

29 So they did eat, and were well filled: for he gave them their own desire;

30 They were not estranged from their lust: but while their meat *was* yet in their mouths,

31 The wrath of God came upon them, and slew the fattest of them, and smote down the chosen *men* of Israel.

32 For all this they sinned still, and believed not for his wondrous works.

33 Therefore their days did he consume in vanity, and their years in trouble.

34 When he slew them, then they sought him: and they returned and inquired early after God.

35 And they remembered that God *was* their rock, and the high God their redeemer.

28 he let them fall in the midst of their
camp,
all around their habitations.
29 And they ate and were well filled,
for he gave them what they craved.
30 But before they had sated their craving,
while the food was still in their mouths,
31 the anger of God rose against them
and he slew the strongest of them,
and laid low the picked men of Israel.

32 In spite of all this they still sinned;
despite his wonders they did not believe.
33 So he made their days vanish like a breath,
and their years in terror.
34 When he slew them, they sought for him;
they repented and sought God earnestly.
35 They remembered that God was their rock,
the Most High God their redeemer.

30-31. Before they had sated their craving: Lit., "They had not become strangers to their desire." On vs. 31 cf. Num. 11:33-34.

4. The Waywardness of the Nation (78:32-39)

The continued sin of the people did not extinguish the Lord's compassion. Yet his repeated clemency brought about no permanent reform in Israel (cf. Num. 14; 16–17).

33. Cf. Num. 14:29, 35; 26:64-65. **Breath** or **vanity:** See Exeg. on 39:4-6. **Terror** rather than **trouble.**

34. Sought . . . earnestly rather than **inquired early after.**

35. The same two appellatives are used for the Lord in 19:14. **Their rock:** See Exeg. on 28:1-2. **Their redeemer:** A title for the Lord appearing thirteen times in Isa. 40–66 (41:14; 43:14; etc.), and four times elsewhere in the O.T. The verb means "to act as a

---

32-66. ***The Mask of Forgetfulness.***—It develops, as we get on with our poem, that the excuse of forgetfulness was a fraud. **They remembered that God was their rock** (vs. 35). The fact was that they were playing moral hide-and-seek with God. In spite of the tragic experience in the wilderness (vs. 31), they served God only when they discovered that for the moment they could not escape him. Hidden behind the mask of forgetfulness was the face of deceit and lying. Vss. 36-37 well sum up the judgment of our poet on the conflict between the law resisters and the Giver of the law and testimony. More evidence is adduced (vss. 36-66) to show that it was nothing less than deliberate rebellion that corrupted their hearts. The catalogue of marvels wrought by **his hand** in Egypt failed to impress them for long; nor did the recollection of their escape from the bondage of serfdom hold their hearts in loyalty to him. The crowning beneficence, a new home in a promised and promising land, evoked only momentary satisfaction. Says our song:

He drove out nations before them,
he apportioned them for a possession
and settled the tribes of Israel in their tents (vs. 55).

With what results?

Yet they tested and rebelled against the Most High God,
and did not observe his testimonies,
but turned away and acted treacherously like their fathers;
they twisted like a deceitful bow (vss. 56-57).

36 Nevertheless they did flatter him with their mouth, and they lied unto him with their tongues.

37 For their heart was not right with him, neither were they steadfast in his covenant.

38 But he, *being* full of compassion, forgave *their* iniquity, and destroyed *them* not: yea, many a time turned he his anger away, and did not stir up all his wrath.

39 For he remembered that they *were but* flesh; a wind that passeth away, and cometh not again.

40 How oft did they provoke him in the wilderness, *and* grieve him in the desert!

41 Yea, they turned back and tempted God, and limited the Holy One of Israel.

42 They remembered not his hand, *nor* the day when he delivered them from the enemy:

43 How he had wrought his signs in Egypt, and his wonders in the field of Zoan:

36 But they flattered him with their mouths;
they lied to him with their tongues.
37 Their heart was not steadfast toward him;
they were not true to his covenant.
38 Yet he, being compassionate,
forgave their iniquity,
and did not destroy them;
he restrained his anger often,
and did not stir up all his wrath.
39 He remembered that they were but flesh,
a wind that passes and comes not again.
40 How often they rebelled against him in the wilderness
and grieved him in the desert!
41 They tested him again and again,
and provoked the Holy One of Israel.
42 They did not keep in mind his power,
or the day when he redeemed them from the foe;
43 when he wrought his signs in Egypt,
and his miracles in the fields of Zo'an.

---

kinsman," "to rescue from distress," and is applied to God in 74:2; Exod. 15:13; etc. The participle **(redeemer)** thus signifies "a friendly helper," "a savior from trouble."

36. According to the Jewish reckoning, the second half of the Psalter commences at this point. **They flattered:** A better translation of the Hebrew is "they deceived" or "they spoke deceitfully to."

37. The **heart** often signifies the mind, but here the will and purpose.

5. The Exodus in Retrospect (78:40-55)

Israel rebelled in the desert, and their rebellion was all the worse because they did not remember the great signs the Lord had wrought for them in Egypt. Thus the psalmist is launched on a review of the Exodus, with special attention to the plagues. In vss. 54-55, however, we find Israel settled in Canaan.

40. They rebelled against rather than **did they provoke.**

41-42. They turned back: The Hebrew is better taken adverbially, **again and again. Provoked** or "pained" is better than **limited. The Holy One of Israel:** This phrase is found twenty-four times in First and Second Isaiah, and only seven times in the rest of the O.T. (see Exeg. on 71:22). If the term originated with Isaiah, its use here may help to date the psalm. **His power: Lit., his hand.**

43-51. The plagues are here cited as illustrations of the Lord's miraculous acts on behalf of his people. The psalmist's account of these events differs considerably from that of Exod. 7:1–12:51 (as does Ps. 105:26-36). Whether the author knew the material of Exodus and treated it with poetic freedom, or whether he had only a limited knowledge

---

Note the sarcastic reference to the bowman's frustration.

The peak of infamy in the rebellion was the establishment of the graven images of heathen neighbors in the place of God. This act was more than ingratitude; it was repudiation, and to that there seemed but one answer: reciprocation. The people had turned away from God and taken the idols of another. He would turn away from them, and deliver to the enemy the symbols of his power and glory. It is not a pretty sight that is described, and it rises to its apex of frightfulness as God is presented as a strong man wakened from a drunken sleep, roaring with anger and scattering his adversaries to everlasting shame.

44 And had turned their rivers into blood; and their floods, that they could not drink.

45 He sent divers sorts of flies among them, which devoured them; and frogs, which destroyed them.

46 He gave also their increase unto the caterpillar, and their labor unto the locust.

47 He destroyed their vines with hail, and their sycamore trees with frost.

48 He gave up their cattle also to the hail, and their flocks to hot thunderbolts.

49 He cast upon them the fierceness of his anger, wrath, and indignation, and trouble, by sending evil angels *among them*.

50 He made a way to his anger; he spared not their soul from death, but gave their life over to the pestilence;

51 And smote all the firstborn in Egypt; the chief of *their* strength in the tabernacles of Ham:

44 He turned their rivers to blood,
so that they could not drink of their streams.
45 He sent among them swarms of flies, which devoured them,
and frogs, which destroyed them.
46 He gave their crops to the caterpillar,
and the fruit of their labor to the locust.
47 He destroyed their vines with hail,
and their sycamores with frost.
48 He gave over their cattle to the hail,
and their flocks to thunderbolts.
49 He let loose on them his fierce anger,
wrath, indignation, and distress,
a company of destroying angels.
50 He made a path for his anger;
he did not spare them from death,
but gave their lives over to the plague.
51 He smote all the first-born in Egypt,
the first issue of their strength in the tents of Ham.

of the Exodus tradition (perhaps in a form similar to that of the J document), are difficult questions to answer. In any case, he does not refer to the third, fifth, sixth, and ninth plagues, and the order of those he does mention is not the order of Exodus.

43-47. The plagues are termed **signs** and **miracles** or **wonders,** as in Exod. 7:3. **Zoan:** See Exeg. on vs. 12. On vs. 44, the water turned into **blood,** cf. Exod. 7:14-25 (the first plague). **Streams** rather than **floods. Swarms of flies:** Cf. Exod. 8:20-32 (the fourth plague). **Frogs:** Cf. Exod. 8:1-15 (the second plague). **Caterpillar:** חסיל (not mentioned in Exodus) is usually assumed to be a kind of locust; Montgomery and Gehman (on I Kings 8:37) take it to be a grasshopper (cf. *ḥsn,* "grasshopper," in Ugaritic). **Locust:** Cf. Exod. 10:1-20 (the eighth plague). **Hail:** Cf. Exod. 9:13-35 (the seventh plague, including thunder and fire). **Frost:** חנמל (not mentioned in Exodus) probably means a "devastating flood" (Ludwig Köhler, *Lexicon in Veteris Testamenti Libros* [Leiden: E. J. Brill, 1948-53]).

48. Their cattle to the hail: As **hail** (ברד) has already been referred to (vs. 47), some scholars believe the text is faulty, and they read with two MSS and Symm., דבר, "pestilence." This latter is the disease that attacked Pharaoh's cattle in Exod. 9:1-7 (the fifth plague). **Thunderbolts:** In the seventh plague of Exod. 9:13-35 thunder and fire accompany the hail. The Ugaritic parallel (רשף) suggests that the word here may mean "pestilence" (cf. Patton, *Canaanite Parallels,* p. 45).

49-51. The death of Egypt's **first-born:** Cf. Exod. 11:1–12:51 (the tenth plague). **A company of destroying angels:** The Hebrew, which is rather unusual, is, lit., "a company of messengers [or "angels"] of evil things." See Exeg. on "angel of the LORD" in 34:4-7. In Exod. 11:4; 12:12, 23, 29, the Lord himself goes through Egypt, but in Exod. 12:23 there is a reference to a "destroyer" (cf. "the destroying angel" in II Sam.

The end of this sort of thing is predictable: either a moral truce between law and rebellion, or a victory of law, or victory of lawlessness. This is to be the issue unless other elements can be introduced into the struggle. The rigor of law could be modified by the introduction of concessions to human frailty; the rebellious heart of man could be turned in contrition toward God; God could overlook men's rebellion, and in an act of forgiveness give him another chance. Short of some such expedient, moral stalemate results.

52 But made his own people to go forth
like sheep, and guided them in the wilderness like a flock.
53 And he led them on safely, so that
they feared not: but the sea overwhelmed
their enemies.
54 And he brought them to the border of
his sanctuary, *even to* this mountain, *which*
his right hand had purchased.
55 He cast out the heathen also before
them, and divided them an inheritance by
line, and made the tribes of Israel to dwell
in their tents.
56 Yet they tempted and provoked the
most high God, and kept not his testimonies:
57 But turned back, and dealt unfaithfully like their fathers: they were turned
aside like a deceitful bow.

52 Then he led forth his people like sheep,
and guided them in the wilderness like
a flock.
53 He led them in safety, so that they were
not afraid;
but the sea overwhelmed their enemies.
54 And he brought them to his holy land,
to the mountain which his right hand
had won.
55 He drove out nations before them;
he apportioned them for a possession
and settled the tribes of Israel in their
tents.

56 Yet they tested and rebelled against the
Most High God,
and did not observe his testimonies,
57 but turned away and acted treacherously
like their fathers;
they twisted like a deceitful bow.

24:16; I Chr. 21:15). **The plague:** Probably not a cattle disease (as in Exod. 9:3), nor a general pestilence (as in Exod. 9:15), but the mysterious ailment which killed off the first-born. **Ham:** Inasmuch as Ham, in Gen. 10:6, is given as the father of Cush, Egypt, and Put (all in northeastern Africa), it is not unnatural that **Ham** should be used here (and four times elsewhere in the O.T.) to designate Egypt and the Egyptians.

53. Cf. Exod. 14:26-31.

54. To his holy land rather than **to the border of his sanctuary. The mountain:** The mountainous country of Canaan, as in Exod. 15:17; Deut. 3:25. The Mishnah, however, interprets this as a reference to Mount Zion (Aboth 6:10). **Had won:** Patton (*ibid.*, p. 44) suggests that קנתה here means "created" (cf. Gen. 14:19, 22).

55. He drove out nations before them: For lists of the peoples who lived in Canaan before the Hebrews see Gen. 15:18-21; Exod. 3:8; Deut. 7:1; etc. **He apportioned them:** Cf. Josh. 23:4.

6. Israel in Canaan (78:56-66)

The scene is now in Canaan, in the period of the Judges and perhaps the early monarchy. The themes, however, are the same: the sinfulness of the people, the Lord's chastisement, and the Lord's mercy (cf. Judg. 2:11-23).

In dealing with this dilemma our author presents two singularly important elements in his quasi-historical poem that provide us with profound truth. The first is the author's description of the development of that state of mind which issues ultimately in rebellion; the second is God's ultimate measure for meeting man's sin. Forgetting the goodness of God is the first step toward rebellion against him; putting him to the test of satisfying our own selfish desires is the second; the third is uttering the lie against God; the fourth is substituting for God at the center of our loyalty idols of our own choosing. This four-stage descent to the Avernus of godlessness may not satisfy our modern attempts to explain the experience, but it is a strong testimony to the moral consciousness of the Hebrew tradition, and proof that at least in so far as God had designed that the law and the testimony were to be passed on to all generations, he has, to that extent, had his will.

Such, as our poet put it, is man's way to his doom. What of the way to redemption? The answer to this gives us the second profound insight. At a point in the poem that breaks boldly into a recital of man's rebellion, we have a reference to God that seems for the moment out of character. Confronted by man's deceit and God's punishment, man's cynical dishonesty and God's anger, one might expect

58 For they provoked him to anger with their high places, and moved him to jealousy with their graven images.

59 When God heard *this,* he was wroth, and greatly abhorred Israel:

60 So that he forsook the tabernacle of Shiloh, the tent *which* he placed among men;

61 And delivered his strength into captivity, and his glory into the enemy's hand.

62 He gave his people over also unto the sword; and was wroth with his inheritance.

63 The fire consumed their young men; and their maidens were not given to marriage.

64 Their priests fell by the sword; and their widows made no lamentation.

65 Then the Lord awaked as one out of sleep, *and* like a mighty man that shouteth by reason of wine.

66 And he smote his enemies in the hinder parts: he put them to a perpetual reproach.

58 For they provoked him to anger with
their high places;
they moved him to jealousy with their
graven images.
59 When God heard, he was full of wrath,
and he utterly rejected Israel.
60 He forsook his dwelling at Shiloh,
the tent where he dwelt among men,
61 and delivered his power to captivity,
his glory to the hand of the foe.
62 He gave his people over to the sword,
and vented his wrath on his heritage.
63 Fire devoured their young men,
and their maidens had no marriage
song.
64 Their priests fell by the sword,
and their widows made no lamentation.
65 Then the Lord awoke as from sleep,
like a strong man shouting because of
wine.
66 And he put his adversaries to rout;
he put them to everlasting shame.

---

58. High places: Local places for worshiping the Lord (e.g., I Sam. 9:12), but sometimes centers for paganistic practices, and hence frequently condemned (I Kings 15:14; 22:43; II Kings 18:4; 23:8; etc.).

60. Shiloh (Seilûn, about twenty to twenty-five miles north of Jerusalem), an early center of the Lord's worship, where the ark was deposited (Josh. 18:1; Judg. 21:19; I Sam. 1:3; 3:21; 4:3; etc.). Its destruction is referred to in Jer. 7:14; 26:6, but no details are recorded. **Where he dwelt:** A repointing of the M.T. with versional support. The Hebrew is "which he established."

61. His power or **his glory:** The reference is to the ark and its capture by the Philistines (I Sam. 4:1-22).

62-64. The defeat of Israel by the Philistines (I Sam. 4:10-11).

63. Fire: Probably war as a consuming fire. **Had no marriage song:** Lit., "were not praised."

65. A bold figure of the Lord awaking from sleep and **shouting** as though stimulated by **wine. Shouting:** Lit., "overcome."

66. Put his adversaries to rout: Lit., "smote his adversaries backward." Probably the allusion is to various victories over the Philistines (I Sam. 7:10-11; 13:3; 14:23; etc.).

---

this contest to go on to exhaustion or stalemate, but unexpectedly there is another note introduced. **Yet he, being compassionate, . . . did not destroy them.** Here in vss. 38-41 is compassion taking the place of justice, with little or nothing to prepare us for the transfer. The Holy One of Israel was provoked, the testimony and the law were affronted, and God **forgave their iniquity.** Why the *non sequitur?* Was the law proved mistaken? No, there was pardon, not the proof of innocence. Basically the reason lay in the nature of God, who is full of justice and mercy. He was angry, but his wrath was under restraint; he was furious, but he **did not stir up all his wrath;** he saw man's forgetfulness, his bickering, his deceit, his idolatry, and yet he remembered that men **were but flesh.** The metaphor changes bluntly: flesh—but not flesh; **a wind that passes and comes not again.** There is a mind of God where law demands justice; there is a heart of God that demands pardon. This is the paradox of law and grace that is encountered by all who are acquainted with the deeps of man's experience with the Eternal.

67 Moreover he refused the tabernacle of Joseph, and chose not the tribe of Ephraim:
68 But chose the tribe of Judah, the mount Zion which he loved.
69 And he built his sanctuary like high *palaces,* like the earth which he hath established for ever.
70 He chose David also his servant, and took him from the sheepfolds:
71 From following the ewes great with young he brought him to feed Jacob his people, and Israel his inheritance.
72 So he fed them according to the integrity of his heart; and guided them by the skilfulness of his hands.

A Psalm of Asaph.

79 O God, the heathen are come into thine inheritance; thy holy temple have they defiled; they have laid Jerusalem on heaps.

67 He rejected the tent of Joseph,
he did not choose the tribe of E'phraim;
68 but he chose the tribe of Judah,
Mount Zion, which he loves.
69 He built his sanctuary like the high heavens,
like the earth, which he has founded for ever.
70 He chose David his servant,
and took him from the sheepfolds;
71 from tending the ewes that had young he brought him
to be the shepherd of Jacob his people,
of Israel his inheritance.
72 With upright heart he tended them,
and guided them with skilful hand.

A Psalm of Asaph.

79 O God, the heathen have come into thy inheritance;
they have defiled thy holy temple;
they have laid Jerusalem in ruins.

---

7. God's Continuing Guidance (78:67-72)

Israel's waywardness receives no further mention, and the poem ends with marked placidity. Much history is covered in these few verses, but it is not presented chronologically. The chief emphasis is upon what the Lord did. It was he who rejected Ephraim and chose Judah, who built the sanctuary on Mount Zion, and who selected David as king. The psalmist leaves unsaid what must have been in his mind: such actions are an earnest of the Lord's continuing beneficence toward his people.

67-68. These verses reflect Judean feelings toward Ephraim, especially after Solomon's death (cf. I Kings 12:1–13:34; II Kings 17:1-23; Isa. 7:1–8:22).

69. Cf. I Kings 6:1-38. **Like the high heavens:** Lit., "like the heights."

70-72. The choice of David: Cf. I Sam. 16:1-23. These concluding verses of the psalm are doubtless an expression of confidence in the Davidic dynasty in Jerusalem. **His servant:** Almost an honorific title, applied in the O.T. to the patriarchs, Moses, Joshua, Caleb, David, Job, *et al.* **With upright heart:** The same phrase is used in reference to David in I Kings 9:4.

LXXIX. Help Us, O God of Our Salvation (79:1-13)

This lament of the community was occasioned by the assault of some unnamed Gentiles upon Judah. The country had been laid waste (vs. 7), Jerusalem ruined, and

---

67-72. ***Conclusion.***—It is on a gentle note that the song ends: Joseph and Ephraim disowned, Judah and Mount Zion beloved again, and David his servant, the shepherd of Jacob his people, guiding Israel with upright heart and skillful hand. The dilemma is not resolved, for there is still the process of disowning the faithless. But there are also love and solicitude and an enduring **sanctuary like the high heavens, like the earth, which he has founded for ever.** Nor is the dilemma likely to be resolved, for it holds the timeless paradox that has made law and grace the primary problem in the education of the mind of man and the primary hope in the redemption of man's soul.

79:1-13. ***Man and His Moral Relationship to God.***—There is strong evidence that the writer who goes by the name of Asaph was not

the temple defiled (vs. 1); blood had flowed like water, and the dead remained unburied (vs. 3). The taunts of Gentile neighbors (vss. 4, 12), who saw in these events the proof of the impotence of Israel's God (vs. 10), only added to the nation's bitter humiliation. Such was the situation that confronted the psalmist, and in the midst of it he rose to voice his people's plea for help. His first word was **God,** for he knew that only in the Lord was there any hope of salvation.

It is manifest that the background of this psalm is very similar to that of Ps. 74, and most commentators find in it a reference to a little-known or an unchronicled attack on Judah in the Persian or early Greek period (Buttenwieser favors 344 B.C. both for this psalm and for Ps. 74). It seems preferable however, for the reasons advanced in Exeg. on 74:1-23, to suppose with Calès that the Babylonian wars of the early sixth century B.C. give the psalm its proper setting. It is noteworthy that in the Christian centuries the Jews recited this psalm on the ninth of the month Ab, a fast day commemorating the two destructions of the temple (587 B.C. and A.D. 70). The practice may point to an old tradition associating the psalm with the Babylonian period.

The poem follows the general pattern of a lament (see Exeg. on 6:4-5 and 13:1-6). It has often been observed that some of the psalmist's language is similar to that found elsewhere (cf. vs. 4 and 44:13; vs. 5 and 89:46; vss. 6-7 and Jer. 10:25; vs. 10 and 115:2; vs. 11 and 102:20). These resemblances do not necessarily mean that our author was always dependent on the other writings, and indeed in the case of Jer. 10:25 the reverse was probably true. The original strophe arrangement may have been as suggested by the RSV. The meter is best described as irregular.

1. Mortification of the Nation (79:1-4)

79:1. Defiled thy holy temple: It has frequently been noticed that the temple is here stated to have been **defiled,** not destroyed, and it has been concluded that the

---

only gifted in producing original poems, but was similarly adept in piecing together, with a composite purpose, fragments of the work of others. This is clearly what has been done here (yet see Exeg.). There are at least fifteen such portions used here that have their parallels in other writings. If today's amenities of authorship had been observed when Asaph was writing, this piece would be liberally adorned with quotation marks or documented with footnotes.

There is no doubt that the poet's concern was deep and his grief genuine, however synthetic his composition may be. He was struggling with a problem that was old long before he had begun his literary career. The major religious and political premise of Israel was the unique relationship to God in which the nation stood. From this derived the idea that a special obligation rested on the Lord for the protection of his favored folk. This was a moral obligation; if it was shirked, some explanation was sought either in his temporary indifference, his anger, or his preoccupation with other matters. The inclination to indict God on moral grounds was doubtless beneath the surface of the other explanations that piety and plausibility could devise, but never in the writings of these ancients was so radical an interpretation hazarded. This is what is meant when it is said that there are no heretics in the O.T.

Unwillingness to confront head on the moral implications of the puzzling behavior of God was one of the reasons for the prevalence of moral immaturity and evasiveness in some of the relationships in which Israel as a nation and Israelites as individuals were involved. From modern perspectives, divine favoritism is morally indefensible. Lacking therefore the major premise of ancient Israel, modern men and nations should be able to arrive at more acceptable moral conclusions, provided of course that their major moral premise is more acceptable.

That our poet borrows the language of others indicates that it was a problem he shared with them. It follows that in so far as his approach to it fails to satisfy us, it must be taken to mean that the whole early treatment of it is unsatisfactory. We can allow ourselves to pass this judgment however only if we recognize that it is through the later developments of the Hebrew-Christian revelationship that moral insights adequate to the solution of our poet's trouble have been made available to us and to the world.

1-4. ***A Lesson Recalled.***—The appalling destruction of the city of Jerusalem, with its complete demoralization of all political and religious order, had once again set forth the problem in stark outline. There is disagreement

2 The dead bodies of thy servants have they given *to be* meat unto the fowls of the heaven, the flesh of thy saints unto the beasts of the earth.
3 Their blood have they shed like water round about Jerusalem; and *there was* none to bury *them*.
4 We are become a reproach to our neighbors, a scorn and derision to them that are round about us.

2 They have given the bodies of thy servants
to the birds of the air for food,
the flesh of thy saints to the beasts of the earth.
3 They have poured out their blood like water
round about Jerusalem,
and there was none to bury them.
4 We have become a taunt to our neighbors,
mocked and derided by those round about us.

---

psalm could therefore not have been written in the sixth century B.C. But the same verb is used in II Kings 23:8 to describe Josiah's defilement of the high places in 621 B.C., a procedure which must have involved their virtual destruction. While the temple was doubtless only defiled in 597 B.C. (II Kings 24:8-17), the physical destruction in Jerusalem was apparently small, and would hardly justify the statement in the last clause of vs. 1. **They have laid Jerusalem in ruins,** rather than **on heaps.** If this statement means that general havoc was wrought in the city, it is most unlikely that so imposing a structure as the temple would have escaped (for 587 B.C. see II Kings 25:8-10; on the contents of this verse cf. Mic. 3:12; Jer. 26:18; 51:51; Lam. 1:10).

2. Thy saints: חסיד, in the singular and plural, is found in a number of psalms. Basically it means "showing loyalty," in nearly all cases loyalty to the Lord. The RSV renders it in the Psalter as "godly," "loyal," "faithful," as well as **saints;** all these words express various aspects of its meaning.

3. This verse is quoted in I Macc. 7:17 with reference to an incident *ca.* 161 B.C. Lack of a proper burial was a great calamity (cf. Deut. 28:26; II Kings 9:10; Jer. 7:33; 8:2; 9:22; 14:16; 19:7).

4. A scorn and derision to them that . . . is a literal rendering of the Hebrew, and is preferable to the RSV. Except for the opening verb, this verse is identical with 44:13. It is also freely quoted in Dan. 9:16.

---

among scholars as to which destruction this refers to, nor do we know why disaster had befallen the city. Presumably there were reasons, but except for the general observation that their tormentors knew not the Lord and called not upon his name (vs. 6), our writer gives no cause for their barbarous aggression. Could Israel have invited it? No hint of this, a fact that in itself qualifies the moral mind of the times.

All we know is that in this atrocity Pelion had been piled upon Ossa by those who wanted to effect the ultimate in destructiveness. The take-over had been complete; to the physical destruction was added the indignity of the profanation of the temple. **O God, the heathen have come into thy inheritance.** This is a despairing summary, a statement of complete defeat. God's inheritance had fallen into the foul hands of the heathen. Here, as in other verses that follow, the loss was God's, even as the shame was his also. This extension of the effect of heathen aggression to God himself derives directly from the moral major premise already referred to; and our poet spares no words in his attempt to bring the realization home to the divine mind. The shame of it all! Unburied bodies, carrion birds and beasts preying on the flesh of God's saints, blood poured out like water, and none left amid the rubble to tidy up the mess or give decent burial to the dead. All this, our poet says, had happened to God. What was the fate of those who were spared?

We have become a taunt to our neighbors,
mocked and derided by those round about us.

To God the loss of city and saints; to them the humiliation and mockery. The taunt was an old one, and it touched the most vulnerable spot of their faith, viz., that they were God's favored ones. What sport the heathen could have with

5 How long, LORD? wilt thou be angry for ever? shall thy jealousy burn like fire?
6 Pour out thy wrath upon the heathen that have not known thee, and upon the kingdoms that have not called upon thy name.
7 For they have devoured Jacob, and laid waste his dwelling place.
8 O remember not against us former iniquities: let thy tender mercies speedily prevent us; for we are brought very low.

5 How long, O LORD? Wilt thou be angry
for ever?
Will thy jealous wrath burn like fire?
6 Pour out thy anger on the nations
that do not know thee,
and on the kingdoms
that do not call on thy name!
7 For they have devoured Jacob,
and laid waste his habitation.

8 Do not remember against us the iniquities of our forefathers;
let thy compassion come speedily to meet us,
for we are brought very low.

2. PLEA FOR THE LORD'S INTERVENTION (79:5-13)

5. **Jealous wrath** is preferable to **jealousy** (cf. Deut. 4:24). One cause of the nation's misfortune is the Lord's anger against his people.

6. The plural (**nations** or **kingdoms**) to designate Judah's foes is probably rhetorical. This verse, contrary to vs. 5, puts the blame for the national calamity on the Gentiles, and prays for their punishment. Such an attitude toward political enemies is common in the O.T. (e.g., Deut. 20:10-18; Zeph. 3:8; Jer. 10:25; Ezek. 25:1-17; see Exeg. on 109:1-31; 139:1-24).

7. Widespread destruction has occurred in Palestine.

8. Here and in vs. 9 another cause of Judah's troubles is brought to light, viz., the people's sins (not specified), and these in turn explain the Lord's wrath of vs. 5. **Former iniquities** is probably what the Hebrew means, rather than **the iniquities of our forefathers** (cf. Isa. 64:9; Deut. 5:9). **Come speedily to meet us** rather than **speedily prevent us, prevent** now being archaic.

that, amid the dust and stench of the demolished city!

5-12. ***Will the Lord Relent?***—Unready yet for modification of the major premise, some other expedient must be resorted to. The assumption that God suffered from this catastrophe of shame and loss was not dubitable. He was angry, and his jealous wrath was like an annihilating fire, but was that enough? God's fury could be a frustrating experience if it was to burn and burn and exhaust itself in flame. It had meaning for his favored people only as it consumed their enemies. **How long, O LORD?** the poet asks. To get the full emphasis we must supply the implication: How long is this sort of thing going to keep up?

Pour out thy anger on the nations
that do not know thee.

This gruesome proposal continues in vs. 12, after an interval of several verses. Here the sense of just requital has been blurred by the desire for vengeance. The suggestion is not that God should serve the mockers according to their deserts, but that they should be recompensed with sevenfold bitterness. Inevitably there comes to mind a more familiar exhortation about the "seventy times seven" forgiveness of one's offenders (Matt. 18:22).

One other verse (vs. 11) emphasizes the calamity. The city was rubble, and its dead inhabitants were exposed to the scavengers. One remnant is left. Can it be salvaged? Perhaps, if the ears of God can be opened to hear the cries of those prisoners on whom the sentence of death lay.

Let the groans of the prisoners come before thee;
according to thy great power preserve those doomed to die!

8-13. ***Prayer for Explanation and Vengeance.***—It seems hardly to have occurred to the writer of the poem that the fate of the city might have been punishment for its own sins, sins of infidelity to God or of aggressive and truculent and overweening attitudes toward neighbor peoples. The sins of their forefathers, however, rose to plague the mind. A scapegoat must always be

9 Help us, O God of our salvation, for
the glory of thy name: and deliver us, and
purge away our sins, for thy name's sake.
10 Wherefore should the heathen say,
Where *is* their God? let him be known
among the heathen in our sight *by* the revenging of the blood of thy servants *which*
is shed.

9 Help us, O God of our salvation,
for the glory of thy name;
deliver us, and forgive our sins,
for thy name's sake!
10 Why should the nations say,
"Where is their God?"
Let the avenging of the outpoured blood
of thy servants
be known among the nations before
our eyes!

---

9. Forgive our sins or **purge away our sins:** See Exeg. on 65:1-3.

10. Where is their God? is asked by the Gentiles in 42:3, 10; 115:2; Joel 2:17; Mic. 7:10. **Avenging** or **revenging:** On the vengeance of God see Exeg. on 94:1. In the second half of this verse the RSV is preferable to the KJV.

---

found by those who will not confess their own failures, and while generally speaking it would seem unfilial to blame one's misfortunes on one's forebears, at the same time even that is preferable to forthright self-indictment. Here was a possible explanation of God's strange behavior: maybe, remembering offenses of earlier evil times, he was bringing delayed retribution to the innocent present.

> **Do not remember against us the iniquities of our forefathers;**
> **let thy compassion come speedily to meet us,**
> **for we are brought very low** (vs. 8).

Following this the author presses back upon God the claim that he cannot afford to allow his name to be traduced. This, as we shall later see, is a claim that looks backward toward the ancient moral major premise and forward to more spacious understanding of the nature of God's relations to all mankind. In the present context it would appear to be concerned only with the backward glance. There is brief reference (vs. 9) to a passing and almost conventionalized sense of sin, but the solid emphasis falls on the fact that God has a reputation to save, honor to defend, a name to protect. How else was this to be done except by an act of summary vengeance? It was preposterous that there should be any question in the heathen mind as to the proprietary claim Israel had on God. If they persisted in asking about it, answer them! Observe that a grisly demonstration such as is set forth in vs. 10 would answer not only the dubiety of the heathen; if it were before the eyes of Israel also, it would help their doubts too.

To bring the matter to conclusion, our author, still keeping close to the moral premise implicit in all he has been saying, makes a promise. It almost has the appearance of being the *quid* offered for the *quo* that has already been asked. If God will save his reputation before the heathen, then his favored flock will recount his praises and give thanks to him forever. **Then we thy people, the flock of thy pasture** [the major premise], **will give thanks to thee for ever; from generation to generation we will recount thy praise.**

The moral difficulties created by the assumption that God has favorites are obvious to those who take time to reflect on them. They became increasingly plain as the experience of Israel with other cultures expanded, and it was the burden of later prophecy that there was as real a universalism in God's relation to the behavior of men as there was in his relation to the behavior of nature. It was against accepting this radical change of outlook that Jonah rebelled. It wounded his stubborn pride to be told that God's moral concern was as great for Nineveh as for Jerusalem. When our poet was taunted, mocked, and derided by those around him (vs. 4), he had no answer. The only language these people could understand was the fury of the Lord poured out on the scoffers (vs. 6).

That God is partisan to nations has long since been repudiated as a premise of our moral code. The reasons are simple. If God, a moral being, confers himself on us whom he has arbitrarily chosen to receive his grace, his favoritism becomes the criterion of his moral behavior. We are likely to place his acts in three categories: the benefits he offers us are good; the ill-fortune we suffer is in some cases tolerable, in many inscrutable; the behavior of God toward the unfavored is amoral. The highest moral level possible in dealing with others is justice; but this is rarely acknowledged because we are convinced, a priori, that only what is good for us, if we are God's favorite, is just. This means of

11 Let the sighing of the prisoner come before thee; according to the greatness of thy power preserve thou those that are appointed to die;

12 And render unto our neighbors sevenfold into their bosom their reproach, wherewith they have reproached thee, O Lord.

13 So we thy people and sheep of thy pasture will give thee thanks for ever: we will show forth thy praise to all generations.

11 Let the groans of the prisoners come before thee;
according to thy great power preserve those doomed to die!
12 Return sevenfold into the bosom of our neighbors
the taunts with which they have taunted thee, O Lord!
13 Then we thy people, the flock of thy pasture,
will give thanks to thee for ever;
from generation to generation we will recount thy praise.

11-12. On God's interest in prisoners cf. 102:20. **Those doomed to die:** Lit., "the children of death," a phrase found only here and in 102:20. **Sevenfold:** Cf. Gen. 4:15; Lev. 26:21, 28; Prov. 6:31.

13. The flock of thy pasture: See Exeg. on 74:1. Possibly between vs. 12 and vs. 13 some temple act was performed or some comforting priestly pronouncement uttered, which would explain the change in the psalmist's tone in vs. 13. In any case this verse is a reiteration of the faith which prompted his initial cry, viz., that the nation's only effective succor would come from God.

---

course that God is under no moral obligation to be good to the heathen. Those who do not know him, those kingdoms that do not call on his name (vs. 6), have no claims on his mercy. Their offense, over and above their ignorance, is that they have **devoured Jacob, and laid waste his habitation** (vs. 7), and such an affront to God's favorite is an affront to him. God's normal response to this affront is "jealous wrath," even though jealousy and wrath combine effectively to negate the impulse and operation of justice. Thus is demonstrated the moral shallowness that expects God to punish those who have injured us. It is vicarious vengeance, the exact opposite of vicarious atonement. Aside from its dubious moral quality, it is psychologically dangerous, for it tends to impart a sense of moral superiority to our satisfaction in the discomfort of those on whom the fury of the Lord has been poured out. Thus we minister both to pride and sadism in the name of righteousness.

This moral log jam gives way only when moral partisanship explodes into a moral universalism in which God has no narrow moral vested interests. His reputation is not tied to the fortunes of one people. **Help us, O God of our salvation, for the glory of thy name** (vs. 9) becomes "Help all, O God of mankind's salvation, for the glory of thy name." And because all mankind is guilty of moral failure, God will deal with all either with summary justice or with the grace of compassion. Thus in our thinking room has been made for the redemptive love that is the heart of the Christian revelation. Here compassion is not allowing to the unfavored the fortunes pre-empted for the chosen; it is the recognition that sin being universal, God's favor in forgiveness must also be universal.

We have noted that the idea of God as partisan to nations has long since been repudiated as a premise of our moral code. Unhappily, however, it has a mischievous way of insinuating itself into modern attitudes. It is an ingredient in all classifications that have reduced humanity to races, nations, and lesser groups. It is often the catalytic that precipitates out of the solution of universality the provincialisms that are from time to time held in suspension. Why? Because religion provides the ultimate sanction for man's quest for group security. He may be sure his fields will provide abundant food, but if there is no confidence that a transcendent moral ratification supports his use of it, he is spiritually insecure. Therefore he will invoke a god to guard his fields, and it is but a short step from concern for crops to the protection of social and political ideals and institutions. Religion is thus betrayed into becoming the proscriptive agent of nationalism, racism, and of all the parochialisms that dim man's realization of his universal identity.

Otherwise, why is it that in times of national difficulty men seize on the familiar words of the Bible that were the testimony of a primitive

To the chief Musician upon Shoshannim-Eduth, A Psalm of Asaph.

80 Give ear, O Shepherd of Israel, thou that leadest Joseph like a flock; thou that dwellest *between* the cherubim, shine forth.

To the choirmaster: according to Lilies. A Testimony of Asaph. A Psalm.

80 Give ear, O Shepherd of Israel,
thou who leadest Joseph like a flock!
Thou who art enthroned upon the cherubim, shine forth

LXXX. Restore Us, O God of Hosts (80:1-19)

This psalm is another testimony to Israel's resolute confidence in God. The people are in dire straits, yet their faith persists that the Lord still tends them like a **Shepherd** and that he can and will save them. As a lament of the community this poem is somewhat less specific than Pss. 74; 79 with respect to the particular circumstances which lie behind it. The people drink their own tears; the neighbors are scornful; the situation is such that the nation is likened to an unprotected **vine** which has become the prey of passers-by. But these complaints are so indefinite that not much history can be deduced from them.

There is some slight evidence that the author had a special interest in the Northern Kingdom. At least the allusions to **Joseph, Ephraim,** and **Manasseh** (vss. 1-2) can be so interpreted. The references to **Israel** and **Benjamin** in the same verses are more ambiguous. Possibly the psalmist was a northerner who, while having a primary concern for Ephraim, had the whole of Israel on his heart; cf. Jeremiah (3:11-13) and Ezekiel (37:15-28), whose interests were not exclusively Judean.

If the psalm comes from the north, it must presumably be dated not later than the eighth century. Both in the ninth and eighth centuries there were numerous occasions when such an appeal as this might very appropriately have been uttered (cf. II Kings 6:24-25; 7:32-33; 13:22; 15:17-22, 27-31; 17:1-6). In this connection we may note that the title of this psalm in the LXX ends with the phrase "Concerning the Assyrian."

The psalm is evidently intended for congregational use, and it may be assumed that at least the refrain (vss. 3, 7, 19) was recited by all the people. Opinions vary about

moral awareness and give them the status of moral finality? Also why is it that men's hearts have always yearned for true universalism and expressed it in utopian hopes and coalitions of peoples? Our poet was puzzled, and there are times when it is easy for us to appropriate his dilemma. There is, however, a higher level of moral apprehension on which our minds can move even in difficult days, and the effort to reach and redefine it is the best way out of difficult times. When we do this, we find the closing words of Ps. 79 expressing our chastened temper as well as they expressed the tentative and contingent faith of the writer.

80:1-19. ***God and the Meaning of History.***—A sense of history, as distinguished from the mere recollection of past events, is a sign of maturity. Without conscious manipulation, the disjunct episodes of the child's life begin to assume the appearance first of continuity and then of significance. This enables the child to make a beginning on the important job of understanding himself and his relation to events he shares with others. It is a paradigm of social growth. The development of broken ejaculations into sentences made continuity of discourse possible. Telling stories made continuity of experience possible. As folk tales became stereotyped, the gaps between episodes filled up, and the first adumbrations of the sense of history were seen. The record of social growth is found in the long process from primitive monosyllable to sophisticated history. Every linguistic and communicative device has been employed to make this possible: from grunt to grammar, from knotted string to reckless metaphor, from blazed forest trail to book index, the movement has gone on. Arnold J. Toynbee tells us that a civilization has reached maturity when it has a military establishment to protect it, a system of propaganda to rationalize it, a highly developed administrative system to give it internal stability, and a money currency to establish its credit. If these are factors in estimating social age, they are also helpful in understanding how mature cultures implement their sense of destiny, which is the moral imperative born of a sense of history. Depending on certain internal factors, it may be sinister or noble, edifying or destructive.

2 Before Ephraim and Benjamin and Manasseh stir up thy strength, and come *and* save us.

2 before E'phraim and Benjamin and
Manas'seh!
Stir up thy might,
and come to save us!

---

the strophic structure of the poem, but the RSV presents as reasonable a scheme as any. The M.T. of vss. 14-15 appears to have suffered somewhat, and the refrain may at one time have appeared after vs. 13. The meter is generally 3+3.

1. Opening Plea to God (80:1-3)

80:1. Shepherd of Israel: This title of the Lord appears only here in the O.T., but the idea is a familiar one (see Exeg. on 23:1-3; cf. 74:1; 78:52; 79:13; Gen. 49:24; Isa. 40:11; etc.). **Israel, Joseph:** The meaning of these terms in their present context is uncertain. Joseph sometimes signifies the Northern Kingdom (as in 78:67-68), as does Israel (I Kings 12:16). But Israel may refer to the whole people, north and south (II Kings 21:7-8), as well as to Judah only (Jer. 2:14; Neh. 10:33). **The cherubim:** A cherub was seemingly a winged lion with a human head; the notion came into Hebrew thought through sculptural practices in Canaan and Phoenicia, and these in turn were dependent on both Egypt and Mesopotamia (cf. Akkadian *karûbu,* "intercessor"). Thus a Byblos sculpture shows a winged sphinx supporting the throne of King Hiram of that city. Ezekiel's description of the cherubim (1:5-13; 9:3; 10:1-22) is an elaboration of the original conception. **Enthroned upon the cherubim** may refer either to the cherubim popularly supposed to bear up the throne of God (as in 18:10; Ezek. 1:1-28) or to the cherubim of Solomon's temple (I Kings 6:23-28; 8:6-7; cf. Exod. 25:17-22; I Sam. 4:4; II Sam. 6:2). We might suppose that the allusion to the cherubim would come most naturally from a Judean, but we do not know to what extent cherubim were used in the furnishings and decoration of sanctuaries in the Northern Kingdom. **Shine forth:** "Show thy power and glory for our salvation" (cf. 50:2; 94:1; etc.).

2. Benjamin: The O.T. sometimes groups this tribe with Judah to form the Southern Kingdom (I Kings 12:21, 23; II Chr. 11:1, 3, 23; cf. Jer. 1:1; 17:26; 32:44; 37:12), and sometimes with the north (cf. "one tribe" in I Kings 11:13, 32, 36). In Num. 2:18-24, Ephraim, Manasseh, and Benjamin are grouped together on the west side of the tabernacle in the march through the wilderness.

These generalizations are pertinent to our study of Ps. 80, for by one of the most familiar and liveliest of metaphors our poet presents—whether by design or poetic inspiration, no matter—what can within limits be called a philosophy of history. There is more in his poem than this; in fact, only four verses deal directly with it, but in a real sense much of the other material is auxiliary to it. Addressed to the choirmaster and set to the tune of "Lilies"—or as it may also be translated, "Anemones"—this clearly is a song written for liturgical purposes. For the most part the mood is somewhat lugubrious, though there are lyric touches of tenderness and beauty, and a refrain repeated three times breaks the doleful monotony with an elevating invocation to the God of hosts. Our author is again said to be Asaph, and his work is called **A Testimony.** This would seem to indicate at least that the earliest editors saw in it more than a song or a psalm.

1-3. *Invocation.*—The opening invocation makes use of one of the oldest images of the divine protector of the people—God, the **Shepherd of Israel.** This is one of five metaphors—God is the leader of the flock, the holy one above the cherubim, the God of hosts, the purveyor of food, and the planter of the vine—indiscriminately used to express varying moods, but following each there is the return to the brief and moving invocation that ends one strophe and allows the introduction of the next.

Give ear, O Shepherd of Israel,
thou who leadest Joseph like a flock!

This is so intimate and simple a figure of speech that it is something of a surprise to have the poet move in vs. 2 to the highly sophisticated idea of formal temple worship. Whatever else it may indicate, this extreme retreat from the pastoral metaphor shows that by the time of the poet a sense of history had become articu-

3 Turn us again, O God, and cause thy face to shine; and we shall be saved.
4 O LORD God of hosts, how long wilt thou be angry against the prayer of thy people?
5 Thou feedest them with the bread of tears; and givest them tears to drink in great measure.
6 Thou makest us a strife unto our neighbors: and our enemies laugh among themselves.
7 Turn us again, O God of hosts, and cause thy face to shine; and we shall be saved.

3 Restore us, O God;
let thy face shine, that we may be saved!

4 O LORD God of hosts,
how long wilt thou be angry with thy people's prayers?
5 Thou hast fed them with the bread of tears,
and given them tears to drink in full measure.
6 Thou dost make us the scorn[k] of our neighbors;
and our enemies laugh among themselves.

7 Restore us, O God of hosts;
let thy face shine, that we may be saved!

[k] Syr: Heb *strife*

---

3. The first appearance of the refrain (cf. vss. 7, 19). **Restore us:** Not necessarily from exile; probably the meaning is "restore us to our former estate." **Let thy face shine:** Cf. the Aaronic benediction in Num. 6:24-26.

2. DESCRIPTION OF THE NATION'S PLIGHT (80:4-7)

4. **LORD God of Hosts:** Although this name for Israel's God is not found in the Pentateuch, Joshua, or Judges, it occurs in the other historical books and is very common in the prophetic writings. It is used as one of the conventional titles for God, and is perhaps the one most expressive of his universal sovereignty, but its original meaning can only be conjectured. Some think it alludes to the Lord as the God of the armies of Israel, others as the Lord of the heavenly hosts, and others as the Lord of the totality of all earthly and heavenly creatures. The title displays minor variations in the O.T., too detailed to be discussed here. **How long wilt thou be angry:** Similar questions occur in 74:1; 79:5.

5. **The bread of tears:** A phrase found only here (cf. 42:3; 102:9; I Kings 22:27; Isa. 30:20). **In full measure:** Probably the meaning of the uncommon שליש.

6. The M.T. is **a strife unto our neighbors.** Many scholars, with the support of the Syriac, emend the first word to מנוד (cf. 44:14), and obtain **the scorn of our neighbors.** The derisive conduct of enemies is referred to in 39:8; 44:13; 79:4; etc.

---

late. From shepherd to the splendid One was a transition, not a break, even as from **flock** to **cherubim** represented an advance, not a reverse. Whether God was to be seen in the field with his flock or in the temple with the cherubim, he was the symbol of the power that could save Joseph the flock or Joseph the congregation. Then, as if to introduce a pause in the swinging rhythm of the song, there comes the first of the three invocative intervals.

Restore us, O God;
let thy face shine, that we may be saved!

4-7. ***Plea for Consideration.***—Again we encounter a sharp shift in metaphor. The enthroned One has been indifferent to the suppliants beneath the cherubim. They have prayed, but that God is still angry distresses them. Vs. 4 preserves the image of worshipers in the temple who wait for the splendor. Then the image of the shepherd tending his flock is changed slightly to that of the purveyor who aliments his charges. But it is cruel provender—both food and drink are one revolting essence, **tears!** It is as if, hoping for bread, a cup of tears was offered; and hoping for drink, more tears in meaningless abundance taunted their thirst. This is worse than an indifferent shepherd or remote splendor, or continuing anger; it is heartlessness. But there is further humiliation: the abandoned flock, the neglected worshipers, and the hungry are delivered over to their

8 Thou hast brought a vine out of Egypt: thou hast cast out the heathen, and planted it.

9 Thou preparedst *room* before it, and didst cause it to take deep root, and it filled the land.

10 The hills were covered with the shadow of it, and the boughs thereof *were like* the goodly cedars.

11 She sent out her boughs unto the sea, and her branches unto the river.

8 Thou didst bring a vine out of Egypt;
thou didst drive out the nations and plant it.
9 Thou didst clear the ground for it;
it took deep root and filled the land.
10 The mountains were covered with its shade,
the mighty cedars with its branches;
11 it sent out its branches to the sea,
and its shoots to the River.

---

3. Israel as a Ravaged Vine (80:8-13)

8. The portrayal of Israel as a **vine** or vineyard is found in Isa. 5:1-7; Jer. 2:21; Ezek. 17:1-10; Hos. 10:1; etc. The metaphor is carried over into the N.T. in Matt. 21:33-42 (cf. John 15:1-8). **The nations:** See Exeg. on 78:55.

10*b*. The Hebrew is unusual, but probably **the mighty cedars with its branches** represents the meaning. **Mighty cedars:** Lit., "cedars of God" (the same idiom in 36:6). **Cedars:** Usually assumed to be *cedrus libani,* which grew in Canaan (cf. Num. 24:6; Isa. 44:14) but which flourished best in Lebanon, whence its timber was imported by Israel (I Kings 5:10; etc.). As to whether the cedar of the O.T. was cedar or some other conifer, see Köhler, *Lexicon.*

11. On the borders of Israel see Exeg. on 72:8.

---

neighbors for their sport, and to their enemies for derision.

Thou dost make us the scorn of our neighbors;
and our enemies laugh among themselves.

These verses, it is important for us to realize, are more than a lament. They represent even in their grim disappointment a progression that holds these episodes together. Between the pastoral life under the eye of the shepherd and the formal temple worship there was a connecting fact: the experience of God. Even such dispiriting factors as are represented by God's anger, a diet of tears and the scorn and laughter of enemies, were not unrelated to the integrating principle of God that somehow informed them all. This is ratified by the second occurrence of the moving invocation (vs. 7). After humiliation at the hands of neighbor and enemy, there is the solemn pause, and then, if we can imagine it as it is sung, the rolling affirmation of unconquerable hope in light beyond darkness, and salvation beyond despair.

8-13. *Recollection of History.*—The lament is done; it has reached depths of bitterness broken twice by the solemn invocation to the God of hosts. The mood changes, and there is throughout the rest of the poem nothing of weeping, though joy is claimed for the future rather than appropriated for the immediate present. We have already noted two aspects of vss. 8-11: lyric beauty and a clear adumbration of a sense of history.

From the nomadic or pastoral phase to the relatively established planting phase is a fairly regular pattern of cultural progress. It is not claimed here that our poet is consciously outlining that direction of development when he begins with an invocation to God the shepherd and advances to a poetic description of God as a vinegrower. Indeed, greater significance may be thought to attach to the fact that he does this without being aware of it. What is important to us is that by the use of a metaphor which at the moment seemed to him to be apt, he introduces the idea of organism. The earliest lore of the Hebrews depicted God as a creator *ex nihilo,* a concept expressed early in the choice of Abram as the agent for the creation of a great people, elaborated by the quantitative simile of the sands of the sea and the stars of the sky (Gen. 22:17). Thus was the divine purpose thought to be fulfilled by direct creative action. Here, however, we see the divine purpose fulfilled by growth or organic action. There is a very great difference between a beach or a galaxy and a growing vine.

More interesting indeed is the statement that the plant which was to grow to such prodigious size was not God's creation; it was a root that had been growing in the fertile soil of Egypt. This, we remind ourselves, is not history; it is poetry. Nevertheless it represents a feeling, if

12 Why hast thou *then* broken down her
hedges, so that all they which pass by the
way do pluck her?
13 The boar out of the wood doth waste
it, and the wild beast of the field doth devour it.
14 Return, we beseech thee, O God of
hosts: look down from heaven, and behold,
and visit this vine;
15 And the vineyard which thy right
hand hath planted, and the branch *that*
thou madest strong for thyself.
16 *It is* burned with fire, *it is* cut down:
they perish at the rebuke of thy countenance.

12 Why then hast thou broken down its
walls,
so that all who pass along the way
pluck its fruit?
13 The boar from the forest ravages it,
and all that move in the field feed on it.

14 Turn again, O God of hosts!
Look down from heaven, and see;
have regard for this vine,
15 the stock which thy right hand
planted.[l]
16 They have burned it with fire, they have
cut it down;
may they perish at the rebuke of thy
countenance!

[l] Heb *planted and upon the son whom thou hast reared for thyself*

---

13. The boar from the forest: The only reference in the O.T. to the wild boar. The boar, as an unclean animal (Deut. 14:8), serves as an appropriate figure for Israel's foes. It would give us a more symmetrical poem if this strophe ended with the refrain found in vss. 3, 7, 19. Vs. 14 starts as though it were the beginning of the refrain, and possibly the text is corrupt. The Amer. Trans., Leslie, and Nötscher therefore introduce the refrain at this point (cf. Briggs, Kittel, Gunkel).

4. The Cry for Help Renewed (80:14-19)

15. Stock or **vineyard:** The word is found only here, and the meaning is uncertain. The RSV omits the second half of the verse **(and the branch that thou madest strong for thyself** KJV; cf. RSV mg.) as belonging properly to vs. 17*b*.

16. They have burned it with fire, they have cut it down: This represents a slightly emended text. The M.T. as set forth in the KJV is, however, passable. The RSV takes the subject of **perish** to be Israel's enemies.

---

not a rationale, for the actions of God. **Thou didst bring a vine out of Egypt.** Comment has been made about the lyric beauty of this section. To describe the agony of the Exodus and the wandering in the wilderness as the transplanting of a tender shoot from one garden to another is to the literalist no description at all, however satisfying it may be to the poet. But he goes on with the development of his imagery. Those who were cultivating their own vines were driven off the land (vs. 8*b*), and the chosen plot was prepared for the chosen vine (vs. 9*a*). Its roots reached down into the rich soil and the plant grew luxuriantly, overspreading the garden (vs. 9*b*). Here is magic growth, an early analogue to a later bean stalk in our own folklore.

There is no hint of doubt that this fertile land and extravagant yield were the doings of a Husbandman who favored Israel above all other plantings on the earth. Greater, then, the puzzlement when he who had brought the vine to such magnificent maturity broke down the walls that protected the garden and exposed it to the passers-by. They saw its value, but dishonored its planter. They despoiled it of its fruit; wild pigs—is this not a suggestion of the indignity of alien usurpation?—from the forest and beasts of the field roamed its broad expanse; and finally men, having exhausted its value to them, burned and cut it down with the wantonness of plunderers.

14-19. ***Prayer for Help.***—We are accustomed to the efforts of our poets to extricate themselves from confusion about the acts of God by assigning forgetfulness or indifference to him. Here the excuse for the vine's unhappy end is supplied by this familiar expedient. God has retreated from his vineyard; he is now the God of hosts in heaven. Nevertheless our poet sees no incongruity in asking that he revisit the vine that once was his delight (vss. 14-15). Of course our poet expects that the despoilers will be punished: **May they perish at the rebuke of**

17 Let thy hand be upon the man of thy right hand, upon the son of man *whom* thou madest strong for thyself.

18 So will not we go back from thee: quicken us, and we will call upon thy name.

19 Turn us again, O LORD God of hosts, cause thy face to shine; and we shall be saved.

17 But let thy hand be upon the man of thy right hand,
the son of man whom thou hast made strong for thyself!
18 Then we will never turn back from thee;
give us life, and we will call on thy name!

19 Restore us, O LORD God of hosts!
let thy face shine, that we may be saved!

---

17. The man of thy right hand: This may be an allusion to Benjamin ("son of the right hand"), though it is difficult to see why that tribe should receive particular mention. It is more probable that the meaning is "the man who has enjoyed thy favor" or "the man who has been nurtured by thy power" (cf. 18:35; 20:6; 21:8; etc.); thus we get good parallelism with the next stich. For **the right hand** as the place of honor see Exeg. on 110:1. **Son of man:** Lit., "a son of mankind," i.e., a human being (see Exeg. on 8:3-4). In both parts of the verse the reference is to Israel. The capitalization of **Man** and **Son** in some editions of the KJV reflects a messianic interpretation.

18. We will never turn back from thee: The only suggestion in the psalm that the people have been religiously perverse. At the same time this is a pledge of more faithful conduct in the future. The Hebrew is "We will not . . ."; there is no basis for the RSV's **never,** although the latter is used by both Calès and Buttenwieser.

---

thy countenance! This would be the just consequence of the discovery of their vandalism.

Whether with deliberate intention we do not know, but it seems that our poet, aware that his metaphor could be mistaken, adds a verse that supplies a key to it. This vine is, after all, **the son of man, the man** of God's **right hand.** In a word—avoiding the effort to extract all the possible implications of these two designations—the vine is God's chosen people Israel. It is they that have been planted and cultivated; it is they that have been cut down. If God will turn and restore them, they will turn again to him (vss. 17-18). The concluding verse returns us to the sonorous antiphon that we have already encountered twice. It is interesting that the frown of God's countenance (vs. 16) was thought to be as destructive to the enemy as the light of his face was salutary to his chosen.

Here we may return briefly to our original proposition: a sense of history is a sign of maturity. There will be little objection to the claim that whatever else its value, this poem is important because it exhibits a sense of history. Our author sees history as an organism; this is a concept generally accepted. History is also an organism planted and cultivated by God; this is a concept less generally accepted, but it lies at the heart of the Hebrew-Christian interpretation of history. No strain is put on the actual words of the poem if we draw from it two central propositions. The first affirms life in the processes of history: the divine design, preparation, planting, nurture, and full growth. This is at polar opposites from the idea of a seabeach of innumerable grains of sand, or a night sky ablaze with discrete and wandering stars. The second affirms that the processes of history can be interrupted by death. Life cannot guarantee its own immortality, whether in a single organism or in a group of organisms united to form a culture. Life and its abatement are God's prerogatives; the same husbandman fetched a vine from Egypt to plant in a favored spot and broke down its protecting walls and let the despoilers in.

This is the pattern that was followed in the life and death of the Hebrew culture as it found its expression in a nation. Were not other data conclusive for other dates (see Exeg.), this might be adduced to prove the poem to have been very late, e.g., at the time when the final destruction of Jerusalem was accurately predictable. Of greater importance is this fact to those who are now studying the history of Western Christian democratic culture within the penumbra of its own possible destruction. The optimism of a few generations ago which saw the vine that was once planted in western Europe, and which literally grew till **the mountains were covered with its shade, the mighty cedars with its branches;** [until] **it sent its branches to the sea, and its shoots to the River**—meaning to our Hebrew poet the known habitable world—this optimism has been rebuked. The walls that have protected the vine

To the chief Musician upon Gittith, *A Psalm* of Asaph.

81 Sing aloud unto God our strength: make a joyful noise unto the God of Jacob.

To the choirmaster: according to The Gittith. A Psalm of Asaph.

81 Sing aloud to God our strength;
shout for joy to the God of Jacob!

LXXXI. God Is Our Strength (81:1-16)

This psalm, sometimes termed a "prophetic liturgy," appears to consist of two independent parts, neither of which is now complete (cf. the structure of Ps. 19). The first, comprising vss. 1-5*b*, is a hymn intended to accompany a musical part of the temple ritual on a feast day. It ends abruptly and it may be only a fragment of a longer work. The second part, vss. 5*c*-16, despite a somewhat uncertain beginning, is in prophetic tenor: the words are spoken on the Lord's behalf, and are a combination of admonition and pleading. The poem reaches an unexpected conclusion on the mundane note of abundant wheat and honey.

According to the Mishnah (Tamid 7:4), this psalm was sung by the Levites in the temple on the fifth day of the week. It is also clear from vss. 1-3 that it was intended for a festival, and later Jewish tradition connects it both with the feast of Tabernacles (Abraham Cohen, ed., *The Psalms* [Hindhead: Soncino Press, 1945], p. 267), and with

---

are broken down and some **who pass along the way pluck its fruit.**

This is not the place to restate the analyses of the predicament of our times, which are being made both by those whose perspective is narrowed by a purely secularistic understanding of the vital forces that animate society and those who see God as the energy that cultivates the fields and breaks down the walls. These latter interpret history as the operation of God in grace (planting) and in judgment (the broken walls). For them there can be no escape from either of these divine offices. If we do not accept his grace in the organization and perpetuation and extension of our cultural inheritance, we shall have to accept his judgment in its destruction. We cannot claim exemption or immortality. In ways that it is never pleasant to realize or easy to confess, we are **the scorn of our neighbors; and our enemies laugh among themselves** (vs. 6). We dare not seek escape by retreat to an easy piety; and yet from our Christian perspective, what more can we claim as our hope than this poem's solemn refrain:

Restore us, O Lord God of hosts!
let thy face shine, that we may be saved!

81:1-16. ***Folk Songs and the Psalter.***—The folk song has been one of the richest sources of the highly technical musical idiom of Western culture. We are familiar with the way in which primitive and simple ritual tunes have been given a symphonic vehicle for thematic presentation, and how folk tales have expanded under the composer's pen into operatic works of great elaborateness. Because of the vagaries of memory and improvisation, these simple mediums of idea and melody are subject to corruption to such an extent that later forms in which they appear may be substantially if not wholly different from the original.

Such certainly was the case in the folk music and lore of the Hebrews. The anthology we are studying shows every sign of the literary vicissitudes through which much of its material passed. This is true in spite of the fact that at various periods efforts were made by learned and devout men to edit the poetic deposit of the centuries, and to give it such order as would make the materials available for all the offices of religion—liturgical, devotional, educational, and historical. How well they did their task depends of course on the literary and religious criteria we bring to its judgment.

We who stand at a point long distant from the early editors can be sure that the Psalter as we now know it served the purposes for which it was devised. It makes very little difference whether it serves our purposes well or ill, though much of it has been incorporated in various ways into the historic and modern church experience. It must be assumed that the composition of the Psalter and the selection of its contents were dictated by the twin factors of utility and survival, the latter deriving largely from the former. Utility is a word of rich connotations, and in the experience of the Jews its basic quality was its value as a vehicle for the profound religious and moral insights with which these great poems are freighted.

Ps. 81, according to the editorial comment that introduces it, is a song to be sung to the

2 Take a psalm, and bring hither the
timbrel, the pleasant harp with the psaltery.
3 Blow up the trumpet in the new moon,
in the time appointed, on our solemn feast
day.
4 For this *was* a statute for Israel, *and*
a law of the God of Jacob.

2 Raise a song, sound the timbrel,
the sweet lyre with the harp.
3 Blow the trumpet at the new moon,
at the full moon, on our feast day.
4 For it is a statute for Israel,
an ordinance of the God of Jacob.

---

the New Year (Talmud, Rosh ha-Shanah 30*b*). The latter reference gives some support to Mowinckel's view that it was used in the "enthronement of Yahweh" ceremonies (*Psalmenstudien,* II, 152-56; cf. Exeg. on 47:1-10; 93:1-5). We do not know precisely how the psalm was fitted into the elaborate ritual of the great festivals, and it is only a surmise that vss. 1-5*b* were sung by the congregation and vss. 5*c*-16 by one of the priests (the successor to the hypothetical "cultic prophet").

There is little in the poem to indicate its date, and there is only the reference to **Joseph** in vs. 5 to support an origin in the Northern Kingdom. We may note that Buttenwieser considers this to be one of the oldest of the pre-exilic psalms. The meter is generally 3+3.

1. Praise to Our God (81:1-5*b*)

81:2. The Levites would normally play the musical instruments in the temple service (for the instruments referred to here and in vs. 3 see Intro., pp. 5-6).

3. Addressed to the priests. **Trumpet** (שופר) is a ram's horn. The horn-blowing at the beginning of the month **(the new moon)** was done with the silver clarion, not the trumpet (cf. Num. 10:10), but on the first of the seventh month (which became New Year's Day) a trumpet (of wild goat's horn) was used (Mishnah, Rosh ha-Shanah 3:3-4; cf. Num. 29:1). **The full moon** is the correct translation of כסה, not **the time appointed. Our feast day:** The word חג, **feast,** is used of all three of the annual festivals, Passover, Weeks, and Tabernacles (Deut. 16:16), but only the first day of Passover and of Tabernacles approximates the middle of the month **(the full moon).**

---

tune of **Gittith.** This word has puzzled critics, but there is fairly general consensus that it indicates a festival song, perhaps sung at the feast of Tabernacles, when the grapes were in the wine press and the spirits of the people were grateful for gathered harvests and for the security promised them for the winter. In its earliest form it was perhaps a vintage song, and sections of the present poem may have been part of the original. It is fairly obvious, however, that elements have been added which are not harmonious with its festal intention, and its abrupt ending is regarded as evidence of patchwork and fragmentary composition.

Nevertheless the psalm served a purpose that can be simply stated: the primary condition on which security, both physical and spiritual, rests is complete and unequivocal faithfulness to the God of Jacob. To us, for whom this is a commonplace of religion, it may appear unexciting and repetitious. Not so to the ancient Jew who was constantly and for good reasons called back to this central datum of history and of his hope. It is a datum indeed to which Western civilization has also been recalled for good reasons in its great periods of crisis and change; and so long as this culture survives, it will always need reiteration.

1-5*b*. *Call to Song.*—The poem opens on a gay festival note as the musical resources of the people are mobilized in a great ensemble. If this was sung at the harvest feast, it was an ascription of praise to the God of field and vine, whose strength had been manifest in an abundant yield. Its rhythm, it would appear, was punctuated by the **shout** of joy, as likely as not an accented emphasis for marching worshipers (vs. 1). All is not the rising crescendo of song and the ecstatic shout; the liturgy modulates into a gentler motif, the **timbrel** with its tinkling disks, **the sweet lyre** with its more sonorous timbre, and the **harp** with its thin and tremulous tone. Since the phases of the moon set the seasons of feasting, it was to be saluted as the celestial monitor of the celebrations. When the **new moon** was first seen shaping its translucent bow against the day's waning light, a trumpeter saluted it, and when the **full moon** rose above the eastern barrier, a horn announced the formal opening of festivities.

5 This he ordained in Joseph *for* a testimony, when he went out through the land of Egypt: *where* I heard a language *that* I understood not.

6 I removed his shoulder from the burden: his hands were delivered from the pots.

7 Thou calledst in trouble, and I delivered thee; I answered thee in the secret place of thunder: I proved thee at the waters of Meribah. Selah.

5 He made it a decree in Joseph,
when he went out over[m] the land of Egypt.

I hear a voice I had not known:
6 "I relieved your[n] shoulder of the burden;
your[n] hands were freed from the basket.
7 In distress you called, and I delivered you;
I answered you in the secret place of thunder;
I tested you at the waters of Mer'ibah. *Selah*

[m] Or *against*
[n] Heb *his*

5*ab*. Joseph, written יהוסף only here, may designate the Northern Kingdom (cf. 78:67; 80:1), but there is no evidence of any of the Hebrew laws being designed particularly for one part of the nation (except provisions dealing with the priesthood). Possibly the word is a synonym for Israel, and its use as such may indicate a writer from the north. **When he went out over the land of Egypt:** Cf. Exod. 11:4.

2. God Yearns for His Wayward People (81:5*c*-16)

These verses purport to be the words of the Lord, and when used liturgically were doubtless rendered by a soloist (cf. the admonition in 95:7*c*-11). They include a reminder of the Exodus experience, a rebuke to a sinful nation, and an expression of God's hope for his people (cf. the more detailed treatment of the same themes in Ps. 78).

5*c*. I hear a voice I had not known: Voice is, lit., **language** or "lip," but the clause as a whole is difficult. Presumably it is meant as an authoritative warrant for vss. 6-16 (cf. the words of Eliphaz in Job 4:12-16).

6-10. A brief review of the Exodus. **Your shoulder . . . your hands:** The RSV follows Duhm *et al.* in changing the M.T. from **his** to **your. The basket** is preferable to **the**

It is a cheerful scene, highhearted and grateful people united in music and laughter. But it was by no means left to spontaneous impulses. Laughter and song cannot be compelled perhaps; but the merrymaking was as much a response to divine ordinance as the solemn processionals in the court of the temple. That the people should unite thus in gaiety was the intention of **statute, ordinance,** and **decree** (vss. 4-5), three words that have significant shades of difference. A statute was an irrevocable act, an ordinance a rule—more particularly religious—and a decree was a formal order. To be sure, these repeated phrases represent a poetic device, but it may be more than that. Some there are who need only an order, some a rule, and some a law to induce their action. There was none exempt from this exercise of celebration. The feast, this seems to say, was not only a seasonal turning to God in thanksgiving; it was a reminiscent enactment of an ancient providence that must never be forgotten. Israel was to rejoice over flowing wine presses, but lest her days of bondage become of no account, she must also recall that God in a day of greater peril had been her sustainer.

5*c*-10. *The Lord's Reply.*—It is a very common human frailty to misuse the holiday occasions that beckon us to play. Relaxation and merriment tend to become the sole interest; and the greater the hilarity, the more obscure the original intent. The evidence of this truth in our own celebration of the great Christian festivals of Christmas and Easter is gravely disturbing, and we have every reason for supposing that the same thing happened during the Jewish feasts. Greed was exploiting the pilgrims to the Passover in the days of our Lord, and the only record of action impelled by his anger was during the great feast when he scattered the money-changers and startled the holidaymakers with a whip of small cords (John 2:13-15).

It was necessary therefore in the midst of this ancient celebration to remind the pilgrims of the meaning of their songs of praise. Joy becomes gaiety, gaiety becomes hilarity, hilarity

8 Hear, O my people, and I will testify unto thee: O Israel, if thou wilt hearken unto me;

9 There shall no strange god be in thee; neither shalt thou worship any strange god.

10 I *am* the LORD thy God, which brought thee out of the land of Egypt: open thy mouth wide, and I will fill it.

11 But my people would not hearken to my voice; and Israel would none of me.

8 Hear, O my people, while I admonish you!
O Israel, if you would but listen to me!
9 There shall be no strange god among you;
you shall not bow down to a foreign god.
10 I am the LORD your God,
who brought you up out of the land of Egypt.
Open your mouth wide, and I will fill it.

11 "But my people did not listen to my voice;
Israel would have none of me.

---

pots: The reference is to a fibrous receptacle for carrying bricks, etc. On the tasks of the Hebrews in Egypt see Exod. 1:11; 5:5-11. **The secret place of thunder:** A phrase found only here. Probably a thundercloud is meant (cf. 18:11, 13), and Mount Sinai may be the locality (Exod. 19:16-19; 20:18). **Meribah:** In the narrative in Exod. 17:1-7, it is the people that test the Lord (cf. Num. 20:1-13). On vs. 9, cf. Exod. 20:3-5. Exclusive devotion to the Lord is the hallmark of the true Israelite. On vs. 10, cf. Exod. 20:2. Israel's very existence was due to God's initial redemptive act. **Open your mouth wide:** Cf. 37:3-4; Matt. 7:7-8, 11.

11-16. The ingratitude of Israel and their subsequent troubles did not diminish the Lord's benevolence. On vs. 11 cf. Exod. 32:1; Deut. 32:15-18. **Their stubborn hearts**

---

becomes revelry, and revelry becomes debauchery if the meaning for one's joy is lost to its indulgence. Our poet uses an interesting and dramatic device to call the pilgrims to remembrance. Nowhere else is the *deus ex machina,* or the ancient analogue to Banquo's ghost, employed to speak the needed word. Apparently it was unlikely that the **voice** that had summoned the people to festivity would be heard if it called them to solemn recollection. So a voice from off stage, so to speak, or the tones of an unfamiliar and therefore arresting interlocutor are heard. In effect it says: Sing aloud, raise a song, blow the horn, but do not forget why you are doing it. The burdens of the summer are now set aside with the gathered harvests; the busy hands now enjoy a respite from the labors of the growing season. The distress of man's unresting toil has found deliverance at summer's close. Rejoice, but remember! The references in vss. 6-7 are clearly reminiscent of the bondage experience in Egypt, but their point here seems to be that escape from slavery did not mean exemption from labor. The burdens and baskets of the Nile Valley were exchanged for the burdens and baskets of the Valley of the Jordan; and when respite came from the latter and the people were called to rejoicing, it was still God who eased the weight off their shoulders and gave them the occasion for feasting. And in vss. 8-10 this unfamiliar but not uninformed voice gives again its admonition, concluding with the promise: **Open your mouth wide, and I will fill it.**

Commentators have found difficulty in fitting this section (6-10) on to the preceding one because of the abruptness of the transition—with good reason. But to early anthologist and liturgist the matter was of little importance so long as the poem in the form they had it served their purposes. Seen in the context of a festival celebration and in the light of the easy prostitution of holiday to the ends of debauchery and forgetfulness, the song's utility is obvious. It is a simple fact that when the song and the timbrel and the harp make music, the ears of strange gods hear, and without any very great display ingratiate themselves to the feasters and soon accept the merrymaking as honor to themselves. For all its figurativeness, this language represents a common human experience against which one must constantly be on guard. The mournful note of the dirge may cause men's minds to question God, but it is the gay note of the dance that causes the hearts of men to forget him.

11-16. ***The Rewards and Penalties of Faith and Rebellion.***—In this final strophe the voice

12 So I gave them up unto their own hearts' lust: *and* they walked in their own counsels.

13 Oh that my people had hearkened unto me, *and* Israel had walked in my ways!

14 I should soon have subdued their enemies, and turned my hand against their adversaries.

15 The haters of the LORD should have submitted themselves unto him: but their time should have endured for ever.

16 He should have fed them also with the finest of the wheat: and with honey out of the rock should I have satisfied thee.

12 So I gave them over to their stubborn hearts,
to follow their own counsels.
13 O that my people would listen to me,
that Israel would walk in my ways!
14 I would soon subdue their enemies,
and turn my hand against their foes.
15 Those who hate the LORD would cringe toward him,
and their fate would last for ever.
16 I would feed you[o] with the finest of the wheat,
and with honey from the rock I would satisfy you."

[o] Cn Compare verse 16b: Heb *He would feed him*

---

rather than **their own hearts' lust.** The psalmist here maintains Israel's freedom to serve or not to serve the Lord (cf. Rom. 1:24, 26, 28). Cohen (*op. cit.*, p. 269) quotes the rabbinical saying: "All is in the hands of God except the fear of God." **O that my people would listen:** The imperfect in the second half of the verse suggests that the verb in the first half should also be imperfect; therefore read ישׁמע instead of שׁמע. The verse expresses the Lord's yearning for his people (cf. Deut. 5:29; 32:29; Isa. 48:18; Matt. 23:37). The Hebrew in vs. 15 is, lit., **their time,** which the RSV renders as **their fate.** Vs. 16 refers to the blessings promised of old which come to obedient hearts (cf. Deut. 28:1-14). The verse in the M.T. commences, **He would feed him** (RSV mg.), but to make the two parts of the verse more harmonious, the RSV emends the first word to read **I would feed you.** For the references to **wheat** and **honey** cf. Deut. 32:13-14.

---

of the interloper at the feast speaks again. It is evident that some of the things against which his solemn warning had been uttered had already got out of hand. Here again scholars have found the development of the poem puzzling; here also it is necessary to point out that the poem served a need felt by those who used it. Pictorially we see the possessor of the unidentified voice turning from the merrymakers to whom his caution had been addressed and indulging in a despairing soliloquy. He speaks as if he were the voice of God. There is judgment followed by wistfulness, and then a flash of that undiscourageable hope that there might be a return to him, and a promise that if there were a return, he would destroy the enemies that had seduced his people and fill his chosen once again with fatness. Properly enough the last verse returns us to the harvest festival setting in which our poem began. The wheat was gathered; sing to God—thus the beginning. If they will still sing to God, the fruitage of the fields and the honey that during the blossoming of summertime had been cached in the rocks will be theirs forever.

Returning briefly to our opening paragraph: from the standpoint of critical scholarship we have here a poem made up of several fragments of folk lore and song put together by early liturgists for use as a festival song. The apparent disparity or distortion of emphasis in its parts did not militate against its effective use as a composite piece. The nature of its utility may be found in two profoundly religious truths that it contains. Attention has already been directed to the way in which the impulse to be gay can grade over into the impulse to be profligate, without the transition being realized. Our poet provides for a warning against this. Two other significant suggestions are made with which we may briefly be concerned.

The first is found in vs. 7, **I tested you at the waters of Meribah,** where reference is to the famous story of rebellion in the wilderness of Zin (Num. 20:2-13) in which Moses and the children of Israel "tested" the Lord. They made compliance with their angry demand for water the test of their continued loyalty. Moses, their spokesman, shared their anger, and for the truculence of his response to the Lord's concession was debarred from the Promised Land. Here, however, the poet represents the situation as reversed; it was not the people who tested God; it was God who tested them. Herein a subtle truth is concealed. The apex of man's pride is reached when he assumes his right to

A Psalm of Asaph.

82 God standeth in the congregation of the mighty; he judgeth among the gods.

A Psalm of Asaph.

82 God has taken his place in the divine council;
in the midst of the gods he holds judgment:

LXXXII. A Scene in Heaven (82:1-8)

In 1888 Thomas K. Cheyne wrote: "No psalm makes a stronger demand than this on the historic imagination of the interpreter. The ideas may be perennial, but their outward forms are no longer understood." (*The Book of Psalms* [New York: Thomas Whittaker], p. 229.) This is a candid recognition of the difficulties of the poem. In truth we do not know very much about this psalm, and we can only trust that our guesses about it are not too wide of the mark.

We may best describe it as a didactic psalm. Vs. 8, whether original to the psalm or not, indicates that the poem served as a hymn, an opinion confirmed by the Mishnah, which records that this psalm was sung in the temple by the Levites on the third day of the week (Tamid 7:4). It also could have been used during the New Year's celebration, or on any other occasion when the moral supremacy of the God of Israel was to be emphasized.

The crux of the interpretation of the psalm is the meaning to be attached to **gods** (אלהים) in vss. 1*b*, 6, and on this point commentators differ widely. The principal meanings proposed are: the lesser gods and angels; the national gods of the heathen; "the wicked governors of the nations holding Israel in subjection" (Briggs, *Psalms,* II, 215); kings and those invested with authority; the judges of Israel (so Targ.). Buttenwieser (*The Psalms* [Chicago: University of Chicago Press, 1938], p. 770) claims that "the author assails the deification of kings in vogue in his day." This variety of interpretation testifies to the paucity and ambiguity of the available data.

The view that the psalmist has in mind a heavenly concourse of gods, demigods, and angels, has much to be said for it. The ancient Near East was well acquainted with

test the Most High and acts upon it. In the lore of Israel it was symbolized in this interesting tale, and its consequence to the career of Moses suggests something of the symbolic importance that attached to it. The modern parallel has less of dramatic intensity perhaps because today man's challenge to God is not addressed to him, but is addressed to his creation. But with an arrogance that outmatches the anger of Moses, modern man, to satisfy himself, has taken up his rod and smitten the rock, and there have gushed forth not only the elements hidden in the rocks that can bless him, but those that can also destroy him, or—to keep the language of the story—bar him from entrance into the promised land. It is not smashing the rocks that is the sin of modern man; it is his arrogant claim that the rock is his, and that what he releases from it is his to use as he wills.

The second insight brings to conclusion the emphasis of what has just been said. **But my people did not listen to my voice. . . . So I gave them over to their stubborn hearts, to follow their own counsels** (vss. 11-12). If history has any one primary lesson to teach, it is that he who strikes the rock in pride finds himself left to the mercy of what he has let loose. Once man denies the counsels of God, he must walk in his own counsel. Some have called this nemesis, others call it fate; some even give it the strange name of the death wish. To all of them our poet has something to say, though he prefers to sing it to the tune of a vintage song:

> **O that my people would listen to me,**
> **that Israel would walk in my ways!**

82:1-8. ***The Problem of Ethical Monism.***—We have seen how the poetry of ancient Israel was used to conserve and pass on to coming generations the epic tales and moral lessons of her history. This is little different from the literary experience of other cultures, but since the stream that has broadened into the ethical and theological estuary of Western thought had its origin in the wilderness of Sinai, these epics and their meaning belong among our most important treasures.

Asaph, whatever the name is taken to mean, is represented in Ps. 82 as making an effort to

assemblies of gods (Patton, *Canaanite Parallels,* p. 24; Pritchard, *Ancient Near Eastern Texts,* p. 386; Gaster, *Thespis,* pp. 177-78), and a priori we should expect the Hebrews to be familiar with such an idea. This supposition is borne out by various references in the O.T. to a heavenly gathering over which the Lord presides (29:1; 58:1; 103:20-21; 148:2; I Kings 22:19-22; Job 1:6-12; 2:1-6; Dan. 7:9-10; 10:13, 20-21), and it throws light upon allusions to the Lord's throne being in heaven (11:4; 103:19; Isa. 66:1; etc.) and to his supremacy over all gods (89:5-8; 95:3; 96:4; 97:7, 9; Exod. 15:11; Deut. 3:24; I Kings 8:23; etc.; cf. Exeg. on 29:1-2; 58:1-2). Ultimately, of course, the Hebrews abandoned the concept that there were lesser gods in heaven, and the heavenly host was thought to consist solely of angels.

In support of the view that the word **gods** refers to human judges or rulers, one may observe that in vss. 2-4 it is juridical iniquity that is condemned, and ordinarily this would involve human beings. Such an interpretation lies behind the use of vs. 6 in John 10:34. Against this exegesis one should urge that in vs. 7 it is implied that those

---

come to grips with a problem which has been a critical issue whenever the minds of men have pondered deeply on the mystery of moral good and evil. Once again it is well to point out that the fact of God was for the pious Jew the *pou sto* from which all his intellectual excursions started and to which he ultimately returned. It is equally important to remember that his excursions took him along all the highways and hedges that invite the speculative mind. We encounter our poet in Ps. 82 standing in a bypath familiar to all intellectual pilgrims. Looking about him, he uses the poetic medium to give shape to one of man's most insistent questions: How can a righteous God be the creator of an unrighteous people? This is the problem of ethical monism.

A minimum of background will help us here. It can be said that Israel started out with monotheistic presuppositions. Abraham, the author of Hebrews tells us, "looked for a city which hath foundations, whose builder and maker is God" (Heb. 11:10). By the time of Moses this inarticulate faith had been formalized in an irreversible divine mandate: "Thou shalt have no other gods before me." This was not a statement of the monotheistic hypothesis that there was only one deity in existence. It said that the children of Israel were to be mono-theists, and that Yahweh was to be the *mono-theos.* Development of this individualistic monotheism to the universal monotheism that is the center of our thought did not follow a direct line. It took devious ways; indeed, it might be said to have almost lost itself at times in the ways of polytheism or even atheism. The fact is, however, that the movement never went so far astray that it could not return to its base. It was the recurrent inspiration of poet and prophet that made this vivid to the people, even in times when they interpreted their ill-fortune as proof of God's indifference, weariness, inconstancy, or anger.

It is not easy for us to sense the tug that pagan neighbors must have exercised on those who never could forget the stern warning of the First Commandment. Israel's national environment was not always conducive to theological security. No more was their social environment conducive to moral security; and the history of Israel from the beginnings of her regular intercourse with neighbor peoples to the time of the Maccabean revolution was generally written from the standpoint of the fortunes that attended theological and moral regularity. The immoralities of Baal and Babylon corrupted both the ideas and the behavior of Israel. There were high places on the hills that bounded Judea, where orgies of the worship of Astarte blacked out the Seventh Commandment, even as there were low places in Babylonian mythology that blacked out the austerity of the First Commandment.

Fluctuation of idea and practice did not go on without leaving their record both in the chronicles of state and in the work of literary men. Ps. 82 obviously is one of the latter records, though as we should expect of a poet, the problem is set up in the language of fancy. The poem in its composition yields a minimum of trouble to critical study. It is brief, its symmetry is preserved, and its text is apparently only slightly corrupted by editorial tinkering. The author constructs an imaginary scene in which his problem is implicit. His solution is much too easy, amounting to little more than an exhortation to God to repossess the portfolios he had apportioned to incompetent deputies and take complete control by himself. Despite these limitations, he is confronting his problem squarely.

1-5. ***The Lord the Judge of the Judges.***—The picture the poet draws may seem odd to us, but to the ancients it was familiar. God was holding a conference with the gods who were his judicial agents on the earth. That the indi-

2 How long will ye judge unjustly, and accept the persons of the wicked? Selah.
3 Defend the poor and fatherless: do justice to the afflicted and needy.
4 Deliver the poor and needy: rid *them* out of the hand of the wicked.

2 "How long will you judge unjustly
and show partiality to the wicked?
Selah
3 Give justice to the weak and the fatherless;
maintain the right of the afflicted and the destitute.
4 Rescue the weak and the needy;
deliver them from the hand of the wicked."

---

addressed are not men, otherwise the forecast of their death **like men** would be meaningless. Further, **gods** nowhere else bears the meaning of "judges" or "rulers"; in Exod. 21:6; 22:8-9; I Sam 2:25, where the word is used, the meaning is "God, represented in his juridical capacity by a human agent."

The psalm will therefore be taken as depicting a scene in heaven, wherein the Lord condemns some of his hierarchy for their abetment of the world's wickedness.

1. The Divine Council (82:1)

82:1. The divine council: Lit., "the congregation of God."

2. The Lord Addresses the Council (82:2-7)

2-4. The indictment. This strikes a familiar note in the O.T., especially in prophetic literature. It may be presumed that these erring members of the heavenly host have been aiding and abetting injustice on earth. The moral is that both heaven and earth are subject to the same searching judgment of God. We may note the suggestion that these verses are not the primary charge leveled against certain members of the Lord's celestial retinue, but a later substitute, and that the original crime was something similar to that now found in Gen. 6:1-4 (Julian Morgenstern, "The Mythological Background of Psalm 82," *Hebrew Union College Annual,* XIV [1939], 29-126). **Show partiality to the wicked** (vs. 2): Cf. Deut. 1:17; Prov. 18:5; etc. On vs. 3 cf. Exod. 22:22; Deut. 10:18; Isa. 1:17; Jer. 22:3; Job 29:12; etc. On vs. 4 cf. Isa. 1:17; 10:1-2; etc.

---

vidual deities in this fancied pantheon are unidentified indicates that the idea was a borrowed one, but back of it we may assume the poet's own perplexity to lie. God, to him, was **the Most High.** There was a good deal of misfeasance in God's world. Why was this? It was easy to assume that God was indifferent or preoccupied or annoyed, but such an assumption involved metaphysical problems as to the divine nature. Was it plausible then to hypostatize a series of deputy deities who, while gods, were less than the Most High? If they failed to measure up to the standards of the Most High, it was his duty to rebuke them. In this way he exercised control. At the same time he could hardly exculpate himself from the failures of his surrogates. This, it is easy for us to see, was an effort to escape the embarrassment of a righteous God in control of unrighteous people —the basic problem of ethical monism.

God, says our poet, is seen in the midst of his deputies holding judgment. They have been empowered to execute justice; it is even intimated that the judges have been suborned by evil men, and that partiality, which is the negation of justice, has been shown the wicked. While we have no right to tamper with our poet's picture, we cannot avoid the wish that he had made room for answers from the gods to the Most High's question. Had he done this, we might have had here all the excuses made by high-minded individuals—as we assume these godlings to have been—for failure to accept and enforce the principles of absolute justice. Circumstances alter cases, ends justify means, people are not all alike, and after all, people are human; these and similar expressions would admirably fit this scene had the opportunity been granted for reply. For these deputy gods were not originally creatures of evil intention or of moral blindness. If they had failed in their high office, there must have been extenuating circumstances.

Instead, however, of granting the opportunity of self-defense, the Most High repeats the orders that he must certainly have given before. What

5 They know not, neither will they understand; they walk on in darkness: all the foundations of the earth are out of course.

6 I have said, Ye *are* gods; and all of you *are* children of the Most High.

5 They have neither knowledge nor understanding,
they walk about in darkness;
all the foundations of the earth are shaken.

6 I say, "You are gods,
sons of the Most High, all of you;

---

5. Almost a soliloquy. On the thought cf. Prov. 2:10-15. **In darkness** must mean "in moral darkness." **All the foundations of the earth:** See Exeg. of "pillars" in 75:3. This third stich in the verse seems unrelated to the context and may be an intrusion into the text. If it is original, the term **foundations** must be metaphorical (cf. Exeg. on 11:1-3) : the evil in heavenly places is jeopardizing the whole moral order.

6. There may be slight irony at this point. **Sons of the Most High:** A phrase found only here (cf. Gen. 6:2, 4; Job 1:6; 2:1; 38:7) .

---

he says therefore may be taken to point up both what were the ideals of justice that were held by the supreme God and the areas in which his agents had failed. If the latter inference is allowed, we have a record of conspicuous and demoralizing incompetence, and the reason for the summary treatment which the judges are subsequently dealt. Had our writer been as much of a metaphysician as he was a poet, he would have had to raise a question more basic than administrative failure; he would have asked how it came about that there were **weak, afflicted, destitute,** and **needy** folk. Beyond that, indeed, he would have sought an explanation of the presence on the earth of wicked men who were responsible for the plight of the needy.

It is possible that vs. 5, which otherwise regarded has bothered commentators, is an oblique reference to this deeper and untouched problem—the origin of inequities, affliction, and wickedness. Some scholars say this verse was added by an editor who sought either to extenuate the failures of the gods or to explain the predicament of the afflicted. Such an explanation gives just as good a reason for assigning it to our poet. If it is taken as a description of the surrogate judges, it also indicts the character of the Chief Judge who engaged them. But as an explanation of the precondition of the needy, the weak, and the destitute, it well serves the practical mind and goes as deep as the reflections of most take them. This of course does not answer the problem of the origin of evil, of which absence of **understanding** and **darkness** are important components; but when our author thinks for a moment of the tottering **foundations of the earth,** he gives evidence that he was aware of a level of insecurity that trembles beneath the tottering foundations of the administration of justice.

6-8. *Judgment Pronounced.*—At this point the poem takes a dramatic turn. The Most High had accused his associates and admonished them to improve their judicial performance; then with almost capricious suddenness he condemns them to death. Who were they? They were **gods.** Why? Because they were **sons of the Most High.** Their office rested upon a unique relationship to God; their performance rested upon a unique obligation to serve his ends; their punishment was therefore to be unique. Here were creatures higher than men, higher even than princes, in a category indeed that should have exempted them from the stigma of mortality—death. But for their failures they were to **die like men, and fall like any prince.** What is the meaning of this? By what standard of justice is the Most High to commit infanticide? Can it be that our poet is saying that the diffusion of justice to agents on a level lower than the Absolute—which means its relativization—tends to corrupt the sense and exercise of absolute justice? Because the Absolute Judge is disappointed in relative justice, does he too succumb to the temptations to injustice? As accomplices to injustice, his sons forfeited the divine perquisite of immortality. If the father is unjust—as certainly slaying one's sons must have been thought to be—by what norm of equity could he retain his own right to immortality?

Such questions are pertinent to those of us who now read the poem, but it is doubtful if they were in the poet's mind. We are perhaps nearer to him if we assume that in vss. 6-7 he is abandoning the hypothesis of ethical pluralism, though not in the way in which modern metaphysics would put it or for the same reasons. If, however, he is dealing with the problem we outlined at the beginning, his failure to solve it might easily have taken the form of

7 But ye shall die like men, and fall like one of the princes.
8 Arise, O God, judge the earth: for thou shalt inherit all nations.

7 nevertheless, you shall die like men,
and fall like any prince."[p]

8 Arise, O God, judge the earth;
for to thee belong all the nations!

[p] Or *fall as one man, O princes*

---

7. It is implied that heretofore either immortality or superhuman longevity had been the lot of the sons of God. **Like any prince:** Like any human ruler. Or is there a reference to an earlier purge of the heavenly host? (Cf. Isa. 14:12-15.)

3. Liturgical Conclusion (82:8)

8. Judge the earth: Cf. 9:8; 58:11; 67:4; Gen. 18:25; etc. The psalmist's words may point to (*a*) some judgment of the world to take place on New Year's Day; (*b*) God's periodic judgments in history; or (*c*) the Lord's definitive judgment at the end of the age.

---

such a summary dismissal of it. This is supported by the peremptory way in which he sweeps away the fancy with which his pen has been engaged, and calls on God to take over the whole operation of justice without assistance of any sort. After all, why should he deputize others? The nations are his own, and he puts them in jeopardy if he allocates the operation of justice to anyone else.

> **Arise, O God, judge the earth;**
> **for to thee belong all the nations!**

This puts the problem back where it was before the gods were called to judgment in the divine assembly. If the nations belong solely to God, he must assume the obligation to be their sole arbiter.

This may be taken to represent the thought of our poet and, since it has been preserved in the literature of his people, to have represented also a fairly responsible segment of the thought of his day. The effort to account for injustice in God's world assigned it to the maladministration of his delegates. This created more problems than it solved, and ended in the ascription of sole responsibility to God. Centuries later the Gnostics propounded a similar solution to the problem of creation. The incorruptible God was able, they said, to produce a corruptible creation by a series of agents whose graduated corruptibility began with a state slightly less than divine and ended with a state slightly more than human. By means of these graded emanations of the supreme being, the material was created by the immaterial (thus Plato), and evil was created by the Good (thus the Gnostics). Ethical monism was preserved by accrediting evil to demiurgic rather than to divine origin.

This notion has been as completely abandoned as is our poet's pantheon of lesser gods, and in so far as the problem exists today, it is dealt with in other ways. Our poet was no metaphysician; his approach to the problem was a practical one, garbed in the language of fancy. So also was his foreclosure a practical one. In the effort therefore to discover the relevance of this piece for the modern mind we shall do well to stick to practical matters.

The philosophical problem of ethical monism exercises very few people today. In a practical way, however, men have created lesser gods who, we may assume, accommodate themselves readily to the evil that men wish to do. Thus ethical pluralism has become a practical moral expedient. It can be rationalized in terms of the paradox of absolute and relative ethics; it can be implemented by the creation of as many gods as the times demand. Thus if we used the imagery employed by our poet, we should see God standing in the divine assembly holding judgment in the midst of the gods, four of whom could be identified as nationalism, power, wealth, and scientism. They might be known by other names; indeed, for practical purposes they have aliases for every occasion. Hear the voice of the Most High as he speaks to them: **How long will you judge unjustly . . . ? Give justice to the weak . . . ; maintain the right of the afflicted and the destitute** (vss. 2-3). What answer would our modern gods give to that?

These gods of the modern world—how far can we trust them to exercise justice? Hear our poet again:

> **They have neither knowledge nor understanding,**
> **they walk about in darkness;**
> **all the foundations of the earth are shaken** (vs. 5).

What then is to be their ultimate fate? Hear our poet once more: **I say, "You are gods, . . . all of you; nevertheless, you shall die like men, and fall like any prince"** (vss. 6-7). We are not

A Song *or* Psalm of Asaph.

83 Keep not thou silence, O God: hold not thy peace, and be not still, O God.

A Song. A Psalm of Asaph.

83 O God, do not keep silence;
do not hold thy peace or be still,
O God!

LXXXIII. Pursue Our Enemies, O God (83:1-18)

This is a lament of the community. After the opening cry to God to break his silence, the psalmist proceeds in vss. 2-8 to describe the perilous situation in which Israel is: she is surrounded by enemies who are set on her extermination. Vss. 9-18 comprise the petition—in this psalm almost an imprecation. As Midian and other foes were destroyed of old, so may Israel's present adversaries perish.

Efforts have been made to date this psalm on the basis of the allusions in vss. 2-8. The ages of Jehoshaphat of Judah (II Chr. 20:1-37), of Nehemiah (1:1-3; 4:7-8), and of Judas Maccabaeus (I Macc. 5:1-68), have all been advocated, but the fact is that at no known time were all the peoples referred to by the author united against Israel. It is probable, therefore, that the references should not be taken too literally. The psalm was doubtless composed at some time of national peril, and, as is well known, in the darker moods of the human soul the whole world seems to conspire against us. The psalmist viewed synoptically all the great dangers of the past, and he found them akin to the situation of his own generation. It was the common aim of all these foes that **the name of Israel be remembered no more.** The meter of the poem is mostly 3+3.

1. Plea to God (83:1)

83:1. A similar cry occurs in 28:1; 35:22; 39:12.

greatly concerned that nationalism, wealth, power, scientism, and the other demigods will in due season die, that they, like any prince, are mortal. So long as they serve practical ends for our times we will worship them.

And yet this is no solution, for the attempt to achieve justice without a transcendental reference becomes mere accommodation. It was Emerson who said:

Heartily know,
When half-gods go,
The gods arrive.[2]

Our ancient poet, as we have noted, abandoned his imagery with an appeal to God to **arise** and **judge the earth,** and that was no solution to his metaphysical problem. But it reflected what, we cannot say too often, was the anchor and the glory of his people's faith: that the predicament of man cannot be understood apart from his relation to the Most High, and that the problem of justice will not ultimately be solved until God has judged the earth. How far beyond that does our best modern understanding of the matter take us?

83:1-18. ***A Passover Song.***—Ancient Jewish ritualists designated this song to be used at the feast of the Passover. This most important of the great festivals occupied seven days in the first month (Nisan) and centered about the idea of deliverance from bondage. Escape from Egypt was the prototype of all such deliverances and was variously dramatized, beginning with the Passover celebration on the fifteenth day of the month. The Christian adaptation of this feast as a memorial of the last meal our Lord had with the disciples, or as a sacrament of the nurture of the soul by mystical partaking of the body and blood of Christ, would hardly permit the use of such a song. The reasons for this did not obtain in the rubrics of the temple liturgies, but we must not forget that Israel was always a small people surrounded and harassed by giant foes, and that deliverance was perhaps the major theme of her history. There were, no doubt, sensitive spirits who were offended by the vindictiveness of such a song as we have here, and this may be the reason for vs. 18, which seems to be a modification of the severity of the foregoing imprecations.

Seen in its historical context, the psalm reflects an actual situation of very great peril for which, if relief was possible at all, extraordinary help had to be summoned. In its religious context it reflects certain attitudes that later Jewish and Christian sentiment could not ratify. At the same time, beneath the surface of the

[2] "Give All to Love."

2 For, lo, thine enemies make a tumult: and they that hate thee have lifted up the head.

3 They have taken crafty counsel against thy people, and consulted against thy hidden ones.

4 They have said, Come, and let us cut them off from *being* a nation; that the name of Israel may be no more in remembrance.

5 For they have consulted together with one consent: they are confederate against thee:

6 The tabernacles of Edom, and the Ishmaelites; of Moab, and the Hagarenes;

2 For lo, thy enemies are in tumult;
those who hate thee have raised their heads.
3 They lay crafty plans against thy people;
they consult together against thy protected ones.
4 They say, "Come, let us wipe them out as a nation;
let the name of Israel be remembered no more!"
5 Yea, they conspire with one accord;
against thee they make a covenant —
6 the tents of Edom and the Ish'maelites,
Moab and the Hagrites,

2. The Dangers Confronting Israel (83:2-8)

2-4. The Lord's enemies are Israel's enemies (vs. 2). **Thy protected ones** or **thy hidden ones:** "Thy cherished ones" is a preferable translation (cf. Ezek. 7:22). On vs. 4, cf. Jer. 48:2.

6-8. An enumeration of Israel's enemies. **Tents** rather than **tabernacles;** the meaning is "people living in tents" (cf. 120:5). **Edom:** South of the Dead Sea. For antipathy to Edom cf. 137:7; Isa. 34:5-6; Ezek. 35:1-15. **Ishmaelites:** Bedouins, who in Gen. 25:18 have a wide range of activity. The only offense recorded of these tribesmen is their share in the disposal of Joseph (Gen. 37:25-28). **Moab:** Located east of the Dead Sea. The Moabites attacked Jehoshaphat king of Judah (II Chr. 20:1-29; cf. II Kings 1:1; 3:4-27), and they are listed as enemies of Jehoiakim (II Kings 24:2). **Hagrites:** Enemies in the days of Saul, living east of Gilead (I Chr. 5:10).

ideas we now repudiate there are feelings we do not disavow. It is true that moral idealism has advanced beyond moral impulses and must therefore always stand in judgment on them. This fact should protect us against the moral superiority that so often characterizes the modern who looks patronizingly at the moral unsophistication of the ancients.

For us the external emphasis of this song is a moral—or if we prefer it—an immoral one. From the national point of view it says that security rests ultimately on protective alliances or massed coalitions. This was the mistake our poet wanted to have pointed out by violent means to those who were combining against Israel. The tradition that an alliance of God and one nation represented the ultimate in power was at the heart of Israel's national consciousness, though it was constantly under assault from the practical-minded who put their trust in princes and their confidence in the sons of men. Integral to the sense of national security by coalition as practiced by the pagans was the more profound feeling that the power of arms was superior to the power of righteousness. Against this the rebuke of God must be registered, even if he had to use the power of arms to do it. Here again, however, the heart of Israel turned, as did that of her foe, toward this subtle and inviting faith. She too needed to be constantly reminded of its folly. **Let them know that thou alone . . . art the Most High over all the earth** (vs. 18). Still further, we encounter here the moral perplexity about the silence of God in the presence of a threat to his people. The identification of God's interests with those of his chosen made his silence little short of complicity with the enemy.

1-8. ***God Alerted.***—The peremptory effort in vs. 1 to wake God up is almost impertinent. The picture is one of God's annoying imperturbability in the face of threat. He might be thought to exhibit the even less worthy aspects of indolence and apathy. A good deal has been said by later writers on the subject of the silence of God, and yet no completely satisfactory answer has been provided for the nonphilosophical victim of his puzzling restraint when a divine syllable might mean rescue. Our poet, however, with a petulant edge to his words, urges that God stir himself and have something to say, not because his silence threatens his friends but because it threatens him.

Once again we see the Hebrew consciousness of their unique status in the sight of God giv-

7 Gebal, and Ammon, and Amalek; the Philistines with the inhabitants of Tyre;
8 Assur also is joined with them: they have helped the children of Lot. Selah.

7 Gebal and Ammon and Am'alek,
Philistia with the inhabitants of Tyre;
8 Assyria also has joined them;
they are the strong arm of the children of Lot. *Selah*

Gebal: Not Byblos on the Phoenician coast, but the region south of the Dead Sea, near Petra. **Ammon:** East of the Jordan River, north of Moab; mentioned as enemies in the days of the judges (Judg. 3:13) and as late as Jehoiakim (II Kings 24:2). **Amalek:** Probably Bedouins in the Negeb region in southern Palestine. They are referred to in Exod. 17:8-16; Deut. 25:17-19, and they appear in the narratives of the conquest of Canaan (Judg. 3:13; 6:3; I Sam. 14:48; etc.). **Philistia:** The maritime plain in Canaan, between Joppa and Gaza. The inhabitants were troublesome foes during Israel's early days in the Promised Land (cf. Judg 3:3, 31; I Sam. 4:1; etc.) and are condemned in Amos 1:8. **Tyre:** The great Phoenician city and seaport, which in the days of David and Solomon was friendly with Israel (II Sam. 5:11; etc.). Censure of Tyre is voiced in Amos 1:9-10; Isa. 23:1-18; Jer. 25:22; Ezek. 26:1-21; etc.

Assyria usually refers in the O.T. to the Assyrian Empire, which ended in 612 B.C. with the fall of Nineveh, but in Ezra 6:22 the word is used loosely to designate Mesopotamia and/or Persia (cf. Judith 2:1). **They have helped:** The M.T. is, lit., "they are an arm to" (cf. RSV). **The children of Lot:** The Moabites and the Ammonites (Deut. 2:9, 19).

---

ing emphasis to what was said. It was the glory of Israel that they could so completely identify their national and personal fortunes with the fortunes of God himself and expect God to react to their peril as if reacting to his own. **For lo! thy enemies are in tumult**—there is no indolence or apathy there!—**those who hate thee have raised their heads**—there is no easy head resting on a comfortable pillow there!

They lay crafty plans against thy people;
they consult together against thy protected ones.

Can it be that our writer intimates that God had been immobilized by the cleverness of enemies who had concealed their conspiracy and thus disarmed his suspicions? If this had been the case, the divine inactivity was doubly culpable, for to the writer their cunning had already been abandoned in a daring and impudent announcement of purpose:

They say, "Come, let us wipe them out as a nation;
let the name of Israel be remembered no more!"

How could God sleep through that?

Who were these conspirators? They have reached a united mind: **Yea, they conspire with one accord;** and they are agreed as to the ultimate focus of their covenanted alliance: **against thee they make a covenant.** Who had dared to do this? We are given eleven names, but they are very little help in determining the effectiveness of the conspiracy. Some scholars delete the names in vss. 6-8 on the grounds that such a miscellany could not have conspired **with one accord** and are therefore a later addition to the poem. This is plausible, though hardly important for us. The Edomites were barbarians from the cave country, and Ishmael was a wild tribe identified sometimes as Midian. The Moabites were descended from Lot and therefore were kin to Israel, though their lands were out of bounds to the chosen people. The Hagrites and Gebal were small tribes west of the Jordan; Ammon, also descended from Lot, had been forbidden entrance to the temple at Jerusalem because they had refused to provision the children of Israel when they encountered them in their wilderness wanderings. Amalek was a powerful nomadic tribe in the Arabian desert, against whom the Lord had declared perpetual war because they had ambushed the Israelites in the wilderness. Philistia was a perpetual feudist with Israel, a people with particularly revolting religious practices; and Assyria (Syria) indicated the plains country, where a respectable culture centering in Nineveh had long flourished. This, we agree, was a tatterdemalion lot, a heterogeneous mélange that would not likely hold together very securely or very long. If we chose to be literalists we might note that, such being the nature of the conspiracy, they were scarcely a threat to God or his people, and he had every good reason therefore for taking his ease and keeping silent in the face of their truculent but innocuous challenge. This view, however, is hardly within the range of our poet's vision.

9 Do unto them as *unto* the Midianites; as *to* Sisera, as *to* Jabin, at the brook of Kison:
10 *Which* perished at En-dor: they became *as* dung for the earth.
11 Make their nobles like Oreb, and like Zeeb: yea, all their princes as Zebah, and as Zalmunna:
12 Who said, Let us take to ourselves the houses of God in possession.

9 Do to them as thou didst to Mid'ian,
as to Sis'era and Jabin at the river Kishon,
10 who were destroyed at En-dor,
who became dung for the ground.
11 Make their nobles like Oreb and Zeeb,
all their princes like Zebah and Zalmun'na,
12 who said, "Let us take possession for ourselves
of the pastures of God."

3. Imprecation (83:9-18)

9-12. The psalmist cites the defeat of the Canaanites and the Midianites as an example of what he craves for Israel's present enemies. Whether the psalmist, in referring to those in the past who have felt the sting of the Lord's power, is following an accepted curse technique we do not know.

Midian: To the east of the Gulf of Aqabah (cf. Num. 31:7; Judg. 6:1–8:28). **Sisera . . . Jabin:** Cf. Judg. 4:1–5:31. **The river Kishon:** A wadi flowing northwest through the Plain of Esdraelon, and emptying into the Mediterranean at modern Haifa. **En-dor:** Toward the east of the Plain of Esdraelon, and south of Mount Tabor. It is not mentioned in Judg. 4:1–5:31. **Oreb . . . Zeeb:** Midianite leaders (cf. Judg. 7:25; 8:3). **Zebah . . . Zalmunna:** Kings of Midian (cf. Judg. 8:1-21). The M.T. in vs. 12 is, lit., **the pastures of God,** and there is no need to paraphrase as **the houses of God.**

9-18. ***Suggested Treatment for Enemies.***—The psalmist is truly frightened, but there is a silver lining to the cloud of his fear. With some of these enemies God had joined battle before, and had victories to his credit. Others not at this moment included in this odd coalition had been just as threatening and just as badly thrashed (vss. 9-12). There is therefore no doubt that God could easily handle all comers if he would only bestir himself to meet the danger. Such confidence derived from some famous tales which proved that God had resources of power far beyond that of any enemy or any combination of enemies. There are no more romantic episodes than those our poet cites. **Do to them as thou didst to Midian** (vs. 9*a*). The phenomenal victory of Gideon, who with three hundred men routed the hosts of Midian and ended seven years of Israel's servitude—this was the way God fought! **Sisera and Jabin,** the former a captain in the latter's Canaanite army who was treacherously killed by Jael, a woman who drove a tent peg through his temple. "So," Judg. 4:23 puts it, "God subdued on that day Jabin the king of Canaan before the children of Israel." **Oreb and Zeeb** were princes in the royal entourage who fled before Gideon's commandos and died, one on the rock that commemorated his death, the other at a wine press that was similarly made famous. A God who could perform military prodigies like these needed only to wake up to make the promise of victory certain.

This psalm is an unedifying and tedious catalogue of bloody violence, however grand it must have sounded to those who sang it as a part of the liturgy that commemorated God's greater victory at the borders of Egypt and the Red Sea. From a literary point of view the spectacle is somewhat improved by a sweeping simile that brings to an end the noisy record of imprecation. Nothing is more grand and terrible than a forest fire, nothing more splendid in its wild fury than a hurricane. The intention is still imprecatory, but the language is more engaging. A wind stirs the chaff of a threshing floor and tumbles a ball of weeds down the path. It picks up an ember under a pot of brewing herbs and tosses it into the dry thicket. There is a burst of flame and a sudden draft, and across the crested hills the tempest of wind and fire races. Before this terror the enemy flees as if pursued by God's firebrands. The idea delights the poet. In vss. 13-15 there is the picture of what could happen to all hostile coalitions if God would bestir himself.

As we read vss. 16-18 we feel that our angry and frightened author relents somewhat. Has he overdone the extremity of horrors to which he has urged the divine hand? He is not sure. Some commentators think these concluding sentiments were appended by a later editor to

13 O my God, make them like a wheel; as the stubble before the wind.

14 As the fire burneth a wood, and as the flame setteth the mountains on fire;

15 So persecute them with thy tempest, and make them afraid with thy storm.

16 Fill their faces with shame; that they may seek thy name, O LORD.

17 Let them be confounded and troubled for ever; yea, let them be put to shame, and perish:

18 That *men* may know that thou, whose name alone *is* JEHOVAH, *art* the Most High over all the earth.

13 O my God, make them like whirling dust,[q]
like chaff before the wind.
14 As fire consumes the forest,
as the flame sets the mountains ablaze,
15 so do thou pursue them with thy tempest
and terrify them with thy hurricane!
16 Fill their faces with shame,
that they may seek thy name, O LORD.
17 Let them be put to shame and dismayed for ever;
let them perish in disgrace.
18 Let them know that thou alone,
whose name is the LORD,
art the Most High over all the earth.

[q] Or *a tumbleweed*

13-18. The petition continued in more general terms. **Whirling dust** rather than **a wheel:** The word means "the wheel-shaped dried calyx of the thistle *Gundelia Tournefortii*" (Köhler, *Lexicon;* cf. Isa. 17:13). The allusion in vs. 15 is either metaphorical, "the **tempest** of thy wrath," or literal, the Lord acting through a thunderstorm (cf. Ps. 29). **That they may seek thy name** suggests the survival of at least some of Israel's enemies, and also some recognition on their part of Israel's God. **Let them know:** As in vs. 16, this implies a limited acknowledgment by the Gentiles of the Lord's supremacy. **Jehovah:** This is one of the four places in the O.T., and the only one in the Psalter, where the KJV thus renders the divine name יהוה. Elsewhere LORD is used. **The Most**

---

modify somewhat the offense to good taste contained in the earlier sections. This, we may recall, is a song sung particularly during the Passover, but we cannot be sure of this judgment. It would seem equally plausible that the poet, with that sense of justice and mercy which was the unique compound of Israel's moral sense, actually felt that God's best interests—and by the same token the best interests of Israel—would be better served by the conversion of the enemy than by their incineration in the flaming mountains. There is clear contradiction between vs. 16 and vs. 17. The former asks that **shame** may suffuse enemy faces in order that they may turn to God; the latter asks that their shame—here called **disgrace**—be the measure of their eternal perdition. If this indicates a divided mind, there is escape from it in vs. 18. Here the hope, so noble and so universal in the Psalter, is expressed that the defeat and debacle of all evil men will finally redound to the glory of God.

Let them know that thou alone,
whose name is the LORD,
art the Most High over all the earth.

From our perspective we feel that this was a costly way of achieving universal acclaim, if not indeed a highly questionable one. These factors are largely responsible for the consensus that regards this psalm as one of the least religious of all the poems in the Psalter. It is so completely given over to irritation and vindictiveness that however much credit we may assign to the pious hope with which it ends, it is all but wholly lacking in any of the overtones of devotion, trust, and godly sorrow that redeem the other imprecatory psalms.

Having said this, we nevertheless can find concealed in the heart of the man who wrote it the congenital religious faith of his culture. It is not surprising that he should be compromised by personal or national exigency. What is notable is that even in such lapses he reveals indigenous moral susceptibilities that are still a part of our Western religious mind. We mention three:

The first is that enmity directed against man is enmity toward God. **Thy enemies are in tumult** (vs. 2), said our poet. Though he was perhaps at the moment more aware of the enemies' threat to himself, nonetheless they were antagonists of God. This was the surety of their doom. Once God was warned and aroused, their defeat was inexorable. Shorn of its imagery of battle, this says simply that man, who may appear sometimes successfully to challenge man, cannot successfully challenge the moral law.

To the chief Musician upon Gittith, A Psalm for the sons of Korah.

84 How amiable *are* thy tabernacles, O LORD of hosts!

To the choirmaster: according to The Gittith. A Psalm of the Sons of Korah.

84 How lovely is thy dwelling place, O LORD of hosts!

High over all the earth: The ultimate end of the psalmist's prayer is that the universal and omnipotent power of the Lord may be exalted (cf. 97:9).

LXXXIV. A SAINT'S DELIGHT IN THE SANCTUARY (84:1-12)

The author of the present psalm, like that of Ps. 73, found in the Lord's dwelling place a blessed peace, and out of the fullness of his heart the lines of this hymn welled forth. One of the features of the poem is that it says almost nothing about the multifarious cultic acts that were centered in the sacred courts. Apart from one casual reference to the **altars** (vs. 3), the only formal aspect of worship that the psalmist mentions is the singing of praises unto the Lord (vss. 2, 4). It is evident that the important thing about the temple, to our author, was that in and through the ritual, and perhaps despite it, men somehow touched the garment of the living God (vss. 2, 7, 11-12). It is in this sense that we must understand Fleming James when he speaks of this psalm as "the supreme Psalm of the Sanctuary" (*Thirty Psalmists,* p. 72).

Opinions differ as to the circumstances under which the psalm was composed. Some (e.g., Herkenne, Terrien) believe that it was written by a devout Judean (a Levite according to Herkenne), who for some reason was prevented from coming to the temple, and who penned these verses from his precious memories of earlier days when he had been in the sanctuary. Most commentators, however, assume that it is the work of one who had just made the pilgrimage to Jerusalem and that, like Ps. 48, it belongs in spirit to the collection of pilgrim songs, Pss. 120–134. If we take this point of view, the psalm offers a striking contrast to the unfulfilled aspirations of the author of Pss. 42–43, although the parallels in thought between the latter and the present psalm may indicate a common author but a different occasion.

If the psalm is a pilgrimage hymn, it betrays little evidence of the particular festival which originally inspired it. The reference to **the early rain** in vs. 6 points at the earliest

---

The second susceptibility is that coalitions of nations, devised by cunning and with unanimous conspiratorial intent to do evil, are also doomed. This has had exact documentation in the last two hundred years of international power politics—for illustration, Hitler's Reich, organized to do precisely and ruthlessly what was described in vs. 4:

They say, "Come, let us wipe them out as a nation;
let the name of Israel be remembered no more."

It is testimony to the moral integrity of the Jewish people that the anti-Semitism recorded in an ancient psalm and cruelly revived in 1933 in Germany has had its nemesis in the plenary ruin of the conspirator. This, we would say, is also because it was out of harmony with the moral law.

The third susceptibility is the often irrational but always indefeasible hope of the redemption not only of God's people but of his enemies also. **Fill their faces with shame, . . . let them perish in disgrace. Let them know . . .** (vss. 16-18). This also is in its way a testimony to faith in the inviolability of the moral law, into harmony with which all men must ultimately come.

If these three generic moral principles are part of the order of man's deliverance, is it not possible that the ancient liturgists sensed this in our poem, and therefore found it suitable for the Passover celebration?

84:1-12. ***A Holiday Song.***—It is a delight to take this poem into our hands, for it brings to us lyric beauty and warm devotion unbroken by the disturbing interludes that mar some of the others we have studied. Its structure has been unimpaired by its long journey, and the purpose both of its writing and its liturgical use is unmistakable. It is a song of holiday to be used at the great autumn festival, the feast of Tabernacles. Our study of Ps. 81 showed us another mood, captured in a very different sort of song, also thought to have been used at this great harvest celebration. It too was to be

to late October, and the only important feast near this time of year is Tabernacles (fifteenth to twenty-first of Tishri). Nor can the date of the psalm be ascertained, although the allusion to the **anointed** in vs. 9 may indicate the period of the monarchy.

The strophic divisions are thought by some (e.g., Oesterley) to be vss. 1-4, 5-8, 8-12. Gunkel favors vss. 1-2, 3-5, 6-7, 10, 11-12, vss. 8-9 being considered an interpolation. The Exeg. follows the arrangement of the RSV. The meter is usually either 3+2 or 3+3.

1. Longing for the Courts of the Lord (84:1-2)

The psalmist longs for the temple, not for its own sake, but for the sake of God's presence to be found there (cf. 63:1-2; 73:17-20).

84:1. How lovely is thy dwelling place is preferable to the KJV. The plural of the M.T. ("dwelling places") is either a plural of majesty or of amplification, or a reference to the various structures in the temple area. **Lord of hosts:** See Exeg. on 80:4.

---

sung to the tune **Gittith,** which apparently was a popular melody. Here we find authorship assigned to the Korahites, from whom we have not heard since Ps. 49, but who will entertain us with three more songs before we are finished with Book III of the Psalter.

Gittith seems to have been a vintage tune. It would be interesting to know how many modern settings this poem has inspired. Because there is in it something irresistibly singable, many composers have fitted its lyric cadence to contemporary harmony, the most familiar and distinguished of which is Brahms's great *German Requiem.* There are few who, accustomed to worship, do not hear the melody of that opening theme whenever these words are read, for the great German master has made his tune as much a part of the words for us as Gittith was for the ancients.

Various schemes for strophic division have been proposed (see Exeg.). But the poem seems to divide itself most naturally into three stanzas, the first two of which end with the musical pause Selah. The final line (vs. 12) has been suggested as properly concluding both the other two stanzas; and it is probable that when it was sung, the final felicitous ascription to **the Lord of Hosts** was used at the end of all three strophes.

Not only is the structure both simple and regular; the development of the theme is as easily detectable. The poet has put together three stages in the development of the religious experience. Since the Korahites were a guild of singers whose vocation kept them in constant service at the temple, it is likely that the first stanza represents their somewhat specialized and professional experience of worship, which is not for that reason any less vital and devoted. The second stanza clearly portrays the mood of the pilgrim who is on his way to the great feast. He is the wayfarer to worship; his experience is therefore less intense than that of those who live within the temple precincts. The third stanza presents one who stands somewhat more remote from the temple than the other two. He neither ministers in the temple ritual nor ascends to the city to celebrate the feast, but he feels nevertheless that he has claims of his own on the divine favor. If he cannot be priest or worshiper, he can still trust in the Lord for the fulfillment of his work.

It hardly needs pointing out that these three conditions or relative positions of the experience of religion have their parallel in all religions, and notably so in our own religious culture. In general there are three classes of people who are said to be within the orbit of formal religion: the celebrant, the worshiper, and the aspirant. In this poem they are represented first as the one to whom dwelling in the temple is as natural for him as for the nesting sparrow and swallow; second, as the one who looks steadfastly toward God in Zion; and third, as the one who, for good reasons denied even a day in the courts, still feels that such a brief interval there is worth more than its multiple by a thousand elsewhere. Presumably there were many in the poet's day, as in ours, who could not be classified in any of these three categories, but he makes no mention of them.

1-4. ***The Delights of the Temple Dweller.***—What is the experience of the temple dweller whose vocation is contained within its portals? These verses describe it; it is satisfying to the sense of beauty, it is a compelling emotional experience, it is natural, and it is felicitous. These four factors were either the cause or the effect of the religious vocation as it was exercised in Israel. We do not wish to make too much of it, but at least it is interesting to note that there is no reference here to the satisfactions that are demanded by the mind as opposed to emotional gratification. This is an early poem; religious ideas were not strictly formulated until much later. God and the satisfactions he provided were taken for granted rather than logically arrived at. For this reason our poet

2 My soul longeth, yea, even fainteth for
the courts of the LORD: my heart and my
flesh crieth out for the living God.
3 Yea, the sparrow hath found a house,
and the swallow a nest for herself, where she
may lay her young, *even* thine altars, O
LORD of hosts, my King, and my God.
4 Blessed *are* they that dwell in thy
house: they will be still praising thee. Selah.

2 My soul longs, yea, faints
for the courts of the LORD;
my heart and flesh sing for joy
to the living God.

3 Even the sparrow finds a home,
and the swallow a nest for herself,
where she may lay her young,
at thy altars, O LORD of hosts,
my king and my God.
4 Blessed are those who dwell in thy house,
ever singing thy praise! *Selah*

---

2. Cf. 42:1-2; 63:1. **Soul . . . heart . . . flesh:** These terms taken together point to the psalmist's whole being. **Sing for joy:** This is the usual meaning of the Hebrew, whereas **crieth out** may suggest anguish. **The living God:** See Exeg. on 42:1-5.

2. THE HAPPINESS OF THOSE DWELLING IN THE TEMPLE (84:3-4)

3. The psalmist envies the birds who nest in the temple grounds. **Sparrow** is the word generally rendered "bird" in the RSV (8:8; 11:1; 102:7; etc.). **At thy altars** cannot mean "upon" the altars (which would hardly be tolerated), but "in the vicinity of" them. There were two altars, the smaller one for incense within the temple itself, and the larger (of bronze, later of stone) for animal sacrifices in the open court before the temple building. A third altar is reported to have been introduced by King Ahaz (II Kings 16:10-16).

4. The blessedness of the priesthood. The Mishnah records that the priests on duty in the temple slept in the "Chamber of the Hearth" (Tamid 1:1), and probably this was an ancient practice; cf. the lodgings in the temple area assigned to Tobiah the Ammonite (Neh. 13:4-9). For similar longings for the security and peace of the temple cf. 23:6; 27:4; 65:4.

---

sets forth here an experience that is intensely emotional and deeply mystical. He is so impressed with the loveliness of the temple that he can do little more than ejaculate ecstatically:

How lovely is thy dwelling place,
O LORD of hosts!

There is a mood of course that regards beauty uncritically, and thinks that it thus does service to religion. The Hebrews were not gifted artistically, or perhaps it is more accurate to say that they did not exercise their gifts in graphic, plastic, or architectural artifacts. This grew out of the proscription of images by the Second Commandment. It was on the temple therefore that aesthetic endowments were lavished. There is little wonder then that the sight of it repeatedly called for raptured comment from the aesthetically impoverished. The word **lovely,** which describes our poet's reaction, says a great deal while saying very little.

Vs. 2 expresses the ecstatic mystical experience in extreme terms as it gives us the second element in the vocational experience of religion. The imagery is as clear as it is intense. Here the soul is described as longing for the experience of God with the acuteness of famishing hunger. Indeed, it is overcome until in a sudden revelation of God both heart and flesh are restored and song breaks involuntarily from the lips.

My soul longs, yea, faints
for the courts of the LORD;
my heart and flesh sing for joy
to the living God.

That, the poet thinks, is no strange or unnatural thing. It is a part of the order of nature with which he was familiar that he, a man, should live in the precincts of God as naturally as the birds that made their nests there. Religion was indeed so indigenous a matter that God's created things found his altars a health-giving environment in which to bring up their families! **Even the sparrow,** that ubiquitous and unprepossessing creature, **finds a home, and the swallow,** a graceful and indefatigable little thing, **a nest for herself . . . at thy altars, O LORD of hosts.**

This experience is not only aesthetically

5 Blessed *is* the man whose strength *is* in thee; in whose heart *are* the ways *of them.*
6 *Who* passing through the valley of Baca make it a well; the rain also filleth the pools.
7 They go from strength to strength, *every one of them* in Zion appeareth before God.

5 Blessed are the men whose strength is in thee,
in whose heart are the highways to Zion.[r]
6 As they go through the valley of Baca
they make it a place of springs;
the early rain also covers it with pools.
7 They go from strength to strength;
the God of gods will be seen in Zion.

[r] Heb lacks *to Zion*

---

3. The Joy of Pilgrims to Zion (84:5-7)

5. The men is a translation of אדם, justified by the context, rather than **the man. The highways to Zion: To Zion** is not in the M.T. but is supplied to give sense. So also Ibn Ezra, ERV, ASV, *et al.*

6. A crux for the commentators. **The valley of Baca:** The name of the valley is thought to come from the Baka shrub or tree, but this has not been identified with certainty. Many think it is the balsam tree. Nor has the valley been located, although II Sam. 5:22-24 may point to a region south of Jerusalem. Presumably it was a comparatively sterile spot through which the road to Zion passed. **They make it a place of springs:** If the text is sound, it possibly means that the pilgrims in their gladness of heart find the valley much less dry than it is reputed to be. **The early rain,** which falls from late October until December, ends the summer drought. **Pools:** A repointing of the Hebrew. The M.T. is "blessings."

7. From strength to strength: The man whose strength is in the Lord grows stronger from day to day, and is not fatigued by his journey to Zion (cf. Isa. 40:31; Prov. 4:18). **The God of gods will be seen in Zion:** This rendering, favored by Calvin, is based on a small emendation, and is supported by the LXX and the Syriac. **Will be seen** virtually means "his presence will be felt during the festival."

---

satisfying, intense, and natural for our court dweller; it is also happy, and endless intonations of praise are the proof of his felicity. This element is necessary, for there is no certain guarantee that the other three components will add up to happiness. There is some satisfaction, to be sure, in contemplating loveliness, but it lacks much of providing deep religious joy. Ecstatic and rapt contemplation can be both fatiguing and depressing, and there is no guarantee that what is natural is also joyous. To our poet, however, there is the experience that he must make explicit. For him, at least, the specialized temple vocation was a happy one. He even acts as proxy for his temple colleagues as he says:

> **Blessed are those who dwell in thy house,**
> **ever singing thy praise!**

5-8. ***The Delights of the Worshiper.***—The celebrant, whether singer or priest, would find a more vivid experience of religious devotion and perhaps express it in a way that differed from the pilgrim worshiper, for whom a visit to the temple was a seasonal or periodic venture. In certain religious cultures temple worship is the sum total of religion, and becomes so perfunctory as to lose all real value. It is a lifeless and often unmeaning routine, and more often than not is little more than a trip to the temple on market day. Not so the pilgrim here described. The season of backbreaking labor is ended. Long days and arduous toil have yielded harvests and the festival of Ingathering promises change and recreation. **Blessed are the men whose strength is in thee,** sings this tired man who feels somehow that his journey to the festival is to be strength-renewing, and he adds, **in whose heart are the highways to Zion.** By this he means that all during the days of toil the prospect of the autumn journey was never out of his heart's hopes. It was a long journey, through lands parched by the late summer heat, but he was undaunted. On the contrary, the gaiety of his own eager spirit seemed to convert a particularly arid valley, where only the rugged balsam tree could grow, into a place of springs. And instead of each day adding cumulative fatigue to his progress, he grows stronger, as if the steadfastness of his purpose to worship were a fillip to tired feet (vss. 6-7). As he plods

8 O LORD God of hosts, hear my prayer: give ear, O God of Jacob. Selah.
9 Behold, O God our shield, and look upon the face of thine anointed.
10 For a day in thy courts *is* better than a thousand. I had rather be a doorkeeper in the house of my God, than to dwell in the tents of wickedness.

8 O LORD God of hosts, hear my prayer;
give ear, O God of Jacob! *Selah*
9 Behold our shield, O God;
look upon the face of thine anointed!

10 For a day in thy courts is better
than a thousand elsewhere.
I would rather be a doorkeeper in the house of my God
than dwell in the tents of wickedness.

4. PETITION (84:8-9)

8-9. These verses, which break the continuity of the psalm, may be due to the adaptation of the original poem to liturgical use.

9. Our shield and **thine anointed** evidently refer to the same person, as the phrasing of the RSV suggests. The reference may be to the high priest, but is more likely to be to the king (cf. Exeg. of "anointed" in 28:8). Patton (*Canaanite Parallels,* p. 41), on the basis of Ugaritic, suggests taking מגננו **(our shield)** as a verb, "We implore."

5. TRUST IN THE LORD (84:10-12)

While a day in the temple brings untold happiness, the supreme blessedness comes to the man, wherever he is, whose trust is in the Lord of hosts. This trust, however, is morally conditioned: one must **walk uprightly.**

10. Elsewhere is not in the Hebrew but appears to be justified by the context. **I would rather be a doorkeeper:** Lit., "I choose to stand at the threshold." The thought may be to act as a humble servant of the temple, perhaps as a porter, although this work could be done only by those qualified by birth to do it (cf. I Chr. 26:1-32); or to be a

along a recurrent strain keeps moving his lips as in a prayer (vs. 8).

9-12. ***The Fulfillment of the Joy of Worship.***—Celebrant and pilgrim—these represent different levels of the religious experience, but our poet brings another impersonation into his song, and though he cannot essay the role of either of the other two, yet he confesses to warmth and wistfulness in his soul. It is quite likely that this person looked on the harvest festival with different eyes. He toiled in no fields; he sang in no temple choir; he wore armor and stood sentinel against the encroachments of the foe. Battlements were more familiar to him than temple altars, and instead of the censer of the priest he carried the shield of the soldier. The nature and rigor of his job allowed him no holiday, and with understandable envy he could wish to stand guard for a day in the temple—one day that would be better than a thousand in the tents of wickedness, or the bivouac of his unresting duty.

He sees, however, even in his drab routine, things that remind him of the God others serve and the temple others can visit. He lifts up his shield as a gesture of devotion, and asks that God's radiance be reflected on him as on others who have his pleasure (vs. 9). He is confident that the dismal work to which he is perforce bound is not a barrier to God's favor or the bestowal of blessing (vss. 10-11). His final *Te deum* (vs. 12), probably sung at the end of each of the other two stanzas, has unique meaning for one engaged as he was in the soldier's precarious trade.

The entire psalm is a bright and gayhearted song which evoked, we may be sure, the hearty participation of the worshiping choruses. Our own delight in singing it is testimony enough to that. But once again we find in it wisdom deeper than its words, and intimations that are more deeply moving than its cadences. This of course is the true meaning of inspiration, and the real reason why these poems have been preserved and used by all those who seek for words to give body to their feelings. Lifted momentarily out of their context, some of these verses are rich in suggestiveness. One recalls, in reading of the anguished longing of the priest for God, another Priest who pronounced that hunger and thirst after righteousness are blessed. What a delightful insinuation is half-concealed in the words about the pilgrim, **In whose heart are the highways to Zion.** Out of the heart "are the issues of life," said the writer of Prov. 4:23, knowing that out of the heart

11 For the LORD God *is* a sun and shield: the LORD will give grace and glory: no good *thing* will he withhold from them that walk uprightly.

12 O LORD of hosts, blessed *is* the man that trusteth in thee.

To the chief Musician, A Psalm for the sons of Korah.

85 LORD, thou hast been favorable unto thy land: thou hast brought back the captivity of Jacob.

11 For the LORD God is a sun and shield;
he bestows favor and honor.
No good thing does the LORD withhold
from those who walk uprightly.
12 O LORD of hosts,
blessed is the man who trusts in thee!

To the choirmaster. A Psalm of the Sons of Korah.

85 LORD, thou wast favorable to thy land;
thou didst restore the fortunes of Jacob.

---

beggar at the temple gates (cf. Acts 3:2); or to be one of the throng of ordinary people who could barely squeeze past the gates on a festive day. **The tents of wickedness:** The reference may be to fellow Hebrews, or to scoffing Gentiles (cf. 42:3; 120:5).

11. A sun and shield: While God as a **shield** is a common figure in the Psalter (3:3; 7:10; 18:2; etc.), nowhere else in the O.T. is he called the **sun** (cf. Mal. 4:2). Possibly this identification was avoided because of the sun worship so prevalent among Israel's neighbors (cf. Deut. 4:19; 17:3; II Kings 23:5; Job 31:26-28; etc.). A somewhat parallel phrase, "my light and my salvation," occurs in 27:1 (cf. Isa. 60:19-20). **Those who walk uprightly:** Who live in moral integrity (cf. Exeg. on 15:2-5*b*, where "blamelessly" of RSV is the same word as **uprightly**).

12. Who trusts in thee: The placing of one's confidence in the Lord is a theme to which the psalms repeatedly return (4:5; 9:10; 13:5; 21:7; etc.).

LXXXV. GRANT US THY SALVATION (85:1-13)

Some describe this psalm as a lament of the community, others as a prophetic liturgy. In either case its three divisions are unmistakable: vss. 1-3 refer to the Lord's past beneficence to Jacob; vss. 4-7 are an urgent plea that the Lord should again save

---

man's impulses walk the highways to Zion or elsewhere. In the somewhat more familiar rendering of vs. 6 we see what the gay heart of a traveler through the barrens of life can do for those who share his journeyings. He is not content to hurry over the desert stretches toward a more hospitable place; he stops and digs a well for those who must travel more slowly than he or must even spend their days in bitterness. It is our feeling that it is because this song is so highhearted that these bright suggestions are voiced by the careful singer; but as already indicated, it is the total structure and volume of the song that make the more profound impression.

We have, then, a picture of three levels of religious inspiration set within the general framework of the great festival occasion. The first is that of the temple dweller, the second the pilgrim, the third the man who finds God by meeting him far away from temple or pilgrim band. Each of these is devout, expressing his own need and its satisfaction in his own way. The mystic rapture, the pilgrim quest, the lonely vigil—these are all familiar, for they have their counterparts in the religious experience of every culture. To each also the spirit of God is mediated by the very things to which one's life is committed. We therefore hesitate to assign to any one a more authentic quality than to another. The lonely sentinel on the outpost sees the Lord God on battlement and shield; the pilgrim digging a well calls on the Lord God of hosts to hear his prayer; and the mystic by the silent altar sings for joy to the living God.

No summary of the matter needs to go any further than the inclusiveness of vs. 12. Each expression of the experience of God stands unimpeachable in its own right. Each man has found his own measure of happiness in his own way.

O LORD of hosts,
blessed is the man who trusts in thee!

85:1-13. ***The Importance of Historical Perspective.***—The Expos. of Ps. 80 commented on the significance of the sense of history as it

his people; vss. 8-13 bring the reassurance that the Lord will indeed deliver his saints. These latter verses are in fact a short hymn whose beauty of diction and thought is almost unmatched in the Psalter. The psalm as a whole is another testimony to the rugged quality of Israel's belief in God.

Many commentators (e.g., Weiser) suppose that the psalmist lived in the sixth century B.C., and that his words reflect the situation in Palestine sometime after 538 B.C. These scholars cite Hag. 1:6-11; 2:15-19 as evidence that about 520 B.C. Judah experienced an economic and spiritual depression. We must observe, however, that the psalmist's words are rather vague, and that unlike many laments, they make no allusion to the machinations of outside enemies. The psalm, in truth, furnishes very tenuous evidence for a specific date (cf. Exeg. of **glory** in vs. 9). The only justifiable conclusion is that the plaint originated on an occasion when some danger threatened the whole community.

The third section of the psalm, vss. 8-13, has been thought to be eschatological (cf. Kittel, Oesterley). It must be admitted that the psalmist's words, dealing as they do with the things of God, necessarily have an absolute character and even an eschatological coloring, and it is these features of the psalm which justify the choice of it in the Book of Common Prayer as a "proper psalm" for Christmas Day. But the circumstances under which we believe the poem was written called for some immediate relief, and there is no reason to suppose that the author himself was looking forward to anything but a speedy demonstration of the Lord's saving power.

Some scholars (e.g., Mowinckel, Leslie) treat this psalm as a prayer for the New Year festival. It is possible that it was so employed, but there is nothing in the psalm to indicate that this was its original purpose or even the commonest use to which it was put. The meter is generally 3+3.

1. The Lord's Past Beneficence (85:1-3)

This strophe, as well as the following, may have been sung by a choir or by the congregation. Vss. 1-3 refer to some past acts of graciousness on the part of the Lord (cf. a similar opening in Ps. 126). A number of occasions could have been in the psalmist's mind (e.g., Jeroboam II's reign, Sennacherib's withdrawal from Judah in 701 B.C., Josiah's reign, Cyrus' edict of 538 B.C.).

85:1. Restore the fortunes of: This is now generally taken to be the correct translation of the phrase שׁבוּת (השׁיב) שׁב, rather than **brought back the captivity of** (cf. Job 42:10). The verse therefore has no necessary reference to a return from exile. **Jacob:** The whole nation.

---

develops in the life of a people. Isolated events are given continuity within an emerging pattern, and the past becomes the monitor of the present. This is an evidence of cultural maturity and gives the rational basis for what becomes sooner or later, with every mature culture, a sense of destiny. As often as not, perhaps, a sense of destiny and the moral energy it supplies to cultural expansion tend to blur the sense of history which was its source. It is then to be corrected by a restoration of an accurate historical perspective. However ruthless or benign history may be, the mind of man has no more patient and infallible teacher.

The historical sense manifest in the poems of ancient Israel is unique in its identification of her vicissitudes with the purposes and acts of God. This salient point created questions beyond the poet's power to answer, but his bafflement never led him to deny the divine agent of his fortunes. If he could not complete his syllogism, he would at least hold on to his major premise. The poem here is a case in point. There is much about it that is unclear to the critical and literary scholar, but in spite of this, it is one of the most interesting and highminded in the Psalter. It was written apparently for rendition by the singers' guild, and cast in such a form as could be used by soloists and chorus in antiphonal response. The three strophes are clearly set off from each other and deal with the different emphases the poet-historian wants to make. The literary quality is exalted, and it has given to our own tongue certain phrases that have long had common usage.

We have here a literary triptych. The first panel presents the writer's recollections of a golden age that is past; the second is a dismal portrayal, in striking poetic parallels to the

2 Thou hast forgiven the iniquity of thy people; thou hast covered all their sin. Selah.
3 Thou hast taken away all thy wrath: thou hast turned *thyself* from the fierceness of thine anger.
4 Turn us, O God of our salvation, and cause thine anger toward us to cease.
5 Wilt thou be angry with us for ever? wilt thou draw out thine anger to all generations?
6 Wilt thou not revive us again: that thy people may rejoice in thee?
7 Show us thy mercy, O LORD, and grant us thy salvation.

2 Thou didst forgive the iniquity of thy people;
thou didst pardon all their sin. *Selah*
3 Thou didst withdraw all thy wrath;
thou didst turn from thy hot anger.

4 Restore us again, O God of our salvation,
and put away thy indignation toward us!
5 Wilt thou be angry with us for ever?
Wilt thou prolong thy anger to all generations?
6 Wilt thou not revive us again,
that thy people may rejoice in thee?
7 Show us thy steadfast love, O LORD,
and grant us thy salvation.

---

2. **Iniquity . . . sin:** See Exeg. on 32:1-2, 5, and cf. 78:38.

3. **Thy wrath:** The anger of the Lord is a reality to the psalmists (2:5, 12; 6:1; 7:6; 21:9; 27:9; etc.).

2. PLEA FOR SALVATION (85:4-7)

4. The present straits of the nation are evidence of the divine anger.

5. Cf. 74:1; 77:7; 79:5; 80:4.

6. On the joy of the godly cf. 9:2, 14; 13:5; 14:7; etc.

---

first, of the unhappy present; and the third is a picture of a golden age that is to come. If we incline to call in question such arbitrary segmentations of time, we must be reminded again that we are reading poetry, not chronicles.

1-3. ***Former Glories.***—The sense of history is not necessarily concerned primarily with accuracy. For this reason it has always had a fondness for fanciful reconstructions of the past in terms of national greatness and glory. Psychologically this is related to the wistfulness for "the good old days," so common with frustrated or disappointed individuals. It is one way to escape the cheerless present. Our author may write with some degree of accuracy, but there is not a great deal in the early records of Israel that can be described as golden. Nevertheless we have here in the first strophe four ideas that, as they were reflected upon, recalled an almost Edenic felicity. It is hardly accidental that they occur in a sequence of ascending importance. One to whom God was the all-important fact would set him at the apex of the scale of values. Thus when we read what God had done in the golden age of Jacob, we find material values, moral values, and spiritual values in an ascending scale. God's favor was first to the land, for land was the basis of Jacob's physical fortunes (vs. 1). But to a God-conscious people the restoration of their former good fortune on the land was of little worth if they were under the blight of moral ruin. It was through their sin that evil days had fallen; restoration therefore would come with forgiveness (vs. 2). Yet even this is not enough. To be forgiven was not an end in itself; it was a means to restored fellowship with the divine friend. What good were fortune and forgiveness without friendliness (vs. 3)?

This was the sort of golden age we should expect a pious son of Israel to recall. In the remote past there had been physical disaster turned into fortune by God's favor, and there had been moral debacle turned into complete forgiveness by God's compassion. These two acts of restoration had been crowned with the love of God displacing his wrath, his kindness setting aside his hot anger. Fortune, forgiveness, and the friendliness of God: these were the outlines of the glorious past within which fancy could fit the alluring details.

4-7. ***The Continuing Providence.***—The second strophe clearly indicates what we mean by the sense of history as the feeling of continuity. The great age of the past was not set off from the present by conditions that could not be reproduced. The Lord God does not change either by a loss of power or a whim of fancy. It is man's folly and sin that bring his misery upon him. Therefore it is in man's own power to create within himself a condition that will release once again God's favor. It was not a

8 I will hear what God the LORD will speak: for he will speak peace unto his people, and to his saints: but let them not turn again to folly.
9 Surely his salvation *is* nigh them that fear him; that glory may dwell in our land.

8 Let me hear what God the LORD will speak,
for he will speak peace to his people,
to his saints, to those who turn to him in their hearts.[s]
9 Surely his salvation is at hand for those who fear him,
that glory may dwell in our land.

[s] Gk: Heb *but let them not turn back to folly*

3. THE LORD'S GOODNESS (85:8-13)

An individual voice is heard, possibly one of the temple staff. Like Second Isaiah, he speaks "comfortably to Jerusalem" (Isa. 40:2). It should be observed, however, that the salvation he promises is for **those who fear** the Lord (cf. a similar qualification in Rom. 8:28). Equally significant is the linking of God's coming with **steadfast love, faithfulness, righteousness,** and **peace.** Where these qualities are, God is (cf. Gal. 5:22-23; I John 4:16).

8. On God's speaking to a psalmist cf. 62:11. **His saints:** See Exeg. on 79:2. The M.T. of the last clause of the present verse probably means, "And let them not return in confidence" (cf. **to folly**). As this makes little sense, most scholars resort to emendations. The RSV adopts **to those who turn to him in their hearts,** which has some support in the LXX.

9. Glory: The glory of the presence of the Lord, especially in the temple (cf. 63:2; Ezek. 10:18; 43:4; Zech. 2:5; etc.). This verse may imply that the psalmist lived at a time when the Lord was not in the temple; in this case, the date might be somewhere between 587 and 516 B.C.

new and different age our poet wanted; it was a restoration of the old, a restoration based on the reciprocal relationship between a righteous God and a righteous people. Thus when our author looked about him, he saw both the condition into which the people had fallen, and by inference, the cause of it. God was not angry for nothing; his kindness was not capriciously withheld. Restoration in the gloomy present could come, but not without reciprocity. Thus as he prayed for a recurrence of the days of old, he certainly had in mind the human defections that once again, as so often in their history, had evoked the indignation of God. In this strophe the chief concern apparently was to escape God's anger. Restoration of fortune to the land—the revival that was his concern (vs. 6)—must wait on moral restoration.

Wilt thou be angry with us for ever?
Wilt thou prolong thy anger to all generations?

This latter question is purely a literary device, a rhetorical question that prepares the way for the third strophe's idealistic picture of a future time of great glory. At this point it serves to emphasize the gravity of Israel's defections, as if they deserved God's endless anger. Once his wrath is abated, they will expect a revival of their depressed fortunes and spirits; and to crown it all, the exhibition again of God's kindness and the grant of his salvation (vss. 6-7).

8-13. *The Fulfillment of Hope.*—The soloist has sung the first strophe, perhaps in a major key, to give musical emphasis to the glories his words recall. The chorus has responded with the second strophe, we assume in a minor key, to give musical color to the somber scene the words represent. What follows? It is generally agreed that vs. 8, introducing the final strophe, was sung by a second solo voice. We can without difficulty imagine the sturdy and confident recitative with which he began his melodic reply to the glories of the past and the prayers for the present. It is a great sentiment, and like others of its unique pattern in Israel's thought, it was predicated upon man's conscious and righteous relations with God. There will be no restoration except to those who acknowledge themselves to be God's people, to those whose lives are his in saintliness, to those who turn from their foolish trust in themselves to him. The prayer for restoration has been uttered, but its answer will be heard only by the deserving.

After vs. 8 there is a dramatic pause and then, as if the singer has heard the word for

KJV	RSV
10 Mercy and truth are met together; righteousness and peace have kissed *each other.*	10 Steadfast love and faithfulness will meet; righteousness and peace will kiss each other.
11 Truth shall spring out of the earth; and righteousness shall look down from heaven.	11 Faithfulness will spring up from the ground, and righteousness will look down from the sky.

10. Cf. 40:11; 89:14; 97:2. The tenses of the verbs in the RSV are justified by the context.

11. This verse, like vs. 10, is sheer poetry, and it may be improper to press the language too closely. But there seems to be an antithesis between **earth** (which is better than RSV's **ground**) and **heaven,** and the point may be that when the Lord's salvation comes there will be perfect harmony between the terrestrial and celestial worlds. The divine attributes of vs. 10 will have become the virtues of mankind.

which he was listening, he says: **Surely his salvation** [man's eager and deathless hope] **is at hand for those who fear him, that glory may dwell in our land.** He has his answer, and he will proceed at once to describe the coming glory. The final strophe is so rich in suggestiveness that down the ages it has been variously employed by those for whom it has had special interest. It has been a vision of utopia, a forecast of the glories of heaven, or a clear indication of an early Jewish belief in immortality. For our purposes it is a poet's dream, an idealization of the full restoration for which he has just been praying. Its imagery is striking: great ideals move about as beatified persons; it is a glory that may dwell in the land, not an eschatological hope. There are, in this preview of the restoration of the fortunes of Jacob, two areas of action: that of human intercourse, and that of physical nature. In the former there are the hypostatized figures of four qualities of ideal human association; in the latter the ideal earth and the sky interact productively.

Steadfast love and faithfulness will meet;
righteousness and peace will kiss each other.

What is this metaphor saying? Was it not that an unnatural estrangement had come about between these four allegorical emblems of human virtue at its highest? Steadfast love and faithfulness, righteousness and peace are natural pairs. Normally one is not seen without the other. In a situation, then, in which they are represented as reunited, it must be that some unnatural circumstance had separated them for a time. Faithfulness is the core of all virtue—that incorruptible, stanch, and fearless integrity the opposite of which is slickness, caprice, calculation. Steadfast love is to faithfulness what consideration is to hardness; it is that quality which keeps integrity aware of the need to restore the disintegrated, that tempers the wind of sternness to the shorn lamb of indecision. If faithfulness is the core of all virtue, peace is the heart of all felicity, and righteousness is its only needed credential. Our poet then has apparently recalled a former situation in which the dark opposites of these shining creatures have interposed their sinister figures between them. Dishonesty and ruthlessness have insinuated themselves into human affairs, giving plausible reasons for their claims to superior virtue. Similarly, because this earlier pair has made a place for them, evil and disorder have established themselves as the normal routine of human relationships. In such distressful circumstance the perfect coalition of steadfast love and faithfulness is dissolved, and each without the other is distraught and relatively impotent. Similarly, the separation of righteousness and peace immobilizes and enfeebles each. Little wonder that in the first two strophes of our poem God's attitude is described in such uncompromising words as **hot anger, wrath, indignation.** Under the conditions, then, in which God's forgiveness and kindness are awarded to those who have turned to him with confidence (vs. 8), there follows glad reunion of the divided virtues. The greeting of the first is duly circumspect; but righteousness and peace embrace each other in the rapture of their reunion.

This is an allegory of restoration on the level of human experience, carried over in similar language to the physical level. Man does not live by peace alone. To a people whose livelihood was largely in the fields under the sun, the ideal of sturdy crops and salubrious weather was perennially inviting. Again the picture we have is set over against capricious weather and the soil's niggardly and grudging yield, but our writer does not forget that he is allegorizing; the crop that springs luxuriously from the soil

12 Yea, the LORD shall give *that which is* good; and our land shall yield her increase.
13 Righteousness shall go before him; and shall set *us* in the way of his steps.

A Prayer of David.

86 Bow down thine ear, O LORD, hear me: for I *am* poor and needy.

12 Yea, the LORD will give what is good,
and our land will yield its increase.
13 Righteousness will go before him,
and make his footsteps a way.

A Prayer of David.

86 Incline thy ear, O LORD, and answer me,
for I am poor and needy.

---

12. Cf. 84:11; Jas. 1:17. **Yield its increase:** Cf. 67:6. The O.T. frequently reiterates that part of the Lord's blessing is of a material kind (cf. Lev. 26:3-13; Deut. 28:1-14; etc.).

13. Make his footsteps a way represents one interpretation of a rather obscure clause. The thought, then, is that **righteousness** is a herald clearing **a way** for the Lord's coming (cf. 89:14; Isa. 58:8).

LXXXVI. A CRY FOR GOD'S SUCCOR (86:1-17)

While some scholars (e.g., Buttenwieser) maintain that this psalm voices the cry of the nation, most commentators consider it to be the lament of an individual. It is impossible, however, to reconstruct the circumstances which elicited his supplication.

---

is the faithfulness that is rejoined to steadfast love in the new Eden, and the rich nurture of the skies is the righteousness that kisses peace. Thus the relationships of human beings with each other, and with the source of their physical livelihood, are re-established in idyllic equilibrium. That this confidence is based on God and on no lesser consideration is made explicit in vs. 12. Here both the human and land levels of experience are recognized and provided for.

The concluding vs. 13 calls up imagery of great power and beauty. It is the pageantry of triumphal advance. The *avant-garde* is not naked power or arrogant pomp. Righteousness and peace go ahead, marking out a highway; and we may properly assume that in our poet's mind there was the realization that the way righteousness would mark out for the Lord's footsteps would be conspicuously different from the direction its opposite would indicate.

We have seen in this specific instance the manner in which a sense of history gives continuity, substance, and idealism to the vicissitudes of national life. From the dim but certain glories of the past, through the valley of humiliation and despair, to the no less certain glories of the future, our poet has sketched the fortunes of his people. He is romantic, to be sure, but his optimism is based on his solid faith in the ultimate triumph of God in which men may, if they will, participate. Nor does his enthusiastic hope for the future dull his realistic understanding of the folly and sin that had invited his people's misadventures in the past.

The enthusiasm with which this song was originally sung can be easily imagined; with certain local and current annotations it can even now be rendered with considerable verve, since it contains assumptions which make it eternally relevant. If utopianism today is as ephemeral as a fad, it may be because it rests upon the promises of science, which shift alternately from predictions of superlative contentment to superlative despair. The reason is obvious: Those promises deal with man in his horizontal relationships alone. Our poet is wiser, for he sees what our culture allows us so easily to forget: that man's fortunes derive ultimately from his relationship to God as expressed in moral imperatives. His utopian dream presents integrity and gentleness, goodness and serenity, as ideal relationships. These are moral ideals, attainable only by moral consent.

Thus the towering hope with which the poem closes is neither idle nor unrealistic to those who have accepted the presuppositions of our poet's religious faith. To deny them is to retreat to amoralism, which means that there are lost the transcendent moral values upon which hope ultimately rests. That the Lord will give what is good, and that righteousness will mark the way for his footsteps, is no small claim to make. If our day declines to make this claim, the reasons for its unhappiness and fear are not far to seek, and the reason for its hopelessness is obvious.

86:1-17. ***The Problem of Trouble.***—It is not necessarily morbid to affirm, as Job did, that

The author describes himself as **poor and needy** (vs. 1), as familiar with **trouble** (vs. 7), as having been on the brink of death (vs. 13), and as surrounded by enemies who seek his life (vss. 14, 17). The reference in vs. 5 to God's readiness to forgive may imply that the speaker felt that he had sinned against the Lord. But nothing more precise can be found in the psalm, and we have simply to conclude that the psalmist was in great personal distress.

It is usually said that although the author was morally earnest, he had few literary gifts. Nearly every verse, or part of nearly every verse he wrote, can be paralleled in either the other psalms or elsewhere in the O.T. (cf. Exeg. below), and it is generally assumed that our psalmist was indebted to these other sources. The variety in the names for God (יהוה, **Lord**; אלהים, **God**; אל, **God**; אדני, **Lord**—the latter being used oftener than in any other psalm) seems to testify to the diverse resources of the author. We can at least grant that the psalmist was steeped in Israel's conventional language of devotion, and that, if he borrowed a good deal of his phraseology from other writings, he displayed considerable individuality as well as good taste in the creation of his own poem.

As a lament usually sets forth near its beginning the grounds of the complaint, it is noteworthy that it is not until vs. 14 that the psalmist's foes are mentioned, whereas vss. 12-13 appear to imply that deliverance from them has already come. Schmidt therefore suggests (being followed by Leslie) that the order of verses in the psalm should be vss. 1-7, 14-17, 8-13. From our point of view this rearrangement would greatly improve the structure of the poem, but we have no way of knowing whether it was the original order, or whether the psalmist would agree with our preference. The meter of the psalm is mixed, with 4+4 much in evidence.

"man is born unto trouble, as the sparks fly upward" (Job 5:7), for that lays no claim to finality as an analysis of the predilections with which man emerges to engage the mortal enterprise. Wordsworth, who knew something about trouble, matched Job's flying sparks with "trailing clouds of glory," a metaphor somewhat more flattering, even if it is no more accurate. Elsewhere we have found in the Psalms an effort to come to an understanding of the relation of trouble to behavior. The result got very little beyond a statement of the dilemma, nor can we be too sure that we have gone much beyond that ourselves. Trouble is part of the forfeit man pays to life.

When a man is in difficulty, he is more likely to ask questions about himself than when he is in clover. Whether he is likely to come up with more accurate answers is another matter, though failure to do so is certainly more generously forgiven by those who sympathize where they do not agree. This is no doubt all to the good, for a rationalization of unmitigated trouble might end in a pessimism as dangerous as the romantic recklessness that is the rationalization of unqualified joy.

Ps. 86 presents us with a man in **trouble.** The editors assigned its authorship to David, though it is manifestly not the work of any single writer. David, whose moods were varied and often extreme, made the allocation easy, particularly since there are some things said here which might have sounded presumptuous on other lips. The poem, whatever its origin and however difficult it is for the literary critic, served a real purpose, else it would not have been preserved in the Psalter. That purpose is manifest. When a man is in trouble, his mind is apt to revolve about three propositions: he will first consider his condition and how it came about; then he will inquire the nature and extent of the help that is available; finally, he will put one and two together in an effort to secure the right help for his already determined condition. To expect his analysis to be accurate, complete, or wholly plausible may be too much, but since all of us in our troubled moments are victims of the same things that bedeviled him, we smile tolerantly, remembering that we are all at one time or another tied up in the same bundle of misfortune. There is another matter about which it is well to be reminded: this poem is a prayer, not an argument. If therefore in his presentation of the three matters suggested above, the poet lacks something of order or even consistency, it will be helpful to remember that he is pouring out his heart in a petition, not disputing a cause.

1-4. ***Man in Trouble.***—Consider the psalmist's condition as he sets it forth in this section. The reason he is invoking the Lord's help is not merely his affliction but his helplessness. It is

2 Preserve my soul; for I *am* holy: O thou my God, save thy servant that trusteth in thee.

3 Be merciful unto me, O Lord: for I cry unto thee daily.

4 Rejoice the soul of thy servant: for unto thee, O Lord, do I lift up my soul.

5 For thou, Lord, *art* good, and ready to forgive; and plenteous in mercy unto all them that call upon thee.

6 Give ear, O LORD, unto my prayer; and attend to the voice of my supplications.

7 In the day of my trouble I will call upon thee: for thou wilt answer me.

2 Preserve my life, for I am godly;
save thy servant who trusts in thee.
3 Thou art my God; be gracious to me, O Lord,
for to thee do I cry all the day.
4 Gladden the soul of thy servant,
for to thee, O Lord, do I lift up my soul.
5 For thou, O Lord, art good and forgiving,
abounding in steadfast love to all who call on thee.
6 Give ear, O LORD, to my prayer;
hearken to my cry of supplication.
7 In the day of my trouble I call on thee,
for thou dost answer me.

1. PRAYERS AMID GREAT TROUBLES (86:1-7)

86:1. Cf. 17:6; 40:17.

2. Cf. 25:20. **For I am godly:** A bold affirmation, unique in the O.T. (cf. Jer. 3:12, spoken by God). On **godly** or **holy** see Exeg. on 79:2. **O thou my God:** The RSV moves these words to the beginning of vs. 3.

3-4. Cf. 57:1. **Daily:** The M.T. is **all the day.** On vs. 4, cf. 25:1.

5-7. Forgiving or **ready to forgive:** A word found only here (cf. 130:4; Exod. 34:6). On vs. 6, cf. 5:2; 28:2; 55:1. On vs. 7, cf. 77:2; 17:6.

this latter fact that gives emphasis to his importunity. He describes his prayer as a **cry of supplication,** and we may infer that his trouble is not some stubborn physical disability he cannot mend, but the design of enemies who seek his destruction. **O God,** he will presently cry in desperation, **insolent men have risen up against me; a band of ruthless men seek my life** (vs. 14*ab*). Insolence was an affront to his pride; his proper self-regard had been assaulted. He had suffered more than insult, however; ruthless men sought to destroy him altogether. It is no doubt this latter threat that induced his sense of helplessness. The affliction he suffered in his soul could be endured, but the jeopardy in which his life stood demanded more effective help than he could muster by himself.

This double indignity, the insolence which was a spiritual wound and the threat against his physical life, gives some help in explaining the case he makes for himself, a claim for divine assistance supported by his sense of rectitude. In coming to his aid, God would not have to overlook some sin or folly which had caused the misfortune. On the contrary, the suppliant was exactly the sort of person God would be expected to help (vs. 2). He is not culpable in the matter of the focus of his devotion or his record of performance, and in vss. 3-4 he continues his prayer.

5-6. ***Why Has This Been Allowed?***—The psalmist, we are forced to observe, has an astonishingly clean bill of health, a claim that demands immediate and thoroughgoing support. What explanation is to be made of the indifference on the part of God that has allowed such a paragon to fall prey to insolent and ruthless men? The problem seems not to have disturbed the petitioner, however. Other poets in other psalms have called on God to explain and justify his averted face when the righteous cry, or his idle hand when his children fall. Not so here. Our poet proceeds at once to describe the God to whom he makes his prayer. Far from questioning him, he exalts him. The effect, as we shall see, is to make his case all the more irresistible. What sort of God is he? **Good and forgiving.** The Exeg. tells us that this use of the word **forgiving** is unique. Nowhere else does it indicate that forgiving is God's trade or occupation, his normal métier.

7-10. ***Faith Falters but Recovers.***—Besides this fact about the nature of God, there is the further specific fact of former experience of his willingness to help. This was obviously not the poet's first contretemps; indeed, one might assume that he thinks the experience had been somewhat constant (vs. 7). It was a ritual

8 Among the gods *there is* none like unto
thee, O Lord; neither *are there any works*
like unto thy works.
9 All nations whom thou hast made shall
come and worship before thee, O Lord; and
shall glorify thy name.
10 For thou *art* great, and doest wondrous things: thou *art* God alone.
11 Teach me thy way, O LORD; I will
walk in thy truth: unite my heart to fear
thy name.
12 I will praise thee, O Lord my God,
with all my heart: and I will glorify thy
name for evermore.

8 There is none like thee among the gods,
O Lord,
nor are there any works like thine.
9 All the nations thou hast made shall come
and bow down before thee, O Lord,
and shall glorify thy name.
10 For thou art great and doest wondrous
things,
thou alone art God.
11 Teach me thy way, O LORD,
that I may walk in thy truth;
unite my heart to fear thy name.
12 I give thanks to thee, O Lord my God,
with my whole heart,
and I will glorify thy name for ever.

2. The Incomparable Lord (86:8-10)

8. Cf. 77:13; Exod. 15:11; Deut. 3:24. **Among the gods:** The meaning is either among the various gods worshiped by the Gentiles, or among the lesser gods of the heavenly host (see Exeg. on 82:1-8).

9. Cf. 22:27. **All the nations:** The God of Israel is the creator of all the nations of mankind (cf. Gen. 10:1-32; Deut. 32:8). **Bow down before thee:** The psalmist sees the day when the Lord will be recognized by the whole world (cf. 22:27-29; 65:2; 66:4; 67:7; 98:4; Isa. 42:6; 45:22-23; 66:23; Zech. 8:20-23; 14:16). This rather obscure saint thus shows himself to be a man of large ideas.

10. Cf. 72:18; 77:14; 83:18. **Thou alone art God:** Cf. Deut. 6:4; Isa. 44:6.

3. Petition and Thanksgiving (86:11-13)

11-12. Cf. 26:3; 27:11. **Thy truth:** In 26:3 the RSV translates the same Hebrew, "in faithfulness to thee." The word אמת signifies both "faithfulness" and **truth.** If the meaning here is **truth,** it must refer to the body of oral and written traditions cherished in Israel and believed to be sanctioned by God. **Unite my heart:** An expression found only here, but presumably meaning "give me single-mindedness" (cf. Jer. 32:39). Many scholars, supported by the LXX and the Syriac, repoint the Hebrew verb to get "let my heart rejoice" (from חדה). On vs. 12, cf. 9:1.

experience rather than an emergency. In vss. 8-9 he continues his estimate of the help he asks. It is unparalleled: **There is none like thee . . . nor are there any works like thine.** So are affirmed both God's rating and his ultimate recognition; and there follows the record:

> **For thou art great and doest wondrous things,**
> **thou alone art God.**

10-15. ***Former Experience.***—Up to this point, as our petitioner presents his claim and God's credentials, we have found ourselves involved in an interesting problem. Why evil men should get into trouble it is easy to see. Why an inept or indifferent Deity should leave them there presents no difficulty. Where, however, we see a godly man and a kindly and powerful God embroiled by man's trouble, we encounter a moral difficulty. The godly man should neither need nor ask for God's help; the kindly God should neither need nor ask man's supplication. If a good man cannot be kept out of the hands of insolent and ruthless men, who then can be saved? And yet, oddly enough, there is no hint of such a dilemma anywhere in this prayer.

The poet has described his predicament and assayed the quality of the help he needed. It remains to ask what he proposes as a way of securing his ally against the machinations of his adversaries. This is introduced with a second petition. He needs help desperately; he proposes to get it by learning more about the ways of God. Such piety in the face of exigent need would seem to be at the expense of safety. It may also appear to involve our poet in contra-

13 For great *is* thy mercy toward me: and thou hast delivered my soul from the lowest hell.

14 O God, the proud are risen against me, and the assemblies of violent *men* have sought after my soul; and have not set thee before them.

15 But thou, O Lord, *art* a God full of compassion, and gracious, long-suffering, and plenteous in mercy and truth.

16 O turn unto me, and have mercy upon me; give thy strength unto thy servant, and save the son of thine handmaid.

13 For great is thy steadfast love toward me;
thou hast delivered my soul from the depths of Sheol.

14 O God, insolent men have risen up against me;
a band of ruthless men seek my life,
and they do not set thee before them.
15 But thou, O Lord, art a God merciful and gracious,
slow to anger and abounding in steadfast love and faithfulness.
16 Turn to me and take pity on me;
give thy strength to thy servant,
and save the son of thy handmaid.

---

13. Cf. 56:13; Deut. 32:22. **The depths of Sheol:** Lit., "the lower [or lowest] Sheol," a phrase found elsewhere only in Deut. 32:22, although "the pit of the lowest parts" occurs in 88:6; Lam. 3:55, and "the lowest parts of the earth" in 63:9; Isa. 44:23 (cf. Ezek. 26:20; 31:14; 32:18). The psalmist is probably using popular phraseology, and it may be doubted whether he or any other O.T. writer conceived of grades within Sheol, as Oesterley suggests.

4. Plea for Help (86:14-17)

14-15. Cf. 54:3. **Insolent men** or **the proud:** See Exeg. on 119:21. **A band of ruthless men** rather than **the assemblies of violent men:** It is not clear whether the psalmist's adversaries are fellow Hebrews or Gentiles. On vs. 15, cf. Exod. 34:6.

16. Cf. 25:16. **The son of thy handmaid:** Either a conventional phrase meaning "thy trusted servant" (cf. 116:16; Gen. 14:14; Exod. 21:2-4), or a reference to the

---

diction, but from another point of view it may turn out to be the essence of saintliness. After all, this poem is a prayer; if that is forgotten, we shall certainly miss its point.

Whatever the way by which the poet proposes to enlist the continued help of God, it will be based upon his experience of God. This has already been mentioned (vs. 7), but it is made more explicit in vs. 13. He has had an experience which is described as deliverance from Sheol. What **Sheol** meant in early Hebrew thought is unimportant here, since what it meant for our poet is clear. His soul had been in **the depths** of the nether world, meaning, we assume, in the grip of uttermost despair. There is a distinction here between his life, threatened by insolent men, and his soul delivered from Sheol. He has the confidence to ask protection for his life because he has known deliverance of his soul. It was this great kindness toward him which gave a fillip to his hopes.

Such rescue as he needs and expects is not, however, wholly the operation of powers external to or independent of himself. It is a co-operative stratagem; and in order to measure up to his obligation, he proposes that he shall learn more of God's **way.** It is God's way of mercy and grace, of patience and kindness and fidelity, that he wants to learn in order that he will be able to conduct himself with constancy and to give his heart with singleness of purpose to reverent devotion to God.

16-17. ***Prayer of Petition.***—These verses supply the traditional ending to a prayer of petition. The situation the petitioner has described, compounded of a threat of immediate peril from men and a long and incessant hope in God, creates a burden of necessity he cannot bear alone. What sort of support he needs he states very simply: he needs **pity, strength,** rescue, and a portent of the divine favor. Such a demonstration would not only serve to imbue him with confidence; conversely, it would shame those who hated him, because they would see in his deliverance the stout aid of the Lord. This is a prayer cast in the mold of a poem. Both of these elements must be kept in mind if its importance for us is to be appropriated. The suppliant first considered his condition, then the resources available, and finally the way

17 Show me a token for good; that they
which hate me may see *it*, and be ashamed:
because thou, LORD, hast helped me, and
comforted me.

17 Show me a sign of thy favor,
that those who hate me may see and be
put to shame
because thou, LORD, hast helped me and
comforted me.

---

piety of the psalmist's mother. A Ugaritic parallel is cited by Pritchard (*Ancient Near Eastern Texts,* p. 143).

17. Cf. 6:10; 35:4. **A sign of thy favor:** Not a favorable oracle in the temple, or a dream of good omen (as Mowinckel would have it), but some demonstration of the Lord's grace and power which will impress the psalmist's foes.

---

in which he could apprehend them, and when that was done, he asked for pity, strength, and deliverance.

There are two ways in which this prayer-poem may be appraised. Its inconsistencies can be pointed out, and the conclusion reached that the petitioner was morally naïve. This sort of judgment has been hinted already. If he was as godly a man as he claimed, was not his predicament a subtle indictment of the godliness of God? If he and God were on the same side of the moral struggle, what had happened to separate them and divide their strength? One could run this sort of criticism to almost absurd and even cynical lengths, and thus completely miss the reason for the poem's preservation in a great anthology of devotional literature. But the Hebrew nation had as few cynics as it had heretics, for good reason: their major premise was the fact of God, and this effectively negated the logic of cynicism or nonconformity.

The second way of looking at this piece sees it within the framework of the authentic experience of saintliness. At first our friend's claim that he was a **godly** man sounds presumptuous. This is because in our times there is a sort of diffidence about using such a claim with reference to others, and a recoil from using it about ourselves. Such was not the case with this man. The term was used generally to denote those who acknowledged and worshiped God, and specifically to indicate a particular body of devout persons in the community. It was not inappropriately applied to the priesthood, but one need not have accepted the priestly vocation to deserve the title. Even among those designated as godly there were grades of achievement and levels of piety. Our poet represents a very high plane of genuine piety. Understanding thus his use of the descriptive adjective, we are in a position to distill from his prayer the essence of devotional excellence.

This saint's problem was with himself and with evil men. It is the paradox of saintliness that the higher the level of spiritual sensitiveness, the greater the feeling of spiritual need or even of failure. This is why the saint can assert his trust and yet cry for help, can claim godliness and yet seek to learn the ways of God. There is no inconsistency here. It is the man who claims godliness and disavows spiritual needs who proves himself a fraud. Thus our poet proposes to deal by ever-extending knowledge of God with the problem that is inside him.

What of the problem with evil men? The psalmist has not abstracted himself from human association, nor has he naïvely assumed that all people are like him and that consequently there can be no insolent or ruthless men. His question then becomes: How shall he deal with them? Since he is a godly man, he must use godly methods, apprehended by learning and practicing the **way** of the Lord. It is not enough to be taught; he must **walk in** [God's] **truth.** Before he engages himself with the fresh instruction he feels need of, he asks God's help in dealing with his antagonists. This he can rightly do because he has committed himself to God's way of handling insolent persons. What is God's way? Here we breathe the rarefied atmosphere of the saint's world, an atmosphere too finely pure for the robust and realistic man of our times. For God's ways are the ways of mercy and grace, of patience and faithfulness.

The cynic will turn from this in disgust, for he has little reason to believe that insolence and ruthlessness ever have yielded to patience, grace, and fidelity. The so-called realist will agree that there is perhaps something to be said ideally for such standards of saintly conduct, but he will say that for the most part the insolent and the ruthless respond better to arrogance and pitilessness than to gentler ways. So he will tell the saint that he lives in an unsaintly world, and of course he will be right.

Is there then to be no acceptance of the saint's way? Perhaps this godly man would point to the ways of the world as an answer—and pray for it.

A Psalm *or* Song for the sons of Korah.	A Psalm of the Sons of Korah. A Song.
87 His foundation *is* in the holy mountains.	87 On the holy mount stands the city he founded;

LXXXVII. A Song of Zion (87:1-7)

This short poem, classified by Gunkel as a Song of Zion, is one of the most striking in the Psalter. On the one hand, it is remarkably terse and enigmatic, almost to the point of obscurity, and on the other, its love for Jerusalem is as deep-seated as that expressed in Ps. 137, and, if we take one possible interpretation of vss. 4-6, its touches of universalism rise almost to the heights of Second Isaiah.

Scholars are divided with respect to the meaning of vss. 4-6. Some believe that in these verses the psalmist has in mind only Jews who are living among the Gentile nations, and that he is asserting that the rights of the Diaspora are equal to those whose homes are in Jerusalem. Others maintain that the author is a person of broad sympathies, that he is thinking of proselytes from paganism, and that he means that such converts are to be treated in Zion as full-born Jews. Taken in the second sense, the verses are an expansion of the thought of 86:9, which may explain why in the Psalter the present psalm follows Ps. 86. This interpretation of the song also makes it one of the O.T. passages that foreshadow such N.T. ideas as are found in Gal. 4:26; Eph. 2:12, 19.

It is an unfortunate feature of the psalm that its text is marked by not a few difficulties which have called forth a variety of emendations. Moreover, many scholars suspect that the original order of the lines has been tampered with, and they propose various rearrangements. Weiser (following Kittel) advocates the following sequences: vss. 1, 2, 3, 6, 4, 5, 7; three other schemes are offered by Gunkel, Herkenne, and Schmidt. As the RSV accepts the M.T. without change, the Exeg. makes no attempt to record, except in two instances, the various alterations in the text proposed by the commentators.

The date of the psalm depends upon the meaning placed on vss. 4-6, and upon our view as to how early less particularistic ideas began to be entertained in Israel. Most scholars place the poem in the exilic or postexilic period. Such a psalm as this might well have served pilgrims coming to one of the festivals. Vs. 7 indicates that it had some connection with a choral group.

1. In Praise of Zion (87:1-3)

87:1. The Hebrew is **His foundation is in the holy mountains,** of which the RSV is a paraphrase. The reference is to Jerusalem and its hills (cf. 125:2; 133:3). On the Lord's founding of Zion see Isa. 14:32. The phrase **the holy mountains** is rare, being found only here and in some MSS of 110:3. In the latter passage, where the RSV adopts the reading of these MSS, the mountains of Palestine are evidently meant.

87:1-7. ***God's Fatherhood; Man's Brotherhood.*** —It is clear that the arrangement of the sequences employed by the editors of the Psalter has nothing to do with the development of ideas expressed by the poets. No better indication of this is needed than the wide separation of mood and emphasis between Ps. 87 and Ps. 88. The first is informed by an unqualified expectation of God's universal dominion; the second is a cry of desperation unrelieved by respite or hope. While this is true, it nevertheless happens every once in a while that poems fall by accident into positions of natural affiliation, so that the mood of one seems continued or complemented by that of another. Some unknown but happy circumstance has united in this way Ps. 87 with Ps. 86. We found that despite certain puzzling irregularities in Ps. 86, the most satisfying interpretation showed it to be an idealized picture of the authentic saint, one who, while describing himself as a godly man, went on to ask for further guidance in the knowledge and practice of the way of God. In the presence of insolent and ruthless men the elevated idealism to which the way of God led the saint was put to formidable tests, but no prospect of testing daunted the saint's spirit.

Ps. 87 is the work of another idealist. Put together as a song, it pairs well with the prayer form of the godly man's idealism. It is an ex-

2 The LORD loveth the gates of Zion more than all the dwellings of Jacob.
3 Glorious things are spoken of thee, O city of God. Selah.

2 the LORD loves the gates of Zion
more than all the dwelling places of Jacob.
3 Glorious things are spoken of you,
O city of God. *Selah*

---

2. **The gates of Zion:** The gates, as the centers of the economic and social life of Jerusalem, are here used to represent the whole city (cf. Ruth 3:11; Isa. 14:31). On the Lord's love of Zion cf. 78:68. **The dwelling places of Jacob:** Any place where Israelites dwell. Primarily the reference is to the towns and villages of Palestine, but if the date of the psalmist permits it, it can refer to the homes of Hebrews in the Diaspora.

3. **Glorious things:** The psalmist may have had in mind (*a*) that "the LORD has chosen Zion . . . for his habitation" (132:13); (*b*) that "his holy mountain, beautiful in elevation, is the joy of all the earth" (48:2); (*c*) that "out of Zion shall go forth the law" (Isa. 2:3); (*d*) that it is a "habitation of justice," a "mountain of holiness" (Jer. 31:23); etc. **Are spoken:** A repointing of this word secures the active participle Piel ("he speaks") and improves the grammar. **City of God:** The same phrase for Jerusalem is found in 46:4, and a similar one in 48:1, 2, 8; 101:8; Isa. 60:14.

---

tension of the idea of God as the center and meaning of the life of the individual to the center and meaning of the life of humanity. This inference has not always been drawn by the religious mind. Individualism and universalism are not in the nature of the case corollary in all theological thought. Even within our Christian tradition the tension between the one and the many has found expression in the controversy between the individual and the social gospel. In other cultures the exercise of the religious impulse has more often than not taken the form of a nationalist universalism, as in Mohammedanism, or of individualist mysticism, as in esoteric Buddhism. It is the glory of the Hebrew tradition that it not only put these two elements of experience together but also made them central in its missionary emphasis. Whenever the Christian tradition has lived up to its best impulses it has done the same. Today its most familiar statement is found in the formula of the fatherhood of God and the brotherhood of man.

The sons of Korah, for whom the authorship of this song is claimed, have to their credit another (Ps. 48) in a somewhat similar vein. This psalm, like the former one, extols the splendor and security of Mount Zion and warns all alien peoples against disputing her primacy. Her claim to universality is based on might and potential dominion; there is a strong ingredient of truculence mixed with her pride. As we shall see, the later Korahite offering makes significant advance on this low-pitched claim. In the latter case universalism is based on common parenthood. To be united thus is a vastly different matter from being united by a threat of domination by force of arms.

1-3. *Glories of Zion.*—It is probably the carelessness of a scribe that has put what is clearly the opening line of the song in the position of vs. 3. The ascription of glory to the **city of God** is the obvious intention of the singer. **Glorious things are spoken of thee, O city of God.** Once this introductory address is set in its proper position, the rest of the song is fairly orderly, though some commentators think it necessary to make other adjustments in the verse sequence (see Exeg.). The first and certainly the most obvious glory of the city is geographical; it was built on an eminence from which it dominated the world, and to which it drew the eyes of the nations of the earth. "You are the light of the world. A city set on a hill cannot be hid" (Matt. 5:14) can well have been an adaptation of our song for the specific needs of the Sermon on the Mount. Not only so; there was glory in the name of the city's founder and builder. Here again is an idea important to a growing group within a later generation of Hebrews who were reminded of a patriarch whose claim to celebrity was that "he looked for a city which hath foundations, whose builder and maker is God" (Heb. 11:10). By this time the dream of universalism had transcended the insubstantial supports of hills and gates and dwelling places which had given it its first substance. The builder, we are told, had special fondness for **the gates of Zion,** at once a synonym for the whole city and a reference to the massive and proudly wrought portals that were its protection. This great city was the Lord's preference of the building achievements of the craftsmen of Jacob. These were the things spoken about Zion: its location, its builder, and his devotion to it. **Glorious** indeed they were.

4 I will make mention of Rahab and Babylon to them that know me: behold Philistia, and Tyre, with Ethiopia; this *man* was born there.
5 And of Zion it shall be said, This and that man was born in her: and the Highest himself shall establish her.

4 Among those who know me I mention
Rahab and Babylon;
behold, Philistia and Tyre, with Ethiopia —
"This one was born there," they say.
5 And of Zion it shall be said,
"This one and that one were born in her";
for the Most High himself will establish her.

---

2. Citizenship in Zion (87:4-6)

4. The speaker is God. **Among those who know me:** This may be the meaning of the Hebrew, and if so, the verse implies the existence of Jews, and possibly of proselytes, among the Gentile nations. In the latter case Israel's inveterate enemies are being won over to the cause of true religion (cf. Isa. 19:24-25). **Rahab:** A term for the primeval dragon (see Exeg. on 89:10), used here, as in Isa. 30:7, as a name for Egypt. **Babylon:** Probably Mesopotamia in general. Long after it ceased to be of political importance (539 B.C.), Babylon remained a cultural and commercial center. **Philistia . . . Tyre:** See Exeg. on 83:7. **Ethiopia:** An O.T. term for the land and people of the Upper Nile, south of Egypt, i.e., south of the first cataract. **This one was born there:** The Diaspora Jew or the Gentile proselyte was spiritually a citizen of Zion. Some take the antecedent of **this one** to be one of the nations just mentioned, not the individual believer.

5. The psalmist speaks, reiterating that the coveted citizenship is open to people of diverse backgrounds. Following the LXX, one may emend the first three words to

---

4-7. *Compare Her Neighbors.*—At this point in the song the voice that has spoken **glorious things** about Zion gives place to the voice of Zion herself. It is as if the city, the symbol of the glory of God, was allowed the opportunity of a few modest words in her own behalf. The claims she makes are, without impropriety, far more important than geography or the excellence of the builder's labors. Three things Zion says about herself: first, that there are some who know her as neighbor; second, that there are some who know her as mother; finally she proudly says that the latter are allowed the claim to a higher distinction by inclusion in the Lord's registry.

Who are her neighbors? **Rahab and Babylon, . . . Philistia and Tyre, with Ethiopia.** She allows that there was proper distinction in having been **born** in such celebrated places. **Rahab,** the emblematical name for Egypt; **Babylon,** the dominant world power when this song was being written; **Philistia and Tyre** (Phoenicia), the former an incessant rival of Israel, the latter a rich seafaring and friendly neighbor; **Ethiopia** (Kush), that vast and romantic hinterland of Egypt—there was distinction of a real sort in all these places, whether their intercourse with Zion had been friendly or not. Indeed, it is significant for the concept of universalism here projected that Zion did not number among those who were known to her only those with whom the traffic had been happy. Narrow nationalistic pride could have crossed Philistia off the list, national jealousy could have refused to speak of Tyre, and racial snobbishness could easily have looked down upon the teeming dark peoples of the land of Kush. There is exhibited here the genial dignity of a great lady who, sure of her position, does not use it as a weapon but as the instrument of her generosity. Can we be faithful both to the context and the time of the poem and say that in this early idea of what we now call universalism it was deeply felt that no allowance could be given to hostility, arrogance, and snobbishness? Or to put it otherwise, are not these national and individual attitudes that divide peoples the as yet unvanquished spiritual enemies of world brotherhood?

This leads us naturally to the second thing Zion has to say for herself. She is not only neighbor to a strange and various clientele, she is mother to an even wider heterogeny. This assumption of the position of universal motherhood is as daring as it is unique. That all the peoples of earth were of the family of God was not infrequently claimed by early seer and prophet. Its implications were not always as ingratiating as the familial idea should be. At certain times ways and means were used

6 The LORD shall count, when he writeth up the people, *that* this *man* was born there. Selah.	6 The LORD records as he registers the peoples, "This one was born there." *Selah*

ולציון אם אמר, "And Zion I call mother." **The Most High himself will establish her:** The same thought occurs in 48:8.

6. This verse assumes that the Lord keeps a kind of register of all the peoples (cf. 56:8; 69:28; 139:16; Exod. 32:32; Isa. 4:3; Dan. 12:1; Mal. 3:16). The idea was doubtless derived from Israel's practice (paralleled in other nations)) of having registers for various purposes (cf. Jer. 22:30; Ezek. 13:9; Ezra 2:62; Neh. 7:5; II Chr. 2:17).

to compel a recognition of the fact of family which destroyed the possibility of it. To put it in the terms not of matriarch but of mother was not common. Eve (Gen. 3:20) was called the mother of all living. This is legendary biology, far removed from the voluntary assumption of maternity for all peoples.

The psalmist's claim—**This one and that one were born in her**—is supported by two other factors. The relationship is not simply assumed as an honorific; she has been established in it by the **Most High** himself, and it is authenticated by the fact of progeny. This comes very close to being the picture of a complete domestic unit out of which the peoples of the world issue. God has established Zion as mother. This may be taken to mean that she is espoused of the Most High; all **peoples** (vs. 6) are in the family registry as having been born of this union. Thus the legitimacy of the offspring was put down in an imperishable and incontestable list.

This is an idealization of an exalted idea, and should therefore not be judged too precisely by the canons of history; i.e., the development of the idea in the poet's mind does not necessarily follow a development in history. Even the most zealous Jew was not likely to claim that Mother Eve was Mother Zion. Granted even that all the nations sprang from one parent stock, that that stock was Hebrew was insupportable. Therefore it was an accommodation of fact to ideal rather than to history that led our poet to say that Rahab and Babylon, Philistia, Tyre, and Ethiopia were the offspring of Zion. Genetically that was not so, though ideally it could be said that they were all the progeny of God. In fact, this domestic figure appears in the N.T. in a form that is both familiar and deeply cherished. The church as the bride of Christ is the mother of a new race, a race that is not identifiable by place or color but by its demonstration of the qualities it inherits from its parents. This also is an idealization that has been falsified too often by the facts of history.

6-7. ***The Word of Praise.***—The corrective that history would have provided our poet if he had been concerned with mere fact cannot be allowed to denigrate the idealism of the poem. The writer was clearly undisturbed on that point. Indeed, as the last triumphant note of the song we hear all the sons of men singing in confident unison as they measure the meter of their melody with the steps of their dance: **All my springs are in you.** If this summarizing coda is allowed to mean all that it says, it will demand recognition as an extraordinary claim. It is not only the residents of the city of God who say the glorious thing; it is all people, symbolized by the cities and nations specified in vs. 4. The final ensemble of dance and song unites all peoples. For them to recognize the Most High and Mother Zion as the universal parents, as the **springs,** so our poet puts it, from which the stream of all their experience has flowed—this is a witness to universalism that has rarely if ever been overtopped in sheer idealism.

If then, as has been claimed, the Korahite song is an idealization of the hope of universalism, it deserves a conspicuous place in the history of the ideas of Western religious culture. That it is put in sublime terms must not encourage the opinion that it was on the one hand mere fantasy, or on the other a description of conditions in the poet's day. The Hebrew mind, it cannot be said too often, established God at the center of Israel's experience, and the implications of this determinative fact every so often broke through other facts that denied it. If God is the Father of all, or, as in this song, Zion is the mother of all, then all men are brethren; and while this allows for variety of culture and behavior within the universal family, it makes no place for a priori favoritism of any sort.

The oneness of the human family has won support from all the sciences that have occupied themselves with the study of man. The data by which anthropologist and sociologist sustain their hypothesis are different from the poet's fancy, but their deductions are the same. **All**

7 As well the singers as the players on instruments *shall be there:* all my springs *are* in thee.

A Song *or* Psalm for the sons of Korah, to the chief Musician upon Mahalath Leannoth, Maschil of Heman the Ezrahite.

88 O LORD God of my salvation, I have cried day *and* night before thee:

7 Singers and dancers alike say,
"All my springs are in you."

A Song. A Psalm of the Sons of Korah. To the choirmaster: according to Mahalath Leannoth. A Maskil of Heman the Ezrahite.

88 O LORD, my God, I call for help[t] by day;
I cry out in the night before thee.

[t] Cn: Heb *O* LORD, *God of my salvation*

3. IN PRAISE OF ZION (87:7)

7. On **singers** cf. 68:25; I Kings 10:12; Ezek. 40:44. **Dancers** is preferable to **the players on instruments.** On religious dancing cf. 30:11; 149:3; 150:4; II Sam. 6:14. A verb seems necessary in the first half of the verse: the RSV supplies **say,** and the KJV **shall be there. All my springs are in you:** Apparently the title or the first line of a hymn addressed to Zion and sung by the aforementioned choristers. **Springs:** Here a figure for the sources of life and joy (cf. 36:9; Isa. 12:3; Hos. 13:15; Prov. 5:16).

LXXXVIII. A STUBBORN FAITH (88:1-18)

The Book of Common Prayer selects this as a "proper psalm" for evening prayer on Good Friday, presumably because, in the words of A. F. Kirkpatrick, "It is . . . a noble example of a faith which trusts God utterly in spite of all discouragement, and

my springs are in you; thus the Korahite. All men spring from one source; thus the scientist. This ought to mean that the minds of modern men can never again be taken in by the nonsense of racism in so far as it is adduced to support claims of one race to innate superiority over another.

It is obvious, however, that no matter how convincing the data must be to the cultivated intellect today, morally and spiritually we seem somewhat unconvinced. This great religious insight that antedates scientific deductions by tens of centuries has often been denied most vehemently by religious folk in the very name of religion. The shaman of the primitive tribe can be indulged his weird unscientific absurdities, but what is to be said for the Christian who, furnished with accurate scientific understanding, holds back by so much as a hair's breadth from his brother because his pigment differs from his own? The least that can be said is that he is a spiritual illiterate.

Think what it meant for the Mother of Zion to claim as her spiritual offspring the dark man of the Ethiopian hinterland, the friendly and successful and sophisticated Phoenician, the suspicious and permanently hostile Philistine, and the Egyptian who worshiped in the temple of the winged bull. It takes nothing from the poet's idealism to say that he in all probability knew little or nothing about the peoples he specified. All the greater wonder that his ignorance did not erect spurious walls instead of tearing them down. Think also what it meant for these so-called alien people to have put upon their lips the confession that God is the ultimate source of all life—physical, spiritual, political, etc. What we actually see here, then, is the claim of Mother Zion to universal motherhood, and the answering acknowledgment of all her progeny. Put in more general terms, we see the universality of man authenticated by both the divine and the human will. Here the idealism of the poet wins the affirmation of God and man. Here also divine paternity and human fraternity are indissolubly united, both in logic and experience.

It is unquestionably spiritually humiliating when we dare to face up to the fact that large segments of so-called Christian groups are not yet ready to admit their spiritual integrity with the modern analogues of ancient Egypt, Tyre, and Ethiopia. It will be unquestionably spiritually ennobling when we are able to sing with all the sons of men: **All my springs are in you.**

88:1-18. ***A Poem About Sickness.***—Heman, Asaph, and Ethan were a committee of three appointed by David to have charge of the music in the house of the Lord. It is no little distinction to have served as members of the first

cleaves to God most passionately when God seems to have withdrawn Himself most completely" (*The Book of Psalms* [Cambridge: Cambridge University Press, 1895; "Cambridge Bible"], II, 524).

While some older scholars (e.g., Wellhausen, Briggs) took this psalm to be a national lament (so, more recently, Berry, Buttenweiser), most modern commentators think that the agonizing situation it reflects is of too personal a character to support such an interpretation, and they view it as the lament of an individual stricken with sickness (cf. Pss. 6; 22; 28; 38). The psalmist appears to have some wasting disease with which he has been afflicted from his youth (perhaps leprosy or palsy). It has cost him his friends who can no longer bear the sight of him, and now he is on the point of death. He complains of no attacks by enemies and he has no sins to confess; yet he looks upon his prolonged experience of suffering as due in some measure to the Lord's wrath. It is therefore to the Lord that his plea is directed. But—and this is what makes it the most somber lament in the Psalter—when the psalm is finished there is no answering voice nor any mitigation of the speaker's plight, and as has often been noticed, the last word in the poem is **darkness.** On the other hand, it is noteworthy that the psalmist's first word is **Lord:** it is to the Lord, as the sole ground of his hope, that he continues to pray in the mornings (vs. 13). In the language of the N.T., "This is the victory that overcometh the world, even our faith" (I John 5:4).

This psalm is also of interest because of the conception of **Sheol** which it assumes. The epithets for Sheol are striking: **Pit** (vss. 4, 6); **regions dark and deep** (vs. 6, cf. vs. 12; **Abaddon** (vs. 11); **the land of forgetfulness** (vs. 12). The references to the dead as **cut off** from the Lord and no longer remembered by him (vs. 5), and as not praising the Lord, whose great works are unknown in Sheol (vss. 10-12), must be kept in mind

---

music committee. Their successors stand in a line of long-suffering and poorly rewarded saints whose patience has been inadequately celebrated, whose exasperation has been too little understood, and whose total contribution to the rich hoard of religious music will almost certainly never be calculated. "These are the men whom David put in charge of the service of song in the house of the Lord. . . . They ministered with song before the tabernacle of the tent of meeting, . . . and they performed their service in due order" (I Chr. 6:31-32).

It is of no importance whether the author of Ps. 88 was the **Heman** of David's appointment. Assuming that he was, his literary and musical output, if the Psalter is his only record, was undistinguished. His colleague Asaph was much more prolific and versatile, being credited with a dozen contributions to the Psalter. Heman and Ethan, if the earliest editors were right, are properly assigned one each, and of the three writers, the first named on the committee puzzles us most.

How such a dismal song was to be sung at all is difficult to see. There is some reason to think the tune **Mahalath** means "sickness." If so, an effort has been made to suit the music to the words. The tune is lost to us, but we may imagine it to have been a very doleful melody. The poem is a Maskil, a teaching poem, and while it is important for men to be taught how demoralizing pain and hopelessness can be, it is from our point of view not very effectively communicated by music. The effort to answer these difficulties, however, belongs to the literary scholars who are well aware of them. As has been often said, those who originally put this Psalter together must have felt this poem deserved a place in it. Our concern therefore is to discover exactly what it is trying to say, and to appropriate it in such measure as is possible for our own uses.

Thus approached, it becomes evident at once that it is unique in that it is a lament almost wholly unrelieved by hope. Almost, it is said, because the fact that out of apparent hopelessness the afflicted man cries to God is an evidence that hope had not been finally abandoned. Hope holds within itself one of the spirit's most interesting paradoxes. Even when one has resigned oneself to hopelessness, one still hopes that hopelessness may be mistaken. There is literally hope beyond hope. "Thou hast made me to hope," said the author of Ps. 119, as if to say that this never altogether extinguished spark is kept alive by the spirit of the Eternal. Job, who some commentators think may have furnished the theme for our poem, said, "Though he slay me, yet will I trust in him" (Job 13:15 KJV; but see Exeg., *in loc.*).

It is important to set our study of this psalm within the perspectives of the problem of man's despair, for in so doing we are likely to come upon its real meaning and the reason for its

2 Let my prayer come before thee: incline thine ear unto my cry;
3 For my soul is full of troubles: and my life draweth nigh unto the grave.
4 I am counted with them that go down into the pit: I am as a man *that hath* no strength:

2 Let my prayer come before thee,
incline thy ear to my cry!

3 For my soul is full of troubles,
and my life draws near to Sheol.
4 I am reckoned among those who go down
to the Pit;
I am a man who has no strength,

---

in reconstructing the O.T. picture of death. These allusions to life in Sheol remind us of similar ideas in the book of Job (7:9, 21; 10:21; 14:18-21; 16:22; 17:13), and this similarity, together with the fact that both the psalm and Job deal with the same basic theological problem, furnishes almost the only basis there is for dating the psalm in the Persian or early Greek period.

The psalm displays no regular strophic structure. The meter is generally 3+3.

1. Appeal to God (88:1-2)

Though God appears to have forsaken him, the psalmist turns to him as the only refuge.

88:1. The Hebrew seems confused. **My God, I call for help by day** rests upon three minor emendations of the M.T., the most important being the change of **my salvation** to **I call for help** (שׁוּעָתִי, as in vs. 13*a*).

2. The Psalmist's Troubles (88:3-9)

4. He is considered to be as good as dead. **The Pit:** A term for Sheol (see Exeg. on 28:1-2). **Strength:** Although this translation of איל is supported by Köhler (*Lexicon*), *et al.*, the Hebrew word and its Syriac counterpart mean "help." The RSV renders a cognate noun in 22:19 as "help."

---

inclusion in the Psalter. God was the central fact of the experience of Israel. When the psalmist cried *de profundis,* he expected help. If help was delayed or denied, he sought for a reason in himself or God, but he never went to the point of denying either the reality of his distress or the reality of God. Job's wife advised him, "Curse God, and die" (Job 2:9). That was as far as she dared to go. It was not as far as some have gone who have denied God and cursed. What, we may ask, would have been the religious deposit of the experience of Israel if hardship—national and individual—had blacked out faith in the centrality of God? This is an idle question if it concerns Israel; it is enormously important if it is asked about ourselves.

The first impulse felt by the modern student of this piece is to dismiss its author either with impatience or with a diagnosis. No one, we may loftily say, could have been as wretched as he and ever lived to write about it. Or we may say, drawing upon our knowledge of the way the mind works, he was not in the predicament he describes; he simply thought he was. He was, in other words, a self-deceived psychopath. Neither of these approaches will serve us. Better to assume first that he was describing his situation accurately and deserved the help he needed; and second, to see that his dilemma propounded two religious problems of great profundity: man's sense of separation from God in life, and the question of immortality. Only by an effort to be sympathetic with our miserable friend will these matters become clear to us.

1-9. ***The Cry to God.***—The poet's address to God is a cry for help. Three times he lifts himself up momentarily from under the crushing weight of tribulation to call for aid. His prayer is a cry; it is not the exchange of quiet confidences between friends. His voice must carry over a great distance; it comes up out of an abyss that separates him from God (vss. 1-2).

His description of himself is not set down in what we would call proper diagnostic order or precision, but it exposes both psyche and soma to be in a state of extreme danger. He has been a chronic invalid since his youth, so constantly ill, in fact, that he had been **ready to die** (vs. 15) ever since he could remember. As he begins his account of his wretchedness, he opens with the sense of the utter desperation of

5 Free among the dead, like the slain that
lie in the grave, whom thou rememberest
no more: and they are cut off from thy
hand.
6 Thou hast laid me in the lowest pit, in
darkness, in the deeps.
7 Thy wrath lieth hard upon me, and
thou hast afflicted *me* with all thy waves.
Selah.
8 Thou hast put away mine acquaintance
far from me; thou hast made me an abomination unto them: *I am* shut up, and I
cannot come forth.

5 like one forsaken among the dead,
like the slain that lie in the grave,
like those whom thou dost remember no more,
for they are cut off from thy hand.
6 Thou hast put me in the depths of the Pit,
in the regions dark and deep.
7 Thy wrath lies heavy upon me,
and thou dost overwhelm me with all thy waves. *Selah*
8 Thou hast caused my companions to shun me;
thou hast made me a thing of horror to them.
I am shut in so that I cannot escape;

---

5. Like one forsaken: Like is either an addition to the M.T. or a very free translation of the Hebrew. **One forsaken** or **free:** The meaning is uncertain and the text may be corrupt. Weiser and Friedrich Nötscher render as "my couch" (cf. Ezek. 27:20). **Like the slain:** Those slain in battle, whose bodies are put in a common grave (cf. Ezek. 32:20-32). **Thou dost remember no more:** Cf. 31:12.

6. The depths of the Pit: Lit., "the pit of the lowest parts," a phrase found also in Lam. 3:55 (see Exeg. on 86:13). **In the regions dark and deep:** Lit., "in the dark places, in the depths" (cf. KJV). On the darkness of Sheol cf. vs. 12; 143:3; Lam. 3:6; Job 10:21-22.

7. The psalmist assumes that his misfortunes are due to the Lord's **wrath** (cf. 6:1; 38:1; etc.), but he does not indicate why the divine wrath should have been thus aroused. **Thy waves:** The same figure for God's judgments and anger appears in 42:7.

8. The psalmist suffers from some loathsome ailment which discourages the approach of even his friends (cf. vs. 18; 31:11; Job 19:13-19). **Caused . . . to shun:** Lit., **put away . . . far. Made me a thing of horror:** Cf. Job 30:10. **I am shut in:** The reference is either

---

his soul. He is literally fed up. This is a phrase far too casually used, for when it represents an honest feeling it describes a deep sickness of the spirit. And yet as here used, it means even more than satiation with life; the psalmist is sated with trouble. He has reached the saturation point; he can absorb no more. This is the nadir of spiritual exhaustion, the point beyond which trouble cannot press without destroying life itself. He sees this clearly, for physical death poises imminent and stark: **my life draws near to Sheol.** To make more vivid and explicit the fact that spiritual exhaustion is the preliminary to physical death, he adds the next descriptive lines (vss. 4-5). His emaciation has reduced him to a shadow; he is already counted among the dying, even indeed as one already dead, lying unidentified in the grave.

So short is the memory of the living; they are always ready to forget those whose lingering pain has been expunged by merciful death. This is bad enough; but to have been forgotten of God as if, once one were dead, he was cut off forever from everything, this was intolerable (vs. 5*cd*). Was death to cut him off from the hand of God, even if the hand had so long neglected to succor him? This was the terrifying question; this was the saturation point of trouble. And yet there was a deeper depth to plumb. Already he has been cast into the abyss (vs. 6); and as if to hound him even in the depths, he is pressed down by the weight of God's anger and drowned in the waves of pursuing fury (vs. 7).

The reproach and banishment that had engulfed him were unrelieved by the compassion of even one understanding friend. He had become odious to all men; companions avoided him (vs. 8). This too was God's doing. There is no hope that he can extricate himself. Indeed, so blinded are his eyes by despair that he cannot even look for a way of escape (vs. 9).

If we thought it would settle the matter to describe his conditions in the terminology of modern psychology, it would not be difficult to do so. Nervous exhaustion and the death wish (vss. 3-4), rejection (vss. 5-7), a sense of

9 Mine eye mourneth by reason of affliction: LORD, I have called daily upon thee, I have stretched out my hands unto thee.

10 Wilt thou show wonders to the dead? shall the dead arise *and* praise thee? Selah.

11 Shall thy loving-kindness be declared in the grave? *or* thy faithfulness in destruction?

12 Shall thy wonders be known in the dark? and thy righteousness in the land of forgetfulness?

9 my eye grows dim through sorrow.
Every day I call upon thee, O LORD;
I spread out my hands to thee.
10 Dost thou work wonders for the dead?
Do the shades rise up to praise thee?
Selah
11 Is thy steadfast love declared in the grave,
or thy faithfulness in Abaddon?
12 Are thy wonders known in the darkness,
or thy saving help in the land of forgetfulness?

---

literal (cf. the quarantine regulations for leprosy, Lev. 13:1-6, 45-46), or metaphorical (cf. Job 3:23; 13:27). **Come forth** or "go out" is better than **escape.**

9. Grows dim or "languishes," rather than **mourneth** (cf. 6:7; 31:9). **Affliction** is preferable to **sorrow** as the translation of עני. The RSV renders this word "affliction" in 25:18; 31:7; etc.

3. THE LORD IS QUESTIONED (88:10-12)

A series of rhetorical questions addressed to the Lord, indicating that death is the absence of everything the psalmist holds most dear (cf. Job 10:20-22).

10. Wonders: Demonstrations of God's great power (cf. 72:18; 77:11, 14; Exod. 15:11). It is implied that such wonders are not performed in Sheol. **The shades** or **the dead:** The Hebrew etymology suggests sinking down (into Sheol) and being powerless. On the inability of the dead to praise the Lord see Exeg. on 94:17 (cf. Ecclus. 17:27-28).

11. Abaddon rather than **destruction:** A synonym for death or the grave. It is cognate to the verb "perish," and it pictures Sheol as the place where all earthly activities and hopes come to ruin. The word appears once in the N.T. as the name of the angel of the abyss (Rev. 9:11).

12. Thy wonders: See on vs. 10. **The darkness:** See on vs. 6. **Saving help** or **righteousness:** The RSV displays some variety in its translation of this word (צדקה) in the

---

inferiority and claustrophobic paranoia (vss. 8-9), and melancholia. This is a formidable diagnosis of spiritual illness. Self-destruction would not have been an unpredictable end to his misery; and yet, as he rests his tension in a moment of relaxation, we hear him repeat his address to the Lord. It seems almost as if, having totted up his symptoms, he adds a final one: his daily call upon the Lord (vs. 9*bc*). For this is as clearly a vital phenomenon of his condition as his feelings of rejection or melancholy. Its difference lies in the fact that for us it is not pathological. It may indeed be regarded as the point at which his cycle had swung from morbidity to an effort, at least, to act rationally in quest of healing.

10-12. ***The Question of Immortality.***—In the light of this possibility vss. 10-12 fit into the poet's mood swing. He had been suffering "the arrows of outrageous fortune," shot from the taut bow of life ever since he was a youth. Life had been his tormentor; he wonders whether death might be a friend. To us for whom life beyond the grave has become an axiom, death as beneficent allows no question; but our sufferer was not so sure as we. Yet for the moment he gives up his preoccupation with the bitterness of life to ask what use God can make of death. There is an ingenuousness in his first question that is touched with pathos. It would have taken a miracle to mend his living frame; perhaps miracles could be worked on his dead body. The sufferer, prostrate in pain, has little impulse and less strength for praise; perhaps the discarnate can manage better. It might be reassuring to know, so he asks.

Dost thou work wonders for the dead?
Do the shades rise up to praise thee?

His question, however, goes deeper than the simple matter of post-mortem survival under somewhat improved conditions for mortal sufferers. He wonders if, with surviving life, consciousness also survives. For him the only intelligible terms for describing the environment within which he may live immortally are charnel words: **the grave,** the world below (**Abaddon,** lit., "place of torture and destruc-

13 But unto thee have I cried, O LORD; and in the morning shall my prayer prevent thee.
14 LORD, why castest thou off my soul? *why* hidest thou thy face from me?
15 I *am* afflicted and ready to die from *my* youth up: *while* I suffer thy terrors I am distracted.

13 But I, O LORD, cry to thee;
in the morning my prayer comes before thee.
14 O LORD, why dost thou cast me off?
Why dost thou hide thy face from me?
15 Afflicted and close to death from my youth up,
I suffer thy terrors; I am helpless.[u]

[u] The meaning of the Hebrew word is uncertain

Psalter. **Righteousness** is the commonest rendition (5:8), but "righteous deeds" (11:7), "deliverance" (22:31), "vindication" (24:5), "salvation" (36:10), "righteous acts" (71:15), "righteous help" (71:24) are also used. **The land of forgetfulness:** A unique term for Sheol. God forgets men who have died (vs. 5); humanity forgets its own dead (31:12; Eccl. 9:5-6); men in Sheol forget God (6:5); cf. the plain of Forgetfulness and the river of Indifference in the Greek Hades (Plato *Republic* X. 621).

4. The Appeal Renewed (88:13-14)

13. In the morning may be an allusion to a conventional time of prayer, coinciding with the morning offering in the temple (Exod. 29:38-42; cf. Pss. 5:3; 59:16). There is a reference in 92:2 to praise offered morning and evening, and in 55:17 to prayer at evening, morning, and noon (cf. three times a day in Dan. 6:10). **Comes before** rather than **prevent:** See Exeg. on 79:8.

14. The Hebrew is **my soul;** cf. **me** (RSV).

5. The Psalmist's Ills (88:15-18)

15. Close to death is preferable to **ready to die.** The psalmist's health has been precarious since his youth. **I am helpless** or **I am distracted:** The Hebrew word is found only here and the meaning is uncertain.

---

tion"); **the darkness;** and **the land of forgetfulness.** Gloomy words all; and yet into his shadowed mind there breaks momentarily the beam of hope that God might possibly invade the darkness with intimations of himself, so that the victim could remember, calculate, understand, and appropriate some healing efficacy.

Is thy steadfast love declared in the grave,
or thy faithfulness in Abaddon?
Are thy wonders known in the darkness,
or thy saving help in the land of forgetfulness?

Would an answer to these desperate questions make life any less insufferable and give to death the aspect of release, healing, and, untroubled by pain, a recognition of God? For a moment the psalmist's eager mind transcends his debilitated body as he awaits an answer.

13-18. ***The Recurrent Cry.***—The moment of relief the poet's questioning brought him was brief, and he was plunged into pain and depression again. Even while reflecting on the possible bliss that the land of forgetfulness might bring him, he is seized with a terrifying paroxysm accompanied by fever. Tortured by these febrile imaginings, he seems to be caught in a whirlpool of anguish, the waters of which circle closer and finally engulf him (vss. 15*b*-17). Before he pronounced this final doom upon himself he had cried again for help. After a night of bewildered questioning, he had made his prayer (vs. 13), but this mood of supplication dies on his lips, and that of wounded petulance follows. Even as he prays he is wracked by pain (vs. 14). And as if to sum up all his despair in one last complaint, he says that God has not only spurned him; he has instigated his rejection by lover and friend. Then he takes his final plunge into the place of darkness, where he finds unrelieved gloom his only comrade.

Of this poem it has been correctly said that nowhere else in the Bible is the problem of uncompensated trouble so hopelessly portrayed. Nevertheless there is even here that modicum of hope suggested by the thrice-repeated cry to God for help. This amounts to saying that nowhere in the Bible is man's hopelessness hopeless. To have said this, however, does not cancel what has been said above: that this man's problem was not doubt of the fact of God; it was his separation from God in life, and his likely

16 Thy fierce wrath goeth over me; thy terrors have cut me off.
17 They came round about me daily like water; they compassed me about together.
18 Lover and friend hast thou put far from me, *and* mine acquaintance into darkness.

16 Thy wrath has swept over me;
thy dread assaults destroy me.
17 They surround me like a flood all day long;
they close in upon me together.
18 Thou hast caused lover and friend to shun me;
my companions are in darkness.

Maschil of Ethan the Ezrahite.

89 I will sing of the mercies of the LORD for ever: with my mouth will I make known thy faithfulness to all generations.

A Maskil of Ethan the Ezrahite.

89 I will sing of thy steadfast love, O LORD,[v] for ever;
with my mouth I will proclaim thy faithfulness to all generations.

[v] Gk: Heb *the steadfast love of the* LORD

16-17. The psalmist's troubles are compared to an engulfing flood (cf. **thy waves** in vs. 7).

16. Thy wrath: See on vs. 7.

17. All day long is better than **daily.**

18. Caused . . . to shun: See on vs. 8. **My companions are in darkness:** This may be the meaning of a doubtful clause, but another possibility is, "Darkness is [constitutes] my acquaintances" (cf. Job 17:14).

LXXXIX. Supplication for a King (89:1-52)

This impressive psalm has four well-defined divisions: (*a*) preface (vss. 1-4); (*b*) hymn in praise of the Lord (vss. 5-18); (*c*) oracle on the Lord's promises to David (vss. 19-37); (*d*) lament on behalf of a Hebrew king (vss. 38-51). While some scholars hold that it comprises two or more quite independent compositions (e.g., Schmidt, vss. 1-18, 19-51 [see below on vs. 52]), it is here assumed that the poem is essentially a unity and is designed as a lament uttered by or on behalf of a Judean king. In a sense therefore it is a royal psalm, and in so far as the welfare of the nation is closely connected with

separation from him in death. The first aspect involves the doctrine of suffering in the divine economy, and has been set forth in the Expos. of Ps. 73. The second involves the doctrine of immortality. In both the experience of hope is vital.

While it is true that this latter doctrine was not formulated by Hebrew thinkers until very late, it is important to note that this tortured poet saw fairly early wherein the essence of the matter lay. It may be, after all, less important to know that immortality is logically more plausible than its opposite than to be assured that the rational capacities that make logical thought possible in life are to be continued post mortem. Not, shall we live after death, but shall we know after death? This is the area into which our poet's mind penetrated momentarily. Does God **work wonders for the dead?** Is his **steadfast love declared in the grave?** Here are knowledge and recollection. Is God's **saving help** known **in the land of forgetfulness?** Here is the projection of God's redemptive grace beyond the limits of mortal life, something for which all men hope.

Our poet has not answered the questions he raises. Who, we may ask, ever has? What he did, however, was to see life and death against the background of a hope that was never wholly extinguished by the dark shadows of suffering. That suffering is an aid to hope is a deep mystery; that it may be an aid to knowledge is less of a puzzle. That suffering may lead hope and knowledge to a deeper apprehension of man's relation to God—*ante et post mortem*—this is the subtle testimony of our author's bitter poem. What better reason can be found for giving it its place in the Psalter?

89:1-52. ***Three Problems About God's Relationship to Man.***—It was pointed out in the Expos. of Ps. 88 that its putative author, Heman, was a member of the music committee appointed by David when the temple worship was in process of organization. He shared his re-

that of its ruler, it may also be described as a lament of the community. Vss. 1-37 constitute a long introduction to the lament properly so called, and indicate the grounds upon which the appeal to the Lord is based. Possibly both the hymn (vss. 5-18) and the oracle (vss. 19-37) once had a separate and prior existence, but if so they were taken up by the psalmist and utilized for his immediate purpose.

Unless their language is highly figurative, vss. 38-45 point to a recent Judean disaster in which the king has suffered military defeat and lost his throne to boot. The only concrete situation that seems to fit these verses is the Babylonian wars of the early sixth century B.C., and accordingly we may date the psalm in its present form shortly after 597 or 587 B.C. The king in question would then be either Jehoiachin or Zedekiah. The poem can hardly have been written long after this time, for it cherishes the hope that the Davidic dynasty will yet be restored.

It is a matter of speculation how this psalm was fitted into the liturgical usage of the temple. Indeed, if it was composed subsequent to 587 B.C., the dislocation in the temple services and religious festivals attendant upon the postwar conditions makes any opinion about the original connection of this psalm with the cult extremely hazardous.

The terms applied by the psalmist to the king (**my chosen one, my servant, the first-born, thy anointed**) have encouraged Christian piety to find a messianic reference in this poem, and account for its selection in the Book of Common Prayer as a "proper psalm" for evening prayer on Christmas Day.

The meter in vss. 1-18 is mostly 4+4, whereas in vss. 19-51 it is mostly 3+3.

---

sponsibilities with Asaph and **Ethan**, both of whom left more distinguished literary remains than he. The early editors of the Psalter assigned a dozen poems to Asaph, and one each to the other two poets. Heman's tortured poem subtly conceals a spark of religious hope under a mantle of all but unmitigated despair; Asaph's twelve poems indicate his many-sided aptitude for form and idea; and what our editors apparently thought was the only creditable product of the pen of Ethan brings Book III of the Psalter to its close.

There is no doubt about the didactic intention of the psalm. It was a Maskil, and there can be no mistaking what it says. That it, like so many other psalms, is a patchwork of borrowings is of no very great importance to the expositor. No matter how the author set about to organize his materials, his result is conspicuously successful.

That God was the major premise of the thought of Israel and the central fact of her life has been pointed out many times. The logic that stemmed from this hypothesis was often confused, even as the life that sought to integrate itself about this fact was not infrequently devious. Nevertheless hypothesis and fact remained, and somehow the people always returned to them for judgment on idea and behavior. To make this explicit was the poet's intention in the first section of his piece.

The second section deals just as specifically with another major fact of Israel's faith. It derived from the first, and in a way may be said to have given body to it. God is not a fact in a vacuum; he wants companionship to fulfill the needs of his nature and to share with him his creative enterprise. Therefore he makes use of men as his agents. This fact also was susceptible of puzzling interpretations, and yet it was never abandoned because of that. This relationship between God and man was not adventitious or unconditioned. It was according to the divine purpose, and was continued only on certain moral conditions.

The third section faces up to another major fact. The literary device employed here leaves the point somewhat less sharply outlined than the other two. Our author discloses a situation by a protest against it and in a quasi-indictment of God; but what he is saying is that God's will can be thwarted by the perverse will of those with whom he has covenanted to work out his creative plan. Again we have a proposition that admits odd questions and curious answers into the arena of thought; and yet again we have a central consideration about the divine and human encounter that lies at a very deep level of the soul of man.

God is eternal; he must have traffic with man to work out his will; man can exalt or subvert God's designs—these are three dominant facts of man's experience as the inspired seers of Israel understood it. Added to this basic metaphysic was the vital religious faith of those who nurtured the ideas. God's will could be subverted by the perverse will of man, but not forever. Man was finite; the perversion of sin

2 For I have said, Mercy shall be built up for ever: thy faithfulness shalt thou establish in the very heavens.

3 I have made a covenant with my chosen, I have sworn unto David my servant,

4 Thy seed will I establish for ever, and build up thy throne to all generations. Selah.

5 And the heavens shall praise thy wonders, O LORD: thy faithfulness also in the congregation of the saints.

2 For thy steadfast love was established for ever,
thy faithfulness is firm as the heavens.
3 Thou hast said, "I have made a covenant with my chosen one,
I have sworn to David my servant:
4 'I will establish your descendants for ever,
and build your throne for all generations.' " *Selah*

5 Let the heavens praise thy wonders, O LORD,
thy faithfulness in the assembly of the holy ones!

---

1. HYMNIC INTRODUCTION (89:1-4)

The **steadfast love** and **faithfulness** of the Lord (both terms occur repeatedly in the psalm) are the guarantee that the promises made to David will be fulfilled.

89:1. Thy steadfast love: Thy is a small emendation of the M.T., supported by the LXX.

2. The RSV translation is obtained by dropping **For I have said** (KJV), adding **thy** to **steadfast love,** and repointing the verb to obtain **is firm.** This produces a pleasing line, but it is conjectural whether it is closer to the original than the M.T. represented by the KJV.

3. Thou hast said: An addition to the M.T. **A covenant** does not occur in II Sam. 7:1-29, but it is found in II Sam. 23:5. The covenant with David must of course be distinguished from that with Israel at Mount Sinai. **I have sworn:** In II Sam. 7:4-17 the promise to David is not accompanied by an oath (cf. 132:11).

2. PRAISE THE LORD (89:5-18)

A hymn praising the Lord for his incomparableness and his creative power as seen in the establishment of the ordered world. These verses bear no direct relation to the troublesome conditions described in vss. 38-45, and they may antedate the age of the psalmist. The references to **Tabor** and **Hermon** (vs. 12) have been thought to point to an origin in northern Israel (perhaps before 722 or 721 B.C.).

5-7. The supremacy of the Lord in heaven. The allusion is to the celestial world peopled by angels (**the holy ones,** vss. 5, 7) and demigods (**the heavenly beings,** vs. 6;

---

was therefore limited. God was eternal; the victory of his will was therefore guaranteed. This in sum is what the author was saying, and for this reason his solitary contribution to the Psalter is highly important. We must be warned, however, against forgetting that he uses the mind and the technique of the poet, rather than that of the metaphysician, to make his point. He teaches by song, not by argument.

1-18. ***God Is Eternal.***—The poet's major premise is given two formulations in the first section. **I will sing of thy steadfast love, O LORD, for ever.** This appears to be positing the nature of God (kindness or love) rather than the fact of God. On the contrary, the implication is clear that the emphasis is more on the eternal existence of God than on his kindness and faithfulness. The iteration **for ever, to all generations, established for ever, firm as the heavens,** has one intent: to establish a hypothesis of the eternal, imperishable fact of God. Having taken this for granted, the poet expects the cosmos to accept and accredit it.

Let the heavens praise thy wonders, O LORD,
thy faithfulness in the assembly of the holy ones!

Here, as also in vss. 6-7, it is expected that the heavens and their ethereal denizens will share the affirmation. The psalmist presents even to the Lord God himself an opportunity to agree (vs. 8). And then without waiting for an answer, he offers God's credentials to him. He is dominant over nature and over the nations of the earth: **Thou dost rule the raging of the**

6 For who in the heaven can be compared unto the LORD? *who* among the sons of the mighty can be likened unto the LORD?

7 God is greatly to be feared in the assembly of the saints, and to be had in reverence of all *them that are* about him.

8 O LORD God of hosts, who *is* a strong LORD like unto thee? or to thy faithfulness round about thee?

9 Thou rulest the raging of the sea: when the waves thereof arise, thou stillest them.

10 Thou hast broken Rahab in pieces, as one that is slain; thou hast scattered thine enemies with thy strong arm.

11 The heavens *are* thine, the earth also *is* thine: *as for* the world and the fulness thereof, thou hast founded them.

12 The north and the south thou hast created them: Tabor and Hermon shall rejoice in thy name.

13 Thou hast a mighty arm: strong is thy hand, *and* high is thy right hand.

6 For who in the skies can be compared to
the LORD?
Who among the heavenly beings[w] is
like the LORD,
7 a God feared in the council of the holy
ones,
great and terrible[x] above all that are
round about him?
8 O LORD God of hosts,
who is mighty as thou art, O LORD,
with thy faithfulness round about thee?
9 Thou dost rule the raging of the sea;
when its waves rise, thou stillest them.
10 Thou didst crush Rahab like a carcass,
thou didst scatter thy enemies with thy
mighty arm.
11 The heavens are thine, the earth also is
thine;
the world and all that is in it, thou hast
founded them.
12 The north and the south, thou hast created them;
Tabor and Hermon joyously praise thy
name.
13 Thou hast a mighty arm;
strong is thy hand, high thy right hand.

[w] Or *sons of gods*
[x] Gk Syr: Heb *greatly terrible*

---

see Exeg. on 82:1-8). **Wonders:** Probably all of God's mighty deeds, not merely his victory over Rahab and his creation of the world. On vs. 6 cf. 86:8. **The heavenly beings** rather than **the sons of the mighty:** Lit., **sons of gods** (RSV mg.). The RSV, supported by the LXX, rephrases vs. 7, and changes **greatly** to **great.**

8. LORD God of hosts: See Exeg. on 80:4.

9. This verse may refer to the Lord's constant control of the sea. It may, however, like vs. 10, be an echo of a myth, in this case Ugaritic, in which Yam, the god of the sea, is conquered by Baal (see Exeg. on 74:13).

10. Rahab ("arrogancy"): Not a name for Egypt as in 87:4, but a reminiscence of the old Akkadian creation myth wherein Tiamat is overpowered by Marduk. The evil force or dragon, conquered according to the Hebrew tradition by the Lord, is here called **Rahab** (cf. Job 9:13; 26:12; Isa. 51:9; see Exeg. on 74:13-15).

12. The north and the south: The extremities of the known world (cf. Job 26:7). **Tabor:** An eminence at the south of Galilee, elevation 1,843 feet. **Hermon:** A snow-capped mountain, northeast of Dan, elevation 9,100 feet. These mountains are cited as striking natural features of Canaan.

---

sea. . . . Thou didst crush Rahab [Egypt] **like a carcass, thou didst scatter thy enemies with thy mighty arm** (vss. 9-10). This is quickly recapitulated in vss. 11-12. The heavens, the earth, the world and all that is in it—these, **north and south,** and **Tabor** and **Hermon** are happy to acclaim his right, by the act of creation, to rule. But there is still more to authenticate the fact: He is power; **arm** and upraised **hand** symbolize it; he is King, **righteousness and justice** support his **throne; steadfast love and faithfulness** are his royal chamberlains (vss. 13-14). To this cosmic affirmation is added (vs. 15) the exultant **shout** of the people. As a grand finale to the overture of acclaim, we have the second of the poet's formulations of the major premise: **For thou art the glory of their strength; . . . our shield belongs to the LORD.**

14 Justice and judgment *are* the habitation of thy throne: mercy and truth shall go before thy face.
15 Blessed *is* the people that know the joyful sound: they shall walk, O LORD, in the light of thy countenance.
16 In thy name shall they rejoice all the day: and in thy righteousness shall they be exalted.
17 For thou *art* the glory of their strength: and in thy favor our horn shall be exalted.
18 For the LORD *is* our defense; and the Holy One of Israel *is* our King.
19 Then thou spakest in vision to thy holy one, and saidst, I have laid help upon *one that is* mighty; I have exalted *one* chosen out of the people.

14 Righteousness and justice are the foundation of thy throne;
steadfast love and faithfulness go before thee.
15 Blessed are the people who know the festal shout,
who walk, O LORD, in the light of thy countenance,
16 who exult in thy name all the day,
and extol[y] thy righteousness.
17 For thou art the glory of their strength;
by thy favor our horn is exalted.
18 For our shield belongs to the LORD,
our king to the Holy One of Israel.

19 Of old thou didst speak in a vision
to thy faithful one, and say:
"I have set the crown[z] upon one who is mighty,
I have exalted one chosen from the people.

[y] Cn: Heb *are exalted in*
[z] Cn: Heb *help*

14. Cf. 97:2*b*. **Righteousness and justice:** An indication of the moral basis of the Lord's sovereignty (as of human kingship, Prov. 16:12). On the Lord's **throne** in heaven see Exeg. on 82:1-8). **Steadfast love and faithfulness** are almost personified as attendant angels (similarly "righteousness" in 85:13).

15. **Who know the festal shout:** The reference is to singing or shouting, to the accompaniment of music, during the religious festivals (cf. 27:6; 33:3; 47:5; I Sam. 4:5; II Sam. 6:15; etc.).

16. **Extol:** A repointing of the M.T., **shall they be exalted.**

17-18. These verses may be due to the adaptation of the hymn to the psalmist's situation. **Our horn:** The reference is to the king (see Exeg. on 75:4). **Our shield:** The king (cf. Exeg. on 84:9). The RSV translates the preposition ל as **belongs to. Holy one of Israel:** See Exeg. on 71:22-24; 78:41.

3. PROMISES TO DAVID (89:19-37)

This oracle on the Lord's promises to David was anticipated in vss. 3-4, and is a poetical expansion of Nathan's words to the king in II Sam. 7:4-17. This part of the psalm, like vss. 5-18, would appear to be prior to the sixth century B.C., and to reflect a period of Judean tranquillity and prosperity. In liturgical use these verses may have been rendered by a soloist.

19. **Of old** or **then:** In Nathan's time. **Thy faithful one** or **thy holy one:** Either Nathan or David. **The crown:** An emendation (נזר, which occurs in vs. 39); the M.T. is **help,** which is in an unusual phrase, but the text is not impossible.

It would be difficult to find anywhere in the Bible so significant a metaphor as that which asseverates the fact of God by calling him the possessor of the **shield** of Israel.

19-37. *God's Compact with Man.*—So much for a poet's presentation of the major premise of his people. He is too wise, however, to leave it in suspension, or to commit it merely to the acclaim of the hosts of heaven and the mighty men of earth. God was a fact, but he was fact plus purpose. Part of his purpose had been worked out in the creation of the cosmos; but part of the cosmos was man, individual and in aggregate. What more obviously deducible fact faced our writer than that man was the chosen agent of God for the advancement of his pur-

20 I have found David my servant; with
my holy oil have I anointed him:
21 With whom my hand shall be established:
mine arm also shall strengthen him.
22 The enemy shall not exact upon him;
nor the son of wickedness afflict him.
23 And I will beat down his foes before
his face, and plague them that hate him.
24 But my faithfulness and my mercy
shall be with him: and in my name shall his
horn be exalted.
25 I will set his hand also in the sea, and
his right hand in the rivers.
26 He shall cry unto me, Thou *art* my
father, my God, and the rock of my salvation.
27 Also I will make him *my* firstborn,
higher than the kings of the earth.
28 My mercy will I keep for him for evermore,
and my covenant shall stand fast with
him.
29 His seed also will I make *to endure*
for ever, and his throne as the days of
heaven.

20 I have found David, my servant;
with my holy oil I have anointed him;
21 so that my hand shall ever abide with him,
my arm also shall strengthen him.
22 The enemy shall not outwit him,
the wicked shall not humble him.
23 I will crush his foes before him
and strike down those who hate him.
24 My faithfulness and my steadfast love shall be with him,
and in my name shall his horn be exalted.
25 I will set his hand on the sea
and his right hand on the rivers.
26 He shall cry to me, 'Thou art my Father,
my God, and the Rock of my salvation.'
27 And I will make him the first-born,
the highest of the kings of the earth.
28 My steadfast love I will keep for him for ever,
and my covenant will stand firm for him.
29 I will establish his line for ever
and his throne as the days of the heavens.

20. Cited in Acts 13:22 (cf. I Sam. 16:12-13; II Sam. 2:4; 5:3; 12:7). **My holy oil:** A phrase found only here (cf. Exod. 30:25).

22-24. Outwit or "deceive," rather than **exact. The wicked:** Lit., **the son of wickedness. His horn:** See Exeg. on 75:4.

25. See Exeg. on 72:8. **The sea:** The Mediterranean. **The rivers:** Probably the Euphrates and its canals, or the Euphrates and the Tigris.

26. **Father:** On the fatherhood of God see Exeg. on 103:13. On the Lord as the father of the Davidic dynasty see II Sam. 7:14. **Rock:** See Exeg. on 28:1-2.

27. **The first-born** enjoys pre-eminence and special favor (cf. Gen. 48:13-20; Deut. 21:15-17). In Exod. 4:22 Israel is called the Lord's first-born (cf. Jer. 31:9).

poses? Already in the first section of the poem (vss. 3-4) the author has given us a forecast of this second great assumption in a bold and unambiguous claim: God, whose integrity is as firm as the heavens, has entered into a compact with man and confirmed it with a sworn oath. He has promised to make David and his posterity and his throne coterminous with himself. Now (vss. 19-21) this solemn fact is repeated. Here God's intention was **of old;** he has **exalted one chosen from the people;** he has promised that his **hand shall ever abide with him.**

It was altogether natural that God's co-operative relationship with mankind should be symbolized in our poet's mind by the figure of **David,** the great king. He was what would have been called in some ages a proletarian king, and his early years at least had been full of romantic and promising adventure. Our writer makes it plain that David's anointing was an agreement between him and God (vss. 26-27). But it was not an unqualified agreement. David and his posterity were promised an endless lineage on conditions. Their compact rested on moral considerations. David knew the divine will as it had been known from ancient times in what are here indicated as **law, ordinances, statutes,** and **commandments.** Violation of these would be recompensed by **rod** and **scourges,** yet—and this is a significant fact—man's disobedience could not falsify either the character or the intention of God. **If his children forsake my law, . . . I will punish their transgression . . . ; but I will not remove from**

30 If his children forsake my law, and walk not in my judgments;
31 If they break my statutes, and keep not my commandments;
32 Then will I visit their transgression with the rod, and their iniquity with stripes.
33 Nevertheless my loving-kindness will I not utterly take from him, nor suffer my faithfulness to fail.
34 My covenant will I not break, nor alter the thing that is gone out of my lips.
35 Once have I sworn by my holiness that I will not lie unto David.
36 His seed shall endure for ever, and his throne as the sun before me.
37 It shall be established for ever as the moon, and *as* a faithful witness in heaven. Selah.
38 But thou hast cast off and abhorred, thou hast been wroth with thine anointed.

30 If his children forsake my law
and do not walk according to my ordinances,
31 if they violate my statutes
and do not keep my commandments,
32 then I will punish their transgression with the rod
and their iniquity with scourges;
33 but I will not remove from him my steadfast love,
or be false to my faithfulness.
34 I will not violate my covenant,
or alter the word that went forth from my lips.
35 Once for all I have sworn by my holiness;
I will not lie to David.
36 His line shall endure for ever,
his throne as long as the sun before me.
37 Like the moon it shall be established for ever;
it shall stand firm while the skies endure."[a] *Selah*

38 But now thou hast cast off and rejected,
thou art full of wrath against thy anointed.

[a] Cn: Heb *the witness in the skies is sure*

30-35. Unfaithfulness on the part of David's descendants will bring punishment, but will not void the divine promise. **Law, ordinances, statutes, commandments:** To be taken as synonyms referring to the general norm of moral and ritualistic behavior demanded by Yahwism. Their use here does not necessarily imply the existence of the Pentateuch. Cf. vs. 32 with Deut. 28:15-68. **Covenant:** See on vs. 3. **I have sworn:** See on vs. 3.

36-37. For the comparison with the **sun** and **moon** see Exeg. on 72:5. **While the skies endure:** A small emendation; the M.T. is **the witness in the skies is sure** (RSV mg.).

4. Plea for God's Help (89:38-51 [52])

The psalmist, having sketched the divine sanctions behind the Davidic house, now proceeds with his lament. Oblivious of any responsibility which might adhere to

him my steadfast love, or be false to my faithfulness (vss. 30-33). As God's part in this cosmic bargain, David (symbol of mankind) was to be allowed extraordinary benefits of wit and power, of a constant sense of the love and integrity of his divine colleague, and of immunities of various sorts (vss. 22-25). There follows a repetition of the promise. Man might violate his pledged word, but the covenant of God, once ratified, was irrevocable. As it appears here, it is put in the symbolic language of the throne of David and his descendants, but the wider implication for us is clear. By his holiness God has sworn. **I will not violate my covenant. . . . I will not lie to David. His line shall endure . . . while the skies endure** (vss. 34-37). In a sense deeper than the imagery of our poem can take us, mankind has come to learn that beyond the petty or prodigious covenant violations of humankind, God's law, his pledged covenant, has endured inviolate.

38-50. ***The Recurrent Doubt.***—The final section of the poem exhibits a violent change of mood. Following a promise, sworn to by the Lord, that the Davidic throne would last as long as sun, moon, and stars, is a series of eight verses describing a complete reversal of such a prospect. This is easily accounted for by

39 Thou hast made void the covenant of
thy servant: thou hast profaned his crown
by casting it to the ground.
40 Thou hast broken down all his
hedges; thou hast brought his strongholds to
ruin.
41 All that pass by the way spoil him: he
is a reproach to his neighbors.
42 Thou hast set up the right hand of his
adversaries; thou hast made all his enemies
to rejoice.
43 Thou hast also turned the edge of his
sword, and hast not made him to stand in
the battle.
44 Thou hast made his glory to cease,
and cast his throne down to the ground.
45 The days of his youth hast thou shortened: thou hast covered him with shame.
Selah.
46 How long, LORD? wilt thou hide thyself for ever? shall thy wrath burn like fire?
47 Remember how short my time is:
wherefore hast thou made all men in vain?

39 Thou hast renounced the covenant with
thy servant;
thou hast defiled his crown in the dust.
40 Thou hast breached all his walls;
thou hast laid his strongholds in ruins.
41 All that pass by despoil him;
he has become the scorn of his neighbors.
42 Thou hast exalted the right hand of his
foes;
thou hast made all his enemies rejoice.
43 Yea, thou hast turned back the edge of
his sword,
and thou hast not made him stand in
battle.
44 Thou hast removed the scepter from his
hand,[b]
and cast his throne to the ground.
45 Thou hast cut short the days of his youth;
thou hast covered him with shame.
Selah

46 How long, O LORD? Wilt thou hide thyself for ever?
How long will thy wrath burn like fire?
47 Remember, O Lord,[c] what the measure
of life is,
for what vanity thou hast created all
the sons of men!

[b] Cn: Heb *removed his cleanness*
[c] Cn: Heb *I*

the royal family for the catastrophe which has come upon Judah, the author describes the low estate of the king (vss. 38-45), and almost reproachfully appeals to God to remember his covenant (vss. 46-51).

38-44. Anointed: The king (see Exeg. on 28:8-9; cf. 84:9). On vs. 40 cf. II Kings 25:10. On vs. 41 cf. 137:7; II Kings 24:2. **The scepter from his hand:** An emended text (מטה מידו); the M.T. is **his glory** (KJV) or **his cleanness** (RSV mg.).

45*a*. The king has become prematurely old; cf. the end of the short reign of the eighteen-year-old Jehoiachin (II Kings 24:8-17).

46. The second **How long** in the RSV has no support in the Hebrew.

47. O Lord: An emendation (אדני) replacing **I** (אני) of the M.T. **The measure of life or time:** In 39:5 the RSV translates the same word "lifetime." **For what vanity**

literary criticism; the section is a borrowed fragment of an early psalm written about the last days of the tottering kingdom of Judah. This leaves unanswered the question of the propriety of its inclusion in this psalm. Was the poet's mind divided as to the integrity of God's promises? Hardly. The explanation must be that he was using a reference to a political debacle, the reasons for which lay not with divine equivocation but with human defection. The onus placed on God by the original poet was not without reason; what God had done was in response to his own inner integrity. The very fact of God's inviolable moral nature made the exercise of judgment inevitable. Indeed, what was described as having happened to the Davidic line was an attestation not of God's moral ambiguity but of his moral steadfastness.

This explanation is supported by the statement that God is exceedingly angry with his anointed. Unless God's anger was capricious or willful—an untenable assumption—it must

48 What man *is he that* liveth, and shall not see death? shall he deliver his soul from the hand of the grave? Selah.
49 Lord, where *are* thy former lovingkindnesses, *which* thou swarest unto David in thy truth?
50 Remember, Lord, the reproach of thy servants; *how* I do bear in my bosom *the reproach of* all the mighty people;
51 Wherewith thine enemies have reproached, O LORD; wherewith they have reproached the footsteps of thine anointed.
52 Blessed *be* the LORD for evermore. Amen, and Amen.

48 What man can live and never see death?
Who can deliver his soul from the power of Sheol? *Selah*

49 Lord, where is thy steadfast love of old,
which by thy faithfulness thou didst swear to David?
50 Remember, O Lord, how thy servant is scorned;
how I bear in my bosom the insults[d] of the peoples,
51 with which thy enemies taunt, O LORD,
with which they mock the footsteps of thy anointed.

52 Blessed be the LORD for ever!
Amen and Amen.

[d] Cn: Heb *all of many*

---

is preferable to **wherefore . . . in vain.** On the vanity of life cf. 39:5, 11; Job 7:6-10; 14:1-2; Eccl. 1:2; etc. On vs. 48, cf. 49:7-10 Ecclus. 41:3-4.

50. The psalmist himself has perforce to share in his people's humiliation. **The insults** or **the reproach:** Some such word seems to be required, although it is not in the Hebrew. The RSV emends כל־רבים, **of all the mighty,** to כלמות, **insults.**

51. Taunt . . . mock: In the Hebrew the same verb is used twice (חרפו). **Anointed:** See on vs. 38.

52. Not a part of the psalm but the benedictory conclusion to Book III of the Psalter (Pss. 73–89; see Exeg. on 41:13).

---

have been justified. How otherwise then than by the malfeasance of his anointed one? The chronicle of collapse is complete; it shows what happens when one uncommonly established in God's favor flouts him. The covenant was abjured, the crown defiled, walls were breached, strongholds ruined. He (Israel) was plundered and scorned by his neighbors and was the victim of the malicious rejoicing of his foes. In battle his sword was blunted, and his only safety was in flight. The symbol of royal office was knocked from his hand and his throne overturned. He was grown old prematurely, and his untimely age was covered with shame.

52. ***The Eternal Question and Testimony of Praise.***—It is, to be sure, a dispiriting record, and yet no indictment is placed against God for what has happened. Had he been the cause of it, the correct moral response of the poet would have been righteous and angry repudiation. Instead, the last section is a cry of bewilderment and despair. Under the sense of God's continuing anger life seems brief, vain, and foredoomed (vss. 46-48). Has God forgotten the plight of his servant, the insult, the taunt, the scorn to which he is abandoned since the kindness of God has been withdrawn (vss. 49-51)? This confession of man's pathetic futility brings us to the end of the song, but it is not the end. With that inextinguishable ember of hope that is the glory of the religious heart of Israel there is a quick and ecstatic apostrophe to God, sung (but see Exeg.) with a vigorous crescendo. This is the sum of Israel's amazing faith:

Blessed be the LORD for ever!
Amen and Amen.

We need only to return to the previously formulated statement to discover the point at which this poem has modern relevance. "God is eternal; he must have traffic with man to work out his will; man can exalt or subvert God's designs." This is the simple formula of ancient Israel's faith. One final component must be added. When man fails God, his only hope is in the compassion that stirs in the Eternal's heart, awaiting always man's return in penitence to release it in pardon and restoration.

Theologically the development of Christian thought has gone no further. It has provided sharpened insights into the nature of sin and the way of redemption, but its basic structure

BOOK IV

A Prayer of Moses the man of God.

90 LORD, thou hast been our dwelling place in all generations.

A Prayer of Moses, the man of God.

90 Lord, thou hast been our dwelling place[e]
in all generations.

[e] Another reading is *refuge*

XC. A Congregational Prayer (90:1-17)

In its present form this psalm can best be described as a congregational prayer; in Gunkel's terminology it is a mixed type. As its use in both Christian and Jewish circles testifies, it is one of the most precious gems in the Psalter. Kittel (*Die Psalmen,* p. 299) speaks of it as "an impressive song of almost unique elevation and power." The O.T., in ascribing the psalm to Moses, traditionally the greatest of the Hebrew prophets, has rendered it Israel's supreme tribute.

Commentators are divided on the question of the psalm's unity. E. A. Leslie, John Paterson, and Artur Weiser argue for a single author, who however voices more than one mood within these seventeen verses. But Gunkel's view seems more attractive, viz., that the poem consists of two parts, vss. 1-12, 13-17, and that these parts have no necessary connection with each other. Possibly the two sections may have come from the same writer, but it remained for a later generation to put them together.

The psalm contains little evidence concerning its date. Its retrospective and reflective tendencies can hardly be earlier than the eighth century. Many scholars place it in the postexilic period.

1. Eternal God and Mortal Man (90:1-12)

The theme is the eternity of God and the mortality of man. The contemplation of the former serves only to bring into relief the transitoriness of human life which is lived under the shadow of the Lord's anger with man's iniquity. The thought is a sober one, and the psalmist can only suggest that in some sense man's true home is in God

---

has been carried over from the older tradition. This is the glory of Israel, and it should be both the joy and the bulwark of the Christian's faith. In what other terms can the Christian gospel be put today and remain Christian? Modern man has reached high levels of power and sophistication, and his ingenuity, plus his avarice, threatens to destroy him. What covenant can be offered him before it is too late to deflect him from self-destruction?

What man can live and never see death?
Who can deliver his soul from the power of Sheol? (Vs. 48.)

This was an ancient question on the lips of one who saw clearly man's predicament. If it arises in the mind of modern man, what better answer shall be given than the ancient one:

Blessed be the LORD for ever!
Amen and Amen.

90:1-17. ***A Mature Man's Song.***—No one preparing an anthology of religious verse can ignore the claims of this well-known psalm. It commands attention not only because of its combined simplicity and stateliness of style, not only because of its sincerity and restraint, but also because of the majesty and abiding interest of its theme. As Alexander Maclaren said, "It preaches man's mortality in immortal words." It does more than that, for it "utters once for all the deepest thoughts of devout men." [3] It is therefore unlike the books we write, most of which are quickly out of date: it endures from one generation to another. Thought changes, interests wax and wane, but this psalm, which has been cited as one of the most sublime of human compositions, one of the deepest in feeling, the loftiest in theological conception, and the most magnificent in imagery, is as powerful and as relevant as ever it was. Not only is its future as secure as any human writing, but its appeal is well-nigh universal. It would be difficult to find men more diverse in faith and disposition than Isaac Watts the Independent, Cardinal Newman the Roman Catholic, Charles V the emperor, and John Hampden the Puritan; yet R. E. Prothero in *The*

[3] *The Book of Psalms* (New York: A. C. Armstrong & Son, 1894), III, 4.

2 Before the mountains were brought forth, or ever thou hadst formed the earth and the world, even from everlasting to everlasting, thou *art* God.

3 Thou turnest man to destruction; and sayest, Return, ye children of men.

2 Before the mountains were brought forth,
or ever thou hadst formed the earth and the world,
from everlasting to everlasting thou art God.

3 Thou turnest man back to the dust,
and sayest, "Turn back, O children of men!"

(vs. 1), and that it is best during this brief span of toil and trouble to live prudently and strive for wisdom (vs. 12).

These verses comprise six couplets, mostly of four stichs each, although vss. 2, 4 have an additional stich, and vs. 10 is a double distich. The meter is 3+3, with the usual variations.

90:1. Dwelling place: Refuge (RSV mg.) is supported by some Hebrew MSS and the LXX.

2. Thou hadst formed: Most of the ancient versions and many commentators favor an emendation which repoints this verb, making it passive, its subject being **the earth and the world. From everlasting to everlasting:** For other references to the One whose "years have no end" see 9:7; 10:16; 29:10; 102:24, 27; 135:13; 146:10; Job 36:26; cf. the eternity of El, the head deity of the Ugaritic pantheon (Patton, *Canaanite Parallels,* p. 16).

3. The dust, rather than **destruction,** is the translation of דכא. The view that man's ultimate destiny is **dust** is reminiscent of Gen. 3:19.

Psalms in Human Life mentions all four, and John Ruskin also, as men deeply indebted to this psalm.[4] Watts was inspired by it to write one of the noblest of Christian hymns, "O God, our help in ages past." Newman, in his *Dream of Gerontius,* inserts part of it at the point where the angel commits his charge to the keeping of the angels of Purgatory. Charles V, who had retired to a monastery, finds comfort in his last moments in this and other favorite psalms. And Hampden, having been mortally wounded at Chalgrove Field, is carried to his last resting place by devoted troopers, who as they march through the leafy lanes of Buckinghamshire sing of men's frailty and God's eternity. These things are recorded; but no human scribe can set down all that this noble song of faith has meant to countless multitudes in many lands. To quote Maclaren again: "Like the God whom it hymns, it has been 'for generation after generation' an asylum."[5]

Though it is essentially a song of faith, it is not the faith that sings with the gaiety of a skylark. It is better compared with the loveliest music of the robin when in the autumn he sits on a branch alone and does nothing but sob a few quiet notes (see Expos. on Ps. 116).

[4] New York: E. P. Dutton & Co., 1903, pp. 248, 234, 96-97, 182-83.

[5] *Loc. cit.*

It reminds us of Wordsworth's likening of poetry to "the still, sad music of humanity."[6] Not without reason did the compilers of the Book of Common Prayer insert it in the burial service, and countless times since 1662 it has been said or sung with tears. Its theme is nothing less than God and the human soul, God's eternity and man's transience, God's righteous anger and man's iniquity, God's mercy and man's prayer for a special demonstration of it.

1-6. ***God's Eternity and Man's Mortality.***—There are numerous references in Scripture to the frail and fleeting nature of human existence. Thoughts of man's mortality run like a sad refrain through many psalms. They touch with pathos the minds and hearts of prophets and inspire pensive passages. "What is man?" asks one who may have watched the glory of sunset, the deepening shadows of evening, the appearance of moon and stars. What is man, who may have temporary dominion over sheep and oxen and the beasts of the field, but who is only a speck in space and appears but for a moment in time? The same thought finds expression here in brief but grand images. Some endowed with health and strength may enjoy life for seventy years. In exceptional cases they may survive without undue weariness to themselves or others for eighty years. To the youth

[6] "Lines Composed a Few Miles Above Tintern Abbey."

4 For a thousand years in thy sight *are*
but as yesterday when it is past, and *as* a
watch in the night.
5 Thou carriest them away as with a
flood; they are *as* a sleep: in the morning
they are like grass *which* groweth up.
6 In the morning it flourisheth, and
groweth up; in the evening it is cut down,
and withereth.

4 For a thousand years in thy sight
are but as yesterday when it is past,
or as a watch in the night.

5 Thou dost sweep men away; they are like
a dream,
like grass which is renewed in the
morning:
6 in the morning it flourishes and is renewed;
in the evening it fades and withers.

---

4. Part of this verse lies behind II Pet. 3:8. **A watch in the night:** The period between sunset and sunrise was divided into three watches (63:6; 119:148; Exod. 14:24; Judg. 7:19).

5. The text is difficult and may be corrupt. **They are like a dream:** Lit., "they are sleep," which may be rendered "they fall asleep"; the reference is to the sleep of death as in Job 14:12. **Is renewed:** The verb here and in vs. 6 may be translated "sprouts up."

---

with everything to learn it may seem time enough and to spare. There comes a point, however, at which it seems like a watch in the night which, however monotonous to the watcher, is gone out of mind when a new day dawns, and to the sleeper is as it were nonexistent. It is **like a dream** which however exciting is quickly forgotten; **like grass** which sprouts in the morning and is scorched by midday; like a **flood** which sweeps everything before it. **Our years come to an end like a sigh.**

There are many references in modern literature also to this feeling of transience. Scientists may promise length of days. Statistics may prove that in civilized countries death is further and further postponed. Yet the inevitable end sooner or later comes in sight. And if science keeps us longer alive, it also gives us a roomier universe with an increasing sense of insignificance. Dwellers in vast cities may not often reflect on stars and planets, but they read of countless light-years and incomprehensible distances. Yet long before astronomers dwarfed men by increasing the frontiers of existence, men had melancholy moods in which they were impressed by their frailty. Among them was Shakespeare, who so often expressed common thoughts in uncommon speech. Consider the grave-digging scene in *Hamlet,* and the half-humorous, half-melancholy conversation of Hamlet and Horatio. Think of the unparalleled burst of language in *The Tempest,* ending with the much-quoted lines:

> We are such stuff
> As dreams are made of, and our little life
> Is rounded with a sleep.[7]

[7] Act IV, scene 1.

Reread some of his sonnets, e.g., the seventy-first, in which the poet bids his friends mourn at his death no longer than they "hear the surly sullen bell" which announces his burial. Men have argued long whether Shakespeare was or was not a religious man, but in these and other places he is one with him who long ago exclaimed: "Man that is born of a woman is of few days and full of trouble. He cometh forth like a flower, and is cut down: he fleeth also as a shadow, and continueth not" (Job 14:1-2).

Is there then no stability? nothing that endures? Modern man may pause and wonder. The psalmist has an answer which is prompt and confident.

Lord, thou hast been our dwelling place in all generations.

Here in the unchanging God, in whom there is no before or after, is the home of man's soul. Here in the Creator, to whom all is present, is the Being in whom the children of men find rest and satisfaction. Before the mountains were brought forth, he was. Though the hills be made low, and all created things should pass away, he will be. The eternity and immutability of God—a rare theme, and few are equal to it; yet the psalmist is as much at home in handling it as in speaking of man's swift-passing days. There is no tedious argument, no strained speculation, no apologetic attitude. As an artist knows beauty, as an unspoiled man or maid knows love, the psalmist knows God and knows that he is the **refuge** in which man may find peace. Again, it is no strange affirmation. It is an assurance that runs throughout the Scriptures, repeated by many voices with varying emphasis but with sustained assurance.

7 For we are consumed by thine anger,
and by thy wrath are we troubled.
8 Thou hast set our iniquities before
thee, our secret *sins* in the light of thy
countenance.
9 For all our days are passed away in thy
wrath: we spend our years as a tale *that is*
told.
10 The days of our years *are* threescore
years and ten; and if by reason of strength
they be fourscore years, yet *is* their strength
labor and sorrow; for it is soon cut off, and
we fly away.

7 For we are consumed by thy anger;
by thy wrath we are overwhelmed.
8 Thou hast set our iniquities before thee,
our secret sins in the light of thy
countenance.

9 For all our days pass away under thy
wrath,
our years come to an end[f] like a sigh.
10 The years of our life are threescore and
ten,
or even by reason of strength fourscore;
yet their span[g] is but toil and trouble;
they are soon gone, and we fly away.

[f] Syr: Heb *we bring our years to an end*
[g] Cn Compare Gk Syr Jerome Tg: Heb *pride*

9. Come to an end: A slight emendation (כלו) of the M.T., with the support of the Syriac. **A sigh** rather than **a tale that is told;** the point is the ephemeral character of man's life.

10. Threescore and ten . . . fourscore: These are the RSV's concessions to traditional phraseology. **Their span:** An emendation (רחבם) with some versional support. The M.T. (רהבם) **their pride** (RSV mg.), meaning "the pride of old age" (cf. Prov. 16:31), is not an impossible text, although the word is found only here.

To know this infinite God is the chief end of man. To fear him is the beginning of wisdom.

What a difference it would make if such a faith ruled men's hearts today! We are deeply concerned about our times. We seek security and peace by improving social conditions and inventing economic systems. Our real need goes deeper. If all social ideals were realized we should still be discontented without a knowledge of him. Augustine was nearer truth when he said that our hearts are restless till they find rest in God. It is not enough to believe that he is, or even to be assured that he is personal and favorable toward man. We must commit ourselves to him, trust him, find in him a refuge in all changing experiences. That is the secret of the saints and heroes of history. They were strong not because they were self-reliant but because they leaned hard upon God. That is what enabled William Ewart Gladstone to stand like a rock through the conflicts of the Victorian Age. The thought with which he rose in the morning and went to bed at night, said John Morley, who did not share his religious convictions, was of the Universe as a sublime moral theater, in which an omnipotent dramaturgist uses kingdoms and rulers, laws and policies to exhibit sovereign purpose for good. And this was the purpose of Jesus Christ—not to demonstrate the existence of God as a mathematician demonstrates a principle, not to make the Father in heaven an article of faith, but to persuade men everywhere to commit themselves and their dear ones to God's gracious keeping.

7-12. *God's Anger and Man's Iniquity.*—The psalmist is troubled, however, with man's sin as well as with his transience. He does not elaborate the point, but he is quite emphatic. The sadness of life is due not to death only but to wrongdoing. And notice that he does not pass immediately, as so many writers ancient and modern have done, to the sins of other people.

Thou hast set our iniquities before thee,
our secret sins in the light of thy countenance.

Finding fault with others, whether they are individuals or congregations or nations, has always been a popular pastime. And it is always the mark of an inferior mind. It is not the saint who sits in judgment upon his fellows: usually he is so concerned with his own transgressions that he has little time for cataloguing the failures of others. It is the hypocrite who makes a habit of condemning them and justifying himself. There are few things Jesus Christ reiterates more than this, and few things that men find easier or more convenient to forget. The true prophet, wherever he appears, begins with himself and the wickedness of his own heart; only then does he turn to observe the evil in those for whom he has responsibility. This is not morbidity, as some would have us believe: it is realism and honesty.

11 Who knoweth the power of thine anger? even according to thy fear, *so is* thy wrath.
12 So teach *us* to number our days, that we may apply *our* hearts unto wisdom.
13 Return, O LORD, how long? and let it repent thee concerning thy servants.

11 Who considers the power of thy anger,
and thy wrath according to the fear of thee?
12 So teach us to number our days
that we may get a heart of wisdom.

13 Return, O LORD! How long?
Have pity on thy servants!

---

11. And thy wrath according to the fear of thee: The meaning is not clear and the text may be corrupt. Gunkel offers the most plausible emendation, changing וכיראתך to ומי ראה תך, and translating the stich "And who perceives the severity of thy wrath?"

12. The wise man uses his limited time to gain a mind stored with **wisdom.**

2. Satisfy Us with Thy Steadfast Love (90:13-17)

This short prayer, possibly a fragment of a longer one, is similar to the sequel of a lament. There are undertones indicative of years of suffering, and the opening question

---

Would there not be greater hope for the modern world if we had more of the psalmist's attitude? Those who live through wars and costly revolutions must expect a spate of self-justification. Men feel that they must defend their cause not only in battle but by argument. They so habitually blame others and excuse themselves that hypocrisy is accepted as a matter of course. Religion itself becomes infected, and its advocates give themselves more to apologetics than to true evangelism. There is little hope for mankind when such an attitude becomes prevalent, unless through prayer and contrition personal confession again becomes genuine. That is where reconstruction must always begin; not so much with houses and peace treaties as in mind and spirit.

Whatever the sins to which any generation is prone, they bring upon themselves the judgment of God. Nor is that judgment uncertain and ineffective. The psalmist speaks of it as **anger** that consumes and **wrath** that overwhelms. Instead of excusing the wrongs we have wrought or permitted, God brings them to light and sets them before him.

There are people who profess difficulty with the whole conception of the wrath of God or explain it as an unworthy anthropomorphism. But can we seriously maintain that God is love unless we also affirm that he resists that which hinders his purpose of love? As W. H. Moberly has well said:

> A certain fierceness against wrong and wrongdoers is involved in a real ardour for goodness: it is necessary for moral health, and, if we have lost it, we need to recover it. . . . The mere amiability of "le bon Dieu" of much modern opinion is but one step removed from the moral indifference of Omar Khayyám's "Good Fellow." The use of "anger" or "wrath" in connection with God is only objectionable, in so far as it suggests an arbitrary, private, and personal emotion.[1]

The life and teaching of Jesus demonstrate that compassion and indignation, far from being contradictory, go hand in hand. His anger is never wayward or capricious, but is consistent in its opposition to sin. It is therefore never to be apologized for, but rejoiced in. Wherever it is found it indicates strength of character and fearlessness of moral judgment. Moberly[2] mentions Richard William Church as one of the gentlest of men, but one capable of intense indignation against anything really vile. That white heat of anger terrified some, but it also reminded them of the phrase "the wrath of the Lamb." Let no one therefore feel that the psalmist has fallen from grace when he says:

> **For we are consumed by thy anger;**
> **by thy wrath we are overwhelmed.**

13-17. ***A Prayer for God's Mercy.***—These fundamental reflections lead the psalmist to a prayer of deep sincerity and importunateness.

> **Return, O LORD! How long?**
> **Have pity on thy servants!**
> **Satisfy us in the morning with thy steadfast love,**
> **that we may rejoice and be glad all our days.**

How quiet and expectant the tone, like the prayer of Elijah on Mount Carmel. There is none of the frenzy we find in the hysterical cries of the priests of Baal; none of the fanaticism that sounds in the speech of bigots. There is in every petition the assurance that God is

1 "The Atonement," in B. H. Streeter, *et al.*, *Foundations* (London: Macmillan & Co., 1912), p. 279.

2 *Ibid.*, n. 1.

14 O satisfy us early with thy mercy; that we may rejoice and be glad all our days.

15 Make us glad according to the days *wherein* thou hast afflicted us, *and* the years *wherein* we have seen evil.

16 Let thy work appear unto thy servants, and thy glory unto their children.

17 And let the beauty of the LORD our God be upon us: and establish thou the work of our hands upon us; yea, the work of our hands establish thou it.

14 Satisfy us in the morning with thy steadfast love,
that we may rejoice and be glad all our days.
15 Make us glad as many days as thou hast afflicted us,
and as many years as we have seen evil.
16 Let thy work be manifest to thy servants,
and thy glorious power to their children.
17 Let the favor of the Lord our God be upon us,
and establish thou the work of our hands upon us,
yea, the work of our hands establish thou it.

(vs. 13) intimates that the darkness of affliction is not yet passed. But the prevailing note is one of confidence in the Lord's kindness and power. The psalmist knows that it is only God's favor that renews the sense of the gladness of life, and it is his benediction that truly prospers the works of men. The meter is mostly 3+3.

13. The troubles and distress, here and in vs. 15, are too vaguely described to be identified. **Have pity,** rather than **let it repent thee.**

17. **Beauty:** Many modern commentators prefer **favor.** In 27:4 both the KJV and the RSV render the same word "beauty." The repetition of **the work of our hands** is most effective rhetorically, and its deletion by many moderns as a redundant doublet is quite unnecessary.

---

not an irresponsible power but is eternally gracious. The language may suggest that God himself must be changed from an attitude of anger to one of favor. And how natural, though imperfect, such a prayer is! Even those who have had many years of Christian training can speak as though they must implore God to return or repent. The change from the KJV, **let it repent thee,** to the RSV, **have pity,** is particularly suggestive. It is the suppliant who must repent and through repentance find peace in the divine purpose. Only so can man find his refuge and abiding place in the Most High. Thus the psalmist brings us back to his starting point, to God who is man's true environment.

Notice the confidence of the psalmist's prayer. (*a*) It is not the confidence of a sanguine temperament. There are people who cannot help believing that "the best is yet to be." [3] They may be as superficial as Mr. Micawber, but they are sure that something good will turn up. We might envy them their optimism were it not that they achieve little in life. The works of genius come not as a rule from men of sunny disposition, but most often from those of melancholic temperament. (*b*) Nor is it the confidence of inexperience. No man who had been immune from suffering could have written this psalm. It is perhaps arguable that Victorian optimism was the result of Victorian security, that such a man as Browning was ready to "greet the unseen with a cheer" [4] because so much of the seen was comforting and comfortable. It is not so here, where we have the confidence of faith proved by experience. Exactly what the experience had been we do not know, but the psalmist had been afflicted, he had fought the specters of the mind, he had passed through deep waters. He found, however, that God has pity upon those who trust him, satisfies them **in the morning with** [his] **steadfast love,** and makes them to **rejoice and be glad all** [their] **days.**

According to G. K. Chesterton, there are two sins against hope—presumption and despair; the presumption which assumes that nothing is being done unless we are doing it, the despair which feels that everything fails when we fail. We need to reassure ourselves that God is on the field when he is most invisible, and that in everything he works for good with those who love him. Note that although unaware of the promise which is in Christ, the psalmist discerns nevertheless in God's sovereign care the abiding-

[3] Browning, "Rabbi Ben Ezra," st. i.

[4] *Asolando,* Epilogue, st. iv.

91 He that dwelleth in the secret place of the Most High shall abide under the shadow of the Almighty.

91 He who dwells in the shelter of the Most High,
who abides in the shadow of the Almighty,

XCI. GOD, MY REFUGE AND MY FORTRESS (91:1-16)

This psalm, which has affinities with Ps. 46, can be taken as a psalm of trust, although as Gunkel, *et al.*, have observed it has certain didactic qualities. Its central thought may be summed up in Paul's words, "If God is for us, who is against us?" (Rom. 8:31.) In a poem of this kind we must not look for a complete theology, and we must accept the fact that the psalmist shows no awareness of the complexity of the problem of evil. The author is a simple soul, but he has a profound faith. Amid the perils of this world he finds his only abiding security in **the shadow of the Almighty.**

It is not clear to what specific dangers the psalmist is alluding. The references to **pestilence** in vss. 3, 6, and to the high mortality rate of the afflicted in vs. 7, have been thought to indicate a disease of epidemic proportions. Another view, not necessarily exclusive of the foregoing, is that many of the allusions are to the work of demons. This line of interpretation is taken by Oesterley (*Psalms,* II, 407) who claims that the psalm is intended to show how to meet the malevolent spirits, viz., "by placing oneself under the protection of Yahweh." John P. Peters had earlier claimed that the poem "was in fact a liturgy against disease produced by the attacks of evil spirits" (*The Psalms as Liturgies* [New York: The Macmillan Co., 1922], p. 363; cf. Mowinckel, *Psalmenstudien,* "Kultprophetie und prophetische Psalmen," III, 102-5). In this

ness of his chosen people and the lasting import of all that he gives their hands to do.

William James sums up much of the teaching of Ps. 90 in a quotation from Charles Voysey, *The Mystery of Pain and Death:*

> It is the experience of myriads of trustful souls, that this sense of God's unfailing presence with them in their going out and in their coming in, and by night and day, is a source of absolute repose and confident calmness. It drives away all fear of what may befall them. That nearness of God is a constant security against terror and anxiety. It is not that they are at all assured of physical safety, or deem themselves protected by a love which is denied to others, but that they are in a state of mind equally ready to be safe or to meet with injury. If injury befall them, they will be content to bear it because the Lord is their keeper, and nothing can befall them without his will. If it be his will, then injury is for them a blessing and no calamity at all. Thus and thus only is the trustful man protected and shielded from harm. And I for one—and by no means a thick-skinned or hard-nerved man—am absolutely satisfied with this arrangement, and do not wish for any other kind of immunity from danger and catastrophe. Quite as sensitive to pain as the most highly strung organism, I yet feel that the worst of it is conquered, and the sting taken out of it altogether, by the thought that God is our loving and sleepless keeper, and that nothing can hurt us without his will.[5]

[5] London: 1892, p. 258. Quoted in William James, *The Varieties of Religious Experience* (New York: Longmans, Green & Co., 1902), pp. 275-76.

91:1-16. ***An Exuberant Song of Faith.***—We have often been advised to read the Bible as we read any other book. But wise men do not read different books in the same way. They approach fiction in one way, philosophy in another, and the daily paper in yet another. As the Bible is not all written in one style, we must try to make the necessary adaptations, or we shall make many mistakes. The book of Psalms is quite different in style and purpose from, say, Deuteronomy or Daniel. Strictly speaking, we ought not to approach every psalm with the same mental attitude, for some are songs of praise, others songs of penitence. There are hymns which are primarily personal, others that are national, and much depends on our ability to repeat them in spirit as well as understanding.

Ps. 91 is a particularly exuberant hymn of praise. It reminds us in many ways of Ps. 90. Both begin with the blessedness of those who find a dwelling place in God. But here the tone is more confident. The faith is not necessarily deeper, or even as deep, but it rises on easy wings and sings spontaneously. Ps. 90 suggests a man of many years who has experienced disappointments and frustrations. Ps. 91 suggests a young man with buoyancy and expectancy. His praise is genuinely religious, i.e., it is the praise not of self-confidence but of one whose hope is rooted in God. He knows that life has many perils; he mentions the fowler's **snare,**

2 I will say of the LORD, *He is* my refuge and my fortress: my God; in him will I trust.
3 Surely he shall deliver thee from the snare of the fowler, *and* from the noisome pestilence.

2 will say to the LORD, "My refuge and my fortress;
my God, in whom I trust."
3 For he will deliver you from the snare of the fowler
and from the deadly pestilence;

---

connection we may note that in the Babylonian Talmud this psalm is referred to as "the song against evil occurrences" and "the song against plagues" (Shebuoth 15*b*). On the other hand it is possible that the psalmist was using his language loosely, and that some of his phrases no longer bore their original meaning, and we may therefore err if we press his words too closely.

How the psalm was used liturgically is a matter of opinion. Schmidt suggests that pilgrims addressed the opening verses to a priest or temple servant who was on duty at the temple gate, that this person then replied to the pilgrims, etc. Leslie, however, following Gunkel, takes vss. 1-13 as a priestly pronouncement directed to the laity. It seems that we can be reasonably certain only that vss. 14-16 were spoken on behalf of the Lord by a priest.

Buttenwieser's remark on the date of this psalm is as apt as any: "Though the ode might have been composed in any age, on analysis it will be seen to be a typical product of the spiritual milieu of post-Exilic Israel" (*Psalms,* p. 818).

Gunkel's strophic division seems the most attractive: vss. 1-2, 3-4, 5-6, 7-8, 9-10, 11-13, 14-16. The meter is generally 3+3.

1. NO EVIL SHALL BEFALL YOU (91:1-13)

91:1. Shelter, rather than **secret place.** As this word (סתר) sometimes designates the temple (as in 27:5; 31:20; 61:4; cf. a cognate in Isa. 4:6), the immediate reference may be to the worshipers in the sanctuary and possibly also to the inhabitants of Jerusalem. It is clear, however, from the usage of the same word in 32:7; 119:114, that it is capable of a metaphorical meaning. **Shadow** (or "shade") is another figure for the Lord's protection, especially in the phrase "the shadow of thy wings" (17:8; 36:7; 57:1; 63:7; cf. 121:5). **Almighty:** A title for God, found elsewhere in the Psalter only in 68:14. This word and **Most High,** both of which are old names for God, help to create a majestic atmosphere appropriate to the psalmist's theme.

2-4. Will say: A small emendation; the M.T. is **I will say. The snare of the fowler:** A metaphor, although it may point to man-made danger. **Deadly pestilence:** Referred

---

the pit of **destruction, the terror by night,** and **the arrow that flieth by day.** Yet his mind is obsessed, not by these things but by the security of those who dwell **in the secret place of the Most High.** It is difficult to decide whether he is thinking primarily of the individual or of the community of Israel, but the emphasis falls not on those who pay fugitive visits, but on those who dwell—who **abide under the shadow of the Almighty.**

This is the language not of prose but of poetry, Oriental poetry which may often seem extravagant to the Western mind. We do not move easily among metaphors drawn from nomad life, with possible references to night demons and magic spells. We are not engaged in watching eagles and their young; nor do we walk warily because of pitfalls and traps that have been set for the careless. Yet we understand when the psalmist sings:

> **A thousand may fall at your side,**
> **ten thousand at your right hand;**
> **but it will not come near you.**

The style is quite different, yet language such as this reminds us of J. E. B. Seely's autobiography *Adventure.* The author begins by telling how each of the elements, earth, air, fire, and water, had threatened him in turn. He had nearly drowned and been revived by artificial respiration; had fallen a distance greater than would be thought possible for survival; had faced a hostile rifle at fifteen yards and been spared. He says nothing about "special providences" and avoids the language of conventional piety. What he does say is all the more impressive:

4 He shall cover thee with his feathers, and under his wings shalt thou trust: his truth *shall be thy* shield and buckler.

5 Thou shalt not be afraid for the terror by night; *nor* for the arrow *that* flieth by day;

6 *Nor* for the pestilence *that* walketh in darkness; *nor* for the destruction *that* wasteth at noonday.

7 A thousand shall fall at thy side, and ten thousand at thy right hand; *but* it shall not come nigh thee.

8 Only with thine eyes shalt thou behold and see the reward of the wicked.

9 Because thou hast made the LORD, *which is* my refuge, *even* the Most High, thy habitation;

10 There shall no evil befall thee, neither shall any plague come nigh thy dwelling.

4 he will cover you with his pinions,
and under his wings you will find refuge;
his faithfulness is a shield and buckler.
5 You will not fear the terror of the night,
nor the arrow that flies by day,
6 nor the pestilence that stalks in darkness,
nor the destruction that wastes at noonday.

7 A thousand may fall at your side,
ten thousand at your right hand;
but it will not come near you.
8 You will only look with your eyes
and see the recompense of the wicked.

9 Because you have made the LORD your refuge,[h]
the Most High your habitation,
10 no evil shall befall you,
no scourge come near your tent.

[h] Cn: Heb *Because thou,* LORD, *art my refuge; you have made*

---

to in vss. 6-7 and apparently in vs. 10. It may be some current epidemic. **Pinions** rather than **feathers. Wings:** See Exeg. on 17:8.

5. The terror of the night: Possibly a reference to night demons; cf. the Liliths of Babylonian magic (cf. also "Lilith" in Isa. 34:14). **The arrow that flies by day:** In 11:2 "arrow" describes the devices of the wicked, and in 64:3 the words of evildoers. Some find in the last reference an allusion to magic spells (see Exeg. on 64:1-10), and this may be the explanation of the present passage. Others believe that here and in vs. 6*b* the psalmist has in mind the heat of the sun, particularly at midday, and the ills popularly associated with the sun's rays (cf. 121:6).

8-10. Vs. 8 expresses the familiar view that God rewards the **wicked** in this world. **Your refuge:** A desirable emendation; the M.T. is **my refuge. Scourge** or **plague:** The word is used of disease in Gen. 12:17; II Sam. 7:14; etc.

"Such experiences have left me with an abiding sense of gratitude to the unseen hand which has protected me so often."[6] Throughout the book runs a feeling of wonder that he had been led as by a guardian angel through a life of great danger.

The psalm reminds us also of William Dobbie, governor of Malta at the most critical part of World War II, who has told his story in restrained prose. From a military point of view the situation in 1940 was hopeless. Malta with 2,700 persons to the square mile was the most densely populated country in the world. Supplies had to be brought by ships through seas controlled by hostile forces. Every convoy that was destroyed renewed the threat of starvation. The defending forces were hopelessly inadequate. There were only four out-of-date airplanes and sixteen antiaircraft guns. When the situation seemed most hopeless, the governor, a deeply religious man, issued a special order of the day which included these memorable words: "It may be that hard times lie ahead of us, but however hard they may be, I know that the courage and determination of all ranks will not falter, and that with God's help we will maintain the security of this fortress. I therefore call upon all officers and other ranks humbly to seek God's help, and then, in reliance upon him, to do their duty unflinchingly." At one desperate moment the chief of the imperial staff in England sent Dobbie a telegram containing a biblical reference: "Deuteronomy, chapter 3, verse 22." When the defenders consulted their Bibles they read the words: "Ye

[6] London: William Heinemann, 1930, p. 1.

11 For he shall give his angels charge over thee, to keep thee in all thy ways.
12 They shall bear thee up in *their* hands, lest thou dash thy foot against a stone.
13 Thou shalt tread upon the lion and adder: the young lion and the dragon shalt thou trample under feet.
14 Because he hath set his love upon me, therefore will I deliver him: I will set him on high, because he hath known my name.
15 He shall call upon me, and I will answer him: I *will be* with him in trouble; I will deliver him, and honor him.

11 For he will give his angels charge of you
to guard you in all your ways.
12 On their hands they will bear you up,
lest you dash your foot against a stone.
13 You will tread on the lion and the adder,
the young lion and the serpent you will trample under foot.

14 Because he cleaves to me in love, I will deliver him;
I will protect him, because he knows my name.
15 When he calls to me, I will answer him;
I will be with him in trouble,
I will rescue him and honor him.

11-12. These verses are quoted by the devil in Matt. 4:6; Luke 4:10-11 (cf. Shakespeare, *The Merchant of Venice,* Act I, scene 3). **His angels:** See Exeg. on 34:7, "the angel of the LORD," and cf. the "destroying angels" (78:49).

13. As the terms here appear to be used metaphorically, the precise identity of the animals mentioned is not important. **Adder** is sometimes translated "cobra." The cobra, even if not found in Palestine, was known in Egypt and Arabia and would serve as a symbol of extreme danger. **Serpent** or **dragon:** Here, as in Deut. 32:33; Exod. 7:10, a large venomous snake, rather than a sea monster (cf. Luke 10:19; Acts 28:1-6).

2. The Lord Speaks Comfortingly (91:14-16)

14-16. These verses represent the words of the Lord, probably in temple use recited by a priest. **Protect:** The basic meaning is **set . . . on high. My name:** On the name of

---

shall not fear them: for the LORD your God he shall fight for you." When in retirement Dobbie published his story, a quotation from Ps. 46 was appropriately on the title page: "God is our refuge and strength, a very present help in trouble." The title of the book is *A Very Present Help.*[7]

Both the psalm and the modern illustrations may quicken difficult questions; e.g., we shall be asked whether it is always or even generally true that good men prosper and evil men are cut down. It must be admitted that for long the orthodox piety of Israel asserted as much; but it must also be made clear that the dogma was frequently questioned and sometimes denied. We must be content here to say that whatever true religion is or is not, it is not an insurance policy against every form of adversity. The history of O.T. saints and the facts of contemporary life should convince us of that. The life and teaching of Jesus Christ should finally dispel any hesitation. He was goodness incarnate, yet he was not only tempted in all points like as we are (Heb. 4:15), but he suffered in mind and body and died upon a cross. True, that was not the last word. The Resurrection, the Ascension, the kingly rule at the right hand of God the Father are reminders of the psalmist's faith:

Because he cleaves to me in love, I will deliver him;
I will protect him, because he knows my name.

But the way was a bloodstained one, and the final victory was not easily bought.

No good pastor sends his young people out into the world with a promise of immunity from temptation, hardship, failure. He speaks of the necessity of endurance and vigilance, of the way of prayer and the ministry of the fellowship of saints. If promise he gives, it is that

More things are wrought by prayer
Than this world dreams of,[8]

and that Jesus Christ, who led his apostles through trial and terror, is "the same yesterday and today and for ever." Amazing things happen to those who walk by faith, even things which may properly be called miraculous.

The protection of which we speak most confidently, however, is that which comes through

[7] Grand Rapids, Mich.: Zondervan Publishing House, 1945.

[8] Tennyson, "Morte d'Arthur."

16 With long life will I satisfy him, and show him my salvation.

A Psalm *or* Song for the sabbath day.

92 *It is* a good thing to give thanks unto the LORD, and to sing praises unto thy name, O Most High:

16 With long life I will satisfy him,
and show him my salvation.

A Psalm. A Song for the Sabbath.

92 It is good to give thanks to the LORD,
to sing praises to thy name, O Most
High;

God see Exeg. on 8:1; 20:1. **With long life:** Lit., "length of days." The longevity of the righteous is referred to in 21:4; 23:6; Deut. 30:20; Prov. 3:2, 16. **My salvation:** See Exeg. on 74:12.

XCII. Praise God for His Works (92:1-15)

This hymn has arisen out of the experience of an unknown saint who has some good reason to praise the Lord. His references, however, are too vague (unless vs. 10 implies recovery from illness) to permit us to say precisely what his blessings are. The psalmist's enemies have been vanquished (vs. 11), and the poet observes in a mood of generalization that while fools and evildoers often appear to flourish, their prosperity is but for a season and in the end they are destroyed. So out of a full heart the words of gratitude to God pour forth.

It is clear from vs. 3 that the hymn was created for use in some form of corporate worship, and according to the Mishnah (Tamid 7:4), the Levites sang this psalm in the temple on the sabbath (cf. the superscription). In the service of the synagogue this psalm, like the others in the group (Pss. 90–99), has continued to occupy a prominent place.

The fact that Duhm (followed by Kittel and Calès), Gunkel, and Schmidt present three different strophic arrangements for this psalm indicates that the basis for any

the reinforcing of inner resources. Whatever may befall us in a dangerous world, the soul of man is inviolable. We can sully it ourselves. We can open the gates and surrender to besetting sins. But no outward circumstances can triumph over those who stand ever on their watch. Paul in prison, Livingstone dying in darkest Africa, Scott writing his last words with frozen fingers—these are not contradictions of the psalmist's faith and testimony. We remember them not with pity but with pride. Such men go down to the valley of the shadow of death saying:

Because you have made the LORD your refuge,
the Most High your habitation,
no evil shall befall you,
no scourge come near your tent.

The modern world has given itself to the pursuit of security. Men and nations have tried to provide for every stage of life and to remove the causes of fear. They have failed. They get wealth, and money loses value. They invent colossal weapons of defense, and find their cities are destroyed overnight. They discover new medicines and progress in surgical skill, and are defeated by the increasing number of the diseases of civilization. No victory in the field, no success at polling booths, no ingenuity in technique can save the world. What is needed is an adequate faith, an assurance that through the chances and changes of life there is a divine protector in whose wisdom and grace we may find peace. Timorous and Mistrust ran into far greater evils when they fled because of lions in the way. Christian by going forward boldly found that perils were not as bad as they seemed.

This hill, though high, I covet to ascend;
The difficulty will not me offend,
For I perceive the way of life lies here:
Come, pluck up, heart, let's neither faint nor fear:
Better, though *difficult*, the right way go,
Than wrong, though *easy*, where the end is woe.[9]

92:1-4. *Goodness and Gratitude.*—Men have always been concerned to know what goodness is and what its effects are. The Greeks of the classical period especially thought much on the cardinal virtues of wisdom, courage, self-control, and justice. They discussed not only the nature of the "high-minded man" but described in some detail the good state in which the good life becomes possible. The psalmists in their

[9] Bunyan, *The Pilgrim's Progress,* Part I, ch. iii.

2 To show forth thy loving-kindness in the morning, and thy faithfulness every night,

2 to declare thy steadfast love in the morning,
and thy faithfulness by night,

such scheme is rather slender. The RSV follows Schmidt's divisions. The meter is generally 3+3. There is nothing in the hymn to indicate a specific date.

I. It Is Good to Give Thanks (92:1-4)

92:2. Morning . . . night: The references may be to temple services, probably the *tāmîdh,* the burnt offering made every morning and evening (Exod. 29:38-42).

own way dealt with the same theme. The book they wrote opens with a vivid description of the good and the bad man. The first is known by what he avoids, by what he does, and by how he fares. He avoids evil companions. He studies his Bible seriously. He flourishes like a tree planted by runlets of water.[1] The wicked, on the other hand, have no stability. They are like chaff driven by the wind. Their end is ruin.

Ps. 92 does not give a detailed picture or even a firm outline, but it cites one of the characteristics of the good man. It emphasizes the importance of gratitude. **It is a good thing to give thanks unto the Lord.** There is of course nothing unusual in such teaching. There is nothing repeated more often by psalmist after psalmist than that "praise is comely for the upright." Like the quality of mercy,

> It is twice bless'd:
> It blesseth him that gives and him that takes.
> 'Tis mightiest in the mightiest: it becomes
> The throned monarch better than his crown.[2]

It increases joy and mitigates sorrow. It is a remedy for depression and spreads good will. Countenances harden in the presence of complaint; they soften under the influence of thanksgiving. Well did Sir Thomas Browne say:

> Make not thy head a grave, but a repository of God's mercies. . . . Register not only strange, but merciful occurrences. . . . Let thy diaries stand thick with dutiful mementos and asterisks of acknowledgment. And to be complete and forget nothing, date not his mercy from thy nativity; look beyond the world, and before the era of Adam.[3]

Praise is due to men and women, for we are debtors "both to the Greeks, and to the Barbarians; both to the wise, and to the unwise" (Rom. 1:14). Our life depends not only on those we know but on the dwellers in many continents. But primarily praise is due to God who works when we sleep and watches over us when we are unconscious of him. Parents do well to teach their children to acknowledge the gifts they receive. They teach them best when they encourage them to praise their Creator. Alexander Whyte[4] used to speak to his Edinburgh congregation about Lancelot Andrewes and his habits of thanksgiving. The thanksgiving for the fifth day was cited in particular, beginning with praise for existence, life, and reason; for nurture, protection, guidance, education, civil rights, religion. The good bishop became more personal as he proceeded, with references to parents and teachers, friends and servants, those who had helped him by their writings, their prayers, their rebukes—"For all these, and all others which I know, which I know not, open, hidden, remembered, forgotten . . . . What reward shall I give unto the Lord for all the benefits which He hath done unto me?"[5]

Praise is not to be left to the mood of the moment. It is good

> **to declare thy steadfast love in the morning,**
> **and thy faithfulness by night.**

There should be order in our devotions as there is in God's gifts. And when can we practice them better than at the beginning and end of each day? To make a habit of praise in the morning will give tone to the whole day and everyone will feel the benefit. Toyohiko Kagawa invariably each morning at four o'clock opened mind and heart to God and to spiritual influences and found it the most joyous period of the day. He says:

> In order to hear the voice of the voiceless God we must be quiet, silent before Him. In man's daily life this is of all things the most important.
>
> It is . . . said that Gandhi, of India, has his devotions at four in the morning and then rests again until early dawn. There is naturally a difference in the religious discipline of the tropics and the religious

[1] J. E. McFadyen, *Old Testament Scenes and Characters* (New York: Doubleday Doran & Co., 1928), pp. 218-19.

[2] Shakespeare, *The Merchant of Venice,* Act IV, scene 1.

[3] *Christian Morals,* Part I, sec. 21.

[4] See *Thirteen Appreciations* (Edinburgh: Oliphant, 1913), pp. 104-5.

[5] *The Private Devotions of Lancelot Andrewes,* tr. John Henry Newman (New York and Nashville: Abingdon-Cokesbury Press, 1950), p. 95.

3 Upon an instrument of ten strings, and upon the psaltery; upon the harp with a solemn sound.
4 For thou, LORD, hast made me glad through thy work: I will triumph in the works of thy hands.

3 to the music of the lute and the harp,
to the melody of the lyre.
4 For thou, O LORD, hast made me glad by thy work;
at the works of thy hands I sing for joy.

3. For the musical instruments see the Intro., pp. 5-6. **The music of:** Supplied by the RSV but not in the Hebrew. **The lute:** Lit., "a ten," hence **an instrument of ten strings.**

4. **Thy work:** Some recent manifestation of the Lord's power on the psalmist's behalf. **The works of thy hands:** All the Lord's deeds both creative and providential. **Sing for joy** is a better translation of the Hebrew than **triumph.**

experience of the Temperate Zone. We would do well, however, to copy India in our religious life.

To observe religious worship in the early morning is man's wisest way. . . .
Jesus also loved the hours before the dawn.[6]

To offer praise again at night is not only a natural conclusion to the day but a fitting preparation for the unconscious hours. Wrote Leslie Weatherhead:

It is almost impossible to exaggerate the importance of the last thoughts at night and the first thoughts in the morning. Our fathers and mothers, who taught us to say our prayers night and morning, were wiser psychologists than they knew. The ideas that are dominant in the mind when the mind is quiescent are the most determining ideas of the personality.[7]

The psalmist gives no instructions in the methods of thanksgiving. It does not follow that forms are unimportant. Each person must find his own way, for what is helpful to one may be harmful to another. Pascal, however, should be heeded when he says:

It is superstition to put one's hope in formalities; but it is pride to be unwilling to submit to them. The external must be joined to the internal to obtain anything from God, that is to say, we must kneel, pray with the lips, etc., in order that proud man, who would not submit himself to God, may be now subject to the creature. To expect help from these externals is superstition; to refuse to join them to the internal is pride.[8]

What is here stressed (vs. 3) is the importance of singing. In this the psalmist is in good company, for in Israel the sons of Jubal were a vigorous race. Other men had other ministries; these made melody to God. They taught Israel not only to sing but to play, to become familiar with lute and harp and lyre. Young men sang and played as they watched their flocks; they sang and played in the king's palace, and especially in the temple. There was a time when in captivity they hung their harps on the willow trees; but they taught Christendom to sing. Their music ranges from the richest notes of triumphant rapture to the saddest minor key. And it was inspired not by natural high spirits but by contemplation of the works of God:

For thou, O LORD, hast made me glad by thy work;
at the works of thy hands I sing for joy.

4-15. ***Gratitude and Divine Goodness.***—The chief difference between Greek and Jewish thinking on the good life is that while for the one ethics is autonomous, for the other it is closely related to theology. For the Greek goodness depended especially upon the earthly environment. For the devout Jew it was the result of faith. It was natural therefore for the psalmist to pass immediately from the common praise of the temple to the goodness of God declared in his mighty acts.

The reference in vs. 5 is not primarily to **works** of creation but to his mercy in providence. If some particular instances of divine power were in the psalmist's mind, there is nothing to indicate what they were. It must be remembered, however, that the Israelite believed as naturally in special providences as we do in universal law. His interpretation of the past and his hopes for the future were colored by them. It was not by the might of Moses that the fathers had been delivered from Egypt, but by the strong hand of God. It was not by the inspiration of Joshua, but by the gracious leadership of the Lord, that they had established themselves in the land flowing with milk and honey.

This conviction appears everywhere in the

[6] William Axling, *Kagawa* (London: Student Christian Movement Press, 1932), p. 135.
[7] *Psychology and Life* (New York: The Abingdon Press, 1935), p. 272.
[8] *The Thoughts of Blaise Pascal* (London: J. M. Dent & Co., 1904), p. 102.

5 O Lord, how great are thy works! *and* thy thoughts are very deep.

6 A brutish man knoweth not; neither doth a fool understand this.

7 When the wicked spring as the grass, and when all the workers of iniquity do flourish; *it is* that they shall be destroyed for ever:

8 But thou, Lord, *art most* high for evermore.

9 For, lo, thine enemies, O Lord, for, lo, thine enemies shall perish; all the workers of iniquity shall be scattered.

10 But my horn shalt thou exalt like *the horn of* a unicorn: I shall be anointed with fresh oil.

5 How great are thy works, O Lord!
Thy thoughts are very deep!
6 The dull man cannot know,
the stupid cannot understand this:
7 that, though the wicked sprout like grass
and all evildoers flourish,
they are doomed to destruction for ever,
8 but thou, O Lord, art on high for ever.
9 For, lo, thy enemies, O Lord,
for, lo, thy enemies shall perish;
all evildoers shall be scattered.

10 But thou hast exalted my horn like that of the wild ox;
thou hast poured over me[i] fresh oil.

[i] Syr: Heb uncertain

2. The Doom of the Wicked (92:5-11)

5-6. Thy thoughts are very deep: Cf. Isa. 55:8-9; Rom. 11:33. **Dull** or **brutish:** See note on "stupid," Exeg. on 73:22. **Stupid** or **fool:** In 49:10; 94:8 the RSV renders the same word (כסיל) "fool." The word is found elsewhere only in the wisdom literature.

7, 9. On the eventual destruction of the wicked see 1:4-5; 5:5-6; 11:5-6; etc.

8. On high: The Hebrew is awkward and some emend מרום to מרומם ("exalted").

10. Horn: See Exeg. on 75:4-5. **Wild ox,** rather than **unicorn,** is the correct translation of ראים (cf. 22:21; 29:6). **Thou hast poured over me:** An emended text, for the M.T. (בלתי) is uncertain. The latter could mean "I have mixed," or on the basis of the Arabic cognate, "I have moistened," but neither makes sense here. The Syriac is "Thou hast moistened me," and this supports the RSV's emendation (בלתני). On anointing with **oil** see Exeg. on 23:5. Possibly the reference is to anointment by oil by a priest in connection with some sickness (cf. the leprosy rite in Lev. 14:10-18).

O.T., but nowhere more clearly than in the story of Joseph. It may have seemed when he was at the bottom of the pit that everything had ended. But God makes use of the Midianites; he is rescued and taken to Egypt, where his great work is done. When family adversity brings his brethren to the land of the Pharaoh, Joseph sees not a train of circumstances but the divine activity. "It was not you that sent me hither, but God" (Gen. 45:8). The same idea finds expression in so many ways, from the beginning of the story to its end, that expositors seem almost to agree on it as an outstanding illustration of Paul's assurance that "all things work together for good to them that love God" (Rom. 8:28).

Not everyone, however, even in Israel, recognized the divine element in history.

> **The dull man cannot know,**
> **the stupid cannot understand this.**

In modern times some who are neither dull nor stupid fail to discover the golden thread. H. A. L. Fisher was in many ways one of the finest flowers of Oxford culture, yet in the preface to his learned *History of Europe* he wrote:

> Men wiser and more learned than I have discovered in history a plot, a rhythm, a predetermined pattern. These harmonies are concealed from me. I can see only one emergency following upon another as wave follows upon wave, only one great fact with respect to which, since it is unique, there can be no generalizations, only one safe rule for the historian: that he should recognize in the development of human destinies the play of the contingent and the unforeseen.[9]

Is this one of the truths that are hidden from the wise and prudent and revealed to babes? It seems certain that neither skill in argument nor the amassing of great knowledge will on the one hand create the psalmist's faith, nor on the other hand dispel it where it is firmly held.

The psalmist believed in the goodness of God because

> **though the wicked sprout like grass**
> **and all evildoers flourish,**
> **they are doomed to destruction for ever.**

[9] London: Edward Arnold & Co., 1936, p. v.

11 Mine eye also shall see *my desire* on mine enemies, *and* mine ears shall hear *my desire* of the wicked that rise up against me.

12 The righteous shall flourish like the palm tree: he shall grow like a cedar in Lebanon.

13 Those that be planted in the house of the LORD shall flourish in the courts of our God.

11 My eyes have seen the downfall of my enemies,
my ears have heard the doom of my evil assailants.

12 The righteous flourish like the palm tree,
and grow like a cedar in Lebanon.
13 They are planted in the house of the LORD,
they flourish in the courts of our God.

---

11. Have seen the downfall of: Lit., "have seen." **My enemies:** The Hebrew word (שורי) is found only here and is unintelligible. Supported by the ancient versions, most scholars adopt the emendation שוררי (lit., "those who watch me"), an expression found in 5:8; 27:11; etc. **My ears have heard the doom of my evil assailants:** The insertion of **doom** or **desire,** neither of which is in the Hebrew, is a recognition of the difficulty of the M.T. The stich seems long, and the idiomatic use of the preposition ב after the verb "to hear" is unique. Most commentators resort to emendations.

3. THE FELICITY OF THE RIGHTEOUS (92:12-15)

12. The palm tree: The date palm, noted for its gracefulness, fruitfulness, and longevity. **A cedar in Lebanon:** A similar phrase, "cedars of Lebanon," is often used in the O.T. (29:5; 104:16; Judg. 9:15; etc.). **Cedar:** Noted for its beauty and strength (see Exeg. on 80:10*b*). **Lebanon:** See Exeg. on 72:16.

13. The psalmist thinks of the righteous as trees planted in the temple **courts** where they flourish in the immediate presence of God. The simile of the righteous as a tree is found in 1:3; 52:8.

This was a part of the orthodoxy of the times, a favorite thought of many wise men, though often questioned or denied by others—e.g., the author of Job—who were neither irreverent nor irresponsible thinkers. That it contains an element of truth few would doubt; but Jesus Christ, who taught that God "maketh his sun to rise on the evil and on the good, and sendeth rain on the just and on the unjust" (Matt. 5:45), did not give the teaching unqualified approval. By accepted standards he himself did not **flourish like the palm tree,** nor did he **grow like a cedar in Lebanon.** If the psalmist speaks from personal experience when he says,

Thou hast exalted my horn like that of the wild ox;
thou hast poured over me fresh oil,

he was more fortunate than some of the best of men who have languished in prisons and died in torment.

The element of truth in the assertion is what Jean Léon Jaurès, the French Socialist, tried to express when he said that he had one great faith, that there is an essential justice at the heart of things which sooner or later brings retribution. The same conviction was affirmed by C. P. Scott, who when under the shadow of great public and private anxiety wrote:

> Of course you're quite right that there is no relation between righteousness and success for nations any more than for individuals. . . . In a very real sense—the deepest—righteousness *is* success. Yet taking the sum of things, is there not something in Matthew Arnold's definition of God (based on the prophets) as "the Power not Ourselves that makes for Righteousness"? . . .
>
> Anyway, if I thought that on the whole the stream of things was towards progressive evil, I should feel it was a Devil's world rather than God's.[1]

The same assurance was expressed in more academic and theological language by William Morgan:

> A man's sin comes back to him and finds him less in what he suffers than in what he misses, and less in its external than in its internal results. It comes back to him in the dulling of the moral intelligence, the deterioration of character, the impairing of the finer sensibilities and energies which are its inevitable consequences. It is only to express the same truth in other words when we say that the real penalty of sin is alienation from God. The soul loses its power to respond to the high, the pure, the generous; moral activity is paralysed, and only the ignoble remains. No external or mechanical order this, but one belonging to the nature of

[1] J. L. Hammond, *C. P. Scott of the Manchester Guardian* (London: George Bell & Sons, 1934), pp. 339-40.

14 They shall still bring forth fruit in old age; they shall be fat and flourishing;
15 To show that the LORD *is* upright: *he is* my rock, and *there is* no unrighteousness in him.

93 The LORD reigneth, he is clothed with majesty; the LORD is clothed with strength, *wherewith* he hath girded himself: the world also is stablished, that it cannot be moved.

14 They still bring forth fruit in old age,
they are ever full of sap and green,
15 to show that the LORD is upright;
he is my rock, and there is no unrighteousness in him.

93 The LORD reigns; he is robed in majesty;
the LORD is robed, he is girded with strength.
Yea, the world is established; it shall never be moved;

---

14. Full of sap: If the figure of the tree is here continued, "juicy" rather than **fat** (KJV) is the sense of רשנים. **Green** rather than **flourishing.**

15. Similar language is found in Deut. 32:4. **My rock:** See Exeg. on 28:1-2.

XCIII. THE LORD IS KING (93:1-5)

This psalm belongs to a group (Pss. 47; 93; 96–99) a characteristic feature of which is the occurrence of the words "Yahweh is king" or "Yahweh has become king." They were sung at the New Year at the solemn ceremony of the accession or enthronement of Yahweh as King over the earth and its peoples (see Exeg. on Pss. 24; 47; 68).

The idea of the kingship of Yahweh was implicit in the early conception of him as the supreme God to whose will his people owed obedience. It comes to expression, for example, in Gideon's words: "I will not rule over you, neither shall my son rule over you: the LORD shall rule over you" (Judg. 8:23); cf. Ludwig Köhler, *Theologie des Alten Testaments* [Tübingen: J. C. B. Mohr, 1936], pp. 12-13). Among the older nations of the ancient East the idea of the kingship of a chief god in their pantheon had a long history. It was born out of a myth that he created the world, bringing order out of the primeval chaos, and thereby establishing his authority over it; and that at the New Year

---

things, and from which there is no escape. Must we not recognize in it a revelation of the Justice that rules at the heart of being? [2]

In this sense the psalmist's conviction survives the most rigorous thinking of the ages, and his words can be repeated without apology. The righteous

still bring forth fruit in old age,
they are ever full of sap and green,
to show that the LORD is upright;
he is my rock, and there is no unrighteousness in him.

To that, Paul in prison and martyrs at the stake and a long succession of humble men and women, in the spirit of Jesus of Nazareth on the cross, cry aloud, "Amen!" It is the secret of praise maintained even in time of humiliation, praise which resounds through the centuries reviving the faith and courage of the saints.

93:1-5. ***King of Kings and Lord of Lords.***—This psalm strikes a note that is continued through the group ending with Ps. 99: **The LORD reigns; he is robed in majesty.** It has been likened to the overture of an oratorio. No one knows precisely when it was written: the probability is that it was used in the temple after the return of the Israelites from Babylon. Such songs were urgently needed by men who had been contending with many difficulties. They had partly rebuilt their city and its walls. They had erected a new temple and dedicated it to the worship of God. They had labored to restore order in every department of community life. There was, however, no prince of the house of David to rule over them. They had leaders and teachers who had faced problems with courage, but there was no king to whom they could look in time of crisis. Time was when that would have been fatal to the peace of the nation, when ambitious men would have fought for supreme authority. But the children of Israel had learned many lessons in the land of their captivity, including this, that all earthly power emanates from above. Even in the days of their independence neither Saul nor David, neither the judges before them

[2] *The Nature and Right of Religion* (Edinburgh: T. & T. Clark, 1926), pp. 97-98. Used by permission.

festival, the annual commemoration of the event, he formally reasserted his kingship and guaranteed afresh the round of the seasons with their products of the field, the flock, and the herd. In consequence, each New Year's festival was marked by a dramatic representation of the events of the myth in sacred processions and rituals of various types, about which we are informed in Egyptian, Babylonian, and Ugaritic (North Canaanite) sources (see S. H. Hooke, ed., *Myth and Ritual* [London: Oxford University Press, 1933]; *The Origins of Early Semitic Ritual* [London: British Academy, 1938]; Frankfort, *Kingship and the Gods,* pp. 313-33; Gordon, *Loves and Wars of Baal and Anat,* pp. 5-26). When the Hebrews settled in Canaan they were influenced by these practices and beliefs of their neighbors and predecessors in the possession of the land, to the extent that they enlarged the scope and character of Yahweh's activities to include in them the roles of the foreign gods. If their neighbors had a King-God, Yahweh was Israel's King-God. In what they heard of the creation myth of other peoples, they substituted Yahweh's name for the names of other gods. Likewise the ritual of the New Year's festival was early introduced among them, and *mutatis mutandis* appropriated. In each of the psalms to which we have referred above, the situation should be interpreted in the light of what has just been said. It is still a matter of discussion, however, whether others of the psalms, and how many, had a place in the enthronement ritual—*tot homines, tot opiniones* (see Mowinckel, *Psalmenstudien,* II; C. C. Keet, *A Liturgical Study of the Psalter* [New York: The Macmillan Co., 1928], pp. 81-104; Gaster, *Thespis,* pp. 73-86, 415-27). But if we keep in mind that the ceremony of enthronement was, even if the most important feature, only one feature in the whole New Year festival, the psalms that can be directly related to it become greatly reduced in number.

The celebration of the New Year festival with its central idea of the kingship of Yahweh began early in Israel's history, and was perpetuated in the postexilic period and beyond it (see Fiebig, *Rosh ha-schana,* pp. 45-56). The hymns and the ritual doubtless suffered changes and readaptations in the course of the years through a growing refinement in religious thought. Hence in Ps. 93 we meet evidences of a late pre-exilic or a postexilic date, e.g., in vs. 5, where **thy house** implies that worship is carried on at one holy place—i.e., Zion—and also in the appearance of such words as תבל, **world,** and עדות, **decrees,** which occur chiefly in the later literature. We note also that the crude elements of the old myth pattern have disappeared because of an elevated spiritual conception of God.

The measure of the first line is 4+4; that of the following lines is 3+3+3.

---

nor the kings after them, had claimed supreme authority. They had been clothed in majesty, but it was majesty which they had received from God. They sat upon a throne; yet they were there not in their own right but as the representatives of the King of kings. This was easily forgotten in times of national prosperity, but it became a reality in Babylon. As anyone could see, even princes had become exiles under the authority of alien rulers. But there was a fact beyond that fact, and every devout Jew remained subject to his invisible King, the Lord seated upon a throne. Thus the people in the land of bondage were prepared for the theocracy which became effective with the return to Jerusalem. They repaired their walls, rebuilt the temple, revised the constitution, but they did not elect a king, for **the Lord reigns; he is robed in majesty.**

There are reasons for believing that this psalm was used as part of the New Year festivals which played a considerable role in Semitic life. Modern research has made us realize that living was for them not dull or individualistic, but full of color and community consciousness and ritual movement. There were high days and holidays, with processions and religious observances. Among them New Year celebrations took a prominent place. It would be foolish to expect uniformity of rite or intention, but normally the celebrations included a repetition of coronation solemnities in which not only priests and rulers and musicians but ordinary citizens participated. We must picture officials, musicians, and representatives of many aspects of community life marching through streets, the people joining in the festive songs and the declaratory acts. They could not all be in the temple for the commemoration of enthronement, but they were all involved in what was happening.

If this is, as we believe, the historic back-

2 Thy throne *is* established of old: thou *art* from everlasting.	2 thy throne is established from of old; thou art from everlasting.

1. His Throne Endures Forever (93:1-2)

This psalm concentrates on the moment when Yahweh assumes his kingship after his victory in the battle with the mythical monsters of the primeval deep (cf. 74:13-17). The ancient account of the conflict has been so modified and refined by our psalmist that its crasser features have disappeared (cf. 74:13-14) and mention is made only of the warring of the waves of the deep. In this fact we have an indication not only of the spiritual stature of the psalmist but also of the process by which Israel characteristically sublimated what it borrowed from its neighbors.

93:1-20. The Lord reigns or "the Lord has become king": The solemn moment has arrived when the Lord is symbolically represented or conceived as seating himself on his **throne** in the most holy place in the temple. As earthly kings at their accession wear magnificent robes of state and bind on weapons symbolic of their power, so **the Lord . . . is robed in majesty, . . . he is girded with strength.** And the consequence of his victorious rule is that **the world is established** immovably and his **throne is established from of old.**

ground of Ps. 93, our attention is called to the place of symbol and ritual in national and religious life. It is indeed a subject in which there is revived interest and upon which serious thinking is required. Our fathers, not without reason, were apt to dwell upon the dangers of "impressive doings." Thomas Carlyle said that it was meritorious to insist on forms—"all substances clothe themselves in forms"—but with him the emphasis fell always, and especially in the lecture on Cromwell, on "the struggle of men intent on the real essence of things, against men intent on the semblances and forms of things."[3] Likewise John Oman in *Grace and Personality,* dealing with "Prayer, Word, and Sacrament," insisted that they are means of grace, "only as they are moral means adapted to moral ends, and not merely as they are devices or vehicles or impressive doings."[4] Never must we forget these repeated and insistent warnings.

Yet not only has recent scholarship emphasized the place of ritual in the use of the psalms and in the public and private life of the Israelites,[5] but modern man shows renewed interest in symbols, in drama, and in both national and religious ceremonies. Every state has its flag, every party its emblem, every church its particular celebrations: all of it rendered quite inevitable by the conditions under which we live, the intensity of our loyalties and antipathies, the demands that are made upon us by the societies to which we belong. There is, however, in our day, more than a revival of partisanship; there is a deepening of Goethe's conviction that the highest cannot be spoken, it can only be acted. Words are important for the exchange of ideas, but the things that are most felt must be expressed by music, by art, by ritual. It is useless to imagine that such expressions can be prohibited by threats or by law; but it is necessary to remember how Carlyle distinguished between "earnest solemnity" and "empty pageant." "Forms which *grow* round a substance, if we rightly understand that, will correspond to the real nature and purport of it, will be true, good; forms which are consciously *put* round a substance, bad."[6]

What the Jews tried to say by public ritual was really what the psalmist put into words. Not only had the Lord girded himself with might but his throne stood firm forever and ever. Vicissitudes might come to them again; enemies might prevail against them and remove

[3] *On Heroes, Hero-worship, and the Heroic in History,* "The Hero as King."

[4] Cambridge: Cambridge University Press, 1917, p. 169; cf. Charles Gore, *The Holy Spirit and the Church* (New York: Charles Scribner's Sons, 1924), p. 25: "Outward forms are notoriously liable to become formal, and religious ceremonies very easily become unspiritual; because the spirit is slumbering or occupied in other regions while the sacred actions are being performed, or because it is relying on the mere performance of a sacred routine, or on the satisfaction of the imagination by splendour of ceremonial. Nothing, in fact, is more conspicuous in the history of the Church than this sort of degradation of sacraments and sacred rites. They easily become charms." How the same evil affected the religion of Israel was pointed out by George Adam Smith, *The Book of the Twelve Prophets* (rev. ed.; New York: Harper & Bros., 1928), I, 22: "The ritual of Israel always remained a peril to the people, the peril of relapsing into Paganism."

[5] See Adam C. Welch, *The Psalter in Life, Worship, and History* (Oxford: Clarendon Press, 1926), pp. 71-74, especially p. 74: "The right form of words was of peculiar significance, and could not, therefore, be left to the will of the offerer, but was prescribed to him by the priest."

[6] *Loc. cit.*

3 The floods have lifted up, O LORD, the floods have lifted up their voice; the floods lift up their waves.

4 The LORD on high *is* mightier than the noise of many waters, *yea, than* the mighty waves of the sea.

3 The floods have lifted up, O LORD,
the floods have lifted up their voice,
the floods lift up their roaring.
4 Mightier than the thunders of many waters,
mightier than the waves[j] of the sea,
the LORD on high is mighty!

[j] Cn: Heb *mighty the waves*

---

2. LORD OF THE PRIMEVAL WATERS (93:3-4)

3-4. The floods [i.e., the primeval deep] **lift up their roaring:** Lit., "crashing," in fierce enmity against the Lord as he proceeds to subdue them to his rule and to bring an ordered world out of their chaos. For the bellowings of the great monster of that deep, variously called Tiamat, Leviathan, or Rahab, and its retinue of "helpers" (cf. 89:10; Isa. 51:9; Job 9:13) the psalmist substitutes the thunderous roar of the waves. **Mightier than the waves:** Lit., "the breakers"; the Lord proves himself in the conflict. **The LORD on high is mighty:** Lit., "majestic" or "kingly." These closing words rise like a loud shout of victory over the raging foes, whose clamor subsides in the silence of defeat. **The LORD reigns.**

---

them once more from Jerusalem: but because God endured, their world was established. It was the faith that Isaac Watts expressed in inspired words,

> Under the shadow of thy throne
> Still may we dwell secure:
> Sufficient is thine arm alone,
> And our defense is sure.[7]

And it is not a baseless faith. It was God who at the Creation reduced the floods to order. It was he who gave the Law to men and ordered the sanctity of the temple. His testimonies are sure, whatever is shaken. The kings of the earth are mortal, and their power is fleeting; but **the LORD on high is mighty.**

There may have been many different conceptions of the divine majesty, but at least the conviction was central to individual and national life and thought. The psalmist's hope was not in man, not in the wisdom of rulers or the courage of the mighty, not in the sobriety or industry of the people, or in his own piety or purity, but in God. Adolf Deissmann divided religion into two types, acting and reacting cults. By acting cults he meant the faiths that emphasize human obligation. It matters little whether in these the stress falls upon ritual duties or personal conduct or any other kind of human achievement; they are wrongly centered. They may lead to deeds of sacrifice and heroic endeavor, but they easily break in time of crisis. They may produce men of courage and tenacity, but there is always a sense of strain: duty becomes a burden, not a delight. By reacting cults Deissmann meant religions that emphasize

[7] "O God, our help in ages past."

divine initiative and succor, that teach men at all times to look up and to behold the God who sits upon the throne. This is the faith that puts a new song upon men's lips, that makes men buoyant even in the midst of danger, that gives "the oil of joy for mourning, the garment of praise for the spirit of heaviness" (Isa. 61:3).

The O.T. generally and the psalms in particular are of the latter type. But religions may degenerate when they seem to flourish. The religion of Israel in time was transformed into the Judaism that crucified Jesus. Pharisees and Sadducees were often sincere and devout men, but even at their best they were too concerned with rites and duties and too little concerned with the God of mercy. The same thing has happened again and again in the history of the Christian church. Men have been anxious about many things, even about their own faith and love and churchmanship, but not sensitive to divine presence and power. They may have labored heroically, but they have not impressed others with a sense of radiant joy and inward peace. They have been succeeded by men who have said less about human responsibility and more about divine strength and grace, and it has been like spring coming to a land held in the grip of winter. Is anything needed in the modern church more than to have the eyes raised from the world's need to God's inexhaustible resources? Let that be done and there will be a new note in our prayers, a new passion in our preaching, a new joy in our service.

The sovereignty of God has often been crudely expressed. There may have been some in the psalmist's time, there have been many since, who imagined a capricious, irresponsible

5 Thy testimonies are very sure: holiness becometh thine house, O LORD, for ever.

5 Thy decrees are very sure;
holiness befits thy house,
O LORD, for evermore.

3. HIS DECREES ARE SURE (93:5)

5. The consequences of the Lord's victory of which the New Year reminds his worshipers are concisely and appositely summed up. **Thy decrees are very sure:** The word **decrees,** often translated **testimonies,** embraces such concepts as "laws," "promises," "warnings." Every utterance of the Lord to his people can be accepted in perfect trust and should be guarded with fidelity, since he alone is the Lord of creation. **Holiness becometh thine house, O LORD, for ever: Holiness** here implies inviolability. The psalmist means to say not so much that the temple should be kept free of unholy things and practices, but that throughout all time the worship of the Lord will endure; for what other god can claim the worship of men, and to what other god can men go with assurance for help? **The LORD reigns:** To him belong dominion, power, and glory forever.

Deity, an almighty Sultan, before whom they must grovel. There were times when even pious Jews thought of a God who sends pestilences and cares nothing about human suffering. They were fortunate if they found the Lord in a good temper, or if they could induce him by prayer and entreaty to consider their condition. They multiplied services and sacrifices in the hope that they might win his attention and be saved.

The same attitude has marked the history of Mohammedanism. The transcendence of God is indeed the central emphasis of the Koran. To such an extent is power vested in Allah that no place is left for the freedom and spontaneous action of man. Attempts have been made to explain that divine omnipotence and human responsibility are compatible, but they have not been well received by the orthodox. God in Mohammedan doctrine has no less than ninety-nine names, including "The Merciful," "The Compassionate," "The Forgiver"; but there remains a monotheism in which every other consideration is subordinated to the unconditioned might of God. "Love and holiness are crowded out by this overmastering conception of absolute might." [8]

There have been Christians who have laid themselves open to the same charge, and without the same excuse. The N.T. takes the work of the great Hebrew prophets and develops it. Amos and Hosea, Isaiah and Jeremiah, had set themselves to moralize the divine autocracy. The N.T. establishes and develops the ideas of righteousness, forgiveness, lovingkindness. It sets forth the patience and mercy of the heavenly Father not in words only, but in the life and death of Jesus, in the suffering and self-sacrifice of the disciples. Paul never surrendered the sovereignty of God, yet when he appeared before Felix he reasoned not in terms of omnipotence but of "righteousness, temperance, and judgment to come" (Acts 24:25). Never in Christian thought has the rule of God been more stressed than by Calvin and his followers. There is, they said, but one true God, and in the Westminster Confession of Faith he is declared to be "most free, most absolute, working all things according to the counsel of his own immutable and most righteous will, for his own glory." [9] Yet never is divine grace belittled, and never under Calvinism at its best did there result, as might have been expected, a race of servile and fawning sycophants. There arose men and women of independent mind, courageous spirit, and adventurous service. Men of faith so virile may make many mistakes; they will never be prudential, hedonistic, or self-centered.

The reconciliation of divine sovereignty and human freedom may still be a problem for the thinker, but we are traveling in the right direction when we remember that "freedom . . . is the power to make the moral law our law, to follow reverence whatever attraction there may be of pleasure or whatever repulsion of fear." [1] The reconciliation in experience is not difficult to discover. It is found in Robert Morrison, who went to China by way of New York, and was asked there by a shipowner if he really thought he could make an impression on so vast a country. "No, sir," replied the undaunted missionary, "but I expect God will." [2] It is found in Kagawa of Japan, who on his return from a world tour received an urgent call for

[8] William Paton, *The Faiths of Mankind* (London: Student Christian Movement Press, 1932), p. 48.

[9] Ch. ii, art. i.

[1] John Oman, *The Problem of Faith and Freedom in the Last Two Centuries* (New York: A. C. Armstrong & Son, 1906), pp. 179-80.

[2] See Archibald McLean, *Epoch Makers of Modern Missions* (New York: Fleming H. Revell, 1912), p. 74.

94 O Lord God, to whom vengeance belongeth; O God, to whom vengeance belongeth, show thyself.

94 O Lord, thou God of vengeance, thou God of vengeance, shine forth!

XCIV. Two Cries for Help (94:1-23)

Some commentators take this psalm as a unity, but it seems preferable, with Gunkel, Schmidt, *et al.,* to find in it two distinct parts, and with Gunkel and Leslie to make the division after vs. 15. It may be noted that the LXX inserts διάψαλμα at this point, although there is no support for this in the M.T. A factor which may have helped to bring the two psalms together, apart from the fact that neither has a title, is that each is a lament, the one of the community, the other of an individual. It is also conceivable that both came from the same author. There is little evidence in either respecting date. Calès suggests the time of Isaiah and Micah, Oesterley the Greek period. The reference to **thy law** (vs. 12) may imply a date after Ezra. According to the Mishnah, this psalm was sung in the temple by the Levites on the fourth day of each week (Tamid 7:4).

A. The Nation Appeals to God (94:1-15)

This is a lament of the community. The chief plaint is the arrogance and oppression of the wicked (vss. 4-6), who appear to disregard the possibility of the Lord seeing them. There is little to help us identify these evildoers, but it is implied in vs. 8 (**O dullest of the people**) that they are members of the Hebrew community. Probably they are politically and socially prominent, and some may be magistrates. The psalm ends, as the lament so often does, on a note of reassurance.

The RSV adopts the same strophe division as Calès. The meter is generally 3+3.

I. God Is Invoked (94:1-3)

94:1. God of vengeance: Lit., "God of vengeances," a phrase found only in this verse (on the vengeance of the Lord see Deut. 32:35, 41, 43; Isa. 35:4; 47:3; Mic. 5:15; Jer. 51:36; Ezek. 25:14; etc.).

---

help from the manager of some co-operative undertaking which Kagawa had initiated. The reply was a sketch of Moses leading the children of Israel through the Red Sea and Pharaoh's host disappearing beneath the waves. With the sketch were some lines from a hymn which, translated, read:

> God will do His gracious will;
> He opens a path through the raging sea,
> And sends down manna in the sandy wastes.

The harassed manager, inspired by the reply, "invented a new line of goods which have made the coöperatives abundantly successful in a financial as well as educational sense." [3]

Thy decrees are very sure;
holiness befits thy house,
O Lord, for evermore.

94:1-23. ***A Relevant Psalm.***—There was a time when a great novelist wrote thus about the Psalms:

> "Do you read your Bible?"
> "Sometimes."
> "With pleasure? Are you fond of it?"
> "I like Revelations, and the book of Daniel, and Genesis and Samuel, and a little bit of Exodus, and some parts of Kings and Chronicles, and Job and Jonah."
> "And the Psalms? I hope you like them?"
> "No, sir."
> "No? oh, shocking! I have a little boy, younger than you, who knows six Psalms by heart: and when you ask him which he would rather have, a ginger-bread nut to eat, or a verse of a Psalm to learn, he says: 'Oh! the verse of a Psalm! angels sing Psalms'; says he, 'I wish to be a little angel here below'; he then gets two nuts in recompense for his infant piety."
> "Psalms are not interesting," I remarked.
> "That proves you have a wicked heart; and you must pray to God to change it; to give you a new and clean one; to take away your heart of stone and give you a heart of flesh." [4]

The passage must not be regarded as Charlotte Brontë's last word on the Bible as a whole or on the psalms in particular. It expresses

[3] *Love, the Law of Life,* tr. J. Fullerton Gressitt (Philadelphia: John C. Winston, 1929), p. 28.

[4] Charlotte Brontë, *Jane Eyre,* ch. iv.

2 Lift up thyself, thou judge of the earth:
render a reward to the proud.
3 Lord, how long shall the wicked, how
long shall the wicked triumph?
4 *How long* shall they utter *and* speak
hard things? *and* all the workers of iniquity
boast themselves?
5 They break in pieces thy people, O
Lord, and afflict thine heritage.
6 They slay the widow and the stranger,
and murder the fatherless.
7 Yet they say, The Lord shall not see,
neither shall the God of Jacob regard *it*.
8 Understand, ye brutish among the people: and *ye* fools, when will ye be wise?
9 He that planted the ear, shall he not
hear? he that formed the eye, shall he not
see?

2 Rise up, O judge of the earth;
render to the proud their deserts!
3 O Lord, how long shall the wicked,
how long shall the wicked exult?

4 They pour out their arrogant words,
they boast, all the evildoers.
5 They crush thy people, O Lord,
and afflict thy heritage.
6 They slay the widow and the sojourner,
and murder the fatherless;
7 and they say, "The Lord does not see;
the God of Jacob does not perceive."

8 Understand, O dullest of the people!
Fools, when will you be wise?
9 He who planted the ear, does he not hear?
He who formed the eye, does he not see?

---

2. Judge of the earth: Cf. 50:4; 98:9; Gen. 18:25; Isa. 33:22. **The proud:** Cf. Isa. 2:12; Job 40:11-12; Prov. 15:25.

2. The Evildoers (94:4-7)

4. They pour out their arrogant words: Lit., "They pour out, they speak an arrogant thing" (cf. 31:18).

5-6. Note the social evils, of which the weak are the easiest victims. **They crush:** As is clear from vss. 6, 8, **they** refers to Hebrew, not alien, oppressors. **The sojourner:** A resident alien, but with certain recognized rights (Exod. 20:10; Deut. 1:16; 10:18; 14:29; etc.).

7. The Lord does not see: The same argument is attributed to Job by Eliphaz in Job 22:13-14.

3. God's Knowledge of Men (94:8-11)

8-11. Dullest: See note on "stupid," in Exeg. on 73:22. **Fools:** See note on "stupid," in Exeg. on 92:6. **Knowledge:** Briggs, *et al.*, emend this word to get "Does he not know?"

---

detestation of certain conventional types of piety, and will be read sympathetically by many who would not agree with all the details of the verdict. There are psalms, and the ninety-fourth may be one of them, which casual readers may pass by as quickly as possible. Men with an instinct for history or literary criticism may indeed find much to detain them. They may become engrossed in problems of date and authorship, in the theological background, or in reconstructing the stage and placing suitable actors upon it. Most readers, however, are primarily concerned with the challenge of life, and it may seem to them that there is little here to help them in their quest for truth and wisdom.

Nevertheless the psalm has relevance to the present age. Those loud and boastful voices with their threats and insolence, of which the psalmist complains, remind us of voices we have heard, and of fears we have had as we have listened. We have seen the rise and fall of such men; as one set of tyrants has perished others have arisen. We find also a reminder of our own reactions to such violence. Like the psalmist's, our first reaction may have been fear; but that has often been followed by answering protests. **Understand, O dullest of the people,** we have cried in tones of indignation: **Fools, when will you be wise?** And after such admonitions addressed to those who have broken the peace, we have turned to God with cries which have not been devoid of querulous complaint (cf. vss. 5-6). We must not lightly condemn the complaint. Great evils have been committed, and the suffering has been grievous and widespread. These words are written immediately after a visit to hospital wards where some were dying and others were longing to die. Among the patients was a man who had been torn from friends and country and had little hope of ever

10 He that chastiseth the heathen, shall not he correct? he that teacheth man knowledge, *shall not he know?*

11 The LORD knoweth the thoughts of man, that they *are* vanity.

12 Blessed *is* the man whom thou chastenest, O LORD, and teachest him out of thy law;

13 That thou mayest give him rest from the days of adversity, until the pit be digged for the wicked.

14 For the LORD will not cast off his people, neither will he forsake his inheritance.

15 But judgment shall return unto righteousness: and all the upright in heart shall follow it.

10 He who chastens the nations, does he not
chastise?
He who teaches men knowledge,
11 the LORD, knows the thoughts of man,
that they are but a breath.

12 Blessed is the man whom thou dost chasten, O LORD,
and whom thou dost teach out of thy law
13 to give him respite from days of trouble,
until a pit is dug for the wicked.
14 For the LORD will not forsake his people;
he will not abandon his heritage;
15 for justice will return to the righteous,
and all the upright in heart will follow it.

(הלא ידע). This is purely conjectural, but it gives excellent parallelism and lengthens the stich. Vs. 11 is quoted by Paul in I Cor. 3:20. **Breath:** See Exeg. on 39:4-6.

4. THE LORD PROTECTS HIS PEOPLE (94:12-15)

12. On God's correction of man see Prov. 3:11-12 (quoted in Heb. 12:5-6); Job 5:17; 33:14-30; Jer. 10:24; 30:11. **Thy law:** Either the Pentateuch or the general body of religious teaching mediated through priest, prophet, and sage.

13. Pit: Frequently used of Sheol (16:10; 49:9; Job 33:24; etc.), but here, as in 7:15; 9:15, of a device for trapping a quarry.

15. The righteous: A slight emendation (צדיק) with some versional support; the M.T. is **righteousness.** Luther's translation of vs. 15*a*, "For right must still remain right," is supported by Kittel and Weiser.

---

seeing his family again. Having been forced to labor in a foreign land, he faced death without a familiar face or the sound of native speech. "It is a reminder," said the doctor who had done his best for him, "of what might have happened to any of us." It would be inhuman to condemn as petulance the prayer **How long shall the wicked exult?**—to denounce a growing acerbity in the demand:

> **Rise up, O judge of the earth;**
> **render to the proud their deserts!**

There have been other moods when the temper has been wiser, when we have been mindful of great mercies, when we have rejoiced in wonderful deliverances, and again the words of our mouth have been similar to those of the psalmist (vss. 18-19). In this sense also the psalm is a contemporary document and full of interest. There are verses appropriate especially in countries where there are solemn celebrations, like Armistice services in Great Britain. In that land early each November there is hardly a city, town, or village without its reading of lists, often long lists, of names—the names of those who laid down their lives in two great wars. But with sad memories and the laying of poppy wreaths on monuments and cenotaphs there is an unspeakable gratitude for deliverance wrought. And much as courageous men and women are remembered and praised, thanksgiving is offered especially to God whose kindness held us up.

14-19, 9-11, 1-2. ***Foundations of a Faith to Live By.***—*1. The Living God.* Times change, and again the nations will rejoice in peace and prosperity. Always, however, men will need a faith to live by, and here they can find at least foundations upon which to build. There is in the first place an assurance that behind the things that appear is a God who presides over the destinies of men and nations (vss. 14-19; 22-23). That assurance is maintained throughout the psalms and indeed almost everywhere in Hebrew literature. On the rare occasions when it was suggested that "there is no God" it was treated as the hasty speech of a fool. In this the mental climate of modern times is different. Even scholars and other men of serious mind in many lands profess atheism. And large numbers

16 Who will rise up for me against the evildoers? *or* who will stand up for me against the workers of iniquity?

17 Unless the LORD *had been* my help, my soul had almost dwelt in silence.

16 Who rises up for me against the wicked?
Who stands up for me against evildoers?
17 If the LORD had not been my help,
my soul would soon have dwelt in the land of silence.

B. An Individual Turns to God (94:16-23)

This lament of an individual is not unlike a psalm of trust. It betrays a more personal experience than that behind vss. 1-15, although in vs. 21 the danger of a miscarriage of justice recalls vss. 5-6. Apparently the psalmist was in peril of losing his life (vss. 17, 21). Whether something is to be understood between vs. 21 and vs. 22, such as a formal verdict of acquittal in a trial or a priestly oracle promising God's help, is a debatable point. In any case the concluding note is one of quiet confidence in **the rock of my refuge.**

There appear to be two strophes, vss. 16-19, 20-23. The dominant meter is 3+3.

1. Who but the Lord Can Help Me? (94:16-19)

17. In the land of silence: Lit., **in silence,** a reference, as in 115:17, to Sheol, where there is no praise of the Lord (cf. 6:5; 30:9; 88:10-12).

who would shrink from making such a confession live without any apparent consciousness of God. Sometimes even those who consider themselves religious are more attached to denominations than they are sure of the Father of mercies. Is this why the world is suffering, not only from divisions and bitter party spirit, but from loss of nerve and confident leadership? It has been said that as the third dimension gives the landscape a quality of "realness," so we need the dimension of the eternal to save us from an air of unreality in life. Is it because men have no dimension of the eternal that they demand so many amusements? Life becomes flat, effort is fruitless, knowledge is vanity if there is no faith in God. There may be material progress and social development, but everything becomes dull and drab without the dimension of the eternal. And relief will come not by argument or exhortation but by the influence of God-intoxicated people.

2. *Omniscience.*—There is, in the second place, an assurance that the Lord is a God of knowledge (vss. 9-11). By some this was denied. "The LORD," they said, "does not see; the God of Jacob does not perceive." He may exist, but he is either ignorant of or indifferent to men's doings. He is like Baal to whom the priests cried on Mount Carmel, perhaps asleep or on a journey, as Elijah suggested, but remote from human needs and prayers. With such a God we can do as we like and need fear no consequences. We have indeed placed ourselves alongside the drunken Rip Van Winkle, as played by Joseph Jefferson, who, as he takes another drink, says: "I won't count this time," and is satisfied that if he does not count no one else will.[5] To drift thus far is at very least to lose reverence for the moral law. Only one thing remains, such cleverness that one will never be found out by any power on earth; i.e., the greatest of virtues is not integrity but secrecy; and the persons to be admired are not those of lofty character but those who are successful in hiding iniquity and manage to live and die with good reputations.

The answer of the psalmist to this is that God knows not only what men do, but what they think and desire.

He who planted the ear, does he not hear?
He who formed the eye, does he not see?

Like the prophet Jeremiah, the psalmist takes refuge in the thought of the omniscience and omnipresence of God.

Am I, saith Jehovah, a God that is nigh,
And not a God afar?
Can any man hide, saith Jehovah,
In secret, where I cannot see him?
Do I not fill heaven and earth? (Jer. 23:23-24.)[6]

John Skinner's comment on the ordinary interpretation of this passage—"that Yahwe is not a near-sighted being, who only sees what is before his eyes, but One who from a remote height surveys all and penetrates every secret place where the false heart seeks to hide itself"—is that it is a little flat and trivial and unsatisfying.

[5] *Rip Van Winkle* (New York: Dodd, Mead & Co., 1895), Act I.

[6] J. E. McFadyen, *Jeremiah in Modern Speech* (London: James Clarke & Co., 1919), p. 93.

18 When I said, My foot slippeth; thy mercy, O LORD, held me up.
19 In the multitude of my thoughts within me thy comforts delight my soul.
20 Shall the throne of iniquity have fellowship with thee, which frameth mischief by a law?

18 When I thought, "My foot slips,"
thy steadfast love, O LORD, held me up.
19 When the cares of my heart are many,
thy consolations cheer my soul.
20 Can wicked rulers be allied with thee,
who frame mischief by statute?

18-19. When I thought: Lit., **when I said. When the cares of my heart are many:** Lit., **In the multitude of my thoughts within me;** the Hebrew word rendered **thoughts** is rare, found elsewhere only in 139:23.

2. THE LORD WILL EXTINGUISH THE WICKED (94:20-23)

20-23. The text of vs. 20 is difficult and may be corrupt. It seems to imply, however, that the reign of law can sometimes be the reign of iniquitous law. **Wicked rulers:** Lit.,

---

He suggests that the best commentary is Ps. 139, and adds that for both prophet and psalmist omnipresence and omniscience are one thing. "Jeremiah is not here denying the nearness of God; he is merely asserting that He is *also* far; that He is both immanent and transcendent, filling heaven and earth as a living conscious mind, setting every event and every secret thought in the light of His countenance." [7]

There is sound philosophical argument in these verses—that there must be as much reality in the efficient cause as in the effect. As Descartes, for example, would say: Not only can nothing be produced from nothing, but what is more perfect cannot be a result of and dependent on what is less perfect. The psalmist's concern, however, was with the practical effect of divine omniscience on human life. Everything will depend upon man's conception of God, and this has often been faulty enough. Even Milton's line about living always in the "great Taskmaster's eye" [8] has been wrongly interpreted, and so has induced fear rather than praise. Rightly understood, it is one of the abiding comforts of religion. Human judgments are faulty because they are the result of inadequate knowledge and are perverted by conscious or unconscious prejudices. The judgment of God is absolute because it is an expression of his omniscience and righteousness. In the light of such reflections how significant become the words of Jesus: "Ye judge after the flesh; I judge no man. And yet if I judge, my judgment is true: for I am not alone, but I and the Father that sent me" (John 8:15-16).

3. The Justice of God.—We have anticipated the psalmist's third contribution to an enduring faith: the justice of God. There were plenty of examples in the ancient world, as there are in modern life, of the fallibility of human justice. Was it not Pascal who said that truth on one side of the Pyrenees was error on the other side? Amiel defined justice as "the right to the maximum of individual independence compatible with the same liberty for others;—in other words, it is respect for man, for the immature, the small, the feeble." [9] But where is such respect to be found? History tells how high-minded men have tried to attain to it; how great states have endeavored to introduce it into international affairs. Usually they have been misunderstood and quickly overpowered by those who have been dominated by self-interest. Even church history, with all its saints and scholars, provides us with innumerable illustrations of prejudice and persecution. Again and again it has been necessary for prophets like Amos to warn and denounce, to declare that the Lord requires not sacrifices and offerings but righteousness and truth. God demands fair play as between man and man. To wrong the poor is diabolical, and no excuse of full churches, of orthodox belief, of active evangelism will avail against it.

There is, however, one place where truth is not perverted, and to that heavenly court of appeal the psalmist lifts his eyes. It cannot be said that even he, steadied as he was with the thought of divine justice, altogether avoided evil. There is a dangerous mood in the opening sentiment (vss. 1-2):

O LORD, thou God of vengeance,
thou God of vengeance, shine forth!

Such feelings, unchecked, will lead men on to the worst forms of retribution. But with the psalmist they are restrained by thoughts of the happiness of those who are corrected and taught by the law of God (vss. 12-13). Lifting

[7] *Prophecy and Religion* (Cambridge: Cambridge University Press, 1922), p. 199.

[8] "On His Having Arrived at the Age of Twenty-three."

[9] *Journal*, tr. Mrs. Humphry Ward (London: Macmillan & Co., 1890), p. 245.

21 They gather themselves together against the soul of the righteous, and condemn the innocent blood.

22 But the LORD is my defense; and my God *is* the rock of my refuge.

23 And he shall bring upon them their own iniquity, and shall cut them off in their own wickedness; *yea,* the LORD our God shall cut them off.

21 They band together against the life of the
righteous,
and condemn the innocent to death.
22 But the LORD has become my stronghold,
and my God the rock of my refuge.
23 He will bring back on them their iniquity
and wipe them out for their wickedness;
the LORD our God will wipe them out.

95 O come, let us sing unto the LORD: let us make a joyful noise to the rock of our salvation.

95 O come, let us sing to the LORD;
let us make a joyful noise to the
rock of our salvation!

"the throne of destruction." **And condemn the innocent blood** is closer to the Hebrew than **and condemn the innocent to death.** On the punishment of the wicked (vs. 23), see 1:4-5; 5:5-6; 11:5-6; etc.

XCV. A Congregational Liturgy (95:1-11)

This psalm consists of two parts quite distinct in character: a hymn (vss. 1-7*c*) and a prophetic admonition (vss. 7*d*-11). Since this latter element marks it off from the normal hymn type, it has been classed by Gunkel and others as a prophetic liturgy such as we meet in Ps. 81, and in some measure in Pss. 15 and 24.

The hymnal part, in turn, is made up of two typical hymns of praise (vss. 1-5, 6-7*c*). It is clear that they were sung in procession; the first as the congregation was moving

mind and heart above himself to him in whom moral goodness exists, he becomes convinced that it ought to be as in heaven so in earth. It was said of C. P. Scott of the *Manchester Guardian* that "when a discussion raged about a fundamental question, when he thought that anyone was proposing to palter with principle, then the eyes flashed and the beard shook and the Commandments came down again in thunder and lightning."[1] He too had been taught **out of thy law** that **justice will return to the righteous, and all the upright in heart will follow it.**

Thus psalmists and prophets prepared the way for the N.T. with its gospel of reconciliation. From the time that Jesus of Nazareth taught not only the holiness but the love of God, and himself died for the sin of the world, the dominating thought in religious faith has been not vengeance but mercy. Without that, even the quest for righteousness is apt to degenerate into pride, hypocrisy, and strife. With it men are led through self-examination to contrition, confession, and mutual understanding. That is why nothing but the spirit of Christ can save a torn and tormented world.

"Blessed," said Harry Emerson Fosdick, "is the life that does not collect resentments."[2] We may add: Blessed is the nation that has no hymn of hate; the man who can say with Job that he has never rejoiced at an enemy's fall, or triumphed when any misfortune befell him (Job 31:29). Edith R. Richards, in the life of her husband Leyton Richards,[3] tells of a visit he paid to South Africa and how he returned to England with copies of inscriptions on two South African monuments. One on a monument erected to a Boer president, Martinus Steyn; a Boer general, Christiaan De Wet; and an Englishwoman, Emily Hobhouse, who by her efforts to relieve the sufferings of prisoners became, in the words of Jan Smuts, "the great symbol of reconciliation between peoples who should never have been enemies." The other erected to thousands of Boer women and children who died during the Boer War: "As your tribute to the dead, bury unforgiveness and bitterness at the foot of this monument for ever." "Blessed are the merciful: for they shall obtain mercy" (Matt. 5:7).

95:1-11. ***Acceptable Worship.***—Having suggested that the book of Psalms was the hymnbook of the Second Temple, we must remind ourselves that hymnbooks are varied in their contents: not only are there hymns which deal with the truths of religion and the abiding needs of the human heart, but there are chants

[1] Hammond, *C. P. Scott,* p. 309.

[2] *Twelve Tests of Character* (New York: Association Press, 1923), p. 165.

[3] *Private View of a Public Man* (London: Allen & Unwin, 1950), p. 56.

toward the temple to **come into his presence,** the second as it was entering into the sacred precincts in response to the invitation, **Oh come, let us worship.** The singing of the hymns may have been led by a single choir or by separate choirs. Since the kingship of the Lord and his creation and ownership of the world are the theme of the first hymn, it seems probable that the psalm was meant for use in the ceremonies related to his enthronement at the New Year festival (see Exeg. on 93:1-5).

At the conclusion of the singing of the hymnal part, a priestly ministrant to whom had fallen the function of the ancient cultic prophets pronounced the second part of the psalm in the solemn form of an oath to the silent throng. The abrupt transition from the joyous anthems of the first part to the grave solo voice of the second must have produced an impressive effect. In the juxtaposition of such contrasting motifs, the purpose doubtless was to waken the people to a sense of the implications of their loud professions in song. Apparently their religious life was characterized by a too easy confidence in their status before God. They were forgetting that their worship of the **great God,** the **great King above all gods,** calls for steadfast loyalty and obedience to his will "today" as much as in the days of Moses. For them to murmur against the Lord or to question his ways, they are told, is to repeat the sin of their forefathers at Massah and Meribah.

Although the author of Heb. 4:7 speaks of this psalm as an inspired utterance of David, we must allow that he was following the common practice of his day, which for purposes of easy reference rather than for registering formal critical judgments ascribed most of the psalms to David. And it is to be noted that in the Hebrew text the psalm is without any ascription. The internal evidences seem to argue for a postexilic date. It is evident in the first part of the psalm that the conception of the universal sway of Israel's God, which is so prominent in Second Isaiah, is well established in the minds of the

---

and anthems, passages of Scripture, and some of the historic creeds. Hymns predominate, but they do not exclude other compositions. The same is true of this O.T. book. There are scholars who maintain that we have here not only the sacred songs of ancient Israel, but remains of liturgies and orders of service. There are meditations for the individual as well as words of praise to be sung by the whole congregation. There are instructions for priests and musicians, some of which have been incorporated into the structure of the psalms. In some cases the intention is clear to the ordinary reader, in others the expert is needed to distinguish between the text proper and comments and explanations which have been added later.

The first part of this psalm is clearly a hymn for congregational singing. It may have been a processional hymn sung by the people as they made their way to the temple. It may have been sung antiphonally, one verse by a priest or by one section of the swelling congregation, another verse by the whole body of worshipers. **O come,** they shout, **let us sing to the LORD; let us make a joyful noise to the rock of our salvation!**

The second part is not so clear. In the middle of vs. 7 both the subject and the style change to a warning against disobedience. It is no longer the **voice** of man, but God himself (or a priest speaking in his name) that breaks in upon the human chorus. There is a note of urgency, almost of reproach, as he cries: **Harden not your hearts, as at Meribah.** The difference is so marked that many have argued that the second part is a fragment from some other writing. There are, however, many hymns, modern as well as ancient, which have abrupt transitions, but certainly come from the same author. There is William Cowper's "Hark, my soul! it is the Lord," which begins with meditation, continues as the voice of God to man, and concludes as man's response to God. Let us then regard the psalm as a unity.

1*a*. *Sing unto the Lord.*—This psalm introduces us again to the subject of worship; and suggests in the first place the value of vocal praise, even of vehement praise. "To every thing," says the Preacher, "there is a season, . . . a time to weep, and a time to laugh; a time to mourn, and a time to dance" (Eccl. 3:1*a*, 4). The psalmist would add that even in worship there is a time to shout and a time to be quiet. A book entitled *The Fellowship of Silence* [4] tells how a few Christian men and women of different communions in New Zealand met together in a church vestry every Saturday and found themselves enriched by silent worship. They had no intention of abandoning their own traditions; they met not to argue, not even to exhort, but in unity to wait upon God. Except for the repetition of the Lord's Prayer at the

[4] Ed. Cyril Hepher (London: Macmillan & Co., 1915). See especially pp. 32-48.

2 Let us come before his presence with thanksgiving, and make a joyful noise unto him with psalms.

2 Let us come into his presence with thanksgiving;
let us make a joyful noise to him with songs of praise!

---

worshipers; and in the second part that the spiritual point of view of the pre-exilic prophets has been appropriated by the priesthood. The solemn emphasis on the sin of murmuring against the Lord may reflect conditions after the Exile at a time when there was a disposition on the part of the people to murmur at their evil circumstances (cf. Hag. 1:2; 2:14-17; Mal. 2:17; 3:14; Isa. 57:11; 58:2; 59:9). But a date still later than the period of the restoration is indicated by the fact that the psalmist in vss. 8-10 seems to be acquainted with the later or canonical form of the text of Exodus and Numbers (cf. Exod. 17:1-7; Num. 20:1-6, 13), which presumes the work of the priestly editors in the fifth century or later.

The meter is for the most part 3+3, but 4+3 occurs in vss. 5, 8, 2+2+2+3 in vs. 7, and 4+4+3 in vs. 10.

1. Let Us Praise the Lord (95:1-7*c*)

95:1-2. O come, let us sing to the Lord: Led by a choir, the worshipers as they move along in procession exhort one another to raise their voices in praise. **Let us sing:** Lit., "Let us raise a joyous, ringing song." **Let us make a joyful noise:** After the manner of Orientals, they mean to express aloud their joyous emotions. They describe the Lord as **the rock of our salvation,** i.e., an invincible defender and helper. **Let us come into his presence:** The verb here, like the "come," lit., "come in," of vs. 6, implies that the throng is in motion. **With thanksgiving:** The festival which they are celebrating is one which awakens gratitude and calls for songs and offerings of thanksgiving.

---

beginning, and perhaps a blessing at the end, it might have been taken as Quaker worship. No one who has read the words of Jesus or studied the lives of the saints will be surprised at the conscious deepening of the spiritual life that resulted. But human nature is complex, and the psalmist reminds us of the complementary truth that we need psalms and hymns and spiritual songs as well as silence. There are churches that would benefit if they would heed the exhortation, **Let us make a joyful noise to him with songs of praise.**

1*b*. ***Make a Joyful Noise.***—The psalmist suggests in the second place that worship should be cheerful in its expressions. True religion is one of the most serious things in life. Its services can become too austere. It can be so intent upon the eternal realities, and especially upon such facts as sin and sorrow and death, that it may frighten normal men and women. The psalmists knew this, but they knew also the joyousness of faith and of community singing. There is a place for mirth in the sanctuary. Browning's disposition was like theirs: he had a natural tendency to revolt against heaviness and morbidity.

> I find earth not gray but rosy,
> Heaven not grim but fair of hue.
> Do I stoop? I pluck a posy.
> Do I stand and stare? All's blue.[5]

It is a blessed corrective to undue severity.

2. ***Into His Presence with Thanksgiving.***—There is yet another suggestion—that thanksgiving must take a prominent place in worship. L. P. Jacks has contrasted the eloquence of criticism with the brevity, almost the speechlessness, of gratitude. If we find fault, words come in a spate: they tumble on top of one another faster than is convenient for orderly speech. But if someone has done us a good turn and we are deeply touched, we may find it impossible to say anything, except by a look or a gesture. It is an interesting contrast, and often true in speech. But in song we repeat the same sentiment in many different ways. We enumerate the blessings we have enjoyed and in wholehearted praise return thanks to God the giver. "Theologians may puzzle their heads about dogmas as they will," wrote Wordsworth to a friend, "the religion of gratitude cannot mislead us."[6] That is the spirit of many a psalmist and certainly of this one. **Let us come into his presence with thanksgiving.** This is indeed the

[5] "At the 'Mermaid,'" st. xii.

[6] William A. Knight, ed., *Letters of the Wordsworth Family* (Boston: Ginn & Co., 1907), II, 257.

3 For the LORD *is* a great God, and a
great King above all gods.
4 In his hand *are* the deep places of the
earth: the strength of the hills *is* his also.
5 The sea *is* his, and he made it: and his
hands formed the dry *land*.
6 O come, let us worship and bow down:
let us kneel before the LORD our maker.

3 For the LORD is a great God,
and a great King above all gods.
4 In his hand are the depths of the earth;
the heights of the mountains are his
also.
5 The sea is his, for he made it;
for his hands formed the dry land.

6 O come, let us worship and bow down,
let us kneel before the LORD, our
Maker!

3-5. In hymn style the grounds for worship follow the summons: (*a*) **For the LORD is a great God, . . . above all gods:** The expression derives from ancient times when the gods of the nations were thought of as real beings, and it persists in use in postexilic times, doubtless because Israel was always menaced by the religions of other peoples who had not come to Israel's way of thinking about the gods. **And a great King:** The emphasis on the Lord's kingship suggests that the psalm was, as has been said above, connected with the enthronement ceremonies. (*b*) The Lord's kingship is seen in the extent of his dominion. **In his hand are the depths of the earth:** The psalmist means that all things in the earth, near and far, high and low, are subject to the Lord's rule. The word translated **depths** (מחקרי) means the parts for searching out and may be an error for "the far-off places" (מרחקי), which the LXX (τὰ πέρατα) seems to favor. In any case, the Lord's power extends to regions where man has never been. The word for **heights** or "peaks" (תועפות) is also rare and vague, and for its meaning we are dependent on the versions. (*c*) The Lord's supremacy over the gods and the earth is grounded on the fact that he is the creator. The sea and the dry land are his because **he made** or **formed** them. This victory of the Lord over the formless waste is a central theme of the New Year festival.

6-7*c*. These verses, brief as they are, conform to the style of a hymn. **Come:** Lit., "come in" or "enter." As the procession moves through the gates at this word of invitation, all are bidden to perform the solemn acts of worship, kneeling and prostrating themselves —a vivid portrayal of a scene of reverent homage in the temple. Such devotion is due to the divine King because **he is our God, and we are the people of his pasture.** This faith evoked their confidence in his guidance of history and in his deliverance of them

---

keynote of the whole book, which is called by the Hebrews not Psalms but "Praises." "Rejoice in the LORD, O ye righteous: for praise is comely for the upright" (33:1).

3-7*b*. ***King Above All Gods.***—But there is more here than suggestions about the spirit of worship. Reason is given why men should worship. Notice the majestic periods:

For the LORD is a great God,
and a great King above all gods.
In his hand are the depths of the earth;
the heights of the mountains are his also.

Explorers in Arctic and other inaccessible regions claim territory for their native lands and proudly place national flags—on Everest there was also the flag of the United Nations—where few if any human eyes will look. In the same fashion, but in a more ambitious manner, the psalmist claims every outlying part of life for God. The mysterious depths and the incalculable heights, the sea and the dry land—all are God's. He made and sustains them: everywhere his writ runs. It may seem to some the utterance of a naïve mind. We should speak of the laws of nature and conceal our ignorance under abstractions. The psalmists, in their boldness or their simplicity, declare that it is God who makes the grass to grow for the cattle and herb for the service of men. Thus they prepared the way for One who saw in the wild flowers of the Nazarene hills a glory that far surpassed the glory of King Solomon. How natural for men who thus looked on nature to cry to one another:

O come, let us worship and bow down,
let us kneel before the LORD, our Maker!

7 For he *is* our God; and we *are* the people of his pasture, and the sheep of his hand. To-day if ye will hear his voice,

8 Harden not your heart, as in the provocation, *and* as *in* the day of temptation in the wilderness:

9 When your fathers tempted me, proved me, and saw my work.

10 Forty years long was I grieved with *this* generation, and said, It *is* a people that do err in their heart, and they have not known my ways:

11 Unto whom I sware in my wrath that they should not enter into my rest.

7 For he is our God,
and we are the people of his pasture,
and the sheep of his hand.

O that today you would hearken to his voice!
8 Harden not your hearts, as at Mer'ibah,
as on the day of Massah in the wilderness,
9 when your fathers tested me,
and put me to the proof, though they had seen my work.
10 For forty years I loathed that generation
and said, "They are a people who err in heart,
and they do not regard my ways."
11 Therefore I swore in my anger
that they should not enter my rest.

---

from all their vicissitudes. For metrical reasons and in accordance with 100:3, the text should be emended to read אנחנו עמו וצאן מרעיתו, "We are his people and the sheep of his pasture" or "tending" (cf. Gunkel).

2. A Warning from the Lord (95:7*d*-11)

7*d*-11. More than songs of praise and acts of worship were needed. Loud professions of faith must be followed by earnest obedience to and acceptance of God's will. **O that today** [in these times] **you would hearken to his voice:** His voice, or what he has to say, is given in the following lines. For the incidents at **Meribah** and **Massah** see Exod. 17:1-7; Num. 20:8-13. The names of these places mean respectively "place of contention" and "place of testing." The murmuring of the forefathers was an evidence that their hearts were hard and unresponsive to the Lord's gracious dealings with them in their deliverance from Egypt. But the hardness of their heart did not cease with the fresh experience of the Lord's goodness; it continued: **For forty years I loathed that generation. Loathed** is a strong word meaning "sickening disgust" or "nausea." Such a reaction against the people was provoked by the conviction that they were so corrupted that their hearts could do nothing else but err. **They do not regard my ways:** More freely, "They have no sympathetic knowledge or appreciation of my ways." So the Lord solemnly resolved not to permit that generation to enter Canaan (Num. 14:22-23), the land which he had promised to give them to rest in security (Num. 14:30; Deut. 12:9) at the end of their wanderings. But in this psalm **my rest** seems to have a new and double meaning:

7*c*-11. ***A Voice of Warning.***—But suddenly into the midst of these cheerful sentiments there breaks another voice, a voice not of mirth but of warning. It is a reminder that some have worshiped and forgotten: have entered into solemn covenants and then broken faith. It is not a fanciful interruption of pious aspiration, but a warning based on history. It is recorded in Exodus how the fathers had been brought out of Egypt with every mark of divine succor, but when adversity came, they murmured and rebelled. The story did not stand alone. It was repeated so often that prophets seemed at times even to denounce worship itself. But it was not worship they complained of, not processions, ecstatic music, convivial feasts. What made them angry was that men should participate in sacrifices and solemn meetings and then live as though they knew not God's demand for righteousness and mercy. To such a man as Amos this was so despicable that he cried with irony in his voice: "Take thou away from me the noise of thy songs; for I will not hear the melody of thy viols" (Amos 5:23).

This kind of thing is always happening—religious profession divorced from morality arousing the indignation of prophetic souls. Robert Lynd in *Dr. Johnson and Company* has

96 O sing unto the LORD a new song: sing unto the LORD, all the earth.

96 O sing to the LORD a new song; sing to the LORD, all the earth!

(*a*) "the place where I shall rest," i.e., Jerusalem and the temple, or (*b*) "a state of peace or rest with me" (cf. 116:7). In this way the lessons from Israel's past are given point for the Israel of "today," for the sin of inconstancy can cost them access both to the temple and to God's favor.

XCVI. A NEW SONG TO THE LORD (96:1-13)

This psalm should be studied in the light of what has been said in the Exeg. on 93:1-5; 95:1-11. There is reason to believe (cf. vs. 10*a*) that, like those psalms, this was meant to be sung during the procession at the ceremony of enthronement, the central feature of the New Year festival. While it can be said to consist of three separate hymns (vss. 1-6, 7-9, 10-13), it is also possible to regard it as a single hymn with three separate motifs, each of which relates to one or more of the principal stages in the solemn proceedings. Through all three of them we are permitted to witness with some vividness, as in Ps. 68, the progress of the action on such an occasion. In the opening part (vss. 1-6) the throng of worshipers, as the voice of the whole earth, are summoned to praise the Lord for his wonderful deeds in creation that set him above all gods. Then (vss. 7-9) as the procession moves on, bearing the offerings to be presented in the temple, the "tribes of the nations" are bidden to join in acknowledging the power and glory due to the God of gods, and on entering the sacred precincts to prostrate themselves in worship before him (cf. 95:6). Finally (vss. 10-13) the high moment of the ceremony arrives, when it is proclaimed **The LORD reigns!** and has come to exercise rule over the earth; appropriately the heavens, the earth, the sea, the plants of the field, and the trees of the forest—all the parts of the ordered world which he brought victoriously out of chaos—are called on to lend their voices to the exultant acclamation of the divine King. Thus, a large portion of the psalm is included in the thanksgiving hymn which, according to the Chronicler (I Chr. 16:1-36; cf. especially vss. 23-33), was to be sung by choirs to the accompaniment of musical instruments before the ark of the Lord. Along with our psalm there are associated in the hymn extracts from Pss. 105–106 which also relate to the cycle of events celebrated in the festivals of the New Year and Tabernacles. Doubtless the Chronicler is recording here what purports to be the historical origin of

much to say about Boswell, the biographer, and some of it is refreshingly frank. Not only is Boswell described as a bundle of contradictions; he is declared to be a stanch friend of religion, yet one who yields to every temptation. "He chuckles amid his pious groans," writes Lynd. "He is like a man married both to vice and to virtue and enjoying playing the one off against the other." [7] It is not to be explained as simply hypocrisy. That is much too facile a verdict. Nevertheless such piety always brings discredit upon true religion. Common worship is far more important than this generation imagines. But if the religious man is not also a good man, the church itself will be brought into condemnation, not only by God but by the multitude. The warning is needed by those who still go with gladness to the place of prayer:

Harden not your hearts, as at Meribah,
as on the day of Massah in the wilderness.

[7] Garden City: Doubleday, Doran & Co., 1928, p. 47.

George Herbert in the seventeenth century might have been inspired by Ps. 95 when he wrote his well-known lines:

Let all the world in ev'ry corner sing
My God and King.
The church with psalms must shout,
No door can keep them out:
But above all, the heart
Must bear the longest part.
Let all the world in ev'ry corner sing
My God and King.

96:1-13. ***An Invitation to Universal Praise.***— The psalm falls into four almost equal parts. Vss. 1-3 assert that Yahweh is to be praised at all times and in all the world. Vss. 4-6 affirm that he alone is worthy of praise and that the idols of the surrounding nations are nothing. Vss. 7-9 call upon the heathen to accept these facts and to come to the temple and take their share in its privileges. In the concluding vss. 10-13 the psalmist calls not only upon the sons

2 Sing unto the LORD, bless his name; show forth his salvation from day to day.
3 Declare his glory among the heathen, his wonders among all people.
4 For the LORD *is* great, and greatly to be praised: he *is* to be feared above all gods.
5 For all the gods of the nations *are* idols: but the LORD made the heavens.
6 Honor and majesty *are* before him: strength and beauty *are* in his sanctuary.

2 Sing to the LORD, bless his name;
tell of his salvation from day to day.
3 Declare his glory among the nations,
his marvelous works among all the peoples!
4 For great is the LORD, and greatly to be praised;
he is to be feared above all gods.
5 For all the gods of the peoples are idols;
but the LORD made the heavens.
6 Honor and majesty are before him;
strength and beauty are in his sanctuary.

---

some New Year observances of his day. The text of the psalm is not altogether uniform with that in I Chronicles.

The psalm belongs to a postexilic date. The ideas stressed in Second and Third Isaiah concerning the nothingness of the gods and the world-wide acknowledgment of the Lord's dominion are dominant throughout (cf. Isa. 40:18-26; 41:23-24; 44:6-8; 56:6-8; 60:14). Further, there is a considerable amount of borrowing from other psalms, e.g., cf. vs. 1 with 33:3; 40:3; 98:1; vs. 3 with 9:11; 105:1; vs. 4 with 48:1; 95:3; vss. 7-9 with 29:1-2; vs. 13 with 9:8; 98:9.

The meter is somewhat irregular; 4+3 occurs in vss. 1, 5, 9, 11; 4+4 in vss. 2, 4, 7, 8, 10, 12; 3+3 in vss. 3, 6; and 2+2+2, 3+2 in vs. 13.

1. The Lord Is Greatly to Be Praised (96:1-6)

96:1-6. Sing . . . a new song: Despite its use of material from elsewhere, the psalm can nevertheless be said to be "new" not only because it recasts an old theme but more especially because of its colorfulness, its jubilant note, and its wide theological horizon. In these respects it bases its claim to surpass older hymns. **Tell of his salvation:** I.e., his victory or triumph which brought about deliverance from chaos. In other words, **his**

---

of men but upon all nature, heaven and earth, sea, plain, and forest, to acknowledge the rule of God and to unite in the universal and joyous act of praise. With such divisions the task of the expositor seems obvious. One may, however, attempt a less beaten track: one may try to make the psalm come alive by picturing the man who wrote it, the musicians who first sang it, and the worshiping congregations who first rejoiced in it.

It is not easy to make great jumps in history. We often carry too much with us and imagine the wrong things. Let us, however, try to see a typical congregation in the temple for the celebration of one of the Jewish festivals. Like most religious assemblies, it is very mixed. The young and the old, with their different interests, are there. Men who have been successful in the battle of life take a prominent place, and others who are conscious of failure appear rather apologetically. Men who are genuinely religious take an intelligent interest in everything that happens, and men who have no spiritual experiences look around them with a curious if not very reverent attitude. But the most noticeable difference is between men of the homeland and Jews who have gathered from distant parts. Some are at home in Jerusalem and take everything for granted. Others have come from remote farms, from distant islands, from foreign cities, and have marks of many cultures upon them. A stranger would be fascinated by the color and confusion of an international assembly.

Yet those differences do not go deep. The apparently cosmopolitan assembly is a real unity. It does not matter where the individuals come from, they know themselves to be one in blood and in faith. They have been trained in many settings, but always in the one law. They speak many tongues, but they are the children of Abraham, and turn instinctively to Jerusalem as their common mother. This sense of unity is fostered and expressed in worship. Not all of them are capable of rising to spiritual heights, not all are conscious of the full significance of these regular festivals; yet they feel themselves to be distinct from the rest of mankind.

7 Give unto the LORD, O ye kindreds of the people, give unto the LORD glory and strength.

8 Give unto the LORD the glory *due unto* his name: bring an offering, and come into his courts.

9 O worship the LORD in the beauty of holiness: fear before him, all the earth.

7 Ascribe to the LORD, O families of the peoples,
ascribe to the LORD glory and strength!
8 Ascribe to the LORD the glory due his name;
bring an offering, and come into his courts!
9 Worship the LORD in holy array;
tremble before him, all the earth!

---

marvelous works are his creative acts among which he **made the heavens.** Hence the Lord **is to be feared above all gods,** for they are mere **idols** or "worthless things" (cf. 97:7; Isa. 40:25; 44:9-20, 24). As earthly kings are served by attendants and housed in fitting grandeur, so the Lord's attendants are that **honor and majesty** of which all earthly regal magnificence is but a pale reflection; and likewise **strength and beauty** fill **his sanctuary,** i.e., his heavenly abode.

2. SUMMONS TO ALL THE EARTH (96:7-9)

7-9. In these verses the psalmist follows closely the opening lines of Ps. 29. **Families of the peoples** are ideally represented by the pilgrims who come to the festival from different parts of the earth and who are an earnest of the fulfillment of such prophecies as Isa. 45:20-25; 60:1-3. **Ascribe . . . glory and strength,** i.e., proclaim in song the glory and power of the Lord in the full measure **due his name** as the God whose supremacy has been revealed in creation. Such praise is to be followed by the presentation of offerings as the worshipers **come into his courts,** where the Levites receive and prepare these offerings for the priests eventually to lay on the altar. **Worship . . . in holy array,** i.e., in garments that are ritually clean (cf. Num. 9:1-14; Lev. 11:24-28) and fitting for the sacred occasion. **Tremble before him:** The reading חילי מפניו may be, according to Ehrlich, a mistake for חלו פניו, "entreat his favor" (cf. 119:58; Zech. 7:2; 8:21; Mal. 1:9).

But while the general assembly may unite in hallelujahs and responses, the psalms depend primarily upon trained musicians. Much of the singing was done antiphonally, one line by one part of the choir, the next by another. The Levites had other duties besides the ministry of song, and the duties varied at different periods; but they were always there to assist the priests and to protect and keep clean the vessels and furniture of the temple. There were also orchestras with instruments of many kinds, cymbals and drums, harps and lyres, horns and clarions. These assemblies were true festivals with many popular elements. They were not like the preaching services of Puritans or the devotional retreats of Quakers. The music might not commend itself to modern ears. But it was joyous and vigorous, and **a new song** must have been received with general delight.

It may be questioned whether Protestants have ever quite realized the influence of music in the religion and life of Israel. Religious services must not be turned into sacred concerts, anthems must not crowd out instruction or exhortation; but it is good advice to "let the people sing." Was he not a wise man who said, "Give me the making of the songs of a nation, and I care not who makes its laws"?[8] And might we not properly add, "Let me write the hymns of the church, and I care not who makes the theology"? Laws and theology are very important, but they are ineffective unless they kindle the imagination; and in singing, if it is well and wisely done, the imagination is kindled. Has there ever been a revival of religion that has not expressed itself in a burst of song? And is there any need greater than this, that some inspired poets should take the truths of the gospel and write them in new and simple lines upon the minds and hearts of the people? Secular music is important, but we are dealing with something still more central when we come to spiritual songs.

O sing to the LORD a new song;
sing to the LORD, all the earth!

But before Levites and other musicians can sing and play in the temple, someone has to prepare the words and the tunes. Let us consider the man who wrote this psalm. In many modern

[8] Andrew Fletcher, "An Account of a Conversation."

10 Say among the heathen *that* the LORD reigneth: the world also shall be established that it shall not be moved: he shall judge the people righteously.
11 Let the heavens rejoice, and let the earth be glad; let the sea roar, and the fulness thereof.
12 Let the field be joyful, and all that *is* therein: then shall all the trees of the wood rejoice

10 Say among the nations, "The LORD reigns!
Yea, the world is established, it shall never be moved;
he will judge the peoples with equity."
11 Let the heavens be glad, and let the earth rejoice;
let the sea roar, and all that fills it;
12 let the field exult, and everything in it!
Then shall all the trees of the wood sing for joy

3. THE LORD'S KINGSHIP ACCLAIMED (96:10-13)

10-13. At the final and high point of the ceremony of enthronement the cultic cry is uttered, **The LORD reigns,** i.e., he has become king or has assumed his kingship. **Say** [it] **among the nations,** for the Lord is the God that "formed the earth and made it . . . that it should be inhabited" (Isa. 45:18). The continuance of his supremacy makes certain that **the world is established, it shall never be moved.** Vs. 10*c* should be deleted as a gloss, since it intrudes into the context and anticipates vs. 13*cd.*

Let the heavens . . . the earth rejoice: With good reason the whole order of the created world is summoned to acclaim the Lord with joyous songs, since through him it was brought into existence and established. Even **the sea,** that remnant of chaos which the Lord "shut in . . . with doors" (cf. Job 38:8), is bidden to **roar** its praises. **For he comes** [better, "he has come"] **to judge the earth:** The reign of the Lord is not some "far-off divine event"; the psalmists mean that it has already begun. His judgments

hymnbooks there are names of authors attached to the hymns with perhaps dates of birth and death. Such information can distract attention. It can, however, be helpful to think of Isaac Watts and Charles Wesley, John Newton and William Cowper, Bernard of Cluny and Francis of Assisi, Ambrose and Gregory. It helps us as we remember not only their aspirations and moods of devotion, but also their struggles and temptations and doubts.

Names appear in the book of Psalms, but most of them were added late and cannot be relied upon. Like most of the others, this psalm is anonymous, in spite of the fact that the LXX refers to it as a "David" psalm. We do not know whether the writer lived in Palestine or dwelt in strange lands. Yet we can discover something about him. We know that he was a man of faith. It was not a borrowed faith, but a personal one; not a faith he had to carry, but one that carried him; not a faith that made him sad, but one that made him joyful. Like Tennyson he would say:

> I do but sing because I must,
> And pipe but as the linnets sing.[9]

It was the faith that inspired the song, not the song that created the faith.

[9] *In Memoriam,* Part XXI, st. vi.

And the faith was not faith in himself, not primarily in his fellow man, but in God. Not in a God who was a tradition, or a necessity of thought, but a Person in whom he could trust. His song is full of theology, but it is the theology of experience, not the formal theology of the schools. The God he worships is a great God, very different from the idols of the surrounding heathen. They are nonentities. The God he lauds and before whom he prostrates himself is the living God who created the heavens. That was a thought never far from the Hebrew mind. The Israelites were not astronomers, but they studied the firmament above and saw through its glories to the Power that made the sun and ordered the course of the moon and caused the morning stars to sing together. They were not concerned to describe or to explain, but they were taught to exclaim: "O LORD our Lord, how excellent is thy name in all the earth! who hast set thy glory above the heavens" (8:1).

This God of unimaginable splendor has shown his power not only in nature but also in human history. He is King, even where his rule is not recognized, with authority over all the nations of the earth. And the characteristics of his dominion are righteousness and truth. That sounds familiar, but we must remember the far-off times when gods generally were capricious, even malicious, and worship was little

13 Before the LORD: for he cometh, for he cometh to judge the earth: he shall judge the world with righteousness, and the people with his truth.

97 The LORD reigneth; let the earth rejoice; let the multitude of isles be glad *thereof*.

13 before the LORD, for he comes,
for he comes to judge the earth.
He will judge the world with righteousness,
and the peoples with his truth.

97 The LORD reigns; let the earth rejoice;
let the many coastlands be glad!

among men and in history are already operative both for vindication and for punishment, since they are dictated by **righteousness** and by **truth** to those who are right. Each New Year's festival therefore reminded Israel that the idea of the Lord's kingship was neither a relic from the past nor a hope deferred to the future, but a present reality. The Lord comes to rule anew in power each New Year.

XCVII. THE KINGSHIP OF THE LORD (97:1-12)

This is commonly designated as one of the psalms of the Lord's enthronement (see Exeg. on 47:1-10; 93:1-5), and in support of this we may note the references to the Lord as king (vs. 1), to his throne (vs. 2), and to the obeisance done him by all the gods (vss. 7, 9). In any case, this is a hymn in praise of the Lord, and its author, while using a familiar vocabulary partly drawn from other psalms, has produced a poem not unworthy of his theme. He advances the following grounds for the rejoicing which the righteous are called upon to make: God's awe-inspiring power, the justice of the divine government of the world, and the universal recognition by both gods and men of the Lord's supremacy.

As the psalmist's words were never literally fulfilled at any New Year's festival or on any other occasion, it is evident that the psalm is partially eschatological, and that it

more than an attempt to buy their good will. Sacrifices were sometimes turned into orgies, or designed to placate deities with uncertain tempers. This affected the common life of the people from top to bottom. What a difference when prophets like Amos began to preach the righteousness of God and to show the implications of the faith! At first they were but voices crying in the wilderness; but gradually the people came to listen, and men like this psalmist put what they heard into song for festive occasions. It was their hearkening that made the Israelites different from other nations. They were not more gifted in the arts and sciences, but they had been laid hold of by the knowledge that there is no pure religion without sound morality.

Such is the picture that paints itself in the mind as we read Ps. 96. It shows how when a man of faith muses the fire within him begins to burn, how one center of real spiritual vitality sends out a glow to others and causes many to rejoice. It shows how common worship maintains unity and deepens a sense of fellowship. Differences are not ironed out, but they do not annoy; they add to the richness of the whole.

Much of it is happening again, especially in the ecumenical movements of the world church. Men come from the far ends of the earth and co-operate in thought and prayer. They come with their own culture, the products of many civilizations; but they find inspiration in common confession and praise. It may be that there is to be found the promise of universal peace. One secular conference after another disappoints; the conferences of the world church, beginning with united contrition, go on to constructive proposals, and end in glad Te Deums. That is a note befitting the church militant, and no one should be surprised that in Christian sanctuaries fear is turned to a hope which expresses itself in songs of praise.

Let the heavens be glad, and let the earth rejoice;
let the sea roar, and all that fills it;
let the field exult, and everything in it!
Then shall all the trees of the wood sing for joy
before the LORD, for he comes,
for he comes to judge the earth.

Already he is on his throne, and the books are in his hands.

97:1-12. ***God's Universal Sovereignty.***—One of the difficulties the expositor faces in the psalms is the repetition he encounters. Having dealt with certain subjects from various points of view, it is embarrassing to find them again in

2 Clouds and darkness *are* round about him: righteousness and judgment *are* the habitation of his throne.
3 A fire goeth before him, and burneth up his enemies round about.

2 Clouds and thick darkness are round about him;
righteousness and justice are the foundation of his throne.
3 Fire goes before him,
and burns up his adversaries round about.

---

points to the end of the present age (so Kittel, Calès, *et al.*). In a poem with this interest, where mundane and extravagant pictures might have bulked large, the psalmist's restraint and sense of values are notable. As Kittel says (*Die Psalmen,* p. 317): "The main point to him . . . is the inner splendor, the spiritual and religious gain from his [the Lord's] coming: the victory over the gods . . . the triumph of the true knowledge of God . . . and above all the victory of righteousness."

The RSV follows Schmidt's strophic divisions. The meter is 3+3, with the usual variations.

1. The Lord on His Throne (97:1-5)

97:1-3. Coastlands: See Exeg. on 72:10, where the RSV translates the same word **isles** (so KJV here). On the **clouds** and **darkness** surrounding the Lord cf. 18:8-12; Exod. 19:9; 20:21; Deut. 4:11; 5:22; I Kings 8:12; Job 22:13-14. **The foundation of his throne:** See Exeg. on 82:1-8; 89:14. **Fire** appears frequently in O.T. theophanies (cf. 50:3;

---

almost the same language. We must remember, however, that there are different kinds of repetition. There is repetition which is sheer monotony, like the constant striking of the same note upon a piano, or the frequent telling of trivial stories. And there is repetition which is sheer delight. The sun rises with great regularity every morning, but no one says that dawn is tedious. The newspapers may be out of date almost as soon as they have been printed, but Shakespeare is still alive, and Dante is always worth rereading, and the poets of classical Greece have perennial youth.

The great thoughts of the book of Psalms belong to this second class. There may be nothing that men call original in Ps. 23, but it is new every morning if a living mind is brought to it. The same is true of Ps. 97. It contains nothing that has not been well expressed in previous psalms. Even its structure has a familiar appearance. Nevertheless the thoughts themselves are like springs of living water to which thirsty men turn with never-failing gratitude.

It is full of the thought of God, and of a consciousness of his all-pervading activity. Everyone knows the difference between an artist who discourses about beauty in a merely professional way or a preacher who talks about sacred things in a detached manner, and the artist or preacher who speaks from the passion of his heart. No one needs to be convinced when he comes to a psalm like this that it is the product not of secondhand religion but of a living faith. The Lord God is not merely one of whom the writer has heard. He is the Lord of his life and the inspiration of every day.

The chief thing the psalmist has to say is that **the Lord reigneth.** The song may have been composed with New Year festivities in mind and may have been used as part of the enthronement ceremonies, but it has universal validity. It will bring humiliation to those who have rebelled against the Lord and paid homage to false gods, but elsewhere it will be the cause of joy and gladness. The remote islands and **the many coastlands** of the sea will hear and rejoice, and the song of praise will be continued from generation to generation.

After the announcement of the main theme in vs. 1, the psalm falls into three parts, each with its dominant thought. Vss. 2-6 tell in highly imaginative language of the cosmic effects of the Lord's enthronement. Vss. 7-9 contrast the shame of idolaters with the rejoicings of Zion. Vss. 10-12 are an exhortation to the faithful to **hate evil,** to **rejoice in the Lord,** and to **give thanks to his holy name.**

2-6. ***Clouds and Thick Darkness.***—The first part may impress us as exaggerated in expression. It may remind us of the "tendency to the gigantesque" which has been referred to as "a fault of the Hebrew genius."[1] If, however, we come to it from a study of Hebrew eschatology, especially from such books as Daniel and Revelation, we shall be impressed by its sobriety. Such

[1] J. D. M. Rorke, *In Search of a Personal Creed* (London: Student Christian Movement Press, 1927), p. 33.

4 His lightnings enlightened the world:
the earth saw, and trembled.
5 The hills melted like wax at the presence of the LORD, at the presence of the
Lord of the whole earth.
6 The heavens declare his righteousness,
and all the people see his glory.
7 Confounded be all they that serve
graven images, that boast themselves of
idols: worship him, all *ye* gods.

4 His lightnings lighten the world;
the earth sees and trembles.
5 The mountains melt like wax before the LORD,
before the Lord of all the earth.

6 The heavens proclaim his righteousness;
and all the peoples behold his glory.
7 All worshipers of images are put to shame,
who make their boast in worthless idols;
all gods bow down before him.

Exod. 3:2; 13:21; 19:18; Deut. 1:33; 4:11; etc.). **And burns up his adversaries round about:** Some scholars, following Wellhausen, emend צריו **(his adversaries) to** צעדיו**,** making vs. *3b*, "and flames about his steps."

4-5. All the verbs here and in vs. 6 are perfects. These must be perfects of experience, some of the basis of the latter being supplied by the Exodus tradition. **The mountains melt:** Cf. Nah. 1:5; Judg. 5:5.

2. THE LORD IS EXALTED OVER ALL (97:6-9)

7. This verse is essentially an expression of religious faith, for from the eighth century B.C. on, Israel actually witnessed a series of political triumphs by the idol-worshiping Gentiles. **Images:** The word פסל, found only here in the Psalter, designates something

---

a theme as the awfulness of God's manifestation, and the irresistible might with which he appears, gave great scope for an imaginative writer and tempts some modern authors as well as many of the ancients to excess. Actually the psalmist expresses himself with considerable restraint. He is influenced by the theophany of Sinai, but he does not become unintelligible. First he speaks of the **clouds and thick darkness** which surround this King of kings. But as Elmer A. Leslie well says, the "awful darkness is lit up from within by blazing fire and great flashes of lightning." [2] The whole passage reminds us of Exod. 19:16, with its thunders and lightnings, and thick cloud and loud trumpet and trembling people. But it helps us to realize the mystery which surrounds the Most High and has caused men of all ages to fall upon their faces in awe and wonder. This enduring sense of mystery may degenerate and become a mere staring into an unfathomable dome. It may, on the other hand, be a corrective to intellectual confidence, a reminder that, much as we may explain, there remains far more that for human minds transcends understanding. Every man who wrestles with the problems of faith comes to the point, and most men come to it early, where he can but confess the inadequacy of reason. Every man who wrestles with the problems of matter does the same. It has indeed been affirmed that the mysteries of religion are child's play compared with those of science. **Clouds and thick darkness are round about** us all, and no one is so conscious of the impenetrable gloom as those who have given themselves to thought on the ultimate realities. This, however, is no cause for despair. Life would lack much of its incentive if we could track down all the hidden secrets. Mystery has been likened to "the half-lifted veil of the sanctuary, through which all life's higher meaning shines, and which is the endless challenge to all our inquiries." [3] Omniscience is God's; it is not meant for man.

> Let knowledge grow from more to more,
> But more of reverence in us dwell.[4]

"It is the glory of God to conceal a thing: but the honor of kings is to search out a matter" (Prov. 25:2; cf. Moffatt's rendering of Eccl. 3:11: "For the mind of man he has appointed mystery, that man may never fathom God's own purpose from beginning to end").

7-9. ***The Sin of Idolatry and the Joy of Pure Worship.***—The second part of the psalm sets a bold contrast between the worshipers of **idols** who are put to shame and the faithful in Zion who hear and are glad. The idol-worshipers are

[2] *The Psalms* (New York and Nashville: Abingdon-Cokesbury Press, 1949), p. 80.

[3] Oman, *The Natural and the Supernatural* (New York: The Macmillan Co., 1931), p. 213.

[4] Tennyson, *In Memoriam*, Prologue, st. vii.

8 Zion heard, and was glad; and the daughters of Judah rejoiced because of thy judgments, O LORD.

9 For thou, LORD, *art* high above all the earth: thou art exalted far above all gods.

8 Zion hears and is glad,
and the daughters of Judah rejoice,
because of thy judgments, O God.
9 For thou, O LORD, art most high over all the earth;
thou art exalted far above all gods.

made by cutting wood, stone, or metal, hence **graven images. Idols:** The physical images of the gods of pagan nations, thus **worthless idols. All gods bow down before him:** The recognition of Israel's God by all the company of man-made idols would not appear to be of much consequence, although the same thought is found in 96:4-5. Possibly the psalmist here and in vs. 9 is referring to the Lord's supremacy over the heavenly host (see Exeg. on 82:1-8).

8. This verse has a close parallel in 48:11. **Zion:** The earthly abode of the Lord and the seat of his sacrificial worship. **The daughters of Judah** are the villages of Judah; the same idiom is found in Num. 21:25; Josh. 15:45; Jer. 49:2; etc. **Thy judgments:** God's vindication of himself and of his people in the events of history. The psalmist may have in mind some recent demonstration of the Lord's power.

9. Most high is better than **high.**

frequently assumed to be dwellers in other lands, but Judah was not free of them. They were often numerous and influential. The idols were not always crude images carved out of wood or stone; but the environment was perilous, and there were many lapses from pure monotheism. Intermarriage with the surrounding peoples introduced strange cults even into Jerusalem, and political relations with great powers led many away from purity of worship. The influence of the shrines of the Canaanites was continually reasserting itself. Idols, though sternly denounced by prophet after prophet, reappeared in domestic worship. There were times when Baalism with its veneration of Astarte, representing the female principle in nature, well-nigh displaced the true worship of God as the established religion. The calf-worship connected with Aaron reappeared in the days of Jeroboam. In Job 31:26-28 we find an allusion to astrolatry, and in II Chr. 34:4; II Kings 23:11, suggestions of sun images and chariots dedicated to the sun. Such practices aroused the wrath of the great prophets, especially the eighth-century prophets, who prepared the way for reformation under Josiah. Severe laws were passed against idolaters, and by the time of the Exile the lesson had been well learned. There are warnings again in the N.T., especially in the writings of Paul. "But idolatry in Christian doctrines has a wider significance than the service of material idols. Anything that interferes between the soul and its God is idolatrous, and is to be shunned." [5]

[5] H. F. B. Compston, "Idolatry," in James Hastings, ed., *Dictionary of the Bible* (New York: Charles Scribner's Sons, 1918), p. 376.

In this larger sense idolatry is still a great evil and cannot be ignored. It is not enough to condemn the images of India and forget the materialism, the militarism, the state-worship of the West. Even humanism in some of its forms can interfere between the soul and God. It does not yet seem that **those who make their boast in worthless idols** are **put to shame;** yet wherever they flourish there will be confusion and frustration. The gods themselves must **bow down** before the Lord if peace and joy are to be found among men.

Such gladness as comes of pure worship is the portion of **Zion** and **the daughters of Judah.** Some scholars understand by **daughters of Judah** the smaller towns and villages around Jerusalem. It might be, however, that the psalmist was thinking of wives and daughters who are involved in the sufferings of idolatry and may benefit especially when their husbands and fathers turn from it to the true God. Leslie reminds us that "in ancient Israel women greeted the Lord's mighty act of Israel's rescue from Egyptian bondage with timbrel, song, and dance. Now their descendants rejoice in the Lord's enthronement as the righteous Judge, and the King of gods and men." [6] Women have certainly been greatly used in evangelism. They have not always occupied conspicuous positions, but their influence has been unmistakable. Scratch history ever so slightly and you come upon the persuasive power of woman. But gladness comes not to women only; it comes to all who have been faithful to the Lord. The righteous community need not see the victory with their own eyes. To hear of it is enough.

[6] *Op. cit.*, pp. 80-81.

10 Ye that love the LORD, hate evil: he preserveth the souls of his saints; he delivereth them out of the hand of the wicked.

11 Light is sown for the righteous, and gladness for the upright in heart.

12 Rejoice in the LORD, ye righteous; and give thanks at the remembrance of his holiness.

A Psalm.

98 O sing unto the LORD a new song; for he hath done marvelous things: his right hand, and his holy arm, hath gotten him the victory.

10 The LORD loves those who hate evil;[k]
he preserves the lives of his saints;
he delivers them from the hand of the wicked.
11 Light dawns[l] for the righteous,
and joy for the upright in heart.
12 Rejoice in the LORD, O you righteous,
and give thanks to his holy name!

A Psalm.

98 O sing to the LORD a new song,
for he has done marvelous things!
His right hand and his holy arm have gotten him victory.

[k] Cn: Heb *You who love the* LORD *hate evil*
[l] Gk Syr Jerome: Heb *is sown*

3. COMFORT FOR THE RIGHTEOUS (97:10-12)

The theme is the general providence of the Lord, although this beneficence is fully apprehended only by **his saints.** Paul has a similar view in Rom. 8:28.

10. The KJV and the RSV mg. give the translation of the M.T. of vs. 10*a*. The RSV, with most commentators, emends the Hebrew in two places to obtain **The LORD loves those who hate evil,** which gives better syntax in the remainder of the verse. The sentiment resembles that in Rom. 12:9. **His saints:** See Exeg. on 79:2.

11. Light dawns: The M.T. reads **light is sown,** but as there is no other instance in the O.T. of light being sown, most commentators since Wellhausen (supported by some of the ancient versions) have changed one consonant to read זרח, "arises" or "shines forth" (cf. 112:4; Prov. 4:18). T. H. Gaster (*Thespis,* pp. 40-41, 423) suggests that the phrase may point to some ancient solar element in the celebration of the autumnal equinox, and that the Lord may here be identified with the rising sun. More probably the word **light** is used loosely by the psalmist (as in 27:1; 36:9; 43:3; etc.) to denote a mental and spiritual enlightenment coming from God (cf. Exeg. on 27:1).

12. To his holy name: A rendition usually justified by the fact that one's name is often what one is remembered by. The Hebrew, however, may mean exactly what it says: **at the remembrance of his holiness.**

XCVIII. PRAISE THE JUDGE OF THE WORLD (98:1-9)

This joyful hymn of praise is often grouped with the psalms of the Lord's enthronement (cf. the reference to **the King** in vs. 6, and see Exeg. on 47:1-10; 93:1-5). If we may judge from vss. 1-3, it has arisen out of some situation in which the Lord's holy arm has been manifested. While the language is too vague to justify a precise identification of the historical background, both the diction and the ideas are similar to those of Second Isaiah, and it is possible that it was the coming of Cyrus which inspired the psalmist's

10-12. ***Love the Lord and Hate Evil.***—The conclusion follows naturally. Those who would share the rejoicings of Zion must not be content to fulfill ritual requirements; they must not simply repeat the recognized observances: they must love the Lord and show that love by hating evil. The greater the love the more passionate will be the hatred. There is no condonation here or elsewhere in Scripture for the Laodicean spirit (Rev. 3:15-16). God does not deliver the lukewarm: he spews them out of his mouth. It is where the love and the hate are intense that **light** will shine forth **for the righteous.** Such men will not hide their candle under a bushel, or fail to lift up their voices in praise.

98:1. ***The Hand of God.***—The purpose of this psalm as a whole is so obvious that it may be left without extended comment (cf. Ps. 96). There are, however, certain words that demand

2 The LORD hath made known his salvation: his righteousness hath he openly showed in the sight of the heathen.	2 The LORD has made known his victory, he has revealed his vindication in the sight of the nations.

words. It is evident from vss. 4-6 that the psalm was designed for temple use, and it may have been first employed on some New Year's Day. Some scholars thus take vss. 4-9 as a call to all creation to acclaim the Lord as he starts a fresh year as Sovereign of the world (e.g., Gaster, *op. cit.*, pp. 423-24). Others believe that the psalmist looked beyond his immediate blessings and proceeded in vss. 7-9 to picture the day when the Lord would come to judge the whole earth. Such an eschatological interpretation (cf. Kittel, Gunkel, *et al.*), with the emphasis in vs. 9 upon the universal and righteous character of the psalmist's God, has given this beautiful little hymn much of its enduring appeal. In the Book of Common Prayer it stands as an alternative to the Magnificat at Evening Prayer.

The RSV follows Kittel's strophic divisions (vss. 1-3, 4-6, 7-9). The meter is rather irregular.

I. Praise for God's Vindication (98:1-3)

98:1. A new song: See Exeg. on 33:3; 96:1.

2-3. Cf. Isa. 52:10. **His victory** or **his salvation:** See Exeg. on 74:12. **His vindication** or **his righteousness:** See note on "saving help," Exeg. on 88:12. On the theological

attention. In vs. 1 it is said that **his right hand, and his holy arm, hath gotten him the victory.** Someone has estimated that in one form or another there are no less than 258 references in the Bible to the **hand** of God. We need not commit ourselves to the exact number, but the idea behind them is important. A close examination would reveal many shades of meaning but one dominant thought. Few events, if any, impressed themselves upon Hebrew minds more than the Exodus from Egypt. It is referred to frequently by different writers, and always the outstanding point is that deliverance was due not to the might of Moses, or to the weakness of the Pharaoh, but to the strong hand of God (Exod. 13:3). That having happened once, nothing is impossible in the future. The position may be humanly hopeless, but "Behold, the LORD's hand is not shortened, that it cannot save" (Isa. 59:1). Sometimes the reference seems to be personal, as though an individual in sore straits had found supernatural protection, as in Isa. 49:2, "In the shadow of his hand hath he hid me." Again, a prophet in explaining his mission to men, instead of protesting that it was not the result of willfulness or ambition, may refer to the work of God in his own heart in such words as these: "So the spirit lifted me up, and took me away, . . . but the hand of the LORD was strong upon me" (Ezek. 3:14). Clearly it is one of the richest O.T. figures of speech, indicating divine protection, guidance, and correction. There are many more instances when we pass to the N.T. The references to the hands of Christ stretched out to heal, lifted in benediction, pierced with nails at Calvary, are a study in themselves. Two of his sayings demand special notice. One refers to the disciples who are to suffer tribulation and persecution, but who have this promise: "No man is able to pluck them out of my Father's hand" (John 10:29). The other is the seventh word from the cross, "Father, into thy hands I commend my spirit" (Luke 23:46). There seems to be a whole gospel in the biblical teaching on the hand of God.

It is right perhaps to remind ourselves that there are references not only to the hand but also to the voice, the words, the ears, the fingers, the eyes, the face of God. There are even references to the shadow of God's wings, which most readers interpret instinctively as poetic expressions of the divine care. There are, however, scholars who connect such expressions with the wings of the sun-god, which was for long a popular idea throughout the ancient Near East. This raises the question whether there was a time when men really believed in a supernatural being with hands and ears, fingers and eyes. We may, however, leave others to search and to speculate in the realms of antiquity. Whatever quaint or superstitious ideas may be discovered, there remains the assurance that God is almighty and that in his right hand we may trust. This was the obvious conviction of King George VI, when in his world-wide radio broadcast on Christmas Day, 1939, he quoted the now famous words of Louise Haskins, from the poem "God knows": how much better it was than any light, and how much safer than any way men know,

3 He hath remembered his mercy and his
truth toward the house of Israel: all the
ends of the earth have seen the salvation of
our God.
4 Make a joyful noise unto the LORD, all
the earth: make a loud noise, and rejoice,
and sing praise.
5 Sing unto the LORD with the harp; with
the harp, and the voice of a psalm.
6 With trumpets and sound of cornet
make a joyful noise before the LORD, the
King.

3 He has remembered his steadfast love and
faithfulness
to the house of Israel.
All the ends of the earth have seen the
victory of our God.

4 Make a joyful noise to the LORD, all the
earth;
break forth into joyous song and sing
praises!
5 Sing praises to the LORD with the lyre,
with the lyre and the sound of melody!
6 With trumpets and the sound of the horn
make a joyful noise before the King,
the LORD!

---

thought cf. Rom. 3:25-26. After **his steadfast love** the LXX inserts "to Jacob," making the line a 3+3 distich, and affording good parallelism. **The ends of the earth:** See Exeg. on 72:8.

2. Let All Men Praise Him (98:4-6)

4. Break forth into joyous song: A felicitous rendering of the Hebrew, which is, lit., "burst forth and sing aloud."

5-6. On the musical instruments here referred to see the Intro., pp. 5-6. **The sound of melody** is better than **the voice of a psalm** (cf. Isa. 51:3). **The King:** This title, to express God's sovereign power, is found elsewhere in the Psalter (5:2; 10:16; 24:7; etc.) Some scholars would omit **the LORD** as a gloss which overloads the line.

---

simply to go out into the darkness with one's hand in God's!

3. *The Mercy of God.*—Men and nations declare themselves in large measure by the words they use. If their language is utilitarian, or if they speak naturally of truth, beauty, and goodness, we know what manner of men they are. This psalmist, in common with many of his race, speaks of mercy or kindness. The Hebrew word is *ḥéṣedh,* a word so rich in meaning that translators are divided when they try to render it in English. The KJV frequently, though not always, employs the word **mercy.** The revisers often chose "lovingkindness." Some would prefer the rather ambiguous and overworked word "love." The RSV reads

He has remembered his steadfast love and faithfulness
to the house of Israel.

The renderings may be questioned, but there is no doubt about the prominence of the idea in Hebrew literature. Pages could be filled with quotations from the psalms alone. Four will suffice. "Thou, O LORD, art a God full of compassion, and gracious, long-suffering, and plenteous in mercy and truth" (86:15). "For as the heaven is high above the earth, so great is his mercy toward them that fear him" (103:11). "O give thanks unto the LORD; for he is good: for his mercy endureth for ever" (136:1). "Let Israel hope in the LORD: for with the LORD there is mercy, and with him is plenteous redemption" (130:7). Similar quotations could be made from the legal and prophetic books and from the wisdom literature.

This quality of kindness is not only attributed to God, it is commended as one of the greatest human virtues. Scholars such as T. H. Robinson assure us that the cultivation of mercy or lovingkindness in the human heart is the highest demand of the prophetic morality. Yet Aldous Huxley speaks of the O.T. as "this treasure-house of barbarous stupidity." Of the God of the O.T. he says: "He was wrathful, . . . he was jealous, he was vindictive."[7] There was therefore no reason why his people should not be wrathful, jealous, and vindictive. It must be admitted that the Jews, like other races, did not always live up to their faith. There were times when they allowed bitterness of heart to blind them. But we cannot believe that Huxley would have written as he did had his own mind been free from tendentiousness. Why is he so

[7] *Ends and Means* (London: Chatto & Windus, 1937), pp. 283-84.

7 Let the sea roar, and the fulness
thereof; the world, and they that dwell
therein.
8 Let the floods clap *their* hands: let the
hills be joyful together
9 Before the LORD; for he cometh to
judge the earth: with righteousness shall he
judge the world, and the people with
equity.

99 The LORD reigneth; let the people
tremble: he sitteth *between* the cherubim; let the earth be moved.

7 Let the sea roar, and all that fills it;
the world and those who dwell in it!
8 Let the floods clap their hands;
let the hills sing for joy together
9 before the LORD, for he comes
to rule the earth.
He will judge the world with righteousness,
and the peoples with equity.

99 The LORD reigns; let the peoples tremble!
He sits enthroned upon the cherubim;
let the earth quake!

---

3. LET ALL NATURE PRAISE HIM (98:7-9)

8. The floods: The reference is not to the primeval deep as in 24:2; 93:3, but to the great watercourses of the earth, and the translation should be "the rivers" (so Amer. Trans.). **Clap their hands:** An indication of joy, a figure used also in Isa. 55:12 with "the trees of the field" as subject.

9. To rule or **to judge:** In the second half of this verse the RSV renders the imperfect of the same verb **he will judge.** The verb should be translated **judge** in both cases. Some scholars emend the text slightly by repeating **for he comes:** this has the support of 96:13 and of the LXXA.

XCIX. THE GOD OF HOLINESS (99:1-9)

This psalm, the last of the psalms of the Lord's enthronement (cf. **the LORD reigns,** vs. 1; **Mighty King,** vs. 4, and see Exeg. on 47:1-10; 93:1-5), may be described as a hymn to the God of holiness. It is clearly intended for use in the temple (vss. 5, 9), and it was probably sung by two or more parties, though the distribution of the lines among them can only be conjectured. We may assume, with Kittel, Schmidt, and Weiser (contra Gunkel and RSV), that the poem comprises three strophes, vss. 1-3, 4-5, 6-9. A pleasing feature is that the concluding verse in the second and third strophes (i.e., vss. 5, 9) is made a little longer than the corresponding verse in the preceding strophe. The meter is irregular.

The psalm is notable on three grounds. First, the Lord's sway is universal in the sense that **he is exalted over all the peoples** (vs. 2), but the extent to which the Gentiles

---

ready to quote passages that support his thesis and to ignore all that contradict it? It is not honest criticism to find evidences of cruelty and spite and to miss the central idea of mercy.

We are wise only if we take the moral to ourselves, and confess how easily we profess an exalted faith and then ignore it when we are hurt and our tempers are roused. The modern world gives too many illustrations of that weakness. We still need to apply in our own conduct the sentiment we have often commended to others: "Love is patient and kind; love is not jealous or boastful; it is not arrogant or rude. Love does not insist on its own way; it is not irritable or resentful; it does not rejoice at wrong, but rejoices in the right. Love bears all things, believes all things, hopes all things, endures all things" (I Cor. 13:4-7). Still more, we need to understand the mind of Christ as it is revealed in the prayer from the cross: "Father, forgive them; for they know not what they do" (Luke 23:34).

99:1-9. ***The Lord Is King.***—Albert Schweitzer in his autobiography, *Out of My Life and Thought,* tells how in September, 1915, when staying on the coast at Cape Lopez, he found it necessary to travel 160 miles up an African river to visit the ailing wife of a missionary. The only means of conveyance was a small steamer towing an overladen barge, which meant creeping upstream slowly for three days. This was a splendid opportunity for thought on fundamentals, and hour after hour his mind was concentrated upon definite questions. On the

engage in his worship is not indicated. Second, the holy King of the world is a **lover of justice** (vs. 4). Third, the psalmist is aware of God's consistency in his dealings with his people. In the days of Moses, Aaron, and Samuel he answered, forgave, and chastened, as the circumstances demanded, and he has done so ever since. He is, in short, "the same yesterday and today and for ever" (Heb. 13:8).

The psalm appears to come from a period of stability in Israel's political and religious life. Calès suggests the time of Zerubbabel.

1. Let the Peoples Praise His Name (99:1-3)

99:1. Peoples rather than **people:** The whole world is in the psalmist's mind (so also in vs. 2). **The cherubim:** See Exeg. on 80:1.

---

third day, at sunset, as they were making their way through a herd of hippopotamuses, there flashed upon his mind the phrase "reverence for life," and he knew that he had discovered what he sought. "The iron door had yielded: the path in the thicket had become visible." [8]

That is how one of the greatest men of modern times sums up his philosophy and his labors. It is a pregnant phrase, but Schweitzer would be the last to claim that it was entirely original. It was original in the way it entered his mind, but in some senses it was similar to Ps. 99. The key word of all these royal psalms (93–99) is the sovereignty of God; but the subject branches out in many directions. Ps. 97 begins with the assertion that "the Lord reigneth," and immediately calls upon the earth to rejoice. Ps. 99 begins with the same assurance, but is followed by the words: **let the peoples tremble!** At first glance it looks like a contradiction. Rejoicing suggests confidence and expectancy. Trembling suggests fear. There are, however, many reasons for trembling, many causes of fear. The guilty man trembles when he stands at the judgment seat. The good man trembles when he contemplates the holiness of God. One is the fear of punishment. The other is reverence as one contemplates the justice and the mercy of God and sees by contrast one's own shortcomings and perversity. Between this kind of awe and spontaneous rejoicing there is no contradiction. "The Lord reigns; let the earth rejoice" (97:1). Surely! What could be more natural than rejoicing in the heart of one who has lived through confusion and crisis and then found stability under sound government? But also **let the peoples tremble,** for they have seen, as Isaiah saw, the Lord sitting upon a throne. The first instinct of many who have thus realized the holiness of God is to be silent; but after the silence comes a song of rejoicing.

This attitude of reverence, common both to the psalmist and to Albert Schweitzer, has been carefully analyzed in recent years. There is no need here to expound the progress of the idea in the O.T. and the N.T., or to attempt an explanation of the numinous, the *mysterium tremendum,* and other technical terms. Let us instead take the word "life" and divide it into convenient parts and see what reverence means in each one of them.

1. *The Earth Quakes.*—There is, to begin with, the life below us, the life of nature, as we call it, not only animal life and plant and bird life, but insect life, even life that is invisible to the naked eye. Too often we take this vast sphere for granted and hardly think of it. But there is a religious attitude which is one of admiration, respect, and wonder. One who possesses this reverence for nature, or is possessed by it, will never think meanly of any creature because it is small, or despise any beast or flower because it is common. It may be necessary sometimes to kill, but there will be no cruelty and nothing less than indignation in the presence of torture. Schweitzer objected even to careless picking of wild flowers or a thoughtless killing of insects.

This may seem exaggerated sensitiveness. But it comes instinctively to men who have appreciated the holiness of God and realized, as so many of the psalmists did, that "the earth is the Lord's" (24:1). It has ever been one of the characteristics of a true saint. Baron von Hügel said that true saints have always revealed four traits: (*a*) they have been loyal to the faith; (*b*) they have been heroic in time of testing; (*c*) they have shown the power to do what ordinarily would seem to be impossible; and (*d*) they have been radiant in the midst of the strain and stress of life. That is good, but it requires an addition: the true saint instinctively adopts an attitude of respect, even of affection, for birds, beasts, and other living creatures. One need only recall Francis of Assisi and the birds, Hugh of Lincoln and the swan, Cuthbert and the seafowl, John Woolman, who has been described as one of "the great lovers of the world," and Sundar Singh, who slept alongside

[8] Tr. C. T. Campion (New York: Henry Holt & Co., 1933), p. 156.

2 The LORD *is* great in Zion; and he *is* high above all the people.
3 Let them praise thy great and terrible name; *for* it *is* holy.
4 The king's strength also loveth judgment; thou dost establish equity, thou executest judgment and righteousness in Jacob.

2 The LORD is great in Zion;
he is exalted over all the peoples.
3 Let them praise thy great and terrible name!
Holy is he!
4 Mighty King,[m] lover of justice,
thou hast established equity;
thou hast executed justice
and righteousness in Jacob.

[m] Cn: Heb *and the king's strength*

---

3. Holy is he is better than **it is holy:** Cf. vss. 5, 9.

2. PRAISE GOD FOR HIS JUSTICE (99:4-5)

4. Mighty King: Cf. Exeg. on 98:5-6. The M.T., **the king's strength,** is obscure and invites emendation. The RSV adopts Gunkel's suggestion (ומלך עז). Kittel *et al.* repoint the Hebrew to obtain "And a strong one reigns."

---

a leopard without any sense of fear. By this test some of the canonized saints may disappear from the ecclesiastical calendar, but others will appear. Even William Blake, who had so much to say not only about lambs and robins, but also about tigers and mongrels, becomes a possible candidate:

> A robin redbreast in a cage
> Puts all Heaven in a rage.
> A dove-house fill'd with doves and pigeons
> Shudders Hell thro' all its regions.
> A dog starv'd at his master's gate
> Predicts the ruin of the State.
> A horse misus'd upon the road
> Calls to Heaven for human blood.
> Each outcry of the hunted hare
> A fibre from the brain does tear.[1]

We must teach little children never unnecessarily to hurt a creature or desecrate a flower. That is the beginning of reverence. And how naturally it grows in minds that worship in sincerity the living God.

> **Extol the LORD our God,**
> **and worship at his holy mountain;**
> **for the LORD our God is holy!**

And the meanest creature on earth reflects in some measure that holiness.

2-4. ***He Is Exalted over All Peoples.***—There is, in the second place, the life around us, i.e., life on the human level. Here the possibilities are enormous. There is to be reverence for the poor as well as for the rich, for the ignorant as well as for the learned, for the handicapped and sinful as well as for the successful and saintly, for black and brown men, women, and children as well as for white ones. Reverence for human life, indeed, goes to the root of most of our social and international problems.

No one has seriously suggested that Abraham Lincoln should take his place among the saints. By this test, however, the idea is not incongruous. It was he who said that "God must like the common people; he made so many of them." Once when he was president he visited the city of Richmond and was received with acclamation. One old Negro so far forgot himself in his excitement as to step out into the road and with the tears rolling down his cheeks to exclaim, "May de good Lawd bless you, President Linkum." Some would have brushed aside such a person—but not Lincoln. He removed his hat and bowed in silence, and one who was present said: "It was a bow which upset the forms, laws, customs, and ceremonies of centuries. It was a mortal wound to caste."

A similar instinct took Schweitzer to Africa. He believed the white man had never been fair to the black man. He felt there was a debt which he could not pay, but toward the payment of which he might make a gesture. So he turned his back upon his life as a university professor. He forsook the advantages of European culture and went where doctors were unknown and disease was rife. There he labored through the years for men, women, and children who came down the rivers and through the bush seeking health and hope. That is the secret of Christian missions to this day. The ignorant say that men go to India, to Africa, to China, to the South Sea Islands in order to thrust their beliefs upon simple minds. Actually it is the instinct to share—the desire to give the best they have to give. It is not a veiled passion to dominate, but reverence for life—all sorts of human life, irrespective of creed or tradition or culture.

[1] "Auguries of Innocence."

5 Exalt ye the LORD our God, and worship at his footstool; *for* he *is* holy.
6 Moses and Aaron among his priests, and Samuel among them that call upon his name; they called upon the LORD, and he answered them.
7 He spake unto them in the cloudy pillar: they kept his testimonies, and the ordinance *that* he gave them.

5 Extol the LORD our God;
worship at his footstool!
Holy is he!

6 Moses and Aaron were among his priests,
Samuel also was among those who called on his name.
They cried to the LORD, and he answered them.
7 He spoke to them in the pillar of cloud;
they kept his testimonies,
and the statutes that he gave them.

---

5. His footstool: This expression in the O.T. always bears a figurative meaning. Here, as in 132:7; Lam. 2:1; I Chr. 28:2, it refers to the temple in Jerusalem. We may note that in the Ugaritic poems the god El is also represented as having a footstool.

3. THE LESSON OF HISTORY (99:6-9)

6. Moses and Aaron are termed Levites in Exod. 2:1; 4:14, but this psalm is the only place in the O.T. where Moses is called a priest (cf. Moses' performance of priestly acts in Exod. 24:6-8; 40:22-27; Lev. 8:1-30). Moses and Samuel are named together in Jer. 15:1. The references to these great figures of the past may be partly intended to add to the prestige of the Jerusalem hierarchy. **They cried . . . he answered:** For Moses, see Exod. 14:15-18; 32:1–34:35; for Aaron, Num. 16:44-48; for Samuel, I Sam. 7:8-9; 12:19-23.

7. The pillar of cloud is connected with God's speaking to Moses (Exod. 33:9) and to Aaron (Num. 12:5), but it does not appear in the Samuel narrative.

And that is the short answer we may give to many of the questions men raise, e.g., the problem of war. No one should be ashamed to say he is afraid of war. We ought to fear what it may do to us personally, to our families, to our countries, and to our churches. But the fundamental reason is not fear for ourselves, it is respect for man as the child of God. The same applies to many of the questions that are raised about sexual relations. Why should we not indulge ourselves? It is useless to meet the question with a random text or mere dogma. Once, however, realize what man is—once see what the apostle meant when he said that the body is "the temple of the Holy Ghost" (I Cor. 6:19), and impurity becomes sacrilege of the highest order. We do not seek to maintain marriage vows or to present ourselves to our life partners unashamed simply because of custom or tradition. We do it because we have caught sight of the holiness of God and some of its implications.

Mighty King, lover of justice,
thou hast established equity;
thou hast executed justice
and righteousness in Jacob.

5. ***He Is Enthroned upon the Cherubim.***—Thirdly, there is the life above us. The assurance that the Lord is enthroned upon the cherubim was instinctive with the psalmist. It is not so spontaneous now. Many of our neighbors may feel, if they do not actually say it, that here we part company. Reverence for man as man is in agreement with much of the best thought of our times. Even reverence for animate and inanimate nature they can appreciate. But the life above of which we speak, this worship of an unseen King—how can they know him, even be sure that he exists?

We must admit that we are moving in a realm of mystery. Mystery, however, abounds in every sphere. The migration of birds is a great mystery, but it is also an undeniable fact. To speak of instinct is not to explain. There is no explanation. Similarly, there is no questioning the fact of worship. All down the ages men have been calling to him who is exalted over all peoples, uniting in his praise, waiting for his guidance. And often we worship in unofficial and almost unrecognized ways. We know what it is to go out, say on some beautiful autumn evening, and watch the swiftly changing colors as the sun sinks into a bank of clouds. We feel the hush that falls upon all nature, and suddenly we find ourselves saying, "Surely the LORD is in this place; and I knew it not" (Gen. 28:16). That is the worship of the "Mighty King, lover

8 Thou answeredst them, O LORD our God: thou wast a God that forgavest them, though thou tookest vengeance of their inventions.
9 Exalt the LORD our God, and worship at his holy hill; for the LORD our God *is* holy.

A Psalm of praise.

100 Make a joyful noise unto the LORD, all ye lands.

8 O LORD our God, thou didst answer them;
thou wast a forgiving God to them,
but an avenger of their wrongdoings.
9 Extol the LORD our God,
and worship at his holy mountain;
for the LORD our God is holy!

A Psalm for the thank offering.

100 Make a joyful noise to the LORD, all the lands![n]

[n] Heb *land* or *earth*

8. Thou didst answer them: There is some uncertainty about the antecedent of **them.** At first glance it appears to be Moses, Aaron, and Samuel, but the psalmist may here be moving from the particular to the general, and he may be thinking of the nation's experience. **A forgiving God:** On the Lord's forgiving nature see Num. 14:17-24. **An avenger:** On the vengeance of the Lord see Exeg. on 94:1. **Wrongdoings** is a better translation than **inventions;** the word appears frequently in Ezekiel (14:22-23; 20:43; etc.). On the **wrongdoings** of Moses and Aaron see Exod. 32:35; Num. 20:12; Deut. 3:23-27; 9:20. Samuel's misdeeds are not recorded. But as is suggested above, the author may be alluding to Israel's sins.

C. Make a Joyful Noise to the Lord (100:1-5)

This simple psalm was sung, as its contents indicate, by a procession of worshipers who were at the point of entering the gates and passing into the courts of the temple (vss. 2*b*, 4*a*) for the service of thanksgiving and thank offerings. The brief title or superscription, **A Psalm for the thank offering,** does not necessarily imply that in later times it was sung contrary to its original purpose during the service. In form it consists of two short hymns (vss. 1-3, 4-5) with the usual hymnal parts, i.e., the call to worship and the grounds for the call. This structure was seemingly meant to serve its liturgical use, the first hymn being sung by a choral body at the head of those who were moving up to the temple gates, the second hymn being a response by another choir within the temple, bidding the worshipers to enter the temple courts.

In content and in purpose the psalm is very similar to Ps. 95, but more concisely than the latter it summarizes the creed of Judaism (vss. 3, 5). This creed, which corrects in measure the conception of Judaism presented in the N.T. is made up of six capital

of justice." We know what it is, especially perhaps in youthful days, to follow the love of truth, to resolve that we will never compromise in our search for truth, never be bought by the promise of temporal gain, never be put off by lies or evasions. That too may be regarded as the worship of the Lord the King. No one can dedicate himself to the love of beauty or truth without in some sense sharing in the worship of the Almighty.

For Christians, however, there is something more concrete than this. Remember how Philip said to Jesus Christ: "Lord, show us the Father, and it sufficeth us," and Jesus replied: "He that hath seen me hath seen the Father" (John 14:8-9). What an amazing thing to say! Yet how true it is. Millions have looked into the face of Jesus and felt themselves looking upon God, have listened to the words of Jesus and felt themselves led into an undying wisdom. To know Jesus is to know God. To obey Jesus is to worship the Father.

Thus it is that the reverence for the life above proclaimed by the sweet singer of Israel finds its complete fulfillment in Jesus of Nazareth, who showed us in word and in life the true attitude of nature, the deepest respect even for sinful men and women, and the blessedness of worship "in spirit and in truth."

100:1-5. ***Sing to the Lord with Cheerful Voice.*** —The book of Psalms is no more an adequate guide to the religious condition of the Jews

2 Serve the LORD with gladness: come before his presence with singing.

2 Serve the LORD with gladness!
Come into his presence with singing!

statements: (*a*) **the LORD is God;** (*b*) he is our creator; (*c*) **we are his people;** (*d*) **the LORD is good;** (*e*) his kindness is everlasting; (*f*) his faithfulness endures to all generations. Such a creed helps us to understand how the Jews were nerved in the Maccabean period to resist the attempts of pagans with their lesser creeds to stamp out their faith; and how, first of all peoples in the world, they took up the cause of religious freedom.

From the standpoint of poetical art the psalm does not rank with the best in the Psalter; but like many modern hymns which lack poetical merit, it has been held in high esteem because it is, as Calès remarks, *plein de vie et riche de sens* (*Livre des Psaumes,* II, 229).

The date is obviously postexilic, for worship is centered at one temple into whose gates and courts the Lord's people seek entrance. The meter is irregular: 3+3+3 (vss. 1-2), 4+4+3 (vs. 3), 3+2+3 (vs. 4), 2+2+3 (vs. 5).

1. SERVE THE LORD WITH GLADNESS (100:1-3)

100:1-2. The occasion is one of giving thanks to the Lord for his blessings at one of the great seasons appointed for Israel to come up to the temple (cf. Exod. 34:22-23; Lev. 7:11-18). Therefore, the people's voices are lifted up to **make a joyful noise to the LORD.** The whole earth is invited to join in the glad song. **All ye lands:** Lit., **all the earth** or **all the land.** It is scarcely probable that the psalmist would limit the summons to the land of Israel alone, as Gunkel and others believe, because in such songs as Pss. 95–99 the universal rule of the Lord is assumed ideally to be at hand. The pilgrims from various lands who gathered to the feast betokened the Lord's world-wide rule. **Serve the LORD with gladness:** The word **serve** is a technical term for performing as servants or subjects what is proper in worship (cf. Exod. 3:12; Mal. 3:14). But **gladness** is the mark of the service rendered to the Lord. The **gladness** expresses itself in jubilant **singing** as his people draw near to his sanctuary (cf. 95:6; 96:8; Deut. 23:2-4).

than a modern hymnbook is to that of our own country; but it leaves us in no doubt regarding the place of the temple in the affections of the people. There may have been exceptions, and at times the exceptions may have been many, but we get the impression that normally men of all ages gladly left their usual occupations and at the time of the great festivals turned their faces toward Zion. Much that was performed there may have been more social than spiritual, more patriotic than ethical, more superstitious than rational; but the temple was a real community center, and for good Jews to neglect it altogether would have been like cutting themselves out of the national life. The services of praise may not have been always deeply religious, but they were participated in without reluctance.

The situation in this respect in many countries is now different. The people have other things to attend to, and they pass by the place of prayer without compunction. Priests and pastors find the reason in the secularization of every department of life. They complain that the mass of the people have lost their instinct for the supernatural, and that anyone who speaks about reverence for the sacred feels that he is using a foreign language. The man in the street, however, has other things to say. He complains that when he does go to church he does not find it convincing. So often the preaching is remote, the hymns and prayers unreal, the congregation listless. He complains further that so far as he can judge, worship makes little difference in life. The churchgoer is not necessarily wiser, juster, or more generous than the nonchurchgoer. He therefore congratulates himself that he is free from the hand of tradition and seeks satisfaction in Sunday excursions.

The whole controversy is not settled in a sentence and will not be concluded here. A consideration of this psalm, however, should help us to understand why the Israelites turned willingly to the temple and how the sanctuary may again make a powerful appeal to the man in the street. Notice that there was one recognized place of prayer, and to it the people turned undisturbed by other loyalties. This does not imply dull uniformity of thought or action. There were many differences of opinion and some of them went deep. The most fundamental difference was that between the prophets and the priests.

3 Know ye that the LORD he *is* God: *it is* he *that* hath made us, and not we ourselves; *we are* his people, and the sheep of his pasture.

3 Know that the LORD is God!
It is he that made us, and we are his;[o]
we are his people, and the sheep of his pasture.

[o] Another reading is *and not we ourselves*

---

3. The inspiration of the glad songs of the congregation is their confidence in what the Lord is. **The LORD is God,** i.e., he alone is God, and there is none beside him. **He . . . made us** and as creator he claims us. But better still, he adopts us, **we are his people,** the special flock which he wishes to shepherd. By such a tender figure the character of the Lord's dominion over Israel is defined. **It is he that hath made us, and not we ourselves** is a translation of a text which was the result of a correction of the scribes confessedly made "from motives of reverence, or to avoid anthropomorphic suggestions." The correction consisted in reading לֹא, **not,** for לוֹ, **his** (cf. Kautzsch, *Gesenius' Hebrew Grammar,* sec. 103*g,* and A. S. Geden, *Outlines of Introduction to the Hebrew Bible* [Edinburgh: T. & T. Clark, 1909], pp. 99-101).

We must not say that this was a conflict of right and wrong; for the prophets were not infallible, and the priests were often gallant and generous. The conflict, however, was important. It was not only theological or ecclesiastical: it was frequently economic and social. But intense as it often became, it did not divide the nation into exclusive and competing parties. And later, when synagogues claimed local loyalties, and learned rabbis developed distinctive tendencies, the body politic was never rent in twain. Men and women without obvious tension attended temple and synagogue and gladly accepted the ministry of both.

The modern scene is a contrast. The church has been split into fragments not only by great principles and traditions but also by relatively unimportant usage and preference. We have accentuated our distinctive contributions out of all proportion to reality, and have confused the public mind with our contentions. With our lips we have prayed for unity, but too often by our deeds we have increased barriers. At last the Christian conscience is rebelling against the sin of schism, but history is not undone in a moment. The urgency of the situation can no longer be ignored. Either the church must learn to speak together for Christ, or the people will continue to go their separate ways.

Notice, second, the cheerfulness of the temple worship. The more one studies the book of Psalms the more one is impressed by this important fact. Not that the hymns of the temple were always pitched to the same note. There are penitential psalms which express men's sorrow for sin. There are moods of shame in which human impurity is contrasted with the holiness of God. There are occasionally bitter cries, protesting against enemies and calling upon God to punish wrongdoers. But it is praise that predominates, common praise, praise expressing the gratitude of different sections for particular mercies, praise accompanied by horn and trumpet, drum and cymbal, praise expressed in ritual acts as well as in words. The temple was a building that started many memories. It was, indeed, history in brick and stone. But it was a center to which men turned primarily because it was the place of praise. This song is one among many contributions to the great ministry of gladness.

Make a joyful noise to the LORD, all the lands!
Serve the LORD with gladness!
Come into his presence with singing!

Such cheerfulness is not altogether lacking in Christian services to this day. But it is not always dominant. Even the psalms, where they are frequently used, do not necessarily lift men from sadness and send them away in joy. They are often gabbled by choirs or read monotonously by ministers and congregations. Some of the metrical versions that have been most familiar have missed the original spirit. Sternhold's rendering pleased Edward VI of England, and subsequent efforts had considerable popularity; yet, according to Prothero, Queen Elizabeth condemned the "Geneva jigs," a Cavalier poet complains of singing "with woful noise," and the Earl of Rochester expressed himself thus:

Sternhold and Hopkins had great qualms,
When they translated David's Psalms,
To make the heart right glad;
But had it been King David's fate
To hear thee sing and them translate,
By God! 'twould see him mad! [2]

[2] *Psalms in Human Life,* pp. 112-13.

4 Enter into his gates with thanksgiving, *and* into his courts with praise: be thankful unto him, *and* bless his name.

5 For the LORD *is* good; his mercy *is* everlasting; and his truth *endureth* to all generations.

4 Enter his gates with thanksgiving,
and his courts with praise!
Give thanks to him, bless his name!

5 For the LORD is good;
his steadfast love endures for ever,
and his faithfulness to all generations.

---

2. ENTER HIS COURTS WITH PRAISE (100:4-5)

4. The service in which the people will participate is here indicated as one of thanksgiving. They enter with songs of thanksgiving on their lips, eager to confess God's providences, individual and communal, and to pay their vows (Deut. 12:11; Lev. 23:37-38).

5. Each of them has in his experience of the Lord's help or deliverance surely come to know that **the LORD is good; his steadfast love endures for ever,** and that he is unchangingly loyal, i.e., **his faithfulness** [endures] **to all generations.**

Nothing need be said here about dismal buildings and dreary preaching and monotonous praying. It is enough to insist that unless we can again make our sanctuaries centers of gladness, men will continue to pass by on the other side.

Notice, third, the healthy objectivity of temple worship. We shall be reminded that there are subjective passages even in the psalms. There was not always the outward look, the uplifted face. The psalmists knew the heart of man, its evil propensities as well as its daring aspirations, its subtleties as well as its simplicities. And without the mood of introspection they would not have had the hold upon the centuries they have had. Their great concern, however, was not the need of man but the greatness of God. Their characteristic expression is not "Woe is me" but:

> **Know that the LORD is God!**
> **It is he that made us, and we are his;**
> **we are his people.**

It might have been expected that with this concentration upon absolute and eternal reality the psalmists would lose themselves in vague speculation. Actually they remain definite in thought and simple in speech. They leave to others the tasks of explanation and definition, but their praise is the expression of a creed which is as clear as it is profound. In private they may have had personal doubts and questions, but these are not brought into public worship. There may have been intellectual conflict in their solitary thought and study, but for the temple there was affirmation. We have seen in the Exeg. above how concisely the creed of Judaism is summarized in this psalm. There is but one God and he is creator. We are his people, and in his goodness, his mercy, and his enduring faithfulness we may trust. It is short, plain, positive. It can be understood by the meanest intelligence, yet it leaves scope for the profoundest thinking. It can be preached by flaming evangelists, yet not exhausted by the most experienced philosophers.

Has it not always been so when religion has been victorious? Has not every great revival of the church been connected with a return to objective, positive, plain speech and unambiguous ritual? And is not this the need of modern Christendom? May not the people be excused their neglect of the means of grace if the preaching is vague and subjective? "If the trumpet give an uncertain sound, who shall prepare himself to the battle?" (I Cor. 14:8.) And the sound will be uncertain if we depend more upon experience, which may be nebulous, than upon the Lord **that made us.** The experience will give point to the truth, it will make our creed live, and give edge to our preaching. But it is no substitute for the truth itself. There is place for plaintive verses, such as Cowper's

> Lord, it is my chief complaint
> That my love is weak and faint;
> Yet I love thee and adore;
> O for grace to love thee more! [3]

But no hymnbook is adequate unless it abounds in songs such as "Praise to the Holiest in the height" and "Now thank we all our God" and "Praise to the Lord, the Almighty, the King of creation." We cannot promise that if our sanctuaries resound to such songs sincerely rendered they will immediately be filled with crowds of eager worshipers. But we shall have more reason for believing that it is not we who have driven men into irreligious ways.

[3] "Hark, my soul! it is the Lord," st. v.

A Psalm of David.

101 I will sing of mercy and judgment: unto thee, O Lord, will I
sing.
2 I will behave myself wisely in a perfect
way. O when wilt thou come unto me? I

A Psalm of David.

101 I will sing of loyalty and of
justice;
to thee, O Lord, I will sing.
2 I will give heed to the way that is blameless.
Oh when wilt thou come to me?

CI. The Moral Ideals of a King (101:1-8)

Luther entitled this psalm *Davids Regentenspiegel*, "David's mirror for reigning princes," and most modern commentators are agreed that it presents a moral code for all those set in authority. While words pointing specifically to royalty do not occur, it is usually presumed that the psalm was written by or for a king, and for some special occasion such as his coronation or a royal anniversary. It is for this reason often classified as a royal psalm (see Exeg. on 2:1-12; 20:1-9). In later years its wholesome tone and the general character of its language secured it a place in the psalmody of Israel. It is possible that vss. 1-2*b* are later additions to the original song, perhaps the result of its adaptation to temple usage (cf. Calès). This supposition takes some of the force from the proposals to make certain textual changes in these verses.

This psalm in a sense is the counterpart to Ps. 15. The latter states the moral principles of a citizen of Zion, as enunciated by or on behalf of the Lord; the former is a solemn affirmation on the part of a human magistrate of his adhesion to those same principles. In his own life, in his household, in his officials, and throughout the land, the speaker will brook no iniquity. As Weiser (*Die Psalmen*, p. 429) observes: "The psalm is infused with all the moral earnestness of Old Testament religion."

The RSV follows the strophic arrangement of Kittel and Gunkel. The meter is generally 3+2.

1. The King's Commitment Before the Lord (101:1-2*b*)

101:1-2*b*. Loyalty or **mercy:** In the psalms the RSV usually renders the Hebrew word by "steadfast love" (5:7; 6:4; 13:5; etc.). **I will give heed to** rather than **I will behave myself wisely. Oh when wilt thou come to me?** The alleged irrelevance of this question has prompted Gunkel *et al.* to change מתי to אמת, which makes the stich, "Let truth come unto me."

101:1-8. ***A Psalm for Rulers.***—Most men are filled with wonder and awe when they visit an ancient cathedral, see the sublimity of planning and execution, and remember that the work was done long before science had put powerful machines into the hands of architects and builders. We are not always so impressed when we turn to O.T. books which are so venerable that by comparison Norman cathedrals are almost modern. We are not always impressed when scholars reconstruct the scene and help us to visualize a civilization quite different from our own. Yet distant as the date is, naïve as in some ways the mentality may appear, these books contain so much wisdom and devotion that it may be questioned how real is the progress of which we so often speak. The sense of wonder should fill our minds especially when we read the book of Psalms, which bears so many marks of antiquity, yet so clearly speaks to our minds and hearts.

These reflections on the book as a whole may be tested not only with universal favorites like Pss. 23; 51; 90, but with a comparatively unknown one like Ps. 101. Some of the psalms are connected with particular vocations. There are shepherds' psalms, priests' psalms, pilgrims' psalms, and others. Ps. 101 is believed to be one for princes and rulers. It is not a treatise on government. It does not move in the same sphere as the writings of John Locke or John Stuart Mill. But it contains ideals that are fundamental to sound government. It is indeed so appropriate to all who exercise authority that at least one ruler, Ernest the Pious, Duke of Saxe-Gotha, would send a copy of it to officials who had been unfaithful. It was sent so often that it became a proverb when any magistrate

will walk within my house with a perfect
heart.
3 I will set no wicked thing before mine
eyes: I hate the work of them that turn
aside; *it* shall not cleave to me.
4 A froward heart shall depart from me:
I will not know a wicked *person.*
5 Whoso privily slandereth his neighbor,
him will I cut off: him that hath a high look
and a proud heart will not I suffer.

I will walk with integrity of heart
within my house;
3 I will not set before my eyes
anything that is base.

I hate the work of those who fall away;
it shall not cleave to me.
4 Perverseness of heart shall be far from
me;
I will know nothing of evil.

5 Him who slanders his neighbor secretly
I will destroy.
The man of haughty looks and arrogant
heart
I will not endure.

---

2. The King's Personal Life (101:2*c*-4)

2*c*-4. Anything that is base: See Exeg. of this phrase in 41:8, where the RSV translates it "a deadly thing." **Those who fall away:** The Hebrew is difficult, and the RSV adopts a small emendation, changing סטים to שטים; the latter form, a participle, is found in 40:4. In vs. 4 רע is either impersonal, **evil,** or personal, **a wicked person.**

3. The King's Subjects (101:5-7)

5-7. I will not endure: The LXX and the Syriac read, "With him I will not eat," which involves two minor changes in the M.T. **I will look with favor: Lit., Mine eyes shall be.**

---

had done wrong, "He will certainly receive the Prince's psalm to read." [4]

The poem begins with a definitely religious note:

> **I will sing of loyalty and of justice;**
> **to thee, O Lord, I will sing.**

Who the singer is we know not. Tradition says that it is a psalm of David, but that may mean no more than that it belonged to a collection of hymns that bore David's name. It is, however, the kind of beginning we should expect from the shepherd-king. Even the word "king" can have many meanings. To one it means supreme sovereignty, to another a constitutional monarchy. David held that Israel was a theocracy. He was the visible ruler, but he reigned not in his own right; he reigned as the Lord's deputy. It was natural therefore that such a reign should start, as Solomon's did, with a prayer for wisdom. Is there any better conception of government than that? Do we not indeed at this point come to the dividing line between governments true and false? We have endless discussions about aristocracies and democracies, dictatorships and plutocracies; but even the best systems can be perversely used. It is the spirit that matters. It is true of democracies as of absolute monarchies, that if they become proud and grasping, selfish and cruel, they will bring strife and misery among the nations. And there is no better way of keeping the spirit right than by the recognition of One to whom every knee must bow.

From the worship of God the singer turns to himself and makes a number of good resolutions. The first is that he **will give heed to the way that is blameless,** or as it is elsewhere rendered, he **will behave** [himself] **wisely in a perfect way;** i.e., he begins to see what a difference it makes when high office is regarded not as a privilege to be snatched at, but as a responsibility demanding personal discipline. How different history would have been if those in authority had begun, continued, and ended their work like that! Instead, we have had vain men like Absalom, who have coveted position for its own sake. We have had them in church and state, in world politics and local affairs, and society has been contaminated from top to bottom.

The next good resolution the psalmist makes is that he will have a well-ordered household and a clean court. Others may surround themselves with flatterers and lovers of frivolity. He

[4] John Ker, *The Psalms in History and Biography* (Edinburgh: A. Elliot, 1888), pp. 126-27.

6 Mine eyes *shall be* upon the faithful of
the land, that they may dwell with me: he
that walketh in a perfect way, he shall serve
me.
7 He that worketh deceit shall not dwell
within my house: he that telleth lies shall
not tarry in my sight.
8 I will early destroy all the wicked of the
land; that I may cut off all wicked doers
from the city of the LORD.

6 I will look with favor on the faithful in
the land,
that they may dwell with me;
he who walks in the way that is blameless
shall minister to me.

7 No man who practices deceit
shall dwell in my house;
no man who utters lies
shall continue in my presence.

8 Morning by morning I will destroy
all the wicked in the land,
cutting off all the evildoers
from the city of the LORD.

4. THE END OF EVILDOERS (101:8)

8. Morning by morning rather than **early:** Probably the reference is to a public hearing of complaints and lawsuits in the ruler's presence every morning.

will expel all who are haughty and disdainful and wasters of time, and in their places he will install men who are capable of high thinking and courageous action. They will not despise amusements, still less the arts, but they will be austere in spirit and habit.

> **I will walk with integrity of heart**
> **within my house;**
> **I will not set before my eyes**
> **anything that is base.**
> . . . .
> **No man who practices deceit**
> **shall dwell in my house;**
> **no man who utters lies**
> **shall continue in my presence** (vss. 2-3, 7).

Compare that with courts we have known! Compare it with the vast retinue that wandered with Louis XIV from countryseat to countryseat, vainly seeking relief from ennui. Only two occupations, we are told, hunting and sexual indulgence, offered Louis himself temporary distraction, and to these he applied himself with all the assiduity of which he was capable. This was the man who told his parliament: "To me alone belongs the power of making laws, absolutely and autocratically. Public order derives entirely from me." [5]

Further, the psalmist set his heart upon justice for all. This is stated definitely in the first sentence and suggested again in vs. 3: **I hate the work of those who fall away,** which may perhaps be better translated, "I hate him that dealeth unfaithfully." It is returned to in vs. 7. The psalmist would have agreed with the voice that murmured in the ears of Socrates: "Think not of life and children first and of justice afterwards, but of justice first, that you may be justified before the princes of the world below." [6] The same demand is made in psalm after psalm and by prophet after prophet. It is repeated in different ways by wise men and lawgivers who cry aloud to the people and say: "Ye shall do no unrighteousness in judgment, in meteyard, in weight, or in measure. Just balances, just weights, a just ephah, and a just hin, shall ye have" (Lev. 19:35-36). These exhortations mean that there were knaves then as there have always been. When cases were brought to the courts, one could not be certain that they would be dealt with impartially. Judges could sometimes be browbeaten by the powerful or bought by the wealthy. But the psalmist will have none of it. **Perverseness of heart shall be far from** him; the slanderer shall be wiped out; the arrogant he **will not endure.**

Is there a touch of self-righteousness in all this? Are we reminded of a Pharisee who in complacency thanks God he is not as other men are (Luke 18:11)? We need to be on our guard against self-pride. Fortunately, though the psalm increases in severity as it proceeds, it begins with mercy as well as with judgment. Never does justice become more religious than when it is tempered with mercy.

> And earthly power doth show likest God's,
> When mercy seasons justice.[7]

The man in authority must have courage to act. Sometimes he must punish. But never will he

[5] Leonard Sidney Woolf, *After the Deluge* (New York: Penguin Books, Inc., 1938), p. 97.

[6] Cf. Plato *Crito* XVI.

[7] Shakespeare, *The Merchant of Venice,* Act IV, scene 1.

A Prayer of the afflicted, when he is overwhelmed, and poureth out his complaint before the LORD.

102 Hear my prayer, O LORD, and let my cry come unto thee.

A prayer of one afflicted, when he is faint and pours out his complaint before the LORD.

102 Hear my prayer, O LORD;
let my cry come to thee!

CII. AN APPEAL TO THE GOD ENTHRONED FOR EVER (102:1-28)

This psalm falls clearly into three parts: vss. 1-11, 12-22, 23-28, and the question arises, What is the relation between them? It has been argued since Duhm that at least two sources must be posited to account for the poem, (*a*) vss. 1-11, 23-28, and (*b*) vss. 12-22 (cf. Schmidt, vss. 1-11, 23-24, and vss. 12-22, 25-28), and separate authors are then made responsible for each section. We must admit that vss. 12-22 are an interruption in their present context, but we can explain their presence in the psalm by assuming that the psalmist himself incorporated these verses into his complaint. Whether the author was here drawing upon some outside source, or whether he was using an earlier hymn of his own, it is impossible to determine.

We have here the lament of an individual, and the title is therefore a fairly accurate description of its contents. While the church selected it as one of the seven Penitential Psalms (the others being Pss. 6; 32; 38; 51; 130; 143), the psalmist nowhere displays

be vindictive, and never will he forget that he too is a sinful man.

> Who made the heart, 'tis He alone
> Decidedly can try us;
> He knows each chord—its various tone,
> Each spring—its various bias.
> Then at the balance let's be mute,
> We never can adjust it;
> What's done we partly may compute,
> But know not what's resisted.[8]

Have we, with all our boasted progress, advanced far in our conception of government? Philosophers have written many learned treatises. Statesmen have experimented with every social doctrine. But have we yet seen that we must begin with the fear of the Lord if we are to continue with true reverence for man? Has every king or president at the time of his coronation or inauguration bowed himself in supplication before the Most High? Has every prime minister, facing the task of constructing a cabinet, sought above everything else men of character and veracity? Have we who are voters in democratic countries chosen men of high principle and sound reputation? One thing is clear: if the fundamental ideals of this psalmist had been honored in word and in deed, history would have had a different story to tell and life would have been more peaceful and blessed.

102:1-28. ***In Times of Trouble.***—It is frequently said that the Bible comes to life in times of trouble. It has certainly come to life for many in this century, which began with extravagant expectations and soon passed to world-wide suffering. Instead of songs of hope there were laments and deep mourning. Instead of a progressive building of the city of God, there were the most destructive of wars. Men left peaceful homes and went forth to hardship, wounds, and death. Women who remained watched and wept, and children were forced to face life as orphans. Authors who had indulged in visions of utopia composed hymns of hate, and orators sank into a spirit of frustration. The faith and courage of millions failed under the strain, and all life seemed to turn gray. There were, however, some who restudied their Bibles and realized that their lot was not unique. They read of men who had passed through deep waters and in the very midst of them had their feet set on a firm foundation. Turning once more to God in prayer and penitence, they found peace and were led on to victory.

Ps. 102 is one of the portions of Scripture that in these circumstances has shone with a new light. Such laments have never been entirely neglected. There have always been some who read with insight, and some who responded with understanding. They may not have known what painful experiences inspired this particular psalm. They may never have heard suggestions that it is a compilation of fragments, one intensely personal, another expressing the sorrows of Jews who looked upon scenes of desolation. It was enough that they sensed human suffering which was no less poignant because the cries rang out from an ancient world. It was enough that they became conscious of the faith that won the victory and put a song of triumph upon troubled lips. They found that

[8] Robert Burns, "Address to the Unco Guid."

2 Hide not thy face from me in the day
when I am in trouble; incline thine ear
unto me: in the day *when* I call answer me
speedily.
3 For my days are consumed like smoke,
and my bones are burned as a hearth.
4 My heart is smitten, and withered like
grass; so that I forget to eat my bread.

2 Do not hide thy face from me
in the day of my distress!
Incline thy ear to me;
answer me speedily in the day when I call!

3 For my days pass away like smoke,
and my bones burn like a furnace.
4 My heart is smitten like grass, and withered;
I forget to eat my bread.

---

anything that can be properly called penitence. The author is suffering from sickness, possibly of an intestinal nature (vss. 4-5), and in addition he has to endure the derision and malice of personal enemies; he interprets all this affliction as being due to the Lord's anger. His mood is somewhat similar to that of Job 7:1-6, but unlike Job, the psalmist does not want to die. It is at this point that we are introduced (vss. 12-22) to a short hymn. Here the contemplation of the eternity of God and of his good purposes for Zion sets human suffering in a truer perspective, and when the poet returns in vs. 23 to his own problems, he is fortified by these high thoughts and finds therein his peace.

There is no indication in the biographical part of the psalm of the date and external circumstances of the psalmist. There are, however, in vss. 13-14, 20, intimations that Zion has suffered some misfortune, and this may point to the Babylonian wars of the early sixth century B.C., or to the disaster of which Nehemiah speaks (1:1-3); otherwise it is some unrecorded calamity. The date would thus appear to be exilic or postexilic. In the Mishnah (Taanith 2:3) this psalm is one of four (the others being Pss. 120; 121; 130) considered suitable for recitation on days of fasting. The dominant meter is 3+3.

1. The Psalmist's Sufferings (102:1-11)

102:3-6. Furnace: The precise meaning is uncertain; **hearth** is supported by Köhler. In vs. 5*a* some, following Baethgen, supply the verb "I am weary" (יגעתי; cf. 69:3*a*).

---

what happened once long ago could happen again, and turning to God in prayer they cried:

> **Hear my prayer, O Lord;**
> **let my cry come to thee!** (vs. 1)
>
> **Thou, O Lord, art enthroned for ever;**
> **thy name endures to all generations** (vs. 12).

1-11, 23-24. ***Personal Troubles.***—For our purposes we can separate the personal experience of the psalmist from the troubles around him. The sufferings set forth in vss. 1-11, 23-24 divide into two groups, physical and mental or spiritual. When the poet says that his whole body is a consuming fire, and that his **bones burn like a furnace,** we suspect that he is referring to some ailment or perhaps to fevers that no physician or medicine could relieve. When he speaks of his **bones** cleaving to his **flesh** so that he forgets **to eat,** he is apparently again describing a physical malady—and it is well that we should pause to consider how great were men's agonies before the development of medical science and how much we are indebted to a long line of patient experimenters. Medical men are often criticized; they are not usually adequately thanked. Yet how great is our indebtedness to doctors, dentists, and nurses! Not only have they ministered to us in our need, but they have gone far to relieve us of the burden of pain. Ought we not occasionally to arrange testimonial meetings in which those who have been helpless and have been restored to health might testify to the ministries of medicine, surgery, and skillful nursing?

But there is reference here to more than sickness of body. When the psalmist likens himself to **a pelican of the wilderness** or an **owl** in the ruins, he seems to be complaining of a mental or spiritual condition. A pelican is a bird that frequents watery places. *The Concise Oxford Dictionary of Current England* describes it as a "large water-fowl with pouch for storing fish." [9] **A pelican of the wilderness** is therefore a bird that is out of its true environment. Again the psalmist likens himself to **a lonely bird on the housetop.** Is there any more convincing picture of destitution than that of a

[9] H. W. and F. G. Fowler, eds. (Oxford: Clarendon Press, 1914).

5 By reason of the voice of my groaning
my bones cleave to my skin.
6 I am like a pelican of the wilderness:
I am like an owl of the desert.
7 I watch, and am as a sparrow alone
upon the housetop.
8 Mine enemies reproach me all the day;
and they that are mad against me are sworn
against me.
9 For I have eaten ashes like bread, and
mingled my drink with weeping,
10 Because of thine indignation and thy
wrath: for thou hast lifted me up, and cast
me down.
11 My days *are* like a shadow that declineth; and I am withered like grass.
12 But thou, O LORD, shalt endure for
ever; and thy remembrance unto all generations.

5 Because of my loud groaning
my bones cleave to my flesh.
6 I am like a vulture[p] of the wilderness,
like an owl of the waste places;
7 I lie awake,
I am like a lonely bird on the housetop.
8 All the day my enemies taunt me,
those who deride me use my name for a curse.
9 For I eat ashes like bread,
and mingle tears with my drink,
10 because of thy indignation and anger;
for thou hast taken me up and thrown me away.
11 My days are like an evening shadow;
I wither away like grass.

12 But thou, O LORD, art enthroned for ever;
thy name endures to all generations.

[p] The meaning of the Hebrew word is uncertain

Vulture or **pelican:** The identity of the bird is unknown; the Amer. Trans. offers "jackdaw."

7-8. I lie awake rather than **I watch:** The first stich is, lit., "I am wakeful and I am," but as this seems incomplete, many scholars since Olshausen have emended "and I am" to "and I moan" (ואהמיה; cf. 77:3). **Bird** rather than **sparrow:** See Exeg. on 84:3. **Use my name for a curse:** Either "take an oath against me" or "use my name in an oath."

11. Like an evening shadow: Lit., "a stretched-out shadow." Some ancient versions (LXX, Jerome, Syriac) read, "My days decline like a shadow" (cf. KJV).

2. THE ETERNAL GOD IS ZION'S SAFEGUARD (102:12-22)

This short hymn, which finds in the Lord's eternity the promise of Zion's salvation, rises in vss. 15, 22 to the thought of the day when all the kingdoms of the world will worship the Lord.

12-18. Art enthroned: Lit., "dwellest." **Thy name:** Better, lit., **thy remembrance.**

bird that has lost its mate, sitting alone on the housetop? Further, he is taunted by enemies who **use** [his] **name for a curse.** Nor can he boast innocence, as Job did, for he knows that he must repent in dust and ashes.

> **For I eat ashes like bread,**
> **and mingle tears with my drink.**
> . . . .
> **My days are like an evening shadow;**
> **I wither away like grass.**

It does not follow that with all these afflictions the psalmist was a mere burden to the community.

It is a curious fact that amongst the greatest workers of the world are large numbers who have had to contend with serious physical defects. Florence Nightingale was a marvel of industry, yet most of her time she was bed-ridden. Richard Baxter lived "in continual expectation of death," yet so did he labour and so did he esteem time "that, if any of it passed away in idleness or unprofitableness, it was so long a pain and burden to my mind." And time would fail to tell of men so diverse as Seneca and John Milton, Charles Darwin, Robert Louis Stevenson, and many others who were both great invalids and great workers. Some of them would understand Paul's own words [II Cor. 12:9, 10 Moffatt]: "It is enough for you to have My grace: it is in weakness that (My) power is fully felt. . . . So I am proud to boast my weakness, and thus to have the power of Christ resting on me. It makes me satisfied, for Christ's sake, with weakness, insults, trouble, persecution and calamity; for I am strong just when I am weak." [1]

12-22. ***Hope Born in Desolation.***—At vs. 12 the psalmist turns to the troubles about him. It makes little difference whether he is in Jeru-

[1] Frank H. Ballard, *Spiritual Pilgrimage of St. Paul* (London: Student Christian Movement Press; New York: Harper & Bros., 1931), p. 96. Used by permission.

13 Thou shalt arise, *and* have mercy
upon Zion: for the time to favor her, yea,
the set time, is come.
14 For thy servants take pleasure in her
stones, and favor the dust thereof.
15 So the heathen shall fear the name of
the LORD, and all the kings of the earth thy
glory.
16 When the LORD shall build up Zion,
he shall appear in his glory.
17 He will regard the prayer of the destitute, and not despise their prayer.
18 This shall be written for the generation to come: and the people which shall be
created shall praise the LORD.
19 For he hath looked down from the
height of his sanctuary; from heaven did
the LORD behold the earth;
20 To hear the groaning of the prisoner;
to loose those that are appointed to death;
21 To declare the name of the LORD in
Zion, and his praise in Jerusalem;
22 When the people are gathered together, and the kingdoms, to serve the LORD.

13 Thou wilt arise and have pity on Zion;
it is the time to favor her;
the appointed time has come.
14 For thy servants hold her stones dear,
and have pity on her dust.
15 The nations will fear the name of the LORD,
and all the kings of the earth thy glory.
16 For the LORD will build up Zion,
he will appear in his glory;
17 he will regard the prayer of the destitute,
and will not despise their supplication.

18 Let this be recorded for a generation to come,
so that a people yet unborn may praise the LORD:
19 that he looked down from his holy height,
from heaven the LORD looked at the earth,
20 to hear the groans of the prisoners,
to set free those who were doomed to die;
21 that men may declare in Zion the name of the LORD,
and in Jerusalem his praise,
22 when peoples gather together,
and kingdoms, to worship the LORD.

The second half of vs. 13 seems both long and awkward. Some emend, with the Syriac, to read, "For the time has come to favor her." There may be a reference in vs. 14 to the desolation of Jerusalem. Ideas of a universalistic character appear not only in vs. 15 but also in vs. 22 and in other psalms (e.g., 22:27; 67:7; 96:7; 138:4). **Prayer . . . supplication:** In the Hebrew the word **prayer** occurs twice (so KJV), but the RSV, to avoid this repetition, emends the second one to תחנתם, **their supplication.** The LXX assumes two different Hebrew words. Vs. 18 shows the psalmist's sense of an obligation to future generations.

19-21. His holy height rather than **the height of his sanctuary.** The reference is to the heavenly world. **The prisoners:** Probably those unjustly condemned; the word does not necessarily point to exiles (cf. 79:11). Vs. 21 alludes to public worship in the temple.

---

salem contemplating the ruined capital or mourning in bondage over news that has reached him. In either case he sees with the eyes of a poet, and recalls how dear those broken stones have been to generations of faithful Jews. He could have named men who planned and built, defended and maintained, who by their deeds showed that they loved Zion more than their own lives. Instead, he lifts his heart to the God who has had pity on his people and whose name endures forever. Had his eyes remained upon chaotic masonry, his heart would have continued in mourning. But turning to him who is **enthroned for ever,** hope is reborn. He has a vision of the Lord appearing in glory and rebuilding the city. He is assured that

The nations will fear the name of the LORD,
and all the kings of the earth thy glory.

There is not a word to suggest his own ability to deal with the situation. Had he been challenged, he might well have said that the Lord would use men, men of many types, men to rule and to obey, men to plan and to work with their hands, men to protect and to feed those who labored with the trowel; but the inspiration to begin and the endurance to continue

23 He weakened my strength in the way;
he shortened my days.
24 I said, O my God, take me not away
in the midst of my days: thy years *are*
throughout all generations.
25 Of old hast thou laid the foundation
of the earth: and the heavens *are* the work
of thy hands.
26 They shall perish, but thou shalt endure: yea, all of them shall wax old like a
garment; as a vesture shalt thou change
them, and they shall be changed:
27 But thou *art* the same, and thy years
shall have no end.

23 He has broken my strength in mid-course;
he has shortened my days.
24 "O my God," I say, "take me not hence
in the midst of my days,
thou whose years endure
throughout all generations!"

25 Of old thou didst lay the foundation of
the earth,
and the heavens are the work of thy
hands.
26 They will perish, but thou dost endure;
they will all wear out like a garment.
Thou changest them like raiment, and
they pass away;
27 but thou art the same, and thy years
have no end.

3. The Appeal Continued (102:23-28)

While in this beautiful finale the psalmist returns to his plaint, the sharpness of his pain is now lessened by his fresh awareness of the God whose **years have no end.**

23-24. The text is difficult and may be corrupt. The RSV disregards the various emendations proposed, and attempts to make sense of the M.T. **In mid-course:** Lit., **in the way. Thou whose years endure:** See Exeg. on 90:2.

25-27. Quoted in Heb. 1:10-12. God outlasts what he has created. The transitoriness of the present world is not a common thought in the O.T. (cf. Isa. 34:4; 51:6), and indeed the contrary idea is found in 78:69; 104:5; Eccl. 1:4. There are numerous references in the N.T. to the end of the age (Matt. 24:35; Mark 13:24-25; I Cor. 7:31; Heb. 12:26-27; etc.). W. F. Albright ("Are the Ephod and the Teraphim Mentioned in Ugaritic Literature?" *Bulletin of the American Schools of Oriental Research,* No. 83 [Oct., 1941], p. 40) quotes a curious parallel to the present verse from one of the Ugaritic poems addressed to the goddess Anath:

> The heavens will wear away and will sag
> like the fastening of thy garment.

But thou art the same is a translation supported by most commentators. But as Berry, Oesterley, Leslie, and Weiser have perceived, the Hebrew is, lit., "Thou art he," which

must come from above. Lacking that directing and sustaining power, they were without hope. With it, all things became possible, for

> **he will regard the prayer of the destitute,
> and will not despise their supplication.**

23-24. See Expos. on vss. 1-11, 23-24.

25-28. ***The Fame of the Lord.***—The central teaching of this psalm, as of the whole book, is the reality and the trustworthiness of God. There is nothing exceptional about the theology. The Lord is creator of heaven and earth. They are temporal, but he is eternal; they are subject to change, but he abides ever the same. These are familiar thoughts. It is here, however, more than doctrine: it is living faith. The words are not just repeated: they have been tested and proved. And the Lord is not an abstract principle for philosophers to discuss, not a vague form which men have raised to the heavens and clothed with human ideals, not a blind force or a God who once acted and then departed from the life he had created, not a God who is struggling to express himself and to achieve an unknown purpose. He is the living God, supreme above all gods, creator of all things, who works in and through nature and man. His mighty deeds in history are manifest. His ultimate victory is sure. This is the conviction that enables the psalmist to lift up his head and dry his tears. The same conviction has led the faithful on through trial and persecution.

28 The children of thy servants shall continue, and their seed shall be established before thee.

28 The children of thy servants shall dwell
secure;
their posterity shall be established before thee.

A Psalm of David.

103 Bless the LORD, O my soul: and all that is within me, *bless* his holy name.

A Psalm of David.

103 Bless the LORD, O my soul;
and all that is within me, bless
his holy name!

---

probably means, "Thou art" or "Thou abidest." It is extremely unlikely that the words point to the immutability of God.

28. The psalmist finds solace in the reflection that the generations to come will also dwell in the security of the same Lord.

CIII. Bless the Lord, O My Soul (103:1-22)

This psalm, as the place it has won in the devotional life of the church testifies, is one of the noblest hymns in the O.T. It appears to have had its genesis in an individual's deep sense of gratitude to God for sins forgiven and for recovery from a desperate illness (vss. 3-4), and thus the psalmist's soul is called upon to bless the Lord. From his own immediate experience the poet passes over to the proclamation of what others have found to be true, viz., that the pity of the Lord constantly hovers over all those who fear him (vss. 6-13). Heinrich Herkenne rightly remarks that "scarcely any other part of the O.T. lets us perceive the truth 'God is love' so intimately as Ps. 103" (*Das Buch der Psalmen* [Bonn: Peter Hanstein, 1936; "Die Heilige Schrift des Alten Testamentes"], p. 331). The psalmist's thankfulness is not diminished by his recognition (vss. 14-18) that the days of the individual are numbered **like a flower of the field,** for against this

---

That it was the faith of the early church is clear from the use the writer of the Epistle to the Hebrews makes of the psalm (Heb. 1:10-12). And through the Christian centuries, through sorrow and defeat, temptation and schism, the same words have been continually upon men's lips:

> **Thou, O Lord, art enthroned for ever;**
> **thy name endures to all generations.**

It was the faith of David Brainerd, whose remarkable *Journal* tells how he grew up in Connecticut, became a missionary to the Indians, labored with amazing devotion and died at the age of twenty-nine. Around his deathbed were gathered faithful friends who sang this very psalm. It has been the faith of thousands through the troubles of our own century, some of whom have suffered in exile or died on battlefields, some have mourned in desolate homes yet turned a brave face to an uncomprehending world. The words have not always been on the lips, but the assurance has been in the heart:

> **thou art the same, and thy years have no end.**
> **The children of thy servants shall dwell secure.**

103:1-22. ***Enduring Mercies.***—Bernard L. Manning, of Jesus College, Cambridge, whose early death was so great a loss both to scholarship and to piety, has told us how he was introduced to a study of hymns.[2] As a small boy he attended a Methodist chapel at Caistor, where sometimes the preaching was too tedious for his active mind. He sought diversion first in the architectural features of the building and the manners of the congregation; but before the long discourses were concluded, he was glad to find further interest in books kept in the family pew. Among them was the Methodist hymnbook. In hundreds of verses the lad found much that puzzled but also much that pleased him, and he began to divide them into good hymns and bad ones. Growing interests never crowded out his fondness for the subject, and whenever he turned aside from the age of Wycliffe, or from other subjects upon which he became an authority, he would lecture with enthusiasm on the praise of the church.

All who would understand a nation or a generation should study its sacred songs. Much can be learned from games and amusements,

[2] *The Hymns of Wesley and Watts* (London: Epworth Press, 1942), pp. 7-8.

temporality of man he places the eternity of God. He concludes his hymn by calling upon both heaven and earth to praise the Lord (vss. 19-22). To paraphrase what Calès has said, the elevation of its ideas, the delicacy of its sentiments, and the nobility and limpid elegance of its expression mark this psalm as one of the most beautiful in the Psalter (*Livres des Psaumes,* II, 256).

There is no evidence within the psalm that it was composed for any liturgical purpose. It is possible, however, that it was publicly recited by the author when he expressed his thanksgiving to God in a temple act, and it may thereafter have passed into general use in the temple and have become part of the repertoire of a temple choir. Schmidt suggests that it was rendered antiphonally, but the internal support for this is weak. If the psalm was used in an enthronement of the Lord ceremony, there is nothing to indicate that it was employed only on such an occasion.

The strophic divisions of Kittel and Gunkel are vss. 1-5, 6-13, 14-18, 19-22 (from which RSV varies slightly). Probably, as in Pss. 33; 38; Lam. 5, the number of verses is

---

from law and humor. But to discover the soul of a people, to understand its deepest convictions and its most cherished aspirations, it is wise to read both the published prayers and the hymns of praise. It is more important in some cases than in others. Even in religious circles it can be more rewarding in some denominations than in others. Here was one of Manning's discoveries. "Hymns," he said, "are for us Dissenters what the liturgy is for the Anglican. They are the framework, the setting, the conventional, the traditional part of divine service as we use it. They are, to adopt the language of liturgiologists, the Dissenting Use." [3] He went on to explain how a great festival in a parish church would be correct so far as the collects were concerned, but the hymns would be a gamble; while in one of the Free Churches the prayers might be uncertain but the hymns would be right.

One could wish that this outspoken Cambridge historian had gone on from *The Hymns of Wesley and Watts* to the psalms of Israel. For here more than anywhere else is where we find the heart of the religion which made the Israelites what they were. It is worth while to study the legal books of the O.T.; for there we see how they ordered their public life. It is better to study the great prophets, for there we find divine inspiration. There indeed we feel ourselves to be at the fountainhead of what was distinctive in O.T. piety. But could the prophets have influenced the minds of the people if there had been no psalmists to turn great truths into popular songs? And they did it for a far larger public than they ever dreamed of; their lines have gone out to all the earth and taken a place in the worship of strange peoples. To take away the book of Psalms is to take away not merely that in which antiquarians rejoice; it is to take away the living book of a creative fellowship.

[3] *Ibid.*, p. 133.

In this collection of hymns stands Ps. 103, which reminds us of Manning's words about Wesley's hymnbook:

> In its own way, it is perfect, unapproachable. . . . You cannot alter it except to mar it; it is a work of supreme devotional art by a religious genius. You may compare it with Leonardo's "Last Supper" or King's Chapel; and, as Blackstone said of the English Constitution, the proper attitude to take to it is this: we must venerate where we are not able presently to comprehend.[4]

Better than labored analysis or prosaic exposition is to read and reread it until we have it by heart, and can repeat it in the dark watches of the night. But as an artist may point out the merits of a great picture and leave it to do its own work, so we may mention some of the qualities of this psalm, assured that it will make its own appeal.

The most obvious thing to say about it is that it is a hymn of praise. And in saying this we are at once placing it among the best of good company. A hymnbook that deserves to capture and retain the affections of multitudes must be catholic in spirit. It must find a place for penitence and resignation, for supplication and intercession. But it cannot be a good book unless praise predominates. Even hymns which start with contrition should end with gladness, for they are inspired by a faith which is nothing if not a religion of redemption. "In every thing give thanks," said the apostle (I Thess. 5:18). And he brought that offering of praise not only when he enjoyed Christian fellowship, but even in prison at night. Exactly what songs he and Silas sang in the Philippian prison is not recorded, but it may well have been this psalm with its bold beginning: **Bless the LORD, O my soul: and all that is within me, bless his holy name.**

Praise does not, however, spring up like a

[4] *Ibid.*, p. 14.

2 Bless the LORD, O my soul, and forget
not all his benefits:
3 Who forgiveth all thine iniquities; who
healeth all thy diseases;
4 Who redeemeth thy life from destruction; who crowneth thee with loving-kindness and tender mercies;
5 Who satisfieth thy mouth with good
things; so that thy youth is renewed like
the eagle's.

2 Bless the LORD, O my soul,
and forget not all his benefits,
3 who forgives all your iniquity,
who heals all your diseases,
4 who redeems your life from the Pit,
who crowns you with steadfast love and mercy,
5 who satisfies you with good as long as you live[q]
so that your youth is renewed like the eagle's.

[q] Heb uncertain

meant to correspond to the number of letters in the Hebrew alphabet. The meter is generally 3+3.

There are no certain evidences within the psalm regarding its time of origin. The pronominal suffix **your** or **thy** (יכי), found in vss. 3-5, may be due to Aramaic influence but this proves little with respect to date.

1. The Psalmist Exhorts Himself (103:1-5)

103:1. All that is within me: Lit., "all my inward parts." The plural of this noun occurs only here, and some scholars change the form to the singular. Either reading signifies the psalmist's whole being.

3-5. You (thee) and **your (thy)** refer to the speaker's soul. **Who forgives all your iniquity:** As is evident from vss. 8-13, the Lord's treatment of the psalmist is of a piece with his graciousness to the whole nation. **Diseases:** Always in its literal sense (Deut. 29:22; Jer. 14:18; 16:4; II Chr. 21:19). **The Pit** rather than **destruction:** Here used as a synonym for Sheol (see Exeg. on 16:9-11). **As long as you live:** The Hebrew (עדיך) is obscure. It does not mean **thy mouth,** and if it signifies "thy ornaments," it is inappropriate to the context. Briggs *et al.* emend to עדכי, "while you still are" (cf. 104:33), and this is

root out of dry ground. Nor can it be taken as evidence of a sanguine temperament. The secret is to be found in men's knowledge of God. Manuals of theology will tell much. Autobiographies and diaries will tell more. "Let thy diaries stand thick with dutiful mementos and asterisks of acknowledgment," wrote Sir Thomas Browne in *Christian Morals.*[5] That is what devout men have done, not only in their diaries and autobiographies but in their hymns. They tell of God's goodness, of his mighty acts to them and to their people and in human history. That is what this psalmist does.

1-5. ***Bless the Lord, O My Soul.***—The psalmist speaks first of what God has done for him personally. Here we stumble upon another of the points always made by the student of hymns. The best hymns are always in some sense personal. There is a place for general praise. We must sing sometimes about what the Lord has done for the nation. There are times when under the inspiration of his universal fatherhood we must rejoice together in the reality of human brotherhood. But usually the best hymns, without being subjective, have yet the intensity of personal experience. They become the songs of all mankind because they express in unforgettable language what one man has seen and felt. They become congregational acts, uniting men and women of many types, because they are in the first place so singular. There is not only good evangelical theology in the familiar hymns

Rock of Ages, cleft for me,
Let me hide myself in thee,

and

Jesus, Lover of my soul,
Let me to thy bosom fly,

but a personal experience that makes dogma the most vital thing in the world.

In the earlier verses of Ps. 103 the personal experience may well be on the physical plane. Some of the expressions seem to suggest the praise of one who has been delivered from a sickness that threatened to be a sickness unto death. There is indeed a reference to the for-

[5] Part I, sec. 21.

6 The LORD executeth righteousness and judgment for all that are oppressed.
7 He made known his ways unto Moses, his acts unto the children of Israel.
8 The LORD *is* merciful and gracious, slow to anger, and plenteous in mercy.
9 He will not always chide: neither will he keep *his anger* for ever.
10 He hath not dealt with us after our sins; nor rewarded us according to our iniquities.
11 For as the heaven is high above the earth, *so* great is his mercy toward them that fear him.

6 The LORD works vindication
and justice for all who are oppressed.
7 He made known his ways to Moses,
his acts to the people of Israel.
8 The LORD is merciful and gracious,
slow to anger and abounding in steadfast love.
9 He will not always chide,
nor will he keep his anger for ever.
10 He does not deal with us according to our sins,
nor requite us according to our iniquities.
11 For as the heavens are high above the earth,
so great is his steadfast love toward those who fear him;

---

followed by the RSV. **Like the eagle's:** The size, strength, and comparative longevity of the eagle explain the simile. Possibly there is a reference to the bird's annual molting, though some detect an allusion to the phoenix legend (cf. Job 29:18; 33:25; Isa. 40:31).

2. GOD'S DEALINGS WITH ISRAEL (103:6-13)

6-13. The psalmist surveys God's gracious acts to the children of Israel, comparing the Lord's mercy to the pity of a father for his children. It is instructive that the poet, while commencing in a very personal way (vss. 1-5), cannot for long separate himself from the larger group, the holy people in whose corporate life the individual finds his true well-being. These verses are also notable for their indifference to the atonement procedures of the Hebrew priesthood.

Vindication: Lit., "righteousnesses," hence **righteousness** (see note on "saving help," Exeg. on 88:12). **The people of Israel:** Lit., **the children of Israel.** This phrase, found over six hundred times in the O.T., appears in the Psalms only here and in 148:14. **Slow**

---

giveness of **iniquities**, but the emphasis falls on the fact that the sinner had been very near **the Pit**, and when hope had almost gone, he had been brought back to health and to his place in the worshiping congregation. Some of us know what that means. We know what it is to feel our grip on life failing. We have seen fear and sorrow in the eyes of those who love us. And then, as it were by a miracle of healing, the decline was arrested, our minds were filled with plans for coming days, and the whole house resounded with cheerful salutations. Yet it is doubtful if any of us has plumbed the depths of the psalmist, for the Pit to him meant Sheol. It meant, not as it means for the Christian, transition to a fuller, freer life, but going down to a dark and dismal place where the departed survived indeed, but in a feeble and ineffectual condition. It is by remembering this that we begin to understand the vigor of the personal praise. **Bless the LORD, O my soul, and forget not all his benefits: who forgiveth all thine iniquities; who healeth all thy diseases.**

6-18. *The Lord Is Merciful and Gracious.*—Ps. 103 has such intensity because it is praise with personal experience in it. But the personal experience quickens the historical imagination, and the psalmist without effort passes from his own deliverance to that of his people. In a moment of time he is back in the days of **Moses.** He is reminded of the Exodus, the long journey through the wilderness, the entry into the land of Canaan, the uniting of the twelve tribes into one nation under the house of David. He could have mentioned men who played prominent parts in the story. He could have compiled a list of teachers and leaders who had sustained the courage of the people at critical moments. But it was more natural for him to go beyond the human agent to the divine power that had moved in and through kings and counselors. The secret of the whole story for him was to be found not in human activity but in divine guidance. And this is what he sings with patriotic pride and religious fervor. The children of Israel had sinned and suffered, but the Lord

12 As far as the east is from the west, *so*
far hath he removed our transgressions from
us.
13 Like as a father pitieth *his* children,
so the LORD pitieth them that fear him.
14 For he knoweth our frame; he remembereth that we *are* dust.
15 *As for* man, his days *are* as grass: as a
flower of the field, so he flourisheth.
16 For the wind passeth over it, and it is
gone; and the place thereof shall know it
no more.
17 But the mercy of the LORD *is* from
everlasting to everlasting upon them that
fear him, and his righteousness unto children's children;
18 To such as keep his covenant, and to
those that remember his commandments to
do them.

12 as far as the east is from the west,
so far does he remove our transgressions
from us.
13 As a father pities his children,
so the LORD pities those who fear him.
14 For he knows our frame;
he remembers that we are dust.

15 As for man, his days are like grass;
he flourishes like a flower of the field;
16 for the wind passes over it, and it is gone,
and its place knows it no more.
17 But the steadfast love of the LORD is from
everlasting to everlasting
upon those who fear him,
and his righteousness to children's children,
18 to those who keep his covenant
and remember to do his commandments.

---

to anger: For another view of the Lord's anger cf. 90:7-9. **Keep:** In the sense of "cherish" or "nurture." **His steadfast love toward those who fear him:** This restriction on the operation of God's love (repeated in vss. 13, 17, 18) raises some important theological questions (cf. Exeg. on 97:10-11). **As a father:** The fatherhood of God is referred to in various O.T. passages (Exod. 4:22; Deut. 14:1; 32:6; Isa. 1:2; 45:11; 63:16; 64:8; Jer. 3:4, 19; 31:9; Hos. 11:1; Mal. 1:6; 2:10; 3:17), but it is not the dominant O.T. view of the Lord (cf. Ecclus. 23:1, 4; Wisd. Sol. 2:16; 5:5).

3. The Everlasting Love of God (103:14-18)

14-18. While man's earthly days are limited, each generation is upheld by the same God whose **steadfast love . . . is from everlasting to everlasting. Our frame:** That which is made or formed. **We are dust:** A reference to Gen. 2:7. On man's eventual return to dust see Gen. 3:19; Eccl. 3:20; 12:7; Job 4:19; 10:9; 34:15. It is significant that in vss. 15-16 the psalmist maintains his faith in God despite the fact that he harbors no hope of personal immortality. Vs. 17 is longer than we might expect; Kittel, Gunkel, *et al.* delete **from everlasting** and **upon those who fear him.** Vs. 18 is rather short, and many commentators suggest small additions to the text. **His commandments:** The RSV usually translates this Hebrew word as "precept" (19:8; 111:7; 119:4; etc.).

---

had shown himself **merciful and gracious, slow to anger and abounding in steadfast love.** It is wonderful in the psalmist's eyes, and as he meditates upon the mercy that had saved them, he rises to such a burst of poetry and such a level of religious thought that his lines (vss. 12-13) take their place among the purest passages in all the O.T.

It is patriotic as well as religious verse; but it is not the narrow nationalism that divides men and sets them in rivalry against one another. It is the patriotism that leads us on to thoughts of God's goodness to all mankind. And the psalm moves toward the end with words that apply to us as much as to those of whom the writer was thinking (vss. 15-17). His language here is familiar, but his thought is both doubted and denied in our time. Is there any divine power in history? The question is debated at many intellectual levels. It is doubted by so serious a scholar as H. A. L. Fisher, who in the preface to his *History of Europe* confesses that in history he can find no rhythm or predetermined pattern. He can see only one emergency following upon another, as wave follows wave. It is denied by the orthodox Communist, who insists that history is nothing but a tension and conflict between class and class. All history, it is said, is a history of class struggle. It is also the working creed of many to whom communism

19 The LORD hath prepared his throne in the heavens; and his kingdom ruleth over all.

20 Bless the LORD, ye his angels, that excel in strength, that do his commandments, hearkening unto the voice of his word.

21 Bless ye the LORD, all *ye* his hosts; *ye* ministers of his, that do his pleasure.

22 Bless the LORD, all his works in all places of his dominion: bless the LORD, O my soul.

19 The LORD has established his throne in
the heavens,
and his kingdom rules over all.
20 Bless the LORD, O you his angels,
you mighty ones who do his word,
hearkening to the voice of his word!
21 Bless the LORD, all his hosts,
his ministers that do his will!
22 Bless the LORD, all his works,
in all places of his dominion.
Bless the LORD, O my soul!

4. PRAISE FROM ALL GOD'S WORKS (103:19-22)

19-22. In this strophe the psalmist urges all creation, including the whole company in heaven, to join with him in blessing the Lord.

19. His throne in the heavens: Cf. Exeg. on 11:4-7.

20-21. An invocation to the celestial assembly (see Exeg. on 82:1-8). **Angels:** See Exeg. on 34:4-7. **You mighty ones** (RSV); **that excel in strength** (KJV): A phrase found only here (cf. Joel 3:11), but apparently a synonym for **angels. Hearkening to the voice of his word:** Kittel, Gunkel, *et al.* omit these words as making the line too long. **His hosts:** As this is a masculine plural, and as "host" elsewhere has a feminine plural (but cf. 148:2), many emend **hosts** to "host." **Bless the LORD, O my soul!** Amid the chorus of the whole universe the psalmist returns to his own humble share in the paean of praise.

is otherwise unacceptable. It has crept into the minds of millions in Europe and the Americas, not to speak of the countries of the East. Is man aimlessly blundering his way through the ages, fancying himself the master of his fate but actually the prey of social and economic forces over which he has little control? Or is there

> a divinity that shapes our ends,
> Rough-hew them how we will? [6]

19-22. ***Ministers that Do the Lord's Will.***—We have noted above one of the fundamental questions to which men are always returning. The Bible's answer is clear. It runs through the O.T. and is repeated with conviction and emphasis in the N.T. To it the church is absolutely committed. Man has traveled far. He thinks he can speak of progress. But it is divine power that has led him and divine grace that has redeemed him when he has fallen. The more religious-minded he is, the more firmly he is convinced that divine love is seeking him and using him for purposes beyond anything that he can guess. It is this conviction which is still inspiring hymns of praise.

> Through the night of doubt and sorrow
> Onward goes the pilgrim band,
> Singing songs of expectation,
> Marching to the promised land.[7]

[6] Shakespeare, *Hamlet,* Act V, scene 2.
[7] B. S. Ingemann.

There is no need to pile up quotations. They are all echoes of the psalmist's praise, but with the added conviction that comes from a knowledge of the divine activity in the life and death and resurrection of Jesus Christ, and in the progressive work of the Holy Spirit. "God's world," Malcolm Spencer said, "deserves from us lyrical praise." [8] The writer of these words was thinking primarily of the beauty and bounty of the earth. But what he says is just as true when we think of God's dealings with us personally, of his goodness to us as a nation, of his kindness to all the sons of men. "There is no virtue, no life, no satisfaction to God or man in praise that is faint or formal." [9] **Bless the LORD, all his works in all places of his dominion: bless the LORD, O my soul.** What a transformation there would be in this generation if the church could so recapture this spirit that men and women would go forth from their sanctuaries with a song like that in their hearts!

> Praise, my soul, the King of heaven,
> To his feet thy tribute bring;
> Ransomed, healed, restored, forgiven,
> Who, like me, his praise should sing?
> Praise him! praise him!
> Praise him! praise him!
> Praise the everlasting King! [1]

[8] *Vitality* (London: Student Christian Movement Press, 1931), p. 50.
[9] *Ibid.*
[1] Henry F. Lyte.

104 Bless the LORD, O my soul. O
LORD my God, thou art very great;
thou art clothed with honor and majesty:

104 Bless the LORD, O my soul!
O LORD my God, thou art very
great!
Thou art clothed with honor and majesty,

CIV. BLESS THE LORD, CREATOR OF ALL (104:1-35)

This is another of Israel's great hymns of praise, and Duhm *et al.* think that it may be from the same hand as Ps. 103. As praise of the Lord often springs from some immediate deliverance in which the divine hand is seen, we cannot rule out the possibility that the psalmist has been moved by some such personal experience to sing. The psalm, however, is noteworthy because it keeps its author in the background (cf. vss. 33-34), and it gives itself to the unstinted blessing of God. Its central theme is the Lord's glory and wisdom as manifested in the created world. There is, in fact, in the psalm a philosophy of the cosmos, for the psalmist recognizes a beneficent providence in the ordering of the world. Nothing is made for itself alone, but each is made for another, so that the needs of all are fully met. The psalmist seems quite familiar with one of the creation stories known to Israel, even though it may not yet have taken on the literary form of Gen. 1. The freedom with which he treats this creation tradition shows his originality and poetic genius. His viewpoint is, however, essentially the same as the compiler of the P document: "And God saw every thing that he had made, and behold, it was very good" (Gen. 1:31).

The extent of extraneous influence on this psalm has been much debated. The theme of the poem, the creation and control of nature by a supernatural power, is one that has inspired writers in various cultures, and the basic natural phenomena being what they are, there is some similarity in the way the subject is handled in the literatures of the ancient Near East. But the Gentile hymn that comes closest to Ps. 104 is the Egyptian "Hymn to the Aton" (the sun disk as the source of life), which dates from the time of Akhenaton (1380-1362 B.C.), a ruler best known for his monotheistic interests. Indeed, the resemblance in places is so striking that it has been argued that our psalmist must have had some knowledge of the Egyptian poem, which may have come into Palestine by way of Phoenicia. The most apposite lines of the Egyptian hymn, as translated by John A. Wilson (in J. B. Pritchard, ed., *Ancient Near Eastern Texts Relating to the Old Testament* [Princeton: Princeton University Press, 1950], pp. 370-71, reprinted here by permission), are as follows:

> When thou settest in the western horizon,
> The land is in darkness, in the manner of death.
> Every lion is come forth from his den [cf. 104:20-21].

104:1-35. ***The Way of Meditation.***—It is interesting to notice how many of the best minds are from time to time driven deeper and deeper into the hidden foundations of life. For years and decades many of those who believe themselves to be in the van of progressive movements are content with the realm of action. They congratulate themselves when they invent complicated machines, multiply possessions, and renovate antiquated societies. Imagining themselves to be the makers of a new world, they replan villages and towns, reshape institutions, and continue to put new patches on old garments.

But how often, just when they seem well on the way to the reorganizing of society from top to bottom, the unexpected happens! Ugly passions well up from unsuspected depths, defying all the old conventions. New ideologies follow and quickly serious rents appear in social structures. The result is a widespread sense of frustration, like that which showed itself in a violent form in H. G. Wells's book *Mind at the End of Its Tether.*[2] In it Wells expressed the belief that the battle not only of Western civilization, but of Homo sapiens himself, was lost. Others, not quite so pessimistic, anxiously sought new foundations on which to build. Gradually attention turned from the seen to the unseen, from the reshaping of things to the explosive power of ideas. Statements appeared,

[2] New York: Didier Publishers, 1946.

2 Who coverest *thyself* with light as *with* a garment: who stretchest out the heavens like a curtain:

2 who coverest thyself with light as with
a garment,
who hast stretched out the heavens like a
tent,

At daybreak, when thou arisest on the horizon,
. . . .
All the world, they do their work [cf. 104:22-23].

How manifold it is, what thou hast made!
. . . .
Thou didst create the world according to thy desire [cf. 104:24].

The ships are sailing north and south as well,
. . . .
The fish in the river dart before thy face;
Thy rays are in the midst of the great green sea [cf. 104:25-26].

Thou suppliest their necessities:
Everyone has his food, and his time of life is reckoned [cf. 104:27].

When thou hast risen, they live,
When thou settest they die.
. . . .
For one lives (only) through thee [cf. 104:29-30].

The parallels between the two hymns may be due, as has been claimed, to some acquaintance on the part of our psalmist with the Egyptian poem, although it is strange that he did not utilize other parts of the hymn which would have served his purpose equally well. It is, however, possible to hold that the resemblances between them can be accounted for by their common monotheistic approach to the world of nature. The differences between the poems are actually more notable than the similarities, not the least of the former being that in the Egyptian hymn the sun is the creator, whereas in the Hebrew psalm the sun is but a part of the handiwork of the Lord.

The strophic analysis appears to be vss. 1-4, 5-9, 10-13, 14-18, 19-23, 24-26, 27-30, 31-35. The meter is 3+3, with some variations.

1. The First Stage of Creation (104:1-4; cf. Gen. 1:1-8)

104:1. Clothed with honor and majesty: Cf. 93:1; 96:6; 145:5; Job 37:22; 40:10.

2. Who coverest thyself with light: Probably the primeval light as in Gen. 1:3 (cf. "who . . . dwells in unapproachable light," I Tim. 6:16), hence the "fire" of the divine

---

sometimes in unlikely quarters, that if the world is to be reformed, it had to be born again in the realm of the spirit.

Among the intellectuals of that day was Aldous Huxley, who showed many of the marks of disillusionment. Weary of the noisy, perspiring West, with its endless programs and its vulgar publicity, he turned to the Far East in the hope that he might there find sanity and peace. But the old civilizations of India and China were also in eruption, spreading their lava far and wide. There were, however, in those ancient lands—there are still—men who let vast movements sweep by them while they cultivated the way of meditation. Year after year they pondered not political theories or national wrongs and aspirations, but eternal realities. Surely, said Huxley, these are the men who are worth knowing; and as Ezekiel went to the Israelites in captivity and "sat where they sat" in order that he might see with their eyes and feel as they felt, so Huxley set himself to understand these men of Oriental detachment. He discovered that the way of the mystic is not easy, that it demands sustained concentration and strict discipline. But he believed that this turning from illusion to reality was bound to be a rewarding effort. And he was not alone. Hugh I'Anson Fausset traveled in the same direction, and in *A Modern Prelude* wrote

3 Who layeth the beams of his chambers in the waters: who maketh the clouds his chariot: who walketh upon the wings of the wind:
4 Who maketh his angels spirits; his ministers a flaming fire:
5 *Who* laid the foundations of the earth, *that* it should not be removed for ever.
6 Thou coveredst it with the deep as *with* a garment: the waters stood above the mountains.

3 who hast laid the beams of thy chambers on the waters,
who makest the clouds thy chariot,
who ridest on the wings of the wind,
4 who makest the winds thy messengers,
fire and flame thy ministers.

5 Thou didst set the earth on its foundations,
so that it should never be shaken.
6 Thou didst cover it with the deep as with a garment;
the waters stood above the mountains.

presence (Exod. 3:2; Dan. 7:9; etc). The notion that God is clothed in unearthly light may be one manner of asserting that while men can apprehend some things about God, his complete nature and being are concealed from them. In Second Isaiah the Lord is to be the light of the New Zion (Isa. 60:19). **Like a curtain** is better than **like a tent,** for the heavens are represented as concealing the aforementioned **light.** Cf. the Ugaritic "Poem of Baal," "The heavens themselves enwrapping thee like a mantle" (Gaster, *Thespis,* p. 186).

3. Thy chambers hardly means, as Briggs (*Psalms,* II, 332) suggests, the successive heights or layers of heaven. The word gives some concrete character to the celestial world, but its literal meaning cannot be pressed. Vs. 13 implies that the **chambers** are the sources of the earth's rain. **The clouds thy chariot:** See Exeg. on 68:4-6; cf. 68:33; Deut. 33:26; Isa. 19:1. **The wings of the wind:** The same phrase occurs in 18:10. The RSV emends the M.T. twice in this verse, and also in vs. 4, in order to get **thy** instead of **his** (KJV). Possibly the psalmist was indifferent to these grammatical niceties.

4. Messengers or **angels:** See Exeg. on 34:4-7. **Winds** rather than **spirits,** though the Hebrew can mean either. **Fire and flame** rests on a small emendation (for grammatical reasons), but the M.T., **a flaming fire,** is not impossible. Jewish tradition, on the basis of this verse, claimed that the angels employed on God's errands are winds, and those forming the heavenly choir are fire (Moore, *Judaism,* I, 405).

2. The Foundation of the Earth (104:5-9; cf. Gen. 1:9-10)

5-9. Thou didst set: A slight emendation, from a perfect to a participle. The RSV takes **mountains** and **valleys** in vs. 8 as the subjects of the verbs. But vs. 9 seems to refer

about his spiritual pilgrimage; he explained the importance of solitude, and described the technique for group meditation.[8] The movement did not win many disciples, but it may be that it was one of the significant signs of the times.

One cannot help wondering, however, why these men found it necessary to wander so far afield. The West may have missed its way, yet it has always had quiet, reflective minds. The church may in large measure have failed, yet there are in it men who know the power of the secret place and the shut door. There are groups—and not all of them are found in Quaker meetings—that have proved the efficacy of the promise that where two or three are gathered together Another would be in the midst of them. There are books on the culture of the devotional life that have for many generations been known as masterpieces. And we can never forget, even though others need to be reminded, that there is a Bible which has more to say than any of the holy men of India. There is in the Gospels much material waiting for the closest examination. And there is the book of Psalms, which though in many ways a contrast to the writings of the mystics, has its own profound contribution to make.

It is worth noticing how more than once meditation and speech are bracketed together. This appears not only in the prayer, "Let the words of my mouth, and the meditation of my heart, be acceptable in thy sight . . ." (19:14), but in the suggestion that it is only as the

[8] London: Jonathan Cape, 1933.

7 At thy rebuke they fled; at the voice of thy thunder they hasted away.

8 They go up by the mountains; they go down by the valleys unto the place which thou hast founded for them.

9 Thou hast set a bound that they may not pass over; that they turn not again to cover the earth.

10 He sendeth the springs into the valleys, *which* run among the hills.

11 They give drink to every beast of the field: the wild asses quench their thirst.

12 By them shall the fowls of the heaven have their habitation, *which* sing among the branches.

13 He watereth the hills from his chambers: the earth is satisfied with the fruit of thy works.

7 At thy rebuke they fled;
at the sound of thy thunder they took to flight.
8 The mountains rose, the valleys sank down
to the place which thou didst appoint for them.
9 Thou didst set a bound which they should not pass,
so that they might not again cover the earth.

10 Thou makest springs gush forth in the valleys;
they flow between the hills,
11 they give drink to every beast of the field;
the wild asses quench their thirst.
12 By them the birds of the air have their habitation;
they sing among the branches.
13 From thy lofty abode thou waterest the mountains;
the earth is satisfied with the fruit of thy work.

---

to **waters** of vs. 6, and in this case the verbs of vs. 8 should also have **they,** i.e., the waters, as subject (so KJV). **That they might not again cover the earth:** An expression of the psalmist's faith that the watery chaos before the earth's beginning will never again hold sway.

3. Springs of Water (104:10-13)

10-13. This provision of water for the earth has no parallel in Gen. 1, but in Gen. 7:11 two sources of water are recognized. The subject of the participles in vss. 10, 13-14 is taken in the RSV to be **thou,** not **he** as in KJV.

13. Lofty abode or **chambers:** In vs. 3 the RSV translates the same word **chambers. Thy** represents a small emendation of the M.T. (**his** KJV). The verse shows an awareness of the function of rain in the economy of God, although **the fruit of thy work** may mean all of the Lord's manifold operations, not merely his sending of rain.

---

heart becomes hot with musing that there is any real freedom (39:3; but see Exeg., *in loc.*). Every literary person or public speaker knows the truth concisely stated in the words, "While I was musing the fire burned: then spake I with my tongue." There would be more inspired poetry, better hymns, and more powerful preaching if there were more meditation. We have tried the way of scholarship. We have read more than we have understood, and in spite of Ruskin and other counselors, have thought it more virtuous to skim many volumes than to dig deep into a few. We have tried the way of conference and talked until many have been bewildered. Is it not time we reminded ourselves that before Jesus began his public ministry he was driven of the Spirit into the wilderness, and that before Paul became either a church builder or a missionary he went out to the silence of Arabia? Churches must still insist upon diligent years in academic training for those who would be ministers of the Word and the sacraments, but the invitation of Jesus is not less necessary, "Come ye yourselves apart into a desert place, and rest a while" (Mark 6:31). It is not enough to say that religion is what a man does with his solitude; but religion without solitude will not avail.

But on what are we to meditate? It is not enough to concentrate on the disorders of the world or on our own personal failures. We must have something that will lift us above ourselves

14 He causeth the grass to grow for the cattle, and herb for the service of man: that he may bring forth food out of the earth;
15 And wine *that* maketh glad the heart of man, *and* oil to make *his* face to shine, and bread *which* strengtheneth man's heart.
16 The trees of the LORD are full *of sap;* the cedars of Lebanon, which he hath planted;
17 Where the birds make their nests: *as for* the stork, the fir trees *are* her house.
18 The high hills *are* a refuge for the wild goats; *and* the rocks for the conies.

14 Thou dost cause the grass to grow for the cattle,
and plants for man to cultivate,[r]
that he may bring forth food from the earth,
15 and wine to gladden the heart of man,
oil to make his face shine,
and bread to strengthen man's heart.
16 The trees of the LORD are watered abundantly,
the cedars of Lebanon which he planted.
17 In them the birds build their nests;
the stork has her home in the fir trees.
18 The high mountains are for the wild goats;
the rocks are a refuge for the badgers.

[r] Or *fodder for the animals that serve man*

4. VEGETATION (104:14-18; cf. Gen. 1:11-13)

14. Plants for man to cultivate: Lit., "herbage for the labor (or service) of man" (cf. KJV). **Fodder for the animals that serve man** (RSV mg.) is supported by Ehrlich *et al.*

15. The psalmist accepts the simple joys of ordinary life as the gift of God. This wholesome view of the nature and needs of the body is characteristic of O.T. piety.

16. The trees of the LORD: Probably trees which grow naturally without human planting or care (cf. Num. 24:6). Some take the phrase to mean "gigantic trees" (cf. 36:6, "the mountains of God"). **Are watered abundantly:** Lit., "are satisfied." On **cedars** see Exeg. on 80:10*b*; on **Lebanon** see Exeg. on 72:16.

17. The fir trees: Probably junipers or cypresses; Buhl *et al.,* to get better parallelism, emend to בראשם, "in the tops of them."

18. This verse has no connection with vegetation, but it illustrates how nature accommodates the animal world. **Badgers** or **conies:** *Hyrax Syriacus,* a small, harelike, ungulate mammal (cf. Prov. 30:26).

and give us wide horizons. Here again the psalmists supply truths of great importance.

One thing they meditated upon was the will of God as it is revealed in the law and the statutes. This is the central theme of the longest of all the psalms; and as we read its 176 verses we see that the study of the law was no barren duty, but a task full of profit and delight. It gave men such personal confidence that they felt themselves to be wiser than many of their teachers. They rejoiced because they believed that they had laid hold of essential truth both for the individual and for the community. That is why in Ps. 119 there are only five or six verses in which there is no allusion to the law of Moses.

There are dangers in this kind of meditation. There is the danger of a legalism which begets external righteousness. The prophets found it necessary constantly to remind men that God requires more than sacrifices, more even than equity; he requires the humble spirit and the contrite heart. These things are repeated by Jesus Christ, who never ceased to warn men against hypocrisy and to plead for a piety that shrinks from ostentation.

There is a place, moreover, not only for the commandments of Moses, but for the fewer and deeper commandments of the gospel. Without them religion becomes vague and preaching becomes indefinite. The world is waiting for a message that sounds forth as a bugle call. We cannot give it unless we return to the Bible and train ourselves in meditation on its commandments as well as its promises.

Another thing the psalmists meditated upon was the power of God revealed in history. They were always going back to the distant past when their fathers were slaves in Egypt. They made sure that each new generation was properly instructed in the emancipating work of Moses, the chief events of the wilderness wander-

19 He appointed the moon for seasons:
the sun knoweth his going down.
20 Thou makest darkness, and it is night:
wherein all the beasts of the forest do creep
forth.
21 The young lions roar after their prey,
and seek their meat from God.
22 The sun ariseth, they gather themselves together, and lay them down in their
dens.
23 Man goeth forth unto his work and to
his labor until the evening.
24 O LORD, how manifold are thy works!
in wisdom hast thou made them all: the
earth is full of thy riches.
25 *So is* this great and wide sea, wherein
are things creeping innumerable, both small
and great beasts.

19 Thou hast made the moon to mark the
seasons;
the sun knows its time for setting.
20 Thou makest darkness, and it is night,
when all the beasts of the forest creep
forth.
21 The young lions roar for their prey,
seeking their food from God.
22 When the sun rises, they get them away
and lie down in their dens.
23 Man goes forth to his work
and to his labor until the evening.

24 O LORD, how manifold are thy works!
In wisdom hast thou made them all;
the earth is full of thy creatures.
25 Yonder is the sea, great and wide,
which teems with things innumerable,
living things both small and great.

---

5. The Moon and the Sun (104:19-23)

19-23. The two great heavenly bodies (cf. Gen. 1:14-19) were widely worshiped as deities in the ancient world, but the psalmist views them as the Lord's creatures, designed to serve the divine purpose.

19. The M.T. "he has made" **(he appointed** KJV) is emended by the RSV to **thou hast made,** as being more agreeable to the context. **The moon,** being pivotal for the Hebrew calendar, is mentioned before **the sun.**

20. It is the Lord, not the absence of the sun, that brings the night.

21. The dependence of the animals upon God's benevolent darkness.

23. The labor of man is part of God's ordering of the world (cf. Gen. 3:17-19).

6. The Sea and Its Animals (104:24-26; cf. Gen. 1:20-23)

24-26. Thy creatures rather than **thy riches:** Cf. the cognate verb in Gen. 14:19, 22. **Which teems with things innumerable:** Lit., "wherein are moving things innumerable" (cf. 69:34). **The ships:** In a list of natural phenomena **ships** seems anomalous; some emend to תנינים, "the sea monsters" (cf. Gen. 1:21), others to אימות, "the fearful things."

---

ing, and the coming at last to the Land of Promise. These things, written not upon perishable stone or parchment, but upon the minds and hearts of the people, became an inspiration and a court of appeal in every crisis.

Not that they thought of history as we do. We call one a romantic, another a scientific, and yet another a philosophical historian. The O.T. writers have affinities with them all, but actually they make another group, a religious school. History for them was not a panorama, often broken and dim, in which are seen the adventures of man on the earth from the earliest beginnings to the last syllable of recorded time. History, as they understood it, was the action of God in and through men and nations. What they rejoiced to discover and set forth was not the wisdom and initiative of man, but the goodness and mercy of God. Is there no place in modern education for such discipline as that? Will not all our attempts to educate go wrong if that concern is not recaptured? Is not our sense of frustration largely due to the fact that we have put our trust in secular education and it has failed us?

Yet another thing the psalmists delighted to meditate upon was the glory of God in nature. They considered the heavens (vss. 2-4), and looked upon the earth (vss. 5-9). They heard the sound of rippling water (vss. 10-13), and described the grass that grew for the cattle (vss. 14-18). They watched the moon and the sun (vss. 19-23), and gazed out at the sea (vss. 24-26). The whole of life (vss. 27-30) spelled out for them the glory of God (vss. 31-35). No one now maintains that theirs was the last word

26 There go the ships: *there is* that leviathan, *whom* thou hast made to play therein.
27 These wait all upon thee; that thou
mayest give *them* their meat in due season.
28 *That* thou givest them they gather:
thou openest thine hand, they are filled
with good.
29 Thou hidest thy face, they are
troubled: thou takest away their breath,
they die, and return to their dust.
30 Thou sendest forth thy spirit, they are
created: and thou renewest the face of the
earth.

26 There go the ships,
and Leviathan which thou didst form to sport in it.

27 These all look to thee,
to give them their food in due season.
28 When thou givest to them, they gather it up;
when thou openest thy hand, they are filled with good things.
29 When thou hidest thy face, they are dismayed;
when thou takest away their breath, they die
and return to their dust.
30 When thou sendest forth thy Spirit,[s] they are created;
and thou renewest the face of the ground.

[s] Or *breath*

Leviathan: In Job 41 this creature is apparently a crocodile, but here and in Job 3:8 (and possibly Ps. 74:14), it seems to be an enormous marine animal (see Exeg. on 74:14).

7. All Life Looks to God (104:27-30; cf. Gen. 1:29-30)

29-30. Thou takest away: Lit., "thou gatherest," i.e., God takes back what he once gave. **Their breath** (רוחם): The animating principle in all life, and the gift of God (Gen. 6:17; 7:15, 22; Job 27:3; etc.); at death it returns to its Giver (Job 34:14; Eccl.

---

in scientific explanation. Perhaps they were not much better even in artistic appreciation. One writer of our time has complained of their "tendency to the gigantesque."[4] They were prone, he says, to pile mountains on mountains, and to glory in thousands, and ten thousand times ten thousand. And this, he suggests, is not imagination but the lack of it. He contrasts it with the way Jesus delighted in little things, not massed mountains but common flowers and sparrows, sheep and trees, not multitudes that no man could number but ordinary persons and little children. This not unsympathetic critic finds many similarities between the transition from the O.T. to the N.T., and the transition from Egyptian to Greek art.

Such criticism is, however, only partly true of Ps. 104. It begins with **the heavens** stretched forth **like a tent,** and the all-pervading **light** with which God covers (envelops; hides?) himself as **with a garment.** It speaks of the **clouds** as his **chariot,** and the **wind** and **the fire** as his **ministers.** The canvas is certainly large, but there is nothing commonplace about the picture. And there is interest in the minute as well as in the immense. Notice the reference to the **springs** that **gush forth in the valleys,** the wild beasts and **asses** that come, perhaps from the hot and arid desert, to **quench their thirst.** Notice the interest in birds that nest among the branches—the natural delight in the coming of spring, bringing beauty where once had been barrenness. Maybe the inspiration for the early verses derived from foreign sources, from Babylonian and Egyptian hymns of praise;[5] but when the psalmist comes to the **wild goats** and the **conies** (or rock badgers) and the beasts of the forest prowling by night and man setting forth in the morning for the work of the day—in all this he is speaking of that which he has himself seen.

And there is more: there is the religious note, the sense of God in things both great and small, the signs of his providence in all that he has made, the willingness to bow the knee in worship and to lift the voice in praise. This is what makes Ps. 104 so solemn and yet so glad, so

[4] Rorke, *In Search of a Personal Creed,* p. 33; cf. Expos. on Ps. 150.

[5] See Exeg., pp. 550-51, where this psalm is suggestively compared with Akhenaton's hymn to the sun-god, composed in the fourteenth century B.C.; cf. also Samuel Terrien, *The Psalms and Their Meaning for Today* (Indianapolis: Bobbs-Merrill, 1952), pp. 61-63.

31 The glory of the LORD shall endure
for ever: the LORD shall rejoice in his works.
32 He looketh on the earth, and it
trembleth: he toucheth the hills, and they
smoke.
33 I will sing unto the LORD as long as I
live: I will sing praise to my God while I
have my being.
34 My meditation of him shall be sweet:
I will be glad in the LORD.
35 Let the sinners be consumed out of the
earth, and let the wicked be no more. Bless
thou the LORD, O my soul. Praise ye the
LORD.

105 O give thanks unto the LORD;
call upon his name: make known
his deeds among the people.

31 May the glory of the LORD endure for
ever,
may the LORD rejoice in his works,
32 who looks on the earth and it trembles,
who touches the mountains and they
smoke!
33 I will sing to the LORD as long as I live;
I will sing praise to my God while I
have being.
34 May my meditation be pleasing to him,
for I rejoice in the LORD.
35 Let sinners be consumed from the earth,
and let the wicked be no more!
Bless the LORD, O my soul!
Praise the LORD!

105 O give thanks to the LORD, call on
his name,
make known his deeds among the peoples!

12:7). **Their dust:** Cf. Exeg. on 103:14-18. **Thy Spirit:** The Hebrew is רוחך, and Luther and many moderns render this **thy breath** (RSV mg.; cf. vs. 29).

8. Concluding Doxology (104:31-35)

34. May my meditation be pleasing to him is preferable to **My meditation of him shall be sweet.**

35. This is not an ideal solution of the problem of evil, but it is a common way for the psalmists to express their conviction that the good will ultimately triumph (cf. 1:4-6; 5:5-6; 37:38; 74:11; see Exeg. on 139:1-24).

CV. God Is Mindful of His Covenant (105:1-45)

This is a hymn of praise, intended, as is clear from vss. 1-4, for use by the congregation, although there is no clue to the occasion which originally called it forth. Like

universal in its appeal and yet so personal in its ministry. The Israelite who wrote it, and the Englishman Gilbert White, who gave us the *Natural History of Selborne*,[6] would have appreciated each other. Someone has said that the whole world did "contract into a span" when the old parson of Selborne saw or heard some newly arrived birds. There is in this psalm the same quiet enjoyment of simple things, the same feeling of wealth and well-being in so rich and beautiful a world. How could so religious a poem end upon any other note than the one we find here,

Bless the LORD, O my soul!
Praise the LORD!

Thus the psalmists meditated and found sweet their fellowship with God. It is hardly necessary to add that the spirit and the methods are not those of the Eastern mystic; he may be an expert in introspection, but he is content if he can penetrate further and further into the mysterious depths of his own mind. He does not often end in praise. He does not make one feel the glory of setting suns, or the peace in which man might live if only he set his heart upon the living God. His gospel, if indeed he finds one, is more like the gloom of Ecclesiastes than the gladness of the N.T. But at least he seeks, believing that he will find. Are we seriously seeking? We cannot hope to minister to the depths of human need unless we are. Only a church that is learning to meditate upon God, only a church that is learning with Christ to sit in the heavenly places, can bring hope and joy to the generation it would try to serve. Only by setting our affections on the things that are above may we help men to exclaim, **The earth is full of thy riches.**

105:1-45. ***Going over Our Knowledge.***—Prothero, in his popular storehouse of historical

[6] New York: D. Appleton & Co., 1895.

2 Sing unto him, sing psalms unto him:
talk ye of all his wondrous works.
3 Glory ye in his holy name: let the heart
of them rejoice that seek the LORD.
4 Seek the LORD, and his strength: seek
his face evermore.
5 Remember his marvelous works that he
hath done; his wonders, and the judgments
of his mouth;
6 O ye seed of Abraham his servant, ye
children of Jacob his chosen.

2 Sing to him, sing praises to him,
tell of all his wonderful works!
3 Glory in his holy name;
let the hearts of those who seek the
LORD rejoice!
4 Seek the LORD and his strength,
seek his presence continually!
5 Remember the wonderful works that he
has done,
his miracles, and the judgments he uttered,
6 O offspring of Abraham his servant,
sons of Jacob, his chosen ones!

Pss 78; 106; 107; 135; 136, it was inspired in part by the contemplation of the nation's history, particularly of that period which commences with Abraham and ends with the conquest of Palestine. The events cited are carefully selected as well as idealized, as is evident from the lack of allusions to the people's waywardness and complaints. The material thus presented serves to illustrate the psalmist's philosophy of history, viz., that in these great events of Israel's past a guiding Hand has been at work. Possibly the times in which the author lived were such as to warrant a review of these familiar facts in order to steady and encourage his contemporaries. His concluding observation, while not elaborated, should not be overlooked: the end of the Lord's merciful dealings with Israel is **that they should keep his statutes.**

This psalm was in existence when the Chronicler worked, for vss. 1-15 appear as vss. 8-22 in the composite poem found in I Chr. 16. There is no strophic structure apart from the divisions in respect of contents. The meter is 3+3, with the usual variations.

1. Summons to Thanksgiving (105:1-6)

105:1-6. Peoples, not **people.** A limited universalism is implied, for the Gentiles are at least to be made aware of the Lord's **deeds** (cf. 9:11). **His presence:** Lit., **his face. The judgments he uttered:** Lit., **the judgments of his mouth. His chosen ones:** Better parallelism is found in some Hebrew MSS which read "his chosen one."

---

facts, reminds us that the opening words of this psalm are inscribed upon the pulpit at Kidderminster, once occupied by Richard Baxter.[7] There are many lines here well fitted to warm the heart of him who has been called to the ministry of the Word and the sacraments. Let us, however, concentrate upon vs. 5, in order to understand the things that were uppermost in the psalmist's mind.

Remember the wonderful works that he has done, his miracles, and the judgments he uttered.

Ernest Dimnet has written some interesting paragraphs on "going over our knowledge." He cites a famous painter who used to take his son on rambles through the country around Boulogne. Now and again they would pause, turn their backs on the landscape, and test each other's recollection of what they had seen. He mentions also two other Frenchmen who relieved the tedium of imprisonment by going over together what they could remember of history, literature, and philosophy. They discovered that though they were deprived of books, pen, and paper, the weariness of imprisonment was thus abated, their knowledge became orderly, their minds freer, and what might have been wasted time became a most profitable experience. Starting thus, the author exhorts his readers to go and do likewise—to fill up leisure moments by recalling the places they had visited, the works of art they had seen, the great men of whom they had read. "Go mentally over what you remember," urges this most practical of writers, and even though at first it may seem a dull mental exercise, you will soon find it to be "the most vitalizing relaxation." [8]

The author of Ps. 105 in his own way had arrived at some of the same conclusions. Especially he knew the value of time spent in

[7] *Psalms in Human Life,* p. 228.

[8] *The Art of Thinking* (New York: Simon & Schuster, 1928), pp. 153, 155.

7 He *is* the LORD our God: his judgments
are in all the earth.
8 He hath remembered his covenant for
ever, the word *which* he commanded to a
thousand generations.
9 Which *covenant* he made with Abraham, and his oath unto Isaac;
10 And confirmed the same unto Jacob
for a law, *and* to Israel *for* an everlasting
covenant:
11 Saying, Unto thee will I give the land
of Canaan, the lot of your inheritance:
12 When they were *but* a few men in
number; yea, very few, and strangers in it.
13 When they went from one nation to
another, from *one* kingdom to another people;
14 He suffered no man to do them
wrong: yea, he reproved kings for their
sakes;

7 He is the LORD our God;
his judgments are in all the earth.
8 He is mindful of his covenant for ever,
of the word that he commanded, for a
thousand generations,
9 the covenant which he made with Abraham,
his sworn promise to Isaac,
10 which he confirmed to Jacob as a statute,
to Israel as an everlasting covenant,
11 saying, "To you I will give the land of
Canaan
as your portion for an inheritance."

12 When they were few in number,
of little account, and sojourners in it,
13 wandering from nation to nation,
from one kingdom to another people,
14 he allowed no one to oppress them;
he rebuked kings on their account,

2. THE COVENANT WITH THE PATRIARCHS (105:7-15; cf. Gen. 12:1-20; 17:1-27; 26:1-35; 28:1-22)

13. The reference is to the migration from Ur and Haran, the movements in Canaan, Abraham's visit to Egypt, Jacob's journey to Haran, etc. (Gen. 11:27-32; 12:1–13:18; 20:1-18; 28:1–29:35).

retrospect, and wanted his countrymen to fortify themselves with a discipline he had found fruitful. Had it been the concern of the moment, he might have urged the individual to go over the years of his own life and to rejoice in every mark of divine protection and guidance. Actually, however, he was concerned with the nation, and with the encouragement to be derived from a survey of the centuries right back to the earliest events of which records or tradition spoke. There was plenty in the long story to hold interest—many remarkable personalities, many perils and dramatic crises, many miraculous deliverances. Some of these he proceeds to mention, beginning with Abraham and Isaac and the solemn covenant that God had made with them. He touches upon their early tribulations, their domicile in Egypt and the privations imposed upon them by the Pharaoh, the deliverance that was wrought by Moses and Aaron, the weariness and special providences of the wilderness. All of it is familiar to us, and must have been still more familiar to him who wrote it—the plagues, the quails, the water from the rock, the bread from heaven—but it is set down with enjoyment and leads up to the splendid conclusion.

So he led forth his people with joy,
his chosen ones with singing.

There are several things here that call for comment. First, notice the fact that the psalmist is quite content to repeat what everyone knew. This would not commend itself to some writers who would be offended if anyone should consider their work conventional or repetitive. But is it necessary always to appear original, and may not anxiety to say something that has not been said before destroy inspiration and lead to barrenness? Is it not true that the best songs come not from those who are afraid of the familiar, but from those who have pondered faithfully the common realities of life and restated them with creative energy? "Great artists," said R. Ellis Roberts, "rarely start as rebels. Shelley, the rebel in morals, was a traditionalist in literature, and all our greatest creative artists have begun traditionally—often by imitation. This is as true of Shakespeare as of Blake, of Tennyson as of W. B. Yeats."[9] There is, of course, a repetition that is maddening, like the continual telling of trivial stories. But there is a repetition which is not only tolerated but welcomed, and is indeed essential in education. A friend's morning greeting may be as regular as dawn or sunset, but if there is sincerity in it, it brings gladness to the heart. The kiss of a parent is not a solitary act, but one that has its

[9] *Christianity and the Crisis,* p. 75.

15 *Saying,* Touch not mine anointed, and do my prophets no harm.
16 Moreover he called for a famine upon the land: he brake the whole staff of bread.
17 He sent a man before them, *even* Joseph, *who* was sold for a servant:
18 Whose feet they hurt with fetters: he was laid in iron:
19 Until the time that his word came: the word of the LORD tried him.
20 The king sent and loosed him; *even* the ruler of the people, and let him go free.
21 He made him lord of his house, and ruler of all his substance:

15 saying, "Touch not my anointed ones,
do my prophets no harm!"

16 When he summoned a famine on the land,
and broke every staff of bread,
17 he had sent a man ahead of them,
Joseph, who was sold as a slave.
18 His feet were hurt with fetters,
his neck was put in a collar of iron;
19 until what he had said came to pass
the word of the LORD tested him.
20 The king sent and released him,
the ruler of the peoples set him free;
21 he made him lord of his house,
and ruler of all his possessions,

---

15. **My anointed ones:** The plural of this noun is found only here and in the parallel passage in I Chr. 16:22. The reference presumably is to the patriarchs and possibly to their families, **anointed** being used in an honorific sense. **My prophets:** In Gen. 20:7 Abraham is referred to as a prophet; the psalmist applies the term "to the patriarchs generally as the recipients of Divine revelation" (Kirkpatrick, *Psalms,* p. 618).

3. THE JOSEPH STORY BEGINS (105:16-22; cf. Gen. 37:1–41:57)

16. **Staff of bread:** The phrase occurs in Lev. 26:26; Ezek. 4:16; etc. (cf. Isa. 3:1), and means the support given by bread, hence the bread supply (Gunkel, *ad loc.,* seems fanciful).

18. **Whose feet they hurt** represents the M.T. and is quite satisfactory. The RSV, following Ehrlich, repoints the verb to get **his feet were hurt.** The Hebrew of vs. 18*b* is "his soul came [into] iron." Wellhausen renders it, "he was put into irons"; cf. **he was laid in iron.** Some think that "soul" here means "neck" (cf. 69:1), and that the reference is to a prisoner's iron chain or collar. Hence, **his neck was put in a collar of iron.**

---

recurring place. The best things cannot be uttered once and then left. They must be reiterated so that aspects not seen at first may be appreciated. In none of this did it occur to the psalmist that apology was needed. And the supreme fact that emerged, the fact of the unfailing goodness and power of God, was one that must be repeated with growing wonder and praise.

Second, notice the psalmist's contentment to take a bird's-eye view of history. Instead of settling down to a particular period he makes a rapid summary of events from the earliest times down to the settlement in the land of Canaan. We may remind ourselves of the saying of the Preacher, "To every thing there is a season, and a time to every purpose under the heaven: a time to be born, and a time to die; a time to plant, and a time to pluck up that which is planted" (Eccl. 3:1-2). Similarly, there is a time for intensive study of a special period and a time for the outline. It is true in dealing with one's personal experience, or with local history, as it is true of nations or indeed of humanity. For certain purposes we use telescopes, and for other purposes magnifying glasses. We are here concerned with one method, and it has obvious merits.

In every story that is worth telling there are outstanding features. They may be catastrophes, with crisis following crisis, and men complaining that there is no one to turn to for salvation, no commanding genius on earth or divine protector in heaven. They may be deliverances, sudden and apparently miraculous deliverances, and men may rejoice in them without understanding their real meaning. In either case, as in both, being in the middle of events, we may not be able to see the forest for the trees. But when we survey the whole landscape, as it were from a high mountain, we may detect signs of supernatural guidance. The psalmist would have found marks of divine leadership had he concentrated upon a part of the story. There was

22 To bind his princes at his pleasure;
and teach his senators wisdom.
23 Israel also came into Egypt; and Jacob
sojourned in the land of Ham.
24 And he increased his people greatly;
and made them stronger than their enemies.
25 He turned their heart to hate his people, to deal subtilely with his servants.
26 He sent Moses his servant; *and* Aaron
whom he had chosen.
27 They showed his signs among them,
and wonders in the land of Ham.
28 He sent darkness, and made it dark;

22 to instruct[t] his princes at his pleasure,
and to teach his elders wisdom.

23 Then Israel came to Egypt;
Jacob sojourned in the land of Ham.
24 And the Lord made his people very fruitful,
and made them stronger than their foes.
25 He turned their hearts to hate his people,
to deal craftily with his servants.

26 He sent Moses his servant,
and Aaron whom he had chosen.
27 They wrought his signs among them,
and miracles in the land of Ham.

[t] Gk Syr Jerome: Heb *to bind*

---

22. To instruct: An emended text (ליסר), supported by the LXX, Jerome, the Syriac, giving better sense and good parallelism. The Hebrew is **to bind. Senators:** The only place in the O.T. where the KJV uses this translation; the Hebrew is usually rendered **elders.**

4. The Migration to Egypt (105:23-25; cf. Gen. 46:1–Exod. 1:22)

23-25. Ham: See Exeg. on 78:51. The RSV supplies **the Lord** as the subject of the verbs in vs. 24. **Their hearts:** I.e., of the Egyptians.

5. Moses and the Plagues (105:26-36)

As in Ps. 78, there is no agreement in detail with the plague traditions of Exod. 7–12.

27. They wrought or **they showed:** Duhm *et al.*, following the LXX, Jerome, and the Syriac, emend to "he wrought" (שם), making the verb more consonant with those in the adjoining verses.

---

no room for hesitation when it came to a review of the whole.

The masters of the devotional life are just as confident in recommending the rapid review in prayer and meditation. The author of *The Interior Life* has a chapter on self-examination, and strongly recommends a brief glance at the end of the day.

> "Do not try to go over in detail all the things you have done or left undone during the day," he says in effect. "It is not what you have done that matters, but the spirit in which you have done it. Ask yourself what has been the *tone* of the day's living. Has it been a *good* day or a *bad* day? Has its tendency been upward, or downward?" It will not take you long to find out. A "glance" will do the work.[10]

Notice further that the psalmist deliberately fixes here upon the more favorable events in the national history. Not that he does this exclusively. He makes mention of trials and hardships, but only in order to show how good came out of evil, and how man's extremity was God's opportunity. There were less pleasing occurrences that might have been cited (cf. Ps. 106): failures through pride and willfulness, defeats through lack of unity, ignominy through lack of faith and sustained purpose (cf. 106:37). But in the main the psalmist avoids a depressing catalogue and allows his eye to rest upon the pleasing.

Was he justified in this? Should we do well to remember our victories and to ignore our defeats? Again we may quote the Preacher of Jerusalem, "To every thing there is a season." There is a time to remember and a time to forget, and blessed is the man who remembers the things that ought to be remembered and forgets the things that ought to be forgotten. There is a time to remember the sorrows as well as the joys, the reverses as well as the successes. But that raises other questions on how we remember, and how we use the lessons that come

[10] Ed. Joseph Tissot (tr. W. H. Mitchell; London: Burns Oates & Washbourne, 1913), pp. 318-21, as cited by William Adams Brown, *The Life of Prayer in a World of Science* (New York: Charles Scribner's Sons, 1927), p. 178.

and they rebelled not against his word.
29 He turned their waters into blood,
and slew their fish.
30 Their land brought forth frogs in
abundance, in the chambers of their kings.
31 He spake, and there came divers sorts
of flies, *and* lice in all their coasts.
32 He gave them hail for rain, *and* flaming fire in their land.
33 He smote their vines also and their fig
trees; and brake the trees of their coasts.
34 He spake, and the locusts came, and
caterpillars, and that without number,
35 And did eat up all the herbs in their
land, and devoured the fruit of their
ground.
36 He smote also all the firstborn in their
land, the chief of all their strength.

28 He sent darkness, and made the land dark;
they rebelled[u] against his words.
29 He turned their waters into blood,
and caused their fish to die.
30 Their land swarmed with frogs,
even in the chambers of their kings.
31 He spoke, and there came swarms of flies,
and gnats throughout their country.
32 He gave them hail for rain,
and lightning that flashed through their land.
33 He smote their vines and fig trees,
and shattered the trees of their country.
34 He spoke, and the locusts came,
and young locusts without number;
35 which devoured all the vegetation in their land,
and ate up the fruit of their ground.
36 He smote all the first-born in their land,
the first issue of all their strength.

[u] Cn Compare Gk Syr: Heb *they did not rebel*

---

28. They rebelled not: This is the Hebrew, but it seems inappropriate. The RSV, supported by the LXX and the Syriac, both of which, however, use another verb, drops the negative. Hitzig *et al.* emend מרו to שמרו and obtain "and they did not keep."

31-34. Gnats or "mosquitos" rather than **lice. Lightning that flashed through their land:** Lit., **flaming fire in their land. Young locusts:** I.e., locusts in the young unwinged stage, hence **caterpillars.**

35-36. Devoured . . . ate up or **did eat up . . . devoured:** These renderings imply two different verbs, whereas the Hebrew uses the same verb (ויאכל) twice. To avoid this unusual repetition, Duhm *et al.* emend the second verb to ויכל, "and consumed." **The first issue** rather than **the chief.**

6. The Exodus and the Wilderness Wanderings (105:37-42)

37-42. Israel: The Hebrew is **them. None . . . who stumbled** is better than **not one feeble person.** Vs. 38 reads, lit., with the KJV, **for the fear of them** [i.e., of the Hebrews]

---

to us when we remember. One thing must be resisted, the dwelling upon failures in such a way that we become the victims of remorse and never proceed to repentance. There are few exercises more debilitating than that, as anyone can see who studies the stories of Nathaniel Hawthorne, to mention but one with a genius for such writing. *The Scarlet Letter* no doubt is more than a demonstration of the pathology of remorse, but that it surely is. *The House of the Seven Gables* makes clear the deep-rooted character of evil by describing the blight that spreads from wrongdoing, not only on wrong-doers but upon generations of innocent folk. It is not so much with the sour grapes eaten by the fathers that Hawthorne was concerned as with the setting of the children's teeth on edge. And we are made to see the corroding effects of insincerity and the depressing effects of shame. Those who have done wrong cannot forget, nor can they repent in the sense of catching sight of the true goal and consciously starting toward it. Better not to remember at all than to live in the past like that.[1]

Notice also the simplicity of the psalmist's philosophy. He must explain the development of the national life, and it never occurs to him to do so by describing the national genius or prowess. They had produced remarkable personalities, men who could take their place with the

[1] So much can be said without making any subtraction from the important role which Hawthorne played in American literature by very reason of his stress on the reality of evil. Editors.

37 He brought them forth also with silver and gold: and *there was* not one feeble *person* among their tribes.

38 Egypt was glad when they departed: for the fear of them fell upon them.

39 He spread a cloud for a covering; and fire to give light in the night.

40 *The people* asked, and he brought quails, and satisfied them with the bread of heaven.

41 He opened the rock, and the waters gushed out; they ran in the dry places *like* a river.

42 For he remembered his holy promise, *and* Abraham his servant.

37 Then he led forth Israel with silver and gold,
and there was none among his tribes who stumbled.
38 Egypt was glad when they departed,
for dread of them had fallen upon it.
39 He spread a cloud for a covering,
and fire to give light by night.
40 They asked, and he brought quails,
and gave them bread from heaven in abundance.
41 He opened the rock, and water gushed forth;
it flowed through the desert like a river.
42 For he remembered his holy promise,
and Abraham his servant.

---

fell upon them [i.e., the Egyptians]. **Cloud . . . fire:** Cf. Exod. 13:21; 14:19-20. **The people asked:** The Hebrew is "he asked," but the RSV, with Duhm *et al.,* and supported by the LXX, Jerome, and the Syriac, emends to **they asked. Quails:** Cf. Exod. 16:12-13. **Bread from heaven:** The manna is thus designated in Exod. 16:4 (see Exeg. on 78:24). **He opened the rock:** Cf. Exod. 17:1-7. Contrary to both the RSV and the KJV, the Hebrew in vs. 42 appears to mean "his holy word [or promise] with [or to] Abraham his servant."

---

heroes of any of the nations. But even he would not have dreamed of ascribing everything to them. Nor could he boast the greatness of the people; for neither in numbers nor in resources were they to be compared with the Egyptians or the Assyrians. The explanation was to be found in God. Everything, as the psalmist understood it, flowed from the fact that through all the chances and changes of life God had been faithful to the covenant he made with their fathers. He had allowed no one to oppress them. When dangers threatened, he had intervened with his own strong hand. The poet had no difficulties when he read of miracles. Food from heaven, water from the rock, a cloud to cover them by day and fire to give them light by night—wonderful, but not perplexing. It is not so easy for us. Being the children of our times, we are glad if we can discover natural explanations of apparently supernatural occurrences. But the main affirmation stands for us as it did for the Israelites, that it was God who sustained them and led them forth with joy, his chosen with glad songs.

One may complain that this is nothing but patriotism with a coating of piety. The answer is obvious: first, that the piety is not a veneer but the spring from which everything that is wholesome flows; second, that patriotism is not a thing to be apologized for. There are those who assume that Dr. Johnson spoke as a wise man when he said, "Patriotism is the last refuge of a scoundrel." [2] Actually he was talking nonsense. For the creation of true internationalism we need more, not less, patriotism. Ought we not to be proud of our own kith and kin, to rejoice in whatsoever is good in our people's traditions and achievements, to thank God for all that he has been able to do through us for his greater kingdom? Edith Cavell was right—"Patriotism is not enough"; but it is something the world needs, and we must cultivate it. There is a place for national, though never for bombastic, histories. There is no need to apologize for anniversaries of national events, always assuming that the celebrations are seemly.

There is, however, for the Christian a more blessed exercise—the remembrance of the specially Christian facts. Here is a story that will bear repetition, that can be told in detail or in outline, and always it deepens wonder and dignifies life. It begins not in Bethlehem but in the purposes of God, not in the birth of a little Babe but in the love that caused the Father to send the Son to be the Savior of the world. It includes much that is depressing, culminating in men's rejection of him who came to save them. But it goes on to the Resurrection, the Ascension, the gift of the Holy Spirit, the creation and spread of the universal church, the unity of severed peoples in the fellowship

[2] James Boswell, *The Life of Samuel Johnson* (New York: E. P. Dutton & Co., 1906; "Everyman's Library"), I, 547.

43 And he brought forth his people with
joy, *and* his chosen with gladness:
44 And gave them the lands of the
heathen: and they inherited the labor of the
people;
45 That they might observe his statutes,
and keep his laws. Praise ye the LORD.

43 So he led forth his people with joy,
his chosen ones with singing.
44 And he gave them the lands of the nations;
and they took possession of the fruit of the peoples' toil,
45 to the end that they should keep his statutes,
and observe his laws.
Praise the LORD!

106 Praise ye the LORD. O give thanks unto the LORD; for *he is* good: for his mercy *endureth* for ever.

106 Praise the LORD!
O give thanks to the LORD, for he is good;
for his steadfast love endures for ever!

7. CONCLUSION (105:43-45)

44-45. The lands of the nations: A reference to the various groups inhabiting Canaan before the Hebrew conquest (see Exeg. on 78:55). **The fruit of the peoples' toil:** Lit., "the toil of the peoples." The aim of the Lord's care for Israel is that there shall be fashioned a people obedient to the divine **laws** (cf. Exod. 19:6)

CVI. HAVE MERCY ON THY SINFUL PEOPLE (106:1-48)

Although some claim that this psalm consists of two separate and independent poems, vss. 1-5, 6-47, this Exeg. assumes that vss. 1-5 are intended to introduce what follows them, and that for practical purposes the psalm is a unity.

Apart from the opening verses, which have the joyousness of a hymn, the mood of the main body of this congregational lament is somewhat lugubrious. As in Ps. 105, we are given a retrospect of the national history, in this case from the Exodus to the settlement in Canaan, but unlike Ps. 105 the present psalm finds in these events a sad tale, and in this respect it is similar to Ps. 78 and Neh. 9:5-37. After the manner of Judg. 1:1–12:15, the period under review is represented as showing a repeating pattern of sin, appeal for help, deliverance, and forgetfulness. The only heartening feature of the recital is found in the allusion to the Lord's great mercy (vss. 8-12, 23, 30, 43-46), and it is this faith in his steadfast love which underlies the appeal for deliverance in vs. 47, with which the psalm ends. It is possible that vss. 1-5 were added by the author to vss.

of the kingdom. Christians cannot too often go over such good tidings. They should visit the places of vision and dedication. They should unite with others in sacraments of remembrance. So will they understand Ps. 105, its spirit of exultation, and its concluding paean: **Praise the LORD!**

106:1-48. ***The Wages of Sin.***—A careless reader might feel that there was in this psalm little to help him in his personal difficulties. But anyone who lingers with it and reads between the lines may find a message that is relevant both to his own needs and to the world situation.

The psalm begins with praise, but quickly passes to a historical review and a confession of sin. In some respects it is like Ps. 105. There we have a patriotic singer who has looked back and seen deliverance after deliverance, and in consequence has found his mouth full of praise to God. Here we have one, whether the same or another, who in his retrospect has been impressed not so much with divine activity as with human failure bringing suffering and disaster. The contrast is as important in significance as in form. It is true that he who contemplates the works of God in nature and history will be filled with the spirit of gladness. But he who concentrates upon the works of man comes face to face with tragedy. There seems to be in human nature a fatal tendency to waywardness leading to futility. There are brilliant achievements, but just as man is ready to put the coping stone upon his highest endeavors, an evil spirit causes confusion, and there is the story of Babel again. Expectation rises as bold

2 Who can utter the mighty acts of the LORD? *who* can show forth all his praise?
3 Blessed *are* they that keep judgment, *and* he that doeth righteousness at all times.
4 Remember me, O LORD, with the favor *that thou bearest unto* thy people: O visit me with thy salvation;
5 That I may see the good of thy chosen, that I may rejoice in the gladness of thy nation, that I may glory with thine inheritance.

2 Who can utter the mighty doings of the LORD,
or show forth all his praise?
3 Blessed are they who observe justice,
who do righteousness at all times!

4 Remember me, O LORD, when thou showest favor to thy people;
help me when thou deliverest them;
5 that I may see the prosperity of thy chosen ones,
that I may rejoice in the gladness of thy nation,
that I may glory with thy heritage.

6-47, either by his own composition or from another source, in order to give more emphasis to the Lord's persistent kindness toward his erring people.

The psalm impresses the reader, especially in vss. 1, 6, 47, as having been written for some liturgical purpose, but apart from vs. 6, which suggests that the public confession of sin is appropriate, there is no indication of the occasion of its origin. No regular strophic structure is apparent, and no division of the lines between two parties (as Kittel advocates) is very convincing. The meter is generally 3+3. The date must be earlier than the Chronicler, for vss. 1, 47-48, are quoted in I Chr. 16:34-36. Vss. 46-47 point to the eighth century B.C. as the *terminus a quo.*

1. HYMNIC INTRODUCTION (106:1-5)

106:3. Blessed are they who observe justice: While the Lord "loves righteousness and justice" (33:5), the need for men to do justly receives a rather limited recognition in the Psalms (cf. 15:1-5; 24:3-5; 72:2; 119:121). **He that doeth righteousness** is the M.T. The RSV (**who do righteousness**) following some Hebrew MSS, as well as the LXX, Jerome, and the Syriac, read עשי.

4. Remember me . . . me is the M.T. Some Hebrew MSS and the LXX read "us" in both cases. **When thou deliverest them:** Lit., **with thy salvation.**

---

spirits set out on great campaigns, but the best-laid plans are wrecked and mouths are full of lamentations.

The psalm is a confession of sin based upon a survey of national history. Not that the writer has no eye for particular instances. Definite occasions are cited when the fathers had been filled with a spirit of revolt. One such occasion was at the Red Sea. God had saved them in that crisis, and it might have been expected that gratitude would never die within them. But they forgot, and because they forgot, there were other revolts, when for example the people murmured for flesh; when again, led by Dathan and Abiram, they envied Moses and Aaron; and yet again, when they made and worshiped a molten image, thus changing their glory for the likeness of an ox. There were other occasions such as those connected with their entrance into the Land of Promise. One was their refusal to enter when the path opened, another was the way they not only mingled with the Canaanites, but adopted the local idolatry. They had even fallen so low as to offer their children as an atonement for sin. It is a depressing catalogue, though it may be questioned whether it is worse than the catalogue to which many modern nations could contribute. Man is like that, we say as we reread the history of nations. Man is like that, we repeat as we consider how we have fallen. In spite of noble aspirations and solemn vows, he seems to be dogged by an innate spirit of evil which causes him to rebel against God and to create strife among men.

But Ps. 106 helps us to see particular evils to which the people of Israel were susceptible. First, there is the sin of forgetfulness. The psalmist would insist upon the necessity of remembrance. If a man or a nation hopes to continue in the way of life, the lessons of the past must be laid to heart. But the Israelites failed. They forgot the covenant God had made with their fathers. They forgot even the miracles

6 We have sinned with our fathers, we have committed iniquity, we have done wickedly.
7 Our fathers understood not thy wonders in Egypt; they remembered not the multitude of thy mercies; but provoked *him* at the sea, *even* at the Red sea.
8 Nevertheless he saved them for his name's sake, that he might make his mighty power to be known.
9 He rebuked the Red sea also, and it was dried up: so he led them through the depths, as through the wilderness.
10 And he saved them from the hand of him that hated *them,* and redeemed them from the hand of the enemy.
11 And the waters covered their enemies: there was not one of them left.
12 Then believed they his words; they sang his praise.

6 Both we and our fathers have sinned;
we have committed iniquity, we have done wickedly.
7 Our fathers, when they were in Egypt,
did not consider thy wonderful works;
they did not remember the abundance of thy steadfast love,
but rebelled against the Most High[v] at the Red Sea.
8 Yet he saved them for his name's sake,
that he might make known his mighty power.
9 He rebuked the Red Sea, and it became dry;
and he led them through the deep as through a desert.
10 So he saved them from the hand of the foe,
and delivered them from the power of the enemy.
11 And the waters covered their adversaries;
not one of them was left.
12 Then they believed his words;
they sang his praise.

[v] Cn Compare 78. 17, 56: Heb *at the sea*

2. Israel at the Red Sea (106:6-12)

6-12. After an acknowledgment that the present generation has sinned as did their fathers, the psalmist turns to consider the nation's unenviable past. He begins with the complaints at the Red Sea. **Thy steadfast love:** A small emendation supported by the LXX, Jerome, and the Syriac. The M.T. has the plural, hence **thy mercies. Rebelled:** Cf. Exod. 14:11-12. **At the sea** is the M.T. (על ים). The RSV adopts a commonly accepted emendation, **the Most High** (עליון; cf. 78:17, 56). **He rebuked the Red Sea:** Cf. Exod. 14:15-31. **The deep:** Lit., "the deeps," as in Exod. 15:5, 8.

by which he had brought them out of the land of bondage. In the wilderness they forgot not only the promises but also the way in which provision had been made for their needs. The same forgetfulness later led them into the iniquity of idolatry even on the mount of revelation. Thus evils multiplied and confusion deepened. Forgetting that God had raised up Moses and Aaron to be leaders of the people, they were guilty of the sin of jealousy. Forgetting the most elementary of commandments, that there is but one God and that they must not make for themselves any graven image, they had even sacrificed innocent children to the lifeless gods of Canaan. Thus the story proceeds to the end—the miserable condition in which they were unable to believe that which was good or to have faith in God or man. So sin corrupts the nature of men and nations and fills the world with despair.

Fortunately there are times when the psalmist lifts his eyes above the doleful scene and thinks of the God who keeps watch above his own. There are references to divine wrath, and in them it may seem as though the psalmist imputes to the Almighty passions like his own. But he passes from divine anger to divine love, and rests in the thought that though the people had forgotten, God had been mindful of his covenant, and had regarded their cry of distress. That is why the psalmist is able to conclude with prayer and doxology, and the psalm may be described as a hymn of praise.

But how can the psalm be described as relevant to our own needs and to the world situation? The first part of the answer is that it brings us back to the reality of sin, a reality to which no interpreter of the modern scene can afford to be indifferent. There was a time when many tried to ignore the somber fact. We knew

13 They soon forgat his works; they waited not for his counsel:

14 But lusted exceedingly in the wilderness, and tempted God in the desert.

15 And he gave them their request; but sent leanness into their soul.

16 They envied Moses also in the camp, *and* Aaron the saint of the LORD.

17 The earth opened and swallowed up Dathan, and covered the company of Abiram.

18 And a fire was kindled in their company; the flame burned up the wicked.

19 They made a calf in Horeb, and worshipped the molten image.

20 Thus they changed their glory into the similitude of an ox that eateth grass.

21 They forgat God their saviour, which had done great things in Egypt;

22 Wondrous works in the land of Ham, *and* terrible things by the Red sea.

23 Therefore he said that he would destroy them, had not Moses his chosen stood before him in the breach, to turn away his wrath, lest he should destroy *them*.

13 But they soon forgot his works;
they did not wait for his counsel.
14 But they had a wanton craving in the wilderness,
and put God to the test in the desert;
15 he gave them what they asked,
but sent a wasting disease among them.

16 When men in the camp were jealous of Moses
and Aaron, the holy one of the LORD,
17 the earth opened and swallowed up Dathan,
and covered the company of Abi′ram.
18 Fire also broke out in their company;
the flame burned up the wicked.

19 They made a calf in Horeb
and worshiped a molten image.
20 They exchanged the glory of God
for the image of an ox that eats grass.
21 They forgot God, their Savior,
who had done great things in Egypt,
22 wondrous works in the land of Ham,
and terrible things by the Red Sea.
23 Therefore he said he would destroy them —
had not Moses, his chosen one,
stood in the breach before him,
to turn away his wrath from destroying them.

---

3. THE WILDERNESS PERIOD (106:13-18; cf. Exod. 15:1–17:16; Num. 11:1-35)

15. What they asked: Lit., **their request. A wasting disease:** Cf. Num. 11:20; Briggs *et al.* emend this word to מזון, "sustenance." **Among them:** Lit., **into their soul.**

16-18. The Dathan and Abiram incident. Korah, who also appears in the narrative in Num. 16, is not referred to by the psalmist.

4. THE GOLDEN CALF (106:19-23; cf. Exod. 32:1-35; Deut. 9:8-21)

19-23. Horeb: Found only here in the psalms; the Deuteronomic name for Sinai. **The glory of God:** Lit., **their glory** (cf. 3:3; Jer. 2:11; Rom. 1:23). Rabbinical tradition ("the corrections of the scribes") claims that the original reading was either "his glory" or "my glory." **Ham:** See Exeg. on 78:51.

---

that life was not perfect, but we thought we were improving. We were like doctors who apply plasters where the malady demands a surgical operation. We recommended a change of conditions when nothing less than a change of heart would do.

But subsequent sufferings cured us of superficialities. "Even in America," as an English theologian told the students of an English university in the middle of World War II, "the romantic illusions of Utopianism are an ebbing tide, as the mystery of iniquity is seen to be a real and an abiding mystery."[3] Easy explanations of evil became unpopular even among secular philosophers. Instead of comforting themselves with words like "evolutionary overhang," or with suggestions that evil is not real in the sense that good is, they began to affirm that iniquity is not merely bestial but devilish. Even businessmen who were as unfamiliar with

[3] J. S. Whale, *Christian Doctrine* (New York: The Macmillan Co., 1941), p. 36.

24 Yea, they despised the pleasant land, they believed not his word:
25 But murmured in their tents, *and* hearkened not unto the voice of the LORD.
26 Therefore he lifted up his hand against them, to overthrow them in the wilderness:
27 To overthrow their seed also among the nations, and to scatter them in the lands.
28 They joined themselves also unto Baal-peor, and ate the sacrifices of the dead.
29 Thus they provoked *him* to anger with their inventions: and the plague brake in upon them.
30 Then stood up Phinehas, and executed judgment: and *so* the plague was stayed.
31 And that was counted unto him for righteousness unto all generations for evermore.

24 Then they despised the pleasant land,
having no faith in his promise.
25 They murmured in their tents,
and did not obey the voice of the LORD.
26 Therefore he raised his hand and swore to them
that he would make them fall in the wilderness,
27 and would disperse[w] their descendants among the nations,
scattering them over the lands.

28 Then they attached themselves to the Ba'al of Pe'or,
and ate sacrifices offered to the dead;
29 they provoked the LORD to anger with their doings,
and a plague broke out among them.
30 Then Phin'ehas stood up and interposed,
and the plague was stayed.
31 And that has been reckoned to him as righteousness
from generation to generation for ever.

[w] Syr Compare Ezek 20. 23: Heb *cause to fall*

5. THE REPORT OF THE SPIES (106:24-27; cf. Num. 13:1–14:3)

26-27. Therefore he raised his hand and swore to them is tautologous. The Hebrew is, lit., "So he lifted up his hand to them" (cf. KJV), which means "So he swore to them" (cf. Exod. 6:8). **And would disperse** represents an emended text (ולהפיץ), proposed by Duhm *et al.*, supported by the Syriac. The M.T. is **and cause to fall** (RSV mg.). A close parallel to the verse is found in Ezek. 20:23.

6. BAAL OF PEOR (106:28-31; cf. Num. 25:1-18; Exod. 34:15)

28-31. Sacrifices offered to the dead: Lit., the sacrifices of the dead. Either **the dead** is an opprobrious epithet for idols (cf. 115:4-7; Wisd. Sol. 13:10; Mishnah, Abodah Zarah 2:3), or the reference is to some mortuary practice (cf. Deut. 26:14; Tob. 4:17; Ecclus. 30:18). **They provoked him: Him** is not in the M.T., but is found in some Hebrew MSS, the LXX, Jerome, the Syriac. The RSV supplies **the LORD. Interposed**

philosophy as with dogmatic theology became conscious of a diabolical energy working in the world thwarting aspirations and reforms.

This more somber reading of life is one of the significant features of spiritual renewal. Always it leads to a new note in Christian preaching and writing. Compare the religious books that were popular at the beginning of the twentieth century with those that were widely read in the years that followed World War II; e.g., D. R. Davies' *Down Peacock's Feathers*. The author himself was a sign of the times. He began, after an apprenticeship in the Welsh mines, as a Christian minister. Like so many other ministers of his generation, he was more concerned to preach external reform than personal repentance. It would not be uncharitable to say that he drew inspiration from parliamentary bluebooks as much as from the Holy Scriptures. But life was too much for him. In spite of all platform promises the world became more dangerous and chaotic. The only way to escape was to go deeper, and there he was challenged by the personal facts he had evaded. The autobiographical details are stated in slight but suggestive books such as Davies' *On to Orthodoxy*[4] and *Secular Illusion or Christian Realism?*[5] The story is taken further in *Down Peacock's Feathers,* which is a study in the "contemporary significance of the General Con-

[4] London: Latimer House, 1948.
[5] New York: The Macmillan Co., 1948.

32 They angered *him* also at the waters
of strife, so that it went ill with Moses for
their sakes:
33 Because they provoked his spirit, so
that he spake unadvisedly with his lips.
34 They did not destroy the nations, concerning whom the LORD commanded them:
35 But were mingled among the heathen,
and learned their works.
36 And they served their idols: which
were a snare unto them.
37 Yea, they sacrificed their sons and
their daughters unto devils,
38 And shed innocent blood, *even* the
blood of their sons and of their daughters,
whom they sacrificed unto the idols of
Canaan: and the land was polluted with
blood.
39 Thus were they defiled with their own
works, and went a whoring with their own
inventions.

32 They angered him at the waters of Mer′-
ibah,
and it went ill with Moses on their
account;
33 for they made his spirit bitter,
and he spoke words that were rash.

34 They did not destroy the peoples,
as the LORD commanded them,
35 but they mingled with the nations
and learned to do as they did.
36 They served their idols,
which became a snare to them.
37 They sacrificed their sons
and their daughters to the demons;
38 they poured out innocent blood,
the blood of their sons and daughters,
whom they sacrificed to the idols of Canaan;
and the land was polluted with blood.
39 Thus they became unclean by their acts,
and played the harlot in their doings.

---

or **executed judgment:** The Hebrew can bear either meaning; Gunkel and Nötscher favor "made atonement." For the reward of Phinehas (vs. 31) see Num. 25:10-13.

7. MERIBAH (106:32-33; cf. Num. 20:1-13)

32-33. They angered him: Him is not in the M.T. **They made . . . bitter** or **they provoked:** Either translation assumes a repointing of the Hebrew verb to obtain the Hiphil of מרר; the M.T. is "they rebelled against" as in 107:11. **He spoke words that were rash:** Lit., "he spoke rashly with his lips" (cf. KJV).

8. THE SINS IN CANAAN (106:34-39)

34. The failure of the Hebrews to exterminate the native Canaanites (Deut. 7:1-2, 16; 20:16-18; Judg. 1:21, 27-36).

36-39. The adoption of Canaanite religious customs (Judg. 2:11-12; II Kings 16:3-4). **They sacrificed their sons:** On child sacrifice see II Kings 3:27; 21:6, 16; Ezek. 16:20. **The demons:** A word of Akkadian origin occurring in the O.T. only here and in Deut. 32:7, and apparently denoting some kind of spiritual being inferior to a god.

---

fession." It contains much about Marx and the Second International and other men and movements. But it maintains that if there was ever a scripture outside the canon that bears the marks of the Holy Ghost, the General Confession can claim to be that scripture. Like the author of this psalm, he is deeply interested in history, though unlike him, he is universal in his range. Looking at the long and tangled story of man's struggles and frustrations, he declares that the one thing in which mankind is united is in sin. He does not, as the psalmist does, attribute this primarily to forgetfulness, but he declares that man who has been created by God in his own image has willed himself out of his subordinate relation, with the result that every individual becomes his own center, until "united in Sin, we become disunited in everything else." He is in sympathy with this psalmist again when he stresses "one peculiar quality of original sin, its levity, its heedlessness, its unintentionalness." [6] Ps. 106 and the General Confession placed thus alongside each other force from us the comment: "Something radically, disastrously wrong somewhere in human nature." "We have erred and strayed from thy ways like lost sheep. We have followed too much the devices and desires of our own hearts. We have offended against thy holy laws."

[6] New York: The Macmillan Co., 1944, pp. 11, 49.

40 Therefore was the wrath of the LORD kindled against his people, insomuch that he abhorred his own inheritance.
41 And he gave them into the hand of the heathen; and they that hated them ruled over them.
42 Their enemies also oppressed them, and they were brought into subjection under their hand.
43 Many times did he deliver them; but they provoked *him* with their counsel, and were brought low for their iniquity.
44 Nevertheless he regarded their affliction, when he heard their cry:
45 And he remembered for them his covenant, and repented according to the multitude of his mercies.
46 He made them also to be pitied of all those that carried them captives.

40 Then the anger of the LORD was kindled against his people,
and he abhorred his heritage;
41 he gave them into the hand of the nations,
so that those who hated them ruled over them.
42 Their enemies oppressed them,
and they were brought into subjection under their power.
43 Many times he delivered them,
but they were rebellious in their purposes,
and were brought low through their iniquity.
44 Nevertheless he regarded their distress,
when he heard their cry.
45 He remembered for their sake his covenant,
and relented according to the abundance of his steadfast love.
46 He caused them to be pitied
by all those who held them captive.

---

9. ISRAEL'S SIN AND GOD'S MERCY (106:40-46)

These verses rehearse the Lord's punishments of a sinful people and his repeated acts of clemency. The psalmist may be thinking of the time of the judges, although a later period could also illustrate his point (e.g., II Sam. 5:22-25).

43. They were rebellious rather than **they provoked him. In their purposes:** Many commentators emend the M.T. to obtain "against his purpose."

46. The captivity referred to need not be confined to that brought about by the Babylonians in the early sixth century B.C. All of Israel's wars, and especially those with Assyria in the eighth century B.C., must have resulted in the taking of Hebrew prisoners.

Some may describe this as reactionary and insist that the sense of sin is a disease which man must rid himself of as quickly as possible. That view, however, has never long prevailed. The sense of sin seems to be the gauge of progress. Wrote Carlyle in *Heroes and Hero-Worship:*

> The greatest of faults, I should say, is to be conscious of none. . . . The deadliest sin, I say, were that same supercilious consciousness of no sin;—that is death; the heart so conscious is divorced from sincerity, humility and fact; is dead: it is "pure" as dead dry sand is pure.[7]

But sin does not stand alone in Ps. 106. There is always the consciousness of God who, mindful of his covenant and moved to compassion by the greatness of his love, hears men's cry and saves them. And this, not merely as it stands here in an O.T. book, but as it is enriched in the N.T., is the message to be preached. Sin has caused almost unparalleled suffering. It has frustrated the dreams of generations, made havoc of schemes for a better order, and brought the world to the edge of despair. Yet there remains forever a way of hope. It is no new way. It is suggested in this psalm, developed by prophet and evangelist, and attested by multitudes of the faithful: it is the way of repentance and forgiveness. There is truth in the grim doctrine of retribution which has been dwelt on so insistently, especially by the novelist and playwright. But there is greater truth in the gospel of grace, truth which has been illustrated and justified in countless men who have rejoiced in the experience of redemption.

Mark Rutherford often maintained the pitiless doctrine of retribution, but had caught a glimpse of the larger truth. In *Catherine Furze* he tells of one who out of jealousy bears false

[7] "The Hero as Prophet."

47 Save us, O LORD our God, and gather us from among the heathen, to give thanks unto thy holy name, *and* to triumph in thy praise.
48 Blessed *be* the LORD God of Israel from everlasting to everlasting: and let all the people say, Amen. Praise ye the LORD.

107 O give thanks unto the LORD, for *he is* good: for his mercy *endureth* for ever.

47 Save us, O LORD our God,
and gather us from among the nations,
that we may give thanks to thy holy name
and glory in thy praise.

48 Blessed be the LORD, the God of Israel,
from everlasting to everlasting!
And let all the people say, "Amen!"
Praise the LORD!

BOOK V

107 O give thanks to the LORD, for he is good;
for his steadfast love endures for ever!

---

10. CONCLUDING APPEAL FOR HELP (106:47[48])

47. Contrary to some commentators, this verse does not necessarily imply that the psalmist was living outside Palestine. The dispersion alluded to can hardly have existed before the eighth century B.C.

48. This verse, which is probably not a part of the original psalm, serves as the doxology which concludes Book IV of the Psalter.

CVII. THANK THE LORD FOR HIS STEADFAST LOVE (107:1-43)

Commentators are not agreed on the unity of this psalm. Some, e.g., Oesterley, maintain that the poem comprises two parts, vss. 1-32, 33-43, which have no real connection with each other. Others, including Nötscher and Weiser, take the view that the psalm comes from a single author. The arguments on either side are not conclusive, and the question must be left an open one.

It is, however, manifest that vss. 1-32 have a distinctive character. They are, in fact, a well-constructed and strikingly original and beautiful litany of thanksgiving. The brief introduction (vss. 1-3) is followed by four strophes of unequal length, each of which uses as a refrain two verses found in the first strophe in vss. 6 and 8. These refrains suggest that the psalm was used antiphonally, but the division of it between two or more parties is a matter of conjecture. Each strophe deals with a distinct reason for gratitude, and possibly the worshipers shared in the singing of that strophe most appropriate to their own condition. Vss. 22 and 32 intimate that the psalm was intended for an occasion when thanksgiving sacrifices were offered. The references to the widespread

---

witness against a fellow workman, charges him with appropriating his master's goods, and thus gets him discharged and disgraced. Hardly has he begun to enjoy his success before the hand of God is laid upon him, his whole world is turned upside down; until at last he stands before his employer and the one he has wronged and confesses the evil he has done. It was fiction, and could have ended there; but the story goes on to tell how the sinner begins to understand the love and forgiveness of God, and spends the rest of his life in the service of his fellows.

Some of the best work in the world has been done by men who have redeemed themselves by the grace with which they have been redeemed. Such facts must not be told apologetically but in bursts of enthusiasm, like that of the psalmist when he concludes:

Blessed be the LORD, the God of Israel,
from everlasting to everlasting!
And let all the people say, "Amen!"
Praise the LORD!

107:1-43. ***Human Need and Divine Succor.***— Here the thought and language are simple and the religious experience common. The psalm begins with an exhortation to praise God. It proceeds to instances of human need and divine succor. The conclusion (vss. 33-43), perhaps added later, summarizes for us the "wisdom"

2 Let the redeemed of the LORD say *so,*
whom he hath redeemed from the hand of
the enemy;
3 And gathered them out of the lands,
from the east, and from the west, from the
north, and from the south.

2 Let the redeemed of the LORD say so,
whom he has redeemed from trouble
3 and gathered in from the lands,
from the east and from the west,
from the north and from the south.

Diaspora of Israel in vs. 3, and to sea-borne commerce in vss. 23-32, favor a date in the Persian or early Hellenistic period. This conclusion is also supported by the resemblances between the phraseology of the psalm and that of Second Isaiah and Job (see Exeg. below).

The second part, vss. 33-43, can be described as a hymn celebrating both the unpredictable dispositions of Providence and the Lord's care for the needy. Its general tone, the absence of any note of thanksgiving, and its lack of the two lines of refrain appearing in vss. 1-32, have been thought to set it apart from the earlier section. As the opening verb in vs. 33 has no nominal subject, it is possible that vss. 33-43, if a separate composition, are a fragment of a longer poem. Those, however, who advocate the unity of the psalm, see in the rather general character of vss. 33-43 a fitting conclusion to the more particular situations dealt with in vss. 4-32.

This psalm is not an exercise in speculative theology, and therefore we cannot censure the author on the ground that he shows no awareness of all the facets of the agelong problem of evil. We may assume that the psalmist was sufficiently familiar with life to realize that circumstances do not always work out, even for the saints, in a happy way. On the other hand, he also knew that many could testify to the Lord's goodness. Their testimony had to do with the facts of their own experience, and it is these facts that are celebrated in the psalm.

In the Hebrew text each of vss. 21-26, 40, has in the margin an inverted Nun (one of the Hebrew consonants), but the significance of these letters has not been satisfactorily explained.

The meter of the entire psalm is 3+3, with the usual variations.

A. A Thanksgiving Litany (107:1-32)

1. Summons to Give Thanks (107:1-3)

107:2-3. The redeemed of the LORD: Cf. Isa. 62:12. **From trouble: From the hand of the enemy** (KJV) is also possible. On a return of Israel from the four quarters of the earth (vs. 3) see Isa. 43:5-6; 49:12. **And from the south** is an emended text (probably ומימין), as the M.T. ("and from the sea," i.e., **and from the west**) is redundant.

---

available to any man. The central part is a beautifully constructed poem, and as we read it pictures take shape before our eyes.

The first is a picture of travelers lost in the **desert.** Most men do not know what it is to be lost. One evening in the Balkans a too brilliant day sank into wet and sullen night. The man who should have known the way stopped and confessed to the little group around him that he had lost his bearings. Never did man seem so puny or nature so grim as then; a handful of the "lost" peered through the gathering gloom and found nothing to help. Perhaps the desert with its pitiless sun and its exasperating mirage is worse. There is only one thing to do in such an emergency: to appeal to "whatever gods there be." [8]

[8] W. E. Henley, "Invictus."

The second picture introduces us to the gloom of the prison house, which also is outside the experience of most of us. We have read about prisons, ancient and modern, and about prison reform. We know that not all **prisoners** who suffer detention are rogues and blackguards. Prisons may contain the greatest as well as the meanest of mankind. The psalmist, however, is concerned with the fact that the people who suffer there are cut off from normal life and doomed to irksome discipline. It is useless to run one's head against stone walls or to hurl the body at bolted doors. The thing to do is to batter the gates of heaven with storms of prayer.

The third picture is nearer our personal experience, for even if we have not been dangerously **sick** ourselves, we know people who have. We have seen them in our own homes. We

4 They wandered in the wilderness in a
solitary way; they found no city to dwell in.
5 Hungry and thirsty, their soul fainted
in them.
6 Then they cried unto the LORD in their
trouble, *and* he delivered them out of their
distresses.
7 And he led them forth by the right way,
that they might go to a city of habitation.
8 Oh that *men* would praise the LORD *for*
his goodness, and *for* his wonderful works
to the children of men!
9 For he satisfieth the longing soul, and
filleth the hungry soul with goodness.
10 Such as sit in darkness and in the
shadow of death, *being* bound in affliction
and iron;
11 Because they rebelled against the
words of God, and contemned the counsel
of the Most High:

4 Some wandered in desert wastes,
finding no way to a city to dwell in;
5 hungry and thirsty,
their soul fainted within them.
6 Then they cried to the LORD in their trouble,
and he delivered them from their distress;
7 he led them by a straight way,
till they reached a city to dwell in.
8 Let them thank the LORD for his steadfast love,
for his wonderful works to the sons of men!
9 For he satisfies him who is thirsty,
and the hungry he fills with good things.

10 Some sat in darkness and in gloom,
prisoners in affliction and in irons,
11 for they had rebelled against the words of God,
and spurned the counsel of the Most High.

---

2. THOSE LOST IN DESERT PLACES (107:4-9)

4. Some wandered: This small emendation (תעי) is made to have the strophe commence with a participle, as in vss. 10, 23. **In desert wastes:** Lit., "in the wilderness, in the waste" (Amer. Trans.). The RSV takes **way** to be part of vs. 4*b*, whereas the KJV puts it in vs. 4*a*.

6. The first part of the refrain, which recurs with slight changes in vss. 13, 19, 28. **And he delivered:** There is no **and** in the Hebrew (except in vs. 28), and the verse is more effective without it.

7. A straight way: Better with the KJV and many commentators, **the right way.**

8. The second part of the refrain, found also in vss. 15, 21, 31.

9. Him who is thirsty: Lit., **the longing soul,** but the context (cf. vs. 5) supports the RSV.

3. THOSE CONFINED IN PRISON (107:10-16)

10-16. On vs. 10 cf. Isa. 42:7; 49:9. **In gloom** or **in the shadow of death:** See Exeg. on 23:4. Vs. 11, like vs. 17, reflects the common O.T. view that misfortune and sickness are due to the individual's sin, here perhaps to certain criminal acts. **Their hearts were**

---

go to hospitals and think of the stories those beds could tell. Things have changed in many ways since this psalm was written. Medical science has made tremendous steps forward. We have outgrown the belief that suffering and **sinful ways** are necessarily connected. We are spared some of the perplexities enumerated in the book of Job. Yet still the question arises: Why should we be singled out for such marks of divine anger?

The fourth picture shows us **ships** in distress at sea. Perhaps those on board were tempted out by smiling skies; but storms had broken, great waves had threatened to swamp the frail craft, and even experienced sailors were helpless. What could they do but cry to the Lord in their trouble?

These are the four pictures. There are several things to be said about them. The first is that they are remarkably relevant. There are times when we think we know the way forward for ourselves and mankind. The course is mapped:

12 Therefore he brought down their heart with labor; they fell down, and *there was* none to help.

13 Then they cried unto the LORD in their trouble, *and* he saved them out of their distresses.

14 He brought them out of darkness and the shadow of death, and brake their bands in sunder.

15 Oh that *men* would praise the LORD *for* his goodness, and *for* his wonderful works to the children of men!

16 For he hath broken the gates of brass, and cut the bars of iron in sunder.

17 Fools, because of their transgression, and because of their iniquities, are afflicted.

18 Their soul abhorreth all manner of meat; and they draw near unto the gates of death.

12 Their hearts were bowed down with hard labor;
they fell down, with none to help.
13 Then they cried to the LORD in their trouble,
and he delivered them from their distress;
14 he brought them out of darkness and gloom,
and broke their bonds asunder.
15 Let them thank the LORD for his steadfast love,
for his wonderful works to the sons of men!
16 For he shatters the doors of bronze,
and cuts in two the bars of iron.

17 Some were sick[x] through their sinful ways,
and because of their iniquities suffered affliction;
18 they loathed any kind of food,
and they drew near to the gates of death.

[x] Cn: Heb *fools*

---

bowed down: A slight emendation of the M.T., supported by the LXX and Vulg. The Hebrew, however, is "so he humbled their heart" (cf. KJV), which makes good sense and is supported by Jerome and the Syriac. On vs. 16, cf. Isa. 45:2, which is almost verbally identical.

4. THE SICK (107:17-22)

17-18. Some were sick: This emendation (חולים) replaces **fools** of the M.T. It gives the strophe a participle at its beginning, as in vss. 4 (emended), 10, 23, and makes the verse more consonant with the succeeding lines. Kirkpatrick defends the M.T. on the ground that folly is a form of moral perversity, and that the O.T. frequently regards sickness as due to sin (cf. vs. 11). On vs. 18 cf. Job 33:20. **The gates of death:** See Exeg. on 9:13.

---

all that is needed is to maintain it in the face of difficulties. We have, if not absolute freedom, at least a large measure of it: it is for us to use it aright and give to others the liberty we enjoy. We possess health of mind and body, not indeed omnipotence; but if the strength and talents we have are pooled, there is little man cannot do. Storms break upon us and tempests threaten to swamp us; but they are sent to test us, and rapidly advancing science will see us through.

This common assumption is then succeeded by the fear that we are lost, and that there is no one capable of leading us to safety, that we are enslaved with no one to deliver us, that we are weak and diseased and tossed about by powers we cannot control. Such a mood was expressed by the drawing of a chessboard found upon the body of a dead soldier. He had relieved the tedium of the trenches by drawing that board with one solitary pawn upon it—indicating, no doubt, his own sense of impotency. Like a pawn in the hand of a player, he was the sport of forces he could not control. There are many who offer themselves as leaders, but we suspect that they are but little wiser than we. We feel ourselves to be travelers in a trackless waste, prisoners in a dark dungeon, voyagers on storm-driven seas. And only here and there are men found with faith enough to cry **to the LORD in their trouble.**

Yet man's extremity is surely God's oppor-

19 Then they cry unto the LORD in their trouble, *and* he saveth them out of their distresses.

20 He sent his word, and healed them, and delivered *them* from their destructions.

21 Oh that *men* would praise the LORD *for* his goodness, and *for* his wonderful works to the children of men!

22 And let them sacrifice the sacrifices of thanksgiving, and declare his works with rejoicing.

23 They that go down to the sea in ships, that do business in great waters;

24 These see the works of the LORD, and his wonders in the deep.

25 For he commandeth, and raiseth the stormy wind, which lifteth up the waves thereof.

19 Then they cried to the LORD in their trouble,
and he delivered them from their distress;
20 he sent forth his word, and healed them,
and delivered them from destruction.
21 Let them thank the LORD for his steadfast love,
for his wonderful works to the sons of men!
22 And let them offer sacrifices of thanksgiving,
and tell of his deeds in songs of joy!

23 Some went down to the sea in ships,
doing business on the great waters;
24 they saw the deeds of the LORD,
his wondrous works in the deep.
25 For he commanded, and raised the stormy wind,
which lifted up the waves of the sea.

---

20. His word: The Lord's **word** is a divine agent at work among men (cf. 147:15, 18; Isa. 55:11). The connection of the **word** with the "wisdom" concept (Prov. 1:20-33; 8:1-36; 9:1-6) and with the later Logos doctrine (as in Philo) is problematic. **Delivered them: Them** is a small addition to the M.T., and is supported by the LXX, some MSS of Jerome, and the Syriac. **Destruction:** Possibly the word means "their pits," but this is uncertain, and the text may be corrupt. The noun occurs elsewhere only in Lam. 4:20.

22. Sacrifices of thanksgiving: Thank offerings were a division of the peace offerings (Lev. 7:11-15; 22:29-30). According to the Mishnah (Zebahim 5:6), the animal was slaughtered in the temple area, but its flesh could be cooked and eaten anywhere in Jerusalem, provided it was consumed by midnight of the same day.

5. Seafarers (107:23-32)

23-32. As the Hebrews were essentially landsmen, the novelty of the nautical theme may account for the longer strophe and the exaggeration in the description. **Some went down to the sea:** Cf. Isa. 42:10. **The waves of the sea** (vs. 25): If this is not an unacknowledged emendation, it is a very free translation of the M.T., which is, lit., "its

---

tunity. Our humiliation may be our salvation. When everything goes well we are tempted to forget God, but when troubles surround us the way of prayer sooner or later is found. There is nothing very virtuous about such praying. It may be mixed with selfishness and superstition. It is like the fear that drives the ungodly to the sanctuary. It may cease when the crisis passes. But it reminds us of the instinct for God that is latent in the human breast. In prosperity men may argue about spiritual values and religious doctrines; face to face with mortal peril they pray with importunity.

But can we continue with the psalmist when he speaks of divine succor? Is it true that when man cries to God, he delivers him? This is a perennial question and we must consider it. There are people ready to repeat the psalmist's refrain quite literally from their personal knowledge. Their interpretation of experience may be questioned, but the last thing an unprejudiced person can do is to brush aside their evidence as worthless. The evidence is from many quarters, continues from one generation to another, and is of great diversity. Consider the story of Dr. Thomas John Barnardo, the friend of "nobody's children." Let us remember how one year winter came early and children were shivering in their cots. There was no money to buy blankets, so Barnardo prayed. On the third day there came a check for almost exactly the sum required, and the covering note

26 They mount up to the heaven, they
go down again to the depths: their soul is
melted because of trouble.
27 They reel to and fro, and stagger like
a drunken man, and are at their wit's end.
28 Then they cry unto the LORD in their
trouble, and he bringeth them out of their
distresses.
29 He maketh the storm a calm, so that
the waves thereof are still.
30 Then are they glad because they be
quiet; so he bringeth them unto their desired haven.
31 Oh that *men* would praise the LORD
for his goodness, and *for* his wonderful
works to the children of men!
32 Let them exalt him also in the congregation of the people, and praise him in the
assembly of the elders.

26 They mounted up to heaven, they went
down to the depths;
their courage melted away in their evil
plight;
27 they reeled and staggered like drunken
men,
and were at their wits' end.
28 Then they cried to the LORD in their
trouble,
and he delivered them from their distress;
29 he made the storm be still,
and the waves of the sea were hushed.
30 Then they were glad because they had
quiet,
and he brought them to their desired
haven.
31 Let them thank the LORD for his steadfast love,
for his wonderful works to the sons of
men!
32 Let them extol him in the congregation
of the people,
and praise him in the assembly of the
elders.

---

waves" (cf. KJV). **Their courage:** Lit., **their soul. And were at their wits' end:** Lit., "And all their wisdom was swallowed up." **He maketh the storm a calm:** A superior rendering to the RSV for it preserves the force of the two nouns. **The waves of the sea** (vs. 29): A small unacknowledged emendation (גלי הים), supported by the Syriac. The M.T. is "their waves."

The assembly of the elders: The elders are prominent from the age of Moses (Exod. 3:16, 18; 12:21; 18:12; etc.) to the time of Ezra (10:8, 14). In Deuteronomy they are assigned certain juridical functions (Deut. 19:12; 21:2, 19; 22:15; 25:7) which may have necessitated their assembling as local groups (cf. Ruth 4:2). Ezekiel (8:1; 14:1; etc.) also refers to gatherings of elders.

---

simply said: "To provide additional clothing needed in consequence of the inclement weather." [9] Or read the life of William Dobbie, governor of Malta during the most critical period of World War II. He tells us that there was a desperate moment in France before he went to the Mediterranean when he needed rolling stock for the removal of troops to a threatened position. When he appealed to the officer responsible, he was assured that no stock was available.

> I hung up the receiver and knelt down in my office at Montreuil, and laid the matter before God. I said to Him: "Lord, I have come to the end of my tether. It is absolutely necessary that we should carry out this move, if we are not to lose the war—please help." Shortly afterward the telephone rang and the officer in charge of rolling stock was speaking. "The most extraordinary thing has happened," he said. "Sufficient rolling stock has suddenly and quite unexpectedly become available, and we can carry out the move as requested." [1]

Such instances are far too common to be dismissed as mere coincidences.

Questions suggest themselves and must not be resisted. Someone wants to know if these are not carefully selected and edited facts. What of the prayers that are not answered? What of men lost in the wilderness or at sea who have perished in their misery? What about prisoners in dungeons and infirm men in hospitals who

[9] A. E. Williams, *Barnardo of Stepney* (London: George Allen & Unwin, 1943), p. 183.

[1] *A Very Present Help*, p. 49.

33 He turneth rivers into a wilderness,
and the watersprings into dry ground;
34 A fruitful land into barrenness, for
the wickedness of them that dwell therein.
35 He turneth the wilderness into a
standing water, and dry ground into watersprings.
36 And there he maketh the hungry to
dwell, that they may prepare a city for
habitation;
37 And sow the fields, and plant vineyards, which may yield fruits of increase.
38 He blesseth them also, so that they are
multiplied greatly; and suffereth not their
cattle to decrease.
39 Again, they are minished and brought
low through oppression, affliction, and sorrow.
40 He poureth contempt upon princes,
and causeth them to wander in the wilderness, *where there is* no way.

33 He turns rivers into a desert,
springs of water into thirsty ground,
34 a fruitful land into a salty waste,
because of the wickedness of its inhabitants.
35 He turns a desert into pools of water,
a parched land into springs of water.
36 And there he lets the hungry dwell,
and they establish a city to live in;
37 they sow fields, and plant vineyards,
and get a fruitful yield.
38 By his blessing they multiply greatly;
and he does not let their cattle decrease.

39 When they are diminished and brought low
through oppression, trouble, and sorrow,
40 he pours contempt upon princes
and makes them wander in trackless wastes;

B. A Didactic Hymn (107:33-43)

1. The Power of God in Nature (107:33-38)

33-38. On vs. 33 cf. Isa. 42:15; 50:2. **A salty waste** rather than **barrenness.** The noun is cognate to the Hebrew word for "salt." On vs. 35 cf. Isa. 41:18; 43:19-20. **By his blessing:** Lit., "then he blessed them" (cf. KJV).

2. The Lord's Steadfast Love (107:39-43)

39-41. There may here be some dislocation of the original order. Some scholars place vs. 39 after vs. 40, and take vss. 39, 41 together. On vs. 40 cf. Job 12:21, 24.

---

have found no release till death has come? These are questions that take us from exposition to apologetics. But this can be said: There are many ways in which prayer is answered. The removal of the distress is one way. Power to endure it and to gain from it is another way. "Who rises from prayer a better man, his prayer is answered." [2] Again the witnesses are beyond number, and they come from every household of faith. One may quote from Jalaluddin Rumi, *A Little Book of Eastern Wisdom,* but the same sentiment appears in all religious literature:

He prayed, but to his prayer no answer came,
And choked within him sank his ardour's flame;
No more he prayed, no more the knee he bent,
While round him darkened doubt and discontent;
Till in his room, one eve, there shone a light,
And he beheld an angel-presence bright,
Who said: "O faint heart, why hast thou resigned
Praying, and no more callest God to mind?"
"I prayed," he said, "but no one heard my prayer,
Long disappointment has induced despair."
"Fool," said the angel, "every prayer of thine,
Of God's immense compassion was a sign;
Each cry of thine, 'O Lord!' itself contains
The answer, 'Here am I'; thy very pains,
Ardour, and love and longing, every tear
Are His attraction, prove Him very near.
The cloud dispersed; once more the suppliant prayed
Nor ever failed to find the promised aid.[3]

It came to Paul the apostle in one brief but gracious promise: "My grace is sufficient for thee." It is a common experience.

He made the storm be still,
and the waves of the sea were hushed.

Should we not try this way of prayer with greater perseverance? Should we not try it for our contemporaries in days of supreme difficulty? We must not expect food where there is famine, or ready-made houses where there is overcrowding, or peace and safety and plenty where men compete and quarrel. God does not relieve us of

[2] George Meredith, *The Ordeal of Richard Feverel* (New York: Charles Scribner's Sons, 1905), p. 75.

[3] Quoted in Wilkinson, *Religious Experience,* p. 193.

41 Yet setteth he the poor on high from
affliction, and maketh *him* families like a
flock.
42 The righteous shall see *it,* and rejoice:
and all iniquity shall stop her mouth.
43 Whoso *is* wise, and will observe these
things, even they shall understand the loving-kindness of the LORD.

A Song *or* Psalm of David.

108 O God, my heart is fixed; I will sing and give praise, even with my glory.

41 but he raises up the needy out of affliction,
and makes their families like flocks.
42 The upright see it and are glad;
and all wickedness stops its mouth.
43 Whoever is wise, let him give heed to these things;
let men consider the steadfast love of the LORD.

A Song. A Psalm of David.

108 My heart is ready, O God,
my heart is ready!
I will sing, I will sing praises!
Awake, my soul!

42-43. On vs. 42 cf. Job 22:19. **Wise:** A common term in the wisdom literature, but found only once elsewhere in the psalms (49:10).

CVIII. Praise and Petition (108:1-13)

This psalm consists of two sections, each of which forms part of another psalm. Vss. 1-5 are found in 57:7-11, and vss. 6-13 in 60:5-12. Whether our author drew his material directly from Pss. 57; 60, or whether he took it from sources upon which Pss. 57; 60 were also dependent, is a moot point. His purpose seems to have been to produce a lament, and this is what we have in vss. 6-13. He then strengthened his appeal to God by prefacing it with a short hymn, and thus we have vss. 1-5. The text of the psalm is almost verbally identical with the corresponding verses in Pss. 57; 60. A few of the relatively minor differences between them are noted below. For a discussion of the contents see the Exeg. on Pss. 57; 60.

1. The Psalmist Gives Thanks (108:1-5)

108:1. The second **my heart is ready** is not found in the M.T., but it is supplied by some Hebrew MSS, the LXX, and the Syriac, and it is present in 57:7. **Even with**

---

responsibility for past crimes or treat us like spoiled children. He will not restore as by magic cities that we have destroyed, or raise from the depths of the sea ships that have been sunk. But he will teach us again the truths by which men live (vss. 33-37); he will give us faith to rebuild, and such an attitude to one another that what we build shall endure. If we will but cry **to the LORD in** [our] **trouble,** he will deliver us **from** [our] **distress**—not perhaps as we hoped or expected, but according to his great love and his everlasting mercy. Then

> **Let the redeemed of the LORD say so** (vs. 2).

> **Let them extol him in the congregation of the people,**
> **and praise him in the assembly of the elders** (vs. 32).

108:1-13. ***Praise and Prayer.***—One's first impression is that this psalm is a unity. Actually it is a composite work, vss. 1-5 being taken from Ps. 57, and vss. 6-13 from Ps. 60. Who put the two parts together and for what purpose it is vain to speculate. There can be no doubt, however, that whether for personal use or as a general hymn it is most effective. The first part is an utterance of praise and adoration; the second part is a prayer for help in time of trouble.

1-5. ***Praise and Adoration.***—Praise is one of the marks of a saint. Baron von Hügel has already been cited (see Expos. on 99:1) as saying that every true saint has revealed four traits: he must have been loyal to the faith, he must have been heroic in times of testing, he must have shown the power to do what ordinarily would be impossible, and he must have been radiant in the midst of the strain and stress of life. That radiance has shown itself in happy faces and cheerful speech. It has been full of the charity that "beareth all things, be-

2 Awake, psaltery and harp: I *myself*
will awake early.
3 I will praise thee, O LORD, among the
people: and I will sing praises unto thee
among the nations.
4 For thy mercy *is* great above the heavens: and thy truth *reacheth* unto the clouds.
5 Be thou exalted, O God, above the
heavens: and thy glory above all the earth;

2 Awake, O harp and lyre!
I will awake the dawn!
3 I will give thanks to thee, O LORD, among
the peoples,
I will sing praises to thee among the
nations.
4 For thy steadfast love is great above the
heavens,
thy faithfulness reaches to the clouds.

5 Exalt thyself, O God, above the heavens!
Let thy glory be over all the earth!

---

my glory: The RSV replaces **even** with **awake** (as in 57:8*a*); **my glory** is used of the inner life of man, hence **my soul** (cf. 7:5; 16:9; 30:12; Gen. 49:6).

3. LORD (יהוה): Cf. "Lord" (אדני) in 57:9.

---

lieveth all things, hopeth all things, endureth all things" (I Cor. 13:7). It has shown itself by a reluctance to criticize. Others may denounce—the saint is more at his ease when commending. It shows itself also in worship, where thanksgiving crowds out complaint. Even the saint may cry, "How long, O Lord, how long?" but the natural attitude is:

> **My heart is ready, O God,**
> **my heart is ready!**
> **I will sing, I will sing praises!**
> **Awake, my soul!**
> **Awake, O harp and lyre!**
> **I will awake the dawn!**

This attitude of spontaneous thanksgiving is characteristic of the life and teaching of Francis of Assisi. Not that he was always the same. There were times when, like Jeremiah, he was a fount of tears. There were other times when, like Amos, he gave utterance to scorching words, especially when one of his brothers accepted money, or when a leper was allowed to pass unhelped. But these outbursts were exceptional. The spirit of the man shines in his hymn of praise. And G. K. Chesterton insists that this sense of gratitude was not a phase or even a sentiment but the very rock of reality: "It was not a fancy but a fact; rather it is true that beside it all facts are fancies. . . . He who has seen the whole world hanging on a hair of the mercy of God has seen the truth; we might almost say the cold truth." Chesterton quotes with approval a remark of Rossetti that "the worst moment for the atheist is when he is really thankful and has nobody to thank." He adds that "the great painter boasted that he mixed all his colours with brains, and the great saint may be said to mix all his thoughts with thanks."[4] Often Chesterton returns to the same reflection in his autobiography. So many, says he, give the impression that they have succumbed to the belief that they were called to be critics; as for himself, he would delight to sing with the congregation:

> **I will give thanks to thee, O LORD, among the**
> **peoples,**
> **I will sing praises to thee among the nations.**

If this sense of appreciation is made a test, we arrive at some strange conclusions. Some who have been prominent in the households of faith fail. It has been said, for example, that Mohammedanism, Stoicism, and some forms of Puritanism, are lacking in praise. The statement will cause protests. Epictetus was a Stoic; yet he takes his place among the men of gladness. Consider such words as these:

> What power of speech suffices adequately to praise, or to set them [the gifts of Providence] forth? For, had we but true intelligence, what duty would be more perpetually incumbent on us than both in public and in private to hymn the Divine, and bless His name and praise His benefits? Ought we not, when we dig, and when we plough, and when we eat, to sing this hymn to God? "Great is God, because He hath given us these implements whereby we may till the soil; great is God, because he hath given us hands, and the means of nourishment by food, and insensible growth, and breathing sleep"; these things in each particular we ought to hymn, and to chant the greatest and the divinest hymn because He hath given us the power to appreciate these blessings, and continuously to use them. What then? Since the most of you are blinded, ought there not to be some one to fulfil this province for you, and on behalf of all to sing his hymn to God? And what else can *I* do, who am

[4] *St. Francis of Assisi* (New York: George H. Doran, 1923), p. 88.

6 That thy beloved may be delivered:
save *with* thy right hand, and answer me.
7 God hath spoken in his holiness; I will
rejoice, I will divide Shechem, and mete
out the valley of Succoth.
8 Gilead *is* mine; Manasseh *is* mine;
Ephraim also *is* the strength of mine head;
Judah *is* my lawgiver;

6 That thy beloved may be delivered,
give help by thy right hand, and answer me!

7 God has promised in his sanctuary:[y]
"With exultation I will divide up Shechem,
and portion out the Vale of Succoth.
8 Gilead is mine; Manas'seh is mine;
E'phraim is my helmet;
Judah my scepter.

[y] Or *by his holiness*

2. A Plea for Help (108:6-13)

6-13. Answer me: Cf. "answer us" in 60:5. **Over Philistia I shout in triumph:** The M.T. of 60:8 is "O Philistia, shout in triumph over me." **The fortified city:** A different word appears in 60:9. **Who will lead me?** is an emendation (ינחני) supported by the LXX and the Syriac. The M.T., here and in 60:9, is "who has led me?"

---

a lame old man, except sing praises to God? Now, had I been a nightingale, I should have sung the songs of a nightingale, or had I been a swan the songs of a swan; but being a reasonable being, it is my duty to hymn God. This is my task, and I accomplish it; nor, so far as may be granted to me, will I ever abandon this post, and you also do I exhort to this same song.[5]

Not all Stoicism, however, rises to this level. The Puritans also vary from genuine, spontaneous praise to worship that is somber and morose, from the spirit of the psalmists to a mood that repels by its severity.

The psalmist's exultation appears among men who make little profession of piety. Lord Grey of Fallodon was one of these shy men, strangely afraid to commit himself. "Today I went to church unintentionally," he wrote one day to a friend, and then proceeded to explain that it was a harvest festival, and that they sang four harvest hymns.

They make me wriggle and purr with enjoyment.
"And keep us in His grace
And guide us when perplexed
And save us from all ills
In this world and the next."
The simplicity gave me such a [*doux*] *attendrissement* that I felt as if I could kiss the whole choir for singing it. But they missed out one verse of "We plough the fields and scatter," and I nearly made a fuss and interrupted the service then. We had too the 118th Psalm and a fine chant for it: do you know that psalm? It is splendid and buoyant and says things two or three or four times over because it is so glad.[6]

[5] *Discourses* I. 16.

[6] G. M. Trevelyan, *Grey of Fallodon* (Boston: Houghton Mifflin Co., 1937), pp. 177-78.

Or consider the writing of W. H. Davies. Davies was not a conventional churchman. He was the "supertramp" of whom George Bernard Shaw said that "if he is to be encouraged and approved, then British morality is a mockery, British respectability an imposture, and British industry a vice." [7] But the spirit of praise appears in poem after poem. It is not the formal praise of the sanctuary, but it compares well with much that in churches is formal and restrained. Think of the poem entitled "A Great Time," in which he sees a rainbow and hears a cuckoo and exclaims:

A rainbow and a cuckoo's song
May never come together again;
May never come
This side the tomb.[8]

Or read "The Green Tent":

Summer has spread a cool, green tent
Upon the bare poles of this tree.[8]

As one reads, one does not feel far from him who wrote:

For thy steadfast love is great above the heavens,
thy faithfulness reaches to the clouds.

6-13. ***Prayer and Intercession.***—Notice now the ease with which the compiler passes from exultation in vss. 1-5 to intercession in vss. 6-13. In both parts we are conscious of the needs of

[7] In the preface to W. H. Davies, *The Autobiography of a Super-tramp* (New York: A. A. Knopf, 1917), p. vii.

[8] From *The Collected Poems of W. H. Davies.* Used by permission of Mrs. W. H. Davies and Jonathan Cape, Ltd., publishers.

9 Moab *is* my washpot; over Edom will
I cast out my shoe; over Philistia will I
triumph.
10 Who will bring me into the strong
city? who will lead me into Edom?
11 *Wilt* not *thou,* O God, *who* hast cast
us off? and wilt not thou, O God, go forth
with our hosts?
12 Give us help from trouble: for vain *is*
the help of man.
13 Through God we shall do valiantly:
for he *it is that* shall tread down our enemies.

9 Moab is my washbasin;
upon Edom I cast my shoe;
over Philistia I shout in triumph."

10 Who will bring me to the fortified city?
Who will lead me to Edom?
11 Hast thou not rejected us, O God?
Thou dost not go forth, O God, with our armies.
12 O grant us help from the foe,
for vain is the help of man!
13 With God we shall do valiantly;
it is he who will tread down our foes.

---

a worshiping community. We should like to know the circumstances the psalmist had in mind. It may have been the return from Babylon, with all its hopes and dangers. It is, however, a common experience that achievements bring new problems. We have found it so in the modern world. Prayers are answered; but even as we rejoice, important questions rise and bring new dangers with them. It is natural therefore to pass from praise to prayer, from an acknowledgment of divine succor to intercession for further guidance.

Prayer in this sense is not easy to expound. It is difficult partly because it has been dealt with so often. There is in all education a place for repetition, but there is also a great danger. There is the difficulty that the points may seem trite. An illustration is found in F. S. Smythe's *The Spirit of the Hills,*[9] in which he expresses himself with indignation about religious services he attended as a boy. It was wartime, and perhaps his own nerves made him critical. But according to his account, visiting ministers talked about the war that was being fought, and proceeded to tell the boys that when their opportunity came they would all be heroes. Meanwhile they could pray—and the impression left was that praying was not equal to fighting, but it was all in the national cause. Have we not all heard references to prayer that made the same suggestion?

Some who set themselves to expound the laws, the methods, and the various parts of prayer, begin by confessing themselves to be novices. This looks like modesty, and it is better than the hypocrisy which leads us to assume that the speaker has really attained. We should not, however, be satisfied with such an attitude in other spheres. If a surgeon began an operation with an apology, it would not induce confidence. If a ship's captain explained before going to sea that he might prove inadequate in a storm, it would not make men eager to sail with him.

[9] London: Hodder & Stoughton, 1935, p. 33.

And book learning is no substitute. The apologetic surgeon and the diffident captain might have all the certificates available, and they would count for little without experience. We need more than a knowledge of what prayer has done for others; we need the heart that is lifted to God in every time of trouble, the life that has been raised to a higher level, the voice that cries with expectancy:

> **O grant us help from the foe,**
> **for vain is the help of man!**

We have used language like the psalmist's; we have sung hymns like "O God, our help in ages past"; but in experience we have looked to men for help. We have done so in national crises. Whatever the professions of our lips, too often our trust has been in force. Even in the realm of organized religion—whatever we have *said,* it is the skill and wisdom of man to which we have turned. Have we not tried new forms of church advertising, more attractive services with better music and more pleasing buildings? But what about a revival of prayer, with its rediscovery of spiritual vision and dynamic?

> Prayer is the Christian's vital breath,
> The Christian's native air.[1]

Prayer, as Luther said, is a powerful thing, for God has bound and tied himself thereto.

> O blessed Lord! how much I need
> Thy light to guide me on my way!
> So many hands, that, without heed,
> Still touch thy wounds, and make them bleed!
> So many feet that, day by day,
> Still wander from thy fold astray!
> . . . .
> Feeble, at best, is my endeavor!
> I see, but cannot reach, the height
> That lies forever in the light,
> And yet forever and forever,
> When seeming just within my grasp,

[1] James Montgomery, "What Is Prayer?"

To the chief Musician, A Psalm of David.

109 Hold not thy peace, O God of my praise;

To the choirmaster. A Psalm of David.

109 Be not silent, O God of my praise!

CIX. Help Me, O Lord My God (109:1-31)

Although Rashi and some modern commentators, e.g., Buttenwieser, maintain that the psalmist is speaking for the nation, most scholars are impressed by the strong personal character of this psalm and take it to be the lament of an individual. It is in fact a very striking poem, marked by vigorous diction and originality of structure.

The psalmist's complaint is described in vss. 1-5, 22-25. It is evident from these verses that while he is suffering from some physical disability, his chief troubles are false accusations directed against him by wicked neighbors who have rewarded his good actions with evil. The plea for God's intervention is contained in vss. 1, 21, 26-29, and so confident is the psalmist of a favorable response, and of his own vindication, that he ends on a note of thankfulness in vss. 30-31.

The crux of the psalm is in vss. 6-19. This section is clearly an imprecation, but since a single person is being addressed, whereas the enemies of vss. 1-5 are a company, the question arises as to the identity of the individual concerned. The Syriac obviates the difficulty by making all the references in these verses plural. Some scholars, e.g., Schmidt, Leslie, Weiser, believe the accursed is the psalmist himself, and they take the verses as a citation of the curses and false charges directed against the psalmist by his foes. It must be admitted, on this view, that in vs. 20 the psalmist calls down upon his adversaries the very evils they hurl at him. A more probable interpretation is that in vss. 6-19 the psalmist himself is speaking, and that for the sake of vividness he refers to his enemies collectively as one person, or else that he selects one of their number, presumably their leader, as the object of his imprecation. It is also possible that the author is using some traditional curse formulas without fully adapting them to his own situation. If his words seem harsh, we must remember that in the O.T. deep piety and a vengeful mood often go hand in hand, as both the Psalms and the book of Jeremiah amply illustrate (Pss. 35:4-8; 58:6-9; 69:22-28; 83:9-17; 129:5-8; 137:7-9; Jer. 11:18-23; 15:15; 17:12-18; 18:19-23; 20:11-12). It is probable that none of these writers was given to a purely personal vindictiveness. Our present psalmist, like the others, undoubtedly

I feel my feeble hands unclasp,
And sink discouraged into night!
For thine own purpose, thou hast sent
The strife and the discouragement! [2]

There have been religious teachers who have spoken with disparagement of petition. They have commended meditation, but have suggested that "all this begging" is on a lower spiritual plane. Yet there is much in the teaching and example of Jesus to encourage us to lift up our hearts. The very prayer he gave us should convince us that petition takes an important if not an unexpected place.

Have we in our worship this transition from praise to supplication? Have we in our daily lives learned the great variety and the immense possibilities of devotional practices? What a deprivation it would be if in music we limited ourselves to particular forms! What an absurdity it would be if in poetry we demanded uniformity of style and sentiment! Even so, in forms of prayer we need to be catholic in sympathy and manner, finding place for a song like Pippa's:

God's in his heaven—
All's right with the world! [3]

as well as for the psalmist when he cries:

**Who will bring me to the fortified city?
Who will lead me to Edom?**

109:1-31. *An Imprecatory Psalm and the Gospel of Forgiveness.*—Anyone who sets himself to expound the book of Psalms will feel that he is like a traveler passing through scenes of the greatest beauty. Sometimes, however, he will find problems as well as delight. There will be psalms he would like to pass by after a single reading, as a traveler hurries by ugly buildings or dreary plains. There are psalms so

[2] Longfellow, *The Golden Legend,* Part II.

[3] Browning, *Pippa Passes,* "Morning."

2 For the mouth of the wicked and the mouth of the deceitful are opened against me: they have spoken against me with a lying tongue.
3 They compassed me about also with words of hatred; and fought against me without a cause.
4 For my love they are my adversaries: but I *give myself unto* prayer.
5 And they have rewarded me evil for good, and hatred for my love.

2 For wicked and deceitful mouths are
opened against me,
speaking against me with lying tongues.
3 They beset me with words of hate,
and attack me without cause.
4 In return for my love they accuse me,
even as I make prayer for them.[z]
5 So they reward me evil for good,
and hatred for my love.

[z] Syr: Heb *I prayer*

identified his cause with that of God, and his faith in the Lord's righteous government of the world demanded that the Lord act in some effective way against the wicked.

As a curiosity of exegesis we may note that both Calvin and some modern Roman Catholic scholars, observing that vs. 8 is quoted in Acts 1:20, take Chrysostom's view that in this psalm we have prophecy under the form of an imprecation. Calvin (*Commentary on the Psalms,* IV, 269) said that "Christ must be principally understood as the person who gives utterance to these lamentations and denunciations, occasioned by the injurious treatment he received from his betrayer and murderers." Herkenne, on the other hand, finds in vss. 6-19 a word of God to the psalmist. The latter's enemy actually prefigures Judas Iscariot, and these verses are then a prophecy of the treachery of Judas and of his unhappy fate (cf. Calès, *Livre des Psaumes,* II, 332, 337).

It is impossible to suggest a definite date for this psalm. If we assume that the psalmist's enemies were fellow Hebrews, the O.T. evidence from Amos to Nehemiah points to persistent tensions within the Hebrew community, and therefore such a psalm as this might have been written at almost any time. The meter is generally 3+3.

1. Appeal to God (109:1-5)

109:2. Wicked and deceitful mouths assumes the repointing of one Hebrew word (רשע) to obtain "wickedness" in the phrase, "a mouth of wickedness." **Are opened:** A small emendation (נפתחו), supported by the LXX, Jerome, and the Syriac. The M.T. is "have opened."

4-5. Even as I make prayer for them: An emended text (ואני תפלתי להם); the M.T. is "and I prayer" (cf. RSV mg.). **They reward me evil:** Similar complaints are found in 35:12; 38:20; Jer. 18:19-20.

full of bitterness that he wonders why they were included in a book of praise, and why he should tarry with them. There is, for example, Ps. 79, which beseeches God to pour out his wrath upon the heathen and to render to neighboring peoples "sevenfold into their bosom." There is Ps. 137, which begins with the fine patriotic lament of exiles who sat down and wept by the waters of Babylon and hung their harps upon the willows and refused to sing the Lord's song in a foreign land. In such circumstances no poet could begin better, but what can we make of the conclusion with its bitter words concerning the Babylonians: "Happy shall he be, that taketh and dasheth thy little ones against the stones"? The Babylonians may have been wicked and cruel, but sentiments like this contradict the best we have learned about religion and life.

Then there is Ps. 109, which is perhaps the most bitter of all. It is not in one mood throughout. There is a great difference between the opening and closing verses, with their prayers for protection and pity, their knowledge that whatever is done must be God's doing, their faith in a Lord who is on the side of the **poor** and **needy**—between all that and the central part which is full of the spirit of retaliation. That the writer and those he speaks for have suffered grievously, that their enemies have in some measure been the Lord's enemies, are doubtless both true. It should also be noticed that the troubles have in part been caused by sins of speech. Slanderers have been busy. Lying tongues have spread so much mischief that the writer feels himself compassed about with words of hatred. Though other trials there were, it was the uncharitable word that wounded so deeply. But however much a man may suffer, is

6 Set thou a wicked man over him: and let Satan stand at his right hand.

7 When he shall be judged, let him be condemned: and let his prayer become sin.

8 Let his days be few; *and* let another take his office.

9 Let his children be fatherless, and his wife a widow.

10 Let his children be continually vagabonds, and beg: let them seek *their bread* also out of their desolate places.

11 Let the extortioner catch all that he hath; and let the strangers spoil his labor.

12 Let there be none to extend mercy unto him: neither let there be any to favor his fatherless children.

13 Let his posterity be cut off; *and* in the generation following let their name be blotted out.

14 Let the iniquity of his fathers be remembered with the LORD; and let not the sin of his mother be blotted out.

6 Appoint a wicked man against him;
let an accuser bring him to trial.[a]
7 When he is tried, let him come forth guilty;
let his prayer be counted as sin!
8 May his days be few;
may another seize his goods!
9 May his children be fatherless,
and his wife a widow!
10 May his children wander about and beg;
may they be driven out of[b] the ruins they inhabit!
11 May the creditor seize all that he has;
may strangers plunder the fruits of his toil!
12 Let there be none to extend kindness to him,
nor any to pity his fatherless children!
13 May his posterity be cut off;
may his name be blotted out in the second generation!
14 May the iniquity of his fathers be remembered before the LORD,
and let not the sin of his mother be blotted out!

[a] Heb *stand at his right hand*
[b] Gk: Heb *and seek*

2. IMPRECATION (109:6-20)

6-8. An accuser or **Satan:** The terrestrial setting favors the RSV. **Bring him to trial:** Lit., **stand at his right hand.** Vs. 8*a* is quoted in Acts 1:20. **His goods** is a possible translation of פקדתו and is supported by Isa. 15:7 as well as by the tenor of the following verses; but **his office** can also be justified (cf. II Chr. 23:18).

9-10. The family must suffer for the sins of the father and husband (cf. Exod. 20:5; 22:24). **May they be driven out:** An emendation (יגרשו, Pual) supported by the LXX. The M.T. is **let them seek.**

13-18. His name: So some Hebrew MSS, the LXX, and Jerome. The M.T. is **their name. In the second generation:** Many scholars follow the LXX and read "in one generation." **The sin of his mother:** Cf. Exeg. on 51:3-5. **And may his memory be cut**

he ever justified in answering back with words like these?

> **May his days be few;**
> **may another seize his goods!**
> **May his children be fatherless,**
> **and his wife a widow!**

Is it surprising that critics point to passages like this, and add the comment, "So this is the book of Psalms about which so much pious nonsense has been talked"?

The critic has been answered, and anyone who studies relevant commentaries can see what the answers are. If justice is to be done to historical characters, they must be judged by the standards of their times. To understand the Victorians we must appreciate their point of view. To be fair to the Puritans we must remember their principles and assumptions. This is still more necessary if we go back, as the psalms take us, into the ancient world. We must remember that the Israelites did not know science as we understand it, and they had not heard the Christian gospel or been taught the maxims of Christian morality. Not that we must think meanly of them. Many of them lived nearer to God than we do. Many of them were more sensitive to moral and spiritual reality than we are. Their very simplicity made it possible for God to speak to them and

15 Let them be before the LORD continually, that he may cut off the memory of them from the earth.

16 Because that he remembered not to show mercy, but persecuted the poor and needy man, that he might even slay the broken in heart.

17 As he loved cursing, so let it come unto him: as he delighted not in blessing, so let it be far from him.

18 As he clothed himself with cursing like as with his garment, so let it come into his bowels like water, and like oil into his bones.

19 Let it be unto him as the garment *which* covereth him, and for a girdle wherewith he is girded continually.

20 *Let* this *be* the reward of mine adversaries from the LORD, and of them that speak evil against my soul.

15 Let them be before the LORD continually;
and may his[c] memory be cut off from the earth!
16 For he did not remember to show kindness,
but pursued the poor and needy
and the brokenhearted to their death.
17 He loved to curse; let curses come on him!
He did not like blessing; may it be far from him!
18 He clothed himself with cursing as his coat,
may it soak into his body like water,
like oil into his bones!
19 May it be like a garment which he wraps round him,
like a belt with which he daily girds himself!

20 May this be the reward of my accusers from the LORD,
of those who speak evil against my life!

[c] Gk: Heb *their*

---

off from the earth: An emended text, with some versional support. The M.T. is represented by the KJV. **To their death:** An emendation, supported by the Syriac. The M.T. is **that he might . . . slay. Oil:** Used as a medicament (Isa. 1:6) and as an unguent (Amos 6:6; Mic. 6:15).

20. There is no magic potency in the preceding curses (vss. 6-19). It is only as the Lord concurs that they become effective.

---

through them to the nation. But he did not speak as he spoke in Jesus of Nazareth. If he had given them then the gospel of redemption, the whole law of mercy, it would have been like putting elementary-school children in a university lecture room. Both in theology and ethics there is growth—not necessarily continuous progress, but leaps forward, and occasional retrogression. Men do not always speak wisely when they talk about "progressive revelation," though the thing itself is a fact. Because the psalmists had personal dealings with God, we go back to them as thirsty men go to perennial springs; but they did not know what their successors have learned. Above all, they did not know "the Word . . . made flesh" (John 1:14).

J. R. Seeley in his epoch-making book *Ecce Homo* tells us that there have been "three stages in the history of the treatment of crime: the stage of barbarous insensibility, the stage of law or justice, and that of mercy or humanity." He illustrates the first point by reference to the *Iliad,* in which "the distinction between right and wrong is barely recognized." There is so little moral indignation that the poet seems incapable of hating evil or of applauding good.[4] How great a step it is from that to the imprecatory psalms with their conception of vengeance and retribution! All the psalms, as has already been said, are not like that. There are spiritual songs that take us into the very presence of God. There are others that anticipate a higher morality, and at least suggest the way of forgiveness. When the psalmists sang, the world was in Seeley's second stage, the stage of law and retribution. There were legal restraints upon the instinct of retaliation. "Eye for eye, tooth for tooth" (Exod. 21:24) meant that there must be measure for measure—one eye for one eye, one tooth for one tooth, not two. And there were times when men defied these legal restraints; nor did the defiance come only from rough men of action, but as well from sensitive and even religious poets. Still, on the whole, putting aside the exceptions, the psalmists lived and moved and had their being in the stage of law and all the penalties of the law.

We come to the third stage when Jesus appears with the gospel of redemption and the

[4] Boston: Roberts Bros., 1886, p. 252.

21 But do thou for me, O God the Lord,
for thy name's sake: because thy mercy *is*
good, deliver thou me.
22 For I *am* poor and needy, and my
heart is wounded within me.
23 I am gone like the shadow when it
declineth: I am tossed up and down as the
locust.
24 My knees are weak through fasting;
and my flesh faileth of fatness.
25 I became also a reproach unto them:
when they looked upon me they shook their
heads.
26 Help me, O Lord my God: O save me
according to thy mercy:
27 That they may know that this *is* thy
hand; *that* thou, Lord, hast done it.
28 Let them curse, but bless thou: when
they arise, let them be ashamed; but let thy
servant rejoice.

21 But thou, O God my Lord,
deal on my behalf for thy name's sake;
because thy steadfast love is good, deliver me!
22 For I am poor and needy,
and my heart is stricken within me.
23 I am gone, like a shadow at evening;
I am shaken off like a locust.
24 My knees are weak through fasting;
my body has become gaunt.
25 I am an object of scorn to my accusers;
when they see me, they wag their heads.

26 Help me, O Lord my God!
Save me according to thy steadfast love!
27 Let them know that this is thy hand;
thou, O Lord, hast done it!
28 Let them curse, but do thou bless!
Let my assailants be put to shame;[d]
may thy servant be glad!

[d] Gk: Heb *they have arisen and have been put to shame*

3. Appeal Continued (109:21-31)

22-25. A further description of the psalmist's plight. **Is stricken:** The M.T. is "and my heart he has pierced within me." Many scholars emend the verb to חולל, obtaining "my heart writhes within me" (cf. LXX, Jerome, and Syriac). **At evening:** Lit., **when it declineth. Like a locust:** As a locust is brushed off a garment. **Are weak:** Lit., "stumble." **My body has become gaunt:** Lit., "my flesh is lean through lack of oil [or fat]." **To my accusers:** Lit., **unto them.**

26-29. The final appeal to God. **Let my assailants be put to shame:** An emended text (קמי יבשו), supported by the LXX. The M.T. is given in the RSV mg.

morality of mercy. We are so used to his words that we can hardly appreciate their significance; but they opened a new era. "Ye have heard that it hath been said, Thou shalt love thy neighbor, and hate thine enemy. But I say unto you, Love your enemies, . . . and pray for them which . . . persecute you; that ye may be the children of your Father which is in heaven" (Matt. 5:43-45). This was not an occasional word but a consistent message and was expressed in the strongest terms. "If ye forgive not men their trespasses, neither will your Father forgive your trespasses" (Matt. 6:15). According to the N.T., Christianity stands or falls by men's willingness or inability to respond to and live by the law of mercy.

It will be seen that this leads us to the heart of a persistent problem. What are we to do with the wrongdoer? The question presses because the enemies of peace are always numerous and powerful. They not only drench the world with blood, they thrust aside every consideration that is not, as they believe, to their own advantage. What are we to do with moral maniacs who spring up one after another in place after place? Various answers have been given, and some of them show that though we live in the Christian Era, it is easy to slip back to pre-Christian standards. It is curious how some who complain about the imprecatory psalms are themselves as violent as any Hebrew. They are not necessarily those who have suffered most. They may be among the most comfortable and secure in a sadly shaken world; but their speech suggests that they are not far from the primitive. They would lynch, or hang, draw and quarter, and expect God to approve. There are others who do not so easily forget N.T. injunctions, though they are often bewildered as to how these are to be applied. There are sentimentalists who would wipe the slate clean for everybody and start again as though nothing had happened. Others hesitate, knowing that an easy condoning may be as injurious as vengeance. There is no quick and simple answer to such questions, and we must resist facile generalizations. It is certain, however, that mere retaliation will not satisfy the Christian conscience. Neither with individ-

29 Let mine adversaries be clothed with shame; and let them cover themselves with their own confusion, as with a mantle.
30 I will greatly praise the LORD with my mouth; yea, I will praise him among the multitude.
31 For he shall stand at the right hand of the poor, to save *him* from those that condemn his soul.

29 May my accusers be clothed with dishonor;
may they be wrapped in their own shame as in a mantle!

30 With my mouth I will give great thanks to the LORD;
I will praise him in the midst of the throng.
31 For he stands at the right hand of the needy,
to save him from those who condemn him to death.

A Psalm of David.

110 The LORD said unto my Lord, Sit thou at my right hand, until I make thine enemies thy footstool.

A Psalm of David.

110 The LORD says to my lord:
"Sit at my right hand,
till I make your enemies
your footstool."

30-31. The psalmist either anticipates his deliverance, or he has received some reassurance, possibly from a priest, that the Lord is indeed with him. **From those who condemn him to death:** Lit., "from those who judge his soul."

CX. ORACLE FOR A KING (110:1-7)

This psalm, like Pss. 2; 18; etc., is to be classified as a royal psalm. A Judean king is being addressed or referred to, and as some military activity is in the offing the ninth

uals nor with nations will it work. Vendettas keep wounds open: they settle nothing. Wrote Arthur Quiller-Couch in his novel *Foe-Farrell,* written during World War I, and dedicated "To Anyone Who Supposes That He Has a Worse Enemy than Himself":

> As I see it, the more you beat Fritz by becoming like him, the more he has won. You may ride through his gates under an Arch of Triumph; but if he or his ghost sits on your saddle-bow, what's the use? You have demeaned yourself to him; you cannot shake him off, for his claws hook in you, and through the farther gate of Judgment you ride on, inseparables condemned.[5]

There were statesmen wrestling with the problems of peacemaking who saw this, though they did not all live up to it. "You and I know," said the French politician Paul Painlevé to an Englishman, "you and I know, as educated men, that France can never recover from war unless she forgives Germany, but that is too hard a truth to-day for the people of France." There were Englishmen who saw it too, and held that it was not too hard a truth for the people of England. Field Marshal Haig said that the peace must be one of reconciliation. C. P. Scott, the famous editor of the *Manchester Guardian,* taught that if the case were properly put to them, the British people would respond. Perhaps he was too optimistic. "Perhaps," says his biographer, "only Gladstone could have succeeded in such an effort." Maybe even Gladstone would have failed; but who can doubt it was such leadership the hour needed, as it has been needed since, and will be needed in the future?[6]

We preach the way of mercy not merely because we believe it will bring peace to a weary world. We preach it because it is God's way. Not that God is an indulgent Father who forgives easily. Even for him it is hard. "God so loved the world, that he gave his only begotten son" (John 3:16). That is the gospel committed to us. There we find hope for our sinful selves. And there only can we find redemption for a sinning and suffering world.

> O brother man! fold to thy heart thy brother;
> Where pity dwells, the peace of God is there;
> To worship rightly is to love each other,
> Each smile a hymn, each kindly deed a prayer.[7]

110:1-7. ***The Ideal King.***—This is one of the royal psalms. It is not easy to expound, and

[5] New York: E. P. Dutton & Co., 1929, p. 324.

[6] Hammond, *C. P. Scott,* pp. 253-54.

[7] John Greenleaf Whittier, "Worship," st. xiii.

or eighth century B.C. gives us the most probable date. Possibly the immediate occasion is the enthronement of a new monarch. Vs. 1 introduces an oracle from the Lord, but it is uncertain how far the oracle extends. Some scholars, e.g., Kittel, Oesterley, restrict the prophetic word to vs. 1, but a good case can be made out for extending it to vs. 4 (so Gunkel). Vss. 5-7 can then be taken as the psalmist's words directed to the king. The language, while marked by some Oriental extravagance, is redolent of a vigorous Hebrew nationalism.

Since Hitzig (1835-36) this psalm has often been considered of Maccabean origin, and indeed Margoliouth and Bickell detected in vss. 1-4 an acrostic on Simon, the Hasmonaean leader. This view of the psalm has now been generally abandoned, although Pfeiffer (*Introduction to O.T.*, p. 630) maintains it.

While the psalm has a primary meaning rich in promise for the age in which it was written, its phraseology and symbolism lend themselves to wider applications, and it is this fact that explains how the church found in these words, as in Isa. 53 and elsewhere in the O.T., prophetic allusions to the ministry and work of Jesus. This psalm is the most often quoted in the N.T. because it was given a messianic interpretation. How early this interpretation arose among the Jews we do not know, but it is clear from the Gospels that it was current at the time of Jesus' ministry (Matt. 22:41-46; Mark 12:35-37; Luke 20:41-44; cf. Matt. 26:64 and parallels). The psalm was employed by the early church in a messianic sense (Acts 2:34-35), and quotations from and echoes of it are numerous in the N.T. (Acts 5:31; 7:55; Rom. 8:34; I Cor. 15:25; Eph. 1:20; Col. 3:1; I Pet. 3:22; Rev. 3:21; and especially in Heb. 1:13; 5:6, 10; 6:20; 7:11, 15, 17, 21; 8:1; 10:12-13; 12:2). It is the N.T. usage that explains Luther's view of this psalm. In 1538 he said: "This is the high and chief Psalm of our dear Lord Jesus Christ, in which His Person, and His Resurrection, Ascension, and His whole kingdom are . . . clearly and powerfully set forth" (quoted in Jane T. Stoddart, *The Psalms for Every Day* [London: Hodder & Stoughton, 1939], p. 267). Among modern scholars, Buttenwieser (*Psalms,* p. 795) claims that "the poet's sire is not a historical king but a visionary figure—the Messiah of his dreams," and he gives the psalm a postexilic date.

The Hebrew presents many difficulties as even the non-Hebraist can infer if he notes the variations within the most recent English translations (cf. RSV, Amer. Trans., Oesterley, and Leslie). The principal obscurities are to be found in vss. 2, 3, 6, 7. The

---

there are questions we shall not discuss. It will be enough to imagine some high court official addressing his king and giving him what purports to be a divine oracle. The oracle develops into a meditation on the ideal King, and it is hard to say where the oracle ends and the meditation begins. The opening is bold and clear:

> **The LORD says to my lord:**
> **"Sit at my right hand,**
> **till I make your enemies**
> **your footstool."**

The **right hand** is obviously the place of honor. The chief guest or the official nearest to the throne will properly sit there. It is the **Lord** himself who sits in the supreme place. Hebrew government was ideally a theocracy. The king was not supreme: he was never more than God's representative. The king could never therefore become an arrogant dictator. He could never be a law unto himself. His power was from above, and he must give an account of his stewardship.

But though in Hebrew thought there was a limitation, there was no lowering of sovereignty. The king was to sit in the place of honor and to rule as the divine representative. To speak disrespectfully of him who had been anointed with oil was to speak against the divine appointment. If a prince should by speech and act show that he had departed from the divine purpose men might remove him, but until that spirit of disobedience was manifest he was to be obeyed. There is a sense, according to the later verses of the psalm, in which the king is not only God's representative in a secular sphere, but he is a king who must be regarded as in some sense a priest.

> **You are a priest for ever**
> **after the order of Melchizedek.**

Into all that was meant by **the order of Melchizedek** we need not enter; it obviously meant exceptional distinction. It meant that whoever was lawfully called to the throne was appointed to an office that was religious as well as secular.

2 The LORD shall send the rod of thy strength out of Zion: rule thou in the midst of thine enemies.

3 Thy people *shall be* willing in the day of thy power, in the beauties of holiness from the womb of the morning: thou hast the dew of thy youth.

2 The LORD sends forth from Zion
your mighty scepter.
Rule in the midst of your foes!
3 Your people will offer themselves freely
on the day you lead your host
upon the holy mountains.[e]
From the womb of the morning
like dew your youth[f] will come to you.

[e] Another reading is *in holy array*
[f] Cn: Heb *the dew of your youth*

RSV adopts a conservative attitude toward the accepted text, and therefore in the following Exeg. it is chiefly the emendations behind the RSV which are recorded.

1. THE LORD SPEAKS (110:1-4)

110:1. The LORD says: This is the only place in the Psalter where the phrase "the utterance of the LORD" (נאם יהוה) occurs (cf. "transgression speaks" in 36:1). In the O.T. it is nearly always used in or at the conclusion of a message purporting to come from God. **My lord:** As a designation of a ruling king see I Sam. 22:12; 26:17; I Kings 1:13; etc. **At my right hand:** The place of honor (cf. 45:9; I Kings 2:19; Zech. 3:1). In a Ugaritic text we read, "And he caused (him) to sit at the right hand of Aleyn Baal" (Patton, *Canaanite Parallels*, p. 30); cf. Wisd. Sol. 9:4. **Till I make** may indicate a time limit to the king's inactivity. Possibly, however, the conjunction עד should be translated "while" as in 141:10. **Your enemies your footstool:** A familiar method in the ancient Near East of treating foes (cf. Josh. 10:24). This verse shows an awareness of the action of God in what seem to be purely human affairs. The verse is also important as reflecting the religious sanction of the Hebrew monarchy. Much of the language here and in the following verses is figurative, and there is nothing to suggest that the king is in any sense a divine ruler (contra Mowinckel, *Psalmenstudien*, II, 302-8). The O.T. view is that the king acts as God's representative (I Chr. 28:5-6; 29:23; for a very sensible discussion of the Hebrew monarchy see Frankfort, *Kingship and the Gods*, pp. 337-44).

3. Your people will offer themselves freely: Lit., "Your people are freewill offerings." **On the day you lead your host:** Lit., "On the day of your host." **Upon the holy mountains** is the reading of some Hebrew MSS, and is supported by Jerome. The M.T. is either **in the beauties of holiness** or "in garments of holiness." **The holy mountains** is an unusual phrase (cf. Exeg. on 87:1). Mount Zion (cf. "the mountains of Zion," 133:3)

And there is much in the historical books and elsewhere to indicate that this idea prevails in the O.T. Thus Saul offered sacrifices in the presence of Samuel; and no one apparently questioned the right of David and Solomon to perform priestly acts in the presence of priests and prophets. This is not the divine right of kings, as it was affirmed by members of the house of Stuart. But it is an august conception of monarchy. It is remote from popular conceptions of government in some modern democracies; but has the progressive exclusion of religious elements from the highest offices made for the peace, the happiness, and the unity of mankind?

The psalm does not maintain this sacerdotal level throughout. In Hebrew thought the king had military as well as sacred duties. He who wore the crown must also wield the sword. He must raise armies, drive out enemies, quell rebellions, and give his people peace. In this duty as warrior there was nothing to apologize for. Time has taken much of the glamour from military life. In many quarters men speak less about heroes on the field of battle and more about the victories of peace. We must, however, beware of reading back modern sentiments into ancient scriptures. There are touches of war weariness even in the O.T., and there are memorable passages in praise of peace. But normally the warrior was honored. No one, however learned or saintly, could satisfy the popular demand if he lacked soldierly virtues and military skill. In this particular case the king is exhorted to remain in **Zion.** He might have preferred the high place on the field, but he must maintain order in the capital while others, in the name of the Lord, made his

4 The LORD hath sworn, and will not repent, Thou *art* a priest for ever after the order of Melchizedek.

4 The LORD has sworn
and will not change his mind,
"You are a priest for ever
after the order of Melchiz'edek."

---

was holy by reason of the temple (cf. 15:1; Ezek. 28:14; Isa. 66:20; etc.), but the O.T. does not elsewhere suggest that the other mountains of Palestine are holy in a comparable sense. **From the womb of the morning:** The morning as the mother of the dew. **Like dew your youth will come to you:** An emended text (תלך לך כטל ילדתיך). The M.T. is, lit., **thou hast the dew of thy youth.** The metaphor suggests the freshness of youthful strength which the king is to enjoy.

4. You are a priest: On the discharge of priestly duties by David see II Sam. 6:12-19; by his sons, II Sam. 8:18; by Solomon, I Kings 8:14, 55-56, 62-63; 9:25; by Ahaz, II Kings 16:12-15. **Melchizedek:** In Gen. 14:18, Melchizedek is described as "king of Salem" (Jerusalem) and "priest of God Most High." It is, however, not necessary to suppose that the present psalm is dependent upon Genesis for its knowledge of this ancient king. The psalmist evidently means that the ruler he is addressing belongs to an illustrious succession of priest-kings who have reigned in Jerusalem for centuries, and of whom **Melchizedek** is one of the best-known representatives.

---

enemies his footstool. There is nevertheless this promise, that the people will go wherever he sends them. Unlike reluctant levies, they will present themselves with enthusiasm—youthful warriors, fresh as the dew of early morning, will fill the hills around Jerusalem.

Much of this will seem remote from modern aspirations. For generations we have been taught to sing Ebenezer Elliott's hymn:

> When wilt thou save the people?
> O God of mercy, when?
> Not kings and lords, but nations;
> Not thrones and crowns, but men!

Not that we are always consistent. Even in the most democratic of countries visiting monarchs may find themselves the idols of the people. The main movement, however, is away from royalty and its accompaniments. H. A. L. Fisher in his *History of Europe* has given a pathetic picture of Francis Joseph, the Austrian emperor, and of his life in Vienna:

> Diligently toiling at his desk, signing and reading, reading and signing, from early morn to night . . . . Under his long rule, the Austrian Empire had sustained so many shattering blows . . . that it seemed to bear a charmed life, even when it was, in fact, fast moving to its dissolution.[8]

Francis Joseph, who "went on his way unmoved, an ascetic, an automaton," did not live to see the tragedy of monarchy as we have seen it; but the story is written by countless hands for the instruction of coming generations. Good kings, and bad ones, representatives of absolute dynasties and of limited monarchies, have been dragged from their thrones and sent as exiles on aimless journeys. No thought of holy oil or solemn consecration has arrested impatient hands. No reverence for the past, no conception of the supernatural, has abated revolutionary fervor. Yet it would be rash to affirm that the new egalitarianism brought happiness or unity. It strewed the path with promises; it did not solve the major problems of government.

Here and there, however, monarchy remains, with the full support of the people. The British royal family exerts an influence and evokes a loyalty as great as ever. This is not because kings are crowned with religious rites or consecrated with national prayers. Ceremonies in Westminster Abbey and elsewhere are apt to be treated as symbols which for historical reasons should not be abolished. Why then is it so difficult to find republican sentiment in the British Commonwealth? Not because of the outstanding ability of recent sovereigns. Not because of gifts of leadership or statecraft. Not because of the political development of the empire, though the crown has become an almost essential symbol of unity. No. The House of Windsor has won its place in the affections of men by the service it has rendered, the duties it has performed, the example that has been set in times of testing. Kings and princes do not now speak of sitting at the right hand of God; but they have called their subjects to prayer, they have led national thanksgiving, they have commended by example the place that worship should take in the life of the community. They have reasoned with men when there was a tendency to levity and called them back to a sense of responsibility. They have not done it

[8] P. 1088.

5 The Lord at thy right hand shall strike
through kings in the day of his wrath.
6 He shall judge among the heathen, he
shall fill *the places* with the dead bodies; he
shall wound the heads over many countries.
7 He shall drink of the brook in the way:
therefore shall he lift up the head.

5 The Lord is at your right hand;
he will shatter kings on the day of his wrath.
6 He will execute judgment among the nations,
filling them with corpses;
he will shatter chiefs[g]
over the wide earth.
7 He will drink from the brook by the way;
therefore he will lift up his head.

[g] Or *the head*

---

2. The Psalmist Addresses the King (110:5-7)

5-6. As the subject of the verbs in these verses is seemingly the king, **your right hand** should probably be emended to "his right hand." Observe that the king is now at the Lord's left hand (cf. vs. 1). **Filling them with corpses:** As the Hebrew is "he fills with the corpses," it is an attractive suggestion that "valleys" (גֵּאָיוֹת) should be added to the text. The KJV supplies **the places,** and the RSV adds **them. Chiefs** or **heads:** The M.T. is **head** (RSV mg.), but the LXX and Vulg. support the plural.

7. The king, as he pursues his foes, will drink from a wayside brook. This seems an inconsequential ending to the psalm, and possibly something has dropped out (so

---

to secure their own positions: that has been an aftereffect. If the British throne is secure, it is not because it rests upon force, but because it has been inspired by spiritual reality. Loyalty is not foisted on the people for reasons of state; it rises spontaneously from the hearts of men and women who are glad to sing:

> Lord God, our monarch bless;
> Girded with righteousness
> Long may she reign!
> Her heart inspire and move
> With wisdom from above;
> Throned on a nation's love,
> Her power maintain.[9]

There is, however, something else to be considered. Who the king was of whom the psalmist wrote, no one knows. It may have been David or one of the Maccabees. It may have been an ideal messiah, the national hero of whom the Hebrews dreamed generation after generation. What we know is that the psalm has been connected with Jesus of Nazareth, and it is to him that the minds of many readers turn. There are, indeed, phrases that do not seem appropriate. No one can think of Jesus as a military leader. The last thing we associate with him is the filling of the nations with **corpses** (vs. 6). But the church has been affirming for centuries that God has set him at his **right hand.** To him and to no other have been given power and authority. It is not an authority that depends upon force, upon earthly dignities, or popularity. It depends, as Christian rule has always depended, not on threats or punishments, but upon love and service, sacrifice and persuasion. In terms of earthly splendor Jesus possessed nothing. When he stood before the representatives of Rome, he seemed to be weakness personified. Yet he confessed that he was a king, though he added that his kingdom was not of this world. Never has ridicule seemed more complete than when Pilate placed above the cross on which he died the words "The King of the Jews." There it was, in the three great languages of the times, for men to read. It was all in keeping with the crown of thorns and the robe of mock majesty that soldiers had put upon him. But if the procurator and those associated with him could have seen the future, how astonished they would have been! That this Lord Jesus, who had no soldiers, and was so easily brought to the place of crucifixion, should reign in innumerable hearts, that tens of thousands should go as his ambassadors and die for his cause, that after twenty centuries his kingdom should make all secular kingdoms seem small—this no one could have predicted or anticipated. Yet the movement still progresses. And still the authority is commended by love and established by deeds of mercy.

> Blessings abound where'er he reigns;
> The prisoner leaps to lose his chains,
> The weary find eternal rest,
> And all the sons of want are blest.[1]

[9] W. E. Hickson, "God bless our native land."

[1] Isaac Watts, "Jesus shall reign where'er the sun."

111 Praise ye the LORD. I will praise the LORD with *my* whole heart, in the assembly of the upright, and *in* the congregation.

111 Praise the LORD.
I will give thanks to the LORD
with my whole heart,
in the company of the upright, in the
congregation.

Cheyne). **His head** (RSV): Lit., **the head** (KJV), but the RSV is supported by some Hebrew MSS and the Syriac.

CXI. PRAISE THE LORD (111:1-10)

This little hymn of praise, which celebrates the Lord's goodness to Israel, is intended for use **in the congregation** (vs. 1), possibly on one of the festivals. Its sentiments and phraseology run along familiar lines and it lacks any clear development of thought, but these features may be due largely to the acrostic form which the psalmist has chosen (cf. Pss. 9; 10; 25; 34; 37; 112; 119; 145). In this instance, however, as in Ps. 112, the acrostic scheme is unusually restrictive, for it is imposed upon the clauses (or stichs), creating a poem of twenty-two very short lines, each of which begins with a new letter of the alphabet. This is an arrangement that makes for considerable artificiality. Weiser's German translation (*Die Psalmen,* p. 462) is an attempt to reproduce the acrostic effect with the German alphabet.

The acrostic form and the echoes of wisdom interest in vs. 10 are the chief evidences of a postexilic date. The meter is 3+3, with variations.

1. INTRODUCTION (111:1)

111:1. Praise the LORD: This heading forms no part of the acrostic arrangement. The verse implies that the psalm is to be sung by an individual before a worshiping **congregation,** the place presumably being the temple.

Thus men with Christian faith in their souls and Christian achievements before their eyes reread the psalm and cry one to another:

> **The LORD sends forth from Zion**
> **your mighty scepter.**
> **Rule in the midst of your foes!**

111:1-10. ***The Necessity of Reverence.***—One of the things that have deepened interest in O.T. study is investigation of the many poetic forms used by Semitic people. The most popular is called parallelism—the repetition of the thought of one line in similar terms in the following lines. Another is the recurrence of a particular sound, consonantal or vowel. Yet another is the alphabetical or acrostic pattern, in which each line or verse begins with successive letters of the Hebrew alphabet. Ps. 111 is one of the best examples of the third style. The advantage of such a usage is that it aids memory, and there are suggestions that this psalm was memorized for the purposes of public worship. The form does not, however, make for a flow of thought or for logical sequence. Whenever the acrostic method is used, one may expect good proverbs but little narrative. Ps. 111 reminds us of this fact. It contains lines that are worth laying to heart; but though there is discernible movement, there is no attempt to develop a particular and consistent theme. There are marks of the kind of mind and spirit so often found elsewhere. There is consciousness of the divine nature and activity (vss. 3-4, 7-8). There is a realization of the fact that man's duty is to respond with gratitude to God's favor (vss. 1, 10). There are references to the national history as indications of a gracious and continuous guidance, of a covenant remembered and unbroken (vss. 5, 9). Then in the final verses there are reflections of a miscellaneous character, including this that should perhaps be chosen for more detailed study: that **the fear of the LORD is the beginning of wisdom,** or as W. O. E. Oesterley translates it, "The zenith of Wisdom is the fear of Yahweh." [2]

Many of the best minds of Israel were concerned with the nature and the way of wisdom, and the psalmist's statement was reaffirmed with equal assurance by others (cf. Prov. 1:7; 9:10; Ecclus. 1:14).[3] In Job 28, which was probably written after most of the psalms, a poet meditates on the mystery of the divine wisdom. First he sets down some of the wonderful things man can do. He can take iron from dust, and smelt

[2] *The Psalms* (New York: The Macmillan Co., 1939), II, 466.

[3] Cf. Frank H. Ballard, *The Undying Wisdom* (London: Student Christian Movement Press, 1935), p. 11.

2 The works of the LORD *are* great, sought out of all them that have pleasure therein.

3 His work *is* honorable and glorious: and his righteousness endureth for ever.

4 He hath made his wonderful works to be remembered: the LORD *is* gracious and full of compassion.

5 He hath given meat unto them that fear him: he will ever be mindful of his covenant.

2 Great are the works of the LORD,
studied by all who have pleasure in them.
3 Full of honor and majesty is his work,
and his righteousness endures for ever.
4 He has caused his wonderful works to be remembered;
the LORD is gracious and merciful.
5 He provides food for those who fear him;
he is ever mindful of his covenant.

---

2. GREAT ARE THE LORD'S WORKS (111:2-4)

2. Studied: Lit., **sought out,** but the seeking is done with the mind.

4. This verse and also vss. 5-6 appear to contain allusions to the Exodus and the conquest of Canaan. **To be remembered:** Lit., "a memorial." Some take this as a reference to the Passover (cf. Exod. 12:14; 13:8-9), but the meaning may not be so circumscribed.

3. GOD'S CARE FOR HIS PEOPLE (111:5-9)

5. He provides food: The classical illustration is the supply of quails and manna at the time of the Exodus (Exod. 16:11-36), but the idea may have a more general application (cf. 34:9-10; 104:14-15; Matt. 6:25-34). טרף is a word commonly meaning "prey" and is not the usual term for **food** (cf. Prov. 31:15). As the first word in the verse, its presence here may be an alphabetical necessity. Peters *et al.,* however, take the noun literally, and assume a reference to the spoils of Egypt and Canaan. **His covenant:** With Israel at Sinai (Exod. 19:5).

---

copper from stone, and cut channels in rock, and bind the streams. But he cannot attain unto wisdom, which is more precious than rubies. The refrain of the poem is the repeated question, "Where shall wisdom be found? and where is the place of understanding?"

Partial answers are to be found scattered throughout several of the O.T. books. In Job 32:9 Elihu says,

> It is not the old that are wise,
> nor the aged that understand what is right.

He had listened to the arguments of Job and his friends and, as befitted youth, had listened in silence; but there came a time when he could be silent no longer. And this was the first thing he had to say. Wisdom may come as a vision in the night or be the fruit of tears, but it is not a state into which one necessarily grows. It was a considerable pronouncement for a Hebrew to make, for they were much inclined to venerate old age. Few today would wish to contradict him. We do not reverence the hoary head as some civilizations have done; we have seen too many foolish old people, and at least some wise young ones. There are, however, ideas which cling to the popular mind though they are not seriously maintained. Traditionally we still associate wisdom with gravity and prudence; and gravity and prudence are believed to be the fruit of years. It is therefore well to point out that wisdom is not necessarily very serious or always deliberate. It is serious enough to know that life is not all levity, but not so serious that it finds no place for humor. The best part of a sense of humor consists in a sense of proportion: it is the ability to see things in perspective and to laugh at things (like oneself in a distorting mirror) that are out of proportion. That is a considerable part of wisdom. Wisdom, again, is often deliberate: it does not let passion run away with us; it does not do mad things for the pleasure of the moment. But it is not so deliberate that it misses opportunities. It knows how to strike while the iron is hot. It takes the tide when it serves. It is daring, as it is cautious. In short, it is not the characteristic of youth or age, but a quality that some possess and others do not.

Another truth to be found in the O.T. is that wisdom is not cleverness or knowledge. A man can be a walking encyclopedia and still act and speak like a fool.

> Knowledge and Wisdom, far from being one,
> Have ofttimes no connection.[4]

[4] William Cowper, *The Task,* Bk. VI.

6 He hath showed his people the power of his works, that he may give them the heritage of the heathen.
7 The works of his hand *are* verity and judgment; all his commandments *are* sure.
8 They stand fast for ever and ever, *and are* done in truth and uprightness.
9 He sent redemption unto his people: he hath commanded his covenant for ever: holy and reverend *is* his name.

6 He has shown his people the power of his works,
in giving them the heritage of the nations.
7 The works of his hands are faithful and just;
all his precepts are trustworthy,
8 they are established for ever and ever,
to be performed with faithfulness and uprightness.
9 He sent redemption to his people;
he has commanded his covenant for ever.
Holy and terrible is his name!

---

6. The heritage of the nations: See Exeg. on 78:55.

7a. Lit., "The works of his hands are faithfulness and justice" (so Amer. Trans.; cf. KJV). The RSV gives the clause a slightly different meaning.

8. Uprightness: The M.T. reads "upright," but the word can be repointed to obtain **uprightness** (so LXX, Jerome, and Syriac).

9. He sent redemption: The reference is not specific. The verb פדה ("deliver" or "ransom"), cognate to **redemption,** is used of God's actions in the Exodus (Deut. 7:8), in David's career (II Sam. 4:9; I Kings 1:29), and in the Babylonian exile (Jer. 31:11).

The point has been made so often that we might well leave it unrepeated, were it not for the many who assume that because we know so much which was hidden from our fathers, we must be wiser than they; and were it not for the many more who pin their faith to what they naïvely call education. We might outgrow that fallacy more quickly if we meditated oftener upon the frailties of philosophers and the limitations of scholars.

Another distinction is that between commonsense and divine wisdom. We all know people who have a knack for sizing up a person or a situation. If they are in business, they seize opportunities that others miss. If they are in politics, they know when to appeal to the country and how to put their case. In the end, however, they are known not as wise leaders but as opportunists. "Horse sense" may be concerned with expediency. Divine wisdom is concerned with eternal principles. It would be foolish to belittle common sense, but it is not the wisdom which is more precious than rubies. The question therefore still faces us: "Where shall wisdom be found? and where is the place of understanding?"

The answer of the poem in Job is at first glance disappointing:

> Man does not know the way to it,
> and it is not found in the land of the living (Job 28:13).

Or again: "It is hid from the eyes of all living" (Job 28:21). But a little later,

> God understands the way to it,
> and he knows its place (Job 28:23).

After such assertions the last verse would seem strange were it not that it is so often repeated in Psalms and Proverbs and other wisdom books: "Behold, the fear of the Lord, that is wisdom; and to depart from evil is understanding" (Job 28:28). Shall we do the words justice if we say that religion is the way of wisdom? It will not be true if we mean a formal religion which asserts creeds without intelligence and multiplies unnecessary rites. But religion which inculcates reverence is the beginning of wisdom (see Expos. on Job 28:28). There are things we strive after, and then we wonder why we wanted them. But reverence, which is too little sought after, is the foundation of the virtues and the condition of life's best attainments. We must not mistake for true reverence the staring into the blue dome of awe that hypnotizes, or the unquestioning submission to authority which makes men the creatures of other wills. True reverence is that which includes and combines the wonder of the scientist, the awe of the artist, and the adoration of the saint. It is not a mere emotion, for it has marked ethical qualities. It is not fear which paralyzes, but contact with reality which slays vanity, gives freedom

10 The fear of the LORD *is* the beginning of wisdom: a good understanding have all they that do *his commandments:* his praise endureth for ever.

10 The fear of the LORD is the beginning of wisdom;
a good understanding have all those who practice it.
His praise endures for ever!

---

4. THE BEGINNING OF WISDOM (111:10)

10. The fear of the LORD is the beginning of wisdom: This sentiment is found elsewhere only in postexilic writings (Job 28:28; Prov. 1:7; 9:10; Ecclus. 1:18). **The fear of the LORD** means "reverence for the LORD," and is a comprehensive term for the worship, ritual, and morality of Israel (found elsewhere in the psalms only in 19:9; 34:11; cf. 5:7; 90:11; 119:38). **The beginning of wisdom:** This translation is favored by Prov. 9:10. Gunkel, Schmidt, *et al.* give ראשית the meaning "chief," and render the phrase "the highest wisdom" or "the supreme wisdom." **A good understanding** is one of the ideals of the wisdom writers (cf. Prov. 3:4; 13:15). **Those who practice it,** i.e., practice **the fear of the LORD.** The RSV, supported by the LXX, Jerome, and the Syriac, adopts a small emendation of the M.T. The latter is "those who practice them."

---

to faculties, and stimulates to fuller service. It is an attitude which enables us to respect the humblest of men, and to set truth above profit or reputation. It is truly called the religious attitude, though it is not always conscious in the professedly religious, and sometimes it is found in men who do not realize that they are religious. It is the beginning and condition of wisdom.

Christianity has far more to say, and the importance of it can hardly be exaggerated. The Christian church points to a historical Figure whose character and teaching can be examined —both of which have, indeed, been scrutinized as no other character or teaching has been. The church points to Jesus Christ and says, "Behold, here is wisdom to be found; at his feet is the place of understanding." It may be a hard saying to many, but notice some of the reasons for it. Even in boyhood our Lord showed such understanding that the very doctors themselves were astonished; and as he developed into manhood, the popular judgment was that he grew in wisdom and stature. When the public ministry began, men said that he taught as no one else had ever taught—"Never man spake like this man" (John 7:46). The disciples went much further. They were reminded of the great prophets; but after years of reflection they spoke of him as the wisdom and the power of God. They even affirmed that in him were "hid all the treasures of wisdom and knowledge" (Col. 2:3). There may be critics who will brush this aside as the verdict of enthusiasts if not of fanatics. Yet the claim is still made by men and women who have tested the Christian way and declare that it is *the* way of life and liberty and truth.

Such a statement could hardly pass unchallenged. There are psychologists who, misunderstanding its spirit, complain that Christianity encourages an unhealthy love of suffering—masochistic is the technical term. There are nationalists who object to its universalism, and worshipers of force who dislike its emphasis on mercy, and practical materialists who fail to appreciate what they call its otherworldliness. The challenge is obvious enough in Britain and the United States; it is even more confident elsewhere. Many of the differences that once seemed important are losing significance; but the difference between those on the one hand who claim that Christ is the wisdom of God and that Christianity is the way of life, and those on the other who preach the way of materialistic Communism or still cling to the superstitions of a hastily revived Nordic romanticism—that is the one controversy which underlies all. People do not always understand what they argue about, but the basic question upon which everything turns is this: are we to cleave to Christ as the wisdom and the power of God, or are we to repudiate him? What the church maintains is that he is our peace, and that to depart from him means chaos; that he is the truth, and to depart from him is darkness. It is not claimed that there is a ready-made answer to all questions. But we do affirm that in this fellowship there is an attitude to life without which knowledge becomes a menace and power becomes a source of self-destruction. Everything awaits the lead which Christian men can give. Politics, economics, industry, the complicated problems of international relations—everything awaits a liberating word, and the word must come from Christian sources or not come at all. What we need is a united attempt to declare the words of eternal life. All have a part; for no

112 Praise ye the LORD. Blessed *is* the man *that* feareth the LORD, *that* delighteth greatly in his commandments.

112 Praise the LORD.
Blessed is the man who fears the LORD,
who greatly delights in his commandments!

CXII. THE RIGHTEOUS WILL NEVER BE MOVED (112:1-10)

Ps. 111 and Ps. 112 are alike in their peculiar acrostic structure (see Exeg. on 111:1-10), and as they have a number of verbal similarities it is probable that they come from the same author. But whereas Ps. 111 is a national hymn, this is a didactic psalm, concerned with the blessedness of the godly individual. A feature of it is that some of the words used of God in Ps. 111 are boldly transferred to Ps. 112 and applied to the pious man (e.g., **righteousness** and 111:3 and 112:3; **remembered** in 111:4 and 112:6; **established** in 111:8 and 112:8). Although Mowinckel has suggested that it has some connection with the temple cult (*Psalmenstudien,* "Die Psalmdichter," VI, 33, 36), the psalm itself lends little support to such a view. Its general theme is akin to that of Ps. 1, and like Deuteronomy it regards the worldly rewards of the righteous and the imminent punishment of the ungodly as fundamental truths. Its concept of what constitutes true piety is more explicit than that found in Ps. 1, and in its social virtues it approximates the moral ideal set forth in Ps. 15.

1. THE SECRET OF BLESSEDNESS (112:1)

112:1. The same thought is found in 1:1-2.

---

progress is likely unless each one does the good he knows. That is the conviction which deepens as the years pass. Wisdom is not something to be sought as men search for hidden treasure. It is waiting for us in the Word made flesh: if we accept him and do his will, we shall know the truth, and the truth will make us free.

112:1-10. ***Characteristics of the Good Life.***—One of the widely read books of the present day is Charles Gore's *The Philosophy of the Good Life.*[5] Its popularity may be due in part to the well-known qualities of the author, but still further to interest in the subject. In an age when everything has been questioned, men want to know what the good life is and how it may be attained. Many answers have been suggested, but they are not all acceptable. Some are too limited in scope, and others too prejudiced by personal bias. One of the reasons Gore has had a respectful hearing is because he has examined the contributions of Zarathustra, Buddha, Plato, Mohammed, and others, with sympathy and understanding and with willingness to give credit where credit is due.

An interesting part of his book is the chapter that deals with the important contribution of Israel.[6] The Jews of ancient times were not philosophers; they were primarily concerned with religion and its practical results. They were not very much interested in science or in metaphysics, in art or political theories; but they produced poets who sang about God and the life that was acceptable to him. The pioneers were the prophets; but they were supported by psalmists who popularized their theological and ethical ideas.

Pss. 111 and 112 are illustrations of this progressive activity. They are very much alike. They are concerned with the same questions and are written in the same acrostic style. They may well have been written by the same man. There is, however, a difference. Ps. 111 is concerned with God, his righteousness, and his compassion; Ps. 112 is concerned with the blessedness of the God-fearing man. This was for the Hebrew a natural progression—to start with the greatness of "the works of the LORD" (111:2) and pass to the character of the true worshiper.

Ps. 112 has been described as a character sketch. From some points of view it is inadequate, and at the end there are phrases that many Christians would delete or hurry over. But the other parts of the psalm give a fair idea of the good life as the teachers of Israel understood it. Notice first the importance of the fixed heart: **His heart is steady.** This is a point which will commend itself in every generation. There are always men who possess all the talents except stability. They raise high hopes; their suggestions of genius arouse sanguine expectations: but, lacking the power to see anything

[5] New York: Charles Scribner's Sons, 1930.
[6] *Ibid.,* pp. 143-68.

2 His seed shall be mighty upon earth: the generation of the upright shall be blessed.
3 Wealth and riches *shall be* in his house: and his righteousness endureth for ever.
4 Unto the upright there ariseth light in the darkness: *he is* gracious, and full of compassion, and righteous.

2 His descendants will be mighty in the land;
the generation of the upright will be blessed.
3 Wealth and riches are in his house;
and his righteousness endures for ever.
4 Light rises in the darkness for the upright;
the LORD[h] is gracious, merciful, and righteous.

[h] Gk: Heb lacks *the* LORD

2. FAMILY FELICITY (112:2-4)

3-4. His righteousness: Probably as in vs. 9, "righteous deeds" (cf. God's "righteousness" in 111:3). **Light rises:** Cf. 97:11; Isa. 58:10. **The LORD is gracious, merciful, and righteous:** The Hebrew of vs. 4*b* has no stated subject, and the KJV supplies **he;** the RSV, **the LORD.** Many commentators since Duhm have struck out the **and** before **righteous** and have obtained "The righteous is gracious and merciful," which is a good parallel to 111:4*b*.

through, they achieve little. They may become the slaves of pleasure or profit, and for the satisfaction of a moment they barter "the vast concerns of an eternal scene." [7] Sometimes it is because a restless intellect finds no foundation upon which it can build. It passes from speculation to speculation without permanent result, there being no abiding conviction or inner assurance. The beginning of wisdom, said the lame philosopher Epictetus, is the finding of a standard.[8] To lack this is to be like a builder without a plumb line or a tailor without a measure.

But what is the standard to be? If the heart is fixed on evil, we shall become evil. If it is fixed upon self, we shall become incurably selfish. If it is fixed upon things, we shall become practical materialists, whatever creed we profess. Here again we are brought face to face with contemporary life. Men in every continent are failing, some of them tragically, because their minds are wrongly centered. Instead of contentment they find disappointment. They may accept it stoically and become hard, expecting little from life. Or they may become so disorganized in their inner selves that the best they can do is creep to psychoanalysts to have their secrets torn out of them. The psalmist was wiser:

Blessed is the man who fears the LORD,
who greatly delights in his commandments!

But when he declared this to be also the way to prosperity, he overstated his case: things do not always turn out as neatly as he expected. The man whose mind is fixed upon God is not unfailingly rewarded with material blessing. In a well-ordered world it would work that way; but the world is not in this sense well ordered. Because it is so seriously disorganized the righteous are often prostrate and the wicked enthroned: "Truth forever on the scaffold, Wrong forever on the throne" [9] is the cry that rings down the ages. It is the problem that makes men question our doctrines of divine sovereignty. The problem lies behind many of the biblical books, Job and some of the psalms in particular. The rigidly orthodox in the face of the bitterest experience maintained that piety worked, even in a business sense, as this psalmist affirms of the godly:

The generation of the upright will be blessed.
Wealth and riches are in his house.

Yet if the poet overstated the case on the material side, in a deeper sense he was right. Virtue is its own reward. Godliness may bring persecution, but it brings blessedness that neither poverty nor opposition can destroy. The psalmist goes on to cite some of the spiritual blessings. The man whose heart is fixed upon God is not an easy victim of fear. **He is not afraid of evil tidings,** though he is not immune from apprehension. Fear comes to all, to the bravest as well as to the cowardly, to the faithful as well as to the faithless. Perhaps it is well that it should; for, like pain, fear has social value. It warns us that danger lurks about our path. But to be watchful is one thing; to be panic-stricken is another. Men whose eyes are on their possessions may run for shelter directly their peace is threatened. Men whose minds are stayed upon God act with sanity and dignity.

[7] Edward Young, *Night Thoughts,* "Night I."
[8] *Discourses* II. 11.
[9] James Russell Lowell, "The Present Crisis," st. viii.

5 A good man showeth favor, and lendeth: he will guide his affairs with discretion.
6 Surely he shall not be moved for ever: the righteous shall be in everlasting remembrance.
7 He shall not be afraid of evil tidings: his heart is fixed, trusting in the LORD.
8 His heart *is* established, he shall not be afraid, until he see *his desire* upon his enemies.
9 He hath dispersed, he hath given to the poor; his righteousness endureth for ever; his horn shall be exalted with honor.

5 It is well with the man who deals generously and lends,
who conducts his affairs with justice.
6 For the righteous will never be moved;
he will be remembered for ever.
7 He is not afraid of evil tidings;
his heart is firm, trusting in the LORD.
8 His heart is steady, he will not be afraid,
until he sees his desire on his adversaries.
9 He has distributed freely, he has given to the poor;
his righteousness endures for ever;
his horn is exalted in honor.

3. THE SOCIAL VIRTUES (112:5-9)

5-9. Hebrew syntax supports **It is well with the man** rather than **A good man. Who deals generously and lends:** The same phrase occurs in 37:26. Lending would normally be to the needy; hence when the borrower is a Hebrew, no interest is to be exacted (Deut. 23:19-20). The Hebrew, followed by the KJV, has **the righteous** in vs. 6*b*, but the RSV moves this word to vs. 6*a*. **Will never be moved:** Frequently said of the godly (15:5; 16:8; etc.). **He will be remembered for ever:** The psalmist's only idea of immortality. **Until he sees his desire:** Lit., "until he looks." Vs. 9 is quoted in II Cor. 9:9. **His horn:** See Exeg. on 75:4-5.

Countless illustrations could be cited. One has only to read *The Pilgrim's Progress* or *Grace Abounding* to see that John Bunyan was no stranger to fear. He had natural shrinking from the indignity of trials and the tedium of imprisonment. He shrank from both not only because of what they meant to him but because of what they meant to his family. But he faced the possibility of banishment, or of death, and went calmly forward. As one of his biographers has said: "He had no sooner ridden up to his Fear, than it was transformed into something full of welcome and gladness and good hope." [1] "Now was my heart full of comfort," said Bunyan himself. "I would not have been without this trial for much; I am comforted every time I think of it, and I hope I shall bless God for ever for the teaching I have had by it." And again, "I have determined, the Almighty God being my help and shield, yet to suffer, if frail life might continue so long, even till the moss shall grow on mine eyebrows, rather than thus to violate my faith and principles." [2] Truly, **light rises in the darkness for the upright.**

And that is not the only blessing that results from finding a standard. The psalmist names also benevolence. **It is well with the man who deals generously and lends.** And almost in the same breath: **He has distributed freely, he has given to the poor.** It is a characteristic of Judaism at its best, as has been set forth by Charles Singer,[3] who cites cases of Jewish liberality and explains that in classical Hebrew the word *çedhāqāh* is equivalent to both charity and justice. Everyone, however, who studies the N.T., and especially the Sermon on the Mount, will find that the deepest word on philanthropy has been spoken and the most perfect example given not by a Jewish rabbi but by the Founder of the Christian church. That true generosity depends not upon the size of the gift but upon the love of the giver has nowhere else been so clearly stated, nowhere else been made incarnate. The supreme example is seen in the cross of Christ.

The death of Christ stands alone, but its spirit has spread far. Not only have men laid down their lives for others, but they have learned to live sacrificially. Bernard Manning of Jesus College, Cambridge, was a modest man who shrank from praise. But when his biography was written, said the colleague who undertook the task:

> No one who turned to him for help of any kind came away empty-handed, no matter who he was or how undeserving he might be. He would move heaven and earth to help anyone in distress. Of

[1] Gwilym O. Griffith, *John Bunyan* (London: Hodder & Stoughton, 1928), p. 156.

[2] *Ibid.*, pp. 156-57.

[3] *The Christian Failure* (London: Victor Gollancz, 1943), pp. 114-15.

10 The wicked shall see *it*, and be grieved; he shall gnash with his teeth, and melt away: the desire of the wicked shall perish.

113 Praise ye the LORD. Praise, O ye servants of the LORD, praise the name of the LORD.

10 The wicked man sees it and is angry;
he gnashes his teeth and melts away;
the desire of the wicked man comes to nought.

113 Praise the LORD!
Praise, O servants of the LORD,
praise the name of the LORD!

4. THE DISCOMFITURE OF THE WICKED (112:10)

10. Cf. 1:4-6. **He gnashes his teeth:** Cf. Matt. 8:12. **Desire:** Since Olshausen many scholars have changed one consonant of this word to get תקות, "hope" (cf. 9:18; Job 8:13; Prov. 10:28; 11:7).

CXIII. PRAISE GOD SEATED ON HIGH (113:1-9)

This simple but pleasing hymn of praise contains in its few verses some of the basic theological ideas of the O.T. The opening verse, addressed to the **servants of the LORD,** may have been spoken to a choir or choirs by an officiating priest in the temple. Vss. 2-4, 5-9 are two strophes possibly sung as a response to vs. 1. The psalm is notable for its peculiar endings on certain Hebrew words in vss. 5-9; these are either genuine or imitation archaisms. The dominant meter is 3+3.

In Jewish practice Pss. 113 118 are known as The Hallel or The Egyptian Hallel (cf. "Egypt" in 114:1), and they have long since established for themselves a place in the liturgy of Judaism's great festivals.

1. EXHORTATION TO PRAISE (113:1)

113:1. The exhortation of a soloist; almost identical with 135:1. **Servants of the LORD:** Either the whole congregation is addressed (cf. 34:22; 69:36; etc.), or only those who serve in the temple, the priests and the Levites (cf. 134:1).

very abstemious habits, he spent little on himself, but was lavish and even reckless with his money in support of any good cause. He frequently helped poor undergraduates, and was equally ungrudging of his time and money to those who had no collegiate or other claim on him.[4]

When an acquaintance got into financial trouble, it was Manning who paid his legal expenses, visited him in prison, and later did everything possible to find him work. So does the psalmist's ideal abide with us to this day.

This then is the good life as it is sketched by the Hebrew poet. It is not a finished portrait. Nor is it a perfect picture. For perfection, let it be said again, we must pass beyond O.T. pages to the strong Son of God, who gave his life a ransom for many. There we find forgiveness without self-righteousness, mercy and magnanimity without condescension or condoning, love that knew no limits, yet never descended to sentimentality.

Jesus, whose lot with us was cast,
Who saw it out, from first to last:
Patient and fearless, tender, true,
Carpenter, vagabond, felon, Jew:
. . . .
Would I could win and keep and feel
That heart of love, that spirit of steel! [5]

113:1-9. ***A Hymn of Praise to God Who Lifts the Needy.***—"And when they had sung a hymn, they went out to the Mount of Olives" (Mark 14:26). These familiar words cause us to think of the "dark betrayal night" when Jesus Christ took the Last Supper with his disciples. The meal itself, with its careful preparation and intimate conversation, with Judas Iscariot stumbling out into the darkness, and especially with the breaking of bread and the passing of the cup—for nearly twenty centuries all this has inspired our tenderest hymns and constituted the central act of Christian worship.

The more the scene is studied the more an attitude of wonder and praise is created within us. The fact that calls for attention here is that in all probability the hymn which was sung before Jesus and his disciples went out to the Mount of Olives was the Hebrew Hallel. There

[4] Fred Brittain, *Bernard Lord Manning: A Memoir* (Cambridge: W. Heffer & Sons, 1942), p. 66.

[5] Author unknown.

2 Blessed be the name of the LORD from this time forth and for evermore.
3 From the rising of the sun unto the going down of the same the LORD's name *is* to be praised.
4 The LORD *is* high above all nations, *and* his glory above the heavens.

2 Blessed be the name of the LORD
from this time forth and for evermore!
3 From the rising of the sun to its setting
the name of the LORD is to be praised!
4 The LORD is high above all nations,
and his glory above the heavens!

2. HIS GLORY IS ABOVE THE HEAVENS (113:2-4)

2-4. The response of a choir: the timeless and universal sway of Israel's God. **From this time forth and for evermore:** The same phrase occurs in 115:18; 121:8; 125:2; 131:3. **From the rising of the sun to its setting:** The same phrase appears in 50:1; Mal. 1:11. The reference is seemingly not temporal but spatial; it reflects the psalmist's view of the wide dispersion of the Lord's worshipers, and may include the Gentiles. Oesterley (*Psalms,* II, 469), however, thinks that the words point to "praise being offered to God the live-long day." **High above all nations** is an affirmation, as in 99:1-2, that Israel's God is supreme over all people.

were several portions of scripture that went by that name, but Pss. 113–118, sometimes known as the Egyptian Hallel, were eminent enough to be referred to simply as the Hallel. They were used at the popular festivals of Passover, Tabernacles, and Weeks, and were so well known that no one needed the help of the written word. What hymns like "Abide with me" and "When I survey the wondrous Cross" are to us, the Hallel was to the pious Israelites. It is not certain how many of these psalms were sung at the conclusion of the Last Supper, but to remember the association is to find light shed both upon the psalms themselves and upon that memorable evening meal.

The word Hallel is derived from the Hebrew *hillēl,* "to praise." That, as we have been reminded again and again, is a note running throughout the O.T. scriptures and finding its climax in the N.T. The Bible is a catholic book representing many needs and many moods, but one might quote as characteristic of the whole the angels' song at the Nativity: "Glory to God in the highest, and on earth peace, good will toward men" (Luke 2:14). We know ourselves to be in the biblical succession when we unite in the "Te Deum," Francis of Assisi's "All creatures of our God and King," or Newman's "Praise to the Holiest in the height."

There are times needed for silence, for penitence and confession. Again and again, weary of speech and excitement, men have sought the intense and quiet listening of Quaker worship. Yet no worship is likely to meet common need, and none corresponds with the biblical tradition unless it gives adequate place for praise, including its expression in hymn and prayer.

But whence this spiritual exuberance? It is not what our knowledge of the Hebrew temperament or history would lead us to expect. One might say that by nature the Jews were inclined to be somber rather than sanguine, more apt to brood upon life's enigmas than to fill the earth with stimulating music. How then account for the prevalence of praise in Hebrew religion and literature?

The answer is that if the Hebrew had no extravagant faith in man, he had an enduring confidence in God. That takes us where the modern man is reluctant to go—into the realm of theology. We must remember, however, that theology is not all of one kind. Much of it—in these days most of it—is the product of the schools. It proceeds from men who may be deeply versed in the development of thought from ancient to modern times, but who may know little of the world. It is often expressed in language more reminiscent of books of philosophy than of the market place. Naturally people who are not academic by training and interest feel that such studies are not meant for them. They may persevere with handbooks of natural science, but they pass by even the more popular books of theology. But not all theology is academic. There is the theology—crude perhaps, but nevertheless very real—of the widow who has to bring up a large family on a small income, and of the sailor who sails many seas and faces the temptations of many ports. In the technical sense one can hardly call it theology at all; it has never been developed into orderly systems or criticized by disciplined minds. But it is theocentric; i.e., it is a faith for life centered in a God who lives and rules and saves.

The O.T. theology is of this latter type. Here and there we find reflective minds dealing with abstract problems, but generally speaking

5 Who *is* like unto the LORD our God, who dwelleth on high,
6 Who humbleth *himself* to behold *the things that are* in heaven, and in the earth!
7 He raiseth up the poor out of the dust, *and* lifteth the needy out of the dunghill;
8 That he may set *him* with princes, *even* with the princes of his people.

5 Who is like the LORD our God,
who is seated on high,
6 who looks far down
upon the heavens and the earth?
7 He raises the poor from the dust,
and lifts the needy from the ash heap,
8 to make them sit with princes,
with the princes of his people.

3. HE LOOKS UPON THE NEEDY (113:5-9)

5-9. A second response, perhaps by another choir: the incomparable majesty of the Lord, who yet concerns himself with the life and needs of humankind. Some scholars, following Buhl, rearrange the stichs in vss. 5-6 as follows: vss. 5*a*, 6*b*, 5*b*, 6*a*. The rhetorical question in vs. 5 implies the uniqueness of the Lord. **Who looks far down upon:** Lit., "who makes low to see," which probably means "who humbles himself to look" (so KJV, Calès, Buttenwieser, *et al.*; cf. 11:4; 14:2; 102:19; 138:6; Phil. 2:5-11). Vss. 7-8*a* are verbally almost identical with the first half of I Sam. 2:8. **Ash heap** (vs. 7) is better than **dunghill.** The verse points to the degradation of the poor who are obliged to ransack the rubbish heaps for sustenance. **To make them sit:** A small emendation (להושיבו) of the M.T., supported by the LXX, Jerome, and the

prophets and psalmists were men who knew the hard realities, and carried the common burdens of life. Only they did not face their difficulties alone. They believed that God was with them, and that because God was with them they need not fear. That is the origin of the note of praise.

There are two outstanding points in this faith that call for mention. The first is the greatness of God, who is **high above all nations, and his glory above the heavens!**

> **Who is like the LORD our God,**
> **who is seated on high,**
> **who looks far down**
> **upon the heavens and the earth?**

It is poetic language, but it means what philosophers and theologians mean when they speak of the transcendence of God. This should not be regarded as spatial in intention. It does not mean that God is bigger than the created universe. Simple-minded as in some ways the ancient Hebrews were, they were not as crude as that. It means that while God is the source of all life, he is not exhausted by or confined in that which he has made. It means also that there are depths in the divine nature which are unfathomed and unfathomable. It affirms the divine absoluteness. God—shall we say, though it is stepping beyond biblical language to use such an expression—is the ultimate Reality, and whatever exists is from him.

It ought to be added that the Hebrews did not think of God as irresponsible or arbitrary Power. In two ways for practical purposes they qualified their affirmation of the divine omnipotence. They qualified it first by maintaining that God's will is the law of nature and is constant and covenanted. He can do nothing foolish, nor can he do wrong, which would be a denial of himself. The point can be made simpler by illustration. A mother holds in her arms a tiny child. It would be easy for her to destroy that tender life. She has the physical power to do it. But she loves the child, and the love controls the power. Tell her to do away with her baby, and even though they were together suffering hardship and facing possible starvation, she would normally exclaim, "Oh, I could not do that." In the same way God cannot act contrary to his purpose of love.

The other way in which prophets and psalmists limited the sovereignty of God was in the recognition of the fact that he had created millions of free beings with liberty to rebel against him. Actually men have rebelled, and continue to rebel, but God has not and will not overrule their liberty. The result is that throughout history he appears not as the sovereign Deity, but as frustrated and defeated. What, however, the Bible dwells upon is not the temporary frustration; it is the certainty of ultimate victory. "Because God is God, He must 'come into His own' in the whole of His universe; and each insolent power in turn must be overwhelmed." [6]

That is one point in O.T. theology which must not be forgotten—the transcendence of God. The other is what theologians call the immanence of God, his nearness to each of us in

[6] Charles Gore, *Belief in God* (London: John Murray, 1921), p. 116.

9 He maketh the barren woman to keep house, *and to be* a joyful mother of children. Praise ye the LORD.

9 He gives the barren woman a home,
making her the joyous mother of children.
Praise the LORD!

Syriac. A similar thought appears in Job 36:7. Probably Hannah is in the psalmist's mind in vs. 9 (cf. Sam. 1:1-28; 2:5), but even such an experience as Hannah's is only a token of God's wondrous power. For the value assigned to children see 127:3-5. **Praise the LORD:** The LXX and Jerome place these words at the beginning of Ps. 114, a practice followed by many scholars.

---

our individual need. Not only is he nearer than the friend to whom we talk, but he is active, guiding us in our thinking, strengthening us in our willing. See how it is put here:

> **He raises the poor from the dust,**
> **and lifts the needy from the ash heap,**
> **to make them sit with princes,**
> **with the princes of his people.**
> **He gives the barren woman a home,**
> **making her the joyous mother of children.**

Such a faith makes a great difference in life. God is high and lifted up, transcending all human thought and imagination. Yet he is with us as we set out upon the day's adventure, and as we commit ourselves at night to sleep; with us when troubles and temptations thicken around us, and when success spreads its more subtle dangers in our path; so near that we need not cry aloud, for he hears our faintest whisper and answers our feeblest prayer.

> Speak to Him thou for He hears, and Spirit with Spirit can meet—
> Closer is He than breathing, and nearer than hands and feet.[7]

No one who forgets that can do justice to Hebrew worship.

This was also the faith that inspired and sustained our Lord. It was the faith he made real and dynamic in the experience of those who followed him. We are in the habit of speaking of him as the author of faith. And that is right. He came into the world, not as a searcher, but as one who was full of wisdom and truth. John says the essential word when he declares, "In him was life, and the life was the light of men" (John 1:4). The witness of the scriptures and the church is that he is the Son of God, standing in a unique relationship with the Father. But the knowledge and the truth which we see in Jesus did not come like a bolt from the blue. It was mediated. Exactly how it was mediated may be more than we can say: it always is more than we can explain when God speaks to the heart of any man. Surely it came in part through the people among whom he lived; it came in part through the scriptures and the church, through the family in which he grew up. Especially it came through prophets and psalmists whose words were continually upon his lips. The first thing to be said about the gospel of Christ is that it is theocentric. It contains guidance for daily living, guidance which man ignores at his peril. But it all begins with the Father of spirits, and without him Jesus has nothing to say.

The two most obvious things in our Lord's revelation of the Father are, first, that he is so great that man must prostrate himself before him: "Our Father which art in heaven, Hallowed be thy name" (Luke 11:2). The second is the emphasis that falls upon the blessed intimacy of the Father, who is not far from any one of us, who cares for us personally, protecting us as a shepherd protects his sheep, communing with us as a man talks to his friend. Even as a boy Jesus insists he must be about his Father's business. Crucified, he cries from the cross, "Father, into thy hands I commend my spirit" (Luke 23:46). This was the faith that made it possible for him with his disciples at the close of the Last Supper to sing the Hallel and then to cross over to the Mount of Olives. They joined the great hymn of the people to whom he came, and it sustained them as they went out into the darkness of the night.

Such a faith makes all the difference in life; and not least, all the difference as one faces the end. "Is there no one here," asked Oliver Cromwell, as he prepared himself for the valley of the shadow, and beheld around him the faces of those who wept, "Is there no one here who will praise the Lord?"

That note will always be heard—**Praise ye the LORD! Praise, O ye servants of the LORD**—whenever there is a living faith in the God **who is seated on high,** yet who **gives the barren woman a home, making her the joyous mother of children.**

[7] Tennyson, "The Higher Pantheism."

114 When Israel went out of Egypt, the house of Jacob from a people of strange language;

114 When Israel went forth from Egypt,
the house of Jacob from a people of strange language,

CXIV. Tremble at the Presence of the Lord (114:1-8)

This, the second of the Hallel group (see Exeg. on 113:1-9), is one of the most original of all the psalms. It refrains from the conventional language of the hymn, and yet it extols the power of Israel's God in an artistic little poem that is a model of concise and vivid description. The psalmist uses as illustrative material some of the great moments of the past, and in his appeal to God's hand in history (contrast the mythology of Egypt and Mesopotamia) we see one of the sources of the strength of Israel's faith. The lyric concludes by calling upon the whole earth to **tremble . . . at the presence of the Lord.**

There is nothing in the psalm to indicate the occasion of its composition. Its contents make it especially appropriate for the Passover celebration, and it may have been written for use in that festival. Schmidt suggests a connection with the enthronement of the Lord ceremony. The date is quite uncertain. The strophic structure is indicated by the RSV, and the meter generally is 3+3.

Dante makes this psalm the hymn sung by the spirits in the boat which brings human souls (in lots of about a hundred at a time) to the shore of Purgatory (*Purgatory,* Canto II, ll. 45-47). The words of the psalm are thus taken to represent mystically the exodus of the soul from this world to the next.

1. Israel's Beginnings (114:1-2)

114:1-2. Of strange language: Cf. Isa. 28:11; 33:19. The Egyptian language was unintelligible to the Hebrews (cf. Gen. 42:23). Probably the terms **Judah** and **Israel**

114:1-8. ***Divine Power in Human History.***— Those who wish to understand Hebrew worship should pay special attention to Pss. 113–118, which together form the Hallel (see Expos. on 113:1-9). As they read and meditate they will begin to see men and women in great numbers, many of whom have traveled long distances for such festivals, uniting in common ritual and singing familiar and favorite hymns of praise. They will understand more clearly why Jerusalem was loved as a religious as well as an administrative center, and why such spiritual exercises made so popular an appeal.

Ps. 114 may also with profit be studied as a characteristic example of Jewish poetry. Poetry is never primarily a matter of structure, though structure is always important. The Hebrews were not interested, as we are, in rhyme or, to the same extent, in meter. They were primarily concerned with parallelism, a statement in one line which is repeated in slightly different language in the following line or lines. Ps. 114, one of the most charming lyrics in the O.T., is an admirable example of this prevailing poetic form. From the first verse to the last the same style is maintained.

Structure, however, though important, is not the essence of poetry. Wordsworth came near to the soul of the matter when he spoke of poetry as "the spontaneous overflow of powerful feelings: it takes its origin from emotion recollected in tranquillity."[1] No one can command it. Like the wind, it bloweth where it listeth. Through long centuries it has been connected especially with man's contact with nature. When individuals, weary of conflict and spent with toil, have turned to the open spaces and sought peace with the earth, the sea, the sky, inspiration has come. It may be a quiet moment at dawn or sunset. It may be a shimmer of light in running water or sun-kissed clouds in the firmament above; but the closed doors of mind and heart have been opened, and sonatas and lyrics have been born.

There are suggestions that Ps. 114 may have been inspired in such a way. The writer has looked with understanding eyes upon the world around him and speaks instinctively of the sea that **looked and fled,** of Jordan that **turned back.** He rises to greater heights of poetic expression in the words that follow:

The mountains skipped like rams,
the hills like lambs.

[1] *Lyrical Ballads,* Preface.

2 Judah was his sanctuary, *and* Israel his dominion.
3 The sea saw *it*, and fled: Jordan was driven back.
4 The mountains skipped like rams, *and* the little hills like lambs.

2 Judah became his sanctuary,
Israel his dominion.

3 The sea looked and fled,
Jordan turned back.
4 The mountains skipped like rams,
the hills like lambs.

---

are used loosely, and no contrast between them is intended. **Judah became his sanctuary** may be an allusion to Exod. 19:6: "You shall be to me a kingdom of priests and a holy nation," and the words may point to Israel's spiritual destiny. Otherwise the reference is to the temple in Jerusalem. **Israel his dominion:** Israel is to be the dominion of God, a realm in which the divine laws operate. **Israel,** here as in vs. 1, designates all the tribes.

2. Nature Recognizes the Lord's Presence (114:3-6)

3-4. The sea looked and fled: Cf. 77:16; Exod. 14:21-22; Hab. 3:10. **Jordan turned back:** Cf. Josh. 3:9-17. Vs. 4 seems to be a poetic treatment of the traditions regarding the theophany at Sinai (cf. 68:8; Exod. 19:18; Judg. 5:5). Vss. 5-6 reveal the psalmist's gentle irony.

But while nature suggests the imagery, the substance of the psalmist's thought is connected with human history. He is not dealing with personal experience except as he has himself imaginatively shared in the history of his people. He goes back to a great event, almost the great event, in the long and dramatic story of Israel, the exodus from Egypt. It was an event that had always been kept alive in the mind of this peculiar people. Perhaps, as so often happens, the story had grown as generation after generation it was retold and reinterpreted. It had become not so much sober history as patriotic poetry. It was not prosaic statement of fact, but part of the romance of a nation. Every nation has its particular memories, its intense celebrations, its songs of deliverance. These are an essential part of its individuality and of its contribution to humanity. But few have such a wealth of tradition as the Jews; and among the many things that cannot be forgotten is the dramatic deliverance from which stemmed their history as a people.

When Israel went forth from Egypt,
the house of Jacob from a people of strange language.

The weakness of patriotic poetry is that it so often becomes boastful. "See," it says, "what we and our fathers have done!" Jewish patriotism rarely falls to this level, for it is naturally religious. Its main theme is not what man has done, but what God has enabled him to do. See how in this psalm there is no reference to Moses or Joshua or any of the mighty men. This was not a lack of appreciation of national heroes. It was not part of the Jewish genius to belittle heroic ancestors. But even Abraham and David, even the prophets and saintly kings, were but instruments of the divine purpose. We may speak of Moses the emancipator. Seers and psalmists more naturally thought of the God who had called him and guided him and crowned his labors with success. That is why vss. 7-8, which form the climax of the poem, are so relevant and indeed so inevitable:

Tremble, O earth, at the presence of the Lord,
at the presence of the God of Jacob,
who turns the rock into a pool of water,
the flint into a spring of water.

This is the theme not of the psalm only, not of the O.T. only, but of the whole Bible. The Lord Jesus Christ did not just emerge. He was sent in the fullness of the times to be the Savior of the world. He came as the dayspring from on high to begin a better day, "to proclaim liberty to the captives, and the opening of the prison to them that are bound" (Isa. 61:1). To this end he labored and suffered and died. To this end, under the guidance of the Spirit, his disciples went out among the nations preaching the gospel of redemption. They had neither wealth nor learning, neither adequate numbers nor conspicuous ability. They had no complex organization, no developed creed, no detailed instructions. They would have been shocked had they been told that they would turn the world upside down. But because they trusted in the Lord who had called them, they suffered defeats without being overwhelmed, and won victories without personal pride. The early expansion of Christianity is often attributed to circumstances—to imperial rule and Roman

5 What *ailed* thee, O thou sea, that thou fleddest? thou Jordan, *that* thou wast driven back?
6 Ye mountains, *that* ye skipped like rams; *and* ye little hills, like lambs?
7 Tremble, thou earth, at the presence of the Lord, at the presence of the God of Jacob;
8 Which turned the rock *into* a standing water, the flint into a fountain of waters.

5 What ails you, O sea, that you flee?
O Jordan, that you turn back?
6 O mountains, that you skip like rams?
O hills, like lambs?

7 Tremble, O earth, at the presence of the Lord,
at the presence of the God of Jacob,
8 who turns the rock into a pool of water,
the flint into a spring of water.

---

3. Apostrophe to the Wide World (114:7-8)

7. As the Red Sea, the Jordan, and the mountains were filled with awe at the approach of Israel's God, so the whole earth is called upon to **tremble** before him (cf. 97:4-5). The word **Lord** (אדון), in an uninflected form and without the article, is found only here in the O.T. in reference to God.

8. Illustrations of God's might and of his solicitude for his people's needs (see Exod. 17:1-6; Num. 20:1-11; Deut. 8:15; cf. Pss. 78:15-16; 107:35; Isa. 41:18). The abruptness of this conclusion to the psalm has led some scholars to believe that the poem in its present form is truncated.

---

roads, to Jewish dispersion and a well-nigh universal Greek speech, to widespread intellectual and moral bankruptcy. It was indeed the hour of opportunity. The world was waiting for a message of hope, and the path of the messenger was to an extraordinary degree made straight. But it was because God had raised up men of faith and courage that the opportunity was seized. Not even Paul with all his native genius could have been equal to the occasion. It was the Power working in and through him that made him the greatest of Christian missionaries.

Christian faith and hope have not always burned so bright. Too often in the history of the church men have trusted human resources rather than divine initiative. The result has always been the same: preaching has become apologetic, and evangelistic activity has been timid and defensive. Yet confidence in a God who brings his people out of Egypt and guides them to the Promised Land has never died. Even when spiritual awareness is at its lowest, it can be found in the prayers of the faithful. It survives in and enriches our books of praise. Philip Doddridge expressed it in the magnificent hymn "O God of Bethel." William Williams reiterated it in "Guide me, O thou great Jehovah." It becomes a prayer memorized by millions in "Lead, kindly Light." How poor hymnbooks would be were there no assurance that now as in the past God redeems and protects.

It is not perhaps the instinctive confession of youth. In the morning of life we are impressed by the possibilities of the future. There is a work for us to do, a battle for us to fight. The important things are the decisions we make, the faithfulness we maintain. We set out on our pilgrimage saying with W. E. Henley, "I am the master of my fate." As the journey moves toward the end, however, there is a change. So often we have paused at the crossroads not knowing which way to take. We have moved this way, not that, because life will not let us pause, not because we have had any assurance that the way was right. We have known the agony of indecision and sometimes of regret. We have envied men of olden times, men like Abraham, who left the land of his fathers because of a divine call. We have contrasted our vague, uncertain way with that of Florence Nightingale, who achieved so much in the ministry of healing because in early years God spoke to her and would not let her rest content with the conventions of her class. We have stumbled out into the darkness, as Captain Oates stumbled out into the snowy wastes. So at least it has seemed. But how often in years of maturity we feel that we have been led when we knew it not, that decisions have been made for us when we were unconscious of making them for ourselves, that, in short, Shakespeare was right when he wrote of the

divinity that shapes our ends,
Rough-hew them how we will.[2]

As William Cowper so aptly expressed it:

God moves in a mysterious way
His wonders to perform.[3]

[2] *Hamlet,* Act V, scene 2.
[3] "Light Shining Out of Darkness."

115 Not unto us, O LORD, not unto us, but unto thy name give glory, for thy mercy, *and* for thy truth's sake.

115 Not to us, O LORD, not to us,
but to thy name give glory,
for the sake of thy steadfast love and
thy faithfulness!

CXV. To Thy Name Give Glory (115:1-18)

This is a liturgical psalm of a mixed type. Vss. 1-2 appear to be the beginning of a lament: they refer to caustic remarks made by Gentiles about Israel's God. Vss. 3-8 constitute a didactic hymn in which the Lord is praised obliquely by pointing out the weaknesses of pagan idolatry. The appeal in vss. 9-11 to **trust in the LORD** and to find in him both **help** and **shield** suggests some perilous situation in which trust in God is the only wisdom. It is conceivable that at this point some cultic action, such as a sacrifice, takes place, for vss. 12-18 breathe a quieter air and the tone is that of a hymn of faith and gratitude.

While it is generally accepted that this psalm was rendered antiphonally (cf. Ezra 3:10-11), there is no agreement about the number of parties or about the division of the psalm between them. Three groups and a soloist are apparently involved in vss. 9-13, and a priest, perhaps the same soloist, in vss. 14-15. What was done with the rest of the psalm is a matter of conjecture.

The internal evidence warrants almost no conclusions about the date of the psalm or the circumstances under which it originated. The prominence given to the **house of Aaron** favors the period of the second temple. Weiser argues that a pre-exilic date is a possibility. The meter is generally 3+3.

In the LXX this psalm is united with Ps. 114 to make one poem of twenty-six verses. There appears, however, to be no sound basis for this union.

It is the final verdict not only of poets like Cowper but of thinkers like Miguel de Unamuno, who exclaims:

> I believe in God as I believe in my friends, because I feel the breath of His affection, feel His invisible and intangible hand, drawing me, leading me, grasping me . . . . Once and again in my life I have seen myself suspended in a trance over the abyss; once and again I have found myself at the cross-roads, confronted by a choice of ways and aware that in choosing one I should be renouncing all the others—for there is no turning back upon these roads of life; and once and again in such unique moments as these I have felt the impulse of a mighty power, conscious, sovereign, and loving. And then, before the feet of the wayfarer, opens out the way of the Lord.[4]

There remains the question: Why—though the divine activity may be recognizable in perspective—why is it not obvious at the moment? Why is it that F. W. Faber is led to say:

> He is least seen when all the powers
> Of ill are most abroad? [5]

The answer of Lord Samuel, one of the most sagacious of British Liberal statesmen, deserves careful consideration. He was speaking in London to a gathering of religious journalists at a fateful hour. The nations were watching to see how governments would act. Was the world heading for Armageddon, or would humanity turn at that late hour to sanity and peace? How gladly in that crisis men would have welcomed guidance from above! But none came. Lord Samuel, who through his long life was known for philosophical caution rather than for religious enthusiasm, dared at that moment to raise again the problem of evil and to affirm that "the reticence of God is his supreme gift to men." God respects the freedom he has granted: he will appeal, suggest, even correct; but he will not compel. "Experience shows that constant intervention is not to be expected, and reflection may reveal that it is not to be desired." The gracious influence of the Eternal never fails, and his resources are infinite, but "a bruised reed shall he not break, and the smoking flax shall he not quench" (Isa. 42:3).

115:1-18. *What Life Taught the Psalmist and What It Teaches Us.*—About the time that this Expos. was written there came to hand a book of essays bearing the title *What Life Has Taught Me.*[6] The writers were well advanced in years, some of them, like William R. Inge, Gilbert Murray and L. P. Jacks, so old that they almost

[4] *The Tragic Sense of Life* (London: Macmillan & Co., 1921), pp. 194-95. Used by permission of St. Martin's Press, Inc.

[5] "The Right Must Win."

[6] Ed. J. Marchant (London: Odhams Press, n.d.).

2 Wherefore should the heathen say, Where *is* now their God?
3 But our God *is* in the heavens: he hath done whatsoever he hath pleased.
4 Their idols *are* silver and gold, the work of men's hands.
5 They have mouths, but they speak not: eyes have they, but they see not:

2 Why should the nations say,
"Where is their God?"

3 Our God is in the heavens;
he does whatever he pleases.
4 Their idols are silver and gold,
the work of men's hands.
5 They have mouths, but do not speak;
eyes, but do not see.

Pss. 115–118, the latter part of the Hallel psalms (see Exeg. on 113:1-9), were sung by the Jews after the Passover meal was finished (Mishnah, Pesahim 10:6-7). If Jesus' Last Supper was a Passover, which is uncertain, the reference to hymn singing in Matt. 26:30; Mark 14:26, is to this psalm and possibly Pss. 116–118. According to Shakespeare, Henry V after the battle of Agincourt, 1415, used this psalm (see *King Henry V*, Act IV, scene 8).

1. A Lament Begins (115:1-2)

115:1. To thy name give glory: The glorification of God and of God's name, which involves the exaltation of justice, truth, and mercy, is the *summum bonum* in the O.T. Hence "man's chief end is to glorify God, and to enjoy him forever" (Shorter Catechism). Some consider this verse to be incomplete. Gunkel suggests inserting "save us from our enemies" after **glory,** while Briggs drops everything after **glory** as a gloss.

2. It is implied that some Gentiles have been vilifying Israel's God (cf. 42:3, 10; 79:10).

2. The Impotence of Idols (115:3-8)

3-8. A didactic hymn in which the psalmist, conscious of the reality and omnipotence of the Lord, derides the idolatry of the nations. Vss. 4-6, 8 have a close parallel in 135:15-18. The general tenor of this part of the psalm is similar to Isa. 40:18-20; 44:9-20;

apologized for writing at all. The longevity may be largely responsible for the wisdom that pervades the volume; it has not abated the diversity, the direction, or the force. Old men may gain sagacity; they still defend themselves with vigor and attack opponents with deft blows.

But why seek guidance only from the living? Why not essays, or indeed volumes, on great historical characters and what life taught them? One can imagine a return of interest to many a listless congregation if preachers announced a series of sermons on what life taught Moses, or David, or Jeremiah, or Paul. Let us adopt the suggestion in the Expos. of this psalm. It is no serious objection that we do not know the name of the writer, or exactly when he lived, or whether he was old or young. We have some of his conclusions, and they are here set forth with vigor and conviction.

The first thing that life had taught him is that it is a good thing to "make a joyful noise unto the Lord" and to "come before his presence with singing" (100:1-2). He has composed a hymn of praise with temple worship in mind, and has done it with real satisfaction. Ps. 114 suggests a poet who casts his mind back over the centuries, and seeing for himself the goodness of God sings because he must. Ps. 115 suggests a hymn writer—and there is a distinct difference between a good poem and a good hymn—writing with equal joy, but with a different purpose, and using a different method. Ps. 114 makes us think of a solitary soul who lifts his spirit to the mountains, and communes with the sea, and through the wonders of nature finds himself in the presence of God. Ps. 115 gives us a picture of one who has in mind the house of God where the people assemble for worship, and sets himself to put a new song on their lips. There are scholars, e.g., Oesterley,[7] who in different parts of the psalm detect liturgical intention—certain parts to be sung by the priests, other parts by the temple choir and the congregation antiphonally (see Exeg.). Even the ordinary reader feels himself in the temple precincts joining with the great congregation in a glad hymn of praise.

It is questionable whether sufficient thought is given to this element in our religious life.

[7] *Psalms,* II, 472.

6 They have ears, but they hear not:
noses have they, but they smell not:
7 They have hands, but they handle not:
feet have they, but they walk not: neither
speak they through their throat.
8 They that make them are like unto
them; *so is* every one that trusteth in them.
9 O Israel, trust thou in the LORD: he *is*
their help and their shield.
10 O house of Aaron, trust in the LORD:
he *is* their help and their shield.
11 Ye that fear the LORD, trust in the
LORD: he *is* their help and their shield.

6 They have ears, but do not hear;
noses, but do not smell.
7 They have hands, but do not feel;
feet, but do not walk;
and they do not make a sound in their throat.
8 Those who make them are like them;
so are all who trust in them.

9 O Israel, trust in the LORD!
He is their help and their shield.
10 O house of Aaron, put your trust in the LORD!
He is their help and their shield.
11 You who fear the LORD, trust in the LORD!
He is their help and their shield.

46:6-7; Jer. 2:26-28; 10:3-15. As late as the first century B.C. idolatrous practices were still subject to Jewish criticism (Wisd. Sol. 13:10-19; 14:12-21; 15:7-17).

3. TRUST IN THE LORD (115:9-11)

9-11. Three groups are addressed: **Israel,** probably the Jewish laity; the **house of Aaron,** the priests; and those who **fear the LORD.** The composition of the third group is uncertain. The phrase seems to have a more specific meaning than "worshipers of the Lord" (cf. 22:23), although Schmidt *et al.* take it to mean the laity and the priests. The words are sometimes thought to signify proselytes (Kittel, Gunkel, *et al.;* cf. I Kings 8:41-43; Isa. 56:6; Acts 10:2; 13:16), but it is improbable, even if the psalm belongs to the Persian or early Greek period, that proselytes were present in the temple in sufficient numbers to form a special group of worshipers. Another possibility is that the term means temple servants (i.e., the singers, porters, Nethinim, and children of Solomon's servants referred to in Ezra 2:41-57; cf. I Chr. 9:2), and may include those

We have many people concerned with theology and organization and missionary expansion; not many concerned with the writing of hymns. Yet is there anything so necessary, especially among people of the Reformed churches? To disparage homiletics or theology would be folly, but whenever there is a revival of religion there is a revival of song. And how enduring are sacred melodies—compared, for example, with music hall tunes which catch men's ears but are quickly forgotten! How sure is the comfort they bring in seasons of distress! Paul and Silas were not the only Christians to sing in prison. How many admit that when no definite prayers will shape themselves in troubled minds, the words of well-known hymns have brought solace and peace! Get some hymns by heart if you would be forearmed for the Slough of Despond.

The second thing life taught this psalmist was that worship which is not pure is poisonous. No sooner has he begun to sing to the praise of God than he turns aside to cast scorn upon idols and idolatry. Now scorn is a dangerous weapon. Life has taught most of us to avoid it, or to use it very sparingly. Yet when the danger is great we may be forced to use it. And the danger in the psalmist's day was so great that he used it with vigor. It did not matter whether the idols were beautiful or hideous, whether they were of silver or gold or cut out of branches of trees or lumps of common stone—it was nonsense anyway. **Our God is in the heavens,** unseen but full of power and wisdom; idols are **the work of men's hands** and are useless.

They have mouths, but do not speak;
eyes, but do not see.
They have ears, but do not hear;
noses, but do not smell.
They have hands, but do not feel;
feet, but do not walk;
and they do not make a sound in their throat.

He used ridicule to save the people from something that had dragged down surrounding nations and was always insinuating itself into the religion of Israel. He was dealing with a deadly disease and could not afford to be too polite.

12 The LORD hath been mindful of us: he
will bless *us;* he will bless the house of Israel; he will bless the house of Aaron.
13 He will bless them that fear the LORD,
both small and great.
14 The LORD shall increase you more and
more, you and your children.
15 Ye *are* blessed of the LORD which made
heaven and earth.

12 The LORD has been mindful of us; he will
bless us;
he will bless the house of Israel;
he will bless the house of Aaron;
13 he will bless those who fear the LORD,
both small and great.

14 May the LORD give you increase,
you and your children!
15 May you be blessed by the LORD,
who made heaven and earth!

---

of impaired priestly stock (Ezra 2:61-62; cf. חלל of the Mishnah, Kiddushin 4:1). The three classes mentioned here, and again in vss. 12-13, appear also in 118:2-4; 135:19-20. In the latter passage the "house of Levi" is found as well (cf. Ecclus. 50:16-19). **He is their help and their shield:** An almost identical clause ("our" instead of **their**) is found in 33:20.

4. The Lord Is Mindful of Us (115:12-18)

Hymnic conclusion. Possibly these verses follow a cultic act or the receipt of some token of the Lord's continued favor.

14-15. These verses perhaps constitute a priestly benediction. **May the LORD give you increase:** Descendants are a coveted blessing (cf. 127:3-5; Deut. 1:11; 28:4). As Kirkpatrick (*Psalms,* p. 686) observes, the maker of **heaven and earth** "has the power to dispense the blessings of earth."

If it is sarcasm, it is sarcasm that concerns us as much as it concerned the people of Israel. Idolatry is a perpetual menace. It is not only a matter of what men worship, but also of how they worship. It is easy for us to pity or deride the people of India and others who still prostrate themselves before images that cannot speak or see or hear or smell. But what of those who in the most civilized of communities have been worshiping wealth, or themselves, or a fashionable ideology? There have been times when men were not considered patriotic if they did not publicly join the emperor or Führer worship. It has been well said that we "make gods now, not out of wood and stone, . . . but out of . . . abstract nouns, which are the most treacherous and explosive things in the world."[8] We can make a god out of our doctrine of the state. We can make a god even out of religious creeds and customs. Whenever self takes the place of God, we are on the path that leads to idolatry. Even prayer may be used as an instrument to make the deity do the will of man. Though our sanctuaries should be swept bare of pictures and images and symbols, yet are we in fellowship with idolaters if we come together with covetousness in our hearts. "Little children," cries a N.T. writer—and surely he is addressing himself to us—"Little children, keep yourselves from idols" (I John 5:21).

Life had taught all this to our psalmist. It appears not only in the scathing references to idols but in the words addressed to God:

Not to us, O LORD, not to us,
but to thy name give glory,
for the sake of thy steadfast love and thy faithfulness!

It may be that the hymn was written to signalize some great deliverance. The temptation at such a moment is always to boast, if not in our own merits at least in the valor and wisdom of our leaders. See what we, or our fathers or sons, have done to defend our shores and to maintain integrity in the earth! It can be found even in churches that proclaim their virtuous records and boast their superiority to all other agencies, sacred or secular.

The truly religious attitude, however, is always that of the psalmist. The deliverance that has come to us, the blessings we have received, the victories that bring us in gladness to Zion's hill—these are not our achievements but God's bounties. We have been his instruments, but it was he who gave the vision and the unity, it was he who gave the courage and the strength to endure. That is the note we should maintain in all our national and ecclesiastical celebrations. We may bestow an honor here, express

[8] Herbert Butterfield, *The Englishman and His History* (Cambridge: Cambridge University Press, 1944), pp. 128-29.

16 The heaven, *even* the heavens, *are* the LORD's: but the earth hath he given to the children of men.
17 The dead praise not the LORD, neither any that go down into silence.
18 But we will bless the LORD from this time forth and for evermore. Praise the LORD.

116 I love the LORD, because he hath heard my voice *and* my supplications.

16 The heavens are the LORD's heavens,
but the earth he has given to the sons of men.
17 The dead do not praise the LORD,
nor do any that go down into silence.
18 But we will bless the LORD
from this time forth and for evermore.
Praise the LORD!

116 I love the LORD, because he has heard
my voice and my supplications.

16-18. The earth he has given to the sons of men: Cf. Gen. 1:28-29; Isa. 45:18. On the thought of vs. 17 and on the meaning of **into silence** see Exeg. on 94:17. The LXX brings out the meaning of vs. 18 by rendering, "But we the living will bless, . . ." (cf. 118:17; Isa. 38:18-19). **Praise the LORD!** belongs, according to the LXX and Jerome, at the beginning of Ps. 116.

CXVI. HE HAS HEARD MY VOICE (116:1-19)

This psalm is an individual's hymn of thanksgiving for deliverance from an illness that brought him to the very brink of death. It is intended for recitation in the temple

---

gratitude there, but such marks of indebtedness are all subordinate to the worship we offer to God.

Exactly how this is to be conveyed may be a matter for theological controversy. Differences manifested themselves, for example, at Amsterdam in August, 1948, at the first general assembly of the World Council of Churches. Karl Barth on the first day declared that "Jesus Christ has already robbed sin, death, the devil and hell of their powers," and that "the care of the church and the care of the world is not our care." He went on to protest against the idea—which he regarded as the final root of human disorder—that "man is the Atlas who is destined to bear the dome of heaven upon his shoulders." And this, as it was generally acknowledged, was "a wholesome warning against the pet schemes of Christian moralists." It was indeed a rebuke to the Christian world, and to the fears and anxieties that spring from the assumption that if we fail everything goes to pieces. That is the kind of atheism which may afflict preachers as they prepare their sermons, and churchmen as they lay their plans for the future. But was not Barth's emphasis a temptation to otherworldliness? Did he not imply that the Christian can be indifferent to the disorders of the world, and even to disturbances in the church? And is not that a dangerous doctrine to preach at a moment when every man ought to be at his post rendering the best service of which he is capable?

There is a question here for theologians to discuss. But Barth has done good service in seeking to save us from the self-centeredness into which we so easily fall. Let nothing be said that will lessen a proper sense of human responsibility; but let us never forget that "the Lord God omnipotent reigneth," and his purpose will endure whether we stand or fall. The psalmist is so intent on saying this that he addresses himself in turn to different groups. He addresses himself to the whole community, the chosen people, elected not to privilege but to service. **O Israel, trust in the LORD!** He addresses himself to the spiritual leaders—and not without reason, for it is fatally easy for priests and prophets to become irreligious even when they are handling sacred things: **O house of Aaron, put your trust in the LORD!** He addresses himself to recent converts—again not without reason, for when the choice is made, and superstition is repudiated, and false worship is repented of, there is always the possibility of slipping back to evil ways. **You who fear the LORD, trust in the LORD!** And to every such exhortation the people are encouraged to respond. **He is their help and their shield.**

That is what the psalmist had learned from life. It was not all he had learned. But this is his main lesson, and it has been passed on to us for our guidance and inspiration.

Not to us, O LORD, not to us,
but to thy name give glory.

116:1-19. *Thanksgiving for Recovery from Sickness.*—As we read this psalm we get a pic-

2 Because he hath inclined his ear unto me, therefore will I call upon *him* as long as I live.

3 The sorrows of death compassed me, and the pains of hell gat hold upon me: I found trouble and sorrow.

4 Then called I upon the name of the LORD; O LORD, I beseech thee, deliver my soul.

2 Because he inclined his ear to me,
therefore I will call on him as long as I live.
3 The snares of death encompassed me;
the pangs of Sheol laid hold on me;
I suffered distress and anguish.
4 Then I called on the name of the LORD:
"O LORD, I beseech thee, save my life!"

---

court in the presence of the congregation, while the psalmist offers his thank offering and fulfills the vows made during his sickness. The poem breathes a spirit of sincere devotion, enhanced by a deep sense of gratitude for mercies received. If its religious tone does not quite reach that of Ps. 73, it is, in Kittel's words, "considerably above the general level of O.T. piety" (*Die Psalmen,* p. 367). In Jewish usage this psalm is another of the Hallel group (see Exeg. on 113:1-9). In the Book of Common Prayer a portion of this hymn is included in The Thanksgiving of Women After Child-birth.

The psalm is marked by some minor literary blemishes. The tenses of the verbs are used in a casual manner; vs. 14 is repeated in vs. 18; and vss. 11, 15 do not seem relevant to their context. These features, added to the fact that the LXX breaks the psalm after vs. 9 into two different poems (to obtain Pss. 114–115 in the LXX), have prompted some scholars (e.g., Schmidt, Buttenwieser) to find here two independent prayers which in liturgical use have become fused together. We cannot, however, assume that an outburst of genuine thanksgiving will always find a flawless literary expression, and as there is no convincing evidence that the alleged parts of the psalm ever had an independent existence, it seems best to treat the nineteen verses as the work of one hand. There are no clearly defined strophic divisions in the poem. The clause "And on the name of the LORD I will call" (vss. 4, 13, 17) occurs too irregularly to be taken as a refrain. The meter is a mixture of 3+2, 3+3, and 2+2. Some Aramaisms in vss. 7, 12, 16 are commonly thought to indicate a postexilic date.

I. The Psalmist's Recent Experience (116:1-11)

116:1. The Hebrew in the first half of this verse is curious (lit., "I love that the LORD hears"), and the text may be faulty. **My voice and my supplications:** This probably should be "the voice [i.e., "sound" or "cry"] of my supplications," as in 28:2, 6; 31:22; 86:6; 130:2; 140:6.

3-9. The snares of death: Lit., "The cords of death." The psalmist's sickness was almost fatal (cf. 18:4-5). **The simple:** Here used in a good sense, young and inexperienced

---

ture of one who has come to the temple to pay his vow and to offer sacrifice. Perhaps he is a provincial farmer who with difficulty has made plans for others to tend his flocks and herds. Perhaps he is a trader from some foreign city who with all his preoccupations has never forgotten that Jerusalem is his spiritual home. What is clear is that he has suffered affliction, and in his hour of need he has vowed that if God would deliver him he would make a pilgrimage to the temple and offer the appropriate sacrifices. Deliverance was granted to him; and now he is in the temple taking **the cup of salvation** to redeem the promise. He is not alone. Friends and neighbors have come to rejoice with him. Around him are others with troubles behind them and numerous reasons for personal thanksgiving, each performing the recognized rites and gladly leaving with the priest the stipulated kid or lamb.

Exactly what the suffering has been is not clear. It looks as though it was a sickness of body which had brought him very near to death.

The snares of death encompassed me;
the pangs of Sheol laid hold on me;
I suffered distress and anguish.

That is common enough. Every generation has its own afflictions to bear. There is, however, this difference between ancient and modern times. Then there was no medical science as we understand it. There were, indeed, physicians,

5 Gracious *is* the LORD, and righteous;
yea, our God *is* merciful.
6 The LORD preserveth the simple: I was
brought low, and he helped me.
7 Return unto thy rest, O my soul; for
the LORD hath dealt bountifully with thee.
8 For thou hast delivered my soul from
death, mine eyes from tears, *and* my feet
from falling.
9 I will walk before the LORD in the land
of the living.
10 I believed, therefore have I spoken: I
was greatly afflicted:
11 I said in my haste, All men *are* liars.

5 Gracious is the LORD, and righteous;
6 The LORD preserves the simple;
when I was brought low, he saved me.
7 Return, O my soul, to your rest;
for the LORD has dealt bountifully with you.

8 For thou hast delivered my soul from death,
my eyes from tears,
my feet from stumbling;
9 I walk before the LORD
in the land of the living.
10 I kept my faith, even when I said,
"I am greatly afflicted";
11 I said in my consternation,
"Men are all a vain hope."

(as in 19:7; Prov. 9:4). **To your rest:** Inner repose, which the ills of the body healed. On vss. 8-9 cf. 56:13.

10. This is a difficult verse and numerous changes have been proposed. The RSV offers an attractive treatment of the M.T., and is supported by Calès, Weiser, *et al.* The first part of the verse is quoted in II Cor. 4:13.

11. In my consternation is better than **in my haste.** Vs. 11*a* is identical with 31:22*a*. **Men are all a vain hope:** Lit., **all men are liars;** cf. 62:9; Rom. 3:4.

---

some of whom were worthy of honor (see Ecclus. 38); but there was also much superstition, and in consequence much unnecessary suffering. Most people nowadays accept without a word of gratitude the privileges that have come to them. Even those who have been brought through illness that once would have proved fatal all too often forget their indebtedness to doctors and surgeons and nurses. Ought we not to praise God for the labors of thousands, most of whom are unknown to us?

There is another difference between the ancient Israelite and ourselves. When he looked into the face of death, he could see nothing to let him close his eyes in hope, nothing to let him sing of a fuller, freer life in the heavenly places. What he saw was Sheol, the dim and dismal abode of the dead, and few could look upon that without trembling. There was no hope of immortality. That came later. It came in one form to the Greek and in another to the Jew. It came with peculiar persuasiveness through Jesus Christ. But there is no hint that it had so much as dawned upon the mind of this Israelite who felt **the pangs of Sheol** lay hold on him, and who therefore suffered distress and anguish that ought not to torment us. Do we lift up the voice of praise for that? The early Christians did, as almost every N.T. page demonstrates. But do we? Or has the Christian hope so lost its power over us that we go down to the grave with no faith to comfort us?

The psalm, however, suggests a recoil from suffering that is still with us. Mencius, the Chinese philosopher who lived in the third century B.C., said that when heaven is about to confer a great office on any man, it first exercises his mind with suffering, and his sinews and bones with toil. Life, he is reported to have said, springs from sorrow. W. H. Davies, the tramp-poet, was expressing the same thought when he referred to the song of the robin as one of the sweetest in nature, and added: "The most effective notes of the robin are not heard in his song, but at that time in Autumn when he sits on a branch alone, and does nothing but sob a few quiet notes."[1] But no matter how much philosophers and poets and others may say, when pain comes either to body or mind we seek deliverance, and will pay a high price to secure it. We will take narcotics and risk the consequences. We will submit ourselves to the psychoanalyst and surrender our wills to the specialist in the quest for peace.

The psalmist did more than accept human help. He **called on the name of the LORD,** and this was his prayer: **O LORD, I beseech thee,**

[1] Thomas Moult, *W. H. Davies* (London: Thornton Butterworth, 1934), p. 73.

12 What shall I render unto the LORD
for all his benefits toward me?
13 I will take the cup of salvation, and
call upon the name of the LORD.
14 I will pay my vows unto the LORD
now in the presence of all his people.
15 Precious in the sight of the LORD *is*
the death of his saints.
16 O LORD, truly I *am* thy servant; I *am*
thy servant, *and* the son of thine handmaid:
thou hast loosed my bonds.
17 I will offer to thee the sacrifice of
thanksgiving, and will call upon the name
of the LORD.
18 I will pay my vows unto the LORD
now in the presence of all his people,
19 In the courts of the LORD's house, in
the midst of thee, O Jerusalem. Praise ye
the LORD.

12 What shall I render to the LORD
for all his bounty to me?
13 I will lift up the cup of salvation
and call on the name of the LORD,
14 I will pay my vows to the LORD
in the presence of all his people.
15 Precious in the sight of the LORD
is the death of his saints.
16 O LORD, I am thy servant;
I am thy servant, the son of thy handmaid.
Thou hast loosed my bonds.
17 I will offer to thee the sacrifice of thanksgiving
and call on the name of the LORD.
18 I will pay my vows to the LORD
in the presence of all his people,
19 in the courts of the house of the LORD,
in your midst, O Jerusalem.
Praise the LORD!

---

2. The Psalmist Goes to the Temple (116:12-19)

12-19. The concrete expression of the psalmist's gratitude. The biblical references cited below suggest that the order of the actions would normally be (*a*) the animal sacrifice; (*b*) the drink offering; (*c*) the payment of the vows. **The cup of salvation:** Probably the drink offering of wine (poured out into a bowl by the altar), one of the concomitants of practically every animal sacrifice (cf. Exod. 29:40; Lev. 23:37; Deut. 32:38; Ezek. 20:28; Ecclus. 50:14-15). Except for the making of the thank offering, the nature of the **vows** in vs. 14 is not disclosed. Vs. 15, which could be an intrusion into the text, presumably means that God will permit the untimely death of his pious followers only when absolutely necessary. As Calvin (*Commentary on the Psalms*, IV, 372) put it: "God does not hold his servants in so little estimation as to expose them to death casually" (cf. 72:14). **His saints:** See Exeg. on 30:4-5. **I am thy servant:** A fresh dedication of the psalmist to the Lord's service. **The son of thy handmaid:** See Exeg. on 86:16. **The sacrifice of thanksgiving:** The thank offering (see Exeg. on 107:22). **In the courts of the house of the LORD:** The altar was in the open court, not within the temple building, and in this area the worshipers were assembled (cf. 96:8).

---

save my life! It may not be the highest kind of prayer. It may be criticized by those who hold that true prayer is communion, not supplication. But asking is a large part of prayer as most of us know it. It found its way even into the prayers of the great Master of prayer, the Lord Jesus Christ. "If it be possible," he cried, when the snares of death compassed him, "let this cup pass from me" (Matt. 26:39). True, he added, and we must add when we are called upon to suffer distress and anguish, "Nevertheless, not as I will, but as thou wilt." With that example before us we shall never be ashamed to come to God not only with intercessions on behalf of others, but for ourselves and our own salvation.

And the psalmist's prayer was answered—perhaps not immediately. The neighbors may have had their own way of accounting for the recovery: the psalmist regarded it as the answer to prayer (vs. 8). Many may have ministered to him in his necessity, but there in the temple, with all its memories and associations, the uppermost thought was the graciousness and the compassion of God (vss. 6-7). This is the psalmist's testimony. And it is supported by a great host of witnesses. God does answer prayer: it is the testimony of all ages. Even when he works through doctors and nurses, it is still his work, for without him they could do nothing.

And because of all he has received this humble yet happy Israelite makes his personal response. Notice how warm and spontaneous it is: **I love the LORD, because he has heard . . .**

117 O praise the LORD, all ye nations: praise him, all ye people.

117 Praise the LORD, all nations! Extol him, all peoples!

CXVII. Extol Him, All Peoples (117:1-2)

117:1-2. The brevity of this poem, the shortest of the psalms, suggests that it is a fragment of a longer hymn designed for temple use. Peters and Schmidt connect it with Ps. 116, and Buttenwieser takes it as the proper conclusion to Ps. 148. The antecedent of **us** in vs. 2 is presumably the worshiping company of Israelites. Vs. 1, in which the

my supplications. Notice too how the response is to be shown not merely in a ritual act but by a maintained relationship: **I will call on him as long as I live. . . . I walk before the LORD in the land of the living.**

Such is the story suggested by this hymn of praise. It is as real and as true as anything we have seen with our own eyes or heard with our own ears. It is not only an ancient incident but contemporary experience. Every day men and women are "Battering the gates of heaven with storms of prayer" [2] and finding emancipation and redemption. It is happening in distant lands and here where we live, in our street, sometimes in our homes. When it happens to us, let us not go our way as though nothing had happened, but let us offer **the sacrifice of thanksgiving** and pay our **vows . . . in the presence of all his people.**

117:1-2. ***The Shortest Psalm.***—This psalm is so short that some scholars (see Exeg.) believe that it is only a fragment detached from its context. There are others, e.g., W. E. Barnes, who maintain that "short as this psalm is, it is complete in itself." [3] Most of us are more interested to learn that Isaac Watts, who set himself to make David the king sing like an eighteenth-century Englishman, managed to get from these two verses a very good hymn—the one beginning "From all that dwell below the skies." It is worth remembering also that it was the psalm sung by Oliver Cromwell and his men after the Battle of Dunbar. The time itself on that occasion was short, and it was convenient that the praise, lacking nothing in gratitude, should be short also.

There are at least three important subjects suggested by these two verses. First there is an ever-necessary exhortation to praise the living God: **O praise the LORD.** Then there is the confident note of universal religion: **O praise the Lord, all ye nations: praise him, all ye people.** Finally there is the reason for this universal attitude of adoration: **For his merciful kindness is great toward us: and the truth of the LORD endureth for ever.**

[2] Tennyson, "St. Simeon Stylites."

[3] *The Psalms* (New York: E. P. Dutton & Co., 1931), II, 555.

1. ***The Necessity of Praise.***—We have on previous pages frequently referred to the necessity of praise. We have dwelt upon the temple as a place of praise, and upon the healing influences that went forth from that center of song. We have pictured the men and women coming from far-off cities and from the little homesteads of Palestine, in due course returning with new hope and inspiration. Not only was national unity deepened; men were more than ever convinced of the mercy of God. We shall consider now the value of praise in everyday life.[4]

Praise is an antidote to depression. Many of us know the dark hour when laughter is folly and even life's good seems ill. W. H. Davies spoke for others besides himself when he confessed that in this mood the rainbow may shine and the cuckoo call, but

> There is no thing in Heaven or Earth
> Can lift my soul.[5]

No one knows where these black hours come from. They may be occasioned by external circumstances or by mental and physical ill-health. Men of action as well as men of thought are prone to them; the deepest and strongest of characters are not exempt. But depression is an enemy to be fought—and one of the best ways of fighting it is to join the praise of singing congregations.

Praise is an antidote also to worry, one of the most prevalent of sins. We worry not only about wars and rumors of wars; we worry about our health, our possessions, our children, even about little things like catching trains, the clothes we wear, or a disparaging remark uttered lightly by a thoughtless neighbor. If we have no worries of our own, we worry about other people's troubles, real or imaginary. If we read our Bibles more and our daily papers less, we should be steadier in crises, and be a steadying influence to others. If we gave a larger place to music,

[4] For some of the points in another setting see Frank H. Ballard, *Does War Shake Faith?* (London: James Clarke & Co., 1940), pp. 58-64.

[5] "The Dark Hour," from *The Collected Poems of W. H. Davies.* Used by permission of Mrs. W. H. Davies and Jonathan Cape, Ltd., publishers.

2 For his merciful kindness is great toward us: and the truth of the LORD *endureth* for ever. Praise ye the LORD.

2 For great is his steadfast love toward us;
and the faithfulness of the LORD endures for ever.
Praise the LORD!

peoples are called upon to **praise the LORD,** is ambiguous. We may infer that the Gentiles are to extol Israel's God either because they cannot deny his power and moral majesty, or because they share with Israel in his worship. In either case the verse has universalistic implications, as Paul recognized when he quoted it in Rom. 15:11. Indeed, this little psalm exhibits ideas that are among the loftiest in the O.T. Two

religious music, and especially the music of praise, we should have more wisdom in times of panic. Paul Sabatier tells of how once when Francis of Assisi was suffering intense pain, he begged a friar to borrow a guitar. The friar was shocked; a guitar seemed hardly the instrument for a saint: but God took pity on Francis. "The following night he sent an invisible angel to give him such a concert as is never heard on earth," and hearing it, Francis overcame the power of pain.[6]

Praise is also a corrective to the spirit of criticism. There are times when we are not much tempted to criticize. Common disaster gives a feeling of unity and mutual dependence. People are so concerned with grave issues that they forget to grumble about trivial annoyances. There are blessings even in great crises! But the danger passes, and once more critics are heard from. They criticize the young and condemn the old. They blame their own government and pour contempt on foreign governments. They magnify the weaknesses of the church and ridicule the Christian ministry. There is much to learn from the critics. Criticism has its uses of course; but it is a dangerous occupation. Faultfinders are a pest. A word of appreciation, on the other hand, is encouraging and constructive. We will learn to praise one another without flattery when we daily lift mind and heart in praise to God.

Praise is never more comely than in the time of adversity. Even the man of melancholy temperament will lift up his voice in the day of victory. It is another matter to find someone saying in all sincerity with the prophet: "Although the fig tree shall not blossom, neither shall fruit be in the vines; the labor of the olive shall fail, and the fields shall yield no meat; the flock shall be cut off from the fold, and there shall be no herd in the stalls: Yet I will rejoice in the LORD, I will joy in the God of my salvation" (Hab. 3:17).

Praise is therefore essential to the purity of religion. Men can be zealous, even fanatical; but without praise they lack radiance, and therefore repel those they would attract. It was the weakness of Stoicism, which with all its admirable qualities depressed and frightened men. Even Epictetus, who had many of the qualities of the good life, lacked the cheerfulness and spontaneity of the Christian apostles. It is a danger to which Mohammedans have always been prone. They too have many virtues. In temperance and missionary enthusiasm they put many Christians to shame. But in fanaticism they turn to force and intolerance. So also Puritanism, though it has produced some of the strongest characters in Christendom, has at times reminded us of Jacob when he wrestled with God and cried, "I will not let thee go, except thou bless me" (Gen. 32:26), more than of Moses when he came down from the mount with his face aglow. There are indeed serious strains and despairing cries in the psalms; but because praise is the dominant note, the singers are continually rising above sorrow and praising God in adversity.

2. ***The Source of Praise.***—Such moralizing may raise obvious objections. In particular it may cause us to complain that good advice is not enough. There never were such planners of the good life as the ancient Greeks, but they had little to say when asked how it was to be made effective. Much modern teaching suffers from that weakness. There are plenty to write books on Utopia, but there remain multitudes repeating the words of Paul to the Romans: "The good that I would, I do not: but the evil which I would not, that I do" (Rom. 7:19).

Such a charge cannot, however, be brought against this shortest of psalms. For here we have set forth not only the necessity but the source of praise. It is to be found not in anything we can do, or in what others may do for us. In this, as in every other sense, our salvation is of God. **His merciful kindness is great toward us: and the truth of the LORD endureth for ever.** Here is at least one difference between morality and religion. Morality may show us the good to which we should move. Religion

[6] *Life of St. Francis of Assisi,* tr. Louise Seymour Houghton (New York: Charles Scribner's Sons, 1901), p. 312.

118 O give thanks unto the LORD; for *he is* good: because his mercy *endureth* for ever.

118 O give thanks to the LORD, for he is good;
his steadfast love endures for ever!

Aramaisms in vs. 1 may point to a postexilic date. In the LXX, **Praise the LORD** of vs. 2 is put at the beginning of Ps. 118.

CXVIII. O GIVE THANKS TO THE LORD (118:1-29)

This psalm, the last of the Hallel group (see Exeg. on 113:1-9), is a litany of thanksgiving. It seems particularly suitable for the feast of Tabernacles (Sukkoth), but the fact that the Jewish community in the early Christian centuries used it on various festive occasions including Sukkoth, as the Mishnah testifies, indicates that it has more than a seasonal appeal. It is in truth one of the great hymns of the Psalter. It was a favorite psalm of Luther, who said of it: "This is the psalm that I love, . . . for it has often served me well and has helped me out of grave troubles, when neither emperors, kings, wise men, clever men, nor saints could have helped me" (quoted by Kittel, *Die Psalmen,* p. 371).

The literary history of the psalm is a matter of conjecture. It is, however, reasonable to suppose with Gunkel that the basis was an individual's hymn of thanksgiving, to which may be ascribed vss. 5-19, 21, 28. This theory at least explains the **I, me,** and **my** which occur in the verses in question. It is evident that the psalmist was delivered from the machinations of certain enemies (vss. 6-13), and from a chastisement that could have been his death (vss. 17-18, 21), and for these mercies he gave thanks to God (vss. 21, 28). The individual concerned may have been a king, and the view of Barnes that it was Hezekiah has some claim to serious consideration. This simple psalm was subsequently adapted to congregational use by the addition of vss. 1-4, 20, 22-27, 29, the I-element in the original hymn being eventually interpreted as the personification of the nation. The psalm, when used in worship, was rendered antiphonally, but the allotment of its verses to various parties, as in the following Exeg., is of course speculative.

There is no conclusive evidence in the psalm that points to a specific date. Barnes, as indicated above, puts its origin in the eighth century B.C., while Baethgen, Kirkpatrick, and Herkenne look to the age of Nehemiah. The meter is generally 3+3.

gives us the desire and power to rise up and hasten toward it. Contrast at this point also the religion of strain and effort with the religion of inspiration and spontaneity. The one results in set teeth and grim countenance; the other declares itself in alacrity and praise. The one may give us occasional heroes, but leaves the ordinary man with a sense of insufficiency; the other gives us many saints who sing as they work, because they know the world rests not on their weak shoulders but upon the absolute grace of God.

A great English essayist has reminded us that in the days of the Commonwealth Bulstrode Whitelock, ambassador to The Hague, full of concern for his country, tried in vain one night to sleep. At length his manservant said:

> "Sir, may I ask you a question?" "Certainly," replied the Ambassador. "Sir, did God govern the world well before you came into it?" "Undoubtedly." "And will He rule the world well when you have gone out of it?" "Undoubtedly." "Then, sir, can you not trust Him to rule the world well while you are in it?" The tired Ambassador turned on his side and fell asleep.[7]

Faith like that has a universal appeal. It wins response in our time no less than in the psalmist's. It appeals to men of all creeds and colors and leads them into a larger unity. It is the secret of an enduring world religion. **O praise the LORD, all ye nations: praise him, all ye people.**

118:1-29. ***Luther's Psalm.***—It may be that no one less than a great composer can do justice to this psalm. Linguists and historians can help by explaining obscure words and phrases, but it needs a musical genius to make us see what the psalmist may have seen—a company of pilgrims or victorious warriors marching toward Zion's hill. Whether they are intent upon military celebrations or religious festivals there is order in their movements, and they sing as they advance. A tuneful voice announces the theme:

[7] W. R. Inge, *Lay Thoughts of a Dean* (New York: G. P. Putnam's Sons, 1926), p. 215.

2 Let Israel now say, that his mercy *en-*
dureth for ever.
3 Let the house of Aaron now say, that
his mercy *endureth* for ever.
4 Let them now that fear the LORD say,
that his mercy *endureth* for ever.
5 I called upon the LORD in distress: the
LORD answered me, *and set me* in a large
place.
6 The LORD *is* on my side; I will not fear:
what can man do unto me?
7 The LORD taketh my part with them
that help me: therefore shall I see *my desire*
upon them that hate me.
8 *It is* better to trust in the LORD than
to put confidence in man.
9 *It is* better to trust in the LORD than to
put confidence in princes.

2 Let Israel say,
"His steadfast love endures for ever."
3 Let the house of Aaron say,
"His steadfast love endures for ever."
4 Let those who fear the LORD say,
"His steadfast love endures for ever."

5 Out of my distress I called on the LORD;
the LORD answered me and set me free.
6 With the LORD on my side I do not fear.
What can man do to me?
7 The LORD is on my side to help me;
I shall look in triumph on those who
hate me.
8 It is better to take refuge in the LORD
than to put confidence in man.
9 It is better to take refuge in the LORD
than to put confidence in princes.

1. LET ISRAEL GIVE THANKS (118:1-4)

118:1. This verse, like vs. 29, may have been rendered by one party or divided among two.

2-4. Probably rendered by a soloist, the responses being made in turn by the laity, the priests, and **those who fear the LORD.** On the meaning of the latter phrase see Exeg. on 115:9-11.

2. THE LORD ANSWERED ME (118:5-9)

5-9. The LORD answered me and set me free: Lit., "The LORD answered me in a broad place." Schmidt and Weiser support the RSV; Leslie translates "answered me with freedom"; Gunkel, emending the text, obtains "led me into a broad place" (cf. KJV). Vs. 6 is quoted in Heb. 13:6. **To help me:** Lit., either "among my helpers" or (with Amer. Trans.) "as my helper." **I shall look in triumph on:** Cf. the same verb in 112:8, where the RSV renders it "he sees his desire on." Possibly the meaning is "when I face." On vss. 8-9 cf. 116:11; 146:3.

O give thanks unto the LORD; for he is good: and the full choir immediately responds, **His mercy endureth for ever.** Again a solitary voice is uplifted in the words, **Let Israel say,** and again the refrain is repeated by the chorus, **His mercy endureth for ever.** The theme is renewed with particular invitations: first to the whole nation, then to the priests, finally to proselytes young and old; and every phrase prompts the united response, **His mercy endureth for ever.** Presently a softer voice suggests a story of suffering: **Out of my distress I called on the LORD. . . . All nations surrounded me. . . . They surrounded me like bees, . . . I was pushed hard, so that I was falling.** And again, full of sympathy and confidence, there is the choral response: **The LORD answered me and set me free. . . . What can man do to me? . . . The LORD is my strength and my song; he has become my salvation.**

By this time the procession has reached the precincts of the temple, where the gates to the temple proper are closed. The gatekeeper is hailed:

> **Open to me the gates of righteousness,**
> **that I may enter through them**
> **and give thanks to the LORD.**

The Levites who guard the gate reply with a challenge:

> **This is the gate of the LORD;**
> **the righteous shall enter through it.**

However, they open the gate, and the procession marches through, still singing. Some of their words have been passed down the centuries and used in many different settings; e.g.,

> **The stone which the builders rejected**
> **has become the chief cornerstone.**

10 All nations compassed me about: but in the name of the LORD will I destroy them.

11 They compassed me about; yea, they compassed me about: but in the name of the LORD I will destroy them.

12 They compassed me about like bees; they are quenched as the fire of thorns: for in the name of the LORD I will destroy them.

13 Thou hast thrust sore at me that I might fall: but the LORD helped me.

14 The LORD *is* my strength and song, and is become my salvation.

10 All nations surrounded me;
in the name of the LORD I cut them off!
11 They surrounded me, surrounded me on every side;
in the name of the LORD I cut them off!
12 They surrounded me like bees,
they blazed[i] like a fire of thorns;
in the name of the LORD I cut them off!
13 I was pushed hard,[j] so that I was falling,
but the LORD helped me.
14 The LORD is my strength and my song;
he has become my salvation.

[i] Gk: Heb *were extinguished*
[j] Gk Syr Jerome: Heb *thou didst push me hard*

3. NATIONS HAD SURROUNDED ME (118:10-14)

10. All nations: An improbable reference in the plight of an individual. Possibly "all the heathen" (with Schmidt) is a better rendering. Both in the O.T. and in later Jewish usage the noun גוים often designates Gentiles. **I cut them off:** This verb, which appears also in vss. 11-12, means "circumcise," and would hardly be expected in the present context. Various emendations have been proposed.

12-14. They blazed: An emended text (בערו), supported by the LXX. The Hebrew is **they were extinguished** (RSV mg.). **I was pushed hard:** An emended text (נדחיתי or דחיתי). The Hebrew is "You indeed pushed me" (cf. RSV mg.), which can be accepted only if an enemy is being addressed. Vs. 14 appears in Exod. 15:2; Isa. 12:2.

This also—which has been on the lips of many a martyr, and is used the world around to call congregations to worship:

> **This is the day which the LORD has made;**
> **let us rejoice and be glad in it.**

At last the worshipers draw near the horns of the altar; as they do so they wave palm branches and beat them on the ground, shouting "Hosannah! Hosannah!" The pageantry concludes with a final chorus in which the main theme is repeated to the accompaniment of appropriate instruments: **O give thanks unto the LORD; for he is good: for his mercy endureth for ever.**

The suggestion thus outlined may appeal to some, especially to those who are interested in ceremonial worship, and more particularly to those who remember the large part that ritualism took in the religion of Israel. The probability is, however, that we shall find a better guide if we turn to Martin Luther, who spent a period of solitude at Coburg studying the psalm and writing a commentary upon it. When the work was completed, Luther dedicated it to Abbot Friedrich and sent it to him, saying that, having searched his possessions, he had come to the conclusion that it was the best he had to give.

> This is my psalm, my chosen psalm. I love them all; I love all Holy Scripture, which is my consolation and my life. But this psalm is nearest my heart, and I have a familiar right to call it mine. It has saved me from many a pressing danger, from which nor emperor, nor kings, nor sages, nor saints could have saved me. It is my friend; dearer to me than all the honors and power of earth.[8]

It is not difficult to name some of the reasons why the psalm made so strong an appeal to such a man as Luther. In the first place it tells the gratitude of one, who having suffered greatly, has been released from his distresses. Exactly what the suffering was, whether it was peculiar to the psalmist, or something that he shared with his people, is not revealed. Whether it was a short sharp crisis or a prolonged affliction is not declared. What is clear is that it was severe enough to try his spirit to the uttermost. **All nations surrounded me. . . . They surrounded me like bees . . . . I was pushed hard, so that I was falling.** It might be the experience of a soldier with enemies closing in on every hand, of a political refugee frustrated at every turn, of a persecuted religious sect watched day and night by police and magistrates. It might be the cry of a Bunyan or a Tyndale cast into foul prisons, haled before judges, sentenced to years of solitude or a martyr's grave. Such things have

[8] Prothero, *Psalms in Human Life*, p. 94.

15 The voice of rejoicing and salvation *is* in the tabernacles of the righteous: the right hand of the LORD doeth valiantly.
16 The right hand of the LORD is exalted: the right hand of the LORD doeth valiantly.
17 I shall not die, but live, and declare the works of the LORD.
18 The LORD hath chastened me sore: but he hath not given me over unto death.
19 Open to me the gates of righteousness: I will go into them, *and* I will praise the LORD:
20 This gate of the LORD, into which the righteous shall enter.
21 I will praise thee: for thou hast heard me, and art become my salvation.

15 Hark, glad songs of victory
in the tents of the righteous:
"The right hand of the LORD does valiantly!"
16 the right hand of the LORD is exalted,
the right hand of the LORD does valiantly!"
17 I shall not die, but I shall live,
and recount the deeds of the LORD.
18 The LORD has chastened me sorely,
but he has not given me over to death.

19 Open to me the gates of righteousness,
that I may enter through them
and give thanks to the LORD.

20 This is the gate of the LORD;
the righteous shall enter through it.

21 I thank thee that thou hast answered me
and hast become my salvation.

---

4. VICTORY FOR THE RIGHTEOUS (118:15-21)

15. Hark, glad songs of victory: This translation suggests some successful military exploit, which may not have been in the psalmist's mind at all. The Hebrew is "the sound of a shout and salvation." The RSV permits itself considerable latitude in the psalms in the translation of the two principal nouns (רנה, **glad songs,** and ישׁועה, **victory**). **Tents:** Unless the reference is a military one, the word is simply a synonym for "dwellings." Most Hebrews lived in houses (often hovels) of mud brick and sometimes of stone.

17-18. Cf. Hezekiah's sickness (II Kings 20:1-11) and Paul's words in II Cor. 6:4-10.

19-20. Cf. 24:7, 9. **The gates of righteousness:** Gates giving entrance to the temple court. They are righteous because they are dedicated to righteous purposes, and lead to the earthly dwelling place of a holy and righteous God (cf. Jer. 31:23). Hence in vs. 20, **the gate of the LORD.** This verse is probably an addition to the original hymn, and was said by a priest at the gate.

---

been common enough and are not yet ended. They happened to Luther, who knew what it was to stand alone before the might of the empire and the wrath of the papacy. Not always are the victims of such persecutions meek and forgiving. Not always do they remember the wisdom of Jesus or his example when he was mocked, insulted, and crucified. Men who have the courage to resist evil and to stand to the end for conscience and for truth are often endowed with hot passions and a reviling tongue. They have strength and often great ability, but they are not perfect. It is not for us, however, to judge them. Least of all should we condemn them if we have lived our days in comfort and security. Nor shall we wish to rebuke them if we ourselves have suffered for righteousness' sake. This is one thing that war has done for us. Standing by night and by day in the place of peril we know how easy it is to threaten, to retaliate, to call down vengeance from on high. With gospel teaching in our ears we may not commend psalmist or reformer who exclaims:

The LORD is on my side to help me;
I shall look in triumph on those who hate me.

But though we may not commend, we dare not judge.

In the second place this psalm appealed to such a man as Martin Luther because from beginning to end it is essentially religious. There are in it human touches, especially references to Israel and to other nations, to **gates of righteousness** and **the stone which the builders rejected,** to enemies who hate, and to wrongs inflicted. These, however, are incidental. The real concern is with the Lord, who heard the cry of distress and gave deliverance. That de-

22 The stone *which* the builders refused
is become the head *stone* of the corner.
23 This is the LORD's doing; it *is* marvelous in our eyes.
24 This *is* the day *which* the LORD hath
made; we will rejoice and be glad in it.
25 Save now, I beseech thee, O LORD:
O LORD, I beseech thee, send now prosperity.
26 Blessed *be* he that cometh in the name
of the LORD: we have blessed you out of the
house of the LORD.

22 The stone which the builders rejected
has become the chief cornerstone.
23 This is the LORD's doing;
it is marvelous in our eyes.
24 This is the day which the LORD has made;
let us rejoice and be glad in it.
25 Save us, we beseech thee, O LORD!
O LORD, we beseech thee, give us success!

26 Blessed be he who enters in the name of the LORD!
We bless you from the house of the LORD.

---

5. Hymn for the Temple (118:22-27)

22-24. Vs. 22 is possibly a proverb: a stone originally rejected for building purposes turns out to be exceedingly useful. **The chief cornerstone:** Probably a bondstone at the corner of the foundation (cf. Isa. 28:16). The psalmist uses the saying to point out that the people which the Gentile world despised has under God become an honorable nation. For the N.T. references, which assume an allusion to Christ in this verse, see Matt. 21:42; Mark 12:10; Luke 20:17; Acts 4:11; Eph. 2:20; I Pet. 2:4, 7. Cf. vs. 23 with the recognition of God's hand in Nehemiah's wall building (Neh. 6:16). The **day** in vs. 24 is the festival, but otherwise is not identified.

25. Save us, we beseech thee: Lit., "Save, I [or "we"] pray." The Hebrew (הושיעה נא) gives us the word hosanna. On the use of this verse in the feast of Tabernacles ceremonies see Mishnah, Sukkah 4:5.

26. A priestly benediction. The first half of the verse is quoted six times in the Gospels. In Matt. 23:39; Luke 13:35, the verse is used by Jesus either as an oblique reference to the forthcoming Passover season (we know that the Hallel psalms were used at Passover), or in an allusion to the imminent establishment of the kingdom of God. The other four citations (Matt. 21:9; Mark 11:9; Luke 19:38; John 12:3) are associated with Jesus' entrance into Jerusalem just before Passover.

---

liverance was not casual or accidental. It was due to the **steadfast love** which **endures for ever** and must never be forgotten.

This was a quality to which Martin Luther responded above most men. Many charges have been brought against him. Some have been admitted even by his stoutest defenders. What cannot be denied is that he was above all a religious man. It was as natural for him as for the psalmist to look beyond himself, beyond all human protectors, and to find in God his refuge and his hope. It will suffice to quote one characteristic sentence. When enemies came and sneeringly asked where he would be when church and state, princes and people, were against him, the answer flashed back: "Where shall I be then? Why, then as now, in the hands of the Almighty God." [1] In sorrow and in joy, in adversity and in success, it was the same.

[1] Quoted in James Stewart, *The Gates of New Life* (New York: Charles Scribner's Sons, 1940), p. 164.

In this respect psalmist and reformer were nearer to each other than we are to either. It would be untrue to say that modern man is unconscious of the spiritual world. One after another, poets and others tell of sudden visitations, of moments when they feel that all life is bathed in mystic splendor, of voices that speak above the din of the world and must not be disobeyed. Yet Wordsworth was right when he said that "the world is too much with us." In our great cities, amid the roar of machinery especially, it is easy to forget God, perhaps to doubt or deny his existence. Even those who spend their lives in religious activities can live for long without spiritual experience, without freshness in prayer or potency in praise. James Martineau felt it in his day and said that men discuss with the lips each other's creeds instead of going into the silence with their own God. R. W. Dale put it more tersely: "God himself is passing out of our life." The military com-

27 God *is* the LORD, which hath showed
us light: bind the sacrifice with cords, *even*
unto the horns of the altar.
28 Thou *art* my God, and I will praise
thee: *thou art* my God, I will exalt thee.
29 O give thanks unto the LORD; for *he is*
good: for his mercy *endureth* for ever.

27 The LORD is God,
and he has given us light.
Bind the festal procession with branches,
up to the horns of the altar!

28 Thou art my God, and I will give thanks
to thee;
thou art my God, I will extol thee.

29 O give thanks to the LORD, for he is good;
for his steadfast love endures for ever!

---

27. He has given us light: In 31:16 the same verb is used with "face" to give "Let thy face shine on, etc.," and a similar construction appears in 67:1; 80:3, 7, 19; 119:135. All these instances are based on the priestly benediction in Num. 6:25. The present clause would therefore seem to mean "He has shone upon us," i.e., "He has shown us his favor." **Bind the festal . . . the horns of the altar:** This part of the verse, in which there is a reference to some cultic act, has been the subject of much discussion. Probably the usage on the feast of Tabernacles gives us the best clue as to what is meant. We learn from the Mishnah (Sukkah 3:4) and Josephus (*Antiquities* III. 10. 4) that on this occasion the worshipers in the temple carried, in addition to citrons, bouquets (lulabs) of palm, myrtle, and willow **branches** (cf. Lev. 23:39-40), and that in the course of the ceremonies they went in a **procession** around the altar. This practice appears to elucidate **Bind the festal procession with branches,** although the Hebrew verb might better be rendered "arrange" or "marshal" (cf. I Kings 20:14). **Up to the horns of the altar: The horns** were the small projections at each corner of the altar. The lulabs were not bound to the altar but the procession bearing the bouquets came near the altar. Some scholars emend **up to** (עד) to procure a verb such as "adorn" (עדו), and Schmidt proposes that the reference is to the putting of blood on the altar's horns by the priest (cf. Lev. 4:7). The suggestion of the KJV that the sacrificial animal was bound with **cords** to the altar is without any support in Jewish tradition.

6. Concluding Doxology (118:28-29)

28-29. The normal ending of a thanksgiving hymn (vs. 29) is preceded by a personal acknowledgment of faith and gratitude (vs. 28).

---

muniqués of World War I have been contrasted with those of Oliver Cromwell. Cromwell was always ready to say that the Lord had given them the victory. Modern generals speak of movements "according to plan." We have come to this, that an Italian philosopher denies to religion any creative place in society and prophesies its ultimate disappearance. Even the Anglican bishops in the Lambeth Report of 1921 sorrowfully confessed that "where God is still acknowledged, he is often regarded as too elusive or remote to be relevant to the practical concerns of life." Not so the soil or the climate which nurtured the psalms.

Finally, Ps. 118 made an irresistible appeal to Martin Luther because it deals with congregational worship and invites men to come as suppliants to the mercy seat. Much had changed in the centuries between Jewish psalmist and Protestant reformer. The temple had been destroyed and the people of Israel scattered. The Dayspring from on high had come bringing new hope to a weary world. Christian missionaries had taken the gospel of peace among the nations. The church had become powerful, even tyrannical. But through all the changes men had sought God, had brought their gifts and waited for a blessing. Luther and his contemporaries turned to the church at the appointed hour as naturally as men had done century after century.

Here again it is different with the modern man. There are indeed millions who still find their way with joy to the sacred place. They do so not because they are the victims of habit, but because they have found peace and strength there. They would no more forsake the Lord's house than they would deny the claims of family

ALEPH

KJV	RSV
119 Blessed *are* the undefiled in the way, who walk in the law of the LORD.	**119** Blessed are those whose way is blameless, who walk in the law of the LORD!

CXIX. THY LAW IS MY DELIGHT (119:1-176)

This psalm is the greatest tour de force in the Psalter. It is not only the longest psalm, but God is addressed or referred to in every one of its one hundred and seventy-six verses. The poem, which has twenty-two strophes of eight lines each, also exhibits a unique application of the acrostic principle (cf. Pss. 9; 10; 25; 34; 37; 111; 112; 145). In the first strophe the first word in each line commences with Aleph, the first letter of the Hebrew alphabet; in the second strophe each line similarly commences with Beth, the second letter of the alphabet; and so on until all twenty-two letters have been utilized. A similar scheme, but with a three-line strophe, is found in Lam. 3.

The psalm is distinguished also by its extraordinary tribute to the **law** of Israel. The author has attempted to have a reference, often eulogistic, to the law in each of his verses, and in only seven cases has he not done so (vss. 84, 90, 121, 122, 132, 149, 156). In five of the latter the word משפט occurs, but not in the usual sense of "ordinance" or "judgment," as in vs. 7. The other words which the psalmist availed himself of are necessarily limited in number, and their frequent recurrence produces a typical Oriental solemnity. Its psychological effect is that of a litany which may appear to some Westerners as monotonous. The repeated words are: **law,** vs. 1; **testimonies,** vs. 2; **ways** (דרכים), vs. 3; **precepts,** vs. 4; **statutes,** vs. 5; **commandments,** vs. 6; **word** (דבר), vs. 9; **word** (אמרה), vs. 11, rendered as **promise** (RSV) in vs. 38. Another synonym, **ways** (ארחת), is used only once (vs. 15). A close parallel to these nouns is found in the six terms for the law found in 19:7-9. While some scholars have tried to find a pattern in the sequence and frequency of the aforementioned ten words, the ordinary M.T. affords little basis for any such scheme (however, see Briggs, *Psalms, ad loc.*).

The psalmist's ten terms must not be pressed too closely for distinctive meanings, but they do suggest the variety of ways in which the law may be considered, and they point to the richness of the revelation. Contrary to some commentators, there is no reason to believe that the author was thinking of the whole of God's revelation to Israel except in so far as it was subsumed in the law. He nowhere alludes to prophecy, and his favorite words, except **precepts** (a word found only in the Psalms) and **ways** (ארחת, vs. 15), are taken from the Pentateuch. As the latter after its completion came to be considered the Lord's supreme revelation to his people, it is probable that only the Law (or Torah) was in the psalmist's mind.

---

or nation. In some lands, however, they have already become a minority, often considered a strange minority. They are surrounded by men and women who prefer to cultivate gardens or enjoy excursions or spend the day of rest in frivolous reading. This is the essential difference between the past and the present: not the discoveries we have made in science, not the machines we have built or the conquest of space, but a loss of the sense of the holy, the failure to understand what common worship means.

No doubt men worship secretly without knowing that they worship. They are suddenly overwhelmed by a sense of beauty and feel a hush falling upon nature and upon their own hearts. They have a vision of truth and vow that they will be true to it and not be tempted aside by money or position. These are experiences from which we can start in an appeal to our contemporaries not to neglect the means of grace. We can go further by making acts of worship so real, so potent, so transforming that neighbors will feel constrained to share such sacred privileges. It is not enough to say that the first day in the week is in a special sense the Lord's. We must show by expression and demeanor that we **rejoice** and are **glad in it.**

119:1-176. ***A Psalmist Praises the Law of God.*** —R. H. Wilenski tells us that John Ruskin "could not write" for the reason that he was addicted from childhood onward to "the emo-

It is impossible to assign this unusual psalm to any of the familiar categories. It has certain didactic qualities, and because of its author's devotion to the law it reminds us of 1:1-6; 19:7-14. The psalmist, however, is not concerned with the minutiae of the law. He neither treats in detail the prescriptions of what we commonly call the moral law, nor does he refer to the temple, temple ceremonies, or Jewish ritual. The only sacrifice he mentions is **my offerings of praise** (vs. 108). He thinks of the law in broad terms as being the truth from God: it is his rule of life and his ground of hope. In one sense therefore the psalm is a hymn in praise of the law, and the psalmist's great passion for the law is evident throughout. On the other hand, the poem has some of the characteristics of a lament. The plea at the end of the first strophe, **O forsake me not utterly** (vs. 8), is the first intimation that the psalmist's portion is not free from distress and trouble. His later references to the **insolent** (vs. 21) or **godless** (vs. 51), the **wicked** (vs. 61); and the **evildoers** (vs. 115), make it clear that his own piety is not shared by all his contemporaries. Indeed, from vs. 21 on there are frequent allusions to the persecution, scorn, and contempt to which the psalmist is subjected. This is vividly portrayed in vs. 83 in the simile **like a wineskin in the smoke.** The identity of these enemies is a matter of opinion, but as the psalmist never mentions Gentiles specifically, it is probable that most of his foes are careless or even apostate fellow countrymen. The author, however, never loses his faith and confidence, and he continues to believe and to pray that his salvation will come from the Lord. Thus in his concluding stanza (vss. 170, 173) he cries:

Let my supplication come before thee;
deliver me according to thy word.

. . . .

Let thy hand be ready to help me,
for I have chosen thy precepts.

The highly artificial structure of the poem, and the selected vocabulary employed to describe the law, have necessarily restricted the literary achievement of the psalmist. The repetition of favorite words and phrases creates an impression of dull uniformity, and the casual reader is apt to conclude, when he has read four or five strophes, that the author's originality is fully exhausted. While there is a difference in emphasis among the strophes, there is little development in the thought, either within the strophes or in the poem as a whole, and a logical analysis of most of the strophes is quite impossible. Despite these weaknesses, the psalm is a notable creation, and it bears testimony to a deep spirituality in one of Israel's anonymous saints. Such words as **The earth, O LORD, is full of thy steadfast love** (vs. 64), and **Thy righteousness is righteous for ever** (vs. 142), reflect the quality of the psalmist's simple but firm faith in God.

The date is probably sometime after Ezra. The meter is 3+2 or 3+3, with some variations.

---

tive language of the Bible."[2] It is not intended in this place either to prove that Ruskin could write or to defend "the emotive language of the Bible." It is true, however, that Ruskin was persuaded to memorize long sections of the scriptures, including Ps. 119.

In order to realize what this means we must remind ourselves that the psalm contains no less than 176 verses. It may further be admitted that the style in which the psalm is written (see Exeg.) is not the happiest. One commentator who rarely allows himself to write critically says that "it would surely be difficult to find in the whole range of literature—real literature—a more artificial arrangement than this."[3] It is difficult to believe that any normal lad could memorize it verse by verse without many wanderings of the mind and inner protests. Not only is there no progressive theme, but there is a great deal of repetition both of words and sentiment. Even the prayers—and the psalm abounds in supplications—are repeated again and again in the same language. What is more, the psalmist quotes, and quotes too frequently.

[2] H. J. and Hugh Massingham, eds., *The Great Victorians* (London: Ivor Nicholson & Watson, 1932), p. 452.

[3] Barnes, *Psalms*, II, 565.

2 Blessed *are* they that keep his testimonies, *and that* seek him with the whole
heart.
3 They also do no iniquity: they walk in
his ways.
4 Thou hast commanded *us* to keep thy
precepts diligently.
5 O that my ways were directed to keep
thy statutes!
6 Then shall I not be ashamed, when I
have respect unto all thy commandments.
7 I will praise thee with uprightness of
heart, when I shall have learned thy righteous judgments.
8 I will keep thy statutes: O forsake me
not utterly.

2 Blessed are those who keep his testimonies,
who seek him with their whole heart,
3 who also do no wrong,
but walk in his ways!
4 Thou hast commanded thy precepts
to be kept diligently.
5 O that my ways may be steadfast
in keeping thy statutes!
6 Then I shall not be put to shame,
having my eyes fixed on all thy commandments.
7 I will praise thee with an upright heart,
when I learn thy righteous ordinances.
8 I will observe thy statutes;
O forsake me not utterly!

---

1. First Strophe (119:1-8)

Seven of the psalmist's ten terms for the law are used in this strophe.

119:1. The happiness of the godly is a familiar theme of the psalmists (1:1; 2:12; 34:8; etc.) and of other O.T. writers (Deut. 28:1-14; Prov. 8:32, 34; etc.). **Those whose way is blameless** is preferable to **the undefiled in the way.**

5. A prayer for constant and steadfast loyalty to the divine requirements.

6-7. Having my eyes fixed on: Lit., "when I look unto." **I will praise thee** (אודך): The RSV often renders this verb as "give thanks to" (7:17; 9:1; 28:7; etc.).

Not that the habit of quoting is to be condemned out of hand. Many of the greatest geniuses have quoted freely and effectively. But it adds to the sense of monotony when ideas and phrases with which one has long been familiar are repeated again and yet again. With all these facts before us, we can hardly imagine a considerate parent or a good teacher setting a child nowadays to learn by heart Ps. 119.[4]

Yet it must not be passed by as sterile and profitless. Alexander Maclaren said that it reminded him of a great violinist who had but one string to play upon, but who out of that one string brought perfect music. It so happens that the psalmist's string is one of the greatest upon which any man can play. His theme is the law of God, not the Ten Commandments, or the Pentateuch, or some other written work. There are verses in which he seems to have Mount Sinai in mind. But he quickly passes to the divine law which works everywhere. He delights in all the divine revelations, those that have come through nature and through history not less than those that have come through scripture.

Notice the different ways in which he describes this ubiquitous law of God. He speaks of the **statutes** of God, of the divine **precepts,** of God's **testimonies** and his **ways,** and again of his **commandments** and his **judgments.** The law is **teaching;** it is **guidance** and **instruction.** The psalmist believes, and would have men everywhere believe, that this law of God is the one thing worth studying. Not only is it his chief delight; it gives him an assurance that he is wiser than teachers who know everything except the Law of God.

> **For ever, O Lord, thy word**
> **is firmly fixed in the heavens** (vs. 89).
>
> **Thy word is a lamp to my feet**
> **and a light to my path** (vs. 105).
>
> **How sweet are thy words to my taste,**
> **sweeter than honey to my mouth!** (vs. 103).

So does he pile phrase on phrase, each full of sincerity and gratitude, and in the most earnest manner pledges himself to keep and to teach

[4] It was different in the medieval church, when the scarcity of copies made it necessary for the clergy to memorize the psalms. W. O. E. Oesterley in *A Fresh Approach to the Psalms* (New York: Charles Scribner's Sons, 1937), pp. 180-82, tells us that Ps. 119 was said daily, and the whole Psalter was repeated weekly by every ecclesiastic. Many people, therefore, including some who were otherwise ill-educated, knew the Psalter by heart. One patriarch of Constantinople would ordain no clerk who could not recite the whole, and Gregory the Great refused to consecrate a bishop for the same reason. Two saints, Patrick and Kentigern, are said to have recited the Psalter daily. This may be heroic, but it conflicts with modern ideas both of holiness and of education.

BETH

9 Wherewithal shall a young man cleanse
his way? by taking heed *thereto* according
to thy word.
10 With my whole heart have I sought
thee: O let me not wander from thy commandments.
11 Thy word have I hid in mine heart,
that I might not sin against thee.
12 Blessed *art* thou, O LORD: teach me
thy statutes.
13 With my lips have I declared all the
judgments of thy mouth.
14 I have rejoiced in the way of thy testimonies, as *much as* in all riches.
15 I will meditate in thy precepts, and
have respect unto thy ways.
16 I will delight myself in thy statutes:
I will not forget thy word.

9 How can a young man keep his way pure?
By guarding it according to thy word.
10 With my whole heart I seek thee;
let me not wander from thy commandments!
11 I have laid up thy word in my heart,
that I might not sin against thee.
12 Blessed be thou, O LORD;
teach me thy statutes!
13 With my lips I declare
all the ordinances of thy mouth.
14 In the way of thy testimonies I delight
as much as in all riches.
15 I will meditate on thy precepts,
and fix my eyes on thy ways.
16 I will delight in thy statutes;
I will not forget thy word.

---

2. SECOND STROPHE (119:9-16)

9-16. The interest in the welfare of youth (vs. 9) is characteristic of the wisdom writers (cf. Prov. 1:4, 8, 10, 15; 2:1; 3:1; Eccl. 11:9; 12:1; etc.). **I have laid up:** Store up as a treasure. **Riches:** On the superiority of wisdom and piety to wealth see vss. 72, 127; 19:10; Job 28:13-19; Prov. 3:14-15; 8:10, 19. **Fix my eyes:** See vs. 6.

---

this way of wisdom to the end. That is why Maclaren likens the psalmist to a master musician drawing sweet music from a single string, and again likens the psalm to "the ripples on a sunny sea, alike and impressive in their continual march, and yet each catching the light with a difference, and breaking on the shore in a tone of its own." [5]

It ought now to be possible to draw a picture of the psalmist himself. He is a student who has set himself to learn the things that are best worth learning and to order his life by them. He is not a poet capable of imaginative flights, nor is he a philosopher intent upon creating a system. But he knows how to lay hold of essential truths, to keep them ever before him, and to commend them to others. His real concern is to know God and his own soul, and to do this he is prepared to sacrifice everything else. It is a concentration that puts him among the wisest of men. No serious quest for knowledge should be disparaged. One can study, as Darwin did, the ways of worms and be led ultimately to a universal law of evolution. It matters less what one studies than the way in which the study is conducted. Not all, however, who join the serious quest for knowledge concentrate upon the most important subjects.

[5] *Psalms,* III, 244.

The psalmist is also a man of deep piety. He is not a spiritual pioneer like Amos, or a commanding personality like Moses or Elijah. There is an element of conventionality both in his convictions and in his practice. But he is a man of humble mind and lowly spirit. There are verses that may seem complacent. There are hints of self-righteousness. Yet he is no hypocrite. His confessions are not formal, but made in a spirit of real contrition. Nor is there anything forced or artificial when he exclaims, **My flesh trembleth for fear of thee; and I am afraid of thy judgments** (vs. 120). The same is true of his prayers. He prays for guidance, for instruction, for revival. Again and again he prays that he may be given an understanding of the law, and be kept from the sin of covetousness. He is very conscious of the temptations that lurk around his path. It may be that his lot is a comparatively secluded one, that he is free from the grosser temptations of life. But there are snares and pitfalls even in learned leisure. One may know nothing of the perils of courts and market places and barracks, but evil creeps into academic halls and quiet cloisters. Some of the most violent struggles of mind and heart have been won and lost in chapels and solitary cells. The religious life is a constant conflict. Nor can it be assumed that

GIMEL

17 Deal bountifully with thy servant, *that* I may live, and keep thy word.

18 Open thou mine eyes, that I may behold wondrous things out of thy law.

19 I *am* a stranger in the earth: hide not thy commandments from me.

20 My soul breaketh for the longing *that it hath* unto thy judgments at all times.

21 Thou hast rebuked the proud *that are* cursed, which do err from thy commandments.

22 Remove from me reproach and contempt; for I have kept thy testimonies.

23 Princes also did sit *and* speak against me: *but* thy servant did meditate in thy statutes.

24 Thy testimonies also *are* my delight, *and* my counselors.

DALETH

25 My soul cleaveth unto the dust: quicken thou me according to thy word.

26 I have declared my ways, and thou heardest me: teach me thy statutes.

17 Deal bountifully with thy servant,
that I may live and observe thy word.
18 Open my eyes, that I may behold
wondrous things out of thy law.
19 I am a sojourner on earth;
hide not thy commandments from me!
20 My soul is consumed with longing
for thy ordinances at all times.
21 Thou dost rebuke the insolent, accursed ones,
who wander from thy commandments;
22 take away from me their scorn and contempt,
for I have kept thy testimonies.
23 Even though princes sit plotting against me,
thy servant will meditate on thy statutes.
24 Thy testimonies are my delight,
they are my counselors.

25 My soul cleaves to the dust;
revive me according to thy word!
26 When I told of my ways, thou didst answer me;
teach me thy statutes!

3. Third Strophe (119:17-24)

19. A sojourner on earth emphasizes man's temporality (cf. 39:12). The psalmist, in the spirit of Deut. 10:19, may also be suggesting his claim as a **sojourner** to the Lord's consideration.

21-23. These verses give the first indication (save in vs. 8*b*) of the psalmist's personal troubles. **The insolent** or **the proud:** Referred to again in vss. 51, 69, 78, 85, 122 (where RSV translates as **godless**). Apparently the reference is to irreligious Jews. **Take away:** The M.T. has to be repointed to get the correct form of the imperative. **Princes:** Also referred to in vs. 161. Probably fellow Hebrews, but of the nobility and magistracy (cf. Jer. 38:4). **Sit plotting against me:** Lit., as in the KJV.

4. Fourth Strophe (119:25-32)

25. The psalmist is in distress (also in vs. 28).

one who lives apart from the busy life of the world, as the psalmist may have done, will necessarily become unpractical. The psalm suggests a man who keeps his feet firmly planted on the earth. He is indeed more practical than many a worldling. There is always the underlying conviction that one will be judged and justified not by fine sentiments but by obedience to God's will.

19. ***A Sojourner on Earth.***—We have considered the general impressions from a reading of the whole psalm. There are however phrases that invite us to return for closer inspection. There is the confession that the psalmist feels himself to be but **a sojourner on earth.** The word is a political one, signifying a resident alien, "A person living in a country to which he does not belong, and excluded therefore from the rights of citizenship in it."[6] It is a word with widespread contemporary significance. Millions of persons have been driven from their native land and have become wandering exiles. Some of them have found accommodation, friends, and interests, and have laid hold on life again. But they cannot forget the old home and youthful com-

[6] James Hastings, ed., *The Speaker's Bible* (Chicago: W. P. Blessing, 1932), IV, p. 58.

27 Make me to understand the way of thy precepts: so shall I talk of thy wondrous works.

28 My soul melteth for heaviness: strengthen thou me according unto thy word.

29 Remove from me the way of lying: and grant me thy law graciously.

30 I have chosen the way of truth: thy judgments have I laid *before me.*

31 I have stuck unto thy testimonies: O LORD, put me not to shame.

32 I will run the way of thy commandments, when thou shalt enlarge my heart.

HE

33 Teach me, O LORD, the way of thy statutes; and I shall keep it *unto* the end.

34 Give me understanding, and I shall keep thy law; yea, I shall observe it with *my* whole heart.

35 Make me to go in the path of thy commandments; for therein do I delight.

36 Incline my heart unto thy testimonies, and not to covetousness.

37 Turn away mine eyes from beholding vanity; *and* quicken thou me in thy way.

38 Stablish thy word unto thy servant, who *is devoted* to thy fear.

27 Make me understand the way of thy precepts,
and I will meditate on thy wondrous works.
28 My soul melts away for sorrow;
strengthen me according to thy word!
29 Put false ways far from me;
and graciously teach me thy law!
30 I have chosen the way of faithfulness,
I set thy ordinances before me.
31 I cleave to thy testimonies, O LORD;
let me not be put to shame!
32 I will run in the way of thy commandments
when thou enlargest my understanding!

33 Teach me, O LORD, the way of thy statutes;
and I will keep it to the end.
34 Give me understanding, that I may keep thy law
and observe it with my whole heart.
35 Lead me in the path of thy commandments,
for I delight in it.
36 Incline my heart to thy testimonies,
and not to gain!
37 Turn my eyes from looking at vanities;
and give me life in thy ways.
38 Confirm to thy servant thy promise,
which is for those who fear thee.

27-32. Meditate rather than **talk. And graciously teach me thy law:** Lit., "And with respect to thy law, be gracious unto me." Buttenwieser proposes, "And grace me with thy law." **I set thy ordinances before me:** The Hebrew is "thy ordinances I have set," but this is an improbable text. Many commentators, with the Syriac, emend the verb to אִוִּיתִי, "I desire." **When thou enlargest my understanding:** Another translation is "For thou enlargest, etc." The fear of the Lord leads to the true enlargement of mind and heart.

5. FIFTH STROPHE (119:33-40)

33. I will keep it to the end: The meaning of עֵקֶב in this context is not perfectly clear, but the rendition **to the end** is supported by the usage of the same word in vs. 112. Presumably the reference is to the end of the psalmist's life. Another translation of the term, favored by many, is "as a reward" (cf. 19:11), the keeping of the law being its own reward.

36-38. Gain: The word means "unjust gain" (cf. **covetousness** KJV). **For those who fear thee:** A slightly emended text, the Hebrew being "for thy fear."

---

panions. News reaches them of the passing of those they loved. More news is brought of homes destroyed, of newcomers with new ways filling familiar streets and dwellings. Even though they call another country theirs, yet part of them belongs and must belong to the soil that bore them.

So the psalmist makes his home on earth; yet there are times when he is reminded of another country from which he came and to which he returns. He is not peculiar in this. Hosts of men and women have confessed that while they move about their various tasks as though these were their whole life, they have

39 Turn away my reproach which I fear: for thy judgments *are* good.

40 Behold, I have longed after thy precepts: quicken me in thy righteousness.

VAU

41 Let thy mercies come also unto me, O LORD, *even* thy salvation, according to thy word.

42 So shall I have wherewith to answer him that reproacheth me: for I trust in thy word.

43 And take not the word of truth utterly out of my mouth; for I have hoped in thy judgments.

44 So shall I keep thy law continually for ever and ever.

45 And I will walk at liberty: for I seek thy precepts.

46 I will speak of thy testimonies also before kings, and will not be ashamed.

47 And I will delight myself in thy commandments, which I have loved.

48 My hands also will I lift up unto thy commandments, which I have loved; and I will meditate in thy statutes.

ZAIN

49 Remember the word unto thy servant, upon which thou hast caused me to hope.

39 Turn away the reproach which I dread;
for thy ordinances are good.
40 Behold, I long for thy precepts;
in thy righteousness give me life!

41 Let thy steadfast love come to me, O LORD,
thy salvation according to thy promise;
42 then shall I have an answer for those who taunt me,
for I trust in thy word.
43 And take not the word of truth utterly out of my mouth,
for my hope is in thy ordinances.
44 I will keep thy law continually,
for ever and ever;
45 and I shall walk at liberty,
for I have sought thy precepts.
46 I will also speak of thy testimonies before kings,
and shall not be put to shame;
47 for I find my delight in thy commandments,
which I love.
48 I revere thy commandments, which I love,
and I will meditate on thy statutes.

49 Remember thy word to thy servant,
in which thou hast made me hope.

6. SIXTH STROPHE (119:41-48)

41-48. Let thy steadfast love come to me is based on a repointing of the verb in the M.T., supported by the LXX. **Those who taunt me:** The plural is due to a small emendation of the Hebrew, supported by the LXX. Many commentators consider **utterly** (vs. 43) an intrusion in the text, for it overloads the line. **For ever and ever:** To the end of the psalmist's life. **At liberty:** Lit., "in a broad space" (cf. 31:8; see Exeg. on 118:5-9). The phrase may suggest freedom both from restraint and from external oppression. **I revere:** Lit., **my hands also will I lift up;** an accompaniment of prayer (cf. 28:2; 63:4), here a symbol of reverence and devotion. **Which I love** overloads vs. 48 and may be a gloss.

7. SEVENTH STROPHE (119:49-56)

49-56. Thy word: Thy is a small emendation with some versional support. **Godless men:** The same word is translated **insolent** in vs. 21 (RSV). **The house of my pilgrimage:**

intimations of a higher world, and in that higher world alone will they find complete satisfaction. Hymnbooks overflow with reiterations of Paul's conviction that his citizenship was in heaven:

Guide us by thy hand
To our fatherland [7]

or

O spread thy sheltering wings around,
Till all our wanderings cease,
And at our Father's loved abode
Our souls arrive in peace! [8]

They all point to the fact that we are here strangers and sojourners who can never quite

[7] Nicholas L. Zinzendorf, "Jesus, still lead on."

[8] Philip Doddridge, "O God of Bethel."

50 This *is* my comfort in my affliction: for thy word hath quickened me.

51 The proud have had me greatly in derision: *yet* have I not declined from thy law.

52 I remembered thy judgments of old, O LORD; and have comforted myself.

53 Horror hath taken hold upon me because of the wicked that forsake thy law.

54 Thy statutes have been my songs in the house of my pilgrimage.

55 I have remembered thy name, O LORD, in the night, and have kept thy law.

56 This I had, because I kept thy precepts.

CHETH

57 *Thou art* my portion, O LORD: I have said that I would keep thy words.

58 I entreated thy favor with *my* whole heart: be merciful unto me according to thy word.

59 I thought on my ways, and turned my feet unto thy testimonies.

60 I made haste, and delayed not to keep thy commandments.

61 The bands of the wicked have robbed me: *but* I have not forgotten thy law.

62 At midnight I will rise to give thanks unto thee because of thy righteous judgments.

63 I *am* a companion of all *them* that fear thee, and of them that keep thy precepts.

50 This is my comfort in my affliction
that thy promise gives me life.
51 Godless men utterly deride me,
but I do not turn away from thy law.
52 When I think of thy ordinances from of old,
I take comfort, O LORD.
53 Hot indignation seizes me because of the wicked,
who forsake thy law.
54 Thy statutes have been my songs
in the house of my pilgrimage.
55 I remember thy name in the night, O LORD,
and keep thy law.
56 This blessing has fallen to me,
that I have kept thy precepts.

57 The LORD is my portion;
I promise to keep thy words.
58 I entreat thy favor with all my heart;
be gracious to me according to thy promise.
59 When I think of thy ways,
I turn my feet to thy testimonies;
60 I hasten and do not delay
to keep thy commandments.
61 Though the cords of the wicked ensnare me,
I do not forget thy law.
62 At midnight I rise to praise thee,
because of thy righteous ordinances.
63 I am a companion of all who fear thee,
of those who keep thy precepts.

Probably this earthly life (cf. vs. 19), although some take it as a literal reference to the psalmist's home. **This blessing has fallen to me:** Lit., "This has been mine," but the meaning of **this** can only be conjectured. Calès suggests "It is my lot."

8. EIGHTH STROPHE (119:57-64)

57-64. Thy ways: An emendation supported by the LXX. The M.T. is **my ways.** The RSV gives a better translation than the KJV in vs. 61*a*. **At midnight:** Cf. vss. 147-48. **Midnight** was not a regular hour for prayer. For the usual times of prayer see Exeg. on 88:13.

---

naturalize ourselves. Other creatures seem to fit into the scheme of nature: man alone is out of harmony with the music of the spheres. **I am a sojourner on earth.**

54. *Statutes and Songs.*—Notice another revealing verse: **Thy statutes have been my songs in the house of my pilgrimage.** Matthew Henry's comment is this: "David was the sweet singer of Israel, and here we are told whence he fetched his songs; they were all borrowed from the word of God."[1] Horace Bushnell sees a picture of an Eastern traveler resting from midday heat, or halting at a caravansary for the night, and soothing his rest with songs of war or love. But the verse suggests a picture of the psalmist singing not of war or of wine but of God's commandments, and thus beguiling the weariness of the journey. J. D. Jones in a volume

[1] *An Exposition of the Old Testament* (Edinburgh: J. Wood, 1858), IV, 387.

64 The earth, O LORD, is full of thy mercy: teach me thy statutes.

TETH

65 Thou hast dealt well with thy servant, O LORD, according unto thy word.

66 Teach me good judgment and knowledge: for I have believed thy commandments.

67 Before I was afflicted I went astray: but now have I kept thy word.

68 Thou *art* good, and doest good: teach me thy statutes.

69 The proud have forged a lie against me: *but* I will keep thy precepts with *my* whole heart.

70 Their heart is as fat as grease: *but* I delight in thy law.

71 *It is* good for me that I have been afflicted; that I might learn thy statutes.

72 The law of thy mouth *is* better unto me than thousands of gold and silver.

JOD

73 Thy hands have made me and fashioned me: give me understanding, that I may learn thy commandments.

74 They that fear thee will be glad when they see me; because I have hoped in thy word.

75 I know, O LORD, that thy judgments *are* right, and *that* thou in faithfulness hast afflicted me.

64 The earth, O LORD, is full of thy steadfast love;
teach me thy statutes!

65 Thou hast dealt well with thy servant, O LORD, according to thy word.
66 Teach me good judgment and knowledge, for I believe in thy commandments.
67 Before I was afflicted I went astray; but now I keep thy word.
68 Thou art good and doest good; teach me thy statutes.
69 The godless besmear me with lies, but with my whole heart I keep thy precepts;
70 their heart is gross like fat, but I delight in thy law.
71 It is good for me that I was afflicted, that I might learn thy statutes.
72 The law of thy mouth is better to me than thousands of gold and silver pieces.

73 Thy hands have made and fashioned me; give me understanding that I may learn thy commandments.
74 Those who fear thee shall see me and rejoice,
because I have hoped in thy word.
75 I know, O LORD, that thy judgments are right,
and that in faithfulness thou hast afflicted me.

9. NINTH STROPHE (119:65-72)

65-72. In vs. 69, as in vs. 71, the corrective value of suffering is alluded to (cf. Job 5:17-18). **Besmear** rather than **have forged. Is gross like fat** is better than **as fat as grease.** The word translated **fat** in the RSV is used of the intestinal fat of a man (Judg. 3:22) and of a sacrificial victim (Lev. 3:3-4); suet is perhaps the best English equivalent. Since the heart is the seat of the intelligence, fatness near the heart impedes comprehension. **Thousands of gold and silver** is the literal translation. No specific monetary unit is mentioned.

10. TENTH STROPHE (119:73-80)

73-80. On vs. 73*a* cf. Job 10:8; on vs. 75 cf. vs. 67. **That they may know** (vs. 79) is based on the consonants, and **and those that have known** on the vowels, of the M.T.

entitled *Watching the Cross* quotes both and says that what the psalmist means is that the statutes inspired the songs.[2] It is a subject inviting extended exposition—the burdens of life become blessings, the demand becomes a pleasure, the obligation becomes a privilege. We are reminded of how Jacob served for Rachel, and how the seven years seemed but a few days because of the greatness of his love. We are reminded also of J. M. Barrie and his mother Margaret Ogilvie, and how boyish obedience developed into delightful anticipation of unspoken wishes. Only in such measure do we

[2] London: Hodder & Stoughton, 1926, p. 254.

76 Let, I pray thee, thy merciful kindness
be for my comfort, according to thy word
unto thy servant.
77 Let thy tender mercies come unto me,
that I may live: for thy law *is* my delight.
78 Let the proud be ashamed; for they
dealt perversely with me without a cause:
but I will meditate in thy precepts.
79 Let those that fear thee turn unto me,
and those that have known thy testimonies.
80 Let my heart be sound in thy statutes;
that I be not ashamed.

CAPH

81 My soul fainteth for thy salvation:
but I hope in thy word.
82 Mine eyes fail for thy word, saying,
When wilt thou comfort me?
83 For I am become like a bottle in the
smoke; *yet* do I not forget thy statutes.
84 How many *are* the days of thy servant?
when wilt thou execute judgment on them
that persecute me?
85 The proud have digged pits for me,
which *are* not after thy law.
86 All thy commandments *are* faithful:
they persecute me wrongfully; help thou
me.
87 They had almost consumed me upon
earth; but I forsook not thy precepts.
88 Quicken me after thy loving-kindness;
so shall I keep the testimony of thy mouth.

LAMED

89 For ever, O LORD, thy word is settled
in heaven.

76 Let thy steadfast love be ready to comfort me
according to thy promise to thy servant.
77 Let thy mercy come to me, that I may live;
for thy law is my delight.
78 Let the godless be put to shame,
because they have subverted me with guile;
as for me, I will meditate on thy precepts.
79 Let those who fear thee turn to me,
that they may know thy testimonies.
80 May my heart be blameless in thy statutes,
that I may not be put to shame!

81 My soul languishes for thy salvation;
I hope in thy word.
82 My eyes fail with watching for thy promise;
I ask, "When wilt thou comfort me?"
83 For I have become like a wineskin in the smoke,
yet I have not forgotten thy statutes.
84 How long must thy servant endure?
When wilt thou judge those who persecute me?
85 Godless men have dug pitfalls for me,
men who do not conform to thy law.
86 All thy commandments are sure;
they persecute me with falsehood; help me!
87 They have almost made an end of me on earth;
but I have not forsaken thy precepts.
88 In thy steadfast love spare my life,
that I may keep the testimonies of thy mouth.

89 For ever, O LORD, thy word
is firmly fixed in the heavens.

---

11. ELEVENTH STROPHE (119:81-88)

81-88. Fail with watching: Lit., **fail. A wineskin in the smoke:** Possibly a reference to the artificial acceleration of the aging process in wine making, in which the wineskin inevitably becomes darker and darker. In any case, the simile points to the psalmist as having been figuratively blackened by an outside agent. **How long must thy servant endure?** Lit., **How many are the days of thy servant?**

12. TWELFTH STROPHE (119:89-96)

89-96. The M.T. of vs. 96, as rendered by the RSV, presumably means that there is a limit or end to everything thought by men to be perfect, whereas the divine law is under no such limitation.

90 Thy faithfulness *is* unto all generations: thou hast established the earth, and it abideth.

91 They continue this day according to thine ordinances: for all *are* thy servants.

92 Unless thy law *had been* my delights, I should then have perished in mine affliction.

93 I will never forget thy precepts: for with them thou hast quickened me.

94 I *am* thine, save me; for I have sought thy precepts.

95 The wicked have waited for me to destroy me: *but* I will consider thy testimonies.

96 I have seen an end of all perfection: *but* thy commandment *is* exceeding broad.

MEM

97 O how love I thy law! it *is* my meditation all the day.

98 Thou through thy commandments hast made me wiser than mine enemies: for they *are* ever with me.

99 I have more understanding than all my teachers: for thy testimonies *are* my meditation.

100 I understand more than the ancients, because I keep thy precepts.

101 I have refrained my feet from every evil way, that I might keep thy word.

102 I have not departed from thy judgments: for thou hast taught me.

103 How sweet are thy words unto my taste! *yea, sweeter* than honey to my mouth.

104 Through thy precepts I get understanding: therefore I hate every false way.

90 Thy faithfulness endures to all generations;
thou hast established the earth, and it stands fast.
91 By thy appointment they stand this day;
for all things are thy servants.
92 If thy law had not been my delight,
I should have perished in my affliction.
93 I will never forget thy precepts;
for by them thou hast given me life.
94 I am thine, save me;
for I have sought thy precepts.
95 The wicked lie in wait to destroy me;
but I consider thy testimonies.
96 I have seen a limit to all perfection,
but thy commandment is exceedingly broad.

97 Oh, how I love thy law!
It is my meditation all the day.
98 Thy commandment makes me wiser than my enemies,
for it is ever with me.
99 I have more understanding than all my teachers,
for thy testimonies are my meditation.
100 I understand more than the aged,
for I keep thy precepts.
101 I hold back my feet from every evil way,
in order to keep thy word.
102 I do not turn aside from thy ordinances,
for thou hast taught me.
103 How sweet are thy words to my taste,
sweeter than honey to my mouth!
104 Through thy precepts I get understanding;
therefore I hate every false way.

---

13. Thirteenth Strophe (119:97-104)

97-104. This strophe has more unity than most of the others: its main theme is the superior wisdom which comes from the study of the law. It is also characterized by the absence of any petition (cf. vss. 161-68). **Thy commandment:** A slight emendation from the plural to the singular. **My teachers:** Human teachers, in contrast to **thy testimonies. The aged:** Lit., "the elders," not **the ancients.** The reference, as in vs. 99, is to human

---

achieve success. If that is what the psalmist meant, he had learned more than books could teach. He had not only committed the law of God to memory; he had tested it in life, tested it in so many ways and upon so many people that the statute now was a song. He had come within sight of the truth our Lord had in mind when he said, "Whosoever shall compel thee to go a mile, go with him twain" (Matt. 5:41).

96. ***Strait Is the Gate.***—Here is a verse which presents difficulties both for the linguist and for the expositor:

> **I have seen a limit to all perfection,**
> **but thy commandment is exceedingly broad.**

Instead of dwelling upon the difficulties, however, it may be more profitable to cite two sermons by representative British preachers.

NUN

105 Thy word *is* a lamp unto my feet,
and a light unto my path.
106 I have sworn, and I will perform *it,*
that I will keep thy righteous judgments.
107 I am afflicted very much: quicken
me, O LORD, according unto thy word.
108 Accept, I beseech thee, the freewill
offerings of my mouth, O LORD, and teach
me thy judgments.
109 My soul *is* continually in my hand:
yet do I not forget thy law.
110 The wicked have laid a snare for me:
yet I erred not from thy precepts.
111 Thy testimonies have I taken as a
heritage for ever: for they *are* the rejoicing
of my heart.
112 I have inclined mine heart to perform thy statutes always, *even unto* the end.

SAMECH

113 I hate *vain* thoughts: but thy law do
I love.
114 Thou *art* my hiding place and my
shield: I hope in thy word.
115 Depart from me, ye evildoers: for I
will keep the commandments of my God.

105 Thy word is a lamp to my feet
and a light to my path.
106 I have sworn an oath and confirmed it,
to observe thy righteous ordinances.
107 I am sorely afflicted;
give me life, O LORD, according to thy word!
108 Accept my offerings of praise, O LORD,
and teach me thy ordinances.
109 I hold my life in my hand continually,
but I do not forget thy law.
110 The wicked have laid a snare for me,
but I do not stray from thy precepts.
111 Thy testimonies are my heritage for ever;
yea, they are the joy of my heart.
112 I incline my heart to perform thy statutes
for ever, to the end.

113 I hate double-minded men,
but I love thy law.
114 Thou art my hiding-place and my shield;
I hope in thy word.
115 Depart from me, you evildoers,
that I may keep the commandments of my God.

wisdom. **Thy words,** in vs. 103, is a small emendation, supported by some Hebrew MSS, the LXX, and the Syriac. The M.T. is "thy word."

14. FOURTEENTH STROPHE (119:105-12)

105-12. My feet: So the LXX and the Syriac. The M.T. is "my foot." **The freewill offerings of my mouth** is a literal translation. **My soul is continually in my hand** is a literal translation (cf. Judg. 12:3). The psalmist's life is constantly endangered. **My heritage:** A repointing of the M.T. securing a noun instead of a verb (cf. Jerome). The Hebrew is, lit., **have I taken as a heritage. For ever, to the end:** Some translate "a reward for ever" (cf. vs. 33).

15. FIFTEENTH STROPHE (119:113-20)

113-20. Double-minded men: This, rather than **vain thoughts,** may be the meaning of the difficult word סעפים (cf. Amer. Trans., "dissemblers"). **And have regard for:** So essentially the KJV. Many scholars, supported by some ancient versions, emend the

W. E. Orchard reminded his congregation that the words may be found inscribed around the tomb of Dean Stanley in Westminster Abbey. Whoever chose them doubtless believed that they represented the spirit of Stanley's ministry and the witness of the Broad-Church movement to which he belonged. But, said Orchard, whatever the exact meaning of the verse may be, it is not that God does not demand perfection, that his commandment is not to be interpreted categorically, that he does not care so very much, that his purposes for us do not outrun our possibilities.

I think it means that though we see an end of all perfection in human affairs, God's law is limitless in its reach, able to cover all the varied application to human need, and has the leisure of eternity to secure its perfect fulfilment. It is not a lowering of its purposes, but an extension of its outlook beyond the narrow confines of human existence. This makes

116 Uphold me according unto thy word, that I may live: and let me not be ashamed of my hope.

117 Hold thou me up, and I shall be safe: and I will have respect unto thy statutes continually.

118 Thou hast trodden down all them that err from thy statutes: for their deceit *is* falsehood.

119 Thou puttest away all the wicked of the earth *like* dross: therefore I love thy testimonies.

120 My flesh trembleth for fear of thee; and I am afraid of thy judgments.

AIN

121 I have done judgment and justice: leave me not to mine oppressors.

122 Be surety for thy servant for good: let not the proud oppress me.

123 Mine eyes fail for thy salvation, and for the word of thy righteousness.

124 Deal with thy servant according unto thy mercy, and teach me thy statutes.

125 I *am* thy servant; give me understanding, that I may know thy testimonies.

126 *It is* time for *thee*, Lord, to work: *for* they have made void thy law.

127 Therefore I love thy commandments above gold; yea, above fine gold.

116 Uphold me according to thy promise,
that I may live,
and let me not be put to shame in my hope!
117 Hold me up, that I may be safe
and have regard for thy statutes continually!
118 Thou dost spurn all who go astray from thy statutes;
yea, their cunning is in vain.
119 All the wicked of the earth thou dost count as dross;
therefore I love thy testimonies.
120 My flesh trembles for fear of thee,
and I am afraid of thy judgments.

121 I have done what is just and right;
do not leave me to my oppressors.
122 Be surety for thy servant for good;
let not the godless oppress me.
123 My eyes fail with watching for thy salvation,
and for the fulfilment of thy righteous promise.
124 Deal with thy servant according to thy steadfast love,
and teach me thy statutes.
125 I am thy servant; give me understanding,
that I may know thy testimonies!
126 It is time for the Lord to act,
for thy law has been broken.
127 Therefore I love thy commandments
above gold, above fine gold.

---

verb to "find my delight in" (cf. vss. 16, 47). **Thou dost count:** An emendation (חשבת) supported by some ancient versions. The M.T. is **thou puttest away.**

16. Sixteenth Strophe (119:121-28)

121-28. With watching . . . the fulfilment of: Not in the Hebrew, but implied by the context. On vs. 127 cf. vs. 14. **I direct my steps by all thy precepts:** The M.T. is in some confusion; the RSV, with some versional support, adopts an emended text (לכל פקודיך ישרתי).

---

it a much safer refuge from disillusionment than the interpretation which seems to lie upon the surface—namely, that God does not require of us so much as we have foolishly imagined. He requires not less, but more, only it is on a grander scale, and is planned on more generous lines.[3]

On Advent Sunday, 1922, W. R. Inge, preaching in St. Paul's Cathedral, linked the words, **thy commandment is exceedingly broad,** with Matt. 7:13-14, "Enter ye in at the strait gate: for . . . strait is the gate, and narrow is the way, which leadeth unto life," setting himself there to consider in what sense the road is broad and in what sense it is narrow. First he affirmed that while the law is broad, the gospel is much broader. He illustrated the point with reference to the ideas of God, of humanity, and of the individual. (*a*) In the ancient world each nation had its exclusive god. Philosophy was narrow and somber in the north, majestic among the Greeks, nebulous among the Romans, sanguinary in Asia. Jesus came and spoke

[3] "A Remedy Against Disillusionment," *Christian World Pulpit,* LXXXVI (1914), 73.

128 Therefore I esteem all *thy* precepts *concerning* all *things to be* right; *and* I hate every false way.

PE

129 Thy testimonies *are* wonderful: therefore doth my soul keep them.

130 The entrance of thy words giveth light; it giveth understanding unto the simple.

131 I opened my mouth, and panted: for I longed for thy commandments.

132 Look thou upon me, and be merciful unto me, as thou usest to do unto those that love thy name.

133 Order my steps in thy word: and let not any iniquity have dominion over me.

134 Deliver me from the oppression of man: so will I keep thy precepts.

135 Make thy face to shine upon thy servant; and teach me thy statutes.

136 Rivers of waters run down mine eyes, because they keep not thy law.

TZADDI

137 Righteous *art* thou, O LORD, and upright *are* thy judgments.

138 Thy testimonies *that* thou hast commanded *are* righteous and very faithful.

139 My zeal hath consumed me, because mine enemies have forgotten thy words.

140 Thy word *is* very pure: therefore thy servant loveth it.

128 Therefore I direct my steps by all thy
precepts;[k]
I hate every false way.

129 Thy testimonies are wonderful;
therefore my soul keeps them.
130 The unfolding of thy words gives light;
it imparts understanding to the simple.
131 With open mouth I pant,
because I long for thy commandments.
132 Turn to me and be gracious to me,
as is thy wont toward those who love thy name.
133 Keep steady my steps according to thy promise,
and let no iniquity get dominion over me.
134 Redeem me from man's oppression,
that I may keep thy precepts.
135 Make thy face shine upon thy servant,
and teach me thy statutes.
136 My eyes shed streams of tears,
because men do not keep thy law.

137 Righteous art thou, O LORD,
and right are thy judgments.
138 Thou hast appointed thy testimonies in righteousness
and in all faithfulness.
139 My zeal consumes me,
because my foes forget thy words.
140 Thy promise is well tried,
and thy servant loves it.

[k] Gk Jerome: Heb uncertain

17. SEVENTEENTH STROPHE (119:129-36)

129-36. I opened my mouth, and panted is a literal translation of the Hebrew. **According to thy promise:** A minor emendation, changing the preposition ב to כ.

18. EIGHTEENTH STROPHE (119:137-44)

137-44. Right or upright: Either translation requires a small emendation of the M.T., a plural instead of a singular adjective. **My zeal:** I.e., for the law. **Small:** Probably the meaning is "insignificant." The **righteousness** of God (vs. 142*a*) is something eternal.

of the time "when ye shall neither in this mountain, nor yet at Jerusalem, worship the Father" (John 4:21), and the writer to the Ephesians followed with the words, "One God and Father of all" (Eph. 4:6). Beyond the N.T. modern thought cannot pass. (*b*) The Greeks, the Romans, and the Jews, in different ways but decisively, divided mankind. Jesus proclaimed that all are brethren. We have often in practice fallen from grace, but the doctrine of the unity of humanity is still an ideal toward which the nations are struggling. (*c*) "The Gospel places before the lowest of human beings only one goal, perfection. It opens before him here on earth eternal life . . . . How it exalts and how it abases us!" [4]

Yet Christianity has been accused of narrowness, not only because of the preachers' limita-

[4] William R. Inge, "Broad and Narrow Ways," *ibid.*, CII (1922), 277.

141 I *am* small and despised: *yet* do not
I forget thy precepts.
142 Thy righteousness *is* an everlasting
righteousness, and thy law *is* the truth.
143 Trouble and anguish have taken
hold on me: *yet* thy commandments *are* my
delights.
144 The righteousness of thy testimonies
is everlasting: give me understanding, and
I shall live.

KOPH

145 I cried with *my* whole heart; hear
me, O LORD: I will keep thy statutes.
146 I cried unto thee; save me, and I
shall keep thy testimonies.
147 I prevented the dawning of the
morning, and cried: I hoped in thy word.
148 Mine eyes prevent the *night* watches,
that I might meditate in thy word.
149 Hear my voice according unto thy
loving-kindness: O LORD, quicken me according to thy judgment.
150 They draw nigh that follow after
mischief: they are far from thy law.
151 Thou *art* near, O LORD; and all thy
commandments *are* truth.
152 Concerning thy testimonies, I have
known of old that thou hast founded them
for ever.

RESH

153 Consider mine affliction, and deliver
me: for I do not forget thy law.
154 Plead my cause, and deliver me:
quicken me according to thy word.
155 Salvation *is* far from the wicked: for
they seek not thy statutes.
156 Great *are* thy tender mercies, O
LORD: quicken me according to thy judgments.
157 Many *are* my persecutors and mine

141 I am small and despised,
yet I do not forget thy precepts.
142 Thy righteousness is righteous for ever,
and thy law is true.
143 Trouble and anguish have come upon
me,
but thy commandments are my delight.
144 Thy testimonies are righteous for ever;
give me understanding that I may live.

145 With my whole heart I cry; answer me,
O LORD!
I will keep thy statutes.
146 I cry to thee; save me,
that I may observe thy testimonies.
147 I rise before dawn and cry for help;
I hope in thy words.
148 My eyes are awake before the watches of
the night,
that I may meditate upon thy promise.
149 Hear my voice in thy steadfast love;
O LORD, in thy justice preserve my life.
150 They draw near who persecute me with
evil purpose;
they are far from thy law.
151 But thou art near, O LORD,
and all thy commandments are true.
152 Long have I known from thy testimonies
that thou hast founded them for ever.

153 Look on my affliction and deliver me,
for I do not forget thy law.
154 Plead my cause and redeem me;
give me life according to thy promise!
155 Salvation is far from the wicked,
for they do not seek thy statutes.
156 Great is thy mercy, O LORD;
give me life according to thy justice.
157 Many are my persecutors and my adversaries,

19. NINETEENTH STROPHE (119:145-52)

145-52. I rise: An emended text (קמתי). The M.T. (קדמתי) means "came to meet," "anticipated," which the KJV renders by **prevented** (cf. Exeg. on 79:8). **The words** and **thy word:** Variants of the M.T. **Are awake before** or **prevent** (vs. 148): The same verb as in the M.T. of vs. 147*a*. **The watches of the night:** See Exeg. on 90:4. **In thy steadfast love . . . in thy justice:** Two cases of changing the preposition כ to ב. **Who persecute me:** A minor emendation, supported by some Hebrew MSS, the LXX, and Jerome.

20. TWENTIETH STROPHE (119:153-60)

153-60. Thy justice: So some Hebrew MSS and the LXX. The M.T. is **thy judgments. Thy commands:** The LXX favors a plural noun, but the M.T. is **thy word** or "thy

enemies; *yet* do I not decline from thy testimonies.

158 I beheld the transgressors, and was grieved; because they kept not thy word.

159 Consider how I love thy precepts: quicken me, O LORD, according to thy loving-kindness.

160 Thy word *is* true *from* the beginning: and every one of thy righteous judgments *endureth* for ever.

SCHIN

161 Princes have persecuted me without a cause: but my heart standeth in awe of thy word.

162 I rejoice at thy word, as one that findeth great spoil.

163 I hate and abhor lying: *but* thy law do I love.

164 Seven times a day do I praise thee, because of thy righteous judgments.

165 Great peace have they which love thy law: and nothing shall offend them.

166 LORD, I have hoped for thy salvation, and done thy commandments.

167 My soul hath kept thy testimonies; and I love them exceedingly.

168 I have kept thy precepts and thy testimonies: for all my ways *are* before thee.

TAU

169 Let my cry come near before thee, O LORD: give me understanding according to thy word.

170 Let my supplication come before thee: deliver me according to thy word.

171 My lips shall utter praise, when thou hast taught me thy statutes.

but I do not swerve from thy testimonies.

158 I look at the faithless with disgust,
because they do not keep thy commands.

159 Consider how I love thy precepts!
Preserve my life according to thy steadfast love.

160 The sum of thy word is truth;
and every one of thy righteous ordinances endures for ever.

161 Princes persecute me without cause,
but my heart stands in awe of thy words.

162 I rejoice at thy word
like one who finds great spoil.

163 I hate and abhor falsehood,
but I love thy law.

164 Seven times a day I praise thee
for thy righteous ordinances.

165 Great peace have those who love thy law;
nothing can make them stumble.

166 I hope for thy salvation, O LORD,
and I do thy commandments.

167 My soul keeps thy testimonies;
I love them exceedingly.

168 I keep thy precepts and testimonies,
for all my ways are before thee.

169 Let my cry come before thee, O LORD;
give me understanding according to thy word!

170 Let my supplication come before thee;
deliver me according to thy word.

171 My lips will pour forth praise
that thou dost teach me thy statutes.

---

promise." **The sum of thy word:** Everything contained in the law. **Sum** is a better translation of ראש than **beginning** (cf. 139:17). **Ordinances:** The plural is supported by some Hebrew MSS, the LXX, and the Syriac. The M.T. reads the singular.

21. TWENTY-FIRST STROPHE (119:161-68)

161-68. This strophe, like vss. 97-104, contains no petition. **Princes:** Cf. vs. 23. **Thy words** and **thy word:** Variants of the M.T. **Seven times a day:** Probably rhetorical, signifying "frequently." On the usual times of prayer see Exeg. on 88:13. **Nothing can make them stumble:** Lit., "they have no stumbling block" (or "occasion for stumbling").

22. TWENTY-SECOND STROPHE (119:169-76)

169-76. Will sing rather than **shall speak. I have gone astray like a lost sheep** may refer to some moral turpitude, but in view of the psalmist's frequent professions of fidelity to the Lord, it seems unlikely. It would appear to be more in keeping with the poem as a whole to suppose that there is an allusion either to a deterioration in the psalmist's

172 My tongue shall speak of thy word: for all thy commandments *are* righteousness.

173 Let thine hand help me; for I have chosen thy precepts.

174 I have longed for thy salvation, O LORD; and thy law *is* my delight.

175 Let my soul live, and it shall praise thee; and let thy judgments help me.

176 I have gone astray like a lost sheep: seek thy servant; for I do not forget thy commandments.

172 My tongue will sing of thy word,
for all thy commandments are right.
173 Let thy hand be ready to help me,
for I have chosen thy precepts.
174 I long for thy salvation, O LORD,
and thy law is my delight.
175 Let me live, that I may praise thee,
and let thy ordinances help me.
176 I have gone astray like a lost sheep; seek thy servant,
for I do not forget thy commandments.

A Song of degrees.

120 In my distress I cried unto the LORD, and he heard me.

A Song of Ascents.

120 In my distress I cry to the LORD,
that he may answer me:

---

circumstances, or to an absence from his own people. In either case, he is **like a lost sheep,** and he needs the protection of his Shepherd.

CXX. DELIVER ME FROM LYING LIPS (120:1-7)

Each of the Pss. 120–134 bears the superscription *Shîr hamma'alôth,* which the KJV renders "A Song of degrees," the RSV calls "A Song of Ascents," and some more recent translations term "A Pilgrim Song," or the like. The differences arise from the different ways in which the second term of the compound have been understood. The older exegetes, noting that in Ezra 7:9 the word *ma'alāh* denotes the return from Babylon, were of the opinion that these fifteen psalms were used by the exiles on their return to Jerusalem (see Theodoret, Kimchi; cf. the use of ἀναβασέων in the Greek versions, Aq., Symm., Theod.). But certain of the psalms postulate a date later than the return; others (cf. Pss. 125; 127–129; 131; 133) reflect the life of Palestine; and still others speak of Zion as a well-established center of Israel's worship (cf. Pss. 122; 132; 134). We may also dismiss the opinion based on the Mishnah tractate Middoth 2:5 (cf. LXX, Jerome) that the psalms were sung by the Levites on the fifteen steps leading from the women's court to the men's court in the temple; this appears to be a late speculation. Equally unacceptable is the view that the reference is to the style of composition of the psalms, which is marked by some instances of climactic parallelism or anadiplosis, e.g., 120:5-6; 121:1-2, 3-4, 7-8, for it is not used in all of them, and there are other psalms outside this group in which this type of parallelism occurs, e.g., 3:1-2; 12:3-4; 25:1-7. Altogether it seems most probable that these psalms formed a collection for the use of pilgrims who came up to Jerusalem to be present at the great feasts (Deut. 12:5-7). In

---

tions, but because there is a sense in which the gospel *is* narrow. It claims to be *the* truth. It is a definite road. It prescribes a way of life. "We have to make our choice, yes, and to search for the narrow gate which does not stand wide open inviting us to enter."

The two sermons thus placed together make us realize how great is the agreement between the different schools of Christian thought. Orchard passed from Protestantism to Roman Catholicism, while Inge remained to the end in the Broad school of Anglicanism; but they stand together affirming:

The world promises joy and gives only disappointment; Christ promises the cross and gives us the crown. The broad way is the way of wandering in the wilderness, while the narrow way leads to heaven. It leads to that true life in which we may ever grow in knowledge, in holiness, and in love, continually renewed in the image of Him who created us.[5]

120:1–134:3. ***The Pilgrimage of Life.***—Every minister knows that congregations can be very sensitive about the hymns they are invited to sing. If the praise is wrong—if favorites are

[5] *Ibid.*

support of this theory we have the evidence of certain of these psalms which are oriented toward Zion as the place "whither the tribes go up," e.g., 122:1-4; 125:1-5; 129:5; 134:1-3. Pss. 120–134 as a whole are characterized by their brevity, felicity, and graphic style. That some of them do not seem directly related to pilgrim motives is to be accounted for by the fact that the collection has in the course of time broadened into something like a handbook of devotions for the use of pilgrims.

Ps. 120 illustrates what has just been said. Its subject matter, if not peculiarly a concern of pilgrims as such, was nevertheless something which was not more strange to pilgrims than to others. The psalm could therefore be appropriately introduced into a pilgrim book of devotions, perhaps with special appositeness because of the reference in vs. 5 to a sojourn in foreign lands. In any case, the psalm is a brief lament in which an unhappy soul pours out a bitter complaint about the distress which he suffers through the lying, backbiting, and quarrelsomeness of men with whom he seeks to live peaceably.

---

omitted or overworked, or an unfamiliar tune is used—both minister and organist will hear about it. There are also strong opinions about the relative merits of various hymnbooks, and every new collection has to run the gantlet. Yet all such books are the results of long and earnest consideration. Vast piles of material had to be examined and sifted and classified. There were long discussions on where the hymns that were accepted should be placed and how far lines should be modernized by the removal of archaic phrases.

Was it not much the same with the editing of the book of Psalms? The material may have been less extensive, but the same kind of question must have been posed. There was little disagreement about "The heavens declare the glory of God," about Pss. 90; 91; 118. But there may have been many doubts about those that breathed a spirit of vengeance. There were others which had been grouped together possibly centuries before the Psalter took its present shape. Some of these must have raised questions: Who wrote them? When and for what purpose? Who first gave them a title or titles? What characteristics have they in common?

The Expos. on Ps. 113, the first of the Hallel psalms, envisaged such a situation. We come to it again with Ps. 120, which is the first of the pilgrim psalms, or as they are frequently called, "The Songs of Ascents" or "The Songs of Degrees." There are fifteen of them—sometimes described as "the psalter within the Psalter"—and for that reason they have been associated with the fifteen steps in the temple that led from the Court of the Women to the Court of Israel. It is further suggested that on each step the worshipers paused and sang one of these songs. Others have maintained that the title derives from a mounting up in the literary style: words and phrases are used and repeated with increasing emphasis, as in a musical crescendo. Again it is argued that they are the hymns used by the children of Israel when they returned to Jerusalem after long exile in Babylon; or—the view held by the Exeg.—that they are the songs of pilgrims who came from far and near for the great festivals in the temple.

There is much in these fifteen psalms that fits in with the regular visits to the temple for the recognized feasts and festivals. But what has all this to do with us? Why trouble our heads with ancient processions and their musical accompaniments? Actually the question may be raised in many other connections. Why study the classics? Why write and read ancient, or indeed modern, history? Why trouble about the excavation of long-buried cities? Why? Because such investigations help us today. There can be no doubt about this with the Songs of Degrees, especially if we think of life itself as a pilgrimage. We are all travelers upon a path which, though trodden hard by those who were before us, is yet new to us with pleasant and unpleasant surprises at every turn.

Let us think further about this matter, noticing first that the idea is a very old and tenacious one. It appears in many parts of the O.T., to say nothing of other ancient scriptures. There is, for example, in Ps. 119, "Thy statutes have been my songs in the house of my pilgrimage" (vs. 54). Again, in the same psalm, there is the confession: "I am a stranger in the earth: hide not thy commandments from me" (vs. 19). There are many other verses that suggest the beauty of the earth and man's place as the crown of creation. But turn a page and read that this is not our real home. We may appreciate it, as a stranger in a foreign land appreciates the country of his adoption; but it is not where we belong. There are feelings, nay, convictions, that we came from another sphere and are traveling to a fairer realm on high. The same thought is reaffirmed in the N.T., especially in the epistle to the Hebrews, where the writer is thinking of the heroes of faith, not

There is nothing in the psalm which clearly indicates its date, though we may conjecture that it presupposes the Diaspora and therefore is postexilic. The meter is 3+2, with the exception of 3+3 in vs. 5.

1. Appeal to the Lord (120:1-2)

120:1-2. In my distress I cried unto the Lord, and he heard me: According to this rendering of vs. 1, the psalmist is recalling an experience already past; and in vs. 2 he records what he said when he cried to the Lord for help. The psalm is then really not a lament but a thanksgiving psalm. But if ויענני ("and he answered me") is repointed to obtain **that he may answer me,** the psalm is in this case a lament. The cry of the psalmist, however, is no less prompted by confidence in what the Lord can do to deliver him

---

only naming them but recalling some of their virtues. To his splendid roll of honor he adds these significant words: "These all died in faith, not having received the promises, but having seen them afar off, and were persuaded of them, and embraced them, and confessed that they were strangers and pilgrims on the earth. For they that say such things declare plainly that they seek a country" (Heb. 11:13-14).

We are here touching something real and abiding. It is not what man grasps that matters so much as what he aims at, what he seeks day and night and pursues even though it is a vision that eludes him. And this persuasion that life is not so much an achievement as a quest, so common in religious literature, is not unknown elsewhere. It will be enough to mention, for example, John Bunyan's immortal allegory, and the hymnbooks which were referred to above. *The Pilgrim's Progress* is popular both with the naïve and untutored and with intellectuals like Dr. Johnson and Lord Macaulay, not only because of its literary genius, certainly not because of its confident Puritan theology; is it not largely because as you watch Christian on his perilous way you see man himself? It is your own soul, or the soul of humanity, that you see in crisis after crisis, struggling through the Slough of Despond or walking through Vanity Fair, always about to be defeated, yet always pressing on toward the Celestial City. As for the hymnbooks, you get the impression that editors were bewildered by the bulk of good material before them. They could not reject this or that, yet the section on "Pilgrimage" was already full to overflowing. They would slip one in under the caption "Conflict and Victory," and another under "Death and Resurrection"—but the problem was never really solved. So many people had written well on aspiration, and on walking with God and man, that the books bulged in those sections, and no literary maneuvering could meet the situation.

There is, however, a possible exception when we come to modern life. T. R. Glover, early in the twentieth century, declared that the word "pilgrim" was dropping out of religious speech, and that Robert Louis Stevenson's sentiment in the *Child's Garden of Verses* was taking its place:

> The world is so full of a number of things,
> I'm sure we should all be as happy as kings.

We are not so much looking for a sphere beyond this bourne of time and place as we are intent on making heaven here and now. John Baillie in a book entitled *Invitation to Pilgrimage* [6] calls attention to the same mental attitude. He hints, however, that the modern mood is again changing, and that men and women are slowly but surely returning to the traditional view. Why did men bring their eyes down from heaven to earth? Partly because of ridicule about "pie in the sky." Much more because they believed in their ability to solve life's problems and to find security on earth. They are beginning to feel that the earthly quest is relatively futile, for the facts of life are against us. Instead of building an ideal world, we achieved chaos and confusion. Instead of peace and security and universal brotherhood, we multiplied hate and division and non-co-operation. In the face of such failure the most confirmed optimist would be silent were it not possible for the tongue to chatter after the brain has ceased to function. But we cannot continue forever with negatives or with tears over damaged castles in the air. We must either go on to darker pessimism or seek again that spiritual purpose by which men have lived in the past and may prosper in the future. Among those supernatural realities is this assurance that the goal lies beyond us in a higher realm, and that toward it the soul aspires as inevitably as migrating birds fly in due season to the lands of light.

There is, however, for all Christians something else to lift the subject beyond vague sentiment to a blessed confidence: we are not left, like blind leaders of the blind, to feel our way, liable at any moment to fall into the ditch.

[6] New York: Charles Scribner's Sons, 1942.

2 Deliver my soul, O LORD, from lying lips, *and* from a deceitful tongue.
3 What shall be given unto thee? or what shall be done unto thee, thou false tongue?

2 "Deliver me, O LORD,
from lying lips,
from a deceitful tongue."

3 What shall be given to you?
And what more shall be done to you,
you deceitful tongue?

---

from lying lips, i.e., persons who employ as their weapons such devices as perfidy, calumniation, duplicity, and other forms of falsehood. **From a deceitful tongue** should be omitted here as a dittograph of the words at the end of vs. 3.

2. PUNISHMENT FOR ENEMIES (120:3-4)

3-4. In vss. 1-2 the psalmist has made his appeal to the Lord and stated the grounds of his complaint. Now, after the manner of a lament, he deals with what is in store for his enemies. **What shall be given to you? . . . What more shall be done?** The usual formula used by a person taking an oath was "God do so to me and more also" (cf. I Sam. 3:17; I Kings 2:23; Ruth 1:17). The psalmist predicts that his perfidious vilifiers will be taken at their word. His prediction is put in the form of a question. Knowing that the agent of the punishment is God, he avoids a declarative statement

---

We have a Guide who has walked through life and has gone to prepare a better place for us. It is not for us to worry about the journey or the heavenly home. Enough for us to live in the spirit of the great pilgrim hymns:

Jesus, still lead on,
Till our rest be won;
Heavenly Leader, still direct us,
Still support, console, protect us,
Till we safely stand
In our Fatherland.[7]

120:1. ***Prayer Answered.***—Wherever a man is, the one thing certain is that troubles will come. Some of them can be dealt with. A child is sick, but the family doctor is equal to the occasion. Harvests fail, but one can buy from foreign lands. In other situations it is different. The sickness is one for which the physician has no remedy. The harvests continue to fail, and resources are exhausted. In such circumstances what can man do but look above himself and seek the help of heaven? This happens even among men and women of secular mind and habit. Having ignored the Father of all mercies, they suddenly appeal to him and expect him to work miracles on their behalf. Deliverance which men recognize as such does not always follow. But again and again things do happen, not perhaps in the way one had hoped or expected; but deliverance comes, and a plain path opens out before the troubled soul. The unthankful may be unthankful still, may fancy that salvation came through his own perseverance or ingenuity; but the pious soul confesses that God heard his prayer and delivered him out of his distresses. This psalmist is such a man. Who he is, or what the nature of his trouble, we do not know; but he has passed through just such an experience as that. **In my distress I cried unto the LORD, and he heard me.**

2-4. *Temptations of the Tongue.*—Having started in this mood, he passes abruptly to prayer for deliverance **from lying lips, and from a deceitful tongue.** It may be that he is thinking of men or nations that surround him and are glad of an opportunity to do him harm. But may it not be a prayer that he may himself be free from such iniquity? Religious teachers in general and the Hebrews in particular have always been conscious of the subtle temptations of the **tongue.** The epistle of James is especially emphatic (3:2-10). Our Lord also gives warnings that must be heeded. Nothing to the thoughtless seems so trivial as a word. It is breathed into the air and disappears. Yet this is not the way Jesus thought of words. Consider some of the sayings recorded in Matt. 12, including these: "How can ye, being evil, speak good things? for out of the abundance of the heart the mouth speaketh. A good man out of the good treasure of the heart bringeth forth good things: and an evil man out of the evil treasure bringeth forth evil things. But I say unto you, That every idle word that men shall speak, they shall give account thereof in the day of judgment. For by thy words thou shalt be justified, and by thy words thou shalt be condemned" (vss. 34-37).

There are many other passages that deserve attention, e.g., from the book of Proverbs: "An

[7] Nicholas L. Zinzendorf, "Jesus, still lead on," st. iii.

4 Sharp arrows of the mighty, with coals of juniper.	4 A warrior's sharp arrows, with glowing coals of the broom tree!

in order not to seem to trespass on divine prerogative. The punishment to be meted out will be in accordance with the *lex talionis*. Their words have been deadly weapons, with the objective of death and devastation (cf. Prov. 25:18-19; 26:18; Isa. 50:11). **A warrior's sharp arrows:** I.e., not the arrows used by hunters but those fabricated especially for a soldier's death-dealing purpose. **Glowing coals of the broom tree:** The white broom (*Retama roetam*) is in the Near East the most popular of the thorny brushwoods collected for burning because it ensures a long, hot fire (Grace M. Crowfoot and Louise Boldensperger, *From Cedar to Hyssop* [New York: The Macmillan Co., 1932], pp. 49-50). The psalmist's prediction implies that his enemies will come to a sudden end, and their houses will be destroyed by fire. The poet is not on the higher level of O.T. religion (cf. Lev. 19:18; Prov. 25:21-22).

evil man is ensnared by the transgression of his lips" (12:13); "There is one whose rash words are like sword thrusts" (12:18); "Lying lips are an abomination to the LORD" (12:22). The psalmists are equally alive to the harm a man may do with his mouth. The human tongue is likened to that of a serpent—"that restless forked organ which is mistaken by the ignorant for the sting itself." "Adders' poison," it is declared, is "under their lips" (140:3). Again, the tongue is likened to a whetted sword, capable of inflicting hideous wounds, and this capacity is said to be found alongside the use of smooth and oily words (55:21): suddenly the suave manner is dropped and we are confronted by speech that is meant to slay. Or truer still to common experience, "The wicked . . . make ready their arrow upon the string, that they may privily shoot at the upright in heart" (11:2). Such references help us to understand the prayer here.

The psalmist repeats the word **deceitful,** assuming this to be the tongue's special characteristic (but see Exeg.). Cunning, artfulness, shooting as it were from a safe ambush—it is one of the commonest of faults, indulged in by the subtle and the weak; not by men who step boldly into the open and say what they have to say so that all can hear, but by wily persons who conceal themselves, as they suppose, from watchful eyes, and like sneaks and cowards shoot their arrows that wound and kill.

A warrior's sharp arrows,
with glowing coals of the broom tree!

is the caustic language used: not merely the arrows of the hunter, but arrows made of the hard wood of the broom and tipped with glowing heat. The danger is not in the sharpness of the words; we know from Jesus that there are times when piercing speech is not only permissible but the only speech that is adequate. The danger is in the motive and the direction. We cannot afford to let a day pass without a prayer that we may be delivered not only from arrows shot by others, but from the desire to employ such weapons ourselves. Pray without ceasing, the apostle would say, for the love that is patient and kind. The prayer and the warning are underlined not in ink but in blood. Better silence than speech if speech is tinctured with selfishness. Maybe that is why Simeon the son of Hillel said: "All my days I have grown up among the Wise, and I have not found anything better than silence; . . . whoso makes many words occasions sin." [8]

Yet speech may be better than silence. Silence is better than the shooting of crafty arrows; but "a word fitly spoken is like apples of gold in pictures of silver" (Prov. 25:11). Wiser than Simeon, if we may read somewhat between her lines, was St. Teresa: "After my vow of perfection I spoke not ill of any creature, how little soever it might be. I scrupulously avoided all approaches to detraction. I had this rule ever present with me, that I was not to wish, nor assent to, nor say such things of any person whatsoever, that I would not have them say of me." Speech too is frequently easier than silence. She says that at times she was so filled with a spirit of anger that she could "eat [some people] up and annihilate them." But she persisted and improved, and if people spoke evil of her, she realized how far they fell short of the truth. When instead of judging others she examined herself, she was driven to prayer in such words as these: "O my Lord, when I remember in how many ways Thou didst suffer detraction and misrepresentation, I know not where my senses are when I am in such haste to defend and excuse myself." [1] More often than not the

[8] Quoted in A. C. Headlam, *The Life and Teaching of Jesus the Christ* (2nd ed.; London: J. Murray, 1927), p. 85.

[1] Quoted by Alexander Whyte, *Bible Characters: Sixth Series, Our Lord's Characters* (4th ed.; New York: Fleming H. Revell, n.d.), pp. 264-65.

5 Woe is me, that I sojourn in Mesech, *that* I dwell in the tents of Kedar!
6 My soul hath long dwelt with him that hateth peace.
7 I *am for* peace: but when I speak, they *are* for war.

5 Woe is me, that I sojourn in Meshech,
that I dwell among the tents of Kedar!
6 Too long have I had my dwelling
among those who hate peace.
7 I am for peace;
but when I speak,
they are for war!

---

3. THE PSALMIST'S PLIGHT (120:5-7)

5-7. Woe is me: The psalmist returns to enlarge on the troubles which assail him. **I sojourn in Meshech . . . the tents of Kedar:** He does not mean to identify by these names the region where he lives. **Meshech** is a nation in Asia Minor (cf. Gen. 10:2; Ezek. 32:26-27; 38:3; 39:1), of which the writers in the O.T. had only vague but unfavorable knowledge. **Kedar** was a region of the Syrian Desert, south of Damascus, where the tribe of Kedar dwelt (cf. Gen. 25:13; Jer. 2:10; 49:28-30). The names are here obviously synonyms of barbarism. The psalmist could not be making his abode in places so remote from each other. He means to say that he is living among people no better than Vandals and Yahoos. Some commentators, however, believing that his words are to be taken literally, ease the geographical difficulty by reading Massa (משא) for Meshech. But though Massa is connected with the region of the North Arabians (cf. Gen. 25:14; Prov. 31:1), its location is indefinite and lends little support to the hypothesis. It is not impossible that in Meshech and Kedar there is a cryptic reference to some well-known center of Jewish population in the Diaspora. **I am for peace,** but those about him are men **who hate peace.** Whenever he speaks and whatever he says, his words are made by his enemies an occasion for **war** against him by methods indicated in the preceding verses.

---

speech that is better than silence is harder than silence!

5-7. ***True and False Peacemaking.***—Unfortunately even charity, if it lacks wisdom, can lead us astray. A man may so govern the tongue that he gives no offense, even where offense is required. He may be silent in the family circle when it would be better to speak. He may be silent because he is afraid, afraid that his comfort may be disturbed and life's routine upset. He may say "peace" when there is no peace, until truth and honor and self-respect are sacrificed and life becomes a miserable quest for the easy way. When such a spirit infects whole populations, one expects governments that are not heroic in policy or distinguished in history. G. G. Coulton unintentionally describes such a situation in his *Studies in Medieval Thought.*[2] He is dealing with the decline of the Roman Empire, and quotes with approval Gibbons' verdict—that from the death of Domitian to the succession of Commodus there was more happiness and prosperity in the world than in any other period in recorded history. But it was a peace purchased by the sacrifice of public spirit. Apathy took the place of self-control. Men asked for peace, peace at any price, even at the price of despotism. The masses were well pleased, but the great families were decimated.

[2] London: Thomas Nelson & Sons, 1940, p. 11.

Much nearer our own times Winston Churchill has described similar dangers. For years he stood almost alone against popular opinion and condemned the policy of appeasement adopted by British governments. Years afterward he told the story as he understood it, and told it with restraint and sincerity. But all through the exciting yet tragic pages there echoes the sad theme of "how the English-speaking peoples through their unwisdom, carelessness, and good nature allowed the wicked to rearm." [3] There are times when idealistic pacifism may be the shortest way to war.

Was this psalmist one who was predisposed to such dangers? The conclusion of the psalm at least suggests it:

Woe is me, that I sojourn in Meshech,
that I dwell among the tents of Kedar!
Too long have I had my dwelling
among those who hate peace.
I am for peace;
but when I speak,
they are for war!

There is personal experience in that confession. It suggests one who had pleaded and labored for sweet reasonableness and had failed. The more he tried to smooth out difficulties, the

[3] *The Gathering Storm* (Boston: Houghton Mifflin Co., 1948), p. ix.

A Song of degrees.

121 I will lift up mine eyes unto the hills, from whence cometh my help.

A Song of Ascents.

121 I lift up my eyes to the hills.
From whence does my help come?

CXXI. The Lord Is Your Keeper (121:1-8)

This psalm is one of the more beautiful, if not the most beautiful, of the pilgrim collection. It is cast in an antiphonal or liturgical form, as the change in the person of the pronouns denotes. But there are differences of opinion as to whether it is a dialogue between a man and his soul, or a layman and a priest in the liturgy of the temple, or a group of pilgrims and their spiritual leader. The third view seems to be the most acceptable, for vs. 1 and the general background of the psalm point to a setting outside the temple, while its thoughts are peculiarly apposite to the circumstances of a perilous pilgrim journey. The text of the psalm as it now stands in vss. 1-2 might appear to favor the second view; but there is a fair consensus among students that **my** in vs. 2 should be "thy," and further, **thy** in vs. 3 should be "my" (see Hermann Gunkel, *Ausgewählte Psalmen* [3rd ed.; Göttingen: Vandenhoeck & Ruprecht, 1911], pp. 188-91), and the verses should be rendered:

I lift up my eyes to the hills;
  whence comes my help?
Thy help comes from the Lord,
  who made heaven and earth.
May he not let my foot slip;
  may my Keeper not slumber!

Whatever decision is made as to the manner of its use, it is clear that this psalm, like others of the collection, has been inspired by some actual situation which the psalmist has witnessed or shared in (cf. Pss. 122; 125; 127; 129; 131; 133). The construction of the *mise en scène* is not difficult. In the long journey to Jerusalem pilgrims had to encamp in the desert or arid regions through which their march lay. At night sentries were set on the top of neighboring hills in order to guard the encampment against sudden attack from robber bands who, knowing only too well the seasons of the pilgrimages, hoped to enrich themselves by raiding the pilgrim camps. In our psalm we have some of the reflections of one of the pilgrims who, before entering his tent for the night, looks toward the hill and sees beside the sentry another guardian, the Lord, who neither slumbers nor sleeps; and who, more than a human sentry, can guard the people in his care from diseases that may afflict them on their travels, like the strokes of the sun or the moon. It is such a situation which has been fashioned into the liturgical form of the psalm.

more men quarreled. Yet it is necessary that someone should play the part of the reconciler, should go on reminding men of the bitterness of strife and the blessedness of forgiveness. Once in a way the Churchills are right. The tyrants must be resisted. But always the peacemakers are right if their motives and their methods are true and honorable. It must, however, be realized that their path is never easy. Is not that the message of the N.T., with its story of rejection and crucifixion? Jesus Christ is the Prince of Peace. He came forth from the Father to save men from their sins and to bring them back to God. But it could be done only by taking the path of service and sacrifice, only by accepting suffering and shame and death. We are always driven back to those hard facts, and never more than when we face our own most urgent needs. There is no way to peace, either among individuals or nations, by clever diplomacy or selfish alliances. There is no way except Christ's way.

121:1-5. ***The Mountains Round About Jerusalem.***—There are many ways of expounding this very suggestive psalm. We may lay hold on the opening sentence and consider its general significance. **I will lift up mine eyes unto the hills.** Much has been written about the bearing

2 My help *cometh* from the LORD, which made heaven and earth.
3 He will not suffer thy foot to be moved: he that keepeth thee will not slumber.
4 Behold, he that keepeth Israel shall neither slumber nor sleep.

2 My help comes from the LORD,
who made heaven and earth.

3 He will not let your foot be moved,
he who keeps you will not slumber.
4 Behold, he who keeps Israel
will neither slumber nor sleep.

The date is post-Deuteronomic (cf. Deut. 12:5; 16:16). The meter is somewhat irregular: 3+3 in vss. 1-2; 2+2+2 in vss. 4-5, 8; 3+2 in the other verses.

1. Whence Does Your Help Come? (121:1)

121:1. The psalm, while functioning as a psalm of trust, is really mixed in type, beginning with the words of a lament and ending with a promise like an oracle (vss. 5-8). **I lift up my eyes to the hills:** Obviously the hills are not the holy hills of Jerusalem or Mount Zion. Otherwise there would be no doubt as to the source of **help.**

2. The Lord as Man's Helper and Keeper (121:2-8)

2. The answer to the question of vs. 1 is given in this verse with the change of the pronouns as indicated above. Can there be a better helper than he **who made heaven and earth?**

3. He will not let your foot be moved: Better, "May he not let my foot slip!" **He who keeps you will not slumber.** Better, "May my Guardian not slumber!" For the idiom see Kautzsch, *Gesenius' Hebrew Grammar,* secs. 107*p*, 109*e*. The clause implies that the Lord, like a human sentry, may fall asleep. This is not a strange thought in the Psalter (cf. 35:23; 44:23; 59:5).

4. The response follows: "Nay, he neither slumbers nor sleeps, the Guardian of Israel." He guards sleeplessly not only the timorous pilgrim but all the faithful in Israel.

---

of geography on character, the encircling sea on the history of Britain, the great forest on the making of Russian peasants, the climate on the character of the Spanish people. George Adam Smith in *The Historical Geography of the Holy Land* has developed the subject with special reference to the religion of the Hebrews. He shows, for example, how, unlike that of Egypt, the climate of Palestine suggests "a personal Providence."[4] He might have written a chapter, even a volume, on the hills and mountains, especially those that were round about Jerusalem. There is a peculiar affinity between souls and hills, as one of the best known of British climbers has confessed: "Some quality in a hill which defies analysis. Call it the spirit of the hill, call it anything you like, but no one has yet explained why it is hills have a power over men, why artists and poets find in them fit subjects for their artistry and poetry."[5] Naturally Palestine, being a hilly country, has cast its spirit upon the Bible. Nearly all the great personal and dramatic national experiences seem to have been connected with mountains. It is enough to mention how at Mount Sinai the tribes, by entering into a covenant with the Lord, became a nation and received the Ten Commandments; how Moses was called in the high places, and at last died upon the top of Pisgah; how Saul and Jonathan were slain on Mount Gilboa, and Elijah in an hour of crisis met and confused the priests of Baal on Mount Carmel. Not only were the hills connected with individual inspiration and dedication, they were often the scene of idolatrous practices against which the prophets protested. The greatness and grandeur of the hills impresses us again when we pass to the N.T. story. How often we have tried to envisage

> Ye fair green hills of Galilee
> That girdle quiet Nazareth.[6]

The Mount of Transfiguration, and the Mount of Olives! How fitting that so much of the training of the twelve took place in quiet spots remote from busy cities, and that at last on a green hill outside Jerusalem's walls the Savior should give his life a ransom for many! Even Wordsworth, having served before the everlasting altars of the high mountains of the

[4] 25th ed.; London: Hodder & Stoughton, 1931, p. 73.
[5] Smythe, *The Spirit of the Hills,* p. 297.
[6] Eustace R. Conder.

5 The LORD *is* thy keeper: the LORD *is* thy shade upon thy right hand.
6 The sun shall not smite thee by day, nor the moon by night.

5 The LORD is your keeper;
the LORD is your shade
on your right hand.
6 The sun shall not smite you by day,
nor the moon by night.

5-8. The rest of the psalm swells the note of confidence sounded in vss. 2, 4, as the leader with glowing assurance enlarges upon his theme. **The LORD is thy keeper; the LORD is thy shade,** or, better, "thy defense" (cf. Num. 14:9; Jer. 48:45, where "shadow" has become "defense" or "protection"); **the LORD is . . . upon thy right hand.** In consequence, the pilgrim may without fear pursue his journey, knowing that the Lord, who made all that is in heaven and on the earth (vs. 2*b*), can protect him from the baleful influences of the **sun** and the **moon,** the works of his hands. The ancients' fear of "sunstroke" was based on the observation of the obvious harmful effects of the sun's rays; their fear of "moonstroke" arose from their belief in a correlation between the activity of certain diseases (e.g., epilepsy and fevers) and the moon's phases (cf.

Lake District, entered upon a priestly ministry international in its power and brought absolution and peace to the souls of erring men. How much more have those who lifted their eyes to the hills of the Holy Land and meditated upon their solemn memories been able to preach pardon and peace to men of all the world through succeeding centuries!

Not that the psalmist's help came from the hills. They may have suggested peace, beauty, and stability, but succor came from the God who made heaven and earth. Above and beyond the majesty of nature was the power of God, the source of all strength. This may seem simple, almost primitive: it is certainly not one of mankind's deepest thoughts, but it is common in every generation. When men consider reverently sun and stars, snow-clad peaks and mighty oceans, they pass easily to thoughts of omnipotence which stretch beyond the limits of human minds. And in days like these, when the eye is fixed more often upon engines that man has made, and upon the atomic energy that science has released, we need to be reminded of the source of all power. We need to be reminded that at the heart of the universe is the power of will. "In the last analysis the stored up energies of the world are the energies of personality. It is the will of God. It is the will of God that drives the stars, it is the will of God that saves the physical world from wreckage, it is the will of God that keeps the smallest child." [7]

But the psalmist saw not only power. He saw divine Love which protects individuals through the ordinary routine of life and guides Israel through extraordinary experiences. He was reassured of a personal God who holds men so that they do not stumble, and watches over them when they sleep, who protects wayfarers from the midday heat and from the magic of the moon. He began with the hills on the way to Jerusalem, but he ended with confidence in divine providence.

5-8. ***A Song of Pilgrimage.***—Or should we have started with the fact that this is a song for pilgrims? The subject will not at first glance appeal to all. We have heard so much about pilgrims and their superstition and fanaticism that prejudice possesses the mind. We think of multitudes traveling to Mecca and the Ganges, or of Russian peasants toiling to Jerusalem, or of devout Roman Catholics turning their faces toward Rome or Lourdes. We think perhaps of the *Canterbury Tales* of Chaucer, and of generations of monks and merchants, soldiers and scholars, who toiled along the pilgrim way. But before we turn aside with a gesture of impatience, it is well to remember that even in our own traditions there are many sacred spots, and that it is a sound instinct which makes denominational leaders plan excursions to such significant places. It is an even safer instinct which causes jaded ministers and others occasionally to leave the normal duties and seek alone the places that for them are full of gracious memories. It may be a little meetinghouse in an obscure village. It may be a deserted glade where the human voice is rarely heard, but where a call from heaven came. What the lakeside was to Peter and John, what the road leading to Damascus was to Paul, that the unpretentious spot is to many a dedicated soul. How foolish is he who never permits himself a visit to such places of inspiration!

It is in this large context that these pilgrim psalms belong. The visits of Jews to Jerusalem have a history of their own which cannot be told here. But we must remember how century after

[7] John MacNeill, "The God of the Pilgrim," *Christian World Pulpit,* LXXXIV (1913), 136.

7 The LORD shall preserve thee from all evil: he shall preserve thy soul.

7 The LORD will keep you from all evil;
he will keep your life.

σεληνιάζεσθαι, "to be moonstruck," Matt. 4:24; 17:15). The popular mind, of course, assumed that a demon in the sun or the moon was the agent of the evil. But **the LORD shall preserve thee from all evil.** Both now and for all time to come unchangingly he will keep you wherever you go and wherever you are—**thy going out and thy coming in** (cf. Deut. 28:6; 31:2).

century the caravans came from far and near. Every year the streets of the city were packed with young and old, all eager to participate in the religious festivities that united them. Once in a lifetime at least it was expected that men and boys would make the journey—a journey which was often crowded with dangers, but also crowned with delight. The pilgrims were frequently exposed to robbers; sometimes the path was barred by enemies. There were deserts to be crossed, and many suffered from the pitiless glare of the sun. There were the sick to be tended and the aged to be supported. But the trials of the way were forgotten when the towers of the city came in sight and the promise of rich fellowship was all but realized. It was in such a caravan, we may suppose, that Jesus of Nazareth when twelve years of age traveled with Joseph and Mary. Their journey was not a long one, but we can believe that it was filled with joys and fears. And millions of other families through the years had trod that pilgrim way and sung as they approached the temple: **I will lift up mine eyes unto the hills.**

Those pilgrimages meant much to devout Israelites. There were surely some to whom they were primarily a social event. There were men of patriotic mind who may have moved hardly at all beyond the satisfaction to be had in such expressions of national unity. But there must have been many who were lifted to the heights of spiritual religion. For them it was not the thrill of the ever-growing company, not merely the splendor of priestly processions and venerable liturgy; it was the deeper realization of the truths that had been passed on from father to son. Above all it was an act of personal trust in the God who had protected them through the perils of the way and guided them through the tedious wilderness. They need not fear for the return journey or for the distant scene. When someone spoke of more troubles and losses, they could reply:

> **The LORD will keep you from all evil;**
> **he will keep your life.**
> **The LORD will keep**
> **your going out and your coming in**
> **from this time forth and for evermore.**

These final words of the psalm deserve special attention. The going out and coming in suggest the common doorstep, which to the Hebrew was not common but highly significant. Even to this day religious Jews hang on their doorposts a small metal cylinder containing parchment upon which is written the great commandment: "Hear, O Israel: the LORD our God is one LORD: and thou shalt love the LORD thy God with all thine heart, and with all thy soul, and with all thy might" (Deut. 6:4-5). It reminds us of the Passover, and of the way in which the doorpost was sprinkled with blood as an indication that the house was protected by the power of God. It reminds us also of the fact that in many parts of the East no one will put his foot upon a doorstep. It must be stepped over, never on.

These things also we may wish to discard as superstitions; but there is homely truth connected with them. The doorstep does indicate a division between the home and the world: the home with its intimacies, and the world with its publicity and its turmoil; the home with its instinctive sharing, and the world with its bitter competition; the home which ought to be and often is a refuge from the storms of life, and the world where one is exposed to trial and temptation. Normally we pass from the one to the other without an immediate sense of change; partly because for us the door is always open, and we expect soon to return. But now and again we pause, knowing that we are passing from one environment to another. A son goes out to war. A daughter leaves to be a foreign missionary. The home is far from perfect. The world outside may provide congenial friendships and tasks. But the going out and the coming in mean a break in old habits, a change for those who go and for those who stay.

The faith of the psalmist, however, is that neither those who go nor those who stay are alone. The way may be long, the dangers many, but **The LORD shall preserve thy going out and thy coming in.** He may not keep us in the way we want to be kept. He may not keep us from sorrow. He may not give us bodily deliverance. "What did Providence do for the martyr Stephen when he was being stoned to death?"

8 The LORD shall preserve thy going out and thy coming in from this time forth, and even for evermore.	**8** The LORD will keep your going out and your coming in from this time forth and for evermore.

The psalm opens (vs. 1) with a troubled soul's petition for **help.** The rest of the psalm (vss. 2-8) rings the changes on **the LORD is thy keeper.** By skillful use of climactic or repetitive parallelism the psalmist, like a musician, builds on this simple theme a rare work of power and beauty; and from generation to generation his words continue to inspire our worship and our song.

asked an agnostic of Joseph Parker while he was still a youth. "What did Providence do in the case of the martyr Stephen?" replied Parker. "He enabled Stephen to say, 'Lord, lay not this sin to their charge.'"[8] God did not save him from stoning, but he saved him from the spirit of hate and a desire to retaliate.

8. ***Acting and Re-acting Religions.***—Both of the possibilities before us lead to important conclusions. Pilgrimage and mountaineering alike mean aspiration. Both demand a distant goal and steady endurance. We cannot set out upon either without personal resolution, and we cannot win through without courage and effort. This is an essential demand in all religious enterprises. The noblest piety always contains an element of sternness. It makes demands not primarily upon others but upon oneself. The O.T. is full of exhortations like that which came to Joshua after the death of Moses: "Be strong and of a good courage" (Josh. 1:6). There is the same insistence in the teaching of Jesus and of Paul. "Not every one who says to me 'Lord, Lord,' shall enter the kingdom of heaven, but he who does the will of my Father who is in heaven" (Matt. 7:21). "Work out your own salvation with fear and trembling" (Phil. 2:12). It appears in the praise of the modern church, as it appeared in the psalms of ancient Israel:

Rise up, O men of God!
  Have done with lesser things;
Give heart and soul and mind and strength
  To serve the King of kings.[9]

Yet essential as this personal note is, it is not the dominant note in biblical teaching. The characteristic word of the Bible appears in its first sentence: "In the beginning God . . . ." The whole burden of the succeeding books is about God. The Israelites are the children of God. Abraham is the friend of God. Jesus Christ is the Son of God. The psalms are hymns of praise to God. This psalm in particular begins and ends with the Lord, from whom comes man's help and who will preserve his going out and coming in forever. The faith of the Bible is what Adolf Deissmann called a "reacting cult," by which he meant a faith in which man's action is a response to the action of God. God speaks, and man says "Amen!" In other words, the Bible in general and this psalm in particular are theocentric, not anthropocentric.

This is so important a matter that frequent references to it in this Expos. are inevitable. Religion in many countries is marked by great earnestness, tremendous activity, and a real desire to conquer evil. It is not, however, marked by a great sense of God. Compare our appeals and reports with the Acts of the Apostles, and see the difference between a church problem-conscious and a church power-conscious. Compare modern preaching with apostolic preaching, and see the difference between men who suggest a point of view and heralds who announce a fact. Or consider our prayers, with their lifting up of anxious hands to grasp God, and the great prayers of the Bible, with their sense of the strong arm of God stretched out to help men. Are we not in the realm of action rather than reaction? We still believe in salvation: but now it is salvation by sacraments, again it is salvation by works or will. We are immersed in schemes for social betterment, and often in our committees and conferences there is an awful sense of responsibility; yet mingling with our seriousness and sometimes our despair is a subtle pride in man's power to set the world right. It insinuates itself even into our worship, so that there is at least a suggestion of the Pharisee who thanked God he was not as other men. Everyone says we are waiting for a revival, but not everyone sees that no revival is possible until we are driven from ourselves to God, from an "acting" to a "reacting" religion.

The forces of modernity are such that the way back will not be easy. We have made a beginning with theology. We are witnessing a changing emphasis in preaching. The real test,

[8] *A Preacher's Life* (London: Hodder & Stoughton, 1899), pp. 249-50.

[9] William Pierson Merrill. Used by permission of *The Presbyterian Tribune.*

A Song of degrees of David.

122 I was glad when they said unto me, Let us go into the house of the LORD.

A Song of Ascents. Of David.

122 I was glad when they said to me,
"Let us go to the house of the LORD!"

CXXII. Pray for the Peace of Jerusalem (122:1-9)

This is the psalm of a pilgrim to Jerusalem. He is one of a company of Jews to whom the privilege of making the journey to join in the feast of Thanksgiving was a rare and soul-stirring experience. It is clear that his pilgrimage has been accomplished; and now, as he is on the eve of departing for the homeward journey, he sums up his impressions of the city as the scene and symbol of Israel's past, the bond that holds the scattered tribes of Israel together; he fittingly concludes by invoking rich blessings on this city of his affections and calling on all his fellows to join with him in praying **for the peace of Jerusalem** and the prosperity of all who love her.

The date of the psalm is postexilic. The fact that Jerusalem is a place to which **the tribes of the Lord** make pilgrimage (vs. 4) points to post-Deuteronomic times (cf. Deut. 12:5). Vs. 5 suggests that the monarchy belongs to the memories of the past. The stress that is laid on the function of Jerusalem in binding Israel together argues for a time when the Jews were scattered in the Diaspora and when the pilgrimage was a well-established feature in Judaism. The language is probably influenced by late Hebrew or Aramaic usage, e.g., in vs. 1 באמרים, if it is not an error for באמרם, **when they said,** reflects the late use of the participle as a tense form, and the periphrastic perfect, עמדות היו, **have been standing,** is more at home in late than in classical usage.

The meter is 3+2, with the exception of 2+2+2 in vs. 5.

1. The Joy of the Jerusalem Pilgrimage (122:1-2)

122:1-2. In the opening verses the psalmist recalls the joy with which he welcomed the invitation of his fellows to go with them to Jerusalem. Because of the dangers of travel

however, comes when we pass from doctrine to life. That is where the psalmist can help us. Seeing how men in other ages have walked with God, we may gradually be brought to form the same habits. We may learn to look above rather than within ourselves, and so to trust Omnipotence that we shall not fear what man can do to us. "When first I stood before this board of directors," said a woman missionary before departing for what might be her last term of foreign service, "I was scared of everyone. Now I am not afraid of anyone. That is what twenty-eight years of missionary work has done for me." It is the experience of multitudes who have not only talked about religion but have lived it.

This is the crux of the matter for the Christian minister. Suppose one day when worship is ended he retires to the vestry and finds waiting for him some broken piece of humanity. When the man begins to talk, he tells how he has been beaten, perhaps by a temper that wrecks the home, perhaps by sexual impulses he cannot control. If the minister has nothing but a word of exhortation to say, he may as well be silent. Or if he is content to repeat phrases that seem remote or archaic both to speaker and hearer, the man will go away as sorrowful as he came. But if in words that seem alive with personal experience he can speak of a God who made and can remake, if he can promise that one who trusts shall be kept, that a foot which has slipped can be made secure, then he will bring new hope to the defeated. It is a message that sets men singing not about what they can do but about what God can do in and through them. All things become possible to those who have **the Lord** as their **keeper.**

122:1-9. ***Worship that Makes the Heart Glad.*** —Of all the pilgrim psalms this is the one that makes us most conscious of the visits to Jerusalem paid on stated occasions by pious and patriotic Jews. It is easy to imagine the preparations that were made in anticipation, the dangers and delights of the journey, the thrill as swelling processions pressed upon the Holy City and the temple itself, and then when the festivities were over, the leave-taking, the return home, and the restarting of old duties.

There may have been some who complained

2 Our feet shall stand within thy gates, O Jerusalem.
3 Jerusalem is builded as a city that is compact together:

2 Our feet have been standing
within your gates, O Jerusalem!

3 Jerusalem, built as a city
which is bound firmly together,

---

journeys to Jerusalem were rare for those who lived in distant parts, and for safety's sake pilgrims went in groups. So the pilgrim band had come to Jerusalem. And now, after

Our feet have been standing
within your gates, O Jerusalem!

and the object of the pilgrimage has been fulfilled, the psalmist is moved to utter a tender farewell to the Holy City.

2. The Meaning of Jerusalem (122:3-5)

3-5. First he speaks of the city itself and its meaning for all who make pilgrimage to it. **Jerusalem, built as a city . . . bound firmly together:** These words signify that the impressiveness of the city is due to its physical conditions, its massive walls enclosing streets of closely packed houses, a sight which might fill a peasant with wonder. But a better translation of the verse is "O Jerusalem, thou that art built as the city by which brethren are united together." The word translated **compact** is used also of the

---

of the expense, the dangers, the interference with normal routine. The general attitude, however, was one of gladness. There were doubtless those who were glad because it brought a welcome change into a dull life. They wanted to see the world, to mix with unknown people, to share the adventures of travel, sometimes by doubtful routes. There were many whose imagination had been stirred by stories of Palestine, and especially of Jerusalem: they would not have been human had they not longed to see the city of David, the walls that had so often been destroyed and rebuilt, the streets where national heroes had walked, the public buildings where leaders had taken counsel in times of crisis. Beyond all this there was the temple, with its courts and pinnacles, its processions and sacrifices, its priests, its music, its vast congregations, and its solemn moments. Of course they responded with alacrity when the word went around: **Let us go into the house of the Lord.**

If we consider Martin Luther's first visit to Rome, we get some idea of the excitement there must have been in the hearts of multitudes of Jews as they made their first journey to Jerusalem.

> At last, after a weary journey in the beginning of summer, under the hot sun of Italy, he approached the city with its seven hills. His heart was moved; his eyes were looking towards the queen of the world and the Church. As soon as he caught sight of the eternal city in the distance, the city of St. Peter and St. Paul, the metropolis of catholicism, he threw himself on the ground exclaiming, "Holy Rome, I salute thee!"[1]

It sometimes happens when we visit an ancient shrine that we are able to read part of its story in stone. We see the Perpendicular and the Decorated styles of architecture, we find an Early English door, a Norman window, possibly the remains of a Saxon tower. Perhaps a guide comes and speaks of incidents and persons, and we are able to people the aisles and chancel with priests, monks, and bishops of many centuries.

What possibilities there were in Jerusalem for Jews who came with minds full of national traditions! They would remember the temple David longed to build, but for which he could do no more than make plans and gather material. They would remember how Solomon achieved what his father planned, how timber was brought from Lebanon and skilled workers from far countries. It was not a great building by modern standards, but it contained the best labor of which the people were capable, and reports of its splendor spread from nation to nation. The details were carefully recorded, the measurements, the decorations, the altar and its furniture. When the building was finished, it was consecrated by Solomon himself with all the splendor and solemnity of which he and his government, the priests and the musicians, were capable.

[1] Jean Henri Merle d'Aubigne, *History of the Reformation of the Sixteenth Century,* Bk. II, ch. vi.

4 Whither the tribes go up, the tribes of the LORD, unto the testimony of Israel, to give thanks unto the name of the LORD.
5 For there are set thrones of judgment, the thrones of the house of David.

4 to which the tribes go up,
the tribes of the LORD,
as was decreed for Israel,
to give thanks to the name of the LORD.
5 There thrones for judgment were set,
the thrones of the house of David.

---

union of associates or members of a group (cf. LXX, Vulg.). Vs. 4 favors the latter sense. The psalmist, then, is moved by the deeper, spiritual significance of Jerusalem for Israel—*la ville où l'on se réunit d'un seul coeur* (Calès, *Livre des Psaumes,* II, 455). And so it is the place **to which the tribes go up, . . . as was decreed for Israel, . . . to give thanks to the name of the LORD.** The decree is given in Deut. 16:16-17, and since the feast of Tabernacles was especially the occasion for giving thanks to the Lord for his bounty in the harvest, it is probably that festival to which our psalmist had made his pilgrimage.

But the psalmist thinks of Jerusalem not only as the city where Israel becomes conscious of its unity, but also as the ancient seat of government where the kings of David's line had reigned and judged. **Thrones for judgment were set, . . . thrones of the house of David.** Recalling the historic past of the city, the psalmist thinks of the

---

There it stood for centuries, the pride of Jews throughout the world. Then in 586 B.C. war came and swept their glory away. Nebuchadrezzar took the city and sacked it, pillaged the temple, and carried the best of the people away in bondage. The story was too deeply ingrained in Jewish minds to be forgotten, and not least the part that told of weary years of exile during which the city of David became a scene of desolation. There came a time, however, when companies were permitted to return, and with great devotion and heroism they began to rebuild. They built protecting walls and houses for the people, but especially they rebuilt the house of the Lord. They could not reproduce the magnificence of Solomon. Where there had been ten golden lampstands there was but one. Where there had been an altar of burnished brass there stood one of unhewn stone. Those who remembered the glory of the past wept aloud when Zerubbabel's temple was dedicated. But others shouted for joy, for their labors were for the moment ended—there in the Holy City stood the symbol of the people's unity in the worship of the Lord, there sacrifices could be offered and psalms sung. The workmanship might be inferior, but again the spirit of the people had expressed itself in traditional and sacred forms.

Sometimes perhaps pilgrims remembered that there was another side to the story. Sometimes they may have remembered that Solomon's temple had been built by forced labor and heavy taxation, and that while the privileged gloried in the architectural achievement, others counted the cost. The burdens on the backs of the poor were largely responsible for the division of the kingdom and centuries of jealousy and warfare. There may well have been such thoughts in men's minds in later times when they came up not to Zerubbabel's temple but to Herod's. There again were the ornate and the extravagant which engendered pride rather than humility, thoughts of human ability rather than an attitude of godly fear. It is likely that true religion owes more to mean buildings than to magnificent ones. Through the centuries inspiration seems to have come to the devout more often in upper rooms than in gorgeous edifices. What Jesus of Nazareth felt about Herod's temple when first he visited it is untold, but we sense a growing attitude of alienation as the ministry proceeded. There are suggestions that it was not there that he found the true development of prophetic faith. In teaching like the parable of the vine and the branches he prepared the way for Paul, for whom the church was not a building, or even primarily an institution, but a mystical body. Perhaps it was no great religious loss when in A.D. 70 Roman legions captured Jerusalem and swept Herod's temple away.

The conclusion to which we come is that the gladness of the people depends upon the extent to which any place of worship is the house of the Lord. If it is the building of men, commemorating the greatness of an individual or the ambition of a people, it may easily become the home of vanity, division, and futility. If, however, it is in intention and practice a real sanctuary of God, it will be through all changing times a symbol of unity, a place of fellow-

6 Pray for the peace of Jerusalem: they shall prosper that love thee.
7 Peace be within thy walls, *and* prosperity within thy palaces.
8 For my brethren and companions' sakes, I will now say, Peace *be* within thee.

6 Pray for the peace of Jerusalem!
"May they prosper who love you!
7 Peace be within your walls,
and security within your towers!"
8 For my brethren and companions' sake
I will say, "Peace be within you!"

---

rule of David and his successors as one of justice. He lives in an age which idealizes things that are past and gone.

3. Prayer for Jerusalem's Welfare (122:6-9)

6-9. Finally, the prophet invites his companions to join with him in a prayer for **the peace** [better, "the prosperity"] **of Jerusalem.** The prayer is a fourfold wish. (*a*) May they **prosper that love thee,** a petition which prompts an active interest in all for which the city is a symbol. (*b*) **Peace be within thy walls,** or "Peace be in thy ramparts," i.e., may war never make breaches in the defenses of the city and may the clamor of war never be heard within its fortifications. (*c*) **And prosperity within thy palaces.** Better, "tranquillity in thy towers." The **towers** were gate towers, and if vs. 7*b* is not synonymous with vs. 7*a*, then the prayer is that sedition and treason may be kept far from the city. (*d*) **For my brethren and companions' sake** [i.e., for all the inhabitants of Jerusalem

---

ship, of inspiration and dedication. In every age the house of the Lord, while it is the work of men's hands and therefore embodies human imperfection, stands for that which is beyond time and space and is beyond human control. It is the meeting place of heaven and earth, the outward and visible sign of the fact that man himself belongs to two worlds, a world of sense and space and an invisible world of spiritual reality. Here men wait for the glory of God to visit them, and putting away all foolish thoughts strive to ascend to the heavenly places. From such places of worship flow grace and power which hallow all life and sanctify all human relations. That is why through all the centuries the church abides. Men may depart from it for a season, either because they have lost consciousness of their higher selves or because the church has so missed its way that people despair of its ministries. But sooner or later they return, because man is made for God, and because God is always seeking the heart of man.

The gladness with which men respond to the invitation is of many kinds; but above all in devout hearts is the desire to know God himself, and through finding him in personal contact to attain newness of life. Without that desire, and its expression in common worship, individual and community life is impoverished and at last starved.

Let us consider three points. First, the true worship of God saves us from the evils of idolatry. The choice that faces us is not shall we or shall we not worship? If we do not worship God, we shall bow the knee, not perhaps to the idols of primitive peoples, but to abstract ideas or personal ambitions, to mammon or even to the image of ourselves. It is not an accident that when the people are tempted from the house of the Lord, they find themselves immersed in ideologies, in war, in state-worship. If we can find nothing else to worship, we shall deify the human race and find ourselves slaves even while we boast our freedom from ancient superstitions. There is every reason why in an age like this we should take to heart the appeal of I John 5:21: "Little children, keep yourselves from idols." We shall do it, not by reforms and iconoclasms, but by worship in spirit and in truth.

Second, the true worship of God unites us in ever-larger unities. The first impression may well be that religion is the great divider. Is not humanity divided into mutually exclusive nations? Are not these nations weakened by rival parties? And are not the causes of separation frequently religious? The answer is in the affirmative because religion has so often been false and worship impure. But religion as it is set forth in the Bible is always drawing men together in spiritual fellowship. So profound is this fellowship that it continues in spite of national, ecclesiastical, and intellectual differences. Wherever is the worship of the universal Father through the one Lord Jesus Christ, there men are conscious of human brotherhood and learn to labor for its complete expression in every department of life.

This is particularly impressive in the modern world, where divisions are so deep and so nu-

9 Because of the house of the LORD our God I will seek thy good.

9 For the sake of the house of the LORD our
God,
I will seek your good.

---

with whom the pilgrims have joined in worship and strengthened the ties of brotherhood] **I will now say, Peace be within thee,** or, better, "I will wish for thee peace." In vs. 9 the prayer is changed into a vow. **Because of the house of the LORD our God**—for this reason even above all others **I will seek thy good.**

This prayer as a form of a blessing on Jerusalem was assumed to have, like all blessings, power to bring about its own fulfillment. It is to be noted that the psalmist seems to believe that the very name of Jerusalem contains within itself an earnest of its peace and prosperity. For in vss. 6-8 he puns on its name by using words of good omen that have an alliterative resemblance to it: *sha'alû,* **pray;** *shālôm,* **peace;** *yishlayû,* **prosper;** *shalwāh,* "tranquillity." And so from line to line he suggests the varied facets of his beloved word, **Jerusalem.**

---

merous. Yet men continue to strive for international peace and world government. There are many agencies assisting them in their persistent efforts, as there are many others frustrating them. It would be optimistic in the extreme to believe in ultimate success if the spiritual depths of life remain untouched. Actually the world has seen conference after conference and ideal after ideal fail because they have been restricted to political, economic, cultural, and recreational interests. At the same time, conference after conference—begun, continued, and ended in Christian faith and united prayer—has succeeded. They have succeeded not because of the excellence of ecclesiastical statesmanship, but because common worship has deepened a sense of common need, of penitence instead of recrimination, of good will instead of hostile judgments—a profound unity of spirit that conquers sectarianism and self-righteousness.

Third, the true worship of God also lifts men's minds above themselves and increases the joy of God-centeredness. One of the evils of secularism is that men are driven in upon themselves: the more obsessed by themselves they become the darker their countenances, the more tragic their literature, the sadder their speech. The place of prayer is forsaken; psychological clinics are overcrowded. The pew is empty; suicide is common. There is no time for meditation; frenzy takes the place of poise. The effects are seen in art, in music, in journalism. Extravagance, sensationalism, impatience, intrude into every sphere of life till minds become jaded, tempers frayed, and energy exhausted. Fidelity in marriage and happiness in domestic life in such an atmosphere become increasingly difficult. Divorce is the easy way out. The family falls apart into separate and sometimes hostile units. It is not an accident. If men have nothing to lift their thoughts to the supreme heights, nothing to appeal to their deepest selves, nothing to help them to see life in perspective, they will become miserable introverts, a torment to themselves and a problem to their friends.

It is the worship of God that gives sanity and peace. It is resting oneself in the divine purpose that saves us from anxiety and fear. To lose oneself in adoration is to find one's true self in God. There is no reformation more needed in the modern world than that which makes men assemble in penitence and then lift their hearts in praise.

Some people who think the Christian religion is gloomy and Christian worship depressing might change their minds if they studied the hymns of the church, especially those written by Isaac Watts, who caught better than most the cheerfulness of the psalmist. It would do us all good to take his verses as a remedy for sadness, even learning by heart such lines as

> Come, let us join our cheerful songs
> With angels round the throne,

and

> Before Jehovah's awe-full throne,
> Ye nations, bow with sacred joy;

but more particularly these, which are strangely omitted from certain hymnbooks,

> How pleased and blest was I,
> To hear the people cry,
> Come, let us seek our God today!
> Yes, with a cheerful zeal
> We haste to Zion's hill,
> And there our vows and homage pay.

A Song of degrees.	A Song of Ascents.
123 Unto thee lift I up mine eyes, O thou that dwellest in the heavens.	123 To thee I lift up my eyes, O thou who art enthroned in the heavens!

CXXIII. Our Eyes Look to the Lord (123:1-4)

This brief psalm opens like an individual lament with the pronoun **I,** but it becomes in vs. 2 a national or congregational lament with the change of the pronoun to **our** and **us.** If we assume that vs. 1 was rendered by a precentor or priest, and the following verses by the worshiping body, we are able to understand why the psalm seems to be a mixture of the two lament types. As in other psalms of the pilgrim collection, a homely scene from everyday life is used as a simile to point the theme.

The experience that has aroused the strong emotions voiced in the psalm points to a time when the Jews are being treated contemptuously by people who regarded themselves as superior to them, i.e., to the time of the Diaspora in the postexilic period. The meter is 3+2, except for 2+2 in vs. 2*b*.

1. Appeal to God for Mercy (123:1-2)

123:1-2. As the eyes of servants look to the hand of . . . master, . . . mistress: A slave may look to the hand of his master either to see how the master handles a tool or performs

---

123:1-4. *Sursum Corda.*—To pass from Ps. 122 to this one is like turning from day to night. The former, with its picture of pilgrims traveling together in a spirit of expectation, fills us with a sense of the joys of life. Ps. 123, with its suggestion of men who endure suffering and who cry aloud for succor, reminds us that our joys are touched with pain. The two psalms are, however, alike in their sincerity. Neither the gladness of the one nor the cry of the other is forced or pretentious. The transition from the one to the other may come swiftly to any of us.

Who these men are who cry from the depths, and what is the cause of their trouble, is not stated. If they suffer from persecution it is not necessarily imprisonment or stripes. There are many forms of torture, and the mental forms can be as wounding as the physical. The body may be fed and housed and protected, but if pride is hurt or the mind depressed, the results can be an agony. The outward man may be treated like a prince, but if beneath the forms of respect there are sarcasm and contempt, the mind may become twisted and the soul embittered.

It is possible that this man (vs. 1) or these men (vss. 2-4) who in distress lift up their eyes to him **that dwellest in the heavens** are the victims of **scorn** (see vss. 3-4). It is indeed so likely that we must consider this common and cowardly method of persecution. John Watson placed it among the "respectable sins." It is a weapon that has been freely employed by men and women who would never stoop to drunkenness or sexual immorality, who would be ashamed to be classed with liars or thieves. One may have a reputation for respectability, occupy an important position in public life, even hold office in the church of God, and still be guilty of the sin of scorn. Such scorn, as John Watson well said,

> is a thing deeper than speech or action; it is a temper of mind which need not in reality be coarse or loud, but which may be subtle and veiled. The scorner may not revile men—very likely he will only ignore them; . . . possibly he will not be proud of speech and gait, but, like the Apothecary in the "Fair Maid of Perth," will veil his haughtiness beneath a cloak of humility.[2]

The sin of scorn takes many forms. Social superiority is one of the commonest, appearing in many different civilizations. The snobbery of the rich can be even more offensive. Neither is cured by declamation or by the proclamation of egalitarian principles. The poor may be relieved and the rich taxed almost out of existence, and even while the foolish congratulate themselves it may be realized that nothing has happened but the removal of privilege from one class to another. Moreover, if pride is suppressed in one place it is likely to assert itself in another. It may show itself where better things might have been expected. It may take the form of intellectual conceit, and it does so whenever men

[2] *Respectable Sins* (3rd ed.; London: Hodder & Stoughton, 1910), p. 242.

2 Behold, as the eyes of servants *look*
unto the hand of their masters, *and* as the
eyes of a maiden unto the hand of her mistress; so our eyes *wait* upon the LORD our
God, until that he have mercy upon us.
3 Have mercy upon us, O LORD, have
mercy upon us: for we are exceedingly filled
with contempt.

2 Behold, as the eyes of servants
look to the hand of their master,
as the eyes of a maid
to the hand of her mistress,
so our eyes look to the LORD our God,
till he have mercy upon us.

3 Have mercy upon us, O LORD, have mercy
upon us,
for we have had more than enough of
contempt.

---

a task or to receive from it food, clothing, and other necessities. The context favors the latter sense. The suppliants here are looking to the Lord not to learn what they need to do but to obtain the favor of his help. **Our eyes look to the LORD . . . till he have mercy upon us.**

2. We Have Had Enough of Contempt (123:3-4)

3-4. The appeal is pressed more passionately in the second strophe, but we note also that it ends without any expression of confidence that the Lord will answer the

---

forget that superior endowment and special educational advantages should be accepted as gifts, not boasted as merit. It may be seen even in religious circles, where denominations boast a better ecclesiastical system, a longer priestly succession, greater missionary activity, even the patronage of the state. Wherever it appears it arouses resentment, creates divisions, embitters society. The reunion of Christendom is made difficult, next door to impossible, not only by different church polities and practices but by generations of contempt. The task of evangelism is frustrated not only by the preoccupations of the busy world but by the personal antipathies of Christians and the rivalries of contending parties. The religious situation being what it is, how intolerable it would be if churchmen presumed to blame politicians for the problems of race that present themselves in almost every part of the world! These racial animosities have revealed themselves in modern times in a particularly truculent manner, and the solution of the trouble is not yet in sight.

The Jew has often been one of the chief sufferers in this respect. He has been slighted and persecuted by peoples and by governments, and sometimes driven from polite society. It is not because he lacks ability. Perhaps it is because he is too able and too industrious and, when opportunity permits, too successful. Men do not enjoy being outclassed: they resent it when they see the instruments of power passing to alien hands. Sometimes the Jews have further offended by flaunting their successes and by acting in antisocial ways. They have not always been the victims of scorn: they have sometimes inflicted it upon others. Not that Gentiles are in a position to admonish or to judge. All we can say is that "all have sinned, and come short of the glory of God" (Rom. 3:23).

Notice in this connection what the psalm does not contain. There is no prayer for punishment. There may be a suggestion of vindictiveness. There is at least a protest:

> **We have had more than enough of contempt.**
> **Too long our soul has been sated**
> **with the scorn of those who are at ease,**
> **the contempt of the proud.**

But there is no demand that the persecutor shall find scorn recoiling upon himself. No one can maintain that hate is absent from the O.T. or even from the Psalter. It took the Jews a long time to learn, as C. G. Montefiore has confessed, that God has no enemies, that his mercy knows no limits, and that the faithful must learn the blessedness of love and forgiveness in all the ways of life. For the downtrodden and the outcast, says Montefiore, "Jesus had a new message; he gave them a new hope; he brought to them a compassion and a love to which they had been unused before." [3] This psalmist seems at least to be looking in that direction; for while there is no savage recrimination there is a prayer for mercy. In the whole psalm there is no more revealing word than that. There have been those

[3] "Contemporary Jewish Religion," in A. S. Peake, ed., *A Commentary on the Bible* (London: Thomas Nelson & Sons, n.d.), pp. 622-23.

4 Our soul is exceedingly filled with the scorning of those that are at ease, *and* with the contempt of the proud.

4 Too long our soul has been sated
with the scorn of those who are at ease,
the contempt of the proud.

---

petition of his servants (cf. 5:12; 13:6). Their complaint is that **we have had more than enough of contempt.** The word **contempt** probably covers such vilifications of the Jews as are summed up by Josephus (*Against Apion* II. 14) and by the Egyptian Manetho (270-250 B.C.; see also H. L. Strack, "Antisemitism," in James Hastings, ed., *Encyclopedia of Religion and Ethics* [New York: Charles Scribner's Sons, 1908-27], I, 594. The principal offenders in heaping contempt on the Jews were men who were **proud,** "puffed up" (גאיונים) and "arrogant," **those . . . at ease** (שאננים), i.e., men who by reason of station, class, and wealth felt secure in their tyranny. In vs. 4 read הלעג לגאיונים, "the scorn of the proud," omitting the other words of 4*b* as a marginal gloss. The *Qerê,* גאי יונים, probably springs from a late attempt to identify the oppressors as "the proud ones of the Greeks" (יונים).

---

who have regarded the consciousness of sin as a disease which man has caught. But we with centuries of religious experience behind us believe that it is the gauge of progress. That man has this sense of failure is an indication that he is rising; the intensity of the sense denotes the height to which he has attained. The natural man is usually ready to excuse himself and condemn others. The man of spiritual sensitiveness and moral integrity confesses his own faults and failures and has little time or inclination for exposing the transgressions of others. Thus it has long been recognized that the holiest of men are the first to strike their breasts and exclaim, "God be merciful to me a sinner" (Luke 18:13). Sometimes, like the apostle who called himself the chief of sinners (I Tim. 1:15), they seem to use the language of exaggeration. To quote a single instance, there is John Bunyan speaking of a family plagued with vermin and

> one or two of the family to be in chief the breeders. . . . I speak by experience. I was one of these lousy ones, one of these great sin-breeders; I infected all the youth of the town where I was born, with all manner of youthful vanities. . . . Wherefore Christ Jesus took me first; and taking me first, the contagion was much allayed all the town over.[4]

Observe what it is that brings about this disposition of the soul. Jacques Maritain has divided the world's teachers into two classes: those who take the horizontal view of life and those who take the vertical. In the first class are many who have excellent reputations. They seem, however, to be untouched by spiritual visions and revolutionary intuitions. Their lives are ruled and their teaching inspired by the mechanisms of human society. They may be counted not only respectable but religious, but they are neither seers nor prophets. They may dominate the religious scene, but in the strict sense of the word they are not spiritual. They were much in evidence in Palestine when in the fullness of the times God sent his Son to be the Savior of the world. The scribes and Pharisees were genuinely concerned for temple and synagogue, for the whole cultus of sacrifices, prayers, and almsgiving. Their devotions and public service were not altogether lacking in sincerity. But they compared sadly with the publican, who may have been neither very scrupulous in ritual requirements nor very reputable in society, but who knew what it means to lift the mind and heart to God.

We know very little about the writer of this psalm, but we have no hesitation in placing him among those who have the vertical view of life. The evidence is found not only in his prayer for mercy but in his initial words:

> **To thee I lift up my eyes,**
> **O thou who art enthroned in the heavens!**

The impression is confirmed when he likens himself to **servants** whose eyes are fixed upon the hand of the master and to the **maid** who watches the hand of the mistress. Such watching may have different causes. It may spring from a desire to learn how things are done by the skillful. It may be sustained by expectation: those hands have often conveyed gifts and may distribute more. Even so devout souls look to God both to learn and to receive, but especially to receive **mercy.** There are many references in the O.T. to the hand of God—the hand that guides and protects, the hand that commands and comforts and chastises. One generation

[4] *The Jerusalem Sinner Saved.* See *The Works of John Bunyan,* ed. George Offor (Glasgow: Blackie & Sons, 1854), I, 78-79.

A Song of degrees of David.	A Song of Ascents. Of David.
124 If *it had* not *been* the LORD who was on our side, now may Israel say;	**124** If it had not been the LORD who was on our side, let Israel now say—

CXXIV. We Have Escaped, Thanks to God (124:1-8)

This psalm is an expression of thanksgiving in recognition of what the Lord did to deliver his people from the fierce assaults of enemies who were resolved on their destruction. In order to show what Israel owes to the Lord the psalmist sets forth by examples of agencies of ineluctable destruction what would have happened "if the LORD had not been for us." Israel would have been "swallowed up alive," "swept away," "submerged," "torn apart," and "trapped in a net" had her enemies worked their wills against her. These images follow one another rapidly, almost breathlessly, to express the sense of sudden crisis and the magnitude of "the danger run and happily escaped," but with a characteristic Hebrew disregard of logical cohesion (Calès). These evidences of strong emotion pulsating in the lines of the psalm suggest that the event to which it refers was a recent one, but we have no means of identifying it more specifically.

Certain linguistic usages in the psalm argue for a late postexilic date, e.g., אזי, ש (Aramaic, אדין, Dan. 7:11), and the structure of the conditional clauses. The fact that the enemy are spoken of as **men** (vs. 2) rather than "peoples" or "nations" may point to a conspiracy or a coup instigated by a faction or party within the country. The history of postexilic Judaism provided situations favorable to political upheavals. The meter is irregular, e.g., 3+3 (vss. 3-4, 8); 2+2+2 (vss. 1, 6); 3+2 (vss. 5, 7*a*); 2+2 (vs. 7*b*); 2+2+3 (vs. 2).

1. If the Lord Had Not Been with Us (124:1-5)

124:1-5. The psalm was meant for liturgical use. Vs. 1*a* was sung probably by a priest or precentor; the words **let Israel now say** were the signal for the congregation

after another, Israelites were reminded of the exodus from Egypt and how "by strength of hand the LORD brought you out from this place" (Exod. 13:3). Always there was the assurance that what had happened in the past was possible still, for "Behold, the Lord's hand is not shortened, that it cannot save" (Isa. 59:1). It is our confidence now. We may despair of ourselves and of one another, yet still hope if we lift up our eyes unto the Lord our God, as servants look to the hand of their master and maidens watch the hand of their mistress.

124:1-8. ***Escape from the Snare of the Fowler.*** —There seems to be progressive experience behind these pilgrim psalms. Ps. 122 makes us think of men who set out on a long journey with great eagerness. Then things go wrong, and while those of stanch heart press steadily onward, the cowards are ready to turn tail. Ps. 123 is not the cry of the feeble who want to turn back; it is a prayer for divine help in the midst of very great troubles. Then comes Ps. 124, with its paean of praise. It may have been a familiar liturgy, composed perhaps after some signal national deliverance. What the pilgrims felt, now that dangers were past, was that the words expressed their own feelings:

If it had not been the LORD who was on our side,
let Israel now say—
if it had not been the LORD who was on our side,
when men rose up against us,
then they would have swallowed us up alive.

It is impossible for us to say who the enemy was, but notice the way in which he is described. He is likened in the first place to a primeval monster who swallows up his helpless victims; then to raging waters which suddenly descend and create chaos; finally to the snare of the fowler so cunningly prepared for the unwary. The pedantic may complain that the metaphors are mixed; at least they are suggestive of destructive powers calculated to strike terror into the bravest hearts. But imminent as the dangers were, the pilgrims passed through them unscathed. No revolting beast devoured them, no flood swept them away, and as for the snare of the fowler, somehow it was broken, and they escaped like a bird on the wing. It was as though a miracle had happened, as though an

2 If *it had* not *been* the LORD who was on
our side, when men rose up against us:
3 Then they had swallowed us up quick,
when their wrath was kindled against us:
4 Then the waters had overwhelmed us,
the stream had gone over our soul:
5 Then the proud waters had gone over
our soul.

2 if it had not been the LORD who was on
our side,
when men rose up against us,
3 then they would have swallowed us up
alive,
when their anger was kindled against
us;
4 then the flood would have swept us away,
the torrent would have gone over us;
5 then over us would have gone
the raging waters.

---

and/or the choirs to take up the singing of the rest of the psalm. **If it had not been the LORD who was on our side:** Better, "If the LORD had not been on our side." The redundant use of the relative ש is characteristic in late usage. **Swallowed us up alive:** The metaphor relates to the action of a monster (cf. Jonah 1:17; Prov. 1:12). **The flood would have swept us away:** A figure suggested by the torrents which after a cloudburst suddenly and without forewarning race down the dry wadies, sweeping to their deaths men and beasts caught in a gorge or narrow passage (see J. A. Montgomery, *Arabia and the Bible* [Philadelphia: University of Pennsylvania Press, 1934], p. 85). **Gone over us . . . the raging waters:** Here the writer is thinking of the hopeless struggles of a man sinking in the turbulent waters of the sea (cf. 42:7; 88:17).

---

invisible hand had interposed. Where could the help have come from? The answer is given with absolute confidence: **Our help is in the name of the LORD, who made heaven and earth.** We too have had experiences, long and terrifying experiences, and one result is that these songs have come to life again.

It is true, for example, on the political plane, as many in Europe and not least in Britain can testify. Suddenly armed nations rose up against us and threatened to obliterate us. They did it not once but twice, and did it with every kind of duplicity and cruelty. There were times when they seemed certain to prevail, when all the watching nations thought we were about to be swallowed up. Yet in that moment of weakness we escaped, not by our own skillfulness or natural resources, but as it seemed by a special Providence. There were not lacking human courage and leadership. The quiet loyalty of men and women was revealed in every station of life. But even the national unity and the words of inspiration and examples of heroism were part of the gift from heaven. Secular historians may content themselves with happenings upon this human level, but others with religious judgment will agree with the psalmist (vss. 1-3).

By way of illustration let us think of one who in these crises took a very prominent place. No one was better known or more widely trusted than Winston Churchill; and no one has done more since to put the story into good literary form. What he gives us is generally a straightforward statement of facts, but now and again there is a suggestion of deeper thought. It may be only a fugitive phrase, but it should be read in the light of confessions made in an earlier book on his experiences in South Africa when he was war correspondent for the London *Morning Post.* Wherever danger was, Churchill seemed to be. He did not hesitate to pray for protection, or to feel grateful when the danger was past. Describing his escape from Pretoria, he used these notable words:

> I realized with awful force that no exercise of my own feeble wit and strength could save me from my enemies, and that without the assistance of that High Power which interferes in the eternal sequence of causes and effects more often than we are always prone to admit, I could never succeed. I prayed long and earnestly for help and guidance. My prayer, as it seems to me, was swiftly and wonderfully answered.[5]

James Grigg, a friend and colleague in peace and war, in an autobiographical volume recalls these instances, and yet another which relates to an escape in France during World War I. On that occasion Churchill spoke of a "strong sensation that a hand had been stretched out to move me in the nick of time from the fatal spot." Adds Grigg:

[5] *A Roving Commission: My Early Life* (new Am. ed.; New York: Charles Scribner's Sons, 1941), pp. 275-76.

6 Blessed *be* the LORD, who hath not given us *as* a prey to their teeth.	6 Blessed be the LORD, who has not given us as prey to their teeth!
7 Our soul is escaped as a bird out of the snare of the fowlers: the snare is broken, and we are escaped.	7 We have escaped as a bird from the snare of the fowlers; the snare is broken, and we have escaped!

2. OUR HELP IS IN THE NAME OF THE LORD (124:6-8)

6-7. The preceding strophe (vss. 1-5) spoke of what the Lord had wrought for Israel. Now the congregation acknowledges it with words of thankfulness. **Blessed be the LORD** means "The LORD be praised." With new figures the peril from which the Lord had delivered them is depicted. Their predicament was comparable to that of victims about to be mangled and torn by the teeth of beasts of prey. **We have escaped as a bird from the snare . . . ; the snare is broken:** The reference is to a snare made of two wooden frames on each of which a net is stretched and so joined together that they can be opened

I had and have no doubt that Winston is a convinced believer in a Higher Power, and, if he also believes that this Higher Power has on occasion intervened in the affairs of this world directly on behalf of Winston Churchill and that He did so on the request of the said Winston Churchill, surely that is a good deal better and even a good deal less crude than the néantisme or behaviourism of so many of the very modern.[6]

May we not say it was that belief which sustained the then prime minister through years of awful responsibility and made him a leader and captain to his people? And may we not say with assurance that when at last national services of thanksgiving were held with pomp and ceremony, this man at least was saying within himself with a depth of feeling he did not reveal in glance or gesture:

If it had not been the LORD who was on our side,
let Israel now say—
if it had not been the LORD who was on our side,
when men rose up against us,
then they would have swallowed us up alive.

Not the nations only but the church has passed through perils that promised to obliterate it. By human calculations it ought to have disappeared long ago. Nothing seemed weaker than the Babe born in Bethlehem: just a little life in a frail body that could so easily have been suffocated. And for guardians no one but Joseph and Mary, who fled to Egypt like any other refugees. No one has ever been more exposed to the malicious than the Prophet of Nazareth, moving among enemies who plotted together and at last had him in their grasp. With comparative ease they planned his death and nailed him to a cross and saw his body sealed in a sepulcher. But, as a bird **escaped . . . from the snare of the fowlers,** he rose again, and with him rose the little Christian community, weak, fugitive, like a flame that a puff of wind could blow out. So it seemed to Jewish authorities. So it seemed to Roman emperors who later set themselves to extinguish it. But the unexpected always happened. The flame could never be put out.

This is ancient history. It is also living memory. If we in favored lands have not yet felt the breath of affliction, others have. Tyrants have arisen in many parts, and they have not only threatened; they have acted. The story can be read, so far as the facts are known, in Kenneth Scott Latourette's *Advance Through Storm,* the seventh volume of his *History of the Expansion of Christianity.*[7] It is a lamentable story, to which there is no parallel in recorded history. Men thought the world was growing kinder and more tolerant; then suddenly found wholesale slaughter and insensate sacrilege and incredible hate. In one country in one year about two thousand churches were closed. Priests and pastors were expelled from their homes and doomed, without economic or political rights, to beggary and slow starvation. Thousands perished. Tens of thousands suffered agonies that remind us of Heb. 11. And in neighboring countries the cruelty blazed up again in violent sentences passed upon Roman Catholic cardinals and evangelical pastors. Is it not the monster, the flood, the snare of the psalm all over again?

But the church was not blotted out. It suffered in some countries almost complete organic ex-

[6] *Prejudice and Judgment* (London: Jonathan Cape, 1948), pp. 212-13.

[7] New York: Harper & Bros., 1945.

8 Our help *is* in the name of the LORD, who made heaven and earth.

8 Our help is in the name of the LORD,
who made heaven and earth.

A Song of degrees.

125 They that trust in the LORD *shall be* as mount Zion, *which* cannot be removed, *but* abideth for ever.

A Song of Ascents.

125 Those who trust in the LORD are
like Mount Zion,
which cannot be moved, but abides for
ever.

---

up booklike and set flat on the ground. When the lure is touched by the bird, a contrivance causes the two parts of the snare to spring up and imprison the luckless creature (cf. Amos 3:5; Prov. 7:23). The snare is destroyed by breaking the frames.

8. The psalm closes with a general conclusion based on the experience of this special deliverance. **Our help is in the name of the LORD:** I.e., when Israel calls on the Lord, he comes to her help. As he **made heaven and earth,** all power belongs to him.

CXXV. THE LORD IS ROUND ABOUT HIS PEOPLE (125:1-5)

A characteristic feature of the pilgrim psalms is their choice of picturesque figures of speech which vividly depict scenes drawn from the everyday life of the times; e.g., the sleeping child (Ps. 131), the watchmen on the city walls (Ps. 130), the weeds on the housetops (Ps. 129), the happy family (Ps. 128), the sower (Ps. 126), the camp sentry (Ps. 121). It is possible that the themes of these psalms were suggested by the poetic mind which sees in the humblest events of the daily round allegories or symbols of spiritual truths.

This psalm, like Pss. 23; 123; 131, is a psalm of trust or comfort. It rises out of a contemplation of **the mountains** which stand like sentries **round about Jerusalem** on the north, the east, and the south. To the man of spiritual insight they symbolize the Lord's protecting presence **round about his people.** The people have need of this consoling thought. For the land which the Lord allotted to his righteous people is under

---

tinction. Yet note what Latourette, who has made the subject especially his own, calls his seventh volume—*Advance Through Storm.* He admits that it is difficult to form a reliable estimate. He agrees to serious losses in many parts of Europe, but he holds that as a force in the contemporary life of the Continent the Christian church was probably more potent at the end than at the beginning of the period with which he is dealing. No one would claim that it is because of the perfection of Christian faith and obedience. The church has often been such a failure that its best friends have wept over it. Our language is the same as the psalmist's:

> **Blessed be the LORD,**
> **who has not given us**
> **as prey to their teeth!**
> **We have escaped as a bird**
> **from the snare of the fowlers.**

Thus Ps. 124 has come to life again. There is, however, a personal application that is still more important. We are all pilgrims. We are journeying to a celestial city. But we cannot maintain the course alone. We slip and fall; we wander and are lost. Again and again, if we are honest, we have to confess it—we are helpless, ensnared, at our wit's end. Nor is there human power or wisdom that can save us. We have tried it all, from the penetrating questions of Socrates to the achievements of the latest scientist, and there is nothing that is adequate to our need.

Yet we are not dismayed, for help is available. The initiative comes from **the LORD, who made heaven and earth,** who through Jesus Christ brought us out of "bondage . . . into the glorious liberty of the children of God" (Rom. 8:21). It is more than we can explain, but we know it, for it is in the realm of our own experience. Not one or two but all the saints of the ages have proclaimed it in glowing words and grateful lives. And though the testimonies take many forms and are repeated in many languages, through it all we can recognize the glad voice of the psalmist:

> **Our help is in the name of the LORD,**
> **who made heaven and earth.**

2 *As* the mountains *are* round about Jerusalem, so the LORD *is* round about his people from henceforth even for ever.

2 As the mountains are round about Jerusalem,
so the LORD is round about his people,
from this time forth and for evermore.

---

the dominion of a **scepter of wickedness.** And the oppression of this government is so cruel and prolonged that the righteous might through loss of faith and in desperation be tempted to put forth their hands to avenge themselves by deeds that are wrong. But things will not come to such a pass, for the Lord has allotted the land to **the righteous,** and therefore he will not permit the wicked rulers to keep possession of it. So to hasten the issue, the psalm ends with a prayer that the good for which **the righteous** are waiting may be realized, and with an imprecation on the oppressors and **their crooked ways.**

The date is postexilic. The psalm reflects a time in which not only is Jerusalem the center of Israel's religion but **the land** and Jerusalem are about synonymous. The time could be any period in Jewish history between 587 B.C and the rise of the Hasmonaeans to power after *ca.* 150 B.C. The godless oppressors might be men like Sanballat and his Samaritans (cf. Neh. 4:7-9; 6:10-14), or the Hellenistic rulers, Egyptian or Syrian, of the third century, or renegade Jews like the Tobiads or pro-Syrians like the high priests, Jason and Menelaus of the second century. As to language, it can be said that the construction ישרים בלבותם (vs. 4), instead of the idiomatic ישרי לב, and the use of למען לא (vs. 3) for פן (Gunkel), point to a postclassical date.

The meter is irregular: 2+2+3 (vs. 1); 3+3+2 (vss. 2, 5); 2+2+2 (vs. 3*a*); 3+2 (vss. 3*b*, 4).

1. THE LORD PROTECTS HIS PEOPLE (125:1-3)

125:1-3. The rhythm, and perhaps the sense, require the omission of **from this time forth and for evermore** (מעתה ועד־עולם) in vs. 2. In vs. 3 read with the LXX, לא יניח, "he will not let rest" for **shall not rest.**

125:1-5. ***Trust and Triumph.***—William James has somewhere told us of a student who began an essay by comparing the world as it often appears in the classroom of a metaphysician with the world as it is known in the experience of practical men. In the one contradictions and difficulties tend to be ruled out or explained away. In the other they remain with all their jagged edges and obstinate antinomies.

Is there not an even sharper contrast between the world as it is portrayed by religion and the world as it is experienced by the man in the street? To the latter life is full of facts, including very unpleasant ones, that cannot be explained but must be tolerated. To the saint the facts can also be unpleasantly real, but they are clothed in a faith that often transforms them. Even such facts as sorrow and pain can in the light of this faith or belief be endured or possibly welcomed as discipline of the mind and soul.

If that were the whole story the advantage would clearly lie with the man of religious faith, always assuming that his beliefs correspond with reality. If they do not, he is living in a world of pretense where the consequences are not likely to be pleasant. It is therefore the duty of theologians and others to be continually examining the beliefs to see how far they can be trusted or how far they need restating.

This psalm brings us face to face with such a task. For centuries there was a popular doctrine in Israel which included the belief that good men flourish as the green bay tree and evil men are destroyed. It is stated again and again in the Psalter as axiomatic. It appears explicitly in Ps. 1, where the man who never follows the advice of the ungodly is contrasted with the man who takes the road of the sinner. The one is like a tree planted by a stream, that bears fruit in due season; the other is like chaff swept away by the wind. We should remember that the psalms were not carefully constructed creeds. Many of them began not even as temple hymns but as folk songs. They were composed by shepherds watching their sheep or by travelers who rested under silent stars. Priests and Levites later collected and edited them and made them available for temple worship; but many of them sprang from the people who labored in the fields or even tended booths in busy bazaars. They therefore represent the hopes and fears, the temptations and deliver-

3 For the rod of the wicked shall not rest upon the lot of the righteous; lest the righteous put forth their hands unto iniquity.
4 Do good, O LORD, unto *those that be* good, and to *them that are* upright in their hearts.

3 For the scepter of wickedness shall not rest
upon the land allotted to the righteous,
lest the righteous put forth
their hands to do wrong.
4 Do good, O LORD, to those who are good,
and to those who are upright in their hearts!

2. RECOMPENSE TO THE JUST AND TO THE UNJUST (125:4-5)

4-5. In the psalm there are two groups of people. On the one hand, there are those **who trust in the LORD,** i.e., those who put their trust in the Lord, and who call themselves **the righteous, those who are good, those who are upright in their hearts.** On the other hand, there are those who are connoted by **the scepter of wickedness** and, along with them, **those who turn aside upon their crooked ways.** Apparently the latter are renegade Jews who have associated themselves with some kind of godless, i.e., foreign or pagan,

ances, of men who were in close contact with the realities of everyday life, who rejoiced when harvests were safely gathered in, who mourned when dear ones died, who reacted as men have always reacted to the processes of nature. And there in the popular mind was the conviction that good men prosper and win the favor of God, but evil men, meriting his displeasure, suffer and perish.

There were indeed some to whom this popular orthodoxy was never acceptable. The classic criticism is to be found in the book of Job, though there are suggestions of it elsewhere in O.T. scriptures. It was not left untouched by Jesus Christ, who declared that God makes the sun to shine on the evil and on the good and sends rain on the just and the unjust. He discusses the matter with his disciples in reference to the man who was born blind. The disciples, under the influence of the popular belief, want to know whether the blindness is due to the man's own sin or to that of his parents. The answer is calculated to turn their minds in another direction: "It was not that this man sinned, or his parents, but that the works of God might be made manifest in him" (John 9:3). The correction has never been lost sight of in the best Christian thinking. The old Jewish belief has often been revived, and naturally, for there is a measure of truth in it. The truth reappears in the writings of Paul, e.g., in Gal. 6:7-8. But it is never the last word in Christian teaching about the problem of pain.

Ps. 125 is a restatement of the popular belief that those who put their trust in the Lord are safe and happy. They are **like Mount Zion,** which stands (or "sits") secure, surrounded by mountains. George Adam Smith in *The Historical Geography of the Holy Land* [8] has shown that Jerusalem was not as impregnable as was imagined. The position was strong, but not so strong that the inhabitants could cease to be vigilant. It had been captured originally, and was again and again to be laid waste. Indeed, if modern scholarship is right, the city at this time was in the hands of invaders. No one can date the psalm with precision or give the name of the author. But the indications are that "God's 'righteous' people are suffering under the heel of foreign occupation." [9] This is important, for it assures us that whoever the psalmist was he was not remote from the trials and torments of life. A city ruled by an invader is not comfortable. To a proud people like the Jews it is intolerable. Yet here is one who is sure that the land will not be left under the sway of knaves (vs. 3), who sings and helps others to sing:

As the mountains are round about Jerusalem,
so the LORD is round about his people,
from this time forth and for evermore.

If we would understand the sublimity of such a faith, it will be well to consider the prose parallel in II Kings 6. There we read of another city, Dothan, besieged by the horses and chariots of Syria. Among the beleaguered people are Elisha the prophet and his servant. How great is the fear of the servant when early in the morning he discovers the encircling host! How calm is the mind of the master because he is sure that the unseen spiritual resources are greater than all those who are drawn up against him! This is the faith that overcomes the world. It is not always an assurance of physical immunity. It is the confidence that whatever hap-

[8] Ch. xiv.

[9] Elmer A. Leslie, *The Psalms* (New York and Nashville: Abingdon-Cokesbury Press, 1949), p. 125.

5 As for such as turn aside unto their crooked ways, the LORD shall lead them forth with the workers of iniquity: *but* peace *shall be* upon Israel.

5 But those who turn aside upon their
crooked ways
the LORD will lead away with evildoers!
Peace be in Israel!

---

ruling class. The identification of the oppressors is beyond us. **Peace be in Israel:** The psalm ends with a liturgical prayer for Israel's peace (cf. 29:11; 122:6-9; 128:6; 131:3; Gal. 6:16).

---

pens to the body the mind can be kept in perfect peace. There was one young minister who, when in August, 1914, war visited Europe, found comfort in the prophetic word: "When thou walkest through the fire, thou shalt not be burned; neither shall the flame kindle upon thee" (Isa. 43:2). The words returned to him later when, sitting in a hospital messroom outside Salonika, he heard an officer tell of being torpedoed in the Mediterranean and saved by an Allied destroyer. They returned yet again when once more war broke in all its fury and threatened to submerge free nations. He was then a pastor in a London suburb where bombs were expected and later came. And once more he spoke to his people, promising them not physical safety but inward peace. Men would die, but truth would prevail. Families might be blotted out, but the church of Jesus Christ would abide. The map of Europe would be changed, but the eternal verities would remain. He continued:

> In the last war a woman assured me that her son would return safely because she had given him a consecrated crucifix and he was wearing it under his tunic. Can we make any promise like that? No. That is superstition and magic, not religion. The rain falleth on the just and on the unjust. And so do the bombs. . . . Yet the promise stands at least in this sense, that the real self is not this bodily presence. The body may be shot or burned or drowned and yet the real self remain untouched. If we are overwhelmed in this proper sense it is only because we ourselves have capitulated. And we invite the enemy to come in whenever we stoop to impurity and deceit and pride. This is the promise of Jesus—not immunity from the physical danger, but peace in the midst of tribulation.[1]

This is the way the N.T. scriptures must be read. We read about Jesus Christ, that he came from God, that he was the Son of God, but he was not exempt from danger and sorrow. In a unique sense he bore the sins of the world. He was tempted and tried. He suffered in body and mind. He was rejected and despised, crucified and buried. Yet—unless it was for a moment upon the cross—he was never alone, never submerged, never defeated. Even in the midst of death agonies he prayed for those who tortured him, forgave those who turned to him, thought of the needs of those he loved, and finally committed himself into the hands of God. The disciples found that following him meant sharing his sufferings, witnessing for him before a hostile world. But while faith held, their hearts were garrisoned by a peace that passed understanding. This is surely the way in which Heb. 11 should be read. The great roll of heroes includes those who "suffered mocking and scourging, and even chains and imprisonment. They were stoned, they were sawn in two, they were killed with the sword," but through all they were "well attested by their faith" (Heb. 11:36-37, 39).

Thus down to our own time divine protection has been a profound reality; but it is the protection a grown son expects from a wise father, rather than that which a helpless babe receives from a mother's arms. It was so with David Livingstone, who started with the faith of psalmist and apostle and continued through African swamps and forests till he died alone in the heart of the Dark Continent. It was so with Mary Slessor, who in spite of natural shrinking pressed on with her service for the children of Calabar, and for the redemption of African slaves. It was so, and still is, with tens of thousands who have never been widely known but who have faced life bravely and carried its burdens courageously. There may be continually changing theories of how God guides and protects, but the facts are beyond dispute.

> If thou but suffer God to guide thee,
> And hope in him through all thy ways,
> He'll give thee strength, whate'er betide thee,
> And bear thee through the evil days;
> Who trusts in God's unchanging love
> Builds on the rock that naught can move.
> . . . .
> Sing, pray, and swerve not from his ways;
> But do thine own part faithfully.
> Trust his rich promises of grace,
> So shall they be fulfilled in thee.
> God never yet forsook at need
> The soul that trusted him indeed.[2]

[1] Frank H. Ballard, *Things Which Cannot Be Shaken* (London: James Clarke & Co., 1939), pp. 16-18. Used by permission.

[2] Georg Neumark, tr. Catherine Winkworth.

A Song of degrees.

126 When the LORD turned again the captivity of Zion, we were like them that dream.

A Song of Ascents.

126 When the LORD restored the fortunes of Zion,[l]
we were like those who dream.

[l] Or *brought back those who returned to Zion*

CXXVI. RESTORE OUR FORTUNES, O LORD (126:1-6)

The psalmist is living in an unhappy time of his people's history. He thinks of the high promise of the period after 537 B.C., when Israel was setting about the rebuilding of the places laid waste by the Babylonians. His conception of that past is colored by what he has read in the prophets (cf. Isa. 55:12-13; Zech. 8:1-23; Hag. 2:1-23) and Ezra, or heard from the lips of the traditionists. In his mind it was a golden age, with so much laughter and joy that the heathen nations were moved to say **the LORD has done great things** for these people. But now all those glad days, as perfect as the visions of a dream, are only a memory. Israel has become as barren of life and hope as the dry wadi beds of the Negeb. However, it is not the purpose of the psalmist to do no more than voice the depression of his people. To his lament over the contrast between Israel's golden age and the present changed fortunes he adds a word of consolation which contains a forecast of a new golden age in which again there will be **shouts of joy:** the tears of the present time are watering the seed of a future harvest of gladness.

This psalm is modeled on the form of the laments which conclude with an oracle giving the divine response to the appeal (cf. 20:6-9; 21:8-12; Hab. 2:1-5; Joel 2:17-19), and should be studied in conjunction with Ps. 85. Such psalms are in structure adapted for liturgical use, and since Israel had frequent experiences of national distress, they served perennially to keep hope alive in the hearts of her people.

The psalm, as shown above, can be understood only in a postexilic setting. For the late use of שׁוב as a Hiphil see 85:1, 4; Deut. 30:3; Nah. 2:2. The meter is 3+2 and 4+2 (or 2+2+2), excepting 2+2 in vs. 5.

1. ZION'S FORMER GLADNESS (126:1-3)

126:1-3. When the LORD restored the fortunes of Zion: There is some divergence in the rendition of the tenses in vss. 1-3. Some (Duhm, Gunkel, Oesterley) believe that

---

126:1-6. *The Poetry of the Full Heart.*—Scholars have explained this psalm in many different ways, but they are agreed that it is one of the most beautiful in the whole of the Psalter. This does not mean that the psalmist has carefully chosen his words and ordered his sentences. It is that he has felt deeply and out of the fullness of the heart the mouth has spoken.

Though the psalm is short, it falls into two parts. The first (vss. 1-3) recalls a great experience in the life of the people, an experience of grief and humiliation from which they had been saved by the goodness of God. The second (vss. 4-6) is a prayer that the Lord will come again and turn their fortunes once more, so that having been like men who sow in tears, they will be like harvesters who come home with ringing cheers and with arms full of sheaves. Thus in a few verses, as J. E. McFadyen says, the psalm passes swiftly through the "vicissitudes of human life—its laughter and tears, sorrow and joy, dejection and exaltation, exile and redemption, spring and autumn, the beautiful dream, and the cruel reality; but the sorrow of it all is swallowed up in the lovely vision with which it ends." [3]

1-3. *Glad Remembrance of Israel's Restoration.*—It is impossible to say with certainty which national deliverance lies behind these verses, but there is general agreement that it points to the conclusion of the Babylonian captivity. The sacking of Jerusalem and the carrying of the flower of the people into exile made a deep impression upon the literature and history of Israel. They could never forget the humiliation of defeat, the hardships of the long journey, the years of homesickness. Families had been scattered, old men had died in a strange land, young people had grown up who had never seen the city of David but who had learned the ancient traditions and idealized

[3] *Studies in Psalms* (London: Student Christian Movement Press, 1916), pp. 112-13.

2 Then was our mouth filled with laughter, and our tongue with singing: then said
they among the heathen, The LORD hath
done great things for them.
3 The LORD hath done great things for
us; *whereof* we are glad.

2 Then our mouth was filled with laughter,
and our tongue with shouts of joy;
then they said among the nations,
"The LORD has done great things for
them."
3 The LORD has done great things for us;
we are glad.

---

the verbs should be translated as futures (cf. Syr.) and that the psalm should be interpreted eschatologically as expressing a hope that in a day to come the promises of Isaiah may be realized. Others (Kittel, Schmidt, Calès, Herkenne) render the verbs as pasts (cf. LXX, Targ., Vulg.). The latter view seems to be preferable on syntactical grounds: all the perfects down to vs. *3b* seem to be relating events that belong to a past experience—e.g., what the heathen said (vs. *2c*)—and the imperfects with the particle אז have the force of perfects (cf. Kautzsch, *Gesenius' Hebrew Grammar,* sec. 107*c*).

The interpretation of the psalm as a sort of lenten liturgy preparatory to the New Year with its promise of revival of life and hope (Mowinckel, Leslie) seems to be oversubtle in reading into the text more than is warranted.

---

what they had learned. Those who in modern times have had contacts with refugees, or who have themselves sent children to places of greater safety, can best understand the heartache, the hopes that wrestled with despair, the joy when at last a return was permitted and once more Jews walked their own streets and rediscovered lost friends. They moved at first like men in a dream. They felt that presently they would awake to discover it was not true. They were dumb with astonishment. Then they became conscious that strange people were saying they were a greatly favored nation, that the Lord had dealt mercifully with them. At last they accepted their restoration with gratitude, their mouths were filled with laughter and their tongues with shouts of joy.

Like all great historical events, the story has its lessons for us. One is that the past, like the present, is very much what we make of it. We can so dwell upon the disasters that the story is sad, even tragic. We can so find good coming out of evil that it is an inspiration for the future. We can so set forth what we have done that men charge us with egoism and conceit. Or we can so tell what has been done to us and through us that men praise our modesty. The differences in autobiographies are not only differences in subject matter; they are differences in interpretation and presentation. It is equally true of history. One man by selecting the mistakes and emphasizing the failures of a nation can minimize its achievements. Another by bringing the best into prominence may inspire heroic action and sustain united effort. The attitude of the religious man to the past is not sentimental or biased. It is an endeavor to state the truth without fear or favor, not only the truth about man's intentions and actions but the truth about God and the working out of his purposes.

Another lesson is that the world is not unconscious of what happens to the people of God. Sometimes the facts are twisted or misinterpreted. But when things happen, conclusions are drawn. If the things are bad, the conclusions will probably be severe. If they are good, sooner or later the verdict will be favorable. The attitude, if it has been hostile, may quickly become friendly. In modern times men may not so easily pass to belief in a supernatural cause as they did in biblical days. But the people of God can never be indifferent to the judgments of those who surround them; for they are passing sentence, for good or evil, not merely upon individuals but upon religion itself. It may sound well when men repeat the words "They say—what say they? Let them say." It may indicate a healthy indifference to rumor and popular clamor. But however indifferent we are to what men say about us, we can never be indifferent to what men say about the faith we profess and the God we worship.

Another lesson is the place of testimony in all life, but especially in the religious life. It is important in domestic life that we should confess indebtedness. If instead of complaints we gave praise where praise is due, there would be fewer family disagreements ending in family tragedies. If instead of taking favors for granted in national life we gave credit to leaders and public servants and remembered how much we owed to the past, there would be greater joy in adding to the common stock and less temptation to demand more than we deserve. Churches too would be transformed if they taught people

4 Turn again our captivity, O LORD, as
the streams in the south.
5 They that sow in tears shall reap in joy.
6 He that goeth forth and weepeth, bearing precious seed, shall doubtless come
again with rejoicing, bringing his sheaves
with him.

4 Restore our fortunes, O LORD,
like the water-courses in the Negeb!
5 May those who sow in tears
reap with shouts of joy!
6 He that goes forth weeping,
bearing the seed for sowing,
shall come home with shouts of joy,
bringing his sheaves with him.

---

2. PRAYER FOR THE LORD'S INTERVENTION (126:4-6)

4-5. Restore our fortunes: The words of vs. 1 are repeated. The prayer is that what once was experienced may be experienced again. **Turn again our captivity:** The KJV is here due to a textual error by which שבית was read for שבות in vss. 1, 4. The error was probably an intentional one by later scribes (see Exeg. on 85:1). **Like the water-courses in the Negeb:** In this region in the south of Palestine the wadi beds (אפיקים) were most of the year waterless, parched, and arid, but when by the mercy of God the rainy season arrived, they ran with streams of life-giving water (cf. Job 6:15-17). Thus may Israel's fortunes be changed so that **they that sow in tears shall reap in joy.**

6. The answer to the prayer of the earlier verses is given like an oracle in a terse and pithy saying of the proverb type (cf. Jer. 12:5). The lesson it communicates is a practical one. There is a law in God's world that first comes the sowing and then follows the harvest. But why is the sowing done with **weeping?** The picture conjured up by the verse is that of a sower who, as he carries his seed sack and does his sowing, at the same time utters a traditional wail or keen, which according to popular belief made the seed

---

in all circumstances to dwell upon the mercies they have received instead of multiplying their troubles. If God did anything for us in our early days, if he has supported us through difficult years and comforted us in bereavement, let us not be silent. Let us tell people not only by the words we speak but by the radiance of our lives. So much of the distress in the world springs from the fact that we want to tell what we have done, not what God has done for us. Afflictions we may keep to ourselves. Blessings we should share. They are neither few nor mean.

The LORD has done great things for us;
we are glad.

4-6. ***Sowing in Tears and Reaping in Joy.***—If the first part of the psalm looks back to great affliction and a great deliverance, the second part suggests first a great need. Life had not been easy for those who returned to Jerusalem. The task of rebuilding the city, the walls, and the temple was enough to test the courage of the best. There was the further task of maintaining the spirit of the people against the allurements and hostility of surrounding enemies. As time passed the sense of a miraculous restoration faded before the constant pressure of such stubborn facts. Even for the leaders the day's work often ended in feelings of despair.

Out of such a need sprang importunate prayer. The faithful turned to God and prayed for another change in fortune. The phrasing of the prayer was suggested by their geographical environment. South of Jerusalem was the thirsty ground known as the Negeb. In the summer the land was barren and the heat pitiless. Every stream was dry, and such men and beasts as remained were faint with thirst. But when autumn came, the rains refreshed the earth and filled the wadies. So, prayed the psalmist and those who repeated his words, so come, O Lord, and change us from frustration to fertility.

They did not however stop with prayer. They were so sure that prayer would be heard and answered that they ventured a bold promise. As the prayer owed something to the physical features of the south land, so the promise owed its form to popular wisdom. They borrowed a familiar proverb and applied it: **They that sow in tears shall reap in joy.** Scholars have found here evidence of a primitive belief that "one must not laugh when he sows, lest he weep when he harvests." [4] They tell us that in Egypt "the sowing of the seed and the covering of it with the soil was like the burying of the god Osiris." [5] We need not dig in the ancient East to know that sowing is always a laborious and often an anxious time. We need go no further than the parable of the sower to learn that

[4] Leslie, *Psalms,* p. 128.
[5] *Ibid.*

A Song of degrees for Solomon.

127 Except the LORD build the house, they labor in vain that build it: except the LORD keep the city, the watchman waketh *but* in vain.

A Song of Ascents. Of Solomon.

127 Unless the LORD builds the house,
those who build it labor in vain.
Unless the LORD watches over the city,
the watchman stays awake in vain.

productive. Back of the custom lay the myth of the death of a god of fertility, e.g., Tammuz, Adonis, Osiris, whose revivification by such a ritual quickened the sown seeds and restored vegetation in the fields (see Gaster, *Thespis,* pp. 50-51). Such a custom could linger on in Israel long after its primitive origin had been forgotten.

Israel was making a sowing with tears. A time of joyous harvesting was confidently predicted for her because of the quality of her sowing (cf. Hos. 10:12). Under the figure of the natural law, the verse alludes to the spiritual law, "Blessed are those who are persecuted for righteousness' sake, for theirs is the kingdom of heaven" (Matt. 5:10).

The text of vs. 6*a* should read הלוך ילך ׃בכה משך הזרע, with the omission of נשא repeated from the following line. The verb משך means to scatter (seed) with a broad cast or sweep; Köhler suggests "carry (in the seed-bag)"; cf. Amos 9:13.

CXXVII. WITHOUT GOD, MAN'S LABOR IS VAIN (127:1-5)

This psalm is to be classed with the samples of wisdom writing which have found a place in the Psalter (cf. Pss. 1; 49; 73; 128). The wisdom writers are concerned with teaching some of the principles and practices the observance of which yields the largest dividends of happiness in this life. Their point of view is secular rather than priestly;

much seed will be wasted. There is, however, some that brings forth plentifully. By an act of faith—and true faith is always venturesome—the psalmist encourages the people to believe that if only they will go steadily on with their sowing they will reap in personal virtue and national advancement.

He that goes forth weeping,
bearing the seed for sowing,
shall come home with shouts of joy,
bringing his sheaves with him.

The psalmist is encouraging men to believe in the happy ending. There are those who will confidently contest the point, saying that it is no more than wishful thinking. In some of its more popular forms it is; yet men persist in the conviction that they are born not for tragedy but for some ultimate good. And in their support they can quote not only the parables of Jesus but his life. Ernest Renan ends his *Life of Jesus* with the Cross. He admits that strange rumors were abroad, but insists that "for the historian the life of Jesus finishes with his last sigh."[6] He is blind to the fact that on such a hypothesis the rise, expansion, and continuance of the Christian church becomes incredible. Actually the N.T. is the most meaningless literature in the world if it does not witness to the happy ending—not only for Jesus Christ but for us. "The central theme of the New Testament," says L. P. Jacks, "is *Immortality*—not the immortality of anybody and everybody, but of *the believer in Christ as risen from the dead.*" If it is not on the surface, it is immediately under it, "the unifying element, holding the parts together and making of the New Testament a unitary whole."[7] The belief may be preached in non-Christian ways, but it is part of the Christian gospel and cannot be discarded as wishful thinking.[8]

Thus Ps. 126 leads us out to great truths which support us in life and comfort us in death. It means that life with God ends in triumph. "Weeping may endure for a night, but joy cometh in the morning" (30:5).

127:1-5. *Unless the Lord Build.*—It may be true that this psalm is made up of two independent fragments of wisdom literature (see Exeg.), but both have the same fundamental thought—that God is working in human affairs, and it is only when man's efforts are in harmony with the divine purpose that true success can be achieved.

The psalmist begins with one of the major concerns of human life, the building of houses. We may assume that one of the chief activities of primitive man was the preparation of rude

[6] Boston: Little, Brown & Co., 1929, p. 402.

[7] *The Confession of an Octogenarian* (London: G. Allen & Unwin, 1942), p. 229.

[8] For an extended treatment of this theme see Frank H. Ballard *Crossing the Bar* (London: James Clarke & Co., 1951), ch. vii.

2 *It is* vain for you to rise up early, to sit up late, to eat the bread of sorrows: *for* so he giveth his beloved sleep.

2 It is in vain that you rise up early, to go
late to rest,
eating the bread of anxious toil;
for[m] he gives to his beloved in sleep.[n]

[m] Another reading is *so*
[n] Or *he gives to his beloved sleep*

they orient themselves to the laity rather than to the cult. Our psalm is in this respect no exception. It appears to be composed of two independent fragments, vss. 1-2, 3-5. But, as in some other examples of wisdom writing, the seemingly disparate elements are really linked together by a common underlying theme (cf. Prov. 11:4-11; 30:24-28), viz., the vanity of human efforts without God (cf. Prov. 10:22).

The presence of the psalm in the pilgrim collection is probably due to the human touch and the freshness and charm of literary expression which it shares with others of the group. In the superscription it is attributed to **Solomon** because **the house** of vs. 1 was understood by later scribal students to be the temple, and the **sleep** of vs. 2 to refer to the incident of I Kings 3:5.

The psalm belongs to a time when teachers of wisdom were inculcating the fear of the Lord as basic to man's happiness and success in life; i.e., the psalm is postexilic. The meter is 3+3 (vss. 1, 3-4); 2+2+2 (vs. 2*a*); 3+4 (vs. 2*b*); 3+2 (vs. 5).

1. Unless the Lord Is There (127:1-2)

127:1-2. The psalmist lists four common human interests which cannot be pursued successfully if God is left out of account. First, **unless the Lord builds the house** the project will come to nought. According to the beliefs of the times, there were mysterious powers

dwellings where he might find shelter, gather his possessions, and maintain his family. And the evolution of the race has been marked by progress in the art of building. There came a time when rich men established themselves in stately mansions, often indifferent to the needs of the poor, who were left to fend for themselves in miserable hovels. Gradually, however, conscience became more sensitive and attempts were made to give all men decent accommodation for growing families. The task has not been easy, especially in recent years when cities and villages have been destroyed in indiscriminate warfare. The building of houses is still one of the major concerns of the race.

What the psalmist has to say about this perpetual activity is **Except the Lord build the house, they labor in vain that build it**—or as we should say, secular services are not enough. It is not enough for architects and town planners and social reformers to take a site, cut it up, and build on it ideal dwellings. That may be done for cows or pigs. But man is a spiritual being with aspirations and feelings that transcend the material world and transport him to realms of mystery. There may be the best of paper schemes, but if the true nature of man is ignored, even the finest of social services will lead to frustration. Let no one imagine that the need of men is met when provision is made for churches where they may worship in freedom, and for schools in which children may be trained in religious knowledge. There is such a thing as building every house in conscious dependence upon the goodness of God. Destroy that spirit, and the plans will defeat themselves. Cultivate it, and they will go on to success. There may seem little difference between the man who builds in a spirit of self-confidence and self-sufficiency and one who remembers that he could do nothing if the material were not provided and he were not endowed with the ability to build; yet that difference is the one thing that matters. Self-confidence leads to pride, pride to selfishness, selfishness to an exaggerated sense of private ownership; reverence leads to personal humility, mutual dependence, and a realization that no man lives or dies to himself. This is the thought that naturally arises in our minds as we read the opening sentence of the psalm. We should have more hope for present plans if it were printed not so much upon the walls of government offices as upon the minds of statesmen and civil servants and local administrators. It is literally and absolutely true that plans made and executed in a purely secular spirit will never satisfy human needs.

Perhaps we are ready now to turn to the second part of the psalm, where the poet is concerned not with the supply of houses but with the families that are to occupy them. This making of homes is an even older occupation

of evil that could curse it with disease, fire, earthquake, or other calamities, but with God as his defense, the builder can build with confidence in the security of the house (cf. 91:9-10; Prov. 21:31).

Second, **unless the LORD watches over the city,** the city in spite of the watchmen's diligence will fall by such things as famine, plague, treachery, or assault (cf. Isa. 26:1; Zech. 2:4-5).

Third, **it is vain for you to rise up early, to sit up late,** for though a man may work from early dawn until late at night, his work will be fruitless unless God crowns it with success. The psalmist is thinking in this case especially of the farmer and his long hours of toil in the fields. מאחרי שבת is, lit., "being late to sit down [to eat]"; the laborer in ancient Israel, like the fellah in modern Palestine, ate his chief meal at the end of the day. **For he gives to his beloved in sleep:** The word כן, here emended to כי, **for,** is difficult to explain. By some it is rendered "what is right" (cf. Prov. 28:2; see Targ. and Franciscus Zorell, *Lexicon hebraicum et aramaicum Veteris Testamenti* [Roma: Pontificium Institutum Biblicum, 1940-], *s.v.*); by others, "such things"; still others would emend it to read אכן, "surely." The reading כי is preferable because (*a*) it is supported by some Hebrew MSS and the LXX (ὅτι=כי); (*b*) כן and כי are elsewhere confused in the M.T. (cf. Jer. 49:19; Hos. 3:4); and (*c*) it suits the context best. These words of the psalmist are not meant to belittle industry but rather to remind men that though (in the words of Matthias Claudius)

> We plough the fields and scatter
> The good seed on the land,
> . . . it is fed and watered
> By God's almighty hand.

(Cf. Mark 4:26-29.) Man's dependence on God is stressed by Jesus (cf. Luke 12:22-31).

---

than the building of houses. Primitive man set about the task in a primitive way; the evolution of the race has largely depended upon domestic progress. There are with us today, it must be confessed, many differences as to the meaning of the ambiguous word "progress." What is not disputed is that in family life there is a great deal of failure. Many people set out too lightheartedly on the great adventure. They fall in love, they marry, they beget children, they set themselves to nourish and train their offspring. Then difficulties arise; there is a clash of wills, sometimes a clash between parents, sometimes between parents and children, and instead of a home to which members of the family return with gratitude, there are "scenes" causing each to go his separate path. We may have progressed in many ways, but we have not been conspicuously successful in the domestic sphere.

The psalmist has a contribution to make to the subject. He tells us in a word that we have no right to expect success if we reduce marriage to a civil contract, and the begetting of children to natural instincts, and the making of homes to chance. We must start with this:

> **Lo, sons are a heritage from the LORD,**
> **the fruit of the womb a reward.**

It makes all the difference to individual and community life if one believes that marriage is not merely for the satisfaction of natural impulses but is a sacred relationship of divine intention and with the highest social ends. We cannot stop the drift to divorce courts by marriage clinics. We must go down with the psalmist to the profoundest realities of life. We must make war on secularism, the great and pervasive enemy of our times, secularism in our own hearts and everywhere in modern society. This is far more vital than most of the matters discussed by our mentors, even in the most select of universities. It is the crying need of our time. Without it we can make no headway.

We must remind ourselves meanwhile, however, that the problem is not simply one of building the city and the home, but of keeping them as well. Maybe the psalmist saw the watchman at the gate or posted upon the walls. Maybe he thought of those who were patrolling the streets and protecting peaceful citizens against evildoers. Men could sleep quietly in their beds knowing that no enemy could approach from outside, no robber could roam at will within the city, without an alarm being sounded.

In our day, when the building is done, we think of the keeping not in terms of isolated

3 Lo, children *are* a heritage of the LORD:
and the fruit of the womb *is his* reward.
4 As arrows *are* in the hand of a mighty
man; so *are* children of the youth.
5 Happy *is* the man that hath his quiver
full of them: they shall not be ashamed, but
they shall speak with the enemies in the
gate.

3 Lo, sons are a heritage from the LORD,
the fruit of the womb a reward.
4 Like arrows in the hand of a warrior
are the sons of one's youth.
5 Happy is the man who has
his quiver full of them!
He shall not be put to shame
when he speaks with his enemies in the gate.

2. SONS, A HERITAGE FROM THE LORD (127:3-5)

3-5. Fourth, if a man will build a family, let him remember that **sons are a heritage from the LORD.** The sons of a man not only ensure the survival of the family line but when they **are the sons of one's youth,** they may be compared to **arrows in the hand of a warrior** for, full grown by the time their father reaches old age, they can defend him against his foes. If he has to answer charges preferred against him before the judges

watchmen but of armies, of conscripted and disciplined youth, of scientists and their inventions, of new forms of massacre and annihilation. We have progressed so far with military science that we are afraid of the weapons we have devised and shrink to think not only of the destruction of enemies but of boomerang effects upon ourselves. Is it not further proof that secular solutions are no solutions, that instead of leading us through to peace and prosperity they raise new fears and problems? The military demands of national defense are no longer rational; they are like the great idols of which we read in childhood days, huge revolting idols that were drawn through crowded streets and beneath whose wheels innocent children were cast by frenzied and superstitious parents. Is it not time we called a halt in this progression toward race suicide? But who will begin? And how can we begin? The answer is here:

Unless the LORD watches over the city,
the watchman stays awake in vain.

It is not that watchmen are wrong and should be abolished, but that the problem of defense takes us far beyond the habiliments of war and includes not only what we have come to call morale but the whole of man, especially the qualities which are distinctive to man. Leave these out, and we exclude the sources of courage and endurance and self-sacrifice, we lose the things that make for unity and co-operation. In short, the one sure line of defense is not in the military sphere. Defense is a spiritual problem. If we had attended to the things of the spirit as carefully as we have attended to guns and gases, battleships and bombers, we might have found ourselves with more friends and fewer foes. We might have found so much less suspicion and hate in the world that, instead of failing to make peace, statesmen would have been able to lead us confidently in the work of reconstruction.

But that is not all the psalmist has to say. In equally simple lines he describes people who rise early and go late to rest, who live day by day in a spirit of anxious toil, and as we read we feel how shortsighted they were. The Hebrews were not prone to inculcate slackness. They were always preaching the gospel of work, and exhorting men to do with their might what their hands found to do. But a strenuous life inspired by a simple faith is one thing; feverish activity incited by a sense of insecurity is another thing.

Unknown to himself, the psalmist was describing the world as it was to be hundreds of years later. He was putting his finger on our besetting sin. Nearly everyone now is tired and excitable. When we are not discussing the causes and possible remedies, we are bracing ourselves to further effort. We refuse to take a lesson from men who have learned to do what they have to do to the best of their ability and then leave the rest to higher hands. So does one come back to the same solution, the religious solution, faith in the power and goodness of God. That, as Jesus of Nazareth made clear many years afterward, is the only effective cure for worry (cf. Matt. 6:25-34).

The concluding line in vs. 2 deserves some comment. The text is probably corrupt and different renderings have been suggested. The rendering in the KJV has been defended by able scholars (e.g., A. F. Kirkpatrick) and in that sense expounded by many preachers: **For so he giveth his beloved sleep.** There is an eloquent sermon in which Charles H. Spurgeon tells how God gives sleep, the sleep of a quiet conscience, of contentment, of freedom from anxiety, and

A Song of degrees.

128 Blessed *is* every one that feareth the LORD; that walketh in his ways.

A Song of Ascents.

128 Blessed is every one who fears the LORD,
who walks in his ways!

---

holding court at the city gate, he will suffer no subversion of justice when he appears with a retinue of stalwart sons. In vs. 5 read with the LXX, לא יבש, **he** [the father] **shall not be put to shame,** and conformably read ידבר, **he** [not the sons] **speaks.**

CXXVIII. BLESSED IS THE GOD-FEARING HOME (128:1-6)

This psalm, like the preceding, is a wisdom psalm. The wisdom writers sought by frequent repetitions and admonitions to impress on their hearers that the fear of the Lord has for its reward prosperity and happiness (cf. Prov. 2:10-22; 3:5-10; 4:5-13). Their writings can be identified both by their style and their themes (cf. 133:1-3; 144:12-15). This psalm is couched in the form of an address to one who belongs to the peasant class. He is told of three blessings that come in the train of his faithful practice of religion: (*a*) the full and peaceful enjoyment of the fruits of his toil; (*b*) numerous offspring; and (*c*) the prosperity of Jerusalem with a long life to rejoice over it.

The date of the psalm is, like that of the other examples of wisdom literature which are impregnated with a religious purpose, postexilic. It should also be noted that **Jerusalem** has become the center of the religious life of Israel (vs. 5). In vs. 3 פריה is an Aramaic form of an active participle. The meter is 3+2, with the exception of 3+3+2 in vs. 5.

1. ENJOYMENT OF THE FRUITS OF LABOR (128:1-2)

128:1-2. The word אשרי, rendered **blessed,** is to be sharply distinguished from the word ברוך, which is also rendered "blessed" (see 1:1). The former, a favorite word of the wise men, has a dynamic and social connotation whereas the latter merely designates an immobile state of "beatitude." **You shall eat the fruit of the labor of your hands:**

---

in which the sleep God gives is contrasted with that which comes from drugs and narcotics. But more recent scholars are almost unanimous in translating the line: **He gives to his beloved in sleep.** The change is slight but significant. There are many gifts which God gives in sleep. He gives physical refreshment. He gives intellectual perception. How often we have gone to bed with unsolved problems and found the answers waiting for us in the morning! He gives peace and moral stability. The fears of nightfall are driven away, and we are able to face life again with new courage. It is easy for us to say that a good sleep made the difference. It was natural for the psalmist to say that God did it in the sleep he gave. In this he was not exceptional. It is the biblical emphasis from Genesis to Revelation. It is the attitude of Jesus, who found it possible to sleep quietly through a storm at sea. It is the teaching of Paul, who is continually saying that man must work out his own salvation and always explaining that it is God who works in him (Phil. 2:12-13), always rendering thanks to God who gives the victory, and always adding "that in the Lord your labor is not in vain" (I Cor. 15:57-58).

This is the conviction of the psalmist. If only the nations could recover that dependence upon God which creates a sturdy independence before men, we should have discovered the secret of peace and contentment, of reconstruction and true progress.

128:1-6. ***Reverence the Basis of the Good Life.*** —This is not a psalm that mothers normally teach their children or enthusiasts select for anthologies. It is not one of the inspired pieces that lift us above ourselves and cause us to sit down in heavenly places. It is more like utilitarian prose than creative poetry, more like O.T. wisdom literature than the work of prophet or seer. We cannot, however, pass it by as of little value, for it is full of sage counsel and makes a strong appeal to practical minds. It has a special message for the man who keeps his feet firmly on the ground, does his daily duty, and leaves to others the great flights of fancy. It helps us also to understand Hebrew mentality. If we would appreciate the genius of the Israelites we must pay special attention to the great dreamers and thinkers, but we must not ignore the shepherd or the craftsman, the worker in the fields or the merchant in the city.

2 For thou shalt eat the labor of thine hands: happy *shalt* thou *be,* and *it shall be* well with thee.

3 Thy wife *shall be* as a fruitful vine by the sides of thine house: thy children like olive plants round about thy table.

2 You shall eat the fruit of the labor of
your hands;
you shall be happy, and it shall be well
with you.

3 Your wife will be like a fruitful vine
within your house;
your children will be like olive shoots
around your table.

Labor means the **fruit** of one's toil. In the history of Israel the peasant farmers often enough went hungry because drought, war, oppression, taxation, or blight deprived them of their normal right to enjoy what they had toiled to produce. For כי, an asseverative particle, in vs. 2, see Kautzsch, *Gesenius' Hebrew Grammar,* sec. 148*d.*

2. Numerous Offspring (128:3-4)

3-4. Your wife . . . within your house: Lit., "in the inner parts of your house," i.e., in the part of the house reserved for women. **Will be like a fruitful vine:** Her children will be numerous, like the clusters hanging from a vine. As her husband looks on his sons

---

We must try to understand their outlook and their habits, the work they did and how they did it. And coming to see the type, which the study of this psalm should help us to do, we should find ourselves in greater sympathy with all those who by their toil still "maintain the fabric of the world."

In every generation men find it necessary to consider afresh the meaning of life. The results have been varied, and the end is not yet in sight. Many have maintained that the chief end of man is to find happiness, but there has been much difference of opinion as to what happiness is and how and where it is to be found. There are those who confuse happiness with pleasure and think it may be found by the immediate satisfaction of the senses. There are others who equate happiness with blessedness and find that the happiness of the individual cannot be envisaged apart from the blessedness of mankind.

The psalmist touches the matter at its deepest point. His concern is not with definition but with the cause. What he says is not original: it is the consistent teaching of the O.T., especially of the wisdom writers.

Blessed is every one who fears the Lord,
who walks in his ways!

Fear, as the psalmist uses the word, means not terror, which is usually destructive of happiness, but reverence. There may be an element of dread in it, but fundamentally it is awe. Hebrew religion passed through many phases, but it was always being brought back to that. There were many superstitions, many forms of idolatry, but it was generally agreed that men must set out upon the great business of life with head and heart bowed before the greatness and the goodness of God.

This instinct of religious awe had some extraordinary developments in Hebrew history. Pious Jews would not so much as repeat the sacred name, nor would their scribes write it. If they met the word as they were copying the scriptures, they would first wash the pen and then write "The Name" or "Adonai." The scrolls themselves were protected with the most scrupulous care. "My son," said one rabbi to a young scribe, "My son, take great heed how thou doest thy work, for thy work is the work of Heaven, lest thou drop or add a letter of the manuscript, and so become a destroyer of the word." [1]

The psalmist, however, is concerned not with this kind of reverence but with that attitude of mind which enables a man to walk uprightly. It includes reverence for truth, for the human soul, for the weakest of God's creatures, for **the labor of your hands.** The Hebrew never doubted the importance of work, especially of manual toil, in the maintenance of society. Worship was essential. But if a man would not work, neither should he eat (II Thess. 3:10). Nor must he be too particular about the character of the work. Greeks and Romans might speak contemptuously of men who worked with their hands, like Cicero, when he said that "the gains of all hired workmen whom we pay for manual toil and not for artistic skill, are ignoble and sordid"; the Jews had had a better training. There were times when they too fell from grace, but Ben Sirach spoke according to the

[1] J. Paterson Smyth, *The Old Documents and the New Bible* (London: Samuel Bagster & Sons, 1890), p. 82.

4 Behold, that thus shall the man be
blessed that feareth the LORD.
5 The LORD shall bless thee out of Zion:
and thou shalt see the good of Jerusalem all
the days of thy life.
6 Yea, thou shalt see thy children's children, *and* peace upon Israel.

4 Lo, thus shall the man be blessed
who fears the LORD.

5 The LORD bless you from Zion!
May you see the prosperity of Jerusalem
all the days of your life!
6 May you see your children's children!
Peace be upon Israel!

---

while they gather about his table, he is reminded of the numerous seedlings that shoot up under a cultivated olive tree. Omit the second word (כי) of vs. 4.

3. PROSPERITY OF JERUSALEM (128:5-6)

5-6. The man who fears the Lord is a man whose happiness is imperfect unless he can see also **the prosperity of Jerusalem.** His interests extend beyond himself and his family to his community, the whole people of the Lord. The promise of the preceding verses becomes in the last strophe a wish, **The LORD bless you from Zion,** perhaps because the use of the psalm in a religious gathering suggested it (cf. Num. 6:24-26).

---

insight of his people when, thinking of manual workers, he said:

They will maintain the fabric of the world,
And in the handiwork of their craft is their prayer
(Ecclus. 38:34).

Both ideas, pagan and Hebrew, passed on into Christendom, and have been contending with one another to this day. Too often Greek and Roman ideas have been conspicuous among ecclesiastics, and sound leadership has come from others like Tolstoy and Carlyle.

There had, however, been many times in Hebrew history when men had worked and not enjoyed the fruit of their labors. In the apparently prosperous times of Jeroboam II rich men treated laborers as slaves and took their produce away. There were other times when foreign foes marched armies into their territory and ransacked the granaries that had so perseveringly been filled. No one can be expected to go on doing his best in the midst of conditions like that. The good life presupposes the maintenance of justice and fair dealing. No land can prosper if there is a widespread fear that all men's labor will be like putting money into a bag with holes (Hag. 1:6).

Look now at vs. 3, which praises fruitful family life, and reads like the main burden of the psalm:

**Your wife will be like a fruitful vine
within your house;
your children will be like olive shoots
around your table.**

This also belonged to the Hebrew ideal. "Marriage," says one O.T. scholar, "was a blessing from God in Israel, and Judaism is the only great faith which has never favoured the moral suicide that bred the monk and the nun."[2] The Christian church inherited this conception of the good life. But elements crept in from other sources and gradually established themselves. We can see the great controversy beginning in the church at Corinth, even in N.T. times. We can see in I Cor. 7 how Paul dealt with it. But in spite of apostolic teaching, ascetic ideas became dominant. In the writings of the Fathers there is frequent insistence upon the glory and the dignity of celibacy. Marriage is not forbidden, but it is referred to as carnal and worldly. In course of time the tendency hardened into the dogma of celibacy of the clergy. "Medieval thought," says G. G. Coulton, "was celibate thought, for good or for evil."[3] It was Martin Luther who turned men's minds once again to the scriptures and proclaimed the innocence and dignity of the married state. He preached it not as something to apologize for but something to rejoice in. And one of the many portions of scripture he cited was Ps. 128. Up to that time expositors had been puzzled. In their perplexity they turned the figure of the **fruitful vine** into an allegory. Even great men like Chrysostom and Augustine did it. The vine, they said, is the church, the spouse of Christ. But truth will out, and it came at length in the Protestant Reformation. Luther was charged with desecrating the cloisters. What he actually did was to sanctify the home. He connected religion once more with the ordinary affairs of

[2] Adam C. Welch, *Jeremiah: His Time and His Work* (London: Oxford University Press, 1928), p. 44.
[3] *Studies in Medieval Thought,* p. 81.

A Song of degrees.

129 Many a time have they afflicted me from my youth, may Israel now say:

A Song of Ascents.

129 "Sorely have they afflicted me from my youth,"
let Israel now say —

May you see your children's children: Two cherished blessings are invoked here, a long life and a family line fortified by many descendants. **Peace be upon Israel:** Once again the prayer for Israel's welfare is repeated because the hopes of all that fear the Lord center in her, for all their springs are in her (cf. 87:5-7). For similar benedictory utterances at the close of psalms see 125:5; 131:3; 134:3.

CXXIX. May Israel's Oppressors Be Put to Shame (129:1-8)

This psalm has been included among the pilgrim psalms because, like others of the group, it relates to a matter which was of concern to the devout souls which made up the pilgrim bands. Many a Jew was depressed when he contemplated the long struggle of his people for survival in the midst of an unfriendly world (vss. 1-2). The psalmist therefore turns the mind of his fellows to the more cheering aspect of their history, viz., that despite its foes, Israel has prevailed by God's grace and lives on (vs. 4).

The psalm is of a mixed type. The first part (vss. 1-4) is a brief song of trust (cf. Pss. 23; 131); the second part (vss. 5-8) resembles an imprecatory psalm (cf. Ps. 137). Like other poets of the Pilgrim collection, the psalmist clothes his thought with lively and original metaphors or similes. He begins by using the metaphor of a plowed field

life and prepared the way for the abandonment of a false distinction between the secular and the sacred. When he, a monk, married Katharina von Bora, the one-time nun, it was like an atomic bomb which shook the ecclesiastical world. We need not oversimplify it to the point of saying that all the good was on one side and all the evil on the other. But it is to be hoped that Christendom will never return to such false asceticism.

These things remind us again of Tolstoy. Reverence, work, especially manual work, the dignity of domestic life—these were thoughts to which he constantly returned. He had his difficulties with them all, especially with the last. He was so plagued by the problems of life that he meditated suicide. At length he discovered, or so he thought, one section of the community, the peasants, to whom life was not an evil thing. He studied them and worked with them and found that their belief in life came from their simple religious faith and their laborious habits. As he shared their lot and entered into their experience he not only came to respect them, he found a gospel to preach and to live by. To fear God, work steadily, and honor all men—that gives life meaning and old age dignity.

Tolstoy is now in the main a neglected prophet. More modern leaders have praised what they call wholesome irreverence. They have something relevant to say. It is necessary to poke fun at things men take too seriously. Someone must expose the shams and ridicule the pomposities we tolerate. "The spirit of irreverence," says so sound a teacher as A. D. Lindsay, then master of Balliol, "a spirit of dry and even cynical humour, is a most wholesome corrective to that sham seriousness to which human nature is so much inclined."[4] It is, however, a dangerous habit to form; so dangerous that without noticing it we may slip into a cynicism that laughs not only at the shams but even at profound realities. It is better to praise the good than to mock the foibles of humanity. Even when we have outgrown primitive ideas and practices, we should be careful not to pour scorn on that which to others is sacred. The time may come when we shall realize that many of the very forms and habits which some are inclined to ridicule may and often do convey truths that have permanent worth. If we revere men as the children of God, we shall not make light of them, though we may have outgrown some of their ways. The foundation of such courtesy is lost if we cease to fear God. There are no limits to the personal and social effects of the psalmist's assurance:

**Blessed is every one who fears the Lord,
who walks in his ways!**

129:1-8. ***Persecuted for Righteousness' Sake.***— This psalm reminds us, not in thought only but in language and structure, of Ps. 124. We see a Hebrew indulging, as so many Hebrews did,

[4] *The Moral Teaching of Jesus* (London: Hodder & Stoughton, 1937), p. 78.

2 Many a time have they afflicted me from my youth: yet they have not prevailed against me.
3 The plowers plowed upon my back: they made long their furrows.
4 The LORD *is* righteous: he hath cut asunder the cords of the wicked.

2 "Sorely have they afflicted me from my
youth,
yet they have not prevailed against me.
3 The plowers plowed upon my back;
they made long their furrows."
4 The LORD is righteous;
he has cut the cords of the wicked.

---

to illustrate the succession of afflictions which Israel has suffered in the course of its history, but the metaphor of the field scarred by furrows becomes itself a metaphor for the ridges raised by the plowman's rod on the flesh of the beast bound to the plow. The one metaphor dissolves into the other. In the second part the psalmist compares the lot of the weed which grows on the walls of Eastern houses with that of the grain in the fields of the farmer. The one grows unwelcome, uncared for, destined to an early end when the hot sun beats upon it; the other is an object of many blessings as men, passing along the way, look on it with interest and hope. In this comparison the psalmist sees mirrored the contrasting fates of the wicked and the righteous.

The date of the psalm is late. The psalmist is living remote from the times when the afflictions of Israel were attributed to its sins and apostasies. The vocabulary betrays late or Aramaic influences: e.g., רבת (vss. 1-2); ל as *nota accusativi* (vs. 3); מענה as "furrow" (vs. 3); שלף "come to stalk" (vs. 6); שקדמת (vs. 6). The meter is 3+2, excepting 4+2 in vs. 7 and 3+3+4 in vs. 8.

1. A Song of Trust (129:1-4)

129:1-4. Sorely have they afflicted me: Lit., "very much" or "very greatly," etc.; i.e., the afflictions have been great both in number and in degree. In a long retrospect of

---

in retrospect: he is concerned less with his own personal life than with the long history of the people of Israel. We imagine him dreaming of Moses and the Exodus, Joshua and the entry into the Land of Promise. He does not pause with these great achievements, but presses on swifter than light or sound through the times of judges, prophets, and kings, through victories and disasters. There are happy incidents upon which it would be pleasant to linger, but what impresses itself most upon his mind is the presence of suffering. Being a man of some originality, he expresses himself in a memorable figure of speech. In a single couplet he suggests the patient plowman driving oxen across the hard field and leaving behind deep and straight furrows. And, he says, Israel's back had been seared as that field is seared: **The plowers plowed upon my back: they made long their furrows.**

No one welcomes suffering like that. Wherever it is found we are prepared for sharp reproaches addressed to those who cause the suffering (vss. 5-8). We may regret the presence of such reproaches in sacred scriptures, but the Bible is always human and truthful, and tells us not what we think we ought to find but what actually is. We do well also to remember that we have been guilty of the same thing, and with far less excuse. We have suffered, or our friends have suffered, and we have given vent to our feelings, or acquiesced when others have poured forth vindictive speech. Why should we be shocked by such expressions in the O.T. if we excuse them in ourselves and our contemporaries? Moreover, we have what the psalmist had not. We have heard from our youth up exhortations to forgiveness. We have had much more: we have had the one perfect example of uncomplaining mercy. We have seen with the eyes of faith One who came in the form of a servant, have seen him persecuted and crucified, yet praying for the men who drove in the nails. How can we find fault with those of ancient times who had no such teaching or example?

But what is said of those who have tyrannized over the people of God?

May all who hate Zion
be put to shame and turned backward!

Then comes another figure of speech that suggests the countryman:

Let them be like the grass on the housetops,
which withers before it grows up.

Wild grasses and cultivated flowers which grow upon the roof are soon destroyed by wind and sun. Let what remains lie where it has fallen,

5 Let them all be confounded and turned back that hate Zion.

6 Let them be as the grass *upon* the housetops, which withereth afore it groweth up:

5 May all who hate Zion
be put to shame and turned backward!
6 Let them be like the grass on the housetops,
which withers before it grows up,

---

history the psalmist, speaking for his people, can recall what Israel has suffered at the hands of Canaanites, Philistines, Aramaeans (I Kings 20; II Kings 6), Assyrians (II Kings 18–19), Chaldeans (II Kings 25), and others such as the Persians and their successors in postexilic times. But **the Lord is righteous** (or "the Lord, the righteous One") because he is loyal to what is right and vindicates the right, redeeming and delivering his people (cf. Isa. 45:24-25; Neh. 9:8). **He has cut the cords of the wicked:** The **wicked** in this instance are the pagan peoples.

2. An Imprecation on Zion's Foes (129:5-8)

5-8. May all who hate Zion: The replacement of **Israel** (vs. 1) by **Zion** here may be explained by assuming that the two parts of the psalm were originally independent compositions. In any case, the psalmist is aware that those **who hate Zion** are not all of the past; it still has to contend with outer and inner foes. **Let them be like the grass on the housetops:** The imprecation is much less passionate than that in Ps. 137; in fact, it may be no more than a prediction of the sorry end of Zion's foes, i.e., "they shall be like the grass" (cf. 1:4). **Before it grows up:** Better, "before it comes to stalk." For the verb cf. the Akkadian *šulpu,* "stalk" and Symm. ἐκκαύλησαι (see G. R. Driver, "Studies in the Vocabulary of the Old Testament," *Journal of Theological Studies,* XXXI [1930], 277).

---

dead and useless. It is not worth harvesting. So, says the psalmist, let the enemies of Israel be: **Like the grass . . . with which the reaper does not fill his hand or the binder of sheaves his bosom.**

And more, let them be like workers in the harvest field who receive no friendly greeting, no pious blessing, from those who pass by. Let them be left alone without neighborly recognition or religious benediction, for they have excluded themselves from such marks of fellowship. Let them be as those whom men pass and never say:

> **"The blessing of the Lord be upon you!**
> **We bless you in the name of the Lord!"**

It is not the language of Jesus, and such rebukes are not seemly upon the lips of his disciples. Yet they have often been there, and still more often are such sentiments found in Christian hearts. We have seen and heard much evidence of it in the modern world: we are still suffering from the evil aftereffects of bitter and widespread hatred.

Alongside such marks of animosity, however, the psalmist confesses to great wonder. Though the people had been persecuted, they had not been obliterated. He might indeed have confessed with many of a later date that "the blood of the martyrs is the seed of the church."[5] It is not always true that persecution is ineffective. Truth can be suppressed by force, if not forever, for a very long time.

> In Spain and Italy in the sixteenth century governments successfully framed public opinion in such a way as to crush Protestantism. In Russia to-day the Government has cut off the recruits to Christian population by its educational campaign; and it is producing a new generation as innocent of Christianity as eighteenth century Spain was of Protestantism.[6]

Yet again and again through the centuries men have marveled, as the psalmist marveled, how enduring truth is, and how in the end those who are persecuted for righteousness' sake prevail. This is not because of their own wisdom or courage or tenacity. In the last analysis it is because **the Lord is righteous.** Just so, as the psalmist marveled at the permanence of a persecuted nation, we too can wonder and rejoice as we think of the continuity of the church. The powers of death have not prevailed against it (Matt. 16:18). As Théodore de Bèze is reported to have said: "The church is an anvil which has worn out many hammers." It is not because the church is above reproach, but because God protects his own.

Attempts have been made to date the psalm.

[5] Tertullian *Apology* L. 13.

[6] Bernard L. Manning, *Essays in Orthodox Dissent* (London: Independent Press, 1939), p. 128.

7 Wherewith the mower filleth not his hand; nor he that bindeth sheaves his bosom.
8 Neither do they which go by say, The blessing of the LORD *be* upon you: we bless you in the name of the LORD.

7 with which the reaper does not fill his
hand
or the binder of sheaves his bosom,
8 while those who pass by do not say,
"The blessing of the LORD be upon you!
We bless you in the name of the LORD!"

His bosom: The **reaper,** holding the stalks by his hand, applies the sickle, and after him comes the binder who gathers the cut stalks into the bosom of his garment until he has enough to bind into a sheaf. **The blessing of the LORD be upon you:** The psalmist gives us a pleasing picture of the exchange of greetings between the passers-by and the harvesters. The blessings are not only polite salutations or conventional courtesies but according to the beliefs of the time, they have real beneficent effects; the more of them pronounced on field and crop, the richer the yield will be. Everyone, the psalmist means to say, has a good wish for the grain but none for the weeds on the housetops.

Some have tried to fit it into the times of Judas Maccabaeus. Others have argued for the exile in Babylon and the ultimate return to Jerusalem. It may be more profitable to take our stand with the modern Jew as he looks back from the twentieth century and ponders the more recent history of his people.

All national records are moving if only we know how to read them, but how inexplicable is this story! In well-nigh every generation the Jews have been a disliked and persecuted race. It is not because they are stupid. It is not extravagant to say that they are among the ablest of mankind. It is not because they are notoriously wicked. Their faults have been many and great, but so have their virtues. Whatever the explanation, they have rarely been strangers to suffering. William R. Inge in one of his essays gives a few high lights—how the Emperor Tiberius banished four thousand of them to Sardinia, causing Tacitus to say that if they died from the unhealthiness of the climate, it would be a cheap loss; how Edward I drove them from England; how batches were burned in the Spanish Inquisition; and how Louis IX of France, later canonized, when asked how a Jew should be answered, replied: "The best answer a layman can make to a contumacious Jew is to run his sword into him as far is it will go." [7]

It would be easy to add details and extend the list. We could recall, for example, how on All Saints' Day, 1290, the day appointed by Edward I for the expulsion from England, one master mariner defied the royal command that the Jews should be allowed to go in peace, dumped his shipload on a sandbank and bade the poor refugees pray to Moses for deliverance. Actually most of them escaped, and the master mariner was hanged; but his action was an indication of popular opinion. We could quote from book after book to show that

> the Jews of the Middle Ages were a people with no rights, because they could not become members of any community. . . . Hence the constantly repeated laws that the Jews must wear distinctive dresses, so that they might never be mistaken for Christians nor enter into familiar relations with the believers.[8]

But never were the records blacker than in recent times. The modern persecution of the Jew did not begin with Hitler, though it became most ferocious under his regime. Some of us cannot forget the exiles who sought refuge in friendlier countries, their poverty, their tales of cruelty, their concern for kinsmen left behind. We can hardly believe that a century which opened with such kindly sentiments, such prospects for reform, such dreams of universal peace, could, before it had half run its course, give itself over to such brutality.

Yet the Israelites not only survive, they seem to flourish. Not only have their sons and daughters taken conspicuous places in government, in learning, in art and music, and particularly in business and finance; they have won a foothold in the Holy Land, have received the recognition of other peoples, and have established themselves in the councils of the nations. They may still be charged with peculiar faults as well as distinctive abilities, but they are not to be placed among the degenerate.

How is it to be explained? Men may hesitate to say with the psalmist that it is the Lord's doing. But their religious faith has been one of the secrets, perhaps *the* secret. We must

[7] Quoted in William R. Inge, *A Rustic Moralist* (New York: G. P. Putnam's Sons, 1937), p. 242.

[8] F. J. Foakes Jackson, "The Rise of the Nations," in A. S. Peake and R. G. Parsons, eds., *An Outline of Christianity* (London: The Waverley Book Co., n.d.), II, 352-53.

A Song of degrees.

130 Out of the depths have I cried unto thee, O Lord.

A Song of Ascents.

130 Out of the depths I cry to thee, O Lord!

CXXX. My Soul Waits for the Lord (130:1-8)

This psalm is universally regarded as one of the gems of the Psalter. Revealing nothing about the concrete situation out of which his cry emerges, the psalmist voices rather the deep distress of his soul as he waits patiently for the Lord's answer to his prayer for relief from the spiritual burden of unforgiven sin. Within the compass of his brief prayer he so genuinely translates into language the poignancy of man's sense of estrangement from God through sin, and of his passionate longing for restoration to divine favor, that his words have throughout the centuries been used as a vehicle of prayer by all who seek anxiously an absolving word from the Lord. Further, separated from their context, vss. 1-2 have served as a word of petition for deliverance from any trial of the flesh or the spirit which it is the lot of humankind to suffer.

A penitential prayer such as this psalm differs from the class of psalms designated laments only in the prominence which it gives to the element of confession of sin (cf. Ps. 51). We do not know in this instance what is the precise form of the affliction or trouble which has brought the psalmist to the point where he despairs of his life as he

---

remember the cohesive power of synagogue worship and fellowship. If this were to decline, as it is reported to be declining, could racial continuity be maintained? The question is important in itself, but it leads on to greater considerations about the place of religion in the progress of the whole human race.

130:1-8. ***Man's Sin and God's Forgiveness.***— When Martin Luther was asked which he believed to be the greatest of the psalms, he replied without hesitation, "The Pauline ones." When invited to be more explicit, he named Pss. 32; 51; 130; and 143.[9] These, it is hardly necessary to say, are four of the penitential psalms. There will be some, perhaps many, who will immediately add that the verdict shows how far the great reformer is removed from the modern world. The modern world, we are told, is not worrying itself about sin.

There we must at once join issue. The modern world does not accept the language of Martin Luther, but there is nothing the world is more worried about than "sin": the thing, if not the word. It may be someone else's sin, which only shows how low we have fallen; but human sin is the ultimate problem, the one subject that is always worth discussing. Pick up the ephemeral writing of the hack journalist, and you will find it there. Turn to the more serious literature of the times, and it is there. The best writing, as in previous centuries, is concerned with man's distress when he compares life as he has made it with life as he has seen it in moments of insight and high seriousness.

Let us consider the subject under four headings: First this, that though as Paul says, "All have sinned, and come short of the glory of God" (Rom. 3:23), all have not realized in any vital or personal sense that they are sinners. They know that they are not perfect. They will say with the great congregation that they are "miserable offenders." But the sense of sin is vague. They class themselves with an imperfect humanity instead of feeling, as this psalmist feels, the burden and the shame of their own weakness and guilt. But it is only as a personal fact that sin can be properly appreciated. We know what sin is only when we know it about ourselves.

Recall the dramatic O.T. chapter which tells how Nathan the prophet came before David the king with a story of outrage and robbery. It was just the kind of story to stir the anger of David: a story of how a rich man with many fine flocks had feasted his visitor, not on a lamb or a calf from his own well-filled fields, but on the one ewe lamb of his poor neighbor, which he had taken and killed. And David exclaimed: "As the Lord liveth, the man that hath done this thing shall surely die" (II Sam. 12:5). We need not look far to find men who speak like that. If, however, a prophet should turn upon them, as Nathan turned upon David, would they seek to excuse themselves? David humbly accepted the accusation. "I have sinned against the Lord," he cried, and never did the nobility of the man so clearly stand revealed as in that prompt and unqualified confession.

Here is a fundamental difference. We divide ourselves at every level—rich men and poor men, conservatives and liberals, Catholics and

[9] Ker, *Psalms in History and Biography*, p. 58.

2 Lord, hear my voice: let thine ears be attentive to the voice of my supplications.

2 Lord, hear my voice!
Let thy ears be attentive
to the voice of my supplications!

sinks in the deep waters of the underworld, the region of the dead. But we are given the reasons by which he hopes to move God to listen to his appeal. First, he pleads the common frailty of man (vs. 3) ; none is free from iniquity. Second, God alone can forgive, and it is through his exercise of his power to forgive that men are moved to fear him as the only source of their peace (vs. 4) . Third, the poet expresses his confidence that help from the Lord, though it may tarry, will come as surely as the morning follows the night (cf. 119:81-88; 138:3; Luke 8:48) . In the concluding strophe his thoughts turn from himself to his people as he urges Israel to learn from him to look in hope to the Lord for the day of her blessedness.

The date is late. It is to be noted that the author makes no mention of atoning sacrifices. His sense of sin is too deep for the old concepts. He views his problem as one of spiritual relationships between himself and God. The vocabulary of the psalm includes two late words: קשבות, **attentive** (vs. 2) and סליחה, **forgiveness** (vs. 4) .

With the omission of אדני, **Lord,** in vss. 2, 3 and of the dittography of שמרים לבקר, **watchmen for the morning** (vs. 6) , the meter is 3+2, except for the instance of 3+3+3 in vs. 7.

1. Appeal to the Lord (130:1-2)

130:1-2. Out of the depths: Cf. Isa. 51:10; Ezek. 27:34. The reference is to the great deep *tehôm,* the engulfing waters of Sheol into which the dead sink (cf. Jonah 2:3) . The psalmist is troubled not so much by the imminence of death, which these words literally imply, as by the spiritual fact of his alienation from God. It is not so much the dying, so to speak, as the why of it that weighs upon his soul. **I cry:** Better than **have I cried** (see Kautzsch, *Gesenius' Hebrew Grammar,* sec. 106*i*) .

Protestants, Baptists and Methodists—but a more significant separation takes place when one comes to such a parable as that of the Pharisee and the publican. On the one hand stands the self-satisfied man, quick to condemn his neighbor, slow to acknowledge faults in himself. On the other hand stands the truly penitent man who is so concerned with crying to God for mercy that he has no time to magnify the wrongdoing of those who surround him.

This is the difference between holiness as the N.T. understands it, and ecclesiastical saintliness as it has been popularly interpreted. It is always the holiest of men who are the most penitent. "When I look at my sinfulness," says Samuel Rutherford, "my salvation is to me my Saviour's greatest miracle."[1] "My daughters," St. Teresa is reported to have said on her deathbed, "do not follow my example; for I have been the most sinful woman in all the world."[2] The confessions often sound exaggerated, as when Paul calls himself "the chief of sinners." But whether we find it here in the penitential psalms, or in the *Confessions* of Augustine or in the *Grace Abounding* of Bunyan, there is always the mark of intensity and a sense of reality. The Nietzschean school of philosophy says that this sense of sin is a disease which man has caught by the way, and of which at all costs he must rid himself. The Christians, with centuries of experience behind them, declare it to be the measure of the soul's growth. It is the true artist who knows how far the labor of his hands falls short of the ideal. It is the amateur who boasts and commends his own work. There is of course a false humility as well as a superficial vanity, and both are morally objectionable. It is none the less true that the sense of imperfection is a mark of progress, and the intensity of it indicates the height to which a man has risen.

Second, though all have sinned, all have not sinned equally. It may be said that the statement is too obvious to need comment. Thinking of our neighbors, we smile at A's weaknesses and pardon them as "foibles." We are not so indulgent with B. We resent his misdemeanors and speak sharply about them. So with ourselves. There are faults that we think of as trivial and quickly dismiss. There are others that hang like a cloud upon the mind and cause prolonged distress.

[1] Quoted in Alexander Whyte, *The Apostle Paul* (Edinburgh: Oliphant, Anderson & Ferrier, 1903), p. 107.
[2] *Ibid.,* p. 108.

3 If thou, LORD, shouldest mark iniquities, O Lord, who shall stand?
4 But *there is* forgiveness with thee, that thou mayest be feared.

3 If thou, O LORD, shouldst mark iniquities,
Lord, who could stand?
4 But there is forgiveness with thee,
that thou mayest be feared.

2. THE LORD'S GREAT MERCY (130:3-4)

3-4. Who could stand? If God should institute judgment, no man would be acquitted (cf. Mal. 3:2) ; rather he would have to fall down and make intercession to his judge (cf. Job 9:15) .

But how valid are these distinctions of which we are so fond? Alfred William Momerie in his book *The Origin of Evil* says that we distinguish between great and little sins after the manner of the law. Sins of the tongue, like rash speech and nasty insinuations, are not likely to lead to law court proceedings; hence the public regard them as "little sins." Legal proceedings are taken against open and violent slander; hence that is considered a "great sin." Actually the senseless scandal may do more harm than the public attack, and certainly the N.T. gives no warrant for regarding it as less heinous. It may be full of deceit and cowardice and malice, while the open attack may at least be heroic and spring from good motives. " 'A little sin' "—if there were such a thing—"would be one that did little harm." But it is exactly the sins commonly called little which are constantly repeated. Hence in the long run it is these sins that do the greatest amount of mischief. "A man cannot commit many murders. He is generally hanged for the first, and there is an end of him. But the sins of temper and of speech and of heart, the sins of unkindness, of unneighborliness, of selfishness, are sins which we can go on committing without fear of punishment, every day, every hour, every moment. The amount of suffering, therefore, which can be inflicted by them is practically infinite." There is no need for us to warn one another against murder, adultery, forgery, rape: these we regard as "big sins" and we are on our guard. We do, however, need to be warned against sins which may be regarded as trivial. "A number of very little sins will make a very great sinner." [3]

With such thoughts in mind it becomes unnecessary to speculate as to the particular sin that lies behind Ps. 130. It may indeed be a great crime. But where the heart is tender and the conscience sensitive, even little deeds of unkindness, even careless and uncharitable speech, even an opportunity of service let slip, will cause the most grievous penitence.

We come now to the third proposition, that though all have sinned, not all have realized the true character of sin. The definitions of sin are legion, and the standards by which men judge what is right and what is wrong are many. The ancient Babylonians thought it wrong to point with a finger at fire or to sit facing the sun. The Pharisees thought it wrong to deviate a hair's breadth from the tradition of the elders. According to Jesus, sin is the contradiction of life's highest law—the law of love. It is more: it is rebellion against God.

That sin is an offense against oneself and against one's fellows is popular sentiment. Suppose we go back to Nathaniel Hawthorne and *The Scarlet Letter,* which is a study in conscience and penitence as well as a remarkable story. We are made to see how sin eats its way into the soul like a cancer, and how it affects others besides the sinner. Hawthorne, perhaps unwittingly, turned his art into a pulpit and preached a sermon on the text: "Be sure your sin will find you out" (Num. 32:23) . What is the use of success as a minister of the Word, or of popularity in a congregation, or anywhere else for that matter, if remorse is eating deeper and deeper into the heart? We might cite many other works in the same field, and fill pages with quotations from Hardy and Galsworthy and Bernard Shaw, etc. There is, however, one aspect of the subject, and this is the essentially religious aspect, upon which they rarely touch. David's cry was: "I have sinned against the LORD." The psalmist's exclamation is

Out of the depths I cry to thee, O LORD!
LORD, hear my voice!

It is this realization that sin is an offense against God which is missing in so much modern writing. And the greatness and the terror of sin never really grip us until we know this—until indeed we see and feel that our transgressions are not merely violations of divine law but the repudiation of divine love. That surely is what the old preachers meant by the solemn phrase, "the extreme sinfulness of sin."

Fourth, though all have sinned, none has sinned beyond forgiveness. Here again the Christian pulpit is left to complete what many a secular writer starts and leaves. Poets and novelists are not satisfied—they never have been satisfied—simply to record the deeds of male-

[3] Edinburgh: William Blackwood & Sons, 1890, pp. 88-89, 93-94.

5 I wait for the LORD, my soul doth wait, and in his word do I hope.
6 My soul *waiteth* for the Lord more than they that watch for the morning: *I say, more than* they that watch for the morning.

5 I wait for the LORD, my soul waits,
and in his word I hope;
6 my soul waits for the LORD
more than watchmen for the morning,
more than watchmen for the morning.

3. The Psalmist Awaits Forgiveness (130:5-6)

5-6. In vs. 5 read **in his word** instead of the M.T. "and for his word." **His word** is the sign of divine pardon and all that follows it. **More than watchmen for the morning:** The **watchmen,** who are on guard on the walls of a city or about a sleeping caravan, find the hours of the night long and look impatiently for the first rays of the morning.

factors. They must show the results. And so again and again we find them returning to the doctrine of retribution. They take a N.T. verse and neglect the context. The thought underlying book after book by George Eliot and her successors is "Whatsoever a man soweth, that shall he also reap" (Gal. 6:7). Preachers and theologians have stressed the fact that the harvest of sin is to be seen in what a man misses more than in what he suffers, and in what he is in mind and heart more than in the external results. It is to be seen in a deterioration of character, a blunting of moral sensibility, confusion in ethical judgment, and failure in sustained effort in noble causes. The secular writers, George Meredith, H. G. Wells, Arnold Bennett, and crowds of lesser men, depict the visible deterioration, the open failures, and the worldly consequences. Someone has said that

> no prophet of righteousness ever bound sin and its consequences more firmly together, or proclaimed with more solemn emphasis the certainty of the evildoer's doom [than George Eliot]. "Our deeds are like children that are born to us," she says, "nay, children may be strangled, but deeds never" . . . . If we have done wrong, it is in vain we cry for mercy. We are taken by the throat and delivered over to the tormentors until we have paid the uttermost farthing.[4]

What a fierce justice there is in *Adam Bede.* Retribution is more certain than that tomorrow the sun will rise. He who sows the wind must reap the whirlwind (Hos. 8:7).

There is a truth here that must be taught in a world like this. There is, however, another truth, a profounder truth, a religious truth—the reality of forgiveness. The psalmist knew it:

> **If thou, O LORD, shouldst mark iniquities,**
> **Lord, who could stand?**
> **But there is forgiveness with thee,**
> **that thou mayest be feared.**

Surely this is one of the deepest notes of religion, too little heard in modern preaching. It is not only gratitude for sins forgiven, but awe in the presence of the God who forgives. It is not a feeling of relief that the burden of guilt has been removed, but holy joy that one can live all one's days in the consciousness of divine mercy.

The same note is repeated with characteristic emphasis by the prophet Hosea, who had been deserted by his own wife, yet found in his heart not resentment but forgiveness, and knew that the instinct to forgive was from above. "How shall I give thee up, Ephraim? how shall I deliver thee, Israel?" (Hos. 11:8.) But the N.T. is the *locus classicus* for the study of the forgiveness of God and its effects upon the penitent sinner. What is so worthy of study as the life and teaching of Jesus in this connection? Where can one better take one's stand than at the foot of the cross, whence "sorrow and love flow mingled down"? What theme more worthy of further attention than the thought and experience of the men who have seen him there, and with Isaac Watts have cried,

> My richest gain I count but loss,
> And pour contempt on all my pride.[5]

What an assurance to offer a despairing generation!

> For the love of God is broader
> Than the measure of man's mind.[6]

We have seen an inadequacy in this respect in secular writers. But let us go back to Mark Rutherford to see one who had a glimpse of this glorious gospel. Rutherford—or William Hale White, to use his proper name—is often referred to as a pessimist, even as a free thinker; but what he took away with one hand he was apt to offer with the other. In *Catherine Furze* he tells how a man out of jealousy and malice bears false witness against one of his fellow workmen. He charges him with robbery, and has him disgraced and discharged. At length the

[4] George Jackson, *The Teaching of Jesus* (New York: A. C. Armstrong & Son, 1903), p. 121.

[5] "When I survey the wondrous cross."

[6] Frederick William Faber, "There's a wideness in God's mercy."

7 Let Israel hope in the LORD: for with the LORD *there is* mercy, and with him *is* plenteous redemption.
8 And he shall redeem Israel from all his iniquities.

7 O Israel, hope in the LORD!
For with the LORD there is steadfast love,
and with him is plenteous redemption.
8 And he will redeem Israel
from all his iniquities.

A Song of degrees of David.

131 LORD, my heart is not haughty, nor mine eyes lofty: neither do I exercise myself in great matters, or in things too high for me.

A Song of Ascents. Of David.

131 O LORD, my heart is not lifted up,
my eyes are not raised too high;
I do not occupy myself with things
too great and too marvelous for me.

4. ISRAEL'S HOPE IS IN THE LORD (130:7-8)

7-8. With him is plenteous redemption: Lit., "redemption abundantly," not "manifoldly" (Ehrlich). The meaning is not that the Lord has various kinds of redemption, but a plenitude of the kindness that operates to deliver men from trouble, danger, and death (see S. R. Driver, *A Critical and Exegetical Commentary on Deuteronomy* [New York: Charles Scribner's Sons, 1895; "International Critical Commentary"], p. 101). **From all his iniquities:** I.e., from all the penalties for his guilt.

CXXXI. QUIETNESS OF SOUL (131:1-3)

This is a song of trust (cf. Pss. 4; 11; 16; 23; 27A; 62). This type of psalm was in its origin a sequel to a lament. After a suppliant had received a favorable answer to his appeal for help, he was sometimes moved in gratitude to tell of the state of peace with the Lord into which he had been brought through his experience of the divine goodness and saving power. Later the song of trust emerged as a distinct type of composition without any immediate dependence on the lament. Still, there are evidences in each of them that the serenity of the psalmist's soul has been won out of some distress or sorrow through which he has passed.

This psalm was written, as Schmidt says, by a hot-blooded man. Once he had a heart that craved wealth, luxury, and pleasure, eyes that were set on power and station, and a mind that busied itself with matters beyond its ability to understand. He was in consequence full of unrest, for pride, envy, and pretentiousness gave him no peace. But now all this has been changed. In contrast to his old restless self, he has become **like a child quieted at its mother's breast.** What has effected the change? Has he become

hand of God is laid upon the conscience-stricken accuser, and one of the most powerful passages in the book is where the man makes confession before his employer and the one he has wronged. In the concluding pages we see him turning from remorse to repentance, coming through repentance to forgiveness, and finally to service. So he ends his life, never slurring over his offense or congratulating himself that he has risen above such meanness, but rejoicing in the love that saved him and giving himself in labor for others till laboring days are done. It is a reminder that much of the noblest work in the world is wrought by men who have fallen but who have redeemed themselves by the love with which they have been redeemed. **There is forgiveness with thee, that thou mayest be feared. . . . Let Israel hope in the LORD: for with the LORD there is mercy, and with him is plenteous redemption. And he shall redeem Israel from all his iniquities.**

131:1-3. ***From the Haughty Heart to the Composed Soul.***—This is one of the shortest of the psalms, but it is also one of the most suggestive. It may be read not as a hymn for common worship but as a page from an anonymous autobiography. The writer exercises the greatest economy in detail. He says nothing about when or where he lived or the position he occupied. Yet he so hints at spiritual experiences that he leaves us wanting to write an essay on the nature of man, his tragedy, and his restoration.

Though he gives no clue to his identity, he suggests a man dangerously full of self-confi-

2 Surely I have behaved and quieted myself, as a child that is weaned of his mother: my soul *is* even as a weaned child.

2 But I have calmed and quieted my soul,
like a child quieted at its mother's breast;
like a child that is quieted is my soul.

---

stoically resigned to life's defeats? Has he given up the former struggle because of old age and weariness? The answer is supplied in vs. 3, **hope in the Lord.** Like the merchant in the N.T. who, after visiting many markets, discovered at length the pearl of great price, he has come through many disillusionments to find in God rather than in things life's highest satisfaction. So come what may, he rests in the Lord and trusts in him for the issue.

The meter is 3+2, excepting 4+3+3 in vs. 2. The date cannot be determined.

131:2. Like a child quieted: The translation **weaned** is due to a misunderstanding of the context. The word so rendered means, lit., "finished" or "completed" and may

---

dence. He does not tell us how this sense of superiority developed, whether it was because of unusual ability, or because of sycophants who persuaded him that he was of no common clay. He does not tell us how his time and talents were spent, though apparently his heart was set on things too lofty and his eyes fixed on things too high. Nor does he say whether he was able to carry it off, or whether men saw through his pretense and left him in his misery. What he does is to leave us with an impression of one who with unusual conceit snatched at the stars. The type is so familiar that it does not matter whether he lived in Jerusalem or London or Washington. His name is legion and his dwelling place is everywhere. One thing we know is that a revolution took place in this vain man so that he was stiff Mr. Loath-to-stoop no longer. What he says is that he soothed and **quieted** his soul, **like a child quieted at its mother's breast.** That, however, only leaves us asking how he did it, for it is exactly what so many of us want to do. We know people who mix marvelous medicines, and when we can do no other we go to them for relief. But the deeper the trouble is the more certain it is to recur, and no soothing will save us from arrogance. Just as we feel that we are improving, an expression of disparagement or an attitude of superiority betrays us. It is easier to tame a lion than to cure a haughty spirit. Only God can do that. But when God and the soul work together, it is impossible to say who is active and who is passive. We can simply accept the fact that what we cannot do alone God can do for us, or enable us to do for ourselves, so that even a prig can become a man or woman of gracious modesty. The final result is not arrogance cloaked with humility, making a man a hundred times more offensive than he was before; the final result is a man who thinks remarkably little about himself or the impression he makes upon others.

The psalm concludes with an appeal to Israel to **hope in the Lord from this time forth and for evermore.** It is not a conventional conclusion. The Israelites had many faults, but is it not true to say that pride was their besetting sin? They were more than once referred to as a stiff-necked people. There were rare souls of course who were always ready to bow themselves before God and to honor all men. But too many of them loved to sit in the seat of the scornful, and especially to despise strangers and foreigners. Others might have military genius. Others might outstrip them in intellectual or aesthetic power. But even the religious leaders of Israel were apt with something like insolence to exclaim, "Stand aside! I am holier than thou!" The bitterness of exile, instead of humbling them, seemed to increase the trouble. National adversity begot spiritual pride. Failing in outer circumstances they sought inner compensation, with the result that at last when God came in the likeness of man they could do nothing but crucify him. How different it might have been if the nation had listened to the psalmist!

To dilate further upon this theme, however, can easily lead us into the error of finding motes in other folks' eyes and remaining unconscious of the beam in our own. That is your temptation and mine. It is everywhere in the world, and it creates insoluble problems. It is not always blatant, as in the person who takes the best seat. There is a pride that is subtle and largely concealed. There is an intellectual pride that quietly assumes pre-eminence. There is social pride, racial pride, class pride. There are many kinds of religious pride. There is the man who has had a spiritual experience which instead of making him humble among his fellows gives him a dangerous sense of superiority. There is another man who glories in and exaggerates the virtues of the particular church of which he is a member. There is still another who has been solemnly set apart for special duties, and in consequence claims special privi-

3 Let Israel hope in the LORD from henceforth and for ever.

A Song of degrees.

132 LORD, remember David, *and* all his afflictions:

3 O Israel, hope in the LORD
from this time forth and for evermore.

A Song of Ascents.

132 Remember, O LORD, in David's favor,
all the hardships he endured;

---

imply either **weaned** or "nursed." But a weaned child is not *ipso facto* a tranquil child. The figure is that of a child which after being suckled is composed.

3. It is not clear whether or not this verse is an addition to suit the psalm to congregational use.

CXXXII. SONG FOR THE HOUSE OF DAVID (132:1-18)

This psalm is a liturgical processional hymn by the rendition of which, with its solo and choral parts, the events connected with David's bringing of the ark to Zion are dramatically presented. The purpose of the re-enactment of that historical occasion was to impress on all who witnessed or participated in it how the fortunes of the city, as the place where the Lord dwells, and those of the house of David, the servant of the Lord, are intertwined. The psalm can therefore be classed as both a royal psalm (cf. Pss. 20; 21; 45) and a song of Zion (cf. Pss. 46; 87).

It may well be, as Mowinckel (*Psalmenstudien,* II, 112-17) *et al.* believe, that in the pre-exilic period at the New Year the anniversary of the reigning king's accession was celebrated conjointly with the annual ceremony of the Lord's enthronement, and that this psalm was used in connection with that occasion. This theory, though not conclusive, offers a reasonable interpretation of the situation to which the psalm relates. In any case, whatever the circumstances, the contents of the psalm are so presented that we can identify the several stages in the unfolding of a liturgical drama in which king and ark are prominent features.

---

leges. We see such things in the world around us. What do we find in church history? We find the saint who has learned of Christ and become content with his lot, whatever it may be and however obscure. But we find also arrogant ecclesiastics, overbearing prelates, proud preachers, and little men climbing to positions of authority. And, God have mercy on us, there is not one among us who is not sometimes enticed by the glamour of it all. As Pascal noted:

> Vanity is so anchored in the heart of man that a soldier, a soldier's servant, a cook, a porter brags, and wishes to have his admirers. Even philosophers wish for them. Those who write against it want to have the glory of having written well; and those who read it desire the glory of having read it. . . . We are so vain that the esteem of five or six neighbours delights and contents us.[7]

Where is the remedy to be found? We must not expect much from secular education, which can indeed intensify the evil. Nor must we pin our faith to popular religion with its obvious deficiencies. Only deep, personal religion can meet the world-wide need. It is surely not an accident that this psalm follows one of the penitential psalms which tells how a contrite soul waited upon God and found peace. Some such experience as that seems to be assumed here. This man too had cried to the Lord out of the depths and so found peace and hope. And the final exhortation to or prayer for Israel springs out of his own deliverance. As his soul has been quieted, so the nation may be like a weaned child with its mother. But it must be real repentance, not a formal act. The people must wait for the Lord as watchers wait for the morning, with the same confidence and the same alertness.

132:1-18. ***The Lord Hath Chosen Zion.***—The historian has an important part to play in modern life. It is for him to show how all history is contemporary history, to make us see how each generation has to face the same problems, to show how leading personalities in different ages have performed the task, and how they fared in the struggle. Everything, however,

[7] *Thoughts,* p. 63.

2 How he sware unto the LORD, *and* vowed unto the mighty *God* of Jacob;
3 Surely I will not come into the tabernacle of my house, nor go up into my bed;
4 I will not give sleep to mine eyes, *or* slumber to mine eyelids,
5 Until I find out a place for the LORD, a habitation for the mighty *God* of Jacob.

2 how he swore to the LORD
and vowed to the Mighty One of Jacob,
3 "I will not enter my house
or get into my bed;
4 I will not give sleep to my eyes
or slumber to my eyelids,
5 until I find a place for the LORD,
a dwelling place for the Mighty One of Jacob."

The date is probably late pre-exilic. Since the king in question cannot be one of the Hasmonaeans, as the latter were not of the line of David, there seems to be no alternative to assigning it to a time when a scion of David was ruling in Jerusalem. The emphasis on Jerusalem as the Lord's **dwelling place** (vs. 7), and the designation of the ark as **his footstool** (vs. 7) in contrast to the older identification of the Lord with the ark (cf. vs. 5; Num. 10:35-36), point to a relatively late, possibly Deuteronomic, date. The historical references also seem to imply that the literature preserving the records of the past was in essentials fairly fixed (cf. vss. 11-12; 89:35, 49; II Sam. 7:4-5, 12-17). The meter is with few exceptions 3+3.

1. Prayer for David's House (132:1-5)

132:1-5. Oriental processions move slowly with frequent halts during which dramatic acts and liturgical rituals may be performed. On this occasion the people, the priests, and the king with his escort are gathered at a point outside the Holy City. The procession is opened with an intercession uttered probably by the king himself, in which he seeks favor for the royal house and by implication for the people by recalling David's zeal to find a resting place for the ark. The words hark back to the story of the loss of the ark in I Sam. 4:1–6:21, and the steps taken by David for its recovery (II Sam. 6:1-11). **Remember . . . all the hardships he endured:** In these words the story of David's vicissitudes in the days before he was king is compressed, as if it had only one motive, the search for a place where the ark might rest. **How he swore to the LORD:** We have no record of such an oath, though in II Sam. 7:1-3 and I Kings 8:17 we are told it was in his heart, nor does the title **Mighty One of Jacob** occur in this connection. The psalmist is either using some haggadic expansion of the material in the historical books or imaginatively recasting the literary tradition. The title is an ancient one (cf. Gen. 49:24; Isa. 49:26; 60:16; also Isa. 1:24) derived from pre-Mosaic Hebrew times; it means "the Champion of Jacob" (see W. F. Albright, *From the Stone Age to Christianity* [2nd ed.; Baltimore: Johns Hopkins Press, 1946], pp. 188-89).

---

depends on the way in which the story is told. If men are offered dull records of distant events they will soon turn away with an expression of weariness. But if to knowledge we can add imagination, if the old writings, the dates, and the persons can be brought to life, so that we see them as men and women like ourselves, fumbling and feeling their way, but striving to do their part honestly and manfully—if we can do this so that the ancient world becomes real and the medieval world important, then people who want to get understanding will pay attention.

This applies to the book of Psalms, in particular to this psalm. And in some respects we are better equipped for the task than were the expositors who preceded us. Scholars have labored long and patiently on Hebrew history, on the place of the psalms in the life of the people, on forms of Hebrew verse and the character of Hebrew worship; one needs only an active mind and a touch of originality to bring it all to life and make it absorbing.

Ps. 132 is described in the KJV and elsewhere as a pilgrim psalm. Some O.T. scholars tell us that it was a processional hymn for popular occasions.[8] We may understand it best if we liken it to the pageants which have become so popular in many countries. A community

[8] See Exeg. and Leslie, *Psalms*, p. 103.

6 Lo, we heard of it at Ephratah: we found it in the fields of the wood.
7 We will go into his tabernacles: we will worship at his footstool.
8 Arise, O LORD, into thy rest; thou, and the ark of thy strength.
9 Let thy priests be clothed with righteousness; and let thy saints shout for joy.
10 For thy servant David's sake turn not away the face of thine anointed.

6 Lo, we heard of it in Eph'rathah,
we found it in the fields of Ja'ar.
7 "Let us go to his dwelling place;
let us worship at his footstool!"

8 Arise, O LORD, and go to thy resting place,
thou and the ark of thy might.
9 Let thy priests be clothed with righteousness,
and let thy saints shout for joy.
10 For thy servant David's sake
do not turn away the face of thy anointed one.

2. THE ARK IN THE TEMPLE PROCESSION (132:6-10)

6-7. A choir representing David and his men re-enact the search for the ark and relate the account of its discovery. **We heard of it in Ephrathah:** While David was living in Ephrathah, i.e., Bethlehem (I Sam. 17:12; Ruth 4:11; Mic. 5:2), he heard that the ark was **in the fields of Jaar,** a poetic variant of the region of Kiriath-jearim (cf. II Sam. 6:2-12; I Chr. 13:1-14). So the choir summons the people to join them in bringing the ark to its place in the temple and to worship the Lord before it. **Let us go to his dwelling place:** It is to be noted here (as in vs. 5) that the ark and the Lord are so closely identified as to be convertible terms (cf. Num. 10:33-36). But the words **let us worship at his footstool** indicate a distinction between them (cf. I Chr. 28:2). A development in the conception of the nature and the media of God's presence accounts for the change. In this verse, however, the two views are set side by side.

8-9. The procession is now prepared to move toward the gates of Zion and the temple. The priests stand ready to bear the ark with which the awful presence is associated. However, it is not proper that men should determine the moment when the Holy One should set forth. So with a loud shout (cf. I Sam. 4:5), after the manner of the ancient acclamation of Num. 10:35-36, the ark as well as Yahweh is addressed: **Arise, O LORD, . . . go to thy resting place, thou and the ark of thy might.** The ark is described as mighty because on this occasion, when the past is being re-enacted, the dread effects of the ark's presence are recalled (cf. Josh. 3:14-17; I Sam. 6:1-21). As the procession advances, the people greet the ark with cries of joy. It is probable that the king, like David, would perform a cultic dance at the head of the procession.

10. The scene changes to the courts of the temple, where after the arrival of the procession, the king offers a sacrifice and prays for divine favor.

wishes to honor its founders and by remembering the past to instruct the present. It therefore sets aside a gifted member whose first task is to gather information, and having mastered the salient facts to prepare speeches for the principal actors and songs for the various choruses. Such festivals seem essentially modern. Actually they are very ancient. They were taking place in Egypt and Babylon many hundreds and even thousands of years before Christ. At some of them the reigning monarch would present himself to the people, perhaps even as a god, not indeed for recoronation but for a repetition of solemn mutual vows. There are reasons for believing that there were similar festivities in Jerusalem, and that they included a procession from the west of the Holy City up to the temple. The king was there in the procession, taking a conspicuous place—but always as the servant of the Most High. Priests and singers were also there, and one of the hymns they sang as they passed through the crowded streets was Ps. 132.

We have only to glance at the psalm to see how suitable it was for such a purpose. For one thing, it recalls the past, which the Israelites were always ready to do. Further, it makes use of religious symbols, which always appealed to the imagination. Still more important, the **ark** of the covenant was included in the procession and pointed references were made to it. It is

11 The LORD hath sworn *in* truth unto David; he will not turn from it; Of the fruit of thy body will I set upon thy throne.

12 If thy children will keep my covenant and my testimony that I shall teach them, their children shall also sit upon thy throne for evermore.

13 For the LORD hath chosen Zion; he hath desired *it* for his habitation.

14 This *is* my rest for ever: here will I dwell; for I have desired it.

15 I will abundantly bless her provision: I will satisfy her poor with bread.

16 I will also clothe her priests with salvation: and her saints shall shout aloud for joy.

17 There will I make the horn of David to bud: I have ordained a lamp for mine anointed.

18 His enemies will I clothe with shame: but upon himself shall his crown flourish.

11 The LORD swore to David a sure oath
from which he will not turn back:
"One of the sons of your body
I will set on your throne.
12 If your sons keep my covenant
and my testimonies which I shall teach them,
their sons also for ever
shall sit upon your throne."

13 For the LORD has chosen Zion;
he has desired it for his habitation:
14 "This is my resting place for ever;
here I will dwell, for I have desired it.
15 I will abundantly bless her provisions;
I will satisfy her poor with bread.
16 Her priests I will clothe with salvation,
and her saints will shout for joy.
17 There I will make a horn to sprout for David;
I have prepared a lamp for my anointed.
18 His enemies I will clothe with shame,
but upon himself his crown will shed its luster."

---

3. The Lord's Purpose for David and for Zion (132:11-18)

11-12. In answer to the king's prayer there comes an oracle. It is couched in the familiar words and style of Nathan's prophetic address to David (II Sam. 7:14-16). It was probably a set form for use in such a ceremony and was both a promise and an admonition (cf. vs. 12*a*).

13-18. The oracle to the king is followed by a second one. The ark has been set in its place within Zion; the prayer in vs. 8 has been answered; and the Lord has come with his ark into the temple. Appropriately, the oracle promises the permanence of his election of Zion as his abode. **The LORD has chosen Zion . . . for his habitation: This is my resting place for ever.** Then follows an enumeration of the blessings that the Lord's presence ensures for Zion: there will be an abundance of food for all including the **poor** (vs. 15); the **priests** will enjoy **salvation;** the whole community of the Lord's people will in consequence **shout for joy;** the royal house will flourish and the **crown** of the reigning king will be a shining one. **I have prepared a lamp for my anointed: My anointed** is the parallel term to **David. A lamp** is to be understood as an heir or successor in accordance with the words of I Kings 11:36; 15:4 (cf. II Chr. 21:7). The house will never be dark and empty. The words therefore are a divine endorsement of the reigning successor of David. Similarly, **a horn . . . for David,** i.e., the bearer of the might of David's line, **I will make . . . to sprout.**

---

difficult for us to imagine the effect the ark would have as it was carried through crowded streets. Nobody presumed to know everything about it; its origin and much of its history were veiled in antiquity. It would remind the onlookers, however, of many national crises. They would think of Moses, and all that he did for the liberation and unification of the tribes. They would think of David and his desire to build a temple in which the ark might be suitably housed. They would think how in times of peril that wooden chest had been an inspiration and a rallying point. As centuries later Christian crusaders carried with them ornamented

A Song of degrees of David.

133 Behold, how good and how pleasant *it is* for brethren to dwell together in unity!

A Song of Ascents.

133 Behold, how good and pleasant it is
when brothers dwell in unity!

CXXXIII. The Blessedness of Brotherly Unity (133:1-3)

This falls into the class of wisdom psalms (cf. Pss. 1; 49; 73; 127). As noted in the Exeg. on Pss. 15; 24, it was not uncommon in the postexilic period to impart at the temple some instruction on matters of moral and spiritual significance. Sometimes the instruction took the form of a homily introduced into the liturgy (cf. 95:8-11); at other times it was given independently of the liturgy by priestly or scribal teachers in or out of the temple courts to help those who were desirous to learn about the way of life which was pleasing to God (cf. prologue to Ecclesiasticus). Some of the fragments of this teaching as preserved in the Psalter reflect the style and interests of the wisdom writers; thus this psalm deals with a practical social matter such as one finds in Proverbs, and like that book it uses apposite similes and arresting words such as **behold, how good,** and **how pleasant** in order to give life and force to what it has to say.

It is not surprising that such a poem was included in the collection of pilgrim psalms, since it had relevance to a concern of every head of a family who pilgrimed to Jerusalem. The solidarity of the family was fundamental to Israel's social and religious structure. It ensured stability and permanence to the family and the preservation of custom and tradition in the community. Such an institution as the levirate marriage was dependent on it (Deut. 25:5). In the old order of things, sanctioned since the days of the forefathers, brothers did dwell together under the parental roof. Under the tutelage of the fathers the several families were held together as one by a sense of the bonds of blood and common interest. But in postexilic times the movement of the Jews to other lands, which the pilgrims themselves evidenced, and the growing commercialization of the economy of the East, worked in various ways against the survival of that old family unity. The psalmist, deploring the weakening of the old custom, sets forth with

crosses, so generation after generation of Israelites had carried their ark—not always to victory, for once at least it had been captured by the Philistines. All this, and much more—history, myth, legend, folklore, some of it mixed with superstition and bordering even on idolatry—all this would excite the emotions as perhaps on the first day of each year the ark was carried in procession through crowded streets and set again in its resting place within Solomon's temple.

133:1-3. *The Concord of Kindred Souls.*—Some of the psalms are difficult to expound. Before anything of value can be said, the central theme has to be discovered, and that is not always easy. There is, however, little difficulty here. The subject is stated in the opening sentence, and what follows is simply an illustration of it:

Behold, how good and pleasant it is
when brothers dwell in unity!

The **brothers** may refer to members of the same family, perhaps men who have traveled from distant parts and find themselves united in religious celebrations in the capital city. Or the writer may be thinking of the whole nation, saying how beautiful it is when the people are one community without dangerous schisms or rival parties. He says it with such emphasis that there must have been particular reasons for stressing it. Whatever the cause or causes, he makes his point, which might have been a tedious commonplace, but which seems to possess many of the qualities of a prayer. If only men would learn to live together in peace how different life would be!

The aspiration is almost too obvious to require comment, but the illustrations deserve attention. In the first place we are reminded of the sacred **oil** used in the consecration of a high priest—or perhaps the **precious oil** which a host poured lavishly on the head of a guest—and how it would trickle down the beard and fall upon the robe. The writer may have started with any high priest and any anointing, but his mind turned to the half-historical, half-mythical figure of **Aaron,** who was believed to be the founder of the hereditary priesthood. Stories

2 *It is* like the precious ointment upon the head, that ran down upon the beard, *even* Aaron's beard: that went down to the skirts of his garments;	2 It is like the precious oil upon the head, running down upon the beard, upon the beard of Aaron, running down on the collar of his robes!

a rare choice of beautiful similes the loveliness and the blessings of the family "where brothers live together."

The psalm, like the others of the pilgrim collection, is postexilic. As noted above, the theme implies a social situation characteristic of Hellenistic times. The use of the relative pronoun ש (vss. 2-3) is also indicative of a late date. The meter, as the text stands, is 3+2, with the exception of 3+3 in vs. 1. At the end of a poem or a strophe the meter not infrequently is subject to alteration.

133:1-3. The text has probably suffered some corruption. The psalmist, like other wisdom writers, is enforcing his maxim about brotherhood by an appeal to something which was within the range of the experiences of his hearers. For Westerners the reference

had grown around the name of Aaron, as they had grown around so many of the fathers of Israel. There were stories about his rod, how it had blossomed and brought forth fruit, and how for that reason it had been deposited in the ark, or as some authorities affirmed, before the ark. There may have been stories about his beard, all the more likely when we remember that while the Egyptians disliked hair upon the face (yet cf. certain of their ritualistic practices), the Jews attached great importance to it. However, what concerns this psalmist is the way the pungent ointment trickled down from head to garment, suggesting the pervasive influence of good will. It cannot be confined to one spot, but spreads fragrance all around.

The second illustration is drawn from nature. The writer leaves the temple and is out among the **mountains** that were so often covered by snow or cloud. The scenery suggested beauty, but it also meant vitality. From those high peaks rain and **dew** proceeded, the moisture that brought refreshment and fertility to parched fields and thirsty vineyards. The concord of kindred souls, says the psalmist, is like that. Wherever brethren dwell together in unity,

> **It is like the dew of Hermon,**
> **which falls on the mountains of Zion!**

The poetic quality of the illustrations need not detain us, but the blessedness of unity and the joy it brings is a subject that cannot be avoided either by the biblical expositor or by anyone who speaks to the needs of the modern situation. Our own illustrations may appropriately be drawn from biography, for while modern literature may not have been conspicuously successful in every department, it has been rich in the lives of men who have played important parts in stirring events. We shall refer to two books that won wide recognition when they were published and must for long retain both personal interest and historical value.

The first is *William Temple, Archbishop of Canterbury: His Life and Letters,* by F. A. Iremonger, Dean of Lichfield. Temple might well be regarded as a typical Anglican. The son of an archbishop, he was trained from childhood in the ways of the national church, and to the end he remained a convinced and consistent Episcopalian. Yet no one would speak of him as a mere denominationalist. He was always looking over party walls and seeking contact with men on the other side. He did it in the secular sphere. Consider the part he played in such organizations as the Workers' Educational Association. He did it still more persistently in church relationships. It did not matter whether he was a student among students, or a bishop among the other leaders of religious thought and action, he was always seeking better understanding and new ways of co-operation. Think of the place he took in Copec—the Conference on Politics, Economics, and Citizenship. Think of the time and inspiration he gave to the World Council of Churches. The ecumenical movement was not something to which he paid lip service: it was a concern that deepened as the years passed, and became at last a consuming passion. When as archbishop of York he visited the United States, the first thing he insisted on was that he was there "not chiefly as a representative of England, not of the English branch of the Catholic Church, but as a minister of the universal Gospel and of the Catholic Church itself." [9] When he was en-

[9] London: Oxford University Press, 1948, p. 380.

3 As the dew of Hermon, *and as the dew* that descended upon the mountains of Zion: for there the LORD commanded the blessing, *even* life for evermore.

3 It is like the dew of Hermon,
which falls on the mountains of Zion!
For there the LORD has commanded the blessing,
life for evermore.

---

to **Aaron's beard** is bathos. The words may be a gloss by someone who recalled the prescriptions of Exod. 30:22-30. The clause **which falls on the mountains of Zion** may also be a gloss. The dews of Hermon do not reach Jerusalem. The gloss cannot be saved to the text by emending **Zion** (צִיּוֹן) to read Ijon (עִיּוֹן), a place mentioned in I Kings 15:20; II Kings 15:29; II Chr. 16:4, and lying southwest of Hermon. With the omission of these glosses the meter is still 3+2. The psalmist accordingly uses just one simile. The brotherhood of which he speaks is compared to the precious perfumed **oil** which a host pours on the head of a guest so lavishly that it flows down to the neck of the guest's robe, fresh and cool **as the dew of Hermon.**

---

throned as archbishop of Canterbury, he was careful to arrange that representatives of other Christian communions were present, and he spoke not as a leader of one church but as a representative of the church universal. The opening verse of this psalm might well be inscribed on the title page of his life story.

The other book is Robert Cecil's autobiography, *All the Way*. Here again is a man who set out from a particular camp. The son of a Conservative prime minister, he bore all his life the marks of his origin. Anyone who listened to his early speeches might have prophesied with confidence that he would end as he began —a Tory of the finest type. But World War I shook him more than most men. The sufferings he saw, the tendencies he watched with growing alarm, the contacts he made with the leaders of many nations, all convinced him that if mankind was to be saved war must be outlawed and the nations must turn from rivalry to comradeship. The result of his thinking was embodied in the covenant of the League of Nations, and especially in the main provision "that there should be no resort to war upon any international grievance until all means of settling it had been tried." The subsequent history of the league is written in blood and tears; but it opened the way for the United Nations. There may yet be many reverses, but the ideal of which Cecil was an outstanding champion will not die. Long after most of the statesmen of the period have been forgotten, he will be remembered and honored as one who took this ancient psalm and set it in a new context, thus giving it new force and meaning.

But the problem of unity is really part of a greater problem, the problem of evil. We are forced to inquire why men fight and quarrel, even to their own destruction; and the answer is because of the sinfulness of the human heart. We are brought face to face not only with division and antisocial behavior, but with such common facts as pride and fear, cruelty and lust, selfishness and a desire to dominate. These troubles cannot be successfully met by a merely conventional religion. A piety which makes institutions more important than spiritual reality may even aggravate the evil. Men are likely to fall still farther apart, with poisoned minds and inherited prejudices, when they are more concerned with customs and rites than with the will of God. The path of those who seek wider fellowship will be littered with failures if they have nothing but their own ability to aid them. We need that which we cannot command, but which comes as naturally as **the dew of Hermon** to those who put themselves in the attitude to receive it. It is the gift of the Holy Spirit, which may indeed, before anything else can happen, make new divisions; for it drives out deceit and malice and all evil: but only so that what remains may be knit more firmly together. That is what we must seek, first in the church of God and then in every human association, the power from on high which casts out evil and creates enduring fellowship. There are many instances of such activities of the Holy Spirit: pre-eminent among them the day of Pentecost, when all were "with one accord in one place." We ought constantly to return to the book of Acts if we want to understand the causes and consequences of that experience. Then pass on to other beneficent revivals—the Montanist movement in the second century, the Franciscan movement in the thirteenth century, the Methodist movement in the eighteenth century, etc.—to study their similarities and their peculiarities, their common experience of power from above, and the liberating, enlarging, uplifting influences that have resulted. At every step of the way, if we walk with humility and spiritual

A Song of degrees.

134 Behold, bless ye the LORD, all *ye* servants of the LORD, which by night stand in the house of the LORD.

A Song of Ascents.

134 Come, bless the LORD,
all you servants of the LORD,
who stand by night in the house of the LORD!

CXXXIV. A NIGHT HYMN FOR THE TEMPLE (134:1-3)

This psalm is the last of the collection of pilgrim songs (Pss. 120–134); it served appropriately as a Nunc Dimittis sung at the end either of one of the nocturnal services of devotion in the temple during a festival or of the last vigil of the festival as the pilgrims were on the point of returning to their homes. It is probable that the psalm belonged to the liturgy of the feast of Tabernacles, since the implication of vs. 1*c* is that the priestly ministrants were on duty in the temple not for one night, as would have been the case on the eve of Passover, but for several nights, and since the presence of the congregation in the temple at night would not accord with the regulation for the observance of the eve of Passover by families in their homes or places of sojourn (cf. Exod. 12:18-20). In the postexilic period the feast of Tabernacles was regarded as "the feast" to which men should "go up from year to year to worship the King, the LORD of hosts" (Zech. 14:16). And we are told in the Mishnah (Sukkah 5:1-4) how in the

awareness, we should be repeating with ever-growing emphasis the psalmist's ejaculation:

Behold, how good and pleasant it is
when brothers dwell in unity!

134:1-3. ***A Benediction from Zion.***—If we were to take a hymnbook from which the names of the writers and their dates had been removed, and then set ourselves to expound the verses in the light of their origin, the results would be highly speculative. Knowing nothing about the author of "Lead, kindly Light," we might assume that he was a traveler in unknown countries. Knowing nothing about such men as Isaac Watts and Charles Wesley, William Cowper and John Keble, having nothing but their hymns, our conclusions as to date and circumstance, purpose and use, might be interesting, even edifying, but we should not expect precision or unanimity.

Yet that, or something like it, is what in the name of biblical exposition we are continually attempting to do with the book of Psalms. There are, it is true, certain headings and traditions; but it is unwise to take them literally. We have information from various sources about the temple in which the psalms were used, and about similar hymns composed in other countries. But we know little about the authors and their dates, the circumstances in which they wrote, and the way in which their compositions were first used. This, however, has not deterred commentators, who have exercised much ingenuity which has often passed into dogmatic assertions and been freely used in theological debate.

These reflections are not out of place in approaching this psalm, for information is meager and expositions numerous. One thing we know is that it is the last in the collection of pilgrim songs; but how the collection was made and why this was included we do not know. There is general agreement that it is an antiphonal psalm, vss. 1-2 being an invitation to the **servants of the LORD** to **bless the LORD,** and vs. 3 the reply sung by an individual or a choir:

May the LORD bless you from Zion,
he who made heaven and earth!

But there is no agreement as to who sang each part and on what occasion. It may be the final song of pilgrims before they left the Holy City. Some would start before dawn. It would therefore be natural that while darkness still reigned, they should approach the temple and receive from the priests and Levites a final blessing. It is at least worth thinking about—a company of Israelites with loins girded and preparations made, seeking from Zion a valedictory benediction.

If this is the right explanation, it brings us to a subject that demands attention. Men have always set apart some of their brethren for religious purposes. They may call them ministers or priests, they may expect them to preach or to offer sacrifices, to expound sacred scriptures or to work miracles. They may look to these trained and separated men for counsel—not for instruction on how to prepare for journeys or on how to govern the state, but on how to please God. They do not expect such ministers to

2 Lift up your hands *in* the sanctuary, and bless the LORD.	2 Lift up your hands to the holy place, and bless the LORD!

brilliantly lighted courts of the temple the Levites, the priests, and the laity joined in songs of praise accompanied by musical instruments; and how they said that whereas their forefathers worshiped toward the sun, "we bow down before the LORD and direct our eyes toward the LORD."

In the liturgy of this psalm vss. 1-2 were sung by the congregation or by the Levitical singers (cf. Sukkah 5:4) on their behalf, and vs. 3 is the response of the priestly ministrants in the form of a benediction. The date of the psalm is, like the collection to which it belongs, postexilic. The meter is irregular.

134:1. All the various orders of those who **stand,** i.e., minister (cf. Deut. 10:8; II Chr. 29:11) in the temple **by night** are called on to **bless the LORD.** The word **bless** here means to praise with words that declare the greatness and goodness of God (cf. 66:8; Josh. 22:33). The opening word, הִנֵּה, **behold,** has probably crept into the text from 133:1.

2-3. The posture of the priests as described here is one which is commonly portrayed on the monuments on which persons are represented in an act of worship. It may be that there was a belief that into the **hands** uplifted in this solemn ritual the priestly power

---

speak as lecturers in divinity, or as commentators on current affairs, but as men who **bless the LORD** and **lift up . . . hands to the holy place;** i.e., men who are called to be ministers in the house of God are set apart for purposes of worship. They are not primarily instructors, but leaders of prayer and praise. This is not to disparage the ministry of the Word or the prophetic element in preaching: it is to include all as an essential part of worship. Rightly understood, there is no conflict between the altar and the pulpit. They represent different attitudes of mind, but they are parts of the one great act—the coming of men together to the throne of the heavenly grace.

Come, bless the LORD,
all you servants of the LORD.

It is not surprising if ministers of religion sometimes become immersed in the technicalities of worship; for there is much that calls for consideration and decision. There is, to start with, the perennial discussion on how to pray, whether in liturgical form or in spontaneous utterance. Closely connected with this are other important questions, including the ordering of services from the opening sentences to the final blessing. These are not matters which can be left to themselves; they demand attention, and whatever tradition is followed it must be practiced as perfectly as possible. As surgeons and physicians must attend to the details of their profession, as artists must pay heed to the niceties of canvas and brush and oils, so priest and pastor must pay heed to the structure of worship—to the progression of ideas, the proportion of penitence and praise, to hymns with subjective and objective attitudes, even to elocution and personal bearing. If such things are neglected, worship will be slovenly, and sensitive worshipers will be offended.

Worship however is one thing; technicality is another. To be a specialist in liturgics is good; it is, however, no guarantee of ability to pray. One may be learned in all the formularies of the church and still be unable to lead a congregation in thanksgiving and supplication. We may draw up the most appropriate orders of service and rehearse them with well-trained choirs, only to have as the result a splendid performance, not divine worship. Or recoiling from such attention to detail, we may cultivate spontaneous prayer and arrive at "ease of utterance." It is difficult to say which of the two is the more offensive; both drive serious-minded men away in anger. There is on record an outburst of righteous indignation from the philosopher Spinoza, which we hope is out of date as well as exaggerated, yet may deserve repetition:

> Every church becomes a theatre where orators, instead of church teachers, harangue, caring not to instruct the people, but striving to attract admiration, to bring opponents to public scorn, and to preach only novelties and paradoxes such as will tickle the ears of their congregation. . . . Verily, if they had but one spark of light from on high, they would not insolently rave, but would learn to worship God more wisely, and would be as marked among their fellows for mercy as they are now for malice.[1]

There are other words too which we must lay to heart, for they are never out of date. Jesus

[1] Quoted by Gwilym O. Griffith, *Makers of Modern Thought* (London: Lutterworth Press, 1948), p. 59.

3 The LORD that made heaven and earth bless thee out of Zion.

3 May the LORD bless you from Zion,
he who made heaven and earth!

to communicate blessing to the laity was received. In any case, the priests answer by bestowing a blessing on the congregation (cf. Lev. 9:22). The word **thee** is here a collective (cf. Num. 6:22-26). The people are in the blessing reminded of two things: the Lord's dwelling place is in **Zion**, and he is the creator of all things.

of Nazareth said much about worship, and his comments are not calculated to make us complacent. He saw much praying in public places, but it did not suggest to him the worship that God requires. It suggested to him spiritual pride rather than dependence upon the Creator. We cannot too often remind ourselves of what he says and of what he leaves unsaid: so little about posture, about the way to make the sign of the cross, about the forms we have thought important; so much about moral and spiritual insight, about willing obedience, about leaving the gift before the altar and going and seeking reconciliation with a brother, about avoiding vain repetition and worshiping the Father in spirit and in truth. That is what the Lord Jesus Christ enjoins.

And if it is to be done successfully in public, it must be done repeatedly in private—when we walk, when we rest, when we suffer and when we enjoy, when we face problems that are too much for us, and when we find light shining into our minds. We are to cultivate not only mystical moods but moral attitudes—thinking with God, reasoning with him, and doing it with candor and courage, sincerity and humility. Prayer is not indulgence in emotional states till we become intoxicated with the Unseen; it is self-examination, meditation, and the praise of God. Men who so live gain spiritual power that no ordination or laying on of hands can give. They become the true spiritual leaders of the nation, who having lived in communion with God have come to know his will. We are reminded of what Carlyle said of Cromwell:

> Cromwell's habit of prayer is a notable feature of him. All his great enterprises were commenced with prayer. In dark inextricable-looking difficulties, his Officers and he used to assemble, and pray alternately, for hours, for days, till some definite resolution rose among them, some "door of hope," as they would name it, disclosed itself. Consider that. In tears, in fervent prayers, and cries to the great God, to have pity on them, to make His light shine before them. They, armed Soldiers of Christ, as they felt themselves to be; a little band of Christian Brothers. . . . They cried to God in their straits, in their extreme need, not to forsake the Cause that was His. . . . Can a man's soul, to this hour, get guidance by any other method than intrinsically by that same,—devout prostration of the earnest struggling soul before the Highest, the Giver of all Light; be such *prayer* a spoken, articulate, or be it a voiceless, inarticulate one? There is no other method. . . . Cromwell's prayers were likely to be "eloquent," and much more than that. His was the heart of a man who *could* pray.[2]

It is that sense of reality which the people seek in their religious leaders—not divinity degrees or ecclesiastical conformity, but suppliants who **lift up . . . hands to the holy place** and **bless the LORD.** Such men give valid benedictions. Many may intone the response, **May the LORD bless you from Zion!** But they will be despised, and even hated, if they repeat their phrases without divine authority or human sympathy. They will not only be ridiculed; they will bring religion itself into ill-repute.

When the benediction is pronounced not only in tones of conviction but with the emphasis of holy living, how effective it becomes! It will live in the hearts of those who receive it, and inspire them when the way is hard. Only a spoken word, but it reawakens memories and comes as a call to renewed effort. Stanley Baldwin tells how one September evening, standing on the terrace of a beautiful villa near Florence, he heard a bell:

> Such a bell as never was on land or sea, a bell whose every vibration found an echo in my innermost heart. I said to my hostess, "That is the most beautiful bell I have ever heard." "Yes," she replied, "it is an English bell." And so it was. For generations its sound had gone out over English fields, giving the hours of work and prayer to English folk from the tower of an English abbey. . . . After four centuries it stirred the heart of a wandering Englishman and made him sick for home.[3]

So a sincere benediction from the holy place in Jerusalem may have brought memories and a sense of the sacred to many a traveling Israelite. It may be heard even yet sounding down the centuries, plucking at the heartstrings, stirring feelings that lie too deep for words, feelings "subconscious and ancestral."

[2] *Heroes and Hero-Worship*, "The Hero as King."

[3] *On England* (New York: Frederick A. Stokes, 1926), pp. 117-18.

135 Praise ye the LORD. Praise ye the name of the LORD; praise *him*, O ye servants of the LORD.

135 Praise the LORD.
Praise the name of the LORD,
give praise, O servants of the LORD,

CXXXV. PRAISE THE NAME OF THE LORD (135:1-21)

This psalm is a liturgical hymn of praise prepared, like Ps. 136 which it closely resembles in content and character, for use at one of the great festivals, probably that of the New Year or Tabernacles. The theme for which it invites the praises of priests and laity is the goodness and greatness of the God of Israel (vss. 3-4, 13-18; cf. 136:1-3), who has manifested himself as Lord of nature and of history in the work of creation (vs. 6), the control of the elements (vs. 7), the events of the deliverance from Egypt (vss. 8-9), the conquest and settlement of Canaan (vss. 10-11), and in his compassionate dealings with Israel from generation to generation (vss. 13-14). Clearly

Whatever the LORD pleases he does
in heaven and on earth,

and in comparison with him the gods of the nations are of no account (vss. 15-18).

The contents of the psalm are for the most part made up of a series of quotations from a variety of sources: cf. vs. 1 with 113:1; vs. 2 with 134:1; vs. 4 with Deut. 7:6; vs. 7 with Jer. 10:13; vss. 10-12 with Ps. 136:17-22; vss. 13-18 with Isa. 44:12-20; Jer. 10:6-10; vss. 15-20 with Ps. 115:4-11. Its effectiveness in providing utterance for the spirit of praise in the congregation was probably heightened by this use of familiar matter, but the skill of the psalmist in the selection and arrangement of the borrowed elements gave the psalm its distinctive quality as a hymn. In short, the psalmist was less a poet than a hymnodist. And it is doubtless for its hymnic qualities that the psalm has been given a permanent place in the Jewish liturgy, being appointed for use in the regular order of the morning service.

It is clear that the psalm was meant to be sung antiphonally. But it achieves its end along different lines from those of its companion piece, Ps. 136, in the distribution of the parts between solo voices, choirs, and congregation. Vss. 5-7, 8-12, 15-17, were probably three independent solo parts. The temple choirs and the congregation had their several parts in the rendering of vss. 1-4, 19-21. Vss. 13-14, 18 seem to be general responses in which both choirs and congregation joined.

Because of its indebtedness to other psalms which are themselves late, a late postexilic date is to be assigned to this psalm. The meter is 3+3 with instances of 4+4 (vss. 16-17, 19-20) and 4+3 (vss. 7, 15).

1. EXHORTATION TO PRAISE (135:1-4)

135:1-4. Praise the LORD and "Bless the LORD" are cultic shouts; in this psalm they must have served as responses, repeated several times, to the exhortation—now to

---

135:1-21. ***Blessed Be the Lord God of Israel.*** —Like every other book of praise, the book of Psalms has its outstanding hymns, the favorites of each succeeding generation. It has also its lesser ones, which no doubt had a useful place in temple worship and are still acceptable in Christian churches, but which appear to be less original, less dynamic, and therefore less known.

Ps. 135 seems to fall into the latter group. Prothero tells us[4] that it was read by David Livingstone before he left his Scottish home to begin his lifework in Africa; but otherwise there are few references to it in ancient or modern literature. It is not one of the passages we are expected to memorize in childhood, nor are its verses in constant use as texts for preachers. No one demands its omission from the Bible, but rarely is it singled out for special mention.

This may be due partly to the fact that its character and purpose have not been widely recognized. It is not intended to be an original poem; it is a hymn prepared for public worship. It may have been constructed with one of the great festivals in mind. It is clearly antiphonal in character, certain parts to be sung by the priests, others by the Levites and by the whole congregation. It might well be used as a proces-

[4] *Psalms in Human Life,* pp. 264-65.

2 Ye that stand in the house of the LORD,
in the courts of the house of our God,
3 Praise the LORD; for the LORD *is* good:
sing praises unto his name; for *it is* pleasant.
4 For the LORD hath chosen Jacob unto
himself, *and* Israel for his peculiar treasure.
5 For I know that the LORD *is* great, and
that our Lord *is* above all gods.
6 Whatsoever the LORD pleased, *that* did
he in heaven, and in earth, in the seas, and
all deep places.
7 He causeth the vapors to ascend from
the ends of the earth; he maketh lightnings
for the rain; he bringeth the wind out of
his treasuries.

2 you that stand in the house of the LORD,
in the courts of the house of our God!
3 Praise the LORD, for the LORD is good;
sing to his name, for he is gracious!
4 For the LORD has chosen Jacob for himself,
Israel as his own possession.

5 For I know that the LORD is great,
and that our Lord is above all gods.
6 Whatever the LORD pleases he does,
in heaven and on earth,
in the seas and all deeps.
7 He it is who makes the clouds rise at the end of the earth,
who makes lightnings for the rain
and brings forth the wind from his storehouses.

---

priests, now to Levites, now to the laity—to praise the Lord. By such means the fervor of the worshipers must have been raised to a high pitch. The goodness and the graciousness of the Lord are themes of praise, but even more, his choice of **Jacob for himself, . . . as his own possession** (KJV, **his peculiar treasure**). Cf. Deut. 7:6-7; 14:2; 26:18.

2. THE LORD'S GREATNESS (135:5-7)

5-7. Another reason for praising the Lord is that he **is above all gods.** The measure of his greatness is to be seen not only in the fact that he created the heavens and the earth in the past, but in that whatever happens now in nature is in accordance with his

---

sional hymn in which clergy and choir exhort the people and the whole assembly responds in joyous unity. How fitting if an Easter morning service should thus begin with loud hallelujahs, with a glad confession of what God has done and still does, with a contrast between worship which lifts the mind and braces the soul and idolatry which depresses and demoralizes! Is there no place for massed instruments and the dramatic note if they rouse us from sleeping acquiescence and bring to life the reality of the words we say and sing?

The writer may have borrowed phrases from many sources, but he compiled them with conspicuous success. Notice the sustained progression of thought. He begins with praise. He passes to reasons why gratitude should be in men's hearts and upon their lips. In the first place, the God they worship is the Lord of nature. In the second place, he is the controlling power in history. These themes are not worked out in detail, but there are references to what he does in heaven and earth and sea, and further references to mighty acts in the deliverance of the fathers from Egypt. The signs and wonders against Pharaoh and his servants were not accidents or coincidence: they were expressions of the divine will, the outward and visible signs of divine favor. The psalmist immediately proceeds then to the contrast between the worship of this mighty God of Israel and the idolatry so common among surrounding peoples. He uses language that prophets have made familiar in describing the idols which his exiled fathers had seen in Babylon, a land that was full of idols, great and small; idols that were crude and repulsive, idols that were cunningly carved and artistically modeled. But they were all alike in this: they were lifeless and useless. They were but images without speech or sight, hearing or smell. Here was a fundamental difference between Israel and the nations that surrounded her, for what men worship they become like. Those who seek the living God who creates, sustains, protects, and guides, become creative beings. Those who pour out their hearts to idols, even though they are of silver and gold, become darkened in mind and distressed in spirit. Thus we come to the final exhortations:

O house of Israel, bless the LORD!
O house of Aaron, bless the LORD!
O house of Levi, bless the LORD!

8 Who smote the firstborn of Egypt, both of man and beast.

9 *Who* sent tokens and wonders into the midst of thee, O Egypt, upon Pharaoh, and upon all his servants.

10 Who smote great nations, and slew mighty kings;

11 Sihon king of the Amorites, and Og king of Bashan, and all the kingdoms of Canaan:

12 And gave their land *for* a heritage, a heritage unto Israel his people.

8 He it was who smote the first-born of
Egypt,
both of man and of beast;
9 who in thy midst, O Egypt,
sent signs and wonders
against Pharaoh and all his servants;
10 who smote many nations
and slew mighty kings,
11 Sihon, king of the Amorites,
and Og, king of Bashan,
and all the kingdoms of Canaan,
12 and gave their land as a heritage,
a heritage to his people Israel.

---

will. **The clouds** that rise out of the Mediterranean horizon (cf. I Kings 18:44-45), the rainstorms that follow with their **lightnings** and **wind,** proclaim his providential rule.

3. The Lord's Mighty Deeds (135:8-12)

8-12. Israel has special reasons for praising the Lord because of the miraculous (vss. 8-9) and mighty deeds (vss. 10-11) by which he gave them their heritage (vs. 12). It is to be noted that Hebrew hymns, different from those of other ancient peoples, appeal to history as an evidence of the greatness of their God. Emend vs. 9*a* to read "who in the midst of Egypt."

Ps. 135 is, however, more than a liturgical hymn of praise. It is a reminder to every generation of some of the essential characteristics of true worship. First, true worship is always objective. It is more than spiritual meditation. It is the offering of a gift, in this case a gift of praise to God. And the God to whom mind and heart are lifted in gratitude and adoration is not just an immanent spirit such as Wordsworth felt—

> The Being, that is in the clouds and air,
> That is in the green leaves among the groves[5]—

not just

> A motion and a spirit, that impels
> All thinking things, all objects of all thought,
> And rolls through all things.[6]

The psalmists believed in a God who is never far from any one of us (see especially Ps. 139). There is no secret that can be hid from his all-seeing eye, and whoever we are and wherever we go we cannot escape his omniscience. The knowledge of such intimacy was too much for men then, as it is too much for us still. But it did not lead to a vague pantheism. As certain as the immanence was the transcendence. God is not only in man; he stands over against him. Like the light of the sun he is above us and beyond us, and to him in highest heaven we must lift thought and speech, and before him we must bow. It does not mean that in worship there is no place for self-examination. There is. But it is knowledge of ourselves as created beings wholly dependent upon the Creator. There are subjective moods in the book of Psalms, but here the emphasis is on the God who is and who creates:

> **He it is who makes the clouds rise at the end of the earth,**
> **who makes lightnings for the rain**
> **and brings forth the wind from his storehouses**
> (vs. 7);

who guides men and nations, and who especially protects his chosen people, leads them out of captivity, and brings them to the Promised Land (vss. 8-12).

Notice the emphatic manner in which the psalmist says that God **has chosen Jacob for himself** (vs. 4). There are times when men themselves must choose. They must be challenged to decide once for all whether they will serve God or Baal, Christ or mammon. They must be given no peace until the confession is made, and their part of the covenant stands plain before the world. But first there is the fact that God has chosen them and will not let them go. This is put so strongly in vs. 6 that it sounds arbitrary until we remember that what God pleases is always consistent with his people's welfare. Indeed, there is no prosperity for men apart from the pleasure of God. Yet though he

[5] "Hart-leap Well," Part II, st. xviii.

[6] "Lines Composed a Few Miles Above Tintern Abbey."

13 Thy name, O LORD, *endureth* for ever; *and* thy memorial, O LORD, throughout all generations.

14 For the LORD will judge his people, and he will repent himself concerning his servants.

15 The idols of the heathen *are* silver and gold, the work of men's hands.

16 They have mouths, but they speak not; eyes have they, but they see not;

17 They have ears, but they hear not; neither is there *any* breath in their mouths.

18 They that make them are like unto them: *so is* every one that trusteth in them.

13 Thy name, O LORD, endures for ever,
thy renown, O LORD, throughout all ages.
14 For the LORD will vindicate his people,
and have compassion on his servants.

15 The idols of the nations are silver and gold,
the work of men's hands.
16 They have mouths, but they speak not,
they have eyes, but they see not,
17 they have ears, but they hear not,
nor is there any breath in their mouths.
18 Like them be those who make them! —
yea, every one who trusts in them!

4. THE LORD VINDICATES HIS PEOPLE (135:13-14)

13-14. All things confirm what the Lord said in Exod. 3:14: his **name . . . endures for ever** [I am that I am] **. . . throughout all ages.** And in all Israel's generations he fulfills the promise of Deut. 32:36 to vindicate his people "when he sees that their power is gone."

5. THE VANITY OF IDOLATRY (135:15-18)

15-18. The greatness of the God of gods is again exalted through a derisive description of what **the idols of the nations** really are. The psalmist uses a favorite argument of the protagonists of Israel's religion to demonstrate the superiority of the Lord by proving the nothingness of his rivals. The gods are by implication equated with their images,

is almighty and all-wise he forces no man, but waits for entrance into human minds and hearts. He sits as judge, yet in mercy he pardons and in love he redeems. It is too wonderful for finite minds to grasp, yet psalmist after psalmist beheld and announced that which was to be fully revealed in the life and death and resurrection of Jesus Christ. This is the God to whom men must turn, and as he is consistently put at the center of man's worship, he takes his proper place at the center of human life.

Second, true worship is common worship. There are, it is true, times for solitary prayer and praise. Just as Jesus Christ would turn aside to a desert place or climb the hills for communion with the Father, so all deeply religious persons find it necessary to be alone with God. This is so essential that one philosopher has declared that "religion is what the individual does with his own solitariness." [7] Yet here as elsewhere we demand fellowship. And God has fashioned it for us because we need it. We need the support of sinners like ourselves as we approach his awful holiness. We need the encouragement of other aspiring hearts as we try to rise above this mundane realm into the heavenly places. We need the guidance of men and women of greater ability and sanctity than ourselves as we endeavor to express the praise we bring. We rarely stop to think how much we depend upon one another when we gather in the place of prayer. We see our indebtedness to those who sing and those who exhort, to those who explain and those who inspire, but we hardly realize how much we owe to worshipers as limited and as sinful as ourselves. A congregation that worships in spirit and in truth is a unity. There are parts we can and should do separately. We cannot all instruct. We cannot all take conspicuous places or perform priestly or musical duties. But we can all participate in the praise. And never is common praise more moving than when every heart, every mind, every voice participates in one glad, solemn chorus of thanksgiving.

Third, true worship expresses itself in praise. It does not always start there. It may begin with silent adoration. It may proceed to a contrite confession of sin. It may and should pass to intercession, in which not only those who are near and dear are remembered but the needs of men everywhere find expression. But if adoration, confession, and intercession are sincere and wholehearted, gratitude will quickly find a

[7] A. N. Whitehead, *Religion in the Making* (New York: The Macmillan Co., 1926), p. 16.

19 Bless the LORD, O house of Israel:
bless the LORD, O house of Aaron:
20 Bless the LORD, O house of Levi: ye
that fear the LORD, bless the LORD.
21 Blessed be the LORD out of Zion,
which dwelleth at Jerusalem. Praise ye the
LORD.

19 O house of Israel, bless the LORD!
O house of Aaron, bless the LORD!
20 O house of Levi, bless the LORD!
You that fear the LORD, bless the LORD!
21 Blessed be the LORD from Zion,
he who dwells in Jerusalem!
Praise the LORD!

136 O give thanks unto the LORD; for *he is* good: for his mercy *endureth* for ever.

136 O give thanks to the LORD, for he is good,
for his steadfast love endures for ever.

---

and then the uselessness and impotence of images is turned into ridicule (cf. 115:3-8; Jer. 10:7-16; Isa. 44:9-18; Wisd. Sol. 15:14-17). Emend vs. 17*b* to read "noses have they but smell not" (cf. 115:6*b*); the **mouths** are mentioned in vs. 16.

6. Final Summons to Praise (135:19-21)

19-20. The psalm ends with a crescendo of antiphonal praises in which laity, priests, Levites, temple servants (cf. I Chr. 9:2) contribute their paeans successively and then in chorus.

21. Read "in Zion" for **from Zion.** The psalm closed with "hallelujah," **Praise the LORD,** and Ps. 136 opened with the same expression (cf. LXX), but through haplography only one "hallelujah" appears in the present text.

CXXXVI. Praise Him Whose Steadfast Love Endures Forever (136:1-26)

This is a liturgical psalm of thanksgiving. It is unique by reason of its thoroughgoing antiphonal character. Every one of its twenty-six verses is constructed of two lines, the first, which carries the theme, being chanted by a choir, and the second by another choir (cf. I Chr. 16:41) or the congregation (cf. II Chr. 7:1-3) as a response. If the responses are removed, the remaining lines constitute a poem closely resembling Ps. 135. The psalm, as it stands, represents an attempt to elaborate a hymn on the simple theme of vs. 1, which was by long tradition a common responsory in the liturgy of the temple (cf. vss. 1-3, 26; 106:1; 107:1; 118:1-4; I Chr. 16:34; II Chr. 20:21; Ezra 3:11; I Macc. 4:24), and its style and manner are honored by imitation in the Hebrew text of Ecclus. 51:12. Because of its general appropriateness for the sacred services at the seasons of

---

place, praise for what God is, for the forgiveness he bestows, for the prayers he answers. It may break through spontaneously in unexpected ways and in different places, but if the worship is intense, it will culminate in a burst of praise. It will express itself in speech and song, very often in antiphonal speech and song, and send men on their homeward way with gladness in their hearts. The sorrows and discords of life will not be ignored, but they will be transcended. The burdens will often remain, but they will be carried more easily. The joy will not be locked up in individual hearts and minds; it will bring a new courage to friends and neighbors and through them pass to men and women unknown. Such worship brings health and happiness to the whole community, and hope to those who are burdened with fear. It is to be regarded not as an emotional indulgence but as an offering to Almighty God which brings peace and blessedness to a needy world.

You that fear the LORD, bless the LORD!
Blessed be the LORD from Zion,
he who dwells in Jerusalem!
Praise the LORD!

136:1-26. ***His Mercy Endureth for Ever.***—Wherever serious-minded people are gathered together one is likely to hear anxious discussions on the present condition of the church. The concern is natural and inevitable, but more thought might well be paid to the cause. Is it because we are deeply interested in religious institutions and are distressed by signs of decline? Or is it because of a deep conviction that man is made for God and apart from him must remain forever unsatisfied?

Before we condemn the institutional approach to the subject, however, we could with

2 O give thanks unto the God of gods: for his mercy *endureth* for ever.
3 O give thanks to the Lord of lords: for his mercy *endureth* for ever.

2 O give thanks to the God of gods,
for his steadfast love endures for ever.
3 O give thanks to the Lord of lords,
for his steadfast love endures for ever;

---

the great festivals its use was perpetuated, and in the Jewish liturgy, either alone or with Ps. 135, it became known as the Great Hallel in distinction from the Little Hallel (Pss. 113–118; see article, "Hallel," *The Jewish Encyclopedia* [New York: Funk & Wagnalls, 1906], VI, 176-77), the epithet "great" deriving from the twenty-six repetitions of the response about the goodness of God.

The psalm, like the *Te Deum,* is the product of some expansions, the original psalm consisting only of vss. 1-9, 25-26, to which later were added vss. 10-24, supplemented with the responses. In the resultant body of verses there are two major themes: the Lord as creator and the Lord as the guide and champion of Israel from the beginnings of its history at the Exodus onward. The psalm was therefore evidently meant for use at the seasons of the Passover and the New Year, two festivals which were closely associated in the postexilic period (Exod. 12:1-20; Lev. 23:5; Num. 28:11; see George Buchanan Gray, *Sacrifice in the Old Testament* [Oxford: Clarendon Press, 1925], pp. 299-300).

The psalm belongs to a late postexilic date. Much of its material is drawn from the Pentateuch in its late form; e.g., cf. vss. 2-3 with Deut. 10:17; vss. 7-9 with Gen. 1:16; vs. 12 with Deut. 26:8; vs. 13 with Exod. 14:29; vs. 15 with Exod. 14:27; 15:4. The use of ל as *nota accusativi* (vss. 19-20, 23) is late. The implied juxtaposition of a New Year festival with the Passover, as noted above, is a late practice. The title **the God of Heaven** occurs only in late postexilic literature such as Chronicles, Ezra, Nehemiah, and Daniel. The meter is almost without exception 3+3.

1. Summons to Give Thanks to God (136:1-3)

136:1-3. The hymn opens with the summons, chanted by a precentor or a choir, to the worshiping congregation to **give thanks to the Lord.** Then follows through the rest of the hymn a series of reasons for rendering this thanksgiving. To each of these reasons the congregation or the whole body of singers repeats the same response, which sets forth with the emphasis of repetition that the fundamental mark of all that God is and does is his never-ceasing *ḥeṣedh,* a word which, though translated "kindness," implies "fidelity" or "loyalty" and has more facets than can be rendered by a single English word. It is in accordance with the hymn style that God is spoken of in the third person throughout the psalm; in a hymn God is usually praised, not prayed to.

The first motif for thanksgiving is what God is: **he is good, . . . the God of gods, . . . the Lord of lords;** i.e., he is a God who because of the goodness of his character deserves the devotion of human beings, who is supreme over all the gods, and who dominates all lords, be they human rulers, angels, or demons (cf. Rom. 8:38-39). Because of his

---

profit turn back to William R. Inge's *Outspoken Essays,* and especially to the chapter entitled "Institutionalism and Mysticism." By mysticism the writer means "immediate communion, real or supposed, between the human soul and the Soul of the World or the Divine Spirit."[8] This he believes, and we must agree, to be the one thing necessary in all true religion. Probably every religious movement which has brought light and liberty to the race has begun with such an experience. Sometimes the experience has been accompanied by extraordinary phenomena. There have been visions and voices, ecstatic speech and miraculous deeds, new social groups and missionary movements. But always the important thing has been the contact with absolute Reality, not the extraordinary accompaniments or the institutional expression.

There are dangers in such experiences. There is the danger of insularity. Some are tempted to keep their visions to themselves, to save their own souls and let the world go its evil way. Even if they do attempt to share the truth that has made them free, they may be guilty of imperfect human sympathy. The result is invariably disappointing. Visions kept secret usually

[8] First series (London: Longmans Green & Co., 1919), p. 230.

4 To him who alone doeth great wonders: for his mercy *endureth* for ever.
5 To him that by wisdom made the heavens: for his mercy *endureth* for ever.
6 To him that stretched out the earth above the waters: for his mercy *endureth* for ever.
7 To him that made great lights: for his mercy *endureth* for ever:
8 The sun to rule by day: for his mercy *endureth* for ever:
9 The moon and stars to rule by night: for his mercy *endureth* for ever.

4 to him who alone does great wonders,
for his steadfast love endures for ever;
5 to him who by understanding made the heavens,
for his steadfast love endures for ever;
6 to him who spread out the earth upon the waters,
for his steadfast love endures for ever;
7 to him who made the great lights,
for his steadfast love endures for ever;
8 the sun to rule over the day,
for his steadfast love endures for ever;
9 the moon and stars to rule over the night,
for his steadfast love endures for ever;

goodness and faithful kindness he will not permit men to be subject to any dominion but his own.

2. God the Creator of All (136:4-9)

4-9. The second motif for thanksgiving is God's work in creation. He made all things without the help of any other being or beings, and so the world is altogether his world. All his creative work manifests understanding, wisdom, and beneficent order. "The world is vivified, not by a multitude of spirits, but by a single Divine Mind. . . . The majesty of the universe, which oppressed Lucretius with a sense of the indifference of the gods and the misery of men, is to the Hebrew poet a revelation not only of the greatness but of the goodness of God" (James Strahan, *The Book of Job* [Edinburgh: T. & T. Clark, 1913], p. 315; cf. Job 38). It is to be noted in this section that the psalmist's description of creation conforms to that of Gen. 1 except in vs. 6, which accords

fade. Even virtues cultivated in solitude may breed vices. We need fellowship to keep us from eccentricities, and fellowship leads to more or less enduring organizations. Thus from personal mysticism we are quickly led to some kind of institution.

But the dangers of institutionalism are also many. There is especially the danger of becoming more zealous for the organization than for the truth it was created to perpetuate. This is the greatest temptation of those who have been called to official positions. We want to maintain numbers and prestige. We want to maintain a worthy place in the community. It may be a laudable ambition; but when we become more anxious about the welfare of the society than about the cause itself, it is lamentable. And how many of us unconsciously fail just here? We go on and on attending meetings, visiting the sick, preaching sermons, and administering sacraments, perhaps winning commendation for our energy and devotion, but doing it for the praise of men more than as an offering to God. We may by ceaseless toil build large congregations, only in the end to find that they are not even religious. We may have theological competence and missionary enthusiasm, but if the institution smothers spiritual life, we need to start all over again.

These reflections, so germane to the present situation, have been prompted by a study of Ps. 136, which in Jewish literature is known as the Great Hallel, the singing of which was a regular part of the Passover and the New Year festivals. It is the one psalm which is liturgical throughout, to every line sung by priest or choir there being the same congregational response: **For his mercy endureth for ever.** Those therefore who read with historical imagination have before the mind's eye a picture of the temple filled with worshipers offering praise and renewing vows. They have come from many parts, representing many vocations and interests and varying states of religious development; but they are united as well in faith and blood as in a common liturgy. It is a picture that suggests institutional religion as it ought to be. The sacred buildings, the priests, the Levites, the musicians and the choristers, cannot guarantee spiritual vision or a living faith; but they belong to the religious cultus and have their necessary place in common worship. The psalm was doubtless composed or compiled for such a festival. It was in that place and to those people

10 To him that smote Egypt in their firstborn: for his mercy *endureth* for ever:
11 And brought out Israel from among them: for his mercy *endureth* for ever:
12 With a strong hand, and with a stretched out arm: for his mercy *endureth* for ever.
13 To him which divided the Red sea into parts: for his mercy *endureth* for ever:
14 And made Israel to pass through the midst of it: for his mercy *endureth* for ever:
15 But overthrew Pharaoh and his host in the Red sea: for his mercy *endureth* for ever.
16 To him which led his people through the wilderness: for his mercy *endureth* for ever.
17 To him which smote great kings: for his mercy *endureth* for ever:

10 to him who smote the first-born of Egypt,
for his steadfast love endures for ever;
11 and brought Israel out from among them,
for his steadfast love endures for ever;
12 with a strong hand and an outstretched arm,
for his steadfast love endures for ever;
13 to him who divided the Red Sea in sunder,
for his steadfast love endures for ever;
14 and made Israel pass through the midst of it,
for his steadfast love endures for ever;
15 but overthrew Pharaoh and his host in the Red Sea,
for his steadfast love endures for ever;
16 to him who led his people through the wilderness,
for his steadfast love endures for ever;
17 to him who smote great kings,
for his steadfast love endures for ever;

---

with the Babylonian story, and that in relating God's attributes and work he employs in Hebrew the hymnic participle (cf. vss. 4-17).

3. God in Israel's History (136:10-22)

10-22. The third motif for thanksgiving is God's work in giving Israel its deliverance from Egypt, its triumphal journey through the wilderness, and its conquest of Canaan—i.e., its nationhood, its land, and its history (cf. Amos 2:9-10; Deut. 8:14-18). The psalmist draws on the traditional sources in describing stage by stage Israel's epic beginnings (cf. Exod. 12:29-37; 13:3; 14:22-29; Num. 21:22-26, 33-35).

---

very much what the Te Deum is in Christian congregations—a community act and a public demonstration.

The most significant thing, however, about this psalm is not its liturgical form but its religious quality. It is a hymn of praise with personal gratitude in every line. There is nothing dubious or hesitating about the opening verses, which suggest a true experience of the living God. **O give thanks to the Lord, for he is good . . . . O give thanks to the God of gods . . . . O give thanks to the Lord of lords.**

It is not necessarily the exclamation of successful men, as the world judges. The most convincing praise comes not from those who have been sheltered and pampered, but from those who have been exposed to the bitter blasts of adversity. Actually there is more than personal experience here: there is a lively appreciation of what God did long before the author looked through wondering eyes. Experience must be narrow and may become narrowing if it is limited to what the individual has seen and felt and heard. But when it is enriched and deepened by an understanding of what God has done to others through the ages, it has the breadth and dignity of vision from a mountain range. And so the psalmist goes back even beyond the human span, beyond the measure of material things, to the Creator who **by understanding made the heavens,** and **spread out the earth upon the waters,** and made **the sun to rule over the day** and **the moon and stars to rule over the night.** Astronomer and geographer may detect an old-world cosmogony in the forms of expression; what is important is that both an instinct for poetry and a feeling for mystical experience lie behind them. But it is not vague poetic instinct nor an otherworldly mysticism, for the writer immediately rejoices in the fact that the Lord who created did not leave the universe to itself. He continued to work in it and through it, through every season and natural law. He had worked especially in and through his people Israel, had brought them out of slavery and established them in the land of Canaan. Had the tribes been left to their own devices they would never have escaped from

18 And slew famous kings: for his mercy
endureth for ever:
19 Sihon king of the Amorites: for his
mercy *endureth* for ever:
20 And Og the king of Bashan: for his
mercy *endureth* for ever:
21 And gave their land for a heritage:
for his mercy *endureth* for ever:
22 *Even* a heritage unto Israel his servant: for his mercy *endureth* for ever.
23 Who remembered us in our low estate: for his mercy *endureth* for ever:
24 And hath redeemed us from our enemies: for his mercy *endureth* for ever.

18 and slew famous kings,
for his steadfast love endures for ever;
19 Sihon, king of the Amorites,
for his steadfast love endures for ever;
20 and Og, king of Bashan,
for his steadfast love endures for ever;
21 and gave their land as a heritage,
for his steadfast love endures for ever;
22 a heritage to Israel his servant,
for his steadfast love endures for ever.

23 It is he who remembered us in our low
estate,
for his steadfast love endures for ever;
24 and rescued us from our foes,
for his steadfast love endures for ever;

---

4. God the Savior (136:23-25)

23-24. The fourth motif for thanksgiving is God's remembrance of Israel from the days of its settlement in Canaan (cf. Judg. 3:7-9; 6:1–8:32), onward through all the distresses which it suffered at the hands of Aramaeans, Assyrians, and Babylonians. It is possible, however, that in these verses the psalmist is thinking only of the Exile and the deliverance from it.

25. The final motif is thanks to God **who gives food to all flesh** (cf. 104:27-29), for he is not a God who has left the world after he created it, nor a God who intermittently

---

Egypt, or if they had, they would have lost themselves in wilderness wanderings. But led on, as they believed, and as the psalmist was assured, even **Sihon, king of the Amorites,** and **Og, king of Bashan,** could not stop them.

Thus we come to those notes of providence and redemption which sound throughout Hebrew literature. The Israelites had not delivered themselves from bondage or guided themselves to a rich heritage. They had been brought out by a strong arm and led by an overshadowing Presence. They had been remembered when they thought themselves forgotten and fed when food failed. They had not by weight of numbers or by military prowess established themselves in the land flowing with milk and honey. It was given to them, the Land of Promise. The wonder of it was ever before them and sprang from their hearts again and again in songs of praise.

It is not strange that John Milton, when he was a young student in Christ's College, Cambridge, made of Ps. 136 a hymn for Christian congregations. Millions have lifted up their hearts in gratitude as they have sung:

> Let us with a gladsome mind
> Praise the Lord, for he is kind.

But kindness is a weak word for such divine activity. Kindness as men know it can be fitful. The mercy of the Lord endures from generation to generation. It is inexhaustible. There can be but one fitting human response: an attitude of praise and adoration. What joy has flowed forth from such worshiping congregations to a humanity still prone to wander, and in wandering to multiply its sorrows!

As a modern illustration of this happy blending of institutionalism and mysticism we might turn to literature of a totally different kind—to Alan Paton's novel *Cry, the Beloved Country.*[9] Critics of certain schools may object to it as too sentimental; but as a study of an unsophisticated mind, and as a picture of African life, it is extraordinarily powerful. It tells of a native pastor who loves his scattered congregation and tends with unswerving devotion his crazy little church. Life is not idyllic in the remote valleys, even though they are free from many of the temptations and sufferings of urban life. There are droughts bringing famine and death to men and cattle and accelerating the drift to the towns. The old men, the women, and the children are left to manage as they can while young men face the dangers, the strange and exciting customs of the crowded cities. Among the latter is the pastor's son, who in the new environment sinks lower and lower until in an unpremeditated act he takes the life of one of the best of the white men. Our concern is not

[9] New York: Charles Scribner's Sons, 1948.

25 Who giveth food to all flesh: for his mercy *endureth* for ever.
26 O give thanks unto the God of heaven: for his mercy *endureth* for ever.

137 By the rivers of Babylon, there we sat down, yea, we wept, when we remembered Zion.

25 he who gives food to all flesh,
for his steadfast love endures for ever.

26 O give thanks to the God of heaven,
for his steadfast love endures for ever.

137 By the waters[o] of Babylon,
there we sat down and wept,
when we remembered Zion.

[o] Heb *streams*

---

intervenes in the course of history, but a God who every day by his care of his creatures gives witness of his presence in his creation.

5. Concluding Doxology (136:26)

26. The psalm is terminated in hymn style by a repetition of the opening theme (vss. 1-3): **Give thanks to the God of heaven.** Some LXX MSS add "Give thanks to the Lord of lords."

CXXXVII. The Song of an Exile (137:1-9)

We are so charmed by the freshness, vividness, and emotional appeal of this balladlike psalm that most of us are blinded to the real purpose which it was meant to serve. It is properly a cursing or imprecatory psalm, the only example of its kind in the Psalter. This type may be viewed as a subclass of the lament, since it is the experience of distress or persecution or bitterness of soul that occasions resort to a curse as a means of defense or revenge.

In the O.T. the history of the curse, like that of the blessing, is one of progress from a time when the curse itself was reckoned as automatically efficacious to a time when the operation of the curse was entrusted to God as the sole source of power in all things. The monotheistic trends in the religion of Israel worked for the eradication of practices that were rooted in primitive beliefs in magic. However, the substitution of

---

with the lad and his inner torments, but with the father who continues to watch over his flock with tender solicitude while secretly he wrestles with God for the soul of his son. It is a poverty-stricken setting, but it represents institutional religion at its best. Without much aptitude for the work, the old man cares for wretched buildings and struggles to balance accounts and deals with tiresome parishioners. It might easily have been so tedious and tiring that joy would have left him altogether. But Kumalo knows what it is to be alone with God. In critical moments, like his Lord, he goes away to the mountains to pray. He is there at the time appointed for his son's execution, and there he finds grace to continue the work God had given him. Behind the pastoral routine and the parental care is the mystical experience which gives poise and endurance even in the midst of tragedy.

This is the cure for empty churches. When it is present, a new note creeps into work and worship, a new spirit even into ecclesiastical business. There is no slackness in duty; the forms are as perfect as diligence can make them. But behind them is reverence, a sense of the sacred, which men feel and to which they respond. Like a tide that covers the rocks and sands and creeps up the rivers, the Spirit of God comes and fills empty hearts and rouses dead congregations, until again from continent to continent the chorus of praise resounds:

O give thanks to the God of heaven,
for his steadfast love endures for ever.

137:1-9. ***True and False Patriotism.***—Many parts of the Bible have "come to life" again in the stirring events of modern times, and not least Ps. 137. We have seen intense patriotism, some of it flamboyant and aggressive, but much of it pure and passionate.[1] And we have seen many exiles in many different lands—men and women fleeing for their lives, leaving behind them friends and property, not knowing whether ever again they would set foot on the soil that gave them birth and the home which

[1] See Ballard, *Does War Shake Faith?* final chapter.

2 We hanged our harps upon the willows in the midst thereof.
3 For there they that carried us away captive required of us a song; and they that wasted us *required of us* mirth, *saying,* Sing us *one* of the songs of Zion.

2 On the willows[p] there
we hung up our lyres.
3 For there our captors
required of us songs,
and our tormentors, mirth, saying,
"Sing us one of the songs of Zion!"

[p] Or *poplars*

God for magic as the agency of evil did not sanctify the ugly thing or transform those who invoked it. In its modified form it lingers in the laments in which the psalmists call on God to execute vengeance on their foes (cf. Ps. 109; Matt. 5:44; Rom. 12:14).

In this psalm we are made intensely aware of the mood of those Jews in the Exile who in spite of their vicissitudes remained loyal to faith, tradition, and country, resisting the temptations to fall away to foreign cults or to give themselves up to the pursuit of business and trade (cf. Ezek. 14:1-11; 16:1–17:24; Isa. 47:13; 65:11). The psalmist belonged to their number, and he translates into burning words the feelings that surged in their souls. But at the time he writes he is no longer in Babylon, as the past tense of the verbs in vss. 1-3 and the word **there** in vss. 1, 3 disclose. Did he escape early in the period of the Exile and find his way to Jerusalem? Is he one of those who returned after Cyrus issued his decree in 538 B.C.? Probably not, for his memory of the experiences of the Exile is still fresh and vivid and his indignation flaming. In addition, according to vs. 8 Babylon is still untouched by the Persians. Thus the psalm belongs to the exilic period and the *terminus ad quem* must be 538 B.C.

The psalm opens with the sad strains of lament (vss. 1-3), then suddenly changes into a curse (*a*) on the psalmist himself if ever his love for Jerusalem grows cold (vss. 4-6), and (*b*) on the peoples who laid it waste (vss. 7-9). The meter is dominantly 3+2. Instances of 2+2+2 occur in vss. 1, 3, 7, but the text is not above suspicion.

1. The Exiles in Babylon (137:1-3)

137:1-3. The psalmist pictures the sad lot of the exiles **by the waters of Babylon,** i.e., by the **streams** or canals which interlaced the land between the Euphrates and the Tigris. **We sat down,** for to sit on the ground was the posture of mourners in the

never seemed so dear to them as when they were snatched from it and forced to go out into a strange inhospitable world. Some of the displaced persons thus thrust forth, like derelicts upon the mighty deep, have found it possible to settle down again, to make new friends and discover new interests; they have indeed been stimulated to great enterprises. Others, and we may surmise that they are the great majority, have pined for old scenes and occupations, have grown listless and languid, have wandered with growing distress from city to city and from country to country. Spiritual reactions have also differed. Some, like the Jews in Babylon, have hung their harps on the willows and declined to sing the songs of the homeland. The national and religious festivals in which they once so gladly participated have come and gone, not indeed without poignant memories, but without so much as a simple hymn or a local assembly. The silence is not to be mistaken for indifference. Strong emotions contend with one another, especially antipathy toward those who have caused such suffering. If only the exiles dared to express themselves, and sometimes they do, what vehemence there would be, what bitterness of denunciation, what promise of reprisals if only an opportunity were to come! Perhaps the language is all the stronger because action is impossible, but the words are frightening enough, words like those at the end of this psalm:

O daughter of Babylon, you devastator!
Happy shall he be who requites you
with what you have done to us!
Happy shall he be who takes your little ones
and dashes them against the rock!

This thing called patriotism, which has so many different attributes and expresses itself in so many different ways, is not the characteristic of an age or a nation or a class. It takes different forms, but it springs from the same root in savage and in savant, in prince and in peasant, in the vast crowds of a modern city and in the primitive dwellings of remote tribes. To try and

4 How shall we sing the LORD's song in a
strange land?
5 If I forget thee, O Jerusalem, let my
right hand forget *her cunning.*
6 If I do not remember thee, let my
tongue cleave to the roof of my mouth; if
I prefer not Jerusalem above my chief joy.

4 How shall we sing the LORD's song
in a foreign land?
5 If I forget you, O Jerusalem,
let my right hand wither!
6 Let my tongue cleave to the roof of my
mouth,
if I do not remember you,
if I do not set Jerusalem
above my highest joy!

---

ancient East, **and wept. On the willows,** a species of **poplars** that grows by streams in the region, **we hung up our lyres,** for in their sorrow the exiles had no heart for music and song. The cause of this sad scene, as the psalmist describes it, was the heartless request of **our captors,** "those who had plundered us," to **sing us one of the songs of Zion.** Perhaps their Chaldean masters had heard some reports of the temple music of Zion, or perhaps they wished, like other conquerors in history (cf. Judg. 16:25), only to extract some amusement from the native songs of the captives.

2. If I Forget You, O Jerusalem (137:4-6)

4-6. How shall we sing the LORD's song? Since for the exiles there are no songs of Zion but the Lord's songs, the cruel request wounds their feelings, stirring afresh grief, homesickness, and indignation. To sing the Lord's songs **in a strange land** would be to

---

analyze it may be a work of supererogation, but some of its ingredients can be identified.

It seems to be an elemental love of the soil that bore us. In this psalm, for example, there is—we feel sure of it even though it is not actually stated—a nostalgia for the hills of Judea and the streets of Jerusalem and especially for the temple which suggested to many an Israelite piety he could not express. These Jewish refugees found the plains of Babylon, pleasant enough no doubt to the Babylonians, sadly different from the mountains and valleys of Palestine, as different as India with its almost unbearable heat is from the fickle climate of England. Their mental attitude, as they pined in the great foreign metropolis, was no doubt something like that of William Carey, who, absorbed in his missionary work in India, yet loved to grow the violets of his own native land. It is the same spirit as was confessed by Tennyson in the great elegy to his friend Arthur Henry Hallam; he found comfort in the thought that the body which had died in Vienna would be moved to the land of its birth, and that ultimately it would be laid to rest by the sea at the familiar and favorite Clevedon.

> 'T is well; 't is something; we may stand
> Where he in English earth is laid,
> And from his ashes may be made
> The violet of his native land.[2]

There is nothing virtuous in it, but also nothing to apologize for. It is one of the elemental sentiments of the human heart, a sort of nature mysticism, if you will, and it is to be respected wherever it is found.

But patriotism is more than a feeling for the soil. It is kinship with one's own people; and that still survives even where there are disagreement and temporary discord. The Pilgrim Fathers, to take a conspicuous incident, felt so out of harmony with both government and public opinion that they determined to seek a home in the New World. But when they arrived in Plymouth, and for many years afterward, they did not cease to be Englishmen. Or take one of the best-known poems in the English language: Gray's "Elegy Written in a Country Churchyard" is instinct with this sense of kinship with the living and the dead. The poet looks with contemplative eye upon the rural graves, and as he reads one inscription after another he sees the succeeding generations and recognizes them as his own people. He sees men of marked individuality, "some village-Hampden, . . . some mute inglorious Milton";[3] but not only solitary individuals. He cannot gaze upon that country churchyard without imagining a continuous procession—babies being brought for baptism and young people for confirmation, brides for marriage and the dead for burial. It stretches back a century, two, three, or four centuries, but they are his people, bone of his bone and flesh of his flesh. Some villager goes up to the capital city and lingers around Westminster Abbey or Bunhill Fields, and there it

[2] *In Memoriam,* Part XVIII, st. i.

[3] St. xv.

7 Remember, O LORD, the children of
Edom in the day of Jerusalem; who said,
Rase *it*, rase *it*, *even* to the foundation
thereof.
8 O daughter of Babylon, who art to be
destroyed; happy *shall he be*, that rewardeth
thee as thou hast served us.

7 Remember, O LORD, against the Edomites
the day of Jerusalem,
how they said, "Rase it, rase it!
Down to its foundations!"
8 O daughter of Babylon, you devastator![q]
Happy shall he be who requites you
with what you have done to us!

[q] Or *you who are devastated*

desecrate them, for foreign lands were profane, "unclean" (cf. Amos 7:17; Hos. 9:3-5). The thought of anyone singing the sacred songs to tickle the ears of a godless people evokes from the psalmist a passionate expression of his love for Jerusalem in the form of a curse on himself should he ever fail in loyalty to her. Sardonically, he offers a song with a string of curses (vss. 5-9) as a grim substitute for the request of the foe. He lays a curse on hand and tongue should they with lyre or song prove traitor to **Jerusalem,** which is higher than **my highest joy.**

3. Imprecation on Edom and Babylon (137:7-9)

7-9. A curse is uttered next against the **Edomites,** who in 587 B.C. had rejoiced over the destruction of the temple and the city on **the day of Jerusalem,** saying, **Rase it . . . down to its foundations** (Obad. 10; Lam. 4:21-22; Ezek. 25:12; 35:5). Since Edom

is before him on a larger scale: the real Hampdens and Miltons, the leaders and geniuses of every sphere of community life; and they all belong to him.

Some of us respond to facts like these as eyes respond to light and ears to sound, and we find the O.T. full of it. There is, to cite but one example, a Jew named Nehemiah, cupbearer to Artaxerxes king of Persia. Surely any man should be satisfied with such a lot. But reports reach him from distant Jerusalem. He hears how the walls are broken down and the gates burned and the people afflicted. And he is sad even in the royal presence. But Nehemiah prays as he weeps, and prays with such good effect that, taking his life in his hands, he pleads with the king that he may be permitted to go back and restore order. Read with any imagination, the book of Nehemiah is a thrilling narrative, for it shows how a brave man at the call of country leaves comfort and prosperity and takes upon himself an almost overwhelming burden of administration and reconstruction. Here is one who accepts the responsibilities as well as the privileges of race and blood, and sacrifices everything at the call of duty. It is not the heights of spiritual religion, but who can apologize for it?

> Our fathers' sepulchres are here,
> And here our kindred dwell,
> Our children too; how should we love
> Another land so well? [4]

[4] John R. Wreford, "Lord, while for all mankind we pray."

If that were all, surely no one could have spoken against it. But every virtue has its vice, and the vices of patriotism are many. Ready to make use of it are pride and selfishness, which too often bring forth the evils of an aggressive imperialism or a grasping industrialism. Whenever patriotism leads to power over others, we may expect arrogance and injustice, racial contempt and color prejudice. And if that develops unchecked, the world will soon be filled with hatred, and wars will defeat the most pacific of politicians and bring to nought the dreams of idealists.

Such bitter nationalism becomes conspicuous not once but many times in O.T. literature. Even Nehemiah oversteps the mark, refuses to co-operate with the surrounding peoples, and commands the Jews to put away foreign wives. Seeds were then sown which were to bear harvests of hate for centuries. The hatred was fanned by many disasters, kept alive by succeeding acts of perfidy and injustice, nursed in solitude, to flame out in violent speech in unexpected places. It appears even in the book of Psalms. It has made many a Christian shudder here in Ps. 137, which begins so nobly and ends so brutally. To defend it is impossible, so contrary is it to the wisdom and example of Christ. The utmost we can do is to see how it came into being, to notice that it is by no means unique, and ourselves to take warning.

We started from one of the songs of ancient Israel; we have been led to the heart of modern problems. The fundamental difficulties of every

9 Happy *shall he be,* that taketh and dasheth thy little ones against the stones.	9 Happy shall he be who takes your little ones and dashes them against the rock!

was a blood brother of Judah (Amos 1:11), being descended from Esau, the brother of Jacob, its treachery was unpardonable and the Jews' hatred of it undying (cf. Oesterley and Robinson, *History of Israel,* II, 341). **O daughter of Babylon:** Lit., "O daughter Babylon" (cf. Isa. 1:8; 47:1). **Who art to be destroyed:** Better, "the destroyer," i.e., שודדה; the M.T. should probably be rendered "who are destroyed" (cf. LXX, Vulg.). **Happy shall he be who requites you:** The curse takes a more ghastly turn as a blessing is invoked on him who in implementing it perpetrates heinous acts of vengeance and **takes your little ones and dashes them against the rock,** wiping out the breed forever (cf. II Kings 8:12; Isa. 13:16; Nah. 3:10).

age are not financial or economic but moral and spiritual. The greatest anxieties arise not from politics or diplomacy but from dark passions and deep-set prejudices. Among them is this spirit of hate, this desire for retaliation, which makes international co-operation impossible, causes colossal waste in military expenditure, and haunts the people with a fear from which often there seems to be no escape. It has been preached from pulpits as well as from secular platforms, the scriptures being interpreted according to the demands of the moment.

In such a generation what are Christians to say and do? Can they do anything to ensure peace and to break down the barriers that divide nations and sects and classes? Certainly it is not their concern to belittle pure patriotism, or to ignore national characteristics. Not only is that unnatural but it leads sooner or later to stagnation and national decay. It has been proved again and again that there is a point beyond which the expansion of loyalties will not work. If water is enclosed in a suitable channel, it will drive a mill: if there are no banks to contain it, it makes a bog. Christian brotherhood is one thing; a vague cosmopolitanism or a theoretical egalitarianism is quite another.

We must cultivate local loyalties, but we must also create respect for other people's loyalties and a mutual regard for public law. And to do this it may be well to go back to some of the great pioneers, e.g., Gladstone. Says a writer in *The Great Victorians:* "Gladstone . . . saw the moral relations of peoples with an imagination more vivid and powerful than any man who took part in the government of Europe in the nineteenth century, unless we count the few hours when Mazzini ruled in Rome."[5] It did not matter whether he was dealing with Ireland or the Sudan or Russia, he saw them all in the light of public law. And he derived his sense of moral unity not, as the writer just quoted suggests, mainly from Dante, but from the N.T. John Morley has told us how one Sunday afternoon in the midst of an international crisis he called on the Old Man at 10 Downing Street. Outside in the streets of London, as in many other cities, minds were tense and people were heatedly arguing or asking what a day would bring forth. Inside the prime minister's house was peace, for the man upon whom the weight of grave responsibility rested was quietly reading from a big family Bible. Gladstone, like the rest of men, made mistakes; but he made less than most of us because he knew where to look for light and truth.

Few things are more necessary than salvation from the spirit of vindictiveness. So long as men pray for the destruction of enemies, for the razing of their cities, and the dashing of their little ones against the rock, all our political reforms and idealistic planning will be in vain. It is a matter not for statesmen and diplomats only; it is essentially a religious problem. If there is no adequate faith in the one God and Father of us all, there will be no achievement of unity. But if once we hear the call of Christ, acknowledge his lordship, and commit ourselves to his leadership, the way will become plain. B. J. Mathews in *The Clash of Colour* tells of a football team on the field of a Syrian college at Beirut. The captain was an Abyssinian, the fullbacks a Turk and an Armenian; the halfbacks and forwards included a Syrian Christian, a Greek, a Persian, and a Copt. The trainer was an Irishman, the principal of the college was an American. Talking to the sports captain, Mathews learned that at the beginning of the training each man wanted to "dribble the ball down the field at his own feet and score the goal himself for his own glory." At last they were all persuaded to play for the side, without losing any of their individuality.[6]

This is a parable of the task before the Chris-

[5] J. L. Hammond, "Richard Cobden," p. 145.

[6] New York: Missionary Education Movement, 1924, pp. 110-11.

A Psalm of David.

138 I will praise thee with my whole heart: before the gods will I sing praise unto thee.

A Psalm of David.

138 I give thee thanks, O Lord,
with my whole heart;
before the gods I sing thy praise;

CXXXVIII. I Give Thee Thanks, O Lord (138:1-8)

It was common practice to conclude a psalm of lament with a vow to offer thanks to the Lord (cf. 7:17; 28:7; 52:9; 56:12; 109:30). Sometimes there was coupled with the vow the hymn to be rendered at its fulfillment (cf. 22:22-24; 31:19-24; 57:7-11), but at other times the thanksgiving hymn was an independent composition (cf. Pss. 18; 30; 32; 34; 41; 66; 116; 118). The number of examples of this type of hymn is much smaller than that of the laments, possibly because among men in general the solicitation of help from God is more regularly practiced than the acknowledgment of benefits received. This psalm is a hymn of thanksgiving by an individual, one of about twenty such preserved in the literature of Israel (see above; see also Isa. 38:10-20; Jonah 2:2-9; Ecclus. 51:1-30; Pss. Sol. 15:1-15; 16:1-15; Odes Sol. 25:1-12; 29:1-11).

The psalmist has come to the temple (vs. 2) to give thanks for deliverance from **the midst of trouble** (vs. 7*a*) which threatened to take his life (vs. 7*b*). The rescue which he experienced was in his eyes so miraculous that all that God had ever done or promised in his gracious dealings with men was exceeded by it (vs. 2). Therefore, with face turned toward the holy of holies, he lifts his voice in praise to the Lord **before the gods.** It is not enough for him to follow the example of other psalmists (cf. 22:26) and call on friends and relatives to swell the volume of praise; he summons **the kings of the earth to sing of the ways of the Lord,** for the story of what the Lord has wrought for him is a gospel for the world. In him kingdoms and nations can see a lasting evidence of the truth that **though the Lord is high, he regards the lowly.** And for himself the psalmist finds comfort and strength in the assurance that what the Lord has done for him in this experience, he will do for him again when trouble comes. For the goodness of the Lord **endures for ever,** and he will **not forsake the work of** [his] **hands.**

tian church. It is not impossible. Nothing is impossible to those who keep near the Savior of the world.

138:1-8. ***Praise for Mercies Past and Future.*** —The book of Psalms is nothing if not a book of praise. Praise, however, is occasioned by many gifts and takes different forms. It may spring from a general consciousness of dependence and express itself in restrained and formal language. It may also arise from an intense and personal consciousness of deliverance and move men to loud and ecstatic utterance. There may indeed be as many forms of praise as there are moods of gratitude.

Ps. 138 is not conventional praise. It is a spontaneous lifting up of the heart to a God who is very real, thanking him for mercies which are recent and vivid. There is room for difference of opinion about the experience that lies behind it and the intention of the psalmist in composing it. It may be intended as a community expression after national deliverance. It may be the cry of an individual who has received great benefits and in gladness of heart sings the goodness of God. Nor can we with any confidence decide the date. The writer may have lived in the early days of the monarchy; much more likely he dwelt in Jerusalem in postexilic times, when much of the glory had departed, but when much had been learned through the sorrows of Babylon and the varying fortunes of the return. What is clear is that there had been a personal or community crisis followed by a great deliverance which was the work not of man but of God.

I give thee thanks, O Lord, with my whole heart; before the gods I sing thy praise.

This vindication was not indeed a cause for surprise; it was the fulfillment of a gracious promise. Nor was it an occasion for scorn: the gods of the heathen were humbled, but how could they hope to stand before the Lord who is great in glory? Even kings shall acknowledge him and sing his ways when they hear his words. Great is the joy of those who have been delivered, but they must not boast before men; because the victory is God's, not theirs, and because all nations will rejoice in Israel's exaltation. The goodness of the Lord endures forever.

2 I will worship toward thy holy temple, and praise thy name for thy loving-kindness and for thy truth: for thou hast magnified thy word above all thy name.
3 In the day when I cried thou answeredst me, *and* strengthenedst me *with* strength in my soul.

2 I bow down toward thy holy temple
and give thanks to thy name for thy steadfast love and thy faithfulness;
for thou hast exalted above everything
thy name and thy word.[r]
3 On the day I called, thou didst answer me,
my strength of soul thou didst increase.[s]

[r] Cn: Heb *thou hast exalted thy word above all thy name*
[s] Syr Compare Gk Tg: Heb *thou didst make me arrogant in my soul* with *strength*

The psalm is one of a small group (Pss. 138–145) belonging to a Davidic collection. Some LXX MSS ascribe it to Zechariah, reflecting an early tradition that the prophet had written it for use at the time of the rebuilding of the temple after the Babylonian exile. The structure argues for a postexilic date, since it has abandoned the form of the simple psalm of thanksgiving (Isa. 12:4-6) and has drawn on other types such as the psalm of trust (cf. vss. 7-8) and the royal psalm of thanksgiving (cf. vss. 4-6). A mixture of types within a psalm, it is assumed, points to a late period in the literary history of its type. It should be noted also that in this psalm no reference is made to a thanksgiving sacrifice, probably because the psalmist has reached such a spiritual level that he regards the hymn of greater importance (cf. 50:7-14). The meter is for the most part 3+3.

1. Before the Gods I Sing Thy Praise (138:1-3)

138:1-3. I give thee thanks, O Lord: In the introduction of a psalm of thanksgiving the psalmist must indicate by name the God to whom he owes and offers his thanks. Our psalmist further singles out his God from among the company of the gods in vs. 1*b*. There is an implication that **the gods** are being put to shame because of their impotence to do what the Lord has done. This word **gods** (אלהים) is variously rendered in the

Inasmuch as his name and his word are steadfast, let those who are frustrated find comfort, and those who are vindicated remain humble.

There may have been many in the psalmist's times, as there are today, who belittle religious institutions and exercises; but what a faith is his to live by! What a difference it makes to men and nations when there is the assurance of divine promise, strong conviction that in all the experiences of life God remains faithful to his declared purpose, a persuasion which nothing can destroy that in his purpose all peoples may rejoice! With such a faith how men are sustained in adversity and restrained in victory! How they are saved from personal vanity and prompted to humble thanksgiving!

There are, however, two points that call for special attention. The first is the splendor of the praise which is prompted by deep personal experience. No one would wish to disparage prayers like the General Thanksgiving. It is right and proper when men who have nothing to be grateful for but

> things unnumbered that we take of right,
> And value first when first they are withheld,
> assemble and return thanks
>
> For light and air; sweet sense of sound and smell;
> For ears to hear the heavenly harmonies;
> For eyes to see the unseen in the seen;
> For visions of The Worker in the work;
> For hearts to apprehend Thee everywhere.[7]

It is altogether good when poets like John Drinkwater turn aside from sensational events to

> Thank God for sleep in the long quiet night,
> For the clear day calling through the little leaded panes,
> For the shining well-water and the warm golden light,
> And the paths washed white by singing rains.[8]

It is a blessed thing when ordinary folk who are called neither poets nor saints join with

[7] John Oxenham, "A Little Te Deum of the Commonplace." From *The Te Deum and the Sacraments.* Used by permission of the Pilgrim Press.

[8] "A Morning Thanksgiving." Copyright 1919 by John Drinkwater. Used by permission of the author's estate and Sidgwick & Jackson, Ltd., publishers of the *Collected Poems.*

4 All the kings of the earth shall praise thee, O LORD, when they hear the words of thy mouth.
5 Yea, they shall sing in the ways of the LORD: for great *is* the glory of the LORD.

4 All the kings of the earth shall praise thee, O LORD,
for they have heard the words of thy mouth;
5 And they shall sing of the ways of the LORD,
for great is the glory of the LORD.

versions and by commentators as "angels" (LXX, Vulg.), "kings" (Syriac), "judges" (Targ.) and **gods** (Jerome, Aq., Symm.). Difficulty in the rendition of the word disappears when one recalls that in spite of its prevailing monotheism, the O.T. shows from time to time that Israel could fall into the language of polytheism, sometimes imaginatively as here (cf. 29:1; 82:1; 97:7; Job 2:1). **The gods,** in our psalmist's flight of imagination, form an entourage of the Lord and so must listen to the psalmist's words. In vs. 1 we should probably add a stich which is preserved in the LXX, "For thou hast heard the words of my mouth." **For thou hast magnified thy word above all thy name:** These words are difficult to understand because of some textual corruption. The simplest emendation is to introduce "and" (ו) and translate, "More than ever [above all] thou hast made thy name and thy word great," i.e., the Lord has surpassed all expectations based on his former renowned deeds and promises. **My strength of soul thou didst increase:** The psalmist's fainting heart was revived (cf. Isa. 40:29).

2. The Kings of the Earth Shall Praise Thee (138:4-6)

4-6. Having introduced his hymn of praise and narrated the reason for his thankfulness (vss. 2*b*-3), the psalmist calls on **the kings of the earth** to **sing of the ways of the LORD.** Such an element doubtless originally belonged to royal hymns of thanksgiving

neighbors as simple-minded as themselves in words like those of Horatius Bonar's hymn:

> Praise in the common things of life,
> Its goings out and in;
> Praise in each duty and each deed,
> However small and mean.[9]

But the act can easily become conventional, so conventional as to lose meaning. We can even repeat such words when we are secretly nursing grievances or magnifying misfortunes. Attention wanders. Praise becomes listless and worship unprofitable.

Suppose, however, there is special cause for gratitude—a harvest festival, perhaps, in a time when food is scarce, in a land where men and women have contended with the vagaries of soil, seed, and weather. Suppose there is a national day of rejoicing after years of wrestling with a foreign foe. At last the danger is removed, the enemy defeated or become a friend. How loud the praise! How large the gatherings! How poor the heart that is not thrilled! Even traditional language assumes new significance: "We bless thee for our creation, preservation, and all the blessings of this life." How much more electric are the familiar words when there are special personal reasons for relief and gratitude! When parents who day by day have been praying for sons exposed in battle join in national rejoicing, the simplest hymns bring a lump to the throat and tears to the eyes. Or if one has lived under the shadow of sickness with a growing certainty of speedy death, and suddenly hope is established in mind and heart, emotion may prohibit speech or song, but there is no questioning the reality of the thanksgiving.

That is why worship instinct with personal experience draws men and will not let them go. The music may be inferior, the building inartistic, the preaching crude, but spiritual reality makes its own appeal. So have evangelical revivals moved the hearts even of the indifferent and the critical. Men and women have felt themselves to be redeemed, have believed that the Spirit has given them liberty, have felt themselves to be the sons of God, and the exuberance of their praise could not be resisted. It is not only a corporate expression of common faith, it is personal religion like that of this psalm. Revivals have great dangers and may have sad aftereffects; yet they are necessary if churches are to be saved from formalism and nations from inertia.

But there is a second point here. Ps. 138 is more than praise: it is an act of anticipation

[9] "Fill thou my life, O Lord my God."

6 Though the LORD *be* high, yet hath he respect unto the lowly: but the proud he knoweth afar off.

7 Though I walk in the midst of trouble, thou wilt revive me: thou shalt stretch forth thine hand against the wrath of mine enemies, and thy right hand shall save me.

8 The LORD will perfect *that which* concerneth me: thy mercy, O LORD, *endureth* for ever: forsake not the works of thine own hands.

6 For though the LORD is high, he regards
the lowly;
but the haughty he knows from afar.

7 Though I walk in the midst of trouble,
thou dost preserve my life;
thou dost stretch out thy hand against the
wrath of my enemies,
and thy right hand delivers me.
8 The LORD will fulfil his purpose for me;
thy steadfast love, O LORD, endures for
ever.
Do not forsake the work of thy hands.

---

and not unfittingly was taken up into the hymns of ordinary men, since the individual saw his deliverance as an event of universal significance (cf. I Tim. 1:15). In vs. 6 the psalmist states the truth made known in him; "the poor have the gospel preached to them" that **the LORD . . . regards the lowly; but the haughty he knows from afar.**

3. THOU DOST PRESERVE MY LIFE (138:7-8)

7-8. In the concluding strophe the psalmist's words take the form of a psalm of trust and can in truth be said to be an epitome of Ps. 23.

---

and preparation. The psalmist looks back, but he does not live in the past. He is like a businessman who, as he takes stock, forms plans for the future, or like a student who, having graduated, sets his eyes on heights yet to be conquered. He does not know, perhaps he does not care, what the years will bring. What he knows is that he need not fear.

The psalmist's confidence is not in himself or in man. There are natural optimists who are persuaded that everything will come right. They may have a necessary place in society, but they are rarely leaders in the realm of the spirit. Prophets and seers do indeed speak words of hope: at critical moments they hold out great promises. But their assurance springs not from man's nature or achievements; it is rooted in the God who gives the victory. That is how they read history, not as the work of giants or heroes, but as the creative activity of God working through the willfulness of men.

Though I walk in the midst of trouble,
thou dost preserve my life;
thou dost stretch out thy hand against the wrath
of my enemies,
and thy right hand delivers me.

In a large London suburb there is a United Free church in which for many years Christians trained in many traditions have worked and worshiped in unity. After surviving two world wars they expressed their continuing fellowship in a pageant in which they remembered the originators of the work and their faithful successors. They remembered them, however, not as pioneers in the cause of reunion, but as men and women who had been raised up and sustained by the Spirit of God. Starting there they went back to the various traditions which for centuries had competed with one another: to Martin Luther making his dramatic pronouncement at the Diet of Worms; to Latimer and Ridley preparing themselves for the stake in Oxford; to Puritans addressed by John Robinson before embarking for the New World; to William Carey starting the modern missionary movement; and many more. It was not a gilding of the tombs of the prophets. It was an illustration of the divine activity in human affairs and an incentive to further evangelism. The words spoken by Luther, by John Wesley to the fashionable residents of Bath, and by others less famous but not less faithful, were words given by inspiration from above. Beginning with the letters to the seven churches in Revelation, the pageant ended with an attempt to understand what the Spirit is saying to the modern church. It was so obviously in harmony with the spirit of the Scriptures that with the aid of dramatic art it was performed in church. It was a call to action as well as a day of remembrance.

There is room for many similar experiments. Let a group of people take the story of any one of these historic figures, study it, and set forth some of the things too often omitted by biographers; e.g., let them concentrate on the life of John Wesley and tell the story of the Epworth rectory, the Holy Club in Oxford, the efforts to

To the chief Musician, A Psalm of David.

139 O LORD, thou hast searched me, and known *me*.

To the choirmaster. A Psalm of David.

139 O LORD, thou hast searched me and known me!

CXXXIX. PRAYER OF A DEVOUT SOUL (139:1-24)

This poem is not only one of the chief glories of the Psalter, but in its religious insight and devotional warmth it is conspicuous among the great passages of the O.T. As a psalm, it is difficult to classify. It has some of the qualities of a hymn and of a psalm of trust, but it is perhaps best considered as a personal prayer. In the words of Schmidt (*Die Psalmen,* p. 245), it is "prayer in a stillness in which the soul and God are alone." It is not surprising that such a psalm shows no trace of any connection with the temple cult. As an exegetical oddity we may note Peters' view (*The Psalms as Liturgies,* p. 474) that the poem is "an incantation to Yahaweh [*sic*] for the purpose of obtaining protection against the wicked."

The psalmist is deeply impressed with the omniscience and omnipresence of the Lord, not however as formal attributes of a sovereign God, but as what he has found to be true in his own experience. The psalm therefore is not an exercise in speculative theology, although "it rises to the very heights of theological inquiry" (Faulhaber, quoted by Calès). It keeps within the range of the psalmist's knowledge and convictions and reflects what his own humble walk with God has taught him. This perhaps is the explanation of the author's indifference to history and to God's wondrous deeds in the past. This man is so wrapped up in the contemporaneous God, and in the wonders at hand, that he shows no interest in the great crises of Israel's earlier days. Hence there is no Hebrew nationalism here to detract from the universalistic appeal which the psalmist's words have had for every generation.

The unity of the psalm is a debatable point, the crux of the matter being vss. 19-22. It can be argued (*a*) that these verses interrupt the close connection between vs. 18

---

evangelize Georgia. During those youthful years there was more frustration than achievement; much courage and perseverance, but elements also of pride and self-assurance. At length there came the moment of absolute surrender in the meetinghouse in Aldersgate Street: henceforward confidence was found not in ecclesiastical tradition, nor in Oxford scholarship, nor in episcopal ordination, but in the grace of God. It can all be read in Wesley's *Journal* and in his sermons. It is put forthrightly in such a hymn as "Jesus, Lover of my soul":

> Other refuge have I none;
> Hangs my helpless soul on thee.

We shall fail if we concentrate upon our learning or organization, upon ordination or tradition, upon our gifts or experience. We shall succeed only if like the psalmist we believe that God is preparing us for greater endeavors.

The LORD will fulfil his purpose for me;
thy steadfast love, O LORD, endures for ever.

139:1-24. ***The Strong Feet that Follow.***—A great Scottish theologian and mystic, Erskine of Linlathen, is reported to have said that the one bit of writing he would wish to have with him on his deathbed was Ps. 139. Others have connected it not with their departure but with the stern battle of life. Never, we may suppose, have men been so destitute of a sense of literary and religious values that they have been indifferent to its beauty and power. It has enabled some to sing in the midst of sorrows, to endure in the face of hardship, and to worship when aspiration had almost failed.

As often happens with the choicest songs, it is anonymous. We might speculate till the end of time and still be unable either to name the author or to state the age in which he lived. But while we should like to name the man who wrote it, we must be content with the words themselves. They suggest the deep thoughts of a rare spiritual genius.

It is written in four equal parts, and each part sets forth a great religious thought. Vss. 1-6 affirm the omniscience of God. It is not stated as a doctrine but as a personal experience. God knows man. He knows the psalmist personally, and equally he knows us. Vss. 7-12 proclaim not only the knowledge but the presence and love of God. Wherever we are, however we may seek to hide ourselves, God is with us and will

2 Thou knowest my downsitting and mine uprising; thou understandest my thought afar off.
3 Thou compassest my path and my lying down, and art acquainted *with* all my ways.

2 Thou knowest when I sit down and when
I rise up;
thou discernest my thoughts from afar.
3 Thou searchest out my path and my lying
down,
and art acquainted with all my ways.

---

and vs. 23; (*b*) that they introduce a third party, **the wicked,** not found elsewhere in the poem; (*c*) that they express sentiments foreign to the general tone of the rest of the psalm. Such facts, when taken by themselves, often lead to the conclusion that vss. 19-22 are not an integral part of the psalm. Buttenwieser, for example, divides the four verses between Pss. 140 and 141. Schmidt, however, assigns vss. 19-24 to a separate psalm, although possibly from the same author. On the other hand, it is true that human nature, even when sanctified by a deep religious faith, displays curious inconsistencies, and the great saint who has given us this beautiful prayer may have been so outraged by the wickedness around him that vss. 19-22 were an inevitable expression of his feelings. Undoubtedly the eventual defeat of evil as represented by his immediate foes, who were considered to be also the enemies of the Lord, was basic to the psalmist's whole religious position (cf. Exeg. on 109:1-31). For similar thoughts in other psalms see 1:4-6; 5:5-6; 37:38; 74:11; 104:35 (cf. Jer. 11:18-23; 18:19-23).

The Hebrew is marred by a number of obscurities and corruptions. The RSV rests upon a minimum emendation of the M.T. Various Aramaisms and some alleged parallelisms to Job are commonly thought to date the psalm in the postexilic period, but these are inconclusive criteria. The age of Jeremiah or of Second Isaiah can be argued, but it seems best to leave the matter of the date an open and somewhat unimportant question. There are four strophes in the poem, as in the RSV, and the meter is generally 3+3.

1. The Lord's Omniscience (139:1-6; cf. Isa. 55:8-9)

139:1-6. My thoughts: A small emendation. The M.T. is **my thought.** The noun means "purpose," "aim," "desire." Buttenwieser translates the stich, "Thou readest my

---

not let us go. In vss. 13-18 there is a meditation upon the fact that God not only knows us; he created us and determined life's development. The fourth part raises nice exegetical questions which need not concern us here. Enough to say that vss. 19-22 to some scholars seem so different in tone and temper that they are removed and added to other psalms (see Exeg.). This leaves us with the final prayer, beginning **Search me, O God, and know my heart: try me, and know my thoughts.**

1-6. *The Omniscience of God.*—The first subject is one to which comparatively little attention is now paid even in religious circles. There is much written and spoken about man's knowledge of and search for God. There is little said about the Almighty's knowledge of and search for us. Perhaps that is partly because it seems to lead straight to a barren realm of speculation. Who shall say what the mind of God is, let alone dogmatize about his thought of creatures like ourselves? Yet there are practical considerations that emerge even here, and we must pause with them.

A common complaint among mortals like us is that we are misunderstood. We act and speak, as we believe, in all sincerity; yet afterward we find that our actions have been misinterpreted and our intentions misjudged. Walter Eccles expresses a common sentiment in the lines:

Not understood,
We move along asunder—
Our path grows wider, as we go down the years.
We marvel and we wonder why life is life,
And then we fall asleep—
Not understood.

. . . .

How many breasts are aching, how many spirits
pass away—
Not understood!
O God, that men should see a little clearer
Or judge less harshly when they cannot see!
O God, that men would draw a little closer
To one another, and they'd be nearer thee—
And understood.[1]

It is not here suggested that people are in the habit of expressing themselves in this querulous

[1] "Not Understood."

4 For *there is* not a word in my tongue, *but,* lo, O LORD, thou knowest it altogether.
5 Thou hast beset me behind and before, and laid thine hand upon me.
6 *Such* knowledge *is* too wonderful for me; it is high, I cannot *attain* unto it.
7 Whither shall I go from thy Spirit? or whither shall I flee from thy presence?
8 If I ascend up into heaven, thou *art* there: if I make my bed in hell, behold, thou *art there.*
9 *If* I take the wings of the morning, *and* dwell in the uttermost parts of the sea;

4 Even before a word is on my tongue,
lo, O LORD, thou knowest it altogether.
5 Thou dost beset me behind and before,
and layest thy hand upon me.
6 Such knowledge is too wonderful for me;
it is high, I cannot attain it.

7 Whither shall I go from thy Spirit?
Or whither shall I flee from thy presence?
8 If I ascend to heaven, thou art there!
If I make my bed in Sheol, thou art there!
9 If I take the wings of the morning
and dwell in the uttermost parts of the sea,

---

mind from afar." **Thou searchest out:** The verb means "scatter," "winnow," though some take it to be another root meaning "determine" (so Köhler, *Lexicon, s.v.*). The KJV of vs. 4*a* is probably closer to the meaning of the Hebrew than the RSV. **Beset:** The verb commonly means "besiege," "shut in." **It is high:** The verb often means "to be inaccessibly or extraordinarily high."

2. THE LORD'S OMNIPRESENCE (139:7-12; cf. Jer. 23:23-24)

7-12. Thy Spirit: A reverent circumlocution for God himself, especially for God as an active presence in the world (cf. 51:11; 104:30; 143:10; Isa. 63:10-11; Hag. 2:5; Zech. 4:6). **Thy presence:** Lit., "thy face." A close parallel to vs. 8 is found in Amos 9:2 (cf. Jer. 23:24). **If I make my bed in Sheol:** The psalmist believes that God's control extends even to Sheol, but he does not elaborate this conviction (cf. 88:5, 10-12; 115:17). **The wings of the morning:** Lit., "the wings of the dawn," a beautiful phrase found

---

manner; but in some measure and form the attitude is prevalent, almost universal. Actually there is more than that. Not only do others misjudge us; we are not very sure of ourselves. In spite of all our excuses, in our most candid moments we admit to mixed motives. Our thoughts are not as straight, our actions not as noble, as they might have been. But if neighbors see the pride, the selfishness, the pretense, we know the moods of abasement, of selflessness, of sincerity. And it is a comfort to be assured that whatever the world thinks and says, there is One above who sees the whole, whose judgment is unerring, whose mercy is unfathomable. This has often found expression, e.g., by Robert Burns:

> Who made the heart, 'tis He alone
> Decidedly can try us;
> He knows each chord, its various tone,
> Each spring, its various bias.
> . . . .
> What's done we partly may compute,
> But know not what's resisted.[2]

[2] "Address to the Unco Guid."

But it has never been better put than here by the psalmist:

> **O LORD, thou hast searched me and known me!**
> **Thou knowest when I sit down and when I rise up;**
> **thou discernest my thoughts from afar.**

7-12. ***The Presence and Love of God.***—These verses take the same thought a step further. Not only does God know us; he is with us wherever we go. Sometimes we resent his presence, for we are complex creatures. We may stand in church and beg the Almighty to take possession of us. We may use the language of scripture and exclaim: "As the hart panteth after the water brooks, so panteth my soul after thee, O God" (42:1). We may say it to the best of our belief, in perfect sincerity, and even invite a congregation to say it with us. Yet in a little time we may be like Adam and Eve in the garden when they covered themselves and tried to hide from him who gave them life. This too has been admirably expressed, notably in Francis Thompson's poem *The Hound of Heaven:*

10 Even there shall thy hand lead me, and thy right hand shall hold me.

11 If I say, Surely the darkness shall cover me; even the night shall be light about me.

12 Yea, the darkness hideth not from thee; but the night shineth as the day: the darkness and the light *are* both alike *to thee*.

13 For thou hast possessed my reins: thou hast covered me in my mother's womb.

14 I will praise thee; for I am fearfully *and* wonderfully made: marvelous *are* thy works; and *that* my soul knoweth right well.

10 even there thy hand shall lead me,
and thy right hand shall hold me.
11 If I say, "Let only darkness cover me,
and the light about me be night,"
12 even the darkness is not dark to thee,
the night is bright as the day;
for darkness is as light with thee.

13 For thou didst form my inward parts,
thou didst knit me together in my mother's womb.
14 I praise thee, for thou art fearful and wonderful.[t]
Wonderful are thy works!
Thou knowest me right well;

[t] Cn Compare Gk Syr Jerome: Heb *fearful things I am wonderful*

---

only here in the O.T. The figure points to the rapidity with which the light of early morning spreads over the entire sky. That there is here an echo of an old pagan belief in a winged sky- or sun-god is doubtful. **The sea:** The Mediterranean. **Cover:** A small emendation (ישׁוּכֵּנִי). The M.T. means "bruise." **Is not dark** is preferable to **hideth not. For darkness is as light with thee:** Some scholars omit this stich as overloading the line. **With thee** is not in the Hebrew but can be justified by the context.

3. The Lord as Creator (139:13-18; cf. Job 10:8-11)

13-15. Thou didst form rather than **thou hast possessed** is the meaning of the verb in this context (cf. Gen. 14:19, 22). **Inward parts** or **reins:** Lit., "kidneys," which to the Hebrews were the seat of the emotions. This word elsewhere in the psalms is translated

---

I fled Him, down the nights and down the days;
I fled Him, down the arches of the years;
I fled Him, down the labyrinthine ways
Of my own mind; and in the midst of tears
I hid from Him, and under running laughter.[3]

Turn where the soul may, however, it can find no rest or peace till at last it confesses that evasion is impossible, that in nothing but surrender is fullness of life to be found. There is a distant parallel among human relationships, in the love of man and maid. The woman desires to be possessed, feels that nothing matters except that someone shall come and claim her. Yet she recoils in fear when one with passionate love presents himself. With conventional wooing she might have been satisfied, but anything so deep and strong and true alarms her and she tries to escape. Just so, a conventional piety we like; but when God breaks in upon us, reveals himself as absolute holiness and love, claims us and all we have—claims us and holds us and will not let us go—then fear rises within us, irrational, speechless fear, and our one impulse is somehow, somewhere, to escape and hide ourselves. Yet—**Whither shall I go from thy Spirit? or whither shall I flee from thy presence?** These are not mere words; they indicate the deepest struggle of which our hearts are capable. And we know what the moment of response is like. The eternal Christ calls us, "Come unto me, all ye that labor and are heavy laden" (Matt. 11:28), and the impulse is there to give ourselves in love and service. Still, even as we profess that for life and in death we will be his, another impulse interferes, holds us back, bids us shut our ears and our hearts to all such divine invitations. Sometimes the experience rises to a crisis and determines everything; to that, followers of the evangelical tradition have given the name "conversion." More often it is a day by day choice between good and bad, between truth and error, between beauty and ugliness, love and selfishness, obedience and rebellion. There is nothing we can say about such deep and frequent struggles but that everything depends upon them, and in comparison nothing else matters.

13-18. ***God Our Maker.***—We have been concerned with great religious thoughts, too great

[3] From *Collected Works*, ed. Wilfred Meynell. Used by permission of Burns, Oates & Washbourne, Ltd., and The Newman Press, publishers.

15 My substance was not hid from thee when I was made in secret, *and* curiously wrought in the lowest parts of the earth.

16 Thine eyes did see my substance, yet being unperfect; and in thy book all *my members* were written, *which* in continuance were fashioned, when *as yet there was* none of them.

17 How precious also are thy thoughts unto me, O God! how great is the sum of them!

18 *If* I should count them, they are more in number than the sand: when I awake, I am still with thee.

15 my frame was not hidden from thee,
when I was being made in secret,
intricately wrought in the depths of the earth.
16 Thy eyes beheld my unformed substance;
in thy book were written, every one of them,
the days that were formed for me,
when as yet there was none of them.
17 How precious to me are thy thoughts, O God!
How vast is the sum of them!
18 If I would count them, they are more than the sand.
When I awake, I am still with thee.[u]

[u] Or *were I to come to the end I would still be with thee*

---

by the RSV as "heart" (7:9; 16:7; 26:2; 73:21). **Thou didst knit me together:** From סכך, stem II, "to weave together," whereas **thou hast covered me** comes from סכך, stem I, "to overshadow," "to cover." **I am fearfully and wonderfully made:** This translation cannot be based on the Hebrew, which is, lit., **fearful things I am wonderful** (RSV mg.). The RSV emends the text to נוראת ונפלאת, **thou art fearful and wonderful. Thou knowest:** A repointing of the M.T. **Me:** Lit., **my soul. My frame:** Elsewhere (e.g., Deut. 8:17) this word means "might," but here it probably signifies "bones." **Intricately wrought in the depths of the earth:** Possibly a reflection of the idea that the human fetus was made by God elsewhere before being introduced into the womb; cf. Plato's Phoenician myth about people being formed and fed in the womb of the earth (*Republic* III 414C-E).

16. This is a difficult verse and scholars have suggested numerous emendations. The RSV adds **for me** and **as yet** to the M.T. **My unformed substance:** This word, found only here in the O.T., means "embryo." **Thy book:** The notion that the Lord keeps a register of the living is found elsewhere in 69:28; Exod. 32:32-33. In Mal. 3:16; Dan. 12:1 the Lord's book appears to contain only the names of the righteous. **The days that were formed for me:** If this represents the psalmist's meaning, it points to some form of predestination (cf. Jer. 1:5; Rom. 8:28-30).

17-18. The sum of them: Lit., "the sums of them." **When I awake:** As this seems unrelated to the first half of vs. 18, some emend the verb to הקצותי (קצץ), "were I to finish" (cf. RSV mg.).

---

to be lightly repeated. But there is a third that must not be omitted. A flippant mind will treat it flippantly. A licentious mind will make it obscene. But here is a religious mind, and as he touches it our hearts are filled with wonder. This God who knows us and is with us is our Maker. He shaped us in our mother's womb. While I was but an embryonic speck he took charge of me and knitted together my bodily frame. The words may be scientifically inadequate, but we are dealing with a religious poem, not with a scientific treatise. And it leads us where most scientific treatises do not lead us, to a sense of wonder which can be more important than knowledge. There must be no belittling of knowledge. The cry is often in our hearts and on our lips: "Let knowledge grow from more to more." But to what end? Simply that we may know? But what is knowledge if it is not guided and controlled? Knowledge of the human frame in particular will be no blessing to us or to those who come after us if it is not dedicated to noble ends. All this Tennyson stated powerfully and reiterated insistently in *In Memoriam:*

> Let knowledge grow from more to more
> But more of reverence in us dwell.[4]

And that is where Ps. 139 brings us:

For thou didst form my inward parts,
thou didst knit me together in my mother's womb.
I praise thee, for thou art fearful and wonderful.

[4] Prologue, st. vii.

19 Surely thou wilt slay the wicked, O
God: depart from me therefore, ye bloody
men.
20 For they speak against thee wickedly,
and thine enemies take *thy name* in vain.
21 Do not I hate them, O LORD, that hate
thee? and am not I grieved with those that
rise up against thee?
22 I hate them with perfect hatred: I
count them mine enemies.
23 Search me, O God, and know my
heart: try me, and know my thoughts:
24 And see if *there be any* wicked way
in me, and lead me in the way everlasting.

19 O that thou wouldst slay the wicked, O
God,
and that men of blood would depart
from me,
20 men who maliciously defy thee,
who lift themselves up against thee for
evil![v]
21 Do I not hate them that hate thee, O
LORD?
And do I not loathe them that rise up
against thee?
22 I hate them with perfect hatred;
I count them my enemies.
23 Search me, O God, and know my heart!
Try me and know my thoughts!
24 And see if there be any wicked[w] way in
me,
and lead me in the way everlasting![x]

[v] Cn: Heb uncertain
[w] Heb *hurtful*
[x] Or *the ancient way*. Compare Jer 6. 16

4. MAY THE WICKED PERISH (139:19-22)

19-22. This part of the prayer is addressed to the Lord as the foe of the wicked, the searcher of the human heart, and the benefactor of the upright. Concerning the authenticity of this passage see Exeg. on vss. 1-24. **Would depart:** A small emendation, from an imperative to an imperfect. The Hebrew of vs. 20*b* is obscure. The RSV emends two words and reads נשאו לשוא עליך. **Them [illegible] rise up against thee:** The M.T. requires a slight change to give this meaning. **I cou[illegible]m my enemies:** Lit., "they have become my enemies."

5. SEARCH ME AND KNOW MY HEART (139:23-24)

23-24. My thoughts: A rare word, found elsewhere in the O.T. only in 94:19, where the RSV renders it "cares." **Any wicked way:** Lit., "a way of pain," an unusual phrase, but presumably meaning a manner of life that brings pain. A repointing of the M.T. could give "the way of idolatry." **The way everlasting:** This phrase is found only here; it describes the way of life which is ordained by God and which is right for all time. Another view is that the words mean "old [or "well-established"] ways" (cf. RSV mg.; Jer. 6:16; 18:15).

23. ***Search Me, O God, and Know My Heart.*** —There is little need to concern ourselves with the technical discussions about vss. 19-22. We may have preferences, perhaps convictions, about literary problems, and feel free to express them. For our purpose, however, it is enough to pass directly to the concluding prayer, which is here taken to be the response of the devout soul to the immanent, active, persuasive appeal of the Holy Spirit. There are indeed those who find in it a suggestion of the self-righteous integrity which sometimes marred Hebrew piety and which found its full expression in the Pharisee who thanked God that he was not as other men. If that is so, it is a serious blemish in so noble a psalm. But it may be understood as a spontaneous prayer to God that he will search out the secret thoughts and bring to light every lurking evil, as a patient might appeal to the surgeon to cut deep and spare nothing so that the hidden trouble may be rooted up and cast away. The complete sincerity of the prayer supports this interpretation, a sincerity which reflects the experience of countless souls when they have tried to pray. They have had no natural fluency. They have possessed no liturgical knowledge. But as in silence they have waited before the mercy seat the ancient cry of the psalmist has met their need.

To the chief Musician, A Psalm of David.

140 Deliver me, O LORD, from the evil man: preserve me from the violent man;

To the choirmaster. A Psalm of David.

140 Deliver me, O LORD, from evil men;
preserve me from violent men,

CXL. DELIVER ME FROM EVIL MEN (140:1-13)

This psalm is one of the less pleasing examples of a lamenting prayer. Like too many of its class it shows no high spiritual aspirations or sense of personal frailty; its cry is only for vengeance. In this respect it does not compare well with Pss. 141; 143. "The good man of the Old Testament believes and hates, and so he prays fervently for the death of his enemy. Even the greatest of them, the prophet Jeremiah, is not always free of this human weakness in prayer (cf. Jer. 18:19-23; 17:17-18)—how much less men of low and lowest degree in Israel." (Willy Staerk, *Lyrik* [2nd ed.; Göttingen: Vandenhoeck & Ruprecht, 1920; "Die Schriften des Alten Testaments in Auswahl"], p. 165). The good man of the N.T., when assailed by evil-plotting men, acts according to the principles expressed by Paul in Rom. 12:14, 17-21.

The psalmist complains of bitter persecution by certain **evil men** whom in their relentlessness he compares now to warriors (vs. 2) and now to hunters (vs. 5). They carry on their attacks not by open deeds of violence but covertly by their words, which are as deadly as **the poison of vipers.** We are not told precisely how **their tongue** or **their lips** are employed as instruments for the psalmist's undoing. It is possible that they were uttering secret curses on him (vs. 9), or that they were whispering slanderous reports about him (vs. 11). In this instance the latter device could itself be as deadly as the former (cf. Prov. 25:18), though it sometimes happened that the two operated conjointly (cf. 10:7-10). The psalmist's stay in his troubles is his assurance that he is under God's aegis—**Thou art my God**—and his confidence that what God has done for him in the past he will again do for him ([illegible]. His fervent appeal to God for protection (vs. 4*a*) and deliverance (vs. 1*a*) and h[illegible]tion to frustrate the plots of his enemies (vs. 8) culminate in a series of passionate [illegible]s on his persecutors. The whole closes (vss.

140:1-13. ***Integer Vitae?***—The O.T. is the natural introduction to the N.T. Without it we should scarcely be able to understand the Gospels or Epistles. The church does well to print them together in one volume and to call that volume the Bible.

Yet there are times when the difference between the two impresses itself even upon the casual reader and makes him feel that they are a contrast rather than a complement one to another. In the one the Messiah is but an expectation, sometimes a confident but often a blurred expectation; in the other he is a glorious reality. In the one length of days is one of life's greatest blessings and death is the chief enemy of man; in the other death is overcome and is a transition from this earthly life to another where the righteous enjoy liberty and peace. So too in the realm of conduct: in the O.T., while the praise of forgiveness is not absent, retaliation is not always regarded as an evil; in the N.T. the emphasis falls consistently on the mercy of God and the forgiveness of injuries among men if the divine love is to be understood and apprehended.

The blessedness of the forgiving heart is not unknown in the Psalter, but there are also maledictions and curses, bitter words that have raised hard questions in many minds, especially in minds that have been trained in certain theories of verbal inspiration; words that have provided material for skeptics and critics, who having quoted them have added obvious comments, usually without explaining that wonderful as the book of Psalms is, it is pre-Christian both in time and sentiment; or that the Bible is in one aspect the record of a progressive revelation, that there has been development in theology and ethics, as in other studies. And so men are not brought to see the difference that Christ has made, or how much we owe to him. It is like passing from one world to another to pass from vss. 9-10 of this psalm to the teaching of Jesus. J. R. Seeley said that the teaching of Jesus on this subject is his "most striking innovation in morality." He also affirmed that "it has produced so much impression upon mankind that it is commonly regarded as the whole or at least the fundamental part of the Christian moral system," so commonly that "when a

2 Which imagine mischiefs in *their* heart; continually are they gathered together *for* war.

3 They have sharpened their tongues like a serpent; adders' poison *is* under their lips. Selah.

4 Keep me, O Lord, from the hands of the wicked; preserve me from the violent man; who have purposed to overthrow my goings.

5 The proud have hid a snare for me, and cords; they have spread a net by the wayside; they have set gins for me. Selah.

2 who plan evil things in their heart,
and stir up wars continually.
3 They make their tongue sharp as a serpent's,
and under their lips is the poison of vipers. *Selah*

4 Guard me, O Lord, from the hands of the wicked;
preserve me from violent men,
who have planned to trip up my feet.
5 Arrogant men have hidden a trap for me,
and with cords they have spread a net,[y]
by the wayside they have set snares for me. *Selah*

[y] Or *they have spread cords as a net*

12-13) with an expression of certainty that the psalmist will be vindicated, and that along with **the righteous** he will offer songs of thanksgiving in the temple.

Little that is positive can be said respecting the date of the psalm. The use of ל (vs. 7) to introduce an object and the appearance of מהמרות (vs. 10), which occurs elsewhere in the Hebrew text of Ecclus. 12:16, suggest a late date. There is no warrant in the language of the psalm for relating it to any of the party feuds in the postexilic period. The meter is a mixture of 4+4 and 4+3, with some disturbances of the pattern due to textual corruptions.

1. Appeal to the Lord (140:1-5)

140:1-5. In these verses occurs a novel mixture of appeal and complaint. The appeal is interrupted at the end of vs. 1 and vs. 4*b* by the description of the work of the enemy. Ordinarily in a lament these two elements form distinct sections. **Deliver me,**

Christian spirit is spoken of, it may be remarked that a forgiving spirit is usually meant."[5] There is, however, one thing more important than the teaching of Jesus: and that is his own practice, including the cry from the cross, "Father, forgive them; for they know not what they do" (Luke 23:34). Jesus could be stern with hypocrites and hypocrisy, but the magnanimity he taught he practiced to the end. How impossible to think of him on the cross praying to the Father:

> **Let the mischief of their lips overwhelm them!**
> **Let burning coals fall upon them!**
> **Let them be cast into pits, no more to rise!**

It is as impossible to reconcile such a cry with the Sermon on the Mount as it is with what Paul writes in Rom. 12:14, "Bless them which persecute you: bless, and curse not."

To admit, however, that this psalm is pre-Christian is not to say that it has nothing to teach us. If we read it with historical imagination, deliberately looking not for the flaws but for the virtues, we can find much in it to admire. Someone has said that we cannot argue from an impression; but the impression the psalm makes is of a certain honesty and integrity. The writer knows the difference between good and evil, and does not try to belittle the one or to excuse the other. This may in part be due to the fact that evil has been done to him, and most of us are conscious of wrongdoing when we are its victims. But it may also be due to the fact that he has not blurred the difference between the two, that he habitually puts truth and error in stark opposition, and calls upon men to see the contradiction between black and white. There are in modern life many who think in terms of relativity; and by it conscience is lulled to sleep. Evil, they say, is a negation. It is nothing but the absence of good. It is not positive, malignant, soul destroying. It is not like a contagious disease which cannot be circumscribed; it is something that should be excused and easily pardoned. The psalmist is more forthright. He faces the fact of evil; sees it as something violent, menacing, constant; describes it in vigorous language. He is himself

[5] *Ecce Homo,* p. 311. See also pp. 303-38.

6 I said unto the LORD, Thou *art* my God: hear the voice of my supplications, O LORD.

7 O GOD the Lord, the strength of my salvation, thou hast covered my head in the day of battle.

8 Grant not, O LORD, the desires of the wicked: further not his wicked device; *lest* they exalt themselves. Selah.

9 *As for* the head of those that compass me about, let the mischief of their own lips cover them.

6 I say to the LORD, Thou art my God;
give ear to the voice of my supplications, O LORD!
7 O LORD, my Lord, my strong deliverer,
thou hast covered my head in the day of battle.
8 Grant not, O LORD, the desires of the wicked;
do not further his evil plot! *Selah*

9 Those who surround me lift up their head,[z]
let the mischief of their lips overwhelm them!

[z] Cn Compare Gk: Heb *those who surround me are uplifted in head*

O LORD, from the evil man, . . . the violent man: Man in each case is a collective, as we see by the use of the plural in the following verses. The psalmist therefore is not singling out one of his antagonists for mention. **Who . . . stir up wars:** Read *yeghārû* (from גרה) for *yāghûrû,* "they sojourn" (KJV, **are gathered together).** A transference of vs. 5*c* to the end of vs. 4 (Gunkel) improves the relation of the metaphors. **The proud have hid a snare for me, and cords:** For *ḥebhālîm,* **cords,** read *ḥōbhelîm,* "those who act corruptly," or *meḥabbelîm,* "those who work ruin."

2. FRUSTRATE THE WICKED (140:6-8)

6-8. Do not further his evil plot: Repoint זממו, a doubtful word, insert אשר, to obtain "what evil they plot," and add with the LXX, לי, "against me."

3. MAY EVIL OVERWHELM MY ENEMIES (140:9-11)

9-11. In these verses the psalmist gives up the "thou" of his appeal for the "he" (indefinite) of a curse. Doubtless he believes that God will effect the curse, but the style of his words is influenced by the primitive curse formulas (cf. 109:6-20). The curse, as he utters it, may be a countercurse, i.e., what the enemy wished for him is

suffering from the evil thoughts, the evil words, the evil deeds of evil men. The issue is alive, concrete, personal: not ignorance but wickedness; not the work of limited intellects but the badness of perverted souls.

It is said the nations drift into war, and so indeed it often seems. We do not, however, so easily rid ourselves of human responsibility. We may often feel that we are but pawns pushed here and there upon the chessboard of life; but it is the language of determinism which omits the element of personal decision. Strife, whether personal or international, does not automatically emerge. It comes and brings with it harvests of suffering because men **plan evil things in their heart.** It is not an accident any more than a garden choked with weeds is an accident: it is there because of sinful decisions; and not only the sinful decisions of rulers and leaders, but those of people like us whose influence seems so restricted.

Actually warfare takes many forms. There are weapons that wound or kill the body; there are also weapons that pierce the mind and the spirit. The psalmist is concerned particularly with the **tongue,** which can be as **sharp as a serpent's.** It can cut through to the quick, whether as private gossip or as national or party propaganda. It can be used as an auxiliary to guns and gas or employed when armies are restrained and what is officially called peace prevails. Whatever the forms or the methods, the work is the work of **evil men.**

The second thing to be said in favor of the psalmist is that when he is thus slandered, he turns to God in prayer. It is not prayer on the highest level. It is not prayer that Christians can copy or commend. Yet it is a cry to God for protection; and protection for self may well involve the punishment of evildoers. If there are low thoughts of the God to whom one prays, such a prayer may actually increase the feelings

10 Let burning coals fall upon them: let them be cast into the fire; into deep pits, that they rise not up again.
11 Let not an evil speaker be established in the earth: evil shall hunt the violent man to overthrow *him*.
12 I know that the LORD will maintain the cause of the afflicted, *and* the right of the poor.
13 Surely the righteous shall give thanks unto thy name: the upright shall dwell in thy presence.

10 Let burning coals fall upon them!
Let them be cast into pits, no more to rise!
11 Let not the slanderer be established in the land;
let evil hunt down the violent man speedily!

12 I know that the LORD maintains the cause of the afflicted,
and executes justice for the needy.
13 Surely the righteous shall give thanks to thy name;
the upright shall dwell in thy presence.

---

stated in reverse. **Let burning coals fall upon them: let them be cast . . . into deep pits.** This language expresses figuratively his wish for the total destruction of the enemy. Such figures of speech derive from the terrible experiences of men in storms, volcanic eruptions, war, and trials by ordeal.

4. Confidence in the Lord (140:12-13)

12-13. It is common to conclude a psalm of this type with an expression of the psalmist's confidence in the vindication of his cause. Such words were on occasion prompted by a priestly announcement of an omen or oracle of favorable import to the suppliant. But in this instance the psalmist is moved simply by his belief that the Lord will not fail him and all like him. **In thy presence,** i.e., in the temple, **the righteous** will ever have cause to be present with songs of praise and thanksgiving on their lips.

---

of self-pity and resentment and vindictiveness. But if as one lifts up one's mind in supplication there are thoughts of the holiness, the justice, even the mercy of God, the mind will be cleansed and the heart purified. He who prays will remember that he too has transgressed the divine law and wounded the Father's heart, and his own feelings of contrition will modify his anger toward arrogant and wicked men.

We are touching here upon a problem that has often troubled religious leaders in times of crisis. As dangers have thickened, and the cruelty of enemies has become more apparent, nations have set aside days for special prayer. Even secular leaders have demanded it. Even the careless and sometimes the irreverent have turned aside from ordinary ways to attend crowded services in public places. Not always have responsible leaders of the church been so enthusiastic. They have hesitated because they have realized the danger. Such popular invocations may but confirm a crude patriotism. They may increase the will to resist, but render more difficult the peacemaking that must ultimately be undertaken. If, however, the impulse to pray can be wisely directed, if there can be Christian teaching on the nature of God and what he requires of men and nations, such national days of prayer may become a means of grace. The instinct is a natural one that leads us unitedly to exclaim:

> **Grant not, O LORD, the desires of the wicked;**
> **do not further his evil plot!**

Those who have been trained in the school of Christ are to see that it becomes more than a religious sanction for personal or national ambitions and antipathies.

The psalmist does not altogether escape that peril, but he learns truths of great importance. He learns that slanderous words recoil upon the speaker, that those who resort to violence meet with violence. It is not Matt. 7:1-5, in all its force and fullness; but the truth is seen, even though it is but a fugitive glance, that "with what judgment ye judge, ye shall be judged; and with what measure ye mete, it shall be measured to you again." The words of Jesus have been repeated so often in our hearing that we assent to them too easily and miss their real significance. We may even see how appropriate they were to scribes and Pharisees and fail to realize how relevant and necessary they are in the modern world and to us in particular. **Evil shall hunt the violent man to overthrow him.** He shall be "hoist with his own petar."

A Psalm of David.

141 LORD, I cry unto thee: make haste unto me; give ear unto my voice, when I cry unto thee.

A Psalm of David.

141 I call upon thee, O LORD; make haste to me!
Give ear to my voice, when I call to thee!

CXLI. INCLINE NOT MY HEART TO EVIL (141:1-10)

This psalm differs from many of its type (cf. Pss. 140; 142–144) in the spiritual elevation of its requests. The psalmist is not crying aloud for deliverance from some desperate plight such as imprisonment, sickness, persecution, or calumny, but is pouring out a petition for protection from the spiritual temptations with which a godless community threatens him. The poem is substantially Ps. 1 put into the form of a prayer. From vs. 2 we deduce that the psalmist, like some other good men of the O.T., made his heart known to God at the time of the evening sacrifice. And since his words in vs. 5*a* imply that he considers himself as one who may be subjected to severe reproof and correction, he is to be accounted a man still in his youth.

We may gather from vs. 4 that the problem with which he as a religious man is confronted is akin to that of Ps. 73. He has been diligent in obeying the commandments of the law in the hope of receiving God's blessings as a reward, but his lot in life has not turned out to be a happy one; in contrast, his godless neighbors, who care not for either the will of God or his precepts, are signally prosperous. In the circumstances he might well ask, "What profit is it that I serve loyally my God?" (cf. Mal. 3:14). The fact that such a question rises in his heart and presses for utterance by his lips (vss. 3-4) shows the strength of the temptation to which he is exposed. The battleground is the heart. So he prays that its thoughts may be kept pure and steadfast. By such inner defenses he will be kept from the snare which is laid for him.

The text, particularly in vss. 5-7, has suffered some corruption, but the argument seems clear and has become the substance of Pss. Sol. 16. The psalm shows the influence of the late wisdom literature in the proverb style of vss. 3-5, and also in some allusions to Aḥiḳar

---

A still more fundamental truth the psalmist learns, suggested more than once, and boldly affirmed in vss. 12-13:

I know that the LORD maintains the cause of the afflicted,
and executes justice for the needy.
Surely the righteous shall give thanks to thy name;
the upright shall dwell in thy presence.

It is not a sudden conviction. Once before God had covered his head with a helmet of salvation (vs. 7). It was no accident or coincidence. The same thing will happen again. It will continue forever, not for a chosen few but for all who turn to him. In other words, the psalmist has discovered not the origin of evil but its remedy. He has found more than an answer to an intellectual problem; he has learned to pray and to trust. He knows now that the plotter of evil is not beyond the reach of God, and the sufferer not without protection. This is to have, in all ordeals, the comfort of a **strong deliverer.** This is to suffer the warfare of men with the peace of God. And how much better that is than to be at peace with men and in conflict with God!

141:1-10. ***The Allurement of the World and the Hunger for God.***—Everywhere in nature the good and the bad are in juxtaposition: that which is good today may be bad tomorrow. Flowers which seem as perfect as anything can be in an imperfect world are soon cast away, fit only for refuse. Fruit which fills us with admiration rots and is repulsive.

It can be so even in religion. Prayer at its best is one of the noblest things man knows on earth. It is a revelation and an ecstasy to him who prays. It is an unforgettable experience also to him who beholds, silencing the scornful and humbling the critic. But prayer can also be a pretense, rousing the ribald to laughter and the profane to derision. Even when it is liturgically correct, it can be so formal and conventional that it merits the condemnation of saints. And he who prays sincerely and humbly today may tomorrow be ostentatious and hypocritical. At its best it may rarely be seen, for like the flower that "is born to . . . waste its sweetness on the desert air," [6] it flourishes in solitude (Matt. 6:6).

[6] Thomas Gray, "Elegy Written in a Country Churchyard," st. xiv.

2 Let my prayer be set forth before thee *as* incense; *and* the lifting up of my hands *as* the evening sacrifice.
3 Set a watch, O LORD, before my mouth; keep the door of my lips.
4 Incline not my heart to *any* evil thing, to practise wicked works with men that work iniquity: and let me not eat of their dainties.

2 Let my prayer be counted as incense before thee,
and the lifting up of my hands as an evening sacrifice!

3 Set a guard over my mouth, O LORD,
keep watch over the door of my lips!
4 Incline not my heart to any evil,
to busy myself with wicked deeds
in company with men who work iniquity;
and let me not eat of their dainties!

---

and Proverbs (cf. vs. 4 with Aḥiḳar [Syriac] 2:16; vs. 5 with Aḥiḳar [Syriac] 73; Prov. 9:8; 27:6; vs. 6 with Prov. 8:7). A late postexilic date is indicated. The pattern of the meter is disturbed because of textual uncertainties, but it seems originally to have varied between 4+4 and 4+3.

1. Appeal to the Lord (141:1-2)

141:1-2. Let my prayer be counted as incense before thee, . . . as an evening sacrifice: The sacrifice referred to is the cereal offering or *minḥāh,* which was regularly offered both morning and evening (Exod. 29:39-41; Num. 28:4-8) along with incense (Jer. 41:5; Lev. 2:1; 6:14-15). It was a custom to offer prayer at the time of this offering (I Kings 18:36; Ezra 9:5; Dan. 9:20-21), and our psalm was doubtless uttered during the performance of the sacrificial rites. The psalmist is at an important stage in the development of Israel's religion. In a former time the sacrifices were the indispensable means of approach to God, but now some religious minds hold the traditional ceremonials in less esteem, and though they have not abandoned them, they are freed from dependence on them and are minded to substitute for them the direct personal outpourings of their hearts to God (cf. 40:6; 51:16-17; 69:30-31; I Pet. 2:5).

2. Prayer for a Righteous Heart (141:3-4)

3-4. In psalms of this class the appeal is usually followed by a description of the situation which provoked the appeal. Here, however, this element is omitted and the

---

Nor is it often seen at its worst; for even those who seem least attentive and reverent have some instinct for truth, some feeling for the holy. The apples on Thomas Hardy's stubbard tree, in the somber story *Tess of the d'Urbervilles,* were "most of them splendid and sound—a few blighted."[7] So are prayers both good and bad. Men turn instinctively from the gabbling and the pretentious, though the words may be admirable. Just as naturally they turn to him who prays with contrite heart and sincere mind, though the supplications may be theologically faulty.

In Ps. 141 we see an Israelite at prayer. His petitions are not perfect. They are not to be compared with the prayers of Jesus. They are not equal to the best recorded prayers of apostles and saints. The psalm is not often quoted in devotional handbooks, nor is there much evidence that it inspired men like Thomas à Kempis, Lancelot Andrewes, or Jeremy Taylor. Yet it is a real prayer, intense, urgent, persistent. It is instinct with sincerity and humanity. It is the utterance of one who knows what it is to come into direct contact with the living God.

We cannot hope to delineate the psalmist; but as we study the words, we seem to see a young man turning aside at the time of the offering of the evening sacrifice to worship in the sanctuary. He cannot immediately cut himself off from the busy world, with its attractions and temptations. Nor is he so conscious of the divine presence that he forgets the instincts which respond to secular allurements. Even as he composes himself to pray, he is aware of inner tension, the longing for communion with God striving with worldly distractions. He watches the priest performing the liturgy of the altar, and doing as all who would worship in spirit and in truth must do, he waits for the demands of the world to subside and turns his mind deliberately to eternal reality. There is at first no conscious asking for particular blessings,

[7] New York: The Modern Library, 1919, p. 30.

5 Let the righteous smite me; *it shall be* a kindness: and let him reprove me; *it shall be* an excellent oil, *which* shall not break my head: for yet my prayer also *shall be* in their calamities.

6 When their judges are overthrown in stony places, they shall hear my words; for they are sweet.

7 Our bones are scattered at the grave's mouth, as when one cutteth and cleaveth *wood* upon the earth.

5 Let a good man strike or rebuke me in kindness,
but let the oil of the wicked never anoint my head;[a]
for my prayer is continually[b] against their wicked deeds.
6 When they are given over to those who shall condemn them,
then they shall learn that the word of the Lord is true.
7 As a rock which one cleaves and shatters on the land,
so shall their bones be strewn at the mouth of Sheol.[c]

[a] Gk: Heb obscure
[b] Cn: Heb *for continually and my prayer*
[c] The Hebrew of verses 5-7 is obscure

---

third element, viz., the petition, comes immediately after the appeal. The second element, had it been brought in, might have dealt with some troubles which the psalmist suffered because of his lapses through failure to set a guard over his mouth and to purify the thoughts of his heart. **Set a guard over my mouth:** The psalmist wishes to be kept innocent of disloyal utterances about God and his ways. He has not in mind here such sins of the tongue as lying, perjury, cursing, calumny. **Incline not my heart to any evil,** because the heart as the seat of thought and will is the primary source of what the lips utter. **To busy myself with wicked deeds:** Lit., "to commit evil deeds through godlessness," or with omission of the preposition, "to commit godless deeds," i.e., התעולל עלילות רשע. The temptation to move in the company of prosperous but godless persons constitutes the spiritual peril of the psalmist. **With men who work iniquity:** Emend את־אישים to בל אשב עם and translate, "Let me not sit with men who do iniquity." **Their dainties:** Lit., "their dainty foods," i.e., their feasts.

3. The Fate of the Wicked (141:5-7)

5-7. Let a good man strike or rebuke me in kindness: Better, "Let a good man wound or a godly man rebuke me," i.e., read חסד as חסיד. The verbs are, lit., "smite" and "chastise." The elder men in the community disciplined errant youths by severe

---

rather a longing that the strain and stress of life may depart and that the suppliant may become conscious of God's peace. As he thus pauses in speechless aspiration words shape themselves in his mind, suggested perhaps by the conventional gestures of the priest and the incense rising from the altar. It is an importunate prayer that God will come quickly and hear him:

I call upon thee, O Lord; make haste to me!
Give ear to my voice, when I call to thee!
Let my prayer be counted as incense before thee,
and the lifting up of my hands as an evening sacrifice!

Such a turning of the soul to God has important effects. One thing it does is to make a man know himself, not as his neighbors see him, nor as at other times he imagines himself to be, but as he really is. Isaiah goes into the temple "in the year that King Uzziah died" and is arrested by a vision of "the Lord sitting upon a throne." At first he thinks of nothing but the holiness and awfulness of God, but his next reaction is to contrast himself and his unclean lips with the absolute purity he has beheld. "Woe is me! for I am undone," he exclaims: "for mine eyes have seen the King, the Lord of hosts." (Isa. 6:1-5.) It is the same with the psalmist, who having been lifted to supernal heights feels with new intensity the evil of his own inner life. Perhaps, like many others who have called themselves the chief of sinners, in the instinctive recoil he exaggerates the evil he feels. It is not however the self-disparagement that certain philosophers so readily condemn; not the morbidity that drives men with sick minds to psychoanalysts. It is the normal reaction when one becomes fully conscious of the

8 But mine eyes *are* unto thee, O GOD the Lord: in thee is my trust; leave not my soul destitute.

9 Keep me from the snares *which* they have laid for me, and the gins of the workers of iniquity.

10 Let the wicked fall into their own nets, whilst that I withal escape.

8 But my eyes are toward thee, O LORD God;
in thee I seek refuge; leave me not defenseless!
9 Keep me from the trap which they have laid for me,
and from the snares of evildoers!
10 Let the wicked together fall into their own nets,
while I escape.

---

punishments (cf. Ecclus. 30:8-13). The psalmist is evidently not an elder. **The oil of the wicked:** Far better is it to suffer the wounds of correction than to have the head anointed with the perfumed oils which the wicked pour on the heads of the guests at their banquets (cf. 133:2; Luke 7:46). **For my prayer is continually against their wicked deeds:** It is possible to emend this difficult line by repointing תפלתי as a verb *tāphálti,* to read, "For soon I should be talking senselessly about their wicked deeds." It must be admitted, however, that the uncertainties of the text of vss. 5*c*-7*b* have not been removed by the current proposed emendations. It is clear in any case that the psalmist means to portray the ghastly end for which the wicked are destined: **So shall their bones be strewn at the mouth of Sheol.**

4. In Thee I Seek Refuge (141:8-10)

8-10. The psalmist turns from the contemplation of such a terrible judgment to the Lord: "As for me [אנכי], my eyes are toward thee." **Keep me from the trap which they have laid for me:** He concludes with a wish frequently repeated in the Psalter (cf. 7:15-16; 9:15; 35:8).

---

reality of the God in whose presence the seraphim cover their faces. We may compare it with the sudden despair of an artist confonted by a picture which is far beyond him, or the abasement of a musician who listens to harmonies of which he is quite incapable. The truer the man, the greater the artist, the more sincere will be the confession of his own imperfections and limitations; yet with the contrition will be joy because he has at least seen or heard that to which he cannot aspire. It is always so with the saint. While others excuse themselves, the holy man strikes his breast and exclaims, "God, be merciful to me a sinner!"

The particular fault that is here immediately confessed is a common one. Who of us when we sincerely examine ourselves by the highest standards can do other than confess to sins of speech? The tongue is "a little member," as a Christian moralist discovered (Jas. 3:5), but it is capable of great harm. Even if we avoid the cruder offenses of slander and blasphemy, cursing and unashamed lying, we do not so easily avoid the subtler offenses of gossip and innuendoes, childish boasting and sharp retorts. Even if we discipline ourselves against the evil of exaggeration, we may still find ourselves guilty of understatement, lacking in expressions of gratitude, silent when we ought to commend, critical when we ought to give thanks. It does not matter who we are, we cannot too often pray to God to **set a guard over my mouth, to keep watch over the door of my lips.** (Yet see Exeg.)

The sins of speech are not accidental or arbitrary. They are an outward expression of evil within. Good desires and intentions are working in our hearts, but they are opposed and often frustrated by evil propensities. It is useless to ignore or belittle this inner conflict. It is equally useless to think that we can save ourselves from it. There are moments when the best in us is released, and we become capable of generosity and heroism. There are, however, too many other moments when the evil instincts get the upper hand and we declare ourselves **with wicked deeds.** The psalmist seems to be particularly susceptible to the temptations of the table and the dainties that are spread upon it and the convivial companions that gather around. No making of good resolutions will save him. It is when he turns aside to seek God that he understands the things that belong to his peace and makes the prayer that liberates and strengthens the noblest aspirations of his heart.

But as the psalmist prays, he also remembers. He remembers that good men have tried to help

Maschil of David; A Prayer when he was in the cave.

142 I cried unto the LORD with my voice; with my voice unto the LORD did I make my supplication.

A Maskil of David, when he was in the cave. A Prayer.

142 I cry with my voice to the LORD, with my voice I make supplication to the LORD,

CXLII. THE CRY OF A LONELY IMPRISONED MAN (142:1-7)

This brief psalm is a fervent prayer uttered by one who is in urgent need of divine help. He is the victim of persecutors (vs. 6) who are too strong for him. They have trapped him by insidious charges falsely made against him and have caused him to be imprisoned (vs. 7). Because of either the semblance of truth in the accusations of his enemies, or fear which they inspired, he is alone, without a friend to stand at his right hand for his defense or even to take notice of him. **No man cares for me** (vs. 4). In his loneliness and distress he cries aloud to God for help. Even as he tells his trouble, his spirit would faint in gloom and despair were it not quickened by a confidence that his prayer will be answered, first, because of his innocence in God's eyes—**thou knowest my way**—and second, because **thou art my refuge, my portion in the land of the living.** He ends the passionate outpouring of his heart by expressing a longing, which is by implication a vow, to make in gratitude for his deliverance an offering of praise and testimony before the congregation of the righteous.

him. Not always perhaps have they been wise in their attitude. Not always, it may have seemed to him, did they speak with fullness of humility and humanity. Good men can become censorious. They may see clearly the perils in a young man's way and not notice his genuine qualities. The blight of Pharisaism is always with us. Such ministries may be well intended, but instead of being gladly received, they arouse a spirit of resentment. Perhaps this young man's repentance includes sorrow for pert answers to the counsels of seniors. In the place of prayer he realizes that it is folly to decline advice, even though the manner of it was unfortunate. Men of many years have much to impart and youth has much to learn. The psalmist remembers also that above all is the counsel of God and his judgment is supreme. The word of the Lord is not merely the verbal expression of a thought; it is moral activity against which evil men break themselves. Evil men who set themselves against eternal truth may seem for a moment to flourish, but in the end **their bones** shall **be strewn at the mouth of Sheol.** Such meditations cause him once more to lift his soul to God with the prayer that he may not perish, that he may be saved from the snares and the traps which evildoers have laid for him; that he may pass on rejoicing, even though the ungodly fall into their own net.

By Christian standards it may be an imperfect prayer; but how do our supplications compare with it? We have been taught in the school of Christ to pray not only for ourselves, but even for those who spread nets against us. But have we this man's urgency and concentration? Being what we are, there will be days when attention is diverted, when other interests crowd the mind even as we repeat sacred phrases, when God himself seems remote. We must not be surprised if on such occasions we go down to our house unjustified. But if we train ourselves to pray in spirit, and with the understanding also, we shall know that it is no vain thing we do. We shall find the answer to prayer in inner strength and peace, even if some of the things we asked for are not granted.

142:1-7. ***A Cry from the Depths.***—First impressions of this psalm are not favorable. The writer tells us that his sufferings are many, his enemies are vindictive, his friends indifferent, and that he is left to endure his tribulations in solitude. It is not an inspiring subject; it might even be the work of a man given to self-pity.

The psalm, however, cannot be so easily dismissed. To start with, the poet's sufferings are real, not imaginary. It is possible that he was shut up in a dungeon (vs. 7*a*), lacking space for movement, and light and air for health of body and mind. In such circumstances even the most patient and heroic may lose serenity, perhaps indeed sanity. Further, the "prisoner" is in the power of crafty enemies who have shown malice in the past and may continue to torture him to the end. His life is in their hands and there is little hope of clemency. He has, or had, friends but they are silent: they neither visit him nor send messages of comfort. Maybe they have forgotten him and become immersed in their own affairs. As he dwells upon his miseries they

2 I poured out my complaint before him;
I showed before him my trouble.
3 When my spirit was overwhelmed
within me, then thou knewest my path. In
the way wherein I walked have they privily
laid a snare for me.

2 I pour out my complaint before him,
I tell my trouble before him.
3 When my spirit is faint,
thou knowest my way!

In the path where I walk
they have hidden a trap for me.

The reference to a **prison in** vs. 7 led late scribal students fancifully to ascribe the psalm to David, **when he was in the cave** at Adullam (I Sam. 22:1). But the date of the psalm is probably late postexilic because of its use of certain words which commonly belong to Aramaic or late Hebrew, e.g., יכתרו (vs. 7); התעטף (vs. 3); שיחי (vs. 2). The meter is mainly 3+3; but 2+2, 2+2 in vs. 6; and 3+2, 3+2 in vs. 7.

1. Appeal to the Lord (142:1-3*b*)

142:1-3*b*. I cry with my voice: The psalmists indicate with no uncertainty that their supplications were not uttered in silence or in low tones (cf. 55:17; 61:1; 102:1). In I Sam. 1:12 we read that because Hannah was whispering her petition in the temple at Shiloh, Eli the priest assumed that she was overcome with wine. Prayer is regarded by the people of ancient times as in the category of an appeal addressed to a royal person. **I pour out my complaint:** Such words imply that prayers were at one time more remarkable for their "much speaking" than their form, since their words went forth like a copious stream. The substance of the psalmist's prayer is called a **complaint** because it consists of the plaintive utterance of his grievances, **my trouble.** He had much to say and much to plead, but what purpose would it serve to prolong his appeal, for **thou knowest my way?** By his **way** he means either the godliness of his life or the troubles through which he has been passing by reason of the calumnies of his persecutors; but the context seems to favor the former sense as implying his innocence of wrongdoing.

2. The Psalmist's Plight (142:3*c*-4)

3*c*-4. The psalmist follows his appeal with a statement of his situation. He has been no match for his enemies who **have hidden a trap for** him, and he has become a victim

---

multiply, until despair settles upon his soul and he concludes that no refuge remains to him.

There is, however, one thing that men in such extremity instinctively do: they look above themselves and seek help beyond human resources. They are not necessarily men of tried piety. They may have denied not only the power of prayer but the existence of a God to pray to. Yet when danger assails they cry aloud in agony of spirit and batter the gates of heaven with storms of prayer. In such moods of importunateness they will make vows: they will reform their ways, they will give to the poor, they will live as dedicated beings. In moments of crisis such promises are as common as are the temptations later to forget.

One detects, however, a deeper note in this supplication. It is not the cry of a coward overwhelmed by fear, but the prayer of one who in the past has often had communion with God and who now, remembering past experiences, lifts up his heart in the words, **Thou art my refuge and my portion in the land of the living.** Enemies may thicken, they may lay traps on every hand. Friends may desert him and excuse themselves with a profession of helplessness. Faith in God still shines like a star in a stormy firmament. Enemies blinded by prejudice may think him guilty. Friends blinded by fear may suspect he has slipped from rectitude. But God knows all; he knows that he is innocent. Were there no more, this would be much. It is not a little to have a clear conscience, to be able to hold high the head when neighbors condemn. It is much more to be convinced that the inner assurance is confirmed by the judgment of heaven. A man can bear trials with greater patience and face the world with fortitude when he believes that the inner monitor is a reflection of God's truth. In such a moment he does not boast or fly into a frenzy; in quiet gratitude he exclaims, **Thou knowest my way.** Such knowledge comforts the strained mind and eases the tortured body and brings peace to prisoners in foul dungeons. It effects a change in attitude even to persecutors. It creates kinder thoughts

4 I looked on *my* right hand, and beheld, but *there was* no man that would know me: refuge failed me; no man cared for my soul.

5 I cried unto thee, O LORD: I said, Thou *art* my refuge *and* my portion in the land of the living.

4 I look to the right and watch,[d]
but there is none who takes notice of me;
no refuge remains to me,
no man cares for me.

5 I cry to thee, O LORD;
I say, Thou art my refuge,
my portion in the land of the living.

[d] Or *Look to the right and watch*

of their wiles. **I look to the right:** The metaphor is of military origin. Since the soldier's left is covered by his shield, he needs in time of peril a protector on his right. **But there is none who takes notice of me** and **no refuge** is open to him since **no man cares for me** (cf. the psalms of lonely souls, 22:11; 38:11; 88:18).

3. The Appeal Renewed (142:5-7)

5-7. I cry to thee, O Lord. The grounds on which the psalmist bases this petition are: (*a*) **thou art my refuge** and all that I possess, **my portion,** this side of the grave **in the land of the living;** (*b*) **I am brought very low.** In asking for deliverance from

toward friends who seem to have forgotten. There grows the assurance that they speak about him, remember him in their intercessions, would act on his behalf if opportunity presented itself. Above all, there is the conviction that God is not indifferent: even in the direst need we are in his hand. A great step toward recovery has been taken when we can say:

> **The righteous will surround me;**
> **for thou wilt deal bountifully with me.**

It is not possible to name or date the psalmist who thus prays in prison. But there are others who have been similarly tried and who in time of crisis have found consolation.

We are reminded first not of individuals but of the children of Israel as a whole. They were not a popular people. There were periods when they lived happily with their neighbors, but more often there was bitter enmity between them, and many of the nations were too strong for them. The Israelites were not guiltless. They were a proud and exclusive race. They could be not only superior in spirit but scornful of others. Guilty or innocent, they found many persecutors. They were driven to their highland capital. They were carried away as captives to strange countries where they were tempted and taunted. Then they cried to the Lord in their trouble, and in pouring out their complaint before him they formed deeper convictions and made new professions. They were not always faithful to promises made in emergency, but they maintained faith in a God of truth and taught other nations to seek the same refuge.

There were many who passed through such vicissitudes and became representative Israelites. Jeremiah especially was a son of affliction who stood among the greatest of the prophets. Called to be a servant of Yahweh, he soon found himself in conflict with his own people who vilified him, dragged him before rulers, cast him into prison, even forced him to escape with them to Egypt. Some of those who owed most to him found it discreet to dissociate themselves from him. If ever anyone might be excused for being a man of tears and loud lamentation, it was this man who longed for a quiet life and found himself forced into controversy. His one comfort was found in prayer. "O LORD," he cried, "thou knowest: remember me, and visit me" (Jer. 15:15). He was a man of tribulation to the end, but he found peace in God.

In the fullness of the times there came one greater than any of the prophets. Jesus of Nazareth is not adequately described as "a man of sorrows, and acquainted with grief" (Isa. 53:3), yet never was there one who stood so utterly alone, never one whose sorrow was like unto his sorrow. He had his friends and disciples, men and women who followed and loved him, but their thoughts were not his thoughts, nor were their ways his ways. They learned much while he was with them, and understood more when he had been taken from them; but they were apt to ask the wrong questions, seek the wrong rewards: when his enemies laid hands upon him and plotted his death, they fled. He had been cast out of the home in Nazareth, out of the synagogue, and at last found himself alone in Gethsemane, alone in the judgment hall,

6 Attend unto my cry; for I am brought very low: deliver me from my persecutors; for they are stronger than I.

7 Bring my soul out of prison, that I may praise thy name: the righteous shall compass me about; for thou shalt deal bountifully with me.

6 Give heed to my cry;
for I am brought very low!

Deliver me from my persecutors;
for they are too strong for me!
7 Bring me out of prison,
that I may give thanks to thy name!
The righteous will surround me;
for thou wilt deal bountifully with me.

A Psalm of David.

143 Hear my prayer, O Lord, give ear to my supplications: in thy faithfulness answer me, *and* in thy righteousness.

A Psalm of David.

143 Hear my prayer, O Lord;
give ear to my supplications!
In thy faithfulness answer me, in thy righteousness!

---

prison, he pleads that his thanksgiving for and testimony to what the Lord shall have done for him will hearten all **the righteous** who are waiting in confidence with him for God's gracious intervention on his behalf. Vs. *7c* is best rendered by assuming that כתר is used in its Aramaic sense of "wait" or "await" rather than in its late Hebrew sense of "crown" (KJV, **compass**). The Targ. avoids the difficulty by a paraphrase: "On my behalf the righteous will offer to thee a crown of praise because thou wilt requite me bountifully," i.e., vs. *7cd* becomes a vow of thanksgiving by the righteous.

CXLIII. My Soul Thirsts for Thee (143:1-12)

This psalm is the last of the so-called Penitential Psalms (Pss. 6; 32; 38; 51; 102; 130; 143) which the Book of Common Prayer lists as proper for Ash Wednesday. It

---

alone on the cross. Yet without complaint he made his solitary way into the comfort of the Father's presence. As the dangers thickened around him, as men taunted him and spat upon him, he entered the more fully into peace. Never was his faith more triumphant than on that darkest of days when the sun was blotted out and the earth quaked. The cup was not taken from him; but in the agony of crucifixion he prayed for those who persecuted him, promised paradise to a repentant thief, and at last in an attitude of perfect trust committed himself into the Father's hands.

Like the first disciples, the multitudes who have followed in his steps have not always caught his spirit. Yet there have been many who have passed through the discipline of suffering and have been vindicated. There was Saul of Tarsus, whose conversion from the synagogue to the church was never forgiven by contemporary Jews. He was driven from one place to another, cast into prisons, brought before magistrates, beaten by Gentiles, and distrusted by fellow Christians. A book might be written on the sufferings of Paul as a man, as a Christian, and as an apostle.[8] But whether it was the thorn in the flesh, the bitterness of religious and sacred authorities, or the care of all the churches, he was sustained by an inner assurance that he dwelt in Christ and Christ in him. He learned in whatsoever state he was therein to be content. He was persuaded that neither life nor death could separate him from the love of God.

The story has never ended. One after another the saints and martyrs of the church rise up before us, telling the same story. It has many variations and compelling interests; but suffering is there, frequently suffering in many forms. Two things made Robert Louis Stevenson, someone has said: pain and work. It might be said of thousands more, especially of great Christians. They have known joy, too, joy so intense, so rare, so pure that it seemed to come as the gift of heaven. They have not always been lifted out of dungeons, but the dungeons have been transformed and they have been transfigured. "In my distress I called upon the Lord, and cried unto my God: he heard my voice out of his temple, and my cry came before him, even into his ears" (18:6). It is a story that has no end.

143:1-12. ***Deliverance Through Prayer.***—This psalm impresses us not by its originality but by

[8] See Ballard, *Spiritual Pilgrimage of St. Paul*, p. 95.

2 And enter not into judgment with thy servant: for in thy sight shall no man living be justified.	2 Enter not into judgment with thy servant; for no man living is righteous before thee.

belongs to the category of a lament and expresses the fervent prayer of one who is imploring God for deliverance from the deadly persecution of relentless enemies (vs. 9), among whom one is singled out for mention because of his truculence (vs. 3). Though the psalm has much in common with others of its type, it stands apart from most of them because, like Ps. 38, it voices a genuinely penitential note. The psalmist has a strong sense of the fact of sin and human frailty, and believes that the troubles which come upon men are not unrelated to men's sin. He seems ready to admit therefore that his enemies may be God's instruments for correcting him (vs. 2), and on this ground he makes none of the usual protestations of innocence in the course of his appeal. At the same time he feels that as a **servant** of God (vs. 12), he can look to God to deliver him from the fierce excess of his enemies' cruelty. But far more than the answer to his request, it is to be noted, he longs to have the guidance of God's good spirit in the days to come so that his path in life may be free of the troubles which arise from failure to know and to do the will of God.

The psalm shows numerous points of contact with other psalms: cf. vs. 1 with 17:1; 39:12; vs. 3 with 7:5; 88:6; Lam. 3:6; vs. 5 with 77:5, 11-12; vs. 6 with 63:1; vs. 7 with 27:9; 28:1; vs. 8 with 25:1-2, 4; vs. 9 with 31:15; 142:6; vs. 11 with 25:11.

The fact that this poem presents so many evidences of acquaintance with other psalms suggests a late date; indeed, it is probably even more recent than other pieces of late date (cf. Pss. 25; 31; 88). The developed sense of sin and of the relation of trouble to sin in the experience of an individual is also indicative of a postexilic date. The meter is 3+3 or 3+3+3, with examples of 3+2 in vss. 7-10; and 4+4 in vs. 11.

1. Appeal to the Lord (143:1-2)

143:1-2. Hear, . . . give ear, . . . answer. This threefold appeal with which the psalm opens reveals the distress and anxiety of the psalmist. In the LXX, Jerome, Vulg.,

its intensity. The subject matter reminds us of other psalms, particularly of Ps. 142, but it is not mere repetition. It is as familiar and as fresh as the dawn of a new day. The psalmist is in dire need. He is not a perfect man: he knows himself to be the frail son of an erring race. He could with entire sincerity utter a prayer of deep contrition, even call himself a "miserable offender." Yet, like Job, he knows that he has done nothing to deserve the exceptional tribulations that have come to him. We therefore find him in one breath confessing that he is a sinful man and in another protesting his innocence (but see Exeg.). He may be compared with scholars who have labored long and well at particular subjects and in their own spheres gained eminence, who nevertheless realize that all their learning, indeed all the accumulated learning of the race, is insignificant compared with the unknown and the unknowable. Men may be counted innocent before the tribunals of earth yet stand without a single boast before the absolute justice of heaven.

The immediate cause of the psalmist's suffering appears to be not his own transgression but the malice of an enemy. Whether the enemy was an individual, a party, or a nation is not clear; what is stated is that the psalmist has been relentlessly pursued and overwhelmed, has had life so crushed out of him that he feels himself left without help or hope. It is useless to expect human aid, equally impossible to raise himself to new courage and effort; he has come to the end of all such expectations.

One thing, however, is still possible: he may try the way of prayer and put his trust in the faithfulness of God. This is not clutching at a chance straw. He has often heard of supernatural deliverances; perhaps he reminds himself of men he has known who had exhausted all human resources and still found a way opening before them. Life has always supplied illustrations of such interpositions, some so quiet and simple as to appear natural, others so dramatic and exceptional as to cause widespread comment. They had happened on national and cosmic planes as well as in individual experience. What was the history of Israel but a long succession of such merciful acts of salvation? The psalmist had been taught in early days

3 For the enemy hath persecuted my
soul; he hath smitten my life down to the
ground; he hath made me to dwell in darkness, as those that have been long dead.
4 Therefore is my spirit overwhelmed
within me; my heart within me is desolate.

3 For the enemy has pursued me;
he has crushed my life to the ground;
he has made me sit in darkness like
those long dead.
4 Therefore my spirit faints within me;
my heart within me is appalled.

---

and certain Hebrew MSS the phrasing of vs. 1*bc* is "Give ear to my supplications in thy faithfulness, answer me with thy righteousness." **In thy faithfulness,** i.e., because of steadfast loyalty to his promises. **In thy righteousness:** As frequently in the Psalter and Second Isaiah, **righteousness** (צדקה) here is better rendered by "deliverance," for it is neither God's retributive justice nor his righteous character, but rather an intervention of God to vindicate the right; sometimes it has for its parallel חסד, "kindness" or "love" (cf. 36:10; 103:17). **Enter not into judgment with thy servant:** Better, "Bring not thy servant into judgment." The psalmist recognizes that if God should bring him to the bar of justice he would not be able to prove himself a man innocent of wrongdoing, **for no man living is righteous before thee.** However, like Job, he believes that he is suffering at the hands of the enemy something worse than a just recompense of his sins.

2. The Psalmist's Situation (143:3-4)

3-4. The psalmist's appeal is followed by the statement of his bitter situation, i.e., technically, his plaint. **The enemy has pursued me, . . . crushed my life to the ground, . . . made me sit in darkness:** Note the crescendo in the description of the enemy's vindictiveness; he pursues, overtakes, tramples to pieces, and sends into the darkness of Sheol; i.e., the enemy has brought the psalmist to the point where he is reckoned as a dead man. The language may connote that the poet is the victim of a legal process which seems about to issue in a death sentence, or that he is in the grip of some deadly physical ill for which he holds the enemy responsible. Indirectly the description of the enemy's bloodthirstiness becomes an argument for God's intervention. Such an excess of brutality is an offense against the ordinary dictates of conscience (cf. Amos 1:11-12).

---

about Abraham and his quest for "a city which hath foundations, whose builder and maker is God" (Heb. 11:10). His mind was stored with traditions of patriarchs and prophets, with legends of Egypt and the wilderness and more precise records of settlement in the Land of Promise. He had learned it as most boys learn history, as something remote and impersonal and not very important. But suffering may open eyes and quicken imagination. Solitude may bring to light deep significance in familiar tales. Perhaps meditating in enforced silence the psalmist began to see that these things had not just happened, nor were they to be attributed to the genius of the race: they had happened because God was and willed and worked.

Perhaps the swift historic survey prompted more personal reflections. There were incidents in his own life which he had accepted too easily and which needed reinterpretation. He had made decisions and they had worked out as he never intended. At other times he found himself at the crossroads, uncertain which way to go. He had ventured here, rather than there, not because of clear conviction but because man is not allowed for long to stand still. Sometimes he had looked back, feeling he had made a mistake and wishing he could start again. But now *in extremis* he begins to realize that he was not as much alone as he had thought. There were influences playing around him; choice was being made for him when he felt incapable of making it for himself. In short:

> There's a divinity that shapes our ends,
> Rough-hew them how we will.[9]

Out of the deepest need there emerges not sullen despair, not a frenzied cry, not irresponsible supplication, but a calm, determined, expectant appeal: **I stretch out my hands to thee.** Perhaps even as he spoke the psalmist looked at those hands lifted in prayer. They had hung so helplessly at his side. The day of action was past. They were as useless as the wings of a bird that had lost the power of flight. But lifted in prayer they were hands of power and purpose. They might even touch the strong hand of God. Why the almighty arm had not

[9] Shakespeare, *Hamlet,* Act V, scene 2.

5 I remember the days of old; I meditate on all thy works; I muse on the work of thy hands.

6 I stretch forth my hands unto thee: my soul *thirsteth* after thee, as a thirsty land. Selah.

7 Hear me speedily, O LORD; my spirit faileth: hide not thy face from me, lest I be like unto them that go down into the pit.

8 Cause me to hear thy loving-kindness in the morning; for in thee do I trust: cause me to know the way wherein I should walk; for I lift up my soul unto thee.

5 I remember the days of old,
I meditate on all that thou hast done;
I muse on what thy hands have wrought.
6 I stretch out my hands to thee;
my soul thirsts for thee like a parched land. *Selah*

7 Make haste to answer me, O LORD!
My spirit fails!
Hide not thy face from me,
lest I be like those who go down to the Pit.
8 Let me hear in the morning of thy steadfast love,
for in thee I put my trust.
Teach me the way I should go,
for to thee I lift up my soul.

3. Reflections on God's Past Mercies (143:5-6)

5-6. The psalmist both argues again for God's coming to his aid and fortifies his trust in the certainty of a favorable answer from God by recalling what God has done in Israel's history. So **I stretch out my hands to thee.**

4. The Appeal Renewed (143:7-12)

7-12. The psalmist's petition is introduced in vs. 7 with a repetition of his appeal and his urgent need of help. **Make haste to answer me, . . . lest I be like those who go down to the Pit.** His petition in particular is **Let me hear** [השמיעני] **in the morning of thy steadfast love,** or, better, "let me be satisfied [השביעני] with thy goodness in the morning" (Duhm, Gunkel). For the phrase **in the morning** see Exeg. on 5:1-3; 57:7-11; cf. 3:5; 4:8; 59:16. The meaning here may be, as in 90:14, no more than "early" or "soon"; on the other hand, it may be strictly "tomorrow." In the latter case the psalmist is expecting by the morning some omen or oracle which will acquit him of the charges of the enemy, or his exculpation in some rite of purgation. A reference to the rite of incubation may be implied (cf. I Kings 3:5-13; Job 33:15-18). Through some such divine

already been made bare, why the lifting of frail hands of flesh should make activity possible —these were mysteries which neither the psalmist nor his successors have fully understood. But his business is not now with mysteries. His business is with one of the declared facts of human life: that man in his distress may cry to God and God in his mercy responds.

Not all prayers are so potent. Men pray, but without the perspective of the years. Their petitions are prompted by present fears more than by remembrance of past mercies. Or if there is memory and a measure of insight, it may be that there is no instinctive lifting of mind and heart in supplication and intercession. And so they sink once more into despondency.

But again the urgency of the situation disturbs the psalmist's reflections and arouses him to importunity. The mills of God have often worked slowly: they must now grind quickly if he is to be saved. The rehearsal of past miracles can embitter if evil continues much longer to triumph:

> **Make haste to answer me, O LORD!**
> **My spirit fails!**
> **Hide not thy face from me,**
> **lest I be like those who go down to the Pit.**

It may not be the note of the maturest piety, but it is a very human petition. We want our prayers answered at once. We cannot understand the patience of God. We cannot see the value of delay either in our individual affairs or in human crises. It only intensifies our exasperation and gives new edge to the gibes of the scornful. We would not allow a son or a brother to continue in suffering if we could interfere. We should make mistakes sometimes,

9 Deliver me, O LORD, from mine enemies: I flee unto thee to hide me.

10 Teach me to do thy will; for thou *art* my God: thy Spirit *is* good; lead me into the land of uprightness.

11 Quicken me, O LORD, for thy name's sake: for thy righteousness' sake bring my soul out of trouble.

9 Deliver me, O LORD, from my enemies!
I have fled to thee for refuge![e]
10 Teach me to do thy will,
for thou art my God!
Let thy good spirit lead me
on a level path!

11 For thy name's sake, O LORD, preserve my life!
In thy righteousness bring me out of trouble!

[e] One Heb Ms Gk: Heb *to thee I have hidden*

---

action the immediate need of the psalmist will be met. **Deliver me . . . from my enemies! I have fled to thee.** The M.T. reads **to thee I have hidden** (כסתי, RSV mg.) for which the LXX reads "I flee" (נסתי) and others would read by emendation **I have fled . . . for refuge** (חסיתי; RSV mg.) or "I have looked" (סכיתי). But the more permanent need of the psalmist is for instruction in and acquaintance with the will of God. **Let thy good spirit lead me:** I.e., through the inner promptings of thy spirit direct me. The psalmist here, as in 51:10, is approaching the N.T. conception of the spirit. By this spirit, reflection on God's good ways in Israel's history (cf. Neh. 9:20) and in the psalmist's own experience will be stimulated, and "a loyal spirit" will be created within

---

it is true. We should pick the fruit before it was ripe. We should perform operations before the appointed time. We should speak when we ought to hold our tongues. But we would do something! Prone to take time by the forelock, we expect Omniscience to do the same.

Fortunately the psalmist does not continue in this mood of impatience. Even as he cries to high heaven he remembers that the divine will is best, and in subdued tones takes to pleading: **Teach me the way I should go** (vs. 8). **Teach me to do thy will, . . . let thy good spirit lead me** (vs. 10). Deliverance, if possible immediate deliverance, is desirable; but most important of all is the knowing and loving of the will of God and the willingness to submit to his wisdom. The further prayer in vs. 12 may be another fall from grace; but if the psalmist's **enemies** are the enemies of God, what can one do but seek their removal? Jesus would have us pray for our enemies that they cease to be enemies, and become friends, not merely our friends but friends of God. That we must not expect to find here. The psalmist is not living at N.T. levels.

One may be reminded of the very different yet essentially similar experience in the life of William Cowper. The story has had many interpreters, but perhaps none more sympathetic than David Cecil, who restates and examines afresh the essential facts. The scene is eighteenth-century England. The chief character is a pitiable scion of a privileged family. There are no external enemies, but serious internal troubles. There is a hypersensitive spirit making the loss of the mother in early childhood an agony. There is such a shrinking from publicity that the ordeal of examination for a public position causes acute mental disturbances. There are friends at their wit's end to know what to advise. Derangement deepens into religious mania. He feels himself an outcast from divine mercy. The verses he wrote in such times of depression are among the saddest in English literature.

Man disavows, and Deity disowns me,
Hell might afford my miseries a shelter;
Therefore hell keeps her everhungry mouth all
Bolted against me.

Hard lot! encompass'd with a thousand dangers;
Weary, faint, trembling with a thousand terrors,
I'm called, if vanquish'd, to receive a sentence
Worse than Abiram's.[1]

Nevertheless he emerged, not indeed for life, but for long, glad, productive periods. Hasty critics have found the cause of the madness in excess of religious zeal. Cecil insists that instead of being responsible for the malady, religion was "the most considerable of the remedies by which he tried to get rid of it." Eighteenth-century Evangelicalism has often been criticized; but "it did seek to fight the enemies of the spirit with spiritual weapons, to expel, not merely to evade them." Argue as men will about causes or cures, there is no questioning the

[1] "Lines Written During a Period of Insanity."

12 And of thy mercy cut off mine enemies, and destroy all them that afflict my soul: for I *am* thy servant.

A Psalm of David.

144 Blessed *be* the LORD my strength, which teacheth my hands to war, *and* my fingers to fight:

12 And in thy steadfast love cut off my enemies,
and destroy all my adversaries,
for I am thy servant.

A Psalm of David.

144 Blessed be the LORD, my rock,
who trains my hands for war,
and my fingers for battle;

---

him. Henceforth he will walk **on a level path.** He concludes his petition by citing four reasons why God should act on his behalf: (*a*) **for thy name's sake,** i.e., for the sake of what is worthy of thy reputation; (*b*) **in thy righteousness,** i.e., in accordance with thy championship of the right; (*c*) **in thy steadfast love,** i.e., according to thy loyalty to thy promises; and (*d*) **I am thy servant.**

His final cry for vengeance on his enemies seems too stark a contrast to his spiritual aspirations if we fail to remember that the creatures against whom his anger tears (vs. 12) are in his mind also the enemies of God, for they are not guided in their ways by his **good spirit.**

CXLIV. Bow Thy Heavens, O Lord (144:1-15)

This psalm consists of two originally independent units which by accident or design were brought together. The two units may be defined as vss. 1-11, 12-15; the one has to do with the concerns of an individual, the other with those of the community.

Vss. 1-11, which in form follow the lines of a lament, express an impassioned appeal to the Lord by one whose mind is occupied by matters of war. We see that he considers himself no mean warrior (vs. 1), and that he fears the onset of foreign foes (vs. 7) whom he accuses of lying and perfidy (vs. 8). He speaks as one on whom the

---

"great wave of joy that had washed all the horrors of madness clean out of his mind, and quickened him to an intensity of spirit he had never known before." "We have not envied you," he was able to write to his friend, the Rev. William Bull, on holiday. "Why should we envy any man? Is not our greenhouse a cabinet of perfumes? It is at this moment fronted with carnations and balsams, mignonette and roses, jessamine and woodbine, and wants nothing but your pipe to make it truly Arabian, a wilderness of sweets." [2]

The lessons for the individual and the nation are obvious. Is there not also a cosmic reference? Again and again the human race has found itself crushed in spirit. Prophets and seers have come in succession, calling upon humanity to break its bonds and step out into liberty. And men have often responded. They have striven so valiantly that their hopes have risen high and more than once they have proclaimed the end of servitude. But just as they seemed to be on the very threshold of mastery there has been another fall. Evil has broken out in unexpected places and unpredictable ways, and again they find themselves sitting in darkness. The worst state is reached when they become content with prison, when hope is surrendered and aspiration ceases.

Man's extremity, however, is found to be God's opportunity. Inspiration comes from above. New messengers are sent to arouse the conscience and nerve the will. God speaks through beauty, calls through goodness and truth. In the fullness of the times he sends his Son. The Incarnation is God's response to man's need. Christ comes not because of human merit but because of divine love. He comes in lowly birth, in perfect life, in sacrificial death, and his coming is vindicated in resurrection and ascension. God still rescues through the ministries of the Holy Spirit, the fellowship of the catholic church, the service of saintly souls. This holy love is our hope in every age: it is mightier than evil, adequate for all our need. Even death cannot triumph over it.

144:1-15. ***Praise and Providence.***—Reference has often been made to the great variety of mood and subject matter to be found in the book of Psalms. There are songs of gratitude

[2] David Cecil, *The Stricken Deer* (London: Constable & Co., 1929), pp. 143, 144, 149, 171.

2 My goodness, and my fortress; my high tower, and my deliverer; my shield, and *he* in whom I trust; who subdueth my people under me.

2 my rock[f] and my fortress,
my stronghold and my deliverer,
my shield and he in whom I take refuge,
who subdues the peoples under him.[g]

[f] With 18. 2 2 Sam. 22. 2: Heb *my steadfast love*
[g] Another reading is *my people under me*

responsibility of leadership in war rests heavily (vs. 10). His language, however, fails to make it clear whether or not he is a king, since in late Hebrew literature appeals to precedent in the Lord's past relations with his people, such as we note in vs. 10, are common (see Norman B. Johnson, *Prayer in the Apocrypha and Pseudepigrapha* [Philadelphia: Society of Biblical Literature & Exegesis, 1948; "Journal of Biblical Literature Monograph Series"], p. 47; also I Macc. 4:30-31; II Macc. 15:22-24). The substance of his prayer is largely made up of borrowings from Ps. 18 and some others; cf., e.g., vs. 1*a* with 18:46; vs. 1*b* with 18:34; vs. 2 with 18:2, 47; vs. 3 with 8:4; vs. 4 with 39:5-6; vss. 5-8 with 18:9-17; vs. 5*b* with 104:32; vs. 9 with 33:2-3; vs. 10 with 18:50. We may assume therefore that the psalm was composed for the suppliant by someone well acquainted with liturgical literature. In its transmission the text has been corrupted: a variant of vss. 7*c*-8 appears as vs. 11*bcd*, and vss. 3-4 are possibly a gloss. Vss. 1-2, 5-10*a* present a normal pattern of a lament.

Vss. 12-15 may have been originally a beatitude or blessing psalm, in the style of the wisdom writers, like Pss. 127 and 128, in which case it is to be assumed as complete in itself. On the other hand, it may be a fragment of a hymn of the type of Ps. 146.

In the Hebrew text the two units of the psalm are given the semblance of a single composition by the presence of the particle אשר, "whose" or "in order that," at the beginning of vs. 12 (contrast Jerome, Vulg., and see Exeg. below). The two units came together possibly through their juxtaposition in some source from which the psalm was drawn into the Psalter.

A. Deliver Me from the Hand of Aliens (144:1-11)

The first unit is to be dated in postexilic times by reason of the following facts: it is a mosaic of borrowings from psalms which are themselves late (see Exeg. on Pss. 8; 18; 33; 104), and its vocabulary contains Aramaic and late Hebrew elements, e.g., קרב (vs. 1), פצה (vs. 7), בני נכר (vs. 11). Those who in the face of these facts assign a pre-exilic date to this unit are influenced by a wrong interpretation of vs. 10 (see above). In the superscription the LXX adds πρὸς τὸν Γολιάδ, "against Goliath," a late conjecture. The meter is generally 3+3.

1. Thanks for Past Mercies (144:1-2)

144:1-2. Blessed be the Lord, my rock: The psalmist begins his lament with words of thanksgiving for what the Lord has already done for him. This use of a hymn motif

and cries of penitence, laments from exiles and prisoners, praise for pilgrims, liturgies for priests and people in the temple. We study one psalm and get a picture of a young man rejoicing in his strength and full of the joy of living. We turn to others and find a poor man wrestling with the soil, a shepherd watching his sheep, or a prince bearing the burdens of state.

1-11. ***A Refuge for Rulers.***—The first part of this psalm suggests, if not a king conscious of royal responsibilities, at least a leader to whom is committed the defense of the country. Whether he is a prince, a statesman, or a soldier, he demands and must deserve the confidence of the people and be skilled in the complexities of government. He must attend to vital preparations, show courage in every crisis. He must be concerned with the moral and spiritual condition of the country as well as with the security of frontiers. He must be with those who pray in the temple as well as with those who sit in council and with those who fight in the field. He must know that national security demands more than popular appeal or skillful diplomacy or wise strategy. He must confess that he is but an instrument in higher hands, that strength

3 LORD, what *is* man, that thou takest knowledge of him! *or* the son of man, that thou makest account of him!

4 Man is like to vanity: his days *are* as a shadow that passeth away.

5 Bow thy heavens, O LORD, and come down: touch the mountains, and they shall smoke.

3 O LORD, what is man that thou dost regard him,
or the son of man that thou dost think of him?
4 Man is like a breath,
his days are like a passing shadow.

5 Bow thy heavens, O LORD, and come down!
Touch the mountains that they smoke!

---

to introduce a lament is more common in the later style (cf. Jer. 17:12-18; Prayer of Manasseh 1–7, Tob. 3:2-3, 11). He gives thanks for two things: (*a*) the skill which he possesses as a warrior in physical prowess (**my hands for war**) and in the wise conduct of campaigns (**my fingers for battle;** cf. Prov. 20:18; 24:6), and (*b*) past military success; **my rock, my fortress, my stronghold, my deliverer, my shield,** are terms which in the context have a military connotation, as we see in vs. 2*d*, which should be read, "who subdues peoples under me" (cf. 18:47).

2. On the Transitoriness of Man (144:3-4)

3-4. If these verses are an integral part of the psalm, they introduce the petition of the psalmist (vss. 5-8) with a confession of his unworthiness. How can the Lord, who is so great, interest himself in any of the race of men who at the best are only **like a breath** or **like a . . . shadow** cast by a moving cloud or a bird in flight? The question is here indirectly an appeal to God's magnanimity. Since God in his goodness does take thought of men, the psalmist is emboldened to make his request with confidence that, unworthy though he is, it will be answered.

3. Prayer for a Theophany (144:5-8)

5-8. Bow thy heavens, O LORD: The psalmist's prayer is that the Lord may come down on the clouds to the mountains of Palestine in a great theophany like that at Sinai of old (see 18:7-15), accompanied by fire and smoke, flashing forth lightning, and

---

comes from God. Blessed is the man, in particular blessed is the man in authority, who believes that the Lord is his rock, his stronghold, and his deliverer. Not the man who trusts to his own ability or the size of his armies, but he who finds his shield and refuge in supernatural resources will see enemies subdued.

In contrast with the Lord of hosts how frail is even the strongest of the sons of men! Whatever his natural gifts, whatever powers the nation has conferred upon him, he is **like a breath, his days are like a passing shadow.** He may attain knowledge that gives him pre-eminence, he may be granted fullness of days, and with it the respect of his contemporaries; he may be loaded with earthly dignities, but

The boast of heraldry, the pomp of pow'r,
And all that beauty, all that wealth e'er gave,
Awaits alike th' inevitable hour.
The paths of glory lead but to the grave.[3]

[3] Thomas Gray, "Elegy Written in a Country Churchyard," st. ix.

How trivial human knowledge or wisdom or skill compared with the omniscience of God! How frail life itself compared with eternity! What are the differences of rank when one considers divine sovereignty! **O LORD, what is man,** whether he lives in palace or cottage, **that thou dost regard him?**

The contrast between divine power and human frailty, however, does not depress the psalmist. It encourages him; for he knows that God can do what man cannot, and that if God is with him, all is well. He can blow with his winds and enemies will be scattered. He can cause earthquakes so that the mountains smoke, or send lightning to break the ranks of the enemy. Did he not divide rivers for the Israelites to pass through dry shod, and were not the pursuing Egyptians engulfed? Had he not again and again stricken the camps of besiegers with panic and fortified the faithful with courage? Some of the language used may suggest those who "praise the Lord and pass the ammunition." But when the psalmist comes to the moral

6 Cast forth lightning, and scatter them:
shoot out thine arrows, and destroy them.
7 Send thine hand from above; rid me,
and deliver me out of great waters, from the
hand of strange children;
8 Whose mouth speaketh vanity, and
their right hand *is* a right hand of falsehood.
9 I will sing a new song unto thee, O
God: upon a psaltery *and* an instrument of
ten strings will I sing praises unto thee.

6 Flash forth the lightning and scatter them,
send out thy arrows and rout them!
7 Stretch forth thy hand from on high,
rescue me and deliver me from the many waters,
from the hand of aliens,
8 whose mouths speak lies,
and whose right hand is a right hand of falsehood.

9 I will sing a new song to thee, O God;
upon a ten-stringed harp I will play to thee,

---

discharging his thunderbolts till the foe is vanquished. **Scatter them . . . and destroy them:** It should be noted that **them** has no antecedent. But doubtless we are right in assuming that **them** is anticipative of the foes described in vs. 7. Otherwise it would refer to **the lightning,** and **thy arrows,** and the translation would be "send forth thy lightnings [ברקיך] and cause them to go zigzag, discharge thy arrows and propel them." **Stretch forth thy hand from on high:** From the chariot of clouds on which he rides, let the Lord reach out his hand and **rescue me and deliver me.** If we compare vs. 7, vs. 11, and 18:16, it becomes clear that the text here has suffered mutilation and should read "stretch forth thy hand from above, draw me [המשני] out of many waters, rescue me [פצני] from the evil sword, and deliver me [הצילני] from the hand of aliens." We know too little of the postexilic period to be able to identify the historical references in vss. 2*d,* 7*c.* Since the psalm is drawing much of its language from Ps. 18, the description of the psalmist's situation may in consequence be less than exact. The foes, whether "foreigners" by race or "foreigners" by alliance (cf., e.g., Neh. 4), are guilty of making false charges (their **mouths speak lies**) and of perfidy, "their oath is a lying oath," two features which are not citations from Ps. 18 and are therefore significant in the situation. Oaths were made by "giving the [right] hand" (cf. KJV; Ezek. 17:18; Ezra 10:3, 19). Since oaths were made under divine auspices, this accusation of the psalmist becomes an additional argument for the Lord's intervention. Were these perfidious foes Samaritans or Hellenizing Jews or their allies?

4. The Psalmist's Vow (144:9-11)

9-11. The psalmist concludes his appeal with a vow to **sing a new song** of thanksgiving for the victory which he believes is at hand. The crisis which confronts the psalmist is so desperate that none of the old songs will be adequate to express his thankfulness

---

resources that are available to those who have a righteous cause, he speaks of something we can understand. We have seen again and again in modern life that men and munitions are not enough. It is the sense of duty, the assurance of justice, that keeps nations united and enables them to continue the struggle whatever the cost. The psalmist uses the language of his age, but he states abiding truth when he affirms that nations are under the sovereignty of God. Even war does not remove God from the earthly scene. The events of history are never outside his active concern. Inspired by such convictions men can look forward not only to victory but to the glad new songs that shall be sung to stringed instruments.

No better illustration of these heartening truths can be found than in the history of the Jews. Egypt, Assyria, and Babylon dominated the Mediterranean world; but their civilizations perished, and today archaeologists dig the fragments out of the dust. The small nation of God, inhabiting a tiny portion of the land, survived the shock of wars, destruction, and captivity. To them through the centuries the Lord revealed himself as almighty Creator, the one true God, holy, righteous, just, merciful, and powerful. Out of their stock he came in Christ to

10 *It is he* that giveth salvation unto kings: who delivereth David his servant from the hurtful sword.

11 Rid me, and deliver me from the hand of strange children, whose mouth speaketh vanity, and their right hand *is* a right hand of falsehood:

12 That our sons *may be* as plants grown up in their youth; *that* our daughters *may be* as corner stones, polished *after* the similitude of a palace:

10 who givest victory to kings,
who rescuest David thy[h] servant.
11 Rescue me from the cruel sword,
and deliver me from the hand of aliens,
whose mouths speak lies,
and whose right hand is a right hand of falsehood.

12 May our sons in their youth
be like plants full grown,
our daughters like corner pillars
cut for the structure of a palace;

[h] Heb *his*

---

for release from it (cf. 33:2-3; 40:3; 149:1). **Upon a ten-stringed harp:** For a description of this musical instrument see Intro., pp. 5-6. **Who givest victory to kings:** The reading **kings** is supported by the LXX, Targ., and Vulg. The divergence from 18:50 with its reading, "his king," has, as noted above, significance in the matter of dating this psalm, since the psalmist is careful not to identify himself as a king.

B. The Blessings of Those Whose God Is the Lord (144:12-15)

The date of vss. 12-15 is postexilic. The vocabulary comprises Aramaic and late Hebrew words, e.g., זוית, תבנית (vs. 12), זן, פוק (vs. 13), צוחה (vs. 14), שככה (vs. 15), and in form and point of view it shows the influence of the wisdom writers (cf. Pss. 1; 127; 128) who teach that godliness as the quintessence of wisdom yields the richest temporal blessings. The meter in vss. 12-14 is for the most part 3+2, and in the concluding verse 4+4.

It seems that the psalmist is giving us in this unit a description of the ideal prosperity which comes to those **whose God is the Lord.** The opening word אשר is either to be dropped as a false connective with the preceding verses or to be read as אשרי. In the former case vss. 12-15 can be construed as a prayer; in the latter case the reading of the LXX, Symm., some Syriac MSS, and Vulg. should be adopted, and the verse rendered "Happy are they whose sons," etc. The LXX may have regarded אשר as an indefinite relative and construed the verses as contrasting worldly happiness and godly happiness: "Those whose sons are like plants . . . are called happy, but how happy are those whose God is the Lord."

12. Our sons . . . like plants full grown: The vigor of the youth is compared to that of flourishing plants in a garden. For בנעוריהם, **in their youth,** Duhm suggests בערוגותם, "in their borders." The daughters are pictured as tall and stately, **like corner**

---

forgive, save, and re-create the world. The coming was the final vindication of the prophetic teaching which proclaimed that the universe has a moral basis. History is not the record of impersonal forces. It is the story of a struggle between good and evil. Not only men but God himself is involved in the plot. The Author of the universe is holy, working in all things for good together with those that love him. The good is creative, the evil is self-destructive. **I will** [yet] **sing a new song to thee, O God.**

12-15. ***Peace and Prosperity Through Obedience.***—The first part of the psalm may seem like a string of quotations. This second part, on the other hand, has originality and power, and suggests the unity of a single mind. The writer may have lived in a period of national difficulty. His message for it is that the way of obedience is the way of peace and prosperity. He could have expanded his theme by showing that the fathers had never found salvation through rebellion, through license or idolatry. He could have insisted that in no age have men found deliverance by material possessions, by luxury or idleness. The blessed people are not those who give themselves to gaiety, not those who surround themselves with slaves, but those **whose God is the Lord.** There is no hope for the nation that worships a cruel, a capricious, or a self-centered deity. There will be zeal for

13 *That* our garners *may be* full, affording all manner of store; *that* our sheep may bring forth thousands and ten thousands in our streets:
14 *That* our oxen *may be* strong to labor; *that there be* no breaking in, nor going out; that *there be* no complaining in our streets.
15 Happy *is that* people, that is in such a case: *yea,* happy *is that* people, whose God *is* the LORD.

13 may our garners be full,
providing all manner of store;
may our sheep bring forth thousands
and ten thousands in our fields;
14 may our cattle be heavy with young,
suffering no mischance or failure in bearing;
may there be no cry of distress in our streets!
15 Happy the people to whom such blessings fall!
Happy the people whose God is the LORD!

---

pillars . . . of a palace. The psalmist's first consideration in an ideal society is for people. Then he turns to speak of full granaries and fields covered with flocks that **bring forth thousands and ten thousands.** Rags and hunger are banished from the scene. In vs. 14 we can see in spite of its textual difficulties that the psalmist envisages a society in which violence and warfare and tumult and wailing over those fallen in battle or smitten by plague (cf. Isa. 24:11-12) shall be known no more. "How happy the people that are in such a case!" It is the happiness of **the people whose God is the LORD.**

---

the formulas of religion, but no open vision and no magnanimity in judgment if men bow down to a God who is primarily concerned with the tithing of mint, anise, and cummin.

> If men think of God as demanding from men a life not true to human instincts, life which is only supposed to be great in proportion as it withdraws itself from itself, and in a false and ascetic way crucifies the flesh, then they will turn their backs upon a God who asks them to deny that which they in themselves find themselves to be.[4]

God is neither capricious nor petty, neither remote nor repressive; but a God of holiness and love, of wisdom and power. The God of the Bible is greater than any man's experience of him, far greater than human powers of expression; but while far above us in majesty and might, he cares for us, deals with us individually, and grants to those who trust him fullness of life. He is the God of light and truth, of strength and beauty and peace. Not only did he create, but he is ever active, working in infinite patience and with endless resources. **Happy** are **the people** who acknowledge such a God, wait for him, live with him, obey him in thought and speech and deed. His peace is in their hearts, his liberty and joy in their minds, his omnipotence at their disposal.

The passage was expounded by Campbell Morgan in London in 1913, a year before the world was cast into the maelstrom of war. His was a characteristic and, in the light of succeeding history, a prophetic utterance. In the last strophe of the psalm he found

> a wonderful description of the experience of happiness in the life of a nation. The singer saw the happy nation in its family life, in its commercial life, and in its social life. Family life—our sons grown up in their youth, the figure of perfect strength; our daughters, fashioned after the similitude of the corner-stone of a palace, at once the figure of strength and beauty. Commercial life—the garners full and the cattle prolific. Change the figures, if you will, for we are no longer living in that district; but changing the figures, remember the underlying principle—that a happy people is a prosperous people commercially. Social life—and here let us change the phrasing of the Psalm, and express its meaning in modern terms. There shall be no breaking in, no invasion; and no going forth, no emigration; and no complaining in the streets, no agitation. The people whose God is the Lord are protected from the invasion of all that destroys and robs and spoils; they are protected from the necessity of sending their sons to the ends of the earth, and thus depleting the nation of its richest strength; they are protected from agitation, because there is nothing to agitate against; all false conditions have been removed, and there is no complaining in the streets.[5]

Utopia is not born out of the labor of war. In war material resources are dissipated, human hatreds are hardened. War is no process for peace. The psalmist perceives the truth concerning peace and prosperity. His final words reveal the true basis of society—obedience to the lordship of God.

[4] G. Campbell Morgan, "Things of Strength in National Life," *Christian World Pulpit,* LXXXIV (1913), 18.

[5] *Ibid.,* p. 20.

David's *Psalm* of praise.

145 I will extol thee, my God, O King; and I will bless thy name for ever and ever.

A Song of Praise. Of David.

145 I will extol thee, my God and King,
and bless thy name for ever and ever.

CXLV. A Hymn of Praise (145:1-21)

This is a hymn of praise. It opens as the hymn of an individual, but as it progresses all God's **works** and **saints** (vs. 10) are summoned to join in. This mixture of individual and congregational elements (vs. 21) is due to the composite character of the psalm, which is much indebted to other psalms for its motifs and material. In addition, like Pss. 9–10; 25; 34; 37; 111–112; 119, it is an acrostic, which by its nature checks freedom in the exercise of the poetic art. However, the psalmist has in measure overcome these limitations by introducing into the psalm such a degree of vigor and logical development that the signs of the mechanical method of its construction are not unduly prominent. His efforts combine to produce a hymn of impressive power and rich spiritual content.

The psalmist's dependence on other writers is seen if we compare vs. 1 with 107:32; vs. *3a* with 48:1; 96:4; vs. 4 with 78:4; vs. 9 with 86:5, 15; Exod. 34:6; vs. 14 with 146:8; vss. 15-16 with 104:27-28. Apart from these close parallelisms, the language of the psalmist manifests a rich acquaintance with the literature of Israel's psalmody.

The date is late, as shown by (*a*) its acrostic character; (*b*) its Aramaisms and late Hebrew usages, e.g., זקף, כפופים (vs. 14); ישבר (vs. 15); ל *nota accusativi* (vss. 14, 16); and (*c*) its use of other psalms, some of which are late. It antedates the Aramaic section of Daniel, since vs. 13 is quoted in translation in Dan. 4:34. The meter is 3+3, with the usual variations.

The verses begin with the successive letters of the alphabet. Through an accident in transcription of the Hebrew text the *nun* verse (between vs. 13 and vs. 14) was at some time omitted. The defect is supplied by the LXX (cf. Syriac, Jerome). The reading was probably as follows: נאמן יהוה בכל־דבריו וחסיד בכל־מעשיו

The Lord is faithful in all his words,
and gracious in all his deeds.

1. The Psalmist's Purpose (145:1-3)

145:1-3. I will extol thee, my God and King: The psalmist opens his hymn with an expression of his purpose to sing the praises of the Lord **every day, . . . for ever and**

145:1-21. ***A Noble Doxology.***—This psalm might easily have given to the reader a sense of artificiality, for it is an acrostic, the verses beginning with successive letters of the Hebrew alphabet. Actually it gives a sense of spontaneity, and has through the ages won widespread and grateful acceptance. It has been in regular use in the Jewish synagogue in morning and evening services. It has taken a prominent place in Christian worship as the psalm for the midday meal in the early church, and as one of the proper psalms for Whitsunday. Reference to Prothero shows the important place it has taken also in private devotion. It inspired such writers as Paul Gerhardt, John Milton, and William Law; was quoted in Augustine's *Confessions;* and one of its verses was prefixed by William Carey to his edition of Roxburgh's *Flora Indica.* Prothero also informs us that words from vs. 13—**Thy kingdom is an everlasting kingdom**—are "written in Greek characters, unobliterated by time or enemies, above the portal of the church at Damascus, once a Christian cathedral, but now, for twelve centuries, a Mahomedan mosque." [6]

Writing with so wide and deep an appeal must have an exalted and universal theme. It would be impossible to find a theme greater or more permanent than this, for it is no less than the glory of God. The words are simple and the style unpretentious; but they suffice to assert God's holiness and his mercy, and to suggest the fear and the love with which he must be worshiped. There is no attempt either to explain or to prove the splendor of the divine majesty: the fact of it is stated and left as self-evident truth in which men may rejoice.

[6] *Psalms in Human Life,* pp. 29-30.

2 Every day will I bless thee; and I will praise thy name for ever and ever.
3 Great *is* the LORD, and greatly to be praised; and his greatness *is* unsearchable.
4 One generation shall praise thy works to another, and shall declare thy mighty acts.
5 I will speak of the glorious honor of thy majesty, and of thy wondrous works.

2 Every day I will bless thee,
and praise thy name for ever and ever.
3 Great is the LORD, and greatly to be praised,
and his greatness is unsearchable.

4 One generation shall laud thy works to another,
and shall declare thy mighty acts.
5 Of the glorious splendor of thy majesty,
and of thy wondrous works, I will meditate.

ever. He speaks of God as his **King** because he has a strong sense of the world-wide rulership of God, to which in the course of the psalm special prominence is given (cf. vss. 11-13). In fact, the theme of the psalm can be said to be a glorification of the King and his kingdom, for **great is the LORD** with a greatness which is beyond man's power to comprehend.

2. God's Mighty Acts (145:4-7)

4-7. This greatness of God is proclaimed by his **works, his mighty acts,** his miraculous deeds or **wondrous works,** his **terrible acts**—i.e., his terror-inspiring theophanies—and his **splendor** and **majesty.** The world and its creation, earthquakes, storm, thunder, lightning, and the glory of the heavens in sun, moon, and stars, all of them declare God's exalted sovereignty, but no more loudly than his **abundant goodness,** and his **righteousness** which are seen in his care of his creatures and his vindication of all who need his saving help. No single tongue, no single generation can compass the volume of praise due to him. So **one generation shall laud thy works to another** and **shall declare, meditate, proclaim, pour forth** in rapturous song the mighty theme.

The subject is not one to which modern writers readily turn. Some refrain because they feel it is beyond them, others because their attention for the time being has been drawn elsewhere. Never have men prayed more earnestly for knowledge than they do now, and rarely if ever have they more persistently sought it. But generally they have been concerned with created things rather than with the Creator. Scientists have set themselves with admirable zeal to explore the mysteries of matter. They have stooped to the smallest and lowest forms of life and brought to light hidden secrets. They have dared with equal courage the immense, not shrinking even from suns and stars and the whole mysterious universe. They have taken us so far that we are awed by the sum of what they have achieved, so much greater than one man's mind can comprehend. Yet with it, instead of growing confidence, there has come intellectual and moral distress; partly because of our inability to fit the pieces together into a satisfactory whole, partly because with the growth of knowledge there is an ever-increasing awareness of the immensity of the unknown and the unknowable.

There have, it is true, been serious attempts to get beyond the material universe. Psychologists have carried their investigations into the mind of man. They have written on instincts and impulses, memory and attention, inherited and acquired characteristics, imagination and will. They have set themselves to comfort the distressed and to heal the deranged in mind and spirit. And they have sometimes achieved successes which in other ages would have been counted miraculous. But the deeper they penetrate the more conscious they become of unsolved problems and the more they are inclined to question the power of man to work out his own salvation.

These scientific investigations properly fill us with wonder; but they have diverted attention from what was the psalmist's chief concern, and will again someday be the chief end of man—the knowledge of God. It may be long before theology is again called the queen of the sciences, but that is what it is. There is no quest more august, nothing that so much demands the labors of the best minds. It is daring enough to set oneself to measure and weigh the stars, to declare the flight of light and sound, to

6 And *men* shall speak of the might of
thy terrible acts: and I will declare thy
greatness.
7 They shall abundantly utter the memory of thy great goodness, and shall sing of
thy righteousness.
8 The LORD *is* gracious, and full of compassion; slow to anger, and of great mercy.
9 The LORD *is* good to all: and his tender
mercies *are* over all his works.
10 All thy works shall praise thee, O
LORD; and thy saints shall bless thee.
11 They shall speak of the glory of thy
kingdom, and talk of thy power;

6 Men shall proclaim the might of thy terrible acts,
and I will declare thy greatness.
7 They shall pour forth the fame of thy abundant goodness,
and shall sing aloud of thy righteousness.

8 The LORD is gracious and merciful,
slow to anger and abounding in steadfast love.
9 The LORD is good to all,
and his compassion is over all that he has made.

10 All thy works shall give thanks to thee, O LORD,
and all thy saints shall bless thee!
11 They shall speak of the glory of thy kingdom,
and tell of thy power,

In vs. 5 אשיחה, **I will meditate,** should be emended to read with the Syriac, ישיחו, "let them meditate."

3. THE LORD'S COMPASSION (145:8-9)

8-9. In these verses the psalmist enlarges on his thoughts in vs. 7, referring more particularly to his dealings with all of humankind. The Lord remembers that man is frail, needy, and erring. Therefore **the LORD is gracious and merciful,** and in his patience he is **slow to anger . . . and his compassion is over all that he has made.**

4. SUMMONS TO BLESS THE LORD (145:10-13*a*)

10-13*a*. Once again the psalmist sends forth a summons to exalt the name of the Lord. Let all his **works,** i.e., his creatures, more explicitly his **saints,** his own people,

demonstrate the laws that govern the movements of heavenly bodies. It is even more daring to proclaim the unsearchable greatness of God. Such an enterprise demands not only the finest intellectual gifts and training, but humility of mind and reverence of spirit. It would be impossible but for the belief that we are the children of One who himself is actively seeking us. This is the fundamental affirmation of all religion worthy of the name. Man seeks and prays, thinks and aspires; but he does it only because

The LORD upholds all who are falling,
and raises up all who are bowed down.

The psalmist begins with a God who is **great . . . and greatly to be praised.** Then he passes to definite marks of the divine activity, e.g., God's work in nature. Reference is made in vs. 15 to the **food** which is given to all creatures **in due season.** Much more might have been said about seedtime and harvest, sun and rain, heat and cold, the light of day and the darkness of night, the seed and the soil, man's labor and God's continuous creation. On some of these matters our knowledge is far greater than the psalmist's, but we need his emphasis upon divine intention and gracious provision.

Thou openest thy hand,
thou satisfiest the desire of every living thing.

There are also the mighty works of God in human history. We study in detail the heroes of the race, their characters and decisions, their adventures and sacrifices, and our hearts glow within us as we rehearse their achievements. But all of them were what they were because of what they had received; all of them were dependent not only upon men and circumstances, but upon innumerable spiritual resources. The psalmist was well aware of those

12 To make known to the sons of men
his mighty acts, and the glorious majesty of
his kingdom.
13 Thy kingdom *is* an everlasting kingdom, and thy dominion *endureth* throughout all generations.
14 The LORD upholdeth all that fall,
and raiseth up all *those that be* bowed
down.
15 The eyes of all wait upon thee; and
thou givest them their meat in due season.
16 Thou openest thine hand, and satisfiest the desire of every living thing.

12 to make known to the sons of men thy[h]
mighty deeds,
and the glorious splendor of thy[h] kingdom.
13 Thy kingdom is an everlasting kingdom,
and thy dominion endures
throughout all generations.

The LORD is faithful in all his words,
and gracious in all his deeds.[i]
14 The LORD upholds all who are falling,
and raises up all who are bowed down.
15 The eyes of all look to thee,
and thou givest them their food in due
season.
16 Thou openest thy hand,
thou satisfiest the desire of every living
thing.

[h] Heb *his*

[i] These two lines are supplied by one Hebrew Ms, Gk and Syr

---

make known the character of the Lord's sovereignty to all **the sons of men.** This notion of the **kingdom** of God holds a central place in the psalmist's view of God and the world. Like others of his fellows in late Judaism, he sees the realization of God's world-wide dominion as the goal of history. Vss. 3-9, which open the psalm, and vss. 13-21, which close it, define what he means by the **glory,** the **power** and the **splendor** of this kingship. In vs. 12 read with the LXX and Syriac, **thy** for **his,** as the context requires.

5. The Lord's Justice and Kindness (145:13*b*-20)

13*b*-20. In this final section the kingship of God is implicitly contrasted with all other kingships with which the sons of men were acquainted. God's rule is one of tender care for all who look to him. He is **faithful, just, kind to all who call upon**

---

invisible resources. He believed in the sovereignty of God as he believed in his own existence. He could doubtless have recited instances in his own life when everything turned not on what he did or failed to do but upon divine providence. He could certainly have done as so many psalmists had done, cited examples of God's guidance in the history of his people, especially in critical events like the escape from Egypt, the wanderings in the wilderness, and the settlement in Canaan. It is likely that if he had, the illustrations would not have been confined to his own people, for a note of universalism runs through the psalm. The Lord is King in Israel, but he is ruler of all the earth:

> **The LORD is good to all,**
> **and his compassion is over all that he has made.**

So was the way prepared for the revelation which was in Jesus Christ, and for the creation of a catholic church transcending the barriers of speech and race and claiming all men as the children of the one Father in heaven. It needs a Christian with the N.T. open before him to interpret fully the psalmist's faith:

> **The LORD preserves all who love him;**
> **but all the wicked he will destroy.**

The psalmist speaks not only of divine majesty but of providential care. God, he says, is no harsh taskmaster. He is patient, kind, compassionate. His glory is seen not in works of creation merely, but in deeds of mercy. He forgives. His pity is over all, even over men who doubt and refuse it. His goodness extends to those who might think themselves too insignificant to be noticed. The belief was not always easy to hold then, nor is it now. People knew in those days, as well as we do, that nature is "red in tooth and claw." [7] They were not indifferent to storm, dearth, disease, death. They

[7] Tennyson, *In Memoriam,* Part LVI, st. iv.

17 The LORD *is* righteous in all his ways, and holy in all his works.
18 The LORD *is* nigh unto all them that call upon him, to all that call upon him in truth.
19 He will fulfil the desire of them that fear him: he also will hear their cry, and will save them.
20 The LORD preserveth all them that love him: but all the wicked will he destroy.
21 My mouth shall speak the praise of the LORD: and let all flesh bless his holy name for ever and ever.

17 The LORD is just in all his ways,
and kind in all his doings.
18 The LORD is near to all who call upon him,
to all who call upon him in truth.
19 He fulfils the desire of all who fear him,
he also hears their cry, and saves them.
20 The LORD preserves all who love him;
but all the wicked he will destroy.

21 My mouth will speak the praise of the LORD,
and let all flesh bless his holy name for ever and ever.

him in truth . . . but all the wicked he will destroy. This psalmist's gospel (cf. vs. 12) of God's love, as he here unfolds it, constitutes a rich element in the Psalter; in sympathy and tenderness it is outstanding in the literature in the O.T. Incidentally, it reveals the spiritual quality of the psalmist's personal religion.

6. CONCLUDING DOXOLOGY (145:21)

21. The psalmist repeats his vow (cf. vs. 1) to **speak the praise of the LORD,** and he summons **all flesh** to join him (vss. 4, 10).

knew enough history, enough of violence, oppression, enslavement, exploitation, to have faith tested. But the faith endured whatever the experience: if it failed in individuals, it flourished in the race in spite of material loss, physical suffering, spiritual distress. At last it was proclaimed and exemplified in One who has often been called the Man of sorrows, who was tempted, betrayed, insulted, crucified, who yet convinced multitudes unnumbered that God is love.

It is this faith that makes the religion of the Bible one of praise. Such a life of dependence begets the gratitude which multiplies joy. Wherever men sincerely return thanks, radiance streams even on darkest hours. Alexander Whyte used to speak about William Law and his habits of thanksgiving. He would tell his Edinburgh congregation about the way Law clothed himself in the morning with a special prayer for every garment.

> For the sun new from his Almighty Maker's hands he had gratitude. For his house over his head he had gratitude. For his Bible and his spiritual books he had gratitude. For his opportunities of reading and study, as also for ten o'clock in the morning when the widows and orphans of King's Cliffe came to his window, and so on. A grateful heart feeds itself to a still greater gratitude on everything that comes to it.[8]

[8] Alexander Whyte, *The Character of Bunyan's Holy War* (London: Oliphant, 1902), pp. 273-74.

And both of them, Whyte and Law, were often found with this psalmist's words on their lips.

> **Every day I will bless thee,**
> **and praise thy name for ever and ever.**

If we followed their examples, we should not be so often cast down, not so often disturbed by petty grudges or imagined slights, by temporary failures, foolish words, stupid deeds. By dwelling upon trivialities like these we lose a sense of proportion, forget the mercies of God, and spread gloom, despondency, and complaint. We become poor in a land of plenty.

All this we need to learn. It needs to be taught, especially to the young. We who deny ourselves so much to give our children secular education, what special pains do we take that they may rejoice in the majesty of God and praise him for his providential care? We can do it only if our days are splendid with the attitude of thanksgiving. Of thy **glorious . . . majesty, and of thy wondrous works, I will meditate.** We can do it only by showing that as a king implies a kingdom, so the sovereignty of God means the rule of God. It means not turning to tyrants and espousing false ideologies and permitting proud dictators to flourish, but submission to One whose standards are perfect, who is at hand before men pray, who keeps those who love, and overcomes the wicked. Hope and peace and joy will find themselves at home in this world only as in sincerity we bow before

KJV	RSV
146 Praise ye the LORD. Praise the LORD, O my soul.	**146** Praise the LORD! Praise the LORD, O my soul!

CXLVI. I WILL PRAISE THE LORD AS LONG AS I LIVE (146:1-10)

This is the first of the collection of five hallelujah psalms which have been set at the end of the Psalter. Pss. 147–150 are clearly congregational hymns of praise. Ps. 146, though included in such a category, arises out of an individual's thoughts on what he had learned about the goodness of the Lord. As Schmidt notes, the psalm is like the song of one who, having discharged his vow of a thank offering and acknowledged the special help which the Lord had given him, proclaims to those assembled at his offering the general conclusion to be drawn from his experience. His theme throughout is that over against God, men, even the greatest of them, are in the human situation a poor source of hope and help (vss. 3, 5). We need not ask therefore whether his trust in princes had in some time of personal need been shattered, or whether he is warning some of his fellows against obsequiousness to temporal powers. Rather, the psalmist is dealing more generally with the fundamental contrast between God and men when it comes to dependence on them for resolving the basic problems of human society. So viewed, the psalm sets forth in its own way a truth which needs fresh emphasis in an era characterized by secularistic trends in culture and taste.

If in the brief compass of his hymn the psalmist touches on a great matter, his style, by contrast, is simple and innocent of literary pretension. A lack of originality is shown by the considerable measure of his indebtedness to other psalms for his material: cf. vs. 3 with 118:8, 9; vs. 4 with 104:29; vs. 7*a* with 103:6; vs. 7*b* with 107:9; 145:15; vs. 8*b* with 145:14; vs. 10*a* with 10:16; 93:1; 97:1; Exod. 15:18. Nor is it a mark of good literary taste that in the Hebrew text the half lines of vss. 7, 8 are rhymed.

However, in spite of these strictures on his style, the psalmist has a special place in the Psalter because like the prophets he is concerned for the lot of the oppressed in the community. With few exceptions (cf. Pss. 10; 15; 24; 37; 72; 94; 103) the psalmists,

---

his eternal throne and give to him the devotion of mind and heart and soul.

146:1-10. ***The Psalms in Common Worship.***—Not yet has justice been done to the book of Psalms in common worship. Priests have memorized and frequently recited the whole, much labor has been given to pointing and choral rendering, boys will sing about such persons as Sihon king of the Amorites, and Og king of Bashan, with minds full of yesterday's cricket or baseball and tomorrow's lessons. Even ministers can be so conventional in preaching that congregations slumber in peaceful inattention.

Something could be done to revivify ancient praises if precentors divided verses between priests, choirs, and people. Perhaps more still could be achieved if ministers encouraged their congregations in responsive readings. Many wandering minds might be held if in such a psalm as this the minister himself began with the words, **Praise the LORD, O my soul!** and the women continued with the second line, **I will praise the LORD as long as I live,** then the men with the third, **I will sing praises to my God while I have being.** Vss. 3-4 might be read by the minister, vs. 5 by the children, vs. 6 by the women, vs. 7*ab* by the men. Finally the whole congregation would read vss. 7*c*-10, concluding with strong assurance:

> **The LORD will reign for ever,**
> **thy God, O Zion, to all generations.**
> **Praise the LORD!**

1-2. ***From Praise to Promise.***—Not only would such united reading hold the attention and deepen the sense of fellowship, but it would bring to many minds truths which preachers often find it difficult to express. Men would see, for example, how naturally praise becomes promise. This psalm starts with veneration and swiftly passes to a vow. A God who is worthy of praise is one to whom men must dedicate themselves with a dedication which lasts for life. It is not a grievous duty, for "man's chief end is to glorify God." Christians have been taught to add, "and enjoy him forever." The psalmist had not progressed so far. Doubtless he believed in Sheol, but that was not an experience to which he could look forward with pleasure. Immortality in the Christian sense was not a part of Hebrew religion. However, he commits himself as far as he knows, and dedicates his earthly life to the praise of

2 While I live will I praise the LORD: I will sing praises unto my God while I have any being.
3 Put not your trust in princes, *nor* in the son of man, in whom *there is* no help.

2 I will praise the LORD as long as I live;
I will sing praises to my God while I have being.

3 Put not your trust in princes,
in a son of man, in whom there is no help.

---

being chiefly interested in the liturgical or the purely personal aspects of religion, do not sound the social note. For our psalmist the thing which evokes his never-ending praises to God is not God's majesty or splendor or dominion or power, as manifested in the world and in history, but God's concern for the hungry, the oppressed, the friendless, the blind, the widow, and the orphan.

The date of the psalm is late as shown by its late or Aramaic words, e.g., ש for אשר (vs. 3*b*), עשתנות (vs. 4*b*), שבר (vs. 5*b*), זקף (vs. 8*b*); its debt to other psalms, some of which are late; and the influence of the wisdom school on its structure (see below and Exeg. on Ps. 1). The LXX ascribes the psalm to Haggai and Zechariah. The meter is generally 3+3, with some variations such as 4+4 (vs. 4), and 4+3 (vs. 5).

1. I Will Extol Thee, My God (146:1-2)

146:1-2. The psalmist begins his hymn by exhorting his soul to **Praise the LORD!** He vows that while he has breath he will never cease to utter the Lord's praises. Obviously his heart is overflowing with gratitude for a signal deliverance from hard circumstances which God has wrought for him. We may gather that he belonged to such a class as he describes in vss. 7-9.

2. Put Not Your Trust in Man (146:3-4)

3-4. The psalmist is not thinking here of the possible capriciousness or deceit of those of humankind to whom one in need looks for help, but of the basic inability of

---

God. He means not only singing but doing and being. Praise, as he understands it, is an attitude of life, not mere words upon the lips.

Two great convictions lay behind this attitude. The first was an assurance that nowhere else but in God could salvation be found. The second was a firm belief that no man who turns in humility and sincerity to God does so in vain.

3. ***Even Princes Fail.***—There was nothing exceptional about the convictions to which reference has just been made. They are two of the fundamental principles of biblical piety. But this psalm suggests much more than conventional teaching. There is a tone in it which implies not hearsay but personal experience. The man who says these things has not learned them by rote; he has proved them in actual living. What the experience was is not stated. There may have been a personal crisis in which he had expected promised help and it had not come. There may have been a national peril in which all the chosen leaders had failed. It is one thing to be born or elected to leadership; it is another thing to be equal to the occasion. When the testing comes, the best that anyone can do may be quite inadequate. Intention may be good, the best advisers available may be heeded, but how limited is human knowledge and how fallible human wisdom! Even the ablest and the best trained may still fail through cowardice or cupidity. They may know what to do and lack the will to make it effective. In any case they are mortal, and how little can be achieved in one short life! Whatsoever the cause the psalmist's conclusion is clear:

Put not your trust in princes,
in a son of man, in whom there is no help.

The conclusion must not be exaggerated. We should go beyond the psalmist's meaning and beyond the truth if we said that mutual confidence between a man and his fellows is unimportant. All good community life depends upon faith, even faith in man. Business becomes impossible without it. Where there is mutual trust, men can buy and sell without fear; where there is none, the bottom has fallen out of commerce and industry, and no office revision or overhauling of executives or expenditure for advertising will save the situation. Family life also becomes impossible if parents and children have little or no confidence in one another. It is

4 His breath goeth forth, he returneth to his earth; in that very day his thoughts perish.
5 Happy *is he* that *hath* the God of Jacob for his help, whose hope *is* in the LORD his God:

4 When his breath departs he returns to his earth;
on that very day his plans perish.

5 Happy is he whose help is the God of Jacob,
whose hope is in the LORD his God,

---

men—even the greatest men—despite their best intentions, to provide a sure answer to the call of human need. The reason is clear, for **when his breath departs he returns to his earth** according to the divine decree of Gen. 3:19; thus he can guarantee no permanency to his plans or purposes, and all that one may have hoped for in him goes to the dust with him. But there is One on whom men can set their hopes with confidence.

3. PLACE YOUR HOPE IN GOD (146:5-7*b*)

5-7*b*. Happy is he whose help is the God of Jacob: The psalmist both in the hortatory style of vss. 3-4, in the beatitude of vss. 5-7, and in the juxtaposition of opposites—God and princes, righteous and unrighteous (vss. 8-9)—is influenced by the manner of

---

useless to redecorate the rooms, to change houses, or to separate for the vacations. Without faith, the home goes to pieces. It is equally true, though perhaps not equally recognized, in the relationships of nations. Conferences and treaties and leagues of nations will get us nowhere without good will. If that is wanting, multitudes may pray for peace and still find their governments piling up armaments. Services of intercession fail unless somehow trust can be fashioned between men and nations. Everywhere and always we live by faith. But we must not expect too much. It is when faith in men is made absolute, when we forget human frailty and ask the impossible, that human confidence fails. Civilized life demands that we trust one another; but we shall find a broken reed if we lean upon our neighbors as we can lean only on God.

3. ***The Failure of Humanism.***—Whether we think of individuals, of democracies, or of the human race, to say that "the voice of the people is the voice of God"[9] is as dangerous in politics as it is in metaphysics; it is to deify man. In both of these areas the psalmist's conclusion is relevant to modern life, though we must here restrict ourselves to the second. In the nineteenth century the philosopher Comte, weary of theological abstractions and subtleties, tried to find a way forward by denying the reality of the supernatural. Accepting the importance of worship, he elaborated colorful ritual and planned churches in which the religion of humanity might be practiced. He was not conspicuously successful in persuading anybody that it was worth while to attend such churches if there was no God to adore. In the twentieth century the Humanists have made similar experiments, denying however both God and the necessity of worship. They have included in their number very able and sincere men who have preached a pure ethic and contributed not a little to social service. By modern methods of propaganda they have persuaded many to forsake religious habits and to regard existing churches as either redundant or museum pieces. But there is no reason to believe that their influence will continue. Some may for a time congratulate themselves that they have discarded ancient taboos: they may laugh at the Ten Commandments, the N.T. beatitudes and Sunday observance, and pride themselves that they have entered into liberty. It does not follow that they will be content for long. There are those that once were leading Humanists who have already begun finding their way back. They are coming to see that it is only a step from the worship of man to the worship of the state, and that that is manifest and open idolatry. They are coming to realize that rulers have no authority and can elaborate no policy worthy to command the total allegiance of their subjects, that the mere assumption of such authority leads men into slavery. Trust, in the sense in which the psalmist speaks of it, belongs to God alone. Humanity's longing for communion with him is too deep set to be easily discarded. The witness of the centuries that only in that communion is peace to be found cannot be set aside.

5-10. ***The Source of Salvation.***—But the psalmist has another conviction. **Happy is he whose help is the God of Jacob.** This is the God of power who created the heavens, the earth and the sea, who throughout the ages has kept faith, executed justice, and fed the hungry. In every

[9] Alcuin *Epistle to Charlemagne.*

6 Which made heaven, and earth, the sea, and all that therein *is:* which keepeth truth for ever:

7 Which executeth judgment for the oppressed: which giveth food to the hungry. The LORD looseth the prisoners:

8 The LORD openeth *the eyes of* the blind: the LORD raiseth them that are bowed down: the LORD loveth the righteous:

9 The LORD preserveth the strangers; he relieveth the fatherless and widow: but the way of the wicked he turneth upside down.

10 The LORD shall reign for ever, *even* thy God, O Zion, unto all generations. Praise ye the LORD.

6 who made heaven and earth,
the sea, and all that is in them;
who keeps faith for ever;
7 who executes justice for the oppressed;
who gives food to the hungry.

The LORD sets the prisoners free;
8 the LORD opens the eyes of the blind.
The LORD lifts up those who are bowed down;
the LORD loves the righteous.
9 The LORD watches over the sojourners,
he upholds the widow and the fatherless;
but the way of the wicked he brings to ruin.

10 The LORD will reign for ever,
thy God, O Zion, to all generations.
Praise the LORD!

---

writing developed in the wisdom school (cf. 1:1-6; 128:1-6; Prov. 3:13-17; 4:14-19). **The God of Jacob:** Cf. Ps. 114:7. The equating of Jacob with Judah is a feature of postexilic literature (cf. Isa. 65:9; Obad. 10). Man's trust **in the LORD his God** will not suffer disappointment because of the Lord's resources of power (vs. 6) and his character and mind (vss. 6-7). He **keeps faith for ever, executes justice for the oppressed,** and **gives food to the hungry** (cf. 145:17-18). In the processes of nature and history the psalmist sees evidences of God's care for those who look to him.

4. The Lord's Gracious Acts (146:7*c*-9)

7*c*-9. In good hymn style, by a series of brief staccatolike participial clauses (vss. 6-9*a*), the psalmist recites the Lord's doings and ways, climaxing the emotional effect by a fivefold utterance of the divine name, Yahweh. It is Yahweh—none other—who in his love delivers the afflicted out of their distresses (cf. Ps. 107). In the interest of logical sequence vs. 8*c* should be set after vs. 9*b* (cf. 75:10).

5. Concluding Doxology (146:10)

10. The psalm concludes with the proclamation that the reign of the God of the psalmist's praises, unlike earthly dynasties, will never come to an end. And the center from which his rule will be exercised will be Zion. **The LORD will reign for ever, thy God, O Zion.**

---

age God has delivered the afflicted, set free the captive, had mercy upon the blind, the widow, the orphan, the resident alien. The wicked, who so often seem prosperous and sometimes grasp earthly power, God resists; but

> **The LORD lifts up those who are bowed down;**
> **the LORD loves the righteous** (vs. 8).

Christians stand in need of this confidence too. For when all is said and done, we are susceptible to contemporary thought even when we set ourselves to refute it. We may repeat biblical texts, praise Christian teaching on love and purity, humility and forgiveness, study the history of Christian thought, and still remain secular in spirit. We may be theologically trained, regularly ordained, experienced in pastoral work, and yet be far from the kingdom of God. We may even be persuaded that no way of life can be adequate until it is theocentric and yet not practice the presence of God. This psalmist can help us to lift hearts and voices in adoration, to see God in nature and history, to feel him in our thinking and willing. It is to the redeemed that redemption is fact, not theory. We may continue to say in the main the

147 Praise ye the LORD: for *it is* good to sing praises unto our God; for *it is* pleasant; *and* praise is comely.

147 Praise the LORD!
For it is good to sing praises to our God;
for he is gracious, and a song of praise is seemly.

CXLVII. PRAISE THE LORD, CREATOR AND SUSTAINER (147:1-20)

This liturgical hymn is the second of the hallelujah psalms with which the Psalter concludes. Each of them is superscribed and subscribed with a hallelujah, which probably signifies that the singing of the body of the psalm was preceded and followed by a series of hallelujahs rapturously cried aloud. As each psalm handles the theme of praise in an independent fashion, it is not improbable that all five of them appropriately composed a part of the liturgy of one or more of the feasts such as the New Year or Tabernacles.

Though it is probable that this psalm was meant to be a unity, it has the appearance of being the composite result of the merging of three psalms—vss. 1-6, 7-11, 12-20—each of which is introduced in hymn style with an invocatory **Praise the LORD!** or **Sing to the LORD.** It is for this reason, no doubt, that in the LXX tradition vss. 12-20 appear as an independent psalm with its own hallelujah superscription.

While the psalmist exhibits almost dithyrambic indifference to a logical ordering of the outpourings of his thoughts, it is not difficult to identify the governing motif which weaves them together: the greatness of the Lord is manifest in his creation and governance of the world and also in his care for his people. The two ideas are set over against each other in such a way that the wonder of the second is heightened. The subject matter of the psalm may be summarized as follows: **Praise the LORD** because, though he made the stars and is immeasurably great in understanding, he

same words, to do the same deeds; but there will be a new intensity in speech, a new vitality in action. We may call upon men in the sanctuary, as of old, to worship and obey the Creator; but there will be a different note and appeal, a deeper reverence, a more commanding grace; and those who listen will know that they are being led into the secret place of the Most High.

147:1-20. *In the Beginning . . . God.*—Why do not men read the Bible? The question was discussed in an English parish with profitable results. Some said they did read it. Others said they lacked time. Such leisure as there was for reading was required for books dealing with contemporary problems. One wondered whether the Bible had been made too cheap. Men prize that which costs much, and neglect the things, however important they may be, that can be easily obtained. Others felt that modern knowledge and the higher criticism had in the popular mind undermined the authority of the Scriptures. The leader dealt with these and other possible objections, proceeding then to argue that everyone should study the Bible, whatever the pressure of life. The reasons he gave were sound and convincing; but years afterward he felt that he had omitted a matter of supreme importance. Men do not turn to the Scriptures as naturally as to contemporary literature because their minds are focused elsewhere. They are concerned with this present world and man's place in it, the secrets that have been won from nature, the machines that have been invented, the systems of government that have been employed. The Bible is also concerned with man, his origin and future, the way he lives and the work he does; but its chief preoccupation is with God, his nature and purpose and creative power. People do not read the Bible as they should because they are living in a different world and have set their affections on different things.

As the Expos. has made clear, the psalmists were obsessed with God. They had many interests: they surveyed the heavens and the birds that flew in them, they considered the sea with its great and small fishes, and particularly they paid attention to the earth with its hills and rivers, trees and deserts, cities and highways. Yet their real concern was not with the things that appeared, but with the God who created and sustained them. They were not unconscious of the order and beauty and beneficence of nature, but instead of aesthetic appreciation they taught mankind to praise the Lord and giver of all. We write nature poems and books of travel; they composed hymns for common

2 The LORD doth build up Jerusalem: he gathereth together the outcasts of Israel.	2 The LORD builds up Jerusalem; he gathers the outcasts of Israel.

thinks of Jerusalem, building it up and bringing home its brokenhearted outcasts (vss. 1-6) ; **Sing to the LORD** who, though he is the providence of the world, has more delight in the humble who fear him than in those whose boast is their might (vss. 7-11) ; **Praise the LORD** who not only directs the elements but also protects and blesses Jerusalem and gives to his people statutes and ordinances such as no other people has known (vss. 12-20) . In the course of the psalm certain religious ideas are prominent: (*a*) the greatness of God as a theme to invoke men's praise; (*b*) confidence in God's care for all his creatures; (*c*) the superiority in God's sight of goodness to might; (*d*) God's special favor to Israel in the gift of its laws and institutions.

The date of the psalm is late postexilic, probably later than 397 B.C. (cf. Exeg. on vss. 2, 20 below) . The influence of Second and Third Isaiah is seen in its language and thought; cf. vs. 2 with Isa. 56:8; vs. 3 with Isa. 61:1; vs. 4 with Isa. 40:26; vs. 14 with Isa. 60:17. Its vocabulary includes some late Hebrew words, e.g., כנס (vs. 2) and שׁבחי (vs. 12) , and a feature of late Hebrew syntax in the use of ל to introduce a direct object (vs. 3) . In its material it shows parallels with other psalms and late writings, e.g., cf. vs. 6 with 146:9; vs. 9 with 104:21; Job 38:39-41; vs. 10 with 33:16-17; vs. 14 with 81:16; vss. 16-17 with Job 38:29-30. It is interesting to note that in the LXX both vss. 1-11 and vss. 12-20 are in the respective superscriptions ascribed to Haggai and Zechariah; evidently certain scribal students assigned them to the period of the restoration. The meter is regularly 3+3.

1. God's Power in History and Nature (147:1-6)

147:1. The text of this verse is a little uncertain. Omit with the LXX from vs. 1*b* נאוה, **seemly,** and introduce vs. 1*a* with הללו יה, **Praise the LORD,** in the style of this type of psalm (cf. Pss. 146; 148–150) . The translation then becomes regular: "Praise the LORD, for it is a good thing to sing to him, our God, for a song of praise is a pleasant thing."

2-3. The LORD builds up Jerusalem: Or "He rebuilds Jerusalem." The psalmist recalls the period of the restoration after the return from the Exile. He knows the story of the work of Nehemiah and Ezra as told by the Chronicler (cf. Ezra 1–2; Neh. 6–7) . The walls went up, and the **outcasts** came home from the Exile. Vs. 3 is a description

worship. We rejoice in the things that please the senses; they were thrilled to adoration as they thought of God from whom all blessings come. The difference is great in thought, in outlook, in habit. It is greatest in worship, which with us is often a duty, but with them was spontaneous delight.

The contrast which appears in so many of these expositions is particularly clear in Ps. 147, which is theocentric from beginning to end. It refers to the city of Jerusalem, to the downtrodden and the outcasts, to stars and clouds, rain and grass, beasts and ravens, the war horse and the city gates, to snow and hailstones, to wind and waters; but it not only begins and ends with praise, the spirit of praise is maintained throughout. The psalmist sang because he must, as a man conscious of the goodness of God. And that goodness he expressed in vivid pictures.

2. *God Builds the City.*—The first picture shows God as a builder. Jerusalem had been destroyed, but the walls, the houses, the temple, had been restored and **the outcasts of Israel** had been gathered into them. Nothing is said about the men and the measures that contributed to so happy a conclusion. There is no mention of Ezra or Nehemiah, Haggai or Zechariah; not a word about the patriots who labored with the sword in one hand and the trowel in the other. Elsewhere it is set down with gratitude. Yet to the psalmist they were all no more than the instruments of the Most High. They suffered and planned and toiled; but it was God who called and commissioned them, gave them minds and hands with which to think and to execute, protected them from enemies and sustained them with food. A city is careful about the way water is conducted to its houses; but its chief care is that the reservoirs shall be adequate and

3 He healeth the broken in heart, and bindeth up their wounds.
4 He telleth the number of the stars; he calleth them all by *their* names.
5 Great *is* our Lord, and of great power: his understanding *is* infinite.
6 The LORD lifteth up the meek: he casteth the wicked down to the ground.

3 He heals the brokenhearted,
and binds up their wounds.
4 He determines the number of the stars,
he gives to all of them their names.
5 Great is our LORD, and abundant in power;
his understanding is beyond measure.
6 The LORD lifts up the downtrodden,
he casts the wicked to the ground.

---

of those exiles in the language of Isa. 56:8; 61:1. Since the date of Ezra may be 397 B.C., the psalm must belong to a still later date.

4. He gives to all of them their names: I.e., **the stars** which were created by him, as according to ancient ideas to name a thing is to call it into existence. The stars therefore are subject to him. Indirectly, the psalmist counters the belief of the Gentile peoples that the stars are gods. The appellations of the stars were invented by those who worshiped and personified them (Wisd. Sol. 13:1-3).

---

full. Likewise the psalmist, while not unmindful of human agents, is primarily concerned with the source of good in God, the creator and giver.

3. ***God Heals the Brokenhearted.***—The second picture shows God as the great physician. This is something we can all appreciate. Perhaps never before has there been greater attention given to broken humanity than in the modern world. We have labored to bring healing to the sick in mind and body. We have a story to tell about surgery and preventive medicine and hospitals and nursing, about social service and progressive health acts and state pensions and comforts for the poor—a record of which we may well be proud. It is not surprising if these applications of scientific investigation are contrasted with what too often happened in the so-called ages of faith. It would not only be surprising, but we should all be knaves if we accepted such ministries without grateful acknowledgment. Yet behind the doctors and nurses and administrators whom we can name and remember there is the infinite mercy and personal care of the Father of us all. Neither the human kindness nor the progressive skill exists in isolation. Each has its cause in the God of all grace to whom praise is due. Ultimately it is he who **heals the brokenhearted, and binds up their wounds.**

4. ***God Names the Stars.***—The mind is next turned from the earth and its suffering to **the stars** above us. Most of us are not very profoundly interested in the stars. Astronomers are, and in their books they tell not only about the names given to the heavenly bodies but about how worlds unseen by the naked eye have been located and measured. Here too is a science that develops with ever-larger instruments and with calculations of increasing complexity. Mathematicians have produced figures of such magnitude that the size of creation is beyond imagination's reach. And the universe, we are told, is still expanding! The galaxies are racing away from one another in every direction. It is all very wonderful and can be flattering to human vanity. But the millions who live in vast cities know little and care less. With eyes fixed on street lights and garish advertisements, they do not see the glory of the clear night or the splendor of the setting sun. For a little while when hostile planes threatened their homes, they considered the heavens; but they were soon back from the vast constellations to illuminated cars and flaming street directions.

It was different with the ancients, who if they lacked modern conveniences yet saw the evening colors from the flat roof of the house or the silent stars from the doors of their tents. In a sense that is no longer true they lived with the stars. Some worshiped them and sought guidance from their movements. But the psalmist was as free from the superstition of the Magi as from the curiosity of the astronomer. He was content to worship the God who created and named the heavenly bodies as he did the earthly ones. In common with others of his day he doubtless believed that to name was to bring into existence, and immediately his mind was full of the wonder of One who was so high and mighty as to create and control so vast a scene.

He determines the number of the stars,
he gives to all of them their names.

6. ***God Lifts Up and Casts Down.***—Again thought returns to the earthly plane, and especially to the inequalities of human life. Instead, however, of moralizing upon the needs of the downtrodden or the arrogance of the wicked,

7 Sing unto the LORD with thanksgiving;
sing praise upon the harp unto our God:
8 Who covereth the heaven with clouds,
who prepareth rain for the earth, who maketh grass to grow upon the mountains.
9 He giveth to the beast his food, *and*
to the young ravens which cry.
10 He delighteth not in the strength of
the horse: he taketh not pleasure in the legs
of a man.
11 The LORD taketh pleasure in them
that fear him, in those that hope in his
mercy.
12 Praise the LORD, O Jerusalem; praise
thy God, O Zion.
13 For he hath strengthened the bars of
thy gates; he hath blessed thy children
within thee.
14 He maketh peace *in* thy borders, *and*
filleth thee with the finest of the wheat.
15 He sendeth forth his commandment
upon earth: his word runneth very swiftly.

7 Sing to the LORD with thanksgiving;
make melody to our God upon the lyre!
8 He covers the heavens with clouds,
he prepares rain for the earth,
he makes grass grow upon the hills.
9 He gives to the beasts their food,
and to the young ravens which cry.
10 His delight is not in the strength of the horse,
nor his pleasure in the legs of a man;
11 but the LORD takes pleasure in those who fear him,
in those who hope in his steadfast love.

12 Praise the LORD, O Jerusalem!
Praise your God, O Zion!
13 For he strengthens the bars of your gates;
he blesses your sons within you.
14 He makes peace in your borders;
he fills you with the finest of the wheat.
15 He sends forth his command to the earth;
his word runs swiftly.

2. THE SUSTAINER OF THE WORLD (147:7-11)

7-11. In this second section the praises of the Lord, as the beneficent providence whose ways can be traced in nature, are proclaimed: **Sing, . . . make melody to our God upon the lyre.** The word **sing** (ענה) here means to sing alternately or antiphonally. The psalmist sets in antithesis, **he covers the heavens with clouds** and **the LORD takes pleasure in those who fear him.** So the weak things can confound the mighty (vs. 10).

3. THE LORD'S SOLICITUDE FOR ISRAEL (147:12-20)

12-20. In this third section the power of the Lord, as seen especially in the meteorological phenomena, is the theme of praise. This power is never still; its seeming

and without exhorting men to protect the one or to beware of the other, the psalmist reminds himself that omnipotence works here as elsewhere. Thus at every step he passes swiftly from the seen to the unseen, from creation to the Creator. But gratitude is due to mercy rather than to omnipotence. The God who determined the number of the stars is not too preoccupied to be concerned with people. Grace is not measured dimensionally. It is pressed down and running over if it covers one sin. God's purpose is not to play with planets. He has made man. His love seeks a child's trust. The winning of human souls is more wonderful than the whirling of meteors. The Cross shines his light brighter than do the stars, and lasts on after suns become dark. This is a paradox of mercy: it is not a problem for mathematics.

8-18. ***Variations on the Same Theme.***—As the psalmist proceeds, he speaks of the God who sends rain to feed animals and birds; of the God who is not pleased with those who trust in war for material ends but with those who obey him and wait for the good things he provides. There would be enough for all if men used the earth's resources unselfishly and in the fear of the Lord. It has been said that the theme which predominates is "the creative activity of God in spring and summer."[1] But autumn appears too. Vs. 14*b* is admirable for a harvest festival: **He fills you with the finest of the wheat.** With us shortage occurs in spite of surplus. World markets and international finance have complicated the sinful process of unequal distribution, but the principle remains unaltered. Economics would be a simpler study if ethics were more advanced. Inequality would be less in evidence if there were deeper piety. The power which produces food for the people is not impersonal. Snow and frost, hail and ice, heat and wind and flowing water all have a place in the divine economy. Behind natural processes is a Person. Human life is not mechanistic. Laws are not

[1] Leslie, *Psalms*, p. 148.

16 He giveth snow like wool: he scattereth the hoar frost like ashes.

17 He casteth forth his ice like morsels: who can stand before his cold?

18 He sendeth out his word, and melteth them: he causeth his wind to blow, *and* the waters flow.

19 He showeth his word unto Jacob, his statutes and his judgments unto Israel.

20 He hath not dealt so with any nation: and *as for his* judgments, they have not known them. Praise ye the LORD.

16 He gives snow like wool;
he scatters hoarfrost like ashes.
17 He casts forth his ice like morsels;
who can stand before his cold?
18 He sends forth his word, and melts them;
he makes his wind blow, and the waters flow.
19 He declares his word to Jacob,
his statutes and ordinances to Israel.
20 He has not dealt thus with any other nation;
they do not know his ordinances.
Praise the LORD!

---

caprices, its inscrutable orderings in the vagaries of snow, hail, hoarfrost, ice, and wind are evidences of a divine spirit (**word**) that never ceases to operate in the world. Israel has learned its beneficent purpose: Zion's **gates** have been made strong against assaults (vs. 13*a*), its inhabitants have enjoyed health and prosperity (vs. 13*b*), its land has been blessed with rich harvests (vs. 14), and its people have been favored with the gift of the law (vs. 20). In all these things the Lord operates through his word. In vs. 15 the Lord's **word** is the issuance of his commands to nature (cf. Gen. 1:3, 6, 9); this word is later viewed as a mediatory agent between an aloof God and his world (cf. the late Jewish *memrā'*). In vs. 19 the Lord's **word** equates with the law. For the notion of the special gift of it to Israel see Deut. 4:8. This particularism acquired fresh emphasis after the work of Ezra.

---

clockwork regulations, but divine guidance and holy will. Thus the psalmist continues his lyrical variation on a constant theme, and calls upon Jerusalem to repeat the strain.

19-20. *God Chose Israel.*—The conclusion is that God **has not dealt thus with any other nation,** and that **they do not know his ordinances.** This is not the voice of arrogant nationalism. It is an acknowledgment of the divine purpose in the choice of Israel. In a peculiar sense Israel is God's people; but if there is privilege in such election, there is also grave responsibility. They have been called not to pride of place but to serve the nations. We can see the divine purpose as we look back over the centuries. We can see progressive revelation and education. Other nations were mightier, more numerous, more cultured. Cretan house hygiene made Israel's tents appear crude. Sumerian handpainted pottery made their goatskin bottles ugly. Egypt's pyramids made their desert graves seem shallow. Assyria's hosts made their guerrilla bands seem puny. Babylon's gardens made their scrubby hills seem arid. Greek sculpture made their temples seem bare. Roman peace made their factions seem intolerable. But the Jewish people survived the empires and, through the changing scene of civilizations' rise and fall, received the revelation of ethical monotheism. Prophetic utterance transcended every culture. Even the speculative question and answer of Greek philosophers sound hesitant and fumbling compared with generation after generation of prophetic "Thus saith the Lord." Israel is chosen to be the servant of God's special acts in history and the proclaimer of his particular words.

Yet the Northern Kingdom failed and disappeared. The Jews were apostate in the south, and there was left only a faithful remnant to return from captivity. Finally the chosen nation chose Barabbas, not Christ. Freely they rejected the Son of God, who chose to share their flesh and blood. Election is therefore not determinism but vocation. Israel can deny her calling and does. But God in Christ has gathered unto himself a new Israel—the Christian church. She is heir to the promise given to the fathers. Again and again must she sing the psalms of restoration. Time and again the faith of men has faltered, but always the Holy Spirit reforms and restores the church. Despite the blemishes upon Christian history that human sin has caused, God continues to call the faithful to renewed service for the world he saves in Jesus Christ. His church is not a society of the perfect. It is the community of the forgiven. It is the body of Christ and the Holy Spirit dwells within it. By God's grace and God's election, for man's faith and man's allegiance, the church is a divine as well as a human society, itself God's

148 Praise ye the LORD. Praise ye the LORD from the heavens: praise him in the heights.

148 Praise the LORD!
Praise the LORD from the heavens,
praise him in the heights!
2 Praise him, all his angels,
praise him, all his host!

CXLVIII. LET HEAVEN AND EARTH PRAISE THE LORD (148:1-14)

This rhapsodic hymn of praise is the third of the five hallelujah psalms with which the Psalter is brought to its close. In modern hymnody its motif finds fresh expression in Maltbie Babcock's well-known hymn, "This is my Father's world." The poet believes that all nature ought to sing to the Lord, and that the worshipers gathered in the temple become for the heavens, the earth, and the underworld, the things that have no power of song, the voice of praise—all nature sings through them.

The psalm falls into two parts which are subdivided severally into two or three strophes. The first part (vss. 1-6) is a fivefold summons to the heavenly creation, made up of the heavenly beings (vss. 1-2) and the heavenly phenomena (vss. 3-4), to praise the Lord. A refrain (vss. 5-6) is sung by the temple choir or choirs as a response to the summons of vss. 1-4. The second part (vss. 7-14*a*) consists of an appeal to the earthly creation, made up of the deep and the things that arise from it (vss. 7-8), the earth and the things on it (vss. 9-10), and the peoples of the earth, high and low, young and old (vss. 11-12), to praise the Lord. A second refrain (vss. 13-14*a*) follows as a response to the second appeal. The parts may each have been sung by a different body of singers, the refrains by all in chorus. The reasons here for the call to praise are compressed within the limits of the brief refrains, in contrast to Ps. 147 where the grounds for praise comprise the major part of the composition. The two psalms represent individual handlings of the hymn form.

The psalmist in addressing his summons in turn to the various parts of nature names them in about the order in which they appear in the creation story of Gen. 1. His cosmology also follows the ancient Oriental conception of the world as a three-storied structure (cf. Ps. 8; Deut. 33:13), with the heavens in the top story, the earth in the lower, and the underworld in the lowest. The attitude of the psalmist to the world is also like that of Gen. 1. The world is good. The government of the world, its purpose, and its order are all for ends that are blessed and deserve praise. And no doubt he believed, differently from the writer of Ecclesiastes, that the goodness of the Creator could be seen and traced in all things.

The psalm may have provided the pattern of the apocryphal song of the three children in Dan. 3:51-90 (LXX), and possibly it is echoed in Rev. 5:13. Its theological

---

continuing and mighty act, whereby **he declares his word . . . , his statutes and** [his] **ordinances. The LORD builds up Jerusalem. Praise the LORD!**

148:1-6. ***Praise to the Holiest in the Heights.*** —Praise is not earth bound. There is a celestial chorus. In heaven the issues are clear; the motives are not mingled. A living face is seen, not an image in a dark glass. Therefore angelic praise is purer, the shouts louder, the phrases triumphant, and the joy exalted.

It is good for men in times marked by human neglect of God to remember that there is a mighty unseen company not merely submissive to his will, but rejoicing in it as the highest happiness and the perfect freedom. One generation of the whole earth in revolt provides not enough voices to drown out the heavenly choir. God could indeed ignore the discord, as if it were but one wrong note in a whole oratorio. But he will not. He has heard from the cross humanity's clamor, that insistent din which forever calls to be subdued in forgiveness. So to the angels of the psalmist the Christian now adds the mighty company of the redeemed, the great clouds of witnesses, saints, apostles, prophets, martyrs. Over all the discordant medley of the earth, that added, harmonious praise in heaven! "Glory to God in the highest, and on earth peace, good will toward men."

Even the **sun and moon** and **shining stars** join with the angels. Behind this appeal to the powers of nature lies the primitive feeling that once they were living beings who could offer conscious praise. To modern man, scientifically analytical, they have no voices, no breath, no

2 Praise ye him, all his angels: praise ye
him, all his hosts.
3 Praise ye him, sun and moon: praise
him, all ye stars of light.
4 Praise him, ye heavens of heavens, and
ye waters that *be* above the heavens.
5 Let them praise the name of the LORD:
for he commanded, and they were created.
6 He hath also stablished them for ever
and ever: he hath made a decree which shall
not pass.
7 Praise the LORD from the earth, ye
dragons, and all deeps:

3 Praise him, sun and moon,
praise him, all you shining stars!
4 Praise him, you highest heavens,
and you waters above the heavens!

5 Let them praise the name of the LORD!
For he commanded and they were created.
6 And he established them for ever and ever;
he fixed their bounds which cannot be passed.[j]

7 Praise the LORD from the earth,
you sea monsters and all deeps,

[j] Or *he set a law which cannot pass away*

and cosmological similarities to Gen. 1 mark the psalm as late postexilic. The meter is generally 3+3, but 3+2 appears in vss. 1-2, and 4+4 in vs. 8.

1. Summons to the Heavenly World (148:1-6)

148:1-6. The Lord is conceived of as a transcendent being, dwelling apart from all his creation; hence praise reaches him **from the heavens.** Such a conception belongs to the developed theology of a late date, to which also belongs the notion that there are several heavens—three or seven—arranged concentrically like a series of walls about a city (cf. II Cor. 12:2, 4), or superimposed one above the other (Heb. 4:14; 7:26). The late emphasis on the holiness of God has fostered the belief in the heavenly gradations by which he is separated from men. **Praise him, all his angels, . . . you shining stars:** The celestial beings and the luminaries, which in the heathen nations were worshiped as divinities and ruling powers in the world (cf. Eph. 1:21; 6:12), are subordinate to the Lord. The reason is that **he commanded and they were created,** and he gave to each of them "a charge which cannot be transgressed." They owe their existence and their functions to him.

2. Summons to the Earth (148:7-14)

7-14*a*. Praise the LORD from the earth: The **earth** here stands for the regions beneath the heavens. The psalmist first turns to the great deep or the *Tehôm* and the

tongues, no lips; but yet they declare the glory of God. The whole inanimate creation in silence witnesses to the power, beauty, and goodness of God. Silence is part of a symphony.

The psalmist writes of an ancient cosmology, for there are no **waters above the heavens.** From their fraction of a hemisphere men see the ether's dome. By day it is drenched in sunlight. At night it is studded with stars, marking a path for the moon which shrinks in modesty as it moves through its sparkling and attentive court. So might it appear to a primitive scientist's eye. He might well assume that waters saddled the dome and undergirded the world. Modern measurement and calculation correct his speculation. The stars are suns soaring to infinity away from one another. Their lights are going out. Yet the psalmist says the truth. They are under God's command. Created by him, they go through no motions that he does not control. They follow no random process. They form a royal procession.

7-10. *And in the Depth Be Praise.*—Now the terrestrial order joins in the paean. His earthly environment tells man of God's glory. The weather is a witness. The contours of the land testify. The earth's fruit, animals, insects, fishes, and birds add telling evidence.

8 Fire, and hail; snow, and vapor; stormy wind fulfilling his word:
9 Mountains, and all hills; fruitful trees, and all cedars:
10 Beasts, and all cattle; creeping things, and flying fowl:
11 Kings of the earth, and all people; princes, and all judges of the earth:
12 Both young men, and maidens; old men, and children:
13 Let them praise the name of the LORD: for his name alone is excellent; his glory *is* above the earth and heaven.

8 fire and hail, snow and frost,
stormy wind fulfilling his command!

9 Mountains and all hills,
fruit trees and all cedars!
10 Beasts and all cattle,
creeping things and flying birds!

11 Kings of the earth and all peoples,
princes and all rulers of the earth!
12 Young men and maidens together,
old men and children!

13 Let them praise the name of the LORD,
for his name alone is exalted;
his glory is above earth and heaven.

---

mythical monsters like Rahab and Leviathan and their "helpers" (Job 9:13), which were associated with the deep at the time of Creation (cf. 74:12-14; 89:10; Isa. 51:9). Out of the deep, which lies under and about the earth, rise the clouds that bring lightning and **hail, snow and frost.** They are now under the Lord's rule and, like the creatures of the heavens, acknowledge him. Lastly, **mountains, trees, beasts, cattle, birds, kings, young men and maidens, old men and children,** all things and persons on the earth must join the anthem of God's world. The reason is that **his name alone is exalted.** He is incomparably great above all "principalities, powers, and dominions." He has

---

There are difficulties for people who believe in creation. All things that God has made may sing of his power, but they do not give conclusive proof of his goodness and mercy. Typhoons strike towns. Volcanoes smother villages. Beasts devour. Insects irritate. Plagues depopulate. The "whole creation groaneth and travaileth" (Rom. 8:22). Nature religions do not see one beneficent being. Fallen man needs another word from God. The Christian trusts not the clerk of the weather but the God of the cross. There he sees the power of holy love unqualified and unlimited. In Christ God speaks his final word.

The psalmist, as he calls upon the whole earth to praise God, would remind men that they are great debtors to the world in which they live. The blessings far outnumber the trials. There is a problem of pain, and the facts of life continually remind us of it. The problem may become most acute when we seek to lift up our hearts in praise. The contrast between the realities we see and feel and the praise we offer is too obvious. Yet as praise continues, a sense of indebtedness overwhelms resentment and complaint. We may even reach the point at which we give thanks for our sorrows, our disappointments, our losses (II Cor. 12:9*b*).

11-13. ***O Loving Wisdom of Our God!***—The final call is to humanity. Stars in the sky, mountains on the earth, powers of the universe, creatures of the land and sea, all these are God's witnesses. Men may be his worshipers. The psalmist lists great and small, the celebrated and the anonymous, the rulers and the ruled, men and women, the old and the young. So is all life set forth as a means of glorifying God. Governments exist to further his justice, and families to fulfill his joy.

Note the imperative of appeal; for human praise is not an established fact. The very exhortation implies the problem of evil. Men are free to worship idols of their own making. And they do. God has honored them, and they enjoy his glory in heaven and earth. All things are given them for good. Above everything and everyone God is high and lifted up. They should require no urging to praise, no reminder to offer thanks, no warning to obey his will. Yet the facts of history tell of what goes on between nations, classes, factions, and even within families. Mankind has exalted itself. A people here and individuals there misuse thought, speech, will, and action. For true praise is more than lip service. The glory is concealed by the dense clouds of human sin. Under the judgment which the facts of this psalm lay upon us, all mankind is found wanting. No person—save One—has used his whole being in praise of God. Wrong motives have blemished good deeds.

14 He also exalteth the horn of his people, the praise of all his saints; *even* of the children of Israel, a people near unto him. Praise ye the LORD.

14 He has raised up a horn for his people,
praise for all his saints,
for the people of Israel who are near to him.
Praise the LORD!

149 Praise ye the LORD. Sing unto the LORD a new song, *and* his praise in the congregation of saints.

149 Praise the LORD!
Sing to the LORD a new song,
his praise in the assembly of the faithful!

---

shown the majesty of his power in that **he has raised up a horn for his people.** For the figure of speech cf. 75:5; 89:17, 23-24. The reference is probably to some historical event of which we are ignorant.

14*b*. This half line is not a part of the psalm but a footnote by some editor or choir leader to indicate the use for which it is intended.

CXLIX. The Triumph of Israel (149:1-9)

This hymn is one of the group of hallelujah psalms (Pss. 146–150) which make up the final addition to the Psalter, providing for it a fivefold doxological conclusion. Each of these psalms begins and closes with a hallelujah. The psalm is said to be **a new song** (cf. 33:3; 96:1; 98:1); it celebrates some fresh experience of God's goodness for which the old traditional hymns did not suffice. It is not an early composition since it has reference to conditions and ideas that are postexilic (cf. vss. 4, 9) and evidences late influence in language and syntax (cf. vss. 6-7). Its interpretation, however, has occasioned much discussion because of the difficulty of integrating vss. 7-9 with vss. 1-6. We may dismiss the view advanced by Schmidt that it was sung at the festival of the Lord's enthronement, since the text, except by arbitrary emendation, is hardly open to such a construction. Others, e.g., Gunkel, Kittel, believe that the psalm is eschatological, being written to celebrate the great day in the future when Israel will in fulfillment of the written promises of the prophets (vs. 9) execute judgment on kings and nations who have oppressed them (vss. 7-8). Against this view one must urge that vss. 1-4 seem to be a fervent expression of an immediate, not an anticipated, experience of the Lord's pleasure in his people (vs. 4). It is best therefore to assume that the psalm was born out of a real historical situation (see below). But the acceptance of this assumption does not preclude the possibility that the psalmist saw in the event a foretaste or the dawn of a greater triumph to come, not simply its immediate realization. In this way both the historical and the eschatological interpretations can be reconciled. However, in the light of the language of I and II Maccabees, the arguments for a purely historical interpretation are weighty.

The date is late, as indicated above. The syntactical construction of vss. 7-9 is loose and late. In vss. 6 and 8 we find the late words, רוממות, **high praises,** and כבל, **fetters.**

Right intentions have been claimed for evil acts. Every man in some measure has exalted his own wishes above the will of God. The psalmist reminds us of our duty, but records no means of deliverance. His is a song for the old Israel.

But that old Israel of which he writes has given way to the new, whose birth the N.T. records. Unable of themselves to draw near to God, men's hope is in the God who has drawn near to them. To be near him is the obedience which the law demands. To believe that he is near is the faith that grace gives. For the Christian it is in Jesus of Nazareth who once and for all **he has raised up a horn for his people,** has restored to them that power which is the praise of all his saints.

149:1-9. ***A New Song.***—As men receive continually new mercies, so they should offer renewed praise. And it can come only from **the assembly of the faithful,** from those who know the restoration of divine grace. The old praise due from the natural man was not forthcoming. Redeemed man must sing **a new song.** By nature

2 Let Israel rejoice in him that made him: let the children of Zion be joyful in their King.
3 Let them praise his name in the dance: let them sing praises unto him with the timbrel and harp.
4 For the LORD taketh pleasure in his people: he will beautify the meek with salvation.

2 Let Israel be glad in his Maker,
let the sons of Zion rejoice in their King!
3 Let them praise his name with dancing,
making melody to him with timbrel and lyre!
4 For the LORD takes pleasure in his people;
he adorns the humble with victory.

There is a strong temptation to assign a late psalm that is found in the last addition to the last book of the Psalter to the Maccabean period, especially as the language of the psalm is remarkably paralleled in Maccabees and Judith (*ca.* 150 B.C.): **the assembly of the faithful** (חסידים) occurs in I Macc. 2:42 (LXX); the situation in vs. 4 resembles that of I Macc. 4:24, 33; the lust for vengeance in vss. 7-8 is like that of I Macc. 7:46-49 (cf. Judith 13:14-15); the words of vs. 6 recall II Macc. 15:27; vs. 4*b* reflects Judith 9:11; for the **new song** see Judith 16:13-17; the singing and the dancing of vss. 3, 6 have a parallel in Judith 15:12-13. However, in spite of the tenor of these citations, we must allow that the psalm may have reference to some earlier event in Jewish history of which we have no record (Oesterley). In any case, for reasons given above, the date cannot be prior to the Greek period. The meter is generally 3+3; in vss. 1, 9 it is 4+3.

1. Let Israel Praise the Lord for Victory (149:1-4)

149:1-4. A great occasion, styled a **victory** (vs. 4), calls for **a new song.** This hymn of triumph (cf. Judith 16:1-17) celebrates a new instance in the long list of the miracles which the Lord has wrought for his people from the times of the patriarchs, of the Exodus, and of the conquest of Canaan down through the years. **The faithful,** or "the loyal ones," i.e., the godly or pious gathered as a congregation or **assembly** in the temple, are summoned to sing it. In vs. 2 they are called **the sons of Zion** and equated with **Israel,** which indicates that in the time of the psalmist the territory of the Lord's people was restricted within narrow limits. The Lord is called their **Maker** and their **King.** For the former of these designations cf. Isa. 51:13; for the latter cf. I Sam. 8:20, where a king's function is said to be to "go out before us and fight our battles." The juxtaposition of the two titles is understood in the light of such a passage as Isa. 44:2. In short, they are the Lord's elect and he is their defender. The kingship of the Lord here gives no support to the eschatological interpretation of the psalm or to the reference of it to the festival of the Lord's enthronement. The singing of the psalm occurs along with a sacred **dance,** accompanied by **timbrel and lyre** (see Ps. 150). The theme of the psalm is the favor which the Lord has shown **his people** by crowning them

---

he sings a discord in reply to God's created gifts. By grace he sings in harmony, **glad in his Maker,** rejoicing in the **King** who has brought deliverance and victory: wholehearted praise, **with dancing, . . . with timbrel and lyre.**

The occasion is one of triumph, quite literal triumph; but the triumph is to be a means of grace. This freedom is Israel's because of God's good pleasure. From Abraham, Joseph, Moses, to the judges, kings, and prophets the nation's destiny depended on the holy purpose of God. Their material resources and their numerical strength were not of themselves sufficient for their preservation throughout centuries of violent imperial conflict. The rationalist may study O.T. history and find in Judah's survival a mystery. The believer sees a miracle. So did the psalmist. It called for some fresh outburst of praise. He would have understood what the helpless prisoners felt when the allied armies broke through into Belsen.

But the mood degenerates. At first exalted, the psalmist soon exults. The music changes key, and it is unpleasant listening for Christian ears. Justice must be done, but not vengeance. Vindictiveness like this is not of the Holy Spirit. Here is no longer a new song. It is the old refrain of feud, retaliation, and revenge. It is

5 Let the saints be joyful in glory: let
them sing aloud upon their beds.
6 *Let* the high *praises* of God *be* in their
mouth, and a two-edged sword in their
hand;
7 To execute vengeance upon the
heathen, *and* punishments upon the people;
8 To bind their kings with chains, and
their nobles with fetters of iron;
9 To execute upon them the judgment
written: this honor have all his saints. Praise
ye the LORD.

150 Praise ye the LORD. Praise God
in his sanctuary: praise him in
the firmament of his power.

5 Let the faithful exult in glory;
let them sing for joy on their couches.
6 Let the high praises of God be in their
throats
and two-edged swords in their hands,
7 to wreak vengeance on the nations
and chastisement on the peoples,
8 to bind their kings with chains
and their nobles with fetters of iron,
9 to execute on them the judgment written!
This is glory for all his faithful ones.
Praise the LORD!

150 Praise the LORD!
Praise God in his sanctuary;
praise him in his mighty firmament!

---

with victory. The victory here is a victory that saves the people from some kind of distress, not a victory in aggressive warfare; "the faithful ones" are **humble,** i.e., bowed down, oppressed.

2. Judgment on the Nations (149:5-9)

5-9. Let the faithful exult in glory: I.e., in trumph (cf. 112:9). **Upon their beds** is a translation of על־משכבותם, which is sometimes conjecturally emended to על־משכנתיו, "in his temple." The singers are still in arms, having **two-edged swords in their hands.** The syntax of the infinitives in vss. 7-9 is not clear. If they are circumstantial, we translate, "As they wreak vengeance, . . . as they bind, . . . as they execute," and understand that the singers, as they sing and dance, are carrying out judgment on their foes. The eschatologists favor this interpretation and therefore refer the whole scene to the messianic future. It seems more natural to construe the infinitives with the final line: "It is glory for his faithful ones to wreak vengeance, . . . to bind, . . . to execute judgment." Such a translation is a warrant for the historical interpretation of the psalm. The victory which **the humble** celebrate is in accordance with "the judgment that is written," i.e., either in prophecy (cf. Isa. 45:14; 49:7, 23) or in the books of heaven (cf. Dan. 7:10).

CL. Let Everything That Breathes Praise the Lord (150:1-6)

This liturgical psalm with its elevenfold exhortation to praise the Lord (framed by the expression "Hallelujah," **Praise the LORD;** vss. 1*a* and 6*b*) was appropriately

---

not the music of mercy, forgiveness, reconciliation. It contains none of the love which suffers long and is kind: the love that is not natural but supernatural; divine love, not sentimental but austere, holy yet forgiving; the love that broke into history in the person of Jesus Christ.

But so, again and again, is the mercy of God forgotten in the moment of triumph. The writer of Revelation faces the cruelty of imperial persecution with an exalted faith in the final victory of God's holy love in Jesus Christ, but he exults more than his Lord in the doom of the evildoers. Every age finds the problem of tempering justice with mercy difficult, the task of matching retribution with reconciliation elusive. To forgive is often to condone, while punishment easily becomes vengeance. There are those who are too soft, others who are too severe. At one moment only in history was the nice balance of justice and mercy maintained. That moment was a divine event. It was God's act on the Cross, where he revealed that his righteousness is his love, and that his love is his righteousness. Those who are in Christ may strive toward what they have seen. But never have they matched it. Nor ever will. Faith is too little, the heart not clean enough. The best of men are yet being saved. It is this, however, precisely this, and nothing else, which is the **glory** of the **faithful.** The best—still being saved.

150:1-6. ***A Fitting Climax.***—In literature, as in music, conclusions are as difficult and usually

chosen by the final editors of the Psalter for its conclusion. The brief doxology with which each of the books of the Psalter is closed expands here into a jubilant hymn. It is possible that this psalm was composed especially for the purpose which it serves, but it is not unlikely that it was one of the praises sung in the temple on the great festival occasions when crowds of worshipers thronged its courts, perhaps even the last one in the ritual of a great feast.

Two motifs dominate the structure. On the one hand, the psalmist follows the traditional form of the introductory section of a hymn with its summons to worship, but in such a way that, as Gunkel observes, he answers four questions: where the Lord is to be praised (vs. 1); why he is to be praised (vs. 2); how he is to be praised (vss. 3-5); and who is to praise him (vs. 6). On the other hand, the psalmist means to effect in the rendition of the psalm a gradually increasing volume of sound until in the closing half line voices and instruments together reach an impressive climax. The handling of these two motifs evidences relatively to his times a measure of artistic skill.

Since the instruments mentioned in the psalm include the horn, which like **the trumpet** was an instrument of the priests (cf. Josh. 6:4; II Chr. 15:14), and the **harp,** the **lute** and the **cymbals,** which were particular instruments of the Levites (Neh. 12:27; I Chr. 15:16; II Chr. 29:25), the division between the priests and the Levites is implied, and this in turn points to a postexilic date. However, it should be noted that the instruments mentioned in the book of Daniel (3:5), and one mentioned in Chronicles—*meçiltáyim* (I Chr. 13:8; 15:19)—do not appear in the psalmist's list, while on the other hand, there are included two—the *minnîm* (**strings**) and the *'ûghabh* (**pipe**)—which do not occur in Chronicles, probably because they were thought by the Chronicler's time to be unworthy for use in the temple. It seems then that the psalm, while postexilic, must antedate both Daniel (166-165 B.C.) and Chronicles (*ca.* 250 B.C). The meter is 3+3.

1. Where the Lord Is to Be Praised (150:1)

150:1. Praise God: Read "Praise the LORD" with the Syriac, Jerome, and 148:1. **In his sanctuary:** I.e., in his earthly habitation. The context does not favor a reference here to the heavenly temple (cf. 102:19). **His mighty firmament:** Lit., **the firmament of his power,** i.e., the heavens (cf. 19:1; Gen. 1:8). Earth and heaven are summoned to lift their voices in praise.

---

as important as beginnings. To begin well is to arrest the attention and to win the respect of the hearer or reader. To end well is to bring a theme to a climax or to clinch an argument. The book of Psalms is successful in both. It begins with the happiness of the good man contrasted with the lot of the wicked, an appropriate portal, as has been said, to the sanctuary of the Psalter. It ends with a universal call to praise. Between are the varied cries of the human heart, some of them marred by doubts and fears and threats, but many others such noble aspirations that they live among the purest prayers of the race. Instructed Christians can find theological and ethical errors; but rarely if ever is there a departure from simplicity and sincerity. If the religion of the psalms is not always religion pure and undefiled, it is at least free from pretense and deceit. And it comes to its climax in a paean toward which the whole creation moves, the very goal of God's redeeming purpose, an eschatology of praise.

Four questions are here suggested and will be considered in the order in which they appear. Where, why, how, and by whom is God to be praised?

1. *Where Praise Is to Be Offered.*—The first question is answered at once: **Praise God in his sanctuary.** The word **sanctuary** can be understood in various senses. There are expositors who make it mean the temple or some other prepared place of worship. This conforms to long and universal usage. If we do not join with others at stated times in the sanctuaries men have built and dedicated, the chances are that we shall soon lose the habit of worship. There are some indeed who assert that they can remain devout in mind and act though they neglect the public offices of prayer and praise. The common experience, however, is that as church attendance declines personal religion also declines. Even if the individual could succeed in maintaining his private devotions, he would lose the corporate realization that comes from

2 Praise him for his mighty acts: praise him according to his excellent greatness.

2 Praise him for his mighty deeds;
praise him according to his exceeding greatness!

2. Why the Lord Is to Be Praised (150:2)

2. **Praise him for his mighty deeds,** which are manifest in the creation of the world. **According to his exceeding greatness:** Lit., "the abundance of his greatness." The measure of his praise is to accord with the measure of his greatness. However, a better reading, favored by the parallelism, is "for his exceeding greatness."

common worship. That is one reason why the broadcast service can never give complete satisfaction. It may prove a channel of grace to many, in hospitals and sickrooms; but it cannot take the place of that assembling together which has always been to Christians the very fellowship of the body of the risen Lord.

It is more likely, however, that the word **sanctuary** should be given a broader reference. It is common biblical teaching that God is not confined within walls that men have built: the whole earth is his temple. He hears our cries and ministers to us wherever we call upon him. He reveals himself to us and gives us his grace not only before altars and sacred tables, but as we journey upon the busy highway or walk beside the still waters. We are to offer praise in shop or office, field or forest, in crowded market place or the vast open spaces, and so to find all of life sacramental,

For thou, within no walls confined,
Inhabitest the humble mind.[2]

The next phrase, **praise him in his mighty firmament,** increases the probability of this rendering. God is everywhere to be adored, in heaven as well as on earth. It is the task therefore not of men only but of angels. Indeed, it is the privilege of all that breathe to swell the universal anthem. It was a Hebrew who wrote, as if he himself had heard the words, that at the beginning of all things "the morning stars sang together, and all the sons of God shouted for joy" (Job 38:7). Many nearer our own time have imagined birds and beasts, trees and flowers, making their contribution to the universal harmony. It is a frequent thought with writers of hymns that the whole creation unites in gratitude and shouts of gladness:

Praise the God of our salvation!
Hosts on high, his power proclaim;
Heaven, and earth, and all creation,
Laud and magnify his Name.[3]

[2] William Cowper, "Jesus, where'er thy people meet," st. ii.

[3] "Praise the Lord, ye heavens adore him," from the Foundling Hospital Collection, 1796.

2. ***Why God Is to Be Praised.***—The second question is answered here:

Praise him for his mighty deeds;
praise him according to his exceeding greatness!

These words, following the reference to the **mighty firmament,** give an impression of immensity and unique power and are characteristically Hebrew. The O.T. writers have a marked tendency to the gigantic. They are prone to pile mountains upon mountains and to rejoice in thousands and ten thousand times ten thousand. This, says one scholar, is not so much imagination as a lack of it. It is mechanical, "like taking a quantity and raising it to the *n*th degree." It makes the transition from O.T. to N.T. in this respect "like the transition from Egyptian art to Greek." Jesus Christ speaks of little things: "He makes us think of God, not as framing the cedars of Lebanon, but as clothing the flowers, not as ruling leviathan, but as caring for the sparrow. Above all, he speaks in terms of the individual—*one* sinner, *one* sheep, *one* sparrow."[4]

The criticism is interesting and may be sound, though there are O.T. passages to which it does not apply. The fact remains that the psalmist, in common with other Hebrew writers, does make us conscious of the majesty and the might of God. Even the most powerful of men are severely limited and are soon at the end of their resources. But God is omnipotent in heaven and upon earth. He is great beyond all human speech and understanding. Again, the emphasis is different when we pass to the N.T. There is in the Christian Scriptures no lessening of divine power, but we are made to marvel at the condescension of God no less than at his creative work. The majesty of the Godhead is to be seen in mercy no less than in the making and sustaining of the spheres. The wonder is not that he is high and holy, but that he stoops to save the human soul. The key words in the N.T. are not **mighty firmament** or **exceeding greatness,** but that Jesus Christ came into the world to save sinners, and that there is joy in

[4] Rorke, *In Search of a Personal Creed,* pp. 34-35.

3 Praise him with the sound of the trumpet: praise him with the psaltery and harp.
4 Praise him with the timbrel and dance: praise him with stringed instruments and organs.
5 Praise him upon the loud cymbals: praise him upon the high sounding cymbals.

3 Praise him with trumpet sound;
praise him with lute and harp!
4 Praise him with timbrel and dance;
praise him with strings and pipe!
5 Praise him with sounding cymbals;
praise him with loud clashing cymbals!

3. How the Lord Is to Be Praised (150:3-5)

3-5. The musical instruments fall into three categories: (*a*) trumpets, possibly blown by priests; (*b*) those of the Levitical musicians, i.e., lutes and harps; (*c*) those used by the laity, men and women who joined in the loud tribute of praise. We can imagine that each group, as it was mentioned, took up its part, and so the volume of sound swelled in a great crescendo. On the instruments here referred to, see Intro., pp. 5-6.

the presence of God over one sinner who repents. Jesus himself is the good shepherd who lays down his life for the sheep. As a woman seeks a lost coin and sweeps her house diligently till she finds it, so divine love seeks the erring heart. This is the ultimate reason for praise; and when we realize how infinite is the grace of God, then we know that no offering we can make is adequate. That is why the whole creation should give thanks, not merely at stated times and in prepared places, but in an undeviating attitude of praise.

> Redeeming love has been my theme,
> And shall be till I die.[5]

3-5. ***How God Is to Be Praised.***—The third question raises many others. There are some who favor the way of silence. They can point to the fact that it is often in solitude that we have our deepest experiences. They can add much about the fellowship of silence as it has been proved in Christian worship. When men gather with one mind and in one place and quietly wait for the Spirit to move them, they can rise to an ecstasy of praise even though in the main it is never expressed by human lips. There are others who rely on ancient forms, on collects and liturgies that have been handed down from the remote past; and still others who trust, perhaps too much, to the spontaneity of the spoken word. Each of these has its serious advocates and also its obvious dangers.

What the psalmist urges is the appropriateness of music, especially instrumental music. He mentions in particular the **trumpet,** the **lute,** the **harp,** the **timbrel, strings and pipe,** and **cymbals,** apparently thinking of them as they played their part in the great festivals of the temple. He speaks also of the **dance,** as though to remind us that things often considered secular can be dedicated to sacred usage. Things are not usually good or bad in themselves but in the way they are used and the motives that prompt them. Even music can be an occasion of evil. Writes a Cambridge professor:

> It can so easily stimulate emotions far beyond any point to which real insight and genuine decision of will would ever take them. . . . I suspect that in church many a man has mistaken the oscillation of his diaphragm in harmony with a ten-foot organ pipe, or the quivering of his heart strings to the melting sweetness of a boy's voice, for a visitation of the Holy Spirit.[6]

We need continually to remind ourselves of Paul's determination to sing with the spirit and with the understanding also. We must remember too that praise must be objective, that it should be directed not to an audience of men and women but to God. "Any piece of music or ritual which is deliberately and primarily designed to stir people's feelings and not to express, and by expressing to deepen, the apprehension of God is dangerous and should be suspect." [7]

Rightly used, however, music, and especially congregational singing accompanied by trumpet and harp, timbrel and pipe, organ and piano, can be a minister of grace. It can be as effective as the spoken word. It may unite and inspire a people where instruction and exhortation fail. Music has played a conspicuous part in evangelism, in revivals, in solemn Eucharists. Bernard Manning, writing on the hymns of Wesley and Watts, maintained that for Free Churchmen hymnbooks are both their liturgy

[5] William Cowper, "There is a fountain filled with blood," st. iv.

[6] H. H. Farmer, *The Servant of the Word* (New York: Charles Scribner's Sons, 1942), pp. 75-76.

[7] *Ibid.*, p. 77.

6 Let every thing that hath breath praise the LORD. Praise ye the LORD.

6 Let everything that breathes praise the LORD!
Praise the LORD!

4. WHO IS TO PRAISE THE LORD (150:6)

6. The climax of the psalm is reached in the final line, **Let everything that breathes praise the LORD,** and is prolonged by a series of glad hallelujahs.

and their devotional manual. W. H. Davies, in common with poets ancient and modern, sings the power of nature's harmonies:

> There's music in the leaves, the shaken tree;
> Aye, in the ocean, cruel though it be.[8]

Many have tried to describe heaven, and in large measure they have disagreed; but it would be difficult to find anyone who has not thought of it as the abode of the purest harmony. James Elroy Flecker, in his poem "Tenebris Interlucentem," thinks of hell and describes a linnet which had lost its way; but its singing on a blackened bough spread transformation.

> And some one there stole forth a hand
> To draw a brother to his side.[9]

6. ***By Whom God Is to Be Praised.***—This praise is to be offered not merely by priests or Levites, by the elect in meetinghouses, or by specially trained choristers, not even by those who have been favored with special blessings. It is to be the offering of men everywhere; in sickness as in health, in the feebleness of old age as in the vigor of youth, in times of trouble and of joy, on our deathbed, as did Oliver Cromwell—"Is there no one here who will praise the Lord?"—or like John Wesley's mother—"Children, as soon as I am released, sing a psalm of praise to God." [1] Epictetus was so crippled that he spoke of himself as "an ethereal existence staggering under the burden of a corpse." [2] Yet in his chapter on contentment he asserts that one must not find fault with the universe "because of one miserable little leg." He continues, and this Exposition may not improperly close with it:

> What else can *I* do, who am a lame old man, except sing praises to God? Now, had I been a nightingale, I should have sung the songs of a nightingale, or had I been a swan the songs of a swan; but, being a reasonable being, it is my duty to hymn God. This is my task, and I accomplish it; nor, so far as may be granted to me, will I ever abandon this post, and you also do I exhort to this same song.[3]

Let everything that breathes praise the LORD!

[8] "Hope Abandoned," from *The Collected Poems of W. H. Davies.* Used by permission of Mrs. W. H. Davies and Jonathan Cape, Ltd., publishers.

[9] Used by permission of J. M. Dent & Sons, Ltd., publishers.

[1] *The Journal of the Rev. John Wesley* (New York: E. P. Dutton & Co., 1907; "Everyman's Library"), I, 385.

[2] Frederic W. Farrar, *Seeker After God* (New York: John B. Alden, 1883), p. 195.

[3] *Discourses* I. 16.

The Book of

PROVERBS

Introduction and Exegesis by Charles T. Fritsch

Exposition by Rolland W. Schloerb

PROVERBS

INTRODUCTION

The book of Proverbs belongs to the wisdom literature of Israel. To this literary genre also belong Job, Ecclesiastes, and some of the psalms (e.g., 1; 19; 37; 49; 73; 112; 119; 127; 128; 133) in the Old Testament; Ecclesiasticus and the Wisdom of Solomon in the Apocrypha; and Pirke Aboth in later Judaism. All of this is part of a great body of wisdom literature which existed throughout the Near East in ancient times.

I. Wisdom Literature in the Ancient Near East

Numerous contacts with the wisdom literature of other lands and with the men who produced it are mentioned in the Old Testament. Balaam son of Beor, who uttered the oracles found in Num. 23–24, "was really a North-Syrian diviner from the Euphrates Valley." [1] In I Kings 4:30-31 we read: "Solomon's wisdom surpassed the wisdom of all the people of the east, and all the wisdom of Egypt. For he was wiser than all other men, wiser than Ethan the Ezrahite, and Heman, Calcol, and Darda, the sons of Mahol; and his fame was in all the nations round about." In this passage at least three extra-Israelitish sources of wisdom are mentioned: the Bedouin Arabs of the East, the land of Egypt, and the sons of Mahol, who were Edomite sages. The wisdom of Edom is again referred to in Jer. 49:7 and Obad. 8.[2] Job and his friends were of non-Israelite extraction, most of them coming from Edom. And the proper name "Massa" in Prov. 30:1; 31:1 may point to an Arabian milieu for those sections. Thus we can see that the Hebrews were familiar with the wisdom of Babylonia, Syria, Edom, Arabia, and Egypt.

Not only were they familiar with these various wisdom literatures, but they actually borrowed quite extensively from them. It is now known that substantial parts of Proverbs are borrowed directly from Phoenician or Canaanite sources. Not only is the conception of hypostatized wisdom, found in Prov. 8–9, of Canaanite origin, but many phrases and words throughout the book can now be traced to Phoenician and especially Ugaritic sources.[3]

It has long been recognized that there are many close parallels between the wisdom literatures of Israel and Babylonia. There is not very much extant material of this kind from Babylonia, but there is enough to show that interaction between the sages of these two cultures was quite extensive. The Babylonian wisdom literature consists mainly of The Babylonian Job, a title bestowed upon the work because of its close similarity with the Hebrew Job, The Babylonian Book of Proverbs, with its frequently recurring phrase, "my son," so common in certain sections of Hebrew Proverbs, and the Proverbs of Aḥikar, a part of the Story of Aḥikar, which ultimately came from Mesopotamia. Between Proverbs and these Babylonian sources W. O. E. Oesterley records over fifty parallels and similarities in thought and words.[4]

[1] W. F. Albright, "The Oracles of Balaam," *Journal of Biblical Literature,* LXIII (1944), 233.

[2] For a full discussion of the wisdom of Edom see R. H. Pfeiffer, "Edomitic Wisdom," *Zeitschrift für die alttestamentliche Wissenschaft,* XLIV (1926), 13-25; but see also W. F. Albright, *Archaeology and the Religion of Israel* (Baltimore: Johns Hopkins Press, 1942), pp. 127-28, where the Edomitic source of these names is challenged.

[3] W. F. Albright, *From the Stone Age to Christianity* (2nd ed.; Baltimore: Johns Hopkins Press, 1946), p. 283.

[4] *The Book of Proverbs* (London: Methuen & Co., 1929; "Westminster Commentaries"), pp. xxxvii-lv. The quotations from Aḥikar and the Babylonian Proverbs are taken from this work, by permission of the publishers.

Do not desire her beauty in your heart,
and do not let her capture you with her eyelashes (Prov. 6:25).
My son, go not after the beauty of a woman,
And lust not after her in thine heart (Aḥikar).

When words are many, transgression is not lacking,
but he who restrains his lips is prudent (Prov. 10:19).
Make not wide thy mouth, but guard thy lips;
The thoughts of thy mind thou shalt not speak at once,
For then quickly what thou hast spoken thou wilt take back again (Babylonian Proverbs).

The wicked are overthrown and are no more,
but the house of the righteous will stand (Prov. 12:7).
My son, the wicked falleth and riseth not; but the just man is not moved, for God is with him (Aḥikar).

He who walks with wise men becomes wise,
but the companion of fools will suffer harm (Prov. 13:20).
My son, associate with the wise man, and thou shalt become wise like him; and associate not with a garrulous and talkative man, lest thou be numbered with him (Aḥikar).

Discipline your son while there is hope;
do not set your heart on his destruction (Prov. 19:18).
My son, subdue thy son while he is yet a boy, before he wax stronger than thee and rebel against thee, and thou be shamed in all his corrupt doing (Aḥikar).

Let your foot be seldom in your neighbor's house,
lest he become weary of you and hate you (Prov. 25:17).
My son, let not thy foot run after thy friend,
Lest he be surfeited with thee and hate thee (Aḥikar).

Your friend, and your father's friend, do not forsake;
and do not go to your brother's house in the day of your calamity.
Better is a neighbor who is near
than a brother who is far away (Prov. 27:10).
My son, remove not from thy father's friend,
Lest perchance thy friend come not near to thee.
My son, better is a friend that is at hand,
Than a brother who is far away (Aḥikar).

Some of these parallels are strikingly close, and there may have been direct borrowing one way or the other. Other examples, which have not been quoted here, are closer in thought than in mode of expression. It is not the purpose here to determine whether the borrowing was done by the Hebrews or the Babylonians. Each example must be studied in its own light. Sometimes there is definite evidence to show who the borrower was, but generally the problem remains unsolved. What is probably true is that both sides drew from a common source and adapted the material to their own culture.

There is much more extant Egyptian wisdom literature than Babylonian, and its influence on Hebrew wisdom literature is much stronger. By far the most important wisdom book from Egypt is The Teaching of Amen-em-ope, written some time after the eighth century B.C.[5] Deuteronomy and Psalms have words and expressions in common with this book, but it is in Proverbs that its influence is most strongly felt. In the two works there are numerous examples of community of thought and expression, but in Prov. 22:17–23:14 the similarities are so striking that one can account for them only by direct borrowing. Only seven verses out of the twenty-seven have no counterpart in the Egyptian, mainly because in those seven verses there is purely Hebraic material which would not be found in Egyptian literature. It should be noted also that the Egyptian parallels do not always follow the order of verses in Proverbs. A number of similar passages are given here to show their close identity: [6]

Incline your ear, and hear the words of the wise,
and apply your mind to my knowledge (Prov. 22:17).
Give thine ear and hear what I say,
And apply thine heart to apprehend (Amen-em-ope).

Have I not written for you thirty sayings
of admonitions and knowledge (Prov. 22:20).
Consider these thirty chapters;
They delight, they instruct (Amen-em-ope).

To show you what is right and true,
that you may give a true answer to those who sent you? (Prov. 22:21.)
Knowledge how to answer him that speaketh,
And (how) to carry back a report to one that sent him (Amen-em-ope).

Do not rob the poor, because he is poor,
or crush the afflicted at the gate (Prov. 22:22).
Beware of robbing the poor
And of oppressing the afflicted (Amen-em-ope).

Make no friendship with a man given to anger,
nor go with a wrathful man (Prov. 22:24).
Associate not with a passionate man,
Nor approach him for conversation (Amen-em-ope).

Do you see a man skilful in his work?
he will stand before kings;

[5] See W. O. E. Oesterley, *The Wisdom of Egypt and the Old Testament* (New York: The Macmillan Co., 1927). This book gives a full account of the Egyptian work and of its relation to the O.T.

[6] Quotations from The Teaching of Amen-em-ope are taken from Oesterley, *Proverbs*, pp. xlvi-l, by permission.

he will not stand before obscure men (Prov. 22:29).
A scribe who is skilful in his business
Findeth himself worthy to be a courtier (Amen-em-ope).

Do not remove an ancient landmark
or enter the fields of the fatherless;
for their Redeemer is strong;
he will plead their cause against you (Prov. 23: 10-11).
Remove not the landmark from the bounds of the field,
Nor shift the position of the measuring-cord.
Covet not (even) a cubit of land,
And violate not the widow's boundary.
A furrow . . . worn by time,
He who wrongfully seizeth it in a field,
Though he claim it with false oaths,
Will be taken captive by the might of the Moon (-God) (Amen-em-ope).

Again the questions arise: Who is the borrower? Which was the original source? There seems to be more evidence this time that Israel was the debtor, although one must not overlook the possibility that Prov. 22:17–23:14 as a unit was in existence long before its incorporation in the present book, and that it might have actually influenced the Egyptian scribe. Regarding this whole problem of interaction between Israel and her surrounding neighbors, however, it can be said definitely that when the Hebrews did utilize outside sources, they made them completely their own and transformed them into something much better.

II. The Wise Men

The cultural life of Israel was molded by three groups of leaders: the prophets, the priests, and the wise men (cf. Jer. 18:18). Of these the prophets and priests were by far the more prominent, since Israel's history was written from both a priestly and prophetic point of view. Although the wise men did not occupy as prominent a position in the life of Israel as the other leaders, their popular style and genial manners attracted a large number of followers among the common people. They did not speak with the authority of the prophet, "Thus saith the LORD," or with the piety of the priest; they were simply earnest seekers of the good life, and it was their aim to teach their disciples what that good life was.

Their origin as a distinct class is probably to be associated with the scribes in governmental service. This was the case both in Egypt and Babylonia, where the wise men were state functionaries who were skilled in writing, the science of government, and the manners and morals of the day. In the Old Testament the scribes are mentioned several times as governmental officials. According to II Sam. 8:17, Seraiah the scribe is one of David's important officers of state. Similar notices are recorded in II Sam. 20:25; I Kings 4:3; II Kings 19:2. In II Kings 22:3-7 the scribe Shaphan is described as a kind of minister of finance, and in Jer. 36:20-21 it appears as though Elishama the scribe had charge of the state archives. In Jer. 8:8-9 the scribes and the wise men are actually equated:

How can you say, "We are wise,
and the law of the LORD is with us"?
But, behold, the false pen of the scribes
has made it into a lie.
The wise men shall be put to shame,
they shall be dismayed and taken;
lo, they have rejected the word of the LORD,
and what wisdom is in them?

It may be that Kiriath-sepher (Josh. 15:15), "the city of the book," was a center for those who pursued the scribal art (cf. LXX *ad loc.;* also Josh. 15:49). The reference to "the wisdom of their wise men" in Isa. 29:14 shows that these men must have existed as a class long before the middle of the eighth century B.C. By the time of Jeremiah the "counsel" of the wise was on a par with the "law" of the priest and the "word" of the prophet (Jer. 18:18).

Strangely enough, the first person with the distinctive title of "wise" in the Old Testament is a woman from Tekoa, the home of the prophet Amos (II Sam. 14:1-20). Another wise woman is mentioned in the story recorded in II Sam. 20:14-22. King Solomon is, of course, the wise man par excellence among the Israelites. His prayer for an understanding heart (I Kings 3:4-15), his clever decisions (I Kings 3:16-28), his sagacity in dealing with the queen of Sheba (I Kings 10:1-10), all add up to make him the most conspicuous representative of Israel's wise men. In the words of his biographer:

"And God gave Solomon wisdom and understanding beyond measure, and largeness of mind like the sand on the seashore, so that Solomon's wisdom surpassed the wisdom of all the people of the east, and all the wisdom of Egypt. For he was wiser than all other men, wiser than Ethan the Ezrahite, and Heman, Calcol, and Darda, the sons of Mahol; and his fame was in all the nations round about. He also uttered three thousand proverbs; and his songs were a thousand and five. He spoke of trees, from the cedar that is in Lebanon to the hyssop that grows out of the wall; he spoke also of beasts, and of birds, and of reptiles, and of fish. And men came from all peoples to hear the wisdom of Solomon, and from all the kings of the earth, who had heard of his wisdom" (I Kings 4: 29-34).

It is almost impossible to understand how

such encomiums could be heaped upon one who made so many foolish mistakes throughout his life in every realm. His faults must have been forgotten early, and in the course of the idealizing process his reputation grew to such an extent that his name became associated with works of wisdom for centuries to come.

Like the Arab sheik, the wise man worked and thought individually, giving forth his counsel publicly in the town gate and privately to whoever came to him for instruction. He was a familiar figure in Israel's life from the earliest times to the Maccabean period. We find two vivid pictures of these wise men in wisdom literature, one belonging to the earlier, the other to the later period when they had set up their schools and their teachings were firmly established. The first one is found in Job 29:7-25, where Job is bemoaning his fate and wishing that he could sit in the gate once again and be respected by both young and old alike:

When I went out to the gate of the city,
  when I prepared my seat in the square,
the young men saw me and withdrew,
  and the aged rose and stood;
the princes refrained from talking,
  and laid their hand on their mouth;
the voice of the nobles was hushed,
  and their tongue cleaved to the roof of their mouth.
When the ear heard it, it called me blessed,
  and when the eye saw it, it approved;
because I delivered the poor who cried,
  and fatherless who had none to help him.
The blessing of him who was about to perish came upon me,
  and I caused the widow's heart to sing for joy.
I put on righteousness, and it clothed me;
  my justice was like a robe and a turban.
I was eyes to the blind,
  and feet to the lame.
I was a father to the poor,
  and I searched out the cause of him whom I did not know.
I broke the fangs of the unrighteous,
  and made him drop his prey from his teeth.
Then I thought, "I shall die in my nest,
  and I shall multiply my days as the sand,
my roots spread out to the waters,
  with the dew all night on my branches,
my glory fresh with me,
  and my bow ever new in my hand."
Men listened to me, and waited,
  and kept silence for my counsel.
After I spoke they did not speak again,
  and my word dropped upon them.
They waited for me as for the rain;
  and they opened their mouths as for the spring rain.
I smiled on them when they had no confidence;
  and the light of my countenance they did not cast down.
I chose their way, and sat as chief,
  and I dwelt like a king among his troops,
  like one who comforts mourners.

The second picture, from Ecclus. 39:1-11, is of a wise man who lived about 180 B.C. He was wise in the ways of the world, yet devout in his religious practices:

It is not so with the man who applies himself,
And studies the Law of the Most High.
He searches out the wisdom of all the ancients,
And busies himself with prophecies;
He observes the discourse of famous men,
And penetrates the intricacies of figures.
He searches out the hidden meaning of proverbs,
And acquaints himself with the obscurities of figures.
He will serve among great men,
And appear before rulers.
He will travel through the lands of strange peoples,
And test what is good and what is evil among men.
He will devote himself to going early
To the Lord his Maker,
And will make his entreaty before the Most High.
He will open his mouth in prayer,
And make intreaty for his sins.
If the great Lord pleases,
He will be filled with the spirit of understanding,
He will pour out his wise sayings,
And give thanks to the Lord in prayer;
He will direct his counsel and knowledge,
And study his secrets.
He will reveal instruction in his teaching,
And will glory in the Law of the Lord's agreement.
Many will praise his understanding,
And it will never be blotted out.
His memory will not disappear,
And his name will live for endless generations.
Nations will repeat his wisdom,
And the congregation will utter his praise.
If he lives long, he will leave a greater name than a thousand,
And if he goes to rest, his fame is enough for him (Amer. Trans.).

The teaching of the wise men was directed to the youth of the nation. It was done orally in public places (Prov. 1:20-21) and privately to individuals. Instruction may have been given gratis (Ecclus. 51:25) although Prov. 17:16 and Ecclus. 51:28 seem to imply the opposite. Perhaps Isa. 55:1 is a taunt of the prophet against the wise men for charging fees. The prophets, as we know from Isa. 29:14; Jer. 8:9, were not too kindly disposed toward the wise men. After the early period, when the wisdom of the sages was given forth at the city gate to those who would hear it, there arose places of instruction where the teacher would sit with his pupils and proclaim his wisdom. These were called the *bêth hammidhrāsh,* i.e., "the house of instruction" or "school," and the *yᵉshîbhāh,* i.e., the "scholar's session," or "academy." There the students came to learn those maxims and principles which

would guide them successfully through life. After the Maccabean struggle the purely ethical teachings of the wise men became less popular with anti-Hellenistic religious leaders of the day, and so the wise men gradually disappeared from Jewish life. Many of their teachings and functions were carried on by the scribes of later Judaism.

III. Types of Hebrew Wisdom Literature

A. Māshāl.—This word is usually translated "proverb," as in the title of this book, but it has many other meanings, as its use in the Old Testament reveals. Its etymology and original meaning have not been definitely established. Most scholars hold the view that the root meaning is "to be like," from which the basic idea of "likeness," "comparison" is derived for the noun. This is also the predominant idea of its cognate roots in the other Semitic languages. To be sure, some proverbs in the Old Testament do have the idea of comparison in them, such as, "Is Saul also among the prophets?" (I Sam. 10:12, and

Like vinegar to the teeth, and smoke to the eyes,
so is the sluggard to those who send him (Prov. 10:26),

but in most cases this is not so. Crawford H. Toy holds therefore that the idea of comparison has to do with the thought of the sentence, that is, "short distiches made by the juxtaposition of related ideas, originally comparisons with familiar objects."[7] Eduard König, on the other hand, holding to the same etymology, believes *māshāl* to be the designation of a clause or combination, so that it is applicable to almost any kind of sentence.[8] In Brown-Driver-Briggs[9] the word is thought to refer simply to the parallelism of clauses. But the word *māshāl* is seldom if ever used to describe poetry as such, or a sentence in general, so that "comparison" can refer only to those proverbs where actual comparisons are made, as quoted above. It must be assumed then that this original use of the word was broadened to include other meanings.

In Gesenius-Buhl[10] the original meaning of the root is given as "to stand for," "to represent," but this is less probable than the one just given, since it is derived from a secondary stem of an Arabic word.

B. Gemser[11] suggests that the noun *māshāl* is connected etymologically with the verb *māshal,* "to rule," because the *māshāl* is a word filled with power that actually creates a new situation. There may be some truth in this idea, since the *māshāl* was "lifted up" by the prophets like a curse and hurled against their enemies and by Balaam like a blessing upon Israel.[12]

As used in the Old Testament, *māshāl* has a variety of meanings. First of all it designates a popular proverbial saying: "And a man of the place answered, 'And who is their father?' Therefore it became a proverb, 'Is Saul also among the prophets?'" (I Sam. 10:12; cf. also I Sam. 24:13; Ezek. 12:22-23; 18:2-3.) As has already been stated, these short statements may have originally contained a comparison, but later on any short saying which contained a general popular truth came to be called a *māshāl.*

In Ezekiel the word is used three times to describe a parable or allegory: "Son of man, propound a riddle, and speak an allegory to the house of Israel; say, Thus says the Lord God: A great eagle with great wings and long pinions, rich in plumage of many colors, came to Lebanon and took the top of the cedar; he broke off the topmost of its young twigs and carried it to a land of trade, and set it in a city of merchants" (Ezek. 17:2-4, with the parable carrying on through vs. 10; also in 20:49; 24:3). If the usually accepted etymology of *māshāl* is correct, it is easy to see how the word came to mean "parable," "allegory."

In other places the word is associated with prophetic oracles which are uttered in blessing or curse against someone. In Num. 23:7, 18; 24:3, 15, 20, 21, 23, the oracles of Balaam are introduced with the formula: "And he took up his *māshāl* and said . . ." and words of blessing as well as of cursing came forth from his mouth. Isa. 14:4 (ASV) reads: "That thou shalt take up this parable against the king of Babylon, and say, How hath the oppressor ceased! the golden city ceased!" In Mic. 2:4 the *māshāl* is lifted up against the prophet's own people: "In that day shall they take up a parable against you, and lament with a doleful lamentation, and say, We are utterly ruined: he changeth the portion of my people: how doth he remove it from me! to the rebellious he divideth our

[7] *A Critical and Exegetical Commentary on the Book of Proverbs* (New York: Charles Scribner's Sons, 1899; "International Critical Commentary"), p. 3.

[8] "Parable," in James Hastings, ed., *A Dictionary of the Bible* (New York: Charles Scribner's Sons, 1900), III, 661.

[9] *A Hebrew and English Lexicon of the Old Testament,* ed. Francis Brown, S. R. Driver, and C. A. Briggs (Boston: Houghton Mifflin Co., 1907), *s.v.* Based on the Lexicon of William Gesenius.

[10] *Wilhelm Gesenius' hebräisches und aramäisches Handwörterbuch über das Alte Testament,* ed. Frants Buhl (17th ed.; Leipzig: F. C. W. Vogel, 1921), *s.v.*

[11] *Sprüche Salomos* (Tübingen: J. C. B. Mohr, 1937; "Handbuch zum Alten Testament"), p. 7.

[12] Cf. August Müller and Emil Kautzsch, *The Book of Proverbs* (tr. Duncan B. Macdonald; Leipzig: J. C. Hinrichs, 1901; "Sacred Books of the Old Testament"), pp. 32-33: "The Hebrew term משל does not mean *simile, parable,* it refers to poetic lines consisting of two parallel halves or hemistichs; cf. Assyr. *mišlu* 'half.'"

fields" (ASV). In Hab. 2:6 the *māshāl* is taken up against the Chaldeans: "Shall not all these take up a parable against him, and a taunting proverb against him, and say, Woe to him that increaseth that which is not his! how long? and that ladeth himself with pledges!" (ASV.) Num. 21:27 seems to indicate that there was a school or group of "mashalists" who composed these oracular poems for special occasions.

From this idea of a warning word, then, the *māshāl* is applied to persons and nations which are to be signs of warning to the world. Israel, because of her backsliding, is especially singled out as a *māshāl* to the world. The writer in Deut. 28:37, speaking of the disobedience of Israel, says, "And you shall become a horror, a proverb, and a byword, among all the peoples, where the LORD will lead you away" (cf. also Pss. 44:14; 69:11; I Kings 9:7; II Chr. 7:20; Jer. 24:9; Ezek. 14:8).

Finally *māshāl,* as used in the title of Proverbs, means the ethical aphorism, poem, and essay, the final and peerless product of the wise man's consummate skill. Starting with the popular proverb as a pattern, the sages of Israel developed the finely polished, succinctly worded ethical proverb which predominates in this book. To test their abilities even further they composed intricate acrostic poems such as the one on the good wife in 31:10-31, or sublime philosophical essays, such as the one on wisdom in 8:22-31. The philosophical drama, as represented by Job, with its penetrating insights and breathless, panoramic outreachings of the heart and mind of man, is the literary zenith of Israel's wisdom literature.

In the Old Testament there are of course many other proverbs which do not have the title *māshāl* attached to them. Some of the more common ones are found in Gen. 10:9; Judg. 8:21; Jer. 31:29; Hos. 8:7.

B. Riddle.—To this type of literature should be added the riddle. The best example of the riddle is found in Judg. 14:14: "And he said to them,

'Out of the eater came something to eat.
Out of the strong came something sweet.'

And they could not in three days tell what the riddle was." And again in the same chapter (vs. 18) Samson replies in the same veiled way, "If you had not plowed with my heifer, you had not found out my riddle," that is, if the men of Timnah had not worked through Samson's wife to get the answer to the riddle given in vs. 14, they would never have known it.

C. Fable.—The well-known fable of the trees, recorded in Judg. 9:7-21, also belongs to the wisdom literature of Israel. Another one is found in II Kings 14:9. To the parables already mentioned in Ezekiel should be added the parable of the prophet Nathan (II Sam. 12:1-6) and the one recorded in I Kings 20:39-40.

IV. Wisdom in the Old Testament

A. The Pragmatic and Religious Origins.—The usual Hebrew word for wisdom is *ḥokhmāh,* which seems to have the primary sense of "firm," "fixed," and then "something which controls or restrains." In early times wisdom was mainly a practical matter. It was that native intelligence or shrewdness by which man performed his tasks skillfully and well. It is used of the artisans who worked on the tabernacle (Exod. 31:3; 36:1-2), and of those who made Aaron's priestly robes (Exod. 28:3). It is applied to women who were professional wailers (Jer. 9:17). Ezekiel uses it of the pilots and shipbuilders of Tyre (27:8-9). And in Prov. 30:24-28 wisdom is ascribed even to small animals such as ants, conies, locusts, and lizards with their amazing instincts and prowess. Thus wisdom for the Hebrew was a pragmatic, empirical thing, not speculative or philosophical. Yet he knew that even this practical wisdom came from the Lord, as several of the passages just noted assert. In view of this fact it may be questioned whether the wisdom of Israel was entirely secular in this early period, as many scholars hold.[13] Truly there are secular proverbs in the Old Testament, as we have seen, which treat of mundane affairs in a nonreligious way, and there must have been a huge reservoir of practical everyday advice in the Near East which each culture took up and treated in its own peculiar way, even as Israel did. But that is not the whole story. One can hardly deny that the ancient oracles of Balaam were divinely inspired, or that Solomon was a religious man who in some way recognized that his wisdom had a divine source. And was not the practical wisdom of these early days, discussed above, many times described as coming from God? Therefore, instead of making such a sharp cleavage between secular wisdom in early Israel and the religious type of later times, would it not be more accurate to say that as Israel fell heir to the common, practical wisdom of the Near East, she used it in her own inimitable way, setting it in her own peculiar context which instinctively related it to God? We cannot emphasize too strongly the difference between the wisdom literature of Israel and that of the pagan countries surrounding her. The emphasis on wickedness and righteousness, and on the fear of Yahweh, can be understood only

[13] Hermann Gunkel, "Vergeltung," *Die Religion in Geschichte und Gegenwart* (Tübingen: J. C. B. Mohr, 1931), V, 1529-33; R. H. Pfeiffer, *Introduction to the Old Testament* (New York: Harper & Bros., 1941), pp. 650-59.

in the light of revealed law and prophetic religion. Israel redeemed the pagan wisdom of her day and made it theocentric.

This of course became more pronounced in later times when *kokhmāh* was almost exclusively applied to the well-ordered moral and religious life, as in Proverbs and the other wisdom books.

I have taught you the way of wisdom;
 I have led you in the paths of uprightness (4:11).

Wisdom is synonymous with moral and religious intelligence; it is filled with a strongly ethical content.

This union of practical wisdom with moral intelligence is expressed by the familiar motto, "The fear of the LORD is the beginning of knowledge" (1:7; cf. also 9:10; Job 28:28; Ps. 111:10; Ecclus. 1:14). The wise men, whose teachings were never too highly regarded by the prophets, as has been seen, are here equating their wisdom with the fear of the Lord, that is, the orthodox religion of Israel, thereby showing that there is no real difference between them. After this step it was not long before wisdom became equated with the law, which was the highest expression of wisdom in later Judaism. Thus the wisdom movement became an integral and respected part of the Jewish religious tradition, as witnessed by Jesus son of Sirach, about 180 B.C.: "He who masters the Law will win her [i.e., wisdom]," and

The fear of the Lord is the sum of wisdom,
And in all wisdom the Law is fulfilled (Ecclus. 15:1; 19:20).

B. The Personification of Wisdom.—Another interesting and widely significant development in the conception of wisdom was its personification and hypostatization. The Hebrew was fond of personifying the things he saw about him. For instance, the prophet says that

the mountains and the hills before you
 shall break forth into singing,
 and all the trees of the field shall clap their hands (Isa. 55:12).

This tendency to personify led the Hebrew to personalize abstract ideas and principles. The process in this particular instance of wisdom is quite clear. The unifying, directing principle of nature and the world, called wisdom, was also found in the individual himself, ordering his mental as well as his moral life. He believed that this wisdom came ultimately from God. It was an easy matter then for the Hebrew to personify this principle, which was in the world about him as well as intimately connected with his own personal affairs. The next step naturally was to regard wisdom as a distinct or separate personality or hypostasis.

The passages in the wisdom literature which show this development will now be discussed. The first glimmer of the personification of wisdom is found in Job 28. Here its mysteriousness is described. It is not to be found in the earth, in the sky, or under the earth. Only God knows where it is.

Whence then cometh wisdom?
And where is the place of understanding?
Seeing it is hid from the eyes of all living,
And kept close from the birds of the heavens.
Destruction and Death say,
We have heard a rumor thereof with our ears.

God understandeth the way thereof,
And he knoweth the place thereof.

. . . .

Then did he see it, and declare it;
He established it, yea, and searched it out.
And unto man he said,
Behold, the fear of the Lord, that is wisdom;
And to depart from evil is understanding (Job 28: 20-23, 27-28 ASV).

This, to be sure, is only a literary personification. But the elaborate description shows that the poet was impressed by the greatness of wisdom.

In Proverbs there are several important passages dealing with this subject. In 1:20-22 wisdom is depicted as crying forth her words of invitation in the busy city marts:

Wisdom cries aloud in the street;
 in the markets she raises her voice;
on the top of the walls she cries out;
 at the entrance of the city gates she speaks:
"How long, O simple ones, will you love being simple?
How long will scoffers delight in their scoffing
 and fools hate knowledge?"

Chs. 2–3 go on in the same vein, the climax being in 3:15-19 where wisdom is connected with God's creation:

She is more precious than jewels,
 and nothing you desire can compare with her.
Long life is in her right hand;
 in her left hand are riches and honor.
Her ways are ways of pleasantness,
 and all her paths are peace.
She is a tree of life to those who lay hold of her;
 those who hold her fast are called happy.
The LORD by wisdom founded the earth;
 by understanding he established the heavens.

In chs. 8–9 is reached the highest stage in the personification of wisdom in the canonical books. The opening verses of ch. 8 again describe wisdom calling to men from the walls and

gates of the city to receive her instruction. In vss. 22-31 wisdom is so distinctly personalized that it is well on the way to being hypostatized. She was brought forth before the world was, and was present at the Creation, watching and sporting before God as he did his work, "delighting in the sons of men" (8:31).

In the apocryphal wisdom books the personification of wisdom is still further developed. In Ecclesiasticus there is not much advance over Proverbs. The two passages that deal with this matter are 1:1-20 and ch. 24. Here are the most significant verses:

Wisdom was created before them all,
And sound intelligence from eternity.
To whom has the source of wisdom been revealed?
And who knows her devices?
There is but one who is wise, a very terrible one,
Seated upon his throne;
The Lord himself created her;
He saw her and counted her,
And poured her out upon all he made;
Upon all mankind, as he chose to bestow her;
But he supplied her liberally to those who loved him (Ecclus. 1:4-10 Amer. Trans.).

The Wisdom of Solomon presents the boldest conception of wisdom. In 1:6-7 she is almost identified with God:

For wisdom is a kindly spirit,
And will not acquit a blasphemer of what he says,
For God is a witness of his heart,
And a truthful observer of his mind,
And a hearer of his tongue.
For the spirit of the Lord fills the world,
And that which embraces all things knows all that is said (Amer. Trans.).

In 6:18-19 she is a source of immortality:

And love for her is the observance of her laws,
And adherence to her laws is assurance of immortality,
And immortality brings men near to God (Amer. Trans.).

But in chs. 7–8 the inspired writer, filled with the deepest admiration for his subject, describes wisdom in the sublimest words he knows:

For wisdom, the fashioner of all things, taught me.
For there is in her a spirit that is intelligent, holy,
Unique, manifold, subtle,
Mobile, clear, undefiled,
Distinct, beyond harm, loving the good, keen,
Unhindered, beneficent, philanthropic,
Firm, sure, free from care,
All-powerful, all-seeing,
And interpenetrating all spirits
That are intelligent, pure, and most subtle.
For wisdom is more mobile than any motion,
And she penetrates and permeates everything, because she is so pure;
For she is the breath of the power of God,
And a pure emanation of his almighty glory;
Therefore nothing defiled can enter into her.
For she is a reflection of the everlasting light,
And a spotless mirror of the activity of God,
And a likeness of his goodness.
Though she is one, she can do all things,
And while remaining in herself, she makes everything new.
And passing into holy souls, generation after generation,
She makes them friends of God, and prophets.
For God loves nothing but the man who lives with wisdom.
For she is fairer than the sun,
Or any group of stars;
Compared with light, she is found superior;
For night succeeds to it,
But evil cannot overpower wisdom (7:22-30 Amer. Trans.).

Jas. 3:17 is strangely reminiscent of the first part of this passage, "But the wisdom that is from above is first pure, then peaceable, gentle, easy to be entreated, full of mercy and good fruits, without variance, without hypocrisy" (ASV). And the words of Wisd. Sol. 7:25-26 are so noble and sublime that the writer of Hebrews uses them almost verbatim to describe the wonder and beauty of our matchless Lord, "who being the effulgence of his glory, and the very image of his substance . . ." (Heb. 1:3 ASV). This is the last stage in the hypostatization of wisdom. Even Philo goes no farther. Wisdom is now ready to take its place with the Spirit and Logos as a great intermediary power between God and man. But even beyond that, in Pauline theology, wisdom is identified with Christ, the only saving, divine wisdom through whom redemption can come into the world, as against the worldly wisdom of the Greeks. "But unto them that are called, both Jews and Greeks, Christ the power of God, and the wisdom of God. . . . But of him are ye in Christ Jesus, who was made unto us wisdom from God, and righteousness and sanctification, and redemption" (I Cor. 1:24, 30 ASV).

V. Date and Authorship

In order to determine the date and authorship of Proverbs one must first of all consider the date and authorship of the individual collections of which it is composed. The divisions of the book are as follows: I. 1:1–9:18; II. 10:1–22:16; III. 22:17–24:34; IV. 25:1–29:27; V. 30:1-33; VI. 31:1-9; VII. 31:10-31. The main sections are I, II, and IV, the rest being appendixes, mostly of foreign origin.

The main themes discussed in Section I (The Excellence of Wisdom, 1:1–9:18) are (*a*) the

merits of wisdom, (*b*) the dangers of associating with the strange woman, that is, the Jewish married woman (2:17) who as an adulteress lures men to destruction with her enticing words and actions, and (*c*) the personification of wisdom. The essay style of this collection differs from the short two-line proverbs which predominate in the rest of the book. The introduction (1:1-6) ascribes these proverbs to Solomon, although he may not necessarily have written all of them. Most scholars hold a postexilic date for this part of the book, mainly because of the highly developed essay style, and the personification of wisdom (8:22-31), which they believe as due to Hellenistic influence. But it is now quite certain that chs. 8–9 are one of the oldest parts of the book, since they are of undisputed Phoenician origin, while many words and grammatical peculiarities throughout the whole section point to strong Ugaritic and Phoenician influence. Therefore to ascribe a Solomonic origin to this collection may not have been as groundless as many have supposed. Certainly the material was reworked and edited in later times, but that does not preclude the possibility that a good deal of the material may have been collected by Solomon, some of it even composed or worked over by him.

Section II (The Proverbs of Solomon, 10:1–22:16) is the core of the book. The 375 proverbs consist of two lines each, except 19:7 (see Exeg.). In chs. 10–15 they are mostly antithetic; in 16:1–22:16 only 33 out of 191 proverbs are antithetic. There seems to be no logical arrangement of the proverbs, although here and there a few consecutive verses seem to be related, as in 16:12-15, which deal with kings, and in 11:9-12, which begin with the consonant ב. Quite a few verses and half verses are repeated in this collection, as the following list shows: 10:1=15:20; 16:2=21:2; 19:5=19:9; 10:2*b*=11:4*b*; 10:6*b*=10:11*b*; 10:8*b*=10:10*b*, etc. The main characters found in these proverbs are the righteous and the wicked, the fool and the wise, the rich and the poor, the proud and the humble, the thrifty and the lazy. This is generally acknowledged to be one of the oldest sections of the book because of the short, single proverbs, and the general political, economic, and social conditions reflected in them. Again, it may be said with certainty that the bulk of these proverbs are Solomonic in origin, many of them probably having been written by him, others having been a part of the collection associated with his name.

Section III (The Sayings of the Wise, 22:17–24:34) is composed of several small collections: 22:17-21, the introduction; 22:22–23:14, similar to The Teaching of Amen-em-ope: 23:15–24:22; and 24:23-24, a second collection of the sayings of the wise. The sentence structure and the threatening tone of these proverbs is reminiscent of Section I. The warnings are quite varied, including those against becoming surety, extravagances in eating and drinking, riches, etc. Since certain of these proverbs show close affinity with the Egyptian wisdom book, The Teaching of Amen-em-ope, which was compiled somewhere between 800 and 600 B.C., the heart of this section can safely be regarded as pre-exilic in origin.

Section IV (Second Collection of Solomon's Proverbs, 25:1–29:27) falls into two parts: chs. 25–27, composed mainly of secular proverbs, and chs. 28–29, with a strong ethical and religious emphasis. This collection is said to have been edited by the men of Hezekiah (25:1), a statement which is generally accepted as authentic (see Exeg.). The collection may be dated near the end of the eighth century B.C.

The authors of Sections V (The Words of Agur, 30:1-33), VI (The Words of Lemuel, 31:1-9), and VII (The Good Wife—an acrostic poem—31:10-31) are unknown. Agur and Lemuel are non-Israelitish rulers, probably of the Arabian tribe of Massa, east of Palestine (see Exeg. on 30:1), but otherwise unknown. The writer of the acrostic poem (31:10-31) is not known at all, although he must have been a Hebrew. It is difficult to determine the dates of these last three sections. They are generally considered to be postexilic, although there is no definite evidence to preclude a much earlier date for the material.

From these observations, then, it appears that most of Proverbs is pre-exilic in origin. In the course, however, of compiling these collections and editing them in their final form and arrangement, many proverbs of a later date became incorporated in the original sources. The first six verses of the book, for instance, were probably added as a general introduction by the compiler and editor of the first two sections. Aramaisms may point to a later date for those proverbs in which they occur. The reference to the law and vision (prophecy) in 29:18 (cf. also 30:5-6) indicates a date long after Ezra for these verses. So that even though the bulk of the material in every section is pre-exilic, the final form of the book, as we know it, was not attained until some time after 400 B.C.

VI. Text and Style

The Hebrew text of Proverbs is in fairly good condition. To be sure, there are errors, difficulties, and corruptions, but in comparison with books like I and II Samuel or Hosea, Proverbs has suffered little in the course of transmission. The most serious textual difficulties are found in 6:26; 7:22*c*; 12:12, 28*b*; 13:23;

14:9*a*; 17:14; 18:19; 19:7*c*, 19, 22*a*, 23*b*; 21:12, 28*b*; 22:21; 25:11, 20, 27*b*; 26:8, 10; 27:9*b*, 16; 28:17; 30:1, 31. In almost all of these cases the Hebrew text is meaningless and emendations, as pointed out in the Exegesis, are purely conjectural. Then, too, there are individual words which defy explanation because they are entirely unknown or not understandable. Some of these are as follows: *'āmôn* (8:30); *yāthēr* (12:26); *ḥibbēl* (23:34); *mānôn* (29:21); *'alûqāh* (30:15); *zarzîr* and *'alqûm* (30:31). These examples point to the remarkable persistence of the consonantal Hebrew text in the course of transmission, even though the words and sentences had long lost their meaning to the Jewish scribe.

The aid of outside sources in determining the meaning of difficult or unknown words has been applied to Proverbs with marked success. Egyptian wisdom sources, for instance, have clarified the difficult *shlshwm* in 22:20 (see Exeg.), and Ugaritic material has already given the clue to the meaning of two expressions in 21:9 and 26:23 (see Exeg.), with the promise of more aid in the future.

The Septuagint is the most valuable ancient version for the study of Proverbs. It must be used with caution, however, in correcting the Hebrew text, since its own text is impaired by corruptions and peculiar modes of translation. Some Hebrew verses are omitted altogether; on the other hand, much material is found in the Greek which is not in the Hebrew. A careful study of these added verses shows that some go back to an original Hebrew source, whereas others seem to be Greek in origin. There are almost one hundred doublets of verses, stichs, phrases, and words in the Greek text of Proverbs, all of which point to the fact that variations of the same proverb, or altogether new ones, were in circulation in postexilic times and were included in the text of Proverbs by the translators of the Septuagint. Many times the Hebrew is freely translated, revealing ignorance on the part of the translator of the Hebrew word or idiom, or an attempt to mold the material into the theological or philosophical position of the person or persons translating. Even the order of chapters from ch. 24 on is different in the Septuagint from the Hebrew. Whatever the reasons may have been for these serious defections and deviations in the Greek text of Proverbs, it is clear that the translator(s) was not bound by a well-established translation tradition, as he would have been if he were rendering the Torah into Greek, or by a sacrosanct attitude toward the Hebrew text.

Proverbs is written in poetic style. That is, each verse is characterized by the parallelism of its members, or stichs, and by a certain number of beats or accents—usually three or four—in those stichs. Paronomasia also plays an important role in the literary structure of the book. The couplet, composed of two stichs, is the most common form of the proverb. The three main types of parallelism in Proverbs are:

1. *Synonymous,* in which the two stichs express the same idea in slightly different ways:

My son, keep my words
 and treasure up my commandments with you (7:1).
Does not wisdom call,
 does not understanding raise her voice? (8:1.)

2. *Antithetic,* in which the truth of the first stich is contrastingly stated in the second:

A son who gathers in summer is prudent,
 but a son who sleeps in harvest brings shame (10:5).
In the path of righteousness is life,
 but the way of error leads to death (12:28).

These two types of parallelism are noted throughout the Exegesis.

3. *Synthetic,* in which the second stich simply carries on the thought of the first, thus forming one whole sentence:

My son, if sinners entice you,
 do not consent (1:10).
If one gives answer before he hears,
 it is his folly and shame (18:13).

The most common meters in Proverbs are 4:3, 4:4, and 3:3, but these are naturally lost in the various translations of the Hebrew text.

VII. Teaching

In Proverbs the teaching of the wise men has become respectably linked with the religion of Israel, or to put it in the proverbial style, the fear of the Lord is the beginning or chief part of wisdom. They were not too closely united as yet, however, since we hear little about the ritual, the priest, the messianic hope, or the prophet throughout the book. It was not until 180 B.C. (date of Ecclesiasticus) that the Law, the supreme expression of religion, and wisdom were equated in Judaism.

The object of the practical instruction given in these proverbs is not the Jewish nation or a special privileged class, but any individual, commonly called "my son," who heeds wisdom's call to listen to her words of advice. This individualistic, democratic approach is characteristic of all of Israel's wisdom literature.

The wise men, in dealing with the practical problems of everyday life, do not resort to creed or revelation for their knowledge, but to human

experience in all its varied forms. There is very little in the world of human affairs that does not come under their critical scrutiny. They know the world of nature too, and from it they draw many illustrations of practical sagacity.

Anyone who reads Proverbs is impressed with the high ethical standard of its teachings. The highest type of family life is extolled; monogamy is taken for granted; the respect for mother and wife is emphasized throughout; chastity and marital fidelity are enjoined for all. The glutton, drunkard, and sluggard, the robber and oppressor of the poor, are all roundly condemned. Those who live in accordance with wisdom's laws are prosperous and happy. A belief in the one true and living God who rewards the righteous and punishes the wicked permeates the book from cover to cover.

In spite of this high standard of ethics, however, it must be admitted that goodness is almost always motivated by personal interest or success. The high-water marks of altruistic behavior, as found in 24:17; 25:21, are sadly marred by the following verse in each case:

Do not rejoice when your enemy falls,
  and let not your heart be glad when he stumbles;
lest the LORD see it, and be displeased,
  and turn away his anger from him (24:17-18);

If your enemy is hungry, give him bread to eat;
  and if he is thirsty, give him water to drink;
for you will heap coals of fire on his head,
  and the LORD will reward you (25:21-22).

In the numerous warnings against illicit dealings with the strange woman, the man is told to abstain because he will be impoverished, or he will be physically weakened, or he will die prematurely. There is no comment on the sinfulness of the act, or on the degradation of the woman who encourages the act. He who is wise will conduct himself in such a way that he will live a long, happy, and prosperous life.

The eschatology of Proverbs is similar to that of the rest of the Old Testament. Sheol is the dismal abode of the departed. Yet there seems to be a slight advance beyond this idea in the book. According to 15:11, for instance, Sheol and Abaddon are said to be before the Lord; that is, he is in some way concerned with the underworld and its inhabitants. This is a foreshadowing of the more highly developed doctrine of later Judaism and Christianity that God has power over both heaven and hell. Then, too, one cannot help feeling that Sheol, as used in Proverbs, refers not just to death alone but to the death of one who has died in his sins before his time. In other words, Sheol seems to be taking on a moral aspect which it fully assumes when it becomes equivalent to hell at a later time.

As to the end of man, Proverbs adds nothing to the general Old Testament idea. The good man receives his rewards of happiness, prosperity, and long life here on earth; the wicked man is punished by a premature or violent death; but in neither case does reward or punishment carry over into the next life (cf. 14:12; 15:24).

VIII. Proverbs and the New Testament

The quotations from Proverbs in the New Testament are few. They are not introduced by any special phrase, such as "it is written," nor are they ascribed to Solomon. They are usually taken from the Greek text of Proverbs rather than from the Hebrew. A comparative list of these quotations, from the American Standard Version, follows:

Be not wise in thine own eyes (Prov. 3:7*a*; cf. 26:12*a*).
Be not wise in your own conceits (Rom. 12:16*b*, with LXX).

My son, despise not the chastening of Jehovah;
Neither be weary of his reproof:
For whom Jehovah loveth he reproveth,
Even as a father the son in whom he delighteth (Prov. 3:11-12).
My son, regard not lightly the chastening of the Lord,
Nor faint when thou art reproved of him;
For whom the Lord loveth he chasteneth,
And scourgeth every son whom he receiveth (Heb. 12:5-6, with LXX).

Surely he scoffeth at the scoffers;
But he giveth grace unto the lowly (Prov. 3:34).
Wherefore the scripture saith, God resisteth the proud, but giveth grace to the humble (Jas. 4:6; I Pet. 5:5*b*, with LXX).

Make level the path of thy feet (Prov. 4:26*a*).
Make straight paths for your feet (Heb. 12:13*a*, with LXX).

But love covereth all transgressions (Prov. 10:12*b*).
For love covereth a multitude of sins (I Pet. 4:8*b*; cf. Jas. 5:20).

This quotation probably came from the Hebrew through some Aramaic translation, or from a different Greek text from ours, since the Septuagint has a different rendition.

Behold, the righteous shall be recompensed in the earth;
How much more the wicked and the sinner! (Prov. 11:31.)
And if the righteous is scarcely saved, where shall the ungodly and sinner appear? (I Pet. 4:18, with LXX.)

In this case the Septuagint is an adaptation of the Hebrew in accordance with the more highly developed doctrine of the future life in later times.

After 22:8 the Greek text has the additional line, "A man who is cheerful and a giver God blesseth," which seems to be a paraphrase of 22:9*a* in the Hebrew. II Cor. 9:7*c* reads, "For God loveth a cheerful giver," which is a condensation of the passage in the Septuagint.

If thine enemy be hungry, give him bread to eat;
And if he be thirsty, give him water to drink:
For thou wilt heap coals of fire upon his head,
And Jehovah will reward thee (Prov. 25:21-22).
But if thine enemy hunger, feed him; if he thirst, give him to drink: for in so doing thou shalt heap coals of fire upon his head (Rom. 12:20, with LXX, except that the last line is omitted).

As a dog that returneth to his vomit (Prov. 26:11*a*).
The dog turning to his own vomit again (II Pet. 2:22*b*).

This proverb must also have come from the Hebrew through the Aramaic, since the Septuagint has paraphrased the verse.

Then, too, there are many proverbs which are the basis of New Testament passages, but are not actually quoted. A brief listing of these follows: 2:4 and Col. 2:3, on the treasures of wisdom; 3:4 and Luke 2:52, regarding the growth of Jesus; 3:28 and Matt. 5:42 and Jas. 2:16 on giving; 9:1-5 and Matt. 22:4, on the invitation to the feast; 10:25; 12:7 and Matt. 7:24-27, on the fool and the wise man who built their houses on sand and rock; 11:4, 28 and Matt. 6:19, on the ephemerality of riches; 11:17 and Matt. 5:7, on the merciful man; 16:1 and Matt. 10:19-20, on trusting God for the right thing to say; 16:19 and Matt. 5:3, on the poor; 18:21 and Matt. 12:36-37, on the power of the tongue; 24:12 and Matt. 16:27 and II Tim. 4:14, on recompense; 25:6-7 and Luke 14:7-11, on humility; 27:1 and Luke 12:16-21, on the uncertainty of the future; 28:24 and Matt. 15:4, 6, on the honoring of parents; 29:23 and Luke 14:11; 18:14*b*, on humility; 30:8-9 and Matt. 6:11, on our daily bread.

Christ links himself with the wisdom of the Old Testament when he says: "The queen of the South will arise at the judgment with the men of this generation and condemn them; for she came from the ends of the earth to hear the wisdom of Solomon, and behold, something greater than Solomon is here" (Luke 11:31; Matt. 12:42). Jesus is not just making a simple comparison, but rather is he saying that the wisdom of the Old Testament, so imperfectly manifested in the character and teachings of Solomon, is now perfectly revealed in the matchless life and words of him who is David's greater son (on the relation of Christ to Prov. 8:22-31 see p. 774).

That Proverbs is part of the Old Testament canon points to the fact that wisdom is the revelation of God's orderly plan in the universe and in the lives of men, rather than merely the accumulation of intelligent observations on life down through the ages. When Jesus identifies himself with wisdom he also confirms this view and brings wisdom into the redemptive plan and purpose of God.[14]

IX. Outline of Contents

I. The excellence of wisdom (1:1–9:18)
- A. Title (1:1)
- B. Purpose of the book (1:2-6)
- C. Motto of the book (1:7)
- D. Exhortation and warning (1:8-19)
  - 1. Exhortation to listen to instruction (1:8-9)
  - 2. Warning against associating with robbers and murderers (1:10-19)
- E. Wisdom publicly proclaims a warning against neglecting her appeal (1:20-33)
- F. Benefits of heeding wisdom (2:1-22)
- G. Blessings of wisdom (3:1-35)
- H. Wisdom commended to scholars (4:1-27)
  - 1. The courting of wisdom (4:1-9)
  - 2. The ways of the wise and the wicked (4:10-19)
  - 3. The straight path of wisdom (4:20-27)
- J. A discourse on marital life (5:1-23)
  - 1. Warning against licentiousness (5:1-14)
  - 2. Exhortation to marital faithfulness (5:15-23)
- K. A group of warnings (6:1-19)
  - 1. Warnings against suretyship (6:1-5)
  - 2. Warnings against indolence (6:6-11)
  - 3. Warnings against perversity (6:12-15)
  - 4. Warnings against seven sins (6:16-19)
- L. Warnings against the adulteress (6:20–7:27)
- M. In praise of wisdom (8:1-36)
  - 1. Exhortation to follow wisdom (8:1-21)
  - 2. Wisdom's exalted position (8:22-31)
  - 3. Concluding words of exhortation (8:32-36)
- N. Contrast between wisdom and folly (9:1-18)
  - 1. Wisdom's invitation (9:1-6)
  - 2. Miscellaneous aphorisms (9:7-12)
  - 3. Folly's invitation (9:13-18)

II. The proverbs of Solomon (10:1–22:16)

III. The sayings of the wise (22:17–24:34)
- A. Introduction (22:17-21)
- B. First collection (22:22–23:14)
- C. Second collection (23:15–24:22)
- D. Third collection (24:23-34)

IV. Second collection of Solomon's proverbs (25:1–29:27)
- A. First section (25:1–27:27)
- B. Second section (28:1–29:27)

[14] See Charles T. Fritsch, "The Gospel in the Book of Proverbs," *Theology Today*, VII (1950-51), 169-83.

V. The words of Agur (30:1-33)
  A. Agur's personal reflections (30:1-14)
  B. Numerical sayings (30:15-33)
VI. The words of Lemuel (31:1-9)
VII. The good wife (31:10-31)

X. *Selected Bibliography*

BOSTRÖM, GUSTAV. *Proverbiastudien.* Lund: C. W. K. Gleerup, 1935.

COHEN, ABRAHAM. *Proverbs.* Hindhead, Surrey: Soncino Press, 1945.

GEMSER, B. *Sprüche Salomos* ("Handbuch zum Alten Testament"). Tübingen: J. C. B. Mohr, 1937.

JAMES, FLEMING. "Some Aspects of the Religion of Proverbs," *Journal of Biblical Literature,* LI (1932), 31-39.

MARTIN, G. C. *Proverbs, Ecclesiastes and Song of Songs* ("The New-Century Bible"). New York: Oxford University Press, 1908.

OESTERLEY, W. O. E. *The Book of Proverbs* ("Westminster Commentaries"). London: Methuen & Co., 1929.

PEROWNE, T. T. *The Proverbs* ("The Cambridge Bible"). Cambridge: Cambridge University Press, 1916.

TOY, CRAWFORD H. *A Critical and Exegetical Commentary on the Book of Proverbs* ("International Critical Commentary"). 2nd ed. New York: Charles Scribner's Sons, 1914.

WILDEBOER, D. G. *Die Sprüche* ("Kurzer Hand-Commentar zum Alten Testament"). Freiburg: J. C. B. Mohr, 1897.

PROVERBS

TEXT, EXEGESIS, AND EXPOSITION

1 The Proverbs of Solomon the son of David, king of Israel;

1 The proverbs of Solomon, son of David, king of Israel:

I. THE EXCELLENCE OF WISDOM (1:1–9:18)

A. TITLE (1:1)

1:1. The words of this verse may serve either as the title of the whole book or of this section (chs. 1–9) alone. The latter is probably the correct assumption, since the other sections of the book have their own titles (10:1; 25:1; 30:1; 31:1). **Proverbs:** See Intro. (pp. 771-72) for the discussion of the word *māshāl.* **Of Solomon:** The ascription of the proverbs in this book or in this section of the book to Solomon does not necessarily mean that he is the author of all of them. Solomon had been a wise king, according to the record, and the author of numerous proverbs (I Kings 3:4-15, 16-28; 4:29-34), and so his name became associated with wisdom literature generally. Its presence in the

1:1. *A Good Way to Be Remembered.*—When a Hebrew sage thought of wisdom he inevitably thought of **Solomon.** King Solomon had achieved the distinction of being remembered as a person who was the source of many wise sayings. His name had become inextricably associated with pithy maxims that had found their way into the common culture of Israel.

Solomon was remembered for other reasons besides his wisdom. He was known for his wealth. His attire was of the best. People who wanted to envisage luxury and magnificence in the time of Jesus turned their thoughts back to this king. "Consider the lilies of the field, how they grow," said Jesus, "they neither toil nor spin; yet I tell you, even Solomon in all his glory was not arrayed like one of these" (Matt. 6:28-29). The grandeur of Solomon's court had become a legend.

Milton thought of Solomon as one who was an easy prey for the wiles of women. The record indicates that he had no dearth of wives and that he did not hesitate to go beyond the borders of his own land to get them.

> For Solomon, he lived at ease, and, full
> Of honour, wealth, high fare, aimed not beyond
> Higher design than to enjoy his state.[1]

There is nothing here about Solomon's wisdom. He is pictured as a pampered man of wealth, at

[1] *Paradise Regained,* Bk. II.

2 To know wisdom and instruction; to perceive the words of understanding;

2 That men may know wisdom and instruction,
understand words of insight,

title therefore indicates the literary genre to which the book belongs. His name is also attached to the Song of Solomon, the Wisdom of Solomon, and other writings (see also the section "Date and Authorship" in the Intro., pp. 774-75). **King of Israel:** The Masoretic accents in the Hebrew text show that this phrase should be attached to Solomon, not David.

B. Purpose of the Book (1:2-6)

The wise men inquire into all things. There is nothing too high or too low that does not come under their inquisitive scrutiny (cf. Eccl. 7:24). Their main interest, however, is not the study of the universe and the laws which govern it, but man and the moral conditions which govern his life. As the writer of 8:22-31 says, wisdom was present at Creation as God's helper, but her "delights were with the sons of men." Therefore the purpose of these proverbs is to bring wisdom and understanding to men so that they may live happily, peacefully, and righteously together.

2. Synonymous. **To know:** The infinitives of vss. 2-4 are all in close syntactical connection with vs. 1. The subject of the infinitives is indefinite, anyone who intends to be instructed by these proverbs being meant. The aim of the proverbs included here is to make men know wisdom; when that is accomplished, it is hoped that men will do that which is right. As Crawford H. Toy points out (*A Critical and Exegetical Commentary on the Book of Proverbs* [2nd ed.; New York: Charles Scribner's Sons, 1914; "International Critical Commentary"], *ad loc.*), the emphasis throughout this book on the intellectual recognition of the right as the basis of the good life is allied to the Socratic conception of morality, which is simply that if one knows what is right, he will do what is right. Conversion, or the change of heart, is not found in Proverbs.

ease in his court, with no higher design than "to enjoy his state." He becomes the symbol of fabulous wealth and of all the temptations that such wealth brings with it. Yet in spite of these other associations, Solomon's name is chiefly connected with wisdom. This is a good way to be remembered.

Evidently Solomon had earned the right to be regarded as a wise man. He must have made some wise judgments in his day, and he is said to have been the author of many proverbs. This does not mean that every saying attributed to him was spoken by him. For centuries after he had lived a process went on that might be called plagiarism in reverse. Teachers who came after him did something quite foreign to present-day practice. Instead of using some saying of Solomon's and purveying it as their own, they took some current maxim or some saying of their own and attributed it to Solomon. What better way to commend the wisdom of a saying than by securing the autograph of Solomon for it? They used his name more than they used his thoughts, because he was remembered as a wise man. In the United States this same kind of process has been at work in stories attributed to Lincoln. He achieved the reputation of telling tales with a flavor of homely wit. Since his day so many stories have been linked with his name that only patient research could ever discover how many of them actually belong to him.

The interesting point in this connection is not whether Solomon wrote all the proverbs ascribed to him, but the fact that people remembered him as a source of wisdom and associated his name with wise dealing. This invites a moment of self-examination. Each one of us, no matter how humble his station, cannot but wonder how he will be remembered. What will people think of first when our name is mentioned? When we think of Job, we think of patience. When we think of Judas, we think of betrayal. Some of these estimates of people that find their way into a stereotype are no doubt unfair and too severely simple, but they accentuate the urgency that each one of us should work for some good way in which to be remembered.

2. ***To Know Wisdom.***—These three words really sound the theme and state the purpose of this collection of writings. They assume that if a person "knows wisdom" he will find his way through life without mishap, and that he will be able to look upon life and call it good. In this and in many other passages wisdom is given the highest praise. Young and old are summoned

Wisdom: See Intro. (pp. 772-73) for a discussion of the word *ḥokhmāh.* In this verse it means moral and religious intelligence, i.e., the knowledge of the moral law of God as it concerns the practical affairs of life. It is not the speculative, philosophical wisdom of the Greeks. **Instruction:** The root meaning of the word *mûṣār* is "discipline," "chastisement." Here, in parallelism with **wisdom,** it means the result of training, the instruction received from submitting oneself to the teaching of the wise men. Endowed with instincts and passions which ever seek to rule and dominate the human spirit, man must learn to submit himself to those in higher authority—father and mother, the wise men, God himself—in order to become truly wise. **Understand:** The root meaning of *bîn* is "to separate," "to divide." It then comes to mean "to distinguish between what is right and wrong" (cf. I Kings 3:9). **Understanding** is from the same root as the preceding verb, to **understand. Words of insight** (RSV) is therefore a more accurate translation.

---

to its pursuit. In fact, in this section no particular person is addressed, so the call is "To Whom It May Concern." Wisdom guards life from pitfalls and holds forth the highest rewards.

This stress on knowing wisdom would seem to indicate that knowing is enough. Both education and religion have wrestled with this very old and yet very new problem. There is evidence to uphold the view that many of the writers of Proverbs believed that "knowledge is virtue"—that knowing what is right will result in doing what is right. There is no doubt that knowledge is power. Knowledge of the laws by which nature works has made it possible for man to harness nature and to put it to work. Knowledge of the ways in which human nature reacts to stimuli has made it possible for propagandists to control masses of people. But does knowledge produce virtue? Experience and observation show that people who know what is right do not necessarily always act according to their knowledge. There is no inevitable connection between knowledge of right and wrong and conduct that is right. If these writers exalted a wisdom that consisted of knowledge which was supposed inevitably to produce good conduct, then many other voices would be raised to oppose this view. Education cannot be content with putting knowledge into people's heads. Neither can it rest back complacently and assume that those who know the most will act the best. This does not call for a headlong retreat into ignorance, but it does sound the warning that no naïve trust in the efficacy of knowledge is warranted.

If knowledge is not everything, it surely is something. Knowledge may not guarantee virtue, but ignorance has a smaller chance to produce a good life. Some of the difficulties into which people fall are due to ignorance. One of the tasks of education is to help people see vividly the consequences of action. If they really perceive the immediate and distant results of a course of action, they will be more apt to choose wisely. Wrong actions may sometimes be the result of inadequate knowledge, even though right action does not necessarily follow adequate knowledge. When Peter was addressing the crowd in Solomon's Colonnade, reminding them of the part they had had in the crucifixion of Jesus, he said to them, "You did not know what you were doing, any more than your leaders did" (Acts 3:17 Goodspeed). These people were acting in ignorance of the true import of their deed. Their comprehension was limited. And we cannot but remember the word of Jesus when men were driving cruel nails into his hands and feet, "Father, forgive them; for they know not what they do" (Luke 23:34). Ignorance has produced a melancholy list of casualties. If knowledge of what is right will not produce a life that is good, how much less will ignorance of what is right issue in good living! The wise man will never abate his quest for knowledge, since virtue has a better chance of thriving where people make an honest attempt to understand the difference between right and wrong.

Some of these writers have thought that wisdom followed knowing. They would all agree that wisdom is more than knowing what is right and wrong. They were not content with a wisdom that consisted in giving the right answers. A wise life was one that expressed itself in attitude and conduct as well as in knowledge. Mere knowledge is not the ultimate goal of endeavor. It is always a means to an end. **To know wisdom** is therefore more than an intellectual achievement or the accumulation of knowledge. It is the expression of that knowledge in conduct toward God and man. When Jesus talked about a wise man he talked of one who not only heard his words but who did them. "Therefore whosoever heareth these sayings of mine, and doeth them, I will liken him unto a wise man, which built his house upon a rock" (Matt. 7:24). Wise living has an intellectual aspect, but it is more than knowing—it is knowing plus doing.

2. *A Genius for Essentials.*—The person who has learned how to **understand words of insight** is one who has learned the art of discrimination.

3 To receive the instruction of wisdom, justice, and judgment, and equity;

3 receive instruction in wise dealing,
righteousness, justice, and equity;

Wisdom is passed on through word of mouth from father to son, from teacher to pupil. It is important, then, that the word is intelligible.

3. **To receive:** Another term used to describe the intricate process of acquiring knowledge. One receives the wisdom derived from past experience and applies it to his own life. The word translated **learning** in vs. 5 is from this root. **Instruction** is the same word as in vs. 2, defined here by its object or aim. **Wisdom,** *haskēl,* means "good sense," as applied to the everyday practical affairs of life. **Wise dealing** (RSV) is therefore a happy combination of both ideas. The next three words in the verse show how **wise dealing** manifests itself.

Justice or **righteousness** ("rectitude" Amer. Trans.): The root meaning of the word *çédheq* is not directly expressed in the O.T., although from such passages as 8:8; Ps. 23:3 it may be inferred to mean "straight." As used in the O.T. it means basically the standard norm of conduct which exists among individuals. In the forensic sense it means "justice"; in the ethical sense it means "right conduct," which later on comes to be identified particularly with right conduct toward the poor, and so "benevolence," "alms." Here it means "right conduct" in general.

Judgment or "justice": The judgment, *mishpāṭ,* or decision, given by the *shôphēṭ* ("judge"), whereby the right relationship was maintained between people, and the precedent set for all succeeding action. Therefore it comes to mean "custom," "manner," and then "way of life." As *çédheq* emphasizes the rightness of the individual character, so *mishpāṭ* expresses the right conduct of the individual in relation to others. **Equity:** The root meaning of *mēshārîm,* a collective plural, is "smooth," "straight." In Isa. 26:7

His is a discriminating mind that knows how to separate and divide the wheat from the chaff, the good from the bad, the essential from the nonessential. He has a genius for essentials.

This art of discrimination is especially essential amid the complexities of modern life. An extremely simple existence would not put the pressure of selection upon people, but an age that confronts everyone with many things to do, with many books and magazines to read, with many places to go and the ability to get there, with many forms of recreation to enjoy—such an age requires men who understand how to discriminate between values. In his essay on "Self-Reliance" Emerson states a problem that has become even more acute since his time: "At times the whole world seems to be in conspiracy to importune you with emphatic trifles. Friend, client, child, sickness, fear, want, charity, all knock at once at thy closet door and say—'Come out unto us.'" Under these circumstances life can become like a room in a clutter. There is crowded confusion. Amid the clamor of many appeals there is need for a high degree of selectivity. Only the person who has a capacity for discrimination, and who has a genius for essentials, can prevent the good from becoming the enemy of the best.

The art of discrimination is made necessary also by the brevity of life. Life's span is not long enough to make it possible for people to do everything they want to do. No man has sufficient years on earth to do everything that he might do. He must choose. He must be discriminating, lest he spend his days inundated by trifles.

When Charles and Anne Lindbergh took their trip by air north to the Orient, they had the task of deciding what to take on their plane. They also had to decide what not to take. Every object had to be weighed, mentally as well as physically. For weeks before their departure their room was covered with large untidy piles of equipment. Each night these objects were rearranged. Because they could not take everything, they had to decide which things were essential. Life has often been compared to a journey. The journey is not long. Only a few things can be taken on this trip. Under the relentless pressure of time, and under the necessity of working within the limitations imposed by the years, each one needs the wisdom of discrimination. Many little pearls may need to be sold in order to secure the pearl of great price.

The irrevocability of our choices adds another incentive to the search for the ability to discriminate between what is good and what is bad. Man does not have a limitless capacity to experiment. A physician may perform an experiment on a human body, but if the patient loses his life the doctor cannot alter the fact of the man's death. He cannot say that he will try

4 To give subtilty to the simple, to the young man knowledge and discretion.
5 A wise *man* will hear, and will increase learning; and a man of understanding shall attain unto wise counsels:

4 that prudence may be given to the simple,
knowledge and discretion to the youth—
5 the wise man also may hear and increase in learning,
and the man of understanding acquire skill,

---

it is used of the path of the righteous, as smooth and level, free of any obstacles. In the moral sense, then, it means "rightness," as here. Our popular idiom, "on the level," expresses the idea exactly.

4. Synonymous. **The simple:** From the Hebrew verb *pāthāh,* "to open," and so one who is open to any influence. The idea of immaturity and inexperience is expressed by the parallel word *na'ar,* **young man,** in the next phrase. **Subtilty** or **prudence:** In Proverbs and wisdom literature generally the word *'ormāh* is always used in the good sense of "shrewdness," i.e., the ability to keep oneself from being misled. In Exod. 21:14; Josh. 9:4 it is used in the bad sense. **Young man:** Used of an infant (Exod. 2:6) or child (II Kings 4:29), and so an immature person without experience in the world. **Knowledge:** From the verb *yādha',* "to know." **Discretion** (*mezimmāh*): Lit., "the power to devise," "to decide one's course." Purposeful planning to gain the right end is signified here. In the O.T. the word is used more often in the bad sense than in the good. In 2:11; 3:21; 5:2; 8:12 it is used in the good sense; in 12:2; 14:17; 24:8, in the bad sense.

5. Synonymous. This verse seems to be parenthetical, the infinitives of the preceding verses giving way to the jussive forms of the verbs. Not only can the young benefit from wisdom, but even those who are wise and intelligent. **Learning:** The Hebrew word *léqaḥ* comes from the verbal root which means "to receive," "to take" (see Exeg. on vs. 3), and so is used to indicate that which is received by being handed down from one generation to another. **Understanding:** Discernment (see Exeg. on vs. 2). **Wise counsels** or **skill:** The Hebrew word is a nautical term, the root meaning being "rope," and then "pulling a rope," "steering," "guiding" (*taḥbûlôth*). The LXX has κυβέρνησιν for this word, and the Vulg., *gubernacula,* from which we get the English word "govern." Here it means the skill of managing one's own affairs. The word occurs five times in Proverbs and once in Job. **Attain:** Better, **acquire** (RSV).

---

again and do better next time. If one could experiment endlessly, he might not be pressed to use his powers of discrimination, but man cannot summon some magic by which time is reversed and past events are blotted out. There is need for the wisdom that enables people to choose a right course before they have tried wrong courses that produce unalterable consequences. Over much that we have done we must write, "What I have written I have written" (John 19:22). This fact constitutes a further urgency to seek earnestly that wisdom that helps men to **understand words of insight.**

4. *Commendable Sophistication.*—Generally it is no compliment to a person to call him sophisticated. This expression usually means that the one referred to is a worldly-wise individual who has experienced much, whom nothing can shock, and who maintains an attitude of bored disillusionment toward life in general. Yet there is a good sense in which wisdom can summon young people to become sophisticated. Since children and young people are open to all kinds of influences, they can easily be misdirected if they are taken off guard. Therefore they need subtlety and shrewdness lest they be led astray by the latest voice that gains their ears. But also they need the open-mindedness to real knowledge which will keep them from being startled when they are confronted with some unfamiliar choice or some novel idea. Someone has said that an educated man is a person who is not embarrassed when he is introduced to a new idea. This is a commendable sophistication, and the writers of Proverbs were tireless in their appeal to those whose minds were open to many influences, that they might learn prudence and discretion before painful experience taught them the hard way.

5. *Never Too Old to Learn.*—This verse is introduced into this passage as a parenthesis, but it is a parenthesis which modern educators

6 To understand a proverb, and the interpretation; the words of the wise, and their dark sayings.

7 ¶ The fear of the LORD *is* the beginning of knowledge: *but* fools despise wisdom and instruction.

6 to understand a proverb and a figure,
the words of the wise and their riddles.

7 The fear of the LORD is the beginning of knowledge;
fools despise wisdom and instruction.

---

6. Synonymous. A continuation of vss. 2-4. This is the scholarly aim of the book. **Interpretation** or **figure** ("parable" Amer. Trans.): The root idea of *m^elîçāh* seems to be "to turn," "to bend." A cognate participle form means "interpreter" (Gen. 42:23; Job 33:23; Isa. 43:27 mg.) and "ambassador" (II Chr. 32:31). In this passage the word probably means a "turned or figurative saying" (Toy), as brought out by the different English versions. In Hab. 2:6, the only other place where this word is found, it means a "mocking poem." **Dark sayings** or **riddles:** The root meaning of *ḥîdhāh* is "to turn aside." The noun therefore refers to a statement which is not straightforward but deflected, and so requires a close examination in order to reveal its meaning. This is the only time it is used in Proverbs.

C. Motto of the Book (1:7)

7. Antithetic. This verse is unconnected with what precedes and what follows. The religion of the priest and prophet, described by the phrase **the fear of the LORD,** is here put on the same level with the religion of the wise men. They are not to be considered antagonistic; rather is the religion of the wise men supplementary to that of the prophet and priest. There can be no true knowledge apart from God, and there can be no true ethic apart from respect for God. Although the idea of **fear** goes back to the terror

---

have underlined. The simple one—the inexperienced youth—is not the only one to profit by the pursuit of wisdom.

The wise man also may hear and increase in learning,
and the man of understanding acquire skill.

The learning process is not something which stops with the passing of the years of youth. One is never too old to learn. Growing up means learning how to learn. The learning process can be cumulative: the more a person knows, the more he knows how to find out the things he does not know. Tests have proved that adults can be taught—they can **increase in learning** and they can **acquire skill.** This makes education a co-operative process. Both teacher and pupil are learners. The teacher may know some things that the student does not know, but the teacher does not need to cease to be a learner himself. The wiser a man is, the more he knows how to become wiser than he is. The book of Proverbs is therefore not restricted to the juvenile section of a library.

7. ***A Life Motto.***—The Amer. Trans. renders this verse, "Reverence for the LORD is the beginning of knowledge." In addition to being a good motto for Proverbs, these words make a good motto for a life. They are a kind of preamble to wise living.

Reverence for the Lord has an ingredient of fear, although it is far more than an abject cringing before some arbitrary and unfriendly power. Religion may have begun in a feeling of terror before the unknown and before the all-powerful, but religious living means more than going through life as a scared person. John Macmurray has rightly said that the eternal task of religion is the conquest of fear.[2] Wise living does not remove fear entirely. It consists in fearing the right things. People today may not fear the same things that troubled their forefathers. A modern man may not ring bells in church steeples to drive devils out of the clouds, nor does he fold his hands as a gesture of self-binding deference to the spirits that move through the trees above him. A modern man may feel he has emancipated himself because he is no longer afraid of a hell of fire after he dies. But modern men have other fears. They are afraid of bacteria that may invade their bodies to produce illness. They are afraid of losing their jobs, of being dependent in their old age, of giving offense to their neighbors, of losing caste. Modern men are afraid of war, afraid of failure, afraid of death.

To add **the fear of the LORD** to these and many other fears that haunt men today seems

[2] *Creative Society* (New York: Association Press, 1936), p. 91.

which was felt in the presence of the Deity, it comes to mean "reverence," "awe," as here. True **knowledge** must start with a recognition of God. Yet it is not just an intellectual assent to Deity that is meant here, but a recognition of God as the self-revealing One, the **Lord** of grace and history who alone can satisfy the longings of the human soul. The Hebrew form of the name of God which was revealed especially to Israel (Exod. 3:14) is composed of four consonants, YHWH, the pronunciation of which has been lost. A suggested pronunciation is Yahweh. The name "Lord" (Adonai) was substituted for this word by the Jews. It means the one, true God who revealed himself to his people in love and grace, the covenant-making and covenant-keeping God who had chosen Israel so that through them he might make himself known to the world.

Beginning or "chief part": The word *rē'shîth* means both the "beginning," "starting point" (Gen. 1:1), and the "chief part," "choice part" (Jer. 49:35; Amos 6:6). The reverence of the Lord is therefore not only the starting point of all knowledge but its chief part. This same idea is expressed in 9:10; Job 28:28; Ps. 111:10; also in Ecclus. 1:14; cf. Pirke Aboth 3:26 (C. Taylor). **Fools:** The root idea of *'ewîl* is "thickness," "dullness." As despisers of wisdom, fools live without taking God into account and so become morally corrupt. This is one of the worst types of fools in wisdom literature.

---

to add to a list of fears that is already too long. Perhaps if we feared God more we would fear everything else less. We can rightly fear the consequences of violating the physical and moral laws through which the creative power of God works. There is something to fear in our flouting of the basic structure of the universe. The foundation of wisdom lies in knowing what we ought to fear. Reverence for the Lord includes an awed regard for the power of God and a sober recognition of the consequences of trying to violate the laws which he has ordained.

Reverence for the Lord is more than a craven bowing before power and mystery.

> Reverence is the response of the soul in the presence of that which has not only power but worth. It is the soul's attitude toward that God in whom goodness and power are one. It is stirred in man whenever he finds those values which he counts as holy, to whose acknowledged claim all else must yield.[3]

Reverence for the Lord is a recognition of man's creaturehood. This is man's way of saying that he knows he is not the creator of this universe, nor is he the sustainer of his own life. Man is dependent upon one greater than himself, and it is the very foundation of wisdom to recognize this fact.

Reverence for the Lord is the highest use of thought. A man may think that he thinks, just because he uses his reason to justify some of the things he wants to do. He must use thought to achieve these ends. But the man who is truly thoughtful recognizes that there is some power greater than himself. This is the basis upon which his life and his knowledge are built. In *Sartor Resartus,* Thomas Carlyle wrote:

> The man who cannot wonder, who does not habitually wonder (and worship), were he President of innumerable Royal Societies, and carried the whole of *Mécanique Céleste* and *Hegel's Philosophy,* and the epitome of all Laboratories and Observatories with their results, in his single head,—is but a Pair of Spectacles behind which there is no Eye.[4]

Reverence for the Lord can be a motive for thought and action. It is the base line from which the religious man proceeds. One needs only to contrast the preamble of another man's life to see the importance of reverence for God as a motive for living. In one of his parables Jesus told the story of a judge "who neither feared God nor regarded man" (Luke 18:2). A man who built his life upon this outlook would be motivated to act quite differently from the man who made reverence for God the foundation upon which he built his thinking and his acting.

Reverence for the Lord means taking God into account. Some people do not despise God —they simply act as if he did not exist. Theirs is the irreverence of thoughtlessness. "I do not know, Sir," said Samuel Johnson in a comment about another man, "that the fellow is an infidel; but if he be an infidel, he is an infidel as a dog is an infidel; that is to say, he has never thought upon the subject." [5] The second part of the verse rightly says that only **fools despise wisdom and instruction**—the kind of wisdom that makes reverence for the Lord the beginning of knowledge.

[3] Harris Franklin Rall, *Christianity* (New York: Charles Scribner's Sons, 1940), p. 11.

[4] Bk. I, ch. x.

[5] James Boswell, *The Life of Samuel Johnson* (New York: E. P. Dutton & Co., 1906; "Everyman's Library), I, 370.

8 My son, hear the instruction of thy father, and forsake not the law of thy mother:
9 For they *shall be* an ornament of grace unto thy head, and chains about thy neck.

8 Hear, my son, your father's instruction,
and reject not your mother's teaching;
9 for they are a fair garland for your head,
and pendants for your neck.

D. Exhortation and Warning (1:8-19)

1. Exhortation to Listen to Instruction (1:8-9)

8. Synonymous. Vs. 8*b*=6:20*b*. The instruction of the wise man was usually oral, and so the exhortation is given to **hear.** According to Hebrew psychology, action was the natural outcome of hearing, and so the verb "to hear" can often be translated "to obey." **My son:** A form of address common to the wisdom literature of both Babylonia and Egypt (see Intro., p. 767). It is found frequently in chs. 1–9. It reflects a rather formal system of education where the teacher imparts his knowledge to the students gathered around him. **Thy father:** The father had the main place in instruction (Deut. 6:6-7; Exod. 12:26 ff.). Wisdom came first from the parents who stood in the place of God for the children. The wise simply carried on the work started by the parents. **Forsake:** Better, **reject** (RSV). **Law:** Rather, **teaching** (RSV), a more accurate rendering of the Hebrew *tôrāh,* which should be so translated wherever found in Proverbs, except in 28:4, 9; 29:18, where it probably refers to the Law or Pentateuch. The legalistic meaning, **law,** represents only one aspect of the word *tôrāh.* **Thy mother:** Proverbs has more to say about respect and love for **mother** than any other book of the Bible. In many instances her claim to consideration is equal with the father's **instruction** (see Exeg. on 31:10-31).

9. Synonymous. Instruction and discipline are not to be looked upon as a burden or shame, but rather as a beautiful adornment. **Ornament of grace** or **fair garland:** A good idiomatic translation of the Hebrew (hendiadys; see Exeg. on vs. 3).

8-9. ***Homemade Religion.***—Life begins at home. Wisdom also, according to this writer, should begin at home. From his father and mother a young man is to learn wisdom that will be as an ornament and a guide for his life.

The home is the primary and most important factor in the education of a young person. The church and the school have a part in bringing him the knowledge he needs and in cultivating the attitudes that will help him to make the most of his life. But the home is supremely important, since it has the child in the formative years, and since a large proportion of the individual's time is spent at home.

A father's instruction is important. A son is summoned to have a high regard for his advice and training. The father is the living link between the wisdom of yesterday and the needs of a youth today. The father has been a son, while the son has not yet been a father. When the father was a son, he learned from his own father, and he is now in a position to see the matter from the viewpoint of both a son and a father. The son has not passed this way before. He is entering new territory. He might learn the hard way, by the costly method of trial and error. The father has passed through the kinds of experiences that the son still must face. A wise son is one who is willing to listen to the father who has walked the way ahead of him.

A mother is here regarded as a second source of wisdom. Proverbs pays high tribute to mothers. Their instruction may be less stern than that of a father, but it may provide the climate of love and affection in which the best attributes can grow. That man is fortunate who has a mother who provides the emotional security which is needed by everyone. He who is sure of his mother's love has a great asset to sustain him during the trying times in his life. In the United States it is the custom to observe the second Sunday in May as Mother's Day. This affords a time for all children to express their appreciation to their mothers and to acknowledge their indebtedness to them. The custom began when Miss Anne Jarvis, whose mother died in 1906, invited several friends to her home in Philadelphia on the first anniversary of her mother's death to honor her memory. This was followed by a movement for the setting apart of a day for the remembrance of all mothers. In 1914 the Congress of the United States gave this day national sanction. But the writer of this proverb would hardly be content to have a child heed his mother's instruction on only one day of the year. Homemade wisdom is not limited

10 ¶ My son, if sinners entice thee, consent thou not.
11 If they say, Come with us, let us lay wait for blood, let us lurk privily for the innocent without cause:
12 Let us swallow them up alive as the grave; and whole, as those that go down into the pit:

10 My son, if sinners entice you,
do not consent.
11 If they say, "Come with us, let us lie in
wait for blood,
let us wantonly ambush the innocent;
12 like Sheol let us swallow them alive
and whole, like those who go down to
the Pit;

2. Warning Against Associating with Robbers and Murderers (1:10-19)

10. The conditions described in this section reveal a lawless state of society. It is difficult to determine whether they belong to the time of the Persian and Greek rule, as Toy and Oesterley believe, or to the pre-exilic period, as Wildeboer holds. Certainly bands of robbers like these were active in the days of Hosea (Hos. 6:9; 7:1). The fact that this evil condition is treated first in the book shows how serious the problem was at the time. **Entice:** The root is connected with the word for "simple" in vs. 4. **Sinners:** The original meaning of the Hebrew word *ḥaṭṭā'* is "one who misses the mark." It is the exact equivalent of the idea expressed by the Greek word ἁμαρτάνω. The form of the noun used here denotes the professional sinner.

11. Triplet. Bloodshed and murder seem to have been the usual accompaniments of robbery. As Toy points out, "Ancient cities were badly lighted at night, and not usually well policed" (*Proverbs*, p. 15). **For blood:** Amer. Trans. renders "for the honest," reading *tām* for *dām*. Many scholars favor this correction, for it preserves the parallelism with **the innocent** in the next clause. However, the Hebrew text as it stands makes good sense. **Without cause** or **wantonly:** The adverb goes with the verb, i.e., as the writer reflects, he notes that the robbers wait to pounce upon their victim even though he has done them no harm.

12. Synonymous. **As the grave** or **like Sheol:** *She'ôl* in the O.T. is the dismal place of departed spirits, both good and bad, where there is no fellowship with God. The proverb means that these bandits destroy their innocent and healthy victims as ruthlessly as death. **Whole:** The Hebrew word *tāmîm* means either physically whole or morally

to one time or to one celebration. Growth in wisdom is something that a filial attitude on the part of a child can assure from day to day, and we therefore pay tribute to the book of Proverbs that elevated mothers to a high position as a daily source of wise living.

10-19. ***Crime Does Not Pay.***—A young man will be invited from time to time to join other people in a common enterprise. This is natural, since he longs for company, and since there are many things that can be accomplished only through common effort. The warning is here sounded against a young man's joining a kind of shared enterprise that is ruthless.

My son, if sinners entice you,
do not consent.

These particular sinners are organized bands of robbers who stop at no form of violence to gain their ends.

According to the wise man, these bandits issue a brazen invitation to a young man. They do not cover up their evil purposes. They commend their cause to him without shame, saying that they **lie in wait for blood** and **wantonly ambush the innocent.** In their minds there seems to be no reason to question the methods they are using.

Perhaps if the bandits themselves were given a chance to speak, they would make a different case for themselves. They would not issue such a shameless summons, but would rather try to give some laudable reasons for entering their adventurous company. At this stage in human history it may not have been necessary to sugarcoat the vocation of bandit. They did not need the hypocrisy that La Rochefoucauld called the "homage vice pays to virtue." [6] Possibly bandits at that time would have recruited members for their robber band in this shameless fashion, but it is safe to say that clever perpetrators of crime today would find some more respectable reasons for their profession than those given above.

One thing is obvious: the chief basis of their appeal to the young man is profit. If he joins

[6] Maxim 218.

13 We shall find all precious substance, we shall fill our houses with spoil:
14 Cast in thy lot among us; let us all have one purse:
15 My son, walk not thou in the way with them; refrain thy foot from their path:
16 For their feet run to evil, and make haste to shed blood.
17 Surely in vain the net is spread in the sight of any bird.
18 And they lay wait for their *own* blood; they lurk privily for their *own* lives.
19 So *are* the ways of every one that is greedy of gain; *which* taketh away the life of the owners thereof.

13 we shall find all precious goods,
we shall fill our houses with spoil;
14 throw in your lot among us,
we will all have one purse"—
15 my son, do not walk in the way with them,
hold back your foot from their paths;
16 for their feet run to evil,
and they make haste to shed blood.
17 For in vain is a net spread
in the sight of any bird;
18 but these men lie in wait for their own blood,
they set an ambush for their own lives.
19 Such are the ways of all who get gain by violence;
it takes away the life of its possessors.

---

perfect. Here, in parallelism with **alive** in the preceding clause, it probably has the former sense. **The Pit:** A synonym of Sheol. From Isa. 14:15; Ezek. 32:23, 25, 28-30 it appears as though **the Pit** were a separate place in Sheol, reserved for the Lord's special enemies.

13. Synonymous. The booty is to be hidden in the **houses** of the robbers, showing that they were city dwellers.

14. Synonymous. **Thy lot:** Originally something cast in order to ascertain the will of the deity; then that which was assigned by the deity in the decision; and finally, one's portion in life, whether good or bad. The inducement here offered to the novice is to become one with the robbers and draw equal shares from the common purse, thus avoiding the probability of small returns if he were left to fend for himself.

15. Synonymous. This verse is the main part of the sentence beginning at vs. 11. **If they say, . . . My son, walk not thou.**

16. Synonymous. Identical with Isa. 59:7*a,* which adds "innocent" at the end (see also Rom. 3:15). The subject of the verb in vs. 16*b* can be either **feet** or **they.**

17. A difficult verse. The Amer. Trans. renders, "As the net is baited in vain in the eyes of any bird." The difficult word is *meᵉzôrāh,* **spread,** "baited." The root *zārāh,* from which it is usually derived, means "to scatter," "to winnow," and is used only here in the sense of "to spread a net." It was evidently from Rashi that the idea of spreading food in the net as bait was derived, since he translated the verse, "In vain is [grain] scattered [on] the net." The Amer. Trans. seems to follow this interpretation. The KJV and the RSV interpret it to mean that unlike birds which do not let themselves be caught when a net is spread before their very eyes, these sinners go to their destruction blindly.

18. Synonymous. These men continue in their crimes even though they are actually bringing about their own destruction.

19. This is the fate of everyone who is **greedy of gain.** This is the way the law of retribution works, a common theme in wisdom literature. Here *béçaʿ* has the sense of

---

them, he will **find all precious goods** and will fill his house **with spoil.** There will be loot enough for all. So he is invited to become one of them, since they **will all have one purse.** The method by which they get the profit may not be altogether to his taste, but the results should be attractive enough for him not to question the means too much. Joining a robber band was a way to some easy money.

How does the wise man deal with this situation? He warns the young man from joining a robber band on the one hand because **their feet run to evil, and they make haste to shed blood.** The means they use are immoral means. They do not regard the rights of other people, nor are they good members of the community. That is one reason why one should resist the invitation when it comes. But the chief reason

20 ¶ Wisdom crieth without; she uttereth her voice in the streets:
21 She crieth in the chief place of concourse, in the openings of the gates: in the city she uttereth her words, *saying*,
22 How long, ye simple ones, will ye love simplicity? and the scorners delight in their scorning, and fools hate knowledge?

20 Wisdom cries aloud in the street;
in the markets she raises her voice;
21 on the top of the walls[a] she cries out;
at the entrance of the city gates she speaks:
22 "How long, O simple ones, will you love being simple?
How long will scoffers delight in their scoffing
and fools hate knowledge?

[a] Heb uncertain

unjust **gain.** It has the simple sense of "profit" in Gen. 37:26; Mal. 3:14; Job 22:3. The subject of **takes** is the unjust **gain** of the preceding clause.

E. Wisdom Publicly Proclaims a Warning Against Neglecting Her Appeal (1:20-33)

In this section wisdom is personified (cf. 3:15-19; 8:1-36; 9:1-6; Ecclus. 1:1-10; 24:1-34; and see Intro., pp. 773-74). She cries aloud to the foolish ones in the noisy streets and the broad places, pleading with them to turn to her. But they do not heed her cry. The dire consequences of this refusal are plainly set forth, with the last verse describing the blessings of those who hearken.

20. Synonymous. **Wisdom:** The Hebrew form *ḥokhmôth,* found here and in 9:1; 14:1; 24:7; Ps. 49:4 (Heb.), is probably not a feminine plural but an abstract singular, corresponding to the Phoenician form of the word. **Cries:** A word used to describe the intensity of feeling, whether of joy (Lev. 9:24; Isa. 12:6; Job 38:7), sorrow (Lam. 2:19), or general excitement (Ps. 78:65). **Cries aloud** therefore expresses the meaning of the word more accurately. **Without:** RSV, **in the street,** gives a better translation since it stands in parallelism with **in the markets** (lit., "wide places") in the next clause. Wisdom is regarded in this and the following verse less as a teacher than as a preacher proclaiming her message in the busy marts of life. Her words of doom which follow from vs. 23 on remind one of the messages of doom which fell from the prophets' lips. In this passage, as well as in 8:1-4 and 9:1-6, wisdom is using the evangelistic method of appeal to the crowds, an approach quite different from her usual method of counseling with the individual.

21. Synonymous. **Chief place of concourse** or **on the top of the walls** (following the Greek): The ASV mg. renders, "At the head of the noisy streets." The Hebrew word *hōmiyyôth,* which is uncertain, has the root idea of "to murmur," "to be boisterous" (cf. Isa. 17:12; 22:2; 51:15; Jer. 5:22; 6:23; 31:35; 50:42), from which certain of the translations given above are derived. Toy favors the Greek rendering here with the RSV. **In the openings of the gates:** This was the center of public life in the Oriental city. Here the prophets prophesied (I Kings 22:10), legal transactions were made (Ruth 4:1), and the wise men proclaimed their teachings.

22. Triplet. The message of wisdom begins with a question, "How long will you

seems to be that the profit promised is never realized. The wise man combats the robbers on their own ground. They invite a young man to join them because he will get much profit from the affiliation. The sage warns the young man that he will lose by the deal. In the long run he will not gain anything. Joining a band of violent men who exploit other people is not even intelligent selfishness. Crime does not pay. Robbers are really robbing themselves. They are doing violence to themselves. They might be partners in getting the loot, but they soon fall apart when the time comes to divide it. Profit becomes loss in the end. Banditry is not successful even as a method of gain. It is self-defeating. So both from a moral and a prudential motive a young man is warned against following a life of crime.

20-33. *Threats and Promises.*—Like a town crier awakening a slumbering populace with an

23 Turn you at my reproof: behold, I will pour out my spirit unto you, I will make known my words unto you.

24 ¶ Because I have called, and ye refused; I have stretched out my hand, and no man regarded;

25 But ye have set at nought all my counsel, and would none of my reproof:

23 Give heed[b] to my reproof;
behold, I will pour out my thoughts[c] to you;
I will make my words known to you.
24 Because I have called and you refused to listen,
have stretched out my hand and no one has heeded,
25 and you have ignored all my counsel
and would have none of my reproof,

[b] Heb *Turn*
[c] Heb *spirit*

---

persist in your foolishness?" The three types of fools mentioned here are the simple one (*pethî*), i.e., the inexperienced simpleton, the scoffer or scorner (*lēç*), i.e., the contemptuous, arrogant one who turns his back on the good, and the fool (*keṣîl*), i.e., the thick, dull person who is insensible, even averse, to moral truth. There are only two other types of fools mentioned in Proverbs, viz., the *'ewîl,* also a thick, dull person, who, if anything, is worse than the *keṣîl,* and the *nābhāl,* found only in 17:7, 21; 30:22, who is a shameless, contemptuous fellow, devoid of any intellectual and religious insight.

23. Triplet. **Turn you:** The Hebrew form of the verb is not an imperative but an imperfect tense, and yet an imperative gives the best meaning. The Syriac, followed by Amer. Trans., has a conditional clause, "If you but turn," but that confuses the issue still more, since vs. 24 assumes that they did not turn. **Reproof:** Admonition, "exhortation tinged with imputation of blameworthiness" (Toy, *Proverbs,* p. 24).

I will pour out my spirit or **my thoughts:** The verb translated **pour out** means, lit., "cause to bubble forth" (*nābha'*), and is used to express the idea of speaking. **Spirit,** which means the inward life or being, must refer to the "mind" or "intention" in this context. In parallelism with the last clause of the verse this second clause corresponds to our idiom, "to speak one's mind." **My words:** Wisdom is here considered the source of the words of salvation for men. They flow forth from her like waters from a spring (cf. John 7:37-39).

24. Synonymous. Wisdom holds in derision those who do not heed her call. The abrupt transition from the gracious invitation in vss. 20-23 to the direful denunciation in this and the following verses is striking. **Stretched out my hand:** She holds forth her hand in order to beckon the people to her. It is a gesture of appeal. Wisdom uses every means to bring people to her, but they refuse to come.

25. Synonymous. **Set at nought** or better, **ignored:** The root idea of the verb *pāra'*

---

urgent message, a personified wisdom is here calling people from ways of simpleness and folly. Wisdom is not dwelling in some ivory tower. She speaks through the very stones of the street. For the young man who has ears to hear, every street corner is vocal with evidence that folly produces death and wisdom yields life.

Wisdom uses every device to awaken people from their lethargy and from following mistaken ways. She threatens. She laughs. She warns. Wisdom is like a dog showing his teeth. Every incentive is appealed to, but in this passage there is strongest emphasis upon the undesirable consequences that follow unwise living. Wisdom is using every effort to tell the truth about consequences. She is urging men to realize the consequences of their wrong acts before they are committed. In a vivid but unappealing picture she portrays herself as gloating over the discomfitures of those who have refused to heed her call. She does not laugh with them—she laughs at them. One can almost hear her say, "I told you so," with no word of comfort or healing. It would seem that there will be rejoicing in wisdom's heaven over every sinner that tastes the bitter fruit of his sin.

Perhaps this is all a method of seeking to awaken a sinner to his evil ways before he follows them. Felix Adler once wrote that "it is characteristic of sin that the fuller knowledge that the harmful deed is sinful *comes after the act.*" [7] Foolish people have to learn the hard way. They have to experience the painful results that come from wrongdoing. Regan describes

[7] *An Ethical Philosophy of Life* (New York: D. Appleton & Co., 1918), p. 172.

26 I also will laugh at your calamity; I
will mock when your fear cometh;
27 When your fear cometh as desolation,
and your destruction cometh as a whirlwind; when distress and anguish cometh
upon you.
28 Then shall they call upon me, but I
will not answer; they shall seek me early,
but they shall not find me:
29 For that they hated knowledge, and
did not choose the fear of the LORD:

26 I also will laugh at your calamity;
I will mock when panic strikes you,
27 when panic strikes you like a storm,
and your calamity comes like a whirlwind,
when distress and anguish come upon
you.
28 Then they will call upon me, but I will
not answer;
they will seek me diligently but will
not find me.
29 Because they hated knowledge
and did not choose the fear of the LORD,

---

is "to let loose" (cf. Exod. 32:25) ; then "to let go free," and so "to neglect," "to avoid," "to ignore." **Reproof:** See Exeg. on vs. 23.

26. Synonymous. Wisdom in turn has her laugh when misfortune befalls those who have disregarded her warnings. **At your calamity:** Better, "in your calamity," with Toy, Wildeboer, and Frankenberg, since it agrees with the designation of time in the next clause. **Mock:** A stronger word than **laugh** of the preceding clause, since it implies utterance. **Fear:** Better, **panic,** since *páḥadh* means "sudden terror." The **panic** results from events which strike fear into the heart. When those who disregard wisdom feel most secure in their own strength, calamity strikes and brings them to ruin. This is a most unappealing picture of wisdom as she gloats over the misfortune of her disdainers. Yet it is not unlike the psalmist and the prophet who likewise exult over the downfall of the sinner.

27. Triplet. **Desolation:** Better, **storm,** because of the parallel word **whirlwind** in the next clause. The reference to storms emphasizes the suddenness with which the calamity comes, as well as its devastating power. **Distress and anguish:** This translation keeps somewhat the assonance of the two Hebrew words *çārāh weçûqāh.* The misfortunes described in vss. 26-27 are physical calamities; they occur in this life (cf. vs. 33) .

28. Synonymous. The fools of vs. 22, whose indifference to wisdom's beck and call brought on calamity, call for her aid in their time of trouble, but are not heard. **Seek me early** or **seek me diligently:** Both of these translations are based on the derivation of the verbal form from a noun meaning "morning," therefore, "to seek early." The adverb in both translations probably should be deleted since, according to the parallelism, "to seek" corresponds more closely with "to call." Although these fools know enough to call upon wisdom in their predicament, they are not delivered. They had refused her pleas earlier; now she is deaf to their cries. They have had ample opportunity to turn to her; now that disaster has come, it is too late.

29-30. Synonymous. The verbs **hated, did not choose, would have none, despised,** are synonymous, revealing the antagonistic attitude of the fools to wisdom and her counsel. The **counsel** of wisdom, or the wise men, is equivalent to the law of the priest and the word of the prophet (cf. Jer. 18:18, "Then said they, Come, and let us devise devices

---

these people to Gloucester in Shakespeare's *King Lear:*

> O, sir, to wilful men
> The injuries that they themselves procure
> Must be their schoolmasters.[8]

There is no gainsaying the fact that foolish living has many unpleasant consequences. Many of these consequences cannot be changed. The drunken driver who kills a child cannot change the fact that the child is dead. The man who in anger kills another man may deeply rue the deed, but he cannot alter the fact that it has happened. That is the truth about consequences: many of them are irrevocable. The Christian gospel has a message even in that hour. It does not picture God as gloating over the sinner who suffers. There is rejoicing over the one who repents, and while there are conse-

[8] Act II, scene 4.

30 They would none of my counsel: they despised all my reproof.

31 Therefore shall they eat of the fruit of their own way, and be filled with their own devices.

32 For the turning away of the simple shall slay them, and the prosperity of fools shall destroy them.

33 But whoso hearkeneth unto me shall dwell safely, and shall be quiet from fear of evil.

2 My son, if thou wilt receive my words, and hide my commandments with thee;

30 would have none of my counsel,
and despised all my reproof,
31 therefore they shall eat the fruit of their way
and be sated with their own devices.
32 For the simple are killed by their turning away,
and the complacence of fools destroys them;
33 but he who listens to me will dwell secure
and will be at ease, without dread of evil."

2 My son, if you receive my words
and treasure up my commandments with you,

---

against Jeremiah; for the law shall not perish from the priest, nor counsel from the wise, nor the word from the prophet").

31. Synonymous. This is God's law of retribution (cf. Gal. 6:7-8). The ways and devices of men are here contrasted with wisdom's counsel and reproof in the preceding verse. **Devices:** Except in 22:20, *mô'ēçāh* is used in a bad sense in the O.T.

32. Synonymous. The punishment is death, presumably an early one, the usual view of retributive punishment in Proverbs. **Turning away:** *Meshûbhāh* is always used in a bad sense in the O.T. Here it refers to the turning away from wisdom and her instruction, which of course leads to an untimely and usually violent death. **Simple:** See Exeg. on vs. 4. **Prosperity** or, better, **complacence:** The root idea is "quietness," "ease," and then "careless security." This is another sign of the foolish man's forgetfulness of God and his laws, which ultimately leads to destruction. **Fools** (*keṣîl*): In this verse, which is a résumé of the section, only two kinds of fools are mentioned, whereas vs. 22, which stands near the head of the section, mentions three kinds.

33. Synonymous. The chapter ends on a happy note. The one who heeds wisdom's call and obeys her teachings will dwell securely, i.e., free from any outward danger. **Evil** refers to external misfortune. Inward peace and security in Proverbs are synonymous with freedom from outward dangers and calamities (cf. vs. 27).

F. Benefits of Heeding Wisdom (2:1-22)

This chapter is an independent poem, really one periodic sentence, divided into six parts. The protasis (vss. 1-4), an appeal to heed wisdom, is followed by a long apodosis which describes the fivefold blessing of wisdom: with her comes the only true knowledge of God (vss. 5-8), life is ordered by wisdom (vss. 9-11), which protects from evil men (vss. 12-15) and evil women (vss. 16-19), and blesses those who walk in her ways (vss. 20-22). In this chapter the teacher, not wisdom, is speaking to the student.

2:1. Synonymous. Similar to 7:1. **My son:** See Exeg. on 1:8. **My words:** The wise man

---

quences that are unalterable, there is still hope for the person who repents and changes his ways. He hears a word of forgiveness and the command, "Go, and sin no more" (John 8:11).

Wisdom seems here to have no assurance for the one who has departed from her ways, but she does hold out the promise that

he who listens to me will dwell secure
and will be at ease, without dread of evil.

2:1-22. *Two Prerequisites for Wisdom.*—Although wisdom is considered a gift from God—**for the Lord gives wisdom** (vs. 6)—it cannot be given to those who do not know how to receive it. There are some things that require a proper attitude on the part of those who are to receive them if the transfer is to be made. A parent would find it difficult to give a boy an education if the lad did not have the desire to be educated.

2 So that thou incline thine ear unto wisdom, *and* apply thine heart to understanding;
3 Yea, if thou criest after knowledge, *and* liftest up thy voice for understanding;
4 If thou seekest her as silver, and searchest for her as *for* hid treasures;
5 Then shalt thou understand the fear of the LORD, and find the knowledge of God.

2 making your ear attentive to wisdom
and inclining your heart to understanding;
3 yes, if you cry out for insight
and raise your voice for understanding,
4 if you seek it like silver
and search for it as for hidden treasures;
5 then you will understand the fear of the LORD
and find the knowledge of God.

---

speaks in his own name and on his own authority, unlike the prophet who says, "Thus saith the LORD." **My commandments:** Not the precepts of the law, to which *miçwôth* usually refers, but the body of teaching which came forth from the wisdom schools. **Hide:** Better, **treasure up** (*çāphan*), as something to be valued (cf. 10:14).

2. Synonymous. A further elucidation of vs. 1, i.e., if one takes wisdom's word seriously by **making . . .** and **inclining. . . .** Every faculty must be employed in the earnest search for wisdom: the **ear** is to hear the words of wisdom; the **heart,** i.e., the mind, is to be applied to the **understanding** of what is heard, and with the voice inquiry is to be made continually for true knowledge. **Heart:** In the O.T. *lēbh* (*lēbhābh*) is the seat of various emotions (cf. 12:25; 13:12; 14:10, 13; 15:13; 19:3); but it figures most prominently as the instrument of man's intellectual and volitional activity, as in this verse and many others. **Understanding** (*tebhûnāh*): Related to the *bînāh* of 1:2 (see Exeg.).

3. Synonymous. A continuation of the protasis.

4. Synonymous. Not only is wisdom **hidden** like some treasure which is put in the ground for safekeeping (Jer. 41:8; Matt. 13:44), but it is extricated with great effort (Job 28:1-11). It must be sought for with diligence, like the kingdom of God, for it is the most important object in life. The things of God are not easily attained. Only by constant meditation on the words of divine wisdom and by rigid discipline can one experience true joy and peace. **Silver:** The "ore" is probably meant here, emphasizing the idea of effort to get it, rather than "money," which would indicate the value set upon it. In each of these four verses the second half is a more emphatic repetition of the first: **receive, treasure up;** [make] **attentive, incline; cry out, raise your voice; seek, search.**

5. Synonymous. The beginning of the apodosis which extends to the end of the chapter. The success of the quest of wisdom is assured by the various benefits or rewards that come with her possession. Most important of all is the fact that when one seeks wisdom he finds God. This is natural, since God is wisdom. There is no other wisdom than that which is with him, and it can come from no other source than from him. He com-

---

One prerequisite for wisdom is a receptive spirit. A person may close his ears to words of wisdom. He may not want to hear what a teacher has to say. He may feel a self-sufficiency that displays itself in a lack of interest in learning anything more. A receptive and teachable spirit is necessary if a person is to gain the desired boon of wisdom.

> **My son, if you receive my words, . . .**
> **making your ear attentive to wisdom, . . .**
> **then you will understand** (vss. 1-2, 5).

It was said of Henry Ford that whenever he heard people criticize the automobile he was making, he listened carefully and jotted down the criticism in his notebook. He was ready to hear, and thus he opened the way to further development in his work. "Let him who has ears listen!" (Matt. 11:15 Goodspeed.)

A second prerequisite for wisdom goes beyond receptivity. An ardent search is necessary if one is to achieve wisdom. Much stronger words are used here. The man who wants wisdom must **cry out for insight,** he must

> **seek it like silver**
> **and search for it as for hidden treasures** (vss. 3-4).

In the previous chapter wisdom is depicted as crying out to the people to listen. Here it is pointed out that the person who wants wisdom

6 For the LORD giveth wisdom: out of his mouth *cometh* knowledge and understanding.

7 He layeth up sound wisdom for the righteous: *he is* a buckler to them that walk uprightly.

8 He keepeth the paths of judgment, and preserveth the way of his saints.

9 Then shalt thou understand righteousness, and judgment, and equity; *yea,* every good path.

6 For the LORD gives wisdom;
from his mouth come knowledge and understanding;
7 he stores up sound wisdom for the upright;
he is a shield to those who walk in integrity,
8 guarding the paths of justice
and preserving the way of his saints.
9 Then you will understand righteousness and justice
and equity, every good path;

---

municates it through the word of his mouth. **The fear of the LORD** is equated with **the knowledge of God,** although they are not identical. As **the fear of the LORD** is "the beginning of knowledge" (1:7), so it is the goal of man's search for wisdom. It is the most important blessing that wisdom can bestow, as its position at the head of the list implies. **Knowledge:** *Dá'ath* is not just intellectual cognition, as the parallelism indicates. True learning has to do with religion and ethics as well as with secular matters.

6. Synonymous. The Lord is the source of wisdom, an idea which is similar to the teaching of the prophets. Only here in Proverbs is God the teacher, not wisdom. **Out of his mouth:** A strong anthropomorphic expression, found only here in Proverbs. The LXX reads "from his face," i.e., his presence.

7. Synonymous. The search for wisdom cannot be fruitless, since he who has hidden it will also reveal it. **Stores up:** The same verb as in 2:1*b*. **Righteous** or, better, **upright:** See Exeg. on 1:3. **Sound wisdom** ("help" Amer. Trans): *Tûshîyyāh* is a technical wisdom literature word, found outside of Job and Proverbs only in Isa. 28:29; Mic. 6:9. Its original meaning is difficult to ascertain as the variety of translations indicates. The translation "help" or "deliverance" (Toy) is derived from the parallelism in this verse. From the context either the Lord or sound wisdom could be the **shield.** It is probably the Lord since that metaphor is common in scripture (Gen. 15:1; Pss. 59:11; 84:11). **Uprightly** or, better, **in integrity:** *Tōm* means "completeness," "perfection," and refers here to right conduct.

8. Synonymous. **Paths of judgment** or **paths of justice:** For **justice** (*mishpāṭ*) see Exeg. on 1:3. The full meaning of the phrase must be that the Lord will guard the paths of those who do justly. **Saints:** The word *ḥaṣîdhîm* is more accurately rendered by "pious ones," since it denotes those who show a steadfast love toward God. In Maccabean times the Hasidim were the legalists of Judaism who opposed the Hellenizing influences which were corrupting the Jews. They were the precursors of the Pharisees. This is the only time the word occurs in Proverbs, although it occurs frequently in the Psalms. Its presence here does not necessarily reflect a late date for the passage.

9. Another reward for heeding wisdom is a successful and happy life in every realm (vss. 9-11). The three nouns, **righteousness, judgment,** and **equity,** occur in the same

---

must cry out for it. One cry meets another. He who ardently searches for wisdom will find it. The miner who wants the silver does not get it by indulging in a passing wish. He must dig for it. He must work hard to get it. "There is . . . in these matters some absolute finding in the seeking," says W. E. Hocking.[9] When once a person wants wisdom enough to cry out for it and to work for it, he will find it. The task is to make him want it, and to make him want it with sufficient ardor that he will pay the price to get it. The achievement of wisdom requires that a person shall be "rich in desire, rich in thirst" for it.

9-22. ***The Company We Keep.***—The teacher in this passage is saying that wisdom helps a man to stay out of bad company and to get into good company. There is both a negative and a positive value here.

Through wisdom a man is delivered from the

[9] *The Meaning of God in Human Experience* (New Haven: Yale University Press, 1912), p. 198.

10 ¶ When wisdom entereth into thine heart, and knowledge is pleasant unto thy soul;

11 Discretion shall preserve thee, understanding shall keep thee:

12 To deliver thee from the way of the evil *man,* from the man that speaketh froward things;

13 Who leave the paths of uprightness, to walk in the ways of darkness;

14 Who rejoice to do evil, *and* delight in the frowardness of the wicked;

15 Whose ways *are* crooked, and *they* froward in their paths:

10 for wisdom will come into your heart,
and knowledge will be pleasant to your soul;
11 discretion will watch over you;
understanding will guard you;
12 delivering you from the way of evil,
from men of perverted speech,
13 who forsake the paths of uprightness
to walk in the ways of darkness,
14 who rejoice in doing evil
and delight in the perverseness of evil;
15 men whose paths are crooked,
and who are devious in their ways.

---

order in 1:3 (see Exeg.). Vs. 9*b* has no verb, which makes for an uneven parallelism with vs. 9*a*. Perhaps the first word *mêshārîm* (**equity**) should be read *tishmōr,* "and thou shalt keep every path of goodness."

10. Synonymous. Wisdom and knowledge enter the heart and bring pleasantness. They are not forced on a man by any external pressure. When he sees the advantages that come to him from a well-regulated life, he willingly accepts the words of wisdom as his guide. **Be pleasant:** The verbal root נעם gave the name Naomi (cf. Ruth 1:20).

11. Synonymous. **Discretion** (see Exeg. on 1:4) and **understanding**—manifestations of wisdom—guard those in whom they dwell.

12. Synonymous. The third benefit derived from following wisdom is protection from perverse and cruel men (vss. 12-15). The two most alluring temptations of the day seem to have been to join up with evil men, especially the highway robber and murderer (as described in 1:10-19), and to associate with lewd women. The wise man who puts his trust in God will not fall into these temptations, which always lead to calamity and destruction. **Evil man** or **evil:** From the context the KJV appears to offer the better translation. The Hebrew has simply *rā'*. **Froward things,** or, better, **perverted speech:** The root of the noun *tahpukhôth* contains the idea of "turning," "overturning," and so the noun really means "that which is turned upside down."

13. Antithetic. A description of the way of wicked men. The path of **uprightness** is illumined, but the path of wickedness is shrouded in **darkness** (cf. Ps. 82:5).

14. Synonymous. Wicked men not only choose evil ways, but they actually take pleasure in them. **Frowardness** or **perverseness:** See Exeg. on vs. 12. **The wicked** or **evil:** See Exeg. on vs. 12. Perhaps the word should be deleted here. It may have come into the text through dittography from the preceding stich.

15. Synonymous. A further description of evil men: they depart from the straight path. There is a problem in the Hebrew as to whether **ways** or **men** is the subject of the sentence. The KJV, following most of the versions, inclines to the former view; the

---

company of evil men on the one hand and from loose women on the other. There come times when a person must bid farewell to company he is keeping, since he is being influenced by them more than he is able to influence them. He is a wise man who will not be closely allied with

> **men of perverted speech,**
> **who forsake the paths of uprightness**
> **to walk in the ways of darkness.**

Wisdom helps people to shun the evil company of men and women who make others over in their own likeness.

More important is it that wisdom helps people to find good company,

> **So you will walk in the way of good men**
> **and keep to the paths of the righteous.**

This is good counsel. A person may be warned about getting into bad company without being led into good company. An individual craves companionship, and if he is not given good companions he will naturally gravitate elsewhere. The famous sermon by Thomas Chalmers, "The Expulsive Power of a New Affection," called attention to the fact that evil can

16 To deliver thee from the strange women, *even* from the stranger *which* flattereth with her words;

17 Which forsaketh the guide of her youth, and forgetteth the covenant of her God.

18 For her house inclineth unto death, and her paths unto the dead.

19 None that go unto her return again, neither take they hold of the paths of life.

16 You will be saved from the loose[d] woman,
from the adventuress[e] with her smooth words,
17 who forsakes the companion of her youth
and forgets the covenant of her God;
18 for her house sinks down to death,
and her paths to the shades;
19 none who go to her come back
nor do they regain the paths of life.

[d] Heb *strange*
[e] Heb *foreign woman*

RSV, the ASV, and most commentators hold the latter. **Crooked** (*ʽiqqēsh*): Used in the O.T. only in the ethical sense, as is also the next word. **Froward** or, better, **devious:** From the root *lûz,* "to turn aside," and so "to turn aside into the wrong path." It is found only in the wisdom literature, except in Isa. 30:12.

16. Synonymous. The fourth blessing of wisdom is her protection from seductive women (vss. 16-19). The problem of vice must have been very grave when this section of Proverbs was assembled, since a great deal of space is devoted to it (5:1-23; 6:20-35; 7:1-27; 9:13-18). This temptation of course has always plagued mankind. It cannot always be treated with such candor and frankness, however, as here. Anyone reading these passages in all of their stark realism is amply warned of the dangers lurking in these forbidden pleasures, but it is only by God's strength and wisdom that he can resist them. **Strange woman** or **loose woman:** The word *zārāh* is not used here of the foreign prostitute, but of the woman who is not one's wife, as vs. 17 clearly indicates. It is synonymous with "another." **Stranger** or **adventuress:** The harlot, or more probably the adulteress, who lures men to their destruction **with her smooth words.** These words are given at length in 7:13-21. This verse is practically identical with 7:5.

17. Synonymous. Monogamy is taken for granted in Proverbs, and the sacredness of marriage and family ties is emphasized throughout the book. **Guide** or **companion:** Cf. Jer. 3:4. The root idea of *'allûph* is "community," "association," and so "one who is allied to another," i.e., her husband. **Covenant:** The marriage relationship is described as a covenant entered into by divine sanction. It is a serious matter which should not easily be forgotten, certainly not broken (cf. Mal. 2:14, where a similar expression is found).

18. Synonymous. The meaning of the verse is clear, although the Hebrew of vs. 18*a* is difficult. It reads, lit., "She sinks down to death, her house." From the parallelism **her house** should be the subject and that can be made possible simply by changing the accent of the verb form, which would then come from *shḥḥ,* "to bow down," rather than from *shûaḥ.* **Her house:** Those who go in to her find that from there the road leads to **death,** i.e., the abode of departed spirits. The punishment implied here is not eternal torment, but premature death. The idea of punishment or reward beyond the grave had not yet taken hold in Proverbs. **Dead** or **shades:** The inhabitants of Sheol.

19. Synonymous. There is no possibility of another chance. The land of death as a place from which no one returns is also a Babylonian figure. **Go unto her:** A sexual expression used here purposely to indicate that illicit intercourse is the one-way road

---

be driven out permanently only by the good. It is said that the following incident brought it to his attention. While he was driving with a man on a pastoral errand, the driver gave the pony a sharp cut with his whip. Chalmers remonstrated. But the driver responded: "Do you see that white post? The pony has a way of shying at it; so when we approach it, I always give him a touch of the whip, to let him have something else to think about." [1] Giving this a positive twist, the preacher pointed out that something positive is needed rather than a mere protest against evil. Wisdom has its negative values in that it keeps people from evil com-

[1] See William P. King, *Motives for Christian Living* (New York: Harper & Bros., 1942), p. 97.

20 That thou mayest walk in the way of good *men,* and keep the paths of the righteous.

21 For the upright shall dwell in the land, and the perfect shall remain in it.

22 But the wicked shall be cut off from the earth, and the transgressors shall be rooted out of it.

3 My son, forget not my law; but let thine heart keep my commandments:

20 So you will walk in the way of good men
and keep to the paths of the righteous.
21 For the upright will inhabit the land,
and men of integrity will remain in it;
22 but the wicked will be cut off from the land,
and the treacherous will be rooted out of it.

3 My son, do not forget my teaching,
but let your heart keep my commandments;

---

to destruction. The expression **paths of life** refers to this life, as in 10:17. No normal, happy life is possible any longer.

20. Synonymous. The fifth and last blessing for those who follow wisdom (vss. 20-22). They will possess the land, whereas the wicked will be cut off. **Righteous** (*çaddîqîm*): Those who do what is right in life (see Exeg. on 1:3).

21. Synonymous. The old idea of reward and punishment is still found in Proverbs, viz., that a man is rewarded or punished in this life in physical terms. **Upright:** See Exeg. on 1:3. The word **land** refers to Canaan (cf. Exod. 20:12). The continuance of God's favor was shown by Israel's dwelling in Canaan. Thus to **dwell in the land** meant to "enjoy God's favor." **Perfect** or **men of integrity:** See Exeg. on 1:12.

22. Synonymous. The violent uprooting of the wicked. **Wicked:** In the wisdom literature the *reshā'îm,* as a class, are always opposed to the righteous (*çaddîqîm*). The root meaning of *rāshā'* is not clear. The word usually means those who are morally bad. In the forensic sense it is the opposite of "just" (see Exeg. on 3:25).

G. Blessings of Wisdom (3:1-35)

This chapter consists of three discourses, each beginning with "My son" (vss. 1-10, 11-20, 21-35). These in turn may be divided into smaller groups of verses which are usually introduced by an exhortation, followed by a recounting of the blessings for those who heed.

3:1. Synonymous. One of the golden words of religion is "remember." There is no spiritual life or growth apart from the great spiritual heritage of the past. No religion recognized this truth more clearly than Judaism, with its strong emphasis on the teaching of its youth concerning the great facts and truths of its holy history (Exod. 12:26-27; Deut. 6). In view of the appalling, continuing ignorance among Christians of the simple biblical facts and Christian doctrines, the church may do well to heed more carefully the message of this verse. **My son:** See Exeg. on 1:8. **Law** or, better, **teaching:** See Exeg. on 1:8. **My commandments:** See Exeg. on 2:1.

---

pany, but it has the positive value of leading them into companionships that are satisfying and constructive.

3:1-4. ***Does Right Living Have Rewards?***—A life devoted to kindness and faithfulness is here commended because of the rewards which it brings. A man is not expected to keep wisdom's commandments for nought. If he writes them **on the tablet of** [his] **heart,** making them an essential part of his being, he is assured that he will experience good results. The rewards of right living are presented as a lure to follow wisdom. They are the bait or the incentive to one who is hesitant. Both the quantity and the quality of life will be enhanced for him who is kind and faithful. He will have **length of days and years of life.** And his years will be full of **abundant welfare.** More than that. He will satisfy one of the deepest hungers of the human spirit: the hunger for approval. He

> **will find favor and good repute**
> **in the sight of God and man.**

His manner of life will bring him a good reputation among his fellows, and will make him acceptable to the eternal God.

One cannot help wondering whether the wise man is overselling his wares. Throughout the

2 For length of days, and long life, and peace, shall they add to thee.
3 Let not mercy and truth forsake thee: bind them about thy neck; write them upon the table of thine heart:

2 for length of days and years of life
and abundant welfare will they give you.
3 Let not loyalty and faithfulness forsake you;
bind them about your neck,
write them on the tablet of your heart.

---

2. The idea that **long life** is the reward of right living is common in Proverbs (cf. vs. 16; 2:21; 4:10; etc.). He who walks in God's path will have his protection and so will live his years to the full without being violently cut off. To the Christian, whose promise of reward for right living is relegated almost entirely to the afterlife, these words may not be too significant. And yet it should be noted that the joys and blessings of this present life are not only God's rewards here on this earth, but also earnests of those fuller and more wonderful joys in the world to come. **Long life** or **years of life:** The expression connotes happy, prosperous years, full of earthly blessing and well-being. **Peace** or **abundant welfare:** The word *shālôm* means "wholeness," and so refers to everything which makes life complete and worth living. Here it again refers primarily to freedom from outward danger, which of course leads to inward serenity.

3. Triplet. **Mercy and truth** or **loyalty and faithfulness:** The first word, *ḥéṣedh,* is usually mistranslated. Perhaps the nearest English equivalent is "piety," although that is not satisfactory either. It really means "loyal love," and describes the relationship which exists between two parties of a covenant. That **loyalty** is an integral part of the meaning of the word is shown by the fact that out of forty-three cases where *ḥéṣedh* is linked to another word with a copula, twenty-three times that other word is *'emeth,* as here, or another form of the same root, *'āman,* which means basically "to confirm," "to support," and then "to trust," "to believe." Together these two words supplement each other, **faithfulness** keeping love from becoming a weak sentimentality, and love preventing faithfulness from becoming a harsh legalism. **Bind them:** Perhaps as an ornament (cf. 1:9), but more probably in order to keep them in mind and so to remember them. The writer is of course speaking metaphorically. The practical application of this idea, however, is found in Exod. 13:9, 16; Deut. 6:8, from which the phylacteries or tephillin of later Judaism are derived. **Write them:** This stich occurs also in 7:3. Since the line is wanting in the LXX, and since the usual form of the proverbs in this section has only two stichs, we may assume that this third line was a later addition (for the idea cf. Jer. 31:33; II Cor. 3:3).

---

book there is this emphasis upon the rewards of right living, that men may be won to wisdom. The difficulty comes when experience fails to validate the promise. Does a life of kindness and faithfulness assure a person **length of days?** A moment's thought will call to mind the many whose days were cut short because of their devotion to such a life. Jesus is a notable example. His life on earth was ended when he was only a young man. Others who were the victims of "man's inhumanity to man" [2] bear testimony to the fact that these rewards of long life and approval by the community do not necessarily follow right living. Job's problem arises when just living does not pay off in **length of days . . . and abundant welfare.**

If long life and prosperity are thought of as the inevitable consequences of right living, many false judgments are possible. Whenever a man is prosperous, this would imply that he is a good man. If a man dies young, this would mean that he was not a good man. A person who is suffering from some reversal of fortune, or who is the victim of an incurable disease, might condemn himself as a monstrous sinner. His fellows might likewise condemn him since ill fortune must be preceded by blameworthy conduct. Later developments in Hebrew and Christian thought and experience made it necessary to revise those categorical equations. Such rewards as wisdom offers may normally follow right living, but they do not inevitably follow it. Perhaps it is good that there is not an inevitable connection between goodness and prosperity, between kindness and longevity. Otherwise goodness would have only prudential motives. A deeper incentive than self-interest must be at

[2] Robert Burns, "Man Was Made to Mourn."

4 So shalt thou find favor and good understanding in the sight of God and man.

5 ¶ Trust in the LORD with all thine heart; and lean not unto thine own understanding.

6 In all thy ways acknowledge him, and he shall direct thy paths.

4 So you will find favor and good repute[f]
in the sight of God and man.

5 Trust in the LORD with all your heart,
and do not rely on your own insight.
6 In all your ways acknowledge him,
and he will make straight your paths.

[f] Cn: Heb *understanding*

4. The reward of obedience. **So shalt thou find.** The Hebrew has the imperative, "find thou." **Good understanding** or **good repute:** The Hebrew word *sēkhel* is related to the word translated "wisdom" in 1:3 (see Exeg.). In this context **understanding** should rather be the cause of the finding, than that which is found. Hence some commentators (Toy, Oesterley) suggest emending the word to *shēm,* meaning "name," "reputation," and so translated in the RSV. This verse is reminiscent of Luke 2:52.

5. Synonymous. In vss. 5-8 the student is told to trust implicitly in God and he will be blessed with health. Human wisdom is imperfect and fallible, even though the young man may think he knows everything. Faith is described here as reliance upon or trust in a person, i.e., God. He is the source of true wisdom and power, and so should be obeyed and acknowledged in all things. **With all thine heart:** The secret of finding God's way and receiving his blessing is to trust him with the whole heart. It is so easy to lean upon our own understanding instead of upon him, to put our plans first and then ask God to co-operate with us in carrying them out.

6. **In all your ways:** Again the emphasis is on the word **all.** God demands absolute obedience and surrender in every realm of life before he can **direct** our **paths.** The

work if true moral stature is to be achieved. The story is told that an old woman was seen in the streets of Strasbourg in the fourteenth century carrying a pail of water in one hand and a torch in the other. "When asked what she was about, she answered that with the pail of water she was going to put out the flames of hell and with the torch she was going to burn up heaven, so that in the future men could love the dear Lord God for himself alone and not out of fear of hell or out of craving for reward."[3]

A life of wisdom is rewarding, but he who devotes himself to kindness and faithfulness with the sole motive of getting long life, abundant welfare, and favor with God and man, may miss the true meaning of wisdom and be denied the rewards that seemed certain.

5-8. ***What Trust in God Does.***—An ancient rabbi, Bar Kappara, once asked this question: "What is the succinct text upon which all the essential principles of Judaism may be considered to hinge?"[4] He answered that the first principle upon which all of our work and hope must depend is this verse: **In all thy ways acknowledge him, and he shall direct thy paths.** That answer can include not only Judaism but the spiritual basis of the whole of humanity.

[3] Douglas V. Steere, *Prayer and Worship* (New York: Association Press, 1938), p. 11.

[4] Israel Goldstein, *Toward a Solution* (New York: G. P. Putnam's Sons, 1940), p. 45.

In all aspects of life God is to be taken into account. The thought of him is not to be limited to special seasons or sacred places. He is to be acknowledged in the home, in business, at work, and at play. In other words, God is to be thought of sufficiently to influence conduct and life. He is not one of the electives in the school of life, nor is the recognition of God one of the frills of existence. Choices should be made in his sight. Actions are subject to his scrutiny.

To acknowledge him requires a fundamental humility. It is the recognition that our wills are subject to a higher will. "He . . . hath made us, and not we ourselves" (Ps. 100:3). His power is prior to our being. Upon him we are dependent for life and breath and everything. Acknowledging him helps a man not to think more highly of himself than he ought to think. Such acknowledgment comes whenever an individual is deeply aware of his creaturehood, and it results in a humble realization that no man has the final answer to all questions and that no person can equate his own opinions and his own judgments with those of God. One who follows this principle of living will be slow to inflict his views on others and equally slow in accepting the views of others as the last word from God. **Be not wise in your own eyes,** for this represents the failure to recognize that there is One whose thoughts are higher than our thoughts, whose ways are higher than our ways.

7 ¶ Be not wise in thine own eyes: fear the LORD, and depart from evil.
8 It shall be health to thy navel, and marrow to thy bones.

7 Be not wise in your own eyes;
fear the LORD, and turn away from evil.
8 It will be healing to your flesh[g]
and refreshment[h] to your bones.

[g] Heb *navel*
[h] Or *medicine*

problem of how we can know God's will for us, or how we can know that God is directing our lives, can be understood only in the light of our trusting him with all our heart and acknowledging him in all our ways.

7. Synonymous. True humility springs from reverence for God (cf. Rom. 12:16).

8. Synonymous. The reward of trusting God is a healthy body. The moral state of a man definitely influences his physical condition. The body, which is the temple of the Holy Spirit according to the Christian view, should in no way be defiled, but should be cared for in temperance and in respect. One who trusts God will have that peace of mind and cheerfulness of soul which make for good health and long life. It is also true, in the author's mind, that the wicked, who do not obey God's laws, are prematurely cut off. Psychosomatic medicine is certainly an old profession. For the rarely used *shōr* (**navel**) the LXX reads *bāsār,* meaning **flesh,** which is more appropriate to the context. **Marrow:** Better, **refreshment,** because the noun comes from the verbal root which means "to drink." In modern speech we would say, "a tonic to thy nerves" (Wildeboer).

To **acknowledge him** results in a trustful attitude. There are many human experiences that are beyond our capacity to explain. Bitterness and cynicism could easily follow the tragedies and frustrations that attend the normal human life on earth. But one who acknowledges God trusts him. He believes that the administration of the universe is in good hands—in trustworthy hands, and although he must often hold this belief through tears and darkness, a religious man seeks and maintains a spirit of trust. This trustful attitude was expressed by William Tecumseh Sherman in a letter written to T. de Witt Talmage shortly after the death of his wife.

> I am sure that you know that the God who created the minnow and who has molded the rose and the carnation, giving each its sweet fragrance, will provide for those mortal men who strive to do right in the world which He, himself, has stocked with birds, animals and man—at all events I will trust Him with absolute confidence.[5]

Times come when this trust seems to be misplaced. The people who saw Jesus suffering on a cross scoffed because his trust in God seemed to be unrewarded. "He trusts in God; let God deliver him now, if he desires him; for he said, 'I am the Son of God' " (Matt. 27:43). For one brief moment Jesus himself felt that God had forsaken him and that he had trusted God in vain. But soon that mood passed. Jesus was able to say at last, "Father, into thy hands I commit my spirit!" (Luke 23:46.) This is the ultimate trust of the religious mind.

[5] Lloyd Lewis, *Sherman, Fighting Prophet* (New York: Harcourt, Brace & Co., 1932), p. 649.

George Macdonald in *Robert Falconer* stated the basis for this spirit of trust in God when he wrote: "This is a sane, wholesome, practical, working faith: first, that it is a man's business to do the will of God; second, that God takes on himself the special care of that man; and third, that therefore that man ought never to be afraid of anything." [6]

Acknowledging God produces tranquillity of mind. There is a comfort, after one has done the best he can, to rest the case with One greater than himself. Our lives are in hands stronger and wiser and better than our own. A person can work as if everything depended upon him, and yet realize that finally he can commit everything to the God in whom "we live, and move, and have our being" (Acts 17:28). In 1888 John Cairns was presented with his own portrait by the synod of the United Presbyterian Church. On that occasion he said:

> Life and labor cannot last long with me. But I would seek to the end to work for Christian truth, and, under the weight of all anxieties and failures and the shadow of separation from loved ones, I would repeat the confession which Time only confirms: "In Thee, O Lord, have I trusted. I shall never be put to confusion." [7]

The storms of life may rock such a faith but they can hardly upset it. The last word is a trust that grows out of the acknowledgment of God's

[6] As quoted in Sherwood Eddy, *A Portrait of Jesus* (New York: Harper & Bros., 1943), p. 76.

[7] Leslie D. Weatherhead, *Thinking Aloud in War-Time* (New York: Abingdon Press, 1940), p. 129.

9 Honor the LORD with thy substance, and with the firstfruits of all thine increase:
10 So shall thy barns be filled with plenty, and thy presses shall burst out with new wine.

9 Honor the LORD with your substance
and with the first fruits of all your produce;
10 then your barns will be filled with plenty,
and your vats will be bursting with wine.

---

9. Synonymous. Vss. 9-10 deal with the right use of wealth. The order of these two verses is significant. If we give to God a portion of our increase, he will abundantly bless us. This is a spiritual law which God-fearing men have found to be valid in all ages. **Firstfruits of all thine increase:** The word **increase** (*tebhû'āh*) means usually agricultural **produce** (RSV). This is one of the rare references to the ceremonial law in Proverbs. The wise men were more interested in practical matters. They simply took for granted the practices of the established religion. To **honor the LORD,** then, is to bring him gifts as to a king (cf. Deut. 18:4; 26:2).

10. Synonymous. **Presses** or, better, **vats:** The wine press consisted of two parts, the upper, or press (*gath*), where the grapes were trodden, and the lower part, or vat (*yéqebh*), as here, in which the juice was received. Obedience to God's laws brings material reward.

---

sovereignty over life, and the confidence that "in his will is our peace." [8]

9-10. ***The Motives and Rewards of Giving.—***

> **Honor the LORD with your substance . . .**
> **then your barns will be filled with plenty,**
> **and your vats will be bursting with wine.**

If it were as simple as that we could adjourn all business services that give advice on how to accumulate wealth. Prosperity would be assured to him who makes his offering to his temple or to his church.

A church treasurer might like to separate the penurious church members from some of their money, and he might resort to an appeal like the one expressed in this proverb. But that summons to giving is not conducted on a very high level. The man who is thinking of his barns when he is giving to his temple might soon confuse barns and temples. He might find that he is tearing down his barns to build larger ones, only to hear a voice that says, "Thou fool, this night thy soul shall be required of thee" (Luke 12:20). When Jesus saw the widow putting her few coins into the temple treasury, he surely did not assume that her sacrificial giving would pay out in bursting barns and overflowing vats of wine. Giving to the church is hardly a way of keeping barns full. Otherwise this would be the simplest way of getting rich quickly.

This does not invalidate the desirability of putting God into the family budget and of carrying the responsibility of a good steward in maintaining the religious institutions of the community. In Pearl S. Buck's novel *The Good Earth* two men are conversing about the gifts which rich men of the town make to the poor.

> [One man asked], "But why should any give like this to the poor and who is it that gives?"
> The man answered then, "It is the rich and the gentry of the town who do it, and some do it for a good deed for the future, that by saving lives they may get merit in heaven, and some do it for righteousness that men may speak well of them."
> "Nevertheless it is a good deed for whatever reason," said Wang Lung, "and some must do it out of a good heart. . . . At least there are a few of these?" [9]

A man may honor God through the giving of his money, notably by meeting human need and by supporting agencies that help people. This may be done for many reasons. Motives may be high or low. Few people today do it because they expect to get rich by doing it. Paul felt that the deepest motive of Christian giving was gratitude for what God had done for him through Christ. He who gives liberally of himself and of his goods will find the true meaning of life. Sir Wilfred Grenfell writes:

> It is not the size nor the gold equivalent of what each of us contributes to the world that is a measure of the value of his gifts. The service we render to others is really the rent we pay for our room on this earth. It is obvious that man is himself a traveller; that the purpose of this world is not "To have and to hold" but "To give and to serve." There can be no other meaning.[1]

Honoring God with our substance is an essential part of religious living, but the motives

[8] Dante, *Paradise,* Canto III, l. 85.

[9] New York: John Day Co., 1931, p. 103.

[1] *A Labrador Logbook* (Boston: Little, Brown & Co., 1938), p. 112.

11 ¶ My son, despise not the chastening of the LORD; neither be weary of his correction:
12 For whom the LORD loveth he correcteth; even as a father the son *in whom* he delighteth.
13 ¶ Happy *is* the man *that* findeth wisdom, and the man *that* getteth understanding:

11 My son, do not despise the LORD's discipline
or be weary of his reproof,
12 for the LORD reproves him whom he loves,
as a father the son in whom he delights.
13 Happy is the man who finds wisdom,
and the man who gets understanding,

11. Synonymous. Another section (vss. 11-20) begins here. It enumerates further blessings of wisdom. Vss. 11-12 deal with the problem of the suffering of the righteous. It is well that this timely warning should be inserted here. Many who trust God and seek his wisdom are not blessed with perfect health, or a life of ease and riches, free from danger and sorrow. These, after all, are the external manifestations of the presence of wisdom in one's life. The highest gift that wisdom can bestow upon a man is such a spirit of trust and devotion that when the sorrows and disappointments of life come they may be accepted from God's hand without rancor or malice (cf. Job 5:17-18). **My son:** See Exeg. on 1:8. **Discipline** (*mûṣār*): See Exeg. on 1:2. **Reproof:** See Exeg. on 1:23.

12. Synonymous. This is the only place in Proverbs where God is compared to a father. The teaching of this verse is different from the old view that suffering is the punishment for sin, which was upheld by the three friends of Job. We find this more advanced doctrine that suffering is the disciplinary action of God's love in Job 4; 5; 33. Vss. 11 and 12 are quoted in Heb. 12:5-6. The N.T. had no better solution than this for the problem of suffering. **As a father:** The LXX, with slight change of consonants, reads "and afflicts," which may have been the original text.

13-18. These verses describe the true joy of the man who has found wisdom. The

and rewards are far more profound than those contained in this proverb.

11-12. ***Using Pain.***—Bodily pain has an important function. It is a warning that something is wrong, and that steps should be taken to correct the difficulty. A leper may hold a lighted cigarette and, if he is not alert, burn part of his hand away because no warning messages of pain come through the nerves of his hand. Pain is beneficent when it brings about correction of what is wrong.

Human suffering can likewise have corrective value. It can be a warning to him who is following a wrong path—a warning that comes soon enough for him to change his ways. Much is said in Proverbs about willingness to accept **reproof** from one's fellows. He is a wise man who does not resent a rebuke. He profits by it. But in this passage the writer thinks of a rebuke administered by the Lord. Suffering may be God's way of awakening a man to his wrongdoing. If the man regards this chastening as the act of a loving father trying to correct his son, he will extract the full value from his pain.

This view is an advance over the idea that suffering is punishment for sin. Even if suffering is the result of sin, that is not the end of the matter. The suffering is not simply punishment, nor is it only the inevitable consequence of departure from the right path. Suffering may have another purpose. It may be corrective, and thus help a person to see the wisdom of leaving an old life and turning to a new one. Eliphaz propounded this view of suffering to Job in these words, "Behold, happy is the man whom God correcteth: therefore despise not thou the chastening of the Almighty: for he maketh sore, and bindeth up; he woundeth, and his hands make whole" (Job 5:17-18). Job was not content to accept this as the full explanation of his pain, but at least it opened the door to a view that he could learn something by the pain which he endured. Suffering cannot be explained completely, but it can be used.

Marcus Dods is quoted as saying: "The world is unintelligible except on the hypothesis that it is for our schooling, and that he that sows in tears is the likeliest to have sheaves worth gathering."[2] Whenever anyone is going through some dark valley of pain, he may never arrive at a satisfactory explanation of his suffering, but he can at least ask himself this question, "What can I learn from this experience of pain?"

13-18. ***The Highest Good.***—Like many other passages in this section, these verses are an enthusiastic commendation of wisdom. The man

[2] Jane T. Stoddart, *The Psalms for Every Day* (Nashville: Cokesbury Press, 1939), p. 322.

14 For the merchandise of it *is* better than the merchandise of silver, and the gain thereof than fine gold.

15 She *is* more precious than rubies: and all the things thou canst desire are not to be compared unto her.

16 Length of days *is* in her right hand; *and* in her left hand riches and honor.

17 Her ways *are* ways of pleasantness, and all her paths *are* peace.

14 for the gain from it is better than gain
from silver
and its profit better than gold.
15 She is more precious than jewels,
and nothing you desire can compare
with her.
16 Long life is in her right hand;
in her left hand are riches and honor.
17 Her ways are ways of pleasantness,
and all her paths are peace.

---

word "happy" or "blessed" is found at the beginning and end of this section. To trust God in every way, to know the secret of the Lord in the bitterest sorrow, to be filled with inward peace even in the face of death, is truly more precious than gold or precious stones.

13. Synonymous. **Happy:** A beatitude proverb, of which there are several in this book. They have to do mainly with the individual moral life. The two verbs in the verse are different tenses: the happy man "has found" **wisdom** (see Exeg. on 1:2), but he must continually "draw forth" or "obtain" **understanding** (see Exeg. on 2:2).

14. Synonymous. **Gold** and **silver** are not to be compared with wisdom. The problem of interpretation here is whether the acquisition of wisdom is better than that of silver, or whether the profit gained from wisdom is better than that gained from silver. The RSV takes the latter view. The author of this proverb cannot be accused of materialistic aims.

15. Synonymous. Precious **jewels** are not to be compared with wisdom. The wise men try to make their picture of wisdom as alluring as possible to the youth of the day, who naturally look upon the possession of earthly treasures like gold and jewels as the ultimate goal of life. **Rubies** or **jewels** ("corals" Amer. Trans.): The meaning of the Hebrew word *penînîm* (found also in 8:11; 20:15; 31:10) is not clear. From Lam. 4:7, where it is modified by the adjective "ruddy," it seems to indicate a red substance.

16. Synonymous. Here again wisdom is personified, holding in her hands priceless treasures. The right hand holds the more precious treasure. The thought of this verse may strike one as materialistic, but there are many more passages which have a higher view (cf., e.g., vss. 2, 14).

17. Synonymous. **Pleasantness** and **peace** must again be taken in the sense of freedom from physical dangers and cares (cf. 2:10).

---

who has found wisdom and gained understanding can count himself happy, since he has found that which is above everything else. **Nothing you desire can compare with her.**

Men have often speculated about the highest good. They have tried to identify the *summum bonum*—that good which is above all others. William R. Inge in *Vale* asks this question: "What are the most precious gifts for which an old man, looking back on his life, ought to thank God?" He then mentions some of the values that men have cherished. The Greeks put health first, but since he had known many men and women who had triumphantly overcome this handicap, he could not rank health as the best thing in life. Recognition and encouragement are valued by many people. Most people need them, although a few proud and heroic natures can do without them. Finally Inge says: "But I have not the slightest doubt that domestic happiness is the greatest of all good gifts, next to that of 'wisdom,' for which Solomon prayed, and which I suppose, may be defined as a right judgment of the relative value of things." [3] One does not need to insist that **long life is in her right hand** and that **in her left hand are riches and honor** to realize that wisdom of the type mentioned above is of the highest value.

Boswell once remarked to Dr. Johnson that he thought admiration was one of the most agreeable of all our feelings. He regretted that he himself had lost much of his disposition to admire, "which people generally do as they advance in life." Dr. Johnson replied, "Sir, as a man advances in life, he gets what is better than admiration,—judgement,—to estimate things at their true value." [4] There is a sense in which

[3] New York: Longmans, Green & Co., 1934, pp. 125-26.
[4] *Life of Johnson,* II, 555.

18 She *is* a tree of life to them that lay hold upon her: and happy *is every one* that retaineth her.

19 The LORD by wisdom hath founded the earth; by understanding hath he established the heavens.

20 By his knowledge the depths are broken up, and the clouds drop down the dew.

21 ¶ My son, let not them depart from thine eyes: keep sound wisdom and discretion:

18 She is a tree of life to those who lay hold of her;
those who hold her fast are called happy.

19 The LORD by wisdom founded the earth;
by understanding he established the heavens;
20 by his knowledge the deeps broke forth,
and the clouds drop down the dew.

21 My son, keep sound wisdom and discretion;
let them not escape from your sight,[i]

[i] Reversing the order of the clauses

---

18. Synonymous. Wisdom is the source of life and happiness. **Tree of life:** This expression is found again in 11:30; 13:12; 15:4; elsewhere in Gen. 2:9; 3:22, 24; Rev. 2:7; 22:2; and allusion in Ezek. 47:12. In Proverbs the term has become a faded metaphor, standing for the source of long life and peace. **Happy:** The last word of the verse, as brought out by the RSV. It is the same word as the one at the beginning of this section (vs. 13).

19. Synonymous. Wisdom is praised for its part in creation. It is not personified, however. The purpose of vss. 19-20 is to show that the wisdom which directs human life and brings such bountiful blessings is the same wisdom by which God created the heavens and the earth. He who surrenders himself to the ways of wisdom will therefore find himself in harmony with the world about him. For that man such phrases as the hostile universe, the great unknown, the laws of chance, hold no terror, since God, who upholds the universe by power and wisdom, is also directing human life and making it meaningful. **Wisdom:** The skill by which God established the earth (see Exeg. on 1:2). The verbs used in this verse reveal the Hebrew cosmogony, in which the earth rests upon foundations, and there is a firmament above the earth. **Understanding:** See Exeg. on 2:2.

20. Synonymous. In this verse two phenomena of nature are ascribed to God's knowledge. **The deeps broke forth:** Referring to Gen. 7:11, when the subterranean waters were released at the time of the Flood. **The clouds drop down the dew:** The tense of the verb refers to the continual, gentle bestowal of moisture upon the earth.

21. Synonymous. Here begins the third main division of the chapter, vss. 21-35. It is a collection of wise sayings. Following Toy and Oesterley, the RSV reverses the two stichs of this verse. Otherwise the subject of the first Hebrew verb is uncertain. **Depart** or **escape:** From the root *lûz* (see Exeg. on 2:15). **Sound wisdom:** See Exeg. on 2:7. **Discretion:** See Exeg. on 1:4.

---

wisdom of this kind is the highest value since it helps an individual to estimate all things at their true value.

19-20. See Expos. on 8:21-36.

21-26. ***Walking Securely.***—The hunger for security is one of the deepest hungers of human life. Nations resort to all sorts of methods to maintain their security, and they often use means that defeat their own ends. Individuals are burdened not only by what happens to them but also by the fear of the evil that might happen to them. This desire for security gnaws at them and robs them of serenity and inner peace. According to this writer, the wise man has an invisible means of support. He has something that will remove fear. He has the assurance that he is working in harmony with the sustaining power of the universe and that this will be his stay no matter what may happen to him.

One could hardly be said to **walk . . . securely** during the bombings of London in World War II. No one knew what a day or a night might bring forth. Many hours were spent in air raid shelters and in tube stations, deep in the earth. In a number of places a doctor placed placards upon which appeared a portion of this passage

22 So shall they be life unto thy soul, and
grace to thy neck.
23 Then shalt thou walk in thy way
safely, and thy foot shall not stumble.
24 When thou liest down, thou shalt not
be afraid: yea, thou shalt lie down, and thy
sleep shall be sweet.
25 Be not afraid of sudden fear, neither
of the desolation of the wicked, when it
cometh.
26 For the LORD shall be thy confidence,
and shall keep thy foot from being taken.

22 and they will be life for your soul
and adornment for your neck.
23 Then you will walk on your way securely
and your foot will not stumble.
24 If you sit down,[j] you will not be afraid;
when you lie down, your sleep will be
sweet.
25 Do not be afraid of sudden panic,
or of the ruin[k] of the wicked, when it
comes;
26 for the LORD will be your confidence
and will keep your foot from being
caught.

[j] Gk: Heb *lie down*
[k] Heb *storm*

---

22. Synonymous. Wisdom is the source of life as well as of graciousness. It manifests itself inwardly in the healthy life of the soul, and outwardly in the gracious, pleasing appearance of the man of wisdom. **Grace or adornment:** See Exeg. on 1:9.

23. Synonymous. Freedom from fear, with which this and the next three verses deal, is one of the greatest blessings that God can bestow upon anyone. He gives it to those who let their lives be regulated and directed by his divine wisdom. They feel secure in their daily walk, they enjoy sweet, peaceful sleep, and they do not fear the sudden calamity which comes to those who do not live in accordance with God's will. Under these conditions the soul flourishes and mind and heart have a peace born of God. **Stumble:** Actually a transitive verb in Hebrew, meaning "to strike."

24. Synonymous. **Liest down** or, following LXX, **sit down:** The latter reading seems the more natural, since it is strange to have the same verb used twice in the same sentence. In Deut. 6:7 we find the following order of verbs, "When thou sittest, . . . when thou walkest, . . . when thou liest down, . . . when thou risest up." The Hebrew text is retained in the KJV and the ASV, but the tenses of the verbs are changed, which is grammatically possible. According to W. O. E. Oesterley (*The Book of Proverbs* [London: Methuen & Co., 1929; "Westminster Commentaries"], p. 25), the sentence could be translated, "When thou shalt lie down thou shalt not be afraid; and when thou hast lain down, sweet is thy slumber."

25. Synonymous. Wisdom is able to cope with any emergency in life. **Ruin of the wicked:** They will be visited by calamities which those who follow wisdom need never fear. The word *rāshā'* is the usual word for **wicked** in Proverbs. It occurs about seventy-five times, mostly in contrast with *çaddiq*, "righteous" (see Exeg. on 2:22).

26. Synonymous. A man is truly wise when he relies on God to direct his paths. With these two verses Oesterley compares The Teaching of Amen-em-ope (see Intro., pp. 768-69):

> Be thou courageous before other people,
> For one is safe in the hand of God.

Thy confidence: The LXX reads "on all thy roads," with a slight emendation of the Hebrew text, making perhaps for a clearer parallelism, but the Hebrew text makes good sense (cf. Job 8:14; 31:24).

---

from Proverbs, a thought that must have helped many people in those dark days: **When thou liest down, thou shalt not be afraid: yea, thou shalt lie down, and thy sleep shall be sweet. Be not afraid of sudden fear, neither of the desolation of the wicked, when it cometh.** There is no telling how many people were given a sense of inner security when they read these words. Sudden desolation was always a threat, and yet those who underwent the privations and horrors of that time must have found an invisible means of support through this faith. "The sovereign

27 ¶ Withhold not good from them to whom it is due, when it is in the power of thine hand to do *it*.

28 Say not unto thy neighbor, Go, and come again, and to-morrow I will give; when thou hast it by thee.

29 Devise not evil against thy neighbor, seeing he dwelleth securely by thee.

30 ¶ Strive not with a man without cause, if he have done thee no harm.

31 ¶ Envy thou not the oppressor, and choose none of his ways.

27 Do not withhold good from those to
whom it[l] is due,
when it is in your power to do it.

28 Do not say to your neighbor, "Go, and
come again,
tomorrow I will give it"—when you
have it with you.

29 Do not plan evil against your neighbor
who dwells trustingly beside you.

30 Do not contend with a man for no reason,
when he has done you no harm.

31 Do not envy a man of violence
and do not choose any of his ways;

[l] Heb *Do not withhold good from its owners*

---

27. One's duty to his neighbor is discussed in vss. 27-30. Wisdom demands uncompromising honesty and justice in human relationships. She cannot endure the withholding of rightful gain or honor, or unnecessary strife or bickering. The curse of the Lord is upon those who because of greed or malicious jealousy despitefully use their fellow men. **From those to whom it is due** ("from the needy" Amer. Trans.; "your neighbour" Moffatt): The literal Hebrew is "from its owners," which is paraphrased in the first rendering given above. The Amer. Trans. follows the LXX; Moffatt follows Toy's emendation. As T. T. Perowne points out, this verse may enjoin either honesty or benevolence (*The Proverbs* [Cambridge: Cambridge University Press, 1916; "The Cambridge Bible"], *ad loc.*).

28. Give promptly, whether wages or help in general. "He who gives quickly gives twice." In Ecclus. 4:3; Jas. 2:16 this idea is expressed in connection with giving to the poor.

29. This verse advises against malicious conduct. **Devise** or **plan:** The verb *ḥārash* means ordinarily "to engrave," "to plow," and then, figuratively, "to devise," usually in a bad sense.

30. A warning against groundless contentiousness. **Strive:** The Hebrew word *rîbh* is a common term for litigation; here it means any unfriendly dispute.

31. Synonymous. As in Ps. 73:3-5, the writer here warns against envying the wicked man who has acquired his wealth by highhanded, unlawful means, and may be prospering at the moment (cf. also Ps. 37:1).

---

cure for worry," wrote William James, "is religious faith. The turbulent billows of the fretful surface leave the deep parts of the ocean undisturbed, and to him who has a hold of vaster and more permanent realities, the hourly vicissitudes of his personal destiny seem relatively unimportant things." [5]

Human life on this planet is always insecure. One can never know what a day will bring forth. He cannot by conscious effort make his heart beat. He cannot be sure that he will turn homeward at set of sun. Yet if he can be delivered from the fear of an uncertain future, he will have the only security that is promised by a faith that is realistic and is persuaded that "neither death nor life . . . shall be able to separate us from the love of God" (Rom. 8:38-39).

[5] Quoted in John Kennedy, *The God Whom We Ignore* (New York: The Macmillan Co., 1938), p. 229.

27-35. ***Living with Our Neighbors.***—Here are some good hints on how to live with other people. This is a major task for every individual. One might live with the world of nature with some measure of appreciation and understanding. He might even have achieved the ability to live at peace with himself, but if he has not learned how to get along with other people, he has still to accomplish one of the important tasks of life.

Sometimes a neighbor needs help. Through no fault of his own he might suddenly find him-

32 For the froward *is* abomination to the
LORD: but his secret *is* with the righteous.
33 ¶ The curse of the LORD *is* in the
house of the wicked: but he blesseth the
habitation of the just.
34 Surely he scorneth the scorners: but he
giveth grace unto the lowly.
35 The wise shall inherit glory: but
shame shall be the promotion of fools.

32 for the perverse man is an abomination
to the LORD,
but the upright are in his confidence.
33 The LORD's curse is on the house of the
wicked,
but he blesses the abode of the righteous.
34 Toward the scorners he is scornful,
but to the humble he shows favor.
35 The wise will inherit honor,
but fools get[m] disgrace.

[m] Cn: Heb *exalt*

32. Antithetic. The wicked man who is prosperous is not to be envied, for actually he is an abomination to the Lord, and a curse rests upon his house. In the long run he shall be disgraced, whereas the wise man will inherit honor. **Froward:** See Exeg. on 2:15. **Abomination:** In earlier literature the word referred to something which was contrary to the religious cult. Later on, as here, it denoted moral offenses. **Upright:** The Hebrew word is *yāshār,* the root of *mēshārîm* in 1:3 (see Exeg.). **Secret** or **confidence:** The word *ṣôdh* originally meant "familiar, confidential intercourse," then "assembly," and finally, the "secret counsel" which emanated from friendly association. Amos says that the Lord will do nothing "without revealing his secret to his servants the prophets" (Amos 3:7).

33. Antithetic. Physical calamity or prosperity comes with the curse or blessing of God. **Wicked:** See Exeg. on vs. 25. **Abode of the righteous:** The Hebrew word *nāweh,* "abode of a shepherd," usually refers to a country dwelling, and so may be used here in contrast with the noisy city where the wicked dwell in their houses (for **righteous** see Exeg. on 1:3).

34. Antithetic. God acts toward men as they act toward him. He is just, not merciful! The LXX reads here, "The Lord resists the proud, but to the humble he shows favor," which is quoted, with variations, in Jas. 4:6; I Pet. 5:5. **Surely** or, better, **toward:** The RSV simply changes one Hebrew consonant and omits another in the following word. **Scorners:** See Exeg. on 1:22.

35. Antithetic. **Glory** or, better, **honor:** Respect is due to the wise on account of their wisdom. **Fools** (*keṣîlîm*): See Exeg. on 1:22. **Get:** The word *mērîm* means, lit., "to lift up," "to carry away," from *rûm,* "to be high." The RSV offers the sense that one would naturally expect (apparently based on an emendation of the text to a form like *môrîshîm,* from *yārash*).

self in desperate need. The suggestion is made here that one should give when it is needed. There is such a thing as timing our philanthropies. Too often in this realm and in others we give too little too late. There is a fine impulsiveness about the person who gives help when it is needed, who does not "weigh the goods so long that he never passes anything over the counter."

Neighbors must be accepted. A man usually hurts himself when he plans evil against his neighbor. The wise man accepts the fact that he cannot isolate himself. A Negro once said to a white group that the Negroes were here to stay, and that it was necessary for both Negroes and whites to accept that fact. Devising evil against one another would not solve the problem. They would have to find some means of living peaceably with each other.

Contentiousness is undesirable in a neighborhood. Some periods in history give birth to the spirit of contention more than others. Nerves are on edge after a war. Fatigue produces irritability. At such times it is doubly necessary to avoid the spirit of contention that is ready for a quarrel even without a cause.

Violence should be avoided. **Do not envy a man of violence,** even though his violence seems to get him what he wants. Force has its uses, but it also has distinct limitations in neighborly relationships.

4 Hear, ye children, the instruction of a father, and attend to know understanding.
2 For I give you good doctrine, forsake ye not my law.
3 For I was my father's son, tender and only *beloved* in the sight of my mother.
4 He taught me also, and said unto me, Let thine heart retain my words: keep my commandments, and live.
5 Get wisdom, get understanding: forget *it* not; neither decline from the words of my mouth.
6 Forsake her not, and she shall preserve thee: love her, and she shall keep thee.

4 Hear, O sons, a father's instruction,
and be attentive, that you may gain[n]
insight;
2 for I give you good precepts:
do not forsake my teaching.
3 When I was a son with my father,
tender, the only one in the sight of my
mother,
4 he taught me, and said to me,
"Let your heart hold fast my words;
keep my commandments, and live;
5 do not forget, and do not turn away from
the words of my mouth.
Get wisdom; get insight.[o]
6 Do not forsake her, and she will keep you;
love her, and she will guard you.

[n] Heb *know*
[o] Reversing the order of the lines

H. Wisdom Commended to Scholars (4:1-27)

1. The Courting of Wisdom (4:1-9)

4:1. Synonymous. Religious instruction in the home. **Instruction:** See Exeg. on 1:22. **Father:** The speaker assumes the character of a father. The wise man himself had received his first instruction from his father. In these verses we get a glimpse into a pious Israelite's home. There is no better place to acquire religious instruction than in the home, and there is no better time than early in life. The child learns not only by precept, but also by the example of the parents around him. These early impressions remain with him throughout life and mold his character. How important it is then that the child is brought up in a home where a religious atmosphere prevails! **Understanding** or, better, **insight:** See Exeg. on 1:2.

2. Doctrine or **precepts:** Hebrew *léqaḥ* (see Exeg. on 1:5). **Law** or **teaching:** See Exeg. on 1:8. According to later Jewish teaching, one can learn nothing beyond that which is delivered to him.

3. Synonymous. A circumstantial clause, subordinate to vs. 4. The sage is using himself as an illustration, i.e., as he learned from his father, so his hearers are to learn from him who is like their father at the moment. The RSV in the first half of the verse brings out the meaning of the Hebrew exceedingly well. **Tender:** Young in years. **Only beloved** or **the only one:** The RSV has the correct rendering of the Hebrew word *yāḥîdh,* but the word **beloved** is "plainly implied in the Hebrew, and necessary in English" (Revisers' Preface, as quoted in Perowne, *op. cit., ad loc.*). The LXX also has **beloved.** This verse presents a beautiful picture of Jewish family life. Even though an only child, he was not spoiled.

4. If one adheres to wisdom's instruction he will secure a long life of happiness on earth. The third stich is identical with 7:2*a,* and may be a later addition here. The LXX has only "keep commandments." **Thine heart:** See Exeg. on 2:2. **Commandments:** See Exeg. on 2:1.

5. The RSV reverses the two stichs of this verse. The repetition of the verb in the first Hebrew stich emphasizes the imperative need of wisdom. **Wisdom:** See Exeg. on 1:2. **Understanding:** See Exeg. on 1:2.

6. Synonymous. In vss. 6-9 the procuring of wisdom is described in terms of getting a wife. **Love her:** Man is to love wisdom (cf. 8:17).

4:1-9. See Expos. on 1:2, 8-9.

7 Wisdom *is* the principal thing; *therefore* get wisdom: and with all thy getting get understanding.

8 Exalt her, and she shall promote thee: she shall bring thee to honor, when thou dost embrace her.

9 She shall give to thine head an ornament of grace: a crown of glory shall she deliver to thee.

10 Hear, O my son, and receive my sayings; and the years of thy life shall be many.

11 I have taught thee in the way of wisdom; I have led thee in right paths.

12 When thou goest, thy steps shall not be straitened; and when thou runnest, thou shalt not stumble.

7 The beginning of wisdom is this: Get wisdom,
and whatever you get, get insight.
8 Prize her highly,[p] and she will exalt you;
she will honor you if you embrace her.
9 She will place on your head a fair garland;
she will bestow on you a beautiful crown."

10 Hear, my son, and accept my words,
that the years of your life may be many.
11 I have taught you the way of wisdom;
I have led you in the paths of uprightness.
12 When you walk, your step will not be hampered;
and if you run, you will not stumble.

[p] The meaning of the Hebrew is uncertain

---

7. This verse seems to interrupt the thought of vss. 6 and 8. It is not found in the LXX, and was probably inserted later as an expansion of vs. 5. **Principal thing** or, better, **beginning:** The Hebrew of the first stich is, "The beginning of wisdom, get wisdom," which is an almost meaningless tautology. The KJV offers an impossible translation of the Hebrew, and the RSV is simply a paraphrase (for **beginning** see Exeg. on 1:7). **With all thy getting** or **whatever you get:** The phrase really means "with all thy possession," i.e., for the price of all your possessions, buy wisdom or understanding.

8. Synonymous. Wisdom exalts those who favor her, honors those who love her, and graces a man's appearance so that he will be admired and respected by those who know him. **Exalt** or **prize . . . highly:** The verb *ṣālal* is difficult here. It means "to cast up a highway," "lift up [a song]." The meaning in both translations is derived from the parallel clause.

9. Synonymous. **Ornament of grace** or **fair garland:** See Exeg. on 1:9. **Crown of glory** or **beautiful crown:** Both expressions in the RSV are examples of hendiadys (see Exeg. on 1:3).

2. The Ways of the Wise and the Wicked (4:10-19)

In vss. 10-19 the paths of wisdom and evil are contrasted. Vss. 10-13 deal with the way of wisdom, which is straight and leads to the abundant life. Vss. 14-17 deal with the way of the wicked, which is filled with violence. Vss. 18-19 epitomize the contrast between the two ways.

10. Years of . . . life: Many happy years on earth are the reward of heeding wisdom (see Exeg. on 3:2).

11. Synonymous. The teachings of the wise men lead those who observe them into the paths of wisdom which are straight and upright. **Uprightness:** See Exeg. on 1:3.

12. Synonymous. The road of those who follow wisdom is broad and free from stumbling blocks. **Straitened** or **hampered:** The root idea of *çārar* is "to be narrow." The Hebrew idea of "broadness" connoted prosperity, general well-being, whereas the idea of "narrowness," expressed by the root of the word used here, connoted distress, adversity, and enmity.

10-19. See Expos. on 3:1-4.

13 Take fast hold of instruction; let *her* not go: keep her; for she *is* thy life.

14 ¶ Enter not into the path of the wicked, and go not in the way of evil *men.*

15 Avoid it, pass not by it, turn from it, and pass away.

16 For they sleep not, except they have done mischief; and their sleep is taken away, unless they cause *some* to fall.

17 For they eat the bread of wickedness, and drink the wine of violence.

18 But the path of the just *is* as the shining light, that shineth more and more unto the perfect day.

19 The way of the wicked *is* as darkness: they know not at what they stumble.

13 Keep hold of instruction, do not let go;
guard her, for she is your life.
14 Do not enter the path of the wicked,
and do not walk in the way of evil men.
15 Avoid it; do not go on it;
turn away from it and pass on.
16 For they cannot sleep unless they have done wrong;
they are robbed of sleep unless they have made some one stumble.
17 For they eat the bread of wickedness
and drink the wine of violence.
18 But the path of the righteous is like the light of dawn,
which shines brighter and brighter until full day.
19 The way of the wicked is like deep darkness;
they do not know over what they stumble.

---

13. Synonymous. The piling up of verbal expressions in this verse shows the earnestness of the sage and the great importance of wisdom. **Instruction:** See Exeg. on 1:2.

14. Synonymous. Vss. 14-17 warn against association with wicked men. **Wicked:** See Exeg. on 2:22; 3:25. **Walk:** Lit., "Go straight on."

15. Synonymous. A repetition of verbs for emphasis.

16. Synonymous. A striking reversal of a common figure. The wicked **sleep** only when they have done something wicked. Ordinarily the guilty conscious is supposed to keep one awake.

17. Synonymous. **Bread of wickedness . . . wine of violence:** The meaning of these expressions is that either their food and drink are wickedness or they acquire their food and drink by wicked means.

18. Wisdom illumines the righteous man's pathway with an ever-increasing light, making him secure in his journey through life. **Shining light** or **light of dawn:** The Hebrew word *nōghah* means "brightness." The rendering of the RSV is implied from the context. **Unto the perfect day** or **until full day:** Lit., "Until the day is established," which may mean either the dawn, or noonday, when the sun stands in the zenith. Most commentators think that the latter is probably correct. The Vulg. "perfect day" is a happy solution of the problem, since it can include any meaning.

19. The way of the wicked is dark, and so they fall because they have no light. In

---

18-19. ***A Problem in Diagnosis.***—It is one thing to pick oneself up after a fall, and another to discover what caused the fall. If one is to profit by his mistakes he ought to know what made him fall. Of the wicked this writer says, **They do not know over what they stumble.** They cannot diagnose their plight; they go on tripping over the same obstacle again and again.

But the path of the righteous is like the light of dawn,
which shines brighter and brighter until full day.

He who walks by daylight can see where he is going. He can discern his way. For him it is possible to see the obstacle over which he might stumble, and thus to avoid a fall. Just as the medical profession needs good diagnosticians—doctors who can distinguish symptoms from causes, who can put their finger on the difficulty that is producing the illness—so the spiritual life needs skillful men of insight who can diagnose the ills of individuals and society. They help us to know over what we stumble. In his "Memorial Verses" Matthew Arnold pays this tribute to Goethe as a diagnostician:

He took the suffering human race,
He read each wound, each weakness clear—
And struck his finger on the place,
And said—Thou ailest here, and here.—

20 ¶ My son, attend to my words; incline thine ear unto my sayings.

21 Let them not depart from thine eyes; keep them in the midst of thine heart.

22 For they *are* life unto those that find them, and health to all their flesh.

23 ¶ Keep thy heart with all diligence; for out of it *are* the issues of life.

24 Put away from thee a froward mouth, and perverse lips put far from thee.

20 My son, be attentive to my words;
incline your ear to my sayings.
21 Let them not escape from your sight;
keep them within your heart.
22 For they are life to him who finds them,
and healing to all his flesh.
23 Keep your heart with all vigilance;
for from it flow the springs of life.
24 Put away from you crooked speech,
and put devious talk far from you.

---

the darkness they do not even know what made them fall. **Darkness** or, better, **deep darkness:** Not the ordinary word for darkness, but one which means "deep obscurity" (*'aphēlāh*), the entire absence of light. The wicked must fall, but what is worse, they do not know why they fall, for they do not recognize wickedness as such, nor are they aware of the punishment which it necessarily brings.

3. The Straight Path of Wisdom (4:20-27)

In these verses ears, eyes, and mouth are all to be used in getting and keeping wisdom.

21. Synonymous. **Depart** or **escape:** The same verb as in 3:21 (see Exeg.). **Heart:** See Exeg. on 2:2.

22. Synonymous. **Life:** See Exeg. on 3:2.

23. The **heart** is the central organ which controls all of man's activities, and so determines the character of his living. As R. F. Horton remarks, it is strange that the Jews should have become so formal in their religious life with all this emphasis on the heart in their Scriptures (*The Book of Proverbs* [New York: A. C. Armstrong & Son, 1903; "The Expositor's Bible"], p. 57). Salvation, after all, is not a matter of living up to a code of ethics. It is a matter of the heart. After the heart is right with God good conduct flows from its hidden springs (cf. Matt. 15:19). To train a child only in outward manners is not sufficient. He must be told of the inward sources of power which will direct him in the right paths.

24. Synonymous. Against dissembling speech and falsification of the truth. **Perverse** or **devious:** See Exeg. on 2:15.

20-27. ***Heart and Health.***—A man's life and health depend in large part upon the condition of his heart. The heart of health is a healthy heart, and this is true even though one uses the word with various meanings. Two references to the heart are made in this section (vss. 21, 23).

The heart may be thought of as an organ of the body. Here it is central in importance. An individual may suffer the loss of other organs, but his body cannot sustain the failure of his heart. In a biological sense it is good advice when the writer says:

> **Keep your heart with all vigilance;**
> **for from it flow the springs of life.**

The heart is also regarded by many writers as the seat of the consciousness and the will. The brain is not mentioned in the O.T. It was evidently not thought of as having intellectual significance. The heart was the center of intellectual activity. The person who hears the words of the wise man is to keep them in sight. He is to keep them within his heart. They are to become an essential part of his thoughts. Wise sayings are to constitute an important part of his intellectual equipment. Right thinking will have an important effect upon his life and health. Ideas are efficacious in producing a healthy body.

By many writers the heart is thought of as the seat of the emotions. If a man has a spirit of compassion and kindness toward other people, he is regarded as a person whose heart is in the right place. On the other hand, a man who cherishes feelings of bitterness or hatred is said to have an ailing heart. There is more than one kind of "heart trouble." Wrong emotions can produce illness. Another proverb states that "a sound heart is the life of the flesh: but envy the rottenness of the bones" (14:30). The spirit of envy may have many serious consequences within human relationships, but it also has damaging consequences in the body and life of the envious person. Bitterness brings pain to other people, but it leaves its worst scars in the one who harbors the bitterness. On the other

25 Let thine eyes look right on, and let thine eyelids look straight before thee.
26 Ponder the path of thy feet, and let all thy ways be established.
27 Turn not to the right hand nor to the left: remove thy foot from evil.

5 My son, attend unto my wisdom, *and* bow thine ear to my understanding:

25 Let your eyes look directly forward,
and your gaze be straight before you.
26 Take heed to[q] the path of your feet,
then all your ways will be sure.
27 Do not swerve to the right or to the left;
turn your foot away from evil.

5 My son, be attentive to my wisdom,
incline your ear to my understanding;

[q] The meaning of the Hebrew word is uncertain

25. Synonymous. **Eyes** that look straight **forward** are evidence of a truthful mind. The modern expression, "To look one straight in the eye," has the same connotation.

26. Synonymous. Likewise, the path of the wise one is level and straight (cf. Heb. 12:13). **Ponder** or **take heed to** ("make level" ASV; "weigh carefully" ASV mg.): The difficult word *pālaṣ* means "to be even," "to weigh," "to ponder," "to make level." Translators and commentators take their choice of meaning. Paul Haupt suggests the Akkadian cognate which means "to regard," "to observe," "to notice," "to consider," and so translates the word the three times it occurs in Proverbs: here and in 5:6, 21 (August Muller and Emil Kautzsch, eds., *The Book of Proverbs,* tr. D. B. Macdonald [Leipzig: J. C. Hinrichs, 1901; "The Sacred Books of the Old Testament"], pp. 38-39).

27. Synonymous. To **swerve** from the straight path is to fall into bad ways.

J. A Discourse on Marital Life (5:1-23)

1. Warning Against Licentiousness (5:1-14)

5:1. Synonymous. **My wisdom:** See Exeg. on 1:2. The only place in Proverbs where **my** is used with **wisdom** and **understanding. My understanding:** See Exeg. on 2:2.

hand, there is healing in cherishing the constructive emotions of hope, peace, love, kindness, and trust. The healing processes have a much better chance to work in the body of one who is tranquil in mind, who refuses to harbor a grudge, and who makes no exorbitant claims that the universe must wait upon his whims.

The heart has also been regarded as the center of all of a man's personal activities. It represents his understanding as well as his emotional nature. When a man's heart is right, it means that his motivation is unselfish and that his innermost longings and desires are in accord with his professions and in harmony with the ways of wisdom. The heart represents the man's true self. A man may be one thing outwardly and something else within. "The LORD trieth the hearts" (17:3). The purity of heart of which Jesus spoke had to do with the inner aspirations and the secret desires of each person. That was what needed to be guarded with all diligence, for from the heart **flow the springs of life.**

Guarding the heart in all these senses has something to do with a healthy body. Many of the diseases which afflict men are not the result of organic difficulty. They are functional. They grow out of the fact that people do not think right thoughts, or cherish proper emotions, or maintain worthy motives. Rightly it has been said that if one is to treat a person who is ill, it is "more important . . . to know what sort of patient has a disease, than what sort of disease the patient has."[6] The health of the body depends in large measure upon the condition of the heart when the heart is thought of as the seat of the emotions and the intellect, the center of all personal motivation and desire.

A national health survey completed in 1938 in the United States made startlingly clear the need of health in a nation. The survey "showed that six million people in the United States are incapacitated by illness or accidents on a typical winter day. In one year there occur twenty-two million illnesses disabling for a week or longer. The average person is disabled approximately ten days out of every year."[7] When we add to these facts the judgment of doctors that from 40 to 60 per cent of the cases that come to them are mental or spiritual in origin, then we can see the importance of keeping the **heart with all vigilance.**

5:1-23. ***Right and Wrong Uses of Sex.***—Much of the book of Proverbs is devoted to warnings

[6] Elsie McCormick, "How Your Mind May Make You Ill," *Reader's Digest,* XLI (1942), 51.

[7] National Education Association of the United States, *The Purposes of Education in American Democracy* (Washington: Educational Policies Commission, *et al.,* 1938), p. 61.

2 That thou mayest regard discretion, and *that* thy lips may keep knowledge.
3 ¶ For the lips of a strange woman drop *as* a honeycomb, and her mouth *is* smoother than oil:
4 But her end is bitter as wormwood, sharp as a two-edged sword.
5 Her feet go down to death; her steps take hold on hell.
6 Lest thou shouldest ponder the path of life, her ways are movable, *that* thou canst not know *them*.

2 that you may keep discretion,
and your lips may guard knowledge.
3 For the lips of a loose woman drip honey,
and her speech[r] is smoother than oil;
4 but in the end she is bitter as wormwood,
sharp as a two-edged sword.
5 Her feet go down to death;
her steps follow the path to[s] Sheol;
6 she does not take heed to[t] the path of life;
her ways wander, and she does not know it.

[r] Heb *palate*
[s] Heb *lay hold of*
[t] The meaning of the Hebrew word is uncertain

---

2. Synonymous. **Discretion:** See Exeg. on 1:4. **Thy lips may keep knowledge:** A difficult expression, since **lips** usually "utter," rather than **keep.** The LXX reads, "And the knowledge of my lips is commanded thee," which is good, but not in parallelism with vs. 2*a*.

3. Synonymous. This is the second of five warnings against immoral women in the first section of Proverbs (chs. 1–9; see Exeg. on 2:16). **Strange woman** or **loose woman:** See Exeg. on 2:16. **Mouth** or **speech:** Lit., "palate." **Smoother:** An example of these enticing words is found in 7:13-21.

4. Synonymous. The contrast between vss. 3 and 4 is striking: **honey** (vs. 3) and **wormwood** (vs. 4); **smoother** (vs. 3) and **sharp** (vs. 4). **End:** The word *'aḥarîth* often involves the idea of final judgment or punishment, as here and in vs. 11 (see Exeg. on 19:20; 23:18; cf. also 14:12; 16:25; 23:32). **Wormwood:** A plant used in the O.T. as a symbol of suffering.

5. Synonymous. Cf. 2:18. **Hell** or, better, **Sheol:** The place of departed spirits (see Exeg. on 1:12). It is from passages like this that Sheol seems to assume in Proverbs a faintly moral tinge, for the word refers here not to death alone but to the death of one who has died before his time on account of his sins. The wicked woman's way of life is fatal to her and to those who consort with her. Note the absence of the purely moral element; the evil results of the action are portrayed merely in the terms of the shortening of life. There is no thought of the moral degradation of the woman, or of the immoral nature of the act.

6. The Hebrew text is uncertain. The subject of the first and last verbs may be either **thou** or **she.** The first stich seems to demand a negative to make sense, and so the versions read. The Hebrew has the particle "lest," which is meaningless. The general sense is that the way of the wicked woman is not straight and does not lead to life. **Ponder** or **take heed:** See Exeg. on 4:26.

---

against illicit sex experience. Sexual sins are considered especially deadly. More space is given to the warnings against this kind of sins than against any other.

These warnings are addressed entirely to men. Here women are the seducers. Men are tempted either by a prostitute or by an adulteress. More often it is a married woman who is using her wiles in involving another married man. One reason why women were not warned against the approaches of men is that the social conventions of the time were believed to protect and guard the woman who wanted to live a chaste life. A stronger reason why these warnings were addressed to men only was that it was an age of male supremacy, and only the men were given the benefit of the instruction of the sages. Today a modern parent would be as eager to warn his daughter against the dangers of illicit sex expression as he would be to instruct his son in the evils of promiscuity.

Sex expression is not considered by the writers of Proverbs to be evil in itself. A satisfying sex experience is a normal part of monogamous marriage, so there is no ascetic condemnation of sex as such. The physical relationship of husband and wife is regarded as a fundamental good. The function of the sex experience is not

7 Hear me now therefore, O ye children, and depart not from the words of my mouth.

8 Remove thy way far from her, and come not nigh the door of her house:

9 Lest thou give thine honor unto others, and thy years unto the cruel:

10 Lest strangers be filled with thy wealth; and thy labors *be* in the house of a stranger;

11 And thou mourn at the last, when thy flesh and thy body are consumed,

7 And now, O sons, listen to me,
and do not depart from the words of my mouth.
8 Keep your way far from her,
and do not go near the door of her house;
9 lest you give your honor to others
and your years to the merciless;
10 lest strangers take their fill of your strength,[u]
and your labors go to the house of an alien;
11 and at the end of your life you groan,
when your flesh and body are consumed,

[u] Or *wealth*

7. Synonymous.

8. Synonymous. **Her house:** See Exeg. on 2:18.

9. Synonymous. The losses which occur from following the immoral woman concern honor, wealth, and health (vss. 9-14). The writer dwells in detail not only on the alluring aspects of sin, but also on its terrible consequences. **Honor:** All of that which has gone into the life of a man to make his position honorable among men. **Cruel:** Those pitiless ones who get possession of the victim's money.

10. Synonymous. Through debauchery the foolish man loses his wealth. He gives everything away in order to satisfy his passions and appetites. He is then unable to buy even the bare necessities of life for himself and for his family. **Wealth** or **strength** ("substance" Amer. Trans.): The word *kōaḥ* means either that which one acquires, or that by which it is acquired. The latter is probably better here in parallel with **labors.**

11. The pangs of remorse which plague the man who refuses instruction (vss. 11-14). This is by far the worst result of sin. At the close of the short life of sin all the warning voices of parent, teacher, friend crowd the memory, but it is too late, for the sinner goes to the inevitable doom which he himself has chosen. **Mourn:** Better, **groan. At the end:**

represented as limited to the procreation of children. This is one aspect of it, but those who share all the experiences of a home are to find the shared sex experience a normal and desirable part of life together. The young man is exhorted to confine his sexual pleasures to the wife of his youth, who is compared to **a lovely hind, a graceful doe** (vs. 19). The author of this passage would hardly agree with Leonardo da Vinci of whom Thomas Craven writes that "there is no record of a single love affair, or indeed of a distant Platonic friendship." Da Vinci once wrote that "the act of procreation and everything connected with it is so disgusting that the human race would soon die out if there were no pretty faces and sensual dispositions." [8] The writers of Proverbs, recognizing sex experience as not evil in itself, pleaded for the confinement of its expression to monogamous marriage.

[8] *Men of Art* (New York: Simon & Schuster, 1931), p. 97.

Illicit sex experience was considered foolish since it led to some very undesirable consequences. Instead of pointing out moral factors and the wrong that is done to others, Proverbs here appeals to self-interest. At the moment when a man is being seduced, he may be under the spell of intense passion—only to find later that he paid too high a price for his moment of pleasure. A number of serious consequences are suggested. An adulterer may lose his wealth.

> If he is caught, he will pay sevenfold;
> he will give all the goods of his house (6:31).

Disease may result from his folly.

> **At the end of your life you groan,**
> **when your flesh and body are consumed** (vs. 11).

Dissolute living takes its toll in disease. Nothing is said of the effect on offspring, but science has shown how seriously venereal disease leaves its scars on children born of parents who are

12 And say, How have I hated instruction, and my heart despised reproof;

13 And have not obeyed the voice of my teachers, nor inclined mine ear to them that instructed me!

14 I was almost in all evil in the midst of the congregation and assembly.

15 ¶ Drink waters out of thine own cistern, and running waters out of thine own well.

16 Let thy fountains be dispersed abroad, *and* rivers of waters in the streets.

17 Let them be only thine own, and not strangers' with thee.

12 and you say, "How I hated discipline,
and my heart despised reproof!
13 I did not listen to the voice of my teachers
or incline my ear to my instructors.
14 I was at the point of utter ruin
in the assembled congregation."

15 Drink water from your own cistern,
flowing water from your own well.
16 Should your springs be scattered abroad,
streams of water in the streets?
17 Let them be for yourself alone,
and not for strangers with you.

See Exeg. on vs. 4. **Flesh:** *Bāsār* is the outside skin. **Body:** *Sheʼēr* is the inner flesh, next to the bones. The man is worn out by dissolute living.

12. Synonymous. **Instruction** or **discipline:** See Exeg. on 1:2. **Reproof:** See Exeg. on 1:23.

13. Synonymous. **My teachers:** The form *môrāy* is from the same root as *tôrāh,* "instruction" (see Exeg. on 1:8). These were the wise men, the heads of the schools.

14. The RSV gives the best translation of a difficult Hebrew original. The second half of the verse has been interpreted in numerous ways. It seems to refer here to the community assembled for judicial purposes, specifically to deal with the sin of adultery. The verse then means that the adulterer had just missed suffering dire punishment at the hands of, and in the presence of, his people.

2. Exhortation to Marital Faithfulness (5:15-23)

15. Synonymous. Exhortation to marital fidelity, and description of the blessings thereof (vss. 15-20). A happy and honorable marriage is the only safeguard against the temptations described in the preceding verses. In Oriental imagery the wife is described in terms of a fountain, and sexual enjoyment in the terms of the drinking of water.

16. Synonymous. A difficult verse. Vs. 16*a* in the Hebrew reads simply, "thy fountains shall spread abroad." According to the KJV, it means that "purity of married life will diffuse itself abroad like streams from a fountain, in a numerous family, and in wholesome influences" (Perowne, *Proverbs,* p. 63). The RSV makes a question out of the sentence in order to bring out the most natural meaning of the words, viz., that the husband, or possibly even the wife, should not be unfaithful. The negative is actually inserted by the LXX in order to take care of the difficulty.

17. Synonymous. The pleasures of sexual enjoyment should be experienced with one's own wife. A strongly monogamistic view, which is taken for granted elsewhere (see Exeg. on 31:10).

---

afflicted with it. The law catches up with the offender. The community applies its sanctions against sexual offenders. In vs. 14 we see a man who barely escaped the wrath of the assembled congregation. The death penalty was applied in some codes to both men and women who were apprehended in the act of adultery. The offender may be the object of the vengeance of an outraged husband. The fury of a jealous husband may cause him to go to all lengths in punishing the man who violated his wife. In short, the man who engages in sexual irregularities is foolish, since he does not properly consider the serious consequences that follow such action. The whole matter could be summed up in this sentence:

> He who commits adultery has no sense;
> he who does it destroys himself (6:32).

Self-interest alone should restrain a man in the hour of his temptation.

Ch. 7 has a vivid picture of a seductive woman behind a lattice enticing men with her smooth offers. But this attractive prospect is contrasted

18 Let thy fountain be blessed: and rejoice with the wife of thy youth.

19 *Let her be as* the loving hind and pleasant roe; let her breasts satisfy thee at all times; and be thou ravished always with her love.

20 And why wilt thou, my son, be ravished with a strange woman, and embrace the bosom of a stranger?

21 For the ways of man *are* before the eyes of the LORD, and he pondereth all his goings.

22 ¶ His own iniquities shall take the wicked himself, and he shall be holden with the cords of his sins.

23 He shall die without instruction; and in the greatness of his folly he shall go astray.

18 Let your fountain be blessed,
and rejoice in the wife of your youth,
19 a lovely hind, a graceful doe.
Let her affection fill you at all times with delight,
be infatuated always with her love.
20 Why should you be infatuated, my son, with a loose woman
and embrace the bosom of an adventuress?
21 For a man's ways are before the eyes of the LORD,
and he watches[v] all his paths.
22 The iniquities of the wicked ensnare him,
and he is caught in the toils of his sin.
23 He dies for lack of discipline,
and because of his great folly he is lost.

[v] The meaning of the Hebrew word is uncertain

---

18. Synonymous. Vss. 18-20 express literally what was metaphorically stated in vss. 15-17. The word **fountain** means **wife** as the parallel clause indicates.

19. Triplet. Throughout these verses the writer is describing the wife as the source of sensual pleasure. **Her breasts** or **her affection:** The change of translation is obtained simply by changing the vowels in the Hebrew word. But the former is preferable because of vs. 20*b* (cf. the imagery of Song of S. 1:13; etc.). **Be ravished** or **be infatuated:** The root meaning of *shāghāh* is "to go astray," "to err."

20. Synonymous. Directed against a vice which was evidently quite prevalent.

21. Synonymous. The fact that God sees all things should make our conduct good. **Pondereth** or **watches:** See Exeg. on 4:26.

22. Synonymous. The description of a man caught in the net of his own wrongdoings (cf. Hos. 11:4, where the same figure is used to express the opposite idea). **Cords** or **toils:** Sin is continuously weaving bands and forging chains around the sinner so that he cannot free himself. Wisdom makes the path of life level and free of obstacles for those who follow her (cf. 4:12), but the sinner or foolish man finds himself inextricably enmeshed in his own net. This is his own doing, for he spurned the warning of wisdom and chose the way of folly.

23. Synonymous. As wisdom brings long life, so the lack of it brings death. **Go astray** or **is lost:** The latter is a more appropriate reading in accord with the parallelism. It of course demands an emendation of the text. Perhaps *yighwa'* is the best one suggested.

---

with the fatal consequences that come to him who succumbs to her wiles:

As an ox goes to the slaughter,
or as a stag is caught fast
till an arrow pierces its entrails;
as a bird rushes into a snare;
he does not know that it will cost him his life
(7:22-23).

Little is said about the sex relationships of a young man before marriage. Apparently this was no great problem in that day, since marriage took place at an early age. The real problem was infidelity after marriage. This problem is still acutely present in our time, but in addition there is the problem of premarital sex relationships. The intensity of sex desire is so great that it can easily get out of hand, causing some of the unhappy consequences mentioned above.

The whole problem of right and wrong sex relationships can be lifted to a higher level than mere self-interest. There are moral factors involved that help to bring this matter into proper perspective. A sex relationship always has the possibility of the birth of a child. With all the contraceptive methods that are used today, none is absolutely certain. Whenever two individuals engage in sexual intercourse, they face the question as to whether they would welcome a child into the situation, and whether the situa-

6 My son, if thou be surety for thy friend, *if* thou hast stricken thy hand with a stranger,

2 Thou art snared with the words of thy mouth, thou art taken with the words of thy mouth.

6 My son, if you have become surety for
your neighbor,
have given your pledge for a stranger;
2 if you are snared in the utterance of your
lips,[w]
caught in the words of your mouth;

[w] Cn Compare Gk Syr: Heb *the words of your mouth*

K. A Group of Warnings (6:1-19)

1. Warnings Against Suretyship (6:1-5)

6:1. Synonymous. Although the Mosaic law advocated financial assistance for those in trouble, with no interest charged, it became the custom in later Judaism to pledge for friends in moments of thoughtless generosity loans which could not be met. This dangerous and unsound practice is frequently warned against in Proverbs (11:15; 17:18; 20:16; 22:26-27; 27:13). **My son:** See Exeg. on 1:8. **Be surety:** The verb *'ārabh* has been taken over into Greek in the form ἀρραβών (II Cor. 1:22; 5:5; Eph. 1:14), meaning "pledge," "earnest." The process of becoming surety was something like this: A man finds that his friend is in debt. With too much sympathy, and without enough thought, he makes a pledge with the creditor that he himself will become responsible for his friend's debt if he cannot pay it. The wise thing to do, of course, is either to pay the debt immediately, if one is so inclined, or if one does not have the money on hand, he should not become implicated in the matter at all. **Friend** and **stranger** are synonymous in this verse. **Stricken thy hand:** Cf. II Kings 10:15. This was the procedure for concluding a bargain. It is like our expression, "shake hands on it."

2. Synonymous. The word **if** should be supplied in both clauses. The figure used here is from hunting—the unsuspecting surety is like an animal caught in a trap. **Mouth** or, better, **lips,** following LXX, since the same noun would hardly occur in parallel stichs.

---

tion is such that a child could grow up without embarrassment. They have a responsibility to the unborn, quite beyond their own self-interest in the matter. And there is this other fact: Illicit sex experience is too often only a method by which two people use each other. There is no deep respect one for the other before the experience, and there is often a loathing for each other after it. The reason is that they have not treated each other as persons. They have only used each other for personal gratification, and this causes the loss of the finer emotions. At its best, the sex experience is not simply a physical relationship. It is the physical aspect of a shared life—a life that is shared at its deepest levels. When two young people are comrades in the joys and sorrows of a home, then the sexual aspect of their life achieves meaning and satisfaction.

6:1-15. *Three Things to Avoid.*—Proverbs is full of danger signals. As red lights warn a motorist of dangerous culverts and hazardous railroad crossings, so men are warned of ways of life that bring disaster and pain. Three things that men ought to avoid are mentioned in this section.

Suretyship should be avoided (vss. 1-5). This word is seldom used in our everyday speech, but it stands here for the too-easy assumption of responsibility for the debts of other people. A person can be too quickly taken in by a stranger who needs a cosigner of a note; and before he knows it, the burden of the debt falls on the man who signed the note. There is no indication here that a person should never help another to carry a debt. Times may come when a great favor can be done to someone who needs to borrow money and who needs someone to underwrite the debt. But such a commitment ought not to be thoughtlessly undertaken. Pledges should not be signed lightly. This is true of all kinds of pledges, for he who signs a pledge under the spell of emotion or a momentary impulse may reprove himself later because he acted too hastily.

This custom of becoming responsible for the debts of another may bring embarrassment to the person who does the signing, and the sages advise him to get rid of that responsibility with all dispatch. Another reason may be given for not assuming the debts of others too quickly and without due consideration: the person assuming the debt is not helped by making it easy for him to go into debt. He should not be encouraged by a gullible cosigner of his note, for he may be tempted to continue to live beyond his

3 Do this now, my son, and deliver thyself, when thou art come into the hand of thy friend; go, humble thyself, and make sure thy friend.

4 Give not sleep to thine eyes, nor slumber to thine eyelids.

5 Deliver thyself as a roe from the hand *of the hunter,* and as a bird from the hand of the fowler.

6 ¶ Go to the ant, thou sluggard; consider her ways, and be wise:

3 then do this, my son, and save yourself,
for you have come into your neighbor's power:
go, hasten,[x] and importune your neighbor.
4 Give your eyes no sleep
and your eyelids no slumber;
5 save yourself like a gazelle from the hunter,[y]
like a bird from the hand of the fowler.

6 Go to the ant, O sluggard;
consider her ways, and be wise.

[x] Or *humble yourself*
[y] Cn: Heb *hand*

---

3. **Humble thyself** or **hasten** ("bestir" ASV mg.): The verb *rāphaṣ* means "to stamp," "to tread," "to foul by treading." The rendering of the RSV is favored, however, by the context and supported by the LXX and the Vulg. (cf. 25:26). **Make sure** or **importune:** Really, "storm him," "besiege him." Although the exact meaning of the two Hebrew verbs is not clear, the general sense is evident, viz., that every effort should be made to be released from one's pledge.

4. Synonymous. The exhortation to importunity in this matter is continued.

5. Synonymous. Cf. vs. 2. **From the hand of the hunter** or **from the hunter:** Lit., "from hand." The RSV reads *çayyādh* instead of *yādh.*

2. Warnings Against Indolence (6:6-11)

6. Here the industry of the ant is set forth as an example for the sluggard; in 30:25 the foresight of the insect is emphasized. We may learn a lot from the animal kingdom. As Job says, "But ask now the beasts, and they shall teach thee; and the fowls of the air, and they shall tell thee" (Job 12:7). **Sluggard** (*'āçēl*): This noun form is found only in

---

means. If he is brought up short in this practice he may later thank the person who did not immediately respond to his frantic overtures for help.

Indolence should also be avoided (vss. 6-11). The lazy man falls into poverty. The accumulation of wealth is not the result of a man's wishes, but of his hard work. In that day, as in others, there must have been the problem of getting the world's work done, and evidently there were many who preferred a life of indolence to a life of industry. Some liked sleep better than work.

> **A little sleep, a little slumber,**
> **a little folding of the hands to rest,**

seemed more desirable than waking up and going to work. Poverty is like a robber who is ready to pounce on the man who forever wants a little more sleep.

The field of the slothful man is eloquent evidence that his laziness makes him a man void of understanding (24:30-31). Thorns soon grow in his garden, and nettles take possession of his vineyard. As a farmer, he must keep everlastingly at his task lest the natural forces of nature break his walls down and the weeds overrun his estate. He cannot sit back and allow nature to take its course. His honest toil is needed if he is not to become the victim of want.

A man who is slack in his work is brother to him who is a destroyer (18:9). He may not actually destroy, but if he refuses to create wealth he is like the person who destroys it. Curtailing production has the same effect as demolishing something which has been produced. The indolent man is one who has left undone those things he ought to have done. In this sense indolence has social implications; it not only brings poverty to the man who is lazy, but it also withholds the product of his labor from the common life. Indolence is shortsighted. The lazy man may have enough to eat today; but the time of want comes, and then he has not saved enough from his industry to supply him in the lean months of the year. He forgets that harvest time does not last forever.

This suggests an important problem for our technological civilization. As long as people have wants, it will be necessary for someone to

7 Which having no guide, overseer, or
ruler,
8 Provideth her meat in the summer,
and gathereth her food in the harvest.
9 How long wilt thou sleep, O sluggard?
when wilt thou arise out of thy sleep?
10 *Yet* a little sleep, a little slumber, a
little folding of the hands to sleep:
11 So shall thy poverty come as one that
traveleth, and thy want as an armed man.
12 ¶ A naughty person, a wicked man,
walketh with a froward mouth.

7 Without having any chief,
officer or ruler,
8 she prepares her food in summer,
and gathers her sustenance in harvest.
9 How long will you lie there, O sluggard?
When will you arise from your sleep?
10 A little sleep, a little slumber,
a little folding of the hands to rest,
11 and poverty will come upon you like a
vagabond,
and want like an armed man.

12 A worthless person, a wicked man,
goes about with crooked speech,

Proverbs. There are numerous passages in Proverbs dealing with the problem of laziness (for a full discussion see Exeg. on 19:24).

7. Modern investigation shows that ants do have an intricate organization. The three nouns in this verse denote the judicial head, the police, and the executive power of a community. **Overseer** or **officer:** The *shôṭēr,* originally a "scribe," was the one who kept the rolls or lists (cf. Exod. 5:6, 14).

8. Synonymous. **Summer** and **harvest** are probably interchangeable terms here. In the LXX several verses follow, which describe the busy bee. They were probably added by a Greek scribe who felt that the industriousness and diligence of the bee should not be slighted.

9. Synonymous. The writer is trying to arouse the lazy man out of his sleep and indolence.

10. Synonymous. Cf. Eccl. 4:5.

11. Synonymous. While the sluggard sleeps, poverty comes upon him suddenly like a highwayman or an armed man.

3. Warnings Against Perversity (6:12-15)

The perverse man is always ready to tell lies with his crooked mouth. He likes to give the impression, by sly glances or cryptic motions, that he knows more than he really does. Wherever he goes he casts suspicion or creates discord among his acquaintances. He is the bane of society.

12. A naughty person or **a worthless person:** Lit., "a man of belial." The word "belial," found also in 16:27; 19:28, is personified in later Judaism and applied to Satan

---

work in order to supply those wants, but there is a real question as to the balance that should be achieved between saving and spending. If too many people save too much, there will be no market for the products of those who work. On the other hand, if too many people spend too much, there will be no accumulation of capital to produce further wealth. A people who have conquered the problem of indolence may be productive, but they still have the problem of distributing the products of their labor equitably.

The lazy man can usually give an excuse for his laziness. "The slothful man saith, There is a lion in the way; a lion is in the streets" (26:13). He convinces himself that there is always some great obstacle in the way, so he turns over in his bed and goes to sleep again "as a door turns on its hinges" (26:14). The sage cries out to the indolent man,

> **Go to the ant, O sluggard;**
> **consider her ways, and be wise** (vs. 6).

An anthill is a busy place. Every member of the colony seems to be at work. Even those little insects are able to prepare for the days of winter. How much more should a man learn the prudence of industry in time of harvest! "None preaches better than the ant," said Poor Richard, "and she says nothing."

Sowing discord is a third practice to be avoided (vss. 12-15). A person who shuffles along through life with little purpose, with no high goal that has captured his imagination, is

13 He winketh with his eyes, he speaketh
with his feet, he teacheth with his fingers;
14 Frowardness *is* in his heart, he deviseth
mischief continually; he soweth discord.
15 Therefore shall his calamity come suddenly;
suddenly shall he be broken without
remedy.
16 ¶ These six *things* doth the LORD
hate; yea, seven *are* an abomination unto
him:
17 A proud look, a lying tongue, and
hands that shed innocent blood,

13 winks with his eyes, scrapes[z] with his feet,
points with his finger,
14 with perverted heart devises evil,
continually sowing discord;
15 therefore calamity will come upon him
suddenly;
in a moment he will be broken beyond
healing.

16 There are six things which the LORD
hates,
seven which are an abomination to
him:
17 haughty eyes, a lying tongue,
and hands that shed innocent blood,

[z] Or *taps*

in the N.T. (II Cor. 6:15). Numerous etymologies of the word have been suggested (see Toy, *Proverbs,* pp. 125-26); it really means "depravity," "degradation." **Froward** or **crooked:** See Exeg. on 2:15. **Speech** is, lit., **mouth.**

13. Three signs of malicious insincerity. **Winketh.** Cf. 10:10. **Speaketh** or **scrapes** (**taps** RSV mg.; "shuffleth" ASV mg.): The renderings of the RSV and the ASV mg. are based upon the rabbinical Hebrew word meaning "to rub ears of corn." "To speak" is the ordinary meaning of the root *mālal,* and is perfectly intelligible in this context. **Teacheth** or better, **points,** which brings out the original sense of *yārāh.*

14. Synonymous. **Frowardness** or, better, **perverted:** See Exeg. on 2:12. **Deviseth:** See Exeg. on 3:29. A verse of two stichs is attained by dividing before **continually** (with RSV).

15. Synonymous. Cf. 1:26. The penalty for this kind of perversity is irremedial. It is death. There can be no gradual punishment for this base creature. It is sudden. He is **broken** to pieces by the hand of God.

4. WARNINGS AGAINST SEVEN SINS (6:16-19)

16. Synonymous. The numerical pattern used here (cf. also ch. 30) is found in the Proverbs of Aḥikar and the Ugaritic literature (see Intro., p. 767; Vol. I, pp. 259-61). The progression, six and seven, is used to denote the full list of things that God hates (cf. Amos 1–2). **Abomination:** See Exeg. on 3:32.

17. Proud look or, better, **haughty eyes:** Cf. 30:13. Note the parts of the body mentioned in these verses.

likely to enjoy devising evil and making life uncomfortable for other people. If he cannot lift himself up, he tries to pull other people down. He is ready to indulge in **crooked speech.** He easily points the finger of accusation at another. Much of his time is given to disapproval of other people, since he does little that can give other people a chance to approve of him. By his sowing discord, people must pay attention to him, although ultimately they will see him as he is and **calamity will come upon him suddenly.** If a worthless man cannot awaken respect for himself by what he does, he ought at least not to become a perverted soul who devises evil and sows discord to get the attention for which he starves.

16-19. *No Indifferent God.*—The God who is described in these verses is no indifferent God who has no preferences. There are some things of which God disapproves. He **hates** them.

The writer is indeed courageous in assuming that he knows what God hates. The probability is that he picked out some human attitudes that were hateful to him and proved damaging in human relations, and then asserted that God also disapproves of them. He could not believe that something could be good in God's sight if it was evil in his human sight. Though years have passed since the writer made this judgment, few would assert that a faithful Creator would not still disapprove of such attitudes as he describes.

18 A heart that deviseth wicked imaginations, feet that be swift in running to mischief,
19 A false witness *that* speaketh lies, and he that soweth discord among brethren.
20 ¶ My son, keep thy father's commandment, and forsake not the law of thy mother:
21 Bind them continually upon thine heart, *and* tie them about thy neck.
22 When thou goest, it shall lead thee;

18 a heart that devises wicked plans,
feet that make haste to run to evil,
19 a false witness who breathes out lies,
and a man who sows discord among brothers.

20 My son, keep your father's commandment,
and forsake not your mother's teaching.
21 Bind them upon your heart always;
tie them about your neck.
22 When you walk, they[a] will lead you;
when you lie down, they[a] will watch over you;

[a] Heb *it*

---

18. Not all crimes are openly committed, nor are their perpetrators apprehended by the police. Only God knows the wicked thoughts of the sinful heart which lead to the ruin and downfall of a fellow man.

19. The crime of bearing false witness against one's neighbor is often condemned in this book (cf. 12:17; 14:5, 25; 19:5, 9). This was a common crime in the days when legal protection was not very strong and the moral conscience of man was not too highly developed (see further Exeg. on 14:25). **Speaketh** or **breathes out,** which is the literal translation of the verb *pûaḥ*. It is a strong expression, occurring again in 12:17; 14:5, 25; 19:5, 9.

L. Warnings Against the Adulteress (6:20–7:27)

This is the longest section in the book which deals with the problem of illicit love (see Exeg. on 2:16). Wisdom speaks frankly about this sin. She does so, however, not to titillate the passions of the reader, as so much modern literature does, but to portray the disillusionment of illicit love and its certain end in unquenchable remorse and bitter death.

20. Synonymous. The instruction of parents is invoked to guard the son against the sin of adultery. The contents of the instruction are those laws and teachings which men in preceding generations have found to be wise and true, and which have been preserved to be passed on to their children. **My son:** See Exeg. on 1:8. **Commandment:** See Exeg. on 2:1. **Law** or, better, **teaching:** See Exeg. on 1:8.

21. Synonymous. See Exeg. on 3:3; 7:3.

22. Triplet. Cf. 3:23-24; Deut. 6:6-8. **They** (RSV) is more natural as the subject after vs. 21. **It** (KJV), following the Hebrew, refers to wisdom.

Five of the seven things hateful to God are pictured in terms of parts of the body: **eyes, tongue, hands, heart, feet.** None of these organs is hateful in itself; the divine disapproval arises when the individual uses his eyes to flaunt his haughtiness, his tongue to lie, his hands to shed innocent blood, his heart (mind) to devise crafty plans, and his feet to run some evil errand. The words of Jesus come to mind, "If your hand or your foot causes you to sin, cut it off and throw it from you; it is better for you to enter life maimed or lame than with two hands or two feet to be thrown into the eternal fire" (Matt. 18:8).

If this picture is left by itself, it presents a God with a blue pencil in his hand. He is more interested in making plain what he hates than he is intent upon indicating what he loves. And yet all love implies rejection of that which harms the loved one. All love of beauty implies a rejection of the ugly. A God who hates nothing could hardly be said to love anything, but we have a God who has the nature to hate and to disapprove the attitudes that frustrate his good purposes for men. The person who searches for the divine approval, who longs to hear the "Well done, good and faithful servant" (Matt. 25:21), will avoid those things which must be disapproved by the Father of all men.

20-35. See Expos. on 5:1-23.

when thou sleepest, it shall keep thee; and *when* thou awakest, it shall talk with thee.

23 For the commandment *is* a lamp; and the law *is* light; and reproofs of instruction *are* the way of life:

24 To keep thee from the evil woman, from the flattery of the tongue of a strange woman.

25 Lust not after her beauty in thine heart; neither let her take thee with her eyelids.

26 For by means of a whorish woman *a man is brought* to a piece of bread: and the adulteress will hunt for the precious life.

27 Can a man take fire in his bosom, and his clothes not be burned?

28 Can one go upon hot coals, and his feet not be burned?

29 So he that goeth in to his neighbor's wife; whosoever toucheth her shall not be innocent.

and when you awake, they[a] will talk
with you.
23 For the commandment is a lamp and the
teaching a light,
and the reproofs of discipline are the
way of life,
24 to preserve you from the evil woman,
from the smooth tongue of the adventuress.
25 Do not desire her beauty in your heart,
and do not let her capture you with her
eyelashes;
26 for a harlot may be hired for a loaf of
bread,[b]
but an adulteress[c] stalks a man's very
life.
27 Can a man carry fire in his bosom
and his clothes not be burned?
28 Or can one walk upon hot coals
and his feet not be scorched?
29 So is he who goes in to his neighbor's
wife;
none who touches her will go unpunished.

[a] Heb *it*
[b] Cn Compare Gk Syr Vg Tg: Heb *for because of a harlot to a piece of bread*
[c] Heb *a man's wife*

---

23. Synonymous. The written law (*tôrāh*) is the light (*'ôr*); the interpretation of the law (*miçwāh*) is the lamp (*nēr*) which is illumined by the light. **Reproofs** and **discipline** in vs. 23*b* correspond respectively to *tôrāh* and *miçwāh* in vs. 23*a*. In Hebrew the order of these four words is chiastic. More than light is necessary to guide one in the path of a long and prosperous life (see Oesterley's discussion of this verse, *Proverbs*, pp. 45-46).

24. Synonymous. Wisdom will keep a man away from the wiles of the evil woman (cf. 2:16).

25. Synonymous. Cf. Matt. 5:28. **Eyelids:** Probably refers to the painted eyelids of Eastern women who enticed men with their lustful looks.

26. The first stich is difficult. The KJV, together with the ASV and the American Jewish Translation, brings out the idea that penury results from harlotry; the RSV and the Amer. Trans. take it to mean that a harlot may be hired for a small sum, whereas an adulteress takes a man's very soul. The basic difficulty lies in the meaning of the Hebrew preposition *be'adh,* which can mean either "on account of," or "in exchange for." Another problem is whether the same woman is meant in both stichs, or whether a harlot is referred to in the first and an adulteress in the second. Although the latter makes good sense (cf. RSV), the fact that this section does not deal with harlots or prostitutes as such militates against such a distinction. **Piece of bread:** Lit., "round loaf of bread," the usual form of bread made in the East.

28. **Coals:** Glowing wood is meant here. The answer to these questions is, of course, "No!"

29. **Innocent** or, better, **unpunished:** There is no escape from the dire punishment that awaits the man who indulges in illicit love.

30 *Men* do not despise a thief, if he steal to satisfy his soul when he is hungry;

31 But *if* he be found, he shall restore sevenfold; he shall give all the substance of his house.

32 *But* whoso committeth adultery with a woman lacketh understanding: he *that* doeth it destroyeth his own soul.

33 A wound and dishonor shall he get; and his reproach shall not be wiped away.

34 For jealousy *is* the rage of a man: therefore he will not spare in the day of vengeance.

35 He will not regard any ransom; neither will he rest content, though thou givest many gifts.

7 My son, keep my words, and lay up my commandments with thee.

30 Do not men despise[d] a thief if he steals
to satisfy his appetite when he is hungry?
31 And if he is caught, he will pay sevenfold;
he will give all the goods of his house.
32 He who commits adultery has no sense;
he who does it destroys himself.
33 Wounds and dishonor will he get,
and his disgrace will not be wiped away.
34 For jealousy makes a man furious,
and he will not spare when he takes revenge.
35 He will accept no compensation,
nor be appeased though you multiply gifts.

7 My son, keep my words
and treasure up my commandments with you;

[d] Or *Men do not despise*

---

30. A difficult verse. As it stands, it does not agree with O.T. teaching. The only way to make any sense out of it is to compare the poor thief with the adulterer who is despised. The question form of the sentence in the RSV and the Amer. Trans. (suggested by many commentators) would mean that if a thief is despised for stealing bread when he is hungry, how much more is a man despised for stealing another man's wife?

31. Synonymous. The robber, if caught, must repay, even if it takes all he has. **Sevenfold:** Actually, according to Exod. 22:1-4, a thief repaid two, four, or fivefold. **Sevenfold** is used here probably to denote full measure, or as a round number.

32. Synonymous. The adulterer pays a heavier price than the robber, viz., his own soul. Note the appeal to self-interest. **Understanding** or **sense:** Lit., "heart" (see Exeg. on 2:2). **Soul** or, better, **himself:** Although the KJV is the literal translation, it "conveys a wrong impression by suggesting moral and spiritual depravation and destruction—an idea correct in itself, but not here expressed" (Toy, *Proverbs,* p. 141). *Néphesh* is used frequently in Hebrew to express the reflexive idea.

33. Synonymous. According to Deut. 22:22-24 and Lev. 20:10, death was the punishment for adultery. Later the penalty seems to have been relaxed. Here the writer may be referring not to legal punishment at all, but to the punishment inflicted upon the adulterer by the outraged husband, as vss. 34-35 indicate.

34. Synonymous. The jealousy of the deceived husband is used as a warning here. Again note the motive of self-interest. **Man:** The word *gébher* emphasizes the strength of man. **Day of vengeance** or **when he takes revenge:** The Hebrew phrase may mean either private or legal revenge. The RSV seems to make it refer to the former.

35. Synonymous. No amount of money will appease the angry husband whose wife has been unfaithful. **Ransom** or **compensation:** Lit., "a covering" (*kṓpher*), and so anything given in lieu of punishment.

7:1. Synonymous. Cf. 2:1; 3:1; 4:1. As in 6:20-23, vss. 1-4 of this chapter introduce the theme of the wicked woman by commending to the youth the teachings of wisdom. **Commandments:** See Exeg. on 2:1.

7:1-27. See Expos. on 5:1-23.

2 Keep my commandments, and live;
and my law as the apple of thine eye.
3 Bind them upon thy fingers, write them
upon the table of thine heart.
4 Say unto wisdom, Thou *art* my sister;
and call understanding *thy* kinswoman:
5 That they may keep thee from the
strange woman, from the stranger *which*
flattereth with her words.
6 ¶ For at the window of my house I
looked through my casement,
7 And behold among the simple ones, I
discerned among the youths, a young man
void of understanding,
8 Passing through the street near her
corner; and he went the way to her house,
9 In the twilight, in the evening, in the
black and dark night:
10 And, behold, there met him a woman
with the attire of a harlot, and subtile of
heart.
11 (She *is* loud and stubborn; her feet
abide not in her house:

2 keep my commandments and live,
keep my teachings as the apple of your eye;
3 bind them on your fingers,
write them on the tablet of your heart.
4 Say to wisdom, "You are my sister,"
and call insight your intimate friend;
5 to preserve you from the loose woman,
from the adventuress with her smooth words.

6 For at the window of my house
I have looked out through my lattice,
7 and I have seen among the simple,
I have perceived among the youths,
a young man without sense,
8 passing along the street near her corner,
taking the road to her house
9 in the twilight, in the evening,
at the time of night and darkness.

10 And lo, a woman meets him,
dressed as a harlot, wily of heart.[e]
11 She is loud and wayward,
her feet do not stay at home;

[e] The meaning of the Hebrew is uncertain

---

2. Synonymous. Vs. 2*a* is the same as 4:4*c*. **Commandments:** See Exeg. on 2:1. **Law** or **teachings:** Hebrew, *tôrāh* (see Exeg. on 1:8). **Apple:** Lit., "little man" (*'îshôn*). In Deut. 32:10; Ps. 17:8 this word is used for something valuable; in vs. 9 and 20:20 it means "center," "core."

3. Synonymous. Cf. 3:3; 6:21. Some think that this is a reference to the phylacteries and the mezuzah of Deut. 6:8-9. The clear meaning is that the teachings of the wise men should be in plain view at all times so that they may be inwardly observed.

4. Synonymous. This verse expresses the intimate relationship that should exist between wisdom and men. The beautiful, happy, and noble kinship of wisdom as sister is suggested here in contrast with the impure, ignoble relationship described in the following verses. **Kinswoman** or **intimate friend:** This word is found only in Ruth 2:1 (cf. also 3:2) where it denotes kinship.

5. Synonymous. See Exeg. on 2:16.

6. In vss. 6-23 the wiles of the adulteress are described in graphic detail. **Casement** or **lattice:** The word refers to a typical Oriental window without glass, protected by an elaborate screen.

7. Simple. See Exeg. on 1:4. **Understanding** or **sense:** Lit., "heart" (see Exeg. on 2:2).

8. Synonymous. He is strolling aimlessly about, not intent on meeting anyone.

9. Four degrees of darkness are described in this verse: **twilight, evening, night,** and **darkness. Black** or **time:** Hebrew, *'îshôn* (see Exeg. on vs. 2). Lit., "in the center of night."

10. The **harlot** here is a married woman (cf. vss. 19-20). For the characteristic attire of the harlot cf. Gen. 38:14. **Subtile** or **wily:** A difficult word. The root *nāçar* means "to guard," "to keep," from which the conjectural translation **wily** might be derived.

11. Synonymous. **Loud:** A difficult word, which, from its use in I Kings 1:41; Isa. 22:2, seems to express the idea of being boisterous and unrestrained. It occurs again in 9:13. **Wayward:** Evidently the RSV reads the word *ṣôrāreth,* **stubborn,** as *ṣôbhābheth,* "going about," "gadding about," with Vulg. (cf. Song of S. 3:2).

12 Now *is she* without, now in the streets, and lieth in wait at every corner.)
13 So she caught him, and kissed him, *and* with an impudent face said unto him,
14 *I have* peace offerings with me; this day have I paid my vows.
15 Therefore came I forth to meet thee, diligently to seek thy face, and I have found thee.
16 I have decked my bed with coverings of tapestry, with carved *works,* with fine linen of Egypt.
17 I have perfumed my bed with myrrh, aloes, and cinnamon.
18 Come, let us take our fill of love until the morning: let us solace ourselves with loves.
19 For the goodman *is* not at home, he is gone a long journey:
20 He hath taken a bag of money with him, *and* will come home at the day appointed.
21 With her much fair speech she caused

12 now in the street, now in the market,
and at every corner she lies in wait.
13 She seizes him and kisses him,
and with impudent face she says to him:
14 "I had to offer sacrifices,
and today I have paid my vows;
15 so now I have come out to meet you,
to seek you eagerly, and I have found you.
16 I have decked my couch with coverings,
colored spreads of Egyptian linen;
17 I have perfumed my bed with myrrh,
aloes, and cinnamon.
18 Come, let us take our fill of love till morning;
let us delight ourselves with love.
19 For my husband is not at home;
he has gone on a long journey;
20 he took a bag of money with him;
at full moon he will come home."

21 With much seductive speech she per-

---

12. Synonymous. The RSV is more accurate and dramatic than the KJV.

13. The present tenses in the RSV are more graphic than the past used in the KJV. **With impudent face:** Lit., "she hardened her face." She makes him believe that she came out purposely to see him. She then offers her allurements in rapid succession.

14. The particular peace offering sacrificed here is made in connection with the fulfillment of a vow, in which case the flesh of the offering had to be eaten the same day or the next (Lev. 7:16). Thus she offers him first of all a sumptuous meal. **With me:** Better, **I had to** (see ASV mg., and numerous commentators). Lit., "upon me," i.e., "incumbent upon me."

15. To seek . . . eagerly: For this word see Exeg. on 1:28.

16. Synonymous. This verse and the following describe the luxurious appointments of the woman's house, which show her position and wealth. She thus plays upon his artistic nature, trying to allure him by describing her beautifully decorated furniture and the sweet-smelling perfumes. **Coverings:** The meaning of this word is derived from the cognate verb used with it here. It occurs again only in 31:22. There is no support for the **tapestry** of the KJV. "Cushions" (ASV mg.) is probably not correct. The meanings of the terms in the second half of the verse are not clear.

17. These aromatic substances were imported by the Jews from foreign lands. **Perfumed:** The verb *nûph* means "to sprinkle."

18. Synonymous. The verbs here express full enjoyment. **Solace:** Better, **delight.**

19. Synonymous. In this verse the wicked woman offers another inducement. Since the husband is away, the young man will not be discovered in his sin and thus will be spared the jealous rage of the husband. **The goodman:** Better, **my husband,** following the LXX. The Hebrew text simply has "the man," which may be a slighting reference to her husband.

20. The husband expects to be away for a considerable time. Since the full moon festival (Ps. 81:3) is in the middle of the month, he must have left home in the first part of the month for, according to vs. 9, it was dark when she went to seek a lover.

21. Synonymous. **Fair speech** or **seductive speech:** The word is *léqaḥ,* for which see Exeg. on 1:5. It is used ironically here.

him to yield, with the flattering of her lips
she forced him.
22 He goeth after her straightway, as an
ox goeth to the slaughter, or as a fool to the
correction of the stocks;
23 Till a dart strike through his liver;
as a bird hasteth to the snare, and knoweth
not that it *is* for his life.
24 ¶ Hearken unto me now therefore,
O ye children, and attend to the words of
my mouth.
25 Let not thine heart decline to her
ways, go not astray in her paths.
26 For she hath cast down many
wounded: yea, many strong *men* have been
slain by her.
27 Her house *is* the way to hell, going
down to the chambers of death.

8 Doth not wisdom cry? and understanding put forth her voice?

suades him;
with her smooth talk she compels him.
22 All at once he follows her,
as an ox goes to the slaughter,
or as a stag is caught fast[f]
23 till an arrow pierces its entrails;
as a bird rushes into a snare;
he does not know that it will cost him
his life.

24 And now, O sons, listen to me,
and be attentive to the words of my
mouth.
25 Let not your heart turn aside to her ways,
do not stray into her paths;
26 for many a victim has she laid low;
yea, all her slain are a mighty host.
27 Her house is the way to Sheol,
going down to the chambers of death.

8 Does not wisdom call,
does not understanding raise her voice?

[f] Cn Compare Gk: Heb uncertain

---

22. Triplet. The third stich is impossible Hebrew. Literally it reads, "As fetters to the correction of a fool." The KJV translates, **as a fool to the correction of the stocks;** the RSV, **as a stag is caught fast;** the ASV, "or as one in fetters to the correction of the fool"; Moffatt, "like a dog cajoled to the muzzle." The KJV inverts the nouns of the clause in order to make sense, although the meaning of **stocks** (fetters) is not certain for *'ékheṣ*. The RSV reads *'ayyāl,* **stag,** for *'ewîl,* "fool," for which the LXX supplies the evidence. Moffatt's "dog" also has LXX support. The ASV is simply a brave attempt to make something out of nothing. To all of this may be added the countless emendations suggested by commentators. The general meaning of the verse is clear, however, from the context. Like a dumb animal, yes, even worse, since he could resist if he wanted to, the fool marches off to his doom.

23. Triplet. The comparison of the fool with the unwary **bird** is added here.

24-25. Synonymous. Cf. vs. 1. Some final warnings against the evil woman.

26. Synonymous. **Strong men:** Better, **mighty host,** since the first clause refers to her numerous victims. She causes premature death.

27. Synonymous. See Exeg. on 1:12; 2:18; 5:5. **Hell** or, better, **Sheol:** In the book's descriptions of doom and punishment which the sinner suffers there is a note of finality and hopelessness which makes the Christian shudder. The law instructs the soul in the right way and warns against the calamities that will befall if its precepts are not followed. But it cannot help him who has not heeded those precepts and finds himself on the road to destruction. In some parts of the O.T., however, especially in Hos. and Isa. 40–55, and in the N.T. we find the message of redeeming love which alone can adequately deal with the sin and the sinner.

M. In Praise of Wisdom (8:1-36)

The chapter divides itself into three main parts: (*a*) An exhortation to follow

---

8:1-36. ***Wisdom's Appeal to Men.***—Few more attractive portraits of wisdom have been painted than the one found here. She is portrayed as a winsome person moving among the crowds. She does not dwell in some secluded spot accessible only to the few. Wherever people are living to-

2 She standeth in the top of high places, by the way in the places of the paths.
3 She crieth at the gates, at the entry of the city, at the coming in at the doors:
4 Unto you, O men, I call; and my voice *is* to the sons of man.
5 O ye simple, understand wisdom: and, ye fools, be ye of an understanding heart.

2 On the heights beside the way,
in the paths she takes her stand;
3 beside the gates in front of the town,
at the entrance of the portals she cries aloud:
4 "To you, O men, I call,
and my cry is to the sons of men.
5 O simple ones, learn prudence;
O foolish men, pay attention.

---

wisdom, and the reward for doing so (vss. 1-21); (*b*) wisdom's exalted position with the Creator (vss. 22-31); and (*c*) concluding exhortations (vss. 32-36).

1. Exhortation to Follow Wisdom (8:1-21)

8:1. Synonymous. Here wisdom, again personified (cf. 1:20), calling from the high and open places, is contrasted with the adulteress who lurks in the dark streets for her prey. Going from ch. 7 to ch. 8 is like passing from a close, oppressive, foul-smelling room into the pure fresh air of God's outdoors. **Wisdom:** See Exeg. on 1:2. **Understanding:** See Exeg. on 2:2.

2. Synonymous. Cf. 1:21.

3. Synonymous. In this verse one place is described in three different ways: the **gates,** i.e., the elaborate gateway; **at the entry of the city,** a more general description; **at the entrance of the portals,** the actual doors in the gateway (see Exeg. on 1:21).

4. Synonymous. Wisdom addresses all men; her priceless treasures are for everyone, if they will but heed her voice and obey her words.

5. Synonymous. **Simple:** See Exeg. on 1:4. **Understand:** See Exeg. on 1:2. **Wisdom** or, better, **prudence:** For the word *'ormāh* see Exeg. on 1:4. **Fools** (*kesîlîm*): See Exeg. on 1:22. **Pay attention:** See Exeg. on 2:2. The RSV renders the sense of the Hebrew.

---

gether—walking through the streets, meeting at the gates, or trading in the market place—her voice can be heard. She makes her appeal to all men.

> **To you, O men, I call,**
> **and my cry is to the sons of men** (vs. 4).

Her ways are not limited to people of one race or nation. Nothing human is outside the pale of her summons. There is nothing provincial about her appeal. She includes all. Her voice can be heard wherever a human community exists. Her appeal is not based on what she expects men to do for her. She summons them to her ways because of what she can do for them. Wisdom has the secret of effective living.

> **Happy is the man who listens to me,**
> **watching daily at my gates,**
> **waiting beside my doors.**
> **For he who finds me finds life**
> **and obtains favor from the Lord** (vss. 34-35).

Wisdom, who here makes her appeal to men, is characterized by truth and righteousness. Hers is a transparent integrity. She has no desire to deceive, no intention to stretch the truth for the sake of expediency. There is nothing twisted or crooked about her words. She speaks in a forthright and straightforward manner.

"Truth" can often become the servant of interest. An individual may speak the words that produce the effect he desires even though he knows that he is not conveying the whole truth to the listener. Wisdom is sincere. In a letter which he wrote to William E. Gladstone in 1882, Charles Spurgeon expressed the belief that the English premier had this characteristic of wisdom: "You do not know how those of us regard you, who feel it a joy to live when a premier believes in righteousness. We believe in no man's infallibility, but *it is restful to be sure of one man's integrity.*"[9]

Wisdom's message is clear

> **to him who understands**
> **and right to those who find knowledge** (vs. 9).

Moral integrity is needed by those who would grasp the meaning of wisdom's words. Some truths are not self-evident. They are understood only by those who are prepared in mind and heart to receive them. Wisdom can be given only to him who has the capacity to receive it and to

[9] John Morley, *The Life of William Ewart Gladstone* (New York: The Macmillan Co., 1903), II, 531.

6 Hear; for I will speak of excellent things; and the opening of my lips *shall be* right things.

7 For my mouth shall speak truth; and wickedness *is* an abomination to my lips.

8 All the words of my mouth *are* in righteousness; *there is* nothing froward or perverse in them.

9 They *are* all plain to him that understandeth, and right to them that find knowledge.

10 Receive my instruction, and not silver; and knowledge rather than choice gold.

11 For wisdom *is* better than rubies; and all the things that may be desired are not to be compared to it.

6 Hear, for I will speak noble things,
and from my lips will come what is right;
7 for my mouth will utter truth;
wickedness is an abomination to my lips.
8 All the words of my mouth are righteous;
there is nothing twisted or crooked in them.
9 They are all straight to him who understands
and right to those who find knowledge.
10 Take my instruction instead of silver,
and knowledge rather than choice gold;
11 for wisdom is better than jewels,
and all that you may desire cannot compare with her.

---

6. Synonymous. **Noble things:** The Hebrew word *neghîdhîm* means "princes." Here it must have an abstract meaning, the only time it is so used. It might be well to emend with Toy and Oesterley (*ad loc.*) to *nekhōḥîm,* "true things," especially in parallelism with **right things. Right:** See Exeg. on 1:3.

7. Synonymous. In vs. 7*b* the **lips** are poetically described as abominating **wickedness.** The LXX reads more naturally, "An abomination before me are false lips." **Mouth:** Lit., "palate."

8. Synonymous. **Righteous:** See Exeg. on 1:3. **Froward** or **twisted:** *Pāthal* is the root from which the noun meaning "cord," "thread" is derived. **Perverse** or **crooked:** See Exeg. on 2:15.

9. Synonymous. **Understands:** See Exeg. on 1:2. **Right:** See Exeg. on 1:3. **Straight:** The word *nākhōaḥ* means "in front of," and then "right," "true" (see Exeg. on vs. 6).

10-11. Synonymous. Wisdom is far more valuable than the most precious earthly possessions (cf. 3:13-15).

---

understand it. This thought lies behind wisdom's strange words:

I love those who love me,
and those who seek me diligently find me (vs. 17).

At first sight wisdom seems to be following a perverted rendition of the Golden Rule: Do unto others as they do unto you. A character who loves only those who love him might be accused of following the common pattern of behavior. Do not even the publicans the same? But deeper meaning must lie behind these words. Only he who hungers and thirsts for righteousness can be filled. Truth and righteousness cannot be purveyed like a bit of merchandise. They can be given only to him who is able to receive them, just as a seed cannot grow without a proper soil in which to germinate. Wisdom has much to give, but she cannot force her gifts upon those who have failed to fulfill the conditions of receiving them.

Good government is possible only when rulers follow the way of wisdom (vss. 15-16). Rulers must make decisions when there is a clash of interests in the community. If justice and righteousness are needed anywhere, they are needed by those who sit in places of authority. The person who feels that his rights have been violated can have no other recourse than appeal to the rulers of his government. If the fountainhead of justice is polluted, there is turmoil and instability in the land.

This passage is characterized by a friendly attitude toward kings and rulers. It would seem that anyone who has acquired power maintains his rule because he follows the precepts of wisdom. **By me kings reign.** This would imply that the possessor of power is in an impregnable position, and that he merits the uncritical loyalty of his subjects. He is a terror only to the evil. But while the writer of this chapter may have had a high regard for people in authority, he no doubt meant that good government is the result of following the ways of wisdom. The crown may lie very uneasy on the heads of some rulers since they cling to power and use ques-

12 I wisdom dwell with prudence, and find out knowledge of witty inventions.

13 The fear of the LORD *is* to hate evil: pride, and arrogancy, and the evil way, and the froward mouth, do I hate.

14 Counsel *is* mine, and sound wisdom: I *am* understanding; I have strength.

15 By me kings reign, and princes decree justice.

16 By me princes rule, and nobles, *even* all the judges of the earth.

17 I love them that love me; and those that seek me early shall find me.

12 I, wisdom, dwell in prudence,[g]
and I find knowledge and discretion.
13 The fear of the LORD is hatred of evil.
Pride and arrogance and the way of evil
and perverted speech I hate.
14 I have counsel and sound wisdom,
I have insight, I have strength.
15 By me kings reign,
and rulers decree what is just;
16 by me princes rule,
and nobles govern[h] the earth.
17 I love those who love me,
and those who seek me diligently find me.

[g] Heb obscure
[h] Gk: Heb *all the governors of*

---

12. Synonymous. Wisdom here describes herself in the terms by which men come to know her. **Wisdom:** See Exeg. on 1:2. **Dwell with** or **in:** The Hebrew here is not clear, although the LXX follows the same text. **Prudence** (*'ormāh*): See Exeg. on 1:4. **And:** Not in Hebrew, but supplied by the versions. **Witty inventions** or, better, **discretion:** See Exeg. on 1:4.

13. Triplet. This verse seems to break the connection between vs. 12 and vs. 14. **Fear:** See Exeg. on 1:7. **The fear of the LORD** is filled with a moral content here. Since the reverse side of **the fear of the LORD** is the **hatred of evil,** wisdom likewise hates everything that is evil. **Pride and arrogance:** Both nouns in the Hebrew are from the same root. **Froward** or better, **perverted:** See Exeg. on 2:12.

14. Synonymous. After saying what she hates, wisdom now goes on to say what she is, what she has, and what can be done through her. **Counsel:** *'ēçāh* is to the wise man what the law is to the priest and the word is to the prophet. These three terms are mentioned together in Jer. 18:18. **Sound wisdom:** See Exeg. on 2:7. **Understanding:** See Exeg. on 1:2.

15. Synonymous. Kings rule by wisdom's guidance. The writer is friendly toward kings (see especially Exeg. on 16:10). **Justice:** See Exeg. on 1:3.

16. Synonymous. **Even all the judges of the earth:** Following the LXX, the RSV renders **govern the earth,** which makes a smoother translation and requires only slight change in the Hebrew text. **Earth:** Many Hebrew MSS have *çédheq,* which may have come about through dittography from the last word in vs. 15. The LXX has γῆς.

17. Synonymous. The rewards of those who love wisdom are enumerated in the following verses. **Seek . . . early** or, better, **seek . . . diligently:** See Exeg. on 1:28.

---

tionable means of holding it. Good government requires men who decree what is just and who speak with honesty and integrity.

Wisdom offers high rewards to those who follow her way. Possessing wisdom is far better than possessing gold or silver, and yet there is assurance that he who is wise and just in his dealing will have gold and silver and much more.

> **Riches and honor are with me,**
> **enduring wealth and prosperity** (vs. 18).

While the wealth which wisdom offers is more than money, there is every evidence that money is included in the reward. Earthly prosperity and a position of honor are held out as inducements. Is wisdom here overselling her wares? Many witnesses could be summoned who did not get wealth and prosperity as a result of living a life of honesty and just dealing. Earthly comforts and prosperity do not invariably follow wise dealing.

The rewards which wisdom offers may be deeper than here depicted. Some satisfactions in life transcend wealth or prosperity. Moral integrity may not always pay off in a bigger bank account, and yet it may bring satisfactions that are greater than earthly wealth. Still the appeal

18 Riches and honor *are* with me; *yea,* durable riches and righteousness.

19 My fruit *is* better than gold, yea, than fine gold; and my revenue than choice silver.

20 I lead in the way of righteousness, in the midst of the paths of judgment:

21 That I may cause those that love me to inherit substance; and I will fill their treasures.

22 The LORD possessed me in the beginning of his way, before his works of old.

18 Riches and honor are with me,
enduring wealth and prosperity.
19 My fruit is better than gold, even fine gold,
and my yield than choice silver.
20 I walk in the way of righteousness,
in the paths of justice,
21 endowing with wealth those who love me,
and filling their treasuries.

22 The LORD created me at the beginning of his work,[i]
the first of his acts of old.

[i] Heb *way*

18. Synonymous. **Enduring:** The root meaning of *'āthēq* is "to advance in years," "to proceed," and then "advanced," "eminent." **Righteousness** or **prosperity:** *Çᵉdhāqāh,* usually rendered as the KJV does here, means in this context the good measure of fortune meted out to man by God.

19. Synonymous. Cf. vss. 10-11; 3:13-15.

20. Synonymous. Wisdom acts in accord with justice, and this conduct is manifested in the lives of those who follow her. **Righteousness:** See Exeg. on 1:3. **Judgment** or **justice:** See Exeg. on 1:3.

21. Synonymous. Since wisdom is just, she will properly reward her followers.

2. Wisdom's Exalted Position (8:22-31)

22. Synonymous. In vss. 22-31 wisdom is exalted as the first thing that God created, and also as his companion in the creation of the world. This is the highest conception of wisdom found in the canonical books. Wisdom therefore should be obeyed not only because of the advantages she brings, but also because of her essential nature and the high place she holds in the universe (see Intro., pp. 773-74, for a general discussion of the concept of wisdom).

Possessed me or **created me** (with LXX): The verb *qānāh* may be translated either way. In view of the statements made in the following verses concerning wisdom, it would seem that the RSV translates correctly; cf. also the following quotations from Ecclesiasticus:

> Wisdom was created before them all,
> And sound intelligence from eternity (Ecclus. 1:4).
>
> The Lord himself created her (Ecclus. 1:9).
>
> Then the Creator of all gave me his command;
> And he who created me made my tent rest (Ecclus. 24:8 Amer. Trans.).

of wisdom may remain on the plane of a high self-interest—a self-interest that desires to know the secret of a satisfying life. The one who follows wisdom is true to his highest self. Wise living is understanding the laws of life and living in accordance with them. The person who sins against wisdom really sins against himself (vs. 36). To **hate** wisdom is to **love death,** and to love wisdom is to love life.

Wisdom is then presented as the master workman with God, having a position of priority in the creative scheme. Wisdom was the first of God's creations. In this role she became a fellow creator with God, one who was beside the Eternal One **like a master workman** (vs. 30). The modern reader of this passage does not need to accept the cosmogony of the writer in order to discover that he was here discussing a perennial question. Looking at the world about him, he tried to explain how it came into existence. He believed that there must have been some creative power adequate to produce the

23 I was set up from everlasting, from the beginning, or ever the earth was.
24 When *there were* no depths, I was brought forth; when *there were* no fountains abounding with water.
25 Before the mountains were settled, before the hills was I brought forth:

[23] Ages ago I was set up,
at the first, before the beginning of the earth.
[24] When there were no depths I was brought forth,
when there were no springs abounding with water.
[25] Before the mountains had been shaped,
before the hills, I was brought forth;

This verse figured prominently in the christological controversies of the early church (cf. I Cor. 1:24, 30).

The beginning . . . before [**first** RSV] **. . . of old:** These three expressions of time, coming one right after the other, emphasize the hoary age of wisdom (cf. Mic. 5:2). **At the beginning** is better than **the beginning,** since the writer is pointing out that wisdom was the first thing created.

23. Synonymous. **From everlasting** [**ages ago** RSV], **from the beginning, or ever the earth was** [**before the beginning of the earth** RSV]: Three more expressions in rapid succession which express the antiquity of wisdom. **I was set up** or "I was fashioned": Two possible translations from two different verb roots which can give the same consonantal form. The translation of KJV, followed by ASV and American Jewish Translation, is from the root *nāṣakh;* that of Amer. Trans. and Moffatt is from *ṣākhakh,* "to weave," "to fashion." W. F. Albright ("The Goddess of Life and Wisdom," *American Journal of Semitic Languages and Literatures,* XXXVI [1920], 285 ff.) holds that the verb root is *nāṣakh,* "to pour out," suggesting that wisdom emanated from God, as later wisdom works describe it; cf. Ecclus. 1:9:

> The Lord himself created her;
> He saw her and counted her,
> And poured her out upon all he made (Amer. Trans.).

Also Wisd. Sol. 7:25:

> For she is the breath of the power of God,
> And a pure emanation of his almighty glory;
> Therefore nothing defiled can enter into her (Amer. Trans.).

24. Synonymous. Vss. 24-26 describe the birth of wisdom before the physical world. **Depths** (*tehômôth*): The primeval waters mentioned in Gen. 1:2. **Abounding with water:** Lit., "heavy in waters," a use of the word *kābhēdh* found nowhere else. Perhaps it is best to omit it with the LXX.

25. Synonymous. **Were settled** or **had been shaped:** According to Hebrew cosmogony the mountains were solid structures resting on deeply sunk foundations.

earth, its forms of life, and its people. He had his particular concept of the waters under the earth, and the waters above that were held in the vault of the skies which we still call the firmament (vss. 28-29). Although our age may not have this picture of the earth and the surrounding universe, we are still confronted with the old problem of discovering how it came to be what it is. Religious faith comes to rest by saying that "in the beginning God created the heaven and the earth" (Gen. 1:1). But children challenge this faith by asking, "If God made the world, who made God?" And to many minds this seems a sufficient refutation to those who affirm their belief in a divine Creator.

Yet before waving aside this ancient faith too glibly, it is well to go on to some other considerations.

Obviously the world as we understand it had a beginning. All evidence points to the fact that this earth did not always exist as it is. People did not always inhabit this planet. Scientists examine fossils and make some estimates concerning the time of the first appearance of men

26 While as yet he had not made the earth, nor the fields, nor the highest part of the dust of the world.

27 When he prepared the heavens, I *was* there: when he set a compass upon the face of the depth:

28 When he established the clouds above: when he strengthened the fountains of the deep:

29 When he gave to the sea his decree, that the waters should not pass his commandment: when he appointed the foundations of the earth:

30 Then I was by him, *as* one brought up *with him:* and I was daily *his* delight, rejoicing always before him;

26 before he had made the earth with its
fields,[j]
or the first of the dust[j] of the world.
27 When he established the heavens, I was
there,
when he drew a circle on the face of the
deep,
28 when he made firm the skies above,
when he established[j] the fountains of
the deep
29 when he assigned to the sea its limit,
so that the waters might not transgress
his command,
when he marked out the foundations of
the earth,
30 then I was beside him, like a master
workman;[l]
and I was daily his[m] delight,
rejoicing before him always,

[j] The meaning of the Hebrew is uncertain
[l] Another reading is *little child*
[m] Gk: Heb lacks *his*

---

26. Synonymous. **Fields:** Lit., "outside places." **Highest part of the dust** or **first of the dust:** The meaning of the Hebrew is not clear. Lit., "the head of the dusts."

27. Synonymous. Vss. 27-31 describe wisdom at the creation of the world. She saw God spread out the firmament like a vault over the earth. She saw the mighty waters of the deep hemmed in at God's command by the great land masses. She was by God's side as he created the universe and the various forms of life that were to inhabit it. **Compass** or **circle:** The term probably refers to the "vault," or solid expanse of the sky which, like a dome, rested on the deep (cf. Gen. 1:6).

28. Synonymous. **When he strengthened** or **when he established:** Both of these renderings result from a slightly emended text. The Hebrew reads, "In the strengthening of the fountains of the deep," which is followed by the ASV, "when the fountains of the deep became strong." The KJV and the RSV are preferable here because their translations are based on a form which is similar to the other verbal forms in vss. 27-29, and also because of versional evidence.

29. Triplet.

30. Triplet. **As one brought up with him** or **a master workman (little child** mg.): These are the most common translations of the difficult Hebrew word *'āmôn,* which is evidently connected with the root *'āman,* "to confirm," "to support." The idea of wisdom

---

on the earth. Living creatures did not always exist here. There was a beginning of plant life and animal life. Astronomers who try to explain the formation of the earth itself venture the hypothesis that the materials of the earth were once a part of the sun. The very nature of the earth is such that we believe it had a beginning and that it will have an end in some near or distant time.

The earth as such had a beginning, and yet we are constrained to believe that something has always existed. It is beyond our imagination to think that once there was nothing and that then something came into being. It is difficult to comprehend the infinite, but it is easier to believe that something has always existed than to believe that once there was nothing and then something came into existence. The religious man is willing to use the word "God" as a name for that which has always existed. Furthermore, the power that existed before the earth was and before the mountains were brought forth must have been great enough and of such a nature to produce this world with its many forms of life, its pulsing human hearts, and its thinking minds. At least this is the belief of those who

31 Rejoicing in the habitable part of his earth; and my delights *were* with the sons of men.

32 Now therefore hearken unto me, O ye children: for blessed *are they that* keep my ways.

33 Hear instruction, and be wise, and refuse it not.

34 Blessed *is* the man that heareth me, watching daily at my gates, waiting at the posts of my doors.

35 For whoso findeth me findeth life, and shall obtain favor of the LORD.

31 rejoicing in his inhabited world
and delighting in the sons of men.

32 And now, my sons, listen to me:
happy are those who keep my ways.
33 Hear instruction and be wise,
and do not neglect it.
34 Happy is the man who listens to me,
watching daily at my gates,
waiting beside my doors.
35 For he who finds me finds life
and obtains favor from the LORD;

---

as a **master workman** is found also in Wisd. Sol. 7:22: "For wisdom, the fashioner of all things, taught me," as well as in rabbinical sources (cf. Oesterley, *Proverbs, ad loc.*). On the other hand, wisdom as a **little child** seems to fit admirably into the context of the whole passage. The versions favor the former translation; modern commentators and translators are about evenly divided in the matter.

His delight: The Hebrew text means that wisdom was the one experiencing the emotion of delight. The KJV and the RSV make wisdom the source of delight (with LXX). **Rejoicing** or, better, "making sport, laughing," as also in vs. 31.

31. Synonymous. Wisdom's main joy is with the sons of men. She sets her heart upon man, the crown of God's creation, for she can disclose herself to his heart and bring him back to God if he obeys her. The laws of wisdom which rule the universe are the same as those which direct the lives of men. Just as wisdom orders the intricate mechanisms of the world about us, so she can order the life of everyone who lives by her words.

3. Concluding Words of Exhortation (8:32-36)

Happy is the man who hears the call of wisdom and follows in her ways. He should attend daily to her instruction, waiting expectantly for the treasures which continually flow from her mouth.

33. Synonymous. **Hear:** See Exeg. on 1:8. **Instruction:** See Exeg. on 1:2. **Refuse** or **neglect:** See Exeg. on 1:25.

34. Triplet. This verse describes one waiting at the doors of a mansion to see a great man. The verse probably suggested the idea of the "house" in 9:1.

35. Synonymous. **Obtain:** Lit., "draw forth" (*pûq*) with the ASV mg. The latter half of this verse occurs again in 18:22*b*.

---

like Darwin contemplate the universe as "that grand sequence of events which the mind refuses to accept as the result of blind chance." [10]

The philosopher Zeno once asked this pertinent question, "Why not admit that the world is a living and rational being since it produces animate and rational entities?" [1] Whatever one's view of that which always was, it must be adequate to account for that which has been produced. The writers of Proverbs were not content to affirm that blind chance had produced wisdom. They put it the other way. They said that wisdom, working with God, produced the earth, and that he who finds the secret of God's creative working will be wise.

"All that exists," wrote Fénelon, "exists only by the communication of God's infinite being. All that has intelligence, has it only by derivation from his sovereign wisdom, and all that acts, acts only for the impulse of his supreme activity." [2]

Wisdom therefore speaks with the authority of one who has true priority, and who was the master workman with God in producing the emergence of this earth, with its drama of living things, and of man, with his hopes and his fears,

[10] Quoted in Alfred Noyes, *Watchers of the Sky* (New York: Frederick A. Stokes Co., 1922), p. x.

[1] Quoted in W. Macneile Dixon, *The Human Situation* (New York: Longmans, Green & Co., 1937), p. 318.

[2] Quoted in J. W. G. Ward, *The God We Need* (Philadelphia: Westminster Press, 1941), pp. 42-43.

36 But he that sinneth against me wrongeth his own soul: all they that hate me love death.

9 Wisdom hath builded her house, she hath hewn out her seven pillars:

36 but he who misses me injures himself;
all who hate me love death."

9 Wisdom has built her house,
she has set up[n] her seven pillars.

[n] Gk Syr Tg: Heb *hewn*

---

36. Synonymous. **Sinneth:** The verb *ḥāṭā'* means, lit., "to miss the mark," and should be so translated here in contrast with vs. 35*a*. **Death:** The doom of those who despise wisdom is sure and unalterable. It is physical death (see Exeg. on 7:27).

N. Contrast Between Wisdom and Folly (9:1-18)

Wisdom invites guests to her own house (vss. 1-6), and so does folly (vss. 13-18; with an intervening section of aphorisms in vss. 7-12). There is a kind of rivalry here between wisdom and folly, the allurements of both of them being set forth intentionally in parallel passages.

1. Wisdom's Invitation (9:1-6)

9:1. Synonymous. **Wisdom:** For the Hebrew form see Exeg. on 1:20. **House:** This may refer to the house of learning which became associated with the wisdom movement (cf. Ecclus. 51:23, 29). **Hewn out:** Better, **set up** (with ancient versions, by a slight change of the Hebrew text). **Seven pillars:** Probably the pillars surrounding the central court of a house, three on each of the two sides, one at the extreme end. The allegorical interpretations of this phrase are numberless.

---

his possibilities and his frustrations. Wisdom does not speak as a tired cynic but as one

> **rejoicing before him always,**
> **rejoicing in his inhabited world**
> **and delighting in the sons of men** (vss. 30-31).

9:1-6, 13-18. ***Two Invitations.***—Wisdom and Folly here issue their invitations to **whoever is simple** (vs. 4). Both are personified as women. Wisdom is presented as a woman who has prepared a feast and invites the young man to dine at her home. Folly is pictured as a wanton woman who **knows no shame** (vs. 13). She invites the simple person to **turn in here** (vs. 16), and to indulge in illicit sex experience. Both of these women make certain assumptions as they extend their invitations to the young man.

Both Wisdom and Folly assume that the young man is without experience. He has not passed this way before. He is **simple** in that he has not yet lived long enough to know which way leads to life and which leads to death. Thus he becomes a candidate to be won. Since he has not yet developed an inner voice to tell him which way to go, he can be appealed to by voices from without. As he begins his journey through life, both voices ring in his ears.

Both Wisdom and Folly assume that they themselves have experience which the young man does not have. They have lived longer. It is not necessary for him to begin with nothing. There is an accumulated reserve of experience upon which he can draw. Others have lived before him. Through the tedious process of trial and error they have arrived at some truths which should help him as he goes forward. **Wisdom has built her house** (vs. 1). She has already erected a place to which the inexperienced can repair. This is indeed fortunate for the young. They can profit by the experiences of others who have gone before them. In his book *Human Destiny* Lecomte du Noüy calls attention to the important place that tradition assumes in evolution:

> The intellectual and spiritual improvement of man is inconceivable without tradition which must now take the place of other mechanisms. The memory of individuals, their experiences, their progress can henceforth be extended in their descendants infinitely more efficaciously and rapidly.[3]

Everyone who begins the adventure of human life has some capital with which to start. His quest for life does not need to be a blind groping along a way that has never been traveled before. Wisdom has already built her house, and Folly is noisy in clamoring for the young man's attention.

The necessity of choice is also assumed by both Wisdom and Folly. The young man is confronted with the task of decision. Each one wants his vote. Both voices sounding in his ears make it clear that he cannot heed both of them. He has the burden of choice. Browning's great

[3] New York: Longmans, Green & Co., 1947, p. 122.

2 She hath killed her beasts; she hath mingled her wine; she hath also furnished her table.
3 She hath sent forth her maidens: she crieth upon the highest places of the city,
4 Whoso *is* simple, let him turn in hither: *as for* him that wanteth understanding, she saith to him,
5 Come, eat of my bread, and drink of the wine *which* I have mingled.
6 Forsake the foolish, and live; and go in the way of understanding.

2 She has slaughtered her beasts, she has mixed her wine,
she has also set her table.
3 She has sent out her maids to call
from the highest places in the town,
4 "Whoever is simple, let him turn in here!"
To him who is without sense she says,
5 "Come, eat of my bread
and drink of the wine I have mixed.
6 Leave simpleness,[o] and live,
and walk in the way of insight."

[o] Gk Syr Vg Tg: Heb *simple ones*

---

2. The feast that wisdom spreads is here described. The **wine** is mixed with spices to make it taste better. The contrast between wisdom as a divine being in ch. 8 and as a busy woman of the house in ch. 9 is striking.

3. Wisdom's **maidens** give the invitation (cf. 1:20-21; 8:1-3). The spaciousness of the house, the lavishness of the banquet, and the generous invitation for all to come and eat are in striking contrast with the private "dinner" described in ch. 7. Compare Jesus' parable in Matt. 22:2-10.

4. Synonymous. This is the street-sermon of wisdom as she calls to those who are in need of her counsel. It is not strange that folly uses the same words in her invitation in vs. 16. **Simple:** See Exeg. on 1:4. **Understanding** or **sense:** Lit., "heart" (see Exeg. on 2:2).

6. Synonymous. The gift of wisdom is a long and prosperous and happy life. An untimely death is the reward of those who spurn her (see vs. 18). **Understanding:** See Exeg. on 1:2.

Pope states the young man's predicament, "Life's business being just the terrible choice."[4] The story is told of a boy who went to an art gallery. He paused before the picture of a young man confronted by a choice. On one side was an angel beckoning him upward; on the other was a woman of intoxicating beauty, crowned with a garland of red roses and holding out a cup of pleasure. When closing time came, the boy was still there. "Oh, don't close yet," he said, "wait and see which will win." Two voices confront the young man with the necessity of choosing one or the other.

Wisdom and Folly both offer some immediate satisfactions. Wisdom offers a feast.

Come, eat of my bread
and drink of the wine I have mixed (vs. 5).

In the N.T., the invitation to enter the kingdom of God is often phrased as an invitation to a feast. Even the memorial act which is done in remembrance of Christ consists of eating the bread and drinking the wine. Folly offers the pleasures of sexual indulgence. She presents the added attraction of a clandestine experience.

[4] *The Ring and the Book,* Bk. X, "The Pope."

Stolen water is sweet,
and bread eaten in secret is pleasant (vs. 17).

For some reason the forbidden act has an added zest because it is forbidden. Perhaps it gives the young man a sense of independence if he flouts convention. His craving for novelty may be satisfied by the secrecy involved.

The difference between the two invitations lies in the ultimate consequences for him who accepts them. The way of Wisdom leads on to fuller life. It has no bitter aftermath. The way of Folly ends in death, for at last **her guests are in the depths of Sheol** (vs. 18). If the young man takes the short view, he might heed the invitation of Folly; but if he takes the long view, he will see the good sense of accepting the invitation of Wisdom. Writes Stephen King-Hall:

> The nature of the problem of Man and Himself, both in its material and spiritual aspects, has always been the same. It has been the need of making a choice between self and selflessness; hatred and love; taking and giving; competition and co-operation; the short view and the long view; nationalism or internationalism.[5]

[5] *Total Victory* (New York: Harcourt, Brace & Co., 1942), p. 246.

7 He that reproveth a scorner getteth to himself shame: and he that rebuketh a wicked *man getteth* himself a blot.

8 Reprove not a scorner, lest he hate thee: rebuke a wise man, and he will love thee.

9 Give *instruction* to a wise *man,* and he will be yet wiser: teach a just *man,* and he will increase in learning.

7 He who corrects a scoffer gets himself abuse,
and he who reproves a wicked man incurs injury.

8 Do not reprove a scoffer, or he will hate you;
reprove a wise man, and he will love you.

9 Give instruction[p] to a wise man, and he will be still wiser;
teach a righteous man and he will increase in learning.

[p] Heb lacks *instruction*

2. Miscellaneous Aphorisms (9:7-12)

7. Synonymous. The **scoffer** (see Exeg. on 1:22) will never be convicted of his errors, neither the godless man. Wisdom therefore directs her entreaties only to the simple and to those who are devoid of understanding (vs. 4). **Shame** or **abuse** (*qālôn*): Originally "littleness," and then "disgrace," "insult." **Wicked man:** See Exeg. on 2:22; 3:25. **Blot** or **injury:** *Mûm* in the O.T. means a physical blot (except here, Job 11:15; and possibly Deut. 32:5). The word in this context is strange. A word like "reproach" or "insult" (so Moffatt) would seem to be more appropriate, but no satisfactory emendation can be suggested.

8. Antithetic.

9. Synonymous. **Learning:** See Exeg. on 1:5. It is revealing that in this verse the **wise man** and the **righteous man** are equated. This is done frequently in the next section of the book (10:1–22:16).

Two invitations! They are constantly being issued to each new generation, and each individual must choose for himself.

7-9. ***Profiting by Reproof.***—He is a wise man who knows when to administer reproof and who knows how to use reproof that is administered to him. Many of the proverbs in this book deal with the contrast between the one who scorns correction and the person who can profit by a rebuke.

Reproof should be administered with discretion. Not everyone knows how to receive correction. In the eyes of some people a rebuke is an unkindly act. They interpret any correction of their own behavior as an attempt on the part of an unfriendly person to undermine their personality. They know nothing of the wounds of a friend, for they cannot imagine a friend inflicting a wound whose ultimate purpose is healing. **Do not reprove a scoffer, or he will hate you** (vs. 8). The scoffer regards reproof as an act of hate toward himself; he therefore responds in kind. And the scoffer may have something on his side; for sometimes rebukes are administered as a blow to the integrity of another's personality. Such rebukes are not directed at errors in judgment or at acts that are blameworthy but are used as weapons to undermine the individual's confidence and self-respect. In fact a man who is uncertain of his own status may find some compensation in being a chronic faultfinder. He rebukes others before they have a chance to rebuke him. This kind of reproof is not an act of kindness, and one can understand why such rebukes would not receive a cordial welcome. Before reproof is administered, the person about to speak ought to ask himself whether the correcting is in a kindly spirit, and whether the person to whom it is directed is mature and secure enough to use the experience of being rebuked.

Refusing correction is a way of despising oneself. "He that refuseth correction despiseth his own soul" (15:32 ASV). A person who refuses correction would appear to despise the judgment of the one correcting him. This may be true, but something more important is also true: he despises his own soul. He does not see the ways in which he might profit by reproof. The man who makes a mistake is not to be despised because he has made a mistake. Anyone who does anything is bound to miss the mark some of the time. The true mistake is to refuse to acknowledge that a mistake has been made. Only an uncertain soul must always be right—in his own eyes. A wise man knows that nobody

10 The fear of the LORD *is* the beginning of wisdom: and the knowledge of the Holy *is* understanding.

11 For by me thy days shall be multiplied, and the years of thy life shall be increased.

12 If thou be wise, thou shalt be wise for thyself: but *if* thou scornest, thou alone shalt bear *it*.

10 The fear of the LORD is the beginning of
wisdom,
and the knowledge of the Holy One is
insight.
11 For by me your days will be multiplied,
and years will be added to your life.
12 If you are wise, you are wise for yourself;
if you scoff, you alone will bear it.

---

10. Synonymous. Cf. 1:7. **Beginning** (*tᵉḥillāh*): A different word from the one found in 1:7. It can only mean the first principle of wisdom, i.e., all wisdom starts with reverence for the Lord. **The Holy** or **the Holy One** (*qᵉdhôshîm*): A plural form which is taken generally to be a name for the Deity (cf. 30:3; Hos. 11:12). **Understanding:** See Exeg. on 1:2.

11. Synonymous. See Exeg. on 3:2.

12. Antithetic. The doctrine of individual responsibility as promulgated in Ezek. 18:4 is found only here in Proverbs. The man who chooses wisdom will reap the rewards of wisdom; the man who turns his back on her will bear the consequences. **Scoff:** The Hebrew verb used here is the one from which *lēç*, "fool," is derived (see Exeg. on 1:22). **Bear:** The LXX and the Vulg. add "evil" to make the sense clear.

---

can be right all the time, and he therefore refuses to despise himself by thinking that his actions and way of life cannot be improved.

The ability to accept correction represents the flexibility necessary to life. "He, that being often reproved hardeneth his neck, shall suddenly be destroyed, and that without remedy" (29:1). A tree that does not bend is in danger of being broken when the storm comes. A tall building that does not sway in the wind might break in a mighty hurricane. Flexibility is needed in personal life as well. When someone "hardeneth his neck" by becoming insensitive to many reproofs, he loses the spiritual resilience that helps him to bend rather than to break.

The truly wise man knows how to profit by reproof. **Reprove a wise man, and he will love you** (vs. 8). He does not interpret a rebuke as an unkindly act. He is more concerned about the content of the criticism than about the motive that prompted it. He sees in it an opportunity to correct himself. "Whoso loveth correction loveth knowledge" (12:1 ASV). This is another demonstration of the truth that to "every one that hath shall be given" (Matt. 25:29). The wiser a man is, the greater is his capacity to become wiser than he is. Confucius once said, "He who seeks learnedness will daily increase."[6] The person who is willing to profit by correction is one who has learned how to learn.

The conclusion of the matter is this: The wise man is not so much the one who administers reproof as the one who can profit by it, not so much a man who gives advice as one who can take it.

10-11. See Expos. on 1:7.

12. *We Are Not Alone.*—This verse is more than the usual statement that every man reaps the consequences of his own deeds. Often the sages in Proverbs state that a man who is wise is wise for himself, and that he who scoffs suffers. This verse is unique in that it affirms that **if you scoff, you alone will bear it.** Or again, "If you are a scoffer, you must bear the consequences alone" (Amer. Trans.).

The writer may be leaning over backward in his attempt to create a sense of individual responsibility. The prophet Ezekiel aimed at the same goal. He saw people who blamed others for their condition. They thought that the fathers had eaten sour grapes and that therefore the children's teeth must of necessity be set on edge. Ezekiel proclaimed the good news, "The soul that sinneth, it shall die" (Ezek. 18:4). This meant that the sins of the fathers could not foredoom a son, that the sins of the son alone can cause his death, and that each person is responsible for his own life. In this proverb the writer is also affirming that the consequences of a man's actions come to him alone. But has he not gone too far? Is it true that our good deeds and our bad deeds have no effect on others whatever? Do we bear all of their consequences alone? Times come when one might wish this were true, for one of the pains of wrongdoing lies in the consciousness of wrongs done to others. If only the bad consequences of our deeds fell on ourselves alone! But "we are members one of another" (Eph. 4:25). If one member suffers,

[6] Lao-Tze, *Tao-Teh-King*, tr. Paul Carus (Chicago: Open Court Publishing Co., 1898), p. 121.

13 ¶ A foolish woman *is* clamorous: *she is* simple, and knoweth nothing.

14 For she sitteth at the door of her house, on a seat in the high places of the city,

15 To call passengers who go right on their ways:

16 Whoso *is* simple, let him turn in hither: and *as for* him that wanteth understanding, she saith to him,

17 Stolen waters are sweet, and bread *eaten* in secret is pleasant.

18 But he knoweth not that the dead *are* there; *and that* her guests *are* in the depths of hell.

10 The Proverbs of Solomon. A wise son maketh a glad father: but a foolish son *is* the heaviness of his mother.

13 A foolish woman is noisy;
she is wanton[q] and knows no shame.[r]
14 She sits at the door of her house,
she takes a seat on the high places of the town,
15 calling to those who pass by,
who are going straight on their way,
16 "Whoever is simple, let him turn in here!"
And to him who is without sense she says,
17 "Stolen water is sweet,
and bread eaten in secret is pleasant."
18 But he does not know that the dead[s] are there,
that her guests are in the depths of Sheol.

The proverbs of Solomon.

10 A wise son makes a glad father,
but a foolish son is a sorrow to his mother.

[q] Cn Compare Syr Vg: The meaning of the Hebrew is uncertain
[r] Gk Syr: The meaning of the Hebrew is uncertain
[s] Heb *shades*

3. Folly's Invitation (9:13-18)

13. Folly is personified as a harlot in vss. 13-18. **Foolish:** The word is connected with the noun *keṣîl* ("fool"); see Exeg. on 1:22. **Noisy:** The same word is used of the wicked woman in 7:11 (see Exeg). **Simple** or **wanton:** In view of the fact that this Hebrew word is found only here, and that it is unnecessary to say that folly is foolish or **simple** (from the root *pethî*), the RSV follows an emended text suggested by Toy. **Nothing** or **no shame:** The RSV follows the LXX here because of an uncertain Hebrew text; the rendering is based on a very slight emendation of the Hebrew.

14-15. Synonymous. Folly, like wisdom, sits in public places and calls to the passers-by.

16. Synonymous. The same words are found in vs. 4.

17. Synonymous. The secret enjoyments of sexual immorality are offered here by folly. Her pleasures cannot be experienced in open daylight but must be enjoyed under the cover of darkness and in secret (cf. 5:15-16).

18. Synonymous. The end of folly's guests is death (cf. 2:18; 5:5; 7:27).

II. The Proverbs of Solomon (10:1–22:16)

This is the largest collection of proverbs in the book. Most of them consist of two stichs each and are antithetic. Outwardly there seems to be no order to their arrangement,

all suffer. Each of us is a part of a web of life that connects us to each other. In "Ulysses" Tennyson said, "I am a part of all that I have met." For better or for worse, the consequences of our acts do not come to us alone.

New meaning is added to human life by this fact of interrelatedness. Nothing is quite so paralyzing to effort as the feeling that what we do makes no difference in the life of anybody else. On the other hand, if a young man knows that what he does will have a profound effect upon the lives of other people, he is given an incentive to take life earnestly and seriously. The truth is that the consequences of good deeds and bad deeds do not come to the doer alone.

13-18. See Expos. on vss. 1-6.

10:1. ***Bringing Joy to Parents.***—Wise living has much to do with family relationships. A son

2 Treasures of wickedness profit nothing: but righteousness delivereth from death.	2 Treasures gained by wickedness do not profit, but righteousness delivers from death.

and so there will be no special divisions of the material except by chapters and verses (see Intro., p. 775, for a detailed description of this section).

10:1. Antithetic. It is significant that the opening proverb of this section deals with the home, which is the first place where wisdom is imparted. The title is omitted in the LXX and the Syriac. **Wise:** *Ḥākhām,* in the double sense of "possessing practical knowledge" and "behaving well." **Foolish** (*k^eṣîl*): See Exeg. on 1:22. **Heaviness** or, better, **sorrow**: A rather uncommon word, *tûghāh.*

2. Antithetic. Vs. 2*b*=11:4*b*. Men cannot put their trust in earthly treasures, especially if they are gained by illegal means. **Righteousness** (*çedhāqāh*) probably means "almsgiving" here, as that was the highest expression of the good life (see Exeg. on 1:3). Ecclus. 29:12 has a similar thought:

> Store up gifts to charity in your storerooms,
> And it will deliver you from all harm (Amer. Trans.).

Death: The premature death of the wicked (see Exeg. on 2:18) The second stich may be found today inscribed on alms boxes in the synagogues.

The subject of wealth is frequently discussed in Proverbs. Since the passages are scattered throughout the book, it may be well to summarize briefly here the main teachings set forth in regard to the possession of wealth. There are certain advantages in having

who is wise brings satisfaction to his father and mother by the way he lives.

> **A wise son makes a glad father,**
> **but a foolish son is a sorrow to his mother.**

Every parent knows that children can bring deep joy or crushing heartache.

In Proverbs consideration for parents is regarded as both a mark of wise living and a motive for it. A people who made much of family loyalty placed the honoring of father and mother high among the list of values. Such loyalty is a mark of wisdom, since he who fails in this regard will be the victim of much that is unpleasant. "Whoso curseth his father or his mother, his lamp shall be put out in obscure darkness" (20:20). Even stronger is the language that is used in another proverb, "The eye that mocketh at his father, and despiseth to obey his mother, the ravens of the valley shall pick it out, and the young eagles shall eat it" (30:17). An important mark of wisdom is filial regard for parents on the part of a young man.

Consideration for parents is also a motive for right living. A young man is invited to think of the effect of his actions on his parents. Parents usually feel that it is their business to bring happiness to their children; in many proverbs children are urged to bring happiness to their parents. They have it in their power to make the hearts of their parents glad. Says one sage, "My son, be wise, and make my heart glad, that I may answer him that reproacheth me" (27:11). A parent may be called to task by the actions of his son. A son's failure becomes in a sense the parent's failure, and so the parent wants his son to act in ways that honor the family name. That desire can easily be pressed too far when parents become more intent upon their own reputations than upon the welfare of their children.

The parent-child relationship is a two-way traffic. Each affects the other. When parents are wise in their living, children are made glad. When children are wise in their choices, a parent's heart is made glad. "The father of the righteous shall greatly rejoice: and he that begetteth a wise child shall have joy of him" (23:24). But deep is the pain that comes to the parents of a wayward son. "A foolish son is a grief to his father, and bitterness to her that bare him" (17:25). The story of the brokenhearted David, mourning over his son Absalom, has been re-enacted many times through the years. Longfellow's "The Chamber Over the Gate" voices a poignant reminder of this fact:

> Is it so far from thee
> Thou canst no longer see,
> In the Chamber over the Gate,
> That old man desolate,
> Weeping and wailing sore
> For his son, who is no more?
> O Absalom, my son!

2. See Expos. on vss. 15-16.

3 The LORD will not suffer the soul of the righteous to famish: but he casteth away the substance of the wicked.

4 He becometh poor that dealeth *with* a slack hand: but the hand of the diligent maketh rich.

5 He that gathereth in summer *is* a wise son: *but* he that sleepeth in harvest *is* a son that causeth shame.

6 Blessings *are* upon the head of the just: but violence covereth the mouth of the wicked.

7 The memory of the just *is* blessed: but the name of the wicked shall rot.

8 The wise in heart will receive commandments: but a prating fool shall fall.

3 The LORD does not let the righteous go hungry,
but he thwarts the craving of the wicked.
4 A slack hand causes poverty,
but the hand of the diligent makes rich.
5 A son who gathers in summer is prudent,
but a son who sleeps in harvest brings shame.
6 Blessings are on the head of the righteous,
but the mouth of the wicked conceals violence.
7 The memory of the righteous is a blessing,
but the name of the wicked will rot.
8 The wise of heart will heed commandments,
but a prating fool will come to ruin.

wealth (vs. 15; 14:20; 18:11, 16, 23; 19:4, 6; 22:7), and there are disadvantages in being poor (14:20; 18:23; 19:4, 7; 22:7). There are many dangers which beset the path of the wealthy man: riches are insecure in themselves (11:28; 23:5); ill-gotten wealth is good for nothing, and even worse, since it brings destruction upon the owner (vs. 2; 15:6; 21:6; 22:16; cf. also 13:11, 22; 28:8). Earthly wealth is insignificant in comparison with spiritual and moral treasures (vs. 22; 11:4; 15:6; 16:8, 16; 19:1; 20:15; 28:6). Wealth is not to be acquired greedily (15:27; 20:21; 23:4; 28:20, 22). One should be generous with his money (11:24-25; 19:17; 21:26; 22:9; 28:27). The prayer of the wise man in regard to riches is found in 30:8-9, where he asks that he be neither rich nor poor, but that he have sufficient food for his bodily needs.

3. Antithetic. God supplies the temporal wants of the righteous (cf. Ps. 37:25). The writers of Job and Ecclesiastes, however, do not agree with this view. **Substance** or, better, **craving:** The word *hawwāh,* when used in this sense, always means "evil desire."

4. Antithetic. Cf. 6:6-11. The RSV rendering of vs. 4*a* is more suitable than the KJV as an antithesis of the thought in vs. 4*b*. **Poor:** Better, **poverty,** by a change of a vowel in the Hebrew word. **Diligent:** The root idea of *ḥārûç* is "to cut," and so the English word "sharp," as used in the figurative sense today, would be a good translation here.

5. Antithetic. Cf. 6:8. On indolence see Exeg. on 19:24.

6. Antithetic. Vs. 6*b*=vs. 11*b*. The KJV, followed by the ASV and the Amer. Trans., differs in vs. 6*b* from the RSV, which follows Moffatt and American Jewish Translation. Both renderings are possible from the Hebrew, the KJV probably being the better one. **Violence,** covering the wicked man like a mantle, controls his life.

7. Antithetic. Vs. 6 describes the earthly life of the righteous and of the wicked; this verse characterizes their lot after death. The memory of the righteous remains as a blessing long after death, whereas the name of the godless becomes rotten and decayed like his bones.

8. Antithetic. Vs. 8*b*=vs. 10*b*. The proverbs which follow deal with the sins of the mouth. **Commandments:** Not the Mosaic law, but the teachings of the wise men, as in 2:1; etc. **Prating fool:** Lit., "foolish of lips," i.e., one who talks foolishly. **Will come to ruin:** The verb *lābhaṭ* is found only here, in vs. 10, and in Hos. 4:14.

3. See Expos. on 3:5-8.
4-5. See Expos. on 6:1-15.
6. See Expos. on 3:1-4.
7. See Expos. on 1:1.
8. See Expos. on 9:7-9.

9 He that walketh uprightly walketh surely: but he that perverteth his ways shall be known.

10 He that winketh with the eye causeth sorrow: but a prating fool shall fall.

11 The mouth of a righteous *man is* a well of life: but violence covereth the mouth of the wicked.

12 Hatred stirreth up strifes: but love covereth all sins.

13 In the lips of him that hath understanding wisdom is found: but a rod *is* for the back of him that is void of understanding.

14 Wise *men* lay up knowledge: but the mouth of the foolish *is* near destruction.

15 The rich man's wealth *is* his strong city: the destruction of the poor *is* their poverty.

9 He who walks in integrity walks securely,
but he who perverts his ways will be found out.
10 He who winks the eye causes trouble,
but he who boldly reproves makes peace.[t]
11 The mouth of the righteous is a fountain of life,
but the mouth of the wicked conceals violence.
12 Hatred stirs up strife,
but love covers all offenses.
13 On the lips of him who has understanding wisdom is found,
but a rod is for the back of him who lacks sense.
14 Wise men lay up knowledge,
but the babbling of a fool brings ruin near.
15 A rich man's wealth is his strong city;
the poverty of the poor is their ruin.

[t] Gk: Heb *but a prating fool will come to ruin*

---

9. Antithetic. The journey of life for the righteous is safe. **Uprightly** or **in integrity:** The root idea of *tōm* is "completeness," "soundness" (see Exeg. on 1:12). **Perverts:** See Exeg. on 2:15.

10. Antithetic. Cf. 6:13. The winking of the eye is the sign of malicious deception. The KJV follows the Hebrew in vs. 10*b* (=vs. 8*b*), but the RSV follows the LXX, which may have been the original text.

11. Antithetic. The one who is righteous, i.e., who lives by the rules of wisdom, is a source of blessing to his fellow men, like a well to a weary traveler, because what he says strengthens and refreshes the soul. **Well:** Better than **fountain** (RSV). On vs. 11*b* see Exeg. on vs. 6.

12. Antithetic. Love overlooks the faults of others (cf. I Pet. 4:8).

13. The contrast between the two stichs is quite clear. **Understanding** and **wisdom:** See Exeg. on 1:2. **Rod:** The fool must be driven like a beast, whereas the wise man is directed by wisdom.

14. Antithetic. **Lay up:** Better, "conceal," which brings out the antithesis more clearly. Wise men, by refusing to speak, avoid many difficulties, whereas fools, by reckless speech, bring on calamities.

15. Antithetic. Vs. 15*a*=18:11*a*. Wealth has its distinct advantages, whereas poverty is fraught with real dangers (see Exeg. on 10:2).

---

9. See Expos. on 18:21.

10. See Expos. on 9:7-9.

11-13. See Expos. on 18:21.

14. See Expos. on 26:1, 3-12.

15-16. ***Where Wealth Accumulates.***—If this proverb were the only comment on wealth and poverty, the sages might be interpreted as giving unqualified approval to the accumulation of wealth. But there are many other observations about wealth in the book of Proverbs. Some emphasize its value. Others call attention to its dangers and liabilities. But all taken together, they offer some pertinent comments about riches.

Poverty in itself is not considered a value. There are some things that money can buy. A poor man often finds doors closed to him. As this proverb states the matter, **the poverty of the poor is their ruin.** Norman E. Richardson has listed poverty as one of the following five major evils that afflict mankind: disease, poverty, ignorance, superstition, and sin.

Few people today would be willing to propose for the world a program aimed to keep everyone

16 The labor of the righteous *tendeth* to life: the fruit of the wicked to sin.

16 The wage of the righteous leads to life,
the gain of the wicked to sin.

16. Antithetic. Riches lead to prosperity for the righteous man, to sin for the wicked one. **Labor** or **wage:** The Hebrew word can mean either the work itself or the recompense for the work. The latter meaning is better here. **Life:** See Exeg. on 3:2.

poor. Money can be instrumental in helping a family to secure proper food and clothing and shelter. These are fundamental human needs, without which it is very difficult to build a good life.

Elsewhere in this book one finds affirmations about the value of wealth. The farmer who has accumulated capital in the form of oxen will have grain (14:4). The rich man has power over the poor man, and the one who borrows is the servant of the lender (22:7). When a man is rich, he has friends. "Wealth maketh many friends; but the poor is separated from his neighbor" (19:4). "The poor is hated even of his own neighbor: but the rich hath many friends" (14:20). However, there is some question as to the value of the friends which are won by wealth. The rich man may many times wonder whether he is being befriended for his own sake, or whether people love his money more than they love him. His experience may drive him to the same conclusion expressed by William Henry Davies:

> When I had money, money, O!
> My many friends proved all untrue;
> But now I have no money, O!
> My friends are real, though very few.[7]

The sages believe that wealth can buy some things, but there are many instances in which they are critical of wealth. Many of their sayings are warnings against false attitudes toward it.

Money cannot buy everything. A time may come when a man's money will not be able to help him.

> Wealth is of no avail on the day of wrath;
> But righteousness saves from death (11:4 Amer. Trans.).

If a man has lived an evil life, or if he has committed a wrong, no money will be able to save him from just retribution. Righteousness is more important than wealth on such an occasion. The man's real asset lies in his character at a time like that. Money cannot buy an education, even though money is needed to pay tuition in a school. A young man may have parents who can pay the fees demanded by a university, but this does not mean that he can therefore acquire an education. One of the proverbs asks this pertinent question,

> Of what use is money in the hand of a fool
> To buy wisdom, when he has no sense? (17:16 Amer. Trans.).

When there is nothing to buy, the possession of money cannot feed hungry mouths. Wars which devastate a nation's productive economy may not prevent the printing of money, but they awaken people to the futility of having money when with bulging pocketbooks they stand before empty shelves in a store.

Among the sages are some who are concerned about the way in which wealth is acquired. They do not ask first how much money a man possesses, but how he got it. The person who has accumulated his wealth by unfair means can hardly expect a blessing from it.

> Treasures gained by wickedness do not profit,
> but righteousness delivers from death (vs. 2).

Wealth that is hastily or easily acquired is seldom of lasting value. "Wealth won in haste will dwindle," writes one sage, "but, gathered gradually it will grow" (13:11 Moffatt). Warnings are heard today against quick easy money that is gathered not by hard work or slow saving, but by scheming and manipulating a market. Such money comes quickly and goes quickly. On the upswing of the market millionaires are created overnight; but the day arrives when they lose everything. "He that hasteth to be rich hath an evil eye, and considereth not that poverty shall come upon him" (28:22). Since the writers of Proverbs placed a strong emphasis upon diligence and industry, they naturally frowned upon the attempt to gain wealth quickly by questionable means and by the exploitation of other people. Their approval did not rest upon the man who had great wealth unless he had come by it through honorable means.

Wealth has some ill effects upon its possessors. Jesus had vigorous words to say about the difficulties that attend the rich in the development of a spiritual life. Their mere possession of wealth is considered a handicap to spiritual living. A man who has wealth tends to become curt in his demands. He is accustomed to getting what he wants because he has the price to pay

[7] "Money," from *The Collected Poems of W. H. Davies.* Used by permission of Mrs. W. H. Davies, and Jonathan Cape, Ltd., publishers.

for it. "The poor useth entreaties; but the rich answereth roughly" (18:23). Wealth may produce conceit. A man who has much money, even though he acquired none of it through his own effort, may feel he is wiser or better than others who have little. "The rich man is wise in his own conceit; but the poor that hath understanding searcheth him out" (28:11). Possibly a wealthy man's apparent bravado is only a method of covering up a sense of inferiority. He may be conscious that all he has is his money, and that he would fare ill in a competition where thought and character are needed.

G. Bromley Oxnam calls attention to the fact that

> E. W. Scripps, who founded the Scripps-Howard chain of papers, spent much time upon a far Western ranch. When queried on the subject, he remarked: "I'm a rich man, and that's dangerous, you know. But it isn't the money that's the risk, it's the living around other rich men. They get to thinking all alike; and their money not only talks, their money does their thinking, too. I come off here on these wide acres of high miles to get away from my sort." [8]

In commenting on Jesus' distrust of wealth, John C. Bennett points out that this is no aberration to be explained away, but an evidence of wisdom. Even more than the writers of Proverbs, Jesus sees the ill effects that wealth may produce on its possessors. According to Bennett, wealth

> does create an artificial sense of self-importance which injures both religious humility and right relations with others. It creates a barrier to fellowship. It causes one to have a stake in the *status quo* which blinds one to the need of change and makes one's mind a nest of rationalizations in the defence of one's own privilege.[9]

Wealth brings worries. People who have possessions are fearful lest they lose them. Thieves may try to get their money away from them. Rich men or their children are in danger of being kidnapped that they might be held for ransom. Of course a man is fortunate if he has the ransom price, but the poor man will probably never be kidnapped since he has nothing to give in exchange for his life.

> A rich man may buy off his life:
> a poor man can ignore the robber's threat (13:8 Moffatt).

Riches are transitory. They are here today and gone tomorrow. Of money it has been said that "you cannot take it with you." A graphic picture of the transitoriness of wealth is presented by a writer in a later chapter: "Labor not to be rich: cease from thine own wisdom. Wilt thou set thine eyes upon that which is not? for riches certainly make themselves wings; they fly away as an eagle toward heaven." (23:4-5.) No man can sit back and be sure that he has his wealth forever. Therefore men are urged to be diligent and watchful in maintaining what they have. A little carelessness in administration, an overconfident assumption that wealth can never be taken away, and a man may find himself in penury. Therefore, "Be thou diligent to know the state of thy flocks, and look well to thy herds: for riches are not for ever: and doth the crown endure to every generation?" (27:23-24.) Men are urged not to trust too highly in their wealth. Money can buy some things, but it is not the object of ultimate trust. "He that trusteth in his riches shall fall: but the righteous shall flourish as a branch" (11:28). The fate of the man who put his complete trust in his money is well described by the writer of Ecclesiasticus:

> One man grows rich by carefulness and greed,
> And this will be his reward:
> When he says, "Now I can rest,
> And enjoy my goods,"
> He does not know when the time will come
> When he will die and leave them to others (Ecclus. 11:18-19 Amer. Trans.).

The writers of Proverbs believed that there was something more important than money or the lack of it. Poverty is not to be cherished for its own sake, since there are some good things that money can buy. Wealth is not to be sought for its own sake, since it brings with it many evils, induces a false sense of security, and often damages the character of its possessors. Izaak Walton quoted a wise man who said that "there be as many miseries beyond riches as on this side of them." [1] With this observation the sages would probably agree. More important than wealth or the lack of it is a "life of integrity."

> Better is a poor man who walks in his integrity
> than a rich man who is perverse in his ways (28:6).

A man may have few of this world's goods and yet be rich in the sight of God. As Tobit said to his son: "And fear not, my son, that we are made poor; for thou hast much wealth, if thou fear God, and depart from all sin, and do that which is pleasing in his sight" (Tob. 4:21).

[8] *Preaching in a Revolutionary Age* (New York and Nashville: Abingdon-Cokesbury Press, 1944), p. 174.

[9] *Christianity—and Our World* (New York: Association Press, 1936), p. 44.

[1] *The Compleat Angler,* ch. xxi.

17 He *is in* the way of life that keepeth instruction: but he that refuseth reproof erreth.

18 He that hideth hatred *with* lying lips, and he that uttereth a slander, *is* a fool.

19 In the multitude of words there wanteth not sin: but he that refraineth his lips *is* wise.

20 The tongue of the just *is as* choice silver: the heart of the wicked *is* little worth.

21 The lips of the righteous feed many: but fools die for want of wisdom.

22 The blessing of the LORD, it maketh rich, and he addeth no sorrow with it.

23 *It is* as sport to a fool to do mischief: but a man of understanding hath wisdom.

24 The fear of the wicked, it shall come upon him: but the desire of the righteous shall be granted.

17 He who heeds instruction is on the path
to life,
but he who rejects reproof goes astray.
18 He who conceals hatred has lying lips,
and he who utters slander is a fool.
19 When words are many, transgression is
not lacking,
but he who restrains his lips is prudent.
20 The tongue of the righteous is choice
silver;
the mind of the wicked is of little
worth.
21 The lips of the righteous feed many,
but fools die for lack of sense.
22 The blessing of the LORD makes rich,
and he adds no sorrow with it.[u]
23 It is like sport to a fool to do wrong,
but wise conduct is pleasure to a man
of understanding.
24 What the wicked dreads will come upon
him,
but the desire of the righteous will be
granted.

[u] Or *and toil adds nothing to it*

---

17. Antithetic. **Instruction:** See Exeg. on 1:2. The disciplined man is the successful man; only a fool is unteachable. **Reproof:** See Exeg. on 1:23.

18. One who hates in secret is really a liar; one who openly slanders is a fool.

19. Antithetic. Much speaking is no virtue; a wise man holds his tongue.

20. Antithetic. **Heart** or **mind:** See Exeg. on 2:2.

21. Antithetic. The good man is a source of blessing to others; the fool cannot take care even of himself. **Die:** An untimely death is meant (see Exeg. on 2:18). **Wisdom** or **sense:** Hebrew, "heart" (see Exeg. on 2:2).

22. Both the KJV and the RSV are possible translations of vs. 22*b*. According to the KJV, the Lord bestows his blessings without the usual sorrows connected with earthly riches; according to the RSV, no human toil can ever produce the riches that God gives. The ASV mg., "toil addeth nothing thereto," is just a slight variation of the RSV. **Sorrow** or **toil** (RSV mg.): The word *'éçebh* may mean either. The words for "work" in Hebrew seem to carry the connotation of pain and sorrow.

23. Antithetic. Just as a fool enjoys doing wrong, so a wise man enjoys right **conduct,** as the RSV translates. In the KJV, as in the Hebrew, the antithesis is not clear. There is no word in the Hebrew to correspond with **pleasure** in the RSV. **Mischief** or **wrong:** The word *zimmāh* is connected with the *mezimmāh* of 1:4 (see Exeg.).

24. Antithetic. In this verse the orthodox view of retribution is presented. **The fear of the wicked** or **what the wicked dreads:** The Hebrew expression, literally rendered by the KJV, may mean either that which the RSV has interpreted it to mean, or the fear that is inspired by the wicked man. It would seem as though the latter would be the better interpretation in this context. **Shall be granted:** The Hebrew reads, "he shall grant," but the passive should be read with the versions.

---

17. See Expos. on 9:7-9.
18-21. See Expos. on 18:21.
22. See Expos. on 3:5-8.
23. See Expos. on 26:1, 3-12.
24. See Expos. on 3:1-4.

25 As the whirlwind passeth, so *is* the wicked no *more*: but the righteous *is* an everlasting foundation.

26 As vinegar to the teeth, and as smoke to the eyes, so *is* the sluggard to them that send him.

27 The fear of the LORD prolongeth days: but the years of the wicked shall be shortened.

28 The hope of the righteous *shall be* gladness: but the expectation of the wicked shall perish.

29 The way of the LORD *is* strength to the upright: but destruction *shall be* to the workers of iniquity.

30 The righteous shall never be removed: but the wicked shall not inhabit the earth.

31 The mouth of the just bringeth forth wisdom: but the froward tongue shall be cut out.

32 The lips of the righteous know what

25 When the tempest passes, the wicked is no more,
but the righteous is established for ever.
26 Like vinegar to the teeth, and smoke to the eyes,
so is the sluggard to those who send him.
27 The fear of the LORD prolongs life,
but the years of the wicked will be short.
28 The hope of the righteous ends in gladness,
but the expectation of the wicked comes to nought.
29 The LORD is a stronghold to him whose way is upright,
but destruction to evildoers.
30 The righteous will never be removed,
but the wicked will not dwell in the land.
31 The mouth of the righteous brings forth wisdom,
but the perverse tongue will be cut off.
32 The lips of the righteous know what is acceptable,

---

25. Antithetic. The proverbs which follow deal with the stability of the righteous. In this verse the wicked are compared with an unstable building which falls when the **tempest** comes; the foundations of the righteous are so deep and strong, however, that they last forever (cf. Matt. 7:24-27).

26. A comparison proverb. A lazy messenger is as irritating as **vinegar** or **smoke** (for the importance of the messenger in those days see Exeg. on 13:17; on the sluggard see Exeg. on 19:24).

27. Antithetic. The accepted doctrine of rewards and punishment in Proverbs: a long, happy, and prosperous life for those who fear God; a short life, cut off by calamity, for those who are wicked (see Exeg. on 2:18; 3:2). **The fear of the LORD:** See Exeg. on 1:7. **Days:** Better, **life. Wicked:** See Exeg. on 2:22; 3:25.

28. Antithetic.

29. Antithetic. Literally, the Hebrew of vs. 29*a* reads, "a stronghold to perfection is the way of the Lord." Following the versions, the KJV and the RSV read **upright** ("perfect") for "perfection," which makes a better contrast with vs. 29*b*. Then either **the way of the LORD** (KJV) or **the LORD** (RSV) may be the subject, with the latter making better sense. **Upright:** See Exeg. on 1:12.

30. Antithetic. The same idea is expressed in vs. 25. **Earth** or, better, **land:** Canaan is of course meant (see Exeg. on 2:21).

31. Antithetic. **Brings forth:** Lit., "bears fruit." The mouth is compared with a tree—its words are like the fruit of a tree. **Froward** or **perverse:** See Exeg. on 2:12.

32. Antithetic. As in the preceding verse, the utterances of the righteous and of the wicked are compared.

---

25. See Expos. on 3:21-26.
26. See Expos. on 6:1-15.
27. See Expos. on 1:7.
28. See Expos. on 13:12.
29. See Expos. on 1:7.
30. See Expos. on 3:21-26.
31-32. See Expos. on 18:21.

is acceptable: but the mouth of the wicked *speaketh* frowardness.

11 A false balance *is* abomination to the LORD: but a just weight *is* his delight.

2 *When* pride cometh, then cometh shame: but with the lowly *is* wisdom.

3 The integrity of the upright shall guide them: but the perverseness of transgressors shall destroy them.

4 Riches profit not in the day of wrath: but righteousness delivereth from death.

5 The righteousness of the perfect shall direct his way: but the wicked shall fall by his own wickedness.

6 The righteousness of the upright shall deliver them: but transgressors shall be taken in *their own* naughtiness.

7 When a wicked man dieth, *his* expectation shall perish: and the hope of unjust *men* perisheth.

but the mouth of the wicked, what is
perverse.

11 A false balance is an abomination to
the LORD,
but a just weight is his delight.
2 When pride comes, then comes disgrace;
but with the humble is wisdom.
3 The integrity of the upright guides them,
but the crookedness of the treacherous
destroys them.
4 Riches do not profit in the day of wrath,
but righteousness delivers from death.
5 The righteousness of the blameless keeps
his way straight,
but the wicked falls by his own wickedness.
6 The righteousness of the upright delivers
them,
but the treacherous are taken captive
by their lust.
7 When the wicked dies, his hope perishes,
and the expectation of the godless
comes to nought.

11:1. Antithetic. Honesty in business is enjoined here, as well as in 16:11; 20:10, 23. The Pentateuch condemns the false balance and unjust weight in Lev. 19:35-36; Deut. 25:13-15. **Just weight:** Lit., "full or correct stone," since stones were used as weights.

2. Antithetic. Pride is condemned and humility is praised in the following proverbs: 13:10; 15:33; 16:18-19; 18:12; 22:4. **Humble:** The word *çānûaʻ* is found only here and in Mic. 6:8, where the verbal form is used of "walking humbly" before God.

3. Antithetic. In vss. 3-6 righteousness is contrasted with wickedness and treachery. At the risk of being trite, the wise men of Israel are continually stating and restating the obvious fact that righteousness is the basis of salvation and a long and happy life, whereas wickedness leads to death and destruction. Yet how well did Israel heed these words, or even more pertinently, how well have we heeded them today? **Integrity:** See Exeg. on 10:9. **Upright:** See Exeg. on 1:3. **Perverseness** or **crookedness:** The noun *ṣéleph* is found only here and in 15:4. The root meaning is "to turn aside" or "upside down." **Transgressors:** Better, **the treacherous,** according to the root meaning of the word.

4. Antithetic. Vs. 4*b*=10:2*b*. See Exeg. on 10:2 regarding riches. **Day of wrath:** Not a day of national calamity, as in prophetic literature, but an individual matter, probably equivalent to death here in the parallel stich. **Death:** I.e., a good man is preserved from an untimely or violent death.

5. Antithetic. Similar to vs. 3. **Perfect** or **blameless:** *Tāmîm,* a cognate of *tōm* (see Exeg. on 10:9). **Direct** or, better, **keeps . . . straight:** See Exeg. on 1:3.

6. Antithetic. Also similar to vs. 3. **Transgressors** or, better, **the treacherous:** See Exeg. on vs. 3. **Naughtiness** or, better, **lust:** For the Hebrew word *hawwāh* see Exeg. on 10:3.

7. A difficult verse. The two stichs mean about the same thing. All that the wicked man had hoped for is blasted at death, usually premature or violent. **Unjust men** or **the godless** ("iniquity" ASV; "strong men" ASV mg.; "success" Amer. Trans.; "the bad man" Moffatt; "strength" American Jewish Translation): A difficult Hebrew word, as the

---

11:1. See Expos. on 21:3.
2. See Expos. on 29:23.
3. See Expos. on 18:21.
4. See Expos. on 10:15-16.
5-6. See Expos. on 1:10-19.
7. See Expos. on 13:12.

8 The righteous is delivered out of trouble, and the wicked cometh in his stead.

9 A hypocrite with *his* mouth destroyeth his neighbor: but through knowledge shall the just be delivered.

10 When it goeth well with the righteous, the city rejoiceth: and when the wicked perish, *there is* shouting.

11 By the blessing of the upright the city is exalted: but it is overthrown by the mouth of the wicked.

12 He that is void of wisdom despiseth

8 The righteous is delivered from trouble,
and the wicked gets into it instead.
9 With his mouth the godless man would
destroy his neighbor,
but by knowledge the righteous are
delivered.
10 When it goes well with the righteous, the
city rejoices;
and when the wicked perish there are
shouts of gladness.
11 By the blessing of the upright a city is
exalted,
but it is overthrown by the mouth of
the wicked.
12 He who belittles his neighbor lacks sense,

---

various translations testify. The Hebrew *'ônîm* can be plural either of *'āwen* ("sorrow," "wickedness") or *'ôn* ("strength"). The LXX reads "ungodly ones" (τῶν ἀσεβῶν= *'ewîlîm*) which seems to be the basis for the RSV.

8. The righteous man is delivered from the trouble into which the wicked one properly falls.

9. Antithetic. By false, slanderous speech the godless man destroys his neighbor; the righteous man is delivered from him, or more probably from death, through his own knowledge. **Hypocrite** or **godless man:** *Ḥānēph* has the root idea of "inclining away from the right," and so "profane," "impure."

10-11. Antithetic. The righteous are a source of praise and blessing to a city; the wicked bring a city to destruction.

12. Antithetic. **Wisdom** or **sense:** Lit., "heart." See Exeg. on 2:2. In contrast with

---

8. ***Vicarious Suffering.***—This proverb seems like a complete reversal of the doctrine of vicarious suffering which is characteristic of the highest conceptions in both the O.T. and the N.T. It implies that the wicked suffer for the righteous, whereas the "suffering servant" passages of Deutero-Isaiah present a chosen one of God who "was wounded for our transgressions, he was bruised for our iniquities: the chastisement of our peace was upon him; and with his stripes we are healed" (Isa. 53:5). Elsewhere we read,

> The wicked is a ransom for the righteous,
> and the faithless for the upright (21:18).

In the light of this proverb the words of Jesus must have sounded strange in the ears of his followers, "Even the Son of man came not to be ministered unto, but to minister, and to give his life a ransom for many" (Mark 10:45). This was hardly an example of a wicked man's giving his life for the righteous. The exact opposite is the case. A supremely good man is suffering because of the sins of others.

The truth being emphasized by these proverbs is something different from vicarious suffering. The truth presented here is not that a wicked man must bear the punishment that rightfully belongs to a righteous man, but the sages are rather pointing out that the suffering that naturally follows wrongdoing is avoided by right living. Some of the suffering which is the lot of human beings is the result of sinful living; the painful results of such living do not fall upon him who lives an upright life.

The implication of this doctrine is the affirmation that wherever there is trouble or suffering there must be sin—a doctrine later challenged by the writer of Job, who saw that many people suffered quite out of proportion to their misdeeds. Innocent people suffer. A closer scrutiny of human experience made impossible the simple statement that evil befalls only the wicked, while the righteous person is always protected against pain and ill fortune. Religious insight became more profound when men not only recognized that suffering comes to good and bad people, just as the rains fall on the just and unjust alike, but when they saw also that suffering has redemptive possibilities. The suffering of a good man might bring help and saving power to another. The triumph of Jesus on the cross lies in great measure in his ability to use that suffering for the redemption of many.

9. See Expos. on 18:21.

10-11. See Expos. on 21:3.

12. See Expos. on 3:27-35.

his neighbor: but a man of understanding holdeth his peace.

13 A talebearer revealeth secrets: but he that is of a faithful spirit concealeth the matter.

14 Where no counsel *is,* the people fall: but in the multitude of counselors *there is* safety.

15 He that is surety for a stranger shall smart *for it:* and he that hateth suretyship is sure.

16 A gracious woman retaineth honor: and strong *men* retain riches.

but a man of understanding remains silent.
13 He who goes about as a talebearer reveals secrets,
but he who is trustworthy in spirit keeps a thing hidden.
14 Where there is no guidance, a people falls;
but in an abundance of counselors there is safety.
15 He who gives surety for a stranger will smart for it,
but he who hates suretyship is secure.
16 A gracious woman gets honor,
and violent men get riches.

---

the wise man who keeps his thoughts to himself, the foolish man speaks openly against his neighbor, which always leads to trouble.

13. Antithetic. Cf. 20:19. Ecclus. 19:7 has the same thought:

> If you never repeat what you are told,
> You will fare none the worse.

14. Antithetic. Vs. 14*b*=24:6*b*. **Counsel** or, better, **guidance:** See Exeg. on 1:5. Many counselors are needed to guide the ship of state.

15. Antithetic. See Exeg. on 6:1 for explanation of the Hebrew words for suretyship. The rendering **is surety** or **gives surety** represents the Hebrew word *'ārabh;* **suretyship** is *tôqeʿîm.* **Shall smart:** A Niphal form from the root *rāʿaʿ,* "to be evil," "bad." The word *raʿ,* which precedes the verb, must be taken as an adverbial accusative, and translated "badly" (cf. 13:20).

16. Antithetic. This verse seems to contrast the use of gracious gentility and brutish

---

13. See Expos. on 18:21.

14. ***Many Counselors.***—A number of reasons could be given to indicate that there is safety in a **multitude of counselors.** An obvious reason is that no one person has all the insight into any situation. He may have a blind spot in his outlook. When any decision is weighed by a number of people, each individual may have something to contribute to the mind of the group. More possibilities are thrown into the common hopper, possibilities that might have been overlooked if one man or a few men had made the decision. Action is sometimes delayed because many counselors are given a chance to speak, but this delay might prevent the taking of foolhardy and shortsighted steps.

When many counselors are participating in a decision, a group process is set in motion. One individual may not make a large contribution to the group mind, but by what he says or by what he asks he may call forth something in the thought of another that never would have been elicited if the group process had not been initiated. In the give and take of group thinking something generally emerges that is better than the conclusion that any one person could have produced by himself.

Consulting many counselors is an important way of securing their loyalty to a program of action. Most people resent having a program forced upon them. No matter how good a decision may be, if they have not had the opportunity of sharing in the task of arriving at it, they will feel little loyalty in carrying it out. Taking others into consultation may not change the decision, but it will do much to secure the loyal support that is needed to make it effective.

When many counselors have a share in the work of the state or in any other enterprise, there is assurance of continuity. One-man rule may be benevolent and wise, but it does little to train others to take over responsibility when the one man is taken away. History affords many instances of weak and divided rule after a strong leader dies. Safety for the future lies in the distribution of responsibility and in giving many an opportunity to express their views and give their counsel.

15. See Expos. on 6:1-15.

16. See Expos. on 31:10-31.

17 The merciful man doeth good to his own soul: but *he that is* cruel troubleth his own flesh.

18 The wicked worketh a deceitful work: but to him that soweth righteousness *shall be* a sure reward.

19 As righteousness *tendeth* to life; so he that pursueth evil *pursueth it* to his own death.

20 They that are of a froward heart *are* abomination to the LORD: but *such as are* upright in *their* way *are* his delight.

21 *Though* hand *join* in hand, the wicked shall not be unpunished: but the seed of the righteous shall be delivered.

22 *As* a jewel of gold in a swine's snout, *so is* a fair woman which is without discretion.

23 The desire of the righteous *is* only

17 A man who is kind benefits himself,
but a cruel man hurts himself.
18 A wicked man earns deceptive wages,
but one who sows righteousness gets a sure reward.
19 He who is steadfast in righteousness will live,
but he who pursues evil will die.
20 Men of perverse mind are an abomination to the LORD,
but those of blameless ways are his delight.
21 Be assured, an evil man will not go unpunished,
but those who are righteous will be delivered.
22 Like a gold ring in a swine's snout
is a beautiful woman without discretion.
23 The desire of the righteous ends only in

---

force in acquiring position and wealth. It is the only place in Proverbs where man and woman are contrasted.

17. Antithetic. Kindness is recommended as being beneficial to the one who practices it; cruelty is detrimental to the one who perpetrates it. **Himself:** Vs. 17*a* in Hebrew has "his soul," vs. 17*b* in Hebrew, "his flesh."

18. Antithetic. It "pays" to be good. **Deceitful work** or **deceptive wages:** Lit., "wages of falsehood" (on **wages** see Exeg. on 10:16). They are **deceptive** in that they will not bring permanent benefit. **Sure reward:** Lit., "wages of truth."

19. Antithetic. The righteous man will have a long and happy life; the wicked will die either an untimely or unnatural death (see Exeg. on 2:18; 3:2). **He who is steadfast:** The difficult word *kēn* (**as**) can mean either "so" or "true," neither of which fits the context. The RSV, together with the ASV, the Amer. Trans., Moffatt, and the American Jewish Translation, attempts a translation which is not in accord with the meaning of the word.

20. Antithetic. **Froward** or **perverse:** For *'iqqēsh* see Exeg. on 2:15. **Abomination:** See Exeg. on 3:22. **Upright** or **blameless:** See Exeg. on vs. 5.

21. Antithetic. The laws of retribution are inexorable. **Though hand join in hand:** The RSV, **be assured,** with the ASV mg., "My hand upon it!" gives the correct meaning of the Hebrew, which literally reads, "hand to hand." The translation of the KJV and ASV is impossible. **Seed:** The reference here is to the righteous people, as the RSV brings out, not to posterity.

22. Two statements describing incongruous conditions. **Jewel of gold** or, better, **gold ring:** Really a "nose ring," a female ornament (cf. Gen. 24:47). **Discretion:** Lit., "taste," including here both intellectual and moral discrimination. The word is used by David of Abigail in I Sam. 25:32-33: "And David said to Abigail, 'Blessed be the LORD, the God of Israel, who sent you this day to meet me! Blessed be your discretion [the word used here in Proverbs], and blessed be you, who have kept me this day from bloodguilt and from avenging myself with my own hand!' "

23. Antithetic. Cf. 10:28. As the RSV translates, the desires and hopes of the

---

17. See Expos. on 3:1-4.
18-19. See Expos. on 3:21-26.
20. See Expos. on 3:1-4.
21. See Expos. on 3:21-26.
22. See Expos. on 31:10-31.
23. See Expos. on 3:1-4.

good: *but* the expectation of the wicked *is* wrath.

24 There is that scattereth, and yet increaseth; and *there is* that withholdeth more than is meet, but *it tendeth* to poverty.

25 The liberal soul shall be made fat: and he that watereth shall be watered also himself.

26 He that withholdeth corn, the people shall curse him: but blessing *shall be* upon the head of him that selleth *it*.

27 He that diligently seeketh good procureth favor: but he that seeketh mischief, it shall come unto him.

28 He that trusteth in his riches shall fall: but the righteous shall flourish as a branch.

29 He that troubleth his own house shall inherit the wind: and the fool *shall be* servant to the wise of heart.

30 The fruit of the righteous *is* a tree of life; and he that winneth souls *is* wise.

good;
the expectation of the wicked in wrath.
24 One man gives freely, yet grows all the richer;
another withholds what he should give, and only suffers want.
25 A liberal man will be enriched,
and one who waters will himself be watered.
26 The people curse him who holds back grain,
but a blessing is on the head of him who sells it.
27 He who diligently seeks good seeks favor,
but evil comes to him who searches for it.
28 He who trusts in his riches will wither,[v]
but the righteous will flourish like a green leaf.
29 He who troubles his household will inherit wind,
and the fool will be servant to the wise.
30 The fruit of the righteous is a tree of life,
but lawlessness[w] takes away lives.

[v] Cn: Heb *fall*
[w] Cn Compare Gk Syr: Heb *a wise man*

righteous and wicked end in good and wrath respectively. The KJV translates the Hebrew literally.

24. Antithetic. Some spend lavishly and get richer; others save every penny and still remain poor. The reason is given in the following verses. **Scattereth:** Better, **gives freely. More than is meet** or **what he should give:** The preposition *min* ("from") may express comparison, as the KJV translates, but here it probably goes with the verb "keep back," and so should read **withholds** with the RSV.

25. Synonymous. One of the few verses in this collection in which the two stichs are synonymous. This verse is an expansion of vs. 24*a*. **Liberal man:** Lit., "soul [person] of blessing." **Shall be made fat** or, better, **will be enriched:** The figure in vs. 25*b* is agricultural.

26. Antithetic. This verse gives an illustration of what the man in vs. 24*b* does. **Grain** was hoarded in order to acquire high prices. This sounds like an ancient version of the black market.

27. Antithetic. **Diligently seeks:** See Exeg. on 1:28. **Procureth** or, lit., **seeks. Favor:** Of God and man.

28. Antithetic. Cf. 10:2. To trust in wealth is false security; the righteous, who trust in God, flourish like a **green leaf** (cf. Ps. 1:3). **Fall:** Better, **wither,** which translation is obtained by a change of only one Hebrew consonant, *yippōl* to *yibbōl*.

29. Two independent lines. **Wind:** The phrase may denote that his possessions will be blown away, or it may suggest their unsubstantial character. **Fool:** See Exeg. on 1:7. By his folly he becomes a slave to the wise man.

30. **Tree of life:** See Exeg. on 3:18. The second stich is difficult. Literally it reads, "And a wise man takes souls." The verb "takes" in this sense always means "destroy,"

24-26. See Expos. on 3:9-10.
27. See Expos. on 3:1-4.
28. See Expos. on 10:15-16.
29. See Expos. on 3:9-10.
30. See Expos. on 3:1-4.

31 Behold, the righteous shall be recompensed in the earth: much more the wicked and the sinner.

12 Whoso loveth instruction loveth knowledge: but he that hateth reproof *is* brutish.

2 A good *man* obtaineth favor of the LORD: but a man of wicked devices will he condemn.

3 A man shall not be established by wickedness: but the root of the righteous shall not be moved.

4 A virtuous woman *is* a crown to her husband: but she that maketh ashamed *is* as rottenness in his bones.

5 The thoughts of the righteous *are* right: *but* the counsels of the wicked *are* deceit.

6 The words of the wicked *are* to lie in wait for blood: but the mouth of the upright shall deliver them.

7 The wicked are overthrown, and *are*

31 If the righteous is requited on earth,
how much more the wicked and the sinner!

12 Whoever loves discipline loves knowledge,
but he who hates reproof is stupid.
2 A good man obtains favor from the LORD,
but a man of evil devices he condemns.
3 A man is not established by wickedness,
but the root of the righteous will never be moved.
4 A good wife is the crown of her husband,
but she who brings shame is like rottenness in his bones.
5 The thoughts of the righteous are just;
the counsels of the wicked are treacherous.
6 The words of the wicked lie in wait for blood,
but the mouth of the upright delivers men.
7 The wicked are overthrown and are no more,

---

which does not fit the context. The KJV understands it to mean that wisdom allures souls to herself. The RSV emends the word *ḥākhām,* "wise," to *ḥāmāṣ,* **lawlessness** (with Toy; cf. LXX).

31. The certainty of retribution which, according to the view of Proverbs, is on this earth. Cf. I Pet. 4:18, which follows the LXX, a free translation of the Hebrew. **Behold** (Hebrew) or **if** (Aramaic): Cf. LXX.

12:1. Antithetic. **Instruction:** See Exeg. on 1:2. **Reproof:** See Exeg. on 1:23. **Brutish:** Lit., "brutishness," and so **stupid,** like a brute animal.

2. Antithetic. **Obtains:** The verb *pûq* means "to bring forth," "to draw forth," and so "to obtain" (see Exeg. on 3:13). **Evil devices:** From the noun *mezimmāh* (see Exeg. on 1:4). **Condemn:** A forensic term, "pronounce guilty"; the opposite of *yaçdîq,* "pronounce righteous."

3. Antithetic. The condition of the wicked man is impermanent and uncertain, whereas the righteous man cannot be torn from the ground in which he is deeply rooted (cf. vs. 7; 10:25; Ps. 1:3-4).

4. Antithetic. See Exeg. on 31:10 concerning woman in Proverbs. **Virtuous** or **good:** Strength of character is meant by the word *ḥáyil.* It is used of women only four times in the O.T. (here; 31:10, 29; Ruth 3:11).

5. Antithetic. **Right:** Hebrew, *mishpāṭ* (see Exeg. on 1:3). **Counsels:** See Exeg. on 1:5, where the word is used of "wise counsels."

6. Antithetic. A strong figure: words lie in wait to destroy their victims. **Them:** The antecedent of the Hebrew suffix in *yaççîlēm* is uncertain. It would naturally refer to **the upright,** but the context does not warrant this supposition. One would expect **the mouth of the upright** to deliver those who are endangered by the wicked. **Men** (RSV) is too general.

7. Antithetic. Cf. 10:25; 12:3; also Matt. 7:24-27.

---

31. See Expos. on 21:3.
12:1. See Expos. on 9:7-9.
2. See Expos. on 3:1-4.
3. See Expos. on 3:21-26.
4. See Expos. on 31:10-31.
5-6. See Expos. on 18:21.
7. See Expos. on 3:21-26.

not: but the house of the righteous shall stand.

8 A man shall be commended according to his wisdom: but he that is of a perverse heart shall be despised.

9 *He that is* despised, and hath a servant, *is* better than he that honoreth himself, and lacketh bread.

10 A righteous *man* regardeth the life of his beast: but the tender mercies of the wicked *are* cruel.

11 He that tilleth his land shall be satis-

but the house of the righteous will stand.

8 A man is commended according to his good sense,
but one of perverse mind is despised.

9 Better is a man of humble standing who works for himself
than one who plays the great man but lacks bread.

10 A righteous man has regard for the life of his beast,
but the mercy of the wicked is cruel.

11 He who tills his land will have plenty of bread,

---

8. Antithetic. To think straight is commended in this verse. **Wisdom** or, better, **good sense:** Hebrew, *sĕkhel* (see Exeg. on 1:3). **Perverse:** From the root *'āwāh,* "to twist," used only here in Proverbs. **Heart** or **mind:** See Exeg. on 2:2.

9. Antithetic. The contrast is between the humble man who honestly earns his livelihood, and the braggadocio who does not have even enough to eat. **Despised** or **of humble standing:** The verb *qālāh* means "to be lightly esteemed," as the ASV translates. **Hath a servant** or **works for himself,** following the LXX: The KJV seems to show that a slave was considered one of the basic necessities of life even for those of humble standing; cf. Ecclus. 10:26-27, which is very similar:

> Do not parade your wisdom when you are at work,
> And do not commend yourself when you are in need;
> It is better to work and have plenty of everything,
> Than to go about commending yourself but in want of bread (Amer. Trans.).

10. Antithetic. Cf. Deut. 25:4 on kindness to animals. **Regardeth:** Lit., "knows." **Life:** Lit., "soul." **Tender mercies:** The root is *rḥm,* from which the cognate form, meaning "womb," is derived.

11. Antithetic. Cf. 28:19. **Vain persons** or **worthless pursuits:** Both translations are

---

8. ***Satisfying the Desire for Approval.***—The hunger for approval is a part of human nature. An important incentive to action is the desire to be approved by others. Few people want to be despised. The longing for approval is raised to high levels when one asks: "Approval for what? Approval by whom?"

Fervently we might wish that popular acclaim would come to the man of wisdom. It does not always so happen. Some far in advance of their time cannot gain the approval of their contemporaries. They must wait for the verdict of history while they suffer the lot of martyrs in their lifetime. The important thing is not to get the approval of the crowd. The best way to satisfy the true desire is so to live as to merit the approval of men of discerning judgment and good will. Tennyson, before his death in 1892, recognized the genius of the young Rudyard Kipling and paid him a compliment. To this word of appreciation Kipling replied, "When the private in the ranks is praised by the general, he cannot presume to thank him, but he fights the better next day." [2]

The desire to leave a good name is another aspect of this same incentive. By some contribution to the wealth of the world, by some addition to its knowledge or its beauty, by some example of courage in the face of adversity, people want to merit the approval of those who come after them. Pasteur marches triumphantly with every child who goes to his inoculation against hydrophobia. The world does not always accord approval to the person who is wise, but each individual can act so as to merit the approval of wise and good men.

9. See Expos. on 29:23.

10. See Expos. on 22:16*a*.

11. See Expos. on 6:1-15.

[2] William Lyon Phelps, *Yearbook* (New York: The Macmillan Co., 1935), p. 446.

fied with bread: but he that followeth vain *persons is* void of understanding.

12 The wicked desireth the net of evil *men:* but the root of the righteous yieldeth *fruit.*

13 The wicked is snared by the transgression of *his* lips: but the just shall come out of trouble.

14 A man shall be satisfied with good by the fruit of *his* mouth: and the recompense of a man's hands shall be rendered unto him.

15 The way of a fool *is* right in his own eyes: but he that hearkeneth unto counsel *is* wise.

16 A fool's wrath is presently known: but a prudent *man* covereth shame.

17 *He that* speaketh truth showeth forth righteousness: but a false witness deceit.

but he who follows worthless pursuits
has no sense.
12 The strong tower of the wicked comes to ruin,
but the root of the righteous stands firm.[x]
13 An evil man is ensnared by the transgression of his lips,
but the righteous escapes from trouble.
14 From the fruit of his words a man is satisfied with good,
and the work of a man's hand comes back to him.
15 The way of a fool is right in his own eyes,
but a wise man listens to advice.
16 The vexation of a fool is known at once,
but the prudent man ignores an insult.
17 He who speaks the truth gives honest evidence,
but a false witness utters deceit.

[x] Cn: The Hebrew of verse 12 is obscure

possible from the Hebrew, but the latter is probably to be preferred. **Understanding** or **sense:** Lit., "heart" (see Exeg. on 2:2).

12. The Hebrew is obscure: "A wicked man desires the net of the evil ones; but the root of the righteous gives." Numerous emendations have been suggested in order to make sense out of the verse. **Net** or **strong tower** ("the prey" ASV mg.): The Hebrew word is *māçôdh.* The LXX omits it. Whether the **net** is that which is spread for others, or that in which wicked men are caught, is not certain. In any event the expression is meaningless in this context. The translation "prey," i.e., that which is caught in the net, is without foundation. The RSV reads *meçādh,* on the basis of the Vulg. **Comes to ruin** comes from a different reading of the first two words in the Hebrew text (cf. 14:11). **Yieldeth** or **stands firm:** To make the Hebrew intelligible, the KJV adds **fruit.** The RSV is based on the LXX, an emendation accepted by many commentators.

13. Antithetic. Evil talk brings calamity. **Is snared:** By a slight alteration of the Hebrew, which reads "is a snare" (ASV).

14. Synonymous. The speech and actions of a man will be rewarded (cf. Gal. 6:7).

15. Antithetic. A fool does not listen to the advice of others. **Fool:** See Exeg. on 1:7. **Right:** A cognate of the word translated "equity" in 1:3 (see Exeg.). **Counsel:** See Exeg. on 8:14.

16. Antithetic. The fool has no self-control. **Fool:** See Exeg. on 1:7. **At once:** Lit., "in the day." **Insult:** A wise man is calm in the face of **shame** when he is insulted. **Prudent:** See Exeg. on 1:4.

17. Antithetic. Most of the proverbs in the rest of this chapter deal with the tongue. There are over one hundred verses in the whole book which have to do in one way or another with the use of the tongue. Even though one of the smallest, weakest, and softest of the organs of the body, it is one of the most powerful, because by it human lives are changed and the course of nature is altered. It is also one of the most difficult organs to control (cf. Jas. 3:3-12). It can be the source of much sorrow and evil. Quarreling words are like the piercings of a sword (12:18); lying words can send a man to his death (14:25); flattering words are like a net set to entrap a man (29:5); whispering

12. See Expos. on 3:21-26.
13-14. See Expos. on 18:21.
15-16. See Expos. on 26:1, 3-12.
17-20. See Expos. on 18:21.

18 There is that speaketh like the piercings of a sword: but the tongue of the wise *is* health.

19 The lip of truth shall be established for ever: but a lying tongue *is* but for a moment.

20 Deceit *is* in the heart of them that imagine evil: but to the counselors of peace *is* joy.

21 There shall no evil happen to the just: but the wicked shall be filled with mischief.

22 Lying lips *are* abomination to the LORD: but they that deal truly *are* his delight.

23 A prudent man concealeth knowledge: but the heart of fools proclaimeth foolishness.

24 The hand of the diligent shall bear rule: but the slothful shall be under tribute.

18 There is one whose rash words are like sword thrusts,
but the tongue of the wise brings healing.
19 Truthful lips endure for ever,
but a lying tongue is but for a moment.
20 Deceit is in the heart of those who devise evil,
but those who plan good have joy.
21 No ill befalls the righteous,
but the wicked are filled with trouble.
22 Lying lips are an abomination to the LORD,
but those who act faithfully are his delight.
23 A prudent man conceals his knowledge,
but fools[y] proclaim their folly.
24 The hand of the diligent will rule,
while the slothful will be put to forced labor.

[y] Heb *the heart of fools*

words cause trouble among friends (16:28); evil things pour out of the mouth of the wicked (15:28); the mouth of the fool is always emitting untimely and harmful speech (15:2). On the other hand, the tongue can be a source of many kinds of blessing (12:25; 15:4, 7, 23; 25:12; 31:8-9). When the tongue is under the control of God, he gives the answer, and blessing will be sure to follow (16:1).

This particular proverb deals with the problem of perjury, a common crime. **Speaks:** A strong word, *pûaḥ,* which means "to breathe," "to blow out" (see Exeg. on 6:19). **Truth:** *'emûnāh* has the root meaning "steadfastness," "fidelity"; cf. our word "amen," which is from the same root. **Righteousness** or **honest evidence:** See Exeg. on 1:3.

18. Antithetic. Thoughtless words wound like a sword, but a wise tongue heals the suffering and saves from trouble. **Speaketh** or **rash words:** The expression "speaketh rashly" (ASV) best translates the uncommon word *bāṭāh* (cf. its usage in Lev. 5:4; Ps. 106:33, the only other places it is found in the O.T.). **Health** or, better, **healing.**

19. Antithetic. Truth, supported by facts, lasts forever; falsehood, which is soon found to be without basis, passes away quickly. **Truth** or **truthful:** A cognate form of the word in vs. 17 (see Exeg.). **For a moment:** Lit., "until I blink."

20. Antithetic. **Devise:** See Exeg. on 3:29. **Peace** or **good:** *Shālôm* means "wholeness," "completeness of being."

21. Antithetic. Retribution takes place in this life. **Evil** or, better, **ill:** No immoral act or condition is meant here, but some outward misfortune.

22. Antithetic. Similar to 11:20 (cf. 12:17). **Abomination:** See Exeg. on 3:22. **Truly** or **faithfully:** See Exeg. on vs. 17.

23. Antithetic. The difference between reticence and forwardness in speech. The rashness of the fool in his speech is a common theme of Proverbs (cf. 10:19; 13:3, 16; 14:23; 15:2; 18:2, 13). **Prudent:** See Exeg. on 1:4. **Fools:** The RSV omits **heart,** which is before this word in the Hebrew text (see Exeg. on 1:22).

24. Antithetic. In praise of industry (cf. vs. 27; 10:4; 13:4; 19:15; 21:5). **Diligent:** See Exeg. on 10:4. **The slothful:** Lit., "slothfulness." The word *remiyyāh* occurs in Proverbs only here; vs. 27; 10:4; 19:15 (cf. also 19:24 on laziness). **Tribute** or **forced**

21. See Expos. on 3:21-26.
22. See Expos. on 18:21.
23. See Expos. on 26:1, 3-12.
24. See Expos. on 6:1-15.

25 Heaviness in the heart of man maketh it stoop: but a good word maketh it glad.

26 The righteous *is* more excellent than his neighbor: but the way of the wicked seduceth them.

27 The slothful *man* roasteth not that which he took in hunting: but the substance of a diligent man *is* precious.

28 In the way of righteousness *is* life; and *in* the pathway *thereof there is* no death.

13 A wise son *heareth* his father's instruction: but a scorner heareth not rebuke.

2 A man shall eat good by the fruit of *his* mouth: but the soul of the transgressors *shall eat* violence.

25 Anxiety in a man's heart weighs him down,
but a good word makes him glad.
26 A righteous man turns away from evil,[z]
but the way of the wicked leads them astray.
27 A slothful man will not catch his prey,[a]
but the diligent man will get precious wealth.[b]
28 In the path of righteousness is life,
but the way of error leads to death.[c]
13 A wise son hears his father's instruction,
but a scoffer does not listen to rebuke.
2 From the fruit of his mouth a good man eats good,
but the desire of the treacherous is for violence.

[z] Cn: The meaning of the Hebrew is uncertain
[a] Cn Compare Gk Syr: The meaning of the Hebrew is uncertain
[b] Cn: The meaning of the Hebrew is uncertain
[c] Cn: The meaning of the Hebrew is uncertain

labor: The root meaning of *maṣ* is unknown. Properly it means "a labor gang." Instead of being in authority over others, the lazy one is forced to work by others.

25. Antithetic. **Heaviness:** Better, **anxiety.**

26. Antithetic. **More excellent** or **turns away** ("a guide" ASV): The meaning of the Hebrew word is uncertain. Ordinarily it is connected with the root *tûr,* "to spy out," "to explore," which makes little sense here. In contrast with the second stich one would expect a translation like that of the RSV, which follows Toy's suggested emendation.

27. The general meaning of the first stich is clear in spite of the fact that the verb is uncertain. The slothful man is too lazy to get his own food. **Slothful man:** Lit., "slothfulness" (see Exeg. on vs. 24). **Roasteth** or **catch:** The verb *ḥārakh* occurs nowhere else in the O.T. The translation of the KJV is derived from its meaning in later Hebrew; the RSV derives its translation from the meaning of the cognate root in Arabic.

The second stich seems to be an unattached line. The order of the words in the Hebrew text is probably wrong. The three different translations of the KJV, RSV, and ASV suggest three different orders of the words. **Diligent:** See Exeg. on 10:4. The ASV adds a preposition, not in the Hebrew, to this word.

28. Antithetic. **Life:** See Exeg. on 3:2. The second stich is unintelligible in the Hebrew. Literally it reads, "the way of a path not death." The KJV, followed by the ASV, is an incorrect translation. The RSV, following most modern commentators, emends the text to read, **but the way of error leads to death,** which is the sense expected in the context.

13:1. Antithetic. Cf. 2:1; 3:1; 4:1. **Heareth:** Added to make sense out of the stich. A good emendation would seem to be to read *'āhabh* for *'ābh,* and so the line would mean, "A wise son loveth instruction" (see Exeg. on 1:2). **Scoffer:** The *lēç* is impervious to advice or instruction (see Exeg. on 1:22).

2. The Hebrew literally reads, "From the fruit of the mouth of a man he eats good, but the desire [soul] of the treacherous is violence." Vs. 2*a* is similar to 12:14*a*.

25. See Expos. on 17:22.
26. See Expos. on 24:15-16.
27. See Expos. on 6:1-15.
28. See Expos. on 3:1-4.
13:1. See Expos. on 9:7-9.
2-3. See Expos. on 18:21.

3 He that keepeth his mouth keepeth his life: *but* he that openeth wide his lips shall have destruction.

4 The soul of the sluggard desireth, and *hath* nothing: but the soul of the diligent shall be made fat.

5 A righteous *man* hateth lying: but a wicked *man* is loathsome, and cometh to shame.

6 Righteousness keepeth *him that is* upright in the way: but wickedness overthroweth the sinner.

7 There is that maketh himself rich, yet *hath* nothing: *there is* that maketh himself poor, yet *hath* great riches.

8 The ransom of a man's life *are* his riches: but the poor heareth not rebuke.

9 The light of the righteous rejoiceth: but the lamp of the wicked shall be put out.

3 He who guards his mouth preserves his life;
he who opens wide his lips comes to ruin.

4 The soul of the sluggard craves, and gets nothing,
while the soul of the diligent is richly supplied.

5 A righteous man hates falsehood,
but a wicked man acts shamefully and disgracefully.

6 Righteousness guards him whose way is upright,
but sin overthrows the wicked.

7 One man pretends to be rich, yet has nothing;
another pretends to be poor, yet has great wealth.

8 The ransom of a man's life is his wealth,
but a poor man has no means of redemption.[d]

9 The light of the righteous rejoices,
but the lamp of the wicked will be put out.

[d] Cn: Heb *does not hear rebuke*

---

3. Antithetic. Against rash speech, which may cost one his **life** (lit., "soul"). Two different Hebrew verbs in vs. *3a* are brought out by the RSV.

4. Antithetic. The lazy man dreams of riches and earthly luxury, but never attains them, since he does nothing about it (for the **sluggard** see Exeg. on 19:24). **Diligent:** See Exeg. on 10:4.

5. Antithetic. **Falsehood:** Lit., "a word of deception." **Is loathesome:** The RSV emends *yabh'îsh,* "he causes to stink," to *yābhîsh,* **acts shamefully.** The last two verbs of the verse seem to express action rather than a state or condition of the wicked.

6. Antithetic. The concrete terms **him whose way is upright** and **the wicked** are in Hebrew "innocence" (see Exeg. on 10:9) and "wickedness" respectively.

7. Antithetic. Two interpretations are possible: According to the KJV, ASV, and Oesterley, the verse means that even though a man is poor he may be rich in spiritual things, and though a man is rich he may be poor in that he is never satisfied. According to the RSV, ASV mg., and most commentators and modern English translations, the verse condemns the fallacious spirit of the spendthrift and the miser.

8. The first clause simply notes the value of wealth which can be used as a means of protection by offering bribes or by buying protection (see Exeg. on 10:2 concerning wealth). The second clause seems unrelated to the first as it stands, unless drastically emended. **Ransom:** See Exeg. on 6:35. **Heareth not rebuke** ("heareth no threatening" ASV): The word *ge'ārāh* means only **rebuke,** and the attempt to make the second stich meaningful in connection with the first by translating this word "threatening" is unwarranted. The RSV **has no means of redemption** is based on a conjectural emendation.

9. Antithetic. Light is symbolic of the joy of the righteous; darkness of the plight of the wicked. The two terms **light** and **lamp** may have been purposely used here to express

---

4. See Expos. on 2:1-22.
5. See Expos. on 18:21.
6. See Expos. on 3:1-4.
7-8. See Expos. on 10:15-16.
9. See Expos. on 3:1-4.

10 Only by pride cometh contention: but with the well advised *is* wisdom.

11 Wealth *gotten* by vanity shall be diminished: but he that gathereth by labor shall increase.

12 Hope deferred maketh the heart sick: but *when* the desire cometh, *it is* a tree of life.

10 By insolence the heedless make strife,
but with those who take advice is wisdom.
11 Wealth hastily gotten[e] will dwindle,
but he who gathers little by little will increase it.
12 Hope deferred makes the heart sick,
but a desire fulfilled is a tree of life.

[e] Gk Vg: Heb *from vanity*

---

a contrast between the divine wisdom of the righteous and the human sagacity of the wicked, just as in 6:23 *tôrāh* is the light and its interpretation is the lamp (cf. also 21:4; Job 18:6).

10. Antithetic. The sin of pride is dealt with quite frequently in Proverbs (cf. 11:2; 16:5, 18-19; 18:12; 21:24; 25:14; 26:12; 27:2; 30:13). As stated in this verse, pride leads to strife, even to warfare (17:19). The proud fool will not allow himself to be corrected, which of course leads to his destruction (15:32). Pride is above all an abomination to the Lord (15:25; 16:5; 21:4). On the other hand, humility is exalted as one of the virtues of a God-fearing man (15:33; 16:19; 22:4). **The heedless:** The RSV emends *raq* **(only)** to *rēq,* with B. Gemser (*Sprüche Salomos* [Tübingen: J. C. B. Mohr, 1937; "Handbuch zum Alten Testament"], p. 48).

11. Antithetic. Cf. 10:2. **By vanity:** Rather, **hastily,** with the LXX and others, which contrasts better with **by labor** in the second stich. In the Hebrew text it requires simply the reversing of two Hebrew consonants *mhbl* to *mbhl.* **By labor** or **little by little:** Lit., "by hand," which in later Hebrew means "gradually."

12. Antithetic. Descriptive of any human disappointment or success. There is no reference here to the moral character of the desire. **Tree of life:** See Exeg. on 3:18.

---

10. See Expos. on 29:23.

11. See Expos. on 10:15-16.

12. ***Hope Deferred.***—This proverb is so obviously a description of a common human experience that it still finds its way many times into contemporary conversation. The person who suffers disappointment because he does not get something he ardently hopes for tends to label his experience with the words: **Hope deferred maketh the heart sick.** If the proverb is read only for what it says, there is little else to be added. But if it is scrutinized for what it suggests, light may be found to illuminate and revise this common experience.

Hope deferred is not an unmitigated evil. Hopes that are too easily realized are hardly worthy of a man whose "reach should exceed his grasp." [3] The glory of some people is the quality of their hopes. They hope for things that cannot be bought at a corner grocery store or made a reality next week. The hope for world peace is an example of a hope that has been cherished and deferred for many generations, and yet it is better to cling to a high hope without seeing its realization than to be content with low hopes that are easily satisfied. A case could even be made for the reverse of the proverb. Hopes deferred keep life interesting, whereas desires fulfilled produce satiety. Anticipation is often better than realization. The person who hopes for something and then gets it often discovers that the thing he received seems less desirable when he gets it than when he hoped for it. Instead of allowing himself to be bogged down in a Slough of Despond because his hope is not realized, an individual can well cling to his hope. He might shrink the size of his disappointment by shrinking the size of his hope, but this is hardly the direction in which human aspiration should go.

Hope deferred is better than hope destroyed. One of the consequences of a defeat in war or of disillusionment concerning its results is a destruction of hope. Many enter such a period as if they were entering the gates that say, "Abandon hope, all ye who enter here." [4] Few pictures are more pathetic than the sight of a dispossessed people accepting their lot blankly and indifferently because they believe there is no hope for improvement. Even the energy to protest against evil conditions is absent. The true hell, as A. J. Cronin states in one of his books, is not when hope is deferred but when people have ceased to hope.

[3] Browning, "Andrea del Sarto."

[4] Dante, *Inferno,* Canto III, l. 9.

13 Whoso despiseth the word shall be destroyed: but he that feareth the commandment shall be rewarded.

13 He who despises the word brings destruction on himself,
but he who respects the commandment will be rewarded.

13. Antithetic. In parallelism with **commandment** in the next stich, **word** must refer to the divine revelation of God to Israel in the law (cf. Deut. 30:11-13). A careful study of 16:20; 19:16; 28:4, 9; 29:18; 30:5-6 shows that the Law and the Prophets were accepted by the wise men of Israel as canonical scripture, and that the Writings, the third main division of the Hebrew canon, were in the course of being compiled, if not entirely completed. The wise men, especially as 30:6 shows, were evidently actively engaged in the formation of the canon. In the practical realm these verses show that the writers and compilers of the wisdom literature based their teaching on the word of God and exhorted their readers, especially the young men, to read this word diligently, for without it they would perish.

Shall be destroyed: With the RSV, ASV, Oesterley, and Toy. But the same Hebrew verb can also mean "to bind," "to pledge" as translated here by the ASV mg. (with

Hope deferred may become an incentive for the re-examination of the hope itself. Perhaps the cherished hope is not a reasonable one. The people who roamed the American continent many years ago searching for a Fountain of Youth by which they could remain perpetually young in body were hardly holding a valid hope. Even "things hoped for" should be critically examined to discover whether this is the kind of world in which such hopes can be realized. If someone had gone to the top of the temple hopeful that God would allow him to drop lightly on the pavement below if he leaped from the pinnacle, he could hardly have expected this hope to be fulfilled. Such action would be flying in the face of reasonable hope. Instead of being heartsick because his hope was not realized (if his heart was still beating after such a fall), the one who jumped from that height could well have re-examined the grounds for his hope. Jesus rejected this suggestion by saying, "You shall not try the Lord your God" (Matt. 4:7 Goodspeed). One of the psalmists spoke a helpful word that is applicable here, "Let me not be ashamed of my hope" (Ps. 119:116). There are hopes that should produce shame because they are selfish or unrealistic rather than heartaches because they are not realized.

True hope requires patience and faith. "Faith is the assurance of things hoped for" (Heb. 11:1). This does not mean that faith is the realization of things hoped for. Such consummation may take a long time. For many heroes of the faith the promised land was never entered. They died in faith while their hope was deferred. Hope is the faith that there are good possibilities in life that are not yet realized. There are also evil possibilities that may be realized. Hope is the devotion of the soul to the unfulfilled good. Instead of becoming heartsick because his hope is not realized in his own experience, or allowing himself to settle down into utter hopelessness, the hopeful man believes that the creative God is always at work to bring the good possibilities to fruition. In order to maintain this kind of hope, patience is needed. "It is good that a man should both hope and quietly wait for the salvation of the LORD" (Lam. 3:26). Such a man will not feel sorry for himself because his hope is not fulfilled; he sees that patience and faith are ingredients that are a part of true hopefulness.

When a person is downcast because his hope is deferred, he may get help in remembering that others went through times of hope's deferment to hope's fulfillment. In 1487 an explorer named Bartolomeu Dias sailed along the west coast of Africa. He had gone farther south than any sailor before him. Finally he came upon a great promontory. He named it "The Cape of Storms." That was what it was to him. While he was there he was conscious of winds and waves. Little he had hoped for had found fulfillment. But when he reported his experience to King John II of Portugal, the monarch saw another significance in what the explorer had discovered. He saw the possibility of a sea route to India, so he called the promontory "The Cape of Good Hope." This was only a hope as yet unfulfilled. In 1497, Vasco da Gama not only entertained this hope—he discovered that it had a basis in reality. He arrived at Calicut, India, by sailing around the cape. For Dias the cape was significant only for its untoward weather; for another it was the promise of a new route to the Orient. Such an experience is hope's fulfillment, and it atones in some measure for the heartache of long delays.

13. See Expos. on 1:5.

14 The law of the wise *is* a fountain of life, to depart from the snares of death.

15 Good understanding giveth favor: but the way of transgressors *is* hard.

16 Every prudent *man* dealeth with knowledge: but a fool layeth open *his* folly.

17 A wicked messenger falleth into mischief: but a faithful ambassador *is* health.

18 Poverty and shame *shall be to* him that refuseth instruction: but he that regardeth reproof shall be honored.

19 The desire accomplished is sweet to

14 The teaching of the wise is a fountain of life,
that one may avoid the snares of death.
15 Good sense wins favor,
but the way of the faithless is their ruin.[f]
16 In everything a prudent man acts with knowledge,
but a fool flaunts his folly.
17 A bad messenger plunges men into trouble,
but a faithful envoy brings healing.
18 Poverty and disgrace come to him who ignores instruction,
but he who heeds reproof is honored.
19 A desire fulfilled is sweet to the soul;

[f] Cn Compare Gk Syr Vg Tg: Heb *is enduring*

Brown, Driver, and Briggs, *ḥābhal;* and Gesenius—Buhl, *ḥābhal*). This latter translation would mean then that just as a debtor gave his creditor an article in pledge until the debt was paid, so the offender of God's word is considered a debtor to it and will be punished if he does not pay his debt, i.e., obedience to the word. **Feareth** or **respects:** See Exeg. on 1:7.

14. Similar to 14:27. The form of this proverb is different from the usual antithetic structure found in the proverbs of this section. The second stich continues the thought of the first one, thus forming one complete sentence. The sentiment is one of the most frequently expressed in the book. **Law** or, better, **teaching:** See Exeg. on 1:8. **Fountain:** See Exeg. on 10:11.

15. The two clauses seem unrelated. **Understanding** or **sense:** See Exeg. on 12:8. **Transgressors** or **faithless:** See Exeg. on 2:22. **Hard** or **their ruin:** With versions, reading *'êdhām* for *'êthān,* which means "perennial," "permanent." The use of the Hebrew word is not clear here.

16. Antithetic. Sobriety versus a display of ignorance. **Every** or **in everything:** Following Vulg. **Prudent:** See Exeg. on 1:4.

17. Antithetic. In the ancient days the nature and results of a message depended to a great extent upon the character of a messenger (cf. 10:26; 25:13). There is an interesting parallel to this verse in the Egyptian wisdom literature, where in the prologue to the Teaching of Amen-em-ope it is stated that one purpose in writing the book was to teach a man "how to return a report to one that has sent him." Both the Hebrew and Egyptian sages are referring to the envoy who was an important government official, or to a scribe who was classified as one of the wise men from the earliest times because he could write and therefore hold a responsible position (see Intro., p. 768; Oesterley, *Proverbs,* p. 103).

Falleth: By changing the verb from *yippōl* to *yappîl,* RSV renders **plunges.** The word **men** (i.e., those who employ the envoy) is supplied by RSV to make sense. **Health:** Lit., **healing.**

18. Antithetic. Failure in business is due many times to the refusal to listen to sound advice. **Refuseth:** See Exeg. on 1:25. The verb is *pāra'.* **Instruction:** See Exeg. on 1:2. **Reproof:** See Exeg. on 1:23.

19. The two clauses seem unrelated. Vs. 19*a* is similar to 13:12*b*, and vs. 19*b* is similar

---

14. See Expos. on 1:2.
15. See Expos. on 12:8.
16. See Expos. on 26:1, 3-12.
17. See Expos. on 20:6.
18. See Expos. on 9:7-9.
19. See Expos. on vs. 12.

the soul: but *it is* abomination to fools to
depart from evil.
20 He that walketh with wise *men* shall
be wise: but a companion of fools shall be
destroyed.
21 Evil pursueth sinners: but to the righteous good shall be repaid.
22 A good *man* leaveth an inheritance to
his children's children: and the wealth of
the sinner *is* laid up for the just.
23 Much food *is in* the tillage of the
poor: but there is *that is* destroyed for want
of judgment.
24 He that spareth his rod hateth his son:
but he that loveth him chasteneth him
betimes.
25 The righteous eateth to the satisfying
of his soul: but the belly of the wicked
shall want.

but to turn away from evil is an abomination to fools.
20 He who walks with wise men becomes wise,
but the companion of fools will suffer harm.
21 Misfortune pursues sinners,
but prosperity rewards the righteous.
22 A good man leaves an inheritance to his children's children,
but the sinner's wealth is laid up for the righteous.
23 The fallow ground of the poor yields much food,
but it is swept away through injustice.
24 He who spares the rod hates his son,
but he who loves him is diligent to discipline him.
25 The righteous has enough to satisfy his appetite,
but the belly of the wicked suffers want.

---

to 29:27*b*. **Abomination:** See Exeg. on 3:32. Since the fools seek that which is morally worthless, they refuse to abhor evil.

20. Antithetic. It is good to choose companions wisely. The influence of one person upon another for good or bad is recognized in several passages (4:14; 16:29; 22:24-25; 23:20; 28:7, 19). **Shall be destroyed** or **will suffer harm** ("shall smart" ASV; "be broken" ASV mg.): A Niphal form from the root *rā'a'*, "to be evil, bad" (cf. 11:15). The ASV mg. should be disregarded.

21. A favorite theme in Proverbs: the misfortune of the wicked and the good fortune of the righteous.

22. The law of retribution. The prosperity of the good man passes on to his children, and the wealth of the sinner also passes over into the hands of the good man.

23. The Hebrew text is meaningless as it stands: "Abundance of food is tillage of poor ones, and substance [existence] is swept away without justice." Neither the versions nor the numerous emendations by commentators clarify it. The standard English translations try unsuccessfully to make sense out of the Hebrew. **Tillage** or **fallow ground:** The Hebrew word *nîr* is found only here and in Hos. 10:12; Jer. 4:3, and means "new, untilled ground." The usual interpretation of the verse, which is arrived at only by free paraphrasing, is that the new land of a poor man, by hard labor, produces much food, whereas the rich man, because of his unjust actions, fails to get nourishment from his land and is destroyed.

24. Antithetic. Corporal punishment was a necessary part of the training of the Jewish child. Even as God punishes those whom he loves (3:12), so a father should punish his son if he really loves him and wants to help him. **Is diligent to discipline him:** Lit., "seeks him with discipline" (for "seek" and **discipline** see respectively Exeg. on 1:28; 1:2).

25. Antithetic. The bodily needs of the righteous are provided for (see Exeg. on 10:3). **Soul** or **appetite:** The word *néphesh* is used here as the seat of desire (cf. 6:30).

---

20. See Expos. on 2:9-22.
21. See Expos. on 3:1-4.
22. See Expos. on 11:8.
23. See Expos. on 21:3.
24. See Expos. on 17:6.
25. See Expos. on vs. 12.

14 Every wise woman buildeth her house: but the foolish plucketh it down with her hands.

2 He that walketh in his uprightness feareth the LORD: but *he that is* perverse in his ways despiseth him.

3 In the mouth of the foolish *is* a rod of pride: but the lips of the wise shall preserve them.

4 Where no oxen *are,* the crib *is* clean: but much increase *is* by the strength of the ox.

5 A faithful witness will not lie: but a false witness will utter lies.

6 A scorner seeketh wisdom, and *findeth it* not: but knowledge *is* easy unto him that understandeth.

14 Wisdom[g] builds her house,
but folly with her own hands tears it down.

2 He who walks in uprightness fears the LORD,
but he who is devious in his ways despises him.

3 The talk of a fool is a rod for his back,[h]
but the lips of the wise will preserve them.

4 Where there are no oxen, there is no[i] grain;
but abundant crops come by the strength of the ox.

5 A faithful witness does not lie,
but a false witness breathes out lies.

6 A scoffer seeks wisdom in vain,
but knowledge is easy for a man of understanding.

[g] Heb *Wisdom of women*
[h] Cn: Heb *a rod of pride*
[i] Cn: Heb *a manger of*

14:1. Antithetic. The verse probably read originally,

> Wisdom has built her house,
> but folly with her own hands is pulling it down.

(Cf. 9:1*a,* where a similar word for wisdom is found; see also Exeg. on 1:20.) "Women" was added later to the text as a gloss in an attempt to elucidate further the word *ḥakhmôth,* whose form had been forgotten. That the noun is singular is shown by the number of the verb.

2. Antithetic. True religion is shown in upright living. As Perowne remarks, piety and probity are intimately related. **Uprightness:** See Exeg. on 12:15. **Feareth:** See Exeg. on 1:7. **Perverse** or **devious:** See Exeg. on 2:15.

3. Antithetic. Pride shoots forth from the mouth of the fool, bringing ruin, whereas the speech of the wise man protects him. **Rod:** More accurately, "branch," "twig." **Of pride: For his back,** reading *gēwō(h)* for *ga'awāh,* with Gemser (*Sprüche Salomos, ad loc.*) and C. Steuernagel ("Die Spruche," in E. Kautzsch, *Die Heilige Schrift des Alten Testaments,* ed. A. Bertholet [4th ed.; Tübingen: J. C. B. Mohr, 1923], II, 297). **Shall preserve them:** The Hebrew form *tishmûrēm* is probably a scribal error for *tishmerûm.*

4. Antithetic. Vs. 4*a* should probably read, "Where there are no oxen, there is no corn," with the RSV, reading *'éphes,* "no," for *'ebhûs,* **crib,** and translating *bār* as "corn," "grain," and not **clean** with the KJV and ASV, since the word is usually used of moral purity. Good crops depend upon the oxen used for plowing.

5. Antithetic. Vs. 5*b*=6:19*a* (see Exeg.). Against perjury in court.

6. Antithetic. **Scoffer:** See Exeg. on 1:22. The **scorner** is no dullard, but is clever and capable of seeking wisdom. He can never attain it, however, because he does not fear the Lord—a prime requisite of true knowledge (cf. 1:7). For the noun **understanding** see Exeg. on 1:2.

14:1. See Expos. on 31:10-31.
2. See Expos. on 1:7.
3. See Expos. on 18:21.
4. See Expos. on 10:15-16.
5. See Expos. on 18:21.
6. See Expos. on 1:2.

7 Go from the presence of a foolish man, when thou perceivest not *in him* the lips of knowledge.

8 The wisdom of the prudent *is* to understand his way: but the folly of fools *is* deceit.

9 Fools make a mock at sin: but among the righteous *there is* favor.

10 The heart knoweth his own bitterness; and a stranger doth not intermeddle with his joy.

11 The house of the wicked shall be overthrown: but the tabernacle of the upright shall flourish.

12 There is a way which seemeth right unto a man; but the end thereof *are* the ways of death.

7 Leave the presence of a fool,
for there you do not meet words of knowledge.
8 The wisdom of a prudent man is to discern his way,
but the folly of fools is deceiving.
9 God scorns the wicked,[j]
but the upright enjoy his favor.
10 The heart knows its own bitterness,
and no stranger shares its joy.
11 The house of the wicked will be destroyed,
but the tent of the upright will flourish.
12 There is a way which seems right to a man,
but its end is the way to death.[k]

[j] Cn: Heb obscure
[k] Heb *ways of death*

7. The Hebrew reads literally,

Go from [or to] a foolish man,
And not dost thou know lips of knowledge.

The general sense is that the sooner one gets away from the company of a fool the better it is, because nothing sensible will be gained from him. The Hebrew phraseology is strange, as witnessed by the variety of translations in the versions.

8. True wisdom consists in the ability to judge present circumstances with the view to future success. To this thought the second stich does not form a direct antithesis. **Discern:** See Exeg. on 1:2. **Deceit** or **deceiving:** The KJV is a literal rendering, but actually self-deceit and deceiving others are the same thing. The LXX here reads "in erring," which may reflect a better reading than the M.T. The second stich might then be, "The folly of fools causes them to err," emending *mirmāh,* **deceit,** to *math'eh,* "causing to err."

9. The Hebrew of vs. 9*a* does not make good sense, "A guilt offering [or guilt] mocks fools." Nowhere else in Scripture is a sacrifice described as mocking an offerer. No help is received from the versions. The many emendations are merely attempts to find a more natural contrast with vs. 9*b* and are not based on textual evidence. The RSV reads *'elōhîm,* **God,** for *'ewîlîm,* and *reshā'îm,* **wicked,** for *'āshām,* with Oesterley.

10. Antithetic. Man's inmost feelings are not known by others. The hidden sorrows (13:12; 15:13; 17:22; 18:14) which almost break a man are many times covered over by a false happiness (14:13). Only God can know man entirely (15:11; 16:2; 20:12; 24:12).

11. Antithetic. The sturdy **house of the wicked will be destroyed,** but the **tent of the upright** will be prosperous and happy (cf. 12:7, where the firmly built house belongs to the righteous). **Flourish:** Lit., "send forth buds." Used figuratively here of a tent, which is strange. The LXX has "stand," a word which makes better sense.

12. Which seemeth right: Better, "is straight before" (ASV mg.). **Seemeth** is from

7-9. See Expos. on 26:1, 3-12.

10. See Expos. on 4:20-27.

11. See Expos. on 3:1-4.

12. ***Seeing Life Through to the End.***—Appearances are often deceitful. A way of living which today seems to be leading toward success and happiness may tomorrow result in pain and death. Seeing life through to its end is more than being faithful unto death—it is the capacity to see the ultimate and logical consequences of a course of action.

A scientific world view cultivates a critical

13 Even in laughter the heart is sorrowful; and the end of that mirth *is* heaviness.
14 The backslider in heart shall be filled with his own ways: and a good man *shall be satisfied* from himself.
15 The simple believeth every word: but the prudent *man* looketh well to his going.

13 Even in laughter the heart is sad,
and the end of joy is grief.
14 A perverse man will be filled with the fruit of his ways,
and a good man with the fruit of his deeds.[l]
15 The simple believes everything,
but the prudent looks where he is going.

[l] Cn: Heb *from upon him*

the LXX; **right** is the Hebrew word *yāshār,* "straight" (see Exeg. on 12:15). The Hebrew says simply, "There is a straight road before man." The way which promises happiness, prosperity, and success may lead for one reason or another to destruction. **End:** See Exeg. on 5:4. This verse is repeated in 16:25.

13. All joy is tinged with sorrow—a rather pessimistic outlook on life, not usual in Proverbs; or it could also mean that even in times of joy there are hidden sorrows which are being suppressed (cf. vs. 10). Toy and Oesterley, following the LXX, interpret the verse to mean the alternation of joy and sorrow in life.

14. Antithetic. **Backslider:** The Hebrew literally reads, "the turned away of heart," and means the one who willfully keeps from the right, not an apostate. A better translation is **perverse man,** or "dissembler." **From himself:** Better, "from his thoughts" (LXX), or with most modern commentators, "from his deeds," reading *mimmaʿalālâw* for *mēʿālâw* (so RSV).

15. Antithetic. The contrast between the credulous fool (*pethî*) and the discerning, prudent man who knows where he is going (see Exeg. on 1:4).

attitude toward appearances. Through the scientific method men have learned not to trust first appearances. The world looks flat to the person who trusts his eyesight alone. By other proofs scholars have learned that the world is round. The earth seems to be standing still while the sun seems to revolve around it. This is only appearance. The world is spinning on its axis, which gives the appearance of the sun's moving around the earth. These are a few illustrations of the fact that science has predisposed men to discount appearances.

A way which appears good today may have undesirable consequences in the future. To be clear-sighted may mean being shortsighted. Attention has been called to the fact that early forms of life were able to adapt themselves to their surroundings too well. They did not reckon with the change of climate and environment that was to come, and were blind to the needs of the future. The creature that survived had not adopted a fixed mode of responding to its surroundings, but had been more flexible in meeting changing conditions. Such a precarious existence might have appeared to be the way of death. In fact, it became the way of life. Too rigid an adjustment meant incapacity to meet new situations, while the sensitive responsiveness of creatures with nerves almost exposed gave those forms of life a better chance to survive than the armored creatures that had apparently made themselves impregnable to attack.

Living by the day therefore has its limitations. Times come when each of us needs to be reminded that each day has enough trouble without borrowing the worries about tomorrow. But this attitude can be carried too far. One can have "peace in our time," and yet be unaware that the course he is following will mean war only too soon. No one can admire the boatman who is on the brink of Niagara Falls, congratulating himself that all is well today, when a few moments hence will find him plunging to his death. Living only for today has little to commend it if people are not examining the inevitable consequences of their actions. He is a wise teacher who can help young people and others to see life through to its end and to its ends. That is a high moment of insight when, as Matthew Arnold writes in "The Buried Life," a man

thinks he knows
The hills where his life rose,
And the sea where it goes.

13. See Expos. on 17:22.
14. See Expos. on 3:1-4.
15-16. See Expos. on 22:3.

16 A wise *man* feareth, and departeth from evil: but the fool rageth, and is confident.

17 *He that is* soon angry dealeth foolishly: and a man of wicked devices is hated.

18 The simple inherit folly: but the prudent are crowned with knowledge.

19 The evil bow before the good; and the wicked at the gates of the righteous.

20 The poor is hated even of his own neighbor: but the rich *hath* many friends.

21 He that despiseth his neighbor sinneth: but he that hath mercy on the poor, happy *is* he.

16 A wise man is cautious and turns away
from evil,
but a fool throws off restraint and is
careless.
17 A man of quick temper acts foolishly,
but a man of discretion is patient.[m]
18 The simple acquire folly,
but the prudent are crowned with
knowledge.
19 The evil bow down before the good,
the wicked at the gates of the righteous.
20 The poor is disliked even by his neighbor,
but the rich has many friends.
21 He who despises his neighbor is a sinner,
but happy is he who is kind to the poor.

[m] Gk: Heb *is hated*

16. Antithetic. Similar to vs. 15. **Feareth:** Not in a religious sense here, as the RSV brings out with the rendering **is cautious. Rageth** ("beareth himself insolently" ASV): The verb *'ābhar* means "to pass over, beyond bounds," and so "to be angry, arrogant." The RSV **throws off restraint** captures the meaning of the verb here. **Is careless:** Hebrew, "trusts."

17. Antithetic. The natural antithesis should be between the quick-tempered man and the more deliberate one, which is actually brought out in the LXX by dropping one consonant in the Hebrew text of vs. 17*b*. The LXX reads, "but a wise man endureth much," reading *yissā'* for *yissānē'* (cf. RSV). Franz Delitzsch, holding to the M.T., with the KJV, claims that the contrast is between the quick-tempered man who suddenly bursts forth in anger, and the man of intrigues who secretly plots against his enemies (*Biblical Commentary on the Book of Proverbs,* tr. M. G. Easton [Edinburgh: T. & T. Clark, 1884], I, 302). **Quick temper:** Lit., "short of nostrils," the feeling of anger being expressed by snorting. **Wicked devices** (*mezimmôth*): See Exeg. on 1:4. The LXX takes this word in good sense here, as does the RSV.

18. Antithetic. **Inherit** or **acquire:** Both renderings are possible, but the RSV suits the context better here. **Are crowned:** This rendering of the verb is unusual, being without parallel in the O.T. One expects an active meaning as in the LXX, which has **acquire.**

19. Evil bows prostrate before moral goodness, or waits humbly at its gates. Moral goodness always wins out in this life, a doctrine which in the course of years proved to be false. It was superseded by the belief that the wicked were punished and the righteous were rewarded in the next world (cf. Wisd. Sol. 2–5).

20. Antithetic. A sad commentary on human nature (see Exeg. on 10:2).

21. Antithetic. **Poor:** From the root *'ānāh,* "to be bowed down, afflicted." Almsgiving in later Judaism was equivalent to righteousness (see Exeg. on 1:3).

17. See Expos. on 16:32.

18. See Expos. on 1:2.

19. See Expos. on 3:13-18.

20. See Expos. on 10:15-16.

21. ***He that Hath Pity.***—Two men are contrasted in this saying. One **despises his neighbor.** He actively loathes the one who lives near him, and he probably has liberal amounts of jealousy, hate, and suspicion in his thought and treatment of his neighbor. Such a man sins because he despises an individual who is a child of God. The other man has toward his neighbor an active and outgoing sympathy and compassion. He has pity on the poor. According to the account in Mark 1:40-41, a leper once came to Jesus seeking help from him. He felt that Jesus had the power to do something for him if he had the will to do so. Mark writes that Jesus, "being moved with pity," stretched out his hand and touched the man, bringing cleansing to him. The capacity to feel with others and to suffer with them, as this thought is expressed in our

22 Do they not err that devise evil? but mercy and truth *shall be* to them that devise good.

23 In all labor there is profit: but the talk of the lips *tendeth* only to penury.

24 The crown of the wise *is* their riches: *but* the foolishness of fools *is* folly.

22 Do they not err that devise evil?
Those who devise good meet loyalty and faithfulness.
23 In all toil there is profit,
but mere talk tends only to want.
24 The crown of the wise is their wisdom,[n]
but folly is the garland[o] of fools.

[n] Cn Compare Gk: Heb *riches*
[o] Cn: Heb *folly*

---

22. Antithetic. The question form in Proverbs is rare; it emphasizes the certainty of the expression. **Devise:** See Exeg. on 3:29. **Mercy and truth:** See Exeg on 3:3. This expression occurs also in 16:6; 20:28.

23. Antithetic. Work, not talk, produces the results. **Labor:** The word *'eçebh* basically means "pain," "hurt." In general the words for "work" in the O.T. have an unpleasant connotation, although work itself was not a curse since it was part of the economy of Eden (Gen. 2:15) and of heaven (Rev. 22:3). The wise men not only condemn indolence (e.g., 6:6-11), but they praise work as the source of legitimate gain.

24. Antithetic. According to the Hebrew text wealth is an ornament possessed by the wise; it not only adorns their appearance but contributes to their influence and power among men. Wealth, however, is usually thought of as a gift of wisdom (3:16; 8:18) and

---

English words "compassion" and "sympathy," will produce ultimate happiness in the person who has the outgoing compassionate attitude.

According to a story found in rabbinical literature,

> While Moses was feeding the sheep of his father-in-law in the wilderness, a young kid ran away. Moses followed it until it reached a ravine, where it found a well to drink from. When Moses reached it, he said, "I did not know that you ran away because you were thirsty. Now you must be weary." He carried the kid back. Then God said, "Because thou hast shown pity in leading back one of a flock belonging to a man, thou shalt lead *my* flock, Israel." [5]

A third attitude toward a neighbor is possible. One needs neither positively to despise a neighbor nor actively to pity him. He can be indifferent toward him, merely tolerating him or completely ignoring him. A man may have a callous heart that makes him unfeeling toward others. He passes by on the other side. In the story of the good Samaritan as told by Jesus (Luke 10:30-37), the robbers were aggressively evil toward the traveler, the Samaritan was positively compassionate in helping the wounded man, while the priest and the Levite were merely indifferent. If they felt for the man, they did not act on his behalf.

Miss Dartle, in Dickens' *David Copperfield,* welcomed the suggestion of Steerforth that underprivileged people were not expected to be as sensitive as other people. "It's so consoling! It's such a delight to know that, when they suffer, they don't feel! Sometimes I have been quite uneasy for that sort of people; but now I shall just dismiss the idea of them altogether. Live and learn." [6]

Love has been described as the capacity to read statistics. Cold figures of hungry people, or sick people, or poor people can be dismissed easily if one does not try to feel with those who suffer. John Woolman was one who cast his lot with the suffering. It was not unnatural that he should have had a dream toward the end of his life in which he thought he was so mixed with the gray mass of suffering humanity that he could no longer reply to his own name when he was called.

The attitude of indifference to the needs and feelings of others is stated in another of the proverbs:

> A good man cares for the rights of the poor;
> a bad man has no interest in them (29:7 Moffatt).

Such a man does not hate the poor. He ignores them. His course of conduct would seem to relieve him of the pain of suffering with others and of sharing their uncertainties. True happiness, according to the sages, does not come to the person who has thus encased himself in a block of ice, but rather to the one whose heart goes out in compassion to his suffering neighbor.

22. See Expos. on 3:27-35.

23. See Expos. on 18:21.

24. See Expos. on 1:2.

[5] C. G. Montefiore and Herbert Loewe, *A Rabbinic Anthology* (London: Macmillan & Co., 1938), p. 45.

[6] Ch. xx.

25 A true witness delivereth souls: but a deceitful *witness* speaketh lies.

26 In the fear of the LORD *is* strong confidence: and his children shall have a place of refuge.

27 The fear of the LORD *is* a fountain of life, to depart from the snares of death.

28 In the multitude of people *is* the king's honor: but in the want of people *is* the destruction of the prince.

29 *He that is* slow to wrath *is* of great understanding: but *he that is* hasty of spirit exalteth folly.

30 A sound heart *is* the life of the flesh: but envy the rottenness of the bones.

31 He that oppresseth the poor reproacheth his Maker: but he that honoreth him hath mercy on the poor.

25 A truthful witness saves lives,
but one who utters lies is a betrayer.
26 In the fear of the LORD one has strong confidence,
and his children will have a refuge.
27 The fear of the LORD is a fountain of life,
that one may avoid the snares of death.
28 In a multitude of people is the glory of a king,
but without people a prince is ruined.
29 He who is slow to anger has great understanding,
but he who has a hasty temper exalts folly.
30 A tranquil mind gives life to the flesh,
but passion makes the bones rot.
31 He who oppresses a poor man insults his Maker,
but he who is kind to the needy honors him.

---

nowhere, except here, as an ornament of the wise. With most commentators the RSV reads *'ormām* **(their wisdom)** for *'oshrām,* and *liwyath* **(garland)** for the first *'iwwéleth* in vs. 24*b,* making for a clearer antithesis.

25. Antithetic. Vs. 25*b* is difficult. Lit., "And he who breathes out lies is deceit." The general sense is clear, however, as the RSV paraphrases. In these early days when everything depended on the testimony of the witness, it was possible for a true witness to save a man's life or for a false witness to condemn an innocent man to death (cf. 6:19; 12:17; 19:28; 25:18). **Utters:** *Pûaḥ* (see Exeg. on 6:19).

26. To fear God means security for a man and for his children. **His children:** ASV mg., "the children of him that hath it" (i.e., the fear of the Lord), a clumsy expression. The antecedent of **his** is the God-fearing man.

27. Similar to 13:14 (see Exeg.), where "the law [teaching] of the wise" is equivalent to **the fear of the LORD** in this verse. They are considered of equal authority by the wise men.

28. Antithetic. A reference to the king and his power in purely secular terms. His strength and permanence depend upon the multitudes who are loyal to him (see Exeg. on 16:10).

29. Antithetic. **Slow to wrath:** Lit., "long of nostrils" (see Exeg. on vs. 17). **Understanding:** See Exeg. on 2:2. **Hasty temper:** Lit., "short of spirit." **Exalteth** ("carrieth away" ASV mg.): Usually *mērîm* takes a material object. Perhaps we should read with the Targ. "increases" (*marbeh*).

30. Antithetic. The wise men were well aware of the influence of mind over body (see Exeg. on 3:8; cf. 15:13; 17:22; 18:14). **Tranquil mind:** Lit., "heart of healing," i.e., a mind that brings composure to the whole body (see Exeg. on 2:2). **Envy** or **passion:** *Qin'āh* may be translated either way. The root meaning is "red," then "inflamed." **Bones:** Together with **flesh** of vs. 30*a* stands for the whole body.

31. Antithetic. To oppress the poor is an offense against God. The influence of the prophets is seen here upon the sages of Israel. The same idea is expressed in 17:5; 19:17

---

25. See Expos. on 18:21.
26-27. See Expos. on 1:7.
28. See Expos. on 16:10-15.
29. See Expos. on 16:32.
30. See Expos. on 4:20-27.
31. See Expos. on 22:16*a*.

32 The wicked is driven away in his wickedness: but the righteous hath hope in his death.

33 Wisdom resteth in the heart of him that hath understanding: but *that which is* in the midst of fools is made known.

34 Righteousness exalteth a nation: but sin *is* a reproach to any people.

35 The king's favor *is* toward a wise servant: but his wrath is *against* him that causeth shame.

15 A soft answer turneth away wrath: but grievous words stir up anger.

2 The tongue of the wise useth knowledge aright: but the mouth of fools poureth out foolishness.

32 The wicked is overthrown through his evil-doing,
but the righteous finds refuge through his integrity.[p]
33 Wisdom abides in the mind of a man of understanding,
but it is not[q] known in the heart of fools.
34 Righteousness exalts a nation,
but sin is a reproach to any people.
35 A servant who deals wisely has the king's favor,
but his wrath falls on one who acts shamefully.

15 A soft answer turns away wrath,
but a harsh word stirs up anger.
2 The tongue of the wise dispenses knowledge,[r]
but the mouths of fools pour out folly.

[p] Gk Syr: Heb *in his death*
[q] Gk Syr: Heb lacks *not*
[r] Cn: Heb *makes knowledge good*

(see Exeg.) and 22:2 (cf. also Job 31:16). **Maker:** On this name of the deity cf. Job 4:17; 35:10; Isa. 51:13; 54:5; Ps. 95:6.

32. Antithetic. **Evil-doing:** Either the evil that the wicked man does, or the "calamity" (ASV mg.) that falls on him. **In his death** (*bemôthô*): Better, with LXX, **through his integrity** (*bethummô*). The Hebrew text seems to reflect too advanced a view of immortality for Proverbs, where death is always thought of as a calamity and Sheol still retains its dismal character (see Intro., p. 777; cf. 15:24).

33. Antithetic. Vs. 33*b* reads, lit., "And in the inward part of fools it is made known," which is unintelligible, at least in this context. The LXX adds a negative, which is a step toward a solution of the problem (see RSV). Toy, followed by Oesterley, suggests emending *tiwwādhēaʿ*, **is made known,** to *'iwwéleth,* "folly." In that case the contrast is between wisdom and folly as the permanent guests respectively of the wise and the foolish. **Understanding:** See Exeg. on 1:2.

34. Antithetic. Impliedly the contrast is between Israel—the only righteous nation since it alone worships the true and living God—and other nations which are idolatrous. **Reproach:** *Ḥéṣedh* is an Aramaism; in Hebrew the word means "goodness," "kindness" (see Exeg. on 3:3). The LXX reads *ḥéṣer,* "need," "want," which is followed by Oesterley and Steuernagel: "Sins bring want to peoples."

35. Antithetic. On the king in Proverbs see Exeg. on 16:10. **Causeth shame:** Better, **acts shamefully,** to sharpen the contrast.

15:1. Antithetic. The most familiar of the many sayings about speech in Proverbs (cf. vs. 23; 24:26; 25:15). "One can discern, speaking generally, four main directions in the treatment of this subject: kindliness of speech, courtesy in reply, the wisdom of silence, and caution in speaking; this last receives most attention. The fundamental guiding principles throughout are consideration for the feelings of others, and self-respect in the speaker, though warnings lest unadvised speech should get a man into trouble also play a part." (Oesterley, *Proverbs,* pp. 117-18.) **Harsh word:** Lit., "word of pain" (see Exeg. on 14:23, where *ʿeçebh* is also used).

2. Antithetic. Knowledge, sent forth in useful channels, is a blessing to all, whereas

32. See Expos. on 3:1-4.
33. See Expos. on 26:1, 3-12.
34-35. See Expos. on 16:10-15.
15:1-2. See Expos. on 18:21.

3 The eyes of the LORD *are* in every place,
beholding the evil and the good.
4 A wholesome tongue *is* a tree of life:
but perverseness therein *is* a breach in the
spirit.
5 A fool despiseth his father's instruction: but he that regardeth reproof is prudent.
6 In the house of the righteous *is* much
treasure: but in the revenues of the wicked
is trouble.
7 The lips of the wise disperse knowledge: but the heart of the foolish *doeth* not
so.
8 The sacrifice of the wicked *is* an abomination to the LORD: but the prayer of the
upright *is* his delight.
9 The way of the wicked *is* an abomination unto the LORD: but he loveth him that
followeth after righteousness.

3 The eyes of the LORD are in every place,
keeping watch on the evil and the good.
4 A gentle tongue is a tree of life,
but perverseness in it breaks the spirit.
5 A fool despises his father's instruction,
but he who heeds admonition is prudent.
6 In the house of the righteous there is
much treasure,
but trouble befalls the income of the
wicked.
7 The lips of the wise spread knowledge;
not so the minds of fools.
8 The sacrifice of the wicked is an abomination to the LORD,
but the prayer of the upright is his delight.
9 The way of the wicked is an abomination
to the LORD,
but he loves him who pursues righteousness.

---

folly, which bursts forth like a torrential flood from the fool, is destructive to all. **Useth knowledge aright** or **dispenses knowledge:** The Hebrew has *têṭîbh,* lit., "makes good." Following the LXX, most modern commentators read *taṭṭîph,* "drops," "utters" (see RSV).

3. God is in his watchtower, keeping watch over the good and bad. This is really a warning that God will punish the wicked, and of course reward the righteous. **Beholding** or, better, **keeping watch:** A word commonly used of the watchman of a city (II Kings 9:17).

4. Antithetic. See Exeg. on vs. 1 regarding the tongue (cf. 12:17). **Wholesome tongue** or **gentle tongue:** The ASV mg. has "the healing of the tongue," a literal rendering of the Hebrew. **Tree of life:** See Exeg. on 3:18. **Perverseness:** See Exeg. on 11:3. The perverseness of the tongue breaks or crushes the spirit of the man to whom or about whom evil things are spoken.

5. Antithetic. Cf. 13:1. **Instruction** ("correction" ASV): See Exeg. on 1:2. **Admonition:** See Exeg. on 1:23. **Prudent:** See Exeg. on 1:4.

6. Antithetic. Virtue is rewarded by prosperity, but the gain of the wicked is ultimately lost since it was gathered by deceitful and unjust means. The form of the expression of the verse is taken from agricultural life. **Trouble:** Not a correct translation, since *ne'kāreth* literally means "a thing troubled." Toy and others emend to *nikhrath,* "is cut off."

7. Antithetic. **Minds:** See Exeg. on 2:2. **Doeth not so:** The ASV mg. has "is not steadfast [or right]."

8. Antithetic. One of the few references to sacrifice in Proverbs (cf. 7:14; 17:1; 21:3, 27). Sacrifice without righteousness is not acceptable to the Lord, according to the prophets and the wise men (cf. Amos 5:22). The sages recognize the importance of the ritual, but they do not stress it. **Abomination:** See Exeg. on 3:32. Two abominations are described here and in vs. 9.

9. Antithetic. This verse complements vs. 8. In the sight of God right living is a necessary concomitant of correct religious practices.

---

3. See Expos. on 3:5-8.
4. See Expos. on 18:21.
5. See Expos. on 9:7-9.
6. See Expos. on 10:15-16.
7. See Expos. on 18:21.
8. See Expos. on 21:3.
9. See Expos. on 3:1-4.

10 Correction *is* grievous unto him that forsaketh the way: *and* he that hateth reproof shall die.

11 Hell and destruction *are* before the LORD: how much more then the hearts of the children of men?

12 A scorner loveth not one that reproveth him: neither will he go unto the wise.

13 A merry heart maketh a cheerful countenance: but by sorrow of the heart the spirit is broken.

14 The heart of him that hath understanding seeketh knowledge: but the mouth of fools feedeth on foolishness.

15 All the days of the afflicted *are* evil: but he that is of a merry heart *hath* a continual feast.

16 Better *is* little with the fear of the LORD, than great treasure and trouble therewith.

17 Better *is* a dinner of herbs where love is, than a stalled ox and hatred therewith.

10 There is severe discipline for him who forsakes the way;
he who hates reproof will die.
11 Sheol and Abaddon lie open before the LORD,
how much more the hearts of men!
12 A scoffer does not like to be reproved;
he will not go to the wise.
13 A glad heart makes a cheerful countenance,
but by sorrow of heart the spirit is broken.
14 The mind of him who has understanding seeks knowledge,
but the mouths of fools feed on folly.
15 All the days of the afflicted are evil,
but a cheerful heart has a continual feast.
16 Better is a little with the fear of the LORD
than great treasure and trouble with it.
17 Better is a dinner of herbs where love is
than a fatted ox and hatred with it.

---

10. Either an early or a violent death is the result of an undisciplined life. **Discipline:** See Exeg. on 1:2. **Reproof:** See Exeg. on 1:23.

11. A rather advanced view of Sheol for the O.T., viz., that God oversees it (cf. Job 26:6; Ps. 139:8). **Hell** or, better, **Sheol:** See Exeg. on 1:12. **Destruction** or **Abaddon:** A synonym of Sheol. In the N.T. it is the name of the angel of the abyss (Rev. 9:11).

12. Scoffer: See Exeg. on 1:22. He is unteachable. **Unto the wise:** Perhaps better with the LXX, "with the wise," in that he has no fellowship with them.

13. Antithetic. See Exeg. on 3:8; 14:30. **A glad heart:** As Toy points out (*ad loc.*) the word **merry** now has more of the idea of movement and utterance than is contained in the Hebrew word used here, which means **glad,** "joyful."

14. Antithetic. A wise man is never satisfied in his quest for knowledge, whereas the fool lies down like a satiated animal and mulls over his folly. **Mind:** See Exeg. on 2:2. **Understanding:** See Exeg. on 1:2. **Mouth:** The reading of the Hebrew margin. The text has "face." The stupid, insensible fool (*k^eṣîl*) is appropriately pictured as an animal ruminating on his folly.

15. Antithetic. Cf. vs. 13. Evidently there is no moral implication here. **Afflicted:** Same root as noun for "poor" in 14:21, where see Exeg. **Cheerful:** Lit., "good."

16. Antithetic. Cf. 16:8, where "righteousness" is used instead of **the fear of the LORD. Fear of the LORD:** See Exeg. on 1:7. **Trouble:** Basically the word means "tumult," "confusion," "disquietude." Spiritual wealth is superior to material wealth.

17. Antithetic. Cf. 17:1. Wealth does not always assure happiness. **Dinner:** More

---

10. See Expos. on 9:7-9.

11. See Expos. on 3:5-8.

12. See Expos. on 9:7-9.

13. See Expos. on 17:22.

14. See Expos. on 2:1-22.

15. See Expos. on 17:22.

16-17. ***Which Is Better?***—These two proverbs, like many others in the collection, recognize that life often confronts an individual with a necessary choice. Sometimes it is a choice between evils. Wise living then consists in accepting the lesser of two evils. Neither alternative seems good, but sometimes there appears to be no other possibility. Human sin and folly bring about conditions in which no solution to a problem is a good one. Men have gone to war not because they thought that this was a good solution to an international dispute, but because recourse to war seemed the lesser of two evils. Fortunately not all choices are of this

18 A wrathful man stirreth up strife: but *he that is* slow to anger appeaseth strife.

19 The way of the slothful *man is* as a hedge of thorns: but the way of the righteous *is* made plain.

18 A hot-tempered man stirs up strife,
but he who is slow to anger quiets contention.
19 The way of a sluggard is overgrown with thorns,
but the path of the upright is a level highway.

---

accurately, "a portion." **Stalled ox:** The expression means an ox fed in the stall and so specially fattened, as the RSV translates.

18. Antithetic. Cf. 14:17, 29; 15:1. **Hot-tempered man:** Lit., "man of heat." The man of anger should be avoided because he is dangerous and the source of much strife (22:24; 26:21; 29:22). That the angry man is a foolish man is often stated in Proverbs (14:17, 29; 20:3); on the other hand, the man who is calm and cool is full of understanding (17:27; 19:11).

19. Antithetic. The road of life is full of obstacles for the sluggard (see Exeg. on 19:24). **Is overgrown:** It is strange to compare a path with **a hedge,** as the KJV does; a verb is needed here, with the LXX, in parallelism with vs. 19*b* (so RSV, with Toy and Oesterley). **Upright:** See Exeg. on 12:15, where the word is translated "right." **Is a level**

---

latter kind. Sometimes there is something good about both alternatives, and the true wisdom is in knowing how to select the better one.

Better is a little with the fear of the Lord than great treasure and trouble with it.

The person who has few material possessions may regard the ownership of wealth as the highest good. Yet wealth is not an unmixed good. The person who has it is constantly afraid that he may lose it. As the Amer. Trans. indicates, a man may have "much treasure, and anxiety with it." A reverent quiet spirit, even though one has little wealth, is better than much money with worry. The accumulation of wealth has a bitter taste if the wealth is secured unfairly. A man must live with himself as well as with his wealth, and if the way in which he acquired his wealth makes him disrespect himself and lose the respect of his neighbors, that wealth loses much of its value.

It is better to be of a lowly spirit with the poor
than to divide the spoil with the proud (16:19).

Why is it better? There are cultures in which recognition is given to the rich, even if they are haughty and proud. Nations in which this takes place are testifying that to them wealth is more important than character. Many years after the writing of this proverb, Oliver Goldsmith reminded the world of the consequences of such an attitude:

Ill fares the land, to hastening ills a prey,
Where wealth accumulates, and men decay.[7]

[7] "The Deserted Village."

Getting wisdom is better than getting gold.

To get wisdom is better than gold;
to get understanding is to be chosen rather than silver (16:16).

The heaping up of earthly goods does not bring the satisfaction that comes with the accumulation of wisdom. In modern terms it can be said that an education which produces appreciation of the beautiful, understanding, and humane feeling is better than a large bank account.

Love is better than luxury.

Better is a dinner of herbs where love is than a fatted ox and hatred with it.

Better is a dry morsel with quiet
than a house full of feasting with strife (17:1).

A heavy-laden stomach is no compensation for a heavy heart. The true value of a meal does not lie in what is on the table; its value comes from the hearts of the people who surround the table. If they are in turmoil and conflict, no lavish diet can make mealtime a desirable occasion. Even where people live in luxury, love is a necessity.

The sages evidently believed that there are many occasions when the good is the enemy of the best. In devotion to some lesser good, a greater good can be missed. The wise person is he who knows the relative value of things, and the sages tried to keep people aware of the better alternatives before them.

18. See Expos. on 16:32.

19. See Expos. on 3:21-26.

20 A wise son maketh a glad father: but a foolish man despiseth his mother.
21 Folly *is* joy to *him that is* destitute of wisdom: but a man of understanding walketh uprightly.
22 Without counsel purposes are disappointed: but in the multitude of counselors they are established.
23 A man hath joy by the answer of his mouth: and a word *spoken* in due season, how good *is it!*
24 The way of life *is* above to the wise, that he may depart from hell beneath.
25 The LORD will destroy the house of the proud: but he will establish the border of the widow.
26 The thoughts of the wicked *are* an abomination to the LORD: but *the words* of the pure *are* pleasant words.

20 A wise son makes a glad father,
but a foolish man despises his mother.
21 Folly is a joy to him who has no sense,
but a man of understanding walks aright.
22 Without counsel plans go wrong,
but with many advisers they succeed.
23 To make an apt answer is a joy to a man,
and a word in season, how good it is!
24 The wise man's path leads upward to life,
that he may avoid Sheol beneath.
25 The LORD tears down the house of the proud,
but maintains the widow's boundaries.
26 The thoughts of the wicked are an abomination to the LORD,
the words of the pure are pleasing to him.[s]

[s] Cn Compare Gk: Heb *pleasant words are pure*

highway: Lit., "is cast up," a road being made by casting up the earth and removing the obstacles (cf. Jer. 18:15; Isa. 40:3; 49:11; 57:14).

20. Antithetic. Cf. 10:1. **A foolish man:** Lit., "a fool of a man"; a construction similar to that in Gen. 16:12, "a wild ass of a man," i.e., a man who acts like a wild ass, and so here, a man who acts like a fool.

21. Antithetic. **Folly:** From the antithesis of vs. 21*b*, this word here has an ethical as well as an intellectual sense. It is practically equivalent to sinfulness. **Wisdom** or **sense:** Lit., "heart" (see Exeg. on 2:2). **Understanding:** See Exeg. on 2:2. **Walketh uprightly** ("maketh straight his going" ASV): The verb *yāshar* has an ethical content here as in 3:6; 9:15. See Exeg. on 1:3, where the noun "equity" which comes from this root is discussed.

22. Antithetic. The value of wise counsel in formulating one's plans (cf. 11:14). **Counsel:** The Hebrew word is *ṣôdh* (see Exeg. on 3:32). **Plans:** Perhaps those of government officials, families, or individuals. There is no religious content in this verse. It is striking how purely secular matters are included in the considerations of the wise men. For them, all things well and wisely done were indications of God's gift of wisdom.

23. Synonymous. Cf. Isa. 50:4. A timely word brings satisfaction to the one who utters it, as well as to the one who receives it.

24. Above or **upward:** Since the O.T. knows of no place in heaven for the souls of men, although the translations of Enoch and Elijah may establish the possibility of exceptions, the expression can only be used here in contrast with the **beneath** of the next clause. The way of wickedness leads down to death, but the path of the righteous is that of a happy and prosperous life to be enjoyed on this earth (cf. 4:18; 12:28). **Hell** or, better, **Sheol:** See Exeg. on 1:12.

25. Antithetic. The Lord is the protector of the helpless and the punisher of the unscrupulous (cf. 22:28; Deut. 19:14). **Proud:** See Exeg. on 13:10.

26. Antithetic. **Abomination:** See Exeg. on 3:32. In vs. 26*b* the M.T. reads, "and pure are the words of pleasantness." The KJV paraphrases and the RSV substantially follows the LXX, which reads, "but the words of the pure are honorable." **Pure** here means ritually clean.

20. See Expos. on 1:8-9; 10:1.
21. See Expos. on 26:1, 3-12.
22. See Expos. on 11:14.
23. See Expos. on 18:21.
24-25. See Expos. on 3:21-26.
26. See Expos. on 18:21.

27 He that is greedy of gain troubleth his own house; but he that hateth gifts shall live.

28 The heart of the righteous studieth to answer: but the mouth of the wicked poureth out evil things.

29 The LORD *is* far from the wicked: but he heareth the prayer of the righteous.

30 The light of the eyes rejoiceth the heart: *and* a good report maketh the bones fat.

31 The ear that heareth the reproof of life abideth among the wise.

32 He that refuseth instruction despiseth his own soul: but he that heareth reproof getteth understanding.

33 The fear of the LORD *is* the instruction of wisdom; and before honor *is* humility.

16 The preparations of the heart in man, and the answer of the tongue, *is* from the LORD.

27 He who is greedy for unjust gain makes
trouble for his household,
but he who hates bribes will live.

28 The mind of the righteous ponders how
to answer,
but the mouth of the wicked pours out
evil things.

29 The LORD is far from the wicked,
but he hears the prayer of the righteous.

30 The light of the eyes rejoices the heart,
and good news refreshes[t] the bones.

31 He whose ear heeds wholesome admonition
will abide among the wise.

32 He who ignores instruction despises himself,
but he who heeds admonition gains
understanding.

33 The fear of the LORD is instruction in
wisdom,
and humility goes before honor.

16 The plans of the mind belong to man,
but the answer of the tongue is
from the LORD.

[t] Heb *makes fat*

---

27. Antithetic. Unscrupulous and unjust means of getting wealth are here condemned, especially bribes given to public officials.

28. Antithetic. The considered answer contrasted with the deluge of evil words (cf. 15:2). **Mind:** See Exeg. on 2:2. **Ponders:** The same word is translated "meditate" in Ps. 1:2.

29. Antithetic. (Cf. vs. 8).

30. Synonymous. From the parallelism with **good report, the light of the eyes** must belong to the one bringing the good news.

31. One of the few verses in this collection consisting of a single sentence. **Ear:** Stands for man by synecdoche. **Admonition:** See Exeg. on 1:23. The **reproof of life** means the admonition which enables one to live prosperously.

32. Antithetic. **Instruction,** "correction" (ASV): See Exeg. on 1:2. **Understanding:** Lit., "heart." See Exeg. on 2:2.

33. There is no practical difference between the divine wisdom and the human wisdom which **the fear of the LORD** produces (cf. 1:7; 9:10). Humility, which is a necessary part of the fear of the Lord, leads to honor. Vs. 33*b*=18:12*b*.

16:1. There is a strong religious note in vss. 1-7, the name of the Lord being found in each one. The KJV, with Oesterley, makes no contrast between the stichs of the first verse. It means then that both the thoughts of man and their utterances are from the Lord. The RSV and the ASV, on the other hand, make a contrast between the two stichs, which would then mean that man's plans and thoughts are contradicted by God-given words (cf. vs. 9, where the meaning is slightly different).

---

27. See Expos. on 18:16.
28. See Expos. on 22:3.
29. See Expos. on 21:3.
30. See Expos. on 17:22.
31-32. See Expos. on 9:7-9.
33. See Expos. on 1:7; 29:23.
16:1. See Expos. on 18:21.

2 All the ways of a man *are* clean in his own eyes; but the LORD weigheth the spirits.
3 Commit thy works unto the LORD, and thy thoughts shall be established.
4 The LORD hath made all *things* for himself: yea, even the wicked for the day of evil.
5 Every one *that is* proud in heart *is* an abomination to the LORD: *though* hand *join* in hand, he shall not be unpunished.
6 By mercy and truth iniquity is purged: and by the fear of the LORD *men* depart from evil.
7 When a man's ways please the LORD, he maketh even his enemies to be at peace with him.
8 Better *is* a little with righteousness, than great revenues without right.
9 A man's heart deviseth his way: but the LORD directeth his steps.
10 A divine sentence *is* in the lips of the king: his mouth transgresseth not in judgment.

2 All the ways of a man are pure in his own eyes,
but the LORD weighs the spirit.
3 Commit your work to the LORD,
and your plans will be established.
4 The LORD has made everything for its purpose,
even the wicked for the day of trouble.
5 Every one who is arrogant is an abomination to the LORD;
be assured, he will not go unpunished.
6 By loyalty and faithfulness iniquity is atoned for,
and by the fear of the LORD a man avoids evil.
7 When a man's ways please the LORD,
he makes even his enemies to be at peace with him.
8 Better is a little with righteousness
than great revenues with injustice.
9 A man's mind plans his way,
but the LORD directs his steps.
10 Inspired decisions are on the lips of a king;
his mouth does not sin in judgment.

---

2. Antithetic. Man's standards of judgment should be tested by God's holy law (cf. 21:2).

3. Just as words, which are the result of thought, come from God (vs. 1), so deeds, which also stem from the mind, ultimately find their origin in God. **Commit:** Lit., "roll" (cf. Ps. 37:5).

4. God controls the universe. Since even the wicked are directed by him, he must have created them for their dismal end. **For himself** or **for its purpose,** "for its own end" (ASV), "his own purpose" (ASV mg.): The RSV and ASV are the correct translations, since the second stich indicates the end to which wicked men are destined.

5. See Exeg. on 11:20, 21; 13:10.

6. Synonymous. In this verse atonement is lifted out of the ceremonial (priestly) realm, and put into the moral (prophetic) sphere of action (cf. Hos. 6:6). **Mercy and truth:** See Exeg. on 3:3. **Is purged** or **is atoned for:** Lit., "is covered" (*yekhuppar*). **Fear of the LORD:** See Exeg. on 1:7.

7. A continuous sentence (cf. Jer. 39:12).

8. See Exeg. on 15:16, which is very similar to this verse. **With injustice:** The noun in Hebrew is *mishpāṭ* (see Exeg. on 1:3).

9. Antithetic. Man proposes, but God disposes. Not quite the same meaning as in vs. 1. **Mind:** See Exeg. on 2:2.

10. Here follow several verses dealing with kingship. The wise men have a lot to say about kings (cf. vss. 10-15; 8:15; 14:28; 19:12; 20:2, 8, 26, 28; 21:1; 22:11; 23:1-3;

---

2. See Expos. on 4:20-27.
3. See Expos. on 3:5-8.
4. See Expos. on 8:1-36.
5. See Expos. on 29:23.
6. See Expos. on 1:7.
7. See Expos. on 3:5-8.
8. See Expos. on 15:16-17.
9. See Expos. on 3:5-8.

10-15. ***Responsible Rulers and Loyal Subjects.***—A large number of the proverbs deal with the relations of a king and his people. In the king was centered the power that made orderly life

11 A just weight and balance *are* the
LORD'S: all the weights of the bag *are* his
work.
12 *It is* an abomination to kings to com-

11 A just balance and scales are the LORD'S;
all the weights in the bag are his work.
12 It is an abomination to kings to do evil,

24:21-22; 25:2-7; 28:15-16; 29:2, 4, 12, 14; 30:22, 27, 31; 31:2-8). The question naturally arises, Are they speaking about Hebrew kings or rulers in general? Some proverbs dealing with kingship seem to be quite general (e.g., 8:15; 30:22; 31:4), and it is not necessary to try to limit their application only to Hebrew kings. When, however, it is said that **inspired decisions are on the lips of a king,** and that "the king's heart is in the hand of the LORD" (21:1), there is very little doubt that the writer is thinking of a Hebrew king. All in all, the O.T. wise men look with favor upon the monarchy as an ideal form of government, beneficial to the nation (29:4, 14), but the king himself may be corrupt or incapable of ruling wisely (29:12; 31:3-5).

Divine sentence or **inspired decisions:** The Hebrew word *qéṣem* always means "divination," "soothsaying" in the bad sense, except here (cf. Deut. 18:10). Since God is the source of the king's oracles, he speaks only with justice. This can refer only to a Hebrew king whose source of righteousness and wisdom is the true and living God. Some think that this verse teaches the infallibility of the theocratic king, but nowhere in the O.T. is such a doctrine expounded or expressed (see discussion in Delitzsch, *Proverbs of Solomon, ad loc.*). **Judgment:** See Exeg. on 1:3.

11. Weight and balance or, better, **balance and scales:** In the Hebrew **just** can belong only to **scales.** The Lord is the giver of all balances, scales, and weights, an idea paralleled in Egyptian sources (see Oesterley, *Proverbs, ad loc.*). As Toy says, "God is the ordainer of the machinery of commercial transactions" (*Proverbs,* p. 324), an idea not expressed elsewhere in the O.T., but none the less not incongruous with the sages' teaching of God and his dealing with men in their everyday affairs. On **weights** in vs. 11*b,* see Exeg. on 11:1.

12. Cf. 25:5; 29:4; and see Exeg. on vs. 10.

---

possible. Government was necessary to maintain order. These proverbs were written in a time when monarchy was the accepted form of government. Power was centered in a king or ruler, and loyal fealty was expected from his subjects.

The need of some governing authority was recognized. Anarchy results when individuals or groups are not prevented from violating the rights of others. The king is therefore a terror to the disobedient. One flouts the king's commands at his own risk.

> The dread wrath of a king is like the growling of a lion;
> he who provokes him to anger forfeits his life (20:2).

In order to maintain a stable society power must be centered in the ruler. Leaders in government are necessary to prevent men from doing what is right in their own eyes to the degree of infringing on the rights of others.

There are good kings and bad kings. The sages did not give uncritical devotion to power. A man might come to a throne by treachery, and he might rule unjustly. Such a king did not elicit the praise of the sages, since they did not glorify power as such. Power must be in responsible hands. They did not believe that the king could do no wrong. He too must cultivate the qualities that go with wise ruling.

> Loyalty and faithfulness preserve the king,
> and his throne is upheld by righteousness (20:28).

Power alone is not sufficient to produce stability of rule. A prince builds on a foundation of sand if he relies on his armies alone.

> By justice a king gives stability to the land,
> but one who exacts gifts ruins it (29:4).

If a king maintains himself in power by accepting bribes he soon ruins the morale of his people. Integrity counts for nothing among them. Each one tries to buy his way to royal favor.

> If a ruler listens to falsehood,
> all his officials will be wicked (29:12).

Why should anyone tell the truth to the king if he closes his ears to it? The coin of language is counterfeited in his realm, and his underlings soon learn that falsehoods get them what they want.

mit wickedness: for the throne is established by righteousness.

13 Righteous lips *are* the delight of kings; and they love him that speaketh right.

14 The wrath of a king *is as* messengers of death: but a wise man will pacify it.

15 In the light of the king's countenance *is* life; and his favor *is* as a cloud of the latter rain.

for the throne is established by righteousness.
13 Righteous lips are the delight of a king,
and he loves him who speaks what is
right.
14 A king's wrath is a messenger of death,
and a wise man will appease it.
15 In the light of a king's face there is life,
and his favor is like the clouds that
bring the spring rain.

13-14. The king loves trustworthy advisers. In vs. 13*a* **kings** is the literal translation, and in vs. 13*b*, **he loves. Right:** See Exeg. on 12:15. Vs. 14*b* means that he who is wise will try to **pacify** or **appease** (lit., "cover over") the wrath of the ruler.

15. Life: I.e., prosperity and happiness (see Exeg. on 3:2). **Spring rain:** The latter part of the rainy season (March-April). It was especially needed for the ripening crops.

Men in places of power often cling to their power with great uncertainty. The head that wears the crown is uneasy lest some other power-hungry individual cut it off. The sages repeat the thought many times that the only security for a person in power is righteousness in its use.

It is an abomination to kings to do evil,
for the throne is established by righteousness (vs. 12).

The good ruler ought to be concerned with the needs and rights of the common people in his domain. Government ought to be the instrument that maintains an approximate justice by which no one group in the community unduly exploits the others.

If a king judges the poor with equity
his throne will be established for ever (29:14).

When the righteous are in authority, the people rejoice;
but when the wicked rule, the people groan (29:2).

Unhappy is the people that has allowed a wicked ruler to gain control over them. In many lands they have little to say in the choice of their governors. They are victims of intrigue among the ruling clique or pawns in the struggle for power.

Like a roaring lion or a charging bear
is a wicked ruler over a poor people (28:15).

In nations where people have a choice of rulers, constant vigilance is necessary to ensure that no exploiting personality achieves a position of power, since power wedded to wickedness can produce oppression and suffering. Such irresponsible power can produce much unhappiness before it is dethroned. That it does not have the requisites of permanence is obvious to the sages. Only power that is guided by righteousness and justice can hope for stability.

The sages are at pains to point out that the king is also a subject. He is subject to the laws of God. His whims or wishes cannot overrule the laws of justice and right.

The king's heart is a stream of water in the hand of the LORD;
he turns it wherever he will (21:1).

He to whom much power is given, from him shall a responsible use of this power be required. His is the greater task since power corrupts the perspective of the one who has it.

The king requires good subjects. A wise citizen recognizes the authority of the ruling powers. He will try not to incur the disfavor of the king.

A king's wrath is a messenger of death,
and a wise man will appease it.
In the light of a king's face there is life,
and his favor is like the clouds that bring the spring rain (vss. 14-15).

Some of the sages seem to counsel the acceptance of the *status quo* in government. "My son, fear thou the LORD and the king: and meddle not with them that are given to change" (24:21). Those in authority would no doubt welcome the kind of subjects who give uncritical allegiance to their rulers. However, too inflexible centers of power are apt to produce rebellion. Only as a government maintains a mechanism of change to meet new conditions can it hope to maintain continuity of power.

Only when both the rulers and the ruled govern their actions by righteousness can there

16 How much better *is it* to get wisdom than gold! and to get understanding rather to be chosen than silver!

17 The highway of the upright *is* to depart from evil: he that keepth his way preserveth his soul.

18 Pride *goeth* before destruction, and a haughty spirit before a fall.

19 Better *it is to be* of an humble spirit with the lowly, than to divide the spoil with the proud.

20 He that handleth a matter wisely shall find good: and whoso trusteth in the LORD, happy *is* he.

21 The wise in heart shall be called prudent: and the sweetness of the lips increaseth learning.

22 Understanding *is* a wellspring of life

16 To get wisdom is better[u] than gold;
to get understanding is to be chosen rather than silver.
17 The highway of the upright turns aside from evil;
he who guards his way preserves his life.
18 Pride goes before destruction,
and a haughty spirit before a fall.
19 It is better to be of a lowly spirit with the poor
than to divide the spoil with the proud.
20 He who gives heed to the word will prosper,
and happy is he who trusts in the LORD.
21 The wise of heart is called a man of discernment,
and pleasant speech increases persuasiveness.
22 Wisdom is a fountain of life to him who

[u] Gk Syr Vg Tg: Heb *how much better*

---

16. Cf. 3:14. The RSV follows the LXX in vs. 16*a*, deleting *mah* in the Hebrew, which may have come about by dittography from the preceding word.

17. The highway of the good man is free from obstacles (cf. 15:19). **Upright:** See Exeg. on 12:15.

18. Pride is spoken of many times in Proverbs. It is considered a religious offense against God (see Exeg. on 13:10).

19. Cf. vs. 18. The figure in vs. 19*b* is taken from military life, the reference being to something taken by violence. **Poor:** See Exeg. on 14:21.

20. Synonymous. **He that handleth a matter wisely** or **He who gives heed to the word:** The reference is no doubt to the written word of the Law and the Prophets, as vs. 20*b* indicates (see Exeg. on 13:13 concerning the wise men's view of Scripture). How the **word** came to be used for the Scriptures is an interesting process. Originally, of course, it meant the word of God, spoken by him as the declaration of his holy will. This is clearly expressed in Gen. 1, where creation is brought into existence by the word of God. Then the word of God is equated with the Decalogue (Exod. 20:1; Deut. 4:13), and finally with all kinds of laws. It was an easy step then to designate the written law and the message of the prophets as the word of God.

21. Synonymous. This advice was good both for the teacher who could impart wisdom more effectively if he possessed a pleasing manner, and for the pupil who was being trained for positions which needed persuasive oratory (cf. 12:17). **Prudent:** I.e., "discerning." The word is *nābhôn* (see Exeg. on 1:2). **Learning:** Here *léqaḥ* really means "persuasion" (see Exeg. on 1:5).

22. Antithetic. **Fountain:** See Exeg. on 10:11. **Wisdom:** See Exeg. on 12:8. Vs. 22*b*,

---

be peace and order in the land. One of the great statements in Proverbs applies to both kings and subjects when it says,

> Righteousness exalts a nation,
> but sin is a reproach to any people (14:34).

Not power, not wealth, not a noble tradition, not a large population—none of these is the secret of a great nation. Only when justice and righteousness make power responsible and loyalty wise does a nation achieve a high status of nationhood.

16. See Expos. on 15:16-17.
17. See Expos. on 3:21-26.
18. See Expos. on 29:23.
19. See Expos. on 15:16-17; 29:23.
20. See Expos. on 3:5-8.
21. See Expos. on 4:20-27.
22. See Expos. on 3:13-18.

unto him that hath it: but the instruction of fools *is* folly.

23 The heart of the wise teacheth his mouth, and addeth learning to his lips.

24 Pleasant words *are as* a honeycomb, sweet to the soul, and health to the bones.

25 There is a way that seemeth right unto a man; but the end thereof *are* the ways of death.

26 He that laboreth, laboreth for himself; for his mouth craveth it of him.

27 An ungodly man diggeth up evil: and in his lips *there is* as a burning fire.

28 A froward man soweth strife: and a whisperer separateth chief friends.

29 A violent man enticeth his neighbor, and leadeth him into the way *that is* not good.

30 He shutteth his eyes to devise froward things: moving his lips he bringeth evil to pass.

31 The hoary head *is* a crown of glory, *if* it be found in the way of righteousness.

has it,
but folly is the chastisement of fools.
23 The mind of the wise makes his speech
judicious,
and adds persuasiveness to his lips.
24 Pleasant words are like a honeycomb,
sweetness to the soul and health to the
body.
25 There is a way which seems right to a
man,
but its end is the way to death.[v]
26 A worker's appetite works for him;
his mouth urges him on.
27 A worthless man plots evil,
and his speech is like a scorching fire.
28 A perverse man spreads strife,
and a whisperer separates close friends.
29 A man of violence entices his neighbor
and leads him in a way that is not good.
30 He who winks his eyes plans[w] perverse
things,
he who compresses his lips brings evil
to pass.
31 A hoary head is a crown of glory;
it is gained in a righteous life.

[v] Heb *ways of death*
[w] Gk Syr Vg Tg: Heb *to plan*

according to the KJV, means that it is a waste of time to instruct fools. According to the RSV, their own folly is their punishment. Both translations are possible (for **instruction** and **chastisement** see Exeg. on 1:2).

23. See Exeg. on vs. 21. Kind, persuasive speech was characteristic of the wise men. **Mind:** See Exeg. on 2:2. **Teacheth** or **makes . . . judicious:** Lit., "makes wise" (*yaskîl*).

24. See Exeg. on vs. 21; 12:17. **Body:** Lit., **bones.**

25. Repetition of 14:12 (see Exeg.).

26. Man's hunger drives him to work, which in turn is a means of gain. **He** or, better, **appetite:** Lit., "soul" (see Exeg. on 13:25). **Craveth:** Better, **urges . . . on.**

27. There follow several verses dealing with mischief-making, especially by means of the tongue (see Exeg. on 12:17). **Ungodly** or **worthless:** See Exeg. on 6:12. **Diggeth** or **plots:** Digs a pit to trap his enemies. **Scorching:** Cf. Ezek. 20:47.

28. Synonymous. **Froward** or **perverse:** See Exeg. on 2:12. **Separates close friends** or **chief friends,** "alienateth his friend" (ASV mg.). **Chief** is unnecessary. The correctness of the KJV and the RSV is shown by the parallel clause.

29. Cf. 1:10-19, where the same Hebrew word for **enticeth** is used.

30. Cf. 6:13-14; 10:10. Two signs signifying malicious intentions. In the second half of the first stich it is perhaps better to read a finite verb form with the LXX for the sake of parallelism with vs. 30*b*, and translate, "He that shutteth his eyes **plans perverse things." Froward** or **perverse:** See Exeg. on 2:12.

31. The RSV with ASV offers an accurate translation. Old age is possible only for

23-24. See Expos. on 18:21.
25. See Expos. on 14:12.
26. See Expos. on 6:1-15.
27. See Expos. on 18:21.
28. See Expos. on 26:21.
29. See Expos. on 3:27-35.
30. See Expos. on 22:16*a*.
31. See Expos. on 20:29.

32 *He that is* slow to anger *is* better than the mighty; and he that ruleth his spirit than he that taketh a city.

32 He who is slow to anger is better than the mighty,
and he who rules his spirit than he who takes a city.

---

those who live righteously. On the other hand, it is assumed generally in this book that the wicked perish prematurely (2:22; 12:7; 29:1).

32. Synonymous. In praise of self-control (cf. 14:29). Aboth 4:1 says: "Who is strong? He who controls his passions, as it is said . . ." and then quotes this verse. **Slow to anger:** See Exeg. on 14:29.

---

32. ***In Praise of Him Who Rules His Own Spirit.***—In many different ways the sages of Proverbs praise the man who is slow to anger and who knows how to exercise self-control. They constantly sound warnings against him who "is soon angry." They have little good to say about the man who is quick-tempered. Temper tantrums have nothing to commend them to intelligent and mature people.

Self-control is better than power. **He who is slow to anger is better than the mighty.** In fact, self-control might be considered the highest kind of power. A man may find himself in a position where he can exercise power over other people, but if he has not learned how to control himself, his power may bring disaster. **He who rules his spirit** is better **than he who takes a city.** Having taken the city, the man without self-restraint may bring it to ruin by some foolish outburst of temper. He can hardly be trusted with rule over others because he has not learned how to rule himself.

Science has put great power into the hands of people. In recent years the discovery of power available through atomic fission has instilled fear into many hearts. People are not afraid that this new power will get out of hand—they are afraid it will fall into the wrong hands. If undisciplined men of power are unable to rule their own spirits, they can destroy not only one city but many. Bursts of temper are also regarded as folly. He is wise who sees the value of controlling his temper.

He who is slow to anger has great understanding,
but he who has a hasty temper exalts folly (14:29).

The individual who gives vent to his indignation in an emotional outburst may momentarily relieve his feelings, but he does not get much light on how to act. As one of the characters in Edwin Arlington Robinson's *The Glory of the Nightingales* has said:

. . . for my only light
Was fire that was in me; and fire like that
Is fire that has no light.[8]

Good sense makes a man slow to anger,
and it is his glory to overlook an offense (19:11).

In a world of complex and close personal relationships it is not difficult to find reasons to take offense. Discretion suggests that one should not cultivate an oversensitive spirit that is ready to fly into a rage over fancied or real affronts. An offense that seems to warrant an emotional torrent at the moment may seem far less serious if one counts to ten or allows oneself a day to think about it. Such self-restraint is not cowardice but good sense.

In a later chapter we come upon the observation,

A fool gives full vent to his anger,
but a wise man quietly holds it back (29:11).

One suspects that not every psychiatrist would give this advice. He would not insist that a person should constantly repress his feelings. Even the wise man might finally get to the point where he had repressed his anger so long that he would suffer a neurosis of one kind or another. The difference is that the fool allows himself a big explosion of feeling whenever he is irritated. The wise man can direct his feelings of indignation into constructive channels. The person who has fits of temper is not necessarily more indignant than another person. The other person may control twice as much feeling, but direct it like the explosions in the cylinders of a gasoline motor.

After an emotional storm is over, it generally leaves destruction in its wake. There are hurt feelings, strained friendships, and often physical damage that must be repaired. Someone must pick up the pieces. Even this is not commended in dealing with one who is a chronic offender:

A man of great wrath will pay the penalty;
for if you deliver him, you will only have to do it again (19:19).

Why do people fly into a rage? "A hot-tempered man stirs up strife" (15:18). He stirs up contention because he wants attention. He has found a way of getting something he wants.

[8] New York: The Macmillan Co., 1930, p. 65. Used by permission.

33 The lot is cast into the lap; but the whole disposing thereof *is* of the LORD.

17 Better *is* a dry morsel, and quietness therewith, than a house full of sacrifices *with* strife.

2 A wise servant shall have rule over a son that causeth shame, and shall have part of the inheritance among the brethren.

3 The fining pot *is* for silver, and the furnace for gold: but the LORD trieth the hearts.

4 A wicked doer giveth heed to false lips; *and* a liar giveth ear to a naughty tongue.

5 Whoso mocketh the poor reproacheth his Maker: *and* he that is glad at calamities shall not be unpunished.

33 The lot is cast into the lap,
but the decision is wholly from the LORD.

17 Better is a dry morsel with quiet
than a house full of feasting with strife.
2 A slave who deals wisely will rule over a son who acts shamefully,
and will share the inheritance as one of the brothers.
3 The crucible is for silver, and the furnace is for gold,
and the LORD tries hearts.
4 An evildoer listens to wicked lips;
and a liar gives heed to a mischievous tongue.
5 He who mocks the poor insults his Maker;
he who is glad at calamity will not go unpunished.

---

33. Antithetic. We may cast the lot, but the decision actually rests with the Lord. **Lap:** The word *ḥêq* means either "breast" or the fold of the garment at the breast. In this verse the latter meaning should be taken, since the lots were thrown into the pocketlike fold and one was taken out. **Disposing** or **decision:** The Hebrew word is *mishpāṭ* (see Exeg. on 1:3).

17:1. Antithetic. Cf. 15:17. The contrast here is between the **dry morsel,** which was eaten in peace, and the feast at which meat was served, a rare and highly significant occasion in ancient times, but one which could not be enjoyed because of tumult and noise. **Sacrifices** or **feasting:** The word *zébhaḥ* means "sacrifice," but since a feast was an integral part of the sacrificial ritual the word came to mean a "feast" in the ordinary sense.

2. Examples of the teaching of this proverb are found in Gen. 15:2-3; I Chr. 2:35.

3. As man refines precious metals in order to reveal their true character, so God tests the hearts of men to bring out their true nature (cf. Isa. 48:10; Ps. 17:3 for this figure). Vs. 3*a*=27:21*a*.

4. Synonymous. For **tongue** see Exeg. on 12:17. **False lips** or **wicked lips:** Lit., "lips of wickedness." **Liar:** Lit., "falsehood." In parallelism with vs. 4*a*, the translation of the KJV and the RSV is expected. Perhaps a participle form, *meshaqqēr,* should be read instead of *shéqer.* **Mischievous tongue:** Lit., "tongue of destruction." The word *hawwāh* means "destruction" here and in 19:13. In 10:3 and 11:6 it means "[evil] desire."

5. Sympathy for the poor is frequently advocated in Proverbs (cf. 14:31, where vs. 5*a* is similar to the first stich of this verse. **Calamities:** I.e., those which befall **the poor.**

Temper tantrums often have their beginnings in childhood experiences. A child who cannot get what he wants in any other way discovers that his parents respond to his wishes when he flies into a tantrum. Or he may come from a home in which his parents never opposed him, only to find his way blocked when he mingles with other children. He then uses the method of flying into a rage when he does not get his way. Having experienced success when he lost his temper, he may never outgrow this infantile reaction to frustration.

If an individual is sincerely trying to overcome a tendency to lose his temper, he may be helped if he tries to understand how he came to regard this as successful conduct. A temper tantrum may momentarily get him what he wants, but it brings so much that he and others do not want that it is worth making every effort to be ruler over his own spirit.

33. See Expos. on 3:5-8.

17:1. See Expos. on 15:16-17.

2. See Expos. on 20:6.

3. See Expos. on 4:20-27.

4. See Expos. on 18:21.

5. See Expos. on 22:16*a*.

6 Children's children *are* the crown of old men; and the glory of children *are* their fathers.
7 Excellent speech becometh not a fool: much less do lying lips a prince.
8 A gift *is as* a precious stone in the eyes of him that hath it: whithersoever it turneth, it prospereth.

6 Grandchildren are the crown of the aged,
and the glory of sons is their fathers.
7 Fine speech is not becoming to a fool;
still less is false speech to a prince.
8 A bribe is like a magic stone in the eyes
of him who gives it;
wherever he turns he prospers.

---

6. Parents and children are the adornment of each other.

7. **Fine speech:** Lit., "lip of excess," from which the meaning of "superiority," "excellence" is derived. The ASV mg. "arrogant" seems to be unwarranted. Some would read *yṓsher* ("uprightness") for the M.T. *yéther.* **Fool** (*nābhāl*): Found only here, vs. 21, and 30:22 in Proverbs. A shameless, contemptuous fellow, devoid of intellectual interest and religious faith (cf. Ps. 14:1). **Prince** (*nādhîbh*): A man of noble character, contrasted here with **fool.**

8. A bribe is a potent means of gaining success. **Bribe** is better than **gift. Precious stone:** Lit., "stone of grace," referring perhaps to an amulet or charm. **In the eyes of**

---

6. ***The Place of Children.***—Nations as well as individuals are tested by their attitude toward children. In many cultures children had little place. They were unwelcome. Infanticide was not uncommon. A culture like that represented by the Hebrew sages, which placed a high worth upon family life, moved upward in its regard for the value of children.

This proverb states that grandchildren are **the crown of the aged.** The world holds few satisfactions comparable to children's children. This was the judgment of the sages, and many have echoed their approval of that judgment through the years. Parents are given one of their deepest joys when they see their children grow and develop into persons of uprightness and integrity. Writes Lin Yutang:

> The rewards of political, literary and artistic achievement produce in their authors only a pale, intellectual chuckle, while the rewards of seeing one's own children grow up big and strong are wordless and immensely real. . . . It is said that a few days before his death, Herbert Spencer had the eighteen volumes of *The Synthetic Philosophy* piled on his lap and, as he felt their cold weight, wondered if he would not have done better could he have a grandchild in their stead.[9]

In the intimate warmth of a happy family, children are the glory of their parents and parents are the glory of their children.

Children need training and correction; this is the view of the sages.

> Train up a child in the way he should go,
> and when he is old he will not depart from it (22:6).

> Folly is bound up in the heart of a child;
> but the rod of discipline drives it far from him (22:15).

These writers saw that each child has impulses and urges that need to be directed and trained. Theirs was hardly the view that a child should be given free rein to express himself as he wishes. They saw the need of discipline and direction, lest a child become a little dictator or an insufferable egocentric in his home. Yet stern discipline can violate personality, and it was inevitable that reminders should be voiced that children are people too. Jesus placed a high value upon children and upon their free and spontaneous responsiveness, their ardent curiosity, their simple directness and unfeigned sincerity. Children have traits that adults can well emulate. Dickens used children as his heroes and heroines, and tried to make his stories appeal to children.

An individual's whole view of life is tested by his attitude toward passing life on to another. He will not be willing to bring children into the world if he feels that life has little meaning or significance. Children are the bearers of the continuity of life on this planet, and if life has gone stale for a man, he will hesitate to bestow it upon another person. A nation's leaders may encourage childbearing to produce the cannon fodder they need for their selfish designs; but only a high faith in life and its possibilities can cause a nation worthily to welcome a new generation of children.

7. See Expos. on 18:21.

8. See Expos. on 18:16.

[9] *The Importance of Living* (New York: Reynal & Hitchcock, 1937), pp. 173-74.

9 He that covereth a transgression seeketh love; but he that repeateth a matter separateth *very* friends.

10 A reproof entereth more into a wise man than a hundred stripes into a fool.

11 An evil *man* seeketh only rebellion: therefore a cruel messenger shall be sent against him.

12 Let a bear robbed of her whelps meet a man, rather than a fool in his folly.

13 Whoso rewardeth evil for good, evil shall not depart from his house.

14 The beginning of strife *is as* when one letteth out water: therefore leave off contention, before it be meddled with.

9 He who forgives an offense seeks love,
but he who repeats a matter alienates a friend.
10 A rebuke goes deeper into a man of understanding
than a hundred blows into a fool.
11 An evil man seeks only rebellion,
and a cruel messenger will be sent against him.
12 Let a man meet a she-bear robbed of her cubs,
rather than a fool in his folly.
13 If a man returns evil for good,
evil will not depart from his house.
14 The beginning of strife is like letting out water;
so quit before the quarrel breaks out.

---

him that hath it probably refers to the briber, rather than to the one who receives the bribe (see RSV).

In vs. 8*b* the subject of the verbs may be either "he," i.e., the briber (RSV, ASV mg.), or "it," i.e., the bribe (KJV, ASV). The meaning remains the same in either case.

9. Antithetic. Cf. 10:12. **Covereth:** Refuses to notice the wrongs done to him by others. The RSV translates **forgives. Repeateth:** "Harpeth" (ASV) is an excellent rendering of the word. Gossip is the evil condemned here. **Very friends:** See Exeg. on 16:28.

10. The problem of education, i.e., the formation of character, is dealt with here. Some are more sensitive to reproof than others. **Goes deeper:** Lit., "descends." **Wise man** or, better, **a man of understanding:** See Exeg. on 1:2.

11. The translation of vs. 11*a* in the KJV, RSV, and ASV is hardly correct unless **rebellion** is taken to mean "revolt against God," as the second stich of the LXX seems to infer. The ASV mg., "a rebellious man [Hebrew, **rebellion**] seeketh only evil," gives better sense, especially in parallelism with vs. 11*b*. The **cruel messenger** refers to some dire disaster which will fall upon the rebel. The verse deals with political rebellion which the king must ruthlessly put down.

12. A fool in his rash folly is more to be feared than a **she-bear robbed of her cubs** (cf. II Sam. 17:8).

13. The law of retribution. The appeal to do good or to refrain from evil is always on the level of self-interest in Proverbs. No mention is made here, for instance, of the harm that is brought on the other person. One should refrain from doing evil simply because in the end he, the evildoer, will have trouble in his own house. In some verses in Proverbs the practical, secular idea of retribution takes on a religious aspect when it is said that the Lord punishes or rewards his children (cf. 10:3; 22:4; 25:21-22).

14. The general sense is clear, but the Hebrew is doubtful. Literally it reads, "The one setting free water is the beginning of strife, and before quarreling leave off contention [or, before contention breaks off, leave off]." **Letteth out:** Never used in this way elsewhere. If the text is retained, it can only refer to making a small opening in a dam through which water will increasingly flow. **Meddled with** or **breaks out** ("is quarrelling" ASV): The verb *gālaʻ* is found only here, 18:1; 20:3. Its root meaning is not certain, but seems to be "to break forth" in a hostile sense.

---

9. See Expos. on 18:21.
10. See Expos. on 9:7-9.
11. See Expos. on 26:21.
12. See Expos. on 26:1, 3-12.
13. See Expos. on 25:21-22.
14. See Expos. on 26:21.

15 He that justifieth the wicked, and he that condemneth the just, even they both *are* abomination to the LORD.

16 Wherefore *is there* a price in the hand of a fool to get wisdom, seeing *he hath* no heart *to it?*

17 A friend loveth at all times, and a brother is born for adversity.

15 He who justifies the wicked and he who condemns the righteous
are both alike an abomination to the LORD.
16 Why should a fool have a price in his hand to buy wisdom,
when he has no mind?
17 A friend loves at all times,
and a brother is born for adversity.

---

15. The terms of this verse are taken from the legal realm. The unjust judge is referred to here (see Exeg. on 2:22; cf. 24:24). **Abomination:** See Exeg. on 3:32.

16. Wisdom cannot be obtained by money; it takes particular qualities of mind to acquire it. It is not certain whether the wise men accepted money for their services. **Mind:** The capacity for learning (see Exeg. on 2:2).

17. The value of friendship is stressed in the wisdom literature (see especially ch. 27). Friends will stand fast together through thick and thin. In this verse **friend** and **brother** are synonymous. The ASV mg., "is born as a brother," means that a friend in time of trouble becomes like a kinsman in his attachment and devotion.

---

15. See Expos. on 21:3; 25:21-22.

16. See Expos. on 10:15-16.

17. ***The High Worth of Friendship.***—He who has a friend is the possessor of one of the best gifts that life can bring to an individual.

A friend loves at all times. Changes in the weather do not change the devotion of the friendly person. Times of adversity only deepen the loyalty of a true friend. This is because friendship is not a method of using other people but a way of appreciating them and respecting them for what they are. Like love, friendship is the fulfillment of the law which calls for the treatment of others as subjects of intrinsic worth rather than as objects of instrumental value.

A friend hurts only that he may help.

> Faithful are the wounds of a friend;
> profuse are the kisses of an enemy (27:6).

A friend does not stoop to the sadistic satisfaction of seeing other people suffer. His intention is not to harm another but to remove all blocks that prevent his being his best self.

> Iron sharpens iron;
> and one man sharpens another (27:17).

He who has a friend has an incentive for living. "So long as we are loved by others," wrote Robert Louis Stevenson, "I would almost say that we are indispensable; and no man is useless while he has a friend." [1] A man's friends do not need to goad him on by their words. They influence his life by the mere fact that they are his friends.

> Once any man has true friends, he never again frames his decisions, even those which are most secret, as if he were alone in the world. He frames them habitually in the imagined company of his friends. In their visionary presence he thinks and acts; and by them, as visionary tribunal, he feels himself, even in his unspoken intentions and inmost feelings, to be judged.[2]

Friendship may bring people closer together than kinship. Unless a blood relationship is founded on a deep sharing of purposes and upon more than the accident of birth, it cannot have the same meaning as a cherished friendship. Jesus was much misunderstood when he said that he who did the will of his Father in heaven was his "brother, and sister, and mother" (Matt. 12:50). There are ties that can be closer even than family ties.

One sage suggests that a neighbor who is near is better than a brother who is far off (27:10). He bids a man not to forsake a friend who has been true to his father. Such friendship is not to be lightly cast aside. Friendship is something that ought to be kept in good repair. In describing the "friend who sticks closer than a brother" (18:24), another sage warns against a superficial approach to the making of friends. Some people make friends easily and lose them quickly because their friendship is not built upon a solid foundation. There is a limit to the number of close friends any one person can have, and it is therefore necessary to observe the disciplines upon which enduring friendship can be built.

Seneca makes an important comment on another aspect of friendship. Life is in danger of

[1] *Lay Morals and Other Papers* (New York: Charles Scribner's Sons, 1911), p. 50.

[2] John MacCunn, *The Making of Character* (New York: The Macmillan Co., 1900), p. 93.

18 A man void of understanding striketh hands, *and* becometh surety in the presence of his friend.

19 He loveth transgression that loveth strife: *and* he that exalteth his gate seeketh destruction.

20 He that hath a froward heart findeth no good: and he that hath a perverse tongue falleth into mischief.

21 He that begetteth a fool *doeth it* to his sorrow: and the father of a fool hath no joy.

22 A merry heart doeth good *like* a medicine: but a broken spirit drieth the bones.

18 A man without sense gives a pledge,
and becomes surety in the presence of his neighbor.

19 He who loves transgression loves strife;
he who makes his door high seeks destruction.

20 A man of crooked mind does not prosper,
and one with a perverse tongue falls into calamity.

21 A stupid son is a grief to a father;
and the father of a fool has no joy.

22 A cheerful heart is a good medicine,
but a downcast spirit dries up the bones.

---

18. See Exeg. on 6:1, where the terms used in connection with becoming surety are discussed. **Sense:** Lit., "heart" (see Exeg. on 2:2).

19. Strife always accompanies a rebellious nature (*pésha'*), and destruction is sure to come upon a proud man (see Exeg. on 13:10). **His gate** or **his door:** This term refers either to a lofty house which was built as a sign of pride or to the mouth, and so to loud and arrogant talk.

20. Life does not go well with those who are morally crooked—a common theme in Proverbs. **Froward** or **crooked** ("wayward" ASV): The Hebrew word is *'iqqēsh* (see Exeg. on 2:15). **Mind:** See Exeg. on 2:2. **Tongue:** See Exeg. on 12:17.

21. The RSV paraphrases the Hebrew in vs. 21*a* while the KJV translates it literally. There are two different words for **fool** here: vs. 21*a* has *kesîl* (see Exeg. on 1:22); vs. 21*b* has *nābhāl* (see Exeg. on vs. 7).

22. Antithetic. A true psychosomatic observation (see Exeg. on 3:8; 14:30; 15:13). **Medicine:** Lit., "healing," "cure."

---

becoming barren for people who are bereft of their friends by death. They no longer have their friends on earth. But the ancient writer makes this reassuring comment: "The comfort of having a friend may be taken away, but not that of having had one. It is an ill construction of providence to reflect only upon my friend's being taken away, without any regard to the benefit of his once being given me. He that has lost a friend has more cause of joy that once he had him, than of grief that he is taken away." [3] The worth of friendship is something that death cannot destroy.

Helen Baker Parker has given us a poem entitled "Discovery." They are the words of a contemporary who shared the view of the sages when they placed high worth upon friendship:

> Today a man discovered gold and fame;
> Another flew the stormy seas;
> Another saw an unnamed world aflame;
> One found the germ of a disease.
> But what high fates my paths attend:
> For I—today I found a friend.[4]

[3] In seeking to comfort Marullus in the loss of his small son, Seneca expresses this thought. See *Moral Epistles* XCIX.

18. See Expos. on 6:1-15.

19. See Expos. on 26:21.

20. See Expos. on 18.21.

21. See Expos. on 26:1, 3-12.

22. ***Good Medicine.***—**A cheerful heart is a good medicine,** or as Moffatt translates it, "A glad heart helps and heals." A number of the proverbs exalt the value of cheerfulness for the person who cultivates a cheerful outlook upon life. Good health is one of the dividends paid.

When a person is ill, God's healing power is at work in his body, but this power is often hindered when the patient becomes deeply anxious, or lonely, or morose, or bitter. A gloomy spirit can make it very difficult for healing power to work. Let the patient experience an inward awareness of this healing force, and let him overcome his heaviness of heart, and he will find his new outlook to be like a medicine. For many generations healers could do very little to help men's bodies by way of medicine. Before the age of scientific medicine the chief

[4] Used by permission of William J. Parker.

23 A wicked *man* taketh a gift out of the bosom to pervert the ways of judgment.

24 Wisdom *is* before him that hath understanding; but the eyes of a fool *are* in the ends of the earth.

25 A foolish son *is* a grief to his father, and bitterness to her that bare him.

26 Also to punish the just *is* not good, *nor* to strike princes for equity.

23 A wicked man accepts a bribe from the bosom
to pervert the ways of justice.

24 A man of understanding sets his face toward wisdom,
but the eyes of a fool are on the ends of the earth.

25 A foolish son is a grief to his father
and bitterness to her who bore him.

26 To impose a fine on a righteous man is not good;
to flog noble men is wrong.

---

23. See Exeg. on vs. 8. **Bribe** is better than **gift. Judgment** or **justice:** See Exeg. on 1:3.

24. Antithetic. The discerning man has his eyes on a goal; the eyes of the fool wander everywhere. **Understanding:** See Exeg. on 1:2.

25. Cf. 10:1; 15:20; 17:21.

26. Also: Perhaps better omitted, with the RSV, since there is no connection with vs. 25. **Punish:** More accurately, "to fine" (see RSV).

Vs. 26*b* is difficult, since it is not usual to smite noble people on account of their uprightness. With Oesterley and others, on the basis of the LXX, we might read "to scourge the upright is not seemly," emending the last two words of the Hebrew text to

---

task of the medicine man was to do something for the spirits of men. For the most part he used various devices to give people new assurance and to build a basis of confidence and joy. Many healers were helpful by dealing directly with men's hearts.

Good news will restore the energies of people. Good news will invigorate the flagging energies of a band of explorers. A homesick child will be changed by an unexpected visit into a dancing elf. Cheerfulness transforms life.

For some it seems like folly to try to be cheerful when there is every reason for gloom and heaviness of heart. They feel that there is a lack of realism in trying to smile when the facts seem to call only for weeping. An individual may affirm that he is temperamentally not the optimistic type, and that he should not be expected to serve the Lord or himself with gladness. But a spirit of cheerfulness is not something that is automatic, or an inevitable result of particular events. The same circumstances may cause one person to be glum and yet not prevent another person from being cheerful. Cultivating a cheerful outlook on life is as much a deliberate act as is the attempt to control one's temper, or the determination to be compassionate toward people in need. The good medicine of a cheerful heart cannot be brewed in an apothecary shop, encased in a capsule, and swallowed. It is the product of a will that refuses to give way to gloom, and it grows from a faith that all things can be made to work to some good end as one co-operates with God. During the pre-war years a group of Christian nurses in the Ellen Mitchell Memorial Hospital in Moulmein, Burma, discussed this question during their Tuesday morning Bible hour: "What does it take to make a Christian?" They agreed that true repentance and acceptance of forgiveness put one into the Christian fold. But then they asked what it takes as the days go on to build up an ever stronger Christian personality. They listed over twenty-five characteristics that are needed. Faith was placed first in the list, followed by service and love. Dr. Martha Gifford, who reported this experience in a communication to the Woman's American Baptist Foreign Mission Society, then wrote:

> Some were convinced that cheerfulness must surely be a part of a Christian personality, especially of those who work among the suffering. Who ever knew a grumpy old grouch who "cranks" all the time helping a sick person to get well? It is the "merry heart [that] doeth good like a medicine," and we decided that no matter what the circumstances, a smile three times a day and at bedtime should be a minimum in a Christian hospital. We also advised a standing order for extras to be given whenever circumstances should demand.

A glad heart of this type helps and heals the body in which it beats; it also helps those who come into the circle of its influence.

23. See Expos. on 18:16.

24. See Expos. on 2:1-22.

25. See Expos. on 1:8-9; 10:1.

26. See Expos. on 21:3.

27 He that hath knowledge spareth his words: *and* a man of understanding is of an excellent spirit.

28 Even a fool, when he holdeth his peace, is counted wise: *and* he that shutteth his lips *is esteemed* a man of understanding.

18 Through desire a man, having separated himself, seeketh *and* intermeddleth with all wisdom.

2 A fool hath no delight in understanding, but that his heart may discover itself.

3 When the wicked cometh, *then* cometh also contempt, and with ignominy reproach.

4 The words of a man's mouth *are as* deep waters, *and* the wellspring of wisdom *as* a flowing brook.

27 He who restrains his words has knowledge,
and he who has a cool spirit is a man of understanding.
28 Even a fool who keeps silent is considered wise;
when he closes his lips, he is deemed intelligent.

18 He who is estranged[x] seeks pretexts[y]
to break out against all sound judgment.
2 A fool takes no pleasure in understanding,
but only in expressing his opinion.
3 When wickedness comes, contempt comes also;
and with dishonor comes disgrace.
4 The words of a man's mouth are deep waters;
the fountain of wisdom is a gushing stream.

[x] Heb *separated*
[y] Gk Vg: Heb *desire*

bal-yāshār (see RSV). **Princes** or **noble men:** In parallelism with **righteous,** *nādhîbh* must mean morally noble (see vs. 7).

27. Cf. 10:19 (see Exeg. on 12:17). **Excellent** or **cool:** The KJV follows the *Qerê* tradition of the Hebrew text; the RSV follows the *Kethîbh,* which is preferable. The translation of this verse in the ASV mg. is also satisfactory.

28. Silence is golden in that it conceals folly. **Intelligent** ("prudent" ASV): See Exeg. on 1:2.

18:1. An impossible Hebrew text for which numerous emendations have been suggested. Literally it reads, "One separated seeks desire, against all wisdom he breaks forth." According to the KJV the verse describes one who pursues wisdom with such avidity that he forsakes everything else; according to the ASV it means that one who holds himself aloof from everyone follows his own selfish desires and opposes all reason. The RSV reads *tō'anāh,* **pretexts,** for *ta'awāh,* **desire,** following the LXX and Vulg. and some modern commentators. The verse then means that an alienated friend **seeks pretexts** to start quarrels with no good reason. **Break out:** See Exeg. on 17:14.

2. Antithetic. The fool, apart from having no delight at all in wisdom, loves to display his ignorance (cf. 12:23; 15:2). **Understanding:** See Exeg. on 2:2. **Discover:** Better, "reveal" (ASV). The RSV gives a free translation.

3. Synonymous. The direction of both **contempt** and **reproach (disgrace)** is uncertain, i.e., whether they are directed by the wicked toward someone else, or by others toward the wicked one himself. It is more naturally the latter. **The wicked:** Better, **wickedness,** with only vocalic changes.

4. The Hebrew literally reads: "The words of a man's mouth are deep waters, a flowing brook, a fountain of wisdom." The ASV mg. substantially follows this translation, which is preferable to the KJV or the RSV. Starting from the impenetrable depths of a man's heart and mind, his words leap forth as **a gushing stream.** This of course refers to the words of a wise man (cf. 20:5). **Fountain:** See Exeg. on 10:11. **Wisdom:** The LXX

27-28. See Expos. on 18:21.
18:1. See Expos. on 1:2.
2. See Expos. on 26:1, 3-12.
3. See Expos. on 12:8.
4. See Expos. on vs. 21.

5 *It is* not good to accept the person of the wicked, to overthrow the righteous in judgment.

6 A fool's lips enter into contention, and his mouth calleth for strokes.

7 A fool's mouth *is* his destruction, and his lips *are* the snare of his soul.

8 The words of a talebearer *are* as wounds, and they go down into the innermost parts of the belly.

9 He also that is slothful in his work is brother to him that is a great waster.

10 The name of the LORD *is* a strong tower: the righteous runneth into it, and is safe.

11 The rich man's wealth *is* his strong city, and as a high wall in his own conceit.

5 It is not good to be partial to a wicked man,
or to deprive a righteous man of justice.
6 A fool's lips bring strife,
and his mouth invites a flogging.
7 A fool's mouth is his ruin,
and his lips are a snare to himself.
8 The words of a whisperer are like delicious morsels;
they go down into the inner parts of the body.
9 He who is slack in his work
is a brother to him who destroys.
10 The name of the LORD is a strong tower;
the righteous man runs into it and is safe.
11 A rich man's wealth is his strong city,
and like a high wall protecting him.[z]

[z] Or *in his imagination*

and some Hebrew MSS read "life," i.e., *ḥayyîm* for *ḥokhmāh* (cf. 10:11, which may have influenced LXX).

5. Condemning injustice in court. **To be partial:** Lit., "to lift the face of," i.e., to show favoritism by looking on the face of the suppliant. An Oriental expression. **Overthrow** or **deprive:** Lit., "to turn aside," i.e., from what are one's rights. **Justice:** See Exeg. on 1:3.

6. Vss. 6-8 have to do with foolish and slanderous talk. In this verse it is stated that foolish talk leads to **strife** and punishment. **Enter:** Better, **bring,** by changing one vowel in the Hebrew word.

8. Repeated in 26:22. The words of the slanderer are greedily picked up by the hearers like dainty morsels and stowed away with gleeful maliciousness. **Wounds** or **delicious morsels:** *Mithlahamîm* is a difficult word, found only here and in 26:22. It may be derived from a stem meaning "to swallow greedily." The KJV follows Rashi's interpretation. **The inner parts of the body:** Lit., "the chambers of the belly," a unique expression found only in Proverbs. As Oesterley points out, it is probably derived from Egyptian sources.

9. A lazy person is kin to a destroyer, not that he is a murderer or robber but simply that he brings ruin on himself and others by not doing his work (see Exeg. on 12:24; 19:24). **Also:** Rightly omitted by the RSV, with the LXX. **Great waster** or **him who destroys:** Lit., "possessor of destruction."

10. In the Semitic world the **name** stood for the person, since it expressed his character and his qualities. Here the name of God, which is a refuge for the righteous, is Yahweh, or **the LORD,** the name by which God revealed himself to Israel (Exod. 3) as the covenant God. By that name God manifested his saving love and his loving care for his people. To this name, i.e., to God who loves and protects, one may flee as to **a strong tower** for shelter from the enemy. **Is safe:** The ASV mg., "is set on high," gives the literal meaning of the verb.

11. The verse simply states a fact that wealth is a source of power, without attaching any stigma to it (see Exeg. on 10:2; cf. 10:15). **In his own conceit:** Better, "in his own

5. See Expos. on 21:3.
6. See Expos. on 26:21.
7-8. See Expos. on vs. 21.
9. See Expos. on 6:1-15.
10. See Expos. on 3:5-8.
11. See Expos. on 10:15-16.

12 Before destruction the heart of man is
haughty; and before honor *is* humility.
13 He that answereth a matter before he
heareth *it,* it *is* folly and shame unto him.
14 The spirit of a man will sustain his
infirmity; but a wounded spirit who can
bear?
15 The heart of the prudent getteth
knowledge; and the ear of the wise seeketh
knowledge.
16 A man's gift maketh room for him,
and bringeth him before great men.
17 *He that is* first in his own cause *seem-*

12 Before destruction a man's heart is
haughty,
but humility goes before honor.
13 If one gives answer before he hears,
it is his folly and shame.
14 A man's spirit will endure sickness;
but a broken spirit who can bear?
15 An intelligent mind acquires knowledge,
and the ear of the wise seeks knowledge.
16 A man's gift makes room for him
and brings him before great men.
17 He who states his case first seems right,

---

imagination" (ASV). A difficult word, *maskîth.* The RSV, **protecting him,** seems to derive it with the LXX and others from *sākhakh,* "to cover," "to lay over."

12. Antithetic. See Exeg. on 13:10 regarding the sin of pride (cf. 16:18). Vs. 12*b*= 15:33*b* (see Exeg.).

13. Against hasty speech (see Exeg. on 12:17); cf. Ecclus. 11:8:

> Do not answer before you hear,
> And do not interrupt in the middle of what is being said (Amer. Trans).

14. Antithetic. We can endure all things if we have will power. If that is gone, then all is lost. **Spirit:** In both cases in this verse the word is *rûaḥ,* the primary, sustaining principle of life which comes directly from God.

15. Synonymous. The **heart,** or **mind** within (see Exeg. on 2:2), and the **ear** without gather knowledge. **Prudent** or **intelligent:** The Hebrew word is *nābhôn* (see Exeg. on 1:2).

16. Synonymous. This verse probably refers to the giving of gifts to influential men or patrons whose friendship and influence were thereby won (see Exeg. on 10:2; cf. 19:6).

17. This verse refers to a court of justice where a kind of cross-examination put the plaintiff's case in a different light. **Searcheth** or, better in this context, **examines.**

---

12. See Expos. on 29:23.

13. See Expos. on vs. 21.

14. See Expos. on 17:22.

15. See Expos. on 2:1-22.

16. ***Giving in Order to Receive.***—The thought here is not that "it is more blessed to give than to receive" (Acts 20:35), but that it is wise to give in order that one might receive. Such giving has a selfish purpose. Gifts are not necessarily the expression of unselfish good will; they may be a method of getting good will from the receiver. Cultures have varied in the effectiveness of gifts to curry favor. In some situations a giver would be suspected of ulterior motives if he came with a gift in his hand. He would appear to be buying something that ought not to be bought with money or a gift. The line between a bribe and a gift is often difficult to draw.

Some of the proverbs commend the giving of gifts. The man who does not come empty-handed can get to places that others cannot reach.

> **A man's gift makes room for him**
> **and brings him before great men.**

The person whose temper has been aroused may be pacified by a gift.

> A gift in secret averts anger;
> and a bribe in the bosom, strong wrath (21:14).

On the other hand, there are times when a gift is obviously an attempt to buy injustice. A wicked man expects to buy his way to immunity against punishment by paying a judge, or a law violator may hope to escape punishment by making a contribution to a policeman. Such a gift is not an expression of good will but a method of avoiding ill will.

> A wicked man accepts a bribe from the bosom
> to pervert the ways of justice (17:23).

17. See Expos. on 21:3.

eth just; but his neighbor cometh and
searcheth him.
18 The lot causeth contentions to cease,
and parteth between the mighty.
19 A brother offended *is harder to be won*
than a strong city: and *their* contentions *are*
like the bars of a castle.
20 A man's belly shall be satisfied with
the fruit of his mouth; *and* with the increase of his lips shall he be filled.
21 Death and life *are* in the power of the
tongue: and they that love it shall eat the
fruit thereof.

until the other comes and examines
him.
18 The lot puts an end to disputes
and decides between powerful contend-
ers.
19 A brother helped is like a strong city,[a]
but quarreling is like the bars of a
castle.
20 From the fruit of his mouth a man is
satisfied;
he is satisfied by the yield of his lips.
21 Death and life are in the power of the
tongue,
and those who love it will eat its fruits.

[a] Gk Syr Vg Tg: The meaning of the Hebrew is uncertain

---

18. Synonymous. The **lot** was used to decide in difficult cases, whether in or out of court. **Decides:** Even though the disputants are powerful, the lot can separate them, i.e., send them away with the dispute settled.

19. An impossible Hebrew text. Lit., "A brother, transgressed against, from [than] a strong city, and contentions like the bar of a fortress." In vs. 19*a* the RSV follows substantially the LXX, and thus certainly improves the text with only a slight emendation. The verb form translated "transgressed against" is found nowhere else in the O.T. Vs. 19*b* means to say that strife makes between those who were once friendly a partition which cannot be broken, i.e., reconciliation is practically impossible.

20. Synonymous (see Exeg. on 12:17; cf. 12:14; 13:2-3). **A man's belly:** A man must take the consequences of his words.

21. Synonymous. The thought of vs. 20 is continued. The word **it** must refer to **the tongue,** and can only mean "to love the use of it."

---

18. See Expos. on 26:21.

19. See Expos. on 17:17.

20. See Expos. on vs. 21.

21. ***The Power of the Tongue.***—Words have tremendous power for good or ill. **Death and life are in the power of the tongue.** One can understand why sages and teachers are conscious of the power of speech, since much of their life is given to communication through words. The sages were especially aware of "speech difficulties." Almost every chapter in the collection of proverbs has something to say about the kinds of speech that get people into trouble, and the kinds that are helpful. Words can hurt or heal those who hear them. Words can harm or help the person who speaks them.

Proverbs makes many suggestions regarding the use of the tongue. Restraint in speech is commended. Persons who speak rashly, who pour forth words before they have given themselves a chance to think, will get into trouble. Words cannot be recalled after they have been spoken, any more than arrows can be called back after they have left the bow. "The mouths of fools pour out folly" (15:2). One can almost hear the cascade of words as they fall from the lips of the garrulous individual.

> When words are many, transgression is not lacking,
> but he who restrains his lips is prudent (10:19).

The rash and voluble talker has the law of averages against him, for sooner or later he will cause damage by some unguarded remark.

Silence is better than glib talk.

> Even a fool who keeps silent is considered wise;
> when he closes his lips he is deemed intelligent (17:28).

To Lincoln is attributed a remark in a similar vein, "Better to remain silent and be thought a fool than to speak out and remove all doubt." In giving his parting advice to his son Laertes, Polonius has several things to say about paucity of words. "Give thy thoughts no tongue," he says, and later he adds this significant word of advice, "Give every man thine ear, but few thy voice."[5] The tongue gets people into trouble when they allow a "multitude of words" (10:19) to pour forth unrestrained and unguarded from

[5] Shakespeare, *Hamlet,* Act I, scene 3.

their lips. Wise living consists partly in being a person of few words.

A lying tongue can do great harm. Through dishonesty speech is counterfeited, and all mutual trust and communication tend to break down. When once a man indulges in falsehoods it is difficult to believe him even if he speaks the truth. Bearing false witness against another man is one of the despicable ways in which the power of the tongue does harm. Even though a man gets a temporary advantage by telling a falsehood, there is nothing stable about his position after that. Sooner or later his deceit will be made known.

Bread gained by deceit is sweet to a man,
but afterward his mouth will be full of gravel (20:17).

Using the power of speech to conceal the truth or to convey untruth is inviting the death of wholesome human relations. An interesting psychological insight is contained in one of the proverbs that deals with lying. "A lying tongue hates its victims" (26:28). This suggests that we hate those whom we hurt rather than hurt those whom we hate. On the positive side it would indicate that we love those whom we help, rather than the usual observation that we help those whom we love.

Unkind gossip about another person is a second deadly use of the tongue. Talebearing is like a dagger thrust at the heart of another individual. There is one kind of gossip that is only the passing on of a rumor. The rumor may have no truth in it, but the talebearer sends it on its damaging way by repeating it. "The words of a whisperer," which to him are "delicious morsels" (26:22), may be a method of compensating for his own sense of inadequacy. By running other people down he hopes to bring them to his own level, or by centering attention upon the weakness of others to withdraw attention from his own shortcomings.

Unkind gossip is not limited to the passing on of falsehoods about other people. The talebearer may be telling the truth about another. No individual is perfect, and some individuals are guilty of the kinds of sin that have greater social disapproval than others. If one is looking for the failures and weaknesses of other men, he will perhaps have no difficulty in finding them. One proverb commends silence rather than glee in conversing about the weakness of others.

He who goes about as a talebearer reveals secrets,
but he who is trustworthy in spirit keeps a thing hidden (11:13).

Taking pleasure in talking about the weaknesses and failures of others is not constructive. Little good is accomplished in this way. A Frenchman has made a good motto to be hung over every hearth, "Here one speaks of evil only to grieve over it and remedy it." Henry van Dyke has proposed three rules which would greatly curtail the output of unkind gossip if they were followed: "Never believe anything bad about anyone unless you positively know it is true; never tell even that unless you feel that it is absolutely necessary; and remember that God is listening while you tell it."

Words have added value when they are properly timed. "A word spoken in due season, how good is it!" (15:23.) The same word spoken out of season or at an inopportune time may do great harm. The wise use of the tongue will include the difficult discipline of proper timing. One might think that truth is truth no matter when it is spoken, but if one is dealing with persons rather than with propositions, he will try to speak the truth when and where it is fitting and needed. The person who calls himself "brutally frank" is one who probably forgets the importance of timing his remarks. He believes he is under necessity to speak the truth no matter what the time or occasion. A woman who had lived a long time once gave this instruction to her grandchildren: "Always tell the truth, but don't always be telling it." The right thing spoken at the wrong time can hardly be called "a word fitly spoken" (25:11).

The tone as well as the content of speech is important. Very often it is not what is said that helps or hurts another—it is the way in which it is said.

A soft answer turns away wrath:
but a harsh word stirs up anger (15:1).

The same words may be spoken in a friendly or in a harsh manner. The person who is addressed curtly does not need to reply in kind. He can give "a soft answer." He does not need to speak as he has been spoken to. Rather than repay curtness with curtness, a considerate individual would try to understand why he was addressed rudely. Instead of repaying people in kind, there is much to be said for repaying them in kindness. No matter what the answer is, if it is given softly and without rancor it will do much to quiet rising tempers and ease strained situations. The emotions that accompany speech are as important as the words spoken.

Since speech has so many hazards, the sages might be expected to urge everyone to join a cult of perpetual silence. This is not the case. They used words, they taught by means of words, and they believed in the efficacy of speech in bringing help and life to people. "The mouth of a righteous man is a well of life" (10:11). "The tongue of the just is as choice silver"

22 *Whoso* findeth a wife findeth a good *thing,* and obtaineth favor of the LORD.

23 The poor useth entreaties; but the rich answereth roughly.

24 A man *that hath* friends must show himself friendly: and there is a friend *that* sticketh closer than a brother.

19 Better *is* the poor that walketh in his integrity, than *he that is* perverse in his lips, and is a fool.

22 He who finds a wife finds a good thing,
and obtains favor from the LORD.
23 The poor use entreaties,
but the rich answer roughly.
24 There are[b] friends who pretend to be friends,[c]
but there is a friend who sticks closer than a brother.

19 Better is a poor man who walks in his integrity
than a man who is perverse in speech, and is a fool.

[b] Syr Tg: Heb *A man of*
[c] Cn Compare Syr Vg Tg: Heb *to be broken*

---

22. Synonymous (see Exeg. on 31:10; cf. 12:4; 19:14).

23. Antithetic. The proud, avaricious, wealthy man and the suppliant, poor man, here contrasted, are well-known characters of the time. **Useth:** Lit., "speaketh."

24. Antithetic. The contrast seems to be between those who are friendly only in a social way and him who stands by in the darkest hours. **A man:** The RSV, following the Syriac and the Targ., reads **there are** (*yēsh* for *'îsh*). **Show himself friendly** or **pretend to be friends,** "to his own destruction (ASV): The KJV and the RSV take the verb form to come from *rā'āh* (with Syriac and Targ.), whereas the ASV takes it from *rā'a'*. The former is better because of the parallelism. Vs. 24*b* is often interpreted messianically (see Exeg. on 17:17); cf. Ecclus. 6:14-16:

> A faithful friend is a strong protection;
> A man who has found one has found a treasure.
> A faithful friend is beyond price,
> And his value cannot be weighed.
> A faithful friend is a life-giving medicine,
> And those who fear the Lord will find it (Amer. Trans.).

19:1. The original form of this proverb is probably 28:6, since the poor man would naturally be contrasted with the "rich" one. But it is questionable whether this version of the proverb here should be made to correspond with 28:6, as in the Syriac. The compiler of the collection in which 19:1 occurs may have had some reason for adapting the original to this form. In other words, 19:1 is not necessarily a textual corruption of 28:6. **Integrity:** See Exeg. on 10:9. **Perverse:** For *'iqqēsh* see Exeg. on 2:15.

(10:20). If ideas are effective in guiding action, they can be communicated through the medium of language. A foreigner who cannot speak the language of the people among whom he lives feels a sense of isolation and helplessness. The particular words of others cannot hurt him, since he does not know what they are saying except as they reveal emotions by the way in which they speak. But neither can he be helped. Through speech we can communicate with each other, and through our words we can instruct and edify one another.

R. Simeon b. Gamaliel said to Ṭabbai his servant: "Go and buy me good food in the market." He went and bought him tongue. He said to him: "Go and buy me bad food in the market." He went and bought him tongue. Said he to him: "What is this? When I told you to get good food you bought me tongue, and when I told you to get bad food you also bought me tongue!" He replied: "Good comes from it and bad comes from it. When the tongue is good there is nothing better, and when it is bad there is nothing worse." [6]

22. See Expos. on 31:10-31.

23. See Expos. on 10:15-16.

24. See Expos. on 17:17.

19:1. See Expos. on 15:16-17.

[6] Midrash Rabbah, Lev. 33:1.

2 Also, *that* the soul *be* without knowledge, *it is* not good; and he that hasteth with *his* feet sinneth.
3 The foolishness of man perverteth his way: and his heart fretteth against the LORD.

2 It is not good for a man to be without knowledge,
and he who makes haste with his feet misses his way.
3 When a man's folly brings his way to ruin,
his heart rages against the LORD.

---

2. Synonymous. A difficult Hebrew construction in vs. 2*a*. The general idea is that it is not good to act without forethought. **Also:** Omitted rightly by the RSV, with the versions. **Soul** or **man** ("desire" ASV mg.): Hebrew, *nĕphesh*. Any one of these translations is correct, and the general meaning of the stich remains the same with each of them. **Sinneth:** Rather **misses his way.** The literal meaning of *ḥāṭā'*.

3. Failure is due to man's folly, not to the Lord. **Perverteth** or **brings . . . to ruin:**

---

2. *A Warning Against Haste.*—The disadvantages of haste are not limited to our streamlined age. **He who makes haste with his feet misses his way** whether he is running breathlessly over a field in the first century or stepping on the accelerator instead of on the brakes in the twentieth century.

In the performance of a physical task haste often destroys good co-ordination. A golfer knows that if he is being pushed, he tends to press. The more he tries to hurry, the more he tends to miss his shots. Friar Laurence saw the difficulty that attends great haste:

> Romeo: O, let us hence; I stand on sudden haste.
> Friar Laurence: Wisely and slow; they stumble that run fast.[7]

A life driven by haste misses much along the way. Important things are passed by unnoticed. The person who drives a car at high speed along a country road has little time or leisure to observe the scenes he is passing.

Haste often results in ill-considered action. When people act too quickly they do not take time to weigh all the consequences. "Every one who is hasty comes only to want" (21:5). The person who refuses to be stampeded by haste may save himself many regrets. When the daughter of Herod danced for her father and his court Herod made a quick, rash promise. He offered to give her anything she wished. His offer was accepted as quickly as it was given. Everything moved with lightninglike swiftness. His daughter rushed to her mother for advice. Her mother had a quick answer ready. She asked for the head of John the Baptist. The record goes on to say: "She came in immediately with haste to the king, and asked, saying, 'I want you to give me at once the head of John the Baptist on a platter'" (Mark 6:25). With feverish haste this deed was done. None of the parties involved took any time to weigh the full consequences of the action.

There is a kind of haste that mistakes quantity for quality. Technological developments have multiplied the number of things a modern man may do, the number of places he may visit, the number of books and magazines he may read, the number of plays or motion pictures he may see. Under these pressures life can easily be measured by the number of things a person does. The difficulty is that a modern man is irritated and develops a driven look. He must hurry to get one thing done so that he can start to do the next thing. Life is too short to do everything we should like to do. None of us can read all the books he would like to read. He cannot attend all the functions that invite his participation. The task of the modern man is to remind himself that life does not consist of quantity but quality. Speaking of the lives of the saints, Emily Herman writes:

> When we read the lives of the saints, we are struck by a certain large leisure which went hand in hand with a remarkable effectiveness. They were never hurried; they did comparatively few things, and these not necessarily striking or important; and they troubled very little about their influence.[8]

Enthusiasts for social change may need to learn to forgo haste. They would like changes to happen quickly; but they must gain the patience of the man who can endure to lose battles because he is confident that the war will eventually be won.

3. See Expos. on 26:1, 3-12.

[7] Shakespeare, *Romeo and Juliet,* Act II, scene 3.

[8] *Creative Prayer* (New York: George H. Doran Co., 1921), p. 28.

4 Wealth maketh many friends; but the poor is separated from his neighbor.
5 A false witness shall not be unpunished; and *he that* speaketh lies shall not escape.
6 Many will entreat the favor of the prince: and every man *is* a friend to him that giveth gifts.
7 All the brethren of the poor do hate him: how much more do his friends go far from him? he pursueth *them with* words, *yet* they *are* wanting *to him*.
8 He that getteth wisdom loveth his own soul: he that keepeth understanding shall find good.

4 Wealth brings many new friends,
but a poor man is deserted by his friend.
5 A false witness will not go unpunished,
and he who utters lies will not escape.
6 Many seek the favor of a generous man,
and everyone is a friend to a man who gives gifts.
7 All a poor man's brothers hate him;
how much more do his friends go far from him!
He pursues them with words, but does not have them.[d]
8 He who gets wisdom loves himself;
he who keeps understanding will prosper.

[d] Heb uncertain

Lit., "overturn." **Fretteth** or, more accurately, **rages:** Ecclus. 15:11-15, 20 enlarges on this idea (cf. also Jas. 1:12-18).

> Do not say, "It was because of the Lord that I fell away,"
> For he will not do things that he hates.
> Do not say, "It was he that led me astray,"
> For he has no need of a sinner.
> The Lord hates anything abominable;
> And it is not loved by those who fear him.
> It was he who made man in the beginning,
> And left him in the hands of his own decision;
> If you will, you can keep the commandments,
> And acting faithfully rests on your own good pleasure.
> . . . .
> He has not commanded anyone to be ungodly,
> And he has given no one permission to sin (Amer. Trans.).

4. Antithetic. See Exeg. on 10:2 regarding the problem of wealth.

5. Synonymous. Very similar to vs. 9 (see Exeg. on 14:25). **Utters:** Lit., "breathes out" (see Exeg. on 6:19). The reference here is to law cases, where many a time the fate of a man hung on the lips of the witness.

6. This verse refers to the generous man of wealth who gives gifts to influence friends (see Exeg. on 10:2). **Seek the favor of:** Lit., "to smooth the face of," probably originally to stroke the face of the idol to gain its favor. It is used here in a secular sense. **Prince** or **generous man:** *Nādhîbh* can mean either. The root meaning of the word has to do with voluntariness. Here the liberal man is probably meant in parallelism with **him that giveth gifts** (lit., "the man of gifts"; cf. 17:7, 26).

7. The only example of a triplet in this section of Proverbs. The third stich seems to be the corrupt remnant of a lost couplet. Lit., "He who pursues words, not are they," or "they are his." The paraphrase of this stich in the KJV and the ASV, text and margin, is not allowed by the Hebrew. Emendations are useless since the line is obviously a fragment (see Exeg. on 10:2 for the general meaning).

8. Synonymous. Intelligence brings prosperity. **Wisdom:** Lit., "heart" (see Exeg. on 2:2). **Understanding:** See Exeg. on 2:2.

4. See Expos. on 10:15-16.
5. See Expos. on 18:21.
6. See Expos. on 18:16.
7. See Expos. on 30:7-10.
8. See Expos. on 3:13-18.

9 A false witness shall not be unpunished; and *he that* speaketh lies shall perish.

10 Delight is not seemly for a fool; much less for a servant to have rule over princes.

11 The discretion of a man deferreth his anger; and *it is* his glory to pass over a transgression.

12 The king's wrath *is* as the roaring of a lion; but his favor *is* as dew upon the grass.

13 A foolish son *is* the calamity of his father: and the contentions of a wife *are* a continual dropping.

14 House and riches *are* the inheritance of fathers: and a prudent wife *is* from the LORD.

15 Slothfulness casteth into a deep sleep; and an idle soul shall suffer hunger.

16 He that keepeth the commandment keepeth his own soul; *but* he that despiseth his ways shall die.

17 He that hath pity upon the poor lendeth unto the LORD; and that which he hath given will he pay him again.

9 A false witness will not go unpunished,
and he who utters lies will perish.
10 It is not fitting for a fool to live in luxury,
much less for a slave to rule over princes.
11 Good sense makes a man slow to anger,
and it is his glory to overlook an offense.
12 A king's wrath is like the growling of a lion,
but his favor is like dew upon the grass.
13 A foolish son is ruin to his father,
and a wife's quarreling is a continual dripping of rain.
14 House and wealth are inherited from fathers,
but a prudent wife is from the LORD.
15 Slothfulness casts into a deep sleep,
and an idle person will suffer hunger.
16 He who keeps the commandment keeps his life;
he who despises the word[e] will die.
17 He who is kind to the poor lends to the LORD,
and he will repay him for his deed.

[e] Cn Compare 13. 13: Heb *his ways*

9. Synonymous. See vs. 5.

10. Two incongruous things are mentioned in this verse: a fool who lives in luxury, and a slave in political power (with vs. 10*b* cf. 17:2; 30:22). **Luxury** is preferable to **delight.**

11. Synonymous. Patience and a forgiving spirit are the earmarks of a wise man (cf. 14:29). **Good sense:** See Exeg. on 12:8. **Deferreth:** **Lit., makes . . . slow.** See Exeg. on 14:29. **Overlook:** For this expression of forgiveness see Amos 7:8; 8:2; Mic. 7:18.

12. Antithetic (see Exeg. on 16:10; cf. 20:2).

13. Calamity or **ruin** (*hawwāh*): See Exeg. on 17:4. With vs. 13*b* cf. 21:9; 27:15.

14. Antithetic. The value of a good wife. Wealth and name are inherited, but a good wife comes from the Lord (see Exeg. on 31:10). **Prudent** (*maskāleth*): See Exeg. on 1:3.

15. Synonymous. Laziness results in hunger (see Exeg. on 12:24).

16. Antithetic. On **commandment** and **word** (emending *derākhâw* [his ways] to *haddābhār*) as relating to scripture, see Exeg. on 13:13.

17. Probably under prophetic influence (cf. Amos 2:6-7; 4:1; 5:15; Isa. 10:1-2; etc.), the Hebrew sages insist that proper care should be taken of the poor. It is not just a passive admonition, viz., that the poor are not to be oppressed, but active measures are to be taken to help them (cf. 14:31; 17:5; 21:13; 22:9, 16, 22, 23; 28:3, 27; 29:7). In this proverb it is said that when one is kind to the poor he is really giving to God, who will repay with long life and prosperity. The danger of making almsgiving atone for sin is quite evident here; cf. Ecclus. 3:30:

9. See Expos. on 18:21.
10. See Expos. on 26:1, 3-12.
11. See Expos. on 16:32.
12. See Expos. on 16:10-15.
13. See Expos. on 1:8-9; 10:1; 31:10-31.
14. See Expos. on 31:10-31.
15. See Expos. on 6:1-15.
16. See Expos. on 3:13-18.
17. See Expos. on 14:21.

18 Chasten thy son while there is hope,
and let not thy soul spare for his crying.
19 A man of great wrath shall suffer punishment: for if thou deliver *him*, yet thou
must do it again.
20 Hear counsel, and receive instruction,
that thou mayest be wise in thy latter end.
21 *There are* many devices in a man's
heart; nevertheless the counsel of the LORD,
that shall stand.
22 The desire of a man *is* his kindness:
and a poor man *is* better than a liar.
23 The fear of the LORD *tendeth* to life:
and *he that hath it* shall abide satisfied; he
shall not be visited with evil.
24 A slothful *man* hideth his hand in *his*
bosom, and will not so much as bring it to
his mouth again.

18 Discipline your son while there is hope;
do not set your heart on his destruction.
19 A man of great wrath will pay the penalty;
for if you deliver him, you will only have to do it again.[f]
20 Listen to advice and accept instruction,
that you may gain wisdom for the future.
21 Many are the plans in the mind of a man,
but it is the purpose of the LORD that will be established.
22 What is desired in a man is loyalty,
and a poor man is better than a liar.
23 The fear of the LORD leads to life;
and he who has it rests satisfied;
he will not be visited by harm.
24 The sluggard buries his hand in the dish,
and will not even bring it back to his mouth.

[f] Heb obscure

As water will quench a blazing fire,
So charity will atone for sin (Amer. Trans.).

18. Cf. 13:24; 23:13. **And let not thy soul spare for his crying:** According to Toy, this translation is derived from medieval Jewish authorities. It certainly does not render the Hebrew text. The RSV **do not set your heart on his destruction** means that punishment should not be neglected lest the child go astray and in fact suffer death on account of his wickedness. It can hardly be a warning to a parent not to kill his child by corporal punishment. **On his destruction:** Lit., "to cause him to die."

19. An impossible Hebrew text. Lit., ". . . of anger, paying a fine, for if thou deliver, and again thou shalt add [increase]." The first word in the M.T. (*gerol-*) is unknown. It may mean "stony," "rough." The margin has *gedhol-* ("great"), and so the usual rendering of vs. 19*a*: "He that is great in wrath pays a fine." All attempts to make sense out of vs. 19*b* are purely conjectural and have no basis in the Hebrew.

20. Advice: See Exeg. on 8:14. **In thy latter end** or, more explicitly, **for the future:** See Exeg. on 5:4; 23:18. Here the idea of the word seems to be "for the rest of thy life."

21. Antithetic. Man's diverse thoughts and plans take on unity and endurance only as they are subjected to the over-all purpose of God (cf. 16:1, 9). **Counsel:** God's **purpose** or plan.

22. The first half of this verse is literally translated in the KJV, but the meaning is uncertain. The RSV and the other English translations are not derived naturally from the Hebrew. There is no apparent connection between vs. 22*a* and vs. 22*b*.

23. As it stands, the verse looks like a triplet, although the text of the second Hebrew stich is probably out of order. Lit., "And satisfied he lodges, not shall he be visited [by] evil." **Fear of the LORD:** See Exeg. on 1:7. **He that hath it:** This phrase is inserted in order to make sense out of the Hebrew.

24. Almost identical with 26:15. The mention of the **sluggard** always seems to evoke a humorous note (cf. 6:6-11; 13:4; 22:13; 24:30-34; 26:13-16). **Bosom,** with ancient

18. See Expos. on 17:6.
19. See Expos on 16:32.
20. See Expos. on 9:7-9.
21. See Expos. on 3:5-8.
22. See Expos. on 15:16-17.
23. See Expos. on 1:7.
24. See Expos. on 6:1-15.

25 Smite a scorner, and the simple will beware: and reprove one that hath understanding, *and* he will understand knowledge.
26 He that wasteth *his* father, *and* chaseth away *his* mother, *is* a son that causeth shame, and bringeth reproach.
27 Cease, my son, to hear the instruction *that causeth* to err from the words of knowledge.
28 An ungodly witness scorneth judgment: and the mouth of the wicked devoureth iniquity.
29 Judgments are prepared for scorners, and stripes for the back of fools.

20 Wine *is* a mocker, strong drink *is* raging: and whosoever is deceived thereby is not wise.
2 The fear of a king *is* as the roaring of a lion: *whoso* provoketh him to anger sinneth *against* his own soul.

25 Strike a scoffer, and the simple will learn
prudence;
reprove a man of understanding, and
he will gain knowledge.
26 He who does violence to his father and
chases away his mother
is a son who causes shame and brings
reproach.
27 Cease, my son, to hear instruction
only to stray from the words of knowledge.
28 A worthless witness mocks at justice,
and the mouth of the wicked devours
iniquity.
29 Condemnation is ready for scoffers,
and flogging for the backs of fools.
20 Wine is a mocker, strong drink a
brawler;
and whoever is led astray by it is not
wise.
2 The dread wrath of a king is like the
growling of a lion;
he who provokes him to anger forfeits
his life.

---

versions and some of the older commentators; **dish,** with RSV, ASV, and the standard lexicons. In this case the sluggard is so lazy he will not bring his food to his mouth with his hand.

25. Antithetic. A fool learns by example, an intelligent man by instruction. Evidently the wise men thought there was a chance for a *pethî* to learn something (see Exeg. on 1:4). **Scoffer:** See Exeg. on 1:22. **Understanding:** See Exeg. on 1:2.

26. A son whose aged parents are dependent upon him is described here. He evidently can maltreat his parents without legal punishment.

27. The words **that causeth** (KJV) and **only** (RSV) are not in the Hebrew. By slight changes in two Hebrew words we get the excellent translation: "[My son], he that ceaseth [*ḥādhēl*] to hear instruction errs [*yishgeh*] from the words of knowledge." **Instruction:** See Exeg. on 1:2.

28. Synonymous. Vs. 28*a* deals with the false witness (see Exeg. on 14:25). In vs. 28*b* it is stated that the wicked gulp down iniquity with great pleasure. **Ungodly** or, better, **worthless:** See Exeg. on 6:12. **Justice:** See Exeg. on 1:3.

29. Synonymous. **Judgments** or **condemnation:** The LXX reads "whips," which may have been the original Hebrew, emending *shephāṭîm* to *shebhāṭîm.* **Scorners** and **fools** (*keṣîlîm*): See Exeg. on 1:22.

20:1. Against excessive drinking (see Exeg. on 23:29). **Mocker:** The Hebrew word is *lēç,* usually translated "scorner." **Brawler** is better than **raging. Is led astray:** "reeleth" (ASV mg.) is most appropriate in this context.

2. See Exeg. on 16:10. Vs. 2*a* is similar to 19:12*a.* The meaning of the Hebrew in vs. 2*b* is not clear. **Provoketh . . . to anger:** Lit., "He that angers himself against him" (with ASV mg.). **Sinneth:** The RSV **forfeits** is probably what the Hebrew phrase means in this context.

---

25. See Expos. on 9:7-9.
26. See Expos. on 1:8-9; 10:1.
27. See Expos. on 9:7-9.
28. See Expos. on 21:3.
29. See Expos. on 26:1, 3-12.
20:1. See Expos. on 23:29-35.
2. See Expos. on 16:10-15.

3 *It is* an honor for a man to cease from strife: but every fool will be meddling.

4 The sluggard will not plow by reason of the cold; *therefore* shall he beg in harvest, and *have* nothing.

5 Counsel in the heart of man *is like* deep water; but a man of understanding will draw it out.

6 Most men will proclaim every one his own goodness: but a faithful man who can find?

3 It is an honor for a man to keep aloof
from strife;
but every fool will be quarreling.
4 The sluggard does not plow in the autumn;
he will seek at harvest and have nothing.
5 The purpose in a man's mind is like deep
water,
but a man of understanding will draw
it out.
6 Many a man proclaims his own loyalty,
but a faithful man who can find?

---

3. Antithetic. It is folly to be quarrelsome. **To keep aloof from:** Lit., "to sit," i.e., to keep quiet, and thus to refrain from any kind of activity that might lead to strife. **Will be quarreling:** See Exeg. on 17:14.

4. The RSV gives the correct sense here; the sluggard refuses to **plow** because of his laziness, not because of the cold, so that when he looks for the harvest it is not there (see Exeg. on 19:24). **Cold** or, better, **autumn** ("winter" ASV): The plowing was done after the reaping of the last crops. **Beg** is not correct. The RSV is better, **he will seek**—i.e., look for food from his fields—but will find none, since he has not prepared the ground.

5. A wise man can fathom another man's thoughts (cf. 18:4). **Purpose:** See Exeg. on 8:14. **Understanding:** See Exeg. on 2:2.

6. Antithetic. The implication of vs. 6*a*, as translated by the KJV and RSV, is that many of these proclamations are mere boastings without much basis in fact. **Will proclaim:** The ASV mg. reads, "many a man will meet one that is kind to him," making *qārā'* ("call") equal *qārāh* ("meet"). The Syriac, the Targ., and the Vulg. read, with a slight change of the Hebrew, "many a man is called a kind man." The same general sense is found in all these renderings. **Faithful:** The same root as that of the word translated "truth" in 12:17 (see Exeg.).

---

3. See Expos. on 26:21.

4. See Expos. on 6:1-15.

5. See Expos. on 1:2.

6. ***A Faithful Man.***—Faithfulness is as essential today as it was when Proverbs was written. In that ancient time, when a man took a message to a distant place, everything depended upon his trustworthiness. There was little possibility of checking on his veracity immediately. He must be an ambassador whose integrity was sure.

The need for faithfulness and trustworthiness takes a different form today. Our life is complex. If one must double-check on every act of every person, no progress can be made. The legal department in a large corporation cannot keep an accurate check on every employee in every operation. There must be faithful performance of duty. Occasionally a scandal is made public in which some civil servant or some person in a responsible position has been untrue to his trust. If such untrustworthiness were to become the rule, organized life would become impossible.

This proverb also calls attention to the person who makes fine pretensions of kindness, but whose actions belie his professions.

Many a man proclaims his own loyalty,
but a faithful man who can find?

Faithfulness is more than words. A man of few words may be a person of great faithfulness. He is at his post when he is needed. He can be counted upon to be in the place of duty.

Faithfulness is more important than success. Not everyone has the good fortune to succeed in what he does. Very few achieve heights of recognition for what they accomplish. However, everyone can aim to be faithful. "We are surely not sent into the world to get credit and reputations," wrote Charles Kingsley, "but to speak such words as are given us to speak; to do such acts as are given us to do; not heeding much, nor expecting to know whether they have effected anything or nothing. Therefore, friends, be of good courage."[9] Our loose and compli-

[9] Quoted in M. B. Reckitt, *Faith and Society* (New York: Longmans, Green & Co., 1932), p. 82.

7 The just *man* walketh in his integrity: his children *are* blessed after him.

8 A king that sitteth in the throne of judgment scattereth away all evil with his eyes.

9 Who can say, I have made my heart clean, I am pure from my sin?

10 Divers weights, *and* divers measures, both of them *are* alike abomination to the LORD.

11 Even a child is known by his doings, whether his work *be* pure, and whether *it be* right.

12 The hearing ear, and the seeing eye, the LORD hath made even both of them.

13 Love not sleep, lest thou come to poverty: open thine eyes, *and* thou shalt be satisfied with bread.

14 *It is* naught, *it is* naught, saith the buyer: but when he is gone his way, then he boasteth.

15 There is gold, and a multitude of

7 A righteous man who walks in his integrity—
blessed are his sons after him!
8 A king who sits on the throne of judgment
winnows all evil with his eyes.
9 Who can say, "I have made my heart clean;
I am pure from my sin"?
10 Diverse weights and diverse measures
are both alike an abomination to the LORD.
11 Even a child makes himself known by his acts,
whether what he does is pure and right.
12 The hearing ear and the seeing eye,
the LORD has made them both.
13 Love not sleep, lest you come to poverty;
open your eyes, and you will have plenty of bread.
14 "It is bad, it is bad," says the buyer;
but when he goes away, then he boasts.
15 There is gold, and abundance of costly stones;

---

7. The best inheritance a child can have is a good name. **Righteous:** See Exeg. on 1:3. **Integrity:** See Exeg. on 10:9.

8. See Exeg. on 16:10. **Scattereth** or, better, **winnows:** I.e., he sifts the evil from the good **with his eyes.**

9. An acknowledgment of human sinfulness. Solomon expressed this thought in his dedicatory prayer (I Kings 8:46). This idea of the sinfulness of the individual human nature is clear in Jeremiah and Ezekiel (cf. also Job 4:17-19; Pss. 51:5; 130:3; Eccl. 7:20).

10. Cf. vs. 23; 11:1; 16:11.

11. Even in childhood character is revealed by conduct. As Toy correctly points out, the word *nà'ar* used here for **child** refers to a mature young man in chs. 1–9, whereas in chs. 10–31 it means one living under the care of parents.

12. The organs of the body and their functions are made by God. Therefore, how great he is; how dependent we are upon him; how we should use that which God has given us to his glory and honor!

13. There is no place for laziness in this world order (cf. 6:9-11).

14. A common practice in Oriental markets is described here. The buyer disparages the article for sale, gets it for a lower price, and then goes his way, bragging about his cleverness in making such a deal.

15. The most natural translation is according to the Hebrew order, "Abundance of [there is] gold, wealth of costly stones, and precious jewels are wise lips." So Toy, Amer.

---

cated life with its anonymity and impersonal relationships calls for people who will honor their own inner integrity. To such as remain true in obscure responsibilities there is the later reassuring word of Jesus: "He who is faithful in a very little is faithful also in much" (Luke 16:10).

7. See Expos. on 21:3.

8. See Expos. on 16:10-15.

9. See Expos. on 28:13.

10. See Expos. on 21:3.

11. See Expos. on 17:6.

12. See Expos. on 8:1-36.

13. See Expos. on 6:1-15.

14. See Expos. on 10:15-16.

15. See Expos. on 18:21.

rubies: but the lips of knowledge *are* a precious jewel.

16 Take his garment that is surety *for* a stranger: and take a pledge of him for a strange woman.

17 Bread of deceit *is* sweet to a man; but afterward his mouth shall be filled with gravel.

18 *Every* purpose is established by counsel: and with good advice make war.

19 He that goeth about *as* a talebearer revealeth secrets: therefore meddle not with him that flattereth with his lips.

20 Whoso curseth his father or his mother, his lamp shall be put out in obscure darkness.

21 An inheritance *may be* gotten hastily at the beginning; but the end thereof shall not be blessed.

but the lips of knowledge are a precious jewel.

16 Take a man's garment when he has given surety for a stranger,
and hold him in pledge when he gives surety for foreigners.

17 Bread gained by deceit is sweet to a man,
but afterward his mouth will be full of gravel.

18 Plans are established by counsel;
by wise guidance wage war.

19 He who goes about gossiping reveals secrets;
therefore do not associate with one who speaks foolishly.

20 If one curses his father or his mother,
his lamp will be put out in utter darkness.

21 An inheritance gotten hastily in the beginning
will in the end not be blessed.

Trans., and Moffatt, substantially. There is no evidence in the Hebrew that the two stichs are antithetical, as the KJV, RSV, and ASV translate. **Rubies** or **costly stones:** See Exeg. on 3:15. **Jewel:** Lit., "article," "vessel" (*k*[e]*lî*), used of household furnishings and personal adornment. The wise men try to compare wisdom with the most precious things they can think of in order to make it attractive to young men (cf. 3:14-15; 8:11; 16:16; 22:1; 28:11).

16. Synonymous. Similar to 27:13; cf. 6:1-5; 11:15; 17:18, where acting as **surety** is condemned. In this verse it is held up to ridicule: any person who assumes a stranger's debt is to be treated as the debtor himself, without any mercy, i.e., his own **garment** is to be taken as pledge (cf. Deut. 24:10-13) and he himself is to stand security if the debt is not paid. **Strange woman:** This is the reading of the Hebrew margin, found also in 27:13. But the parallelism favors the Hebrew text, **foreigners.**

17. Antithetic. The untruthful man who gains his possessions by **deceit** enjoys them because they have come to him with little effort. Soon, however, when he is found out and punished, they turn to **gravel** in his mouth.

18. Synonymous. All things, including war, should be carried on with skilled planning and advice (cf. 24:6). **Counsel:** See Exeg. on 8:14. **Advice** or **guidance** (*taḥbûlôth*): See Exeg. on 1:5.

19. Cf. 11:13*a*. **Flattereth with his lips** or **speaks foolishly** ("openeth wide his lips" ASV): The word *pāthāh* can mean either "to be open" or "to be simple." The RSV is figurative (cf. 13:3*b*, where the verb is different).

20. Utter darkness: Lit., "the pupil of darkness" with the *K*[e]*thîbh* (see Exeg. on 7:2). The word in the *Qerê* is not known.

21. The Hebrew *Qerê* is preferable for the verbal form in vs. 21*a*, reading *m*[e]*bhôhéleth,* **gotten hastily,** with the ancient versions, most modern commentators, and the standard English translations, instead of the form found in the Hebrew text, *m*[e]*bhôḥéleth,* whose meaning is uncertain. **End:** The issue, or final outcome, with possibly a connotation of divine punishment (see Exeg. on 5:4; 19:20).

---

16. See Expos. on 6:1-15.
17. See Expos. on 18:21.
18. See Expos. on 11:14.
19. See Expos. on 18:21.
20. See Expos. on 1:8; 10:1.
21. See Expos. on 14:12.

22 Say not thou, I will recompense evil; *but* wait on the LORD, and he shall save thee.

23 Divers weights *are* an abomination unto the LORD; and a false balance *is* not good.

24 Man's goings *are* of the LORD; how can a man then understand his own way?

25 *It is* a snare to the man *who* devoureth *that which is* holy, and after vows to make inquiry.

26 A wise king scattereth the wicked, and bringeth the wheel over them.

27 The spirit of man *is* the candle of the LORD, searching all the inward parts of the belly.

22 Do not say, "I will repay evil";
wait for the LORD, and he will help you.

23 Diverse weights are an abomination to the LORD,
and false scales are not good.

24 A man's steps are ordered by the LORD;
how then can man understand his way?

25 It is a snare for a man to say rashly, "It is holy,"
and to reflect only after making his vows.

26 A wise king winnows the wicked,
and drives the wheel over them.

27 The spirit of man is the lamp of the LORD,
searching all his innermost parts.

---

22. A noble verse (cf. 24:29). Vengeance against the wrongdoer is here condemned, evidently, as vs. 22*b* has it, on the ground that the Lord will save his followers from the evil-doings of the enemy (cf. Rom. 12:19).

23. Synonymous. See vs. 10.

24. Trust in God and he will make the way plain (cf. 16:9). The absolute sovereignty of God is recognized here, although throughout Proverbs man's free will and initiative are much more emphasized. There is no attempt made to reconcile the two views. **Understand:** See Exeg. on 1:2.

25. A difficult verse. **Who devoureth that which is holy** (KJV; ASV mg.) is an improbable translation. The RSV is better, **to say rashly, "It is holy,"** with most of the standard English translations. The meaning seems to be that it is not good for one to consecrate something without thinking. **To make inquiry** or **to reflect:** *Bāqār* ("to seek," "to inquire") is a difficult word here. The context favors the rendering of the RSV, but it is a question whether the Hebrew root can bear that meaning. The general meaning of the stich seems to be that all things should be considered before a vow is made.

26. Synonymous. See Exeg. on vs. 8. **Wheel:** Probably the wheel of the threshing cart which was driven over the grain on the threshing floor. This was a severe kind of punishment, to be sure (cf. Amos 1:3).

27. Spirit: Hebrew, "breath" (*neshāmāh*) which was breathed into man (Gen. 2:7) and made him a complete living soul. As Delitzsch says, "If the O.T. language has a separate word to denote the self-conscious personal human spirit in contradistinction to the spirit of a beast, this word according to the usage of the language, . . . is נשמה" (*Proverbs of Solomon,* II, 58). It seems to be equivalent here to the conscience which is God's **lamp** that searches out the innermost recesses (see Exeg. on 18:8) of man.

---

22. See Expos. on 25:21-22.

23. See Expos. on 21:3.

24. See Expos. on 3:5-8.

25. See Expos. on 19:2.

26. See Expos. on 16:10-15.

27. ***The Lamp of Conscience.***—Moffatt translates this proverb:

> Man's conscience is the lamp of the Eternal,
> flashing into his inmost soul.

This inner monitor calls a man to do as he ought, and it is here named the light of God in a human life. Conscience is a peculiar endowment of man, an imperative that bids him to do right. Various interpretations have been given of this inner urge to do right. For some the theory is that conscience is due simply to the acceptance under various forms of social pressure of the traditional moral ideas of the community or some group within it. There is a conflict between what the individual wants and what the group expects him to do. However, there are many times when a man's conscience bids him to depart from group standards. He lays down his life for the sake of conscience

28 Mercy and truth preserve the king: and his throne is upholden by mercy.
29 The glory of young men *is* their strength: and the beauty of old men *is* the gray head.

28 Loyalty and faithfulness preserve the king,
and his throne is upheld by righteousness.[g]
29 The glory of young men is their strength,
but the beauty of old men is their gray hair.

[g] Gk: Heb *loyalty*

28. This verse should probably be connected with vs. 26. It is stated here that the king is kind (see Exeg. on 16:10). **Mercy and truth** or **loyalty and faithfulness:** See Exeg. on 3:3. **Mercy** in vs. 28*b* is probably better translated **righteousness** with the RSV and LXX, since it would be strange to have the same quality repeated twice in the same verse.

29. Antithetic. Cf. 16:31.

because he feels he ought to oppose the will of the group.

No matter how one interprets the fact, men are aware of right and wrong, and something within them says, "Do right!" This voice does not tell a man what is right. His judgment, his training, his surroundings will all have something to do with what he considers right. In the name of conscience many wrongs have been done, since conscience itself only tells a man to do as he ought, but does not give him an infallible answer concerning what he ought to do. William H. Lecky says that during the Inquisition, "Philip II. and Isabella the Catholic inflicted more suffering in obedience to their consciences than Nero or Domitian in obedience to their lusts." [1]

A man has to live with his conscience. He cannot easily indulge in conduct that is unacceptable to himself. There is a brake on his action and a loss of zest in his living when he continues to do what he regards as wrong.

> The wicked flee when no one pursues,
> but the righteous are bold as a lion (28:1).

Mental and emotional health can be preserved only as the individual tries to close the gulf between what he does and what he feels he ought to do, and as he accepts the assurances of forgiveness for his wrongdoing.

28. See Expos. on 16:10-15.

29. ***Old Age Also Has Its Glory.***—Youth is not better than old age, nor is old age better than youth. Each has a glory of its own. Each has its handicaps and its temptations, each has its triumphs in a well-ordered life.

In a moment of nostalgic longing an aged person may wish he were young again. He may try to emulate young people and start the vain search for the Fountain of Youth. Lin Yutang has made some vigorous comments about this tendency which he finds in the West:

> The desire of American old men and women for action, trying in this way to gain their self-respect and the respect of the younger generation, is what makes them look so ridiculous to an Oriental. Too much action in an old man is like a broadcast of jazz music from a megaphone on top of an old cathedral. Is it not sufficient that the old people *are* something? Is it necessary that they must be forever *doing* something? [2]

The glory of old age is different from that of youth. A young man's strength draws people to him. Through the proper functioning of well-co-ordinated muscles he can run a race or wield an ax. He can respond almost intuitively to the steering wheel of a swiftly moving automobile. The glory of an old man lies in another area. Old age is more than remembering happier days. Advancing years are a time for the thinking of interesting thoughts which have accumulated through the decades, and for an increased understanding of what is happening in the present. Growing old has been likened to climbing a tower; the view halfway up is better than the view from the base, and it steadily becomes finer as the horizon expands.

In England there is an inscription on the grave of the seventeenth-century poet, Edmund Waller, written by the poet himself:

> The soul's dark cottage, battered and decayed,
> Lets in new light through chinks that Time has made.
> Stronger by weakness, wiser men become
> As they draw near to their eternal home.[3]

One of the proverbs states that old age is the reward of upright living.

[1] *History of European Morals* (New York: D. Appleton & Co., 1869), I, 266.

[2] *Importance of Living*, p. 164.

[3] "Of the Last Verses in the Book."

30 The blueness of a wound cleanseth away evil: so *do* stripes the inward parts of the belly.

21 The king's heart *is* in the hand of the LORD, *as* the rivers of water: he turneth it whithersoever he will.

2 Every way of a man *is* right in his own eyes: but the LORD pondereth the hearts.

3 To do justice and judgment *is* more acceptable to the LORD than sacrifice.

30 Blows that wound cleanse away evil;
strokes make clean the innermost parts.

21 The king's heart is a stream of water
in the hand of the LORD;
he turns it wherever he will.
2 Every way of a man is right in his own
eyes,
but the LORD weighs the heart.
3 To do righteousness and justice
is more acceptable to the LORD than
sacrifice.

---

30. Chastisement is good for the evil man. Just how the chastisement cleanses the evil is not said. It may deter him from further wrongdoing. **Blueness:** I.e., "the bruise of the wound." **Blows** is better. **Make clean** repeats the verb of vs. 30*a* which is not present in the Hebrew of vs. 30*b*. **Innermost parts:** See Exeg. on 18:8.

21:1. God controls the actions and decisions of the king (see Exeg. on 16:10). **Stream:** The reference here is to artificial irrigation canals (*peḻāghîm*) which can be controlled by the irrigator.

2. Antithetic. Similar to 16:2. **Right:** See Exeg. on 12:15. **Weighs** is probably more accurate than **pondereth.** This figure of weighing the heart or spirit (also in 16:2; 24:12) is probably taken over from Egyptian religion, where Thoth is said to weigh the hearts of men.

3. This verse shows prophetic influence (cf. Amos 5:22-24; Hos. 6:6; Mic. 6:6-8; also I Sam. 15:22). The wise men felt that the sacrificial system was necessary because

---

A hoary head is a crown of glory;
it is gained in a righteous life (16:31).

This is a generalization that can hardly survive careful examination. Jesus of Nazareth, who was acknowledged to be supremely good, was not allowed to live beyond his early thirties. Many who have been loyal to truth have been judged by their fellows to be unfit to live. When one considers the fate of martyrs he cannot affirm that righteousness always is rewarded by a long life on earth.

Yet righteousness may be said to have survival value when one lives a temperate and sober life. Dissolute living burns the candle at both ends. Debauchery breaks down body resistance and predisposes the body to attacks of disease. As a general observation it may be said that he who lives a sober and upright life has a better chance to arrive at old age than he who wastes his life in loose and fast living. The remark has been made that old people get the faces they deserve. Through the years character has had a chance to etch itself on the countenance.

Old age is not something to be feared. Advancing years bring corresponding compensations. To make the most of old age is a worthy aspiration, since a radiant old age is one of the best gifts a person can give to those around him. In his "Rabbi Ben Ezra," Robert Browning sounds the clarion call that has not been silenced:

Grow old along with me!
The best is yet to be,
The last of life, for which the first was made:
Our times are in His hand
Who saith "A whole I planned,
Youth shows but half; trust God; see all nor be afraid!"

30. See Expos. on 9:7-9.

21:1. See Expos. on 3:5-8.

2. See Expos. on 4:20-27.

3. ***What Is Justice?***—Justice is a virtue that is easier to acclaim than to clarify. More difficult than either is the ability to practice justice in concrete situations.

Justice is elevated to a high place not only in biblical writings but in other sources as well. Ethical teachers in many cultures have tried to explain what it means. Many of the proverbs praise the just man. Some of them give examples of just or unjust actions. In Proverbs justice is given a high place as an example of wise living. In addition to finding its way into our religious thought and practice, justice is a part of our contemporary American culture. Citizens of this country work for what they call "a just and durable peace." When children salute the American flag, they reaffirm their loyalty to a

commanded by the Law, but at all times the sacrifices were subordinate to the spirit in which they were offered; i.e., the ethical demands were more important than the ritual itself (see vs. 27; 15:8). **Righteousness:** See Exeg. on 1:3.

---

nation "indivisible, with liberty and justice for all."

What does **justice** mean? When is a person just? There is a recurring note heard in many of the discussions of the meaning of justice. Perhaps Justinian has phrased it as well as anyone, "Justice is the firm and continuous desire to render to everyone that which is his due."[4] Writing to the Romans, Paul emphasizes the same idea: "Pay all of them their dues, taxes to whom taxes are due, revenue to whom revenue is due, respect to whom respect is due, honor to whom honor is due" (Rom. 13:7). The point at which perplexity arises is when one tries to find out what is due an individual or a group. What is due a child in the home? What is due the widow who is a stockholder in a company? What is due the laborer who works at a machine? Is a prisoner of war receiving what is due him? The mere exhortation that each person shall give everyone his due is very general, but it can be a base line from which the man who desires to practice justice may work. Various proverbs afford insight into ways of giving others what is due them; they also give instances of the failure to give others their due. Sometimes it is easier to state what justice is not than to say what it is. Even a negative assertion about justice can clear the ground for progress toward a clearer idea of the meaning of just living.

To do righteousness and justice
is more acceptable to the Lord than sacrifice.

This is a straightforward statement of the prophetic affirmation that just living is more important in God's sight than ritual correctness. The people who tried to approach their Creator in worship often wondered how they could best come to him. They came with sacrifices, sometimes even sacrificing their own children, giving the fruit of their bodies for the sin of their souls (Mic. 6:7). A long forward step was taken in both religion and ethics when men began to think of God as desiring **justice . . . more . . . than sacrifice.** God was more pleased with men who tried to give their fellow men what was due them than he was with ardent worshipers who burdened the temple altars with sacrifices. This proverb gives concise expression to a prophetic note which is given memorable phrasing in Mic. 6:8.

An obvious example of refusing to give other people their due is the use of false weights and measures.

A false balance is an abomination to the Lord:
but a just weight is his delight (11:1).

When a housewife purchases a pound of butter, she ought to have the assurance that she will receive a pound of butter. That is her due. No amount of devotion to the temple can compensate for a lack of justice in business matters. In modern times, the state aims to supervise the weights and measures used by buyers and sellers, so that the purchaser may be confident that he is receiving just treatment. This principle is pressed somewhat further in the matter of advertising and labels on containers. Firms are expected to state accurately what a package contains so that the buyer may know what he is getting. Unfounded claims in advertising are also unjust, since it is not expected that everyone can take the time to make a chemical analysis of everything he buys to make sure that he is getting what is due him.

Impartiality in human relationships is necessary if each person is to get his due.

It is not good to be partial to a man,
or to deprive a righteous man of justice (18:5).

Untold damage is inflicted on the children in a family when parents show partiality. One child is unduly inflated because he gets more than his due; another may resort to retaliatory methods because he feels he has not received what is owing to him. The picture of justice as a young woman holding a scales and having a blindfold over her eyes at least emphasizes the need of impartiality in judgment. If she is to give everyone his due, she may need good eyesight as well as insight, but if she cannot see the person whose case is being weighed, she will at least be able to remain impartial in her decisions.

Peter took a great step forward in his religious life when he became convinced through his experience with Cornelius that God shows no partiality (Acts 10:34). Justice therefore means that people in the same situation ought to be accorded the same treatment. The administration of justice results in chaos when the wicked are justified and the righteous condemned (17:15). Such perversions of equity are an abomination to the Lord and a menace to the state.

Justice must be more than the rule of the strong. A person may be strong enough to im-

[4] *Institutes* I. 1.

4 A high look, and a proud heart, *and* the plowing of the wicked, *is* sin.

5 The thoughts of the diligent *tend* only to plenteousness; but of every one *that is* hasty only to want.

6 The getting of treasures by a lying tongue *is* a vanity tossed to and fro of them that seek death.

7 The robbery of the wicked shall destroy them; because they refuse to do judgment.

8 The way of man *is* froward and strange: but *as for* the pure, his work *is* right.

9 *It is* better to dwell in a corner of the housetop, than with a brawling woman in a wide house.

4 Haughty eyes and a proud heart,
the lamp of the wicked, are sin.
5 The plans of the diligent lead surely to abundance,
but every one who is hasty comes only to want.
6 The getting of treasures by a lying tongue
is a fleeting vapor and a snare of death.
7 The violence of the wicked will sweep them away,
because they refuse to do what is just.
8 The way of the guilty is crooked,
but the conduct of the pure is right.
9 It is better to live in a corner of the housetop
than in a house shared with a contentious woman.

---

4. Two unrelated, fragmentary lines; all attempts to connect them are forced. **Plowing** (*nîr*) or, better, **lamp** (*nēr*), with ancient versions and most modern commentators and translations.

5. Antithetic. Cf. 28:20. The reference in vs. 5*b* is to those who hasten to be rich. **Diligent:** See Exeg. on 10:4.

6. See Exeg. on 10:2. Literally, vs. 6*b* reads, "a driven vapor, seekers of death," a meaningless construction. The RSV, based on the LXX, reads for the latter phrase of the stich, **snare of death,** emending $m^{e}bhaqq^{e}sh\hat{e}$ to $m\hat{o}q^{e}sh\hat{e}$, which really is plural.

7. The translation of the RSV is more accurate. It is the picture of the wicked being swept away like fish in a net because they do not do justly. **Violence** is more accurate than **robbery. Judgment** or **what is just:** See Exeg. on 1:3.

8. Antithetic. Bad men are crooked in their dealings; pure men are straightforward. **And strange:** The RSV, the ASV, and others take the word *wāzār* to mean **guilty** (with the standard lexicons), from a cognate Arabic root. The difference in the interpretation of this word causes the difference in the translations of the KJV and RSV in vs. 8*a*. **Right:** See Exeg. on 12:15.

9. Repeated in 25:24. The meaning of the verse is that peace with any kind of privation or discomfort is better than strife with luxury (cf. vs. 19; 19:13; 27:15). **A house shared:** Lit., "house of a companion." The KJV and the ASV read, with the LXX,

---

pose his will on another, but this does not mean that he is giving the other his due. In Plato's *Republic,* Thrasymachus gives expression to the view that justice is nothing else than "the interest of the stronger."[5] Might makes right. If a weakling allows a stronger one to dominate him, then the weakling is getting exactly what is due him. He deserves nothing better. Such a cynical devotion to violence is rejected by the writers of Proverbs.

> The violence of the wicked will sweep them away,
> because they refuse to do what is just (vs. 7).

Instead of being "realists" who believe that one may as well acknowledge that the mighty will get their way, this proverb affirms that those who practice violence will be defeated. In the long run only justice endures.

In the present world there is a search for order among nations. Many contend that there can be no peace without order. Order can come if one nation or group of nations rules the others by force—by violence. But that kind of order cannot live. It violates something basic in the structure of human relationships. He who trusts in might alone builds on sand. Only a just order can be an enduring order.

4. See Expos. on 29:23.
5. See Expos. on 6:1-15; 19:2.
6. See Expos. on 18:21.
7. See Expos. on vs. 3.
8. See Expos. on 3:21-26.
9. See Expos. on 31:10-31.

[5] I. 338C.

10 The soul of the wicked desireth evil: his neighbor findeth no favor in his eyes.

11 When the scorner is punished, the simple is made wise: and when the wise is instructed, he receiveth knowledge.

12 The righteous *man* wisely considereth the house of the wicked: *but God* overthroweth the wicked for *their* wickedness.

13 Whoso stoppeth his ears at the cry of the poor, he also shall cry himself, but shall not be heard.

14 A gift in secret pacifieth anger: and a reward in the bosom, strong wrath.

15 *It is* joy to the just to do judgment: but destruction *shall be* to the workers of iniquity.

16 The man that wandereth out of the way of understanding shall remain in the congregation of the dead.

10 The soul of the wicked desires evil;
his neighbor finds no mercy in his eyes.
11 When a scoffer is punished, the simple becomes wise;
when a wise man is instructed, he gains knowledge.
12 The righteous observes the house of the wicked;
the wicked are cast down to ruin.
13 He who closes his ear to the cry of the poor
will himself cry out and not be heard.
14 A gift in secret averts anger;
and a bribe in the bosom, strong wrath.
15 When justice is done, it is a joy to the righteous,
but dismay to evildoers.
16 A man who wanders from the way of understanding
will rest in the assembly of the dead.

---

rāḥābh **(wide)** for *ḥābhēr* (M.T.). W. F. Albright renders the term *bt-ḥbr* "granary," from a Ugaritic parallel (see "A New Hebrew Word for 'Glaze' in Proverbs 26:23," *Bulletin of the American Schools of Oriental Research,* No. 98 [April, 1945], p. 25, n. 3).

10. Synonymous. The fruits of wickedness extend beyond the wicked one to his neighbor.

11. Antithetic. The simple fool, who does not benefit by instruction like the wise man, learns by seeing the scorner punished for his wickedness (cf. 19:25). **Scoffer:** See Exeg. on 1:22. **Simple:** See Exeg. on 1:4. **Is instructed** (*haskîl*): See Exeg. on 1:3.

12. This difficult verse probably consists of two unconnected lines. Lit., "A righteous one regards the house of the wicked, overturning wicked ones to evil [ruin]." **The righteous man:** "One that is righteous," referring to God, with the ASV mg., Amer. Trans., Moffatt, and the American Jewish Translation, since only God can ruin the wicked (as stated in vs. 12*b*). But this designation of God is found only in Job 34:17. It is very uncertain here. **But God:** The KJV tries to solve the difficulty by inserting **God** as the subject of vs. 12*b* only. The translation of vs. 12*b* in the RSV and the ASV does not follow the Hebrew.

13. See Exeg. on 19:17 for the wise men's attitude toward the poor. **Not be heard:** Hebrew, "shall not be answered."

14. Both lines refer to the power of the bribe with men in position. This is a mere statement of fact; no moral implications are considered here, as in 17:23. **Pacifieth,** with the ASV, Amer. Trans., Moffatt, and the American Jewish Translation, reading *yekhappēr* or *yekhabbeh* ("extinguishes") instead of the verb of the Hebrew text, *yikhpeh,* **averts** (or "subdues").

15. Antithetic. **Joy** belongs to those who do justice; it cannot belong to evildoers because they know that if justice is done to them they will end in ruin. **Justice:** See Exeg. on 1:3. **Destruction: Dismay** is also a possible translation of *meḥittāh,* and probably a better one in contrast with **joy** of the first stich.

16. A fool, as well as a sinner, dies prematurely—the standard doctrine of that day. **Understanding** (*haskēl*): See Exeg. on 1:3. **Dead:** The inhabitants of Sheol.

---

10. See Expos. on 3:27-35.
11. See Expos. on 9:7-9.
12. See Expos. on 3:1-4.
13. See Expos. on 22:16*a*.
14. See Expos. on 18:16.
15. See Expos. on vs. 3.
16. See Expos. on 3:1-4.

17 He that loveth pleasure *shall be* a poor man: he that loveth wine and oil shall not be rich.

18 The wicked *shall be* a ransom for the righteous, and the transgressor for the upright.

19 *It is* better to dwell in the wilderness, than with a contentious and an angry woman.

20 *There is* treasure to be desired and oil in the dwelling of the wise; but a foolish man spendeth it up.

21 He that followeth after righteousness and mercy findeth life, righteousness, and honor.

22 A wise *man* scaleth the city of the mighty, and casteth down the strength of the confidence thereof.

23 Whoso keepeth his mouth and his tongue, keepeth his soul from troubles.

24 Proud *and* haughty scorner *is* his name, who dealeth in proud wrath.

25 The desire of the slothful killeth him; for his hands refuse to labor.

17 He who loves pleasure will be a poor man;
he who loves wine and oil will not be rich.
18 The wicked is a ransom for the righteous,
and the faithless for the upright.
19 It is better to live in a desert land
than with a contentious and fretful woman.
20 Precious treasure remains[h] in a wise man's dwelling,
but a foolish man devours it.
21 He who pursues righteousness and kindness
will find life[i] and honor.
22 A wise man scales the city of the mighty
and brings down the stronghold in which they trust.
23 He who keeps his mouth and his tongue
keeps himself out of trouble.
24 "Scoffer" is the name of the proud, haughty man
who acts with arrogant pride.
25 The desire of the sluggard kills him
for his hands refuse to labor.

[h] Gk: Heb *and oil*
[i] Gk: Heb *life and righteousness*

17. Synonymous. Against self-indulgence, especially at the table, which brings poverty. **Wine and oil** were used at a feast. The oil was used for personal adornment.

18. Synonymous. The bad suffer for the good; the idea is related to that of 11:8. **Ransom** (*kōpher*): The price of atonement, and then generally, as here, the means of reconciliation which atones for anyone. **Transgressor** or **faithless:** See Exeg. on 2:22.

19. See Exeg. on vs. 9. **Desert land:** *Midhbār* may refer to a sparsely settled pastureland.

20. Antithetic. **And oil:** The RSV omits, reading in its place, with LXX, something like *yishkōn,* **remains.** It makes for a smoother translation. The verse seems to refer to a wise man's provident amassing of wealth and a fool's squandering of it, although the Hebrew is obscure.

21. Righteousness: See Exeg. on 1:3. In vs. 21*b* this word is correctly omitted by the RSV with the LXX, since it probably slipped into the Hebrew text through a copyist's error. **Mercy** or **kindness:** See Exeg. on 3:3. **Life:** A long and happy life.

22. Synonymous. The power of wisdom is superior to that of human strength and material things.

23. Cf. 12:13. The **tongue** can get a man into all sorts of trouble (see Exeg. on 12:17).

24. According to the RSV and the ASV, the verse is a definition of the **Scoffer** (cf. 24:8). He sets himself up against the moral law (see Exeg. on 1:22).

25. In a humorous vein. The **sluggard** practically commits suicide by his refusal to provide for himself (see Exeg. on 19:24). **Desire:** For rest and ease.

17. See Expos. on 23:29-35.
18. See Expos. on 11:8.
19. See Expos. on 31:10-31.
20. See Expos. on 26:1, 3-12.
21. See Expos. on vs. 3.
22. See Expos. on 1:2.
23. See Expos. on 18:21.
24. See Expos. on 29:23.
25. See Expos. on 6:1-15.

26 He coveteth greedily all the day long: but the righteous giveth and spareth not.

27 The sacrifice of the wicked *is* abomination: how much more, *when* he bringeth it with a wicked mind?

28 A false witness shall perish: but the man that heareth speaketh constantly.

29 A wicked man hardeneth his face: but *as for* the upright, he directeth his way.

30 *There is* no wisdom nor understanding nor counsel against the LORD.

31 The horse *is* prepared against the day of battle: but safety *is* of the LORD.

26 All day long the wicked covets,[j]
but the righteous gives and does not hold back.
27 The sacrifice of the wicked is an abomination;
how much more when he brings it with evil intent.
28 A false witness will perish,
but the word of a man who hears will endure.
29 A wicked man puts on a bold face,
but an upright man considers[k] his ways.
30 No wisdom, no understanding, no counsel,
can avail against the LORD.
31 The horse is made ready for the day of battle,
but the victory belongs to the LORD.

22 A *good* name *is* rather to be chosen than great riches, *and* loving favor rather than silver and gold.

2 The rich and poor meet together: the LORD *is* the maker of them all.

22 A good name is to be chosen rather than great riches,
and favor is better than silver or gold.
2 The rich and the poor meet together;
the LORD is the maker of them all.

[j] Gk: Heb *all day long he covets covetously*
[k] Another reading is *establishes*

---

26. Coveteth greedily: Lit., "he desires desire," which is obscure. The RSV, with the LXX, supplies **the wicked** as subject and omits the noun "desire" which may have crept in by dittography. This rendering makes the antithesis more pointed.

27. The first stich is similar to 15:8*a*. Sacrifice without righteousness is an abomination (see Exeg. on 3:32) ; the more so when brought merely with the **evil intent** of being absolved from the punishment of his sin (with ASV mg.) . **Wicked mind** or **evil intent:** Lit., "plan" (*zimmāh*) , used in the O.T. in a bad sense.

28. Cf. 19:5, 9. Vs. 28*b* is obscure. Lit., "And a man who hears will speak for ever." The RSV and ASV have no basis in the Hebrew.

29. Antithetic. The brazen-faced person is inconsiderate of anyone else, doing whatever he wants without regard for the other fellow. The good man, anxious to do right, carefully considers his ways. **Directeth** or **considers:** With the LXX, reading *yābhîn* for *yākhîn;* both make good sense. **Upright:** See Exeg. on 12:15.

30. The three nouns in this verse are practically synonymous. No human wisdom can avail against God, who is the source of all true wisdom. **Can avail** is added to make better sense.

31. Antithetic. Victory is decided by God, no matter how strong the army may be. The **horse** was not too favorably looked upon by the religious leaders of Israel (cf. Ps. 20:7; Hos. 1:7; Zech. 9:10) . **Victory** is better than **safety.**

22:1. Synonymous. In regard to a good name, Pirke Aboth 4:17 reads: "There are three crowns, the crown of the Torah, the crown of the priesthood, and the crown of kingship, but the crown of a good name excels them all."

2. All men, no matter what their social status may be, are created by God (cf. 29:13) .

---

26. See Expos. on 18:16.
27. See Expos. on vs. 3.
28. See Expos. on 18:21.
29. See Expos. on 29:23.
30-31. See Expos. on 3:5-8.
22:1. See Expos. on 12:8.
2. See Expos. on 3:5-8.

3 A prudent *man* foreseeth the evil, and hideth himself: but the simple pass on, and are punished.

4 By humility *and* the fear of the LORD *are* riches, and honor, and life.

5 Thorns *and* snares *are* in the way of the froward: he that doth keep his soul shall be far from them.

6 Train up a child in the way he should go: and when he is old, he will not depart from it.

3 A prudent man sees danger and hides himself;
but the simple go on, and suffer for it.
4 The reward for humility and fear of the LORD
is riches and honor and life.
5 Thorns and snares are in the way of the perverse;
he who guards himself will keep far from them.
6 Train up a child in the way he should go,
and when he is old he will not depart from it.

---

3. Antithetic. Repeated in 27:12. A prudent man keeps himself out of trouble, whereas the fool (*pethî*) continues along the way in which danger lurks. **Prudent** (*'ārûm*): For the noun form of this root see Exeg. on 1:4. **Are punished** or **suffer:** Lit., "are fined."

4. **By humility** or, better, **the reward for humility: Humility** and **fear of the LORD** (see Exeg. on 1:7) are practically synonymous here. There is no copula between these two expressions in the Hebrew. The root meaning of the noun for **humility** (*'anāwāh*) is "to be bowed down," "afflicted"; see Exeg. on 14:21 (cf. also 15:33; 18:12). **Life:** See Exeg. on 3:2.

5. **Froward** or **perverse:** For *'iqqēsh* see Exeg. on 2:15.

6. This verse expresses one of the strong points of the Hebrew sages, viz., their insistence on the moral training of the child by the parents. This training must start early when the mind of the child is impressionable. The use of the rod is encouraged as part of the educational process (13:24; 19:18; 23:13-14). The greatest joy that parents can have is a wise son (23:15-16, 24); the most tragic sorrow is to have a foolish one (17:21, 25). **Train up:** The verb *ḥānakh* means "to dedicate" (cf. the feast of Hanukkah, celebrating the rededication of the temple in Jerusalem under the Maccabees in 165 B.C. [I Macc. 4:52 ff.]), and here only in the O.T., "to train."

---

3. ***Caution Is Sensible.***—A sensible man senses danger and avoids it. He uses caution. A simple man takes no precautions. He acts as if he were afraid of nothing. The result is that he may be the victim of circumstances which he should have feared and against which he should have prepared himself.

A lack of caution may be rooted in the commendable desire to overcome fear. Too many people go through life paralyzed by fear. Primitive man was haunted by many threats to his existence; modern man is not exempt from fears of many kinds. People are afraid of pain, of failure, of sickness and death. They are afraid of being unloved or unrecognized. They fear unemployment and poverty. Fear can go beyond the dread of particular evils and become a state of mind and a cast of character. A man may be fearful even when he cannot locate the object of his fear.

In an effort to conquer fear a man may become foolhardy. He may lose his capacity to distinguish between what is a true threat to his life and what is an imagined enemy of his welfare. So he goes forward as if he had nothing to fear, with the result that he is not prepared to avoid danger. Overcoming fear is more than becoming foolhardy and throwing caution to the winds.

Obviously there are some things that every man ought to fear. A wholesome respect for danger will give a man the incentive to avoid it. Fear has biological value when it impels a creature to avoid danger and to flee from it. Starbuck in *Moby Dick* stated the case simply when he said, "I will have no man in my boat who is not afraid of a whale." [6] The mere overconfident assertion that he is afraid of nothing will hardly give a man the caution that is needed in the presence of real danger.

4. See Expos. on 3:1-4; 29:23.

5. See Expos. on 3:21-26.

6. See Expos. on 17:6.

[6] Ch. xxvi.

7 The rich ruleth over the poor, and the borrower *is* servant to the lender.

8 He that soweth iniquity shall reap vanity: and the rod of his anger shall fail.

9 He that hath a bountiful eye shall be blessed; for he giveth of his bread to the poor.

10 Cast out the scorner, and contention shall go out; yea, strife and reproach shall cease.

11 He that loveth pureness of heart, *for* the grace of his lips the king *shall be* his friend.

12 The eyes of the LORD preserve knowledge; and he overthroweth the words of the transgressor.

13 The slothful *man* saith, *There is* a lion without, I shall be slain in the streets.

14 The mouth of strange women *is* a deep pit: he that is abhorred of the LORD shall fall therein.

7 The rich rules over the poor,
and the borrower is the slave of the lender.
8 He who sows injustice will reap calamity,
and the rod of his fury will fail.
9 He who has a bountiful eye will be blessed,
for he shares his bread with the poor.
10 Drive out a scoffer, and strife will go out,
and quarreling and abuse will cease.
11 He who loves purity of heart,
and whose speech is gracious, will have the king as his friend.
12 The eyes of the LORD keep watch over knowledge,
but he overthrows the words of the faithless.
13 The sluggard says, "There is a lion outside!
I shall be slain in the streets!"
14 The mouth of a loose woman is a deep pit;
he with whom the LORD is angry will fall into it.

---

7. Synonymous. See Exeg. on 10:2.

8. Synonymous. The law of retribution. **Vanity** or **calamity:** The KJV is better than the RSV here on account of the parallelism, although both renderings make good sense. **Rod of his anger:** The rod which the sower of iniquity makes another one feel. After this verse the LXX inserts two lines, the first of which reads, "A man who is cheerful and a giver God blesseth." This seems to be a paraphrase of vs. 9*a* in the Hebrew text. It is the basis of Paul's words in II Cor. 9:7, "For God loveth a cheerful giver."

9. See Exeg. on 19:17. **Bountiful eye:** Lit., "good of eye."

10. Synonymous. **Scoffer:** See Exeg. on 1:22.

11. An apparently defective Hebrew text. Lit., "He who loves purity [the pure] of heart, the grace of his lips a king is his friend." **Whose speech is gracious:** *Ḥēn sᵉphāthâw* has no grammatical connection in the sentence. The RSV seems to make the best sense out of the text.

12. Antithetic. Vs. 12*a* is difficult. The **eyes of the LORD** usually "rest upon" or "are directed toward" an object; to say that the eyes **preserve,** or "guard," an abstract thing like **knowledge** is indeed strange; the translation of the ASV, "him that hath knowledge" for *dă'ath,* is impossible. No satisfactory solution of these problems seems to be at hand. **Transgressor** or **faithless:** See Exeg. on 2:22.

13. In a humorous vein. Similar to 26:13. This is an excuse that the sluggard gives for remaining at ease (see Exeg. on 19:24).

14. Cf. 23:27. **Strange women** or **loose woman:** See Exeg. on 2:16. **Abhorred** or, better, **angry:** The Lord is angry with the one who consorts with the adulteress.

---

7. See Expos. on 10:15-16.
8. See Expos. on 3:1-4.
9. See Expos. on 3:9-10.
10. See Expos. on 26:21.
11. See Expos. on 18:21.
12. See Expos. on 3:1-4.
13. See Expos. on 6:1-15.
14. See Expos. on 31:10-31.

15 Foolishness *is* bound in the heart of a child; *but* the rod of correction shall drive it far from him.

16 He that oppresseth the poor to increase his *riches, and* he that giveth to the rich, *shall* surely *come* to want.

17 Bow down thine ear, and hear the words of the wise, and apply thine heart unto my knowledge.

15 Folly is bound up in the heart of a child,
but the rod of discipline drives it far from him.
16 He who oppresses the poor to increase his own wealth,
or gives to the rich, will only come to want.

17 Incline your ear, and hear the words of the wise,
and apply your mind to my knowledge;

---

15. Cf. 13:24. In regard to the problem of education see Exeg. on 22:6. **Discipline:** See Exeg. on 1:2.

16. A difficult verse because of the ambiguity of the Hebrew. Numerous interpretations have been given to it. The KJV, RSV, and ASV mean that both the oppression of the poor and the courting of the rich lead to poverty.

III. The Sayings of the Wise (22:17–24:34)

This part of Proverbs resembles chs. 1–9 in that the pupil or son is addressed mainly in strophes of four lines rather than in the form of the couplet which characterized 10:1–22:16. It may be divided as follows: A. Introduction (22:17-21); B. First collection (22:22–23:14); C. Second collection (23:15–24:22); and D. Third collection (24:23-34).

A. Introduction (22:17-21)

17. The expression **the words of the wise** stands at the head of the verse in the LXX, and probably served as a heading for the section. After **hear** should come "my words" (*debhāray* instead of *dibhrê* of M.T.) with the LXX. The parallel from Amen-em-ope reads:

---

15. See Expos. on 17:6.

16a. The Exploitative Personality.—Here is a typical example of the exploitative personality. He uses people for his own ends. He treats people as objects to be used, rather than as subjects to be respected. History has many instances of "man's inhumanity to man" stemming from the lack of regard for the rights of others. There is nothing commendable about exploiting the resources of nature, but there is something far less commendable when one individual exploits another. Such human exploitation achieves a demonic dimension when individuals are exploited by groups, or when a state treats its citizens only as objects to be used for the glorification of the nation.

Immanuel Kant saw in this relationship between persons, each of whom is an end in himself, an unconditional command upon everyone. "So act as to treat humanity," he said, "whether in thine own person or in that of any other, in every case as an end withal, never as means only." [7] In commenting on this maxim, W. E. Hocking says:

> This is one of the most impressive formulations of our moral common sense that has ever been made. We recognize at once its force and its effect. Besides defining accurately that element of underlying equality (running through all the inequalities among men) which is the basis of all legal right, and therefore of all equity and justice, it forbids all forms of what we call "exploitation." [8]

The sages further affirmed that those who have been exploited will be defended by God.

> Do not rob the poor, because he is poor,
> or crush the afflicted at the gate;
> for the Lord will plead their cause
> and despoil of life those who despoil them (vss. 22-23).

God helps those who cannot help themselves. When human beings are exploited, an affront has been committed against God, since he has made them as ends and not as objects to be used.

17-21. See Expos. on 2:1-22.

[7] *Fundamental Principles of the Metaphysics of Morals*, tr. T. K. Abbott (6th ed.; London: Longmans, Green & Co., 1909), p. 47.

[8] *Types of Philosophy* (New York: Charles Scribner's Sons, 1929), p. 311.

18 For *it is* a pleasant thing if thou keep them within thee; they shall withal be fitted in thy lips.

19 That thy trust may be in the LORD, I have made known to thee this day, even to thee.

20 Have not I written to thee excellent things in counsels and knowledge,

21 That I might make thee know the certainty of the words of truth; that thou mightest answer the words of truth to them that send unto thee?

22 Rob not the poor, because he *is* poor: neither oppress the afflicted in the gate:

18 for it will be pleasant if you keep them
within you,
if all of them are ready on your lips.
19 That your trust may be in the LORD,
I have made them known to you today,
even to you.
20 Have I not written for you thirty sayings
of admonition and knowledge,
21 to show you what is right and true,
that you may give a true answer to
those who sent you?

22 Do not rob the poor, because he is poor,
or crush the afflicted at the gate;

Give thine ear, and hear what I say,
And apply thine heart to apprehend.

18. Within thee: Lit., "in thy belly." **All of them:** Lit., "together" **(withal).** The word is meaningless here in the Hebrew. The Egyptian parallel also has a word whose meaning is not clear. It is translated "peg" (Gressmann) or "mooring-mast" (Griffith), as quoted by Oesterley. The corresponding passage in Amen-em-ope reads as follows (see Oesterley, *Proverbs,* p. 189):

It is good to place them in thine heart,
—Woe to him that refuseth them—
Let them rest in the casket of thy belly,
That they may be a threshold in thy heart;
That if a hurricane of words arise,
They may act as a peg upon thy tongue.

19. In vs. 19*b* the addition of **them** (RSV) makes the sense clearer.

20. Excellent things: More correctly, **thirty sayings.** The meaning of the heretofore unknown שלשום is now clear from the Egyptian parallel in Amen-em-ope, which reads, "Consider these thirty chapters." It has been pointed out that there are exactly thirty sayings in the section 22:22–24:22 (see *ibid.,* p. 192).

21. Obviously a corrupt text. "To make thee know truth, words of truth, to return words, truth, to thy sender." The first **truth** is an Aramaic word (*qōshṭ*) which was doubtlessly a marginal gloss that slipped into the text. **Truth** in vs. 21*b* also seems to overcrowd the line, and probably crept in by dittography from the first stich. The verse should probably read: "To make thee know words of truth so that thou mightest answer [lit., return words] those who send you," the latter phrase usually interpreted to mean the parents who send the child to school. In the light of Amen-em-ope, however, it seems to refer simply to the messenger who is to bring a true report back to those who sent him (see Exeg. on 13:17). The Egyptian parallel reads:

Knowledge how to answer him that speaketh,
And (how) to carry back a report to one that hath sent him.

B. First Collection (22:22–23:14)

These proverbs are closely similar to those in The Teaching of Amen-em-ope (see Intro., pp. 768-69).

22-23. Synonymous. It would be a dastardly act to rob the poor of the little he has.

22-23. See Expos. on vs. 16*a*.

23 For the LORD will plead their cause, and spoil the soul of those that spoiled them.

24 Make no friendship with an angry man; and with a furious man thou shalt not go;

25 Lest thou learn his ways, and get a snare to thy soul.

26 Be not thou *one* of them that strike hands, *or* of them that are sureties for debts.

27 If thou hast nothing to pay, why should he take away thy bed from under thee?

28 Remove not the ancient landmark, which thy fathers have set.

29 Seest thou a man diligent in his business? he shall stand before kings; he shall not stand before mean *men*.

23 When thou sittest to eat with a ruler, consider diligently what *is* before thee:

23 for the LORD will plead their cause
and despoil of life those who despoil them.
24 Make no friendship with a man given to anger,
nor go with a wrathful man,
25 lest you learn his ways
and entangle yourself in a snare.
26 Be not one of those who give pledges,
who become surety for debts.
27 If you have nothing with which to pay,
why should your bed be taken from under you?
28 Remove not the ancient landmark
which your fathers have set.
29 Do you see a man skilful in his work?
he will stand before kings;
he will not stand before obscure men.

23 When you sit down to eat with a ruler,
observe carefully what[l] is before you;

[l] Or *who*

Afflicted: See Exeg. on 14:21; 22:4. **Gate:** The place where justice was dispensed. **Despoil:** The exact meaning of *qābha'* is unknown. From its contexts in the O.T. (here; Mal. 3:8-9) it must mean something like "to rob." The Egyptian parallel to vs. 22 reads:

> Beware of robbing the poor,
> And of being valorous against the afflicted.

Vs. 23 has no parallel in Amen-em-ope since it is a peculiarly Hebrew observation.

24. Synonymous. See Exeg. on 15:18. **A man given to anger:** Lit., "owner of anger." **Wrathful man:** Lit., "man of wraths," the plural of the noun being used to denote intensity. The Egyptian parallel is very close:

> Associate not with a passionate man,
> Nor approach him for conversation.

25. **Learn:** A rare word, *'ālaph,* "to learn by association," found only here and three times in Job.

26. Synonymous. See Exeg. on 6:1 for these terms.

27. **Take away:** The RSV reads different vowels in this verbal form, **be taken.**

28. This is a simple couplet, very rare in this section. A boundary was held to be sacred in the ancient world (cf. Deut. 19:14; see Exeg. on 23:10-11 for the Egyptian parallel).

29. Triplet. **Diligent** or, better, **skillful:** The word *māhîr* is used of a scribe in Ps. 45:1 and Ezra 7:6, and so evidently here. The Egyptian parallel corroborates this view:

> A scribe who is skilful in his business
> Findeth himself worthy to be a courtier.

Mean men or **obscure men:** The root meaning is "to be dark."

23:1-3. Concerning good table manners. **What is,** with ancient versions and the

24-25. See Expos. on 16:32.
26-27. See Expos. on 6:1-15.
28. See Expos. on 10:1.
29. See Expos. on 6:1-15.
23:1-3. See Expos. on 16:10-15.

2 And put a knife to thy throat, if thou *be* a man given to appetite.
3 Be not desirous of his dainties: for they *are* deceitful meat.
4 Labor not to be rich: cease from thine own wisdom.
5 Wilt thou set thine eyes upon that which is not? for *riches* certainly make themselves wings; they fly away as an eagle toward heaven.

2 and put a knife to your throat
if you are a man given to appetite.
3 Do not desire his delicacies,
for they are deceptive food.
4 Do not toil to acquire wealth;
be wise enough to desist.
5 When your eyes light upon it, it is gone;
for suddenly it takes to itself wings,
flying like an eagle toward heaven.

Egyptian parallel; the ASV "him that . . ." is possible, but evidently not what is meant here. **Put a knife:** A figurative way of expressing self-restraint in eating. **Appetite:** Lit., "soul" (see Exeg. on 13:25).

Vs. 3*a*=vs. 6*b*. The hospitality of a ruler cannot always be trusted, for he may have ulterior motives. **Deceptive food:** Lit., "bread of lies."

The Egyptian parallel passage (*ibid.*, p. 198) reads:

> Eat not bread in the presence of a ruler,
> And do not lunge forward (?) with thy mouth before a governor (?).
> When thou art replenished with that to which thou hast no right,
> It is only a delight to thy spittle.
> Look upon the dish that is before thee,
> And let that (alone) supply thy need.

There are obviously many differences between this passage and the one in Proverbs, yet there is also a basic similarity between them. In Ecclus. 31:12-18 there is a similar passage dealing with table manners:

> Do you sit at a great table?
> Do not gulp at it,
> And do not say, "How much there is on it!"
> Remember that an envious eye is wrong.
> . . . .
> Do not reach out your hand wherever it looks,
> And do not crowd your neighbor in the dish;
> Be considerate of him of your own accord,
> And be thoughtful in everything.
> Eat like a human being what is served to you,
> Do not champ your food, or you will be detested.
> Be the first to leave off for good manners' sake,
> And do not be greedy, or you will give offense.
> Even though you are seated in a large company,
> Do not be the first to help yourself (Amer. Trans.).

See also Ecclus. 41:19*c*, "Be ashamed to lean on your elbow at table."

4. Synonymous. See Exeg. on 10:2. **Toil** is better than **labor. From thine own wisdom:** The RSV **be wise enough** makes the sense clearer if the Hebrew text is retained.

5. The RSV evidently deletes the first consonant of the Hebrew text, which is the sign of a question. The transitoriness of riches is here described. Vs. 5*a* reads, lit., "Shall thine eyes [eye] fly to it, and it is gone?" Toy and Oesterley think that the whole stich may be a gloss. If omitted, vss. 4-5 would then be composed of the usual four lines. The Egyptian passage (translated by Oesterley, *op. cit.*, p. 200) which seems to have suggested this thought to the Hebrew sage is much longer. Only the lines directly connected with the thought in the Hebrew text are given here:

4-5. See Expos. on 10:15-16.

6 Eat thou not the bread of *him that hath* an evil eye, neither desire thou his dainty meats:
7 For as he thinketh in his heart, so *is* he: Eat and drink, saith he to thee; but his heart *is* not with thee.
8 The morsel *which* thou hast eaten shalt thou vomit up, and lose thy sweet words.
9 Speak not in the ears of a fool: for he will despise the wisdom of thy words.
10 Remove not the old landmark; and enter not into the fields of the fatherless:
11 For their Redeemer *is* mighty; he shall plead their cause with thee.

6 Do not eat the bread of a man who is stingy;
do not desire his delicacies;
7 for he is like one who is inwardly reckoning.[m]
"Eat and drink!" he says to you;
but his heart is not with you.
8 You will vomit up the morsels which you have eaten,
and waste your pleasant words.
9 Do not speak in the hearing of a fool,
for he will despise the wisdom of your words.
10 Do not remove an ancient landmark
or enter the fields of the fatherless;
11 for their Redeemer is strong;
he will plead their cause against you.

[m] Heb obscure

Toil not after riches
When thy needs are made sure to thee.
. . . .
(Or) they have made for themselves wings like geese,
And have flown into the heavens.

6. Synonymous. **An evil eye:** The RSV gives the sense of the phrase, **who is stingy** (cf. 28:22).

7-8. Concerning the greedy man. Vs. 7*a* is obscure. The verb *shāʿar* is unknown except in later Jewish sources, where it means "to reckon," "to estimate." The Amer. Trans. substitutes here a line from Amen-em-ope.

According to the Egyptian parallel the references to food here should be taken figuratively. One would hardly suspect that from the Hebrew text alone. Only vss. 6 and 8 seem to have Egyptian parallels (*ibid.*, pp. 201-2):

Covet not the goods of a dependent,
And hunger not after his bread.
. . . .
When thou failest before thy chief,
And art embarrassed in thine utterances,
Thy flatteries are answered by curses,
And thy obeisances by beating.
Thou swallowest (indeed) thy too great mouthful, and must vomit it forth again,
And thus art emptied of thy good.

9. A single couplet. **Wisdom:** See Exeg. on 12:8. The Egyptian parallel is:

Empty not thine inmost soul to everybody,
Nor spoil (thereby) thine influence.

10. Synonymous.

11. Cf. 22:28. The sacred boundary prevents the poor from being encroached upon. The Lord is called the *gôʼēl* here, i.e., the one who redeems his kinsman's land (cf. Lev. 25:25; Ruth 4:1-8). The corresponding passage in Amen-em-ope has some interesting parallels (see Intro., p. 769). It will be noted that just as God is the protector of the

6-8. See Expos. on 22:16*a*.
9. See Expos. on 26:1, 3-12.
10-11. See Expos. on 22:16*a*.

12 Apply thine heart unto instruction, and thine ears to the words of knowledge.
13 Withhold not correction from the child: for *if* thou beatest him with the rod, he shall not die.
14 Thou shalt beat him with the rod, and shalt deliver his soul from hell.
15 My son, if thine heart be wise, my heart shall rejoice, even mine.
16 Yea, my reins shall rejoice, when thy lips speak right things.
17 Let not thine heart envy sinners: but *be thou* in the fear of the LORD all the day long.
18 For surely there is an end; and thine expectation shall not be cut off.
19 Hear thou, my son, and be wise, and guide thine heart in the way.
20 Be not among winebibbers; among riotous eaters of flesh:
21 For the drunkard and the glutton shall come to poverty: and drowsiness shall clothe *a man* with rags.

12 Apply your mind to instruction
and your ear to words of knowledge.
13 Do not withhold discipline from a child;
if you beat him with a rod, he will not die.
14 If you beat him with the rod
you will save his life from Sheol.
15 My son, if your heart is wise,
my heart too will be glad.
16 My soul will rejoice
when your lips speak what is right.
17 Let not your heart envy sinners,
but continue in the fear of the LORD all the day.
18 Surely there is a future,
and your hope will not be cut off.

19 Hear, my son, and be wise,
and direct your mind in the way.
20 Be not among winebibbers,
or among gluttonous eaters of meat;
21 for the drunkard and the glutton will come to poverty,
and drowsiness will clothe a man with rags.

---

weak in the Hebrew passage, so the Egyptians depended upon the moon-god (Thoth) for protection against the violator of property rights.

12. Synonymous. A similar appeal is found in 22:17. **Instruction:** See Exeg. on 1:2.

13-14. Cf. 19:18; on the education of children see Exeg. on 22:6. **Discipline:** See Exeg. on 1:2. **Hell** or, better, **Sheol:** See Exeg. on 1:12.

C. Second Collection (23:15–24:22)

These proverbs are addressed to "my son," and the style of composition changes from the single proverb to the longer discourse composed of several verses.

15-16. My son: See Exeg. on 1:8. **Reins** or **soul:** Lit., "kidneys," regarded by the Hebrews as the seat of the emotions. In this verse the teacher is rejoicing at the progress his pupil is making (cf. 27:11*a*). **Right things:** See Exeg. on 1:3, where the word is translated "equity."

17. Antithetic. **Be thou:** The RSV supplies **continue** to make a smoother translation. **Fear of the LORD:** See Exeg. on 1:7.

18. Cf. Pss. 37; 73. **End** or **future** ("reward" ASV): Here the word *'aḥarîth* denotes the outcome of the righteous man's life, i.e., reward. It is the end which crowns all that has gone before (see Exeg. on 5:4; 19:20). Vs. 18*b*=24:14*b*. **Expectation** or **hope:** I.e., for long life and prosperity.

19-21. Synonymous. See Exeg. on 23:29 in regard to drunkenness. **Mind:** See Exeg. on 2:2. **The way:** Cf. John 14:6. This is the only time that this term is used in an undefined sense in Proverbs. **Gluttonous eaters:** Lit., "those who are lavish with flesh," as also in vs. 21. **Drowsiness** comes from overeating and overdrinking.

12-14. See Expos. on 17:6.
15-16. See Expos. on 1:8-9; 10:1.
17-18. See Expos. on 1:7; 27:4.
19-21. See Expos. on vss. 29-35.

22 Hearken unto thy father that begat
thee, and despise not thy mother when she
is old.
23 Buy the truth, and sell *it* not; *also*
wisdom, and instruction, and understanding.
24 The father of the righteous shall
greatly rejoice: and he that begetteth a wise
child shall have joy of him.
25 Thy father and thy mother shall be
glad, and she that bare thee shall rejoice.
26 My son, give me thine heart, and let
thine eyes observe my ways.
27 For a whore *is* a deep ditch; and a
strange woman *is* a narrow pit.
28 She also lieth in wait as *for* a prey, and
increaseth the transgressors among men.
29 Who hath woe? who hath sorrow? who
hath contentions? who hath babbling? who
hath wounds without cause? who hath redness of eyes?

22 Hearken to your father who begot you,
and do not despise your mother when she is old.
23 Buy truth, and do not sell it;
buy wisdom, instruction, and understanding.

24 The father of the righteous will greatly rejoice;
he who begets a wise son will be glad in him.
25 Let your father and mother be glad,
let her who bore you rejoice.

26 My son, give me your heart,
and let your eyes observe[n] my ways.
27 For a harlot is a deep pit;
an adventuress is a narrow well.
28 She lies in wait like a robber
and increases the faithless among men.

29 Who has woe? Who has sorrow?
Who has strife? Who has complaining?
Who has wounds without cause?
Who has redness of eyes?

[n] Another reading is *delight in*

22-23. Synonymous.

24-25. Wise children make parents happy. On education in Proverbs see Exeg. on 22:6.

26-28. Synonymous. Against harlotry. This vice is dealt with at great length in the first section of the book, chs. 1–9, especially chs. 5; 7; 9. **Heart:** The mind or the attention of the youth (see Exeg. on 2:2). **Observe** is the reading of the Hebrew margin. The text has **delight in** (so RSV mg.). **Strange woman** or **adventuress:** Cf. 22:14. The rendering **for a prey,** with ASV mg., may be ignored. The RSV, **robber,** is correct.

29-35. Drunkenness condemned. The wise men of Israel were keenly aware of the dangers that lurk in strong drink. It should be generally avoided as a bad thing (20:1). The physical tortures of the alcoholic are graphically described in these verses. Excessive drinking brings poverty and disgrace (vss. 20-21). Strong drink should be avoided by

---

22-25. See Expos. on 1:8-9; 10:1.

26-28. See Expos. on 5:1-23.

29-35. ***The Plight of the Alcoholic.***—The writer of this poem paints the plight of the drunkard in vivid terms. The excessive use of alcohol was a problem in that day as well as in this. By picturing the unhappy condition of the intoxicated man, the sage hoped to provide the incentive for leaving the sparkling cup alone.

Intoxicating liquor may give some momentary pleasure, but it has so many unpleasant consequences that only folly would make a man persist in its use. It may go down **smoothly;** but

**At the last it bites like a serpent,
and stings like an adder.**

The thrill of the moment hardly compensates for the dreary prospect of the aftermath that follows drunkenness.

The resort to the excessive use of alcohol is generally more than the satisfying of a physiological craving. Alcoholism is usually a form of escape from an unpleasant or intolerable situation. When life becomes unduly burdensome, when the individual is crushed by a sense of inferiority or frustration, when circumstances seem to place too heavy a load upon him, he looks for some way of escape. He hungers for temporary oblivion. He wants "to get away from it all." An English laborer for whom life had become meaningless said that getting drunk was "the quickest way out of Manchester." Intoxica-

30 They that tarry long at the wine; they that go to seek mixed wine.
31 Look not thou upon the wine when it is red, when it giveth his color in the cup, *when* it moveth itself aright.
32 At the last it biteth like a serpent, and stingeth like an adder.

30 Those who tarry long over wine,
those who go to try mixed wine.
31 Do not look at wine when it is red,
when it sparkles in the cup
and goes down smoothly.
32 At the last it bites like a serpent,
and stings like an adder.

---

men in high places who need their mental faculties in times of decision (31:4-5). Yet the Hebrew sage also believed that wine was a source of joy and comfort for the despairing and the dying (31:6-7). Notice likewise how the author of Ecclus. 31:25-30 discusses in the same passage the curses and benefits which come from wine:

Do not play the man about wine,
For wine has been the ruin of many.
The furnace proves the steel's temper by dipping it;
So wine tests hearts when proud men quarrel.
Wine is like life to men
If you drink it in moderation;
What life has a man who is without wine?
For it was created to give gladness to men.
An exhilaration to the heart and gladness to the soul
Is wine, drunk at the proper time and in sufficient quantity;
Bitterness to the soul is much drinking of wine
Amidst irritation and conflict.
Drunkenness increases the anger of a foolish man to his injury,
Reducing his strength and causing wounds (Amer. Trans.).

29. The effects of drunkenness are graphically described. The first line has interjections in the Hebrew, "Who has Oh! Who has Alas!" (with ASV mg.). **Redness:** A slightly different form of the word occurs in Gen. 49:12. It may also refer to the "dimming" of the eyes (cf. ASV mg.).

30. Synonymous. **Seek:** Better, **try,** as a connoisseur. **Mixed:** With spices.

31. Giveth his color or, better, **sparkles:** Lit., "gives its eye" (cf. Ezek. 1:4, 7). **Moveth . . . aright** or **goes down smoothly:** Lit., "goes straight" (cf. Song of S. 7:9). The word translated "straight" here is the same one that is translated "equity" in 1:3.

32. Synonymous. **At the last:** Lit., "its end" (see Exeg. on 5:4). **Stings:** The meaning of *pārash* is unknown; from the parallelism it must mean something like "bites" or "poisons" (LXX).

---

tion makes a man temporarily insensitive to trouble. The writer of the poem here discussed depicts a man who can be struck without feeling pain. He may be beaten without knowing it. For all practical purposes he has indulged in some self-anesthetization. For the time being he is "out," so that he is no longer conscious of an unbearable situation.

Another writer, while emphasizing the thought that rulers and people in positions of authority ought not to use strong drink, suggests that one ought to give wine "to him who is perishing," and "to those in bitter distress" (31:6).

That as he drinks he may forget his poverty,
And think no more of his misery (31:7 Amer. Trans.).

"As he drinks he may forget." This is the incentive for much drinking. It is a method of forgetting when life becomes too burdensome; but bitter is the return to the world of reality. The method of combating such alcoholism can hardly be limited to portraying the ill effects of a drunken spree. There is need to help people understand their feelings of inferiority and defeat, to help find more adequate ways of dealing with them. Some forms of escape mean only jumping from the frying pan into the fire. While the alcoholic can forget for a little time, he always comes back to face life again through eyes that are blurred with redness. A change in drinking habits can hardly occur unless such a man has a change in his life philosophy.

The problems of alcoholism take on new

33 Thine eyes shall behold strange women, and thine heart shall utter perverse things.

34 Yea, thou shalt be as he that lieth down in the midst of the sea, or as he that lieth upon the top of a mast.

35 They have stricken me, *shalt thou say, and* I was not sick; they have beaten me, *and* I felt *it* not: when shall I awake? I will seek it yet again.

24 Be not thou envious against evil men, neither desire to be with them:

33 Your eyes will see strange things,
and your mind utter perverse things.
34 You will be like one who lies down in the midst of the sea,
like one who lies on the top of a mast.[o]
35 "They struck me," you will say,[p] "but I was not hurt;
they beat me, but I did not feel it.
When shall I awake?
I will seek another drink."

24 Be not envious of evil men,
nor desire to be with them;

[o] Heb obscure
[p] Gk Syr Vg Tg: Heb lacks *you will say*

33. Synonymous. **Strange women** or, better, **strange things:** The word *zārôth* can mean either, but the context seems to favor the latter. **Perverse:** See Exeg. on 2:12.

34. Synonymous. The ground heaves up and down like the sea. The drunkard can no longer stand up. **Mast:** The meaning of *ḥibbēl* is unknown. The translation is merely a conjecture.

35. The drunkard had a fight but he does not feel any bad effects. In fact, he starts looking for the next drink immediately upon becoming a bit sober. **Shalt thou say:** Not found in the Hebrew text, but the versions have it.

24:1-2. Cf. 3:31; 23:17. **Heart** or **minds:** See Exeg. on 2:2. **Destruction:** Better, **violence.**

dimensions in a machine age. The social consequences of drinking are more serious when the drinker is at the wheel of a fast-moving automobile, or when he is an engineer guiding a speeding streamlined train, or when he is a surgeon with a sharp instrument in his hand. The sage who insisted that rulers and princes should refrain from drinking wine saw that their position of responsibility made it necessary for them to have clear minds. They might too easily pervert justice if they were under the influence of liquor. Today the number of those in positions where they can affect the lives of others is vastly increased. The evil consequences of drunkenness do not fall on the drunken man alone. The very lives of innocent people are jeopardized by those whose minds are darkened and whose reactions are impaired under the influence of alcohol.

The problem of alcoholism is made more serious in nations where liquor is sold for private profit. The distiller and the brewer must sell their products. They must try to produce consumers for their goods. Their aim is to make attractive the taking of strong drink. The resources of the printer's art and the advertising writer's cleverness are used to make drinking socially acceptable and the mark of a stalwart man's accomplishments. The O.T. prophet would hardly be impressed by the modern presentation of portraits of users of liquor.

Woe to those who are brave—
at drinking!
mighty at—mixing a bowl! (Isa. 5:22 Moffatt.)

One method of resisting the trend toward alcoholism is to make it impossible for anyone to derive a profit by selling alcoholic beverages. It may be a man's business as to whether or not he wants to drink, but it ought not to be somebody's business to encourage him to drink in order to produce a profit for the liquor merchant. No single method has been able to solve this whole perplexing problem. Prohibiting the sale of liquor by law is not effective if there is no general disposition to support the law. Only as there is an undergirding of a legal enactment by a community sentiment can law be effective in dealing with the small proportion of violators who might try to fly in the face of the wishes of a large majority.

The writer of the poem in this chapter of Proverbs seems to be advocating total abstinence. **Do not look at wine when it is red** (vs. 31). The best way to avoid the evil consequences of drinking too much is not to drink at all. Winston Churchill says he once asked Bernard Shaw, "Do you really never drink any wine at all?" Shaw replied, "I am hard enough to keep in order as it is." [6]

24:1-4. See Expos. on 27:4.

[6] *Great Contemporaries* (New York: G. P. Putnam's Sons, 1937), p. 35.

2 For their heart studieth destruction,
and their lips talk of mischief.
3 Through wisdom is a house builded;
and by understanding it is established:
4 And by knowledge shall the chambers
be filled with all precious and pleasant
riches.
5 A wise man *is* strong; yea, a man of
knowledge increaseth strength.
6 For by wise counsel thou shalt make
thy war: and in multitude of counselors
there is safety.
7 Wisdom *is* too high for a fool: he
openeth not his mouth in the gate.
8 He that deviseth to do evil shall be
called a mischievous person.
9 The thought of foolishness *is* sin: and
the scorner *is* an abomination to men.
10 *If* thou faint in the day of adversity,
thy strength *is* small.
11 If thou forbear to deliver *them that
are* drawn unto death, and *those that are*
ready to be slain;

2 for their minds devise violence,
and their lips talk of mischief.
3 By wisdom a house is built,
and by understanding it is established;
4 by knowledge the rooms are filled
with all precious and pleasant riches.
5 A wise man is mightier than a strong man,[q]
and a man of knowledge than he who has strength;
6 for by wise guidance you can wage your war,
and in abundance of counselors there is victory.
7 Wisdom is too high for a fool;
in the gate he does not open his mouth.

8 He who plans to do evil
will be called a mischief-maker.
9 The devising of folly is sin,
and the scoffer is an abomination to men.

10 If you faint in the day of adversity,
your strength is small.
11 Rescue those who are being taken away to death;
hold back those who are stumbling to the slaughter.

[q] Gk Compare Syr Tg: Heb *is in strength*

3. Synonymous. **Wisdom** and **understanding:** See Exeg. on 1:2.

4. Cf. 9:1; 14:1. Literally, as well as figuratively, wisdom helps to build a house.

5-6. Synonymous. Wars are won by wisdom. With the LXX, the RSV reads both stichs of vs. 5 as comparisons, which makes better sense. Vs. 6*a* is similar to 20:18*b*, and vs. 6*b*=11:14*b* (see Exeg.). **Victory:** The word *teshû'āh* means basically "deliverance," "salvation." Where there is deliverance from the enemy, there is **victory,** and thus **safety.**

7. A difficult verse. **High:** Reading *rāmôth* for the M.T. *rā'môth* ("corals"). It must be further interpreted to mean **too high. Wisdom** (*ḥokhmôth*): See Exeg. on 1:20. **Gate:** See Exeg. on 1:21.

8. Mischief-maker: Lit., "lord of plans" (see Exeg. on 1:4, where the word "plans" is translated "discretion").

9. Synonymous. **Thought** or **devising:** Lit., "plan," a play on words here with *zimmāh* in this verse and *mezimmāh* in vs. 8 (see Exeg. on 21:27 for the former word). **Abomination:** See Exeg. on 3:32. **Scoffer:** See Exeg. on 1:22.

10. If one is lax in difficult times, he does not have much strength. **Faint:** Lit., "show thyself slack." **Small:** Lit., "narrow" (*çar*). Again a play on words, since adversity is *çārāh.*

11. Synonymous. Does this verse refer to the oppressed or to those who are condemned to death because of political intrigue or judicial sentence? Probably the former, since

5-6. See Expos. on 11:14.
7-9. See Expos. on 26:1, 3-12.
10. See Expos. on 6:1-15.
11-12. See Expos. on 14:21.

12 If thou sayest, Behold, we knew it not; doth not he that pondereth the heart consider *it?* and he that keepeth thy soul, doth *not* he know *it?* and shall *not* he render to *every* man according to his works?

13 My son, eat thou honey, because *it is* good; and the honeycomb, *which is* sweet to thy taste:

14 So *shall* the knowledge of wisdom *be* unto thy soul: when thou hast found *it,* then there shall be a reward, and thy expectation shall not be cut off.

15 Lay not wait, O wicked *man,* against the dwelling of the righteous; spoil not his resting place:

16 For a just *man* falleth seven times, and riseth up again: but the wicked shall fall into mischief.

12 If you say, "Behold, we did not know this,"
does not he who weighs the heart perceive it?
Does not he who keeps watch over your soul know it,
and will he not requite man according to his work?

13 My son, eat honey, for it is good,
and the drippings of the honeycomb are sweet to your taste.
14 Know that wisdom is such to your soul;
if you find it, there will be a future,
and your hope will not be cut off.

15 Lie not in wait as a wicked man against the dwelling of the righteous;
do not violence to his home;
16 for a righteous man falls seven times, and rises again;
but the wicked are overthrown by calamity.

---

nothing much could be done about the latter class and since the wise men have a lot to say about the poor and oppressed (see Exeg. on 19:17). The KJV is not correct here; cf. the strong language of the prophets in regard to the oppressed (Amos 2:7; Hos. 4:2). **Those who are stumbling** is more accurate than **those that are ready.**

12. Probably to be taken with vs. 11. This is a specific example of one who has failed to help his brother in distress, because, as he says, he knew nothing about his brother's need; but God, who observes the hearts of men, knows that such an excuse is not valid, and he will repay accordingly. **Pondereth:** Lit., **weighs.** This figure is probably drawn from Egyptian religion where Thoth weighs the heart of man in a balance (see Exeg. on 21:2).

13-14. Cf. 16:24. Wisdom is to the mind what honey is to the mouth. Vs. 14*b*=23:18, from which it probably has been copied (see Exeg.). **Knowledge of wisdom** or **know that wisdom . . . :** A difficult stich; lit., "so know wisdom to thyself," out of which the RSV makes the best sense. **Reward** or **future:** Lit., "end" (see Exeg. on 5:4).

15. Synonymous. **Dwelling** and **home** are both rural terms: lit., "pasture" and "lair."

16. Antithetic. Those who molest the private homes of the righteous will suffer punishment at the hands of God. **Fall** or **are overthrown:** Lit., "stumble."

13-14. See Expos. on 3:13-18.

15-16. ***The Fall and Rise of the Righteous Man.***—Familiar words seem to be reversed in this passage. Usually we think of the rise and fall of an individual or an empire. Rome rises to its height and then we read of *The History of the Decline and Fall of the Roman Empire,* as the title of Gibbon's monumental work puts it. In this proverb we read of the fall and rise of an upright man.

An ominous finality is implied in the rise and fall of an individual or a nation. **The wicked are overthrown by calamity.** This is the conclusion that is written over an evil life. At the last some catastrophe strikes such a person and he falls. The righteous man, on the other hand, falls only to rise again. He has many experiences of falling and rising again. The righteous person is not described as an individual who never falls. The best man makes mistakes. He commits errors of judgment and makes wrong decisions. He sins. But his fall is not the end of him. He falls only to rise again. He is a person who makes no high pretenses on his status, for in acknowledging his wrongs and in profiting by his mistakes he makes a new start.

17 Rejoice not when thine enemy falleth, and let not thine heart be glad when he stumbleth:
18 Lest the LORD see *it*, and it displease him, and he turn away his wrath from him.
19 Fret not thyself because of evil *men*, neither be thou envious at the wicked;
20 For there shall be no reward to the evil *man;* the candle of the wicked shall be put out.
21 My son, fear thou the LORD and the king: *and* meddle not with them that are given to change:
22 For their calamity shall rise suddenly; and who knoweth the ruin of them both?
23 These *things* also *belong* to the wise. *It is* not good to have respect of persons in judgment.

17 Do not rejoice when your enemy falls,
and let not your heart be glad when he stumbles;
18 lest the LORD see it, and be displeased,
and turn away his anger from him.

19 Fret not yourself because of evildoers,
and be not envious of the wicked;
20 for the evil man has no future;
the lamp of the wicked will be put out.

21 My son, fear the LORD and the king,
and do not disobey either of them;[r]
22 for disaster from them will rise suddenly,
and who knows the ruin that will come from them both?

23 These also are sayings of the wise.

Partiality in judging is not good.

[r] Gk: Heb *do not associate with those who change*

17-18. Synonymous. A beautiful expression, but somewhat marred by the last sentiment. We are not to rejoice in the misfortune of our enemies lest the Lord become angry at us and turn his anger away from them. All attempts to twist the meaning of the verse in order to achieve a more altruistic view are unsupported by the Hebrew text (cf. 17:5; 24:29; 25:21-22, where a similar spirit of forgiveness and deep concern for others is enjoined).

19-20. Synonymous. **Reward** or **future:** See Exeg. on 23:18.

21-22. Obedience to God and king is enjoined here (cf. I Tim. 2:1-2; Tit. 3:1). **Meddle not with:** The RSV, with the LXX, **disobey,** possibly reads the verbal root *'ābhar* instead of *'ārabh.* **Given to change:** The RSV, with LXX, reads *shenêhem* for *shônîm* and renders **either** [both] **of them.** The KJV means that one should not associate with those who are of a revolutionary character, whether in religion or politics. In vs. 22 the best sense seems to be obtained if the pronouns are taken as subjective, with the RSV. In vs. 22*b* the translation of the ASV mg., "of their years" for **of them both** may be disregarded.

D. THIRD COLLECTION (24:23-34)

23-26. Against partiality in the courts. **Have respect of persons** or **partiality: Lit.,** "to regard faces" (cf. 18:5; 28:21).

A righteous man falls seven times, and rises again. The number of times is hardly significant. This is not a limiting number. Jesus might add that he falls seventy times seven times and still rises again. The righteous man's experience need not be the dismal repetition of the same mistakes again and again. He may conquer one evil habit or correct one mistake, but always there are new areas in which he fails and fresh ways in which he misses the mark. But he keeps on trying. The biblical record is full of this kind of picture of man. Man falls—but he does not stay fallen. He who comes to God with a humble and contrite heart can have a right spirit renewed within him (Ps. 51). His past mistakes are steppingstones to a better self. For him the greatest failure is not falling, but failing to rise again.

The man who never falls is either a god or a self-deluded creature. The good news of Christianity accepts the fact that men fall because they are human, but it also affirms that men do not need to stay down. A divine hand is always ready to help a man to his feet again if he hungers and thirsts for righteousness.

17-18. See Expos. on 25:21-22.

19-20. See Expos. on 1:7; 16:10-15.

23-25. See Expos. on 21:3.

24 He that saith unto the wicked, Thou *art* righteous; him shall the people curse, nations shall abhor him:
25 But to them that rebuke *him* shall be delight, and a good blessing shall come upon them.
26 *Every man* shall kiss *his* lips that giveth a right answer.
27 Prepare thy work without, and make it fit for thyself in the field; and afterward build thine house.
28 Be not a witness against thy neighbor without cause; and deceive *not* with thy lips.
29 Say not, I will do so to him as he hath done to me: I will render to the man according to his work.
30 I went by the field of the slothful, and by the vineyard of the man void of understanding;

24 He who says to the wicked, "You are innocent,"
will be cursed by peoples, abhorred by nations;
25 but those who rebuke the wicked will have delight,
and a good blessing will be upon them.
26 He who gives a right answer
kisses the lips.

27 Prepare your work outside,
get everything ready for you in the field;
and after that build your house.

28 Be not a witness against your neighbor without cause,
and do not deceive with your lips.
29 Do not say, "I will do to him as he has done to me;
I will pay the man back for what he has done."

30 I passed by the field of a sluggard,
by the vineyard of a man without sense;

---

24. Wicked and **righteous** are forensic terms. Better, "guilty" and **innocent** (see Exeg. on 2:22).

25. The RSV adds **the wicked** to make the sense clear. This verse, which praises those who convict the wicked, is in sharp contrast with vs. 24, which condemns those who falsely declare a wicked man to be innocent.

26. The RSV gives the correct rendering of the M.T. here. **Kiss the lips:** A sign of true friendship. This is the only place in the O.T. where this practice is mentioned (yet see Song of S. 4:11; 5:1). Oesterley makes the interesting suggestion that the verb *nāshaq* may be used here in the postbiblical sense of "to equip," "to arm," and so figuratively, "to equip the lips" with knowledge, or some word like it which seems to have dropped out here (cf. Ps. 78:9; I Chr. 12:2; II Chr. 17:17, where the word is used in this sense). **Right:** See Exeg. on 8:9, where the translation is "plain." **Answer:** Lit., "words."

27. The moral of this verse is to get everything in order before getting married and starting a family. **Build your house:** Usually taken in the sense of rearing a family (cf. Ruth 4:11).

28. For the problem of the false **witness** see Exeg. on 14:25, and the verses alluded to there. **Deceive:** See Exeg. on 1:10, where the verb is translated "entice."

29. With this verse we reach one of the high points in the moral and ethical teachings of the O.T. (cf. 17:5; 20:22; 23:17; 25:21-22). The parallel Babylonian proverb in Amen-em-ope reads:

> Unto him that doeth thee evil shalt thou return good,
> Unto thine enemy justice shalt thou mete out.

30-34. Regarding the **sluggard** (see Exeg. on 19:24). Laziness is strongly censured by

---

26. See Expos. on 18:21.
27. See Expos. on 6:1-15.
28-29. See Expos. on 18:21.
30-34. See Expos. on 6:1-15.

31 And, lo, it was all grown over with
thorns, *and* nettles had covered the face
thereof, and the stone wall thereof was
broken down.
32 Then I saw, *and* considered *it* well: I
looked upon *it, and* received instruction.
33 *Yet* a little sleep, a little slumber, a
little folding of the hands to sleep:
34 So shall thy poverty come *as* one that
traveleth; and thy want as an armed man.

25 These *are* also proverbs of Solomon, which the men of Hezekiah king of Judah copied out.
2 *It is* the glory of God to conceal a
thing: but the honor of kings *is* to search
out a matter.
3 The heaven for height, and the earth
for depth, and the heart of kings *is* unsearchable.

31 and lo, it was all overgrown with thorns;
the ground was covered with nettles,
and its stone wall was broken down.
32 Then I saw and considered it;
I looked and received instruction.
33 "A little sleep, a little slumber,
a little folding of the hands to rest,"
34 and poverty will come upon you like a
robber,
and want like an armed man.

25 These also are proverbs of Solomon which the men of Hezekiah king of Judah copied.

2 It is the glory of God to conceal things,
but the glory of kings is to search things out.
3 As the heavens for height, and the earth for depth,
so the mind of kings is unsearchable.

---

the Hebrew sages; cf. 6:6-11, the last verses of which are similar to the last verses of this section (cf. 10:4; 12:24, 27; 13:4; 15:19; 18:9; 19:15; 20:4, 13; 21:25).

30. Synonymous. **Understanding** or **sense:** Lit., "heart" (see Exeg. on 2:2).

31. Triplet. **Thorns** and **nettles** are rare Hebrew words whose meanings are not quite certain.

32. Synonymous. **Considered:** Lit., "set my heart [mind]" (see Exeg. on 2:2). **Instruction:** See Exeg. on 1:2.

33-34. See Exeg. on 6:10-11. **As one that traveleth:** The RSV, **like a robber,** reads *kīmehallēkh* for *mithhallēkh* with 6:11.

IV. Second Anthology of Solomon's Proverbs (25:1–29:27)

This anthology is composed of two sections: chs. 25–27, which resemble Part III (22:17–24:34), and chs. 28–29, which are more like Part II (10:1–22:16). The first section deals more particularly with worldly wisdom, whereas the latter has a more religious tone (see Intro., p. 775; cf. pp. 772-73).

A. First Section (25:1–27:27)

25:1. Title. **Hezekiah,** king of Judah from 721 to 693 B.C., was a man of literary ability and a patron of the arts (cf. II Kings 18:18, 37; 19:2-3; Isa. 38:10-20). **Copied:** This use of the verb *'āthaq* ("to remove") is very late, pointing to a late date for the title but not necessarily for the whole section.

2-7. Regarding kings. The numerous references to kings in this section (28:2, 15-16; 29:4, 12, 14, 26) point to a pre-exilic date for the collection (see Exeg. on 16:10 for the Hebrew sages' views on kingship).

2. Antithetic. The ways of God are inscrutable, but a king's glory rests in his investigation of difficult problems and their solution. In these verses the king is looked upon with favor (see Exeg. on 16:10).

3. Mind: See Exeg. on 2:2. The superior wisdom of the king is taken for granted by the writer.

25:1-3. See Expos. on 3:5-8.

4 Take away the dross from the silver, and there shall come forth a vessel for the finer.

5 Take away the wicked *from* before the king, and his throne shall be established in righteousness.

6 Put not forth thyself in the presence of the king, and stand not in the place of great *men:*

7 For better *it is* that it be said unto thee, Come up hither; than that thou shouldest be put lower in the presence of the prince whom thine eyes have seen.

8 Go not forth hastily to strive, lest *thou know not* what to do in the end thereof, when thy neighbor hath put thee to shame.

9 Debate thy cause with thy neighbor *himself;* and discover not a secret to another:

10 Lest he that heareth *it* put thee to shame, and thine infamy turn not away.

4 Take away the dross from the silver,
and the smith has material for a vessel;
5 take away the wicked from the presence of the king,
and his throne will be established in righteousness.
6 Do not put yourself forward in the king's presence
or stand in the place of the great;
7 for it is better to be told, "Come up here,"
than to be put lower in the presence of the prince.

What your eyes have seen
8 do not hastily bring into court;
for[s] what will you do in the end,
when your neighbor puts you to shame?
9 Argue your case with your neighbor himself,
and do not disclose another's secret;
10 lest he who hears you bring shame upon you,
and your ill repute have no end.

[s] Cn: Heb *lest*

---

4. According to the KJV a vessel comes forth merely by removing the dross from the silver, which is not possible. The RSV adds **material for** in vs. 4*b* to make the desired sense. The LXX reads, "it will be purified wholly pure," which may presuppose in Hebrew, "and it cometh forth wholly purified."

5. Cf. 16:12.

6. Synonymous.

7. This refers to a royal feast where the guests are seated according to rank or royal favor (cf. Luke 14:8-11). Vs. 7*c* belongs to vs. 8, with the RSV. Ecclus. 7:4-5 gives a similar warning:

> Do not ask the Lord for pre-eminence,
> Or the king for a seat of honor.
> Do not justify yourself in the sight of the Lord,
> Or show off your wisdom before the king (Amer. Trans.).

8-10. Do not come to hasty conclusions concerning another's acts, lest you may be wrong and look foolish in the eyes of the one you have falsely accused.

8. With the RSV, vs. 7*c* becomes the first line of vs. 8, making excellent sense and solving an otherwise difficult problem. **Go not forth:** The RSV, by the change of one vowel, reads **bring. To strive:** The verb *rîbh* is the technical word for court action and is so translated in the RSV. **Lest:** RSV emends *pen* to *kî* and reads **for.**

9. To discuss a disputed matter in private, and to try to settle it there, is better than to bring it into court.

10. Put thee to shame: The verb is the same as the noun translated "reproach" in 14:34 (see Exeg.).

4-5. See Expos. on 16:10-15.
6-7. See Expos. on 29:23.
8-10. See Expos. on 19:2.

11 A word fitly spoken *is like* apples of gold in pictures of silver.

12 *As* an earring of gold, and an ornament of fine gold, *so is* a wise reprover upon an obedient ear.

13 As the cold of snow in the time of harvest, *so is* a faithful messenger to them that send him: for he refresheth the soul of his masters.

14 Whoso boasteth himself of a false gift *is like* clouds and wind without rain.

15 By long forbearing is a prince persuaded, and a soft tongue breaketh the bone.

16 Hast thou found honey? eat so much as is sufficient for thee, lest thou be filled therewith, and vomit it.

17 Withdraw thy foot from thy neighbor's house; lest he be weary of thee, and *so* hate thee.

11 A word fitly spoken
is like apples of gold in a setting of silver.
12 Like a gold ring or an ornament of gold
is a wise reprover to a listening ear.
13 Like the cold of snow in the time of harvest
is a faithful messenger to those who send him,
he refreshes the spirit of his masters.
14 Like clouds and wind without rain
is a man who boasts of a gift he does not give.

15 With patience a ruler may be persuaded,
and a soft tongue will break a bone.
16 If you have found honey, eat only enough for you,
lest you be sated with it and vomit it.
17 Let your foot be seldom in your neighbor's house,
lest he become weary of you and hate you.

---

11. A difficult verse. The lines are transposed in the English translations. **Fitly:** The Hebrew word is unknown. The meaning is derived from Symmachus, and by inference from 15:23. **Apples of gold:** The meaning is not certain, although "apple," as we know it, is hardly correct. Most likely some kind of fruit is meant, maybe quince, made of gold as part of an artistic decoration. **Pictures** or **setting** ("network" ASV) : Another difficult word whose precise meaning is not known. It is some kind of carved work (cf. Lev. 26:1; Num. 33:52) .

12. To be able to take advice is as valuable as the most costly ornament. **Earring of gold** or **gold ring:** See Exeg. on 11:22. **Reprover:** See Exeg. on 1:23.

13. On the importance of sending a trustworthy messenger cf. 22:21 (in contrast cf. 10:26) . The answer he brings back is as refreshing as a cold drink on a hot day. **Cold of snow:** Refreshing in time of heat, whether of drinks made cool by mixing snow with them, or of an actual snowfall. The **harvest** extended from March to September, according to the crops.

14. The RSV follows the Hebrew order. **Clouds:** Really, "mists," "vapors," which rise (*nāsā'*) . The word **like** is not in the Hebrew. **A gift he does not give:** Lit., "gift of falsity." The proverb speaks about the braggart who does not come through with his promised gifts.

15. Synonymous. Patience and gentleness are powerful weapons. **Patience:** Lit., "length [slowness] of anger" (see Exeg. on 14:29) . **Persuaded:** Cf. 1:10; 16:29, where the verb has the meaning "to entice."

16. Self-control and moderation were virtues that the Hebrew sages held in high regard (cf. vs. 27) .

17. Withdraw or **let . . . be seldom:** Lit., "make rare," "make precious," from the root *yāqar*.

---

11. See Expos. on 18:21.
12. See Expos. on 9:7-9.
13-14. See Expos. on 20:6.
15. See Expos. on 18:21.
16-17. See Expos. on 3:27-35.

18 A man that beareth false witness against his neighbor *is* a maul, and a sword, and a sharp arrow.

19 Confidence in an unfaithful man in time of trouble *is like* a broken tooth, and a foot out of joint.

20 *As* he that taketh away a garment in cold weather, *and as* vinegar upon nitre, so *is* he that singeth songs to a heavy heart.

18 A man who bears false witness against his neighbor
is like a war club, or a sword, or a sharp arrow.
19 Trust in a faithless man in time of trouble
is like a bad tooth or a foot that slips.
20 He who sings songs to a heavy heart
is like one who takes off a garment on a cold day,
and like vinegar on a wound.[t]

[t] Gk: Heb *lye*

---

18. The KJV and the RSV transpose the Hebrew stichs. The metaphor (with KJV) describes the seriousness of the crime (see Exeg. on 14:25). **Maul or war club:** Reading with the LXX, and most commentators and English translations, *mappēç* instead of *mēphîç* ("a scatterer").

19. The KJV and the RSV transpose the Hebrew stichs. **Faithless man:** See Exeg. on 2:22. **Broken:** From *rāʿaʿ,* in which case it would be better to read *nirʿāh.* The RSV, **bad,** demands merely the change of a vowel point in the M.T., reading *rāʿāh.* **Out of joint** or, better, **that slips:** From the root *māʿadh,* "to slip," "to totter." Probably *môʿādheth* should be read instead of *mûʿādheth.*

20. Triplet. Mirth and sadness do not go together. The KJV follows the Hebrew order. **Taketh away** or **takes off:** The Hebrew word is uncertain. With the LXX and most modern commentators (and Amer. Trans. and Moffatt) this first strophe of the Hebrew text is omitted as a dittogram of the last strophe in vs. 19. **Nitre:** The RSV, with the LXX, reads *nétheq* or *péçaʿ,* **wound.** According to the KJV, the **vinegar** on the soda, which is what is meant by the word translated **nitre,** causes effervescence and so brings about a disturbing condition. According to the RSV **vinegar** in a **wound** causes smarting and pain. It is difficult to determine the exact meaning from the present state of the Hebrew text.

18-20. See Expos. on 18:21.

20. ***Timing Our Actions.***—Singing **songs to a heavy heart** is an example of ill-timed action. Wisdom would indicate that it is not enough for a man to consider what he says and does—he must also ask himself whether he is choosing the proper time for his speaking and his acting. William Penn, in his meditations and maxims, has a paragraph on what he calls "right-timing." There is a proper time to speak and to act, if a person is to achieve his purposes.

Timing what we say is important. At first sight it appears that the truth is the truth no matter when one says it, and that he who proclaims it should sound it forth at all times and in all places. Jesus did not follow such a course. "I have yet many things to say to you," he remarked to his disciples, "but you cannot bear them now" (John 16:12). He was dealing with persons, not with propositions. His purpose was to give these people the ideas that would help them at the time. If he had given them the whole truth in a lump sum they might have lost it all.

A family needs to pay attention to the importance of timing words and actions. People who live in the intimacy of a family can be of great help to each other by calling attention to each other's imperfections and shortcomings. But such criticisms need to be well timed. The difference between a nagging wife and a gentle wife is that the latter knows how to time properly her suggestions to her husband. To put it crudely, the one nags all the time while the other times her nags.

The principle of timing can be applied to actions as well as to words. A person must choose when he is to do a thing as well as what he is to do. One comes upon the remark of Jesus in which he says, "My time has not yet come" (John 7:6). The request of his mother at the marriage feast seemed to push him into public activity faster than his judgment warranted. His brothers wanted him to manifest himself publicly in Jerusalem, but he went quietly because he said that his time had not yet come. There were times when he evaded death, and there was

21 If thine enemy be hungry, give him bread to eat; and if he be thirsty, give him water to drink:
22 For thou shalt heap coals of fire upon his head, and the LORD shall reward thee.

21 If your enemy is hungry, give him bread
to eat;
and if he is thirsty, give him water to
drink;
22 for you will heap coals of fire on his head,
and the LORD will reward you.

21-22. Again the sentiment is spoiled by the last line. Do good because it will bring reward (cf. 17:5; 20:22; 24:17-18, 29). **Coals of fire:** This expression probably refers to the vengeance that will be taken on the enemy by returning good for evil. The pain thus inflicted may bring the enemy to repentance (cf. Rom. 12:20).

---

another time when he would not evade it. He apparently chose the time at which his death might serve the largest interests of God's purpose for man.

21-22. ***On the Treatment of Enemies.***—The treatment of enemies is here lifted to a relatively high level. These sages do not have the mood of the writer of Ps. 109, who utters a malediction against his enemy and prays that his enemy's days may be few—that his wife should be left a widow and his children should become fatherless (Ps. 109:8-9). Nor do we find here the fear of infection if enemies are allowed to live. In earlier Hebrew history there was the command to annihilate enemies completely, lest their gods call forth the loyalty of their conquerors. "And thou shalt consume all the people which the LORD thy God shall deliver thee; thine eye shall have no pity upon them: neither shalt thou serve their gods; for that will be a snare unto thee" (Deut. 7:16). The sages present more advanced ideas than these in the treatment of a foe.

Rejoicing when an enemy falls is not in place.

> Do not rejoice when your enemy falls,
> and let not your heart be glad when he stumbles:
> lest the LORD see it, and be displeased,
> and turn away his anger from him (24:17-18).

Gloating over an enemy's discomfiture cannot be the attitude of a wise man. During the Battle of Santiago on July 3, 1898, the battleship "Texas" swept past the burning Spanish ship "Vizcaya." When his men began to cheer, Captain John Woodward Philip restrained them by saying, "Don't cheer. The poor devils are dying."[1] It is obvious that the refusal to take pleasure in the suffering of enemies lifts the treatment of enemies to a high level; but the motive given in Proverbs is still the motive of self-interest. The reason that people are not to gloat over the defeat of a foe is that such action may displease the Lord, causing him to withhold his wrath against the enemy. The suffering which the Lord inflicts on the enemy may be turned on the person or nation who takes pleasure in the pain of a fallen foe.

The proverb under consideration here goes beyond refusing to rejoice when an enemy falls; it urges feeding a hungry enemy and giving drink to him who is thirsty. An enemy should be helped instead of hated. Yet again there is the motive of self-interest to which appeal is made. Do this, says the sage, **and the LORD will reward you.** Treating enemies well is a method of getting a reward from God.

These sayings on the treatment of enemies have found their way into the heart of Christian teaching. Paul quotes this thought when he summons the Christians at Rome to forgo vengeance against enemies. "If your enemy is hungry, feed him; if he is thirsty, give him drink: for by so doing you will heap burning coals upon his head" (Rom. 12:20). Paul does not add that this is a way to get a rich reward from God. Treating an enemy with kindness may **heap coals of fire on his head,** which may be interpreted to mean that such treatment will kindle in him a feeling of shame and self-reproach. This in turn can bring about a new relationship. The real reason for treating an enemy with kindness is to change him from an enemy into a friend! A Chinese sage has put the same thought in these words: "I meet good with good, that good may be maintained; I meet evil with good that good may be created."[2]

In the struggle against slavery in the United States, William Lloyd Garrison was ardent in his opposition to the evil. But as John T. McNeill points out, Garrison was more impatient and violent than some other lesser known opponents to the system of slavery. Notable among these was Theodore Dwight Weld, who worked within Presbyterianism. He and those associated with him received support not only from their own denomination, but from other churches as well, in a way that was denied to Garrison.

[1] Henry Cabot Lodge, *The War with Spain* (New York: Harper & Bros., 1899), p. 150.

[2] Quoted in Hocking, *Meaning of God in Human Experience,* p. 205.

23 The north wind driveth away rain: so *doth* an angry countenance a backbiting tongue.

24 *It is* better to dwell in the corner of the housetop, than with a brawling woman and in a wide house.

25 *As* cold waters to a thirsty soul, so *is* good news from a far country.

26 A righteous man falling down before the wicked *is as* a troubled fountain, and a corrupt spring.

27 *It is* not good to eat much honey: so *for men* to search their own glory *is not* glory.

23 The north wind brings forth rain;
and a backbiting tongue, angry looks.
24 It is better to live in a corner of the housetop
than in a house shared with a contentious woman.
25 Like cold water to a thirsty soul,
so is good news from a far country.
26 Like a muddied spring or a polluted fountain
is a righteous man who gives way before the wicked.
27 It is not good to eat much honey,
so be sparing of complimentary words.[u]

[u] Cn Compare Gk Syr Tg: Heb *searching out their glory is glory*

---

23. The KJV means that the slanderer is reproached by the angry look of the listener. The RSV, with practically the same meaning, says that slander produces **angry looks** on the maligned person. **North wind:** Usually the harbinger of nice weather, and so interpreted by the KJV. It may refer to general northwesterly winds which bring rain (see RSV). **Driveth away:** With the Vulg. The RSV **brings forth** is better, from the root *ḥûl*. **Backbiting:** Lit., "secret."

24. See Exeg. on 21:9.

25. It was difficult to get news from a distant country in those early days. Any report from friends far away was **like cold water to a thirsty soul** (cf. 25:13 and 15:30). **Thirsty:** Lit., "weary."

26. When a good man falls it is a catastrophe, especially when he falls in the presence of the wicked who point the finger of scorn at him. The KJV transposes the Hebrew stichs. **Falling down** or **gives way:** The verb *môṭ* means "to totter," "to slip." In Ps. 17:5 it is used in the sense of slipping morally, which seems to be the meaning here. This is one of the most profound statements in Proverbs, since the writer deals not with misfortune but with the sin of a righteous man. **Troubled** or **muddied:** Lit., "trampled."

27. The two stichs of this verse do not belong together. With vs. 27*a* cf. vs. 16. The Hebrew of vs. 27*b* makes no sense, "The searching of their glory is glory." The RSV, following most modern commentators (and Amer. Trans, and Moffatt), reads *hôqar* (from *yāqar;* see vs. 17) for *ḥēqer,* and *dibhrê* ("words of") for *kebhōdhām.*

Perhaps the reason is revealed in a remark made by one of Weld's hearers, who wrote after one of his most powerful speeches in 1834, "His great soul was full of compassion for the oppressor and the oppressed."[3] Such an attitude was more promising in winning over an enemy than a less kindly approach to him.

The Sermon on the Mount contains a high point in the treatment of enemies. Instead of adopting the simple formula of loving a neighbor and hating an enemy, Jesus says, "Love your enemies and pray for those who persecute you, so that you may be sons of your Father who is in heaven; for he makes his sun rise on the evil and on the good, and sends rain on the just and on the unjust" (Matt. 5:44-45). A new motive for the kindly treatment of enemies is brought to light in this N.T. teaching. Enemies are to be treated with kindness, not in order to get a reward from God but in order that one may share the purposes and nature of God. God seeks the good of all his children. When people become enemies through hostile acts on the part of one or both, there is need to restore fellowship. This is what God is always trying to do, and he who engages in this effort can rightly feel that he is working with God. No higher motive for kindly treatment of enemies can be imagined; none is more difficult to achieve.

[3] *Christian Hope for World Society* (Chicago: Willett, Clark & Co., 1937), p. 185.

23. See Expos. on 18:21.

24. See Expos. on 31:10-31.

25. See Expos. on 17:22.

26. See Expos. on 3:27-35.

27. See Expos. on 18:21.

28 He that *hath* no rule over his own spirit *is like* a city *that is* broken down, *and* without walls.

26 As snow in summer, and as rain in harvest, so honor is not seemly for a fool.

2 As the bird by wandering, as the swallow by flying, so the curse causeless shall not come.

3 A whip for the horse, a bridle for the ass, and a rod for the fool's back.

28 A man without self-control
is like a city broken into and left without walls.

26 Like snow in summer or rain in harvest,
so honor is not fitting for a fool.

2 Like a sparrow in its flitting, like a swallow in its flying,
a curse that is causeless does not alight.

3 A whip for the horse, a bridle for the ass,
and a rod for the back of fools.

---

28. The KJV and the RSV transpose the Hebrew stichs. Self-control, one of the most important virtues in the eyes of the wise men, is enjoined here. **Self-control** means the rule of the spirit (see KJV) which is the source of man's passionate energies.

26:1-12. These verses deal with the fool (*keṣîl*), the type most detested by the wise men (see Exeg. on 1:22).

1. Snow in the heat of summer in Palestine is unheard of; likewise **rain** in the harvest season, i.e., from March to September. These unseasonable elements are descriptive of the unsuitability of a fool for high office.

2. The only verse in this section which does not contain the word "fool." Curses uttered without cause have no power. In the ancient world curses and blessings were thought to have inherent power and, when uttered, to speed to their destination with certainty and force. This proverb breaks down the ancient view in so far as it says that unjustified curses will not find their mark.

3. A fool cannot be controlled by reason (cf. 10:13; 19:29). Toy suggests that there may be a reason for making a distinction here between the **whip for the horse** and the **bridle for the ass.** The ass, the favorite riding animal, hardly needed the whip, whereas

---

28. See Expos. on 16:32.

26:1, 3-12. ***About Fools.***—A fool is not necessarily a knave. He is a person who lacks good sense. His eye may not be evil—only blind. Sages who are proclaiming the value of wisdom would have fools as their special target, since fools are people who do not guide their actions by wisdom.

A lack of fitness characterizes a fool's actions; e.g., he does not know how rightly to use a proverb. Wise words fall helplessly from his lips as the legs of a lame man dangle and fail to bear him up (vs. 7). As a stick in the hands of a drunken man, so a proverb in the mouth of a fool may do much "more harm than good" (vs. 9). A fool seldom learns by experience. Everyone makes mistakes, but a fool does not learn by his mistakes. He repeats his folly.

Like a dog that returns to his vomit
is a fool that repeats his folly (vs. 11).

He is obtuse, for the bludgeonings of experience leave him untaught.

Crush a fool in a mortar with a pestle,
along with crushed grain,
yet his folly will not depart from him (27:22).

Life repeats a melancholy succession of painful experiences, and yet the foolish man never learns by what happens to him.

Many of the proverbs are addressed not to fools but to those who must live with them. Wise living implies the ability to live with people who are not wise. Honor should not be granted lightly to a fool. He does not know what to do with it. He misunderstands it, and inflates himself unduly. He who gives too much recognition to a fool is like a person who fastens a stone too tightly in a sling (vs. 8). The stone is supposed to lie loosely in the sling so that it may be hurled at a target. A fool clutches appreciative recognition to himself and loses his sense of proportion. Even the praise that he rightly deserves is blown up so large that wisdom prompts the withholding of honor from a foolish individual. The line between silence and answering a fool in his folly is not an easy one to draw. In this matter the sages almost contradict themselves, for they suggest that one degrades himself to the level of a fool if he answers him in his own language (vs. 4); on the other hand, they say that one cannot leave a fool unanswered, lest he construe silence as the inability to reply to him.

4 Answer not a fool according to his folly, lest thou also be like unto him.

5 Answer a fool according to his folly, lest he be wise in his own conceit.

6 He that sendeth a message by the hand of a fool cutteth off the feet, *and* drinketh damage.

7 The legs of the lame are not equal: so *is* a parable in the mouth of fools.

8 As he that bindeth a stone in a sling, so *is* he that giveth honor to a fool.

9 *As* a thorn goeth up into the hand of a drunkard, so *is* a parable in the mouth of fools.

10 The great *God* that formed all *things* both rewardeth the fool, and rewardeth transgressors.

4 Answer not a fool according to his folly,
lest you be like him yourself.
5 Answer a fool according to his folly,
lest he be wise in his own eyes.
6 He who sends a message by the hand of a fool
cuts off his own feet and drinks violence.
7 Like a lame man's legs, which hang useless,
is a proverb in the mouth of fools.
8 Like one who binds the stone in the sling
is he who gives honor to a fool.
9 Like a thorn that goes up into the hand of a drunkard
is a proverb in the mouth of fools.
10 Like an archer who wounds everybody
is he who hires a passing fool or drunkard.[v]

[v] The Hebrew text of this verse is uncertain

---

horses, used mostly in war and on the plain, had to be controlled many times by the whip (*ad loc.*).

4-5. These two verses are antithetic of each other. The first verse means that one should not descend to the level of a fool; the other, that one should answer a fool in order to show him his folly and thus rebuke him.

6. The KJV and RSV transpose the Hebrew stichs. To send a **message by . . . a fool** is as good as sending none at all (cf. 22:21; 25:13; also Exeg. on 13:17).

7. A fool can make as little use of a proverb (*māshāl,* see Intro., pp. 771-72) as a lame man of his legs. **Are not equal** or **hang useless:** A difficult verb. The RSV and many other translations take it from the root *dālal,* "to hang," "to be low."

8. The meaning of vs. 8*a* is not clear because some of the words are obscure. Perhaps to fasten **a stone** so firmly in **a sling** that it cannot be thrown out is as absurd as to give **honor to a fool. He that bindeth:** With the LXX. The Hebrew word *çerôr* means "bundle," "bag." **Sling:** With the LXX. It also means "stone heap."

9. Goeth up: The verb *'ālāh* in later Hebrew means "to come into," i.e., "to come into the hand of" (see RSV). The comparison is obvious: a thorn bush or stick in the hands of a drunkard is like a proverb in the mouth of a fool. More harm than good is done by both of them.

10. Probably the most obscure verse in Proverbs. Lit., "Much wounds all, and he who hires a fool, and he who hires passers-by." Out of the numerous suggested translations and emendations given by Toy (*ad loc.*) not one is satisfactory. **The great God** is unwarranted. The Hebrew simply has *rabh,* which can mean "much," "chief," or perhaps **archer,** as

---

Rough treatment is suggested for people who lack wisdom.

> **A whip for the horse, a bridle for the ass,**
> **and a rod for the back of fools** (vs. 3).

That is apparently the only language they understand. They are not reasonable enough to understand reasonable treatment, so they must be given the "shock treatment" that is more vigorous.

In spite of the apparently hopeless position of the fool, there is another position more hopeless. This is occupied by the man **who is wise in his own eyes.** There is **more hope for a fool than for him** (vs. 12). The fool is a person who does not know that he does not know; the man who is wise in his own eyes thinks he knows when in reality he does not know. The sages sometimes glibly divide people into fools and wise men. Observation reminds us that not everyone is a fool all the time, and not everyone is a wise

11 As a dog returneth to his vomit, *so* a fool returneth to his folly.

12 Seest thou a man wise in his own conceit? *there is* more hope of a fool than of him.

13 The slothful *man* saith, *There is* a lion in the way; a lion *is* in the streets.

14 *As* the door turneth upon his hinges, so *doth* the slothful upon his bed.

15 The slothful hideth his hand in *his* bosom; it grieveth him to bring it again to his mouth.

16 The sluggard *is* wiser in his own conceit than seven men that can render a reason.

17 He that passeth by, *and* meddleth with strife *belonging* not to him, *is like* one that taketh a dog by the ears.

11 Like a dog that returns to his vomit
is a fool that repeats his folly.
12 Do you see a man who is wise in his own eyes?
There is more hope for a fool than for him.
13 The sluggard says, "There is a lion in the road!
There is a lion in the streets!"
14 As a door turns on its hinges,
so does a sluggard on his bed.
15 The sluggard buries his hand in the dish;
it wears him out to bring it back to his mouth.
16 The sluggard is wiser in his own eyes
than seven men who can answer discreetly.
17 He who meddles in a quarrel not his own
is like one who takes a passing dog by the ears.

---

the RSV and ASV translate (cf. Job 16:13). In vs. 10*b* the KJV and ASV try to follow the order of the Hebrew text. The RSV emends considerably without any basis. The ASV mg. has an interesting interpretation, but it is not according to the Hebrew text: "A master worker formeth all things; but he that hireth the fool is as one that hireth them that pass by" (i.e., unskilled laborers).

11. The fool never learns (cf. II Pet. 2:22).

12. Against self-conceit. Hope is here expressed for the fool, who is elsewhere given up as hopeless, except in 29:20*b*.

13-16. Concerning the **sluggard** (see Exeg. on 19:24).

13. This is a good excuse to stay at home and sleep (cf. 22:13). **Lion** is used to translate two different Hebrew words in the verse (see Job 4:10-11 for the many names of this animal).

14. The sluggard never gets up. Like a door on a hinge he turns over on his bed for another nap, and gets nowhere.

15. Nearly identical with 19:24 (see Exeg.).

16. The sluggard is also mentally lazy. This is aggravated by the fact that he thinks he is **wiser . . . than seven men** (a round number). **Conceit: Lit., eyes. Render a reason:** Better, **answer discreetly.**

17. The KJV and RSV transpose the Hebrew stichs. **Passeth by:** The word **passing,** which modifies **dog,** should probably be deleted, as in the LXX, because its omission makes for better rhythm. It may have got into the text by dittography, *'ôbhēr mith'abbēr*. **Meddleth:** This translation presupposes a change of text, with Syriac and Vulg., reading *mith'ārēbh* instead of the M.T. form *mith'abbēr,* which literally means, "to put oneself in a fury." The ASV retains the M.T. form.

---

man all the time. There are foolish actions and wise actions, and it is hardly in place to look at one person and say, "Thou fool!" when as a matter of fact no person has achieved the status of choosing and acting wisely in everything he does.

The ability to achieve wisdom is a lifelong enterprise, since people are often more foolish than bad. Robert Louis Stevenson speaks of one hardship that everyone must struggle incessantly to overcome: "We speak of hardships, but the true hardship is to be a dull fool, and permitted to mismanage life in our own dull and foolish manner." [4]

13-15. See Expos. on 6:1-15.

16. See Expos. on 29:23.

17. See Expos. on vs. 21.

[4] *Travels with a Donkey,* "The Monks."

18 As a mad *man* who casteth firebrands, arrows, and death,

19 So *is* the man *that* deceiveth his neighbor, and saith, Am not I in sport?

20 Where no wood is, *there* the fire goeth out: so where *there is* no talebearer, the strife ceaseth.

21 *As* coals *are* to burning coals, and wood to fire; so *is* a contentious man to kindle strife.

18 Like a madman who throws firebrands,
arrows, and death,
19 is the man who deceives his neighbor
and says, "I am only joking!"
20 For lack of wood the fire goes out;
and where there is no whisperer, quarreling ceases.
21 As charcoal to hot embers and wood to fire,
so is a quarrelsome man for kindling strife.

18-19. It is not a joke when one deceives his neighbor. **Like a madman:** A difficult form. The Hebrew word may be the Hithpalpel of *lāhāh,* "to be faint," "to be amazed," "startled." Some commentators emend the word to *mithhôlēl,* "one who acts like a madman," from *hālal.*

20. Talebearer or, better, **whisperer:** On this word cf. 16:28; 18:8.

21. Coals or **charcoal:** A difficult word. The RSV affords a better parallel with **wood** in the following clause, but the meaning is not certain.

18-20. See Expos. on 18:21.

21. *The Contentious Man.*—Apparently there are people who enjoy contention. If there is no fight going on, they would like to start one; and if there is a fight going on, they would like to get into it. The sages have little praise for the contentious man.

> He who meddles in a quarrel not his own
> is like one who takes a passing dog by the ears
> (vs. 17).

Some periods in history are more productive of contentiousness than others. Any time of fatigue, especially after weary years of conflict, tends to make people irritable and ready for controversy and contention. Insight is needed to understand why people easily resort to altercations if contentiousness is to be reduced to a minimum.

A man who is very uncertain of himself may stir up strife. This is a method of getting the attention that he cannot get in any other way. Or, paradoxically, he may use the method of stirring up a quarrel to direct attention away from his own inadequacies. If he can cause people to fight each other they will have no time or energy to fight him. Anyone who helps a man to understand why he likes to stir up strife may give him guidance in overcoming this tendency.

Men who seek power may use the method of stirring up contentions to gain their ends. They thrive on chaos. If a man seeking power can discredit those who are in power, and if he can arouse suspicion toward them and among them, he may cause them to oust each other from power and thus give himself a chance to achieve it. Stirring up strife becomes a political enterprise by which power may be secured.

Men become contentious when they can find no satisfactory way of settling their disputes. One of the proverbs states, "It is an honor for a man to keep aloof from strife" (20:3). Any fool can start a quarrel, but to settle a controversy requires wisdom and patience. Contentiousness becomes a substitute for good argument. One can always hurl epithets at his opponent when he cannot think of an answer to the other's arguments. A bully can resort to physical violence when someone disagrees with him. A man of honor does not feel that this settles the controversy. The incident is related that "a man who held different views from Aristotle, once hit the philosopher and knocked him down. Aristotle arose and wiped the blood from his nose. 'Now, my friend,' he said, 'let us proceed with the argument.' "[5]

Differences of opinion will always exist among men. Conflicts of interest are unavoidable. If life is to be more than one long drama of bickering and quarreling, there is need of agreeing upon some equitable method of settling controversies. By formulating laws to govern conduct, and by accepting the decisions of law courts, many contentions can be ended. Life is orderly when people believe in the validity of law and in the need of governing their lives in obedience to the law.

A saying reveals the method of deciding doubtful cases which was used during the period when Proverbs was written:

> The lot puts an end to disputes
> and decides between powerful contenders (18:18).

[5] Otto Eisenschiml, *The Art of Worldly Wisdom* (New York: Duell, Sloan & Pearce, 1947), p. 24.

22 The words of a talebearer *are* as wounds, and they go down into the innermost parts of the belly.

23 Burning lips and a wicked heart *are like* a potsherd covered with silver dross.

24 He that hateth dissembleth with his lips, and layeth up deceit within him;

25 When he speaketh fair, believe him not: for *there are* seven abominations in his heart.

26 *Whose* hatred is covered by deceit, his wickedness shall be showed before the *whole* congregation.

27 Whoso diggeth a pit shall fall therein: and he that rolleth a stone, it will return upon him.

28 A lying tongue hateth *those that are* afflicted by it; and a flattering mouth worketh ruin.

27 Boast not thyself of to-morrow; for thou knowest not what a day may bring forth.

22 The words of a whisperer are like delicious morsels;
they go down into the inner parts of the body.
23 Like the glaze[w] covering an earthen vessel
are smooth[x] lips with an evil heart.
24 He who hates, dissembles with his lips
and harbors deceit in his heart;
25 when he speaks graciously, believe him not,
for there are seven abominations in his heart;
26 though his hatred be covered with guile,
his wickedness will be exposed in the assembly.
27 He who digs a pit will fall into it,
and a stone will come back upon him who starts it rolling.
28 A lying tongue hates its victims,
and a flattering mouth works ruin.

27 Do not boast about tomorrow,
for you do not know what a day may bring forth.

[w] Cn: Heb *silver of dross*
[x] Gk: Heb *burning*

---

22. See Exeg. on 18:8.

23. The KJV transposes the Hebrew stichs. **Burning:** The RSV, with the LXX, reads *ḥalāqîm,* **smooth,** for *dôleqîm.* **Silver dross:** The RSV, **like the glaze,** is correct. See H. L. Ginsberg, "The North-Canaanite Myth of Anath and Aqhat," *Bulletin of the American Schools of Oriental Research,* No. 98 (April, 1945), p. 21, n. 55; and Albright, "A New Hebrew Word for 'Glaze' in Proverbs 26:23," pp. 24-25, where it is shown from Ugaritic that the Hebrew words כסף סיגים should be read כספסיג(ים), meaning, "like glaze."

24-26. He who hides his hatred behind his words nourishes **deceit** within himself.

25. When he speaks graciously: Lit., "when he makes gracious his voice." **Seven:** A round number, denoting the countless **abominations** in his heart (see Exeg. on 3:32).

26. Congregation or, better, **assembly:** The concealed hatred will in time make itself known in some outward act of violence, and the culprit is brought to trial before the assembly.

27. Harm perpetrated against others recoils on the one who devises it.

28. Its victims: Lit., "its crushed ones." A peculiar expression.

27:1. In Amen-em-ope a similar idea is expressed (see Oesterley, *Proverbs,* p. 237):

> Of a truth thou knowest not the design of God,
> Thou can'st not realize the morrow.

And:

> Man knoweth not how the morrow will be,
> The events of the morrow are in the hands of God.

Cf. also Jas. 4:13-16.

When no decision could be arrived at, there was—and still may be—the possibility of using some method like casting lots or "tossing a coin."

22-26. See Expos. on 18:21.

27. See Expos. on 3:1-4.

28. See Expos. on 18:21.

27:1. See Expos. on 29:23.

2 Let another man praise thee, and not
thine own mouth; a stranger, and not thine
own lips.
3 A stone *is* heavy, and the sand weighty;
but a fool's wrath *is* heavier than them both.
4 Wrath *is* cruel, and anger *is* outrageous; but who *is* able to stand before envy?

2 Let another praise you, and not your own
mouth;
a stranger, and not your own lips.
3 A stone is heavy, and sand is weighty,
but a fool's provocation is heavier than
both.
4 Wrath is cruel, anger is overwhelming;
but who can stand before jealousy?

---

2. Synonymous.

3. Cf. Ecclus. 22:15:

> Sand and salt and a lump of iron
> Are easier to bear than a man without understanding (Amer. Trans.).

4. Vs. 4*a* reads, lit., "cruelty of wrath, flood of anger." **Anger** and **wrath** do not last long, but **jealousy** burns on until it consumes him who is its object. The jealousy referred to here is that of a jealous husband (cf. 6:34). **Outrageous** or **overwhelming:** Lit., "flood" (ASV mg.). **Envy** or **jealousy:** See Exeg. on 14:30.

---

2. See Expos. on vs. 21.

3. See Expos. on 26:1, 3-12.

4. ***Overcoming Jealousy.***—Jealousy, which has been defined as the "suspicious apprehension of being supplanted by a rival in some coveted position," is one of the corrupting influences in human relationships. This proverb states that jealousy is worse than wrath or anger.

> **Wrath is cruel, anger is overwhelming;**
> **but who can stand before jealousy?**

Anger is like a torrent. It is like a storm that rages for a short time and leaves ruin in its wake. Jealousy is more continuous and persistent. Jealousy is like the incessant dropping of water on a stone. The person who lives with an envious individual has no relief.

Several of the proverbs mention a particular kind of envy.

> Let not your heart envy sinners,
> but continue in the fear of the LORD all the day.
> Surely there is a future,
> and your hope will not be cut off (23:17-18).

When one sees the apparent success of unprincipled men he is impelled to envy their lot. They are not oppressed by a sensitive conscience. Life seems to give them rewards in spite of their wrongdoing. But the sages come back to their oft-repeated observation. The wicked may be successful for a time, but there is no future in their way of life.

> Fret not yourself because of evil-doers,
> and be not envious of the wicked;
> for the evil man has no future;
> the lamp of the wicked will be put out (24:19-20).

If one can quiet his rising envy long enough, he will see that the fate of the evildoer is nothing to covet.

Jealousy sometimes expresses itself in the enjoyment of the misfortunes of others. This feeling may be present among the closest of friends. Each is fearful of his own status and is afraid that he may not be properly recognized. When he feels low, he gets a subtle satisfaction out of seeing his companions brought low. Bacon once wrote that "whoso is out of hope to attain to another's virtue, will seek to come at even hand by depressing another's fortune." [6] The way in which to combat such an attitude is to determine never to glory in the misfortunes of others, and to discipline oneself against being a purveyor of anything which damages the reputation or standing of another. The fact can be frankly recognized that one never builds oneself up by tearing other people down.

Another way in which a person displays jealousy is by being made unhappy by the successes of others. The uncertain person's lack of success will be made more manifest to himself by the successes of those with whom he shares his life. Their achievements seem to be a threat to his standing. Wives may be jealous of the successes of their husbands, and husbands may be envious if their wives achieve distinction. The triumphs of their mates seem to accentuate their own lack of stature. The ability to enjoy the successes of others is an important mark of maturity. Usually it is easier to weep with those who weep than to rejoice with those who rejoice. Aeschylus wrote centuries ago in *Agamemnon:*

[6] Essay "Of Envy."

5 Open rebuke *is* better than secret love.
6 Faithful *are* the wounds of a friend; but the kisses of an enemy *are* deceitful.
7 The full soul loatheth a honeycomb; but to the hungry soul every bitter thing is sweet.
8 As a bird that wandereth from her nest, so *is* a man that wandereth from his place.
9 Ointment and perfume rejoice the heart: so *doth* the sweetness of a man's friend by hearty counsel.

5 Better is open rebuke
than hidden love.
6 Faithful are the wounds of a friend;
profuse are the kisses of an enemy.
7 He who is sated loathes honey,
but to one who is hungry everything bitter is sweet.
8 Like a bird that strays from its nest,
is a man who strays from his home.
9 Oil and perfume make the heart glad,
but the soul is torn by trouble.[y]

[y] Gk: Heb *the sweetness of his friend from hearty counsel*

5-6. A good friend tells one his faults. **Rebuke:** See Exeg. on 1:23, where the word is translated "reproof." **Hidden love:** Love which does not make itself known in some outward act of rebuke or correction.

6. Antithetic. Cf. vs. 14. **Faithful:** See Exeg. on 3:3. **Deceitful** or **profuse:** The meaning of the Hebrew word is not certain, as witnessed by the way the versions and English translations handle it. The KJV is based on the Vulg., but it demands a change in the text, reading possibly *ne'eqāshôth* (see Exeg. on 2:15). The RSV derives its translation (with ASV) from an Aramaic stem עתר, "to be abundant." But since the Hebrew equivalent, עשר, is commonly used in the O.T., there would be little need to introduce its Aramaic cognate. Certainly the KJV gives the sense expected in the antithesis of the two stichs.

7. Antithetic. Hunger is the best cook. **Soul:** See Exeg. on 13:25. **Loatheth:** Lit., "tramples on."

8. The sage may be alluding to his own experience, for the wise men of Israel were great travelers, as their knowledge of other lands seems to show, and as we are told in Ecclus. 39:4:

> He [the wise man] will serve among great men,
> And appear before rulers.
> He will travel through the lands of strange peoples,
> And test what is good and what is evil among men (Amer. Trans.).

And 51:13, "When I was very young, before I went on my wanderings" (Amer. Trans.).

9. Oil and perfume: The text of vs. 9*b* is corrupt and reads, lit., "and sweetness of his neighbor from the counsel of the soul." It is impossible to tell whether this stich is to be synonymous with or antithetic to the first one. Out of the numerous emendations which have been suggested no one is satisfactory. The RSV, with the Amer. Trans., seems to give the best sense, but it does not stem from M.T.

> . . . Few are they who have such inborn grace,
> As to look up with love, and envy not,
> When stands another on the heights of weal.[7]

Instead of producing envy in us, the success of others should develop emulation. Jealousy can be overcome if one determines to rejoice not with iniquity but with the truth, and if one determines to appreciate accomplishments in others no matter what the relative effect may seem to be on one's own position.

[7] See *Harvard Classics*, ed. Charles W. Eliot (New York: P. F. Collier & Son Co., 1909), VIII, 34.

A high standard of conduct is proclaimed in one of Paul's letters to the Corinthians. According to Moffatt's translation we read: "Love knows no jealousy. . . . Love is never glad when others go wrong, love is gladdened by goodness, always slow to expose, always eager to believe the best, always hopeful, always patient" (I Cor. 13:4*b*, 6-7).

5. See Expos. on 9:7-9.
6. See Expos. on 17:17.
7. See Expos. on 3:9-10.
8. See Expos. on 10:1.
9-10. See Expos. on 17:17.

10 Thine own friend, and thy father's friend, forsake not; neither go into thy brother's house in the day of thy calamity: *for* better *is* a neighbor *that is* near than a brother far off.

11 My son, be wise, and make my heart glad, that I may answer him that reproacheth me.

12 A prudent *man* foreseeth the evil, *and* hideth himself; *but* the simple pass on, *and* are punished.

13 Take his garment that is surety for a stranger, and take a pledge of him for a strange woman.

14 He that blesseth his friend with a loud voice, rising early in the morning, it shall be counted a curse to him.

15 A continual dropping in a very rainy day and a contentious woman are alike.

16 Whosoever hideth her hideth the wind, and the ointment of his right hand, *which* bewrayeth *itself*.

10 Your friend, and your father's friend, do
not forsake;
and do not go to your brother's house
in the day of your calamity.
Better is a neighbor who is near
than a brother who is far away.
11 Be wise, my son, and make my heart glad,
that I may answer him who reproaches
me.
12 A prudent man sees danger and hides
himself;
but the simple go on, and suffer for it.
13 Take a man's garment when he has given
surety for a stranger,
and hold him in pledge when he gives
surety for foreigners.[z]
14 He who blesses his neighbor with a loud
voice,
rising early in the morning,
will be counted as cursing.
15 A continual dripping on a rainy day
and a contentious woman are alike;
16 to restrain her is to restrain the wind[a]
or to grasp oil in his right hand.

[z] Vg and 20. 16: Heb *a foreign woman*
[a] Heb obscure

---

10. Triplet. The three stichs are loosely connected. Vs. 10*b* seems to be a contradiction of 17:17. The general sense is that one is not to forsake old family friends. Two passages from the Proverbs of Aḥikar, as quoted by Oesterley (*ibid.*), are obviously the source of the ideas expressed in this verse:

> My son, remove not thy father's friend,
> Lest perchance thy friend come not near to thee.

And:

> My son, better is a friend that is at hand,
> Than a brother who is far away.

11. The teacher who speaks here is responsible for the mistakes of the pupil (cf. 23:15).

12. See Exeg. on 22:3.

13. Almost identical with 20:16 (see Exeg.).

14. "Ostentatious professions of regard, like the profuse kisses of an enemy (v. 6), justly incur the suspicion of sinister design" (Perowne, *Proverbs, ad loc.*). **Blesseth:** The verb here means "to salute," "to greet" (cf. Gen. 47:7; II Kings 4:29).

15. Cf. 19:13.

16. An impossible Hebrew text. Lit., "*Those* who hide her, *he* hides wind [or, spirit], and oil meets [or, calls] his right hand [or, his right hand meets oil]." Possibly vs. 16 is to be connected with the preceding verse, the general sense then being that the shrewish

---

11. See Expos. on 1:8-9; 10:1.
12. See Expos. on 22:3.
13. See Expos. on 6:1-15.
14. See Expos. on 17:17.
15-16. See Expos. on 31:10-31.

17 Iron sharpeneth iron; so a man sharpeneth the countenance of his friend.

18 Whoso keepeth the fig tree shall eat the fruit thereof: so he that waiteth on his master shall be honored.

19 As in water face *answereth* to face, so the heart of man to man.

20 Hell and destruction are never full; so the eyes of man are never satisfied.

21 *As* the fining pot for silver, and the furnace for gold; so *is* a man to his praise.

17 Iron sharpens iron,
and one man sharpens another.
18 He who tends a fig tree will eat its fruit,
and he who guards his master will be honored.
19 As in water face answers to face,
so the mind of man reflects the man.
20 Sheol and Abaddon are never satisfied,
and never satisfied are the eyes of man.
21 The crucible is for silver, and the furnace is for gold,
and a man is judged by his praise.

woman is as unsteady as the **wind,** and as slippery as **oil.** All attempts to make sense out of the Hebrew text are conjectural.

17. In praise of social intercourse. The RSV deletes **countenance** in vs. 17*b*. This verse states one of the most important aspects of the educational process, viz., the influence of one's fellows upon his character (see Exeg. on 22:6; cf. 13:20; 22:24-25).

18. Synonymous. A diligent servant is rewarded by his master. The wise men were interested in all classes of society.

19. Literally the Hebrew reads, "Like water, face to face, so the heart [mind] of man to man." The verse is taken to mean either that men are similar in their spiritual and mental make-up (KJV; ASV), or that the heart of a man reflects his true character (RSV; ASV mg.). **As in water:** It is possible that with the **LXX** the phrase *kammáyim* should be read simply *kemô,* "like," translating then, "as face to face, so the heart of man to man," i.e., as men recognize each other by their exterior appearance, so they recognize the inner character of each other. **Mind:** See Exeg. on 2:2.

20. Man's desires are insatiable. **Hell and destruction** or, better, **Sheol and Abaddon:** See Exeg. on 15:11; cf. the parallel passage in the Proverbs of Aḥikar, as quoted by Oesterley (*op. cit.,* p. 245):

> My son, the eye of man is like a fountain of water,
> And it is not satisfied with riches until filled with dust.

21. The first stich equals 17:3*a*. Vs. 21*b* reads, lit., "and a man according to his praise," to which the RSV adds **is judged** to clarify the sense that one is tested by the praise given to him by others.

17. See Expos. on 17:17.

18. See Expos. on 20:6.

19. See Expos. on 4:20-27.

20. See Expos. on 2:1-22.

21. ***Tested by Praise.***—A man is tested by his praise. He is tested when he is praised—and by what he praises! A test does not produce weakness; it only reveals it if it is present.

When an individual is praised, he tends to reveal the kind of person he is. This may make him exaggerate his own importance. Because someone thinks highly of what he has done, he may easily lose his perspective about himself, and think of himself more highly than he ought to think. The person who suddenly rises to fame by doing something brilliant on the athletic field, in the arena of politics, or on the stage, is being tried like silver in a refining vessel. Under the blaze of that adulation he may easily fall victim to a false estimate of himself. Few people can retain a balanced view of themselves when they are suddenly elevated to a high pinnacle in the public mind by becoming the heroes of the hour. Being praised often puts a more severe strain on character than being persecuted.

In one of his epistles, Seneca rightly said, "You can tell the character of every man when you see how he gives and receives praise." [8] The praised person may lose his imaginative sympathy for other people. His attention is being centered upon himself, and it will take genuine self-discipline to remember how others feel. When Jesus was being acclaimed on the occasion of his triumphal entry into Jerusalem, he was objective enough to see what was happen-

[8] *Moral Epistles* LII.

22 Though thou shouldest bray a fool in
a mortar among wheat with a pestle, *yet*
will not his foolishness depart from him.
23 Be thou diligent to know the state of
thy flocks, *and* look well to thy herds:
24 For riches *are* not for ever: and doth
the crown *endure* to every generation?
25 The hay appeareth, and the tender
grass showeth itself, and herbs of the mountains are gathered.
26 The lambs *are* for thy clothing, and
the goats *are* the price of the field.
27 And *thou shalt have* goats' milk
enough for thy food, for the food of thy
household, and *for* the maintenance for thy
maidens.

22 Crush a fool in a mortar with a pestle
along with crushed grain,
yet his folly will not depart from him.
23 Know well the condition of your flocks,
and give attention to your herds;
24 for riches do not last for ever;
and does a crown endure to all generations?
25 When the grass is gone, and the new
growth appears,
and the herbage of the mountains is
gathered,
26 the lambs will provide your clothing,
and the goats the price of a field;
27 there will be enough goats' milk for your
food,
for the food of your household
and maintenance for your maidens.

28 The wicked flee when no man pursueth: but the righteous are bold as
a lion.

28 The wicked flee when no one pursues,
but the righteous are bold as a lion.

---

22. A fool and his folly are hard to part. **Along with crushed grain:** This phrase should probably be deleted, as it overburdens the line.

23-27. A bucolic interlude, included here perhaps to persuade Jewish young men to turn from trade and business, with their temptation to grow rich quickly, to agricultural pursuits which were less fraught with worldly allurements.

23. Synonymous. **Condition:** Lit., "face," "appearance."

24. Synonymous. **Crown:** This makes little sense in the context. One expects a synonym of **riches** in the first stich. Toy suggests reading *'ōçār,* "wealth," for M.T. *nēzer,* **crown.** Vs. 24*b* then reads, "nor wealth from generation to generation."

25-27. These verses should probably go together, as in the RSV. Vss. 26-27 describe the lasting nature of wealth attained by agriculture, thus implicitly contrasting it with the uncertainty of that gained in the business world.

B. Second Section (28:1–29:27)

28:1. Antithetic. A good conscience makes one unafraid. **Are bold:** In Hebrew the verb is singular but the subject is plural. It is probably better, with the LXX, to make the subject singular, as it is in vs. 1*a*.

---

ing. He was not swept off his feet by the applause. He could not forget the plight of the city into which he was going. He wept over it while others praised him.

An individual is also tested by what he praises. In a sense this means that each of us is judged by what he worships, by what he holds of highest worth. Civilizations as well as individuals differ from one another in what they praise. One nation applauds the man who can accumulate much wealth; its people do not scrutinize too closely his method of getting it. Another nation may not be impressed at the outset by a man's possessing many earthly goods. Its people are more concerned with the kind of person he is, by the way in which he made his money, by the contribution he has made to his generation.

What a man considers good is a good measuring rod to discover the kind of man he is. The values which a nation cherishes are a better indication of the quality of its people than the size of its army or the magnitude of its annual income.

22. See Expos. on 26:1, 3-12.

23-27. See Expos. on 6:1-15; 10:15-16.

28:1. See Expos. on 20:27.

2 For the transgression of a land many *are* the princes thereof: but by a man of understanding *and* knowledge the state *thereof* shall be prolonged.

3 A poor man that oppresseth the poor *is like* a sweeping rain which leaveth no food.

4 They that forsake the law praise the wicked: but such as keep the law contend with them.

5 Evil men understand not judgment: but they that seek the LORD understand all *things.*

6 Better *is* the poor that walketh in his uprightness, than *he that is* perverse *in his* ways, though he *be* rich.

7 Whoso keepeth the law *is* a wise son: but he that is a companion of riotous *men* shameth his father.

8 He that by usury and unjust gain increaseth his substance, he shall gather it for him that will pity the poor.

2 When a land transgresses
it has many rulers;
but with men of understanding and knowledge
its stability will long continue.
3 A poor man who oppresses the poor
is a beating rain that leaves no food.
4 Those who forsake the law praise the wicked,
but those who keep the law strive against them.
5 Evil men do not understand justice,
but those who seek the LORD understand it completely.
6 Better is a poor man who walks in his integrity
than a rich man who is perverse in his ways.
7 He who keeps the law is a wise son,
but a companion of gluttons shames his father.
8 He who augments his wealth by interest and increase
gathers it for him who is kind to the poor.

---

2. Unstable government is due to the wickedness of the people; men of wisdom preserve good government. **Understanding:** See Exeg. on 1:2. **State** or **stability:** The word *kēn* also can mean "the right." The Hebrew text may be corrupt here; cf. the LXX which reflects a better Hebrew text than we have now. It reads:

> Through the sins of the unholy ones crises arise,
> But a man of understanding quenches them.

3. For a poor man to oppress the poor is a strange situation. Instead of *rāsh,* **poor,** it is possible to read either *rāshā',* "wicked," or *'āshîr,* "rich," and translate, "A wicked [or rich] man who oppresses the poor."

4. Antithetic. **Law** (*tôrāh*): Either the instruction of the wise, as usually used in Proverbs (see Exeg. on 1:8), or the law of Moses, in the technical sense of later Judaism. It is probably the latter here (as also in vs. 9 and 29:18; see Exeg. on 13:13).

5. Antithetic. Evil men do not know what is right since they do not seek the will of the Lord as revealed in his law. **Justice:** See Exeg. on 1:3.

6. The first stich is identical with 19:1*a* (see Exeg.). In regard to riches see Exeg. on 10:2. **Uprightness** or **integrity:** See Exeg. on 10:9. **Perverse:** See Exeg. on 2:15, where the word is translated "crooked." **Ways:** Dual number in the Hebrew, although it probably should be pointed as plural, with Vulg.

7. Law: Here the instruction of the wise (see Exeg. on vs. 4; also 1:8).

8. Interest was forbidden among Israelites but could be taken from foreigners (cf. Exod. 22:25; Lev. 25:35-37). **Unjust gain:** Lit., **increase.** The difference between the two Hebrew terms in this verse is not clear; cf. Lev. 25:35-37, where the first term, **interest,** means interest taken in money, and the second, **increase,** means interest taken in kind

---

2. See Expos. on 16:10-15.
3. See Expos. on 22:16*a*.
4-5. See Expos. on 21:3.
6. See Expos. on 10:15-16.
7. See Expos. on 1:8-9; 10:1.
8. See Expos. on 10:15-16.

9 He that turneth away his ear from hearing the law, even his prayer *shall be* abomination.

10 Whoso causeth the righteous to go astray in an evil way, he shall fall himself into his own pit: but the upright shall have good *things* in possession.

11 The rich man *is* wise in his own conceit; but the poor that hath understanding searcheth him out.

12 When righteous *men* do rejoice, *there is* great glory: but when the wicked rise, a man is hidden.

13 He that covereth his sins shall not prosper: but whoso confesseth and forsaketh *them* shall have mercy.

9 If one turns away his ear from hearing the law,
even his prayer is an abomination.
10 He who misleads the upright into an evil way
will fall into his own pit;
but the blameless will have a goodly inheritance.
11 A rich man is wise in his own eyes,
but a poor man who has understanding will find him out.
12 When the righteous triumph, there is great glory;
but when the wicked rise, men hide themselves.
13 He who conceals his transgressions will not prosper,
but he who confesses and forsakes them will obtain mercy.

(food). But this distinction cannot be pressed, as Deut. 23:19 shows that the first term can be used for general interest also. God will take the ill-gotten gain and give it to a kind man.

9. The prayer of him who turns from God's will as revealed in his law must necessarily be insincere. **Law:** See Exeg. on vs. 4; 13:13. **Abomination:** See Exeg. on 3:32.

10. Triplet. The law of retribution. **Upright:** See Exeg. on 12:15. **Blameless:** See Exeg. on 10:9.

11. The rich man is not always wise. The poor man who is intelligent can usually "see right through him" (see Exeg. on 10:2). **Conceit: Lit., eyes. Has understanding:** See Exeg. on 1:2.

12. Antithetic. Cf. vs. 28. The text is uncertain. **Rejoice** is the correct translation. **Triumph** (RSV, ASV) is an attempt to make sense out of a difficult text, but is not correct. **A man is hidden** or, better, **men hide themselves** in fear. Lit., "are searched for."

13. Antithetic. God's mercy is dependent upon a contrite heart, not sacrifice. Confession must be followed by the forsaking of sin. Cf. Ecclus. 21:1-2:

> My child, if you have sinned, do not do it again,
> And pray over your former sins.
> Flee from sin as from the face of a snake;
> For if you approach it, it will bite you.
> Its teeth are lion's teeth,
> And destroy the souls of men (Amer. Trans.).

---

9. See Expos. on 21:3.

10. See Expos. on 3:1-4.

11. See Expos. on 10:15-16.

12. See Expos. on 21:3.

13. ***Open Confession Is Good for the Soul.***—Repressed feelings of guilt can produce havoc in a person's life. Little wonder that religions have tried to construct a system by which men might be delivered from the haunting sense of wrongs done or good deeds left undone! One man even asked the terrible question: "Shall I give my firstborn for my transgression, the fruit of my body for the sin of my soul?" (Mic. 6:7.) The answer which this proverb gives is pitched on a high ethical level. Feelings of guilt are not to be removed by some magic formula or by observing some complicated system of rites. The transgression is to be confessed. It is to be brought into the open, so that the transgressor hears himself admit his wrong. Such confession may be made to another individual, or the heart can be poured out before God. The important thing is not that somebody else condemns an individual for pain he has caused, but that he sees his wrong in its true light. While this may seem to be a humiliating experience,

14 Happy *is* the man that feareth always: but he that hardeneth his heart shall fall into michief.

15 *As* a roaring lion, and a ranging bear; *so is* a wicked ruler over the poor people.

16 The prince that wanteth understanding *is* also a great oppressor: *but* he that hateth covetousness shall prolong *his* days.

17 A man that doeth violence to the blood of *any* person shall flee to the pit; let no man stay him.

18 Whoso walketh uprightly shall be saved: but *he that is* perverse *in his* ways shall fall at once.

14 Blessed is the man who fears the LORD always;
but he who hardens his heart will fall into calamity.
15 Like a roaring lion or a charging bear
is a wicked ruler over a poor people.
16 A ruler who lacks understanding is a cruel oppressor;
but he who hates unjust gain will prolong his days.
17 If a man is burdened with the blood of another,
let him be a fugitive until death;
let no one help him.
18 He who walks in integrity will be delivered,
but he who is perverse in his ways will fall into a pit.[b]

[b] Syr: Heb *in one*

14. Antithetic. **Fears:** Lit., "dreads" (*pāḥadh*). It has no object in the Hebrew. The RSV supplies **the LORD** as object, although "sin" may also be meant. **Hardens his heart:** Against God and the things of God (cf. 29:1).

15. See Exeg. on 16:10.

16. In vs. 16*a* the Hebrew reads simply, "A prince lacking in understanding and great in oppression." The ASV mg. makes the verse one continuous sentence. On kingship in general see Exeg. on 16:10. **Understanding:** The form of the noun is plural. It is connected with the root *bîn* (see Exeg. on 1:2). **Unjust gain** is better than **covetousness.**

17. An impossible Hebrew text. Lit., "A man oppressed by the blood of a soul [person] flees unto a pit, let them not grasp [support] him." The sentence is not in the style of Hebrew poetry. It seems to deal with the problem of a murderer, fleeing for his life, perhaps to one of the cities of refuge (Num. 35:26 ff.). All emendations are purely conjectural. **Doeth violence to** or **is burdened:** The word *'āshûq,* "oppressed," can in no way bear either of these meanings. The word *bôr* (pit) can hardly mean **death** here since it would be impossible to help one fleeing to death or the grave.

18. Antithetic. **Uprightly** or **in integrity:** See Exeg. on 10:9. **Perverse:** See Exeg. on 2:15. **Ways:** Dual in the Hebrew. It probably should be pointed as a plural, with LXX

it is also a healing experience. Bramwell Booth, who spent many years in dealing with the spiritual ills of people, once said:

> Few things surprise me more, either in my public work or in my personal dealing with souls, than the evidences I meet of unconfessed sin. It would be no exaggeration to say that fully half the misery, uncertainty, and weakness I come across arise from this cause. The fact is, man's nature was not constructed to harbor evil.[9]

This proverb states that **He who conceals his transgressions will not prosper.** Things will not go well with his spirit. Psychologists are underlining this point, for they can see the misery which endless self-reproach produces. Speaking of transgressions, the proverb goes on to say that **he who confesses and forsakes them will obtain mercy.** Confession is not enough. The individual must confess *and forsake* them. One could easily resort to a repetition of words of confession without touching the true springs of conduct. The person who really confesses his sins will take steps to forsake them as well. Confession is incomplete if it does not include the intention to turn from a course that is wrong.

14. See Expos. on 1:7.

15-16. See Expos. on 16:10-15.

17. See Expos. on 3:27-35.

18. See Expos. on 3:1-4.

[9] "Confession of Sin," *Christian Century,* XLIII (1926), 444.

19 He that tilleth his land shall have plenty of bread: but he that followeth after vain *persons* shall have poverty enough.

20 A faithful man shall abound with blessings: but he that maketh haste to be rich shall not be innocent.

21 To have respect of persons *is* not good: for, for a piece of bread *that* man will transgress.

22 He that hasteth to be rich *hath* an evil eye, and considereth not that poverty shall come upon him.

23 He that rebuketh a man, afterward shall find more favor than he that flattereth with the tongue.

24 Whoso robbeth his father or his mother, and saith, *It is* no transgression; the same *is* the companion of a destroyer.

25 He that is of a proud heart stirreth

19 He who tills his land will have plenty of bread,
but he who follows worthless pursuits will have plenty of poverty.
20 A faithful man will abound with blessings,
but he who hastens to be rich will not go unpunished.
21 To show partiality is not good;
but for a piece of bread a man will do wrong.
22 A miserly man hastens after wealth,
and does not know that want will come upon him.
23 He who rebukes a man will afterward find more favor
than he who flatters with his tongue.
24 He who robs his father or his mother
and says, "That is no transgression,"
is the companion of a man who destroys.
25 A greedy man stirs up strife,

(see vs. 6). **At once** or **into a pit:** Lit., **in one** (RSV mg.). The KJV cannot be justified in any way from the M.T. The RSV emends according to the Syriac. The expression probably should be omitted, with the LXX. It may have crept in from vs. 10.

19. Antithetic. Cf. 12:11. Here again the wise men idealize the life of the farmer (see Exeg. on 27:23). **Vain persons** or **worthless pursuits:** Either is possible, with the latter being the more probable. Cf. a parallel passage from Amen-em-ope (quoted by Oesterley, *Proverbs,* p. 256):

> Plough thine own fields, then wilt thou find what is,
> And wilt obtain bread from thine own threshing floor.

20. Antithetic. Hastening to get rich implies the use of dishonest procedures for which one will be held guilty (see Exeg. on 10:2).

21. Synonymous. Cf. 18:5; 24:23. The smallest thing may be used to tempt a man to show partiality in the court.

22. The selfish man will suffer want in the end. On the subject of wealth see Exeg. on 10:2. **A miserly man:** The RSV gives sense to an obscure Hebrew phrase, **that hath an evil eye** (see Exeg. on 23:6).

23. On the benefits of reproof and the evils of flattery cf. 15:5, 12; 25:12; 27:5-6; 29:5. **Rebukes:** See Exeg. on 1:23. **Afterward:** The Hebrew text has, lit., "after me." It should probably be deleted, with the Syriac, as a gloss.

24. Triplet. Cf. Matt. 15:4-6. A rather brutal practice is described here of robbing the parents, a crime that must have been defended on some ground as vs. 24*b* infers. **Destroyer:** A technical term of which we know nothing, or it may mean here simply one who destroys family and home (cf. 18:9).

25. Antithetic. The greedy man stirs up strife against himself, thus causing ruin to come his way, whereas the man who trusts God for his daily needs will prosper. **Proud**

---

19. See Expos. on 6:1-15.
20. See Expos. on 20:6.
21. See Expos. on 21:3.
22. See Expos. on 10:15-16.
23. See Expos. on 9:7-9.
24. See Expos. on 1:8-9; 10:1.
25. See Expos. on 3:5-8.

up strife: but he that putteth his trust in the LORD shall be made fat.

26 He that trusteth in his own heart is a fool: but whoso walketh wisely, he shall be delivered.

27 He that giveth unto the poor shall not lack: but he that hideth his eyes shall have many a curse.

28 When the wicked rise, men hide themselves: but when they perish, the righteous increase.

29 He, that being often reproved hardeneth *his* neck, shall suddenly be destroyed, and that without remedy.

2 When the righteous are in authority, the people rejoice: but when the wicked beareth rule, the people mourn.

3 Whoso loveth wisdom rejoiceth his father: but he that keepeth company with harlots spendeth *his* substance.

4 The king by judgment establisheth the land: but he that receiveth gifts overthroweth it.

but he who trusts in the LORD will be enriched.

26 He who trusts in his own mind is a fool;
but he who walks in wisdom will be delivered.

27 He who gives to the poor will not want,
but he who hides his eyes will get many a curse.

28 When the wicked rise, men hide themselves,
but when they perish, the righteous increase.

29 He who is often reproved, yet stiffens his neck,
will suddenly be broken beyond healing.

2 When the righteous are in authority, the people rejoice;
but when the wicked rule, the people groan.

3 He who loves wisdom makes his father glad,
but one who keeps company with harlots squanders his substance.

4 By justice a king gives stability to the land,
but one who exacts gifts ruins it.

---

heart or, better, **greedy man:** Lit., "wide of soul [appetite]." **Shall be made fat:** Better, **will be enriched.**

26. Antithetic. To trust in one's own abilities is utter foolishness. A wise man trusts in God. **Mind:** See Exeg. on 2:2. But here it could readily be translated "self," as the word is often used to express the reflexive idea by synecdoche. **Be delivered:** I.e., from any danger which may befall him, because he has the intelligence to deal with it.

27. Antithetic. See Exeg. on 19:17 regarding the care for the poor. Vs. 27*b* means that he disregards human needs.

28. Antithetic. A variation of vs. 12. The reference is to public officials (cf. 29:2).

29:1. The Hebrew literally reads, "A man of reproofs who hardens his neck shall suddenly be broken, and no healing." The obstinate man refuses to learn. **Reproved:** Lit., "reproofs" (see Exeg. on 1:23).

2. Antithetic. Cf. 28:12, 28. **Are in authority:** Lit., "in the increasing of the righteous," with the ASV. "Increasing" in number may carry with it the idea of authority belonging to the larger group, but the same idea may be obtained by reading *bīredhôth* ("to rule") for *bīrebhôth.*

3. Antithetic. This verse is reminiscent of the many warnings against licentiousness in Part I of the book of Proverbs (cf. chs. 2; 5–7; 9; for the thought in vs. 3*a* cf. 10:1; 23:15, 24; 27:11). **Squanders:** Lit., "causes to perish."

4. Antithetic. Regarding the king in Proverbs see Exeg. on 16:10. **Justice:** See Exeg. on 1:3. **He that receiveth gifts** or **one who exacts gifts:** Lit., "a man of exactions." The word

---

26. See Expos. on 29:23.
27. See Expos. on 22:16*a*.
28. See Expos. on 16:10-15.
29:1. See Expos. on 9:7-9.
2. See Expos. on 16:10-15.
3. See Expos. on 10:1.
4. See Expos. on 16:10-15.

5 A man that flattereth his neighbor spreadeth a net for his feet.

6 In the transgression of an evil man *there is* a snare: but the righteous doth sing and rejoice.

7 The righteous considereth the cause of the poor: *but* the wicked regardeth not to know *it*.

8 Scornful men bring a city into a snare: but wise *men* turn away wrath.

9 *If* a wise man contendeth with a foolish man, whether he rage or laugh, *there is* no rest.

10 The bloodthirsty hate the upright: but the just seek his soul.

11 A fool uttereth all his mind: but a wise *man* keepeth it in till afterward.

5 A man who flatters his neighbor
spreads a net for his feet.
6 An evil man is ensnared in his transgression,
but a righteous man sings and rejoices.
7 A righteous man knows the rights of the poor;
a wicked man does not understand such knowledge.
8 Scoffers set a city aflame,
but wise men turn away wrath.
9 If a wise man has an argument with a fool,
the fool only rages and laughs, and there is no quiet.
10 Bloodthirsty men hate one who is blameless,
and the wicked[c] seek his life.
11 A fool gives full vent to his anger,
but a wise man quietly holds it back.

[c] Cn: Heb *upright*

terûmāh usually means ritual offerings, but here it is used in a nonritual sense. The translation of the KJV here makes good sense in that a corrupt king who receives gifts will overthrow the land. According to the RSV, *terûmāh* would have to refer to taxes or similar demands for money.

5. Flatters: In the sense of "deceive" (cf. 26:28; 28:23) .

6. Antithetic. The KJV renders literally the Hebrew of vs. 6*a*, which is a poetic expression. It cannot literally be said that a **snare** lies in a **transgression.** The RSV follows the Syriac.

7. Antithetic. The verse refers to a court of justice. Vs. 7*b* literally reads, "a wicked man does not understand knowledge," which makes no sense in this context. Both the KJV and RSV try to force a meaning out of the text by adding words not present in the Hebrew. Toy suggests reading "the wicked does not plead for the needy." This requires little emendation of the Hebrew text and has some support in the LXX.

8. Antithetic. **Bring . . . into a snare** or, better, **set . . . aflame:** The root is *pûaḥ* (not *pāḥaḥ*, as KJV translates) , meaning "to blow," i.e., "to fan [a fire]." The word is used elsewhere in Proverbs of "uttering," i.e., breathing out (lies) . See Exeg. on 6:19. The passions of men are fanned by these scoffers until they burst forth in fury and rage, and the city is in an uproar.

9. Has an argument: I.e., in court. The subject of vs. 9*b* may be the fool (with KJV, RSV, and ASV mg.) who refuses to listen to the arguments of the wise man, or the wise man (with ASV) who in no way can put his arguments across. The verbs more naturally describe the reactions of the fool.

10. Blameless: See Exeg. on 10:9. Vs. 10*b* reads, lit., "and upright ones seek his soul," which is impossible. Either *yeshārîm* can be emended to read *reshā'îm* "wicked ones," or *yebhaqqeshû* to read *yebhaqqerû* "to seek (in care for) ." The RSV follows the former emendation.

11. Antithetic. **Mind** or **anger:** Lit., "spirit" (*rûaḥ*) . Vs. 11*b* literally reads, "and a

5. See Expos. on 27:21.
6. See Expos. on 3:1-4.
7. See Expos. on 14:21.
8. See Expos. on 16:10-15.
9. See Expos. on 26:21.
10. See Expos. on 22:16*a*.
11. See Expos. on 16:32.

12 If a ruler hearken to lies, all his servants *are* wicked.
13 The poor and the deceitful man meet together: the LORD lighteneth both their eyes.
14 The king that faithfully judgeth the poor, his throne shall be established for ever.
15 The rod and reproof give wisdom: but a child left *to himself* bringeth his mother to shame.
16 When the wicked are multiplied, transgression increaseth: but the righteous shall see their fall.
17 Correct thy son, and he shall give thee rest; yea, he shall give delight unto thy soul.
18 Where *there is* no vision, the people perish: but he that keepeth the law, happy *is* he.
19 A servant will not be corrected by

12 If a ruler listens to falsehood,
all his officials will be wicked.
13 The poor man and the oppressor meet together;
the LORD gives light to the eyes of both.
14 If a king judges the poor with equity
his throne will be established for ever.
15 The rod and reproof give wisdom,
but a child left to himself brings shame to his mother.
16 When the wicked are in authority, transgression increases;
but the righteous will look upon their downfall.
17 Discipline your son, and he will give you rest;
he will give delight to your heart.
18 Where there is no prophecy the people cast off restraint,
but blessed is he who keeps the law.
19 By mere words a servant is not disciplined,

---

wise man afterwards [?] stilleth it." The word "it" grammatically refers to the anger of the fool, but probably designates the wise man's wrath. Conceivably the wise man may succeed at last in quelling the fool's **anger.**

12. On the **ruler** see Exeg. on 16:10. With this verse cf. Ecclus. 10:2:

> Like the judge of a people are his officers,
> And like the governor of a city are all who live in it (Amer. Trans.).

13. Deceitful or, better, **oppressor:** Lit., "man of oppressions." God causes his light to shine on all classes (cf. 22:2).

14. Faithfully or **with equity:** Lit., "in truth" (see Exeg. on 16:10).

15. Antithetic. Cf. 13:24; see Exeg. on 22:6. **Left to himself:** Lit., "sent away," so as not to be bothered with him.

16. The orthodox doctrine that the wicked will fail and the righteous prosper is still taught here, even though actual experience proved otherwise. **Are multiplied** or **are in authority:** See Exeg. on vs. 2.

17. See Exeg. on 22:6. **Delight:** Lit., "dainties."

18. Antithetic. Another important verse which throws light on the problem of the canonization of the O.T. (see Exeg. on 13:13 for a full discussion). **Vision** or, better, **prophecy:** This term probably refers to the prophetic books in the canon, as **law** in vs. 18*b* refers to the Pentateuch. The LXX translates this word by ἐξηγητής, "guide," "interpreter" (exegete). **Perish** or **cast off restraint:** The root is *pāra'*, "let go."

19. Corporal punishment is recommended for slaves. Cf. Ecclus. 33:24-28:

> Fodder and a stick for an ass,
> Bread and discipline and work for a servant.
> Put your slave to work, and you will have rest;
> Leave his hands idle, and he will seek his liberty.

---

12. See Expos. on 16:10-15.
13. See Expos. on 22:16*a*.
14. See Expos. on 16:10-15.
15. See Expos. on 17:6.
16. See Expos. on 16:10-15.
17. See Expos. on 9:7-9.
18. See Expos. on 16:10-15.
19. See Expos. on 9:7-9.

words: for though he understand he will not answer.

20 Seest thou a man *that is* hasty in his words? *there is* more hope of a fool than of him.

21 He that delicately bringeth up his servant from a child shall have him become *his* son at the length.

22 An angry man stirreth up strife, and a furious man aboundeth in transgression.

23 A man's pride shall bring him low: but honor shall uphold the humble in spirit.

for though he understands, he will not
give heed.
20 Do you see a man who is hasty in his
words?
There is more hope for a fool than for
him.
21 He who pampers his servant from childhood,
will in the end find him his heir.[d]
22 A man of wrath stirs up strife,
and a man given to anger causes much
transgression.
23 A man's pride will bring him low,
but he who is lowly in spirit will obtain
honor.

[d] The meaning of the Hebrew word is uncertain

The yoke and the strap will bend his neck,
And racks and tortures are for a servant who is a wrongdoer.
Put him to work, so that he will not be idle,
For idleness teaches much evil.
Set him such work as is suited to him,
And if he does not obey, load him with fetters (Amer. Trans.).

20. This verse should probably follow vs. 21. There is no question in the Hebrew of vs. 20*a* (see Exeg. on 26:12, of which this verse is a variation).

21. A difficult verse. **Delicately bringeth up** or **pampers:** The word is found only here in the O.T. It is a strange expression to use with **servant. His son** or **his heir:** The word *mānôn* is unknown. These two translations connect it with *nîn,* "offspring," "posterity." The LXX reads differently from the M.T., "He who lives luxuriously from a child will be a servant, and finally shall be grieved with himself."

22. Synonymous. Cf. 15:18.

23. Antithetic. Cf. 15:33; 18:12. **Low** and **lowly:** A good play on words, as in the Hebrew.

---

20. See Expos. on 18:21.

21. See Expos. on 17:6.

22. See Expos. on 16:32.

23. ***Arrogant Pride or Sincere Humility.***—Arrogant pride, which expresses itself in inordinate self-esteem in the presence of God and man, receives repeated and unqualified condemnation from the writers of Proverbs.

A man's pride will bring him low,
but he who is lowly in spirit will obtain honor.

Pride produces instability. A conceited person may fool some of the people some of the time, but sooner or later he is discovered in his true light. By sheer arrogance he may push himself to the chief seat at the feast, but chagrin follows when he is asked to step down from his high position (25:6-7).

Pride goes before destruction,
and a haughty spirit before a fall (16:18).

These familiar words are a reminder that pride does not have longevity. "Pride goes. . . ." One who builds his house on conceit is building on shifting sands.

Pride prevents growth. When a person is sure that he knows everything there is to be known he is not in a frame of mind to learn anything from others. A man who is blind to his own defects has little chance to correct them. The sages have little good to say about a fool, but they think that there is more hope for a fool than for "a man wise in his own conceit" (26:12). The fool may stumble upon some bit of wisdom in his wandering, but the arrogant man is sure he knows all there is to be known. The vain man is undeterred by facts and unhampered by ignorance, since he feels a self-sufficiency in his own opinions. Folly has achieved rigidity in him. Pride produces contention.

By insolence the heedless make strife,
but with those who take advice is wisdom (13:10).

24 Whoso is partner with a thief hateth his own soul: he heareth cursing, and bewrayeth *it* not.
25 The fear of man bringeth a snare: but whoso putteth his trust in the LORD shall be safe.
26 Many seek the ruler's favor; but *every* man's judgment *cometh* from the LORD.
27 An unjust man *is* an abomination to the just: and *he that is* upright in the way *is* abomination to the wicked.

24 The partner of a thief hates his own life;
he hears the curse, but discloses nothing.
25 The fear of man lays a snare,
but he who trusts in the LORD is safe.
26 Many seek the favor of a ruler,
but from the LORD a man gets justice.
27 An unjust man is an abomination to the righteous,
but he whose way is straight is an abomination to the wicked.

30 The words of Agur the son of Jakeh, *even* the prophecy: the man spake unto Ithiel, even unto Ithiel and Ucal,

30 The words of Agur son of Jakeh of Massa.[e]

The man says to Ith'i-el,
to Ith'i-el and Ucal:[f]

[e] Or *the oracle*
[f] The Hebrew of this verse is obscure

24. A partner in crime is impeding justice if he says nothing in court when it is asked whether anyone knows anything about the case in question. **Curse:** "Adjuration" (ASV) is probably better. The word *'ālāh* can mean both "curse" and "oath," since part of the oath was the curse against the violator of the agreement (cf. Lev. 5:1).

25. Antithetic. **Fear of man:** The fear caused by what other men may think of one's actions. **Safe:** Lit., "shall be set on high."

26. Antithetic. This verse condemns reliance on mere human power because God ultimately overrules all things. **Ruler's favor:** Lit., "face of a ruler." The phrase may mean to seek the presence of the ruler, "face" standing for "presence," as in Exod. 33:14; or it may mean to seek his recognition (see Exeg. on 16:10). **Justice:** See Exeg. on 1:3.

27. Antithetic. **Abomination:** See Exeg. on 3:22. **Upright** or **straight:** See Exeg. on 12:15.

V. THE WORDS OF AGUR (30:1-33)

The title may belong to the whole chapter or simply to vss. 1-14. This collection

When an individual is fearful of his own status and arrogantly affirms his own worth he will resent opposition and threats to his position. Contention comes when each one wants to be the greatest and to occupy the position of honor.

Pride toward God is the ultimate sin. Such pride is a man's assertion of his self-sufficiency. The conceited man lacks the profound self-knowledge that he is dependent on God, that he is a creature, not the Creator. A humble man recognizes his creaturehood. This does not mean that he thinks meanly of himself—he thinks objectively, recognizing that another is the sovereign of this universe, not himself.

Young Benjamin Franklin, when he went to visit Cotton Mather, had an experience that illustrates the teaching in Proverbs. Franklin recounts the event in these words:

> He received me in his library and, on my taking leave, showed me a shorter way out of the house through a narrow passage, which was crossed by a beam overhead. We were still talking as I withdrew, he accompanying me behind, when he said hastily; "Stoop, stoop!" I did not understand him, till I felt my head hit against the beam. He was a man that never missed any occasion of giving instruction, and upon this he said to me: "You are young, and have the world before you; stoop as you go through it, and you will miss many hard bumps." [1]

There are dangers in carrying the head too high, both in relation to other men and in relation to God. For this reason the sages commend the man who walks humbly with his God and who refuses to be haughty in spirit toward others.

24. See Expos. on 22:16*a*.

25-26. See Expos. on 3:5-8.

27. See Expos. on 21:3.

30:1-6. ***A Man Aware of His Ignorance.***—He is a wise man who is aware of his ignorance. The

[1] Carl Van Doren, *Benjamin Franklin* (New York: Viking Press, 1938), pp. 43-44.

2 Surely I *am* more brutish than *any* man, and have not the understanding of a man.
3 I neither learned wisdom, nor have the knowledge of the holy.

2 Surely I am too stupid to be a man.
I have not the understanding of a man.
3 I have not learned wisdom,
nor have I knowledge of the Holy One.

---

consists of two parts: Agur's personal reflections (vss. 1-14) and numerical proverbs (vss. 15-33, except vss. 17, 20, 32-33).

A. Agur's Personal Reflections (30:1-14)

30:1. The title. A difficult verse. The proper names **Agur** and **Jakeh** are found nowhere else in the O.T. They are not Hebrew names, but may be connected with Arabic roots (see Gemser, *Sprüche Salomos,* p. 79). **Massa:** "Burden," "utterance." A term frequently used of prophetic utterance or oracle. It is obviously connected with *nāsā'* ("to lift"). Cf. Isa. 14:4; Mic. 2:4; Hab. 2:6, where this verb is used with *māshāl* ("proverb") and so is brought into the wisdom tradition. The word might refer, as in 31:1, to the Arabian tribe of **Massa,** east of Palestine (cf. Gen. 25:14; I Chr. 1:30). The LXX finds no proper names in this first stich, and reads, "Fear my words, son, and receiving them, repent," which actually represents a Hebrew text very similar to the M.T. except for the last word. It is probably better, however, to retain the proper names as we find them in the KJV and the RSV. Vs. 1*b*, which looks like a second title, is quite unintelligible. Of the proper names, **Ucal** is entirely unknown, and **Ithiel** occurs in Neh. 11:7. The LXX again has no proper names in this stich, but the translation gives no help in the understanding of the Hebrew text. The Greek reads, "These things says the man to those who believe God, and I cease." The ASV mg., "I have wearied myself, O God, I have wearied myself, O God, and am consumed," may be obtained from the present consonantal M.T., but so may other translations, depending upon the way the text is manipulated. **Says:** The word *ne'ûm* is another technical prophetic term (see above), although it may be used to introduce any kind of formal communication.

2. Synonymous. Is the writer sarcastic in these opening verses, claiming that he is not like those who know everything, or is he really humble before God who can be comprehended not by human reason, but by revelation alone (vss. 5-6)? The latter is probably the correct interpretation. **Brutish** or **stupid:** The RSV gives the correct meaning of the Hebrew. **Understanding:** See Exeg. on 1:2.

3. Synonymous. **The holy** or **Holy One:** See Exeg. on 9:10.

---

sage who speaks in this passage is unidentified, even though his name is given, but he reveals an attitude that easily can be identified. He is conscious of his ignorance of God and his ways. The little he does understand is but a tiny island in an ocean of mystery. The reflective person shares this view. He sees how little he knows about the divine governance of the universe. He knows he is not the Creator. As a creature he cannot fathom the intentions of the God who made him.

The text of the second part of the first verse is hopelessly corrupt, but attempts have been made to get rid of the proper names and find other meanings for the words (see Exeg.). In his commentary Crawford H. Toy [2] calls attention to a translation suggested by Cocceius in 1669: "These things says the man: I have wearied myself about God, I have wearied myself about God, and I have pined away." In these words Agur expresses his complete failure in his effort to comprehend God's nature and mode of procedure. Even though there is scant warrant to use an obscure passage to describe man's inability to understand God, there is a fundamental truth expressed here that is a fitting introduction to what follows.

Some of the statements of the sage may be sarcastic comment (yet see Exeg.) on those who think they understand divine things. **Surely I am too stupid to be a man,** he says, implying that if he were a man like other men he would have easy answers for the perplexing questions of human existence. He then wants to know who it is that has ascended to heaven and brought the answers to the problems of understanding God. Surely those who profess to know God's

[2] *A Critical and Exegetical Commentary on the Book of Proverbs* (New York: Charles Scribner's Sons, 1899; "International Critical Commentary"), p. 520.

4 Who hath ascended up into heaven, or descended? who hath gathered the wind in his fists? who hath bound the waters in a garment? who hath established all the ends of the earth? what *is* his name, and what *is* his son's name, if thou canst tell?

5 Every word of God *is* pure: he *is* a shield unto them that put their trust in him.

6 Add thou not unto his words, lest he reprove thee, and thou be found a liar.

4 Who has ascended to heaven and come down?
Who has gathered the wind in his fists?
Who has wrapped up the waters in a garment?
Who has established all the ends of the earth?
What is his name, and what is his son's name?
Surely you know!

5 Every word of God proves true;
he is a shield to those who take refuge in him.
6 Do not add to his words,
lest he rebuke you, and you be found a liar.

---

4. No man can do all these things. Only God can do them (cf. Job 38:4 ff.). **Garment:** The clouds (cf. Job 26:8). **Son's name:** Is there anyone to whom God has imparted his nature and attributes? This question reveals the longing in men's hearts for a fuller and clearer revelation of God, which of course was fully answered in the Incarnation.

5. This verse is taken from Ps. 18:30 (Hebrew 18:31). **Pure** or **proves true:** The word *çerûphāh* refers to the refining of metals.

6. Cf. Deut. 4:2; Rev. 22:18. **His words:** The writer is referring to the words of scripture, including the Law, the Prophets, and the Writings. The Law and the Prophets are mentioned in 29:18. The Writings may also be included now since the preceding verse is a quotation from the Psalms. This threefold division of the Hebrew Bible is first explicitly mentioned in the Prologue to Ecclesiasticus (132 B.C.; see Exeg. on 13:13). **Rebuke:** See Exeg. on 1:23.

---

ways can identify the emissary who has come from him. While acknowledging that he does not know the divine purposes, he has little patience with those who think they know when they are equally ignorant.

This consciousness that we know in part, and that in regard to many things we must see as through a glass darkly (I Cor. 13:9, 12), is not foreign to religion. Our faith is what we do with our ignorance, and the first thing to do with ignorance is to acknowledge it and to recognize that it reminds us of our creatureliness. Herbert Spencer gave expression to this same sense of mystery when he wrote:

> But one truth must grow ever clearer—the truth that there is an Inscrutable Existence everywhere manifested, to which he [the man of science] can neither find nor conceive either beginning or end. Amid the mysteries which become the more mysterious the more they are thought about, there will remain the one absolute certainty, that he is ever in presence of an Infinite and Eternal Energy, from which all things proceed.[3]

[3] *The Principles of Sociology* (New York: D. Appleton & Co., 1896), III, 175.

Vss. 5-6 seem to give some reassurance to the man who is aware of his ignorance of God. He may not know all the answers to the riddles of existence, but he can trust in the God who has given him sufficient light to guide his steps. If a man has only his ignorance there is little hope for him. But here is something more. He has the assurance that there is knowledge with God. His mood changes from a sense of ignorance to a sense of mystery. W. E. Hocking has said: "Religion is bound up in the difference between the sense of ignorance and the sense of mystery: the former means, 'I know not'; the latter means 'I know not; but *it is known.*'"[4] We may not know God, but he knows us.

Awareness of ignorance alone becomes a depressant. But a sense of mystery releases effort and places our little lives in the more ample framework of One who knows us altogether.

> The fact that God is greater than anything we can understand, that His Being is a mystery which we can never fathom, that all begins and ends in mystery, suggests the richness and wonder of the

[4] *Meaning of God in Human Experience,* pp. 235-36.

7 Two *things* have I required of thee; deny me *them* not before I die:
8 Remove far from me vanity and lies; give me neither poverty nor riches; feed me with food convenient for me:
9 Lest I be full, and deny *thee,* and say, Who *is* the LORD? or lest I be poor, and steal, and take the name of my God *in vain.*
10 Accuse not a servant unto his master, lest he curse thee, and thou be found guilty.

7 Two things I ask of thee;
deny them not to me before I die:
8 Remove far from me falsehood and lying;
give me neither poverty nor riches;
feed me with the food that is needful for me,
9 lest I be full, and deny thee,
and say, "Who is the LORD?"
or lest I be poor, and steal,
and profane the name of my God.

10 Do not slander a servant to his master,
lest he curse you, and you be held guilty.

7-9. From vs. 7 on, with the exception of vss. 10, 17, 20, 32-33, the proverbs of ch. 30 are of the numerical type; cf. 6:16-19; Amos 1:3–2:6; and examples from the Canaanite material found at Ugarit (from about the fifteenth century B.C.).

8. Vanity or, better, **falsehood:** The word *shāw'* literally means "emptiness," but as a synonym of **lies** it must be translated as in the RSV. It has this meaning in other places in the O.T. **Lying:** Lit., "word of falsehood." **Food convenient for me** or **food that is needful for me:** Lit., "the bread of my portion." Nothing more, nothing less.

9. The dangers of wealth and poverty are here stressed (see Exeg. on 10:2). **Take . . . in vain** or **profane:** Lit., "lay hold of," "grasp," and so figuratively here, "handle the name lightly or profanely" (ASV mg.).

10. Accuse or **slander:** Lit., "do not tongue." The RSV is probably too strong here in this context. The expression may refer to simple gossip or tongue-wagging.

Being of God. As we gaze upwards into that Bright Cloud of Unknowing we worship the Mystery of God with a kind of delighted ignorance. For if we could comprehend God He would be God no longer.[5]

7-10. ***Neither Poverty nor Riches.***—A small boy living in the twentieth century arrived at a conclusion similar to that of the writer of these words. He told his parents that he wanted to be "middle-size." When they asked him what he meant by this remark, he said that he did not want to be too poor, since in that event he would not have enough to eat and to wear; but he did not want to be too rich, since in that case he would live in constant fear of robbers who might try to take his money away from him. The boy's remark might be branded as a typical child's reaction in a bourgeois culture. He was an incipient middle-class man, seeking the security of the golden mean. At least he found himself in a good literary tradition, for in Cowper's translation of a passage from Horace we read these words:

He that holds fast the golden mean,
And lives contentedly between
The little and the great,
Feels not the wants that pinch the poor,
Nor plagues that haunt the rich man's door,
Imbittering all his state.[6]

The program of a proletarian may have much in common with this view. It seeks greater equity in the distribution of this world's goods. Greater equity generally moves in the direction of greater equality. A society may divide the products of the efforts of its members in such a way that too much is given to too few and too little is given to too many.

The desire of the man who wrote this passage in Proverbs need not be limited to an individual's aspirations. A whole society can hold this goal before itself. The O.T. story of the gathering of the manna had a truth which commended itself to Paul. A good society might have these same words said of it, "The man who got much did not have too much, and the man who got little did not have too little" (II Cor. 8:15 Goodspeed).

[5] Olive Wyon, *The School of Prayer* (Philadelphia: Westminster Press, 1944), p. 113.

[6] *Odes* II. 10.

11 *There is* a generation *that* curseth their father, and doth not bless their mother.

12 *There is* a generation *that are* pure in their own eyes, and *yet* is not washed from their filthiness.

13 *There is* a generation, O how lofty are their eyes! and their eyelids are lifted up.

14 *There is* a generation, whose teeth *are as* swords, and their jaw teeth *as* knives, to devour the poor from off the earth, and the needy from *among* men.

15 The horseleech hath two daughters, *crying,* Give, give. There are three *things that* are never satisfied, *yea,* four *things* say not, *It is* enough:

16 The grave; and the barren womb; the earth *that* is not filled with water; and the fire *that* saith not, *It is* enough.

17 The eye *that* mocketh at *his* father, and despiseth to obey *his* mother, the ravens of the valley shall pick it out, and the young eagles shall eat it.

11 There are those who curse their fathers
and do not bless their mothers.
12 There are those who are pure in their own eyes
but are not cleansed of their filth.
13 There are those—how lofty are their eyes,
how high their eyelids lift!
14 There are those whose teeth are swords,
whose teeth are knives,
to devour the poor from off the earth,
the needy from among men.

15 The leech[g] has two daughters;
"Give, give," they cry.
Three things are never satisfied;
four never say, "Enough":
16 Sheol, the barren womb,
the earth ever thirsty for water,
and the fire which never says, "Enough."[h]

17 The eye that mocks a father
and scorns to obey a mother
will be picked out by the ravens of the valley
and eaten by the vultures.

[g] The meaning of the Hebrew word is uncertain
[h] Heb obscure

11-14. Four types of evil men. Each verse in the Hebrew begins simply with **A generation that. . . .** The word **generation** here means a class of men. With vs. 11 cf. 20:20. Vs. 14 describes the rapacious ones who oppress the poor. **Teeth:** The Hebrew has two synonyms for teeth in vs. 14.

B. Numerical Sayings (30:15-33)

15-16. Four insatiable things. Vs. 15*a* literally reads, "To *'alûqāh* are two daughters, Give, Give." This seems to have been added later as an introductory statement to these two verses and seems to have no connection with the following lines, except that the numeral **two** may have been thought to have some connection with the **three** and **four** that follow. **Horseleech** or **leech** is the meaning of *'alûqāh* in Syriac and rabbinical Hebrew (see the ancient versions). The connection of this word with allegorical or mythological figures is philologically unsound. **Enough:** The word *hôn* means "wealth."

16. Grave or **Sheol:** See Exeg. on 1:12 (cf. 27:20). **Barren womb:** Lit., "restraint of womb." **The earth:** Better, "the land." The soil in Palestine was parched and dry except in the comparatively short rainy season.

17. An isolated verse which is probably out of place here, since its form is different from the numerical proverbs around it. **To obey:** A difficult Hebrew word whose meaning and form are questionable. The LXX reads, "the old age of," i.e., *tiqnath* for יקהת (?), which the Amer. Trans. and Moffatt follow. **Young eagles** or, better, **vultures:** The body of the disobedient son is left unburied and birds of prey attack it.

11. See Expos. on 1:8-9; 10:1.
12-13. See Expos. on 29:23.
14. See Expos. on 22:16*a*.
15-16. See Expos. on 13:12.
17. See Expos. on 1:8-9; 10:1.

18 There be three *things which* are too wonderful for me, yea, four which I know not:
19 The way of an eagle in the air; the way of a serpent upon a rock; the way of a ship in the midst of the sea; and the way of a man with a maid.
20 Such *is* the way of an adulterous woman; she eateth, and wipeth her mouth, and saith, I have done no wickedness.
21 For three *things* the earth is disquieted, and for four *which* it cannot bear:
22 For a servant when he reigneth; and a fool when he is filled with meat;
23 For an odious *woman* when she is married; and a handmaid that is heir to her mistress.
24 There be four *things which are* little upon the earth, but they *are* exceeding wise:
25 The ants *are* a people not strong, yet they prepare their meat in the summer;

18 Three things are too wonderful for me;
four I do not understand:
19 the way of an eagle in the sky,
the way of a serpent on a rock,
the way of a ship on the high seas,
and the way of a man with a maiden.

20 This is the way of an adulteress:
she eats, and wipes her mouth,
and says, "I have done no wrong."
21 Under three things the earth trembles;
under four it cannot bear up:
22 a slave when he becomes king,
and a fool when he is filled with food;
23 an unloved woman when she gets a husband,
and a maid when she succeeds her mistress.

24 Four things on earth are small,
but they are exceedingly wise:
25 the ants are a people not strong,
yet they provide their food in the summer;

18-19. Four wonderful things. The flight of a great bird **in the sky;** the reptation of a snake without feet or wings; the sailing of a ship through the trackless deep; and the mystery of sexual union, or possibly defloration (see Exeg. on vs. 19).

19. "Vulture" is better than **eagle. Midst of the sea** or **on the high seas:** Lit., "in the heart of the sea." **Maid** (*'almāh*): A marriageable young girl, probably referring to a virgin, here as elsewhere (cf. Gen. 24:43; Exod. 2:8; Ps. 68:25; Song of S. 1:3; 6:8; and perhaps Isa. 7:14).

20. This verse is taken by many to be a gloss. It is linked to vs. 19 by the word **way.** It might also have been suggested by the last line of vs. 19, although no immoral act is implied there. **Wipes her mouth:** Showing her indifference to the immoral act.

21-23. Four unbearable types of persons, two from each sex, are described here. They are people of inferior rank who, because they have been raised to higher positions, are out of place and reveal arrogant and generally disagreeable dispositions.

22. Cf. 19:10. **Fool:** See Exeg. on 17:7.

23. Odious woman or **unloved woman:** Lit., "a hated woman." **Is heir to** or **succeeds:** Comes into possession of her mistress' inheritance when the husband divorces the wife and marries her maid.

24-28. Four small but wise things.

24. Exceeding wise: Lit., "wise, they are made wise."

25. See Exeg. on 6:6-8, describing the industry of the ant.

18-19. See Expos. on 8:1-36.

20. See Expos. on 5:1-23.

21-23. See Expos. on 16:10-15; 26:1, 3-12; 31:10-31.

24-28. ***The Great in the Small.***—The man who wrote these words was not bowled over by bigness. He saw the significance of small things. The ant, the badger, the locust, the lizard—these are not in the class of the giants of the jungle, nor can they be compared to the armor-clad monsters that once were monarchs of the animal world. Yet these little creatures survived.

The writer of Ecclesiasticus says, "The man who despises little things will gradually fail" (19:1 Amer. Trans.). People who live in the atomic age do not need a reminder of the importance of the apparently insignificant elements in our world. Their experience only

26 The conies *are but* a feeble folk, yet make they their houses in the rocks;
27 The locusts have no king, yet go they forth all of them by bands;
28 The spider taketh hold with her hands, and is in kings' palaces.
29 There be three *things* which go well, yea, four are comely in going:
30 A lion, *which is* strongest among beasts, and turneth not away for any;
31 A greyhound; a he goat also; and a king, against whom *there is* no rising up.

26 The badgers are a people not mighty,
yet they make their homes in the rocks;
27 the locusts have no king,
yet all of them march in rank;
28 the lizard you can take in your hands,
yet it is in kings' palaces.

29 Three things are stately in their tread;
four are stately in their stride:
30 the lion, which is mightiest among beasts
and does not turn back before any;
31 the strutting cock,[i] the he-goat,
and a king striding before[j] his people.

[i] Gk Syr Tg Compare Vg: Heb obscure
[j] The meaning of the Hebrew is uncertain

26. Conies or, better, **badgers:** This word does not refer to the rabbit as we know it but to a species of badger which lives in the rocks. According to Lev. 11:5; Deut. 14:7, this animal chews the cud; this mistaken assumption is derived from the observation that it moves its jaws from side to side while eating.

27. Locusts: For a vivid description of the locust bands and their devastating work cf. Joel 2. **By bands** or **in rank:** Lit., "dividing."

28. Spider: Better, **lizard. Taketh hold** (so the ASV and the Amer. Trans.): I.e., **the lizard** can take hold of any surface and make its way even into kings' palaces. The phrase **you can take** (RSV, ASV mg., Moffatt, American Jewish Translation) refers to the smallness of the animal, and it better suits the context.

29-31. Four stately things.

29. Go well . . . comely in going or **are stately . . . are stately:** Lit., "well-doers of step, . . . well-doers of going."

31. A difficult verse. Lit., "Girt in the loins, or a he-goat, and a king *'alqûm* [?] with him." All emendations and translations are purely conjectural. One can merely say that

serves to underline the central thought being stressed by the writer of this section of Proverbs. By turning their attention to the microscopic facts, students of atomic research have shed light upon the ultimate nature of reality. In order to find out what the universe is made of, it has not been necessary to get mountains or stars in their grasp. They have turned to the unpromising area of the very small.

One does not need to get the whole sun into his spectroscope in order to discover what the sun is made of. One ray of light is sufficient for this purpose. The sun's nature is revealed in this infinitesimal emanation from its heart. This simple fact is a reminder of the importance of apparently trivial matters in revealing human character. One does not need to know everything about a person in order to find out what kind of man he is. Some small act of his will open the door to understanding his nature. Plutarch, who has given us a number of short biographies of important personalities, has made a classic statement in this connection in his life of Alexander the Great:

> It must be borne in mind that my design is not to write histories but lives. And the most glorious exploits do not always furnish us with the clearest discoveries of virtue or vice in men; sometimes a matter of less moment, an expression or a jest, informs us better of their characters and inclinations, than the most famous sieges, the greatest armaments, or the bloodiest battles whatsoever.[7]

Christians are often accused of an audacious act of faith. Many feel that it is an unwarranted credulity. Christians believe that in very truth God was in Christ. This does not mean that they believe the whole creative power of the universe was confined to the body and spirit of one man, but it does mean that in this man they learn best what the creative and redeeming power of God is like. As one clear, unobstructed ray from the sun can tell us what the sun is like, so one human life can show forth the nature of God. Paul can even say "in him dwelleth all the fulness of the Godhead" (Col. 2:9).

29-31. See Expos. on 29:23.

[7] *Alexander* I.

32 If thou hast done foolishly in lifting up thyself, or if thou hast thought evil, *lay* thine hand upon thy mouth.

33 Surely the churning of milk bringeth forth butter, and the wringing of the nose bringeth forth blood: so the forcing of wrath bringeth forth strife.

31 The words of king Lemuel, the prophecy that his mother taught him.

2 What, my son? and what, the son of my womb? and what, the son of my vows?

3 Give not thy strength unto women, nor thy ways to that which destroyeth kings.

4 *It is* not for kings, O Lemuel, *it is* not for kings to drink wine; nor for princes strong drink:

32 If you have been foolish, exalting yourself,
or if you have been devising evil,
put your hand on your mouth.
33 For pressing milk produces curds,
pressing the nose produces blood,
and pressing anger produces strife.

31 The words of Lemuel, king of Massa,[k] which his mother taught him:

2 What, my son? What, son of my womb?
What, son of my vows?
3 Give not your strength to women,
your ways to those who destroy kings.
4 It is not for kings, O Lemuel,
it is not for kings to drink wine,
or for rulers to desire[l] strong drink;

[k] Or *King Lemuel, the oracle*
[l] Cn: Heb *where*

---

three stately things are being described here. **Greyhound** or **cock** (following LXX; "warhorse" ASV mg.): The Hebrew expression, translated above, "girt in the loins," is unknown. **Against whom there is no rising up** or **striding before his people** ("when his army is with him" ASV mg.): These translations are hopeless attempts to make something out of the unknown word *'alqûm*.

32-33. The verses offer an admonition to exercise self-restraint.

32. Thou hast done foolishly: The verb is *nābhal,* connected with the noun for "fool" found in 17:7 (see Exeg.). **Devising evil:** The verb *zāmam* is connected with the noun *zimmāh* (see Exeg. on 21:27). **Hand upon thy mouth:** Be silent in view of your wrongdoing.

33. Churning, . . . wringing, . . . forcing are all the same Hebrew word, as the RSV brings out. **Nose** and **wrath** are the same Hebrew word (see Exeg. on 14:17). It is good to avoid unnecessary strife.

VI. The Words of Lemuel (31:1-9)

Warnings against lust and strong drink (vss. 2-7), and an exhortation to rule justly (vss. 8-9).

31:1. The title. The M.T. reads, "The words of Lemuel, king, oracle, which his mother taught him."

Lemuel: An unknown king. The name does not occur in the LXX. **Prophecy** or **Massa:** See Exeg. on 30:1. **Taught:** Lit., "corrected," "set in the right way."

2. Son of my vows: A son given because of the vows that were made (cf. I Sam. 1:11). The word for **son** in each case in this verse is Aramaic, not Hebrew.

3. Synonymous. The wiles of the wicked woman are described at length in Part I of the book of Proverbs (cf. chs. 2, 5–7, 9). **That which destroyeth** or **those** [fem.] **who destroy:** By changing a vowel in the Hebrew form the RSV makes a better parallelism with vs. 3*a*. **Kings:** The form is Aramaic.

4. The general meaning is clear, but the text is corrupt. The opening word *'al,* a negative, ordinarily goes with a verb, which is missing here. **It is not for kings, O Lemuel,** has probably gotten into the Hebrew text by dittography of the following words. On

---

32-33. See Expos. on 16:32.
31:1-3. See Expos. on 5:1-23.

4-7. See Expos. on 16:10-15; 23:29-35.

5 Lest they drink, and forget the law,
and pervert the judgment of any of the
afflicted.
6 Give strong drink unto him that is
ready to perish, and wine unto those that
be of heavy hearts.
7 Let him drink, and forget his poverty,
and remember his misery no more.
8 Open thy mouth for the dumb in the
cause of all such as are appointed to destruction.
9 Open thy mouth, judge righteously,
and plead the cause of the poor and needy.
10 ¶ Who can find a virtuous woman?
for her price *is* far above rubies.

5 lest they drink and forget what has been
decreed,
and pervert the rights of all the afflicted.
6 Give strong drink to him who is perishing,
and wine to those in bitter distress;
7 let them drink and forget their poverty,
and remember their misery no more.
8 Open your mouth for the dumb,
for the rights of all who are left desolate.[m]
9 Open your mouth, judge righteously,
maintain the rights of the poor and
needy.

10 A good wife who can find?
She is far more precious than jewels.

[m] Heb *are sons of passing away*

strong drink see Exeg. on 23:29. **O Lemuel:** Hebrew, *lemô'el.* **To desire:** The RSV and ASV mg. read *'āwōh* for the M.T. או. The ASV and RSV mg. read, with Hebrew mg., **אי, where.**

5. Synonymous. All the verbs are singular in the Hebrew. The LXX makes them plural. **Law: Lit., what has been decreed. Afflicted:** See Exeg. on 22:4.

6-7. Synonymous. Strong drink evidently has its proper use, according to the wise men, although they deprecate overindulgence (see Exeg. on 23:29).

7. The verbs are singular in Hebrew. The LXX makes them plural.

8. Synonymous. **Dumb:** Figuratively used here, meaning one who cannot plead his case. **All . . . appointed to destruction** or **all who are left desolate** (with ASV): Lit., **sons of passing away** (RSV mg.). A difficult expression, interpreted by the KJV to mean "those who disappear," i.e., "perish," and by the RSV, "those who are left behind."

9. See Exeg. on 19:17 for the gnomic view of the poor and the help that they need.

VII. The Good Wife (31:10-31)

In Proverbs woman is portrayed in a bad light as well as in a good one. A contentious woman is referred to in 19:13; 21:9; 25:24; 27:15 as an undesirable companion. The wicked woman who lures young men to the sins of the flesh is frequently mentioned throughout the book, especially in chs. 1–9 (see also vs. 3; 22:14; 23:27; 27:13; 29:3). On the other hand, we also find in Proverbs the most complimentary picture of woman in the O.T. As wife (vss. 10-31; 12:4; 18:22; 19:14) and as mother who helps with the training of the children and thereby demands their respect and obedience (1:8-9; 10:1; 17:25; 23:25; 28:24), she holds an important place with the father in the household. Although polygamy was allowed by law, it is not even hinted at in Proverbs. The ideal of the wise men was monogamy, which is definitely encouraged in 5:15-19.

This eulogy of the good wife is written in the form of an acrostic poem in which the first letter of each verse follows the order of the Hebrew alphabet. By this device the writer may be indicating that he is dealing exhaustively with the subject in an orderly way. It also facilitates the memorization of the passage (cf. Ps. 119; Lam. 1–4; etc.).

10. Virtuous or **good:** See Exeg. on 12:4. **Rubies** or **jewels:** See Exeg. on 3:15.

8-9. See Expos. on 21:3.

10-31. ***A Good Wife.***—The concluding passage of Proverbs is an acrostic poem in praise of a good wife. In the Hebrew each of these twenty-two verses begins with a different letter in alphabetical order. The writer summons the whole

11 The heart of her husband doth safely
trust in her, so that he shall have no need
of spoil.
12 She will do him good and not evil all
the days of her life.
13 She seeketh wool, and flax, and worketh willingly with her hands.
14 She is like the merchants' ship; she
bringeth her food from afar.
15 She riseth also while it is yet night,
and giveth meat to her household, and a
portion to her maidens.
16 She considereth a field, and buyeth it:
with the fruit of her hands she planteth a
vineyard.

11 The heart of her husband trusts in her,
and he will have no lack of gain.
12 She does him good, and not harm,
all the days of her life.
13 She seeks wool and flax,
and works with willing hands.
14 She is like the ships of the merchant,
she brings her food from afar.
15 She rises while it is yet night
and provides food for her household
and tasks for her maidens.
16 She considers a field and buys it;
with the fruit of her hands she plants a
vineyard.

---

11. Heart: If the word is taken in its usual meaning in Proverbs as "mind" (see Exeg. on 2:2), the verse does not refer to the husband's affection for her but to his confidence in her ability to manage things so that she will not squander the money he has earned. **Spoil** or **gain:** The word *shālāl* means booty taken in war. Here it means general wealth.

13. With willing hands: Lit., "in the delight of her hands," i.e., whatever her hand chooses.

14. She gets her supplies from distant lands.

15. Food: The word *ṭéreph* literally means "prey." **Portion:** Whether the word refers to allotted work (so ASV and RSV) or to food (so KJV and ASV mg.) is uncertain. The third stich was probably added later as a gloss on the preceding one, since no other verse in the poem has three stichs.

16. If taken literally, this verse reveals a remarkably high status of woman in the economic world. Some exegetes believe that this detail represents an exaggeration, since it appears that the man would have to do the actual buying. **The fruit of her hands:** That which has been earned with her hands.

---

alphabet to expound the virtues of a worthy woman. Crawford H. Toy has called this poem the "Golden ABC" of the perfect wife.[8]

There is no indication that this kind of wife is easy to find. He who has found a good wife has found a treasure that is worth more than many jewels (vs. 10). Evidently there were other types of wives against whom a warning was sounded by other writers. One needs only to place this poem against the background of many other sayings concerning women in the collection of Proverbs to discover that such a good wife shines with exceptional splendor.

One writer implies that every wife is good.

> He who finds a wife finds a good thing,
> and obtains favor from the Lord (18:22).

Whether these are the words of one who found a wife, or the longing of one who was looking for one, is difficult to say. He seems to feel that having a wife would be enough. Others are not so certain. They are more concerned about getting the right kind of wife than being content with any wife. There are some qualities in a woman that make her an unworthy wife; e.g., she may be a contentious or nagging person. One sage says,

> It is better to live in a corner of the housetop
> than in a house shared with a contentious woman (21:9).

Another says,

> It is better to live in a desert land
> than with a contentious and fretful woman (21:19).

A fair countenance is no substitute for a lack of discretion. One writer senses the incongruity that exists in a woman who is beautiful but lacking in good taste.

> Like a gold ring in a swine's snout
> is a beautiful woman without discretion (11:22).

[8] *Proverbs*, p. 542.

17 She girdeth her loins with strength, and strengtheneth her arms.
18 She perceiveth that her merchandise *is* good: her candle goeth not out by night.
19 She layeth her hands to the spindle, and her hands hold the distaff.
20 She stretcheth out her hand to the poor; yea, she reacheth forth her hands to the needy.
21 She is not afraid of the snow for her household: for all her household *are* clothed with scarlet.
22 She maketh herself coverings of tapestry; her clothing *is* silk and purple.
23 Her husband is known in the gates, when he sitteth among the elders of the land.
24 She maketh fine linen, and selleth *it;* and delivereth girdles unto the merchant.

17 She girds her loins with strength and
makes her arms strong.
18 She perceives that her merchandise is
profitable.
Her lamp does not go out at night.
19 She puts her hands to the distaff,
and her hands hold the spindle.
20 She opens her hand to the poor,
and reaches out her hands to the needy.
21 She is not afraid of snow for her household,
for all her household are clothed in scarlet.
22 She makes herself coverings;
her clothing is fine linen and purple.
23 Her husband is known in the gates,
when he sits among the elders of the land.
24 She makes linen garments and sells them;
she delivers girdles to the merchant.

---

17. Synonymous. She gathers up her skirt and sleeves for serious work.

18. Perceives: Lit., "tastes" (cf. Ps. 34:8). **Candle** or, better, **lamp:** A sign of her industriousness, the good wife working late at night and early in the morning.

19. Synonymous. The RSV, with the ASV, has the correct order of nouns: **distaff . . . spindle.** The Hebrew word for **distaff** is found only here. Its meaning is not certain.

20. Synonymous. See Exeg. on 19:17.

21. Scarlet: The household of the good wife is dressed in warm clothing. The LXX and the Vulg. read "double" (*shenáyim*) for this word (*shānîm*), probably referring to "double" garments.

22. Coverings: See Exeg. on 7:16. This word occurs only in Proverbs. **Silk:** Correctly, **linen. Purple:** Garments dyed with this coloring matter were very costly. Her wardrobe is luxurious.

23. Gates: See Exeg. on 1:21.

24. Synonymous. **Linen garments:** A different word from the one in vs. 22. It probably refers to a larger cloak worn over a dress or used at night. **Merchant:** Lit., "Canaanite." The Phoenicians or Canaanites were such noted traders that their name became a synonym for merchant.

The writer of this poem realizes that

Charm is deceitful, and beauty is vain,
but a woman who fears the LORD is to be praised
(vs. 30).

A good wife is to be admired as well as loved. The man who cannot respect his wife because of her manner of life is without one of the ingredients of a truly happy home.

A good wife is the crown of her husband,
but she who brings shame is like rottenness in his bones (12:4).

A worthy woman does not need someone to speak words of praise on her behalf. Her own **works praise her in the gates** (vs. 31).

The good wife whose portrait is painted in this chapter has a full-time job. If she does all the things attributed to her, she indeed **does not eat the bread of idleness** (vs. 27). In that early time many economic activities were a part of her function as a wife and mother: to provide food and clothing for her family and herself; even to engage in buying and selling, often making the business deals that displayed prudence and good management (yet see Exeg.). Little is said about the husband's part in the home. Apparently his energies were devoted to political matters outside the home.

Her husband is known in the gates,
when he sits among the elders of the land (vs. 23).

25 Strength and honor *are* her clothing; and she shall rejoice in time to come.

26 She openeth her mouth with wisdom; and in her tongue *is* the law of kindness.

27 She looketh well to the ways of her household, and eateth not the bread of idleness.

28 Her children arise up, and call her blessed; her husband *also*, and he praiseth her.

29 Many daughters have done virtuously, but thou excellest them all.

30 Favor *is* deceitful, and beauty *is* vain: *but* a woman *that* feareth the LORD, she shall be praised.

31 Give her of the fruit of her hands; and let her own works praise her in the gates.

25 Strength and dignity are her clothing,
and she laughs at the time to come.
26 She opens her mouth with wisdom,
and the teaching of kindness is on her tongue.
27 She looks well to the ways of her household,
and does not eat the bread of idleness.
28 Her children rise up and call her blessed;
her husband also, and he praises her:
29 "Many women have done excellently,
but you surpass them all."
30 Charm is deceitful, and beauty is vain,
but a woman who fears the LORD is to be praised.
31 Give her of the fruit of her hands,
and let her works praise her in the gates.

---

25. **Rejoice:** Better, **laughs** at the future, unafraid because of her secure social and financial position.

26. Synonymous. Her attainments extend also into the intellectual realm. **Teaching** is better than **law. Kindness:** See Exeg. on 3:3.

29. This verse, according to the RSV, is the expression of praise from the lips of the good wife's husband. **Daughters** or **women:** The KJV has the literal rendering of the Hebrew here. As Toy says (*ad loc.*) this custom of using the word "daughter" for "woman" may be a survival from the time when a woman, even after marriage, remained a member of her father's family, and so was called daughter. **Virtuously** or **excellently:** This is the same Hebrew word as the one found in vs. 10, translated there "virtuous."

30. Charm is often treacherous, beauty is ever transitory. **That feareth the LORD:** Lit., "a fearer of the Lord" (see Exeg. on 1:7). In vs. 30*b* the LXX has a doublet which reads, "An intelligent woman is praised, and she praises the fear of the Lord." It may be that the LXX preserves the original text in the expression "intelligent woman," and that the religious element was added later.

31. **Fruit of her hands:** The recognition which she deserves. Vs. 31*b* is perhaps an exaggeration, since domestic and womanly virtues would hardly be the subject of discussion in the **gates** of the town (see Exeg. on 1:21).

While a good wife looks well to the needs of her own family,

She opens her hand to the poor,
and reaches out her hands to the needy (vs. 20).

Her life is home-centered, but it is not confined to her own home alone. She has interests that take her into the community, where her influence is felt for good. Through her prudence and industry she gives reassurance to all members of her family. She gives to them a sense of security, not only because she is a good provider for their physical needs, but because of the kind of person she is.

Strength and dignity are her clothing,
and she laughs at the time to come (vs. 25).

She is a teacher. Evidently much of the teaching activity in that time took place in the home. A good mother is one who

opens her mouth with wisdom,
and the teaching of kindness is on her tongue (vs. 26).

Little wonder that both her children and her husband rise up and call her blessed!

Since Proverbs is full of warnings against the seductive powers of a licentious or simple-minded woman, it is significant that in this same collection there are high tributes to women who have qualities of integrity and honor.

House and wealth are inherited from fathers,
but a prudent wife is from the LORD (19:14).